Ilocano Dictionary and Grammar

PALI Language Texts
Department of Linguistics
University of Hawai'i

Byron W. Bender
General Editor

Ilocano Dictionary and Grammar

Ilocano-English, English-Ilocano

Carl Ralph Galvez Rubino

University of Hawai'i Press

© 2000 University of Hawai'i Press
All rights reserved
Printed in the United States of America

10 09 08 07 06 05   7 6 5 4 3 2

Library of Congress Cataloging-in-Publication Data

Rubino, Carl R. Galvez.
    Ilocano dictionary and grammar : Ilocano-English, English-Ilocano / Carl Ralph
Galvez Rubino.
        p.   cm. — (PALI language texts. Philippines)
    ISBN-13: 978-0-8248-2088-6 (paper : alk. paper)
    ISBN-10: 0-8248-2088-6 (paper : alk. paper)
    1. Iloko language—Dictionaries—English.   2. English language—Dictionaries—Iloko.
3. Iloko language—Grammar.   I. Series.

PL5753 .R83   2000
499'.21—dc21   99-085745

University of Hawai'i Press books are printed on acid-free paper and meet the guidelines
for permanence and durability of the Council on Library Resources.

Printed by Edwards Brothers Incorporated.

Dedicated with love to my family: Grace, my brothers, parents, and grandparents,

Siaayatko nga iruknoy daytoy a pagitarusan kadagiti adingko,
    Paul, Alan and Earl

kadagiti nagannak kaniak
    Ralph Daniel Rubino and Erlinda Galvez Rubino

ken kadagiti nagannak kadakuada
    Florence Tomisek Konvalinka and Robert E. Konvalinka
    Josefa Mallare Galvez ken daydi Catalino Hidalgo Galvez

CONTENTS

ACKNOWLEDGMENTS * PANAGYAMAN

Special thanks are due to four people who have reviewed the first manuscript of my dictionary and have subsequently helped me with my linguistic research and travels in the Philippines every year since. They are Mrs. Josefa Mallare Galvez, Dra. Geraldine Galvez, Mrs. Maria Roldan, and Mrs. Elizabeth Tadina of San Fernando, La Union. I would also like to thank my parents, Florence Konvalinka, Carmen, Edwin, Benedict, and Carol Villanueva, Melissa Deleissegues, and Alex Gonzales for their support and encouragement in all my work. Thanks to the faculty and graduate students of the Department of Linguistics at the University of California–Santa Barbara for all the wonderful times and to the Linguistics faculty and graduate students of the Australian National University. I also greatly appreciate the efforts of the Sanglay Law Office in San Fernando, La Union, Galvez Clinic, Cristy Borja, DZNL radio, Liw Agbayani, APGSA Santa Barbara, and the Superior Court of Laoag for accommodating my research with such warm hospitality. Atty. Aurora Sanglay and Dr. Imelda Quilala graciously supplied me with *Bannawag* magazines for which I am most grateful. I must also express my deep gratitude to some Ilocano writers and pressmen for their gracious help with my inquiries: Roy V. Aragon, Dr. Godofredo Reyes, Ramon Pagatpatan, Prescillano Bermudez, Lorenzo Tabin, Elnora Manangan, Severino A. Pablo, Pelagio Alcantara, Ethelwaldo Madamba, D. Nicasio Asuncion, and Redentor Santos. They are, of course, not responsible for any shortcomings in the manuscript. In preparing this dictionary, I have read the works of hundreds of Ilocano writers from different regions in order to collect the sample of words in this present volume. I cannot thank them all personally, but I wish them continued success in propagating the beauty of the Ilocano language through literature. *Maraming salamat* to Kenneth Chang and Nick Kibre for their computer help. I am also very grateful to all the linguists who have commented on my work in linguistics, especially to my mentor Marianne Mithun, Laurie Reid, Nikolaus Himmelman, Andy and Medina Pawley, Wallace Chafe, Steven Fincke, Susanna Cumming, Sandra Thompson, Byron Bender, Bob Dixon, Sasha Aikhenvald, Geoff Haig, Alec Coupe, Agnes Kang, Tony Davis, Peter Fitzgerald, and to the Ilokano department in Hawai'i: Josie Paz Clausen and Precy Espiritu. I would like to thank Mrs. Hilda Manansala for allowing me to use the Market scene painting on the cover of this book. Maria Victoria Herrera was extremely helpful in contacting the members of the Philippine art community for me. In closing, I would like to give special thanks to my family in America and the Philippines (the Rubinos, Galvezes, Villanuevas, Konvalinkas, Carbonells, and Lita Aquino) and to Maria Gracia Tan Llenado for their untiring support and understanding of my work in lexicography and linguistics.

INTRODUCTION

Ilocano is a Western Austronesian language spoken by about nine million people in Northern Luzon, Philippines. It is the most widely spoken Philippine Cordilleran language, and constitutes its own branch within the Cordilleran language family as indicated in the following genetic reconstruction by Lawrence Reid (1989:57):

CORDILLERAN LANGUAGES

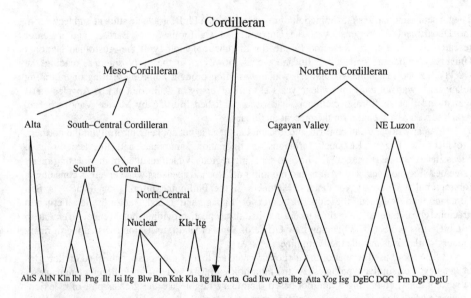

Key to Cordilleran Languages: AltN Northern Alta; AltS Southern Alta; Blw Balangaw; Bon Bontok; DgtC Casiguran Dumagat; DgtEC East Cagayan Dumagat; DgtP Palanan Dumagat; DgtU Umirey Dumagat; Gad Gaddang; Ibg Ibanag; Ibl Ibaloi; Ifg Ifugao; Ilk Iloko (**Ilocano**); Ilt Ilongot; Isg Isneg; Isi Isinay; Itg Itneg; Itw Itawis; Kla Kalinga; Kln Kallahan; Knk Kankanaey; Prn Paranan; Yog Yogad.

During early Spanish contact, the Ilocano-speaking areas were confined to the provinces of Ilocos Norte, Ilocos Sur, Abra, and La Union, but the Ilocano people have populated many other areas in the Philippines and even predominate in many areas of the provinces of Pangasinan, Benguet, and Tarlac. There are also sizable communities in many other Philippine provinces and the islands of Mindoro and Mindanao. Because the original Ilocano region borders the mountainous interior of Luzon, where members of linguistic minority groups prevail, Ilocano has been used for centuries as the lingua franca of the region and in legal documents and proceedings of the various mountain peoples. Many of these ethnic groups still use Ilocano today to communicate among themselves, despite the fact that Tagalog has been declared the national language of the Philippines.

Ilocanos are the most migratory of the Philippine ethnic groups. They have settled in many other parts of the world, forming sizeable communities in Brunei, Singapore, Hong Kong, Saudi Arabia, Kuwait, and most urban centers in the United States, Canada, and western Europe. The largest concentrations of Ilocanos in the United States are in California, Alaska, and especially Hawai'i, where nearly one-fifth of the total population can claim Ilocano descent (Espiritu 1977; Foronda 1978). In Hawai'i, Ilocano has been taught in the schools in bilingual education programs as the medium of instruction and in universities as a foreign language.

THE DICTIONARY

The present dictionary is a culmination of my research as a Ph.D. graduate student and lecturer in the Department of Linguistics at the University of California–Santa Barbara and a senior research associate at the Research Centre for Linguistic Typology at the Australian National University. I began "collecting" Ilocano words, however, in the early eighties, reading the weekly Ilocano magazine, *Bannawag*, which was often brought home by visiting or migrating relatives. It was not until my college years at the University of California at Los Angeles that I was aware that an Ilocano dictionary had been published in 1956 by Morice Vanoverbergh, which served as a skeleton for the present dictionary.

As any Ilocano can confirm, the Ilocano language is not spoken uniformly in the northern provinces of Luzon. Regional variations in intonation, grammar, and the lexicon have necessitated several trips to all the Ilocano speaking regions, which resulted in my meeting many esteemed Ilocano poets and writers and monolingual Ilocano speakers who served as consultants for regional and literary vocabulary. Members of the Philippine Information Society in San Fernando and Bangued, the Superior Court of Laoag, and DZNL radio in San Fernando graciously volunteered their time to aid me in this respect, providing much encouragement to complete this project. The Sanglay Law Office of San Fernando, La Union assisted me in many matters while I was outside the Philippines.

The root-based format of the dictionary matches that of previously published dictionaries of languages of similar typologies. As the morphology (affix system) in Philippine languages is rather complex, compiling a nonroot-based dictionary might take the greater part of a lexico-grapher's life before a good portion of the important words in the language were documented. It is my belief that a root-based dictionary would be more beneficial to native Ilocanos, students of Ilocano, linguists, and anthropologists because it allows the users to see affixal permutations and better understand the essence of the complex morphological system.

The grammatical affixes were put into the dictionary in the same section as lexical roots. This was done merely for convenience in word searching by the user who is not expected to determine the morpheme class before looking up each word. It may also be a useful method of arranging lexicons of languages with highly prefixing typologies such as Ilocano.

Common Ilocano words or bases where the boundary between the root and affix has been phonetically fused may be found in the dictionary under independent entries to simplify dictionary searches. For instance, the word *sumrek* 'to enter' from the root *serrek* 'enter' may be found under both entries. Even native Ilocano speakers experience some difficulty determining the lexical roots in these cases.

A short introduction to Ilocano grammar has been included to outline rudimentary aspects of Ilocano phonology, morphology, and syntax as an aid to natives and nonnatives alike. As the

short grammar is merely a brief synopsis of the system, it is broken down in terms of morphological classes, exemplifying paradigms that may aid users of the dictionary in their lexical searches or in constructing simple sentences. It is by no means to be taken as a thorough representation of the grammar of the language. Those interested in seeing the most thorough grammar of the language are encouraged to try to acquire a copy of my Ph.D. dissertation or Morice Vanoverbergh's 1955 Iloko grammar.

Nonnative Ilocano speakers using this dictionary will find the Affix Cross-Reference List useful when looking up polymorphemic (derived and inflected) words. It lists the most common prefixes and all suffixes, infixes, reduplications, and enclitics, which are written in Ilocano orthography as joined to their roots. Since derivational morphology in Ilocano is extremely productive, not all derivations are given with each root. I have tried to include the most common derivational patterns with the most high-frequency roots for users who are not yet familiar with the morphological system of the language, and also to show that the resulting meanings of many derived items are not always semantically transparent. The introductory phonology section outlines the pronunciation of native words and also introduces the user to the basics of Ilocano phonology, including stress (vowel length), stress shift, morphophonemics, and syllabification. Stress is shown with each root, but not with the derived forms unless it is idiosyncratic. Tagalog equivalents are given for many of the entries, as are equivalents in many of the important languages of Northern Luzon for a large number of basic words to aid comparativists.

As this is the first edition of a root-based dictionary written without financial support for adequate field editing or typing/research assistance, it fails to be as thorough as I would have desired. I welcome all comments, criticism, and suggestions, and encourage the users to contact me regarding the dictionary or any aspect of the Ilocano language they find interesting. It is my hope that the dictionary can be improved and expanded one day in the future from the comments of the users so as to be of greater value. I can be reached via electronic mail at ilocano@philippines.to or through regular mail at the Department of Linguistics, University of California, Santa Barbara, CA 93106 USA.

Although the Ilocano language is spoken as a lingua franca of Northern Luzon and in large communities outside the Philippines, it has no official status in the Philippines. No particular body that I am aware of is presently working to modernize the language or create materials for its instruction in the Philippines. It is my fervent hope that such a committee will evolve to research the role of the Ilocano language in the twenty-first century and perhaps decide how the language can effectively deal with the changing world into the third millennium. If such a committee were to develop, I would be honored to be able to offer my time, research, and suggestions to help propel its worthy cause.

A Note on the Orthography

In orthographic systems that have been used to write Ilocano since the 1600s, two systems have predominated. The older system is based on Spanish orthography and the newer system is the standardized alphabet accepted for the Tagalog language, as used in the weekly Ilocano magazine, *Bannawag*. The orthography is mostly phonemically based for the consonants, but not for the vowels. Among the five vowels (a, e, i, o, u) used in Ilocano writing, the letter *e* corresponds to two separate phonemes in the southern dialects, a mid front vowel, and a high back unrounded vowel. The orthographic symbols *o* and *u* originally represented one phoneme with alternative pronunciations in specific environments (*o* word-finally). Due to the large number of foreign loans in the language and high degree of bilingualism, however, these letters now represent two contrastive vowel sounds, e.g. *oso* 'bear' vs. *uso* 'use, in fashion'.

The older Spanish system vs. the modern system

Although perhaps the majority of Ilocanos continue to use the older Spanish spelling system, I choose to abide by the conventions accepted in most modern publications and the *Bannawag* magazine. Here, I briefly outline the two systems:

Vowels are the same in both: *a, e, i, o, u*; where *e* represents two distinct sounds in the southern dialects (see Phonology).

Consonantal representation varies as follows. Differences between the systems are highlighted in boldface. The starred consonants in the second (Spanish orthography) column are used only in loanwords:

Ilocano sound [IPA]	Spanish orthography	Standardized orthography
p	p	p
	*f	**p**
b	b	b
	*v	**b**
t	t	t
d	d	d
k	c	k
	qu	k
kk	ck	kk
g	g	g
ge, gi	**gue, gui**	**ge, gi**
s	s	s
	*z	s
se, si	**ce, ci**	**se, si**
ch [tʃ]	**ch**	**ts, ti + vowel**
j [dʒ]	**di + vowel**	**di + vowel, dy**
h	*j	h
he, hi	**ge, gi**	**he, hi**
l	l	l
ly + vowel [lj]	***ll**	**li + vowel**
r	r	r
	*rr	**r**
m	m	m
n	n	n
ny + vowel	**ñ**	**ni + vowel**
ng [ŋ]	**ñg, nĝ**	**ng**
w	o, u, w	w
y	y	y

Examples of words:

Old Spanish spelling	Modern Ilocano spelling	Gloss
acero	asero	steel
tucac	tukak	frog

dackel	dakkel	big
achara	atsara	pickles
fiesta	piesta	party, fiesta
ginebra	hinebra	gin
daguiti	dagiti	plural article
trabajo	trabaho	work
taller	talier	car repair shop
ñgata	ngata	perhaps
vaca	baka	cow
zapatos	sapatos	shoes
pizarra	pisara	chalkboard

The idiosyncrasies of the older Spanish-based system are eliminated in the modern system as follows:

The letters *c* and *g* used in the older Spanish spelling system no longer represent two sounds. In the old system, *c* and *g* before a front vowel (*i*, *e*) represented [s] and [h] respectively. In other environments, they represented [k] and [g], respectively:

Old Spanish spelling	Modern Ilocano spelling	Gloss
gelatina	helatina	gelatin
ginebra	hinebra	gin
hacendero	asendero	estate owner

The velar stops [k] and [g] before front vowels used to be represented in Spanish orthography as '*qu*' and '*gu*', respectively. They are now represented without the '*u*'.

Old Spanish spelling	Modern Ilocano spelling	Gloss
daguiti	dagiti	plural article
manggued	mangged	worker
naganaquen	naganaken	gave birth already
baquet	baket	old lady

The Pre-Hispanic Syllabary

Before the arrival of the Spaniards in the sixteenth century, the Ilocanos employed a syllabary resembling the Vedic scripts of India used in various other languages found throughout the Philippines and Indonesia. It is similar to the scripts used by the Tagalogs and Pangasinenses, although unlike these, the Ilocano script was innovated to designate coda consonants. In the Tagalog script, readers were expected to supply the coda consonants from the context, as only consonants in initial syllable position were written, with a diacritic representing the appropriate vowel. Although this script is no longer in use in modern Ilocano, I show it below, taken from the Ilocano *Doctrina Cristiana* of 1621.

The Ilocano Syllabary

a e — i o — u

ba be — bi bo — bu b ka ke — ki

ko — ku k da de — di

do — du d ga ge — gi go — gu g

nga nge — ngi ngo — ngu ng la le — li

lo — lu l ma me — mi mo — mu m

na ne — ni no — nu n pa pe — pi

po — pu p ha he — hi ho — hu h

sa se — si so — su s ta te — ti

to — tu t va ve — vi vo — vu v

ya ye — yi yo — yu y

Affix Cross-Reference List

Successful word searching in a root-based dictionary of a morphologically complex language such as Ilocano requires the ability to separate the root morpheme from the affixes. Native speakers of Ilocano and trained linguists are usually able to do this quite easily in most cases, but for students of the language, this cross-reference list may prove most helpful. The affixes alphabetized below are separated by category: prefixes, infixes, suffixes, and enclitics (which are written in Ilocano orthography as suffixes). Users of the dictionary must also keep in mind that many of these affixes may be used with root reduplication of various types:

Reduplication Patterns[1] in Ilocano

-V- [-ʔV-]	kumra*a*d	creak
	manalba*a*ng	fire (sound of gun)
	kanalpa*a*k	slapping sound
	lumtu*o*g	burst, explode
-C-	la*l*laki	boys
	ba*b*bai	girls
	a*d*di	younger siblings
CV-	aga*a*rab [ʔagaʔarab]	cattle rustler
	agin*da*dalus	pretend to be clean
	*nu*nuang	water buffalo (plural)
CVC-	ag*ad*-adal [ʔagadʔadal]	studies (continuative)
	nag*sang*sangit	was crying
	*bat*bato	stones
	*dag*dagitoy	only these
CVC(C)(V)V-	ag*taplia*tapliak	splash repeatedly/intermittently
	*buttua*buttuag	rocking chair
	*tapi*tapiken	pat repeatedly
	*bugka*bugkawan	startle repeatedly
CVCVN-	*rupan*rupa	face to face
	*patem*pateg	mutual caring
	*gurang*gura	mutual hatred
	ayan-ayat	mutual love, lover
Full root	*saka*saka	barefoot
	*ima*ima	barehanded
	*tapok*tapok	covered in dust
	*dara*dara	drenched in blood
	*silaw*silawan	light up various locations
	ag*rikus*rikos	go around in circles
	*pisang*pisangen	tear to shreds

For grammatical explanations and examples of the use of these affixes, please refer to the dictionary. Prefixes marked with an asterisk maintain the initial glottal stop (or in rapid speech, a syllable break) when affixed to underlyingly vowel-initial words, e.g. *ag-* [ʔag-] + *úni* [ʔú:ni] 'to sound' > *agúni* [ʔa.gú:.ni]; but *sinan** [sinan-] + *allawági* [ʔallawá:gi] 'fake carpenter' > *sinan-allawagi* [si.nan.ʔal.la.wá:.gi].

---

[1] Onset consonants may be complex or an underlying glottal stop [ʔ]. Most Ilocano reduplicants are prefixes, except -*V*- used with roots of onomatopoetic origin and -*C*- animate pluralization.

PREFIXES

ag-
aga-
agat*-
agi-
agin*-
agipa-
agka-
agkai-
agkara-
agkarai-
agkaraipa-
agkinna-
agmara-
agpa-
agpagin*-
agpai-
agpaipa-
agpaka-
agpinna-
agpinnai-
agpinnaipa-
agsi-
agsin-
agsinan-
agtagi-
agtagipag-
agtagipagi-
agtagipagipa-
agtagipagpa-
agtagipagpai-
agtagipagpaipa-
akim-
akin*-
aking-
apag-
apagka-
apagpa-
ari-
arig-
arim-
arin*-
aring-
bise-
de-
di-
i-
im-
impa-
in-
iny-

ipa-
ipami-
ipin*-
ka-
kai-
kaka-
kanika-
kapi-
kapin*-
kara-
kina-
kumara-
kon-
kunsi-
ma-
magsi-
mai-
maika-
maipa-
maka-
makai-
makaipa-
makapa-
makapag-
makapagin*-
makapagpa-
makapagpai-
makapagpaipa-
makapagtagi-
makapagtagipag-
makapagtagipagi-
makapagtagipagipa-
makapagtagipagpa-
makapagtagipagpai-
makapagtagipagpaipa-
makapai-
makapaipa-
makapamin-
makapaN-
maki-
makika-
makin*-
makipa-
makipag-
makipagi-
makipagin*-
makipagpa-
makipagpai-
makipagpaipa-
makipai-

makipaipa-
makipaN-
mama-
mamag-
mamai-
mamaipa-
mamaka-
mamaki-
mamaN-
mamang-
mami-
mamin-
mamimpin*-
mamm-
mammag-
mammai-
mammaipa-
mammaka-
mammaki-
mammaN-
mammang-
mammangi-
man-
maN-
mana-
manag-
managsinan-
managtagi-
manama-
manamag-
manamai-
manamaipa-
manamaki-
manamaN-
manamang-
manamangi-
manamangipa-
manaN-
manang-
manangi-
manangpa-
manangpag-
manangpai-
manangpaipa-
manangpaka-
manangpaki-
manangpaN-
manangpang-
manangpangi-
mannaka-

mannaki-
mang-
mangi-
mangipa-
mangpa-
mangpag-
mangpai-
mangpaipa-
mangpaka-
mangpaki-
mangpang-
mangpangi-
mapa-
mapag-
mapagpa-
mapai-
mapaki-
mapaN-
mapang-
mapangi-
mapangipa-
mara-
maran*-
mari-
masi-
masin*-
may-
na-
nag-
nagi-
nagin*-
nagipa-
nagka-
nagkara-
nagkarai-
nagkaraipa-
nagkinna-
nagmara-
nagpa-
nagpagin*-
nagpai-
nagpaipa-
nagpaN-
nagpinna-
nagpinnai-
nagpinnaipa-
nagsinan*-
nagtagi-
nagtagipag-
nagtagipagi-
nagtagipagipa-
nagtagipagpa-

nagtagipagpaipa-
nai-
naipa-
naka-
nakai-
nakapa-
nakapag-
nakapagi-
nakapagpa-
nakapagpai-
nakapagpaipa-
nakapagtagi-
nakapagtagipag-
nakapagtagipagipa-
nakapagtagipagpa-
nakapagtagipagpai-
nakapagtagipagpaipa-
nakapai-
nakapaipa-
nakapamin-
nakapaN-
nakapara-
nakasag-
nakatagi-
naki-
nakin-
nakipa-
nakipag-
nakipagin*-
nakipagpa-
nakipagpai-
nakipagpaipa-
nakipai-
nakipaN-
nama-
namag-
namai-
namaipa-
namaka-
namaki-
namaN-
namang-
namangi-
namangipa-
nami-
namin-
naN-
nang-
nangipa-
nangpa-
nangpag-
nangpai-

nangpaipa-
nangpaka-
nangpaki-
nangpaN-
nangpang-
nangpangi-
nangpangipa-
napa-
napag-
napai-
napaipa-
napaka-
napaki-
napangi-
napangipa-
nasinan*-
ni-
pa-
pag-
paga-
pagat*-
pagin*-
pagka-
pagpa-
pai-
paikapin*-
paipa-
paipi-
paipin*-
paka-
paki-
pakipag-
pam-
pama-
pamag-
pamai-
pamaipa-
pamaka-
pamaki-
pamaN-
pamang-
pamangi-
pamangipa-
pami-
pamin-
pamma-
pammag-
pammaipa-
pammaka-
pammaki-
pammaN-
pammang-

pammangi-
pammangipa-
pan-
paN-
panag-
panagin-
panama-
panamag-
panamai-
panamaipa-
panamaka-
panamaki-
panamaN-
panamang-
panamangi-
panamangipa-
panaN-
panang-
panangi-
panangipa-
panangpa-
panangpag-
panangpai-
panangpaipa-
panangpaka-
panangpaki-
panangpang-
panangpangi-
panangpangipa-
pannaka-
pannakai-
pannakapa-
pannaki-
pannakipag-
pang-
pangi-
pangipa-
pangpa-

pangpag-
pangpai-
pangpaipa-
pangpaka-
pangpaki-
pangpaN-
pangpang-
pangpangi-
pangpangipa-
para-
pi-
pimmi-
pimmin*-
pin*-
pinag-
pinagin*-
pinai-
pinaipa-
pinaikapi-
pinaikapin*-
pinaipi-
pinaipin*-
pinaka-
pinaki-
pinama-
pinamag-
pinamai-
pinamaipa-
pinamaka-
pinamaki-
pinamaN-
pinamang-
pinamangi-
pinamangipa-
pinaN-
pinang-
pinangi-
pinangipa-

pinangpa-
pinangpag-
pinangpai-
pinangpaipa-
pinangpaka-
pinangpaki-
pinangpaN-
pinangpang-
pinangpangi-
pinapi-
pinapin*-
pinin-
pinnaka-
pinnaki-
puma-
pumi-
sag-
sagga-
sagpami-
sagpamin-
sanga-
sangsanga-
sangka-
sangsangka-
si-
sin*-
sinag-
sinam-
sinan*-
sinin*-
sumag-
tagi-
tagtagi-
tari-
tarin-
tinagi-
y-

SUFFIXES

-ak
-akon
-akto
-am
-amon
-amto
-an

-ek
-ekon
-ekto
-em
-emon
-emto
-en

INFIXES

-C-
-V-
-an-
-im-
-imm-
-in-
-inn-
-um-
-uman-

ENCLITICS

-ak	-kayon	-nan
-akon	-kayonto	-nanto
-akto	-kayto	-nsa
-da	-ko	-nto
-dan	-kon	-sa
-danto	-konto	-ta
-en	-m	-tan
-k	-mi	-tanto
-ka	-min	-tayo
-kan	-minto	-tayon
-kanto	-mo	-tayonto
-kami	-mon	-tayto
-kamin	-monto	-to
-kaminto	-n	-ton
-kayo	-na	

PHONOLOGY AND PRONUNCIATION

Phonology refers to the sounds and sound systems of a language. This section outlines the pronunciation of the various sounds of Ilocano and then introduces the rules of stress, stress shift, reduplication, and syllabification.

1. The Consonants

Ilocano has fifteen original phonemes (contrastive consonants), one loan consonant /h/, and two complex affricates as seen in the chart below:

	Labial	Dental	Alveolar	Alveopalatal	Palatal	Velar	Glottal
Stops	p	t				k	- [ʔ]
	b	d				g	
Fricatives			s	(si + V/ [ʃ])			(h)
Affricates				(ts /ti + V/ [tʃ]) (dy /di + V/ [dʒ])			
Lateral			l				
Tap/trill			r				
Glides	w				y		
Nasals	m	n				ng [ŋ]	

1.1 The stops

Stops are produced by a complete closure in the oral cavity, followed by an immediate release of air. They are differentiated by *place of articulation* (the exact place in the mouth where the closure takes place) and *voicing* (whether or not the vocal chords vibrate during their articulation).

Ilocano stops are contrastive for voicing and have four places of articulation: bilabial, dental, velar, and glottal. Voiceless stops in Ilocano are not articulated with aspiration (a puff of air). As syllable codas (final consonant of the syllable), they are usually unreleased and not articulated with full force.

Bilabial stops

The bilabial stops are /p/ (voiceless) and /b/ (voiced). They are unaspirated.

*Note: In the three columns below, the first column shows segments as they are spelled in Ilocano, and the second column reflects the pronunciation in simplified IPA. The IPA pronunciation reflects the dialect spoken in San Fernando, La Union, Philippines. In the northern dialects of Ilocos Norte and Ilocos Sur, the high back unrounded vowel [ɯ] is pronounced as a mid front vowel [ɛ].

ápay	[ʔá:.pay]	why
napnó	[nap.nó]	full
pangláw	[paŋ.láw]	poor
bála	[bá:.la]	bullet

| úbet | [ʔú:.bɯt] | buttocks |
| nababá | [na.ba.bá] | short |

Dental stops

The dental stops are /t/ (voiceless) and /d/ (voiced). They are pronounced with the tip of the tongue touching the teeth. Like all stops in Ilocano, they are unaspirated and not released in final position.

matá	[ma.tá]	eye
tastásen	[tas.tá:.sɯn]	rip garments
tumáud	[tu.má:.ʔod]	originate
táta	[tá:.ta]	father
díla	[dí:.la]	tongue
adú	[ʔa.dú]	many
didíng	[di.díŋ]	wall
agbeddabéd	[ʔag.bɯd.da.bɯ́d]	snuffle

Before the glide [y], /t/ and /d/ become [tʃ] and [dʒ], respectively. See Palatalization, section 1.7.

idiáy	[ʔi.dʒáy]	there
diáket	[dʒá:.ket]	jacket
tiémpo	[tʃém.po]	time, weather

Velar stops

The velar stops in Ilocano are /k/ (voiceless) and /g/ (voiced). They are never aspirated, and in final position are usually unreleased. The voiceless stop /k/ often fricates to /kˣ/ between vowels, or is pronounced as a glottal stop [ʔ] before consonants:

káka	[ka:.kˣa]	elder sibling
Ilokánoka?	[ʔi.lo.kˣá:.no.kˣa]	Are you Ilocano?
árak	[ʔá:.rak]	wine, alcohol
pukráy	[puʔ.ráy]	ripened squash
nagagét	[na.ga.gɯ́t]	industrious
aggátang	[ʔag.gá:.taŋ]	to shop, purchase
gumatél	[gu.ma.tɯ́l]	to itch
aragáag	[ʔa.ra.gá:.ʔag]	transparent

Glottal stop

The glottal stop /ʔ/ is produced with a quick closure and release in the glottal area. Due to the constraints of human anatomy, it is always voiceless. Vowel-initial words in Ilocano have the glottal stop as their initial consonantal onset. For further discussion of the glottal stop, see section 4.

apró	[ʔap.ró]	bile
agsay-á	[ʔag.say.ʔá]	clear one's throat
masig-átan	[ma.sig.ʔá:.tan]	be dried up
nasam-ít	[na.sam.ʔít]	sweet

1.2 The fricatives

Ilocano has one native voiceless alveolar fricative [s], and a nonnative glottal fricative [h]. The voiceless alveolar fricative is pronounced like the *s* in *soda*. Like the stops, it may geminate:

málas	[má:.las]	bad luck
súsay	[sú:.say]	species of fish
assawa	[ʔas.sá:.wa]	married couple
susó	[su.só]	snail

Before the glide [y] or its counterpart (vowel *i* followed by another vowel), the fricative /s/ palatalizes to [ʃ]:

siémpre	[ʃém.prɛ]	of course
siák	[ʃak]	I
ísyu	[ʔí:.ʃu]	issue

The glottal fricative [h] is not native to the Ilocano language and does not geminate. It often appears in borrowings from languages like Spanish, English, Chinese, or Tagalog. The only native word with a glottal fricative is *haán* 'no', a spoken variant of *saan*.

haán	[ha.ʔán]	no
éhe	[ʔé:.hɛ]	axle (f. Spanish)
húsi	[hú:.si]	pineapple fabric (f. Chinese)

1.3 The affricates

Although there are no contrastive affricate consonants in Ilocano, affricates do occur in the language as a result of palatalization in certain phonological environments or in foreign language borrowings.

The voiced alveo-palatal afficate [dʒ], like the English *j* in *juice*, is represented in the orthography by *dy* or *di* + a vowel.

mandiák	[man.dʒák]	I don't
dióga	[dʒó:.ga]	breast, slang
dyús	[dʒús]	juice (f. English)
diós	[dʒós]	god (f. Spanish)

The voiceless alveo-palatal affricate [tʃ], like the English *ch* in *China* is represented in the orthography by *ts* or *ti* + a vowel in borrowed words:

tsokoláte	[tʃo.ko.lá:.tɛ]	chocolate (f. Spanish)
atsára	[ʔat.tʃá:.ra]	pickles (f. Malay)
itsúra	[ʔit.tʃó:.ra]	figure (f. Spanish)
tianggí	[tʃaŋ.gí]	store (f. Chinese)

In native words, the alveo-palatal affricate [tʃ] results from the palatalization of *t* occurring before the glide *y* or its equivalent (vowel *i* followed by another vowel).

tián	[tʃan]	stomach
agtiád	[ʔag.tʃad]	protrude the belly

1.4 The liquids

Ilocano has two liquid consonants, /r/ and /l/. /l/ is pronounced as a dental lateral in all environments. It does not have a velarized variant like the English 'l' in syllable-final position.

lalláki	[lal.lá:.ki]	boys
agílo	[ʔa.gí:.lo]	wipe the anus
nagádal	[na.gá:.dal]	studied

The consonant [r] is a dental tap pronounced like the Spanish r in araña. In careful speech, it is often trilled like the Spanish rr of perro.

diário	[dʒá:.ryo]	newspaper
agrugárog	[ʔag.ru.gá:.rog]	grunt
naríri	[na.rí:.ri]	noisy; complaining

1.5 The glides

Ilocano has two glides, /w/ and /y/. For their use in diphthongal codas, see section 2.1.

The labio-velar glide /w/ is formed with rounded lips and some obstruction at the velar part of the mouth.

agbariwengwéng	[ʔag.ba.ri.wɯŋ.wɯ́ŋ]	whirl
waláwal	[wa.lá:.wal]	dibble
nawadwád	[na.wad.wád]	abundant, plentiful
sílaw	[sí:.law]	light

The palatal glide /y/ is pronounced like the y in yes. It is the consonantal counterpart of the high front vowel i.

layá	[la.yá]	ginger
nalayláy	[na.lay.láy]	withered
yo	[yó]	shark

1.6 The nasals

Ilocano has three nasal consonants, differentiated by the place of articulation in which the oral airstream is blocked. The three nasals in Ilocano are /m/, /n/, and /ng/.

The bilabial nasal /m/ is formed by closing the airstream at the lips. It is equivalent to the English m in mother.

umáy	[ʔu.máy]	to come
amá	[ʔa.má]	father
medmedán	[mɯd.mɯ.dán]	loosen, slacken
káma	[ká:.ma]	bed

The dental nasal [n] is formed by obstructing the airflow in the mouth with the tongue touching the upper teeth or the alveolar ridge slightly behind the upper teeth. It is equivalent to the Spanish n in no.

iná	[ʔi.ná]	mother
nengnéng	[nuŋ.núŋ]	simpleton
intán	[ʔin.tán]	let's go (dual)

The velar nasal [ng] is formed by obstructing the airflow in the mouth at the velum. It is equivalent to the English *ng* in *sing*. The velar nasal may appear in syllable-initial position.

ngatá	[ŋa.tá]	maybe
singsíng	[siŋ.síŋ]	ring
agmangísit	[ʔag.ma.ŋí:.sit]	wear mourning clothes

1.7 Palatalization

The obstruents /t/, /d/, and /s/ all palatalize before the glide /y/ or its equivalent, i.e. the high vowel /i/ followed by another vowel.

The dental stops /t/ and /d/ form alveo-palatal affricates before the glide /y/, [tʃ] and [dʒ] respectively.

buttióg	[but.tʃóg]	large abdomen
diák	[dʒák]	I don't
diammó	[dʒam.mó]	don't know
idiáy	[ʔi.dʒáy]	there
dyip	[dʒíp]	jeep

The alveolar fricative /s/ forms an alveo-palatal fricative [ʃ] before the glide [y] or its equivalent, i.e. the vowel *i* followed by another vowel.

siák	[ʃák]	I
Asia	[ʔá:.ʃa]	Asia
siúman	[ʃú:.man]	stepchild

2. The Vowels

Ilocano has six contrastive vowels (five in the northern dialect) represented in the orthography by five letters /a, e, i, o, u/ based on the borrowed Spanish system. The use of a Spanish writing system to represent the vowels is one of the few instances of nonphonemic orthographic practice in the language, as shown in the chart below.

	Front	Central	Back	
			Unround	Round
High	i		e [ɯ]	u
Mid	e [ɛ]			o
Low		a		

/a/. The low central vowel is the most common vowel in the language. Of all the vowels, this one is least subject to variation:

bása	[bá:.sa]	reading
alawági	[ʔa.la.wá:.gi]	carpenter
atsára	[ʔat.tʃá:.ra]	pickles

/e/. The orthographic symbol 'e' in Ilocano constitutes two separate sounds in southern speech, and one sound in the northern dialects. In the northern dialects (Ilocos Norte, Ilocos Sur), it corresponds to a front, central lax vowel [ɛ] similar to the *e* in *pet*.

In the southern dialects, the letter 'e' represents two separate vowel sounds. In Spanish loanwords, it is equivalent to the northern pronunciation. In native words, however, it is pronounced as a high to high-mid, centralized back unrounded vowel [ɯ] that does not occur in word-final position.

Spanish loanwords

kalésa	[ka.lé:.sa]	horse-drawn carriage
Presidénte	[pre.si.dén.te]	president
késo	[ké:.so]	cheese
éhe	[ʔé:.hɛ]	axle

Native words

suráten	[su.rá:.tɯn]	to write something
tabbéd	[tab.bɯ́d]	stupid
nabengbéng	[na.bɯŋ.bɯ́ŋ]	thick
met	[mɯt]	also

/i/. The vowel 'i' is pronounced as a high front vowel, not quite as tense as the English *ee* in *meet*. In unstressed environments, it has a lax variant a little higher than the English [i] in 'pick'.

itlóg	[ʔɪt.lóg]	egg
sángit	[sá:.ŋɪt]	cry
lasí	[la.sí]	dandruff

/o/ and /u/. Historically, the vowels *o* and *u* did not meaningfully contrast. In the native syllabary, they were both represented by one character (or by a small dot underneath the syllabic character corresponding to their consonantal onset). After the arrival of the Spaniards and the incorporation of many Spanish loanwords in Ilocano vocabulary, native Ilocanos were able to distinguish these vowels and chose to do so in subsequent orthographic practice. The [o] vowel is a rounded upper mid vowel similar to the Spanish *o* in *no*, while the [u] vowel is a rounded high back vowel similar to the Spanish *u* in *azul* with a more lax interpretation in unstressed environments.

Word-finally, /u/ is realized as [o], while in word-medial positions and stressed environments, as [u]. In Spanish loanwords, the Spanish pronunciation is retained for these vowels.

úlo	[ʔú:.lo]	head
súrat	[sú:.rat]	letter
agtútor	[ʔag.tú:.tor]	be patient
nabló	[nab.ló]	sprained

An /o/ vs. /u/ distinction has arisen due to a few words of Spanish origin:

| bólo | [bó:.lo] | machete (from Spanish) |
| búlo | [bú:.lo] | bamboo |

2.1 Diphthongs

The glides /w/ and /y/ may combine with certain vowels to form the following diphthongs:

/aw/	[aw]	
lawláw	[law.láw]	surround, area around
sílaw	[sí:.law]	light

/iw/	[iuw]	
kissíw	[kis.siúw]	epilepsy
riwríw	[riuw.riúw]	million

/ay/	[ay]	
aráy	[ʔa.ráy]	exclamation of pain
únay	[ú:.nay]	very
matáy	[ma.táy]	die

/ey/ (variant of /ay/)	[ey]	
didiéy	[di.dʒéy]	that
idiéy	[ʔ.dʒéy]	there
meysá	[méy.sa]	one

/oy/, /uy/	[oy], [uy]	
sallóy	[sal.lóy]	weak, frail
ditóy	[di.tóy]	here
apúy	[ʔa.póy]	fire

2.2 Stress and vowel length

Stress may occur on the open penultimate or final syllable in Ilocano. It is contrastive, as it may contribute to a change of meaning in a few words. Stress assigned to an open syllable (syllable ending in a vowel) entails that the vowel is long:

| ások | [ʔá:.sok] | my dog |
| asók | [ʔa.súk] | smoke |

| síka | [sí:.ka] | dysentery |
| siká | [si.ká] | you (singular, familiar) |

| ábut | [ʔá:.but] | reach; catch up with |
| abút | [ʔa.bút] | hole |

| padáya | [pa.dá:.ya] | go to the east |
| padayá | [pa.da.yá] | party |

sapáen	[sa.pá:.ʔɯn]	to do early
sapaén	[sa.pa.ʔúɪn]	to spit out chewed betel leaf
basáan	[ba.sá:.ʔan]	to read to someone
basaán	[ba.sa.ʔán]	to wet someone

Although stress is contrastive in Ilocano, the following patterns can be observed:

Stress in Ilocano falls on the last syllable if the penultimate syllable is closed, i.e., if the last vowel is preceded by two consonants or a consonant followed by a glottal stop (written '-' in Ilocano orthography when in word-medial position):

basnót	[bas.nót]	whip
takkí	[tak.kí]	excrement
kulbét	[kul.búɪt]	tough, chewy (meat)
kulagtít	[ku.lag.tít]	jerking movement
uksób	[ʔuk.sób]	naked from the waist up
kaw-ít	[kaw.ʔít]	hook
lis-á	[lis.ʔá]	nit, egg of a louse
sam-ít	[sam.ʔít]	sweet
al-aliá	[ʔal.ʔal.yá]	ghost

Exceptions to this rule include stems in which the last vowel is preceded by *ngk*, or in words of foreign origin.

lángka	[láŋ.ka]	jackfruit
bibíngka	[bi.bíŋ.ka]	rice cake
súngka	[súŋ.ka]	kind of native game
karámba	[ka.rám.ba]	jar (from Spanish)
kuárto	[kwár.to]	room (from Spanish)
líbro	[líb.ro]	book (from Spanish)
ókra	[ʔók.ra]	okra vegetable (from Spanish)

Stress also falls on the last syllable if the last vowel is preceded by a consonant and glide (produced by the vowels *i*, *u*, or *o*):

sadiá	[sa.dʒá]	renowned
isbuán	[ʔis.bwán]	to urinate on
aniá	[ʔa.nyá]	what
al-aliá	[ʔal.ʔal.yá]	ghost
bituén	[bit.wúɪn]	star
basiluág	[ba.sil.wág]	type of plant used for poison

Exceptions to this rule include borrowed words:

aránia	[ʔa.rán.ya]	chandelier (from Spanish)
hópia	[hóp.ya]	Chinese bean cake (from Chinese)
mília	[míl.ya]	mile (from Spanish)

Orthographic double vowels [phonetically *aʔa, eʔe, iʔi, uʔo*] following two consonants usually take stress on the first vowel, with an intervening glottal stop.

manabtúog	[ma.nab.tú:.ʔog]	thump
arináar	[ʔa.rin.ná:.ʔar]	moonlight
manatbáag	[ma.nat.bá:.ʔag]	slam; thump
manabsúok	[ma.nab.sú:.ʔok]	splash
rebbáas	[rɯb.bá:.ʔas]	aftermath of flood

Words that include two identical CVC sequences separated by a vowel usually will carry the stress on the vowel separating them.

arimasámas	[ʔa.ri.ma.sá:.mas]	red skies at moonrise
arimukámok	[ʔa.ri.mu.ká:.mok]	slight drizzle
basíbas	[ba.sí:.bas]	hurl a long object
bugábog	[bu.gá:.bog]	to be mixed sorts (rice)
bukíbok	[bu.kí:.bok]	overturn; scatter
gusúgos	[gu.sú:.gos]	scrub, rub hard
guyúgoy	[gu.yú:.goy]	suggestion, convincing
ngurúngor	[ŋu.rú:.ŋor]	cut throat
salísal	[sa.lí:.sal]	contest, competition
supúsop	[su.pú:.sop]	lengthen; join, add

Exceptions to this rule include:

| yakayák | [ya.ka.yák] | sieve |
| pidipíd | [pi.di.píd] | closely set together; joined |

Words that do not fit into the above categories must be learned separately with regard to stress placement, as in the following set of words with an open penultimate syllable:

báles	[bá:.lɯs]	revenge
síkap	[sí:.kap]	sly, cunning
tíkaw	[tí:.kaw]	confuse
turéd	[tu.rɯíd]	courage
burís	[bu.rís]	diarrhea
pasét	[pa.sɯít]	part

2.2.1 Secondary stress

Aside from underlying stress assigned to polymorphemic enclitics and affixes (see section 2.2.4), there are a few different environments that attract secondary stress.

a. Vowels preceding a geminate consonant receive inherent secondary stress (shown with the grave accent below):

babbái	[bàb.bá:.ʔi]	girls
pannakatúrog	[pàn.na.ka.tú:.rog]	ability to sleep
kappó	[kàp.pó]	clam

mannániw	[màn.ná:.niw]	poet
aggayyém	[ʔag.gày.yúm]	mutual friends
dakkél	[dàk.kúíl]	big
keggáng	[kùg.gáng]	dried crust of a scab

b. When a reduplicated root results in an open syllable of CV structure, the vowel of the open reduplicated syllable is lengthened with inherent secondary stress:

nakabàbaín	cf. naka- CV- baín	shameful
kìkiám	root word	kind of native sausage
agbìbiág	cf. ag- CV- biág	characters in a script
dàdaíten	cf. CV- dáit -en	things to be sewn

2.2.2 Stress shift

Each root carries an underlying stress on the penult or final syllable. The placement of the stress may shift to the following syllable under the following conditions:

a. For stems ending in a consonant or the vowel *a*, the stress shifts one syllable to the right with suffixation (the *-en* or *-an* suffixes). The stress does not shift one syllable to the right if the stressed vowel of the root is preceded by two different consonants, a consonant and a glide (vowel *i*, *u*, or *o* + another vowel), or a consonant followed by a glottal stop:

Stress shift:

kalawáen	cf. ka- láwa + -en	widen
ragawán	cf. ragáw + -an	prune (trees)
basáen	cf. bása + -en	read something
in-inúten	cf. in-ínut + -en	do intermittently

No stress shift:

amiánan	cf. amián + -an	north
Kainsíkan	cf. ka- insík + -an	China town, China
lat-óngan	cf. lat-óng + -an	toilet hole
pultíngen	cf. pultíng + -en	cut, sever at stem
rabsúten	cf. rabsút + -en	snatch

If the stressed vowel of the root is *e*, the stress shifts with suffixation, regardless of environment:

kasingpetán	cf. ka- singpét + -an	most virtuous
kadak(ke)lán	cf. ka- dakkél + -an	biggest, largest
panggepén	cf. panggép + -en	aim, plan, intend
pangremán	cf. pangrém + -an	pout at
kapangtedán	cf. ka- pangtéd + -an	turn, opportunity
paglangdetán	cf. pag- langdét + -an	scapegoat; accuse wrongly
pespesén	cf. pespés + en	squeeze

If the stressed vowel of the root is preceded by a geminate consonant, stress shifts one syllable to the right with suffixation:

ikkatén	cf. ikkát + -en	remove, take away
annadén	cf. annád + -en	beware of
ibbatán	cf. ibbát + -an	let go of, release

The only exceptions to the above rules occur with a few roots beginning with the vowel *i*: *imbág* 'good', *itlóg* 'egg', and *istáy* 'almost'.

nagistayán	cf. nag- istáy + -an	almost
pagitlogán	cf. pag- itlóg + -an	nest
iitlogán	cf. CV- itlóg + -an	uterus of birds
pagimbagán	cf. pag- imbág + -an	interest; benefit
kaimbagán	cf. ka- imbág + -an	best
paimbagén	cf. pa- imbág + -en	make better, cure

b. For stems ending in a vowel other than *a*, the suffix will always bear the stress.

punnuén	cf. punnó + -en	fill
kaasián	cf. kaási + -an	have pity on
talién	cf. talí + -en	twist into a rope
sangkaaduán	cf. sangka- adú + -an	majority
kikién	cf. kíki + -en	tickle
lutuén	cf. lúto + -en	cook something

2.2.3 Regression of stress

The stress may shift one syllable to the left under the following conditions:

a. Certain kinship terms that refer to specific relatives (related to the speaker or addressee) such as *amá* 'father', *iná* 'mother', and *apó* 'grandparent' shift their stress one syllable to the left following the personal article *ni* or any of its variants (*ken, kada*, or *da*):

ni áma	cf. ni + amá	father
ken ína	cf. ken + iná	to mother
da ápo	cf. da + apó	grandma and grandpa

b. The infix *-an-* used for onomatopoetic purposes may change an ultimate stress to a penultimate stress provided that the stressed vowel of the derived word is preceded by a single consonant:

rumanípak	cf. ripák + -uman-	slam, break (plate)
tumanául	cf. taúl + -uman-	bark repeatedly
lumanípak	cf. lipák + -uman-	slap repeatly

2.2.4 Stress in prefixes and enclitics

Although prefixes and enclitics may not contribute to a stress change in stems, polysyllabic prefixes and enclitics may carry secondary underlying stress (indicated with the grave accent in the glosses):

   paggatángantayó
   pag-gátang-an=tayò
   LOCATIVE-buy-NOMINALIZER=1p.INCLUSIVE
   'the place where we buy'

   pánnakangíwattayó
   pànnaka-ngíwat-tayò
   NOMINALIZER-mouth-1p.INCLUSIVE
   'our spokesperson'

3. Consonant Gemination[1]

Consonant gemination in Ilocano occurs both in root words and as a result of productive derivational affixation. All Ilocano consonants may be geminated (except the glottal fricative). In many roots, consonants are underlyingly geminate.

ittíp	crust of rice that sticks to the bottom of the pot
pittagáw	species of bird
lammín	cold
sammakéd	prop; support
ikkát	remove, take away
kappó	clam
ballígi	victory, triumph

Some consonants may geminate as a result of derivational affixation.

laláki	boy	lalláki	boys
babái	girl	babbái	girls
asáwa	spouse	assáwa	spouses, couple
baró	bachelor	babbaró	bachelors

Geminate consonants (*t, d, k, m,* and *n*) may result from encliticization:

Agdáitto.	He/she will sew.
Tabbédda.	They are stupid.
Nagragsákkan!	How happy you are!
Sardámmo.	It is your evening.
Ayánna?	Where is he?

Gemination may also transcend prefix boundaries, where the coda consonant of the prefix matches the onset consonant of the root or following prefix.

   Naggatángam?   /nag-gátang-an=mo/
   'Where did you buy it?'

   pagattáo a sarmíng   /pagat-táo a sarmíng/
   'full-length mirror'

---

[1] In some cases, consonants will geminate due to their environment, such as intervocalically preceding two vowels and especially before the sequences *ia* and *ua*. No orthographic conventions have been established to reflect this gemination, so in the body of the dictionary, words will be spelled as they are most often found in texts. Common words like *takiág* 'arm' are pronounced [*tak.kiag*] but written with a single *k* in modern publications.

Certain prefixes may trigger consonant gemination, such as *agaC-/agat-* 'to smell like' or *pagaC-/pagat-* 'to reach until'.

> Pagabbarúkongnak.
> pagaC -barukong=na=ak
> reach-chest=3s=1s
> 'She reaches my chest'.

> Agattakkída.
> agaC -takki=da
> smell-excrement=3p
> 'They smell like excrement'.

Geminate nasals may be triggered by fusing a homorganic nasal [N] prefix to certain roots, in which the onset consonant appears as a nasal in the appropriate place of articulation.[2]

taráy	run	mannaráy	runner
dániw	poem	mannániw	poet
sugál	gamble	mannugál	gambler
duríken	mollusk	mannuríken	collector of mollusks
dáit	sew	mannáit	seamstress
bagí	body	pammagí	physique
páti	believe	pammáti	faith
umá	clear land	mangngumá	slash and burn farmer
saó	speak	pannaó	word

4. Glottal Stop

The glottal stop may occur in syllable-initial position or in onset position word-medially. As a variant of *k* or *t* before another consonant, the glottal stop may also appear in coda position. Unlike in Tagalog, there is no word-final glottal stop. In the orthography, word-initial glottal stop is never written, and word-medial glottal stop after a consonant is written with a hyphen.

As all syllables in Ilocano must have a consonantal onset, words that orthographically begin with a vowel are actually articulated with an initial glottal stop (See also section 6).

áso	[ʔá:.so]	dog
itá	[ʔi.tá]	now
úken	[ʔú:.kɯn]	puppy

Orthographic double vowels are articulated with an intervening glottal stop, as all syllables take a consonantal onset. In rapid speech, this may reduce to a mere audible syllable break.

mabiít	[ma.bi.ʔít]	short time
naalás	[na.ʔa.lás]	ugly
mapuóran	[ma.pu.ʔú:.ran]	be burned

---

[2] These actor (*maNN-*) and instrumental (*paNN-*) nominalizations result from the regular loss of an unstressed vowel following affixation of *maN-/paN-* + CV-: *Mannaray* < **mananaray*; *pammati* < **panamati* (Lawrence Reid, p.c.).

kées	[kúː.ʔúís]	crazy
agtaúl	[ʔag.ta.ʔúl]	bark
nagsaó	[nag.sa.ʔó]	spoke
daíten	[da.ʔíː.tʊɯn]	sew something
táo	[táː.ʔo]	man
saán	[sa.ʔán]	no
rúot	[rúː.ʔot]	grass

An initial glottal stop may be seen as an underlying consonant, as in the following reduplications of ʔVC sequences:

ad-addá	[ʔad.ʔad.dá]	more likely
ay-áyam	[ʔay.ʔáː.yam]	toy, game
kaing-íngas	[ka.ʔiŋ.ʔíː.ŋas]	resembling
in-ínut	[ʔin.ʔíː.nut]	gradually
ag-al-al-ál	[ʔag.ʔal.ʔal.ʔal]	panting

Fully reduplicated words or roots that begin with a glottal stop must commence with a glottal stop before the second reduplicated segment:

| maùlit-úlit | [ma.ʔúː.lit.ʔú.lit] | do repeatedly |
| inùlit-úlit | [ʔi.núː.lit.ʔúː.lit] | done repeatedly |

Word-medial glottal stop may be underlying. In this instance, it is written with a hyphen.

agug-óg	[ʔa.gug.ʔóg]	cry noisely
nasam-ít	[na.sam.ʔít]	sweet
agdiram-ús	[ʔag.di.ram.ʔús]	wash the face
agbariw-ás	[ʔag.ba.riw.ʔás]	turn abruptly
al-ó	[ʔal.ʔó]	pestle
buy-óng	[buy.ʔóng]	large belly

The consonants *k* and *t* may be pronounced as glottal stops before another consonant, the only environment where the glottal stop may appear in coda position.

pukráy	[puʔ.ráy]	ripening (squash)
pokló	[poʔ.ló]	angle brace
agtakdér	[ʔag.taʔ.duír]	stand up
itlóg	[ʔit.lóg]	egg
litnáw	[liʔ.náw]	clear, transparent

Certain prefixes when used before vowels require that the vowel be articulated with an initial glottal stop (see page xvii).

sinan-abógado	[si.nan.ʔa.bo.gáː.do]	fake lawyer
akin-úken	[ʔa.kin.ʔúː.kʊɯn]	owner of the puppy
makin-unég	[ma.kin.ʔu.núíg]	in the interior, inner
agin-uúlaw	[ʔa.gin.ʔù.ʔúː.law]	pretend to be dizzy

5. Morphophonemics
(Phonological Changes Due to Affixation)

a. The infix -*in*- may metathesize to *ni*- before *l* or *r* due to Tagalog influence. Both forms are found in spoken Ilocano but the non-metathesized form is preferred in writing.

nirugián	= r*in*ugián	started
nilúto	= l*in*úto	cooked
nilukatán	= l*in*ukatán	opened

b. The vowel *e* of many roots is often lost with affixation that causes it to become unstressed.

itdán	cf. itéd + -an	give to someone
ulsán	cf. ulés + -an	cover with blanket
pagablán	cf. pag- abél + -an	loom

c. With certain roots, single vowels may be lost with affixation:

kanén	cf. kaán + -en	eat something
tarimnén	cf. tarimáan + -en	fix
luktán	cf. lukát + -an	open

d. Many roots containing geminate consonants usually undergo two changes under affixation. The geminate consonant becomes single, and the unstressed or de-stressed vowel (often *e*) is lost:

maikatló	cf. maika- talló	third
lumtég	cf. lettég + -um-	swell
kadaklán	cf. ka- dakkél + -an	largest
pannakatnág	cf. pannaka- tinnág	act of falling
napnó	cf. na- punnó	full
nalpás	cf. na- leppás	finished
nakalpéng	cf. naka- leppéng	deafening
pannakapnék	cf. pannaka- pennék	satisfaction
bumták	cf. betták + -um-	crack; explode
rumsuá	cf. russuá + -um-	emerge
parsuá	cf. pa- + russuá	creation
sumgár	cf. seggár + -um-	bristle

e. Certain roots may add epenthetic consonants when affixed:

pas*r*ekén	cf. pa- serrék -en	let in, allow to enter
sum*b*rék	cf. serrék + -um-	enter
bis*r*áden	cf. bisrád + -en	spread open

f. The homorganic nasal (represented as *N* in the dictionary) assimilates to the first consonant of a root (N > -*ng* before velars *k*, *g*, sonorants *r*, *l*, *w*, *y*, and vowels; *m* before labials *m*, *p*, *b*; and *n* elsewhere). In some cases, the initial consonant of the root becomes a nasal:

pa*ng*ulotén	cf. paN- kulót -en	rather curly
ma*mm*áti	maN- páti	to believe
ma*ng*apkappó	maN- CVC- kappó	gathering clams
pan*n*áit	paN- dáit	thread

na*m*ituén	naN- bituén	starry
na*n*aksí	naN- saksí	witnessed
pa*m*igát	paN- bigát	breakfast
pa*ngng*eddéng	paN- keddéng	decision

g. In a few rare cases, high frequency roots with *t/d* onsets preceding an unstressed vowel may lose a syllable (*starred forms are not synchronically parsable):

manggéd	maN- teggéd	work
panggedán	paN- teggéd –an	employment
mangngég	maN- dengngég	hear, listen
makangég	maka- dengngég	be able to hear
pangngegán	paN- dengngég –an	insinuate, hint
mambí	maN- tibbí	cotton spinner
pagpagténg	pag- CVC- daténg	experiences
mapagténg	mapag- daténg	experience, undergo
makagténg	maka(pa)g- daténg	be able to arrive
pamkuátan	paN- *takkuát –an	reason for doing
pambár	paN- *tebbár	excuse

h. Some roots undergoing onomatopoetic affixation undergo internal modification resulting in the reduplication of their second vowel [V_2?V_2]. These affixes include: Voice affix + -V_2-, commonly seen with the following forms: *m{an}a*- -V_2-, *p{an}a*- -V_2-, *CaC*- -V_2-, *k{an}a*- -V_2-, and permutations thereof (Rubino 1999).

tumpáak	tupák -um- -V_2-	fall down with a thump
rumsíit	rissít -um- -V_2-	sizzle, hiss (burning meat)
palbaágen	pa- libág -V_2- -en	slam a door
palsuótan	pa- lisút -V_2- -an	shoot someone with a pop gun
dadpúor	CaC- dipór -V_2-	crumbling, rumbling sound
kaktúol	CaC- kitól -V_2-	clicking sound of heels
makakréeb	ma- CaC- kiréb -V_2-	crash (waves)
pababtuógen	pa- CaC- bitóg -V_2- -en	slam a door
mababséet	ma- CaC- bisét -V_2-	dart out; swish
kanadlúog	k{an}a- dilóg -V_2-	continuous thunder
kanakláang	k{an}a- kiláng -V_2-	successive clattering sounds
manarsíit	m{an}a- rissít -V_2-	produce a hissing/crackling sound
agkanarsibók	ag- k{an}a- rissibók -V_2-	make a loud splash
panalpaáken	p{an}a- lipák -V_2- -en	slap someone in the face
panarsaáken	p{an}a- rissák -V_2- -en	crush dry leaves
ipanabráang	i- p{an}a- biráng -V_2-	slam

6. Syllabification

Every syllable in native Ilocano words is composed of a consonantal onset and vowel, with an optional consonantal coda [CV(C)]. Geminate consonants cross syllable boundaries.

árak	[ʔá:.rak]	wine, alcohol
agsángit	[ʔag.sá:.ŋit]	to cry
nasam-ít	[na.sam.ʔít]	sweet

pagabbarúkong	[pa.gab.ba.rú:.koŋ]	reaching the chest
arasáas	[ʔa.ra.sa.ʔas]	whisper

Each vowel in Ilocano maintains its own syllable, except word-finally with a suffix in which the vowel becomes a glide. This rule holds true for all vowel combinations except *i* followed by *a, e, o,* or *u;* or *u* followed by *a, e,* or *i.*

babbái	[bàb.bá:.ʔi]	girls
agsaó	[ʔag.sa.ʔó]	speak
lakién	[lak.kyuín]	tomboy
babawién	[ba.baw.yuín]	regret
agintutúrog	[ʔa.gin.tù.tú:.rog]	pretend to sleep
rúot	[rú:.ʔot]	grass

but

siák	[ʃák]	I
diák	[dʒák]	I don't
siémpre	[ʃém.prɛ]	of course
diós	[dʒós]	god
siúman	[ʃú:.man]	stepchild
muák	[mwák]	without antlers (deer)
suér	[swuír]	bronze
suítik	[swí:.tik]	cheat

Two nondiphthongal vowels followed by vowel-initial suffixes become glides but do not lose their consonantal onset, except in high-frequency words such as *sao* 'speak' in rapid speech.

bai*én*	[ba.ʔyuín]	effeminate male
katatao*án*	[ka.ta.ta.ʔwan]	fiend, nonhuman spirit

but

saoén	[sa.ʔwuín]	say
or sawén	[sa.wuín]	"

GRAMMAR OUTLINE

This grammar outline is aimed primarily at introducing the fundamentals of Ilocano word formation that may assist readers in using this dictionary.[1] I will break up the grammar outline into grammatical classes and discuss morphological forms. For a more complete treatment of Ilocano morphology and a discussion of issues in Ilocano syntax, please see Rubino (1997).

SYNOPSIS FOR LINGUISTS: Ilocano, like its sister Philippine languages, is a predicate-initial language with a complex, head-marking, highly-prefixing morphology. Affixes denote a wide range of grammatical categories including aspect, focus, number, volition, transitivity, reciprocity, and some lexical categories such as pretense, smell, and relative size. Noun phrases may function as predicates and arguments. As arguments, they are usually preceded by noun markers (articles or demonstratives) that inflect for case (core vs. oblique), number (singular vs. plural), and time. Articles also inflect for reference (common vs. personal). Pronouns inflect for person, number, and case (ergative, absolutive, and oblique). There is an inclusive/exclusive distinction in the first person plural forms. When core (non-oblique) pronouns are used with predicates, they are enclitic. There is a pervasive particle (*nga/a*) used to link related constituents (heads and attributes) called a ligature (§12), and a number of uninflecting adverbial particles (§7.2). All roots (non–p/articles) may be nominalized or verbalized by morphology or syntactic function.

1. Pronouns

Ilocano has five sets of pronouns: independent absolutives, independent possessives, enclitic absolutives, enclitic ergative forms, and obliques. Pronouns in Ilocano encode person and number. The first person plural pronouns differentiate inclusivity (including the addressee: I/we + you) and exclusivity (excluding the addressee: we, but not you). Second person pronouns encode respect. Pronouns do not mark gender distinctions.

1.1 The independent absolutive pronouns are summarized below:[2]

siák	First person singular (I)
siká	Second person singular, informal pronoun (you)
isú(na)	Third person singular (he, she, it)
datá	First person dual inclusive (you and I)
dakamí	First person plural exclusive (we not you)
datayó	First person plural inclusive (I/we and you)
dakayó	Second person plural; second person singular formal (you sir or maam)
isúda	Third person plural (they); second person formal (more formal than *dakayo*).

Independent pronouns may stand alone in an utterance as full predicates. When a nominal appears in predicate position, it usually serves to identify or contrast a referent:

Asíno ti napán?	Who went?
Siák.	I (did).

[1] Special thanks to Nikolaus Himmelmann, Marianne Mithun, Lawrence Reid, and Chikao Yoshimura for their helpful comments on a previous version of this grammar outline.

[2] The regional variants *sitá, sikamí, sitayó,* and *sikayó* may replace *datá, dakamí, datayó,* and *dakayó*, respectively.

Isúna.	He/she (did).
Isúda.	They (did).
Siák ti napán idiáy Tagudín.	I (was the one who) went to Tagudin.
cf. Napának idiáy Tagudín.	I went to Tagudin.
Isúda ti nasadút.	They (are the ones who) are lazy.
cf. Nasadútda.	They are lazy.

When partially reduplicated, the independent pronouns express uniqueness:

sisiák	Only I
siksiká	Only you
Is-isú(na)	Only he/she
Dakdakamí.	Only us (exclusive).

1.2 The enclitic absolutive pronouns (=ak series)

The enclitic absolutive pronouns are referred to in the dictionary as the =ak series pronouns to avoid confusion among many linguistic traditions of naming them (absolutive, nominative, focus). In this grammar sketch, we will refer to them as absolutives, as they encode both single arguments of intransitive verbs and patient (object) arguments of transitive verbs, the absolutive category. As second position enclitics, they usually attach to the first constituent of their phrase. The absolutive (=ak series) paradigm is as follows:

Independent	=ak series pronoun	English gloss
siák	=ak[3]	I
siká	=ka	you
isú, isúna	Ø, isu	he, she
datá, sitá	=ta	you and I
dakamí	=kamí	we, not you
datayó	=tayó	we and you
dakayó	=kayó	you (pl); you (formal)
isúda	=da	they; you (very formal)
laláki	boy	
lalákiak	I am a boy	
nangán	ate	
nangánka	you ate	

Idí napánda idiáy Bacnótan, nagsángitkamí.
'When they went to Bacnotan, we cried'.

In negative constructions, the absolutive pronouns encliticize to the negative particle (saan or di) in the verb phrase, the first constituent of the verb phrase:

Saánda a nangán.	They did not eat.
Dída nangán.	They did not eat.

---

[3] The enclitic =ak takes the form =akó before the enclitic =(e)n, reflecting its origin.

1.3 The ergative enclitic pronouns

The ergative enclitic pronouns are used to indicate possession of a nominal (concrete noun or nominalization) and to indicate the actor of a transitive verb (see section 6). In the body of this dictionary, they are also referred to as the =ko series pronouns to avoid confusion in the many linguistic traditions of naming them (actor, nonfocus subject, genitive). As enclitics, they have the same morpho-syntactic properties as the =ak series pronouns. With verb phrases, they attach to the first constituent.

The =ko series paradigm is outlined below:

Independent	=ko series	English gloss
siák	=ko, =k	my
siká	=mo, =m	your
isú, isúna	=na	his, her
datá	=ta	our (dual, inclusive)
dakamí	=mi	our (exclusive)
datayó	=tayó	our (inclusive)
dakayó	=yo	your (plural); your (polite)
isúda	=da	their

The first and second person singular pronouns have two forms =ko, =k; and =mo, =m, respectively. The forms =k and =m are used after vowels and fuse with the suffixes =en or =an where the final -n of the suffix is lost, making these pronouns more like affixes than clitics:

baláyko	my house (f. baláy 'house')
púsam	your cat (f. púsa 'cat')
inumék	I (will) drink something. (f. inumén 'to drink something')
Intédko kenkuána.	I gave it to him.

Ilocano transitive verbs and possessed nouns may express both the actor and patient (or possessor/possessed) pronominally with enclitics. In this case, the =ko pronouns express the agent (or possessor) and the =ak pronouns express the patient (or possessed entity). Some of the forms have fused together and are now portmanteau enclitics that neutralize certain combinations, i.e. -mo/-na + -ak = -nak, -yo/-da + ak = -dak, -na + -ka = -naka, -da/-kami + -ka = -daka, etc.[4]

ACTOR ↓			←	P A T I E N T			→	
	siak	sika	isu	data	dakami	datayo	dakayo	isuda
siak	REFL	=ka	=k(o)	-	-	-	=kayo	=k(o) idá
sika	=nak	REFL	=m(o)	-	=nakami	-	-	=m(o) idá
isu	=nak	=naka	REFL/=na	=nata	=nakami	=natayo	=nakayo	=na idá
data	-	-	=ta	REFL	-	-	-	=ta idá
dakami	-	=daka	=mi	-	REFL	-	=dakayo	=mi idá
datayo	-	-	=tayo	-	-	REFL	-	=tayo idá
dakayo	=dak	-	=yo	=data	=dakami	-	REFL	=yo idá
isuda	=dak	=daka	=da	=data	=dakami	=datayo	=dakayo	REFL/=da idá

---

[4] Reflexive forms in this table are marked REFL. They are discussed in section 1.6.

Examples:

Tulóngandak man.	Please help me (you people).
Riingénnak intóno álas saís.	Wake me up at six.
Nakítadakamí idiáy simbáan.	They saw us in the church.
Díka pilíten nga ayaténnak.	I don't force you to love me.
Aw-awísendak nga agahedrés.	They are inviting me to play chess.
Abogádoka.	You are my lawyer.
Kasinsínnak.	I am your first cousin.
Lakáyko (isúna).	He is my husband.
Kayátka a manúgangen.	I want you as a son/daughter-in-law.

1.4 The oblique pronouns

The oblique pronouns are formed by adding the enclitic ergative (=*ko* series) pronouns to the stem *kania*- or with the personal oblique articles *ken* (singular) or *kadá* (plural).

Independent pronoun	Oblique pronoun	English gloss
siák	kaniák	to me
siká	kaniám, kenká	to you
isú	kaniána, kenkuána	to him, to her
datá	kaniáta, kadatá	to us (you and I)
dakamí	kaniámi, kadakamí	to us (not you)
datayó	kaniátayó, kadatayó	to us (and you)
dakayó	kaniáyo, kadakayó	to you (pl; polite)
isúda	kaniáda, kadakuáda	to them/ (or you polite)

Oblique pronouns are used to indicate direction toward a person or persons or transference of an object toward the party specified by the oblique pronoun:

Kinunána kadakamí.	He told it to us.
Napán kadakayó.	He went to you.
Naláwa kaniák.	It is loose on me.
Intédna kaniána.	He gave it to him/her.
Isu ti immáy kaniák.	He is the one who came to me.
Addá kaniák.	I have it. (It is with me.)
Adú kadakayó.	You people have a lot. (There is much with you.)

1.5 The independent possessive pronouns

There are two sets of independent possessive pronouns formed by attaching the =*ko* series pronouns to either of the stems *kukuá*- or *bági*- as shown in the following paradigm:

Independent	*bági*- GENITIVE	*kukuá*- GENITIVE	Gloss
siák	bágik	kukuák	mine
siká	bágim	kukuám	yours
isá, isúna	bágina	kukuána	his, hers
datá	bágita	kukuáta	ours (dual, incl)

dakamí	bágimi	kukuámi	ours (excl)
datayó	bágitayo	kukuátayo	ours (incl)
dakayó	bágiyo	kukuáyo	yours (pl; pol)
isúda	bágida	kukuáda	theirs

Makimbági daytóy?	Whose is this?
Bágik daytá.	That's mine.
Bágimon no kayátmo.	It's yours if you want it.
Kukuáda ti baláy.	The house is theirs.
Kukuámi ti dakkél a nuáng.	The large water buffalo is ours.

1.6 The reflexive pronouns

Reflexive pronouns in Ilocano are formed from the root *bagí* 'body' and an ergative enclitic. Notice the difference in stress between the reflexive pronouns and the independent pronouns outlined in section 1.5 from the stem *bági*.

Independent pronoun	Reflexive pronoun	English gloss
siák	bagík	myself
siká	bagím	yourself (singular)
isú	bagína	himself; herself; itself
datá	bagíta	ourselves (you and I
dakamí	bagími	ourselves (not you)
datayó	bagítayo	ourselves (and you)
dakayó	bagíyo	yourselves (pl; polite)
isúda	bagída	themselves (or you polite)

Ibílangyo ti bagíyo a nagásat.	Consider yourselves lucky.
Nakítana ti bagína iti sarmíng.	He saw himself in the mirror.
Bag-útem 'ta gayáng ken salakníbam ta bagím!	Unsheathe that spear and save yourself!
Pinatáyna ti bagína.	He killed himself.

2. Nouns

Ilocano nouns may be classified into personal nouns and nonpersonal nouns based on their morpho-syntactic behavior, the articles they take (see article section 3.1), and their plural formation. They may also consist of a simple root or a morphologically complex derived form (see section 2.3).

Nouns may appear in discourse as predicate arguments, oblique referents, and even predicates. Postpredicate nominal slots are introduced by determiners (articles or demonstratives).

| Napán ni Maria idiáy simbáan. | Mary went to church. |
| Ni Maria ti napán idiáy. | Mary is the one who went there. |

Nouns in initial position are predicative and must take a determiner if they are personal nouns.[5]

| Simbáan. | Church. It's a church. |
| Ni Maria. | Mary. It is/was Mary. |

---

[5] This excludes nouns used vocatively, which do not take articles.

2.1 Plural of nouns

Nouns are usually pluralized simply by introducing them with the appropriate plural form of the article or demonstrative.[6]

To emphasize plurality or distributiveness, however, nouns may be pluralized by CVC (consonant-vowel-consonant) reduplication of the initial sound sequence of the root, e.g. *sab-sábong* 'flowers (each individual flower; several flowers, different varieties of flowers; flowers here and there)', *balbaláy* 'houses', *tugtugáw* 'chairs', *púspuso* 'hearts', *bakbákes* 'monkeys'.

Nouns beginning with vowels are articulated with an initial glottal stop, since no Ilocano word may begin phonetically with a vowel. These nouns are pluralized by reduplicating the initial glottal stop, vowel, and following consonant of the root. Ilocano orthography does not represent the initial glottal stop; it is represented word-internally with a hyphen.

áso [ʔá:.so]	dog
as-áso [ʔas.ʔá:.so]	dogs

Nouns that begin with a CVV (consonant-vowel-vowel) sequence form their plural by reduplicating the initial consonant and vowel of the root. The plural form thus begins with an open syllable with a long vowel:

nuáng	water buffalo
nunuáng [nu:.nuáng]	water buffalos

Many kin terms and proper nouns (nouns taking the article *ni*) form their plural simply by reduplicating the initial CV (consonant-vowel) of the root, resulting in an open initial syllable.

baknáng → babaknáng	rich men
dakkél → dadakkél	parents
gayyém → gagayyém	friends
íkit → iíkit [ʔi.ʔi:.kit]	aunts
ípag → iípag [ʔi.ʔí:.pag]	sisters-in-law
kaarúba → kakaarúba	neighbors
kabsát → kakabsát	siblings
kailián → kakailián	townmates
kasinsín → kakasinsín	cousins
káyong → kakáyong	brothers-in-law
komádre → kokomádre	*komadres* (see dictionary)
masírib → mamasírib	wise men
ulitég → uulitég [ʔu.ʔu.li.tég]	uncles
siúman → sisiúman	stepchildren

The following terms denoting human referents form their plural simply by geminating (doubling) the first consonant of the second syllable of the root:

ádi → addí	younger siblings
amá → ammá	fathers
anák → annák	children
apó → appó	grandparents; grandchildren; gentlemen, etc.

---

[6] Verbs, nominalizations, and adjectives may also specify derivational plurality, with initial CV reduplication of the stem, which may be a root as in *Napipintasda* 'They are (all) pretty' or *Nagaabayda a naguray* 'They waited side by side'; or prefix as in *panagiinnapal ken panagpipinnadakesda* 'their envying and slandering one another'.

asáwa → assáwa	spouses
babái → babbái	girls
iná → inná	mothers
ingá → ingngá	girlfriends
laláki → lalláki	boys
ubíng → ubbíng	children

Finally, some common animate nouns have irregular plurals:

bakét → babbakét	old ladies
balásang → babbalásang	maidens (unmarried women)
bálo → babbálo	widows; widowers
baró → babbaró	young men
lakáy → lallakáy	old men
táo → tattáo	people

Plural articles or demonstratives preceding nouns also indicate plurality. They may be the sole indicator of plurality in a clause:

Nagsángit dagití lalaki/lalláki.	They boys cried.
Immáy dagití ulitégko/uulitégko.	My uncles came.

2.2 Gender of nouns

Ilocano has no grammatical gender. However, many Spanish loanwords have been introduced into the language that typically end in -a to indicate feminine gender:[7]

doktór	male doctor
doktóra	female doctor
emperadór	emperor
emperatrís	empress
mánong (Spanish *hermano* + -ng)	older brother
mánang (Sp. *hermana* + -ng)	older sister

Gender in nouns is sometimes expressed in Ilocano by separate lexical items:

amá & iná	father and mother
bakét & lakáy	old woman and old man
baró & balásang	bachelor (young man) and bachelorette (maiden)
bulá & takóng	boar and sow
kawítan & úpa	rooster and hen
káyong & ípag	brother-in-law and sister-in-law
laláki & babái	boy and girl
lólo & lóla	grandfather and grandmother
ulitég & íkit	uncle and aunt
tátang & nánang	father and mother

---

[7] Some words borrowed from colloquial Tagalog also indicate gender, -*oy* 'masculine' and -*ay* 'feminine'. These are recently innovated forms that reflect Spanish influence: *Pinoy* 'male Filipino', *Pinay* 'female Filipino', *Tisoy* 'fair-complexioned Filipino man', *Tisay* 'fair-complexioned Filipino woman'.

In order to differentiate gender, the appositives *a laláki* or *a babái* may be used to designate masculinity or femininity respectively.

kabsát a laláki	brother
kabsát a babái	sister
áding a laláki	younger brother
áding a babái	younger sister
anák a laláki	son
anák a babái	daughter

2.3 Morphological formation of nouns—nominal derivation

So far I have outlined only simple noun roots. Ilocano has two ways of forming nominals. Any lexeme in a nominal position (i.e., after an article or demonstrative) functions as a noun:

immáy	came
dagití immáy	the ones who came
nasingpét	well behaved, virtuous
ti nasingpét	the well-behaved person

Ilocano also has very productive derivational affixes that may nominalize a root that is typically not substantival. I will list a few of the most common and useful of these prefixes here.

2.3.1 Abstract nouns

Abstract nouns may be formed with the prefix *ka-* (with roots expressing quantity or dimension) or *kina-* (with stative roots). These substantives may be further elaborated with additional morphology (morpheme boundaries shown with hyphens):

adu	much, a lot
ka-adú	quantity
kina-adú	abundance
na-ngáto	high
ka-ngáto	height
kina-ngáto	highness
dákes	bad
kina-dákes	the badness, evil
ayát	love
manag-ayát	loving
kina-manag-ayát	loving nature

Some abstract nouns are formed by the prefix *ka-* with initial CV reduplication of the root morpheme:

bagás	rice	kababagás	meaning, essence
sáad	place	kasasáad	position
táo	man	katatáo	human nature
nákem	mind, will	kananákem	idea, opinion

2.3.2 Locative nouns

Location may be designated with the circumfix *pag- -an* (with a past form of *nag- -an*):

| ádal | study |
| pagadálan | school, place where one studies |

| langóy | swim |
| paglangoyán | swimming place, swimming pool |

The circumfix *ka- -an* is used to indicate the place where the entity denoted by the root exists in great quantities:

dárat	sand	kadarátan	sandy place
bayábas	guava	kabayabásan	guava orchard
úbas	grape	kaubásan	vineyard
manggá	mango	kamanggáan	mango plantation

2.3.3 Comitative/sharing nouns with *ka-*

The notion of concomitance or shared participation/possession is denoted by the prefix *ka-*. The perfective form is *kina-*. The prefix *ka-* may co-occur with reduplication or the suffix *-an*:

amá	father	kaamá	one having the same father
íli	town	kailián	townmate
ádal	study	kinaádal	former classmate
baláy	house	kabbaláy	housemate
rúpa	face	karuprúpa	one with a similar face
páyong	umbrella	kapáyong	one with whom an umbrella is shared

2.3.4 Reciprocity

The notion of reciprocity or rivalry is indicated by the infix *-inn-* placed before the first vowel of the root. These forms may also be nominalized with the suffix *-an*:

lemméng	hide	linnemmengán	hide-and-seek game
taráy	run	tinnaráy	racing with one another
pítak	mud	pinnitákan	throwing mud at one another
sírib	wise	sinniríban	competition of wits

The prefix *ag-* with kin terms indicates mutual relationship:

| amá | father | agamá | father and son |
| asáwa | spouse | agasáwa | married couple |

iná	mother	aginá	mother and child
siúman	stepchild	agsiúman	stepchild and stepparent
ulitég	uncle	agulitég	uncle and nephew (or niece)

2.3.5 Resemblance

The prefixes *sinan-* and *mara-* are used to indicate the resemblance of the derived word to the entity designated by the root morpheme. Most words with these prefixes are lexicalized:

táo	man	sinantáo	like a human being, humanoid
bilóg	outrigger	sinambilóg	toy outrigger boat
balitók	gold	sinambalitók	fool's gold, goldlike substance
baláy	house	sinambaláy	play house
pána	arrow	sinampána	pointing arrow (not a real arrow)
allawági	carpenter	sinan-allawági	novice carpenter
dágum	needle	maradágum	young cowpea (like a needle)

Reduplication may also be employed to indicate resemblance, as shown by the following lexicalized items:

anák	child	an-annák	doll (like a child)
bató	stone	batbató	shell
bánga	pot	bangabánga	skull
dágum	needle	dagumdágum	sting (of a bee, etc.)
tukák	frog	túkaktúkak	wart

2.3.6 Ownership

Ownership is expressed in Ilocano by the prefixes *akin- (akim-)* or *makin-*:

kuá	thing	akinkuá	owner
manók	chicken	akinmanók	owner of the chicken
anák	child	makin-anák	(father or mother) of the child
baláy	house	akinbaláy	owner of the house

2.3.7 Origin

Origin or nationality is expressed by the prefix *tagá-*. A hyphen is used in Ilocano spelling between the prefix and root if the root noun is capitalized. In some Ilocano localities, this prefix has the regional variant *i-*.

amiánan	north	tagáamiánan	person from the north
Ilókos	Ilocos region	tagá-Ilókos	person from the Ilocos region
Amérika	America	tagá-Amérika	American
Espánia	Spain	tagá-Espánia	Spaniard, person from Spain

2.3.8 Kinship

The prefix *kapi(n)-* is used with numerical roots over one to indicate the exact degree of kindred.

duá	two	kapiduá	second cousin
talló	three	kapitló	third cousin
uppát	four	kapimpát	fourth cousin
limá	five	kapinlimá	fifth cousin
sangapúlo	ten	kapinsangapúlo	tenth cousin

2.3.9 Complex nominalizations of verbs

Ilocano morphology allows extensive nominalization of verbs through various affixes. The major verb classes and their most frequent nominalization patterns, formed off intransitive verbs, are outlined below. Please refer to the body of the dictionary for further explanations of the various affixes:

Mode	Verbal Affix	Gerund (Manner)	Instrument	Locative/Reason	
				Neutral	Perfective
Dynamic	ag-	panag-	pag-	pag- -an	nag- -an
	-um-	iCV-	-	-um- -an	-imm- -an
	mang-	panang-	pang-	pang- -an	nang- -an
	mangi-	panangi-	pangi-	pangi- -an	nangi- -an
	mangipa-	panangipa-	pangipa-	pangipa- -an	nangipa- -an
	mangpa-	panangpa-	pangpa-	pangpa- -an	nangpa- -an
	mangpai-	panangpai-	pangpai-	pangpai- -an	nangpai- -an
	mangpag-	panangpag-	pangpag-	pangpag- -an	nangpag- -an
Potentive	maka-	pannaka-	paka-	paka- -an	naka- -an
	makai-	pannakai-	pakai-	pakai- -an	nakai- -an
	makaipa-	pannakaipa-	pakaipa-	pakaipa- -an	nakaipa- -an
	makapa-	pannakapa-	pakapa-	pakapa- -an	nakapa- -an
	makapai-	pannakapai-	pakapai-	pakapai- -an	nakapai- -an
	makapag-	pannakapag-	pakapag-	pakapag- -an	nakapag- -an
	makapagi-	pannakapagi-	pakapagi-	pakapagi- -an	nakapagi- -an
Social	maki-	pannaki-	paki-	paki- -an	naki- -an
	makipag-	pannakipag-	pakipag-	pakipag- an	nakipag- -an
	makipagi-	pannakipagi-	pakipagi-	pakipagi- -an	nakipagi- -an

agsúrat	write
panagsúrat	act of writing
pagsúrat	writing implement
pagsurátan	place where someone writes
nagsurátan	place where someone wrote
pannakisinnúrat	writing to one another
sumangpét	arrive
isasangpét	arrival
makikúyog	accompany
pakikúyog	companion
pakikuyógan	reason for accompanying
matúrog	sleep
pakaturógan	reason why someone sleeps
pagturógan	place where someone sleeps

3. Articles and Demonstratives

3.1 Articles

Articles in Ilocano encode number (singular and plural), two cases (core and oblique), and differentiate personal nouns (names, vocatives, etc.) from non-personal nouns as shown in the following paradigm:

Non-personal articles

	Core	Oblique
Singular	ti	ití
Plural	dagití	kadagití

Personal articles

	Core	Oblique
Singular	ni	kenní (ken ni)
Plural	da	kadá

The core and oblique distinction in Ilocano can be summarized in the following way. Core nouns may be morphological arguments of verbs. They may be replaced by an enclitic pronoun of either the =ko or =ak series. Oblique nouns, however, are not verbal arguments in that they cannot be replaced by enclitic pronouns, although they may play an essential role in the semantic frame of a verb.

Grammatically intransitive verbs in Ilocano may take one enclitic pronoun in the =ak series. When this particular argument appears as a full noun phrase, it takes core case marking:

nangán; nagsángit	ate (intransitive); cried (intransitive)
Nangának.	I ate.
Nangán ti babái.	The girl ate.
Nagsángitda.	They cried.

Intransitive verbs may take an indefinite notional patient or object in the oblique case.

Nangának iti dinadaráan.	I ate blood pudding.
Nangán ti babai iti pariá.	The girl ate bittermelon.

Transitive verbs, on the other hand, take two core arguments. When encoding two arguments by enclitic pronouns, the actor of the action is encoded by the =ko series pronouns (ergative case), while the non-actor takes absolutive case (=ak series pronouns). All noun phrases in these cases are given core case marking; all other nouns are peripheral and encoded in the oblique.

nakíta	saw (transitive)
Nakítanak.	She saw me.
Nakítanak ni Maria.	Maria saw me.
Nakíta ti babái ti laláki iti madióngan.	The girl saw the boy at the mahjong parlor.
itéd	give (transitive)
Intédko ti kuartá kenní Juan.	I gave the money to Juan.
Intédko kadakuáda.	I gave it to them.
kinnán	ate (transitive)
Kinnán dagití babbái ti baradibód.	The girls ate the sweet potato porridge.

3.2 Demonstratives

Ilocano demonstratives, like the articles, also inflect for plurality and case. There are no special forms, however, to differentiate personal nouns from non-personal ones. Ilocano demonstratives are traditionally classified with regard to three degrees of space and time.

3.2.1 Spatial demonstratives

Ilocano demonstratives mark three degrees of spatial orientation: proximal, medial, and distal. Proximal demonstratives mark nouns near the speaker, medial demonstratives mark nouns near the addressee, or slightly far from both, while distal demonstratives are used to indicate the distance of the noun to the speech event. The forms are given in the following paradigm:

	Proximal	Medial	Distal
Core			
Singular	daytóy	daytá	daydiáy
Plural	dagitóy	dagitá	dagidiáy
Oblique			
Singular	iti daytóy	iti daytá	iti daydiáy
	kadaytóy	kadaytá	kadaydiáy
Plural	kadagitóy	kadagitá	kadagidiáy

The singular demonstratives *daytóy, daytá,* and *daydiáy* have abbreviated forms *'toy, 'ta* and *'diay,* respectively, which are used in Ilocano discourse like the articles. The full demonstratives may be connected to their nouns with the ligature *(ng)a*, while the abbreviated articles may not:

Naglúto daydiáy (a) laláki.	That boy cooked.
Naglúto 'diáy laláki.	The/That boy cooked.
Intédko ti baláy kadagidiáy lallakáy.	I gave the house to those old men.
Nailét ití daydiáy a balasáng.	It's tight on that maiden.

3.2.2 Past (out of sight) demonstratives

Past demonstratives indicate nouns that are not visible at the time of the speech event. These are called recent past and remote past demonstratives and are detailed in the following chart:

	Recent past	Remote past
Core		
Singular	daytáy ('tay)	daydí ('di)
Plural	dagitáy	dagidí
Oblique		
Singular	kadaytáy	kadaydí
	iti daytáy	iti daydí
Plural	kadagitáy	kadagidí

Recent past demonstratives are used with specific referents that are not immediately accessible or visible during the speech event:

Aniá daytáy náganna?	What was her name (again)?
Ayán dagitáy tulbékko?	Where are my keys? (I had them just a while earlier).

Remote past demonstratives are often used with people who are deceased or things that no longer exist:

Nalipátak ti nágan daydí gayyémko.	I forgot the name of my (long lost) friend.
Nagparáng daydí lólom.	Your (deceased) grandfather appeared (in an apparition, etc.).

3.2.3 Future marker

Ilocano has a marker used to form temporal expressions with future time reference. The marker usually appears in one of the four forms: *intón, intóno, tóno,* or *ton.*

bigát	morning	intóno bigát	tomorrow
rabií	night	intóno rabií	tonight
malém	afternoon	intóno malém	in the afternoon

4. Adjectives

Adjectives[8] in Ilocano may be predicative or attributive. Many Ilocano adjectives are formed with the prefix *na-*. This form is identical to the perfective aspect of the stative *ma-* verb:

laíng	intelligence	nalaíng	intelligent
alsém	sourness, acidity	naalsém	sour
ángin	wind	naángin	windy
pigsá	strength	napigsá	strong

---

[8] The lexical class of adjectives differs formally from verbs since members of the class do not inflect for aspect and do not assign focus. Adjectives, unlike verbs, may also follow the modifying adverb borrowed from Spanish *medio* 'somewhat' > *medio natangkén* 'somewhat hard'.

káyo	tree	nakáyo	with many trees
kaldíng	goat	nakaldíng	with many goats
singpét	virtue	nasingpét	virtuous, well behaved
baknáng	wealth	nabaknáng	rich
asúk	smoke	naasúk	smoky

Some Ilocano adjectives denoting an intrinsic quality begin with a fossilized (no longer productive) prefix *a-*:

ababá	short	akába	broad
abábaw	shallow	akíkid	narrow
adálem	deep	atiddóg	long

Some adjectives are formed with the prefix *ma-*. Notice the meaning changes in the first three when the same adjectives are used with the prefix *na-*:

maíngel	valiant (*naíngel*: strong [liquor, tobacco]).
masakít	sick (*nasakít*: sore, aching)
maúyong	crazy, insane (*naúyong*: cruel, mean)
mabíleg	strong, full grown, potent
manákem	reasonable, logical, judicious
masírib	wise, educated

Finally, a few adjectives are simple roots. Many adjectives in this class refer to physical attributes or defects:

Basic adjectives:

baró	new
bassít	small
dáan	old
dakkél	large
puráw	white

Physical/mental attributes:

buldíng	blind in one eye
bulsék	blind
bungí	toothless
kusipét	with almond eyes
kuskós	bald
leppáp	flat nosed
pangkís	cross-eyed
páwad	with one arm or hand
putót	without a tail
rísay	with ears torn
rukapí	with coupled teeth
suriáb	with deformed upper lip
tabbéd	stupid
tammí	with protruding chin
túleng	deaf
tuppól	with missing teeth

4.1 Placement of adjectives

Adjectives may either precede or follow the noun they attribute, separated by the ligature *(ng)a*. Adjectives used to contrast nouns usually follow.

ti nasingpét nga ubíng	the well-behaved child
ti ubíng a nasingpét	the well-behaved child (as opposed to the naughty ones)
ti áso a nalaíng	the intelligent dog

Adjectives indicating the composition or material of the qualified noun also follow:

ti tulbék a balitók	the gold key
ti ruángan a bató	the stone door
ti tugáw a landók	the iron chair

4.2 Intensification and derivation of adjectives

The quality of an adjective may be intensified by adding the prefix *nag-* and the enclitic *=(e)n* to the root. This form is usually used to express wonder or admiration:

adú	much, a lot	nagadún	so many!
napintás	beautiful	nagpintásen	how beautiful!
nalukmég	fat	naglukmégen	how fat!

Adjectives may also be intensified with the prefix *nakaCVC-* or with the adverb *unay*:

naángot	smelly	nakaang-ángot, naangot unay	stinking very much
nasakít	sore	nakasaksakít, nasakit unay	very sore
katáwa	laughter	nakakatkatáwa	funny

The affix *paN- -en* is used to moderate the degree of the adjective:

nalukmég	fat	panglukmegén	rather stout
kulót	curly	pangulotén	curly, wavy
dakkél	big	panakkelén	quite big, large

The affix *nain- -an* derives abstract adjectives.

kappiá	peace	nainkappiáan	peaceful
púso	heart	naimpusuán	sincere

4.3 Comparatives and superlatives

4.3.1 The comparative degree

The comparative degree of the adjective is formed by reduplicating the first CVC sequence of the root:

dákes	bad	dakdákes	worse
naimbág	good	naim-imbág	better

nakuttóng	thin	nakutkuttóng	thinner
narugít	dirty	narugrugít	dirtier

The disjunctive conjunction *ngem* 'but' links two nouns in a comparative construction.

Naluklukmégka ngem ni Sergio.	You are fatter than Sergio.
Nabakbaknángak ngem siká.	I am richer than you.

Ilocano has a conditional superlative formed with the prefix *sumangka-*.

No napúdaw ni Gloria, sumangkapúdaw ni Maria.
If Gloria is fair complexioned, Maria is even more so.

No tabbéd ti lakáymo, sumangkatabbéd ti bakétko.
If your husband is stupid, my wife is even stupider.

4.3.2 The superlative degree

The superlative degree is expressed with the circumfix *ka- -an*:

nasadút	lazy	kasadután	laziest
naimbág	good	kaimbagán	best
dakkél	large, big	kadak(ke)lán	largest, biggest

Isú ti kasadután nga ubíng.	He is the laziest child.
Siká ti kaimbáganda ámin.	You are the best of them all.
Asíno ti kasingpetán?	Who is the most virtuous?

5. Numbers

5.1 Cardinal numbers

Ilocano numbers follow a decimal system (of base ten). The cardinal numbers from one to nine are: 1. maysá; 2. duá; 3. talló; 4. uppát; 5. limá; 6. inném; 7. pitó; 8. waló; 9. siám.

Numbers over nine are formed by counting in terms of the following base-ten groups:

púlo	group of ten
gasút	group of one hundred
ríbo	group of one thousand
laksá	group of ten thousand
riwríw	group of one million

Decimal groups are counted by the cardinal numbers from one to nine, separated by the ligature *(ng)a* if the base number ends in a consonant. One group of a particular decimal number is represented by the prefix *sanga-* attaching to the unit.

sangapúlo	ten (one group of ten)
sangapúlo ket maysá	eleven

duapúlo	twenty
tallopúlo	thirty
uppát a púlo	forty (four groups of ten)
limapúlo	fifty
inném a púlo	sixty
pitopúlo	seventy
walopúlo	eighty
siám a púlo ket maysá	ninety-one
sangagasút duapúlo ket inném	one hundred twenty-six
siám a riwríw, sangapúlo ket pitó.	nine million seventeen

As adjectives, numbers are linked to the nouns they count by the ligature *(ng)a*:

inném a riwríw, siám a gasút, tallopúlo ket limá a pisos
six million nine hundred thirty-five pesos

5.2 Ordinal numbers

Ordinal numbers are formed by joining the prefix *maika-* to the cardinal number. 'First' is represented by the word *umuna* (past: *immuna*), from the Spanish loanword *una*.

Immunáak.	I was first; I went first.
Aláem ti maikapát.	Get the fourth one.
Siká ti maikasangapúlo a táo.	You are the tenth person.

Note the phonological alternations with this prefix when used with the numbers having geminate consonants: *tallo, uppat,* and *innem*:

talló	three	maikatló	third
uppát	four	maikapát	fourth
inném	six	maikaném	sixth

5.3 Counting in groups

The prefix *sanga-* is used to specify one group of or one unit of. It is used for all units of length, capacity, time, etc., as well as numbers. When used for units, its variant is *sangka-*:

púlo	group of ten	sangapúlo	ten (one group of ten)
ríbo	one thousand	sangaríbo	one thousand
ígup	swallow	sangkaígup	one swallow of, draught
deppá	armspan	sangad(ep)pá	one armspan
kabán	twenty-five gantas	sangakabán	one unit of twenty-five gantas
íwa	slice	sangaíwa	one slice of
lámut	put in mouth	sangalámut	one mouthful

The suffix *-an* may be attached to the *sang(k)a-* measurements to nominalize the concept of measurement. Many of these formatives are lexicalized:

pútot	father a child	sangaputútan	one generation
baláy	house	sangkabbalayán	one household

| sapátos | shoes | sangasapatósan | one pair of shoes |
| lúbong | world | sangalubóngan | whole world, universe |

5.4 Indefinite numbers

Indefinite (nonspecific) numbers are formed by the prefix *sumag-* with initial CV reduplication of the root:

sumagpapátda a nagtálaw	about four of them escaped
sumaglilimá ti nagáwid	about five went home
Sumagmamanóda?	About how many are they?

5.5 Limitative numbers

Cardinal numbers have reduplicated limitative forms. The prefix *sang(k)a-* may also be reduplicated to express limitation:

maymaysá	only one
sangsangakabán	only one kavan (of rice)
Duduáda ti napán.	Only two of them went.

5.6 Fractional numbers

Fractional numbers are formed by prefixing the denominator of the fraction with *pagka-*.

maysá a pagkaném	one-sixth
limá a pagkawaló	five-eighths
maysá a pagkagasút	one percent (1/100)

The prefix *agka-* (perfective: *nagka-*) is used with numerical roots to indicate into how many parts something is divided:

| Agkalimánto ti kaldíng. | The goat will be divided into five parts. |
| Agkalimá ti bálonmi. | Our provisions will be divided into (will have) five parts. |

5.7 Multiplicatives

Multiplicative adverbial numbers are formed by adding the prefix *mami(n)-* (past: *nami(n)-*) to the numerical root. The numerical root undergoes the same phonological alternations with this prefix as with the prefix *maika-* in section 5.2.

maminsán	once
maminduá	twice
mamitló	three times
mamimpát	four times
maminlimá	five times
mamin-adú	often

Naminpitóak a nangán.	I ate seven times.
Naminwalóda a nagayáb.	They called eight times.

The multiplicative ordinal numbers are formed by the prefix *kapami(n)-*. These particular numbers take the *=ko* series pronouns:

Kapamitlóna ti mapán.	This is his third time to go.
Kapaminlimádansa ti mangán.	I think this is their fifth time to eat.

5.8 Distributives

Distributive cardinal numbers are formed by the prefix *sag-*, usually with CV reduplication, as shown below:

maysá	one	saggaysá	one each
duá	two	sagduduá	two each
talló	three	saggatló	three each
uppát	four	sagpapát	four each
limá	five	saglilimá	five each
inném	six	sagniném	six each
pitó	seven	sagpipitó	seven each
waló	eight	sagwawaló	eight each

Sagwawaló ti innálami.	We took eight each.
Sagpapátkayó.	Go in groups of four; Take four each.
Sagpipísos ti sabá.	The bananas are one peso each.

Distributive multiplicatives are formed by the prefix *sagpami(n)-*:

Sagpaminlimá.	each five times
Sagpamintallopúloda.	They did it each thirty times.
Sagpaminwalónakamí a binaútan.	He beat us each eight times.

6. Verbs

An interesting feature about Ilocano (and other Philippine languages) is that every root in the language that can act as a noun can also be transformed into a verb by means of syntactic placement or verbalizing morphology. Because the initial position is reserved for the predicate, any noun in that position may take on a predicative function. Conversely, verbs may occur in nominal functions (after articles or demonstratives). Ilocano does not have a copular (*to be*) verb:

káyo	tree; It is a tree.
Napán.	He went.
ti napán	the one who went

daytóy káyo	this tree
Káyo daytóy.	This is a tree.

laláki	boy.
Laláki.	He is a boy.

There are numerous morphological affixes that combine with roots to give them verblike qualities (i.e., aspect [tense], mode, volition, transitivity). Words with these particular morphemes will be considered 'verbs' in this grammar sketch, forming a separate lexical class from nouns.

6.1 The categories of verbs

6.1.2 Focus (verbal orientation) and transitivity

One notable distinction present in every affixed verb is the encoding of what has been termed 'focus' in Philippine linguistics, referring to formal marking that reflects the privileged syntactic status of the absolutive noun phrase. Ilocano verbs assign 'focus' to their absolutive nominal (=ak pronoun NP), the nominal in the most syntactically privileged position in terms of the semantic and grammatical relationship the nominal has with the verb. Simple intransitive verbs such as ag-, -um- and mang- verbs, for instance, take at most one core nominal as the argument whose semantic relationship to the verb is usually 'actor' or single-argument 'experiencer'.

Nagsángit ti balásang.	The unmarried woman cried.
Timmugáwda.	They sat down.
Nangánkamín.	We already ate.
Agap-ápada.	They are fighting.
Ngimmísitdan.	They got dark (from the sun).

Certain affixes, however, such as -en and -an, encode transitive frames that may assign two nominals in core case, an agent (actor) encoded in the ergative case, and a nonactor (patient, location, recipient, benefactor, reason, or theme, etc.) encoded in the absolutive case. Since the absolutive argument in focus for these verbs is a nonagent/actor, they are called "goal focus verbs". Because these verbs can take two core nominals, they are grammatically transitive.

Nakítanakán.	Tinákawda ti nuáng.
'He already saw you'.	'They stole the water buffalo'.
Kayátdaka.	Ay-ayaténnak?
'They want you'.	Do you love me?

Verbs are thus classified in semantic terms, by the semantic relationship between the verb and the role of the referent indicated by their absolutive argument. The following table illustrates these classifications with a brief overview of their use.

Summary of Major Focus Types

Macro Role	Semantic Role	Transitivity	Focus Affix
Actor	Various, usually actor	Intransitive	ag- -um-
		Detransitive	mang-
Goal (nonactor)	Patient	Transitive	-en
	Directional		-an
	Theme		i-
	Benefactive		i- -an
	Instrumental		pag-
	Comitative		ka-

Actor focus

Actor focus verbs take at most one core argument in the absolutive case whose relationship to the verb is that of 'actor' (semantic agent or experiencer). Actor focus verbs may be formed with the prefixes *ag-* (durative), *ma-/maka-* (stative or potentive), or the infix *-um-* (punctual or inchoative). Transitive verbs may be detransitivized with *mang-* (distributive).

Naglútokamí.	We (without you) cooked.
Naglúto dagití ansisít	The dwarfs cooked.
Naglayláy ti sábong.	The flower wilted.
Ngimmísitkan!	You got darker!
Naglayláyda.	They wilted.
Naglayláy ti sábong.	The flower wilted.
Nangánakón.	I already ate.
Nangán diáy balásang.	The unmarried woman ate.
Limmukmégdan!	They got fat!
Natúrogak idiáy siléd ni Akong.	I slept in Akong's room.

Many verbs denoting natural phenomena do not take formal arguments in Ilocano but they are classified as actor focus verbs because they do not vary in form.

Nagtúdo.	It rained.
Nagkimát.	Lightning flashed.
Nagbagió.	It stormed.
Nagarbís.	It drizzled.
Naglayós.	It flooded.

Goal focus distinctions

Goal focus verbs are classified by affix type on the basis of what semantic relationship the argument in the absolutive case has with the verb.

Patient focus

Patient focus verbs take an argument in the absolutive case whose semantic role with respect to the verb is that of a 'patient' (an affected entity or target of the action of the verb). The patient focus suffix is *-en* (perfective *-in-*). The suffix *-en* typically forms transitive verbs in which the absolutive argument is directly affected by a volitional actor.

Root	Patient focus verb	English gloss
súrat 'write'	suráten	to write something
kaán 'eat'	kanén	to eat something
kíta 'see'	kitáen	to look at something
dáit 'sew'	daíten	to sew something
bása 'read'	basáen	to read something

Sinipátna diáy ubíng.
'She spanked the child'. (Perfective form of *sipatén*)

Sinúratko ti sarsuéla.
'I wrote the opera'. (Perfective form of *suráten*)

Aniá't kinnánmo?
'What did you eat?' (Perfective form of *kanén*)

Directional focus

The directional focus is formed with the suffix *-an*. It indicates that the absolutive argument is a locative of some kind or some kind of partially affected patient. The suffix *-an* may also be used with certain verbs to indicate addition or removal. It is used with many roots to indicate a human patient in the case frame, i.e., *takáwen* 'to steal something' vs. *takáwan* 'to rob someone'. The morphological cover term *directional focus* is reserved for the *-an* verb class, not because of the semantic properties shared by all the members of the class, but due to certain semantic changes that may indicate the direction or location of an action with a number of roots, i.e., *sagáden* 'to sweep (dirt)' vs. *sagádan* 'to sweep (the floor)'.

Root	*-an* verb	English gloss (verb)
adayó 'far'	adaywán	to get away from
túlong 'help'	tulóngan	to help someone
aluád 'care'	aluádan	to heed
ságad 'sweep'	sagádan	to sweep (the floor)
bása 'read'	basáan	to read to someone
súrat 'write'	surátan	to write to

Sinagádanna ti datár.
'He swept the floor'.

Sinurátamon ni lólom?
'Did you write your grandfather already?'

Theme focus

The prefix *i-* forms theme focus verbs, putting the 'theme' in absolutive position. The theme is the entity whose location is at issue (Foley and Van Valin 1984:51). Absolutive arguments of theme focus verbs are typically objects that are transferred, implemented, or affected (physically or psychologically) by means expressed in the root. Among the major verbs in this focus category are:

Root	Theme focus verb	Gloss
pan 'go'	ipán	to bring
ruár 'outside'	iruár	to put outside, take outside
áwid 'go home'	yáwid	to take home, bring home
ted 'give'	itéd	to give
kastóy 'like this'	ikastóy	to do like this
bolsa 'pocket'	ibolsa	to put in the pocket

Inyáwidna ti suká ken buggóong.
'He brought home the vinegar and fish paste'.

Itédmo ti pansít kenni kabsátmo.
'Give the noodles to your sibling'.

Benefactive focus

The absolutive argument of benefactive verbs is usually the beneficiary of an action, but in some cases the person encoded in the absolutive case can be seen as having the action of the verb done in his/her place rather than for his/her benefit. It is formed with the circumfix *i- -an* (past: *in -an*), morphologically a combination of a theme prefix and a directional suffix.

Root	Benefactive verb	English gloss
dáit 'sew'	idaítan	to sew for someone
lúto 'cook'	ilutuán	to cook for someone
arámid 'do, make'	yaramídan	to do, make for someone
ála	yaláan	to get something for someone

Indaítak ni Maria ití bádo.
'I sewed a dress for Mary'.

No kayátmon ti mangán, ibagám ta idasárankan.
'If you want to eat already, say so and I'll set the table for you'.

Instrumental focus

The instrumental focus places the instrument or tool used to carry out the action in the absolutive case. It is formed by the prefix *pag-* (past: *pinag*). Because of the semantic and pragmatic nature of this particular focus, derived *pag-* words usually appear in discourse as non-predicative nouns.

Root	Instrumental verb	English gloss
tugáw 'chair; sit'	pagtugáw	to use as a chair; chair
súrat 'write'	pagsúrat	to use for writing; pen
dáit 'sew'	pagdáit	to use for sewing; sewing materials
báut 'thrash'	pagbáut	to use for thrashing; whipping stick

Pinagdáitna ti dágum. Awán ti pagbádok.
'He used the needle to sew'. 'I have nothing to wear' (use as clothes).

Comitative focus

The comitative focus places the party with whom the action is performed in the absolutive case. It is formed by the prefix *ka-* (past: *kina-*). Like verbs in instrumental focus, these *ka-* lexical items behave more like prototypical nouns but may also appear predicatively and denote aspect.

Root	Comitative verb	English gloss
saó 'speak'	kasaó	speak with someone; talking partner
tugáw 'sit'	katugáw	sit with someone; seatmate
ay-áyam 'play'	kaay-áyam	play with someone; playmate

túrog 'sleep'	katúrog	sleep with someone; sleepmate
páyong 'umbrella'	kapáyong	share an umbrella with
lúgan 'ride'	kalúgan	share a ride with

Kinasaók ni Maria.	Asíno ti kinatungtúngmo?
'I spoke with Maria'.	'With whom did you converse?'
Ni Pedro ti kinatugáwko.	Kasaóm iti Ilokáno.
'I sat with Pedro'.	'Speak with him in Ilocano'.

6.1.3 Potentive and stative mode

The prefixes *maka-* (intransitive) and *ma-* are used to form potentive verbs. Verbs in the potentive mode can designate a variety of distinctions: the ability or opportunity to perform an action, coincidental activity, accidental activity, and involuntary activity (activities performed without control or prior intent).

Contrast the following verbs in potentive mode (*ma(ka)-*) with their dynamic (unmarked) counterparts (shown with the roots *gatang* 'buy' and *dungpar* 'crash, collide'):

gum*átang*	to buy (intentionally)
ag*gátang*	to go shopping, buy
*maka*gátang	to be able to buy; to happen to buy; to purchase accidentally
dungpár*en*	to crash into someone (on purpose)
*ma*dungpár	to crash into someone (on accident)
*Ina*tálak ti billít.	I ran over the bird (on purpose).
*Naa*tálak isúna.	I accidentally ran over him.
*Iná*watko ti kuartá.	I got the money (with effort).
*Naá*watmo ti súratko?	Did you receive my letter?
*Naá*ngotko ti pabanglóna.	I smelled her perfume.
*Iná*ngotko ti pabanglóna.	I sniffed her perfume.

The prefix *ma-* (perfective form *na-*) is also used to form involuntary or stative verbs (and adjectives) that take only one core argument in the absolutive case.

*ma*ldáang	to be sad
*ma*úyong	to be crazy
*ma*lmés	to drown
*ma*tnág	to fall

With the suffix *-an*, the prefix *ma-* indicates nonvolitional or abilitative agency. The resulting verbs can be intransitive resultatives (in many cases where the agent is expressed in the root) or transitive potentives, where the agent is expressed in the ergative case.

Intransitive verbs:

*ma*rabiiyán	to be overtaken by the night
*ma*pudótan	to be warmed up
*ma*atálan	to be run over
*ma*gasángan	to be affected by spice
*Naa*tálanak idí kalmán.	I was run over yesterday.
*Naga*sánganak.	I was affected by the spice.

Transitive verbs:

*maa*tálan	to be able to run over someone; accidentally run over
*maa*wát*an*	to (be able to) understand
*ma*sabidóng*an*	to be able to poison; happen to poison
Saánko a *maa*wát*an*.	I don't understand it.
Dinak *ma*sabidong*an*.	You can't poison me.
*Naa*tala*k* isúna.	I accidentally ran over him.
*Na*puór*an*na ti baláy.	He accidentally burned down the house.

6.2 Detransitivizing strategies for goal focus verbs

All goal focus (grammatically transitive) verbs in Ilocano can be changed into actor focus (grammatically intransitive) verbs with detransitivizing affixes. This strategy is employed either to form the antipassive, whereby an unindividuated patient (grammatical object) is put into the oblique case and rendered indefinite, or it is used when the verb must be detransitivized as required by the syntax, as in relative clause formation (see section 13.1). Note the differences between the following sentences with transitive verbs and their detransitivized counterparts:

Kinnánko ti sabá.	I ate the **banana**. (Transitive verb, core patient)
Nangának ití sabá.	I ate bananas. (Intransitive verb, oblique patient)
Ginatángna ti sidá.	He bought the fish. (Transitive verb, core patient)
Gimmátang ití sidá.	He bought fish. (Intransitive verb, oblique patient)

The following chart shows the particular affixes used to detransitivize a transitive verb:

Focus type	Transitive	Detransitive/*Intransitive
patient	-en	mang-
directional	-an	mang-
theme	i-	mangi-
benefactive	i- -an	mangi-
instrumental	pag-	*ag-
comitative	ka- (comitative)	*agka- (mutual); *maki- (social)

6.3 Aspect

Ilocano verbs inflect for a number of aspectual distinctions: The perfective (completive) aspect is used for actions that are initiated and completed; the continuous aspect denotes continuous, repetitive, or habitual actions; and the future aspect is used for actions that have yet to be initiated. The unmarked infinitive form of the verb does not specify whether an action has been initiated or completed.

The perfective aspect is formed with a prefix (or infix) as shown below. The continuous aspect is formed by initial CVC reduplication of the stem,[9] and the future is formed by the adverbial clitic =*to* after consonants and =*nto* after vowels.

---

[9] Stems in Ilocano may be polymorphemic, as opposed to roots. Examples of reduplicated stems are: *ma-túrog* 'sleep' > *mat-matúrog* 'sleeping', *pa-síkal* 'labor pains' > *ag-pas-pa-síkal* 'suffer labor pains', *mangán* /maN-kaan/ 'eat' > *mang-mangán* 'eating'.

Infinitive (unmarked for aspect)	Perfective	Continuous	Future
Actor focus verbs			
agsúrat 'write'	nagsúrat	agsursúrat	agsúratto
gumátang 'buy'	gimmátang	gumatgátang	gumátangto
mangtákaw 'steal'	nangtákaw	mangtaktákaw	mangtákawto
matúrog 'sleep'	natúrog	matmatúrog	matúrogto
Goal focus verbs			
ikábil 'put'	inkábil	ikabkábil	ikábilto
suráten 'write'	sinúrat	sursuráten	surátento
punásan 'wipe'	pinunásan	punpunásan	punásanto

Continuous verbs may be complete or in progress, depending on whether they are formed off the perfective aspect (n-/-imm-/-in-) form of the verb; e.g., *agsursúrat* 'is writing' vs. *nagsursúrat* 'was writing'.

Ilocano verbs may also be derived for aspectual distinctions with CVCV or full reduplication to express the iterative, durative, continual, distributional, intermittent, or intensive nature of the action expressed by the root. Because this morphology is derivational, it is not equally productive on all action verbs.

agbanníkes	arms akimbo
agbannibanníkes	repeatedly (scold) with the arms akimbo
agkabúkab	grit the teeth
agkabukabúkab	continuously and intensively grit the teeth; gossip
agtilmón	swallow
agtilmotilmón	repeatedly or forcefully swallow
siláwan	light up a place
silawsiláwan	light up various places
naisiglót	to be tied in a knot
naisiglosiglót	to be tied up in knots

6.3.1 The recent past

Ilocano has a recent past construction to designated actions completed just prior to the speech event. This construction is formed by the prefix *ka-* and CV reduplication of the initial syllable of the root. The actor of verbs in the recent past appears in the ergative case:

kasasangpét	just arrived (from the root *sangpet* 'arrive')
Kasasangpétko.	I just arrived

Words denoting a recently completed action or achieved state can also be designated by the prefixes *kapag-* or *kaCVC-/kaC-*:

itlóg	egg	kait-itlóg	freshly laid (egg); just laid
lúto	cook	kal(ut)lúto	freshy cooked (food); just cooked
asáwa	spouse	kapagas-asáwa	recent marriage; just married
agasáwa	marry	kapagasawáan	newlywed couple, recently married
serrék	enter	kasserrék	newcomer; just entered

purós	pick	kappurós	just picked
raép	transplant	karraép	just transplanted (rice)
tugáw	chair	kattugáw	just appointed
sibét	depart	kassibét	just departed

6.3.2 Inchoativity

The concept of 'becoming' a state or quality is expressed by the infix -um-; the perfective aspect counterpart is -imm- (historically *-inum- > *inm > imm):

táyag	tall
tumáyag	to grow tall
timmáyag	grew tall(er)
baknáng	wealth
bumaknáng	to become wealthy
bimmaknáng	became wealthy
guápo	handsome
gumuápo	to become handsome
gimmuápo	became handsome

The verb agbalín 'become' may also be used for this purpose, usually for actions that are more controllable by the actor or involve more energy exerted by the actor:

Nagbalínda a nabaknáng.	They became rich.
Nagbalín a nasingéd kenkuána.	He became close to her.

No kanáyon a mayúperka iti taltálon, agbalín nga umamarílio dagití sákam.
'If you are always soaking in the fields, your feet will become yellow'.

6.3.3 Frequentatives with -an-

Ilocano –an-[10] frequentatives are formed from intransitive verbs in different ways for different verb classes. Unlike the more prototypical verbs examined earlier, the Ilocano frequentatives do not have perfective forms, they cannot be transitivized; and they are readily used as nouns. Unlike adjectives, they do not have comparative or superlative forms. They may, however, take the reciprocal infix -inn-. They are shown in the table with their corresponding gerunds due to their formal similarities.

---

[10] The infix -an- is also productively used in roots to form derivational iterative/intensive stems: saó 'speak', sanaó 'chatter, gossip', sumanaó 'to chatter, gossip'; taúl 'bark', tanaúl 'repeated, loud barking'. Likewise, the infix -ar- with the prefix ka- is used to form iterative stems: umay 'he comes', agkaraumay 'he often comes'; agkara-kanalduok 'he often noisily swallows' (Rubino 1999).

Mode		Verbal Affix	Gerund (Manner)	Frequentative
Dynamic	Durative	ag-	panag-	manag-
	Punctual	-um-[11]	iCV-	CumV-
	Distributive/ Detransitive	mang-	panang-	manang-
		mangi-	panangi-	manangi-
		mangipa-	panangipa-	manangipa-
		mangpa-	panangpa-	manangpa-
		mangpai-	panangpai-	manangpai-
		mangpag-	panangpag-	manangpag-
	Potentive	maka-	pannaka-	mannaka-
		makai-	pannakai-	mannakai-
		makaipa-	pannakaipa-	mannakaipa-
		makapa-	pannakapa-	mannakapa-
		makapai-	pannakapai-	mannakapai-
		makapag-	pannakapag-	mannakapag-
		makapagi-	pannakapagi-	mannakapagi-
	Social	maki-	pannaki-	mannaki-
		makipag-	pannakipag-	mannakipag-
		makipagi-	pannakipagi-	mannakipagi-

managsángit	always crying, frequently crying; crybaby
mannakidangádang	frequently engaging in warfare; warrior
managtagipang-or	always carrying a club
Mannakisaludsódda.	They are always asking questions.
Mannakiápa ti anákko.	My child is always fighting.
Managtaúl diáy ásoda.	Their dog is always barking.
Managtinnulongtúlongda.	They frequently help each other.
Managluálo ni bakétko.	My wife often prays.
Managinnápalda.	They always envy each other.
Managuntón ni Choring.	Choring is very inquisitive (always asks questions).

Saánkami a managnaténg, ngem bin-íg a bulbulóng pay láeng ti linútona.
'We are not vegetarians (fond of vegetables), but she still only cooked pure leaves anyway'.

---

[11] The paradigmatic discrepancies with the infix *-um-* allude to the possibility that the infix was not originally a voice affix, but an aspectual one. In modern Ilocano, it maintains its aspectual nature with some roots, e.g., *agtakder* 'to stand (durative)' vs. *tumakder* 'to stand up (punctual)'.

6.3.4 Habituals with *sangka-*

The prefix *sangka-* may be used to indicate habitual events. The actor of these formatives is encoded in the ergative case.

Sangkasaónaka.	He is usually/always talking about you.
Sangkadámagnak.	She keeps on asking about me.

6.3.5 Immediacy with *apag-*

The prefix *apag-* is used to indicate immediate fulfillment of an action or state. When denoting the English concept *as soon as,* the actor is encoded in the ergative case. With stative roots, it may indicate a state not fully attained.

bángon	get up	apagbángon	just up (from bed)
biít	moment	apagbiít	in just a moment
sangpét	arrive	apagsangpétna	as soon as he arrives
bingngí	open	apagbingngí	slightly ajar

6.4 Causation (indirect action) and direction: the prefix *pa-*

Ilocano verbs have corresponding causative (indirect) forms in which the action of the verb is caused to be done, not directly done by the actor. The causative morpheme in Ilocano is *pa-* and is used with the verbal affixes as exemplified in the following chart.

Verb form	Causative/indirect form
ag-	agpa- (intransitive); pag- -en, pa- -en (transitive)
agi-	agipa-; agpai- (intransitive); pagi- -en (transitive)
mang-	mangpa-
-en	pa- -en
-an	pa- -an
i-	ipa-
pag-	pagpa-
maka-	makapa-
ma-	mapa-
mai-	maipa-

Nagpapúkisak idí kalmán.	I had my hair cut yesterday.
Makapasalun-át ti salúyot.	*Saluyot* leaves are healthy (cause health).
Napasaplítmi ti pádi.	We managed to have the priest whipped.
Pinagimpipílaynak.	He made me pretend to be lame.
Pastrekém idá.	Let them come in.
Paturógam diáy ubíng.	Put the child to sleep (make him sleep).

With locative roots, the prefix *pa-* also specifies the direction in which an object is transferred for goal focus verbs or the direction in which the actor nominal moves for actor focus verbs.

Impaamiánanmi.	We sent it to the north.
Nagpa-Bauángkamí.	We went to Bauang.

| Impasúlik dagití alikámen. | I put the furniture in the corner. |
| Agpaabagátandanto. | They will go to the south. |

6.5 Pretense

The prefix *aginCV-* (perfective *naginCV-*, gerund *panaginCV-*) indicates that the action expressed by the root is feigned:

Aginsasángitda.	They are pretending to cry.
Aginsisingpét ti lakáyna.	Her husband is pretending to be virtuous.
Nagimpapangláw.	He/she pretended to be poor.
Managimbabaknángda.	They are always pretending to be rich.
Pinagimpipílaynak.	He made me pretend to limp.
Nakapagintútuleng.	He managed to pretend to be deaf.

6.6 Smell

The prefix *agaC-* or *agat-* is used to designate smell. It has no perfective form:

báwang	garlic	agabbáwang	smell of garlic
layá	ginger	agat-layá, agallayá	smell of ginger
tsíko	sapodilla	agattsíko	smell of sapodilla

Agatdára ti al-aliá.	The ghost smells like blood.
Agatnatáy a baóka.	You smell like a dead rat.
Agat-árak 'ta sang-áwmo.	Your breath smells of wine.
Agabbarániw ditóy.	It smells like lemon grass here (indicates a scandal).
Agattsíko ta sang-áwmo.	Your breath smells like sapodilla fruit (indicates intoxication).

6.7 Social verbs

The prefix *maki-* (transitive *ka-*) is used to form social verbs. Social verbs are used to indicate shared participation of an action (actions performed in the company of other people) or verbs used to ask permission to perform an action that is usually comitative.

Inkayó makiápit.	Go participate in the harvest.
Intán makisála.	Let's go join the dance.
Makiinúmak man?	May I have a drink (with you)?
Makisindíkamí man?	May we borrow some fire?
Mabalín ti makikatugáw?	May I sit (with you)?
Nakitinnúlagda idí kalmán.	They signed a mutual contract yesterday.

With kin terms, the prefix *maki-* indicates the way the relative expressed by the root is treated, and with food and commodities, *maki-* indicates a request.

| Makiinátayo kenkuána. | We treat her like our mother. |
| Inkayó makisidá. | Go ask for some food. |

6.8 Reciprocals

Reciprocity is expressed with the infix -inn-, placed before the first vowel of the root. The prefix ag- may also be used with verbs that are inherently reciprocal with plural actors.

Naglinneméngkamí.	We hid from each other.
Ammók nga aginníliwdantó.	I know that they will miss each other.
Kanáyonda nga agap-ápa.	They are always arguing (with each other).
Nagkítakamí idiay kabayábasan.	We saw each other in the guava grove.

6.9 Root verbs

Almost all Ilocano verbs are formed by affixing verbalizing morphology to a root. However, a few frequent verbs can be considered morphologically simple (some of which can be constructed to be bimorphemic historically):

ammó	know	goal focus, no perfective form
in-	go	actor focus, no perfective form
ikkán	give	goal focus, perfective: inikkán
itéd (*i-ted)	give	goal focus, perfective: intéd
kayát (*ka-ayat)	want	goal focus, perfective: kinayát
kuná	say	goal focus, perfective: kinuná
madí (*ma-di)	to be unwilling	actor focus, perfective: nagmadí
mayát (*ma-ayat)	be willing	actor focus, perfective: nayát
yeg	bring	goal focus, perfective: inyég
sidá	eat	goal focus, perfective: sindá

Kayátko a mapánka.	I want you to go.
Kayátko ti mapán.	I want to go.
Aniá ti kinunám?	What did you say?
Ikkánnak man iti gundáway.	Please give me a chance.
Ania't sindáyo?	What did you eat?

7. Adverbs and Particles

Ilocano has many different ways of modifying predicates, from enclitics (varying in their placement and bondedness) and invariant adverbial particles to derivable morphemes.

Agsangsángiten.	He/she is *already* crying. (fusional enclitic)
Nabaknáng kanó.	He/she is supposedly rich. (nonfusional, enclitic-like particle)
Nangándan itáy.	They ate *just a while ago*. (invariant particle)
Nagistayánda natáy.	They *almost* died. (derivable adverb)

The prefix siCV- specifies manner:

Sipapardásda a nagtaráy.
They ran fast.

Silalagípka pay láeng kenkuána.
You are still thinking about him.

As in many other languages, adjectives may also modify predicates.

Nagtaráyda a napardás.	They ran fast.
Aglulúto a nalaíng.	He cooks well.

Ibalunétmi a naimbág dagití rídaw.   We bar (lock with a bar) our doors well.

7.1 Temporal adverbials

Ilocano has temporal adverbs that mark three degrees of past time, a present time marker, and one future time marker used with time expressions in the future. These are *itattay* for the immediate past, *itay* for the recent past, *idi* for the remote past, *itatta* for the immediate present, *ita* for the present time 'now' or 'today', and *intono* + temporal noun for future time:

Immáyda itáy.	They came just now.
Kasasangpétna itáy bigát.	He just arrived earlier this morning.
Nagsángit idí.	He cried then (a while back).
Natáyda idí kalmán.	They died yesterday.
Umáy kanó intóno bigát.	He says he'll come tomorrow.
Agádalak idiáy intóno umáy a tawén.	I'll study there next year.

Some temporal nouns may take the infix -*in*- to express habituality:

aldáw	day	inaldáw	every day
bigát	morning	binigát	every morning
rabií	night	rinabií	every night
tawén	year	tinawén	every year

Umáy ditóy ití binúlan.	He comes here every month.
Agbasbásada ití binigát.	They read every morning.

Other common temporal adverbs are:

agnanáyon	always
agpatnág	all night long
apagbiít	in a short while
apagdarikmát	in an instant, in a short while
dandaní	almost, nearly
kanáyon	always
madamdamá	later
mamin-adú	often
maminpinsán	once and for all
masansán	often
no daddúma	sometimes, occasionally
nagistayán	almost, nearly
nganngáni	almost, nearly
pasaráy	sometimes, occasionally
patináyon	all the time, always
sagpaminsán	now and then, occasionally

7.2 Adverbial particles

Ilocano also has a separate closed class of adverbial particles that are commonly used to elaborate clauses and/or specify certain clausal relationships. Many of these particles function as second position enclitics to a predicate.

bassít	polite particle, particle expressing brief duration
biít	for a short time
di	negative particle, no, not
=(e)n	already, perfective aspect; change of state particle; now; contrastive enclitic
gáyam	expresses sudden realization, surprise, so
kadí	interrogative particle; counters a claim
kanó	hearsay particle: it is said; they say, supposedly
kas(la)	like; seemingly
kastóy, kastá, kasdiáy	like this, like that (medial), like that (distal)
ketdí	anyway, on the other hand
komá (kumá)	optative particle: must, should, hopefully
la	limitative particle: only, just (*laeng*)
láeng	limitative particle: only, just
lattá	just
=(n)to	expresses uncertainty or future time
úray	even (if)
man	please; marker of counterfactuality/expectation
manén	again
met	also, emphatic particle
ngamín	causal or emphatic particle: because, in that sense; in fact
ngarúd	resultative: then; indeed
ngatá	possibly, maybe; do you think?
ngay	particle of elicitation (solicits information)
pay	particle of addition: more; too; first
píman	unfortunately, too bad

Immáyda met laeng.	They came anyway.
Ilukátmo man.	Please open it.
Asíno ngatá ti nangábak?	Who do you think won?
Laláki ngamín.	It's because he's a boy.
Siká gáyam!	So it's you! (I wasn't expecting it to be you.)
Wen ngarúd.	Yes indeed.
Mapánka kumá.	You should go.
Nagsángit láeng ni Blueberry.	Blueberry (name of dog) just cried.
Nabaknángda kanó.	They are supposedly rich.
Isúna ngay?	What about him?
Mangánka pay.	Eat first.
Manó pay ti kasapúlam?	How many more do you need?

The enclitic =(*n*)*sa*[12] attaches to verb phrases to express uncertainty on behalf of the speaker. It attaches to the first constituent of the phrase and has two variants =*sa* after consonants and =*nsa* after vowels:

---

[12] Some Ilocano writers prefer to write -*sa* as a separate word, although its variant -*nsa* is phonologically conditioned.

Napándan*sa*.	I think they went.
Agtagtagainépka*nsa*.	I think you are dreaming.

The enclitic =(e)n has two variants: =*en* after consonants and =*n* after vowels. After the pronouns *siak*, =*k*, and =*m*, the original form of the pronoun is retained with this enclitic, preserving the final *o* (from **si-ako*, **ko* and **mo*).

Nabsúg*en*.	He is already full.
Addáda*n*.	They're here already.
Siák*on*.	It's my turn; I'll do it. (Me now)
Innálak*on*.	I already took it.
Aláem*on*!	Take it (already)!
Kaném*on*!	Eat it (now)!

8. Existentials and Locatives

8.1 *Addá* and *awán*

There are two existential particles in Ilocano: *addá* 'there is, there are' and *awán*, the negative counterpart. They may be used to express the existence or location of an entity or absence thereof. Ilocano has no equivalent to the English copular verb 'to be'.

Addáak ditóyen. (Addáak*ón*)	I am here already.
Awánda pay.	They are not (here) yet.

Notice how definite noun phrases are usually preceded by an article or demonstrative in the *addá* existential construction:

Addá kaldíng.	There is a goat (here).
Addá ti kaldíng.	The goat is (here).

When these existentials are used with possessed nominals, they express possession.

Addá anákmo?	Do you have a child?
Addá ásoda.	They have a dog.
Awán kuarták.	I have no money.

When *addá* precedes a verb, it functions like an English indefinite pronoun (in absolute position). Notice the difference in meaning when the verb frame is intransitive versus transitive:

Addá immáy.	Somebody came (*addá* = actor).
Addá kinnánda.	They ate something (*addá* = patient).
Addá nakítana.	He saw something (*addá* = patient).
Addá nakakíta kaniána.	Someone saw him (*addá* = actor).
Adda insúratna.	He wrote something down (*addá* = theme)

8.2 Locatives

Ilocano locatives differentiate three degrees of spatial orientation: proximal (near speaker), medial (near hearer, or close to speech participants), and distal (far from both speaker and hearer):

ditóy	here
ditá	there, medial
idiáy, sadiáy	there, distal
Ditákan.	Stay there (Good bye).
Agúrayka ditá.	Wait there.

The locatives are also used to introduce locative nouns with reference to the location of the speaker:

Napánda idiáy Pagdar-áoan.	They went to Pagdar-aoan.
Addáda idiáy padayá.	They are at the party.
Addáak ditóy Laoág.	I am (here) in Laoag.
Nalam-ék ditóy Australia.	It's cold (here) in Australia.

9. Conjunctions and Subordinators

Ilocano has a wealth of conjunctions and subordinators used in both speech and literature. As in English, they precede their subordinate clauses (see section 13). Please refer to the dictionary for the specifics of each of the following.

abús ta	while, also, besides
aginggána(t)	until
aglálo	especially
agsípud ta	because
anansá ta	therefore
báreng	hopefully
báyat ti	during
gapú ta	because
idí	when (remote past time)
imbés	instead
intóno	if, when (future time)
isú nga (invariant *nga*)	so (resultative)
itáy	when (recent past time)
kadá	and (sometimes used to replace *ken* when used with plural nouns)
kalpasán	after
kas	like, as
ken	and
ket	and; introduces a predicate
maipapán	about, concerning
maipanggép	about, concerning
malaksíd	except, unless
maysá pay	besides, furthermore

ngem	but
no	if, when; (with *kuma*) counterfactual if
no di ket	but rather
numóna ta	since, because
núpay	although, even though
núpay kastá	nevertheless
sa	then
sakbáy	before
ta	because
tángay	since, because
tapnó	so that
tunggál	every time, each time
úray	although
wennó	or
yantángay	since, because

Kayátmo ti tsa wennó kapé?
Do you want tea or coffee?

Nagtaráyda, sáda naglemméng.
They ran, then they hid.

Agsángit tunggál umáyka.
He cries whenever you come.

Tángay dímo impángag dagití balákadko, panáwankanto.
Since you didn't heed my advice, I will leave you.

Saának a nakatúrog báyat ti kaaddáda.
I wasn't able to sleep while they were here.

Tapnó agballígika, tulúngankanto.
So that you will succeed, I will help you.

No umáyka ditóy, agpartíkaminto ití kaldíng.
If you come here, we'll slaughter a goat.

Adú ti inápitmi, isú nga nasalun-átkamí pay láeng.
We had a big harvest, so we are still healthy.

10. Interrogatives

Ilocano interrogatives appear in initial predicate position in questions:

Asíno ti immáy?	Who came?
Aniá ti imbagána?	What did he say?
Apay a kastáka?	Why are you like that?
Manó ti ginátangmo?	How many did you buy?

The following is a list of the most frequent interrogative particles in the language:

aniá	what
ápay	why; what
asíno	who
ayán	where (is located)
inton-anó	when (future time)
kaanó	when
kasáno	how
manó	how many
sadíno	where (an action is performed)
siasíno	who
síno, sinnó	who

There are also morphologically complex interrogatives, sometimes specifying concepts that are not expressed lexically in English. Notice how the interrogatives are created with prefixes and the 'dummy' root -*ano*:

agpaanó	in what direction?
kapín-anó	how related (in kin terms)?
maikamanó	in what ordinal number? (first, second, third, etc.)
mamin-anó	how many times?
sagmamanó	how many each?
sagpamin-anó	how many times each?
tagá-anó	where from?

The interrogatives *kaanó, inton-anó,* and *sadíno* appear in predicate position and take nominalized verbs as their complements:

Inton-anó ti yaáymo?	When will you come? When is your coming?
Sadíno ti papanám?	Where are you going? Where is your going?

Many interrogatives in predicate position must appear as absolutive arguments of their verbal complements; an actor will take an actor focus verb and a patient will take a patient focus verb, etc.

Sinnó ti nakítam?	Who did you see? Who was your seeing? (patient)
Sinnó ti nakakíta kenka?	Who saw you? (actor)
Manó ti innálam?	How many did you get? (patient)
Aniá ti limtég?	What got swollen? (actor)
Ania ti pinagiwana?	What did he use to slice it with? (instrument)

Interrogatives can function as indefinite pronouns in embedded questions. They are preceded by the complementizer *no* in this case:

Ammók no sinnó ti nagturpós.
I know who graduated.

Ammóm no ápay a kasdiáy?
Do you know why he is like that?

Saánda nga imbagá no manó ti kayátna.
They didn't say how many he wants.

Umanáyen ti létra a rugí ti apeliédom a mangipakdáar no taga-anóka.
The first letter of your last name is enough to reveal where you come from.

There are three important interrogative particles in the language that are used as second position enclitics of the verb phrase: *kadí, ayá,* and *ngay. Kadí* is used to form simple interrogatives and to soften commands, *ayá* is used to express wonder, surprise, or doubt in the interrogative, and *ngay* is used to verbally elicit response in any statement:

Siká ngay?	What about you?
Naúyong ayá?	Is he really cruel (seems surprising)?
Sinnó kadí?	Who is it?
Napangláw kadí?	Is he poor?

11. Negation

Ilocano has two negative adverbs used to negate clauses or constituents: *sáan* (dialectal variant: *haán*) and *di*. With declarative sentences lacking enclitic pronouns, the negative counterparts are formed by the negative adverb *sáan* or *di* preceding the full declaration. With the adverb *saán,* the declaration must be joined with the ligature (*ng*)*a*; no ligature is required with *di. Saán* is preferred to *di* when negating noun phrases.

Nagallikúbeng ti ángin.	The wind blew around.
Saán a nagallikúbeng ti ángin.	The wind did not blow around.
Di nagallibkúbeng ti ángin.	The wind did not blow around.

diáy kabsátko	my sibling
saán a diáy kabsátko	not my sibling
saán a ni Carmel	not Carmel

With declaratives containing second position enclitic pronouns, the enclitic pronouns attach to the negative adverbs *saán* or *di. Saán* takes the ligature (*ng*)*a* before the negated constituent, while *di* does not:

Ay-ayaténka.	I love you.
Saánka nga ay-ayatén.	I don't love you.
Díka ay-ayatén.	I don't love you.

After the negative adverb *di*, the enclitic particle =*ak* is found where =*k(o)* would normally be positioned. This is due to the fossilization of the forms *diak, indiak,* and *mandiak*.

Kayátko.	I want/like it.
Diák kayát. Indiak kayát. Mandiák kayát.	I don't want/like it.
Saánko a kayát.	I don't want/like it.

Negative commands (prohibitives) are identical in form to negative declaratives. They are differentiated only by intonation. Unlike in Tagalog, there is no prohibitive morpheme:

Adaywánnak!	Get away from me!
Saánnak nga adaywán.	Don't leave me.
Dínak adaywán.	Don't leave me.

Existential phrases (expressing existence, location, or possession) are negated by replacing the positive existential *addá* 'there is, there are' with its negative counterpart *awán* 'there is/are not'.

Addáda idiáy Pagdalagán.	They are in Pagdalagan.
Awánda idiáy Pagdalagán.	They are not in Pagdalagan.
Addá ások.	I have a dog.
Awán ások.	I don't have a dog.

A negative response to a polar (yes/no) question or imperative is formed with the negative adverb *saán*, never with *di*. *Saán man* is used to negate a negative question, to affirm the realization of an action that is contrary to the expectation of the addressee. It may be contracted in speech to *sammán*.

Nalaíngda?	Are they smart?
Saán.	No.

Dímo kayát no addákamín?	Don't you want us to be here?
Saán man, a.	On the contrary, (I want you to be here).

12. The Ligature *(ng)a*

The ligature (or linker) is a connective particle used in Philippine languages to connect various syntactic parts of a sentence (heads and attributes). The Ilocano ligature has two written variants: *nga* before vowels and *a* before consonants. However, in speaking, the ligature *nga* is usually preferred regardless of phonetic environment.

Among the many uses of the ligature are the following: connect adjectives and nouns, introduce complements or appositional constituents of all syntactic categories, separate the negative particle *saan* from the verb in negative declarations, and separate repeated words in emphatic constructions:

Saó a saó ni Kondring.	Kondring is always talking.
naímas a digó	delicious broth
Saánkamí a napán.	We didn't go.
Nalaká a daíten.	It is easy to sew it.
ti kabsátko a laláki	my brother
ti nuáng a napigsá	the strong water buffalo

When the ligature *(ng)a* joins non-predicative syntactic elements, notice that the two conjoined constituents do not predicate:

Naímas ti bibíngka.	The rice cake is delicious.
naímas a bibíngka	delicious rice cake

Ni Erlinda ti maéstra.	Erlinda is the teacher.
ni Erlinda a maéstra	Erlinda, the teacher

13. Clause Combining

Various processes are involved when Ilocano clauses are combined. In certain combinations, one clause becomes a well-integrated (dependent) constituent of another. These include relative clauses and complement clauses. Clauses may also combine where neither is the superordinate clause; both may function independently. Such is the case with coordinate clauses. This section will discuss the following clause types:

    13.1   Relative clauses
    13.2   Complement clauses
    13.3   Adverbial clauses
    13.4   Coordination

13.1 Relative clauses

A relative clause is a clause that modifies the head of the noun phrase (NP) to which it belongs; it 'relates' a piece of information to its head noun. Relative clauses are linked to their head noun in Ilocano with the ligature *(ng)a*: NP = head noun + ligature *(ng)a* + relative clause.

ti táo a manákem	the man that is wise
ti balásang nga agur-úray kaniák	the maiden who is waiting for me
ti al-aliá a nakítana	the ghost that he saw

The head noun taking a relative clause must be in the absolutive position with respect to the predicate of the relative clause. A head noun that functions as an actor will take an actor focus verb, a head noun that functions as a patient will take a patient focus verb, etc.

ti táo a nagsúrat	the man who wrote (actor)
ti mannála a sinurátanna	the dancer to whom he wrote (direction)
ti sarsuéla a sinúratna	the opera he wrote (patient)
ti nágan nga insúratna	the name he wrote down (theme)
ti ubíng a nagsángit	the child who cried (actor)
ti balásang a nakítak	the maiden I saw (nonactor)
ti al-aliá a nakakíta kaniák	the ghost that saw me (actor)
ti tukák nga innálada	the frog that they got (patient)
diay babái a kinasaók	the girl with whom I spoke (comitative)

13.2 Complement clauses

Complement clauses are those that can be considered as embedded arguments of a matrix predicate. Most complement clauses have the potential to stand alone as a complete phrase, except those that are 'reduced', sharing a co-referential argument with the matrix clause that is only overtly expressed in the matrix clause.

Kayátko nga agáwidka.	I want you to go home. (no shared argument)
Kayátko ti agáwid.	I want to go home. (shared argument)

Agáwidka.	Go home! You go home.
Agawidak.	I go home.
Agáwid.	He goes home.

There are three main types of complement clauses in Ilocano that can be categorized by their form: nominal *ti* complementation, ligature *ta* complementation, and ligature *nga* complementation. Nominal *ti* complementation is used when the verb of the main clause is transitive. The pivot of the two clauses is the ergative actor. It is an argument of both the matrix and the embedded predicate but it is overtly expressed only in the main clause.

Masápulko ti mangán.	I need to eat.
Kayátmo ti aglangóy?	Do you want to swim?
Insardéngnan ti mapán idiáy tálon.	He stopped going to the field.
Rinugiánmi manén ti agkáli.	We started digging again.
Diákon natúloy ti nangán.	I could no longer continue eating.
Mabalínko pay láeng ti agárem kenká?	Can I still court you?

The verb of a *ti* complement clause may take perfective morphology for completed actions.

Inan-ánatna ti timmakdér.	He carefully stood up.
Inagawáanna ti nagpakléb.	He hastily fell prone.
Dína pay pinádas ti simrék idiáy.	He still hasn't tried to go in there.
Inggaédko ti nagádal idiáy koléhio.	I earnestly studied in college.

This type of complementation can be compared to nominalized arguments of transitive verbs, except that the arguments are usually overtly expressed with the nominalization as an ergative enclitic or full noun phrase:

Dina intúloy ti yuúlogna.	He didn't continue descending (his descent).
Tinaliáwna ti naggapuán ti áwag.	He looked back at where the call came from.

Ta complementation involves complement clauses preceded by the ligature-like element *ta*. *Ta* complement clauses are always finite; co-referential arguments are not deleted in the complement clause. Furthermore, the verb of the main clause does not have to be transitive. Predicators that take *ta* complement clauses can be considered lexicalized expressions that require *ta* in their case frames: e.g., *(na)imbág ta* 'it's good that', *sapay komá ta* 'I hope that', *pagammuán ta* 'suddenly...', *pangngaásim ta* 'please', *sáyang ta* 'it's a shame that', *bay-án ta* 'let, allow'. The matrix clauses may be personal or impersonal.

Impersonal main clauses:

Sapáy komá ta agballígiak.	Hopefully (I hope) I'll succeed.
Imbág ta nakaumáyka.	It's good that you could come.
Sáyang ta díka nakapán.	It's a shame you didn't go.

Personal main clauses:

Ibagám ta umáy.	Tell him to come.
Agúrayka ta idasaránka iti meriéndam.	Wait and I'll prepare you an afternoon snack.
Pangngaásim ta isardéngmo ti panggépmo.	Please (have mercy to) stop your plan.

Nga complementation, in which the complement clause is preceded by the ligature *nga*, is the most versatile of complementation types. Both the verbs of the main clause and complement clause can be personal or impersonal, transitive or intransitive. There are no restrictions on the grammatical role of the co-referential argument in the main clause. That is, the co-referential argument may function as either an ergative or an absolutive argument of the matrix predicate.

Impersonal main predicates:

Naskén nga aginanákayo.	You need to rest.
Masápul a mabuniáganka itan.	You need to be baptized now.
Pudnó nga ay-ayaténka.	It's true that I love you.
Nabayágen a birbirókenka.	I have been looking for you for a long time.
Di mabalín a sumrékak?	Can't I come in?

Personal main clause predicates:

Addákamí a mangsarábo kenká.	We are here to welcome you.
Nagsardéngda nga agwáyat.	They stopped casting their fishing nets.
Diák mabalín nga ibagá kenká.	I cannot tell you.
Aw-awísendak nga agahedrés.	They are inviting me to play chess.
Mabaínak a makisaríta kenkuána.	I am ashamed to speak with him.

Clauses sharing an argument (may or may not be expressed twice if the verb of the complement clause is transitive):

Padásekto a kasaríta ni Anching.	I'll try to speak with Anching.
Ingagárak nga inlímed kenká.	I purposely hid it from you.
Ikarík a pasiárek ti tanémmo iti inaldáw.	I promise to pass by your tomb every day.
Inkeddéngko a kasarítak ni Beng.	I decided to speak with Beng.
Kayátka a manúgangen.	I want you to be my son-in-law.
Bay-ánnak nga agsángit.	Let me cry.
Napuyátanak a nagur-úray kenkuána.	I stayed up all night waiting for him.

Clauses that do not share an argument:

Pagarupék a saántantón nga agkíta.	I suppose we won't be seeing each other now.
Kayátko a patayém ni Berníng.	I want you to kill Berning.
Intulókyo ngarúd nga agkakallaútangtayo.	You let us drift aimlessly then.

13.3 Adverbial clauses

Adverbial clauses are sentential or phrasal adjuncts. They provide modificatory information that relates to their main clauses, and they are not required by the syntax of the language. Adverbial clauses are formed with some type of adverb or overt subordinator that may be followed by a variety of constituents ranging in form from simple nouns or nominalizations to independent predicates (finite verbs). Among the various adverbial clause types are the following:

Temporal

Nalúton idí sumangpét ti asáwana.	It was already cooked when his wife arrived.
Inarámidko sakbáy ti panagáwidda.	I did it before they went home.

Nagpalpá pay, sa nagáwid.   He rested after eating first, then went home.
Agsángit tunggál umáyka.   He cries whenever you come.

Locational

Inggasanggásatda iti dagá a sinaldáda.   They tried their luck in the land they mortgaged.
Innálana iti lamisáan a pagmakmakiniliáak.   He took it from the table where I was typing.

Manner

Saánmo nga aramíden a kasití inarámidna.   Don't do it like he did.
Nagsángit a kas kaldíng a natuduán.   He cried like a goat that got rained on.

Reason/purpose

Agsangsángitda ta nabáutda.   They are crying because they were whipped.
Inarámidna tapnó makaáwid.   He did it so he can go home.

Circumstantial

Naduáyaka ití panagkantána.   You were lulled to sleep by her singing.
Nakapán babaén ti pannakatúlongda.   He was able to go with their help.

Simultaneous

Saának a nakatúrog báyat ti kaaddáda.   I wasn't able to sleep while they were here.
Nagáwidda nga agkatkatáwa.   They went home laughing.

Conditional

No umáyka ditóy, agpadayátayontó.   If you come here, we'll have a party.
No nabaknángak komá, mangasáwakamí.   If I were rich, we would get married.

Concessive

Maawátanka úray dímon baliksén.   I understand you although you do verbalize it.
Núpay narusepkami, naragsakkamí.   Although we are drenched, we are happy.
Úray agluáka ití dára, díkanto taliáwen!   Even if you cry blood, I will not look back at you!

Substitutive

Isú ti maanupán imbés nga isú ti aganúp.   He will be the hunted instead of the one who hunts.

Additive

Awánen ti maarámidna no di agulímek.   There was nothing she could do but be quiet.
Abús ta sadút, naalás.   Aside from being lazy, she is ugly.

Resultative

Natuduán ngamín, isú nga natáy.   It got rained on, so it died.
Agngíwatka ket matáyda a duá.   You breathe a word and the two of them will die!
Umasidégka ket papolíska!   You come near and I'll call the police.

Optative

Báreng no umáy.   I hope he comes.

Kayátko a makíta ni mánong báreng maallúkoyko nga agáwid idiáy Pilipínas.
I want to see older brother in the hope that I can convince him to return to the Philippines.

13.4 Coordination

In coordination, constituents of equivalent syntactic function are linked together. Clauses can be combined by simple intonational breaks or with coordinating conjunctions, of which Ilocano has three: *ken* 'and', *ngem* 'but', or *wenno* 'or'.

Coordination with no overt coordinator:

Nasadút, naalás pay.	He is lazy (and he is) ugly too.

Phrase level coordination:

Nalínis ken naláwa ti kalapáwna.	His hut is clean and spacious.
Naragsák ken mannakigayyém ni Beng.	Beng is happy and friendy.
Insík da Wei ken Yi.	Yi and Wei are Chinese.
Agsublát ti sagawísiw ken dayyéngna.	His humming and whistling alternated.
Aniá ti kayátmo, danúm wennó tsa?	What do you want, water or tea?
wennó naimbág wennó dákes	either good or bad
babái man wennó laláki	both boys and girls, either boys or girls

Clause level coordination:

Nagáwiddan ngem nalipátanda ti tulbék.	They went home already but forgot the key.
Ináremnak ngem diák pay sinungbátan.	He courted me but I still haven't answered him.

Numbers are traditionally linked with *ket*, although the coordinator *ken* is used now by most speakers for this purpose. *Ket* most often marks inversed predicates or resultative/reason adverbial clauses.

sangapúlo ket limá	twenty-five
duapúlo ket inném	twenty-six

Isúda ket nabangsít.	They are smelly.
Dítaka pay láeng ket addá papanák.	Good-bye (stay there), for I am going somewhere.
Agannádkayo ket simmangpéten ti bagtít.	Beware, for the crazy man has arrived.

ABBREVIATIONS USED IN THIS DICTIONARY

a.	adjective	Kal.	(Lubuangan) Kalinga
abbr.	abbreviation	Kan.	Kankanay
adj.	adjective	Kpm.	Kapampangan
adv.	adverb	Jap.	Japanese
alt.	alternate form	lig.	ligature (linker)
AmSp.	American Spanish	lit.	literally; literary
art.	article	masc.	masculine
Aus.	Australian English	mus.	music
Bik.	Bikol	myth.	mythology
Bol.	Bolinao	n.	noun
Bon.	Bontok	N	nasal
C	Consonant	num.	number
Ch.	Chinese	obs.	obsolete
circum.	circumfix	opp.	opposite
contr.	contraction	orig.	originally
dim.	diminutive	part.	particle
coll.	colloquial	perf.	perfective
conj.	conjunction	Pil.	Pilipino, common to major
dem.	demonstrative		Philippine languages
exp.	expression (idiomatic or	pl.	plural
	proverbial)	Png.	Pangasinan
f.	from	pref.	prefix
fam.	familiar	pron.	pronoun; pronounced
fem.	feminine	PSp.	Philippine Spanish
fig.	figurative	reg.	regional
Hok.	Hokkien	Sam.	Sambal
Ibg.	Ibanag	sp.	species
Ibl.	I(ni)baloy	Sp.	Spanish
Ibn.	Ibanag	suf.	suffix
Ifg.	Ifugao	Tag.	Tagalog
interrog.	interrogative	v.	verb
Itb.	Itbayaten	V	vowel
Itg.	Itneg	var.	variant
Ivt.	Ivatan	vulg.	vulgar

ILOCANO-ENGLISH

ILOKO-INGGLES

A

a₁: *lig.* A ligature that links various syntactic parts of a sentence (heads and complements). It is a literary allomorph of *nga* used mainly before consonants. Among its many uses are the following: **1.** Connects complement clauses to main clauses: **Kayatko a mapanka.** I want you to go. **Palubosanda a mangan.** They permit her to eat. **Nakitada a kinayatna.** They saw that she liked it. **Maawatak a nangabakka.** I understand that you won. **2.** Connects adjectives and nouns: **naimas a kankanen.** tasty sweets. **dua a babbai.** two girls. **3.** Connects adverbial clauses to main clauses: **Kitaem a nalaing.** Look at it carefully. **Sitatalna a nagadal.** He studied quietly. **4.** Introduces infinitival complements: **Nalaka a daiten.** It's easy to sew it. **5.** Introduces nominal complements: **Dimteng a bagio.** It came as a storm. **6.** In negative constructions, separates *saan* from the verb: **Saanka a makaluto.** You cannot cook. **7.** Precedes appositions: **Ni Carmen a kantante.** Carmen, the singer. **8.** Follows certain interrogatives: **Apay a nalukmeg?** Why is she fat? **Ania a tao.** What kind of man. **9.** Connects relative clauses to their head nouns: **ti bado a kimres.** the dress that shrank. **10.** Separates fully reduplicated verbs in emphatic constructions: **sao a sao.** (He is) always talking. [Png. *ya, a, –n*, Tag. *na, -ng*]

a₂: *part.* Particle expressing confirmation: **Wen, a.** Yes indeed (I agree).

a-: fossilized prefix (no longer productive) used with a closed class of common adjectives: **akaba.** wide. **atiddog.** long. **akikid.** narrow. **ababa.** short.

aabírat: *n.* plural of *abírat*: same generation in-laws.

aabukáyen: (f. *abukay*) *n.* erogenous zone; *a.* excitable; causing one to be aroused.

aaddí: plural of *adi*: *n.* younger sibling.

aagkán: (f. *agek*) *n.* kissable lips.

aak: *n.* (children's talk) dirty thing (*ak-ák*). [Bon. *a-a*]

aamkán: (f. *amek*) *n.* fearful, dreaded thing. **Awan met ti aamkak ta kuna ti gayyemko nga awan ti managdakdakes ditoy yanda.** I have nothing to fear because my friend says there are no criminals here in their place.

aán: *coll.* version of *saan*: no.

aanakán: (f. *anák*) *n.* womb, uterus. [Knk. *bal-bal-éy*, *belbeluá*, Tag. *bahay-batà*]

aandáran: (f. *andár*) *n.* the way something runs; the way a person manages himself.

aannák: (f. *anák*) *n.* children (distributive plural of *anák*).

aangótan: (f. *angot*) *n.* mucus membrane; nasal cavity.

aangsán: (f. *anges*) *n.* windpipe, respiratory track. **Limmawa ti aangsanna.** His breathing became easier (*lit*: loosened).

aapálan: (f. *apal*) *n.* that which is envied; that which causes envy or jealousy.

aapóng: (f. *apóng*) *n.* grandparents.

aappó: (f. *apó*) *n.* grandchildren; descendants (distributive plural of *apó*).

aarakén: (f. *arák*) *a.* attractive; charismatic; magnetic.

aariekán: (f. *ariek*) *n.* ticklish zones of a person's body; sensitive erogenous zones.

aayatán: (f. *ayát*) *n.* like; desire; condition of liking. **Awan a pulos ti aayatak kenkuana.** I don't like him at all.

aayúsan: (f. *ayus*) *n.* gutter for water flow; part of upper lip under nostril where mucus flows.

ába: *n.* taro, *Colocasia esculenta.* **aba-aba.** *n.* variety of the taro plant which is cultivated for decorative purposes. **kaabaan.** *n.* taro field. [Knk. *ammoáng*, *písing*, Png. *abá*, *lokó*, Tag. *gabi*; Knk. *ába* = banana skin]

abáab: *n.* a half coconut shell (lower half), (used for drinking, etc.) (*ungot*, *sabut*; *sudo*, *surusor*, *tebteb*); indistinct vocalization. (*anabaab*) **ag-anabaab.** *n.* echo; produce a faded, faint sound. **abaaban.** *v.* to hold something between the lips. [Tag. *bao*, *lumbó*]

ab-áb: **umab-ab.** *v.* to drink while kneeling (from a faucet); to drink from the palms of the hands; to drink without a cup. **sangkaab-ab.** *n.* one draught (of water or wine).

ababá: *a.* short (objects); low. *n.* brevity (*biit*); shortness. **umababa.** *v.* to become shorter or lower. **paababaen, yababa.** *v.* to shorten. **kaababa, kinaababa.** *n.* brevity; shortness. **pangyababaan.** *n.* abbreviation. **iti ababa a pannao.** in short; in other words. **Pulitiagan ti pangyababaan ti Puli-ti-Tiagan.** *Pulitiagan* is the abbreviation of People-from-*Tiagan*. [Ibg. *abebba*, Ifg. *atikke*, Itg. *atubbat*, Kal. *agobbya*, Knk. *amtík*, *baég*, Kpm. *makúyad*, Png. *abebá*, *antikey*, Tag. *babà*]

abábaw: *a.* shallow (*rabaw*, *gádang*); dull, without meaning. **umababaw.** *v.* to become shallow. **pagababawan.** *n.* shallow region in the ocean, etc. [Png. *tapéw*, Tag. *babaw*]

abábet: *n.* a kind of edible freshwater fish.

ábad: (Eng.?) *n.* abbot.

abáda: *n.* mermaid; sea cow. (*duyong*)

abáday: *n.* sling for broken arm; object held swung over the shoulder. **agabaday.** *v.* to carry something over the shoulder slung in a band. **yabaday.** *v.* to sling a band over the shoulder.

Adda abadayna a kuribot. He has a *kuribot* basket swung over his shoulder.

abága: *n.* shoulder (of person or garment). **yabaga.** *v.* to place on the shoulder; bear responsibility. **maabaga.** *n.* a kind of jar smaller than the *burnay.* **abagaen.** *v.* to put the arm over another's shoulder. **nakayabaga.** *a.* (resting, hanging, etc.) on the shoulder. **pagat-abaga.** *a.* reaching the shoulder, shoulder length. **Natnag ti pagat-abaga a buokna kadagiti pingpingna.** Her shoulder length hair fell on her cheeks. [Bon. *pókel*, Ibg. *avága*, Ifg. *pukul*, Ivt. *pakuh*, Kal. *abyaÿa*, Knk. *púke*, Kpm. *pago*, Png. *abalá*, Tag. *balikat*]

abagá: *(obs.) interj.* Interjection expressing wonder.

abágat: *n.* the south wind. **abagatan.** *n.* south. **abagatan a daya.** *a.* south east. **abagatan a laud.** *a.* south west. **makinabagatan, akinabagatan.** *a.* in the south. **kaabagatánan.** *n.* southernmost. **agpaabagatan.** *v.* to go to the south. **taga-abagatan.** *n.* southerner; person from the south. [Ivt. *kasumlaan*, Kal. *kapun cheÿa*, Png. *abalaten, dapit-ilog*, Tag. *timog, habagat* = west or southwest wind]

abágay: *(obs.)* see *abaga*: interjection expressing wonder.

abáho: *(Sp. abajo:* below, under, underneath, down) *interj.* down with! (used in Spanish expressions) **Abaho los tíranos!** Down with the tyrants! [Spanish antonym: *arríba*; Ilocano antonym: *agbiág* (long live)]

ábak: *n.* loss, defeat; losses in gambling (*inabak*). **abaken.** *v.* to defeat; win; overcome. **umabak, abaken.** *v.* to defeat; overcome; triumph over. (*atiw; paksiat; parmek; parukma; sebbet*) **mangabak, agabak.** *v.* to win. **maabak.** *v.* to lose. **paabak.** *v.* to let oneself lose. **inabak.** *a.* winning, (winning number); *n.* winnings. **ipaabak.** *v.* to forfeit, let someone lose. **panangipaabak.** *n.* forfeiture. **makiinnabak.** *v.* to compete. **agabanabak.** *v.* to win some and lose some. **panagabak.** *n.* winning, victory. **agpaabak.** *v.* to give away a victory, allow the opposing team to win. **agin-innabak.** *v.* to alternately win and lose; to be at odds with each other. **ipangabak.** *v.* to try one's best to win. [Ibg. *affut*, Ivt. *nahumis*, Kal. *abyak*, Knk. *ábak*, Kpm. *sambut*, Png, Tag. *talo*]

abaká: *n.* Manila hemp. [Ibg., Kpm. Png., Tag. *abaka*, Ivt. *avakaq*, Ifg. *polwak*]

ábako: *(Sp. abaco:* abacus) *n.* abacus (bead calculator). **agabako.** *v.* to use an abacus.

ábal: abal-abal. *n.* a kind of June bug. (*barrairong*) **agabal-abal.** *v.* to cluster around like the *abal-abal*; to catch June bugs. **abalen.** *n.* a kind of white larva destructive to plants. [Bon. *lissing*, Png. *sibbawéng, simmawá*, Tag. *salagubang*]

abalayán: *n.* the relationship between the parents of a married couple; term of address used to express this relationship. **agabalayan.** *v.* to be of this relationship. [Bon. *aliwíd*, Kal. *abeÿyan, kaatummang*, Png. *abalayán*, Tag. *magbalae*]

abalbaláy: *n.* toy. (*ay-ayam*) **abalbalayen.** *v.* to play with; trifle with; finger. **No adda lalaki a mangisarita kaniak, abalbalayek laengen.** If there is a man who speaks to me, I just play with him. **Saan a mabalin nga abalbalayen ti apuy.** One cannot play with fire. [Tag. *larô*]

abálen: *n.* a kind of white larva that lives on roots. **inabalen.** *a.* attacked by the *abalen.*

abáleng: *var.* of *abalen*: white larva.

abalório: *(Sp. abalorio:* glass bead) *n.* colored silver beads used in decorating clothes; bead work on a costume, bag, etc. [Tag. *abaloryo*]

abandonádo: *(Sp. abandonado:* abandoned) *a.* abandoned.

abanéra: *(Sp. habanera:* kind of dance) *n.* kind of slow dance; tune that accompanies the *habanera* dance.

abaníko: *(Sp. abanico:* fan) *n.* (folding) fan. **agabaniko.** *v.* to use a fan, fan oneself.

abáno: *(Sp. habano:* Havana cigar) *n.* rectangular shaped cigar with *bayág* tobacco. **agabano.** *v.* to smoke a cigar. **makiabano.** *v.* to ask for a cigar.

abánon: *n.* Scrofula (tuberculosis of the lymph glands characterized by swelling), king's evil. (*biel, buklong*); goiter. **pangabanon.** *n.* a kind of vine whose roots are used to cure scrofula. [Tag. *bosyò*]

abánse: *(Sp. avance:* advance) *n.* **agabanse.** *v.* to go ahead, advance (army). **miting de abanse.** *n.* last political rally before the election.

abánte: *(Sp. avante:* ahead) *interj.* Move on! Hurry up! (*aria, sige*) **agabante.** *v.* to go forward, go ahead. **maabantean.** *v.* to be left behind. **yabante.** *v.* to move something forward (a car, etc.).

ábang: *n.* rent; interest; lease; landowner's share of yearly crop. **agabang.** *n.* renter; tenant; leasee. **abangan.** *v.* to rent, hire out, lease out. **ipaabang.** *v.* to lease, rent out. **pagpaabang.** *v.* to rent a house. **agpapaabang.** *n.* landlord; one who leases a property. **paabangan.** *v.* to hire; rent. **pagab-abang.** *n.* rental payments, **pagabangen** *v.* to lease out. [Kal. *abyang, lawos*, Png. *ábang*, Tag. *upa*]

abáng: **abangan**. *v.* to wait for. (*urayen*, *tambang*) **umabang, abangan**. *v.* to ambush (*saneb, saed, sada*). [Tag. *abáng*]

abangbangígan: *n.* a kind of large bee whose wings are used in decoration (*barrairong*). [Tag. *uwáng*]

ábar: *n.* a kind of tree whose leaves are used to cure *barkes*, Santiria; *Hymenodictyon excelsum.*

abarngís: *n.* unsuitable; placed on the wrong side (*buttons*); dissimilar. (*abbigit*; *sungani*; *supadi*) **agabarngis**. *v.* to be slightly dissimilar; place on the wrong side. **-pagabarngisen**. *v.* to place on the wrong side. **agabarngis ti botones**. *v.* having buttons placed in the wrong buttonhole.

ábas: *n.* animal mouth tumor, foot and mouth disease.

abásto: *n.* supply; provisions; baggage. **abastuen**. *v.* to supply; provide with. [Tag. *panustós*]

ábat: see *salbat*: intercept; stop on the way. [Tag. *abát*]

abatík: *n.* cloth woven from *abaka* fiber, usually of a finer texture than *sinamay.*

abátir: *n.* remorse; a grub that attacks wood. (*bukbuk*) **inabatir**. *a.* attacked or infested by the *abatir.* [Tag. *bukbók*]

ábay: *n.* side, unison (of voices); best man in a wedding; (*coll.*) friend. **iti abay**. *prep.* beside. (*ampir, asibay, denna, sibay*) **agabay**. *v.* to stand side by side; to sing in unison. **yabay**. *v.* to place at the side of. **kaabay**. *v.* to stand by the side of. **agkaabay**. *v.* to stand side by side. **abayen**. *v.* to stand by the side of; stand beside; escort. [Kal. *cheeg*, Png. *abay*, Tag. *tabí*]

abáya: **umabaya**. *v.* to fester (wounds) (*rettab*). [Tag. *naknák*]

abáyon: *n.* sling for a broken arm, support. **yabayon**. *v.* to support (a broken arm). [Tag. *sakbát*]

abbál: **agabbal**. *v.* to carry in/with the mouth (dogs). (*ammal*; *tangal*) **abbalen**. *v.* to carry something in the mouth, hold something with the lips.

abbát: **apagabbat**. *a.* not thoroughly cooked due to lack of water (rice). **abbatan**. *v.* to let the water evaporate when cooking; dry up. **naabbatan**. *a.* dried up (rice fields, poorly cooked rice); suffering from draught. (*maatianan*) **apagabbat**. *a.* evaporated (rice) before it is thoroughly cooked. **Di maabbatan ti ubbog a paggapuan ti kuartana**. *exp.* His wallet never runs out (*lit*: the spring where his money comes from does not dry up). **Maabbatan ti baybay.**

The sea will dry up first (said to indicate impossibility).

abbéd: *n.* preventive measure; obstacle; hindrance. (*bangen*; *lapped*) **abbedan**. *v.* to obstruct; hinder. **pangabbed**. *n.* tourniquet; any device used to stop the flow (of blood, current, etc.), manmade obstacle. **Inlimedko a nagtomarak iti pildoras tapno maabbed ti panaganakmi.** I concealed the fact that I was taking birth control pills. [Tag. *bará*]

abbéng: *n.* obstacle, hindrance, something in the way of something else. (*arbeng*; *lapped*; *tiped*; *tubeng*) **abbengan**. *v.* to obstruct; hinder; prevent; intercept. **yabbeng**. *v.* to obstruct, use something to shield oneself (from excessive sunlight, etc.). **Nasamsam-itto ti panaglangenyo apaman a mawaknit ti ulep a nayabbeng iti langityo.** Your relationship will be sweeter as soon as the clouds obstructing your sky clear. [Png. *makasbél*, Tag. *hadláng*]

abbiáng: *n.* buri palm. (*abiang*; *anaaw*; *labíg*)

abbigít: *a.* unsuitable; not similar in size or fit; unadaptable. **agabbigit**. *v.* to be unsuitable; to not fit. (*abarngis*)

abbít: *n.* a kind of fish the shape of a silver dollar coin; glutton (*rawet*).

abbúkay: *n.* persuasion; suggestion; that which causes excitement. (*sulisog*) **abbukayen**. *v.* to persuade; excite; arouse; remind. **aabbukayan**. *n.* the erogenous zone (body part that is aroused when stimulated) **makaabukay**. *a.* arousing; stimulating; exciting. **Makaabbukay dagiti tokar manipud kadagiti banda.** The music coming from the bands was stimulating. [Tag. *antíg*]

abbóng: *n.* cover, lid, wrapper. (*akkub*; *kalúb*) **abbongan**. *v.* to cover, put a lid on. **yabbong**. *v.* to cover with. **maabbongan**. *v.* to be covered with. [Png. *takúp, sakób, dakib*, Tag. *takíp*]

abbúngot: *var.* of *abungot.*

abbútaw: *n.* hole. (*abut*) **abbutawan**. *v.* to pierce, bore a hole through. **naabbutawan**. *a.* pierced, having a hole.

ábe: (Sp. *ave, avemaría*: Hail Mary, rosary bead) **abe Maria**. Hail Mary.

abél: *n.* textile; web; woven fabric. **agabel**. *v.* to weave. **ablen**. *v.* to weave something (in the *pagablan*). **inabel**. *n.* woven fabric. **pagablan**. *n.* loom for weaving; textile mill. **mangngabel, umaabel**. *n.* (good) weaver. **ab-abel**. *n.* a kind of large hairy spider. (*abel-abel*) **abel-Iloko**. *n.* Ilocos weaving. [Ibg. *talapig, manikol*, Ivt. *tuminom*, Kal. *bilala, laga*, Kpm. *lála*, Knk. *káma, kambéy*, Png. *lagá, abel*, Tag. *habi*]

abeliána: (Sp. *avellana*: hazelnut) *n.* hazelnut colored leather, tan; tan leather shoes.

abenída: (Sp. *avenida*: avenue) *n.* avenue, wide street. **agpaabenida.** *v.* to go to the avenue. **pangabenida.** *n.* that which is used to take to the avenue, Sunday's best clothes used to show off.

abentúra: (Sp. *aventura*: adventure) *n.* adventure, exciting incident. **agabentura.** *v.* to have an adventure. [Tag. *pakikipagsapalaran*]

abenturéro: (Sp. *aventurero*: adventurer) *n.* explorer, adventurer. (*managbaniaga*)

ábér: *n.* a sardine sized marine fish of the *Clupeidae* family.

abér: (Sp. *a ver*: let's see) *exp.* let's see.

abería: (Sp. *avería*: vehicle trouble) *n.* vehicle damage; mechanical trouble; cause of delay.

abesedário: (Sp. *abecedario*: spelling book) *n.* alphabet; beginning alphabet book. **naabesedario.** *a.* in alphabetical order.

abestrús: (Sp. *avestruz*: ostrich) *n.* ostrich.

abí: *n.* insult (*daridar*, *yagyag*); contempt; hatred, despise (*gura*; *uyaw*). **ab-abien.** *v.* to insult. **maab-abi.** *v.* to be despised, hated, condemned. [Kal. *amsiwon*, Tag. *apí*]

abiadór: (Sp. *aviador*: aviator) *n.* aviator, pilot.

abiasión: (Sp. *aviación*: aviation) *n.* aviation.

abíday: *n.* shawl. **yabiday.** *v.* to throw something over the shoulder. **maabidayan.** *v.* to be wrapped, covered with (a curtain). **agabiday.** *v.* to wrap oneself over the shoulder. [Png. *abaráy*, Tag. *sagbát*, *salakbát*]

abiérta: (Sp. *abierta*: open) *n.* open necked (coat); open (store, window).

ábig: *n.* illicit coitus, adultery; infidelity. (*kamalala*) **makiabig.** *v.* to commit adultery. **pannakiabig.** *n.* adultery. **kaabig.** *n.* the person one commits adultery with. [Tag. *apíd*]

abígay: see *abiday*: wrap over shoulder; throw over shoulder; shawl; bandana. [Tag. *alampáy*]

abíit: *n.* ghost, spook. (*al-alia*)

abilidád: (Sp. *habilidad*: skill + English ability) *n.* ability, skill; talent; ingenuity. (*kabaelan*)

abinár: *n.* hobby; something repeatedly done by someone. **Isu laeng ti abinarenna nga aramid.** That's all he does with his time.

abíngay: see *bingay*: share; portion.

abír: *n.* term of direct address, short for *abírat*.

abírat: (pl. *aabirat*) *n.* term applied to the relationship between two unrelated men (or women) who marry siblings. **agabirat.** *v.* to be of this specified relationship (co-in-laws of the same generation, two people who have married siblings). [Bon. *abilat*, Kpm., Tag. *bilás*]

abíso: (Sp. *aviso*: warning) *n.* written notice; warning; information. **yabiso.** *v.* to forewarn;

give advance notice. (*ballaag*; *pakdaar*) **naabisuan.** *a.* notified, informed. [Tag. *patalastás*]

abistrána: *n.* a kind of shrub with violet-edged leaves.

ábit: **abit-abit.** *n.* affidavit; document. [Tag. *pahayag*]

abíto: *n.* habit; nun's outfit. **nakaabito.** *a.* wearing a habit. [Tag. *sutana*]

abitsuélas: (Sp. *habichuela*: white bean) *n.* lima bean, *Phaseolus sp.*

ablá: (Sp. *habla*: talk) *n.* idle talk; romantic talk. **agabla.** *v.* to propose; to verbally express one's love; to talk idly, speak nonsense. [Tag. *diga*]

ablát: **ablaten.** *v.* to throw something against; to whip from above. (*batbat*; *baut*) **yablat.** *v.* to whip something; thresh rice. **panangyablat.** *n.* manner of speaking. **naablatan.** *a.* whipped, lashed, flogged; threshed. **pagablatan.** *n.* old-fashioned thresher for rice. **Kasla naablatan nga uleg ti ayus ti karayan.** The flow of the river was like a whipped snake. [Tag. *hagupít*]

áblig: **maabligan.** *v.* to be looked down upon with contempt by the spirits. (*amling*)

abló: *n.* alley cat; wild cat. (*musang*) **abluen.** *v.* to knead a muscle or dislocated tendon.

ablóg: *n.* a kind of tree with edible fruit and whose leaves are used in curing rheumatism. **ablugen.** *v.* to drive away (*bugaw*). [Tag. *bugaw*]

ablón: **ablunen.** *v.* to massage; set a dislocated bone. (*ilut*; *bullo*) **mangngablon.** *n.* massage therapist; medicine man. [Tag. *hilot*]

ablusión: (Sp. *ablución*) *n.* ablution, moral purification.

abnormalidád: (Sp. *abnormalidad*: abnormality) *n.* abnormality.

ábo: *n.* a variety of awned rice. **abuen.** *a.* gray; *n.* a gray cock with a red tail (*dapuen*). [Tag. *abó* = ash]

abubília: (Sp. *abubilla*: hoopoe) *n.* hoopoe bird.

abubút: *n.* a basket with a long neck; knick-knacks. [Tag. *abubot*]

ábug: **abug-abug.** *a.* without notice or warning; sudden.

ábug: **abugen.** *v.* to drive away (*bugaw*); incite. **yabug.** *v.* irrigate a rice field; cajole; encourage someone to fall in love. **pangabug.** *n.* that which is used to drive away animals, goad. **pangabugan.** *n.* main source of water used to irrigate a rice field. [Tag. *bugaw*]

abogadílio: (Sp. *abogadillo*: petty lawyer) *n.* minor, petty lawyer; third-rate lawyer.

abogádo: (Sp. *abogado*: lawyer) *n.* lawyer, attorney; government solicitor. **agabogado.** *v.*

to be a lawyer; to become a lawyer. **pangabogado.** *n.* lawyer fee. **yabogaduan.** *v.* to defend in court (as a lawyer) **mangabogado.** *v.* to hire a lawyer. **ipaabogado.** *v.* to send someone to a lawyer; to take to an attorney. [Tag. *manananggól*]

abogágo: (Pil., *slang*, f. *abogado* 'attorney' + *gago* 'stupid') *n.* derogative appellation for lawyers.

abogásia: *n.* law course, law degree; the law profession. **pagabogasiaan.** *n.* where one attained his law degree; where one studies law.

abokádo: *n.* avocado, used in native medicine against diarrhea and wounds. **kaabokaduan.** *n.* avocado orchard.

abúkay: *n.* Job's tears: *Coix lachrymajobi*; necklace made of the seeds of the *abukay* plant.

abúlog: *n.* bamboo fence around bamboo houses; bamboo fence that encloses the space between the floor of the house and the ground. **abulugen.** *v.* to fence the space under the house. **mayabulog.** *v.* to be controlled; prevented; fenced in. [Tag. *kulong*]

abúloy₁: *n.* agreement, consent (*anamong*). **abuloyan.** *v.* to approve; agree with; acquiesce to. **yabuloy.** *v.* to donate to charity; contribute. [Png. *abóbon*, Tag. *payag* (agree), *abuloy*]

abúloy₂: *n.* help, aid, assistance; contribution. (*tulong*) **agabuloy.** *v.* to help, aid. **panaginnabuloy.** *n.* cooperation, the act of helping one another.

abonádo: (Sp. *abonado*: guaranteed, paid for (debt)) *n.* person responsible for paying a debt of someone else, guarantor. **agabonado.** *v.* to pay someone else's debt.

abunár: **pangabunar.** *n.* money to cover an emergency loss. **abunaran.** *v.* to disperse emergency money; to add the necessary money to cover a shortage of funds.

abúnaw: *a.* plentiful, abundant; *n.* abundance (*adu*, *narway*). **Nupay abunaw ti agkakaimas a sida ken makmakan, kasla diak mabsog no awan inabraw wenno binugguongan.** Even though there is abundant food and fish, I do not get satisfied if there are no boiled vegetables or shrimp paste dishes.

abúno: (Sp. *abono*: manure; security for a debt) *n.* fertilizer; dung (*ganagan*); money contributed by one to pay another's debt; advanced payment. **agabuno, abunuan.** *v.* to fertilize; pay in advance. **pagabuno.** *v.* to use as fertilizer. [Tag. *patabâ*]

ábong: *n.* hut; school of mudfish. **abong-abong.** *n.* repository used in processions, hut; toy house for children. **agabong-abong.** *v.* to live

in a hut. **abong-abongan.** *v.* to build a hut (*kalapaw*). [Tag. *kubo*, *barongbarong*]

abúngol: **abungolan.** *v.* to surround, crowd around, gather around. (*aribungbong*)

abúngot: *n.* kerchief; mask; blindfold. (*dalungdong*) **agabungot.** *v.* to wear a mask, veil, blindfold, etc. **yabungot.** *v.* to cover the head or the eyes with cloth. **abungotan.** *v.* to blindfold someone. **nakaabungot.** *a.* wearing a blindfold; wearing a veil. [Tag. *talukbóng*]

aborsión: (Eng.) *n.* deliberate abortion of fetus. (*paraspa*)

abúos: *var.* of *buos*: species of red stinging ant whose eggs are edible. [Kal. *tiyongan*]

abúroy: *n.* a female that has given birth to twins, triplets, etc. of the same sex; (*reg.*) twins, triplets of the same sex.

aburrído: (Tag. also, Sp. *aburrido*: bored) *a.* perplexed, troubled, worried (mind); bored; upset; obsessed. (*alalaw*; *danag*) **agaburrido.** *v.* to become worried, perplexed. **pagaburriduan.** *n.* worry, cause of one's worries.

abús: **abus man, abus ta.** *conj.* while, besides. **abus man pay.** *conj.* in spite of; in addition to. **Abus man pay ta tuleng, umel pay.** Besides being deaf, he is also dumb. [Tag. *yamang*]

abusádo: (Sp. *abusado*: abusive) *a.* stubborn; abusive; overbearing. **agabusado.** *v.* to abuse; be stubborn, overbearing. (*bangad*)

abusár: (Sp. *abusar*: abuse) **abusaren.** *v.* to abuse.

abuséro: (Sp. *abuso*: abuse, + *-ero* borrowed Spanish nom. actor suffix) *n.* abusive person; person who takes advantage of another; troublemaker.

abúso: (Sp. *abuso*: abuse) **agabuso.** *v.* to abuse; bother, irritate. **abusuen.** *v.* to irritate someone, annoy someone. **abusero.** *n.* troublemaker.

abústra: *n. Arcangelisia flava* tree. (*abutra*)

ábut: **maabut.** *v.* to reach; understand; overtake. **maabutan.** *v.* to be on time for; to be caught (by the rain); to be able to overtake someone; to be short of supply. **agaabut.** *v.* to come one after another (a woman who gives birth yearly, short breaths, etc.) **yabut.** *v.* to bring to one's reach; extend. **agaabut.** *v.* to touch; come one after the other. **agab-abut.** *v.* to catch up with; regain one's losses. **umabut.** *v.* to reach; be sufficient (until next harvest season, etc.); to be able to catch up with. **abut-palad.** *a.* within reach. **ababuten ti anges.** *v.* to gasp for breath. **Tallo a puntos ti pangabutanda kadakami.** They are three points behind us. **Immabut iti dua a**

tawen ti sakitna. Her sickness lasted up to two years. [Ibg. *battá, avvúq,* Png., Tag. *abót*]

abút: *n.* hole; pit; perforation. (*abbutaw, butbot; buttaw, lussok; tubbaw*) **abutan.** *v.* to pierce; bore a hole into. **yabut.** *v.* to drop something into a hole. **mayabut.** *v.* to step into a hole; fall into a hole. **agabun-abut.** *v.* to defend oneself by exposing another's mistakes or faults. **abut-abut.** *a.* with many holes; potholed. **mangngabut.** *n.* term for insects or other creatures that dwell in holes. **Abutek koma ti bilogda tapno lumnedda iti sabangan.** I should put holes in their canoe so it will sink in the mouth of the river. [Ivt. *balusut,* Knk. *lúkaw,* Kpm. *busbus,* Png. *abót, labó; butáw, botbot,* Tag. *butas*]

abútra: *n. Arcangelisia flava* tree.

ábuy: abuyan. *v.* to incite; stimulate. (*sugsog*) **yabuy.** *v.* to encourage; invite to do; direct; cajole. [Tag. *buyó*]

abúyan: *n. Harpullia sp.* plant whose bark is used to poison fish.

abúyo: *n.* jungle fowl. **agabuyo.** *v.* to not obey orders to go to a certain place. **pangngabuyo.** *n.* a kind of large striped bird with a large bill. [Tag. *labuyò*]

abrá: (Sp. *abra:* open) *n.* mountain gap; bay; cove; province east of Ilocos Sur.

abrása: *n.* embrace. (*arakup*) **abrasaen.** *v.* to embrace. **Nagiinnabrasa dagiti babbai.** The girls embraced each other.

abrasadéra: (Sp. *abrazadera:* clasp) *n.* iron strap for clasping posts.

abrasadór: (Sp. *abrazador:* embracer) *n.* side pillow; leg pillow. (*sap-al*) **agabrasador.** *v.* to use a side or leg pillow.

abrasiéte: (Sp. *de bracete:* arm in arm) *a.* walking arm in arm.

abráw: (Northern dialect) **agabraw.** *v.* to cook vegetables. (*dengdéng*) **inabraw.** *n.* vegetable dish. [Knk. *dengdéng*]

ábre: (Sp. *abre:* open) **abrean.** *v.* to open; operate on. **nakaabre.** *a.* open. **mangabre.** *v.* to open (mass); operate on; start.

abreláta: (Sp. *abrelatas:* can opener) *n.* can opener.

Abrénio: (f. *Abra* + borrowed Spanish suffix *-eño* denoting origin) *n.* native of Abra Province. (*taga-Abra*)

abresíto: (Sp. *abrazo:* embrace + *-ito* Spanish *dim. suffix*) *n.* embrace (said of children). **abresituen.** *v.* to embrace (*arakup*). [Tag. *yakap, yapós*]

abrí: (Sp. *abrir:* open) **abrian.** *v.* to open; pry open; to expose one's feelings.

abridór: (Sp. *abridor:* opener) *n.* can opener. (*abrelata*)

abrigádos: (*obs.*) settler in a foreign place.

abrígo: (Sp. *abrigo:* overcoat) *n.* thick scarf. (*dalungdong*) **nakaabrigo.** *a.* wearing a thick scarf.

abriguár: (Sp. *averiguar:* find out) **abriguaren.** *v.* to investigate; inquire about. (*usig*)

Abríl: (Sp. *abril:* April) *n.* April. [Kal. *akeÿ*]

abrisiéte: agabrisiete. *v.* to hold each other around the waist; walk arm in arm. (*abrasiete*) **abrisieten.** *v.* to hold around the waist.

abrót: abrúten. *v.* pull out; recover; regain losses. **makaabrot.** *v.* to be able to regain; get back. **maabrot.** *v.* to profit; gain; able to be regained (*subbot*). **umabrot.** *v.* to regain; recover; pull out (a nail). **Masapul nga abrutenna ti panagpuyatna.** He must recover (his sleep) from staying awake all night. [Tag. *bawì*]

absénte: (Eng.) *a.* absent (*langan*). [Tag. *liban*]

abséso: (Sp. *absceso:* abscess) *n.* abscess. (*bukol*)

absuélto: (Sp. *absuelto:* absolved) *a.* absolved; acquitted. **absueltuen.** *v.* to absolve; acquit. [Tag. *pawaláng-salà*]

absolbér: (Sp. *absolver:* absolve) **absolberen.** *v.* to absolve, set free from obligation, guilt or sin; acquit.

absolusión: (Sp. *absolución;* absolution) *n.* absolution; forgiveness, pardon; acquittal. (*pakawan*)

abstinénsia: (Sp. *abstinencia:* abstinence) *n.* abstinence. **agabstinensia.** *v.* to abstain.

abtó: umabto. *v.* to change one's mind; renounce (*likudan*); break a promise; abandon a fight (in cockfighting); to move abruptly, jump. [Tag. *bago*]

adáan: *n.* a kind of tree whose bark is used to poison fish, *Albizzia procera.*

ad-ád: *n.* sharpening with a stone; moving up and down while lying prone. **ad-adaen.** *v.* to sharpen on a stone. (*asa*) **pangad-adan.** *n.* anything used for sharpening a knife. [Tag. *hasà*]

ad-addá: *a.* more probable. **umad-adda.** *v.* to increase; fester (wounds). **yad-adda.** *v.* to add more to; increase; (*fig.*) to add a worse thing to an already bad situation. [Tag. *higít*]

ad-adú: *a.* more (see *pay*). [Tag. *mas marami*]

adág: *var.* of *addag:* weigh down, press down.

adák: agadak. *v.* to stroll; ramble, saunter; to swim back and forth (fish); trespass; encroach. **agadak-adak.** *v.* to trespass. (*basak*)

ádal: *n.* learning; education; knowledge; degree; vocation; profession. **agadal.** *v.* to study, learn.

(*suro*; *basa*) **adalen.** *v.* to study; investigate. *n.* homework; assignment. **adalan.** *v.* to teach; influence. *n.* student. **deadal.** *a.* educated; literate. **kaadalan.** *n.* fellow disciple; classmate. **maadal.** *a.* able to be learned; able to be studied. **managadal.** *a.* studious, diligent. **mapagadal.** *v.* to be able to put through school, to have the means to educate. **pagadal.** *n.* money used for one's education. **pagadalan.** *n.* book; school; college; university. **pagadalen.** *v.* to put through school, pay for one's education. **agpaadal.** *v.* to send to school; afford an education. **awan adalna.** *exp.* he is illiterate, not educated. **yadal.** *v.* to lecture; teach something. **Iti pintas ti apitna, napagadalda dagiti annakda.** Because of their good harvest, they were able to put their children through school. [Ibg. *gigiyammu*, Ivt. *macinanauq*, Kal. *achëÿ*, Png. *ádal*, Kpm., Png., Tag. *aral*]

adálem: *a.* deep, profound. (*liweng*) **umadalem.** *v.* to become deep. **kaadalem.** *n.* depth, profoundness. **pagadalman.** *n.* the point where water begins to become deep. **adalem a sardam.** *n.* late evening. [Bon. *adalem*, Ibg., Png. *aralém*, Itg. *uneg*, Ivt. *marahem*, Knk. *adáem*, *adáek*, *adallém*, *adálek*, *biéng*, Kpm. *malálam*, Tag. *lalim*]

adália: (Sp. *dalia*: dahlia flower) *n.* dahlia.

adambagin: *n. Adenanthera intermedia* plant.

Adán: (Sp.) *n.* Adam (in Bible stories).

adaní: *a.* near. (*asideg*) **umadani.** *v.* to come near, approach. **yadani.** *v.* to bring near. **No ni gasat ti umadani, uray iliktadan umuli.** *exp.* When fate comes, you cannot ward it off (it will climb up even if you remove the ladder). [Bon. *takdol*, Tag. *lapit*]

ádap: **umadap.** *v.* to begin to walk (infants). **adapen.** *v.* to visit every spot in a certain place; doubt; suspect; have second thoughts about something. [Tag. *angpáng*]

adaptár: (Sp. *adaptar*: adapt) **mangadaptar**, **adaptaren.** *v.* to adapt to; fit. **panagadaptar.** *n.* adaptation, act of adapting.

ádar: **naadar.** *a.* well-shaped; graceful. (*libnos*) **adaren.** *v.* to arrange nicely; do well (*urnos*; *dalimanek*). [Tag. *sinop*]

ádas: **adasen.** *v.* to glean (in a harvest). (*tudtod*) **adasan.** *v.* to drain.

adás₁: **naadasan.** *a.* faint through loss of blood; suffer from hemorrhage. **naadasan ti dara.** *n.* profuse bleeding. [Tag. *agas* = miscarriage]

adás₂: **agad-adas.** *v.* to be almost the same. (*pada*) **pagad-adasan.** *n.* points of similarity. [Tag. *hawíg*]

adasay: *n. Vernonia vidalii* plant.

ádat: *n.* aftertaste, bad taste. **naadat.** *a.* bad tasting. **umadat.** *v.* to become bad tasting. **Ti adatna.** *exp.* the bad thing about it. [Kal. *lagakÿak*, Tag. *paklá* = tart taste]

ádaw: **umadaw.** *v.* to borrow fire from a neighbor (*makisindi*). **adawan.** *v.* to take out, extract something (from a place). **adawen.** *v.* to take out from; extract; remove (from the fire); quote, copy. **naadaw.** *a.* taken out, extracted. **yadaw.** *v.* to take out of the pot, extract. **innadaw.** *n.* a children's finger game. **yadawan.** *v.* to draw something out of a pot for someone. [Tag. *hangò*]

adáwar: **adawaran.** *v.* to leave; go away from. **yadawar.** *v.* to remove; pull away from (*ikkat*). [Tag. *layò*]

adawáy: *n.* species of tree.

adayó: *a.* far, distant. (*sulinek*, *watiwat*; *wawwek*) **yadayo.** *v.* to take away, remove. (*ikkat*) **naadayo.** *a.* distant (in personal relationship). **adaywan.** *v.* to go far away from; get away from, keep one's distance. **agaddayo.** *v.* to be far away from each other. **yad-adayom**, Apo. *exp.* prayer asking for God's protection. **kaadayo.** *n.* interval; distance. **karkardayo.** *a.* far off; remotely possible. **pagaddaywen.** *v.* to place apart from each other. **Adayo a napimpintas ngem ni Irena.** She is by far prettier than Irena. **Iti yaadayona, nakitak ti panangpunasna kadagiti matana.** As she went away, I saw her wiping her eyes. [Ibg. *arayyu*, Ivt. *marayiq*, *ateng*, *vawa*, Kal. *achayu*, Knk. *adawí*, *dayodáyan*, *kaysán*, Kpm. *maráyuq*, Png. *dawí*, *arawi*, Tag. *layò*]

adbentísta: (Eng.) *n.* Adventist.

adbiénto: (Sp. *adviento*: advent) *n.* advent (period including the four Sundays before Christmas).

addá: Existential that expresses the concepts of possession or location, loosely translated into English as "to have" and "to be located." The negative counterpart is *awán*. 1. *Adda* used with possessed nouns expresses possession: **Adda asom.** You have a dog. **Adda kuartana.** He has money. *Adda* can also be used to express location: **Addadan.** They are already (here). **Adda ti kuarta 'toy pitakak.** The money is here in my wallet. **Addakami ditoy.** We are here. 2. When used with verbal complements, *adda* represents an indefinite argument in absolutive case: **Adda agsala.** Someone is dancing (is going to dance). **Adda nakitana.** He/she saw something. **Adda intedyo?** Did you guys give anything? **Adda kayatna nga ibaga.** He has something he wants to say. 3. When used with CVC reduplication of the following lexeme, *adda* attenuates the degree. **Adda bakbaknangmo.** You are somewhat rich. **Adda kekeesna.** He is a bit crazy. **Adda gasgastadora ni Ulay.** Ulay is a bit of a spendthrift. **agadda.** *v.* to become existent. **ad-adda.** *a.* more; more probable. **umad-adda.** *v.* to increase; augment; enhance. **maaddaan.** *v.* to have in one's possession. **addaan.** *a.* having, possessing; wealthy. **umad-adda.** *v.* to increase, augment; worsen. **paaddaen.** *v.* to produce, cause to exist. **pannakapaadda.** *n.* the creation (of); ability to produce. **kaadda.** *n.* act of existing; act of being at a certain location; having. **Baloak ken addaanak iti anak.** I am a widow with children. **Saanak nga agluto bayat ti kaaddana.** I won't cook while he is here. **Siak ti kaunaan a naaddaan iti ragadi.** I was the first to have a saw. [Knk. *wáda*, Png. *walá*, Tag. *may, mayroón*]

addág: *n.* weight; burden; load. (*pandag*) **addagan.** *v.* to press down, overrun; put a heavy weight on something; exert one's influence; (*reg.*) surpass, excel. **yaddag.** *v.* to lay on, put a weight on; pressure into. [Tag. *dagán*]

addagidiáy: [*adda + dagidiay*]. There they are. [Tag. *hayon*]

addagitá: [*adda + dagita*]. There they are (near addressee). [Tag. *hayan*]

addagitóy: [*adda + dagitoy*]. Here they are. [Tag. *heto*]

addán: [*adda + -en*] She/he/it is here; has arrived. **Addadan?** Are they here yet? [Tag. *nandíto na*]

addanási: naaddanasi (*obs.*) *n.* loiterer.

addaní: see *adaní*: close intervals (of events). (*asideg*)

addáng: *n.* step; gait; footstep; pacing; measure; project; plan. **agaddang.** *v.* to step; walk; to walk for the first time (babies). **mangad-addang.** *v.* to pace with regular steps. **addangen.** *v.* to step over; make it in one step; measure by steps. **agadda-addang.** *v.* to pace; walk step-by-step. **ipaaddang.** *v.* to measure by pacing. **umaddang.** *v.* to step forward. [Png. *koráng*, Tag. *hakbáng*]

addaydiáy: [*adda + daydiay*] There it is. [Png. *níman, wadmán*, Tag. *naroón, nandoón*]

addayó: *var.* of *adayo*. *a.* far. **panaginaddayo.** *n.* act of being far from each other.

addaytá: [*adda + dayta*]. There it is (near addressee). [Png. *nítan, wadtán*, Tag. *nandiyán, hayan*]

addaytóy: [*adda + daytoy*] Here it is. [Png. *nía, wadiá*, Tag. *nandito, naritó, heto*]

addí: pl. of *adi*: younger siblings.

addiwásiw: agaddiwasiw. *v.* to patrol, reconnoiter.

addúkay: maaddukayan. *a.* renewed; renovated; restored to life, invigorated.

adelantádo: (Sp. *adelantado*: done beforehand) *a.* unsure; uncertain; bold; fast (clock); progressive (*rang-ay*); advanced, ahead of time; developed too early.

adelantár: (Sp. *adelantar*: progress) **agadelantar.** *v.* to progress, advance; be fast (watch). **yadelantar.** *v.* to set a watch forward.

adelánte: (Sp. *adelante*: forward) *adv.* forward. (*agpasango*) **yadelante.** *v.* to set a clock forward.

adelánto: (Sp. *adelanto*: advance) *n.* down payment; advanced watch.

adélpa: (Sp. *adelfa*: oleander, rosebay) *n. Nerium oleander*, oleander shrub with red, white, or pink flowers.

adéntro: (Sp. *adentro*: inside) *n.* term used in the *rigodon* dance for a step involving an inward motion.

ádi: *n.* younger brother or sister; younger person in the same generation frequently addressed as *ading*. **adien.** *n.* next to the elder sibling. **maki-adi.** *v.* to treat like a younger sibling. **agadi.** *n.* the elder brother or sister. [Bon. *ódi*, Ivt. *adekey*, Knk. *alín, ugtán*, Kpm. *wali*]

ádi: mayadi. *v.* to age (*boggoong*); to be robust (plants); to bear many fruit (trees).

adí: agadi. *v.* to go back on one's word, to not like. **madi.** *v.* to refuse, not want. **aginmamadi.** *v.* to pretend to not want. **agmadimadi.** *v.* to be undecided. [Tag. *ayaw*]

adiáy: regional variant of *daydiay*: that (far from speaker and hearer).

adídas: (*coll.*, from the company name) *n.* barbecued chicken feet.

adígi: *n.* post; pillar. (*bayabay; dugo; singit; suray*) **yadigi.** *v.* to use as a post. **adigian.** *v.* to put posts on. [Bon. *tolkod*, Ibg. *kelleng, arigi*, Itg. *taldek*, Ivt. *parey*, Kal. *aliki*, Knk. *kubkub*, *túkud*, Kpm. *asyas*, Png. *losék*, Tag. *haligi*]

adín(o): *var.* of *sadino*. *interrog.* Where? [Tag. *saán*]

áding: *n.* younger brother or sister; term of address used for younger person of the same generation of the speaker. [Bon. *ódi*, Ivt. *adekey*, Knk. *ugtán, alín*, Png. *agí*]

adiós: (Sp. *adiós*: goodbye) *n.* goodbye, farewell.

adípen: *n.* slave; servant. (*bag-en; baon; tagabo*) **adipnen.** *v.* to enslave. **naadipen.** *a.* enslaved. **pannakaadipen.** *n.* slavery.

No kasapulan nga agpaadipen tapno makatulong a mangisakad iti pamilia, aramidenna dayta. If it is necessary to be a servant to be able to help support the family, he will do that. **Nauman a maad-adipen.** He is tired of being a servant. [Ibg. *ezzifen*, *wásin*, Ifg. *himbut*, Itg. *talaken*, Ivt. *pacirawatan*, Kpm. *ípus*, Png. *aripén*, Tag. *alipin*; Knk. *adípen* = service, use]

adirángot: *n.* stench, diffused odor. **umadirangot.** *v.* to diffuse (bad smells), stink. **Napalalo ti pungtotna iti umadirangot a rugit dagiti pusa iti balay.** He was excessively angry about the stench of the cats' litter in the house. [Tag. *amóy*]

adiwará: *n.* diffusion (of odor, fame, news, etc.). **agadiwara.** *v.* to spread; diffuse. (*arinuor*) **Nagadiwara ti ayamuom ti pabanglo nga insapsapona iti bagina.** The fragrance of the perfume he smeared on his body diffused. [Tag. *halimuyák*; *laganap*]

adíwas: umadiwas. *v.* to increase the intensity (wind, rain). [Tag. *lakás*]

adiwás: *n. Aglaia llanosiana* plant.

administrasión: (Sp. *administración*: administration) *n.* administration; (politics) regime, government; management of a dead man's property.

admitír: (Sp. *admitir*: admit) **admitiren.** *v.* to admit, recognize as factual; concede.

adú: *adv.* many, much, plenty. (*maruay*; *burnok*; *wadwad*) **nagadu.** *adv.* very much. **umadu, agadu.** *v.* to increase, augment. **kaadu.** *v.* total number; quantity. **ad-adu.** *adv.* more. **kaaduan, sangkaaduan.** *n.* majority. **makaadu.** *v.* to have more than usual. **makiinnadu.** *v.* to have the same quantity, match in quantity. **managadu.** *a.* multiplying; *n.* variety of mushroom. **paaduen, kaaduen.** *v.* to add to; increase. **mamin-adu.** *adv.* many times. **makapamin-adu.** *v.* to have done many times. **pagad-aduan.** *v.* to outnumber. **panagpaadu.** *n.* multiplication; reproduction. **pangaduan.** *n.* business, etc. in which one gains or profits much. **saggadu.** *a.* many for each. **Nayaduk.** I took a lot. **Agpayso nga adda dagiti kanito a kayattayo ti agmaymaysa ngem kaaduanna nga agsapultayo iti kaduatayo.** It is true that there are times when we want to be alone, but most times we need companionship. **Dagiti Ilokano ti kaaduan nga agindeg iti lugar.** The Ilocanos are the majority of the inhabitants of the place. [Bon. *edda*, *angsan*, Ibg. *aru*, Ifg. *dakol*, Ivt. *áruq*, *yavung*, Kal. *achu*, *amod*, Knk. *adá*, *goknót*, Kpm. *dakal*, Png. *dakél*, *amayámay*, Tag. *dami*]

aduána: (Sp. *aduana*: customs) *n.* customs, government department that collects duties on imports. **naaduana.** *a.* inspected by customs. [Tag. *adwana*]

aduanéro: (Sp. *aduanero*: customs officer) *n.* customs officer.

adóbe: (Sp. *adobe*: dried mud brick) *n.* quarry stone.

adubár: adubaren. *v.* to alleviate; restrain, repress; mitigate; conceal, camouflage. **maadubar.** *v.* to be alleviated; repressed; restrained; mitigated; concealed, camouflaged. **Inyisem ni Paquing a pinangadubarna iti riknana.** Paquing smiled to conceal his feelings. (*ep-ep*)

adóbo: (Sp. *adobo*: type of marinade) *n.* Filipino national dish made of pork and chicken seasoned with vinegar, garlic, salt (soy sauce), and sometimes bay leaves (*laurel*). **agadobo.** *v.* to cook this dish, pickle pork. **adobuen.** *v.* to pickle food the *adobo* style. [Tag. *adobo*]

ádug: see *ullok*: insist courteously.

adukág: *n. Dysoxylum ilocanum* plant.

adólpo: *n.* felt hat. (*dolpo*)

adulterádo: (Sp. *adulterado*: adulterated) *a.* adulterated.

adúngor: umadungor. *v.* to weep out loud; groan (*dung-aw*; *ug-og*). [Tag. *hagulgól*]

adoradór: (Sp.) *n.* adorer, one of the sacraments.

adorár: (Sp.) *n.* adoration; homage. **adorasion.** *n.* adoration. **adorasion nokturna.** *n.* nocturnal adoration.

adúray: (*obs.*) *part.* of course; it is evident; indeed. (*uray a*; *wen*, *a*; *la ketdi*)

adórno: (Sp. *adorno*: adornment) *n.* decoration; adornment. **agadorno.** *v.* to adorn oneself.

ádut: *n.* a variety of rice with a red kernel.

adú't: contraction of *adu* + *ti* = *adu't*: There is/are a lot of: **Adu't pusa ditoy.** There are a lot of cats here.

adtá: Contraction of *addayta*: there it is.

adtó: see *into*: marker of future.

adtóy: [*adda* + *ditoy*] It's here; here it is.

adyós: *var.* of *adiós*: goodbye. (*Dios ti kumuyog*; *Dios ti agbati*; *Ala ngaruden*; *kasta pay*)

ag-: *pref.* very frequent general intransitive verbalizing prefix that takes the *-ak* pronouns and marks the actor focus in the verb (perfective form is *nag-*): **1.** It verbalizes actions in which the actor exerts complete control: **agkatawa.** to laugh. **agisem.** to smile. **aglangoy.** to swim. **agdigos.** to bathe. **2.** However, it may also form verbs where the agent experiences the action of the root without exercising any control: **aglati.** to rust. **agukrad.** to bud. **3.** With some roots, it may indicate habitual occurrence of the action denoted by the verbal root: **aginum.** to habitually drink (alcohol) (vs. *uminom* 'to drink'). **4.** May indicate a state or condition (physical or mental): **agsakit.** to be in a state of pain. **agsarut.** to have tuberculosis. **5.** With sports and musical instruments, it carries the meaning of playing or use. **agtenis.** to play tennis. **agpiano.** to play the piano. **6.** With natural phenomena (meteorological roots) it expresses occurrence: **agkimat.** to strike (lightning). **agtudo.** to rain. **7.** With certain occupations it indicates study or practice: **agabogado.** to be a lawyer; to study to be a lawyer. **agallawagi.** to be a carpenter. **8.** With clothes, it designates wearing or putting on: **agtsinelas.** to wear slippers; put on slippers. **agbado.** to wear a dress; to change into a dress. **9.** With fruits and vegetables, it expresses collection: **agubas.** to gather grapes. **agtarong.** to gather eggplant. **10.** With certain implements, it verbalizes the action typically associated with that instrument: **agmartilio.** to hammer. **agragadi.** to saw. **11.** With condiments, it carries the meaning of use or seasoning with the condiment: **agsili.** to season with *sili*. **12.** It verbalizes stative roots: **agdakkel.** to be large. **agbayag.** to take a long time. **13.** With full reduplication of the root, it expresses continuous or reiterative occurrence: **aglamo-lamo.** to go around naked. **agsaka-saka.** to go around barefoot **14.** With languages it indicates speaking or proficiency: **ag-Kastila.** to speak Spanish. **15.** With certain kin terms and family names, it expresses reciprocal relationship. **agama.** father and son. **agasawa.** married couple. **agama.** father and son. **dagiti ag-Galvez.** the Galvez family. **16.** With numbers, it indicates the count: **Agduapulo ngata dagiti Mehikanos.** There were probably twenty Mexicans. **17.** May be also used to indicate reciprocal relationships taking plural absolutive subjects. **Agamammokamin.** We already know each other. **Nagapada.** They fought with each other.

ag- -inn-: Intransitive affix of reciprocity: to do to each other. Perfective form is *nag- -inn-*. To further specify plural actor, the root undergoes CV reduplication **agtinnulong.** to help each other. **agsisinnaranay.** to save, guard each other. **ayat.** love. **aginnayatda nga agassawa.** husband and wife that love each other, loving married couple. **Agkinnaawatankami.** We understand each other.

agaC-: *pref.* attaches to nominal roots to indicate the particular odor designated by the root, also *agat-*: **agassabong.** to smell like a flower. **agatlaya.** to smell like ginger. **Agabawang diay baket.** That old lady smells like garlic. **Agasabongka.** You smell like a flower. This prefix may also attach to full noun phrases: **agat-natay a baoka.** You smell like a dead rat. With certain roots, the meaning becomes lexicalized, as in the following: **agattsiko.** *v.* to smell like sapodilla fruit (*fig.* to have alcoholic breath) (*agat-arak*) **agappugot.** *v.* to smell like a bogeyman (*fig.* to have strong underarm odor) (*anglit*) **agabbawang.** *v.* to smell like garlic (*fig.* to feel as if a wedding is approaching). **agabbaraniw.** *v.* to smell like lemon grass (fig: to seem scandalous; to seem as if a wedding is near). [Bal. *paggaCVCV-*, Ibg. *magaC-*, Ivt. *maya-*, Png. *magkaka-*]

agáag: *n.* very slight crack (in a jar, etc.); faint ray of light. **agagaag.** *v.* to crack slightly (*agbirri, agrekka, agbettak*). [Tag. *lamat* (crack); *anag-ág* (glimmer of light)]

agáal: see *agal*: moan; lament.

ágab: *n.* stealing of livestock (cattle or goats); (*fig.*) enriching oneself furtively; theft; **agaagab.** *n.* livestock thieves. **umagab.** *v.* to steal cattle. **Maibusen dagiti kalding dagiti kaarrubak nga ag-agaben dagiti managdakdakes.** My neighbors' goats that the criminals stole are all gone. [Knk. *ágab* = covet, said of wealthy]

agábe: (Sp. and English *agave*) *n.* the agave plant of the *amaryllis* family.

agabís: *n.* a kind of minute, edible marine shrimp, smaller than the *armang*. [Tag. *agahis*]

agabuét: *n.* a kind of delicious marine fish.

ágad: *n.* track; trail; path. (*bit-ang, daná, sebbang, desdes, basbas*) **yagad.** *v.* to encourage; suggest; propose; recommend. [Tag. *daán*]

agáging: (*coll.*) *n.* hiding place; faraway place.

ágal: **umagal, agagal.** *v.* to moan; lament; complain. **agalen.** *v.* to complain (*angal; asug*). **ag-agalen.** *n.* sickness. **Inagal ti inana ti panagruar iti takki iti mabagbagina imbes koma nga iti ubetna.** His mother complained about the expulsion of her feces through her genitals instead of through her anus. [Tag. *angal*]

agáma: *n.* a kind of large, white crab. [Bon. *agma*, Ibg. *akayaq*, Itg. *agamma*, Ivt. *cituh*, Knk. *gaki*, Kpm. *éma*, Png. *alama*, Tag. *alimango, alimasag*]

agamá: (f. *amá*) *n.* father and son. [Tag. *mag-amá*]

agámang: *n.* granary. (*sarúsar, kamalig*) **yagamang.** *v.* to store in a granary. [Tag. *kamalig*]

agámid: *n. Ficus palawanensis* plant.

aganáy: *adv.* approximately (used with numbers). [Tag. *halos*]

agandóng: *n. Pipturus arborescens* plant.

aganiáng: *n.* a kind of medicinal herb.

agangáy: (f. *angay*) *adv.* eventually; finally, in the end; at last; as a result. **pagangayán.** *n.* end; result; outcome (*pagbanagan*). **Idi agangay, nangabakda met laeng.** At long last they won, they finally won. [Tag. *sa wakás*]

ágap: **agagap.** *v.* to slice thinly. (*iwa*) **agapen.** *v.* to cut something into thin slices.

agápad: **agapaden.** *v.* to mention in passing; refer to; make use of; include. [Tag. *banggít*]

agapagáwan: *n.* young chicken. (*pagaw*)

agaró: *n. Dysoxylum turczaninowii* plant. (*pupuut*)

agarúp: *a.* seemingly; to seem. (can be used with verbs); almost (used with numbers). (*arig; ngani*) **Agarup agkatawenda.** They seem to be the same age. [Tag. *halos, parang*]

ágas: *n.* medicine; cure, remedy. **agasan.** *v.* to cure, heal; treat with medicine. **mangngagas.** *n.* doctor, physician; faith healer. **pannaka-agas.** *n.* medication. **panangyagas.** *n.* treatment. **yagas.** *v.* to apply medicine to. **managagas.** *n.* person prone to taking medication; habitual medicine consumer. **kinamangngagas.** *n.* doctorate, medicine (field of study). **maiparit nga agas.** *n.* illegal drugs. [Ibg. *urú*, Ivt. *tuvatuvaq*, Kal. *lugem*, Knk. *súmang*, Kpm. *panúlu*, Png. *tambál*, Tag. *gamót*; Tag. *agas* = miscarriage; Knk. *ágas* = boil]

agásem: *part.* Just imagine. (plural *agasenyo*). **Agasem ti panagmaymaysanton ti lakay idiay kabakiran.** Just imagine how lonely the old man in the forest will be. [Tag. *akalain mo*]

agas-móro: *n. Vernonia cinerea* plant.

agat-: *var.* of the prefix *agaC*- denoting smell. **bawang.** garlic. **agat-bawang.** smelling of garlic. **Apay ngata nga agat-sorbetes ti puloy?** Why do you think the breeze smells like ice cream? [Bal. *paggaCVCV-*, Ibg. *magaC-*, Png. *magkaka-*]

agáta: (Sp.) *n.* agate.

agatól: *n.* a kind of freshwater crab with one large claw. [Kal. *agoma*, Tag. *alimango*]

ágaw: **agawen.** *v.* to snatch off (*bigsot, gursot; rabsut; rabnis; sibbarut*); carry off. **agawan.** *v.* to snatch from someone, rob someone. **agagaw sipnget lawag.** *n.* dawn; dusk; twilight. **aginnagaw.** *v.* to scuffle; wrestle to obtain an object; overcome. **kainnagaw.** *n.* rival. **yagaw.** *v.* to interpose. **Awan ti siasinoman a parsua**

a makaagaw kenka kaniak. Nobody can take you away from me (*lit*: no creation). [Png. *labnót, sikwát*, Tag. *agaw*]

agáwa: *n.* diligence, industry (*gaget*); anxiety, eagerness; greed; ambition. **naagawa.** *a.* ambitious; greedy for money; industrious. **agawaan.** *v.* to be diligent; be fast, hasten. **Inagawaanna ti nagpakleb.** *v.* He immediately (with diligence) fell prone. **Agawaakto ti agtrabaho tapno makaurnongak iti kuarta.** I will be diligent in work so I can save money. [Tag. *sipag*]

agáwi: **agawien.** *v.* to allure (*sulisog*); invite; take the opportunity.

agay-ayám: (f. *ayám*) *n.* reptiles, creeping animals.

agbulígan: (f. *búlig*) *n. Clerodendron macrostegium* plant.

agdamá: (f. *dama*) *adv.* currently; at the present time, right now. **agdinama.** *a.* present (time).

agdán: *n.* ladder, stairs. **umagdan.** *v.* to go up or down stairs. **agdanan.** *v.* to use a ladder; add stairs to. **maagda-agdan.** *v.* to do one step at a time; *adv.* going up like a staircase. **pagagdanan.** *n.* stairway. (*arsadanan ti agdan*) **iliktad ti agdan.** *v.* to pull up the ladder (of a house high over the ground). [Bon. *teytey, saklang*, Ibg. *addán, eddan*, Ifg. *téte*, Ivt. *iskalíraq*, Kal. *echen*, Knk. *tétey*, Kpm. *eran*, Png. *takáyan*, Tag. *hagdán*]

agdanpársa: *n.* long ladder.

ageb-éb: *n.* a kind of small freshwater shrimp.

agék: *n.* kiss. (*bisung, besito, agep, ungngo*) **agkan, umagek.** *v.* to kiss. **aagkan.** *n.* kissable lips. **agpaagek.** *v.* to allow oneself to be kissed. **aginnagek.** *v.* to kiss one another. **yagek.** *v.* to say it with a kiss; do with a kiss. [Ibg. *ummoq*, Ivt. *mayarek*, Kpm. *úmaq*, Png. *angób*, Tag. *hagkán, halík*]

agép: *n.* kiss of respect for elders. **umagep.** *v.* to kiss (usually said of sniffling while embracing elders).

agi-: *pref.* Intransitive prefix used with theme focus *i*- verbs that takes the *-ak* pronouns, similar to *mangi-*. Perfective form is *nagi*-. **Saanka koma nga *agi*lunod iti masakbayanna.** You should not curse her future.

agíbas: *n.* hitting, striking; passing by; flash. **umagibas.** *v.* to pass by; to go to a place and return quickly; to suddenly flash (light); flash in one's mind; to hit, strike. **agibasen.** *v.* to pick up something fast; pass by. **Narumektayo koma no saan a naalibtak ti piloto iti yaagibas ti yelo.** We would have been smashed to pieces if the pilot was not clever when we hit the ice.

agiína: *n.* plural of *agina*; mother with children.

agíing: *n.* species of tree. **umagiing.** *v.* to be shy, timid, lack self-confidence (*agbabain*). [Tag. *dungô, hiyâ*]

ágila: (Sp. *águila*: eagle) *n.* eagle. **agila ti taaw.** *n.* seagull. [Bon. *koling, banog*, Kal. *tuÿayan*]

agimó: *n.* a kind of herb.

agimpapa-: Pretentative prefix for causative *pa-* stems. **agimpapangina.** to play hard to get; to pretend to show off wealth one doesn't have.

aginCV-: *pref.* Pretentative prefix. As an intransitive prefix, it takes the *-ak* series pronouns. Perfective form is *nagin*CV-. **Aginsisingpet.** He pretends to be virtuous. **Aginsasangitda.** They are pretending to cry. **aginnanakem.** to do voluntarily. **agindidi.** insincere.

agína: *n.* mother and child, from *ina.* (plural is *agiina*).

agináldo: (Sp. *aguinaldo*: Christmas bonus) *n.* Christmas gift. (*regalo*; *sagut ti Paskuá*)

agindidí: (f. *di*) *v.* to be insincere; pretentious.

áging: *n.* hidden place, remote place.

aginggá: see *aginggana*: until. **agingga't inggana.** *exp.* forever, for eternity. [Tag. *hanggáng*]

aginggána: **aginggana ti.** *prep.* until.

agipa-: *pref.* Causative or directional form of the *agi-* verb. Perfective form is *nagipa-*. As an intransitive affix, it takes the *-ak* series pronouns. **awat.** understand. **agipaawat.** to make something understood.

ágir: **naagir.** *a.* oversensitive; timid. **yagir.** *v.* to watch over; protect; refrain. **kinaagir.** *n.* sensitiveness; sensitivity.

agír: **umagír.** *v.* to snore (*urok*; *gerrek*). [Tag. *hilík, harok*]

ágis: *n.* narrow strip. **sangkaagis.** *n.* one strip of. **agisan.** *v.* to make narrower. **agisen.** *v.* to cut in order to maker narrower. [Tag. *kayas*]

agít: *n.* a kind of small fish.

agíto: *n. Tagetes erecta* ornamental plant, (*Sp. amarilyo*).

ágiw: *n.* cobweb (*kulalabat*). [Tag. *agiw* = soot]

agka-₁: Prefix used to form fractional numbers. **agkapito.** It is divided into seven parts. **agkasangagasutda.** They are divided into one hundred parts.

agka-₂: Prefix of equality indicating that the actors of the verb have the quality expressed in the root to an equal degree or rank, share the entity denoted by the root, or perform the action expressed by the root together: **agkapintas.** to be of equal beauty (f. *pintas* beauty). **Agkadakkelta.** I am as tall as you (You and I are of equal height). **agkarupa.** to have the same face; to look like; resemble.

agkabunggoyan. to be from the same neighborhood. **agkamaris.** to be of the same color; **agkalugan.** *v.* to ride together, share a ride in a car. **Agkalinongkami iti payongna.** We shared the shade of his umbrella. **Agiinnammo dagiti agkakadaraan.** Countrymen (*lit.* people with the same blood) know each other. **-Agkabagbagikami.** We are of the same build (have the same body).

agka- -an: Affix of reciprocity, taking only plural subjects. Perfective form is *nagka- -an.* **agkaayatanda.** They love each other.

agka- -an-: Prefix and infix combination used with certain onomatopoetic roots to indicate continuous or repetitive sounds; see also *-uman-* where the sound is produced in quick succession. Perfective form is *nagka- -an-* **bitog.** thumping sound, root **agkabanitog.** to produce thumping sounds several times at regular intervals. **bumanitog.** to produce a thumping sound several times in quick succession.

agkabannuág: *n.* youth. (*kinaagtutubo*)

agkaCkaC-: Prefix of distributive equality. **Agkatkatayag dagiti agkapkapuner a kabalio.** The muscular horses are equally tall.

agkai-: Intransitive prefix indicating distributivity of the action expressed in the stem (past is *nagkai-*): **agkaiwaris.** to be scattered everywhere **agkaisubli.** to come back repeatedly.

agkaka-: Intransitive prefix used with plural actors to denote the performance of an action or the achievement of a state to a similar degree; see *agka-*. Perfective form is *nagkaka-* **agkakanginada.** They are all equally expensive. **dagiti agkakalapsat a bastonera.** The equally well endowed majorettes.

agkamanó: (f. *manó*) *interrog.* Into how many parts is it divided? **Agkamanokayo?** Into how many groups are you divided? **Agkamanoda?** Into how many groups are they divided?

agkán: *v.* [*agek + -an*] to kiss (*bisung, agep, bisito*). [Tag. *halík*]

agkana- +V$_2$: Prefix used with onomatopoetic roots to indicate the occurrence of a succession of sounds indicated by the root. The first root vowel may drop while the second root vowel may double when used with this prefix. Perfective form is *nagkana- +* V$_2$. **agkanalbuong.** (f. *libóng*) succession of firing (gunshots). **agkanaltuok.** (f. *litok*) succession of hollow metallic sounds. **agkanalsitak.** sound of clashing swords. **agkanalpaak.** sound of repeated slapping. **agkanalpuot.** sound of flatulence. **agkanalpiit.** sound of clashing heels or slippers.

agkanika-: *pref.* used with numerical bases to indicate that the amount is approximately that which is specified by the base. Perfective form is *nagkanika-*. **Agkanikaduapuloda.** There are about twenty of them.

agkara-: Frequentative prefix used with *ag-* verbs. Perfective form is *nagkara-*. **tinnag.** fall **agkaratinnag.** to fall down repeatedly, continuously; **agkaraapan.** to be always on the go; **agkarauyekda.** They are coughing continuously. **Agkaralipak dagiti kanion.** The cannons fire repeatedly. **Agkarasuyaabak ngem diak met makaturog.** I keep yawning but I can't sleep.

agkarai-: Frequentative prefix used with *i-* verbs specifying repeated or continual action. Perfective form is *nagkarai-*: **agkaraisubli.** He always brings it back.

agkinna- -an: Reciprocal affix denoting that the action of the stem is performed by a plural subject to each other. Perfective form: *nagkinna- -an*: **Nagkinnaawatanda.** They understood each other.

aglálo: (f. *lalo*) *adv.* especially.

Aglipáy: *n.* a Philippine church, *Iglesia Filipina Independiente*. **Aglipayano.** *n.* member of the Aglipayan church.

agmaka-: *pref.* used with temporal roots to indicate one period of the time frame designated by the root. Perfective form is *nagmaka-*. **Agmakabulanakto idiay.** I will spend a month there. **Agmakalawasen.** It has been a week already.

agmara-: Intransitive prefix *ag-* + similarity prefix *mara-*. Perfective form is *nagmara-* **agmaratubbog.** to water (eyes), be like juice.

agmúy: **agagmuy.** *v.* to bend the tops of trees (to shade a path, etc.); to arrange the hair, fall on one side (hair). **agmuyen.** to arrange hair; bend the tops of trees. **Narakab ti rupana nga inagmuyan ti lampong a buokna.** He had a long face with shaggy hairs falling on the sides. **Agmuyem ti aringkuloten a buokna.** Arrange her wavy hair. [Tag. *hapay*]

agnanáyon: *adv.* always; forever; eternally; perpetual. **kinaagnanayon.** *n.* eternity. [Tag. *magpakailán man*]

agnás: *n.* kind of freshwater fish.

agnéb: **umagneb.** *v.* to ooze; become damp; percolate. **naagneb.** *a.* damp, moist (*alunapet*); fertile. **kapaagneb.** *v.* to fertilize (render fertile). **makapaagneb.** *v.* to be able to impregnate or fertilize. **naagneban.** *a.* overwhelmed; overburdened; dispirited. **Inaprosanna ti**

immagneb a rupana. He wiped his moist face. [Tag. *tagas*]

agnóstiko: (Sp. *agnóstico*: agnostic) *a.* agnostic.

água: (Sp. *agua*: water) *n.* water (*danum*); deodorant (*pabanglo*). **agua bendita.** *n.* holy water. **agua burikada.** *n.* boric lotion. **agua potable.** *n.* drinking water. **agua pataranta.** (*coll.*) *n.* liquor (*arak*). **agua plorida.** *n.* rose water; scented water. **agua-asahár.** *n.* orange flower water. **agua-poso.** *n.* well water. **agua-rehia.** *n.* mixture of nitric acid and hydrochloric acid. **agua-oksihenada.** *n.* hydrogen peroxide. [Tag. *tubig*]

aguádo: (Sp. *aguado*: watered-down) *n.* dulce, fruit cocktail; *a.* melted; liquefied.

aguadór: (Sp. *aguador*: water carrier) *n.* water carrier. (*parasakdo*)

aguáhe: (Sp. *aguaje*: wake of a ship) *n.* wake of a ship.

agúanta, aguantár: (Sp. *aguanta*: endure) **ag-aguanta, maaguantaran.** *v.* to cope; endure; put up with; do fast. **Iti agtultuloy a panagadu ti tao, diyonto la ketdi maaguantaran ti kasapulanda.** With the continued population growth, you won't be able to cope with their needs. [Tag. *tiís*]

aguardiénte: (Sp. *aguardiente*, from *agua ardiente*: burning water) *n.* gin (*hinebra*); hard liquor.

aguárras: (Sp. *aguarrás*: oil of turpentine) *n.* oil of turpentine. (*trementína*)

aguás: *n.* a kind of freshwater fish, large-scaled mullet.

aguasíl: (Sp. *alguacil*: peace officer) *n.* peace officer during the Spanish time.

aguatiémpo: (Sp. *agua* 'water' + *tiempo* 'time') *n.* staple beverage besides water, usually given to a sick person to hasten a cure.

águb: *n.* odor of stored grains. (*bang-eg*) **naagub.** *a.* smelling of rotten rice or stored grains.

águd: *n.* scraping the edge of something with a tool to make it smooth; knead; smooth out creases in clothes. **agudan.** *v.* to scrape; scrape into smoothness; smoothen out. [Tag. *hagod*]

aguday: *n. Crypternia sp.* plant.

agúha: (Sp. *aguja*: needle) *n.* needle; hypodermic needle; hand of a watch; needle of a compass.

aguhília: (Sp. *aguja*: needle + *-illa* dim. suffix) *n.* hairpin.

aguhón: (Sp. *agujón*: large needle) *n.* very large needle; drawing compass needle.

águm: *n.* ambition, greed; envy. (*buklis; garamugam; apal*) **aguman.** *v.* to crave for, covet;

be envious. **naagum.** *v.* covetous; greedy. [Png. *agum*, Tag. *inggít, hilì*]

agundalagap: *n. Ixora cumingiana* plant.

agonías: (Sp. *agonías*: death agonies) *n.* tolling of church bells for the dying or dead.

agunoy: *n. Wedelia biflora* plant found along the beach and streams.

agóng: *n.* nose; funnel shaped entrance of a bow net. **agongan.** *a.* having a large nose. **impaagong.** *a.* nasal. **ipaagong.** *v.* to say nasally. **Kasano ti pannakaag-agongna ta maangotna pay ti sangpetko.** Must be some nose he has if he can even smell my arrival. [Bon. *engel*, Ibg. *igung*, Ifg. *olong*, Ivt. *mumudan*, Kal. *ongeÿ*, Knk. *eng*, Kpm. *árung*, Png. *eléng*, Tag. *ilóng*]

agóo: *n.* a kind of pine tree; *Casuarina equisetifolia* found along sandy seashores (*aroo*). [Tag. *aguhô*]

agúot: *n.* a kind of tasty marine fish.

agúpa: (f. *upa*) *n.* tenant, renter; *v.* to rent, lease.

agúrong: *n.* a kind of marine fish; kind of shellfish with a black, elongated shell of spiral design.

águs: *n.* current; white water of a stream. **ipaagus.** *v.* to throw with the current. **mayagus.** *v.* to be carried off with the current. **sumurot iti agus.** *exp.* to go along with the crowd. [Png, Tag. *agos*]

Agósto: (Sp. *agosto*: August) *n.* August. [Kal. *bisbis*]

agustíno: (Sp.) *n.* Augustinian monk.

águt: agutan, aguten. *v.* to knead; massage by kneading. [Tag. *masa*]

agúyan: *n.* cloth used in fishing to trap fish from the bottom.

agúyong: (f. *uyong*) *a.* crazy; insane (*bagtit*). [Tag. *ulól*]

agpa-: *pref.* 1. Causative or indirect form of the prefix *ag-*. Perfective form is *nagpa-*. **pukis.** haircut. **agpapukis.** to have a haircut. **pintas.** beauty **agpapintas.** to beautify one's self. 2. directional prefix indicating motion toward the place named by the locative root: **Agpaabagatanda.** They are heading south. **Nagpa-Bauangkami.** We went to Bauang. May also indicate that the actor is asking for the action of the stem to be done: **Agpagatangak iti hopia kenkuana.** I am going to ask him to buy (me) *hopia*.

agpá: *n.* armspan (*deppa*). **agpaen.** *v.* to measure by extending the arms. **sanga(a)gpa.** *n.* one armspan; the length of two extended arms. (*sangadpa*)

agpaCpa-: Continuous aspect form of the *agpa-* prefix. **agpappapatay.** *n.* murderer, one who

murders. **dagiti agpaspasukmon.** *n.* wine vendors.

agpai-: Actor focus, causative instrumental prefix. Indicates that the actor of the verb has the action designated by the verb root carried out using an unspecified implement. Perfective form is *nagpai-*: **agluto.** to cook. **agpaluto.** to have something cooked. **agpailuto.** to have something cooked with other ingredients.

agpaka-: Actor focus prefix of causation. Perfective form is *nagpaka-*. **agpakaasi.** to beg; plead; ask for pity. **agpakalukmeg.** to become fat (with control).

agpalpalamá: *n.* beggar, pauper.

agpáng: *n.* bamboo strip used in netting; a measure; standard; guidepost. **agkaagpang.** *v.* to be of the same class or standard; to be suitable. **umagpang.** *v.* to be about time to do something; to be suitable; to be of the same class, level; to be in season. **maagpangan.** *v.* to be one's turn to do something. [Tag. *agpáng* = fitted; adequate]

agpapán: *prep.* until, till. **agpapan pay.** even, with regard to; despite. **agpapan-agawid.** *n.* roundtrip. **agpapan ita.** until now. [Tag. *hanggáng*]

agpáw: umagpaw. *v.* to jump over an obstacle; to surmount; to jump one step higher (*lagto*; *layaw*). [Tag. *igpáw*]

agpaysó: *a.* true, factual; genuine. (*pudno*) **ipaypayso, paypaysuen.** *v.* to fulfill one's word; to be serious. **kinaagpayso.** *n.* truth; fact. **Awan kinaagpaysuananna.** There is no truth to the matter. [Tag. *totoó*]

agpi(n)-: Prefix used with numeric roots to indicate how many times an action is done. Perfective form is *nagpi(n)-* **Siak ti nagpimpat.** I am the one who did it four times. **Nagpinlimada.** They did it five times.

agpinna-: *pref.* indicating a reciprocal causal relationship between the plural actors of the verb. Perfective form is *nagpinna-*: **Agpipinnabasolda.** They are blaming each other.

agpipinna-: Intransitive prefix taking plural actors to specify reciprocal causation. Plural form of *agpinna-*. Perfective form is *nagpipinna*. **agpipinnabasol.** to blame one another, to blame each other

agrabiádo: (Sp. *agraviado*: injured; offended) *a.* offended, aggrieved; injured; treated unfairly. **maagrabiado.** *v.* to be offended; aggrieved; upset; treated unfairly. **agrabiaduen.** *v.* to offend, treat unfairly.

agráman: *prep.* with; including (*pati*). [Tag. *pati*]

agrário: (Sp. *agrario*: agrarian) *a.* agrarian, pertaining to agriculture.

agrasiádo: (Sp. *agraciado*: rewarded) *a.* having a work scholarship in school, having work study.

agráw: *n.* a kind of shrub with small white flowers: *Sambucus javanica*; *Premna nauseosa*.

agresíbo: (Sp. *agresivo*: aggressive) *a.* aggressive.

agridúlse: (Sp. *agridulce*: sweet and sour) *a.* sweet and sour (sauce); bittersweet. **sarsa agridulse.** *n.* sweet and sour sauce.

agrikultúra: (Sp. *agricultura*: agriculture) *n.* agriculture. (*panagtaltalon*)

agrimensór: (Sp. *agrimensor*: land surveyor) *n.* land surveyor.

agrimensúra: (Sp.) *n.* science of land measuring.

agsápa: *n.* early morning. (*sapa*; *bigat*) **ipa-agsapa.** *v.* to wait until morning to do something. **kaagsapáanna.** *adv.* the following morning. [Kal. *makawisngit*, Png. *buás*, Tag. *umaga*]

ágsaw: *n.* skimmer (used in skimming *basi*). (*pagagsaw*) **agsawen.** *v.* to skim, collect, scoop whatever is left; snatch away; pick out the good ones; study. **sangkaagsaw.** *n.* handful; bundleful; *a.* meagerly.

agsép: *n.* osmosis, absorption. (*agneb*, *sagepsep*) **agsepen.** *v.* to absorb. **naagsep.** *a.* absorbent. [Png. *sepsép*, Tag. *sipsíp*]

agsi-: Actor focus prefix used to express concomitance or distribution of the action of the stem. Perfective form is *nagsi-*: **agsiwara.** to scatter in all directions (many people).

agsinCV-: (*obs.*) prefix of reciprocity. **Agsintu-tulongkami.** We (*excl.*) help each other.

agsinan-: Intransitive prefix combination of the intransitive verbalizing prefix *ag-* and the *sinan-* prefix of similarity or untruth: **agsinan-abogado.** to be a fake lawyer. **agsinan-inheniero.** to take engineering type courses, to be a quasi-engineer.

agsípud: *prep.* because, on account of. (*gapu ta*) **agsipud ta.** because. [Png. *sipor*, Tag. *dahil sa*]

agsít: *n.* thatchwork, layer of grass or leaves for thatching. **pagagsit.** *n.* bamboo (or other material) used to hold the thatching. **agsitan.** *v.* to thatch (*atép*). [Tag. *atíp*]

Agtá: *n.* Negrito; the language of the Negritos. (*Aeta*, *Ayta*)

agtagi-: Prefix used to indicate possession or general interest or concern over the entity designated by the root (may be used with some roots to indicate the habitual action of a profession expressed by the stem). Perfective form is *nagtagi-* **agtagibuneng.** *v.* to carry a machete. **agtagikua.** to own; *n.* the owner. **agtagibalay.** to keep house; *n.* housewife. **agtagilako.** to be a salesperson. **Dimmarup ti uppat a lallaki a nagtagipang-or.** He approached in an attacking manner four men carrying clubs.

agtás: **agtasan.** *v.* to clear one's way by hacking. (*raat*)

agtungpál: *prep.* until, to, till (*aginggana*), see also *tungpal*. [Tag. *hanggáng*]

agtutúbo: *n.* youth. see *tubo*.

ahedrés: (Sp. *ajedrez*: chess) *n.* chess. **agahedres.** *v.* to play chess. **ahedresista.** *n.* chess player.

ahénsia: (Sp. *agencia*: agency) *n.* agency, organization existing to promote the exchange of goods and services. **ahensia de empenios.** *n.* pawnshop.

ahénte: (Sp. *agente*: agent) *n.* agent; sales representative; travelling salesman; middleman. (*pannakabagi*) **yahentean.** *v.* to act as an agent.

ahíngko: (Sp. *ajenjo*: wormwood; absinthe) *n.* wormwood.

ahíto: (Sp. *ajo*: garlic) *n.* a kind of yellow flower, marigold.

áire: (Sp. *aire*: air) *n.* tune.

-ak: **1.** First person enclitic used with actor focus verbs, adjectives, and nouns: I (am). **Mangmangan***ak*. I am eating. **Natayag***ak*. I am tall. **Lalaki***ak*. I am a boy. **2.** Combination of the enclitic *-ak* and suffix *-an*. **Idiay ti pagpa-pukis***ak*. That's where I get my haircut. [Png. =*ak*, Tag. *akó*]

akába: *a.* wide, broad. **akabaen.** *v.* to widen. **agakaba.** *v.* to have the same length. **kaakaba.** *n.* breadth; width. **pangakabaen.** *a.* somewhat wide. **paakabaen.** *v.* to make wider, widen. [Ibg. *alawa*, Ifg. *ambílog*, Ivt. *uvung*, Png. *lapar*, Kpm., Tag. *lapad*]

akád: *n.* agility in walking.

akadémia: (Sp. *academia*: academy) *n.* academy, place for studying or training in a specific field.

akadémiko: (Sp. *académico*: academic) *a.* academic, pertaining to school.

ákak: *n.* double chin (*akat*); goiter (*buklong*). **agakak.** *v.* to have or develop a double chin; to be affected with goiter. [Tag. *bosyò* (goiter)]

ak-ák: baby talk denoting anything unclean or worthless. [Bon. *a-a*]

akapúlko: (Sp. *acapulco*) *n.* candle bush, a common, small tree of the bean family with yellow flowers.

ákar: agakar-akar. v. to move from place to place. umakar. v. to move (to another house); change one's position or job. yakar. v. to transfer; infect with a disease. naakaran. v. to be infected (with disease); contaminated; influenced. payakar iti nagan ni. v. to transfer something into the name of. Kasla umang nga agakar-akar. exp. He continually changes residence (like a hermit crab). Inyakarna ti kanal iti damdamag. He changed the channel to the news. [Png. akár, Tag. lipat]

ákas: akasen. v. to collect, gather (drying clothes) (urnong). naakas. a. collected, gathered. Inakasen ti baket dagiti ikamenmi ta managisbo ti buridek. The old lady gathered up our sleeping mats already because the youngest child urinates frequently. [Tag. likom]

akásia: n. acacia tree, raintree, also algarrubo. [Tag. akasya]

akasít: n. species of freshwater crab.

ákat: n. double chin. (akak) agakat. v. to have a double chin.

ákay: n. herd. (pangen) akayen. v. to guide; to herd. yakay. v. to drive into a herd. sangaakay. n. a herd, flock. [Tag. akay]

akbáb: see sakrab: bite, seize with teeth.

akbáy: (Tag.) umakbay, akbayen. v. to put one's arm around another's shoulder.

ákem: akem-akem. n. opening and closing of the hands (kemmakem)

akém: n. duty, task; responsibility, obligation. (takem; rebbeng). agakem. v. to fulfill a position, assume the responsibility for a certain role. akmen. v. to take charge of, be responsible for, discharge one's duty. agak-akem. v. to take charge of, be in an acting capacity. ipaakem. v. to entrust a duty to another. Iti iririgat ti biag, nanayonan pay ti akem ti babai. In the hardships of life, the duty of the woman is further increased. [Png. kábtang, Tag. tungkól]

akíkid: a. narrow. (kipet; aripusok, lengsat; ngepngep; tupitop) kaakikid. n. breadth. akikid ti panagpampanunotna. He is narrow-minded. [Ibg. atezziq, Ivt. idid, Kal. lalipit, Knk. agígid, dagíus, Kpm. makiput, Png. ingét, Tag. kitid, kipot]

akíli: var. of aklili: yakili, akilien. v. to carry under the armpit.

akílis: n. strips of rattan used to tie bamboo in flooring. inakilis. n. wickerwork. akilisen. v. to weave, intertwine with cotton. (kayyamet)

akim-: var. of the prefix akin- before labial consonants m, p, and b. akimmanok. the owner of the chicken.

akin₁- prefix indicating ownership. Perfective form is nakin- akimmanok. owner of the chicken; akimbalay. owner of the house; akintalon. owner of the ricefield; Akin- may also indicate the person responsible for the entity named by the nominal root: Mabalin ti sabali ti akin-aramid. Maybe somebody else did it (was responsible for the act). [Bon. kan-]

akin₂- Prefix used with place nouns to indicate relative position, var. of makin-: akindaya. (somewhere) in the east. akinabagatan. (somewhere) in the south. akinsango a pilid. front wheel.

akìnkuá, akinkùkuá: (f. kua) interrog. whose? [Tag. kanino]

aking-: var. of the prefix akin- before k, g, and ng (also spelled akin- + word).

akíp: inakip. a. covering each other (said of bamboo used in construction.) pagakipen. v. to place one over another. [Tag. takíp]

akkáb: n. excavation. akkaban. v. to excavate.

akkál: akkalen. v. to squeeze (a body); take by force; remove (ikkat). naakkal. a. removed by force; taken away; separated. Saannan a naakkal iti liday ken babawi. He couldn't banish the sadness and regrets. [Tag. alís]

akkáng: a. with legs wide apart, straddling; term applied to Japanese soldiers during World War II. (sakkang; askaw; kayang; pakkang; baddakaw) agakkang. v. to straddle; walk with legs far apart. [Bon. wákang, Tag. bukakà, sakáng]

akkát: akkaten. v. to remove, take away. (akkal; ikkat)

akkáw: agakkaw. v. to walk in haste; stride (askaw). [Tag. hakdáw]

akkúb: n. cover (usually temporary, contrast kalúb (lid)); wrapper; pillowcase; shell of a crab; joined hands in praying; cover page (of a magazine). akkuban. v. to cover (kalub; abbóng (cloth cover, shroud)); protect. yakkub. v. to use to cover with. paraakkub. n. cover girl; cover model in a magazine. [Tag. takíp, saklób]

Aklánon: n. a. people and language of Aklan Province, Panay.

akléng: akleng-parano. n. Albizzia procera plant. (adaan)

aklí: var. of kali: dig, bury.

aklíli: aklilian. v. to hold by the arm (an escorted woman); to carry under the arm or armpit (igpil). paaklili. v. to ask for someone's help, care, etc. [Tag. akbáy]

aklimatádo: (Sp. aclimatado: acclimatized) a. acclimatized.

akló: n. ladle. ak-aklo, aklo-aklo. n. shoulder blade (aliwadáng). akluen. v. to ladle out; hit with a ladle. [Ibg. *kuwig*, Ivt. *pákul* (shoulder), *ariwadang* (shoulder blade), Kal. *ichus*, Knk. *bakkóng*, *tagáong*, Kpm. *sandok*, Png. *akló*, Tag. *kawot*, *sandók*]

aklúlo: *n.* care; guidance; protection. (*aywan*) **akluluen**. *v.* to care for; help; sympathize with. [Tag. *lingap*]

aklón: *n.* acceptance; refuge, protection. (*ako*) **aklonen**. *v.* to accept under one's responsibility; to protect; agree; admit. **paaklon**. *v.* to ask to be loved in return. **pannangaklon**. *n.* acceptance (of affection). **Uray tagabuennakto iti agnanayon, basta aklonennak.** Although he may enslave me forever, at least he accepts me. [Tag. *tanggáp*]

akó: **akuen**. *v.* to admit; to admit one's error; to receive graciously; get an award. **panangako**. *n.* acceptance (*awat*, *aklon*). **Akuek a talaga a siak met la ti gapu dagiti nagparikutantayo.** I admit that I am the reason for our problems. [Tag. *amin*]

akuário: (Sp. *acuario*: aquarium) *n.* aquarium; Aquarius.

akuát: **akuaten**. *v.* to dig out, exhume (*kali*) **maakuat**. *v.* to be exhumed, to be dug out.

akuaréla: (Sp. *acuarela*) *n.* watercolor; watercolor painting. **akuarelista**. *n.* watercolor artist.

akuátiko: (Sp. *acuático*) *a.* aquatic.

akób: **pangakuben**. *v.* to join together; clasp the hands. **agakob**. *v.* to join; join in business. (*sugpon*) **akoban**. *v.* to substitute something for. **yakob**. *v.* to compensate with. **nagakob**. *a.* clasped, joined together. **saan nga agakub ti sabut ken pinggan**. *exp.* A rich man and poor woman (or vice-versa) can never be compatible (*lit*: a plate and coconut shell do not go together). [Tag. *taklób*]

akompaniadór: (Sp. *acompañador*: accompanist) *n.* accompanist.

akompaniár: (Sp. *acompañar*: accompany) **akompaniaran**. *v.* to accompany (in music). (*pasakalie*) **akompaniamiento**. *n.* accompaniment (music).

-akón: [*-ak* + *-(e)n*]. Indicates recently performed action by a first person singular subject. *Nanganakon*. I already ate.

ákup: **agakup**. *v.* to amass; collect. (*urnong*) **akupen**. *v.* to collect; scoop, gather. **pagakup**. *n.* dustpan. **sangkaakup**. *a.* one handful. [Tag. *dakót*]

ákup-ákup: *var.* of *akut-akut*: kind of slender bumblebee-like insect.

akórde: (Sp. *acorde*: chord; harmony) *n.* chord in music, three or more notes in a musical harmony.

akorré: (Sp. *ocurrir*: occur; *acorrer*: succor) **agakorre**. *v.* to appear (disease). **yakorre**. *v.* to use, apply. (*ikurri*)

akusár: (Sp. *acusar*: accuse) **akusaran**. *v.* to accuse. **akusado**. *n.* the accused. **akusasion**. *n.* accusation.

akústika: (Sp. *acústica*: acoustics) *n.* acoustics, factors that affect the quality of sound in an enclosed place.

ákut: **akut-akut**. *n.* a kind of slender bumblebee-like insect; term applied to slender people.

ákoy: **akuyen**. *v.* to gather. (*kuykoy*) **yakoy**. *v.* to gather by pushing toward someone. [Tag. *ukuy*]

akóy: *n.* person with abnormal hands and/or feet.

aksáw: *var.* of *askaw*: stride, large step. [Png. *kupbáng*, *kutdáng*, Tag. *kulakdáng*]

akseptár: (Eng.) **akseptaren**. *v.* to accept. (*awat*)

aksesória: (Sp. *accesoria*: outworks, outbuilding) *n.* tenement, apartment house, or building for rent.

aksidénte: (Sp. *accidente*: accident) *n.* accident. (*disgrasia*) **maaksidente**. *v.* to have an accident; to injure in an accident.

aksión: (Sp. *acción*: action; stock) *n.* action; stock; share (in stocks); bet; lottery ticket. **umaksion**. *v.* to act upon. **aksionista**. *n.* shareholder, stockholder. **naaksionan**. *a.* acted upon.

ákta: (Sp. *acta*: act) *n.* act; law. [Tag. *batás*]

aktibísta: (Sp. *activista*: activist) *n.* activist.

aktíbo: (Sp. *activo*) *a.* active (*siglat*). **miembros aktibos**. *n.* active members.

aktitúd: (Sp. *actitud*: attitude) *n.* attitude. (*nakem*)

-akto: [*-ak* + *-(n)to*]. Indicates future action of verb in the first person singular: I will. **Mapanakto**. I will go.

ákto: (Sp. *acto*: act) *n.* act; meeting. **aktuan**. *v.* to act on.

akyát-bahay: (Tag. *akyát* 'climb; go up' + *bahay* 'house') *n.* robbery, burglary; holdup of a residence.

ála₁: **alaen**. *v.* to get, take; go and get; catch; willfully accept. **aginnala**. *n.* tag (a children's game); *v.* to be at odds with one another; (*fig.*) make love, copulate; compare. **makaala**. *v.* to be impregnated; conceive. **umala**. *v.* to resemble in looks, take after. **pagala**. *n.* trap; bait; instrument used to get something. **agala**. *n.* the person who is *it* in children's games; (*coll.*) copulate. **maala**. *v.* to be taken; to be caught; chosen, selected. **alaan**. *v.* to get something from someone. **makiinnala**. *v.* to copulate, have sexual intercourse. **pannakiinnala**. *n.* coitus. **maala ti turog**. *v.* to be able to catch some sleep. **Agkaalaanda iti pintas.** They are equally beautiful. **Ammok a nasaririt ti anakko, immala met la kaniak.** I know my child is bright, he takes after me. [Ibg. *mangaq, eppen,* Ivt. *manghap,* Kpm. *kuwaq,* Png. *alá,* Tag. *kuha*]

ála₂: (Sp. *ala:* at (used with *una*)) the form of *alas* used before *úna.* **Ala una.** It's one o'clock.

alá: Interjection used in saying good-bye. **Ala wen.** All right. **Alanto** (*obs.*) Woe to. **ala kadi, ala koma.** *exp.* used in asking a favor. **ala latta.** go on; keep on going. **Ala ngarud.** all right; OK.

alaál: *n.* neap tide. **Awan ita dagiti mangngalap gapu iti kinaalaal ti danum.** There are no fishermen today because the water is at neap tide.

alaála: (borrowed from Tagalog *alaala:* remember) *n.* indecision. **agalaala (*ti panunotna*).** *v.* recollect; to take a while to decide.

alabáab: *n.* unappeasable thirst. (*waw*) **alabaaben.** *v.* to be affected by an unappeasable thirst. [Tag. *uhaw*]

alabár: (Sp. *alabar:* praise, extol) **alabaren.** *v.* to atone, make amends. (*allangon*)

alabástro: (Sp. *alabastro:* alabaster) *n.* alabaster.

álad: *n.* fence; hedge. **aladan.** *v.* to put a fence around. **agalad.** *v.* to make a fence. **inaladan.** *a.* surrounded by a fence; *n.* backyard. **yalad.** *v.* to use to make a fence with. **pagalad.** *n.* materials used in making a fence. [Bol. *darekdek,* Ibg. *gutuk,* Ivt. *ahad, adimut,* Kal. *aÿed,* Png. *alár,* Kpm., Tag. *bakod*]

aladág: see *addag:* press down; surpass; excel.

aladán: *n. Scleria scrobiculata* plant.

alágad: *n.* model, example, guide, pattern; standard. **pagalagaden.** *n.* set of rules; Constitution; design, plan; norm; regulation. **umalagad.** *v.* to follow the rules; follow a plan. **alagaden.** *v.* to imitate, copy; reproduce; follow the rules. [Png., Tag. *tuntón*]

aláhas: (Sp. *alajas:* jewels) *n.* jewels; jewelry. (*saniata*) **agalahas.** *v.* to wear jewelry. **alahero.** *n.* jeweler.

alahéro: (Sp. *alajero:* jeweler) *n.* jeweler.

alák: *interj.* expressing wonder or surprise.

alakán: *n.* a kind of mollusk.

alákre: (Sp. *lacre:* lacre) *n.* sealing wax.

al-ál: agal-al. *v.* to pant; breathe heavily. (*upal; sung-ab, tunglab*) **Agal-al nga umuli iti mai-kadua a kadsaaran.** He panted going up to the second floor. [Ibg. *aggág,* Tag. *hingál*]

alála: alala pay. What a pity. (*sayang; kailala*)

alalagát: *n. Uvaria lancifolia* plant.

alalási: *n. Leucosyke capitellata* plant.

alálaw: agalalaw. *v.* to be confused, troubled, perturbed.

alalawígan: *n.* small bird with a white breast; term applied to flirtatious females.

alaláy: (Tag.) *n.* nursemaid; (*fig.* bodyguard; gentle way of caring for the sick) (*yaya*)

alalék: alalek pay. How much! How many!

al-aliá: *n.* ghost. (*katataoan, pugot; alingaas; atros; aniwaas; bambanig; aningaas*) **al-aliaen.** *v.* to haunt, be visited by a ghost. **maal-alia.** *v.* to be visited by a ghost. **Al-aliaen ti basolna.** *exp.* He is haunted by his sins. [Knk. *aliliá,* Png. *aniáni,* Tag. *multó, mumò*]

alalináw: *n. Grewia multiflora* plant.

alalindáy: *n.* carrying things on the head without holding them.

álam: *n.* opinion, view (*pamanunotan*); custom, habit. (*ugali*)

alamáam: see *allinga:* echo; turning head to hear better.

alamáno: (Sp. *a la mano:* by hand) *n.* handshake. **agalamano.** *v.* to shake hands. (*agdakulap*) **Awan innalamanuan kadagiti Hapones.** There is no mutual handshaking among the Japanese. [Tag. *kamáy*]

alamangá: *var.* of *amanga:* awe, wonder.

alámbre: (Sp. *alambre:* wire) *n.* wire. (*bárut*) **naalamrean.** *a.* wired. [Knk. *palténg,* Tag. *kawad*]

alambréra: (Sp. *alambrera:* wire netting) *n.* wire netting; screen (of a chicken coop, etc.).

alamén: *n.* lowermost dry leaves (banana stalks, etc.).

álamo: (Sp. *alamo:* poplar) *n.* poplar tree.

alán: Interjection used to ask a favor. **naalan.** *a.* tipsy, dizzy (from betel chewing or drinking). [Tag. *langó* (tipsy)]

alaná: umalana. *v.* to swell moderately (rivers); become deeper; heat up (passion).

alan-án₁: alan-anen. *v.* to pull (string of a kite); unroll (toilet paper). [Tag. *hila*]

alan-án₂: umalan-an. *v.* to subside; ease up; simmer down.

alánas: see *aranas:* to do carefully.

alánay: yalanay. *v.* to level; be in solidarity with and support; sympathize with.

alangaáng: *n.* sacrum bone: upper thigh (bikini line).

alangán: Alangan met. of course. **Alanganen.** It is doubtful (something will fit, etc.).

alang-áng: *n.* whine of a dog. (*anang-ang*) **agalang-ang.** *v.* to whine (said of the dog.)

alángi: *n. Canarium luzonicum.*

alangígan: *n. Canangium odoratum,* a kind of plant with fragrant flowers. (*ilang-ilang*)

alángon: *var.* of *allangon*: compensate, atone, make up for.

alap-áp: **alap-apen**. *v.* to skin; flay (*kulanit*); (*coll.*) to get all (awards).

aláped: *n.* threshold, bar used to keep animals from escaping. **alapedan**. *v.* to obstruct with an *alaped* (*sagiped*). [Tag. *hadláng*]

alarákas: (Sp. *alharacas*: clamor) *n.* fuss, much ado about nothing.

alárma: (Sp. *alarma*: alarm) *n.* alarm. **alarmado**. *a.* alarmed, forewarned; afraid.

álas₁: *n.* inclined beam used to lift heavy objects; (*obs.*) stick attached to a rope or chain placed near an animal's mouth to prevent it from biting. **alasan**. *v.* to gag; muzzle. [Tag. *sikang*]

álas₂: (Sp. *a las*: at [used with time expressions]) With Spanish numerals, *alas* is used to give the time: **Alas dos**. Two o'clock. **Alas dose**. Twelve o'clock. Normally when used with prefixes, *alas* is written joined to the numeric root: **Agalaskuatro idi bumangonak**. It was four o'clock when I woke up.

álas₃: (Sp. *el as*: the ace) *n.* ace in cards. [Tag. *alas*]

alás: **naalas**. *a.* ugly; disgusting; obscene; impure; shameful; shocking. **alasen**. *v.* to consider something indecent, obscene, improper, etc. **tagialasen**. *v.* to consider something ugly or indecent. [Ibg. *fea, nakasisinnan*, Itg. *alas*, Ivt. *marahet*, Kal. *bulikis, lawwik*, Knk. *sapé, saséw, bakáud, koláit*, Kpm. *matsura*, Png. *aliwá, kápuy*, Tag. *pangit*]

alasáas: *n.* the soft sound of water or the breeze. (*arasaas*)

alasán: (Sp. *alazán*: sorrel) *n.* sorrel.

alas-ás: *n.* fallen dry leaves (*as-as; kariskis*); (*fig.*) excess matter, residue. **alas-asen**. *v.* to remove dry leaves from; to pick out the bones; tear off; to clean. [Png. *alasas* = dried banana leaves, Tag. *pagaspás*]

alas-kuátro: (Sp. *a las cuatro*) *n.* four o'clock; a branching herb of the bougainvillea family with yellow or white flowers and dark green oval leaves said to open at four in the afternoon.

álat: (borrowed from Tagalog) **itlog nga maalat**. *n.* salted red egg. (*naapgad nga itlog*)

alát: *n.* a kind of cylindrical basket used by fishermen. **agalat**. *v.* to carry the *alat* by tying it around the waist. **yalat**. *v.* to put into the *alat*; succeed in a contest, argument, etc.; to win a prize or girl's favor. **adda inalatna**. *exp.* he has something up his sleeve. [Kal. *búyun, agguwong*, Tag. *pangnan*]

al-át: *var.* of *sal-at*: mild curse word.

alatáat: *var.* of *alat-at*.

alat-át: **alat-aten**. *v.* to snatch off; tear off (*lapsi*). **Rumuarkayo, no saan, alat-atek dagiti punieta nga aritosyo**. Get out, otherwise I will tear off your damn earrings. [Tag. *balták*]

álaw: **agalaw**. *v.* to be large enough for so many people; to work assiduously; enlarge.

aláw: *n.* rescue; method of getting back a lost spirit by putting water in a white bowl, dekernel 27 pieces of plain rice, pray the Apostle's creed. At resurrection, 27 pieces of rice are put in the water with bubbles; the rice that floats is collected with cotton and pinned on a person's inside clothes or on his pillow. The person then drinks some of the water. **alawen**. *v.* to aid; save; rescue; get. **Nupay kuna dagiti akinkabagian a naalawda met la ti lungon, dida kanon nabiroken ti bangkay**. Although the relatives say that they were able to rescue the coffin, they supposedly didn't find the corpse. [Tag. *ligtás*]

alawáaw: *a.* empty; meaningless; without purpose. **agal-alawaaw**. *v.* to evaporate; wander aimlessly; waste one's life.

alawáo: *n.* noise of the hornbill (*kalaw*).

aláwig: *n.* whirlwind; cyclone; hurricane (*bagio*); (*fig.*) hardships in life. (*allawig*) **naalawig**. *a.* destroyed by a whirlwind. **agalawig**. *v.* to have a cyclone or hurricane. [Tag. *buhawì, ipuipo*]

alawígan: *n.* a kind of black and white small bird with a long tail.

alayaáy: see *alay-ay*: cook slow over low heat.

alay-áy: *n.* cooking over a slow fire. **alay-ayan**. *v.* to cook over low heat. **naalay-ay**. *a.* soft and tender; tenderly slow. **naalay-ayan a sungrod**. *n.* slow flame.

álba: (Sp. *alba*: alb) *n.* alb, long white robe worn by a priest at mass.

albáab: *n.* Tinguian death dirge.

albág: *n.* the reverse side. **kaalbag**. *n.* opposite.

albaháka: (Sp. *albahaca*) *n.* a kind of aromatic plant used to facilitate menstruation. (*erbaka*)

Albanés: (Sp. *albanés*) *n., a.* Albanian, *fem*: *Albanésa*; Albanian language.

albankóke: see *kasoy*: cashew.

albásia: *n.* marital matchmaking; talks between the parents and/or relatives of a prospective couple. (*alud*) **mangalbasia**. *n.* matchmaker. **yalbasia**. *v.* to match a partner for marriage. **Yalbasiam ta barom bareng saan a mapurnada**. Match your bachelor so he won't be wasted. [Tag. *albasya*]

albasiadór: *n.* marital matchmaker. (*mangalbasia*)

albát: **albatan**. *v.* to whip; belt; beat (*ablat, baut*). [Tag. *hagupít*]

albayálde: (Sp. *albayalde*: white lead, ceruse) *n.* white lead powder.

albolário: *n.* quack doctor (*erbolario*). [Kal. *aalisig*, Tag. *albularyo*]

albór₁: (Sp. *arbol*: tree) *n.* pole for electric wires. (*tulos*). **albor de puego.** *n.* fire tree.

albór₂: (Sp. *labor*: labor) **alburen**. *v.* to seek (a position); to be after (money, votes).

albor₃: *n.* dawn (*bannawag*); whiteness; beginning.

albór₄: (*reg.*) *n.* souvenir given by a friend.

albornós: (Sp. *albornoz*: burnoose) *n.* burnoose; woolen cloth.

alboróto: (Sp. *alboroto*: tumult) *n.* uproar. tumult; outcry; tantrum. (*gulo*) **agalboroto.** *v.* to make trouble, disturb, cause an uproar.

aldába: (Sp. *aldaba*: knocker, hitching ring) *n.* latch (for fastening a door). **yaldaba.** *v.* to latch.

aldáw: *n.* day; daytime. **aldawan.** *v.* to work or hire on a daily basis. **inaldaw.** *adv.* everyday. **mangaldaw.** *v.* to eat lunch. **pangaldaw.** *n.* lunch; midday meal. **pangngaldaw.** *n.* lunch, luncheon. **maaldawan.** *v.* to be late. **idi kasangaldaw.** *n.* the day before last. **ka-aldawan.** *n.* day of; birthday. **kanikadua nga aldaw.** two days ago. **ita nga aldaw, aldaw itoy.** today. **aldaw ken rabii.** day and night. **nangina nga aldaw.** *n.* holy week. **Addanto aldawmo!** Your day will come! **Ditoyka a mangaldawen tapno makapagpakadata met kenkuana.** Have lunch here so we can bid farewell to him (see him off). [Ibg. *aggáw*, *eggáw*, Itg. *wákas*, Kal. *egew*, Kpm. *aldo*, Knk., Png. *ágew*, Ivt., Tag. *araw*]

alég: **agaleg, agal-aleg.** *v.* to do in a hurry; roam (*alleg*). [Tag. *dalî*]

alegasión: (Sp. *alegación*: allegation) *n.* allegation.

alegoría: (Sp. *alegoría*: allegory) *n.* allegory, representation by a figurative story.

alégre: (Sp. *alegre*: joyful) *a.* joyful; cheerful; funny; pleasing.

alegría: (Sp. *alegría*: joy) *n.* songs performed at the death of a child that alternate with readings. **agalegria.** *v.* to sing songs at a child's death.

alégro: (Sp. *alegro*: allegro) *n.* allegro, lively part of a musical composition; *a.* lively (*mus.*).

alehandría: (Sp. *alejandría*: Alexandria) *n.* a thorny shrub with small roselike flowers.

álem: *n.* a kind of shrub with greenish yellow flowers.

Alemán: (Sp. *alemán*: German) *n. a.* German. (fem: *alemana*) **agaleman.** *v.* to speak German.

Alemánia: (Sp. *Alemania*: Germany) *n.* Germany. **agpa-Alemania.** *v.* to go to Germany.

alembóng: *a.* wanton, loose; silly (said of girls). (*garampang*)

áleng: **aleng-aleng.** *a.* absent, absent-minded; careless, unobservant; inattentive; insincere. **aleng-engen.** *v.* to do carelessly. (*liway*) **yaleng-aleng.** *v.* to neglect; not give proper care to. [Tag. *pabayà*, *walang-bahalà*]

alep-ép₁: *n.* plaster, bandage; anodyne. (*tapal*) **alep-ep.** *v.* to plaster; place a bandage on. [Tag. *tapal*, *panapal*]

alep-ép₂: **alep-epen.** *v.* to make amends; soothe out bad feelings, alleviate. (*ep-ep*)

alep-ép₃: *var.* of *dalepdep*: sprinkle water on dusty or dry ground.

alep-ép₄: *n.* banana leaf placed at the bottom of a rice pot to prevent the rice from burning. (*ápin*)

aléro: (Sp. *alero*: eaves) *n.* eaves; gable end of a building.

alérto: (Sp. *alerto*: alert) **naalerto.** *a.* alert, clever. (*siglat*)

algarrúba: *syn.* of *algarrúbio*: acacia tree.

algarrúbio: *n.* carob tree; acacia tree. (*akasia*)

alguasíl: (Sp. *alguacil*: peace officer; bailiff) *n.* sheriff; peace officer.

álhebra: (Sp. *álgebra*: algebra) *n.* algebra.

áli: **naalian.** *a.* stained, discolored. (*mansa*) **makaali.** *v.* to be capable of staining or discoloring. **alian.** *v.* to stain, discolor. [Tag. *mantsá*]

alí: *var.* of *ala* interjection.

aliá: **al-alia.** *n.* ghost. (*mamaw*, *pugót*; *di katataoan*, *alingaas*) **maal-alia.** *v.* to be visited by a ghost; to be affected by a ghost's visit. **naal-alia.** *a.* haunted. [Png. *aniáni*, Tag. *multó*]

aliádo: (Sp. *aliado*: ally) *n.* ally.

aliamár: (Sp. *llamar*: call) **aliamaren ti atension.** *v.* to call the attention of.

aliánsa: (Sp. *alianza*) *n.* alliance.

aliás: (Eng.) *n.* alias, assumed name; nickname (*birngas*). [Tag. *alyás*]

aliáw: *n.* horror, fright (*amés*, *buteng*; *alingget*); a kind of tree. **makaaliaw.** *v.* to startle; frighten. **maaliaw.** *v.* to be scared, frightened. [Png. *tágnaw*, *takót*, Tag. *takot*]

alibadáw: *var.* of *amangaw*: delirium.

alibadbád: *a.* suddenly; unexpectedly (*apagdarikmat*; *bigla*). [Tag. *biglâ*]

alibágo: *n.* kind of shady tree.

alibangbáng: *n.* a tree with sour leaves used in cooking. (*ariwat*)

alibáta: (Tag.) *n.* the Arab alphabet.

alibét: **mangyalibet.** *v.* to kill or knock down at the first stroke.

alibnúno: *n.* whirlpool; eddy of water. (*alikuno*) **agalibnuno.** *v.* to eddy.

alibudábod: *n.* sediment; dregs (*ared-ed*; *intaer*; *lissaad*; *lued*; *parek*; *ureb*; *rinsaed*; *basabas*). [Tag. *latak*]

alibúdbud: *var.* of *alibudabud.*

alibukáy: *var.* of *libukay*: beginning of menstruation.

alibunó: *var.* of *alikuno*: whirlpool. (*alinuno*)

alibungúbong: *n.* vapor, steam. (*sengngaw*, *alingasaw*) **naalibungubong.** *a.* cloudy; overcast. **maalibungubongan.** *v.* to be affected by steam or vapor; to be steamed up. [Tag. *singáw*]

alibúob: *n.* steam. (*sengngaw*, *alingasaw*) **agalibuob.** *v.* to steam up; emit steam. **alibuuban.** *v.* to steam (a place). [Tag. *singáw*]

alibút: *n.* a kind of shiny wild lizard. [Tag. *bubuli*]

alibúyong: **naalibuyong.** *a.* cloudy; overcast (*lulem*; *naulpan*; *langeb*; *daguyemyem*; *kuyem*). [Tag. *kulimlím*]

alibták: **naalibtak.** *a.* clever. (*alisto*; *ladino*; *saldet*; *sikap*; *tarem*; *siglat*) **agalibtak.** *v.* to get busy; be quick, clever.

alibtók: **agalibtok.** *v.* to disappear; lose oneself in a crowd (*agawan*); *n.* tramp; vagabond (*baligawgaw*; *bayanggudaw*). [Tag. *mawalâ*]

alidabdáb: *var.* of *alidukdok*: feel nauseous.

alidengdéng: *n.* a kind of small blue and white marine fish.

alidukdók: *n.* nausea, nauseous feeling. **agalidukdok.** *v.* to feel nauseous; to be about to vomit (*sarua*). **Nagsasaruno ti uyekna ta alidukduken.** He started coughing repeatedly because he was nauseous.

alidungdóng: *n.* head cloth, bandana. (*dalungdong*) **alidungdongan.** *v.* to cover the head with a piece of cloth. [Tag. *talukbóng*]

alidungét: *n.* moodiness; boredom; gloominess. (*alipunget*; *sidunget*) **naalidunget.** *a.* moody; sad; gloomy; sullen. **agalidunget.** *v.* to be bored, gloomy; moody; irritable. [Tag. *sungit*]

áligı: *n.* a kind of small bee with a poisonous sting, smaller than the *uyokan*, which stores its honey in small holes it bores in trees.

álig2: *n.* a variety of awned *diket* rice with a speckled hull and white kernel.

aligagáw: *n.* fear, fright. (*buteng*, *amak*; *aligaget*; *alingget*) **agaligagaw.** *v.* to be afraid. **makapaaligagaw.** *a.* horrible; frightful; dreadful. [Png. *takót*, Tag. *takot*]

aligagét: *n.* sudden terror; shock. (*aliáw*) **agaligaget.** *v.* to shudder from fright. **makapaaligaget.** *v.* to be shocking; horrible. [Tag. *sindák*]

aligamén: *n.* Zizyphus talanai plant.

aligawgáw: *var.* of *aligagaw*; fear. (*buteng*; *amak*; *aligaget*)

aligusgús: *coll. var.* of *alipuspus*: whorl in the hair. [Tag. *puyó*]

alikád: *var.* of *alikadkad.*

alikádkad: *n.* restlessness; mischief. (*alikuteg*) **agalikadkad.** *v.* to be mischievous. [Tag. *likót*]

alikáka: *n.* concern, care. **agalikaka.** *v.* to be careful. **yalikaka.** *v.* to be careful of; keep from harm; prevent. **naalikaka.** *a.* careful, wary; excessively delicate.

alikaká: *n.* timidity, shyness; excessive care. (*annad*) **naalikaka.** *a.* careful; bashful. [Tag. *hiyâ*]

alikámen₁: *n.* furniture; tools; implements. [Kal. *alikamon*, Tag. *kagamitan*]

alikámen₂: *n.* magical charm; amulet. **al-alikamen.** *n.* amulet, charm. (*anting-anting*; *babato*; *tagiruot*) **Adda alikamenna.** *exp.* He knows black magic (*lit.* has magical charms).

alikawkáw: *var.* of *salikawkaw.*

alikenkén: *n.* a kind of dance. **agalikenken.** *v.* to wind, coil; crouch, curl up in fright. **alikenkenen.** *v.* to gather misplaced things and arrange them (*alikomkom*). [Tag. *yukyók* (crouch)]

alikeskés: **umal-alikeskes.** *v.* to cower in the corner; to shrink in cowardice (shy children); embrace someone's bosom for protection. **Immalikeskes kaniak ni baket ngem piniselko ti takiagna a kasla pangpatibkerko kenkuana.** My wife embraced me in fear but I squeezed her arm to give her courage.

alikubéng: *n.* eddy. (*alipugpog*) **agalikubeng.** *v.* to fly round about. **Nagalikubeng ti tapok iti kapanagan.** The dust flew around the plain.

alikubkób: *n.* encircling whirlwind. **alikubkuban.** *v.* to fence around; surround; encircle (*lawlaw*; *likmot*). **Naregtada latta a mangibaba kadagiti bilog tapno alikubkubenda dagiti salmon.** They are alert in lowering the boats to circle the salmon. [Tag. *kubkób*]

alikubnéng: (*obs.*) **agalikaubneng.** *v.* to fly round about. (*allikubeng*)

alikubóng: *var.* of *alikubeng*: eddy. (*alipugpog*)

alikudóg: *n.* sound of trampling feet; stampede. **umalikudog.** *v.* to romp, frolic; stampede. [Tag. *dabóg*]

alikumkúm: **alikumkumen.** *v.* to gather up without order; gather together ends of a skirt (*arikomkom*); curl up (clouds before a storm). [Tag. *likom*]

alikunnóg: **agalikunnog.** *v.* to walk to and fro, pace; tack; wiggle (*kinni*). **alikunnugen.** *v.* to shake. [Tag. *alóg*]

alikunó: *n.* whirlpool; dimple. **umalikuno.** *v.* to do things without planning. **mayalikuno.** *v.* to be caught in a whirlpool; (*fig.*) be in a passionate love affair. **agalikuno ti kallid.** *v.* to form a dimple (when smiling). **Makakayaw ti alikuno ti bugbugtong a kallidna.** His sole dimple is charming when it forms. **Nagalikuno ti asi, ladingit, ken pungtot iti barukongko.** Pity, sadness, and anger whirled in my chest. [Png. *alimpokapok, alauli,* Tag. *alimpuyó*]

alikúteg: naalikuteg. *a.* restless; mischievous; adept in stealing. (*alikadkad; alimegmeg; aliwegweg; pilio; welwel*) **umalikuteg.** *v.* to be restless; mischievous. **kinaalikuteg.** *n.* mischief; restlessness. **Alikuteg latta dagiti matana.** He just has roaming eyes. [Tag. *likót*]

alíla: *n.* maid, servant. (*katulong, baon; adipen*) **agpaalila.** *v.* to serve as a maid. [Png. *alíla,* Tag. *alilà*]

alíleg: (*obs.*) see *aleg*: bee.

alílek: *n.* very fine cotton.

alíli: *n.* either of the two wooden handles of the bellows. (*putan*)

alílis: **yalilis.** *v.* to postpone, delay (*igábay; sanud; tantan*). [Tag. *liban*]

álim: **umalim.** (*obs.*) *v.* to be suspicious of; suspect. (*atap; ilem; inap; sadap*)

alimadámad: *n.* gossip; rumor; speculation. (*sayangguseng*) **umalimadamad.** *v.* to listen to gossip. **maalimadamad.** *v.* to hear gossip; catch ear of something that is not completely certain. [Tag. *higing, tsismis*]

alimadámag: **maalimadamag.** *v.* to remember vaguely; hear indistinctly. [Tag. *higing*]

alimadmád: *var.* of *alimadamag*: to hear vaguely.

alimámad: *n.* hearsay, rumor. **maalimamad.** *v.* to hear a rumor, be informed by hearsay. (*alimadamad, sayangguseng*)

alimani: *n. Vaccinium myrtoides*.

alimangmáng: *n.* conclusion; result; finale. (*gibus*) **agalimangmang.** *v.* to be nearly finished; draw to a close. [Tag. *wakás*]

alimáseg: *n.* very sharp pain in the stomach. **agalimaseg.** *v.* to have an acute abdominal pain (*bisaleg*). [Tag. *kalám*]

alimátek: *n.* generic term for leech (*linta* is used in Pangasinan and *biled* is the smaller mountain leech). **No matay ti alimatek, dumteng ti napigsa a bagio.** When the leeches die, a strong storm will come. [Bon. *mátek,* Ibg. *alitta,* Ibg., Kal. *alinta,* Ifg. *bilábil,* Kal. *matok,* Knk. *mátek,* Png. *linta,* Kpm., Tag. *lintâ*]

alimbádaw: **agalimbadaw.** *v.* to turn in sleeping; grope; be uncertain. [Tag. *hibáng*]

alimbanagén: (f. *banag*) *a.* about to ripen (bananas). (*apagluom, darangidang*)

alimbangágan: *n.* a variety of maize with speckled kernel; semibaritone voice (*bangag*). **agalimbangagan.** *v.* to resound. [Tag. *alingawngáw* (resound)]

alimbásag: *n.* restlessness in bed, insomnia. **alimbasagen.** *v.* to have insomnia, have trouble sleeping; be uneasy.

alimbatóng: *n.* clog; drag; weight tied to an animal or man to prevent escape; burden. **alimbatongan.** *v.* to weigh down (something thrown in the water to prevent it from surfacing).

alimbawángan: *n.* variety of rice.

alimbayágan: (*obs.*) **al-alimbayagan.** *n.* death struggle (of drowning persons, fish out of water, etc.). (*bugsot; tunglab*)

alimbáyong: *n.* sling used in hurling stones (*pallatibóng*). **alimbayúngan.** *n.* a kind of poisonous horsefly.

alimbubúdo: *n.* a kind of large, dark, hairy caterpillar (*budobuduan*). [Tag. *higad*]

alimbubungáw: see *bungaw*: kind of dragonfly.

alimbubúyog: *n.* bumblebee; wasp; (*fig.*) male actor. [Bon. *moyóngan,* Ibg. *avariyúngan,* Ivt. *davugan,* Kal. *biyugen, tikkakaÿong,* Knk. *áleg,* Kpm. *tatabwan,* Png. *ampingílan,* Tag. *bubúyog*]

alimbukáy: *n.* a vine with gray fruits used in medicine; the seeds of this plant are used to play *sungka*.

alimbuyógen: *n.* a cock with dark red plumage.

alimegmég: **naalimegmeg.** *a.* naughty. (*aliwegweg, welwel*)

alímek: **agalimek.** *v.* to keep silent. (*ulimek*)

alimekmék: see *alumamek*: keep silent; cease to do.

alimugmóg: see *mulumog*: gargle.

alimugtóng: see *dalimugtong*: heap up; pile up. [Tag. *salansán*]

alimúken: *var.* of *alimúkeng*.

alimúkeng: *n.* a kind of wild gray dove; a variety of thin-skinned greenish banana. **immalimukeng.** *a.* resembling a wild dove, beautiful but wild; with a sexy body. **immalimukeng a mata.** small, sharp eyes.

alimúking: *n. Caesio sp.* fish.

alímon: **alimunen.** *v.* to swallow; engulf; suppress one's tears; (*fig.*) to accept without question. **Maalimonto kadi dagiti libbi ken uyaw gapu iti daydiay a bayanggudaw?** Can he take the despisement and criticism resulting from that tramp? **Nagalimon iti barreta.** He swallowed a crowbar (said of proud or strong people) [Png. *akmon,* Tag. *lunók*]

alimunmún: *v. var.* of *alimunumon*.

alimunúmon: *n.* last signs of a trail or track; fading memory; fleeting glimpse of something disappearing in the distance. [Tag. *latak*]

alimúom: *n.* sick feeling arising from transferring between extreme degrees of temperature; exhalation, vapor, steam (*alingasaw*); haze, mist (*angep*). **maalimuoman.** *v.* to feel sick (or nauseous) from transferring between extreme degrees of temperature; to be affected by exhalations. [Tag. *singáw* (vapor)]

alimúteng: *n.* irritation; annoyance; impatience. (*alidunget*; *alipunget*). **alimutngen.** *v.* to be angry (*intransitive*); to irritate (*transitive*). **makaalimuteng.** *a.* irritating; impatient. **pagalimutngan.** *v.* to anger, irritate. **No adda parikut ken sagubanit a sumangbay kenka, dika koma agalimuteng ken agdukot.** If sickness and trouble befall you, you shouldn't be irritated and distressed. [Tag. *bugnót*, *yamót*]

alim(pa)pátok: *n.* summit, peak, top; climax; orgasm. (*pantók*; *aringgawís*; *toktok*; *alintotok*; *tapaw*) **umalimpapatok.** *v.* to climb to the top. **agalimpapatok.** *v.* to reach the climax; have an orgasm. [Knk. *alintayók*, *mayukmúkaw*, Tag. *tuktók*]

alimpawér: **umalimpawer.** *v.* to hurl, fly away, fly through the air. (*awer*)

alimpáyag: **agalimpayag.** *v.* to hover around; soar (birds) (*ampáyag*). [Tag. *lipád*]

alimpayáng: **agal-alimpayang.** *v.* to wander (said of the mind, thoughts, etc.); hover about (*ampáyag, alimpáyag*).

alimpayéng: **maalimpayeng.** *v.* to be dazed, stunned. (*pelleng*; *riweng*) **Naalimpayengak gapo iti panagriawna kaniak.** I was stunned at his yelling at me. [Tag. *tulíg*]

alimpék: **naalimpek.** *a.* chubby (*lukmeg*). [Tag. *tabâ*]

alimpupúsa: *n.* a kind of grub; the larva of the rhinoceros beetle.

alín: **al-alin man** (*obs.*) Interjection expressing wonder.

alinaáy: **umalinaay.** *v.* to become smooth, gentle; flow gently. (*talna*) **naalinaay.** *a.* smooth, peaceful, calm (*talinaay*). [Tag. *payapà*]

alinága: *n.* illumination; ascending ray of the sun at sunrise. (*anaraar*) **maalinagan.** *v.* to be illuminated, enlightened; understand. **Lawag-pagsaingan ti alinagami.** Our illumination comes from artificial lamp light. [Tag. *aninag*]

alinagá: **agalinaga.** *v.* to imprint in the mind.

alínam: **naalinam.** (*obs.*) *a.* tasteless (*lupta*; *labay*; *tamnay*). [Tag. *tabáng*]

alinamnám: **alinamnamen.** *v.* to enjoy immensely; to be long in swallowing food.

naalinamnam. *a.* delicious; flavorful (*imas*). [Tag. *namnám*]

alinápet: **naalinapet.** *a.* sticky; greasy; sweaty (clothes) (*alunapet*). [Tag. *lagkít*]

alinápog: *n.* dust created when pounding the mortar. **naalinapog.** *a.* dusty; polluted (*natapok*). [Tag. *alikabok*]

alinár: (Sp. *llenar*: fill) **alinaran.** *v.* to fill (blanks); settle (accounts).

alínaw: *n.* Juss, a kind of shrub whose bark is used in making ropes.

alinayánay: *n.* slight movement. **umalinayanay.** *v.* to move slightly (grass being treaded on by a snake). (*agin-inayad*) **naalinayanay.** *a.* calm; tranquil; peaceful. [Tag. *alumanay*]

alindadáw: **maalindadaw.** *v.* to be affected by vertigo; to be dizzy from looking down (people with fear of heights) (*alindaw*). [Tag. *hilo, lulà, liyó*]

alindadáy: *n.* railing of a bridge (for hand support). **alindadayen.** *v.* to carry something on the head without support from the hands. **agalindaday.** *v.* to walk on a bridge without help of the hands. **pangalindadayan.** *n.* railing; hand support.

alindádo: (Sp. *arrendado*: leased) *a.* rented; leased.

alindáw: **maalindaw.** *v.* to be dizzy from looking down (*ulaw*). **makaalindaw.** *v.* causing dizziness (high elevation). **Maalindaw ti riknana no luktanna wenno saan ti ridaw.** He feels dizzy whether or not she opens the door. [Tag. *hilo, lulà, liyó*]

alindáyag: **agalindayag.** *v.* to float in the air; soar; hover over prey. (*ampayag*) **uleg alindayag.** *n.* a kind of large poisonous snake. [Tag. *lipád*]

alindayág: *var.* of *dayag*.

alinduaán: (f. *dua*) *a.* unsure; doubtful.

alinednéd: *n.* negative state of being: utter darkness; acme of misfortune. **agalinedned.** *v.* to settle to the bottom. **naalinedned.** *a.* sunken; settled to the bottom. [Tag. *sukdól*]

alinegnég: *n.* depth of a body of water; resort; accumulation of sorrows, sicknesses, etc; forum, assembly. **agalinegneg.** *v.* to accumulate; settle; congregate. **pagalinegnegan.** *n.* outcome; net result (*pagbanagan*). [Tag. *lalim* (depths)]

alinkudóg: **agalinkudog.** *v.* to stampede; stamp the feet. (*baragsot*)

alíno: *n.* strong sensation or emotion (can range in degree of pleasantness from a tingling pain in the teeth to a sensual emotion). **maalino.** *v.* to be affected by a strong emotion; have a tingling pain in the teeth from cold food; to feel passionate; be lustful. **makaalino.** *a.* causing a strong feeling or emotion: sensual; sexually attractive; causing a tingling sensation or tooth pain; provocative; pleasing; irritating. **Nangngeg ti balud dagiti makaalino a karasakas dagiti ruot a mayapra-apras iti bakrang dagiti berdugo a mangguyguyod kenkuana.** The prisoner heard the irritating noise of the grass brushing against the sides of the executioners pulling him. [Tag. *ngiló*]

alinúno: *n.* whirlpool. (*alipono*) **agalinuno.** *v.* to eddy, cause whirlpools.

alipúdos: alipudusen. *v.* to gather (with a cloth).

alinsaéd: *var.* of *arinsaed*: sediment.

alinsánag: *n.* watchfulness. (*siglat*)

alinsáwad: alinsawaden. *v.* to grope for; look for by feeling. (*arikap*) **dika agal-alinsawad.** *exp.* keep your hands to yourself (when sleeping with members of the opposite sex, etc.). [Tag. *kawág*]

alinsukág: agalinsukag. *v.* to create confusion; disarrange; vomit. [Tag. *kalat* (disorder); *suka* (vomit)]

alintá: *n.* earthworm; (*reg.*, Pangasinan) leech. [Bon. *kelang*, Ivt. *dwati*, Kal. *alinta*, Tag. *bulati* (earthworm); *lintâ* (leech)]

alintatáo: *n.* pupil of the eye (*taotao*); imagination. [Bon. *kaminatagowen*, Kal. *kalimattagu*, Knk. *bokbokká*, *bokbokkáeg*, Tag. *balintatao* (pupil of eye)]

alintúbong₁: *n.* bamboo tube for storage; mouthpiece; weight for the *tumbali* of the loom. **mayalintubong.** *v.* to reach one's ears indistinctly.

alintúbong₂: *n.* candle socket; gasoline torch. [Tag. *sulô*]

alintungúgan: *n.* the depth of a body of water; depression on land; (*reg.*) abandoned channel. **agalintungugan.** *v.* to resound; reverberate (*aweng*). [Tag. *lunas*]

alintúto: agalintuto. *v.* to swim on the back; do the backstroke. (*tata*, *tagintudo*)

alintútot: *n.* top; peak; summit. (*patok*; *sampa*; *alimpapatok*; *toktok*; *tapaw*) **agalintutok.** *v.* to reach the summit; attain one's goal. [Tag. *toktók*]

alínga: see *allinga*: echo; turning the head to hear better.

alingáas: *n.* a kind of spirit or ghost. (*al-alia*; *aningaas*; *pugot*; *aniwaas*; *bambanig*) **Adda alingaasna pay ditoy.** There is still the feel of someone's presence here.

alingagngág: *n.* echo (*alingawngaw*; *allungugan*). [Tag. *alingawngáw*]

alinganágan: agalinganagan. *v.* to abstain from drinking or smoking.

alingásaw: *n.* exhalation of steam or odor. (*alibungabong*, *alimuom*, *sengngaw*, *ubuob*) **agalingasaw.** *v.* to steam; reek. **umalingasaw.** *v.* to emit an offensive odor. **No maangotda ti alingasaw ti malutluto, agtataraydan a sumrek iti kosina.** When they smell the fumes of what she is cooking, they'll run into the kitchen. [Bon. *alingásog*, Tag. *alingasaw*]

alingék: *var.* of *aligaget*: horror; fright.

alinggagét: *n.* horror; fright. **agalinggaget.** *v.* to be scared, frightened (from high places). [Tag. *sindák*, *hindík*]

alinggék: *var.* of *alingget*: fright, horror. **nakaal-alinggek.** *a.* frightful; horrible; hideous.

alinggét: *n.* fright; horror. (*aligaget*; *alinggek*; *buteng*; *amak*) **nakaal-alingget.** *a.* scary, horrible, frightening; hideous.

alingkudóg: agalingkudog. *v.* to stampede; stomp the feet.

alíngo: *n.* wild boar. [Bon. *láman*, Knk. *bangó*, Tag. *bulugan*, *baboy-damó*]

alingúbong: *var.* of *alibungubong*: vapor, steam.

aliúg: mangaliug. *v.* to flatter. (*altit*; *sugsog*, *lamiong*)

alipága: *n.* dirt, soot; fire flake, ember; cobweb; radioactive fallout. **agalipaga.** *v.* to emit embers; fly around and about.

alipása: *n.* girandole; chandelier web.

alipáwen: *n. Alstonia scholaris.*

alipuápo: agalipuapo. *v.* to move; mill about; crowd.

alipúdas: alipudas, alipudásen. *a.* restless, uneasy; worried; bothered (*alusiis*, *alikuteg*). [Knk. *alipugá*, Tag. *balisa*]

alipugpóg: *n.* whirlwind. (*alikuno*; *bagio*) **agalipugpog.** *v.* to have a whirlwind. **babato ti alipugog.** *n.* magical amulet consisting of a stone with supernatural powers. **Kasda la alipugpog nga aggargaraw.** They move like whirlwinds (fast). [Kal. *alipuspus*, Png. *alimpokapok*, Tag. *alimpuyó*, *ipuipo*]

alipunó: *n.* whirlpool. (*alinono*) **agalipuno.** *v.* to revolve, spit, eddy, whirl (*tayyek*; *uddog*). [Tag. *ipuipo*]

alipúngat: maalipungatan. *v.* to be taken by surprise.

alipúnget: naalinpunget. *a.* angry; irritable, touchy; passionate. **umalipunget.** *v.* to get angry. [Tag. *galit*]

alipuspús: *n.* whorl in the hair; a type of cotton cloth with whorls. **alipuspusan.** *a.* multiwhorled. **yalis ti alipuspus.** *exp.* to cheat; fool. **uray maukas ti alipusposko.** *exp.* used to attest the truth of a statement. **bangking ti alilpusposna.** *exp.* denotes abnormal behavior. [Knk. *togtog-ó*, Kal *alipuspus* = whirlwind]

aliptók: (*obs.*) *a.* restlessness. (*alusiis*)

ális: **umalis**. *v.* to move, shift; move (change residence). (*akar*) **yalis**. *v.* to move, shift, displace, transfer. **makaalis**. *a.* contagious (disease), catching. **agalis-alis**. *v.* to constantly move. **maalisan**. *v.* to be infected, contaminated. [Png. *pangekel*, Kpm. *yáwa*, Tag. *alís*]

alís: *n.* abortion, miscarriage; the product of an abortion. **maalisan**. *v.* to miscarry, abort. (*regreg*) **kasla nayanak nga alis**. *exp.* referring to frail, sickly people. [Tag. *agas*]

aliseksék: *a.* half-cooked; *n.* hideaway; remote place. **umaliseksek**. *v.* to shrink with shame; be shy or cowardly. (*bain, takrot*)

alisó: *n.* a kind of tasty fish, gray snapper, *Lutianus sp.*

alisuáso: *n.* steam, vapor. (*sengngaw, alingasaw*) **agalisuaso**. *v.* to steam up. [Tag. *singáw*]

alisugásog: *n.* vapor rising from the ground after rain; steam. [Tag. *singáw*]

alisón: *n.* container; receptacle. **yalison**. *v.* to transfer from one container to another (*alis, akar*). [Tag. *lalagyán* (container)]

alísto: (Sp. *listo*: smart, clever) *a.* clever, smart; talented; quick, fast (*partak*); alert, wide awake. **agalisto, alistuan**. *v.* to do fast. **Dina namnamaen a kastoy ti kaalisto dagiti pasamak.** He didn't expect things to happen this fast. [Tag. *listó*]

alít: *n.* putty; paste; plastic cement. **alitan**. *v.* to patch; mend; paste. **yalit**. *v.* to patch with. **maalitan**. *v.* to be patched, mended. [Tag. *pandikít*]

alít: **agalit-alit**. *v.* to move to and fro; be indecisive.

al-ít: *var.* of *sal-it*: mild curse word.

alitadtád: *a.* restless (from the heat), ill at ease; unable to sleep. **Idi rabii, diak makaturog, alitadtadenak.** Last night, I couldn't sleep; I was restless. (*alimbásag, alusíis*)

alitakták: **umalitaktak**. *v.* to try to walk after being confined in bed.

áliw: *n.* comfort, consolation; amusement; relaxation. **aliwen**. *v.* to comfort; console (*liwliwa*). [Tag. *aliw*]

aliwá: *n.* head ax used by Igorots.

aliwadáng: *n.* collar bone; clavicle. [Ivt. *ariwadang*, Kal. *papadchange*]

aliwaksáy: **umaliwaksay**. *v.* to amuse oneself, to have leisure time; to migrate to a distant place; travel for pleasure to a distant place. **managaliwaksay**. *a.* restless; adventurous. **pagaliwaksayan**. *n.* place of recreation;

better place to raise a family (place of intended migration). **Saan a pulos nga immaliwaksay iti lugar a nakayanakanna iti unos ti panagbiagna.** He hasn't ever wandered in his lifetime from the place he was born.

aliwangáwang: *a.* uncertain; vague (news); *n.* gossip, rumor. (*sayangguseng*) **agaliwangawang**. *v.* to be uncertain, mistrustful; (*reg.*) to signal approach.

aliwaswás: **aliwaswasen**. *v.* to untie; unravel; let loose. (*waswas*) **maaliwaswasan**. *v.* to have leisure time (*aliwaksay*); to understand fully; be able to see through a difficult problem. **agaliwaswas ti pudot**. *v.* to release heat (from body).

aliwaték: *n.* wisdom; intelligence; (*reg.*) vagrant. **kinaaliwatek**. *n.* wisdom; mental brilliance. (*saririt; kinasirit*)

aliwegwég: **naaliwegweg**. *a.* restless; mischievous; naughty; messy; stubborn; immodest. (*alikuteg, welwel*) **Dakes ti ubing a nasukir ken aliwegweg.** Children that are restless and disobedient are bad.

alíwid: (*lit.*) *n.* old friend.

aliwít: *n.* shadow; tail end of something; last signs of something disappearing into the distance. **aliwit ti bagio**. *n.* tail end of the storm. **umaliwit**. *v.* to move away fast into the distance. [Tag. *buntót*]

alkaguéte: (Sp. *alcahuete*: go-between) *n.* go-between; pimp; conniver; slanderer.

alkáyde: (Sp. *alcaide*: warden) *n.* warden of a prison.

alkálde: (Sp. *alcalde*: mayor) *n.* mayor. **ipaalkalde**. *v.* to refer a case to the mayor.

alkaldésa: (Sp. *alcaldesa*: mayoress) *n.* mayoress; wife of the mayor.

alkalí: (Sp. *álcali*: alkali) *a.* alkali; lye; soda ash.

alkampór: (Sp. *alcanfor*: camphor) *n.* mothball; camphor; henna. **agalkampor**. *v.* to use mothballs.

alkamporádo: (Sp. *alcanforado*: camphorated) *a.* camphorated. **asiete alkamporado**. *n.* camphorated oil.

alkansár: (Sp. *alcanzar*: reach) (*obs.*) *n.* having time for.

alkánsia: *n.* piggy bank; money box. **yalkansia**. *v.* to put into the piggy bank or money box. [Tag. *alkansiyá*]

alkantarília: (Sp. *alcantarilla*: culvert) *n.* culvert, drain crossing under a road; sewer.

alketrán: (Sp. *alquitrán*: tar) *n.* tar. (*briá*)

alkilá(r): (Sp. *alquilar*: rent) *n.* hire; rent. **alkilaen**. *v.* to rent, hire out. **umalkila**. *v.* to go rent.

alkiládo: (Sp. *alquilado*: rented) *a.* chartered, rented (vehicle).

alkilér: (Sp. *alquiler*: rent) *n.* hire. (*abang*)

alkitrán: (Sp. *alquitrán*: tar) *n.* liquid pitch, tar. **alkitranan.** *v.* to tar, cover with liquid pitch.

alkohól: (Eng.) *n.* alcohol (*arak*). **alkohalada.** *a.* mixed with alcohol.

allá: *n.* an interjection of wonder or threatening, see also *alla-alla*. **Allaka!** Watch out!

alla-allá: *n.* nomad, wandering person. **agallaalla.** *v.* to be undetermined, unresolved (*duadua*); vacillate; to wander from place to place, roam. [Tag. *galà* (wander)]

allábat: **allabaten.** *v.* to contradict; intercept; (*reg.*) meet by chance (*angat*; *kabbatil*; *suppiat*; *supapak*). [Tag. *salungát*]

alladán: *n.* a type of vine.

allagádan: *n.* a kind of small black bird.

allágat: *n.* a shrub with red fruits and edible flowers; *Uvaria rufa*. (*al-allagat*)

allagáw: *n.* a kind of shrub, *Premna odorata*, with a fragrance that drives away chicken ticks and is used in medicine for fever, cough, stomachache or headache. (*annubrang*)

allakápa: **agallakapa.** *v.* to be undecided; wander aimlessly. **Mabang-aran no agallakapa dagiti lorona.** His parrots will be relieved if they can wander free. [Tag. *alangán*]

allakattá: interjection expressing warning or threat. (*allaka tatta!*)

allangígan: *n.* a tree, *Canangium odoratum*, with fragrant flowers used for *ilang-ilang* perfume. **agallangigan.** *v.* to be known for one's fragrance, glamour, etc. [Tag. *ilang-ilang*]

allangúdan: *var.* of *allangugan*: echo.

allangúgan: *n.* echo. **agallngugan.** *v.* to echo. [Png. *alinag*, Tag. *alingawngáw*]

allángon: **allangonen.** *v.* to make up for; compensate; atone for. **maallangon.** *v.* to keep in; conceal inside oneself; hide one's feelings, intelligence, etc. **Pampanunotek ti pannakaallangonna.** I am thinking about her compensation. **Sika ti paallangon ti dayawna.** You will make up for her honor. [Tag. *magbayad-pinsalà*]

allátiw: **umallatiw.** *v.* to move, shift; visit a neighbor (without a reason); change the subject; change one's profession. **aginnalatiw.** *v.* to visit one another (neighbors). **yallatiw.** *v.* to move, shift, displace; tarnish someone's reputation. **agallaallatiw.** *v.* to go from one to another; *a.* transferable. **Nasaona pay a sangkadamagnak ni Fe no umallatiw iti balayda.** He also said that Fe always is asking about me when she visits their house. **Nalawag pay a mangngeg ditoy ti uni dagiti nadumaduma a** billit nga agalla-allatiw iti napuskol a kakaykaywan. It is also easy to hear here the sound of various birds moving around in the thick wooded areas. [Tag. *lipat*]

alláw: *n.* kite. (*ulláw*)

alláwa: (*reg.*) *n.* kite.

allawági: *n.* carpenter. (*karpintéro*) **agallawagi.** *v.* to be or become a carpenter. **yallawagian.** *v.* to make a false excuse to get out of work. [Ivt. *vada*, Kpm. *aluwagi*, Tag. *alwagi*, *anluwagi*]

alláwat: **yallawat.** *v.* to pass on; transmit; pass a ball. **allawaten.** *v.* to fetch; understand; to interrupt someone speaking; hand down from one generation to another. **aginnallawat.** *v.* to exchange (gifts, ideas, etc.); pass on; transmit. **Naginnallawat ti nagubsang a balikas ti kutsero ken ti agtutubo.** The coach driver and the youth exchanged coarse words. [Tag. *saló*]

alláway: **agallaway.** *v.* to cheer up (*ray-aw*); relax; gain confidence.

alláweng: **agallaweng.** *v.* to wander vagrantly.

alláwig: *n.* whirlwind; calamity; turmoil. **allawigen.** *v.* to cajole; mislead, dupe. **Kasla allawig ti kapardas dagiti pasamak.** Things happened so fast (as a whirlwind). [Tag. *ipuipo*]

allég: **agalleg.** *v.* to hurry up; do quickly.

allék: Particle of admiration. How + ADJ.!

allí: *var.* of *allá*, *alá*.

allíd: *n.* beeswax; paste. **allidan.** *v.* to apply wax on. [Knk. *alíd*, Bik., War. *taro*, Tag. *pagkít*]

allígang: *n.* look out from a high place. **agalligang.** *v.* to be on the lookout. [Tag. *bantáy*]

allikúbeng: *n.* small eddy of air. **agallikubeng.** *v.* to fly round about. **Nagallikubeng ti tapok iti kapanagan.** The dust flew around the plain.

allílaw: **allilawen.** *v.* to confuse, deceive; puzzle; cheat; mislead; swindle. **maallilaw.** *v.* to be confused; mistaken. **manangallilaw.** *n.* one who habitually cheats or deceives; confusing. **No diak maallilaw, asideg ti gameng iti pagkalkalianyo.** If I'm not mistaken, the treasure is close to where you are digging. [Tag. *darayà*]

allín: *n.* rolling away. **agallin.** *v.* to roll away; overflow. **allinen.** *v.* to propel; roll away; move a heavy object; remove the intestines of a slaughtered animal. **agallin-allin.** *v.* to move back and forth without direction; be idle.

allínga: *n.* echo; turning the head to hear a sound better. **agallinga.** *v.* to turn the head toward the speaker to hear better. **maallinga.** *v.* to hear confusedly. [Tag. *alingawngáw*]

allíngag: **maalingag.** *v.* to hear indistinctly. **allingagen.** *v.* listen to a faint sound; try to focus one's hearing; eavesdrop. (*timud*) **Naallingag-**

ko laengen ti panagbambaningrotna. I just heard her sniffling. [Tag. *ulinig*]

allíngang: *n.* lookout from a high place to guard below.

allít: *n.* string used for spinning a top. **yallit.** *v.* to spin the spinning top from the side forward. [Tag. *pisi*]

allitálit: *n.* multitude of moving people or animals, insects, etc; kind of shrub with violet flowers. **agallitalit.** *v.* to move about in a big throng; to move with hustle and bustle. [Tag. *magkalibumbón*]

allitán: (f. *allít*) *n.* string of the spinning wheel or sewing machine.

allíwit: *n.* track (of tire, animal, etc.); trail; alternate route. **agalliwit.** *v.* to detour; to keep away from someone or something (*silliwasiw*). **Ammomi ti alliwitna a darasudos.** We know his daring trail. [Tag. *bakás*]

alluálod: *var.* spelling of *alualod*: prepare for marriage ceremonies.

alluás: *n.* large bone of the arm or leg (one of twelve). (*barawas*) **naalluas ti saksakana.** He has long legs.

allúbog: *var.* of *alubog*.

allúdan: *n.* a basket larger than the *labba* and smaller than the *rangaya*. **yalludan.** *v.* to place something in the *alludan*.

allúday: *n.* a kind of earring; rope for carrying. **alludayan.** *v.* to carry with a rope.

allúdoy: **agalludoy.** *v.* to move in groups; to move in single file; to walk slowly as to not be noticed. (*aludoy*)

allók: **agallok-allok.** *v.* to ripple (waves in ocean); be wavy.

allúki: (*reg.*) *n.* earthworm. (*alinta*)

allúkud: **allukuden.** *v.* to lead; guide (*bagnos*); conduct; sponsor a measure or proposition. [Tag. *akay*]

allukón: *var.* of *alukon* plant.

allúkoy: **agallukoy.** *v.* to lean, incline; convince (*ammuyot*). **allukuyen.** *v.* to lead; guide; conduct; convince; explain. **Allukoyek ida a tumulong kadakayo.** I will convince them to help you. **Masapol a mapadakkel ti maganar iti panagtalon tapno maallukoy dagiti agtutubo a mangigubetto met iti kiredda iti agrikultura.** It is necessary to increase the farming salaries to encourage young people to put their strength in agriculture. [Tag. *hikayat*]

allulúsi: *n.* a kind of shiny shrub.

allón: *n.* large water wave that forms no breakers, unlike the *dalluyon*, which breaks near the coast. **agallon.** *v.* to swell in small waves; breathe heavily; ripple (in the wind, waves, etc.). **mayallon.** *v.* to be carried off by the waves; float on the waves. **panguloten-agalloallon a buok.** *n.* curly, wavy hair. [Kal. *tuppiyak*, Tag. *alon*]

allungkít: **al-allungkitan.** *v.* to use with care. (*annad*)

allúngog: *n.* hollow sound. (*aweng*) **agallungog.** *v.* to be dry (said of cough); to resonate a hollow sound, reverberate. [Tag. *alingawngáw*]

allúp: **agallup, allupen.** *v.* to invite someone to dance. (*kortisia*) **kaallup.** *v.* partner in dancing (girls).

allúsob: *n.* replenishing a container by emptying another; transferring of contents between containers. **yallusob.** *v.* to replenish a container by emptying the contents of another. **pagallusoben.** *v.* to put two containers together in order to transfer the contents.

allót: **agkaallot.** *v.* to live in harmony. **yallot.** *v.* to conform; suit; fit. (*bagay*) **mayallot.** *v.* to be suitable, fitting; appropriate. [Tag. *tugmâ*]

allután: *var.* of *alutuot*.

allúy: *n.* a kind of elongated marine fish.

almá: (Sp. *armar*: arm; mount; make a mess; make a fuss) **agalma.** *v.* to run wild, scamper (horses). (*buatit*) **yalma.** *v.* to hitch, harness (an animal) (*pako*).

almadón: *n.* pillowcase; square cushion.

almágre: (Sp. *almagre*: red earth) *n.* red ochre; red-colored earth.

almán: *n.* desire, craving (*tarigagay*); envy (*apal*) **almanen.** *v.* to desire a reward; wish; crave, long for. **naalman.** *a.* envious. [Tag. *inggít*]

almanáke: (Sp. *almanaque*: almanac) *n.* almanac.

almasíga: (Sp. *almáciga*: mastic; nursery of trees) *n.* mastic tree; large evergreen tree of the mango family; resin yield from this tree used to fill holes in masonry or walls.

almasén: (Sp. *almacén*: warehouse) *n.* warehouse (*sarusar*); department store. **almasenero.** *n.* warehouse keeper; owner of a department store.

almasón: (Sp. *armazón*: framework, skeleton, mounting) *n.* pillow rack; cabinet; mold.

alméndras: (Sp. *almendra*: almond) *n.* almond; almond tree.

almendrília: (Sp. *almendrilla*) *n.* almond-shaped carpenter's file.

almidór: (Sp. *almidón*: starch) *n.* starch. (*gawgaw*) **almidoran.** *v.* to starch clothes. **Saan a makapagna gapu iti kasikkil ti pannaka-almidor ti pantalonna.** He can't walk because of the stiff starching of his pants. [Tag. *almiról*]

almiránte: (Sp. *almirante*: admiral) *n.* admiral, captain of a ship.

almíres: (Sp. *almirez*: mortar) *n.* small stone mortar (*alsong*). [Tag. *almiris*]

almískle: (Sp. *almizcle*: musk) *n.* musk.

almohadón: (Sp. *almojadón*: cushion) *n.* cushion; soft pillow. [Tag. *kutsón*]

almóndigas: (Sp. *albóndigas*: meatball) *n.* meatball. **agalmondigas.** *v.* to make meatballs.

almonída: (Sp. *almoneda*: auction) *n.* auction. (*subasta*) **yalmonida.** *v.* to put for sale at an auction.

almoránas: (Sp. *almorranas*: hemorrhoids) *n.* hemorrhoids (*busigit, tubél*). [Bon. *bitbitli*, Tag. *almoranas*]

almosár: (f. Old Spanish *almorzar*: have breakfast) *n.* breakfast. (*pamigát*) **agalmosar.** *v.* to eat breakfast.

almoséda: (Sp. *almoseda*) *n.* tax on water for land irrigation.

alnáab: **agalnaab.** *v.* to dampen; become humid or moist. **naalnaab.** *a.* damp, moist; humid (*alunapet*).

alnág: **yalnag.** *v.* to publish. (*iwarnak*).

alnó: *n.* alder bush.

alnók: *n.* moisture. **naalnok.** *a.* moist; damp. **kaalnokan.** *n.* wet, shady place.

alngóg: *var.* of *allángog*: resound, reverberate.

aló: *n.* leap; copulation with a female animal. **agalo.** *v.* to be in heat. (*maya*) **ipaalo.** *v.* to have animals copulate. (*yot*)

al-ó: *n.* pestle (mortar is *alsong*). **immal-o.** *a.* shaped like a pestle (body). **natukkol ti al-o.** *exp.* the pestle is broken (preparations are consumed). [Ibg. *alu, ellu*, Ivt. *ahuq, tutuhan*, Kal. *eÿ-u*, Knk. *lay-ó, al-ó*, Kpm. *álu*, Png. *aló*, Tag. *halo*]

aluád: **agaluad.** *v.* to beware, be careful, take precautions; warn. **aluadan.** *v.* to take care; be careful; look out for; beware; be cautious. **agaluad.** *v.* to be careful. (*annad*) **agaluanaluad.** *v.* to look after each other. **ti Dios ti aluadna.** the dead, the late that rest in peace. [Png. *aluár*, Tag. *ingat*]

aluálod: (f. *alod*) **yalualod.** *v.* to prepare for marriage ceremonies (parents of bride and groom).

alúbag: **makialubag** (*obs.*) *v.* to meet by chance on the way.

alubaybáy: *n.* kind of *bugguong*.

alubíd: *n.* hem; ridge; border. (*lebleb*) **alubidan.** *v.* to hem; edge; put a border on.

alúbog: **agalubog.** *v.* to be suited to each other; conform. **pagalubugen.** *v.* to balance; equalize; compare. **umalubog.** *v.* to be proper, suitable (*bagay*). **mayalubog.** *prep.* in accordance with, in consonance with (*annatup*). [Tag. *bagay, akmâ*]

alúd: *n.* embryo, fetus (*sab-uk*); shoot of a tree; small compartment inside a chest. **alud-alud, mangyalud-alud.** *n.* proxy; matchmaker. **yalud-alud.** *v.* to recommend a man for marriage. **Linuktak ti maysa nga alud ti tokador.** I opened up a drawer in the dresser. [Tag. *bilíg* (embryo)]

aludáb: **yaludab.** *v.* to slant; to chisel slantwise. (*dalubdob*)

aludáid: **agaludaid.** *v.* to scuffle; drag oneself while sitting or lying (*allin, alud-od, alunain, ilas, kunail, uyas, iwas, isin*). **Imbaddekna ti preno ti kasla masikog a nuang nga agalaludaid a kotsena.** He stepped on the brakes and the car scuffled like a pregnant water buffalo. **Nagaludaid a bimmaba iti papag.** He dragged himself off the bamboo bench. [Tag. *hilahod*]

alúdig: *n.* a kind of tree with yellow fruits, *Streblus asper*.

alud-ód: **agalud-od.** *v.* to glide down intermittently, slowly shuffle; to slide forward; to run (the nose). **yalud-ud.** *v.* to delay, postpone. (*tantan*) **Inyalud-odna ti asmangna iti ungto ti pagsalaan.** He glided his partner to the end of the dance floor. **Yalud-odta koma ti panagpaprobinsia.** We should delay our going to the province. [Tag. *hilahod*]

alúdoy: **agal-aludoy.** *v.* to walk away without being seen; pass unnoticed; walk away without capturing attention (*aludaid*). **Idi ngannganin agbannawag, nagal-aludoyak nga immulog.** When it was almost daybreak I climbed up (to the house) without being seen.

álog: *n.* low land; puddle; swamp.

alúgal: **agal-alugal.** (*obs.*) *v.* to move from place to place. [Tag. *lipat-lipat*]

alugangián: *n.* rice straw, called *arutang* when dried (*lugangian, garami*). [Tag. *pasiyók*]

alogbáti: *n.* malabar nightshade; species of plant with edible leaves and reddish stems.

alug-óg: *n.* small fence to enclose plants, building materials, etc. **alug-ugen.** *v.* to enclose with a fence (*alad*). [Tag. *bakod*]

alugúog: *n.* marsh, swamp; (*reg.*) quicksand (*gayong*). [Tag. *kumunoy*]

Alóha: (Hawai‘i) *interj.* Hawaiian greeting of welcome or farewell.

alukáp: *n.* a kind of small bird living near freshwater. **al-alukap.** *n.* water strider.

alukén: *n.* a kind of freshwater fish.

alukón: *n.* a kind of tree, *Allaeanthus glaber*; Warb. (*allukon, bungón*)

alúkop: **agalukup.** *v.* to embrace while lying down (*arakup*); to lie close; cuddle up. [Tag. *yakap*]

alúla: *n.* a kind of basket wider at the top.

alúloy: agaluloy. *v.* to be content; rest in the shade.

alumamáni: *n.* Walp, tall, long leafed shrubs with dark-red fruits and bright red flowers, *Lea manillensis.* **pangalumamamien, immalumamani.** *a.* light brown; fair complexioned.

alumámay: naalumamay. *a.* kind, gentle; considerate; mild; sweet natured; soft; soft-spoken. **agalumamay.** *v.* to do gently; act in a gracious manner. [Png. *imsáy,* Tag. *hinay*]

alumámek: *n.* silence; stillness; quietness. **agalumamek.** *v.* to keep silent; cease to do (*arimekmek*). [Tag. *tahimik*]

alumár: (Sp. *alomar*: become strong) **agalumar.** *v.* to distribute equally (load on a horse); plow in furrows; become strong. **alumaren.** *v.* to fortify, strengthen; invigorate; (*fig.*) let out one's feelings. **Alumarenna koma ti riknana ngem nagteppel.** He should have expressed his feelings but he restrained himself.

alumaymáy: see *alumamay*; kind; soft; gentle; soft spoken.

alumbáyad: (*reg.* Pangasinan.) *n.* earthworm (*alinta*). [Tag. *bulati*]

alumígas: (Sp. *hormiga*: ant) *n.* a kind of large, red ant; a kind of nettle vine; *Tragia irritans.* [Tag. *hantík*]

alumíim: *n.* timidity, squeamishness. **naalumiim.** *a.* squeamish; lacking self-confidence, with an inferiority complex; cowardly; afraid; prudent, suspicious; cautious. **umalumiim.** *v.* to not feel at home. (*aripapa; bain*) **Adda panagalumiim ti balasang.** The girl is shy (does not feel quite at home). **Nakababain ngem diak maalumiim a mangipudno kenka.** It is shameful but I can't be timid in confessing to you. [Tag. *hiyâ*]

alumínio: (Sp. *aluminio*: aluminum) *n.* aluminum.

alúmno: (Sp. *alumno*: pupil) *n.* pupil, student. (*agadadal, estudiante*)

alumpipínig: *n.* wasp. [Bon. *iyókan,* Knk. *lulúkaw, ngípil,* Png. *ákot,* Tag. *putaktí*]

álon: agalon-alon. *v.* to gasp for breath. (*tunglab*) **alon-alon.** *n.* rheumatism (*rayuma*). [Tag. *hingalô*]

alunáin: *var.* of *kunail*: slow movement.

alunápet: naalunapet. *a.* dank, damp (dirty clothes) (*dulpet*); soggy half-cooked rice. [Tag. *masá-masâ*]

alunét: *n.* young betel nut. **agalunet.** *v.* to start forming (fruits). [Tag. *bunga*]

alunít: *n.* a painful skin boil (on knee or anus), usually *al-alunit.* **agalunit.** *v.* to form into a boil (*letteg*). [Tag. *pigsá*]

alunkín: *n.* (*obs.*) molding.

alun-ón: *n.* greedy eater; (*fig.*) greedy person. **alun-unen.** *v.* to gobble up; gorge down; eat voraciously, swallow food; engulf. **In-inut nga inalun-on ti sipnget.** The darkness slowly engulfed (us). [Tag. *lulón*]

alúnos: *n.* immodest person; greedy person; overeating. **agalunos, alunusen.** *v.* to eat without rice or bread; overeat; gobble up. **Diak kayat dagiti kasla mangal-alunos a panagkitkitana kaniak.** I don't like his devouring look toward me. **Dimo alunosen ti pasayan.** Don't eat too many shrimps. [Tag. *takaw*]

alunggigít: *n.* something that easily slips out of the hands; something not firmly held. **alunggigitan.** *v.* to hold something carelessly; to not have a firm grasp on something.

alúngkat: mangalungkat. *v.* to begin; start.

alungmaman: *n. Leea quadrifida.*

álup: alupen. *v.* to add by jointing (making a plow). **alupan.** *v.* to lengthen by jointing. **mangngalup.** *n.* plow maker. **ipaalup.** *v.* to have a plow made or repaired.

alupá: *reg. var.* of *lupa*: species of stinging shrub.

alupási: *n.* dry sheath of the banana leaf; when fresh it is referred to as *ubbak.*

alupúop: *n.* exhalation from the earth. (*alingasaw*) **maalupuopan.** *v.* to be affected by earth exhalations, the result being weak or sick in the stomach. **alupuopan.** *v.* to cook by steaming (*salapusop*). [Tag. *singáw*]

álus: *a.* used, secondhand. (*segunda mano, talibugnay*) **alusen.** *v.* to receive secondhand; *a.* used previously. **naalus.** *a.* discarded, secondhand; no longer a virgin.

alusibsíb: umalusibsib. *v.* to nibble at the bait. (*arusibsib*)

alusíis: *n.* feeling cramped and restless. (*alimbasag; alipudas*) **umalusiis.** *v.* to feel cramped and restless. **Alusiisenak iti sumuno a rabii.** I was restless the next night. [Tag. *balisa*]

alus-ús: *n.* sliding down; fall behind in a contest; have a bad season in business; (*coll.*) loser; one who doesn't dare to make important decisions. **agalus-us.** *v.* to slide down. **yalus-us.** *v.* to slide down with. **alus-usen.** *v.* to pull down (the pants). [Tag. *dausdós*]

alutáit: (*obs.*) **umalutait.** *v.* to be dizzy (*maulaw*). [Tag. *hilo, lulà, liyó*]

alutén: *n.* firebrand, half-burned wood. (*atong*) **al-aluten.** *n.* a kind of small, blackish marine fish with a white belly. **Timmingra ti matana a kasla aluten a pinal-idan ti angin.** Her eyes lit up like a firebrand fanned by the wind.

alutí: *var.* of *lanutí*: white-wooded tree.

alutíit: *n.* lizard (usually the common house lizard). **al-alutiit.** *n.* temporary flexing or protruding of muscles resulting from a blow. **agalutiit.** *v.* to rise up (muscles) from being hit. **Kaska la agpuspuso nga alutiit.** *exp.* You have the heart of a lizard (have no mercy). [Ibg. *alifaq*, Ifg. *banbanaggu*, Ivt. *geget*, Knk. *kammulitílit*, Kpm. *lupisák*, Png. *tikí*, Tag. *butikî*]

alutúot: maalutuotan. *v.* to be tainted (meat). **alutuotan.** *n.* spinning wheel axle; bamboo used as shutter, door, or window supports.

alut-ót: alut-uten. *v.* to pull to loosen (*parut*); disentangle; extort; pry out. **alut-utan.** *n.* the part of the head above the ear, auricularis superior. [Tag. *hugot*]

alóy: aluyan. *v.* to send the dog after unwelcome intruders or animals.

alúyo: *n.* tidal wave. **agaluyo.** *v.* to have tidal waves. [Tag. *dalúyong*]

aluyúoy: *n.* slough, quagmire, bog. **aluyuoy.** *v.* to wallow in the mud; wither (leaves).

alúyos: *n.* tidal wave, tsunami. (*aluyo*)

aluyúoy: *n.* slough, quagmire, bog. (*gayong*) **agaluyuoy.** *v.* to wallow. [Tag. *pusalì*]

aluy-óy: see *uy-oy*.

alpabétiko: (Sp. *alfabético*) *a.* alphabetized, alphabetical.

alpabéto: (Sp. *alfabeto*) *n.* alphabet.

alpahól: (Sp. *alfajor:* sweetmeat) *n.* sweet dish made of sweet potatoes, coconut, sugar, and milk. **agalpahol.** *v.* to make *alpahol*.

alpáka: (Sp. *alpaca*) *n.* wool made from the alpaca anima; suit made out of alpaca wool; cream-colored woven fabric for men's suits.

alpálpa: (Sp.) *n.* alfalfa, lucerne.

alpargátas: (Sp. *alpargatas:* hemp sandal) *n.* hemp sandal.

alperés: (Sp. *alferez*) *n.* town official during the Spanish regime.

alpiág: *n.* a variety of awned rice with a small, white kernel.

alpíl: (Sp. *alfil:* bishop) *n.* bishop in chess.

alpilér: (Sp. *alfiler:* pin) *n.* brooch; safety pin (*perdible*).

alpómbra: (Sp. *alfombra:* rug) *n.* rug; carpet. **alpombraan.** *v.* to carpet a floor.

alponsíno: (Sp. *alfonsino:* Alphonsine) *n.* style of haircut with a part.

alpórhas: (Sp. *alforja:* saddlebag) *n.* saddlebag; knapsack. **agalporhas.** *v.* to use a saddlebag or knapsack.

alpormayór: (Sp. *por mayor*) *n.* wholesale dealer.

alprésia: (Sp. *alferecia:* infant epilepsy) *n.* beri-beri.

alsá: (Sp. *alzar:* rise) *interj.* Rise! Revolt! **alsaen.** *v.* to lift; raise; erect; revolt. **umalsa.** *v.* to rise up; revolt; become puffed up (boxer's eyelids).

alsaan. *v.* to take away, take off; unharness; take out a water buffalo or horse. **yaalsa.** *n.* revolution. **kaal-alsa.** *a.* just finished (work). [Tag. *himagsík*]

alsáda: (Sp., *obs.*) *n.* height; elevation.

alsádo: (Sp. *alzado:* height; raised) *a.* high (mountains) (*ngato*); disobedient and semiwild (cattle, buffalo). (*kaliado*)

alsamiénto: (Sp. *alzamiento:* revolt) *n.* insurrection, rebellion. (*yaalsa*)

alsék: (*coll.*) **al-alsek.** *n.* mutual oral-genital stimulation, sixty-nine.

alsém: *n.* sourness, acidity. **naalsem.** *a.* sour, tart. **apagalsem.** *a.* sourish, not yet fully ripe. **pagalsem.** *n.* anything used in cooking to make sour. **kaalsemen.** *v.* to make extra sour. **kasla nakakita iti alsem.** *exp.* used to show someone's excitement upon seeing something excitable. [Ibg. *nassem*, *nattem*, *assúq*, Ivt. *mangalabicit*, Kal. *silom*, *sampot*, Knk. *pakgeláng*, Kpm. *maslam*, Png. *akseng*, *anapseng*, Tag. *asim*]

alsóng: *n.* mortar, used chiefly for husking rice that has been threshed; fat and chubby (like a mortar) (*tibong*, *almires*). [Ibg. *ettung*, Ivt. *husung*, Kpm. *ásung*, Png. *lasung*, Kal., Knk., Tag. *lusóng*]

álta: (Sp. *alta:* high) *a.* high. (*ngato*) **alta sosiedad.** *n.* high society. (*nangato a gimong*)

altapresión: (Sp. *alta presión:* high pressure) *n.* high blood pressure.

áltas: *n.* declaration of property. **yaltas.** *v.* to declare property.

alternatíbo: (Sp. *alternativo:* alternative) *n.* alternative.

altésa: (Sp. *alteza:* highness, *obs.*) *n.* highness (address of respect for royalty).

altít: *n.* convincing talk; talk with an ulterior motive; **al-altíten** *a.* gullible, easily convinced or deceived; **altiten.** *v.* to try to persuade someone.

altipít: *a.* gullible, easily convinced or deceived.

altó: (Sp. *alto:* stop) **altuen.** *v.* to stop; cease; halt. (*sardeng*)

altóg: *n.* a kind of small marine fish with a flat body.

altót: maaltótan. *v.* to have something caught in the throat.

-am: Combination of the second person singular ergative enclitic *-mo* and the suffix *-an.* **Papan***am***?** Where are you going? **Naggapu***am***?** Where did you come from?

áma: *n.* term of respect for an older man (said by men); interjection denoting surprise, wonder, etc. **ni áma**. (f. *amá*) (my) father.

amá: *n.* father; respectful term used to address males one generation above the speaker. (*tatang*) **pannakaama**. *n.* foster father. **ama ti bunyag**. godfather. **ama ti kasar**. sponsor at a wedding. **agama**. father with child (*pl. agaama*). **immama**. *a.* taking after one's father in features, manners, etc. **kaama**. *a.* having the same father, but different mothers. **kaamaan**. *n.* relatives on the father's side; clan. **maka-ama**. *a.* very close to one's father. **ipaama**. *v.* to consider an elderly man as one's father. **naamaan**. *a.* fatherly. **ni áma**. (my) father. [Ivt. *amaq*, Kpm. *tata*, Ibg., Kal., Png., Tag. *amá*]

amáam: **umamaam**. *v.* to worsen (*karo*; *degdeg*). [Tag. *samâ*]

amaayá: Interjection expressing amazement. (*ámaya*)

ámad: *n.* essence; sense; meaning; topic, news. **amaden**. *v.* to determine; understand; construe. **umamad, agamad**. *v.* to inquire about (news, information, etc.). **Masuronak iti daydiay a laklakayan, sangkaamadna no nobioka.** I'm fed up with that old man, he keeps asking if you are my boyfriend. [Tag. *tanóng* (inquire)]

ámag: *n.* a reddish intestinal worm about two inches long; cambium; mold; soft, external part of a tree.

amák: **amken**. *v.* to fear. (*buteng*) **umamak**. *v.* to be afraid. **naamak**. *a.* feared. **nakaam-amak**. *a.* frightening. **kaamak**. *v.* to be afraid of. [Kal. *latayak*, Knk. *ínget*, Tag. *takot*]

amáka: (Sp. *hamaca*: hammock) *n.* hammock. **agamaka**. *v.* to sleep in a hammock (*indayon*). [Tag. *duyan*]

amálit: *n.* a variety of awned rice with white kernel.

am-ám: *n.* usury; (baby talk: food). **mangngam-am**. *n.* usurer. **agam-am**. *v.* to practice usury, lend money at a high rate of interest. **naam-am**. *a.* greedy. [Tag. *usura*]

amámang: How ADJ! , also *amamángan*.

amamgíd: *n. Scleria scrobiculata* (*aladan*).

am-ammó: *v.* to know a person, see *ammo*.

amanó: *var.* of *amangán*.

amános: (Sp. *a manos*: even) *a.* even (in gambling, paying off a debt, etc.). **nayamano**. *a.* settled (debt), even. [Knk. *delkák*]

amansít: *n. Physalis minima* weed (*tultullaki*)

amántes: (Sp. *dos amantes*: two lovers) **dos amantes**. *n.* bleeding heart flower and plant.

ámang₁: *n.* refuge, shelter; protection. **um-amang**. *v.* to take refuge; seek shelter. **yamang**.

v. to take to a shelter. [Tag. *kanlungan*, *tagakupkóp*]

ámang₂: *adv.* by far. **am-amang**. *a.* far removed; remote. **nasasayaat nga amang**. it is far better.

ámang₃: (f. *amá*) *n.* address used toward one's father, dad.

amangá: *n.* reverence; awe; surprise. (*ammanga*) **agamanga**. *v.* to be stunned or stupefied with surprise or awe. [Tag. *taká*]

amangán: *adv.* it is possible that; indicates doubt or possibility that the action of its complement will occur: **Amangan a tumaray.** He might run away. **amangan no**. just in case. **Agdaluska amangan no umay.** Clean up in case he comes. **Nagsaganaak nga aganawa amangan no agdinnuklapda.** I prepared to be alert to prevent a fight in case they fight each other. **Nangato met ti sueldo ket amangan no makaipatakderto ketdi iti bukodna a talier.** The salary is high so he might be able to put up his own workshop.

amangáw: **am-amangaw**. *n.* delirium. **agam-amangaw**. *v.* to be stunned, stupefied, delirious. [Tag. *hibáng*]

amapóla: (Sp. *amapola*: poppy) *n.* poppy, species of plant with medicinal properties whose leaves and flowers can be used as an expectorant or as an antidote to certain poisons.

amaránto: (Sp.) *n.* amaranth.

amáras: *n. Piper retrofractum* plant. (*lilít, kamára*).

amargóso: (Sp.) *n.* old name for the bittermelon vine (*pariá*). [Tag. *ampalayá*]

amaríles: (Sp. *amarilis*: amaryllis) *n.* belladonna lily.

amarílio: (Sp. *amarillo*: yellow) *a.* yellow (*kiaw, duyaw*). **amarilio ti itlog**. *n.* egg yolk.

amáris: *n.* slight shower of rain. **agamaris**. *v.* to shower slightly.

ámas: *n.* thin (rice in the fields); scarce. **naamas**. *a.* yielding a poor rice harvest (*kisang*). [Tag. *dalang*]

amasóna: (Sp. *amazona*: Amazon) *n.* Amazon, mannish woman (*lakien*). **Adda am-amasona-na.** She has Amazon characteristics.

amatísta: *n.* amethyst.

ámay: *n.* uncivil word; uncouth act; insolence. **naamay**. *a.* insolent; uncouth. [Tag. *kawaláng-galang*]

amayá: interjection expressing amazement.

ambabasit: *n. Eugenia parva*.

ambág: **pagambagan**. *n.* company; association. (*gunglo*) **makiambag**. *v.* to associate; enter in a partnership. **pagambagan**. *v.* to make a joint purchase; contribute money to a charity. [Tag. *ambág*]

ambagél: *n.* insane, lunatic person (*balla, bagtit, mauyong*). [Tag. *ulól*]

ambál: **naambal.** *a.* brackish; tasteless water. (*tabáng*) **umambal.** *v.* to become brackish; lose original taste.

ambálag: *n. Mischocarpus fuscescens* plant.

ambalangá: *n.* a kind of skate. [Png. *ambalangá* = red]

amballóg: (*reg.*) *n.* decrepit male beast of burden.

ámbas: (Sp. *ambas*: both, plural and feminine gender) **makiambasan.** *v.* to be matched (abilities). **ambas pareho.** on equal level, matched.

ambáyon: see *abayon*: band; support.

ambiáw: *n.* fear, fright. **maambiaw.** *v.* to be afraid. (*amak; buteng*)

ambíng: *a.* impatient for food, with mouth watering (dog). **agambing, umambing.** *v.* to have the mouth water when seeing someone else eat food; to desire to have; be envious. **paambingan.** *v.* to make the mouth water. **naambing.** *a.* envious. [Tag. *inggít*; Knk. *ambíng* = interrupt]

ambisión: (Sp. *ambición*) *n.* ambition.

ambisióso: (Sp. *ambicioso*: ambitious) *a.* ambitious.

ambubunót: *n.* a kind of plant.

ambúdo: *var.* of *embudo*: funnel. (*sarangusong*)

ambúg: **naambug.** *a.* proud; haughty; vain; arrogant; one who easily influences. **agambug.** *v.* to brag (*pangas*). [Tag. *yabang, hambóg*]

ambulánsia: (Sp. *ambulancia*: ambulance) *n.* ambulance.

ambulánte: (Sp. *ambulante*: ambulatory) *n.* itinerant; peddler.

ambulígan: *n.* corncob, cob. **am-ambuligan.** *n. Clerodendron minahassae* plant (*ayam-ayam*). [Tag. *busal*]

ambúlong: *n. Rhaphidophora merrillii* plant.

ambón: *n.* assemble; concourse. **ambonen.** *v.* to join in fighting against the enemy. **innambonan.** *n.* game of catching one another.

ambungáw: see *bungaw*.

ámbus: (Sp. *ambos*: both) *n.* sweepstakes ticket winning the lowest prize, consolation prize. **makaambus.** *v.* to win the lowest prize; be the last in a race of contest. **pagaambusan.** *v.* to share a small amount among many people. [Tag. *ambós*]

ambús: *n.* vulva of young girls (under seven years of age).

ambuywán: *n.* timber whose ashes are used for making soap.

ambrósia: (Sp.) *n.* ambrosia, dish of sliced fruits, sugar, and milk.

ámen: see *ameng*: covet; greed; selfishness.

amén: (Eng.) *n.* amen. **Awan ti aglualo a di agamen.** *exp.* No one prays without saying amen (no one will fail to complete an easy and beneficial task).

amendár: (Eng., Sp. *enmendar*) **amendaran.** *v.* to amend (a law).

ámeng: *n.* greed; envy; selfishness. **naameng.** *a.* covetous; greedy; stingy, miserly, selfish, parsimonious. **agameng.** *v.* to covet. [Tag. *sakím*]

América: *n.* America. **Amerikano.** *a.* American.

amerikána: (Sp. *americana*: coat) *n.* coat. **agamerikana.** *v.* to wear a coat.

Amerikáno: *n. a.* American, feminine counterpart: *Amerikana*. (*taga-Amerika*) **Amerikanista.** *a.* Americanist, person in favor of American policies.

amés: *n.* fright. (*buteng; amak*) **amsen.** *v.* to frighten; intimidate. **amsan.** *v.* to treat mercifully. **am-ames.** *n.* scarecrow. (*bambanti*) **nakaam-ames.** *a.* scary, frightening. **iyames.** *v.* to be afraid of; *n.* that which is feared. **kaames.** *n.* that which is feared. [Bon. *egyat*, Png. *takót*, Tag. *takot*]

ametraliadóra: (Sp. *ametralladora*: machine gun) *n.* machine gun.

amgíd: *n.* a slender grass, *Leersia hexandra.* **maamgidan.** *v.* to be affected with an itch caused by the *amgid*; receive a small portion of a loot. [Png. *talamít*]

amián: *n.* north wind. **amianan.** *n.* north. **agpaamianan.** *v.* to go to the north. **makiamianan.** *a.* on the north side. **Nasalemsem ti amian nga aggapu iti akinlaud a bakrang ti bantay.** The north wind coming from the western side of the mountain was invigorating. [Ivt. *kaydawran*, Kal. *kapun lagud*, Png. *amianen*, Tag. *hilagà*]

amígo: (Sp. *amigo*: friend) *n.* friend (*gayyem*). **amiguen.** *v.* to befriend.

ámil: *n.* mucous membrane of the upper lip. **agamil.** *v.* to lick the lips. (*dilpat*) **pangamil.** (*coll.*) *n.* lips including the tongue. **Naamilna ti subsobna.** He licked his snout (said of someone who sees something delicious). [Tag. *dilà* (lick)]

amiliaramiénto: (Sp. *amillaramiento*: tax assessment) *n.* land taxes. (*buis ti daga*)

amilíng: **paria-amiling.** *n.* species of the bittermelon vine.

ámin: *adv. a.* all, entire, whole, complete. **amin no.** whenever. **isu amin, dagup amin.** all; every; entirely; completely. **amin nga awan labasna.** *exp.* everybody. **Basolna aminen a mapasamak a di naimbag iti balay.** Everything not good that happens in the house is his fault. [Bon. *ngonon, wasdin,* Ibg. *ngámin,* Ivt. *atávuq,* Kal. *losan,* Knk. *am-ín, idín, ngam-ín, ngámos,* Kpm. *eganagana, sablaq, ngansaping,* Png. *amín, tálba,* Tag. *lahát*]

ámin: **agamin.** *v.* to kiss the hand of elders to show respect. [Tag. *mano*]

amín: (Tag.) **aminen.** *v.* to confess one's guilt or error *(akó);* admit defeat, concede. **umamin.** *v.* to admit one's mistake. [Tag. *amin*]

aminádo: (f. *amín*) *a.* admitted, conceded; confessed; certain, sure.

amíngan: *n.* hut, shed. *(kalapaw)*

amír: *n.* fear. *(amak)* **kaamir.** *v.* to be afraid of.

amíris: **amirisen.** *v.* to determine *(amísig, arísit, asáas, bukíbok, nákem, panúnot, tingíting);* perceive; tell (construe); pick carefully; *(reg.)* to pulverize between the fingers. **maamiris.** *v.* to be able to understand; scrutinize; discern; determine. **pannakaamiris.** *n.* observation, study; determination. **Naamirisko a talaga nga ay-ayatennak.** I determined that you truly love me. **Inkari met dagiti manarawidwid nga amirisenda dagitoy a dawat dagiti obrero.** The managers promised that they would study the demands of the workers. [Tag. *surì* (examine); *hatol* (determine); *pilì* (choose)]

amísig: **amisigen.** *v.* to observe carefully; pay attention to. *(amiris)*

amistád: (Sp. *amistad:* friendship) *n.* friendship. *(pannakigayyem)*

ámit: **maamitan.** *v.* to be caught, overtaken. **makaamit.** *v.* to reach; suffice until; be enough until *(umdas).* [Tag. *kasya*]

amít: *n.* load; burden; responsibility. **amiten.** *v.* to carry, bear (while moving). **innamit.** *n.* carrying one another on a bamboo pole. (young boys game) **maamit.** *v.* to be able to carry or bear. **Napeggad unay ti maamitan iti tudo iti bantay.** It is very dangerous to be carried away by the mountain rain.

amitáw: *n.* monorchid animal, animal or man with only one testis; man who has one testicle smaller than the other. *(búdi, bukáw)*

amíto: (Sp. *amito:* amice) *n.* amice. **nakaamito.** *a.* wearing an amice.

amkén: (f. *amak*) *v.* to fear.

amlíd: **agamlid.** *v.* to wipe with the arm or hand. *(ammusay)* **yamlid.** *v.* to wipe on. **Inyamlidna ti gayadan ti garitan a pandilingna.** She wiped (her nose) with the hemline of his striped skirt. **Nadlawko nga am-amlidan itay ni tatang dagiti matana.** I noticed that father was wiping his eyes a while ago (with his hands). [Kpm. *saping*]

amlíng: *n.* supernatural visit. **maamlingan.** *v.* to become sick due to a supernatural visit.

makaamling. *v.* to cause the sickness of the *amling.*

amlóy₁: **agamloy.** *v.* to wash the face around the mouth after eating *(ammusay);* to oil or wet the hair to set it in place, comb hair with the fingers *(amuy).*

amlóy₂: **amluyen.** *v.* to rub softly; caress; flatter. *(lailo)*

ammá: *pl.* of *ama, n.* fathers.

ammadáng: *n.* a kind of shoe, clog. **pagammadang.** *n.* stilt. **am-ammadang.** *n.* improvised play shoe with strings attached to the hands, used by children. [Tag. *bakyâ*]

ammál: **agammal.** *v.* to hold between the lips. *(ammimi; tangal)*

ammangáw: **agam-ammangaw.** *v.* to be delirious; worry with convulsions as an insane person. [Png. *luang, manitaw,* Tag. *hibáng*]

ammáray: **ammarayen.** *n.* cold cooked rice dried in the sun.

ammásit: *(coll.) n.* crybaby; sissy. *(mangit, managsangit)*

ammími: **ammimian.** *v.* to hold with the mouth; treasure dearly. *(sammimit; abbal; ammal)*

ammimiráy: **agammimiray.** *v.* to come to; recover; get well; recover from a hangover. **maammimirayan.** *v.* to recover from a spell; return back to normal; regain composure *(usaw; munaw).* [Tag. *himasmás* (regain consciousness)]

ammímit: *var.* of *ammimi:* hold with the lips.

ammingáw: **umammingaw.** *v.* to make a brief appearance; peer. **ammingawan.** *v.* to look over briefly; glance at. [Tag. *sungaw*]

ammít: **naammit.** *a.* slow; done little by little; seldom, rarely.

ammó: *v.* (defective, takes *-ko* pronouns) to know; *n.* knowledge; experience. **ammok.** I know. **am-ammo.** *v.* to know a person; *n.* acquaintance. **aginnammo.** *v.* to get acquainted with; get to know. **makiam-ammo.** *v.* to make the acquaintance of. **yam-ammo.** *v.* to introduce someone to. **ammuen.** *v.* to acknowledge; recognize. **maammuan.** *v.* to come to know; find out. **agpakaammo.** *v.* to notify. **makaammo.** *v.* to be responsible for. **mannakaammo.** *a.* knowledgeable; educated; literate; experienced. **ipakaammo.** *v.* to notify; make known, publish. **agin-aammo.** *v.* to pretend to know. **Indiak ammo, Ammok pay, Ammok kadi.** I don't know. **ammok pay.** I don't know. How should I know? **agtagtagiammo.** *v.* to be uncertain. (takes *-ak*) **pagam-ammuan.** *adv.* all of a sudden; suddenly. **pagam-ammo.** *v.* to introduce. **panaginnammo.** *v.* to get to know each other. **paggaammuen.** v. to introduce several people to each other. **siam-ammo, siaammo.** a. aware; cognizant. **Pagaammok.** I am aware; I am well informed. **Sika ti maka-ammo.** exp. It's up to you; You are responsible. **Siak ti makaammo a mangisagana iti padaya.** I will be the one responsible to prepare for the party. **Siak ti makaammo iti pagpletem.** I will be the one to take care of your fare. **Sangakaarrubaan a di agammo-ammo, di aginnallatiw iti sarsardam tapno agpapatang koma.** It is a neighborhood where nobody knows each other, they do not go around visiting in the evenings to talk. **Ti babai a yam-ammo ti baro kadagiti dadakkelna ket isu ti kayatna nga asawaen.** The girl that the bachelor introduces to his parents is the one he wants to marry. [Ibg. *emmu*, Ivt. *masulib*, Kal. *ammuwon* (fact), *tagtagammu* (person), Kpm. *biása*, Png. *amtá* (fact); *kábat* (person), Tag. *alám, dunong* (fact); *kilala* (person)]

ammuán: n. wad of cotton to catch sparks while striking flint; tinder, materials used to start a fire.

ammúd: n. a curse. (*lunod*) **maammudan.** v. to be cursed. **maam-ammudanka koma.** curse. May you die! [Tag. *sumpâ*]

ammúgod: **ammuguden.** v. to investigate. scrutinize. (*amiris, usisa*)

ammól: **agammol.** v. to hold in the mouth (*mulmol*), play or toy with something in the mouth. **naammolan.** v. to be held in the mouth. **Nginatngatna ti naammolan ti tabakona sana intupra.** He chewed on the cigar in his mouth and then spit it out.

ammóng: n. group of people. (*ummong*) **ammongen.** v. to collect, gather, accumulate. [Tag. *tipon*]

ammúsay: **agammusay.** v. to wipe the face or mouth (*amloy*). **ammusayen.** v. to wipe the face and mouth of a baby (or other person); (*fig.*) to have lost much money in gambling. **Inammusayanna ti pamuskolen a subsobna.** He wiped his rather thick snout.

ammútil: n. Adam's apple; nipple; button; knob; top of the banana fruit; protruding growth; (*coll.*) teat; clitoris. **am-ammutil.** n. cartilage, appendix, appendage; xiphisternum (posterior part of the sternum). [Tag. *gulunggulungan* (Adam's apple)]

ammúyo: **agammuyo.** v. to work together. (*tagnawa*) **ammuyuen.** v. to ask the help of someone else. **innammuyo.** n. mutual work, cooperation. [Kal. *abbuyug*, Png. *tagnawa*, Tag. *bayani*]

ammúyot: **ammuyotan.** v. to convince, persuade; arouse.

amnáw: n. tastelessness (*lab-ay, tamnay*). **na-amnaw.** a. weak (liquor); flat (food); slipshod. **umamnaw.** v. to recover; grow well; lose flavor. **Nalagipna ti naamnaw a pannaki-langen ni Charito kenkuana.** He remembered Charito's weak relationship with him. [Tag. *tabáng*]

amnésia: (Sp. *amnesia*: amnesia) n. amnesia (*tagilipat*). **agamnesia.** v. to suffer from amnesia.

amnestía: (Sp. *amnestía*: amnesty) n. amnesty, pardon for an offense against the government.

amnút: **naamnut.** a. solid, tough, hardy; logical and clear (speech). **umamnut.** v. to become tough, pliant (*lap-it*); to convince gently another person to change his mind. [Tag. *lambót*]

ámo: (Sp. *amo*: lord) n. master, lord; chief; boss. (*apo*) **umam-amo.** v. to bootlick; to maintain a sycophantic relationship with the boss. [Tag. *amo*]

ámo: n. civilized people. **naamo.** a. tame, gentle; domesticated. **panagamo.** n. reconciliation. **yamo.** v. to reconcile people. **pagamuen.** v. to make enemies friends as before, make people reconcile. **paamuen.** v. to tame; domesticate; temper; subdue. **umamo.** v. to reconcile; like something not liked before. **tagiamo.** n. see *tagiroot*: talisman. **pangpaamo.** n. love potion, talisman. [Png. *ámo*, Tag. *amò*]

amugá(w)en: n. a kind of plant; *Sapindus sapponaria* tree whose seeds are pounded and used as a fish poison.

amúgod: see *ammugod*: investigate; scrutinize.

amúlong: n. a kind of shrub that roots in trees, *Epipremnum medium.*

amoniáko: (Sp. *amoníaco*: ammoniac) n. ammonia water.

amúog: **amuugen.** v. to appreciate; be pleased with; attracted to.

ámong: var. of *amo*: master, lord.

amór: (Sp. *amor*: love) n. morning dew (*lin-naaw*); love, affection (*ayat*). **agpaamor.** v. to stay outdoors in the cold mornings. **kasla naamoran ti rupana.** exp. face as fresh as the morning. **amor propio.** n. self-love. [Tag. *hamóg* (dew)]

amóras: (Sp. *mora* (fruit), *morera* (tree): mulberry) n. mulberry, *Morus alba*; *Andropogon zizanioides;* the boiled leaves are used to cure rheumatism.

amóres: (Sp. *amor*: love) n. love affairs or escapades; unpleasant odors.

amurát: *n.* fibers of fibrous vegetables; variety of fibrous sweet potato. **pagamuratan.** *n.* discarded fibers when eating. **yamuratan.** *v.* to discard fibers (from root crops) before eating; cull (*amurít*). [Tag. *hiblá, himaymáy*]

amurít: *n.* the root of the sweet potato next to the vine. **yamuritan.** *v.* to cull.

amorítis: (*coll.*) *n.* lovesickness; affection; passion. **agamoritis.** *v.* to be lovesick.

amorósa: (Sp. *amor* 'love' + *rosa* 'flower') *n.* species of tasty banana; (*fig.*) light complexioned skin.

amoróso: (Sp. *moroso*: delinquent, late) *a.* late in paying taxes.

amúrot: **amuruten.** *v.* to pull up; uproot; pull up hair; get rid of excess matter from a bunch; scrutinize; take out foreign particles or pieces that do not belong. [Tag. *bunot*]

amorséko: (Sp. *amor seco*: dry love) *n.* burry lovegrass. (*puriket*)

amortisasión: (Sp. *amortización*: amortization) *n.* mortgage installment.

amútil: see *ammutil*: Adam's apple; knob; nipple; appendage.

amutong: *n. Hoya meliflua*, commonly growing on trees at low altitudes.

ámuy: **amuyen.** *v.* to influence, move; prompt; assemble; gather; comb the hair with the hands. [Tag. *hikayat*]

amúyo: **agamuyo.** *v.* to work in a group.

ampág: (*reg.*) **maampag.** *v.* to be consumed (drinks).

ampák: see *sipát*: slap; spank.

ampáng: *a.* wanton, loose, silly (women). (*dangnga, garampang*)

ampapagét: *n.* species of marine fish with an ugly face.

ampapáok: *a.* simple, naive, ignorant, too trusting, innocent. [Tag. *tangá*]

ampára: (Sp. *parar*: stop) *interj.* stop! **agampara, amparaen.** *v.* to stop (work); to catch something falling.

ampás: *var.* of *angpas*: animal tick.

ampát: **ampaten.** *v.* to glean (*tudtod*); gather what is left after reaping.

ampáw: *n.* simpleton, fool; empty shell; kind of sweet rice ball; popcorn; *a.* foolish; ignorant; dull; empty; worthless, nonsubstantial. **nagampaw.** *a.* foolish, simple minded.

ampáyag: *n.* hovering, gliding flight; casting upwards. see *ampayog*. (*alimpayag, ampayog, salingkob*) **agampayag.** *v.* to float about; hover. **yampayag.** *v.* to cast upwards, fling. **agamampayag a panunot.** *n.* stray thoughts. **Nagampayag ti panunotko dagiti aldawmi iti**

unibersidad. Our days in the university hovered in my thoughts. **agampayag-agdisso.** *v.* to take off and land. [Tag. *alindayag*]

ampáyog: **agampayog.** *v.* to glide, hover. (*ampayag*) **ampayugen.** *v.* to throw; toss; cast upwards.

ampép: *var.* of *angpep*: stench of rotten fish.

ampiág: *n.* a kind of vine whose leaves are used to cure wounds.

ampiáng: *var.* of *ampang*.

ampipít: *n.* a kind of small stinging black ant. [Tag. *hantík*]

ampír: **umampir.** *v.* to approach, come close to something. **yampir.** *v.* to place something near. **Nagtugawak iti papag a nakayampiran ti telepono.** I sat on the bamboo bench adjacent to the telephone. [Tag. *lapit, tabí*]

ampít₁: *n.* a kind of vine whose fruit is used in medicine.

ampít₂: *n.* person having one foot smaller and shorter than the other. **agampit.** *v.* to walk limping. [Tag. *pilay* (limp)]

ampít₃: **ampiten.** *v.* to cheat at cards. (*kusit*) **agampit ti rabii.** It's midnight. **naampit ti anges.** *n.* hard breathing.

ampiteátro: (Sp. *ampiteatro*) *n.* amphitheater.

ampó: *n.* a kind of small, blackish freshwater fish with poisonous fins. **ampuen.** *v.* to be pricked by the fins of an *ampo*. **naampo.** *a.* hot-tempered, hasty, touch-me-not. (*kasla ampo*) **agpaampo.** *v.* to play hard to get (women); to be a hypocrite. **kasla sumpeg nga ampo.** *exp.* fighting with tooth and nail. **Sumngaren nga ampo ti babai.** The lady bristled furiously.

ampólia: (Sp. *ampolla*: vial) *n.* vial (usually used for medicines).

ámpon: *n.* adopted child. **amponen.** *v.* to adopt a child; rear an adopted child. [Tag. *ampón*]

amsít: *a.* crybaby, sissy. (*mangit, managsangit*) **amsiten.** *v.* to stop a baby from crying by amusing him.

amták: *n.* a variety of cowpea with large seeds.

amték: *n.* tin.

amtík: **agamtik.** *n.* nightshade plant, *Solanum nigrum.*

-an-: Infix used with onomatopoetic roots to indicate continual repetition or intensity of the sound or action associated with the root. **banitog.** series of thumping sounds. **ranitrit.** series of creaking or rustling sounds. **ranipak.** crackling sounds. **tanaul.** repeated, loud barking of dogs.

-an₁: Verbalizing suffix with the following uses: 1. Verbalizing transitive suffix taking the *-ko* ergative pronouns that specifies directional focus. **suratan.** to write to (someone) **aday-wan.** to move away from (someone) **iwaan.** to slice (a piece) from/off something **kaluban.** to cover something; 2. The *-an* suffix can also be used to denote an action performed by the actor on behalf of someone else (in focused object position): **Sinaksiak ti ubing.** I testified for (on behalf of) the child. 3. The *-an* suffix is used with certain roots to express augmentation or diminishment: **silpuan.** to connect something. **putolan.** to cut off a head. **kartiban.** to cut off a piece with scissors. **nayonan.** to add to something. 4. Sometimes the *-an* suffix specifies human patients. Notice the meaning differences between the following roots when used with the patientive *-en* as opposed to the directional *-an*: **suro: suruen.** to learn something. **suruan.** to teach someone. *takaw:* **takawen.** to steal something. **takawan.** to rob someone. 5. The *-an* suffix can also be used to express payment or offering: **Talloam.** Offer three for it. **Manuanda ti balay.** How much do they offer for the house? **Winaluanmi.** We paid eight (pesos) for it. 6. May indicate that something is earned by the action designated by the root. **Pisos ti dinaitak.** I earned one peso by sewing. **Mano ti tinalonam?** How much did you earn farming?

-an₂: Affix used with body parts to denote their existence or unusual size: **barbasan.** bearded, having a beard. **saraan.** having antlers. **sa-ongan.** with tusks, tusked. With general body parts inherent to the species, the *-an* suffix may also indicate the abnormal size of the body part designated by the root. This affix is also used for naming certain species renowned for a large body part. **ipusan.** with a large tail; kind of fish with a long tail. **mataan.** with large eyes; kind of fish with large eyes.

-an₃: Nominalizing suffix used for instrumental purposes: **gilingan.** grinder. **sagatan.** strainer.

-an₄: Nominalizing suffix used for finite verbs (forms aspectual gerunds). **naggatangan.** *n.* place where something was bought. **limma-kayan.** *n.* having grown old (said of a man) **Idiay ti dimmakkelanna.** That's the place where he grew up. **Idiay ngamin ti masansan nga umiananna.** It's because there is where he usually stays.

-an₅: Nominalizing suffix that forms agentive nouns, usually denoting occupation: **babúyan.** pig dealer. **manokán.** chicken dealer. **adalan.** disciple.

CV- -an₆: With initial CV reduplication, indicates suitability: **aasinan a mangga.** mango good for salting. **susukaan a singkamas.**

jicama fruit good for eating with vinegar. **baka a gagatasan.** *n.* dairy cow. May also form instrumental nouns: **iideppan.** turnoff switch.

aná: (*reg.*) *var.* of *ania*: what. [Tag. *anó*]

anáaw: *n.* a kind of tall palm, *Livistona rotundifolia.* **inanaawan.** *n.* a kind of hat made with *anaaw* leaves. **kaanaawan.** *n.* palm grove. [Tag. *anahaw*]

anabáab: *n.* sound not heard distinctly, background noise; chatter. **umanabaab.** *v.* to be noisy (*ariwawa*). **Madamdama pay, nakangngegkami iti adu nga anabaab.** Afterwards, we heard a lot of noise. [Tag. *ingay*]

anábo: *n. Malachra capitata* weed.

anabó: *n. Abroma augusta.*

ánag₁: *n.* flavor; meaning; savor, characteristic property; substance; essence. **naanag.** *a.* nutritious; nourishing; flavorful; **anagen.** *v.* to study; analyze; understand; savor. **Adda anagna.** It is meaningful, substantial. **No an-anagek, ad-adda a dagiti ubbing ti agsagaba.** When I think about it, it's probably the children who are suffering. [Tag. *lasà, linamnám* (taste); *lamán* (substance)]

ánag₂: *n.* odor of human feces. **naanag.** *a.* odorous.

anág: **umanag.** *v.* to court; make love (*arem*). [Tag. *ligaw*]

anagép: *n.* a kind of hard timber; *Beilschmiedia cairocan* (*kalangíking*); *Eriobotrya ambigua.*

anák: (pl. *annak, aannak; an-anak* for fish). *n.* offspring, child, son, daughter; earning of interest. **aganak.** *v.* to give birth (*sengngay*). **anaken.** *v.* to stand as a sponsor at a baptismal or wedding; wield political power. **anakan.** *v.* to father a child illegitimately. **maanakan.** *v.* to be impregnated; deliver ahead of a scheduled time. **yanak.** *v.* to give birth. **inanak.** *n.* offspring. **naganak.** *n.* parent, father, mother. **kaanakan.** *n.* nephew, niece. **an-anak.** *n.* doll; fry; young of birds. **manganganak.** *n.* kind of small crab; fertile female; person or animal with numerous offspring. **manganak.** *n.* godparent, sponsor. **aanakan.** *n.* womb, uterus. **pangganakan.** *n.* fertile female for breeding. **sangaanakan.** *n.* litter (of born animals); one family. **anak ti bunyag.** *n.* godchild. **anak ti ruar.** *n.* child born out of wedlock, lovechild. **anak ti sal-it.** curse expression: thunder child. **mamagpaanak.** *v.* to induce childbirth or abortion. **agpaanak.** *n.* midwife. **kaiyanak, apag-anak.** *n.* newly born baby. **ipaanak.** *v.* to consider oneself as a son or daughter of someone else. **kinaanak.** *n.* filiality. **nakayanakan.** *a.* native. **pannakaanak.** *n.* stepchild. **No agar-arbis nga agin-init, agan-anak ti**

mangmangkit. *exp.* When it drizzles in sunny weather, an elf is giving birth. [Ifg. *ambabale*, Kal. *alak*, Png. *ilálak*, *anák*, *ogáw*, Ivt., Knk., Kpm., Tag. *anák*; Knk. *kaplís* (child of second marriage)]

anák: *n.* interest. **aganak.** *v.* to earn interest. **paanakan.** *v.* to impose interest. **agpapaanak iti kuarta.** *n.* loan sharks, usurers; people who loan money with interest.

anákki-: (Plural *annakki-*) contraction of *anak ti* 'child of' as used in certain curse expressions: **anakkisal-it.** son of lightning. **annakkidiables.** sons of the devil.

anakónda: (Sp. *anaconda*: anaconda) *n.* anaconda, kind of very large boa.

análisis: (Sp. *análisis*: analysis) *n.* analysis.

ánam: umanam. *v.* to do little by little, discontinuously (*inut*); do with no set schedule or deadline. [Tag. *pauntí-untí*]

anám: *n. Glochidion philippicum* plant.

anamá: apaganama. *a.* scarcely; hardly; barely (*apáman*). [Png. *dagdaiset*, Tag. *bahagyâ*]

anamír: kaanamir. *v.* to be afraid of; fear. (*amák*, *buténg*)

anámong: umanamong. *v.* to agree; consent; conform; approve; affirm; adhere to; be willing. **aganamong.** *v.* to agree with each other. (*abúloy*, *annúgot*, *annúrot*, *kanúnong*, *túboy*) **Immanamongak a nagkallaysakami.** I agreed we would get married. [Bon. *tan-oy*, Ivt. *panmu*, Kal. *iteun*, Knk. *abúyug*, Png. *abóbon*, *kitáw*, Tag. *payag*, *sundô*]

anampáy: *var.* of *apay*: why. [Tag. *bakit*]

ananat: *n.* plant with hemplike leaves that are used for making mats.

anannáy: interjection expressing pain. (*annáy*) **agananay.** *v.* to moan from pain.

an-annóng: (f. *annong*) *n.* attack of an evil spirit. **an-annongan.** *v.* to make someone ill by use of spirits. **maan-annongan.** *v.* to be made ill by spirits. **makaan-annong.** *v.* to be able to make someone ill by use of spirits. **Napukawna ti sukal ti an-annong.** He lost the antidote for the evil spirits.

an-anó: (f. *anó*) **agan-ano.** *v.* to be the matter with; to happen, to do. **maan-ano.** so what; who cares; never mind. **Naan-ano?** *interrog.* What happened? **pagan-ano.** *v. interrog.* what to do with, what to use for. **an-anuen.** *v. interrog.* what to do with or use for.

ananuán: umananuan. *v.* to worsen; intensify. (*degdeg*; *karo*)

anansá: *conj.* therefore, wherefore; also *anansa ta*, *anansa ngarud*; *yantangay.*

anang-áng: aganang-ang. *v.* to howl; whine (dog). (*alang-ang*) **Napaanang-ang a napa-**

lagto ti napalsiitan a pusa. The cat hit with a slingshot made a whining jump. [Tag. *ungol*]

anangká: *n.* jackfruit (*langka*). [Tag. *langkâ*]

anangkí: *n.* a kind of tree that bears *pilis* fruit.

anangsáb: umanangsab. *v.* to breathe heavily; sigh.

ánap1: *n.* slight fever. (*gurigor*) **umanap.** *v.* to rest; be still (when sick).

ánap2: umanap. *v.* to hint, insinuate (*ripirip*); to have a feeling that something may happen.

anáping: *n.* porcupine; wild boar; hairy person; simpleton.

anaráar: *n.* dawn; ray of the sun; first light of dawn. (*alinaga*; *arimasamas*) **aganaraar.** *v.* to emit light; glow. **Nadlawna met ti anaraar ti pagsilawan a rummuar iti ruangan.** He noticed the glow of the light coming out of the door. [Tag. *liwaywáy* (dawn)]

anarep: *n. Terminalia calamansanai* plant.

anarkía: (Sp. *anarquía*: anarchy) *n.* anarchy, absence of government. **anarkiko.** *a.* anarchical. **anarkismo.** *n.* anarchism. **anarkista.** *n.* anarchist.

anatomía: (Sp. *anatomía*: anatomy) *n.* anatomy; structure of an animal or plant.

ánas: *n. Pentacme contorta* plant; itch from a skin rash. **anasen.** *v.* to have itchy eruptions on the skin. [Tag. *an-an*]

anás: *n.* shedding (palay). **aganas.** *v.* to shed palay. **anasen.** *v.* to cause a sharp pain.

anasáas: *n.* rustling sound; murmur; whisper. (*arasaas*) **aganasaas.** *v.* to whisper. **Nakataltalna ti baybay ket naumbi ti anasaas dagiti babassit a dalluyon nga agkaradap iti darat.** The sea was quite calm and the sound of the small waves crawling on the sand was lovely. [Tag. *anás*]

anasánas: maanasanas. *v.* to be chafed by friction.

anas-ás: aganas-as. *v.* to pant, breathe heavily. (*al-al*, *tunglab*)

ánat: naanat. *a.* calm, serene, peaceful, tranquil; careful. **anaten.** *v.* to do something calmly or carefully. **Inan-anatna ti timmakder.** He stood up carefully. [Tag. *dahan*]

anátad: kaanatad. *v.* equal, peer, match. **agkaanatad.** *v.* to be of the same level; equally matched. [Tag. *pantáy*]

anátup: umanatup, mayanatup. *v.* to be enough, sufficient; to be appropriate; to agree. **anatupen.** *v.* to be deserved, merited. **kaanatupan.** *v.* to correspond to. *n.* equivalent. **agkaanatup.** *v.* to correspond to each other. [Tag. *bagay*, *ayon*]

anáwa: anawaen. *v.* to quiet; prevent fights; admonish noisy children. **aganawa.** *v.* to prevent, stop (fight); mediate; quiet down (children). **maanawa.** *v.* to be silenced; prevented. **yanawa.** *v.* to prevent; avoid. **Nagsaganaak nga aganawa amangan no agdinnuklapda.** I prepared to prevent a fight in case they fought each other. **Wagasyo a pananganawa kadakami?** Is that your way of admonishing us? [Bon. *óyam*, Tag. *awat*]

anáwang: *n.* a kind of underground furnace use for processing sugar, made with four holes. [Tag. *pugón*]

anaw-áw: (f. *aw-aw*) *n.* repeated barking of dogs. **aganaw-aw.** *v.* to bark repeatedly (dogs). (*tanaul*)

ánay: *n.* termite; white ant. **anayen.** *v.* to be attacked by *anay*; to be termite ridden. **inanay.** *a.* infested by termites. [Bon. *áney*, *lákey*, Ibg., Ivt. *anay*, Kal. *lakoy*, Knk. *bukbuk*, *lákey*, Kpm. *áne*, Png. *tabuney*, Tag. *anay*]

anáy₁: *n.* part added to complete what is lacking; total; sum. **umanay, makaanay.** *v.* to be enough, sufficient. **anayen.** *v.* to add. **aganay.** *adv.* almost; nearly; approximately. **naan-anay.** *a.* sufficient; enough. **anayan.** *v.* to full up; complete. **an-anay.** *n.* circumstances; qualifications. **pagan-anay.** *n.* clothes; attire; wardrobe. **ti pagan-anay bassit.** more or less. **yananay.** *v.* to set aside in order to make a supply last longer. **Umanay kanon a pakaragsakanna ti pannaktulongna iti sabali a tao.** They say he is happy enough just to be able to help another man. [Bon. *keneg*, *ag-o* (enough), Tag. *sapát*]

anáy₂: *n.* silt; sand by seashore.

anáyad: *n.* a kind of marine jellyfish that stings. [Tag. *dikyâ*]

andadasí: *n.* a kind of herb whose leaves are used to cure skin diseases of the *Cassia sp.*, *Cassia tora*, *Cassia occidentalis*.

andadéras: *obs.* variant of *andador*: baby stroller; crutches.

andadór: *n.* baby walker (consisting of a hoop, strap, and wheels used to aid a baby in walking). **agandador.** *v.* to use a baby walker.

andámio: *n.* ladder of a ship (*agdan*); gangplank.

andán: *n.* small bridge (*tatay*). [Tag. *tuláy*]

andánte: (Sp. *andante*: andante) *a.* moderately slow (said of musical compositions).

andáp: *n.* glow, luminescence. (*raniag*) **agandap.** *v.* to glow, be luminous; dazzle (light on water). **Agandap ti pudawna iti kasipngetan.** Her whiteness glowed in the dark. [Tag. *kisláp*]

andapí: *n.* a slender vine, *Hewittia sublobata*.

andár: (Sp. *andar*: pace; walking; functioning) *n.* action; working, operation; functioning; run-

ning. **agandar.** *v.* to be running (engines). **pagandaren.** *v.* to turn a device on, turn on the electricity. **mangpaandar.** *v.* to operate a machine. **mapaandar.** *v.* to start an engine. **Pinagandarna ti pirakna.** He put his money to work.

ándas: (Sp. *andas*: bier) *n.* bier; frame for a religious image.

andáy: see *onday*: straight; long.

andén: (Sp. *andén*: train platform) *n.* platform at a railway station.

andí: (*coll.*) **andiandi.** *a.* henpecked (husband); under the *saya*.

andídeng: **agandideng.** *v.* to take the first steps (babies), stand erect for the first time. (*indereng, antok*)

andidikén: *n.* millipede (see *gayaman*). [Tag. *alupihan*]

andídit: *n.* cicada. (*kundidit*) **andidit sanud-sanud umuli nga umulog.** rhyme uttered to entice cicadas to climb down the tree trunk when catching them. **Naimbag ta adda pay danum iti gripo nupay kasla isbo laengen ti andidit.** It's good that there's still water in the faucet although (the water pressure) is just like the urine of a cicada. [Knk. *yáyak, yáyes*, Png. *piyaes*, Tag. *kuliglíg*]

andíngay: *n.* solace; comfort. (*liwliwa*) **andingayen.** *v.* to console; sympathize with; entertain, keep company; tolerate, support; prop; back up; protract. **Nariknak a kasla masursurok ti makalipaten kenka gapu iti naragsak a panangan-andingayna kaniak.** I feel that I am just about over you because of his happy support and consolation for me. **Nakian-andingay tapno mayaw-awan ti buteng.** They console each other to escape the fear. [Tag. *aliw*]

andó: **yandoando.** *v.* to do something dawdling (not finishing work immediately); to put off work (*tongkua*). [Tag. *tayong-tayong*]

anduduál: *n.* a kind of insect living in coconut trees.

andór: *n.* endurance, perseverance. **naandor.** *a.* strong, tough, resistant. **maandoran.** *v.* to endure, bear. (*ibtur*) **immandoran.** *n.* a variety of awned rice with white kernel. [Tag. *tatag, tibay, tiís*]

andúro: **naganduro.** *a.* deformed, misshapen. (*riwis*)

andúyan: see *indayon*: cradle.

andúyas: **aganduyas.** *v.* to slide down.

anek-ék: *n.* sobbing out of pain; cry; lament. (*araraw; gawawa*) **aganek-ek.** *v.* to cry; beg; implore; plead from the heart. [Tag. *hinaíng*]

anel-él: *n.* growling of dogs; moan; groan.

anem-ém: **apaganem-em**. *a.* lukewarm. **anem-emen**. *v.* to make hot, heat up. [Tag. *ligamgám*]

anémia: (Sp. *anemia*: anemia) *n.* anemia.

anémiko: (Sp. *anémico*) *a.* anemic.

anémone: (Sp. *anénoma*) *n.* anemone, windflower.

aneng-éng: *n.* moan; whine of a dog. (*alang-ang*) **aganeng-eng.** *v.* to whine, moan. [Tag. *ungol*]

anép: *n.* diligence; industriousness. (*gaget*; *regget*; *siseg*) **naanep.** *a.* fond of; diligent, hard-working, industrious; active. **anepan.** *v.* to do with diligence. **Nagbungan ti anepna nga agtrabaho iti daga.** *exp.* He reaped the fruits of his labor. [Png. *kolí*, Tag. *sipag*, *sikap*]

ánes: *n.* a kind of thin bamboo, *Schizostachyum hallieri.*

anes-és: *n.* swishing sound (letting out air of tires, etc.). **aganes-es.** *v.* to fit. (~ **ti anges**) *v.* to sniffle when breathing as when sick; to make a swishing sound.

anestésia: (Sp. *anestesia*: anesthesia) *n.* anesthesia.

anestétiko: (Sp. *anestético*: anesthetic) *n.* anesthetic.

anét: *n.* five yards. **umanet-anet.** *v.* to be overburdened; weighed down.

anet-ét: *n.* sharp sound of door hinges or of pliant material being compressed or wound. **aganet-et.** *v.* to creak (door hinges). [Tag. *ingít*]

áni: *n.* rice harvest; (generic harvest is *ápit*). **agani, anien.** *v.* to harvest (grain). **makiani.** *v.* to join in harvesting; help out with the harvest. **Malpas ti ani, awan garami.** *exp.* denoting nothing left at all, all evidence destroyed (*lit*: after the harvest there is no straw). **Sadiay ti pakikianian dagiti dadduma a kapurokanmi.** That's where some of our fellow villagers harvest the crops together. [Png., Tag. *áni*]

aniá: *interrog.* What? Which? So. **aniaman.** whatever, anything. **Awan ti aniamanna.** You're welcome. **Ania ngay? Ania ngarud?** What now? What can be done? **ania la ketdi.** lest. **uray ania.** no matter what. **Aniakan?** You're too much. **Aniatay,** abbreviation of *ania daytay*: What do you call it, What was that? **ket ania.** *exp.* so what. **ania aya.** *exp.* what is it? **anian.** *interj.* oh my; how great it is; wow. **ania metten.** expression of disgust. **ania ngata no.** what if; so what if. **Ania, mapanka manen?** So, are you going again? [Bon. *sino*, *ngag*, Ibg. *anni*, Ivt. *angu*, Png. *antó*, Tag. *anó* (*what*); *alín* (*which*)]

aniá: interrogative tag question used to ask for confirmation of a statement. **Napintas, ania?** She's pretty, isn't she?

aniád: *n.* old, superstitious beliefs.

anianiá: (f. *ania*) *interrog.* why; what for (emphatic).

ánib: *n.* amulet; charm, talisman; defensive weapon; herbs having power against evil; antidote. (*anting*) **aniban.** *v.* to place an *anib* near a sick child to help cure him; to put a good luck charm in one's pocket or wallet. [Tag. *anting-antíng*]

anibáar: **aganibaar.** *v.* to chirp (birds).

anibersário: (Sp. *aniversario*: anniversary) *n.* anniversary. (*panagtinawén*)

aníbong: *n.* fish-tail palm, *Caryota cumingii.*

anibúos: *n.* vapor, fumes, exhalation. (*alingasaw, sengngaw*) **aganibuos.** *v.* to grunt; exhale vapor. [Tag. *singáw*]

aniddág: (*obs.*) see *atiddag*, *atiddog*: long.

aniého: (Sp. *añejo*: aged) *n.* aged wine.

anigkí: *var.* of *anikkí*: grunt.

anií: *n.* a kind of tree with purplish red flowers, *Erythrina fusca,* Lour.

aniíl: *n.* whimper. **umaniil.** *v.* to whimper.

aniíit: *n.* smell of burning rice, wax or leather; prickly feeling (when hot, etc.). **naaniit.** *a.* smelling of burned wax or leather; with a prickly feeling.

anikbáy: *n.* diffusive smell (of a burning candle, gunpowder, etc.). (*inakbáy*) **aganikbay.** *v.* to diffuse (said of smells such as gunpowder).

anikkí: *n.* grunt. (*angék*) **agan-anikki.** *v.* to feel pain or exertion due to lifting heavy objects or being constipated; grunt. [Knk. *dogóek*, Tag. *igík*]

aníl: (Sp. *añil*: indigo) *n.* indigo dye (*tayum*). [Tag. *anyíl*]

aniláw: *n.* *Grewia sp.* plant.

anil-íl: *n.* sob; crybaby. **aganil-il.** *v.* to whimper.

aniliádo: (Sp. *anillado*) *a.* ringed, provided with a ring.

anílio: (Sp. *anillo*: ring) *n.* ring (*singsing*); small hoop. **huego-de-anilio.** *n.* kind of game involving the piercing of a ring.

animádo: (Sp. *animado*: animated) *a.* animated, lively.

animál: (Sp.) *n.* animal, beast; brutal person; women's curse expression. **kaanimalan nga aramid.** *n.* malicious act.

ánimas: (Sp. *ánima*: soul; sunset ringing of bells) *n.* ringing the church bells at eight P.M. to remind the faithful to pray for the dead in purgatory.

anínag: see *saragasag*: thin; transparent; gauzy; *n.* shadow. (*anning*) **maaninagan.** *a.* blurry; shadowy; with an unclear vision of; *v.* to perceive indistinctly. **Awan naaninaganna.** He didn't perceive anything.

anínaw: *n.* reflection, outline. (*anninaw*) **aganinaw.** *v.* to shadow. **maaninawan.** *v.* to be visible due to clearness. **paganinawan.** *n.* mirror. **yaninaw.** *v.* to insinuate, hint. **Naaninawanda ti kinaliday iti rupana bayat ti panangibuksilna ti riknana.** His sadness reflected in his face as he poured out his feelings. [Png. *aníno*, Tag. *anino*]

aníneng: **aganineng.** *v.* to resound; echo softly in the background (music, etc.).

aniníwan: *n.* shadow, image. **yaniniwan.** *v.* to insinuate, hint (*aninaw*). [Bon. *áew*, Ivt. *anyinu*, Png., Tag. *anino* (shadow)]

aningáas: *n.* a kind of ghost; haunting voices from the past. (*al-alia*; *pugot*; *aniwaas*; *bambanig*)

aníngat: *n.* a large tree that yields resin; *Parinarium corymbosum.*

ánio: (Sp. *año*: year) *n.* year (used with Spanish numerals). (*tawén*)

anipó: *n.* vitriol or sulfuric acid, used to burnish gold.

anís: (Sp. *anís*: anise) *n.* anise, *Pimpinella anisum.*

anisádo: (Sp. *anisado*: aniseed; mixed with aniseed) *n.* anise liquor, aniseed brandy.

anitay: *n. Columbia mollis* plant.

anit-ít: **aganit-it.** *v.* to creak. (door) **Kasla nasam-it a samiweng iti panagdengngegna dagiti anit-it dagiti andidit iti kakawatian.** His hearing the creaks of the cicadas in the cacao grove is like sweet music (to the ears).

aníto: *n.* spirit of the forefathers, ghost. **aganito.** *v.* to worship the spirits. **managanito.** *n.* superstitious person. [Tag. *anito*]

aniwáas: *n.* supernatural character: ghost, elf, fairy (*al-alia*). [Tag. *multó*]

aniwaráwar: *n.* red skies at sunset or sunrise. **aganiwarawar.** *v.* to have a colorful sky at sunrise or sunset.

annabó: *n.* a kind of shrub whose bark yields a valuable fiber, *Abroma fastuosa*; offspring; shoot (of plants).

annád: **agannad.** *v.* to be careful, cautious. **annadan.** *v.* to take care of; be cautious about. **naannad.** *a.* cautious, careful. **di naannádan.** *a.* not taken care of; uncontrolled. **Imbilinna nga annadan ken sayaatenmi ti panagtrabahomi.** He ordered us to be more careful and better our work. **Annadam ti agsarsarita no iti kabusor asideg kenka.** *exp.* Be careful what you say when an enemy is near. (*aluad*) [Ivt. *hawa*, Png. *aluár*, Tag. *ingat*]

annagáw: *var.* of *bannagáw*: chameleon.

annák: plural of *anak*: children.

annákki-: plural of *anakki-.*

annám: *n.* a kind of vine that yields a substance for coating fishing nets; *Bridelia stipularis.*

annanáyo: *n.* a kind of black songbird.

annanayó: *n.* indisposition; feeling ill at ease.

annangá: *n.* woven palm tree leaf raincoat (*labig*). **an-annanga.** *n.* a variety of awned early rice. **Adayo pay ti natutudo magtengan, isaganamon ti annangam.** *exp.* Long before the rainy season comes, prepare your *annangá* raincoat.

annaráar: see *anaraar*: ray of sunlight.

annáwag: *a.* perceptible. **annawagen.** *v.* to perceive; visualize. **maannawagan.** *v.* to be perceptible; visible; perceivable. [Tag. *tanáw*]

annáwid: *n.* customs; mores; habits of a certain area. (*ugali*) **kaannawidan.** *v.* to do something habitually, regularly according to custom or the normal mode of conduct. [Tag. *kaugalian*]

annawíl: see *annawir*: pronounce imperfectly; stutter (*beddal*). [Tag. *utál*]

annawír: **agannawir.** *v.* to stutter; pronounce imperfectly; be out of tune; (*obs.*) to be undecided. [Tag. *utál*]

annawíri: see *annawir*: pronounce imperfectly.

annáy: *Interj.* Ouch! **agannay.** *v.* to moan from pain. see *ananay*. **an-annayen.** *n.* pain, illness; suffering. [Tag. *aráy*]

annayángan: *n.* conduit of a sugar mill.

annáyas: **naannayas.** *a.* calm, smooth (said of traffic; politics, leadership, etc.); orderly. (*naurnos*) [Tag. *kaayusan*]

annáyat: *var.* of *annáyas*: smooth, calm; *var.* of *ináyad*: slow.

annayásan: *n.* situation, progress, state of affairs; mast of a ship, usually *pagannayasan.* [Tag. *kalagayan*]

annínaw: *n.* reflection; outline; shadow. **anninawan.** *v.* to mirror; visualize; see through clearly. **maanninawan.** *v.* to be seen clearly; to be able to visualize. **pagannninawan.** *n.* model; standard; mirror. **yanninaw.** *v.* to reflect, mirror. **Saan a nakatimek ngem agan-anninaw ti ragsak ti rupana.** He didn't say a word, but the happiness was reflected in his face. [Ibg. *aninu*, *alínaw*, Ivt. *añinuq*, Knk. *alídung*, *alin-ew*, Kpm. *alíno*, Png. *aníno*, Tag. *anino*]

annínek: **agannínek.** *v.* to be drowsy; sleep soundly; be calm; still; quiet. [Tag. *tahimik*]

anniníwan: *n.* shadow; image; reflection. [Bon. *áew*, Png., Tag. *anino* (shadow)]

anniríir: (*obs.*) *n.* fragrance. (*banglo*)

annó: *conj.* or; lest. (*wenno*) **anno la ketdi no.** lest.

annuád: *n.* a slender vine that climbs by its leaves, *Flagellaria indica*. (*way ti wak*)

annubráng: *n.* medicinal herb, *Callicarpa sp.* whose boiled leaves are used for the flu and to cure coughing spells; *Berria ammonilla*; *Cordia subcordata.* (*allagáw*).

annúgot: **umannugot.** *v.* to obey; consent. (*tungpal*; *sungput*; *surot*; *tulnog*; *annurot*) **naannugot.** *a.* obedient; submissive. **annuguten.** *v.* to obey, consent; accept; acknowledge. **annugotan.** *v.* to allow; agree to. **Annungotek a nagbasolak.** I accept that I was at fault. [Tag. *sang-ayon*]

annóng₁: *n.* occupation; duty; obligation; responsibility. **annongen.** *v.* to fulfill one's duty or responsibility. **nagannong.** *a.* perfect. **maannongan.** *v.* to be competent, qualified to do. **kaannong.** due to, equivalent to.

annóng₂: *n.* kind of illness believed to be caused by spirits. **maan-annongan.** *n.* kind of mild illness caused by invisible spirits (see *anannong*). **Nabirtud kano ti sukal ti anannong.** The antidote for the evil spirits is supposedly powerful.

annúper: *n.* a vine used in medicine to induce perspiration.

annúrot: **umannurot.** *v.* to agree, consent; comply. (*annungot*) **annuruten.** *v.* to follow, obey. **pagannurotan.** *n.* rules and regulations. **paannurot.** *v.* to implement. **maannurot.** *v.* to be followed (rules). **Agkaannurotanda.** They are compatible, in harmony. **Saan a mayannurot iti kasta nga aramid.** He will not consent to that sort of act. [Knk. *abúyug*, Tag. *sunód*]

annuyóp: *n.* a kind of shrub with poisonous lavender fruits, used to poison animals. **maannuyopan.** *v.* to be poisoned by the *annuyop*.

anngáb: **anngaban.** *v.* to take with the mouth.

áno: *n.* pus (*nána*). [Ibg., *nána*, Ivt., Kpm., Tag. *nanà*, Knk. *laléng*, *yayéng*, *deng*, Png. *negna*]

anó: **an-anuen.** *interrog.* How? What is the use of? **agan-ano?** What can I do? Why? What's happening? What's wrong? **pagan-ano.** *v.* to be of use or interest to; **naan-ano.** *a.* impaired; spoiled; tainted. **Naan-ano?** What happened? What's wrong? **agpaano.** In what direction? **kaano.** *interrog.* when. **uray (no) ano (man) saan.** never. **Maan-ano kadi.** so what; who cares. **di magan-ano.** *a.* docile; harmless. **mamin-ano.** *interrog.* how many times? **kapin-ano.** *interrog.* how related? **sangkaano.** *v.* to tease, bother repeatedly. **Naan-anoka?** What happened to you? **Pakaanoan dayta?** Of what use is that? **anuen.** in what direction from. **Kapin-ano?** How is X related? **Agkaananokayo?** How are you related? **Taga-anoka?** Where are you from? **sagpamin-ano?** how many times each? **Uray kaskasano, mamit-**

lokami a mangan iti agmalem. No matter how poor we are, we still eat three times a day. **di mangano.** it will not harm. **Diak pagan-ano.** I don't care; It is of no interest to me. **Dinaka an-anuen.** He won't do anything to you; He won't hurt you. **Inan-anom?** What did you do to him? **Yanoka?** Where will I bring you? **Saanna a pagan-ano ti ibubusnag a kas iti kalkalikaguman ti dadduma.** He doesn't care about her fair complexion as others would desire. [Tag. *anó*]

anubráng: *var.* of *annubrang*.

ánud: **maanud.** *v.* to drift with the current; float along. **yanud.** *v.* to throw in a current; float something. **maiyanud.** *v.* to be carried away by the current. **agan-anud a lungon.** *n.* floating coffin (superstitious belief). **Adda pay malagipko a balsa a nayanud gapu iti kadakkel ken kapegges ti danun.** I also remember a raft that drifted because of the swift and mighty current. [Ibg. *mévuruq*, *agiq*, Ivt. *ñilyud*, Kal. *alod*, Kpm. *dela ne ning águs*, Png. *anór*, Tag. *anod*]

anug-úg: *n.* weeping, wailing, loud crying. **aganug-ug.** *v.* to weep, wail. (*ngugngug*)

anomália: (Sp.) *n.* anomaly.

anónang: see *anonas*: custard apple; *Annona reticulata.*

anónas: *n.* custard apple, *Annona reticulata.* [Tag. *atis*]

anónima: (Sp. *anónima*: anonymous) *n.* anonymous letter.

anunsiadór: (Sp. *anunciador*: announcer) *n.* announcer (radio or television).

anunsiánte: (Sp. *anunciante*: advertiser; announcer) *n.* advertiser, announcer.

Anunsiasión: (Sp. *anunciación*: annunciation) *n.* Annunciation, Catholic festival held on March 25 in memory of the Annunciation.

anúnsio: (Sp. *anuncio*: announcement) *n.* advertisement, announcement. **yanunsio.** *v.* to announce. (*warragawag*)

ánong: **paganongan.** *n.* yard used to repair in weaving.

anóng: (*coll.*) *n.* term of address for a young male given by elders. (*inong*)

anúngo: *n.* G-string. (*baag*; *bayakat*; *pallak*)

anúngos: **naanungos.** *a.* used up. (*ungkos*) **anungusen.** *v.* to use up; consume completely.

anúp: *n.* hunter; hunting dog. **manganup.** *v.* to hunt with dogs. **inanupan.** *n.* game; quarry; variety of awned *diket* rice. **mangnganup.** *n.* hunter. **panaganup.** *n.* the hunt; chase. **maanupan.** *v.* to be hunted. [Ibg. *manganuq*, Ivt. *mamulaw*, Kal. *alop*, Kpm. *manáyup*, Png. *anóp*, Tag. *hanap*, *baríl*] ánus: *n.* patience; perseverance; kindness. (*tutor*) **naanus.** *a.* kind; mild; considerate; patient, nice, good; gentle; friendly; lenient. **anusan.** *v.* to bear with patience. **kinaanus.** *n.* patience; kindness. **aganus.** *v.* to be patient; endure. **aginnanus.** *v.* to be patient with one another. **yanus.** *v.* to endure; do patiently. **Saan a makaan-anus a makisarsarita.** He cannot converse nicely (with diplomacy). **Agananuskayo ta naimbagto no makapagkasarkayo kenkuana.** Persevere because it will be good if you marry her. **Yanusmo ta kasta ti biag ditoy.** Bear it because that's the way life is here. **Aganuska, bagi, ta dika met nagpadi.** *exp.* Have patience body, since you did not choose to be a priest (said of poor men who do manual labor). [Ibg. *sippóq*, Itg. *anus*, Ivt. *masisiyen*, Kal. *alos*, *bibiyu*, Knk. *ammá*, *emnáy*, Kpm. *maganaka*, Png. *ánus*, *maong*, Tag. *baít* (*kind*); *tiís*, *tiyagâ* (*patient*, *enduring*)]

anús: **paanusan.** *v.* to have something gilded.

ánut: *n.* sinewy meat. (*pennet*)

anuyop: *n.* *Callicarpa cana*; *Callicarpa formosana.* (*anuyut*)

ansád: *n.* slope; hillside (*induyas*; *bakras*; *arisadsad*). [Tag. *gilid*]

ansí: (*coll.*) *adv.* negative adverb used to deny or refuse (*saan*). [Tag. *hindî*]

ansiáno: (Sp. *anciano*: elder) *n.* expert.

ansíket: *n.* a variety of awned *diket* rice; *sansanniket.*

ansisít: *n.* dwarf; elf. (*kaibaan*; *banig*)

antá$_1$: *n.* rancid odor. **naanta.** *a.* rancid, having changed flavor after being stored for a long time.

antá$_2$: *conj.* since, whereas (*yanta*). [Tag. *yamang*]

antá$_3$: **yanta.** *v.* to soak, immerse, steep. (*uper*)

antábay: **antabayan.** *v.* to support; guide by the hand; comfort. [Tag. *alalay*]

antángay: *conj.* whereas; since. (*yanta, anta, atangay, tangay*)

antár: *n.* lagoon, pond; (*obs.*) cut off from the main body. **naantaran** (*obs.*) *v.* to be aground (boats).

Antártiko: (Eng.) *n.* Antarctic, the south polar region.

ántas: (Sp. *llanta*: wheel) *n.* iron hoop, band of a wheel.

antatádo: *n.* a kind of blackish freshwater fish about one foot long.

antatádul: *n.* species of butterfly larvae. [Png. *antatáro* = destructive worm]

antatáteg: *n.* a kind of white larva, grub.

antáteg: *var.* of *antatateg*: kind of white larva.

antél: *n.* *Canarium villosum.* (*anténg*)

antemáno: (Sp. *antemano*: beforehand) *n.* payment in advance; *adv.* beforehand, in advance. **yantemano.** *v.* to tell beforehand. **antemanuan.** *v.* to deposit money in advance.

antén: *n.* *Canarium calophyllum* plant.

anténg: *n.* a large tree with long leaves, *Canarium villosum.*

anteóhos: *var.* spelling of *antiohos*: eyeglasses. (*sarming*) **aganteohos.** *v.* to wear glasses. **nakaanteohos.** *a.* wearing eyeglasses. **anteohos de grado.** *n.* prescription lenses. **anteohos de color.** *n.* sunglasses. [Tag. *salamín*]

ántes: (Sp. *antes*: before) *adv.* before. (*sakbay*)

antí: (Sp.) *a.* against. **agkaraanti.** *v.* to be always opposed or against.

antígo: (Sp. *antiguo*: old). **naantigo.** *a.* of good quality; genuine antique. **antigo a korte.** old-fashioned.

antígua: (Sp. *antigua*: old) *n.* antique.

antihuélas: (Sp. *antijuelas*: spangle) *n.* spangle, sequins, tiny disk of glittering metal sewn into a garment for decorative purposes.

antikuélas: *var.* of *antihuelas*: sequin.

antikrísto: (Sp. *anticristo*) *n.* Antichrist.

antimáno: (Sp. *antemano*: beforehand) *adv.* immediately, right away (*darikmat*), beforehand.

antimónia: (Sp. *antimonio*) *n.* antimony.

antinagan: *n.* *Diospyros parva.*

antíng: *n.* *Sterculia sp.* plant. (*ginnamol*) **antinganting.** *n.* amulet, charm, talisman.

antipárra: *n.* eyeglasses (*anteohos*); goggles. **agantiparra.** *v.* to wear eyeglasses or goggles. **antiparra de kolor.** sunglasses. **Insuotna ti antiparrana ket nanabsuoken iti danum.** He put on his goggles and dived in the water.

antipatía: (Sp. *antipatía*: antipathy) *n.* antipathy, dislike.

antipátiko: (Sp. *antipático*: unfriendly) *a.* unfriendly; displeasing; disagreeable.

antipólo: (Tagalog also) *n.* species of tree.

antífona: (Sp. *antífona*: antiphony, anthem) *n.* antiphony, musical response.

antisípo: (Sp. *anticipo*: down payment) *n.* down payment; advance payment. **antisipuan.** *v.* to make an advance payment; deposit an advance.

antó: *var.* of *intono*: future article.

antók: **agantok.** *v.* to take the first steps (infants) (*indereng*). [Tag. *antók* = drowsy]

antúkab: *a.* voracious (*ráwet*). **kinaantukab.** *n.* voracity. **Isuda dagiti antukab nga alimatek ditoy.** They are the voracious leeches here. [Knk. *tayabbán*, Png. *labláb*, *sibá*, Tag. *takaw*, *sibà*]

antolohía: (Sp. *antología*: anthology) *n.* anthology, collection of literary or musical pieces.

antón: see *inton*: future marker.

antutúngal: *n.* a kind of large, black ant. [Tag. *langgám*]

antropolohía: (Sp. *antropología*: anthropology) *n.* anthropology, science dealing with the origin, development, customs, language, and beliefs of mankind.

antropólogo: (Sp. *antropólogo*: anthropologist) *n.* anthropologist.

anyíl: (Sp. *añil*: indigo) *n.* indigo powder. **anyilen.** *v.* to color blue with indigo.

ángad: **yangad.** *v.* to lift the head, raise the face. (*tangad*, *tag-ay*) **Adda nagayus ti pingping ti lakay idi yangadna ti rupana.** The old man's cheek flowed a bit when he raised his head.

ángal: **agangal.** *v.* to moan softly; complain. [Tag. *angal*]

Angálo: *n.* mythological giant, the first male of the Ilocano creation myth, the husband of *Aran*.

ang-áng: **nagang-ang.** *a.* weakling; crybaby; stupid, dumb, idiotic. (*tabbed*; *gago*; *langgong*; *maag*; *tungngang*; *laglag*) **umang-ang.** *v.* to fall apart; disintegrate.

angangék: **agangangek.** *v.* to whine (dogs).

ángat: **agangat.** *v.* to fight with each other; to bite, claw (animals fighting). **agaangat.** *a.* to be contradictory (statements); *n.* vicious fight. **ka-angat.** *v.* to quarrel, fight with. **mannakiangat.** *a.* quarrelsome. **pagangaten.** *v.* to goad two animals (dogs, spiders, etc.) to fight each other. **pinnaangat.** *n.* spider fight. **Tratarentayo met ita ti panagtaraknan ken panagpaangatan ti lawwalawwa.** We are also trying now to raise and fight spiders. [Tag. *salungát*]

angát: *n.* a type of plow.

angáw₁: *n.* joke; jest. (*rabak*; *sutil*) **naangaw.** *a.* joking, lewd, lustful, dishonest; playful. **ag-angaw.** *v.* to joke, joke around; banter, toy, play, frolic. **angawen.** *v.* to joke about, make fun of, tease. (*durog*; *sutil*; *parato*) **mannakiangaw.** *a.* playful; friendly; gregarious. **pag-angawan.** *v.* to make a fool of; to not take seriously; to be lustful. [Bon. *otyok*, *angaw*, *lag-as*, Png. *lurey*, *sulon*, *galaw*, Tag. *birò*]

angáw₂: **agangaw.** *v.* to grow larger than normal (well-fertilized plants, etc.). (*langpaw*)

ángay: *n.* visitor. (*bisíta*) **angayen.** *v.* to invite; call a meeting. **umangay.** *v.* to be near (in time). **pangangayan.** *n.* reason for calling a meeting, reason for assembling. **pakaangayan.** *n.* meeting place, place of assembly (*paka-urnongan*). **Adda kadi pakainaiganyo iti daytoy nakaangayantayo?** Do you have something to add to this meeting? [Tag. *tipon*]

angáy: *n.* (*obs.*) misgiving. **idi agangay.** in the end, eventually, as a result (*banag*). **pangang-**

ayan. *n.* result, outcome; effect. **Bay-am ida a gumura ta inton agangay, dayawendaka.** Let them get angry, because in the end they will respect you. **Naparnuay ti sayangguseng idi agangay.** As a result, the gossip started.

angbáb: **naangbab.** *a.* brackish (water). **kina-angbab.** *n.* brackishness (*tabang*). **umangbab.** *v.* to become brackish. [Tag. *alát-alát*]

angdód: *n.* stench, bad smell. **naangdod.** *a.* having a bad smell. [Tag. *bahò*]

ánged: *n.* nasal mucus, snot. (*buteg*) **naanged.** *a.* snotty; with running nose. **aganged.** *v.* to have a running nose. [Tag. *uhog*]

angék: **agangek.** *v.* to yelp, grunt (when hit in stomach, etc.). (*anikki*) **Angek nga angek ti aso, kasla agballa.** The dog keeps yelping, it seems to be crazy.

angél: *var.* of *ungel*.

angén: (*obs.*) *n.* sharp pain in the eye.

angép: *n.* mist, fog. (*alimuom*, *libbuob*) **na-angep.** *a.* foggy; misty; overcast; hazy. **ma-angepan.** *v.* to be in the fog; to be lonely; gloomy. [Kal. *mambubulot*, Png. *kelpá*, Tag. *ulap*, *labò*]

angér: *n.* boiled meat. (*lingta*) **angren.** *v.* to boil. **inanger.** *n.* boiled dish; that which is boiled. [Knk. *ágas*, Png. *lambóng*, Tag. *lagà*]

ánges: *n.* breath; (*fig.*) life. **aganges.** *v.* to breathe; respire. **angsen.** *a.* asthmatic. **angsan.** *v.* to administer mouth-to-mouth resuscitation. **paanges.** *n.* drain of a dike. **umanges-anges.** *v.* to breathe fast (in crying, etc.). **aangsan.** *n.* windpipe, respiratory track. **maangsan.** *v.* to be short of breath; to be overwhelmed, to be in awe. **umang-anges.** *v.* breathing and full of life. **pagangsan.** *n.* nose; mouth. **yanges.** *v.* to exhale. **yangsan.** *v.* to ascertain the presence of breath in a dying person. **nailet ti aangsan.** *exp.* to have a hard, poverty-stricken life. **ngudo ti anges.** *n.* end of life. **Inggana't adda pay angesko.** As long as I'm still alive. [Ibg. *inángoq*, Ifg. *yahya*, Ivt. *minawaq*, Kal. *angos*, Kpm. *pangisnáwa*, Png. *ánges*, Tag. *hingá*]

anggá: (*reg.*) **angga-angga.** *n.* kind of long, freshwater insect.

anggálog: (*slang.*) *n.* Tagalog language.

anggápan: *n.* lobster. (*udang*)

anggápang: *n.* crust in cooking (sticking to the pot); limy silt; a kind of freshwater fish. [Tag. *tutóng* (rice crust)]

anggarília: (Sp. *angarillas*: handbarrow) *n.* handbarrow basket for carrying tobacco.

anggéd: *a.* in former times; ancient; *n.* distant past. **angged a pammati.** *n.* ancient beliefs. **inton angged.** *n.* distant future (when one does not intend to fulfill a deed, etc.). [Tag. *noóng unang panahón*]

anggímo: (*obs.*) *n.* desire, longing for.

anggó: angguen. *v.* to kiss (*agek, bisung, bisito*). [Tag. *hagkán*]

ánggulo: (Sp. *ángulo*: angle) *n.* angle.

anggúyot: angguyoten. *v.* to comfort, caress, deal with someone tenderly (*appúyot, laílo*); appease, calm down; pacify.

ánghel: (Sp. *ángel*: angel) *n.* angel. **immanghel.** *a.* angelic (in appearance). **anghelito.** *n.* little angel; species of plant with fragrant flowers used against snake bites.

anghína: (Sp. *angina*: angina) *n.* angina, angina pectoris; tonsillitis with pus.

ángid: naangid. *a.* sensitive; easily irritated; prone to crying (babies). (*arsagid*)

ángil: *n.* a kind of large fish like the corvina.

ángin: *n.* air; wind; draft (of air). **agangin.** *v.* to be windy; to blow (wind). **anginen.** *v.* to suffer a stroke from a heart attack. **ipaangin.** *v.* to place in the wind and shade to dry; expose to the wind. **maangin.** *v.* to be caught in the wind. **maanginan.** *v.* to be affected by the wind; affected by gas in the chest. **mayangin.** *v.* to be carried away by the wind; (*fig.*) to go back on one's promise; to be 'full of hot air'. **naangin.** *a.* windy. **agpaangin.** *v.* to go out to get some fresh air. **mangngangin.** *n.* liar, deceitful person. **Kari nga intayab ti angin!** *exp.* useless promise (*lit*: promise taken away by the wind). **Naanginan ti ulona.** He is crazy (*lit*: winded in the head). [Ibg. *paddág*, Ivt. *salawsaw*, Kal. *angin, bidbid*, Kpm. *ángin*, Knk., Png. *dagém*, Tag. *hangin*; Ivt. *anyin* = typhoon]

ángit: *n.* wailing cry of a baby. **ang-angit.** *n.* crybaby. (*mangit, managsangit*)

angkás: (Sp. *anca*: croup) *n.* haunch of a horse, croup; load. **yangkas.** *v.* to carry a load.

angkát: *n.* merchandise bought on credit; importation; consignment. **angkaten.** *v.* to borrow, take on credit; import. **agpaangkat.** *v.* to lend. **ipaangkat.** *v.* to consign, lend. **agang-angkat.** *n.* wholesaler; importer. **Angkatem man laengen ti ikanko.** Just take my fish on credit. [Png., Tag. *angkát*]

angkáy: *n.* term of address for an elder man. (*lakáy*).

angkét: *n.* term of intimate address for an elderly woman.

angkít: *n.* asthma. **angkiten.** *a.* asthmatic. **ag-angkit.** *v.* to have asthma; to have an asthma attack. **managangkit.** *a.* asthmatic. [Png. *singáp*, Tag. *hikà*]

angklá: (Sp. *ancla*: anchor) *n.* anchor. **agangkla.** *v.* to cast the anchor.

angláb: *n.* smell of smoke or burning (*anglem*), odor produced by a burning substance that is said to revive a pregnant woman; **maanglab.** *v.* to smell a burning substance.

anglém: *n.* stench of burning cotton; incense; twined cloth (burned to keep bad spirits away). **aganglem.** *v.* to burn cotton to keep the spirits away. **naanglem.** *a.* smelling of burning cotton or cloth. **Nagtantanamitim a nangisuob iti anglem iti kadaklan ti kalapaw.** She muttered to herself as she smoked the living room of the hut with incense.

anglikáno: (Sp.) *n.*, *a.* Anglican.

anglít: *n.* underarm odor; odor of a goat. **naanglit.** *a.* having body odor; having offensive armpit smell. **aganglit.** *v.* to have strong underarm odor. **Agatibuor ti anglitna.** His underarm smell is diffusing. [Bon. *angseg*, Kal. *ang-it*, Tag. *anghít*]

angló: maanglo. *v.* to work hard; toil; bootlick. **mangmanglo.** *n.* daily wage earner; ordinary laborer. **angluen.** *v.* to earn one's living. [Tag. *maghanap-buhay*]

angngáb: angngaban. *v.* to hold in the mouth. (*ammal*)

angngó: (*obs.*) see *anggo*: kiss. (*bisung, bisito, agek*)

ángol: *n.* epidemic, pest; (*lit.*) sacrifice on many lives. **agangol.** *v.* to be attacked by an epidemic (*didigra*). [Tag. *peste*]

ángot: *n.* smell, odor. **angoten.** *v.* to smell, sniff. **naangot.** *a.* smelly, stinking, reeking. **aangotan.** *n.* nasal cavity; pituitary membrane. **aginnangot.** *v.* to sniff each other (dogs). **makaangot.** *v.* to be able to smell; to smell something fishy. **maangotan.** *v.* to smell something (usually bad); (fig.) to smell something fishy, start to notice something is wrong. **ipaangot.** *v.* to have something be smelled. [Bon. *ágob*, Ibg. *agug*, Ivt. *angut*, Kal. *sungsung*, Knk. *seng-éw, akóo*, Kpm. *báu*, Png. *angób*, Tag. *amóy*]

anguyób: *n.* blowpipe; horn; bellows. **ang-anguyób.** *n.* windpipe; trachea. **anguyoban.** *v.* to blow the fire. **Gistay natilmon ni Edwin ti ang-anguyobna iti pannakakellaatna.** Edwin almost swallowed his windpipe in his surprise. [Tag. *tambulì* (horn); *lalagukán* (windpipe)]

angpás: *n.* a kind of animal tick (*ampas*). **inangpas.** *a.* infested with ticks. [Ivt. *liplip*, Kal. *apngot*, Tag. *garapata*]

angpép: *n.* stench of fermenting meat or fish; stench of a woman's soiled undergarments.

naangpep. *a.* smelling of soiled undergarments or fermented meat.

angráb: *n.* semidry condition of leaves during draught.

angrág: naangrag. *a.* dry. (*maga*) **umangrag.** *v.* to become dry. **No lumabas ti bagio, maangrag amin a bulong.** When the storm passes, all the leaves dry up.

angráp: *n.* thinning out something by beating. **naangrap.** *a.* thin. (*batbat*)

angrát: *n.* a kind of large fish like the corvina; a variety of awned early rice.

angrén: (f. *anger*) *v.* to boil something, cook by boiling.

angrí: *n.* stench of fish or bats. **naangri.** *a.* smelling like fish. **ang-angri.** *n.* *Azima sarmentosa*; *Clerodendron inerme*.

angrít: *n.* stench of putrid urine of aged fish. **naangrit.** *a.* smelling of putrid urine or aged fish. **Nakaang-angrit ti isboda.** Their urine smells putrid.

angsáb: agangsab. *v.* to pant. (*al-al*, *tunglab*) **angsaben.** *a.* at a loss for breath. **maudi nga angsab.** *n.* the last gasp; last breath. [Tag. *hingál*]

angsán: see under *anges*: breath.

angsáw: *n.* stench, powerful smell (of sewers); odorous vapor. **maangsawan.** *v.* to be affected by a powerful smell. **Mariknana ti nabara nga angsaw dagiti imbornal.** She can feel the odorous vapor of the sewers.

angség: *n.* the smell of human urine. **naangseg.** *a.* smelling like urine. [Bon. *angteg*, Kpm. *balíng*, Png. *baléng*, Tag. *panghí*, *palot*]

angsén: [*anges* + *-en*] *a.* asthmatic. (*angkit*)

angsét: *n.* the smell of burning rice, meat; *Guioa koelreuteria*. **naangset.** *a.* smelling of burned rice. [Knk. *angílit*]

angsít: *var.* of *angset*: the smell of burned rice or meat.

angsúot: *n.* smell of burning grass or wet garbage. **naangsuot.** *a.* with a burnt and sooty smell. (*banniit*)

angsót: *n.* work; business (*sapul*); duty; task; occupation. **angsoten.** *v.* to do, accomplish. **paangsoten.** *v.* to have someone else do the work.

angtém: *n.* the smell of burning resin or flesh. **naangtem.** *a.* smelling of burning resin or flesh.

angtít: *n.* the smell of fermenting fish or meat. **naangtit.** *a.* smelling like this.

angtóol: *n.* the smell of burned bones or a corpse. **naangtool.** *a.* smelling of a corpse.

angtót: *n.* stench, odor. **agangtot.** *v.* to smell; (*coll.*) to fool around. **Dita ti pagang-angto-**

tanmi no malpas ti klase. That's where we horse around after class.

aú: Interjection of dismissal. **umauau.** *v.* to grumble, murmur.

auditíbo: (Sp. *auditivo*: earpiece of a telephone) *n.* receiver of a telephone.

áok₁: *n.* a disease affecting the scalp of children. **agaok.** *v.* to be afflicted with a scalp disease. [Tag. *galís*]

áok₂: *n.* (*coll.*) moron; clumsy person.

auménto: (Sp. *aumento*: increase) *n.* addition; increase; raise in salary. **naaumentuan.** *a.* having received a raise in pay.

áon: aonen. *v.* to pull up from; to draw out, scoop, extract (*ádaw*, *gaó*); quote; cite; bail out of jail; (*reg.*) translate (*tarús*). **umaon.** *v.* to come up from; climb out of. **yaon.** *v.* to pull up from, scoop from. [Tag. *hangò*]

Australiáno: *n.* Australian.

autokrasía: (Sp. *autocracia*: autocracy) *n.* autocracy, absolute authority or government.

autókrata: (Sp. *autócrata*: autocrat) *n.* autocrat, ruler with unlimited power.

automátiko: (Sp. *automático*) *a.* automatic.

autonomía: (Sp. *autonomía*: autonomy) *n.* autonomy, self-rule.

autópsia: (Sp.) *n.* autopsy, post-mortem.

autoridád: (Sp. *autoridad*: authority) *n.* authority.

autorisádo: (Sp. *autorizado*: authorized) *a.* authorized.

ápa₁: (Jap.) *n.* thin rolled wafer of rice starch and brown sugar, used as an ice-cream cone.

ápa₂: *n.* fight; quarrel. **agapa.** *v.* to fight, quarrel, dispute. **apaen.** *v.* provoke a fight, quarrel with someone. **yapa.** *v.* to forbid. **mannakiapa.** *a.* quarrelsome, always fighting. **kaapa.** *n.* opponent; person with whom one fights. **Ti balasang a makiapa, mapukaw ti guddua ti nginana.** *exp.* A young lady who quarrels loses half her value. [Ibg. *damán*, Ivt. *diman*, Kal. *subog*, Knk. *íbaw*, Kpm. *pate*, Png. *kolkól*, Tag. *away*]

apá: apaan. *v.* to plaster (*tapal*). **yapa.** *v.* to apply (medicinal) plaster to. [Tag. *apâ* = grope; steal]

apaáp: *n.* a reef fish with an offensive odor.

apag-: Prefix used with verbal roots indicating concept of 'as soon as'. Takes *-ko* series pronouns **Apagsangpetna, nagtudon.** As soon as he arrived (Upon his arrival), it rained. With certain temporal roots, it indicates immediate time, with *isu*, preciseness: **apagdarikmat, apagbiit.** in a moment, immediately. **apagisu.** precisely. With stative verbs, it expresses a state not fully achieved. **apagbingngi.** slightly open, ajar.

apág: *n.* share; portion. (*bingay*; *binglay*) **apag-apagen**. *v.* to divide in equal shares. **pag-apagan**. *v.* to share equally. **yapagan**. *v.* to give a share to someone. [Tag. *hatì, bahagi*]

apagdarikmát: *adv.* in a moment.

apagisú: *adv.* precisely the right amount. **Apagisu ti apittayo kadatayo, awan ti mailakotayo.** Our harvest is precisely the right amount (for our needs), we have nothing to sell.

apagka-: Prefix used to form fractional numbers; see *pagka-* **apagkalima**. one-fifth. **apagkanem one sixth.**

apagkatló: [*apagka-* + *tallo*] *n.* one-third.

apagpa-: Prefix indicating that the action denoted by the stem has been done to a sufficient degree: **pintas**. beauty. **apagpapintas.** sufficiently made beautiful.

apaká: (*obs.*) Interjection expressing wonder.

ápal: *n.* envy; jealousy; greed. **naapal.** *a.* envious; greedy. **umapal, apalan.** *v.* to be envious of, envy. **pagapalan.** *n.* source of envy or greed. **ipaapal.** *v.* to show a possession in order to make someone envious. [Png. *ibeg, inglit*, Tag. *inggít, hilì*]

apáleng: *n.* a tree used to cure *supotsupot* (hives), *Osmoxylon pulcherrimum.*

apáman: *a.* barely, scarcely, hardly; as soon as; right away. **apagapaman.** *a.* scarcely, barely; hardly distinguishable. **Apaman a nalpaskami a nangaldaw, rinugianmi manen ti agkali.** As soon as we finished eating lunch, we started digging again. [Png. *dagdaiset*, Tag. *bahagyâ, kaagád*]

apán: *var.* of *appán*: bait.

apán: *v.* to go. **agapan.** *v.* to go, see *pan, mapan.* **managapan.** *v.* to frequent a place. **agpapan.** *v.* to be on the way. **papanan.** *n.* destination; place where one is going. **agpapan-agawid.** round-trip. [Tag. *puntá*]

ap-áp: *n.* tablecloth, ground cloth; cover, wrapper; layer; lower pillowcase (under the *akkub*); saddle cloth. **ap-apan.** *v.* to spread cloth over something. **yap-ap.** *v.* to use to spread on. [Tag. *sapín*]

ap-apéra: (f. *apa*) *n.* troublesome woman.

apár: *n.* small shop; hut; temporary seashore shelter for fishermen.

aparadór: (Sp. *aparador*: dresser) *n.* dresser; chest of drawers. **aparador dagiti libro.** *n.* bookcase.

aparáto: (Sp. *aparato*: apparatus) *n.* apparatus, implement; tackle; equipment; gear; machine. **aparatista.** *n.* operator of a machine.

apárte: (Sp. *aparte*: apart; aside) *n.* aside (in a play). **yaparte.** *v.* to separate from.

ápas: *n.* aversion; disgust; dislike; envy. (*gura; apal*) **maapas.** *v.* to be annoyed, irritated, to be a poor sport; hate. **mangngapas.** *n.* teaser. **Iti barukongna, kayatna nga ibulos ti rumurusing nga apas.** In her chest, she wants to unleash the growing irritation. [Tag. *suklám*]

apasionádo: (Sp. *apasionado*: impassioned) *a.* passionate; impassioned; devoted.

apasótes: (Sp. *apasote*) *n.* a kind of grass whose leaves are used in seasoning and whose plasters cure colic.

ápat₁: *n.* shortcut. (*buntáyak*) **apaten.** *v.* to take a shortcut. [Kpm. *baltáng*, Tag. *tuwirang daán*; *apat* = four]

ápat₂: **apat-apat.** *n.* tapeworm. (*kuyamkúyam*)

apatía: (Sp. *apatía*: apathy) *n.* apathy.

apátot: *n.* a kind of shrub whose fruit may be used as soap and whose roots yield a red dye, *Morinda bracteata.* **ap-apatot.** *n.* kind of edible marine shellfish.

ápaw: **umapaw.** *v.* to overwhelm; overflow (*lupias*). [Tag. *apaw*]

ápay: *interrog.* Why?; What? (in answering a call). **umapay.** *v.* to be affected by a light; approach; attack; lean; come to mind (*sekken*), recall; incline, lean (trees). **Apay ngay?** How come? [Ibg. *ngatta*, Ivt. *untaa, angu*, Kpm. *obát, bakit*, Png. *ákin*, Tag. *bakit*]

apáy: *n.* leaves spread on the ground for a slaughtered animal. [Tag. *panapín*]

apáya: *n.* saltpeter. (*salitre*) **inapaya, maapaya.** *a.* invaded by salt water (rice fields). **No agatab, maapaya dagiti pagay.** In the flood tide, the rice gets invaded with salt water. [Tag. *salitre*]

apayá: *var.* of *apay*: why. [Tag. *bakit ba*]

Apayáo: *n.* ethnic group of Apayao Province; their language.

apayyá: (f. *apay* + *aya*) emphatic version of *apay*: why.

apdáy: *n.* heavy sea; spring tide. (*arabaab*) **agapday.** *v.* to bend down; to decline.

apektár: (Sp. *afectar*: affect) **naapektaran.** *a.* affected; infected.

apéla: (Sp. *apelar*: appeal) *n.* appeal to a higher court of justice. **agapela.** *v.* to appeal.

apelasión: (Sp. *apelación*: appeal) *n.* an appeal to a higher court.

apelyído: (Sp. *apellido*: surname) *n.* last name, surname. (*nagan*)

apéndise: (Sp. *apéndice*: appendix) *n.* appendix; addition at the end of a book or document.

apéra: **ap-apera.** *a.* stingy; *n.* troublemaker.

apgád: **naapgad.** *a.* salty; stinging and sarcastic (said of speech). **umapgad.** *v.* to get salty. **na-**

apgad ti panagsasaona. *exp.* stinging (sarcastic) speech. [Ibg., Png. *asín*, Ivt. *payit*, Kpm. *malát*, Tag. *alat*]

apgés: *n.* stinging pain, sharp pain. makaapges. *v.* to cause sharp pain. naapges. *a.* sharp, stinging (said of pain). Naapges dagiti matak iti puyatko. My eyes were stinging from staying awake all night. [Ibg. *feggi, benniq*, Ivt. *mandetden*, Kal. *bed-ik, bogla*, Kpm. *maplas*, Png. *ápges*, Tag. *hapdî*]

ápgod: apgudan. *v.* to polish; knead; smooth out hair with the fingers (*as-as*). [Tag. *kinis* (polish)]

apí: apien. *v.* to cut at a slant; slash (*singtaw*). [Tag. *apí* = oppress]

apiadóres: (Sp. *fiador* (*afianzador*): guarantor) *n.* bondsmen; guarantor.

apiáng: (Hok. *â p^hian*) *n.* opium; opiate. naapiang. *a.* addicted to something; under the influence of an opiate. apiangen. *v.* to seduce to the point of addiction. Naapiangen a súnggo. He has a monkey addiction. Inapiangnak ti banglo. The fragrance seduced me (to the point of addiction).

apíd: (*coll.*) *n.* term of address for a second cousin (*kapidua, kapid*). [Tag. *apíd* = fornication]

apidábit: (Eng.) *n.* affidavit.

apíg: apigen. *v.* to clear a path through grasses; part the hair; layer nipa roofs; bundle tobacco. inapigapig, naapig-apig. *a.* well bundled and arranged (tobacco leaves); perfectly layered (nipa roofs). [Tag. *hawì*]

apígod: *var.* of *appigod*: lefthanded; clumsy; injured; not feeling at ease.

apíla₁: *syn.* of *ap-ap*: cover; wrapper; bedding.

apíla₂: (Sp. *en fila*: in line) *n.* line. agapila. *v.* to stand in line.

ápin: *n.* banana leaf that lines the bottom of a clay pot for cooking rice. apinan. *v.* to place the *apin* at the bottom of a pot (*alep-ep*). [Tag. *sapín*]

apinádo: (Sp. *afinado*: tuned) *a.* tuned.

apinadór: (Sp. *afinador*: tuner) *n.* tuner (of a piano, etc.).

apinidád: (Sp. *afinidad*: affinity) *n.* affinity, relation by marriage; close link or connection.

apiráng: *n.* a kind of bamboo basket.

apíras: maapiras, umapiras. *v.* to search for by feeling (*arikap*); touch indecently; finger; pass the hand over to feel. apirasen. *v.* to smoothen, level the contents of; polish; finger, grope. Tengnga't aldaw ngem narigat a marikna ti darang ti init gapu iti apiras ti nalamuyot nga angin. It is midday but it is difficult to feel the heat of the sun because of the touch of the

smooth wind. Immapiras ti nasalem nga angot. He felt the tart smell. [Tag. *haplós*]

apíring: agapiring. *v.* to be similar; to stand close together. umapiring. *v.* to cling to, stay close to. yapiting. *v.* to put close to. nayapiring. *a.* adjacent, next to; close to (*bangibang; sidíran; tapíl; kasigkay*). [Tag. *katabí*]

apirmár: (Sp. *afirmar*: affirm) apirmaren. *v.* to affirm.

apís: *n.* netlike appendages at the base of the leaf of the coco palm.

apisión: (Sp. *afición*: hobby) *n.* inclination to, liking, hobby. apisionado. *n.* fan, one who is devoted to, interested in; amateur; *a.* talented, inclined.

ápit: *n.* harvest; yield; produce; (*fig.*) outcome. (*gapas*) agapit. *v.* to harvest; reap; benefit from one's acts. apiten. *v.* to harvest, reap. ipaapit. *v.* to have one's crop harvested. Agmulakayo tapno adda pagapitanyo. Plant so you will have something to harvest. [Kpm. *agtál, pálut*, Png., Tag. *ani*]

apítong: *n.* species of hardwood tree used in construction.

aplág: yaplag. *v.* to spread, unfurl. (*bikrád, bisrád; ukrád*) nakaaplag. *a.* spread out, unfurled. Inyaplagna ti tualiana iti kadaratan. He unfurled his towel on the sand. [Knk. *abilá*, Tag. *latag*]

aplás: *n. Ficus blepharostoma* shrub. (*uplas*)

aplát: *n.* a kind of aphid destructive to plants; a plant disease brought upon by the *aplat*. inaplat. *a.* affected by aphids. [Tag. *dapulak*]

apláw₁: (*reg.*) *n.* superstition that attributes illness to the intervention of bad invisible elements. maaplawan. *v.* to be caught in the draft; affected by invisible spirits. (*amling, annong*)

apláw₂: aplawen. *v.* to flap; sweep off dirt. aplawán. *v.* to drive away insects. (*saplid*) yaplaw. *v.* to wave something with the hands. [Tag. *palís*]

apláya: (Sp. *playa*: beach) *n.* beach (usually sandy) (*igid ti baybay*); coastline.

aplí: see *ap-ap*: tablecloth; cover; spread.

áplid: *var.* of *aplaw* or *saplid*.

aplikár: (Sp. *aplicar*: apply) agaplikar. *v.* to apply. aplikante. *n.* applicant.

aplikasión: (Sp. *aplicación*: application) *n.* application.

aplít: aplitan. *v.* to whip in a slashing way; flap (a tail). (*saplit*) yaplit. *v.* to whip something in a slashing way; influence. [Tag. *haplít*]

apnít: *n.* the *palosapis* and white *lauan* trees, *Anisonptera thurifera, Pentacme contorta, Shorea malaanonan*. apnitan. *v.* to skin a vine to make into rope.

apnút: **apnutan**. *v.* to wax; compress, squeeze by pressure. **naapnut**. *a.* strong, resilient. [Tag. *hagod*]

ápo: *n.* term of address to show respect, sir; ma'am. **Wen, apo**. Yes, sir (ma'am). **agapo**. *v.* to call the attention of the occupants of a house be calling out *apo*. [Tag. *ginoó*]

apó: *n.* (pl. *appo*, *aappó*) kinship term for relatives two generations apart: grandparent or grandchild; master, mistress. **apo iti dapan**. *n.* great-great-grandchild. **apo iti tumeng**. *n.* great-grandchild. **apo iti siko**. *n.* child in the fifth degree of descent. **apo iti pingil**. *n.* child in the sixth degree of descent. **apuen**. *n.* boss; gang leader. **umapo**. *v.* to be one's grandchild; to bootlick; enslave oneself. **apo-apo**. *n.* boss; gang leader. [Kal. *apú*, Bon., Png., Tag. *apó* (grandchild)]

ápug: *n.* lime. **pagapugan**. *n.* a kind of small jar to hold lime (by betel chewers). [Bol. *litúen*, Ibg. *áfug*, Ivt. *amed*, Kal. *apuÿ*, Kpm. *ápiq*, Png. *dená*, Tag. *apog*]

apóko: *n.* grandchild; grandson, granddaughter. **agapoko**. *n.* grandparent and grandchild. **apoko ti túmeng**. *n.* great-grandchild. **apoko ti dapán**. *n.* great-great-grandchild (fourth degree of descent). [Png., Tag. *apó*]

apúlas: *n. Ficus glareosa.*

apúlid: *var.* of *buslig*: *Eleocharis sp.* sedge.

ápon: *n.* pen (for animals), chicken coop, horse stable. **agapon**. *v.* to roost (chickens); go into the coop or stable. **kaapon**. *n.* sharing the same coop or stable; (*fig.*) companions. **yapon**. *v.* to coop, herd. **umapon**. *v.* to go home (*awid*) **panagaapon**. *n.* time for animals to return to their stables or pens before dusk. **Ungtannakto ni ikitko no awan ti agyapon kadagiti baka**. My aunt will get angry with me if nobody brings in the cows to their pen. [Tag. *kulungan*]

apúnte: (Sp. *apunte*: prompting) *n.* prompt (on stage). **agapunte**. *n.* to prompt. **apuntador**. *n.* prompter.

ápong: (pl. *aapong*) term of address for *apo*; grandparent. **apong a baket**. *n.* grandmother. (*lola*) **apong a lakay**. *n.* grandfather. (*lolo*)

apoúnayen: (*apo* + *unayen*) exclamation denoting mild disgust or alarm: what's the matter?

apúngol: *n.* embrace. **apungulen**. *v.* to hug, embrace. (*arakup*; *rakep*) **agapungol iti silag**. *v.* to remove the pith or unopened leaves of palm trees. (*ubog*) **Simrekda iti siled ket inapungolda ti agsasaibbek nga inada**. They entered the room and embraced their sobbing mother. [Tag. *yakap*]

apúra: (Sp. *apura*: quick) *n.* quick action. (*daras, paspas, dagdag*) **agap-apura**. *v.* to hurry up, be in a hurry. **pangapuraan**. *n.* fast way to do something; alternative. [Kal. *cheÿson*, Tag. *paspás*]

apurá(r): (Sp. *apurar*: hurry) *v.* to hasten. (*daras*) **apurado**. *a.* in a hurry. **yapurado, apuraduen**. *v.* to hasten. [Tag. *dalî*]

apuradór: (Sp. *aforador*: appraiser; gauger) *n.* one who classifies tobacco leaves.

apóro: (Sp. *aforro*: lining) *n.* lining (of a dress, coat, etc.); the classification of tobacco leaves. **aporuan**. *v.* to line (a dress, etc.). **yaporo**. *v.* to use for lining.

apúro: *n.* diaper. (*lampin*)

apúrot: **agapurot**. *v.* to dive; swim underwater. (*batok*)

aportunádo: (Sp. *afortunado*: fortunate) *a.* fortunate. (*nagasat*)

apostól: (Sp.) *n.* apostle. **kinaapostol**. *n.* apostleship. **inapostol**. *n.* variety of rice.

apostóliko: (Sp. *apostólico*) *a.* apostolic.

apóy: *n.* fire. **agapoy, apuyen**. *v.* to cook rice, cook a meal. **in(n)apoy**. *n.* cooked rice. **in-inapoy**. *n.* the depression of the cheek while gaping. **umapoy**. *v.* to give off sparks. **naapoy**. *a.* easy to burn. **agapoy-apoy**. *v.* to play house (cooking rice, etc.) **Umap-apoy ti pungtotna**. *exp.* His anger flared up. **Sangkasapulan, sangkaapuyan**. *exp.* denoting poverty-stricken conditions: cooking what is found. **Agurayka ngarud ta ikkankayo ti bagas ta adda apuyenyo**. Wait then and I'll give you rice to cook. [Ibg. *afi*, Ivt., Png., Tag. *apóy*, Knk. *apéy*, Kpm. *apiq*]

apuyár: (Sp. *apoyar*: support) **apuyaren**. *v.* to support, back up. **apuyaren ti rason**. *v.* to back up one's reasoning.

appán: *n.* bait. **appanan**. *v.* to set bait. **yappan**. *v.* to use as bait. [Ibg. *eppan*, Itg. *appan*, Ivt., Kal. *papan*, Knk. *pápan*, Kpm. *apan*, Png. *tapang*, Tag. *pain*]

appaúnay: **Appaunayka metten**. *exp.* You're too much; What's the matter with you?

appáyaw: *n.* being just about to do something; on the verge of; coming near. (*ampayag*) **umappayaw**. *v.* to have the urge to do something; come to mind. **appayawan**. *v.* to hover; fly swiftly.

appéd: see *lapped*: obstruction (*tiped*). [Tag. *pigil*]

appéng: **yappeng**. *v.* to apply to; include. **mayappeng**. *v.* to be applied; to be included.

appigúd: *a.* left-handed. **maappigud**. *v.* to do something in a way deviating from the normal; to be clumsy; to not feel at ease. **Inwalinna ti kutsilio ken kubiertosna ta appigud kano.** He threw aside his knife and silverware because he is supposedly not normal. [Tag. *kaliwete*]

appípi: *n.* tender care. **appipien.** *v.* to care for tenderly. **ipaappipi.** *v.* to have someone taken good care of.

appít: (*coll.*) *n.* vulva. (*uki*)

appó: *n.* ancestor; also, plural of *apo*. **appuen.** *n. pl.* descendants.

appuág: see *appuap*: caress.

appuáp: **appuapen.** *v.* to caress. (*lailo*; *arakup*)

appukó: (*obs.*) **appukuen.** *v.* to straighten; corner.

appón: *n.* collection; sum; total; ring a conjurer uses to protect himself from animals. **appunen.** *v.* to gather; collect; assemble (*taripnong*). [Tag. *kabuuan*]

appúpo: *n.* holding with care. **agappupo.** *v.* to join the hands in a cup. **appupuen.** *v.* to hold in the cup of one's hands; hold with care; to take into one's care.

appút: *n.* pieces of timber under the ceiling. **agapput.** *v.* to cover the genitals with the hands; cover any part of the body with the hands. **apputen.** *v.* to cover with the hands. **maapput.** *v.* to catch someone hiding in the act; to be exposed. **Naganug-og ket inapputna ti rupana.** He wept and covered his face. [Tag. *takíp* (cover)]

appúyot: **appuyuten.** *v.* to lift up tenderly (*sappúyot*); comfort, caress.

aprád: **makaaprad.** *v.* to cause hoarseness of the voice (by eating or drinking). (*suprad*) **naaprad.** *a.* bitter; acidic; salty. **maapradan.** *v.* to be affected by salty foods (causing a hoarse voice).

apragáta: *var.* of *alpargatas*: hemp sandals.

apráng: **nakaap-aprang.** *a.* horrible, shocking, hideous (*alingget*). [Tag. *hindík*]

aprás: *n.* gathering out of reach fruits with a stick. **aprasen.** *v.* to beat, strike (fruits) so they fall. **yapras.** *v.* to beat down (fruits). **aprasan.** *v.* to clean an area with a sweeping movement. [Tag. *hampás*]

aprendís: (Sp. *aprendiz*, *obs.*) *n.* apprentice; newcomer.

aprés: *n.* speed and sound of rushing water. (*pegges*) **naapres.** *a.* strong flowing (river current).

apresiár: (Sp. *apreciar*: appreciate) **apresiaren.** *v.* to appreciate, esteem.

apréta: (Sp. *apretar*: tight; press) **naapreta.** *a.* excessive. (*napalalo*) **apretaen.** *v.* to speed up, hurry up.

apretár: (Sp. *apretar*: tighten) **apretaren.** *v.* to speed up, accelerate; strain the eyes; constrain. **naapretado.** *a.* quick; excessive.

aprí: **maaprian.** *v.* to bump the head while walking. (*dalápus*)

apriák: **maapriakan.** *v.* to dry by spreading in the shade (fish).

Áprika: (Sp. *África*) *n.* Africa. **Aprikáno.** *n.*, *a.* African.

aprít: **apriten.** *v.* to beat down (*apras*); hit with a stick; cause to fall down. **maaprit.** *v.* to fall down; drop in large numbers (fruit during a storm). [Tag. *lagas*]

apritáda: (Sp. *fritada*: fry) *n.* achiote meat stew.

apró: *n.* bile. (*papait*) [Ibg. *aggu*, *ádu*, Ivt., Kpm. *apdu*, Kal. *apchu*, Knk. *pidis*, Png. *apgó*, Tag. *apdó*]

aprobár: (Sp. *aprobar*: approve) **agaprobar.** *v.* to approve. **maaprobaran.** *v.* to be approved. **aprobado.** *a.* approved. **aprobasion.** *n.* approval.

aprobétsar: (Sp. *aprovechar*: take advantage) **agaprobetsar.** *v.* to profit; take advantage (*gundawayan*). [Tag. *samantalá*]

apropiár: (Sp.) **apropiaren.** *v.* to appropriate. **yapropiar.** *v.* to allot.

aprós: *n.* light touch (*lailo*). **aprosan.** *v.* to rub softly; touch tenderly. **pagapros.** *n.* massage ointment. **yapros.** *v.* to stroke, touch gently (with the hand). **Inaprosak ti takiagna a mangipaneknek iti pannakipagrikna.** I gently touched his arm to demonstrate my sympathy. [Ibg. *guggufan*, Itg. *too*, Ivt. *pahputan*, Kpm. *aplus*, Png. *aplus*, Tag. *haplos*]

apsáy₁: *n.* straight hair (as opposed to wavy). (*unnat*) **agapsay.** *v.* to sit down with stretched-out legs. **yapsay.** *v.* to straighten the hair; stretch out.

apsáy₂: *n.* a kind of small marine fish.

apsí: *var.* of *lapsi*.

apsút: **maapsut.** *v.* to slide, slip, get loose; be removed; to be singled out. **apsutan.** *v.* to press, squeeze; separate from a group; take away. [Tag. *talilis*; *tanggál*]

aptá: *n.* a fish that is born in the sea but spawns in rivers, called *apta* in the sea stage and *bursian* or *bagset* in the rivers.

aptáng: *n.* remainder. (*udi*)

ará: Interjection used to drive animals. **maara.** *v.* to copy, imitate. (*túlad*)

árab: **agarab.** *v.* to graze, pasture. **pagaraban.** *n.* pasture, grazing land. **narabraber a pagaraban.** *n.* (*fig.*) place where the grass is greener. **Bay-am lattan 'ta nuang nga agarab.** Just let that water buffalo graze. **No sadino ti pakaiwaywayan ti kabalio, isu't pagarabanna.**

exp. Where the horse is tied, that's where it grazes. [Bon. *angteb, atlab,* Knk. *anglúd,* Tag. *pastól* (Sp.)]

arabáab: *n.* spring tide. (*apdáy*)

arábas: *n.* a kind of speckled yellow, green, blue, and black larva destructive to rice plants, armyworm. **arabasen.** *v.* to be infested with armyworms. **Tumaud dagiti arabas kalpasan a mapaksiat dagiti lukton.** The armyworms will emerge after the grasshoppers are killed off.

Arabiáno: (Eng.) *n., a.* Arabian.

arábika: *n.* variety of coffee.

Arábiko: (Sp. *arábico:* Arabic) *a.* Arabian; Arabic.

arabís: *var.* of *arrabis:* back-handed slap (*sipat*); diagonal.

Arábo: (Sp. *árabe:* Arab) *n. a.* Arab. (*arabiano*)

arábong: *n.* the tip of a bunch of cotton arranged in a knot.

arad-ád: *n.* lamentation, supplication. (*araraw*) **umarad-ad.** *v.* to lament; supplicate, plead.

aradáng: **agaradang.** *v.* to creep, crawl slowly; begin to walk (*karadap, karayam*). [Tag. *gapang*]

arádas: **agaradas.** *v.* to go and rape a sleeping woman (*rames*). **aradasen.** *v.* to fondle in the dark. [Tag. *gahasà*]

arádo: (Sp. *arado:* plow) *n.* plow. (*ringkon*) **agarado.** *v.* to plow. **ipaarado.** *n.* land to be plowed. **kaar-arado.** *a.* recently plowed. [Kal. *manchelok,* Tag. *araro*]

aradón: *var.* of *arandong:* species of plant with small yellow flowers.

aradór: (Sp. *arador:* one who plows) *n.* water buffalo used for plowing.

aragaág: *a.* transparent; porous; spongy; *n.* shafts of light coming through gauzy material. **agaragaag.** *a.* transparent; gauzy; loose; (*reg.*) spongy, porous. (*saragasag*) **naaragaag.** *a.* old (tools); having holes (pots, etc.). **Aragaag kenka ket awan ti mailangaam.** It is transparent to you so you can't recognize anything. [Tag. *aninag*]

arágan: *n.* a type of edible brown seaweed; (*fig.*) disheveled hair. **aragan-tamnay.** *n. Najas graminea* seaweed. **immaragan.** *a.* wavy (hair). **mangaragan.** *n.* (*lit.*) wind that travels close to the earth. **Nagparang la ket ngarud dagiti aragan kadagiti kilikilina.** The untidy hair of her armpits appeared.

árak: *n.* generic name for alcohol; wine, whisky. **ar-arak.** *n.* nest egg. **ar-arakan.** *v.* to entice; allure; bait. **agat-arak.** *a.* smelling of liquor. [Ibg. *binaráyang, binaráyeng,* Ifg. *baya,* Ivt. *palek,* Kal. *beyyas,* Kpm. *álaq, básiq,* Png. *álak, káwat,* Tag. *alak*]

arák: **agarak.** *v.* to gather, assemble, come together (*taripnong*); collect. **naarak.** *a.* wanting to accompany somebody. **aaraken.** *a.* attractive; charismatic; magnetic. **managarak.** *a.* easily attracted to. **ar-arak.** *n.* nest egg; decoy; something used to allure. [Png., Tag. *tipon*]

arakattót: **maarakattot.** *v.* to be surprised; do hurriedly.

arakáyan: *n.* a thin green freshwater alga.

arakiák: **agarakiak.** *v.* to cackle (hens). (*kutak*) **Naarakiak dagiti lampong nga agiinum iti serbesa iti arubayan.** The wild neighborhood drinkers cackled. [Tag. *putak*]

arákup: *n.* embrace, hug. **arakupen.** *v.* to embrace (*apungol; kepkep; rakep*). **aginnarakup.** *v.* to hug, embrace each other. [Ibg. *gakkó,* Ivt. *kepkep,* Kpm. *kaúl,* Png. *lakáp,* Tag. *yakap*]

aramáng: *n.* small marine shrimp used in *buguong,* also called *armáng;* variety of awned early rice. [Tag. *alamáng*]

arámat: **aramaten.** *v.* to use; employ (*dakamat, dakawat, gakat*). **maaramat.** *v.* to be necessary, to need. **paaramat.** *v.* to lend to someone; to allow oneself to be taken advantage of. [Tag. *gamit; alamát* = legend, myth]

arámid: *n.* work; business; occupation; action; deed. **agaramid.** *v.* to make, construct. **aramiden.** *v.* to do; make, manufacture; accomplish. **maaramid.** *v.* to be able to do; to happen. **akin-aramid.** *n.* the person responsible. **maaramid.** *v.* to be able to do, make; makeable; doable. **yaramidan.** *v.* to do/make for someone. **ipaaramid.** *v.* to have something done. **pagaramid.** *v.* tool used to make something. **pagaramidan.** *n.* workshop, factory. **Saan nga agpada ti sao ken aramid.** Words are not the same as actions. **Ti aramidmo no ubingka, kastanto met no lakayka.** *exp.* What you do when you're young you will also do when you're old. **Diak ammo no kasano ti pannakaaramidna nga adda ditoy.** I don't know how it happened to get here. [Bon. *gáeb, ikkan, amma, angnen, kam,* Ibg. *kuwan, meppedday, magengnguwa,* Ivt. *parin,* Png. *gawá,* Kpm., Tag. *gawâ*]

áran₁: *n.* sorcerer, witch; magician; the "Eve" of Iloko mythology. **immaran.** *a.* giantlike (women).

áran₂: *n.* variety of awned *diket* rice.

arána: *var.* of *harana:* serenade (*tapat*). [Tag. *harana*]

aranáar: *var.* of *anaraar:* moonlight; natural light.

aránas: **aranasen.** *v.* to do carefully.

arándi: **agarandi**. *v.* to be similar; be of the same social standing, position, etc. (*ariring*, *pada*). [Tag. *wangkí*]

arandóng: *n.* a kind of shrub with yellow flowers, *Wikstroemia ovata*. **pangarandongen**. *n. Trema orientalis* shrub.

aránia: (Sp. *araña*: spider; chandelier) *n.* chandelier, branched holder for several lights or candles, suspended from a ceiling.

arániw: *n.* a kind of vine with medicinal leaves.

aranúor: *n.* droning or roaring sound of the ocean or machine.

aransél: (Sp. *arancel*: tariff) *n.* list of church fees; tariff, customs duty.

árang: **arangen**. *v.* to block, obstruct, blockade; seize by surprise, ambush, waylay (*sada*, *tambang*); loot.

aráng: **arang-arang**. *n.* coxcomb, popinjay. *a.* selfish; conceited. [Tag. *yabang*]

arángan: *n.* a type of aquatic fern, *Najas graminea*.

aranggawís: *var.* of *aringgawis*: tree top.

arangín: *n.* a kind of tree with valuable lumber.

arangkáda: (Sp. *arrancada*: sudden departure) *n.* sudden departure, sudden start; spurt; burst of speed; voyage; trip; travelling. (*biahe*; *baniaga*) **agarangkada**. *v.* to go on a trip; travel; speed up a car.

arangúong: see *gunggong*: ignorant; *v.* resound.

arapáap: *n.* aspiration, dream; vision. (*darepdep*) **arapaapen**. *v.* to imagine; dream of; aspire for; observe with misgiving. **managarapaap**. *n.* dreamer; one who usually daydreams. **Ar-arapaapenda a no makakalida iti gameng, mangbangonda iti asienda**. They aspire to put up a plantation if they are able to dig up the treasure. [Png. *gunaét*, Tag. *arap*]

arapéep, **arapíip**: *var.* of *arapaap*: dream; vision; aspiration.

ar-ár: *n.* rivulet; branching off from the main river; tributary; irrigation ditch (*banawang*). **ar-aran**. *v.* to make or provide with an irrigation ditch or rivulet. [Tag. *agusan*]

ar-árak: *n.* bait to lure something. **ar-arakan**. *v.* to lure someone to do something, entice.

ararásan: *n.* a kind of large, black ant.

aráraw: **umararaw**, **ararawen**. *v.* to wail, cry, lament; beg, implore. (*gawawa*, *anek-ek*) **ag-araraw**. *v.* to chant prayers during All Saint's Day. **Nagbalin a tuleng iti ararawda**. He was deaf to their pleas. [Tag. *pakiusap*]

araráwan: *n.* a kind of cicada-like gray insect that makes noises at night. [Kal. *yayas*]

araró: *n.* kind of blackish freshwater fish.

ar-arusip: *n.* a kind of grapelike seaweed, *Antidesma ghaesembilla*.

áras₁: (Sp. *arras*: dowry of thirteen coins given by a bride to a groom on their wedding) *n. arrha*, coins in the wedding used for good luck and prosperity. **aras ti atang**. *n.* eggs or coins added to the sacrifice to the spirits. **yaras**. *v.* to give the *arrha*.

áras₂: *n.* painful disease of the mouth characterized by pearl-colored flakes (usually suffered by children); the visible effects of the *aras* disease. **agaras**. *v.* to suffer from *aras*. **Isapsapom ti tawas iti rabaw ti dilam tapno marunaw ti arasmo**. Smear talcum powder over your tongue so the *aras* will melt.

arasáas: *n.* whisper; murmur. **agarasaas**. *v.* to whisper; rustle softly (leaves). **yarasaas**. *v.* to whisper something to. **aginnarasaas**. *v.* to whisper to each other. [Bon. *todtodo*, *alasáas*, Ivt. *akaak*, Kal. *iyagasaas*, Knk. *ayásak*, *tibí*, *tallugítib*, Kpm. *bulúng*, Png. *esaes*, Tag. *anás*, *bulóng*]

arasagát: *n. Scheflera odorata*.

arasagaysáyan: *n.* mouse gray.

arasalígaw: *n. Croton verreauxii*.

arásaw: *n.* water used in rinsing rice. **arasawen**. *v.* to rinse rice or vegetables. **maarasaw**. *v.* to be rinsed. (*bilnas*) **Ninayonanna ti ar-arasawenna a bagas**. She added the rice she was rinsing. [Knk. *gawgáw*, Tag. *hugas*]

arasiés: *n.* a kind of mollusk. **umarasies**. *v.* to swarm, wiggle in a mass. (*ariyamyam*)

arawáaw: *n.* babbler. (*salawasaw*, *tarabitab*) **agarawaaw**. *v.* to babble; gossip. [Tag. *tsismoso*]

áray: *n.* row, line (of plants) (*batug*); plot. **agaray**. *v.* to prepare the ground in rows for planting. **arayen**. *v.* to plant in rows, make into rows. [Tag. *hanay*]

aráy: Interjection expressing pain. **managaray**. *a.* in the habit of saying *aray*, overly sensitive to pain. (*annay*)

aráya: *n.* variety of children's game.

aráyat: *n.* a kind of spiny shrub; *Capparis sepiaria*; help; aid. **ar-arayat**. *n.* a multi-headed sea animal resembling a sea cucumber. **umarayat**. *v.* to gather; assemble, come together; aid, rescue. **arayaten**. *v.* to help, aid, save, rescue (*salakan*, *tulong*). **yarayat**. *v.* to help, provide assistance. [Tag. *saklolo*, *tulong*]

aray-áy: *n.* loose array, loose ends. **naaray-ay**. *a.* torn. **ar-arayen**. *v.* to tear (*pigis*). [Tag. *himulmól*]

arbaáka: *n.* an aromatic plant used as a diuretic and to facilitate menstruation.

arbán: *n.* flock, herd; young *tokling* bird. **sangaarban**. *n.* one herd; one flock (*pangen*). [Tag. *kaban*]

arbás: agarbas. *v.* to prune; cut against the grain. [Tag. *tagpás*]

arbéng: *n.* hindrance; obstacle; temporary fence. **arbengan.** *v.* to protect temporarily (plants) with a fence. **paarbengan.** *v.* to have something fenced in temporarily. **saan a maarbengan.** *v.* it cannot be prevented. [Tag. *harang*]

arbís: *n.* drizzle, light rain. **agarbis.** *v.* to drizzle. **maarbisan.** *v.* to be caught in the drizzle. **arbis la ti nabagida.** *exp.* they only got the crumbs. **Nariknak ti arbis a mangrugin nga agtinnag.** I felt the drizzle start to fall. **No agar-arbis nga agin-init, agan-anak ti mangmangkit.** When it drizzles during sunny weather, an elf is giving birth. [Bon. *lagoy, lagyot, og-ogmoy, op-oplot*, Kal. *appuput*, Knk. *dámoy, lageyléy, lagúy*, Png. *mayamayá*, Tag. *ambón*]

arbobuéna: (Sp. *hierbabuena*: mint) *n.* mint. (*yerbabuena*)

árbol: (Sp. *árbol*: tree) *n.* fire tree.

arbulário: *var.* of *erbulario*: herb doctor; quack doctor.

arbór₁: (Sp. *árbol*: tree) *n.* fire tree.

arbór₂: *n.* decoration (*arkos*); embroidery (*bordado*).

ardáng: see *aradang*: to begin to walk (infants); creep; crawl.

ardiáy: *var.* of *addaydiay*: it's over there.

ardiód: *n.* excessive makeup or jewelry. **nakaardiod.** *a.* wearing excessive makeup or jewelry. **konsi-ardiod.** *n.* person prone to wearing makeup excessively or during inappropriate occasions. **naardiod.** *a.* showy; ornate; with a lot of makeup and/or jewelry.

areb-éb: *n.* bubble; gurgling sound; (*coll.*) drunkard. **agareb-eb.** *v.* to burp; gurgle; gulp down (*tig-ab*). [Tag. *bulubok*]

aredák: *n.* (*reg.*) first rains.

ared-éd: *n.* sediment; dregs. (*alibudabud; rinsaed; intaer; lissaad; basabas; lued; ureb*) **agared-ed.** *v.* to settle. [Tag. *latak*]

arégla: (Sp. *arreglar*: arrange) *n.* arrangement. **agaregla.** *v.* to arrange, make arrangements.

aréglo: (Sp. *arreglo*: arrangement) *n.* arrangement; agreement. **areglado.** *a.* arranged; settled; adjusted.

arek-ék: *n.* noise of a rooster of hen scratching; (*fig.*) murmur, indistinct sounds.

árem: agarem. *v.* to be in love; lust; court. **armen.** *v.* to desire; court a girl. **arem-matá, bain-bagá.** expression said of a person who is too shy to court the girl he wants. **innarem.** *n.* mutual courting. **umarem.** *v.* to court, express one's love. **Di makaarem ta kabuteng dagiti babbalasang a makaam-ammo kenkuana.** He cannot court anyone because he is afraid of the ladies that know him. [Bon. *gelwi, salwit, ángo*, Knk. *sim-án*, Kpm. *lólo*, Png. *káraw*, Tag. *ligaw*]

aréna: (Sp. *arena*: arena) *n.* field of battle.

arendádo: (Sp. *arrendado*: leased) *a.* leased, hired.

arendár: (Sp. *arrendar*: lease) **arendaren.** *v.* to hire.

arendém: maarendem. *v.* to discern. descry; perceive; detect in the distance or in the darkness. [Tag. *pansín*]

aren-én: agaren-en. *v.* to shrink; shrivel (*karenken*). [Tag. *urong*]

arenóla: *n.* small container used as a toilet. (*pagisbuan*)

areng-éng: *n.* moan; groan; complaint. **agarengeng.** *v.* to whinny (horses); moan, groan. **yareng-eng.** *v.* to moan for something; complain in a childish way. **sangkayareng-eng.** *a.* always asking for something in a childish way; vocally insistent, persistent. **Mano kadakuada ti addaan kabaelan a mangurnos iti arengengda.** How many of them are able to organize their complaints? [Tag. *halinghíng*]

arengkék: see *rengkek*: bull-necked.

arep-ép: *n.* premonition. (*partaang*) **arep-epen.** *v.* to visualize. [Tag. *salagimsím*]

arestádo: (Sp. *arrestado*: arrested) *a.* arrested. (*natiliw*)

aret-ét: *n.* creaking sound. **umaret-et.** *v.* to shrink, contract under a load. **Iti pannagnana, nagaret-et ti inakilis a kawayan a datar.** As he walked, the bamboo floor strips creaked and buckled. [Tag. *laginít*]

argólia: (Sp. *argolla*: ring, hoop) *n.* swinging rings in gymnastics; hoop. **agargolia.** *v.* to play with gymnastic hoops; do pull-ups on suspended rings.

arguménto: (Sp. *argumento*: argument) *n.* argument; debate.

ari-: *pref.* taking the *-ak* pronouns indicating that the subject is about to undergo or experience the action or state specified by the verbal stem, usually used with the suffixes *-an* or *-en* and oftentimes used with reduplication: **Arintutuduen.** It is about to rain. **Ar-arinpatayanka.** You (sing) are on the verge of dying. **Arinturogen.** He seems to be about to sleep. **arikabusen a bulan.** a nearly full moon. **Arinsadutenak a bumangon nupay rabiin.** I am rather lazy to get up although it's already night. **Arintapusen ti Mayo.** May is about to end.

ári: *n.* king, emperor. **pagarian.** *n.* kingdom; monarchy. **agari.** *v.* to reign as king; rule;

dominate. **naarian.** *a.* kingly. [Png. *ári*, Tag. *harì*]

ariá: (Sp. *arriar*: slacken) expression used to incite or goad: go on; carry on; go ahead; giddy-up. (*sige*) **umaria, ariaan.** *v.* to let loose (an animal); let go; untangle; slacken. **ariaen.** *n.* main work. **Naariaan ti angkla.** The anchor was released.

ariák: agariak. *v.* to gather, assemble, convene. (*taripnong*) **mangyar-ariak.** *v.* to spread, disseminate (gossip). [Tag. *tipon*]

ari- -an: see under *ari-*.

arianggá: *n.* noise made by a crowd. **Kaibibusna ti pansitna idi pagammuan la ta adda kasla nagariangga iti agdan.** He had just finished his noodles when all of a sudden it seemed there were people crowding around the staircase. [Ibg. *tennug*, Itg. *natbag*, Ivt. *liak*, Kpm. *mangye*, Png. *ingal*, Tag. *ingay*.

ariawyáw: *n.* a kind of small marine fish.

aríba: (Sp. *arriba y abajo*: up and down) **ariba i baho.** *n.* dealing cards from the top of the pack and from below; rapid discharging at both ends of the digestive tract (vomiting accompanied with loose bowel movement). **agaribaibaho.** *v.* to have diarrhea accompanied with vomiting.

aribái: (coined from *ari* 'king' and *babái* 'female') *n.* queen; muse; goddess. (*reyna*) [Png. *binári*]

aribasá: agaribasa. *v.* to start to tear (eye); perspire.

aribásay: agaribasay. *v.* to leak, ooze out; flow out of (tears, sweat, etc.). [Tag. *tagas, daloy*]

aribawbáw: *n.* a kind of small destructive insect.

aribáyan: see *arubayan*: surroundings; neighborhood.

aribéngbeng: *n.* floodgate, sluice; temporary fence. **agaribengbeng.** *v.* to clothe oneself, cover oneself. **aribenbengan.** *v.* to surround; crowd; overwhelm; dam the floodgate. [Tag. *agusan*]

aribuábo: agaribuabo. *v.* to seed; grain. **naaribuabo.** *a.* not yet mature.

aribúbo: *n. Dioscorea luzonensis.* (*kamangeg*)

aribúdbud: *n.* sediment, dregs, things settling to the bottom. (*aribudabud; rinsaed; intaer; lued; basabas*)

aribugbúg: *n. var.* of *aribukbúk.*

aribukbúk: *n.* a kind of vine with small red berries, *Deeringia baccata; Deeringia amaranthoides;* whirlpool. **agaribukbuk.** *v.* to bubble (boiling water) (*burek, barukbok*). [Tag. *bulâ*]

aribungbóng: *n.* crowd. **aribungbungan.** *v.* to surround in a crowd; crowd around. **Nagkakatawa dagiti nagaribungbong nga mannalon.** The farmers crowding around laughed.

Aribungbunganen dagiti tao iti igid ti kalsada a kasta unay ti siddaawda. The people crowded around the edge of the road very surprised. [Tag. *kulumpón*]

aribúob: *var.* of *arubúob*: raging of the sea; violent gust of wind.

aribusábos: *n.* final portion; end; last part. **agaribusabos.** *v.* to draw near the end. [Tag. *hulihan*]

aributantán: aributantanen. *v.* to do consecutively; to attack without letup (*arisadsad*). **Inaributbutannan daytoy a dinanogdanog.** He punched without letup.

aributéd: *n.* impurities (in water); the smallest of the bunch. **naaributed.** *a.* unclear (water) (*rituer*). [Tag. *dumí*]

aribúyot: agaribuyot. *v.* to throng, hustle; stampede; overwhelm (*aribungbung*). **Ninamnamak nga agaribuyotda a mangpadaan iti panagpababa ti eroplanok.** I was expecting them to gather around to prepare for the landing of my airplane.

aridaéd: *var.* of *arinsaed*: sediment.

aridakdák: *n.* haunt; hangout (*ayuyang*); noise of approaching feet. **umaridakdak.** *v.* to stamp the feet while walking; appear, show oneself (*parang*); be present, come, go. [Tag. *pugaran* (hangout)]

aridamdám: aridamdaman. *v.* to spy; observe stealthily. (*arendem, siim*)

aridenggán: *n.* noise. **awan ti aridenggan.** *exp.* no quiet; too much noise. **umaridenggan.** *v.* to make a lot of noise. [Tag. *ingay*]

aridóndo: (Sp. *redondo*: round) *a.* round. (*timbukel*) **nagaridondo.** *a.* round; cut around.

ariék₁: *n. var.* of *ariet*: intestinal roundworm. [Kal. *kuÿang*]

ariék₂: maariek, or **mariek.** *v.* to be tickled; to nauseate, feel disgust. **kaariek.** *n.* that which is repulsive. **makaariek.** *a.* causing someone to be repulsed. **aariekan.** *n.* sensitive erogenous zone; ticklish part of a person's body. **Naariekak kadagiti nagadu nga ipes a naglemmeng kadagiti sirok dagiti alikamen.** I am repulsed by the many cockroaches hiding under the furniture. [Knk. *dúgis*, Tag. *alimbukáy*]

ari- -en: see under *ari-*.

ariésgo: (Sp. *arriesgar*: risk) *n.* danger. (*peggad*) **naariesgo.** *a.* dangerous.

ariesyés: see *arasies*: *n.* kind of mollusk; *v.* squirm; wiggle.

ariét: *n.* a kind of intestinal roundworm. **agariet.** *v.* to be infected with roundworms. [Kal. *kuÿang*]

arig-: Prefix of similarity applied to certain nouns. (*sinan-*) **arigbituen.** starry (*sinam-*

bituen). **arigbituen a mata.** starry, beautiful eyes. **Arig-arasaas ti saona.** His words were soft (like a whisper).

árig: *a.* like, as if. **yarig.** *v.* to compare; contrast. **pagarigan.** *n.* example. **kas pagarigan.** for example. **kayarigan.** *n.* example, instance; comparison. **pangarig.** *n.* parable. **no ar-arigen.** *exp.* If I'm not mistaken. (*no diak agbiddut*) **ar-arigen.** *v.* to expect; anticipate good results. **arigna't manok a saan a makaitlog.** *exp.* denoting a woman who refuses to perform her duties (like a chicken that doesn't lay eggs). **Awan kayariganna iti pagtaengan a tinalawanna.** There is no comparison to the house he escaped from. [Png. *égpang (compare)*, *alimbawá (example)*, Tag. *hambíng (compare)*, *halimbawà (example)*]

arigenggén: **agarigenggen.** *v.* to shiver, tremble, shake (*pigerger, tigerger*). [Tag. *kiníg*]

arígi: see *adigi*: post, pillar.

arikáaw: *var.* of *arikiáw*: scream.

arikaká: see *alikaka*: carefulness; timidity.

arikamkám: **arikamkamen.** *v.* to sweep garbage.

aríkap: **arikapen.** *v.* to feel with the hand or finger; touch; fondle; understand. **agar-arikap.** *v.* to be at a loss for words; to be unprepared for debate; (~ *ti sungbat*) to search for an answer. **yarikap.** *v.* to bribe. **maarikap.** *v.* to be able to touch; (*fig.*) to be able to comprehend. **mangngarikap.** *n.* lewd, immodest person. **aginnarikap.** *v.* to fondle one another. **Awan ti maarikapko a balikas.** *exp.* I am at a loss for words. [Png. *diwít, akapkap, kapá*, Tag. *hipò, kapkáp, kapâ, apuhap, halughóg*]

arikattót: **maarikattot.** *v.* to be in a hurry.

arikawkáw: **agarikawkaw.** *v.* to shake something with the hands (to remove rice, etc.), to remove rice from the stems by shaking and sifting with the palms up (*sariwagwag*); to mix, stir with the hands; (*reg.*) to meddle in someone else's affairs. **Nagarikawkawda iti nagango a ruot sada binunton iti sirok ti kamantiris.** They shook the dry grass (to remove the dirt) and then piled it under the *damortis* tree. [Tag. *halò* (mix)]

arikaykáy: *n.* leisure time. **agarikaykay, umarikaykay.** *v.* to travel for adventure or fun, spend time leisurely (*aliwaksay*).

arikenkén: *n.* nineteenth-century version of the *dallot*, ancient chant. **agarikenken.** *v.* to shake, tremble.

arikeskés: **agarikeskes.** *v.* to cover, wrap oneself (in a blanket). **arikeskesen.** *v.* to cover with, clothe with; shudder from cold or fear; to be restless. (*aribengbeng*)

ariketkét: **ar-ariketketan.** *v.* to be afraid; suspicious; have second thoughts (*buteng*). [Tag. *mangambá*]

arikiák: **umarikiak.** *v.* to chirp (sparrows, etc.); make noises (chickens at night).

arikiáw: *n.* scream, shout (*láaw*). **agarikiaw.** *v.* to scream, shout.

arikumkóm: **agarikumkom.** *v.* to collect the lower ends of one's skirt when climbing stairs, etc.; to contract (certain animals when disturbed); coil (worms); shrink (animals). **arikumkumen.** *v.* to sweep, gather, collect in disarray.

arikunók: **agarikunok.** *v.* to assemble in one place; cluster together.

arikuykúy₁: **arikuykuyan.** *v.* to sweep garbage in one place. (*kuykoy*)

arikuykúy₂: *n.* a variety of awned early rice with white kernel.

arim-: *var.* of the prefix *arin-* before labial consonants *m*, *p*, and *b*.

arimadéng: **agarimadeng.** *v.* to hesitate, vacillate; be afraid. (*sarimadeng, maredmed*)

arimanáan: *n.* frame of a scoop net. (*baringring*)

arimándo: *n.* the soursop fruit. (*bayubána*; Tagalog *guyabáno*)

arimaóng: *n.* a kind of speckled wildcat.

arimasá: **agarimasa.** *v.* to be moist, damp, slightly wet. **agar-arimasa.** *v.* to be almost dry (creeks, rivers, etc.); damp. **Kasano nga aggurigorka no agar-arimasa ti kilikili ken mugingmo a bimmangon?** How can you have a fever if your armpits and forehead were not very wet when you woke up?

arimasámas: *n.* red skies at moonrise. **naarimasamas.** *a.* coarse; misground, ground badly. (*gaspang*) **agarimasamas.** *v.* to have a reddish glow. [Tag. *gaspang* (coarse)]

arimáta: *n.* bamboo pole used to carry heavy objects, used by two people (*assiw*); variety of early rice with striped hull. **pagarimataan.** *v.* to carry a load together. [Tag. *pingga*]

arímay: *n. Boehmeria nivea.*

arimayáng: **agarimayang.** *v.* to spread, flow (liquids, tears, etc). (*arubos*) **Nagarimayang ti luana.** Her tears flowed.

arimbaáw: **arimbaawen.** *a.* subsiding (fever); cooling off (hot water).

arimbángaw: *n.* the noise made by a crowd. (*ariwawa*) **umarimbangaw.** *v.* to be noisy, boisterous. **Immarimbangaw dagiti agbuybuya iti ragsakda.** The spectators were boisterous in their happiness. [Tag. *ingay*]

arimbará: **agarimbara.** *v.* to be about to ripen. (*luom, darangidang*)

arimbubúkod: (f. *bukod*) **arimbubukóden**. *a.* greedy. (*managimbubukod*)

arimbukal: *n. Terminalia nitens.*

arimbukél: **arimbuklen**. *a.* not perfectly round, somewhat round; near completion.

arimbukéng: *n.* a kind of edible nocturnal shore crab; *a.* short and stocky. [Ibg. *akayaq*, Itg. *agamma*, Ivt. *cituh*, Knk. *gaki*, Kpm. *éma*, Png. *alama*, Tag. *alimango*]

arimekmék: *n.* soft noise, quiet sound; murmur. **agarimekmek**. *v.* to make a slight noise.

arimukámok: *n.* slight drizzle. **agarimukamok**. *v.* to drizzle lightly; shower. [Tag. *ambón*]

arimunúnom: see *aritemtem*: ripple (liquids).

arimungámong: *n.* junction, crossroads; intersection; adipose tissue cleaving to the small intestine. **pagaarimungamongan**. *n.* meeting place; melting pot.

arimungmóng: *n.* multitude, crowd; gathering. **agarimungmong**. *v.* to crowd, flock together, assemble, congregate; come together; encircle. **arimungmungan**. *n.* particles of fat under the skin or abdomen of swine. *v.* gather around; encircle. (*aribungbung*). **pagarimungmungan**. *n.* place of assembly. **Nagarimungmong ti pungtot iti karabukobna.** His anger built up in his throat. [Tag. *kalumpón*]

arimuran: *n.* species of tree.

arimutmót: *var.* of *sarimutmot*: glean.

arimutóng: *n.* group; gathering (*taripnong*); lump of bamboos. **agaarimutong**. *v.* to be in a group; assemble. **panagaarimutong**. *n.* gathering. **Kunam no alimbubuyogda nga aga-arimutong.** You would think they were bees gathering. [Tag. *tipon*; *libumbón*]

arimúyos: see *arinunos*: approach; draw near the end.

arimpadék: *n.* the sound of passing horses; footsteps. (*danapeg*) **agarimpadek**. to stamp, walk noisily (*tabbuga*). [Tag. *yabág*]

arimpanásan: *n.* walking to and fro; irritability. **agarimpanasan**. *v.* to be fidgety, irritable (with worries).

arimpayáng: **agarimpayang**. *v.* to totter off balance.

arimpunók: *var.* of *aripuno*: multitude, crowd.

arimpongápong: see *arimongamong*.

arin-: Prefix taking *-ak* series pronouns to indicate that the subject is about to undergo the action of the verbal stem. It may co-occur with the suffixes *-an* or *-en*. **Arintutuduen.** It is about to rain. **Ar-arimpatayanka.** You are on the verge of dying. **Arinturogen.** He seems to be about to sleep.

arinCV-: Affix used with natural phenomena indicating that they are about to or likely to take place. **tudo**. rain. **arintutuduen.** It is about to rain.

arin- -en: Affix denoting similarity or manner of the state, condition, or action specified by the root: **arintulengen**. somewhat deaf. **arimbainen**. shamefully.

arín: **agarin**. *v.* to gather, come together, assemble.

arína: (Sp. *harina*: flour) *n.* flour (*belláay*); starch. **arinaan**. *v.* to sprinkle flour on something, add flour to.

arináar: *n.* moonlight. (*aranáar*) **naarinaar**. *a.* bright (moon).

arinakáwen: *n.* a variety of awned rice.

arínat: *n. Ampeloscissus pauciflora*; *Tetrastigma harmandii* plant.

arínaw: **maarinaw**. *v.* to perceive the outline of; perceive vaguely.

arinawnáw: **arinawnawan**. *v.* to look back. (*taliaw*)

arináya: *n. Scyphiphora hydrophyllacea* plant growing in swamps and streams.

arindaráen: (f. *dara*) *a.* light red, pink, reddish. (*pangindaraen*)

arindúyog: *a.* oblong.

arinebnéb: **agarinebneb**. *v.* to dive; plunge in water. **maarinebneb**. *v.* to sink (*lumnéd*). **Dandani maarinebneb ti nalupoy a bilog gapu ta nadagsenda.** The weak outrigger almost sank because they were heavy.

arinednéd: *var.* of *arinebneb*: plunge in water.

arinkawáy: *a.* long shanked (legs or arms). (*bangkawas*)

arinkonádo: (Sp. *arrinconado*: cornered) *n.* fandango dance.

arinuán: *n.* a kind of tame bee.

arinoknók: **agarinoknok**. *v.* to pirouette; collapse from weakness. (*salungayngay*) **Naarinoknok iti lona.** He collapsed onto the floor of the ring. **Pinang-orna ket naarinoknok ti beklat.** He clubbed it and the cobra collapsed. [Tag. *lugmók*]

arinóla: *var.* of *arinola*: urinal bowl, bedpan. (*pagisbuan*)

arinúnos: *n.* the latter period of; ending part of; finale. **agarinunos**. *v.* to draw near the end of. **arinunos ti lawas**. *n.* the end of the week; weekend. [Note: some speakers use this word to designate the extremities of a season, the latter part or the beginning]

arinúor: *n.* odor; nonfragrant smell. **agarinuor**. *v.* to smell bad; diffuse (odor). [Tag. *amóy*]

arinusnós: *var.* of *arinuknók*: collapse from weakness; fall to the knees. **Agikkis koma nga agpaarayat, ngem naarinusnos.** She should have screamed for help, but she collapsed.

arinsaéd: *var.* of *rinsaed*: settlings; sediment. agarinsaed. *v.* to settle, sink (sediments, dregs). pagarinsaedan. *n.* result; outcome. [Tag. *latak*]

arinsáwad: *var.* of *alinsawad*: grope for; search by feeling.

arinsayád: *n.* lower end or trail of gown. (*saringgayad*) arinsayeden. *v.* to trail behind.

arintiddóg: *var.* of *karantiddog*: elongated.

arintúmeng: agarintumeng. *v.* to curl (eyelashes); to kneel. (*parintumeng*)

aring-: *var.* of the prefix *arin-* before the velar consonants *k*, *g*, and *ng*.

áring: agaring. *v.* to be almost similar. (*asping*) aringan. *v.* to influence. maaringan. *v.* to be influenced; to be changed (due to influence). **Naar-aringanen ti ugali ditoy Hawaii.** (Our) ways are already influenced and changed here in Hawai'i.

aringawngáw: *a.* noisy; boisterous. (*ariwawa, tagarí*)

aringgawís: *n.* treetop; high branches of a tree. naaringgawis. *a.* with long branch tips; too far out at the tip of the branch. [Tag. *dulo*]

aringgunáy: *n.* slight movement. agaringgunay. *v.* to move slightly (by the wind).

aring-íng: *n.* neighing; boisterous noise of a crowd. agaring-ing. *v.* to neigh (*garaigi*). [Tag. *halinghíng*]

aringkayám: agaringkayam. *v.* to crawl. (*karayam*)

aringkék: *n.* bull-necked.

aringkét: *var.* of *aringkek*.

aringkulotén: (f. *kulot*) *a.* somewhat curly (hair); wavy.

aringkuyót: agaringkuyot. *v.* to weigh down (loaded fishing net). **Adu nga ikan ti inaringkuyot ti iketda.** Their net was loaded down with a lot of fish.

árip: *n.* a curved knife shaped like a sickle. aripen. *v.* to slice (*iwa, galip*). [Tag. *hiwà* (slice)]

aripapá: *n.* stillness; quietness; timidity; shame. umaripapa. *v.* to be timid, shy; very quiet. **Adu ti agaripapa nga umasideg gapu iti amak a mapabainan.** Many people are shy to approach others because of fear of embarrassment. **Dikayo umaripapa a mangikabbalay iti daydiay balo a diyo inkasar?** Aren't you ashamed to live with that widow you didn't marry? [Png. *baing*, Tag. *kimî*]

aripaspás: see *kuripaspas*: struggle in pain; writhe in agony.

aríping: *a.* near, close to; beside. agariping. *v.* to stand close together. nagkaaripping. *a.* joined together. yaripping. *v.* to place close to. **Ti laeng barong a kaaripingda ti**

naulimek ita. Only the rattlesnake next to them was quiet now. [Png. *abay*, Tag. *nugnóg, lapit, tabí*]

arípit: *n.* hairpin; pliers (*ipit*); small canal (*banawang*); ditch. aripiten. *v.* to clip with a hairpin; make a small waterway. [Tag. *pangipit*]

aripunó: *n.* crowd, mass of people; large quantity. agaripuno. *v.* to throng; congregate; crowd (*taripnong*). [Tag. *kalumpón*]

aripunók: *var.* of *aripono*.

aripungsán: *n.* end; stop; cessation. agaripungsan. *v.* to be about to end. [Tag. *katapusan*]

aripusók: *n.* a very narrow place. (*akikid, lengsat*) pagaripusokan. *n.* place where something becomes narrow. [Tag. *kipot*]

aripúyot₁: *n.* muscle of the buttocks, gluteus maximus. aripuyot ti takkiag. *n.* biceps humeri of the arm.

aripúyot₂: aripuyoten. *v.* to pinch between the fingers and thumb. (*kuddot*)

ariríng: *n.* slight difference. agariring. *v.* to be very similar to each other. yariring. *v.* to compare. pagariringan. *n.* point of difference. [Tag. *halintulad* (compare)]

arirít: *a.* excellent, perfect, very fine. (*sarírit*) aririten. *v.* to do carefully.

arisadsád₁: *n.* foot, base, lowest part of something; slope. (*lansad; bakras*) agarisadsad. *v.* to form a slope; slope down. [Tag. *paanán*]

arisadsád₂: arisadsaden. *v.* to attack repeatedly (*aributantan*). aginnarisadsad. *v.* to grapple, attack each other. **Arintarayen a nangarisadsad iti padi tapno uloyannan.** He ran to attack the priest to give him his final death blow. [Tag. *daluhong*]

arisagaysáyan: *n.* mousegray; new moon (shape of a comb).

arisaksák: *n.* thrashing sound; sound of many voices. arisaksaken. *v.* to thrash, beat harshly. agarisaksak. *v.* to flounder (a fish); babble; burst (unthreshed dry beans); resound (bullets).

arisamsám: arisamsamen. *v.* to cut grass by hand and throw it aside.

arisangásang: *n.* spark; fire flake. umarisangasang. *v.* to spark (*rissik*). [Tag. *kisláp*]

arisaysáy: *n.* teardrop. agarisaysay. *v.* to flow (said of tears only). (*aglua*)

arisgá(r): umarisga, arisgaan. *v.* to do something beyond the limit of one's ability; to be diligent (*gaget*).

arisgádo: (Sp. *arriesgado*: risky) *a.* risky.

arísgo: (Sp. *riesgo*: risk) *n.* risk. naarisgo. *a.* met with an accident. yarisgo. *v.* to risk.

arisíes: agarisies. *n.* the sound of locusts; to be restless (insects).

arísit: **arisiten**. *v*. to pour off gently; decant; examine carefully; choose. **yarisit**. *v*. to pour gently into a container in order to remove the sediments from. [Tag. *tigis*]

aristokrasía: (Sp. *aristocracia*: aristocracy) *n*. aristocracy, nobility.

aristókrata: (Sp. *aristócrata*: aristocrat) *n*. aristocrat, person belonging to the nobility.

árit: **ariten**. *v*. to provoke; anger, irritate; excite; stir up; challenge; entice, tempt; move. **pangarit**. *n*. temptation; bait; bribe money. **Adun dagiti naarit nga agkameng.** Many were enticed to become members. [Tag. *buyó*]

arítag: *n*. fishing snare.

aritemtém: *n*. circular ripples on the surface of a liquid. **agaritemtem**. *v*. to ripple in rings (liquid surfaces). [Tag. *saluysóy*]

aritúer: see *aributed*: impurities (in water).

aritóndal: *n*. variety of small sweet yellow banana.

aritongtóng: *n*. *Terminalia pellucida*. **agaaritongtong**. *v*. to gather, assemble in one place.

arítos: (Sp. *arete*: earring) *n*. earrings. **agaritos**. *v*. to wear earrings. **nakaaritos**. *a*. wearing earrings. **ar-aritos**. *n*. a hairy weed with lavender flowers used in medicine, *Heliotropium indicum*. [Ibg. *sissing*, Ivt. *huvay*, Kal. *lubey*, Knk. *sengág*, Png. *íkaw*, Tag. *hikaw*]

ariwagwág: *n*. gesticulation, exaggerated movement shaking of the body when speaking (*sariwagwag* = shake; fluff); fidgeting. **agariwagwag**. *v*. to gesticulate; move hastily, fidget. **Kasta unay ti ariwagwagna.** She was excessively fidgety.

ariwáiw: *n*. species of fish.

ariwakwák₁: **umariwakwak**. *v*. to rise from a bed (the sick). **naariwakwak**. *a*. restless; wandering.

ariwakwák₂: *n*. sound made by birds or a group of chatting people. **umarikwakwak**. *v*. to be boisterous.

ariwánas: *n*. Milky Way; galaxy; group of stars, constellation. **naariwanas**. *a*. clear; bright (sky). **Awan ti ariwanas a tanda ti kaadda ti pangen ti ipon.** There was no celestial sign that there were schools of *ipon* fish (such as a cloud formation). [Knk. *aggiwánas*]

aríwat: *n*. a long vine whose fruits are used in seasoning, *Tetrastigma harmadii*, Planch.

ariwátang: *n*. crowd, multitude; large number of things. **agariwatang**. *v*. to assemble; crowd (*aripuno, taripnong*).

ariwáwa: *n*. confused speech of several people talking at the same time; outburst; (in Batak) edible frog. (*arimbángaw, aringawngaw*) **ag-**

ariwawa. *v*. to be noisy; sound (alarm clock); burst (sound). **umariwawa**. *v*. to be noisy. **Simmardengda iti panagaariwawada.** They stopped their commotion. [Kal. *atingeÿ*, Tag. *ingay*]

ariwegwég: see *ariwekwek*: abound; be plentiful. (*marway*)

ariwekwék: *n*. secluded place; hideaway. **umariwekwek**. *v*. to be plentiful, to abound, teem. (*marway*)

aríweng: see *riweng*: stunned; dazed and confused. **ariweng ti dalanna**. *a*. lost one's way. **makaariweng**. *v*. to confuse, stun. **makaariweng**. *a*. stunning, confusing. **Makaariweng dagiti taguob.** The howling was stunning. (*alimpayeng*)

ariwengwéng: *n*. buzzing sound. (*wengweng*) **agariwengweng**. *v*. to buzz.

aríwis: **mangariwis**. *v*. to hunt; fish with a baited line. [Tag. *bingwít*]

ariyakyák: *n*. chirping of birds; cackling of fowls. **umariyakyak**. *v*. to chirp (birds); to make noises (chickens). **Ariyakyakannak a kasla salaksak.** He is cackling at me like a kingfisher.

ariyamyám₁: **agariyamyam**. *v*. to squirm (lice on head).

ariyamyám₂: **iyariyamyam**. *v*. to spread, scatter; disperse over a place. (*wara*)

ariyawyáw: *n*. kind of small marine fish; meat eaten raw.

ariyesyés: *var*. of *arasíes*: squirm.

árka: (Sp. *arca*: ark) *n*. ark (Biblical).

arkabála: (Sp. *alcabala*: excise, sales tax) *n*. municipal tax paid on market merchandise.

arkás: **markas**. to become loose; loosen up. (*rekkas*)

arkéd: **agarked**. *v*. to be equal or equivalent. (*patas; pareho; patad; anatup; padpad; katitimbeng*) **mayarked**. *v*. to match, fit; correspond to; conform (*bagay*). [Tag. *katulad*]

arkeólogo: (Sp. *arqueólogo*) *n*. archaeologist.

arkilá: (Sp. *alquilar*: rent) *v*. to rent; hire. (*ábang*) **arkilado**. *a*. hired, rented.

arkilér: *var*. of *alkiler*: rent, hire.

arkitékto: (Sp. *arquitecto*: architect) *n*. architect.

arkitektúra: (Sp. *arquitectura*: architecture) *n*. architecture.

árko: (Sp. *arco*: arch) *n*. arch. (*sillók*) **agarko**. *v*. to arch. **nagarko**. *a*. arched. [Tag. *arkó*]

árkos: *n*. decoration, adornment. **arkosan**. *v*. to decorate, adorn. **yarkos**. *v*. to decorate with. **maarkosan**. *v*. to be decorated with. **arkos ti dila**. *n*. flowery expression. [Tag. *palamuti*]

arkuyanyám: (*obs*.) **agarkuyanyam**. *v*. to spread (an itch).

armáda: (Sp. *armada*: navy) *n.* the armed forces. (*buyot*)

armádo: (Sp. *armado*: armed) *a.* armed with a weapon. (*siiigam*)

ármalait: *n.* M-14 rifle; general term for machine gun. (*masinggan*)

armaménto: (Sp.) *n.* armament.

armáng: *var.* of *aramang*: small shrimp used in *bogoong*. [Png. *agamáng*, Tag. *alamáng*]

armár: (Sp.) **armaren.** *v.* to arm, provide with weapons.

ármas: (Sp. *arma*: weapon) *n.* weapons, arms. (*ígam*) **agtagiarmas.** *v.* to carry weapons, be armed. **armas ti kilabban.** *exp.* teeth.

armén: (f. *arem*) *v.* to court; woo.

Arménio: (Sp. *armenio*: Armenian) *n. a.* Armenian (*tagá-Armenia*).

armidól: *var.* of *almidor*: starch.

armistísio: (Sp. *armisticio*: armistice) *n.* armistice, cease of warfare. **agarmistisio.** *v.* to have an armistice, agree to cease warfare.

armónia: (Sp. *armonía*: harmony) *n.* harmony, sounding together of musical notes in a cord.

armónio: (Sp. *armonio*: harmonium) *n.* organ; harmonium instrument.

armosár: *var.* of *almosár*: breakfast.

arnák: **agarnak.** *v.* to wander around the yard (domestic animals).

arnáp: *var.* of *ránap*: covered evenly with.

arnás: **arnasen.** *v.* to glean (*tudtud*). [Tag. *himaláy*]

arníbal: *n.* syrup made of sugar boiled in water.

árnika: (Sp. *árnica*: arnica, wolfsbane) *n.* arnica, species of flowered herb.

arnís: *n.* native martial art of fencing. (*arnis de mano*) **kaarnis.** *v.* to fence with. **agarnis.** *v.* to fence with each other.

arngéd: *a.* beside; near; in front of; adjoining. **umarnged.** *v.* to go near, approach; to be comparable. **mayarnged.** *v.* to match, fit, suit; conform. **iti arnged.** *prep.* in front of, before. **pagarngedan.** *n.* degree of contrast; point of similarity (*arngi*; *asping*). [Tag. *sa tabí*]

arngí: see *asping*: resemblance; comparison. **umarngi.** *v.* to be similar, resemble. **agka-kaarngi.** *v.* to be similar; to resemble. **pagka-arngian.** *n.* similarity; resemblance. (*arnged*)

áro₁: **yaro.** *v.* to haul, drag; pull; trail (*ulod; guyod*). [Tag. *hila*]

áro₂: **ar-aro.** *n.* a kind of freshwater fish. **Kasla adda agkulkulipagpag nga ar-aro iti baru-kongko bayat ti panangmingmingko ken-kuana.** *exp.* It seems there are squirming fish in my chest (from excitement) when I look at her.

aró: interjection expressing cynicism. **yaro.** *v.* to goad, heckle.

aruát: *n.* personal accessories; clothes; gear. **agaruat.** *v.* to wear; use, employ. **aruaten.** *v.* to use, employ; wear; to begin, start, commence. **maaruat.** *v.* can be used, worn. **yaruat.** *v.* to use for (a certain purpose). **Naisaganakon dagiti aruatem.** I have prepared your gear. [Tag. *gamit*]

árub: **aruben.** *v.* to make over, repair, redo.

arubáka: *var.* of *erbaka*: *albahaca* plant.

arubáyan: *n.* trench formed by water falling from eaves; yard; premises; surroundings. **arubayan ti ili.** outskirts of town. **arubayan ti dalan.** wayside. **mangar-arubayan, umar-arubayan.** *v.* to be about to fall (said of tears); to loiter around the premises; trespass around. **ar-arubayan.** *n.* the front yards or backyards of neighboring houses. (*paraangan*)

arobéte: (Sp. *ribete*: trimming) *n.* neckline of a dress; strap of a chemise. (*lebleb*)

arub-ób: *n.* sipping, gulping; (*coll.*) drunkard. **arub-uben.** *v.* drink immoderately; gulp (*areb-eb*). **Nagimas man ti panagarub-obko iti digo ti manok itay pangaldaw.** It was delicious sipping the broth of the chicken for lunch.

arubuób: *n.* the first downpour after a long, hot summer; violent gust of wind; raging of the sea. **agarubuob.** *v.* to rage (ocean); blow violently (wind); rain heavily. **arubuoben.** *v.* to fumigate, smoke. **umarubuob.** *n.* violent gust of wind. **kaarubuob.** *n.* raving of the sea.

arúbos: **agarubos.** *v.* to trickle, flow (sweat, tears); unravel. **arubosan.** *v.* to unravel; expose. [Tag. *tulò*]

arudáid: *var.* of *aludaid*.

arúdok: *n.* stooped motion; secret action. **ag-arudok.** *v.* to stoop; to escape observation by stooping. **arudoken.** *v.* to attack stealthily. **ipaarudok.** *v.* to have something done stealthily. **yarudok.** *v.* to give something to someone stealthily. **Kaltaang kanon ti rabii idi sumangpet a nagar-arudok iti siledna.** They say it was midnight when he arrived and sneaked into his room.

arúg₁: *n.* dare, challenge, dare, also: *var.* of *arem*. **arugen.** *v.* to challenge; court; copulate (animals); dare. [Png. *oyot*, Tag. *hamon*]

arúg₂: **umarug.** *v.* to gather, assemble; collect.

arugá: **arugaen.** *v.* to take care of a person. (*aywan*)

arukattót: *var.* of *arakattot*: confused; scampering.

arúkong: *a.* stooping; bent. **agarukong.** *v.* to stoop while entering. **Nagarukong iti panag-turongna iti agdan.** He stooped as he directed his way to the staircase. [Tag. *yukód*]

arúkot: *agarukot.* *v.* to stoop, bend. [Tag. *yukód, hukót*]

arumádi: *n.* (*reg.*) border of a basket. (*lebleb*)

arumúom: *var.* of . *ayamuom.*

arumoy: *n. Shorea guiso.*

arún: *n.* burning firewood; dry material used to ignite a fire. **arunan.** *v.* to feed the fire; put on fire, inflame; anger (*rasok*; *rubrub*; *segged*). **pangarunan.** *n.* anything flammable used for starting a fire (*sungrod*). **Arunanyo ti siliasi sayonto paburken ti basi.** Put the pot on the fire and then boil the sugarcane wine. [Tag. *gatong*]

arúnsa: **yarunsa.** *v.* to delay, postpone.

arungáing: *n.* begging, pleading. **arungaingan.** *v.* to beg someone, implore. **yarungaing.** *v.* to express; plead, beg, implore. (*gawawa*)

arunggawís: see *aringgawis*: top; peak; summit.

arunggáy: *var.* of *maronggay*: horseradish plant whose leaves are used in cooking.

aroó: *n.* a leafless tree with oblong cones whose roots and bark are used to make medicinal tea, *Casuarina equisetifolia.* (*agoo*)

arúp: *n.* similarity. **umarup.** *v.* to resemble.

arúpag: *n.* a tree used for its timber.

aruráyan: *var.* of *arurúyan*: meowing of a cat in heat. [Tag. *ngiáw*]

aroro: *var.* of *arraro-baybay*, a species of fish.

arúrub: **aruruben.** *v.* to gulp down. (*arub-ob*)

aruruéro: *n.* Maidenhair fern, *Adiantum sp.*, used in medicine to purify the blood.

arúrog: *n.* sipping continually. **arurugen.** *v.* to sip continuously.

arurúyan: *n.* noise a cat makes while in heat. **agaruruyan.** to meow loudly and continuously (cats in heat).

árus: **arusen.** *v.* to drift, carry away (currents). **maarus.** *v.* to lag behind; be surpassed; drift away. **pakaarusan.** *n.* point of defeat. **arus-arus.** *n.* a kind of whitish June bug. **agarus-aros.** *v.* to catch *aros-aros* bugs. **Ti agsakbay, maarus pay.** *exp.* Even the one who plans ahead may end up lagging behind. [Png., Tag. *agos*]

arós: *var.* of *arrós*: rice (Sp.).

arusadánan: *n.* courtyard; front yard. (*arubayan*)

arusadúsan: *n.* landing of stairs.

arosáos: see *kiraos*: measuring cup.

arusibsíb: *n.* greedy, uncouth person. **arusibsiben.** *v.* to overuse the mouth (in eating, drinking, kissing, etc.). **No siak ni sika, nabayagen nga inarusibsibko ni Perla.** If I were you, I would have been heavily into Perla for a long time already.

arusíes: see *arasies*: *n.* mollusk; **agarusies.** *v.* squirm; wiggle.

arusíp: *n. Antidesma ghaesembilla* tree with panicled spikes and small, white flowers. **ar-arusip.** *n.* a kind of clustering seaweed.

arosít: *n. Fluggea virosa* plant. (*barusík*)

aroskáldo: (Sp. *arroz caldo*: rice broth) *n.* rice porridge with chicken broth and ginger. (*lugaw*)

arus-ós: *agarus-os.* *v.* to slide down.

árot: **maarutan.** *v.* to be ravaged, deprived of everything; lose leaves (plants); fall out (hair). (*urot*); lose vigor, vitality. **maarutan ti dara.** hemorrhage.

arutáit: *n.* small strips of wood.

arutáng: *n.* bundle of degrained rice straws used to make shampoo; rice stalk. (*garami*)

áruy: **aruyen.** *v.* to pull, drag, haul. **ar-aruyen.** *v.* to do gradually (in degrees of difficulty). **aruyan.** *n.* rope for carrying things; rattan ring where the spindle of the spinning wheel rests. **pangaruyanan.** *n.* wooden peg that the *aruyan* of the spinning wheel is attached to. [Tag. *hila*]

arúyot: *n.* gush, spurt. **agaruyot.** *v.* to gush out, flow out; ooze. (*arubos*) **paaruyotan.** *v.* to drain, empty. **mangaruyot.** *v.* to be numerous, to abound. **agaruyot a dara.** *n.* bloodshed. **Agar-aruyoten ti dara iti takkiagko.** The blood is already gushing out of my arm. [Tag. *tulò*]

aruy-óy: *n.* hanging decoration; medallion; species of plant whose flowers hang towards the ground. **Insublina ti panagkitana iti sirok ti bato a pagar-aruy-oyan ti lumot.** He looked again under the stone from which moss was hanging.

árpa: (Sp. *arpa*: harp) *n.* harp.

arpád: *n.* side of (*denna*, *abay*). **umarpad.** *v.* to come to the side; to be comparable. **makiarpad.** *v.* to stand at the side; go to the side. **mayarpad.** *v.* to be at the side of, alongside. **yarpad.** *v.* to compare; place alongside. **awan arpadna.** *exp.* it has no comparison. **iti arpad.** in the midst of, among. **Maragsakanka kadi iti kaaddada iti arpadta?** Are you happy that they are at our side? [Png. *ábay*, Tag. *paligid*]

arpád₂: *n.* a kind of vine used in medicine.

arpáp: *a.* not being able to see at night, *var.* of *korarap.*

arpáw: *n.* temporary cover or shield. **arpawan.** *v.* to cover. (*sarpaw*, *kalub*) **yarpaw.** *v.* to cover with, use as a cover. [Tag. *sapaw*]

arrá: see *ara*: Interjection used to drive away animals.

arrabál: (Sp. *arrabal*: suburb) *n.* suburb.

arrábas: *n.* a kind of destructive two-inch worm; *var.* of *arrabis*: diagonal cut. **mangarrabas, arrabasen.** *v.* to cut imperfectly or diagonally.

arrabís: (Sp. *al reves*: reverse) *n.* backhanded slap; spank; diagonal cut. **arrabisen.** *v.* to slap; spank (*sipat*). **iti paarrabis.** diagonally.

arráp: see *kurarap*: with bad eyesight. **agarrap.** *v.* to be blinded by light; to be short-sighted. **Arrapen ti baket no kastoy a nasipnget.** The old woman is short of sight when it is this dark. [Knk. *buligawgáw*, *kóap*, *kudap-éng* (myopic), Tag. *silaw* (dazzled by bright light)]

arráro: *n.* climbing perch fish, *Anabas testudineus*. **arraro-baybay.** *n.* rock pilot fish of the *Pomacentridae* family.

arráste: (Sp. *arrastre*: drag) *n.* the act of playing a lower card in order to make an opponent play a higher card that the opponent will lose to the partner of the player with the lower card. **agarraste.** *v.* to deceive an opponent by having him play a high card that he will lose.

arráyan: (Sp. *arrayán*: myrtle field) *n.* myrtle shrub with fragrant white flowers and aromatic berries.

arréglo: (Sp. *arreglo*: arrangement) *n.* arrangement. (*urnos*)

arróba: (Sp. *arroba*: arroba) *n.* twenty-five pounds.

arrós: (Sp. *arroz valenciana*: Valencian rice) **arros balensiana.** *n.* paella, dish made of cooked rice colored with *atsuete* and various bits of meat, eggs, vegetables, seafood, beans and raisins. **arroskaldo.** *n.* chicken rice porridge.

arsáb: *n.* glutton, voracious eater. (*ráwet*, *antukab*) **naarsab.** *a.* gluttonous. [Tag. *takaw*]

arsád: *n.* bottom of something. **arsadanan.** *n.* base of something, threshold; foot of a mountain (*sakaanan*).

arsagíd: *a.* sensitive. **nagarsagid.** *a.* sensitive, touchy, easily hurt. **kinaarsagid.** *n.* sensitiveness, sensitivity.

arsáman: *n.* the pulp of the *damortis*. [Tag. *kamatsile*]

arsáng: *n.* ashes at the end of a cigarette. **arsangan.** *v.* to snuff a candle; remove the ash of a cigarette. **naarsang.** *a.* with a lot of ashes. **yarsang.** *v.* to knock down cigarette ashes. **pagarsangan.** *n.* ashtray. [Tag. *abó*]

ársaw: **yarsaw.** *v.* to rinse haphazardly (fruits). [Tag. *hugas*]

arsenáto: *n.* kind of poison. (*arsinit*)

arséniko: (Sp. *arsénico*) *n.* arsenic.

arsísio: (Sp. *ejercisio*: exercise) *n.* training drill, exercise. (*watwat*) **agarsisio.** *v.* to perform a drill, exercise.

arsép: *n. var.* of *arosíp* tree.

arsinít: *n.* rat poison. **arsiniten.** *v.* to poison with *arsinit*.

arsobíspo: *n.* archbishop. **arsobispado.** *n.* archbishopric.

artá: *reg. var.* of *addayta*: there it is.

arták: **umartak.** *v.* to compete, have a contest with (*batara*; *balubal*; *dayondayo*; *pasil*; *salisal*; *salip*). [Tag. *sali*]

artáp: **artapan.** *v.* to do better; surpass; outdo; go a step further. **umartap.** *v.* to go down, descend. (*reg.*) *var.* of *artak*. **maartapan.** *v.* to outdo, surpass. **aginnartap.** *v.* to compete with one another. (*salisal*) **Mangngegna ti aginnartap nga urokda nga aggapu kadagiti siled.** He hears their competing snores coming from the rooms. **Iti agdama, awan makaartap iti kabaelanna.** At present, nobody can outdo what she can do. [Tag. *daíg*, *higít*]

árte: (Sp. *arte*: art) *n.* art; skill; role of an actor (*papel*). **naarte.** *a.* stylish; artistic; refined; see *maarte*. **maarte.** (Tagalog also, *coll.*) artificial in manners, insincere. **Kolehio ti Artes Liberales.** College of Liberal Arts.

arték: *n.* drunkard. (*bartek*, *mamartek*)

artém: *n.* pickle. **artemen.** *v.* to pickle. (*paksiw*; *atsara*) **pagartem.** *n.* marinade used for pickling. **naartem.** *a.* pickled. [Tag. *atsara*]

arténg: see *parteng*, *banteng*: line; cord.

artesiáno: (Sp. *artesiano*: pump well) *n.* pump well, also *poso artesiano*. (*poso*)

artikulánte: (f. Old Spanish *articulante*: articulate) *a.* articulate; talkative, loquacious.

artíkulo: (Sp. *artículo*: article) *n.* article.

artiók: *n.* clownish person. **artiokan.** *v.* to tease; make fun of; heckle. **aartiokan.** *n.* easily flattered person, someone who easily gives in to requests or demands.

artipisiál: (Eng.) *a.* artificial. (*parbo*; *peke*)

artísta: (Sp. *artista*: artist) *n.* actor, actress; artist. **artista ti pelikula.** *n.* movie star.

artók: see *aliug*: flattery. **agartok.** (*reg.*) *v.* to walk for the first time.

artóy: *reg. var.* of *addaytoy*: here it is.

artsíbo: (Sp. *archivo*) *n.* archive. **yartsibo.** *v.* to archive, deposit in the archives.

artyók: **artyoken.** *v.* to provoke, incite, tease. (*suron*; *pídas*; *sutil*; *dúrog*)

arwát: **arwaten.** *v.* to use, to wear (*aruat*). [Tag. *gamit*]

ása: **asaen.** *v.* to grind, whet; polish, burnish; chafe; study; learn. **ipaasa.** *v.* to have a blade sharpened with a honing stone. **mangngasa.** *n.* knife sharpener. **pangasaan.** *n.* whetstone; oilstone; hone. **Pamrayanda metten ti agkape**

no kasdiay nga agas-asada. They just have coffee when they grind blades like that. [Ibg. *iteq*, Ivt. *tadmen*, Knk. *pálid*, Kpm. *táis*, Png. *oból*, Tag. *hasà*]

asáas: agasaas. *v.* to learn, study. **asaasen.** *v.* to learn thoroughly; to repeat; to chafe the groin; study. [Tag. *pagaralan*]

asabátse: (Sp. *azabache*: jet) *n.* black and shiny (horse).

asád: *n.* a rake; pitchfork. **asadan.** *v.* to till; make holes with the *asad* in which to plant seeds. **as-asad.** *n.* a wickerwork trap for mudfish. **agasad.** *v.* to prepare ground for planting, putting holes in the ground for seedlings or raking. [Png. *kalaykay, kaladkad,* Tag. *kalaykay, asaról*]

asádo: (Sp. *asado*: roasted) *n.* meat roasted with salt, vinegar, and lemon juice; *a.* roasted. **yasado.** *v.* to roast something. **asador.** *n.* spit used for roasting. **agasado.** *v.* to roast, fry (meat).

asadór: (Sp.) *n.* spit for roasting. **yasador.** *v.* to roast on a spit. **agasador.** *v.* to use spits in roasting.

asahár: (Sp. *azahar*: orange blossom) *n.* orange blossoms worn by brides.

asák: asaken. *v.* to pass between; make one's way through. **maasak.** *v.* to be passable. **agasak-asak.** *v.* to stampede. **Masapul nga asakem lattan ti karuotan.** You have to just make your way through the grass field.

asálto: (Sp. *asalto*: assault) *n.* assault; surprise attack (*duklos*); surprise party. **asaltuan.** *v.* to assault.

asambléa: (Sp. *asamblea*: assembly) *n.* assembly.

asánas: maasanas. *v.* to be abraded, chafed, worn down by friction. [Tag. *gasgás*]

asanória: (Sp. *zanahoria*: carrot, *obs.*) *n.* carrot.

ásang: *n.* gill; glands inside the throat. **naasang.** *a.* gilled; with sharp gills. [Ibg. *átang, barangasang,* Ifg. *hípe,* Ivt. *arang,* Kpm., Png. *ásang,* Tag. *hasang*]

asáng: *n.* term of address given by elders to a young girl. [Tag. *ineng*]

asaprán: (Sp. *azafrán*: saffron) *n.* saffron.

ásar: see *kiléb*: fish trap.

asár: (Sp. *asar*: roast) **asaren.** *v.* to roast. (*tuno*) **inasar.** *n.* roasted or barbecued meat. **maka-asar.** *a.* (*coll.*) irritating, disgusting. [Tag. *ihaw*]

as-ás: *n.* dry leaves. (*alas-as*) **as-asen.** *v.* to pound a second time. **as-asan.** *v.* to polish by rubbing. [Tag. *dahong tuyô*]

asáwa: [pl. *assawa*] *n.* spouse, husband, wife; one part of a pair; counterpart, match. **agasawa.** *v.* to get married. **agassawa.** *n.* husband and wife. **apagasawa.** *a.* newlywed. **asawaen.** *v.* to wed, marry someone; sexually assault; copulate. **kaasawa.** *v.* to get married to. **mangasawa.** *v.* to marry (men). **makiasawa.** *v.* to marry (women). **mangyasawa.** *v.* to marry off one's daughter. **pangasawa.** *n.* dowry. **sangapagasawaan.** *n.* married couple, pair. **pangasawaan.** *n.* reason for getting married; place where a man will get married. **pakiasawaan.** *n.* the person someone will marry. **yasawa.** *v.* to marry off. **siaasawa.** *a.* married (*kasado*). **pakaasawaan.** *n.* place where one will get married. **Agkaasawaanda.** They are suitable for each other. **Adun ti nadamagtayo nga agassawa a nagsina gapu laeng iti bassit a di panagkinnaawatan.** We heard a lot of reports of married couples separating just because of a slight misunderstanding. [Ibg. *atáwa,* Ifg. *inayan,* Ivt. *kakuvut,* Knk. *desán,* Png. *asawá,* Knk., Kpm., Tag. *asawa*]

asbáng: *var.* of *isbáng*: plan, scheme.

asébo: (Sp. *acebo*: holly) *n.* holly.

asél: aslen. *v.* to dread, fear; distrust. (*buteng*)

aseleradór: (Sp. *acelerador*: accelerator) *n.* accelerator.

asembléa: (Sp. *asamblea*: assembly) *n.* assembly (*asamblea, ummong, tipon*). **asembleado.** *a.* assembled.

asendéra: (Sp. *hacendera*: lady estate owner) *n.* lady estate owner; the wife of an estate owner.

asendéro: (Sp. *hacendero*: estate owner) *n.* estate owner; owner of a large amount of land or plantation; landlord.

asénso: (Sp. *asenso*: credit) *n.* advancement; promotion. **umasenso.** *v.* to improve (conditions of life). **asensado.** *a.* promoted; advanced; *n.* someone who has become rich or improved his social standing.

asensór: (Sp. *ascensor*: elevator) *n.* elevator.

asénta: (Sp. *asentar*: affirm; settle; set up) **agasenta.** *v.* go into the correct position. **yasenta.** *v.* to adjust; set up. **asentado.** *n.* sharpshooter.

asentáda: (Sp. *asentar*: fix, lay down; hone) *n.* structure of hollow blocks; the layer of mortar between hollow blocks.

asentádo: (Sp. *asentar*) *n.* sharpshooter, person who aims well.

asentár: (Sp. *sentar*: sit; *asentar*: fix, lay down; hone) **agasentar.** *v.* to be alert, quick; sit up straight; stand erect. **asentaran.** *v.* to pay attention to, be attentive to. **naasentar.** *a.* attentive.

asép: *n.* perfume; fragrance; incense; beauty; elegance; renown. **aspan.** *v.* to perfume. (*pabanglo*) **naasep.** *a.* fragrant; renowned; elegant. [Tag. *bangó*]

aséro: (Sp. *acero*: steel) *n.* steel (*paslep*); point of a ballpoint pen. **aserado.** *a.* made of steel. **agasero.** *v.* to use a pen.

áses: (Eng.) *n.* ace in cards (*alas*). **umases.** *v.* to be a political candidate.

aséte: *var.* of *asiete*: oil. **asetera.** *n.* oil can.

asetisísmo: (Sp. *ascetismo*: asceticism) *n.* asceticism, life of an ascetic; extreme self-denial.

asetúna: (Sp. *aceituna*: olive) *n.* pickles. (*atsara*)

ási: *n.* mercy, compassion; charity; clemency. **kaasi.** *n.* pity, mercy, compassion; charity. **kakaasi.** *a.* having hardships; pitiful. **nakakakaasi.** *a.* pitiful. **nakaasi.** *a.* merciful, kind. **ikakaasi.** *v.* to do something for someone as an act of mercy. **asi pay.** woe to. **maasian.** *v.* to have pity; have mercy on someone. **naasi.** *a.* compassionate, charitable, merciful. **kumakaasi.** *v.* to beg, plead for mercy. **kumakaasian.** *n.* person to whom one begs for mercy. **asinto.** (*obs.*) woe to. **agpakpakaasi.** *v.* to ask for pity or a favor, to humbly request. **Ipakpakaasik kenka.** I have a favor to ask of you. **kinamanangngaasi.** *n.* compassion. **makikakaasi.** *v.* to implore, plead; ask for pity and understanding. **Kakaasiak.** Poor me (I have suffered much). **pangngaasi.** please. **pangngasian.** *n.* reason for pitying. **ipakaasi.** *v.* to plead, beg for mercy. **pakákaási.** *v.* to implore, beseech. **pakakaasian.** *n.* reason for being pitied. **balay ti kaasi.** *n.* charitable institution. **Pangngaasim ta saanmo a rakraken ti biagko.** Please do not destroy my life. [Bon. *seg-ang*, Ibg. *kabbiq*, *abbíq*, Ifg. *hómok*, Ivt., Png. *kási*, Knk. *seg-áng*, *bey*, *sóag*, Kpm. *lúnus*, Tag. *awà*]

así: see *asiasí*.

asiáb: **umasiab.** *v.* to inflame; burn; get angry; flee from danger. [Tag. *liyáb*]

asi-así: (Sp. *así así*: so so) *a.* of low class; not of good quality; bogus; not genuine; untidy. **asiasien.** *v.* to do haphazardly; to belittle. [Tag. *wardi-wardí*]

asíbay: *var.* of *assibay*: beside.

asidég: *n.* vicinity, *a.* near. **agasideg.** *a.* close, intimate. **agassideg.** *v.* to be close to one another; (*fig.*) to be intimate. **umasideg.** *v.* to approach, come near. **kaasitgan.** *a.* nearest; closest. **yasideg.** *v.* to put close to; bring within reach. **assitgan.** *a.* giving birth yearly; *v.* to happen at very close intervals. **assitgen.** *v.* to plant at close intervals. **kaasideg.** *n.* distance; proximity. **kaasideg.** *n.* distance, proximity. **kinaasideg.** *n.* proximity. **maasidegan.** *v.* to be able to go near. **makapaginnasideg.** *v.* to be near one another. **pangasidegén.** *a.* a bit near. [Ibg. *arenni*, Itg. *adanni*, Ivt. *asngen*, Kal.

achali, Knk. *anggéy*, *tudadá*, *sagulát*, *sag-én*, Png. *asinggér*, Tag. *lapit*]

ásido: (Sp. *ácido*: acid) *n.* acid. **naasido.** *a.* acidic. **yasido.** *v.* to dip in acid. **asido burikada.** boric acid. **asido moriatiko.** muriatic acid. **asido nitriko.** nitric acid. **asido silisiko.** silicic acid. **asido solporiko.** sulphuric acid.

asiénda: (Sp. *hacienda*: estate) *n.* plantation; estate; large tract of land consisting of a landlord (*asendero*) and workers. **asiendero.** *n.* plantation owner; landlord of a large estate.

asiéte: (Sp. *aceite*: oil) *n.* cooking oil. **agasiete.** *v.* to use oil. **asiete de bakalaw.** *n.* cod liver oil. **asiete de alkamporado.** *n.* camphorated oil. **asiete de mansanilia.** *n.* chamomile oil.

ásig: (*obs.*) *n.* appreciating.

asignatúra: (Sp. *asignatura*: subject) *n.* subject in school.

asikalláw: **agasikallaw.** *v.* to wander aimlessly (*ballog*). [Tag. *lagalág*]

Asikapay!: Interjection. Woe to you!

asikáso: (Sp. *hace caso*: pay attention) **asikasuen.** *v.* to pay attention to; take good care of; handle; finish (*taripato*; *pangag*). [Knk. *esét*, Tag. *asikaso*]

asimbúyok: *n.* smoke; fume. (*asuk*) **agasimbuyok.** *v.* to smoke. **pagasimbuyokan.** *n.* chimney. (*tambutso*) [Png. *aséwek*, Tag. *usok*, *asó*]

asín₁: *n.* salt (salty is *naapgád*). **pagasinan.** *n.* salt cellar; salt marsh. **asinan.** *v.* to add salt to. **agasin.** *v.* to use salt with food. **awan as-asin ti kulot.** *exp.* denoting something not honorable. **managasin.** *a.* fond of salty food. **awan as-asin ti panagsasaona.** *exp.* disrespectful and blunt talk; talk without substance. [Ibg., Ivt., Kal., Kpm., Png., Tag. *asín*, Ifg. *ahin*, Knk. *agít*]

asín₂: *contr.* of *asino*: who.

asíno: *interrog.* Who? (*sino*) **uray asino.** no matter who. **asino man.** whoever; anyone. **Awan kalinteganna a manpapanaw iti asino man ditoy a balay.** He has no right to have anyone leave this house. [Ibg. *sinni*, Knk. *sinó*, Png. *siópa*, Bon., Tag. *sino*]

asinúso: see *assinúso*.

asintár: **agasintar.** *v.* to get ready. (*rubbuat*)

ásing: **naasing.** *a.* harsh, cruel, bullying. (*dawel*; *ulpit*; *ranggas*) **asingan.** *v.* to think bad of someone; cast a spell; look at someone with the evil eye. **agasing.** *v.* to make faces, make grimaces. **mangasing.** *v.* to look with the evil eye. **maasingan.** *v.* to be influenced by bad company (*guyyó*); to be under an evil spell.

asipakpák: *n.* fragrance; aroma; fame due to beauty. (*asep*) **agasipakpak.** *v.* to spread fragrance; be renowned. **naasipakpak.** *a.* fragrant; renowned (*banglo*). [Tag. *bangó*]

asísaw: *var.* of *assisaw*: roam.

asisténsia: (Sp. *asistencia*) *n.* attendance; attendance card; assistance.

asistír: **asistiran.** *v.* to attend to; be present at; assist. **naasistir.** *a.* frequently attending.

asíte: *var.* of *asiete*: oil.

asitgán: *v.* [*asideg* + *-an*] *v.* to go close to, approach. **kaasitgan.** *a.* closest.

asíwar: **asiwaren.** *v.* to search for, explore (*sawar*); consider carefully; examine. **Inasiwar ti panunotna no asino a kabagianna ti nangisurat kenkuana iti aramidna.** He pondered in his mind which relative wrote her as to what he did.

askáw: *n.* stride; big step. (*addang*) **agaskaw.** *v.* to straddle. (*akkang*; *kayang*; *pakkang*; *baddakaw*; *sakkang*) **askawen.** *v.* to go over in one big step; step over. **Inrugina ti nagaskaw a rummuar iti simbaan.** He started to leave the church in big strides. [Tag. *hakbáng*]

áskay: **askayen.** *v.* to patrol; reconnoiter.

askuéte: *var.* of *atsuete*: annatto.

askól: **maaskol.** *v.* to meet by chance. (*agrana*; *askul*; *tummo*)

aslég: *n.* timidity; bashfulness (*madleg*, *sileg*). [Tag. *hiyâ*]

asmá: (Sp. *asma*) *n.* asthma (*angkit*). **agkara-asma.** *v.* to have frequent asthma attacks.

asmáng: *n.* partner; companion; counterpart. **kaasmang.** *n.* counterpart; partner, companion; teammate. **agasmang.** *v.* to team together. **naasmangan.** *v.* to go well together. **yasmang.** *v.* to pair; match. **sangaasmang.** *n.* one pair; one couple. **Insuotna ti kamisa nga inasmanganna iti maong a pantalon.** He put on his shirt that went well with his denim pants. [Tag. *pareha*]

asmátiko: (Sp. *asmático*) *a.* asthmatic.

asmeríl: (Sp. *esmeril*) *n.* emery. **de-asmeril.** smoked glass.

asnó: (Sp. *asno*: ass) *n.* donkey.

asngáw: *n.* vapor; steam (*sengngaw*); visible breath in the cold; emission; barely inaudible words emitted from the mouth. **agasngaw.** *v.* to steam, vaporize; steam up; emit. [Tag. *asngáw* = smell of liquor]

asngí: see *asping*: resemblance.

áso₁: *n.* dog, canine. **asuen.** *v.* to be attacked by dogs. **Di malamut ti aso ti saona.** The dog can't eat his words (referring to insincere talk). **asosena.** *n.* dish of dog meat. **mangngaso.** *n.* person fond of eating dogs. **aso-aso.** *n.* henchman of a politician. [Ibg. *kítu*, Ifg. *áhu*, Ivt. *cituq*, Png. *asó*, Kal., Kpm., Tag. *aso*]

áso₂: **yaso.** *v.* to match; urge, incite (*sulisog*, *sugsóg*); instigate; prod. **Agsasaruno dagiti**

nagannak a mangyaso kadagiti babbaroda. The parents one by one matched up their bachelors.

asuáng: (Tag.) *n.* evil mythological demon.

asúd: **agasud.** *v.* to help one another pounding rice. **pagaasudan.** *v.* to work together. [Tag. *makipagbayó*]

asuéro: *var.* of *suero*: serum; dextrose.

asuéte: *var.* of *atsuete*: annatto.

ásug: *n.* complaint; entreaty. **agasug.** *v.* to moan; complain; beg, entreat, plead; pray. **yasug.** *v.* to complain about; petition. [Tag. *daíng*]

asóge: (Sp. *azogue*: mercury) *n.* magnet, magnetic power (*batumbalani*); mercury.

asók: *n.* smoke, steam, vapor. (*sengngaw*) **agasok.** *v.* to smoke, steam. **naasok.** *a.* smoky, steamy. **paasukan.** *v.* to fumigate. (*suob*) **pagasukan.** *n.* chimney. **ipaasuk.** *v.* to smoke something, fumigate. **agpakaasukán.** *v.* to stay in the smoke. **Kasla asok a nagpukaw.** He disappeared like smoke. **Kasla umas-asok ti aglawlaw gapu iti pigsa ti tudo.** It seems to be smoking around because of the strong rain. [Ibg. *atuq*, Ivt. *ahub*, Kpm. *asuk*, Png. *aséwek*, Tag. *asó*, *usok*]

asúkar: (Sp. *azúcar*: sugar) *n.* sugar. **managasukar.** *a.* sweet toothed, fond of using sugar. **naasukaran.** *a.* sprinkled with sugar. [Kal. *intí*, Knk. *intí*, Tag. *asukal*]

asukaréra: (Sp. *azucarera*: sugar refinery; sugar bowl) *n.* sugar bowl; sugar refinery.

asukaréro: (Sp. *azucarero*: sugar merchant) *n.* sugar merchant, dealer in sugar.

asúl: (Sp. *azul*: blue) *a.* blue. (*balbág*)

asulého: (Sp. *azulejo*: tile) *n.* blue-glazed floor tile.

asúnto: (Sp. *asunto*: matter) *n.* lawsuit; affair, business. **yasunto.** *v.* to file a court case.

asúngot: *n.* tag along, person who follows a group although he is not necessarily welcome.

asúpre: (Sp. *azufre*: sulfur) *n.* sulfur. **agat-asupre.** *v.* to smell like sulfur. [Kpm. *ubát*]

asoséna: (*aso* + Spanish *cena*: dinner) (*coll.*) *n.* dog meat.

asuséna: (Sp. *azucena*: white lily) *n.* white lily.

ásut: **asuten.** *v.* to unsheathe; take out of one's pocket. **agasut.** *v.* to take a deep breath, sigh; exclaim. **aginnasut.** *v.* to draw a weapon at each other. **asutan.** *v.* to draw (a gun, etc.) at someone. [Tag. *bunot*]

asutár: (Sp. *azotar*: whip) **asutaren.** *v.* to whip, flog. (*baut*, *saplit*)

asútea: *n.* second-story balcony; roofless veranda over the porch. **agpaasutea.** *v.* to go to the balcony.

aspálto: (Sp. *asfalto*: asphalt) *n.* asphalt. **aspaltado.** *a.* asphalted.

asperína: (Sp. *aspirina*: aspirin) *n.* aspirin. **agasperina.** *v.* to take aspirin.

aspéto: (Sp. *aspecto*) *n.* aspect.

aspíki: *n.* lever, pry. (*suag*; *battuil*) **aspikien.** *v.* to pry with a lever.

aspilí: (Sp. *alfiler*: pin) *n.* pin, straight pin. [Kal. *ispili*, Tag. *aspilí*]

aspíng: umasping. *v.* to resemble. **yasping.** *v.* to compare with. **kaasping.** *n.* one's likeness, something that is similar. **pakayaspingan.** *n.* comparison; likeness; resemblance. **umasasping.** *a.* comparable, resembling. [Tag. *katulad*]

aspiránte: (Sp. *aspirante*: aspiring) *a.* aspiring (politician, etc.). **agaspirante.** *v.* to aspire for, vie for; compete for (a political position).

assád: *n.* base; bottom. (*arsad*)

assáwa: pl. of *asawa*: spouses. **agassawa.** *v.* to be husband and wife.

assáway: (*obs.*) *n.* doubt. (*duadua*)

assí: Interjection expressing disgust. (*aysi*)

assiáy: Interjection expressing disgust and wonder.

assíbay: *prep.* near; close; alongside; by the side of. (*abay*) **agassibay.** *v.* to put the arm on another's shoulder. **assibayan.** *v.* to stay by the side of. **umassibay.** *v.* to stay around; be at hand; put the arm around. **mangassibay.** *v.* to court. **yassibay.** *v.* to put or bring beside. **umas-assibay.** *v.* to loiter, hang out; stay near. [Tag. *tabí*]

assidég: see *asideg*: near.

assinúso: (f. *suso*) **agassinuso.** *v.* to be infantile; immature; young; (*lit.* still suckling).

assísaw: *n.* reconnaissance, examining a certain place; wandering. **agas-assisaw.** *v.* to roam around, wander, stroll; examine; reconnoiter. **managassisaw.** *n.* vagabond. **Di met adda agas-assisaw a buaya idiay?** Aren't there crocodiles roaming there?

assitgén: see *asideg*: near.

assíw: *n.* pole used to carry loads on the shoulder. **assiwan.** *v.* to carry a load with a pole. **panginnassiwan.** *n.* pole used to carry a load between two persons. **Kabaelanna ti agassiw ti dua a lata ti danum a pagsibog iti minuyonganna.** He is able to carry two cans of water on a pole over his shoulder to use to water his garden. [Tag. *pingga*]

assíwar: agassiwar. *v.* to wander, roam around.

astáy: see *istay*: almost (*dandani*). [Tag. *halos*]

astít: (*coll.*) **nakaas-astit.** *a.* overjoyed; glad; delighted.

astrólogo: (Sp. *astrólogo*: astrologer) *n.* astrologer.

astrolohía: (Sp. *astrología*: astrology) *n.* astrology.

astronomía: (Sp. *astronomía*: astronomy) astronomy, the study of the universe.

astrónomo: (Sp. *astrónomo*) *n.* astronomer.

astronóto: (Eng.) *n.* astronaut.

áta₁: *conj.* since, whereas (*yata*).

áta₂: *n.* unripeness; rawness. **naata.** *a.* immature, unripe, raw; not thoroughly cooked. **ata-ata.** *n.* raw meat. [Ibg. *náta*, Ivt. *mátaq*, Kpm. *sagíwa*, Png. *eta*, Tag. *hilaw*]

atáat₁: ataatan. *v.* to lessen, diminish (*kissáy*); slacken, relax (*lukáy*). **saan nga ataatan.** *v.* to maintain the pressure without letting up. [Tag. *hinà*]

atáat₂: naataat. *a.* bitter (*napait*); sour (*naalsem*).

atáat₃: ataatan. *v.* to whip moderately, beat; attack; kill trees by girdling.

ata-áta: *n.* raw meat. (*kilaw*)

atáb: *n.* flood tide, high tide; flow. (ant. *úgot*) **umatab.** *v.* to rise (body of water). **agatab.** *v.* to rise (said of the tide). **panagaatab.** *n.* seasonal high tide. **Talaga a malayustayo no sumabat ti atab ti baybay.** We will really flood if the high tide of the ocean meets us.

atáday₁: yataday. *v.* to adjust; conform; fit. **agkaataday.** *v.* to be suitable; fit each other. **pannakayataday.** *n.* conformity. [Tag. *bagay*]

atáday₂: *n.* delay, postponement. **yataday.** *v.* to delay, postpone. (*tantan*)

atádo: (Sp. *atado*: tied) *n.* bundle, bunch; parcel. **sangaatado.** *n.* one bundle; one bunch (of things sold in the market). **ataduen.** *v.* to divide into equal bundles.

átag: agatag. *v.* to lie down in pairs (animals, young children). **atagen.** *v.* to lie by the side of. **yatag.** *v.* to lay down in pairs, or alongside each other.

atakár: (Sp. *atacar*) **atakaren.** *v.* to attack.

atákay: *n. Coix sp.* plant.

atáke: (Sp. *ataque*: attack) *n.* attack. (*duklós*) **umatake.** *v.* to attack; have an attack. **atake ti puso.** *n.* heart attack. **maatake.** *v.* to be attacked.

átal: *n.* roller for moving heavy objects. **paatalan.** *v.* to run over. **naatalan.** *a.* run over by a roller, run-over. [Tag. *gulong*]

atánud: *n.* term used interchangeably between the godparents of one's children and the parents who chose them. [Png. *astanor*]

átang: *n.* food offered to the dead. (*paniáng*) **yatang.** *v.* to offer food to the dead. **payatangan.** *v.* to have food offered to the dead (by an *herbulario*, quack doctor, etc.). [Kal. *pusik*, Png. *átang*, Tag. *alay*; *atang* = placing load on someone else's head or shoulder; Ivt. *atang* = buttock]

atáng: umatang. *v.* to quit; withdraw; cease; retreat. (*lusulos*) **atangen.** *v.* to pull out a nail, etc. [Tag. *tigil*]

atángay: see *yata*: since; whereas. ((*an*)*tangay*).

átap₁: *n.* suspicion, misgivings, doubt. **naatap.** *a.* savage, wild; suspicious. **atapen.** *v.* to suspect. **managatap.** *a.* suspicious. **Adda atapko nga isuda met laeng.** I have a hunch that it was them. [Png. *átap, ínap*, Tag. *hinalà*]

atáp₂: *n.* wedge (*sanat, tingal*). [Tag. *kalsó*]

átar: **ataren.** *v.* to level a new rice field.

at-át: **agat-at.** *v.* to diminish; lessen; lose (strength, smile, etc.); lessen the pressure; go easy. **at-atan.** *v.* to maintain the pressure. (*ataat*)

átay: **atayen.** *v.* to divide, apportion, share.

ateísmo: (Sp. *ateísmo*: atheism) *n.* atheism.

ateísta: (Eng., Hispanicized from *ateismo*) *n.* atheist. (*ateo*)

átel: *n.* someone who speaks imperfectly (changing the *r* into *l*). **agatel.** *v.* to speak imperfectly.

atendér: (Eng.) **atenderen.** *v.* to attend. **na-atender.** *a.* attentive.

atendído: *a.* paying attention to, interested. **agatendido.** *v.* to pay attention to. (*asikaso*)

atenéo: (Sp. *ateneo*) *n.* athenaeum.

aténto: (Sp. *atento*: attentive) *n.* attentive. (*asikaso*)

atéo: (Sp. *ateo*: atheist) *n.* atheist.

atép: *n.* roof, roofing. **agatep.** *v.* to build a roof; thatch (*agsit, bubóng*). **aatepan.** *a.* scheduled to be roofed. **atapan.** *v.* to put a roof on. **yatep.** *v.* to use as roofing. **pagatep.** *n.* roofing materials. [Ibg. *vuvvung, atóp*, Itg. *palsa, atep*, Ivt., Png. *atép*, Kal. *otop, tabongan*, Kpm. *bumbúngan*, Tag. *atíp, bubong*]

atí₁: *n.* low tide. **agati.** *v.* to ebb; subside; abate. [Tag. *kati* (low tide)]

atí₂: **agat-ati.** *v.* to dry up. (*atian; maga*)

atián: **naatianan.** *a.* dried out, evaporated (said of an exhausted supply of liquid). **atianan.** *v.* to dry out. **paatianan.** *v.* to drain. **Awan ti bubon nga saan a maatianan.** *exp.* There is no well that does not dry up. [Tag. *tuyô*]

ati-atíhan: (Tag.) *n.* festival in Panay celebrating the Aeta tribes, formerly the war dance of the Aetas.

atibangráw: umatibangraw. *v.* to hum; buzz; croak (crows). [Tag. *hugong, ugong*]

atíbay: atibayen. *v.* to assist; help; aid. (*tulong*) **atibayan** (*obs.*) *v.* to equalize loads. **Inasitgak tapno atibayek ngem inwadagnak.** I ap-

proached to help him but he threw me aside. [Tag. *tulong*]

atibelbél: *n.* attacking in groups (insects, crowd, etc.); overwhelm. **umatibelbel.** *v.* to swarm around, crowd (*aribungbong*); overwhelm. **Naatibelbelankami ti lamok.** We were attacked by swarms of mosquitoes.

atiberbér: umatiberber. *v.* to blow strongly (wind). **Umatiberberen ti angin.** The wind is already blowing strongly.

atiberrét: umatiberret. *v.* to spin around; revolve around (a theme); be abundant (joy).

atibúor: *n.* smell; odor. **agatibuor, umatibuor.** *v.* to blow around (dust); diffuse, spread around (odor) (*arinuor*). **naatibuor.** *a.* having a strong smell. **Agatibuor ti anglitna.** His underarm odor is diffusing. [Tag. *amóy*]

atiddág: *var.* of *atiddog*: long. [Tag. *habà*]

atiddóg: *a.* long. **umatiddog.** *v.* to lengthen, become longer; stretch. **ikaatiddog.** *v.* to stretch; elongate. **pangatiddogen.** *a.* rather long. **marantiddog.** *a.* straight; stretchable. **maiyatiddog.** *v.* to be elongated, made longer. **kaatiddog.** *n.* length. **ipaatiddog.** *v.* to have something lengthened. **pagatiddogan.** *n.* the difference in length of two objects. **iti nagatiddogan ti.** *prep.* along. **Atiddog ti anusna.** *exp.* He has a lot of patience. [Ibg. *afeddu*, Itg. *ataddu*, Ivt. *anaruq, ayyid*, Kal. *anchu* (Sp.), Knk. *andókey, andó, ulanguéy*, Kpm. *makábaq*, Png. *dukéy*, Tag. *habà*]

atigíd: (*obs.*) *var.* of *kanigid*: left side.

átik: *kinaatik*. *n.* instinctive talent; endowed aptitude.

atík: (*coll.*) *n.* money. (*kuarta*) **maatik.** *a.* having much money. (*baknang*)

atikábok: umatikabok. *v.* to fly around (dust). **umatikabok ti apa.** *n.* fierce fighting.

átil: *var.* of *tiltil*: weaken. **makaatil.** *a.* exhausting, wearisome; weakening. **naatil.** *a.* weak, tired, exhausted. **Talaga a makaatil ti agtubero.** Plumbing is really exhausting.

atimálon: *n.* chewing with both sides of the mouth; have a mouthful. **agatimalon.** *v.* to chew with both sides of the mouth.

atiman: *n.* incantation, act performed to ward off evil spirits. **agat-atiman.** *v.* to ward off spirits with incantations.

atimarmár: atimarmar. *v.* to recover; smear the face with food (*pulágid*). [Tag. *himasmás* (recover)]

atimbukéng: *a.* chubby, fat; round. (*arimbukeng*)

atimbúyok: *n.* smoke, fume (*asúk*). **umatimbuyok.** *v.* to smoke, smoke up, fume. **Im-matimbuyok ti naanglem a nanglemmes iti**

pagangsanna. The smell of burning cloth fumed up and drowned his windpipe.

atímon: at-atimon. *n.* a kind of vine that grows in marshes whose fruits are used in medicine.

atimúrong: agatimurong. *v.* to wind; meander.

atimpáraw: *var.* of *atipáraw:* hoarse.

atimpáyok: umatimpayok. *v.* to fly around (dust in a whirlwind, etc.).

atimpáyok: *n.* climax, height (of an event). **umatimpayok.** *v.* to reach the climax; soar to the height of.

atimpék: *a.* stocky, stout; muscular (*baneg; puner*). [Tag. *tipunò*]

atíng: see *pagating.*

atíngal: *n.* a kind of small fish that kills sardines by sticking to their gills; bootlicker. **umatingal.** *v.* to panhandle; bootlick; be like a parasite; live off someone else.

atingáw: agatingaw. *v.* to stray.

atíngig: see *allinga:* echo; turning the head to hear better.

atingír: see *tingig:* leaning.

átip: *n.* overlapping. (*saknib; takip*) **pagatipen.** *v.* to overlap; arrange in an overlapping manner. [Tag. *sudlong*]

atípa: atipaen. *v.* to tap the shoulder of someone else.

atipá: atipaen. *v.* to hinder, impede; mitigate, abate; moderate. **di maatipa.** *exp.* it cannot be prevented. **pangatipa.** *n.* preventative measure; hindrance. **Tulongannakami a mangatipa iti pannakadadael ti pagarian.** Help us hinder the destruction of the kingdom. [Tag. *pigil*]

atipadá: *n.* a water buffalo with small horns.

atipáraw: *n.* hoarseness of voice due to colds. **agatiparaw.** *v.* to suffer from a hoarse voice (*páraw*). [Tag. *malát, paós*]

atipatápok: (*obs.*) *n.* dust on clothes.

atiperpér: *a.* numerous; swarming. **umatiperper.** *v.* to swarm.

atípil: atipilan. *v.* to lean on; press against; stick together; cling to.

atipokpók: *n. Vernonia patula* weed; *Erigeron sumatrensis*; cloud of dust. **agatipokpok.** *v.* to blow around (dust); to fly with the wind. **umatipokpok ti apa.** *exp.* to heat up an argument (intensify into a whirlwind). [Tag. *alimbukáy*]

atipurápor: *n.* cloud of dust. (*atipokpok; payugpog*)

atippukéng: *n.* short-bodied, small in stature, but well built (*búkeng, atimpek*). [Tag. *tipunò*]

atír: atiren. *v.* to arrange side by side. **agaatir.** *v.* to fall in line. **naatir.** *a.* arranged side by side; dry, seasoned (timber); well structured. [Tag. *hilera*]

átis: *n.* sweetsop, kind of tropical fruit similar to the *cherimoya* and *anónas*, Arnona squamosa. [Ibg. *attíq*, Ivt. *antis*, Kpm. *anátis*, Tag. *atis*]

átiw: *n.* loss; disadvantage. **atiwen.** *v.* to defeat. (*abak; parmek; sebbet; parukma*) **agpaatiw.** *v.* to let oneself be defeated. **mangatiw.** *v.* to win. **maatiw.** *v.* to lose, be defeated. **pakaatiwan.** *n.* disadvantage. **pangatiwan.** *n.* advantage. [Png., Tag. *talo*]

atiwekwék: umatiwekwek. to abound, be plentiful. (*ariwekwek*)

atiwerrét: umatiwerret. *v.* to speak a language imperfectly.

atléta: (Sp. *atleta:* athlete) *n.* athlete.

atmospéra: (Sp. *atmósfera*) *n.* atmosphere.

átud: atudan. *v.* to trim, prune. (*paad*)

atóle: (f. Mexican Spanish atole: corn flour gruel) *n.* starch; paste made from flour. (*gawgaw*) **atulien.** *v.* to starch the clothes.

átong: *n.* firebrand (for burning). **atongan.** *v.* to leave a firebrand burning; arouse; incite. [Tag. *gatong*]

atúngol: agatungol. *v.* to heap, pile up. (*penpen*)

atúped: *n. Schismatoglottis merrillii* plant that grows along stream banks.

atúpi: atupian. *v.* to cover (harvested rice); fall over.

átor: aturen. *v.* to straighten, amend, correct. **agator.** *v.* (*coll.*) to have an erection. **pangator.** *n.* corrective measures. [Tag. *ayos*]

atorgár: (Sp. *otorgar:* grant) **agatorgar.** *v.* to agree. **atorgaren.** *v.* to consent to; accept, admit. **Maaturgaryo ti dinawatda.** Can you accept what they are asking for?

atót: naatot (*obs.*) *a.* ill tempered. [Png. *atót* = fart]

atrakár: (Eng. attract + borrowed Spanish verbal suffix –*ar*) **atrakaren.** *v.* to attract. (*atraer*)

atraér: (Sp. *atraer:* attract) **maatraer.** *v.* to be attracted. (*kayaw*) **umatraer.** *v.* to attract.

atrás: (Sp. *atrás:* backwards) **agatras.** *v.* to move backwards; back up. **atrasan.** *v.* to get behind someone. **atras abante.** back and forth. **yatras.** *v.* to back out. **Ammok a saanmo nga atrasan ti karitko.** I know you will not withdraw from my challenge.

atrasádo: (Sp. *atrasado:* slow) *a.* slow; late, delinquent (payment); behind; backward; unprogressive.

atrasár: (Sp. *atrasar:* delay) **atrasaren.** *v.* to delay.

atráso: (Sp. *atraso:* delay) *n.* delay; act of being late or behind; unpaid due debt.

atrebído: (Sp. *atrevido:* daring) *a.* daring. (*tured*)

atríl: (Sp. *atril:* lectern) *n.* lectern; music stand; easel. **yatril.** *v.* to place on the easel.

átrio: (Sp. *atrio*: porch, atrium) *n.* courtyard; patio.

atrubír: (Sp. *atribir*) **atrubiren**. *v.* to accept, take the initiative.

atropía: (Sp. *atrofia*: atrophy) *n.* atrophy, wasting away of the muscles.

atrós: (Sp.? *atroz*: atrocious) *n.* a supernatural ghost that brings sickness with the wind, usually rides horses, and dresses elegantly.

atrosidád: (Sp. *atrocidad*: atrocity) *n.* atrocity.

atsára: (Tag. also) *n.* pickled vegetables. **atsaraen**. *v.* to pickle. (*artem*)

atséro: (Sp. *hachero*: lumber man) *n.* lumberjack.

atsíbar: (Sp. *acíbar*: aloes) *n.* native bitter concoction taken by pregnant women to induce abortion, aloes.

atsuéte: (f. Mexican Spanish *achuete*: annatto) *n.* annatto, *Bixa orellana*, used to color food red.

attán: **attanan**. *v.* to reserve for future use; reserve; withhold; refrain from; be wary, cautious (*annad*). **awan ti attananna**. *a.* he has no fear. **At-attanak ti panagsubangmi**. I refrained from (prevented us from) quarreling. **Awan ti at-attanam a sumarang iti uray asino**. You are unafraid to face anyone.

attási: (*reg.*) *n.* species of freshwater fish similar to the *dalag*. **Kasla agkulkulipagpag ti attasi iti barukongko**. *exp.* denoting extreme excitement (like squirming fish in my chest).

atténg: **agatteng**. *v.* to abstain from certain foods in times of sickness; to abstain from sex.

attít: (*coll.*) *n.* sissy; clown; fool. **attiten**. *v.* to jest; make a fool of.

attó: see *into*: future marker.

attuáng: **agattuang**. *v.* to gallop; run in all directions. (*buatit*)

attúbaw: see *abbutaw*: hole; pierce.

attuíl: *n.* counterbalance, counterweight. (*battuon*) **attuilen**. *v.* to apply a counterweight. [Tag. *panimbáng*]

attúkaw: *n.* a peck in a fruit from a bird.

attóno: *var.* of *intono*: future article.

attóy: *var.* of *adtoy*: Here it is.

áwa₁: yawa. *v.* to keep from injury, preserve.

áwa₂: *n.* a variety of long banana; *var.* of *aba* taro.

áwa₃: *n.* a kind of large spiny fish whose young is called *banglot*; milkfish *Chanos chanos*.

awáaw: **umawaaw**. *v.* to die; go flat (liquor) (*tamnay*). **panagawaaw**. *n.* emptiness, void. **manipud iti panagawaaw ti mugingna**. from the void of his mind (*lit*: forehead). **Nagawaaw sa pay ketdin ti utekko gapu ken ni ayat**. I think my mind went numb because of love.

awák: *n.* variety of *diket* rice.

awakan: (myth.) *n.* water in southern Mindanao where merfolk take their victims.

áwag: *n.* calling; name (*nagan*); nickname (*birngas*); military draft. **umawag**. *v.* to call; summon; implore (in praying). (*ayab*) **awagan**. *v.* to call, invoke. **yawag**. *v.* to proclaim; publish. **pangaw-awag**. *n.* nicknaming. **paawagan**. *v.* to have oneself called. **parayawag**. *n.* crier; barker; toastmaster. [Kal. *ayag*, Knk. *awáaw*, Png., Tag. *táwag*]

awán: Existential. Negative of *adda*. to not have; nothing, nobody; there is not, there are not. **Awan ti lapisko**. I don't have a pencil. **Awan tao idiay**. Nobody is there. **Awan ti kuarta**. There's no money. **Awanda ditoy**. They are not here. **awanan**. *a.* deprived of; poor. **agawan**. *v.* to vanish; disappear. **agawan-awan**. *v.* to come and go; vanish; fade on and off. **kaawan**. *n.* absence; state of nothingness. **kinaawan**. *n.* absence; nothingness; void. **maawan**. *v.* to be lost, misplaced; disappear, vanish; err, forget. **mayaw-awan**. *v.* to forget; not remember correctly; lose one's way; be unfortunate; be unhappy. **nagawan**. *n.* the dead; the deceased. **mangyaw-awan**. *a.* misleading, deceiving; confusing. **nayaw-awan**. *a.* lost, unfortunate, unlucky, miserable. **yaw-awan**. *v.* to confuse, deceive, mislead, baffle. **makaiyaw-awan**. *a.* confusing, deceiving, misleading, baffling. **maawanan**. *v.* to lose. **umaw-awan**. *v.* to diminish. **pagawanen**. *v.* to make something disappear; cause something to vanish. **paawanen**. *v.* to annihilate; make something disappear; forgive. **apag-awan**. it has just disappeared. **awan ti adda**. *exp.* don't mention it; all right. **Awan as-asin ti saona**. What they say has no substance (*lit*: salt). **Naawanak iti puot**. I lost consciousness. [Bon. *maid*, Ivt. *arava*, Knk. *maíd*, Png. *anggapó*, Tag. *walâ*]

awanagin: *n.* Siderxylon parvifolium plant.

awanán: *n.* tiebeam (in construction).

áwang: *n.* plot of land (*áray*). [Tag. *lote*]

awáng: *a.* vacant; *n.* emptiness; void. **awangan**. *v.* to provide some space; empty. **nagawangan**. *a.* empty. (*gáwang*, *awan nagyán*)

awangáp: (*obs.*) nowhere.

áwar: *a.* far, remote. (*adayo*)

awáray: *n.* anything abnormally larger or more numerous, a sixth finger, a double fruit, etc. (*síping*)

áwas: *n.* a tall, straight tree or log.

awás: **maawas**. *v.* to miss an opportunity. (*kapis*) **aginnawas**. *n.* a boy's game consisting of slapping hands.

áwat: *n.* job contract; amount agreed upon by contract. **awaten**. *v.* to get, accept. **maawat**. *v.* to receive, get (unintentionally or non-volitionally); pick up (radio waves). **maawatan**. *v.* to understand, comprehend. **kinamannakaawat**. *n.* understanding; reasonable; intelligent. **makiinnawatan**. *v.* to reconcile, settle differences. **yawat**. *v.* to give; deliver, hand to. **yawatan**. *v.* to hand something to someone. **umawat**. *v.* to receive, accept. **panagkinnaawatan**. *n.* agreement; understanding. **mannakaawat**. *a.* reasonable; intelligent. **pagkikinnaawaten**. *v.* to have people reconcile their differences (understand each other). **agipápaawat**. *n.* translator; teacher. **ipaawat**. *v.* to have something accepted, translate; explain to someone. **payawatan**. *v.* to order something to be given to someone. **Agyamanak ta maawatannak**. I am thankful that you understand me. [Ivt. *rawat*, Png. *awát*, Tag. *tanggáp*]

áwat: **awat-awat**. *n.* a type of self-defense; native martial art.

awáw: *var.* of *waw*: thirst. [Png. *pegá*, Tag. *uhaw*]

aw-áw: (*coll.*) *n.* dog meat; dog. **agaw-aw**. *v.* to spill out. **anaw-aw**. *n.* repetitive barking. **immabat ti anaw-aw dagiti aso idi lumaemkami iti purok**. The repeated barking of the dogs greeted us as we entered the village.

áway: *n.* outskirts of town, boondocks; rural country. (*wayaway*) **umaway**. *v.* to go to the *away*. **taga-away**. *a.* from the *away*. **yaway**. *v.* to take to the village. [Tag. *nayon*]

áwel: (Eng. AWOL) **agawel**. *v.* to be absent without leave; to be idle.

áweng: *n.* resonance, echo; indigenous music. **agaweng**. *v.* to resound, ring. **papaaweng**. *n.* a bamboo bow that rings when attached to kites. **naaweng**. a resonant, sonorous. **Maymayat ti aweng ti Ilokano para kaniak**. Ilocano sounds better to me. [Tag. *tunóg*]

áwer: *n.* the sound of strong wind or water; object whizzing in the air. **agawer**. *v.* to roar (the wind, streams, etc.); to vanish. **naawer**. *a.* noisy (roaring sound); alert, clever (thoughts). **Mangmangkik gayam, umawertan!** It's a goblin, let's get out of here. [Tag. *dagundóng*]

awés: **umawes**. *v.* to make a whishing sound.

áwet: **awet-awet**. *n.* sound of gulping.

awét: **umawet-awet**. *v.* to shrink or contract under a heavy load.

áwid₁: *n.* custom, habit; going home; tradition; character; personality; manners (*ugáli*). **aawidan**. *n.* mood. **aw-awid**. *n.* customs, habits, mores. **agawid**. *v.* to go home. **yawid**. *v.* to bring something home. **pagawidan**. *n.* place of residence. **pangawidan**. *n.* place where one is taken home. **panagawid**. *n.* homecoming. **panagaawid**. *n.* time of dismissal from work or school. **Pagawidam?** Where do you live? **mangpaawid**. *v.* to send someone home. **Agawidka iti naggapuam!** Go back to where you came from! **Dakes ti awidmo**. You have bad manners. [Ibg. *lubbéq*, Ivt. *sumavat*, Knk. *bésaw*, Kpm. *múliq, uliq*, Png. *isempet, onpawil*, Tag. *uwî* (go home)]

áwid₂: **awiden**. *v.* to divert water to a field. **pangawidan**. *n.* turnout of an irrigation structure.

áwid₃: **sangkaawid**. *n.* 1/25 of a *labay* of cotton.

áwid₄: **awiden**. *v.* to keep back; turn a steering wheel; win someone over; convince.

awíngan: (*obs.*) *n.* workman in a silversmith's shop.

awingí: *a.* awry, wry. (*tirítir, píwis, nadawíris*).

awír: **awiren**. *v.* to take care of; rock, quiet babies. **paraaw-awir**. *n.* baby-sitter. [Ivt. *unung*, Tag. *iwi, alagà*]

áwis: *n.* invitation. **awisen**. *v.* to invite; allure; move; advise; persuade. **makaawis**. *a.* enticing, inviting; alluding. **ipaawis**. *v.* to have someone invited or persuaded. **pannakaawis**. *n.* invitation. **yawis**. *v.* to invite. **makaawis iti imataing**. catching the attention. **Inyawisen ti baket ti isasarungkarda iti pagmulmulaanda**. The old lady already invited them to visit their garden. **Ditay koma agar-aramid kadagiti banag a pakaawisan dagiti dikatataoan**. We shouldn't do anything that would invite the spirits. [Kal. *ayeg, bulliti*, Tag. *anyaya*]

awít: *n.* load; burden; duty; responsibility; problem. **awiten**. *v.* to carry (*amít, bagkat, baklay, bitbit, bunag, dagensen*); (*fig.*) bear (pain, grief). **awit-awit**. *n.* a kind of black bird that cries at dusk. **sangkaawit**. *a.* always carrying something. **umawit**. *v.* to carry a load. [Ibg. *kattu, ivuluq, ekkaten*, Ivt. *raraq*, Kal. *agtu, bukuchon*, Kpm. *dala*, Png. *awit*, Tag. *dalá*]

awtór: (Sp. *autor*: author) *n.* author (fem. *awtora*). (*mannúrat*)

awtoridád: (Sp. *autoridad*: authority) *n.* authority. (*pannakabalín, singkéd*)

ay₁: **umay**. *v.* to come. **makaumay**. *v.* to be able to come. **ayen**. *v.* to go to. *a.* coming. **agin-aay, agin-uumay**. *v.* to pretend to come. **paay**. *n.* use, benefit, utility. **ipaay**. *v.* to present, use as, offer. **ippaymo nga ayat**. please. **kakaumay, agkaraumay**. *v.* to come often. **kaipaayan**. *n.* utility, use. **kapápaayán, kapaypay-an**. *n.*

result, consequence, outcome. **pamaayan.** *v.* to treat in a certain way, *n.* means, procedure. **pakapay-an.** *n.* result, outcome; situation; condition. **agpaay.** *v.* to be for someone. **maipaay.** *a.* to be convenient, reasonable; to be intended for; to be for. **makaipaay.** *v.* to be able to give. **makapagpaay.** *v.* to be of service. **yaay.** *n.* coming. [See also *umay*, which functions now as a root. Bon. *áli*, Png. *la, gala*, Tag. *datíng*]

ay₂: Interjection expressing wonder or pain.

ayá: Interrogative particle implying wonder. **Apay aya?** Why? Emphatic. **Sinnoka aya nga aginsisingpet?** Who do you think you are, pretending to be virtuous?

ayáb: *n.* call; summons; invitation. **ayaban.** *v.* to call. **pagayaban.** *n.* telephone. **yayab.** *v.* to call someone for. **Ayabannakto no sumangpetka.** Call me up when you arrive. [Bon. *ayag*, Ibg. *ágal*, Kal. *ayag, pokaw*, Knk. *áyag*, Kpm. *áus*, Ivt., Png., Tag. *tawag*]

áyam₁: **ay-ayam.** *n.* game, sport, play, amusement, toy. **agay-ayam.** *v.* to play; amuse oneself. **ayaman.** *v.* to play with; fool with; do with ease. **kaay-ayam.** *v.* to play with someone. **agkaayaman.** *n.* playmates. **ay-ayamen.** *v.* to amuse, play with. **pagay-ayaman.** *n.* playground. *v.* (*fig.*) to fool around with a girl; take it easy. **paay-ayam.** *n.* sponsored game. **Agbalinka a natibker, dimo ipalubos nga ayayamennaka ti gasat.** Be strong, don't let luck play with you. [Ibg. *gáyam*, Ivt. *yáyam*, Kpm. *piálung*, Png. *galáw*, Tag. *larô*; Ibg. *ayam* = animal]

áyam₂: **ayam-ayam.** *n.* a tree with violet leaves used in medicine; *Clerodendron minahassae.*

ayám: *n.* chicken tick. **umayam.** *v.* to creep, crawl. (*karayam*) **agay-ayam.** *n.* reptile, anything that crawls. **inayam.** *n.* infested with chicken ticks. [Kal. *alikammot*, Knk. *tilalagá, atilalagá*, Tag. *hanip*]

ayambán: *n. Dipterocarpus philippinensis.*

ayamúom: *n.* fragrance, aroma, perfume; pleasant smell. (*banglo; sayamusom; sumusum*) **agayamuom.** *v.* to diffuse fragrance. **naayamuom.** *a.* fragrant. **pagayamuomen.** *v.* to beautify the fragrance of something. [Tag. *halimuyák*]

ayán: *n.* place, location; Interrogative used with nouns and *-ko* pronouns, Where (is located)? **Ayanmo?** Where are you? [Png. *kulaan, pásen*, Tag. *dako (place); nasaán (interrogative)*]

ayan-ayát: (f. *ayát*) *n.* mutual love, sweetheart. **kaayan-ayat.** *n.* person with whom one is in love.

ayaúnay: *Interj.* Good grief; expression uttered while sighing (*ayaunayen, ayaunay metten*)

ayás: **umayas.** *v.* to slide down, glide (*alus-os*); spread. **paayas, pak-yas.** *n.* ditch; trench. [Tag. *salimbáy*]

áyat: **ayatan.** *v.* to entice; bribe someone. **yayat.** *v.* to face two gamecocks together; bribe; entice; bait a trap. **yayatan.** *v.* entice someone with a bribe. **umayat.** *v.* to be quarrelsome, pugnacious. **paayatan.** *v.* to entice, allure.

ayát: *n.* love; liking; affection. **ayan-ayat.** *n.* love story; love affair. **kaayan-ayat.** *n.* sweetheart; lover. **agayan-ayat.** *n.* sweethearts. **agayat.** *v.* to fall in love; love, be pleased. **ayaten.** *v.* to love, be pleased with. **ay-ayaten.** *v.* to love (a person). **Ay-ayatenka.** I love you. **kinamanagayat.** *n.* compassion. **naayat.** *a.* lovable, loving. **nakaay-ayat.** *a.* lovely. **makaayat.** *v.* to be happy, pleased; excited. **maayatan.** *v.* to be pleased with, happy. **managayat.** *a.* fond. **kinamanagayat.** *n.* lovingness. **pagayatan.** *n.* loving, desire; preference; will. **mayat.** *v.* to want, like; agree; consent. *a.* good. **agmayat.** *v.* to agree, be willing. **siaaayat.** *a.* willingly; lovingly. **bunga ti ayat.** child. [See also *kayat*. Bon. *layad*, Ibg. *ayaten, mangayaq*, Ivt. *maddaw*, Knk. *layad*, Kpm. *buri*, Png. *áro*, Tag. *mahál, ibig*]

ayáw: *n.* rice growing wild. **agayaw.** *v.* to grow excessively, much taller than normal. (*langpaw*)

ay-áy: **naay-ay.** *a.* pitiful, sad. **ay-ayen.** *v.* to pity. **manangay-ay.** *a.* charitable; merciful. **kinamanangay-ay.** *n.* kindness; mercifulness. **panangay-ay.** *n.* sympathy, compassion, feeling of pity. **Kayatna laeng a lemmesen iti basi ti panagay-ayna iti kinapimpimantayo.** He just wants to drown the sorrows of our misfortune in sugarcane wine. [Tag. *habág*]

ayed-éd: **agayed-ed.** *v.* to walk energetically (*baddakaw*). **umayed-ed.** *v.* to do a strenuous activity, exert oneself.

ayek-ék: *n.* controlled laughter. **umayek-ek.** *v.* to laugh softly; try to hold back laughter but laugh by shaking the body.

ayeng-éng: *n.* soft whining (hungry dogs), groan. (*alang-ang*)

ayná: *Interj.* expressed wonder and admiration. [From the expression *ay, nakú*, literally, oh! my child]

áyo: **ay-ayuen.** *v.* to flatter; please; persuade, convince. **nakaay-ayo.** *a.* pleasing, attractive; flattering; comforting. **kaay-ayo.** *n.* cause of one's pleasure or enjoyment, what one is fond of. **pannakaay-ayo.** *n.* interest in something or someone. **Kaay-ayona ti agbaniaga, agkakangina nga aruaten ken alahas.** She is fond of traveling, expensive clothes, and jewelry. **Naay-ayoda iti kinamannakigayyemna.** They were pleased by her friendliness. [Tag. *hibò*]

ayó: *n.* the first to start a game. **agayonayo.** *v.* to compete. **mapanen ti ayona.** *exp.* the time has come.

áyon: *n.* right timing in music; vinelike strings that grow on fig trees. **ayonan.** *v.* to favor, incline toward; agree with. **umayon.** *v.* to favor; suit; agree; fit, conform. **umayon-ayon.** *v.* to bend by an external force. **Diak ayonan ti kapanunotanna.** I do not agree with what he is thinking. [Tag. *sang-ayon*]

ayós: (Tag.) *adv.* it's done; it's all right.

aysiáy: Interjection expressing mild irritation.

Aysús: Interjection. *contr.* of *Ay Hesús*: Oh, Jesus!

ayúbo: **agayubo.** *v.* to move to and from meeting one another (ants in a colony); tat. **ayubuan.** *v.* to cover with tatting (ropes). **inayubo.** *a.* tatted (not braided), said of ropes.

ayúd: *n.* antlers.

ayúda: (Sp. *ayuda*: aid) *n.* aid, help (*tulong*); supplementary food (given to babies). **agpaayuda.** *v.* to ask for help.

ayudánte: (Sp. *ayudante*: helper) *n.* assistant; aide-de-camp.

ayudár: (Sp. *ayudar*: help) *n.* prayers at the foot of the altar during mass.

áyug: *n.* accent in speaking, intonation (*bengngat*); implication (hidden meaning of a statement); lasting long; protracted illness. **yayug.** *v.* to stress, prolong; hum the tune of a song. **ayug-Paskua.** *n.* Christmas cheer. [Tag. *punto*]

ayúkan₁: *n.* honeybee. [Kal. *iyukan, alig*, Knk. *yúkan*, Tag. *pukyutan*]

ayúkan₂: *n.* variety of awned *diket* rice.

ayúkos: *var.* of *ayyukos*: stooping posture (*kubbo*). [Tag. *ukô*]

ayúma: *n.* a kind of mouth infection with blisters; reparation of fishnets. **agayuma.** *v.* to repair nets; have blisters around the mouth.

ayumúdong: (*obs.*) *n.* moneybag.

ayumúom: see *ayamuom*: fragrance; aroma (*banglo, sayamusum*). [Tag. *bangó*]

ayunár: (Sp. *ayunar*: fast) **panagayunar.** *n.* fasting.

ayúno: (Sp. *ayuno*: fast) *n.* fast. **agayuno.** *v.* to fast (refrain from eating).

ayungín: (Tag. also) *n.* a kind of small blackish fish.

áyup: *n.* animal, beast. **kinaayup.** *n.* bestiality, brutality. **inaayup.** *a.* beastly, of an animal nature. **Inaayup ti kababalinna.** He has a beastly nature. **Ayupka!** You beast! **Idi nalasag pay, kanayon a puoran dagiti inaayup a kalikagum.** When he was still lustful, his animal desires were always burning. [Ibg. *ayam*, Ifg. *amayu*, Ivt. *viñay*, Kpm. *animál*, Png. *áyep*, Tag. *háyop*]

áyus: *n.* current, flow; stream; arrangement (of hair). **agayos.** *v.* to flow, run (water); to speak fluently. **ayusan.** *n.* stream. **aayusan.** *n.* the part of the upper lip under the nostril where mucus hits; gutter for water flow. **maiyayus.** *v.* to be carried away by the current. **apagayus.** *a.* just enough to flow (said of meager supplies). **paayos.** *n.* blowout. **Pinunasna ti ling-etna a nagayus iti igid ti matana.** He wiped off the sweat flowing from the corner of his eye. [Ibg. *mangiyámug*, Ivt. *umuyug*, Kpm., Png., Tag. *agos*]

ayúyang: *n.* haunt; place for recreation, resort; hang out, place where one frequents. (*aridakdak*) **agayuyang.** *v.* to frequent a place; linger. **Daytoy ti ayuyang dagiti adda kuartana.** This is the place where the rich frequently visit. **Agay-ayuyang iti panunotna ti napasamak.** What happened is haunting his thoughts. [Tag. *pugaran*]

ayúyeng: *n.* a kind of freshwater fish.

aywán: *n.* ward; guard; protection; custody. (*bantáy*) **aywanan.** *v.* to baby-sit, take care of; guard; watch; have custody of. **ipaaywan.** *v.* to entrust in the care of. **mangaywan.** *n.* guardian, custodian; *v.* to take care of. [Tag. *kalingà*]

aywáy: (*obs.*) *n.* length. (*atiddóg*)

aywén: (f. *ayo*) **ay-aywén.** *v.* to flatter.

ayyamá: (*ay* + *ama*) exclamation denoting mild surprise: oh my!

ayyapón: (*ay* + *apo*) exclamation denoting mild surprise: Oh my! Oh my god!

ayyúkos: *n.* slightly stooping posture. **naay-yukos.** *a.* slightly stooping.

B

ba: Interjection used to startle or scare, or to make children laugh.

baág₁: *n.* G-string. (*bayakat, anungo, kuba, pallak*) **agbaag.** *v.* to wear the G-string. **baagan, agbabaag.** *n.* person who wears a G-string, G-string-wearing mountain dweller. [Bon. *wanes*, Ibg. *bag*, Ivt. *saguut*, Kal. *beÿ-eÿ*, Knk. *wanés, kúba*, Kpm. *baag*, Png. *beel*, Tag. *bahág*]

baág₂: **babaag.** *n.* a kind of large eel that shrinks when approached. **ibaag ti ipusna.** *exp.* to hide one's tail (coward dogs). **nakabaag ti ipusna.** *exp.* with the tail between one's legs (cowards).

báak₁: *a.* old, very old (*lakáy; bakét*); aged (rice, wine, grains, etc.). **nabaakan.** *a.* very old (person); ancient. **baaken.** *v.* to age (wine, rice, etc.) **apo a baak.** great-grandparent. **lolo báak.** *n.* great-grandfather. **lola báak.** *n.* great-grandmother. **balasang a baak.** *n.* old maid; spinster (*bayóg*). **bumaak.** *v.* to become old, age; become seasoned. **Saanda kano a kayat ti agbaak a kas kenkuana.** They say they don't want to get old like her. [Tag. *tandâ*; Ivt. *vaak* = old preserved yam]

báak₂: **baakan.** *n.* a kind of tree, *Litsea sp.* whose leaves seem to be scorched.

baám: *var.* of *bay-am*. Let it be; Never mind.

baámon: *var.* of *bay-amon*: Never mind. Let it be; Forget it.

baán: Contraction of *bay-an*: to let be.

baár: **sangabaar.** *n.* one-tenth an *úyon*, ten bundles of rice.

báaw: *n.* left over, cold rice; tepidity; coolness. **agbaaw.** *v.* to cool off; decrease; simmer down; become tepid. **arimbaáwen.** *a.* cooling off (hot water); subsiding (fever). **nabaaw.** *a.* lukewarm, cool; indifferent, uncaring. **pabaawen.** *v.* to let cool off. **bumaaw.** *v.* to cool down; decrease; abate. **pamaawen.** *v.* to be uninterested, indifferent; *a.* not very hot. **panagbaaw ti panagayat.** *exp.* losing interest in love. **Ururayennan sa a bumaaw ti umas-asuk a sangatasa a kape.** I think he is waiting for the smoking cup of coffee to cool down. [Bon. *baew*, Knk. *tená*, Tag. *hupâ* (decrease, diminish)]

baáy: *n.* a kind of shrub whose bark is used in net making.

babá: *n.* downstairs; lower part of something; underneath; lowlands. **iti baba.** *prep.* below. **ababa.** *a.* short; low. **agbaba.** *v.* to go down (in social status); become poorer. **agpababa.** *v.* to descend; go down; go downstairs. **nababa.** *a.* short; low. **bumaba.** *v.* to descend, go down; go downstairs. **babaen.** *prep.* by means of. **ibaba.** *v.* to take down; take downstairs; lower. **kinababa.** *n.* lowliness. **pababaen.** *v.* to let someone go down; to send something down. **panagbaba.** *n.* lowering (one's social status, etc.). **nababa ti tayabna.** *exp.* flying low (said of promiscuous women). **Nupay nababa ti timekna, saan a mapagbiddutan dagiti balikasna iti nabannayat a panagsaona.** Although his voice was soft, his words did not falter in his careful speech. [Bon. *gowab*, Kal. *cheÿa, sokbya*, Knk. *dáo* (under), *amtík* (low), Png. *bebá*, Tag. *babà*]

babaén: *prep.* through, by means of; underneath. **Adda met dagiti saludsod a masungbatan laeng baben ti panagulimek.** There are questions that are just answered through silence. [Tag. *sa pamamagitan ng, ayon sa*]

babái: (pl. *babbai*) *n.* girl, woman, female; concubine, mistress; socket for a plug. **binabai.** *a.* womanlike, effeminate; *n.* a castrated rooster. **baien.** *a.* effeminate; homosexual. **agbabai.** *v.* to have a concubine. **babaien.** *v.* to court; treat badly; keep as one's concubine. **kababai.** *n.* the smaller part of a pair; shorter of the two handles of the *sayot* net. **nababaian.** *n.* the relatives of the bride. **agkababai.** *v.* to have female characteristics. **managbabai.** *n.* womanizer; person having many women or concubines. (*babairo*) [Ibg. *vakes*, Kal. *bebyai*, Knk. *básang*, Kpm. *babayi*, Png. *bíi*, Tag. *babae*]

babaíro: (*f. babai*) *n.* womanizer; ladies' man. (*managbabai, palikero*)

bábak: *n.* fault; moral sin. (in prayers). (*biddut*) **nakababak.** *a.* sinning; *n.* committed sin. **Ti adda babakna, adda aluadanna.** *exp.* He who has guilt (sin) has something to beware of. [Tag. *kasalanan*]

babaláw: (*f. baláw*) *n.* correction; reprimand; reproof. **babalawen.** *v.* to reprimand, criticize.

babantót: *n.* bad feelings. **agbabantot.** *v.* to be sick; to be pregnant.

bábang: *n.* powder, dust of pounded rice. (*tapok*)

babaonén: *n.* servant; maid.

babaóng: (*obs.*) *n.* waiting while the meal is on the table.

babará: *n.* buboes; inflammatory swellings in the groin (*pannakalen*). [Tag. *kulanì*]

babás: **mababas.** *v.* to miss (after aiming). (*tawás*) **pakababasan.** *n.* fault, defect. (*pílaw*)

babásil: *n.* whitlow, felon. **agbabasil.** *v.* to have a *babasil* on the finger.

babató: (*f. bato*) *n.* talisman.

bábaw: *n.* a kind of small, poisonous snake.

babáwi: *n.* regrets; repentance, self-reproach. **agbabawi.** *v.* to repent; regret. **babawien.** *v.* to regret, repent; take back, withdraw (a statement). **ibabawi.** *v.* to rescind; recant; go back on one's word. **makapagbabawi.** *v.* to be able to repent. **Ti nalabes a panagtalekmo, agbabawikanto.** *exp.* You will regret if you trust too much. **Pagbabawyak ti amin a napasamak ken pakawanendak.** I repent everything that happened so forgive me. [Ibg. *bavawi*, Ivt. *manehseh*, Kal. *chachauli*, *byabyawi*, Png. *babáwi*, Kpm., Tag. *sisi*]

bábay: (Eng.) *interj.* good-bye. [Tag. *paalam*]

babáyo: *n.* a kind of large, edible marine fish, barracuda.

babayóte: *n. var.* of *babayo*: barracuda.

babbáb: *a.* with sunken lips (due to lack of teeth). (*bebbeb*)

babbái: *n.* Irregular plural of *babai*: girls; women; females.

babbakét: *n.* Irregular plural of *baket*: old ladies.

babbaró: *n.* Irregular plural of *baro*: young men. **babbarito.** *n.* plural of *barito*.

babék₁: *n.* a variety of short banana.

babék₂: *a.* short (in stature), term for short people or stunted plants. (*pandek*)

báber: **ibaber.** *v.* to throw away in anger; hurl something to the floor.

babéra: (Sp. *babera*: beaver (of a helmet); bib) *n.* bib. **nakababera.** *a.* using a bib, wearing a bib. **ibabera.** *v.* to put a bib on (a baby).

babéro: *var.* of *babera*: bib.

bábes: **agbabes.** *v.* to drool.

babumbáboy: see under *baboy*.

babór: (Sp. *babor*: larboard) *n.* larboard, port side of a ship; the starboard is called *estribor*.

báboy: *n.* pig, hog, swine; dirty person. **agbaboy.** *v.* to raise pigs. **agabbaboy.** *v.* to smell like a pig. **baboybaboy.** *n.* pill bug; a kind of fish; a kind of grass. **agbabumbaboy.** *v.* to move on the hands and knees. **binababuyan.** *n.* a kind of boat. **pagbabuyan.** *n.* piggery, pig farm. **agbinnaboy.** *n.* a children's race on all fours, crawling race. **kababuyan.** *n.* filth, foul odor (nature of a pig). [Ibg. *bávi*, Itb. *kuyis*, Itg. *íyas*, Ivt. *baguq*, Kal. *beýok*, Knk. *píkat*, Kpm. *bábiq*, Png. *babóy*, Tag. *baboy*]

Babúyan: *n.* island located north of Cagayan and south of Batanes.

babséet: **mababseet.** *v.* to dart out; leave immediately. **pababseeten.** *v.* to slap (on the back or buttocks).

babtúog: **agbabtuog.** *v.* to make successive thumping sounds. (*bitog*) **pababtuogen.** *v.* to slam a door. **No gasat ti dumteng, mababtuog**

met laeng. *exp.* When fortune comes, it comes suddenly and unexpectedly.

badáho: (Sp. *badajo*: bell clapper) *n.* clapper of a bell.

bádal: *n.* leather sandals. **agbadal.** *v.* to wear leather sandals.

bádang: *n.* help, aid. (*tulong, batak, arayat, tarabay, takonaynay*) **agbinnadang.** *v.* to help each other. **badangan.** *v.* to help, aid, assist, save someone. **binnadang.** *n.* cooperation, helping one another. **ibadang.** *v.* something given to help solve a problem. **kabadangan.** *n.* bailiff (*bilonggo, agbaras*); helper; companion; aid. **Asino kadi ti kangrunaan nga agbibinnadang no saan a dagiti agkakaaruba?** Who assists each other the most if not neighbors? **No badangam koma ti kinagaget diay asawam, narang-aykayo koman.** If you would only cooperate with your industrious wife, you should prosper. [Tag. *tulong*]

badáng₁: *n.* a kind of broad knife with a pointless blade. **agbinnadang.** *v.* to engage in a *bolo* fight. **nagbadang, nakabadang.** *a.* armed with this knife. **badangen.** *v.* to hit or threaten someone with a *badang*. **nagbadang.** *a.* armed with this type of *bolo*. [Kal. *gaman, paching*]

badáng₂: **badbadang.** *n.* a kind of large mollusk.

badáng₃: **badangbadang.** *n.* a pink-flowered vine with edible pods, *Canavallia ensiformis*.

bad-áy: *n.* bamboo spit used for hanging and drying tobacco leaves. **agibad-ay.** *v.* to hang tobacco leaves on bamboo to dry.

baddakáw: (*coll.*) *a.* long-legged (*bangkawas*); taking long strides. **agbaddakaw.** *v.* to straddle vigorously; walk in big strides. (*akkang, kayáng, askaw, pakkang*)

baddál: *n.* clumsiness at being overweight. **nabaddal.** *a.* to be clumsy as a result of being obese. **nabaddal nga agsao.** *a.* being slow in speech.

baddék: *n.* footprint; step; sound of footsteps. **baddeken.** *v.* to step on, trample, tread on. (*payat*) **bumaddek.** *v.* to step in (a house). **ibaddek.** *v.* to step on something; kill an insect by stepping on it; downgrade. **maibaddebaddek.** *v.* to be continually trampled (one's rights). **Ti tao a manakem, dina buyaen ti panagdisso ti sakana iti daga, kitaenna ketdi ti sumaruno a baddekanna.** *exp.* Wise men don't see where their feet are on the ground, they see their next step instead. [Png. *koráng*, Tag. *habkáng*]

baddí: *n.* fairy; goddess; muse. [Tag. *diwatà*]

baddúngal: **kabaddungalan.** *n.* contemporary, peer; equal (in age or height). **agkabaddung-**

alan. *v.* to be equal, *n.* colleague; peer. [Tag. *kasamahan*]

baddút: *n.* mistake, error, sin, fault. (*biddut, kammali*)

badéng: *n.* lovesick ditty; ballad. **agbadeng.** *v.* to sing a lovesick song. [Tag. *kundiman*]

badidít: *n.* salacious, indecent, or lewd song.

badíl: (*obs.*) *n.* cannon shot.

badíng: (Pil., *slang*) *n.* homosexual male.

bádo: *n.* dress; coat; shirt; jacket; clothes, attire. **agbado.** *v.* to dress, put on one's clothes. **ibado.** *v.* to put on or wear a particular garment. **pagbado.** *v.* to wear. **baduan.** *v.* to clothe someone. **sibabado.** *a.* dressed; clothed. (*pelles*) **badobado.** *n.* a girl's hopping game consisting of hopping around a dresslike figure drawn on the ground and divided into seven parts. **Nakabado iti pagturog ket madlaw ti sukog ti bagina.** She was dressed in her sleepers and the shape of her body was noticeable. [Bon. *saping*, Tag. *damít*]

badobádok: *n.* kind of pond reed used for nipa hut walling, cattail flag, *Typha angustifolia.*

badúd: *n.* gate crasher, person who attends a function uninvited.

bádok₁: *n.* roof thatching, ridging of a roof.

bádok₂: badobadok. *n.* cattail flag, *Typha angustifolia*; reed used for nipa huts.

bádok₃: *n.* a species of herb with yellow flowers.

badól: boda-badol. *n.* extravagant wedding. (*en grande a kasar*)

bádong: badongbadong. *n.* a kind of edible, elongated mollusk.

badús: nabadus. *a.* lazy; reluctant to work (*sadut*). **Pinagtalawnaka ti bados a lakaymo?** Your lazy husband eloped with you. [Tag. *tamád*]

badúy: (Tag.) *n.* not in style; embarrassingly out of fashion.

badúya: *n.* a kind of flat rice cake cooked with bananas. **baduyaen.** *v.* to make into rice cake.

Badyáw: *n.* sea gypsy; *Bajao*, ethnic group from the Sulu Archipelago.

bádyet: (Eng. budget) *n.* budget. **agbadyet.** *v.* to budget.

báed: *n.* person who speaks nasally; (*reg.*) mute person. **agbaed.** *v.* to speak nasally; snuffle; nasalize. **agbibinnaed.** *v.* to speak through the nose in competition (a boy's game). **nagbaed.** *a.* talking through the nose. **kasla nakaraman a baed.** *exp.* to be starving. [Tag. *ngongò*]

baél: *n.* strength; appropriateness, suitability, fitness. **baelen.** *v.* to carry a heavy load. **babaelan.** *v.* to do what one can; (*reg.*) to do haphazardly. **mabaelan.** *v.* to be able, can. **kabaelan.** *n.* capability, ability; power. *v.* to be able to do. **ibael.** *v.* to carry. **mannakabael.** *a.* fit; strong; intelligent; capable. **Mabaelam?** Can you carry it? Can you do it? **No kabaelam, kabaelak met.** If you can do it, so can I. [Knk. *ánge, kibíl*, Png. *sarág, yári, aliméng*, Tag. *kaya*]

baén: *n.* sneeze. (*bang-es*) **agbaen.** *v.* to sneeze. **managbaen.** *a.* frequently sneezing. **makapabaen.** *a.* causing one to sneeze. **agkamkamakam a panagbaen.** *n.* continuous sneezing. [Ibg. *abbán*, Kal. *boon*, Knk. *báis, bing-ís*, Kpm. *atchíng*, Png. *básis*, Tag. *bahín*]

baéng: *n. var.* of *baen:* sneeze. **Makababaengak iti ingel.** I feel like sneezing from the strong liquor smell. **No agbaeng ti baka, umayen ti nepnep.** When the cows sneeze, a strong rain is coming.

baeng-éng: *n.* slow motion.

baét: *n.* interval; space between; time interval. **iti baet.** *prep.* between; despite. **iti pagbaetan.** *prep.* between. **ibaet.** *v.* to place between. **ibabaet.** *v.* to intercede for someone. **baetan.** *n.* southeast wind; main road. **makibaet.** *v.* to stay in between. **mangibabaet.** *v.* to intervene; intercede; mediate. **bumaet.** *n.* traveler, passenger; *v.* to intervene; go between. **iti nagbibinnaetánda.** in between them. **Laglagipennak bassit nga ibabaet kadagiti kararagmo.** Please remember to include me in your prayers. **Dakkel ti baetmi iti tawen.** We have a lot of years between us (we differ much in age). [Knk. *bet-áng*, Png. *leét*, Tag. *pagitan, patláng, siwang*]

bag: short for *naimbag: bag no:* it's good if.

bága: bagabaga. *n.* kite. (*ullaw*) **agbagabaga.** *v.* to hover like a kite; fly a kite. [Tag. *saranggola*]

bagá: *n.* notice; announcement; bulletin. **ibaga.** *v.* to say, tell, declare, utter; inform on. (*kuna; sao*) **bagaan.** *v.* to inform; notify; **bagabaga.** *n.* emcee; one who announces ceremonies; informer. **bagbaga.** *n.* advice. **bagbagaan.** *v.* to advise; admonish. **bagaan.** *v.* to inform; notify; be corrigible, docile. **mamagbaga.** *v.* to advise, counsel. *n.* advisor; counselor. **paibaga.** *v.* to relay a message, send information through someone. **pammagbaga.** *n.* advice, counseling. (*balakad*) **pabagbagaan.** *v.* to go for advice or counseling. **panagbibinnaga.** *n.* the spreading of news (from one person to another). **Ti madi a pagbagbagaan, agturong iti pagrigatan.** *exp.* He who refuses advice is headed for hardship. [Kal. *bega*, Knk. *báag, kawáni*, Png. *bagá*, Tag. *sabi (tell)*, *payo (advice)*]

bagabaga: *n.* Cardinal fish, *Amia sp.*

bagabúndo: (Sp. *vagabundo*: vagabond) *n.* vagabond, tramp; homeless person.

bagáhe: (Sp. *bagaje*: baggage) *n.* baggage (*maleta*), luggage; freight. **ipabagahe.** *v.* to send as freight.

bakáhe: (Sp. *bagaje*: baggage) *n.* Igorot bag.

bagamúndo: *var.* of *bagabundo*: vagabond.

bagánsia: (Sp. *vagancia*: vagrancy) *n.* vagrancy; truancy.

bagangán: *n.* a kind of newt that jumps like a frog; salamander; *a.* rich.

bagás₁: *n.* uncooked rice; seed; kernel; tuberous root (of taro); bulb; contents; objective, aim, goal; edible animal inside a mollusk shell, mollusk meat. **bagasan.** *v.* to put something in between (sandwich); *n.* market location where the rice vendors are. **ibagasan.** *v.* to cull; extract; explain, give meaning to; interpret; give the contents of. **agbagas.** *v.* to bear fruit. **kababagas.** *n.* essence, meaning. **nabagas.** *a.* important, substantial; meaningful; fruitful; useful; meaty; full. **pagbagasan.** *n.* rice container; provider. **bagas ti kamote.** *n.* kamote tuber. [Ibg. *beggaq*, Ivt. *paray*, Kal. *bilayu*, Kpm. *abyas*, Png. *belás*, Tag. *bigás*]

bagás-lingét: *n.* prickly heat, type of skin rash. [Png. *balyangét*, Tag. *bungang-araw*]

bagás₂: (*coll.*) **bagasbagas.** *n.* clitoris. (*tuldi*)

bagáso: (Sp. *bagazo*: bagasse) *n.* bagasse of sugarcane, pulpy sugarcane refuse after the juice has been extracted.

bagát: see *bagel*: perform superstitious acts.

bagáwa: **bagbagawa.** *n.* puppet (*munieka*). [Tag. *manikà*]

bagawál: **mabagawal.** *v.* to be embarrassed; perplexed. (*bain*)

bagawwéng: *n.* species of tree.

bágay: *n.* state of harmony; *a.* proper, fit, well suited. **agbagay.** *v.* to be well matched; well suited; fit. **bagayan.** *v.* to help in a project; accompany on a musical instrument; encourage. **maibagay.** *v.* to agree; fit; be suitable, proper. **ibagay.** *v.* to do properly; adjust, fit; make suitable. **pannakibagay.** *n.* conformity. **agkabagaykayo.** *exp.* you guys go well together; you are suited for each other. **Binagayan ti panagkallugongna iti bistukol.** His *bistukol* suited him as a hat. [Png. *nepég,dúga,angáy*, Tag. *bagay*]

bagaybáy: **agbagaybay.** *v.* to encircle hunting game with a rope.

bagbág: *n.* a kind of tree with red flowers and leaves used to cure headaches, *Etythrina indica*. **bagbagen.** *v.* to unravel, disentangle; demolish old buildings (*rakrak*); clear underbrush. [Tag. *wasák*]

bagbagá: *n.* advice. (f. *bagá*) **mamagbaga.** *v.* to advise, counsel.

bagbagútot: *n.* a shrub with black, edible fruits.

bagél: *n.* witch; moron; crazy person. **agbagel.** *v.* to perform superstitious acts. **baglan.** *n.* quack doctor, witch doctor, sorcerer. **agbagla-baglan.** *v.* to act as a witch doctor.

bag-én: *n.* slave. (*adipen*) **agpabag-en.** *v.* to work as a slave. **nabagbag-en.** *a.* enslaved. [Ibg. *ezzifen*, *wásin*, Ifg. *himbut*, Itg. *talaken*, Ivt. *pacirawatan*, Kpm. *ípus*, Tag. *alipin*]

baggák: *n.* (~ *ti agsapa*) morning star, daystar; Venus; beauty queen (*kabuntala*). [Kal. *ambigaton*, Tag. *talà*]

baggíing: *n.* pumice, porous stone.

bági: *n.* share, portion, lot, part; offspring, child; used to show possession: **Bagim dayta**. That's yours. **bagián.** *v.* to share with others. **bumagi.** *v.* to have a share; to have a chance. **ipabagi.** *v.* to offer to share, leaving something for others. **mabagbagi.** *n.* genitals. **pabagian.** *v.* to let someone have a share, to let someone have a chance. **nalmeng a bagbagi.** *n.* private parts of the anatomy. **pannakabagi.** *n.* share. **Bassit laeng ti dawatek a pannakabagik.** I am only asking a small amount for my share. [Png. *apág*, Tag. *kabahagi* (share)]

bagí₁: *n.* body; structure; relative. **agbagi.** *v.* to take the form of, develop into (something else). **agbabagi.** *v.* to be related. **agkabagi.** *v.* to have the same body type; to be similarly built. **bagi ti pirak.** *n.* cash. **bumagi.** *v.* to increase in corpulence; fatten up. **nabagi.** *a.* stocky, corpulent. **ibagi(an).** *v.* to represent, stand for. **pannakabagi.** *n.* representative. **kabagian.** *n.* relative. **kababagi, pammagi.** *n.* condition of the body, body build, physique; physical condition. **sangkabagi.** *n.* stranger, foreigner. (*gannaet*) **agkabagian.** *v.* to be related. **panagkakabagian.** *n.* relationship; affinity. **Adda panagkabagianda.** They are related to each other. **Nabagbagi ngem siak.** He has a bigger body than me. [Bon. *áwak*, Ibg. *baggí*, Ivt. *karakuhan*, Kal. *long-eg*, Knk. *áwak*, *balángen*, Kpm. *katáwan*, Png. *lamán*, Tag. *katawán*]

bagí₂: *n.* self (used in reflexive constructions), **bagik** = myself, **bagim** = yourself, **bagina** = himself, herself, etc. **Ibilangko ti bagik a nagasat.** I consider myself lucky. **Inyam-ammok ti bagik.** I introduced myself. **Nakitana ti bagina iti sarming.** She saw herself in the mirror. **Ngem ti met la bagbagim ti un-unaen ngem ti pamiliam.** But you just put yourself ahead of your family. **Bagbagik ti pinabasol-ko.** I only blamed myself. [Ibg. *beggiveggi*, Ivt. *karakuhan*, Kal. *long-eg*, Kpm. *sarili*, Png. *búkur, díli*, Tag. *sarili*]

bagiát: *n.* a ribbon worn around the calf to prevent cramp or rheumatism.

bagígir: (*obs.*) *n.* small feathers of a rooster.

bagíing: *n.* pumice, porous stone.

bagilawláw: *n.* roaming, wandering. (*awel*) **agbagilawlaw.** *v.* to roam, wander.

baginánay: (*obs.*) *n.* cast of characters.

bagingét: *n.* large pincers. (*ipit*)

bagió: *n.* storm, typhoon. **bagbagio.** *n.* a kind of small long-legged spider that shakes when resting. **naibagio.** *a.* carried away by a storm; destroyed by a storm. [Ibg. *badiyu, bagyu*, Ivt. *añin*, Kal. *byali*, Knk. *pewek, lemlém, báli*, Png., Tag. *bagyó*]

bagiús: (*obs.*) *n.* dagger.

bágis: *n.* intestine, gut; wick of a candle; spindle of a loom; catgut; term of address between siblings. **ibagisan.** *v.* to spill the guts; remove the guts. **kabagis.** *n.* sibling: brother, sister; address between a godchild and the children of the godparents. **makibagis.** *v.* to be related through a religious ceremony (baptism, confirmation, etc.). **bagisan.** *v.* to murder brutally, butcher. [Ibg. *sinay, bitúka*, Ifg. *putu*, Ivt. *cináyiq*, Kal. *byagis*, Png. *páit*, Kpm., Tag. *bitúka* (intestine, gut)]

bágiw₁: bagiwen. *v.* to shake; shudder; tremble (*pigerger*). [Tag. *kiníg*]

bágiw₂: (*reg.*) *n.* freshwater algae. [Knk. *bágiw*]

bagkál: *n.* rice cake. (*kankanén*)

bagkát: bagkaten. *v.* to lift up and carry. (*awít*) **sangkabagkat.** *n.* one load. **pabagkaten.** *v.* to have a load carried. **Saan a panagbagkat iti bukod a banko.** To not be able to carry one's own load. [Tag. *buhat*]

bagkét: bagketen. *v.* to bind tightly.

bagkóng: *n.* stabbing, stab. **agbagkong, bumagkong.** *v.* to stab. (*duyok*) **nabagkong.** *a.* stabbed. **bagbagkong.** *n. Yucca aloifolia* plant with a sharp rigid point at the apex sometimes used as a protective hedge. [Ibg. *dukkayalen*, Ivt. *rawahen*, Kpm., Png., Tag. *saksák*]

baglán: (f. *bagél*) *n.* quack doctor; medicine man; herb doctor. **agbaglabaglan.** *v.* to perform services of a *baglan*.

bagnáw: bagnawan, ibagnaw. *v.* to rinse; wash; clean. (*balnaw*)

bagnét: *n.* pieces of fat used to extract lard; semi-moist wood that is difficult to burn; (*fig.*) person who is difficult to convince or influence. **nabagnet.** *a.* half-dried. **bagneten.** *v.* to dry.

bagnós: *n.* leader, guide; landmark. **ibagnos.** *v.* to guide, lead, conduct; advise. **nabagnos.** *a.* stubborn. [Png. *bagnos*, Tag. *patnubay*]

bágo: (f. Tag) *a.* new; having been in a certain condition for a short time; newly installed; newly settled; **bagíto.** (*coll.*) *n.* neophyte, novice.

Bágo: *n.* highlander; member of a highland tribe in the province of La Union (*Kankanay*); half-breed person of half-Ilocano and half-highlander extraction.

Bag-ó: *var.* of *Bágo.*

bagó: *n.* strips of bark for tying; a kind of small bird with a yellow breast and black back. **binago.** *n.* a large bundle of unhusked rice.

baguén: *n.* a tall tree used in boat making, *Parkia sp.*

bágok: (*obs.*) *n.* contingency.

bagúl: (*coll.*) *n.* tall, dumb man; simpleton (*tabbed*). [Tag. *tangá*]

baguléng: agbaguleng. *v.* to loaf; wander about aimlessly (*ballog*). [Tag. *lakuwatsa*]

bagón: (Sp. *vagón*: wagon) *n.* wagon; railway coach. **agbagon.** *v.* to go by wagon, to ride in a wagon. **bagonero.** *n.* driver of a *bagon.*

bagonéta: (Sp. *vagoneta*: truck; trolley) *n.* small open freight car.

bagungon: *n.* funeral gathering. **makibagungon.** *v.* to participate in a funeral gathering. **Sibibiag koma pay ita ti baket no saan a mannakibagungon.** The old lady would have still been alive today if she didn't participate in so many funeral gatherings.

bagusó: agbaguso. *v.* to stamp the feet in discontent. (*tabbuga, baragsut*)

bagusót: *var.* of *bagusó, baragsút*: stamp the feet.

bagót: *n.* leaves of the *karay*; *var.* of *bag-út*: pull out.

bag-út: bag-uten. *v.* to pull out; uproot. **agpabag-ut.** *v.* to have one's tooth extracted. **Bagutem 'ta gayang ken salaknibam 'ta bagim!** Take out that spear and defend yourself! [Png. *bagót*, Tag. *bunot*]

bag-óy: (*reg.*) *n.* carrying; carried load. **bagoyen.** *v.* to carry.

bagútot: bagbagutot. *n.* a shrub with small green flowers and purple and black fruits that yield an ink that is used in medicine, *Phyllanthus reticulatus.*

baguybóy: (*reg.*) *var.* of *baruyboy*: fringe decoration.

bagrás: *n.* species of tree commonly used in reforestation projects.

bagsák: (Tag.) *n.* sudden fall of something heavy; drop with force. **bumagsak.** *v.* to fall down heavily, to tumble. **ibagsak.** *v.* to throw down heavily.

bagsáng: *n.* a kind of small, fat fish, glass fish, *Ambassis sp.*; a variety of awned rice.

bagsét: *n.* the *apta* fish in freshwater; a variety of awned late rice with a dark hull.

bagsiáw: see *ariyawyaw*: kind of small, edible, marine fish.

bagsól: bagsulen. *v.* to stab, pierce. **agbagsolbagsol.** *v.* to stamp the feet (as in a tantrum). **Imbagsobagsolna ti buneng iti padi a nangtulaw iti kinalalakina.** He repeatedly stabbed the priest that disgraced his manhood with a machete.

bagsót: *var.* of *bagusot*: stamp the feet. (*tabbuga*)

bagtíkan: *n.* species of tree, *Parashorea malaanonan*.

bagtín: agbagtin, bagtinen. *v.* to estimate the weight of by lifting. **mabagtin.** *v.* to be able to be lifted. [Tag. *bintáy*]

bagtíng: *var.* of *bagtin*: estimation of weight by lifting.

bagtít: *a.* crazy, mad, lunatic. (*ballá*; *kuírong*; *kées*) **agbagtit.** *v.* to become crazy, go insane. **imbagtit.** *n.* the reason for going crazy. **nagbagtitan.** *n.* cause of insanity. **Ania ti imbagtitna?** What made him go insane? [Kal. *latingang*, Knk. *tongngók*, *tángo*, *túge*, *tugallá*, Png. *bágel*, *tiwél*, Tag. *balíw*, *ulól*]

bagtó₁: bumagto. *n.* a kind of small mollusk or cuttlefish.

bagtó₂: *var.* of *lagto*: jump.

bagyó: *var.* of *bagió*: typhoon, hurricane, storm. **agbagyo.** *v.* to have a storm. **bagyuen.** *v.* to be hit by a storm. **mabagyo.** *v.* to be demolished by a storm. **bagbagyo.** *n.* a kind of long-legged spider that continuously shakes when resting. [Png. *bágio*, Tag. *bagyó*]

baháda: (Sp. *bajada*: descent) *n.* descent (of a slope). **agbahada.** *v.* to descend; fall (prices). **nabahada.** *a.* steep. **ibahada.** *v.* to bring down; lower prices.

bahár: *n.* (Sp. *bajar*: lower) *v.* to lower. (*pababa*)

bahília: (Sp. *vajilla*: dishes) *n.* dinner set.

bahísta: (Sp. *bajista*) *n.* bass player.

báho: (Sp. *bajo*: bass) *n.* tuba; bass; lowest part in music; voice of a low singer. **baho de arko.** *n.* fiddle bass.

bahón: (Sp. *bajón*: bassoon) *n.* bassoon. **agbahon.** *v.* to play the bassoon.

bái: *n.* bow; bowlike device used for fluffing cotton; homosexual; (Pangasinan) term for old woman (see *babái*). **baien.** *v.* to fluff cotton with the *bai*; *a.* effeminate (said of men); homosexual (men).

baién: (f. *bai*) *n.* homosexual man, see *bai*. [Knk. *baién* = henlike cock]

bailáble: (Sp. *bailable*: danceable) *a.* suitable for dancing (music).

báile: (Sp. *baile*: dance) *n.* dance; ball. (*sala*)

bailita: *n.* rice plant cut and laid out to dry with grains.

baín: *n.* shame; timidity; embarrassment; guilty feeling. **mabain.** *v.* to be ashamed; shy. **nabainan.** *a.* shamed, disgraced, humiliated. **agimbabain.** *v.* to pretend to be shy. **kabain.** *v.* to be ashamed of. *n.* person one respects. **kababainan.** *n.* embarrassment. **ibain.** *v.* to feel embarrassed or ashamed of. **ibabain.** *v.* to shame; insult; humiliate; disgrace; embarrass. **ibainan.** *v.* to respect one's feelings; to not embarrass. **nakababain.** *a.* shameful, disgraceful. **babainen.** *v.* to shame someone. **bainbain, babain.** *n.* a kind of plant whose leaves curl up upon touch, *Mimosa pudica.* **pabainan.** *v.* to disgrace someone; insult. **managpabain.** *a.* continually insulting or disappointing. **mapabainan.** *v.* to be refused and disgraced. **pakaibabainan.** *n.* source of shame or disgrace. **agpipinnabain.** *v.* to insult one another. [Bon. *enel*, Ibg. *pasiran*, Ivt. *masnek*, Kal. *biin*, *kimot*, Knk. *baín*, *lúpa*, Kpm., *marine*, Png. *baíng*, Tag. *hiyâ*]

baína: (Sp. *vaina*: sheath) *n.* sheath of a knife. (*kalúban*) **ibaina.** *v.* to sheathe. **nakabaina.** *a.* sheathed. [Ibg. *kellebban*, Ifg. *híkot*, Ivt. *suhut*, Knk. *sitáp*, *sikét*, Kpm., Png., Tag. *kalúban*]

bainíka: (Sp. *vainica*: hem-stitch) *n.* hem stitching.

baínte: *var.* of *beinte*: twenty.

báir: *n.* scarecrow. (*bambanti*; *ames*) **ibair.** *v.* to hang cloth (to use as a scarecrow); to hang cloth on a hook as a magical charm. [Bon. *sápol*, Png. *tootoó*, Tag. *balián*, *pátakót*]

báis: ibais. *v.* to entrust; charge against what one owes; beat around the bush; imply; give what is due; insinuate. **Imbaisna ti saona kaniak.** He intended his words for me.

báka: (Sp. *vaca*: cow) *n.* cattle, cow. **karne ti baka.** *n.* beef. **baka a (ga)gatásan.** *n.* dairy cow. **binnakabaka.** *n.* a boys' game consisting of passing under a row of legs. **agbakabaka.** *v.* to walk on all fours. **bimmaka.** *a.* resembling a cow; *n.* type of grass. **agbakabaka iti delleg.** (*fig.*) *a.* extremely poor. [Kal. *byaka*, Knk. *tainá*, Tag. *baka*]

báka: bakabaka. *n.* small brown and orange flying insect that fights fellow insects; a game played by children consisting of fighting the *bakabaka*.

baká: (Tag. also) *adv.* maybe, perhaps; might be. (*ngatá, sigúro*) **agbakabaka.** *v.* to be vague; perplexed; anxious; stupid; hesitant. **bakbaka.** *n.* a herb resembling dog grass. **Baka adda idiay ngato.** Maybe it's up (on the high shelf).

bakábak: *n.* a kind of boring weevil that feeds on timber. **bakabakan.** *v.* to be bored away by the *bakabak*; to remove the rotting part of timber. **binakabak.** *a.* destroyed or eaten by the *bakabak*.

bakág: *a.* obese, fat, corpulent. (*lukmeg*) **nabakag.** *a.* puffed up, bulging. **binakag.** *n.* a stout herb, *Hygrophila angustifolia*. [Tag. *tabâ*]

bákak: (Ibaloi) *n.* ritual performed by the Ibaloi before the opening of the harvest season.

bákal: *n.* fight; battle, war. (*gubát*) **makibakal.** *v.* to fight with; (*fig.*) struggle against death. **bakalen.** *v.* to fight; throw a missile in war. **ibakal.** *v.* to throw, toss; throw a missile in war. **mannakibakal.** *n.* warrior; soldier. **pagbabakalan.** *n.* battlefield. **kabakal.** *n.* enemy. (*kabusor*) **Imbakalna ti panagkitana iti amianan.** He threw his glance to the north. [Tag. *digmâ*]

bakaláw: (f. Spanish *bacalao*: codfish) *n.* a kind of tree with pinnate leaves, *Euphoria cinerea*.; a kind of marine fish (codfish); (*coll.*) the smell of a vagina. **agbakalaw.** *v.* to fish for codfish. **agabbakalaw.** *v.* to smell like codfish.

bakánte: (Sp. *vacante*: vacant) *a.* vacant. **bakantien.** *v.* to vacate, make vacant. **mabakantian.** *v.* to be vacated.

bákang: *a.* bandy legged. (*akkang, pakaw, sakang*)

bakár: *n.* a kind of large basket used for laundry.

bakará: *n.* a kind of small freshwater fish, smaller than the *boktó*.

bákas₁: *n.* end of mourning; period of time after a funeral; nine-day wake. **agbakas.** *v.* to be the period of the *bakas*.

bákas₂: **agbakas.** *v.* to bet jointly in gambling. (*sugpon, pusta*)

bákas₃: **mabakasan.** *v.* to be stripped off; unroofed; naked. **bakasen.** *v.* to strip off (a wall, roof, etc.). [Tag. *alís*]

bakása: *n.* salt deposits; sweat stain in a garment. **nagbakasa.** *v.* to be sweaty (clothes); stained due to perspiration.

bakasión: (Sp. *vacación*: vacation) *n.* vacation. **agbakasion.** *v.* to have a vacation; vacation. **ibakasion.** *v.* to take on a vacation. **bakasionista.** *v.* vacationer, person on vacation.

bákat: **agbakat.** *v.* to leave a trace, mark, impression.

bakáwan: *n.* handle; handle of a slingshot.

bakayáw: *n.* a tree used for its timber and whose fruit yields oil.

bakbák₁: **agbakbak.** *v.* to fade; lose color. (*kupas*) **mabakbakan.** *a.* crustless; badly fired (pottery). **bakbaken.** *v.* to knock down; strip off, detach; strip off. **pagbakbak.** *n.* tool used to remove or strip off something. **Binakbak dagiti allawagi ti bobeda ti munisipio.** The carpenters detached the roof of the municipal building. [Tag. *kupas* (fade); *bakbák* (detach)]

bakbak₂: (*coll.*) **bakbakan.** *n.* fight.

bakéd: *n.* body build; body structure. (*pammagi*) **nabaked.** *a.* strong, robust; muscular; strengthened; nice, pleasing; dignified. **bumaked.** *v.* to become muscular; strong. **pamakeden.** *a.* somewhat strong; robust. **Kalalainganna ti bakedna.** His body build is just right. [Tag. *tipunò* (robust)]

bakéro: (Sp. *vaquero*: cowboy) *n.* dealer in cows or water buffalo; herdsman, cowboy. **agbakero.** *v.* to be a cowboy; work as a herdsman; deal in cows.

bákes: *n.* monkey, ape. (*sunggo*) **bakenbakes.** *n.* an herb with pink flowers, *Malachria fasciata*; a kind of bluish wood louse. [Bon. *káag, bolángen*, Ibg. *ayong*, Itg. *káag*, Ivt. *cungguq*, Knk. *káag, akkí*, Kpm. *matsín*, Png. *bakés*, Tag. *sunggo, matsíng, unggóy*]

bakét: *n.* old woman; wife. **agbaket.** *v.* to marry an older woman; have an older woman. **agbakbaket.** *v.* to grow old (women). **bumaket.** *v.* to grow old (women) **bakbaketan.** *a.* very old (women) **agbabaket.** *a.* fond of older women. **apo a baket.** *n.* grandmother. **nakabakbaketen.** *a.* already looking like an old lady. **agbabaket.** *v.* to prefer an older woman for a wife. **agabbaket.** *n.* husband and wife. **nabaketan a balasang.** *n.* spinster. **baket a bullilísing.** *n.* old mistress. **agbaketbaket.** *v.* to appear like an old woman; clown. **pagbaketen.** *v.* to cause one to become old. [Ibg. *bakavákoq*, Kal. *byakbyakot*, Knk. *alapó, bakés, mad-án, sikdé*, Png. *akuláw*, Tag. *matandáng babáe*]

bakéta: (Sp. *baqueta*: ramrod) *n.* ramrod, cleaning rod for firearms.

bakí: *n.* chicken coop, manmade nest for eggs (where hens lay eggs), open-worked basket with a flat square bottom and round rim in which hens lay their eggs; nest. **ibaki.** *v.* to place inside the *baki*. [Kal. *bubukÿutan* (chicken coop), Tag. *pugad* (nest)]

bakiá: (Hok. *bàk kʰiáq* wood clog) *n.* wooden shoe, clog (*suekos*); (*coll.*) term applied to common, low-class, or unsophisticated things. **Awan ganasko ti agbuya iti kasdiay ti**

kabakiana a pabuya. I have no desire to watch a show that low class. [Tag. *bakyâ*]

bak-iás: see *bakas*: disarrange; stripped off.

bákid: (Tagalog also) *n.* large basket used by farmers to carry their goods to the market. **sangabakid.** *n.* one basketful of goods.

bákig: sangabakig. *n.* group of ten inanimate objects. **bakigen.** *v.* to do by tens, group by tens.

bakília: *n.* whispered croaker fish, *Umbrina sp.*

bak-iús: bak-iusan. *v.* to spindle.

bákir: *n.* woods, forest, jungle. **agbakir.** *v.* to cut down trees in the forest. **mamakir.** *v.* to cut down trees in the forest. **bakiren.** *v.* to deforest; work diligently for a living. **kabakiran.** *n.* jungle. **mammakir.** *n.* lumberjack. **tsa ti bakir.** *n.* medicinal herbal concoction used to treat diarrhea and stomach upsets. **Opisina ti Panagbakir.** *n.* Bureau of Forestry. [Bon. *tálon*, Ibg. *kakayiwan*, Ivt. *kakaywan*, Kal. *gilubyat*, Knk. *pagpag, kada*, Png. *takél*, Tag. *gubat*]

bakiwelwél: *a.* twisted, crooked, bent; disfigured. (*killo*) **agbakiwelwel.** *v.* to twist; contort. [Tag. *pilipit*]

bakká: *n.* a kind of basin for washing; very large vulva; (*coll.*) term used to tease obese women. **bimmakka.** *a.* resembling a *bakka.*

bakkawéng: *a.* curved, crooked, twisted; deformed. [Tag. *pilipit*]

bakkuár: *var.* of *bakuar:* vomit.

bakkúg: *a.* curved, crooked, twisted, bent. (*killo*) **agbakkug.** *v.* to curve, bend; cower; shrink. **bakkugen.** *v.* to curve; bend; twist something. [Tag. *baluktót*]

bakkuít: *n.* a spiny shrub whose boiled roots are said to cure Asiatic cholera, *Harrisonia sp.*

bakkúko: *n.* bamboo hoop or rib of the *balawbaw; a.* curved, arched (*bakkug*); bent. **agbakkuko.** *v.* to arch; bend; curve; contort the body. **Pinagbakkuko ti ikan ti bagina sa kellaat a nagkulipagpag.** The fish contorted its body and abruptly squirmed.

bakkúg: *a.* bow-shaped; not straight.

baklá: (Tag.) *n.* homosexual man (*baien, mahó*). [Tag. *baklâ*]

baklád: *n.* spindle; first two threads of a woof; fish trap made of stripped bamboos. **pamakladan.** *n.* selvage (weaving term), edge of woven fabric where the first two threads of the weft are inserted.

baklág: agbinaklag. *v.* to be scarred by bruises or bites.

bakláy: *n.* load carried on the shoulders; duty; responsibility. **baklayen.** *v.* to carry on the shoulder. **binaklay.** *n.* colored ring around the nipple, areola. **pabaklayan.** *v.* to put a load on someone. **pamaklayan.** *n.* pole used for carrying a load over the shoulder. **Bukodakto nga ibaklay.** I will assume the responsibilities alone (carry the burden alone). [Ibg. *vuttungen*, Ivt. *isabhay*, Kpm. *pusánan*, Png. *sakbat*, Tag. *pasan*]

baklíng: *n.* a catch used in traps, trigger device for snares. **baklingan.** *v.* to put a trigger device to a snare or trap; *n.* an effeminate boy.

baklís: *var.* of *baksil.*

baklóg: *n.* testicle. (*ukel-ukel, lateg*)

baknád: *n.* reef; shoal. (*kadili*)

baknáng: (pl. *babaknang*) *n.* the rich, wealthy. **nabaknang.** *a.* rich, wealthy; noble, aristocratic; progressive (countries); advanced; productive (field); fruitful (year). **bumaknang.** *v.* to get rich. **pamaknangen.** *n.* influential man. **pabaknangen.** *v.* to enrich; progress; improve. **agimbabaknang.** *v.* to pretend to be rich. **babaknang ken nagadal.** the rich and literate (social elite class). **Awan ti kinabaknang a kas pateg ti natalna a panunot.** No riches are as valuable as peace of mind. [Png., Tag. *yáman*]

baknér: *a.* bruised, black-and-blue. (*litem*)

baknís: baknisan. *v.* to tear with the teeth. (*kinnit*)

baknós: baknosan. *v.* to remove the outer skin of bamboos. (*káyas*)

báko: *n.* species of shrub. (*tuka, aradon*)

bakó: babako. *n.* a kind of basket carried on the back. (*pasiking*)

bakuár: agbakuar. *v.* to vomit. (*sarwa, bel-a*) **ibakuar.** *v.* to spew (something); vomit. **makabakbakuar.** *v.* to feel like vomiting. [Tag. *suka*]

bakúbak: *n.* dry shell of a gourd used as a container or hat. **nakabakubak.** *a.* wearing a calabash hat.

bákud: *n.* wall; stockade; halo of the moon. **nabakudan.** *a.* fenced, walled in. (*naaladan*) **Pagatsiket ti bakudda a sinako a darat.** Their wall of sandbags is waist high. [Tag. *bakod*]

bakuít: *n.* refugee; *Harrisonia sp.* shrub. **agbakuit.** *v.* to evacuate. **bakuitan.** *n.* refugee camp; evacuation center. [Tag. *likas*]

bakúka: *n.* hair band. **nabakukuan.** *a.* wearing a hair band.

bakúkong: nabakukong. *a.* bulky; overloaded (wallet).

bakúl: binakul. *a.* twilled (bamboo strips in weaving); a kind of blanket with a different colored border. **bakulen.** *v.* to weave; twill.

bakúlaw: (Tag. also) *n.* a kind of large long-haired ape; (*fig.*) ugly person.

bakuláw: *n.* a kind of freshwater fish.

bákulo: (Sp. *báculo*: staff, walking stick, crosier) *n*. staff, crosier. **agbakulo.** *v*. to hold a staff, use a staff.

bakúlod: *n*. hillock. (*túrod*)

bakúna: (Sp. *vacuna*: vaccine) *n*. vaccine, vaccination. **agpabakuna.** *v*. to get a vaccination. **bakunador.** *n*. vaccinator. **bakunasion.** *n*. vaccination.

bákong: *n*. a fragrant, white-flowered ornamental plant, *Crunium asiaticum.*

bákur: **nabakuran.** *a*. having been twisted or bent. **bakuren.** *v*. to twist; bend; contort. (*killo*)

bakúrut: (*obs.*) *n*. high ground.

bakút: **agbakutbakut.** *v*. to carry a lot of objects at the same time; to strain under a heavy load; to be heavily burdened.

bakutók: **ibakutok.** *v*. to insert under the shirt; insert in the waist region. **nakabakutok.** *a*. tucked in the shirt; inserted into the shirt.

bakúyad: **nabakuyad.** *a*. sluggish, slow; listless; indolent. **agbakuyad.** *v*. to move slowly or sluggishly. (*bontog*)

bakráng: *n*. side of the body; slope of a hill. **bakrangen.** *v*. to feel pain in the side of the body. **pabakrangan.** *v*. to strike sideways, at the side. [Tag. *tagiliran*]

bakrás: *n*. slope; hillside. (*ansad*; *induyas*; *arisadsad*; *barikir*; *liday*) [Kal. *challug*, Png. *alosarsar*, Tag. *dahilig*]

bakrát: (*coll.*) *a*. bankrupt; unstable; having no direction.

bakrís: *var*. of *bakras*: hillside. (*ansad*)

bákriw: **bakriwen.** *v*. to carry in the crook of the arm (*bakróy*). **Sumagmamano a lallaki ti nagbakriw iti sangakuribot a ruot.** A few men carried in their arms a basket of grass.

bakrúy: **bakruyen.** *v*. to carry on the shoulders. **binakruy.** *n*. a variety of awned late rice. **sangabakruy.** *n*. one armful.

baksáy: *n*. hillside; mountainside. **baksáyen.** *v*. to climb; ascend; cross mountains. [Tag. *gulód*]

baksiát: *n*. a kind of gun.

baksíl: *n*. other side of a high object (mountain, cliff, etc.) **bumaksil.** *v*. to go to the other side. [Tag. *kabilâ*]

baktád: *n*. pole used to bar a fence or gate, etc. **baktaden.** *v*. to obstruct, bar (animals from crossing). **pamaktadan.** *n*. one of the two posts on which the bar is held. [Tag. *halang*]

baktáw: *n*. omission. **bumaktaw.** *v*. to skip over. (*labas*) **bagtawen.** *v*. to jump over, omit; skip over. **baktabaktaw.** *a*. with many intervals or omissions. **nabaktawan.** *a*. skipped, omitted. [Tag. *laktáw*]

baktéria: (Sp. *bacteria*: bacteria) *n*. bacteria, microbe; germ.

bakwít: see *bakuit*: evacuate.

bála₁: (Sp. *bala*: bullet) *n*. bullet; ammunition; keel of the *baloto* boat. **balaan.** *v*. to load bullets. **nabalaan.** *a*. loaded with bullets. **ibala.** *v*. to use as a bullet or missile.

bála₂: **balabala.** *n*. thought; idea; guess; apprehension; plan; plot; guideline. **balabalaen.** *v*. to plan; conceptualize; trim; to ponder about; guess.

bála₃: *n*. gobi fish.

bála₄: *n*. keel of the *baluto* boat.

balábag: *n*. single-barbed harpoon; (*obs.*) getting a share at a distribution. **balabagen.** *v*. to throw something at; hit with something, harpoon. **ibalabag.** *v*. to cast, hurl, throw. **Pimmidot ti balasang iti binalsig ket impennekna nga imbalabag iti baro.** The young lady picked up the ax and threw it at the young man with all her might.

balabág: (*obs.*) *n*. getting one's share of a distribution of goods.

balábal: *n*. scarf; muffler. (*dalungdong*) **balabalan.** *v*. to cover snugly; to swarm over. **i-balabal.** *v*. to wrap with. **nakabalabal.** *a*. wrapped with (a towel, etc.). [Tag. *balabal*]

balabála: see under *bala*: plot, plan, course of action. [Tag. *balak*]

baláda: (Sp. *balada*: ballad) *n*. ballad.

baládang: *n*. bracelet (*pulseras*). [Tag. *pulseras*]

baladbád: *var*. of *baludbód*: luxuriant growth.

baláding: *a*. bulky; corpulent, stout.

baládong: *n*. a disease affecting swine; hog cholera.

bal-ág: *n*. obese woman. **bumal-ag.** *v*. to become obese (women). (*lumukmeg*)

balagbágan: *n*. a kind of hammerhead shark, *Sphyrna zygaena.*

balagebég: *n*. the sound made by running feet. (*danapeg, tabbuga*)

balagibág: *n*. temporary fence. **balagibagan.** *v*. to surround with a temporary fence.

balagúbag: *n*. bark, soft wood around the *bugas* of trees that is often peeled and discarded.

balagubóg: *var*. of *dalagudog*: sound of running or stamping the feet.

balágot: *n*. kind of small edible leaves that grow in the rice field. (*balángeg*)

Balagtás: *n*. pseudonym of Francisco Baltazar, the father of Tagalog poetry. see *Bukaneg.*

balagtóng: **bumalagtong, agbalagtong.** *v*. to jump, leap over; trip; stamp the feet. [Tag. *dambá*; *talón*]

baláis: *n*. bamboo used to strengthen the shaft of a cane mill; bow and arrow trap. **agbalais.** *v*. to put out a snare.

balákad: *n.* advice; admonition. **agpabalakad.** *v.* to ask for advice. (*patigmaan*) **balakadan.** *v.* to advise; council; admonish. **ibalakad.** *v.* to give advice. **pammalakad.** *n.* advice. **pabalakadan.** *v.* to receive advice, ask for advice. **mamalbalakad.** *n.* counselor; advisor. **Tangay dimo impangag dagiti balakadko, panawankanto.** Since you did not pay attention to my advice, I will leave you. [Bon. *tógon*, Knk. *atúb*, Png. *ópit, bilín*, Tag. *payo*]

balakdáy: *n.* burden; load; suffering; obstruction. **bumalakday.** *v.* to weigh down; overcast; shroud. **ibalakday.** *v.* to bear the burden, shoulder the responsibility. **ipabalakday.** *v.* to put the burden on someone else's shoulders.

baláki: *n.* a kind of white, pink, and yellow marine fish with yellow-colored lips, goatfish from the *Mulidae* family. **pagbalakien.** *v.* to make an assortment, assort. **agbalaki.** *v.* to turn the opposite way (from joy to sorrow). [Tag. *saramulyete* (goatfish)]

balakídang: (*obs.*) *n.* peddler's traffic.

balakkád: maibalakkad. *v.* to obstruct a path. (*lapped, bangen*)

balaknúd: *n.* provisional rice field fence. **balaknuden.** *v.* to surround with a temporary fence.

balála: *n.* plan for a project. (*balabala; gakat; sikat; ranta; gandat; daremdem*) **balalaen.** *v.* to plan, set for a course of action. [Tag. *balak*]

balambalay: (f. *balay*) **balambalayen.** *v.* to go from house to house.

balának: *n.* a tree with poison sap; a kind of fish.

balandániw: (newly coined word from *balay ti daniw*) *n.* theater.

balándra: (Sp. *balandra*: sloop) *n.* bar; obstacle, hindrance; piece of wood placed at the entrance of a passenger jeep for riders to sit on; sailing vessel with a single spar. **agbalandra.** *v.* to bounce; ricochet; boomerang. **ibalandra.** *v.* to put an obstruction in the way. **balandraan.** *v.* to block the way. [Tag. *talbóg*]

balanét: *n.* flotsam, twigs, and grass floating in the water.

baláni: (Tag. *balanì*) *n.* magnet. (*batumbalani*) **mabalani.** *v.* to be charmed; attracted to. [Tag. *balanì*]

balanióg: *n.* leaf of the coco palm.

balánsa: (Sp. *balanza*: balance, scales) *n.* weighing scale. [Tag. *timbáng*]

balánse: (Eng.) *n.* balance; *a.* balanced; equally proportioned. **balansien.** *v.* to balance.

balanséro: (Sp. *balancero*: weigh-master) *n.* weigh-master, part of a weighing scale used to balance two things being weighed.

balánsia: (Sp. *balancear*: balance) *n.* equilibrium, balance. **balansiado.** *a.* balanced.

balantád: *var.* of *balangtad*: lying lengthwise; spread out; inert, lying still (*balát*). **ibalantad.** *v.* to lay out in the open; spread out; (*fig.*) divulge a secret.

balánti: *n. Homalanthus fastuosus* plant whose leaves are used for poisoning fish.

balantík: *n.* being hit by twigs while crossing a path. **agbalantik.** *v.* to flick. **mabalantikan.** *v.* to be hit by a flicked twig. [Tag. *talsík*]

bálang: *n.* marauder; wild animals or insects; a variety of awned early rice. **agbalang.** *v.* to go crazy; become wild; be absent from classes.

balángan: *n.* obstruction; hindrance. (*bangen*) **balanganan.** *v.* to obstruct physically. [Tag. *hadláng*]

balángat: *n.* wreath; garland; crown. (*korona*) **balangatan.** *v.* to crown. **mabalangatan.** *v.* to be crowned. [Png. *balangét*, Tag. *putong*]

balangawán: *n.* a kind of medium-sized fish.

balángeg: *n.* a kind of vine with edible leaves, hollow stems, and purple flowers, *Ipomoea reptans*; swamp cabbage. **bimmalangeg.** *n.* a variety of sweet potato with white meat. **Saankayo koma a kas iti dayta a balangeg a nakaluklukmeg a kitkitaem ngem awan met nagyan iti unegna.** Don't be like the *balangeg* plant that looks substantial but has nothing inside. [Tag. *kangkóng*]

balanggawísan: *n.* fishing tackle. (*banniit*)

balánggot: *n.* hat (*kallugong*); *Scirpus grossus* aquatic reed used in making bags and sleeping mats. [Png. *balánggot*, Tag. *balanggót*]

balang-ít: see *bulang-it*: curvet, leap, prance.

balangkád: balabalangkad. *n.* field not properly plowed. **agbalangkad.** *v.* to skip (said of a plow).

balangkantís: *a.* deceitful; always bargaining; counterfeit; not genuine; *n.* whore. **balangkantisen.** *v.* to swindle; cheat. [Knk. *bagayyáng, daytákan* (whore)]

balangkát: *n.* hoop, rim; plaster cast.

balangkóy: *n.* cassava.

balangtád: ibalangtad. *v.* to put down something lengthwise; spread out. (*balat*) **maibalangtad.** *v.* to lie lengthwise; be spread out; (*fig.*) to be inert, lie still. **Agkaraibalangtad dagiti matmaturog a kaduana.** His sleeping companions were spread on the floor lengthwise.

balár: (Sp. *varal*: long pole) *n.* long piece of wood used by construction workers for measuring.

balása: (Sp. *baraja*: deck of cards) *n.* shuffle; the shuffling of government employees, usually under a new administration. **balasaen.** *v.* to shuffle (cards, government employees). **nabalasa.** *a.* shuffled.

balásang: (pl. *babbalasang*) *n.* bachelorette; unmarried woman; virgin lady. **agbalasang.** *v.* to grow up to be an unmarried lady. **balasitang.** *n.* young bachelorette. **bumalasang.** *n.* maid; young single lady; female animal. **balasangen.** *v.* to flatter; court; employ as a maid. **panagbalasang.** *n.* womanhood; female adolescence. **pabalbalasang.** *v.* to work as a housemaid. **balasang a baak.** *n.* spinster; old maid. **balasang-a-nalasang.** *n.* sexually experienced girl. **Bimmalbalasangankayo la nga awan manaknakemna.** You are just grown up ladies with no sense. [Bon. *balásang, maggit*, Ibg. *magingánay,* Ivt. *kanakan a mavakes,* Kal. *bebeÿasang,* Knk. *longaybán, madáan,* Kpm. *dalága,* Png. *marikít,* Tag. *binibini, dalaga*]

balasbás: *n.* species of weed similar to cogon grass. **balasbasan.** *v.* to go out of the way of; turn away from; trim; beat, whip. **pabalasbas.** *v.* to do haphazardly. [Tag. *putol*]

balasiáng: *var.* of *takuli*: small boat made out of hollowed tree trunk.

balasítang: (f. *balasang*) teenage girl, very young lady. **bumalasitang.** *n.* a young female animal. **kinabalasitang.** *n.* female puberty. [Tag. *dalagita*]

balasúbas: *n.* charlatan. **nagbalasubas.** *a.* insincere, not fulfilling promises.

bálat: *n.* birthmark; skin blemish.

balát: *n.* a kind of black sea worm, sea cucumber. **ibalat.** *v.* to throw down; put down lengthwise; defeat; overcome. **maibalat.** *v.* to be able to throw down; to lie down at full length. **nakabalbalat.** *a.* haughty, arrogant. **Awan ti nakaibalat kaniak iti linnangoyan.** No one was able to defeat me in the swimming competition.

balatbát: *n.* bamboo rafters that run along the roof; bamboo edge of woven bamboo products. **balatbatan.** *v.* to brace a roof.

baláto: *var.* of *barato*. [Tag. *balato*]

balátong: *n.* mungo bean, *Phaseolus radiatus*; a dish prepared with mungo beans. **balbalatong.** *n.* wood louse. **balatongen.** *v.* to flatter; swindle. **balbalatongen.** *v.* to lie to; fib to. (*ulbod*) **makibinnalatong.** *v.* to flatter each other; to swindle each other, dupe each other, deceive. [Kal. *beÿatong,* Png. *balatóng,* Tag. *munggó*]

bálaw: *n.* a kind of tree, *Dipterocarpus sp.* **balawbalaw.** *n.* a kind of miniature freshwater shrimp.

baláw: **agbalaw.** *v.* to startle; wonder; notice; become aware of, realize; to realize a wrong-doing. **babalawen.** *v.* to wonder about; notice; correct, rectify; blame; reprimand; criticize (*uyáw, umsá, dilláw*). **pammabalaw.** *n.* criticism; correction; censorship; blame. **pamababalawan.** *n.* cause for censorship or rebuke. **managbabalaw, mammabalaw.** *n.* person who is prone to criticize or find faults. **Babalawennakami ti kapitan gapu kano ta naliwaykami.** The captain reprimanded us because we were supposedly negligent. [Png. *balaw*, Tag. *surì, pintás, pulà*]

balawbáw: *n.* awning, canopy (usually over a cart). **agbalawbaw.** *v.* to use a canopy (*tambubong, langub*). [Tag. *sibi, ambí*]

baláy: *n.* house; residence; stable (for horses); pen (for pigs); any kind of dwelling; beehive; turtle shell; book cover; case; hive (for bees); sheath of a sword; hall. **abalayán.** *n.* relationship between the two sets of parents of a married couple; term of address employed to this relationship. **agbalay.** *v.* to start a family; build a house; to freeze, coagulate, curdle. **agkakabbalay.** *n.* members of a household. **agtagibalay.** *n.* housekeeper; housewife. **balay íli.** *n.* house in town. **balay tálon.** *n.* house in the country. **bumalay.** *n.* house owner; *v.* to occupy a new house. **ibalay.** *v.* to encase, surround with casing; sheathe a bolo. **ibabalay.** *n.* housewarming. **ibalayan.** *v.* to build a house for somebody; maintain a house for a mistress. **kabbalay.** *n.* housemate. **mamalaybalay.** *v.* to go from house to house; to campaign house to house; canvass. **sangkabalayan, sangakabbalayan.** *n.* one household. **binalayan.** *a.* engrained, embodied. **balay lamók.** *n.* a tree whose leaves are used for sprains, *Crataeva religiosa.* **binnalayan.** *n.* a two-player boys game: steal the stone. **kabalbalayan.** *n.* residential area of a community. **balambalayen.** *v.* to go from house to house. **sibabalay.** *a.* sheathed, encased. **Balay ni Dayaw.** Hall of Fame. **balay a pagtaraknan.** orphanage. **Ti balay no inka agindeg, ti bumalay agalipunget.** *exp.* If you stay too long in a house the hostess will frown. **Ti balay nga dua ti agtagikua, asideg ti pannakarbana.** *exp.* The house with two owners will soon be neglected. **Saan a balay ti kitaen, no di ket dagiti tao nga agtaeng.** *exp.* It is not the house the guest visits, but the inhabitants. **Ti tao a makikabkabbalay, tinembeng amin a gunay.** *exp.* The man who lives in another's house must be careful with his manners and movements. [Ibg. *balay,* Ivt. *vahay,* Kal. *beÿoy,* Knk. *baéy,* Kpm. *bale,* Bon., Png. *abóng,* Tag. *bahay*]

baláyang: *n.* a variety of seedy, yellow, large thick-skinned banana. **binalayang.** *n.* a variety of awned early rice.

balaybáy: *n.* anything hung out to dry. (*salapay*) **ibalaybay.** *v.* to hang in order to dry. **balaybayan.** *n.* a kind of tree, *Pterosperum sp.*; wire or rope used to hang out things to dry. **Agakakas iti balaybay a linabaan iti paraangan.** He is collecting his wash hanging in the yard. [Tag. *sampáy*]

balbáag: ibalbaag. *v.* to slam (the door, etc.). (*banalbaag*)

balbág: *n.* color of the sky; blue. (*asul*) **bumalbag.** *v.* to become blue. [Tag. *bugháw*]

balbál: *n.* young pod of the mungo plant. (*barawbaw*) **balbalan.** *v.* to rinse.

balballúsa: (f. *ballúsa*) *n.* a spiny, white-flowered herb resembling the eggplant.

balbaltík: (f. *baltik*) *n.* wriggler; mosquito larva; restless child. [Tag. *kitikití*]

balbíki: *var.* of *barbeki*: brace and bit.

bálbula: (Sp. *válvula*: valve) *n.* valve.

baldá: mabalda. *v.* to sprain; be rejected outright. **baldaen.** *v.* to injure.

baldádo: (Sp. *baldado*: crippled; worn-out) *a.* seriously injured; with a dislocated bone; disabled; defective from overuse. **baldaduen.** *v.* to seriously injure; cripple. **Baldadonsa ti lakay ta adda muletana iti kotse.** I think the old man is seriously injured because he has crutches in his car.

baldadór: *n.* one who frequently hurts or injures fellow players in sports.

baldák: mabaldak. *v.* to fall on one's back (*tuang*). [Tag. *tumbá*]

baldakíno: (Sp. *baldaquino*: baldachin) *n.* baldachin, canopy for the sacrament.

baldát: *n.* meat of the *langka* (jackfruit).

bálde: (Sp. *balde*: pail) *n.* pail; bucket. (*tímba*) **ibalde.** *v.* to put in a pail. **agbalde.** *v.* to use a pail; (*reg.*) to mop a floor.

baldés: balbaldes. *n.* a kind of burweed with large fruits.

báldi: (Sp. *balde*: pail) *n.* a large can; kerosene can; pail.

baldíit: *n.* slingshot; catapult (*palsiit*). [Tag. *tiradór* (Sp.)]

baldíki: *var.* of *barbeki*: brace and bit.

baldóng: *n.* kind of machete.

baldósa: (Sp. *baldosa*: floor tile) *n.* floor tile. **agbaldosa.** *v.* to place tiles. **baldosin.** *n.* small paving tile. **agpabaldosa.** *v.* to have a floor tiled.

baldosín: (Sp. *baldosín*: small tile) *n.* small, square tile.

bále: (Sp. *vale*: it is worth) *n.* value; importance; significance; I.O.U. **agbale.** *v.* to write an I.O.U. to acknowledge a debt. **saan nga bale.** It doesn't matter. **bumale.** *v.* to buy on credit. **bale-awan.** *v.* disregard; ignore. **bale-bale.** very good. **ipabale.** *v.* to give on credit.

baléd: *n.* welt; circlets of embossed ornaments; punishment consisting of flicking the shin with the thumb; (*reg.*) *var.* of *balunet*: bar used to lock a door. **agbinaled.** *v.* a game whose loser is punished by the *baled*. **baleden.** *v.* to scrape someone's shin bone with the thumb. [Tag. *latay* (welt)]

baledbéd: *n.* a kind of spiny fish; binding. **baledbedan.** *v.* to bandage a wound with cloth; to screen a window or door (*balengbéng*); bind.

balediktórian: (Eng.) *n.* valedictorian. **agbalediktorian.** *v.* to be the valedictorian.

báleg: *a.* big; large; enormous. (*dakkel*)

balegbég₁: *n.* swelling; wale. (*batlag*)

balegbég₂: **maibalegbeg.** *v.* to pierce; penetrate; run aground (boats) (*sadsad*).

balembén: *n.* screen; dam; temporary obstruction. **mabalembenan.** *v.* to be hindered, obstructed.

balensiána: (Sp. *valenciana*: Valencian) **arros balensiana.** *n.* paella, Valencian rice dish.

balengbéng: balengbengan. *v.* to screen; protect with a screen. **maibalengbeng.** *v.* to be unable to move; obstructed.

baleriána: (Sp. *valeriana*) *n.* valerian, a plant with white or pink flowers and medicinal roots, used as a nerve sedative and antispasmodic.

báles: *n.* revenge; retribution; remuneration. **bumales.** *v.* to take revenge; make remuneration; reward; to survive transplantation (plants). **agbabales.** *v.* to change; alter; alternate. **ibales.** *v.* to seam and hem; take revenge on. **balsen.** *v.* to avenge. **manangibales.** *a.* vengeful. **mangibales.** *n.* avenger. **balembales.** *n.* act of continually avenging one another. **agbalembales.** *v.* to continually avenge each other (as in a feud). **Inkarik nga agibalesak.** I vowed to take revenge. **Diak makaarikap iti maibalesko a balikas.** I cannot think of a rebuttal. [Knk. *báes*, Png. *balés*, Tag. *gantí*]

bal-ét: bumalbal-et. *v.* to go (be inserted) in between. (*ratíp*) **makibalbal-et.** *v.* to interrupt a conversation. (*ballaet*). **bal-eten.** *v.* to intersperse; insert between. [Tag. *patláng*]

baléte: *var.* spelling of *baliti*: banyan tree.

balétse: *var.* of *buritse*.

baliád: ibaliad. *v.* to resell; retail; transfer from one shoulder to another. **agbaliad.** *v.* to resell; to do something contrary to normal; fall backwards; go back on one's word. **mabaliad.** *v.* to fall backwards; be thwarted.

baliádo: (Sp. *variado*: varied) *a.* changed. (*baliw*)

baliáng: *n.* species of taro root. (*aba*)

baliásat: baliasaten. *v.* to cross a field, road, etc. (*ballasiw, daliasat*). [Tag. *tawíd*]

balibád: mabalibad. *v.* to mispronounce; make a mistake. **agbalbalibad.** *v.* to revolve; move around (boats.) [Tag. *kamalí*]

balibág: ibalibag. *v.* to slam down an object.

bálibol: (Eng.) *n.* volleyball. **balibolan.** *n.* volleyball court. **balibolista.** *n.* volleyball player.

balidbíd: *var.* of *baledbed*: binding.

bálido: (Sp. *válido*: valid) *a.* valid.

baliéna: (Sp. *ballena*: whale) *n.* whale. [Ivt. *ruyung*, Tag. *balyena*]

balíga: *n.* a kind of edible freshwater fish; bar used in weaving to help insert the *buluan*. **balbaliga.** *n.* a kind of bean with large pods; silver bar fish (*Chirocentrus dorab*). **bimmaliga.** *a.* with a sharp ridge.

baligawgáw: *n.* tramp, vagabond. (*bayanggudaw; alibtok; patotot*) **maibaligawgaw.** *v.* to be distracted; lose one's way. [Tag. *hampaslupà*]

baligáya: *n.* person who pounds rice with acrobatics; acrobat. **balbaligaya.** *n.* show-off.

balík: *n.* scrappy garment. **agbalik.** *v.* to change; turn; make a *balik*. **agbalikbalik.** *v.* to move to and fro. **baliken.** *v.* to retract, recant. [Tag. *balík* = return]

balikangkáng: *n.* chignon in platted hair; bun. (*pinggol*) **agbalikangkang.** *v.* to become contorted; twist. [Tag. *pusód* (bun)]

balikás: *n.* word; syllable; pronunciation, speech. **agbalikas.** *v.* to utter; pronounce. **agbalbalikas.** *v.* to be meaningful. **nabalikas.** *a.* clearly articulated. **balikasen, baliksen.** *v.* to pronounce. **sangkabalikas.** *n.* syllable; always uttering. **sangabalikas.** one word. **apagbalikas.** *adv.* in a short time. **ibalikas.** *v.* to utter, say, pronounce. **iti maymaysa a balikas.** *adv.* briefly. **Ania man a baliksen wenno isawangmo mabalin a maaramat kontra kenka iti pagukoman.** Whatever you say or utter may be used against you in a court of law. [Png. *balikás*, Tag. *salitâ*]

balikawkáw: see *salikawkaw*: do in a roundabout way.

balikawwét: *a.* twisted, spirally coiling (vines); clawlike. (*barikawwet*)

balik-báyan: (Tag.) *n.* Filipino who returns home to the Philippines after a stay abroad. **agbalikbayan.** *v.* to go home to the Philippines. **Nagbalikbayan kano tapno sumapul metten iti kapunganna.** He went home to the Philippines supposedly to look for a mate.

balíkid: *n.* reverse side, other side (*ballikid*); wrong side. **bumalikid.** *v.* to roll over; turn over. **balikiden.** *v.* to turn over to the reverse side. **ibalikid.** *v.* to turn over; put the wrong side up. **Agbalbalikid iti iddana, kasla masinsinit ti bagina.** He keeps turning as he lies like his body is on fire. [Tag. *baligtád*]

balikongkóng: **nabalikongkong.** *a.* twisted, contorted. (*riwis*) **binalikongkong.** *n.* a round, twisted bread loaf. [Tag. *pilipit*]

balikuskús: see *balikutkut*: stoop; bend the body.

balikutkút: agbalikutkut. *v.* to bend the body; stoop; wriggle; squirm. [Tag. *mamaluktót*]

balikutsá: (Sp. *melcocha*: taffy) *n.* sugar used to make confections, taken from the boiled sap of the sugarcane and coiled; taffy. **Naibuang ti bimmalikutsa nga isemna.** She broke into a sweet (taffylike) smile. [Tag. *panutsá*]

baliktád: *a.* inside out; upside down; reversed; inverted; *n.* reverse, other side. **baliktaden.** *v.* to turn over; make inside out; turn upside down; invert. **balibaliktad.** *a.* disorganized; messy; topsy-turvy. [Png. *biyék, benég, baligtád* (reverse side); *pigár* (inside out); *balintuwág* (upside down); Tag. *baligtád*]

baliling-ét: *n.* prickly heat. (*bagas-ling-ét*)

balímbing: *n.* kind of sweet yellow-green fruit.

balín: mabalin. *a.* possible; allowed, permitted; *v.* to be able, can; *adv.* maybe, perhaps; possibly. **agbalin.** *v.* to become, be (in the negative command); to turn into; to be possible or effective. **balinen.** *v.* to change, transform. **ibabalin.** *n.* the act of becoming. **kababalin.** *n.* habit, custom; kind, sort. **kabalinan.** *n.* ability; capability; competence. **mabalinan.** *v.* having the ability to do. **mabalbalin.** *adv.* maybe, perhaps. **mannakabalin.** *a.* all-powerful. **pagbalinan.** *n.* outcome, result; effect. (*pagbanagan*) **pagbalinen.** *v.* to create; make possible. **balbalinen.** *v.* to do what can be done under the circumstances. **pannakabalin.** *n.* power; influence. **Awan ti mabalinmi no di makirupak.** There is nothing we can do but fight. **Agbalin amin a kalman a tagainep ti ragsak.** All yesteryears become happy dreams. [Tag. *kaya, puwede* (Sp.)]

balinawnáw: *n.* vomit with bile. (*sarua*) **agbalinawnaw.** *v.* to vomit with bile. [Tag. *suka*]

balinó: *n.* water lily.

balinsuék₁: *a.* upside down (*baluknóg*). **agbalinsuek.** *v.* to do something upside down. **balinsueken, ibalinsuek.** *v.* to place upside down; to suffer losses; be bankrupt; turn against in treason. **mabalinsuek.** *v.* to fall head first. [Tag. *tiwarík*]

balinsuék₂: *n.* variety of bean with yellow flowers.

balintawák, balintawág: *n.* a kind of checkered or cross-barred pattern.

balintuág: *a.* inverted; *n.* somersault. **agbalintuag.** *v.* to somersault; tumble. **balintuagen.** *v.* to turn upside down, roll over. **mabalintuag.** *v.* to roll over. [Tag. *taób*]

balínga: mabalinga. *v.* to mishear something.

baling-ád: mabaling-ad. *v.* to be pulled back violently. (*baliad*; *balungiad*)

balingagtá: *n.* a kind of ebony, *Diospyros sp.*

balingásay: *n.* a kind of tree with red edible fruits, *Buchanania arborescens.*

baling-át: *var.* of *baling-ad*: pull back violently.

balingató: *n.* a kind of mudfish trap. (*bangkat*; *bukatot*) **balingatuan.** *v.* to trap fish in a *balingato* trap.

balingegngég: nabalingegngeg. *a.* stubborn, obstinate. (*galasugas*; *bengngeg*; *punged*; *suber*; *sukir*; *suer*; *suweng*; *pakutibeg*, *bangad*)

balinggás: *n.* a variety of awned early rice with speckled hull.

balinggása: *n.* a kind of large mollusk.

balinggi: see *linggi*: seesaw; rock.

balinghóy: (Tag.) *n.* species of cassava.

balingiád: *var.* of *balungiad.*

balíngit: balbalingitan. *v.* to shake someone by the shoulder.

balingkanáway: *n.* an omen of seeing something extraordinary.

balinglíng: *a.* inverted. **balinglíngen.** *v.* to turn around in the opposite direction or location. **balibalinglingen.** *v.* to turn over on all sides. **Nagbalingling ti baketna a nangakkal iti naikalladay a tabungaw.** His wife turned around to remove the bottle gourd hanging from the shoulder strap. [Tag. *pulingling*]

baliúdong: *n.* carefree person with no responsibilities or work. **agbaliudong.** *v.* to roam around. (*sulpeng*; *ballog*)

balísa: (Sp. *valija*: valise) *n.* nameplate of a street; crosslike sign.

balisák: see *barsiat*: break; snap. (*maspak*)

balisóng: *n.* butterfly knife; big knife. **sibabalisong.** *a.* armed with a butterfly knife.

balisongsóng: *n.* cone; funnel. (*sungusung*; *sarongosong*) **balisongsongen.** *v.* to make cone shaped. **binalisongsong.** *n.* kind of rice cake. [Tag. *balisongsóng*]

balítang: *n.* bamboo seat (*papag*; *dalagan*); box where grass for water buffalo is kept.

balítaw: *n.* a kind of native dance.

balíti: *n.* *Ficus sp.* trees (*sanglaw*), banyan tree. **pamalitien.** *n.* tree with valuable timber.

bimmaliti a ramay. thick fingers (resembling the *balite* tree). [Tag. *balitè*]

balitók: *n.* gold. **balitokan.** a kind of speckled marine fish. **binalitokan.** *n.* different varieties of maize mixed together. **nabalitokan.** *a.* golden. **Nabalitokan ti pusona.** *exp.* He has a heart of gold. **Naipasngay nga addaan balitok iti ngiwatna.** *exp.* to be born rich (born with gold in the mouth). **bimmalitok nga init.** golden sun. [Kal. *buÿawan*, Knk. *lapúgan*, *buláwan*, Png. *balitók*, Tag. *gintô*]

balitungég: *n.* a kind of worm (common to sweet potatoes); portion of worm-eaten produce. **binalitungeg.** *a.* worm-eaten; rotten; (*fig.*) corrupt. **Binalitungeg 'ta utekmon!** *exp.* Your head has become rotten (worm infested). [Tag. *bulók*]

balittád: *var.* of *baliktad*: inside out; wrong side up; inverted.

báliw: *n.* opposite shore; opposite side. **agbaliw.** *v.* to change, alter; fade; to be unstable; go across, traverse; lose value. **agbaliwbaliw.** *v.* to be unstable; fickle. **ibaliw.** *v.* to take across (to the other side). **baliwen.** *v.* to cross, wade across. (*ballasiw*) **baliwan.** *v.* to change; replace; alter; repeat, do again; correct, mend. **managbalbaliw.** *a.* prone to change; fickle. **Talaga a dakkel ti namnamana a mapagbaliwna ti panunotko.** He really has high hopes of changing my mind. **Binaliwanna a pinunno ti barukongna iti angin sa bimmatok.** He filled his chest again with air and then dove. [Png. *omán*, *máliw*, Tag. *ibayo*; *bago*]

balíwas: *n.* turn (in motion). **ibaliwas.** *v.* to turn in the opposite direction. (see also *bariw-as*)

baliw-ás: *var.* of *baliwas.*

baliwáto: (*coll.*) *n.* dragonfly. (*tuwato*) **tuwato baliwato, aluadam ta ipusmo ta dinto itaray ti soldado.** children's chant (dragonfly, watch out for your tail so the soldier doesn't run off with it).

baliwegwég: *a.* obstinate (*bangad*); hardheaded (said of men); naughty, wayward. **agbaliwegweg.** *v.* to spend time idly. **Innem a baliwegweg nga ubbing ti annak da Meding ken Pablo.** Meding and Pablo have six stubborn children.

baliwengwéng: (*obs.*) *n.* depth of a chasm. (*bariwengweng*)

baliweswés: *n.* a tree whose fruit is used as a laxative; sound of a strong breeze.

balkásia: (f. *balkat*) *n.* derogative appellation given to a fat woman, fatty, fatso.

balkát: *a.* stout, fat (usually applied to old people), see also *balkasia*. (*lukmeg*)

balkón: (Sp. *balcón*: balcony) *n.* balcony, porch.

balkonáhe: (Sp. *balconaje*: range of balconies) *n.* terrace, space covered by a whole balcony.
balkút: *n.* bundle, package; roll; wrapping. **balkuten.** *v.* to roll up, bundle up; wrap up. **balkutan.** *n.* wrapper (differs from *abbong*, as *abbong* indicates wrapping for the sake of protecting). **nabalkut.** *a.* wrapped. [Tag. *balot*]
ballá: *n.* madness, frenzy; rabies; lunatic; a kind of gray freshwater fish; white gobi, *Glossogobius giurus*; *a.* mad, insane. **agballa.** *v.* to go crazy; become demented. [Tag. *balíw, ulól*]
balláag: *n.* preface, introduction (of a book); comment; explication, explanation; oration, discourse; argument; warning; threat. **agballaag.** *v.* to argue loudly with each other; scream for help. **iballaag.** *v.* to notify, warn; threaten. **ballaagan.** *v.* to threaten (*pangta*). [Tag. *babalâ* (notice)]
ballaayáng: see *ballayang*: kind of sedge.
ballábag: **agballabag.** *v.* to share a pillow when sleeping; to bet at opposite extremes. **kaballabag.** *n.* the opposition. [Tag. *kalaban* (opposition)]
ballaballaét: see *ballaet*: intersperse crops in planting.
ballád₁: *n.* idler; loafer. (*ballog, baliudong*) **agballad.** *v.* to idle around.
ballád₂: **binallad.** *n.* a kind of round, gold bracelet.
balladáw: *n.* large machete, long soldier's bolo. **nakaballadaw.** *a.* carrying a machete. **iballadaw.** *v.* to hurl a machete or long object.
ballaét: *n.* interval; space between. (*baet; bal-et*) **iballaet.** *v.* to intermix, intertwine; interlace; intersperse. **iballaballaet.** *v.* to plant crops interspersed in a row (one kind after another). **bumallaet.** *v.* to intervene; interrupt; interfere; get between (two fighting people). **makiballaet.** *v.* to interfere. **ballaetan.** *v.* to insert between two things. **Ala, tapno agtalnakayo, agbibinnalaet ti pagtugawan dagiti babbai ken lalaki.** Okay, so you (children) will calm down, sit boy-girl-boy-girl. **No dika kuma bimmalaet, naragsak kukma ti panagdennami kenkuana.** If you hadn't interfered, we would have been happy together. [Png. *salét*, Tag. *pagitan, patláng*]
ballág: *a.* slightly cross-eyed. **agballaballag.** *v.* to appear intermittently; to have wandering eyes; to be very slightly cross-eyed.
ballagúbag: *n.* alburnum, sapwood, splintwood.
ballaibá: *n.* eel grass, *Vallisneria gigantea* with edible roots (*gurgurmot*).
ballaibí: *n.* spleen; pain in the spleen. **agballaibi, ballaibien.** *v.* to have splenalgia, pain in the spleen. [Tag. *palí*]

ballaibó: *n.* evildoer; imposter. **ballaibuen.** *v.* to cheat; fraud; deceive; slander; swindle. **mamallaibo.** *n.* imposter; swindler; cheater (*kusit*). **Pagsardengmon ti ubing a mangballaibo kadakami!** Stop the child from deceiving us! [Tag. *dayà*]
ballaígi: see *balligi*: victory; triumph. [Tag. *tagumpáy*]
ballaílaw: *n.* rainbow. (*bullalayaw*) **bimmallailaw.** *a.* resembling a rainbow (arched). **agsinanballailaw.** *v.* to resemble a rainbow, to arc like a rainbow. [Ibg. *vunnung*, Ivt. *rayiñorang*, Kal. *tileg*, Knk. *balingkáog, bulanglámg*, Kpm. *punináriq*, Png. *kabulalákaw*, Tag. *bahagarì*]
ballangán: **agballangan.** *v.* to block; cut off someone (in driving).
ballangawán: *n.* a kind of marine fish larger than the *baramban*; hardtail fish, *Megalaspis cordyla*. (*ballangawán*)
ballaulíng: *n.* a kind of small fish.
ballásat: **agballasat.** *v.* to cross over; roll over.
ballásiw: *n.* opposite side of; place across. **agballasiw.** *v.* to cross to the other side; change political parties or affiliations. **bumallasiw.** *v.* to pass; go across; get across. **iballasiw.** *v.* to take to the other side. **pagballasiwan.** *n.* crossing; pedestrian lane. **ballasiwen.** *v.* to cross, ford. **ballasiw-taaw.** *a.* overseas. **agballasiwtaaw.** *v.* to go overseas. [Kal. *chomang*, Knk. *tupák, súpang, lasín*, Png. *beltang*, Tag. *kabilâ, ibayo*]
ballasúg: *n.* a kind of shrimp.
ballasóy: *n.* a kind of shrimp living in holes near the seashore.
ballát: *n.* inner wood of the bamboo or rattan. **ballatan.** *v.* to strip the inner part of bamboo; skin; (*coll.*) mulct. **pagiballatan.** *n.* the inner part of bamboo stripped from the outer skin. [Tag. *balát* = skin]
ballatád: **ballataden.** *v.* to throw a big knife at. **agballatad.** *v.* to somersault; rebound. **pagballatadan.** *n.* effect; outcome. **maballatadan.** *v.* to be hit back. [Tag. *balibág*]
ballaték: **agballatek.** *v.* to bounce off; rebound; boomerang. **paballatekan.** *v.* to be hit back; to be at the receiving end. **agballaballatek.** *v.* to continually roll over. **Siak ti pagbalballatekan ti pungtotna.** *exp.* I am usually the victim of his anger. [Tag. *talbóg*]
ballátik: **maballatikan.** *v.* to be hit or scratched by a chip or splinter. **agballatik.** *v.* to splinter. [Tag. *sipák, salubsób*]
ballatináw: *n.* *Diospyros sp.* ebony; a variety of awned *diket* rice; a variety of maize with dark

kernel. **bimmallatinaw.** *a.* like ebony (dark and hard); brown (hair).

ballatiní: *n.* variety of gray-colored *diket* rice.

ballato: *n.* plowing instrument.

ballawáng: *n.* gap, space; void (*balláway*). **naiballawang nga ulimek.** prolonged silence.

balláwas: *n.* internode; limb. **naballawas.** *a.* long-limbed. [Tag. *biyás* (internode)]

balláway: **naballaway.** *a.* with long intervals or time between. (*battaway*)

ballawés: *n.* stroke of the hand; fancy end of a signature. **agballawes.** *v.* to swing the hand; miss a target.

ballawitán: *n.* the young of the *bulong unas* fish.

balláyang: *n.* kind of coarse edge (*Cyperus radiatus*)

balláyon: **agballayon.** *v.* to continue; prolong; extend further; go beyond the deadline; be in surplus.

balliád: see *baliad*: retail.

balliásat: **agballiasat.** *v.* to get across; pass to other side.

ballibí: see *ballaibi*: spleen.

ballígi: *n.* victory, triumph; success. **agballigi.** *v.* to triumph; be victorious; succeed. **panagballigi.** *n.* success. **managballigi.** *a.* always winning, always successful. **naballigian.** *a.* victorious; triumphant. **Naimballigian nga abogado.** He is a successful lawyer. **Awan ti derosas a dalan nga agturong iti balligi.** There is no flowery path that leads to success. [Knk. *bal-ó*, Png. *alignas*, *impanalo*, Tag. *tagumpáy*]

ballikbá: *var.* of *ballaiba*: eel grass.

ballíkid: *var.* of *balikid*: reverse.

ballikúg: *n.* treason, faithlessness. **agballikug.** *v.* to be corrupt; to be unfaithful. **ballikugen.** *v.* to recant; be hypocritical in one's actions or words; distort what someone has said.

balliling-et: *n.* prickly heat rash (*bagas-ling-et*). [Tag. *bungang araw*]

ballíng: *a.* small. (*bassit, battit*) **sangkaballing.** *n.* a small amount (of). [Tag. *katiting*]

ballíngaw: **balballingaw.** *n.* a kind of small bird.

balliúdong: *var.* of *baliudong*: idler; tramp; vagrant. **agballiudong.** *v.* to be idle. (*ballóg*)

ballít: (*coll.*) *a.* small; meager; tiny. **sangkaballit.** just a bit; just a little. [Tag. *bulilít*]

ballitungég: *var.* of *balitungég*: sweet potato worm.

ballóg: *n.* loafer; idler (*baliudong*). **agbalballog.** *v.* to look aimlessly for fun; to always go out to have fun. **Nangrugi ti panagballogko idi agtawenak iti kinse.** I started loafing around when I was fifteen years old. [Png. *bulakból, ngíras*, Tag. *bulakból, lakuatsa, aligandó*]

ballúgo: *n.* bud of the *lipay* vine.

ballók: *a.* curved (poles). **balluken.** *v.* to curve; bend.

ballukánag: *n.* a kind of tree whose fruit is used for oil.

ballukáti: **agbalballukati.** *v.* to be fickle, unstable, wishy-washy, always changing, inconsistent. (*balukattit*)

ballukattít: **agballukattit.** *v.* to change one's mind; be fickle; unstable.

ballúkog: **agballukog.** *v.* to swell (eyes after crying).

ballúkok: *n.* a kind of tree with sour fruit.

ballúkot: *a.* swollen; temporarily abnormally enlarged. **agballukot.** *v.* to swell (eyes after crying). [Tag. *magâ*]

ballúlong: *n.* stroke of the hand; top of door frame. **agballulong.** *v.* to put the hand on the head (when lying down, etc.); to put both hands on the head or forehead (with crossed fingers); to get set to start a race. **Nakaballulong ken nakaammal iti pipa.** He had his hands on his head and a pipe in his mouth. **Nagdata ket imballulongna ti kanawan a takiagna iti mugingna.** He fell on his back and stroked his forehead with his right arm.

ballóng: *n.* colloquial term of address given by elders to young males.

ballosángi: *Solanum sp.* spiny herbs with white flowers.

ballúsa: **balballúsa.** *n.* a spiny herb with eggplant like fruits, *Solanum cumingii.*

ballúsong: **agballusong.** *v.* to wear a jacket; (*reg.*) to wear an inverted jacket or shirt.

ballutó: *var.* of *balutó*: small boat.

ballúyan: *n.* quality of a sound. **agballuyan.** *v.* to resound; persist (sounds); linger.

balnás: **balnasan.** *v.* to rewash; rinse soaped dishes. (*bilnas, balnaw*) **Nagbalnas tapno di napigket ti bagina iti apgad.** He rinsed himself so his body won't be sticky with salt. [Ibg. *sinnáw*, Png. *begnáw*, Tag. *banláw*]

balnáw: see *bugnaw*: rinse (*bilnas, balnaw*). [Tag. *banláw*]

balnukóy: *n.* species of tall tree.

bálo: *n.* widow, widower. **baluen.** *v.* to cause someone to become a widow(er). **mabalo.** *v.* to be widowed. **babaluen.** *n.* family of widows. **manangibalo.** *a.* having a lot of widows or widowers in one family. **Tallopulo kano idi mabalo.** She was supposedly widowed at thirty. [Ibg., Kpm. *bálu*, Knk. *lasáng*, Ivt. *viúdaq*, Png., Tag. *balo, biyudo* (Sp.)]

baló: *n.* upper stalk of sugarcane; stake. **agbalo.** *v.* to stake holes in the soil for planting (as when planting sugarcane). **pagbalo, inbabalo.** *n.* stake used for making holes. **maibalo.** *v.* to step or fall into a hole. **ibalo.** *v.* to cause to sink or fall into a hole; to cause to fall into debt.

baluár: (Sp. *valuar*: value, appraise) *n.* value. (*ngina*; *bayad*; *pateg*) **baluaran.** *v.* to rate, appraise. **Ngimmato ti baluar ti ginatangda.** The value of what they purchased went up.

baluárte: (Sp. *baluarte*: bulwark) *n.* respected man in a locality in charge of defense; watchtower, bulwark; bastion; defense.

balúbal: *n.* half pounded rice; rivalry; opponent. **agbalubal.** *v.* to be rivals. **makibalubal.** *v.* to compete against someone. **kabalubal.** *n.* opponent; opposition. **binnalubal.** *n.* competition. **agbalbalubal a paksion.** *n.* rebel faction. **Napintas dagiti nakabalubalna.** Her opponents were beautiful.

bálud: *n.* prisoner. **pagbaludan.** *n.* prison, jail. **ibalud.** *v.* to pawn, gage; imprison; enclose; incarcerate. **baluden.** *v.* to imprison; confine; seize; bind, tie. **sibabalud.** *a.* incarcerated. **nabalud nga agsao.** *exp.* to be tongue-tied, at a loss for words. [Tag. *bilanggô*]

balúd: agsimbalud. *v.* to trip the legs when tangled; stammer.

baludbúd: agbaludbud. *v.* to grow vigorously. (*rukbos*) **nabaludbud.** *a.* growing vigorously. [Tag. *bulas*]

bálog: *n.* a kind of wild pigeon.

balúga: (Tag. *balugà*) *n.* Aeta, Negrito; person with a predominant Negrito phenotype.

balúkag: *n.* second plowing. **balukagen.** *v.* to twist; twine, bind ropes around. [Tag. *pilipit*]

balukattít: *a.* inconstant; fickle; always changing one's mind. **agbalukattit.** *v.* to be fickle; change one's mind; back out of an agreement. [Tag. *bagu-bago*]

baluknás: baluknasan. *v.* to remove; take away the top of.

baluknít: balukniten. *v.* to turn inside out; to turn a page; to smash. **babaloknit** (*obs.*) *n.* feud between towns. [Tag. *baligtád*]

baluknóg: mabaluknog. *v.* to turn upside down (*balinsuék*); empty by turning upside down. [Tag. *taób*]

balúlang: *n.* a large coverless basket used to hold tobacco; a kind of thin seaweed; high flying rooster. **balbalulang.** *n.* a pungent edible hairthin seaweed; kind of marine mollusk.

bálon: *n.* sack lunch; food for a journey; provisions. **balonan.** *v.* to supply with food. **agbalon.** *v.* to bring food along. **mamalon.** *v.* to carry provisions to. **managibalon.** *v.* to eat a lot in anticipation or before a late meal. [Ibg. *bálun*, Ivt. *mavaw*, Kpm. *bakál*, Png. *bálon*, Knk., Tag. *baon*]

balón: (Sp.) *n.* air balloon; bale of paper or fabric; wide skirt, balloon skirt; long pants.

balunábid: balunabiden. *v.* to appropriate land (a small plot near one's own).

balúnay: *n.* a kind of tree. **nabalunay.** *a.* long, straight (logs). (*tanos*)

balunét: *n.* ward of a lock; bar used to fasten doors or windows from the inside. **ibalunet.** *v.* to bar a door from the inside. [Tag. *trangká*]

balónok: *n.* a strip of bamboo used to help weave mats.

balóng: *n.* term applied to young bachelors. (*baró*)

balungási: *n.* counterpoise of a steelyard.

balungiád: *a.* pulled backwards. **balungiaden.** *v.* to move backward (body part). **mabalungiad.** *v.* to be pulled backwards; pulled back. [Tag. *balinghát*]

balúngos: (Pil., Tag. *balungos*: snout of a fish) **kuskus balungos.** *exp.* potpourri, large assortment; trifles; many things to do; a lot of paperwork or red tape; idle talk. (*tsetse buritse*)

balór: (Sp. *valor*: price, value) *n.* price, value (*bayad*; *ngina*); importance; worth; power. **nabalor.** *a.* gallant, elegant; costly. **pabaloran.** *v.* to have something priced; to make someone appraise something.

balusbús: *n.* merchandise. **balusbusen.** *v.* to buy, purchase. (*gatang*; *sakada*) **agbinnalusbus.** *v.* to exchange mutually.

balusingsíng: *a.* inappropriate; inverted. **balusingsingen.** *v.* to disguise; convince; find fault with; inspect; persuade. **mabalusingsing.** *v.* to be repudiated; changed; reversed; broken (law). **pamalusingsingan.** *n.* reason for repudiating; reason for changing one's statement. **Narigaten a mabalusingsing ti riknana.** It is hard to change his feelings. **Saan a mabalusingsing ti pangngeddeng ti ukom.** The decision of the judge cannot be reversed.

balustráda: (Sp. *balustrada*: balustrade) *n.* banisters, balustrade. (*barandilia*)

balústre: (Sp.) *n.* banister; support for a railing.

bálut: baluten. *v.* to roll up (*lukot*); gather. [Tag. *lukot*]

balút: *n.* a delicacy made from a nearly hatched duck egg. [Tag. *balót*]

balóta: (Sp. *balota*: ballot) *n.* ballot.

baluták: *n.* adipose tissue around the small intestine of pigs.

balutbút: ibalutbut. *v.* to drive into the ground. **balutbuten.** *v.* to pull up, pull out; take out, extract.

balotó: *n.* a small *bilog* without outriggers. **balbaloto.** *n.* toy boat. (*sinambilog*)

báloy: *n.* alternative name for the *bároy* tree.

balóy: agbaloy. *v.* to spawn (said of the *buttiog* fish). **pabaloy.** *n.* water lilies used as spawning grounds for the *buttiog* fish. **panagbabaloy.** *n.* time for the *buttiog* fish to spawn in the water lilies.

baluybúy: *n.* a large net used to catch mudfish.

bálsa: (Sp. *balsa:* raft) *n.* raft, float (*rakit*); harrow. **agbalsa.** *v.* to ride a raft. **balsaan.** *v.* to cross the river on a raft. [Kal. *beÿsa*]

balsamár: (Sp. *embalsamar:* embalm) **balsamaren.** *v.* to embalm, preserve a corpse from decay by use of chemicals. **balsamador.** *n.* embalmer.

bálsamo: (Sp. *bálsamo:* balsam) *n.* balsam, balsam oil. (*subusob*) **nabalsamo.** *a.* embalmed. **balsamuen.** *v.* to embalm.

bálse: (Sp. *valse:* waltz) *n.* waltz. **agbalse.** *v.* to dance the waltz. **balse-kawiwit.** slow dance in which the dancers are hooked together.

balsén: (f. *bales*) *v.* to avenge.

balséro: (f. *balsa*) *n.* raftsman, ferryman. (*rakit*)

balsíg: balsigen. *v.* to chop wood; ax (*wasay*). **balbalsig.** *n.* praying mantis. [Tag. *sibák* (chop wood)]

balsóg: *a.* chubby, stout; obese (*lukmeg*). [Tag. *tabâ*]

balták: ibaltak. *v.* to throw. (*bato*)

baltáw: bumaltaw. *v.* to float (*tapaw; lumtaw*). [Tag. *lutang*]

baltík: baltiken, ibaltik. *v.* to flip. (*piltik*) **balbaltik.** *n.* mosquito larva; a kind of shrimp; restless person. **balbaltik ti ulo.** *exp.* crazy in the head. [Tag. *pitík, paltík*]

baltóg: ibaltog. *v.* to throw down forcibly. **agbaltog.** *v.* to slump down; rock back (in a chair). **Imbaltogna ti bagina iti nalukneng a kama.** He threw down his body on the soft bed.

baltóng: *n.* a kind of ballad.

baltúog: *n.* sound made from a crashing or heavy dropping object. **ibaltuog.** *v.* to slam down; thrust down an object.

balyéna: (Sp. *ballena:* whale) *n.* whale; term applied to obese people. [Tag. *balyena*]

bambán: *n.* bamboo strip for tying. (*banban*) **bambanen.** *v.* to make into thin strips of bamboo. (*kerker*) **marabamban.** *a.* nearly ripe (bean); *n.* young bean pod. **maribamban a buok.** *n.* hair that has just started growing (beard, pubic hair). **Linabsanda ni Amangda nga agbambanban iti sango ti agdan.** They passed their father tying bamboo strips under the staircase.

bambánti: *n.* scarecrow. (*am-ames*) [Bon. *sápol*, Png. *toótoó*, Tag. *balián, pátakót*]

bambáng: *n.* drain, gutter (*bannawang*); kind of medicinal plant.

bámbo: *n.* wooden club (*pang-or*). **bambuen.** *v.* to hit with a club. [Tag. *bambo*]

bámos: (Sp. *vamos:* let's go) Let's go (used to entice someone to play one's hand in cards, etc.).

bampíra: (Sp. *vampira:* vampire) *n.* vampire.

baná: agbanabana. *v.* to differ slightly; be nearly identical. **pagbanabanaan.** *a.* similarity; slight difference. [Tag. *pagkakaibá*]

ban-á: agbanban-a. *v.* to think deeply; think seriously; glean. **Marigatan ti utek nga agbanban-a no maminsan.** It is difficult for the mind to think seriously sometimes.

banáal: *n.* a kind of tree with good timber, *Lagerstroemia speciosa*; stench. **nabanaal.** *a.* smelling like feces, or starched clothes that are not properly dried in the sun. [Tag. *bahò*]

banaáw: *n.* lake; pond; river pool.

banabá: *n.* a kind of tree, *Lagerstroemia speciosa.* (*bagbag*)

banabbáb: *n.* sound of a machine gun; popping sound; bubbling sound; sound of a faulty engine. **agbanabbab.** *v.* to make the sound of a machine gun; pop; bubble. (*banagbag*)

bánag: *n.* thing, object; matter; result; effect. **agbanag.** *v.* to result into; end; reach completion; settle down; marry. **banagen.** *n.* resulting effect. **ibanag.** *v.* to conclude; implement. **pagbanagan.** *n.* result; conclusion. **panangibanag.** *v.* to resolve; conclude. **pangibanagan.** *v.* to use. **Anianto man ti pagbanagan daytoy, bukodakto nga ibaklay.** Whatever comes out of this, I alone will take on the burden. [Png. *bengatla*, Tag. *bagay*]

banág: *n.* a kind of spiny vine, *Smilax bracteata.*

banagbág: agbanagbag. *v.* to make the sound of continuous firing. (*panippip*)

banák: (*reg.*) *n.* plateau.

bánal: *a.* of regular size.

banalbáag: agbanalbaag. *v.* to slam the door.

banángar: *n.* a variety of banana.

banangbáng: *n.* sound of gunfire.

banang-és: *n.* short, strong breathing; snort. **agbanang-es.** *v.* to pant; have this type of breathing; to snort; to clean one's nose when clogged.

bánar: banáran. *n.* sea shore; wide space with no shade. (*kabanaran, kapanagan*) **ibanar.** *v.* to put out in the sun; lay something out in the sun.

banarbár: *n.* sound of broken bells or a broken voice, huskiness of the voice; grating, rasping sound. **agbanarbar.** *v.* to make this sound. [Tag. *garalgál*]

bánas: *n.* high rice field, not reachable by irrigation. **kabanasan.** *n.* plain, wide field.

banasák: *n.* mud skipper fish, *Periophthalmus barbarus*. (*bannasak*)

bánat: *n.* stroke of a whip; lengthening by forging. **ibanat, banatan**. *v.* to strike with a whip; lengthen by forging.

banáta: *n.* common property. **sangabanata**. *n.* a piece, coil.

banatábat: *n.* glow; radiance; light. (*raniag*) **panagbanatabat**. *n.* the brightening of the horizon at daybreak. (*bannawag*) **Agbanata-baten**. The horizon is brightening. [Tag. *liwanag*]

banatbát: *n.* sound of a dropping object. **ma-banatbat**. *v.* to fall from a high place.

ban-áw: *n.* pool in a stream; lake; pond (*dan-aw*). **Inabogda dagiti nuang iti ngarab ti bimman-aw ken pangadalmen a waig.** They drove the water buffalo to the edge of the deep, lakelike stream. [Tag. *dagatan*]

banáwag: *n.* gate; pass in the mountains. (*bessang*)

banáwang: *n.* ditch; small canal. [Tag. *kanál*]

banawbáw: **agbanawbaw**. *v.* to speak vociferously.

bánay: *n.* aromatic reed or medicinal root; slight indisposition. **banay ti bagí**. *n.* slight illness.

ban-áy: *n.* string connecting meshes of a net.

banayábay: **nabanayabay**. *a.* sluggish. (*buntog*)

banbán: *n.* strips of bamboo; a kind of bamboo strip hat. **marabanban**. *n.* young pod of the cowpea.

bánda: *n.* sash, ribbon from shoulder to hip; band; part (of a municipality or body); side (of town); place; billiard cushion. **ibanda**. *v.* to carry a purse with the strap going from the shoulder to the hip.

bandála: *n.* assessment; a kind of coarse cotton blanket.

bandalísmo: (Sp. *vandalismo*: vandalism) *n.* vandalism.

bandéha: (Sp. *bandeja*: tray) *n.* tray; platter; dish. **bandeho ti orno**. *n.* griddle; cover of a suction pump.

bandehádo: (Sp. *bandeja*: tray) *n.* tray; platter. **sangabandehado**. *n.* one trayful; one platterful.

bandéra: (Sp. *bandera*: flag) *n.* flag (*wagayway*); standard. **agbandera**. *v.* to hoist the flag. **nabanderaan**. *a.* ready for auction. **ibandera**. *v.* to inform; divulge; announce. (*waragawag*) **banderado**. *n.* flag bearer. [Tag. *bandilà*]

banderéta: (Sp. *bandereta*: bannerette) *n.* bannerette; small flag, pennant.

banderília: (Sp. *banderilla*: banderilla) *n.* small, colored barbed dart used in bullfighting.

banderín: (Sp. *banderín*: small flag; railway signal) *n.* small flag used for signaling airplanes or trains.

banderítas: (Sp. *banderetas*: bannerettes) *n.* small flags hung for decoration.

bandído: (Sp. *bandido*: bandit) *n.* bandit; robber. (*tulisan*)

bandíli: *n.* blade of a saw. (*ragadi*)

bandílio: (Sp. *bando*: proclamation + *-illo* dim. suffix) **ibandilio**. *v.* to announce to the townspeople (after beating a drum).

bándo: (Sp. *bando*: faction; proclamation) *n.* publicly announced ordinance, proclamation. **ibando**. *v.* to announce something publicly.

bandúg: see *bindug*: kind of large speckled black and white bird.

bandoléra: (Sp. *bandolera*: female bandit) *n.* woman bandit; wife of a bandit; bandoleer, shoulder belt used for carrying ammunition. **nakabandolera**. *a.* wearing a bandoleer.

bandoléro₁: (Sp. *bandolero*: bandit) *n.* flagman; highwayman.

bandoléro₂: (Sp. *bando*: proclamation) *n.* town crier; town announcer.

bandolín: (Sp.) *n.* pandore, mandolin.

bandória: (Sp. *bandurria*: bandore) *n.* mandolin. **bandurista**. *n.* mandolin player.

bandús: *n.* comet; ornament of feathers. **No adda bandus, adda kano angol.** If there is a comet, there will supposedly be a plague. [Tag. *kometa*]

banég: **nabaneg**. *a.* broad-chested; muscular, strong. **bumaneg**. *v.* to become muscular. (*puner*) **Nabaneg ken kalalainganna ti katayag.** He is muscular and just the right height. [Tag. *tipunò*]

banegbég: **agbanegbeg**. *v.* to thump regularly. **banegbegen**. *v.* to knock on.

banel: **bumanel**. *v.* to harden, stiffen; clench the teeth or jaw. [Png. *banél* = loin]

banér: **kabanbaneran**. *n.* adult age. **nabaner**. *a.* strong and husky; powerfully built. **kabam-baneran**. *a.* in the prime of life. [Tag. *tipunò*]

banerbér: *n.* sound of a strong wind or river current; sound of sipping liquids. **bumanerber**. *v.* to sound like a strong wind or river current. **Nagpabanerber iti kapena.** He sipped his coffee.

banesbés: **bumanesbes**. *v.* to move quickly, dart (cars, etc.). **Pinagbanesbesko ti bisikletak.** I sped up my bicycle.

banetbét: *n.* sound of continuous whipping. **banetbeten**. *v.* to continually whip.

baní: *n.* a kind of tree with oblong pods, *Pongamia mitis*, whose leaves and bark are used to cure cough.

baniadéro: (Sp. *bañadero*: watering hole) *n*. bathing resort.

baniága: *n*. commerce, trade; travel; trip. **agbaniaga**. *v*. to travel abroad; wander. (*daliasat*; *biahe*) **Adun ti nagbaliwam ta nakapagbaniagakan iti ballasiw-taaw.** You have changed a lot since you were able to travel overseas. [Knk. *gákay*, Png. *bároy*, Tag. *lakbáy* (travel); *banyagà* = stranger, foreigner]

baniagáw: *var*. of *bannagáw*: chameleon.

baniákaw: *n*. a kind of tree with poor timber.

baniás: *n*. a kind of iguana with edible eggs; variety of awned early rice with striped kernel. [Knk. *kal-ís*, Png. *tiláy*, *basakay*, Tag. *bayawak*, *banyás*]

banidád: (Sp. *vanidad*: vanity) *n*. vanity; something useless or worthless.

banidóso: (Sp. *vanidoso*: vain) *a*. vain; proud. (*pasindayag*)

baniéra: (Sp. *bañera*: wash tub) *n*. large basin (larger than a *palanggana*); wash tub.

bánig: **banbanig**. *n*. elf, fairy; ghost (*al-alia*; *pugot*; *alingaas*; *aningaas*; *atros*). [Tag. *duwende*]

baniít: *n*. smell of burned wax; itchiness caused by heat. **nabaniit**. *a*. smelling like burned wax, hair, food; overcooked; (*reg*.) hot and itchy. (*aniit*)

baniked: **nabaniked**. *a*. husky, strong.

banílag: *n*. bamboo kitchen shelf.

ban-ílat: **maiban-ilat**. *v*. to fall on the back (*baliad*), fall backwards.

banília: (Sp. *vainilla*: vanilla) *n*. vanilla.

baningrút: (f. *bingrot*) **bumaningrut**. *v*. to sniff, sniffle.

bánio: (Sp. *baño*: bath) *n*. bathroom. **pagbanio**. *v*. to use as a bathroom. [Kal. *oomsan*, Tag. *banyó*]

baniomaría: (Sp. *baño de María*: bain-marie) *n*. double boiler or sponge bath.

bánios: (Sp. *baño*: bath) *n*. sponge bath. **agbanios**. *v*. to wash oneself with a washcloth, (as opposed to bathing).

banipbíp: *n*. continual beeping noise. **bumanipbip**. *v*. to repeatedly make beeping sounds.

banírong: *n*. coconut beetle (living also in bamboos). (*bannirong*) **agbanirong**. *v*. to rotate, revolve; turn.

baníto: *n*. a kind of large fish.

banítog: *n*. thumping sound of a falling coconut.

bánko: see *bangko*.

bánlon: *n*. synthetic cloth used in making shirts and sweaters.

bannaási: *n*. a kind of shrub with hard wood and fragrant white flowers, *Murraya exotica*.

bannagáw: *n*. a kind of chameleon; dragon. [Tag. *hunyangò*]

bannakaláw: *n*. a tall tree, *Sterculia crassiramea*.

bannákaw: (*reg*.) **agbannakawan**. *v*. to be worried, anxious, uneasy; restless.

bannasák: *n*. a kind of two-legged tadpole; person who walks in a strange way; jumping fish.

bannatíran: *n*. a kind of dark bird; variety of awned rice.

bannáwag: *n*. dawn; name of an Ilocano magazine. **agbannawag**. *v*. to approach dawn. **ibannawag**. *v*. to publish or publicize in the *Bannawag* magazine. [Ivt. *maysehsehdang*, Knk. *wisngít*, Tag. *liwaywáy*]

bannáwil: **bannawilen**. *v*. to rein; pull reins of. (*bannáwir*)

bannáwir: **bannawiren**. *v*. to rein (a horse or *nuang*).

bannáy: *n*. act of frightened animals scattering in a frenzy. **agbannay**. *v*. to scatter in a frenzy.

bannayabéd: **nabannayabed**. *a*. clumsy; awkward; uncouth. **agbannayabed**. *v*. to be clumsy or awkward; to stutter. [Tag. *lampá*]

bannáyad: *var*. of *bannayat*: slow; gentle.

bannáyat: **nabannayat**. *a*. slow; gentle. **sibabannayat**. *adv*. slowly; gently. **bummanayat**. *v*. to be slow; gentle. **Imbannayatna tapno saan a nalaka a mabannog.** He did it slowly so he wouldn't tire easily. [Png. *tayam*, *aga*, Tag. *dahan*, *hinay*, *yumì*]

bannayét: *a*. slow (*bannayat*); retarded; helpless; pathetic.

banníit: *n*. fishing tackle, hook and sinker. **agbanniit**. *v*. to fish with a hook and line. **mabanniitan**. *v*. to be hooked; seduced. **Daytoyen ti gundawaymo a makabanniit.** This is your chance to catch something (a girl). [Kal. *bungwit*, *bentak*, Tag. *kawíl*]

banníkes: *n*. arms akimbo. **agbannikes**. *v*. to stand with hands akimbo (on waist). **bannikesan**. *v*. to confront someone with hands akimbo. **Idi agsubli, binannikesannakon a nakatudo ti tammudona iti rupak.** When she returned, she stood with arms akimbo pointing her finger in my face. [Tag. *nakapamaywáng*]

bannírok: *n*. coconut beetle. (*es-es*)

bannírong: *n*. species of beetle destructive to bamboo.

bannuág: **agkabannuag**. *a*. middle-aged; youthful. **kinaagkabannuag**. *n*. adulthood; prime of life. **idi kabambannuaganyo**. when you were young, in your prime.

bannuár₁: *n.* hero, idol; invention. **managbannuar.** *n.* inventor. **naimbannuaran.** *a.* courageous; heroic. [Tag. *bayani* (hero)]

bannuár₂: *n.* funnel-shaped fishnet for shallow waters.

bannóg: *n.* fatigue; weariness; labor, toil. **nabannog.** *a.* tired; weary; sleepy. **banbannog.** *v.* to be useless; fruitless; *n.* (lit) birdlike dragon). **agbambannog.** *v.* to do without purpose. **agbannog.** *v.* to tire; wear oneself out; labor. **bannogen.** *v.* to tire; make exhausted. **makabannog.** *a.* tiresome, boring. **bambannogmo.** *exp.* It's a waste of your time; it's useless for you. **pagbannogan.** *n.* endeavor; fruit of one's labor. **sibabannog.** *v.* tired; fatigued. **Agbambannogka no ituloymo ti agayat kenkuana.** You are wasting your time if you continue loving her. **Bayadam ti bannogko!** Pay for my labor! [Bon. *belay,* Ibg. *benneg, vennag,* Ifg. *naátu,* Ivt. *hupag,* Kal. *laungeÿ,* Knk. *ámud, beáy,* Kpm. *pagal,* Png. *alál, banál, kesáw,* Tag. *pagod*]

bannúgis: *n.* outline; form, shape.

bannúyat: *var.* of *ban-uyat:* sprawl.

banuár: *n.* a kind of funnel-shaped fish bag net.

banogbóg: **bumanogbog.** *v.* to be boisterous; sounds of drumming or of the shoes on the floor.

banugsó: *n.* snorting grimace showing disgust *(banang-és)*; stamping of the feet. **agbanugso.** *v.* to make a snorting grimace when disgusted; stamp the feet in disgust.

banúog: *a.* rotten fruit; *(slang)* lazy sleeper.

banúor: **ibanuor.** *v.* to expose to the elements. **maibanuor.** *v.* to be exposed to the elements.

banúot: *n.* stench, unpleasant smell. *(bangsit)*

bánor: *n.* strip of dried meat or fish; variety of cowpea; term applied to long beans.

banurbúr: *n.* sound of a strong wind or river; sound of an airplane. **agbanurbur.** *v.* to make a roaring sound.

bánus₁: *n.* long, narrow strip of farmland.

bánus₂: **nabanus.** *a.* ungovernable (animal); stubborn; unmanageable. *(bangad)*

bánut: **banutan.** *v.* to peel, pare *(ukis).* [Tag. *talup*]

banútan: *n. Hopea plagata* tree. *(yakal)*

ban-úyat: **agban-uyat.** *v.* to lie on one's back; sprawl. **iban-uyat.** *v.* to stretch in a line. **maiban-uyat.** *v.* to fall flat; be sprawled. [Tag. *hilatà*]

banság₁: **ibansag, bansagen.** *v.* to throw something. [Tag. *hagis*]

banság₂: *n.* waiting for the opportune time; rack for kitchen objects; pantry; measure (in music). **bansagan.** *v.* to fall in step, dance to the music; do what is popular, go with the flow. **bansagam ti mapan.** Wait for the right time to go. [Tag. *banság* = motto; slogan; famous]

banság₃: *var.* of *bangsal.*

bansawáy: *n.* a kind of speckled *rasá* crab with long claws.

bansí: **agbansi.** *v.* to kick someone in the ham.

bansúroy: *n.* a variety of awned late rice with red kernel.

bantá: **agbanta.** *v.* to glean. *(agsaw)*

bantág: **bantagen.** *v.* to peer curiously; notice; view; look cautiously.

banták: *n.* raft with sail used in fishing; fishhook and line. **agbantak.** *v.* to catch fish with a hook. **agbambantak.** *n.* fisherman *(mangngalap).*

bantáy₁: *n.* mountain; hill. **bambantay.** *n.* mountain chain; rough and pathless place. **kabambantayan.** *n.* mountain ranges. **ipabantay.** *v.* to take to the mountains; abduct a person and take to the mountains. **tagabambantay.** *n.* mountain person; *(fig.)* guerilla in hiding in the mountains. **Kasla nagsang-at iti pito a bantay.** It seems he climbed seven mountains. **Napalalo ti panangtagibassittayo kadagiti taga-bantay a kakabsattayo.** We excessively belittle our brothers from the mountains. [Bon. *bílig,* Ibg. *bakúlug, vukíg,* Ifg. *bílid,* Ivt. *tukun,* Kal. *bilig,* Knk. *bílig,* Kpm. *bunduk,* Png. *palandéy,* Tag. *bundók*]

bantáy₂: *n.* guard, caretaker. **bantayan.** *v.* to guard; defend; watch; protect. **agbantay.** *v.* to guard; be on watch; stay home alone. **agbanbantay.** *n.* guard, sentinel. **parabantay.** *n.* caretaker; babysitter. **bantay-sabút.** *n.* "it" in a game *(lit:* guarder of coconut shell). [Knk. *áug,* Png., Tag. *bantáy*]

bantáyog: *(Tag.) n.* monument. *(batonlagip)*

banténg: *n.* clothesline; line. *(salapay)* **bantengan.** *v.* to stretch out a line (between two points); to surround with wire, etc. **ibanteng.** *v.* to make a clothesline. [Tag. *sampáy*]

bantí: **bambanti.** *n.* scarecrow. *(bair; pakdaar)* **kaska la agkawkawes a bambanti.** *exp.* ridiculing someone's attire (you dress like a scarecrow). [Bon. *sápol,* Knk. *eg-egiát,* Png. *toótoó,* Tag. *balián, pátakót*]

bantíl: **bantilen.** *v.* to hit or pinch a dying person in order to resuscitate or make the blood circulate. [Tag. *tampál; bantíl* = light stroke with the open hand]

bantó₁: *n.* mixture (watered-down wine). **bantuan.** *v.* to mix; adulterate; dilute. [Tag. *bantó*]

bánto₂: **bantuen.** *v.* to attack, overwhelm; bet (many against one). **pabanto.** *n.* missile, projectile; artillery.

bantó₃: *n.* immigrant, newly arrived foreigner.

bantóg: *n.* lowland; plain.

bantók: **agbantok**. *v.* to flounder when caught in a net.

bantolay: **nagbantolay**. *a.* unbalanced, unstable.

bantót: *n.* weight. **babantot**. *n.* load; weight; burden; loneliness. **nabantot**. *a.* heavy; serious; sluggish, lifeless; stinking, having a bad smell; weighty. **agbabantot**. *v.* to be unwell, indisposed. **mamagbabantot**. *v.* to cause to feel lazy. **pamantot**. *n.* heaviness; weight. **Nabantot dagiti askawna a nagpangato.** He made heavy strides going up (the stairs). [Png. *belát*, Tag. *bigát*]

báng: *n.* sound of a firecracker or gunshot. **bumanangbang**. *n.* rapid fire. **banangbangen**. *v.* to riddle with bullets.

bánga₁: *n.* a clay pot used for cooking. **agkabanga**. *v.* to have a mutual *banga*; to share meals when living together (from the same pot). **agkabbanga**. *v.* to play house. **pagbabangaan**. *n.* part of the *bansal* where the *banga* are washed. [Ibg. *bánga*, Ivt. *vangaq*, Kal. *byanga*, Knk. *palsu*, Kpm. *balangaq*, Png. *sayáp*, *banga*, Tag. *palayók*]

bánga₂: **bangabanga**. *n.* skull. **Patayabek ti bangabangana**. *exp.* I will blow his brains out (*lit*: I will make his skull fly). [Png. *lapislapis*, Tag. *bungô*, *bao ng ulo*]

bánga₃: **bangabanga**. *n.* swarm of insects. **agbangabanga**. *v.* to swarm (insects); *n.* a game where June bugs are tied and fluttered by strings. **Agbangabanga dagiti lamok iti arubayan ti ridaw idi agtoktokak.** The mosquitoes were swarming around the door when I knocked. [Png. *olup*, Tag. *kawan*, *langkáy*]

bángad: *n.* back of a knife. **nabangad**. *a.* stubborn, obstinate; disobedient. **bangaden**. *v.* to strike with the back of a knife.

bángag: **nabangag**. *a.* low pitched, deep voiced; changing pubescent boy's voice; harsh sounded. (*singgit*) **bumanag**. *v.* to become low pitched (changing male's voice at puberty, etc.). **Nakigtot ni Mariana iti nabangag a boses iti likudanna.** Mariana was startled by the deep voice behind her.

bángal: **maibangal**. *v.* to compete, contend. (*salisal*)

bángan: *n.* fire saw.

bangár: *n.* a kind of tree with bad-smelling flowers, *Sterculia foetida*.

bang-ár: *n.* relief; comfort. (*gin-awa*) **mabangaran**. *v.* to be relieved; comforted; lessened (pain). **makabang-ar**. *a.* relieving, comforting; relaxing. [Png. *papakasil*, Tag. *ginhawa*]

bang-ás: *n.* a variety of awned *diket* rice.

bángaw: *n.* a kind of tree whose timber is used for boards; (*coll.*) get-together party. **bangbangaw**. *n.* *Cissampelos sp.* plant with poisonous roots.

bangáw: *n.* long-haired person (*lampong*); male goat; downy (cloth); hairy raincoat.

bangawísan: *n.* a kind of thick-skinned banana.

bangbáng: *n.* a kind of herb used to cure rheumatism and skin diseases. **bangbangan**. *v.* to make a hill (for plants). (*ringkon*)

bangdól: **agbangdol**. *v.* to butt; shoulder; collide with each other. (*dalapus*, *dugpa*; *dunget*; *dungpar*; *dungso*; *salapon*; *sangdo*; *timog*; *kintol*; *pokkool*) **bangdulen**. *v.* to collide with. [Tag. *suwág*]

bangéd₁: *n.* hunting dog.

bangéd₂: *n.* mountain site.

bangéd₃: **agbabanged**. *v.* to be worried, unquiet; annoyed, bothered. (*pulkok*)

bángeg: *n.* hoarse voice; harsh sound. (*bangag*, *paraw*) **nagbangeg**. *a.* having a hoarse voice.

bang-ég: *n.* stench of rotten wood or spoiled grains. **nabang-eg**. *a.* smelling of rotten wood or spoiled grains.

bangén: *n.* small fence to cover doors and stairs when children are present, any device that prevents one from passing by; obstruction. (*lapped*) **bangenen**. *v.* to obstruct; hinder; deter. **maibangen**. *v.* to be blocked; hindered; obstructed. [Tag. *hadláng*]

bang-és: *n.* snort. **agbang-es**. *v.* to snort; sneeze; blow the nose noisily (usually said of animals). (*baen*)

bangét: *n.* stench of fermenting fish, dirty diapers or an unwashed vulva. **nabanget**. *a.* smelling of fermenting fish, etc.

banggá: *n.* large number of things, multitude. **agbabangga**. *v.* to fence; fight with side arms; collide head on. **agbanggaabangga**. *v.* to fight. [Tag. *banggâ* = collide]

banggál: **agbanggal**. *v.* to tie a handkerchief over the head. **ibanggal**. *v.* to tie around the head of someone.

banggáw: *n.* a variety of rice with elongated spike and kernel.

banggéra: *var.* of *bangkera*: backyard porch; place in kitchen where dishes are drained and kept.

banggiáw: *n.* fuss.

banggilát: *a.* cross-eyed. (*pangkis*)

banggól: see *bangdol*: to shoulder, butt.

bángi: *n.* native dance. **agbangibangi**. *v.* to dance in a circle.

bang-í: *n.* smell of toast. **nabang-i**. *a.* smelling of toast. **Adda bang-i ti kaddaripespes a daga a yarakup ti berber ti angin iti pameggesen a**

taray ti kotse. There is the smell of just-watered soil embraced by the rushing wind through the rather swift running of the car.
bangíbang: **agbangibang.** *v.* to be nearby, adjacent. (*apiring*; *sidiran*; *kasigkay*; *tapíl*) **kabangibang.** *n.* someone close or adjacent; suburb. [Tag. *karatig*]
bangiét: (*obs.*) *n.* torsion of the neck through sleeping on the pillow in a wrong position.
bangíg: *n.* kind of tongue-shaped dagger.
bángir: *n.* opposite side; side. **bumangir.** *v.* to go to the other side. **bangiren.** *v.* to use the other side for doing something. **bangiran.** *a.* unmatched, unpaired. **bangbangir.** *n.* one-half of; only one part; only one side; *a.* having some parts cooked and others not fully cooked. **agbangbangir.** *v.* to have uncooked parts in. **ipabangir.** *v.* to place on the opposite side. **kabangiran.** *n.* collateral relative. **kasumbangir.** *n.* opposite side; counterpart. **pasumbangiran.** *v.* to flank. [Kal. *chomang, biik*, Png. *biyek, basil*, Tag. *kabilâ*]
bángka: *n.* a kind of large *bilog* without outriggers; dealer in a card game; the banker in a gambling game, the bank of a casino. [Ibg. *barangay*, Ivt. *tatayaq*, Kal. *byangka*, Kpm., Tag. *bangkâ*]
bangkág: *n.* upland field; dry land; vacant land; vegetable garden. **bumangkag.** *v.* to go ashore; travel by land. **agbangkag.** *v.* to have a vegetable garden. **bangkagen.** *v.* to make into a vegetable garden. **ibangkag.** *v.* to put ashore. **sairo't-bangkag.** *n.* nuisance. **Napanda kinita no adda naala dagiti nakaibangkag.** They went to see if the fishermen coming ashore had caught anything. **No bumangkag ti tukak, umay ti layos.** *exp.* When frogs go ashore, a flood is coming.
bangkáraw: *n.* a kind of legged wooden bowl.
bangkaróta: (Sp. *bancarrota*: bankruptcy) *n.* bankruptcy; *a.* bankrupt.
bangkát: see *bokatot*: kind of basket or fish trap.
bangkáw: *var.* of *bangkawas*: having long legs.
bangkawás: *a.* having long legs. (*baddakaw*)
bangkáy: *n.* corpse; body; box; framework; frame of a cart. [Kal. *lecheg*, Png., Tag. *bangkáy*]
bangkéra: *n.* place in the kitchen where dishes are washed and drained; backyard porch.
bangkéro₁: (f. *bangka*) *n.* boatman, driver of a *banca* outrigger.
bangkéro₂: (f. *bangko*) *n.* banker; dealer in gambling.
bangkéta: *n.* sidewalk; embankment; concrete path.

bangkéte: (Sp. *banquete*: banquet) *n.* banquet. (*padaya*)
bangkíl: *n.* handlelike device for carrying jars between two persons; hoop that keeps doors and windows shut from inside; piece of wood used to twist a rope used for a clamp.
bangkília: (Sp. *banca*: Philippine canoe + -*illa* dim. suffix) *n.* small boat; small bolt.
bangkíng: *a.* different; unbalanced; unequal; unmatched, odd, inconstant; having only one eye, arm, leg, etc.); unstable. **agbangking.** *v.* to tilt; be uneven; be unbalanced. **binnangking.** *n.* a children's coin game where children must guess outcome of two spinning coins, *paris* (same side) or *bangking* (different sides). [Tag. *tagilíd*]
bangkíra: *n.* bamboo shelf used for kitchen utensils (*bangkera*). [Tag. *banggera*]
bangkírig: *a.* sloping, slanting, lopsided. **nabangkirig.** *a.* sloping. (*tingíg*) **bangkirigen.** *v.* to cause to slope. [Tag. *tagilíd*]
bangkíto: (Sp. *banquito*: small bench) *n.* small, low bench; stool.
bángko₁: (Sp. *banco*: bench) *n.* bench.
bángko₂: (Sp. *banco*: bank) *n.* bank. **Saan a panangbagkat iti bukod a bangko.** *exp.* to not be able to carry one's own load. **Nawadwaden ti imbangkona.** He put a lot in the bank.
bangkuáng: (Tag. *bangkuwáng*) *n.* coarse, aquatic herb used in mat weaving, mat or bag made out of the *bangkuang* herb. **Adda imetna a panakkelen a bay-on a bangkuang.** He's holding a large *bangkuang* sack.
bangkúdo: *n.* red cotton.
bangkók: *n.* species of catfish; species of sweet *santol* with large seeds, named after the place from which it comes.
bangkulóng: *n.* kind of fish trap.
bangkúrog: *var.* of *bingkurog*: mound.
bangláw: **apagbanglaw.** *a.* tipsy. (*bartek; alan; ulaw; sinít*)
banglés: *n.* a kind of tree; rancid stench; foul smell of spoiled food; rancid smell. **nabanglés.** *a.* rancid, spoiled; sour smelling; fermented. **bumangles.** *v.* to ferment; become rancid; spoil. [Bon. *bang-es*, Knk. *bidaddéy*, Png. *bangles*, Tag. *panís*]
banglíg: *n.* stench of rancid oil. **bumanglig.** *v.* to turn rancid. **nabanglig.** *a.* smelling of rancid oil. [Tag. *antá*]
bangló: *n.* fragrance. (*ayamoom; sayamusum; sumusum; dangiir; ayumoom*) **nabanglo.** *a.* fragrant, aromatic. **bangbanglo, pabanglo.** *n.* perfume. **agpabanglo.** *v.* to wear perfume; perfume oneself. **kinabanglo.** *n.* fragrance; popularity. [Ibg. *vangúg*, Ivt. *mayababanguq*,

asdep, Kal. *byangu*, Knk. *sum-út, sengáag, sengáeg*, Kpm. *banglu*, Png. *balingít*, Tag. *bangó*]

banglót: *n.* a small *awa* fish. (*bangus*)

bangól: *n.* tusk. **bangulan**. *n.* wild boar with protruding teeth; old animal; see also *bangulán*; *v.* to attack (like a wild boar). **bangol-bangulan**. *n.* big, tough man. **No saan a ni Inang, siak ti pagbabangolanna a kabilen no awan mainkankano kenkuana.** If not mother, I am the one he attacks to hit if nobody is minding him.

bangulán: (f. *bangól*) *n.* veteran; professional (at a trade); old timer. **bangbangulan**. *n.* species of tree.

bángon: bumangon. *v.* to rise, become erect. **bangunen**. *v.* to raise, erect; elevate; nominate; found, originate. **kabbangon**, **kabambangon**. *a.* newly built, just erected. **mabangunan**. *v.* to be affected by or aware of something happening while waking up. **makabangon**. *v.* to be able to start again. **tarimbangon**. *n.* something that startles. **panagbangon**. *n.* construction; erection; establishment of something. **pagbangunan**. *n.* construction site. **-pabangonen**. *v.* to let someone rise. **nabangunan a sao**. native tongue. **agbangon iti negosio**. *v.* to put up a business. **apagbangon**. *a.* convalescent; recently awaken. **Unaentayo pay a bangonen ti gunglotayo.** Let us found our organization first. [Ivt. *yukay*, Png. *bangón*, Tag. *tatag, bangon*]

bangúngot: (Tag.) *n.* nightmare. (*batibat*)

bangós: (Tagalog also) *n.* milkfish. **agbabangos**. *n.* milkfish dealer.

bangsá: (Tag. *bansa*) *n.* country; nation. (*pagilian*)

bangsál: *n.* backyard porch; platform near kitchen used to clean pots. [Kal. *byangseÿ*, Tag. *batalán*]

bangsí: **agbibinnangsi**. *v.* to kick at one another. (*kugtar*)

bangsít: *n.* stench, foul smell. **bumangsit**. *v.* to stink. **nabangsit**. *a.* rancid, reeking, with a bad smell. **bangbangsit**. *n.* an herb with blue flowers, *Hyptis suaveolens* used against rheumatism. [Ibg. *vuyuq*, Ivt. *mayuyuk*, Kal. *byangtit*, Knk. *angbéb, anggí, bangsít*, Kpm. *buluk*, Png. *bangét*, Tag. *baho*]

bangtál: *n.* species of evergreen tree.

bangyód: *n.* appellation applied to namesakes. (*tokayo, kanaganan*)

baó: *n.* rat, mouse; any rodent. **babao**. *n.* a kind of rat with a short tail. **binao**. *a.* eaten by rodents. [Bon. *ótot, kantib, motkal*, Ibg. *uleg, balakeg*, Ivt. *karam*, Knk. *baltút, mágan, útut*,

Kpm. *dagis*, Png. *otót*, Tag. *dagâ*, Png. *baó* = vagina]

baúd: *n.* gamecock; *a.* tied to a post (domesticated animal); (*coll.*) henpecked. **agbaud**. *v.* to keep a gamecock. **ibaud**. *v.* to tie, attach, fasten to. **Patpatgekto a kas iti panangipateg ni amang kadagiti baudna.** I will cherish it as father cherishes his gamecocks. **Nagsarungikngik a kasla ubbing dagiti baudmi a kalding.** Our tied-up goats whined like children. [Tag. *tinalî*]

báog: *a.* seed that did not germinate due to lack of water; odor of stored grains. **nabaog**. *a.* spoiled and smelling due to lack of air and moisture (rice and seeds).

baóg: (Tagalog also) *a.* infertile (people). (*lupes*) **pamaog**. *n.* sterilizer. **kinabaog**. *n.* sterility, impotence.

báukok: *n.* a kind of tree, *Garcinia binucao*.

baúl: (Sp. *baúl*: trunk; chest) *n.* trunk; chest. locker. **ibaul**. *v.* to place in the *baul*.

baón: agbaon. *v.* to order someone to do something. **baonen**. *v.* to send a messenger; send. **babaonen, mabaon**. *n.* messenger, errand boy. **nabaon**. *n.* person chosen to be the messenger or to run a certain errand. **managbaon**. *n.* person who always orders someone else to do errands for him. **pababaon**. *n.* servant. **Naumaakon a kankanayon a baonenyo.** I am tired of you always sending me on errands. [Bon. *báal*, Ibg. *meddog*, Ivt. *macirawat*, Kpm. *utus*, Png. *gan-gan*, Tag. *utos*]

báor: baoran. *v.* to mix ordinary rice with *diket* rice. [Tag. *halò* (mix)]

baór: *n.* switch of an automatic snare. **pabaoran**. *v.* to ensnare. [Tag. *bitag*]

báut: *n.* stick for beating, whip; whipping, beating; a kind of poisonous vine. **agbaut, bauten**. *v.* to whip, beat. (*saplit; basnut; betbet; latiko*) **pamaut**. *n.* stick used in beating. **ibaut**. *v.* to beat on; (*coll.*) to kick in; contribute to a fund; invest (money). **binnaut**. *n.* game consisting of trying to whip one's opponent while dodging his whips. **pagbautan**. *n.* place where one is beaten; ladderlike contrivance used to thresh rice. [Bon. *sapágot, báig, saplat*, Ibg. *pisi*, Knk. *sákab*, Kpm. *baróg*, Png. *dampalís*, Tag. *palò*]

baútek: *n.* door post; side piece of a bamboo ladder.

bautisár: (Sp. *bautizar*: baptize) **bautisaran**. *v.* to baptize. **bautisado**. *a.* baptized. (*buniag*)

bápa: (*reg.*) *n.* title of respect for person one generation older than the speaker.

bapór: (Sp. *vapor*: ship) *n.* ship; vapor. **agbapor**. *v.* to go by ship. **bapor de gera**. *n.* warship. [Kal. *byapuÿ*]

bára₁: (Sp. *vara*: yardstick) *n*. yardstick, 80 cm. long.

bára₂: (Sp. *barra*: bar) *n*. bar; encumbrance.

bára₃ *n*. heat; warmth (*pudot*). **baraen**. *v*. to measure something by the *bara*. **na(g)bara**. *a*. red hot. **bumara**. *v*. to become red hot; angry, violent. **agbabara**. *v*. to be hot with fever. **agbara**. *v*. to block, prevent; to be very hot. **makapabara a pelikula**. *n*. hot, steamy movie. **agbinnara**. *v*. to argue heatedly. **pabaraen**. *v*. to heat up. [Tag. *init*]

bára₄: **barabara**. *n*. freestyle swimming. **agbarabara**. *v*. to swim freestyle. [Tag. *barabara*]

bará₁: *n*. lung. [Ibg. *baga*, *lettaq*, Ivt. *pwaw*, Kal. *beÿá*, Knk. *ballá*, Bon., Png. *balá*, Kpm., Tag. *bagà*]

bará₂: **babara**. *n*. buboes, swellings in the groin. (*pannakalen*) **agbabara**. *v*. to have buboes, swellings in the groin. [Tag. *kulanì*]

bará₃: **aginbara**. *a*. ripening, red plum. (*karimbara*, *darangidangan*)

bará₄: **babaraén**. *v*. to be timid, cowardly. (*bain*)

barábad: *n*. binding, wrapping a part of the body; shawl. **barabadan**. *v*. to put a bandage around something; put a shawl on someone. **nabarabadan**. *a*. wrapped up; bandaged; blindfolded. **Nagsangit idi madlawna ti nabarabadan a rupa ken takkiagna.** She cried when she noticed his bandaged face and arms. [Tag. *benda*]

barabaddáw: *n*. haphazard work; carelessness; *a*. careless, haphazard. (*barubaddut*)

barabbáb: *n*. popping sound, sound of a faulty engine. **agbarabbab**. *v*. to make a popping sound.

barad-áy: *n*. clothes being dried in the sun. **ibarad-ay**. *v*. to hang in the sun to dry. (*salapay*)

baradéro: (Sp. *varadero*: shipyard) *n*. shipyard, dockyard. [Tag. *dahikan*, *dalahikan*]

baradibúd: *n*. porridge made from beans and/or tubers.

barádo: (Sp. *barrado*: barred) *a*. clogged; plugged up (so contents cannot come out).

barág: *a*. rotating unevenly (spinning top); faltering. **bumarag**. *v*. to rotate unevenly; falter (when speaking).

baragúbay: see *barayubay*: fringe; decoration.

baragsót: *n*. joker; abrupt jerking movement made when upset. **agbaragsot**. *v*. to jerk.

baráha: (Sp. *baraja*: deck) *n*. deck of cards.

baraírong₁: **agbarairong**. *v*. to revolve, rotate; turn; become wayward; become restless. **nabarairong**. *a*. restless, unquiet.

barairong₂: *var*. of *barrairong*: coconut borer; (*fig*.) troublemaker, wayward person.

barákang: *n*. girdle (placed around hogs, etc. so they cannot escape); binding; belt. **agbarakang**. *v*. to girdle; bind one's chest. [Tag. *paha* (girdle)]

barakbák: see *barakubak*: withered leaf, small leaf of the bittermelon vine. (*laylay*; *barakubak*)

barakílan: *n*. horizontal rafter used in construction.

baráko: (Sp. *varraco*: boar) *n*. stud, male animal used for breeding; (*fig*.) tough guy, bully; variety of native-grown coffee.

barakúbak: *n*. withered leaf; dandruff (*lasí*). **agbarakubak**. *v*. to wither. (*laylay*)

barákus: *n*. tie for binding. (*reppet*) **barakusan**. *v*. to net up; close the top of a basket, sack, etc. **ibarakus**. *v*. to tie around.

baraksút: **baraksuten**. *v*. to snatch away. (*agaw*)

baralíti: *n*. red snapper, a kind of fish. (*baraniti*)

barambán: *n*. a kind of fat silver-colored marine fish.

barán: *n*. a kind of mollusk similar to the *gosipeng*, but with a rougher shell.

barandál: (Sp. *barandal*: hand railing) *n*. the upper part of a balustrade, top railing.

barandílias: (Sp. *barandillas*: balustrade) *n*. stairway railing; playpen railing; crib railing; door railing; balustrade.

barándis: *var*. of *burandis*: strew, scatter. **Nalawag a nakitak dagiti naibarandis a tultulang ti nayaw-awan a kamelio a nakadalpus iti minas.** I clearly saw the scattered bones of the lost camels that stepped on the land mines. [Tag. *sabog*]

baraníbud: *n*. tapered part of a pole narrowed at a point.

baraníti: *n*. *var*. of *baraliti*: red snapper fish.

barániw: *n*. lemongrass; *Andropogon citratus*, used in native medicine against stomachaches. **barbaraniw**. *n*. young, edible branches of vines. **ginelgel a baraniw**. *n*. euphemism for scandalous matters. **agbabbaraniw**. *a*. stinking; scandalous; (*reg*.) sensing a wedding is near. **nabaraniwan a bisokol**. *n*. native dish of shellfish cooked in lemongrass. [Ivt. *varanuy*, Tag. *tanglád*]

baranúbor: *n*. roar, rumbling sound; sound of falling water. **agbaranubor**. *v*. to roar, rumble.

baránoy: *var*. of *baraniw*: lemongrass.

baransiágaw: *n*. a kind of tree with aromatic wood.

barangábang: **ibarangabang**. *v*. to simmer, boil softly; keep warm; place near the fire.

barángan: *n*. a kind of small, gray freshwater fish, *Teuthis virgatus*.

barangáw: *n.* a tree with long fruits.

barangáy: *n.* kind of boat (usually with sails); ship.

barangbá: *var.* of *barangbang.*

barangbáng: *n.* a kind of freshwater bitter herb; sound of rapid fire.

barangét: **agbaranget.** *v.* to argue offensively. **nabaranget.** *a.* peevish, querulous. **Nagbaranget dagiti kabagianna ket kayatda nga ibales.** His relatives argued viciously and they want to take revenge. [Tag. *away*]

baranggáwid: **maibarbaranggawid.** *v.* to wind around, coil, entangle, hang around indiscriminately.

baranggáy: (Tag.) *n.* section of a barrio; municipality; political division of a town; clan. (*abbr.* brgy). **bumaranggay.** *n.* residents of a *baranggay.*

baranggúday: **agbarangguday.** *v.* to hang around in a slovenly manner (clothes). **ibarangguday.** *v.* to hang (clothes) improperly.

baranghás: *n.* orange.

barangkás: *n.* pomelo; *Citrus decumana* (*sua*). [Tag. *suhà*]

barangúbong: *n.* the sound of a waterfall.

baraúngan: *n.* a kind of freshwater black and white-striped fish; the gruntfish, *Therapon jarbua.*

barára: *n.* salt deposit; unwashed raw salt.

baráro: *a.* blue-eyed.

báras: (Sp. *barra*: bar) *n.* bars (in gymnastics); bailiff. (Sp. *vara*: pole) **agbaras.** *n.* bailiff. (*kabadangan*)

barasábas: *n.* sound of falling water, heavy rain. (*bayakábak*)

barasbás: *n.* fast reading, skimming over when reading. **barasbasan.** *v.* to skim over when reading, lightly read.

barasíbis: *n.* sound of soft rain or a drizzle; sound of a shower or splashing (*tarakitik*). **Nangngegna ti barasibis ni Tutsang nga agdigdigos.** She heard the sound of Tutsang taking a bath.

barasiksík: *n. Fluggea virosa* plant.

baráso: (Sp. *brazo*: arm) **nabaraso.** *a.* sturdy. (*lagda*)

barasubós: *n.* extravagant spender, spendthrift. (*gastador, barayuboy*)

barasungiád: *n.* hardheaded child. **agbarasungiad.** *v.* to be hardheaded; to contradict; oppose.

barasút: *n.* a kind of blackish marine fish, halfbeak fish of the *Hemiramphidae* family.

barasuwéng: *n.* ill-behaved person.

bárat: *n.* a variety of greenish banana.

barát: *n.* porous pebbles found on the beach; (Tag.) haggler. **nagbarat.** *a.* bargaining hard to pay the lowest price; stony, graveled. **baraten.** *v.* to buy at the lowest price. [Tag. *barát*]

baratabát: *n.* sound of following one another in rapid succession. (*paratupot*) **bumaratabat.** *v.* to follow in quick succession, come one right after the other (bowels, drops, etc.).

baratiktík: *n.* a kind of small, red fish with hard scales.

baratílio: (Sp. *baratillo*: bargain counter) *n.* bargain; sale (in store). **agibaratilio.** *v.* to sell at a low place, have a sale. **ibaratilio.** *v.* to put on sale, sell at a low price.

baráto: (Sp. *barato*: cheap; money given by winning gamblers) *n.* money given by gambling winners to bystanders. **bumarato.** *v.* to ask for *barato.* **agpabarato.** *v.* to give away a small portion of one's winnings. [Tag. *balato*]

barawábaw: *n.* large hole (in a jar). (*abut*) **barawabawan.** *v.* to enlarge a hole; provide something with a large hole. [Tag. *butas*]

baráwang: *n.* a kind of large marine fish.

baráwas: *n.* large arm of leg bone. **kabarawasan.** *n.* grove. **nabarawas.** *a.* long-limbed; straight-limbed.

barawbáw: *n.* a kind of kidney bean.

baráwid: *n.* additional rope used to reinforce. **barawidan.** *v.* to reinforce; tie. [Tag. *panalì*]

báray: *a.* with swollen breasts (after childbirth). [Tag. *bintóg*]

baraybáy: **agbaraybay.** *v.* to start earring (sorghum, corn, etc.); to start growing horns.

barayúbay: *n.* hair falling on forehead; fringe of cloth; decoration; trimmings. **barayubayan.** *v.* to decorate (*arkos*). [Tag. *palamuti* (decorate)]

barayúboy: *n.* spendthrift. (*barasubos, gastador*) **agbarayuboy.** *v.* to be a spendthrift. **nagbarayuboy.** *a.* wasteful, extravagant.

barbakíso: *n.* halter without a headstall placed around the nose of the cow or water buffalo.

barbakuá: (f. Am. Spanish *barbacoa*: barbecue) **barbakuaen.** *v.* to roast leaving the skins on; broil. [Tag. *ihaw*]

barbangísit: *a.* with a very dark complexion. (*pugot*)

barbár: *n.* hoarse voice; cracked jar. **agbanarbar.** *n.* sound of male's pubescent voice, or broken bells.

bárbaro: (Sp. *bárbaro*: barbarian) *n.* barbarian, uncivilized person.

barbaridád: (Sp. *barbaridad*: barbarity; stupid thing to do) *n.* rudeness; barbarity. **que barbaridad!** (Sp.) what nonsense!

bárbas: (Sp. *barba*: beard) *n.* beard. (*íming*) **barbasan.** *a.* bearded. **agibarbas.** *v.* to shave. **igat a barbasan.** *n.* a kind of whiskered eel.

barbas ni tatangmo a Bombay. *exp.* denoting pubic hair. [Tag. *ahit* (shave)]

barbása: *n.* dictation. **ibarbasa.** *v.* to dictate. **ipabarbasa.** *v.* to have something dictated.

barbekí: (Sp. *berbiquí*: carpenter's brace) *n.* carpenter's brace and bit.

bárbekiu: (Eng.) *n.* barbecue. **agbarbekiu.** *v.* to barbecue, roast.

barbería: (Sp. *barbería*: barbershop) *n.* barbershop. (*pagpapukisan*)

barbéro: (Sp. *barbero*: barber) *n.* barber. (*mammukis*) **agbarbero.** *v.* to become a barber.

barbília: (Sp. *barbilla*: chin; ranula) *n.* tumor between the legs of animals.

bárbula: *var.* of *balbula*: valve.

bárbon: (Sp. *barbón*: full beard) *n.* body hair. (*dutdot*) **barbonan.** *a.* hairy.

bardáy: **ibarday.** *v.* to hang on a clothesline (*salapay*, *birdáy*). **Ipasimudaag ti agkaraibarday a lupot a puraw ken nalabaga.** The hanging white and red clothes were displayed.

baredbéd: baredbedan. *v.* to wrap up, bandage.

bárek: *n.* tall and thick rattan. (*way*) **kabarekan.** *n.* rattan grove. [Tag. *yantók*]

barekbék₁: *n.* a kind of bow net used to catch freshwater lobsters.

barekbék₂: *n.* bubbling water; bad reception in a radio. **agbarekbek.** *v.* to bubble; to have bad reception (television or radio). (*barokbok*)

baréna: (Sp. *barrena*: auger) *n.* drill, auger. **barenaen.** *v.* to drill with an auger.

báreng: hoping, in the hopes of; hopefully. **bareng no.** I hope; possibly, perhaps; if. **bareng pay no.** so it will be possible that. **ipabpabareng.** *v.* to hope; suppose; attempt; make an effort to do. **barengbareng.** *a.* false; useless; unworthy, worthless; futile; superficial; trivial; vain;. **barengbarengen.** *v.* to belittle, give little credit to; cheapen; not care. **kinabarengbareng.** *n.* uselessness. **No adda bareng ania.** If something bad happens. **Saan a barengbareng ti ayat.** Love is not trivial. **Intalmegna ti rusokna bareng maep-ep ti bisinna, ngem limmanlan ketdi.** He pressed on his stomach hoping to relieve his hunger, but it worsened instead.

barengbéng: *n.* materials used to reduce the flow of a current. **barengbengan.** *v.* to stem; reduce the force or flow of a current.

baréra: (Sp. *barrera*: barrier; tollgate) *n.* tollgate.

baresbés: *n.* brook, creek; marshy soil; swamp; stream. [Tag. *sapà*]

baréta: (Sp. *barreta*: bar) *n.* crowbar. (*barreta kabra*)

barguéla: *n.* old name for the guitar. (*kutibeng*)

barí: magical word used to drive away various spirits, see under *baribari*. **baribari.** *n.* shaman, medicine man; magical word. **agbaribari.** *v.* to drive away evil spirits by uttering the *baribari* magical words.

bariá: (Sp. *variar*: vary) *n.* loose change, coins (as opposed to paper money); small denominations of paper money. **ipabaria.** *v.* to break a bill into smaller denominations.

baríbar: *n.* diagonal or oblique position; drunkard. **ibaribar.** *v.* to turn around a half circle. **agbaribar.** *v.* to totter; turn on one's side when sleeping or drunk. **agbanaribar.** *v.* to make the sound of heavy rain. **baribar a panunot.** *n.* muddled thought. **baribar a tao.** *n.* not well disciplined person. **baribar ti alipusposna.** *exp.* denoting someone mildly crazy or illogical (diagonal whorl). [Tag. *pahalang*]

baribarí: Interjection used to drive away evil spirits. **Baribari (dika) tagtagari (agkadkaduatay met laeng idi).** *exp.* used to drive away spirits.

baridéro: (Sp. *barridero*: sweeper) *n.* streetsweeping machine.

barigsót: *var.* of *baragsot*: jerking movement.

barikáda: (Sp. *barricada*) *n.* barricade.

barikakkák: *n.* loud cry of a baby. **agbarikakkak.** *v.* to cry loud (said of a baby).

barikattót: agbarikattot. *v.* to squirm and stamp the feet to show resentment.

barikawwét: *a.* crooked; zigzag. (*kawerkawer*) **agbarikawwet.** *v.* to curve; zigzag.

baríkes: *n.* girdle; sash; belt; boards that form the skeleton of a house. **agbarikes.** *v.* to wear a belt around the waist. **bariksan.** *v.* to put a belt around. **Napintas ti lalat ti beklat a maaramid a barikes.** The skin of the *beklat* snake is good for making belts. [Kal. *takyed*]

barikigkíg: *var.* of *sarukigkig*: limp, walk as a cripple.

baríkir: *n.* hillside; base of a mountain. (*bakras*; *liday*; *ansad*) **bimmarikir.** *a.* like a hillside.

barikogkóg: *n.* nagger. **mabarikogkog.** *v.* to shake off balance; lean from side to side when traveling.

baríl: (Sp. *barril*: barrel) *n.* barrel of a gun; gun. **mabaril.** *v.* to be shot accidentally.

baríles: (Sp. *barril*: barrel) *n.* barrel.

barília: (Sp. *barrilla*: small bar) *n.* glass stirring rod; small metal bar.

barinatnát: *n.* a kind of vine with medicinal powers, *Cissus trifolia.*

barin-áwas: *n.* branchless tree. **agbarin-awas.** *v.* to be naked. **nabarin-as.** *a.* naked (*labus*).

barínit: *n.* a kind of vine with edible shoots.

barinudnúd: *n.* magical words used to incite the ant lion larva (*taptapuyo*) to move in the dirt: *sunsunod barinudnod.*

barinsáway: **agbarinsaway.** *v.* to fidget. **nabarinsaway.** *a.* fidgety.

báring: **baringbaringen.** *v.* to scrutinize. (*bilíng*)

baringawngáw: *a.* loquacious; gossipy; chattering. (*salawasaw*)

baringgáwid: *n.* frenum on the underside of the tongue; short rope kept under the neck of the water buffalo to keep the yoke in place.

baríngit: see *baranget*: querulous; peevish.

baríngkuas: *n.* sudden awakening; swaying while waking up. **mabaringkuas, bumaringkuas.** *v.* to suddenly awaken. **Kellaat a nabaringkuas idi mariknana a kasla adda nangreppet iti siketna.** He immediately awoke when he felt that there was something tying his waist. [Tag. *balikwás*]

baringkukúrong: *n.* a kind of tree, *Cratoxylon blancoi*; a kind of speckled black and white bird.

baringríng: *n.* a kind of scoop net; walking with the body leaning to one side. **agbaringring.** *v.* to stagger, totter. (*basing, bariring*) **baringringen.** *v.* to invert; reverse the position of. **Pinabaringringannak a kinita ni Marissa sakbay a simmungbat.** Marissa turned to look at me before answering.

baríring: **agbariring.** *v.* to stumble; rock; stagger; sway. (*daweng; dawiris; duir; dungay; gudday; ibar; lupay; sabbadaw; tiwed*) **maibariring.** *v.* to sway from side to side. [Tag. *suray*]

barírong : see *barrairong*: kind of rhinoceros beetle.

báris: **barisbaris.** *n.* a purple seaweed found in rivers.

barisangá: see *barsanga*: kind of sedge.

barisawsáw: *n.* vain, idle talk, gossip. **agbarisawsaw.** *v.* to gossip.

barisugsóg: **agbarisugsog.** *v.* to grumble in discontent.

barisungiád: *var.* of *barasungiad*: stubborn.

barisuwéng: *a.* hardheaded; obstinate; stubborn.

bárit: *n.* a variety of short sugarcane; a red variety of rattan.

baríto: (f. *baró*) *n.* young man. [Kal. *bebeÿu*]

bariwakwák₁: *n.* a kind of large-mouthed marine fish; loudmouth. **ibariwakwak.** *v.* to declare in a loud voice; announce, proclaim to a group of people.

bariwakwák₂: *var.* of *bariwawa*: spacious, extensive.

bariw-án: *n.* a kind of small tree, *Grewia eriocarpa.*

bariwangwáng: *n.* open space.

bariw-ás: *n.* act of laterally moving from place to place. **agbariw-as.** *v.* to go out and gather; roam, wander, range; migrate to a faraway place; make an abrupt turn (*baliw-as*). **Nagdakiwas ti namariw-as a lagipna.** His roaming memory drifted. [Tag. *galà*]

bariwáwa: *a.* extensive; very spacious. [Tag. *lawak*]

bariwengwéng: *n.* bamboo square that buzzes when whirled. **agbariwengweng.** *v.* to whirl; rotate; be stunned; make the noise of the *bariwengweng.* **Agbarbariwengweng pay laeng ti ulona.** His head is still spinning (as when drunk or stunned).

bariweswés: *n.* kind of tree with good timber; profile; a device used to drive away *maya* birds.

barkáda: (Sp. *barcada*: boat load, Tag. also) *n.* clique, social group; gang; group of friends; shipload of passengers. **kabarkada.** *v.* to gang up with; *n.* fellow gang mate, friend. **makibarkada.** *v.* to join a small group of friends. **Dika makibarbarkada kadagiti di-matalek a tattao.** Don't hang around untrustworthy people.

barkadéro: *a.* sociable, having a lot of friends.

barkéro: (Sp. *barquero*: boatman) *n.* ferryman; bargeman.

barkés: *n.* a skin disease usually caught on the waist with blisters. **agbarkes.** *v.* to be afflicted with the *barkes* skin disease. **barkesen.** *v.* to tie into a bundle. **binarkes.** *n.* six bundles of *palay* bundled into one.

barkília: (Sp. *barquilla*: wafer mold) *n.* shuttle of a loom (*bartilia*). [Knk. *sikuán*]

barkílios: (Sp. *barquillos*: thin rolled wafer) *n.* thin wafers in cylindrical rolls.

bárko: (Sp. *barco*: boat) *n.* barge, cargo boat. (*bapor*)

barná: *n.* one-half *labay* (of cotton).

barnís: (Eng.) *n.* varnish. **barnisan.** *v.* to varnish.

baró₁: (pl. *babbaró*) *n.* unmarried man, bachelor; youth (*bannuag*). **bumaro.** *n.* young male animal; variety of awned early rice with dark hull. **agbaro.** *v.* to become a male adolescent. **kinabaro.** *n.* bachelorhood. **panagbaro.** *n.* adolescence. **Nasuroken a tallopulona ngem baro pay laeng.** He is over thirty but still a bachelor. [Kal. *bebeÿu*, Knk. *baló*, Png. *balólakí*, Tag. *binatà*]

baró₂: *a.* new; fresh; recent; *n.* virgin soil. **kabarbaro.** *a.* new; different. **kabaruanan.** *a.* latest in style; latest news. **pabaruen.** *v.* to remodel; renew; renovate. **panagbaro.** *n.* renovation. **panangbaruanan.** *n.* renovation; change; reformation. **mapabaro.** *v.* can be renovated or renewed. [Ibg. *bagu*, Ivt. *vayuq*, Kal. *kàaÿa*, Kpm. *báyu*, Png. *bálo*, Tag. *bago*]

baró₃: *n.* variety of rice with a dark hull.

baruáng: *n.* (*reg.*) a kind of tree with hard timber.

barubaddút: barobaddutan. *v.* to do haphazardly (*barabaddaw*). **agbarubaddut.** *v.* to be lazy and stubborn.

barubása: *n.* interpreter. **agbarubasa.** *v.* to interpret; translate.

bárog: see *balog*: kind of wild pigeon.

barugsót: *n.* jerking movement made when upset. (*biragsot*) **agbarugsot.** *v.* to jerk.

barogsóy: *a.* fat, obese. (*lukmeg*)

baruíng: (*obs.*) **agbaruing.** *v.* to slip while sitting.

barokbók: agbarokbok. *v.* to make a bubbling sound (bamboo joint dipped in water), bubble out; make bubbles in water (*barekbek*). [Tag. *bulubok*]

barúkong₁: *n.* chest; bosom (*suso*: breast); (*fig.*) seat of emotions. **barukongan.** *n.* a kind of large marine fish; *a.* broad-chested. **barukongen.** *v.* to suffer from chest pains. **barukong ti daga.** *n.* center of the earth. **pagabbarukong.** *a.* up to the chest; reaching the chest. [Bon. *keg-ew, takeb, palagpag,* Ibg. *gákaw,* Ivt. *kalangángan, kabedberan,* Kal. *byaÿukong,* Knk. *agabíab, pagáew* (of men), *págew* (of animals), Kpm. *sálu,* Png. *pagéw,* Tag. *dibdíb*]

barúkong₂: *n.* species of large marine fish. **barukongan.** *n.* species of edible marine fish.

barumbádo: (Sp. *barrumbada*: boastful thing to say) *a.* coarse, uncouth; disrespectful, shameless. (*tarantádo*)

barómetro: (Sp. *barómetro*) *n.* barometer.

barón₁: (Sp. *barón*: baron) *n.* baron.

barón₂: (Sp. *varón*: male) *a.* male (used in civil registration records only).

barunáas: *n.* a tall, branchless tree trunk.

baronésa: (Sp.) *n.* baroness; wife of a baron.

baruníbod: *n.* species of medicinal plant.

bárong₁: *n.* rattlesnake.

bárong₂: barongbarong. *n.* small house; squatter house.

baróng: *n.* Filipino dress shirt for men usually made of *husi*, pineapple fabric with embroidery, also called *barong Tagalog*.

barungisngís: *a.* cut slantwise (cloth).

barongóbong: see *barangobong*: sound of waterfall.

barongróng: *n.* a kind of mollusk.

báros: *n.* nausea associated with seeing blood or a corpse. **mabaros.** *v.* to die in the act of killing; to become sick supernaturally; become

nauseated upon seeing a corpse. **makabaros.** *a.* nauseating, sickening, horrible.

barusbús: agbarusbus. *v.* to revive (plants); grow well (*rukbos*); shoot up again. [Tag. *lagô*]

barusik: *n. Fluggea virosa* plant.

barusngí: *a.* contradictory. **mabarusngi.** *v.* to be out of place; contradict; be done wrongly. **ibarusngi.** *v.* to put in an improper position. **barubarusngi.** *a.* improperly placed. **barusngien.** *v.* to contradict; do the opposite of what is expected. **barusngi a panagpampanunot.** *n.* negative attitude. **Pasig a barusngi ti ammom.** You only know wrong things. **Ammona a saanna a mabarusngi ti pangngeddeng ni apongna.** He knows he should not go against the will of his grandfather.

barúso: (Sp. *barroso*: pimply) *a.* with a reddish and pimpled complexion. (*kamuro*)

barúsok: *n.* (*reg.*) handle of a shovel. **Asaenda dagiti barusokda tapno naal-alistak ti panagsudakda.** They are sharpening their spades so their digging will be faster.

bárut: *n.* wire. (*alambre*) **baruten.** *v.* to make bamboo into thin strips for weaving. **pagbarutan.** *n.* silversmith tool used to thin silver bars. [Bon. *walteng,* Knk. *palténg,* Tag. *alambre*]

barutbút: barutbuten. *v.* to grub up. **agbarutbut.** *v.* to break wind noisily and frequently (*uttot*). [Tag. *utót*]

barutiktík: *n.* a kind of large, black and white, edible bird.

bároy: *n.* a kind of tree with white flowers, *Pterospermum diversifolium.*

baruybóy: *n.* threads at the end of a piece of material used for decoration; fringe border; tassel.

barraírong: *n.* coconut borer, a kind of rhinoceros beetle whose larva is called *alimpupusa*; (*fig.*) good-for-nothing person; idler; lazy bum; bad person; criminal. **Adu dagiti barrairong a mannukmon idiay balayda.** There are a lot of good-for-nothing alcoholics at their house. [Kal. *ewod,* Tag. *uwáng*]

barraúngen: *var.* of *baraúngan*: species of fish.

barréna: (Sp. *barrena*: drill) *n.* drill, brace (*laput*). [Kal. *balila*]

barréta: (Sp. *barreta*: bar) *n.* crowbar, often called *barreta kabrá*; bar (of soap or chocolate). **barretaen.** *v.* to open with a crowbar. **Kasla barreta ti kadakkel ti tudo.** *exp.* To rain very heavily (like crowbars).

bárrio: (Sp. *barrio*: part of town) *n.* barrio, suburb of a town; division of a town. **ipabarrio.** *v.* to send to the barrio. **kabarrioan.** *n.* barrio mate. **bumarrio.** *n.* residence of a barrio,

barrio people. **mangbarrio-barrio.** *v.* to go from barrio to barrio.

barruáng: *n.* kind of tree with hard timber.

barrúga: *n.* a boy's stick game. **barrugaen.** *v.* to throw a stick at.

barrukáya: *n.* prostitute; streetwalker; slut; cheap woman. (*balangkantis*; *babai a kalapati*)

barróte: (Sp. *barrote*: iron bar) *n.* windowsill; ledge of timber.

barsák₁: *n.* distribution of people or materials for work; force of a throw; distance covered by a throw. **barsabarsaken.** *v.* to apportion, distribute.

barsák₂: **ibarsak.** *v.* to drop, let fall; fling; cast. **maibarsak.** *v.* to drop, fall; to be thrown, flung, cast. [Png. *basileng, opak*, Tag. *balabág, halibas*]

barsangá₁: *n.* a kind of sedge with brown spikes, *Cyperus rotundus*. **tumangad iti barsanga.** *exp.* to die and be buried six feet under (look up at the *barsanga* weed from the grave below). **Ti agtangtangad, makatangad-barsanga.** *exp.* He who looks up only sees withered branches of *barsanga* (one doesn't gain anything by being idle).

barsangá₂: *n.* variety of awned rice with a hard white kernel.

barséro: *var.* of *balsero*: raftsman, ferryman.

barsiák: *n.* splintered bamboo (*barsiat*); chip; splinter; crack. **mabarsiak.** *v.* to snap, break; splinter; crack. [Tag. *tipák*]

barsiát: *var.* of *barsiák*: crack, chip, snap.

barsík: *n.* a kind of tree with oval fruits from whose shoots is made plaster, *Mimusops sp.*

barsiók: *var.* of *barsak*: distribution; apportionment. **barsioken.** *v.* to hurl (*basibas*); throw sticks at. **binnarsiok.** *n.* game played by children consisting of throwing sticks or bundles of grass.

bartáy: *n.* scattered dirty clothes; line. **bartayen.** *v.* to arrange, file, put in order. **bumartay.** *v.* to fall into place. **ibartay.** *v.* to stretch a rope by tying; arrange in a line; set in place. **Adu dagiti pagan-anay a naibartay kadagiti tawa.** There is a lot of clothing hanging from the windows. [Tag. *hanay*]

barték: *n.* drunkard; *a.* drunk. **barteken.** *v.* to get somebody drunk. **nabartek.** *a.* drunk, tipsy. **agbartek.** *v.* to get drunk. **kinamammartek.** *n.* drunkenness. **mammartek.** *n.* drunkard. **mabartek.** *v.* to become drunk. **agbarbartek.** *v.* to go on a drinking spree. **makabartek, makapabartek.** *a.* intoxicating. **Kayatnak a barteken no malpas ti pasala.** She wants to get me drunk when the ball is over. [Bon. *bóteng*, Ibg.

illáw, Itg. *naúlaw*, Ivt. *navuq, vuuk, diñat*, Kal. *buuk*, Png. *buék*, Tag. *lasíng*]

bartekéro: *n.* drunkard. (*artek*)

bartília: *n.* shuttle of a loom (*gettay*). [Bon., *sikwán*, Knk. *sikuán*]

bartín: *n.* poisonous snake with variegated skin.

bartolína: (f. Am. Spanish *bartolina*: dungeon) *n.* dungeon, underground prison; jail. (*pagbaludan*)

bartília: *n.* shuttle of a loom.

bartín: *n.* a kind of green poisonous snake.

bása: **agbasa.** *v.* to read; study; learn; go to school. **basaen.** *v.* to read something. **basabasa.** *n.* cook rice with water. **makabasa.** *v.* to be able to read; to be literate. **pagbasaan.** *n.* book; school. **ipabasa.** *v.* to have something read. **pagbasaen.** *v.* to put through school. **ibarbasa.** *v.* to dictate. **managbasa.** *n.* avid reader; bookworm. **konsibasa.** *n.* person who reads for the wrong purpose (to impress, although he does not understand, etc.). **pakabasaan.** *n.* book. **mangibasa.** *n.* reader. **Idin ti pannakaammok a saanakon a makapagtuloy nga agbasa.** That is to my knowledge the time when I was not able to continue studying. [Ibg. *bibbig*, Ivt. *maylir*, Kal. *byasa*, Kpm., Png, Tag. *bása*]

basá: **nabasa.** *a.* wet. **mabasa.** *v.* to get wet; become wet. **agbabasa.** *v.* to get oneself wet. **basaen.** *v.* to wet, drench. **babasaen.** *v.* to wet something dry. **sibabasa.** *n.* rainy season; *a.* soaking wet. **pagbabasaan.** *n.* puddle. **kabasaan.** *n.* marshy soil. **pagbabasa.** *n.* clothing for rainy days. [Ibg. *basa, vasa*, Ifg. *tína*, Ivt. *vasaq*, Kal. *bes-al*, Png. *basá*, Kpm., Tag. *basâ*]

basábas: *n.* dregs, sediment. (*ared-ed*; *rinsaed*; *intaer*; *lissaad*). **agbasabas.** *v.* to rub the body with a wet cloth. **ibasabas.** *v.* to sponge someone with.

basák: **basakbasak.** *a.* clumsy, uncouth, unrefined. **agbasakbasak.** *v.* to trespass; walk with heavy footsteps. (*adak*) **Awanen ti makaitured nga agbasakbasak iti paraanganda.** No one dares trespass on their yard. **Addaanda iti karbengan iti pribado a biagda a saan koma a rumbeng a mabasakbasak.** They have the right to their private lives that shouldn't be violated.

basaklá: *n.* variety of tree, *Ficus payapa*.

básal: *n.* fertilization of the soil before planting; (f. Tag.) virgin forest. **agbasal.** *v.* to fertilize the soil before planting.

basálio: (Sp. *vasallo*: vassal) *n.* soldier, subject, vassal.

básang: *n.* term of address used by adults to young girls or women.

basangál: *n.* hardwood.

básar: *n.* a kind of bamboo flooring. **pagibasaran.** *n.* a kind of gridiron. **basarbasar.** *n.* a shrub with white flowers and red fruits, *Randia cumingiana.*

basár₁: *n.* (*reg.*) mayor; bazaar.

basár₂: (Sp. *basar*: base) **ibasar.** *v.* to base on. (*ikugnal*) **pangibasaran.** *n.* basis. (*pangikugnalan*)

básat: *n.* swimming underwater. **agbasat.** *v.* to swim underwater. **agbasanbasat.** *v.* to vie in staying underwater. **Bimmasat a nangsurot iti ayus a kasla ikan.** He followed the current underwater like a fish. [Tag. *sisid*]

básaw: *n.* open land, wide land; prairie, field; pond.

basbás: *n.* footpath; alley. **basbasan.** *v.* to unroof for repairs; create a path. [Tag. *daán*]

báse: (Sp. *base*: base) *n.* base; basis. **ibase.** *v.* to base on. (*ibasar, ikugnal*)

baselína: (Sp. *vaselina*) *n.* Vaseline; lubricant.

baséng₁: *n.* wild ginger (*laya*).

baséng₂: *n.* (*reg.*) homosexual (*baien*).

baséng₃: *n.* garbage (*basura*).

bási: *n.* sugarcane wine that is boiled with the bark of the Java plum (*lungboy*) for coloring and then fermented in earthen jars with yeast (*búbod*), popular in the Ilocos region. **basi ti lalaki.** *n.* potent *basi.* **basi ti babai.** *n.* sweet *basi.* [Ivt. *palek*, Png. *basí*, Tag. *basi*]

basiár: (Sp. *vaciar*: to empty) **basiaren.** *v.* to sharpen (tools). **basiador.** *n.* someone who sharpens tools.

basíbas: **basibasen.** *v.* to hurl a noncircular object (*palapal*). [Tag. *pukól*]

basíkang: *n.* frame of the *gagan-ayan.*

basíkaw: *n.* wood hoop; rim of a wheel; round frame, hoop; parenthesis. **agbasikaw.** *v.* to make round. **basikawan.** *v.* to hoop, loop. [Tag. *buklód*]

basíkut: *n.* arsenic.

básil₁: *n.* wedge. (*tingal*) **basilan.** *v.* to drive a wedge. [Tag. *kalsó*]

básil₂: **agbabasil.** *v.* to have whitlow, boils on the hands and fingernails.

basiluág: *n.* *Dysoxyllum sp.* plant used as a fish poison.

basíng: **maibasíng.** *v.* to totter, not stand straight. [Tag. *suray*]

basingkáwel: *n.* vagrant, vagabond; election time; political campaign. **agbasingkawel.** *v.* to be absent without official leave. [Png. *basingkáwel*]

básio: (Sp. *vacío*: empty) *n.* empty bottle. (*gawang*)

básiok: **basioken.** *v.* to hurl a noncircular object. (*palapal*)

basísaw: *n.* urinary bladder. **basisawen.** *v.* to feel or hear water moving in the belly; to feel bloated. **bumasisaw.** *v.* to bloat; grow fat. [Bon. *bidong*, Kal. *bichung*, Knk. *bidúng*, Png. *birong*, Tag. *pantóg*]

basíto: (Sp. *vasito*: small glass) *n.* small glass.

baskág: *n.* frame. **agbaskag.** *v.* to swell, bulge; jut out, protrude. **ibaskag.** *v.* to stretch; frame. **naibaskag, sibabaskág.** *a.* framed. [Tag. *balangkás*]

baskét: (Eng.) *n.* basket with a handle.

basketból: *n.* basketball. **agbasketbol.** *v.* to play basketball.

basketbolísta: *n.* basketball player.

báskula: (Sp. *báscula*: platform scale) *n.* platform scale.

baslát: **ibaslat.** *v.* to tumble down, topple down (*baldák*); defeat, overcome.

basnég: *n.* a kind of grass with red spikelets.

basnút: *n.* whip; whiplash. **agbasnut, basnutan.** *v.* to beat someone with a cane; thrash (winds, etc.). (*saplit*; *baut*; *betbet*) **Imbasnotna ti sayana iti pagsalapayan.** She whipped her skirt on the clothesline. [Png. *bakbák*, Tag. *haplít, palò*]

báso: (Sp. *vaso*: drinking glass) *n.* glass (for drinking), cup.

basó: *n.* experimental trial before slapping the calf of the leg in games.

básol: *n.* sin, fault; mistake, error. (*biddut*; *kammali*) **agbasol.** *v.* to sin; err. **ibasol.** *v.* to do wrong. **pabasolen.** *v.* to blame, accuse. **bumasol.** *v.* to err, make a mistake. **pakabasolan.** *n.* occasion of sin. **agpinnabasol.** *v.* to blame each other. **naimbasolan.** *a.* sinful. **no diak pakabasolan.** *exp.* if you don't mind. **no diak bumasol.** *exp.* if I am not mistaken. **sibabasol ti langana.** *exp.* He has a guilty face. **Agpipinnabasolda gapu iti pannakatayna.** They blame each other for his death. [Kal. *byasuÿ*, Png. *tetél*, Png., Tag. *kasalánan*]

basúra: (Sp. *basura*: garbage) *n.* garbage. (*dalupitpit*) **ibasura.** *v.* to throw away; throw in the garbage. **basurero.** *n.* garbageman.

básut: **nagbasútan.** *a.* empty. (*awan nagyan, gawang*)

basúyak: **nabasuyak.** *a.* soft (cooked rice); flabby.

bassát: see *basat*: **agbassanbassat.** *v.* to vie in staying underwater.

bassáwang: *n.* cussword; blasphemy. **agbassawang.** *v.* to talk arrogantly; blaspheme; utter cusswords. **Nagbassabassawang dagiti ubbing ket agkakarugit a balikas ti inturongda**

kadagiti pulis. The children swore and uttered dirty words directed at the police. [Tag. *tungayaw*]

bassíkaw: *var*. of *basikaw*: hoop; loop.

bassiók: see *barsak*: distribution, apportionment.

bassiusít: *a*. very small, very few; diminutive. (*battit*)

bassísaw: *var*. of *basísaw*: *n*. urinary bladder. **bimmassisawen a gobierno**. *n*. baloney government.

bassít: *a*. small, little; few, scarce. (*obs*.) *n*. half centavo piece. **man bassit**. *part*. a moment please. **bumassit**. *v*. to decrease, shrink. **ikabassit**. *v*. to diminish; shorten; lessen, lower the number of. **sangkabassit**. *a*. very little; a little bit. **tagibassiten**. *v*. to belittle, deprecate. **bassitan**. *adv*. almost; nearly; more than, over (an amount). **apagbassit**. *adv*. just a little. **makabassit**. *v*. to do a little; to do bit by bit. **bassit-bassiten**. *v*. to do little by little. **Inka bassit turongan ti danum dagitay raeptayo.** Please go change the direction of the water flow to what we were transplanting. [Ibg. *beddiq*, Ifg. *ittay*, Itg. *battikit* (small), *ettey* (few), Ivt. *dékey* (small), *mayahaw*, *pere* (few), Kal. *paat* (small), *paat*, *akit* (few), Knk. *atík*, *amtekéw*, Kpm. *malati* (small), *ditak* (few), Png. *daisét* (*few*), *melág* (*small*), Tag. *muntî*, *liít*]

bassit-usít: *a*. very small, diminutive, miniature.

bassuíl: see *battuil*: lever.

bástaₗ: (Sp. *basta*: enough) *a*. enough, sufficient; used in alerting someone when to stop: *huston*; nevertheless, just; as long as. **basta sika**. *exp*. as long as it's you. **bastabasta**. *a*. ordinary, banal; not respectable (family, person, etc.). **Basta ikarim nga agsingsingpetka.** Just promise you will behave.

básta₂: (Sp. *bastear*: baste) **bastaen**. *v*. to baste in sewing; pack; bale (tobacco).

bastánte: (Sp. *bastante*: enough) *a*. enough, sufficient. (*umanay*, *umdas*)

bastárdo: (Sp. *bastardo*: bastard) *n*. bastard (*anák ti ruár*); hybrid. [Knk. *tupúg* (child with unknown father)]

bastéd: **nabasted**. *a*. turned down; rejected (person). **basteden**. *v*. to turn down someone, reject (*paay*). **Binastedna met aminen dagidi nagrayo kenkuana manipud nagnobioda.** She turned down everyone who courted her since they were going steady.

bastidór: (Sp. *bastidor*: stretcher for canvas) *n*. round frame used for embroidery; stretcher for canvas.

bastipúr: *n*. a bamboo and palm-leafed sun helmet.

bastón: (Sp. *bastón*: cane; baton) *n*. cane. (for walking); orchestra conductor's rod; baton.

bastonéra: (f. *bastón*) *n*. majorette, baton twirler.

bastonéro: (f. *bastón*) *n*. conductor of an orchestra.

bástosₗ: (Sp. *bastos*: clubs (in cards)) *n*. suit of clubs in a Spanish deck of cards; the other three suits are *oros*, *kopas* and *espadas*.

bástos₂: *n*. a kind of earthenware plate.

bastós: (Sp. *basto*: rude) *a*. rude, impolite; clumsy. **bastosen**. *v*. to act rudely; treat impolitely.

bátaₗ: (Tag. *batà*) *n*. sweetheart; fiancé(e). (*ayan-ayat*)

báta₂: (Sp.) *n*. nightgown, gown. **bata de banio**. bathing suit.

batáan: *n*. follower; aid; protégé.

bataáno: *n*. a kind of tree whose sap makes the face swell.

batábat: **batabaten**. *v*. to overtake by a cutoff (*salikbay*); guess; surmise (*palatpat*); check.

batád: **nabatad**. *a*. clear, plain; candid; public, evident. (*latak*) **ibatad**. *v*. to state clearly; be frank; explain (*lawag*). **kinabatad**. *n*. frankness; candidness; evidentness; clearness, clarity. **Impariknana met, impadlawna met, ngem dina met imbatad iti sangonsango, iti rupanrupa.** He alluded and suggested to it but did not frankly state it in the open, face-to-face.

bátak: **bataken**. *v*. to help, lend a hand; pull; lift (*badang*; *tulong*). [Tag. *batak* = pull]

bátal: *n*. hump under one's back when lying down.

batalán: *n*. in Ilocano houses, the waiting room or dining room of a house.

batália: (Sp. *batalla*) *n*. battle (*bakal*, *gubat*); joust, fencing joust; frame of a bicycle.

batáno: *n*. *Excoecaria agallocha* plant.

bátang: *n*. turn (in a game); chance; opportunity. **mabatangan**. *v*. to be chosen by chance to do something. **maibatang**. *v*. to happen by chance. **ibatang**. *v*. to assign; schedule. **ipabatang**. *v*. to put someone in charge of, assign someone to a task. **batang a trabaho**. assigned work. **nabatang-batang**. *a*. taking turns. **Dumteng ti batangna nga agsuot iti trahe-de-boda.** Her turn will come to wear a wedding gown. [Kpm. *bagút*, Tag. *pagkakataón*]

batángal: *n*. muzzle. **batangalan**. *v*. to muzzle, halter. (*busal*)

batángan: *n*. sawhorse; wood used to place objects on over the floor; one of the four horizontal beams of the granary.

batanggá: *n*. horizontal piece of wood used as a support.

batánggas: (f. *Batangas*, Tagalog speaking region) *n*. butterfly knife. (*balisóng*)

Batanggénio: (Sp. *batangueño*) *n.* native of Batangas province.

batangtáng: *n.* tolling of bells. **batangtangen.** *v.* to ring a bell. (*tangtang, rupiki*)

bátar: *n.* a kind of white larva. (*bátir*) **binatar.** *a.* infested by the *batar* larva.

batára: *n.* free labor; communal work (*bataris*). **agbatara.** *v.* to work together for a common good; work for the community without wages. (*tagnawa*; *ammuyo*) **agbabatara.** *v.* to compete, contend. **makibatara.** *v.* to join in a community project (as a volunteer). [Ivt. *yaru*, Tag. *bayanihan*]

batáris: *var.* of *batara*: free labor, communal work. **makibataris.** *v.* to join in a communal volunteer project. **batarisen.** *v.* to have someone work for free. **No awan ti papanam no bigat, mabalin a batarisenka?** If you aren't going anywhere tomorrow, can I ask you to do some work for me (for free)? [Ivt. *yaru*, Tag. *bayanihan*]

batáy: *n.* stand, support on which objects are placed; stepping-stone. **pabatay.** *n.* stick used to catch chickens. **agbatay.** *v.* to stand on something in order to reach something else. **ibatay.** *v.* to set on for support; perch on; base on. **pangibatayan.** *n.* basis; model. (*kugnal*) **agbatay iti dila.** *exp.* to be on the tip of one's tongue. **Dika pagpannakkel ti nagbatayam, tapno dika maikuyog nga matnag.** *exp.* Do not boast of your support, for you may fall with it. [Tag. *batay*]

batbát: *n.* striking with the hand. **batbaten.** *v.* to strike, whip the shoulder; fluff cotton by beating; thresh rice. **ibatbat.** *v.* to throw down. **pamatbatan.** *n.* mat for cotton to be scutched on. **mabanatbat.** *v.* to fall from a high place, drop, sink, lower one's social status. **Kasla kabbatbat a kapas ti ummong ti ulep.** The gathering of the clouds was like cotton that was just threshed.

baték: *n.* tattoo; glass bead; white spot on tobacco leaves. **batekbatekan.** *a.* spotted; tattooed. [Tag. *batik* = spot]

batél: *n.* interisland vessel.

baténg₁: *n.* a kind of net used in hunting; scoop net for fishing (also *batbaténg*). **agbateng.** *v.* to hunt wild animals with a net. **mabatengan.** *v.* to catch with a net. **Rinabii a mapan agpana wenno agbatbateng.** They go hunting every night with bow and arrow or with the *bateng*.

baténg₂: *n.* length of rope used as an obstruction; boundary rope. **batengen.** *v.* to obstruct the way of (with a rope). **batengan.** *v.* to mark off a place, mark off a limit.

batería: (Sp. *batería*: battery) *n.* battery.

báti: **agbati.** *v.* to stay; wait, linger. **batibati.** *n.* homemade pulley for lifting. **ibati.** *v.* to leave behind, cause to remain, abandon. **batibatien.** *v.* to bind a post to take it out of a hole. **mabati.** *v.* to be left behind; *n.* remainder, left over. **makabatbati.** *v.* to stay (said of evil spirits causing sickness). [Ibg. *panawan*, *gikkáng* (leave behind), *vuna* (left over), Ivt. *vidiñen* (leave behind), *mavaw* (left over), Kpm. *lakwan* (leave behind), *tágan* (left over), Png. *itilak* (leave behind), *kera* (left over), Tag. *iwan* (leave behind), *tira* (left over)]

batiá: (Sp. *batea*: washing trough) *n.* basin for washing or kneading. **ibatia.** *v.* to put something in the *batia*.

batíbat: *n.* nightmare. (*bangungot*) **batibaten.** *v.* to have a nightmare. [Bon. *lemam*, Png. *leplep*, Kpm., Tag. *bangungot*]

batibáti: *n.* homemade pulley.

batído: *a.* specialist; experienced; expert.

batidór: (Sp. *batidor*: eggbeater; beater) *n.* stick for beating raw cotton; eggbeater; whisk.

batík: *n.* white spot on leaves. **batikbatik.** *a.* spotted.

Batikáno: (Sp. *Vaticano*: Vatican) *n.* Vatican.

batíkang: *n.* a kind of tree, *Dracontolmelum cumingianum*; a variety of awned late rice.

batikén: *n.* a box with soil to be used as a hearth; pad for jars. (*diken*; *sagapa*)

batikóla: (Sp. *baticola*: crupper) *n.* crupper, part of the harness that passes under a horse's tail.

batikuléng: *n.* chicken gizzard. **bimmatikuleng.** *a.* having the shape of a gizzard; hardened. **Anian a bimmatikuleng a kinabuisit!** *exp.* What awful luck! [Bon. *batikkol*, Knk. *bantikóen*, *bitlí*, Tag. *balumbalunan*; *batikulíng* = species of tree with yellow wood]

batikóngkong: *n.* beating bamboos to warn the neighborhood of present danger; hollow sound; *a.* hollow. **batikongkongen.** *v.* to sound the alarm; beat a hollowed-out instrument to produce a hollow sound.

batíkos: (f. Tag. *batikos*: cudgel) **batikosen.** *v.* to criticize severely, attack verbally. **Binatikosda ti turay.** They criticized the government.

batíl: (Sp. *batir*: beat) **batilen.** *v.* to beat (eggs). **agbatil.** *v.* to beat; (*reg.*) masturbate. [Tag. *batí*]

batílid: *n.* swell; surge; wave before breaking (*dalluyon*). [Tag. *alon*]

batillóg: *n.* testicle (*ukel-ukel*). [Tag. *bayág*]

batingtíng: (Sp. *batintin*: Chinese gong) *n.* bell (*kampana*); musical triangular bar. **batingtingen.** *v.* to ring a bell. [Png. *kalingkalíng*, Tag. *baimbî, kulilíng*]

bátir: *n.* a kind of larva, white worm. **batiren.** *n.* plant disease caused by the *batir*.

batiwáak: *a.* wide, big, large (wounds, plots, etc.)

batiwáwa: sibabatiwawa. *a.* always open (*silulukat*); completely exposed. [Png. *akatindá*, Tag. *tiwangwáng, bukangkáng*]

batiwelwél: *n.* rotating, spinning, whirling action. **agbatiwelwel.** *v.* to rotate; whirl.

batiwerwér: *var.* of *batiwelwel*: whirl. **Agbatbatiwerwer a nagpatnga iti salas.** She whirled into the center of the living room.

batkán: *n.* a kind of edible fish.

batlág: see *baklag*: welt; bruise. **agbinatlag.** *v.* to bruise; welt (*belled*). [Tag. *pasâ*]

batláng: (*obs.*) *n.* passengers. (*paseros*)

batná: agbatbatna. *v.* to pick up leftover grains; harvest a second crop of rice.

báto: *n.* the stone or coin used in games to hit other stones or coins; quoit. **pammato.** *n.* quoit; leader; vanguard.

bató₁: *n.* stone, rock, pebble. **batuen.** *v.* to stone. **binato.** *a.* made of stone; variety of awnless rice. **batbato.** *n.* generic name for shellfish or mollusks or shells. **batobato.** *n.* weight, lead, clock plum bob. **bimmato.** *a.* stony; hardened; indifferent; apathetic. **Kasla puspuso a bato.** *exp.* having a heart of stone. [Ivt. *vatuq*, Kal. *betu, patungaw*, Knk. *engát*, Png. *batingtíng, batu*, Ibg., Knk., Kpm., Png., Tag. *bató*]

bató₂: *n.* kidney. [Knk. *batíl*, Png. *batók*, Tag. *bató*]

bató₃: bato-bato. *n.* grouper fish, *Serranidae* family.

bató₄: **ibato.** *v.* to fling, hurl, throw, toss. **bumato.** *v.* to throw stones. [Ibg. *itebbaq*, *ipettu*, Ivt. *pagsiden*, Kpm. *atsa*, Png. *túpak*, Tag. *hagis*]

batuág: *n.* lever for drawing water from a well; a person who gulps down a bottle of *basi* without stopping to take a breath. **batuagen.** *v.* to upturn; tilt. **batuabatuag.** *n.* rocking chair; seesaw. [Tag. *tiwaík*]

batúbat: agbatubat. *v.* to rest for a short while. **di agpabatubat.** *a.* continuous; unrelenting. **Di agbatubat ti iliw dagiti kabbalaymo.** Your housemates' nostalgia is unrelenting. [Tag. *pahingá*]

bátug: *n.* row, line (*aray*); file; part opposite or in front of; *prep.* across; opposite. **agbatug.** *v.* to match; be in line with each other. **kabatug.** *n.* area in front of which something stands; something on the opposite side of. **maibatug.** *v.* to be put in a row or line. **mabatugan.** *v.* to be across, opposite. **binatog.** *n.* line, passage; sentence. **kaibatugan.** *n.* equal worth, equivalence; price, value. **binnatugan.**

n. a girl's version of hide-and-seek. **sangabatog.** *n.* one row, line. **dita a batog.** *exp.* in that direction; somewhere there. **Adda pay laeng kaibatogam iti pusok.** You still have the same place in my heart. [Png. *dásig*, Tag. *hanay*]

bat-úg₁: *n.* a kind of elongated marine fish; (*reg.*) a kind of big-bellied toad (*battog*).

bat-úg₂: agbat-ug. *v.* to stamp, hit the ground. (*tabbuga*) **ibat-ug.** *v.* to throw down violently. [Tag. *dabóg*]

bátok: *n.* diving; a kind of scoop net for fishing. **bumatok, agbatok.** *v.* to dive; (fig.) purposely lose in a game or race. **binnatok.** *n.* diving and catching one another in the water. **batuken.** *v.* to look for something diving. **pagbatok.** *n.* diving equipment. **Kapamitlonan ti bumatok idi masirpatna ti napuskol a pangen.** It was his third dive when he perceived the thick school of fish. [Kal. *lumtop*, Tag. *sisid*; *batok* = nape, *pamatok* = yoke]

batukanág: *n.* a kind of thick tree with edible red fruit.

batukót: *n.* bulge, hump under clothes. **agbatukot.** *v.* to bulge. **nagbatukot.** *a.* bulging (clothes). [Tag. *bukol*]

batuláng: see *sakkub*: kind of basket placed over the mother hen to restrain her.

batumbaláni: *n.* magnet; magnetic attraction. **makabatumbalani.** *v.* to be attracted to someone. **Ti nakasamsam-it nga isemna ken ti makapasalibukag a rimat dagiti matana dagiti nangnangruna a pakabatombalaniak.** Her sweet smile and invigorating sparkle in her eyes are what especially attracted me. [Tag. *batubalanì*]

batón: *n.* conductor's rod. (*baston*)

batonéro: *n.* conductor of an orchestra. (*bastonero*)

batonlagíp: *n.* monument (*artificially created word, bató-n + lagíp: stone memory*)).

batón siléng: *n.* diamond.

bátong: agbatong. *v.* to fight (hogs); hunt (said of hogs). [Tag. *bangay*]

batúngol: *n.* chicken pox; disease of humans and animals characterized by skin eruptions; kind of insect living in salted meat. **agbatungol.** *v.* to have the *batungol* disease. [Tag. *bulutóngtubig*]

batúta: (Sp. *batuta*: conductor's baton) *n.* police stick. (*pang-or*) **batutaen.** *v.* to beat with a *batuta*. [Tag. *batutà*]

batútay: binatutay. *n.* sausage. (*longganisa*)

batsiliér: (Sp. *bachiller*: bachelor) *n.* bachelor (*baró*); bachelor's degree; holder of a bachelor's degree.

batsiliéra: (Sp. *bachillera*: female bachelor's degree recipient; loquacious) *n.* bachelorette, female bachelor (*balásang*); prattling woman.

batsóy: (Ch.) *n.* kind of Chinese soup dish with pig entrails. **batsoyan.** *n.* place where *batsoy* is served.

battád: *var.* of *batád*: clear, plain, evident.

battál: *var.* of *bátal*: hump under one's back when lying down.

battálay: *n.* period of time. **nabattalay.** *a.* occurring at regular distant intervals; slow, deliberate; with long intervals. **ibattalay.** *v.* to lengthen the period between intervals. [Tag. *bagál*]

battári: **agbattari.** *v.* to move on the hands with legs upturned.

battáway: *n.* period; great distance between. (*battalay*) **nabattaway.** *a.* far apart. **ibattaway.** *v.* to set things far apart. **Bimmataway ti panagpitik ti pusona.** His heartbeats came at slower intervals. [Tag. *pagitan*]

battiá: *n.* pail. (*timba*)

battíng: (*coll.*) *a.* small (*battit*). **'Nia ket nga anusmon kadagiti nagbabatting a duriken?** Why are you so patient (in eating, collecting) tiny *duriken* mollusks?

battít: *a.* very little, diminutive; very few. **battit-usit.** *a.* very small. **battit-battiten.** *v.* to do little by little.

battuág: *n.* windlass, lever for drawing water; a person who empties a jug of wine without stopping. **agbattuag.** *v.* to seesaw; rotate. **nagbattuag.** *a.* unbalanced; tilting backwards. **battuagen.** *v.* to tilt backwards. **battuagan.** *n.* lever for drawing water from a well. **battuabattuag.** *n.* rocking chair.

battóg₁: *n.* thud, sound of something falling heavily. **maibattog.** *v.* to drop, fall from a high place. [Tag. *bagsák*]

battóg₂: **battobattog.** *n.* a kind of bush frog. (*tukak, bat-ug*)

battuíl: **battuilen.** *v.* to lever (*suíl*); move something with a pole or oar. **battuilan.** *v.* to apply a counterweight. [Tag. *panikwás*]

battúlay: *n.* uneven ground. **agbattulay.** *v.* to be unbalanced. **maibattulay.** *v.* to turn over, tilt, capsize; tip over.

battúog: **batuogen.** *v.* to drop from a high place. **mabattoog.** *v.* to drop, fall.

battúon: *n.* load; burden; weight. **battuonan.** *v.* to counterweight; weight down. (*attuil; paktangen; salensen*) **agbattoon.** *v.* to become heavy; oppressive. **ibattoon.** *v.* to put a weight on. [Tag. *bigát*]

battúri: **agbatturi.** *v.* to run wild. (*buatit*)

battútay: **battutayen.** *v.* to carry a person by both hands and legs; carry by the neck.

battúto: *n.* leap, jump. (*lagto; layaw; lokso*) **agbattuto.** *v.* to spring, leap, jump. **battutuen.** *v.* to jump over something. **binnattuto.** *n.* jumping in competition. [Tag. *talón, kandirít*]

battúyang: *var.* of *battútay*: carry, lift or swing by the neck; carry by the hands and legs; carry by the edges. **Binattuyangna ti natay a wak, sana impisok iti bay-on.** He picked up the dead crow by its feet, then threw it in the sack.

báwang: *n.* garlic, used in native medicine against high blood pressure. **agbabawang.** *a.* smelling of garlic; (*fig.*) to be about to get married. **agbabawang.** *n.* garlic vendor. **bawangan.** *v.* to season a dish with garlic. **kabawangan.** *n.* garlic field. **Kasla adda maangotko nga agbabawang.** *exp.* said when expecting a wedding soon (*lit*: it seems as though I smell garlic). [Ivt. *akus*, Kal. *byawang*, Png., Tag. *báwang*]

baw-áng: *n.* gorge, ravine. (*báwek*) **maibawang.** *v.* to fall into a ravine. [Tag. *bangín*]

baw-ás: **baw-asen.** *v.* to lessen; diminish; mitigate. (*kissay*) [Png. *bawás*, Tag. *bawas*]

báway: *n.* long stalk of fruits; cord of a bow.

bawbáw: *n.* gaping hole; large hole; manhole (*barawabaw*). [Tag. *butas*]

bawbáw: *a.* flat, insipid. **bumawbaw.** *v.* to become flat (drinks) or tasteless; (*reg.*) evaporate, abate. **agbanawbaw.** *v.* to talk loudly; to become tasteless, fade.

báwed: **naibawed.** *a.* hooked; hindered, restrained. **Nagbinnawed ti imada.** Their hands were hooked.

bawég: **agbaweg.** *v.* to strive to do; twist; deform. **Nabaweg ti aglikmut.** They made strong efforts to surround (us). [Tag. *sipag; pilipit*]

báwek: *n.* base of a mountain; ravine; gorge; restless person.

bawél: *n.* corporal punishment in a boy's game (*baled*). **bawelen.** *v.* to punish a loser in a boy's game by striking the calf of the loser's leg with a stick. [Tag. *paltík*]

bawér: see *pabawer*.

báwi: **makabawi.** *v.* to win one's money back; disown; disclaim one's promise. **babawi.** *n.* remorse; regret. **agbabawi.** *v.* to regret. **bumawi.** *v.* to regain one's losses. **bawien.** *v.* to redeem, regain losses, win back. **Diak met mabalin nga ibabawi dagiti sinaok.** I cannot take back what I said. [Ibg. *bavawi*, Ivt. *manehseh*, Kal. *chachauli, byabyawi*, Png. *babáwi*, Kpm., Tag. *sisi*]

baw-íng: *n.* changing of one's course. **agbawing.** *v.* to turn the head; change direction;

withdraw. **apagbaw-ing.** *v.* to make a brief appearance; *adv.* briefly; in a moment; *adv.* in a moment. **ibaw-ing.** *v.* to turn one's attention to; look in another direction. **baw-ingen.** *v.* to turn away from; change, change one's mind. **Mababain a nangibaw-ing iti rupana.** He turned his face away in shame. **Pinilitna a maibaw-ing ti panunotna.** He forced her to change her mind. [Tag. *baling*]

báwir: see *bannawir*: to rein a horse or water buffalo.

baw-ít: *n.* air plant; hanging decorative plant.

bay-á: **(bay)bay-an.** *v.* to permit, allow, let; cease, stop; leave alone; neglect. **agbaybay-a.** *v.* to neglect, disregard. **managbaybay-a.** *a.* careless; negligent; uncaring. **kinamanagbaybay-a.** *n.* neglectfulness, carelessness. **panagbaybay-a.** *n.* laissez-faire; abandonment; act of letting something be; negligence. **Bay-am latta.** Just let him be; Never mind; Let it be, leave it alone. [Png. *paulyán*, Tag. *bayà*]

bayábas: (Sp. *guayaba*: guava) *n.* guava, used in native medicine for diarrhea, itching, wounds, toothaches and stomachaches. [Bon. *kaybas*, Ibg. *bayáboq*, Kal. *geyait*, Knk. *gey-ábas*, Png. *bayáwas*, Tag. *bayabas*]

bayábay₁: *n.* a net used to scare fish into another net.

bayábay₂: *n.* escort; coronation celebrants; bridesmaids and ushers; additional support. **bayabayen.** *v.* to escort, flank, guard, protect. **Saan a makapan iti kayatna a papanan no awan ti mangbayabay kenkuana.** He cannot go where he wants to if no one will escort him. [Tag. *abay*]

bayábay₃: *banayabay.* *a.* slow, sluggish. [Tag. *bagal*]

bayábay₄: *n.* two tugs extending from the neck of a water buffalo to the thing to be hauled; post of a house.

báyad: *n.* cost, price; payment; tone in speaking; fare. **agbayad, bayadan.** *v.* to pay. **agpabayad.** *v.* to request payment. **babayadan.** *n.* remainder of a debt. **nabayadan.** *a.* paid. [Ibg. *paga*, Ivt. *mamagaq*, Kal. *tangchen, byayed*, Png. *báyar*, Kpm., Tag. *bayad*]

bayág: *n.* late rice; plant giving a second harvest; variety of tobacco used in *abano* cigars. **mabayag.** *v.* to take a long time in doing. **nabayag.** *a.* for a long time. **agbayag.** *v.* to tarry, delay; take a long time in doing; linger. **ibaybayag.** *v.* to procrastinate. **kabayag.** *n.* duration, length of time. **makapagbayag.** *v.* to be able to stay long. **makipagbayag.** *v.* to stay a long time in a certain place with others. **di pay nabayag.** *exp.* not long ago. **Nabayagen a**

birbirokenka. I have been looking for you for a long time. [Bon. *liwa*, Ibg. *bayag, vayag*, Ivt. *kaycúwaq*, Kal. *beyeg*, Kpm. *malambat*, Png. *bayág*, Tag. *tagál*; Tag. *bayág* = testicle]

bayakábak: *n.* heavy rainfall, downpour. **bumayakabak.** *v.* to pour, splash (said of rain).

bayakán: *n.* sloping side of a roof.

bay-ákan: *n.* speckled hog.

bayákat: *n.* G-string. (*baag*)

bay-ámon: (f. *bay-a*) *exp.* Never mind it. Let it be.

bay-án: (f. *bay-a*) *v.* to let, allow, permit; neglect, leave alone, abandon. **Adu ti gaygayyemmo no adda kuartam, no awanen baybay-andakan.** You have a lot of friends when you have money, when you don't they abandon you.

báyang₁: *bayangbayang.* *n.* a kind of marine fish with a flattened body.

bayáng₂: *n.* portion of the wall from the tiebeam (*sekkeg*) to the roof (gable end of roof).

bayangbáng: *a.* open (*lukat*).

bayangbáyang: *n.* gable end of a roof.

bayanggúdaw: *n.* tramp. (*baligawgaw; alibtok; agpalpalama; patotot*); *a.* lazy, idle. **Kimmaro ti kinabayanggudaw ti anakko manipud idi adda relasionyo.** My child's laziness has worsened since your relationship (with him).

bayangúbong: see *bayongobong*: diarrhea; cholera.

bayás: *n.* baptismal party. [Tag. *binyág*]

báyat: *bayat ti, kabayatan ti.* *prep.* during, while (*bulon*). **nabayat.** *a.* slow, sluggish; stressed (word); unprepared. **pagbayatan.** *n.* interval. **Bayat ti panagmeriendami, sinaludsodna no sino ti amak.** While we ate our snack, she asked who my father is. [Png. *anggán, légan*, Tag. *habang*]

bayaténg: *n. Anamirta cocculus* plant used in fish poisons, fish poison. **nabayateng.** *a.* poisoned (said of fish).

bayatíng: *var.* of *bayateng.*

bayáw₁: (Tagalog also) *n.* brother-in-law (*káyong*). **agbayaw.** *n.* two brothers-in-law.

bayáw₂: *n.* corn granary. (*sarusar; garong*) **ibayaw.** *v.* to put into the granary.

bayáwak: *n.* scorpion. (*manggagama*)

bayáwas: (*reg.*) *n.* guava. (*bayabas*)

baybáy: *n.* sea; beach, shore; side. (*taaw*) **agbaybay.** *v.* to line up properly; stand, sit, etc. side by side. **agbabaybay.** *v.* to fall in line. **igid ti baybay.** *n.* beach (*aplaya*); seashore. [Ibg. *bébay*, Ivt. *táaw*, Knk. *daúyen*, Kpm. *dáyat*, *málat*, Png. *baybáy, dáyat*, Tag. *dagat*]

baybóy: *bumayboy.* (*obs.*) *v.* to abate (sickness).

bayén: (f. *bai*) *binabayen.* *n.* a kind of bow net.

bayengbéng: *a.* drunk. **bimmayengbeng.** *a.* full and elongated (fruits); straight and erect (body).

bayengyéng: *n.* thick bamboo nodes used for carrying water or rice.

báyle: (Sp. *baile:* dance) *n.* dance. (*sala*)

baylíta: ibaylita. *v.* to spread newly harvested rice in order to dry.

báyo: *a.* reddish brown; milling of rice. **agpabayo.** *v.* to have rice milled **bayuen.** *v.* to mill rice; crush; bruise. **binayo.** *n.* milled (uncooked) rice. **panagbabayo.** *n.* season after harvest in which farmers start to mill rice. **pagbaywan.** *n.* rice mill. **Nangipatakder iti pagbaywan.** He put up a rice mill. [Ivt. *mangsad*, Ibg., Kpm., Png., Tag. *báyo*]

bayubána: *n.* soursop used in native medicine to cure dizziness. [Tag. *guyabano*]

báyog: *n.* signal of occupation; cause; movement. **ibayog.** *v.* to hoist; found a movement; spearhead. **nabayog.** *a.* craggy (mountain); broad; large (chest, muscles, etc.). **kinabayog.** *n.* broadness, bigness, largeness. **Ibayogmo ti barukongmo.** Heave your chest.

bayóg: *n.* old maid, spinster; bamboo used for flooring; rattan strip used for tying. **nabayog.** *a.* tall and slender (bamboo).

bayúkan: *n.* a kind of tree.

bayokbók: *n.* ornament of a hat; bulging of a garment. **agbayokbok.** *v.* to swell, bulge, become erect; rise.

bayukyók: *a.* bent; hunched (under heavy weight). (*apday*) **agbayukyok.** *v.* to bend under heavy weight.

bay-ón: *n.* a kind of bag made of *silag* leaf strips; shopping bag with a handle. **sangabay-on.** *n.* one bagful.

bayonéta: (Sp. *bayoneta:* bayonet) *n.* bayonet. **bayonetaen.** *v.* to hit or stab with a bayonet.

bay-óng: *var.* of *bay-ón*. sack, bag.

bayungúbong: *n.* diarrhea; cholera. (*buris; suyot*) **agbayungubong.** *v.* to have diarrhea or cholera.

bayúngon: *n.* a kind of edible reef mollusk with a pointed shell.

bayúot: *n.* stench of dried urine. (*angseg*) **nabayuot.** *a.* smelling of putrid urine. [Tag. *panghí*]

bayúyang: *var.* of *bayyuyang:* hang upside down; carry while hanging upside down (pigs tied to a pole).

bayyábas: *n.* guavas. (*bayabas*) **agbayyabas.** *v.* to pick guavas.

bayyát: *n.* a kind of mussel. **sibabayyabayyat.** *a.* caught unexpectedly while naked.

bayyaténg: *n.* fruit of the *labtang* vine used to poison fish. **mabayyateng.** *a.* to be poisoned with *bayyateng*.

bayyék: *n.* tadpole, polliwog; chubby person; restless person. **agbayyek.** *v.* to catch tadpoles. [Kal. *bayyok*, Knk. *piéng*, Tag. *ulouló*]

bayyét: *n.* thread used to tie the spur of a gamecock.

bayyúyang: bayyuyangen. *v.* to carry a person on both hands and feet (*kullalong*); to hang something upside down.

beáta: (Sp. *beato:* overly pious) *n.* kind of nun; pious woman.

bebbéb: *a.* short; cropped; snub-nosed; chubby; with sunken lips (toothless person). **bebbeben.** *v.* to crop. [Tag. *pangô* (snub-nosed)]

bebedór: (Sp. *bebedor:* drinker) *n.* feeding bottle. **agbebedor.** *v.* to bottle feed.

bédak: *n.* flower of the screw pine.

bedbéd: *n.* bandage, band. **bedbeden.** *v.* to bandage, bind, tie (*galut*). **ibedbed.** *v.* to use to tie or bind. **dua a kabedbed.** two bundles. **sangkabedbed.** one bundle. [Tag. *tali*]

beddabéd: agbeddabed. *v.* to nasalize, snuffle.

beddál: *n.* rude person; steelless blade; untattooed; person who has difficulty in pronouncing words. **agbeddal.** *v.* to stammer (*annawil; annawir; bede*). [Kal. *gole*, Tag. *utál*]

beddáng: nabeddang. *a.* out of tune. **beddangen** (*obs.*) *v.* to stretch oneself to the limit.

beddéng₁: *n.* limit, boundary; share, portion; territory; assignment of work. **pagbeddengan, pagbedngan.** *n.* boundary, border; limit. **kabeddeng.** *n.* owner of the adjacent lot. **ipabeddeng.** *v.* to have borders drawn, land surveyed. **iti beddeng ti.** *prep.* in matters of, concerning (*maipapan*). **Nagkakabeddengda.** They have subdivided the land between them. [Tag. *hangganan*]

beddéng₂: bumdeng. *v.* to hesitate to do; be apprehensive; to fear; be doubtful of or timid. [Png. *manduwaruwa*, Tag. *atubili*]

bedé: *n.* stutterer. (*beddal*) **agbede.** *v.* to stutter, stammer. [Knk. *aslé, bagiwbíw, enen-é,* Kpm. *kakák*, Tag. *utal-utál*]

bedéng: bumdeng. *v.* to waver; falter; be shy. [Tag. *alangán, atubilí*]

begbég: nabegbeg. *a.* minced, ground up, milled. **agbanegbeg.** *n.* sound of pestle in mortar. **begbegen.** *v.* to grind, pulverize. **banegbeg.** *n.* the sound of pounding. [Tag. *durog*]

beggáng: *n.* live coal; ember. **bumeggang.** *v.* to glow like a live coal. **Impuorna ti buneng agingga a bimmeggang.** He placed his machete in the fire until it glowed like live coal. **Adda beggang kadagiti mata ni Tutsang**

tunggal maipalagip kenkuana ti amana. There is a live coal in Tutsang's eyes every time he is reminded of his father. [Ibg. *baga, beggang,* Ivt. *inmaya,* Knk. *gabbáng, baggáng,* Kpm. *báya,* Png. *ngalab,* Tag. *baga*]

beggáy: (*obs.*) *n.* chasing the devil.

begkés: *n.* protective covering: cover of a jar, abdominal band placed over a baby's navel for protection. **ibegkes, begkesen.** *v.* to wrap around (a towel, etc.), tie together. **Naukarkar ti nakabegkes a tualia iti bagina.** The towel wrapped around her body unfurled.

begkét: *n.* protective covering of a jar (paper, cloth, wood, leaves, etc.) (*begkes*). **begketen.** *v.* to cover a jar. **nabegket.** *a.* tightly covered.

begnás: *n.* feast celebrated among mountain peoples.

begnát: *n.* relapse. **mabegnat.** *v.* to relapse (a sickness). **pakabegnatan.** *n.* cause of relapse. [Tag. *binat*]

behíkulo: (Sp. *vehículo:* vehicle) *n.* vehicle (*lugan*). **behikulo a pakigubat.** war vehicle.

behúko: (Sp. *bejuco:* rattan) *n.* rattan.

bekbék: nabekbek. *a.* stocky, stout; muscular (*baneg; puner*). [Tag. *tipunò*]

bekká: bumekka. *v.* to vent one's feelings; burst out laughing; burst, crack. **nabka.** *a.* broken, cracked (*bettak*).

bekkág: *n.* cotton boll (fruit of cotton). **agbekkag, bumkag.** *v.* to burst open (cotton bolls).

bekkáng: bumkang. *v.* to burst open; snap; crack. **mabkangan.** *v.* to crack; suffer a broken rib. **nabkang.** *a.* cracked. **Nabkangansa 'toy barukong.** I think my chest cracked.

bekkás: bumkas. *v.* to dart, burst out; burst open; snap (snare). **ibkas, yebkas.** *v.* to dart, burst out doing something; vent one's feelings. [Tag. *buká*]

bekkáy: see *bekkas*: dart; declare.

bekkél: *n.* kidney (*bató*); goiter (*biél, buklóng*). **agbekkel.** *v.* to hang oneself; to be numb. **bekkelan.** *n.* goiter. **bekkelen.** *v.* to strangle, choke. **bebekkelan.** *n.* the part of the trachea in the throat. **nabekkel.** *a.* strangled. **kasla nabekkel (a nakabasa iti surat).** *exp.* to be shocked (to read a letter). [Tag. *bató* (kidney); *sakál* (strangle)]

bekkér: *n.* tiebeam; pole placed on cloth to prevent shrinking.

bekkóg: *n.* depressed part on a surface. **bekkugen.** *v.* to bend, curve (*bakkug*). [Tag. *balikukô*]

bekkór: *n.* protuberance, bulge. **agbekkor.** *v.* to bulge. [Tag. *uslî*]

beklát: *n.* a large nonpoisonous snake; python. **bimmeklat.** *a.* like a python.

bel-á: *n.* vomit of babies. **agbel-a.** *v.* to vomit, throw up (babies). **maibel-a.** *v.* to belch out (soldiers out of the trenches); be vomited out. [Ivt. *hanu,* Png. *etyák,* Tag. *suka, lungad, luwâ*]

beláda: (Sp. *velada:* night program, soirée) *n.* vigil; evening program; entertainment, evening concert. **agbelada.** *v.* to give or present a program. **makibelada.** *v.* to participate in a vigil or evening program.

belasiónes: (Sp., *obs. velación*) *n.* time during which the church in the Philippines prohibited pompous weddings.

belbél₁: *n.* soggy rice cooked in too much water; end of a cold. [Tag. *latâ*]

belbél₂: *n.* attacking in groups. **belbelan.** *v.* to attack (many against one); stuff the mouth.

belbél₃: *var.* of *bilbil*: large belly, adipose tissue that hangs over the belt. (*buttiog*)

beldát: *n.* a kind of river mollusk.

Belén: (Sp.) *n.* Bethlehem; manger, Christmas stable.

Bélga: (Sp. *belga:* Belgium) *n.* Belgian. **Belhika.** *n.* Belgium.

bèliadóna: (Sp. *belladona*) *n.* belladona, deadly nightshade plant with reddish bell-shaped flowers and shining black berries. **asiete de beliadona.** kind of ointment applied to ulcers.

bélias: (Sp. *bella:* beautiful woman) *n.* nightclub dancer; woman with excessive makeup.

bélias-ártes: (Sp. *bellas artes*) *n.* fine arts.

belláak: *n.* uproar, turmoil, rebellion, pandemonium; (*reg.*) rumor. **bumlaak.** *v.* to be tumultuous; riot. **pablaak.** *n.* notice, announcement. **ipablaak.** *v.* to announce; publish. **Adda pay ngata gundawayna a maipablaak?** Do you think there still is a chance for it to be published? [Tag. *guló*]

belláay: *n.* flour (rice flour); dough. **bellaayen.** *v.* to make into dough. [Tag. *masa* (Sp.)]

bellád₁: *n.* puffiness of cereals in water. **bumlad.** *v.* to swell from being in liquid; expand (rice or beans in water), bloat. **agbelladan.** *v.* to be full (in the stomach). **agbellad.** *v.* to die of indigestion. **mabladan.** *v.* to suffer from indigestion. **pinablad.** *n.* water-cooked corn, grains cooked in water until they puff up. **agpablad.** *v.* to boil corn to make *pinablad*. **pabladen.** *v.* to cook cereals in water; (*fig.*) to insinuate. [Tag. *magâ; alsá*]

bellád₂: *n.* a kind of reef mollusk.

belláng: *n.* hard wood of the *palma brava*; long wooden rod. **bellangan.** *n.* very hard palm wood.

bellát: *n.* core (of fruits); fiber of fruits or reeds.

belléd: *n.* welt. **bumled.** *v.* to welt; fester. [Tag. *latay*]

belléng: **ibelleng**. *v.* to throw out, throw away; dispose of; deport; vanish. **maibelleng**. *v.* to spill, run out, fall out. **agibleng**. *v.* to defecate; have diarrhea. **ipabelleng**. *v.* to have something thrown away. **pagibellengan**. *n.* trash can; garbage dump. [Ibg. *ivuttu, itebboq*, Ivt. *ipuhaq*, Kpm. *ugse*, Png. *bantak*, Tag. *tapon*]

bellés: *n.* sprain. (*bullo*) **nables, nablesán**. *a.* sprained. **mammelles**. *n.* one who cures sprains. [Knk. *siklí*, Tag. *pilay*]

belnás: see *balnas*: rinse. [Tag. *banláw*]

bélo: (Sp. *velo*: veil) *n.* veil. **nakabelo**. *a.* wearing a veil. **agbelo**. *v.* to wear a veil.

belosidád: (Sp. *velocidad*: speed) *n.* speed, velocity; might. **nakabelosidad**. *a.* very fast. **kontodo belosidad**. with all one's might.

belták: *n.* crack, fissure. **beltaken**. *v.* to crack, split, break. **mabeltak**. *v.* to be cracked; split open. [Tag. *biták*]

béna: (Sp. *vena*: vein) *n.* vein. (*urat*)

benbén: **benbenen**. *v.* to prevent; hold back, restrain. **makabenben**. *v.* to have enough money to buy; to be able to hold.

bénda: (Sp. *venda*: bandage) *n.* bandage; binding. **bendaan**. *v.* to apply a bandage to.

bendáhe: (Sp. *vendaje*: bandage; gratuity) *n.* bandage; commission of a broker.

bendesír: (Sp. *bendecir*: bless) **bendesiren**. *v.* to bless. [Tag. *biyayà*]

bendisión: (Sp. *bendición*: blessing) *n.* benediction, blessing. **bendisionan**. *v.* to bless. [Tag. *biyayà*]

bendíta: (Sp. *bendita*: holy) *n.* holy water. (*nasantuanan a danum*) **benditaan**. *v.* to sprinkle with holy water. **nabenditaan**. *a.* blessed.

benditár: *var.* of *bendita*: bless.

bendíto: (Sp. *bendito*: blessed) *a.* blessed.

benepisiar: (Sp. *beneficiar*: benefit) **mabenepisiaran**. *a.* to benefit from. [Tag. *pakinabang*]

benepisiário: (Sp. *beneficiario*: beneficiary) *n.* beneficiary.

benepísio: (Sp. *beneficio*: benefit) *n.* benefit; benefit show.

bennál: *n.* sugarcane sap or juice.

bennát: **bennaten**. *v.* to stretch; extend; stretch a supply. **agbennat**. *v.* to shoot up (in growing); extend; expand. **bumbumnat**. *v.* resounding; reverberating. **mamnat**. *v.* to stretch. [Png. *pínat, onát*, Tag. *inát, banat*]

bennég: *n.* section; partition; aisle; beam used in a partition; department; division; chapter; portion; corridor; newspaper column. **bennegen**. *v.* to apportion; divide into parts; subdivide. [Tag. *bahagi*]

bennék: *n.* a kind of small freshwater clam (*bukaig*). [Tag. *tulya*]

bensá: *n.* chapter; paragraph. **bensabensaen**. *v.* to speak or read clearly. [Tag. *kabanatà* (chapter)]

bensído: (Sp. *vencido*: conquered) *a.* due and payable; controlled, subdued, conquered.

bénta: (Sp. *venta*: sale) *n.* article for sale. **debenta**. *a.* for sale. **ibenta**. *v.* to sell.

bentáha: (Sp. *ventaja*: advantage) *n.* advantage. [*Bentahe* is more common nowadays]

bentáhe: (Sp. *ventaja*: advantage + -*e* English word termination) *n.* advantage (*gundaway*). **nabentahe**. *a.* advantageous. [Tag. *pakinabang, samantalá*]

bentahéro: (Sp. *ventaja*: advantage + -*ero* agentive suffix) *n.* one who buys or sells stocks at a low price.

bentána: (Sp. *ventana*: window) *n.* window. (*tawa*). **agbentana**. *v.* to look out a window; lean out a window. [Tag. *bintanà*]

bentanília: (Sp. *ventanilla*: ticket window, small window) *n.* ticket window (*takilia*); peephole, small window.

bénte: (Sp. *veinte*: twenty) *num.* twenty. (*beinte*)

bentiliadór: (Sp. *ventilador*: ventilator) *n.* ventilator, electric fan.

bentósa: (Sp. *ventosa*: cupping glass) *n.* cupping glass used to improve the circulation of blood. **bentosaen**. *v.* to cure someone with a cupping glass. **agbentosa**. *v.* to undergo cupping glass treatment.

bentrilokía: (Sp. *ventriloquía*: ventriloquism) *n.* ventriloquism.

bengbéng: *n.* thickness; curtain; drapery. **nabengbeng**. *a.* thick; close-woven; thick-skinned, disobedient. **kabengbeng**. *n.* thickness. **bengbengan**. *v.* to cover an opening. **mabengbengan**. *v.* can be concealed. **nabengbeng ti rupana**. *a.* thick-skinned (*napuskol*). [Tag. *kapál* (thick)]

benggadór: (Sp. *vengador*: avenger) *n.* avenger. (*bales*)

benggánsa: (Sp. *venganza*: revenge) *n.* revenge, vengeance (*bales*). [Tag. *higantí*]

benggatíbo: (Sp. *vengativo*) *a.* revengeful, vindictive. **kinabenggatibo**. *n.* vindictiveness (*bales*). [Tag. *mapaghigantí*]

bengkág: *n.* field (not of rice). (*bangkag*)

bengngabengngét: (*obs.*) *n.* sling.

bengngál: *n.* wedge. (*sanat, tingál*)

bengngát: *n.* accent in speaking (*ayug*); intonation; word repeated frequently in talking; intonation. **agbengngat**. (*reg.*) *v.* to start to talk (children). **Bengngat-bantay ti ayugna**. He has a mountain accent. [Tag. *punto* (accent in speaking)]

bengngáw: nabngaw. *a.* pierced, perforated; destroyed.

bengngáy: *n.* a large crack in the ground. (*rengngat*)

bengngéd: (*obs.*) *a.* preferring, mending.

bengngég: *a.* hard of hearing, almost deaf; obstinate, stubborn, disobedient. **ipabpabengngeg.** *v.* to refuse to heed.

bengngél: benglan. *v.* to swarm around, throng, crowd upon; overwhelm; *a.* stony, hardened.

bengngét: see *panget:* stick to.

bengráw: *n.* a large greenish fly.

beránda: (Eng.) *n.* veranda, high porch.

berbakan: (*lit.*) *n.* shark. (*yo; pating*)

berbéna: *n.* species of flowering decorative plant with large flowers.

berbér: *n.* draft of air; sound of wind. **agberber.** *v.* to expose oneself to the wind. **maiberber.** *a.* fully exposed to the wind or current. **berberan.** *v.* to restrain; hold back (boats). **bumanerber.** *n.* sound of strong wind or a river. **paberberen.** *v.* to drive fast.

bérbo: (Sp. *verbo*) *n.* verb.

bérde: (Sp. *verde:* green) *n. a.* green. **pamerberdien.** *a.* somewhat green. [Ibg., Kpm. *berdi,* Ifg. *maáta,* Ivt. *árem,* Kal. *lanti,* Png., Tag. *berde*]

berdéng: naberdeng. *a.* tense, taut (*irténg*); rigid; serious (face).

berdigónes: (Sp. *perdigón:* pellet) *n.* lead pellet for shotguns.

berdigrís: (Eng.) *n.* verdigris, a greenish blue poisonous pigment obtained by the reaction of acetic acid on copper.

berdúgo: (Sp. *verdugo:* hangman) *n.* executioner; torturer; hangman; villain; kind of yellow and black bird.

berdúras: (Sp. *verdura:* green vegetable) *n.* vegetables. (*nateng*)

bérhas: (Sp. *verja:* grating) *n.* grating on doors; iron railing.

berína: (Sp. *vitrina:* glass case) *n.* glass bell, glass cover.

berkák: *a.* wide-mouthed. **agberkak.** *v.* to swell (said of the throats of certain snakes and frogs). **ígat berkakan.** *n.* a kind of large eel, lamprey; painted moray, *Gymnothorax pictus.*

berkákak: *var.* of *berkak:* wide-mouthed (with throat expanded).

berkakók: *n.* a kind of speckled bird; variety of awned early rice.

berlína: (Sp.) *n.* limousine; car with a closed body. **agberlina.** *v.* to ride in a *berlina.*

bermúda: (Sp.) *n.* Bermuda onion.

bernáng: (*obs.*) *a.* fierce, savage; severe.

berráak: bumraak. *v.* to be about to vomit; suffer stomach discomfort before vomiting; crack like gunfire; be deafening.

berráat: *n. var.* of *berraak.*

berrúko: *n.* a kind of small bird living near water.

bersíkulo: (Sp. *versículo:* versicle) *n.* verse, versicle; short division of a chapter in the Bible.

bérso: (Sp. *verso:* verse) *n.* verse; type of firecracker; light cannon fire salute.

besbés: sangkabesbes. *n.* one bundle. (*reppet*) **bumanesbes.** *n.* sound of people running, moving fast (*berber*). [Tag. *hagibis*]

béses: (Sp. *veces:* times) *n.* times. (*mamin-, daras*)

béso: (Sp. *beso:* kiss) **besobeso.** *n.* kisses upon greeting. **agbesobeso.** *v.* to kiss upon greeting.

besság: *n.* paleness. **agbebessag.** *v.* to be pale (from sickness). **bumsag.** *v.* to turn pale, pallid. **nabessag.** *a.* pale; lifeless. [Tag. *putlâ*]

bessáng: *n.* mountain pass; tear, rip; *a.* hamstrung. **bebessangan.** *n.* hamstring in animals; Achilles tendon. **binsang.** *n.* (*reg.*) window.

bessát: *n.* equality in length. **sangkabessat.** *a.* of the same length.

bessíl: nabsil, nakabsil. *a.* sprained. [Knk. *siklí*]

bestí: *n.* ornament; clothing. (*kawes*) **bestian.** *v.* to adorn; dress up. [Tag. *palamuti*]

bestída: (Sp. *vestido:* dress, fem. *a. vestida:* dressed) *n.* dress; gown. **nakabestida.** *a.* wearing a dress.

bestído: (Sp. *vestido:* dress) *n.* dress; gown. **agbestido.** *v.* to wear a dress.

bestidúra: (Sp. *vestidura*) *n.* vesture; vestment.

bet-áng: *n.* lane, narrow dirt road; pathway.

betbét: *a.* lazy; stupid; slow. (*sadut; bontog; tabbed*) **agbanetbet.** *v.* to produce a whipping sound. **betbeten.** *v.* to whip (*basnut; saplit; baut*). [Tag. *kupad* (slow)]

beteráno: (Sp. *veterano:* veteran) *n.* veteran.

beterinário: (Sp. *veterinario:* veterinarian) *n.* veterinarian, animal doctor.

béto: (Eng.) *n.* veto. **ibeto.** *v.* to veto (a bill, etc.). **betobeto.** *n.* a game of dice.

betón: (Sp. *betún:* shoe polish) *n.* shoe polish. **betunen.** *v.* to polish shoes. [Tag. *bitón*]

betsín: *n.* Monosodium glutamate, MSG.

bettáang: *n.* the cessation of rain. **agbettaang.** *v.* to stop raining.

bettád: *n.* kind of sledgehammer. **agbettad.** *v.* to forge; crush stones.

betták: *n.* cracking, bursting, breaking. **bumtak.** *v.* to burst open, crack, explode, break; be wounded. **bettakan.** *v.* to buttonhole. **mabtak.** *v.* to crack; be caused to crack; go flat (tire). **marabettakan.** *a.* full of cracks. **ibebettak ti**

bulkán. *n.* volcanic eruption. **bettaken.** *v.* to burst something open; to pop a pimple; smash; break. **dakkel a panagbettak.** *n.* outburst; the big bang theory of creation. **apagbettak nga isem.** *n.* slight smile. **Kasla saan a makabtak iti bulong.** He seems incapable of breaking a leaf (said of someone who does something very surprising). **Bettakek ta bangabangam no tungpalem ti bilinna.** I'll smash your skull if you follow his orders. [Kal. *laplaptak*, Png. *paltog*, Tag. *putók*]

bettéd: *n.* cramp in the muscles. (*betteg*, *tortub*) **agbetted.** *v.* to have a cramp in the muscles. [Tag. *pulikat*]

bettég₁: *n.* cramp (*tortúb*). **agbetteg.** *v.* to have a cramp. [Tag. *pulikat*]

bettég₂: *a.* slow, sluggish. (*buntog*)

bettég₃: mabetbettegan. (*obs.*) *v.* to be seen distinctly.

bették: *n.* band, string, strip used to bind; bundle of *palay*. **betteken.** *v.* to bundle (rice stalks for thatching). **sang(k)abtek.** *n.* one bundle of *palay*, usually made of four smaller bundles. [Tag. *panalì*]

bettiág: *a.* (*obs.*) proud. (*pannakel; ambug; pasikat; pusong; tangsit*)

biáda: (Sp. *virada*: turn, veering) *n.* wiggling of wheels; wiggling of a revolving object.

biág: *n.* life. **agbiag.** *v.* to live; survive. **agbibiag.** *n.* characters, personage. **biagen.** *v.* to vivify, enliven; recall; refresh (memories). **pagbibiag.** *n.* livelihood; staple food. **panagbiag.** *n.* biography, life; lifestyle; way of life. **sibibiag.** *a.* alive. **pagbiagan.** *n.* livelihood; means of living. **tungpal-biag.** *a.* for the rest of one's life. **tungpal biag a pannakabalud.** *n.* life imprisonment. **kabibiag.** *n.* biography. **mangbiag.** *v.* to provide livelihood for, support, earn a living (for one's family, etc.). **nabiag.** *a.* lively, full of life; full of water (spring). **Panggepdakami a puoran a sibibiag.** They plan to burn us alive. **Rumbeng laeng a tulongak a mangbiag iti pamiliami.** I just need to help support our family. **Saanmo kuman a biagen dagiti napalabas.** You shouldn't revive the past events. **Ti napudpudno nga agbibiag, saanna nga ibaga nga isu ti biag.** The real hero doesn't tell that he is. **Agbiag kuma ti Ari!** Long live the King! [Ibg. *tólay*, Ifg. *tágu*, Ivt. *viay*, Knk. *lemía*, Kpm. *bye*, Png. *biláy*, Tag. *buhay*]

biáhe: (Sp. *viaje*: trip; travel) *n.* journey; travel. (*baniaga*) **agbiahe.** *v.* to travel. **biahero, managbiahe.** *n.* one who likes to travel. **ibiahe.** *v.* to transport to; take on a trip. **Adda bukodna a lugan a pagibiahena kadagiti magatangna.** He has his own car to take for his purchases. [Knk. *gákay*, Png. *bároy*, Tag. *lakbáy*]

biahedór: (f. *biahe*, Sp. *viajador*) *n.* traveler.

biahéro: (Sp. *viajero*: traveler) *n.* traveler, one who likes to travel; traveling merchant (*managbiahe, managbaniaga*)

biakrúsis: (Sp., from Latin *via crucis*) *n.* stations of the cross.

biála: *n.* a kind of large black marine fish.

biámbo: *n.* curtain; partition.

biáng: *n.* responsibility, concern; charge, care; condition, state. **bumibiang.** *v.* to concern oneself with. **biangan.** *v.* to meddle; mediate; interfere. **ibiang.** *v.* to involve. **mannakibiang.** *n.* meddler; gossiper. **pannakabiang.** *n.* one's share of responsibility. **kaniak a biang, iti biangko.** *exp.* as far as I'm concerned; in my opinion. **Saannakon a biangan.** Don't meddle in my affairs. **Awan ti biangmo.** It doesn't concern you. It's none of your business. [Kpm. *bálaq*, Tag. *pakialám*]

biángot: (f. *biang*) *n.* someone who always interferes in other people's business. **Dakayo a biangot, apay a kitkitaendakami?** You meddlers, why are you staring at us?

biát: biaten. *v.* to shoot an arrow. **sibibiat.** *a.* stretched, drawn (bows). **ibiat.** *v.* to release; let an arrow fly from a bow. **Kasla imbiat a pana ti luganda.** Their car is like a shot arrow (very fast). [Tag. *pakawalán*]

biátiko: (Sp. *viático*: viaticum) *n.* viaticum, Eucharist given to someone on the verge of death.

bíba: (Sp. *viva*: long live) Long live!

biberón: (Sp. *biberón*: nursing bottle) *n.* nursing bottle, rubber nipple (*mamador*). **Saan kadi nga imbati ni inangmo tay bibironmo?** Didn't your mother leave you your bottle?

bibíg: *n.* lip. **bibigan.** *a.* thick lipped; big mouthed. (*amil*) [Ibg. *bivig, bibig*, Ivt. *viviq*, Kal. *subin*, Knk. *súbil*, Kpm. *lábiq*, Png. *bibíl*, Tag. *labì*]

bibílan: *n.* wooden turntable used by pottery makers.

bibíneg: (f. *bineg*) **agbibineg.** *v.* to be numb. **bibinegen.** *v.* to make numb; anaesthetize. **nabibineg.** *a.* numb. [Knk. *pikét*, Tag. *manhíd*]

bibíngka: *n.* a kind of sweet rice cake cooked with coconut, the specialty of Vigan, Ilocos Sur; (*coll.*) female genitals. **bibingkaen.** *v.* to make into rice cake. [Tag. *bibingka*]

bibír: (*obs.*) *var.* of *bibig*: lip.

bibirán: *n.* a kind of marine fish.

bíblia: *n.* Bible. **Santa Biblia.** Holy Bible.

bibliotéka: (Sp. *biblioteca*: library) *n.* library.

bíbo₁: (Sp. *vivo*: edging, colored seam) *n.* edging or fabric; stripes on trousers running from the hips to the ankles.

bíbo₂: (Sp. *vivo*: alive) Go ahead; hurry up; follow suit with a lower card in *burro*.

bída: (Sp. *vida*: life) *n.* protagonist of a movie; hero or heroine of a movie or book. **kontrabida.** *n.* antagonist of the *bida*.

bídang: *n.* apron; tapis, sash. **agbidang.** *v.* to wear a *bídang*. **bidangan.** *v.* to put an apron or sash around someone. [Tag. *tapis*]

bidáw: **bidawbidaw.** *n.* a kind of tasty, bony marine fish.

bidáy: *n. Ocimum sanctum*, a plant with small pink fragrant flowers and chewable leaves used in native medicine for toothaches or swollen gums. Its fragrant leaves are sometimes used in bathwater.

biddáng: **biddangen.** *v.* to stretch. **nabiddang.** *a.* stretched to the limit.

biddáy: **biddayen.** *v.* to clean cotton (by shaking out extraneous matter before removing seeds).

biddít: (*obs.*) *n.* margin. (*igid*)

biddút: *n.* mistake, error, fault, blunder. (*kammali*) **bumiddut.** *v.* to think incorrectly. **no diak bumiddut.** *exp.* if I'm not mistaken. **agbiddut iti ikakapet.** lose one's grip. **Biddutna kadi ti panangasawana iti ubing?** Is it her fault that she married a child? [Knk. *kesáw*, Png. *lingó*, Tag. *kamalî*]

bíding: *n.* a kind of kingfisher; a black wart.

bidíng: **bidingen.** *v.* to handle repeatedly; (*fig.*) examine, study, scrutinize. **No adda met ngarud tumawar, bidbidigenda sada pay ram-uyen.** Then when there's a haggler, they handle (the merchandise) repeatedly, then bargain. [Tag. *lamutak*]

bidugól: *n.* bruise (*litem*, *labneg*); hematoma. **agbidugol.** *v.* to bruise. [Tag. *pasâ*]

bidsáy: *n.* small oar (*gaud*). [Tag. *sagwán*]

biého: (Sp. *viejo*: old) *n.* old man (*lakay*); (*obs.*) Chinese.

biél: *n.* goiter, enlargement of the thyroid gland, swelling in neck (*buklong*). [Knk. *ákak*, *baséy*, *buséy*, Kal. *bikkok*, Tag. *bosyò*]

bién: (Sp. *bien*: good) *n.* good deed; benefit. **mas bien.** better. (*nasasayaat*) **esta bien.** very good. **bienbenida.** *n.* welcome party. **bienbenido.** *n.* welcome.

biénes: (Sp. *bienes*: real estate) *n.* property, real estate; possessions (*tagikua*); taxes (*buis*).

Biérnes: (Sp. *viernes*: Friday) *n.* Friday. **Biernes Santo.** Good Friday. **Biernes de dolores.** Friday before Palm Sunday. **Biernes Santo a rupa.** *n.* solemn, gloomy face. [Kal. *kalima*]

Bietnamís: (Eng.) *n. a.* Vietnamese. **agbietnamis.** *v.* to be Vietnamese; to speak Vietnamese.

bietnamrós: (Eng. Vietnam rose) *n.* species of flowering plant used as decor.

bíga: *n.* Elephant's ear plant, *Alocasia indica*.

bigáo: *n.* winnowing basket. **agbigao.** *v.* to winnow. [Kal. *liblak*, Png. *bigaó*, Tag. *bilao*]

bigát: *n.* morning (*agsapa*); morrow. **pamigat.** *n.* breakfast. **pammigat.** *n.* time for breakfast. **mamigat.** *v.* to eat breakfast. **makipamigat.** *v.* to join someone for breakfast. **bigbigat.** *n.* early morning. **agbigbigat.** *v.* to last until early morning. **agkabigatan.** *v.* to stay until the next morning. **bigbigaten.** *v.* to do in the early morning. **mabigatan.** *v.* to be overtaken by the morning; stay until the next morning. **binniganbigat.** *adv.* every morning. (*binigat*) **bumigat.** *adv.* at dawn. **inton bigat.** tomorrow. **bigat kalman.** Yesterday morning. **binigat.** *adv.* every morning, (*biniganbigat*). **ipabigat.** *v.* to put off until morning, postpone until the next day. **kabigatanna.** *n.* next morning (future). **bigat-kasangaldaw.** *n.* the day after tomorrow. **kinabigatanna.** *n.* next morning (past). **Naimbág a bigatyo.** Good morning (polite). **Inton sangabigaten ti panagkasangayna.** The day of his birthday. **Timmawagak iti kabigatanna, ngem awan kanon.** I called the next morning, but he supposedly wasn't there. **Mamigmigat ni Sinting a nadanon ni Pepay.** Sinting was eating breakfast when Pepay arrived. **Diak maipabigat ti damag.** I cannot put off the news until morning. [Ibg. *umma*, Itg. *agsapa*, Ivt. *mavekhas*, Kal. *bigbigat*, Kpm. *ábak*, Png. *buás*, Tag. *umaga* (morning), *bukas* (tomorrow); Tag. *bigát* = heavy]

bigbíg: *n.* act of recognizing. **bigbigen.** *v.* to recognize; scrutinize, inspect closely; consider; claim object as one's own. **mabigbig.** *v.* to recognize (someone) identify; *a.* outstanding; renowned for; famous. **pammigbig.** *n.* recognition. **pamigbigan.** *n.* mark, characteristic; clue; identity. **agpabigbig.** *v.* to identify oneself. **bumigbig iti utang a naimbag a nakem.** acknowledge one's debt of gratitude. **Adu ti limmakayanna, ngannganin diak nabigbig.** He aged so much, I hardly was able to recognize him. **Mabigbig ti siudad ti San Fernando gapu iti pintas ti aplayana.** The city of San Fernando is renowned for the beauty of its beach. **Dida maipaay ken ni Bago dagiti pammigbig a maipaay iti dadduma a puli.** They do not grant the recognition to the Bagos that is given to other peoples. [Png. *birbír*, Tag. *kilala*]

biggáng: *n.* fireball (*agtutulid nga apuy*).

bigkás: *n.* syllable. **agbigkas.** *v.* to pronounce.

bigkét: **bigketen.** *v.* to cover with cloth.

binnigket. *n.* a girl's blindfolding guessing game.

biglá: *a.* sudden, suddenly. (*kellaat*) **biglaen.** *v.* to do suddenly; surprise. **biglaan.** *v.* to startle; surprise. [Tag. *biglâ*]

bignón: *n. Kleinhovia sp.* tree. (*biknong*)

biguélas: (Sp. *vihuela*: cithern) *n.* big guitar. **biguelista.** *n. biguelas* player.

bigór: (Sp. *vigor*) *n* vigor, strength. **agbigor.** *v.* to grow strong, thrive; be effective; be in vogue.

bigórnia: (Sp. *begonia*) *n.* begonia.

bigót: **biguten.** *v.* to starve; famish. (*bisin*) **mabigot.** *v.* to be starved; famished. [Tag. *gutóm*]

bigóte: (Sp. *bigote*: moustache) *n.* moustache. **agbigote.** *v.* to grow a moustache. [Bon. *semsem*]

bigotílio: (f. *bigote* + *-illo* depreciative suffix) *n.* small moustache; moustached man; (*fig.*) macho man.

bigsá: (*obs.*) *n.* beam of a threshold.

bigsót: **bigsuten.** *v.* to jerk; yank out; pull violently; snatch; stamp the feet in frustration. **binibigsot a panagsungbat.** *n.* hasty, rude answer. **Imbigsotna ti bagina iti akinlikud a bangko ti simbaan.** He threw down his body on the bench in the back of the church. [Tag. *hablót*]

bígta: *a.* sudden; instantaneous. (*bigla*) **mabigta.** *v.* to die instantaneously; to do in one sweep. **Adda pamigtana.** *exp.* He has something up his sleeve.

bihilánte: (Sp. *vigilante*: vigilant) *n.* vigilante, watchman; *a.* watchful, vigilant.

bihília: (Sp. *vigilia*: vigil) *n.* porgy fish, *Lethrinus atkinsoni*; eve; vigil. **bihiliaan.** *v.* to have a vigil in honor of.

bíhon: (Hok. *bì hùn*: rice flour) *n.* thin, transparent rice noodle.

biíg: *a.* purely, all, solely. (*bin-ig*)

bíik: **agbiik.** *v.* (*obs.*) to carry a two-piece load on the shoulder.

biít: *adv.* for a short moment; *n.* generic name for early rice; short duration. **mabiit.** *adv.* for a short time. **apagbiit.** *adv.* immediately, in a short while; for a short while; promptly. **bibbiiten.** *v.* to do shortly. **nabiit.** *n.* the recent pass; *n.* briefly; easy; swift, quick. **itay nabiit.** a short while ago. **iti kabiitan a panawen.** *exp.* as soon as possible. **Apagbiit a nagdigos.** He took a bath in a short time. **Gapu ta asidegak iti dalikan, apagbiitak a naugingan.** Because I am close to the stove, I get soot on myself immediately. [Tag. *sandalî, saglít*]

bikág: **ibikag.** *v.* to scold; say in a frightful manner in order to shame. **bikagen.** *v.* to scold; scare and shame someone.

bíkal: *n.* species of climbing bamboo, *Schrizonstachyum acutiflorum.* **kabikalan.** *n.* grove of *bikal* bamboo.

bikarbonáto: (Sp. *bicarbonato*: bicarbonate) *n.* bicarbonate.

bikário: (Sp. *vicario*: vicar) *n.* vicar, Roman Catholic clergyman who represents a bishop or the Pope.

bíkas: **nabikas.** *a.* strong, robust; sturdy; vigorous. **bumikas.** *v.* to become strong; robust. [Tag. *tipunò*]

bikkél: see *bekkel*: *n.* kidney; *v.* strangle.

bikkiás: **bumkias.** *v.* to slack, loosen; burst open. **bikkiasen.** *v.* to flip a stick by bending.

bikkiát: *var.* of *bikkias.*

bikkóg: see *bekkog*: hollow, depressed part of something; *v.* curve, bend.

bikkóng: *a.* concave, with raised sides.

biknóng: *n.* a kind of tree with pink flowers whose bark is used in rope making, *Kleinhofia hospita.* (*bitnong*)

bíko: (Hok. *bì ko*: rice cake) *n.* coconut rice cake made with brown sugar.

Bíkol: *n.* native of the Bikol region of southern Luzon; the language of the Bikol people, also referred to as Bikolanos. **Kabikolan.** the Bikol provinces.

Bikoláno: *n.* native of the Bikol region of southern Luzon.

bikong: *n.* a type of flowering plant.

bikrád: see *bisrad*: spread, open.

bíktima: (Sp. *víctima*: victim) *n.* victim. **Dandani biniktimanak ti tulisan.** The robber almost victimized me.

biktória: (Sp. *victoria*) *n.* victory. (*balligi*)

bil-á: *var.* of *bel-a.*

Biláan: *n.* ethnic group from the interior of Davao and Cotabato in Mindanao; the Austronesian language of the *Bilaan* people.

biláda: (Sp. *velada*: evening entertainment) *n.* celebration, entertainment (usually in evening). (*padaya*)

bilág: *n.* sunny place; things placed under the sun to dry. **ibilag.** *v.* to dry in the sun; put under the sun. **agbilag.** *v.* to sunbathe; stay under the sun (*inar*). [Bon. *sap-ey*, Ibg. *bilág*, Ivt. *rakayan*, Kal. *bileg, saoy*, Knk. *beknág*, Kpm., Tag. *bilad*, Png. *págew*; Ibg. *bilág* = sun]

bilágot: *n.* a kind of marsh herb with blue flowers and edible leaves, *Monochoria vaginalis.*

bilák: *n.* glow; radiance; glitter. (*raniag*) **bumilakbilak.** *v.* to glow; glitter. [Tag. *kináng*]

bílang: *n.* number; sum; date. **agbilang.** *v.* to count. **bilangen.** *v.* to count; compute; reckon. **ibilang.** *v.* to count; account; judge. **ipabilang.** *v.* to have something counted. **mabilang.** *v.* to be counted; *n.* date. **no bilang (ta).** *exp.* in case; suppose. **di ibilang.** *v.* to not count; not include or consider. **no bilang adda.** in case of. **Inaldaw nga agbilbilang iti poste.** *exp.* denoting someone idle without anything constructive to do (*lit:* counting posts everyday). **Awan ti pakaibilbilanganna.** He is useless. **No ibilangnak met la a kas manongmo, dimo kuma pagkedkedan ti tulongko.** If you consider me like your brother, you shouldn't refuse my help. **No bilang pudno, panawankan.** In case it's true, I will leave you. [Bon. *iyap,* Ivt. *vidang,* Kal. *iyap,* Png. *bilúng,* Knk. *biáng,* Ibg., Kpm., Tag. *bilang*]

bilánggo: *n.* bailiff (*agbaras*; *kabadangan*). [Tag. *tagapamahalà*; *bilanggô* = prisoner]

biláw: bumilaw. *v.* to jeer, make faces at. **pamilawan.** *v.* to criticize. [Tag. *ismíd*]

bilbíl: *n.* double fold in the upper stomachs of stout women. [Tag. *bilbíl* = dropsy]

biléd: *n.* mountain leech. (*alimatek*)

bíleg: *n.* power, force, strength. (*pigsa*) **nabileg.** *a.* strong, powerful; influential; potent. **bumileg.** *v.* to become strong; powerful; potent. [Knk. *bisíl,* Png. *biskég,* Tag. *lakás*]

biliáko: (Sp. *bellaco:* sly) *a.* sly; artful.

biliáno: (Sp. *villano:* rustic) *n.* nobleman in the *Moro-moro* play disguised as a commoner.

biliansíko: (Sp. *villancico:* carol) *n.* Christmas carol.

biliár: (Eng.) *n.* pool, billiards. **pagbiliaran.** *n.* pool house, billiard saloon.

bilíb: (*coll.,* f. Tag. via Eng. *believe*) *v.* to be impressed. **Talaga a bilibak kenka!** I am really impressed by you!

bílid: *n.* outer edge, border; angle; pulpy carpel of an orange; furrow. **bilidan.** *a.* furrowed; edged. [Tag. *gilid*]

biliéte: (Sp. *billete:* ticket) *n.* ticket; bank note; love letter.

bílin: *n.* order, command, mandate; commandment (in the Bible). **agbilin.** *v.* to order, command; send a message through someone. **ibilin.** *v.* to order, command; send a message or delivery through an errand person. **bilinen.** *v.* to instruct; counsel. **pabilbilin.** *n.* slave; follower; messenger. **Bilbilennak ti panunotko tapno arakupek ngem igawgawidnak ti riknak.** My thoughts are ordering me to embrace her but my feelings are restraining me. [Ibg. *dorob,* Ivt. *yukuyukud,* Kal. *buulon, bililon,* Knk. *pong,* Png. *gangán,* Tag. *utos*]

bilíng: bilingen. *v.* to scrutinize by turning over a few times. [Tag. *biling*]

bilión: (Sp. *billón:* billion) *n.* billion. **sangabilion.** *n.* one billion.

bílios: biliusen. *v.* to kiss. (*agek, ungngo, bisito*)

bilís: *n.* a kind of sardine.

billagút: *n.* a kind of striped shell mollusk.

billíing: *syn.* of *uwao*.

billít: *n.* bird; used for small birds, songbird; flying fish (*coll.*) young boy's genitalia. **billittuleng.** *n.* a kind of sparrow harmful to rice fields, *maya* bird. **billiten.** *n.* cock with red plumage; variety of awned late rice; *v.* to be attacked by birds. **billit baláy.** *n.* house bird. **billit-tsína.** *n.* kind of ordinary sparrow-sized bird. **billit a sangsangkaburik.** birds of a feather. **Agal-al-al ti sipupusok a billitna ngem di pay la agsardeng nga agtayabtayab.** The caged bird was panting from exhaustion but did not stop fluttering around. [Bon. *inyólan,* Ibg. *memmánuq,* Ifg. *hamuti,* Itg. *balbalay,* Ivt. *manumanuk,* Kal. *sissiwit,* Knk. *tála, kúyat, ít-ít,* Kpm. *áyup,* Png. *manók,* Tag. *ibon*]

billitén: *n.* brown (or red) cock.

billók: nabillok. *a.* bent, twisted; deformed. **billuken.** *v.* to twist, bend; deform; contort. **Malaksid ti pannakabettak ti sarming iti sango ti motorsiklo, nabillok pay ti manibela ken ti kambiona.** Aside from the front mirror of the motorcycle cracking, the steering wheel and gearshift bent out of shape too.

billós: bibillosen (dagiti bibig) *n.* red, kissable lips.

bimól: (Sp. *bemol:* flat in music) *n.* flat (in music).

bilnás: *var.* of *balnás:* rinse.

bilóg: *n.* outrigger; a boat with two outriggers. **agbilog.** *v.* to ride in an outrigger. **sinambilog.** *n.* toy boat; *a.* in the shape of a boat. [Kal. *byangka,* Tag. *bangkâ*]

bilukóg: *n.* large swelling, bump, welt. **bumilukog.** *v.* to swell up; puff up (eyes).

bilúng: kanabluong. *n.* explosions. **manabluong.** *v.* to explode.

bílot: *n.* cylindrical roll of paper. **agbilot, biluten.** *v.* to roll up (cigarettes); roll up in.

bilsíg: see *balsig:* chop.

bimbiár: see *ibniar:* allowing young locusts to pass.

bimpó: (Ch.) *n.* face towel. (*dimpo*)

binaklág: agbinaklag. *v.* to swell due to bites or injury.

bin-ás: *var.* of *bun-ás:* healthy, robust (plants), leafy.

bindóg: *n.* a kind of large black and white bird.

bindúngo: (*pron. bindunggo*) *n.* native dish made of beef innards cooked in broth.

bíneg: **bibineg.** *n.* numbness. **agbibineg.** *v.* to be numb; insensible. **bibinegen.** *v.* to anesthetize. **pagbibineg.** *n.* anaesthetic (*pikel*), something used to cause numbness. **-makabibineg.** *a.* causing numbness. **makabibineg a lamiis.** *n.* bitter cold. **Naut-ot ti bagbagina ken agbibbineg ti laslasagna.** His whole body ached and his muscles were numb. **Agpigpigerger dagiti ramramayna a bimbinegenen iti ut-ot.** His fingers trembled, numbed from the pain. [Knk. *pikét*, Tag. *manhíd*]

bínes: (Sp. *bienes*) *n.* taxes (*buis*).

bin-í: *n.* selected seed for planting. **ibin-i.** *v.* to reserve a seed for planting purposes. **bin-ien.** *v.* to use for seeding purposes. **pamin-ian.** *n.* healthy crops whose seeds will be saved for sowing the next season. **bin-i a lames.** *n.* fingerlings. [Ibg. *bini*, Ifg. *binung-o*, Ivt. *vutuh*, Kal. *sington*, Kpm. *biniq*, Png. *biní*, Tag. *binhî*]

biniás: *n.* gold necklace.

biniát: *var.* of *bennat*: stretch.

binibóy: (*slang*, Tag. *bihibini* = young lady + Eng. boy) *n.* hermaphrodite; transsexual.

bin-íg: *a.* pure, nothing but (*pasig; panay*). [Tag. *puro, taganás, pawà*]

binnát: **binnaten.** *v.* to stretch something. (*bennat*)

binnúbo: (*obs.*) *n.* gold ears.

bíno: (Sp. *vino*: wine) *n.* wine. **bino blangko.** *n.* white wine. **bino roho.** *n.* red wine.

binuélos: (Sp. *buñuelo*: fritter) *n.* fritter, kind of native pastry.

binogbóg: (f. *bogbog*) *n.* leftovers for the pigs.

binokbók: (f. *bokbok*) *n.* cavity; tooth with a cavity.

binong: *var.* of *biknóng* tree.

bínor: **binuren.** *v.* to straighten (something still growing). **bininor.** *n.* (*reg.*) cleaned rattan. [Tag. *hubog*]

binsá: **ibinsabinsa.** *v.* to clarify in detail; enumerate; explain one by one. **Isu nga imbinsabinsami dagiti nadumaduma a makailuod a droga.** So we explained in detail about various harmful drugs. [Tag. *isa-isá*]

binsír: (Sp. *vencer*: defeat) **binsiren.** *v.* to observe, examine carefully; outdo, surpass; defeat, conquer.

binsót: **binsuten.** *v.* to jerk a rope. (*bigsot*)

bínta: (f. Old Spanish *vinta*: vinta) *n.* kind of small sailboat, vinta. **agbinta.** *v.* to ride in the vinta.

bintáan: *n.* a kind of marine fish.

bintána: (Sp. *ventana*: window) *n.* window. (*bentana, tawa*) **bintanilia.** *n.* little window, ticket window. [Tag. *bintanà*]

bintíng: *n.* twenty-five centavos.

bintór: **agbintor.** *v.* to wander, roam.

bintúrod: *a.* hilly.

bingaló: *n.* large *aramang* shrimp when fully grown.

bíngat: (*coll.*) *n.* vulva. (*uki*) **bingaten.** *v.* to open wide something; dilate (*bingit*). **nabingat.** *a.* dilated, open wide. [Tag. *hilat*]

bíngay: *n.* share; portion (*binglay*). **agbingay.** *v.* to share; divide. **bingayen.** *v.* to divide, share; split. **bingay-bingayen.** *v.* to divide into portions, apportion. **mabingay.** *v.* to be shared; divided. **pagbibingayan.** *v.* to share among many. **mabingay ti rikna.** *exp.* to have mixed feelings. **Pagbibingayanda dagiti gastos uray pay iti agassawa no dadduma.** They share the expenses, even married couples once in a while. [Tag. *bahagi*]

binggás: *n.* fiber, grain (of meat); streak; vain; sinew. **binggasen.** *v.* to add a streak, color, tone, etc. **maibinggas.** *v.* to be intermixed. [Tag. *hilatsá*]

binggáw: **agbibinggaw.** *v.* to wrangle, compete for the same thing. **binggawen.** *v.* to burn part of a forest. [Tag. *pag-agawan*]

bíngit: (*coll.*) *n.* vulva. **bingiten.** *v.* to open with the hands; separate; dilate (*bingat*).

bingkuál: *var.* of *bingkol*: lump of soil, clod.

bingkól: *n.* lump of soil, clod; hardened plowed soil. **bumingkol.** *v.* to harden into lumps (plowed soil). **nabingkol.** *a.* cloddy, lumpy. **no agtaraok ti bingkol.** *exp.* expressing no hope, 'when the clod crows'. [Tag. *tigkál*]

bingkúlog: *n.* clod of clay or mud. **maibingkulog.** *v.* to stumble by hitting a clod of earth. **bumingkulog.** *v.* to hump; gather into a mound of earth.

bingkúrog: see *bingkolog*: clod of clay or mud. [Tag. *umbók*]

bingláy: *n.* share, portion. (*bíngay*) **binglayen.** *v.* to share; divide, distribute, apportion. **pagbibinglayan.** *v.* to share with one another. **Kayatko met nga ibinglay kadagiti sabsabali pay a tao.** I also want to share it with other people. [Tag. *bahagi, hatì*]

bingngí: *n.* opening; *a.* open; dilated. **agbingngi.** *v.* to break open, burst open. **bingngien.** *v.* to open. **apagbingngi.** *a.* slightly ajar. [Tag. *buká*]

bingngít: **bingngiten.** *v.* to part the hair. (*bisngáy*)

bingráw: *n.* a kind of large green fly. **bingrawen.** *v.* to be attacked by a swarm of flies. [Tag. *bangaw*]

bingrút: bumaningrut. *v.* to suck, sip; lick the nasal mucus; to cry noisily while sucking up nasal mucus. [Tag. *singhót*]

bingsíran: *n.* old, red bamboo. (*lungugan*)

bió: *n.* a kind of tree with good construction timber.

biúda: (Sp. *viuda*: widow) *n.* widow; masculine counterpart is *biudo*. (*balo*) **nabiuda.** *a.* widowed.

biúdo: (Sp. *viudo*: widower) *n.* widower (*balo*). **nabiudo.** *a.* widowed.

biograpía: (Sp. *biografia*: biography) *n.* biography (*pakasaritaan ti biag*). [Tag. *talambuhay*]

bióla: (Sp. *viola*: viola) *n.* viola; leapfrog game.

bioléta: (Sp. *violeta*: violet) *n.* violet.

biolín: (Sp. *violín*: violin) *n.* violin. (*labér, inging*) **agbiolin.** *v.* to play the violin. [Tag. *biyolín*]

biolinísta: (f. *biolin*) *n.* violinist.

biólogo: (Sp. *biólogo*: biologist) *n.* biologist.

biolohía: (Sp. *biología*: biology) *n.* biology.

biolón: *var.* of *biolonsélo*: cello.

biolonsélo: (Sp. *violoncelo*: cello) *n.* cello.

biombó: (Sp. *biombo*: folding screen) *n.* booth; polling booth; folding screen.

bióng: *n.* sampan.

biopsía: (Sp. *biopsía*: biopsy) *n.* biopsy.

biór: biuren. *v.* to control; bend; flex. **mabior.** *v.* to be flexible, easily bent. [Tag. *hutok*]

bipbíp: (Eng. beep) *n.* sound of an automobile horn or beeping pager. **banipbip.** *n.* continuous honking or beeping.

bir: (Eng.) *n.* beer. (*serbésa*)

bira: *n. Alocasia macrorrhiza* plant.

birá: (Sp. *virar*: turn, veer) *Interj.* go ahead. (*aria; sige*); *n.* pull with force; beating as punishment. **agbira.** *v.* to tighten a rope; cut cards; box; lift a load; crank a vehicle; box, punch. **biraan.** *v.* to eat a lot. **biraen.** *v.* to tug; hit, punch, box, strike; beat.

birábid: *n.* a kind of round freshwater mollusk. **mabirabid.** *v.* to feel sick and dizzy after eating *birabid* out of season.

birád: *n.* kind of mollusk with big lips; (*coll.*) gossiping mouth.

biráda: agbirada. *v.* to take cards from a pack.

biradór: (Sp. *virador*: turner; viol) *n.* screwdriver; wrench; engine crank.

birág: kanabraag. *n.* loud or continuous banging sound. **manabraag.** *v.* to bang, slam the door. **ipanabraag.** *v.* to slam the door.

biragsót: *var.* of *baragsot*: jerking movements made when upset.

bir-ák₁: *var.* of *bir-it*: angry shout.

bir-ák₂: *var.* of *per-ák*: break.

birákak: *a.* expanded, inflated (neck of reptiles). **bumirakak.** *v.* to puff out the neck (snakes ready to attack, etc.) (*berkakak*). **ibirakak.** *v.* to scold.

birákat: agbirákat. *v.* to sing with all one's might.

biráng: kanabraang. *n.* continuous explosions. **manabráang.** *v.* to explode (gunfire). **Adda nanabraang iti uneg ti pagadalan.** There were gunshots inside the school.

biráw: birawbiraw. *a.* with too much broth. (*labnaw*)

biráy: *n.* a small boat with a flat bottom and rudder. **Agpatpataaw pay laeng ti biray.** The boat is still drifting off to sea.

birayán: *n.* kind of small boat with a flat bottom. (*biráy*)

bir-áyon: *var.* of *birrayon*: hanging aloft.

birbír: *n.* (*obs.*) rim of a jar. **agbirbir.** *v.* to swell, puff (said of face); to talk with a fowl mouth. **nabirbir** (*reg.*) *a.* foul-mouthed; gossiping. [Tag. *magâ*]

birdáy: ibirday. *v.* to hang in order to dry. (*salapay*)

birék: *n.* Scrofula, swelling of the lymph nodes of the neck.

biréta: (Sp. *birreta*: biretta, *obs.*) *n.* biretta, kind of hat worn by clergy, cardinal's cap.

biréte: (Sp. *birrete*: biretta, cap) *n.* small cap.

bírhen: (Sp. *virgen*: virgin) *n.* virgin. **kinabirhen.** *n.* virginity. **Ti kinabirhenko ti sagutko kenka.** My virginity is my gift to you.

birína: (Sp. *vitrina*: glass case) *n.* glass shade for candles; glass cover for statues (of saints, etc.).

birhínia: (Eng.) *n.* Virginia tobacco. **agbirhinia.** *v.* to plant Virginia tobacco.

bir-í: *n.* crack. (*birrí*) **agbir-i, bumri.** *v.* to crack. [Ibg. *meggenna, bakkí*, Ivt. *apsahen*, Kpm. *lamat*, Png. *betag*, Tag. *bitak*]

biría: (Sp. *brea*: tar) *n.* tar, pitch. **biriaan.** *v.* to patch, mend; to tar. [Tag. *alkitrán*]

biríndis: (Sp. *brindis*: toast, dedicate) **agbirindis.** *v.* to throw money to the crowd. (*burandis*) **maibirindis.** *v.* to be scattered, dispersed.

biríng₁: *n.* nasal septum, frenum.

biríng₂: *n.* strips of rattan used to bind a post. **pamiringan.** *n.* a hole in a post. **biringen.** *v.* to bind.

birís: birbiris. *n.* trifles, small inconsequential things; (*reg.*) gift giving (from house-to-house). **agbirbiris.** *v.* to give gifts (from house-to-house). **Agbirbiris dagiti katalonan ti tunggal piesta.** The farmers that tend to the ricefields come to the house every fiesta to give gifts.

biriská: (Sp. *brisca*: card game) *n.* kind of card game. **agbiriska.** *v.* to play a biriská.

bírit: *n.* a scar or scab on the eyelid; scar face; curled up scarred eyelid. **biriten.** *v.* to make a small slit in; to dilate slightly.

bir-ít₁: *n.* shout. **bir-iten.** *v.* to shout; scold, upbraid. (*kariar*; *dayengdeng*; *luya*)

bir-it₂: *var.* of *bir-i*: crack. **Nabir-it ti pantalonna.** His pants cracked (seam opened). [Tag. *biták*]

birkákak: *var.* of *berkakak*: with a puffed neck (snakes before attack). (*birakak*)

bírko: *n.* belt; waistband. (*barikes*) **nabirko.** *a.* wearing a belt. **ibirko.** *v.* to insert in one's belt.

birkúg: *n.* vagrant. vagabond; thief. (*tulisan*; *takaw*) **agbirkug.** *v.* to steal; rob. **nagbirkug.** *a.* always absent; negligent. [Png., Tag. *bulakból*, Tag. *dambóng*]

birnít: **birniten.** *v.* to smooth, unwrinkle. **agkaibirnit.** *v.* to hang in disarray.

birngás: *n.* nickname. **birngasen.** *v.* to call by one's nickname; address impolitely. **panangbirngas.** *n.* name calling. **birngasan.** *v.* to nickname someone, call by one's nickname. **Binirngasandak iti Amboy.** They nicknamed me Amboy. [Kpm. *bánsag*, Png. *balingás*, Tag. *palayaw*]

biruá: *var.* of *bel-a*: spew, vomit, eject forcefully; overflow.

bírok: *n.* salary; wages. **agbirok.** *v.* to look for; earn by working. **biruken.** *v.* to look for, search for. **mabirokan.** *v.* to find; discover. **agbibinnirok.** *v.* to play hide-and-seek. **pagbirokan.** *n.* business; employment. **sangkabirok, sangkakaan.** *exp.* denoting meager existence (*lit*: eating what one finds). [Ibg. *alerén*, *magalég*, Ivt. *citahen*, Kal. *sington*, Knk. *ánap*, Kpm. *paintunan*, Png. *anap*, Tag. *hanap*]

birurúko: *var.* of *birruruko*: land snail.

birurúkong: see *biruruko*: land snail.

birúrot: **nabirurot.** (*obs.*) *a.* big bellied. (*buttiog*)

bírus: (Eng.) *n.* virus.

birút₁: *n.* worn-out knife; (*coll.*) woman's vagina).

birút₂: *n.* kind of freshwater fish, the young *burarog*, *Eleotris melanosoma*.

birráaw: *n.* shout. **bumraaw.** *v.* to shout. **biraawan.** *v.* to shout at someone. (*pukkaw*, *laaw*)

birráyon: **agbirrayon.** *v.* to hang aloft. **birrayunen.** *v.* to carry aloft. **Nupay nabagas ti piskel ti lakay, addan birrayonnan.** Although the old man's muscles were substantial, there was some hanging flesh.

birrí: *n.* crack. **agbirri.** *v.* to crack, burst; fissure (*bir-i*). [Knk. *bissát*, *bissít*, Tag. *biták*]

birrurúko(ng): *n.* kind of large snail; mild curse word. **Kasla agruprupa a birruruko, talaga**

nga awansa ti babainmo. You have the face of a snail, I really think you have no shame.

birtúd: (Sp. *virtud*: virtue) *n.* virtue. **nabirtud.** *a.* virtuous; potent (medicine, poison).

bísa: (Eng.) *n.* visa.

bisádra: *var.* of *bisagra*: door hinge.

biság: **bisbisag.** *n.* a kind of small bird that nests by rivers.

biságra: (Sp. *bisagra*: hinge) *n.* door or window hinge. **bisagraan.** *v.* to put a hinge on.

bísak: see *busak*: cracked, splintered in two; halve; divide. **Tinaraigidna ti kalsada a naipasurot iti waig a nangbisak iti ili.** He went around the street following the creek that divided the town. [Ibg. *gedduwan*, Ivt. *asbiden*, Kpm. *aspák*, Png. *pisag*, Tag. *biyák*]

bisaklák: see *dupakpak*: bowlegged.

bisáleg: *n.* acute abdominal pain. **agbisaleg.** *v.* to feel pain in the stomach from eating something bad or from starving. **Makapabisaleg dagiti angot ti taraon iti panganan.** The smells from the food in the dining room are causing stomach pains. [Tag. *kalám*]

bisár: **bumisar.** *v.* to take effect; flourish (well-maintained plants).

Bisáya: *n. a.* Person of the Visayan Islands (islands between Luzon and Mindanao); name applied to any of the Visayan languages; usually refers to Cebuano, Waray, or Hiligaynon (Ilonggo).

Bisayáno: *n.* Visayan, native of the Visayan region; language spoken in the Visayas.

bíse-: *pref.* (Sp. *vice-*) vice- prefix in loanwords. **bise-presidente.** *n.* vice-president. **bise-mayor.** *n.* vice-mayor. **bise-bersa.** vice-versa.

biséra: (Sp. *visera*: visor) *n.* top of a dining table; footboard; headboard; visor.

bisíbis: *n.* sprinkle, sprinkling. **bisibisan.** *v.* to sprinkle with water (*sibog*). [Tag. *dilíg*]

bisík: *n.* secret (*palimed*); speech. **ibisik.** *v.* to whisper, mention privately; explain, utter.

bisikléta: (Sp. *bicicleta*: bicycle) *n.* bicycle. **agbisikleta.** *v.* to ride a bicycle. **bumibisikleta.** *n.* cyclist.

bísil: *n.* pebbles, gravel. (*graba*) **kabisilan.** *n.* soil where pebbles abound.

bisín: *n.* hunger; famine. **agbisin.** *v.* to go hungry. **bisinen, pabisinan.** *v.* to starve. **mabisin.** *a.* hungry. **mabisinan.** *v.* to be starving. **panagbisin.** *n.* famine; period of starvation; hunger. **No ammom ti agidulin, adayo ti inka panagbisin.** *exp.* If you know how to save, you will never go hungry. [Bon. *ólat*, Ibg. *bisin*, Itg. *bitil*, Ivt. *mapteng*. Kal. *bitin*, Knk. *óat*, Kpm. *danúpan*, Png. *erás*, Tag. *gutom*]

bísio: (Sp. *vicio*: vice) *n.* vice. **bisioso, nabisio.** *a.* having many vices.

bisióso: (Sp. *vicioso*) *a.* vicious.

bisíro: (Sp. *becerro*: young bull) *n.* young male pony.

bisít: kanabsiit. *n.* sound of thunder; continual lightning; crack. **agkanabsiit.** *v.* to have continuous lightning. **manabsiit.** *v.* to whip, lash. **panabsiiten.** *v.* to whip someone continuously.

bisíta: (Sp. *visita*: guest) *n.* guest, visitor. (*sangaili*) **bumisita, bisitaen.** *v.* to visit.

bisíto: (Sp. *besito*: small kiss) *n.* kiss (*agek*). [Tag. *halík*]

biskár: biskaren. *v.* to spread on the ground.

biskéd: *n.* handsomeness, manliness. (*taer*; *taraki*; *guapo*) **nabisked.** *a.* handsome, manly; strong, powerful. **Bagayna ti duyaw a roba ti monghe a naputipot iti nabisked a bagina.** The yellow robe suited the monk, coiled around his powerful body.

biskég: nabiskeg. *a.* strong, powerful. (*bakéd*)

biskél: *n.* goiter (*biel*). [Knk. *ákak, baséy, buséy*, Kal. *bikkok*, Tag. *bosyò*]

bískir: (*obs.*) **bumiskir.** *v.* to pass through a crowd. (*bislin*)

biskúlog: bimmiskulog. *a.* swollen (eyes after crying). (*ballukog*)

biskónde: (Sp. *vizconde*: viscount) *n.* viscount. **biskondesa.** *n.* viscountess.

biskótso: (Sp. *bizcocho*: biscuit) *n.* toasted bread.

bislák: *n.* sliver, splinter; piece of split bamboo.

bislín: bumislin. *v.* to pass through; squeeze in; stand in a crowd. **pakaibislinan.** *n.* one's worth or value. **ibislin.** *v.* to interpose. **Bumisbislin ti ladawanna iti panunotna.** Her image is passing through his mind.

bismúto: (Sp.) *n.* salt of bismuth.

bisngár: agbisngar. *v.* to turn up the nose; prude; to expand the nostrils of the nose; flare up (nose). (*busingar*)

bisngát: var. of *bisngit*: open.

bisngáw: nabisngaw. *a.* blatant, loud-mouthed. (*salawásaw*)

bisngáy: *n.* part in the hair. **bisngayen.** *v.* to part the hair; part; separate; pass through. [Knk. *búsig*, Tag. *hatì ng buhók*]

bisngít: bisngiten. *v.* to open, part; to pass through, insert. **apamisngit.** *n.* a snout that begins to grow tusks. **apagbisngit.** *a.* slightly ajar. [Tag. *buká*]

bisúdak: *n.* species of plant whose leaves are used to embalm corpses.

bisúgo: *n.* species of fish.

bisúk: *n.* sound of splashing in the water. **manabsuok.** *v.* to fall in the water with a splash. **ipanabsuok.** *v.* to throw something in the water with a splash. **agkanabsuok.** *v.* to splash in the water.

bisukól: *n.* a kind of mollusk, snail. **marabisukol.** *n.* young buck with velvet; *a.* small breasted. **Kasla nagsultopan a bisukol dagiti matana.** His eyes are like sucked snails. [Kal. *bisukuÿ*, Tag. *kuhól*]

bísung: *n.* children's kiss. (*agek*; *bisito*) **bisungen.** *v.* to kiss. [Tag. *halík*]

bisóng: ibisong. *v.* to throw, cast; plant in the ground.

bisút: *n.* sound of farting (*uttót*). **kanabsuot.** *n.* sound of flatulence or continuous farting. **bumsuot.** *v.* to fart. [Knk. *kibbát, kippús*]

bísperas: (Sp. *víspera*: eve) *n.* eve. **Bisperas ti Paskua.** *n.* Christmas Eve. **Umayto makibisperas.** He is coming to spend Christmas Eve with us.

bisrád: bisraden. *v.* to spread open; open (book, eyes). (*bistrad*)

bissáng: see *bessang*.

bissáyot: agbissayot. *v.* to hang (animate beings); droop. **bissayuten.** *v.* to keep aloft; hold aloft; carry overhead. **Nagbissayot ti kuentas iti barukongna.** The necklace hung on his chest. **Nagawidda a kasla awitdan ti krus a pakaibissayotanda met laeng.** They went home as if they were carrying a cross to hang themselves on.

bísta: (Sp. *vista*: court hearing) *n.* court hearing; court case; view; landscape; extent to which the eye can see. **agbista.** *v.* to attend a court hearing. **parabista.** *a.* for display. **mabista.** *a.* presentable (in church, etc.); to be investigated. **bistaen.** *v.* to try a case.

bistádo: (Sp. *visto*: obvious + *-ado* borrowed Spanish adjectival suffix) *a.* obvious; certain; seen.

bistí: (Sp. *vestir*: dress) **agbisti.** *v.* to dress oneself. **bistian.** *v.* to dress. **pagbisti.** *v.* to dress oneself with. [Tag. *damít*]

bísto: (Sp. *visto*: obvious, evident) *n.* prospect; knowledge; *a.* obvious, clearly seen; discovered. **mabisto.** *v.* to be found out (usually in bad circumstances); to be discovered; seen; obvious; prospected. **nakabisto.** *a.* well dressed, dressed to kill.

bistukól: *n.* native hat made of a squash shell or bamboo strips. (*kattukong*) **nakabistukol.** *a.* wearing a squash hat. [Tag. *salakót*]

bistrád: var. of *bisrad*: spread out; lay open; open wide.

bítad: bitaden. *v.* to spread, open; spread tobacco to dry.

bitaél: *n.* stomach fat.

bitalidád: (Sp. *vitalidad*: vitality) *n.* vitality. (*pigsa*)

bitamína: (Sp. *vitamina*) *n.* vitamin. **agbitamina.** *v.* to take vitamins.

bit-áng: *n.* small dirt road; path. (*bet-ang*)

bitánga: *n.* a kind of large mollusk. **kabitangaan.** *n.* place abundant with *bitanga* mollusks.

bitáog: *n. Calophyllum inophyllum*, kind of tree whose fruits are boiled to extract oil for lamps. (*pamitaogen*) **kabitaogan.** *n.* grove of *bitaog* trees.

bítay: *n.* hanging by the neck; capital punishment. **agbitay.** *v.* to hang oneself. **bitayen.** *v.* to hang by the neck; execute (in any manner). **pagbitayan.** *n.* gallows; capital punishment. [Png., Tag. *bítay*]

bitbít: *n.* hand luggage. **bitbiten.** *v.* to carry in the hand; hand carry. **pagbitbitan.** *v.* to carry mutually. **pamitbitan.** *n.* handle for carrying. **parabitbit.** *n.* porter. [Tag. *bitbít*]

biték: *var.* of *bitik*: pulse (*giteb; pitik*). [Tag. *pitík*]

bitíbit: *n.* buoy. **bitibiten.** *v.* to carry in the hand, lift up; sustain. **agpabitibit.** *v.* to plead for love or understanding; ask for help. **Binitbitdak a pinatakder.** They carried me up (until I was standing). [Tag. *angát* (raise)]

bitík: *n.* pulse; pulsation; beat (of a heart); throb. (*giteb; pitik, bitek*) **agbitik.** *v.* to throb, palpitate. **bitikbitik.** *n.* noise of a throbbing heart.

bítin: *n.* medallion; hanging adornment; rope attached to rafters on which baskets are hung. **agbitin.** *v.* to hang oneself; hang on. **ibitin.** *v.* to hang, suspend (*birrayon, bissayot, bittayon, kalumbitin*). **mabitin ti anges.** to be out of breath. **bitinbitin.** *n.* scale hanging from a balance; anything hanging. **pabitin.** *n.* game of young children played at parties in which participants compete in reaching for hanging gifts suspended in midair and drawn by a rope. **sarumbitin.** *n.* adornment. **agkarasarumbitin.** *v.* to be hanging in disarray. **nakabitin.** *a.* hanging, dangling; (*fig.*) in suspense. **mabitin ti anges.** *exp.* to be out of breath; be in awe. [Tag. *bitin*]

bitín: (Pil.) *n.* hanging in suspense, expression said after seeing or hearing a movie or story that comes to a confusing or unexpected end.

bitlá: *n.* speech; discourse; address. **agbitla.** *v.* to speak, address, discourse. **ibitla.** *v.* to accuse, denounce; address. **pagbitlaan.** *n.* podium; platform from which one addresses speeches. [Tag. *talumpati*]

bitlóg: (*coll.*) *n.* testis, testicle (*ukel*). **bitbitlog.** *n.* testicles.

bitnél: *a.* muscular; stocky. (*baneg; puner*) **bumitnel.** *v.* to exceed; to become muscular. [Tag. *tipunò*]

bitnóng: *n.* a kind of tree with pink flowers and whose bark is used to make ropes, *Kleihofia hospita.* (*biknong*)

bíto: *n.* pit, hole; well; waterhole (*bubón*). [Tag. *balón* (water well)]

bituén: *n.* star. **bituen baybay.** *n.* starfish. **marabituen.** *n.* a variety of awned early rice. **namituen.** *a.* starry (sky at night). **kabituen.** *n.* star (in a movie). [Ibg. *bitun*, Ivt. *vituhen*, Kal. *bituwon*, Knk. *taláw*, Kpm. *batwin*, Png. *bitéwen*, Tag. *bituín*]

bitóg₁: *n.* species of wild banana that reproduces by seeds.

bitóg₂: *n.* fist; cuff. **bitugen.** *v.* to strike with the fist; knock down. **mabitog.** *v.* to be knocked down. **banitugen.** *v.* to overthrow someone, defeat someone. [Tag. *upak*]

bitóg₃: *n.* thumping sound, sound of pounding. **kanabtuog.** *n.* sound of trampling feet or thumping objects. **ibabtuog.** *v.* to throw down with a thump. **mabanitog.** *v.* to fall down. **Agbitogbitog ti barukongko iti danagko.** My chest pounded from my anxiety.

bitúka: *n.* stomach; intestine. [Bon. *bowang*]

bitúki: *n.* missile of a blowgun.

bitúkol: **agbitukol.** *v.* to thrust forward; protrude.

bitón: *n.* shoe polish. **agbiton, bitunen.** *v.* to polish the shoes.

bitúog: (f. *bitog*) **agkababtuog.** *n.* sound of a heavy falling object. **nabtuog.** *v.* to fall down.

bitór: *n.* applause accompanied by throwing coins; the throwing of money to newlyweds. **agibitor.** *v.* to throw into the crowd (money, etc.); to throw (rice, etc.) at newlyweds. **Idi malpas ti puni, nangrugi ti bitor.** When the fiesta was over, the throwing of money started.

bítso: **bitso-bitso.** *n.* kind of Chinese cake made of rice flour.

bitsuélas: (Sp. *habichuela*: bean) *n.* Baguio beans, variety of short string bean. [Knk. *bokílas*]

bittagáw: *n.* a kind of bird.

bittákal: see *barruga*: kind of boy's game.

bittáug: *n.* a kind of tree with white flowers, *Callophyllus inophyllum.* **pamittaugen.** *n. Callophyllum sp.* trees.

bittáyon: **agbittayon.** *v.* to hang, dangle. **ibittayon.** *v.* to hang, dangle through an opening.

bittíg: *n.* wart (*tukaktúkak*). [Tag. *kulugó*]

bíwag: *a.* overused, old. **nagbiwag.** *a.* distorted, deformed.

bíwig: *var.* of *biwag.*

blángko: (Sp. *blanco*: blank) *a.* blank. **bino blangko.** white wine.

blg.: abbreviation of *bilang*, number; year (of a magazine).

blúsa: (Sp. *blusa*: blouse) *n.* blouse. **nakablusa.** *a.* wearing a blouse. **agblusa.** *v.* to wear a blouse.

blsng.: abbreviation of *balasang*, young lady.

buá: *n.* the betel nut palm, *Areca catechu.* **agbua.** *v.* to chew betel nuts. [Ibg. *vuwa, huwa, va,* Ivt. *vwaq,* Kal. *buwa,* Kpm. *lúyus,* Png. *bwá,* Itg., Tag. *búnga*]

buábo: *n.* trot; rocking motion, swinging movement. **agbuabo.** *v.* to swing the body when running (said of the *nuang*); to trot. **nabuabo a palangka.** *n.* rocking chair. [Tag. *tumbá-tumbá*]

buák: **agbuak.** *v.* to flutter, shake, tremble. **bumuak.** *v.* to lead, be first; speak with high intonation. **mabuak.** *v.* to scamper in fright. **buaken.** *v.* to shoo away animals. **Nabuak ti panagpipinnatangda nga agina idi adda danapeg ken agsasaruno a tugtog iti ridaw.** The conversation of the mother and daughter stopped abruptly with the sound of heavy footsteps and the successive knocks at the door.

buákag: *var.* of *buakaw*: greedy.

buákaw: (Tag. also) *n.* monopolizer of an action; someone who hogs the ball in a game, someone who exclusively controls or monopolizes a conversation, etc; *a.* greedy. *(reg.)* *n.* braggart.

buál₁: *n.* voile, a kind of silk cloth.

buál₂: **bualen.** *v.* to cause to fall down by uprooting. **mabual.** *v.* to fall down (by being uprooted); to be knocked down; to be uprooted.

buáng: *n.* opening; *a.* open. **ibuang, buangan.** *v.* to permit, allow; open (clear obstruction), open (faucet); set loose (animal); let newly hatched chicks out of the nest. **Bigla a naibuang ti di naibalunet a ridaw.** The unbarred door suddenly opened. [Tag. *buká*]

buángay: *n.* mood; attitude. *(buat)* **agbuangay.** *v.* to do on one's own. **buangayen.** *v.* to do something on one's own; be responsible for; put into writing (for records); to form (an organization). **kabbuangay.** *a.* newly formed; newly established. [Tag. *tatag*]

buanggér: *n.* masculine strength and aptitudes; machismo. **agbuangger.** *v.* to heat up (excitement); speed up; get a rush of adrenaline; make the sound of heavy rain on a roof.

buángil: **mabuangil.** *v.* to change, alter. *(mabaliwan)*

buárit₁: **agbuarit.** *v.* to run and scamper *(buatit).* [Tag. *yagyág*]

buárit₂: **nabuarit.** *a.* tilted, upturned. *(batuag)*

buás: *n.* Mallotus philippensis plant. *(pangaplasin)*

buát: *n.* behavior, conduct. **naimbag ti buatna.** *a.* elegant, nice, fine. **buaten.** *v.* to lift, raise. **buatan.** *v.* to help raise (a load off someone's shoulder). **ibuat.** *v.* to lift something on the head or shoulder. [Tag. *buhat* (lift)]

buátit: **agbuatit.** *v.* to scamper, run wild. *(buarit)* **Inaplitanna manen ti nuang ket nagbuatit daytoy.** He whipped the water buffalo again and it scampered.

buáya: *n.* crocodile. *a.* *(fig.)* cunning; greedy; corrupt. **binubuaya.** *n.* head knee, a boy's crocodile game. **kinabuaya.** *n.* greediness. **buaya ti sang-at.** *n.* usurer, greedy person. [Ibg. *vuwaya,* Ivt. *vuwayaq,* Kpm. *dápu,* Png., Tag. *buwaya*]

búbas: (Sp. *buba*: pustule, small tumor) *n.* pustule; small tumor.

bóbida: (Sp. *bóveda*: vault) *n.* ceiling. **bobidaan.** *v.* to provide with a ceiling. [Kal. *chopeg,* Tag. *kísame, taluktók*]

bobína: (Sp. *bobina*: bobbin, reel) *n.* spool; reel.

bóbo: (Sp. *bobo*: fooling, silly) **konsuelo de bobo.** *n.* consolation prize.

búbo: *n.* bag of a seine; a kind of shrimp net made of fine bamboo splints; *a.* stupid. **ibubo.** *v.* to expose to the wind; dry in the wind. **maibubo.** *v.* to be exposed to the wind.

búbod: *n.* yeast that is fermented to make *basi* or *binubudan.* **binubodan.** *n.* alcoholic beverage made with *bubod* yeast and rice; fermented rice. **bubodan.** *v.* to prepare rice for fermentation. [Png. *bubor*]

bubód: *(obs.)* *n.* something laid by and lost by theft.

bubón: *n.* well (for water) *(bito);* cistern; oil rig. **Panggepna ti agbubon.** He plans to build a well. [Png. *bubón,* Tag. *balón*]

bubóng: *n.* thatch, ridge of a roof. **bubongan.** *n.* beam of a roof ridge; *v.* to make a roof. **pagbubong.** *n.* roofing materials. **sangabubong.** *n.* household; married couple. [Tag. *bubóng* (thatch roof)]

búbor: **maibubor.** *v.* to be fully exposed to (the elements, etc.) *(berber, banuor)*

búbos: **bubusen.** *v.* to exhaust, consume, use up *(ibus).* [Tag. *ubos*]

bóda: (Sp. *boda*: wedding) *n.* wedding (used in certain contexts). *(kasar)* **boda-badol.** *n.* extravagant wedding. **boda de plata.** *n.* silver wedding anniversary. **boda de oro.** *n.* gold wedding anniversary. **makiboda.** *v.* to attend a wedding.

Búda: (Eng.) *n.* Buddha.

bodabíl: (Eng.) *n.* vaudeville, stage play

budák: *var.* of *buddák*: imprint; engrave; instill. [Tag. *ukit*]

buddák: ibuddak. *v.* to imprint; engrave; instill; clarify. **maibuddak.** *v.* to be clearly imprinted. **Dagiti naganda ket maibuddakda kuma iti Balay ni Dayaw.** Their names should be engraved in the Hall of Fame. [Tag. *ukit*]

buddóng: *n.* exclusive property; (*reg.*) wrestling (*gabbo*). **agbuddong.** *v.* to make an exchange (*súbor*); to wrestle.

bodéga: (Sp. *bodega*: cellar) *n.* warehouse. **bodegero.** *n.* warehouseman.

búdi: *n.* animal with only one testicle. (*amitaw*)

budí: *n.* mixture; extraneous matter; rice mixed of different qualities. **maibudi.** *v.* to be different; to be mixed into; interspersed. **mabudian.** *v.* to err, mistake in choosing.

Budísmo: (Sp.) *n.* Buddhism.

Budísta: (Sp.) *n.* Buddhist.

búdo: *n.* hair of insects; bristle of plants; itch. (*gatel*) **agbudo.** *v.* to itch. **mabuduan.** *v.* to itch. **makabudo.** *a.* causing itchiness. **nabudo.** *a.* itchy. **budobudo, buduabuduan.** *n.* kind of hairy caterpillar. **Diak maawatan 'toy bagik ta kasla mabudbuduanak no kadendennak.** I can't understand myself because my body seems to itch when you are with me. **Ammom metten ti kinabudo ti ngiwat ti tattao.** You know how itchy people's tongues are (are prone to gossip). [Tag. *balahibo* (fine body hair)]

budobudoán: *var.* of *bodobodo*: kind of hairy, stinging caterpillar.

budóng: *n.* peace pact; peace conference; truce. **agbudong.** *v.* to make a peace pact; negotiate peace. **pagbudongan.** *n.* place where a peace treaty is declared. **Nagpirma dagiti Pangasinense, Ilokano ken Igorot ti budong idiay Bangar idi 1820.** The Pangasinenses, Ilocanos, and Igorots signed a Peace Pact in Bangar in 1820.

buélas: *n.* ruffle.

buélo: (Sp. *vuelo*: flight) *n.* the right time to do something; proper timing; strength; speed, momentum; rotation of a bell on its axis; soaring flight; pendulum. **ibuelo.** *v.* to do with force and accuracy.

buélta: (Sp. *vuelta*: turn) *n.* turn. **agbuelta.** *v.* to turn back, return; overturn; capsize. **ibuelta.** *v.* to cause to go back; turn something back. **bueltaen.** *v.* to do for a second time. [Tag. *buwelta*]

buéna: (Sp. *buena*: good) **buena mano.** *n.* first one to do something; first sale of the day. (*mangbusat*) **buenabista.** *n.* species of ornamental shrub with colored, speckled leaves.

buénas: (Sp. *buenas*: good, *pl. adj.*) *n.* good luck (in gambling, etc.). **agbubuenas.** *v.* to be always lucky. **ag(de)buenas.** *v.* to have good luck.

buéno: (Sp. *bueno*: good) *Interj.* good; well; all right.

buéstra: (Sp., *obs. vuestra*: your) **buestra altesa.** your highness. **buestra mahestad.** your majesty.

búga₁: *n.* a kind of edible yam, *Dioscorea sp.* **panagbubuga.** *n.* season for digging yams.

búga₂: **bubugaen.** *v.* to plow for the first time. **panagbubuga.** *n.* season for plowing the fields.

búga₃: *n.* pumice.

bugá: **ibuga.** *v.* to cause; have an effect upon.

bugábog: **mabugabogan.** *v.* to be mixed (with different qualities). **bugabogan.** *v.* to mix (bad-quality ingredients with good ones).

bugadór: *n.* able-bodied man used for lifting heavy objects.

bugagáw: *n.* albino; blue or gray eyes; blond; auburn. [Png. *bugagew*, Tag. *bulagáw*]

bugák: **agbugak.** *v.* to scamper; scatter due to fright. **nabugak.** *a.* scampered; dispersed; scattered. **bugaken.** *v.* to frighten and cause to disperse.

bugambília: (Sp. *buganvilla*) *n.* bougainvillea plant.

bogár₁: (Sp. *boga*: vogue) **parabogar.** *a.* intended for household use (dress).

bogár₂: (Sp. *bogar*: row) **agbogar.** *v.* to row a boat with oars. (*gaud*)

búgas: *n.* core (fruits); central part of a tree trunk or stem; essence; principle; central theme; contents of a sandwich; main idea. **agbugas.** *v.* to develop a core (fruits). **bugasan.** *a.* half-cooked. **binugasan.** *n.* a kind of G-string with an indigo stripe running through the middle. **ibugas.** *v.* to mix different foods together; to insert something in clothes to make them bulge. **Kasla kayo nga awan bugasna ti tao nga awan prinsipiona.** A man without principles is like a tree without a trunk. [Png. *apongol*, Tag. *ubod* (core of fruits)]

bugáso: (Sp. *bagazo*: bagasse) *n.* bagasse, remains of pressed fruits or sugarcane refuse; something used as fertilizer (*usang*). [Tag. *bagaso*]

búgaw: (*coll.*) *n.* pimp. **bugawen.** *v.* to startle; scare away; drive away. **bugawan.** *v.* to evade, avoid. **agbuganbugaw.** *v.* to be at variance. [Ibg. *vugaw, deddag*, Ivt. *vuyawen*, Kpm. *tábiq*, Tag. *taboy, bugaw*]

búgay: *n.* drippings on the table when eating. (*murkat*)

bugayóng: *n.* a kind of bitter-tasting vine, *Abrus precatorius*; a seed of this vine.

bugbóg₁: *n.* a kind of spiny rattan.

bugbóg₂: *a.* mauled, mashed into a pulp, soft by overcooking. **agbugbog.** *v.* to maul. **bugbugen.** *v.* punch; to cause to become pulpy; maul. **mabogbog.** *v.* to pulp; become soft from cooking. [Kal. *chutayok*, Tag. *bugbóg*]

bugbóg₃: *n.* cooked hog feed. **agbugbog.** *v.* to cook food for the pigs. **pamugbogan.** *n.* container for used food for the hogs. **binugbog.** *n.* cooked hog feed.

bogbóg₄: *n.* hollow sound. **agbanogbog.** *n.* sound of a drum, trampling feet.

bugbugtóng: *a.* only, sole; unique. from *bugtong*.

búged: **bugdan.** *v.* to destroy, kill in revenge; pillage.

bugel: **nagbubugel.** *n. Caranx sp.* cavalla fish.

bugelgél: **agbugelgel.** *v.* to writhe; contort the body.

bugéy: (*obs.*) **nabugey.** *a.* overturned (boats).

buggí: **buggibuggi.** *n.* a kind of herb that grows in rice fields.

buggó: *n.* washing the hands or feet. **agbuggo.** *v.* to wash a part of the body. **bugguan.** *v.* to wash, cleanse; baptize. **pagbugguan.** *n.* bowl of water at the table for washing hands. **pammuggo.** *n.* baptism. [Ibg. *beggaw*, Ivt. *mavanaw*, Kal. *beÿbeÿ*, Kpm. *manos*, Png. *uras*, Tag. *hinaw*, *hugas*]

buggúong: *n.* salted fermented fish or shrimps used to season food; fish silage; fish sauerkraut. **agabbugguong.** *v.* to smell like fermented fish or shrimps. **pamugguongan.** *n.* hollow dish used for dissolving fish in making *bugguong*. **mamguong; mamuguong.** *v.* to dissolve sated fish on a cup by adding boiling water. **bugguongan.** *v.* to season a dish with *bugguong*. **binugguongan.** *n.* dish seasoned with *bugguong*. **bubugguongan.** *n.* good for making into *bugguong*. **Bugguong ti utekna.** His brain is fermented fish (denotes a dull mind). [Tag. *bagoóng*]

búgi: *n.* spawn; roe, fish eggs; fuse of homemade bombs. **mabugi.** *v.* to be pregnant, full of eggs. **agbugi.** *v.* to begin to bud (said of palay); to spawn. **bugibugi.** *n.* water bug. **bugbugian, nabugi.** *a.* full of eggs; *n.* roe, roe sack. **Nalukmeg dagiti takkiagna sa nabugi dagiti gurongna.** Her hands were fat and her legs were fully developed. **Bugbugianda ta nalulukmeg ken puraw ti tianda.** They have roe because they are fat and their stomachs are white. [Knk. *etléy*, *itléy*, Kpm. *pugá*]

bugiás: *n.* a kind of double-edged knife. **nakabugias.** *a.* carrying a double-edged knife.

bugiáw: **bugiawen.** *v.* to shoo away by shouting (*bugaw*). **nabugiaw.** *a.* scared away (animal). **Kapilitan a kinayumkomda ti naipakaten nga iket gapu iti pannakabugiaw dagiti ikan.** They were forced to collect the nets they set because the fish were scared away. [Tag. *bugaw*]

bugíbog: *n.* main road. **maibugibog.** *v.* to be mixed.

bogimbília: (Sp. *buganvilla*) *var.* of *bugambília*: bougainvillea plant.

búgis: **agbugis.** *v.* to burn underbrush. (*puor*)

bugkál: *n.* knot in wood. (*duguldugul, mata ti kayo*) **bugkabugkal.** *a.* knotty. [Tag. *bukó*]

bugkaláw: **bugkalawen.** *v.* to prosecute; to follow until the end; hail.

Bugkalót: *n.* member of the Ilongot tribe from Sierra Madre; language of the Ilongots; (*fig.*) pagan. **Bugkalot pay idi ti pammatimi.** Our religion was pagan before.

bugkáw₁: *n.* a kind of owl.

bugkáw₂: *n.* shout; command. **agbinnukaw.** *v.* to shout at each other (when arguing). **bugkawan.** *v.* to yell at; startle, frighten. **Agbimbinnukaw a bigat-aldaw-malem dagiti dadakkelna.** His parents yell at each other morning, noon, and night. [Tag. *bulyáw*]

bugkóng: **bugkong.** *n.* bunch, bouquet (of flowers).

bugnáw: **ibugnaw.** *v.* to rinse. (*belnas*) [Png. *begnáw*, Tag. *banláw*]

bugnáy: *n.* a kind of tree with red, acidic edible fruits, *Antidesma bunius* whose wood is made into charcoal. **mamugnay.** *v.* to gather the fruits of the *bugnay* tree. [Tag. *bignáy*]

búgno: *n.* second helping; second serving. **agbugno.** *v.* to have a second helping. **bugnuan.** *v.* to offer a second serving.

bug-óy: *n.* overleaping bounds of right conduct; failing to behave with good manners **agbug-oy.** *v.* to fail to act with good manners, overstay one's welcome.

bugsá: *n.* a kind of small marine fish.

bugsí: *n.* a kind of small inch-long freshwater fish with delicious meat.

bugsóng: *n.* bundle. **bugsongen.** *v.* to wrap in a large sheet, tying the four ends together.

bugsót₁: *n.* death struggle (of an animal being slaughtered); agony. **agbugsot.** *v.* to convulse (near death); to agonize near death; (*fig.*) to have anger written on one's face. **bugsotan.** *v.* to injure fatally. **nagbugsotan.** *n.* place of one's agony; (*fig.*) place of one's death. [Png. *panpanabos*, Tag. *kisáy*, *hingalô*]

bugsót₂: *n*. kind of cylindrical basket.
bugsót₃: **bubugsuten.** *n*. a kind of small marine fish.
bugták: *n*. scolding, shout; harsh command. **agbugtak.** *v*. to scold; talk rudely; drive away animals. **bugtaken.** *v*. to scold someone; berate; disturb. **binubugtak.** *a*. crude; harsh; rude. [Tag. *bulyáw*]
bugtóng: *n*. one of its kind. (*kakaisuna*) **bugbugtong.** *a*. only, sole, single; unique. [Png., Tag. *bugtóng*]
bohémio: (Sp. *bohemio*: Bohemian) *n*. playboy (*palikero*); *a*. Bohemian.
buhía: (Sp. *bujía*: spark plug) *n*. spark plug; candle, candlestick.
búi: *n*. Manila hemp plant.
buís: *n*. tax. **agbuis.** *v*. to pay taxes. **ibuis ti biag.** *v*. to sacrifice one's life. **buis ti bisio.** *n*. luxury taxes taken from alcohol and cigarettes. **buisan.** *v*. to tax someone. **mabuisan.** *a*. taxable, subject to tax. **pagbuisen.** *v*. to impose a tax. **pagbuis.** *n*. something used as tax. **panagbuis.** *n*. taxation. **Kaykayat ti turay a dakdakkel ti buis nga awidenna kadagiti babaknang.** The government prefers to take higher taxes from the rich. **Rumbeng nga agbuiskayo iti apagkapat nga apitenyo.** You need to pay taxes with one-fourth of your harvest. [Ibg. *vugít*, Png. *buis*, Tag. *buwís*]
buísit: (Hok. *bo uî sít*: no clothes or food) *n*. bad luck; *a*. unlucky. (*daksangasat*) **agbubuisit.** *v*. to suffer from bad luck. **buisiten.** *v*. to cause someone to be unlucky. [Tag. *malas* (Sp.)]
buítre: (Sp. *buitre*: vulture) *n*. vulture. **lumabaga a buitre.** *n*. buzzard; hawk.
búka: **agbuka.** *v*. to give birth (*pasngay*).
buká: *a*. not tied or fastened together. (*warwar*) **agbuka.** *v*. to open (flower); bloom; (*reg.*) give birth. **bukaen.** *v*. to untie, undo, unfasten; unzip. **bukaan.** *v*. to liberate (a prisoner); set free. [Ibg. *vukáq* (open), Tag. *buká* (open)]
bokádo: (Sp. *bocado*: bit) *n*. bit of a bridle.
bokadúra: (Sp. *embocadura*: mouthpiece; jumping the first hurdles) *n*. mouthpiece (of an instrument); enunciation.
búkag: *n*. gathering cotton balls. (*bukar*) **agbukag.** *v*. to pick cotton; pluck, cull; open.
bukáig: **bukbukaig.** *n*. a kind of very small mollusk. (*bennek*)
boka-inséndio: (Sp. *boca* 'mouth' + *incendio* 'fire') *n*. fire hydrant.
bukáit: **bukaitan.** *v*. to open slightly (as in customs checks) to peek inside at the contents.
bukákaw: *n*. sorghum, *Andropogon sorghum*.
bukál: *n*. wild boar; big louse. (Sp. *vocal*: voter) *n*. provincial board member; vowel.

bukál: (Sp. *brocal*: curbstone of a well) *n*. fountain, natural spring; well (*poso*); reservoir.
bokamángga: (Sp. *bocamanga*: cuff) *n*. cuff attached to shirt sleeves, butterfly sleeve.
Bukanég: *n*. father of Ilocano literature, his name derives from *nabukaan nga Itneg*: Christianized pagan. **bukanegan.** *n*. impromptu poetical joust. **agbukanegan.** *v*. to engage in a poetical joust. **makibukanegan.** *v*. to attend a poetical joust. **ibukaneg.** *v*. to recite in a poetical joust.
bukangkáng: *n*. bamboo musical instrument. **nabukangkang.** *a*. big bellied. (*buttiog*)
búkar: **agbukar.** *v*. to open; break open; to bloom. **panagbukar.** *n*. blooming season. [Tag. *bukadkád*]
bukarkár: **bukarkaren.** *v*. to undo; unfasten; untangle. (*buka*; *warwar*)
bukasít: see *buttiki*: small cowry shell.
bukát: *n*. mouse, rat. (*bao*) **binukat.** *a*. infested by rats; eaten by rats. **pamukat.** *n*. mousetrap.
bukatíng: *n*. a variety of rice with a light-colored hull and white kernel.
bukátot₁: *n*. a kind of basket for holding fish.
bukátot₂: *n*. glutton; greedy person; long, basket-like fish trap used in streams. **nagbukatot.** *a*. greedy, avaricious; gluttonous (*rawet*).
bukáw₁: *n*. skull; empty ear of palay (*eppés*); animal with only one testicle (*amitaw*); empty pod; empty shell. **nabukaw.** *a*. grainless, empty (ear of palay); having only one testicle. **agbukaw.** *v*. to grow grainless (rice); become empty, contentless. **No maapaya dagiti pagay, adu ti agbukaw.** When the rice is invaded with salt water, a lot of the plants grow with empty ears. [Tag. *bungô* (skull)]
bukáw₂: *n*. small green flying insect.
búkay: **makabukay.** *n*. type of bitter vine whose boiled infusion is used for aborting pregnancies.
bukaykáy: **mabukaykayan.** *v*. to spill (contents) (*burayray*); fall. **bukaykayan.** *v*. to cut open and spill out the contents. [Tag. *bubô*]
bokáyo: (Tag. *bukayò*) *n*. a coconut sweet, nougat. **bokayo a lengnga.** *n*. sesame nougat sweet.
bukbók₁: *n*. woodworm, larva of grain beetle. **bukbuken.** *v*. to be attacked by the *bokbok*. **binukbok.** *n*. cavity (of teeth) *a*. wormeaten. [Kal. *luÿuk, bubuk*, Tag. *bukbók*]
bukbók₂: **ibukbok.** *v*. to pour out, spill. **bukbokan.** *v*. to pour into; fill up. **ibukbok.** *v*. to do without letup, e.g., devote one's time, express one's anger. **Ibukbok amin nga orasko iti X.** I devote all my time to X. **Ibukbokmo ti amin a kabaelam para iti panagrang-ay ti nego**

siom. Do all that you can for the prosperity of your business. [Tag. *buhos*]

búke: (Sp. *buque*: bulk; capacity) *n.* ship; capacity of a ship, bulk. **buke de gerra.** *n.* warship.

bukekkék: *n.* a variety of short-eared corn.

bukél: *n.* seed; nut; circle, round shape. **agbukel.** *v.* to form (a body); grow into a seed or embryo; become round; take shape. **arimbuklen.** *adj.* not perfectly round; (*fig.*) near completion. **buklen.** *v.* to form (an idea); create; form a club; to blame someone rashly. **buklan.** *a.* having many seeds. **ibuklan.** *v.* to remove the seeds from. **makabukel.** *v.* to be able to create; to arrive at a decision. **nabukel.** *a.* whole; round and solid; loud and clear; formed; assembled. **mangbukel.** *v.* to make up (a larger entity), form, organize, conceive. **mapagbukel.** *v.* to be able to make out; to perceive entirely. **pagbuklén.** *v.* to make into a circle; cut something into a circular shape. **pakabuklán.** *n.* the entire body; the whole thing; result, outcome. **sibubukel.** *a.* whole, entire, complete. **sangabukel.** *n.* one count of a group; *a.* single; not divided. **bukelbukel.** *n.* eyeball; testicle (*ukel*). **agpammukel.** *v.* to become pollinated (rice plants); to become protuberant (breasts of females and males at puberty). **pamukelen.** *a.* a little round. **Nakita ti dua bukel a matak ti panaginnarakupyo nga agsinsinnippit.** I saw you embracing and pecking each other with my own two eyes. **Ammo ti sibubukel nga ili dayta.** The whole town knows that. **Aggargaraw dagiti bibigda ngem diak mapagbukel ti kayatda a sawen.** Their lips are moving but I can't make out what they are trying to say. **Paseten ni Perlita iti pakabuklak.** Perlita is already a part of me. **Pasig a nataengan a babbai ti nangbukel itoy a klase.** It is all elderly ladies that make up this class. [Bon. *bola*, Ibg. *vukel, vullung*, Ivt. *vutuh*, Kal. *bukeÿ*, Kpm. *bútul*, Png. *bokél*, Tag. *butó, binhî*]

búkeng₁: *a.* short and stocky.

búkeng₂: *n.* variety of maize with a short, thick ear.

bukengkéng: *var.* of *bukeng*.

bukíbok: bukibuken. *v.* to overturn (contents of suitcase, etc.); research; develop; exploit natural resources. **agbukibok.** *v.* to grow spontaneously; shoot up. **ibukibok.** *v.* to scatter seeds (*wara*). **di mabukbukibok a dagdaga.** *n.* neglected lands. [Tag. *saliksík* (research)]

búkid: dalagan-bukid. *n.* kind of large, red, fleshy marine fish.

bukiéng: *n.* small boat.

bukíg: (*obs.*) *n.* asthma (*angkit*); (*reg.*) potbellied. (*buttiog*)

bukík: (*obs.*) *n. var.* of *bukíg*: asthma. (*angkit*).

bukílad: *var.* of *bukírad*: opened wide. **Bimmukilad ti mulagatna iti sarming.** His eyes enlarged as he stared in the mirror.

bukiláw: *n.* prolapse of the vagina (*butiláw*). [Tag. *buwà*]

bokília: (Sp. *boquilla*: mouthpiece) *n.* mouthpiece of a musical instrument. **bokiliado.** *a.* having both ends tapered (cigar).

buking: (Pil., *slang*) **mabuking.** *a.* caught red-handed, discovered while doing something inappropriate.

bukingking: *n.* stroke with the back of the hand. **bukingkingen.** *v.* to hit with the back of the hand.

bukírad: *a.* opened wide. **agbukirad.** *v.* to break open, burst open; open wide. **bukiraden.** *v.* to open wide something. **Bukiradem dagiti matam tapno makitam dagiti mapaspasamak.** Open your eyes so you can see what's happening. (*bukilad, bukiras, bulikad*)

bukíras: *var.* of *bukirad*: open, burst; break forth.

bukirkír: *var.* of *bukitkit*.

bukitkít: bukitkiten. *v.* to seek for by groping (with the hand). **bukitkitan.** *v.* to force open slightly; open slowly (birthday presents). **Binukitkitanna ti awitko a supot.** He went through the bag I was carrying with his hands. [Tag. *halungkát*]

bukkáig: *var.* of *bennék*.

bukkárot: *n.* a kind of crocodile; kind of wild bird; (*fig.*) immodest woman. [Tag. *alembóng* (immodest woman)]

bukkáw: *n.* a kind of vine.

bukkél: bumukkel. (*obs.*) *v.* to swell; form an abscess.

bukkuál: bukkualen. *v.* to dig up, uproot by digging (*kali*). [Tag. *hukáy*]

bukkól: agbukkol. *v.* to dig up earth. (*bukual*)

bukláw: nabuklaw, buklawan. *a.* gluttonous, greedy. (*rawet*) **kinabuklaw.** *n.* greed; gluttony. [Tag. *takaw*]

buklís: nabuklis. *a.* greedy, voracious. *var.* of *buklaw* (*rawet*). [Tag. *sukáb, sakím*]

buklóng: *n.* goiter. (*biel*) **agbuklong.** *v.* to have goiter. **buklongan.** *a.* having an oversized neck because of a goiter. [Knk. *ákak, baséy, buséy*, Kal. *bikkok*, Tag. *bosyò*]

buknág: maibuknag. *v.* to be spilled (non-liquids).

buknáy: ibuknay. *v.* to stick out (the tongue); to spill. **maibuknay.** *v.* to be stuck out (tongue, intestines, etc.); to be spilled out. **buknayan.** *v.*

to spill someone's guts (by slashing the abdomen). **naibuknay a sikóg.** fully developed pregnancy. **Natuang ti indissona a kalupit ket sumagmamano a kannateng a saluyot ti naibuknay iti rabaw ti lamisaan.** The basket he put on the table fell over and some freshly gathered jute leaves spilled out.

búkno *n.* swelling; inflammation. **bumukno.** *v.* to swell (said of the eyes when weeping); swell; inflame (*letteg*). [Tag. *magâ*]

buknót: buknuten. *v.* to uproot (a nail).

bukó$_1$: *n.* knuckle, node; bud; joints (of bamboo etc.). **agbuko.** *v.* to meet a misfortune. **panagbuko.** *n.* misfortune. **maibuko.** *v.* to be repaid; requited. [Tag. *bukó*]

bukó$_2$: bukobukuan. *n.* a kind of herb.

búkual: see *bukkuál.*

bukuár: *n.* jet; gush of water. (*kubbuar*) **agbukuar, bumkuar.** *v.* to jet, gust (water). [Tag. *bulwák*]

bukúbok: *n.* tree used as a vermifuge.

búkod: *n.* exclusive property; *a.* alone. **bukbukod.** *a.* alone, only; exclusive. **agbukod.** *v.* to stay alone; live alone; be alone; do on one's own. **agbukbukod.** *v.* to want to own everything; *a.* independent. **bumukod.** *v.* to live separately from (one's family). **bukodan.** *v.* to do exclusively; to own by oneself; to monopolize over. **kabukbukodan.** *a.* exclusively owned, own. **mangbukod.** *v.* to own; monopolize. **managbukbukod.** *n.* loner, introvert; greedy, prone to monopolize. **agimbubukod.** *v.* selfish, self-centered; greedy; voracious. **managimbubukod.** *a.* covetous, wanting to possess everything. **kinamangimbubukod.** *n.* greediness; possessiveness. **managimbubukodan.** *a.* selfish; possessive. **mabukodan.** *v.* to do on one's own. **arimbubukóden.** *a.* greedy, covetous. **agbukbukod a pagilian.** *n.* independent nation. **Bukodakto nga ibaklay.** *exp.* I alone will assume the responsibility. **Bukbukodko ti agtakuat.** I will find out on my own. **Ladladingitenna a bukbukod.** He is grieving about it all by himself. **Napan a bukbukodna.** He went on his own. [Png. *bókor*, Tag. *tangi*]

búkol: *n.* hump; swelling; any projecting bone (wrist bone). **bukolan.** *v.* to cause to swell or form a hump (by hitting, etc.). **bumukol.** *v.* to start forming (said of a hump or swelling).

bukún: see *bulagaw.*

búkot$_1$: *n.* back. (*likud*) **agbukot.** *v.* to have back pains. **bukot ti saka.** *n.* back of the foot. **iti bukot.** *prep.* in back of, behind. **ibukot.** *v.* to do to the utmost; to bear; shoulder. **agbinnukot.** *v.* to lie back-to-back. **kabinnukot.** *n.* sleepmate;

live-in mate. **bukot ti dakulap.** *n.* back of one's hand. **Mangibukot iti pudot ken mangkepkep iti lamiis.** He bears the heat and embraces the cold. [Ibg. *likug*, *vullug*, Itg. *dútug*, Ivt. *dicud*, Kal. *ochog*, Kpm. *gúlut*, Png. *benég*, Tag. *likód*]

búkot$_2$: bukotan. *n.* a kind of shrimp with a blackish back.

bukót: *a.* humpbacked; humped. **agbukot.** *v.* to hump; have a humped back (*kubbo*). [Tag. *hukót*]

bukrá: bukraen. *v.* to untie, untangle; undo; unfasten (*ukrad*). **agbukra.** *v.* to untangle; (*reg.*) to give birth. **nabukra.** *a.* untangled, untied, unfastened. **bukraan.** *v.* to set free. [Tag. *kalás*]

bukrád: see *ukrad.*

bukró: ibukro. *v.* to spill.

bukrós: *a.* fat, obese, corpulent, stout (*lukmég*). **mabukros.** *v.* to be unfastened and let fall (pants). **Nabukrosanak.** My pants fell down on me. [Tag. *tabâ*]

buksíl: *n.* outer covering of seeds; black bean recipe. **buksilan.** *v.* to husk, peel; remove seeds from. **ibuksilan, ibuksil.** *v.* to explain; state succinctly; express. **ibuksilan ti rikna.** *v.* to express one's feelings. **nabuksilan.** *a.* shelled; husked. **Ibuksilanyo ti gagarayo.** Explain your intentions. [Tag. *balatán*]

bóksing: (Eng.) *n.* boxing; boxing match. **agboksing.** *v.* to box; engage in a fistfight.

boksingéro: (*pron. boksinggéro*) *n.* boxer. (*sulong*)

buksít: *n.* belly (below umbilicus); umbilical region. (*tian; buy-ong; buttiog*) **agbubuksit.** *v.* to suffer from gas pains. **buksitan.** *a.* having a large belly. [Knk. *bogsít*, Png. *egés*, Tag. *pusón*]

boktó: *n.* a kind of fat freshwater fish; goby, *Chronophorus melanocephalus.* [Tag. *biyâ*]

buktól: nabuktol. (*obs.*) *n.* dead drunk.

bóla: (Sp. *bola*: ball; deceit) *n.* ball; (slang) bluff; pretense; not serious matter; draw. **agbola.** *v.* to play ball. **bolaen.** *v.* to flatter; draw the winning number. **bolabola.** *n.* wound thread; flattery. **bolabolaen.** *v.* to flatter; make into balls; roll into balls. **bola de niebe.** *n.* snowball. **binola.** *n.* wound thread used for sewing.

bulá: *n.* male pig (used in breeding); boar. **agbula.** *v.* to be in heat (*maya*). [Knk. *bullá*, Tag. *bulá*]

boláda: (f. Mex. Spanish *volada*: lie) *n.* trick, deception; bluff.

bulábog: (Tag. *bulabog*: tumult; scatter; disturb) **mabulabog.** *v.* to disperse in all directions; scatter; scamper (frightened animals). **bula-**

bugen. *v.* to scare animals, causing them to scatter. **Nabulabogda gapu iti kanabruong.** They dispersed because of the sound of thunder.

buládas: *n.* joker; liar; cheat. **buladasen.** *v.* to joke; cheat.

boladéro: (Sp. *voladero*) *n.* float (of a water wheel).

boladór: (Sp. *volador*: flyer) *n.* kite; skyrocket; kind of small flying fish.

bulág: *a.* blind. (*bulsek*) **agtagibulag.** *v.* to practice legerdemain; make something disappear through magic; to be invisible. **tagibulag.** *n.* talisman that renders the wearer invisible. [Ivt. *vuta*, Png., Tag. *bulág*]

bulagáw: *n.* clown; comedian; jester. **agbul-ibulagaw.** *v.* to play the clown. [Tag. *payaso* (Sp.); *bulagáw* = with gray eyes]

bulagí: (*obs.*) *n.* gonorrhea.

bulákbol: (Tag.) *n.* lazybones; idler, vagrant person. **agbulakbol.** *v.* to loaf around. (*ballog*; *baliudong*)

bulála: *n.* a kind of white-flowered tree, *Sarcocephalus orientalis.*

bulalákaw: *n.* meteor.

bulála: *n.* species of large tree with round, yellow-green, inedible fruits.

bulalát: *n.* a variety of awnless late rice.

bulallék: *n.* a variety of awned early rice with a light-colored hull and white kernel.

bulálo: *n.* bobbin of thread; small balls of rice or flour cake (*tambong*). **binulalo.** *n.* bobbin of thread. **agbulalo.** *v.* to roll into a ball. **bulaluen.** *v.* to roll into balls. **Nagbalin a kas maysa a bola dagiti nagbubulalo nga alinta.** The earthworms coiled themselves into a ball. [Tag. *bulalo*, Tag. *bulalô* = kneecap]

búlan₁: *n.* moon; month; menses. **agbulan.** *v.* to menstruate, have menses. **binulan.** *a.* every month, monthly. **binulan-bulan.** *adv.* monthly; monthly. **bulambulanen.** *a.* moonstruck, lunatic. **makabulan.** *adv.* for one month. **mabulanan.** *v.* to reach a full cycle; reach a full nine months (fetus). **kabulanan.** *n.* the expected month of giving birth. **agkabulanan.** *v.* to be born in the same month. **panagbinulan.** *n.* menstruation; monthly period. **immindayon a bulan.** crescent moon. **bumulan.** *v.* to spend a month. **Pamulananto daydi Lolo toy baboy.** This pig will be slaughtered to commemorate the month anniversary of Grandfather's death. **Uray no kabulanannan, simrek latta nga agtrabaho.** Even though she is expecting this month, she went to work anyway. **Pasaray bumulanda ket inton dumanon ti panag-awidda, awan a pulos ibatida a pakalag-**

lagipan ti bakasionda. They often spend a month here and when the time for them to go home comes, they do not leave any souvenir of their vacation. [Ibg. *vulan*, Ivt. *vuhan*, Kal. *buẏan*, *seẏeg*, Knk. *buán*, Kpm. *búlan*, Png. *bolán*, Tag. *buwán*]

búlan₂: bulambulan. *n.* a kind of fish, tarpon fish, *Megalops cyprinoides*; kind of children's circular tag game.

bulandáy: *n.* fruit of the *buri* palm.

bulános: nabulanos. *a.* voluntary; spontaneous; willing; flowing freely (blood). **agbulanos.** *v.* to volunteer; do until satisfied. **pagbulanusen.** *v.* to let someone do to his heart's content; to let be, not mind; let loose. **sibubulanos.** *adv.* willingly. **Nabulanos ti dara iti sugatna.** The blood flowed freely from his wound.

bulansióg: *a.* boastful. (*bulastog*)

bolánte: (Sp. *volante*: *n.* flywheel; *a.* flying) *a.* usable in all places; going all places; *n.* flywheel; circular letter; wide ruffle on a dress. **lisensia bolante.** *n.* peddler's license.

búlang: *n.* cockfight. (*pallót*) **bulangan.** *n.* cockpit for cockfights. **ibulang.** *v.* to match a gamecock in a fight. **makibulang.** *v.* to go to a cockfight; have a cockfight. **pagbubulangan.** *n.* cockfight arena. **Kasda la agbulbulang iti balay.** It's like they're having a cockfight in the house (noisy children). [Kal. *pallot*, Tag. *sabong*]

bulang-ít: agbulang-it. *v.* (*reg.*) to curvet, leap; bend down with the buttocks up.

bulangkóg: *a.* boastful, conceited, pompous (*lastog, bulastog*).

bulangláng: *n.* variety of sweet potato. [Tag. *bulangláng* = vegetable stew]

bólas: *n.* a kind of bird.

bulastóg₁: (Tag. also) *n.* liar (*ulbod*); braggart, boastful person (*lastog*). **Adu ti pinangbul-bulastogko.** I lied to her a lot.

bulastóg₂: *n.* variety of awned *diket* rice.

bulátaw: *a.* boastful, bragging. (*lastog, bulastog*)

bulatsíng: (*coll.*) **bulatsingen.** *v.* to joke with, tease, make fun of (*angaw*). **Bulbulatsingen-nak sa metten.** I think she is joking with me.

buláw: *n.* cock with dark brownish yellow plumage; drab color. [Tag. *buláw* = reddish color; suckling pig]

búlay: ibulay. *v.* to spill (rice, cereals, etc.). **makabulay.** *v.* to escape (animals, game). [Tag. *bulay* = strip of palm leaf; *bulaybulay* = reflection, meditation]

bulay-óg: (*coll.*) *a.* boastful. (*bulastog*)

bulból: mangbulbol, bulbolan. *v.* to harass; bother; fight with. [Tag. *bulból* = pubic hair]

bulbullagáw: (f. *bullagaw*) *n.* clown, funny person, jester. **agbulbullagaw.** *v.* to act like a clown. **Bulbullagawenna ti kalabanna tapno mapukaw ti konsentrasionna.** He is joking around with his opponent so he will lose his concentration.

buldák: (*reg.*) *var.* of *pultak*: bald spot; bald. (*kalbo*) **agbuldak.** *v.* to blot (pen).

buldíng: *a.* one-eyed; blind in one eye. **bulbulding.** *n.* the *kuribetbet* shrub. **buldingan.** *v.* to blind someone in one eye; injure one eye of someone else. **mabuldingan.** *v.* to lose sight in one eye. [Kal. *busking, bussok*]

buldóg: *a.* stout, fat, huge, large-bodied; cumbersome; pug-nosed; *n.* bull dog.

buldók: **bulbuldok.** *n.* round freshwater alga.

buldóser: (Eng.) *n.* bulldozer. **agbuldoser, buldoseren.** *v.* to bulldoze.

buldót: *n.* down (soft hairy undergrowth); hair growing at the nape of neck. (*muldot*)

búleg: *n.* (*reg.*) rancid smell.

bulelékong: (*coll.*) *n.* joker. **agbulelekong.** *v.* to joke; to be insincere about an undertaking.

boléro: (Sp. *bolero*: bolero) *n.* kind of dance; ballplayer; (*coll.*) flatterer.

bulgár: (Sp. *divulgar*: divulge) **ibulgar.** *v.* to divulge; make known. **Ibulgarko nga aw-awisennak iti balayyo no awan dagiti katugangam.** I will tell (people) that he invites me to your house when your in-laws aren't home.

bulgaridád: (Sp. *vulgaridad*: vulgarity) *n.* vulgarity.

Búlgaro: (Sp.) *n.*, *a.* Bulgarian.

bulí: *n.* lead; sinker for fishing, fishing weight. **bulian.** *v.* to attach lead weights to. **pakanen iti buli.** *exp.* to riddle with bullets. **bumuli.** *v.* to turn cold like lead. **Kas kalamiis ti buli ti timekna.** Her voice was as cold as lead. [Tag. *tinggâ* (lead)]

buliála: *n.* yellow-colored cock.

bulíbog: **agbulibog.** *v.* to act against one's will. **mabulibog.** *a.* inclined to do something.

bólibol: (Eng.) *n.* volleyball.

bulíbul: *n.* remuneration; payment; payment of *palay* used to pay the wages of the harvester; instrument used for perforating wood. **bulibulen.** *v.* to caulk; perforate. **mabulibul.** *v.* to receive something (nonmonetary) for services rendered.

búlig₁: *n.* banana stem; cluster; bunch. **agbulig.** *v.* to carry together, between two. **agbinnulig.** *v.* to help each other; do together. **sangkabulig.** *n.* one banana cluster. **panagbinnulig.** *n.* community development; mutual cooperation. **kabulig iti biag.** spouse. [Ibg. *vúlig*, Knk. *sápad*, Kpm. *búlig*, Png. *munil*, Tag. *buwig*]

búlig₂: **nagbuligan.** *n.* a kind of tree whose leaves are purple on the underside, *Clerodendron macrostegium.*

bulíg: **agbubulig.** *n.* several pairs of godparents of one baptized infant. [Tag. *bulíg* = mudfish not fully grown]

buligagáw: *var.* of *buligawgáw.*

buligawgáw: **agbuligawgaw.** *v.* to roll, turn (eyes of a dying person); to widen the eyes showing the whites; amuse by comedy. **ibuligawgaw.** *v.* to entertain, amuse. [Knk. *buligawgáw* = dim, dull; myopic]

buligengén: *n.* a small close-woven basket.

bulíkad: **bulikaden.** *v.* to open wide; fix the eyes upon. (*bukirad*)

buliliáso: (Pil. *slang*) *a.* failed; mild curse word.

bulilíkong: *var.* of *bulelekong*: joker.

bolílio: (Sp. *bolillo*: iron pin; small ball) *n.* bowling pin; small ball.

bolîlio: (Sp. *bolillo*: bars of sweet paste) *n.* kind of small, round, fried rice cake.

bulilísing: *var.* of *bullilising*: a kind of green parrot; mistress.

bulilít: *n.* a kind of small, silver marine fish called *palápal* when fully grown; *a.* short, dwarfish, small. [Tag. *galunggóng* (fish); *bulilít* = dwarfish, tiny]

Bolinawon: *n.* language and ethnic group from Bolinao, Pangasinan.

Bolinayen: (*myth.*) *n.* ancient Ilocano mountain god.

bulintík: *n.* marble; game of marbles (*holen, koriendo*); eyeball (*bukelbukel*). **agbulintik.** *v.* to play marbles.

boliós: (Sp. *bolillo*: bobbin) *n.* lace, bobbin lace. [Tag. *puntás*]

bulisangsáng: *n.* brown sugar that fails to harden into a coconut shell mold, loose brown sugar. (*panutsa*)

bolítas: (Sp. *bolitas*: small balls) *n.* ball bearing; meatball; small round pellets used in a cartridge.

bolkániko: (Sp. *volcánico*: volcanic) *a.* volcanic.

bulkanisádo: (Sp. *vulcanizado*: vulcanized) *a.* vulcanized.

bulkanólogo: (Sp. *vulcanólogo*: vulcanologist) *n.* vulcanologist.

bulkanolohía: (Sp. *vulcanología*: vulcanology) *n.* vulcanology.

bulláaw: **bumlaaw.** *v.* to digest with difficulty; to have indigestion (*bellad, lisay*). **Naibullaawak iti panaglangoylangoyko itay.** I have indigestion from my swimming around earlier.

bullád: *n.* big round eyes. (*buragat; mulagat*) **bulladan.** *v.* to look at someone with rounded, widened eyes. **ibullad.** *v.* to open the eyes

wide. **Immuyong dagiti pammulladen a matana.** Her large rounded eyes got angry.
bullagáw: *var.* of *bulagaw*: clown.
bullakáyan: *n.* very old man.
bullaláyaw: *n.* rainbow. (*ballaílaw*) **agbullalayaw.** *v.* to arc like a rainbow. **bimmullalayaw.** *a.* like a rainbow, arched. [Ibg. *vunnung,* Ivt. *rayiñorang,* Kal. *tileg,* Knk. *balingkáog, bulanglång,* Kpm. *punináriq,* Png. *kabulalákaw,* Tag. *bahagarì*]
bullaló: *var.* of *bulaló*: bobbin of thread. **agbullalo.** *v.* to roll into a ball.
bullán: bullabullan. *n.* hallucination; blindness; scapegoat; imposter; two-faced person. [Tag. *guní-guní* (hallucination)]
bulláwit: *n.* branch of bamboo; (*reg.*) tip of a post.
bullígit: nabulligit. *a.* badly dyed.
bullilísing[1]**:** *n.* a kind of green parakeet. [Tag. *kulasisì*]
bullilísing[2]**:** *n.* variety of rice; variety of red banana.
bullilísing[3]**:** *n.* kind of marine fish.
bullilísing[4]**:** *n.* (*coll.*) mistress. **pamullilisingen.** *n.* a tree with good timber. [Tag. *kulasisì*]
bulló: *n.* bone dislocation; dislocation of joints. (*belles*) **bullubulluen.** *v.* to set dislocated bones; to break someone's bones. **nablo.** *a.* dislocated. **mammullo.** *n.* setter of dislocated bones; native chiropractor. **Bulbulluem ta gunggonana!** Break his bones because he deserves it! [Kal. *lalis-u,* Png. *potér,* Tag. *lisók, linsád, balî*]
bulluák: bulbulluakan. *n.* afterbirth. (*kadkadua*)
bullóng: bumlong. *v.* to swell; turn over. **Bimbimlong dagiti dadduma a paset ti bagina.** A few parts of his body swelled.
bulnóg: nabulnog (*obs.*) *a.* excellent.
bulnós: *n.* payment; remuneration; payment given to person who helps with the harvest. (*bulibul*) **bulnusen.** *v.* to select the best from the harvest. **bulnusan.** *v.* to pay in kind for work performed.
bólo: *n.* a kind of large machete.
búlo[1]**:** *n.* kind of bamboo, highland bamboo. **binulo.** *a.* made of *bulo* bamboo. **kabuluan.** *n.* bamboo forest. **mamulo.** *v.* to cut and gather highland bamboo. [Tag. *buhò*]
búlo[2]**: buluan.** *n.* inedible mollusk with an elongated shell.
búlo[3]**:** *n.* horizontal bar of the *pagtagudan* combing frame of the loom; two internodes of bamboo inserted in the warp to keep threads in place while weaving
búlod: bumulod, buluden. *v.* to borrow. **agpabulod, ipabulod.** *v.* to lend. **ibulodan.** *v.* to borrow for someone. **pabulodan.** *v.* to lend to

someone. **agbinnulod.** *v.* to lend and borrow mutually. **managpabulod.** *a.* always lending things; charitable. [Bon. *bólod,* Ibg. *magikkaw;* *pekkáw* (lend), Ivt. *macivuhud,* Kal. *gawat, bulud,* Knk. *tengél,* Kpm. *dam,* Png. *bayés,* Tag. *hirám*]
bulóg: *n.* uncastrated male animal; (*coll.*) immodest man.
bulók: (*coll.,* Pil.) *a.* spoiled; rotten; old (cars), of poor quality; corrupt. **mabulok iti pagbaludan.** to rot in jail.
bóloman: (Eng.) *n.* guerilla guard during the second world war. [coined from the words *bolo* 'machete' + man]
búlon: *n.* favorable wind for sailing; accompaniment; *prep.* as; along with; while. **agbulon.** *v.* traveling companion. **bulonan.** *v.* to make easier; to take with; do with, accompany. **bulunen.** *v.* to take advantage of; go with the chance. **ibulon.** *v.* to make favorable or easier; to let something be accompanied by something else. **maibulon.** *v.* to go with; to be carried by. **kabulon.** *v.* to do while, to do at the same time, be accompanied by. **pagibulon.** *n.* appetizer; chaser. **Maipabulon ti tsa ti almusarmi a binigat.** Tea goes along with our breakfast every morning. **Insungbatna a bulon ti panangbarikesna iti bunengna.** He answered as he put the machete in his waistband. **Nagrukob a bulonna a nagsanud.** He bowed as he moved back. **Dua a tableta ti bulonam iti adu a danum.** Take two tablets with lots of water.
bulón: (Tag.) *n.* choking. **mabulonan.** *v.* to choke, have food or water stuck in the mouth. (*maaltotán*).
boluntád: (Sp. *voluntad*: will) *n.* volition, will.
boluntário: (Sp. *voluntario*) *n.* volunteer; *a.* voluntary (*bulanos*). **agboluntario.** *v.* to volunteer.
bulóng[1]**:** *n.* leaf; page of a book; blade of grass; brim of a hat. **agbulong.** *v.* to develop leaves. **nabulong, nakabulbulong.** *a.* leafy. **bulong ti bapor.** *n.* sail of a ship. **bulong kalúnay.** *n.* spinach leaves. **Kasla saan a makabtak iti bulong.** He seems incapable of breaking a leaf (said of someone who does something surprising he did not seem capable of doing before). [Ibg. *don,* Itg. *túbu, dáon,* Ivt. *vuhung,* Kal. *tubu,* Knk. *ananguá, túbo,* Kpm. *bulung,* Png. *bolóng,* Tag. *dahon; bulóng* = whisper, murmur; Knk. *bulúng* = cabbage]
bulóng[2]**: bulongan.** *n.* a kind of elongated marine fish. **bulong-unas.** *n.* a kind of flattened, elongated marine fish, cutlass fish of the *Trichiuridae* family.
bulungnás: *var.* of *bulong unas*: cutlass fish.

bolóri: *n.* a kind of marine fish.

búlos: *a.* free; loose; stray; liberated (animals, not person); profuse bleeding. **agbulos.** *v.* to flow out; gush out; flow profusely. **bulosan.** *v.* to unleash (anger, etc.); let go; bid farewell to one who is leaving. **ibulos, bulosan.** *v.* to liberate; let loose (feelings). **makabulos.** *v.* to break loose; be able to flow out; be able to escape (bird from a cage). **Insanggirna ti rupana iti abagak ket imbulosna ti saibbekna.** She leaned her face on my shoulder and let out her sobs. [Tag. *layà*; *bulos* = gust of air; open space; complete trust; second helping of food]

búlos₂: *n.* slender cane used for beating.

bulóy: *n.* term of address given to a person with the same name or nickname. **agbuloy.** *v.* to have the same nicknames (*katokayo*). [Tag. *tokayo*, Sp. *tocayo*]

bólsa: (Sp. *bolsa*: purse, bag, pocket; stock exchange) *n.* pocket; stock exchange. **ibolsa.** *v.* to place something in the pocket; illegally pocket money. **butbot ti bolsa.** *n.* a hole in the pocket (referring to someone who always spends money). **bolsa de yelo.** *n.* icecap; ice bag. [Kal. *buÿsa*, Knk. *luy-óng* (pocket)]

bulsék: *a.* completely blind. (*bulag*) **agimbubulsek.** *v.* to pretend to be blind; to refuse to see and understand. **bulseken.** *v.* to make blind; pluck out the eyes. **ipabpabulsek.** *v.* to do something, pretending not to see; to go ahead and do something prohibited. **Sangkasao daydi nanangna a saan a matmaturog no nabasa ti buokna ta pakaalaan kano ti panagbulsek.** His deceased mother used to always tell him not to sleep with wet hair for it supposedly causes blindness. **Bulsekka a simamata.** You are blind even with your eyes open. [Ibg. *vulling*, Ivt. *vutaq*, Kal. *kuÿap*, Knk. *buldíng*, *budiké*, *kulláw*, *budsék*, *budkáw*, Knk., Kpm., Png., Tag. *bulág*]

bulsílio: (Sp. *bolsillo*: pocket) *n.* small pocket.

bolsísta: (Sp.) *n.* stockbroker.

bolsíto: *n.* small pocket.

bulsó: ibulso. *v.* to launch. **bulsuan.** *v.* to let go; let loose. [Tag. *bunsód*]

bólta: (Sp. *volta*: volt) *n.* volt.

boltáhe: (Sp. *voltaje*: voltage) *n.* voltage.

bulták: *n.* forceful throw. **ibultak.** *v.* to fling; throw (*ibato*); (*fig.*) implicate; blame.

búlto: (Sp. *bulto*: religious figurine) *n.* religious image of a saint or the Virgin Mary (also *rebulto*); pile; bulk. **ibulto.** *v.* to pile up (cloth).

bumagtó: *n.* a kind of shellfish; kind of cuttlefish.

bumalásang: (f. *balásang*) *n.* girl, young girl.

bumaró: (f. *baró*) *n.* boy, young man. **agbumaro.** *v.* to be near the age of puberty (boys).

bómba₁: (Sp. *bomba*: pump; bomb) *n.* pump, pump well; bomb; fire engine; water hose; attack made in a political speech; bomb; thunderbolt. **agbomba, bombaen.** *v.* to pump (a well); bomb.

bómba₂: (*coll.*) *n.* nudity, show with a lot of nudity; *a.* nude. **kontodo bomba.** completely nude.

Bombáy: (Eng.) *n. a.* Asian Indian.

bombéro: (Sp. *bombero*: fireman) *n.* fireman. **agbombero.** *v.* to become a fireman.

bombília: (Sp. *bombilla*: lightbulb) *n.* lightbulb.

bombísta: (f. *bombo*: drum + *-ista* agentive suffix) *n.* drummer.

bómbo: *n.* drum. (*tambór*) **agbombo.** *v.* to beat a drum. [Knk. *solíbaw*]

bómbra: *n.* adult anchovy fish, *Stolephorus commersoni.* (*bumra*)

bumdéng: (f. *beddeng*) *v.* to hesitate to approach someone or enter a room; be apprehensive. **Dika bumdeng nga umasideg kaniak.** Don't hesitate to come to me.

bumkuár: (f. *bukuár*) *v.* to jet; gush out; flow out freely.

bumláaw: (f. *bulláaw*) *v.* to digest with difficulty, have indigestion.

bumlíng: (*obs.*) *n.* pusillanimity.

bumlóng: (f. *bullóng*) *v.* to swell; turn over.

bumrá: *n.* the *munámon* fish when fully grown.

bumráak: (f. *berráak*) *v.* to be nauseous; about to vomit.

bumrí: (f. *birrí*) *v.* to burst, explode from being overfilled; rupture; crack.

bumság: (f. *besság*) *v.* to turn pale, pallid.

bumsóg: (f. *bussóg*) *v.* to become full.

bumták: (f. *betták*) *v.* to crack open, burst open; explode.

bumtó: (f. *buttó*) *v.* to be ready to be born.

bumrá: *n.* large *munámon* fish, adult anchovy.

búna: *n.* residue, remnant, residue.

bunábon: ibunabon. *v.* to distribute; share; apportion. (*bíngay*) **makabunabon.** *v.* to be enough (said of things being apportioned); to be sufficient (shared food supply).

búnag: *n.* act of transporting. **ibunag.** *v.* to carry to; haul. **bunagen.** *v.* to transport; carry somewhere; haul. **ipabunag.** *v.* to have something hauled, transported. **makibunag.** *v.* to help in transporting. **agbumbunag a trak.** *n.* pickup truck. [Tag. *hakot*]

bunannág: *n.* proclamation. (*waragawag*) **ibunannag.** *v.* to publish; glorify, praise; proclaim. [Tag. *pahayag*]

bonánsa: (Sp. *bonanza:* prosperity) *n.* prosperity; fair weather; rich vein of gold (mining).

búnar: *n.* red ant. **binunar.** *a.* attacked by red ants. **kabunaran.** *n.* nest of red ants.

bunár: pabunar. *n.* feast, celebration. (*pasken, padaya*) **agpabunar.** *v.* to host a feast. **makipabunar.** *v.* to attend a celebration.

bun-ás: *n.* tall, straight, healthy branchless tree. **nabun-as.** *v.* healthy and robust (*rukbos*). [Tag. *lagô*]

bunatan: *n.* striped mackerel fish, *Tastrelliger chruysozonus.*

bun-áy: maibun-ay. *v.* to protrude (guts from the belly when wounded); to be spilled. (*burayray*)

bundáw: *n.* spot in the pupil of the eye.

búneg: *n.* a kind of tree whose fruits are fed to swine. **kabunegan.** *n.* place abundant with *buneg* trees.

búnel: *n.* base of a banana stalk whose upper portion is sliced and cooked for hog feed.

bunél: clot, lump in badly ground flour; fragment of badly burned lime; uncooked particles or seeds; corn that doesn't pop when fried, dud. (*fig.*) person or animal that is retarded in growth.

bunéng: *n.* large machete-like knife, *bolo.* **agbuneng.** *v.* to carry a *buneng.* **bunengan.** *a.* armed with a *buneng.* **buneng ti agkakayong.** *n.* dull *buneng* (*buneng* of brothers-in-law, as brothers-in-law are not supposed to fight in Ilocano culture). [Bon. *kantíla, beneng,* Ibg. *badang,* Ivt. *lukuy,* Kal. *pachin,* Kpm. *palang,* Png. *baráng,* Tag. *gulok*]

bonéte: (Sp. *bonete:* bonnet) *n.* bonnet. **nakabonete.** *a.* wearing a bonnet.

búni: *n.* Pagan god, see *Kabunian.*

buniág: *n.* baptism; baptismal. **agbuniag.** *v.* to have a baptism; baptize. **buniagan.** *v.* to baptize; christen; name. **ibuniag.** *v.* to bestow a name or an alias. **ipabuniag.** *v.* to have someone baptized. **agbibinnuniag.** *v.* to play at nicknaming people. **anak ti buniag.** *n.* godchild. **mamuniag.** *n.* priest at a baptism. **naibuniag a nagan.** *n.* Christian name. **Nasapa a napan timmulong iti balay ti kabsatna nga agpabuniag no rabii.** He went to help at the house of his brother early for the evening baptism. [Kal. *bunyeg,* Png., Tag. *binyág,* Tag. *bunyág* = expose]

boníte: *n.* small baby's hat, bonnet.

bunnék: *n.* a variety of small banana.

bunnóng: bunnongen. *v.* to store in times of shortage; to check, arrest (water in rice field); dam. **In-inut a napapintasda ti dagada babaen ti danum ti ubbog a binnunnong ken pinagayusda iti talonda.** They gradually improved their land with springwater that was checked and made to flow in their fields. [Tag. *saplád*]

búno: (Sp. *bono:* bond) *n.* bond; bond issue.

bunuán: *n.* kind of fish trap. (*tárik*)

bunúbon: *n.* seedling; plant ready for transplantation. **agbunubon.** *v.* to grow plants from seedlings by transplanting them. **pagbunubonan.** *n.* seedbed. **panagbubunubon.** *n.* season for sowing seeds. [Kpm. *sinábud,* Tag. *punlâ*]

bunuélos: (Sp. *buñuelo:* fritter) *n.* fritter, doughnut. (*binuelos*)

búnog: *n.* large *bokto* fish.

bunóg: mabunog. *v.* to move to and fro (food in stomach); shake (contents).

búnong: ibunong. *v.* to distribute, apportion; deal out cards. **bunongan.** *v.* to distribute to someone. **agibunong.** *v.* to serve food to guests. **mabunongan.** *v.* to be served. **ipabunong.** *v.* to have something served. **pabunongan.** *v.* to have someone served. **Intuloydan a nagibunong iti kape.** They continued serving coffee.

búnot: *n.* uprooting; unsheathing. **bunuten.** *v.* to pick out; pull out; unsheathe. **ibunotan.** *v.* to draw for someone. **agbibinnunot.** *v.* to draw lots. **nabunot.** *a.* picked, drawn out. [Tag. *bunot*]

bunót₁: *n.* outer husk of a coconut. **ibunotan.** *v.* to husk (*banut*). **bunuten.** *v.* to scrub the floor with a coconut husk. [Kal. *tetagon,* Png., Tag. *bunót*]

bunót₂: bunótan. *n.* a kind of large marine fish, striped mackerel. [Tag. *alumahan*]

bunsó: (Tag. *bunsô*) *n.* youngest child. (*inaudi; buridek; kimmot*). **ibunso.** *v.* to wrap up. (*balkot*)

búntal₁: *n.* stroke of the fist. **buntalen.** *v.* to strike with the fist. **binnuntalan.** *n.* boxing. **bumuntal.** *v.* to box. [Tag. *suntók*]

buntál₂: *n.* species of palm tree yielding a fine fiber; hat made out of the *buntal* fiber.

buntála: kabuntala. *n.* morning star.

bontáni: *n.* goblin; bugbear.

bontár: *n.* bamboo raft, longer than the *rakit.*

buntatóg: *n.* slow, sluggish. (*buntog*)

buntáyak: bumuntayak. *v.* to take a shortcut. (*ápat*)

buntayán: *n.* still for *nipa.*

buntáyog: *n.* variety of awned late rice; coin toss (usually flipped by two players simultaneously, with the head side winning). **agbuntayog.** *v.* to flip the coin.

buntiék: *n.* young of the *dalag* fish. *a.* big bellied.

buntílog: *n.* variety of awned late rice.
buntitíkeng: *n.* a kind of vine with edible pods.
buntó: **agbubunto.** *v.* to buy one thing among many. **makibunto.** *v.* to contribute to a common expense.
buntóg: **ibuntog.** *v.* to slow down; immerse in water. **agbuntog.** *v.* to anchor. **bumuntog.** *v.* to be slow, sluggish. **nabuntog.** *a.* slow; clumsy; lazy. [Ibg. *mavayag*, Ivt. *mawadiq*, Kpm. *malamlam*, Png. *kálna, tantán*, Tag. *bagal*]
búntok: *n.* additional thing given free to a purchase (extra banana, egg, etc.) (*nayon*) **buntokan.** *v.* to give something extra to a buyer free of charge. **Awan buntokna? Awan nayonna?** Isn't there a *buntok*? [Tag. *dagdág*]
buntón: *n.* heap, pile; stack; small hill; anthill; (myth.) home of the *ansisít*. **ibunton.** *v.* to place things in a pile or heap. **maibunton.** *v.* to be heaped, placed in a pile. [Png. *átip*, Png., Tag. *buntón* (pile); *punsó* (anthill)]
buntúon: *var.* of *bunton*.
buntutúyan: *n.* slow-footedness; slow walker. (*buntóg*)
bunyág: *n.* baptism. see *buniag*.
bóng: *n.* sound of an explosion; firecracker. **bumanongbong.** *a.* exploding; resounding.
búnga: *n.* fruit; berry; offspring; pod; nut; advantage; benefit. **binunga.** *n.* child, offspring. **agbunga, bungaen.** *v.* to bear fruits. **ibunga.** *v.* to cause; result. **bungabunga.** *n.* fruit of the *ubi* yam; small round growth on the eyelid. **bunga ti mata.** *n.* sore on the eyelid; sty. **bunga ti tian.** *n.* child. **bunga ti nagrigrigatanna.** fruit of one's labor. **Ti kamatis, di agbunga't manggá.** The tomato plant does not bear mango fruit (not all siblings will be the same). [Ibg. *vunga*, Ivt. *asiq*, Knk. *begas, lames*, Png. *bongá*, Kpm., Tag. *bunga*; Knk. *búnga* = young pine tree]
bungábong: **ibungabong.** *v.* to announce, publish; declare. [Tag. *pahayag*]
búngag: *n.* embryo; germ of seeds; corncob.
bungál: (Tag.) *var.* of *kabúl, tuppól*: with decayed teeth.
bungánga: *n.* barrel of a gun; mouth of a cave. **Indeppelna ti bunganga ti paltog iti darangidong ni Nhoe.** He pressed the barrel of the gun against Nhoe's bridge of the nose.
búngar: *n.* the act of drinking alcohol as a cure for a hangover. **agbungar.** *v.* to drink alcohol in order to cure a hangover. **bungaren.** *v.* to cure drunkenness or a hangover by drinking again. **bungaran.** *n.* first alcoholic batch of *nipa*.
bungáw₁: *n.* scrotal hernia. **agbungaw.** *v.* to suffer from a scrotal hernia. [Tag. *luslós*]
bungáw₂: *n.* kind of large dragonfly. (*tuwato a bungaw*)

bungbóng: *n.* explosion; dynamite; sound of an explosion; firecracker. **bungbongen.** *v.* to explode (with dynamite).
bungdól: *a.* tipless and blunt (horns). **bungdulen.** *v.* to attack with the horns; blunt the horns. [Tag. *suwág*]
bungéd: *n.* trunk (of a tree, man); torso.
bunggá: *a.* lavish; extravagant.
búnggalo: (Eng.) *n.* bungalow.
bunggóy: *n.* group, band, troop; faction; company. **agbubunggoy.** *v.* to unite, group, join together. **bunggobungguyen.** *v.* to divide into groups. **makibunggoy.** *v.* to join with, associate. **kabunggoyan.** *n.* colleague; associate; peer. [Tag. *samahan*]
bungí: *a.* with missing teeth. [Knk. *gib-áw*, Tag. *bungî*]
búngil: *n.* hard betel nut; rachitic undeveloping person. **nabungil.** *a.* stunted in growth; hard. **bumungil.** *v.* to become hard; to be stunted in growth; to overstay an office.
búngis: **nabungisan.** *a.* with uncovered pubic region (women); bare bottomed (*labus*). [Tag. *lantád*]
bungísngis: *n.* torn wrappings showing the inside of a package. [Tag. *bungisngís* = giggle]
bungkákeng: *n.* a percussion musical instrument made of bamboo.
bungkaló: *n.* hook bones.
bungkatól: *n.* hard protuberance; bunion. **nabungkatol.** *a.* protruding; with humps; coarse. [Tag. *umbók*]
bungkítan: *n.* variety of *diket* rice.
bungkók: **agbungkok.** *a.* lice-infected. (*kinuto*)
bungkól₁: *n.* large bone (for dogs). **ibungkolan.** *v.* to separate meat from the bones. **pagbubungkolan.** *v.* to wrangle for bones (said of dogs).
bungkól₂: *n.* pretentious woman.
bungkól₃: *n.* (coll.) feast. (*padaya, pasken*) **pagbubungkolan.** *n.* festivities, place of festivities.
bungkól₄: *n.* variety of awned late rice.
bungkóng: *n.* bulge. **nabungkong.** *a.* massive, bulky; large. (*padiwakal*) **bumungkong.** *v.* to bulge. **Nadlawko ti nabungkong iti bolsana.** I noticed a bulge in his pocket. [Tag. *tambók*]
bungkós: (Tag.) *n.* bundle. (*reppet*)
bunglóg: *n.* stench of rancid lard, rotten meat. **nabunglog.** *a.* smelling of rotten meat. **bumunglog.** *v.* to become rancid; stink. **Nasaprianak iti bunglog ti ngiwatna.** I was sprayed by the stench of his mouth. [Tag. *antá*]
bungúbong: **bungubungan.** *v.* to fill up containers (with liquids). **maibungubong.** *v.* to accidentally step in a crevice. [Tag. *buhos*]

búngol: **bungolan**. *v.* to attack in groups; kind of spotted fragrant banana. **pagbubungolan**. *v.* to overwhelm (many against one); swarm. **No adda inaramidko a dakes, dakay amin pagbubungolandak.** If I do something wrong, you all gang up on me.

bungúlan: *n.* a kind of yellow spotted fragrant banana.

bungón₁: *n.* wrapper, covering; package. (*balkot*) **bungunen**. *v.* to wrap up, pack; bundle up. **binungon**. *n.* food wrapped in leaves. **ibungonan**. *v.* to wrap for someone. **ipabungon**. *v.* to have something wrapped. **Imbungonan ni nanangna iti innapuy ken layalay.** His mother wrapped him rice and *layalay* fish. [Ibg. *vungunen*, Ivt. *pungusan*, Kpm, Tag. *balot*, Png. *púngus*]

bungón₂: *n.* tree with yellow flowers, *Allaeanthus luzonicus.*

bung-ór: *n.* swelling; protruding awry. **bumungor**. *v.* to become swollen (body part). [Tag. *magâ*]

bungró: *n.* wilderness, jungle. **kabungruan**. *n.* dense forest, jungle.

bungsót: **nabungsot**. *a.* rotten, spoiled; putrid; decomposing. **bungsuten**. *v.* to cause to become *nabungsot*. [Ibg. *darál*, Png., Tag. *bulók*]

bungtíl: **bungtilen**. *v.* to break off (*sep-ak*).

bungtól: *n.* broken stick or needle. **bungtulen**. *v.* to break off (horns, branches). **nabungtol**. *a.* broken. [Tag. *balî*]

bungtót: *n.* stench of dung; rotten meat. **nabungtot**. *a.* smelling of rotten meat; rotten; rancid; decomposing. **bumungtot**. *v.* to smell (as when rotting). **Bungbungtot sino ti immuttot, isurom ti nagkauttot.** Ilocano version of eenie meenie miney moe, a child's verse. [Tag. *baho*]

buók: *n.* hair (of the head); horse's mane. **agbuok**. *v.* to grow hair. **buokan**. *a.* having long hair. (*lampong*) **ibuokan**. *v.* to remove the hair of. [Ibg. *vuq*, Ivt. *vuwuk*, Kal. *buuk*, Knk. *bagbágo*, Kpm. *bwak*, Png. *buék*, Sbl. *sabut*, Tag. *buhók*]

búong: *n.* break, crack; broken vessel. **buongen**. *v.* to break. **nabuong**. *a.* broken (by cracking, shattering or bursting). **buong ti ulo**. *n.* problem, perplexity. **buong ti ulo nga anak**. *n.* problem child. **kasla di makabuong iti pinggan**. *exp.* seemingly innocent; pretentious. [Ibg. *navekka*, Ivt. *napsaq*, Kpm. *balbal*, Png. *betág*, Tag. *sirâ, basag*]

búos: *n.* a large red ant with edible eggs.

búot: *n.* mildew, mold. (*ratikratík*) **buoten**. *v.* to be moldy. **bumuot**. *v.* to grow mold; (*fig.*) age. **Saan a bumubuot ti kuartada.** Their money

does not grow mold (it is spent fast). [Bon. *bóot*, Ibg. *uppig, kúleg*, Ivt. *uhapung*, Kal. *buut*, Kpm. *kulapu*, Png. *abuútan*, Sbl. *balutabot*, Tag. *ámag*]

búpalo: (Eng.) *n.* buffalo.

bupánda: (Sp. *bufanda*: muffler) *n.* lady's muffler; neckerchief. **nakabupanda**. *a.* wearing a muffler.

bupéte: (Sp. *bufete*: bureau) *n.* law firm; law office. **agkabupete**. *v.* to be in the same law firm.

bópis: *n.* buffet service; kind of *pulutan* made from spicy, sliced pieces of meat, liver, and tripe.

burá: (Sp. *borrar*: erase) **buraen**. *v.* to erase; wipe out; efface; delete. **pagbura**. *n.* eraser.

burábor: *n.* sting of a stingray; rudderstock; instrument used for flushing out insects; disturbance. **naburabor**. *a.* sick by the sting of a *burabur*. **buraburen**. *v.* to flush out insects; disturb the peace. **Nagkaanda kadagiti tukak ken dudon a maburabor iti panagarabda.** They ate the frogs and locusts that disturbed their grazing. [Tag. *bulabog* (disturb)]

buradíng: (*reg.*) *n.* catfish. (*paltat*)

buradór₁: (Sp. *borrador*: rough draft) *n.* flying fish, *Cypselurus oligolepsis*; outline (of a project); rough draft.

buradór₂: (Sp. *borrador*: eraser) *n.* eraser. [Kal. *gusugus*]

burág: *a.* having an eye disease when the iris becomes white. [Tag. *bulág* = blind]

buragát: *a.* with eyes opened wide. (*bullad*)

buragsót: **agburagsot**. *v.* to stamp the feet. (*baragsot, tabbuga*)

buraíkaw₁: *n.* *dalag* fish larger than the *burikikkik*.

buraíkaw₂: **binuraikaw**. *n.* variety of rice.

buráis: *n.* something scattered. (*wará, burandis*) **naiburais**. *a.* scattered.

buraít: *var.* of *burais*: scatter. (*burandis*)

búrak₁: **buraken**. *v.* to break, shatter, crush. **agburak**. *v.* to separate, part company. **maburak**. *v.* to be crushed, shattered, smashed. **naburak**. *a.* broken. [Tag. *basag*]

búrak₂: **buraken**. *v.* to shake in order to collect the fish caught in the *pamurak*. **pamurak**. *n.* kind of scoop net. **binurakan**. *n.* catch of fish. **ipaburak**. *v.* to shoot at random; abandon a ship to be shipwrecked.

burándis: **iburandis**. *v.* to scatter; spill; throw around. **maiburandis**. *v.* to be scattered; spilled (*wara*). [Tag. *kalat*]

burangén: *n.* old male monkey; term applied to people with scary, malevolent faces.

burang-ít: agburang-it. *v.* to raise the buttocks. (*pugiit; duriri*) **burang-iten, iburang-it.** *v.* to place something with the bottom up, upside down; upturn. **naburang-it a kotse.** *n.* overturned car. [Png. *abalintuwág, bungitngit*, Tag. *tuwád*]

burangítan: *n.* a kind of marine eel.

borár: (Sp. *borrar*: erase) **agborar.** *v.* to erase something; efface; delete. **boraren.** *v.* to erase, eradicate; delete; efface.

buraráwit: *n.* long branch of bamboo. (*bullawit*)

burárog₁: *n.* large *birut* fish.

burárog₂: agburarog. *v.* to drink too much water.

búras: *n.* fruit harvest, grain harvest (not used for rice) (*apit*). **burasen.** *v.* to reap, harvest, gather fruits, not rice. **iburasan.** *v.* to harvest, gather for someone. **maburas.** *v.* can be harvested. **panagbuburas.** *n.* harvesting season. **makiburas.** *v.* to help with the harvest. **No kasta nga agburas ni Lelang, ilasinna dagiti napipintas tapno ilakona, dagiti naruker, isu ti kanenmi.** When grandmother reaps the harvest, she separates the good stuff to sell; the worm-eaten vegetables is what we eat. [Tag. *pitás*]

burasí: *n.* species of fish.

boratséro: (Sp. *borracho*: drunk) *n.* drunkard. (*bartek*)

búray: *n.* share. **iburay.** *v.* to divide; deal out, apportion, distribute. **burayan.** *v.* to throw at; hurl. **panangiburay iti kapanunotanna.** sharing of one's thoughts. [Tag. *bahagi*]

burayuán: *n.* turkey. (*pabo*)

buráyok: *n.* fountain; spring (of water). **agburayok.** *v.* to gush out. [Tag. *bukál* (Sp.)]

burayóngan: *n.* axle of a *palakapak.*

burayráy: naburayrayan. *a.* slashed or cut open so contents can come out (i.e. cut in an animal's stomach to let the intestines out.).

buraywán: *var.* of *burayuan*: turkey. (*pabo*)

burbór₁: burboren. *v.* to spend; to overcook until mushy; destroy completely. **naborbor.** *a.* spent; destroyed completely; overcooked.

burbór₂: *n.* fur, shag; moth; shaggy dog; heavy woven blanket; sound of engine or large mechanical instrument. **burburan.** *n.* a kind of small hairy dog. *a.* having a lot of *burbur*. **binurburan.** *n.* kind of cotton cloth; towels. **bumanurbor.** *n.* sound of strong wind or current. **naburbor.** *a.* finely ground; strong (wind or current). **paburburen.** *v.* to rev up an engine. [Tag. *balahibo* (body hair)]

burburtiá: *n.* riddle; puzzle. **agburburtia.** *v.* to tell a riddle. **burburtiaan.** *v.* to tell a riddle to.

bórda: (Sp. *bordar*: embroider) *n.* embroidery. **naiborda.** *a.* embroidered. **mangborda.** *v.* to do embroidery. **bumoborda.** *n.* embroideress.

bordádo: (Sp. *bordado*: embroidered) *a.* embroidered.

bordadór: (Sp.) *n.* embroiderer.

bordalésa: (Sp. *bordelesa*: from Bordeaux) *n.* kind of woven fabric.

bordár: (Sp. *bordar*: embroider) **agbordar.** *v.* to embroider.

burdít: nagburdit. *a.* ugly. (*laad, alás*)

bordón: (Sp. *bordón*: bass string) *n.* bass string.

burék: *n.* bubble; foam; lather; breaking part of a wave. **agburek.** *v.* to boil. **bumurek.** *v.* to simmer. **impaburek.** *n.* boiled water. **napaburkan.** *a.* boiled (sterilized utensils). **Agburburek ti darana.** His blood is boiling (denotes anger). [Ibg. *lúwag*, Ifg. *bayakbak*, Ivt. *kumbuwal*, Kpm. *bukal*, Png. *lambung*, Tag. *kulô* (boil), *bulâ* (bubble)]

burgís: (Sp. *burgués*: bourgeois) *n.* middle class, bourgeois.

búri: *n.* wild goat. (*kalding*)

burí: *n.* buri palm, *silag.*

bur-í: *n.* giving sparsely what one has in abundance. **ipabur-i.** *v.* to give sparsely what one has in abundance.

buriás: *n.* young hog; variety of awned *diket* rice. **buriasan.** *a.* having many piglets (said of a sow). **mamurias.** *v.* to get a piglet. [Bon. *ammogit*, Kal. *iyas*, Knk. *lablab-ó*, Png. *belék*, Tag. *biik*]

buribód: *n.* porridge (not made of rice). **maburibod.** *v.* to pulp; cook to excess. **binuribod.** *a.* pulped; mashed.

buríbor: *n.* trouble (of the mind), disturbance (*burabor, ribuk, singa, yengyeng*). **maburburibor.** *v.* to be muddled (said of the mind). **mangburburibor.** *v.* to trouble the mind. **buriburen.** *v.* to trouble, bother. **pakaburiboran ti panunot.** *n.* mental torment. **Kasla maburburiboranka, anak.** You seem to be troubled, child. [Tag. *abala*]

burídek: *n.* youngest child (*inaudi; kimmot*); sediment in broth (*rinsaed*). **Silulukat ti balayko kadagiti ubbingmo, nangnangruna ti buridek.** My house is open to your children, especially your youngest child. [Bon. *alílis*, Ivt. *dékkey*, Kal. *uchichi*, Png. *kayogtanán*, Tag. *bunsô*]

buridíbod: *var.* of *buribod*: pulp, mash.

búrik: *a.* with different colors, dappled, variegated in color; tattooed all over the body. *n.* a bird or fowl with variegated plumage. **kaburburik.** *a.* similar or the same in color variegation. **Agkukuyog dagiti agkakaburik.** Birds of a feather flock together. [Tag. *batik-batík*]

búrik: burikan. *v.* to carve, engrave, sculpture; emboss; design, sketch.

burík: *n.* a kind of bird with variegated plumage.

buríki: agburiki. *v.* to flare up in anger, become angry. **Sapay ta di agburikinto ni Pepay no matakuatanna daytoy.** I hope that Pepay doesn't get angry when she discovers this.

burikák: (Tag. also) *n.* prostitute. (*pampam*)

buríkaw: *n.* the *dalag* fish when not fully grown. **binurikaw.** *n.* variety of awned late rice.

burikayákay: naiburikayakay. *a.* dry, non-sticky (rice). (*marayamay; parayapay*)

buríki: *n.* hollow pipe device used to stick into rice to check the condition of the rice in the middle.

burikikkík: *n.* small *dalag* fish.

buringetngét: *a.* frowning, with a scowling face. **agburingetnget.** *v.* to grumble; murmur with discontent; to have a temper (*rupanget*). [Tag. *simangot*]

buring-ít: naburing-it. *a.* with raised buttocks or bottom. (*burang-it, pugiit, duriri*)

buringusngós: agburingusngos. *v.* to rub the sides with the forearms; to grumble by stamping the feet (impatient children).

buringutngót: *var.* of *buringusngos.*

buríraw: iburiraw. *v.* to give for free; give as a favor. **Namin-adun a nagpaw-it iti pagguduaanta kuma ngem burburirawem met amin.** He sent us a lot of things that we should have shared equally between us, but you gave everything away.

buríri: naburiri. *a.* with protruding buttocks. (*pugiit, turirit, duriri, burang-it*) **agburiri.** *v.* to stoop in order to lift; protrude the buttocks. **ipaburiri.** *v.* to give away for free.

buririnték: *n.* a variety of rice with speckled hull.

burís: *n.* diarrhea, loose bowels. **agburis.** *v.* to have diarrhea. **makapaburis.** *a.* causing diarrhea. (*agtakki, agbayangubong*) [Bon. *poyok, ógos, ogyok,* Kal. *koyas,* Knk. *pog-úy,* Kpm. *tílis,* Png. *mantai, empatelo,* Tag. *kursó, bululós*]

burisangsáng: *n.* brown sugar with clods in it.

buritekték: *a.* multicolor, variegated. **bumuritektek.** *v.* to smile or laugh by tickling. **buritekteken.** *v.* to be tickled. [Tag. *makulay*]

buritiktík: *n.* kind of card game.

buritrít: naburitrit. *a.* overturned, capsized. (*burayray*)

burítse: see *tsetse buritse.*

bórlas: (Sp. *borla:* tassel) *n.* bangs; tuft; crest of feathers.

burlés: (Eng.) *a.* burlesque; *n.* striptease. **agburles.** *v.* to perform a striptease.

búrley: *n.* variety of tobacco.

burnabó: *n.* jack of all trades; one well versed in many things.

burnáy: *n.* a kind of deep jar. **iburnay.** *v.* to pour something into a *burnay.* [Tag. *tapayan*]

burníl: *n.* road roller; obese person.

burnít: makiburnit. *v.* to share (goods); attend a banquet. **burnitan.** *n.* banquet. **agpaburnit.** *v.* to give a banquet.

burnók: agburnok. *v.* to abound. **burnokan.** *v.* to release all at once; let out string in a kite. **naburnok.** *a.* abundant, plentiful (food at meals). **kinaburnok.** *n.* plentifulness. **iburnok.** *v.* to do without reservation. **Burnokam ta ullawmo.** Slacken your kite. [Tag. *saganà* (abundant)]

burnót: burnuten. *v.* to pull (weeds, hair, etc.); snatch out of someone's hands; rob. (*gurnot*)

búro₁: *n.* food preserved in salt, (meat, fruits, etc.). **agburo.** *v.* to make *buro.* **buruen.** *v.* to preserve something in salt. [Kal. *ilasilan,* Tag. *buro*]

búro₂: (Eng.) *n.* bureau. [Tag. *kawanihan*]

buró: *n.* mistake; error in a game; stepping offsides in a game. **naburo.** *a.* mistaken. [Tag. *malî*]

buruáng: *var.* of *burruang:* unleash, release.

burúbor: *n.* creek; gorge; sound of swollen streams. **bumanarubor.** *v.* to stampede. [Tag. *sapà* (stream)]

buróg: *n.* lazy fellow; bum.

boróka: (Sp. *bruja:* witch, *myth.*) *n.* organ-sucking vampire.

burokrásia: (Sp. *burocracia*) *n.* bureaucracy.

buróna: *n.* hide-and-seek game (*binnatugan*). **agburona.** *n.* to play hide-and-seek.

búrong: bumurong. *v.* to miscarry; fail; suffer a casualty. **di bumurong.** *exp.* without fail; certain, sure.

buróng: agburong. *v.* to be responsible for the preparation of. **burong-burong.** *n.* gatherings, celebrations.

buróngko: *n.* quarrel, fight, brawl; tantrum. **agburongko.** *v.* to quarrel; fight; brawl; tantrum.

burraráwit: *n.* long bamboo branch. (*bullawit*)

burráwit: see *burrarawit.*

búrro: (Sp. *burro:* donkey) *n.* donkey; kind of card game; error in a game. **naburro.** *a.* mistaken. **agburro.** *v.* to commit a mistake in a game. **burrista.** *n.* player of the *burro* card game.

burruáng: burruangan. *v.* to open; release. **ipaburruang.** *v.* to have something opened or

released. **Kellaat a maiburruang ti ridaw sa naibel-a dagiti polis.** The door suddenly opened and the police spewed in.
burruát: *var.* of *burruáng*.
burrúong: agburruong. *v.* to drink to excess an unalcoholic beverage. **Agannadkayo no puro wiski ti pagburburruonganyo.** Be careful if you are drinking pure whisky.
burrós: *n.* young *kappi* crab.
bursí: *n.* shade; color. (*maris*) **naburbi.** *a.* very colorful; multicolored. [Tag. *kulay*]
bursián: *n.* the *apta* fish found in rivers.
bursigí: (Sp. *borceguí*: half-boot) *n.* half-boot; shoe with laces.
bursók: maburbok. *v.* to be well filled (ears of sorghum). (*messek*)
burták: burburtak. *n.* Bidens pilosa plant, eaten to cure goiters due to its high iodine content.
burtiá: burburtia. *n.* riddle; puzzle; mystery. **binnurtiaan.** *n.* game of riddles. **binnurtia.** *n.* game of mutual riddles, riddle contest. [Kpm., Tag. *búgtong*]
burtóng: *n.* smallpox; *a.* pock-marked. **agburtong.** *v.* to have smallpox. **burtongan.** *a.* pock-marked. [Bon. *bolattong*, Kal. *toku*, Knk. *bultóng*, Tag. *bulutong*]
burwáng: *n.* sandbar; see also *burruang*: release, unleash. **namurwang.** *a.* having formed a sandbar.
bus: (Eng.) *n.* bus. **agbus.** *v.* to ride the bus.
busá: *n.* cataract of the eye. (*boskaw*)
buság: (*reg.*) *n.* eldest born in a family (*inauna*). [Tag. *panganay*]
búsak: nabusak. *a.* cracked, split (wood). **nagbusak.** *a.* with groups of three stripes with the middle stripe being darker than the other two; *opp.* *nagkiday*. **busaken.** *v.* to crack; split; halve. [Tag. *biyák*]
busál: (Sp. *bozal*: muzzle) *n.* muzzle. (*dangal*, *padun*; *sungo*) **busalan.** *v.* to put a muzzle on. **No ditayo agkuti, mabusalanton ti ngiwat dagiti napanglaw iti agnanayon.** If we don't act, the mouths of the poor will be muzzled forever.
busáli: *n.* boil, furuncle. (*lettég*) **agbusali.** *v.* to have boils. [Tag. *pigsá*]
busangél: *var.* of *busanger*: mean person.
busangér: *n.* mean, cruel person. (*naúyong*)
Busao: *n.* ethnic group living between Abra and Ilocos Sur in the mountain of *Siguey*.
busasáw: ibusasaw. *v.* to utter; voice out; tell.
busasót: *n.* loudmouthed; braggart; loquacious. **agbusasot.** *v.* to gossip. **binnusasot.** *n.* a card game similar to Old Maid, but using a withdrawn jack.

búsat: *n.* first sale of the day or of the product.
busatan. *n.* first buyer (*buena mano*); *v.* do for the first time; pioneer; devirginize a girl.
busatsát: *n.* gossip. (*tsismis, sayanguseng*)
busbús₁: busbusen. *v.* to use up (*ibús*); spend; invest. **mabusbusan.** *a.* consumed, used up, exhausted. **managbusbus.** *a.* spendthrift; extravagant. **Sangariwriw a pisos ti nabusbosmi iti dayta.** We spent a million pesos for that. [Tag. *gastá* (Sp.)]
busbús₂: busbusen. *v.* to loosen, slacken. **mabusbus.** *v.* to become loose, slack. [Tag. *luwág*]
búsel₁: *n.* flower bud of pistillate flowers; young squash, coconut, etc; raised belly button. **agbusel.** *v.* to bud; (*fig.*) develop. **bumusel.** *v.* to be inflamed (eyes). **kaibbusel.** *n.* newly formed bud. **panagbubusel.** *n.* season when budding occurs. **sinanbusel.** *n.* gourd, dry shell of fruits; *a.* resembling a bud. **Nupay ubingka iti tawenmo, saanka laeng a busel no di ket nagukradkan a sabong.** Although you are young, you are no longer a bud, but rather an opened flower. [Tag. *buko*]
búsel₂: buselbusel. *n.* a kind of tree with good timber.
bóses: (Sp. *voz*: voice) *n.* voice (*timek*); part (in a musical piece). [Tag. *tinig*]
busí₁: *n.* popped corn or rice formed into sugar balls. **agbusi, bumusi.** *v.* to pop corn or rice; to crack open (skin of beans when boiled); spit out (words out of mouth). **pabusien.** *v.* to cook by popping. **Nagbusi ti ngiwatna.** His mouth popped (denotes loquacity). **Agbusbusi ti bitukana.** *exp.* referring to someone with misgivings (*lit*: his stomach is popping). [Tag. *busá*]
busí₂: busbusi. *n.* a kind of herb with greenish white flowers, *Sphaeranthus africanus*.
busigít: *n.* hemorrhoids (*almoranas*); anus; *a.* scarred. **agbusigit.** *v.* to have hemorrhoids; scar; deform. **nabusigit.** *a.* scarred, deformed. [Tag. *almoranas* (Sp.)]
busílag: *var.* of *busílak*.
busílak: *n.* a kind of large tree. **busbusilak.** *n.* a white flowered shrub.
busilinggí: *n.* a variety of awned early rice with red kernel.
busína: (Sp. *bocina*: horn) *n.* horn (of a car). **agbusina.** *v.* to blow the horn (of a car). **businaan.** *v.* to blow the horn for (to call attention). [Kal. *busila*]
busingár: *a.* scarred; puckered; popped; with protruding lips; with flared nostrils. **agbusingar.** *v.* to pucker up; burst open; flare (nostrils). **pagbusingaren.** *v.* to pucker up. **Indeppelna ti busingar a subsubna iti lapayagko.**

He pressed his flaring snout into my ear. [Tag. *ngiwî*]

bósio: (Sp. *bocio*: goiter) *n*. goiter. [Knk. *ákak*, *baséy*, *buséy*, Kal. *bikkok*, Tag. *bosyò*]

busísaw: *var*. of *basisaw*: bladder.

busiséra: **nagbusisera**. *a*. fastidious; unruly (child).

busísi: (Tag. *busisì*) *a*. fastidious; meticulous. **busisien**. *v*. to make a fuss about, be fastidious about. **Busisienna amin a babassit ken awan kuentana a banag.** She makes a fuss about everything little and unimportant.

busitsít: see *pussuak*: to bubble.

buskáw: see *busa*: cataract of the eye.

busláyog: *n*. testicle. (*ukel-ukel*, *lateg*)

buslíg: *n*. water chestnut; *Eleocharis sp*; edible stems rising from a bulb. (*apulig*)

busló₁: **bubuslo**. *n*. a kind of large marine fish; (*coll*.) crybaby.

busló₂: *n*. variety of awned rice with elongated spikes.

buslóg: **nabuslog**. *a*. robust; fast-growing. **buslogan**. *n*. puffer fish.

buslón: **nabuslon**. *a*. wasteful, spendthrift; generous, liberal; abundant; excessive. **agbuslon**. *v*. to waste, use more than necessary. **buslonen**. *v*. to be generous; wasteful. **No ayat ti buslonen, no sapulen awanen.** *exp*. Love vanishes when ones loves to excess.

busnág: *n*. light complexion. (*púdaw*) **nabusnag**. *a*. light-colored (skin). **pamusnagen**. *a*. rather light complexioned. **Kayumanggi ti kudilna ngem pinabusnag ti lawag ti silaw iti ngatuen ti entablado.** Her skin is brown but the light from above the stage made it fair. [Tag. *maputî*]

busnáy: (*obs*.) **busnayan**. *v*. to agree to go someplace.

busnóy: **nabusnoy**. *a*. abundant, plentiful.

busngál: *n*. wedge for disjointing (*tingal*). [Tag. *kalang* (Sp.)]

busngót: *n*. mauling, thrashing. **busngoten**. *v*. to maul, thrash, batter. [Tag. *bugbóg*]

búso: (Sp. *buzo*: diver) *n*. sea diver with helmet.

busól: *n*. mountain savage; mean person.

busón: (Sp. *buzón*: mailbox) **ibuson**. *v*. to mail letters. **maibuson**. *v*. to be mailed. **pagbusonan**. *n*. mailbox.

busóng: (*obs*.) **mabusong**. *v*. to suffer a curse; turn bad.

búsor: **kabusor**. *n*. enemy. (*saranget*) **agbusor**. *v*. to cause trouble; oppose. **busuren**. *v*. to oppose; war against; disagree; repudiate. **bumusor**. *v*. to oppose; revolt. **busoran**. *n*. a girder supporting floor joists. **agbinnusor**. *v*. to be at odds with one another. **managbusor**. *a*. rebellious; persistent; prone to disagreeing. **Kabusorda unay ti alingasaw ti magustuantayo a sidaen.** They are really offended by the fumes of what we like to eat. [Bon. *bósol*, Knk. *bóso*, Png. *bosól*, Tag. *tunggalî*, *laban*]

busóran: *n*. girder made of timber or heavy bamboo to support the floor joists.

búsoy: *a*. pampered; spoiled. **ibusoy**. *v*. to pamper.

bus-óy: **agpabus-oy**. *v*. to share; let out (feelings, words); give out freely; give way (to cars on the freeway); consent to, allow; grant. **ipabus-oy**. *v*. to grant, consent to (*anamong*); permit (*palubos*). **managpabus-oy**. *v*. generous, prone to sharing. **agpinnabus-oy**. *v*. to tolerate one another. **kinamanagpabus-oy**. *n*. generosity. **Pabus-oyem ti riknam.** Let out your feelings.

bussuág: *n*. water and rice thrown out from the pot when boiling; volcano debris. **agbussuag**. *v*. to overflow (boiling rice). **agibussuag**. *v*. to eject, spit out (volcano lava, etc.)

bussuáng: **bussuangan**. *v*. to release; liberate; let go. (*burruang*)

bussóg₁: *n*. state of being full (from eating); *a*. inflated. **agbussog**. *v*. to fill oneself when eating. **bubussogan**. *n*. appetite; part of a flank of a quadruped that bulges when the animal is satiated. **nabsog**. *a*. full (after eating); satisfied, convinced. **bumsog**. *v*. to swell; increase in volume. **agbubussog**. *a*. with a pot belly (children). **makabsog**. *v*. able to fill (satisfy hunger); *n*. a variety of awned early rice. **pabussugen**. *v*. to inflate. **pabpabussog**. *n*. something that becomes inflated when blown up. [Ibg. *battúg*, Ivt. *absuy*, Kal. *lassug*, Knk. *bisták*, Png. *napsel*, Tag. *busóg*]

bussóg₂: **pabpabussog**. *n*. a kind of herb with yellowish flowers, *Physalis angulata*.

bussúot: (f. *bisót*) *n*. the sound of a fart. (*uttot*) **bumsuut**. *v*. to break wind. [Tag. *utót*]

bústo: (Sp. *busto*: bust) *n*. bust.

bustón: *n*. metal heel clip.

bóta: **botabota**. *n*. a kind of elongated marine fish.

buták: see *maldit*: imprint; print.

butáka: (Sp. *butaca*: armchair) *n*. armchair; orchestra seat or section of a theater.

butákal: *n*. bamboo offshoot; slender twigs of bamboo not suitable for construction.

butakták: *n*. exposé; divulging. **maibutaktak**. *v*. to be spread, divulged; to be exposed. **ibutaktak**. *v*. to expose; divulge. [Tag. *siwalat*]

butál: *n*. loose change; small change; excess of round numbers; small hidden cost. **Adda ngamin butal dagiti presio ti tagilako.**

There's a small excess fee in the prices of the merchandise.

botánika: (Sp. *botánica*: botany) *n.* botany.

botaniko. *n.* botanist; *a.* botanical.

botánte: (Sp. *votante*: voter) *n.* voter, elector.

butáng: butangen. *v.* to attack; beat up; gang up on. [Tag. *upak*]

butangéro: (f. *butáng*) *n.* tough guy; gangster; bully.

butárga: (Sp. *botarga*: loose breeches) *n.* trousers; pants; jeans. (*pantalon*)

bótas: (Sp. *botas*: boots) *n.* boots. **agbotas.** *v.* to wear boots.

butáw: *n.* hole. (*abut*; *abbutaw*) **butawan.** *v.* to perforate; make a hole in. [Knk. *gáladek*, *gádek*, Tag. *butas*; *butaw* = membership fee]

butawtáw: *n.* puncture. **butawtawen.** *v.* to put a hole in, puncture, perforate. **Nasken nga umdas ti kadakkel ti butawtaw ti balsa tapno lumned iti lima a minuto.** The puncture must be big enough so the raft will sink in five minutes. [Tag. *butas*]

butáy: *n.* coarse rice; granule of badly ground flour; additional free item asked for when purchasing. **binutay.** *n.* pulverized or powdered rice. **nabutay.** *a.* with coarse particles (said of pulverized grains). [Tag. *butil*]

butáyong: *n.* spathe of the coco palm.

butbút₁: *n.* hole, puncture. (*butaw*) *a.* full of holes, holy; with stuffing showing. **butbut ti bolsa.** *n.* hole in the pocket (referring to someone who spends a lot of money). **parabutbut ti tugaw.** *n.* wallflower (someone who remains seated the entire time at a dance). **Agbutbut iti tugaw.** *exp.* He is stuck to the chair (said of 'wallflowers' at a dance, etc.). **butbutan.** *v.* to pierce; perforate. [Tag. *butas*]

butbút₂: butbuten. *v.* to pick cotton.

bóte: (Sp. *bote*: bottle) *n.* bottle; can of sheet metal; small boat. **agbote.** *v.* to feed from a bottle. **panagbote.** *n.* bottle feeding.

búteg: *n.* snot, nasal mucus. **agbuteg.** *v.* to snivel; to discharge nasal mucus. **marabuteg.** *n.* young fruit; young, tender meat of the coconut; young betel nut. *a.* like nasal mucus. **Agbutbuteg pay laeng.** *exp.* referring to someone immature or very young (*lit*: still snotty). [Bon. *saleysey*, Kal. *angod*, Knk. *múteg*, Kpm. *kulangot*, Png. *motég*, Tag. *uhog*]

botélia: (Sp. *botella*: bottle) *n.* bottle. **ibotelia.** *v.* to bottle. **ipabotelia.** *v.* to have something bottled. **naibotelia.** *a.* bottled, placed in a bottle. **boteliado.** *a.* bottled. [Knk. *palanggó*, Tag. *botelya*]

buténg: *n.* fear. (*amak*) **agbuteng.** *v.* to be afraid, alarmed. **butbuteng.** *n.* fear, alarm. **butbu-**

tengen. *v.* to frighten, scare. **ibutngan.** *v.* to fear for (another's safety). **mabuteng.** *v.* to be afraid; timid; panicky. **managbutbuteng.** *a.* fearful; cowardly. **mapabutngan.** *v.* to be startled; frightened. **nakabutbuteng.** *a.* scary, frightening, fearful. **kabuteng.** *v.* to be afraid of; dread. **kabut(e)ngan.** *a.* the most fearful. **pamut(e)ngan.** *n.* reason for frightening. **pamutbuteng.** *n.* threat. **Awan ti rumbeng a pagbutnganyo.** There is nothing you should be afraid of. **Kabutengtayo ti saantayo nga ammo.** We fear what we do not know. [Ibg. *assíng*, Ivt. *amuq*, Kal. *umugyat*, Knk. *egyát*, Png. *takót*, Kpm., Tag. *takot*]

botéte: (Tag. *butete*) *n.* puffer fish of the *Tetraodontidae* family.

butiák: *n.* incision. **butiakan.** *v.* to open the belly; operate on; make an incision. [Tag. *tistís*]

bútig: *n.* a kind of wart on the face. [Tag. *kulugó*]

butígi: *n.* pumice.

butík: *n.* spots. (*batek*) **butikbutik(an).** *a.* spotted, speckled, marbled.

botíka: (Sp. *botica*: drugstore) *n.* drugstore.

butikangkáng: *a.* oversatiated, full (with food). (*bussog*)

botikário: (Sp. *boticario*: apothecary) *n.* druggist; chemist.

botikéro: (f. *botika* + *-ero* agentive suffix) *n.* pharmacist, druggist.

botikín: (Sp. *botiquín*: medicine chest) *n.* medicine chest in a home; small dispensary.

butiktík: agbutiktik. *v.* to be overcrowded; to be gorged. **nabutiktik.** *a.* overcrowded, gorged.

butíl: *n.* grain of rice; lowermost coin of the *saliona* game.

butiláw: *n.* fallen womb, protrusion of the uterus into the vagina, prolapsed uterus. **agbutilaw.** *v.* to suffer from a prolapsed uterus. [Bon. *bolágay*, *botbotlog*, Tag. *buwà*, Bon. *bottiláw* = prolapsed rectum]

butillóg: (*coll.*) *n.* testicles (*láteg*). [Knk. *butillog* = false, untrue]

butinggán: *n.* *Lycopersicum esculentum*: wild tomato; a variety of awned late rice.

butíngting: agbutingting. *v.* to toy with in order to fix. (*kutingting*)

bútir: *n.* a sweet potato-like tuber of the *gabi* plant.

butiróg: (*coll.*) *n.* boy; guy; tough guy; see *butillóg*.

butít: *n.* child with protruding abdomen from intestinal worms, nickname for child who eats much. **marabutit.** *n.* newborn mouse; small mouse. (*utot*)

butíti: *n.* a kind of fat marine fish covered with spines on the back with poisonous gall, puffer fish; short, big-bellied person. **Kasla la ngaruden butiti ti langana, lamut pay la ti adda iti ulona.** He looks like a puffer fish, food is the only thing on his mind. [Tag. *botete*]

botítos: (Sp. *botito*) *n*. ladies' gaiters, high boots.

butittít: **agbutittit**. *v*. to eat little by little. **mamutittit.** *v*. to be oversatiated; to overeat.

butnég: *n*. a variety of small banana. **kabutnegan.** *n*. field of *butneg* banana trees.

butnéng: *var*. of *butneg*.

butnóng: *n*. alternative name for the *biknong* tree.

búto: *n*. penis; tongue of a bell; either of the two pins of the upper beam of the lathe of the loom. **butobuto.** *a*. with uncovered genitals. **pabutuan.** *v*. to kick someone in the penis. [Bon. *lósi, láday, óti,* Ibg. *usin,* Ivt. *gutay,* Knk. *lúsi, ladáy, ayokán,* Kpm. *bútuq,* Png. *útin,* Tag. *titi* (penis); Knk. *búto* = female genitalia]

butuág: *a*. tilted; upturned. **butuagen.** *v*. to tilt; upturn. **butuabutuag.** *n*. rocking chair. **Nabutuag ti kidayna.** Her eyebrow raised. [Tag. *tiwarík*]

butuán: *n*. callous; long-tailed fish. **butuabutuan.** *a*. full of calluses. **Butuabutuan dagiti rungbeb a ramayna.** His short fingers have many calluses. [Tag. *kalyó* (Sp.)]

butúbot₁: *a*. chubby; having round and fleshy buttocks (*lukmeg*); (*coll*.) short person.

butúbot₂: *n*. a kind of freshwater fish, *Bunaka pinguis*.

butúbot₃: *n*. hole. (*abut*) **butubutan.** *v*. to make a hole in; perforate. [Tag. *butas*]

butóg: (*coll*.) *n*. tough guy. (*butangero*)

bútol: *n*. pad on the feet of fowl; snag in ropes. **butolbutol.** *v*. with plenty of snags.

butól: *n*. plague; syphilis; leprosy; gonorrhea; buboes.

botónes: (Sp. *botón*: button) *n*. button. **agbotones, ibotones.** *v*. to button (clothes). **botbotones.** *n*. a kind of ornamental herb. [Bon. *pot-ik,* Kal. *byatulis, besulit, kuttitis*]

bútong: **butongen.** *v*. to combine; unite in; join; crowd around. **pagbubutongan.** *v*. to do together for one common purpose; *n*. place where work is done together.

bótos: (Sp. *voto*) **agbotos, bumotos.** *v*. to vote. **ibotos.** *v*. to vote for. **panagbobotos.** *n*. election time. **mabotosan.** *v*. to be elected. (*pili*) **Iti yaasideg ti panagbubutos, inaramid dagiti agsalip ti ammoda a wagas a pangabakanda.** When election time drew near, the competitors did the things they knew that would help them win. [Tag. *boto*]

bútot: (*obs*.) *a*. bucolic, rustic. (*taga-away*)

butóy: *n*. calf of the leg (*gurong*). [Tag. *kalamnán ng bintí*]

bútsi: (Ch.) *n*. sesame rice cake filled with bean paste.

butsíti: *a*. proud; arrogant; show-off.

buttáw: *a*. pierced, perforated; no longer a virgin (said of girls). **nabuttawan.** *a*. perforated. **bubuttawan.** *n*. depression above both clavicles. **ipabuttaw.** *v*. to have something pierced. **pagbuttaw.** *n*. hole puncher, instrument for perforating. **Aglatlati ken buttabuttaw ti atepda.** Their roof is rusting and full of holes.

buttiák: *n*. incision; stab in the belly. **buttiakan.** *v*. to operate; cut open the abdomen (Caesarian operation); cut open, slash. **nabuttiakan.** *a*. with a wounded abdomen.

buttikí: *n*. cowry shell.

buttióg: *a*. having a potbelly, beer belly (males); species of fat freshwater fish with gold scales. **mamagbuttiog.** *v*. to cause someone to become fat in the stomach. **Limtaw ti buttiogna iti turikturikan a kamisetana.** His large potbelly appeared through his spotted shirt. **Agbalin a taba a mamagbutiog kenka.** It will become fat that will cause you to have a big stomach. [Knk. *bulidkéng*]

buttó₁: *n*. tendon.

buttó₂: **bumto.** *v*. to be ready to be born.

buttó₃: **buttuan.** *n*. a kind of freshwater fish with a long tail and large eyes.

buttó₄: **butto-butto.** *n*. flower cluster of the breadfruit.

buttuág: **agbuttuag.** *v*. to seesaw, rock; tilt; upturn. **butuabuttuag.** *n*. rocking chair. *var*. of *battuag*.

buttuán: *n*. wart; corn on the foot; callus; freshwater fish resembling the *talakitok* with a long tail. **agbuttuan.** *v*. to have a wart or corn. **buttubuttuan.** *n*. unripe breadfruit.

buttúon: *n*. load; burden; responsibility. **butuonan.** *v*. to overload; burden; press down.

buttúor: **mabtuor.** *v*. to move suddenly; startle. **buttuoren.** *v*. to announce, do, etc. at once. **nabtuor.** *a*. badly roasted (raw meat inside).

buttót: *n*. a kind of gallinule; person excused from doing housework.

bóya: (Sp. *boya*: buoy) *n*. buoy, floating device.

búya: *n*. spectacle, performance, entertainment; appearance; scenery; face. **pabuya.** *n*. performance, show; appearance. **agbuya.** *v*. to watch, look at; see a show; watch television; *n*. spectators; audience. **agbuybuya.** *n*. spectator. **buyaen.** *v*. to watch; look at; contemplate. **ipabuya.** *v*. to show (a play, performance).

makapagbuya. *v.* to be able to watch (a performance). **pamuyaan.** *n.* the way a person looks. **pagpabuyaan.** *n.* theater; stage. **Awan ti buyana.** *exp.* She is not good looking. **Kaanonto nga ibuyanak iti sine?** When are you going to take me to see a movie? [Ivt. *talamad*, Png. *bántag, bantáy*, Tag. *noód*]

buyág: *a.* lean and unprofitable (said of harvest, catch, etc.).

buyangyáng: *a.* exposed and unprotected (genitals). (*lukais*)

buyasyás: *n.* kind of brown mantislike insect, named after its night song.

buyát: *n.* spilled or poured water; water thrown away. **ibuyat.** *v.* to pour out. **maibuyat.** *v.* to spill, pour out accidentally. **agbuyat.** *v.* to pour; **bumuyat.** *v.* to take a short bath; shower. **Nagbuyat, nagsabon, sa nagbuyat laeng.** He poured the water, soaped himself, then poured again. **Naibuyat ti tudo.** It was pouring rain. [Knk. *suyát*, Tag. *buhos*]

buyáyong: ibuyayong. *v.* to pour out; spill. **maibuyayong.** *v.* to spill out suddenly; to be spilled, poured out. [Tag. *buhos*]

buybúy₁: ibuybuy. *v.* to recriminate; expose; divulge. **Pagbusingaren ti lawwalawwa ti kerretna ket agpabuyboy iti napino a saput a paglibasanna.** The spider puckers his anus and stealthily exposes a fine web. [Tag. *siwalat*]

buybúy₂: *n.* fringe; shoot, sprout; a type of coarse grass, *Thysanolaena maxima*; broom made out of *buybuy*. **agpabuybuy** (*obs.*) *v.* to sow at weeding time. **buybuyan.** *a.* with fringes.

buybúy₃: *n.* kind of bamboo fish trap.

buyúbuy: *n.* a kind of coconut shell cup made of half a coconut shell (*sabut, sudo, ungot*). **agbuyubuy.** *v.* to drink out of a coconut shell cup. [Bon. *buyuboy* = bulging buttocks)]

búyog: *n.* empathy. **bumuyog.** *v.* to follow; agree. **buyogan.** *v.* to sympathize with; do along with (singing while dancing, etc.), accompany. **buyugen.** *v.* to follow; agree with, consent; comply. **maibuyog.** *v.* to have empathy for; be moved, touched, impressed. **nabuyogan.** *a.* accompanied by. **Maulawak iti sang-awna, ngem buybuyogak lattan.** I am dizzy from his breath, but I just go along with him anyway.

buyók₁: *n.* smell of rotten flesh; fetid smell. **nabuyok.** *a.* fetid, smelling, stinking. **Dagiti tao a saan a mangayat ti nakayanakanna a pagsasao ket nabuybuyok pay ngem iti nalaes nga ikan.** People who do not love their native language are more rotten than spoiled fish. [Kal. *buyok*, Tag. *baho*]

buyók₂: buybuyok. *n.* a blue-flowered, spiked herb, *Parosela glandulosa.* **binnuyok.** *n.* a variety of the *lipay* game.

búyon₁: *n.* divination; magic charm. **agbuyon.** *v.* to practice divination; to tell a fortune. **ipabuyon.** *v.* to have someone find something out through divination. **mammuyon.** *n.* one who practices divination, fortune teller. [Tag. *hulà*]

búyon₂: buyunen. *v.* to sell out; buy up (everything).

buy-óng: *n.* large belly (said of women only; for men: *buttióg*) **buy-ongan.** *a.* big bellied. [Tag. *buyón*]

búyot: *n.* army; forces, troops; followers; attendants; companions. **agbuyot.** *v.* to accompany. **siiigam a buyot.** *n.* the armed forces. [Tag. *hukbó*]

buyyábo: *n.* heaving; seesaw motion, rocking motion; (*fig.*) thrill. **agbuyyabo.** *v.* to rock, seesaw; heave.

brá: (Eng.) *n.* bra, brassiere. **agbra.** *v.* to wear a bra. **nakabra.** *a.* having a bra on.

brábo: (*coll.*, Sp. *bravo*: brave, valiant, manly) **nabrabo.** *a.* courageous (with women), not shy; brave. **Kayatna koma tay agbalin a nabrabo.** He wants to become valiant.

bráha: (Sp. *baraja*: deck) *n.* deck of cards. [Kal. *lipis*, Tag. *baraha*]

brása: (Sp. *braza*: fathom; brace) *n.* fathom; strap to a post.

bráso: (Sp. *brazo*: arm) *n.* arm. (*takkiag*) **nabraso.** *a.* having strong arms. **braso-de-Mercedes.** *n.* type of pastry. [Tag. *bisig*]

bréa: (Sp. *brea*: tar) *n.* resin; white paste used for repairing holes in pottery; sealing wax; red seal of a ballot box. **breaan.** *v.* to apply *brea* to.

brebiario: (Sp. *breviario*) *n.* breviary.

briát: mabriat. *v.* to be torn open; dislocated; ripped. **briaten.** *v.* to rip, tear open; split apart. **Kasla mabriat ti bibigna iti kalawa ti isemna.** Her lips seem to split from the width of her smile. [Tag. *buká*]

brigáda: (Sp.) *n.* brigade.

briliánte: (Sp. *brillante*: brilliant) *n.* diamond; *a.* brilliant; glossy.

bríndis: (Sp. *brindis*: toast, dedication) **agbrindis.** *v.* to throw candy, money, etc. to the crowd. **maibrindis.** *v.* to scatter; disperse.

brío: (Sp. *brío*: vigor) *n.* vigor, animation; spiritedness.

Británia: (Sp. *Bretaña*: Britain) *n.* Britain.

brúas: (Sp. *broa*: biscuit) *n.* ladyfinger cookie.

brúha: (Sp. *bruja*: witch) *n.* witch; sorceress; evil woman; (*coll.*) obstinate girl.

brúhula: (Sp. *brújula*: magnetic needle; compass) *n.* dial (of a clock); magnetic needle, compass.

brómo: (Sp.) *n.* bromine.

bromúro: (Sp.) *n.* bromide.

brónse: (Sp. *bronce*) *n.* bronze.

brúsko: (Sp. *brusco*: brusque) *a.* brusque; rude; rough, coarse in manner.

brúto: (Sp. *bruto*: brute) *a.* brute; ferocious. (*wagnet*; *ranggas*; *wagteng*) **brutos.** *n.* gross weight.

brútsa: (Sp. *brocha*: brush) *n.* painter's brush; (*coll.*) mustache; cunnilingus, oral sex. **brutsaen.** *v.* to brush; perform cunnilingus.

D

-da₁: Enclitic third person ergative and absolutive plural pronoun: they, they are; their: Note that this form may also be used in the second person singular to show extreme respect. **Babbaida.** They are girls. **Napandan.** They went already. **'diay asoda.** Their dog. **Kayatdaka.** They like you. **isuda.** third person plural, nonenclitic pronoun, they. [Png. *da/ra, ira,* Tag. *silá; nilá*]

-da₂: Enclitic ergative pronoun used in double enclitic pronoun constructions to designate both a third person plural agent, or a first person plural agent: **Kayatdaka.** They like you; We like you. **Patayendakayonto.** They/We will kill you. [Tag. *nilá* (3p), *namin* (1p exclusive), *natin* (1p inclusive)]

da₁: *art.* Plural of the personal article *ni.* **ni Juan.** John. **da Juan.** John and company. **da Juan ken Erlinda.** John and Erlinda; *adv.* confirmatory particle. [Tag. *siná; niná*]

da₂: *part.* confirmatory particle. **Iyegmo man da.** Bring it here quick. **da man.** let me be, leave me. **Da man ta siak ti agtugaw.** Move away, I will sit (there).

dáak: *n.* spit, spittle. (*sarkak, tupra*) **agdaak.** *v.* to spit, expectorate. [Tag. *dahak* (clear throat of phlegm)]

dáal: *adv.* inasmuch as.

dáan₁: *a.* old, ancient; obsolete; stale; *n. Albizzia procera* plant. **dumaan.** *v.* to get old, be old. (things). **kadaanan.** *a.* old-fashioned; outdated; antique. **Idi kadaanan nga aldaw.** In the olden days. [Ibg. *dána,* Ivt. *adan,* Kal. *chachaan,* Kpm. *laun,* Png. *dáan,* Tag. *lumà*]

dáan₂: **madadaan, sidadaan.** *a.* ready, prepared. **masindadaan.** *v.* to be ready; be willing; assured. **daanan.** *v.* to wait for; drop by. **padpadaanan.** *v.* to expect; wait for. **agpapan iti madaan.** from now on. **di makapakpakadaan.** *a.* unexpectedly; suddenly. **mapadaanan.** *v.* to be aware of; be able to discern. **Madadaanak a paikallaysa kenka uray dika ay-ayaten.** I am ready to marry her off to you although I do not love you. **Pinadpadaandaka manipud idi.** They waited for you since then. [Knk. *dadána,* Tag. *handâ* (prepared); *daán* = pass by]

dabiána: (Tag. also, *coll.*) *n.* stout girl. (*lukmeg*)

dabúg: **agdabugdabug.** *v.* to stomp the feet repeatedly.

dadáel: *n.* destruction, damage; deterioration; ruin. **nadadael.** *a.* broken, ruined, damaged, destroyed. **dadaelen.** *v.* to destroy, ruin; damage. **madadael.** *v.* to be destroyed, ruined. **makadadael.** *v.* destructive; injurious; dam-

aging. **dadaelen ti oras.** *v.* to waste time. [Ibg. *nadarel,* Ivt. *nararayaw,* Kpm. *síraq,* Png. *gebá, bagbág, aderal, atak-atak,* Tag. *walat, sirâ*]

dádag: *n.* ripening pods. **dumadag.** *v.* to mature, ripen (said of pods).

dádak: **nadadak.** *a.* wasteful, spendthrift. (*barayuboy*)

dadál: *var.* of *dedal*: thimble.

dadáli: *n.* a kind of elongated marine fish, *Psettodes erumei.*

dadanés: (f. *danes*) **idadanes.** *v.* to insult; belittle; be cruel to, mistreat. (*lupit*) **maidadanes.** *v.* to be insulted; despised; molested; enslaved; mistreated. **manangidadanes.** *a.* cruel, vicious; mistreating.

dadanúgen: (f. *danog*) *n.* variety of yellow fragrant banana.

dadáng: *n.* warmth of a fire; warming by a fire. **agdadang.** *v.* to go near a fire, go near the heat. **idadang.** *v.* to heat, warm at a fire. **indadang.** *a.* re-warmed (food) (*damdam; darang*). [Ibg. *daddang,* Ivt. *dangdangen,* Knk. *bánag, dangdang,* Kpm. *sálab,* Png. *dangdang,* Tag. *darang*]

dadaúlo: (f. *ulo*) *n.* leaders; heads; chiefs.

dadapílan: (f. *dapil*) *n.* sugar mill.

daddán: **madaddan.** *v.* to be habitual, customary; frequent. (*sarday; masansan; daraddan*) **daddanen.** *v.* to do frequently. [Tag. *dalás*]

daddúma: *n.* some; others. **idadduma.** *v.* to favor; prefer. (*kaykayat*) **maidadduma.** *v.* to be favored; preferred. **no dadduma.** once in a while, sometimes. (*pasaray*) **Nangngeg dagiti dadduma ket nagkakatawada.** A few of them heard and they laughed. [Tag. *ibá*]

dadí: *contr.* of *daydi,* remote past, singular demonstrative; that; (used with names) the late, deceased.

dádo: (Sp. *dado*: die) *n.* die, dice. **agdado.** *v.* to play dice; to throw the dice.

dadpúor: see *dappuor*: stumbling sound.

dadsúor: **madadsuor.** *v.* to fall to the ground with a thump.

daég: *n.* honor (*dayaw*); grace; beauty. (*darisay, libnos*) **nadaeg.** *a.* grand, stately, majestic, elegant, graceful, fine. **daegen.** *v.* to honor; excel, outdo (*artap, atiw, rimbaw, addag, saliw-an, aladag, abak*). **madaegan.** *v.* to be disturbed, confused, alarmed. **agdinnaeg.** *v.* to outdo each other. **pangpadaeg.** *n.* point of beauty, something that makes something else beautiful. [Tag. *gandá*]

dáel: *adv.* it is well that (*imbag ta*); scarcely; see also *dadael.*

daép: *n.* fetid smell. **agdaep.** *v.* to smell bad; to be fetid. **daepen.** *a.* fetid, reeking (*bangsit*). [Tag. *bahò*]

daér: daeren. *v.* to do to the utmost; to overcome. **di madaeran.** *v.* to be unable to bear; be overwhelmed. **Dandani diak madaeran ti riknak.** I almost cannot bear my feelings. [Tag. *kaya*]

dáes: (*obs.*) *var.* of *dakes:* bad; wicked.

dága: (Sp. *daga:* dagger) *n.* dagger. [Tag. *patalím*]

dagá: *n.* soil, land, ground; Earth. **dagadaga.** *a.* with dirt on the skin. **dumaga.** *v.* to turn into soil (decaying matter). **ipadaga.** *v.* to plant cuttings; knock down violently, send to the ground. **kadadaga.** *n.* nature of the soil. **kadagaan.** *a.* fertile, productive (soil); suitable (climate). **naindagaan.** *a.* earthly; materialistic; worldly. **lubuag ti daga.** *n.* illegitimate child, bastard. **sangadagaan.** *n.* the whole earth. **Saanda a kadagaan ditoy.** *exp.* They are not accustomed to this place, They do not feel at home here. [Ibg. *devvún*, Ivt. *tanaq*, *takey*, Kal. *pita*, Kpm. *gabun*, Png. *dalín*, Tag. *lupà*]

dagáang: *n.* sultry weather. **agdagaang.** *v.* to feel sultry. **dumagaang.** *v.* to be sultry. **nadagaang.** *a.* sultry, very hot. **Nupay nadagaang, nakakaskasdaaw ti ulimek.** The cold is surprising in spite of the fact it is sultry. [Tag. *alinsangan*]

dagádag: idagadag. *v.* to suggest; urge, insist. (*deldel; ullok; singasing, dagdag*) **dagadagen.** *v.* to hurry up, hasten, speed, urge upon. **dumagadag.** *v.* to blaze, flame (*rasok; gil-ayab; rubrub; rangen*). [Tag. *giít*]

dágas: nadagas. *a.* slow, sluggish (*dúgos; buntog*). [Tag. *kupad*]

dagás: *a.* quickly. **dagasen.** *v.* to stop by for; stop by and pick up; drop by; fetch. (*daw-as*) **dumagas.** *v.* to make a brief stop when passing by, drop by. **idagas.** *v.* to deliver in passing. **Immayko indagas ti ginatangko a balut.** I came to drop by the duck eggs I bought. [Bon. *dag-os*, Tag. *daán* (drop by)]

dágaw: *n.* light-colored hair; striped shoat.

dagdág: dagdagen. *v.* to hurry, hasten, speed. (*dagadag; darasen*) **Ibagak nga agsakitak tapno madagdag ti yaayna.** I'll say I'm sick so he will come fast. [Tag. *apurá* (Sp.)]

dagél: dumagel. *v.* to get worse (sickness), increase in intensity. (*káro*) **idagel.** *v.* to make feel worse. **naidagel.** *a.* overwhelmed, burdened, crushed; bedridden. [Tag. *lalâ*]

dagém: *n.* pain; suffering; misery. **idagem** *v.* to do something intensely; attack, oppress; tire. [Tag. *lubhâ*]

dagensén: *n.* load; grief; burden; heartache. **dumagensen.** *v.* to oppress; weigh down. **Diakon kabaelan nga awiten ti dagensen ti konsiensiak.** I can no longer carry the burden of my conscience.

dági: dagidagi. *n.* hammock (*indayon*); improvised stretcher; sling for carrying things over the back.

dagidí: *dem.* Plural remote past demonstrative adjective: those (referring to objects with relevance long ago, deceased people, etc.) Singular is *daydi.* **Malagipmo dagidi panagsampedro ken panaglilinnemmengtayo idi ubbingtayo?** Do you remember playing *San Pedro* and hide-and-seek when we were young?

dagidiáy: *dem.* Plural demonstrative denoting objects far from both the speaker and hearer: those (far off). Singular is *daydiay.* [Png. *saráman*, Tag. *mga iyón*]

dagimesmés: dumagimesmes. *v.* to get soaked. (*daripespes; rusep*) **madagimesmes.** *v.* to be soaked, drenched.

dagínot: agdaginot. *v.* to be frugal, use sparingly. (*inut, salimetmet*)

daginsén: agdaginsen. *v.* to settle down due to weight. **daginsensen.** *v.* to squeeze, compress, press down. **idaginsen.** *v.* to jam, pack tightly, crowd.

dágir: see *padagir:* to offend, hurt the feelings of.

dagitá: *dem.* Plural demonstrative denoting objects near the addressee: those (near you). Singular is *dayta.* [Png. *sarátan*, Tag. *mga iyán*]

dagitáy: *dem.* Plural recent past demonstrative denoting objects with relevance to the recent past: those. Singular is *daytay.*

dagití: *art.* Plural article for common nouns: the Singular is *ti.* With the plural article marking, the plural noun does not have to appear in reduplicated plural form: **ti babai.** the girl. **dagiti bab(b)ai.** the girls. [Png. *saray*, Tag. *mga*]

dagitóy: *dem.* Plural demonstrative denoting objects near speaker: these. Singular is *daytoy.*

dagmél: nadagmel. *a.* stupid, dense, dull (*dugmél*). [Kal. *latuntu* (Sp.), Tag. *tangá*]

dagnáy: *n.* addition, increase. (*nayon*) **dagnayan.** *v.* to add to, augment.

dagó: *n.* class; classes. **dumago.** *v.* to attend class. (*adal*)

daguldól: idaguldol. *v.* to insist, press on; be persistent about. **daguldolen.** *v.* to insist. **madaguldol.** *v.* to be repetitive; to be redundant; insistent. (*dagullit*)

dagullít: *n.* repeater; *a.* repetitious; bothersome (due to repetitiousness) (*ulit*) **dagulliten.** *v.* to do often. **nadagullit.** *a.* overly persistent; *adv.* again. **madagdagulit.** *adv.* again and again; said of someone who keeps repeating the same thing over and over. [Tag. *kulít*]

dágum: *n.* needle. **dagumdagum.** *n.* sting of a bee, wasp, etc. **maradagum.** *n.* young pod of the cowpea. **Kasla adda naitudok a dagum iti barukongna.** It seemed like a pin stung his chest (deep emotion). [Ifg. *bílat*, Ivt. *rayem*, Ibg., Kal. *talud*, Knk. *dágum, alámid*, Png. *dágom*, Kpm., Tag. *karayom*]

dagúmpo: *n.* pile. (*penpen*) **maidagumpo.** *v.* to be piled up. **sangadagumpo.** *n.* one pile of, one stack of. **Nasangpetanna ti sangadagumpo a surat.** A stack of letters arrived for him. [Tag. *buntón, salansán*]

dágun: see *dagum:* needle. [Tag. *karayom*]

dagúon: *n.* heap; mound; pile. (*penpen, dagumpo*) **idaguon.** *v.* to pile up; heap. **sangadaguon.** *n.* one heap; one pile. [Tag. *buntón*]

dágup: *n.* total, sum; all. **dagupen.** *v.* to total, sum up; unite, combine. **dagup amin.** all. **dagup ti.** out of; very. **kadagupan.** *n.* total, sum; net result; summary; resume. [Png. *dágop*, Tag. *buô; lahát*]

dágus: *adv.* immediately, right away. **dagusen.** *v.* to do immediately. **Saan a nakasungbat a dagus.** He wasn't able to answer right away. [Tag. *agád; dagos* = sudden departure]

dagús: *n.* temporary lodging place (*sangbay, yan*); dormitory; hotel room. **agdagus.** *v.* to stay, lodge temporarily. **pagdagusen.** *v.* to let someone board. **pagdagusan.** *n.* boarding house; place to stay. **kadagusan.** *n.* fellow boarder. **makidagdagus.** *n.* boarder; lodger. **managpadagus.** *a.* hospitable, always offering a place to stay. **kinamanagpadagus.** *n.* hospitality. [Tag. *kasera* (Sp.)]

dagútay: **agdagutay.** *v.* to run, flow (mucus, saliva). (*uy-oy*)

daguyemyém: *n.* gloom; overcast weather. **nadaguyemyem.** *a.* cloudy, overcast, darkened (*ulep; langeb; alibuyong; kuyem; lulem*). [Tag. *kulimlím*]

dagsáng: **nadagsang.** *a.* sultry, warm. (*dagaang*)

dagsén: *n.* weight; burden; counterbalance; heaviness; gravity; importance. **idagsen.** *v.* to make heavier; stress, emphasize. **nadagsen.** *a.* heavy, burdensome; serious, grave; weighty, important; trustworthy. **agdadagsen.** *v.* to be indisposed; heavy with child. **agpadagsen.** *v.* to get heavier (by force). **makapadagsen.** *n.* burden. **padagsen.** *n.* weight; paperweight. **padagsenan.** *v.* to weigh down; oppress. **pa-**

dagsenen. *v.* to add more weight to, make something heavier. **dumagsen.** *v.* to become heavy; (*fig.*) to become burdensome, oppressive; worsen. **panagsenen.** *a.* somewhat heavy. [Ibg. *arammoq, mademmoq*, Bon., Itg. *dagsen*, Ivt. *marahmet*, Kal. *chegson*, Kpm. *mabáyat*, Png. *belát*, Tag. *bigát*]

dagyót: *var.* of *dugyót:* filthy, untidy, messy.

dái: (*obs.*) *n.* uncle, aunt, stepfather.

dáib: (Eng.) **dumaib.** *v.* to dive. (*bumátok*) **daiben.** *v.* to dive for, dive and get. [Tag. *sisid*]

dáig: *n.* tuberculosis, consumption. (*sárut*) **agdaig.** *v.* to have tuberculosis. [Tag. *tisis*]

daík: *n.* turtle egg. (*itlog ti pag-ong*)

dáing: (Tagalog also) *n.* salted and sundried fish. (*káring*) **daingen.** *v.* to salt and dry in the sun. [Ivt. *pawpaw*, Kal. *bilis*, Png. *daíng*]

daípit: *n.* narrow space between many things (people, buildings, etc.). **agdaipit.** *v.* to crowd, conglomerate, stick together. **idaipit.** *v.* to place in a crowd; place among many things.

dáir: *n.* antidote. (*suma*) **dairen.** *v.* to treat (animals who do not fatten).

dáit: *n.* sewing; manner of sewing; style of sewing. **agdait.** *v.* to sew. **daiten.** *v.* to sew something. **dadaiten.** *n.* cloth for sewing. **mannait.** *n.* sewer, seamstress, tailor. **nagdaitan.** *n.* seam. **pagdait.** *n.* needle; sewing thread (*sinulid*). **panait.** *n.* sewing thread. **pagdaitan.** *n.* sewing machine. **makidait.** *v.* to earn by sewing; to sew with another's machine. [Ibg. *dageq*, Ivt. *heneb*, Kal. *kibiton*, Kpm. *tayiq*, Bon., Png. *dait*, Tag. *tahî*; Tag. *daít* = put together, make objects touch]

dákal: **dinakal.** *n.* variety of awned rice.

dakámat: *n.* need (*masapol*); mention. **madakamat.** *v.* to need; be able to make use of; mention. **dakamaten.** *v.* to make use of; use; mention. [Tag. *banggít* (mention)]

dakamí: *pron.* First person exclusive plural pronoun, nonenclitic: We, but not you. (*sikamí*) The enclitic forms are -*kami* and -*mi*. [Png. *sikamí*, Tag. *kamí*]

dakáp: **dinakap.** *a.* pointed (spears). (*tirad, murdóng*)

dákar: **agdakar.** *v.* to cast a net. (*saruag*)

dakáwat: see *dakamat:* need.

dakáy₁: *n.* contraction of *dakayo:* you (plural or polite).

dakáy₂: *n.* animal copulation. **dakayan.** *v.* to leap (a female animal). (*dakep*)

dakayó: *pron.* 2nd person plural, or 2nd person polite nonenclitic pronoun. You guys, you (formal). Enclitic forms: ergative: -*yo*; absolutive: -*kayo*. [Png. *sikayó*, Tag. *kayó*]

dakáyos: *var.* of *dayákos.*

dakdák₁: (*obs.*) *n.* sod. **maidakdak.** *v.* to be brought ashore. **idakdak.** *v.* to wash ashore; dribble. **padakdak.** *n.* a kind of snare with noose for birds. **ipadakdak.** *v.* to set a trap, ensnare. [Tag. *sadsád*] **dakdák₂**: **dinakdakan.** *n.* native dish made of pork brains, tongue ears, and garlic.

dakép: *n.* copulation between animals (*iyot*). **agdakep.** *v.* to embrace; catch; copulate (animals). **dakpen.** *v.* to catch, seize, capture. **padakepan.** *v.* to copulate; breed.

dákes: *a.* bad; evil, wicked, immoral, wrong; unfit; annoying; injurious; incorrect; invalid, void. **dumakes.** *v.* to worsen; become serious. **padpadaksen.** *v.* to slander; bear false testimony against. **kadakes.** *n.* badness, the degree of badness. **kinadakes.** *n.* wickedness; immorality. **kadaksan.** *a.* worst. **panakésen.** *a.* somewhat bad. **makadakes.** *v.* to be harmful; cause trouble. **naindaksan.** *a.* vicious; evil. **pagdaksan.** *n.* trouble; disadvantage; calamity. **tagidaksen.** *v.* to take in a bad light. **ti pagdaksanna.** *exp.* the bad thing about it. **agpinnadakes.** *v.* to slander one another. **Adda dakesna?** Is there something wrong with it? **Ti makadakes.** The bad thing about it. **Awan met dakes nga ar-aramidenmi.** There is nothing wrong with what we are doing. [Ibg. *dákay*, Itg. *ul-úlay*, Ivt. *marahet*, Knk. *baség*, *kaláw*, *kalút*, Png. *ogés*, Kpm., Tag. *samá*]

dákir: **agpadakir.** see *damlit*: accuse indirectly.

dakíwas: *n.* search. **agdakiwas.** *v.* to go to one after the other with intention; prowl searching; roam. **dakiwasen.** *v.* to search for something; go through. **Agdakdakiwas dagiti matana.** His eyes are looking around. **Adda kano lima a sindikato nga agdakdakiwas ita idiay Abra.** There are supposedly five gangs roaming around Abra. [Tag. *galà*]

dakkél: *a.* big, large; great. **dumakkel.** *v.* to grow, grow up, become large. **dadakkel.** *n.* parents. **kadaklan.** *a.* largest, biggest. *n.* principal part of a house. **mangpadakkel.** *v.* to enlarge. **naindaklan.** *a.* great, illustrious. **pannakel.** *n.* pride. **padakkelen.** *v.* to rear (a child); make something bigger or more serious than it actually is; enlarge. **idakdakkel.** *n.* traits in which one grew up since childhood. **ikadakkel.** *v.* to enlarge. **agdinnakel.** *v.* to swell (rivers). **sipapannakel.** *a.* proud. **ipannakel.** *v.* to be proud of, boast of, show off something. **ipagpanakkel.** *v.* to boast of, take pride in. **madakkelan.** *v.* to outgrow; overcome a bad condition in the past; get over a bad habit. **managpannakel.** *a.* proud, prone to boast. **Indakdakkelna ti agkalap iti kastoy a wagas.**

He grew up fishing this way (since childhood). **Kabaelak a padakkelen ken pagadalen ti ubingko.** I am able to raise my child and put him through school. **Ipagpampannakkelka!** I'm proud of you! [Bon. *dakel*, Ibg. *dakál*, Ifg. *ongal*, Itg. *nalakay*, Ivt. *rakuh*, Kal. *chakeÿ*, *laotong*, Knk. *daké*, Kpm. *maragul*, Png. *báleg*, Tag. *lakí*]

daklág: **idaklag.** *v.* to drive ashore (by waves). **maidaklag.** *v.* to be washed ashore. (*dakdak*, *sanglad*)

daklín: (*obs.*) *n.* steelyard. **idaklin.** *v.* to drive ashore. (*daknir*, *sanglad*, *dakdak*)

daklís: *n.* kind of rectangular fishing net with bamboo sinkers and poles to keep it in place. **agdaklis.** *v.* to fish with a net. **dumadaklis.** *n.* *daklis* fishermen. **makidaklis.** *v.* to join in a fishing exhibition, take part in *daklis* fishing. **dakdaklis.** *n.* boy's river game in which the boys take turns filliping water. The boy whose water fillip is weak must go to the center of a circle and try to swim through the surrounding players. **madaklisan.** *n.* fish catch. **Apay a datdayta ti nadaklisanyo?** Why is that all you were able to net?

dakmól: **maidakmol.** *v.* to trip, fall on one's face. (*daramudom*)

daknáy: **naidaknay.** *a.* left dead; left dead in the middle of the road.

daknír: **idaknir.** *v.* to drive ashore (by current). **maidaknir.** *v.* to be washed ashore. **Naidaknirda iti nadumaduma a pagilian ti lubong.** They went ashore in various nations of the world.

dakuáda: (*obs.*) *pron.* they.

dakúlap: *n.* palm of the hand with fingers (palm without fingers: *pálad*). **idakulap.** *v.* to shake the hand. **makidinnakulap.** *v.* to shake hands with someone. **sangadakulapan.** *n.* one palm (size). **sinandakulap.** *n.* iron gloves. **Agtinnagka iti dakulapko.** *exp.* I'll have you (you'll fall in the palm of my hands). **Nairut ti panagdidinnakulapmi.** Our handshake was firm. **Nalukay ti dakulapna.** *exp.* He is generous (*lit*: his palm is loose). [Kal. *appe*, Png. *dakúlap*, Tag. *palad*]

dakúmo: *n.* a kind of freshwater crab. **Kasla kinirog a dakumo ti pangaan a rupana.** His large-jawed face was like a fried crab.

dákor: **agdakor.** *v.* to be the time for; be prevalent, prevail; reign; to be widespread, frequent.

daksanggásat: [*dakes nga gasat*] *n.* misfortune, bad luck. **Kadagiti rabii, mapampanunotko latta ti kinadaksanggasatko.** Each night I just think of my misfortune. [Tag. *malas*]

dalabdáb: *var.* of *dalapdap:* creep (vines).
daládal: *n.* track, trail; passageway. (*dalan; desdes, dana*)
dalág: *n.* a kind of freshwater mudfish, called *borikikkik* when very small or *borikaw* when small, *Ophicephalus striatus.* **daldalag.** *n.* lizard fish of the *Synodontidae* family. [Kal. *palispis,* Kpm. *bulíg,* Png. *gelegelé,* Png., Tag. *dalág*]
dalága: (Tag. *dalaga:* maiden, unmarried lady) **dumalaga.** *n.* young hen; pullet; (*slang*) virgin.
dalagádag: dalagadagan. *v.* to take a look at to detect robbers; look around. **madalagadagan.** *v.* to be observed briefly in passing. [Tag. *tingnán*]
dalágan₁: *n.* kind of inclined bed used by women in confinement (*papag*); the period after childbirth when the woman is confined to rest. **agdalagan.** *v.* to be in this period (after childbirth).
dalágan₂: dimmalagan. *n.* rapids; cascade.
dalagúdog: *n.* a kind of leguminous herb, *Desmodium micyophyllum.*
dalagudóg: *n.* stampede; sound of rolling thunder. **agdalagudog, dumalagudog.** *v.* to run noisily; stampede. **nadalagudog.** *a.* with boisterous running; noisy throbbing; stomping. **agdalagudog a barukong.** *n.* throbbing chest (during excitement). [Tag. *kalabóg. dabóg*]
dalaidí: *n.* school of small fish. **agdalaidi.** *v.* to school (fish). (*gateb; rotok; taklong*) **dalaidien.** (*obs.*) *v.* to smooth (metals).
dalakdák: agdalakdak. *v.* to spread (branches in growth, etc.). **maidalakdak.** *v.* to be spread around; to be spread out. **idalakdak.** *v.* to spread out.
dalákit: *n.* a kind of raft (*rakit*); stem; small branch. **daldalakit.** *n.* taro roots.
dalakúdug: (*obs.*) **madalakudug.** *v.* to go together in a pair.
daláli: see *dalallien:* kind of edible seaweed.
dalallién: *n.* species of edible seaweed resembling the *kulót.*
dalamgís: *var.* of *damgis:* graze, hit slightly.
dalam-ít: idalam-it. *v.* to utter, say, declare. (*ebkas, baga, kuna*)
dalampiáw: *n.* species of marine bird that feeds on *ipon.*
dálan: *n.* road, street; path; passage; track.; corridor; aisle. **agpadalan.** *v.* to give way, make room for; go to the road. **agpaidalan.** *v.* to ask for advice. **dalanen.** *v.* to follow a road. **idalan.** *v.* to advise; guide; influence. **madalanan.** *v.* to pass by. **padalanan.** *v.* to run over; excuse, apologize. **dumalan.** *v.* to pass through. **padalanen.** *v.* to give way; make way. **pag-**

dalanan. *v.* to run over; run through; do haphazardly; *n.* passageway; pathway. **agdalan iti korte.** *v.* to settle in court. [Ivt. *rarahan,* Kal. *chaÿan,* Png. *dalán,* Tag. *daán*]
dalándan: (Tagalog also, Sp. *naranja:* orange) *n.* orange. (*narangha; baranghas; darukis*) [Png., Tag. *dalandan*]
dalanés: dumalanes. *v.* to pile up; accumulate (*penpen*); to be at hand (seasons, cycles). [Tag. *ipon*]
dalangádang: *n.* light at sunrise or moonrise. **idalangadang.** *v.* to toast (on a spit). **maidalangadangan.** *v.* to be warmed over the fire; to be overcome by sunrise or moonrise.
dalangdáng: *n.* large fish cut open and dried in the sun; a variety of awned rice with green hull.
dalanghíta: (Tag.) *n.* orange. (*baranghás*)
dalangíding: idalangiding. *v.* to place near the fire to warm (*dadáng*); to place on the stove.
dalapádap: *var.* of *dalapdáp:* creep; encroach.
dalapánas: *a.* without exception. **dalapanasen.** *v.* to do without exception; to apply the same treatment to everybody. [Tag. *lahát*]
dalapdáp: *n.* runner, creeping shoot. **dumalapdap.** *v.* to crawl (said of vines); creep; spread out; encroach. **madalapdapan.** *v.* to be covered with vines; to be blanketed by nuclear fallout. [Tag. *dalapdáp* = prune trees]
dalápus: dalapusen. *v.* to trip, stumble; meet accidentally; hit with the feet while running. **dumalapus.** *v.* to bump, collide with. (*tim-og; pagat; dungpar; kintol; bangdol*) **agdalapus.** *v.* to jostle; hustle; scramble. **makadalapus.** *v.* to become sick due to colliding with a ghost; catch a disease. **padaldalapus.** *v.* to be around idling when not needed; to be in the way. [Tag. *banggá* (bump)]
dalatídet: (*obs.*) **nadalatidet.** *a.* sticky. (*pigket*)
dálaw: *n. Acorus calamus,* sweet flag; a kind of small, white marine fish similar to the *ariawyaw.* [Tag. *dalaw* = visit]
dalawádaw: *n.* protruding; projecting. (*dawadaw*) **agdalawadaw.** *v.* to penetrate; pass through; protrude; pierce; exceed in dimensions. [Tag. *uslí*]
dalawát: dalawaten. *v.* to speak; chatter. **Ti la daldalawatém.** You don't know what you're talking about.
dalawídaw: *n.* gossipmonger; loudmouth. **nadalawidaw.** *a.* blatant; loudmouthed.
dalawít: *var.* of *dalawat:* chatter. **Ti la nadaldalawit ti dilana!** What a chattering mouth he has! [Tag. *dalawit* = lever; pry]
daláy: (*obs.*) *n.* short breath.
daláyap: *n.* a kind of shrub with lemonlike fruits, *Citrus lima,* used in native medicine to cure

fever. **panalayapen.** *n. Champereia manillana* shrub. [Png. *dalayáp*, Tag. *dayap*]

dalaydáy₁: **idalayday.** *v.* to hang in a careless way; to soil, smear. **naidalayday.** *a.* hung in a careless way; soiled; smeared.

dalaydáy₂: **padalayday.** *n.* either of the two shafts of a cart between which an animal is hitched.

dalayúdoy: **agdalayudoy.** *v.* to be spongy; pulpy; bruised (fruits); soft; (*fig.*) flabby. **Agdaldalayudoy ti buy-ongna iti panagsagkisagkingna.** Her large stomach shook flabbily as she hobbled.

daldál₁: (Tagalog also: loquacity) *n.* talking idly; gossipmonger; speaking with the mouth full. **daldalen.** *n.* subject of useless talk. **nadaldal.** *a.* talkative; rambling on. **daldalera.** *n.* gossipmonger, idle talker.

daldál₂: **idaldal.** *v.* to soil, stain, smear (trailing garments). **madaldalan.** *v.* to be soiled, smeared, stained. (*pulagid*)

Dále: (Sp. *dale*, *darle*: go ahead; *obs.*) *Interj.* Go ahead! (*sige*)

daléb: **agdaleb.** *v.* to fall prone. (*dapla*; *rugma*; *dugmam*; *pakleb*; *daramudom*; *tikleb*; *sakoba*) **idaleb.** *v.* to invert, turn upside down; cause to fall prone, cause to fall on one's face. **maidaleb.** *v.* to fall on one's face; be overpowered.

dáleg: *n.* rough sea. **nadaleg.** *a.* rough (sea).

dálem: *n.* liver. **dalman.** *n.* a large freshwater mollusk. **dimmalem a daga.** *n.* reddish brown soil. [Bon. *agtey*, Ibg. *agél*, Ivt. *atay*, Kal. *ogtoy*, Knk. *átey*, Kpm. *ate*, Png. *altéy*, Tag. *atáy*]

dalemdém: *n.* watershed, wet, moist place; deep forest, jungle; secluded place.

dal-én: **maidal-en.** *v.* to crowd, pile up, accumulate (due to waves). **Agdal-en ti adu a baro iti biagmo ita.** Lots of new things will accumulate in your life now.

dalepdép: **dalepdepen.** *v.* to press down; lay, lower, settle; press a *buneng* handle on a sick person to prevent his sickness from becoming worse; verbally soothe the emotions. **Imbagto la a mangdalepdep ti wawna no makainum manen.** It will be good to quench his thirst if he drinks again.

dalgét: **idalget.** *v.* to press against; pressure. **maidalget.** *v.* to be pressed against; to be pressured; to be singled out (in a court case).

dalgís: **ipadalgis.** *v.* to imply; insinuate. (*ipasagid*)

daliágot: **madaliagot.** *v.* to meet by chance. (*rana*)

daliásat: **agdaliasat.** *v.* to pass, go across; go through, move in crowds; travel. (*ballasiw*;

baniaga) **daliasaten.** *v.* to cross, traverse (something). **idaliasat.** *v.* to carry across, transport. **pagdaliasatan.** *n.* road, path; place where one travels. **Inturedna ti namin-adu a panagdaliasatna iti nadawel a taaw.** He often ventured to travel the cruel seas. [Tag. *lakbáy*]

dálig: *n.* dam. **daligen.** *v.* to dam up.

dalíg: *n.* wooden wheel of a cart; tire. (*pilid*) **padaligan.** *v.* to run over. [Tag. *gulong*]

dalígan: *n. Averrhoa carambola* tree, (Tagalog *balimbing*). (*obs.*) **daliganen.** *v.* to square logs, stones. [Tag. *balimbíng*]

dalígaw: (*obs.*) **dumaligaw.** *v.* to become spiritless (liquor).

daligdíg: *n.* species of fanlike mollusk. **dumaligdig.** *v.* to roll (ball, wheel).

daligét: **nadaliget.** *a.* flowing, running (said of sweat). **dumaliget.** *v.* to sweat profusely. (*kalimduos*; *degges*)

dalikán: *n.* hearth where jars are placed for cooking. **pagdadalikanan.** *n.* place around the *dalikan*. **Ti asideg ti dalikan, isu ti mapudotan.** *exp.* He who is nearest the stove gets the heat. [Ibg. *kalan*, Ivt. *rapuyan*, Knk. *wangaán*, Kpm. *kalang*, Png. *dalikán*, Tag. *dapóg*, *kalán*]

dalikén: *n.* coiled cloth placed on the head for holding jars. **agdaliken.** *v.* to wear a cloth on the head when transporting jars.

dalikenkén: **agdalikenken.** *v.* to curl up; coil (*kawíkaw*); amass, collect in a pile. [Tag. *mamaluktót*]

dalikepkép: *n.* crossing the arms on the chest. **agdalikepkep.** *v.* to cross the arms on the chest. **Kabaelak met ket ti agdalikepkep ken siuulimek a dumngeg.** I am able to cross my arms and listen quietly. [Tag. *halukipkíp*]

dalikonkón: *var.* of *dalikenkén*: curl up; coil; amass, collect or gather in a pile. **Dinalikonkonko dagiti narugit a bado.** I gathered the dirty clothes (in a pile).

dalimánek: **idalimanek.** *v.* to arrange, put in order; tidy up. (*urnos*) **maidalimanek.** *v.* to be arranged; put in order. **kinadalimanek.** *n.* orderliness; neatness. **Inagawaanda nga indalimanek dagiti in-inumenda.** They diligently arranged what they were drinking. [Tag. *ayos*]

dalimánet: *var.* of *dalimánek*: arrange, put in order.

dalimugtóng: **dalimugtongen.** *v.* to pile up, heap up (*penpen*). [Tag. *salansán*]

dalimpakó: *n.* frizzy hair, maidenhair. **nadalimpako.** *a.* curly, wavy. (*kulot*)

dalinepnép: see *dalepdep*: settle; press down.

dalinesnés: **agdalinesnes.** *v.* to settle; retire; withdraw; flee. (*lusulos*)

dalingdíng: *n.* drapery, hangings; walling. **dalingdingan.** *v.* to provide with a temporary partition. **dalingdingen.** *v.* to overprotect (a child).

dalipáto: *n.* flake of fire. (*alipaga*) **agdalipato.** *v.* to fly around (flakes of fire).

dalipáwen(g): *n.* kind of tree.

dalipempén: **dalipempenan.** *v.* to muffle up with blankets. **dalipempenen.** *v.* to pile up. [Tag. *buntón* (pile)]

dalipespés: **maidalipespes.** *v.* to be saturated, drenched. (*rusep*)

dális: *n.* pancreas; sweetbread. **padalisan.** *v.* to run over (*atalan, padaligan*). [Tag. *lapáy* (pancreas)]

dalisungsóng: *n.* depression at the foot of a cataract.

dálit: **idalit.** *v.* to crush. **naidalit.** *a.* crushed; bedridden. **pannakaidalit.** *n.* period of time in which someone is bedridden. **Maidalit iti malaria dagiti nakapsut ti salun-atna.** The ones with weak health are bedridden with malaria. [Tag. *datay* (bedridden)]

dallaáso: **daldallaaso.** *n.* a kind of small bluebird.

dalláng: (myth.) *n.* Ilocano goddess of beauty; folksong, *var.* of *dalleng.* **dumadallang.** *n.* folksinger. [Tag. *awit*]

dallawít: *var.* of *dillawit*: chatter.

dalléng: *n.* a kind of song.

dallimúkeng: *n.* utter laziness (*sadut*). [Tag. *tamád*]

dallipáwen: *n.* a kind of tree with white flowers, *Alstonia scholaris.*

dallót: *n.* a kind of chanting song and dance; pulling one another by the hands. **agdallot.** *v.* to sing the *dallot.* **daldallot.** *n.* a variety of awnless *diket* rice. **dinnalotan.** *n.* singing joust.

dallúyon: *n.* breaker wave; variety of rice with much straw. **agdalluyon.** *v.* to swell into waves (ocean waters). **maidalluyon.** *v.* to be carried away by a wave. **kimmapilia a dalluyon.** *n.* large breaker wave (like a chapel). **pagdalluyon ti piskel.** *v.* to flex a muscle. [Ibg. *palung*, Ivt. *abkas*, Kal. *challuyon*, Kpm. *álun*, Png. *dalóyon*, Tag. *daluyong, alon*]

dalmán: (f *dalem*) *n.* a kind of large, freshwater mollusk.

dalmátika: (Sp. *dalmática*: dalmatic) *n.* solemn sung Dalmatic mass; special vestment worn by the deacon at a solemn sung Mass.

dalmít: *n.* mention; *var.* of *damlit.* **Sangkadalmityo dayta a babai.** You keep mentioning that lady.

dalubdúb: *n.* prick (in the finger); simple stitch. **dalubduben.** *v.* to stitch. **idalubdub.** *v.* to prick (*dalukdok; aludab; sarait*). [Tag. *hilbana* (Sp.)]

dalúdal: *n.* creeping shoot, runner (of a vine).

dalugúdug: see *dalagudug*: sound of running or trampling.

dalúk: (*obs.*) **daluken.** *v.* to fatten a hog.

dalukappá: **madalukappa.** *v.* to collapse; fall unconsciously to the ground. (*kusbo*)

dalukappí: *n.* sitting with the legs crossed in a lotus position. **agdalukappi.** *v.* to sit with the legs crossed; squat. **nakadalukappi.** *a.* squatting. **Agdaldalukappi laengen a mangur-uray iti anak ti kuartana iti banko.** He is just sitting cross-legged on the ground waiting for the interest of his money in the bank.

dalukappít: *var.* of *dalukappi.*

dalukdók: *n.* prick of a needle; kind of grass that sticks to clothing, *var.* of *salsalpot.* **idalukdok.** *v.* to prick. **daldalukdok.** *v.* a kind of small bird. [Tag. *tusok*]

dalumpapá: *n.* textile factory; loom.

dalumpínas: *n.* flag, flagstone.

dalumpináy: see *lupinay*: crouch, sit with legs bent to one side.

dalundón: **madalundonan.** *v.* to increase in number. (*nayon*)

dalunít: see *pangarandongen.*

dalungdóng: *n.* head cloth; kind of veil. (*alidongdong*) **agdalungdong.** *v.* to cover the head with a head cloth. **dalungdongan.** *v.* to cover someone with a veil. [Tag. *talukbóng*]

dalunggiás: *var.* of *damgis.*

dalunggó: **dalungguen.** *v.* to pile up, heap up (*penpen*). [Tag. *buntón*]

dalupakpák₁: *a.* sitting with the legs crossed; crippled. (*lupisák*)

dalupakpák₂: (*reg.*) **agdalupakpak.** *v.* to sprawl, lay with the body extended. **nakadalupakpak.** *a.* sprawling, lying on the stomach with the body extended. (see *pakleb*)

dalúpang: *n.* a kind of shrub with yellow flowers, *Thespesia lampas.*

dalupásay: **nadalupasay.** *a.* knocked down, fallen down (from losing one's balance).

dalupídip: **idalupidip.** *v.* to arrange, put away neatly.

dalupináy: see *lupinay*: crouch; sit with the legs bent to one side.

dalupingpíng: **dalupingpingen.** *v.* to press, squeeze together, compress; draw up a skirt.

dalupisák: **agdalupisak.** *v.* to squat. (*lupisak*) **madalupisak.** *v.* to fall on the buttocks; to be thrown to the ground. **Madalupisak ti babai no lukayan ti lakayna ti panagiggemna kenkuana.** The woman will fall flat on her rump if her husband loosens his hold of her. [Tag. *lupagì, tingkayád*]

dalupitpít: *n.* garbage, waste, rubbish; a kind of small marine fish. **dalupitpiten**. *v.* to batter, flatten, crush. [Tag. *pipî*]

dalupó: dalupuen. *v.* to pile up in a disorderly way; knock down. **maidalupo**. *v.* to collapse, fall helplessly; to be knocked down; (fig.) become involved in, fall into (politics). **nadalupo**. *a.* collapsed, knocked down; crushed. **Naimatanganna ti nakakaasi a langa ti lalaki a nadalupo iti daga**. She observed the pitiful face of the man that collapsed to the ground. **manipud pannakadalupona iti politika**. from the time he became involved in politics.

daluppíit: nakadaluppiit. *a.* sitting with legs crossed and buttocks on ground (Indian style). (*dalupisak, lupisak*)

dalús: *n.* clean space; clearing (of a forest); completed work. **nadalus**. *a.* clean. **dalusan**. *v.* to clean; cleanse; make way. **idalus**. *v.* to finish; complete; finalize. **pagdalus**. *n.* cleanser; anything used for cleaning. **managdaldalus**. *a.* habitually clean; sanitary. [Ibg. *rénu*, Itg. *dawes*, Ivt. *marahus*, Png. *dalós*, Kal. *mampekas*, Knk. *kagam-ís*, Kpm., Tag. *linis*]

dalusápi: *n.* a cock with light red plumage.

dalúson₁: *n.* heap, pile (*penpen*). **dalusunen**. *v.* var. of *daluponen*. **agdadaluson**. *v.* to throng, crowd. **idaluson**. *v.* to bring together, gather up. **nadaluson**. *a.* abundant, plentiful. [Tag. *buntón*]

dalúson₂: *n.* variety of awned early rice.

dalutaytáy: agdalutaytay. *v.* to be weak; collapse, faint. **maidalutaytay**. *v.* to be weak; collapse. [Tag. *handusáy*]

dalpák: *a.* flat. **dumalpak**. *v.* to become flat. (*kuppit*)

dalpíg: *a.* flat (objects). (*kuppit*)

dáma: (f. Am. Spanish *dama*: checkers) *n.* checkers; bridesmaid. **agdama**. *v.* to play checkers. **kadama**. *v.* to play checkers with; *n.* checker partner. **dama de noche**. *n.* kind of night-blooming shrub with sweet-scented white flowers, *Cestrum nocturnum.*

damá: agdama. *adv.* now, at this moment, presently, modern; this current (month). **agdinama**. *a.* presently, at the current time. **ipadamdama**. *v.* to do in a little while. **madama**. *adv.* just now, at this moment. **nagdama**. *adv.* at this time. **madamdama**. *adv.* later, soon, in a short while. **agpadama**. *v.* to brag, boast. **Madamdamakan nga agsaludsod**. Ask later. [Tag. *sa ngayón*]

dámag: *n.* news; report. **dumamag**. *v.* to ask for news. **madamag**. *v.* to be reported to hear;

come to learn about. **damagen**. *v.* to ask about, question, inquire. **agdindinamag**. *a.* famed, renowned, illustrious. **agdinamag**. *v.* to be popular; known in town. **makidamag**. *v.* to ask for information. **padamag**. *n.* news release; press release; *v.* to have someone else ask or inquire. **agpadamag**. *v.* to inform. **ipadamag**. *v.* to make known, report; announce; relate. **padamagan**. *v.* to inform somebody about. **ulbod a damag**. *n.* false report. **sangkadamag**. always asking. **Madamdamag idin**. It has been heard before. **Nakadamagam?** How have you come to learn about it? Where did you hear it? **Idi nakapangrabiikamin, inserreknak iti salas tapno ituloymi ti agpinnadamag**. When we were finished eating dinner, he had me enter the living room so we could continue asking the news about each other. [Ivt. *vahey*, Png. *damag*, balita, Tag. *balità*]

damahuána: (Sp. *damajuana*: demijohn) *n.* demijohn, large bottle.

damára: var. of *ramada*: improvised shelter (for wedding ceremonies).

damás: *n.* a kind of white marine fish.

dam-ás: var. of *dap-aw*: step in.

damásko: (Sp. *damasco*: damask) *n.* damask, rich silk fabric woven with elaborate patterns. **agdamasko**. *v.* to put flags under the windows of buildings on certain holidays.

dámay: agdamay. *v.* to stay up all night to watch over the newly dead; diffuse; spread. **damayan**. *a.* having calved more than twice.

dámay: dumamay. *v.* to penetrate; spread, diffuse. **damayan**. *a.* having calved more than once.

damáyo: (*obs.*) *n.* tarrying purposely.

damdám: idamdam. *v.* to bake in hot ashes; heat up. (*dadang*) **madamdaman**. *v.* to heat up; get hot.

damég: damegdameg. *n.* the sound of running.

dam-ég: *n.* moisture; fertility. **nadam-eg**. *a.* moist, wet (soil, wood, etc.); fertile. **padamegen**. *v.* to moisten; make the soil fertile.

damgís: *n.* scratch; slight scrape. (*kudias*) **dumamgis**. *v.* to make a brief rest stop in passing. **madamgisan**. *v.* to scratch, brush against. **padamgisan**. *v.* to hit; slightly brush against. [Tag. *daplís*]

dámi: damien (*obs.*) *v.* to fling in someone's face.

damíli: *n.* pottery, earthenware. **agdamili**. *v.* to make pottery. **agdamdamili**. *n.* potter. **damilien**. *v.* to mold into pottery; to rear children properly. **Naidamili iti ugali ni Pilipino**. It is molded into Filipino ways. [Tag. *pagpapalayók*]

damílig: *n.* kind of banana. (*dippig*)

dámit: damiten. *v.* to collect, receive the reward of one's labor; profit from; enjoy the benefits of; receive.

damká: nadamka. *a.* wicked, vicious, malicious; destructive; violent. (*damsak*; *dangkok*; *ulpit*) **agdamka.** *v.* to be cruel; violent; pillage. [Tag. *lupít*]

damlíng: *n.* wild orchid.

damlít: agpadamlit. *v.* to utter accusations, reproaches for the benefit of a listening third person; to berate indirectly.

dammáng: *n.* other side of a river, opposite shore; bank of a river. **agdammang.** *v.* to go ashore (to the bank of the river). **dumammang.** *v.* to cross a river.

dámo: *a.* former. *n.* beginning, opening, initiation; threshold; first time to do a certain thing. **(Dam)damok ti umay.** It's the first time I came. **damoan.** *v.* to begin; do for the first time. **iti damona.** at first. **agdadamo.** *n.* beginner, novice. **pagdadamuan.** *v.* to do for the first time. [Tag. *simulâ*]

damuága: damdamuaga. *n.* a kind of herb.

damortís: *n.* a kind of tree with spiny branches and white flowers, *Pithecolobium dulce*; an earring the shape of a *damortis* pod.

dampág: see *lampad*: breadth (of a log, etc.).

dampíg: dampidampig. *n.* a kind of small herb.

dampíl: *n.* boys game that consists of sitting on the haunches with intertwined legs and trying to knock each other down. **agdampil.** *v.* to play the game of *dampil*.

dampílag: *a.* flat; level; even. (*kuppit*) **pagdampilagen.** *v.* to make flat; flatten. [Tag. *patag*, *pantáy*]

dampír: *n.* wall; side (of a cave). **dumampir.** *v.* to lean against a wall.

damrós: *var.* of *diram-us*: to wash the face.

damsák: *n.* violence; cruelty; viciousness; wickedness; maliciousness. (*damka*; *dangkok*) **nadamsak.** *a.* vicious; cruel; wicked; violent; spendthrift, wasteful; dissolute; sacrilegious. **agdamsak.** *v.* to be cruel; wicked; violent. [Tag. *lupít*]

daná: *n.* trail, path (beaten by the feet); track. (*desdes*) **dana ti law-ang.** *n.* space orbit.

dánag: agdanag. *v.* to worry. (*pulkok*) **madananagan.** *v.* to be worried, restless, anxious. **nadanag.** *a.* easily worried. **sidadanag.** *a.* worried; fearful. **makapadanag.** *v.* to cause anxiety. **pakadanagan.** *n.* worries. **idanagan.** *v.* to worry for; feel anxious for. **Saanka a madanagan, adda agasnan dayta.** Don't worry, there is a cure for that. [Kal. *chaleg*, Kpm. *abalá*, Png. *pága*, Tag. *alaalá*]

danaldál: dumanaldal. *n.* talkative person. (*daldal*; *tarabitab*, *salawasaw*)

danapég: *n.* sound of a horse's galloping hooves. **agdanapeg.** *v.* to walk with heavy footsteps. [Tag. *yabág*]

danapídip: *n.* sound of light footsteps on a bamboo floor. **agdanapidip.** *v.* to tiptoe; walk silently. [Tag. *kaluskós*]

danapísip: *var.* of *danapidip*.

dánar: *n.* wound (*dunor*). **danaren.** *v.* to wound, injure. **nadanar.** *a.* injured, wounded.

danarúdor: *var.* of *daranudor*: sound of an engine or wind. **Pagammuan ta nakangeg iti danarudor iti dakkel a makina.** He suddenly heard the roaring sound of the big machine.

danás: *n.* clothes press. **idanas.** *v.* to press clothes.

danasádas: dumanasadas. *v.* to rustle (leaves in the wind).

dánaw: *n.* lake, pond (*dan-aw*). **danawan.** *n.* adult female animal.

dan-áw: *n.* lake, pond. [Ibg. *lebbeng*, Ifg. *lobong*, Itg. *taaw*, Kal. *eÿwan lobong*, Png. *lóok*, Tag. *lawà*]

dánay: see *dumanay*.

dandaní: *adv.* almost, nearly; *a.* near, almost hear. (*nganngani*) **Nangngeg ti dandani sibubukel a sangapagilian ti makapasangit a lualo ti pangulo.** Almost the entire nation heard the tearful prayer of the president. **Dandanitan kabaelan ti gumatang iti bukodta a balay.** We are almost able to buy our own house. [Bon. *ngaanngáni*, *tegang*, Png. *ngalngalí*, Tag. *halos*]

danekdék: *n.* continuous pounding; insistence; persistence. **idanekdek.** *v.* to insist, press on, be persistent about; urge; emphasize (*daguldol*, *pilit*). **Indanekdek ni Beling iti pangukomanmilitar a yetnagna ti sentensiana a patay.** Beling insisted that the military court pass the death sentence. [Tag. *pilit*, *giít*]

danéng: idaneng. *v.* to take seriously; mind; level; bring lower, bring down. **agdaneng.** *v.* (*obs.*) to plot, conspire; be of the same color.

danengdéng: *n.* muttered scolding. **danengdengan.** *v.* to insult, reprimand, rebuke; scold; affront; mumble; mutter. [Tag. *bulóng*]

danés: maidadanes. *v.* to be despised; insulted; to suffer loss. **idadanes.** *v.* to insult; despise; belittle; oppress; be cruel to. **panangidadanes.** *n.* cruelty; oppression; injustice. [Tag. *lupít*]

Danés: (Sp. *danés*: Danish, feminine: *danesa*) *n.* Danish person; Danish language; *a.* Danish.

daní: dandani. *adv.* almost, nearly; a little short of. **umadani.** *v.* to approach (in time); come soon. [Png. *ngalngalí*, Tag. *halos*]

daníir: *n.* foul smell of animals or cadavers or from being under the sun. **nadaniir.** *a.* foul smelling.

daníkag: *n.* brazier to warm oneself.

dánios: (Sp. *daño*: damage) *n.* damage. **danios ken perhuisios.** (Sp. *daños y perjuicios*: damages and injuries) *n.* damages and injuries (as applied to court cases).

danísor: agdanisor. *v.* to sound (canons, etc.).

dániw: *n.* poem; poetry; (*lit.*) song. **agdaniw.** *v.* to write poetry; sing. **mannaniw.** *n.* poet, poetess. **sarindaniw.** *n.* narrative poetry. **idaniw.** *v.* to poeticize. **daniwan.** *v.* to praise in poetic verse; dedicate a poem to. **naindaniwan.** *a.* lyrical; poetic. **maradaniw.** *a.* poetic, flowery (prose). **Nalaingka gayam a dumaniw.** So you are good at writing poetry. [Png. *anlóng*, Tag. *tulâ*]

daniwangáw: [coined from *daniw* + *angaw*] *n.* humorous poem.

daniwarwár: nadaniwarwar. *a.* clear, open (land).

dannóg: nadannog. *a.* asking questions that have already been answered; repetitious.

dánog₁: *n.* fist; blow with the fist. **danugen.** *v.* to cuff; box with the fist. **dinnanugan.** *n.* boxing bout. **madanog.** *v.* to be hit with a fist; suffer a blow. [Knk. *dongápil*, Tag. *suntók*]

dánog₂: dadanugen. *n.* a variety of thick-skinned, large banana.

danúm: *n.* water; pus (*áno*). **agdanum.** *v.* to liquefy, turn to water. **danuman.** *v.* to add water to. **dinanuman.** *n.* Ilocano version of *sinigang*; a dish with boiled fish seasoned with sour ingredients such as *pias*. **dadanum.** *n.* an herb growing near the water. **padanum.** *n.* irrigation. **agpadanum, padanuman.** *v.* to irrigate. **kadandanuman.** *n.* marsh. **taridanum.** *n.* itchiness of fingers or toes due to prolonged immersion in water. **agtaridanum.** *v.* to suffer from *taridanum*. **Kasla nadanuman a tukak.** *exp.* like watered frogs (describing a situation where everyone is talking at once). **agdanum ti bara.** suffer from pneumonia. [Ibg., Ifg., Kpm., Png. *danom*, Kal. *chelum*, Ivt. *ranum*, Itg. *liting*, Tag. *tubig*]

dánon: *n.* report; marriage custom of dowry negotiation and wedding date agreement. **danonen.** *v.* to reach; come to, get to; meet with; attain; understand; touch; ask for the hand in marriage. **dumanon.** *v.* to come inside, enter a house. **madanon.** *v.* to reach, arrive at. **pananon.** *v.* to be sufficient until. **nadanon.** *a.* reached; attained; contemporaneous, living at the same time. **agidanon, idanon.** *v.* to inform, report, tattle; take to (causative of reach).

idadanon. *n.* arrival; negotiations for a wedding. **makadanon.** *v.* to be able to reach; extend up to; last until; attain. **nadanonan.** *a.* extremely, exceedingly, very. **pagdadanonan.** *n.* meeting place. **padanonen.** *v.* to let someone come in. **pananon.** *n.* relief goods, additional supplies given during a crisis. **Nakadandanonkami iti nadumaduma nga ili.** We reached various towns. [Tag. *pamanhikan* (marriage custom); *abót* (reach)]

danúor: *n.* stench. **nadanuor.** *a.* stinking, odorous. (*naangot*)

danuprá: *n.* a kind of tree.

-danto: [-*da* + -(*n*)*to*] enclitic expressing third person plural subject and future time. **Agsaladanto.** They are going to dance.

dangádang: *n.* battle, fight. (*bakal, gubat*) **agdangadang.** *v.* to scuffle; fight; battle (with each other) **kadangadang.** *v.* to fight with; compete with. **dadangadangan.** *n.* battlefield. **mannakidangadang.** *n.* warrior. [Tag. *digmâ*]

dángal: *n.* muzzle placed in the mouth. (*busal; padun; songo*) **maipadangal.** *v.* to get stuck in the throat; to be obstructed. **agdangaldangal.** *v.* to obstruct; crowd someone. **padangal.** *n.* baited fishhook; muzzle. [Tag. *busál*]

dángalay: *n.* stand, support (to keep things off the floor) (*batay*). [Tag. *katang*]

dángan: *n.* handspan. **sangadangan.** *n.* measure of the palm of the hand. **danganen.** *v.* to measure with the hand measurement. **dangandangan.** *n.* a kind of green larva destructive to beans. **Agarup sangadeppa ken agakaba ngata iti dua a dangan.** It is about one armspan (long) and as wide as two measurements of the hand. [Ibg., Png. *dangan*, Ivt. *rangan*, Kal. *changan*, Kpm. *karángan*, Tag. *dangkál*]

dángas: *n.* handsomeness. (*taráki, taer, guapo*; *bisked*; *pogi*; *saldit*) **nadangas.** *a.* handsome.

dang-ás: *n.* arrogance; conceit; selfishness. **nadang-as.** *a.* arrogant; conceited; selfish. **Nadang-as ti tigtignayna.** She has an arrogant gait. **Sidadang-as a nakipinnereng kenkuana.** She arrogantly stared back at him. [Tag. *pagmalakí, yabang*]

dángaw: *n.* a kind of stinkbug. **dangawen.** *v.* to be attacked by stinkbugs.

dangép₁: *n.* palliative; intermittent overcast. **idangep.** *v.* to apply (a palliative). (*dengngep*)

dangép₂: dumangep. *v.* to get angry.

dangér: *n.* arrogance. **nadanger.** *a.* mean; proud, conceited; cheerful; witty; facetious. **kinadanger.** *n.* arrogance, haughtiness; pride, conceit. [Tag. *yabang*]

danggáy: *n.* harmony; accompaniment. **agdanggay.** *v.* to sing, chant together; do two things at one time. **dumanggay, danggayan.** *v.* to accompany with a musical instrument; go along with. **idanggay.** *v.* to suit, fit; match. **makidanggay.** *v.* to accompany a group; go along; (*coll.*) go with the flow. **danggayanna kumá ti panawén.** *exp.* go with the flow. **Makapagdanggaykayo nga agkatawa?** Are you able to laugh together? [Tag. *salíw*]

danggíl: *var.* of *dangil*.

danggól: *var.* of *danggil*; fool; stupid person.

dangíir: *n.* fragrance of fruits.

dangíit: *n.* stench of dry animal waste.

dángil: **dangilen.** *v.* to hit; hurt; do cruelly; elbow, push, shove. **Basta dakami ken Bluebsi ti agkuyog, awanen ti makaitured a mangdangil kadakami.** As long as I go with Bluebsi, no one will dare to hurt us.

dángin: *n.* side stroke. **danginen.** *v.* to punish by beating.

dangkáw: *a.* long-legged (*dangkawas*); *n.* monster with long legs. [Tag. *tikbalang*]

dangkawás: *a.* long-legged (*bangkawas*); tall and lanky. [Tag. *tangkád*]

dangkés: *n.* wickedness. **nadangkes.** *a.* bad, evil, wicked; obscene; lewd. **agdangdangkes.** *v.* to do evil deeds. [Tag. *lupít*]

dangkíl: *n.* bump. **agdinnangkil.** *v.* to bump into each other, collide.

dangkók: **nadangkok.** *a.* bad, evil; wicked; rude. **kinadangkok.** *n.* cruelty; wickedness. **Nakadangdangkok la unay dagiti turayen a Kastila kadagiti Pilipino.** The Spanish rulers were very cruel to the Filipinos.

danglá: *n.* an aromatic shrub with blue flowers, *Vitex negundo*, the boiled leaves are used as a disinfectant for wounds and the fresh leaves are used to keep away bedbugs. **agpadangla.** *v.* to pester (wounds); suffer from a sensation of being drugged; nurse a wound. **agpadangladangla.** *v.* to be like *dangla* (referring to a person who takes a long time in dying). **Agas ti tarindanum ti nalebbek a dangla.** The crushed *danglá* leaves are a cure for the *tarindanum* skin condition.

dangngá: *a.* dumb, stupid (said only of girls). [Tag. *tangá, gaga*]

dangngó: see *dungngo*: beloved. [Tag. *giliw*]

dang-ól: **agdang-ol.** *v.* to howl (*taguub*)

dangpíl: **dangpilen.** *v.* to compress, press; hang from a gallows.

dangrán: **dangran, dangranan.** *v.* to hurt, injure. **maidangran.** *v.* to be hurt, harmed. **makadangran.** *a.* harmful. **nadangran.** *a.* injured, harmed. **mangdangran.** *v.* to injure, harm. **panangdangran.** *n.* harm, injury. **Kayatmi a maammuan no asino ti nangdangran kenkuana.** We want to know who hurt him. [Tag. *saktán* (hurt)]

dangró: **nadangro.** *a.* smelling of spoiled meat or fish, sharks, crocodiles; smelling like foul breath. **Ti nasadot a baró, kas karne a nadangro.** A lazy young man is like rotten meat.

dángwa: *var.* of *tangwa*: to look up.

daó: *n.* a kind of tree with valuable timber, *Dracontomelum sp.*

daúlo: (pl. *dadaulo*) *n.* leader. **agdadaulo.** *v.* to direct, lead, be first. **idaulo.** *v.* to lead, direct, guide. **panangidaulo.** *n.* leadership. [Tag. *pangulo*]

daóng: *n.* a kind of large boat, ark. **daongan.** *n.* pier; harbor. **dumaong.** *v.* to dock at the harbor.

dapádap: **dapadapen.** *v.* to feel (touching). **apagdapadap.** *n.* slight touch with the hand. **Siaannad a nangdapadap iti tian ti asawana.** He carefully felt the belly of his wife. [Tag. *hipò, damá*]

dápag: *n.* gust of wind. **agdapag.** *v.* to suddenly gust (wind).

dapág: *n.* plain; heavy footstep; *a.* flat. (*kuppit*) **agdapag.** *v.* to drop heavily; fall flat. **dumapagpag.** *v.* to walk with heavy footsteps. **idapag.** *v.* to place solidly on. **nadapag.** *a.* flat. **pagdapagen.** *v.* to flatten. **pagdadapagan.** *n.* fortune, luck in life. [Tag. *yabág*]

dapák: **agdapakdapak.** *v.* to make a galloping sound; walk with heavy footsteps. (*padak*)

dapálet: *n.* a variety of awned early rice.

dapán: *n.* sole of the foot. **dapandapan.** *n.* a kind of cake the shape of a sole; *a.* barefoot. **agdapandapan.** *v.* to go barefoot. (*sakasaka*) **kadapan.** *n.* foot (in measuring). **padapan.** *n.* runner of a sledge, pedal, foot of a mechanical device. **appo ti dappan.** *n.* great-great-grandchildren. **Masolok ti tumakder iti kabukbukodak a dapan nga awan ti kibinak.** *exp.* I can stand on my own two feet without assistance. [Ibg. *dafuwan*, Ifg. *guppak*, Ivt. *tatakad*, Kal. *chapan*, Png. *dapán*, Kpm., Tag. *talampakan*]

dap-ás: *n.* the action of punching. **agdap-asdap-as.** *v.* to beat up, maul; attack.

dápat: *n.* plain, flat land. (*dapag*) **nadapat.** *a.* full, with abundant supply of; flat (land). **kadapat.** *n.* owner of a field coterminous with one's own.

dap-áw: **dumap-aw.** *v.* to step lightly; pay a short visit. **madap-awan.** *v.* to be stepped on; to be stepped on by flies. **Saanka a makadapaw iti uneg ti balayko.** *exp.* You are no longer welcome in my house (can no longer step in).

dap-áy: idap-ay. *v.* to let out; express (thoughts, idea, etc.) **dap-ayan.** *v.* barrio hall; community center.

dapdáp₁: dumapdap. *v.* to stamp and whirl in dancing.

dapdáp₂: idapdap. *v.* to wipe gently (sweat on forehead with a handkerchief).

dapét: agdapet. *v.* to grapple; seize one another; (*reg.*) marry.

dapián: *n.* board put at the entrance of a house: threshold, doorsill; foot rest; doormat.

dapídip: *var.* of *dapisip*. **danapidip.** *n.* light walking (as on one's tiptoes).

dápig: dapigen. *v.* to strike (with the flat of a sword or flat side of something); strike from the side. **Nagalang-ang ti nadapig nga aso.** The struck dog whined.

dapíg: *a.* semicircular, half rounded.

dapíkan: *n.* a variety of awned late rice with double awns.

dápil: *n.* sugarcane milling. **dadapílan.** *n.* sugar mill machine. **agdapil.** *v.* to press the juice out of sugarcane using the *dadapilan*. **dapildapilen.** *v.* to thrash violently. **Inyuldagna lattan iti ulnas iti abay ti dadapilan a landok.** He just laid it on the sled next to the iron sugar mill machine. [Tag. *kabyáw*]

dapil: *var.* of *dapig*. *a.* semicircular.

dapílag: *n.* a kind of shallow bamboo basket, two inches deep. **dapdapilag.** *n.* a kind of freshwater fish.

dapílos: *a.* crumbling; limping; sagging; disabled. **madapilos.** *v.* to collapse (due to weakness or flimsiness); sag. **dapilusen.** *v.* to cause to collapse.

dapíros: *var.* of *dapilos*: collapse.

dapísip: agdanapisip. *v.* to tiptoe; walk quietly. (*til-ay*; *yatyat*)

dap-ít: makadap-it. *v.* to fall on; stumble on top of; hit against. **Nadap-itanda ti baldado a takiagna.** They accidentally hit his injured arm.

daplá: agdapla. *v.* to spread (news, disease); lie prone with the arms spread. (*waras*) **maidapla.** *v.* to fall prone. (*daleb*; *pakleb*; *daramudom*; *dugmam*; *rugma*; *sakoba*; *tikleb*)

daplág: madaplag. *v.* to fall dead.

daplák: *n.* flat. **agpadaplak** (*obs.*) *v.* to start a fire windwardly; fall flat. **agdaplak.** *v.* to fall flat; sway with the wind.

daplát: *n.* layer of woven bamboo for flooring and roofing purposes; *a.* flat; level. **agdaplat.** *v.* to become flat.

daplís: *n.* slight touch. **daplisan.** *v.* to slightly touch someone.

daplót: nadaplot. *a.* razed, leveled to the ground (by fire, etc.); bedridden. **dapluten.** *v.* to raze.

dapnás: idapnas. *v.* to press clothes, iron. **dapnasen.** *v.* to massage (a woman after childbirth for nine consecutive months).

dapnís: dapnisan. *n.* beach (*igid ti baybay*; *aplaya*); (*reg.*) *var.* of *sanggir*.

dapó: *n.* ashes; remains. **dapoen.** *a.* ash-colored, gray. **dapdapo.** *n.* a tree with good construction timber. **dimmapo.** *a.* burned to ashes. **kolordapo.** *a.* ashen-colored, gray. **padapuen** *v.* to pulverize; destroy. [Bon. *dapol*, Ibg. *avu*, Ivt. *avuq*, Png. *dápol*, Kpm., Tag. *abó*]

dapúg: *n.* firebrand. (*átong*) **dapugán.** *n.* receptacle for ashes, makeshift stove; open fire. [Ibg. *dafug*, Ivt. *rapuyan*, Kpm., Tag. *dapog*]

dapúl: *a.* gray; ash-colored. (*dapo*)

dápon: agdadapon. *v.* to meet (*taripnong*); converge; get together. **pagdadaponan.** *n.* meeting place; melting pot. **madaponan.** *v.* to be overtaken by light.

dap-ór: see *dappuor*: crumbling down; resound.

daput: daput no. *conj.* provided that.

dapúyos: agdapuyos. *v.* to lean, incline (about to fall).

dappáak: *n.* the cracking sound of bamboo. **agdappaak.** *v.* to crack; crash.

dappág: *n.* homestead.

dappát: *n.* level plot of ground; (*obs.*) creek adjoining a town or farm; virgin land claimed for agricultural purposes. **agdappat.** *v.* to land; set foot on the soil for the first time; pioneer; leave one's native land to settle somewhere else. **pagdappatan.** *n.* settlement area.

dappíg: see *dapig*: strike with the flat of a sword.

dappúor: *var.* of *dippuor*. **agdappuor.** *v.* to resound; stomp on the ground; walk heavily; crumble down (buildings). [Tag. *dabóg*]

dapráy: madapray. *v.* to faint, fall down swooning. (*dalutaytay*)

dára: *n.* blood. **agdara, dumara.** *v.* to bleed. **agpadara.** *v.* to vomit blood, pass blood, expectorate blood; hemorrhage. **agkadara.** *v.* to be of the same blood type. **agkadaraan.** *v.* of the same race; to be kin; suitable; compatible. **dardara** (*obs.*) *n.* fortitude. **agarindaraen.** *v.* to blush; redden. **dinardaraan.** *n.* Ilocano version of *dinugoan*, a dish of meat cooked in blood; blood pudding. **daradara.** *n.* a kind of herb used to cure wounds, *Euphorbia hirta*; *a.* bloody. **nadara.** *a.* bloody. **pangindaraen.** *a.* light red. **padaraen.** *v.* to bleed an animal or person; (*fig.*) mooch. **dara ti panniki.** *n.* bat blood; (*fig.*) sugarcane wine, *basi*. **Adda ti kinamauyong iti darada.** There is lunacy in their bloodline. **Saanmo a mapadara ti awan**

darana. You cannot squeeze blood from the bloodless. **No agtartaray ti dara, addanto iruruarna.** If it runs in the blood, it will show in due time. [Bon. *dála*, Ibg. *dága*, Ivt. *rayaq*, Kal. *cháÿa*, Knk. *basa, dadá*, Kpm. *dáyaq*, Png. *dalá*, Tag. *dugô*]

darádar₁: *n.* summer, hot season; heat. (*bara, pudot*) **nadaradar.** *a.* hot (said of the sun).

darádar₂: **idaradar.** *v.* to explain, make clear. (*palawag*)

daraddán: **agdaraddan.** *v.* to occur frequently. **daraddanen.** *v.* to do successively; to do frequently. **Agdadaraddanen ti taraok dagiti kawitan.** The crows of the rooster were continuous (one after another). **Pinagdaraddannan ti nagtilmon ta kasla adda dumakdakkel a nagtimbukel iti karabukobna.** He swallowed rapidly and repeatedly because it was as if he had a round object growing in his throat. [Tag. *dalás*]

darágang: daragangan. *a.* immodest, indiscreet, lewd, (said of a woman). **Daragangang a babai, tengnga ti bangbangkag ti pakisaysayyetanna!** That immodest woman, she is fooling around in the middle of the fields! [Tag. *halay*]

daragúp: **agdaragup.** *v.* to unite; pile up; accumulate. [Tag. *buntón, salansán*]

darákan: *n.* a kind of tree that yields guttapercha, *Palaquium oleiferum.*

daram-ég: **agdaram-eg.** *v.* to tumble down headfirst.

daramuángan: *n.* entrance; gate; door. [Tag. *pasukan*]

daramúdum: maidaramudum. *v.* to fall prone; stumble, trip. **agdaramudum.** *v.* to bow; incline the head; stoop.

darán: dumardaran. *v.* to supervene; intensify. **maidaran.** *v.* to increase in intensity; worsen. [Tag. *lalà*]

daranúdor: **agdaranudor.** *v.* to make a rumbling sound (before a storm, etc.). [Tag. *ugong*]

daráng: *n.* flame; heat (of the sun). (*pudot; gilayab; rangrang*) **dumarang.** *v.* to become hot; become aroused. **padarangen.***v.* to heat; inflame. [Ivt. *dangdang*, Tag. *init*]

darangádang: *n.* light at sunrise or moonrise. **agdarangadang.** *v.* to begin to light up.

darangés: dumaranges. *v.* to gush out; flow.

daranghíta: *var.* of *naranghita.*

darangidángan: *n.* ripening fruit just changing color; half ripe. **agdarangidangan.** *v.* to reach maturity. [Tag. *manibalang*]

darangídong: *n.* the middle of the nose, from the bridge to the tip. **darangidongan.** *a.* endowed with a pronounced bridge of the nose. [Tag. *balingus*]

daraudó: *n.* profuse menstrual bleeding. **agdaraudo.** *v.* to have a strong menstrual discharge; (*reg.*) to menstruate. [Tag. *pagdurugô*]

darápat: agdarapat. *v.* to lie side by side. **kadarapat.** *a.* adjacent. **Immayda nagdappat iti kadarapat ti balay daydi manongna.** They came to settle in the house adjacent to his late brother. [Tag. *karatig*]

darapdáp: see *pandaras*: carpenter's adz.

darapúyo: agdarapuyo. *v.* to lean, incline. [Tag. *hilig*]

dáras: *n.* times, instances; rate; frequency. **agdaras.** *v.* to recur periodically. **kadaras.** *n.* frequency. **mamindua a daras.** *adv.* twice. **mamitlo a daras.** *adv.* three times. **mamin-ano a daras?** how many times? [Tag. *ulit*]

darás: *a.* quick; rapidly. (*paspas, partak, pardas*) **nadaras.** *a.* quick, fast, rapid; hasty; ready; easy. **darasen, dardarasen.** *v.* to hasten, hurry up. **dumaras.** *v.* to become often. **managdardaras.** *a.* restless; lively; hyperactive. **panarasan.** *v.* to make do; take a shortcut. [Itg. *siglat*, Png. *gánat, pugá, maples*, Tag. *dalás, bilís*]

darasádas: dumarasadas. *v.* to rustle (said of the rain). see *dayasadas.*

darasúdos: nagdarasudos. *a.* overhasty; uncouth; disrespectful (*sabrak*). **agdarasudos.** *v.* to do hurriedly; to be disrespectful; do without planning; dare to do. **Asino koma kadakami ti agdarasudos nga umarayat?** Who among us dares to help? [Tag. *bastós*]

dárat: *n.* sand; silt. **dimmarat.** *a.* sandy, resembling sand. **kadaratan.** *n.* sandy place. (*karagatan; paratong; ruburub; tap-oy*) **panaraten.** *a.* sandy. [Ibg. *dágeq*, Ivt. *anay*, Kal. *legen*, Knk. *ladég*, Kpm. *balas*, Png. *buér*, Tag. *buhangin*]

dáraw: *n.* short visit. **dumaraw.** *v.* to make a short visit (*dar-aw*).

dar-áw: *var.* of *dar-aw*: visit; looking down from a high place. **agdar-aw.** *v.* to visit; look down from a high place (*tamdag*). **Nasayaat no madar-awanyo met dayta a paset ti probinsia.** It would be nice if you could drop by that part of the province. [Tag. *tanáw*]

darawádaw: *a.* protruding, jutting out (*dawadaw, dalawadaw*). **Nakitak dagiti rungo ti udang a nakadarawadaw.** I saw the antennae of the crayfish jutting out.

darawdáw: *var.* of *dawdaw*: species of mollusk with brown elongated shell.

darawídaw: *n.* talkative person. **nadarawidaw.** *a.* talkative, loquacious. [Tag. *daldál*]

darawiswís: *n.* a kind of freshwater mollusk with a sharp, elongated shell.

dar-áy: **dar-ayan.** *v.* to help, assist; participate in a meeting. **makidar-ay.** *v.* to cooperate. **dumar-ay.** *v.* to attend (*tabunó, taripnong*); assist. **makadar-ay.** *v.* to be able to attend, participate. **Inta dumagas idiay Bauang tapno darayanta ti kasarda.** Let's drop by *Bauang* to attend their wedding. [Tag. *daló* (attend)]

darayán: *n.* a variety of thick-skinned banana. (*daray-an*)

daray-án: *var.* of *darayán.*

darekdék: *n.* stake. (*pasok*) **mannarekdek.** *n.* a vine used to cure boils; *v.* to cut down bamboo for stakes. **maidarekdek.** *v.* to be firmly rooted (like a post); to be staked down. **Kasla naidarekdek ti nagtakderanna.** He stood straight like a post. [Tag. *haligi* (stake)]

daremdém: *n.* project; design; plan. (*panggep*; *gandat*; *ranta*; *ngayangay*; *gakat*; *balala*) **daremdemen.** *v.* to perceive indistinctly.

darepdép: *n.* imagination; dream; aspiration; daydream. **agdarepdep.** *v.* to imagine; dream; daydream. **darepdepen.** *v.* to imagine; picture in the mind. [Tag. *pangarap*]

darídar: **idaridar.** *v.* to insult; despise (*abi, pabain; uyaw*). [Tag. *pahiyâ*]

daríket: **nadariket.** *a.* healthy; strong. (*nasalunat*) **dariktan.** *v.* to do fast. [Tag. *lusóg*]

darikmát: *n.* instant, moment. (*kanito*; *biit*; *siwet*) **iti apagdarikmat.** in a moment. [Tag. *saglít*]

darikmakmák: **agdarimakmak.** *v.* to eat eagerly; to do without constraint.

darimángan: *n.* entrance into a narrow passage; small gate. (*wangawangan*; *ruangan*)

darimesmés: *var.* of *daripespes*: thoroughly wet. **agdarimesmes.** *v.* to sweat profusely. (*kalimduos*; *ling-et*)

darimusmús: *n.* end of play. **madarimusmusan.** *v.* to catch a glimpse of; just miss an opportunity. **Madarimusmusak ti likudanna idi lumabas.** I just caught a glimpse of his back when he passed.

darínas: **maidarinas.** *v.* to suffer a relapse; feel dizzy from the heat of the sun.

darinasnás: **darinasnasen.** *v.* to take the whole thing, everything. (*kayuskos*)

darináwar: *var.* of *dariwanáwar*: first light of the sun or moon; plain; evident.

darinesnés: see *dalinesnes*: settle down; retire; withdraw.

daringgár: **idaringgar.** *v.* to insist; persist (*pilit*); propose. [Tag. *pilit, giít*]

daringúngo: *n.* nosebleed. **agdaringungo.** *v.* to have a nosebleed (*sang-or*). **daringunguen.** *v.*

to give someone a bloody nose. **Pagdaringunguekto ket dagiti sinalbag!** I will give those damn people a bloody nose! [Knk. *dalingong-ó*, Tag. *balinguyngóy*]

daripespés: **madaripespes.** *v.* to be thoroughly wet. (*rusep*) **Nupay nasapa pay, nadaripespesen iti ling-et.** Although it was still early, he was drenched in sweat. [Tag. *basâ*]

darírag₁: *a.* hot and dry; *n.* heat of the sun. **madarirag.** *a.* to suffer a relapse for having walked in the sun. (*begnat*)

darírag₂: **idarirag.** *v.* to propose; sponsor; insist (*pilit*); remind; spread secret news. **Agtultuloyda a mangidardarirag iti pannakaaramat kadagiti makadangran a pestisidio.** They continue to warn about the use of dangerous pesticides. [Tag. *giít*]

darís: **nadaris.** *a.* long-haired; long-stemmed. (*lampong*; *raber*)

darísay: *n.* beauty; excellence; black and white rooster. **nadarisay.** *a.* excellent, superior. **darisayen.** *n.* a black and white cock. **Uray sadino ti yanko ket ipudnok latta ti darisay a panagayatko kenka.** Wherever you are I will reveal my true love for you. [Tag. *lantáy*]

darisdís: *n.* slope. **nadarisdis.** *a.* sloping. (*bangkirig*) **ipadarisdis.** *v.* to put in a horizontal position. [Tag. *dahilig*]

daríson: **agdarison.** *v.* to squeeze in; push in a crowd, hustle. **idarison.** *v.* to crowd; press; cram into a corner; squeeze in. **pagdadarisonan.** *n.* melting pot; crowded area. **Nagdadarison nga immulog dagiti rebelde iti paglugananda.** The rebels squeezed in as they entered their vehicle. [Tag. *magkalumpón*]

dariwanáwar: *n.* first rays of light of the sun or moon. **nadariwanawar.** *a.* evident, clearly seen; bright. [Tag. *liwanag*]

dariwangwáng: *n.* rugged, steep place; abyss; chasm; hell. **nadariwangwang.** *a.* fearful. **idariwangwang.** *v.* to open wide. **maidariwangwang.** *v.* to fall into a hole. [Tag. *bangín*]

daríway: *n.* a variety of awned early rice; also, see *bansaway.*

daríwis: *a.* diagonal, slanting.

darmós: *var.* of *damros*: wash the face (*diramos*). [Tag. *hilamos*]

darnáp: **agdarnap.** *v.* to spread. **idarnap.** *v.* to spread out (*aplag*). **madarnapan.** *v.* to be covered with. **Aglanglangay dagiti sabong a naidarnap iti igid ti dalan iti nalailo nga apros ti pul-oy.** The flowers spread along the edge of the road were growing lustily in the caressing touch of the breeze.

darnás: **maidarnas.** *v.* to be present at a particular time (said of stars and celestial bodies).

darúdar: *n.* the third night of the full moon. **madarudaran**. *v.* to be overcome by moonrise while having supper during the third night of the full moon (sign of bad luck). **darudaran**. *v.* to meet by chance; inspect; go and see; take a look at; inspect.

darúgas: *var.* of *durogas*: swindle; cheat. (*kusit*)

darugsóy: **madarugsoy**. *v.* to be drenched with sweat. (*kalimduos*)

darúk: **madaruk**. *v.* to have the stomach burned by liquor. **daruken**. *v.* to add salt to (fruits); pickle (*atsara*).

darúkis: *var.* of *dalandan*.

darukmáma: **maidarukmama**. *v.* to bow deeply; bend to the ground; fall prostrate; to be overburdened by unbearable odds.

darúm: *n.* lawsuit; charge, indictment; accusation. **idarum**. *v.* to confess; accuse; squeal; bring to the attention of. **yuli ti darum**. bring up a charge (in court). **Adu ti nangidarumanmi kenkuana.** We have filed many lawsuits against him; We have accused him of many things. **Napigsa ti pruebak iti panangidarumko kenka.** I have strong proof to indict you. [Bon. *dalom*, Kal. *chiÿum*, Png. *dalém*, Tag. *sakdál*]

darumaká: *n.* a kind of plant with large leaves used to make baskets, *Donax cannaeformis*.

darumisá: **agdarumisa**. *v.* to spill food or drinks. **nadarumisa**. *a.* dirty; messy; lazy. [Tag. *kalat*]

darúmog: **agdarumog**. *v.* to bend down one's head. (*dúmog*) **nakadarumog**. *a.* stooping, bending; inclining.

darumpapék: *n.* a kind of elongated marine fish; a variety of rice. **nadarumpapek**. *a.* stocky; with a broad base and tapering off at the top like a pyramid.

darumpít: (*obs.*) *n.* black lead.

darundón: *n.* second harvest of the year; *a.* producing a second crop; not yet mature (fruits); second child born after a long interval. **agdarundon**. *v.* to follow one another face-to-face; to bear fruit for the second time in one season; to attack forward; to push someone in line or in a crowd. **darundunen**. *v.* to attack at full speed (*daruros*). **idarundon**. *v.* to push back (an enemy); defeat. [Tag. *sugod* (plunge into an attack)]

darúp: **dumarup**. *v.* to approach eagerly; to prepare to attack (*raut*). **darupen**. *v.* to feed in order to fatten (*seksek*); approach. **Darupdarupenda ti ruangan ti pagadalan.** They are approaching the door of the schoolhouse. [Tag. *sugod*]

darupdúp: *var.* of *darup*: sudden movement forward, attacking, advancing.

darúros: **darurusen**. *v.* to attack, forward charge (dogs, etc.). (*duklos, darup*)

dar-ós: **agdar-os**. *v.* to assemble; do after finishing something else. (*reg.*) drop by, visit (*dar-aw*). **pagdadar-usan**. *n.* meeting place; melting pot. **Nagdar-osda idi kalman iti yanmi.** They dropped by our place yesterday.

darusdús: *n.* a kind of hoe for weeding, trowel. **agdarusdus**. *v.* to slide down a slope or tree. [Tag. *dausdós*]

darusepsép: **nadarusepsep**. *a.* wet, soaked (*rusep*). [Tag. *basâ*]

daróy: **nadaroy**. *a.* thin; weak (food) (*lasaw, taroy*). **dumaroy**. *v.* to become thin; weaken. **Kasapulanna ti agas a pangpadaroy iti napalet a darana.** He needs medicine to thin out his thick blood. [Tag. *labnáw*]

darsí: **maidarsi**. *v.* to trip; fall; be knocked sideways. (*obs.*) **nadarsi**. *a.* humble. (*nanumo*)

das: **umdas**. *v.* to be enough, adequate. (*umanay*)

dasádas: *n.* rustling sound of leaves. **dumanasadas**. *v.* to rustle (*darasadas, anasaas*). [Tag. *pagaspás*]

das-ál: **idas-al**. *v.* to shake the contents; to put down heavily; heap on something; shake in order to settle; transfer the blame to someone else. **agdas-al**. *v.* to settle (many inhabitants in one place); to suffer stomach pains. **pagidasalan**. *n.* scapegoat, person who receives the blame or punishment (*langdét*). **pagdas-alan**. *n.* person who will bear the burden; scapegoat, person who will be punished. **Dakkel ti panagamakna amangan no isu ketdi ti pagdas-alan ti pungtot ti ari.** He was very afraid in case he would be the one punished by the wrath of the king.

dasár: *n.* food set on the table. (*puní*) **dasaram**. *v.* to set the table. **idasar**. *v.* to set out for use, set the table. **No kayatmon ti mangan, ibagam ta idasarankan.** If you want to eat already, say so and I will set the table for you. [Kal. *choslog*, Tag. *hain*]

dásay: **maidasay**. *v.* to be weakened; faint; prostrate from sickness. **Nasarakandaka a naidasay dita salas.** They found you prostrate in the living room. [Tag. *lupaypáy*]

dasdás: *n.* stubble; trail. **dasdasan**. *v.* to make a path; make way. [Tag. *landás*]

dasí₁: **maidasi**. *v.* to fall on the back (*tuang, darsi*). **agkaidasi**. *v.* to stagger, totter. [Tag. *giray*]

dasí₂: *a.* strange, alien; awkward.

dásig: *n.* row, line; file. **maidasig**. *v.* to be segregated into classes, classified. **idasig**. *v.* to classify, separate into classes; compare; segregate. **dasigen**. *v.* to classify; segregate; grade. **kaidasigan**. *n.* category; class; value; worth; importance. [Tag. *hambíng* (compare)]

daskól: maidaskol. *v.* to trip forward (*daramudom*). [Tag. *tisod*]

dasúdas: agdasudas. *v.* to abound, be plentiful (at one time); to bear many fruits; happen all at once.

das-ól: agdas-ol. *v.* to collapse suddenly (while stepping in a hole, etc.). **agdas-oldas-ol a panaganges**. *n.* hard, hollow breathing.

-data: enclitic expressing third plural or second plural agent on first dual patient. **Kayatdata.** They like us (you and me).

dáta: *a.* face up. **agdata, agpadata.** *v.* to lie on the back, lie with the face up. **idata.** *v.* to cause someone to lie on the back. **mapadata.** *v.* to fall on the back. **padataen.** *v.* to place on the back. **agdadata.** *v.* to stand uncovered; be evident, obvious, clear. **nakadata.** *a.* lying with the face up. **Naim-imbag ti agdadata a kabusormo ngem ti gayyem nga saan a pudno.** Better an open enemy than a false friend. **Ti tao nga saanna a matungpal ti karina, salawasaw nga agdadata.** He who cannot fulfill his promises cannot be trusted (is a liar on the back). [Tag. *tihayà*]

datá: *pron.* Siak series independent pronoun for the first person dual: We two; enclitic form is *-ta*. [Png. *sita*, Tag. *tayong dalawá*]

datág: idatag. *v.* to bring forward, report, submit; allege; deliver; present. **dumatag.** *v.* to present oneself; appear in person; give up; surrender. **Padasenta nga idatag ti singasingmo kadakuada.** Let's try to present your suggestion to them. [Tag. *haráp, tanghál*]

datáo: *pron.* Indefinite pronoun usually denoting the speaker: one. **kadatao.** oblique pronoun of *datao*: to me, for me. **Bagay met datao a maawagan iti kasta.** It also suits me well to be called like that.

dátar: idatar. *v.* to present, display, exhibit; expose; deal out, apportion. **agidatar.** *v.* to hand out food. [Tag. *pakita, tanghál*]

datár: *n.* floor (*basar, dissaar, suelo*); bamboo flooring. **agdatar.** *v.* to make a bamboo floor. **padatar.** *n.* a kind of automatic trap for wild birds. **agpadatar.** *v.* to use the *padatar* trap. [Ibg. *datág*, Ifg. *dulong*, Ivt. *tapiq*, Kal. *gittagon, tabla*, Knk. *dáu, det-á*, Kpm. *lande*, Png. *datal*, Tag. *sahig*]

datáy: *var.* of *datayo*: we (inclusive).

datayó: *pron.* First person independent (*siak* series) inclusive plural pronoun: We and you, I and you plural. Enclitic form is *-tayo*. [Knk. *daitakó*, Png. *sikatayó*, Tag. *tayo*]

datdát: datdaten. *v.* to give everything; include everybody; get all.

daténg: *n.* arrival. (*sangpet*) **dumteng.** *v.* to arrive, come; reach one's destination. **datngan.** *v.* to come upon; befall. **makagteng.** *v.* to be able to arrive. **madatngan.** *v.* to reach; be able to find out; arrive on a person, come upon a person (while he is doing something else); be overtaken by; have menstrual flow. **magteng, madateng.** *v.* to reach, come to; attain. **magtengan.** *v.* to be able to reach; (*fig.*) afford a certain price. **pagteng.** *n.* experience, happening. **ipagteng.** *v.* to cause to happen. **mapagteng.** *v.* to happen, occur; get; undergo. **pannakagteng.** *n.* the way in which someone is able to arrive. **idadateng.** *n.* arrival. **Adu a talaga a pannubok ti idateng ti biag.** There are a lot of trials that life brings. [Bon. *dátom*, Ibg. *lebbeq*, Ivt. *mawaraq*, Kpm. *dátang*, Png. *sabí, daténg*, Tag. *dating*]

dáti: (Tag. also) *a.* former; original. **Nagbalinen a bayakabak 'tay dati nga arbis.** The former drizzle has already turned into a heavy downpour. [Kal. *si chamu*]

datíbo: (Sp. *dativo*: dative) *n.* dative case; indirect object.

dátiles: (Sp. *dátil*: date) *n.* the date tree; date fruit.

datlág: datdatlag. *n.* phenomenon; wonder; miracle; fashion; mystery. **kinadatdatlag.** *n.* miracle, wonder, marvel. **makadatdatlag.** *a.* phenomenal, wondrous. [Tag. *hiwagà*]

dáto: *n.* Muslim ruler.

dáton: *n.* sacrifice; gift, offering. **idaton.** *v.* to offer; sacrifice to; present. **agdaton.** *v.* to court; offer love. **Pasig a tirong dagiti agdatdaton kenkuana.** Those that court her are all pirates. [Png. *miter, ibagat*, Tag. *handóg, alay*]

datúng: (*coll.*) *n.* money. (*kuarta*)

dátos: (Sp. *datos*: data) *n.* data.

dátoy: *var.* of *daytoy* when reduplicated. **datdatoy.** *n.* only this one.

dáwa: *n.* ear of grain; blade of a knife. **agdawa.** *v.* to develop spikes (rice). **managdawa.** *a.* fruitful. **panagdadawa.** *n.* season for the appearance of rice stalks. **Nakadawa aminen dagiti pagayko.** All my rice stalks have developed ears. [Tag. *uhay*]

dawádaw: agdawadaw. *v.* to protrude, project; exceed in height or length. **idawadaw.** *v.* to project, cause to protrude (*dalawadaw*). [Tag. *uslí*]

dawádaw: dawadawen. *v.* to take food out of the pot early for someone who prefers his food less cooked. **idawadawan.** *v.* to take food out of the pot early for someone.

dáwang: agdawang. *v.* to buzz (bees).
daw-ás: dumaw-as. *v.* to stop by briefly in passing; to exaggerate. **idaw-as.** *v.* to make a brief stop in order to deliver something. **dawasen.** *v.* to make a brief stop in passing in order to get something. [Tag. *saglít*]
dáwat₁: *n.* request; petition. (*kiddaw*; *unnoy*) **agdadawat.** *n.* moocher; one who always asks for something. **dumawat.** *v.* to ask for; request, beg. **dawaten.** *v.* to ask for something; demand; claim; expect. **idawdawat.** *v.* to request, ask for. **idawatan.** *v.* to request on behalf of someone. **madawat.** *v.* to get, obtain; *n.* something that is obtained (for free). **padawatan.** *v.* to give to someone what someone requests. **Ulitek manen ti dumawat iti pammakawan.** I will again ask for forgiveness. [Ibg. *mekkiddaw*, Ivt. *iyahes*, Kal. *kochewon*, Kpm. *nyáwad*, Png. *keréw*, Tag. *hingí*]
dáwat₂: dawatdawat. *n.* uvula of the palate. [Bon. *oklong*, Knk. *il-ilók*, *ak-aklóng*, Tag. *tilaó*]
dáway: (*obs.*) **dinaway.** *n.* singing of drunkards.
dawdáw: *n.* a kind of marine mollusk with a brown elongated shell. **dumawdaw.** *v.* to be too long; not fit. **idawdaw.** *v.* to make longer; brighten by raising the wick.
dawél: agdawel. *v.* to be cruel (person or weather). **nadawel.** *a.* cruel, merciless, harmful; strong (sea or wind). (*asing*; *ulpit*; *ranggas*; *rungsut*) **Rabii ken nadawel ti taaw.** It is night and the sea is strong. [Tag. *lupít*]
dáweng: agdawengdaweng. *v.* to be dizzy; to stagger (*ulaw*). [Tag. *liyó*]
dawér: *n.* a kind of woody vine with yellow flowers, *Caesalpinia crista*.
dáwi: nadawi. *a.* usual, common, customary; frequent. **dumawi.** *v.* to be trapped (people), hooked (fish). **kadawyan.** *n.* custom, habit. *a.* normal, customary, usually. **Kadawyan nga alas nuebe ti luas ti lantsa.** The departure of the boat is usually at nine.
dawí: *n.* a kind of tree.
dawíris: agdawiris. *v.* to stagger. (*bariring*; *daweng*; *dungay*; *lupay*; *sabbadaw*; *tiwed*) **nadawiris.** *a.* twisted, crooked, contorted (*killo*, *riwis*). [Tag. *baluktót*]
dáwis: *n.* narrow strip of land projecting into the sea; strip used for stringing fish, fruits, etc.; sharp point; tongue; amount of tobacco leaves to be speared on a stick. **nadawis.** *a.* pointed. **dawisen.** *v.* to string (fish); pierce. **dadawisan.** *n.* the depression between the branches of the lower jaw, under the chin. **sangadawis a lames.** one line of strung fish. **Dinawisna a siu-**

ulimek ti pasilio. He thrust through the hall quietly. [Tag. *tulis*]
dáwit: idawit. *v.* to include. (*raman*) **maidawit.** *v.* to be included.
day: (*obs.*) **dumay.** *v.* to frighten birds.
dáya: *n.* east. **makindaya.** *a.* on the east side. **agpadaya.** *v.* to go to the east. **ipadaya.** *v.* to point to the east. [Ibg. *lalassangan*, Itg. *tadaya*, Ivt. *valugan*, *pangaditan*, Kal. *kapun amiyanan*, Knk. *beskáan*, Kpm. *aslagan*, Png. *bokíg*, Tag. *silangan*]
dayá: daya, padaya. *n.* party, feast, banquet. **sidadaya.** *a.* exposed to view, laid bare. **agdaya, agpadaya.** *v.* to have a party, feast. **padayaan.** *v.* to celebrate. **makidaya.** *v.* to attend a feast or party. [Tag. *pigíng*]
dayáas: dumayaas. *a.* to rain heavily. (*bayakabak*)
dayág: *n.* glory; beauty. (*dayaw*; *ngayed*; *tan-ok*) **nadayag.** *a.* grand, elegant, fine, majestic. **Kasano koma a malipatak ti maysa a nalasbang a dayag?** How could I ever forget such an exuberant beauty? [Bon. *dáyaw*, Tag. *gandá*, *dangál*]
dayákos: *n.* a kind of fishing net. **madayakos.** *v.* to trip, stumble. (*dalápus*) **dayakusen.** *v.* to take all; include all; sweep everything, accumulate everything.
dayamúdum: *n.* mumbling, muttering. **agdayamudum.** *v.* to mutter, mumble. (*dayengdeng*; *danengdeng*) **dayamuduman.** *v.* to mutter at; growl at (with disrespect). [Tag. *bulóng*]
dáyang: *n.* name given to a Muslim princess; open; bare, uncovered. **dayangdayang.** *a.* without walls. **agdayangdayang.** *v.* to be without walls; roam, wander.
dayangdáng: *n.* *Lunasia amara* plant. (*paitan*)
dayánggos: *n.* hustle. **dayanggusen.** *v.* to hit the foot against; bump into. **makadayanggos.** *v.* to accidentally bump; collide with. (*dalapus*) **padayanggos.** *n.* poorly done work. **pagdayanggosan.** *v.* to do a job poorly. **Pasaray dayanggusen ti sapatosna a goma dagiti bato a pangipeksaanna iti gurana iti lakay.** He often strikes his rubber shoes on the rocks to express his anger at the old man. [Tag. *banggâ*]
dayangkí: *n.* fish trawl net. **maidayangki.** *v.* to be caught in a fish trawl net.
dayás: dayasan. *v.* to cleanse wounds. **idayas.** *v.* to wash with, cleanse with.
dayasádas *n.* sound of showering; torrential downpour. (*bayakabak*) **dumayasadas.** *v.* to shower (said of rain). [Png. *beyebeyé*, Tag. *lirit*]
dáyaw: *n.* honor, glory; respect; reputation, fame. (*dayag*; *ngayed*; *tan-ok*) **agdaydayaw.** *v.* to pay respects to; venerate. **nadayaw.** famed,

honored; polite; respectful. **dayawan.** *v.* honor; award; recognize. **dayawen.** *v.* to honor, respect, glorify, praise. **madaydayaw.** *a.* honorable; famous. **managdaydayaw.** *a.* respectful. **pammadayaw.** *n.* acknowledgements; award. **padayawan.** *v.* to be courteous to. **padayaw.** respect; homage; (*obs.*) *n.* animal foot. **agpipinnadayaw.** *v.* to honor each other. **padayawan.** *v.* to reward; honor; recognize officially. **ipadayaw.** *v.* to boast about, be proud of, show off. **manangdaydayaw.** *a.* respectful. **agkakadayaw.** *v.* to be equal in fame or status; salutation or opening address given to a crowd: respected people. **Sitataya ti dayawna.** *exp.* Her honor is at stake. **Nasaysayaat ti matay a sidadayaw ngem ti mabiag nga mauy-uyaw.** It's better to die with honor than live with shame. [Ibg. *dayaw*, Png. *dáyew*, Kal. *chayaw* (honor), *lanchilongeÿ* (famous), Kpm. *dangal, damlaq,* Tag. *puri, dangál, galang,* Tag. *dayaw* = chirping of birds]

daydáy: **idayday.** *v.* to spread out in order to air. **maidayday.** *a.* completely exposed (without protection); laid bare.

daydí: *dem.* Singular remote past demonstrative: that (long ago). With people it implies that the person has deceased; plural is *dagidi.* **daddaydi.** that only, nothing but that (*daydi*). **kadaydi.** oblique of *daydi.* **Kaano pay daydi panangpaspasusok ken panangsuksukatko iti lampinna?** Just how long ago was it when I breast-fed him and changed his diapers? **Siak daydi nangisalakan kenka, malagipmo?** I was the one who saved you (a long time ago), do you remember? [Tag. *yaon*]

daydiáy: *dem.* Singular present tense demonstrative referring to objects far from both the speaker and hearer: that. Plural is *dagidiay.* **daddadiay.** that only, nothing but that. [Knk. *sidéy*, Png. *sáman*, Tag. *iyón*]

dayég: **madayeg.** *v.* to shake, shiver, tremble. (*tigerger*) **apadpadayeg.** *v.* to wobble.

dayegdég: see *dayasadas*: showering rain. (*bayakabak*)

day-éng: *n.* humming; wordless song. **agdayeng.** *v.* to sing a wordless song, hum. **agpadayeng.** (*obs.*) *v.* to pucker the face.

dayengdéng: **dayengdengan.** *v.* to scold, reprimand. (*kariar; luya; bir-it; danengdeng*)

dáyo1: *n.* guest from another town. (*sangaili*) **dumayo.** *v.* to go to another place (for livelihood).

dáyo2: **agdayondayo.** *v.* to compete, rival. (*pasil; salisal; salip; artak*) **dayoan.** *v.* to outdo, better, exceed. **dinnayo.** *n.* tournament, athletic match; athletics.

dayúday: *n.* wood shelf on the wall to hold mats, pillows, etc. **idayuday.** *v.* to place on a shelf.

dayúsdos: **agdayusdos.** *v.* to scrape. **dayusdusen.** *v.* to scrape; take all.

daytá: *dem.* Singular present tense demonstrative referring to objects close to the hearer: that. Plural is *dagita.* **datdata.** that only, nothing but that (*dayta*). [Bon. *sána*, Png. *sátan*, Tag. *iyán*]

daytáy: *dem.* Singular recent past demonstrative: that. Plural is *dagitay.* **datdatay.** that only, nothing but that (*daytay*). [Tag. *yaon*]

daytóy: *dem.* Singular present tense demonstrative: this. Plural is *dagitoy.* **datdatoy.** this only, nothing but this. [Knk. *sináy, tuná*, Png. *sáya, áya*, Tag. *itó*]

dayyáng: **idaydayyang.** *v.* to show. (*ipabuya*)

dayyég: **agdayyeg.** *v.* to quake; tremble; vibrate. **madayyeg.** *v.* to be shaken; to be stunned. **Pagpigsaenna ti namnamana iti baet dagiti kanalbuong a mangdayyeg iti aglawlaw.** He is strengthening his hopes in the midst of the cannon fire shaking the world around. **maysa a makadayyeg-utek a kugtar.** *n.* one head-spinning kick. [Tag. *kiníg*]

dayyéng: *n.* humming; sound; melody. **agdayyeng.** *v.* to hum or mumble a song; (*reg.*) gossip. [Png. *amingaw*, Tag. *higing, huni*]

de-: (Sp. *de:* of; by) *pref.* 1. Prefix indicating the use of, wearing, or being equipped with the entity denoted by the stem: **de-armas.** *a.* equipped with weapons. **desarming a ridaw.** *n.* mirrored door. **de-uniporme.** *a.* wearing a uniform. **derehas a balay.** *n.* house with railing. **deadal.** *a.* literate, educated (with an education). 2. may also denote measurements or dimensions, used with Spanish numbers. **de-tres a lansa.** three-inch nail.

deádal: *a.* finished with schooling; scholarly.

debáak: *n. Ternstroemia sp.* tree.

debáte: (Sp. *debate:* debate) *n.* debate. (*rupir; subang*) **agdebate.** *v.* to have a debate.

debatísta: (f. *debate*) *n.* orator, master of rhetoric. (*agdedebate*)

debér: (Sp. *deber:* duty) *n.* right; obligation; duty. (*kalintegan*)

debilidád: (Sp. *debilidad:* debility) *n.* debility, physical weakness. (*kapsut*)

debú: (Eng.) *n.* debut.

debómba: *n.* type of gun that must be pumped before use.

debosión: (Sp. *devoción:* devotion) *n.* devotion, loyalty. **debosionado.** *a.* devout, pious. **debosionado.** *n.* devotee. **debosionario.** *n.* prayer book.

debutánte: (Sp.) *n.* debutante, one making a formal entrance into society.

debóto: (Sp. *devoto*: devotee) *n.* devotee; devout client.

dedál: (Sp. *dedal*: thimble) *n.* thimble.

déde: (Tag. also, *coll.*) *n.* baby's milk bottle; mammary glands. **agdede.** *v.* to suck.

dedikádo: (Sp. *dedicado*) *a.* dedicated.

dedóse: (Sp. *doce*: twelve + prefix *de-*) *n.* kind of gun that spits twelve ball bearings from its exploded bullet.

deg-ás: *n.* the second pounding of rice. **deg-asen.** *v.* to re-pound rice.

degdég: **manegdeg, degdegan.** *v.* to increase, add to; worsen; intensify. **dumegdeg.** *v.* to increase in intensity or degree. **padegdegen.** *v.* to make something worse. **Degdegam laeng ti saem ti napalabas a diak pay laeng malipatan agingga ita.** You are just increasing the pain of the past that I still am not able to forget until now. [Tag. *lalà*]

deggá: **agdegga.** *v.* to increase (rain); become abundant. **nadga.** *a.* abundant; lavish. **dumdumga.** (*obs.*) *v.* to be anxious, arrogant.

deggáng: **nadeggang.** *a.* noble, aristocratic; bright, radiant. **kinadeggang.** *n.* renown; glamour; nobility; fame. [Tag. *bantóg, tanyág, bunyî*]

deggés: **dumges.** *v.* to gush out. **agdegges.** *v.* to be at its height (meal). **agpadegges.** *v.* to be at its height; do with intensity; to suckle. **agpadpadegges.** *v.* to emit a flow of (milk). **Dumdumges ti sakit ti pakinakemko.** My hurt feelings are gushing out. [Tag. *bulwák*]

deggét: *a.* sticky. (*pigket, dekket*) **dumget.** *v.* to stick to, adhere to. [Tag. *dikít*]

degnáy: (*obs.*) *syn.* of *degdeg*: increase.

degrádo: (Sp. *grado*: grade + prefix *de-*) *a.* graded (eyeglasses); calibrated.

dehádo: (Sp. *dejado*: left behind) *n.* underdog; outsider (in a game); unexpected winner; horse or roster with the least bets; *a.* deficient; weak. (ant: *liamado*)

dehár: (Sp. *dejar*: abandon, neglect) **deharan.** *v.* to neglect. (*bay-a*)

dekáda: (Sp. *decada*: decade) *n.* decade. (*sangapulo a tawen*)

dekadénsia: (Sp. *decadencia*: decadence) *n.* decadence.

dekalidád: (Sp. *calidad*: quality + prefix *de-*) *a.* quality.

dekálogo: (Sp. *decálogo*: decalogue) *n.* decalogue, basic set of rules carrying binding authority.

dekáno: (Sp. *decano*: dean) *n.* council head; barrio head; dean of a college or university.

dekár: *var.* of *kedar*.

dekaréra: (Sp. *carrera*: career + prefix *de-*) *a.* having a career or profession; *n.* a professional.

dekdék: **dekdeken.** *v.* to pound; re-pound; grind. **dumekdek.** *v.* to recur intermittently. **nadekdek.** *a.* ground; pounded. [See also *danekdek.* Tag. *dikdík*]

dekkét: *n.* paste; adhesive; glue. **agdekket.** *v.* to stick; stick to each other. **idket, idekket.** *v.* to paste; glue. **dumket.** *v.* to stick to, adhere; fit nicely. **nadket.** *a.* fitting nicely; clinging; agreeing, sticky; close; intimate; affectionate. **nadketan.** *a.* nicely dyed. **madket.** *a.* dark brown, blackish. **awan ti dumket a rikna.** *exp.* cold personality, having no warm feelings toward anything. **Mayat ti dekketda kenkuana.** They suit him well. **Ti kadekketan a gayyemmo ti ad-adda a mangpasakit kenka.** Your closest friend is most likely to be able to hurt you. [Png. *pekét*, Tag. *dikít*]

deklamár: (Sp. *declamar*) **agdeklamar.** *v.* to declaim. **deklamasion.** *n.* declamation.

deklarádo: (Sp. *declarado*: declared) *a.* declared; stated.

deklarár: (Sp. *declarar*) **ideklarar.** *v.* to declare; proclaim.

deklarasión: (Sp. *declaración*) *n.* declaration.

deklíbe: (Sp. *declive*: slope) *n.* slope; amount of a slope.

dekuátro: (Sp. *cuatro*: four + prefix *de-*) **agdekuatro.** *v.* to sit with the legs crossed with one foot dangling over the knee, forming a square between the legs. The term *sikkawil* is used for when the legs are tightly crossed. **nakadekuatro.** *a.* sitting with the legs crossed in a *dekuatro* position. **Kanayonka nga agdekdekuatro.** *exp.* You are always sitting with the legs crossed (*fig.* you are always sure of yourself).

dekolór: (Sp. *color*: color + prefix *de-*) *a.* colored.

dekorádo: (Sp. *decorado*: decorated) *a.* decorated. **dekoratibo.** *a.* decorative.

dekorasión: (Sp. *decoración*: decoration) *n.* decoration. **dekorasionan.** *v.* to decorate.

dekurión: (Sp. *decurión*: decurion) *n.* group of ten students who act as monitors.

dekréto: (Sp. *decreto*: decree) *n.* decree.

del-á: (*obs.*) *var.* of *bel-a*.

del-ág: **agdel-ag.** *v.* to shout in order to startle.

delantál: (Sp. *delantal*: apron) *n.* apron.

delantéra: (Sp. *delantera*: front) *n.* front, frontage; façade.

delástiko: (Sp. *elástico*: elastic + prefix *de-*) *n.* stretchable substance; accordion.

deláta: (Sp. *de lata*: canned) *n.* canned food. *a.* canned. **pagidelataan.** *n.* cannery.

deldél: deldelen. *v.* to move something to one's advantage; put nearer to. **dumeldel.** *v.* to insist; be persistent; refuse to compromise. **ideldel.** *v.* to stick into; insist; persist. **Uray no kasano ti panangideldelko ti bagik kenkuana, saannak nga ikaskaso.** No matter how strong I force myself upon him, he doesn't pay any attention to me.

delegádo: (Sp. *delegado*: delegate) *n.* delegate.

delegasion. *n.* delegation.

delegasión: (Sp. *delegación*: delegation) *n.* delegation.

delikadésa: (Sp. *delicadeza*: delicacy) **delikadesa.** *n.* delicacy; considerateness; refinement; tact. **agdelikadesa.** *v.* to have tact.

delikádo: (Sp. *delicado*: delicate) *a.* weak, sickly; fragile; delicate; serious (sickness); crucial; critical; risky; aristocratic; fussy, fastidious.

deliniánte: (Sp. *delineante*: draftsman) *n.* draftsman.

delingkuénte: (Sp. *delincuente*: delinquent) *n.* delinquent.

delírio: (Sp. *delirio*: delirium) *n.* delirium (*ammangaw*). **agdelirio.** *v.* to be in a state of delirium.

dellég: *n.* girder, bamboo floor joists.

dellúog: see *dulluog*: thunder. (*gurrood*)

delúbio: (Sp. *diluvio*) *n.* deluge, flood (*layos*). [Tag. *bahâ*]

delpín: (Sp. *delfín*: dolphin) *n.* dolphin. [Ivt. *gaganam, lumbalumba*]

demákina: (Sp. *máquina*: machine + prefix *de-*) *a.* mechanized. **demakina a pagarado.** *n.* mechanized plowing equipment.

demálas: (Sp. *malas*: bad things + prefix *de-*) **agdemalas.** *v.* to have bad luck. (*daksangasat*; *buisit*)

demánda: (Sp. *demanda*: demand, petition, request) *n.* lawsuit; legal claim; demand. (*darum*) **idemanda.** *v.* to charge in a court of law. **agdemanda.** *v.* to file a lawsuit. [Tag. *sakdál*]

demandádo: (Sp. *demandado*: accused) *n.* the accused in court, respondent.

demandánte: (Sp. *demandante*: accuser) *n.* the accuser, complainant.

demdém: *n.* rancor, grudge; ill will. **demdemen.** *v.* to repress anger; harbor a grudge. **agdemdem** (*obs.*) *v.* to disobey.

demmáng: *adv.* on opposite sides; armspan; twice orphaned; blind in both eyes; deaf in both ears; paralyzed in both legs. **agdemmang.** *v.* to lift with both hands; to be twice orphaned; blind in both eyes; deaf in both ears, etc. **demmangen.** *v.* to do with both (hands). **Ulilan a demmang.** He was already twice orphaned.

demokrásia: (Sp. *democracía*: democracy) *n.* democracy. (*wayawaya*) **demokratiko.** *a.* democratic.

demókrata: (Sp. *demócrata*) *n.*, *a.* democrat.

demónio: (Sp. *demonio*: devil) *n.* devil, demon. (*sairo*) **agdemonio.** *v.* to go wild (as when drunk). **makapademonio.** *a.* having the potency to make one go wild (alcohol). **markademonio.** *n.* gin.

demonstradór: (Sp. *demostrador*: demonstrator, *n* from English influence) *n.* demonstrator.

demoralisádo: (Sp.) *a.* demoralized.

demo(n)strasión: (Sp. *demostración*: demonstration) *n.* demonstration.

dendén: dumenden. *v.* approach, go nearer to. **idenden.** *v.* to put close to; slide to. [Tag. *lapit*]

dennái: *n.* side. (*denna*) **dumna.** *v.* to stand by the side of, near; to follow immediately; put by the side of. **agdenna.** *v.* to stay close together, be side by side; stick together; (*fig.*) marry. **kadenna.** *a.* adjacent, next to; *n.* spouse. **makidenna.** *v.* to live with, deal with. **denaan.** *v.* to stay close to; live with someone. **makapagdenna.** *v.* to be able to live together. **nadenna.** *a.* close, near the side of. **idenna.** *v.* to put beside, put close to. **Mabudbuduanak no kadendennak.** I feel a tingling sensation when she is beside me. **No apay ketdi a dikay makapagdenna a nasayaat, awan dumayo iti aso ken pusa.** Why can't you live together well, you're no different from cats and dogs. [Png. *diking, ábay*, Tag. *tabí*]

denná₂: padna. *n.* piece of rope that connects the tug rope to the nasal septum of a water buffalo.

dennés: agdennes, apagdennes. *v.* to slightly touch, rub against. **Nagdennes dagiti barukongda.** Their chests rubbed against each other. [Tag. *daít*]

dennét: idennet. *v.* to steep; dip; dunk; to put in contact with. **maidennet.** *v.* to come in contact with. **agdendennet iti asin.** *exp.* denoting poverty (dipping in salt).

denominadór: (Sp. *denominador*: denominator) *n.* denominator (in fractions).

denominasión: (Sp. *denominación*: denomination) *n.* denomination.

denúnsia: (Sp. *denuncia*: accusation) *n.* denunciation; accusation. **agdenunsia.** *v.* to make an accusation or denunciation; to make a claim against someone with the police.

dentadúra: (Sp. *dentadura*: set of teeth) *n.* dentures, false teeth. (*postiso*)

dentísta: (Sp. *dentista*: dentist) *n.* dentist. **agpadentista.** *v.* to go to the dentist.

dengdéng: agdengdeng. *v.* to boil vegetables. (*abraw*) **dinengdeng.** *n.* boiled vegetable dish, usually with *boggoong*. **agdinengdeng.** *v.* to cook *dinengdeng*, boil vegetables. [Knk. *dengdéng*, Png. *pisíng*, Tag. *bulanglang*]

déngge: (Sp. *dengue*) *n.* dengue fever.

denggén: (f. *dengngeg*) *v.* to hear, listen to; respond to. **Madi no dina denggen ti agas.** It's bad if it doesn't respond to medicine. **dengngég**: **denggen.** *v.* to hear, listen to (*allingag, imdeng, indeng, lapayag, timud*); respond to; react to. **dumngeg, mangngeg.** *v.* to hear. **madengngegan, mangngegan.** *v.* to hear something. **makangeg.** *v.* to be able to hear. **dedengngegan.** *n.* auditory canal. **pangpangngegan.** *v.* to cause to hear; to say something to someone with the intention of being heard by a third party. **nagdenggan.** *n.* what was heard or understood. **pangngeg.** *n.* insinuation, hint. **kangkangngeg.** *a.* just heard. **makangkangngeg.** *v.* usually hear. **agipadengngeg.** *v.* to hint, insinuate, let be heard; broadcast. **pangngegan.** *v.* to insinuate; hint. **padengngegen, pangngegen.** *v.* to make someone listen. **Dumngegka!** Listen! **Mangngegko laeng ti baresbes ti danum.** I just hear the sound of running water. [Ibg. *ginna*, Ivt. *adngey*, Kal. *chongeÿ*, Kpm. *damdam*, Bon., Png. *dengél*, Tag. *diníg*]

dengngép: *n.* palliative. **dengngepen.** *v.* to apply ointment on (a wound, etc.); alleviate; soothe; ease. **Agsudor dagiti babai ti away tapno madengngep ti matrisda.** The country girls sit on warm water so their womb can be relieved (after pregnancy). [Tag. *bawa* (alleviate)]

deodoránte: (Sp.) *n.* deodorant.

departaménto: (Sp. *departamento*: department) *n.* department. **departamento ehekutibo.** executive department.

depdép: **depdepen.** *v.* to put out, extinguish; alleviate. **makadepdep.** *v.* to ease, relieve; remedy. **Nadepdep dagiti lua iti baet dagiti isem ken innabrasa.** The tears dried up between the smiles and the embraces.

depektíbo: (Sp. *defectivo*) *a.* defective; faulty.

depékto: (Sp. *defecto*: defect) *n.* defect, flaw, imperfection; weakness; blemish.

depénde: (Sp. *depende*: depends) *n.* depending on; it depends.

dependér: (Sp. *defender*: defend) **dependeran.** *v.* to defend (in court or in battle).

dependiénte: (Sp. *dependiente*: dependent) *n.* dependent.

depénsa: (Sp. *defensa*: defense) *n.* defense; fender, bumper of a car.

depié: (Sp. *de pie*: on foot) *a.* powered by the foot (sewing machine, paddleboat, etc.).

deplá: *var.* of *dapla*: spread (fire, news, etc.).

depláto: (Sp. *plato*: plate + prefix *de-*) *n.* rifletype gun with platelike bullet storage.

deponénte: (Sp.) *n.* deponent, one who testifies under oath.

depormádo: (Sp. *deformado*) *a.* deformed.

depórta: (Sp. *deportar*) **ideporta.** *v.* to deport. **deportasion.** *n.* deportation.

deposisión: (Sp. *deposición*: deposition) *n.* testimony, legal deposition.

depositánte: (Sp. *depositante*: depositor) *n.* depositor.

depositário: (Sp.) *n.* depository, place where something is deposited for safe keeping.

depósito: (Sp.) *n.* deposit; reserve; reservoir. **ideposito.** *v.* to deposit.

deputádo: (Sp.) *n.* deputy.

deppá: *n.* armspan. **sangadpa.** *n.* measurement of the arms extended, about six feet. **agdeppa.** *v.* to extend the arms. **deppaen.** *v.* to measure with the arms extended; extend. **ideppa.** *v.* to extend the arms; hang on a cross. **padeppa.** *n.* arm of a cross. **Armek la ketdi, uray asino ti agdepdeppa.** I will court her anyway, no matter who stands in the way. **Depdeppaek ti panagbabawik.** I extend my regrets. [Ibg. *lakeg, eppa*, Ivt. *adpaq*, Kal. *sinchopa*, Kpm. *kagpa*, Png., Tag. *dipa*]

deppáag: **madpaag.** *v.* to collapse; cave in (something burning). **dumpaag.** *v.* to collapse. **deppaagen.** *v.* to cause to collapse. [Tag. *guhò*]

deppáar: *n.* side of an object; region; area; coast. **sangadeppaar.** *n.* one region; one area. **Tubo iti deppaarko.** He grew up in my region.

deppáas: **dumpaas.** *v.* to increase (rain); intensify. **deppaasen.** (*obs.*) *v.* to force one's way through.

deppél: *n.* thumbprint; imprint; touch; press. **agdeppel.** *v.* to imprint one's thumbprint. **deppelen.** *v.* to squeeze; compress. **ideppel.** *v.* to print; impress; stamp. **makina a pangideppel.** *n.* punching Braille machine. **di maideppel iti lagip.** *exp.* to not be able to recall. **Agdeppelda iti asin.** *exp.* denoting poor, hungry people (putting their thumb in salt to eat). [Tag. *taták*]

deppér: **madper.** *v.* to become blunt (knife blade) (*ngudel*). [Tag. *puról, pudpód*]

deppés: *a.* leaning; prostrate; flat. **agdeppes.** *v.* to bend downward. **deppesen.** *v.* to cause to bend backward, push down. **ideppes.** *v.* to press down; flatten. **madpes.** *v.* to fall down; lie prone; lean toward. [Tag. *hilig*]

deppúor: see *dappuor*: crumbling down.

depresión: (Sp. *depresión*: depression) *n.* depression; hollow in the ground; financial depression; low spirits.

der-án: *n.* species of durable timber.

derdér: **maderder.** *v.* to become mushy (from being overcooked); decomposed; disordered; pulverized. **iderder.** *v.* to overdo; do over and over. **derderen.** *v.* to cause to become pulpy or mushy; mash; pulverize; batter; mutilate. **Derderek ti bagiyo iti buli!** I will mutilate your bodies with lead! [Tag. *durog*]

deréhas: (Sp. *rejas*: rails + prefix *de-*) *a.* with railings; with bars (said of windows).

derepénte: (Sp. *de repente*: sudden) **naderepente.** *a.* sudden (death).

derétsa: (Sp. *derecha*: right) *n.* right-hand side. (*kanawan*)

derétso: (Sp. *derecho*: law; straight; direct) *var.* of *diretso*: straight; *n.* law; duty, fee; direct; plain (without decoration). **deretso a biahe.** *n.* direct trip (nonstop).

derétsos: (Sp. *derechos*: rights, *obs.*) *n.* fee, toll.

dermatólogo: (Sp. *dermatólogo*: dermatologist) *n.* dermatologist.

dermatolohía: (Sp. *dermatología*: dermatology) *n.* dermatology, study of the skin.

derósas: (Sp. *rosa*: rose + prefix *de-*) *a.* rosy; pink. **dumerosas.** *v.* to become rosy (face).

derráas: *n.* cliff, precipice. (*rangkis*; *kayas*; *garangugong*) **maiderraas.** *v.* to fall down a cliff; (*fig.*) succumb to temptation, bring someone down morally. [Ibg. *gatág*, Kal. *angit*, *chigchig*, Png. *alosarsar*, Tag. *talampás*]

derráaw: *n.* tumult, uproar. **agderraaw.** *v.* to shout; agitate; complain. [Tag. *guló*]

derrém: *n.* gloom; misfortune; darkness. **dumrem.** *v.* to dim. **naderrem.** *a.* gloomy; overcast; foreboding. [Tag. *dilím*]

derrép: *n.* passion, emotion; lust; strong desire. **naderrep.** *a.* lustful. **nainderrepan.** *a.* lustful, sensual. **pangderrep ti lasag.** *n.* lust, sexual desire. [Tag. *libóg*]

dersá: **agdersa.** *v.* to rot; putrefy; decay; decompose; detach from the bone when well cooked. [Tag. *bulók*]

dersáy: **madersay.** *v.* to rot; decay; decompose; detach from the bone (cooked meat).

desábog: *n.* kind of gun. (*paltog*)

desekadór: (Sp. *secador*: drier) *n.* drier; drying room.

desakáto: (Sp. *desacato*: disrespect; contempt) *n.* contempt; disrespect of authority.

desapinádo: (Sp. *afinado*: tuning + prefix *de-*) *a.* out of tune. (*sintunado*)

desapío: (Sp. *desafío*: challenge) *n.* duel; challenge. (*aróg*)

desaprobádo: (Sp. *desaprobado*: disapproved) *a.* disapproved.

desaregládo: (Sp. *desarreglado*: disarranged) *a.* disarranged; disordered.

desbentáha: (Sp. *desventaja*: disadvantage) *n.* disadvantage.

desbokádo: (Sp. *desbocado*: wide-mouthed) **agdesbokado.** *v.* to be out of tune; to have poor pronunciation.

desdés: *n.* trail, path; **desdesan.** *v.* to cut a path into the forest; make a path. **madesdesan.** *v.* to stream with sweat (have trails of). [Ibg. *dallen*, *dalan*, Ivt. *rarahan*, Kpm., Png. *dalan*, Tag. *daán, landás*]

desénso: (Sp. *descenso*: demotion) *n.* demotion.

desénte: (Sp. *decente*: decent) *a.* decent.

desesperádo: (Sp. *desesperado*: desperate) *a.* desperate.

desétso: (Sp. *desecho*: reject) *n.* reject, product with a defect (usually sold at a lower price); *a.* rejected (said of defective products).

desgáste: (Sp. *desgaste*: wear and tear) *n.* wear and tear of machine parts.

desgrásia: (Eng.) *n.* disgrace; automobile accident, mishap; misfortune. **madesgrasia.** *v.* to be disgraced; have a mishap, automobile accident. **maidesgrasia.** *v.* to meet a mishap.

desgrasiádo: (Sp. *desgraciado*: disgraced) *a.* unfortunate, unlucky; violated; disgraced (said of women losing virginity before marriage); risky.

desidído: (Sp. *decidido*: decided) *a.* decided, with the mind made up.

desiérto: (Sp. *desierto*: desert) *n.* desert.

designár: (Sp.) **designaran.** *v.* to designate; appoint.

desisión: (Sp. *decisión*: decision) *n.* decision.

deskansádo: (Sp. *descansado*: rested) *a.* rested; comfortable (shoes); carefree.

deskansár: (Sp. *descansar*: rest) **agdeskansar.** *v.* to rest; stay for a while.

deskánso: (Sp. *descanso*: rest) *n.* rest. (*inana*) **ideskanso.** *v.* to put down a load.

deskárga: (Sp. *descarga*: unload) *n.* unloading. **deskargaen.** *v.* to unload.

deskárgo: (Sp. *descargo*: plea; discharge) *n.* excuse; apology.

deskaríl: (Sp. *descarril*: derailment) *n.* derailment. **nadeskaril.** *a.* derailed (train).

deskárte: *var.* of *diskarte*.

desklabadór: (Sp. *desclavador*) *n.* claw wrench; nail puller.

deskubrimiéntos: (Sp. *descubrimiento*) *n.* discovery.

deskubrír: (Sp. *descubrir*) **agdeskubrir.** *v.* to discover, invent.

deskuénto: (Sp. *descuento*: discount) *n.* discount.

deskomulgádo: (Sp.: *descomulgado*: ex-communicated) *a.* ex-communicated.

deskompasádo: (Sp. *descompasado*: out of time, out of tune) *a.* out of time, out of step (in dancing).

deskonektár: (Sp. *desconectar*) **ideskonektar.** *v.* to disconnect.

desmáya: (Sp. *desmayar*: faint) **madesmaya.** *a.* feeling faint.

desordenádo: (Sp. *desordenado*: disordered) *a.* disordered, in disorder.

desorganisádo: (Sp. *desorganizado*: disorganized) *a.* disorganized.

despalkadór: (Sp. *desfalcador*: embezzler) *n.* embezzler.

despálko: (Sp. *desfalco*: embezzlement) *n.* embezzlement. **despalkuen.** *v.* to embezzle.

despánta: (Sp. *espanta*: frighten) **nadespanta.** *a.* startled; amazed.

despásio: (Sp. *despacio*: slow) *a.* slow. **agdespasio.** *v.* to slow down.

despatsádo: (Sp. *despachado*: dispatched) *a.* dispatched; sold. **despatsador.** *n.* salesperson; dispatcher.

despatsár: (Sp. *despachar*: dispatch) **despatsaren.** *v.* to sell; dismiss; dispatch; discharge.

despátso: (Sp. *despacho*: dispatch) *n.* dispatch, official communication; counter (of a store or bank, etc.); ticket office; office.

despedída: (Sp. *despedida*: farewell party) *n.* farewell party. **agdespedida.** *v.* to have a going away party. **pagdespedidaan.** *n.* place where one will celebrate his farewell party.

despertadór: (Sp. *despertador*: alarm clock) *n.* alarm clock.

despetsár: *var.* of *despatsar*.

después: (Sp. *después*: after) *adv.* afterwards; next; then.

desposáda: (Sp. *desposada*: newly wed lady) *n.* betrothal; wedding ceremony. **makidesposada.** *v.* to be betrothed.

desposório: (Sp. *desposorio*: betrothal) *n.* deed of sale.

desprésio: (Sp. *desprecio*) *n.* contempt; disdain.

destakaménto: (Sp. *destacamento*) *n.* detachment of troops; military outpost.

destempládo: (Sp. *destemplado*: out of tune; harsh) *a.* out of tune; annealed.

destiér(r)o: (Sp. *destierro*: exile) *n.* exile, banishment (*pammatalaw*). **maidestiero.** *v.* to be exiled. **Naidestiero idi agsubli iti pagilian.** He was exiled when he returned to the country. [Tag. *pagtatapon*]

destiládo: (Sp. *destilado*: distilled) *a.* distilled. **destilador.** *n.* distilling apparatus.

destíno: (Sp. *destino*: destiny) *n.* place of work; destiny; appointment; assignment. **destinado.** *a.* destined; intended for.

destorniliadór: (Sp. *destornillador*: screwdriver) *n.* screwdriver.

destrongkár: (Sp. *destroncar*) **destrongkaren.** *v.* to dismantle.

detálie: (Sp. *detalle*: detail) *n.* detail, fine point. **detaliado.** *a.* detailed.

detenído: (Sp. *detenido*: detained) *a.* detained.

detensión: (Sp. *detención*) *n.* detention.

detenér: (Sp. *detener*) **deteneren.** *v.* to detain; confine.

detítulo: (Sp. *título*: title + prefix *de-*) *a.* with a degree; professional.

di₁: Adverb of negation. **Dika mangan.** Don't eat. **di pay.** not yet. **di kad uray.** even so. **Di pay ket nangrabiin ta urayennaka kano.** He hasn't even eaten dinner yet because he says he is waiting for you. [Negative statement: Png. *ag-*, Tag. *dî, hindî*; Negative command: Png. *alég*, Tag. *huwág*]

di₂: abbreviation of *daydi* or *idi*.

día: (Sp. *día*: day) *n.* day (*aldaw*). **por dia.** by the day (payment). **makipordia.** *v.* to work for the day, be a day laborer.

diá: **agdidia.** (*obs.*) *v.* to try one's strength. **idia.** *v.* to forget; let pass; not mind.

diáas: **dumiaas.** (*obs.*) *v.* to rain heavily. (*bayakabak*)

diabétiko: (Sp. *diabético*: diabetic) *n, a.* diabetic, suffering from diabetes.

diábles: *n.* cursing form of *diablo*.

diáblo: (Sp. *diablo*: devil) *n.* devil, demon. (*sairo*) **maniablo.** *n.* pagan priest. **Diablokayo a babbai!** You evil women! **Diablo'ttoyen.** Damn this! **Anak ti diablo!** mild curse (son of the devil).

diáging: (Eng.) **agdiadiaging.** *v.* to jog.

diák: [*di* + *-ak*] Negative adverb and first person singular absolutive enclitic: I (do) not. **Diak ammo.** I don't know. (*saanak*) [Replaces *di*-ko, see also *indiák* and *mandiák*]

diáket: (Eng.) *n.* jacket. **agdiaket.** *v.* to wear a jacket.

diakonádo: (Sp. *diaconado*) *n.* deaconship.

diákono: (Sp. *diácono*: deacon) *n.* deacon.

diákpat: (Eng.) *n.* jackpot. **agdiakpot.** *v.* to strike a jackpot.

dialékto: (Sp. *dialecto*: dialect) *n.* dialect. (*ayug*)

diálogo: (Sp. *diálogo*: dialog) *n.* dialog.

diálusi: (Eng. jalousie) *n.* jalousie, window blind with adjustable horizontal slats used to let in the wind while keeping out the sun and rain.

diamánte: (Sp. *diamante*: diamond) *n.* diamond.

diámbol: **agdiambol**. *v*. to jump for the ball (in basketball at the start of the game).

diamétro: (Sp. *diametro*: diameter) *n*. diameter.

diammó: (f. *di* + *ammo*) don't know. **agindidiammo**. *v*. to pretend not to know. [Png. *áwey*, Tag. *aywan*, *ewan*]

diamóntre: (Sp. *demontre*) *n*. the deuce.

dián: **idian**. *v*. to drop a bad habit and reform; to let bygones be bygones. [Tag. *waksí*]

diána: (Sp. *diana*: reveille) *n*. reveille.

dianitór: (Eng.) *n*. janitor.

diántre: (Sp. *diantre*: devil) *Interj*. curse word used toward a bad, disobedient person.

diár: *n*. appearance, look; the way someone is; countenance; bearing; posture. (*itsora*, *langa*)

diário: (Sp. *diario*: daily) *n*. newspaper. (*pagiwarnak*) **maidiario**. *v*. to be published in a newspaper (story). **madiario**. *v*. to be published in the paper (person or news event). **nakadiario**. *a*. made out of newspapers; with a newspaper.

diás: (Eng.) *n*. jazz music.

diáske: *syn*. of *diables*: devil.

diáy: *art*. distal article corresponding to the distal demonstrative *daydiay*; definite noun marker. **Natay diay anakna**. Her child died. [Png. *sámay*, Tag. *iyón*, *yung*]

diáya: *n*. gift, offering (*regalo*; *aginaldo*; *sagut*; *parabur*); proposal. **idiaya**. *v*. to expose, put out to view; offer gifts. **agdidiaya**. *v*. to manifest; be evident; obvious. **sididiaya**. *a*. offered. **Insungbatmi a didakami pakadanagan a bulon ti panagyamanmi iti panagdiayada**. We answered that they needn't worry about us as we thanked them for their offering. [Tag. *alay*]

dibidendáso: (Sp. *dividendo*: dividend + Spanish augmentative suffix -*azo*) *n*. tips in horse racing.

dibidéndo: (Sp. *dividendo*: dividend) *n*. dividend; interest on investment or share of stock.

dibinidád: (Sp. *divinidad*: divinity) *n*. divinity.

dibíno: (Sp. *divino*: divine) *a*. divine.

dibisión: (Sp. *división*) *n*. division; partition.

dibisór: (Sp. *divisor*: divisor) *n*. divisor in math.

dibuhánte: (Sp. *dibujante*: drawer) *n*. draftsman.

dibúho: (Sp. *dibujo*: drawing) *n*. drawing; illustration; sketch; pattern. **agdibuho**. *v*. to draw, make a drawing.

diborsiádo: (Sp. *divorciado*: divorced) *a*. divorced.

dibórsio: (Sp. *divorcio*: divorce) *n*. divorce. (*panagwinnaswas*) **agdiborsio**. *v*. to divorce.

dibusionádo: (Sp. *devocionado*: devoted) *a*. devoted. (*napeklan*)

didál: (Sp. *dedal*: thimble) *n*. thimble. (*dadál*) **agdidal**. *v*. to wear a thimble; use a thimble.

didigrá: *n*. disaster, catastrophe. **madidigra**. *v*. to be scared, frightened.

didíng₁: *n*. wall; side of a cart. **agdiding**. *v*. to put up a wall. **didingan**. *v*. to provide with walls. **pagdiding**. *n*. partition; materials used for making a wall. [Kal. *chingching*, Png., Tag. *dingding*, *padér*]

didíng₂: **dinnidingan**. *n*. variety of the girl's *kudo* game.

dídiok: *n*. a kind of vine with edible fruits.

didiósen: (pl. of *dios*) *n*. deities; gods; minor idols.

diém: *var*. of *giem*: friend (also used as adverb of emphasis).

diés: (Sp. *diez*: ten) *num*. ten; *n*. ten centavos, ten pesos. (*sangapulo*) **alas dies**. Ten o'clock. **sagdidies**. *a*. ten pesos each; ten each.

diéta: (Sp. *dieta*: diet) *n*. diet. **agdieta**. *v*. to diet.

díga: (Sp. *diga*: say, Tag. also) *n*. verbal expression of love. **dumiga**. *v*. to declare one's love. **digaan**. *v*. to declare one's love to someone. **Agkutukot dagiti tumengko no gamdek ti dumiga**. My knees shake when I try to express my affection. **Kaykayatko met ti makangkangngeg iti diga**. I also like to hear words of love.

dígek: *n*. a blue-flowered shrub with edible fruits, *Memecylon ovatum*.

dígem: **dumigem**. *v*. to fit nicely.

dignidád: (Sp. *dignidad*: dignity) *n*. dignity.

dignitário: (Sp. *dignitario*: dignitary) *n*. dignitary.

digó: *n*. broth; juice (of coconut). **mamadigo**. *v*. to share one's food; feed. **ipadigo**. *v*. to share a portion of one's food with another. **padiguan**. *v*. to share a dish. **No adda sidam, pagdiguam 'ta kaarubam**. If you have food, share it with your neighbor. [Ibg. *zigú*, *kaldo*, Ivt. *asuy*, Kal. *beÿat*, Knk. *sibó*, Kpm. *sabo*, Png. *digó*, Tag. *sabáw*]

digulló: **agdigullo**. *v*. to neck, fondle one another; make love.

dígom: (*obs*.) **digomdigoman**. *v*. to add to.

digungón: (*obs*.) *n*. idleness.

dígos: **agdigos**. *v*. to take a bath; bathe. **digusen**. *v*. to bathe; apply water to. **pagdigusan**. *n*. bathtub, place where one takes a bath. **padigusen**. *v*. to bathe animals; lead animals to a waterhole. **digos ti wak**. *n*. crow's bath, bathing wetting only the head. **nadigos iti**. bathed in, enveloped in. [Bon. *emes*, Ibg. *zigúq*, Ivt. *mariyus*, Knk. *diamsán*, Kpm. *díluq*, Png. *amés*, Tag. *ligò*]

digrá: madigra. *v.* to startle; be frightened. **didigra.** *n.* disaster, catastrophe; calamity. **didigraen.** *v.* to frighten; threaten; inflict suffering. **makadidigra.** *a.* disastrous, calamitous. [Tag. *sakunâ*]

digsí: *n.* brisk jump.

díka: [*di* + *-ka*] negative, second person singular particle. **Dika agsangit.** Don't cry.

dikálut₁: *n.* variety of awnless *diket* rice.

dikálut₂: dikalutan. *v.* to smear; scrape up with (food on bread); spread with the finger. **sangkadikalut.** *n.* one finger-smear full of. **idikalut.** *v.* to spread with the finger or spoon.

dikár: dumikar. *v.* to reoccur; come back. (*sumro manen*) **panagdikar ti angkit.** *n.* recurrence of asthma; asthma attack.

díkay: (*obs.*) **dikaydikayen.** *v.* to part while passing though; contraction of *dikayo*.

dikayó: [*di* + *-kayo*] negative, second person plural particle. **Dikayo agapa!** Don't fight with one another!

dikáyos: *var.* of *dayakos*.

dikay-ós: *var.* of *dayakos*.

díke: (Sp. *dique*) *n.* dike; dam.

dikén: *n.* pad placed on the head to put loads upon. **dikendiken.** *n.* millipede. **Kasla nagkarenken a dikendiken ni Addong idi mapanunotna.** Addong reacted like a folded millipede when he thought of it. [Bon. *gíken*, Png. *dikén*, Tag. *sapín*]

díket: *n.* generic name for soft rice, often used for making rice cakes and native sweets; variety of red-kernelled maize; variety of purple sugarcane; variety of coconut with soft, sweet meat. [Kal. *cheÿkot*, Png. *kulnét*, *sapkét*, Tag. *malagkít*]

dikídik: dikidiken. *v.* to regrind, re-pound.

dikkáyos: *var.* of *dayákos*.

dikkí: *n.* tartar of the teeth. **nakadikdikki.** *a.* full of tartar.

dikkúmer: agdikkumer. *v.* to be languid (*taramnay*); slothful, lazy; all alone; to lack self-confidence, withdraw from shame. **Nadatngan ti lakay ni Kundring a nakadikkumer iti talon.** The old man found Kundring languishing in the field. [Tag. *tamláy*, *lupaypáy*]

dikkúmor: *var.* of *dikkúmer*.

dikkúong: agdikkuong. *v.* to gather around (to spend time idly); hang around. (*tukkuong*)

diklát: *n.* a kind of tree with green fruits, *Zizyphus trinervia*.

dikláwit: dumiklawit. *v.* to make a brief stop in passing. **idiklawit.** *v.* to involve; include; deliver something when passing by.

díkol: dikulen. *v.* to beat with the knuckles, knuckle the head (*katós*).

dikongkóng: agdikongdikong. *v.* to stand together idly. (*mattider*, *tukkuong*)

dikútsa: *n.* species of yellow cooking banana, larger than the *dippig* variety.

diksionário: (Sp. *diccionario*) *n.* dictionary (*pagitarusan*). [Tag. *talatinigan*]

diktadór: (Sp. *dictador*: dictator) *n.* dictator.

diktadúr(i)a: (Sp. *dictadura*: dictatorship) *n.* dictatorship.

dil: agdil, agidil, idil. *v.* to help someone sell something.

díla: *n.* tongue; native language; arrowhead. **diladila.** *v.* kind of soft rice cake in the shape of a tongue; bowstring hemp, *Sansevieria zeylanica*; kind of brown slug. **padila.** *n.* wooden handle fitting iron socket; tong of knife; front flap of a shoe. **dilaan.** *v.* to lick. **Nagasang ti dilana.** *exp.* He is sharp tongued. **Nagatel ti dilana; Aggagatel ti dilana.** *exp.* He is a chatterbox (*lit*: his tongue itches). **Adda siding ti dilana.** *exp.* He is loquacious (*lit*: has a mole on his tongue). [Bon. *díla*, Ibg. *zilá*, Itg. *híla*, Ivt. *ridaq*, Kal. *chila*, Png. *dilá*, Tag. *dilà*]

dil-ág: *n.* loud, threatening voice. **idil-ag.** *v.* to yell something in a threatening voice.

dilámut: dilamutan. *v.* to take from a small supply; lick.

dilána: (Sp. *de lana*: of wool) *a.* made of wool.

diláng: *n.* ray of light passing through a hole; brilliance; elegance. **padidilangen.** *v.* to feed the fire.

dílap: *var.* of *dilat*: to stick out the tongue.

diláp: *n.* flood (*layos*); the lapping of the sea on the shore. **agdilap.** *v.* to have a flood, inundation. **dilapen.** *v.* to lap (sea lapping the shore).

dílat: agdilat. *v.* to stick out the tongue. **dilatan.** *v.* to stick out the tongue at someone. [Png. *dilát*]

diláw: (Tag.) *n.* turmeric (*kuliáw*). [Png. *kulalaw*, Tag. *dilâw*]

dildíl: dildilan. *v.* to lick. **agdildil.** *v.* to live meagerly. **agdildildil iti asin.** *exp.* to lick salt (live as a pauper). [Tag. *dildíl*]

dilég: madileg, madleg. *v.* to be shy; embarrassed; lack confidence. [Tag. *hiyâ*]

diléma: (Sp. *dilema*: dilemma) *n.* dilemma, problem. (*parikut*)

díli: *n.* reef; (*reg.*) cliff, rock. **nadili.** *a.* stony, rocky. **kadilian.** *n.* reef area; coral reef. **mangngadilian.** *n.* reef fisherman.

dilíg: idilig. *v.* to compare (*pada*). **pakaidiligan.** *n.* comparison; value; worth. **Karissabong ni Maria no idilig iti tawenko.** Maria is just an immature flower when you compare her to my age. [Tag. *hambíng*]

dilihénsia: (Sp. *diligencia:* diligence) *n.* diligence; (*coll.*) having expertise in finding ways of getting what one wants. **dilihente.** *a.* diligent.

dillaáso: see *dallaaso:* kind of small bird.

dilláw: dildillaw. *n.* something extraordinary or unusual. **dillawen.** *v.* to observe, perceive, notice; criticize (*baláw*). **agdillaw.** *v.* to make a remark; criticize. **madlaw.** *a.* noticeable. *v.* to notice by chance. **ipadlaw.** *v.* to show, display; cause to notice. **dumlaw.** *v.* to notice; wonder; show; disagree; be unsuitable or harmful; not be able to take (food, cold, etc.). **nakadkadlaw, nakadidillaw.** *a.* strange; unusual; extraordinary; suspicious. **agpadlaw.** *v.* to manifest one's presence (ghosts); call attention to oneself. **apagdillaw.** a little, slight. **Nadlawko ti danag ken buteng iti rupana.** I noticed the worry and fear in his face. **Bambannog ti agdildillaw, no kadua ti agtaktakaw.** It is useless to be careful if your companion is a thief. **Dumlaw ti tianko iti pasayan.** I cannot stomach shrimps. [Png. *imano,* Tag. *pansín*]

dilláwit: *n.* instant, moment, very short period of time. **apagdillawit.** *a.* immediately, in an instant. **Saan a nagparang uray apagdillawit la koma.** She didn't appear, even for an instant.

dillawít: idillawit. *v.* to chatter; talk.

dillút: *var.* of *dallot:* kind of native chant.

dílmut: dilmutan. *v.* to burn something. (*sinit*)

dilnák: idilnak. *v.* to scald. (*lamaw; tapliak; loptoy*) **nadilnakan.** *a.* scalded. [Png. *lunák,* Tag. *pasò, banlí*]

dilút: nadilut. *a.* damp; soiled; unclean.

dilpág: *n.* light touch or tap. **dilpagen.** *v.* to tap lightly, touch.

dilpát: dumilpat. *v.* to lick one's lips. **dilpatan.** *v.* to lick. **agdildilpat iti asin.** *exp.* denoting poverty (licking salt for food). [Tag. *dilà*]

dimisión: (Sp. *dimisión:* resignation) *n.* resignation. **agdimision.** *v.* to resign.

dímpo: *n.* face towel; washcloth.

dinámiko: (Sp. *dinámico:* dynamic) *a.* dynamic; energetic; active; forceful.

dinamíta: (Sp. *dinamita:* dynamite) *n.* dynamite, explosive.

dínang: dinangdinang. (*obs.*) *n.* idleness.

dinastía: (Sp. *dinastía:* dynasty) *n.* dynasty.

dinengdéng: (f. *dengdeng*) *n.* boiled vegetables.

dínep: (*obs.*) **madinep.** *n.* well-eared palay.

dinéro: (Sp. *dinero:* money) *coll. n.* money. (*kuarta*)

dinná: *var.* of *denná:* side; next to.

dinnó: (usually baby talk) short for *sadino:* where.

dínos: (*reg.*) *n. dallot* song and dance.

dinwá: *var.* spelling of *dinua:* saronglike piece of clothing consisting of a cloth wrapped around the waist and usually worn over the *pandiling* skirt.

dingáay: (*obs.*) **agdingaay.** *v.* to cleave through earthquakes.

díngal: (*obs.*) *n.* weak respiration.

dingdíng: *n.* iron moldboard of a plow.

dingíding: see *barangabang:* place near the heat, keep warm. **Idingidingmo iti pammagbaga, gaoem iti patigmaan.** Keep counsel warm and extract advice.

dingkál: *var.* of *dingkol:* nudge; elbow. **Timrem ti luana gapu iti ragsak a nangdingkal iti kaungganna.** Her tears flowed from the happiness nudging insider her.

dingkól: agdingkol. *v.* to nudge with the elbow. (*kidág*)

díngo: dingoen. *v.* to raise animals (usually hogs.) *n.* animals (hogs) raised for meat.

díngol: agdingol. *v.* to growl; howl.

díngpil: dingpilen. *v.* to press, squeeze; compress. [Tag. *pikpík*]

dingpít: see *dangpil:* compress.

díngra: nadingra. *a.* bright red.

díngraw: *n.* large black fly.

dingség: (*obs.*) **agdingseg.** *v.* to shrink, contract.

dióga: (Tag. also, *slang*) *n.* breast. (*suso*)

diók: *n.* a kind of herb used in medicine. **didiok.** *n.* species of vine with edible fruits. **dioken.** *v.* to stab.

dióker: (Eng.) *n.* joker, extra playing card in certain games.

dión: *n.* a kind of legendary bird.

diós: (Sp. *diós:* god) *n.* god. (*Namarsua*) **padidiosen.** *v.* to treat like a god. **padiodios.** *n.* person who acts like a god (always demands respect, etc.). **madidios.** *a.* respected, revered. **ag-Dios ti bumales.** *v.* to thank. (*agyaman*) **Dios ti agngina.** Thank you. (*agyamanak*) **kaasi ni Apo Dios.** *exp.* by the mercy of God; thank God. **Dios ti agbati.** *exp.* God stay with you. Goodbye (said by person leaving). **Dios ti kumuyog.** *exp.* God go with you. Goodbye (said by person being left behind). **agdios unay iti agngina kenka.** I thank you very much. **pordiós!** *interj.* by God! **Diay yanmi, saanmi a didiosen ti nakitikitan a kayo.** In our place, we do not venerate engraved woodcarvings as gods. **Dios mio!** My God! [Png., Tag. *diyós*]

diósa: (Sp. *diosa:* goddess) *n.* goddess.

diósen: (pl. *didiosen*) *n.* minor deity; idol.

dipág: madpaag. *v.* to collapse, cave in; settle. **nadpaag.** *a.* collapsed, caved in; settled. **kanadpaag.** *n.* crumbling down, collapsing.

dipák: *n.* cracking sound (of bamboos), breaking branches. **dumpaak.** *v.* to crack (bamboos); break (branches). **kanadpaak.** *n.* cracking, breaking, snapping.

dipás: apagdipas. in a very short time (*apagbiit*). [Tag. *sandalî*]

dipáy: dipayen. *v.* to put off; postpone. (*tantan; gabay*)

diperénsia: (Sp. *diferencia*: difference) *n.* difference; indisposition; malfunctioning; ill feeling; rancor.

diplóma: (Sp. *diploma*: diploma) *n.* diploma.

diplomasía: (Sp. *diplomacía*: diplomacy) *n.* diplomacy, management of relations between nations.

diplomátiko: (Sp. *diplomático*: diplomatic) *a.* diplomatic.

dipúr: *n.* sound of crumbling or collapsing. **madpuor.** *v.* to collapse, crumble down. **dumpuor.** *v.* to collapse, crumble down. **kanadpuor.** *n.* succession of rumbling or crumbling sounds.

diputádo: (Sp. *diputado*: representative) *n.* delegate, representative.

dipúyos: agdipuyos. *v.* to lean; bend.

dippíg: *n.* variety of small banana; *a.* flattened. **nagdippig.** *a.* flattened, compressed. [Tag. *pipî*]

dippít: dippiten. *v.* to compress in order to flatten, crush; crowd together. **agdidippit.** *v.* to crowd, press together, be crushed. **dumippit.** *v.* to come close to; lean; stick to. [Tag. *pipî*]

dipsománia: (Sp. *dipsomanía*: dipsomania) *n.* dipsomania, craving for alcohol.

diptéria: (Sp. *difteria*: diphtheria) *n.* diphtheria. **agdipteria.** *v.* to suffer from diphtheria.

diptónggo: (Sp. *diptongo*: diphthong) *n.* diphthong, gliding sequence of two vowels.

diráan: *n.* species of oak, *Quercus caudatifolia.*

díram: see *siram*: scorch.

diram-ós: *n.* washing of the face. **agdiram-os.** *v.* to wash one's face. **diram-usan.** *v.* to wash the face of; flatter. **kaddiram-os.** *a.* refreshed; newly washed. [Bon. *dal-op*, Ibg. *magammuwaq*, Ivt. *mayramun*, Kal. *cheop*, Kpm. *ímu*, Png. *dilamós*, Tag. *hilámos*]

direksión: (Sp. *dirección*: direction) *n.* direction.

direktíba: (Sp. *directiva*: board of directors) *n.* board of directors; management.

dirékto: (Sp. *directo*: direct) *a.* direct; straight.

direktór: (Sp. *director*: director) *n.* director. **direktorio.** *n.* directory.

direktório: (Sp. *directorio*: directory) *n.* telephone directory.

dirém: *var.* of *derrem*: dim.

dirétso: (Sp. *derecho*: straight; direct) *a.* straight (direction). **agdiretso.** *v.* to go straight; go directly to a place. **Dina maidiretso ti rupana kadagiti bisitana.** He cannot look at his guests straight in the face.

dir-í: *n.* shout; applause; shriek. **agdir-i.** *v.* to shout (*riaw, pukkáw*); hail; applaud. **dir-ian.** *v.* to yell at. **agdirdir-i.** *v.* to keep on yelling. **Itag-aymo ti kanawan nga imam ket idir-im nga patiennak.** Raise your right hand and shout that you believe me. [Tag. *ipagbunyî*]

diríg: *n.* a kind of shrub with red fruits, *Otophora fruticosa.*

dirihe, dirihír: (Sp. *dirigir*: direct) **idirihir.** *v.* to direct; guide, lead.

dirís: *var.* of *ridis.*

dirnás: dirnasan. *v.* to enlarge, widen.

diró: *n.* honey; (*fig.*) fragrance, sweetness. **dumiro.** *v.* to turn into honey; become sweet. **nadiro.** *a.* sweet like honey. **Nadiro ti isemna.** Her smile is sweet (like honey). [Kal. *chílu*, Tag. *pulút-pukyutan*]

díros: dirusen. *v.* to push, shove; thrust.

dis-ál: see *das-al*: shake in order to make contents settle.

disekadór: (Sp. *disecador*: one who stuffs animals) *n.* taxidermist, person who stuffs animals.

disénio: (Sp. *diseño*: design) *n.* design.

disentería: (Sp. *disentería*) *n.* dysentery (*síka*).

disertasión: (Sp.) *n.* dissertation.

disgánas: (Sp. *desgana*: reluctance) **madisganas.** *v.* to not be in the mood to do, to have no desire to do.

disgústo: (Sp. *disgusto*: disgust) *n.* disgust; displeasure. **nadisgustado.** *a.* disgusted. **makapadisgusto.** *v.* to cause disgust, be disgusting.

disgrásia: (Sp. *desgracia*: mishap, misfortune; disgrace) *n.* accident, mishap; misfortune. **madisgrasia.** *v.* to be injured, have an accident; be raped (*rames*). **disgrasiaan.** *v.* to harm, injure; rape. (*danger; rames*)

dísi: napadisi. *a.* deposed; ousted; put aside. **pannakadisi.** *n.* deposition of a politician.

disidénte: (Sp. *disidente*: dissident) *n.* dissident.

disíembre: (Sp. *diciembre*: December) *n.* December. [Kal. *kililing*]

disimuládo: (Sp. *disimulado*: concealed; pretended) *a.* pretended, feigned; covered up.

disimulár: (Sp. *disimular*: pretend; conceal) **agdisimular.** *v.* to dissemble; pretend, feign; conceal (ugliness with makeup, etc.); conceal artfully.

disintería: (Sp. *disentería*: dysentery) *n.* dysentery. **agdisinteria.** *v.* to have dysentery. (*sika*)

disiótso: (Sp. *diez y ocho*: eighteen) *n.* eighteen. (*sangapulo ket walo*)

disipádo: (Sp. *disipado*: dissipated) *a.* dissipated; dissolute.

disiplína: (Sp. *disciplina*: discipline) *n.* discipline. (*singpet*) **disiplinado.** *a.* disciplined.

disípulo: (Sp. *discípulo*: disciple) *n.* disciple.

diskalér: **nadiskaler.** *a.* out of order; stuck on the side of the road.

diskánso: (Sp. *descanso*: rest) *n.* rest. (*inana*) **agdiskanso.** *v.* to rest; be steady.

diskarádo: (Sp. *descarado*: brazen) *a.* out of place (not dressed well enough at a formal occasion).

diskárga: (Sp. *descargar*: unload) **diskargaen.** *v.* to unload. **agdiskarga.** (*fig.*) *v.* to urinate or defecate. **diskargado.** *a.* unloaded.

diskárgo: (Sp. *descargo*: unload) **agdiskargo.** *v.* to apologize.

diskaríl: (Sp. *descarrilar*: jump the track) **nadiskaril.** *a.* fallen off; cut off; fired (from a job); derailed.

diskárte: (Sp. *descarte*: discard; cast aside) **dumiskarte, diskartien.** *v.* to remedy a situation; find a way to get to somebody; express one's love to (a girl). **Narigatanak a dumiskarte kenkuana.** It is hard for me to find a way to get to her.

diskíta, diskitár: **agdiskitar.** (Sp. *desquitar*: compensate) *v.* to look for (money); procure. **madiskitaan.** *v.* to find. (*birok*)

dísko: (Sp. *disco*: disk, record) *n.* disk; discothèque; (*obs.*) record. **diskuán.** *n.* disco house, discothèque.

diskórte: (Tag.) **madiskorte.** *a.* deformed; with no figure.

diskuénto: (Sp. *descuento*: discount) *n.* discount. **diskuentuan.** *v.* to discount.

diskumpiádo: (Sp. *desconfiado*: untrustworthy) *a.* untrustworthy.

diskúrso: (Sp. *discurso*: speech) *n.* speech; discourse. (*bitla*) **agdiskurso.** *v.* to make a speech. [Tag. *talumpatì*]

diskursonáda: (f. *kursonada* + Spanish prefix *dis-*) **nadiskursonada.** *a.* discouraged; disgusted.

diskutír: (Sp. *discutir*: discuss) **agdiskutir.** *v.* to discuss. **makidinniskutir.** *v.* to argue.

diskriminasión: (Eng.) *n.* discrimination.

dislokasión: (Sp. *dislocación*: dislocation) *n.* dislocation; sprain.

dismayá: (Sp. *desmayar*: faint) **dismayaen.** *v.* to upset, distress; discourage. **madismaya.** *v.* to be upset, distressed. *a.* feeling faint.

dismenoréa: (Sp. *dismenorrea*: dysmenorrhoea) *n.* dysmenorrhoea, painful menstruation. **agdismenorea.** *v.* to have painful menstruation.

dismulár: (Sp. *disimular*: conceal; pretend) **madismular.** *v.* to cover up (a social faux pas, the face with makeup, age, etc.). **dismulado.** *a.* feigned (occupation, position); in disguise.

dismontár: (Sp. *desmontar*: dismount) **dismontaren.** *v.* to unsaddle a horse; dismount; dismantle a machine.

disnúdo: (Sp. *desnudo*: bare) *a.* set on doing something, determined; plain, mere, sheer (vegetables without meat). **agdisnudo.** *v.* to volunteer; to be set on doing something. **Nagdisnudo dagiti soldado a nangisuko kadagiti paltogda.** The soldiers volunteered to surrender their guns. [Tag. *boluntaryo* (Sp.)]

disnóg: *n.* knuckle; fist. **disnugen.** *v.* to punch, box with the fist. **dinnisnogan.** *n.* fistfight; boxing match. **Makadisdisnogak pay kenkuana.** I even feel like punching him. [Tag. *kamaó* (fist), *suntók* (punch)]

disól: *n.* a kind of herb with aromatic rootstocks used in medicine, *Kaempferia galanga*. **disulen.** *v.* to hit lightly with the hand or elbow.

dispálko: (Sp. *desfalco*: embezzlement) *n.* embezzlement; bankruptcy; loss in business. **nadispalko, dispalkado.** *a.* bankrupt; embezzled. **dispalkador.** *n.* embezzler.

disparáte: (Sp. *disparate*: rubbish) *a.* unbelievable; superstitious; *n.* blunder, mistake; nonsense.

dispatsadór: (Sp. *despachador*: dispatcher) *n.* salesman; dispatcher. **dispatsaen.** *v.* to sell; complete; kill.

dispénsa: (Sp. *dispensa*: dispensation) *n.* certificate granting a dispensation; *var.* of *dispensar*: forgiveness, pardon; pantry.

dispensár: (Sp. *dispensar*: excuse, forgive) **dispensaren.** *v.* to forgive, excuse. **agpadispensar.** *v.* to apologize; excuse oneself. **Dispensarennak.** Excuse me. **Dispensarem la-engen ti dimi pannakaumay iti luasmo.** Please excuse us that we weren't able to come to your departure.

dispensário: (Sp. *dispensario*: dispensary) *n.* rural public health clinic.

dispenséra: (Sp. *despensera*: housekeeper of a priest) *n.* housekeeper of a priest; variety of *diket* rice.

dispenséro: (f. *dispensa* + Spanish agentive suffix *-ero*) *n.* steward, superintendent; butler.

disponér: (Sp. *disponer*: displace) **mangdisponer, disponeren.** *v.* to displace; dispatch.

disposisión: (Sp. *disposición*: disposition) *n.* opinion; disposition; capacity; aptitude; condition.

dissáag: *n.* floor; downstairs. **dumsaag.** *v.* to dismount; get down from; get off. **idissaag.** *v.*

to take down; unload; unpack. **pagdissaagan.** *n.* unloading zone; destination. **Pagdissaagam?** Where are you getting off? [Kal. *logsed, chessaeg,* Tag. *babâ*]

dissáar: *n.* floor of a building. **idisaar.** *v.* to place on the floor. **kadsaaran.** *n.* floor; bottom of (cart, etc.); back of a pickup truck. [Tag. *palapá g*]

dissó: *n.* place, location, site; position. **agdisso.** *v.* to land (birds, airplanes); fall down. **panagidisso.** *n.* manner of saying or doing things. **idisso.** *v.* to put down, set down, place. **dissuan.** *v.* to unload; hit. **agidisso.** *v.* to place; put down food for the ancestors. **madisso.** *v.* to do at intervals. **madissodisso.** *a.* scattered. **mapadso.** *v.* to fall (animate beings). **dissodissuen.** *v.* to do at intervals; to arrange in bunches; arrange in a scattered way. **pagdissuan.** *n.* landing place, place where someone settles or something is put down. **dumisso.** *v.* to land; alight (birds); fall down. **kadisso.** *n.* one's share. **sangkadisso.** *n.* one portion of. **padsuen.** *v.* to tumble down; overthrow; defeat. **napadso.** *a.* defeated; fatigued; knocked down. **ipadso.** *v.* to put down; knock down. **pagdissuán.** *n.* place where something will be put down; landing place. **Karbengam a dissuannak ngem awan ti denggek itan a palawagmo.** You have the right to hit me but I don't hear any explanation. **Nasaganaak ta amkek a dissuannak manen.** I prepared myself because I feared he would hit me again. [Png. *pásen,* Tag. *dako* (place)]

dissúon: *n.* lump; mound; heap. (*penpen*) **dissuonen.** *v.* to pile up; heap. [Tag. *buntón*]

dissúor: *n.* waterfall; sound of falling water. **agdissuor.** *v.* to happen suddenly; sound of moving water; to fall suddenly. **idisuor.** *v.* to cause to suddenly fall; rage; bring about, carry out; put into effect. [Ivt. *katutulaq,* Kal. *teub,* Knk. *pey-as,* Kpm *saug,* Tag. *talon* (waterfall)]

distánsia: (Sp. *distancia*: distance) *n.* distance (*kaadayo*); disparity; interval of time or space.

distiliría: (Sp. *destilería*) *n.* distillery.

distúrbo: (Sp. *disturbo*: disturb) *n.* trouble, disturbance. (*istorbo*) **disturbuen.** *v.* to disturb, bother.

distorniliadór: (Sp. *destornillador*: screwdriver) *n.* screwdriver. **distorniliador estrelia.** *n.* Phillips screwdriver.

distrása: (Sp. *de estraza*: brown paper) **papel distrasa.** *n.* kind of white, absorbent paper.

distríto: (Sp. *distrito*: district) *n.* political district.

distrungkádo: (Sp. *destroncado*: detruncated) *a.* broken (applied to locks).

díta: *n.* snake venom; artificial poison. **ditaan.** *n.* hard rattan. [Png. *ditá*]

ditá: *deic.* There (near person addressed). [Ibg. *tátun,* Png. *ditán,* Tag. *diyán*]

ditáan: *n.* variety of hard rattan.

ditóy: *deic.* Here. **iditoy.** *v.* to place something here. **tagadtoy.** from here. [Ibg. *taw,* Knk. *siná,* Png. *diá,* Tag. *dito*]

dítso: (Sp. *dicho*: saying) *n.* lines of an actor in a play or movie.

diwákal: see *padiwakal.*

díweng: **agdiweng.** *v.* to sway; totter; stagger (*basing*). [Tag. *suray, hapay*]

díwer: *n.* crookedness. (*killo*) **agdiwer.** *v.* to go crooked, zigzag. **Agdiwerdiwerda ken nalabbasit dagiti matada ket ammok lattan a nakainumda.** They were staggering with red eyes and I just knew they had been drinking. [Tag. *pilipit*]

díwig: *a.* awry, deformed; distorted. **nadiwig.** *a.* crooked, twisted, deformed. **Kasla nakangalngal iti sili ti sairo iti panagdiwigna.** His crooked expression looks like he chewed on hot peppers. [Png. *wiswis, piwis,* Tag. *ngiwî*]

do: (Sp.) *n.* first note of a musical scale; first string of certain musical instruments.

duá: *num.* two. **dudua.** *num.* only two. **kadua.** *n.* companion, mate; one of a pair. **kadkadua.** *n.* afterbirth. **kapidua.** *n.* second cousin. **kapamindua.** *a.* second time around. **maikadua.** *a.* second. **dinua.** *n.* kind of apron apron, tapis wrapped around twice over the upper *saya* skirt. **duaen.** *v.* to take two. **pagduaen.** *v.* to do two at the same time; divide into two. **paminduaen.** *v.* to multiply by two. **pidua.** *n.* second crop. **piduaen.** *v.* to do twice. **sagdudua.** *a.* two each. **sinagdudua.** *a.* consisting of two strings twisted together. [Bon. *dowa,* Kal. *chuwa,* Png. *duá,* Tag. *dalawá*]

duaduá: *n.* doubt, hesitation; uncertainty. **agduadua.** *v.* to be in doubt; to be undecided. [Tag. *alinlangan*]

duág: *n.* porch, balcony; penthouse. **Nagtalinaed a nakamulengleng iti duag.** He kept on staring at the penthouse.

duál: **idual.** *v.* to heave and push.

duanáig: (f. *dua* 'two' + *naig* 'piece') *n.* two-piece; two folds in a fabric.

duayá: *n.* lullaby. **agduaya.** *v.* to sing a lullaby. **makaduaya.** *a.* lulling; soothing. [Tag. *hele, uyayi*]

duayyá: *var.* of *duaya*: *n.* lullaby.

dobár: **makiduban-dubar.** *v.* to vie, strive for superiority, compete with each other.

doblá: (Sp. *doblar*: fold; toll the death knell) *n.* toll for a dead adult. **doblaen.** *v.* to roll (tobacco); fold. **doblado.** *a.* repeated, doubled.

agdobla. *v.* to roll a cigar. **pagdoblaan, panoblaan.** *n.* wrapper for a cigarette.

dobladéra: (Sp. *doblar:* fold) *n.* female cigar roller (occupation).

doblár: (Sp. *doblar:* double) **doblaren.** *v.* to double; *var.* of *dobrar:* enjoy, take advantage of.

dóble: (Sp. *doble:* double) *n.* double. **agdoble.** *v.* to double. **doble trabaho.** *n.* double the workload. **iti doble espásio.** *a.* double spaced.

dóbles: (Sp. *doblez*) *n.* bells tolling for the dying.

dublí: (Sp. *doble:* double) *a.* double. **dublien.** *v.* to repeat. (*dupag; ulit; sunot; surnad*)

dúbar: makidubandubar. *v.* to try to overcome (win).

dobrár: (Sp. *doblar*) **dobraren.** *v.* to double; enjoy, take advantage of.

dubság: dubsagen. *v.* to push against; beat repeatedly. (*timpag*)

dubsák: dubsaken. *v.* to drive away (animals, etc.). (*dugsak*)

dúda: (Sp. *duda:* doubt) *n.* doubt; skeptical attitude, suspicion. **agduda.** *v.* to be doubtful, suspicious. (*duadua*)

dudóg: dudugen. *v.* to beat repeatedly; overwhelm; overused. **madudog.** *v.* to be beaten; crushed; broken to pieces; overwhelmed; overdone. **Dina kayat nga ibaga ti nadudogen a rason a "panagserbi ti panagiliak".** He doesn't want to say the excessively used reason "to serve my country." [Tag. *bugbóg*]

dudól: *n.* a kind of rice pudding made with coconut milk and sugar. **agdudol.** *v.* to make rice pudding.

dudomén: *n.* immature rice roasted before pounding. [Tag. *pinipig*]

dúdon: *n.* locust. **duduonen.** *v.* to be swarming with locusts. **agdudon, manudon.** *v.* to catch locusts. **pagdudon.** *n.* something used to flush out locusts. **agpadudon.** *v.* to flush out locusts. [Itg. *luktun,* Ivt. *lulun,* Kal. *sintok, chuchun,* Kpm. *dúrun,* Png. *durón,* Tag. *luktón, balang, tipaklóng*]

duduogán: (f. *duog*) *a.* very old; decrepit. [Tag. *tandâ*]

dudóso: (Sp. *dudoso:* doubtful) *a.* doubtful (*ngatangata*); hazardous, dangerous; courageous, brave; daring. [Tag. *tapang* (brave)]

duék: *n.* wanderer. **agduek.** *v.* to stroll, wander, roam. (*ballog*)

duélo: (Sp.) *n.* duel. **agduelo.** *v.* to duel; fight one-on-one. (See -*inn-* infix). [Tag. *duwelo*]

duénde: (Sp. *duende:* hobgoblin) *n.* (hob)goblin, elf, fairy; dwarf; ghost. [Tag. *duwende*]

duéto: (Eng.) *n.* duet. **agdueto.** *v.* to sing or play as a duet. [Tag. *duweto*]

dúgal: *n.* dart. **dugalan.** *v.* to hit with a dart; to notch; indent. **madugalan.** *v.* to be notched, indented. **dinnugal.** *n.* children's pencil fight game. **nadugal.** (*obs.*) *a.* frivolous. **kaddugal.** (*coll.*) *n.* girl who has recently lost her virginity.

dugáng: *n.* ugly person; long-legged boogeyman. [Tag. *tikbalang*]

dugayóng: dugdugayong. *n.* sting, bite. (insects) (*silud*)

dugdúg: madugdug. *v.* to dissolve; decay, rot; decompose. **dugdugen.** *v.* to decay; chop up; mash; beat into a pulp.

dugél: *n.* simpleton, fool (*tabbed, nengneng*). [Tag. *gago, tangá*]

dúges: see *banus:* ungovernable (animals); disobedient.

duggóng: *n.* booger, dry nasal mucus. **agiduggong.** *v.* to peel off dried nasal mucus. **iduggongan.** *v.* to remove dried nasal mucus from (children). **kadugduggong.** *a.* unkempt, messy (said of children). [Knk. *ngúe,* Png., Tag. *kulangot*]

dúgi: *n.* large sewing needle.

dugkál: dugkalen. *v.* to stab, pierce. (*bagsol, bagkong*)

dugkík: *var.* of *tugkík:* nudge; prick, stab.

dugmám: maidugmam. *v.* to fall prone; to strike the face against something (ground, etc.) (*pakleb; tikleb; sakoba; rugma; dapla; daramudum*) **idugmam.** *v.* to cause to fall prone. **Ammom no apay a naidugmam ti ekonomia?** Do you know why the economy has collapsed? [Tag. *dapâ*]

dugmél: nadugmel. *a.* lazy; stupid. (*betbet; sadut; tabbed; ginad; kamol; tamleg; lunakol*)

dugmón: *n.* nest of the wild boar (or any other animal that is not a bird); *a.* dirty. **agdugmon.** *v.* to make a nest (said of pigs); wallow; to not make one's bed.

dugmóy: see *dugnoy:* decompose; decay; rot; become pulpy. (*lungsot; dersay; tubeg; tumuy; rupsa; dor-oy; duted; timming*)

dugnóy: madugnoy. *v.* to decay, rot, decompose; become mushy.

dúgo: *n.* corner post of a house (one of four); backbone; foundation; monument. [Tag. *haligi, bantayog*]

dugúdug: *n.* northeast wind; deep rumbling sound. **dugudugan.** *n.* northeast. **dugudugen.** *a.* dried up (lips). **agdugudug.** *v.* to rumble.

dúgol: *a.* with cysts (nose, scalp, etc.) *n.* hump. **dugoldugol.** *n.* knot in wood. (*bugkal, mata ti kayo*) *a.* full of humps. **agpadugol.** *v.* to host a banquet. **dugoldugolan.** *n.* type of unagressive spider. [Tag. *bukol* (lump); *bukó* (knot in wood)]

dúgos: **nadugos**. *a.* sluggish; slow (said of animals). see *banus*.

dugpá: **agdugpa, dugpaen**. *v.* to butt. (*bangdol*; *dalapus*; *donget*; *dungpap*; *dungpar*; *kintol*; *pagat*; *pokkool*; *rupak*; *salapon*; *sangga*; *timog*; *tum-ong*) **maidugpa**. *v.* to collide, bump into, clash. [Tag. *banggâ*]

dugpák: *var.* of *dugpa*.

dugsák: **dumugsak**. *v.* to frighten, scare away (animals). **nadugsak**. *a.* scared, frightened. **Nainayad ti yaasidegko iti rama tapno diak madugsak ti lamesna**. I slowly approached the branches in the water so I wouldn't frighten the fish in them. [Tag. *gulat, takot*; Knk. *dugsák* = annoy]

dugsít: **dugdugsit**. *n.* species of jumping spider.

dugsól: *n.* anything with a sharp end or point. **dugsolen**. *v.* to jab (with a pointed instrument, finger, etc.). **idugsol**. *v.* to stab, pierce; stick something into, thrust. **Indugsdugsolna a sikukusilap ti tammudona iti ladawan nga ig-iggamanna**. He repeatedly jabbed the picture he was holding with an angry stare. (*bagkong*; *durudor*). [Tag. *saksák*]

dugyót: **nagdugyot**. *a.* filthy, untidy, piggish (person).

dúir: **agduir**. *v.* to stagger, totter. (*bariring*; *daweng*; *dawiris*; *dunggay*; *gudday*; *lupay*; *tiwed*; *sabbadaw*)

duká: **maduka**. *v.* to soften, become tender; become moved by compassion (*tignay*); melt. **dukaen**. *v.* to soak the soil before planting.

dukakká: *var.* of *duyaya*.

dukál: see *sukal*: discover; inspect; detect.

dukáng: **nadukang**. *a.* bulky; heaped up in a disorderly way.

dókar: *n.* auto *calesa*.

dúkay: **dukayen**. *v.* to prepare ground for planting.

dukayyáng: *n. Digitaria sp.* slender grasses.

dukdók: **dukdoken**. *v.* to push into a hole. **padukdok**. *n.* long fishing rod for deep fishing.

dúke: (Sp. *duque*: duke; fem: *dukesa*) *n.* duke, a nobleman ranking below a prince.

dukém: *n.* frustration; disheartened feeling. **maidukem**. *v.* to fall on one's face. **makaidukem**. *a.* frustrating; disheartening. **sidudukem**. *a.* dejected, disheartened; frustrated; prostrated. **Linemmesna iti arak ti dukem ti barukongna**. He drowned the sorrows in his chest with wine. [Tag. *tamláy*]

dukésa: (Sp. *duquesa*: duchess) *n.* duchess; the wife or widow of a duke.

dukínar: **idukinar**. *v.* to scatter; turn over. **naidukinar**. *a.* scattered; strewn (*wara*). [Tag. *kalat*]

dukít: **dukiten**. *v.* to handle; touch lightly; mention again. **idukit**. *v.* to mention; recall, remind (*palagip*). **dukitdukiten**. *v.* to do all over again. **Sangkaidukitna ti anak**. He keeps handling the child.

dukkúong: **agdudukkuong**. *v.* to stand shrunk up when body is ill. (*kurot*)

dukláp: **duklapen**. *v.* to attack. (*duklos*; *pengngel*; *raut*) **Nagsaganaak nga aganawa amangan no agdinnuklapda**. I prepared to defend in case they fought. [Tag. *salakay, lusob, sugod*]

dúklaw: **dumuklaw**. *v.* to peck like birds; to strike with fangs (snakes). [Tag. *tukláw*]

dukláwit: *var.* of *diklawit*: make a brief stop in passing; involve someone in a situation.

duklós: *n.* attack, forward charge. (*duklap*; *pengngel*; *raut*) **dumuklos, duklusen**. *v.* to assault, attack. **agdinnuklos**. *v.* to attack one another. [Tag. *sugod, salakay, lusob*]

duklóy: **dukloyen**. *v.* to wound with an upward thrust.

dukmál: **dukmalen**. *v.* to thicken (ropes, thread).

dukmám: see *dugmam*: fall prone; strike the face against something.

dukmén: **agkaidukmen**. *v.* to nod, droop the head while sleepy. [Tag. *antók*]

dukmól: *var.* of *dugmam*.

dukó: **dumuko**. *v.* to declare oneself, show one's presence; recur (*surro*); bite at the bait (fish).

dúkol: **dumukol**. *v.* to stick out, protrude, jut out. (*dusol, tukol, tadul*)

dokumentádo: (Sp. *documentado*: documented) *a.* documented, supported by written references or legal papers.

dokuménto: (Sp. *documento*: document) *n.* document. **idokumento**. *v.* to document, write into a document.

dúkot: **dukuten**. *v.* to pick someone's pocket.

dukót$_1$: *n.* uneasiness; inconvenience. **madukutan**. *v.* to grieve; be sad; anxious. **madukot**. *a.* inconvenient, uncomfortable. **sidudukot**. *a.* worried; anxious; impatient.

dukót$_2$: **idukot**. *v.* to connect, join. **dumukot**. *v.* to draw near; approach.

dukráng: (*obs.*) **dukdukrang**. *n.* a kind of rattle.

dukrarián: (*obs.*) **agdukrarian**. *v.* to flutter, hover.

duktál: **duktalan**. *v.* to detect, find out; make an effort to catch someone in the act. **maduktalan**. *v.* to detect; discover. **pannakaduktal**. *n.* discovery. **naduktalan**. *a.* discovered; noticed; caught in the act. **Dina ninamnama a kastoy ti maduktalanna a palimed**. He didn't expect his secret would be discovered in this way. [Bon. *góka*, Kpm. *tuklas*, Tag. *duklás*]

doktór: (Sp. *doctor*: doctor) *n.* male doctor. (*mangngagas*) **doktora**. *n.* female doctor. **ipadoktor**. *v.* to send someone to the doctor. **doktorado**. *n.* doctorate (degree).

doktrína: (Sp. *doctrina*: doctrine) *n.* doctrine; dogma; tenet.

dukyáng: *n.* a kind of small freshwater clam.

dúlang: *n.* low table. **padulang**. *n.* machine used to pulverize the soil. [Png., Tag. *dulang*]

dularéng: *n. Grewia bilamellata* shrub.

dúlaw: (*obs.*) *n.* tailed comet. **dulawen**. *n.* variety of awned early rice with red kernel.

duláw: **duldulaw**. *n.* kind of shrub. **dulawen**. *n.* variety of awned early-maturing rice with red kernel.

duldóg: *n.* dog's mange. (*gudgud*) **naduldog**. *a.* dirty, nasty; despicable; dumb; lazy; tyrannical; blunt, dull. **Mabalin a kunaen a ti panagsurat iti Filipinas ket maysa a naindaklan a kinaduldog.** It is possible to say that writing in the Philippines is pure trash. [Tag. *galís* (mange)]

duldól: **iduldol**. *v.* to refuse to give up; force feed; insist upon; urge. **dinuldol**. *n.* (*reg.*) var. of *dudol*: rice pudding. **Sangkaduldolna a saankon a kakuykuyog ni Fe.** He keeps insisting that I don't accompany Fe. [Tag. *pilit*]

dúli: (*obs.*) *n.* blemish. (*ganna*; *pílaw*; *tukí*)

dulián: **dulianan**. *v.* to distinguish between; abate; check. **duldulianan**. *n.* difference, distinguishing trait. (*duma*)

doliár: (Eng.) *n.* dollar. **ipadoliar**. *v.* to exchange into dollars.

dulídol: *n.* food given to patients. **idulidol**. *v.* to urge, incite; animate; insist (*sugsóg*). [Tag. *giít*]

dúlin: *n.* safe place; savings. **idulin**. *v.* to keep; put away; kill; bury, inter. **paidulin**. *v.* to entrust for safekeeping. **ipadulin**. *v.* to condemn for. **agpadpadulin**. *v.* (*reg.*) to accuse one another. **Insabalina iti nangidulinanna.** He changed the place where he kept it. **No kayatmo ti agragsak, agidulinka ti adu a pirak.** If you want to be happy, keep a lot of money. [Kpm. *sínup*, Png. *amot*, *akastol*, *átol*, Tag. *ligpít*]

dulinát: **agdulinat**. *v.* to wipe the fingers or feet, rub off dirt. (*pigad*)

dulíng: *a.* slightly cross-eyed. see *gilab*. **agduling-duling**. *v.* to be cross-eyed. [Png., Tag. *dulíng*, Tag. *duklíng*]

dúlit: *n.* remains of a crushed bug. **maidulit**. *v.* to adhere, stick to.

dullít: **dullidulliten**. *v.* to repeat many times. (*dagullit*)

dullúog: (*reg. var.* of *gurruod*) *n.* thunder. (*gurruod*) **agdulluog**. *v.* to thunder. **nadulluog**.

a. struck by thunder; killed by thunder. [Tag. *kulóg*]

dulmén: see *dulpet*: damp; dank.

dulnó: **dumulno**. *v.* to start, commence, begin (tide, throw up, etc.). (*rukuas*; *rugi*; *rusat*; *ussuat*)

dul-ó: **agdul-o**. *v.* to throw up, vomit (*dul-ok*, *bel-a*, *sarwa*). **makapadul-o**. *a.* nauseous, causing one to vomit. **Makapadul-o ti buyokna.** Its stench is nauseous. [Tag. *suka*]

dul-ók: **agdul-ok**. *v.* to vomit (*sarwa*); (*reg.*) to hiccup (*saiddek*). [Tag. *suka*]

dúlon: *n.* limit, boundary; monument, landmark. (*beddeng*) **agkadulon**. *a.* adjacent; bordering. **pagduldulonan**. *v.* to set a demarcation line. **kadulon a mannalon**. *n.* neighboring farmer. [Tag. *hangganan*]

dúlong: *n.* bow, stem; prow (*purua*).

doloróso: (Sp. *doloroso*: sorrowful) *a.* sorrowful. (*makapaladingit*)

dúlot: **idulot**. *v.* to offer. **agidulot**. *v.* to wait a table, serve.

dulpák: *a.* flat, flattened; flat nosed. **agdulpak**. *v.* to become flat; to be snubnosed. [Tag. *pangô* (flat nosed)]

dulpáp: *var.* of *dulpak*.

dulpét: *n.* stench of dirty clothes. **nadulpet**. *a.* damp, dank (clothes). (*alunapet*)

dulpó: *n.* felt hat.

dulséra: (Sp. *dulcera*: dessert bowl) *n.* bowl for desserts.

dúlsi: (Sp. *dulce*: sweet) *n.* candy; sweets. **pagdulse**. *n.* what can serve as dessert.

dúma: **agduma**. *v.* to differ (*giddiat*; *salumina*; *sabali*; *supadi*). **agduduma**. *a.* various, several; different. **maiduma**. *v.* to be different. **maidumduma**. *v.* to stand out; to be unique; distinguishable. **nadumaduma**. *a.* different; various. **idumduma**. *v.* to prefer; to excel. **pakaidumaan**. *n.* preference; difference; uniqueness. **ipadpaduma**. *v.* to prefer, favor. **Ania ti nagdumaan ti manok ken ti piek?** What is the difference between the chicken and the chick? [Png. *dumá*, Tag. *kaibá*]

dumadára: *n.* tuna (*Thunnidae* family).

domadór: (Sp. *domador*: tamer) *n.* tamer (of animals); trainer.

dumalága: (f. *dalaga*) *n.* young hen.

dumánay: *n. Homonoia riparia* shrub whose roots are used in medicine; variety of awned late rice with red kernel.

dumbál: (*obs.*) **madumbal**. *v.* to retrograde (boats).

dumbér: **nadumber**. *a.* dull, blunt (*ngudel*, *dusber*; *rungbeb*). [Tag. *puról*]

dumég: see *tomég*: bump against; knock, strike against.
dominádo: (Sp. *dominado*: dominated) *a.* dominated.
dominánte: (Sp. *dominante*: dominant) *a.* dominant, domineering.
dominár: (Sp. *dominar*: dominate) dominaran. *v.* to dominate; domineer.
domíniko: (Sp. *dominico*) *n., a.* Dominican; robin.
dómino: (Sp.) *n.* domino. agdomino. *v.* to play dominoes.
domínggo: (Sp. *domingo*: Sunday) *n.* Sunday; week. makadominggo. *n.* one week. dinominggo. *a.* weekly. Domínggo Ramos. *n.* Palm Sunday (*palaspas*). Agmakadominggotayonto idiay. We will spend a week there. [Kal. *chuminggu*, Tag. *linggó*]
dumgés: (f. *degges*) *v.* to gush out (sweat, etc.).
dumkét: (f. *dekket*) *v.* to stick to, adhere. (*pigket*; *kumpet*; *luyak*; *kulamat*; *kidkid*)
dumláw: (f. *dilláw*) *v.* to notice, take note; be aware of; wonder; show, reveal; disagree; be unsuitable. Satayto dumlaw no maimpeksionda ket lumtegda. Then we will take note if they get infected and swell.
dúmmog: agdummog. *v.* to stoop the head.
dummóg: *n.* forehead; upper lip; (*obs.*) bottom of gums or jaws.
dummón: (*reg.*) *n.* pomelo. (*sua, lukban*)
dumná: (f. *denna*) *a.* next (*sumarunó*); next to, close to, beside (*abay*).
dumngég: *v.* [*dengngeg* + -*um*-] *v.* to listen, hear, (progressive: *dumdumngeg*).
dumúdom: *a.* bent forward. maidumudom. *v.* to fall prone. idumudom. *v.* push forward, press down violently; thrash the face of an opponent on the ground. Indumudomko ti rupak iti barukongna. I pushed my face against her chest. [Tag. *dapâ*]
dúmog: agdumog. *v.* to bow the head; incline, lean. idumog. *v.* to cause to bend down, bow. dumugan. *v.* to bend over something; concentrate on what one is doing. Immirteng ti rupana sa nagdumog. He stretched his face and then bowed. Dumoganyo ti mangan. Concentrate on eating. [Tag. *yukô*]
dumparí: *n.* *Trianthema portulascastrum* herb, see *tabtabukol*.
dumsáag: *v.* [*dissaag* + -*um*-] *v.* to get down, get off; go down.
dumténg: *v.* [*dateng* + -*um*-] *v.* to come, arrive.
dumyáas: (f. *dayaas*) *v.* to rain heavily. Dumyaas pay la ngamin ti tudo a nangrugi idi sumangpetda. Because the rain started to pour down heavily when they arrived.

don: (Sp. *don*: sir) *n.* title of respect, sir; distinguished gentleman. agpadondon. *v.* to pretend to be a rich man.
dunál: madunal. *v.* to be felt again (wound); recur (*surró*).
donár: (Sp. *donar*: donate) idonar. *v.* to donate.
dundún: dundunen. *v.* to reclaim; repay a mortgage. (*tunton*)
dónia: (Sp. *doña*: madam) *n.* Madam, Mrs.; distinguished woman; upper-class woman; rat, mouse.
dúnor: *n.* external injury, wound. (*sugat*) nadunor. *a.* injured, harmed, hurt. (external injury). dunoren. *v.* to hurt; injure; wound; harm. Tay aso a managtaul, saan a makakagat ken makadunor. *exp.* A barking dog does not bite or harm. [Png. *lagás*, *sugát*, Tag. *sugat*]
donsélia: (Sp. *doncella*: maiden) *n.* maiden; virgin; female calf.
dung-áw: *n.* dirge; cry for the dead; lamentation. agdung-aw. *v.* to lament, sing a dirge; wail. makidung-aw. *v.* to keep vigil over a dead body. [Bon. *ádog*, Tag. *panangis*]
dúngay: manungay. *v.* to stagger, sway, totter (*bariring*; *dawiris*; *duir*; *dungay*; *tiwed*; *gudday*; *lupay*; *sabbadaw*). [Tag. *suray*]
dungbáb: *a.* blunt; stocky; flattened. maidungbab. *v.* to knock the mouth against something. idungbab (*obs.*) *v.* to blow on a fire.
dongdóng: *n.* a kind of large *banga* pot. dinnongdong. *n.* a girl's game similar to *binnatugan*.
dungér: agdunger. *v.* to shake the head continuously and rapidly without control (from old age). maidunger. *v.* to drop the head involuntarily due to drowsiness. Sumagmamanon ti agdudunger nga agkatkatay iti bartekda. A few of them shook their heads uncontrollably and drooled in their drunkenness.
dungét: idunget. *v.* to put close to. agdunget. *v.* to collide, bump each other. (*dungpar*) maidunget. *v.* to trip, stumble.
dunggiál: *n.* top. (*kampuso*) agdunggial. *v.* (*reg.*) to be in love. dunggialan. *var.* of *dunggiár*: to hurt, injure. madunggialan. *v.* to be hurt, be injured.
dunggiár: *n.* bruise; slight wound. (*dunor*) dunggiaran. *v.* to wound; bruise. [Tag. *galos*]
dunggóp: *n.* joint. agdunggop. *v.* to join; unite; attach (*silpo*). [Tag. *dugtóng*]
dúngir: *n.* wound, injury; bruise. dungiran. *v.* to hurt, injure. madungiran. *v.* to be hurt, injured, bruised. Nasaem dagiti dungir ken kammuol iti ulok. The bumps and bruises on my head are painful. [Tag. *saktán, gasgás*]

dúngis: *a.* (*reg.*) disobedient, unmanageable. (*sukir, bángad*)

dungkít: dungkiten. *v.* to hit; bump; goad (an animal into moving).

dungkóg: *a.* slightly hunchbacked.

dungngó: *n.* loved one; love; compassion; tender care; sweetheart (*ayat*). dungnguen. *v.* to love. nadungngo. *a.* loving, affectionate; tender. Dungdunguenkanto. I will love you. [Tag. *mahál*]

dúngon: *n.* *Heritiera littoralis* tree whose bark is used to dye nets.

dungpáp: *a.* flattened, crushed. agdungpap. *v.* to collide, bump. (*dungpar*)

dungpár: agdungpar. *v.* to collide, crash. agdinnungpar. *v.* to crash into each other. dungparen. *v.* to bump, collide (*dalapus*); hit with the fist. madungpar. *v.* to accidentally bump into, meet by chance. [Bon. *songpel*, Png. *banggá*, Tag. *bundól, banggâ*]

dungpér: see *depper*: blunt (*ngudel*). [Tag. *puról*]

dungráraw: *var.* of *dungraw*: stick out, protrude. Dimmungraraw iti ridaw. She stuck out of the door.

dungráw: dumungraw. *v.* to stick out, protrude the head (turtles) (*tungraraw*). [Tag. *dukwáng*]

dungrít: nadungrit. *a.* filthy, dirty (face.) (*rugit*) Nagparang ti nakuttong a balasang a nagubba iti nadungrit nga ubing. A thin lady appeared carrying a filthy child.

dungsá: agdungsa. *v.* to nod; doze off; fall asleep outside of one's bed. makadudungsa. *a.* sleepy, drowsy (*tuglep*). [Ibg. *tuttummoq*, Ifg. *tumog*, Ivt. *maduhuq*, Kpm. *makatukba*, Png. *temeg*, Tag. *antók*]

dungsél: *var.* of *dungsa*.

dungsó: dungsoen. *v.* to crash into, collide with. (*dungpar; bangdol; salapon; pokkool; dunget; kintol; dugpa*) maidungso. *v.* to collide.

dungsól: *n.* blacksmith's hammer. (*dugsol*) dungsolen. *v.* to batter with a *dongsol*.

dúog: duduogan. *a.* decrepit; ancient. dumuog. *v.* to age. [Tag. *tandâ*]

dúol: *n.* handout; food given to young birds by their mother. duolan. *v.* to give out, give for free; feed directly to someone's mouth. (birds to their young). paduolan. *v.* to live on somebody's support, be dependent upon someone else. Adda koma idiay Pilipinas nga agpampannuray iti iduol dagiti dadakkelna. He should be in the Philippines depending on the handouts of his parents.

duóm: duomen. *v.* to eat immature or uncooked rice. duduomen. *n.* rice about to mature.

dúong: see *bingalo*: large *aramang* shrimp.

dúoy: *n.* babyish action; *a.* unkempt; unclean; slothful. (*dugyot; dulpet*) naduoy. *a.* unkempt; unclean. agduoy. *v.* to act like a baby. [Tag. *dungis*]

dúpag: *n.* work; job. dupagen. *v.* to repeat (*ulit; surnad; sunot*); approach, come toward; come upon. idupag. *v.* to repeat; interpose; remind. madupag. *v.* to come toward; approach; to be just ahead of. Pul-oy a dumupdupag iti kaunggan ti balay a nangalli-allin kadagiti atitiddog a buokna. It was a breeze that approached the inside of the house, making her long hair sway.

dupák: *a.* flat, flattened.

dupakpák: nadupakpak. *a.* bowlegged (*pakkang*). [Tag. *sakáng*]

dupálit: madupalit. *v.* to drop down (from wind, etc.). dupaliten. *v.* to knock down; crash into; cause to crumble.

dupáp: *var.* of *dungpap*.

dupdúp: idupdup. *v.* to extinguish by hitting against floor or wall. [Tag. *sulsól*]

dupiatyát: see *duyayat*: open (said of something that is usually closed).

dupír: *n.* corner; brink; edge; dead end. dupiren. *v.* to shove; strive; make efforts to do; overwhelm. idupir. *v.* to push, shove. agdidinnupir. *v.* to attack one another; throng. Kasla dadakkel a gurruod a mangdupdupir ti barukongna. It seems like heavy thunder pounding at his chest.

duplikádo: (Sp. *duplicado*: duplicate) *n.* duplicate. ipaduplikado. *v.* to have something duplicated.

dupúdup: *n.* crowd; meeting place; resort. nadupudup. *a.* crowded. agdupudup. *v.* to go to a *dupudup*; meet. agdudupudup. *v.* to come together to do. makidupudop. *v.* to join a crowd. pagdudupudupan. *n.* meeting place. Dupudupdan kadagiti lamisaan a pagsusugalan. They are all crowded around the gambling tables. Saan a maisala ti baro ta mabain ngata a makidupudop. The young man can't dance with her probably because he is shy to join a crowd. [Tag. *gitgít*]

dupóng: dupongen. *v.* to attack head on. agdudupong. *v.* to crowd. [Tag. *lusob* (attack)]

dúpoy: madupoy. *v.* to collapse from weakness (*lupóy*). kinadupoy. *v.* weakness.

duppó: *n.* time before the rainy season, May and June. tagidpoan. *n.* beginning of the rainy season. panagduduppo. *n.* blooming season. [Tag. *taglagás*]

duppúor: see *dappuor*: crumbling down.

duprák: dupraken. *v.* to demolish; tear down, dismantle; ruin. naduprak. *a.* destroyed; torn down; dismantled; ruined. **ramramit a pagduprak.** *n.* siege engines, demolishing devices (like bulldozers, etc.). **Nadupraken daydi daan a kalapaw ni Lelong.** Grandfather's old hut is demolished. [Tag. *gibâ*]

dupyatyát: see *dupiatyat*.

-dor: (Sp. *–dor*: agentive suffix) suffix denoting the agent of an action. It is used mainly with Spanish loanwords but may also be incorporated with some Ilocano roots, feminine form: *-dora*: **tayador.** gambler, one who places bets (from Pilipino root *tayá*). **sugador.** gambler (from Spanish word *jugador*). (*-ero*, *agCVC-*, *CumV-*, *maNCV*)

doprado: *n.* species of large, tunalike marine fish with tough meat. [Ivt. *arayu*]

duráb: **duraben.** *v.* to hit, punch in the face (usually in the region of the mouth); knock in the chin (*tibab*). [Png. *tibeb*]

durág: **agdudurag.** *v.* to be haggard looking.

dúran: **duran-duran.** *n.* pupa of the dragonfly. [Knk. *os-ósung*, *súngan*, *tultulbá*, *pekpéke*]

durandál: (Fr. *durendal*) *n.* small stone with magic power.

durás: **durasdurasen.** *v.* to do often. (*darasdarasen*)

dur-ás: *n.* progress; modernity (*rang-ay*). **naduras.** *a.* progressive, modern, advanced; developed (country). **agdur-as.** *v.* to progress. **dumurdur-as a pagilian.** *n.* developing country. [Tag. *unlád*]

durbáb: *a.* rough, ill mannered. (*sabrak*)

dúrek: *n.* earwax. (*yuyek*) **agdurek.** *v.* to run (the ear). [Kal. *attay chi inga*, Knk. *lúek*, *túeng*, Kpm. *lúgaq*, *tulúk*, Png. *olilek*, Tag. *tutulí*, *lugâ*]

dúri: *n.* spinal column; backbone; bone of the finger; keel of a ship. **duri ti lulod.** *n.* tibia (shinbone). **durduri.** (*obs.*) *n.* large water pitcher. **iduri.** *v.* to bear. **naduri.** *a.* courageous. **tumakder ti adda durina.** *exp.* let anyone with a backbone stand up. **Awan durina.** *exp.* He has no spine (is a weak coward). **Timpuar ti init iti duri ti bantay.** The sun appeared from the spine of the mountain. [Bon. *dólig*, Ivt. *vukut*, Kal. *taliti*, Knk. *talidtíd*, Kpm. *galudgód*, Png. *tenten*, Tag. *gulugód*]

durián: *n. Dioscorea batatas*, wild yam; also a popular, stinky fruit with sharp spikes and white flesh.

dúrik: **durikan, duriken.** *n.* a kind of mollusk like the *gosipeng*. **mannuriken.** *n.* collector of the *duriken* mollusk; *a.* resembling a *duriken*.

duríkan: *a.* spotted.

duríri: *a.* having protruding buttocks. (*turirit*) **agduriri.** *v.* to protrude the buttocks; project.

iduriri. *v.* to insist; persist. [Knk. *toád* (large buttocks), Tag. *uslî* (protrude)]

dúris: **agduris.** *v.* to transpire, come into being (*dukó*, *sumró*).

dúrit: (*obs.*) *a.* horrible.

durkó: **nadurko.** *a.* crooked; crooked-backed (*killo*). [Tag. *hukót*]

durkóng: *n.* slight crook in the neck. **nadurkong.** *a.* having a slight curve in the neck.

durmáng: **agsidurmang.** *v.* to sit (or do) at both sides of something; to be at both ends of. (*sipungto*)

durmém: **makadurmem.** *a.* nauseous; sickening, disgusting (*ariek*). **Agingga ita ket kadurmemdaka.** Even until now they are sick of you.

durubása: see *barubasa*: interpret.

durúdor: *n.* fruit with pointed base; bamboo spit. **duruduren.** *v.* to prod, poke from below; put on a spit. [Tag. *panundót*]

dúrog: *n.* species of sparrow.

duróg: *n.* teaser, tease; a kind of sparrow. **durogan.** *v.* to tease (*suron*; *artiok*; *parato*; *angaw*); incite; goad; prod. **madurogan.** *a.* sensitive to teasing. **dinnurogan.** *n.* teasing one another. [Png. *sutíl*, Tag. *tuksó*]

durógas: (*coll.*) *n.* cheater; grafter (*kusit*) **agdurogas.** *v.* to cheat, swindle.

durugísta: (f. *drogas*; Sp. *drugista*: cheat) *n.* drug addict; cheater, grafter.

durón: *n.* impulse; emotion. **iduron.** *v.* to push, shove. **pagiduron.** *n.* chaser (for alcoholic drinks); that which entices someone to do more than he normally would. **duronduron kapetkapet.** *n.* an old Ilocano song and dance. **Kasla adda mangidurduron kenka nga agawid.** It seems something is pushing you to go home. [Bon. *tolod*, Ibg. *irubbaq*, *itubbaq*, Ivt. *pasuysuyen*, Kpm., Png., Tag. *tulak*]

dúros: *n.* short-shafted hunting spear. (*píka*; *gayang*); *a.* steep; straight; drooping. **agduros.** *v.* to fall; drop. **durusen.** *v.* to prick with a *durus*; poke; wound. **maduros.** *v.* to fall straight down. **Ta pudno a kasla madurduros ti pusok nupay siak ti nagintangtangken.** Because it's true that it seems like my heart is falling, although I was the one pretending to be tough. [Tag. *tarik* (steep)]

dur-ús: **dinur-us.** *n.* kind of *wasig* cloth.

dur-óy: **madur-oy.** *v.* to rot, decay, putrefy (*dersay*; *lungsot*; *rupso*; *tubeg*; *tumuy*; *dugmuy*; *duted*; *timming*). [Tag. *bulók*]

durpá: (*obs.*) **madurpa.** *v.* to be covered with blood.

dursá(n): **idursan.** *v.* to shove, push into. **agdursan.** *v.* to fall back.

dursók: agdursok. *v.* to be rude, impolite. **nadursok.** *a.* impulsive, fervent; bold; forward; abrupt; rude, ill mannered. **kinadursok.** *n.* rudeness, impoliteness; violence. **Iwallagesda dagiti agdursok a mangipaddek iti patpatgenda a nakayanakanda a daga.** They throw down anyone who dares to trample on the land of their birth.

dos: (Sp. *dos*: two) *num.* two. (*dua*) **A las dos.** two o'clock. **dos grados.** *n.* two stories (buildings). **dos amantes, dos korasones.** *n.* bleeding heart.

dúsa: *n.* punishment; penalty; discipline; fine. **agdusa, dusaen.** *v.* to punish, discipline. **pannusa.** *n.* means of punishment; penalty. **pakadusaan.** *n.* cause for punishment. **dusa a bitay.** *n.* capital punishment, death by hanging **ipadusa.** *v.* to have someone punished **mapadusaan.** *v.* to be made to suffer. **Masapol a madusa ti nagbasol.** The guilty must be punished. **No dika agdusa, sika ti madusa.** If you do not punish, you will be the one punished. [Kal. *chusa, kaÿu*, Png. *dosá*, Tag. *dusa, parusa*]

duság: dusagen. *v.* to elbow; drive away. **madusag.** (*obs.*) *v.* to fall and mangle one's face. **Nakigtotak a nakariing idi adda natangken a banag a nangdusag iti timidko.** I woke up startled when a hard thing hit my chin. [Tag. *siko*]

dusáng: madusang. *v.* to come upon by chance. **Adda baro a kapadasan a madusdusangko.** I have a lot of new things to try out. **Simmaruno ti pannakadusangmi iti kuartel.** Next we came upon the barracks.

dusár: dusaren. *v.* to visit a foreign land, tour. **idusar.** *v.* to submit money.

dusáy: *a.* careless of one's belongings. (*liway*)

dusbér: (*reg.*) *a.* blunt, dull (*ngudel, ngelngel, dumber*). **kinadusber.** *n.* bluntness, dullness. [Tag. *puról*]

dusdús₁: *n.* a kind of scoop net for fishing. **dusdusan.** *v.* to clear cotton of seeds with a roller. **dusdusen.** *v.* to level (land). **idusdus.** *v.* to push forward (a roller, scoop). **padusdusan.** *v.* to flatten, level.

dusdús₂: padusdusan. *v.* to do negligently, to do a haphazard job.

dóse: (Sp. *doce*: twelve) *num.* twelve. **Alas dose.** Twelve o'clock; *n.* kind of flower.

dosél: (Sp. *dosel*: canopy) *n.* canopy.

doséna: (Sp. *docena*: dozen) *n.* dozen. **sangadosena.** *n.* one dozen.

dusír: *var.* of *duris*: become apparent, come into being, transpire. (*sumkén*)

dósis: (Sp. *dosis*: dose) *n.* dose.

dosmános: (Sp. *a dos manos*: by two hands) *n.* sledgehammer.

dusnóg: dusnogen. *v.* to prod, poke someone.

dusngí: *a.* wry-mouthed. **agdusngi.** *v.* to contort the mouth; grin; laugh. (*ngirsi*) **nakadusngi.** *a.* with a contorted mouth. **Nadusngi a nagturong iti agdan.** He went to the stairs with a wry-mouthed grimace. [Tag. *ngiwî*]

dusngíit: *n.* grimace of laughter (*ngirsi*); contortion of the mouth. **agdusngiit.** *v.* to grimace.

dusngó: maidusngo. *v.* to strike against something. **idusngo.** *v.* to shove; push; gesture with the nose. [Tag. *tulak*]

dusúdos: *n.* landslide. (*duyos; korokur; ludulud*) **agdusudos.** *v.* to form a landslide. **dusudusen.** *v.* to make flat, level.

dúsol: *var.* of *dukol*: protrude, stick out.

dussúor: see *dissuor*: happen suddenly and at once.

dutdút: *n.* body hair, fur; wool; feather; plumage; down. **dutdutan.** *a.* full of body hair or plumage; *v.* to deplume, remove the feathers of a chicken. **dutduten.** *v.* to pick out; extract; excite; entice, allure, induce, stir up. **dumutdut.** *v.* to draw out, extract. **dinnutdutan.** *n.* drawing lots (straws); raffle. **agkadutdut.** *v.* to be sympathetic; to be congenital; of the same beliefs and loyalties. **kadutdutan.** *a.* having similar feelings, beliefs. **dudutdutan.** *n.* kind of large elongated mollusk. **idutdutan.** *v.* to strip of hair, fur, wool, or plumage. **dinnutdut.** *n.* raffle; drawing lots. **dutdutenna ti dilana.** she is a chatterbox. **awan ti dumket a dutdot.** *exp.* not sympathetic or in agreement. **Nakatakder ti dutdutna.** He was petrified (*lit*: his body hair bristled). **no asino ti agkadutdut, isu ti agkakuyog.** *exp.* birds of a feather flock together. **Awan ti rumkuas a dutdutko kenka.** *exp.* You don't excite me; I have no feelings for you (*lit*: my hair does not stand up because of you). **Dimmutdut iti kuarta iti petakana.** He took some money out of his wallet. [Ibg. *dudduq*, Ivt. *bubuh*, Kal. *chutchut*, Kpm. *bulbul*, Png. *bagó*, Tag. *balahibo*]

dóte: (Sp. *dote*: dowry) *n.* dowry. (*sab-ung*)

dúted: naduted. *a.* rotten, decayed, putrefied (*dersay; lungsut; rupso; tubeg; tumuy; dugmuy; duted; timming*). [Tag. *bulók*]

dútok: dutuken. *v.* to designate, appoint; assign (*tuding*). **kaddutok.** *a.* just designated, just appointed. **madutokan.** *v.* to be designated, appointed. [Png. *getár*, Tag. *takdâ*]

dútsa: (Sp. *ducha*: shower) *n.* shower head, sprinkler in a shower bath. **Kasla nabang-aran iti apaganem-em a danum manipud iti dutsa.** He seemed to be relieved by the lukewarm water coming from the shower.

duyakyák: *var.* of *duyatyat.* **Maipaduyakyaken ti ap-apalanda a relasionmi.** Our relationship that they are envious of is out in the open.

dúyan: (Tag.) *n.* rattan stretcher; hammock. (*indáyon*)

duyangyáng: **nakaduyangyang.** *a.* exposed and unprotected (breasts, etc.).

duyas(yás): paduyasyas. *a.* slippery. **agduyasyas.** *v.* to slide, slip.

duyatyát: *a.* open (something that is usually closed). **nakaduyatyat.** *a.* open (said of shirts that should be buttoned, etc.); laid bare; exposed. **iduyatyat.** *v.* to expose; open; declare.

duyáw: *a.* yellow, golden-colored. (*kiaw, amarilio*) **dumuyaw.** *a.* yellowish. [Ibg. *ngíla*, Ivt. *mañuhamaq*, Kpm. *dilo*, Png. *duláw*, Tag. *diláw*]

duyáya: *n.* straddling. **agduyaya.** *v.* to straddle. (*kayang*)

duyáyat: (*reg.*) *a.* shallow (pans).

duyayyát: iduyayyát. *v.* to display; expose; lay bare. **nakaduyyayat.** *a.* exposed; laid bare. **Iti igid ti baybay, naiduyayyat ti pagturistaan a nakaipasdekan ti otel.** Along the waterfront, the tourist spots where the hotels were built were displayed. [Tag. *lantád*]

duydúy: duyduyen. *v.* to mash. **dinuyduyan.** *n.* a kind of sweet made with coconut, sugar, and boiled ripe squash.

dúyog: *n.* small dish made of a coconut shell for food other than rice, or for drinking; bowl. **sangaduyog.** *n.* one dishful. [Kal. *peÿatu*]

duyók: *n.* thrust; stab. **dumuyok.** *v.* to stab; cause a stabbing pain. **duyuken.** *v.* to stab; pierce (*bagkóng*). **Kasla maduyduyok ti puso ti baak.** The heart of the old lady seemed to be pierced (from sadness). [Tag. *ulos*]

dúyong: (Tagalog also) *n.* manatee, dugong; (myth.) mermaid. (*abada; sirena*)

dúyos: *n.* landslide. (*dusudus; korokor; ludulud*) **agduyos.** *v.* to shield, safeguard; favor; side with; slip, slide; to be interested in; prefer; like. **pagduyusan.** *n.* inclination, interest; favorite; that which causes sympathy. **agduyos ti rikna.** *v.* to fall in love. [Tag. *hilig*]

dragón: (Sp.) *n.* dragon. **dumaragon.** to be wild (animals).

drakoniáno: (Sp. *draconiano*) *a.* draconian.

dráma: (Sp. *drama*: drama) *n.* drama, play. (*pabuya*) **pagdramaan.** *n.* playhouse. **naindramaan.** *a.* dramatic. **ipadrama.** *v.* to stage (a play).

dramátiko: (Sp. *dramático*: dramatic) *a.* dramatic.

dramatúrgia: (Sp. *dramaturgia*: dramaturgy) *n.* dramaturgy, dramatic art.

dramatúrgo: (Sp. *dramaturgo*: dramatist) *n.* dramatist; playwright.

dróga(s): (Sp. *droga*: drug) *n.* drug. **agdrogas.** *v.* to take drugs. **agpadrogas.** *v.* to get drugs. **drogista.** *n.* druggist, pharmacist.

dyínggel: (Eng. jingle, *slang*) **agdyinggel.** *v.* to urinate. (*isbo*)

dyíp: (Eng.) *n.* jeep. **agdyip.** *v.* to ride in a jeep; go by jeep. [Kal. *talak* (Eng.)]

E

ébano: (Sp. *ébano*: ebony) *n*. ebony.

ebanghelísta: (Sp. *evangelista*: evangelist) *n*. evangelist, preacher.

ebanghélio: (Sp. *evangelio*) *n*. gospel.

ebaporáda: (Sp. *evaporada*: evaporated) *n*. evaporated milk.

ebaporasión: (Sp. *evaporación*: evaporation) *n*. evaporation.

ebbá₁: agebba, **ebbaen**. *v*. to carry (a baby) on the hip (*ubba*).

ebbá₂: **umba**. *v*. to be dismayed; let down, disheartened; daunted; intimidated; frightened.

ebbáas: **umbaas**. *v*. to subside; decrease (rivers, tide, etc.)

ebbák: *n*. sheath of a banana leaf. (*ubbak*)

ebbál: *n*. beriberi; muscle swelling. **umbal**. *v*. to swell, tumefy; to have dropsy, beriberi. [Png. *manás*, Tag. *manás, panás* (beriberi)]

ebbás: **umbas**. *v*. to subside, abate, decrease (rivers, etc.) (*umbaas*). [Tag. *hupâ*]

ebbát: **ebbaten** (*obs*.) *v*. to expend at once what should have served twice.

ebbáw: see *ubbaw*: vain; empty; worthless.

ebbés: see *ebbas*: subside; abate (rivers, etc.).

eb-éb: **umeb-eb**. *v*. to seep; spread. (water through parched earth). **eb-eban**. *v*. to drink little by little (bottle, coconut, etc.). [Tag. *tagas*]

ebidénsia: (Sp. *evidencia*: evidence) *n*. evidence, proof. (*pamaneknek*)

ebidénte: (Sp. *evidente*: evident) *a*. evident. (*latak*)

ebkás: **mangyebkas, yebkas**. *v*. to state, say, utter, express. **panagyebkas**. *n*. manner of speaking. **umebkas**. *v*. to spring out; set free. [Original root word is *bekkas*, transmuted as *ibleng < belleng*]

ebolusión: (Sp. *evolución*: evolution) *n*. evolution; gradual development. **ebolusionario**. *a*. evolutionary.

Ebréo: (Sp. *hebreo*: Hebrew) *n*. Hebrew.

edád: (Sp. *edad*: age) *n*. age. (*tawen*) **agedad**. *v*. to be as old as. **menor de edad**. *n*. minor (in age). **kaedad**. *n*. of the same age, contemporary.

eddáng: see *addang*: pace; step; walk.

eddék: *n*. grunt; heave. **umdek, ageddek** to exert one's strength; grunt (while defecating or giving birth). [Knk. *wik*, Tag. *irí*]

eddét: *var*. of *eddék*: grunt.

eddúkay: **eddukayen**. (*obs*.) *v*. to spill, to spread out. **maeddukayan**. *v*. to choke; have a lump in the throat. [Tag. *hirin*]

edéma: (Sp. *edema*: edema) *n*. edema, swelling, tumor.

edipikár: **maedipikaran**. *v*. to cultivate (land).

edipísio: (Sp. *edificio*: building) *n*. building, edifice. (*pasdek*)

édit: (Eng.) **editen**. *v*. to edit something. **editor**. *n*. editor. **inedit ni**. edited by.

edukádo: (Sp. *educado*: educated) *a*. educated (*deadal*); well bred, well brought up; with good manners.

edukár: (Sp. *educar*: educate) **edukaran**. *v*. to educate. (*sursuroán*)

edukasión: (Sp. *educación*: education) *n*. education. (*panursuro*)

edtí: **yudti, umedti**. *v*. to grunt (when giving birth, defecating, under a heavy load, etc.); groan.

eggéd: *n*. omen, presage; prognostic; portent; augury; sign; token; premonition. (*labeg*) **yegged**. *v*. to fear, dread (*buteng*); apprehend. [Tag. *salagimsím*]

egoísmo: (Sp. *egoísmo*: egotism) *n*. egotism; exaggerated sense of self-importance. **egoista**. *n*. egoist; *a*. egoistic.

egotísmo: (Eng.) *n*. egotism; selfishness. **egotista**. *n*. egotist, selfish person.

éhe: (Sp. *eje*: axle) *n*. axle. see *burayongan*.

ehekusión: (Sp. *ejecución*: execution) *n*. execution; rendition; putting into effect; performance.

ehekutíbo: (Sp. *ejecutivo*: executive) *n*. executive.

ehekutór: (Sp. *ejecutor*: executor) *n*. executor (of a will), testator; executioner (of capital punishment).

ehemplár: (Sp. *ejemplar*: model) *n*. model; example. (*pagwadan, pagarigan*)

ehémplo: (Sp. *ejemplo*: example) *n*. example. (*pagarigan*) **por ehemplo**. for example (*kas pagarigan*). [Tag. *halimbawà*]

ehersísio: (Sp. *ejercicio*: exercise) *n*. exercise (*watwat*); drill, military exercise; performance of the duties of one's office.

ehérsito: (Sp. *ejército*: army) *n*. army.

Ehípsio: (Sp. *egipcio*: Egyptian) n, *a*. Egyptian.

Ehípto: (Sp. *Egipto*: Egypt) *n*. Egypt.

ek-ék: see *anek-ek*.

ekilíbrio: (Sp. *equilibrio*: equilibrium) *n*. equilibrium, balanced state.

ekipáhe: (Sp. *equipaje*: baggage) *n*. baggage. (*maleta*)

ekípo: (Sp. *equipo*: equipment) *n*. equipment.

ékis: (Sp. *equis*: x) *n*. the letter x. **ekisan**. *v*. to mark with an x; cross out.

ekkék: *n*. giggle. (*ellek*) **umkek**. *v*. to laugh with subdued laughter. [Tag. *bungisngís*]

eklípse: (Sp. *eclipse*: eclipse) *n*. eclipse.

ekuadór: (Sp. *ecuador*: equator) *n*. equator.

ekualidád: (Sp. *igualdad*) *n*. equality.

ekuasión: (Sp. *ecuación*: equation) *n*. equation.

ekolohía: (Sp. *ecología*: ecology) *n*. ecology.

ekonomía: (Sp. *economía*: economy) *n*. economy.

ekonómiko: (Sp. *económico*: economic) *a*. economic; economical.

eksaherádo: (Sp. *exagerado*: exaggerated) *a*. exaggerated. **eksaherasion**. *n*. exaggeration.

eksákto: (Sp. *exacto*: exact) *a*. exact. (*apagisu, maitutop*) **yeksakto**. *v*. to do exactly; put in the right place.

eksámen: (Sp. *examen*: exam) *n*. examination, test. (*suut*) **ageksamen**. *v*. to take a test. **eksamenen**. *v*. to give a test to. **eksaminado**. *a*. examined; experienced. [Tag. *sulit*]

eksaminádo: (Sp. *examinado*: examined) *a*. examined; passed, approved; accredited (after examination).

eksélsa: (Sp. *excelsa*) *n*. variety of coffee.

ekséma: (Eng.) *n*. eczema, inflammation of the skin with itching and formation of red patches.

ekskomunión: (Sp. *excomunión*: ex-communication) *n*. ex-communication. (*panagtálaw*)

ekskursión: (Sp. *excursión*: excursion) *n*. excursion. (*bassit a biáhe*)

ekspektár: (Eng.) **ekspektaren**. *v*. to expect. (*daanan, namnamaen*)

ekspektoránte: (Sp. *expectorante*: expectorant) *n*. expectorant.

eksperiénsia: (Sp. *experiencia*: experience) *n*. experience. (*pádas, lásat*)

eksperiménto: (Sp. *experimento*: experiment) *n*. experiment. (*padas*)

ekspérto: (Sp. *experto*: expert) *n*. expert.

eksplanasión: (Eng.) *n*. explanation.

eksplikár: (Sp. *explicar*: explain) **eksplikaren**. *v*. to explain. (*palawag*)

eksploradór: (Eng.) *n*. explorer.

eksplosíbo: (Sp. *explosivo*: explosive) *n*, *a*. explosive.

eksplosión: (Sp. *explosión*: explosion) *n*. explosion.

eksplotasión: (Sp. *explotación*: exploitation) *n*. exploitation.

eksponénte: (Sp. *exponente*: exponent) *n*. exponent.

ekstérno: (Sp. *externo*) *n*. day pupil; non-boarding student in a sectarian school.

ekstranghéro: (Sp. *extranjero*: stranger, fem: *ekstranghera*) *n*. stranger; foreigner.

ekstraordinário: (Sp. *extraordinario*: extraordinary) *a*. extraordinary; unusual.

ektária: (Sp. *hectares*: hectare) *n*. hectare. (*rukud ti daga*)

elaborasión: (Sp. *elaboración*: elaboration) *n*. elaboration. (*panagpalawag*)

eládo: (Sp. *helado*: frozen) *a*. frozen; icy. **makina a pangelado**. *n*. freezer.

elástiko: (Sp. *elástico*: elastic) *a*. elastic; *n*. rubber band.

elegánsia: (Sp. *elegancia*: elegance) *n*. elegance. (*kinangayed*)

elegánte: (Sp. *elegante*: elegant) *a*. elegant. (*ngayed*)

elehía: (Sp. *elegía*) *n*. elegy.

eleksión: (Sp. *elección*: election) *n*. election. (*panagbubutos*) **ageleksion**. *v*. to have an election; to vote.

elékto: (Sp. *electo*) *n*. elect.

elektór: (Sp. *elector*: elector) *n*. elector, voter.

elektrisísta: (Sp. *electricista*: electrician) *n*. electrician.

elektrisidád: (Sp. *electricidad*: electricity) *n*. electricity. (*koriente*)

elektrokutádo: (Sp. *electrocutado*) *a*. electrocuted. (*nakuriente*)

elektróniko: (Sp. *electrónico*) *a*. electronic.

el-él: *n*. furrow; notch; temporary line in the skin produced by pressure; groove at the base of the glans penis; groove at the inner thighs. **kaelelan**. *v*. to rot, decay in the ground; *n*. inner part of a groove; center; midst. **el-elan**. *v*. to etch or engrave on. **mael-elan**. *v*. to have something engraved on. **umel-el**. *v*. to tighten; dig into. [Tag. *ukà*]

elementária: (Sp. *elementaria*: elementary) *n*. elementary school.

eleménto: (Sp. *elemento*: element) *n*. element; forces of nature.

elepánte: (Sp. *elefante*: elephant) *n*. elephant (*gadia*). **elepantino**. *a*. elephantine, huge.

elepantíasis: (Sp. *elefantíasis*) *n*. elephantiasis, disease caused by *filaria* worms characterized by the enlargement of tissues of the body.

eléra: (Sp. *hilera*: row, line, file) *n*. row (of plants); line.

élie: (Sp. *elle*) *n*. the pronunciation of the Spanish letter *ll*.

eliminádo: (Sp. *eliminado*: eliminated) *a*. eliminated.

élise: (Sp. *hélice*: propeller, helix) *n*. propeller.

elláw: see *alláw*: kite.

elláy: **umlay**. *v*. to tire, become exhausted; to droop; to become flaccid, said of the penis. [Tag. *layláy*]

ellék: *n*. unrestrained laughter. **umlek**. *v*. to be dumb, mute, speechless (with anger, laughing, weeping, etc.); laugh unrestrainedly. **agellek**. *v*.

to laugh continuously. [Png., Tag. *galakgák*, Tag. *hagikgík*]

em: (*obs.*) see *ngem*: but.

embaháda: (Sp. *embajada*: embassy) *n.* embassy.

embahadór: (Sp. *embajador*: ambassador) *n.* ambassador.

embalsamádo: (Sp. *embalsamado*: embalmed). *a.* embalmed.

embalsamadór: (Sp. *embalsamador*: embalmer) *n.* embalmer.

embárgo: (Sp. *embargo*: seizure; embargo) *n.* distress; seizure or detention (confiscation) of goods of another by way of pledge for the reparation of an injury or the performance of a duty; embargo; foreclosure. **embarguen**. *v.* to seize, commandeer; foreclose. **maembargo**. *v.* to be seized, confiscated, captured; foreclosed. **No agkibaltangtayo, maembargo amin a sanikuatayo.** If we make a mistake, all of our possessions will be confiscated.

embáse: (Sp. *envase*: bottling, packing, canning) *n.* bottling, canning; packaging.

embés: (Sp. *en vez de*: instead) *prep.* instead of.

embestidúra: (Sp. *envestidura*: investiture) *n.* investiture; ceremony of wearing the graduation cap and gown.

embléma: (Sp. *emblema*: emblem) *n.* emblem. (*tanda, kayarigan*) **emblematiko**. *a.* emblematic; symbolic.

embúdo: (Sp. *embudo*: funnel) *n.* funnel.

emboláda: (Sp. *embolada*) *n.* piston stroke.

émbolo: (Sp. *émbolo*: piston) *n.* piston; plunger.

embolsá(r): (Sp. *embolsar*: pocket) **embolsaran**. *v.* to reimburse someone.

embolsádo: (Sp. *embolsado*: pocketed) *a.* obliged to reimburse; forced to pay in the name of someone else.

embornál: *var.* of *imburnal*: sewer opening, scupper hole.

embutído: (Sp. *embutido*: sausage) *n.* sausage, minced meat.

embráso: (Sp. *embarazo*: hindrance) *n.* obstacle, hindrance. (*lapped*)

emdúk: **emduken**. *v.* to spend wisely, judiciously, economically. (*inut; tipit*) **mangemduk**. *a.* stingy in spending.

em-ém: **agem-em**. *v.* to compress the lips. **ememan**. *v.* to hold with the lips; suppress emotions. **naem-em a sangit**. *n.* crying with the mouth closed. [Tag. *tikóm*]

emerhénsia: (Sp. *emergencia*: emergency) *n.* emergency.

emigránte: (Sp. *emigrante*: emigrant) *n.* emigrant.

emigrasión: (Sp. *emigración*: emigration) *n.* emigration.

emisário: (Sp. *emisario*: emissary) *n.* emissary.

emmá: *n.* kindness. (*ánus*) **naemma**. *a.* kind, gentle, mild, meek, affable. [Knk. *ammá*, Tag. *yumì, baít*]

emmák: **agemmak**. *v.* to bleat (said of sheep); also, to moo (said of the cow.) [Png. *alangab*, Tag. *ungâ*]

emulsión: (Sp. *emulsión*) **emulsio de Skot**. cod-liver oil.

empáke: (Sp. *empaque*: packing) *n.* packing; wrapping. **agempake**. *v.* to pack; wrap up.

empanáda: (Sp. *empanada*: pie) *n.* crescent-shaped pie filled with meat, vegetables or fruit.

emparedádo: (Sp. *emparedado*: sandwich) *n.* sandwich.

émpasis: (Sp. *énfasis*: emphasis) *n.* emphasis.

empátso: (Sp. *empacho*: indigestion) *n.* indigestion. **empatsado**. *a.* suffering from indigestion.

empénio: (Sp. *empeño*: pawning; pledging) *n.* request, favor asked; pawn, mortgage. **ahensia de empenios**. *n.* pawnshop.

emperadór: (Sp. *emperador*: emperor) *n.* emperor. (*ari*)

emperatrís: (Sp. *emperatriz*: empress) *n.* empress; wife of an emperor.

empiséma: (Sp. *enfisema*) *n.* emphysema.

emplásto: (Sp. *emplasto*: plaster) *n.* plaster; poultice.

empleádo: (Sp. *empleado*: employee) *n.* employee. (*mangmangged*)

empléo: (Sp. *empleo*: employment) *n.* employment. (*panggedán, pagsapulan*) **mangiyempleo**. *v.* to employ.

empliár: (Sp. *emplear*: employ) **agemplear**. *v.* to employ.

empório: (Sp. *emporio*: emporium) *n.* emporium.

empresário: (Sp. *empresario*: contractor, showman) *n.* impresario; theatrical manager.

=en: *adv.* [Adverbial enclitic with the variant -*n* after vowels. After the enclitics =*ak*, =*m*, and =*k*, the original *o* of the pronoun is retained: =*akon*, =*mon*, =*kon*] *encl.* already, sooner than expected (when used with a completed verbal aspect (past)); now (with continuative verbs); may also indicate change of state or contrast a referent: **Nanganako*n***. I already ate. **Napane*n***. He/she already went. **Umayka*n***. Come now. **Siako*n***. Now it's my turn; I'll do it; Me (as opposed to someone else); *adjectival enclitic*. Combined with the prefix nag-, -*en* is used as an admirative intensifier: **Naglaade*n*!** How ugly! **Nagsipngete*n*!** How dark! [Ibg. *nganá*, Png. *la*, Tag. *na*]

-en₁: (Perfective form *-in-*). Transitive patient focus verbal suffix. As a transitive verbal suffix, *-en* takes the *-ko* series pronouns. **suraten.** to write something, *perf. sinurat.* **basaen.** to read something, *perf. binasa.* **alaen.** to get something, *perf. innala.* *-en* verb Paradigm in first person singular: **basaen:** [*basa* + *-en*] 'to read something'. **Basaek.** I read (Present) it. **Basbasaek.** I am reading it. **Binasak.** I read (past) it. **Binasbasak.** I was reading it. **Basaekto.** I will read it. With adjectival (stative) roots, may denote attaining or fulfilling a quality or state. **Ragsakem kadi no pumusay?** Will you be happy about it if he dies? **Siertuem a makapanka.** Make sure you can go.

CV- -en₂: The initial CV reduplication of the root of *-en* verbs indicates suitability: **lulutuen a saba.** bananas good for cooking. **tutunuen a sida.** fish good for barbecuing. **gigisaen a nateng.** vegetables good for frying. **lilitsonen.** pig good for roasting. **Talaga a kukuraben dagiti lupponá!** Her thighs are really devourable (good for eating).

-en₃: (Perfective form *-in-*). Affix used with certain animate roots to indicate infestation, destruction, or negative affect. **iggesen.** to be infested with worms, may be worm infested. **kutonen.** to be infested with ants, may be infested with ants. **karominasen.** to be affected (negatively) by the sting of a jellyfish.

enáguas: (Sp. *enaguas*: petticoat) *n.* underskirt, petticoat.

enamorádo: (Sp. *enamorado*: enamoured) *a.* in love with, enamoured of.

enáno: (Sp. *enano*: dwarf) *n.* dwarf. (*ansisit*)

endémiko: (Sp. *endémico*: endemic) *a.* endemic.

endiápi: *n.* a kind of rebec.

endórso: (Sp.: endorsement) *n.* endorsement.

énema: (Eng.) *n.* enema. (*labatiba*) **agpaenema.** *v.* to get an enema.

enemígo: (Sp.) *n.* enemy. (*kabusor*)

enerhía: (Sp. *energía*: energy) *n.* energy.

Enéro: (Sp.) *n.* January. [Kal. *kiyang*, Knk. *lúya*]

-énia: feminine form of *-enio*: **Currimaoenia.** female from Currimao.

-énio: (Sp. *-eño* derivational suffix denoting origin) suffix borrowed from Spanish that denotes origin (*taga-, i-*); the feminine form is *-enia*. **Abrenio.** person from Abra. **Sarratenio.** person from Sarrat. **Currimaoenio.** person from Currimao.

enkomendéro: (Sp. *encomendero*) *n.* commissioner of an estate or piece of land given by the Spanish kings.

enmiénda: (Sp. *enmienda*: amendment) *n.* Constitutional amendment.

enná: *n.* sandy salt water from which salt is extracted through a filtering process.

ennék: *var.* of *eddék*: grunt due to physical exertion.

ennép: ennepen. *v.* to keep, to conceal one's feelings, especially rancor.

enorabuéna: (Sp. *enhorabuena*: congratulations) *n.* congratulations.

ensaláda: (Sp. *ensalada*: salad) *n.* salad. **agensalada.** *v.* to prepare salad; to have salad.

ensaymáda: (Sp. *ensaimada*: bun) *n.* puff cake.

ensáyo: (Sp. *ensayo*: rehearsal) *n.* rehearsal; training, practice. **agen-ensayo.** *v.* to train, practice; rehearse. **ensayado.** *a.* rehearsed, practiced.

enséma: *n.* additional money given when two items of unequal value are traded. **agensema.** *v.* to trade in; give an extra amount of money when trading an object of better value.

ensepalítis: (Sp. *encefalitis*) *n.* encephalitis, inflammation of the brain.

ensiáno: (Sp. *anciano*) *n.* expert; something that is well known.

ensigida: *var.* of *insigida*: immediately.

ensiklopédia: (Sp. *enciclopedia*: encyclopedia) *n.* encyclopedia.

entabládo: (Sp. *entablado*: stage) *n.* stage, raised platform.

entendído: (Sp. *entendido*: understood) *a.* wise, understanding; learnèd. (*manakem*)

enteraménte: (Sp. *enteramente*: entirely) *a.* entirely. (*pulos, bin-ig*)

enterár: (Sp. *enterar*: learn; inform) **makienterar.** *v.* to consult with, make an agreement.

entéro: (Sp. *entero*: entire) *a.* entire, complete, whole (*dagup amin*); quite.

entiérro: (Sp. *entierro*: burial) *n.* burial, interment.

entonasión: (Sp. *entonación*: intonation) *n.* intonation; modulation.

entónses: (Sp. *entonces*: then) *adv.* then; therefore.

éntra: (Sp. *entra*: enter) *n.* opening of classes; beginning of work. (*serrek*)

entráda: (Sp. *entrada*: entrance) *n.* entrance; admission; entree, course at dinner; entry (in a dictionary); beginning of a speech or book.

éntre: (Sp. *entre*: between) *adv.* more or less, somewhat (*medio*); almost; among. **entre pamilia.** among relatives. **entre nangisit.** more or less black. **entre nalipatak.** I almost forgot.

entreákto: (Sp. *entreacto*: intermission) *n.* intermission at a show.

entrédos: (Sp. *entre dos*: between two) *n.* strip of lace sewn in between a lower and upper part of a skirt.

entréga: (Sp. *entrega*: delivery) *n.* delivery. (*panangyawat*) **yentrega.** *v.* to deliver, hand over.

entregado. *a.* given to; addicted to.

entremés: (Sp. *entremés*: canapé) *n.* canapé; side dish, appetizer.

entremetído: (Sp. *entrometido*: meddlesome) *a.* officious, interfering, meddlesome.

entrepánio: (Sp. *entrepaño*: panel) *n.* panel (of wood).

entresiéte: (Sp. *entre siete*: card game) *n.* kind of card game played in pairs whose highest cards are the ace, two, and three, which are called *politana*.

entresuélo: (Sp. *entresuelo*: mezzanine) *n.* mezzanine, second floor.

entretéla: (Sp. *entretela*: interlining) *n.* buckram, coarse cloth made from hemp.

entsúpe: (Sp. *enchufe*: socket joint) *n.* socket joint, electric socket. (*pagsaksakan*)

eng-éng: ageng-eng. *v.* to grumble, mutter, mumble, stutter. **aganeng-eng.** *v.* to whimper, whine. [Tag. *haluyhóy*]

enggánio: (Sp. *engaño*: deceit) *n.* deceit; fraud; disappointment. **maenganio.** *v.* to be flattered; deceived. **engganioso.** *a.* deceitful.

enggáste: (Sp. *engaste*: setting of gems) *n.* setting of gems.

enggranáhe: (Sp. *engranaje*: gearing) *n.* mechanical gear.

enggránde: *var.* of *engrande*.

engkáhe: (Sp. *encaje*: lace) *n.* lace, lacework.

engkantadóra: (Sp. *encantadora*) *n.* enchantress; fairy; kind of flower.

engkánto: (Sp. *encanto*: charm) *n.* charm. (*ginammol, ánib, mutia*; *kayaw*) **maengkanto, engkantado.** *a.* enchanted. **engkantador.** *n.* enchanter; sorcerer. **Ta uray karurodko a denggen ket kasla maengkantoak.** Because even if I am angry hearing it, I seem to be charmed too.

engkargádo: (Sp. *encargado*: in charge) *n.* person in charge, caretaker. (*manarawidwid*)

engkarnasión: (Sp. *encarnación*: incarnation) *n.* incarnation.

engkuéntro: (Sp. *encuentro*: meeting) *n.* meeting; encounter.

engngát: agengngat. *v.* to separate while engaged in a fight.

engranáhe: (Sp. *engranaje*: gear) *n.* toothed wheel, gear.

engránde: (Sp. *en grande*: grand) *a.* grand. (*ngayed*) **kasar engrande.** *n.* grand wedding.

eukalípto: (Sp. *eucalipto*: eucalyptus) *n.* eucalyptus tree.

eukaliptól: (Sp. *eucalipto*: eucalyptus) *n.* eucalyptus oil.

eunóko: (Sp. *eunuco*) *n.* eunuch; chamber attendant.

Európa: (Sp. *Europa*: Europe) *n.* Europe. **agpa-Europa.** *v.* to go to Europe. **Europeo.** *n. a.* European; feminine: *Europea*.

epátika: (Sp. *hepática*) *n.* liverwort.

epékto: (Sp. *efecto*: effect) *n.* effect; chemical reaction.

ep-ép: ep-epen. *v.* to restrain, hold back; to check, repress, bridle; curb; control; soothe; alleviate; subdue; inhibit; dim, shade. **maep-ep.** *a.* repressed, checked; mitigated. **di maep-ep.** *a.* unrepressed; uncontrolled; unrestrained; uninhibited. **pagep-ep.** *n.* palliative; temporary relief. [Tag. *bawa*]

epidémia: (Sp. *epidemia*: epidemic) *n.* epidemic, rapid spreading of disease.

épika: (Sp. *épica*: epic) *n.* epic story, epic poetry.

épiko: (Sp. *épico*: epic) *a.* epic; heroic.

epiléptiko: (Sp. *epiléctico*: epileptic) *n.* epileptic. (*kissiw*)

epílogo: (Sp. *epílogo*: epilogue) *n.* epilogue.

Epipanía: (Sp. *Epifania*: Epiphany) *n.* Epiphany, the feast of the coming of the Wise Men to Christ.

episódio: (Sp. *episodio*: episode) *n.* episode. (*paset ti pabuya, kapitulo*)

epístola: (Sp. *epístola*: epistle) *n.* epistle.

epitápa: (Eng.) *n.* epitaph.

epitéto: (Sp. *epiteto*: epithet) *n.* epithet.

epítome: (Sp. *epítome*: epitome) *n.* epitome; abstract; summary.

époka: (Sp. *época*: epoch) *n.* age, era, epoch.

eppáaw: umpaaw. *v.* to abate, decrease (wind).

eppég: *n.* parcel of land. **eppegen.** *v.* to allot, distribute, apportion, divide, share (plots of land).

eppél: yeppel. *v.* to suffocate (by applying pressure to the nose and mouth); (*coll.*) to force inside (penis). **naeppelan.** *v.* to suffer from the inability of the fetus to leave the womb; to suffer from the inability of the egg to leave the hen, resulting in the egg breaking in the hen's body.

eppén: *n.* two-barbed spear. (*gayang*)

eppés: *a.* empty (ears of grain, words, etc.); meaningless; without air (balls); flat (tires); hollow. **umpes.** *v.* to reduce, subside, unswell; become flat (tires, balls). [Tag. *hungkág* (hollow)]

eppét: (*obs.*) *a.* dry, without milk.

epsút: see *apsut*: slip out; squeeze out.

eramiénta: (Sp. *herramienta*: tools) *n.* tools.

eráta: (Sp. *errata*: errata) *n.* errata, list of errors.

erb(a)áka: see *albahaka*, *arbaka* or *erbaka*.

erbulário: (Sp. *herbolario*: herbalist) *n.* herb doctor; quack doctor. [Tag. *albularyo*]

ére: *n.* air, middair (*angin*). **nakaere.** *a.* suspended in midair. **Timmayab ti buokna iti ere.** Her hair flew in the air.

eredéro: (Sp. *heredero*: heir) *n.* heir, heiress (*tawid*). **bugbugtong nga eredero.** sole heir.

eréhe: (Sp. *hereje*: heretic) *n.* heretic. **erehía.** *n.* heresy.

er-ér: *n.* accumulated dirt in perspiration. **agerer.** *v.* to accumulate dirt with sweat; to be ostentatious, pompous.

érgo: agergo. *v.* to argue, reason, dispute. (*apa, susik*; *tubar*; *baranget*) **erguen.** *v.* to argue with someone.

eringgília: *var.* of *heringgilia*: syringe.

ermána: (Sp. *hermana*: sister) *n.* woman presiding officer of certain confraternities.

ermíta: (Sp. *ermita*: hermitage) *n.* hermitage; chapel in which mass is held. **ermitanio.** *n.* hermit, person who lives alone in a solitary place sometimes practicing religious mediation.

ernít: (*obs.*) **maernit.** *v.* to be awed.

eruá: (*obs.*) **eruaen.** *v.* to exhume. (*kutkuten iti tanem*)

eronáutika: (Sp. *aeronáutica*: aeronautics) *n.* aeronautics, the science or art of aviation.

eropláno: (Eng.) *n.* airplane. **ageroplano.** *v.* to ride an airplane; go by plane. [Bon. *doplano*, Kal. *loplalu*]

eropuérto: (Sp. *aeropuerto*: airport) *n.* airport.

erupsión: (Sp. *erupción*: eruption) *n.* eruption.

erpéng: mayerpeng. *v.* to fit, be suitable, proper, becoming (*maiyasping*). [Tag. *akmâ*]

errádo: (Sp. *errado*: erring) **agerrado.** *v.* to err, make a mistake. (*kammalí*)

errés: umres. *v.* to shrink (clothes), to contract (wood), to droop, decline; languish (persons, animals, plants); lose weight (*kessén*). **panagerres ti bagi.** weight loss.

ersán: (*obs.*) **agersan.** *v.* to do all together.

erténg: yerteng, ertengen. *v.* to tighten by stretching.

eséna: (Sp. *escena*: scene) *n.* scene. (*buya*; *parang*)

esénsia: (Sp. *esencia*: essence) *n.* essence. **esensia de trementina.** *n.* oil of turpentine.

es-és: *n.* black and brown flying insect with small antlers that is destructive to coconuts. (*bannirok*) **umes-es.** *v.* to shrink, contract (*umres*); ebb, subside; level; evaporate. **es-esen.** *v.* to put closer together. **pages-esan.** *n.* shrinkage. **Tunggal ages-es ti mapupuoran a taep, nayonan laeng tapno saan a masinga ti darang ti dalikan.** Whenever the burning husk subsides, just add more so the heat from the stove is not affected.

eskabétse: (Sp. *escabeche*: pickled fish) *n.* pickled fish. (*pinaksiw a sida*)

eskála: (Sp. *escala*: scale; stepladder) *n.* scale, measuring marks of a scale or measuring instrument; dock, port; step; turning away from a regular route. **ageskala.** *v.* to make a stopover; turn away or deviate from the regular route.

eskaléra: (Sp. *escalera*: staircase) *n.* ladder, staircase (*agdan*); three consecutive cards of the same suit in one hand.

eskalón: (Sp. *escalón*) *n.* street; block of houses.

eskán: see *kaes-eskan*.

eskándalo: (Sp. *escándalo*: scandal) *n.* scandal. **ageskandalo.** *v.* to create a scandal, uproar. **eskandaloso.** *a.* scandalous.

eskantilión: (Sp. *escantillón*: gauge; template) *n.* printer's template; pattern mold.

eskapár: (Sp. *escapar*) **ageskapar.** *v.* to escape; dodge; flee. **mangeskapar.** *v.* to save from danger.

eskaparáte: (Sp. *escaparate*: showcase) *n.* showcase; show window of a store.

eskápe: (Sp. *escape*) *n.* exhaust; escapement of a watch or clock.

eskápula: (Sp. *escápula*) *n.* scapula.

eskapulário: (Sp. *escapulario*: scapular) *n.* scapular.

eskarapéla: (Sp. *escarapela*) *n.* cockade worn by the policemen during the Spanish regime.

eskarláta: (Sp. *escarlata*: scarlet) *n.* scarlet; red rose; scarlet fever.

eskarlatína: (Sp. *escarlatina*) *n.* scarlatina, mild form of scarlet fever; red or crimson woolen fabrics.

eskayóla: (Sp. *escayola*: plaster) *n.* plaster of Paris.

eskiláda: (Sp. *esquilla*: small bell) *n.* ringing of church bells. (*rupiki*)

eskiládo: (Sp. *esquilado*: sheared) **eskiladuen.** *v.* to cut hair with clippers. **eskilador.** *n.* clippers.

eskína: (Sp. *esquina*: corner) *n.* street corner (*suli*); cutting of hair on the neck and on the face. **ageskina.** *v.* to cut hair.

eskiníta: (Sp. *esquina*: corner + dim. suffix *-ita*) *n.* street corner turning into an alley; alley. (*suli*)

eskiról: (Sp. *esquirol*: scab) *n.* strike breaker, scab.

esklabína: (Sp. *esclavina*) *n.* pelerine worn by churchgoing women in the olden days.

esklabitúd: (Sp. *esclavitud*: slavery) *n.* slavery. (*adipen*)

eskuádra: (Sp. *escuadra*: squad) *n.* squad; squadron; carpenter's square; motorcycle frame.

eskuadrón: (Sp. *escuadrón*: squadron) *n.* naval squadron.

eskuála: (Sp. *escuadra*: carpenter's square) *n.* carpenter's square. **eskualado.** *a.* right-angled.

eskuáter: (Eng.) *n.* squatter; slum dweller. **ageskuater.** *v.* to squat; live in a slum; build a makeshift house on property not owned. **kaeskuateran.** *n.* slum area, squatting area.

eskóba: (Sp. *escoba*: brush) *n.* brush. (*sugígi*) **eskobaen.** *v.* to brush.

eskobília: (Sp. *escobilla*: small brush) *n.* whisk broom; species of shrub with pale hairs and yellow flowers; burr or irregular protuberance on certain herbs.

eskudéro: (Sp. *escudero*: squire) *n.* squire, shield bearer.

eskúdo: (Sp. *escudo*: shield) *n.* shield; coat of arms; escudo, monetary unit of Portugal.

eskuéla: (Sp. *escuela*: school) *n.* school. (*pagadalan, pagbasaan*) **ageskuela.** *v.* to attend school.

eskueláan: see *eskuela.* (*pagadalan, pagbasaan*)

eskólar: (Eng.) *n.* scholar. (*agad-adal a masirib*)

eskólta: (Sp. *escolta*: escort) *n.* military escort, convoy.

eskultór: (Sp. *escultor*: sculptor) *n.* sculptor. **eskultura.** *n.* sculpture, sculpting.

eskómbro: (Sp. *escombro*: debris) *n.* crushed stones used in pavement.

eskomulgádo: (Sp. *excomulgado*: ex-communicated) *a.* ex-communicated.

eskopéta: (Sp. *escopeta*: shotgun) *n.* shotgun. (*paltog*) **eskopetilia.** *n.* toy gun.

eskupidór: (Sp. *escupidero*: spittoon) *n.* spittoon. (*pagtupraan*)

eskorbúto: (Sp. *escorbuto*: scurvy) *n.* scurvy. **ageskorbuto.** *v.* to have scurvy.

Eskosés: (Sp. *escocés*: Scottish) *n.* Scotch, Scottish; feminine: *Eskosesa.*

eskosésa: (Sp. *escocesa*: Scottish) *n.* Scotch plaid cloth; Scottish female.

Eskósia: (Sp. *Escocia*: Scotland) *n.* Scotland.

eskóta: (Sp. *escota*) *n.* stonecutter's chisel.

eskotáda: (Sp. *escotada*: low cut) *n.* low cut in the neck of a dress.

eskotadúra: (Sp. *escotadura*: low neckline) *n.* low cut in the neck of a dress.

eskotília: (Sp. *escotilla*: hatchway) *n.* hatchway, rectangular opening in the desk of a vessel for passage below.

eskríba: (Sp. *escriba*: scribe) *n.* scribe. (*eskribiénte*)

eskribánia: (Sp. *escribanía*: writing desk) *n.* rolltop desk; office of a notary or clerk.

eskribáno: (Sp. *escribano*: court clerk) *n.* court clerk. (*eskribiénte*)

eskribiénte: (Sp. *escribiente*: clerk) *n.* clerk; scribe. (*sumusurat*)

eskríma: (Sp. *esgrima*: fencing) *n.* fencing, sword fighting. (*arnis*) **eskrimador.** *n.* one who fences. **makieskrima.** *v.* to fence with, join in fencing. **Saan a nakieskrima iti saritaan ni Ama.** Father did not join in the vicious debate (*lit.* fencing conversation). [Kal. *byabbyakeg*]

eskritório: (Sp. *escritorio*: desk) *n.* writing desk.

eskrúpulo: (Sp. *escrúpulo*: scruple) *n.* scruple. (*alikaká*) **eskrupuloso.** *a.* scrupulous.

eskrutínio: (Sp. *escrutinio*: scrutiny) *n.* canvassing of ballots; scrutiny.

Eslábo: (Sp. *eslavo*) *n.*, *a.* Slav.

eslabón: (Sp. *eslabón*: link of a chain) *n.* link. (*kalangkáng ti káwar*)

esmálte: (Sp. *esmalte*: enamel) *n.* enamel. **esmaltador.** *n.* one who lays enamel.

esmárte: (Eng.) *a.* smartly dressed, well dressed.

esmelína: *n.* the *gmelina* tree.

esmerálda: (Sp. *esmeralda*: emerald) *n.* emerald.

esmól: (Eng. small, *coll.*) **esmolen.** *v.* to belittle (*tagibassit*).

esngáw: (f. *sengngaw*) **yesngaw.** *v.* to express; utter; say; voice. **makasngaw.** *v.* to be able to talk; express oneself. **saan a makayesngaw.** *v.* to be unable to express oneself; be speechless.

esópago: (Sp. *esófago*: esophagus) *n.* esophagus.

espáda: (Sp. *espada*: sword) *n.* sword; spade in playing cards; swordfish.

espadánia: (Sp. *espadaña*: belfry; reed-mace) *n.* fantail.

espadón: (Sp. *espadón*: large sword) *n.* broadsword.

Espánia: (Sp. *España*: Spain) *n.* Spain. **agpaEspania.** *v.* to go to Spain.

Espaniól: (Sp. *español*: Spanish, *fem*: *Espaniola*) *n.* Spaniard; *n.* & *a.* Spanish. (*Kastíla*)

espanióla: (Sp. *española*: Spanish) *n.* Spanish woman; oxtongue preparation.

espásmo: (Sp.) *n.* spasm.

espasmódiko: (Sp. *espasmódico*) *a.* spasmodic.

espátula: (Sp.) *n.* spatula.

espediénte: (Sp. *expediente*) *n.* important papers kept at home.

espého: (Sp. *espejo*: mirror) *n.* mirror. (*sarming*) agespeho. *v.* to look at oneself in the mirror. [Tag. *salamín*]

espéransa: (Sp. *esperanza*: hope) *n.* hope (*namnama*). [Tag. *pag-asa*]

esperiénsia: (Sp. *experiencia*: experience) *n.* experience.

espérma: (Sp. *esperma*: sperm) *n.* spermaceti, a waxy solid obtained from the sperm whale and used in making cosmetics; white candle usually made from spermaceti (*kandéla*); semen, sperm (*kissit*).

espérto: (Sp. *experto*: expert) n, *a.* expert.

espesiál: (Sp. *especial*: special) *a.* special.

espesialidád: (Sp. *especialidad*: specialty) *n.* specialty.

espesialisasión: (Sp. *especialización*: specialization) *n.* specialization.

espesialísta: (Sp. *especialista*: specialist) *n.* specialist.

espía: (Sp. *espía*: spy) *n.* spy. (*tiktik*) espiaen. *v.* to spy on. maespiaan. *v.* to be spied on.

espiadóra: (f. *espia*) *n.* female spy, meddler.

espiár: (Sp. *espiar*: spy; *especializar*: specialize) espiaren. *v.* to spy; skulk; sample, test; master, specialize, do well; *var.* of *estimar*: fix; arrange.

espíga: (Sp. *espiga*: spike) *n.* spike or ear of grain. (*dawa*)

espína: (Sp. *espina*: spine, fishbone) *n.* spine; thorn; splinter; fishbone. (*siit*)

espináka: (Sp. *espinaca*: spinach) *n.* spinach.

espínghe: (Sp. *esfinge*) *n.* sphinx.

espioháhe: (Sp. *espionaje*: espionage) *n.* espionage. (*panagsiim*)

espiritísmo: (Sp. *espiritismo*: spiritualism) *n.* spiritualism, the belief that the dead can communicate with the living.

espiritísta: (Sp. *espiritista*: spiritualist) *n.* spiritualist, one who believes that the dead can communicate with the living.

espíritu: (Sp. *espíritu*: spirit) *n.* spirit; soul. (*kararua, aníto*) espíritu sánto. *n.* holy spirit.

espuélas: (Sp. *espuelas*: spur) *n.* spur.

espués: (Sp. *después*: after) *conj.* then; afterwards. (*kalpasan*)

espolín: (Sp. *espolín*: silk brocade; small spur) *n.* silk brocade.

esponsáles: (Sp. *esponsales*: betrothal) *n.* espousal or betrothal ceremonies.

espóngha: (Sp. *esponja*: sponge) *n.* sponge; powder puff. esponghoso. *a.* spongy; porous. esponghado. *a.* puffed-up. esponghera. *n.* sponge holder.

espóra: (Sp.) *n.* spore.

esporádiko: (Sp. *esporádico*: sporadic) *a.* sporadic.

espósa: (Sp. *esposa*: wife) *n.* wife. (*asáwa, bakét*)

esposáda: (Sp. *desposada*: newlywed) agesposada. *v.* to marry without mass.

espóso: (Sp. *esposo*: husband) *n.* husband. (*asáwa, lakáy*)

espúma: (Sp. *espuma*: foam) *n.* foam; lather; spume (*lutab, labutab*). [Tag. *bulâ*]

espóngha: (Sp. *esponja*: sponge) *n.* sponge.

espúting: agesputing. *v.* to dress up; to dress formally. nakaesputing. *a.* dressed up; sharply dressed.

essék: umsek. *v.* to fit; be of an appropriate size to wear. kaes-eskan. *n.* use, utility; meaning, sense, significance. Mayessek ti sakak iti sapatos. My feet can fit into the shoes. Awan ti kaes-eskanna. It is useless.

essém: *n.* desire, wish; passion; compassion. (*kalikagum, tarigagay*) esman. *v.* to desire, covet, long for. naessem. *a.* greedy, covetous. umsem. *v.* to copy, imitating others through simulation pagesman. *n.* object of desire. [Knk. *sitém*, Png. *linawá, ibég*, Tag. *nais, nasà*]

está: (Sp. *está*: is) esta bien. very well; all right.

estabilidád: (Sp. *estabilidad*: stability) *n.* stability.

establesimiénto: (Sp. *establecimiento*: establishment) *n.* establishment.

establisádo: (Eng.) *a.* established.

establisár: (Eng. + Sp. *–ar*; Sp. establish = *establecer*) mangestablisar. *v.* to establish.

estádio: (Sp. *estadio*: stadium) *n.* stadium.

estadísta: (Sp. *estadista*: statesman) *n.* statesman.

estadístika: (Sp. *estadística*: statistics) *n.* statistics.

estádo: (Sp. *estado*: state) *n.* state; situation; estate; civil status, married status; condition, appearance; aspect. Estados Unídos. The United States. naestaduan. *a.* married; settled; (*coll.*) accounted for.

estáka: (Sp. *estaca*) *n.* stake. estakaan. *v.* to stake out.

estakáda: (Sp. *estacada*: stockade) *n.* stockade, prison for insurgents or rebels.

estámbre: (Sp. *estambre*: stamen) *n.* yarn, spun thread; stamen (botany).

estámpa: (Sp. *estampa*: dry seal; print; image) *n.* image, dry seal; picture of a saint.

estampíta: (Sp. *estampita*: small picture) *n.* holy picture, small religious picture or holy card. (*búlto*)

estandárte: (Sp. *estandarte*: banner) *n.* banner. (*wagayway*)

estaniadór: (Sp. *estañador*: solderer) *n.* welder, solderer; tinsmith.

estánio: (Sp. *estaño*: tin) *n.* tin (used in soldering).

estánsia: (Sp. *estancia*: farm; habitation) *n.* grassland, pasturage.

estánte: (Sp. *estante*: shelf) *n.* bookshelf, showcase.

estangkádo: (Sp. *estancado*: watertight) *a.* stagnant; checked.

estángko: (Sp. *estanco*: state tobacco shop, *obs.*) *n.* common cigar.

estápa: (Sp. *estafa*: swindle) *n.* swindle. (*agkallid*; *sikapan*; *sauren*) **estapador.** *n.* swindler. [Tag. *tansô*]

estasión: (Sp. *estación*: station) *n.* station; institution of study. **pagestasionan.** *n.* parking place. **agestasion.** *v.* to stop at a station.

estátua: (Sp. *estatua*: statue) *n.* statue. (*búlto*)

éste₁: (Sp. *éste*: east) *n.* east. (*daya*)

éste₂: (Sp. *este*: this [used as a hedge]) hedge used in speaking: um.

estebedór: (Sp. *estibador*: stevedore, docker; longshoreman + English stevedore) *n.* stevedore; longshoreman.

estéla: (Sp. *estela*: wake) *n.* wake of a ship.

esterlína: (Sp. *esterlina*: sterling) *a.* sterling. **libra esterlina.** *n.* pound sterling.

estero: (Sp.) *n.* estuary. (*sabangan*, *luob*)

estéropon: (Eng.) *n.* Styrofoam.

estétika: (Sp. *estética*) *n.* aesthetics.

estetoskópio: (Sp. *estetoscopio*: stethoscope) *n.* stethoscope.

estibadór: (Sp. *estibador*: stevedore) *n.* longshoreman, cargo man, stevedore, man who loads and unloads ships.

estílo: (Sp. *estilo*: style) *n.* style. (*móda*) **naestilo.** *a.* elegant; tasteful; refined. **Bambannogyo ti agestilo, no nalabesen ti tiempoyo.** It is useless to beautify yourself when you're past your prime.

estimá(r): (Sp. *estimar*: estimate; esteem) *n.* attention given to or entertainment of guests. **agestimar.** *v.* to take care of (*awir*); do with care. **estimado.** *a.* esteemed, respected. **estimaren.** *v.* to arrange, fix; take care of. **naestimar.** *a.* neat, orderly; diligent. **Estimarem ti bagim.** Take care of yourself.

estimasión: (Sp. *estimación*) *n.* estimate.

estimulánte: (Sp. *estimulante*: stimulant) *a.* stimulating, exciting; *n.* stimulant.

estímulo: (Sp. *estímulo*: stimulus) *n.* stimulus; prompt; encouragement.

estudiánte: (Sp. *estudiante*: student) *n.* student (*agad-adal*). **estudiantilia.** *n.* little girl student.

estudiár: (Sp.) **estudiaren.** *v.* to study (*adal*).

estúdio: (Eng.) *n.* studio.

estoisísmo: (Sp. *estoicismo*: stoicism) *n.* stoicism.

estokáda: (Sp. *estocada*: thrust) *n.* parry and thrust, lunge in fencing.

estóla: (Sp. *estola*: stole) *n.* stole (worn by clergy). **nakaestola.** *a.* wearing a stole.

estopádo: (Sp. *estofado*: stew) *n.* stew. (*lauya*, *inanger*)

estupidés: (Sp. *estupidez*) *n.* stupidity.

estúpido: (Sp. *estúpido*: stupid) *a.* stupid. (*tabbed*)

estórbo: *var.* of *istorbo*: bother, nuisance; hindrance.

estória: (Sp. *historia*: story) *n.* story. (*estoriaan*) **ngem sabali daytan nga estoria.** *exp.* but that's another story.

estoriadór: (Sp. *historiador*: historian) *n.* historian; storyteller.

estútse: (Sp. *estuche*: box, case; kit) *n.* case or bag for instruments, usually surgical instruments.

estráda: (Sp. *estrada*: road) *n.* paved road.

estranghéro: (Sp. *estrangero*: stranger) *n.* stranger; foreigner (*gannaét*). [Tag. *dayo*]

estratéhia: (Sp. *estrategia*: strategy) *n.* strategy. (*síkap*)

estrélia: (Sp. *estrella*: star) *n.* star (*bituén*); variety of pig with a long body and big ears. **estreliado.** *n.* fried egg whose yoke is intact.

estreliádo: (Sp. *estrellado*: fried egg) *n.* fried egg (sunny-side up usually).

estríbo: (Sp. *estribo*: stirrup) *n.* spur; stirrup; running board of a vehicle. **estribo ti bus.** *n.* suitcase rack in a bus. (*kargadera*)

estribór: (Sp. *estribor*: starboard) *n.* starboard, right side of a ship.

estríkto: (Sp. *estricto*: strict) *a.* strict (*nainget*, *natimbeng*, *nairut*). [Tag. *higpít*]

estruktúra: (Sp. *estructura*) *n.* structure.

estrópa: (Sp. *estrofa*: stanza) *n.* stanza; verse of a poem.

eswés: *var.* of *espues*: then; afterwards (*sa*; *kalpasan*); that's why (*isu nga*).

eternidád: (Sp. *eternidad*: eternity) *n.* eternity.

et-ét: **maet-etan.** *v.* to be constricted (by a rope, etc.) **naet-et.** *a.* tight. (*ilét*) **et-etan.** *v.* to tighten. [Tag. *higpít*]

étika: (Sp. *ética*: ethics) *n.* ethics, the principles or science of proper conduct.

etikéta: (Sp. *etiqueta*: label) *n.* label; ticket indicating price; etiquette.

étiko: (Sp. *ético*: ethical) *a.* ethical, moral.

etimolohía: (Sp. *etimología*: etymology) *n.* etymology, an account of the origin and history of a word.

etnág: **yetnag.** *v.* to say with finality; proclaim. **kayyetnag.** *a.* just proclaimed. **Kaanonto pay ti panangyetnagmo ita nasam-it a wen-mo kaniak.** When will you utter your sweet yes to me?

étniko: (Sp. *étnico*) *a.* ethnic.

etnolohía: (Sp. *etnología*: ethnology) *n.* ethnology, science dealing with the origin, customs, beliefs, etc. of different ethnic groups.

étsar: (Sp. *echar*: throw) **etsaran.** *v.* to strike, hit.

étso: (Sp. *hecho*: done) *n.* position; *a.* done; exact. **ti etso a lugar.** the exact place. **Di ma-etso-etso.** It cannot be ascertained.

etsúra: (Sp. *hechura*: form) *n.* figure, form, appearance; aspect, the way someone looks. (*langa*) **kasano ti etsurana?** How does he look?

ettúkaw: *n.* a bird peck in a fruit; also *attukaw*.

G

gáang: (*obs.*) **magaang**. *v.* to crack over the fire. **aggaang**. *v.* to wear a chemise with lace over the breast.

gaás: (Eng.) *n.* gas.

gábang: **ginnabang**. *var.* of *sámak*: *Macaranga tanarius* tree whose bark is used to color *basi*.

gabára: (Sp. *gabarra*: barge) *n.* barge, shallow flat-bottomed boat with square ends.

gabardín: *n.* kind of stretchable cloth.

gábat: *n.* flotsam; debris; stray; straggler; loot. **aggabtat**. *v.* to loot; pick out loot from a flood. **gabaten**. *v.* to loot, rob a house; gather anything usable from flotsam. [Tag. *layák*]

gábay: *n.* delay; lateness. (*ladaw*) **magabay**. *v.* to be late; miss an opportunity. [Png. *liwag*, *bayag*, Tag. *abala*, *antala*]

gabbál: *n.* bare-handed fight. (*gabbo*) **aggabbal**. *v.* to wrestle. [Ibg. *gabbál*, Ivt. *rakep*, Kal. *popoot*, Knk. *awét*, *púged*, Png. *garapal* (Eng.), Tag. *bunô*]

gabbáy: *n.* putting the arm over another's shoulder. **gabbayen**. *v.* to put the arm over another's shoulder. [Tag. *akbáy*]

gabbék: **gumabbek**. *n.* flat, round, white fish. When small, it is called *turingturing* and *sapsap*.

gabbí: *n.* mumps. **aggabbi**. *v.* to have mumps. [Knk. *kamísil*, Tag. *bikì*, *baikì*]

gabbó: *n.* wrestling match. **aggabbo**. *v.* to wrestle. **gabbuen**. *v.* to wrestle with someone. **gumagabbo**. *n.* wrestler. **igabbo**. *v.* to do while wrestling. **Ingabbok nga inanawa.** I broke up the fight (wrestling). (*buddong*) [Ibg. *gabbál*, Ivt. *rakep*, Kal. *popoot*, Knk. *awét*, *púged*, Png. *garapal* (Eng.), Tag. *bunô*]

gabbuát: synonym of *rubbuat*: prepare; get ready.

gabbuáy: *var.* of *gebbuay*: increase.

gabbós: *n.* swarm of wild bees.

gabén: **magabenan**. *v.* to be able to do all. **kagabenan**. *n.* power; capability.

gabés: **gumabes**. *v.* to intrude, trespass.

gabí: **aggagabi**. *v.* to thrust forward.

gábia: (Sp. *gavia*: topsail) *n.* main topsail of a small boat.

gabílan: (Sp. *gavilán*: iron hook) *n.* spokeshave, drawknife.

gabinéte: (Sp. *gabinete*: cabinet) *n.* cabinet.

gabión: (Sp. *gavión*: gabion) *n.* grub hoe for digging. **gabionen**. *v.* to dig something with a hoe. [Tag. *piko* (Sp.)]

gabís: *n.* failure to be present; absence. **maigabis**. *v.* to be disappointed, frustrated; to miss a successful event. **naigabis**. *a.* absent.

gábo: (*obs.*) natural father of a child born out of wedlock. **gabuen**. *v.* to join stalks of sugar-cane.

gabuát: synonym of *rubbuat*.

gabúr: *n.* fillings; filler; pile. **gaburan**. *v.* to fill up, stuff, cram; plug up, close up, block (a hole); cover; bury. **gaburgabur**. *n.* a kind of bird the size of the quail that cries when ill and covers its dead with dirt. **paggabur**. *n.* filling materials. **magaburan**. *v.* to be buried under.

gábut₁: **gabuten**. *v.* to pull up, uproot (*pag-ut*; *gunot*). [Tag. *bunot*]

gábut₂: **gagabuten**, **gabutgabut**. *n.* the yard grass, *Eleusine indica*.

gabráng: *var.* of *gamrang*: unruliness.

gabsáw: **gabsawen**. *v.* to tread over, trample; (*fig.*) degrade, belittle. **magabsagabsaw**. *v.* to be trampled over; to be degraded; thoroughly insulted. **Itulokyo latta kadin a magabsagabsaw ti dayaw ken kalinteganyo?** Do you just let your honor and rights be trampled on?

gabsúon: *n.* pile; heap. (*penpen*) **gabsuonen**. *v.* to heap up, pile up (trash, etc.). **igabsuon**. *v.* to pile. **maigabsuon**. *v.* to be piled up. **magabsuon**. *v.* to pile up, accumulate (hardships, etc.). **magabsuonan**. *v.* to be heavily burdened; to have piles of work to do. **ginabgabsuon**. *a.* piled up; (*fig.*) abundant, too much. **sangagabsuon**. *a.* plentiful. **Adu a surat ti naigabsuon iti lamisetak.** Many letters were piled on my desk. [Png. *átip*, Tag. *buntón*, *tambák*]

gabyón: *var.* spelling of *gabion*: hoe.

gadágad: *var.* of *dagadag*: urge; insist upon.

gádang: *n.* wading; *a.* short (pants) (*kiting*); shallow (*ababaw*). **nagadang**. *a.* short. **magadang**. *a.* shallow, water not reaching the waist. **gadangen**. *v.* to wade across. [Tag. *iklî*]

gádas: **aggadas**, **gadasen**. *v.* to top with a sickle (grass).

gádaw: **gadawen**. *v.* to cut the top of. (*tadaw*)

Ga'dang: *n.* upland ethnic group from the Mountain Province of northern Luzon; the language of the Ga'dang people.

Gaddáng: *n.* lowland ethnic group from the provinces of Isabela and Nueva Vizcaya; the language of the Gaddang people.

gaddíl: *n.* itch, mange; scab. **aggaddil**. *v.* to itch; have an itching disease. [Knk. *sígab*, Tag. *galís*]

gadgád: *n.* grater; coconut meat scraper; whetstone used to smooth spindles. (*igad*) **aggadgad**. *v.* to grate. **igadgad**. *v.* to whet, smoothen. **gadgadan**. *n.* whetting stone. [Tag. *gadgád*]

gádia: (Malay *gajah*, Tagalog also, *obs.*) *n.* elephant. (*elepante*)

gáding: (*obs.*) *n.* ivory. [Tag. *garing*]

gádol: *n.* hook in the spur or gaff of gamecock. (*tádi*)

gaéd: *n.* earnestness; eagerness; diligence. (*gaged*) **igaed**. *v.* to do eagerly, with much effort. **nagaed**. *a.* industrious; diligent; persistent. [Png. *manpilpilalek*, Tag. *sabík*]

gága: (Tag. also) *a.* flirtatious; stupid; simpleton (said of girls).

gága: **igaga**. *v.* to esteem, value, prize; benefit; protect from.

gagan-áyan: *n.* frame for sorting thread before passing it through the loom.

gagángay: *a.* ordinary, usual (*kadawyan*); habit; trait; nature; custom (*ugali*). **kagagangay**. *n.* custom; habit.

gágar: *n.* intent, enthusiasm; excitement; eagerness. (*ganaygay*, *tarigagay*) **aggagar**. *v.* to crave, desire strongly. **gagaran**. (*obs.*) *n.* foolish talk. **gagaren**. *v.* to strongly wish for. **makapagagar**. *a.* exciting. **magagaran**. *v.* to be eager about. **nagagar**. *a.* enthusiastic. **paggagaren**. *v.* to enthuse, excite. **Ti rabii a nasipnget, silaw dagiti gagarda a dakes.** A dark night is light to those who plot evil. [Png. *pilalek*, Tag. *sabík*]

gagára: *n.* aim, objective, intention, purpose. (*ranta*; *panggep*; *gagém*; *gandat*) **igagara, gagaraen**. *v.* to do on purpose (*ranta*); overwhelm; intensify; intend; beat. **gumagara**. *v.* to increase; worsen. **nagagara**. *a.* strongly, vigorously; to be affected by, overexposed to; overwhelmed; defeated. **magagara**. *a.* to be overused; overwhelmed. **nagagaraan**. *a.* overused, overworked (*napalaluan*). [Bon., Png. *gagala*, Tag. *tangkâ*, *sadyâ*]

gagayyém: Plural of *gayyem*: friends.

gagéd: *var.* of *gaed*: earnestness; eagerness.

gagém: *n.* bad intention, ulterior motive; evil purpose, objective. (*gagara*; *gakat*; *panggep*; *panagém*) **gageman**. *v.* to desire something with an ulterior motive. **Ginagemko ti agibales.** I planned to take revenge. [Tag. *masamáng tangkâ*]

gagét: *n.* industry, diligence. **nagaget**. *a.* hardworking, diligent, assiduous, industrious. (*siseg*; *anep*; *regget*) **kinagaget**. *n.* industry, diligence. [Bon. *bíkas*, Ibg. *lappoq*, Ifg. *mahlu*, Ivt. *pangtuq*, Kal. *pangngog*, Knk. *kámet*, Png. *kolí*, Kpm., Tag. *sipag*]

gágo: (Tag. also) *n.* idiot, imbecile. (*ang-ang*; *laglag*; *lampangog*; *langgong*; *maag*; *tungngang*; *tabbed*) **naggago**. *a.* idiotic.

gáho: (Sp. *gajo*: fruit segment, *obs.*) *n.* each division of an orange.

gáik: **gaikan**. *v.* to clear, open (roads); to weed. **paggaik**. *n.* instrument used for weeding.

gáit: *var.* of *gaik*: clear vegetation.

gákab: *var.* of *kágab*: wide-brimmed chicken coop.

gákap: (*obs.*) *n.* bamboo spear.

gákat: *n.* plan, project; proposal; bill. (*gandat*; *gagara*; *ranta*; *panggep*; *ngayangay*; *daremdem*; *gannuat*; *sikat*) **gakaten**. *v.* to plan, intend, use, design. **igakat**. *v.* to equip, arm, fit; sponsor a proposal. **paigakat**. *v.* to recommend a proposal for approval. [Png. *kanonotan*, Tag. *balak*, *panukalà*]

gakgák: *n.* a kind of large duck. **aggakgak**. *v.* to croak (frogs); change voice at puberty. **agganakgak**. *n.* the sound of broken bells; quacking of ducks. [Tag. *kurók*; *gakgák* = idle talk]

gakká: *n.* a large, edible, black mollusk found in brackish waters.

gáko₁: *n.* a kind of vessel.

gáko₂: **igako**. *v.* to save, safeguard; rescue; protect; entrust, commit; deliver.

gáko₃: *n.* a kind of edible frog commonly found in the rice fields during the rainy season.

gála₁: *n.* the *almasiga* tree.

gála₂: **galagala**. *n.* cement. (*semento*; *galém*)

gála₃: (Sp. *gala*: gala) *n.* gala, festive celebration; wedding ritual of pinning money on the bride and groom.

galád: *n.* lineage, rank, pedigree; surname; habit, custom; ability. **maigalad**. *v.* to have virtue or authority. [Tag. *katangian*]

galakgák: *n.* the spreading growth of grass or ground cover. **aggalakgak**. *v.* to spread in growth (grass).

galanéd: **nagalaned**. *a.* both dying on the same day, gone in one day.

galánte: *a.* extravagant, excessively generous; gallant, chivalrous, knightly.

galantería: (Sp. *galantería*: gallantry) *n.* gallantry.

gálang: **igalang**. *v.* to honor, respect (*raem*; *dayaw*; *daeg*; *ragpat*; *takneng*; *tandudo*). **galangen**. *v.* to respect, treat with respect. [Png., Tag. *galang*]

galáng: *n.* a kind of thin handcrafted bracelet.

galangúgang: *var.* of *galangúgong*: echo, hollow sound; sound of falling into a deep place.

galangúgong: *n.* *var.* of *garangugong*: fall into a deep place; resound; echo.

galapón: *n.* rice flour, rice powder. [Png. *tapóng*, Tag. *galapóng*]

gálas: *var.* of *alas*.

galasúgas: **aggalasugas**. *v.* to be firm, determined; obstinate, stubborn. (*balingegngeg*;

bangngeg; *pakutibeg*; *punged*; *subeg*; *suer*; *sukir*; *suweng*) **naggalasugas.** *a.* stubborn.

galatgát: *n.* a kind of herb eaten by deer and used in medicine to cure boils.

galawgáw: *n.* movement.

gálba: (Sp. *galvanizado*: galvanized) *n.* galvanized iron used in roofs. (*sim*) **ginalba.** *a.* with an iron sheet roof. **galbanisado.** *a.* galvanized.

galdí: *n.* chink; crack; notch; bruise. **magaldian.** *v.* to be nicked; cracked; have a chink. [Tag. *biták*]

galeón: (Sp. *galeón*: galleon) *n.* galleon, large ship with several decks formally used for war or commerce.

galém: *n.* native cement. **igalem.** *v.* to make *galem* cement; add cement to for patching.

galéra: (Sp. *galera*: galley) *n.* galley, long narrow ship with oars and sails; galley of type (in printing); rowboat.

galeráda: (Sp. *galerada*: galley proof) *n.* galley proof; galley (in printing); type set in a galley tray.

galería: (Sp. *galería*: gallery) *n.* gallery; lobby.

galgál: aggalgal. *v.* to chew dry (*ngalngal*); (*coll.*) to butcher a language by speaking it badly. **Kakaasikami la a manggalgalgal iti Inggles.** We are pitiful (trying to) speak English. [Tag. *nguyâ*; *galgál* = foolish]

galgaling: *var.* of *galing-galing*: amulet; charm.

galiáb: *a.* slightly cross-eyed.

galiáng: *n.* the *biga* plant.

galiéra: (Sp. *gallera*: cockpit) *n.* cockpit arena (*pagpallotan*; *bulang*). **makigaliera.** *v.* to bet on a cockfight.

galiétas: (Sp. *galleta*: cookie) *n.* biscuit; cracker; cookie; flat round bread.

galímba: *n.* species of large red coconut.

galimbán: (*obs.*) *n.* a coconut shell from a rare species of coconut.

galimúsaw: ginagalimusaw. *a.* unsatisfactory, inadequate, inferior, defective; mediocre. **galimusawen.** *v.* to do something haphazardly.

galinéra: *n.* storage chest.

galing-galíng: *n.* amulet, charm (*anting-anting*). [Tag. *anting-antíng*, Tag. *galíng* = skill, ability]

gálio: (Sp. *gallo*: rooster) *n.* rooster (*kawitan*); species of bluish flower (*botbotones*).

gálip: *n.* slice. **galipen.** *v.* to slice (*iwa*). **panggalip.** *n.* slicing instrument. **sangkagalip.** *n.* one slice. [Png. *gálip*, Tag. *hiwà*]

galís: nagalis. *a.* slippery. **maigalis.** *v.* to slip, slide. **gumalis.** *v.* to become slippery. **pannakaigalis ti dila.** *n.* slip of the tongue, accidental divulging of a secret. [Bon. *kadlis, kadilas, lapisot, damílos*, Ibg. *dalúq*, Ivt. *rakpes*,

Kal. *byabyagiw, mangngaÿutoy*, Png. *galís*, Tag. *dulás*, Tag. *galís* = sarna infection]

galliáb: *adj.* semicross-eyed. [*pangkís, dulíng* = cross-eyed]

galumpápa: see *abubot*: kind of bottle-shaped basket.

galón: (Sp. *galón*: gallon) *n.* gallon; worsted fabric used for dress trimmings; epaulets on the shoulders; chevron; officer's arm badge or stripes.

gálong: galonggalong. *n.* rack for kitchen utensils; swing for children; cable made for crossing rivers.

galunggóng: (Pil.) *n. bulilít* fish.

galópe: (Sp.) *n.* gallop of a horse.

gálut: *n.* tendon; tie, anything used for tying. **igalut.** *v.* to tie; hitch. **paggalut.** *n.* something used to tie, binding. **galugalut, galutgalut.** *n.* Bermuda grass, *Cynodon dactylon.* **nakagalut.** *a.* tied. **Igalutyo a nasayaat amangan no makalibas.** Tie him well so he can't escape. [Ibg. *gáluq*, Ivt. *pakedkeren*, Kpm., Tag. *talì*, Png. *singer*]

galút: *n.* frame, mold. **maigalut.** *a.* inclined to do something, having the disposition to do.

galpák: *n.* beating, spanking. **galpaken.** *v.* to hit someone (when punishing). (*baut*)

galyéra: *var.* of *galiera*: cockpit.

galyétas: *var.* of *galietas*: cookies.

galyinéro: (Sp. *gallinero*: poultry basket) *n.* large bamboo chest; hen coup.

gamá: manggagama, panggagamaen. *n.* scorpion. [Png., Tag. *alakdán*]

gamágan: *n.* the first symptoms of fever. **gumanamagan.** *v.* to show first signs of fever, chills.

gámal: *n.* handful. **sangagamal.** *n.* one handful. [Tag. *sandakót*]

gamál: gamalen. *v.* to gather, summon together, muster up. **makigamal.** *v.* to do with a cooperative spirit (*ammuyo*; *tagnawa*). [Tag. *tipon*]

gámas: *n.* mixture. **gamasen.** *v.* to mix, blend. (*ramas*) **maigamas.** *v.* to be mixed with other things. [Tag. *halò*]

gámat: *n.* tentacle; tendril (*gammat*). [Tag. *galamáy*]

gamáw: *n.* bamboo floats used for fishing nets. **gamawan.** *v.* to provide with floaters.

gámay: *n.* 22-karat gold. **gamayan.** *n.* first calving.

gamáy: *n.* mixture of flour and water. **gamayen.** *v.* to knead flour. [Tag. *masa* (Sp.)]

gambáng: *n.* copper; variety of small, red, fragrant, thick-skinned banana. [Knk. *galák, langiús*, Tag. *tansô* (copper)]

gambóng: *n.* a large *karamba* (jar).

gamdír: (*obs.*) maigamdir. *v.* to slip out of place. (*kamlos*; *kabsiw*; *labsin*; *labsiw*; *ligsay*)
gaméd: *n.* desire, want. gamdan. *v.* to desire, wish, want. (*kalikagum*; *kayat*; *tarigagay*) gam(e)den. *v.* to try; make an effort. Dimo gamden a kasarita ti di-katataoan. Do not attempt to speak with the supernatural beings. [Tag. *hangád*]
gámeng: *n.* treasure; wealth; anything precious to the owner. nakaisigudan a gameng. *n.* natural resources. [Tag. *kayamanan*, Knk. *gámeng* = movable property]
gamér: *n.* mixture; ingredient; pollutant. gameran. *v.* to mix, blend; knead; pollute. igamer. *v.* to mix up with. maigamer. *v.* to be imbued; to be deeply involved in; to be impregnated. nagameran. *a.* mixed with. [Tag. *halò*]
gamét: *n.* a brownish green edible seaweed.
gamgám: *n.* desire to own what is not yours (especially land). gamgaman. *v.* to wish to obtain (an educational degree, property, etc.). gamgamen. *v.* to desire, covet; long for. managgamgam. *a.* greedy. [Tag. *kamkám*]
gamígam: *n.* tools; utensils; implements (*reminta*). [Knk. *gamígam*, Tag. *kagamitán*]
'gamín: *var.* of *ngamín*: so, for that reason.
gam-ís: *var.* of *damgis*: hit in a grazing manner. Nagam-is ti pilid ti kalesa ti bakrang ti agtutubo. The wheel of the coach grazed the back of the youth.
gámit: gumamit. *v.* to gather, used when a populace collects in one place to form a village. gamgamit. *n.* stranger, passerby. igamit. *v.* to entrust; secure, put away.
gammál: gammalan. *v.* to grip, clasp, grasp. (*iggam*) sangagammal. *n.* one handful. [Tag. *dakmâ*]
gammaróng: *n.* a kind of mud crab.
gammát: *n.* handful. also, *var.* of *gammal*; tentacles; claws; paws, hands. gammatan. *v.* to grab, get ahold of. Ginammatanna ti naklaat a tulisan. He took ahold of the surprised thief. [Kal. *gammat* = finger]
gammogammót: *n.* array of seaweed.
gammók: gammok, gammogammok. *n.* medley, potpourri, mingling. (*aglalaok*) aggammogammok. *v.* to gyrate (wind).
gammól: ginammol. *n.* bezoar (found in some fruits and used in charms).
gamnút: gumamnut, gamnuten. *v.* to snatch from; rip off, tear off.
gamó: *n.* bark of the Java plum boiled with sugarcane juice when making *basi* to color the *basi*. gamuan. *v.* to season with the bark of the Java plum.

gámud: *n.* black magic. gamuden. *v.* to bewitch. manggagamud. *n.* witch; witch doctor. magamudan. *v.* to be the victim of witchcraft. nagamud. *a.* poisoned. gamudgamud. *n.* black magic, witchcraft; actions or implements used in bewitching. [Kal. *kochot*, Png. *gamór*, Tag. *kulam*]
gam-úd: magam-udan. *v.* to overtake, catch up with; to obtain, attain, get. gam-uden. *v.* to obtain, get. gumam-ud. *v.* to arrive early for; catch up with. makagam-ud. *v.* to be sufficient until; to be able to overtake. [Tag. *tamó* (obtain); Knk. *gam-úd* = bad luck]
gamuló: aggamulo. *v.* to manage everything (in business, etc.) gamuluen. *v.* to turn over something; to drag; manage a business; work the land.
gamúsa: (Sp. *gamuza*: chamois) *n.* chamois; leather; suede. (*lalat*)
gamút: *n.* poison (vegetable); drugs. (*sabidong*) makagamut. *a.* poisonous. gamuten. *v.* to poison. magamut. *v.* to be poisoned. [Tag. *lason*, Knk. *gamút* = edible red mushroom]
gampáng: gampang, garampang. *n.* easy girl. *a.* frivolous; unchaste. maragampang. *a.* frivolous. [Tag. *alembóng*]
gampápaw: gampapawan. *v.* to fill up to the brim.
gampáw: gampawen. *v.* to fill to the brim (*gampapaw*). gamgampawan. *a.* overflowing; overloaded. [Tag. *apaw*]
gampól: *n.* a brown dye from the bark of the Java plum used by fisherman to camouflage their nets and clothing. ginambol. *a.* brown colored.
gampór: *n.* different varieties of rice mixed together, see *kampor*. gampuran. *v.* to mix; blend; dilute.
gampót: *n.* reward; gain. magampot. *v.* to achieve; gain; attain.
gamráng: *n.* unruliness; boldness, daring (cats taking food). nagamrang. *a.* bold, daring.
gamrúd: *n.* greed; ambition for the unjust procurement of material things. (*agum*) nagamrud. *a.* greedy; materialistic. gamruden. *v.* to take away one's possessions in an unjust way.
gamsáw: gamsawen. *v.* to acquire, procure unjustly. gumamsaw. *v.* to meddle in other people's business (*sampitaw*, *biang*). Madi no gamsawenyo ti kukua ti pada a tao. It is bad if you snatch the possessions of a fellow man.
gána: (Sp. *gana*: appetite) *var.* of *gánas* in certain words. pampagana. *n.* appetizer; something used to stimulate pleasure (liquor, party; aphrodisiac, etc.).
gánab₁: *n.* hereditary disease or custom; hereditary instinct; end; result; profit, benefit.

gumanab. *v.* to gain, profit; to act on instinct; follow the ways of one's parents, inherit behavior. **ganaben.** *v.* to expect to acquire. **Maganabna!** *exp.* That's what she/he gets! [Tag. *palâ*]

gánab₂: *n.* animal breeding. **paganaban.** *v.* to breed animals. [Tag. *pakasta* (Sp.)]

ganadéro: (Sp. *ganadero*: cattle owner) *n.* cattle owner.

ganádo: (Sp. *ganado*: livestock) *a.* excited; enthusiastic; interested; having a good appetite; *n.* sure win (player); herd; flock; livestock.

ganadór: (Sp. *ganador*: winner) *n.* winner; fighting cock that has many wins. (*abak*)

ganágan: *n.* fertilizer. (*abuno*) **ganaganan.** *v.* to fertilize; apply compost. [Tag. *patabâ*]

ganáka: *n.* sheet metal for making cans.

ganakgák: agganakgak. *v.* to ring loud, resonate. (cars, etc.); quack (said of ducks); to croak (frogs). [Tag. *kakak*]

ganamágan: (*reg.*) **gumanamagan.** *v.* to feel the first symptoms of fever.

ganánsia: (Sp. *ganancia*: profit) *n.* profit; gain. **agganansia.** *v.* to profit; gain.

ganáp: *a.* general; widespread. **gumanap a sakit.** *n.* epidemic. [Tag. *laganap*]

ganár: (Sp. *ganar*: earn) *n.* earnings. **agganar.** to earn. **gumanar.** *v.* to thrive (plants).

gánas: (Sp. *gana*: desire; appetite) *n.* desire, willingness; appetite; pleasure. **naganas.** *a.* pleasing. **agganas.** *v.* to enjoy. **ganasen.** *v.* to enjoy something, relish. **pampagana.** see under *gana*. **Napukaw ti ganasna a mangan.** She lost her desire to eat. **Awan ganasko nga agtrabaho.** I don't feel like working. [Tag. *kasiyahán*]

ganásio: gangganasio. *n.* job done in a slovenly manner. **agganganasio.** *v.* to do in a slovenly manner.

gánat: *n.* hurry; haste. **gumanat.** *v.* to be in a hurry; to be impatient. **agganat.** *v.* to hasten; be impatient. [Tag. *dalî*]

gan-áy: *n.* warp, warping frame; twist. **gan-ayen.** *v.* to fix fibers to weave, warp yarn. **gaganayan.** *n.* warping frame for yarn; either of the two bamboos that run across the upper border of a cart or *bangkáy*; Constellation Orion.

ganaygáy: *n.* spirit, vigor; movement; liveliness. **gumanaygay.** *v.* to be enthusiastic. **agganaygay.** *v.* to be full of life, to be high spirited; walk with difficulty. **ganaygayen.** *v.* to animate, make lively; cheer up. **iganaygay.** *v.* to force oneself to move. **Naganaygayak a napan nageskuela iti kabigatanna.** I went to school enthusiastically the next day. [Tag. *siglá*]

gandát: *n.* purpose; plan; business. (*panggep*; *gakat*) **gandaten.** *v.* to plan, intend, design; contrive; to do something on purpose; plot. **Adda manen gandatna a tumaray.** He is planning on running again (in the election). [Png. *kanonotan*, Tag. *balak, panukalà*]

gandióng: ganggandiong. *n.* costume jewelry; something feigned; counterfeit.

ganéb: gumaneb. (*obs.*) *v.* to pass the night in the open (animals.)

ganét: naganet. *a.* active, busy.

ganetgét: *n.* fervor. (*gaget*; *anep*; *regget*; *siseg*) **naganetget.** *a.* diligent. **ganetgetan.** *v.* to do diligently, earnestly. **ipaganetget.** *v.* to impress upon one's mind; insist. **Impaganetgetna nga mapanda idiay ili.** He insisted that they go to town. [Tag. *sipag*]

ganiádos: *var.* of *gandát*: intention, intent.

ganiákaw: ganganiakaw. *n.* kind of bird that is supposed to fly away with naughty children.

ganilgíl: *n.* flirt, immodest woman (*sayyét*; *garampáng*).

gánná: *n.* defect, flaw, blemish; anything imperfect physically. [Tag. *lamat*]

gannaét: *n.* foreigner, stranger. **ganggannaet.** *n.* foreigner, alien, stranger. **utang iti ganggannaet.** *n.* foreign loans.

gannéb: gumanneb. *v.* to stay in the open air at night. (*ganeb*)

gannuát: *n.* project (*gakat*; *sikat*). **aggannuat.** *v.* to invent. **igannuat.** *v.* to start a project; push through with a plan. **Igannuatna ti pannakakali ti sumagmamano a bubon iti sakaanan ti bantay.** His project is to dig a few wells at the foot of the mountain. [Tag. *panukalà*]

gannogannót: *n.* melting-pot nation.

ganokgók: *n.* the repeated squealing and crying of hogs. **agganokgok.** *v.* to squeal (hogs).

ganunggóng: *n.* sound of an echo. **gumanonggong.** *v.* to resound.

ganús: *n.* immaturity; youthfulness. **naganus.** immature (plants and people), unripe; young. **kinaganus.** *n.* immaturity; youthfulness. **gumanus.** *v.* to become delicate. [Png. *maeta*, *sabóng*, Tag. *bubót*]

gánot₁: *n.* membrane that surrounds the flesh of the jackfruit.

gánot₂: ganuten. *v.* to pull up, uproot; eradicate (*parut*). [Tag. *bunot*]

gansá: (Sp. *gansa*: female goose) *n.* gong; female goose. [Tag. *gansâ* (goose)]

gansál: *n.* flaw (in music, speech, fabrics, etc); remainder in mathematical division (*sása*). **aggansal.** *v.* to have a defect; miss a note.

gansílio: (Sp. *ganchillo*: crochet needle) *n.* crochet hook; crocheting. **aggansilio.** *v.* to crochet.

gánso: (Sp. *ganso*: goose) *n.* goose. [Tag. *gansâ*]

gansúa: (Sp. *ganzúa*: picklock; burglar) *n.* skeleton key.

gánta: *n.* three-liter measure (for rice, etc.)

gántil: **gantilen.** *v.* to joke (*angaw*); play with; jest. **aggantil.** *v.* to be playful; to jest. **Napaikkis a nakakita iti dua nga uleg nga aggingginnantil.** She screamed when she saw the two snakes playing with each other. [Tag. *larô*]

gantília: (f. *ganta*) *n.* one-sixth of a *ganta*.

gantíng: *n.* balance; weighing scale; steelyard; (*fig.*) taking advantage of inexperienced people. **gantingen.** *v.* to weigh. **gagantingan.** *n.* scales, balance. [Tag. *timbáng*]

gántong: *n.* large pot for *basi*.

gantsó: (Sp. *gancho*: hook) *n.* hook. (*kaw-it*) **manggagantso.** *n.* rustler.

gangá: **makaganganga.** *a.* horrible, terrible, hideous. [Tag. *hindík*]

gángab: (*obs.*) *n.* cave.

gángal: *n.* large stone, rock; boulder. **gangalan.** *v.* to hinder, obstruct physically.

gángat: *n.* kindling. **gangtan.** *v.* to light (candles). **igangat.** *v.* to kindle, light. **nakagangat.** *a.* kindled; lit up (lights, signs, candles, etc.). **Alas diesen ngem sigagangat pay laeng ti silaw ti balayda.** It's already ten but the light in their house is still lit. [Tag. *sindí*]

gángay: *n.* habit; nature; custom; characteristic. **gagángay.** *a.* common; ordinary; not special; *adv.* usually; habitually. **kagagángay.** *n.* custom; habit. **Saan a gagangay a panangpakan.** He does not usually feed people. [Png. *iluwam*, Tag. *gawì*, *daniw (karaniwan)*]

gángen: *n.* kind of bow net.

gángga: (Sp. *ganga*: bargain) *n.* bargain sale.

ganggók: *var.* of *ganggóng*: stupid.

ganggóng: *a.* stupid.

ganggréna: (Sp. *gangrena*: gangrene) *n.* gangrene.

gángi: *n.* crucible.

gángo: **nagango.** *a.* dry; withered; wilted; unsympathetic. **ginango.** *n.* dried banana leaves. **ipagango.** *v.* to dry. [Tag. *tuyô*]

gangó: *n.* poison (*gamut*; *sabidong*). [Tag. *lason*]

gaó: **aggao.** *v.* to draw, extract food (usually rice) from the pot. **naggao, nakagaon.** the table is ready. **gaoen.** *v.* to take food out from the pot to serve. **igaoan.** *v.* to draw out food for someone. **Inikkatna ti kalub ti kaldero ket rinugiannan ti aggao iti sida.** He took the cover off the pot

and started to scoop out the food. [Bon. *sekwat*, Tag. *sandók*]

gáud: *n.* oar; paddle. **aggaud.** *v.* to paddle, oar. **gaudan.** *v.* to paddle, propel a boat. **Kamkamatenna ti angesna ket sumaggaysa laengen ti panaggaudna.** He caught his breath and oared just once per breath. [Ibg. *láfag*, *tegguwan*, Ivt. *kaud*, *yutap*, Kal. *gaud*, Kpm. *baksé*, Png. *begsay*, Tag. *gaod*, *sagwán*]

gapágap: **gapagapen.** *v.* to cut round, to shape on a potter's wheel; to thinly slice.

gápak: *n.* scrap metal; bracelet.

gapák: *n.* variety of awned rice with an elongated white kernel.

gápas: *n.* rice harvest by use of a sickle. (*ani*) **aggapas.** *v.* to harvest rice with a sickle. **gapasen.** *v.* to gather (harvest) by cutting; to top with a sickle (rice that has to be transplanted). **panaggagapas.** *n.* harvest season. [Tag. *gapas*]

gapgáp: *n.* slice cut parallel to cutting board. **gapgapen.** *v.* to slice parallel to the cutting board.

gapó: *n.* reason, cause; motive. (*gapuna*, *pakaigapuan*) **gapo ta.** because. **gapo ta kasta.** therefore, consequently. **aggapo.** *v.* to come from, originate. **ania ti gapona?** Why? **manggapo.** *v.* to start. **kagagapo.** *n.* origin, source, root. **kagapgapo.** *v.* just arrived from. **gapuanan.** *n.* deed; act; accomplishment. **Naggapuam?** Where have you been? **igapo.** *v.* to do for the sake of, on account of; to start from; originate from; take form somewhere. **makagapo.** *n.* motive; reason; cause. **maigapo.** *v.* to be done for the sake of; because of, due to. **singgapo.** *n.* ancestor. **isu't gapuna.** that's why. **iti ania a gapo?** For what reason? **Manggapo nga agsabong.** It is starting to bloom. [Ibg. *gafu*, Png. *lapó*, Tag. *dahil*, *layon*]

garád: **maigarad** (*obs.*) *v.* to knock against something (boats.)

garabiádo: **nagarabiado.** *a.* losing (in gambling; games, etc.). (*atik*, *abak*); *var.* of *agrabiado*: aggrieved.

garadgád: *n.* scratch, slight wound. **magaradgadan.** *v.* to be scratched; bruised. [Tag. *galos*]

garadugód: *n.* rumbling sound (of hungry stomach, thunder, etc.). **aggaradugod.** *v.* to gurgle, make a gurgling sound (in the stomach, distant thunder, etc.) [Tag. *dagundóng*]

garágar: *n.* fervent wish (*kalikagum*). **gumaragar.** *v.* to be eager for (*gaed*). **aggaragar.** *v.* to desire strongly. **nagaragar.** *a.* desirous of. [Tag. *sabík*]

garáhe: (Sp. *garaje*: garage) *n.* garage. **igarahe.** *v.* to put in the garage.

garaigí: aggaraigi. *v.* to neigh (horses, goats, etc.) [Knk. *galikgík*, Png. *aring-ing*, Tag. *halinghíng*]

garakgák: *n.* loud laughter. (*paggáak*) **aggarakgak.** *v.* to loudly laugh. [Png., Tag. *galakgák*, Tag. *halakhák*]

garalgál: *n.* stammerer; stutterer.

garamgám: *n.* type of large fishing net smaller than the *daklís*.

garámi: *n.* rice stalk; straw, rice hay. **kagaramian.** *n.* field (of hay) where rice has been harvested. [Bon. *om-ang*, *dagámi*, Ibg. *ákaw*, Ifg., Itg. *dagámi*, Kal. *chagammi*, *uÿot*, Knk. *alláng*, *gum-áng*, *gus-áng*, Kpm. *áre*, Png. *usang*, Png., Tag. *dayami*]

garamúgam: nagaramugam. *a.* greedy; sensual, lustful, voluptuous, lascivious; impure; rash; unruly; evil (*agum*). [Tag. *sakím*]

garampáng: *n.* easy girl; immodest girl; unchaste; flirtatious (*sayét*; *sarampiting*; *sarampingat*). [Knk. *gayádok*, Png. *talandit*, *talandéw*, *garampingat*, Tag. *landî*, *kirí*]

garampingát: *syn.* of *garampang*.

garampitíng: *syn.* of *sarampiting*: restless; fidgety (said of girls).

garánay: ginaranay. *n.* variety of rice.

garanión: (Sp. *garañón*: stallion) *n.* stallion.

garantía: (Sp. *garantía*: guarantee) *n.* guarantee. **garantiaan.** *v.* to guarantee.

garantisádo: (Sp. *garantizado*: guaranteed) *a.* guaranteed. **garantisador.** *n.* guarantor.

garantisár: (Sp. *garantizar*: guarantee) **aggarantisar.** *v.* to guarantee.

garáng: *a.* half-filled. (*gudua*)

garangúgong: *n.* echo; abyss; sound of something falling into a deep place. **aggarangugong.** *n.* sound of something falling into a deep place. *v.* to echo; slide down a pit. (*galangugong*) **gumarangugong.** *v.* to fall into an abyss. **igarangugong.** *v.* to drop something down a deep hole; (*fig.*) to tempt into evil. **maigarangugong.** *v.* to fall into a deep hole; (*fig.*) to be overcome by temptation; fall into sin. **No agsuksukirkayo, igarangugongnakay no kua idiay impierno.** If you are disobedient, he will throw you down into hell. **Dikan makalung-aw iti abut a nakaigarangugongam!** You can no longer escape (redeem yourself) from the deep pit you fell into. [Tag. *bangín*]

garápa: (Sp. *garrafa*: carafe) *n.* wide-mouthed bottle, decanter.

garapál: (Sp. *garrafal*: whooping, big) *a.* ill mannered, shameless.

garapáta: (Sp. *garrapata*: sheep tick) *n.* tick.

garapiñéra: (Sp. *garapiñera*: ice cream freezer; wine cooler) *n.* ice cream container.

garapón: (Sp. *garrafón*: large carafe) *n.* jar; wide-mouthed bottle.

garasigásan: *n.* ripening betel nut.

garasó: see *darasudos*: to do hurriedly.

garatigít: *n.* half-repressed laughter, giggling; animated state. **nagaratigit, nagarutigit.** *a.* vivacious, lively; frivolous. **gumaratigit.** *v.* to giggle; be frivolous. [Tag. *alembóng*]

garáw: *n.* wild animal; unruliness; movement; action; (*obs.*) toy. **aggaraw.** *v.* to move, stir. **garawen.** *v.* to move; to touch, molest; (*coll.*) copulate. **nagaraw.** *a.* lively, restless, active, wild (animals); unruly; lewd; immodest. **Saanmi pulos a ginaraw ti dinengdeng.** We didn't touch the boiled vegetables at all. [Tag. *galáw, kilos*]

garaw-át: gagaraw-aten. *n.* part of back below the shoulder blade.

garawígaw: nagarawigaw. *a.* snoopy, always moving about and touching things; not refined; unruly (superlative of *garaw*); immodest; meddling. **Adda gargarawigaw daytoy no maipapan iti babai.** This (man) is a bit lewd when it comes to women.

garáyaw: nagarayaw. *a.* thin, lean; frail. [Tag. *payatot*]

garaygáy: *n.* tassel; plume; a variety of rice; pendant; earlobe of a rooster. [Tag. *palawít* (tassel), *borlas* (Sp.)]

garbánso: (Sp. *garbanzo*: chickpea) *n.* chickpea.

garbí: see *abbigit*: unsuitable; not fitting.

garbó: (Sp. *garbo*: gracefulness, ease) *n.* gracefulness; elegance. **nagarbo.** *a.* grand; lavish; elegant; graceful. (*rongbo; ngayed*)

gardáng: *n.* drum. (*tambor*) **gardang a kawayan.** *n.* bamboo tambourine. [Tag. *tamból* (Sp.)]

gardínia: (Sp.) *n.* cape jasmine.

garém: *n.* species of prickly weed. **kagaremán.** *n.* place abundant with *garem* plants.

garéng: garenggareng. *n.* a vine used in medicine for boils.

garés: nagares. *a.* watery, soft; friable (potatoes, squash, etc.) (*marasamas*). **naggares ti ngiwat.** *exp.* to have a loose, gossiping tongue. [Tag. *labsák* (soft from cooking)]

garét: gargaret. *n.* furniture, jewels; tools, utensils. [Tag. *kagamitán*]

gargantília: (Sp. *gargantilla*: choker) *n.* choker, necklace worn close to the neck; decorative pin; long-necked water jar.

gargár: *n.* hoarse voice. **gargaren.** *v.* to hurry, hasten; urge on.

gargarét: (f. *garet*) *n.* kitchen utensils; furniture; jewels.

gári: gargari. *n.* attraction. gargarien. *v.* to incite, stir up, arouse, provoke, urge on. gumargari. *v.* to goad, provoke. magargari. *v.* to be seduced. [Tag. *bunsód, tuksó*]

garikgík: aggarikgik. *v.* to neigh (horses), to bleat (goats). [Knk. *galikgík,* Tag. *hagikhík*]

garimungamóngan: see *arimongamong.*

gáring: *n.* false teeth; dentures (*postiso*). [Tag. *garing* = ivory]

garinggíng: aggaringging. *v.* (*obs.*) to straddle. (*baddakaw; askaw; kayang; akkang*)

gárit: *a.* striped, streaked; color; shade. kagargarit. *a.* of the same color, creed, loyalties, etc. garitan a pandiling. *n.* striped skirt. [Png. *gulis,* Tag. *guhit*]

garíta: (Sp. *garita*: sentry box.) *n.* sentry box; (*reg.*) var. of *garreta:* (*reg.*) small store by the roadside.

garítan: (f. *garit*) *n.* pampano fish, *Gnathanodon speciosus.*

garníl: (Sp. *gramil*: marking gauge) *n.* joiner's marking gauge.

garnót: var. of *gurnót*: pull, uproot; snatch.

'garúd: var. of *ngarud*: so, then, in that case.

garugád: *n.* a file (instrument). garugaden. *v.* to file something. [Kal. *gaÿuged*]

garomáto: *n.* bullcart. garomatero. *n.* driver of a bullcart.

garuméte: (Sp. *grumete*: cabin boy) *n.* sailor, crewman.

garumiád: *n.* scratch on the skin; superficial wound. garumiadan. *v.* to scratch someone, inflict a superficial wound on. garugarumiad. *a.* full of scratches. magarumiadan. *v.* to be scratched on the skin. [Tag. *galos*]

garumpápeng: *n.* large green pepper (not pungent).

garóng: *n.* woven basket used to store *palay.*

garungíging: *n.* sound of the cowbell.

garúp: pagarup. *n.* guess; presumption. ipagarup. *v.* to guess; suppose; assume; expect. pagarup. *n.* suspicion; presumption. panangipagarup. *n.* assumption; presumption.

gárot: garuten. *v.* to snap, break in two; break loose (tied animal). gumarot. *v.* to let loose, unleash. makagarot. *v.* to escape, break away (animals) by breaking the tethering rod. gumagarot. *n.* an animal who has the habit of breaking away or escaping. Kasla la agsapul met no kuan iti nakagarut a nuangmo. You seem to be looking for your escaped water buffalo.

garóte: (Sp. *garrote*: club) *n.* stick used in beating, cudgel, bludgeon; garrote. garotien. *v.* to cudgel; bludgeon, beat; garrote.

garutigít: var. of *garatigit:* lighthearted laughter.

garpá: *n.* craziness due to full moon. (*bulanbulanen*) aggarpa. *v.* to go crazy.

garpét: *syn.* of *garpa*: craziness due to the full moon.

garutigít: nagarutigit. *a.* joyous, vivacious, animated, spirited, lively. gumarutigit. *v.* to laugh indecently.

garrapón: *n.* jar. (*garapón*).

garréta: *n.* small village store. (*tiánggi, terséna*)

garrúmay: *n.* a kind of children's game.

garróte: (Sp.) *n.* bludgeon, cudgel.

gársa: (Sp. *garza*: heron) *n.* heron; stork.

garsíta: (Sp. *garceta*: lesser egret) *n.* seagull.

garsút: var. of *gursót.*

gartéb: magarteb. *v.* to be gathered, collected, picked, harvested.

gartém: *n.* desire, craving; passion. aggartem. *v.* to desire, wish for. garteman. *v.* to crave for something. nagartem. *a.* desirous; (*fig.*) lustful, passionate. [Png. *ibég, linawá,* Tag. *nais, nasà*]

gas: (Sp. *gas*: gas) *n.* gas. (*sedden*)

gása: (Sp. *gasa*: gauze) *n.* gauze; wick of lamp; armband.

gásad: *n.* border, margin, edge. (*igid*)

gaságas: *n.* sieve. (*yakayak, salawasaw; sigi; yokoyok; tar-ap*) gasagasen. *v.* to sift *ipon* fish from the sand, by floating; strain; pan gold. Impalagipna ti panangiparit dagiti soldado nga aggasagas iti balitok. He reminded (us) of the prohibition of the soldiers to pan gold. [Tag. *salà*]

gásal: *a.* rough; coarse (*kersang*). [Tag. *gaspáng*]

gásang: *n.* spiciness, pungency. agasang. *a.* hot (piquant food), spicy. gumasang. *v.* to become pungent. Nagasang ti dilana. *exp.* He is sharp tongued. Ti agsili, magasangan. He who uses chili pepper gets burnt. [Ibg. *feggi, napeq,* Ivt. *mamcit, abchit,* Kal. *man-agat,* Knk. *suyágat,* Kpm. *maparas,* Png. *gasáng,* Tag. *angháng; gasang* = undertow, surf; small chip or piece of a stone or shell]

gasanggasáten: (f. *gasat*) (ga)gasanggasaten. *exp.* Leave it to fate.

gásat₁: *n.* luck, fortune; chance; accident. nagasat. *a.* lucky, fortunate. gasaten, gumasat. *v.* to be lucky, fortunate. makigasangasat. to adventure, take the chances, risk. kagasat. *n.* one's life partner. mannakigasanggasat. *a.* adventurous; prone to take risks. daksanggasat. *n.* bad luck. kinadaksangasat. *n.* bad luck, misery; misfortune. kinadaksangasat. *n.* misfortune; bad luck; misery. igasatan. *v.* to tell the fortune of. **naingasatan.** *a.* fortunate. **makagasat.** *v.* to have good luck; *n.* one's life partner. **napagasatan.** *a.* blessed with good fortune. **pannakigasanggasat.** *n.* adventure. **naipagpagasat.** *a.* luckily; opportunely. **igasanggasat.** *v.* to risk. **Dagiti nabati, inanusanda ti nakigasanggasat a nagtalon ken nagbangkag.** Those who remained tried their luck in rice farming and planting. **Nasaysayaat a maysa laeng a lalaki ti pakigasanggasatem.** It's good that you are only venturing on one man. [Kal., Knk. *gasat*, Png. *pálar*, Tag. *palad*]

gásat₂: gasatan. *n.* kind of tree (*Basia sp.*) yielding valuable timber.

gasátan: *n. Palaquium luzoniense* plant. [Tag. *dulitan, bagalangit*]

gásaw: gasawgasawen. *v.* to do futilely, uselessly, inadequately (*galimusaw*); to belittle, degrade; dishonor; insult; intimidate. **Dinakam magasawgasaw nga agkabsat.** You cannot insult us siblings.

gas-bá: (slang *baliktad* of *bagas*) *n.* uncooked rice.

gaséla: (Sp. *gacela*: gazelle) *n.* gazelle.

gaséra: (Sp. *gasera*: gas lamp) *n.* gas lamp.

gaséta: (Sp. *gazeta*: gazette) *n.* gazette.

gasgás: *n.* scratch. **magasgas.** *v.* to wear out (by friction). **gasgasen.** *v.* to scrape off. [Kal. *lakulitan*, Tag. *galos*]

gásiang: (*coll.*) *n.* girl; female. (*babai; mayyang*)

gásiong: (*coll.*) *n.* boy; guy. (*lalaki*)

gásid: gasidan. *v.* to part, separate (jungle while passing); to avoid mixing. **nagasid** (*obs.*) *a.* excusing oneself from work.

gásig: gasigan. (*obs.*) *v.* to counterbalance.

gasolína: (Sp. *gasolina*: gas) *n.* gas, gasoline. **mangpagasolina.** *v.* to fill one's tank.

gasonília: *n.* gas stove.

gasút: *n.* hundred. **sangagasut.** one hundred. **dua a gasut.** two hundred. **ginasut.** *a.* many hundreds; *adv.* by the hundreds. [Kal. *gasut*, Png. *lasós*, Tag. *daán*]

gaspáng: nagaspang. *a.* coarse; rough (*kersang, gásal, arimasámas*); vulgar. [Kal. *sageÿaseÿ*, Tag. *gaspáng*]

gassék: (*coll.*) *n.* seedlings. (*bunubon*) **igassek.** *v.* to sow seedlings.

gastádo: (Sp. *gastado*: spent) *a.* worn out.

gastadór: (Sp. *gastador*: spendthrift) *n.* spendthrift. (*barayuboy*)

gastáy: *var.* of *gistáy*: almost.

gastí: see *nagastián*: almost.

gastó: (Sp. *gasto*: expense) **gastuen.** *v.* to spend.

gástos: (Sp. *gasto*: expense) *n.* expense, cost. **magastos.** *a.* expensive. **gagastosen.** *n.* money intended to be spent.

gatá: (Tag.) *n.* coconut milk. (*getta*)

gátab: aggatab. *v.* to test two knives edge to edge. **nagataben.** to cut (metals), to serrate edges (knives, saws, etc.) **gataben.** *v.* to serrate; cut (metals). **paggataben.** *v.* to test two knives edge to edge.

gatád: *n.* price, value. (*ngina; bayad*) **gatadan.** *v.* to set a price to. **manggatad.** *v.* to price, appraise. **nagatadan.** *a.* priced, with fixed price. **agkagatad.** *v.* to have the same value. [Png. *kakanaan*, Tag. *halagá*]

gátang: *n.* coconut shell measurer; purchase. (*balusbus; sakada; gatang*) **gagatangen.** *n.* consumer goods; merchandise. **gumatang.** *v.* to purchase, buy. **gatangen.** *v.* to buy something. **ginnatang.** *n.* commerce; trade. **Dakkel ti maigatgatangko iti agasko.** I spent a lot on my medicine. **Makagatangka iti agas, ngem dimo magatang ti salun-at.** You can buy medicine, but you can't buy health. **Ti dayaw, saan a magatang.** Honor cannot be bought. [Ibg. *gatang*, Itg. *ngina*, Ivt. *manadiw*, Kal. *ngila*, Knk. *sekéb*, Kpm. *sáliq*, Png. *salíw*, Tag. *bili*]

gátas: *n.* milk. **gatasan.** *v.* to milk. **maragatas.** *a.* like milk (very pale skin); milky; species of medicinal plant used to cure wounds. **baka a gagatasan.** *n.* dairy cow, cow for milking. [Ibg. *pappóq* (milking), Kal. *beÿat chi susu*, Png., Tag. *gatas*]

gatbáng: aggatbang. *v.* to stir water, agitate. (*gáteb*)

gatbáw: *var.* of *gutbaw*: pierce; bore a hole in; perforate.

gáteb: *n.* school of fish. (*dalaidi; pangen; rotok; taklong*) **aggateb.** *v.* to come up for air (fish); school (fish).

gat-éb: *n.* fear, fright; *var.* of *gitéb*: throb.

gatél: *n.* itch; (*fig.*) sexual desire. **aggatel.** *v.* to itch; (*fig.*) have a sexual desire. (*bodo*) **nagatel.** *a.* itchy; sexually stimulated. **makakagagatel.** *n.* object that causes one to itch. **kinagatel.** *n.* itchiness; lewdness. **gatel a lakay.** *n.* dirty old man. **Nagatel ti dilana; Aggagatel ti dilana.** He is talkative (*lit*: has an itchy tongue). **Nakagatgatelen dagiti nagkagatan ti lamok.** The mosquito bites are already really itchy. [Ibg. *katel*, Ifg. *munkiyákit*, Ivt. *kateh, hateh*, Kal. *gete*, Knk. *sígab*, Kpm. *gatal*, Bon., Png. *gatél*, Tag. *katí*]

gatílio: (Sp. *gatillo*: trigger) *n.* trigger.

gáto: (Sp. *gato*: jack) *n.* vise; lifting jack; *var.* of *garomato*. **gato de mano.** *n.* piece of wood used as a lever; hand lathe.

gátud: gatuden. *v.* to cull, pluck; pick (tobacco leaves). **gagatuden.** *v.* to be ready for picking (*puros*). **kaggatud.** *a.* freshly picked; freshly culled. [Tag. *pitás*]

gatút: nagatut. *a.* rash, impatient, overhasty. **gatutan.** *v.* to buy something hastily (losing money in the process). [Tag. *dalî*]

gaw-án: (f. *gao*) *v.* to extract food from the pot.

gáwang: (*obs.*) *a.* noseless; full of holes; oppressed heart. **gawanggawang.** *a.* full of holes; oppressed with grief. **gawangan.** *v.* to perforate. **magawangan.** *a.* to be perforated. [Tag. *butas-butas*]

gáwat: *n.* famine, scarcity (of food); drought (when food is scarce). **aggawat.** *v.* to suffer from a famine. [Png. *gáwat*, Tag. *salát*]

gaw-át: magaw-at. *v.* to be able to reach, to understand. **gaw-aten.** *v.* to get, obtain; reach for. **gumaw-at.** *v.* to be enough, sufficient; reach for; reach out; extend the hand for. **igaw-at.** *v.* to hand to; extend. **makagaw-at.** *v.* to be adequate; sufficient (supplies). **mannakagaw-at.** *a.* wise. **Igaw-atannak man iti atis.** Please reach for some custard apple for me. **Sitatangsitak a nanggaw-at iti dakulapna ket nagkibinkamin a napan naglugan.** I arrogantly reached for her hand and we held hands to ride together. **Agsubliak tapno tulunganka a manggaw-at iti arapaapmo.** I will return to help you achieve your dreams. [Tag. *abót*]

gawáwa: gawawaam. *v.* to ask for something earnestly. **gumawawa.** *v.* to ask earnestly. [Tag. *magmakaawà*]

gáway: *n.* physical power; strength; capability. **gawayen.** *v.* to respect (*raem*). **makagaway.** *v.* to withstand, be able to resist; to be able to manage, get along; be strong. **saan a gagawayen.** *v.* to not take lightly. **adda gawayna.** *exp.* He is strong, capable. [Tag. *kaya*]

gawéd: *n.* betel pepper, used in native medicine to cure wounds, stomachaches and bone dislocations. People combine *gawed*, *apug* (powdered lime) and *buá* (betel nut) to make *mama*, a concoction for chewing. **maragawed.** *n.* tree with white flowers, *Ehretia navesii*. [Ibg. *gog*, Ifg. *hápid*, Ivt. *samuh*, Kal. *lawod*, Kpm. *samat*, Png. *lawer*, Tag. *ikmó*]

gawgáw₁: *n.* cornstarch (used in starching clothes) (*almidor*). [Tag. *gawgáw*]

gawgáw₂: gawgawan. *v.* to rinse, clean in water. **Inkamadana dagiti ginawgawanna a bunubon iti igid ti tambak.** He stacked the rice seedlings he rinsed in the water at the edge of the dike. [Kal. *chaliw-as*, Tag. *banláw*]

gáwid: igawid. *v.* to hold back, detain; check, restrain; hinder, impede; curb. **taringgawid.** *n.* restraining force. **makagawid.** *n.* hindrance; impediment. **Bimmangon tapno alaenna ti** pana ngem inggawid ti baketna. He got up to get the arrow but his wife held him back. [Png. *pamatondá*, *baat*, Tag. *pigil*]

gaw-ís: *n.* flick, flip. **gaw-isen.** *v.* to take something fast when leaving; flick; flip; wound with the tip of a whip. **magaw-is.** *v.* to make a glancing hit; be hit; to be within reach.

gawwáwa: *var.* of *gawawa*.

gay-áb: *a.* torn, ripped. **gay-aben.** *v.* to tear, rip by pulling (*pisang*; *ray-ab*). [Tag. *punit*]

gay-ábang: magay-abang. *a.* torn into shreds. **gayabbáng:** *var.* of *gay-ábang*: torn to shreds.

gáyad: *n.* length of a garment. **nagayad.** *a.* long, trailing (attire). **gayadan.** *n.* hemline; foot of a hill. **gumayad.** *v.* to trail (garments); become long. **Napaisem a nagayad.** He smiled a long smile. [Tag. *habà*]

gayágay: *n.* beginnings of a coming rain. **gayagayen.** *v.* to attempt, begin to do, undertake. (*ngayangay*) **igayagay.** *v.* to extend the hand to give or receive; to be about to rain.

gay-ák: see *gay-ab*: tear; rip.

gáyam: *part.* Implies sudden realization of something not previously known; particle expressing surprise (counterexpectation), so. **Sika gayam!** So it's you! **kasta gayam.** *exp.* so that's the way it is. **Saannak gayam a nalipatan.** So you didn't forget me (I thought you had). **Nadismaya idi maduktalanna a babai gayam.** He was upset upon discovering that it was a girl. [Png. *manáya*, Tag. *palá*]

gayáman₁: *n.* centipede. **gimmayaman.** *a.* like a centipede. **gimmayaman a karayan.** *n.* centipedelike river. **saringgayaman.** *n.* crawling, slithering like a centipede. **Kasla nasinit a gayaman daytay nalap-it a bagina.** Her flexible body is like a scorched centipede. [Ivt. *didipwan*, Kal. *gayyaman*, Knk. *gayáman*, Png. *gayamán*, Tag. *alupíhan*]

gayáman₂: gayyaman. *n.* marine shrimp resembling a *gayaman*. **maragayaman** (*obs.*) *n.* a jar with a long neck.

gayámat: *n.* arm (of cuttlefish). (*gamat*) **gumayamat.** *v.* to spit (cats); clutch; grasp, seize. **Immapras ti nasalemsem a pul-oy ket manipud iti rupana gimmayamat ti lamiis a simmuknor kadagiti tulangna.** The cool breeze struck and from his face, the cold clutched his bones.

gayammát: *var.* of *gayámat*.

gayamó: *n.* chicken tick. **ginayumo.** *a.* infested by chicken ticks. **Kasla gaygayamuen ti pingpingna.** His cheeks seem to be infested with chicken ticks.

gayamúdaw: *n.* look, appearance, aspect. (*langa*; *itsora*)

gayáng: *n.* pointed weapon: spear, lance; arrow. (*gusud*; *pika*; *durus*; *turag*) igayang. *v.* to throw a spear. gayangen. *v.* to spear. Kasla inggayong a nagawid. He went home immediately (like a spear). [Bon. *tóbay, solkod*, Knk. *bábeg, bagsáy*, Png. *gayáng*, Tag. *sibát*]

gayanggáng: aggayanggang. *v.* to roam, wander aimlessly; spend time idly roaming around. (*sorsor*)

gáyat: gayaten. *v.* to slice into thin strips; cut tobacco.

gay-át₁: gay-aten. *v.* to reach for to grasp something.

gay-át₂: *n.* purpose; aim; goal (*gandat, gagara*). igay-at. *v.* to start to do. gay-aten. *v.* to start to do something; try. [Tag. *balak*]

gáyaw: see *istay*: almost.

gayáw: aggayaw. *v.* to melt (metals).

gaybáng: *a.* shredded, torn. nagaybang. *a.* shredded; torn (*gay-ab*; *pisang*; *ray-ab*). gaybagaybang. *a.* tattered. [Knk. *gaybáng*, Tag. *punit*]

gayebgéb: *n.* fire, blaze. gumayebgeb. *v.* to burn. nagayebgeb. *a.* flammable, easily set on fire. [Tag. *lagabláb*]

gaynán: (*obs.*) *n.* daily ration.

gaynék₁: *n.* whirling; spinning; twisting. aggaynek. *v.* to whirl; spin. [Tag. *ikot*]

gaynék₂: gaygaynek. *n.* variety of rice with white kernel.

gayubána: *n. var.* of *guyabano*.

gayógoy: agganayogoy. *v.* to shake (ground).

gayúma: (Tag. also) *n.* kind of drug used as an aphrodisiac; sensual magic or charm; allurement; spell. gayumaan. *v.* to charm someone by use of a drug. Ginayumaannak. She secretly gave me an aphrodisiac.

gayóng: gayonggayong. *n.* fat of obese people moving while in motion; quicksand; marsh kind of seaweed. maigayonggayong. *v.* to fall in quicksand; (*fig.*) to become deeper involved in. [Tag. *kumunoy*]

gayonggák: aggayonggak. *v.* to croak (said of frogs).

gayót: *a.* worn down, threadbare; frayed.

gayyém: *n.* friend (plural: *gagayyem*). makigayyem. *v.* to befriend. pakigayyem. *n.* means used to win a friend. mannakigayyem. *a.* friendly. kinamannakigayyem. *n.* friendliness; sociability. aggayyem. *n.* mutual friend. *v.* to be friends. paggayyeman. *n.* reason for starting a friendship. Nadekketkami nga aggayyem. We are close friends. [Bon. *káyong, gagáyam*, Ibg. *piggoq*, Ivt. *kayvan*, Kal. *geyyom*, Knk. *alíwid, kabién, káyong*, Kpm. *kalugúran*, Png. *kaáro, amigo*, Tag. *kaibigan*]

gayyét₁: *n.* line on skin where skin folds (elbow, etc.).

gayyét₂: *a.* whirling, spinning; wavy (hair). gumagayyet. *v.* to spin; whirl; twist (*gaynek, tayyek*). [Tag. *inog*]

gebbá: *n.* burning coals; fired clay. gebbaen. *v.* to fire ceramics. ginebba. *a.* burnt, fired (ceramics).

gebbuáy: (*obs.*) *n.* increase.

gebgéb: magebgeban. *v.* to be able to do the whole thing; hold back; control. gebgebam ti riknam. *exp.* control your emotions. magebgeban. *v.* to be able to do everything. di magebgeban. *a.* overwhelming.

geddás: nagdas. *v.* to die promptly; do on short notice. (*pettat*) gumdas. *v.* to be done quickly, promptly. Gineddasna ti biagna. He killed himself all of a sudden.

geddáy: *n.* mountain slide. aggedday. *v.* to erode. magday. *v.* to cave in; crash in. (*reggaay*) geddayen. *v.* to level (a mountain).

gedgéd: *n.* line; groove; cut. gedgeden. *v.* to cut, carve, saw. ipagedged. *v.* to inculcate, urge in one's mind; insist. [Tag. *giít*]

gedtéd: ipagedted. *v.* to give special care or emphasis to.

geggéd: *var.* of *gedged*: cut, slice, injure with a knife. Kasla gumegged nga imuko ti panagsasaom. What you say cuts like a knife.

gekgék: gumekgek. *v.* to penetrate, go to the innermost part of a cave, the forest, etc.

gelgél: aggelgel. *v.* to crumple. (*kuleng*; *kumon*; *kunes*; *lunes*) igelgel. *v.* to rub between the hands. gelgelen. *v.* to knead, squeeze, rub. paggelgelan. *n.* strainer; rectangular bag used in making starch out of rice. ginelgel a baraniw. *exp.* scandalous matter (*lit*: mashed lemongrass). [Tag. *kusót*]

gellúong: gumluong. *v.* to resound (when slamming a door).

gemelína: *n.* species of tree used in construction and for making electric posts.

gemgém: *n.* fist. (*petpet*) aggemgem. *v.* to clench the hand. gemgeman. *v.* to clutch, grasp, clasp; seize. sangkagemgem. *n.* handful. [Kal. *sasantok*, Png. *gemgem*, Tag. *kamaó*]

genná: *n.* defect, flaw, blemish; crack.

gennéd: *n.* enclosure; division, partition. gen(ne)dan. *v.* to enclose, confine. genneden. *v.* to divide, partition (a field). [Tag. *palibot*]

genggén: *n.* driftwood. genggen ken gábat. *n.* flotsam (of a river or ocean, etc.).

geólogo: (Sp. *geólogo*: geologist) *n.* geologist.

gepgép: aggepgep, gepgepen. *v.* to cut through a cylindrical object (cut a pole in two, etc.).

geppák: geppaken. *v.* to persecute; treat cruelly; dominate.

geppás: geppasen. *v.* to cut in one stroke, slash. (*sigpat*)

geppéng₁: *n.* a piece cut off of something; trimming; trimming blade. **geppengen.** *v.* to trim. **agpageppeng.** *v.* to get a trim.

geppéng₂: *n.* clove (of garlic).

gergér: *n.* line, groove. **gergeran.** *v.* to mark with a line; to groove.

gerília: (Sp. *guerrilla*: guerilla) *n.* guerilla. (*geriliéro*)

geriliéro: (Sp. *guerrillero*) *n.* guerilla fighter.

gérra: (Sp. *guerra*: war) *n.* war. (*gubát*) **aggerra.** *v.* to wage a war. **mannakigerra.** *a.* warlike.

gerrék: *n.* snoring. (*urok*; *agír*) **aggerrek.** *v.* to snore.

gerréro: (Sp. *guerrero*: warrior) *n.* fighter in a battle, warrior.

gerrét₁: *n.* slice; chisel for grooving hot iron. **gerretan.** *n.* something with many grooves or notches. **gerreten.** *v.* to slice; slit the throat (*iwa*). **tallo a kagerret ti layalay.** three slices of *layalay* fish. [Tag. *gilít*]

gerrét₂: gerretan. a kind of edible, marine mollusk with a wedge-shaped shell.

gertém: see *getteng*: scissors; shears. (*kartib*)

gesgés: *n.* two-handed saw for chopping down trees; clogged nose. **gesgesen ti anges.** *v.* to have a clogged nasal passage.

gessáad: *n.* flat land, plain, level land at the foot of the mountain.

gessát: magsat. *v.* to snap; cut. (*pugsat*) **magsatan.** *v.* to die; expire. **nagsat ti anges, nagsat ti biag.** *v.* to emit the last breath, to die. **Kasla magsaten dagiti urat ti tengngedko iti dagsen ti inassiwak.** The veins in my neck seem to be pulled from the heavy weight I carried over my shoulders on a pole. [Tag. *lagót*]

gesséb: (*reg.*) **igesseb.** *v.* to do fervently (*pasnek*); throw together in one place.

gesséd: gesdan. *v.* to control; check one's feelings. **di magesdan.** *a.* uncontrollable. [Tag. *pigil*]

get: obsolete form of *ket*.

getgét: see *gerger*: line; groove.

gettá: *n.* coconut milk. **ginettaan.** *n.* dessert made of coconut milk and tropical fruits. **ginettaan nga ikan.** *n.* fish cooked in coconut milk. **gettaan.** *v.* to season with coconut milk. **nagetta.** *a.* milky. [Ibg. *piggoq*, Itg. *ládek*, Ivt. *gataq*, Kal. *luchog*, Kpm. *pigaq*, Png. *gatá*, Tag. *gatâ*]

gettáng: *n.* flaw, crack (in plates, etc.)

gettáy: *n.* netting needle, shuttle of a loom. (*bartilia*)

gettéb: *n.* teeth or claw of crustaceans. **getteben.** *v.* to break, snap with the teeth. **Nagbuteng ti asona ta nagistayan ginetteb ti alingo ti tengngedna.** His dog was frightened because the wild boar nearly bit off his neck. [Tag. *ipit*]

getténg: *n.* scissors, shears. (*kartib*) **gettengen.** *v.* to cut with scissors. [Knk. *kantíb*, Png. *katli*, Tag. *guntíng*]

geyyét: (*reg.*) *n.* middle; center. (*tengnga*)

gía: (Sp. *guía*: guide) *n.* guide. (*bagnos*)

giád: gigiad. *n.* small spider with long legs.

giák: *n.* hornet. **aggiak.** *v.* to sound the alarm.

gián: (f. *yan*) **aggian.** *v.* to live, dwell, reside.

gíbak: *n.* potsherd, fragment of broken pottery thinner than a *ribak*.

gíbus: *n.* end, finish, conclusion, close. (*turpos*) **gibusan.** *v.* to end; conclude; finish. **paggibusan.** *n.* finale; conclusion. **manipud rugi inggana't gibusna.** from start to end. [Ivt. *kavus*, Knk. *langdét*, Kpm. *patád*, Png. *sangpót*, Tag. *tapos*, *wakás*]

gidágid: aggidagid. *v.* to rub the body against something. (itchy back to a wall, etc.) **igidagid.** *v.* to rub part of the body against something.

giddán: *adv.* simultaneously; at the same time. **igiddan.** *v.* to do at the same time, simultaneously. **aggiddan.** *v.* to so at the same time. **makigiddan.** *v.* to go together. **Nagistayanda naggigiddan.** They just about did it at the same time. **Naggiddanda a timmaliaw.** They looked back at the same time. [Bon. *geglat*, Png. *banság*, Tag. *sabáy*]

giddáto: *n.* sudden happening; *adv.* instantly. **igiddato.** *v.* to do instantly. **gumiddato.** *v.* to act instantly. [Tag. *agád*]

giddí: giddigiddien. *v.* to break or cut into small fragments.

giddiát: *n.* difference; inequality; dissimilarity. (*supadi*; *sabali*; *salumina*) **aggiddiat.** *v.* to be different, unequal; separate. **igiddiat.** *v.* to distinguish; discriminate. **pakaigiddiatan.** *n.* point of difference. **paggidiatan.** *n.* differences. **Maigiddiat ti tao iti ayup.** Man is different from animals. [Tag. *kaibhán*]

gidgíd₁: igidgid, magid. *v.* to cling to, hold on tight to; rub the body against. **aggidgid.** *v.* to rub the body against. (*gidigid*)

gidgíd₂: *n.* sore eyes. (*magid*) **aggidgid.** *v.* to have sore eyes.

gidiát: *n. var.* of *gidiat*: difference.

gidígid: aggidigid. *v.* to rub, chafe (against the wall). (*gudugod*)

giém: (*coll.*) contraction of *gayyem*: pal; buddy; friend.

giérra: *var.* of *gerra*: war. (*gubat*)

gigián: *n.* a variety of rice with dark hull and white kernel. **aggigian**. *n.* dweller (from *aggian*: to dwell) (said also of haunting spirits). **paggianan**. *n.* place where someone lives; house; boarding house. [Tag. *tirá*]

gigiót: *n.* small restless bird. (*giot*; *kinod*; *lawlawigan*)

gígir: **aggigir**. *v.* to be apprehensive, fearful of what is coming; be careful. **igigir**. *v.* to shelter, shield; protect, guard, take care of (*aywan*, *taripato*); defend. **Dimo ammo nga igigir ta bagim**. You do not know how to take care of yourself.

gigís: *n.* corner of the mouth; gum. (*gisgis*, *ngisngis*; *gugot*)

giém: particle expressing uncertainty, lack of confidence.

giíng: **giingen**. *v.* to estimate the weight of by lifting. (*bagting*)

giít: *n.* piece of betel nut ready for chewing; midrib section of a tobacco leaf; small piece. **giiten**. *v.* to cut into small pieces. **sangkagiit**. *n.* one piece of (garlic, betel nut). [Tag. *kapiraso* (Sp.); *giít* = insist, assert]

gikgík: *n.* a kind of bird with a white breast and black beak; varieties of rice with a hard kernel. **aggikgik**. *v.* to cry as birds do; to make the sound of a hawk.

gílab: *a.* having a slight squint in the eye. **aggilab**. *v.* to squint the eyes.

gilágid: *var.* of *gidágid*: rubbing the body against something.

gílan: *n.* strip used to tie together coconuts.

gílap: *n.* flash. **aggilap**. *v.* to reflect light. **gumilap**. *v.* to flash.

gil-áyab: *n.* flame. (*segged*; *darang*; *rubrub*; *dagadag*) **gumil-ayab**. *v.* to flame. [Png. *liáb*, *daláng*, Tag. *liyáb*, *alab*, *sikláb*]

gíling: **gilingen**. *v.* to grind. (*asa*; *muli*) **gilingan**. *n.* grinder, mill. **giniling**. *n.* ground meat. **gilinggilingen**. *v.* to beat to a pulp (an opponent). [Png. *ligíg*, Isg. *mahirid*, Knk. *getmá*, Ibg., Ivt., Knk., Kpm., Tag. *giling*, Kal. *ledled*]

gilóng: **gumluong**. *v.* to thunder, roll (said of thunder). **kanagluong**. *n.* succession of loud, thundering sounds. **managluong**. *v.* to thunder.

gilotína: (Sp. *guillotina*) *n.* guillotine; paper cutter.

giltí: **giltigilty**. see *giray*: serrated; dented.

gimbál: *n.* war drum; war.

gimbara: *var.* of *karimbara*: fruit at the time of ripening.

gímong: *n.* meeting, crowd; gathering; assembly; society, company, community, council, congress, convention. **kagimongan**. *n.* society. **ag-**

gigimong. *v.* to congregate. **mannakigimong**. *a.* sociable. **paggigimongan**. *n.* place of assembly; meeting place. **nangato a gimong**. *n.* high society. (*alta sosiedad*) **Inigges a gimong dagiti aginsisingpet**. Those that pretend to be virtuous are a worm-infested lot. [Png. *tugyóp*, *olúp*, Tag. *lipunan*]

gimpápaw: *var.* of *gimpaw*.

gimpás: *n.* roll of cloth; one piece. **sangagimpas**. *n.* one piece of cloth to make a garment.

gimpáw: *n.* height of a heap. **gumimpaw**. *v.* to surpass, transcend. **gimgimpawan**. *a.* overloaded; brimming. [Tag. *apaw*]

gimpéd: **aggimped**. *v.* to slow down one's expenditures; be economical (*salimetmét*). [Tag. *tipíd*]

gína: **igingina**. *v.* to feel, be affected by, mind, bother; pay attention to. **di iginggina**. *v.* to grin and bear it. **Diak igingina ti pudot**. I can bear the heat.

gínad: **naginad**. *a.* slow, lazy, listless, sluggish. (*sadut*; *lunakol*; *kamol*; *tamlag*; *kuliwengweng*; *kudat*; *bantot*) **guminad**. *v.* to slow down; become sluggish. [Tag. *kupad*]

ginammól: *n.* bezoar, substance found in certain fruits that is supposed to have curative properties; charm from leaves or stones. [Tag. *antíng-antíng*]

gin-áwa$_1$: *n.* relief, comfort, ease, rest, relaxation. **nagin-awa**. *a.* comfortable. **gumin-awa**. *v.* to become comfortable. **makagin-awa**. *a.* comforting; to be comfortable. **pagin-awaen**. *v.* to relieve, soothe, calm; comfort, console. **Kabigatanna, nakagin-awa ni Akong ta di unay nakaro ti didigra**. The next morning, Akong was relieved because the disaster wasn't too serious. [Png. *ináwa*, Tag. *ginhawà*]

gin-áwa$_2$: **gingin-awa**. *n.* variety of awned late rice.

gin-áy: see *gan-ay*: warp; twist.

gíno: *n.* mark, target. **ginuen**. *v.* to shoot at.

ginsáad: *n.* brink, brow (of a hill).

ginséd: *n.* group; pile. **ginseginsed**. *a.* distributed into groups, piles, etc. **ginseginseden**. *v.* to distribute.

gintóng: *n.* pounding rice in the mortar, noise of pounding rice with pestles. **aggintong**. *v.* to pound rice in the same mortar. **gintong-gintongan**. *v.* to row with oars in a repetitive motion.

gínga: *n.* kind of purple mollusk smaller than the *palloki*.

gíngas: *n.* kind of marine fish similar to the *purong*.

gingét: *n.* cave; dense thicket. **iginget**. *v.* to ram, force down. [Tag. *bangín*]

ginggína: (f. *gina*) **igingginga.** *v.* to mind; bother; pay attention to.

ginggíng: ginggingan. *v.* to be envious of. **igingging.** *v.* to spend money unnecessarily.

gingginamól: *n.* magic charm. (*galing-galing*)

ginginéd: *n.* earthquake. **aggingined.** *v.* to have an earthquake, quake, tremble. [Bon. *gido, oliwan,* Ibg. *lunig,* Ivt. *ñiqñiq,* Kal. *chita,* Knk. *káyeg,* Kpm. *ayun,* Png. *yegyég,* Tag. *lindól*]

gión: (Sp. *guión:* hyphen) *n.* hyphen; small silver standard carried in a procession before the blessed sacrament.

giút: gigiut. *n.* a kind of small, gray bird similar to the *tarakatak,* named for its constantly moving tail.

gípang: *n.* a type of popped and fried rice cake made with *diket.* (*ampaw*)

gipás: apaggipas. *adv.* in a very short time; see *dipas.*

gípi: *n.* offshoot of palay. (*sagibsib*) **aggipi.** *v.* to grow shoots.

gipít: magipit. *v.* to lack; be insufficient.

gípo: *n.* dried twigs (used as fuel).

girád: see *garad:* knock against something.

giráng: (*reg.*) *var.* of *burnay:* earthen jug. **sangagirang.** *n.* one jugful (of *basi,* etc.).

giráy: nagirayan. *v.* to serrate, make teeth into. **magiray.** *a.* slanted, tilted.

girét: giniret (*obs.*) *n.* a narrow bracelet.

girgír: igirgir. *v.* to take care of (sickness), be careful about (something serious).

girír: (*obs.*) cold chisel; buttocks; anus. **gigiriran.** *n.* bottom (of jars, etc.).

girít: *n.* cold chisel; hide-and-seek game. **aggirit.** *v.* to play hide-and-seek.

giród: gurruod. *n.* thunder. **gumruod.** *v.* to thunder, rumble. **agkanagruod.** *v.* to roll (thunder) continuously, rumble. [Root no longer used by itself]

girsáy: see *persay:* torn; lacerated. (*pigis*) **girsayen.** *v.* to tear; shred. [Tag. *punit*]

girtíw: *n.* partial cut. **girtiwen.** *v.* to sever partially, partially cut off. **magirtiwan.** *v.* to be partially cut, sliced (*iwa, galip, ilap*). **girtiwan.** *v.* to cut a small piece off.

gisá: (Sp. *guisar:* sauté) **igisa.** *v.* to stir fry, sauté. **ginisa.** *a.* sautéed; fried. [Kal. *intumon,* Tag. *gisâ*]

gisádo: (Sp. *guisado:* stir fried) *a.* sautéed; fried; stewed.

gisántes: (Sp. *guisante:* pea) *n.* peas.

gisáy₁: gisayen. *v.* to slice (*iwa, galip*). [Tag. *hiwà*]

gisáy₂: gisayen. *v.* set free, give independence to; divide, separate.

giséd: *n.* a dense fence of stakes. **gumsed.** *v.* to sink, descend into the ground. **gisedan.** *v.* to enclose with stakes, surround with stakes.

gisgís: *n.* corner of the mouth. (*gigis*) **gisgisan.** *v.* to make a small dent in, to tear off a small part of. **gisgisen.** *v.* to tear up. (*pigis*)

gisígis: *n.* toothbrush. (*sipilio*) **aggisigis.** *v.* to brush the teeth (*sugigi*). [Tag. *sepilyo* (Sp.)]

gísit: gisitgisit. *a.* uneven, spun irregularly. **gisitan.** *v.* to spin irregularly.

gislá: *n.* shred. **gislaen.** *v.* to shred. **ginisla.** *n.* shred, thin strip of bamboo.

gisúd: gimmisgisud. *a.* uneven, rough, rugged.

gissáad: *n.* center. (*tengnga*)

gissíng: igissing. *v.* to remove a part from; take a portion from. **maigissing.** *v.* to be removed. (*ikkat*)

gissít: *n.* small, thin glass.

gistáy: *adv.* about to, almost, *abbr.* of *nagistayan.* **magistayán.** *v.* to be almost; to nearly do; to have a close shave. **Nagistayánda naggigiddan.** They almost did it at the same time. [Notice stress shift after heavy syllable. Traceable from *istáy > nagistáy > nagistayán*] Png. *ngalngalí,* Tag. *halos*]

git: gitgít. *n.* groove.

gíta: *n.* snake venom; poison used in arrows. **nagita.** *a.* venomous; deadly. [Tag. *lason, kamandág*]

gitá: nagita. *a.* oily to the taste (certain nuts, coconut milk, etc.). **gumita.** *v.* to become oily. [Tag. *langís*]

gitáb: *n.* clattering teeth. **aggitab.** *v.* to clatter the teeth, as when feverish.

gitára: (Sp. *guitarra:* guitar) *n.* guitar (*kutibeng*). **aggitara.** *v.* to play the guitar. **gimmitara a pammagi.** *n.* guitarlike physique, referring to the body of a shapely woman. **gitarista.** *n.* guitar player.

gitéb₁: *n.* throb; pulsation. (*pitik*) **aggitebgiteb.** *v.* to throb; palpitate. [Png. *parók,* Tag. *tibók*]

gitéb₂: *n.* bar of timber.

gítiw: *n.* wound or scar near the mouth.

gitúb: *n.* gorge; defile. **igitub.** *v.* to close, shut by joining.

gitól: aggitol. *n.* sound of object moving in a clay jar.

gittá: *n.* sudden confiscation. **gittaen.** *v.* to snatch.

gittáy: *n.* net-making device with a spool for thread.

gittém: (*obs.*) like that. (*kasdiay*)

giwáng: *n.* gap; breach. (*siwang*) **giwangan.** *v.* to breach, make a hole in. **Limmawa ti giwang iti baetda.** The gap between them widened. [Tag. *awáng*]

giwgíw: (*reg.*) *n.* cobwebs. **Nabayagen a kinumotan ida ti giwgiw ken tapok.** The cobwebs and dust have covered them for a long time. [Tag. *agiw*]

gíya: (Sp. *guía*: guide) *n.* guide. (*bagnos*)

gladióla: (Sp. *gladiolo*: gladiolus) *n.* gladiolus.

glándula: (Sp. *glándula*: gland) *n.* gland.

gliserína: (Sp. *glicerina*: glycerin) *n.* glycerin.

glóbo: (Sp. *globo*) *n.* air balloon; globe.

glukósa: (Sp. *glucosa*: glucose) *n.* glucose.

glória: (Sp. *gloria*: glory) *n.* glory, praise; honor; heaven; fame; honor. (*tan-ok*; *dayaw*; *dayag*; *langit*)

gloriéta: (Sp. *glorieta*: summer house) *n.* lawn; flower garden; summer house; bandstand, raised platform in a plaza; kiosk.

glosário: (Sp. *glosario*: glossary) *n.* glossary, list of definitions at the back of a book.

gmelína: *n.* species of hardwood tree.

guád: **pagguadan.** *n.* model; example.

guáno: (Sp. *guano*: guano) *n.* guano, dung of bats or seabirds high in nitrates that is used in fertilizer. (*lugit*)

guántes: (Sp. *guante*: glove) *n.* gloves. **nakaguantes.** *a.* wearing gloves.

guápo: (Sp. *guapo*: handsome) **nagguapo** *a.* good-looking, handsome. (*taraki*; *bisked*; *dangas*; *pogi*; *saldit*; *taer*)

guardabóske: (Sp. *guardabosque*: ranger) *n.* keeper of the forest, ranger.

guardádo: (Sp. *guardado*: guarded) *a.* guarded. (*nabantay*)

guardakósta: (Sp. *guardacosta*: coastguard) *n.* coastguard.

guárdia: (Sp. *guardia*: guard) *n.* guard, watchman (*bantay*); outpost. **guardiaan.** *v.* to watch over something. **agguardia.** *v.* to stand guard.

guardílias: (Sp. *guardilla*) *n.* police during the Spanish regime.

guarní: (Sp. *guarnir*: trim) **iguarni.** *v.* to tie with a rope (ship, log, etc.).

guarnisión: (Sp. *guarnición*: harness) *n.* harness, leather fittings for a horse connecting it to a cart.

guatló(ng): (*slang*) *n.* wayward person, idle person.

guayabáno: (Sp. *guanábano*: custard apple tree) *n.* soursop fruit, *Annona muricata.* (*bayubana*)

gúba: **agguguba, gugubaen.** *v.* to re-plow.

gúbal: **aggubal.** *v.* to wrestle. (*gabbo*) **makigubal.** *v.* to wrestle with. **paggugubalan.** *n.* wrestling arena. **igubal.** *v.* to do wrestling. [Knk. *púged, awét*, Png. *garapál*, Tag. *bunô*]

gubál: **nagubal.** *a.* coarse, rough, harsh; unrefined, vulgar (*gubsang*); uneducated; rude (*sabrak*).

gúbang: *n.* sandstone used to scour leather. **gimmubang.** *a.* burnt, nearly charred. **nagubang.** *a.* coarse (texture), unpolished; burnt. [Tag. *sunog*]

gubát: *n.* war, battle; combat. (*bakal, gérra*; *dangadang*) **aggubat.** *v.* to go to war. **makigubat.** *v.* to wage war with. **paggugubatan.** *n.* battlefield. (*gubatan*) **pakigubat.** *n.* armor; ammunition; war equipment. **mannakigubat.** *n.* warrior. **pakigubat a barko.** *n.* warship. [Kal. *papatoy, bibïyuklit, leÿapun,* Png. *bakál,* Tag. *digmâ*]

gubbó: see *gabbo*: wrestle.

gubbuáy: *n.* result of an effort; reason, cause; source; start, beginning. **gubbuayan.** *a.* lucky, successful. **gubbuayen.** *v.* to cause; bring about. **aggubbuay.** *v.* to originate, spring up, start. **paggubbuayan.** *n.* source. **Aduda ti saan a mangayat iti lasona gapu iti angot a gubbuayenna.** Many do not like onions because of the smell that comes from them. [Tag. *simulâ*]

gobernadór: (Sp. *gobernador*) *n.* governor. [Kal. *gubillachuÿ*]

gobernadorsílio: (Sp. *gobernadorcillo*) *n.* municipal mayor during the Spanish regime.

gobernár: (Sp. *gobernar*: govern) **gobernaren.** *v.* to govern. **gobernaran.** *v.* to govern over; do work skillfully. **magobernaran.** *v.* to be able to cope with something.

gubés: **igubes.** *v.* to do to one's utmost; to work hard; beat; thrash; damage. **maigubes.** *v.* to be overburdened or overworked. **Igubgubesna ita ti panawen iti panagtalon.** He is busily spending all his time farming.

gubét: *var.* of *gubes.*

gubgób: **aggubgob.** *v.* to keep to one's bed. **igubgob.** *v.* to shelter, protect from cold.

gúbia: (Sp.: *gubia*: gouge, *obs.*) *n.* gouge.

gobiérno: (Sp. *gobierno*: government) *n.* government. (*panagturay*) **aggobierno.** *v.* to rule.

gubláng: *n.* scar formed after the scab has fallen off. **nagublang.** *a.* having formed a scar after the scab has fallen off. **aggublang.** *v.* to scar after the scab has fallen off.

gubuáy: see *gubbuáy.*

gubsáng: **nagubsang.** *a.* rough, coarse; having bad manners (*sabrak*). **kinagubsang.** *n.* bad manners; vulgarity. [Tag. *gaspáng*]

gubsí: **gubsien.** *v.* to contradict, oppose.

gudágod: **igudagod.** *v.* to rub something against a smooth surface. (*gudugud*)

gudák: **manggudgudak.** *v.* to start, commence; introduce.

gúdas: **gudasen.** *v.* to forget, erase from the mind, put an end to, eradicate; liquidate; salvage; assassinate, kill. **gudasan.** *v.* to take by force; ravish; violate. **nagudas.** *a.* killed, assassinated. **Gudasennakon, total, nabayagakon nga agsagsagaba.** Kill me, anyway, I have suffered for a long time. [Tag. *utás*]

guddatél: naguddatel. *a.* coarse. (*gubsang*)

guddáy: agguddagudday. *v.* stagger, sway (*tiwed*; *ibar*; *kudday*; *dungay*; *duir*; *dawiris*; *daweng*; *bariring*). [Tag. *suray, hapay, giray*]

gudduá: *n.* half. **kaguddua.** *n.* half of two parts **agguddua.** *v.* to share. **gudduaen.** *v.* to cut into two. **gudduagudduaen.** *v.* to divide into several parts. **ingguddua.** *n.* act of sharing fifty-fifty. **makiguddua.** *v.* to have a share (50/50). **maiguddua.** *v.* to be half-full; half-finished. **paggudduaen.** *v.* to halve. [Kal. *gudwa*, Png. *palduá*, Tag. *hatì*]

gúdeng: aggudenggudeng. *v.* to totter from fatigue; to be hesitant, reluctant. **Aringgudengenak a sumrek.** I hesitated to enter.

gudgúd: *n.* itchy exanthema on the skin; herpes; mange. **aggudgud.** *v.* to have this disease; to be mangy.

gúdil: *n.* solution to a problem. **nagudilan.** *a.* notched, nicked, indented; having contributed a little part to a larger job; accomplished. **Masapol nga adda magudilak iti uneg dayta a tiempo.** I need to have something accomplished within that time. **Awan ti nagudilanna.** He did not accomplish anything. [Tag. *gatlâ* (notch)]

gudóg: *n.* beat, throb, pulsation. **aggudog.** *v.* to beat, throb. (*pitik*)

gudúgod: aggudugod. *v.* to rub the body against a post or wall. **igudugud.** *v.* to rub or squeeze violently. (*gidigid*)

gueddáy: *n.* stony soil.

gúgo: *n.* a kind of tree whose bark may be used for shampoo.

gugúba: *n.* land prepared for cultivation.

gúgur: *n.* test of faith; (hardship of life). **guguran.** *v.* to refine (metals), purify; to put under severe trial; purge the body in penitence. **igugor.** *v.* to devote oneself fully to. **maigugur.** *v.* to be put to a severe test; to be overburdened; inflicted. **naguguran.** *a.* refined; purified; tested; overburdened with work, saddled with responsibilities. [Tag. *dalisay* (pure)]

gugót: *n.* gum of teeth (*gigís*). [Ivt. *ngares*, Kal. *nguÿtangot*, Kpm., Tag. *gilágid*]

gukáyab: *n.* cave. (*rukíb*) [Kal. *gongeb*, Knk. *gangáb, gangéb, liáng*, Png. *ongib*, Tag. *yungíb*]

gukgók: *n.* the cry of the hog. **aggukgok.** *v.* to cry (said of the hog).

gulágol: aggulagol. *v.* to struggle; squirm. **Aggugulagol ti kaunggan.** *exp.* to have an excited feeling inside. **Impanna amin a pigsana a naggulagol.** He put all his might in struggling.

guláman: (Tag.) *n. agar-agar.* see *guraman.*

gúlay: (Tag.) *n.* vegetable; salad. (*nateng*) **ginulay.** *n.* a vegetable dish of boiled vegetables seasoned with vinegar. **gulayen.** *v.* to prepare vegetables.

gulgól: *n.* a kind of native shampoo; act of washing the hair. **aggulgol.** *v.* to wash the head. **gulgulan.** *v.* to shampoo the hair. **panaggulgol.** *n.* shampooing; (*reg.*) act of shampooing the hair in the process of burying the dead. [Kal. *logÿog*, Tag. *gugò*]

gulíb: nagulib. *a.* treacherous, disloyal, unfaithful. **guliban.** *v.* to betray; cheat; bear false witness. **kinagulib.** *n.* treachery. [Kpm. *sukab*, Png. *pakl áp*, Tag. *taksíl*]

gulímba: *var.* of *galimba*: red coconut.

gulintáng: gulgulintang. *a.* tattered, threadbare. [Tag. *gulanít*]

gulíng: gulingguling. *n.* throwing mud at someone; placing ashes on the foreheads of the faithful on Ash Wednesday.

gúlis: *n.* line dug by a plow; furrow; mark. **gulisan.** *v.* to make a hill (for cultivating); make a row for cultivation. **inggulis.** *n.* manner of planting in which seeds are furrowed instead of scattered (*kilas*). [Tag. *guhit*]

gulló: *n.* persuasion, induction; influence. **igullo.** *v.* to persuade; influence; induce. [Tag. *himok, hikayat*]

gullúong: (f. *gilóng*) *n.* sound of thunder. **gumluong.** *v.* to resound.

guló: *n.* disorder; revolt, rebellion; insurrection. **aggulo.** *v.* to create disorder. **guluen.** *v.* to make disorderly; create trouble. **nagulo.** *a.* disorderly; dangerous; riotous. **Maguluanak unay.** I am so confused. [Kal. *ngumolot*, Png., Tag. *guló*]

gúlong: gulonggulong. *n.* a kind of bracelet.

golósa: aggolosa (*obs.*) *v.* to trill, sing with a trill.

gólpe: (Sp. *golpe:* blow, strike) *n.* sudden blow; strike; *adv.* all at once; wholesale. **a golpe.** *adv.* suddenly, unexpectedly. **agpreno a golpe.** *v.* to suddenly step on the brakes. **golpe de estado.** *n.* coup d'état.

gulpí: (Sp. *golpe:* blow, strike) **gulpien.** *v.* to do all at once; to buy everything at once, buy in bulk; hit; whip. **No trabaho, gulpiem, no kanen, in-inutem.** If it's work do it all at once, if it's food, do it little by little.

gólpo: (Sp. *golfo:* golf) *n.* gulf, large bay.

géma: (Sp. *goma:* rubber) *n.* rubber; rubber tire; eraser; rubber band; condom. **gomaen.** *v.* to stiffen a fabric; to erase mistakes.

gumbá: *n.* small rectangular bamboo device used as a fish scoop.

gumabbék: *n.* the slip-mouth fish, *Leiognathidae* family.

gumaméla: *n.* the hibiscus plant; the hibiscus flower. (*kayanga*)

gumbá: *n.* bamboo device used for siphoning water of a river and catching fish.

gumés: igumes. *v.* to wash (clothes) by squeezing them in water.

gúmi: *n.* ear of corn; boll of cotton.

GÚMIL: *n.* Ilocano writer's association (acronym of *Gunglo dagiti Mannurat nga Ilokano*).

gumintáng: *n.* kind of native dance. **aggumintang.** *v.* to move the hands in different directions, as in dancing (*kumintang*). **igumintang.** *v.* to do with hand gestures. **Aggumgumintang latta ni manong ta sangkasiputna ti panagdarup ni tatang kenkuana.** Older brother is flailing his arms, vigilant against the attacks of father toward him. [Tag. *gumintáng*]

gumlúong: (f. *gulluong*) *v.* to resound, reverberate.

gumón: maigumon. *v.* to become addicted to (drugs, etc.).

gumpápa: *n.* a small basket (for *dudumén*).

gumpapék: *n.* a variety of maize.

gumpápeng: *n.* green pepper; variety of maize with a dark red kernel. (*garumpapeng*)

gumpéd: *n.* the blunt tip of anything pointless. **gumpeden.** *v.* to make blunt (*ngudel*). [Tag. *puról*]

gúmpo: *n.* cut of wood; (*reg.*) var. of *dagumpo*: pile. **maigumpo.** *v.* to be piled up.

gumpól: *n.* mix, mixing (of various ethnic groups, etc.). **maigumpol.** *v.* to be mixed. **igumpol.** *v.* to mix with.

gumrád: [*gurad* + *-um-*] *n.* skin scratch.

gumriád: *n.* slight scratch on the skin. **nagumriadan.** *a.* scratched.

gumróod: (f. *gurruod*) *v.* to thunder; to make the sound of machine guns.

gúnad: magunad. *v.* to relapse. (*begnat*)

gúnam: gunamgunam. *n.* explicit order; persuasion; (*obs.*) medley. **igunamgunam.** *v.* to express, manifest, declare clearly; reiterate; stress. [Tag. *diín*]

gunáy: *n.* movement; action, activity. **aggunay, agunggunay.** *v.* to move. (*kuti; tignay*) **gunayen.** *v.* to move (someone or something). **makagunay.** *v.* to be able to move. [Png., Tag. *galáw*, Tag. *kilos*]

gundáway: *n.* privilege; chance; distinction; superiority. **magundawayan.** *v.* to be privileged. **gundawayan.** *v.* to take the opportunity; take advantage of an opportune moment. **naigundawayan.** *a.* opportune. **mananggundaway.** *n.* opportunist. **Ginundawayandaka.** They took advantage of you. **Agyamanak ta dinak ginundawayan.** I am thankful that you did not take advantage of me. [Png. *kagter*, Tag. *pagkakataon, samantalâ*]

gunés: *n.* gust, squall. **nagunes.** *a.* crumbled.

gunnót: *n.* fiber; fibrous seed of the mango. **gunnuten.** *v.* to shake by the hair. **nagunnot.** *a.* fibrous. **igunnutan.** *v.* to strip clean of fibers. [Png. *kánot, lánot,* Tag. *himaymay*]

gun-ód: *n.* success. **magun-od.** *v.* to obtain, get, attain; secure; earn; achieve; win. (*ragpat*) **igun-od.** *v.* to take more than enough. **di magun-od.** *a.* unattainable; unreachable. **dagiti gunggunuden.** *n.* goal; aim. **Kasla nakagun-od-langit.** As if he reached heaven. [Png. *pakala,* Tag. *kamít*]

gonoréa: (Sp. *gonorrea*: gonorrhea) *n.* gonorrhea. **aggonorea.** *v.* to suffer from gonorrhea.

gunsí(s): *n.* figure-eight knot; chain knot (used in plowing, etc.). **gunsien.** *v.* to tie in a figure-eight knot.

gungo: *n.* bundle of rice stalks.

gúnggon: aggunggon. *v.* to shake; sway; rock. **Ginunggonna ti ima ti kaabayna.** He shook the hand of the person beside him. [Tag. *ugà*]

gunggoná: *n.* reward, recompense; profit, benefit; advantage. **gunggunaan.** *v.* to reward, repay. **gunggonana.** *a.* well deserved; *n.* one's due. **Gunggonam!** That's what you get! [Png. *gongóna,* Tag. *gantimpalà*]

gunggunáy: (f. *gunay*) **aggunggunay.** *v.* to move (*kuti*). [Tag. *kilos*]

gunggóng: *a.* ignorant, stupid. **gumanunggong.** *v.* to resound, echo, reverberate. **Maysaka met gayam a gunggong.** So you really are an idiot. [Tag. *tangá*]

gúnglo: *n.* association. (*pagambagan*) **makigunglo.** *v.* to join a group or association. **kagungluan.** *n.* fellow member of an organization. **sangagungluan.** *n.* the whole association. [Tag. *samahán*]

gungúgong: *n.* hollow cavity, area deep inside. **maigungugong.** *v.* to fall into a deep hole.

gungón: aggungon. *v.* to shake (a house). **magungon.** *v.* shakable. **gungunen.** *v.* to shake something. **Ti nalamuyot a sao, gungunen ti puso.** *exp.* Soft words are convincing.

gunguná: *var.* of *gungguná*: prize, reward.

gungtúb: *n.* smell and taste of burnt food. **magungtuban.** *v.* to be burnt (food, grains).

gupang: *a.* feeble minded and crazy.

gup-áng: igup-ang. *v.* to delay, detain (*tantan*); hold back, restrain.

gúped$_1$: gupden. *v.* to cut breadthwise; quit, desist from; shorten, eradicate. **maguped.** *v.* to be cut; curtailed. [Tag. *putol*]

gúped₂: *n.* obstruction. (*típed*; *lapped*) **makaguped.** *v.* to obstruct, hinder, impede; stop.

gúpeng: **gupngen.** *v.* to slice, cut breadthwise. (*íwa*)

gupgúp: **gupgupen.** *v.* to summarize; compile; take all; embrace; make blunt. **pakagupgupugan.** *n.* summary. **Balitok ti tunggal darikmat a panaggupgupmo iti pirak.** You can always buy gold with silver (money). [Tag. *buód*]

gúpi: *n.* dish made of meat cooked in lard and vinegar.

gupít: *n.* treasure, riches; storehouse of unthreshed rice; characteristics, attributes. **maigupit.** *v.* to have refined characteristics. **Kadagitoy a gupit ken saguday ni Filipina ket kalkalikaguman dagiti lallaki kadagiti sabali a pagilian.** These characteristics and qualities of the *Filipina* are what men from other nations desire. [Tag. *katangian, kayamanan*]

gúpud: see *gupeng*: cut tree.

gupúgop: **gupugupen.** *v.* to saw crosswise (*ragadi*). **pakagupugopan.** *n.* part that will be sawn crosswise; summary. **nagupugop.** *v.* cut, sawn.

gúpong: see *gupeng*: cut tree. **gupungen.** *v.* to cut. (*puted*)

guppápaw: **iguppapaw.** *v.* to do gently, lightly (with little interest).

gúra: *n.* anger; hate. (*pungtot*) **kagura.** *n.* anger. **guraen.** *v.* to hate, abhor. **gumura.** *v.* to be angry, hate. **mananggugura.** *a.* easily provoked. **makagura.** *a.* angry, mad. **makapagura.** *a.* offensive, irritating. **kagurgura.** *n.* enemies. **guranggura.** *n.* mutual hatred; mutual disgust. **No dika agpudno, guraenka.** If you don't confess the truth, I'll get mad at you. [Ibg. *poray, lussaw,* Ivt. *maqket, suli,* Kal. *mulit,* Kpm. *mua,* Png. *pasnók,* Tag. *galit*]

gurabáng: *n.* ugly, haggard face. (*kuggangí*)

gurábis: *n.* matches (*posporo*); matchbox. **gurabisan.** *v.* to light with a match.

gúrad: *n.* mark, line on something. **igurad.** *v.* to scrape the shoes on the doormat. **naguradan.** *a.* scratched.

guráman: *n.* a slippery seaweed found in river mouths.

gurámi: *n.* gourami fish.

guráng: *n.* wild pigeon; (*coll.*) old, mature (animal). **Nalaing a talaga ti ayup a gurang.** A mature animal is really intelligent.

gurárab: *n.* ghost. (*al-alia*)

gordión: *var.* of *akordion*: accordion.

gurdó: *n.* selling short; losing in a sale. **nagurdo.** *a.* rough; coarse; poorly ground.

gurgór: **gurgoran.** *v.* to refine, take out impurities.

gorgoríta: *n.* earthen jug.

gurgurmút: *n.* the edible roots of the eel grass (*ballaiba*).

guríd: *n.* a kind of skin disease; eczema (for dogs). (*gudgud*)

guridéng: (*obs.*) *a.* dropsy.

gurígor: *n.* fever. **aggurigor.** *v.* to have a fever. **Aggurigor a di agpudot, agsakit ti ulona a di agut-ot.** *exp.* Having a fever that doesn't get hot, having a headache that doesn't hurt (describing someone in love). [Ibg. *kulikug,* Ivt. *maynguhat,* Kal. *man-atong,* Knk. *pudot,* Png. *petang, golígol,* Tag. *lagnát, sinat*]

gorília: (Sp. *gorila*: gorilla) *n.* gorilla.

gurión: (Sp. *gorrión*: sparrow) *n.* small kite.

gúrit: *n.* the first furrow; stripe; groove. **aggurit.** *v.* to dig furrows in the soil. **guritguritan.** *a.* striped. **Kaduaennakto nga aggurit.** You will dig furrows with me. [Tag. *guhit*]

gúrlis: (Pil.) *n.* line; stripe; mark. **gurlisan.** *a.* striped; *v.* to make a line; stripe; underline.

gurmút: **gurmut, gurgurmut.** *n.* the edible roots of the eel grass (*ballaiba*).

gúrnot: **gurnuten.** *v.* to uproot; weed; pull (hair). **Adda pay ngata tiempoda a mapan manggurnot iti uggot ti niog.** They perhaps have time to go uproot coconut sprouts. **Nariknana a kasla magurgurnot dagiti uratna.** He felt as if his veins were being pulled.

goró: **gorogoro.** see *goso*.

gur-ón: *n.* heddle of the loom, parallel sets of cotton yarns that compose the harness of a loom suspended from both ends of bamboo sections lying across the tiebeams (*awanán*) of the loom. **igur-on.** *v.* to heddle.

gúrong: *n.* shank, shin, lower leg between knee and ankle. **agginnurong.** *n.* game played by two boys who try to knock each other down with their shins while squatting (*dampil*). [Kal. *butuy,* Png. *bikkíng, saláp,* Tag. *bintí*]

górra: (Sp. *gorra*: cap) *n.* cap.

gurráyon: *var.* of *gunggon*: shake, sway.

gurrúod: *n.* thunder. (*dulluog*) **aggurruod.** *v.* to thunder. **gumruod.** *v.* to make a rumbling sound like thunder. [Bon. *kidol,* Ibg. *arugug,* Ifg. *kidul,* Ivt. *adey,* Kal. *kuchuÿ,* Knk. *kidó,* Kpm. *duldul,* Png. *karól,* Tag. *kulóg*]

gursót: **igursot.** *v.* to violently snatch something. (*agaw*)

gusáb: *a.* with the lips cut; with a harelip (*gusíng*). **gusaban.** *v.* to cut the lips of someone. **magusaban.** *v.* to accidentally have one's lips cut.

guságos: *var.* of *gusugos*: rub.

gusanílio: (Sp. *gusanillo*: small worm) *n*. small worm (*igges*); bit of an auger; twist stitch embroidery.
gusáno: (Sp. *gusano*: worm) *n*. worm (*igges*); small winding spring of a watch or clock.
gúsi: (Ch.) *n*. china vase or jar; burial jar. **Inruarna ti gusina a naglaon iti tapuy.** He took out the vase containing the rice wine.
gusíng: *a*. harelipped; notched at the rim (plates, etc.). **magusingan.** *v*. to be chinked; have one tooth missing. [Bon. *gisla, góngis*, Ibg. *gusing*, Ifg. *nagihe*, Ivt. *lísay*, Kpm. *bungiq*, Png. *bungis*, Tag. *bingót, bungì* (harelip)]
gusipéng: *n*. kind of small, brown-shelled, edible mollusk.
gusó: **nagusoguso.** *a*. disorderly, messed up, disheveled, without form. **gusogusuen.** to make disorderly. (*kuso*)
gúsud: **gusuden.** *v*. to spear. (*gayang*) **igusud.** *v*. to thrust into the ground, drive into the ground. **Inggusodna a dagus ti kanawanna iti rusok ti kalabanna.** He immediately thrust his right hand in his opponent's abdomen.
gusúgus: **gusugusan.** *v*. to rub; scrub hard. **igusugus.** *v*. to rub something on; browbeat; beat a weaker opponent. [Png. *goragor*, Tag. *kuskós*]
gósos: (Sp. *gozo*: joy) *n*. hymn of praise where certain words or phrases are repeated after every couplet.
gusút: (Tag.) *n*. wrinkle. (*kuretret*) **nagusut.** *a*. crumpled.
gustó: (Sp. *gusto*: desire) *n*. like; want; desire. (*kayat*) **agginnusto.** *v*. to like each other; fall in love. **pagustuan.** *v*. to favor; condescend; play along. **magustuan.** *v*. to like. **napagustuan.** *a*. satisfied. **Dayta ti magustuak kenka.** That is what I like about you. **Namnamaek a magustuam daytoy.** I feel that you like this.
gútab: *a*. unfinished, incomplete. *n*. bad habit; bad haircut. **ginutaban.** *a*. half-eaten. **gutában.** *v*. to chip, chip off a piece; to unevenly cut the hair. **magutában.** *a*. chipped, chipped off; not smoothly cut. **gutabgutáb.** *a*. badly cut; notched; not properly done.
gutád: *n*. jerk; pull. (*guyod, aruy*) **makagutad.** *v*. to remind. **gutaden.** *v*. to pull (a rope). **aggutad.** *v*. (*coll.*) to masturbate. **Gutadgutadem ti saput a nagbitinan ti lawwalawwa babaen ti tammudom.** Pull the web that the spider is hanging from with your forefinger. [Tag. *halták*]
gutágot: *a*. inconsistent. **aggutagot.** *v*. to be inconsistent. **gutaguten.** *v*. to pull and push; seesaw.

gutapértsa: (Sp. *gutapercha*) *n*. gutta-percha, the thickened juice of the gutta-percha tree.
gutbáw: *a*. perforated, pierced. **gutbawan.** *v*. to pierce, perforate, bore a hole in. [Tag. *butas*]
gutbóng: see *gupeng*: cut tree.
gúted: *var*. of *guped*.
gotéra: (Sp. *gotera*: dripping) *n*. dripper; pipette.
gutígot: *var*. of *gutugut*: provoke; rouse; excite. **makagutigot.** *a*. provoking; exciting.
gótiko: (Sp. *gótico*) *a*. Gothic.
gutúgot: **gutuguten.** *v*. to provoke, move, excite, stir up, stimulate, rouse; persuade. (*guyugoy*) **makagutugot.** *v*. convincing; stimulating; believable. **Ginutugotda nga umakarkami ditoy.** They persuaded us to move here. [Tag. *hikayat*]
gutók: *n*. heartbeat. (*bitek, giteb, pitik*) **aggutok-gutok.** *v*. to throb, pulsate violently; feel remorse. [Png. *parók*, Tag. *tibók, pitík*]
gútong: *n*. hidden rocks and stones that make the ground rugged.
guttá: **guttaen.** *v*. to tug (*guyod, aruy*). [Tag. *halták*]
gúyab: **agguyab.** *v*. to grimace, make faces; stick out tongue. **guyaban.** *v*. to make a face at someone; stick out the tongue at someone.
guyabáno: (Tag.) *n*. soursop fruit. (*bayubana*)
guy-ád: **agguy-ad.** *v*. to squirm; move the legs and arms in the water to keep afloat.
gúyod: *n*. variety of awned rice; pull; jerk; tug. (*aruy*) **guyuden.** *v*. to pull, draw, haul, drag, tug; trail. **aggiginnuyod.** *n*. to play tug of war. **guyudan.** *n*. rope used to pull a plow. **makaguyod.** *v*. to be capable of pulling; to be sufficient; be of use; capable of drawing a crowd. **paringguyuden.** *v*. to drag; haul. **paguyuden.** *v*. to haul a load (with help of the water buffalo, etc.). **sangapaguyudan.** *n*. bundle of thirty bamboos. **No agsasao kasla maguyguyod a lata iti kabatuan a kalsada.** When they speak, it's like a can being hauled over a rocky road. **panaggiginnuyod ken panagdidinnuron.** *n*. mutual push and pull. [Bon. *goygoy*, Ibg. *guggunan, meggugun*, Ivt. *palangen*, Kpm. *gulyut*, Png. *goyór*, Tag. *hila, batak, hatak*]
guyúguy: *n*. suggestion to do something. **guyuguyen.** *v*. to convince; float; invite, attract, allure; persuade. **makaguyuguy.** *a*. inviting, alluring. **makaguyuguy-rikna.** *a*. interesting. **Talaga a makaguyuguy ti sam-it ti timekna.** The sweetness of her voice is really attractive. **Mabalinnaka pay nga makaguyugoy kadagiti babbai.** It makes you attractive to girls. [Tag. *himok, hikayat*]

guyyó₁: guyyoguyyo (*obs.*) *n.* fright. **agguyyoguyyo.** *v.* to shake the shoulders, to sway, rock. [Tag. *ugóy*]

guyyó₂: iguyyo. *v.* to influence. **maiguyyo.** *v.* to be influenced.

grába: (Sp. *grava*: gravel) *n.* mound; gravel; coal.

grabádo: (Sp. *grabado*: engraved) *n.* illustrations in printed matter; cut; engraving. **grabador.** *n.* engraver.

grabadúra: (Sp. *grabadura*: engraving) *n.* engraving, carving.

grábe: (Sp. *grave*: serious) *a.* serious. **grabeka!** (*coll.*) *exp.* You're too much.

grabedád: (Sp. *gravedad*: gravity) *n.* gravity; seriousness.

grabiádo: (also *agrabiado*) *a.* losing (financially); in a bad position; dissatisfied; wronged; aggravated.

grádo: (Sp. *grado*: grade) *n.* grade; degree; intensity; story (of a house); rank; interval of measurement; shelf.

graduádo: (Sp. *graduado*: graduated) *a.* graduated. (*turpos*)

granáda: (Sp. *granada*: grenade; pomegranate) *n.* hand grenade; pomegranate. **Sagduduada laeng iti granada.** They only had two grenades each. [Kal. *sanggalilit*]

granadília: (Sp. *granadilla*: passion fruit) *n.* passion flower vine; passion fruit.

granáte: (Sp. *granate*) *n.* garnet; dark red color.

gránde: (Sp. *grande*: grand) *a.* great; grand. **engrande.** *a.* lavish, grand.

graníto: (Sp. *granito*: granite) *n.* granite.

gráno: (Sp. *grano*: grain; pimple) *n.* grain, cereal; pimple (*kamuro*). **grano maldito.** *n.* kind of ulcer.

grápa: (Sp.) *n.* cramp (used in sawing).

grása: (Sp. *grasa*: grease) *n.* grease. (*sebo*; *taba*; *kábut*; *lanit*)

grásia: (Sp. *gracia*: grace) *n.* grace; grace period (for paying a debt).

grasióso: (Sp. *gracioso*: gracious) *a.* gracious; pleasant; friendly.

grátis: (Sp. *gratis*: free) *a.* free of charge. **aggratis.** *v.* to do free of charge.

gratitúd: (Sp. *gratitud*: gratitude) *n.* gratitude.

grenáte: (Sp. *granate*: garnet) *n.* maroon red, violet; garnet.

Griégo: (Sp. *griego*: Greek) *n.* Greek. *a.* Greek. **aggriego.** *v.* to be Greek; to speak Greek.

griliéte: (Sp. *grillete*: shackle, fetter) *n.* shackle. (*posas*)

grípo: (Sp. *grifo*: faucet) *n.* faucet, tap.

gris: (Sp. *gris*: gray) *a.* gray. (*kolordapo*)

grúa: (Sp. *grúa*: crane) *n.* crane (mechanical device used for lifting heavy things).

gruésa: (Sp. *gruesa*: gross) *n.* gross; twelve dozen.

gruméte: (Sp. *grumete*: cabin boy) *n.* crewman, sailor.

grúpo: (Sp. *grupo*: group) *n.* group (*timpuyog*; *ummong*).

grúta: (Sp. *gruta*: grotto) *n.* grotto; cavern. (*gukáyab*)

H

Originally not a sound in the Ilocano language, the glottal fricative [h] does occur in a few loanwords and one native word, *haan*, the dialectal version of *saan*. In old Ilocano writings, words with this glottal fricative sound were written with a [j] based on Spanish orthography.

haán: variant of *saan*: no. **haan man.** see *saan man*.

Habanés: (Sp. *javanés*: Javanese; fem: *Habanesa*) *n*. Javanese.

habládas: (Sp. *habla*: speak) *n*. gossip, empty talk, impertinent talk.

habonéra: (Sp. *jabonera*: soap dish) *n*. soap tray. (*sabonera*)

habonéro: (Sp. *jabonero*: soap maker; fem: *habonera*) *n*. soap maker. (*sabonero*)

habonéte: (Sp. *jabonete de olor*: toilet soap) *n*. toilet soap. (*sabonete*)

hagábi: (Ifugao) *n*. throne or symbol of authority among mountain tribes; feast sponsored by the wealthy.

hágad: (Tag.) *n*. motorcycle cop.

háiskul: (Eng.) *n*. high school. **aghaiskul.** *v*. to go to high school.

hakulatória: (Sp. *jaculatoria*: ejaculation) *n*. ejaculation; short prayer.

haléa: (Sp. *jalea*: jelly) *n*. jelly.

háloblak: (Eng. hollow block) *n*. hollow concrete block (used in construction). **hinaloblak.** *a*. made out of hollow blocks.

halo-hálo: (Tag. *halo-halò*) *n*. a dessert made of crushed ice mixed with tropical fruits, sweet beans, and milk, popular in the hot weather.

hámba: (Sp. *jamba*: jamb) *n*. door frame; window frame.

hammét: (*abbr*. of *haan met*) Not at all; not really; it's not so.

hampáy: (*abbr*. of *haan pay*) Not yet.

hamón: (Sp. *jamón*: ham) *n*. ham.

hanabále: (*abbr*. of *haan nga bale*) It doesn't matter; it is of no importance.

hánimon: (Eng. honeymoon) *n*. honeymoon. **paghanimunan.** *n*. the place where a couple spends their honeymoon.

Hanunoó: *n*. ethnic group from southern Mindoro; the Mangyan language of the *Hanunoo* people.

Hapón: (Sp. *Japón*: Japan) *n*. Japan, Japanese person; Japanese language. **Haponésa.** *n*. a Japanese woman.

harakíri: (Jap. *hara-kiri*: abdomen-stabbing suicide) *n*. suicide by slicing the abdomen with a knife. **agharakiri.** *v*. to perform *harakiri* on oneself.

harána: (Sp. *jarana*: small guitar) *n*. serenade. **agharana.** *v*. to serenade. **Ania ti kunam ta mapantayo haranaen ni Linda ita a rabii?** What do you say we serenade Linda tonight?

hardín: (Sp. *jardín*: garden) *n*. garden. (*minuyongán*) **hardinero.** *n*. gardener.

harína: (Sp. *harina*; flour) *n*. flour. (*bellaáy*)

hárra: (Sp. *jarra*: jug) *n*. jug, jar.

hásag: *n*. oil lamp.

hasínto: (Sp. *jacinto*: hyacinth) *n*. turquoise; hyacinth.

hasmín: (Sp. *jasmín*: jasmine) *n*. jasmine. **agathasmin.** *v*. to smell like the jasmine flower.

haspé: (Sp. *jaspe*) *n*. jasper; fluidity of texture; draping; *a*. lustrous, polished, glossy; draping.

Hawáy: *n*. Hawai'i. **Hawayáno.** *n*. *a*. Hawaiian. (*taga-Hawaii*)

háwla: (Sp. *jaula*: cage) *n*. birdcage. (*kulungan*)

hebília: (Sp. *hebilla*: buckle) *n*. buckle; clasp.

hektária: (Eng.) *n*. hectare. (*ektaria*)

helatína: (Sp. *gelatina*: gelatin) *n*. gelatin.

hemélos: (Sp. *gemelos*: cuff links) *n*. cuff links.

heneradór: (Sp. *generador*: generator) *n*. generator.

henerál: (Sp. *general*: general) *n*. *a*. general.

henerasión: (Sp. *generación*: generation) *n*. generation. (*kaputotan*)

henerosidád: (Sp. *generosidad*) *n*. generosity. (*kinamanagparabur*)

heniéro: (Sp. *inheniero*: engineer) *n*. engineer.

hénio: (Sp. *genio*: genius) *n*. genius. (*sirib*)

Hentíl: (Sp. *gentil*: gentile) *n*. gentile; person who is not Jewish.

heograpía: (Sp. *geografía*: geography) *n*. geography.

heográpiko: (Sp. *geográfico*: geographic) *a*. geographic.

hépe: (Sp. *jefe*: chief) *n*. chief; chief of police. (*pangulo*)

heránio: (Sp. *geranio*: geranium) *n*. geranium flower or plant.

herarkía: (Sp. *jerarquía*: hierarchy) *n*. hierarchy.

heringgília: (Sp. *jeringilla*: syringe) *n*. syringe, vaccination needle.

hermáno: (Sp. *hermano*: brother) *n*. brother. (usually used religiously) (*kabsat*)

héro: (Sp. *hierro*: iron, brand) *n*. brand on cattle. **panghero.** *n*. branding iron.

heroglípiko: (Sp. *jeroglífico*: hieroglyphic) *n*. hieroglyphic, ancient writing of the Egyptians.

Hesuíta: (Sp. *jesuita*: Jesuit) *n*. Jesuit.

Hesukrísto: (Sp. *Jesucristo*: Jesus Christ) *n.* Jesus Christ.

higánte: (Sp. *gigante*: giant) *n.* giant.

Higaónon: *n.* ethnic group from Misamis Oriental, Mindoro.

hilátsa: (Sp. *hilacha*: loose thread) *n.* thread unraveled from cloth.

hilbána: (Sp. *hilvanar*: baste) *n.* basting; tack; stitch used as a temporary fastening.

hílig: (Tag.) *v.* to like; be inclined to. (*kayat*)

Hiligaynón: *n.* ethnic group from Panay and western Negros island; alternate name for the *Ilonggo* people and their Visayan language. **Hiligaynonen.** *v.* to say in Hiligaynon, to translate into Hiligaynon.

himnásio: (Sp. *gimnasio*: gym) *n.* gym, gymnasium.

hímno: (Sp. *himno*: hymn) *n.* hymn. (*kansión*) **hímno filipíno.** Filipino national anthem.

hímog: (Ifugao) *n.* death ritual dance of the Ifugaos of northern Luzon.

Híndu: (Eng.) *n.* Hindu person; Hindu religion; native of India.

hinébra: (Sp. *ginebra*: gin) *n.* gin.

hinekolohía: (Sp. *ginecología*) *n.* gynecology.

hinekólogo: (Sp. *ginecólogo*) *n.* gynecologist.

hinéte: (Sp. *jinete*: jockey) *n.* jockey.

hipnotísmo: (Eng.) *n.* hypnotism. **hipnotista.** *n.* hypnotist.

hipokóndria: (Eng.) *n.* hypochondria.

hirasól: (Sp. *girasol*: sunflower) *n.* sunflower. (*mirasol*)

hírit: (Tag.) *n.* asking for more. (*ponggá*) **aghirit.** *v.* to ask for more.

híro postál: (Sp. *giro postal*: money order) *n.* money order.

história: (Sp. *historia*: history) *n.* history. (*istoria*) **historiador.** *n.* historian.

hitáno: (Sp. *gitano*: gypsy) *n.* gypsy.

Hudhód: (Ifugao) *n.* Ifugao epic poem.

hudikatúra: (Sp. *judicatura*: judiciary, judicature, dignity of a judge) *n.* judiciary; judgeship; magistracy.

Húdio: (Sp. *judío*: Jew) *n.* Jew. *a.* Jewish.

hudisiária: (Sp. *judicial*: judicial, judiciary + Sp. locative suffix *-ria*; Sp. *judiciaria* = astrologer) *n.* law court offices.

Huébes: (Sp. *jueves*: Thursday) *n.* Thursday. [Kal. *kapat*]

huégo: (Sp. *juego*: set) *n.* set; gambling.

hués: (Sp. *juez*: judge) *n.* judge. (*ukóm*) **aghues.** *v.* to judge. **Nagkasardan iti hues.** They had a civil wedding.

huéteng: (Hok. *huê teng*: flour space) *n.* kind of lottery gambling game consisting of guessing

two numbers from one to thirty-seven, yielding 400:1 in payoff. **huetengero.** *n.* *hueteng* player.

hugadór: (Sp. *jugador*: gambler) *n.* gambler. (*agsugsugal*)

huísio: (Sp. *juicio*: trial; sense) *n.* court trial (*pannakausig, sakláng*); common sense.

huk: (Tag. *hukbalahap*) *n.* member of the Communist *hukbalahap* movement.

húla: (Tag. *hulà*: guess) *n.* fortune-telling. (*panangipalad*) **agpahula.** *v.* to have one's fortune told. (*agpadles, agpapalad*)

hólen: (Eng. hole in) *n.* playing marble. **agholen.** *v.* to play marbles. (*bulintik*)

Húlio: (Sp. *julio*: July) *n.* July. [Kal. *waÿu*, Knk. *óao*]

Húnio: (Sp. *junio*: June) *n.* June. [Kal. *kitkiti*]

húnta: (Sp. *junta*: board, council) *n.* board (of directors); council; junta. **aghunta.** *v.* to have a board meeting. **huntaen.** *v.* to discuss something in a board meeting.

hópia: (Hok. *hò pià*: good cake) *n.* sweet bean cake.

hurádo: (Sp. *jurado*: jury) *n.* jury; board of judges; sworn statement; *a.* sworn in.

huramentádo: (Sp. *juramentado*: sworn in; cursed) *a.* amuck; running in a frenzy. **aghuramentado.** *v.* to run amuck. **Ad-addanto manen nga aghuramentado dagiti nakullaapan ti panunotna no maipupokda.** The people thinking wicked thoughts will most probably run amuck again if they jail him.

huraménto: (Sp. *juramento*: oath) *n.* oath of office. (*sapata*)

hurár: (Sp. *jurar*: swear) *n.* oath. (*sapata*) **aghurar.** *v.* to swear in; take an oath.

hurísta: (Sp. *jurista*: jurist) *n.* jurist, expert in law.

hornál: (Sp. *jornal*: daily wage) *n.* installment (of a debt); daily wage.

hórno: (Sp. *horno*: oven) *n.* oven. (*paggebbaán*)

husgá: (Sp. *juzgar*: judge) **manghusga.** *v.* to judge; sit in judgment.

húsgado: (Sp. *juzgado*: court of justice) *n.* court of justice. (*pagukoman*) **Agkitatayonto idiay husgado.** I'll see you in a court of law. [Tag. *húkuman*]

husgar: (Sp. *juzgar*: judge) **husgaran.** *v.* to judge. **mahusgaran.** *v.* to be judged. (*ukom*)

húsi: (Hok. *hò se*: rich, good cotton yarn) *n.* pineapple and silk fabric.

hustipikár: (Sp. *justificar*: justify) **hustipikaran.** *v.* to justify. **mahustipikaran.** *v.* to be justified.

hustísia: (Sp. *justicia*: justice) *n.* justice. (*kinalinteg*)

hústo: (Sp. *justo*: enough) *a.* enough, just right. (*kusto*) **humusto.** *v.* to be just right. **apaghusto.** *a.* just enough; suitable. **huston!** Enough already! That's just right.

hóta: (Sp. *jota*: j; kind of dance) *n.* the letter *'j'* in the Spanish alphabet; kind of Aragonese dance adapted in the Philippines. **aghota.** *v.* to dance the *jota*.

I

i-: *pref.* common theme focus verbalizing prefix that takes the *-ko* series pronoun endings and expresses the instrumental or thematic nature of the absolutive argument, perfective: *in-* before consonants and *iny-* before vowels: **Gatangenna.** He buys it. **Piso ti inggatangna.** He bought it with one peso; The prefix *i-* may also indicate physical or psychological conveyance, to bring, to carry, or to put the referent designated by the stem in a certain place: **Iruarmo ti basura.** Take out the garbage. **Iyasidegyo daytoy.** Put (you pl.) that nearer. **Iditoymo.** Put it here. **Awan ti inyawidna.** He didn't bring home anything; The perfective form of the prefix *i-* is *in-* before consonants or *iny-* before vowels: **Iyalisna ti lugan.** He moves the car. **Inyalisna ti lugan.** He moved the car.

i-: *pref. var.* of *taga-*. **i-Laoagda.** They are from Laoag.

iCV-: Nominalizing affixation for *-um-* verbs. **sangpet.** arrival. **isasangpet.** act of arriving, arrival.

i- -an: *circumfix.* Transitivizing circumfix that takes the *-ko* series pronoun endings and expresses a beneficiary action, that the action expressed in the root is done for someone else (perfective form is *in- -an*): **Igatangannak man dayta.** Please buy that for me. **Inlutuannakami ti adobo.** She cooked *adobo* for us. **Indaitannaka daytoy.** She sewed this for you.

ián: **umian.** *v.* to spend the night at somebody's house. **umianan.** *n.* place where one lodges for the night. [Tag. *makitulog*]

ibáar: aganibaar. *v.* to chirp (birds).

Ibabao: *n.* ethnic group from northern Samar.

Ibalói: *n.* ethnic group from southern Benguet Province (also called *Nabaloi* or *Benguet Igorot*); language of the *Ibaloi* people. Dialects include *Daklan, Kabayan,* and *Bokod.*

Ibanág: *n.* ethnic group from northwestern Luzon; the Cordilleran language of the Ibanag people with two major dialects, northern and southern. **ag-Ibanag.** *v.* to be Ibanag; to speak Ibanag.

íbar: *adj.* out of position, askew; *n.* staggering, swaying. **agibar-ibar.** *v.* to stagger; sway. (*bariring*; *dawiris*; *duir*; *dungay*; *gudday*; *lupay*; *sabbadaw*; *tiwed*) **pagibaren.** *v.* to lean sideways; place diagonally. **Nagibar-ibar a nagturong iti sasakyan.** He staggered on his way to the ship. [Tag. *suray, hapay, giray*]

Ibatán: (Sp. *Ivatán*). *n.* ethnic group from the Batanes Islands, north of Luzon; the Austronesian language of the Ivatan people. Dialects of Ivatan include *Basco* and *Itbayaten.*

íbaw: agibaw. *v.* to go around, compass. (*rikos*) **ibawan.** *v.* to encircle; encompass. [Tag. *paligid*]

ibbát: ibattan. *v.* to release, let go of; drop; loosen; set free; yield. **yibbat.** *v.* to drop; let go. **umibbat.** *v.* to release, stop holding on to. **makaibbat.** *v.* to lose one's hold; let go accidentally. **panagibbat.** *n.* manner of speech, delivery; manner of doing something. [Ibg. *ibbót*, Png. *ikbán*, Tag. *bitíw*]

ibbét: *n.* house arrest; person confined to a cell; *var.* of *ibbat*. **yibbetna ti saona.** he releases his thoughts.

ibbóng: *a.* said of eggs with the chicken nearly developed; vain, worthless, spoiled (eggs); sterile (said of men). **agibbong.** *v.* to become spoiled (eggs) (*luang*). **Awan ti puonmi nga ibbong.** We have no sterility in our blood.

íbeng: *n.* the body of the bellows.

íbit: agibit. (*reg.*) *v.* to weep, to cry (children) (*sangit*). [Knk. *ebék*, Tag. *iyák*]

ibléng: *n.* human excrement. **umibleng.** *v.* to have a bowel movement. **agibleng.** *v.* to have diarrhea. (*buris*) **pagiblengan.** *n.* toilet. **yibleng.** *v.* to defecate out. [Png. *taí*, Tag. *tae*]

ibniár: (*obs.*) *a.* allowing young locusts to pass by mutual agreement.

íbo: *n.* awn of rice. **agibo.** *n.* to develop awns (rice). **iboan.** *n.* variety of awned late rice with red kernel.

íbon: *n.* young calf of carabao; (*obs.*) large bird.

ibús: ibusen. *v.* to finish up, finish off, use up; eat completely; conclude. **maibus.** *v.* to be consumed, exhausted; finished, concluded. **maibus.** *v.* to be used up, consumed. **yibus.** *v.* to use up, use everything. **di maibusan.** to have enough, be sufficient in quantity. **maibusan iti bala.** to run out of bullets. **aginnibus.** *v* to finish each other off. **Nakaibusakon iti lima a botelia.** I was able to finish off five bottles. [Ibg. *nófuq, nafúnu*, Kal. *amin*, Kpm. *gísan*, Png. *uput*, Tag. *ubos*]

ibtúr: maibturan. *a.* tolerable; endurable. *v.* to tolerate, endure, bear. (*andur*) **makaibtur.** *v.* to be able to bear, to be able to put up with, tolerate. **ibturan.** *v.* to bear; endure; suffer; withstand. **managibtur.** *a.* durable; tolerant; enduring. **naibtur.** *a.* tolerant, patient; resistant, lasting; durable, tough. **Diak maibturanen ti bisinko.** I can no longer take this hunger. **Adda pagpatinggaan ti panagibtur.** *exp.* There is a limit to one's endurance. [Knk. *ánus, sóot*, Png. *tepél, irap*, Tag. *tiís*]

idá: *enclitic oblique pron.* to them, used in transitive double pronoun constructions: **Tinulonganmi ida.** We helped them. **Apay a diyo padasen a sarungkaran ida?** Why don't you try to visit them? [Tag. *silá*]

idád: (Sp. *edad*: age) *n.* age. (*tawen*)

idál: *n.* object (such as a fish bone) that gets stuck in the throat. **maidalan.** *v.* to have an object stuck in the throat.

ídam: (*obs.*) *a.* rejecting.

ídat: *a.* writhing (from pain), twisting. **agidat.** *v.* to writhe in pain.

ídaw: *n.* black and white cock with black feet; heathen sacrifice or superstition; disposition of a newly awakened person. **madi ti idawna.** *exp.* indisposed. **idawen.** *v.* to do something due to superstition.

iddá: *n.* couch; bed; where one lies. **agidda.** *v.* to rest, lie down. **agkaidda.** *v.* to lie together; make love. **ipaidda.** *v.* to lay something down. **maipaidda.** *v.* to fall prostrate; be stretched out. **makikaidda.** *v.* to lie with someone. **agkaidda.** *v.* to lie down together. **kaidda.** *n.* sleepmate. *v.* to sleep with someone. **iddaen.** *v.* to lay down something. **pagiddaan.** *n.* resting place, where one lies down. **siiidda.** *a.* prostrate; lying down. (*ilad; atag*) **umidda.** *v.* (*fig.*) to be bedridden. **Nagidda iti rakit a nakakayang ken nakadeppa.** He lay on the raft with his arms and legs fully extended (spread-eagle). [Ibg. *idda*, Itg. *emeg*, Ivt. *maypeptad*, Kpm. *kéra*, Png. *akarokól, dukul*, Tag. *higâ*]

iddál: *n.* food caught in the throat. **naiddalan.** *a.* having the throat blocked with something, a fish bone, etc.

iddék: *var.* of *eddek*: grunt, exert strength verbally.

iddép: **iddepen.** *v.* to turn off (lights); extinguish, put out. **maiddep.** *v.* to be turned off (lights); extinguished, put out. (*depdep; patay*) **pagiddep.** *n.* fire extinguisher. **iidepan.** *n.* extinguisher, light switch. **Nalawag iti uneg nupay naiddepen ti bombilio iti ruar.** It was bright inside although the lightbulb outside was already out. [Bon. *ádep, epa*, Ibg. *addóq*, Ivt. *usep*]

iddúg: **umdug.** *v.* to spin. (*tayyek*)

idéa: (Sp. *idea*: idea) *n.* idea. (*panunot*)

idealísmo: (Sp. *idealismo*: idealism) *n.* idealism.

idealísta: (Sp. *idealista*: idealist) *n.* idealist.

identidád: (Sp. *identidad*: identity) *n.* identity. (*kinasiasino*)

idí: *adv.* shows former past time; at that time, then; in those days. *conj.* before; at that time in

the past, while (past); *prep.* relates temporal nouns to the past: **idi kalman.** yesterday. **idi napan a bulan.** last month. **idi Mierkoles.** last Wednesday. **idian.** *v.* to give up; cease, stop; quit. **idinto.** *adv.* whereas; since. **Idi agsinakami, impalagipna ti tulagmi.** When we parted ways, he reminded (me) of our contract. **Awan ti damagda maipanggep kaniak manipud idi.** They had no news from me since then. [Png. *nen*, Tag. *noón* (past time marker); *waksí* (give up)]

idiár: (Sp. *idear*: think up, devise) *v.* to teach, direct.

idiáy: *adv.* there (far from the speaker and the hearer); *prep.* in, at, to, on, into. **Napanda idiay eskuela.** They went to the school. [Ibg. *tári*, Knk. *sidí*, Png. *dimán*, Tag. *doón* (distal demonstrative), *sa* (oblique noun marker)]

idín: *adv.* then (in the past).

idínto: (f. *idi*) *conj.* whereas; as, since (in the past). **Iti amianan, daan ken marmarpuog dagiti balay idinto nga iti abagatan, pimmalasio.** In the north, the houses are old and dilapidated, whereas in the south, they are palatial.

idná: **agpakaidna.** *v.* to remain calm, stay peaceful. **makaidna.** *v.* to be quiet, calm, peaceful; still. **di makaidna.** restless.

ídog: *n.* a kind of gray dog; a variety of late rice with dark straw.

idolatría: (Sp. *idolatría*: idolatry) *n.* idolatry, worship of idols.

ídolo: (Sp. *ídolo*: idol) *n.* idol; (Tag.) gigolo.

ídos: *n.* spoon; spoonful. (*kutsara*) **idusen.** *v.* to spoon. **sangkaidos.** *n.* one spoonful.

ídra: (Sp.) *n.* hydra, kind of freshwater polyp.

idtá: *var.* of *dita*; there (near the addressee).

idtóy: *var.* of *ditoy*; here.

Ifugao: (*pron. Ifugáw*) *n.* ethnic group from northern Luzon that speaks the following languages: *Batad Ifugao, Mayoyaw Ifugao* and *Tuwali Ifugao*; the language of the Ifugao peoples.

igáaw: *n.* drought. (*kalgaw, tíkag*) **umigaaw.** *v.* to stop raining; be clear (weather). [Ivt. *apseng*, Png. *kebet*, Tag. *bisì, baisì, tagtuyót*]

ígad: *n.* coconut scraper, sometimes made with a chair. **igaden.** *v.* to grate coconut meat (*gadgad*). **naigad.** *a.* grated (coconut meat). [Ibg. *igad*, Knk. *kutkut*, Kpm. *adjar*, Png. *ígar*, Kal. *iged, igachun, gasagas*, Ivt., Kpm., Tag. *kudkud*]

ígado: (Sp. *hígado*: liver) *n.* dish consisting of liver, meat, peas, raisins, garlic, onions, heart, and spices.

igágaw: *n.* dry season. (*kagaw, igaaw*)

ígam: *n.* weapon; arm. (*armas*) **igaman.** *v.* to arm; provide with weapons. **siiigam.** *a.* armed. **siiigam a buyot.** armed forces. [Knk. *gamán*, Tag. *sandata*]

igáo: *var.* of *bigao*: winnowing basket.

ígat: *n.* eel whose young is called *kíwet.* **igat berkakan.** *n.* fish resembling the lamprey. **Kasla nagalis nga igat.** He is slippery like an eel. [Ibg. *kíwoq*, Ifg. *dalit*, Ivt. *aymang*, Kal. *chalit*, Knk. *dalít*, Png. *egát*, Kpm., Tag. *igat*]

igéra: (Sp. *higuera*: fig tree) *n.* fig tree.

igét: *n.* strictness; sternness. **igtan.** *v.* to strictly follow; to compel to do, urge. **naiget.** *a.* strict, rigid; severe. [Tag. *sungit*, *higpít*]

iggám: *n.* hold; grasp; clasp. (*iggem*) **iggaman.** *v.* to hold in the hand, clutch. **pagiggaman.** *n.* handle; handhold. [Tag. *hawak*]

iggém: *var.* of *iggam*: grasp; clench; holding in the hands. **agiggem.** *v.* to grasp, clench, cling on to something. **sangkaiggem.** *n.* one grasp of, one handful of. **siiiggem.** *a.* holding, grasping. **No agig-iggemka kadagiti sabidong, liklikam ti mangan.** If you are handling poisons, refrain from eating. **Adda iggemmo dita?** *exp.* Do you have it there? Do you have it on you? Are you carrying any? [Ibg. *tammiten*, Ivt. *pundanan*, Kpm. *talnan*, Png. *benben*, *akóp*, Tag. *hawak* (grasp), *dakót* (handful)]

iggés: *n.* worm; caterpillar; larvae; anything resembling a worm. **agigges.** *v.* to breed worms. **inigges.** *a.* worm-infested. **Iggesen kuma 'ta ngiwatmo, salawasaw!** *exp.* may your mouth become worm infested, you gossiper! **igges-seda.** *v.* silkworm. [Ibg. *tuggiq*, Ivt. *uhed*, Kal. *tuwing*, Knk. *gége*, *kuwang*, *keáng*, Kpm. *úlad*, Png. *bigis*, *alombáyar*, Tag. *uod*, *bulati*]

ígid: *n.* edge, border, margin; limit, bound. **umigid.** *v.* to reach the shore; to defecate outside. **ipaigid.** *v.* to put aside; put to the side. **iti igid ti.** *prep.* beside; at the side of. **agpaigid.** *v.* to come to the shore; reach the side of; land; go to the side; pull over (car on the road). **akinigid.** nearest to the edge, shore, etc. **Dimo ipaigid ti awis ti babai.** Do not put aside the invitation of the girl. [Kal. *igid*, Knk. *iplí*, Png. *gilíg*, Tag. *gilid*]

ígid ti baybáy: *n.* beach (*aplaya*). [Ibg. *eggig nabbévay*, Ivt. *kanayan*, Kpm. *pampang*, Png. *gilig na baybay*, Tag. *dalampasígan*, *tabíng-dagat*]

ígis: **agigis.** *v.* to widen (smiles).

iglésia: (Sp. *iglesia*: church) *n.* church. (*simbaan*) **Iglesia ni Kristo.** Church of Christ. **anak ti santa iglesia.** (*fig.*) illegitimate child (*anak ti ruar*).

ígo: (Sp. *higo*: fig) *n. fig.* **igéra.** *n.* fig tree.

iguáles: (Sp. *igual*: equal) *n.* equal, the same (*pada*); even (*amanos*).

ígup: **sangkaigup.** *n.* one sip, one swallow. (*tilmon*; *arub-ub*; *lamdok*) **umigup, igupen.** *v.* to sip (liquids); to sip slippery substances: *suloy.* **igupan.** *n.* coconut shell dish. [Kal. *singgip*, *sisipon*, Png. *ilóp*, Tag. *higop*]

Igorót: *n.* name for the natives of the interior provinces of Luzon, especially Mountain Province and Benguet; the language of the *Igorot* people.

igút: **naigut.** *a.* thrifty, saving money. (*salimetmet*) **igutan.** *v.* to save (on expenditures), spend wisely. [Png. *igót*, Tag. *tipíd*]

ígpaw: **umigpaw.** *v.* to jump over (*lagto*). [Tag. *talón*]

igpíl: **igpilan.** *v.* to carry under the arm (*akili*). [Tag. *kipkíp*]

íha: (Sp. *hija*: daughter) *n.* daughter (used as an endearing term of address). (*anak*) **ihada.** (*obs.*) *n.* goddaughter.

ího: (Sp. *hijo*: son) *n.* son. (*anak*, *putot*) **ihong.** term of address for one's son.

ií: Interjection expressing wonder.

iíkit: Plural of *ikit*: aunts.

iíl: **umaniil.** *v.* to whimper. (*ibit*; *il-il*)

iípag: Plural of *ipag*: sisters-in-law.

iít: *n.* the central rib of the coco leaf, midrib used for the *kaykay* broom. **yiitan.** *v.* to remove the central rib from the leaf (for making brooms, etc.). [Tag. *tingtíng*]

iitlogán: (f. *itlog*) *n.* uterus of birds. (*rarasá*)

ika-: *pref.* (perfective *inka-*) used to form distributive or multiplicative verbs or volitional increase of dimension. **adu.** many. **ikaadu.** *v.* to make many. **atiddog.** long. **ikaatiddog.** *v.* to make something long. **Diyo met panggep aya nga ikalawa ken ikadakkel ti kapiliatayo?** Isn't it also your aim to make our chapel larger and more spacious? [Tag. *ika-* ordinal prefix]

íkab: **agikab.** *v.* to eat secretly. **ikaben.** *v.* to eat something secretly.

ikamén: *n.* mat (for sleeping on). **agikamen.** *v.* to sleep on a mat; use a mat. [Bon. *aplag*, Ibg. *dafen*, *dapán*, Ivt. *apin*, Kal. *obok*, Knk. *kamen*, *ápis*, Kpm. *dáse*, Png. *ikamén*, Tag. *baníg*]

ikán: *n.* fish. (*sidá*; *lames*) **mangikan.** *v.* to buy fish. **mangngikan.** *a.* fond of fish, frequently eating fish. **pangikanan.** *n.* fishing grounds. **ikan-tamnay.** *n.* freshwater fish. [Ibg. *sira*, Itg. *lames*, Ivt. *amung*, Knk. *ikán*, Kpm. *asan*, Png. *sirá*, Tag. *isdâ*]

ikapi(n)-: Prefix used with numeric roots to indicate how many times something is to be done. Perfective form is *inkapi(n)*-. **pito.** seven. **ikapimpito.** to do for a seventh time.

íkas: umikas. *v.* to fade; cease.

ikát: *n.* certain design in Ilocano weavings.

íkay: umikay. *v.* to go away; drift from; stay away from. **ikayan.** *v.* to avoid; veer away from. **Nagikayak iti kinaliday dagiti matana.** I turned away from the sadness of her eyes.

ikáy: *n.* displeasure, disgust, resentment. (*gura*)

ikdál: see *iddal*: with throat obstructed by something sharp.

íker: agiker. *v.* to become breathless (from a dry cough) (*kelkel*). [Tag. *ihít*]

íkes: agikes-ikes. *v.* to totter, stagger (*diwer*). [Tag. *suray, hapay, giray*]

ikét: *n.* net. **agiket.** *v.* to weave nets; (*spider*) make a web. **iniket.** *a.* netted. [Png. *ikét*, Tag. *lambát*]

ikgáy: *n.* egg yolk. (*nalabaga ti itlog*)

ik-ík: *n.* sound made by rats. **agik-ik.** *v.* to cry (said of rats).

íking: *n.* edge; edge of a cart. (*igid*) **ikingan.** *v.* to give an edge to, provide with edges. **yikingan.** *v.* to remove the edges. [Tag. *gilid*]

íkit: (plural *iikit*) *n.* aunt. (*tia*) **agikit.** *n.* niece and aunt. [Png. *nana*, Tag. *tiya* (Sp.)]

ikkán: *v.* to give; grant; place, put; respect; add to; confer; (*coll.*) to give what is due. **pa(n)gikkan.** *n.* container. **di ik-ikkan.** *v.* to belittle; degrade; not respect. [Png. *itér*, Tag. *bigáy*]

ikkát: ikkaten. *v.* to remove, take away; fire from a job. **ikkatan.** *v.* to take away from, lessen, diminish. **maikkat.** *v.* to be able to be removed; to be removed, taken away. **agikkat.** *v.* to quit; withdraw; resign. **paikkat.** *v.* to have something removed; fire from a job. **umikkat.** *v.* to move away from; quit. **agpaikkat.** (*fig.*) *v.* to have an abortion (*alis*). [Bon. *káan*, Ibg. *ari*, Tag. *alís*]

ikkís: agikkis, um(ik)kis. *v.* to scream, shout. (*riaw*) **ikkisan.** *v.* to shout at someone. [Ibg. *aggay, kallí*, Kal. *akikis*, Tag. *sigáw, hiyáw*]

iklóg: *reg. var.* of *itlog*: egg. [Ibg. *illug*, Kal. *ipÿug*, Kpm. *ébun*, Png. *iknól*, Bon., Tag. *itlóg*]

ikúb: *n.* a hutlike enclosure for freshly harvested rice; **iti ikub.** *prep.* inside; within. **ikuban.** *v.* to enclose with a fence (*alad*). [Tag. *bakod*]

ikonoklásta: (Sp. *iconoclasta*: iconoclast) *n.* iconoclast, person opposed to worshipping holy images.

ikúran: *n.* a kind of white freshwater fish.

ikút: *n.* possession, ownership. **ikutan.** *v.* to possess; own (*kua, kupikop*); hold; take care of, guard. **agikut.** *v.* to own; possess. **paikutan.** *v.* to surrender; entrust; let oneself be possessed.

Timmaud iti ikut daytoy a balay. He was raised in this house. **panagikut iti paltog.** *n.* gun possession. [Tag. *arì*]

ikráw: (*obs.*) *n.* subdued weeping.

ikráy: maikrayan. *v.* to be ravaged, devastated, laid to waste. (*kerraay*)

íla: *n.* first word of a lullaby; loneliness; nostalgia. **ilaen.** *v.* to gather together; summon together. **mail-ila.** *v.* to be lonely; long for; be nostalgic. **Simgiab ti ila iti barukongna.** The loneliness flared up in his chest. [Tag. *lumbáy*]

ílad: *a.* prostrate, supine; stretched. **agilad.** *v.* to rub the body against something or someone; to lie on the floor while rubbing. **yilad.** *v.* to cause a garment to rub against the floor. [Tag. *hilatà*]

iláil: see *iliil*: swaying the hips while walking.

ilalá: ilala pay, kailala pay. What a shame! It's a pity! **kailalaan.** *v.* to appreciate, value, esteem; use with care. **mailalaan.** *v.* to regret, feel sorry for. **panangilala.** *n.* loving care. **ilalaen.** *v.* to value; appreciate. [Tag. *sayang*]

ílang: *ilang-ilang.* *n.* a tree with fragrant flowers.

ílap: (*reg.*) *n.* slice. (*iwa, galip*) **ilapan.** *v.* to cut a slice from something. **ilapen.** *v.* to slice. **sangkailap.** *n.* a slice. [Tag. *hiwà*]

ílas: *n.* crawling, slithering, dragging movement, walking along on the body. **agilas.** *v.* to crawl, slither. [Png. *ilás*]

ílek: *n.* a kind of large spotted marine fish with tasty meat, rudder fish, *Kyphosus sp.*

ílem: *n.* jealousy, suspicion; timidity. (*imon*; *apas*) **umilem.** *v.* to be shy, timid. **nakaiilem.** *a.* suspicious. **agilem.** *v.* to be jealous; suspicious. **nailem.** *a.* jealous; suspicious. **managilem.** *a.* prone to suspicion or jealousy. **umilem.** *v.* to be suspicious, jealous; shy, timid. **panagilem.** *n.* suspicion, jealousy; envy. **Agilemak kenka ta agparikutak ita.** I am envious of you because I am troubled now. [Tag. *panibughô*]

ilét: *n.* tightness; narrowness. **nailet.** *a.* tight; narrow; difficult. (*irút*) **umilet.** *v.* to become tight. **paileten.** *v.* to tighten; make narrow. **Immilet ti barukongna.** *exp.* He could hardly breathe. [Bon. *silet*, Knk. *ipét*, Png. *ipét*, Tag. *sikíp*]

iletrádo: (Sp. *iletrado*: illiterate) *a.* illiterate; uncultured; ignorant.

ilgát: ilgatén. *v.* to slice. (*iwa*; *irap*; *galip*) **sangkailgat.** *n.* one slice.

íli: *n.* town; municipality. **pagilian.** *n.* country, native land. **kapagilian.** *n.* countryman. **sangapagilian.** *n.* one country; one community. **sangkailian.** *n.* the whole town, the whole country; *a.* nationwide. **umili.** *n.* citizens, residents of a particular place; inhabitants; *v.* to live in town; go to town. **mangili.** *v.* to visit another town. **kailian.** *n.* town mate, of the same town. **agkailian.** *v.* to be from the same town. **inilin-ili.** *n.* every town; town to town. **agpaili.** *v.* to go to town. **ipaili.** *v.* to take something to town. **sangaili.** *n.* foreigner, stranger; menses. **agsangaili.** *v.* to have a guest; menstruate. **managsangaili.** *a.* hospitable. **kinamanagsangaili.** *n.* hospitality. **agpasangaili.** *v.* to have oneself treated as a guest. **pakipagilian.** *n.* town where one intends to live. **makipagili.** *n.* citizen. **pannakipagilin.** *n.* citizenship. **nailian a sabong.** *n.* national flower. **pumaili.** *v.* to go to town. [Kal. *ili*, Knk. *íli*, *táon*, *babéy*, Png. *báley*, Tag. *báyan*]

ilíil: umiliil. *v.* to sway the hips while walking. (*kinnikinni*); to be slothful. [Tag. *kendéng*]

il-íl: see *iil*: whimper, demanding affection or attention.

íliw: *n.* homesickness, nostalgia. (*ila*) **mailiw.** *v.* to be homesick, long for something. **managiliw.** *a.* longing for a loved one. **iliwen.** *v.* to enjoy being with a long-absent person. **il-iliwen.** *n.* fondest wish. **umiliw.** *v.* to visit a person who is missed. **kailiw.** *n.* person who is missed. **aginniliw.** *v.* to renew the bonds of love or friendship. **Mailiwak kenka.** *exp.* I miss you. **Kinulding ti iliw iti pannakalagipna kadagiti dadakkelna.** He felt nostalgia upon remembering his parents. **Kayatko nga umayka iti kabiitan a panawen tapno makapaginniliwta.** I want you to come as soon as possible so we can be with each other again (after a long absence). [Kal. *umayu*, Png. *ilíw*, Tag. *sabík*]

illá: agilla, illaen. *v.* to pull logs (or trees) by use of a water buffalo.

illáw: *var.* of *ulláw*: kite.

illín: *var.* of *allin*.

illón: (*obs.*) fashioning something.

illós: *var.* of *ilos*: crawl, crawl on the buttocks.

ílo: ilo, pagilo. *n.* toilet paper, something used to wipe the anus after defecating. **agilo.** *v.* to wipe the anus after defecation. **iloan.** *v.* to wipe (a child's) anus after defecation. **pailuan.** *v.* to have the anus (of a baby) wiped after defecation. [Bon. *angílo*, Tag. *iwang*]

ílog: *n.* saltwater creek; river (*waig*; *karayan*). [Tag. *ilog* = river]

Ilokándia: *n.* the Ilocos provinces, region in the Philippines where Ilocano is spoken natively.

Ilokanísta: (Sp. *ilocanista*) *n.* specialist in the Ilocano language.

Ilokáno: (Sp. *ilocano*) *n.* a native of the Ilocos region (fem: *Ilokana*); the language of the Ilocos region, the lingua franca of northern Luzon. **ag-Ilokano.** *v.* to speak Ilocano. (*samtoy*) **y-Ilokano.** *v.* to translate into Ilocano.

Ilóko: (Sp. *iloco*) *n.* Native of the *Kailokuan*; the provinces of Ilocos Norte, Ilocos Sur, and La Union; the language of the Ilocano people (Ilokano). **sailoko.** *a.* of Iloko origin. **Kailokuan.** *n.* the region of the Ilocano people. **yiloko.** *v.* to translate into Ilocano. (*samtoy*)

ilón: ilon-ilon. *n.* variety of awned late rice.

Ilónggo: *n.* Visayan ethnic group from the islands of Panay and Negros; the Visayan language of the *Ilonggo* people, (also called *Hiligaynon*.)

Ilónggot: *n.* mountain tribe from Nueva Vizcaya.

Ilóngot: *n.* ethnic group from the provinces of Nueva Vizcaya and Quirino, also called *Bugkalot*. Dialects of Ilongot include *Abaka*, *Egongot*, *Ibalao*, *Italon*, and *Iyongut*.

ílus: *a.* lame; crippled. (*pilay*) **agilus.** *v.* to crawl on the buttocks (like a baby).

ílut: *n.* massage. **mangngilut.** *n.* one who massages; midwife; bone setter. **iluten.** *v.* to massage; rub; knead. **ipailut.** *v.* to have someone give a massage; to have somebody rub something; (*fig.*) to have an abortion. **yalut.** *v.* to rub something on. [Kal. *uleÿ*, *bya-ug*, Png. *ilót*, Tag. *hilot*]

ilpuét: (*obs.*) *a.* covering an entire field (locusts).

-im-: *var.* of the infix *-imm-* before consonants, when a root vowel is dropped. The vowel is usually but not always an 'e,' and it frequently is deleted before underlying geminate consonants: **sim**rek. entered, from root *serrek*. **kim**raang. dried, from root *kerraang*. **lim**teg. swelled, from root *letteg*.

im-: *var.* of *in-* before labial consonants (p and b). **imbaga** (*in-* + *baga*). said. **impan** (*in-* + *pan*). brought to.

íma: *n.* hand; arm; sleeve. **imaen.** *v.* to hit. **imaan.** *v.* to attach sleeves to. **ima-ima.** *a.* empty-handed (*pauy*); unarmed. **paima.** *v.* to hand over. **surat-ima.** *a.* handwritten. **Atiddog ti imana.** He is a thief (*lit*: has a long arm). **Saanmo a kadakkelen ti imam no awatem ti mabatayam.** Don't enlarge your hands when you receive your share. [Ibg. *limá*, Ivt. *tanuruq*, Kal. *ima*, Knk. *ledeng*, Kpm. *gámat*, Png. *limá*, Tag. *kamáy*]

imá: maima. *v.* to be thwarted, foiled; to miscarry. (*paay*)

imáhen: (Sp. *imagen*: image) *n.* image (*ladawan*). [Tag. *larawan*]

imáid: agimaid. *v.* to be neat; take care of one's belongings.

imáig: naimaig. *a.* elegant, graceful.

imáim: umimaim. *v.* to be timid, shy. (*bain*) **naimaim.** *a.* timid; shy; bashful; demure. [Tag. *kimî*]

imáno: imanuén. *v.* to recognize (*lasin*); see carefully.

ímar: naimar. *a.* clear (music, sounds, etc.).

ímas: *n.* deliciousness; flavor; delight; goodness; pleasure. **naimas.** *a.* tasty, delicious; pleasing; satisfying (sleep, etc.); pleasurable. **imasen.** *v.* to enjoy, relish. **maimasan.** *v.* to enjoy, take delight in; be enjoyable. **agimas.** *v.* to reach orgasm. **kaimásen.** *v.* to make something tasty, delightful, pleasant. **ti imasna.** the good thing about it. **umimas.** *v.* to become delicious, pleasant. **tagiimasen.** *v.* to enjoy, take delight in. **Nagimasen a buya inton agkikitakami.** It will be a nice sight when we see each other. **Napukawen ti iimasanna a mangan.** He lost his appetite. [Ibg. *singngóq*, Ivt. *asdep*, Kal. *piya*, Knk. *mam-is*, *sídek*, *engáy*, Kpm. *manyáman*, Png. *nanám*, Tag. *saráp*]

imátang: *n.* attention; mind; notice; point of view, opinion; observation. **imatangan.** *v.* to bear in mind; consider; heed; regard; notice; observe. **iti imatang.** *prep.* in the presence of; in view of; in the opinion of. **panangimatang.** *n.* way of seeing things. **manangimatang.** *a.* observant. **Sairokayo amin iti imatangko.** You are all devils in my opinion. [Tag. *paningín*]

imatón: imatonan. *v.* to care for; attend to, guard, watch over, manage. **umimaton.** *n.* overseer. **panagimaton.** *n.* way a person performs his job; way one manages. **mangimaton.** *n.* manager; caretaker; overseer. **iti imaton ti.** *prep.* under the care of; under the administration or management of. [Tag. *bahalà*]

imbág: *n.* goodness; good. **naimbag.** *a.* good, kind; respectable; skillful; enjoyable; proper; helpful; healthy. **umimbag.** *v.* to become good, healthy. **kaimbagán.** *a.* best. **paimbagén.** *v.* to make well; heal. **naimbagán.** *a.* cured; made well. **agimbag.** *v.* to be lucky; successful; fortunate. **pagimbagán.** *n.* benefit; advantage; improvement; good; well-being. **utang a naimbag a nakem.** debt of gratitude. **Naimbag a gasatmo.** Good luck to you. **Naimbag a bigat.** Good morning. **nadaras a yiimbag.** *n.* speedy recovery. [Note the stress shift following the closed syllable. Kpm. *kayapan*, Png. *maóng*, *ábig*, Tag. *butì*]

imbálido: (Sp. *inválido*: invalid) *a.* invalid.

imbárgo: (Sp. *embargo*: seizure) *n.* seizure, confiscation. **imbarguen.** *v.* to seize, confiscate.

imbáyon: *n.* slingshot. (*palsiit*)

imbénto: (Sp. *invento*: invention) *n.* invention. (*parsua*) **imbentor.** *n.* inventor. **imbension.** *n.* invention.

imberná(r): maimberna. *a.* to be delayed, stop a while (*taktak*); to dock (ship).

imbérso: (Sp. *inverso*) *n.*, *a.* inverse.

imbertebrádo: (Sp. *invertebrado*) *n.*, *a.* invertebrate, with no backbone or internal skeleton.

imbés: (Sp. *en vez de*: instead) *prep.* instead of (*ketdi*). **Isu ti maanupan imbes nga isu ti aganup.** He was the one hunted instead of the hunter.

imbestidúra: (Sp. *investidura*: investiture) *n.* investiture; act of installing into an office.

imbestíga: (Sp. *investiga*: investigate) **imbestigaan.** *v.* to investigate. **imbestigasion.** *n.* investigation. **imbestigador.** *n.* investigator.

imbihília: (Sp. *vigilia*: vigil) **maimbihilia.** *a.* given funeral rites. **mangimbihilia.** *v.* to give funeral rites.

imbisíble: (Sp. *invisible*: invisible) *a.* invisible.

imbisibilidád: (Sp. *invisibilidad*: invisibility) *n.* invisibility.

imbíta, imbitár: (Sp. *invitar*: invite) **imbitaran.** *v.* to invite. (*kumbida*) **imbitasion.** *n.* invitation. **imbitado.** *a.* invited. [Tag. *anyaya*]

imbúdo: (Sp. *embudo*: funnel) *n.* funnel (*sarangusong*). [Tag. *balisongsóng, imbudo*]

imbúko: *n.* a boys' game of knocking down sticks driven into the ground by beating them with a piece of wood. **agimbuko.** *v.* to play *imbuko*.

imbúlsa: (Sp. (*re*)*embolso*: reimbursement) *n.* reimbursement.

imbornál: *n.* water passage; sewer; aqueduct; manhole; culvert; scupper hole.

imdáng: *var.* of *imdéng*.

imdéng: see *indeng*: heed, pay attention to; listen to. (*pangag*) **Adda kararagko a rumbeng met a maimdengan.** I have a prayer that also should be heeded. [Tag. *pakinggán*]

ímeng: *n.* sweater. **naimeng.** *a.* safe, snug, cozy. **agimeng.** *v.* to wear a sweater. **pagimeng.** *n.* sweater.

imét: *n.* load; burden. **sangkaimet.** *n.* one load (to be carried). **imeten.** *v.* to carry. (*awit*) **pagimet.** *n.* something used for carrying a load. [Tag. *dalá*]

imigránte: (Sp. *inmigrante*: immigrant) *n.* immigrant. **imigrasión.** *n.* immigration.

im-ím: (*obs.*) *n.* forgetting without concern. **imiman.** *v.* to forget. (*lipat*)

im-ima: im-imaen. *v.* to thwart. **maim-ima.** *v.* to be thwarted.

imímit: **kaimimitan** (*obs.*) *n.* friendly acquaintance.

im-immoko: (*lit.*) *n.* a bolo-like shell from an edible mollusk.

íming: *n.* beard (*barbas*); whiskers; moustache (*bigote*). **agiming**. *v.* to grow a beard. **agimiming**. *v.* to shave. **imingan**. *a.* bearded. [Bon. *ógem*, Kal. *iming*, Tag. *balbás* (Sp.)]

imíray: **im-imiray**. (*obs.*) *a.* unexpectedly showing signs of life.

ímis: **naimis**. *a.* affected; squeamish; fastidious; delicate; overnice. **agimis**. *v.* to be choosy (usually applied to food) (*napili*; *kusim*). [Tag. *selang*]

imitasión: (Sp. *imitación*: imitation) *n.* imitation. (*tulad*) **imitador**. *n.* imitator.

imló: (*obs.*) *n.* nice trimming.

imlóy: **imluyan**. *v.* to take good care of; treasure something.

-imm₁-: *infix.* Perfective form of the infix *-um-*. It is used before the first vowel of the root. **Tumakder**. He stands up. **Timmakder**. He stood up. **Umayakto**. I will come. **Immayak**. I came. [Knk. *-in(u)m-*, Png. *-inm-* Tag. *-um-*]

-imm₂-: *infix.* adjectivalizing resemblance infix used before the first vowel of the root denoting a characteristic quality, i.e., shape, appearance, size, aptitudes, etc. **timmigre**. like a tiger, i.e., ferocious. **gimmayaman**. like a centipede. **dimmagum a bulong**. needlelike leaves. **Impakitana ti pimmusa nga isemna**. She showed her catlike smile.

-imm- -an: Affix forming perfective nominalizations of *-um-* verbs. May indicate the attainment of a state: **lukmeg**. fat. **limmukmegan**. state of having fattened up, the act of having gained weight. **baknang**. rich. **bimmaknangan**. state of having achieved much wealth; having gotten rich. **Adu ti kimmuttongan ken limmakayan ti ulitegna, ngannganin diak nabigbig**. Her uncle has aged and lost a lot of weight, I almost did not recognize him. **Ditoy ti dimmakkelanna**. Here is where he grew up.

immaradú: *n.* spotted guitar fish, *Rhynchobatus djiddensis.*

immík: *n.* bleating of goats of sheep. **agimmik**. *v.* to bleat.

immús: **agim-immus**. *v.* to taper (become gradually more slender at the end). **nagimmus**. *a.* tapered at the end.

imnás: *n.* muse; pleasure; delight; elegance. **naimnas**. *a.* handsome, elegant; graceful; sweet; pleasurable.

imnét: **naimnet**. *a.* solid, strong, firm. (*amnut*) **umimnet**. *v.* to become firm, solidify.

ímno: (Sp. *himno*: hymn) *n.* hymn; anthem.

imnós: (*obs.*) *n.* prompt conclusion.

imó: **kaimuan**. *n.* acquaintance.

ímud: *n.* talisman; charm (*anting-anting*; *galing*). [Tag. *antíng-antíng*]

ímog: *n.* bait for June bugs.

imukó: *n.* knife; dagger. **im-immuko**. *n.* a kind of long, edible mollusk. **imokuan**. *v.* to sharpen (pencils, knives, etc.). [Knk. *gípan*, Tag. *patalím*]

ímul: *a.* having a very small tail; *n.* tail end of rhizomes.

ímon: *n.* jealousy, envy (about matters of the heart, as opposed to *apal*, which concerns material goods). **naimon**. *a.* jealous, envious. **pagimunan**. *v.* to be jealous of. **managimon**. *a.* envious; jealous. (*apal*; *ilem*) **Adda imon a rimmusing iti kaungganna**. Jealously sprouted inside him. [Png. *guyaét*, *damág*, *ébeg*, Tag. *inggít*, *bughô*]

imón: *n.* a variety of rice with large white kernel.

imúnan: (Png., see *imon*) *n.* courtship dance from San Jacinto, Pangasinan, depicting a love triangle.

ímor: **naimor**. *v.* to be on fire, to burn; be combustible. (*segged*; *puor*)

imoralidád: (Sp. *inmoralidad*: immorality) *n.* immorality; wrongdoing. **imoral**. *a.* immoral.

imortalidád: (Sp. *inmortalidad*: immortality) *n.* immortality. **imortal**. *a.* immortal.

ímus: *var.* of *imul*: tail end of rhizomes.

ímut: **agimut**. *v.* to be stingy. **naimut**. *a.* stingy, tight with money. (*kirmet*) **iimutan**. *n.* the groove at the back of the neck. **yimut**. *v.* to be selfish with something, not share with others. **yimut ti kabaelan**. *exp.* to perform less than one's abilities. [Png., Tag. *kuripot*, Tag. *damot*]

impa-: Perfective form of *ipa-*: **Impakitanak iti ladawanna**. He showed me his picture. **Impa-Bauangda**. They brought it to Bauang.

impá: **naimpa**. *a.* ended, over with.

impaka-: Perfective form of *ipaka-* prefix. **Impakaammok kadagiti dadakkelko ti panagtayabko**. I let my parents know about my flight.

impákto: *n.* evil spook, ghost.

impalibilidád: (Sp. *infalibilidad*: infallibility) *n.* infallibility.

impami-: Perfective form of *ipami-* verbs indicating how many times an action was done. **Impamitlomi ti lumagto**. We jumped for a third time.

impánte: (Sp. *infante*: infant) *n.* infant. (*ubing*)

impantería: (Sp. *infantería*: infantry) *n.* infantry, soldiers who fight on foot. (*buyot*)

impardóble: (Sp. *imperdible*: safety pin) *var.* of *perdible*: safety pin.

impáte: (Sp. *empate*) *n*. tie, draw in a game. (*tabla*)

impátso: (Sp. *empacho*: indigestion) *n*. stomach-ache due to overeating; indigestion. (*lisay*; *sakit ti tian*) maimpatso. *v*. to suffer a stomachache; to have indigestion. impatsado. *a*. suffering from indigestion.

impeksión: (Sp. *infección*: infection) *n*. infection. impektado. *a*. infected.

impén: im-impén. *n*. grudge, ill will harbored against someone. im-impenen. *v*. to bear a grudge, have ill feelings toward. Bulbulseken-naka laeng ti naimpen nga imon ken luksaw iti barukongmo. The jealousy and disgust you bear in your chest is blinding you

imperdíble: *var*. of *perdible*: safety pin.

império: (Sp. *imperio*: empire) *n*. empire. (*pagarian*).

impermeáble: (Sp.) *a*. waterproof.

impernál: (Sp. *infernal*) *a*. infernal.

impiérno: (Sp. *infierno*: hell) *n*. hell.

impinidád: (Sp. *infinidad*) *n*. infinity.

impinitibo: (Sp. *infinitivo*) *n*. infinitive.

impirmária: (Sp. *enfermería*: infirmary) *n*. infirmary, place where the sick are taken care of.

implasión: (Sp. *inflación*: inflation) *n*. inflation.

implikádo: (Sp. *implicado*) *a*. implicated.

impluénsia: (Sp. *influencia*) *n*. influence. impluente. *a*. influential.

impuél: (*obs*.) *a*. secretive; patient.

impulsíbo: (Sp. *impulsivo*) *a*. impulsive.

impúlso: (Sp.) *n*. impulse.

impormalidád: (Sp. *informalidad*: informality) *n*. informality.

impormánte: (Sp. *informante*: informant) *n*. informant.

impormár: (Sp. *informar*) impormaran. *v*. to inform someone (*ipakaammo*). maimporma-ran. *v*. to be informed.

impormasión: (Sp. *información*: information) *n*. information. (*damdamag*)

impórme: (Sp. *informe*) *n*. account; report.

imporsár: (Sp. *forzar*, Eng. *enforce*) maimporsar. *v*. to be enforced.

importánsia: (Sp. *importancia*) *n*. importance.

importánte: (Sp. *importante*) *a*. important. (*ngruna*)

importasión: (Sp. *importación*) *n*. importation.

importunadór: (Sp.) *n*. importuner, peeve.

imposibilidád: (Sp.) *n*. impossibility.

imposíble: (Sp.) *a*. impossible.

impoténsia: (Sp.) *n*. impotency.

impoténte: (Sp.) *a*. impotent.

impraestruktura: (Sp. *infraestructura*) *n*. infra-structure.

imprénta: (Sp. *imprenta*: printing) *n*. printing press; printing shop. naimprenta. *a*. printed; *v*. to be imprinted.

imprudénte: (Sp. *imprudente*: imprudent) *a*. imprudent.

imtúod: *var*. of *intuod*: ask; inquire.

in-: *pref*. Perfective form of the prefix *i*- Iyawidmo ti pansit. Take home the *pansit*. Inyawidna ti pinakbet. He took home the *pinakbet*. Inruarna ti basura. He took out the garbage.

in- -an: *circumfix*. Perfective form of benefactive *i*- *-an* verbs. Indaitannak iti badok. She sewed a dress for me.

-in-: *infix*. 1. Perfective infix of *-en* and *-an* verbs and many complex verbs with these endings: With *-en* verbs, *-in-* is infixed before the first vowel of the root, and the *-en* suffix drops. buyaen. to watch something. binuya. watched something; With *-an* verbs, the *-in-* is infixed before the first vowel of the root, but the *-an* suffix is *not* dropped. suratamto. You will write somebody. sinuratamon. You already wrote (a person); 2. With numeric roots, *-in-* indicates by how many (+ specified quantity) something is done or divided. rinibu. by the thousand. ginasut. by the hundred. 3. with agents of infestation, the infix *–in-* may indicate negative effect: inigges. eaten by worms, worm infested. kinarominas. stung by jellyfish. binao. infested with rats, eaten by rats. 4. May indicate habitualness: inaldaw. every day. tinawen. every year. 5. With CV reduplication, may indicate plurality: dinadakes nga ugali. evil ways. kinikillo a linteg. crooked laws. [This infix was also originally used for *-um-* verbs but it has fused with the *-um-* infix in the following way for the perfective form: *-*inum*- > *-*inm*- > -*imm*-]

-in- -an: Perfective form of *-an* verbs. Nabayag a minulenglengannak. She looked at me with a blank face for a long time.

-CinV-: *infix*. indicates a characteristic quality. inuubing. childish, like a child. ginagaram-pang. frivolous; unchaste, like a *garampáng*. Pasig nga inaangaw ti sasawem. What you are saying is pure jest (not serious).

in: *v*. to go (*mapán*), with the enclitic pronoun *-ak*, the *n* geminates: innakon I'm already going. Inkan! Go now!

ína: (*obs*.) *n*. decreasing in quantity.

iná: *n*. mother; a female one generation older than the speaker. pannakaina. *n*. person acting as one's mother. agina. *n*. mother and child. agkaina. *v*. to have the same mother. ina ti bunyag. *n*. godmother. panginaen. *n*. stepmother; woman leader; aunt. **kaina**. *a*. of the same mother, but having different fathers. **sangkainaan**. *n*. mother and children. **umina**. *v*. to take after one's mother; favor one's mother. [Kal. *ila*, Png., Knk., Tag. *iná*, Ivt. *inaq*]

ínad: **nainad**. *a*. slow; taking a long time to do something.

** inaín**: *n*. flour from the *silag* palm.

inaká: **nakain-inaka**. *a*. pitiful; serious; dangerous; delicate. **kainaka**. *v*. to dislike; hate; detest. **aginaka**. *v*. to start to grow tired of one's companion.

inakbáy: **aginakbay**. *v*. to spread, diffuse (odors; popularity) (*anikbay*). **Agin-inakbay ti naangdod a pay-odna**. His reeking scent diffused. [Tag. *halimuyák*]

inaládan: (f. *alad*) *n*. anything surrounded by a fence.

ínam: **inamen**. *a*. well deserved. **makipaginam**. *v*. to become used to something. **mapainaman**. *a*. pleased, delighted. **inamen**. *v*. to receive a due penalty. **kainaman**. *v*. to become fond of. **uminam**. *v*. to become used to; to accustom oneself to. [Tag. *hirati* (accustomed)]

inaná: *n*. rest. **aginana**. *v*. to rest (sleep). **paginanaen**. *v*. to allow to rest; retire. **mainanaan**. *v*. to be rested, comfortable. **Dimmagaskami a naginana biit**. We dropped by to rest a while. [Ivt. *nahah*, *wayam*, Knk. *ingángay*, Png. *ináwa*, Tag. *pahingá*]

inanák: (f. *anak*) *n*. offspring.

inanáma: *n*. hope; confidence, trust. (*namnama*) **inanamaen**. *v*. to hope for. **manginanama**. *v*. to hope; rely on; trust. **nakainanama**. *a*. hopeful; trustworthy; confident. **pangnamnamaan**. *a*. reliable; trustworthy. [Png. *ilálo*, Tag. *pagasa*]

ínang: *n*. term of address for one's mother, or a motherly figure (*nanang*). [Tag. *ináy*]

inaúdi: (f. *údi*) *n*. youngest child. (*burídek*) **inaudian**. *n*. youngest child. [Ivt. *dekkey*, Tag. *bunsô*]

inauná: *n*. firstborn child. **inaunaan**. *n*. firstborn child. **Inauna ngem siak iti nasurok a dua a tawen**. He is older than me by over two years. [Kal. *panguÿu*, Knk. *beság*, Png. *panguloan*, Tag. *panganay*]

ínap: *n*. doubt; suspicion. (*átap*) **aginap**. *v*. to suspect; doubt. **managinap**. *a*. suspicious; doubtful; doubting. [Tag. *hinalà*]

ináp: **inapen**. *v*. to make into layers. (*apít*) **sangkainap**. *n*. one layer.

inapóy: (f. *apóy*) *n*. cooked rice.

ínar: **kainaran**. *n*. scorching heat of the sun. **agkainaran**. *v*. to stay under the hot sun.

ikainaran. *v*. to put out under the sun to dry (*bilag*). **mainaran**. *v*. to be scorched by the heat of the sun. **Ngimmisiten gapu iti kanayon a kaaddana iti kainaran**. He got dark because he is always under the hot sun.

inasár: (f. *asar*) *n*. roasted pig, *letson*.

ínat: **aginat**. *v*. to stretch oneself (as when waking up). [Tag. *unat*]

ínaw: *n*. the appetite of a pregnant woman. **aginaw**. *v*. to suffer the syndrome of pregnant women. **paginawan**. *n*. the object of desire a pregnant woman craves for. **mainaw**. *v*. to be conceived; created; conceptualized. **inawen**. *v*. to conceive; visualize; conceptualize; conceive (a child). **panaginaw**. *n*. conception. **Idi madlawko nga inawek daytoy anakko, nagbaban ti salun-atko**. When I was aware that I conceived this child, my health failed. **Inton aginaw, pasigto a napintas a ipakitak ken ipakanko tapno napintasto ti anakmi**. When I'm pregnant, I only eat and show nice things so our child will be beautiful. [Kal. *bosway*, Tag. *lihí*]

inawgurasión: (Sp. *inauguración*: inauguration) *n*. inauguration.

ináyad: **nainayad**. *a*. slow; careful; gentle. **inayaden**. *v*. to do slowly. **aginayad**. *v*. to move slowly; slow down. **In-inayadna nga inrikep ken imbalunet ti ridaw**. He slowly and carefully closed and barred the door. [Tag. *dahan-dahan*]

indág: **agindag**. *n*. overseer, supervisor, inspector, foreman. **indagan**. *v*. to oversee; mind; pay attention to.

indáng: *var*. of *indag*: oversee; inspect; mind.

indás: **indasen**. *v*. to conclude, finish.

indáyog: *var*. of *indayon*.

indáyon: *n*. hammock; cradle; swing. (*talabong*; *anduyan*) **agindayon**. *v*. to swing. **indayunen**. *v*. to rock somebody in a hammock or cradle. **immindayon a bulan**. crescent moon. [Png. *andóyan*, Itg. *dáyug*, Ibg., Ivt., Tag. *duyan*]

indég: **agindeg**. *v*. to stay long; *var*. of *indag*. **pagindegan**. *n*. place of residence. **dagiti agindeg**. *n*. the inhabitants. **makipagindeg**. *v*. to reside with others. [Tag. *tirá*]

indéng: **indengan**. *v*. to heed; listen attentively to. (*pangag*; *imdeng*)

independiénte: (Sp. *independiente*: independent) *a*. independent. (*wayawaya*) **independensia**. *n*. independence.

indéreng: *a*. erect; standing; straight. **agindereng**. *v*. to stand erect for the first time (babies).

indiák: *part.* Negative particle of the first person singular: I don't want to; I refuse. **Indiak ammo.** I don't know.

indibidualísta: (Sp. *individualista*: individualist) *n.* individualist, one who lives his life for himself.

indienéro: (*coll.*) *n.* someone who backs out of promises.

índio: *n.* Indian; term applied to native Filipinos under Spanish occupation.

indiperénsia: (Sp. *indiferencia*: indifference) *n.* indifference. **indiperente.** *a.* indifferent.

indíreg: *var.* of *indereng*.

índise: (Sp. *índice*: index) *n.* index.

indisénte: (Sp. *indecente*: indecent) *a.* indecent.

induksión: (Sp. *inducción*) *n.* induction; installation.

indulhénsia: (Sp. *indulgencia*: indulgence) *n.* indulgence, remission of punishment for a forgiven sin. **indulhente.** *a.* indulgent.

indúlto: (Sp. *indulto*: pardon) *n.* pardon; amnesty. **naindultuan.** *a.* pardoned.

indonár: *var.* of *donár*: donate.

Indonés: (Sp. *indonés*: Indonesian; fem: *Indonesa*) *n*, *a.* Indonesian.

indúrog: **agindurog.** *v.* to whirl; reach the top; reach the height of.

indós: **agindos.** *v.* to amble (horses); walk like a woman (with affect).

indústria: (Sp. *industria*: industry) *n.* industry.

indúyas: *n.* slope (*bakras*; *ansad*; *arisadsad*); slant. **naginduyas.** *a.* sloping.

inéng: *n.* term of address given by elders to a young girl. [Tag. *nene*]

inép: *n.* dream; ambition. **inpen.** *v.* to intend; have in mind; bear a grudge. **im-impen.** *n.* dreams; grudge; ambition. [See also *tagainep* and *impén*. Tag. *pangarap*]

inheniéro: (Sp. *ingeniero*: engineer) *n.* engineer. **inhenieria.** *n.* engineering.

inhénio: (Sp. *ingenio*: ingenuity) *n.* ingenuity; inventive faculty. **inhenioso.** *a.* ingenious.

inhustísia: (Sp. *injusticia*: injustice) *n.* injustice.

inhústo: (Sp. *injusto*: unjust) *n.* unjust.

iníin₁: **aginiin.** *v.* to waddle; wiggle. **iniinen.** *v.* to shake a container so the contents will settle. **Sinimpana ti agin-iniin a lampara.** He fixed the waddling lamp.

iníin₂: *n.* a kind of brownish flour made from the pith of the *silag* palm, used in native rice cakes.

inípis: *var.* of *nipis*: playing cards.

inisiál: (Sp. *inicial*: initial) *n.* initial.

inisiatíba: (Sp. *iniciativa*: initiative) *n.* initiative.

ínit: *n.* sun. **nainit.** *a.* sunny. **aginit.** *v.* to shine (said of the sun). **mainitan.** *v.* to be exposed to the sun. **agkainitan.** *v.* to sunbathe; stay under

the sun. **ipainit.** *v.* to put under the sun. [Bon. *algew*, Ibg. *bilág*, *mata*, Ifg. *algo*, Kal. *ilit*, Knk. *sugit*, *agew*, Png. *ágew*, *bánwa*, Kpm. *aldo*, Ivt., Tag. *araw*; Tag. *init* = hot]

inka-: Perfective form of *ika-* **Inkaubinganna ti panagayatna kenkuana.** He loved her from the time he was very young.

inkapin-: Perfective form of *ikapi(n)-* prefix taking numeric roots and indicating how many times an action was done. **Inkapimpatna ti agadal.** He studied four times.

inkatár: (Sp. *inquietar*: restless, disturb) **mainkatar.** *v.* to be restless, uneasy; to worry.

inkíwar: (f. *kiwar*) *n.* a type of rice pudding.

inkubadóra: (Sp. *incubadora*) *n.* incubator.

-inn-: Infix of reciprocity or rivalry. It is used with other affixes (actor or goal focus) and placed before the first vowel of the stem. **Naglinnimedda.** They hid from one another. **Agsinnuratda.** They write one another. **pinnintas.** beauty competition **Ammokon ti aramidenta tapno dita agbinnain.** Now I know what we should do so we won't be ashamed of ourselves.

inn: *var.* of the irregular verb *in*, used before the first person singular enclitic *-ak*. **innak.** I am going. **inka.** you go.

inná: *pl.* of *iná*: *n.* mothers.

innádaw: *n.* a children's finger game.

ínnak: *v.* [*in + -ak*] *v.* I'm going. (*mapanak*)

innapóy: (f. *apoy*) *n.* cooked rice. **in-innapoy.** *n.* depression in the cheek. [Bon. *makan*, Ibg. *inafi*, Ifg. *hinamal*, Ivt. *inapuy*, Kal. *isla*, Knk. *ingsád*, Kpm. *násiq*, Png. *nilutu*, Tag. *kanin*]

innát: *var.* of *unnát*: stretch; sprawl.

innáw: *n.* dishwater, rinsing water. **aginnaw.** *v.* to do the dishes; rinse plates. **paginnáwan.** *n.* dishwasher (machine). **parainnaw.** *n.* person responsible for doing the dishes. [Ibg. *magúgaq*, *mabeggay*, *mabbebbel*, Ivt. *manuyas*, Kpm. *wásan*, Png. *uras*, Tag. *hugas*]

inném: *num.* six; with certain prefixes, *innem* shortens to *-nem*: **maikaném.** sixth. **sagneném.** six each. **pagkaném.** one-sixth. [Bon. *enem*, Kal. *olom*, Png. *aném*, Tag. *anim*]

innípis: *n.* playing cards; deck of cards. **aginnipis.** *v.* to play cards. [Tag. *baraha* (Sp.)]

innó: see *silno*; dialectal variant of *ania*: what.

innúrog: **aginnúrog.** *v.* to spin (tops). (*indurog*, *tayyek*)

inúdo: **aginudo.** *v.* to warm oneself by the fire. **paginuduan.** *n.* bonfire.

inodóro: (Sp. *inodoro*: toilet) *n.* toilet. (*kasilias*)

inúgot: **mainugot.** *v.* to conform with (*alubog*; *annugot*). [Tag. *ayon*]

inúm: *n*. drink. **uminum**. *v*. to drink. **inumen**. *n*. to drink a beverage. **inuman**. *v*. to drink from (a glass). **aginum**. *v*. to drink (alcohol). **mangnginum**. *n*. alcoholic, habitual drinker. (*artek*) **inninuman**. *n*. drinking spree. **ipainum**. *v*. to feed (liquids); make someone drink. **nakainum**. *a*. drunk. **makiinum**. *v*. to ask for a drink. **paginumán**. *n*. drinking vessel; source of water. **pagpápainumán**. *n*. drinking trough. [Bon. *inom*, *saldok*, Ivt., Kpm. *minum*, Kal. *ilum*, Png. *lagók*, Ibg., Png., Tag. *inóm*]

inóng: *n*. colloquial term of address given by elders to a young boy (*anong*). [Tag. *totoy*]

inorgániko: (Sp. *inorgánico*) *a*. inorganic.

inosénte: (Sp. *inocente*: innocent) *a*. innocent. **inosensia**. *n*. innocence.

ínut: *a*. thrifty, economic. (*salimetmet*) **agininut**. *v*. to be thrifty. **in-inuten**. *v*. to do at intervals, to do (or eat) a little at a time. **in-inutan a bayadan**. *v*. to pay by installments. **inut-inut**. *adv*. gradually; little by little; step-by-step. **nainut**. *a*. thrifty, economical. **makainut**. *v*. to be able to do a little at a time. **In-inut a pimmanglawda**. They gradually got poorer. **Madanagan iti in-inut a pannakarba ti nabaneg a pammagina**. He is worrying about the gradual decay of his stocky body. **Ti bassit nga bassit, mangin-inut**. Little by little will soon be too much. [Png., Tag. *inót*, Tag. *untí-untí*]

inútil: (Sp. *inútil*: useless) *a*. useless; infertile; impotent.

insán: *n*. cousin (see also *kapin-*). (*kasinsin*) **aginsan**. *v*. to be cousins. [Tag. *pinsán*]

insarabásab: (f. *sarabasab*) *n*. broiled meat.

inseguridád: (Sp.) *n*. insecurity.

insékto: (Sp. *insecto*: insect) *n*. insect. **insektisidio**. *n*. insecticide.

insénso: (Sp. *incienso*: incense) *n*. incense. **insensario**. *n*. censer; container in which incense is burned.

insentíbo: (Sp. *incentivo*: incentive) *n*. incentive.

insiár: **insiaren**. *v*. to memorize; train; rehearse; accustom. **nainsiar**. *a*. trained; rehearsed; accustomed.

insidénte: (Sp. *incidente*: incident) *n*. incident. (*pasamak*)

insiénso: (Sp. *incienso*) *n*. incense.

insigída: (Sp. *en seguida*: immediately) *adv*. right away, immediately. (*apagdarikmat*; *sigud*)

insignár: (Sp. *enseñar*: teach, *asignar*: assign) **mainsignaran**. *a*. assigned.

Insík: *n*. *a*. Chinese (*sanglay*); (*fig.*) someone cunning in business. **ag-Insik**. *v*. to speak the Chinese language. **ka-Insikan**. *n*. Chinatown; Chinese neighborhood.

insineradór: (Sp.) *n*. incinerator.

insubordinasión: (Sp. *insubordinación*: insubordination) *n*. insubordination.

insulár: (Sp. *insular*: insular) *a*. insular, having to do with islands. **gobierno insular**. national government (term used by the Spanish for the colonial Philippine government).

insúlto: (Sp. *insulto*: insult) *n*. insult.

insómnia: (Eng.) *n*. insomnia, inability to sleep. (*puyat*)

insupisiénte: (Sp. *insuficiente*: insufficient) *a*. insufficient.

insureksión: (Sp. *insurección*: insurrection) *n*. insurrection; revolt; rebellion.

insurékto: (Sp. *insurrecto*: insurgent) *n*. insurgent.

insurhénsia: (Sp. *insurgencia*: insurgency) *n*. insurgency.

inspirádo: (Sp. *inspirado*: inspired) *a*. inspired. **inspirasion**. *n*. inspiration.

instalasión: (Sp. *instalación*: installation) *n*. installation; act of being installed.

instánsia: (Sp. *instancia*: instance) *n*. instance.

instigadór: (Sp. *instigador*) *n*. instigator.

instínto: (Sp. *instinto*: instinct) *n*. instinct.

institusión: (Sp. *institución*: institution) *n*. institution.

institúto: (Sp. *instituto*: institute) *n*. institute; place of education.

instruktór: (Sp. *instructor*: instructor) *n*. instructor, teacher.

instruménto: (Sp. *instrumento*: instrument) *n*. instrument.

intaér: *n*. sediments, settlings. (*ared-ed*; *rinsaed*; *lissaad*; *basabas*; *aribudabud*; *lued*) **agintaer**. *v*. to settle.

intán: *n*. variety of hard rice; *v*. let's go (dual form).

intár: *n*. row; line file. (*batug*; *aray*) **agintar**. *v*. to stand in a row. **intaren**. *v*. to place in a row; to arrange in a series, file. **yintar**. *v*. to arrange in rows or lines. [Tag. *hanay*]

intayón: (f. *in*) Let's go (inclusive). [Png. *tíla la*, Tag. *tayo na*]

integrál: (Sp. *integral*: integral) *n*. integral; whole, complete.

integrasión: (Sp. *integración*: integration) *n*. integration.

integridád: (Sp. *integridad*: integrity) *n*. integrity.

inték: **agintek**. *v*. to stay, remain, reside; persist. **Nagkaradap dagiti bibigna iti pingpingko sa naginтек kadagiti bibigko**. Her lips crawled on my cheeks and then remained on mine. **Inyintekna dagiti nalennek a matana kaniak**. She kept her deep-set eyes on me.

intelihénsia: (Sp. *inteligencia*: intelligence) *n.* intelligence. (*laing, sirib*) **intelihente**. *a.* intelligent.

intensión: (Sp. *intención*: intention) *n.* intention. (*panggep, gagara*) **intensional**. *a.* intentional, on purpose.

intér: see *intaer*: sediments; settlings.

interés: (Sp. *interés*: interest) *n.* interest. (fond of: *anep*, money: *anak*)

interesádo: (Sp. *interesado*: interested) *a.* interested, enthusiastic.

interíno: (Sp. *interino*: pro tempore, for the time being; provisional, temporary) *n.* temporary appointee; acting chief.

interesánte: (Sp. *interesante*: interesting) *a.* interesting.

interiór: (Sp.) *a.* interior; *n.* inner part of a building; remote place; inner tube.

intermédia: (Sp. *intermedia*: intermediate) *n.* intermediate (school).

intérno: (Sp. *interno*: intern) *n.* intern; boarding student.

interupsión: (Sp. *interrupción*: interruption) *n.* interruption.

intérprete: (Sp. *intérprete*: interpreter) *n.* interpreter. (*mangyulog*) **interpretasion**. *n.* interpretation.

intimidasión: (Sp. *intimidación*: intimidation) *n.* intimidation.

intó: *adv.* indicating future time. **into la ketdi no.** lest. **into ngarud no.** if. **uray inton kaano man.** *adv.* never.

intuisión: (Sp. *intuición*: intuition) *n.* intuition.

intoksikasión: (Sp. *intoxicación*: intoxication) *n.* intoxication. (*panagbartek*)

intoleráble: (Sp. *intolerable*: intolerable) *a.* intolerable.

intoleránte: (Sp. *intolerante*: intolerant) *a.* intolerant.

intón: *var.* of *intono*.

inton-anó: When? At what time? How soon? **Inton-ano ti panagawidtayo?** When are we going home? **uray inton-ano.** *adv.* never. **Uray inton-ano diakto asawaen diay baket.** I will never marry that old woman.

intóno: *conj.* indicates the future: when, if. **uray inton kaano man.** Never. **intono kuan.** then; sometime in the future. **intono kien.** never.

intón(o) bigát: *adv.* tomorrow. [Bon. *wákas*, Ivt. *amyan*, Png. *nabuás*, Tag. *bukas*]

intonár: (Sp. *entonar*: tune) **intonaren**. *v.* to tune into; focus on, pay close attention to; concentrate.

intúod: **intuoden**. *v.* to ask; inquire about, question. (*imtuod, damag; saludsod*) **managintuod**. *a.* inquisitive, always asking questions.

Idi agrubuatda a mapan sumarungkar, inintuod ti kaanakanna no ania ti sagut a kayatna. When they were preparing to go visit, his nephew asked what present he wants. [Tag. *tanóng*]

intóy: short for *sadino ditoy*: where (in this place).

intríga: (Sp. *intriga*: intrigue) *n.* intrigue.

intrigánte: (Sp.) *n.* intriguer.

intrimís: (Sp. *entremeter*: meddle) **intrimisen**. *v.* to meddle. (*biang*)

intrimitído: (Sp. *entremetido*: meddlesome) *a.* meddlesome; inquisitive; curious.

iny-: Variant of the prefix *in-* before vowels. **Inyawidna ti adobo.** He took home the *adobo*.

inyóg: *n.* coconut, variant of *niog*.

ing-: *var.* of *in-* before velar consonants: (*k, g* and *ng*).

ingá: (pl. *ingngá*) *n.* woman friend (of a woman); best friend. **nainga**. *a.* friendly. (*gayyem*)

íngab: **ing-ingab**. *n.* very remote place; mountain cave.

íngar: **umingar**. *v.* to growl; get angry; to face, stand up to, defy; rise to the emergency; to break out again (illnesses). **naingar**. *a.* extravagant in dress; mad; rebellious, defiant. [Tag. *suwaíl* (defiant)]

íngas: **agkaingas**. *v.* to resemble someone in features. **umingas**. *v.* to take after (in looks). **kaing-ingas**. *a.* resembling; similar to. **panagkaingas**. *n.* resemblance, similarity in features. **Adda pagkaingasanda ken ni tatangko.** They look a bit like my father. [Tag. *hawig*]

ingát: *n.* toothpick. **agingat**. *v.* to pick the teeth. **ingatan**. *v.* to insert between the teeth or between any opening. **maingatan**. *v.* to be removed by a toothpick. [Png. *ingát*, Tag. *pantingá*]

íngel: *n.* strength; strength of liquor. **maingel**. *a.* brave, courageous. **naingel**. *a.* strong (alcohol, tobacco, etc.). **umingel**. *v.* to age (liquor); to become narcotic. **kinamaingel**. *n.* bravery; courage; heroism. **kamainglan**. *a.* bravest; most courageous. **Makababaengak iti ingel.** I feel like sneezing from the strong smell of alcohol. [Tag. *tapang*]

ingép: **ingpen**. *v.* to imagine; daydream (*inep*). [Tag. *hagap*]

ingét: **nainget**. *a.* strict, severe, firm; determined. (*iget*) **ingetan**. *v.* to discipline; strictly enforce. [Tag. *higpít*]

inggá: *n.* end, ending; conclusion, termination (*gibus*); *prep.* **ingga't, inggana't, aginggana't, agginggana't.** until; *conj.* until, since. **ingaan.** *n.* boundary; limit; *v.* to end; stop. **ingga ti.** *var.* of *aginggana ti*: until. **awan inggana.** *a.*

eternal; infinite. **umingga.** *v.* to stop; cease.
pagingaan. *n.* finish line; end of the road.
inggat-inggana. *adv.* forever. **Saan nga ining-**
gaan dagiti agama ti panagaywanda iti daga.
The father and son did not stop taking care of
the land. [Tag. *katapusan*]

inggána: *prep.* until. **inggana't inggana.** *exp.*
until the very end. **Tinarabaynak a magna**
inggana iti ridaw. He guided me (walking) to
the door. [Tag. *hanggáng*]

inggarília: *var.* of *angarilia*: handbarrow
basket.

inggét: *adv.* used to form absolute superlatives of
adjectives: extremely; absolutely. **ti ingget**
dalus a balay. the very clean house.

Ingglatéra: (Sp. *Inglaterra*: England) *n.*
England.

Inglés: (Sp. *inglés*: English) *n.* Englishman;
English language. **ag-Inggles.** *v.* to speak
English. **maka-Inggles.** *v.* to be able to speak
English.

inggréso: (Sp. *ingreso*: ingress, admission) *n.*
receipts; income; ledger entry; part of a breadwinner's salary given to the spouse.

ing-íng: *n.* violin. **aging-ing.** *v.* to play the violin.
ing-ingen. *v.* to cut in a seesaw movement; play
on the violin.

ingkilíno: (Sp. *inquilino*: tenant) *n.* tenant.
(*abang*)

ingkompléto: (Sp. *incompleto*: incomplete) *a.*
incomplete.

inkompórme: *var.* of *komporme*: in conformity
with; whatever.

ingkorporádo: (Sp. *incorporado*: incorporated)
a. incorporated.

ingngá: plural of *inga*: woman friends.

ingúngot: ingunguten. *v.* to love dearly. **kai-**
ngungot. *n.* sweetheart. **agkaingungot.** *v.* to be
sweethearts, lovers. [Tag. *mahál*]

ingpís₁: naingpis. *a.* thin (inanimate objects).
ingpisen. *v.* to thin out; to cut thin; make thin.
Naingpis ti kudilna. He is sensitive (*lit*: has
thin skin). **Naingpis ta lapayagmo.** *exp.*
ridiculing someone who has had excessive sex.
[Ibg. *neppiq*, Ivt. *mataripis*, Kal. *manyapit*,
Knk. *yápit*, Kpm., Png. *ímpis*, Tag. *manipís*]

ingpís₂: maingpis. *n.* a kind of marine mollusk
with a very thin shell.

ingráto: (Sp. *ingrato*: ungrateful) *a.* ungrateful,
thankless; *n.* ungrateful person, ingrate.

ingréso: (Sp. *ingreso*: ingress, entrance) *n.*
income; receipts; part of a husband's salary
given to the wife. (*inggreso*)

ingsáy: ingsayan. *v.* to thin.

ingsét: agingset. *v.* to dry, dry up; settle to the
bottom. (*bessag*)

ipa-: *pref.* Causative applicative verbal prefix
of theme focus construction; perfective form
impa-. **kita.** see. **ipakita.** show to someone.
ipa-Manila. to bring something to Manila.
Kunada a naim-imbag no ipa-Manilami.
They say that it would be better if we brought
it to Manila.

ipaanó: ipapaano. *v.* to mind.

ípag: (pl. *iipag*) *n.* sister-in-law. **ipagen.** *v.* to be
a prospective sister-in-law. [Knk. *aydó*, Png.
ípag, Tag. *hipag*]

ipáip: umaipaip. *v.* to approach; prowl around (a
thief).

ipaka-: Causative affix used with certain verbs.
Perfective form is *impaka-* **ipakaammo.** to tell,
let someone know **Umaykonto ipakaammo ti**
damag. I will come let (you) know the news.
Ipakaasikton kenkuana ti pannakidagusmi
ken ni Inang idiay balayna. I will ask him that
Inang and I pass by her house.

ipami-: prefix used with numerical stems to
indicate the number of times an action is done;
perfective form is *impami-*. **tallo.** three.
ipamitlo. to do a third time.

ipapaanó: see *uray*.

ipás: makaipas. *a.* sharp, able to wound. **naipas.**
a. wounded. **ipasen.** *v.* to wound somebody.
(*dunor*)

ipdók: maipdukan. *v.* to choke. **Kasla nai-**
pdukan ni papang iti sinao ti lakay. Father
seemed to choke from what the old man said.
[Tag. *hirin*]

ipdúok: *var.* of *ipdok*: choke.

ípel: *n.* sacrum bone.

ípeng: umipeng. *v.* to take refuge, shelter. (*ka-*
mang)

ípes: *n.* cockroach. **inipes.** *a.* infested with
cockroaches. [Bon. *tamiing*, Ibg. *kími*, Ifg.
balaingan, Ivt. *ipes*, Kal. *langgangan*, Knk.
sipyuk, takí, Kpm. *ípas*, Png. *asípet*, Tag. *ipis*]

ípig: ipigen. *v.* to hold; put the arm around
someone. **agipig.** *v.* to do side by side (two
people). **umipig.** *v.* to stay close; cling to
closely.

ípil: *n.* a kind of tree used for its timber, *Intsia*
bijuga.

ipin-: verbal prefix, see *pi-*.

ípit: *n.* claw, pincer (of crabs, lobsters, etc.); vice;
monkey trap. **ipiten.** *v.* to pinch; claw. **maipit.**
v. to be pinched; to be clawed. **umipit.** *v.* to
claw; pinch. **paipit.** *n.* carpenter's vice;
bamboo trap for catching monkeys; clamp.
Also: **sipit.** *n.* tongs. **sigpit.** *n.* hair clip. **sirpit.**
n. clip. [Png. *angkop*, Tag. *sipit*]

iplóg: *var.* of *itlóg*: egg. [Ibg. *illug*, Kal. *ipyug*,
Kpm. *ébun*, Png. *iknól*, Bon., Tag. *itlóg*]

ípog: inipog, naipog. *a.* worm-eaten.

ipókrita: (Sp. *hipócrita:* hypocrite) *n.* hypocrite. **kinaipokrito.** *n.* hypocrisy.

ípol: see *sípol:* cut from the bottom; do from the beginning.

ípon: *n.* a kind of fish used in *boggoong,* less than one inch in length. **agipon.** *v.* to catch the *ipon* fish. **inip-ipon.** *a.* with indigo stripes (cloth). **inipon.** *n.* variety of rice. [Tag. *ginamos; hipon* = shrimp]

ipupúsay: (f. *púsay*) *n.* passing death.

ípor: see *imor:* set on fire.

ípus: *n.* tail (of animal, of letters, etc.); postscript; end. **ipusan.** *a.* with a large tail; also: tailless; *v.* to conclude, come to the end of; *n.* kind of freshwater fish with a large tail. **ipusan.** *v.* to add a tail to; to end, finish; a kind of fish with a long tail; the *labtang* vine. **ipusen.** *v.* to hold by the tail; ask recommendation from an important person; (*ip-ipusen*) to lag behind. **mangipus-ipus.** *v.* to follow the pleas of parents. **umipus.** *v.* to follow after. **umip-ipus.** *v.* to tail; lag behind. (*arus*) **maraipus.** *n.* the *labtang* vine. **nakabaag ti ipusna.** *exp.* with the tail between one's legs (cowards). **ipus ti pagi, ipus ti pusa.** *n.* kinds of orchids. **paraipus.** *n.* trainbearer. **Ip-ipusen ti aso ti kabalio.** The dog is trailing behind the horse. [Ibg. *ifuq,* Ifg. *íwit,* Ivt. *ipus,* Knk. *íko,* Kpm. *íkiq,* Png. *ikól,* Tag. *buntót*]

ippél: yippel. *v.* to insert in an opening.

ipriák: naipriakan. *a.* dry; parched (*maga; na-atian*). [Tag. *tuyô*]

iráir: *n.* whispering sound of leaves in a soft wind; crying of hogs or babies; aspirations; sentiments. **agirair.** *v.* to make this sound; murmur; cry (hogs or babies), let out one's feelings.

írang: *n.* rampart, sentry box; outpost. **agirang.** *v.* to rest on the *dalagan* bamboo bed; sit on the branches of a tree.

írap₁: *var.* of *sirap:* dazzle.

írap₂: irapen. *v.* to cut; slice. (*ilgat; iwa*) **sangkairap.** *n.* one slice. [Tag. *hiwà*]

íras: agir-iras. *v.* to plow rows. (before planting)

irasionál: (Sp. *irracional:* irrational) *a.* irrational.

íray: *n.* row (of plants); *a.* inclining; leaning. **agiray.** *v.* to align plants; to bend down, lean, bend; align with, lean toward a particular group or political party. **yiray.** *v.* to lean something, make something slant. **pagirayan.** *n.* preference. **Adda kano pulong kadakuada nga agir-irayka kadagiti kabusor ti turay.** There supposedly is information from them that you are leaning toward the enemies of the government. [Png. *ísarál,* Tag. *hilig, hapay*]

Iráya: *n.* ethnic group of northern Mindoro, the language of the Iraya people.

irbás: *var.* of *arbas:* trim, prune.

íren: *n.* wrinkle in the skin. **agiren.** *v.* to wrinkle; furrow. [Tag. *kulubót*]

iresponsáble: (Sp. *irresponsable:* irresponsible) *a.* irresponsible.

íri: agiri. *v.* to scream very loud, shriller than *ikkis.* **Ti tao nga iri nga iri, saona't di-mapati.** No one believes the words of a noisy man. [Tag. *tilî*]

iriág: agiriag. *v.* to shout. (*pukkaw, riaw*)

iriák: *var.* of *iriag.*

iridiíd: iridiiden. *v.* to squeeze, crush, or pulverize in a circular pressing manner (such as a mill).

írig: agirig. *v.* to lean, bend (trees, plants); to throw oneself down to rest. **yirig.** *v.* to bend something; to lean something. [Png. *sarál,* Tag. *hilig, hapay*]

irigasión: (Sp. *irrigación:* irrigation) *n.* irrigation.

iriíd: iriiden. *v.* to squeeze, crush; mill; pulverize.

irík: *n.* unhusked rice. (*palay*) **irik-iriken.** *v.* to trample; thrash. (*payat; sadak*) **iriken.** *v.* to thresh (rice). **pagirik.** *n.* thresher. [Kal. *paguy,* Png. *ilík, pagéy,* Tag. *giík*]

iríng: see *ariring:* differ slightly; be similar.

ir-ír₁: *a.* insensitive to hunger; **agir-ir (ti bisin).** *v.* to be weak for lack of nourishment.

ir-ír₂: *a.* dry; decorticated; withered. **pair-iran.** *v.* to put out to dry (tobacco).

ir-ír₃: *n.* dirt, filth. (*rugit*) **nair-ir.** *a.* dirty, filthy. **Umir-ir ti ngisitna a sumileng.** Her dirty dark complexion shines.

íris: *n.* green stool of babies. **agiris.** *v.* to defecate green stool.

Irlánda: (Sp. *Irlanda:* Ireland) *n.* Ireland. **Irlandés.** *n. a.* Irish; fem: *Irlandesa.*

irnáad: umirnaad. *v.* to decrease, become less. (*kissay*) **irnaaden.** *v.* to decrease something. **Nagirnaad ti sardam.** The evening came to an end.

íro: *n.* soot. [Itg. *pálat,* Ivt. *aliw,* Knk. *págit, ágiw,* Kpm. *ágiq,* Png. *suul,* Tag. *ágiw*]

írub: iruban. *v.* to roast immature rice. **ini-ruban.** *n.* roasted immature rice. [Kal. *chuum*]

írud: irudan. *v.* to trim the edges of; round off corners. **nairudan.** (*obs.*) *n.* oval. [Tag. *bilóg*]

irók: *n.* doubt. **ir-iruken.** *v.* to bear a grudge; be aware of, worried by something wrong, have a feeling. **mairok.** *v.* to be left as a trace, an aftertaste. **mairuk-irok.** *v.* to be reluctant; fearful to do wrong. **iruken.** *v.* to have bad feelings toward someone; harbor a grudge.

Apay kuma a dida bay-an dagiti tao a mangipeksa kadagiti ir-irukenda. Why don't they let the people voice out their grievances? **íron₁: irunen.** *v.* to draw back; fold. *(karenken)* **íron₂: agiron.** *v.* to crowd; throng. *(aribungbong)* **ironía:** (Sp. *ironía:* irony) *n.* irony. **irút: nairut.** *a.* tight *(ilet);* tense; stretched. **iruten.** *v.* to tighten; stretch. **irutan.** *v.* to press; to urge. **nairut a barukong.** *n.* tense feelings. **Gapu iti nairut a panaggagayyemtayo ket aramidenmi.** Because of our close friendship, we will do it. **Nairut ti turog ti tagibida iti dagidagi.** The sleep of their maid on the hammock was tense. [Png. *málet,* Tag. *sikíp*] **irúy:** *n.* a variety of awned *diket* rice. **irténg:** *n.* tension; stretching. **nairteng.** *a.* stretched; tense; strained. **irtengen.** *v.* to stretch; strain. **Nakair-irteng pay laeng ti panesna.** *exp.* to be still in mourning. [Knk. *ipét,* Tag. *igtíng*] **ísa:** (Sp. *izar:* hoist, haul up) **isaen.** *v.* to hoist the flag; raise the flag. **maisa.** *v.* to be hoisted, raised. **isá: inisa.** *n.* a kind of thin cloth. **is-isa.** *n.* the *Scoparia dulcis* plant. **ísar: agisar.** *v.* to fray; become unwoven; run (fabrics). [Tag. *gahî*] **isbáng₁: isbangan.** *v.* to plan, devise, scheme ahead *(balabala).* [Tag. *balak*] **isbáng₂: kaisbang.** *n.* look alike, one similar in features. **kaisbangna ti ugsa.** She looks like a deer. **isbó:** *n.* urine. **agisbo.** *v.* to wet one's bed. **makais-isbo.** *v.* to be on the verge of urination; feel like urinating. **umisbo.** *v.* to urinate. **iisbuan.** *n. Meatus urinarus,* urethra. **isbuan.** *v.* to urinate on something. **pagisbuan.** *n.* urinal; bedpan *(arenola).* **yisbo.** *v.* to urinate out. **Arin-isbuenak.** I feel like urinating. **Nakangatngato ti isbona.** His urine is rather high (said of an ill-mannered person). [Bon. *isbo,* Ibg. *píseg,* Ivt. *peteg* (of men), *upis* (of women), Kal. *isbu,* Knk. *ibsú, isbú,* Kpm. *imiq,* Png. *sírit,* Tag. *ihî*] **isék:** *n.* a kind of early rice. **isél: islen.** *v.* to wring. **ísem:** *n.* smile. **naisem.** *a.* always smiling. **umisem.** *v.* to smile; *(coll.)* urinate (said of women). **aginnisem.** *v.* to smile at each other. **isman.** *v.* to smile at someone. **siiisem.** *adv.* smiling. **makais-isem.** *a.* about to smile. **Napaisem iti pannakalagipna iti dayta.** She smiled upon remembering that. **No rigat ti iseman, agbalinto a liwliwan.** If it is at hardship that one smiles, it will become one's consolation. **Kasla agis-isem a kasapuego.** He

is like a smiling match (said of a person with an insincere smile). **isem ti adipen.** *n.* obsequious smile. [Bon. *bíngil,* Kal. *maimis,* Png. *ímis,* Tag. *ngitî*] **ísen:** *n.* grin, broad smile. **isiág: umsiag.** *v.* to shout; scream. **isiagen.** *v.* to shout at; yell at someone. [Tag. *sigáw*] **isiák: umsiak.** *v.* to burst out laughing *(paggaak; katawa).* [Tag. *tawa*] **isíis: yisiis.** *v.* to stabilize, steady. **agisiis.** *n.* the movement of a wriggling person; *v.* to constantly shift in one's seat. **isiisen.** *v.* to sift flour. **ísin: umisin.** *v.* to move, shift out of the way. **maisin.** *a.* movable. **isinen.** *v.* to move something. **Isináy:** *n.* ethnic group from the southern portion of *Magat* Valley in Nueva Vizcaya; the central Cordilleran language of the Isinay people. **isíng:** *(obs.)* *n.* a small piece of wood. **ísip:** *n.* mind, intellect; intelligence. *(utek; panunot; nakem)* **isipen.** *v.* to consider, think about; reflect; contemplate. **maisip.** *v.* to comprehend; be able to think. **naisip.** *a.* intelligent; understanding. [Png., Tag. *isip*] **is-ís:** (Pil.) **is-isen.** *v.* to rub clean. **is-íso:** (f. *iso*) *n.* stone used to scrub the skin while bathing. **is-isú:** *pron.* Reduplicated form of *isu.* Only he, only she. **ísit: isiten.** *v.* to tickle or tease someone (by touching the buttocks); *(fig.)* to provoke. **iská:** *n.* coconut fibers; palm fiber (used as kindling when starting a fire). **iskíl: naiskil.** *a.* rigid, unyielding, firm *(sikkil).* [Tag. *tigás*] **iskiníta:** (Sp. *esquinita:* street corner) *n.* street corner turning into an alley, narrow passage. **iskuála:** *var.* of *eskuala:* carpenter's square. **ísla:** (Sp. *isla:* island) *n.* island. *(púro)* **isláan: naislaanan.** *a.* having too much work, overburdened; occupied. **islaanan.** *v.* to pay attention to, mind. **islóte:** (Sp.) *n.* barren islet. **ismágel:** *n.* slippers, thongs. *(tsinelas)* **naka-ismagel.** *a.* wearing slippers. **ismágler:** (Eng.) *n.* smuggler. **ismáy:** *(obs.)* *n.* brass; copper *(gambáng);* alchemy. **isnáb:** (Eng.) *n.* snob. *(suplado)* **isnabero.** *a.* snobbish; *a.* snob. **Isnág:** *n.* ethnic group from northern Apayao, Luzon; the Ibanagic language of the Isnag people with the following dialects: *Ayag, Dibagat-Kabugao, Calanasan, Karagawan (Daragawan), Talifugu-Ripang (Tawini).*

Isnég: *n.* ethnic group from Abra, the Ilocano term for the *Tinguian* people and language from *Tineg*, Abra.

íso: *n.* stone used to scrub the skin. **nagiso.** to wipe, scrub oneself. **is-isoan.** *v.* to wipe; remove body dirt by rubbing with the *iso* stone. [Kal. *igud*, Tag. *hilod*]

isú: *pron.* Third person singular independent pronoun: He, she, it. **apagisu.** *a.* just enough; just right. **agin-iisu.** *a.* conceited; arrogant; overbearing. **isu met laeng.** the same. **isunan.** It's enough now. **isuna laeng ta.** *conj.* it's just that. **isu ti gapona.** therefore. **is-isu.** Only he, only she. **isuda.** they. **kakaisuna.** only, just one. **isu amin.** all. **aginiisu.** *v.* to be presumptuous, self-confident. **umisu.** *a.* reasonable, appropriate, convenient; enough, sufficient; right; exact. **kaisuan.** *n.* identity; correctness; reasonableness. **isu nga.** so (in that case). **isu laeng no.** unless. **Kalleppas manen ti arbis isu a mariknam latta ti kinadam-eg ti aglawlaw.** The drizzle has just ended so you can feel the moistness around. **Inkarik a tulonganka isu a bay-annak kuma.** I promised to help you so you should just let me. **Ay-ayatennaka, isuna laeng ta saan a makapagpudno ta kanayonmo kano met nga apaen.** He loves you, it's just that he cannot admit it because you supposedly always fight with him. [Knk. *siá*, Png. *sikató*, Bon., Tag. *siyá*]

isúda: *pron.* Third person plural of the *siak* pronoun series: They. [Knk. *daidá*, Png. *sikará*, Tag. *silá*]

isúna: independent pronoun, spoken variant of *isu*: he, she. [Png. *sikató*, Tag. *siyá*]

isópo: (Sp. *hisopo*: hyssop; aspergill, sprinkler) *n.* aspergill.

ispá: **maispaan.** *v.* to be satiated; satisfied. (*pennek*)

ispál₁: **ispalen.** *v.* to defend; guard; protect; save; rescue. (*salakan*) **maispal.** *v.* to be rescued; saved; guarded.

ispál₂: *var.* of *ispel*: choke on food.

ispániko: (Sp. *hispánico*) *a.* Hispanic.

ispél: **maispelan.** *v.* to choke on something stuck in the throat; have the throat blocked. [Tag. *hirin*]

ispía: (Sp. *espía*: spy) *n.* spy. (*tiktik*)

issék: (*obs.*) *n.* scattering.

issiág: **umsiag.** *v.* to shout; scream. (*riaw, pukkaw*)

issiák: **umsiak.** *v.* to sprint, burst out.

issiáy: Interjection expressing disgust and wonder.

istádo: (Sp. *estado*: state) **maistaduan.** *a.* married and settled, spoken for.

istaltópe: *interj.* expressing mild reproach and disbelief.

istambáy: (Eng. stand by) *n.* stand by, person who idles around and does nothing. (*ballog*) **agistambay.** *v.* to spend time idly in one place.

istampóko: *a.* sure of oneself.

istapíd: **agistapid.** *v.* to stop (talking). (*sardeng*)

istáy: *a.* nearly, almost. (*dandani, nganngani*) **nagistayán.** *a.* almost. **Nagistayánnakon kinagat.** It almost bit me. [Notice stress shift after the preceding closed syllable. Tag. *halos*]

isténg: (*slang*) *a.* drunk. (*bartek*)

istibís: *n.* annoyance, disturbance. **istibisen.** *v.* to meddle in someone's business. (*biang*) **Saanmo a pagis-istibisan.** Don't meddle in that (it is none of your business).

istík: (*coll.*, Eng. stick) *n.* cigarette. (*sigarilio*)

istórbo: (Sp. *disturbo*: disturb) *n.* annoyance; disturbance; hindrance. (*buribor*)

istória: (Sp. *historia*: story) *n.* story. (*sarita*) **agistoria.** *v.* to tell a story. **istoriaen.** *v.* to narrate to someone, tell a story to. **istoriador.** *n.* historian; storyteller.

istríkto: (Sp. *estricto*: strict) **naistrikto.** *a.* strict. (*igét*)

itá: *adv.* now, at this moment; this; oblique of *dayta*: that (near hearer). **itatta.** right now. **itanto.** *adv.* in a moment. **ita ta.** *conj.* whereas; since; while. [Bon. *wáni*, Ibg. *sangáw*, Kal. *sala* (now), *salaoy* (just now), *salan egew* (today), Knk. *ganígan*, Png. *nátan*, Tag. *ngayón*]

itág: (*reg.*) *n.* pork preserved in lard and stored in a bamboo tube.

Itália: (Sp. *Italia*: Italy) *n.* Italy.

Italiáno: (Sp. *italiano*: Italian) *n.* Italian person; Italian language; *a.* Italian. **ag-Italiano.** *v.* to speak Italian.

itáliko: (Sp. *itálico*) *a.* italic.

ítang: *n.* a kind of fern, *Asplenium phyllitidis*.

itáng: *n.* a term of address given to a father by his children. [Tag. *itáy*]

itattá: *adv.* right now, at this very moment, see *ita*. **itatta ta.** *conj.* whereas (absolute present).

ittatáy: *adv.* marks the immediate past: just a short while ago, just a moment ago. *conj.* when (immediate past). [Kal. *geled*]

Itáwit: *n.* ethnic group living in southern Cagayan; the Ibanagic language of the Itawis people with the following dialects: *Malaweg, Itawis.*

itáy: *adv.* a short while ago, a little while ago; implies the near past, as opposed to *idi,* which implies the remote past. **itattay.** *adv.* just a moment ago.

itdál: *var.* of *iddal*: obstruction in the throat.

itdén: *v.* [*ited* + *-en*] to give to.

itéd: *v.* to give, grant. Takes the *-ko* pronouns. **mangted, itden.** *v.* to give to. **paited.** *v.* to give through somebody else. **pangitedan.** *n.* the receiver. **pakaitedan.** *n.* person to whom something is given. **pannakaited.** *n.* manner of giving. [Ibg. *yáwaq,* Ivt. *tumuruh,* Kpm. *ibye,* Png. *itér,* Tag. *bigáy*]

iték: *n.* a kind of early rice that needs little water.

ití: *prep.* the oblique of the article *ti; prep.* with regard to, concerning; *conj.* because of, due to.

ítib: *n.* whitlow, panaris. (*basil*)

itíit: **umitiit.** *v.* to force one's way through a crowd. **agitiit.** *v.* to creak shrilly. **itiitan.** *n.* a break in the crowd; space where one can pass through. **awan ti itiitan.** *a.* overcrowded; overloaded; overflowing. [Tag. *siksík*]

ítik: *n.* a kind of freshwater duck. **ítik-itik.** *n.* native dance that resembles the movements of the duck. [Knk. *pepá,* Png., Tag. *itik*]

itinerário: (Sp. *itinerario*: itinerary) *n.* itinerary.

it-ít₁: *n.* a tree with large leaves.

it-ít₂: **agit-it.** *v.* to cry (said of rats, snakes, etc.); chirp.

itlóg: *n.* egg. **agitlog.** *v.* to lay an egg. **kait-itlog.** *n.* fresh egg. (*apagitlog*) **iitlogan.** *n.* uterus of birds. **itlog ti lalaki.** *n.* sperm. (*kissit*) **pagitlogán.** *n.* nest. **pagitlogén.** *v.* to keep hens for egg laying. **mangngitlog.** *n.* egg thief; egg-laying hen. **immitlog.** *a.* resembling an egg, oval. **Immitlog ti tabas ti rupana.** He has an oval-shaped face. [Note stress shift with suffixes despite the preceding closed syllable; in certain dialects, this stress shift does not take place. Ibg. *illug,* Kal. *ipÿug,* Kpm. *ébun,* Png. *iknól,* Bon., Tag. *itlóg*]

itmó: (*obs.*) *n.* coincidence.

Itnég: (f. *Tineg,* place in Abra) *n.* a native of the provinces of Abra and Kalinga-Apayao; the language of these people, which includes the following dialects: *Binongan, Masadiit, Inlaod,* and *Southern Itneg;* (*lit.*) pagan.

itnéng: **agitneng.** *v.* (*obs.*) to be quiet. (*talna, ulimek*)

itúm: **itumen.** *v.* to close the mouth.

itóy: the oblique of *toy,* abbreviated form of *daytoy*: this.

itsá: *n.* tea. (*tsa, tsaa*)

itsóra: (Sp. *hechura*: form, figure) *n.* figure, form, the way someone looks; appearance; shape. **Awan met itsoraenna.** He's not good looking at all.

ittá: *n.* defective utterance; writing error; unhusked kernel of rice mixed with cooked rice; black sheep in the family; error in speaking. **ittaan.** *v.* to remove unhusked grains from milled rice. **naitta.** *a.* full of unhusked kernels, hence coarse or unclean. [Kal. *gusseÿang*]

ittíng: *a.* little, small. (*bassit*) **sangkaitting.** *n.* a small amount.

ittíp: *n.* crust of rice that sticks to the bottom of the pot when cooked. (*kidkid*) **immittip.** *a.* hardened; crusty. [Ibg. *kikkid,* Knk. *dekét, agápang,* Png. *garól,* Tag. *tutóng*]

íwa: *n.* slice. **sangakaiwa.** *n.* one slice, one cut. **iwaen.** *v.* to cut open, slice; dissect. **iwaan.** *v.* to carve, cut, take a slice out of. [Bon. *agis, géged, tágip,* Ibg. *gelliq, gappó,* Ivt. *haripen, aktekteven,* Kpm. *gili,* Png. *gálip, tegteg,* Tag. *hiwà*]

I-wak: *n.* ethnic group from Benguet Province, Luzon; the Pangasinic language of the I-wak people.

íwas: **agiwas.** *v.* to ramble; roam; move from side to side. **iwasen.** *v.* to move aside.

iwés: **agiwes.** *v.* to zigzag; move swiftly. **Nagiwes ti nabengbeng nga asuk manipud iti uneg ti rukib.** The thick smoke zigzagged out from the inside of the cave.

íwet: *n.* the young of the eel, *var.* of *kiwet.*

iwét: *var.* of *iwes.*

iw-íw: *n.* cut; slice. (*puted; galip, iwa*) **naiw-iw.** *a.* cut; sliced.

iy-: Variant of *i-* before a vowel; in this dictionary, these words are normally spelled *y-.* **iyawid = yawid.** to bring home. **iyuper = yuper.** to soak.

iyaáy: *n.* coming, the nominalization of *ay.*

iyás: **paiyas.** *n.* drainage; drain.

iyó: *n.* shark (*pating*). [Tag. *patíng*]

iyót: *var.* of *yot*: copulate.

K

-k: var. of enclitic *-ko* after vowels or *n*: transitive first person singular I, or genitive my: **basaen + -ko = basaek.** I'll read it. **pusa + -ko = pusak.** my cat.

-k: Enclitic suffix. first singular patient occurring after *-na* and *-da*: **Nakitanak.** He saw me. **Kinayatdak.** They wanted me.

ka₁- 1. Transitive verbal prefix indicating companionship of the action expressed by the root. Perfective form is *kina-* and the intransitive counterpart in actor focus is *maki-kasala.* to dance with someone **kasao.** to speak with someone **Sino ti kinasaom?** Who did you speak with?; 2. Nominalizing prefix used to form nonconcrete substantives. Sometimes occurs with the suffix *-an*: (Perfective form is *kina-*) **mabaelan.** to be able. **kabaelak.** what I can do. **mayulog.** to be translated. **kayulugan.** meaning. **malintegan.** to be straightened. **kalintegan.** right, privilege; **kaattidog.** length. **kangato.** height. **kabassit.** smallness; 3. With the particle *idi* the *ka-* prefix with an adjectival root translates that the quality of the adjective is at the highest level: **pintas.** beauty. **idi kapintas(na).** at the height of (his/her/its) beauty.

ka₂: ligature used with certain counted nouns: **dua katao.** two people. **sangkabassit.** a little bit (*maysa + ka + bassit*). **tallo kagalip.** three slices. **Tallo kasilong laeng ti tinawidna.** He only inherited three rice paddies.

kaC-: *affix*. Indicates recent completion of the event expressed by the root, whose initial consonant is geminated, see also *kaCV-*: **kattiliw.** just caught. **kassangpet.** just arrived. **kalluto.** just cooked.

kaCV-: *affix*. With reduplication of the first open syllable of the stem, this affix forms abstract nominals: **kasasaad.** condition (f. *saad*: place). **katatao.** human nature (f. *tao*: human). **kada-daga.** nature of the soil (f. *daga*: soil).

kaCV(C)-₁: *prefix*. Denotes the recently completed action of the verbal stem; this form takes the *-ko* pronouns, see also *kaC-*: **labas.** pass. **kalablabas.** recently passed; just passed by. **Kasapsapulnaka.** He has just found you.

kaCVC-₂: *prefix*. Denotes near identity of two entities. **karuprupan.** having the same (very similar) face. **kabagbagi.** having the same body build. **kamatmata.** having identical eyes. **Ka-matmatam.** He has the same eyes as you. **Karuprupak.** He has the same face as I do.

-ka: *enclitic pron*. Second person singular (familiar) absolutive enclitic pronoun. **Ilokanoka.** You are Ilokano. **Makasalaka.** You can dance. [Png., Tag. *=ka*]

-ka: *Enclitic*. Attached to transitive verbs, this enclitic denotes that the action of the verb is performed by the first person subject onto the second person (singular, informal), Underlyingly *=ko=ka*: I to you. **Ay-ayatenka.** I love you. **Makitakanto.** I will see you. After the ergative pronominal enclitics, *-na* and *-da*, this enclitic implies that the receiver of the action is second person singular informal: **Kayatdaka.** They want you. **Kasapulannaka.** He needs you. **Kukuakan!** You are mine! [Png. *taká*, Tag. *kitá*]

ka- -an: (Perfective form *kina- -an*) 1. circumfix expressing the superlative adjective: **kaimbagán.** best. **kababaan.** lowest; 2. locative circumfix indicating a place where the referent expressed in the nominal stem exists in great abundance: **kadaratan.** sandy place. **karuotan.** grassy place; **kaubasan.** vineyard. **kapiniaan.** pineapple plantation. 3. nominalizing circumfix indicating companionship, or shared or mutual participation: **kanaganan.** namesake (sharing same name). **katugawan.** seatmate (sharing seat). **kailian.** townmate. **katrabahuan.** workmate; 4. circumfix used with cardinal numbers indicating that the number must be increased: **kalimaam.** Make it five. **kinatluam dagiti pisos.** You increased the number of pesos to three; also: see under *ka-*. 5. With locative roots, it may also indicate general area: **Kailokuan.** *n*. Ilocos region. **Katagalugan.** *n*. Tagalog region. **Kamanilaan.** *n*. vicinity of Manila. 6. may nominalize stative roots (Tag.): **kalanggongan.** *n*. foolishness. 7. May indicate preference or fondness. **Kagatanganmi ti sapin.** We are fond of buying underwear. **Kainumanda ti gatas.** They are fond of drinking milk. **KapanganAna ti kalding.** He is fond of eating goat.

kaCV- -an: *affix*. forms absolute superlatives: **pintas.** beauty. **kapintasan.** most beautiful. **kapipintasan.** most beautiful of them all.

káad: kaadan. v. to clean the ashes from the furnace.

kaád: ikaad. v. to warn, caution; inform. (*ballaag*)

kaadalmán: (f. *adalem*) n. the deep sea; deep part (of a pool, etc.).

káag: n. young monkey; a kind of bird; stupid or foolish person. **kakaag.** n. a wasplike insect; *Helicteres hirsuta* herb with purple flowers.

kaaldawán: (f. *aldáw*) n. the very day, the same day.

kaamaán: (f. *ama*) *n.* family, the father and his family. **sangkaamaan.** *n.* one family. [Tag. *mag-anák*]

kaán: agkaan. *v.* to feed, prey on; devour. **mangan.** *v.* to eat. **kanen.** *v.* to eat something; devour, consume; *n.* food. **kankanen.** *n.* sweets; rice cakes. **kumakaan.** *v.* to eat well; *n.* gourmet. **kakaanan.** *n.* appetite. **kankanen.** *n.* sweet (usually rice cakes) **agpakan.** *v.* to give out food, host a banquet, give a party. **mangpakán, pakanén.** *v.* to feed. **pakanán.** *n.* feast; banquet. **makan.** *v.* to be able to eat; *n.* variety of rice. **makakaan.** *v.* to be able to eat. **makakàkaán.** *v.* to crave for. **makikaan.** *v.* to have a free meal. **makipangan.** *v.* to eat with someone. **ipangan.** *v.* to eat something with something else. **kinnaanan.** *n.* eating contest. **mannangan.** *n.* gourmet; good eater. **pannangan.** *n.* time to eat. **pakakákaanán.** *v.* to crave for a food. **ipakan.** *v.* to feed; shoot, pick, throw. **panganan.** *n.* dining room. **agkapangan.** *v.* to eat together. **pakikinnaanan.** *v.* to share food together. **kapangpangan.** *v.* to have just finished eating. **kapanganan.** *v.* to be fond of eating a certain thing. **Kakakaanmi.** We have just eaten. **pakakákaanán.** *v.* to crave for a certain food. **agkapangan.** *v.* to eat together. **No narigat ti pannakaalana, naimbag ti pannakakaanna.** *exp.* If it is hard to get, it is good to eat (the harder the struggle, the more glorious the triumph). [Bon., Knk., Png. *kan*, Knk. *labáy*, Tag. *kain*]

kaanakán: (f. *anák*) *n.* nephew; niece. [Kal. *amulakon*, Knk. *kamonakén*, Tag. *pamangkín*]

kaanó: *interrog.* when?, at what time? see *intonano* **inton kaano, kaanonto?** How soon? **kaano pay.** since when? **kaanoman.** whenever. **uray kaanoman.** anytime; until eternity. [Ibg. *kanni*, Ivt. *anmangu*, Kal. *kapiga, kam-amman*, Kpm. *kapilán*, Png. *kapigán*, Tag. *kailán*]

kaappón: see *kappón*: contribution; portion; joining.

kaa(r)rúba: (pl. *kakaarúba*) *n.* neighbor. *a.* neighboring, adjoining. **sang(k)aarrubaan.** *n.* the whole neighborhood. **kumaaruba, mangarruba.** *v.* to visit with a neighbor. **agpakaarruba.** *v.* to go to the neighbors. [Bon. *kabay-bay, saggong*, Knk. *alép, sagúgung*, Kpm. *kasíping-bale*, Png. *kaabay*, Tag. *kapit-bahay*]

kaási: (f. *ási*) *n.* mercy, pity, compassion, leniency, charity. **kaasian.** *v.* to pity, have mercy on. **nakaasi.** *a.* merciful, kind, humane. **nakakaasi.** *a.* pitiful, pathetic. **ikaasi.** *v.* to plead for, beg for. **pakakaasi.** *v.* to beg, implore, plead, entreat. **pakaaasian.** *v.* to be pitied. **ipakaasi, ipakpkaasi.** *v.* to beg for; plead. **kaasi met.** *exp.* what a shame; poor thing. **manangngaasi.** *a.* compassionate; merciful; charitable. **balay ti kaasi.** *n.* charitable institution. **Kayatna a maammuan no siasino ti agtagikua iti talon ta isun ti pagpakpakaasianna.** She wants to know who is the owner of the rice field, because he will be the one to implore. [Png. *kasi*, Tag. *awà*]

kaasitgán: (f. *asideg*) *a.* nearest, closet. **Nagapapura a kimmamang iti kaasitgan a paglinongan.** He hurried to seek shelter in the nearest shady spot.

kaayan-ayát: (f. *ayát*) *n.* sweetheart.

kába: *n.* honeycomb. (*kalába*) [Knk. *tánug*, Png. *kalaba*, Tag. *saray*]

kabá: agkabakaba. *v.* to be anxious; perplexed. (*pulkok*)

kababagás: (f. *bagás*) *n.* meaning, essence.

kababalín: (f. *balín*) *n.* habit, custom.

kabaddungál: agkabaddungal. *v.* to be of the same age. (*kasadar*)

kabádo: *a.* hesitant; fearful.

kabaelán: (f. *baél*) *n.* capability; power; *v.* to be able to.

kábag: *n.* gas pain; flatulence. **kabagan.** *v.* to have gas pains. [Png. *lebág*, Tag. *kabag*]

kabagián: (f. *bagí*) *n.* relative. [Ivt. *lipus*, Kal. *agi*, Knk. *tun-úd*, Png. *kanáyon*, Tag. *kamaganak*]

kabágis: (pl. *kakabágis*) *n.* sibling: brother, sister. (*kabsát*) **kabagis iti bunyag.** *n.* sibling by baptism, the child of one's godparents. [Png. *agí*, Tag. *kapatíd*]

kabákab: kabakaben. *v.* to dig up, unearth, exhume (bones of the dead). [Tag. *hukay*]

kabakián: (f. *baki*) *n.* hen; (*fig.*) female animal.

kabál: *n.* breastplate; armor; bulletproof vest. (*kalasag*) **kabkabalan.** *n.* surgeonfish, *Acanthurus triostegus.*

kabaliás: (Sp. *caballa*: mackerel) *n.* short-bodied mackerel; saddlebag.

kabalería: (Sp. *caballería*: cavalry) *n.* cavalry.

kabalierísa: (Sp. *caballeriza*: stable) *n.* stable. (*kuádra*)

kabaliéro: (Sp. *caballero*: gentleman) *n.* gentleman; a kind of ornamental plant, *Caesalpinia pulcherrima.*

kabaliéte: (Sp. *caballete*: little horse; ridge; stand for saddles; gallows; trivet; horse used for torture. *n.* bridge of the nose (*darangídong*); easel; gable, ridge, end of a ridged roof; gallows of a printing press; sawhorse.

kabálio: (Sp. *caballo*: horse) *n.* horse; queen (in cards); ironing board. **kumakabalio.** *n.* horseman. **agkabalio.** *v.* to ride a horse. **nakakabalio.** *a.* riding horseback, on a horse.

maipakabalio. *v.* to straddle (a horse). **pakabalio.** *n.* ridgepole of a roof. **sinankabalio.** *n.* toy horse. **kabkabalio.** *n.* horses; game of jumping horse. **kabalio de paso.** *n.* ambling horse. **ipakabalio ti tabako.** to stick tobacco leaves in the fashion of the letter x with the ribs inward. **kumabalio ti bibigna.** *exp.* denoting extremely big lips. [Kal. *kabyayu*, Tag. *kabalyo*]

kabálio moréno: (Sp. *caballo*: horse + *marino*: marine) *n.* seahorse, often used as an amulet placed under the ladder of a residential entrance to ward off evil.

kabalyería: variant spelling of *kabalieria*: cavalry.

kabalyerísa: variant spelling of *kabalierisa*: horse stable.

kabán: n. 75 liter dry measure; cavan. **kabanen.** v. to place in sacks; measure in cavans.

kabánia: (Sp. *cabaña*: cabin) n. cabin; hut.

kabarbáras: (obs.) n. heathen practices.

kabási: n. a kind of large marine fish; gizzard shad, *Anodontostoma sp.*

kábat: kabaten. v. to package, bundle, pack up. (*balkot*; *bungon*)

kabatíti: n. *Luffa cylindrica*, vine with edible, long cylindrical fruits; variety of rice with fragrant soft kernel. [Ivt. *kabatiti*, Tag. *patola* (cylindrical fruit of the *Luffa cylindrica* vine)]

kábaw: a. n. senile; weakness of tobacco or liquor. **agkabaw.** v. to go senile; dote; to be always forgetful. **nakabaw.** a. mild, weak (tobacco, wine, etc.) **kumabaw.** v. to become senile; to lose strength (liquor). [Png. *kabaw*, Tag. *huklób*, *nahúhulì*, *ulián*]

kabáy: awan kabayna. without delay.

kabayán: (f. *bai*) n. female animal. (*dánaw*)

kabáyo: *var.* of *kabalio*: horse. **kabáyo moréno.** (Sp. *caballo marino*) n. seahorse, *Hippocampus sp.*, sometimes used as a good luck charm. **ipakabayo.** v. to put something astride. **maipakabayo.** v. to straddle. (*askaw*; *akkang*; *sakkang*; *kayang*) **pakabayo.** n. ridgepole. **kabayo a moreno.** n. seahorse. **kabaywan.** v. to straddle; sit astride. [Tag. *kabalyo*]

kabbáb: *a.* toothless.

kabbaláy: (f. *baláy*) n. housemate; concubine. **makikabbalay.** v. to live in the same house with; to be someone's mistress. **Makabulanen nga agkabbalaykami kenni Jane.** Jane and I have been living together for one month already. [Ibg. *kabaláy* = relative by marriage]

kabbangá: n. game of playing house. **agkabkabbanga.** v. to play storekeeper; to play house (girl's game).

kabbángon: (f. *bángon*) a. recently established, just founded; just put up, just erected. **kabbangon nga ili.** a city just founded.

kabbatíl: agkabbatil. v. to contradict one another (*allabat*; *suplat*; *supapak*; *sungani*). [Tag. *salungát*]

kabbég: (obs.) a. secretive; cautious.

kabbéng: var. of *kebbeng*: claw. **Sikakabbeng iti natadem a kukona.** He is clawed by her sharp nail.

kabbét: kabbeten. v. to grip; clutch. (*gemgem*, *iggem*)

kabbí: n. mumps. (*gabbí*) **agkabbi.** v. to have mumps. [Tag. *bikì*]

kabbíbaw: a. wry mouthed; with a twisted, contorted mouth. (*diwig*, *riwis*) **kumabbibaw.** v. to become *kabbibaw*; to swell as a result of a bump. **Pinagkabbibawdaka.** They gave you a contorted mouth (punched your mouth).

kabbó: kinnabbuan. n. variety of hide-and-seek with two teams and a base camp.

kabbúkar: (f. *búkar*) n. recently opened flower; *a.* just opened.

kabbukuál: (f. *bukuál*) a. just uprooted, just dug up. **Kasla kabbukual a kamote.** He is like a sweet potato just dug from the ground (dirty).

kabbukrá: (f. *bukrá*) a. just unfastened, unwound; (*reg.*) just born.

kabbuksíl: (f. *buksíl*) a. just husked, shelled, peeled.

kabbót₁: agkabbot. v. to make the puffing sound of boiling rice.

kabbót₂: ikabbot. v. to consume all (food). (*íbus*)

kabélio-de-ánghel: (Sp. *cabello de angel*: angel hair) *n.* cypress vine cultivated for ornamental purposes.

kabén: see *tampípi*: large rectangular basket with flat sides.

kabéng: n. homemade wine.

káber: n. muffled sound of a drum.

kabésa: (Sp. *cabeza*: head) **ikabesa.** v. to memorize, learn by heart. (*yúlo*, *tandaanán*) **kabesa túrko.** n. variety of edible flower. **kabesada.** n. headgear, harness. [Tag. *saulo* (memorize)]

kabesádo: (f. *kabesa*) **kabesado.** a. memorized, learned by heart; skilled. **ikabesado.** v. to memorize.

kabeséra: (Sp. *cabecera*: head of table) n. capital; head of the table. **agkabesera, mangabesera.** v. to sit at the head of the table; occupy the seat of honor. **pangabeseraan.** n. head of the table.

kabesília: (Sp. *cabecilla*: ringleader) *n.* leader of a group; banker in cards; chief investor in a business partnership. **mangikabesilia.** *v.* to lead.

kabíbi: n. kind of large, brown mollusk; kind of elongated river fish with delicious meat. [Tag. *kabibe*]

kabibiág: (f. *biág*) n. biography.

kábig: kabigen. v. to turn (a steering wheel).

kábil₁: ikabil. v. to put, place, lay, set. **pagi-kabilan, pangikabilan.** n. container. **Nangi-kabilam ti tulbekko?** Where did you put my key? [Ibg. *ikuwa, mangipay*, Itg. *ikwa*, Ivt. *pangayen*, Kpm. *ike*, Png. *iyan*, Tag. *lagáy* (put)]

kábil₂: agkabil. v. to fight one another; maltreat; punish. **kabilen.** v. to fight someone; beat, hit, strike. **kakabil.** v. to fight with. **kinnabil.** n. fight; scuffle; commotion. **kumabil.** v. to hit; box (*danog*); beat. **pakabil.** v. to hire someone to hurt another. **pangngabil.** n. violent disposition. [Tag. *suntók, laban*]

kabília: (Sp. *cabilla*: dowel) n. dowel; belaying pin.

kabisáda: (Sp. *cabezada*: cord, headstall) n. bridle; head part of a horse's harness.

kabisádo: (f. *kabésa*) a. memorized; very familiar with. **Kabisadok ti ugali ti lakay.** I know the habits of the old man by heart.

kabisília: *var.* of *kabesilia*: head of a *baranggay*; banker in gambling; chief investor in a business partnership.

kabisóte: (Sp. *cabezote*: obstinate, obs.) a. obstinate; stupid, mentally slow.

kabít₁: n. small box; *Caesalpinia nuga*, shrub with yellow flowers and one-seeded pods. **kabiten, ikabit.** v. to connect; fasten, hook (*kab-it*)

kabít₂: (Tag.) n. mistress, lover. (*bullilising, babai*)

kab-ít: n. hook. (*kalláwit, kalub-ít; for fish: síma, banníit*) **ikab-it.** v. to hook, fasten; entangle, entrap, ensnare. **maikab-it.** v. to be hooked, caught. [Png. *sagór*, Tag. *kawit*]

kabíte: n. retaining stone wall. **kinabite.** a. made of stone (fence, wall, etc.). **kabitero.** n. builder of retaining walls.

kabitég: n. bruise; wale. (*batlag*) **agkabiteg.** v. to be marked with welts, bruises, etc. [Kal. *betlog*, Tag. *pasâ*]

kabiténio: (Sp. *caviteño*) n. resident of Cavite Province. **kabitenia.** n. female resident of Cavite Province; variety of awned early rice.

kabíti: kabitien. v. to cement.

kabkáb: n. body dirt. **nakakabkabkab.** a. full of dirt on the body. **kabkaben.** v. to dig up an already buried corpse. [Png. *muringis*, Tag. *amol, dungis, libág*]

kabkabánga: n. skull (*bangabánga*). [Tag. *bungô*]

kabláaw: n. greeting; compliment; visitation of a spirit believed to cause sickness. **agkablaaw.** v. to salute; address; compliment; congratulate. **kumablaaw.** v. to greet; congratulate. **nakab-kablaawan.** n. disease causing debility, perspiration and softening of the ears (literally from being greeted by a dead relative). **Kabla-awandaka.** (fig.) The bad spirits will attack you. **Kablaawandaka iti panangabakmo.** We congratulate you on your victory. [Png. *piam-begya*, Tag. *batì*]

káble: (Sp. *cable*) n. cable; heavy rope.

kablegráma: (Sp. *cablegrama*: cablegram) n. cablegram.

kablíng: n. *Pogostemon cablin.* species of aromatic herb with pink-purple flowers.

kábo: (Sp. *cabo*: corporal) n. corporal; foreman. **ikabuan.** v. to command.

kabúgaw: n. a kind of seedy lemon, larger than the *daláyap* (*kaburaw*). [Tag. *kabuyaw*]

kabúkab: agkabukab. v. to gnash, grind the teeth; (coll.) gossip. **kabukaben.** v. to grind something with the teeth. [Tag. *ngalót*]

kabúl: agkabulkabul. v. to have difficulty in chewing (due to lack of teeth).

kabonégro: (Sp. *cabo negro*: black ropes) n. sago palm; black fibers taken from the sheathing of the leaves of the sago palm.

Kabunián: n. (*myth.*) Ilocano supreme being.

kabuntála: n. morning star (*bagsák*).

kábur: agkabur. v. to boil (water agitated by fish); to worsen; intensify (anger). **Nagkabur ti kinaguyongna.** His lunacy intensified. [Tag. *bulâ*]

kabúraw: n. variety of the *kabugaw* lemon.

kaborráta: n. a kind of whip.

kábus: n. full moon; period of the full moon; (*fig.*) lunatic. **agkabus.** v. to be full (said of the moon). [Kal. *langanggangsa*, Tag. *kabilugan ng buwán*]

kabúsor: (f. *búsor*) n. enemy. [Knk. *ngílan*, Tag. *kaaway*]

kábut: n. lard, fat, grease (of animals); epicarp, outermost layer of the pericarp of fruits.

kabotít: n. kind of girl's game played with the feet, hands, and words: *kabotít kabotít, ikkatém ti lugít.*

kabrá: (Sp. *cabra*: goat) n. female goat. (*kalding*) **barreta-kabra.** n. crowbar.

kabríto: (Sp. *cabrito*: small goat; fem: *kabríta*) n. young male goat.

kabrón: (Sp. *cabrón*: adult male goat) n. adult male goat. (*kalding*)

kabsát: (f. *bessát*, pl. *kakabsát*) n. sibling; brother, sister (*kabagis*); kinsman. **agkabsat.** v. to be siblings. **ipakabsat.** v. to consider as a brother or sister. **nainkabsatan, inkakabsatan.** a. brotherly, sisterly. **kabsat ti ama.** n. half sibling with the same father. **kabsat ti ina.** n. half sibling with the same mother. **panagkakabsat.** n. brotherhood. **Maymaysaak a lalaki iti lima nga agkakabsat.** I am the only boy out of five siblings. **Nainkabsatan laeng ti riknak kenka.** My feelings toward you are only brotherly. [Bon. *agi, eta*, Ibg. *wagi*, Ifg. *túlang*, Ivt. *kakteh*, Kal. *sulud*, Kpm. *kapatad*, Png. *agí*, Tag. *kapatíd*]

kabsíw: **agkabsiw.** v. to be uneven, unbalanced; unequal; slip; miss (a step, a target, etc.) (*kaglis, galis*). **Pasaray maitik-ol ti tumengna iti pasamano no maikabsiw dagiti saka kadagiti pimmariok a likkaong.** He often hits his knees against the armrail if his feet miss a step from the panlike potholes. [Tag. *dulás*]

kad: var. of *kadí*.

káda: (Sp. *cada*: each) a. each; every (*tunggal*). **kada rabii.** each night. [Kal. *kacha*, Tag. *tuwíng*]

kadá: Plural of *ken*. 1. Oblique of the personal plural article *da*. **da Carmen ken Juan.** Carmen and Juan. **kada Carmen ken Juan.** to (for) Carmen and Juan. 2. connective particle of addition usually linking plural or indefinite nouns (and): **dagiti lallakay kada babbaket.** old men and women. **Kitaem man ta langam, pinagkabbibawdaka kada pakkangka pay ket a magnan!** Just look at yourself, they boxed in your mouth and you even are walking as a bowlegged person. **Orkidia met kada rosas ti pakakumikoman ti inana.** His mother keeps herself busy with orchids and roses. [Tag. *kiná* (plural article); *at saká, at* (and)]

kadagidí: Oblique of *dagidí:* to those (remote past).

kadagidiáy: Oblique of *dagidiáy.* to those (far from addresser and addressee).

kadagitá: Oblique of *dagita.* to those (near addressee).

kadagití: Oblique of *dagiti.* to the (plural). **Kasla awanak iti bagik a simmurot kadagiti tao.** It was like I was beside myself following the people. **Intedna kadagiti baboy.** He gave it to the pigs.

kadagitóy: Oblique of *dagitoy.* to these.

kadakám: var. of *kadakamí.*

kadakamí: Oblique of pronoun *dakami:* to us (exclusive). **Nailet kadakami.** It is tight on us. [Png. *ed sikamí*, Tag. *sa amin*]

kadakáy: var. of *kadakayó.*

kadakayó: Oblique of pronoun *dakayo:* to you (plural). **Dayta la kadakayo.** It's up to you. [Png. *ed sikayó*, Tag. *sa inyó*]

kadakkél: (f. *dakkél*) n. parent. [Png. *ateng*, Tag. *magulang*]

kadaklán: n. principal part of the house (f. *dakkél*); a. largest, biggest; principal (superlative of *dakkel*).

kadakuáda: Oblique of pronoun *isuda:* to them. **Intedna kadakuada.** He gave it to them. [Png. *ed sikará*, Tag. *sa kanilá*]

kadáli: n. two beams on which rest the body of a cart.

kádang: n. eight timber pieces that form the Saint Andrew's cross of the granary; building with a lower story higher than the upper one. **kadangkadang.** n. stilt; coconut beetle. **agkadangkadang.** v. to walk on stilts. [Ivt. *kalasag*, Knk. *akkád*, Tag. *tayakád, takyaran* (stilts)]

kadáng: **nakadang.** a. straddling (in walking) (*kayang*). [Tag. *bukakà*]

kadapá: **agkadkadapa.** v. to drag oneself forward; to walk blindly; grope in the dark. **kumadapa.** v. to drag; live miserably. **kumadkadapa.** v. to move with light, quick steps.

kadapán: (f. *dapán*) n. foot (used for measuring).

kadaráto: (Sp. *cata rato*: each period of time) adv. immediately; at once; (reg.) time and again. [Tag. *kaagád*]

kadás: **kadasan.** v. to sweep, brush up. [Tag. *kalos*]

kadatá: Oblique of the pronoun *datá:* to the two of us.

kadatáo: Oblique of the pronoun *datáo:* to one (person); to me; to us. **Kanayonka la nga adda iti ruar a mangpaspasungad kadatao.** You are just always outside waiting for me. **Gunggonana a manglokloko kadatao.** That's what he gets for deceiving (us).

kadatáy: var. of *kadatayó.*

kadatayó: Oblique of the pronoun *datayó:* to us (inclusive). [Png. *ed sikatayó*, Tag. *sa atin*]

kadawyán: (f. *dawi*) n. custom; habit; usage; menstrual flow. a. regular, normal. **agkadawyan.** n. to have a menstrual flow. **maipakadawyan.** v. to become habitual. **ipakadawyan.** v. to make it a habit. **No dimo am-ammo, ipatom a kadawyan laeng a mintalon.** If you didn't know him, you would assume he were just an ordinary farmer. [Tag. *ugalì*]

kadáy: n. knapsack. (*pasiking*)

kadaydí: *pron.* oblique of *daydí.*

kadaytá: *pron.* oblique of *daytá.*

kadaytáy: *pron.* oblique of *daytáy.*

kadaytóy: *pron.* oblique of *daytóy*.

kaddígos: (f. *digos*) n. one who has recently bathed; just washed.

kadduá: (f. *dua*) Irregular plural of *kadua*: companions.

kaddóg: n. old, mature man. (*lakáy, lakaddóg*)

kaddúgal: (f. *dugal*) (*coll.*) n. girl who has recently lost her virginity; *a.* just nicked, just notched or indented.

kaddútok: (f. *dútok*) *a.* just assigned, recently designated or appointed.

kadéna: (Sp. *cadena*: chain) n. chain (*kawar*); fetters, shackles; necklace. **kadena de amor.** n. vine with pink flowers. **nakakadena.** *a.* chained up.

kadenéta: (Sp. *cadeneta*: small chain) n. small chain; chain stitch.

kadenília: (Sp. *cadenilla*: small chain) n. part of the rigodon dance; small chain.

kadénsia: (Sp. *cadencia*: cadence) *n.* cadence.

kadéte: (Sp. *cadete*: cadet) n. cadet.

kadí: interrogative particle; particle of entreating. **Agurayka kadi, manang.** Wait, older sister. **Talaga kadi a saannakon a kagura?** Are you really not angry with me? [Tag. *ba*]

kadióg: **kadiogen.** *v.* to maul, box; thrash, punch or beat excessively. **Kinadugkadiogdak a kinugtakugtaran sadak pinungo.** They mauled me by kicking, then they bound me.

kadiúl: (*coll., Eng. cajole*) **agkadiul.** v. to copulate. (*yot*)

kadiós: *var.* of *kardís*: pigeon pea.

kadís: n. the spotted moonfish, *Mene maculata*.

kádit: **kaditen.** v. to cut off the head of a palm; extract the sap from; poll; bleed a wound; open a boil.

kadkád: **ikadkad.** v. to remove ashes, rake ashes. **kadkadan.** *v.* to clean a furnace of ashes. (from a stove, etc.) **pagkadkadan.** n. ash pit.

kadkaduá: (f. *kaduá*) n. placenta, afterbirth.

kaduá: [f. *duá*, pl. *kadduá*] n. companion; mate; one of a pair. **agkadua.** v. to be a companion; accompany. **agkakadua.** n. partners; colleagues; peers. **kumadua.** v. to pair with; join with; accompany. **kaduaan.** *v.* to escort, accompany; stay with someone overnight; second a motion. **kaduaen.** v. to accompany someone. **kadkadua.** n. afterbirth, placenta. **makikadua.** v. to join a group; associate. **maikadua.** *num.* second. **pagkaduaen.** v. to divide in two. **panagkaduata.** adv. since the time you and I were together. **pakikaduaán.** *v.* to associate socially with, deal with; request to have someone accompanied. **Saanka pay a pumanaw, kaduaennak biit ditoy.** Don't leave yet, stay with me a while here. [Bon. *dáit*, Ibg.

kavulúq, Kal. *biÿun, kadwa*, Knk. *ib-á*, Png. *ibá*, Tag. *kasáma*]

kádos: n. sack, saddlebag.

kadús: n. condom. [Tag. *goma*]

kádre: (Sp. *cadre*: cadre) n. cadre; skeleton drill.

kadsaáran: n. story, floor (of a building).

kadtá: [*umaliska dita*] get away from there, *kadta man ta.*

káeg: **nakaeg.** *a.* boastful, braggart; blustering; dull; ignorant. [Tag. *tangá*]

kaém: **agkaem.** v. to close, shut (two things together: mouth, clams, etc.); come together (pl. subject). **nagkaeman.** n. joint. **Nagtalinaed a sikakaem ti bibigko.** My lips remained sealed. [Tag. *tikóm*]

kaes-eskán: n. use, utility. **Dimo dadaelen ti orasmo kadagiti awan kaes-eskanna a banag.** Don't waste your time on useless things.

kágab: see *kalálaw*: kind of basket with small opening.

kagát: n. bite. **agkagat, kumagat, kagaten.** v. to bite. **ipakagat.** v. to cause to bite. **pakagat.** n. peg, pin; tap. **sikakagat.** *a.* biting; carrying between the teeth. [Ibg. *kagaq, kagat*, Ivt. *suñiten*, Kal. *kotob*, Knk. *bangét, ketkét*, Kpm. *ket*, Png. *kalát, ketket*, Tag. *kagát*]

kágaw: n. germ; itch mite. [Kal. *okkeb*, Knk. *kágew*, Tag. *kagaw*]

kagáwat: n. scarcity of food; famine; crisis. [Tag. *tagsalát, taggutóm*]

kagáy: n. cape, cloak, mantle; shawl. **agkagay.** v. to wear a cape. **ikagay.** v. to wear as a cape. **kagayan.** *v.* to cloak someone, cover with a cape or shawl. [Png., Tag. *balabal*]

Kagayáno: *n.* native of Cagayan Province.

kagdíl: var. of *kakdil*: to affect; be notched, dented.

kaggátud: (f. *gátud*) *a.* just picked (leaves).

kaggó: n. species of shell similar to the *tukmem* scallop.

kagimóngan: (f. *gímong*) n. society; group; organization.

kagkág: **agkagkag.** v. to bask in the sun. **ikagkag.** v. to shake, beat dirt off something. **kumanagkag.** v. to shine bright (said of the moon); make the sound of something being beaten. **kagkagan.** *v.* to hit with something woven (a basket). **Adda tallo nga ayup idiay nga agkagkagkag.** There are three animals there basking in the sun. [Tag. *pagpág* (shake off dirt)]

kaglís: **maikaglis.** v. to slip, slide. (*galís*) **kumaglis.** v. to deflect, swerve, move from side to side. **Iti apurok, naikaglisak iti agdan.** In my haste, I slipped on the staircase. [Knk. *kidlís*, Tag. *dulás*; *lihís*]

kágud: ikagud. v. to finish one's work on time; to do lavishly. **makagud.** v. to be barely on time. **kaguden.** v. to catch up; hurry up. [Tag. *habul* (hurry, pursue)]

kaguduá: (f. *dua*) n. half.

kagumáan: agkagumaan. v. to make an effort, endeavor. **ikagumaan.** v. to take time to do something; endeavor. **makagumaan.** v. to obtain with little effort. **Ikagumaanna latta a kanayon nga adda yawidna a pakalaglagipan dagiti dadakkelna.** He makes an effort to always bring home souvenirs to his parents. [Png. *seseg, seét*, Tag. *punyagí*]

kágun: agkagun. v. to consent to doing a bad thing. **kagunan.** v. to tolerate.

kagpaáyan: n. *Kibatalia blancoi*; *Kickxia sp.* tree. (*pasnit*)

kagsíit: n. strike of lightning; fluency in the delivery of a speech. **agkagsiit.** v. to strike (lightning); to strike as eloquent (in delivering a speech, conversing, etc.).

kagténg: n. kind of striped marine fish larger than the *birút*. **makagteng.** v. to arrive; be able to make a deadline. **magtengan.** v. to reach a deadline. [Tag. *datíng, abót*]

káha: (Sp. *caja*: box) n. box, case; cashbox; pack; small packet; frame of a building; typecase. **ikaha.** v. to put into a box. **sangakaha.** n. one pack; one box of. **kaha de yero.** n. iron lockbox.

kahabíba: (Sp. *caja viva*: snare drum) n. snare drum.

kahél: (f. Tag. *via* Sp. cajel) n. species of orange tree with sweet or sour fruit (*dalandan*). **kakahelan.** n. orange orchard. **kahelada.** n. orangeade. [Kal. *aÿagen*]

kahéro: (Sp. *cajero*: cashier) n. cashier, fem: *kahera.*

kahetília: (Sp. *cajetilla*: packet of cigarettes) n. small box, packet of cigarettes.

kahísta: (Sp. *cajista*) n. typesetter; compositor.

kahíta: (Sp. *cajita*: small box) n. small box.

káho: (Sp. *cajo*) n. bookbinder's groove.

kahón: (Sp. *cajón*: large box) n. large box; drawer; total of five votes used to facilitate vote counting. **ikahon.** v. to put in a box. **kinahon.** a. in boxes; in heaps, in abundance.

káhoy: (Tag. *kamoteng-kahoy*) n. cassava. [Kal. *kastila*, Tag. *kahoy* = wood]

kaiCVC-: *affix.* attaches to *i-* verbs to denote recency of action: **ikabil.** to put, place. **kaikabkabil.** recently installed. **ipaw-it.** to send. **kaipawpaw-it.** recently sent.

kaibaán: n. mythological elf; (Tinguian) mythological spirit that watches over the crops. (*ansisit*; *banig*)

kaibatúgan: (f. *bátog*) n. equivalence, equal worth, equal value. **Isuda met ti kaibatugan ti rinibu a panagungar.** They are equivalent to thousands of resurrections.

kaída: (Sp. *caída*: fall) a. leaning (tree); n. corridor leading from the head of the staircase to the rear of the building; (*music*) modulation.

kaído: (Sp. *caído*: fallen) **agkakaido.** v. to worsen. (*karo*)

kailalá: (f. *ilala*) *exp.* what a shame; what a pity (*sayang*; *isu pay*). [Tag. *sayang*]

kailián: (f. *ili*) n. townmate; countryman. [Tag. *kababayan*]

Kailokuán: (f. *Iloko*) n. the Ilocos region, native region of the Ilocano people. **agpa-Kailokuan.** v. to go to the Ilocos region.

kaimíto: (Tag.) n. star apple tree; star apple fruit, used in native medicine to treat diarrhea.

káin: n. long skirt. (*pandiling*) **nakakain.** a. wearing a long skirt. [Tag. *saya*]

káing: n. a large open-worked basket. **ikaing.** v. to place in the *kaing* basket.

kaingéro: var. of *kainginero*: slash-and-burn farmer.

kaíngin: (Tag.) n. clearing of a forest for cultivation. **agkaingin.** v. to practice slash-and-burn agriculture.

kaínginéro: n. slash-and-burn farmer.

kaingúngot: n. spouse. (*asawa*; *ingungot*)

kaippasngáy: (f. *pasngay*) a. newly born. **Nasken nga agibit ti kaippasngay a maladaga tapno agbiag.** The newly born babe must cry in order to live.

kaír: (Sp. *caer*: fall) **agkair.** v. to be for; to befall, take effect. **pagkairan ti dalan.** n. crossing.

kaka-: var. of *apagka-* fractional prefix. **kakapát.** *num.* one fourth. (*apagkapat*)

káka: (Ch.) n. elder sibling; kind of lasso for animals. **agkaka.** n. two siblings together. **kakaen.** v. to be the elder of the two. [Knk. *yon-á*, Tag. *kakâ*]

kákab: n. chicken cage. **mangngakab.** n. a kind of small speckled bird.

kákab: n. grouper fish, *Serranidae* family.

kakaisúna: (f. *isú*) a. unique, sole, one and only. (*bugbugtong*) *conj.* since, now that. [Tag. *nag-iisá*]

kákak: agkakak. v. to cry (said of hens) (*kutak*). [Tag. *putak*]

kákang: n. term of address used for an older sister. (*manang*)

kákap: n. kind of edible marine fish.

kakapát: [*kaka-* + *uppat*] *num.* one-fourth. (*apagkapat*)

kakaptán: (f. *kapet*) n. rail of stairs.

kakatló: [*kaka-* + *talló*] *num.* one-third. '*apagkatlo*) **kakatluen.** v. to divide in three parts.

kakáw: (Sp. *cacao*: cacao) n. cacao. **madre kakaw.** n. a kind of tree with edible flowers and durable timber used in construction and hardwood flooring.

kakawáte: n. the *madre cacao* hardwood tree. [Tag. *balokbalok*]

kakdíl: kakdilan. v. to affect. **makakdil.** v. to be notched, indented, chipped.

kakdipás: makakdipas. v. to be done in a very short time.

káki: (Sp.) *n.* khaki.

kakísid: n. crisis.

kakitkíta: (f. *kita*) a. similar to.

kakkák: *n.* croaking of frogs. **agkakkak.** v. to croak (frogs), cry (hens) (*kakak*).

kakkáli: (f. *kali*) a. just dug up, just unearthed.

kakkirús: (f. *kirús*) a. just scraped; *n.* freshly scraped coconut meat.

kákok: kakoken. v. to knock on the head. **agkakok.** v. to make the sound of knocking something on the head. [Tag. *tuktók*]

kakók: n. kind of black cuckoo. **Kasla umok ti kakok ti buokna.** Her hair is like a cuckoo nest.

kaktúol: n. sound of clicking heels on the ground. **kumaktuol.** v. to click (heels on the ground when walking).

kalá₁: n. kind of gray hen with large bill and legs. **kalkala.** a. slow, sluggish. **kalkala pay.** a long time ago. **kalakala.** a. easy; with no worry. **kalakalaen.** v. to do with ease. **Saan met a kalakala a malipatak ti nabayag a relasionta.** It is not easy for me to forget our long relationship.

kalá₂: n. sandpaper. (*líha*)

kaláad: n. *Cissampelos pareira.* a vine with red fruits whose leaves are used to cure skin diseases. (*kalkalaad*; *kuskusipa*)

kaláan: n. indentation made on something: (foothold cut in the side of a pit, etc.); notch. [Tag. *gatlá*]

kaláb: kumalab. v. to stay put; cling to. [Tag. *kapit*]

kalába: n. honeycomb. (*kaba*) [Png. *kalába*, Tag. *saray*]

kalabása: *var.* of *karabasa*: squash, pumpkin. [Tag. *kalabasa*]

kalabéha: *var.* of *klabeha*: peg of a stringed instrument.

kalab-ít: var. of *kab-it*: hook.

kalabkáb: n. adipose tissue around the viscera. **kumalabkab.** v. to adhere to; cling to; stick to; climb up with hands and feet (*kaladkad*).

kalábus: (Sp. *calabozo*: prison) n. jail, prison. **ikalabus.** v. to imprison.

kalabóso: *var.* of *kalábus*: jail.

kalachuchí: n. the *frangipani* tree with white and pink flowers.

kaláday: *var.* of *kalláday*: slung on the shoulder; Dutch wife.

kaladkád: kumaladkad. v. to climb (using hands and feet). **kaladkaden.** v. to climb over something using hands and feet. [Tag. *akyát*]

kaládo: (Sp. *calado*: open work, fretwork) n. fretwork (used on top of walls for ventilation); open work in metal, cement, stone, wood, or cloth.

kaladúkad: n. the sound of heavy steps.

kálag₁: agkalag. v. to be obliged to do; to be compelled, bound. **ikalag.** v. to bump against the ground to remove dirt.

kálag₂: kalagen. v. to cut cards; divide deck. **nakakalag.** ready to show one's hand in cards.

kalagí: (obs.) **kumalagi.** v. to overcome.

kalaígid: kalkalaigid pay idi. It was a long time ago.

kalaíseg: kumalaiseg. v. to move from place to place.

kalákag: kumalakag. v. to be aggressive, persevering. **ikalakag.** v. to do to one's utmost; to work hard; care for; support. [Tag. *sipag*]

kalákal: kalakalen. v. to transplant.

kalakalá: (f. *kalá*) a. easy; with no worries. **kalakalaen.** v. to do without difficulty. [Tag. *dalí*]

kalakián: (f. *lalaki*) n. male animal; a. masculine; male.

kalalaingán: (f. *laing*) a. just the right amount; superlative of *laing*: smartest; one who knows everything. **Kalkalaingan ti ramanna.** The flavor is just right. **Kaska la kalalaingan.** It appears you know everything.

kalálaw: n. basket with small opening used to transport chickens. (*tiklis*; *baki*; *kagab*)

kalamansí(ng): n. *Citrus mitis.* the Philippine lemon, smaller than the *daláyap* lemon; the tree of the lemon. [Kpm. *kalamundíng*, Tag. *kalamansí*]

kalamáos: mangalkalamaos. a. miserable, wretched (*kuranges*). [Tag. *hirap*]

kalamár: (Sp. *calamar*) n. calamary, squid. (*pusít*)

kalámay: (Tag. also) n. kind of sticky coconut sweet made of rice.

kalambuáya: n. *barringtonia sp.* tree.

kalambukáy: see *alimbukáy*: a kind of slender vine with gray fruits.

kalámbre: (Sp. *calambre*: cramp) n. cramps, painful muscle contraction. **agkalambre.** v. to suffer from cramps. [Tag. *pulikat*]

kalamiát: **kumalamiat.** v. to clamber up (*kaladkad*). [Tag. *akyát*]

kalamidád: (Sp. *calamidad*: calamity) n. calamity. (*didigra*)

kalamíkam: **kumalamikam.** v. to interpose; meddle; intrude. **ikalamikam.** v. to mix up; say something irrelevant.

kalam-ít: **maikalam-it.** v. to involve someone in a plot, case; to get involved in a plot; participate. **kumalam-it.** v. to intrude, intermeddle. [Tag. *dawit*]

kalamíta: (Sp. *calamita*: loadstone) n. loadstone; magnetic needle of a compass.

kalamkám: var. of *kayamkam*: pervasive spreading.

kalamuáy: **ikalamuay.** v. to overturn.

kalamóko: (Sp. *calamoco*: icicle) *n.* icicle.

kalamón: (Sp. *calamón*: purple water hen) n. cormorant bird.

kalamundíng: (Tag.) *n.* Chinese orange, Panama orange; citrus tree bearing small, sour fruits.

kalámos: (Sp. *cálamo*: calamus) n. calamus reed; quill of a feather.

kalampág: n. slapping or knocking sound. (not on door) **kalampagen.** v. to knock on something (not door).

kalampít: see *kampít*: meddle; interfere.

kalámre: *var.* of *kalambre*: cramp, spasm.

kalandiáwan: n. kind of spiny vine with olive-like fruits.

kalannióg: n. egg white; albumen. [Tag. *putî ng itlóg*]

kalanútsi: *var.* of *kalatsutsi*: frangipani plant.

kalantangán: n. bull (male cattle).

kalantás: n. *Cedrela sp.* Philippine cedar tree.

kalantáy: n. bridge. (smaller than a *rangtay*) **agkalkalantay.** v. to clamber up. (as a monkey) **kalantayen.** v. to walk over a bridge. **ipakalantay.** v. to make a bug walk from one stick to another (as when spider fighting). [Png. *taytáy*, Tag. *tuláy*, *taytáy*]

kálang: **ikalang.** v. to kill. (*patayen*) **maikalang.** v. to be left to die (on road, battlefield, etc.). [Tag. *patay*]

kaláng: **agkalang.** v. to become loose; crack, fissure. (*lumkang*) **nakalang.** a. loose-jointed, shaky; rickety. [Tag. *luwág*]

kalangákang: n. overripe tamarind with skin sticking to the seed; shaken contents. **kumalangakang.** v. to become overripe; make the sound of a nut in its shell.

kalángay: n. kind of multicolored parrot.

kalanggíking: *n.* shrill cry.

kalangián: n. variety of late rice.

kalangíking: n. variety of awned *diket* rice. **agkalangiking.** v. to make a jingling sound or sound of shaken contents. **Kinaamakna ti uray bassit la a kalangiking.** He was afraid of even the slightest jingling. [Tag. *tagintíng*]

kalangkáng: **kalangkangen.** v. to form into a ring; catenate, connect in a series of links or rings.

kalangúgan: **agkalangugan.** v. to echo; produce a deep, hollow sound.

kalangúkong: n. deep, hollow sound. **agkalangukong.** v. to make a deep rattling sound like a coconut shell in a clay jar; produce the sound of a drum.

kalangtáy: var. of *kalantay*: bridge.

kalaúsig: **kumalausig.** v. to wring; squirm; be tormented, tortured. (*kulaiseg*)

kalaútot: n. a kind of tree.

kálap: **agkalap, mangalap.** v. to fish. **kalapen.** v. to catch fish. **mangngalap.** n. fisherman. **panagkalapan.** *n.* fishing season. **Inikkatnakami iti pakalapna.** He removed us from his fishing team. [Kal. *malaÿop*, Tag. *isdâ*]

kalapáti: (f. Sanskrit) n. pigeon; dove; wedding dance. **babai a kalapati.** *exp.* easy girl; whore. [Png. *malapati*, Knk. *kalupáti*, Kal., Tag. *kalapati*]

kalapáw: n. hut; shed; temporary shelter or covering; small house. (*abong*) **agkalapaw.** v. to put up a hut. **kalkalapaw.** n. playhouse. [Kal. *sigey*, Knk. *dugmám, kullúb, sagakbá, sagok-ó*, Tag. *bahay-kubo*]

kalapiáw: n. native raincoat made from palm leaves. (*annanga*) **nakakalapiaw.** a. wearing a *kalapiaw* raincoat.

kalapíni: n. kind of gray bird; the *kalupini* tree.

kalapkáp: **kalapkapen.** v. to trim fat off meat; deduce, conclude; guess. **mangalapkap.** v. to surmise; deduce; grope mentally. **pangalapkapan.** n. ways; means; strategy. **Awan ti pangalkalapkapanna.** He has no idea; is unskilled. [Tag. *sapantahà*]

kalár: n. features. (*panaglanglanga*)

kalásag: n. shield; defender; defensive covering. **agkalasag.** v. to wear a shield; use a shield. [Png. *kinlóng*, Tag. *kalasag*; Ivt. *kalasag* = stilt]

kalasákos: n. kind of *bibingka*-like rice pancake.

kalásaw: **agkalkalasaw, agkalasawan.** v. to be sparsely distributed in a wide space (few people in a large house, etc.). **No nalmesda, agkalkalasawda itan iti baybay.** If they drown, they will be lost in the vast sea.

kalasiáw: n. kind of long *bolo* (made in *Calasiao*, Pangasinan). (*buneng*)

kalasíkas: n. hoop; wall of a well; rim of a wheel. **kinalasikasan**. a. enchased.

kalaskás: n. rope to which coconut shells are attached, used in fishing like the *udáud*. **agkalaskas**. v. to fish. **kalaskasen**. v. to gather up scattered things.

kalasúgan: *n*. rain gutter; rain pipe; aqueduct.

kalát: n. limit; boundary; goal; ambition; end. **maipakalat**. v. to lag behind; be at the end.

kalatió: see *malabáto*: one-fourth of a Spanish real.

kalatkát: **kumalatkat**. v. to climb (said of vines and plants). **pakalatkat**. n. support made for climbing plants. **Nagitugkel iti saggaysa a pasok iti asideg ti puon ti paria tapno adda pagkalatkatanna**. He drove into the ground one stake next to each bittermelon plant so they will have something to climb on. [Png., Tag. *gapang* (crawl, creep)]

kalatukót: **agkalatukot**. v. to crack (said of knee joints); shake, tremble (knees). **agkalatukót ti túmengna**. he is very weak.

kalatsútsi: (Tag. also) n. frangipani plant with fragrant red or white flowers.

kálaw: n. kind of hornbill. **agkalkalaw**. v. to be absent at a meeting; fail to appear at an appointed time. **kakálaw**. n. kind of plant. [Kal. *kangaw*, Knk. *káew*]

kaláw: **kalawkalaw**. a. loose fitting (garments) (*labunglabúng*). [Tag. *luwáng*]

kaláwag: n. shelf made to hold dishes. **kalkalawag**. *Rivea sp*. twining shrub with globose fruits. [Tag. *banggera*]

kalawákaw: n. simpleton; moron; a. empty. **agkalawakaw**. v. to become empty; loose. **kalawakawen**. v. to dip the fingers in.

kalawásan: **agkalawasan**. v. to have more than enough room (with plural subject). **agkalkalawasan**. v. to stray; wander.

kalawákaw: a. empty, void; dull, simpleminded; loose, shaky; n. moron, simpleton. **kalawakawen**. v. to dip the fingers in. **Kalawakaw ti ulona**. She is simple minded; at a loss for words.

kalawíkaw: n. young edible branches of the cowpea. **kalawikawen**. v. to coil a rope. (*kawikaw*)

kalawíkiw: n. wagging of the tail. (*kiwkiw*) **kumalawikiw**. v. to wag the tail. **Nagkalawikiw ti asok a kimmarab-as**. My dog wagged his tail as he jumped up on his hind legs. [Png. *pilík*, Tag. *kawág*]

kalawkáw: **kalawkáwen**. v. to extract food without a utensil; stir liquid with the hand.

kaláy: (slang, *baliktad* of *lakay*) n. old man; husband.

kalay-áb: see *kalay-at*: climbing with difficulty.

kalayákay: see *kayákay*.

kalay-át: **agkalay-at**, **kumalay-at**. v. to climb with difficulty. **kalay-aten**. v. to climb something with difficulty. **No kayat ti kumalay-at, anusan ti garadgad**. If you want to climb, you must endure the scratches. [Tag. *akyát*]

kalbarió: (Sp. *calvario*: place where Jesus was crucified) n. cavalry; suffering, with many problems.

kalbít: n. touch; nudge. **kalbiten**. v. to nudge; pluck; make plucking motion of fingers to call someone's attention; touch, tip; pull the trigger of a gun. (*sagid, koldit, kolding*) **ikalbit**. v. to catch one's attention by touching. **kakalbitan, pangalbitan**. n. trigger. [Png. *kablit*, Tag. *kalbit, kalabít, kulbít*]

kalbó: (Sp. *calvo*: bald) a. bald (completely: *puridasdás, polinangnang*, with the forehead bald: *ludingás*). **kalbuen**. v. to shave off all the hair of someone; (fig.) deforest (a mountain, etc.). **nakalbo**. a. deforested. [Png. *koskos*, Tag. *panót, kalbó*]

kalbúro: (Tag.) *n*. carbide. (*karburo*)

kaldáang: (f. *leddaang*) **nakakalkaldaang**. a. pitiful; sorry; sorrowful.

kaldéra: (Sp. *caldera*: kettle) n. steam engine, boiler.

kalderéta: (Sp. *caldera*, with native employment of Spanish suffix) n. Philippine beef or goat stew. [Kpm. *kalgaríta*, Tag. *kalderéta*]

kaldéro: (Sp. *caldero*: cauldron) n. cauldron; kettle; pot.(*banga*) **Napattog ti kaldero**. *exp*. He lost everything, has no more work (*lit*: the kettle turned over). [Kal. *kanchilu*]

kalderón: (Sp. *calderón*: cauldron) n. large kettle, cauldron.

kaldiás: var. of *kuldias*: deflect; bounce off.

kaldíng: n. goat. (*buri*) **mangngalding**. n. goat thief; one who is fond of goat meat. [Bon. *gelding*, Ibg. *kazzí*, Kal. *keÿching*, Knk. *kaldí*, Png. *kandíng*, Tag. *kambíng*]

kaldít: **kalditen**. v. to bleed; open an abscess or boil.

káldo: (Sp. *caldo*: broth) n. soup; broth. (*digó*; *sopas*) **kalduen**. v. to make into broth (bones). **aroskaldo**. n. rice gruel cooked with chicken and ginger. [Tag. *sabáw, sopas* (Sp.)]

kalég: **makakaleg**. v. to be satisfied, content (used ironically); gratified (*pennek*). [Tag. *siyá*]

kalendário: (Sp. *calendario*: calendar) n. calendar. **ikalendario**. v. to write in the calendar.

kalenkén: **kalenkenen**. v. to draw aside (curtain; clothes hanging to dry); plait; ruffle; make a fold in clothes.

kaléra: (Sp. *calera*) *n.* limekiln; lime pit.

kalésa: (Sp. *calesa*: carriage) *n.* horse-drawn carriage. **mangalesa**. *v.* to drive a carriage. **kalesaen**. *v.* to transport in a carriage.

kaleséro: (f. *kalésa*) *n.* driver of a *kalesa*; maker of a *kalesa*. (*kutséro*)

kalesín(g): (f. *kalésa*) *n.* baby car; light horse-drawn carriage.

kalgáw: *n.* dry season; drought (*igáaw, daradar*). [Bon. *tiyágew*, Ivt. *rayuun*, Kal. *chegun*, Knk. *tiágew*, Tag. *tag-araw*]

káli: *n.* hole; pit; ditch; dike; drainage. **agkali**. *v.* to dig. **kumali**. *v.* to dig into. **ikali**. *v.* to bury something; dig up; inhume. **nakali**. *a.* dug out. **kalien**. *v.* to dig out; exhume. **nagkalian**. *n.* that which was exhumed. **pagkali**. *n.* digging instrument. **No diak maallilaw, asideg ti balitok iti pagkalkalianyo.** If I'm not mistaken, the gold is near where you are digging. [Bon. *káob*, Ibg. *kokkog, kokkob*, Ivt. *maycadiq*, Knk. *kaúb*, Kpm. *kulkul*, Png. *kotkót, seká, uká*, Tag. *hukay* (dig)]

kalí: *n.* kind of speckled brown and white hawk. **kinnalikali**. *n.* girl's game consisting of mother hen trying to defend her chicks from the hawk. [Kal. *bukaw, beÿlug*, Knk. *koáwi*, Tag. *lawin*]

kalí: *n.* pond, lagoon; reservoir. (*dan-aw*)

kaliádo: *a.* disobedient, semiwild (horse, cow, etc.) (*alsado*); hard to satisfy.

kaliát: *n.* finish line of a race.

kaliáw: *n.* braces of the yards of ships.

kalíbo: *n.* variety of awnless rice.

kalibúyog: (obs.) *n.* group of people with a leader. (*gimong*)

kalibúyot: **kumalibuyot**. *v.* to spread over the ground (plants).

kalíbre: (Sp. *calibre*: caliber) *n.* caliber (*kita; dásig*); top military officer; capacity or mental ability.

kalidád: (Sp. *calidad*: quality) *n.* quality (*kababalin*). **makalkalidad**. *a.* arranged according to quality.

kálie: (Sp. *calle*: street) *n.* street (*dalan*). **kaliehero**. *n.* street loafer.

kaliehón: (Sp. *callejón*: alley) *n.* alley; lane; narrow pass.

kalígid: **kalkaligid**. *v.* to differ; be distinct; to be far off; to be from a time in the past. (*salumina*) **ikaligid**. *v.* to evade; make excuses.

kaligrapía: (Sp. *caligrafía*: calligraphy) *n.* calligraphy, handwriting; penmanship.

kalígrapo: (Sp. *calígrafo*: calligrapher) *n.* handwriting expert, person with good penmanship.

kalikágum: *n.* wish, desire. (*kayat; tarigagay; essem*) **kalikaguman**. *v.* to desire; wish for; want; crave. **ikalikagum**. *v.* to propose; recom-

mend. **Awan ti panangikalikagumna nga agkasarda, idinto ta namansaanen ti dayawna.** He has no desire that they marry now that her honor is stained. [Knk. *dalimetmét*, Png. *inawá, ebég*, Tag. *nais, nasà*]

kalílis: *a.* unlawful; illegitimate. **kumalilis**. *v.* to avoid, evade; postpone. [Tag. *iwas* (evade)]

kalimbatóg: *n.* commotion, noise of many people; throb, palpitation; loud sound (*kulimbatóg*). **Nangngegmi ta kalimbatog idiay ngato.** We heard the commotion upstairs. [Tag. *karambola*]

kalimbukáy: see *alimbukáy*: a kind of slender vine with gray fruits.

kalimbunóg: see *maragawéd*: a kind of tree with white flowers, *Ehretia navesii*.

kalimduósan: **agkalimduosan**. *v.* to sweat profusely (*ling-et*). [Png. *sabáy*]

kalimusót: *a.* newly opened.

kalimpayáng: **kumalimpayang**. *v.* to hover (*alimpáyag*); keep on moving.

kalindário: (Sp. *calendario*: calendar) *n.* calendar.

kalintáyag: **agkalintayag**. *v.* to stretch oneself to reach for something; climb to the top.

kalintegán: (f. *lintég*) *n.* legal right; privilege. **nainkalintegan**. *a.* righteous. **Mamatiak a nainkalintegan ti inaramidmi.** I think what we did was righteous. **Siak ti dakdakkel ti kalinteganna.** I have more rights (to it). [Tag. *karapatán*]

kalintúdo: **agkalintudo**. *v.* to walk outside in the rain without covering. **agkalintuduan**. *v.* to stay in the rain. [Tag. *paulán*]

kalintúto: **agkalintuto**. *v.* to swim on the back.

Kalínga: *n.* mountainous province of north-central Luzon; the people of this province, the language of the *Kalinga*.

kalíngag: *n.* echo; resonance. (*áweng; allangúgan; allíngag*)

kalingagngág: *n.* echo; reverberating, amplified sound. **agikalingagngág**. *v.* to resound; speak through a loud horn. [Tag. *tunog*]

kalingíking: see *kalangíking*: jingling sound.

kalió: (Sp. *callo*: corn on foot, callus) *n.* corn (hardened surface on the foot); callus. [Kal. *bute*, Kpm. *galigúg*, Tag. *lipák*]

kálios: (Sp. *callos*: tripe) *n.* dish consisting of tripe, beans, pepper, and tomatoes.

kaliót: *n.* kind of tree with good timber, *Hopea acuminata*. (*dalingdingan*)

kalipikasión: (Sp. *calificación*: qualification) *n.* qualification. (*galád, sagúday, kabaelán*) **kalipikado**. *a.* qualified.

kalipkíp: *n.* precipice; edge, brink. **agkalipkip, kumalipkip**. *v.* to climb; creep; crawl; (reg.) to walk along a cliff or hillside. **kalipkipen.** v. to ascend (a mountain, etc.)

kaliptán: n. *Cerbera sp.* plant common to the seashore.

kális₁: (Sp. *cáliz) n.* chalice.

kális₂: agkalis. v. to fence, practice fencing; cross the hands or feet (while rubbing) due to cold.

kalís: agkalis. v. to excuse oneself. **ikalis.** v. to dissemble; dissimulate; disguise; express oneself unsatisfactorily; make excuses.

kalít: *var.* of *kallít:* dimple; cheat.

kaliwáweng: ikaliwaweng. *v.*to ignore, not pay attention to. (*kaliwengwéng*)

kaliwengwéng: see *paliwengweng:* ignore, not heed; avoid; escape; wander idly.

kaliwéte: (Tag.) *n.* left-handed person. (*kanigíd*)

kalká: kinalka. n. kind of red cotton yarn imported from Europe.

kalkág: ikalkag. v. to bump something against the ground (in order to remove the dirt). **kalkagan.** v. to bump somebody against the ground; hit someone on the head (with a basket, box, etc.). **No ikalkagna met ti kanawanna, agling-ika iti apagapaman samo ikawit ti kanawanmo iti pispisna.** If he hits you with his right hand, avert the blow and give him a left hook in his temple.

kalkál: agkalkal. v. to be sexually stimulated; to be in heat (*maya*); to walk behind a lady with desire and lewd thoughts. **kalkalen.** v. to move; seduce; incite, instigate, prompt; rummage through a pile or stack (of papers, clothes, etc.). **kalkalan.** v. to massage the genitals of a female animal to calm her down. [Tag. *landî*]

kalkalá: a. happening a long time ago; being present a long time ago.

kalkulár: (Sp. *calcular*) **kalkularen.** *v.* to calculate, compute. **kalkulasion.** *n.* calculation.

kálkulo: (Sp. *cálculo*) *n.* calculation; computation; estimate.

kallabá: (f. *laba*) *a.* just laundered.

kallábay: ikallabay. v. to put the arm around another's shoulder. (*sallabay*) **kallabayen.** *v.* to carry on the back. **Nagmasngaad ni Bong iti sikigan ti amana a nangikallabay ti kanawan a takkiagna.** Bong was squatting on the ground at the side of his father, who had his right arm over his shoulder. [Tag. *akbáy* (arm over another's shoulder)]

kallabés: (f. *labés*) *a.* last; past. **kallabes a bulan.** last month. [Tag. *nakaraán*]

kalláday: n. Dutch wife. (*sap-al*) **ikalladay.** v. to carry something suspended from a band slung over the shoulder.

kallaigí: ikallaigi. v. to baffle; disappoint; frustrate; foil.

kallaikí: var. of *kallaigi.*

kallamó: n. fish in *boggóong* that has not totally fermented; newcomer; apprentice; novice. [Tag. *baguhan* (novice)]

kallangán: n. kind of shed without walls.

kallangúgan: n. echo. **agkallangugan.** v. to echo; resound.

kallaútang: agkallautang. v. to drift; float at random; to be a stowaway.

kallaútit₁: n. *Terminalia sp.* tree.

kallaútit₂: a. very remote, far away (*adayó*); last (*údi*).

kallásaw: agkallasawan. v. to be overfilled (with fruits). **Nagkalkallasawan pay ti koloretena.** She overdid the rouge.

kallátik: *n.* rebound. **agkallatik.** v. to rebound; (*fig.*) echo; deflect, bounce off (*ballatek*). **Nagkallatik ti nalamuyot nga ayugna.** Her soft accent echoed. [Tag. *talbóg*]

kalláting: ikallating. v. to transmit; pass on; hand down. **agkallating.** v. to rebound (branches being flicked).

kallatók: n. deep; hollow sound. **agkallatok.** v. to drop; bounce off; fall on; to miss (fail to hit); make a deep, hollow sound.

kalláw: n. kind of large yellow waterbird with a long neck.

kallawásan: agkallawasan. v. to move at random, wander; be alone.

kalláwit: n. hook. (*kab-ít, káwit*) **kumallawit, kallawiten.** v. to catch with a hook; hook. **Narigat ti kallawitan ti di pay nataldengan.** *exp.* It is hard to catch with a hook what is not yet perforated. [Png. *sagór,* Tag. *kawit*]

kallaysá: n. marriage. (*kasár*) **ikallaysa.** v. to wed, marry someone. **agkallaysa.** v. to get married; *n.* husband and wife. **kumallaysa.** v. to be in agreement with; to be in harmony with. **mangallaysa.** n. person who officiates at a wedding ceremony (usually a priest). **paikallaysa.** v. to marry off. **pagkallaysaan.** v. force a marriage; have someone marry. **apagkallaysa.** n. newlywed. **Agkinnari dagiti agkallaysa iti sango ti altar a ni patay laeng ti mamagsina kadakuada.** Those getting married promise to each other in front of the altar that only death can separate them. [Png., Tag. *kasál* (Sp.)]

kallíd: n. dimple. **agkallid.** v. to cheat (*kusit*); deceive, trick; swindle. **kallidan.** a. dimpled. [Kal. *piyuk,* Knk. *tamíek,* Png. *abat na aping,* Tag. *biloy* (dimple)]

kallído: var. of *kallid.*

kallikí: var. of *kallaigí.*

kallíngag: n. echo. (*allungog*) **agkallingag**. v. to echo; vibrate. [Tag. *alingawngáw*]

kallingtá: (f. *lingtá*) *a*. just boiled.

kallít: n. cheek dimple. (*kallíd*)

kallukát: (f. *lukát*) *a*. just opened.

kallugóng: n. hat (generic term). **agkallugong**. v. to wear a hat. **kallugongen**. v. to cover with a hat. **nakakallugong**. *a*. wearing a hat. [Ivt. *tavahus*, Kal. *betukung*, Tag. *sambalilo* (Sp.)]

kalluít: n. kind of large mollusk with long red and white shell.

kallukmó: (f. *lukmó*) n. crustacean without a shell; newly hatched insect; a. invalid; weak; cowardly.

kallúlot: n. extra claw of a cock.

kallóng: *n*. stealing of food. **agkallong**. v. to eat food surreptitiously between meals; steal food. **mangngallong**. *n*. thief; (*fig*.) person who takes another's wife. **mangkakallong**. *n*. stealer of food; kind of bird. **kallongen**. v. to steal food; (fig.) to commit adultery with another's wife. **Kalkallóngenda daydiay asawana**. They are committing adultery with his wife. **Nagtarusak ti nagkallong iti kosina**. I went directly to the kitchen to steal food.

kallúop: *var*. of *kulluop*: cover; encase, enclose; surround.

kallútang: **agkallutang**. v. to drift; float at random. (*kallautang*)

kallúto: (f. *lúto*) a. just cooked. (*kalutlúto*, *apaglúto*)

kallóy: **nakalloy**. a. weak (*kapsut*). [Tag. *hinà*]

kalmá: (Sp. *calma*: calm) **nakalma**. a. calm, tranquil. (*talna*) **kalmado**. a. calmed; soothed from pain. **pagkalmaen**. *v*. to calm down, subdue, bring under control.

kalmán₁: n. the day before; yesterday. **idí kalmán**. yesterday. **idi bigat kalman**. yesterday morning. **Dumteng ti aldaw nga agbalinak a paset dagiti kalmanmo**. The day will come when I become a part of your yesteryears. [Bon. *gogga*, Png. *karomán*, Tag. *kahapon*]

kalmán₂: **marakalmán**. n. herb eaten by horses.

kalmánte: (Sp. *calmante*: sedative) n. sedative. (*mangpatalna*) **agpakalmante**. v. to take a sedative.

kalnaawán: (f. *linnaaw*) n. outdoors, open air. **agkalnaawan**. v. to be outdoors.

kalnuód: (f. *linód*) a. recently deceased. **Kalkalnuodna**. He just died.

kalnguópan: (f. *lungngúop*) n. enclosed place; hothouse, warm storage place used to hasten the ripening process of fruits; heart of the forest.

kaló: **kaluen**. v. to preserve fruits by cooking. **kaluan**. n. to enclose in wickerwork (bottles, etc.).

kaluát: n. kind of tray or basket hanging from the ceiling to keep food out of the reach of animals.

kalúb: n. cover; lid; kind of boy's coin-tossing game: (*páris*: even or *bangkíng*: odd). **kalúb ti matá**. n. eyelid. **ikalub**. v. to use to cover with. (*abbong*) **kaluban**. v. to cover, put a lid on. **pagkaluben**. see *pagakuben*. **kaluban ti sal-at**. *exp*. to cover up a bad thing. **agkinnalub**. *v*. to cover each other (two facing surfaces such as plates of shells). **de-kalub**. with a cover. **Nagkalub dagiti matana**. His eyes closed; (*fig*.) He is dead. **Padpadasenna laengen a kaluban ti basolna**. He is just trying to cover his mistake. [Ibg. *tekkeb*, *takkeg*, *kallág*, Ivt. *tuhung*, Kpm. *takap*, Png. *kolób*, Tag. *takíp*]

kalúb ti matá: *n*. eyelid. [Knk. *kúyup*, Tag. *takípmatá*, *talukapmatá*, *takubmatá*]

kalúban: n. sheath (covering knives or blades) (*baína*) **ikaluban**. v. to sheath. **sikakaluban**. a. sheathed. [Knk. *sitáp*, *sikét*, Png., Tag. *kaluban*]

kalubbába: see *kalumbába*: rest the chin on the hand.

kalub-ít: see *kab-it*: hook. (*kalláwit*, *káwit*; (*for fish*): *síma*, *banníit*)

kalubkúb₁: a. masked, disguised. **kalubkuben**. v. to plate; enclose. **kalubkuban ti dakes**. *exp*. to hide the bad.

kalubkúb₂: n. mudfish trap. (*lab-óg*)

kálod: n. young coconut with soft meat. **agkalod**. v. to gather young coconuts.

kálog: n. young coconut fruit; fool; silly person. [Ibg. *kálug*, Ivt. *maunged a nyuy*, Kpm., Tag. *buko*, Png. *malangwer* (young coconut)]

kalóg: (*coll*.) n. fellow who is easy to get along with; mischievous person. **kalogen**. v. to shake. (*wagwag*, *arigengén*) **agkalogkalog**. v. to waggle, wobble; wiggle. [Png., Tag. *kalóg*]

kaluít: n. kind of edible, small, conch-shaped shellfish.

kalúlot: n. ferrule; ring of scales on the legs of some cocks. **kalulutan**. v. to put a ring around the handle of a blade.

kalumámit: **agkalumamit**. v. to conclude, finish; end (*leppas*); be accomplished, achieved. **maikalkalumamit**. v. to be about to be finished. **ikalumamit**. v. to complicate, make difficult. [Tag. *tapós*]

kalúmay: n. a kind of plant whose fruits are used to make *tuba*.

kalumbába: **agkalumbaba**. v. to rest the chin on the arms. (*pannimid*, *kubbaba*, *kulimbaba*, *kalubbaba*, *kalimbaba*)

kalumbayá: n. kind of tree with edible olivelike fruits.

kalumbíbi: *var.* of *kalumbaba*: rest the chin on the arms.

kalombída: n. rope fastening the cart to the yoke.

kalumbítin: (f. *bitin*) **agkalumbitin.** v. to hang on; cling on to. [Tag. *lambitín*]

kalumiát: *var.* of *kalamiát*: climb, clamber up (*kalay-at*)

kalumínga: n. kind of fruit tree.

kalúmnia: (Sp. *calumnia*: calumny) n. calumny; slander.

kalumpagí: **agkalumpagi.** v. to move sideways; do something sideways. [Tag. *pataligíd*]

kalúmpio: *var.* of *kulumpio*: rocking chair.

kalunádsi: var. of the *kulalatsi* tree.

kalunákon: **nakalunakon.** a. sluggish, inactive; slow; indolent. [Tag. *burarâ*]

kalúnay: n. *Amaranthus spinosus,* spinachlike herb. **bulong-kalunay.** n. spinach leaves. **kalkalunay.** *n.* *Spinacia oleracea* plant with hollow stems, edible and fleshy leaves.

kaluníkon: a. curled up (snakes, etc.). (*kawíkaw*)

kalunkón$_1$: **agkalunkon.** v. to clear the table after meals. **kalunkonen.** v. to put away after using, gather plates after eating. [Tag. *samsám*]

kalunkón$_2$: **agkalunkon ti anges (biag)** v. to be on the point of death. **Nagkalunkonen.** He died.

kalóng: **kalongkalong.** a. loose (not fitting) (*lawa*). [Tag. *luwáng*; *kalong* = lap]

kalongíking: see *kalangíking*.

kalongkóng: **agkalungkong.** v. to collect and stack dishes after eating; fix, arrange.

kalupápis: **ikalkalupapis.** v. to talk or do in a roundabout, indirect way, beat around the bush in talking. (*palikawkáw*)

kalupí: n. kind of basket with rectangular bottom used to store rice.

kalupíni: n. *Avicennia officinalis.* a tree with yellow flowers living in mangrove swamps.

kalupípis: **ikalupipis.** v. to do in a roundabout way; beat around the bush. (*kalupápis*) **Awan ti maikalkalupipis a sao.** He does not beat around the bush (gets straight to the point) when talking.

kalupít: var. of *kalupi*.

kalupkúp: n. gold plating; overlay; gilding. **kalupkupan.** v. to cover; plate; overlay; gild; put a shoe on (a horse). **ikalupkup.** v. to encrust on. **makalupkupan.** v. to be encrusted with something. **Dimmerosasen ti langit ket ngangnganin makalupkopan amin a natda nga asul ti rabii.** The sky is pink already and

all of the remaining blue sky is overlaid by the night. [Tag. *kalupkóp*]

kaloría: (Sp. *caloría*: calorie) n. calorie.

kálus: n. strickle (used in striking grain). **kalusen.** v. to level off. [Tag. *kalos*]

kalút: **kumalut.** (obs.) v. to cut badly.

kalutákit: (obs.) **kumalutakit.** v. to keep one's inherited property.

kalúya: **ikaluya.** v. to hinder, obstruct; prohibit; protect; guard; cover; shield; help in a fight (*kanawa*). [Kal. *isaÿak*, Tag. *alagà* (protect, attend to)]

kalpás: (f. *leppas*) **kalkalpas.** a. just finished. **kalpasán.** prep., adv. after, afterwards; n. period after. **kalpasanna.** adv. afterwards.

kalpót: **kalputan.** v. to engulf with a web (said of spiders); enwrap, envelop; involve (*sáput*); *var.* of *karámut*: scratch; (*fig.*) copulate. **makalputan.** v. to be enwrapped, engulfed (in a web). **makakalkalpot.** v. to have the urge to enwrap food, spin a web. [Knk. *kilpút*]

kalsáda: (Sp. *calzada*: road) n. paved street, road. (*dalan*) **agkalsada.** v. to build a road. **pagkalsada.** *n.* money for building a road; road materials. **mangkalsada.** *v.* to follow a road; construct a road. [Kal. *keÿsa*, Tag. *daán*]

kalsádo: (Sp. *calzado*: footwear, obs.) n. footwear.

kalsadór: (Sp. *calzador*: shoehorn) n. shoehorn.

kalséb: a. cowardly; shy, timid; **agkalseb.** v. to be cowardly; shy; to have an inferiority complex. **pangalseben.** *a.* rather shy (*bain, madleg*). [Tag. *hiyâ*]

kalsetín: (Sp. *calcetín*: socks) n. socks; stockings.

kálsio: (Sp. *calcio*: calcium) n. calcium.

kalsó: (Sp. *calzo*: wedge) n. prop (*túkal*); wedge. **kalsuan.** v. to prop; hold by using a wedge; *n.* folded piece of cloth used as a girdle for the abdomen of a woman who has just delivered a baby.

kalsón: (Sp. *calzón*: long trousers) n. trousers with buttons going to the ankle; short pants; men's underwear.

kalsonsíllo: (Sp. *calzoncillo*: pants) n. knee breeches; men's underwear with strings around the waist.

kaltáang: n. midnight; middle of the night. **Kaltaang kanon ti rabii idi sumangpet a nagararudok iti siledna.** It was supposedly midnight when she returned, sneaking into her room. [Ivt. *mavak*, Knk. *kámag labí*, Tag. *hatinggabí*]

kaltás: **kumaltas.** v. to leave a group; remove oneself from. **kaltasen.** v. to take without permission, take from.

kaltí: n. sugar syrup. **agkalti**. v. to cook sweet potatoes, unripe bananas, etc. in boiling sugar. **kaltien**. v. to slice and cook in boiling sugar. **kinalti**. n. unripe fruits or sweet potatoes cooked in sugar. [Tag. *minatamís*]

kálye: *var.* spelling of *kalie*: street, road.

kalyísta: (f. *kalyo*) n. person specializing in the removal of calluses.

kalyó: *var.* spelling of *kalio*: corn hardening on skin.

-kam: var. of *-kami*.

káma: (Sp. *cama*: bed) n. cushioned bed; cot (*pagturogan*; *kátre*); native dam made usually of trees. **pakamaen**. v. to dam up.

kamáda: (Sp. *camada*: layer; litter; brood) n. litter of animals; small flock; band of thieves; gang; heap, pile. **ikamada**. v. to pile up; stack. **nakamada**. a. pile up, stored up. **kamador**. n. one who stacks inventory in a warehouse. **pagkamadaan**. *n.* storehouse. **kamkamada**. *n.* stockpile.

kamadór: (f. *kamada*) n. person who stocks merchandise in a warehouse.

kamágong: see *mabólo*.

kamákam: **makamakam**. v. to overtake, catch up with; be on time for. **agkamakam**. v. to grab, touch, overreach. **kamkamakamen**. v. to try to reach. **agkakamakam**. v. to follow closely; to occur in rapid succession. **ikamakam**. v. to catch up with; do in time; rush to do something; bring something to someone who has just left. **maikamakam**. *v.* to be able to do on time. **makamakam**. *v.* to catch up with; be on time for. **pakamakam**. *n.* postscript. **agkamakam iti oras**. to hurry in order to be on time. **Di mabayag, agkakamakamen dagiti kirayna**. In just a short while, her winks were already occurring in rapid succession. **Makamakamyo pay la ti umuna a biahe idiay Vigan**. You can still catch the first trip to Vigan. **Agkakamakamen ti panagangesna**. He is short of breath. [Tag. *habol*]

kamalála: n. concubine, person committing adultery. (*abig*) **makikamalala**. v. to commit adultery. **pannakikamalala**. n. adultery. **Nasakit a makita dagiti tao a makikamkamala ti asawana**. It is sickening to see the people that commit adultery with his wife. [Kal. *chegchegas*, Tag. *apíd*; *kalaguyò*]

kamaleón: (Sp. *camaleón*: chameleon) n. chameleon, lizard that changes color.

kamalí: (Tag., Ilocano version is *kammalí*) n. mistake, error; sin. **agkamali**. v. to err, make a mistake.

kamálig: n. kind of low granary or warehouse, lower than the *agamang* but with a larger

capacity (*sarusar*). **ikamalig**. v. to store in the granary. [Png. *kamálir*, Tag. *kamalig*]

kamálit: n. *Merremia sp.* vines with yellow flowers.

kamalmán: (f. *malém*) n. (the very) afternoon. **kamalmanna**. n. yesterday afternoon. **kamalmannanto**. n. tomorrow afternoon.

kamán: n. family, household (*sangaputotan*; *pamilia*); lineage; descendants.

kamánaw: n. patches of discolored pale skin. **agkamanaw**. v. to be affected with the *kamanaw* skin affliction. [Png. *kaménew*, Tag. *an-án*]

kamantígi: n. *Impatiens balsamina*, balsam, touch-me-not, used in native medicine against boils.

kamantirís: (f. *Camanchiles*, Mex. *quamochitl*) see *damortís*. [Tag. *kamatsili*]

kamantsíle: n. *Pithecolobium duke*, type of tree.

kámang: n. asylum, refuge; shelter; protection. **kumamang, kamangen**. v. to take refuge. **agkamang**. v. to join, unite; connect, combine; be joined in marriage; to be joined by affinity. **kamangan**. n. joint. **ikamang**. v. to connect, join; bring to a court; to live in with a lover. **maikamang**. v. to be joined or related by marriage; be joined to. **pakaikamangan**. n. in-laws, the new members of the family acquired by a marriage bond. **agkakamang**. v. to be joined, interlaced; intersecting. **napagkakamang**. a. joined together. **pagkamangan**. n. refuge. **Maikamkamangka laeng**. *exp.* You are just related (to our family) through marriage. **Nasaysayaat ngarud no ikamangta iti husgado**. It would be better then if we bring it to court. **Nagbakwit dagiti dayo malaksid dagiti naikamangen itoy nga ili**. The strangers evacuated this city, except the people with marriage ties. **Alut-otenmi ti saput ti dugoldugolan manipud iti ubetna sami ibantebanteng nga ikamangkamang kadagiti bulbulong ken sangsanga**. We pulled the web of the *dugoldugolan* spider from its anus, then we stretched it out to connect it to the leaves and branches. **Sika laeng ti mabalinmi a pagkamangan**. You are the only one with whom we can seek refuge. [Tag. *kupkóp*; Knk. *kámang* = crawl]

kamángeg: n. kind of yam, *Dioscorea sp.* (*tugi*)

kamangián: n. kind of Chinese incense.

kamaúdi: (f. *údi*) n. hind leg. **kamaudiánan**. n. end, conclusion.

kamauná: (f. *uná*) n. foreleg.

kámara: (Sp. *cámara:* chamber, house in senate) n. house in a senate; house of representatives; hall, parlor; chamber; photographic camera.

kamará: n. *Piper retrofractum* climbing vine with edible leaves.

kamaréra: (Sp. *camarera*: waitress) n. waitress; stewardess; chambermaid, female servant.

kamaréro: (Sp. *camarero*: waiter) n. steward; waiter; valet; servant.

kamarín: (Sp. *camarín*: granary) n. barn; granary. (*kamálig, sarúsar, agámang*) **ikamarin.** v. to store in the barn.

kamáro: see *kamíro*: look after; take care of. (*awir*)

kamarón: (Sp. *camarón*: prawn) n. prawn. **kamaron-rebosado.** n. breaded prawns.

kamaróte: (Sp. *camarote*: ship cabin) n. ship cabin, berth; stateroom.

kamás: n. jicama. (*singkamas*)

kamasoén: n. cock with black and white plumage.

kámat: kamaten. v. to chase, pursue; run after. **agkakamat.** v. to follow at close range. **makamat.** v. to become dry, empty of water (wells) **kamatkamaten.** v. to drive away. **ikamat.** v. to run after. **pakamat.** n. chase with a dog. **kamkamaten ti angesna.** *exp.* to catch one's breath. **Tallo a puntos ti pangamatanmi kadakuada.** We are three points under them. **Ti aso a mannaul, adayo ti pakamatna.** The dog that barks is far from its pursuit. [Ibg. *kamat, daddág,* Ifg. *pudgon,* Ivt. *lakatan,* Kpm. *tagal,* Png. *abut, pangosil,* Tag. *habol*]

kamatá: (f. *mata*) n. eye infection; ophthalmia, inflammation of the eyes; sore eyes. **agkamata.** v. to have an eye condition with red eyes and gum discharge; to have sore eyes. [Knk. *mayangmáng,* Png. *kamata*]

kamátis: (Sp. *tomate*) n. tomato. **agkamatis.** v. to become swollen like a tomato (said of a circumcised penis). **kamatisan.** *v.* to add tomatoes to. **ti kamatis, saan nga agbunga't tarong.** *exp.* The tomato does not bear eggplant fruit, referring to the unlikelihood of a bad family raising a good child. [Knk. *gubgubbáw*]

kamató: n. kind of large poisonous spider; kind of shrimp with small mouth parts.

kamatsíle: *var.* of *kamantsile*: damortis tree.

kam-áw: n. kind of broad-mouthed jar used for holding lard.

kámay: n. young head louse. (egg: *lis-a,* fully grown: *kuto*) **kamayan.** (obs.) v. to do slowly. [Kal. *pàimayan* (young head louse)]

kambál: a. having two yokes (eggs); twin (*singin*); n. variety of rice with large kernel. [Tag. *kambál* = twin]

kámbas: (Eng. canvass) **agkambas, kambasen.** v. to go from store to store in search of the lowest price; solicit (votes, opinions); inquire from place to place; canvass.

kambiár: (Sp. *cambiar*: change) **agkambiar.** v. to do together; to be in a partnership. **makambiaran.** v. to be reshuffled (employees).

kambíng: n. frenum. **kambingen.** v. to unite, join; put together (edges of a wound). [Tag. *kambíng* = goat]

kámbio: (Sp. *cambio*: change) n. gearshift; change (money); work shift. **agkambio.** v. to change gears in a vehicle; work in shifts.

kambuáw: n. kind of large, nocturnal green grasshopper. (*riari*)

kambóng: n. large cooking jar.

kambór: *n.* mixing. **agkambor.** *v.* to mix together (various substances) (*laok*). **kamboran.** *v.* to blend, mix. [Tag. *halò*]

kambút: see *karomsí*: white dove orchid, *Dendrobium crumenatum.*

kambráy: (Sp. *cambray*: cambric) n. cambric, fine linen material.

kamélia: (Sp. *camella*: female camel) n. female camel; camellia, an ornamental greenhouse shrub.

kamélio: (Sp. *camello*: camel) n. camel.

kámeng: *n.* genitals. [Tag. *bayág*]

kaméng$_1$: n. member, delegate, representative. (*pannakabagí*). **panagkameng.** n. membership. **maikameng.** v. to become a member of; become a part of. **kamkameng.** *n.* members; all the parts of the body. **Disinuebe ti tawenna idi kimmameng iti gunglo.** He was nineteen when he joined the organization. [Png. *móyong,* Tag. *sapì*]

kaméng$_2$: n. limb of crustaceans; mouthparts, pincers, antennae; tendril; limbs. **kamkameng.** *n.* limbs; organs of the body.

kámera: (Eng.) n. camera. (*kodák, pangretratuan*)

kamerón: (Sp. *camarón*: shrimp) *n.* shrimp (used to name certain recipes).

kamés: *var.* of *kammés*: hand cleaning by removal.

kamét: **agkamet.** v. to stick together. **agkakamet.** v. to stick together in a disorderly way. [Tag. *dikít*]

-kamí: *pron.* exclusive first person *-ak* series pronoun: we (*-kam*). [Png., Tag. *kamí*]

kamiá: n. species of fragrant white flower.

kamíding: n. large mole.

kamília: (Sp. *camilla*: small bed) n. small bed; stretcher for carrying the sick.

kamíling: **kinamiling.** v. variety of awned late rice.

kaminéro: (Sp. *caminero*: street sweeper) n. person responsible for repairing roads; street sweeper.

kamíno: (Sp. *camino*: road) n. road; avenue; street. **kamino real**. n. main highway.

-kaminto: enclitic expressing first person plural exclusive actor and future action (*-kamto*). **Mapankaminto**. We will go.

kam-ír: **kam-iren**. *v*. to snatch, grab; grasp and pick up, gather.

kamíring: n. *Semecarpus cuneiformis* shrub that yields a rash-causing poison; juice of an unripe mango. **makamiríngan**. v. to have nettle rash, hives, urticaria; be affected by the *kamiring* plant.

kamíro: **kamiruen**. v. to take care of; be in charge; look after.

kamísa: (Sp. *camisa*: shirt) n. shirt, jacket. **kamisa déntro**. n. men's shirt. **kamisa tsíno**. n. type of men's T-shirt with buttons in the front and tight sleeves.

kamisadéntro: (Sp. *camisadentro*: undershirt) n. dress shirt.

kamisería: (Sp. *camisería*: shirt store) n. shirt store.

kamiséta: (Sp. *camiseta*: undershirt) n. sleeveless undershirt.

kamisóla: (Sp. *camisola*: blouse) n. chemise; women's undergarment of upper body. **No kas kenka laeng ti mangidatdaton iti panagayatna kaniak, agbakbaketak laengen ditoy kamisola**. If only people like you offer their love to me, I will just grow old in my chemise.

kamisón: (Sp. *camisón*: chemise) n. chemise, slip; half-slip; petticoat.

kámit: see *kalomámit*: finish, complete, end. (*gíbus*, *leppás*)

kamít: **kamiten**. v. to profit, benefit from, gain from.

kamkám: *a*. greedy (*agum*). **kamkamen**. v. to acquire unjustly or illegally. **Narigat a pagtalkan ti tao nga kamkam**. Greedy people are hard to trust. [Png., Tag. *kamkám*]

kamkampílan: n. tree with big pods; the fruit of this tree.

kamlát: **mangamkamlat**. v. to be destitute (*agpanglaw*). [Tag. *hirap*]

kamlós: **agkamlos**. v. to slip, slide out of place. (*gamdir*; *labsin*; *kasiw*; *ligsay*; *labsiw*) **kumamlos**. v. to slide out of place; loosen; untie. [Tag. *dulás*]

kamlóy: *a*. clumsy; weak; negligent. **kamluyan**. v. to drop out of clumsiness.

kammá: **kammaen**. v. to take without permission; snatch (*gammat*). [Tag. *dakmâ*]

kammáal: see *gammál*: grip, clasp, grasp. (*iggem*, *kapét*)

kammáboy: *var*. of *mammáboy*: heron.

kammadáng: n. kind of wooden shoe with a high heel used in rainy weather. **agkammadang**. v. to wear high-heeled shoes.

kammágay: n. kind of small locust. (*dudon*)

kammalí: n. mistake, error. (*biddut*) **agkammali**. v. to commit a mistake; err. [Knk. *báki*, *bangsá*, Png. *lingó*, Tag. *kamalî*]

kammán: Contraction of *kano man*.

kammáng: n. kind of small net used in freshwater fishing.

kammaúdi: *var*. of *kamaudi*: hind leg.

kammaúlaw: **kamkammaulaw**. *Datura alba* herb with long white flowers and poisonous spiny fruits. **agkamkammaulaw**. *v*. to go crazy; be very dizzy.

kammauná: *var*. of *kamauna*: foreleg.

kammatalék: n. confidence; trust. (*talék*) **agkammatalek**. v. to rely on; depend on; confide in; have confidence in. [Tag. *tiwalà*]

kammayét: **agkammayet**. v. to differ (ideas, etc.). **Nairut ti panagkakammayet dagiti Pilipino**. The differing opinions of the Filipino people are deep. **Saanko a pabasolen ida no agkakammayetda**. I don't blame them if they differ in opinion.

kammél: **agkammel**. v. to fish with the hands; fish in a river. **mangngammel**. *n*. fisherman. **makakammel**. v. to be able to catch fish with the hands. [Knk. *sílib* (fish with hands), Tag. *mangisdâ* (fish)]

kammés: **agkammes**. v. to remove weeds by hand (*lámon*); clean rice fields.

kammét: n. clutch; grip; hold; handful (of cooked rice). **agkammet**. v. to eat with the hands. **kammeten**. v. to grasp with the fingertips. (rice) **kumammet**. v. to have a quick meal before leaving the house. **sangkakammet**. *n*. handful. [Png. *kamót*, Tag. *magkamáy*]

kammó: (coll.) *abbr*. of *indiak ammó*: I don't know; *abbr*. of *ikkanmo*: give it. [Png. *awey*, Tag. *ewan*, *aywán* (don't know)]

kammúol: n. welt; bump from a blow. (*dúnor*; *dugol*) **agkammuol**. v. to swell; form a welt. [Tag. *bukol*]

kammúor: *var*. *of* kammúol*: bump, welt.

kámo: **ikamo**. v. to persuade, influence. **kumamo**. v. to set the pace; take the lead; show the example. [Tag. *himok*, *hikayat*]

kámol₁: **nakamol**. *a*. slow, sluggish (*bontog*); inactive; lazy (*sadut*). [Tag. *kupad*]

kámol₂: **agkamolkamol**. *v*. to eat without teeth.

kamuntatála: n. morning star, Lucifer, Venus. (*kabuntala*, *baggak*)

kamúras: n. measles, rubella (*karibnás*); plant used for binding purposes. **agkamuras.** v. to have measles. (*agkaribnás*) [Bon., Knk. *kamólas*, Bon. *kalagnas*, Kpm. *ípe*, Png. *barís*, Tag. *tigdás*]

kamúro: n. pimple. (*taramídong*) **agkamuro.** v. to break out, develop pimples. **kamukamuro.** *a.* pimply, full of pimples. [Bon. *kamólo*, Kal. *chaliwaat*, Knk. *dalliwáat*, Kpm. *dalyáwat*, Png. *kamúro*, Tag. *tagihawat*]

kámos: n. scratch mark (*karámut*). [Tag. *kalmót*, *gasgás*]

kamotál: (Sp. *camotal*) n. sweet potato field.

kamóte: (AmSp., also *kamotit*) n. sweet potato, *Ipomoea batatas*; (*fig.*) poor showing. **kamoteng-kahoy.** (Tag.) *n.* cassava, manioc. **kamote-cue.** *n.* barbecued sweet potato on a stick (*kamotit*). **kamote-de-moro.** *n.* yucca tuber. **Kasla kakkali a kamote.** He is like a freshly dug up sweet potato (said of a dirty person). [Ibg. *kamósi*, Ifg. *gattok*, Itg. *katíla*, Ivt. *wakay*, Kal. *katila*, Knk. *luktu*, *lutúd*, Kpm., Png., Tag. *kamote*]

kamótig: see *kamótit*.

kamótit: n. *Ipomoea batatas*, sweet potato.

kamotít: n. last hand of the banana fruit stem.

kamúyaw: n. kind of wild lemon.

kampá: n. *Rhyacicthys aspra*, kind of white freshwater bottom-dwelling fish.

kampaménto: (Sp. *campamento*) n. camp, encampment.

kampána: (Sp. *campana*: bell) n. bell. (*batingting*) **kamkampana.** n. a bell-shaped flower. **pagkampanaan.** n. bell tower.

kampanário: (Sp. *campanario*: bell tower) n. bell tower.

kampanéro: (Sp. *campanero*: bellman) n. bell maker; bell ringer.

kampánia: (Sp. *campaña*: campaign) n. political campaign. **agkampania.** v. to campaign.

kampanília: (Sp. *campanilla*: small bell) n. small bell. (*kililíng*) **Apaguni ti kampanilia, dimmuklusen.** As soon as the bell rang, he attacked.

kampaniliéro: (Sp. *campanillero*) *n.* bell ringer; public crier.

kampáy: *abbr.* of *kanó pay*: also as they say.

kampeón: (Sp. *campeón*: champion) n. champion. (*nagballigi*)

kampeonáto: (Sp. *campeonato*: championship) n. championship.

kampí: **kumampi, kampien.** v. to join, offer allegiance to.

kampiár: (Sp. *campear*: pasture) **agkampiar.** v. to pasture, be in the field. **agkikinnampiar.** v. to intermingle with each other.

kampílan: n. sword; saber. (*badáng*) **kamkampilan.** n. *Canavallia ensiformis* beans.

kampís: see *baknís*: to tear with the teeth; n. scallop.

kampít₁: n. kitchen knife. (*immokó*)

kampít₂: **kumampit.** v. to interfere, meddle (*makibiang*); talk beside the point. **ikampit.** v. to get entangled; openly sympathize with the person being investigated. [Tag. *makialám* (meddle)]

kámpo: (Sp. *campo*: camp) n. camp (*pagsangbayan*; *pagsardengan*); quarters; bunkhouse. **pagkampuan.** n. campgrounds; camping area. [Tag. *himpilan*]

kampór: n. mixture, medley. (*laók*) **pagkamporen.** v. to mix. [Tag. *halò*]

kamposánto: (Sp. *camposanto*: holy field) n. cemetery. (*yan dagiti tantaném*) **agpakamposanto.** v. to go to the cemetery. [Tag. *libingan*]

kampúso: n. top (spinning), peg top. (*sunay*; *trumpo*) **kimmampuso a rupa.** n. oval face (like a top). [Tag. *trumpo* (Sp.)]

kamráy: see *kambray*.

kamrít: **nakamrit.** a. quarrelsome; conceited. **kamriten.** v. to quarrel with.

-kamto: var. of *-kaminto*.

kamtúd: **makamtud.** a. to be short, in short supply, to be deficient. **nakamtud.** *a.* short in supply, lacking, deficient. **pagkamtudan.** n. shortage (*kiddít*, *kurang*). [Tag. *kulang*]

kan: var. of *kanó*. [Tag. *daw*]

kana- (*ka-* + *-an-* *-V-*) prefix used with onomatopoetic roots to indicate a quick succession of sounds. **kanadpaak.** succession of crackling sounds. **kanakráad.** sound of continuous scraping. **kanalbuong.** succession of explosions. **agkanalbuong.** to produce these sounds. **kanalpaak.** succession of clapping or slapping sounds. **agkanalpaak.** to produce these sounds. **kanalpiit.** succession of snapping sounds; slipper on floor; clashing heel. **kanalpuot.** succession of windy sounds, storm; successive flatulence. **kanalsitak.** succession of clashing swords. **kanaltaak.** succession of popping sounds; sound of rain on a tin roof. **kanaltiik.** succession of snapping sounds; falling gravel. **kanaltuok.** succession of hollow metallic sounds.

kána: **nakana.** a. acute, sharp, pungent (pain), biting, harmful; serious. **Apay met a ti pudno a ragsak agramut iti nakana a liday?** Why does true joy take roots in utter sadness? [Tag. *lubhâ*]

kaná: (Tag.) **kanaen.** *v.* to attack with a deadly weapon.

kanáat: **nakanaat**. a. slow, sluggish. (*bontog*) **agkanaat**. v. to prepare oneself.

kanabláag: n. sound of thumping on wood. **agkanablaag**. v. to thump on a wooden board.

kanabláang: (f. *biláng*) n. var. of *kanabraang*: resounding noise.

kanablúong: (f. *bilóng*) n. sound of explosions.

kanabráang: (f. *biráng*) n. resounding noise, sound of a gong, hitting metal, scraping a can, etc. **agkanabraang, kumanabraang**. v. to resound loudly (gong).

kanabrúong: (f. *biróng*) **agkanabruong**. v. to make the sound of gunfire.

kanabséet: var. of *kanabsiit*: sound of lightning.

kanabsíit: (f. *bisit*) n. sound of thunder or whiplash. **pagkanabsiiten**. v. to whip resoundingly.

kanabsúok: (f. *bisok*) n. sound of splashing in the water.

kanabsúor: n. resonant sound of roaring or rumbling; thump. **Natukaykami idi adda agkanabsuor iti danum.** We were agitated when there was a heavy thumping splash in the water.

kanabsúot: (f. *bisot*) n. hollow sound; sound of a balloon releasing air or a person farting.

kanabtúog: (f. *bitóg*) n. stomping noise. **agkanabtuog**. v. to make a stomping noise; fall down with a heavy thud. **manabtuog**. v. to fall down with a thud. **Nakigtotak iti kanabtuog iti bangir.** I was startled by the thump next door. [Tag. *kalabóg*]

Kánada: (Sp. *Canadá*: Canada) n. Canada. **Kanadiano**. n. Canadian.

kanáda: **maikanada**. v. to be proper, appropriate, suitable; reasonable; correct. [Tag. *akmâ*]

kanadlúog: (f. *dilúg*) n. sound of thunder. **agkanadluog**. v. to rumble (thunder).

kanadpáag: (f. *dipág*) n. sound of crumbling (buildings). **agkanadpaag**. v. to crumble; to collapse.

kanadpáak: (f. *dipák*) n. sound of continuous crackling. **agkanadpaak**. v. to crackle.

kanadpúor: (f. *dipór*) n. the sound of continuous crumbling (buildings). **agkanadpuor**. v. to make a succession of crumbling or collapsing sounds.

kanagkág₁: n. bright moonlight. (*sellág*) **kumanagkag nga bulan**. n. bright moon.

kanagkág₂: n. dull sound of things being beaten.

kanaglúong: (f. *gilúng*) n. sound of continuous rumbling or thunder. **agkanagluong**. v. to make the sound of continuous rumbling or thunder.

kanagpáak: (f. *gipák*) n. sound of loud laughter or stomping feet.

kanagrúod: (f. *girúd*) n. sound of continuous thunder or loud rumbling.

kanagtúog: n. sound of fireworks or violent knocking on a door.

kanáig: (f. *naig*) **kanaig ti**. prep. aside from; in addition to.

kanáka: (Hawaiian use only) n. Native Hawaiian. (*Hawayano, taga-Hawaii*)

kanákan: **ikanakan**. v. to anticipate, do before the normal time.

kanakiáas: n. clanging sound; rustling sound; scampering from fear.

kanakláang: (f. *kiláng*) **agkanaklaang**. v. to make the sound of an object rattling in a tin can.

kanaklíing: (f. *kilíng*) **kumanakliing**. v. to make the sound of shattering glass. (*kanarpaak*)

kanaklúong: (f. *kilóng*) n. sound of a rattling object in an earthen jar. **agkanakluong**. v. to rattle in an earthen jar.

kanakráad: (f. *kirád*) n. sound of continuous scraping. **agkanakraad**. v. to scrape continuously. [Png. *kidkid, kadkad*, Tag. *kayod*]

kanakráas: (f. *kirás*) n. sound of continuous crashing of falling heavy objects.

kanakríis: (f. *kirís*) n. succession of shrill sounds.

kanaktéek: (f. *kitek*) n. sound of continuous ticking. **agkanakteek**. v. to click continuously.

kanakteél: n. sound of falling rain; continuous hitting; tinkling sound. **kumanakteel**. v. to happen continuously; happen one after another.

kanaktíil: n. the sound of gravel falling down a slope. **agkanaktiil**. v. to make the sound of falling gravel.

kanaktúol: (f. *kitól*) n. sound of heels hitting the floor. **agkanaktuol**. v. to click (heels against the floor). **Napardas ti kanaktuol ti sapatos nga immadayo.** The sound of the shoes running away was fast. [Tag. *kalatók*]

kanál: (Sp. *canal*: canal) n. canal. **agkanal**. v. to make a canal. **ikanal**. v. to drive into a canal; dump, throw into a canal.

kanaládo: (Sp. *canalado*: corrugated) a. grooved, corrugated.

kanalbúog: (f. *libóg*) n. sound of a gun; gunshot. (*kanalbuong*) **manalbuog**. v. to explode (gun). [Tag. *puták*]

kanalbúong: (f. *libóng*) n. sound of continuous explosions. **agkanalbuong**. v. to resound (said of explosions). [Tag. *puták*]

kanaldúok: (f. *lidok*) n. sound of swallowing. **agkanalduok**. v. to swallow noisily. **agkarakanalduok**. v. to swallow noisily and repeatedly as when tasting delicious food.

kanaléro: (f. *kanal*) n. irrigation man.

kanalón: (Sp. *canalón*: gutter) n. eaves; trough.

kanalpáag: (f. *lipág*) n. sound of crumbling down. **agkanalpaag.** v. to crumble down (many buildings, etc.).

kanalpáak: (f. *lipák*) n. continuous slapping sound.

kanalpíit: (f. *lipít*) n. sound of the slipper hitting the heel of the foot, or of a slap with the palm of one's hand.

kanaltáak: (f. *liták*) n. sound of heavy rain; sound of continuous bursting. **agkanaltaak.** v. to burst; rain heavily.

kanaltíik: (f. *litík*) n. sound of continuous ticking. **agkanaltiik.** v. to tick continuously.

kanaltúog: (f. *litóg*) n. sound of a gun or thunder.

kanapé: (Sp. *canapé*: canapé) n. sofa (usually rattan) (*sopá*); appetizer, canapé.

kanápon: see *kappón*: contribution.

kanaplíing: (f. *pilíng*) n. succession of shrill sounds (as those produced by the rice culm).

kanarbúos: (f. *ribós*) n. hustle and bustle. **agkanarbuos.** v. to hustle and bustle.

kanárem: see *kitakita*: *Bischofia javanica* tree that yields valuable timber.

kanário: (Sp. *canario*: canary) n. canary; light yellow color. [Tag. *diláw* (yellow)]

kanarkár: **agkanarkar.** v. to have a raspy voice due to colds or excessive smoking.

kanarpáak: (f. *ripák*) n. the sound of shattering glass. **agkanarpaak.** v. to shatter loudly (glass).

kanarpúok: (f. *ripók*) n. succession of smashing or crashing sounds. **agkanarpuok.** v. to shatter to pieces; to smash to pieces.

kanarsáak: (f. *rissák*) n. sound produced by dry leaves being crushed. **agkanarsaak.** v. to get crushed (dry leaves).

kanarsibák: (f. *rissibák*) n. sound of falling rocks.

kanarsibók: (f. *rissibók*) n. sound of splashing in the water. **agkanarsibok.** v. to make splashing sounds, splash in the water.

kanarsíik: (f. *rissík*) n. succession of crackling sounds.

kanarsíit: (f. *rissít*) n. succession of hissing sounds (roasting meat). **agkanarsiit.** v. to hiss (in frying lard, etc.).

kanarsúod: (f. *risód*) n. sound of continuous crumbling down. **agkanarsuod.** v. to crumble down continuously.

kanartúok: (f. *rittók*) n. sound of continuous crackling.

kanásta: (Sp. *canasta*: basket) n. crate; hamper.

kanástro: (Sp. *canasto*: basket + *r*) n. woven basket worn on the back.

kanát: **agkakanat.** a. unrelated; unsympathetic. **pagkakanaten.** v. to do unsystematically; to speak nonsense.

kanátad: **nakanatad.** a. proper; regular, orderly; accurate; straight; level; correct. **maikanatad.** v. to put in order; straighten out; be proper, right; to fit, be in harmony with; be righteous. **Maikanatad kadi a pulagidanna iti lugit iti tuktukko a kas pangbales kaniak?** Is it right that she smear guano on my head as a means of revenge? [Tag. *akmâ, darapat*]

kanatíkat: **agkanatikat.** v. to make oneself ready for a journey (*rubbuat*).

kanatpáak: (f. *tipák*) n. sound of continuous falling with a thump.

kanáw: **kanawen.** v. to dissolve.

kanáwa: **ikanawa.** v. to shield, shelter, protect, guard, defend. **maikanawa.** v. to be protected (*kaluya*). [Tag. *tanggól*]

kanawán: n. right side. a. right, referring to the right hand. **agpakanawan.** v. to go to the right; turn right; from left to right (as when reading captions on photos). **makakanawan.** n. rightist; loyalist. **pannakakanawanna.** n. one's right-hand man. **kakanawanan.** a. farthest to the right, far right. **makinkanawan.** a. on the right side. **Naut-ot pay laeng ti kanawan nga imak a nagalaanda iti darak.** My right hand is still sore from where they took out my blood. [Ibg. *ziwanan*, Ivt., Ifg. *wawwan*, Itg. *kannawan*, Kal. *chuwalan*, Knk. *kanawán*, Kpm. *wanan*, Png. *káwanán*, Tag. *kanan*]

kanáyon: adv. always, n. part, integral part. **ikanayon.** v. to do until the end, to do always. **kankanayonen.** v. to persevere, persist in doing. **agkakanayon.** v. to do without letup; *adv.* continuously, repeatedly. **kanayonen.** *v.* to do persistently, frequently, repeatedly, continuously. [Kal. *iyeegew, pappasig*, Kpm. *pane, parati, púrus*, Png. *láwas*, Tag. *parati*]

kandádo: (Sp. *candado*: lock) n. lock. **ikandado.** v. to lock. [Kal. *lichakig*]

kandaróma: n. *Cinnamomum pauciflorum* aromatic tree; perfume of the flowers of the *Mimosa farnesiana*. **kakandaromaan.** n. grove of *kandaroma* trees.

kandarúpa: **agkandarupa.** v. to be confused; disoriented.

kandéla: (Sp. *candela*: candle) n. candle. (*espérma*) **kimmandela (ti ramay)** *exp.* said of long, attractive women's fingers. **sikakandela.** a. holding a candle. **agtakandila.** *n.* smell of a candle; (*fig.*) feeling of being in touch with a dead person. [Kal. *kanche*, Tag. *kandilà*]

kandelábra: (Sp. *candelabra*: chandelier) n. candle stand; candle chandelier.

kandelábro: (Sp. *candelabro*) n. candelabrum, hearse.

kandelária: (Sp. *candelaria*) n. candle mass.

kandeléro: (Sp. *candelero*: candlestick) n. candle holder.

kandidáto: (Sp. *candidato*: candidate) n. candidate; fem: *kandidata*. **kumandidato.** v. to become a candidate. **kinakandidato.** n. candidacy.

kandidatúra: (Sp. *candidatura*: candidacy) n. candidacy.

kandíling: n. curtain ring. **kandilingen.** v. to begin sewing or stitching; n. first stitches in sewing.

kandúli: n. a kind of freshwater fish resembling the *paltát*.

kandúman: n. pouch used by anglers to carry things in.

kandóng: n. *Memecylon umbellatum* tree with deep blue or purple flowers.

kanéla: (Sp. *canela*: cinnamon) n. cinnamon.

kanén: (f. *kaan*) n. food (*taraon*); v. to eat something. **pakanen.** v. to feed. **kankanen.** n. sweets (rice cakes). [Tag. *pagkain*]

kanengkéng: **nakanengkeng.** a. well built, stocky.

kánia: (Sp. *caña*: reed) n. reed; sugarcane.

kaniáda: *pron.* oblique of *isuda*: to them (*kadakuáda*). [Png. *ed sikará*, Tag. *sa kanilá*]

kaniák *pron.* oblique of *siak*: to me. [Png. *ed siák*, Tag. *sa akin*]

kaniamáso: (Sp. *cañamazo*: canvas) n. canvas or burlap cloth used for embroidery.

kaniám: *pron.* oblique of *siká*: to you (singular, informal) (*kenka*). [Png. *ed siká*, Tag. *sa iyó*]

kániamo: (Sp. *cáñamo*: hemp) n. hemp.

kaniána: *pron.* oblique of *isu*: to him, to her, to it. (*kenkuána*) [Png. *ed sikató*, Tag. *sa kaniyá*]

kaniáw: n. Igorot marriage ritual; (*fig.*) heathen practice; something done that leads to evil. **Kaniawenda.** They are doing something evil. [Tag. *kanyáw*]

kanibás: **agkanibas.** v. to be uneven, unequal.

kaníbor: (f. *kibor*) n. trouble; agitation.

kaníbos: n. end (*gibus*). [Tag. *tapos*]

kanibusánan: (f. *kanibos*) n. end (of life, of the world, etc.). **agkanibusanan.** v. to come to an end; to die. **Kanibusanamon!** This is the end for you!

kanigíd: *var.* of *kannigíd*: left. [Kal. *chuwigi*, Knk. *kanigíd*, *igíd*, Tag. *kaliwâ*]

kanika-: *prefix.* Forms ordinal numbers (*maika-*). **kanikapat.** fourth. **kanikalima.** fifth. [Tag. *ika-*, *pang-*]

kanikatló: (*kanika-* + *-tallo*) num. third (*maikatlo*). [Tag. *pangatló*, *ikatló*]

kanílias: (Sp. *canilla*: bobbin) n. bobbin used to hold woof threads.

kanimbásar: see *kimbasar*.

kanión: (Sp. *cañón*: cannon) n. cannon. **kanionen.** v. to hit something with a cannon.

kanít: n. kind of small black stinging ant. **kinanit.** a. attacked by black stinging ants.

kanitó: n. instant, moment. (*darikmát*) **iti apagkanito.** in a moment. **Dimtengen ti kanito nga ited ti supli iti gimmatang.** *exp.* The time has come to give what is due (*lit*: give the change to the purchaser). [Png. *bektá*, Tag. *saglít, sandalî*]

kaniwás: **agkaniwas.** v. to be in opposition to; to be contrary to; to be opposed. (*suppiat*; *labsing*) **maikaniwas.** v. to be opposed to; to be against. **kaniwasen.** v. to violate, fail to obey or fulfill. [Tag. *labág*]

kaniwásiw: **agkaniwasiw.** v. to be contrary; opposed. (*kaniwás, suppiát*)

kannág: n. shore; moonlight; outdoors. **Napanna ginuyod ti ulnas ket daytoy ti nagikargaanmi kadagiti alikamenmi a maturog idiay kannag.** He went to drag the sled and that is what we used to load our furniture to sleep in the outdoors. [Ibg. *kannág* = scab]

kannapí: var. of *kanape*: rattan sofa.

kannásiw: see *kaniwásiw*: to be contrary to, opposed to (*suppiat*)

kannaténg: (f. *nateng*) a. just picked (said of vegetables only); n. freshly picked vegetable.

kannáwag: **ikannawag.** v. to announce; proclaim. (*waragawag*)

kannawán: *var.* of *kanawán*: right (hand, side).

kannáway: n. kind of white heron, egret; swan. **Kimmanaway ti tengngedna a nakanganga a mangkitkita kaniak.** Her neck lengthened like a swan as she looked at me with her mouth agape. [Knk. *danggáak, dawwáak*, Tag. *tagák*]

kannawídan: (f. *tawid*) n. customs; tradition; culture; habits. [Tag. *kaugalian*]

kannél: **nakannel.** a. strong and forceful (blow).

kannigíd: adv. left, n. left side. (*katigid*) **kannigiden.** v. to do left-handed. **agpakannigid.** v. to turn left. **makakannigid.** n. leftist. **kakannigidan.** a. far left, farthest to the left. [Ibg. *zimigi*, Ifg. *iggid*, Ivt. *huliq*, Kal. *chuwigi*, Knk. *kanigíd, igíd*, Kpm. *kaili*, Png. *kawigí*, Tag. *kaliwâ*]

káno: *pagkanuan*. n. the line in which money is thrown in gambling (*pagmanuan*). **Kanok.** It is my *kano* (I am the winner since the money I threw is nearest the *pagkanuan*).

kanó₁: (f. *Amerikano*) n. term for American males.

kanó₂: *part.* marks indirect speech and/or doubt, it is said; they say; supposedly, allegedly; according to. **ikankano**. v. to heed, mind, care about; respect. **Adda kano mangmangngegna nga agsasao iti uneg.** He said he heard someone talking inside. **Iparitna ta mangdadael kano ti oras.** He forbids it because it is said to be a waste of time. [Bon., Knk. *kano*, Png. *konó*, Tag. *daw*]

kanúbog: n. main activity; monopolization of time. **idi kanubog.** *conj.* while.

kanugkúg: (f. *kugkúg*) **kumanugkug.** v. to make a repeated pounding sound; sound of a kettle lid jumping on a kettle.

kanukkók: n. sound produced by continually striking something hollow. **agkanukkok.** v. to make the sound of striking a hollow object.

kanúmay: n. *Diospyros multiflora* tree.

kanumsíit: n. species of plant.

kanon: (Sp. *canon*: land tax; royalty) *n.* fee for use. **makikakanon.** *v.* to use someone else's property to perform work (usually applied to borrowing ovens for drying Virginia tobacco).

kanúnay: n. *Croton sp.* shrubs.

kanonisádo: (Sp. *canonizado*: canonized) a. canonized. **kanonisasion.** n. canonization.

kanúnong: n. air plant; itchy parasitic vine that feeds on trees; fellow worker; fellow sufferer. **agkanunong.** v. to take sides with. **kanunongan.** v. to yield to; acquiesce to; agree; consent. **kumanonong.** v. to agree; comply; yield to. **pagkakanunongan.** v. to approve unanimously. **makikanunong.** v. to go along with. [Tag. *sang-ayon*]

kanungkóng: (f. *kungkóng*) *n.* hollow sound, echo, reverberation. [Tag. *alingawngáw*]

kanuskús: *n.* sound of scratching, shuffling. **agkanuskus.** v. to scratch the head; scratch the floor (slippers, etc.). **Nakigtot a nakangeg iti kanuskos ti bobeda.** He was startled to hear the sound of scratching on the roof. [Tag. *kaluskós*]

kánot: n. kind of children's game; long hair. **ikanot.** v. to entangle the feet. **kanotkanot.** n. kind of seashore plant, agar-agar.

kanutílio: (Sp. *canutillo*) *n.* small reed used in music; small tube.

kanseládo: (Sp. *cancelado*: cancelled) a. cancelled. **kanselasion.** n. cancellation.

kánser₁: (Sp. *cancel*: ironwork door or screen used in churches) *n.* movable screen or partition. **ikanser.** *v.* to partition, screen off.

kánser₂: (Sp. *cáncer*: cancer) n. cancer.

kansiáw: *var.* of *kantiaw*: joke; tease. (*tangkiaw*)

kansiliér: (Sp. *canciller*: chancellor) n. chancellor.

kansión: (Sp. *canción*: song) n. song. (*kanta*) **kinnansionan.** n. singing competition. [Tag. *kantá* (Sp.)]

kánsir: var. *of* kanser: movable partition that divides a room.

kánta: (Sp. *cantar*: sing) n. song (*kansión*; *daniw*); melody; tune. **agkanta.** v. to sing. **kantaen.** v. to sing a song. **pakantaen.** v. to have someone sing. **ikantaan.** *v.* to sing for, sing in honor of. **Bayat ti kinnantaan, naininut met a naibus ti arak.** While they were singing to each other, the alcohol was gradually consumed. [Ibg., Png. *kansion*, Ivt. *kanta*, Kpm. *dálit*, Tag. *awit*]

kantád: **nakantad.** a. meaningful, of significance.

kantádo: (Sp. *cantado*: sung) a. sung; chanted. **misa kantada.** *n.* sung mass.

kantadóra: *var.* of *engkantadora*: fairy, enchantress; kind of flower.

kantamísa: n. first mass of a newly ordained priest.

kantár: (Sp. *cantar*: sing) **ikantar**. v. to announce; count; consider.

kantarídas: (Sp. *cantaridas*: cantharides) n. Spanish fly, powdered drug used as an aphrodisiac. (*gayúma*) **Pakantaridasmo?** Are you going to give him an aphrodisiac?

kantáy: **agkantay.** *v.* to ford, cross (a river).

kantería: (Sp. *cantería*: art of hewing stone) n. masonry.

kantéro: (Sp. *cantero*: stonecutter) n. mason, cement worker; stonecutter.

kantiáw: (Tag. also) n. teasing, banter; making fun of someone. (*surón*) **kantiawan.** v. to tease someone, make fun of. **Kinantiawandakami dagiti makaammo nga agayan-ayatkami.** The people who knew we were lovers teased us.

kantidád: (Sp. *cantidad*: quantity) n. quantity.

kantíga: (Sp. *cantiga*: troubadour poem) **makikankantiga.** v. to join in (a dance).

kántiko: (Sp. *cántico*: canticle, hymn) *n.* canticle.

kantilión: (Sp. *cantillo*) *n.* adjustable steel square.

kantimplóra: (f. Am. Spanish *cantimplora*: canteen) n. canteen, flask.

kantína: (Sp. *cantina*: canteen; station buffet) n. general store. **kantinero.** n. storekeeper.

kantinéla: (Sp. *cantinela*: ballad) *n.* ballad.

kantíng: (coll.) **kantingen.** v. to weigh.

kantíngen: n. *Cedrela sp.* tree with good timber. **pangantingen.** n. tree similar to the *kantingen.*

-kanto: enclitic expressing future action and second person singular (familiar) actor. **Makapankanto.** You will be able to go.

kánto: (Sp. *canto*: edge) n. street corner (*suli*); angle. **kuatro kantos.** edge of a file; (*coll.*) locally made gin.

kántoboy: (*slang*, f. *kanto* 'corner' + Eng. boy) *n.* street loafer, idle boy.

kantón(g): n. thin wheat noodle (usually yellow in color).

kantonéra: (Sp. *cantonera*: corner plate) n. corner bracket; angle iron.

Kantonés: (Sp. *cantonés*: Cantonese; *fem*: *Kantonesa*) n. Cantonese.

kantór: (Sp. *cantor*: singer) n. male singer. (*fem*: *kantóra*)

kanyá-: *prefix. var.* spelling of *kania-*. Combines with *-ko* pronouns to form the obliques.

kangáwan: n. variety of awned *diket* rice with red kernel.

kángel: a. clumsy; foolish; stupid. **Dimo kunaen a kangelka!** Don't say that you're stupid! [Tag. *lampá*]

kánggarú: (Aus.) *n.* kangaroo.

kanggréna: (Sp. *cangrena*: gangrene) n. gangrene.

kangkáng: **kumangkang.** v. to separate; part; open; peel off. [Tag. *tukláp*]

kángkaro: (Sp. *cancro*: canker) n. canker. (*letteg nga agnunog*)

kangkóng: (Tag.) n. water spinach (*balangeg*). [Png., Tag. *kangkóng*]

kangngég: (f. *dengngeg*) **agkangkangngeg.** v. to hear. (*dumngeg*)

kangrunáan: (f. *nangruna*) a. primary, principal, most important. **umuna ken kangrunaan.** first and foremost. **Sika ti kangrunaan a pagyamanak.** I would especially like to thank you. [Tag. *pang-uná*]

kaóba: (Sp. *caoba*: mahogany) n. mahogany.

káod: n. small cup or scoop used for drawing water from a container. **kauden.** v. to take out; extract. (*ikkat*) **Timmapogda iti pagattumeng a danum sada kimmaud iti inumenda.** They dove into the knee-high water and then scooped out some to drink. [Tag. *tabò*]

káog: **kumaog.** v. to bend, curve, fold together; stoop; become hollow.

kaulpán: (f. *ulep*) n. cloudy part of the sky; clouds. **Kasla tumtumpawak iti kaulpan.** It seems like I am floating in the clouds.

káong: see *kamótit*: sweet potato; (Tag.) n. palm fruit. **moro kaong.** *n.* variety of sweet potato with very starchy rhizomes.

kaóng: n. mussel. [Tag. *tahóng*]

kaunggán: (f. *uneg*) n. depth; inside; core; subconscious.

káor: var. of *saur*: cheat, swindle; lie.

káos: **kausen.** v. to clean by scraping or raking; scrape the bottom of an empty container.

kaút: **kumaut.** v. to take contents out of an empty opening. **kauten.** v. to stick in one's hands in order to take out what is inside, draw from a hole or empty place. **naikaut.** a. nicked, notched. **kautan.** n. cut of cloth (sleeve sewn to coat). **Kinautko ti petakak.** I took out my wallet (out of my pocket).

kautíbo: (Sp. *cautivo*: captive) n. captive. **kautibuen.** v. to capture; confiscate. **Kinautiboda dagiti kameng ti Konseho.** They confiscated the Counsel's treasures.

kápa: (Sp. *capa*: cape) n. cape; cloak (*kagáy*); wrapper for a cigar.

kapaCpa- prefix that denotes recently completed indirect actions (with *pa-* verb stems). **Kapatpaturogko.** I just put him to sleep.

kapadés: n. height of a season (harvest, etc.); period of time; times.

kapádo: (Sp. *capado*: castrated) n. castrated bull. (*kaponado*) **kapado a pukis.** n. crew cut.

kapag- (CV-): pref. denotes recency of action: **asawa.** spouse **kapagasawáan.** recently married; (recently married couple). **kapagasasawa.** recent marriage.

kapami(n)-: n. pref. to form multiplicative ordinal numbers; takes *-ko* pronouns: **Kapaminsiamna ti immay.** This was the ninth time he came. **Kapamitlomi.** This is our third time.

kapanágan: n. plain; open space outdoors. (*tanáp, tay-ák*)

kaparangét: n. neighbor, something situated near. **agkakaparanget.** v. to be adjacent to each other.

kápas: n. cotton; cotton ball. **marakapas.** n. *Pterocymbium tinctorium* tree. **kapaskapas.** n. kind of fish with bony meat. **kimmapas nga ulep.** n. cottonlike cloud. [Ibg. *kafoq, kapoq*, Ivt. *dájiq*, Kal. *kapas*, Png. *kapés*, Knk. *kápes*, *kastíl*, Kpm., Tag. *bulak*]

kapasangláy: n. *Ceiba pentandra*, silk-cotton tree. (*kapok*)

kapaséte: (Sp. *capacète*) *n.* sun helmet.

kapasidád: (Sp. *capacidad*: capacity) n. capacity, ability to contain.

kapatádan: n. contemporary, person of the same age. (*kasadar*) **agkapatadan.** v. to be of the same age. (*agkatawen*)

kapatás: (Tag. also) n. overseer, supervisor. (*mangimatón, agbantáy*)

kapátor: n. the height of something; eminence.

kapay-án: (f. *pay-an*) n. manner of doing something.

kapé: (Sp. *café*: coffee) n. coffee. **agkape.** v. to have coffee, drink coffee. **pagkapean.** *n*. café. **managkape.** *a*. fond of coffee, always drinking coffee.

kapelián: (Sp. *capellán*: chaplain) n. chaplain.

káper: n. smegma; term used insultingly for uncircumcised men. **agkaper.** v. to produce smegma. **kaper ti musang.** n. civet, used as a perfume. [Tag. *kupal*]

kapét: kumpet. v. to hold, cling to, stick, adhere. (*dumket; pigket; kidkid; kulamat; luyak*) **kapten.** v. to cling to; to transfer; infect (disease) **ikapet.** v. to fix, make firm, stable; wear (clothes) **kaptan.** *v*. to attach something to. **kakaptan.** n. rail of stairs. **kapkapét.** n. spider nest. **nakapet.** *a*. sticky, easy to adhere to. **pagkapetan.** n. handrail; handrest; *v*. attach to something, use a handrail; (*fig*) inflict harm. **Nagbiddut iti ikakapetna ket nanabtuog iti daga.** She lost her grip and fell to the ground. [Knk. *kawwá*, Png. *pekét*, Tag. *kapit*]

kapetéra: (Sp. *cafetera*: coffee pot) n. coffee pot.

kapí: var. of *kapé*: coffee.

kapi(n)-: Prefix indicating degree of kindred. **Kapin-ano?** How is X related? **kapidua.** second cousin. **kapitlo.** third cousin. **Agkapin-anoda?** How are they related? **Dika kapkapin-ano.** You are not related to me.

kapiá: nakapia. a. calm, tranquil, quiet. (*talná*)

kapíd: n. informal term used in addressing a second cousin. (*kapidua*)

kapiduá: n. second cousin. (*kapin-* + *dua*)

kapíged₁: n. variety of awned late rice.

kapíged₂: n. kind of flat saucerlike freshwater fish.

kapilaridád: (Sp. *capilaridad*) *n*. capillary.

kapília: (Sp. *capilla*: chapel) n. chapel. **kimmapilia a dalluyon.** n. large (*lit*: chapel-like) breaker waves.

kapin-anó: *interrog*. What is your relation to? How are you related to? **Agkapin-anokayo?** How are you guys related? **Kapin-anom ni Gracia?** How are you related to Gracia? **Dinak kapkapin-ano tapno isakitnak.** I am not related to you for you to defend me. [Tag. *kaanu-anó*]

kápis₁: maikapis. v. to miss an important event. **pakaikapisan.** *n*. missed event. **ikapis.** *v*. to attend an event somebody else missed. **Inkapiska.** I went to the event you missed.

kápis₂: *a*. empty; flat; flat chested.

kapís: (Tag.) n. seashell ornaments, scallop.

kapít: n. term used in addressing a third cousin (*kapitlo*) **kapiten.** v. to fold; (reg.) to stack up.

kapitalísmo: (Sp. *capitalismo*: capitalism) n. capitalism. **kapitalista.** *n*. capitalist.

kapitán: (Sp. *capitán*: captain) n. captain. (*pangúlo*)

kapitló: [*kapin-* + *tallo*] n. third cousin.

kapitólio: (Eng.) *n*. capitol (building). (*ngúlo, kabeséra*)

kapítulo: (Sp. *capítulo*: chapter) n. chapter. (*pasét*)

kapkáp: agkapkap. v. to grope in the dark. (*karapkáp*) **kapkapan.** v. to frisk.

kapón: (Sp. *capón*: castrated animal) n. sterilized human or animal not able to bear children; castrated male. **agpakapon.** v. to get a vasectomy; to get a tubal ligation (as to not bear children); get castrated. **kaponen.** v. to give a sterilizing operation to. **Kaska met la kakapkaponen a nuang nga agpaspasanaang.** You are just like a recently castrated water buffalo in pain. [Tag. *kapón*]

kapóna: agkapona. v. to play at odd or even.

kaponádo: (f. *kapon*) n. castrated bull. (*kapado, nakapon*)

kaponéro: (f. *kapón*) *n*. castrater; gelder.

kápor: kapuren. v. to whitewash a wall.

káput: n. kind of baglike fishing net. **kumakaput.** n. kind of pelican.

kaputótan: (f. *putot*) n. generation; descendant. [Kal. *galak*]

kapóte: (Sp. *capote*: poncho) n. raincoat. **nakakapote.** *a*. wearing a raincoat.

kapútsa: (Sp. *capucha*: hood) n. hood; circumflex accent.

kápuy: *n*. weakness. **nakapuy.** a. weak (*kapsút*); fragile; slow. **agkakapuy.** v. to feel weak. **kumapuy.** v. to become weak. **pagkapuyan.** n. personal weakness; weak point. **di agkakapoy.** *a*. fast, swift; aggressive; quick witted. [Png. *kapoy, gápil*, Tag. *hinà*]

kapúyo: n. blister. (*lapúyot, lapúyok; lapitog*) **agkapuyo.** v. to become blistered. [Kal. *bumti, labtakan*, Knk. *bidúng*, Png. *lanók*, Tag. *paltós*]

kappá: kappakappá. n. *Drynaria sp.* ferns.

kappellés: (f. *pelles*) v. to have just dressed (changed clothing).

kappéng: kumappeng. v. to convert from one religion to another; join, associate. **Suksukimatenna kano pay dagiti gunglo a nakaikappengam iti napalabas.** He supposedly will also check out the organizations you were a member of in the past.

kappessá: (f. *pessa*) *n*. just hatched.

kappí₁: n. kind of small crab. **utek-kappi.** *n*. the brain of a crab (said of a stupid person). [Knk. *gakí, gakíming*, Png. *alamá, daliwéy*, Tag. *talangkâ*]

kappí₂: **agkappi**. v. to sit down with crossed legs.

kappiá: (f. *pia*) n. peace; harmony. **agkappia**. v. to reconcile. **makikappia**. v. to negotiate for peace. **nainkappian**. *a*. peaceful. **pagkappiaen**. v. to make two enemies agree to peace; pacify. (*amo*) **panagkakappia**. n. time of peace. **Patienna nga agballigi ti panggepna babaen iti nainkappian a wagas**. He believes that his plan will succeed through peaceful means. [Png. *kareenan, maligén*, Tag. *payapà*]

kappintá: (f. *pinta*) *a*. freshly painted.

kappísi: (f. *písi*) just cut; just divided. **Naimas ti kappisi a naluom a sandia**. The fresh watermelon that was just cut is delicious.

kappó: n. clam. **kapkappo**. n. type of mollusk smaller than the *kappó*. **agkappo**. n. a boys' game consisting of throwing up coins and claiming all the ones that land on a particular side. **kimmapo**. a. term applied to large vaginas. (ant. *kimmartíb*) **Kitaem ti dalan kunak itay kenka, selleng a kappo**. I just told you to keep your eyes on the road, you dumb clam. **In-inut nga immasideg iti pangapkappuan ti balasang**. He gradually approached the place where she was clamming. [Png. *gilitán, dukiáng*, Tag. *kabyâ, lukán*]

kappúkan: (f. *pukan*) *a*. newly cut; newly chopped.

kappúkis: (f. *pukis*) *a*. just cut (hair).

kappón: n. contribution; share; stock; member. **ikappon**. v. to add to, put together with. **kakappon**. n. associate. **agkakappon**. *v*. to form a partnership. **kumappon**. v. to join a (group of people) **iti kappon**. prep. with, in company with. [Tag. *sapì*]

kappusíng: (f. *pusing*) n. novice; rookie; inexperienced person; child who has just stopped suckling. (*kabarbaro*)

kappusót: (f. *pusot*) n. animal who has just stopped breast feeding.

kaprá: **nakapra**. a. fidgety; not well behaved.

kápre: n. size-changing magical demon.

kaprítso: (Sp. *capricho*: whim) n. whim. **kaprítsoso**. a. whimsical, capricious.

kapsít: n. sperm (*kissit*). [Tag. *tamód*]

kápsula: (Sp. *cápsula*: capsule) n. capsule.

kapsút: *n*. weakness. **nakapsut**. a. weak, feeble, frail. (*kápuy*) **agkakapsut**. v. to feel weak. **agkapsut**. v. to be a weak person. **kumapsut**. v. to weaken. **pakapsuten**. *v*. to weaken, make weak. **pagkapsutan**. n. personal weakness; Achilles' heel. **Pakapsuten ti iliw ti pakinakem**. Nostalgia weakens the mind. [Ibg. *kafi*, Ivt. *makahaq*, Kal. *baksiwot, pat-ig*, Knk. *pígo*, Kpm. *mainaq*, Png. *kápoy*, Tag. *hinà*]

kapsóy: var. of *paksuy*.

kara-: *prefix*. denotes frequency or habitual action:. **agkaraumay**. to come all the time. **agkarasubli**. to frequently return. **agkarapanateng**. to always have a cold.

kára: (Sp. *cara*: face) n. heads (in a coin toss). **karakrus**. n. heads or tails. **maikara**. v. to be written on one's face.

karáag: var. of *angrág*: dry.

karáang: see *tagáang*: kind of underground furnace. (*anáwang*)

karabá₁: **kumaraba**. v. to ask, plead, beg (*gawawa*). [Tag. *magmakaawà*]

karabá₂: **agkaraba**. v. to start to climb (vines). **apagkaraba a bantay**. n. ridged hillock.

karábab: n. kind of pinkish fish.

karab-ás: n. *act of climbing over with the forelegs (or arms); lifting the forelegs*. **agkarab-ás, kumarab-as, karab-asen**. v. to put the hands or forelegs heavily on something (dogs on the door, etc.). **Limmagto iti tambak sa kimmarab-as iti bukot ti nuang**. He jumped out of the dike and hopped on (with the help of his arms) the back of the water buffalo.

karabása: (Sp. *calabaza*: squash) n. pumpkin or similar-type squash: *Cucurbita pepo*. **karkarabasaen**. v. to cut the hair poorly. **kimmarabasa**. a. like a pumpkin (round). [Knk. *kumbása*, Png. *kalobása*, Tag. *kalabasa*]

karábay: n. companion (participating in the same event). [Tag. *kasama*]

karabína: (Sp. *carabina*) *n*. carbine.

karabíyanna: (f. *rabíí*) n. the night before.

karabnís: *n*. scratch, stroke. **karabnisen**. *v*. to scratch; stroke.

karábo: n. inopportune event, happening at the wrong moment; time of plenty; kind of bird. **kumarabo**. v. to happen at the wrong time.

karabúkab: n. blister on fried food; greedy person. **agkarabukab**. v. to blister (fried food); to be greedy. [Tag. *sakím* (greed)]

karabukób: n. throat; esophagus. (*luludoókan*) **karabukuben**. v. to have a sore throat. **mangarabukob**. v. to be oversatiated with food (filled to the throat). [Ibg. *barukkaw*, Ivt. *tehnan*, Kal. *ekuuk*, Knk. *inum*, Kpm. *akmúlan*, Png. *kolókolóng*, Tag. *lalamunan*]

karábus: **maikarabus**. v. to be late; miss an opportunity. (*kapis*)

karabúyo: n. kind of red mussel shell used to curl hair.

karád: n. kind of tree with good building timber.

karadákad: n. sound of walking over gravel. **agkaradakad, kumaradakad**. v. to make a sound similar to that of passing over gravel; rattle like a cart.

karádap: agkaradap, kumaradap. v. to crawl; creep (vines). (*karayam*) **karadapen.** v. to reach a place by crawling; crawl to; crawl stealthily into a woman's bed. (*aradang*) **agikaradap iti kuarta.** *exp.* to hand money under the table, sneak money to. **Nagkaradap dagiti atitiddog ken napino a ramayna iti rabaw dagiti tekla.** Her long, fine fingers crawled over the keys. [Knk. *kámang*, Tag. *gapang*]

karadíkad: n. net used to catch freshwater shellfish.

karáding: n. mysterious magical charm in a person; man living with a concubine. **makikarading.** v. to take in a mistress. (*kamalala*) **Adda karadingna.** He has some magical aura about him. **mangngarading.** n. sorcerer, witch; a. with many extramarital affairs.

karadkád: n. health. (*pia, salun-át*) **nakaradkad.** a. healthy, robust. **kumaradkad.** v. to become alive, animated. **karadkadan.** v. to do actively (with spirit). [Png. *buná, aligwás*, Tag. *lusóg*]

karadúkod: n. rumbling sound. **agkaradukod.** v. to make a rumbling sound.

karág: karagkarag. a. rickety.

karagátan: n. sandy or gravelly place. (*kadaratan; paratong; ruburub*)

karáho: (Sp. *carajo*) n. shameful young man, good for nothing; brat (mild curse word).

karai-: pref. denotes frequency or repetition of an action (used with *i-* verbs): **isubli.** v. to return something. **karaisubli.** v. to continually return something. **karaikuddotdak.** They continually pinch me.

karáid: n. rake (*karaykay, pagkaykay*); broom made of coconut leaves. [Tag. *walís-tingtíng*]

karaínas: agkarainas. v. to trail a garment. **ikarainas.** v. to clean and arrange. **kumarainas.** v. to be restless; uneasy.

karáis: karaisan. v. to scratch, scrape by fingernails or claws. (*karamut*) **nakaraisan.** a. scratched by nails or claws. [Tag. *kalmót, gasgás*]

karákar₁: karakaren. v. calculate; estimate; anticipate. **ikarakar.** v. to intend, propose, design.

karákar₂: makarakar. v. to be eroded. (*kurukor*) **karakaren.** v. to erode. [Tag. *agnás*]

karákar₃: agkarakar. v. to hurry. (*daras*) **karakaren.** v. to do something fast.

karákar₄: karakaran, kinarakaran. n. craw of stomach of fowls, crop.

karakátak: n. snare drum.

karakattít: n. silly, wanton girl. (*garampang*)

karakrús: (Sp. *cara o cruz*: heads or tails) n. game of heads or tails. **agkarakrus.** v. to toss a coin in a heads or tails game.

karáma₁: kumarama. v. to join again temporarily, (a musician joining his former band for a day); participate, partake in.

karáma₂: n. weapon, arm. (*igam*) **agkarama.** v. to use a weapon.

karamákam: n. kind of small marine crab.

karamatília: var. of *karomatilia*: wheelbarrow.

karamayát: (f. *mayát*) **agkaramayat.** v. to be always agreeing.

karámba₁: n. broad-mouthed jar for holding water. **pagkakarambaan.** n. stand for the *karamba* jar. **Kasla karamba ti ulok.** I was really scared. (My head was like a pot). [Ibg. *emmutu, angang,* Ifg. *buwod,* Ivt., Kpm. *bangaq,* Kal. *sakchuwan, bilongka ÿawan,* Tag. *bangâ*]

karámba₂: (Sp. *caramba*) *interj.* mild exclamation: Oh my!

karambuáya: var. of *karimbuaya*.

karambóla: (Sp. *carambola*) *n.* carambole; stupid person (*karamboles*).

karambóles: (Sp. *carambola*: fluke; trick) n. stupid person.

karamélo: (Sp. *caramelo*: caramel) n. caramel.

karamkám: agkarkaramkam. v. to bring together, collect. (*urnóng*)

karamukóm: n. hard fruit (guava) before ripening. a. hard, not ripe. **kumaramukom.** v. to be hard and crunchy.

karámot: agkaramot. v. to scratch. (*gurád, úged, úges, garadgád; karais, kudkod*) **nakaramutan.** a. scratched, clawed. **Nagkinnaramotda.** They clawed at each other. [Kal. *lagalidgichen,* Png. *kogkor, gúgo,* Tag. *gasgás, kalmót*]

karandíkang: a. crispy; overdry. (*gango*) **kumarandikang.** v. to be crispy. [Tag. *tuyót*]

karanúkon: ikaranukon. v. to dump something; drop something into a heap.

karansíwa: kumaransiwa. v. to roam about; prowl.

karantiddóg: a. elongated. **kumarantiddog.** v. to become elongated.

karantíng: nakaranting. a. alert; nimble; fast moving (*karting*). **Sikakaranting a timmulong kenni Linda a nangiserrek kadagiti gargaretna.** He nimbly helped Linda put in the belongings. [Tag. *bilís*]

karantitíway: *var.* of *karantíway*.

karantíway: a. long legged; tall and thin; slender stalked; lanky.

karanggúkong: *n.* sound of a can being dragged over a paved road.

karangíkang: **kumarangikang**. v. to become overdry.

karangkáng: **kumarangkang**. v. to act immodestly (women).

karangúkong: var. of *garangugong*: cliff, precipice. (*derráas*) **kumarangukong**. v. to make the sound of a can being dragged over a road. **maikarangukong**. v. to fall into a deep place; to be overcome by temptation. **Kalintegan nga agadal ken rumkuas manipud iti gayonggayong ti pannakaadipen a nakaikarangukongna**. It is his right to study and break free from the quicksand of servitude in which he is buried deep.

karapét: **kumarkarapet**. v. to (take) steal as much as possible while fleeing.

karapkáp: see *kapkáp*: grope for in the dark; search by feeling. **Agkarkarapkaptayo iti kadaanan nga ugali**. We are still crawling in our old customs.

karappét: *var.* of *karapét*.

karárag: n. prayer. (*lualo*) **agkararag**. v. to pray. **ikararag**. v. to pray for something to happen. **kararagan**. v. to pray; implore; beg; beseech. **kumararag**. v. to beseech; beg. **pagkararagan**. n. church; place of worship. **Ikarkararagandak bassit ta bareng awan ti dumdumteng a sagubanitko**. Please pray for me not to get sick. [Kal. *luwalu*, Png., Tag. *dasál*]

kararáwi: n. *Bridelia stipularis* shrub with greenish flowers dotted with purple.

kararét: n. wheel; pulley; imaginary animal heard in times of sickness. [Png. *mutón*, Tag. *mutón, tangkálag, kalò* (pulley)]

kararuá: n. soul; spirit. **ikararua**. v. to embody; imbue. **mangkararua**. v. to serenade a house on the eve of All Souls' Day for money or food. **Aginana kuma ti kararuana iti kappia**. May his soul rest in peace. [Ivt. *pahad*, Kal. *kalichodwa*, Kpm. *kaladuwá*, Png. *kamarérua*, Tag. *káluluwá*]

kararwá: see *kararua*: soul.

káras: **agkaras**. v. to catch fish by scooping; to draw water with a scoop and throw it overboard (from a boat). **karasen**. v. to bail out of; dip from. **karasan**. v. to bail out (a pond). [Tag. *limás*]

karasaén: n. poisonous snake, Philippine cobra; also used in cursing; evil person. [Ibg. *bálaq*, Tag. *ulupóng*]

karasákas: n. rustling sound; shuffling sound of feet on floor; crumpling sound. **agkarasakas**. v. to make a rustling sound. **Ti karasakas dagiti lupotda ti dimanggay ti panaglantip dagiti bibigda**. The crumpling sound of their clothes accompanied the joining of their lips. [Png. *kalasukos, kalasikas*, Tag. *kaluskós, agahás*]

karasíkis: n. thin, crispy sound. **agkarasikis**. v. to make a crispy sound, e.g., a lizard passing through bamboos.

karasúkos: *n.* slope. **kumarasukos**. v. to slide down; shoot, dart; rush; move swiftly. **agkarasukos**. v. to slide down a slope. **Maikarasukos a matnag iti nalibeg ken narugit a waig**. (They) swiftly fall into the turbid and dirty stream.

karassábong: see *karissábung*: young mango or guava just formed.

karát: (obs.) **pakaraten**. v. to add salt to. (*asinan*)

karatákat₁: n. large tree with good timber.

karatákat₂: **agkaratakat**. v. to make a jingling, rattling, or rustling sound, e.g., wheels over gravel, coins in pocket; rattle.

karatáw: *n.* line of the *tabukol* net. (*kuratáw*)

karatáy: n. kind of basket carried on the back. **ikaratay**. v. to carry something on the back. **nakakaratay**. a. with something carried on the back. **No kayatmo, ipurosanka iti lima raay nga ipakaratayko kenka no agawidkayo**. If you want, I will pick five bundles for you to carry back when you go home.

karatéla: (Sp. *carretela*: stage coach) n. two-wheeled vehicle with three parallel benches for passengers.

karatéra: (Sp. *carretera*: highway) n. highway, national road, road for vehicles.

karatíkit: *n.* jingling sound. **agkaratikit**. v. to make a jingling sound such as coins (*karotikit*). **Nagkaratikit ti nalettat a posas**. The slackened handcuffs jingled. [Tag. *kalansíng*]

karatília: (Sp. *carretilla*: pushcart) n. wheelbarrow. (*karamatilia, karomatilia*)

karatísta: (Eng. karate + -*ista*) n. karate fighter.

karatúkok: n. song of the turtledove (*pagaw*). **agkaratukok**. v. to sing (said of the turtledove).

karatúkot: n. cracking sound. (*kalatokot*) **agkaratukot**. v. to produce a cracking sound; to shake, tremble (said of the knees). [Tag. *kalatóg*]

karátula: (Sp. *carátula*: mask) n. signboard.

karat-óm: **nakarat-om**. a. crunchy. (*karemkem; karut-om*) **agkumarat-om, kumarat-om**. v. to crunch. [Tag. *ngalót*]

karattót: **nakarkarattot**. a. in a hurry; hurriedly. (*daras, dagdag*) **Makarkarattot dagiti mangmangged iti konstruksion**. The construction workers moved around in a hurry.

karáw: **karawkaraw**. n. young wingless cricket.

karáwa: n. groping touch. **agkarawa**. v. to feel with the hand. (*kapkap, karapkáp; karadap*)

karawaen. v. to touch indecently; grope, feel with the hand. **ikarawa.** v. to hand over surreptitiously; hand over bribe money. **karkarawaen ti tengnged.** *exp.* to live in fear. **Ti la nakarkarawam nga impambar.** You are just searching for an excuse. [Png. *kapá*, Tag. *apuhap, hagilap*]

karawáwi: n. willow.

káray: n. kind of large-leafed aquatic plant.

karáy: n. plastron, turtle shell. (*kasíkas*)

karayám: agkarayam. v. to creep, crawl. (*úyas*) **ikarayam.** v. to grope with the hands; secretly hand over; pay for with money under the table. [Ibg. *mekkaray*, Itg. *karadap*, Ivt. *maycababakaq*, Kpm., Tag. *gápang*, Png. *kurung*]

karayán: n. river. **agpakarayan.** *v.* to go to the river. [Bon. *wangwang*, Ibg. *deppaq, bánnag*, Ifg. *wangwang*, Ivt. *ahsung*, Kal. *chewwang*, Knk. *gináwang, wané*, Kpm., Png., Tag. *ílog*]

karayapán: kumarayapan. n. flock. (*purók, pangén*)

karáyat: (obs.) makakarayat. v. to show one's pleasure in seeing something.

karaykáy: n. foot of a bird; rake (*karaid*). **agkaraykay.** v. to scratch, burrow (rodents and chickens) **Kasla kinaraykay ti manok ti suratna.** His writing is like chicken scratches. [Tag. *kalmót, gasgás* (scratch)]

karáyo: *n.* craving, longing; affection; love. **kumarayo.** v. to crave, long for, yearn for (*kalikagum, ayat, tarigagay*). **sikakarayo.** *adv.* affectionately [Png. *pitamitam, pilalek*, Tag. *sabík, nais, pithayà*]

karbengán: (f. *rebbeng*) n. duty, responsibility; privilege, right. **Adda karbenganda a mangammo.** They have the right to know. [Tag. *karapatán; tungkulin*]

karbín: n. carbine; M1 rifle.

karbón: (Sp. *carbón*: carbon) n. carbon paper; coal.

karbonáto: (Sp. *carbonato*: carbonate) n. carbonate.

karbunkulo: (Sp. *carbunclo*: carbuncle) *n.* garnet, carbuncle (precious stone).

karburadór: (Sp. *carburador*: carburetor) n. carburetor.

karbúro: (Sp. *carburo*: calcium carbide) n. calcium carbide, element used to speed up the ripening of fruits. **Kabuteng kano dagiti dikatataoan ti angot ti karburo.** The supernatural beings are supposedly afraid of the smell of calcium carbide. [Tag. *kalburo*]

kardayó: karkardayo. a. farfetched; remotely possible, impossible.

kardelína: (Sp. *cardelina*: goldfinch) n. goldfinch.

kardenál: (Sp. *cardenal*: cardinal) n. cardinal.

kardéro: *var.* of *kaldero*: cauldron, kettle.

kardílio: (Sp. *cardillo*: golden thistle) *n.* stewed fish in scrambled egg sauce.

kardís: n. *Cajanus cajan*, pigeon pea. **pangardísen.** n. *Dipterocarpus grandiflorus* tree. [Kal. *keÿchis*, Knk. *kídis*]

karekkék: n. sound produced by a hen when calling her chicks for food.

karemkém: *n.* crunch. **kumaremkém.** v. to crunch (in eating). (*karat-om*) **karemkemen.** v. to grind something with the teeth. **karkaremkem.** n. kind of herb. **Kinaremkemko ti nabati a pulutan.** I crunched up the remaining beer snacks. [Tag. *ngalót*]

karenkén: n. crease, fold; wrinkle. (*kupín, pliéges; kuretret*) **karenkenen.** v. to plait, make a fold in clothes; coil (worms). **nakarenken.** *a.* wrinkled, creased. [Tag. *kulubót*]

karenténa: *var.* of *kuarentena*: quarantine.

karengkéng: n. wanton or flirtatious girl (*garampang*); lewdness. **agkarengkeng.** *v.* to be lewd, sexually immoral. **Imbes nga ayonannak, siak pay ti pabasolen a kumarengkeng.** Instead of siding with me, she blamed me for being a tramp. **Agkikinnarengkengda ngata?** Do you think they are involved sexually?

karéra: (Sp. *carrera*: career) n. career, profession; degree; race (competition). **kumarera.** v. to pursue a profession, degree. **kakarera.** v. to run a race with. **agkarera.** v. to race against each other. **de-karera.** *a.* professional, with a career. **kinakarera.** *n.* professional life.

karerísta: (Sp. *carrerista*: racer) n. racer; racing fan.

karerákit: (coined term used in Abra) n. raft race. (*rinnakitan*)

karesón: see *karetón*: kind of dump cart.

karéta: (Sp. *carreta*: cart) n. kind of small, long, hand-pushed cart.

karéte: (Sp. *carrete*: spool) *n.* spool; bobbin.

karetéla: (Sp. *carretela*: dogcart) n. kind of dogcart. (*karomata*)

karetéra: (Sp. *carretera*: highway) n. highway; freeway.

karetília: (Sp. *carretilla*: wheelbarrow) n. wheelbarrow, small cart.

karetkét: var. of *karenken*; also kind of poisonous snake. **kumaretket.** v. to wrinkle; contract, shrink, shrivel. **karetketen.** v. to cause to wrinkle. [Tag. *kulubót*]

karetón: (Sp. *carretón*: pushcart) n. kind of dump cart. **karkareton.** n. pushcart. [Tag. *karitón*]

kárga: (Sp. *carga*: load) n. load; cargo, freight; capacity. **agkarga, kargaen.** v. to carry (*awít,* *búnag, bagkát*); load; transport. **kumarga.** *v.* to become a load; lie in a hammock. **ikarga.** v. to load into. [Kal. *keÿga*]

kargáda: (Sp. *cargada:* cargo) n. load, cargo (*maipaawít*). **nakargadaan.** *a.* loaded; supplied with.

kargadéra: (Sp. *cargadera:* suitcase rack) n. carrier; suitcase rack. (*pagbunagan, pagawitan*)

kargádo: (Sp. *cargado:* loaded) a. full of, with much; plenty. **kargaduen.** v. to load; put too much in; drink too much.

kargadór: (Sp. *cargador:* porter) n. porter, carrier.

kargaménto: (Sp. *cargamento:* cargo) n. cargo, luggage; freight. (*maipaawít; maléta*)

kargéra: *var.* of *kargadera:* luggage rack.

kargét: (f. *regget*) *n.* diligence; perseverance; zeal; *v.* to be enthusiastic about. **Dina unay karget a kadkadua dagiti puraw.** He is not really enthusiastic about accompanying the whites.

kárgo: (Sp. *cargo:* charge) n. charge (in account); obligation; ward.

karí: n. promise, vow. **ikari.** v. to promise. **maikari.** v. to deserve; to be proper, just, right. **kaikarian.** n. merit; destiny; worth. **karian.** v. to threaten. **karikari.** n. native dish made with oxtail cooked in a red peanut sauce, colored with *assuete.* **pagkarien.** v. to compel one to take a vow. **karinkari.** n. mutual promises, promises made to each other. **itungpal ti kari.** to carry out a promise. **agkinnari.** *v.* to promise each other. **Ikkandaka iti dakkel a gatad no ikarim a dika agipulpulong.** We will pay you a big price if you promise not to tell on us. **Ti panagtungpal ti kari, isu't birtud.** The fulfillment of a promise is a virtue. [Kpm. *panátaq*, Png. *sipán*, Tag. *pangakò*]

kariáda: (Sp. *acarrear:* convey; transport) n. load to be transported; transporting of goods by several people. **kariadaen.** v. to transport by vehicle, convoy. **nakakariada.** a. transported by vehicle.

kariáp: (obs.) n. flock of chickens.

kariár: kariáran. v. to scold; punish; threaten (*dayengdeng; luya; bir-it; danengdeng*). **kariaren.** *v.* hurry someone up. **Nagbalinen a sabidong dagiti matana no makitkitana ti asawana aglalo no kariarenna no mabartek.** His eyes become like poison when he sees his wife, especially when she scolds him when he is drunk. [Tag. *parusa*]

karibál: (f. *ribal*) n. rival (usually for a woman).

karibnás₁: n. measles (*kamúras*). [Kpm. *ípe*, Png. *barís*, Tag. *tigdás*]

karibnás₂: *var.* of *kuribnas:* gather food or vegetables. **Bantayanyo a naimbag dagiti mani amangan no karibnasen ida dagiti aliwegweg.** Guard the peanuts well in case the mischievous people gather them.

karibusó₁: n. kind of herb used to cure wounds, tumors, etc.

karibusó₂: n. commotion, noise made by hustling and bustling; confusion. **kumaribuso.** v. to do rapidly; to hustle and bustle; have many people doing different things at once. **Napnuan-segga dagiti ikkis dagiti nagkakaribuso a tao.** The screams of the scuffling people were full of anxiety. **Kunam no nagkaribuso a marabutit a nakasaep iti keso.** You would think he was a scrambling mouse that smelled cheese. [Tag. *abalá*]

karibuyó: n. tapered portion (*immus*). **karibuyuen.** *v.* to taper; *n.* tapering at the end.

karidád: (Sp. *caridad:* charity) n. charity. **agkaridad.** *v.* to be charitable; have pity on.

karidkíd: karidkiden. v. to scrape off (burned rice from the bottom of the pot, etc.).

kárig: (f. *arig*) a. like, similar to. **karig pay ta, karig kad ta.** therefore.

karigá: (obs.) **maikariga.** v. to be adequate. (*umdas; umanay*)

karikatúra: (Sp. *caricatura:* caricature) n. caricature, exaggerated drawing of a face; cartoon. **karikaturista.** n. cartoonist.

karikkík: karikkiken. v. to tickle. (*kiki*)

karílio: (Sp. *carillo:* beloved, obs.) n. shadow play.

karilión: (Sp. *carillón:* carillon) n. set of chiming bells played by machinery or by finger keys.

karimbanasá: *var.* of *karibusó:* commotion; hustle and bustle.

karimbará: n. fruit when it starts to ripen. **agkarimbara.** v. to start to ripen (fruit).

karimbúbo n. long-necked earthen water container.

karimbubuá: n. tree with small (1cm) red fruits.

karimbuáya: n. *Euphorbia trigona* cactuslike plant with winged branches. (also *karimbubuaya*)

kar-ín: kar-inen. v. to separate (brush) in order to pass. **ikar-in.** v. to turn over food with a spatula; wash ashore; place aside. **agkar-in.** v. to trim the soil around the plant.

karindéria: n. eatery, small native restaurant.

karínio: (Sp. *cariño:* affection) n. affection. (*dungngo*) **nakarinio.** a. affectionate.

karinióso: (Sp. *cariñoso:* affectionate) a. affectionate. (*fem. karinyosa*)

karintár: (Sp. *calentar:* heat) **agkarintar.** v. to hurry; exchange bad words. **karintaren.** v. to

make someone hurry; yell words or orders at someone. **makarintar.** *v.* to be in a hurry.
karintitíway: *var.* of *karintiway*.
karintíway: *var.* of *karantiway*: long-legged.
káring: *n.* dried fish (*daing*). [Knk. *kigíng*, Png. *káing*, Tag. *daing*]
karingkíng: (Tag.*)* **kumaringking.** *v.* to flirt.
kário: (Sp. *careo*: confrontation) *n.* act of putting two roosters beak to beak to incite them to fight. **ikario.** *v.* to pit roosters.
kariskís: *n. Albizzia lebbeckoides* tree whose leaves are used to dye nets and cure headaches; dry bark. **kariskisen.** *v.* see *karosákis*: scrape (tree bark); scrape the outside of a pot. [Png. *kidkid, kadkad*, Tag. *kayod* (scrape)]
karisón: (Sp. *carretón*: cart) *n.* cart. **karisonero.** *n.* cart driver; cart maker.
karissábong: *n.* young guava or mango just forming; girl reaching puberty; (fig.) immature, inexperienced person.
kárit: *n.* challenge; dare; defiance. **nakarit.** *a.* bold, daring; overconfident; too forward; rude. **kariten.** *v.* to dare; challenge; provoke; irritate. **kumarit.** *v.* to stand up and fight; defy; provoke. **Karitanna ti agtrabaho.** He is persistent in his work. **Nabayagak ditoyen ngem awan pay maikaritko a balligik.** I have been here for a long time already but I still cannot challenge my success. [Kal. *gaygayon, ay-ayyatan*, Png. *oyot*, Tag. *hamon*]
karitíkit: *n.* sound of a running mouse or a shuffling hen; sound of rain; sound of jingling. **Awan ti agkarkaritikit iti bolsana.** Nothing is jingling in his pocket.
karit-óm: **nakarit-om.** *a.* crunchy. (*karemkém*). **karit-umen.** *v.* to crunch. [Tag. *ngalót*]
karitón: (Sp. *carretón*) *n.* cart (*karisón*). **karitunero.** *n.* cart driver; cart maker.
kariwawwét: **kumariwawwet.** *v.* to form rings (tendrils of the bittermelon vine).
karkár: **kumarkar.** *v.* to erode. (*kurukor*) **makarkaran.** *v.* to be eroded. [Tag. *agnás*]
karkardayó: *a.* remotely possible; too far off; denotes degree of comparison implying both extremes (much less; much more).
kárkulo: (Sp. *cálculo*: calculation) **agkarkulo.** *v.* to calculate (*pattapatta*)
karlóta: **la karlota.** *n.* variety of avocado.
karmá: *n.* soul, spirit. (*kararuá*) **karkarma.** *n.* vigor, strength, energy; kind of ghost. **makarkarma.** *v.* to be visited by a spirit of the dead. [Kpm. *kaladuwá*, Png. *kamarérua*, Tag. *káluluwá*]
karmáy: *n. Glochidion rubrum* shrub with clustered fruits. **karmáy a lugkáw.** *n.* kind of

tree with medicinal bark. **kumarmay ti ling-et.** *v.* to sweat in large droplets.
karmelítos: (Sp. *carmelitos*) *n.* white loaf sugar.
kármen: (Sp. *carmín*: carmine) *n.* a kind of cookie; variety of slender sugarcane with red skin; scapular badge.
karná: **karkarna.** *a.* extraordinary; mystical; strange; incredible; phenomenal; out of this world; unusual. **agkarna.** *v.* to incidentally meet. **kinarkarkarna.** *n.* strangeness; extraordinariness. **karkarna a pasamak.** *n.* supernatural or extraordinary event. **Saan a karkarna kenkuana.** It is familiar to him. [Tag. *kataká-taká*]
karnabál: (Sp. *carnaval*: carnival) *n.* carnival. **pagkarnabalan.** *n.* carnival grounds.
karnál: (Sp. *carnal*) *a.* carnal, sensual; related by blood; (Catholic calendar) referring to the time of the year when meat can be eaten.
kárne: (Sp. *carne*: meat) *n.* meat, flesh. (*laság*) **karne ti baboy.** *n.* pork. **karne ti baka.** *n.* beef. **karnien.** *v.* to butcher; raise for meat. **karkarnien.** *a.* ready for butchering. **managkarne.** *a.* fond of eating meat. [Bon. *watwat*, Knk. *dáot, dawdáw, kuawwá, móa* (meat); *wáwak* (pork)]
karnélia: (Sp. *cornelina, cornalina*) *n.* carnelian gem.
karnéro: (Sp. *carnero*: sheep) *n.* sheep; mutton. **karnero negro.** *n.* black sheep; black sheep in the family (*itta*). **Kasla karnero a sumursurot lattan iti kayatda.** He just follows what they want like a sheep. [Ivt. *kañiru*, Tag. *tupa*]
karnesería: (Sp. *carnecería*: butcher shop) *n.* butcher shop.
karníboro: (Sp. *carnívoro*: carnivorous) *a.* carnivorous, meat eating.
karniséro: (Sp. *carnicero*) *n.* butcher.
káro: **nakaro.** *a.* serious, excessive, exceptional. **kumaro.** *v.* to worsen, get more serious. **ikaro.** *v.* to atone for; pay in kind; compensate. **agikaro.** *v.* to compensate, pay for; pay for one's wrongdoings; (fig.) take a beating. **agkaro.** *v.* to recur (sickness). **agpakaro.** *v.* to have temper fits. **pagikaruen.** *v.* to take revenge on. **pakaruen.** *v.* to make worse. **kakarona.** at the worst or most serious stage. **Agikaronto met dagiti anak ti sal-it.** Those damn children will pay for what they've done! [Tag. *lalà*]
karuáhe: (Sp. *carruaje*: carriage) *n.* four-wheeled, horse-drawn carriage.
karuás: *n.* kind of bamboo ladle used as a strainer; triangular net for fishing. **agkaruas.** *v.* to fish with a *karuas*.

karudákid: n. sound of scraping the bottom of a rice pot. **agkarudakid.** v. to remove the last bits of rice from a pot by scraping.

karudkúd: n. kind of harrow. (*moriskí, palpal, pak-ól*) **karudkuden.** v. to dig by scraping.

karúkay: *n.* scratching (the soil). **agkarukay.** v. to scratch as chickens. (*karaykay*) **karukayen.** v. to scratch something; scrape the soil when cultivating. [Tag. *kalmót, gasgás, kalaykáy*]

karukbába: **agkarukbaba.** v. to kneel (*parintúmeng*); var. of *kalumbába*: to rest the chin on the arms. **kumarukbába.** v. to kneel before someone (*agparintúmeng*); fall prostrate in pleading. [Tag. *tirapâ*]

karúkod: n. seine smaller than the *daklís*.

karomáta: (Sp. *carromato*: covered wagon + -*a*) n. kind of two-wheeled horse-drawn carriage. (*karetéla*) **karomatero.** n. driver of a *karomata*.

karomatília: (Sp. *carromato*: covered wagon + dim. suffix -*illa*) n. wheelbarrow.

karomáto: (Sp. *carromato*: covered wagon) n. pushcart, bull cart.

karomínas: n. jellyfish. (*korimínas*) **agkarominas.** v. to be sick (from eating jellyfish). **kinarominas.** *a.* affected perversely from a jellyfish; stung by a jellyfish. [Tag. *dikyâ*]

karumsí: n. *Dendrobium crumenatum*, white dove orchid.

karuníkon: **agkarunikon.** v. to put everything in one place; to arrange in one place.

karunúkon: var. of *karanukon*.

karuprúpan: (f. *rupa*) a. having a similar face to; with the same face.

karuráyan: n. yellow-legged chicken believed to have healing powers.

kárus: n. scraper; strickle. **ikarus.** v. to scrape; (fig.) to insist. **karúsen.** v. to scrape; level with a strickle. **karusan.** v. to card (maguey fibers). **kinarus nga mangga.** n. scraped mango. **Urnongenyo dagita makarusyo a semento ta sayang.** Save that scraped cement of yours because it is a waste. [Png. *kidkid, kadkad*, Tag. *kayod*]

karósa: (Sp. *carroza*: coach; carriage) n. float in a parade; coach, stagecoach; hearse, funeral car.

karusakés: n. kind of brown worm found in *boggóong*; rough (not properly ironed) surface.

karosákis: **pagkarosakisen.** v. to scrape (bark off trees) **karusakusen.** v. to scrape off (*karus*). [Png. *kidkid, kadkad*, Tag. *kayod*]

karuskós: **agkaruskos.** v. to slide down. [Tag. *dausdós*]

karót: n. *Dioscorea daemona*, wild yam. **kakarutan.** n. place abounding with the *karot* yam.

karutakét: n. rough surface (not yet sandpapered).

karutíkit: **agkarutikit.** v. to make a jingling sound.

karutukót: n. sound of cracking joints. (*rituok*) **agkarutukot.** v. to crack (said of joints).

karut-óm: *n.* crunching (*karit-om*). **karut-umen.** v. to crunch, grind with the teeth (*karemkem*). **makarut-om.** *n.* crunchy foods. **Mangraem iti makarut-om.** He idolizes crunchy (junk) food. [Tag. *ngalót*]

káruy: **karuyen.** v. to scoop out; scrape out coconut meat. **kakaruyen.** n. soft coconut meat; (fig.) younger flesh of sexual desire. [Kal. *laotong* (soft coconut meat)]

kárpa: n. carp fish.

karpéta: (Sp. *carpeta*: portfolio, folder) n. pocketbook; wallet.

karpintería: (Sp. *carpintería*: carpentry) n. carpentry; carpenter's shop.

karpintéro: (Sp. *carpintero*: carpenter) n. carpenter. (*allawagi*)

kárpio: (Eng.*)* n. curfew. [Tag. *kurpiyo*]

karrá: **karrakarra.** n. spinning awry (tops), wobbling while spinning. (*barág*)

karráang: n. underground furnace.

karraép: (f. *raép*) a. just transplanted (rice).

karréra: *var.* spelling of *karera*: career; race.

karréte: (Sp. *carrete*: spool) n. spool. **karretean.** v. to wind thread on a spool.

karretéro: (Sp. *carretero*) *n.* carter, carman.

karretón: (Sp. *carretón*) n. cart; cartload. **sangakarreton.** one cartload.

kárro: (Sp. *carro*: cart) n. cart, four wheels with no body; funeral coach.

karrúba: var. of *kaaruba*: neighbor.

karrosería: (Sp. *carrocería*) *n.* coachbuilder's shop, cartwright's shop.

karsáda: var. of *kalsada*: street, road. (*dalan*)

kársel: (Sp. *cárcel*: jail) n. jail; prison. (*pagbaludan*) **ikarsel.** v. to imprison. (*ikulung*)

karseléro: (Sp. *carcelero*: jailer) n. jailer, warden.

karsibók: (f. *rissibok*) **kanarsibok.** *n.* sound of splashing water.

karsó: n. hamlet; temporary quarters; hut. (*abong*) **pakarso.** n. temporary country residence. [Tag. *kubo*]

karsonsílio: (Sp. *calzoncillo*: underwear) n. men's underwear, briefs. **nakakarsonsilio.** a. wearing briefs. [Tag. *kalsonsilyo*]

kárta: (Sp. *carta*: letter) n. love letter; charter; (*reg.*) playing card (*inipis*). [Tag. *saligangbatás* (charter)]

kartamonéda: (Sp. *portamoneda*: wallet, coin purse) n. pocketbook; purse.

kartél: (Sp. *cartel*: placard) n. show bill; placard; handbill.

kartéles: (Sp. *carteles*: placards) *n.* streamers.

kartelón: (Sp. *cartelón*: poster) n. poster, placard.

kartéra: (Sp. *cartera*: wallet) n. ladies' handbag; female mail carrier.

kartéro: (Sp. *cartero*: mailman) n. mailman; postman.

kartíb: n. scissors; shears. (*getténg*) **karkartib, pangngartib, mangngartib.** n. kind of flying insect with scissorlike jaws and destructive to vegetation. **kartiben.** v. to cut with scissors. **kimmartib.** a. term applied to small vaginas. (ant. *kimmappo*) [Knk. *kantíb*, Png. *kátli*, Tag. *gunting*]

kartília: (Sp. *cartilla*: primer book) n. syllabary; primer book of kindergarten or first grade.

kartíng: nakarting. a. alert, active (*siglat*); agile; brisk (*paspas*). (*karanting*) **kartingan.** v. to do fast; do promptly. **Ikartingmo ket matektekan dagiti mangur-uray kenka.** Hurry it up because the people waiting for you are anxious. [Tag. *tulin*]

kartulário: (Sp. *cartulario*) *n.* archives; registry, public records.

kartolína: (Sp. *cartulina*: thin cardboard) n. cardboard.

kartón: (Sp. *cartón*: box) n. cardboard; cardboard box. **ikarton.** v. to place in a box. **sangakarton.** n. one boxful.

kartún: (Eng.*)* n. cartoon. **kartunen.** v. to make into a cartoon.

kartútso: (Sp. *cartucho*: cartridge, roll of coins) n. roll of coins wrapped in paper; cartridge.

karwáhe: (Sp. *carruaje*: carriage) n. carriage.

karyáda: var. of *kariada*: transport.

kas: adv. like, as (usually *kasla*) **no kas (no)** if. **kas kaniada.** like them. **Saanak a kas karugit ti panangipagarupmo.** I am not as dirty as you think. **Apay a kayatnakon nga ibelleng a kas tulang wenno siit a nagsidaan?** Why do you want to throw me away like eaten bones? [Bon. *kag, kas-on*, Knk. *anég*, Png. *singá*, Tag. *parang, gaya, tulad*]

kása: (Sp. *casa*: house) n. house (of a casino, of *sungka* game); business firm. **ipakasa.** v. to send home (in games such as *sungka* or *simbara*).

kasá: (Sp. *cazar*: hunt; shoot) **ikasa.** v. to cock a gun. **kumasa.** v. to prepare to fight; gamble. **Inkasana ti paltogna sa nangngegko ti danapegna nga immuneg.** He cocked his gun and I heard his footsteps entering.

kasabá: n. *Carthamus tinctorius*, safflower. **agkasaba.** v. to preach. **kasabaan.** *v.* to preach

to someone. **mangaskasaba.** n. preacher. **ikaskasaba.** v. to indoctrinate, proselytize.

kasábang: n. kind of spiny tree with medicinal bark used to cure abdominal pains.

kasábay: n. *Sapindus saponaria* tree.

kasáda: (Sp. *cazada*: hunted) n. match, opponent (in a game). [Tag. *kalaban*]

kasádar: n. contemporary, of the same age. (*kataengán*) **agkasadar.** v. to be of the same age.

kasádo₁: (Sp. *casado*: married) a. married (*naikallaysa*). [Tag. *may-asawa*]

kasádo₂: (Sp. *cazado*: hunted) *exp.* Agreed! (used in cockfights).

kasadór: (f. *kasa*) *n.* hunter; person in charge of betting or gambling; person in charge of a brothel.

kaság: n. dome-shaped fish trap. **agkasag.** v. to catch fish with the *kaság*. **makasag.** v. to be able to catch fish with the *kaság*.

kasákas: kasakasen. v. collect; gather (what is left out to dry). (*akas*)

kasakbáyan: (f. *sakbay*) n. period before.

kasamák: (f. *samák*) n. sharecropper, tenant farmer.

kasamiénto: (Sp. *casamiento*: wedding) n. wedding; part of the *rigodon* dance.

kasanó: *interrog.* How? **no kasano.** *conj.* how; as, like. **uray kasano.** however; anyway. **Kasano ti pannakaammmom?** How do you know? **Kasanottan?** What now? [Ivt. *mangwangu*, Png. *pánon*, Tag. *paano*]

kas-áng: *n.* painfulness; gravity of a bad situation (*sanaang, panaas*). **nakas-áng.** a. painful; serious; vulgar, rude; mean, ugly, improper. **nakakaskas-ang.** a. sorrowful; pitiful. **kasangen.** v. to scorn, condemn; despise. **Anian a nakas-ang a panunuten.** What a painful thing to think about. [Tag. *habág*]

kasangaaldáw: (f. *aldáw*) n. the day before.

kasangáy: n. birthday; patron saint. **agkasangay.** v. to celebrate one's birthday. **panagkasangay.** n. birthday celebration. **Nakaammuam a kasangayko ita?** How did you know it was my birthday today? [Root word *sengngay*. Knk. *daúmna*, Png. *aiyanakan*, Tag. *kaarawan*]

kasangoánan: (f. *sángo*) n. period before.

kasáor: n. northeast wind. **agkasaor.** v. to blow in from the northeast.

kasapígo: var. of *kasapuego*: matchbox.

kasapuégo: (Sp. *casa de fuego*: house of fire) n. matchbox; matches. [Knk. *andúlus, kulígo*]

kasapúlan: (f. *sapul*) n. something needed; need.

kásar: (obs.) **kumasar.** v. to be very tired.

kasár: (Sp. *casar*: marry) n. wedding. (*kallaysa*) **agkasar.** v. to marry, wed. **kasaren.** v. to wed off; officiate at a wedding. **ikasar.** *v.* to marry a woman. **makikasar.** v. to marry (said of women); to attend a wedding. **kakaskasar.** *a.* newly wed. **kakasar.** *n.* marriage partner. **pakasar.** *n.* wedding party, wedding feast. **agpakasar.** *v.* to give a wedding celebration. [Png., Tag. *kasál* (Sp.)]

kasasaád: (f. *saad*) n. condition; position; situation; social standing.

kásaw: n. layer of *nipa* leaves used in thatching. **kasawen.** v. to arrange into rows.

kásay: n. debility due to lack of nourishment. (*kapsut*)

kasburán: *var.* of *kasiburán*: time of plenty; height of a season.

kasdí: [*kas* + *daydi*] like that (remote past) **ikasdi.** v. to do like that (remote past) **kaskasdi.** a. same as before. **gapu ta kasdi.** because of what happened.

kasdiáy: [*kas* + *daydiay*] like that; so. **ikasdiay.** v. to do like that. (*daydiay*) **no kasdiay.** in that case. [Kal. *katlat*, Png. *onmán*, Tag. *ganoón*]

kaséra: (Sp. *casera*: landlady) n. landlady; boarding house. **kakaseraan.** n. fellow boarders. **pagkaseraan.** n. boarding house. **Agkakaseraan ken agkabangakami.** We are fellow boarders and we share food.

kaséro: (Sp. *casero*: landlord) n. landlord; boarding house; boarder. **agkasero.** *v.* to board; *n.* boarder. **agpakasero.** *v.* to take boarders. **kakasero.** *n.* fellow boarder.

kaseróla: (Sp. *caserola*: saucepan) n. saucepan; casserole.

kaséta: (Sp. *caseta*: cabin) n. cottage, hut.

kasí: *n.* wild fowl. [Kal. *kasi* = parrot, Tag. *labuyò*]

kasia: (Sp. *casia*: cassia; bastard cinnamon) *n.* cassia, a tropical leguminous plant.

kasibag: n. var. of *kasibeng.*

kasíben(g): n. *Sapindus saponaria tree* with poison bark used in killing fish. (*kusibeng*)

kasiburán: n. height of a season, time of plenty, season with abundant produce. **agkasiburan.** v. to be bountiful.

kásig: kasigan. v. to put a border around the rim of. (*lebleb*)

kasíkas: n. plastron, shell of a turtle.

kasíke: (Sp. *cacique*) *n.* cacique, chief.

kasíli: n. kind of cormorant.

kasílias: (Sp. *casilla*: cabin) n. toilet; outhouse; stall. **mangasilias, agpakasilias.** v. to go to the toilet. [Kal. *aattayan, iisbuwan*, Png. *pátiang*, Tag. *kubeta* (Sp.)]

kasilóng: (f. *silóng*) n. division of land equal to five *kinelleng*; large rice paddy.

kasimpungálan: n. mate; spouse. (*asawa*) **Kayatko a sika ti agbalin a kasimpungalak.** I want you to be my spouse. [Tag. *asawa*]

kasinsín: (pl. *kakasinsin*) n. cousin. (usually first) **agkasinsin.** v. to be cousins. [Bon. *kasingsing*, Ivt. *kataysa*, Kal. *kapingsan*, Png., Tag. *pinsán*]

kasinggáy: n. bamboo shaft put over two parts of repaired pole.

kásir: kasiren. v. to provoke, irritate; threaten. **nakasir.** a. vicious; ruthless. **Dina inkasir daydi nabaybay-an a sapata.** The neglected oath did not bother him.

kasír: agkikinnasir. *v.* to compete with each other; aspire against one another. **makikinnasir.** *v.* to vie, contend.

kasíray: n. kind of tree with light building timber.

kasísaw: agkaskasisaw. v. to run around busily.

kásiw: n. vegetable amulet used for fleeing or hiding; kind of edible sea mollusk. **kumasiw.** v. to miss the mark; deviate; slide out of place. (*gamdir; kamlos; ligsay*; *kabsiw*)

kaskabél: (Sp. *cascabel*: jingle bells) n. jingle bells.

kaskarí: a. easy; without difficulty. **saan a kaskarina.** to be very difficult.

kaskarón: (Sp. *cascarón*: thick rind) n. puffed rice sweet boiled in sugar.

kaskás$_1$: kaskasen. v. to gather in one place; scour (in cleaning). **kaskasan.** v. to clean out all one's money in gambling.

kaskás$_2$: kaskasán. v. to do swiftly; do fast. **kaskasero.** n. habitually fast person; speeder on the freeway. [Tag. *paspás*]

kaskasdí: adv. nevertheless; same as before.

kaskenán: a. most important; primary. **Ti salunat ti kaskenan iti tao.** Health is the most important thing to man.

kásko: (Sp. *casco*: helmet) n. barge; cask; headpiece; horse's hoof; base, bottom. **nakasko.** *a.* flat-hoofed.

kaslá: adv. like; as; as though; similar to; *v.* seem (*kas*). **Apay a kasla makasangsangitka?** Why do you look like you are about to cry? [Knk. *kamán, anég*, Png. *singá*, Tag. *gaya, parang*]

káso$_1$: (Sp. *caso*: case) n. court case; case; value, importance. **kasuan.** *v.* to file a court case against someone.

káso$_2$: (Sp. *hacer caso*: pay attention) **ikaskaso, kaskasuen.** v. to mind, care about; appreciate; pay attention to. **mangikaso.** v. to heed; listen. (*pangag*; *asikaso*)

kasuáy: n. a kind of tree with light building timber.

kasuéla: (Sp. *cazuela*) *n.* earthen cooking pot.

kasúgpon: (f. *sugpon*) *n.* helper in farming; partner; tenant.

kasukát: (f. *sukat*) *n.* substitute, successor.

kasúkob: (f. *sukob*) *n.* relative. (*kabagian*)

kasúlia: (Sp. *casulla*: chasuble) *n.* chasuble, vestment worn by a priest at mass.

kasumbá: *n. Carthamus tinctorius*, safflower.

kasunó: *n.* substitute, successor.

kasuóran: *n.* part of the roof over the hearth. **Kaska la narba a kasuoran.** *exp.* You are like a collapsed *kasuoran* (look very depressed and pouting).

kásoy: *n.* kind of shrub.

kasúy: *n.* cashew nut, whose fruit is used for toothaches (*sambaldoke*). [Tag. *kasóy*]

kaspél: (f. *ispel* with *ka-* prefix) **makaspel.** *v.* to choke.

kasserrék: (f. *serrek*) *n.* newcomer; recently enrolled person; person who has just entered.

kassibét: (f. *sibét*) *a.* just departed, just left.

kassibbó: (f. *sibbó*) *a.* just used for the first time; just tried.

kassiból: (f. *sibbol*) *a.* just plucked with a pole (fruits from a tree).

kassít: var. of *kissít*: semen; sperm. [Tag. *tamód*]

kassulnót: (f. *sulnot*) *a.* just pulled, just picked; just drawn out.

kastá: [*kas + dayta*] like that. **ikasta.** *v.* to do like that. **gapo ta kasta**, therefore, as it is so, because of that. **nopay no kasta.** however, although it is so. **no kasta.** thus, hence, in that case. **kasta unay.** excessively so, very much; really. **sapay kuma ta kasta.** so be it, amen. **ikasta.** *v.* to do like that. **kastakasta.** *a.* worthless; fake; *n.* prostitute. **dika agkasta.** Don't be like that. **iti kasta.** in that way. **Saannak nga angawen iti kasta.** Don't joke with me like that. **Kasta unay ti agawa dagiti kaadalanna.** His classmates are very diligent. [Png. *ontán*, Tag. *ganyán*]

kastánias: (Sp. *castaña*: chestnut) *n.* chestnut.

kastaniétas: (Sp. *castañeta*: castanets) *n.* castanets.

kastánio: (Sp. *castaño*: hazelnut) *n. a.* brown.

kastanuélas: (Sp. *castañuela*: castanets) *n.* castanets.

kastáy: [*kas + daytay*] like that (recent past). **ikastay.** *v.* to do like that (recent past). **kastay nakairuaman.** *exp.* as is customary; as tradition permits.

kastigádo: (Sp. *castigado*: punished) *a.* punished. (*nadusa*)

kastigár: (Sp. *castigar*: punish) **kastigaren.** *v.* to punish.

kastígo: (Sp. *castigo*: punishment) *n.* punishment. (*dusa*) **kastiguen.** *v.* to punish someone.

kastigador. *n.* punisher.

kastiguár: *var.* of *kastigar*: punish.

kastíla: (Sp. *Castilla*: Castile, pl. *kakastila*) *n. a.* Spanish. **agkastila.** *v.* to speak Spanish. **kastilaen.** *v.* to translate into Spanish; utter something in Spanish. **kimmastila.** *a.* with Spanish features. [Tag. *kastilà*]

kastília: (Sp. *castilla*) *n.* Castile soap, soap made from olive oil and soda.

Kastiliáno: (Sp. *castellano*: Castilian) *n.* Spanish person, Spanish language.

kastiliého: (Sp. *castillejo*: small castle; scaffolding) *n.* scaffolding; platform.

kastílio: (Sp. *castillo*: castle) *n.* castle. **kastilio a darat.** *n.* sand castle.

kastína: (Sp. *castina*: flux) *n.* flux.

kastíso: (Sp. *castizo*: pure blooded) *n.* pure blooded, thoroughbred; faultless (language).

kastóli: *n.* kind of marrow whose root is used as a diuretic.

kastónay: [*kasta + unay*] very much like that.

kastór: (Sp *castor*: beaver) *n.* castor-oil plant; beaver.

kastoría: (f. *kastor*) *n.* castor oil.

kastóy: [*kas + daytoy*] like this. **ikastoy.** *v.* to do like this. **kastoy latta.** *exp.* just like this; just fine. **agpakastoy.** *v.* to come this way. **Apay nga inkastoynak?** Why did you do this to me? [Kal. *katla, katchi*, Png. *onyá*, Tag. *ganitó*]

kastrádo: (Sp. *castrado*) *a.* castrated.

kastrénse: (Sp. *castrense*) *n.* chaplain.

katá: **kumatakata.** *v.* to make the sound of a restive crowd.

katákat: **katakatan.** *v.* to lessen, diminish. **makatakatan.** *v.* to lessen, become fewer in number.

katakúmba: (Sp. *catacumba*: catacomb) *n.* catacomb.

katálogo: (Sp. *catálogo*: catalog) *n.* catalog.

katám: (Tag. also) *n.* carpenter's plane, jack plane. **katamen.** *v.* to shave with a plane. **nagkatamán.** *n.* shavings.

kátang: **agkatangkatang.** *v.* to drift, randomly float; to not have a permanent house to live in; to live from house to house. **yarigka 'tay billit nga agkatangkatang.** *exp.* you are always on the move. [Tag. *tangáy*]

katangkátat: (obs.) *n.* bustle; resonance.

katáo: (f. *tao*) *n.* number of persons (used to count people); individuality. **kinatao.** *n.* character; personality; individuality. **katatao.** *n.* lineage; race; personality; social status. **agpakatao.** *v.* to act as a human; respect people as humans should. **sangkataoan.** *n.* human race;

humanity. **di katataoan.** n. invisible spirits; demons. **Innem a katao ti nasugatan.** Six people were injured.

kataó: n. cage; gauge (for measuring); horizontal bamboos for thatching roofs.

katár: (Sp. *catar*: sample) **kataran.** v. to sample, taste; examine; judge. **kataren.** v. to examine; investigate;

kataráta: (Sp.) n. cataract of the eye. (*busa*; *boskaw*)

katastrál: nakatastral. a. registered (property).

katástro: (Sp. *catastro*: fiscal property register) n. land registry.

katát: agkatat. v. to stutter (*bede*; *beddal*). [Tag. *utál*]

katatáo: (f. *tao*) n. human nature; one's nature as a human.

katataoán: (f. *tao*) n. evil demon. (usually headless and dwelling in trees).

katátos: n. strips of jerked meat.

katáwa: n. laugh; laughter; hilarity. **agkatawa.** v. to laugh. **katawaan.** v. to laugh at. **ikatawa.** v. to laugh off. **managpakatawa.** a. funny; humorous. **nakatawa.** a. funny, joyful, laughable, amusing. **nakakatkatawa.** a. funny, humorous, comical. **pagkakatawaan.** n. humor. [Bon. *iyek*, Ibg. *galóq*, Ivt. *ma-yak*, Kal. *mayokyok*, Knk. *síyek*, Kpm. *ili*, Png. *elék*, Tag. *tawa*]

kátay₁: n. saliva; spittle; web (of a spider); venom (of snakes). **agkatay.** v. to drivel; have one's mouth water. **ikatay.** v. to spin a web (spiders, silkworms). **katay ti lawwalawwá.** n. spiderweb. **katay ti uleg.** n. snake venom. **agkakatay.** v. to dribble saliva; slobber. **katayan.** v. to drip saliva; apply saliva to. **pagkatayan.** *n.* bib. **Sumagmamano ti agdudunger nga agkatkatay iti kinabartekda.** A few of them shook their head and drooled in their drunkenness. [Ivt. *ngahay*, Kal. *angiw*, Knk. *ngáiw*, Png. *katáy*, Tag. *laway*]

kátay₂: **katayan.** n. kind of freshwater fish with black and white stripes.

kátay₃: **kataykatay.** n. kind of slug.

katáy: (obs.) a. avaricious, grasping.

katdól: (obs.) see *kitdól*: to gather the first.

katedrál: (Sp. *catedral*: cathedral) n. cathedral. **agpakatedral.** v. to go to the cathedral.

kategoriá: (Sp. *categoría*) n. category.

katék: agkatek. v. to throb, palpitate.

katekísta: (Sp. *catequista*: catechist) n. catechist.

katelán: (Sp. *catalán*) **papel katelan.** *n.* thin, brittle paper.

katesísmo: (Sp. *catecismo*: catechism) n. catechism. **agkatesismo.** v. to have catechism, go through catechism.

káti: n. pound; weighing scale (*pagkilluán*). **kakatian.** n. steelyard. **katien.** v. to weigh. [Tag. *timbáng*]

katigíd: a. left; left-handed; n. left side. (*kanigíd*) **agpakatigid.** v. to go to the left. **kakatigidan.** *a.* far left, farthest to the left. [Knk. *kanigíd*, Png. *kawigí*, Tag. *kaliwâ*]

katíkat: n. ball of thread. **katikaten.** v. to wind thread. **agkanatikat.** v. to prepare oneself for a journey.

kátil: n. animosity, rancor, ill will, resentment. **agkatinkatil.** v. to fight (children). **katilen.** v. to fight with. [Tag. *away*]

katilmón: (f. *tilmon*) n. gulp; swallow.

katíng: n. leprosy. **agkating.** v. to have leprosy (*kutel*). [Ivt. *dipad*, Png. *kating*, *lipra* (Sp.), Tag. *ketong*]

katipúnan: (Tag.) *n.* name of the revolutionary society organized by Andrés Bonifacio against the Spanish government. **katipunero.** member of the *katipunan.*

katít: *var.* of *kutit*: last (in a succession).

katkatnág: (f. *tinnag*) *a.* just fallen.

katkuáti: var. of *kakawate*: the *madre cacao* tree.

katúd: n. *Eclipta alba*, herb with reddish stems and white flowers. **marakatud.** n. kind of plant.

katúday: n. *Sesbania grandiflora*, tree with large white edible flowers; variety of awned early rice. **katkatuday.** n. kind of herb with small yellow flowers. **mangatúday.** n. *sawsaw-it* bird. **kimmatuday.** a. long, slender bolo. [Tag. *katuray*]

katugángan: (f. *tugang*) n. father-in-law; mother-in-law. (pl. *kakatugangan*). **agkatugangan.** n. relationship between a person and parents-in-law. **makikatugangan.** v. to be related by marriage (*kamang*). [Kal. *katuganga, med-an, maÿong-eg*, Kpm. *katuángan*, Png. *katólangán*, Tag. *biyanán*]

katók: (Tag.) a. crazy. (*bagtit*) **agkatok.** v. to knock.

katól: n. mosquito coil (burned to repel mosquitoes). **katolen.** v. to ward off mosquitoes by burning a coil. **Kinatolko ida.** I killed them (the mosquitoes) with a *katol.*

katulágan: (f. *tulag*) n. agreement; contract.

katóliko: (Sp. *católico*) n. a. Catholic.

katolisismo: (Sp. *catolicismo*) *n.* Catholicism.

katumbáw: n. herbal plant whose leaves are used to cure rheumatism and stem is used to heal dislocations.

katón: (Sp. *catón*: primer) n. alphabet (*abakáda*), primer spelling book during Spanish occupation.

katórse: (Sp. *catorce*: fourteen) n. fourteen. (*sangapulo ket uppat*)

katós: *n.* knock on the head. **agkatos, katusan.** v. to strike the head; hit the head with a hard abrasion (in punishment).

katút: (obs.) **ikatut.** v. to be unable to utter. **katutan.** v. to do something hasty.

katuwáw: n. kind of tree used for its red timber. **kakatuwawan.** n. grove of *katuwaw* trees.

kátoy: n. kind of hammer made with a horn.

kátre: (Sp. *catre*: cot) n. bed, cot. (*káma, pagturogan*)

katsá: n. coarse-woven cloth material, unbleached muslin cloth.

katsáro: (Sp. *cacharro*: worthless thing) n. broken piece of pottery; worthless thing.

kattaldéng: (f. *taldeng*) n. novice; apprentice.

kattapóg: (f. *tapóg*) a. just begun, just commenced. **Kattapog pay la ti bulan ti Oktubre, nabukelen dagiti komite ti piesta.** The month of October has just begun and the fiesta committees have already formed.

kattilíw: (f. *tiliw*) a. just caught; just arrested; n. beginner (in politics).

kattugáw: (f. *tugaw*) a. just sat down; just appointed; just inaugurated.

kattukóng: n. bamboo-woven hat. (*bistukol*) **nakakattukong.** a. wearing a bamboo-woven hat.

kattungból: n. sprout.

káwa: n. large kettle for making *sinublán* or *bási*.

káwa: **maikawa.** v. to happen to do, do accidentally or inadvertently; feel strange or lost for being in a place with someone; feel nostalgia for; to err through negligence; fall down; regret with sorrow. **ikawa.** v. to fail, disappoint; lead into temptation. **maikawkawa.** v. to feel out of place (in a strange land). **Maikawakami la ketdi iti pannakapukawmi kenkuana.** We nevertheless feel regret about losing him, we miss his loss. **Maikawa unayen nga ag-Iloko.** She doesn't feel at home speaking Ilocano (after not having spoken it for a long time).

káwad: n. second bunch of tobacco harvest after the *palaspás*; wooden pegs stuck in the posts of a house to prevent them from wobbling. **agkawad.** v. to try to grab on to something while falling; to use as a support while losing balance or getting up; flail the arms when swimming.

kawág: a. very tall. (*táyag, káwas*)

kawákaw: a. foolish; silly; n. kind of winged brownish insect; top layer of cooked rice. **kawakawan.** v. to remove the top of, top.

káwal: **kawalen.** v. to stick the fingers in to take something out; to touch something with the fingers; thrust. **ikawal.** v. to thrust the fingers into. **kawalen ti bagí.** v. to touch oneself indecently (women). **kumawal.** *v.* to take out with the hands. **Kimmawal iti dinengdeng.** He stuck his fingers into the boiled vegetables. [Tag. *dukot*]

káwang: (obs.) **kumawkawang.** n. shoal of marine fish.

káwar: n. chain. (*kadena*) **kawaran.** v. to chain. **nakakawar.** a. chained. [Ibg. *káwag*, Tag. *kadena* (Sp.)]

káwas: **nakawas.** a. tall. (*kawág, tayag*)

káwat: n. anchor (*ángkla, sinipéte*). [Tag. *angkla*]

kawatán: n. robber; thief. (*tulisan*)

kawáti: **kawkawati.** n. a kind of tree. (*dalagudog*)

kawáw: n. foolish person; empty coconut. **agkawaw.** v. to become empty. **kawaw ti panunotna.** a. empty minded, thoughtless. [Tag. *hungkág*]

kawáy: **ikaway.** v. to signal with the hand; wave the hand in greeting or summoning.

kawáyan: n. bamboo. **kawkawáyan.** n. *Panicum crusgalli* grass. **mangawayan.** v. to cut down bamboo. [Ibg. *pasíngen, kawayan*, Ivt. *kawayan*, Knk. *kawwáyan*, Kpm. *kuáyan*, Png. *kawayán*, Tag. *kawayan*]

kawér: **kawerkawer.** a. crooked; curved. **agkawerkawer.** v. to curve. (*barikawwet*)

kawés: n. clothes; attire. (*bádo*) **nakakawes.** a. clothed; dressed. **kawesan.** v. to clothe; fit; decorate. **makawesan.** *v.* to be dressed; to be bestowed; to be vested. **ikawes.** *v.* to dress; bestow. **maikawes.** *v.* to be dressed; to be bestowed upon. **Ti agkawes iti dina kukua, uray iti dalan labusanda.** He who wears borrowed clothes will be stripped even in the street. **Adu a pammadayaw ti naikawes kenkuana.** Many honors were bestowed upon him. [Ivt. *unay*, Kal. *silup*, Png. *kawés*, Tag. *damít*]

kawíkaw: n. coil (of rope, wire, etc.). **agkawikaw.** *v.* to coil up, twist; entwine. **kawikawen.** v. to twist; coil a rope. **Nagampayagda iti ngatuen dagiti kumawkawikaw a waig.** They hovered over the twisting streams. [Tag. *ikid*]

kawíl: n. Dutch wife. (*sap-al*) **agkawil, agkakawil.** v. to cross the legs; interlace, intertwine. **pagkawilen.** v. to form into a chain; interlace; wrap the legs around. **kawilen.** v. to hold fast with the legs. **Kawilanna ngata met laeng ti salladayna?** Do you think he wraps his legs around the pillow?

kawíli: agkawili. v. to come back the same day. makawili. v. to be able to reach a destination and return on the same day.

kawíng: a. crooked, knock-kneed; with crooked toe or thumb. agkawing. v. to bend, curve.

káwit: n. hook. (kab-ít, kalláwit, kalub-ít; for fish: síma, banníit) kawiten. v. to hook something. [Ivt. sayrin, Png. sagór, Tag. kawit]

kaw-ít: var. of kawit: hook.

kawítan: n. rooster, cock (fowl); (slang) penis. [Bon. kawítan, ka-ol, Kal. kawitan, Png. lalóng, Tag. tandáng, tatyaw]

kawíwit: n. cockspur turning upward (kawwet); leg hook; karibusó plant. kumawiwit. v. to clasp with the legs; embrace. kawiwitan. v. to hold something with the arms and legs; clasp on to someone (a child seeking protection from his mother). Dayta a kinakuttongna, siguro kasla lanut a nakair-irut iti kawiwitna. Because of his thinness, perhaps the tightness of his clasp is like a vine. Kasla adda lamiis a kimmawiwit iti barukongko. It is like the cold is embracing my chest.

kawkáw: n. kind of black bird; washing of private parts with water. agkawkaw. v. to wash the vagina. (pawpaw) kumawkaw. v. to dip the fingers in water. ikawkaw. v. to dip in water.

kawkawan. v. to touch or stir something with the fingers. [Bon. ípaw, Png. kawkaw (wash vagina)]

kawwéng: a. half-circular shape (crescent moon, bent finger, bowlegged person, etc.). nagkawweng. a. crooked, curved; deformed, bent like a hook. pangawwengen. a. curved, bent, rather crooked. [Knk. kawét, Tag. kilô, likô, balikukô]

kawwét: n. cockspur, spur. (tadi) kawweten. v. to claw. barikawwet. a. twisted; clawlike; hooklike. [Png. balongkawitan, Tag. tahíd (cockspur)]

-kay: encl. pron. var. of -kayo: you (pl.); you (formal).

káya₁: (Tag.) n. ability to do something (bael). kayam dayta? Can you do (manage) that? (kabaelan)

káya₂: nakaya. a. advantageous; profitable.

káyab: kumayab. v. to flutter, flap in the wind. agkayabkayab. v. to flutter in the air. Iti ilalabasna iti sango ti bentilador, naikayab ti gayadan ti pantalonna. When she passed in front of the fan, the hemline of her pants fluttered. [Tag. pagaspás]

kay-áb: ikay-ab. v. to be borne by the wind. kay-aban. v. to flutter around. pakay-aban. v. to shoot overhead.

kayabáng: n. large, woven, funnel-shaped basket used for produce. (kayyabang) ikayabang. v. to place in the kayabang basket.

kayábas: n. rain shower. (arbis; tarakitik) agkayabas. v. to shower (rain). [Tag. ambón]

kayabkáb: n. foul smell of women. agkayabkab. v. to flap the wings, flutter (hens). [Tag. wagaywáy (flutter)]

kayáding: n. variety of awned late rice with soft kernel.

kayákay₁: kayakayen. v. to lift; keep away from. nakayakay. a. remote; withdrawn; indifferent; lonely. kumayakay. v. to go away; withdraw; stay at a distance. Mariknak a nakayakay ni tatangmo kaniak gapu ngata ta saanak a kasla kadakayo a nalawa ti talonna. I feel that your father is distant with me probably because I am not like you, owning wide expanses of rice fields.

kayákay₂: sikakayakay. v. to be ready, all set.

káyam: kayaman. v. to bewitch, cast a spell on. makayaman. v. to be bewitched.

kayamkám: kumayamkam. v. to spread. (kalamkam, salnap; ramram) kayamkamen. v. to spread over, engulf (fire, etc.). [Tag. laganap]

kayammét: n. clutch; clasp. agkayammet. v. to intertwine, interlace, tangle. agkinnayammet. v. to come in quick succession (one after another). kayammetan. v. to clutch, clasp; claw. Immet-et ti kayammetna. His clasp tightened. Pirmi ti panagkinnayammet ken panagkinkinnagatda no mapupokda iti baso. Their clasping and biting each other is firm and constant when they are caged in a glass. [Tag. kuyóm]

kayámut: agkayamut. v. to scratch (with nails or claws) (karamut, kayammet). [Tag. kalmót, gasgás]

kayanákas: see karasákas.

kayáng: a. straddling, with the legs wide open. agkayang. v. to straddle the legs. (akkang; pakkang; askaw; baddakaw) nakakayang. a. sitting with open legs. kayangen. v. to force open the legs of someone else. pakpakayang. n. person prone to opening legs wide (young girls with no etiquette, etc.).

kayánga: n. Hibiscus rosainensis, hibiscus; variety of awned early rice with red kernel. kakayangaan. n. grove of hibiscus plants. [Png. kayanga, Tag. gumamela]

káyap₁: n. variety of banana.

káyap₂: n. the setting in of day or night. agkayap. v. to start (to darken, lighten), dawn. agkayap ti sipnget. exp. to start to get dark. kayapkayapen. v. to be doubtful; uneasy. pakayapan. v. to shoot overhead. apagkayap

ti lawag. the light of day has just appeared. **Kumayapen ti sipnget idi dumtengak idiay.** The night was already falling when I arrived there.

káyap₃: agkayapkayap. v. to flutter. [Tag. *pagaspás, wagaywáy*]

kayápas: n. variety of orange.

kayapkáp: agkayabkab. v. to flutter (chickens). (*kayabkáb*).

káyas₁: n. smoothed-out strips of bamboo. **kayasan.** v. to thin; whittle; scrape.

káyas₂: nagkayasan. n. kind of fine edible seaweed; thin strips of bamboo or rattan removed while smoothing out the bamboo. [Tag. *kayas*]

kayás: n. cliff, precipice. (*rangkis*; *derraas*; *teppang*) **agkayas.** v. to slide. **ikayas.** v. to throw something in a sliding manner. **kayas-kayas.** n. sound of slippers shuffling on floor. [Kal. *iwas*, Tag. *kaluskós*]

kayaskás: n. sound of slippers on the floor; *Harpulia sp.* tree. **agkayaskas.** v. to scrape the floor when walking (said of slippers). **kayas-kasen.** v. to gather scattered objects. [Tag. *kaluskós*]

káyat: kumakayat. n. kind of mollusk with a round, brown shell.

kayát: (perfective form: *kinayát*, transitive verb which takes the *ko* pronouns) v. to want, like, wish, desire; be willing. n. wish, desire, something wanted. **kaykayat.** n. something preferred. v. to prefer. **mayat.** v. to be willing; a. willing; good; suitable. **pangayatan.** *n.* reason or cause for liking. **Kayatmo ti mapan?** Do you want to go? [Original root is *ayát*. Kal. *pion*, Png. *gabáy*, Tag. *labáy*]

kay-át: var. of *kuy-át*: swim with the legs.

kayatúkot: *n.* penetration of temperature (*kinnit*). **kumayatukot.** *v.* to penetrate (temperature).

káyaw: n. charm; charisma; glamour; elegance. **mangayaw.** v. to headhunt. **kayawan.** v. to charm; capture (prisoner); captivate, fascinate. **makakayaw.** a. captivating; fascinating. **pangayaw.** n. charm; allure (*sulisog*); enchantment. **Makakayaw ti agsumbangir a kallidna.** His dimples on both cheeks are charming. **Nalaing a kumanta ken gumitara ket nakayawanna ti balasang.** He is good at singing and playing the guitar so the ladies are charmed by him. [Png. *ayat*, Tag. *akit*]

kayaw-á: var. of *kayaw-at*: flap the air.

kayaw-át: kumayaw-at. v. flap the arms (to call someone's attention); (*lit.*) beat the air. **ikayaw-at.** v. to move the hands to and fro. [Tag. *palág*]

kaybaán: n. kind of small dwarf that inhabits white ant nests or coconut groves that helps farmers and inflicts skin diseases.

kayetkét: agkayetket, kumayetken. v. to shrink; cower; crouch in hiding; hold on tightly to the legs (children holding on to a parent's leg). [Tag. *pulupot*]

kaykáy: n. outdoor broom made of coconut midribs. **kaykayan.** v. to sweep a place with a *kaykay.* **kaykayen.** *v.* to sweep dirt. [Tag. *walís-tingtíng*]

káyo: n. tree; wood; timber; trunk; stem. **mangayo.** v. to gather firewood. **sangakayo.** n. one piece (of cloth) **kayuen.** *v.* to cut into firewood. **tarikayo.** n. log; timber, lumber. **agtarikayo.** v. to gather lumber or firewood; log a forest. **manartarikayo.** n. wood vendor; lumberjack. **kakaykaywan.** n. woods; forested area; jungle of trees. **pagtarikayuan.** *n.* logging concession. **Ti bassit a kayo, nalaka a lintegen, ngem no dakkel narigaten.** *exp.* A small tree is easy to straighten, but once it has grown, it is difficult. [Bon. *káew, pagpag,* Ibg., Kal. *kayu,* Ivt. *kayuq,* Knk. *muyóng,* Kpm. *dútung,* Png. *kiéw,* Tag. *punò* (tree); *káhoy* (wood)]

kayo: n. roll of cloth woven in a native loom.

-kayó: *pron.* second person plural *-ak* series enclitic pronoun, or second person singular polite: you (pl.). **Umay***kayo***n.** Come (you plural). **in***kayo***n.** Go already! **kayokayo, umadayokayo.** expression uttered when throwing something or urinating in a strange place to avoid offending spirits.

-kayó: *pron.* enclitic of *dakayó* after the ergative pronominal enclitics *-na* and *-da*, used as a second person formal or plural object. **Naki-tana***kayo***.** He saw *you*. (pl. or formal). **Suro-tenda***kayo***.** We'll follow you. After transitive verbs, *-kayo* is used to denote that the action is performed by the speaker onto the second person plural or second person formal: (I to you) **Tulongan***kayo***.** I'll help *you*.

kay-ó: ikay-o. v. to clean (remove trash from). **kay-uan.** v. to clean.

kayubbót: *var.* of *kayumot*: to cover entirely; blanket. **nakayubbotan.** *a.* to be covered, shrouded, engulfed in, blanketed; engulfed. **kumayubbot.** *v.* to cover, engulf, blanket.

kay-ód: (reg.) var. of *kay-o*.

kayumanggí: (Tag. also) n. having brown skin; brown-skinned race. **Natayengteng a kayumanggi ti kudilna.** His skin is very dark brown. [Tag. *kayumanggí*]

kayumkóm: kayumkumen. v. to gather; take clothes off a line; lift a trailing dress.

kayúmot: kayumutan. v. to cover entirely (*kayubbot*). **nakayumutan.** a. covered entirely.

kayumpáw: n. kind of edible mollusk.

-kayonto: enclitic expressing second person plural (or polite) actor and future time. **Umaykayonto.** You (pl.) will come.

káyong: (pl. *kakayong*) n. brother-in-law (fem. *ipag*). **agkayong.** n. the relationship between brothers-in-law. **buneng ti agkakayong.** *bolo* of brothers-in-law (with a dull blade, as brothers-in-law are not supposed to fight in Ilocano culture). [Knk. *kas-úd*, Png., Tag. *bayáw*]

kay-óng: n. lasso. (*sílo, lab-ong; lasta; kaka*) **kay-ongen.** v. to lasso. [Tag. *silò*]

kayuskús: kayuskusen. v. to sweep, gather all.

kayotkót: kumayotkot. v. to climb a tree while embracing it with hands and feet; to cling to like a leech.

kayrél: (Sp. *cairel*: fringe trimming; wig; flounce, furbelow) n. watch chain.

kaysá: (f. *maysa*) **agkaykaysa.** v. to unite, agree; become one; agree.

-kayto: abbreviation of *-kayonto*.

kayyabáng: n. kind of two-handled basket used for transporting fish. **agkayyabang.** v. to rain in heavy, scattered drops.

kayyabéng: n. variety of awned early rice.

kayyanák: (f. *anak*) a. newly born.

kdp(y).: abbreviation of *ken dadduma pay*: et cetera, (etc.).

kebbá: n. throb; pulsation; excitement shown by physical tension. **agkebbakebba.** v. to gasp for breath; be out of breath; to rise and fall strongly (said of a chest out of breath). [Tag. *kabá*]

kebbáal: kumbaal. v. to become dry and hard (said of dough, paste, cooked rice, etc.) (*magá*). [Tag. *tuyô*]

kebbéng: a. bent; clawlike. **kumbeng.** v. to claw; stand one's ground by planting the feet firmly; bristle (animals). **kebbengen.** v. to claw something, scratch; bend. **ikebbeng.** v. to claw, sink the nails into. [Tag. *kalmót*]

kebbés: kebsen. v. to measure something by grabbing a handful; measure the thickness of a round object.

kebbét: (coll.) n. poor harvest, season of scarcity; a. withered; wrinkled, shriveled; parched, dry. **kumbet.** v. to shrink; contract; reduce; unswell; wrinkle up. **makbetan.** v. to run out of water (in the field). **pakebbeten.** v. to make something shrink, contract. **pinakbet.** n. Ilocano vegetable dish (made of vegetables that shrink and wrinkle when cooked). [Tag. *kulubót* (wrinkle)]

kebbó: agkebbo, kumbo. v. to bend; make crooked; warp. **mapakbo.** v. to overturn; tip over; capsize. **pumakbo.** n. kind of flat, triangular marine fish.

kebbúot: n. kind of hemp used in rope making.

kebília: (Sp. *hebilla*: buckle) n. buckle.

kebkéb: agkebkeb, kumebkeb. v. to embrace; clasp tightly; claw; shrink, crouch in hiding.

kébra: (Sp. *quebra*: break) n. mistake, error; disorder; weakness; malfunctioning; wrong card. (*biddut*) **agkebra.** v. to make a mistake, commit an error.

kebráda: (Sp. *quebrada*) n. fraction.

kebradúra: (Sp. *quebradura*) n. (bone) fracture.

kéda: (Sp. *queda*: remain) n. remainder (in subtraction); money kept on the table after an unfair game of *burro*.

kedár: (Sp. *quedar*: stay) **agkedar.** v. to result; come back (disease) (*sumro*).

keddáar: n. noise of wood clapping. **kumdaar.** v. to make the sound of bamboo, wood, or water; to make a clapping sound.

keddél: n. pinch. (*kuddot*) **agkeddel.** v. to pinch. **keddelen.** v. to pinch; claw; dig with the nails; take a small piece. **Malagipko ti kanayon a panangkeddelna kaniak.** I remember him always pinching me. [Kal. *kitingon*, Png. *karót*, Tag. *kurót*]

keddéng₁: n. resolution; decision; judgment; end of everything; limit; wish, desire. **ikeddeng, kedngan.** v. to determine, decide; settle; judge; decree; direct; limit; resolve. **makaikeddeng.** v. to be able to decide. **pakedngan.** v. to stand and be judged; have someone sentenced. **mangeddeng.** v. to decide; judge. **nakapangngeddeng.** a. decided. **pangngeddeng.** n. decision; sentence; verdict. **saan a makedngan.** limitless, unlimited. **Kedngandak kuma iti kaunggan iti barukongyo.** You should judge me inside your heart (*lit*: chest). **Karbenganda ti mangeddeng iti bagbagida.** They have the right to decide for themselves. [Tag. *pasiyá*]

keddéng₂: n. kind of tree with valuable timber.

kedém: (obs.) n. burned spot.

kedkéd: agkedked. v. to refuse to pay or give what is due. **kedkedan.** v. to refuse to give something. **Pinagkedkedak ti awisna.** I turned down his invitation. **Nagkedkedak met a nagsaludsod.** I refused to ask questions. **Diak makapagkedkedan ti mandar ti pusok.** I cannot refuse the command of my heart. [Tag. *umayaw*]

kedmán: var. of *kedngan*: limit; condemn; dare; settle.

kedrés: (obs.) n. counterpoise of a mechanism.

kées: n. slight craziness. **Adda kekeesna.** He is a bit crazy. [Knk. *kées* = chronic cough]

keggáng: n. scab; crust. **agkeggang.** v. to form a scab. **keggangan.** v. to remove a scab. [Ibg. *kannág*, Tag. *langíb*]

kegkég: **agkegkeg.** v. to brag, boast. (*agpangás, agpasindayag*)

kegsál: **ikegsal.** v. to shove, push; poke; stick somebody.

kegtár: var. of *kugtár*: kick.

kéha: (Sp. *queja*: complaint) n. complaint. (*reklamo*) **agkeha.** v. to complain, make a charge. **ikeha.** v. to complain against.

kekkék: **kumekkek.** v. to cry (said of the hen); make the sound of a broken bell, cluck. **kekkekan.** v. to call chickens by imitating their cries.

kekkés: (obs.) **keksan.** v. to whiten with rice.

kel-án: **kel-anan.** v. to do excessively; lessen, diminish. **di kel-anan.** *exp.* without letup.

kelgá: **kelgaen.** v. to confuse; stun; startle. **nakelga.** *a.* confused, stunned, startled.

kelkél: n. whooping cough. **kelkelen.** v. to cough repeatedly (*letlet*). **Nakelkel ken naipdukan pay ti lakay iti kellaat a pannakalagipna iti pasamak.** The old man coughed and choked when he suddenly remembered the event. [Tag. *ubó* (cough)]

kellá: n. slime (of eels, catfish, etc.).

kelláat: *adv,* a. sudden, instantly; abrupt. (*apagdarikmát*) **kellaaten.** v. to surprise; come upon suddenly. **maklaatan.** v. to be surprised. **maklaat.** v. to be surprised; do something unexpectedly (die). **makaklaat.** *a.* surprising, astonishing. **kumlaat.** *v.* to appear suddenly; (obs.) cut awry. **kumlaat ti angin.** n. violent gust of wind. **Kellaat nga inwagtengna ti petpetko a dakulapna.** She abruptly shook off my grasp of her palm. **Saan a nakatimek gapu iti pannakakellaatna.** He couldn't say a word because of his surprise. [Png. *biglá*, Tag. *biglâ*]

kellád: **ikellad.** v. to strike, do treacherously (*liput*); cheat, **kelladan.** v. to bite, gnaw off (*kibkib*).

kelláng: (obs.) **agkellakellang.** v. to languish.

kelléb: n. cover of a jar; lid of a pot. **kelleban.** v. to cover with a *kelleb.* **agpakleb.** v. to fall prone; lie on the stomach. **ipakleb.** v. to throw prone; invert; turn over, upside-down. **letteg a pakleb.** n. abscess; boil with pus inside. **pakpakleb.** see *kappakappá.* **Di makalawlaw (iti) kelleb.** *exp.* He cannot keep a secret. **kumleb.** v. to seek cover; hide; dig in. **Itedna amin a kelkellebanna.** He gives everything that he can cover. [Png. *kolób*, Tag. *takíp*]

kelléng: n. rice field; square. **kinelleng.** n. rice field; kind of tissue. **sangkakelleng.** n. one square plot of ground. **kinellekelleng.** a. checkered (pattern). [Tag. *pitak*]

kellép: n. period of having no moon, new moon. **maklep.** v. to black out; be knocked down. **kellepen.** v. to hit with a strong blow; knock out; enclose. **naklepan iti danum.** surrounded by water.

kelnát: *n.* parboiling. **kelnáten.** v. to parboil, broil. **kinelnát.** n. dish of slightly boiled meat or fish. **Naimas ti beklat a makelnat iti rangaw ti bayawas sa maadobo.** The *beklat* snake is delicious boiled with the upper guava stalks and marinated *adobo* style.

kelnét: *var.* of *kilnet*: chewy; firm.

keltáy: **keltayen.** v. to cut; frustrate; ruin; defeat; balk. **nakeltay.** a. dried (leaves); frustrated; cut. **nakeltay nga ayat.** frustrated love. **Itanemta ti napalabas ta isu laeng ti mangkeltay ti masakbayan.** Let's bury the past because that is what will hurt the future. **Natalinaay ket nadayaw kuma ti kasasaadmi no diyo kineltay ti kakaisuna a paglainganna nga aramiden.** Our condition would be calm and honorable if you wouldn't have destroyed the one thing he is good at doing.

kemkém: **kemkemen.** v. to chew; clench the jaw; bear a grudge. **pakemkeman.** v. to bridle; put something in the mouth; give money to a godchild. **pakemkem.** n. money given to a godchild after baptism. **pakemkeman.** v. to give money to a godchild. **sikekemkem.** *a.* clenched (jaws). **Dinagdagullitna a sikekemkem dagiti sangina.** He repeated it with clenched jaws. [Tag. *kimkím*]

kemmá: **kemmaen.** v. to feel lightly; to examine and treat (a sore eye, etc.). **nakmaán ti nákem.** v. to know one's own mind.

kemmákem: **agkemmakem.** v. to open and close the hands quickly.

kemmég: **kemmegen.** v. to catch someone; seize, capture. **kumemmeg.** *v.* to catch. **kinnemmegan.** n. tag game. **nakemmeg.** a. captured; seized; caught. **pakemmeg.** *v.* to order the arrest or capture of. **Nakemmeg idi Abril.** He was caught last April. [Tag. *hulí*]

kemméng₁: **kemmengen.** v. to scratch with the nails (*kudkod*). [Tag. *kalmót, gasgás*]

kemméng₂: **kemmekemmeng.** n. *Capparis horrida,* spiny shrub with pink flowers.

kemmét: see *kayammét*: tangle; intertwine.

ken₁: *conj.* and (disjunctive or conjunctive). **Napankami ken Berong.** Berong and I went. [Bon. *ya,* Ibg. *anna,* Knk. *yan,* Png. *tan,* Tag. *at*]

ken₂: *oblique marker*. forms the oblique of the article *ni* and certain enclitic pronouns: **kenni**. to, at, with (personal noun) **kenkuana**. to him, to her. **kenká**. to you. [Png. *ed*, Tag. *kay*]

kenká: *pron*. oblique of *siká*. to you. **adda kenka, dayta la kenka**. *exp*. It's up to you. [Png. *ed siká*, Tag. *sa iyó*]

kenkén: see *kalenkén*.

kenkuána: *pron*. oblique of *isú*. to him, to her. [Png. *ed sikató*, Tag. *sa kaniyá*]

kenná: **mak(en)ná**. v. to catch, trap; to be caught by surprise. **kumna**. v. to fall into a trap; attack (disease) **kennaen**. v. (*obs*.) entrap; beguile a person.

kennáy: **maknay**. v. to rot, decay, decompose. (*rupsa*)

kenní: (*ken + ni*) *art*. oblique singular personal article, plural is *kadá*. **Intedko kenni Juan**. I gave it to Juan. [Ibg. *kani*, Tag. *kay*]

kengkéng: see *pilát*: kind of potbellied toad; appellation given to obese people. [Tag. *kengkeng* = sound of a bell or beating a pan]

kepkép: n. kind of speckled bird. **agkepkep**. v. to fold the arms over the chest. **kepkepán**. v. to hug, embrace. (*arakup*; *rakep*) **kumepkep**. v. to cling tightly to (clothes, etc.); hug. [Tag. *yakap*]

keppá: **kumpa**. v. to abate, subside, calm down. (*kirpa*)

keppál: n. economy; thriftiness. **nakeppal**. a. not easily consumed, economized.

keppéng: (*obs*.) **kumpeng**. v. to stop raining.

keppés: a. empty (seeds; fruits; grains). (*eppes*) **kumpes**. v. to shrink from fear; cower.

keppét₁: n. flower bud; a. shut; wrinkled. **agkeppet**. v. to shut (eyes); close; join by closing; heal together (wound); dry up (fruits). **kumpet**. v. to cling, attach to. **pagkeppeten**. v. to unite; close, shut; coalesce (wounds). **Immirut ti pannakakeppet dagiti matana iti pannakatitilengna kadagiti kanalbuong**. He shut his eyes tighter from the deafening sounds of the gunfire. [Tag. *tikóm* (close)]

keppét₂: **kepkeppet**. n. *Flemingia strobilifera* shrub. (*kopkopies*)

kerád: var. of *keras*: stomping the feet.

kerás: **kumerskeras**. v. to stomp the feet.

kerdát: **nakerdat**. a. firm, consistent. **kumerdat**. v. to become firm; strengthen. **nakerdat a rikna**. n. uncomfortable feeling, not in a good mood. **Naikkaten daytay nakerdat a riknana itay makapagmaga ti ling-et ti bagina**. His uncomfortable mood went away when he was able to dry off the sweat on his body. [Tag. *kunat*]

kerél: *var*. of *kayrel*: watch chain.

kerélia: (Sp. *querella*, *obs*.) n. complaint; accusation.

kerída: (Sp. *querida*: sweetheart) n. sweetheart, lover (female).

kerído: (Sp. *querido*: sweetheart) n. sweetheart, lover (male).

kerkér: **sangakerker**. n. one bunch. **kerkeren**. v. to bunch (things together); bundle.

kerubín: (Sp. *querubín*: cherubim) n. cherubim, angel. **kimmerubin a rupa**. n. angelic face.

kerráad: **kumraad**. v. to creak (noise); scrape. **manakraad**. v. to slam a door shut.

kerráang: a. withered; dry. **kumraang**. v. to dry (*magá*). [Tag. *tuyô*]

kerráay: **makraayan**. v. to be depleted; ravaged; devastated. **kerraayen**. *v*. to ravage, deplete, devastate.

kerrás: **kerrasan**. v. to level with a strickle, top off; lessen. **kumerras**. v. to decrease. **Idi sumiplot manen iti mugingna ti ladawan ti nobiana, kas man nakerrasan ti ut-ot a marikriknana**. When the image of his girlfriend flashed again in his mind, he felt the pain cutting him. [Tag. *bawas*]

kerréet: a. wrinkled, shriveled. (*kuretret*) **kumreet**. v. to shrivel up; become wrinkled.

kerrém: **agkerrem**. v. to close the eyes; bite the lips in anger. **mangrem, agpangrem**. v. to bite the lip. **agpakrem**. v. to gleam with anger; drink liquor for encouragement. **pangreman**. *v*. to look at someone with a sharp glance.

kerrép: (*obs*.) a. n. half-witted.

kerrét₁: n. anus. (*ubet*)

kerrét₂: **kumret**. v. to wrinkle; pucker. (*kuretret*)

kerrúod: var. of *kerraad*.

kerrúom: **kumruom**. v. to crunch (*karemkem*, *karut-om*). [Tag. *ngalót*]

kersáng: *n*. coarseness, roughness. **nakersang**. a. coarse, rough. (*rusangér*, *gubál*, *kersang*) **kerkersang**. n. vine used to make ropes. **pangersangen**. *a*. rather coarse, rough. **Ti nakersang a dakulap, isu't dalan ti pirak**. The rough hand is the way to wealth. [Ivt. *payas*, Kal. *sageÿaseÿ*, Png. *gasal*, Tag. *gaspang*]

keskés: **keskesen**. v. to scorch, singe; hold tightly to. [Tag. *darangín* (scorch)]

késo: (Sp. *queso*: cheese) n. cheese. **keso de bola**. n. ball cheese.

kessén: **kumsen**. v. to contract, warp; shrink. (*erres*)

kessét: **makset**. v. to burn. **kesseten**. v. to burn; char; singe; scorch. **nakset**. a. burnt. **inpakset**. n. meat burned (on purpose) to be placed in a glass of water to drink for indigestion; food burned on purpose. **Nakset iti init ti kudilna**. He got sunburned. **pakseten**. *v*. to singe, put in the fire. **agatnakset.** the smell of something burning. [Ivt. *temtem*, Png. *pool, angsit*, Tag. *sunog*]

kessuák: n. splashing sound. **kessuakan.** v. to splash, splatter something. [Tag. *wisík, saboy*]

ket: *conj.* and; although; but; resultative conjunction, so; topicalizing predicate marker (used to signal an upcoming predicate not in initial position). **no la ket ta.** for fear that. **sangapulo ket lima.** *num.* fifteen. **daytoy ket nga ubing.** because of this child. **Nakainumen ket kasla kinirogen a pasayan ti rupana.** He had drunk so his face was like a toasted shrimp. **Agkantaka ket patayenka.** You sing and I'll kill you.

ketdí: adv. particle that implies opposition: but; on the contrary, anyway. **ania la ketdi.** *conj.* lest. **no la ketdi no.** *conj.* provided that. **Riingem ketdi ta mangankayo a dua.** Wake him up anyway so the two of you can eat. **Dikayo agsangsangit, ikararagyo ketdi a nakaradkadak laeng uray sadino ti yanko.** Do not cry, pray instead that I will be healthy no matter where I am.

ketég: ketegán. n. boundary; limits. (*dulon*)

kettá: kettaén. v. to part, disjoint, disunite. **makta.** v. to be taken apart, disassembled.

kettáb: n. bite. (*kagat*)

kettáng: n. fatigue; weariness. **maktang, maktangán.** v. to tire; be bored for being in the same place for a long time. **makaktang.** a. tiresome, tiring, boring. **paktangén.** v. to weigh down, press in order to straighten. **Inilutna ti naktangán a teltelna.** She massaged his tired nape. [Tag. *antók*]

kettát: kumtat. v. to rebound; recoil (shy children); ricochet. **kettatán.** v. to refuse to do because one is not up to it. [Tag. *talbóg*]

kettéb: n. bite. (*kagat*) **ketteben.** v. to bite.

kettél: n. pinch. **agkettel.** *v.* to pick with the fingers. **kettelen.** v. to pick, pluck; pinch; cut short; snap off; spoil; frustrate. **agpakettel.** (*fig.*) *v.* to have an abortion. [Tag. *kurót*]

kettér: kumter. v. to wrinkle, shrivel; shrink (genitals) (*kuretret, kebbet*). [Tag. *kaligkíg*]

kiáas: *n.* rustling sound; clanging sound. **kanakiaas.** *n.* clanging, rustling; scampering from fear. [Knk. *kiáas*]

kiád: a. with protruding abdomen; n. walking with protruding belly, (e.g. pregnant women). **agkiad.** *v.* to walk or stand with the belly protruding. [Png. *sikár*, Tag. *liyád*]

kiág: makiag. v. to wake up with a start.

kiák: n. cry of a chicken. **agkiak.** v. to shriek (said of chickens when being caught, etc.);

squeal (talk under pressure). [Knk. *tagák*, Tag. *puták*]

kiám: kiamkiam. *n.* spark. **agkiamkiam.** v. to see stars (from a blow); to be extremely famished; to sparkle. **Sumsumngaw ti kiamkiam iti maur-uram a daga.** The sparks were emitted from the burning land.

kiaóng: n. lasso (*sílo, kay-óng*). [Tag. *silò*]

kiápet: kumiapet. *v.* to be terrified, paralyzed by fear.

kiásan: n. species of frog with long, slender legs.

kiát: kimmiat. a. fast, swift (*paspas, pardas*). [Tag. *bilís*]

kiáw₁: n. kind of yellow and black oriole; color orange or yellow; a. orange; yellow. [Ibg. *ngilá*, Tag. *diláw* (yellow)]

kiáw₂: kiawkiaw. a. talkative; gossipy. **agkiawkiaw.** v. to gossip; talk out of turn. [Tag. *kiyáw*]

kibaán: n. (myth.) kind of elf. (*kaybaán*)

kibaltáng: a. with too many troubles. **agkibaltang.** v. to err, make a mistake. **Nagkibaltang ti panagbitek ti pusona.** His heart missed a beat.

kibát: n. groove. [Tag. *ukit, ukà, bakat*]

kibbá: *var.* of *kebba*: throb, palpitate.

kibbaél: (obs.) **kumibbael.** v. to squirm, wiggle.

kibbásiw: kumbasiw. v. to deviate, swerve; miss the mark (*kabsiw, kaglis*). [Tag. *lihís*]

kibbakól: *var.* of *kibbatól*: potholed road.

kibbatól: n. rough, rocky road; potholed road. **kibbakibbatol.** *a.* full of potholes. **Nagalis iti panawen ti nepnep ken natangken a kibbakibbatol iti kalgaw.** In the times of heavy rain it is slippery, and it is hard and potholed during the summer.

kibbáyo: *var.* of *tibbáyo*: shudder.

kibbó: a. bent; twisted. (*killó*) **agkibbo, kumibbo.** v. to bend. **kibbuen.** v. to bend something, cause to bend.

kibéb: n. slapping sound. **makakbeb.** v. produce a slapping sound.

kibília: *var.* of *kebilia*: buckle.

kíbin: n. guide; guardian. **kibinen.** v. to lead with the hand (a blind person, child, etc.); guide. **agkibkibin.** v. to hold hands. **kibinkibin pakaalaan iti ubing.** *exp.* denoting that holding hands may end up in pregnancy. **Adda pasaray mangkibin kenkuana no adda kayatna a papanan.** She often has someone to escort her if she wants to go someplace. [Tag. *akay*]

kíbis: (obs.) **kibiskibis.** see *kíbit*.

kíbit: agkibit. v. to draw near the end. **agkibitkibit ti anges.** v. to be on the verge of death.

kibkíb: kibkiben. v. to nibble, gnaw. (*kitkit; kurib*) **kibkiban.** v. to nibble a part of. [Tag. *ngatngát*]

kibnór: (reg.) n. eddy; whirlpool. (*alikuno*; *alinuno*) **ikibnor**. v. to shake; agitate.

kíbol: a. short-tailed.

kíbong: **kibongkibong**. n. upper part of the buttocks as they inflect at the back. **agkibongkibong**. v. to be very loose (clothing). (*kalaw*)

kíbor: a. obstinate; tough (troublemaker); disturbed, agitated. **kiburen**. v. to disturb, confuse; stir, agitate; confuse. **makibor**. v. to be disturbed, confused, upset; dismayed. [Tag. *guló*]

kibút: n. kind of funnel-shaped trap for catching fish.

kibróng: n. (*obs.*) old practice of kidnapping a person to sacrifice him for a newly constructed bridge; stealing (*takaw*). **kibrongen**. v. to kidnap; steal. **Impulongna a kinibrongmo kano ti ganadorna.** He informed that you supposedly stole his fighting cock. **Siak itan ti masuspetsa a mangkikibrong.** Now I am the one suspected of stealing. [Tag. *nakaw*]

kidág: n. kick; shove; push; goading. **kumidag**. v. to kick, hit with the knee or elbow. **kidagen**. v. to hit something with the knee or elbow; prod. **Nakidag ti riknak a mangibaga koman iti ayatko ngem kasla nasarait ti bibigko.** My feelings tried to prompt me into declaring my love for her, but my lips were sealed. [Tag. *sipà* (kick)]

kidár: var. of *kedar*: remainder.

kídas: **kumidaskidas**. v. to move about too much and disturb another person.

kíday: n. eyebrow; crest. **ikidayan**. v. to trim bamboo. **nagkiday**. a. with equal groups of two or more stripes of different colors. **bimmullalayaw a kiday**. n. arched (rainbow) eyebrow. [Bon. *gídey*, Ibg. *kiray*, Ivt. *ciray*, Kal. *kímit*, Knk. *kídey*, Kpm. *kíle*, Png. *kirép*, Tag. *kilay* (eyebrow)]

kiddámol: **nakiddamulan**. n. leftover food to be shared. **pakiddamulan**. v. to share a person.

kiddáw: n. request; plea; petition. **agkiddaw**, **kiddawen**. v. to request, ask for; beg. **Kiddawek ti panangitulnogko kenka iti papanam.** May I request to escort you where you are going. **No gayyem ti agkiddaw, saan nga iladladaw.** If it is a friend who asks, do not be late. [Bon. *kedaw*, Tag. *hilíng*]

kiddáy: **agkidday**. v. to wink with the eyebrow (*kidmát*). **kiddayan**. v. to wink at. **agkinnidday**. v. to wink at each other. [Bon. *kedyat*, Png. *kindat*, Tag. *kindát*, *kisáp*, *kuráp*]

kiddél: var. of *keddel*: pinch. (*kuddót*)

kiddém: **makdem**. v. to tarnish; become dull (*láti*). **mapakdemán**. a. to be made dull, tarnish.

kiddiás: **kumdias**. v. to deflect; bounce off; glaze.

kiddís: n. pinch (*kuddót*). **sangakiddis**. n. one pinch of. **kiddisen**. v. to pinch off. **kiddisan**. v. to pinch off a part of. **Kasla nakiddis ti pusona iti panagmingmingda kenkuana.** She felt their staring at her in her heart (as if her heart was pinched). [Tag. *kurót*]

kiddít: **nakiddit or nakdit**. a. with a small yield (cows, wells, etc.). **kumiddit**. v. produce little; to yield little. [Tag. *kakauntí*]

kiddó: **kiddokiddo**. n. kind of tadpole. **agkiddokiddo**. v. to be anxious. [Tag. *sikdó*]

kiddúor: **agkidduor**. v. to throb, palpitate. (*kibbá*)

kidém: n. first night after the full moon; a. closed (eyes). (see *kirem*) **agkidem**. v. to close the eyes; be new (moon). **kumidkidem**. v. to sleep, take a nap. **kideman**. v. to close one's eyes to; look the other way around. **nakidman**. a. orphaned in babyhood. **Inkidemko ti naguray iti sumaruno a mapasamak.** I closed my eyes to wait for what would happen next. [Tag. *pikít* (close eyes)]

kidiablés: contraction of *anakkidiables*: son of the devil.

kidiáp: var. of *kudias*.

kidiás: var. of *kudias*.

kidkíd: n. crust of rice that sticks to the pot after the *ittip* has been removed. **ikidkidan**. v. to remove the crust. **kumidkid**. v. to adhere, stick. (*dumket*; *kumpet*; *kulamat*; *luyak*; *pigket*) **Kimmidkid ti tutungna.** exp. flat-chested (women).

kidmát: n. wink. (*kiddáy*) **kumidmat**. v. to wink. **apagkidmat**. adv. in a wink; in a twinkling of an eye. [Png. *kindát*, Tag. *kindát*, *kuráp*, *kisáp*]

kidóg: n. uproar, confusion, disturbance. (*gulo*) **kidugen**. v. to agitate; disturb. [Tag. *sulsól*]

kidól: **kidulen**. v. to hit with the elbow (*kidag*). [Tag. *siko*]

kidsér: **nakidser**. a. robust, vigorous, strong; tough; resistant. **Sisiak laeng ti makapagbalin a nakidser iti masakbayanko.** Only I can become tough in my future. [Tag. *kunat*]

kiéme: (Pil.) n. feigned disinterest. **agpakieme**. v. to pretend to show disinterest, play hard to get. **Awanen adu pay a kieme, wen kinunak a dagus.** There was no playing hard to get, I said yes immediately. [Tag. *kiyeme*]

kién: (Sp. *quién*: who) **intono kien**. never.

kíet: **agkiet**. v. to shrug the shoulders. **napakiet**. a. with shrugged shoulders.

kiét: a. bent; drawn. **kumiet**. v. to bend the knees to lower the backside.

kígaw: n. fawn, young deer; young calf; hermitlike person who tries to avoid people. **Nakigaw ni ridep kaniak kadayta a nagpatnag.** Sleep was a stranger to me that night of staying awake. [Knk. *kigkígaw*, Tag. *muntíng usa*]

kiggét: (obs.) n. bundle (*reppét, bungón*). [Tag. *balutan*]

kiglá: **kiglaen.** v. to scare; startle; frighten (*buteng*). [Tag. *gitlá*]

kigmát: **apagkigmat, saan a kakigmatan.** in a short moment. (*biit*)

kigpál: n. dry, parched soil (hard to plow). **kumigpal.** v. to become parched and hardened (soil). [Tag. *tuyô*]

kigténg: **nakigteng.** a. poor, inadequate; inferior; inefficient; tight.

kigtót: n. fright; surprise. **kigtuten.** v. to startle, surprise. **makigtot.** v. to be startled. **managkigkigtot.** n. coward, person prone to be startled. **makakigkigtot.** a. surprising, startling. [Bon. *kibtot*, Png. *kilaw*, Tag. *gulat, gitlá*]

kíki: **kikien.** v. to tickle (*ariek, kili, karikkik*); tingle. **makakiki.** a. tickling. [Bon. *bágay*, Knk. *gítik, yákat*, Png. *kiki*, Kpm., Tag. *kilití*]

kikiám: (Tag.) n. kind of salty pork sausage.

kíkil: n. bootlicker. **kikilen.** v. to do favors and expect something in return. **kikilan.** (Pil.) v. to ask someone forcibly.

kíkir: n. saw (tool). (*ragadi*) **agkikir.** v. to saw. **kikir a sarutso.** ripsaw. [Tag. *lagarì*]

kikít: n. smallest finger, little toe; (*fig.*) matter of extreme unimportance; least favored. **pakikít.** n. jack rafter; fetlock; dewclaw, nonfunctional claw in dogs. **kikiten.** v. to do easily. **Kikit dagiti agar-arem.** He is the least favored of the suitors (*lit*: the small finger). [Kal. *pàikking*, Png. *kikíng*, Tag. *kalingkingan*]

kíkiw: **agkikiw.** (obs.) v. to wag the tail (*kalawíkiw*). [Tag. *payipoy*]

kikkík: n. kind of marine fish. **agkikkik.** n. the cry of the *gikgík* bird.

kilabbán: n. cold cooked rice; leftovers (of a meal). **agkilabban.** v. to eat between meals with cold rice. **kilabbanen.** v. to eat cold rice with something between meals. **Dida kayat ti agkilabban ta saan kano a makapasalun-at.** They do not like to eat small meals with cold rice because it is supposedly unhealthy. [Bon. *teda*, Kal. *labun-an*]

kiladóra: *var.* of *triliadora*: thresher.

kil-ág: **kil-agen.** v. to startle; scare. (*kigtot*)

kílang: n. kind of tree whose bark is used in the fermentation process of *bási*. **ikilang.** v. to toll the bells for the dead. **maikilang.** v. to announce a death by tolling the bells.

kiláng: n. sound of metal containers, bells. **agkilangkilang.** v. to resonate (metal sounds).

kiláp: *n.* shine; brilliance (*raniág*). **kumilap.** v. to gleam, glitter; shine; be brilliant. **pakpakilap.** n. burning glass; gathering the rays of the sun with the aid of a lens. **nakilap.** a. shining, glittering, sparkling. (*gilap*) [Png. *kidláp*, Tag. *kisláp*]

kílas: n. furrow dug on the ground by a plow. (*gulis*)

kílat: n. with lower eyelids stretched downward.

kilát: Interjection of mocking; cry of fishermen: *kilát, kilát, punnoém ti pagikkák:* fill my net; (obs.) n. first fruit of a tree.

kilátis: (Sp. *quilate*) n. carat (gold). **kilatisen.** v. to perceive (*amiris*); appraise the value of. **Pangato-pababa ti panagkita ti babai kenkuana a kasla mangilkilatis.** The girl looked up and down at him as if she were appraising him. [Tag. *kilates*]

kiláw: **kilawen.** v. to eat raw meat, n. raw meat dish. **kilawén ti dálem.** v. to cuckold. **kilawkiláw.** n. staring, gazing at a fixed object. **kumilaw.** v. to stare at someone with intense, sharp eyes; to eat something raw; to be vicious, ruthless. **makakilkilaw.** v. to crave for raw food. **Kasla kumilaw dagiti matana.** She is staring intensely (like her eyes are eating raw). [Ivt. *mata*, Knk. *bágis*, Png. *éta*, Tag. *bagís, kiláw*]

kilawét: (coll.) n. lightning (*kimat*). **Nagpigsan ti kilawet ken gurruod.** The lightning and thunder were very strong.

kiléb: n. kind of fish trap. (*asar*) **mangngileb.** n. fisherman who uses the *kileb* trap.

kilép: n. (obs.) fine piece. **maklep.** v. to languish; droop; faint (from a strong blow).

kílga: **kilgaen.** v. to confuse; disturb (animals); frighten, scare.

kilí: **kilikilí.** n. armpit. **kilikilien.** v. to tickle (*kikien*). [Bon. *yekyek, sekang*, Ivt. *kekedwan*, Kal. *oyok*, Knk. *yekyék*, Png. *kilikilí*, Tag. *kilikili* (armpit)]

kília: (Sp. *quilla*) n. keel, the main timber or steel piece at the bottom of a ship or boat.

kilíkil: n. lightning. (*kimát*) **kumilkilikil.** v. to contort the body; writhe (snakes); waddle (people). **kimmilkilikil.** a. twisted.

kililíng: n. small bell. (*kampanílya*) **agkililing.** v. to ring. (said of a *kililing*) **kililingen.** v. to ring a small bell.

kíling: **agkiling.** v. to lean; be about to capsize. [Tag. *kiling*]

kilíng: n. *Bambusa vulgaris* spineless bamboo; variety of awned rice with striped kernel; small bell. **agkiling.** v. to make a tinkling sound (bells) **agkanakliing**. n. jingling sound of glasses. **makakliing**. v. to be resonant, sonorous. (see *kililing*)

kílit: n. person with half-closed eyes; person with one eye smaller than the other. **kumilit**. v. to be half-closed (eyes). **ipakilit**. v. to look with a side glance.

killá: (obs.) interjection.

killabót: n. pothole, depression in the ground. **killa-killabot**. *a.* full of potholes. (*likkaong*)

killáwang: **kinillawang**. a. rusty, rusted. (*kalawang*, *lati*)

killawít: n. kind of small bird resembling the *bannatíran*.

killíng: **killiing**. *n.* continuous ringing. **kumilling**. v. to ring (bell). [Tag. *tagintíng*]

killít: n. acute voice; sharp voice. **killíit**. *n.* very shrill sound, sharp sound.

killó: **nakillo**. a. winding, meandering; twisted; crooked; distorted; broken (talk). **makillo**. v. to become bent, twisted. **ikillo**. *v.* to turn. **ipakpakillo**. v. to worsen (said of sickness); to beat around the bush. **killuen**. v. to bend, curve. **pagkilluan**. *n.* turning point. [Png. *kiwét*, Tag. *kilô*]

kilnát: n. parboil (*kelnát*). **Naimas a makilnat sa masukaan**. It's delicious to be parboiled, then seasoned with vinegar.

kilnáw: *n.* rinsing. **kilnawen**. *v.* to rinse.

kilnét: *n.* firmness; consistency. **nakilnet**. a. firm, solid, stiff. (*tibkér*, *talinaéd*) **kumilnet**. v. to be stiff, firm. [Tag. *kunat*]

kilnó: **agkilno**. v. to shake (liquids in a container). **Namrayanna a kinilnokilno ti yelo iti basona**. He impulsively shook the ice in his glass. [Tag. *ligwák*]

kilnóg: **agkilnog**. v. to rinse. (*ugas*, *uper*)

kílo: n. kilo; (construction) ordinary rafter. **sobrekílo**. see *ladét*. **kiluen**. v. to weigh something with a machine. **pagkiluan**. n. a weighing machine. **sangakilo**. n. one kilo.

kílog: n. *Gleichenia linearis* fern used in basketry.

kilóg: **agkilogkilog**. v. to rattle (said of shaken contents).

kilómetro: (Sp. *kilometro*: kilometer) n. kilometer.

kilóng: **agkanakluong**. v. to make the sound of an object moving in a clay jar. **kumilongkilong**. v. to make the sound of water swishing in a container or a stomach.

kimár: **kimaren**. v. to take all (in the *sungka* game, referring to when one player lands his last shell in a hole of the *sungka* board opposite his opponent's hole, which contains shells. In this case, the player who dropped his last shell claims all of the shells in the opponent's hole opposite from the dropped shell for his bank). (*kayuskos*)

kímat: n. eyelash (*kurimatmat*). [Png. *sagumay-(may)*, *kolimatmát*, Tag. *pilikmatá*]

kimát: n. lightning. **agkimat**. v. to have lightning; to strike (said of lightning) **makimat**. v. to be struck by lightning. **kimaten**. v. to be struck by lightning. [Bon. *kelyat*, Ibg. *kilaq*, *tallíq*, Itg. *sil-it*, Ivt. *cidat*, Kal. *kilat*, Kpm. *kildap*, Png. *kirmát*, Tag. *kidlát*]

kimáw: **agkimaw**. v. to jump over the water (said of fishes), swim up for air. **kimawen**. v. to flash (lightning), strike suddenly.

kimbásar: **kanimbasar**. *n.* commotion, sound of many people, hustle and bustle (*karibusó*). **agkanimbasar**. v. to make the sound of many people; hustle and bustle; stampede.

kímeng: n. kind of large China jar. **agkikimeng**. v. to be stiff with cold; contract (nerves); suffer cramps.

kímika: (Sp. *química*: chemistry) n. chemistry.

kímit: n. buckle, hook and eye; clasp. **ikimit**. v. to buckle, fasten (garment)

kimkím: **nakimkim**. a. frugal in eating (*kusim*). [Tag. *kimkím* = held in the fist]

kimmáy: **agkimmakimmay**. v. to be blinking (eyes) (*kirmed*; *kirem*; *kuyep*). [Tag. *kuráp*]

kimmí: **kimmien**. v. to shut, part, compress, close with the hands.

kimmó: **agkimmo**. v. to meet unexpectedly along the way.

kimmól: n. coccyx. (*moriit*) **agkimmolkimmol**. v. to pucker (anus of chickens). [Tag. *tumbóng*]

kimmót₁: n. youngest child (*buridek*). [Png. *bulirek*, Tag. *bunsô*]

kimmót₂: n. anus. (*kimmol*; *moriit*; *kirret*; *merret*) **kumimmot**. v. to dilate and contract (said of anus) **kimmuten**. v. to contract the anus. **Ken sinanlakay a kinimmutan ti kappo**. And the clam dilated and contracted like an old man. [Ibg. *uvoq*, Ivt. *dacan*, Kal. *allutong*, Knk. *kimút*, Kpm. *pitakan*, Png. *ebét*, Tag. *puwít*, Png., Tag. *tumbóng*]

kímo: **kimuen**. v. to pick up with the fingers. **kimkimuen**. v. to toy with, finger.

kímuen: (obs.) var. of *kímeng* jar.

kimóna: n. native blouse made of transparent material. **nakakimona**. a. wearing a *kimona*.

kimóno: (f. Japanese) n. kimono, Japanese lounging robe; woman's loose dressing gown.

kímos: **agkimos**. v. to curve (road, path, river, etc.).

kimós: a. pyramidal. **agkimos**. v. to taper.

kina-: *prefix*. 1. Perfective form of comitative *ka*-formatives. **Kinasaonaka**. He spoke with you.

Kinasalanak. He danced with me; 2. Prefix used to form abstract nouns: **kinalagda** durability. **kinatao.** humanity. **kinadakes.** badness. **kinaagpayso.** as a matter of fact.

kinalká: n. kind of red cotton yarn.

kinamanag- (CV-): pref. nominalizing prefix used with frequentative stems: **agsao.** to speak **managsasao.** to be talkative. **kinamanagsasao.** act of being loquacious. **Kinamanagsagubanit.** condition of being sickly.

kinamanagpaN-: Abstract nominalizing prefix used with frequentative *managpaN-* stems: **kinamanagpanakkel.** arrogance, act of always being proud.

kinamannaka-: Abstract nominalizing prefix for *mannaka-* stems. **Agyamanak iti kinamannakaawatyo.** I thank you for your understanding.

kinamannaki-: Abstract nominalizing prefix for *maki-* frequentative stems. **Kayatda ti kinamannakigayyemna.** They like the way he is always friendly (his friendliness).

kindúyos: agkinduyusan. v. to be chaotic; in a turmoil; perplexed, confused. [Tag. *guló*]

kinét: n. snake eel of the *Ophichthyldae* family.

kiniéntos: (Sp. *quinientos*: five hundred) n. five hundred. (*lima a gasut*)

kiníit: kumniit. v. to stunt, dwarf.

kiníkin: agkinikin. v. to sway the hips when walking. (*iliil; kinni*)

kinína: (Sp. *quinina*: quinine) n. quinine.

kinís: makakniis. v. to disperse (said of crowds). (*wara*)

kinní: agkinni, agkinnikinni. v. to wiggle the hips in walking. [Tag. *kendéng*]

kinníkin: agkinnikin. v. to shiver, shake, tremble (*pigerger*). [Tag. *katóg*]

kinníit: (f. *kinnit*) **kumniit.** v. to grow stunted, be dwarfed in growth. [Tag. *bansót*]

kinnít: n. heat; pulling with the teeth (*baknis, ngetnget, kampis*); penetration of temperature (*kayatukot*). **agkinnit.** v. to pull with the teeth. **sangkakinnit.** n. one bite. **kuminnit.** *v.* to penetrate (temperature). **kumniit.** *v.* to grow stunted. **Kimminnit ti pudot.** v. to penetrate (heat). **Kuminnit ti lamiis ngem saan a rinikna ti gumilgil-ayab a barukongna.** The cold was penetrating but her flaming chest did not feel it. [Tag. *ngabngáb*]

kinnó: see *silnó*: spill over; undulate, wave (liquids).

kinód: *n.* movement in sexual intercourse. **agkinod.** v. to become erect (penis); to move the pelvic region back and forth as during coitus.

kinudan. v. to move the pelvic region back and forth in the direction of someone. **kinudkinod.**

n. (coll.) the *lawlawigan* bird. **napakinod.** a. moved up and down or back and forth.

kínon: nakinon. a. scarcely; scantily; sparsely; seldom.

kinón: a. arrogant; unconcerned; indifferent. **kuminon.** v. to become arrogant; indifferent. [Tag. *mapagmataás*]

kinúng: agkinung. v. to make waves (liquids). (*silnó*) **nagkinung.** a. sensitive. [Tag. *ligwák*]

kinotán: n. Ilocano ant dance.

kínse: (Sp. *quince*: fifteen) *num.* fifteen (*sangapulo ket lima*). [Tag. *labin-limá*]

kinsénas: (Sp. *quincena*: fifteen days) n. fifteen days (*sangapulo ken lima nga aldaw*); middle of the month.

kínsi: kinsikinsi. n. decoration on walls consisting of designs of small pieces of timber. (*kadang*)

kínta: (Sp. *quinta*: fifth) n. fifth. (*maikalima*) **kintuen.** v. to take one-fifth.

kintál₁: *n.* firmness; good consistency of root crops. **nakintal.** a. sticky and firm (squash meat). **Dina nagawidan ti nakakinkintal a panagrasawna.** She did not restrain her firm insolence. [Tag. *ligat*]

kintál₂: (Sp. *quintal*: native measure) n. measure of 100 kilograms (used to measure tobacco, etc.). **por kintal.** sold by the *kintal*. **kumintal.** *v.* to be approximately a *kintal*, approximate a *kintal* in weight.

kintayég: n. fear; shudder; (obs.) sensual delight. **agkintayeg.** v. to shake, tremble, quiver. **nakintayeg.** a. jerky. **makapakintayeg.** a. dreadful; horrifying. [Tag. *kiníg*]

kínto propúgo: (Sp. *quinto profugo*: fifth refugee) *n.* unmarried man who refuses the army service draft.

kintól: agkintol. v. to collide (round objects). **kintolan.** v. to knock the head. [Tag. *untóg*]

kintóng: var. of *gintong*: pound rice in a mortar.

kintsáy: (Hok. kʰín cʰài) n. Chinese celery (used in seasoning).

kínga: kuminga. n. tree with valuable dark colored timber.

kíngki: (Sp. *quinqué*: kerosene lamp) n. kerosene lamp.

kingkíng₁: n. hopscotch. **agkingking.** v. to hop. **kingkingen.** v. to walk by hopping on one foot. [Png. *kitkít*, Tag. *pikô, kandirít*]

kingkíng₂: (reg.) n. kind of native musical instrument made of bamboo. **agkingking.** v. to play the *kingking*.

kió: n. sediment, dregs of vat dyes.

kiók: *n.* cry of a hen (*kiak*); singing out of tune; term applied to a cock when losing a cockfight. **agkiok.** *v.* to sing out of tune.

kióng: **kiongkiong**. *n.* tottering, swaying. **agkiongkiong**. *v.* to totter, sway (drunks, liquids in a container, etc.). **Agkiongkiong iti bartekna ti lakay**. The old man is tottering from his inebriated state.

kiósko: (Sp. *quiosco*: kiosk) *n.* kiosk, newsstand, small structure with one or more sides open for selling merchandise.

kióte: *n.* light cinnamon color; yellow. [Tag. *diláw* (yellow)]

kiúteks: (f. English brand name *cutex*) *n.* nail polish remover. **agkiuteks**. *v.* to remove nail polish.

kipás: **ikipas**. *v.* to kill; do away with; conclude; finish. **nakipas**. *a.* ended, concluded, terminated. [Tag. *ligpít*]

kípet: var. of *kiput*: tight fitting (*ilét*). [Knk. *tipék*, *suymút*, Tag. *sikíp*]

kípis: *n.* miniskirt; jockey cap. **nakakipis**. *a.* wearing a miniskirt; wearing a jockey cap.

kipkíp: *n.* kind of small fish; (obs.) cry of frogs, snakes, etc.

kípot₁: **nakipot**. *a.* tight fitting (*ilet*). [Png., Tag. *pitís*, Tag. *sikíp*]

kípot₂: (Pil) **pakipot**. *n.* feigning disinterest (*kieme*), playing hard to get. (*aginmamadí*)

kippál: **nakippal**. *a.* not consumed fast (grains); economical.

kippí: (*reg.*) var. of *kappí*: crab.

kippíng: **kinipping**. *n.* variety of awned rice.

kippít: *a.* flattened sideways (said of the head). **kippiten**. *v.* to flatten (*kuppit*). [Tag. *pipí*]

kiraá: *n.* noise of the *bakes* monkey.

kírab: var. of *kurab*.

kirád: **makirad**. *v.* to accidentally hit against something. **kiraden**. *v.* to hit, strike, rub against. **kumraad**. *v.* to creak, grate. **manakraad**. *v.* to continuously creak; slam.

kiráid: *n.* sound of scraping the bottom of a container. **ikiraid**. *v.* to scrape the bottom of a container.

kiráis: *n.* slight wound, scratch. **nakiraisan**. *a.* scratched. [Tag. *kalmót*, *gasgás* (scratch)]

kírang: *n.* scarcity; paucity; deficiency (*kisang*; *kurang*). **agkirang**. *v.* to be scarce. **nakirang**. *a.* scarce, scanty; deficient. **kinakirang**. *n.* scarcity; hard times. [Png., Tag. *kulang*]

kiráod: *n.* cuplike instrument for dipping or measuring; (reg.) sound of an object moving in an earthen jar. **ikiraod**. *v.* to scrape out of the bottom of a container. **kirauden**. *v.* to scrape. **Nadadagsen nga anges a kasla mangkirkiraud iti diding ti barukongna**. He has heavy breathing as if his chest were scraping the wall. [Tag. *kayod* (scrape)]

kiráos: *n.* sound of a grumbling stomach; noise coming from the throat. **agkiraos**. *v.* to grumble (stomach). **mangirkiraos**. *a.* miserly; destitute.

kirás: **agkiras**. *v.* to make the sound of walking slippers; to walk by dragging the feet. **ikiras**. *v.* to scrape against the ground in walking. **mangiras**. *v.* to strike a match. **kumiraskiras**. *v.* to make the sound of slippers. **kumraas**. *v.* to make a crashing sound (as a tree falling). **kanakraas**. *n.* continual crashing sounds. [Tag. *kaluskós*]

kirát: adv. all at once; (all killed) with one blow. **kiraten**. *v.* to kill or knock down in one stroke. **makirat**. *v.* to be killed or knocked down in one blow. **kumiratkirat**. *v.* to rattle. [Tag. *kalantóg*]

kiráy: *n.* twinkling. (*kirem*; *kirmed*; *kiray*; *kuyep*; *kuridemdem*) **agkiray**. *v.* to twinkle, flicker; wave. **agkiraykiray**. *v.* to blink; wink; twinkle; sparkle. **Agkiraykiray dagiti bituen iti paset nga awan ti ulepna**. The stars are twinkling in the cloudless part (of the sky). [Tag. *kuráp*]

kírbas: *n.* (myth.) *n.* hideous maiden snatcher. **kirbasan**. *v.* to trim lawns, cut grass along the edge.

kirbáy: *n.* shoreline; rim of a pool; side of a hill.

kirbót: **ikirbot**. *v.* to consume all (*kulet*, *ibus*). **nakirbot**. *a.* consumed.

kirdát: var. of *kerdat*: firm; consistent.

kiré(e)b: **makakreb, makakréeb**. *n.* to produce the sound of a crashing wave or door slam.

kiréb: *n.* sound produced by breakers on the shore.

kíred: *n.* strength, vigor (*pigsa*); endurance; ferrule. **nakired**. *a.* strong, robust; hardy, durable; solid. **kinakired**. *n.* strength, endurance. **kumired**. *v.* to become strong. **pangirdán**. *n.* pole (for vaulting). **pakirden**. *v.* to strengthen; (~ *ti nakem*) have courage. **Kayatko ti agpudno kenkuana inton maaddaanak iti kired**. I want to confess the truth to him when I have the strength. **Pakirdem kuma ta nakemmo a mangsango iti didigra**. You should have the courage to face disaster. **Ti tao nga di mabain nga mangged, biagna ti nakired**. He who is not ashamed to work has an enduring life. [Tag. *lakás*]

kirek: *n.* kind of small frog.

kirém: **agkirem, kumirem**. *v.* to wink; blink; twinkle. (*kirmed*; *kiray*; *kuyep*; *kuridemdem*; *kimmay*) **kirman**. *v.* to wink at someone. **iti apagkirem**. adv. in a flash. **Napakiremak iti kawesna**. I winked at her clothes. [Bon. *kimkim*, Png., Tag. *kindát*, Tag. *pikít*]

kiremrém: *a.* with eyes half closed, with slit eyes (*kidem*: blink); *n.* wink, twinkling of the eyes. [Knk. *kudimdím*, Tag. *kurát, kindát, kisáp*]

kiriket: var. of *girit.*

kiríkir: n. saw; carpenter's file (*kirkir*) (obs.) **kinirkir.** a. lead earring.

kirikkík: n. tickle. (*kiki*) **kirikkiken.** v. to tickle.

kir-ín: agkir-in. v. to move slightly, stir. **kirinen.** v. to move something. [Tag. *kislót*]

kiríno: n. kind of small drab bird, buff flower pecker.

kíring: n. quaillike bird; period between October 20 and 25 that has superstitious significance, possibly from atmospheric disturbances happening at this time; uncontrollable shaking of the head. **ikiring.** v. to have a shaking palsy. **makiring.** v. to be plagued with bad luck.

kiríng₁: kiringkiring. n. kind of rice sweet; variety of early rice with reddish kernel.

kiríng₂: n. sound of ringing bells. **agkiringkiring.** v. to ring (bells). **kiringen.** v. to ring a bell. **kanakriing.** n. continuous ringing. [Tag. *kililíng*]

kiriríng: n. telephone ring. **agkiriring.** v. to ring (said of the phone). [Tag. *kililíng*]

kiririt: agkiririt. v. to jingle (coins in pocket).

kirís: n. soft sound (walking lizard, writing of a pen). **kumirriis, manakriis.** v. to produce a soft sound.

kirít: agkikinnirit. v. to cry *kirít* (all are hidden) in the hide-and-seek game. **kiritkirit.** n. jingling sound of coins. **kumiritkirit.** v. to jingle.

kirkír: n. carpenter's file. **kirkiran.** v. to scrape, file with a *kirikir* (*karudakid*); (*fig.*) clean thoroughly.

kirkír: kirkiran. v. to scrape, scrub. (*karus; kirus; kiskis; kuskus; sapsap*) **maikirkir.** v. to knock the head against something. [Png. *kidkid, kadkad*, Tag. *kayod* (scrape)]

kirmát: var. of *kigmát*: moment, instant.

kirméd: agkirkirmed. v. to wink; twinkle; blink (*kiray; kimmay; kuyep; kuridemdem; kirem*). [Tag. *kindát*]

kirmét: n. stinginess. **nakirmet.** a. stingy, tight with money, miserly. (*imut*) **kirmetan.** v. to deny someone (money, help, etc.), to be stingy with someone. [Knk. *íkut, bitíeg*, Png., Tag. *kuripot*]

kirnád: mangirnad. v. to abstain, have self-control; stop a habit.

kiró: nakiro. v. confusing; disorderly. **kiruen.** v. to disorder, disarrange; confuse; mislead. **kirokiro.** n. *pl.* disturbances, problems. [Tag. *guló*]

kiróg: agkirog, kirugen. v. to roast; fry. (*asado; asar; tuno; lutti; uttom; sarabasab*) **kinirog.** n. anything roasted; popped corn,

popped rice. **nakirog.** *a.* roasted. **kinirog a lagdaw ti rupa.** *exp.* with a blushing face (*lit:* with a fried prawn face). [Ibg. *itélaq*, Ivt. *mananghag*, Kpm. *mayangle*, Png. *sanglel*, Tag. *sangág*]

kirús: n. strickle; scraper for cleaning, smaller than the *kárus*. **kirusan.** v. to level with a strickle. **kirusen.** v. to scrape off (*karudakid*). **kakkirus.** *a.* just scraped (coconut).

kir-ós: n. rice pounded for a third time. **agkir-os.** v. to pound rice a third time. (*lib-ok*)

kirót: see *kiró*: confusing, disorderly.

kírpa: agkirpa. v. to cease (said of rain, storm, noise, etc.); subside. **Nakirpan ti apuy ti essemna.** The fire of his desire abated. **Di agkirpa ti riknak a sibabasol.** My guilty feelings do not cease. [Tag. *hupâ*]

kirpó: maikirpo. v. to trip, stumble. (*agtibkól*)

kirréb: (obs.) n. bustle; restlessness.

kirrét: n. anus. (*busigit; kimmut; merret; moriit; tatakkian*)

kirriáw: agkirriaw. v. to cry out (in complaining) (*riaw*). [Tag. *sigáw*]

kirríis: (f. *kiris*) **kumirriis.** v. to make the sound of a pen when writing; to make a shrill sound (lizard walking on grass).

kirríit: n. impaired person or animal; withered skin; dried plants or fruits. **kumriit.** v. to tan (in the sun); dry up. **kirriiten.** v. to dry up something under the sun.

kísame: n. ceiling. (*bóbeda*)

kisáng: nakisang. a. scanty, deficient, insufficient; inadequate; few. (*kirang; takkon*) **dagiti nakisang a bulan.** n. months in which the food supply is short. **Kumiskisangen ti suratda.** Their letters are already getting scarce. [Tag. *untî*]

kisáp: a. flat-nosed, snub-nosed (*lugpak*); bare; shorn (with all hair cut off). **ikisap.** v. to cut at the root; consume entirely. **kisapen.** v. to consume entirely. **maikisap.** v. to be completely consumed; destroyed. [Tag. *panot* (shorn head)]

kísaw: n. acute abdominal pain, stomach disorder. **agkisaw.** v. *to have stomach pain (as a person with diarreha)*; grumble (stomach).

kisíkis: see *pisípis*: little movement left to something confined in a small place. **agkisikis.** v. to clean the side part.

kísing: kisingkising. n. kind of small marine fish; kind of small mollusk with a round shell, smaller than the *kusíling.*

kiskís₁: agkiskis. v. to shave; scrape. (*kirkír; kuskús*) **kiskisen.** v. to shave off. **kiskisan.** v. to shave someone; n. barbershop; [Tag. *ahit* (shave)]

kiskís₂: **kiskisan.** *n.* rice mill, corn mill, mill. **ipakiskis.** *v.* to have rice milled. (*pabayo*) **pagkiskisen.** *v.* to cause friction; strike a match.

kisláp: n. glimpse; glance. (*taldiáp, palúdip*)

kismáy: makakismay. *v.* to be able to move. **agkismay.** *v.* to move involuntarily (twitch, on being revived, etc.).

kisút: var. of *kúsit:* cheat. [Tag. *dayà*]

kissáy: agkissay. *v.* to reduce one's possessions. **kissayan.** *v.* to reduce, lessen, diminish; decrease. **kissayen.** *v.* to remove, deduct, take away from in order to lessen. **maksay.** *v.* to be lessened, subtracted from. **maksayan.** *v.* to be cut off, shortened. **agpaksay.** *v.* to move the bowels (*ibléng; takkí*); have slight bloody discharges when pregnant. **awan naksay.** complete. [Tag. *bawas* (diminish)]

kissiál: kumsial. *v.* to harden, become tough; have muscle cramps (*tumangken*). [Tag. *tigás*]

kissiát: maiksiat. *v.* to deflect. (*taldiap, kisláp, palúdip; kudiás*) **mapaksiatan.** *v.* to be hit by a glancing missile. **paksiaten.** *v.* to defeat, overpower; overcome; exterminate.

kissíim: *n.* whisper (*arasaas*); secret scheme. **agkiskissiim.** *v.* to talk secretly. **ikissiim, kissiiman.** *v.* to whisper something to; forewarn by whispering. **agkinnissiim.** *v.* to speak to each other in whispers. **Amkek nga adda nakaikissiim kenka iti maipapan kenkuana.** I fear that somebody told you something secretly about her. [Tag. *bulóng*]

kissít: n. semen. (*itlóg ti laláki; kapsít; kassít*) **agkissit.** v. to ejaculate; produce semen. [Bon. *gisit*, Ivt. *hapit*, Knk. *kisít, daliwádew, áyot*, Tag. *tabód, tamód*]

kissíw: n. epilepsy; cramp. **agkissiw.** v. to have epilepsy; to have an epileptic seizure. **kumsiw.** v. to warp (timber); suffer from cramps or epilepsy. **pagkissiwén.** *v.* to throw into an epileptic fit. [Bon. *keldas*, Kal. *keÿtoy*, Knk. *kédas*, Kpm. *sóning*, Tag. *himatáy*]

kíta₁: n. kind, class; appearance (*itsóra*); species; shape; aspect; look. **kumita.** v. to look, see. **agkita.** v. to see each other. **makita.** v. to see; notice; a. able to be seen. **kitaen.** v. to look at; examine; seek; watch over; pay attention to; watch out for. **ipakita.** v. to show, display, reveal, indicate. **agpakita.** v. to appear; materialize. **agkita.** v. to meet; meet by chance. **pagkita.** n. eyes; organs of sight. **pakakitaan.** n. evidence; proof. (*paneknék*) **pakakitkitaan.** n. souvenir; memoir. **kakitkita.** a. belonging to the same class; of the same kind. **nadumaduma a kita ti sabong.** n. various kinds of flowers. **Panagkitak, nasaysayaat kuma no**

nangasawakayo. In my opinion, it would be better if you married. **Awan ti napintas a makita ni Helena iti nangisit a suako.** Helen doesn't see anything beautiful in the black pipe. [Bon. *íla*, Ibg. *singen, inná*, Ifg. *tibon*, Ivt. *vuyaq*, Kal. *tollong*, Kpm. *ákit*, Png. *nengneng*, Tag. *kita* (see), *urì* (kind; sort)]

kíta₂: (Sp. *quitación:* salary, income) n. wages, salary. (*suéldo, tegdén*) **kumita, kitaen.** v. to earn as wages. **kumitaan.** *n.* earnings, livelihood.

kitá: **kitakita.** n. *Bischofia javanica* tree with good timber and trifoliate leaves. (*kanaran*)

kitákit: agkitakit. v. to excuse oneself from; evade an obligation; refuse. [Tag. *tanggí*]

kitáng: n. trawl, long fishing line with many hooks. **agkitang.** v. to fish using the *kitang.*

kitdól: kitdulan. v. to gather the first. (*sula*) **kitdulen.** (obs.) v. to pick.

kíteb: n. bedbug. **kiniteb.** *a.* infested with bedbugs. **kakitkiteb, nakakitkiteb.** a. full of bedbugs. **singpet-kiteb.** *exp.* insincere person; person who looks innocent on the inside but is in fact hiding something. [Ibg. *kenniq*, Ivt. *tatumuk*, Kal. *kitob*, Kpm. *suldut*, Png. *piséng*, Tag. *surot*]

kitéb: agkiteb. v. to beat, throb, pulsate, palpitate (*pitik*). [Tag. *kitíg*]

kitég: n. boundary (*patinggá, pagbeddengán*). **Nalaka a linasatna ti bassit a waig a nagkitegan dagiti dua a turod.** It was easy for him to cross the small brook that bounded the two hills.

kiték: *n.* ticking. **agkitekkitek.** v. to tick (clocks) (*bitek*). **kanakteek.** *n.* continuous ticking.

kitém: *var.* of *kitúm:* close, shut. **Awan ti sumrek a kuriat iti sikikitem a ngiwat.** Crickets do not enter a closed mouth.

kití: (f. Tag. *kitikiti:* mosquito larvae) **kitikiti.** *a.* fidgety; *n.* mosquito larvae (*balbaltík*).

kitík: n. sound of ticking (clocks). **agkitik.** v. to tick (said of a clock).

kitíkit: n. groove (*gúrit*); carving; sculpture. **agkitikit.** *v.* to carve; sculpt. **ikitikit.** v. to engrave; carve; notch. **agkitkitikit.** n. wood carver. **Saan kano met nga immala kenni lakayna, uray sangatukel laeng koma a sallapiding ti naikitikitna.** He (the baby) supposedly didn't take after her husband one bit, not even a single little mole sculpted into him. [Kal. *tikitik*, Tag. *lilok*]

kitíl: agkanaktiil. v. to make the sound of gravel falling. [Tag. *kitíl* = barracuda; nip off; kill]

kíting: nakiting. a. short (clothes); narrow, restricted. **ikiting.** v. to shorten. **nakiting a panunot.** *a.* narrow-minded; brainless. **Naka-**

ing-ingpis ken nakakitkiting ti badoda. Their dresses are very thin and short. [Tag. *iklî*]

kitíw: **kitkitiw.** n. kind of bird; cry of certain birds.

kitkít: **kitkiten.** v. to nibble; gnaw (*kinnít*, *kittíb*, *kibkib*, *kúrib*). **kitkitan.** v. to nibble at, knaw at. [Tag. *ngatngát*]

kitóg: n. blow, strike. **agkitog.** v. to wave, undulate; shake. **agkitogkitog.** v. to shake, tremble, shiver, quiver. **kitogen.** v. to strike, hit, give a blow to. [Tag. *kalóg*]

kitól: n. sound of walking shoes. **agkitol.** v. to knock the heel of the shoe on the floor (*kanaktuol*). **kitolan.** v. to knock the head. **kanaktuol.** n. continuous sound of heels.

kitúm₁: **kinitumán.** n. variety of early rice with hard kernel.

kitúm₂: var. of *kit-um*: shut; close. **kituman.** v. to keep something secret; nourish a feeling, harbor in the mind. **kitumen.** v. to shut the mouth. **pagkitumen.** v. to shut, close (lips, etc.). [Tag. *tikóm*]

kit-úm: *var* of *kitúm*: shut, close.

kitós: *var.* of *katós*: knock on the head.

kitsí: (Ch.) n. lead washer (for roofing nails).

kitsíng: (*fam.*) young lady.

kittáb: n. bite. (*kagat*) **agkittab, kumittab.** v. to take a bite; nibble. **kittaban.** v. to bite something off. **sangkakittab.** n. one bite. [Tag. *kagát*]

kittíb: **kittiben.** v. to nibble. (*kitkít*, *kúrib*, *kinnít*, *kibkib*) **kittiban.** v. to nibble at, eat bit by bit. [Tag. *ngatngát*]

kittíig: **kumtiig.** v. to wither, shrink, shrivel up. (*layláy*)

kittíng: (obs.) **kumting.** v. to clear up (weather)

kiwákiw: n. zigzagged form, curved form. **agkiwakiw.** v. to zigzag, curve.

kíwar: n. instrument for mixing, ladle, mixer. **kiwaren.** v. to stir; stir up; plow a second or third time. **inkiwar.** n. kind of pudding. [Bon. *kíwal*, Kal. *kiwkiw*, Png. *kiwál*, *kanáw*, Tag. *halò*]

kíwas: see *dakíwas*: roam, prowl searching.

kiwáweg: *a.* contorted, twisted. **agkiwaweg.** v. to contort the body; writhe; warp; twist; squirm. [Tag. *baluktót*]

kiwér: a. curved at the top (tails of some dogs, etc.). (*kiwerkiwer*) **agkiwer.** v. to curve; twist. [Tag. *baluktót*]

kíwet: n. young of the eel. [Knk. *galumbík*]

kiwét: a. bend; crooked; twisted. **agkiwet.** v. to bend; curve; twist. **agkiwetkiwet.** v. to zigzag; writhe. [Tag. *kiwít*]

kiwíkiw: n. wagging of the tail. **agkiwikiw.** v. to wag the tail (*kalawikiw*). [Tag. *payipoy*]

kiwíng: **nagkiwing.** a. crooked, bent; curved. (*killó*) **kiwingen.** v. to curve; bend slightly.

kiwkíw: n. caudal fin; tail. **kiwkiwan.** v. to paddle, incite; instigate; urge, persuade; trap. **agkiwkiw.** v. to wag the tail (*kalawikiw*). **pagkiwkiw.** n. oar, paddle. **Nabayag a kiwkiwkiwandak tapno isinak ti kasimpungalak.** They have been urging me for a long time to separate from my spouse. [Tag. *payipoy* (wag the tail)]

kiyáw: n. yellow (*duyáw*). [Tag. *diláw*]

kiyyét: shrugging of the shoulders; *var.* of *kiet*: lower backside by bending the knees. **nakakiyyet.** a. with shrugged shoulders.

klábe: (Sp. *clave*: code) n. clue; *var.* of *klabiha*: peg; dowel.

klabéha: *var.* of *klabiha*: peg (of a stringed instrument); dowel.

klabél: (Sp. *clavel*: carnation) n. pink carnation.

klabéte: (Sp. *clavete*: tack) n. small nail; tack.

klabíha: (Sp. *clavija*: pin, peg) n. peg; dowel.

klábo: (Sp. *clavo*: nail) n. roofing nail (*lansa*); see *klabo-de-komer*. **klabos.** n. cloves (spice).

klábo-de-komér: (Sp. *clavo de comer*: clove) n. clove.

kláusula: (Sp. *cláusula*: clause) n. clause.

klára: (Sp. *clara*: white of an egg) n. white of an egg (*puraw ti itlóg*).

klaréte: (Sp. *clarete*: claret) n. claret wine.

klarín: (Sp. *clarín*: bugle) n. bugle, clarion; bugler.

klarinéte: (Sp. *clarinete*: clarinet) n. clarinet.

kláse: (Sp. *clase*: class) n. class; kind, sort (*kita*); grade; variety. **kaklase.** n. classmate. **primera klase.** first class. **segunda klase.** second class. **tersera klase.** third class. **kaklase.** of the same class, of the same kind. **mangklase.** v. to teach. **pagklaseklaseen.** v. to sort by class, assort. **klinase.** a. classified, divided into classes. **sangkaklase.** of one class, of the same quality.

klasipikádo: (Sp. *clasificado*: classified) a. classified (*klinase*).

klasipikasión: (Sp. *clasificación*: classification) n. classification.

klátsbag: (Eng. clutch bag) n. strapless purse. **nakaklatsbag.** a. with a strapless purse.

kléro: (Sp. *clero*: clergy) n. clergy.

kliénte: (Sp. *cliente*: client) n. client.

klientéla: (Sp. *clientela*: clientele) n. clientele.

klíma: (Sp. *clima*: climate) n. climate. (*tiémpo*, *panawén*)

klínika: (Sp. *clínica*: clinic) n. clinic.

klise: (Sp. *clisé*) n. cut (printing).

klobéra: (Sp. *clovera*) n. clove tree.

kloropórmo: (Sp. *cloroformo*: chloroform) n. chloroform, a colorless liquid that, when inhaled, renders a person unconscious.

-ko: *pron.* ergative first person singular enclitic pronoun: I, my. Changes to *-k* after vowels and the suffixes *-an* and *-en*. **balayko.** my house **arakko.** my wine **asok.** my dog. **aramidek.** I'll do it. **inaramidko.** I did it. [Grammatical note: Before the enclitic *=en*, *ko* retains its full form and does not contract to *=n* after a vowel, e.g. *asokon.* it is already my dog. *Ko* does not occur before the enclitic *=ka*, e.g. *Bautenka.* I'll beat you. Png. *=ko*, *=k*, Tag. *=ko*]

kuá: n. term used to replace nouns or roots that the speaker cannot name by word due to lack of memory: whatchamacallit. With the *-ko* pronouns, *kuá* forms possessive pronouns: **kukuak.** mine. (*bagik*) **kukuam.** yours. (*bagim*) **kukuana.** his/hers/its., etc. (*bagina*) **agkua.** *v.* to do; (fig.) to have sexual intercourse; make love. **kuaen (kueén).** *v.* to do, make. **ikua.** *v.* to put, place somewhere, do, etc. **ipakua.** *v.* to have something done. **makikua.** *v.* to have intercourse. **akinkukua, tagikua.** n. owner. **agtagikua.** *v.* to be the owner. **tagikuaen.** *v.* to own, possess. **ipatagikua.** *v.* to bequeath. **kukua.** n. possession; goods. **panagkukua.** n. manner, way; conduct, behavior. **makipagkukua.** *v.* to participate; join in. **sanikua.** *n.* goods; property, commodities. **idi kua.** then. (remote past) **intono kua.** sometime in the future, later on, afterwards. **intono kuan!** warning exclamation. **Intono kuan, binautka.** You better watch out or I'll beat you. [Phonological note: Stress shift with the suffixes is regional, *kuáen* and *kuaén* are both heard. Ibg. *kwá*, Png. *kién*, Tag. *kuwán*]

kuadérno: (Sp. *cuaderno*: notebook) n. notebook, writing book.

kuádra: (Sp. *cuadra*: stable) n. stable. (*kabalierísa*) **ikuadra.** v. to put into the stable.

kuadrádo: (Sp. *cuadrado*: square) n. square; cube. **pie kuadrada.** n. square foot. [Kal. *lapampalasku*, Tag. *parisukát*]

kuadránte: (Sp. *cuadrante*: carpenter's square) n. carpenter's square (*eskuala*); sundial.

kuádre: (Sp. *cuadro*: square of troops) n. police force (during the Spanish regime).

kuadrília: (Sp. *cuadrilla*: squad) n. squad; patrol of four; group of four persons.

kuadriliéro: (Sp. *cuadrillero*) *n.* rural guard; mountain patrol man.

kuádro: (Sp. *cuadro*: frame) n. framed picture; frame (*sukogán*, *bangkay*). **kuadros.** four of a kind: four cards of the same value belonging to different suits in one hand. **ikuadro.** *v.* to frame

a picture. **maikuadro.** a. to be framed; (fig.) cornered. **agkuadro-alas.** v. to get four aces in one hand of cards. **Naikuadro ni Macario a nakabidang iti tualia iti ruangan.** Macario was cornered at the door with a towel wrapped around him.

kuadrúple: (Sp. *cuadruple*) *a.* fourfold, composed of four parts.

kuágo: (Tagalog also) n. owl. (*kulláaw*)

kuála: n. harbor; pier; haven; port; estuary of mud; mouth of river.

kuansít: kukuansit. v. to play make believe; *a.* pretense (*kundit*). [Tag. *kunwari*]

kuantóng: n. *Amaranthus viridis* edible spinach-type herb.

kuarénta: (Sp. *cuarenta*: forty) *num.* forty. (*uppát a púlo*)

kuarenténas: (Sp. *cuarentena*: quarantine) n. quarantine. (*pannakaipútong*)

kuarésma: (Sp. *cuaresma*: lent) n. lent; summer, dry season (*kalgáw*). [Tag. *tag-araw*]

kuárta: (Sp. *cuarta*: fourth) n. fourth; fourth gear. **kuarta clase.** n. fourth class. [See also *kuarto*, the masculine form]

kuartá: (Sp. *cuarto*: a copper coin) n. money (*pirák*). **makakuarta.** *v.* to have money; earn money. **kuartaen.** v. to pay in money for. **kuartaan.** v. to mooch; get money from; bribe someone with money. **makuarta.** a. wealthy; rich. (*baknáng*) **Awan bibiangmo iti gatgatangek ta kuartak ti inggatangko kadagitoy.** You have no business in what I'm buying because I bought these things with my money. [Kal. *pilak*, Png. *kuárta*, Tag. *pera*, *kuwaltá*]

kuartáis: (Sp. *cuarto*: a copper coin) n. commission; market fee. **agkuartais.** v. to pay a market or stall fee. **kuartaisan.** v. to collect a market tax. **kuartaisen.** v. to sell on commission. [Tag. *buwís*]

kuartél: (Sp. *cuartel*: army quarters) n. army quarters; precinct. [Tag. *himpilan*]

kuarteláda: (f. *kuartel*) *n.* military coup d'état.

kuarteléro: (f. *kuartel*) *n.* soldier given the task of keeping the barracks clean.

kuartília: (Sp. *cuartilla*: quarter; sheet of writing paper) *n.* sheet of paper; original copy for the typesetter.

kuartílio: (Sp. *cuartillo*) *n.* pint, one-eighth of a gallon.

kuartíto: (Sp. *cuartito*: small room) *n.* small room. (*bassit a siled*)

kuárto₁: (Sp. *cuarto*: room) *n.* room. (*siled*) **kakuartuan.** n. roommate. **agkakuarto.** *v.* to share a room. **mangkuarto.** *v.* to occupy a room. **nakuartuan.** *a.* divided into rooms.

Nagkakagiddanankami a nagadal ken agka-kuartuankami pay. We studied at the same time and we were roommates also. [Kal. *kuweÿtu, susuyyopan*, Tag. *silíd*]

kuárto₂: (Sp. *cuarto*: fourth) *a.* fourth (*maikapat*); quarter of the moon; quarter; quarter of an hour. **kuarto grado.** fourth grade. **kuarto anio.** fourth year.

kuásit: *var.* **kukuasit.** *a.* make-believe (*kuansit*). [Tag. *kunwarì*]

kuáso: kuasokuaso. *n.* poorly done work; job poorly performed.

kuát: pangkuatan, pamkuatan. *n.* reason, excuse; motive. (*pambár*) **Ania ti pamkuatam a mangtagibassit kaniak.** What is your reason for belittling me? [Tag. *dahilan*]

kuátit: var. of *buatit*.

kuátro: (Sp. *cuatro*: four) *num.* four. (*uppat*) **alas cuatro.** four o'clock. **kuatrosientos.** *num.* four hundred.

kuatroáguas: (Sp. *cuatro aguas*: four slopes) *n.* roof with four corners on top, forming four slopes.

kúba: *n.* band used as a G-string by women. (*bayakat; anungo; pallak*)

kubálan: *n.* species of marine fish.

kubalbág: agkubalbag. *v.* to fade, discolor.

kubálig: (obs.) **kubaligen.** *v.* to rudely push.

Kubáno: (Sp. *cubano*) *n., a.* Cuban.

kúbang: kubangkubang. *n.* buttock (of animals). (*pingping ti ubet*)

kub-áw: *var.* of *kubbáw*: foreleg kick. [Tag. *dambá*]

kúbay: *n.* species of vine with edible tops.

kub-áy: *n.* kick, flying kick.

kubbáal: *n.* kind of large marine mollusk. **kubkubbalan.** *n.* kind of very large marine mollusk.

kubbába: see *kalumbába*: to rest the chin on the arms.

kubbaóng: *n.* kind of freshwater mollusk with speckled shell. (*leddangan*)

kubbáw: *n.* foreleg kick. **agkubbaw.** *v.* to strike with the forelegs (horses) (*kub-áw*). [Tag. *dambá*]

kubbó: *a.* humpbacked, hunchbacked; with a crooked back; *n.* variety of awned early rice. **agkubbo.** *v.* to become humpbacked or stooping. **pagkubbuen.** *v.* to bend. [Ivt. *vukut*, Knk. *bakúg, yákug, odang-ó*, Tag. *kubà*]

kubbuár: *n.* jet, gust of water, spout. **agkubbuar.** *v.* to gush out, spout out, jet, spurt, rise and crack (soil where tubers are growing). **kubbuaren.** *v.* to stir water strongly. **Agkubkubbuar ti barukongna iti pungtotna.** His chest is stirring with anger. [Tag. *bulwák*]

kubéng: agpakubeng. *v.* to turn a deaf ear, pretend not to hear (*agpatúleng*).

kubéta: (Tag. via Sp. *cubeta*: toilet bowl) *n.* public restroom; latrine. (*kasilias*)

kubiérta: (Sp. *cubierta*: deck) *n.* deck of a ship. **Dagus met a bimmaba ni Beng iti kubierta.** Beng went down immediately to the deck of the ship.

kubiértos: (Sp. *cubiertos*: silverware) *n.* silverware. **kubiertosan.** *n.* table service.

kúbiko: (Sp. *cúbico*) *n.* cubic meter.

kubitér: agkubiter. *v.* to contract, shrink (*umres*). [Tag. *urong*]

kubkób: kumubkób. *v.* to surround, lay siege on. **kubkuben.** *v.* to surround; dig with the hands or forelegs. **agkubkob.** *v.* to dig scratching. [Tag. *kutkót*]

kubláng: *n.* a kind of herb. **kubla-kublang.** *a.* with light-colored spots (plates, skin after burns have healed).

kublás: *var.* of *kubrás*: slide down, slip.

kubó: *n.* hut, cottage; kind of mudfish trap. [Tag. *kubo* (hut)]

kubuár: see under *kubbuar*. [Tag. *bulwák*]

kubúkob: agkubukob. *v.* to curl up (from sickness, cold, etc.); hunch the body (when planting rice, etc.). **Ikarkaritko iti kabsatko nga agkubkubukob lattan iti kalapawna.** I challenged my brother to just curl up in his hut. **Kumubkubukob a nagmula iti birhinia.** She was hunched over planting Virginia tobacco. [Tag. *kulóng*]

kúbong: kubongkubong. *n.* mosquito net, bed curtain; kind of bamboo dog trap; hut.

kubóng: *n.* fence built around a young tree to protect it. **kubongen.** *v.* to enclose with a fence.

kóboy: (Eng. cowboy) *n.* cowboy; (*fig.*) person who is able to handle himself well in any situation, person who fits in with any type of crowd.

kóbra: (Sp. *cobra*: collect) **agkobra.** *v.* to collect a payment, the rent, etc. (*singír*) **kobraen.** *v.* to collect payment from.

kobradór: (Sp. *cobrador*: collector) *n.* bill collector; collector of gambling debts (*pasingír*).

kobránsa: (Sp. *cobranza*: collection) *n.* money collected (for debts).

kobrár: (Sp. *cobrar*: collect) **kobraren.** *v.* to collect (a bill). (*singír*)

kubrás: maikubras. *v.* to slip, slide down (*alusos*); miss a step and fall. **agkubras.** *v.* to slide down. [Tag. *dulás*]

kóbre: (Sp. *cobre*: copper) *n.* copper; ferrule.

kobrekáma: (Sp. *cubrecama*: bedspread) *n.* bedspread; quilt.

kubrír: (Sp. *cubrir*: cover) **kubriren**. v. to complete, make up; cover for (an obligation).

kudáap: (reg.) **agkudaap**. v. to faint, suffer a fainting spell (*talimudaw*); to turn white (said of the eyes). **ikudaap**. *v*. to do to the utmost, do to excess.

kúdad: **nakudad**. a. lazy; slow; awkward; clumsy; half-witted; dull; unlucky; unsuccessful; not in demand.

kúdag: n. kind of bird net. **agkudagkudag**. v. to use hands and feet in subduing a person or animal lying on the ground; flail the arms and legs (while lying on one's back).

kúdag: *var*. of *kudad*: **nakudag**. a. slow (said of sale)

kudág: **agkudagkudag**. *v*. to flail the arms (*kúdag*).

kudáil: *n*. fluttering motion, flailing motion (of a baby throwing a tantrum). **agkudail**. *v*. to flutter, squirm restlessly (*kulaídag*).

kodák: (Eng.) n. camera. (*pagretratuan*) **kodaken**. v. to take a picture of.

kudapís: a. thin, slender, slim; empty; meager. **agkudapis**. v. to become thin; empty. [Tag. *impís*]

kuddáy: **manguddakudday**. v. to sway, totter; be weary. [Tag. *suray, hapay*]

kuddó: n. kind of snapping beetle.

kudduág: **ikudduag**. v. to throw, furl, toss upward; fling. **agkudduag**. v. to rumble violently.

kuddúor: *n*. rumbling sound. **agkudduor**. v. to produce a sound in the throat (drinking, coughing, etc.); rumble.

kuddót: n. pinch using the nails, *keddel* is used for pinches without the use of the nails. **kudduten**. v. to pinch between the fingers. [Png. *karót*, Tag. *kurót*]

kudét: var. of *kudit*: tree ear fungus. [Ivt. *amuhung*, Tag. *kabuté*]

kudetá: (Eng.) n. coup d'état, forceful overthrow of the government.

kudetdét: n. kind of bracket fungi.

kúdi: **ikudi**. v. to dedicate; devote, do something with all one's attention; find time to do something; consecrate. [Tag. *laán*]

kudiáp: n. discolored blotch of skin (lighter than normal).

kudiápi: (obs.) n. lyre, kind of violin with two wire strings. [Tag. *kudyapî*]

kudiás: n. deflection; superficial wound of a deflected missile or bullet. **kumdias**. v. to deflect; bounce off. **makudiasan**. v. to be deflected off; to suffer a superficial wound from a deflection, to be scraped by a bullet. [Tag. *lihís*]

kudídit: n. slow, stunted growth. **nakudidit**. a. dwarfed, stunted; puny, rickety. [Tag. *bansót*]

kódigo: (Sp. *código*: code) n. code. **kodigo sibil**. civil code.

kódiko: (Sp. *código*: code) n. memorandum; (coll.) cheat sheet.

kúdil: n. skin; hide. (*ukis*) **ikudilan**. v. to skin; flay; peel (*kulanit*). **kakudkudil**. a. belonging to the same race. **Naingpis ti kudilna**. *exp*. He is sensitive (*lit*: has thin skin). **Napuskol ti kudilna**. *exp*. denoting lack of refinement (*lit*: he has thick skin). [Ibg. *tebbiq*, Ivt. *kudit*, Kal. *kublit*, Knk. *ukis*, *kupkúp*, Png. *báog*, Kpm., Tag. *balát*]

kudíng: **kumuding**. v. to do something for entertainment. **kudingen**. v. to tinker with something.

kúdis: **kudisan**. v. to skin; peel. **nakudisan**. a. peeled, skinned, flayed. [Tag. *talop*]

kudís: **nakudis**. a. in short supply (money); having a small amount of (*atado*; flesh on meat).

kud-ís: *var*. of *kúdis*: skin, flay, peel.

kudíser: **kumudiser**. v. to harden in cooking (rice, beans). [Tag. *kunat*]

kudísi: n. a kind of children's game. **makikudisi**. v. to join in a game of *kudisi*.

kodísia: (Sp. *codicia*: greed) **nakodisia**. a. hard to please. (*napili*)

kudít₁: n. kind of bracket fungi with an ear shape (*kudet*). [Tag. *kabuté*]

kudít₂: **agkudit**. v. to be active, diligent; to be restless, unquiet; putter around. **kuditan**. v. to scratch, rub. **kumudit-kudit**. *v*. to putter around. **managkudkudit**. *a*. always moving; diligent. **No adda kuditem**. If you have work. **Saan met nga agtalna dagiti ubbing a mangkudkudit kadagiti insangpet ti amada nga ay-ayam**. The children wouldn't calm down as they puttered around the toys that their father brought home.

kuditdít: var. of *kudit*: bracket fungi, tree ear fungus. [Ivt. *amuhung*]

kudkúd: n. scratching instrument; scratching. **agkudkud**. v. to scratch oneself. **kudkuden**. v. to scratch an itch; pet (an animal). [Ibg. *kebbeng*, Ivt. *kadkaren*, Kpm. *gámus*, Png. *kogkor*, *gugu*, Tag. *gasgás*, *kalmot*, *kamot*]

kudlás: **nakudlas (ti gasat)**. a. ill fated (luck). (*malas*)

kódo: (Sp. *codo*: angle) *n*. angle.

kudó: n. pebbles used as jack stones. **agkudo**. n. a kind of girl's game resembling knucklebones.

kuduág: var. of *kudduay*: hurl; throw upward. **agkuduag**. v. to rumble violently.

kúdog: **ikudog ti bagí.** v. to ingratiate oneself; win one's way into favor. **nakudug.** a. selfish, self-seeking.

kudóg: n. stampede; stomping of the feet. **agalinkudog.** v. to stomp the feet; stampede. **kudugen.** v. to control, restrain (one's feelings, etc.). **kudogkudog ti barukong.** n. pounding of the chest. [Tag. *dabóg*]

kudór: (obs.) n. placing at a distance.

kudrép: **nakudrep.** a. dim; overcast; obscure; indistinct; not easily understood. **kumudrep.** v. to become dim, overcast. **pakudrepén.** v. to make dim. **Kumudkudrepen ti lampara.** The lamp is getting dimmer. [Tag. *lamlám* (dim), *kulimlím* (overcast)]

kudsól: var. of *kugsol*: thrust; stamp.

kudsón: (Sp. *colchón*: mattress) n. foam mattress.

kué: (coll., f. kua) **kueen.** v. to do. (kua) **Kukueem?** What are you doing? [Tag. *gawâ*]

kuéba: (Sp. *cueva*: cave) n. cave (*rukib, gukayab*)

kuélio: (Sp. *cuello*: collar) n. collar.

kuénta: (Sp. *cuenta*: account) n. account; bill; worth, value. **agkuenta.** v. to count; calculate; compute. **ikuenta.** v. to consider, regard; to include. **makikuenta.** v. to settle accounts. **panagkuenta.** n. counting; mathematics. **kuentana.** seemingly, apparently. **awan kuentana.** exp. worthless. **kuenta de libro.** n. account book, ledger. [Tag. *kuwenta*]

kuentadór: var. of *kontadór*: bookkeeper; cashier; computer; counter; gas meter.

kuèntagótas: (Sp. *cuentagotas*: medicine dropper) n. medicine dropper.

kuèntapáso: (Sp. *cuentapaso*) n. odometer.

kuéntas: (Sp. *cuentas*: beads) n. necklace; beads; rosary. **agkuentas.** v. to wear a necklace. **kuentasan.** v. to put a necklace around the neck of. **ikuentas.** v. to wear around the neck. **kuentas a bendita.** holy rosary. [Bon. *boyáya,* Ivt. *saryu,* Kal. *bongeÿ,* Png. *kolíndas,* Tag. *kuwintás*]

kuentísta: (Sp. *cuentista*: storyteller) n. storyteller; short-story writer. [Tag. *kuwentista*]

kuénto: (Sp. *cuento*: story) n. story, narration (*sarita*). [Tag. *kuwento*]

kuéngka: (Sp. *cuenca*: river basin) n. basin of a river; deep valley surrounded by mountains.

kuérat: **kinakuerat.** n. mild lunacy, anger or delirium. **agkuerkuerat.** v. to go on a rampage or mean streak.

kuérdas: (Sp. *cuerda*: cord) n. string of a musical instrument. **kuerdasan.** v. to wind a clock; provide with a string, put a guitar string on; n. spring of a watch; tiebeam. [Tag. *kuwerdas*]

kuéro: (Sp. *cuero*: leather) n. leather, rawhide (*lalat*). [Tag. *kuwero, katad*]

kuérong: **agkuerong.** v. to go crazy, wild (*uyong*). [Tag. *ulól*]

kuérpo: (Sp. *cuerpo*: body, corps) **kuerpo ti polisia.** n. police corps.

kuestionár: (Sp. *cuestionar*) **kuestionaren.** v. to interrogate.

kuestionário: (Sp. *cuestionario*: questionnaire) n. questionnaire.

kuétes: (Sp. *cohete*: rocket) n. kind of rocketlike firecracker.

kúgab: n. a kind of slender close-jointed rattan.

kugan: n. threadfin fish of the *Polynemidae* family.

kúgaw: n. a kind of fish resembling the *puróng*.

kuggangél: a. stupid; slow. (*tabbed*)

kuggangí: a. ugly, hideous; bad, wicked. (*dakes; alas, laad*) **Uray kuggangi ta rupam no la ket propesionalka ket adda bassit mabalinmo.** Even though you have a hideous face, you are professional and can do a few things. **Ti pili nga pili makapili iti kuggangi.** He who is choosy picks the ugly one.

kúgit: a. circumcised. **kugiten.** v. to circumcise. **agpakugit.** v. to get circumcised. [Bon. *segyat,* Knk. *luptík, segiát,* Png. *galsim,* Kpm., Tag. *tulì*]

kugmél: **kugmelen.** v. to sprinkle water at something dry; (reg.) wring something dry.

kugmés: var. of *gumes*.

kugnál: (Sp. *cuñar*: wedge) **ikugnal.** v. to base on. **maikugnal.** v. to be based on. **pangikugnalan.** n. basis, model; reference. [Tag. *salig*]

kugsól: **ikugsol.** v. to drive, thrust in the ground (*gusod*); plant. **kugsulen.** v. to rap, pound, thump, hammer.

kugtár: n. kick. **kumugtar.** v. to kick. **ikugtar.** v. to kick something toward something. **kugtaren.** v. to kick something. **kinnugtar.** n. boy's game consisting of kicking to defend a square. **kukugtaren.** n. the *dadanúgen* banana. **Kugtar ni kabaian, ilot ni kalangangan.** The kick of the female carabao is the caress to the male. [Ibg. *ikappeq,* Ivt. *sariñan,* Kpm. *paldak,* Png. *depák, sípa,* Tag. *sipà*]

kuidáw: (Sp. *cuidado*: careful!) interj. Look out!

kuíng: (AmSp. *cuí*) n. guinea pig.

kuírong: **agkuirong.** v. to be crazy; insane. (*bagtit; kees*)

kuítis: var. of *kuetes*: rocket.

kokaína: (Sp. *cocaína*) n. cocaine.

kukarátsa: (Sp. *cucaracha*: cockroach) n. kind of foreign dance with castanets.

kukbúot: makokbuot. v. to produce the sound by slapping with an open hand.

kukkók: n. knock; cluck. agkukkok. v. to cluck (chickens); knock. agkanukkok. v. to produce the sound of striking something hollow. kukkókan. v. to knock against someone's head. [Tag. katók]

kóko₁: (Sp. coco: muslin) n. white muslin.

kóko₂: (Sp. coco: coconut) yema de koko. coconut macaroon.

kukó: n. nail (of finger or toe); claw; hoof. agikuko. v. to cut the nails. ikukuan. v. to cut someone's nails; to manicure. pakuko. n. notched lower part of a rafter. [Bon. koko, Ivt. kukuq, Kal. kuku, Knk. kiwi, Ibg., Kpm., Png., Tag. kukó]

kukua-: (f. kua) n. goods; owned items; property; possessions; things; used with -ko pronouns to form the possessive pronouns (sometimes shortened to kua-): (ku)kuak. mine. kukuam. yours. kukuana. his, hers. kukuada. theirs, etc. panagkukua. n. manner; behavior; conduct. akinkukua. n. owner. tagikukuaen. v. to make something one's own property unjustly (i.e., borrowed items). Kukuakto ti maudi a katawa. The last laugh will be mine. Kukuana tatta, kukuakto no bigat. It is his today and mine tomorrow. [Tag. ari-arian (possessions)]

kúkod: n. shank, shin.

kúkok: n. the cry of the turtledove.

kukulbén: n. kind of large basket for holding clothes or yarn.

kokomáre: plural of komare.

kukumér: (f. kumer) agkukumer. v. to walk slowly and unsteadily; to feel indisposed.

kokompádre: n. plural of kompadre.

kukót: agkukot. v. to huddle up; cower; shrink. (kulmeg) ikukot. v. to bend, fold (arms or legs). [Tag. baluktót]

kukútel: (f. kutel) n. leprosy. (kating) agkukutel. n. leper; v. to have leprosy. [Ivt. dipad, Png. kating, Tag. ketong]

kokrétas: (Sp. croqueta: croquet) n. croquet.

kóla₁: (Sp. cola: glue) n. glue, paste; adhesive (piket). kolaan. v. to seal with glue; glue; paste. nakolaan. a. pasted, glued. [Tag. pandikít]

kóla₂: (Sp. cola: tail) n. train of a dress; tail of a coat. de-kola. n. mestisa dress with a train.

kóla₃: (Eng.) kimmolakola. a. in the shape of a Coca-Cola bottle (referring to a shapely woman's body).

kulába: n. film; pellicle on a liquid; cream (scum) on milk; sweat stain on collar. agkulaba. v. to be stained (collars).

kulabbét: a. aged; withered; wrinkled; dried up (fruits). agkulabbet. v. to wither; dry up. [Tag. kulubót]

kolaboradór: (Sp. colaborador: collaborator) n. collaborator (enemy).

koláda: (Sp. colada: bleaching in lye). n. clothes to be bleached. koladaen. v. to bleach clothes; to comb cotton yarn. ikolada. v. to bleach; comb hanging cotton yarn. [Tag. kulá (Sp.)]

kuládong: nakakulkuladong. a. skinny, extremely thin (kuttong). [Tag. payatot]

kulagtít: n. jerk, frisk, quick movement. agkulagtit. v. to jerk, frisk (from being tickled, etc.); gambol; move feet while lying on the floor; move while sleeping. kulagtit a kulagtit. a. always moving. Adda nagkulagtit iti panunotna. Something flashed in his mind. [Tag. igtád]

kulaídag: n. squirming motion. agkulaidag, kumulaidag. v. to struggle (by flaying the arms); squirm (person in pain or a fish out of water); flutter (birds). Lallayak ti agkulkulaidag nga ubing a makipalpalama met iti ayat. I sing a lullaby to the squirming child begging for love. [Tag. alumpihít, pilipit]

kulaíseg: n. restlessness. agkulaiseg. v. to be restless; uneasy; fretful in bed. Nagkulaiseg ti rusokna. exp. denoting an uneasy feeling (lit. his abdomen is restless).

kulákob: n. small hut (to keep chickens or pigs).

kulalábang: n. kind of large gray owl that feeds on chickens.

kulalábat: n. cobwebs. agkulalabat. v. to be full of cobwebs. [Tag. agiw]

kulalantí: n. firefly; glowworm; variety of awned diket rice with red kernel; flickering. agkulalanti. v. to flicker (like fireflies). kimmulalanti a silaw. n. light like a firefly (flickering). [Knk. kubkubiatí, kulkuldíat, Png. kankánti, Tag. alitaptáp]

kulalángaw: n. the búkaw insect.

kulalátsi: n. tree whose bark is used to cure skin diseases and flowers are used in bouquets for the dead. [Tag. kulanadsí]

kúlam: (Tag.) n. witchcraft. mangkukulam. n. witch. (manggagamud) kulamen. v. to bewitch; enchant; lay a spell on. [Png. kólan, Tag. kulam]

kulámat: n. first layer of coconut meat; gum of the eyes. maikulamat. v. to stick to; cleave; adhere. nakulamatan. a. covered, veiled. [Tag. lambóng (covered, veiled)]

kulámaw: apagkulamaw. n. bit, particle, speck, small part. kulamawen. v. to do bit by bit; a little at a time. Awansa met kimmulamaw a

pangut-utekna. He doesn't have a bit of common sense. [Tag. *untí-untí*]

kulámbo: (Tag. kulambô*)* n. mosquito net. (*moskitero*) **agkulambo.** v. to use a mosquito net. **kulambuan.** v. to put a mosquito net over someone.

kulanadsí: var. of *kulalatsi.*

kulanagsí: var. of *kulalatsi.*

kulanét: agkulanet. v. to wither due to lack of water. (*laylay*)

kulánit: n. membrane; skin of egg; lining of gizzard; tissue of some fruits (oranges). **kulanitan.** v. to skin a frog; skin squid.

kulannáy: *n.* sluggishness; weakness; frailty. **nakulannay.** a. slow, sluggish; effeminate; frail and clumsy. **Inaplagan ti kulannay a silaw ti kalsada.** The weak light spread over the street.

kulantóng: n. hollow sound. **kumulantong.** v. to produce a hollow sound.

kulántro: (Sp. *culantro*: coriander) n. coriander. **agatkulantro.** v. to smell like coriander.

kuláng: n. spadix of the betel palm. **kulangán.** n. variety of long, curved sugarcane.

kulanggít: nakulanggit. a. easily moved; sensitive; lively; vivacious (*paragsit, siglat*). [Tag. *siglá*]

kulangít: n. *bunotán* fish before it completely matures; variety of awned rice with a depressed white kernel.

kulangtót: agkulangtot. v. to lovingly caress; grovel. **panagkinnulangtot.** v. act of caressing each other. **Kanayon kano a maduktalanna ti lakayna a makikulkulangtot iti katulongda.** She supposedly always finds her husband caressing their maid.

kulapís: n. inner lining of bamboo.

kulapnít: *n.* outer membrane (skin of a frog, thin membrane of lima beans, etc.) (*kulanit*). **kulapnitan.** v. to skin a frog; remove the skin of. **makulapnitan.** *v.* to be removed (skin). **No makulapnitan ti imana iti agburburek a danum, nakabasol.** If the skin comes off his hand in the boiling water, he is guilty. [Tag. *balát*]

kulápot: n. membranes of the fetus (chorion and amnion); sheaths of the muscles; tendon; skin of the egg; lining of the gizzard; skin of fish; skin of peanut; tissue; spiderweb. **ikulaputan.** v. to peel; skin. **kulaputan.** v. to enwrap with a spiderweb. [Kal. *ayabya*]

kullapít: var. of *kullapit*: thin, skinny. [Tag. *payát*]

kulár: *reg. var.* of *koral*: corral.

kulás: kulaskulas. n. pupa of the dragonfly.

kulásay: ikulasay. v. to leave out, omit; give up; abandon; quit. [Tag. *waksí*]

kolasión: n. fast (food) (*ayunar*). **agkolasion.** v. to fast.

kulasísi: (coll.) n. mistress. (*babai*) **agkulasisi.** v. to have a mistress. [Tag. *kulasisì*]

kúlat: n. bracket fungi; var. of *kúdad*. [Tag. *kabuté, kulat*]

kuláta: (Sp. *culata*: rifle butt) n. butt of a rifle. **kulataen.** v. to hit with the butt of a rifle. **Nangkulata kaniak idi tiempo ti gubat.** He hit me with the butt of his rifle during the war.

kulatlát: kulatlatan. v. to peel off; skin, flay. **nakulatlatan.** a. peeled, skinned; flayed. [Tag. *balát*]

kulay-óng: n. depression in the flank of a quadruped; emaciation. **mangulay-ong.** v. to be famished (said of animals with emaciated stomachs); emaciated. **nakakulay-ong, kulay-ongan.** *a.* emaciated. **nangulay-ong a pingping.** emaciated cheeks. **Nasaysayaat a mangulay-ong ti ayup ngem ti agpukaw lattan a kasla asuk iti waywayan.** An emaciated animal is better than a loose animal that is lost like smoke. [Knk. *kulay-óng* = breast, chest of the water buffalo]

kulbá: (Sp. *curva*: curve) n. wooden brace placed on the upper side of a plow's beam at the curve where the beam is connected with the landslide.

kulbén: kulkulben. n. large basket with a square bottom and round rim.

kulbét: nakulbet. a. tough (meat); fibrous (wood). **kumulbet.** v. to become tough and chewy (boiled meat, etc.) (*kerdat*). **nakulbet a gasat.** tough luck. [Tag. *kunat*]

kulbó: ikulbo. v. to do inaccurately, unreliably; endanger; betray; deceive; cheat. **manangikulbo.** v. to be false, deceitful (*kusit; liput*). [Tag. *dayà*]

kulbóng: n. kind of deep chest made of bark for tobacco leaves.

kuldém: agkuldem. v. to sleep with the eyes open.

kuldiás: n. deflection; slight (deflected) wound, scrape. **agkuldias.** v. to deflect; bounce off (*kudias*). [Tag. *lihís*]

kuldíng: n. light touch. (*sagid, salgid*) **kuldingen.** v. to touch lightly (a part of the body). **Adda nakulding iti kaunggak.** *exp.* denoting sensitive feeling inside (i.e. upon remembering pleasant memories, etc.). **Nakulding ti barukongko.** My heart (*lit.* chest) was touched. [Tag. *kalabít*]

kuldít: kuldíten. v. to tap someone lightly with the fingers.

kulébra: (Sp. *culebra*: snake) n. skin disease characterized by fever and spreading dark spots; ringworm. (*kúrad*) **agkulebra**. v. to be afflicted with the *kulebra* disease.

kolehiála: n. female college student.

koléhio: (Sp. *colegio*: college) n. college; boarding home. **agkolehio**. v. to go to college.

kolékta: (Sp. *colecta*: collection) n. church collection; collection. **kolektaen**. v. to collect.

koleksionísta: (Sp. *coleccionista*: collector) n. collector.

kolékta: (Sp. *colecta*) n. collection (*singir*). **kolektor**. n. collector. **kolektibista**. n. collectivist.

kolehiádo: (Sp. *colegiado*: collegiate) a. collegiate, college level.

kulélat: a. slow moving.

kuléleng: (*slang*) a. crazy, insane.

kulemlém: n. variety of rice with olive kernel.

kuléng₁: **nakulengkuleng**. a. crumpled; wrinkled. (*kuretret*) **kulengen**. v. to crumple; wrinkle. **Kasla nakulengkuleng a papel ti luganda**. Their car is like crumpled paper.

kuléng₂: **maikuleng**. v. to be shocked, speechless, stunned. (*kigtot*) **maikulkuleng**. v. to do without concentrating; to be out of one's mind when doing.

kulengléng: **agkulengleng**. v. to be idle; sit around and do nothing. (*sadut*; *bantot*; *lunakol*; *tamleg*; *ballog*)

kulép: n. almond eyes with folded-in eyelids. (*kusipét*)

kólera: (Sp. *cólera*: cholera) n. cholera. **makolera**. v. to have cholera, suffer from cholera.

kuleráw: n. kind of edible fish with barbells.

koleró: (Tagalog also) n. counterfeit money.

kulét: **ikulet**. v. to finish off; spend all; consume everything. **Ikuletmo amin ta sida**. Finish off all that fish.

kuléta: (Sp. *coleta*: small tail) n. small tail or queue of hair; braided hair of a *matador*; short addition to a letter.

kolgadóra: (Sp. *colgadura*: hangings) n. hangings.

kuliáp: n. drinking straw; cigar holder. (*kulisep*) **kuliapen**. v. to drink using a straw. [Tag. *panghithít*]

kuliápis: a. empty (ears of rice, beans, etc.).

koliár: (Sp. *collar*: necklace) n. collar; necklace.

kuliáw: n. jaundice. **agkuliaw**. v. to have jaundice.

kulibagtít: **agkulibagtit**. v. to jerk; make an instant motion. (*kulibagtóng*)

kulibagtóng: n. jerking movement. **Adda agkulkulibagtong nga paltat 'toy barukongko**. *exp*. denoting strong, excited feelings (*lit*: I have frisking catfish in my chest). **Agkulkuli-**

bagtong toy pusok a makipagrikna kenka. My heart heaves to sympathize with you.

kulibangbáng: n. butterfly; moth; butterfly fish; female star, actress; (*coll*.). politician who frequently changes his political party. **kulkulibangbang**. n. species of tree with sour leaves (*alibangbang*). [Bon. *kopap-ey*, Ibg. *kulivabbang*, Itg. *ambubulaw*, Ivt. *kudibábang*, Kal. *kullapoy*, Knk. *pakpakiáw*, *maymay-á*, Kpm. *mariposa*, Png. *kompápey*, Tag. *paroparó*]

kulíbaw: **ikulibaw**. v. to smuggle.

kulidabdáb: **agkulidabdab**. v. to turn white (said of the eyes of dying persons). (*kudaap*)

kulidagdág: **agkulkulidagdag**. v. to tremble the body (in agony).

koliér(a): (Sp. *collera*: collar) n. animal collar, usually with bells attached.

kuliglíg: n. small motorized vehicle used in plowing (*pugpog*). **agkuliglig**. v. to use a *kuliglig*, ride a *kuliglig*. [Tag. *kuliglíg* = cicada]

kulikák: n. fake coin; (reg.) prostitute. [Tag. *peke* (Sp.)]

kulikóg: n. hollow; concavity; counterfeit money; refusal, denial; fat, unresistant body. **kulikugen**. v. to deny a former utterance.

kulíkol: n. tubelike instrument used by toothless people to grind their *mamaén*.

kulíli: n. fire saw; person who goes to and fro. **kulilien**. v. to bore a hole; cause friction. [Tag. *lagarì*]

kulilíng: n. small bell (*kililing*). **agkuliling**. v. to ring.

kulimáw: n. snake, serpent. (*uleg*)

kulimbába: see *kalumbába*.

kulimbásag: n. restlessness; hustle and bustle. (*alimbaságen*)

kulimbatóg: n. throb, palpitation; loud sound. **agkulimbatog**. v. to throb, palpitate strongly.

kulimbítin: **agkulimbitin**. v. to dangle, hang on something with the hands. **kulimbitinen**. v. to dangle something; cause to dangle.

kulimpág: n. clanking noise, scraping sound of wood and iron.

kuliníkon: **agkulinikon**. v. to coil up (snakes) (*kunikon*). [Tag. *pulupot, ikid*]

kulintabá: n. firefly, glowworm. (*kulalanti*) **agkulintaba**. v. to glow; radiate; (fig.) to see stars before blacking out (*siamsiam*). **Ti tao kas kulintaba, ngumato, bumaba**. Man is like a firefly, he soars and dives. [Bon. *kolkoldong*, Png. *kankánti*, Tag. *alitaptáp*]

kulintáng: n. kind of musical instrument.

kulintípay: n. conch, piece of shell used for window glass; mollusk the conch comes from. **mangulintipay**. v. to become light and translucent. **Impanalbaagna nga inrikep ti kulintipay a tawa.** He slammed the *kulintipay* window shut.

kulintítin: kulintitinen. v. to lift up, hold up in the air.

kúling: n. kind of *paráw* propelled by oars.

kulinglíng: kulinglingen. v. to do on all sides; scrutinize (*pulingling*). [Tag. *butingtíng*]

kulípag: nakulipag. a. dehydrated, dried up; with half-filled ears (rice); devoid of nutrients.

kulipagpág: agkulipagpag. v. to flutter (birds being killed); shake frantically. **Naregreg ti alotiit itay nagkulipagpagak.** The lizard fell off me when I shook frantically. [Tag. *palág*]

koliplór: (Sp. *coliflor*: cauliflower) n. cauliflower.

kulíreng: n. kind of speckled black and white freshwater fish.

koliséo: (Sp. *coliseo*) n. coliseum.

kulísep: n. drinking straw. (*kuliap*)

kulísip: n. var. of *kulisep*: drinking straw; cigar holder. [Tag. *panghithít*]

kulislís: kulislisan. v. to scratch. **nakulislisan.** a. scratched; lined. [Tag. *kalmót, gasgás*]

kúlit: kulitan. v. to peel, decorticate (sugarcane); bite off the rind of sugarcane.

kulít: (obs.) n. diacritical mark of the ancient Ilokano alphabet that represented vowels; above the letter, it represented the sounds now denoted by the letters *e* or *i*, and below, the sounds now denoted by *o* or *u*. **bassít kulít.** a little, a bit. **sangkakulit.** a little bit.

kulitadtád: n. jerking movement of animals on the verge of death. (*kuripaspas, bugsot*) **agkulitadtad.** v. to twitch in agony; convulse; flutter; squirm in pain.

kulitangtáng: *n.* tolling of bells. **agkulitangtáng.** *v.* to toll (bells).

kulitiágang: n. mountain person, person from the uplands, member of one of the various mountain tribes of the Cordilleras.

kulitiáno: var. of *kulitiagang*: mountain person.

kolítis: (Sp. *colitis*) n. colitis; amaranth.

kuliwengwéng: agkuliwengweng. v. to idle; be lazy (*kulengleng*). [Tag. *bulakból*]

kulkól: agkulkol. v. to litigate. **kulkulan.** v. to alarm, disturb; tumult; entangle. **makulkulan.** v. to be disturbed, upset, entangled. **nakulkol.** a. entangled, intertwined; troubled. **nakulkulisip.** a. troubling the mind, mentally agitated.

kulkulanióg: n. cartilage.

kulláap: makullaapan. v. to dim; become overcast; become dull, stupid; to lose clear vision. **Nakullaapan ti panunotna.** His thoughts were unclear. [Tag. *labô, lamlám; kulimlím*]

kullaási: kulkullaasi. n. *Commelina nudiflora*, spiderworts.

kulláaw: n. a kind of owl whose night cry is considered a bad omen (*puek*). **Addaytan ti kullaaw a mulagatna.** There's his owl stare. **Kuna dagiti lallakay a no aguni dagiti kullaaw iti sardam wenno parbangon, adda sakit wenno didigra a sumangbay.** The old men say that if the owls sound in the evening or at dawn, sickness or catastrophe is approaching. [Bon. *kóop*, Ivt. *bantuluk*, Knk. *kup*, Png. *kolayot*, Tag. *kuwago* (Sp.); Knk. *kulaaw* = hornbill]

kullabót: *var.* of *kulabbét*: wrinkled, withered (*kuretret; kurayappet*).

kullálong: kullalongen. v. to lift up by both hands and feet.

kullangán: n. *Tylophora sp.* twining vines used in rope making.

kullaóng: n. dugout; depression in the ground. (*lukkaong*)

kullapít: n. young fruit; young pod of the *damortís*; a. very thin (*kuttong*). **agkullapit.** v. to become thin; to fail to develop fully. **Napintas uray no adda kulkullapitna gapu ngata iti panagkurkurangda iti taraon.** She is pretty although she is a bit thin, probably because of their lack of food. [Tag. *patpát*]

kullawít: (obs.) **agkullawit.** v. to knock the head of someone who is asleep sitting.

kulláyaw: agkullayaw. v. to be frightened all of a sudden, gasp when startled. **Kellaat a nagkullayaw idi kinitana ti relosna.** He suddenly gasped when he saw his watch. [Tag. *kabá*]

kulláyot: n. whip. (*baut*) **nakullayot, kummullayot.** a. slim, slender. **kullayuten.** v. to whip. [Tag. *palò, haplít*]

kulló: kullokullo. n. kind of fruit.

kulluób: n. wall-less shed. **makulluob.** v. to be surrounded; encased; enclosed. **Tunggal malpas a sumala, mapan makitungtong iti kulluob.** Every time he is finished dancing, he goes to converse in the wall-less shed.

kullúong: n. wooden trough used to feed pigs; hollowed-out log used to pound rice grains. [Bon. *atotong*, Kal. *atatúng*, Tag. *sabsaban* (trough)]

kullót: kullokullot. n. *Urena lobata*, shrubby plant with pink flowers.

kulmán: n. petromax, kerosene gas.

kulmég: n. introvert; position of head resting or arms (on a desk). **agkulmeg.** v. to crouch down, be huddled up; cower. (*kul-ób*)

kuluág: *var.* of *kudduág*: hurl, throw, shove off.

kul-ób: agkul-ob. v. to bend toward the ground, prostrate (*rukob; ruknoy*); crouch over (a computer) (*kulmeg*). **No di nakapagkul-ob, nadugolan la ketdi ti pultakna.** If he didn't happen to bend down, his bald head would have been struck. [Tag. *patirapâ*]

kúlod: n. colored, woven sleeping mat.

kul-ód: *var.* of *kolbó*: cheat, deceive.

kulóg: kulugen. v. to shake contents. **agkulogkulog.** v. to shake repeatedly (e.g. the contents of a hollow vessel). [Tag. *kulóg* = thunder]

kolokár: (Sp. *colocar*: place) **naikolokar.** a. placed; assigned.

kulúkol₁: n. auger; drill (*kutúkut*). **kulukulen.** v. to bore a hole with an auger. [Tag. *balibol*]

kulúkol₂: n. irrigation canal (*banáwang*).

kolumbína: (Sp. *columbina*) *n.* columbine, species of flowering plant.

kulumbítin: *var.* of *kalumbitin*: hang, cling.

kolúmna: (Sp. *columna*: column) n. newspaper column. **kolumnista.** n. columnist.

kulúmpio: (Sp. *columpio*: rocking chair) n. rocking chair; swinging chair.

kolón: (Sp. *colón*: colon) n. colon. **semikolon.** n. semicolon.

kulunákol: n. very slow movement; slothful movement.

kolónia: (Sp. *colonia*: colony) n. colony.

kolonisádo: (Sp. *colonizado*: colonized) a. colonized.

kolóno: (Sp. *colono*: colonist) n. colonist.

kulóng₁: ikulong, kulungen. v. to imprison, confine. (*ipupok*) **kulungan.** n. cage; jail. **Iti kulungan, dida pakanen, painumen ken paturogen dagiti baludda.** In prison, they don't feed or let their inmates drink or sleep.

kulóng₂: kulongkulong. n. Adam's apple.

kul-óng: var. of *kulluong*: hollowed-out log used for pounding rice grains, trough.

kulúong: see *kulluong*: trough (for feeding pigs); crib.

kolór: (Sp. *color*: color) n. color. (*maris*) **koloran.** v. to color.

koloránte: (Sp. *colorante*: coloring) n. coloring, food coloring.

kolordapó: [*kolor* + *dapó*] a. ash gray, ashen colored. (*uspák*)

koloréte: (Sp. *colorete*: rouge) n. rouge.

kolórum: *n.* name given to rebels who fought the established government in Tayug, Pangasinan during the Commonwealth regime; a. illegal; unauthorized. [Tag. *kulurom*]

kulós: n. brook, creek. (*waig*)

kulót: n. curl; Negrito; kind of edible seaweed; variety of late *diket* rice; a. curly; kinky. **kuloten.** v. to curl. **agpakulot.** v. to have a perm (curl the hair). **mangngulot.** n. beautician; hairdresser. [Ibg. *kuluq*, Ifg. *nakilkili*, Isi.

nakulíku, Ivt. *makaden*, Kal. *kullong*, Png. *kólot*, Kpm., Tag. *kulót*]

kúlpa: (Sp. *culpa*: blame) n. blame (*basol*).

kulpá: agkulpa. v. to calm down; cease. **Agdanagda gapu iti panagkulpa ti ekonomia.** They are worrying because of the slow economy. [Tag. *kasalanan*]

kulpí: *n.* fold. **kulpien.** v. to fold. (*kupin*) **agkulpi.** v. to fold up (oneself). [Tag. *lupî*]

kultáb: n. poorly cut hair. (*gutab, sarawsaw*) **kultaban.** v. to give an incomplete haircut.

kultáp: n. small bald spot in hair (*pultak*). **kultapkultap.** a. having bald spots. **Apay a di nakultapan ti alipusposna kas iti kultap ti kimmastila a padi?** Why doesn't his whorl go bald like the bald heads of the Spanish priests?

kultibádo: (Sp. *cultivado*: cultivated) a. cultivated. **kultibasion.** n. cultivation.

kultó: (Sp. *culto*: cult) n. cult; religious ceremony among certain sects. **makikulto.** v. to attend a religious ceremony. **libre kulto.** religious liberty.

kultóng: agkultong. v. to poll; cut the tops of plants. (*uggot*)

kultóp: a. with a very small penis.

kultúra: (Sp. *cultura*: culture) n. culture. (*kannawidan*)

koltsón: (Sp. *colchón*: mattress) n. mattress. (*kudson*)

kóma: (Sp. *coma*: comma) n. comma.

kumá, komá: particle expressing conditional, optative or hypothetical (contrary to fact) situations. **Sápay kuma.** I hope so. **ania kuma.** so what. **Imbagaka kuma.** *exp.* I should have told you. **No ammok la kuma idi ti ammok itan, saanka kuma a natay.** If only I knew then what I know now, you wouldn't have died. **Ania kuma no adda suratmo?** So what if you have a letter? **Adda kuma ipudnok kadakayo.** I have something to confess to you. **Bayat ti panangruotna iti talonna, ikararagna a di kuma agpigsa ti bagio iti purokda.** While he was cutting the grass of his field, he prayed for the storm not to be strong in their village. **Pangaasim ta isardengmo kuman ti panggepmo.** Please stop your plan. [Tag. *sana*]

komádre: (Sp. *comadre*: fellow godmother; midwife) n. term of address used between the mother of a godchild and the godmother (one's female sponsor at a baptism); friendly term of address for close social peer (used by women). (*ina ti buniag*)

komadróna: (Sp. *comadrona*: midwife) n. midwife (usually referring to illegal abortion-performing midwives). (*partera*)

kúman: n. farming soil; ground. **agkuman.** v. to clear land for cultivation.

komandánsia: (Sp. *comandancia*: command; commander's office) *n.* command; commander's office. **komandansia-probisional.** *n.* provisional command.

komandánte: (Sp. *comandante*: commander; playmaster) n. comedy; long Ilocano play combining music and poetry with the Christians and Muslims as cast; commandant, high-ranking officer.

kumara-: *prefix.* forms intransitive frequentative verbs. **kumarasubli.** He continually comes back.

komáre: (pl. *kokomare*) n. term of address for *komadres*.

kúmaw: n. imaginary boogeyman monster in Ilocano mythology with the following forms: evil kidnapper; dragon responsible for sudden death; ogre that sacrifices children. **nakumawan.** a. ruined, devastated; completely depopulated.

kumbábuy: n. pillbug, sawbug. (*babuybábuy*)

kombáte: (Sp. *combate*) n. combat.

kumbató: (Sp. *con*: with + *bato*: stone) n. children's hopscotch-type game consisting of throwing a stone and jumping around four squares. **agkumbato.** v. to play *kumbato*.

kombatséros: n. band consisting of about five players on strings with a cymbal and a rattle. (*kombo*)

kumbawá: (f. Japanese *komban wa*: good evening) **agkumbawa.** v. to bow.

kombeniénte: (Sp. *conveniente*) a. convenient, opportune.

kombénio: (Sp. *convenio*: agreement, convention) n. agreement. (*tulag*)

kombensér: (Sp. *convencer*: convince) **agkombenser.** v. to convince. **kombensido.** a. convinced.

kombensión: (Sp. *convención*: convention) n. convention. **agkombension.** v. to have a convention.

kombensír: *var.* of *kombenser*: convince.

kombénto: (Sp. *convento*: convent) n. convent; rectory.

kombentuál: (Sp. *conventual*: monastic) n. retired priest or nun. **agkombentual.** v. to live in seclusion.

kombertír: (Sp. *convertir*: convert) **agkombertir.** v. to change one's mind. **kombertiren.** v. to convert.

kumbét: (f. *kebbet*) v. to shrink; contract; wrinkle up (by losing liquid while cooking).

kumbidá(r): (Sp. *convidar*: invite) *n.* invitation. **agkumbida.** v. to invite. **kumbidados.** n. invited guests. (*bisita*) **Kumbidarenka la kuma iti maminsan.** I should invite you one time.

kombiéne: (Sp. *conviene*: fit, agree) a. proper, appropriate. **naikombiene.** *a.* adapted to.

kombinár: (Sp. *combinar*) **kombinaren.** v. to combine, join; mix drinks.

kombinasión: (Sp. *combinación*: combination) n. combination.

kumbinsído: (Sp. *convencido*: convinced) *a.* convinced.

kumbíte: (Sp. *convite*: banquet) n. special party that requires an invitation.

kombó: n. var. of *kombatseros*. **kumombo-kombo.** v. to become inflated; puff up; spread (itch, rash).

kombulsión: (Sp. *convulsión*) n. convulsion.

kombóy: (Eng.) n. convoy. **agkomboy.** v. to travel in a convoy.

komédia: (Sp. *comedia*: comedy) n. comedy; musical play.

komediánte: (Sp. *comediante*: comedian) n. comedian; player.

komedór: (Sp. *comedor*: dining room) n. dining room. (*panganan*)

kumég: *var.* of *kulmeg*: hide, cower; stay in one's room. **agkumeg.** v. to stay indoors, to stay in one's room, to stay at home; hide, cower. **Kellaat a nagkumeg a bulon ti pannakapilko dagiti tumengna.** He instantly cowered as his knees bent. **Saan a nasken nga ikumegmo ti kinamanagbabainmo.** It is not necessary for you to stay home out of shyness.

kúmel: *a.* crumpled, wrinkled (*kuléng*). **Insuotna ti kumel a polona.** He put on his wrinkled polo shirt.

kumél: **nakumel.** a. slow, sluggish; cowardly; fainthearted. **agkumel.** v. to work slow and lazily. [Tag. *batugan*]

komentário: (Sp. *comentario*: commentary) n. commentary, comment; criticism.

komentarísta: (Sp. *comentarista*: commentator) n. commentator.

kúmer: **agkukumer.** v. to walk slowly; to be indisposed.

komér: (Sp. *comer*: eat) *excl.* Time to eat! **klabo-de-komer.** *n.* clove (spice).

komersiánte: (Sp. *comerciante*: merchant) n. merchant. (*tagilako*)

komérsio: (Sp. *comercio*: trade, business) n. business (*pagsapulan*, *aramid*); trade. **agkomersio.** v. to trade, engage in business. **ikomersio.** v. to invest. [Tag. *kalakalan*]

kométa: (Sp. *cometa*: comet) n. comet.

komída: (Sp. *comida*: meal) n. meal (*kanén, pannangán*); cuisine, food. **libre komida.** n. free board.

kómik(o): (Sp. *cómico*: funny) a. funny. (*nakakatkatawa, nakaang-angáw*)

kumíkom: makumikom. a. busy, occupied. **pakakumikoman.** *n.* something that keeps one busy; worries. **Di makaturpos iti panagadalda gapu iti adu a pakakumikomanda.** They can't graduate because of the many things keeping them busy.

komílias: (Sp. *comillas*: quotation marks) n. quotation marks.

kumíno: (Sp. *comino*: cumin) n. cumin, species of small plant with an aromatic, seed-like fruit.

kumintáng: (Tag. *kumintang*: battle songs of ancient *Kumintang* warriors) *n.* swinging the arms in dancing; native dance in which arms are swung. **agkumintang.** v. to swing the arms in dancing (*gumintang*).

komisária: (Sp. *comisaria*: commissary) n. commissary.

komisión: (Sp. *comisión*: commission) n. commission. **komisionado.** a. commissioner, agent; person in charge of a public department; *a.* commissioned. **komisionista.** n. commission agent.

kumít₁: kumitan. v. to shield, guard, defend; look after; take care of. **ikumit.** v. to entrust, put in charge. [Tag. *ipagkatiwalà* (entrust)]

kumít₂: kinumit. n. kind of cloth with twilled basketwork texture.

komité: (Sp. *comité*: committee) n. committee.

komitíba: (Sp. *comitiva*: retinue) *n.* retinue.

kumléb: (f. *kelleb*) v. to lie on one's stomach. **kumkumlebka latta dita arubayan ti agong-mo.** *exp.* you never get out of the house.

kumlíing: (f. *kilíng*) *v.* to ring; tinkle; jingle.

kummó: n. kind of edible marine crab.

kúmna: (f. *kenna*) v. to affect, take effect; attack; fall into a trap.

kumníit: (f. *kinit*) *v.* to grow stunted.

kómo: (Sp. *como*: since, because, inasmuch) prep. since, as.

komulgár: (Sp. *comulgar*: receive communion) *n.* receiving communion. **agkomulgar.** v. to receive communion.

kúmon: kumunen. v. to crumple; improperly fold. (*gelgel; kuleng; kunes; lunes*) **nakumon-kumon.** a. crumpled; improperly folded. [Tag. *gusót*]

kumón: n. toilet; outhouse. (*kasilyas, inodoro*)

komún: (Sp. *común*: common) a. common. **makikomun.** v. to join a group. **komun de dos.** two-seater.

komunál: (Sp. *comunal*: communal) n. land owned by the community; common property (of heirs).

komunidád: (Sp. *comunidad*: community) n. community.

komunión: (Sp. *comunión*) *n.* communion.

komunísmo: (Sp. *comunismo*: communism) n. communism.

komunísta: (Sp. *comunista*: communist) n. communist.

kumustá: (Sp. *cómo está*: How are you?) *interrog.* used in asking condition of a person. **Kumustaka?** Hello; How are you? **agkumusta.** v. to send regards. **agpakumusta.** v. to send regards through someone else; have someone else greet a third party on one's behalf. **kumustaen.** v. to greet; hail; inquire about someone's well being. **pakumustaan.** *v.* to extend regards to someone. **Kumusta ti gasatmo 'di rabii?** How was your luck last night?

kúmut: agkumut. v. to wrap oneself completely in a blanket. **ikumut.** v. to use to wrap oneself in. **kumutan.** *v.* to cover entirely. **sikukumot.** *a.* covered; (*fig.*) engulfed. [Png. *kómot*, Tag. *kumot*]

kompádre: (Sp. *compadre*: fellow godfather, pl. *kokompadre*) n. vocative term for one's godfather, male sponsor at a wedding; vocative term for one's social peer (used among males). (*ama ti bunyag, ninong*)

kompaktoderétro: (Sp.) n. mortgage. (*salda*)

kompánia: (Sp. *compaña*) *n.* company; common pipe tobacco. **sangkakompania.** one company.

kompaniam(i)énto: (Sp. *acompañamiento*) *n.* musical accompaniment.

kompaniár: (Sp. *acompañar*) **agkompaniar.** *v.* to accompany (with a musical instrument). (*pasakalie*)

kompaniéro: (Sp. *compañero*: companion) n. companion; partner; friend. (*kadua*) (fem: *kompaniéra*)

kompáng: *n.* container for *saíngan*; joint venture; receptacle used by silversmiths to hold metals to be melted. **agkukumpang.** v. to share (costs); form a business partnership. (*palwagan*)

komparár: (Sp. *comparar*) **ikomparar.** *v.* to compare.

kompáre: var. of *kompadre*: vocative term for godfather. (*ama ti bunyag*)

kompársa: n. string band.

kumpás: (Sp. *compas*: rhythm; compass) n. compass; rhythm; compatibility; harmony; gesticulation, expressive motion. **agkumpas.** v. to keep rhythm; harmonize; beat time; be well

matched (couple). **ikumpas**. *v*. to keep to the rhythm; synchronize. **maikumpas**. *v*. to be synchronized. **kontra-kumpas**. out of rhythm. **Kumkumpasanna gayam ti kanta**. She is following the rhythm of the song.
kompatrióta: (Sp. *compatriota*) *n*. countryman, fellow citizen (*kailian*).
kumpáy: n. sickle with toothed blade. **kumpayen**. v. to cut with a sickle. **Nabaknang man wenno napanglaw, kumpayen ni patay**. Whether rich or poor, death will strike (with a sickle). [Png. *kómpay*, *kárit*, Tag. *lilik*]
kumpéng: **agkumpeng**. v. to stop raining. (*sirnaat*)
komperénsia: (Sp. *conferencia*: conference) n. conference; meeting. **makikomperensia**. v. to join a conference; confer with (*pannakisao*). **ikomperensia**. *v*. to confer on, discuss at a meeting.
kompesár: (Sp. *confesar*) **agkompesar**. *v*. to confess sins. **pagkompesaran**. *n*. confessional box. **mangompesar**. *v*. to hear confessions.
kumpés: (f. *keppes*) *v*. to shrink.
kompesión: (Sp. *confesión*: confession) n. confession. **kompesionario**. n. confession booth, confessional. **kompesor**. n. confessor.
kumpét: (f. *kapet*) v. to adhere; stick to; hold. (*kidkid*; *dumket*; *kulamat*; *luyak*; *pigket*) **kumpet a kasla tekka**. v. to cling on tight like a lizard; hold on tightly.
kompeténsia: (Sp. *competencia*: competition) n. competition; rivalry.
kompeténte: (Sp. *competente*: competent) a. competent, apt; able.
kompiánsa: (Sp. *confianza*: confidence) n. confidence, trust (*talék*). **agkompiansa**. *v*. to trust.
kumpiáng: n. cymbal. (*piangpiáng*) **kumpiangen**. v. to strike with a cymbal.
kumpiár: (Sp. *confiar*) **agkumpiar**. *v*. to rely on; have confidence in. **Nagkumpiarda nga agassawa**. The married couple relied on each other.
kumpíl: **nakumpil**. a. folded; bent.
kompilasión: (Sp. *compilación*: compilation) n. compilation. **kompilado**. a. compiled.
kompírma: (Sp. *confirmar*) **agkompirma**. *v*. to receive confirmation (religious ceremony). **kompirmasion**. *n*. confirmation.
kompiskádo: (Sp. *confiscado*: confiscated) a. confiscated. **kompiskasion**. n. confiscation.
kumpiskár: (Sp. *confiscar*: confiscate) **kumpiskaren**. *v*. to confiscate. **Wagas dayta a mangkumpiskar iti wayawayana agingga a malpas ti kaso**. That's a way to take away his freedom until the case is finished.

kumpítis: (Sp. *confites*: confetti) n. *Clitorea ternatea*, the *samsampíng* vine; confetti.
kómple: (Sp. *cumplir*: fulfill) **agkumple**. v. to be discharged from the army after having served the required time.
kompleánio: (Sp. *cumpleaño*: birthday) n. birthday. (*kasangay*)
kompléto: (Sp. *completo*: complete) a. complete, whole. (*sibubukél*) **kompletuen**. v. to complete, finish. **nakakompleto**. *a*. finished, completed, through with.
komplikádo: (Sp. *complicado*: complicated) a. complicated.
komplikasión: (Sp. *complicacción*: complication) n. complication. (*parikút*)
komplontádo: (Sp. *confrontado*) **ikomplontado**. *v*. to compare; check on.
kumplót: (Sp. *complot*: plot) **agkumplot**. v. to connive to do; conspire; plot. **pannakikumplot**. *n*. conspiracy.
kumpóg: **makikumpog**. *v*. to join, associate; get together, mix socially in a crowd (*ummóng*).
komponénte: (Sp. *componente*) *n*. component.
komponér: (Sp. *componer*: compose) **agkomponer**. v. to arrange, prepare (a table, etc.).
kompórme: (Sp. *conforme*: conforming) adv. whatever, in conformity with; agreeable. **komporme ti kayatmo**. whatever you want.
kompormidád: (Sp. *conformidad*: conformity) n. conformity; agreeableness.
kompositór: (Sp. *compositor*) *n*. composer in music; typesetter.
komputasión: (Sp. *computación*) *n*. computation.
kómpra: (Sp. *comprar*: buy) **kompraen**. v. to buy, purchase. (*gatang*) **agkompra**. v. to buy in bulk. **ipakompra**. *v*. to sell in bulk.
komprabénta: (Sp. *compraventa*: buying and selling) n. bargain sale.
kompradór: (Sp. *comprador*: buyer) n. buyer; trader, merchant. (*aggatgátang*)
kompramiénto: (Sp. *compramiento*: buying) n. purchase contract.
komprangkésa: (Sp. *con franqueza*) *a*. frank, sincere.
komprobánte: (Sp. *comprobante*: proof; certificate) n. voucher; proof (in printing).
komprometér: (Sp. *comprometer*: compromise; bind, put under obligation) **makikomprometer**. v. to take part in, participate. **maikomprometer**. *v*. to be involved in.
komprometído: (Sp. *comprometido*: compromised; bound) a. engaged, affianced; pledged; placed in a compromising situation; implicated, involved.

kompromíso: (Sp. *compromiso*: compromise) n. compromise; appointment; engagement; agreement.

komprontár: (Sp. *confrontar*: compare; confront) **agkomprontar.** *v.* to be equal, the same. **ikomprontar.** *v.* to adjust, set one's watch. **komprontasion.** *n.* confrontation.

kumráang: (f. *kerraang*) v. to dry. (*maga, kumriit*)

kumrét: (f. *kerret*) v. to wrinkle; pucker up.

kumríit: (f. *kirriit*) v. to dry in the sun. **kumriit ti balor.** v. to lower in price.

kumsén: (f. *kessen*) v. to shrink; contract.

kumsí: (obs.) **nakomsi.** a. soft, smooth. (*nalamúyot; nalukneng*)

kumsiál: (f. *kissial*) v. to harden. (*tumangkén*)

kumsíw: (f. *kissiw*) v. to warp (timber); to suffer from cramps.

kumtát: (f. *kettat*) v. to recoil; rebound; ricochet, deflect.

kumtér: **kumkumter.** v. to shake from the cold; to dip meat in vinegar.

kon: (Sp. *con*: with) with, using, holding. **kon singsing.** with a ring. **kon bandera.** holding a flag. **kon de.** used to indicate some sort of negative association (pretense or inappropriateness), see also *kunsi-*. May be spelled *konde* or *konde-*. **kon de lualo, uray no demonionto met laeng.** He keeps praying, although he will nevertheless become a devil again. **kon de alahas.** wearing jewels unnecessarily or too extravagantly. **kon de tsinelas.** wearing slippers on an inappropriate occasion. **kon de sobre.** wrapped unnecessarily in an envelope (small amount of money given back as a friendly loan). **Kondesaoka.** You keep talking (but you don't know what you're talking about).

kúna: (Sp. *cuna*: cradle) n. rattan crib, cradle.

kuná: v. (transitive, takes -*ko* enclitic pronouns): to say (*baga*; *sao*); utter; believe; suppose; mean. (*perf. kinuna*). **ikuna.** v. to do like this (using gestures) **pakpakuna.** v. to pretend; talk randomly. **aginkukuna.** v. to pretend, feign; counterfeit. **managinkukuna.** *a.* pretentious; *n.* hypocrite. **panaginkukuna.** *n.* pretension; hypocrisy. **Panagkunak.** What I'm saying. **pakpakuna.** v. to pretend; talk in trifles. **managinkukuna.** a. pretentious; selfish; greedy. **pagkukuna.** n. saying; proverb. **pagkunaan.** n. cause or source of something being said; remark; comment; criticism. **sangkakuna.** *v.* to often say. **Kunak no.** I thought that. **Adda pagkunaanda kenka.** They have something against you. **Ania ti makunayo?** What do you think? **Awanan panaginkukuna iti panagpa-**

bus-oyna. There was no pretense in what she was giving out. [Ibg. *kagiyen*, Ivt. *vatahen*, Knk. *kaná*, Png. *kuan*, *baga*, Kpm., Tag. *sabi*]

kunáil: n. slow movement (of sick persons, etc.) **di makakunail.** v. cannot move. **Awaganmi iti "agkukutel" ta agkakapsut ngamin wenno di makakunail.** We call him 'leper' because he is weak and can hardly move.

kundápis: a. with hollow, sunken cheeks (said of skinny persons).

konde-: see under *kon*.

kónde: (Sp. *conde*: count) n. count. **rosa konde.** n. species of large pink rose.

kondenár: (Sp. *condenar*: condemn) **kondenaren.** v. to condemn. **kondenado.** a. condemned.

kondensáda: (Sp. *condensada*: condensed) n. condensed (milk).

kondésa: (Sp. *condesa*: countess) n. countess.

kundídit: n. cicada. (*andídit*). **Naduayada iti singgit dagiti agsasinnungbat a kundidit.** They were lullabied to sleep by the sounds of the conversing cicadas. [Png. *andírit*, Tag. *kuliglíg*]

kundilíng: n. variety of rice with dark hull and white kernel.

kundíman: (Tag.) *n.* love song.

kondinár: var. of *kondenar*: condemn.

kundíng: n. bit; part; particle; speck.

kondisión: (Sp. *condición*: condition) n. condition; situation; circumstance; terms; prerequisite.

kondít: **konkondit.** a. with pretense, insincere. (*kuansit, agin-*)

kondúkta: (Sp. *conducta*) *n.* conduct, behavior. **konduktor.** *n.* conductor.

kundúyot: n. children's hand game.

konébre: *var.* of *punebre*: funeral march.

koného: (Sp. *conejo*: rabbit) n. rabbit. **kimmuneho a lapayag.** n. rabbit ears (said of people who are good at hearing what they are not meant to). [Kal. *labit* (Eng.)]

konektádo: (Sp. *conectado*: connected) a. connected. **koneksion.** n. connection.

kúnem: **nakunem.** a. overcast, cloudy; dull; weak minded (*kuyem*). [Tag. *kulimlím*]

kúneng: **nakuneng.** a. dull, slow-witted, ignorant, stupid. (stronger than *nakunem*) **kinakuneng.** n. ignorance. [Tag. *mangmáng*]

kunés: **kunesen.** v. to wrinkle, crumple. (*lunes; gelgel; kuleng; kumon*) **Nakunesna ti surat iti sakit ti nakemna.** He crumpled the letter because of his ill feelings.

kúnia: (Sp. *cuña*: wedge) n. wedge; mouthpiece of a musical instrument.

kuniáp: (obs.) **mapakpakuniap.** v. to lose one's bearings.

kúnig: n. *Circuma zedoaria*, plant that yields a yellow dye. **kunigan.** n. variety of awned rice with yellow hull. **kimmunig.** a. yellowish. **kayumanggi-kunig.** a. yellowish brown. **marakunig.** *a.* not yet fully developed (rice). [Tag. *diláw* (yellow)]

kuníkon: *n.* coil. **kunikunen.** v. to twist; wind; contort; curl; bend; roll; coil; n. small intestine of the chicken. **sangakunikon.** n. one coil of. **agkunikon.** v. to curl up (*kawikaw*). **nakunikon.** *a.* coiled, curled up. [Tag. *ikid*]

kuníng: n. kitten. (*kuting*).

konkísta: (Sp. *conquista*) *n.* conquest; **konkistado.** *a.* conquered. **konkistadór.** *n.* conqueror.

konkréto: (Sp. *concreto*: concrete) n. concrete.

kunnayét: *n.* slowpoke; weak, effeminate, or frail person (*kulannáy*); *a.* slow, slow moving. **Agkabaw ket ngatan ti sadut a kunnayet.** And maybe that lazy weakling is also senile.

kunníber: n. large mythological bird that carries off men; graft and corruption. **agkunniber.** v. to be corrupt; run away with the cash and goods; stroll; roam around; steal; cheat. **panagkunniber.** n. corruption. **kinukunniber.** n. corruption; graft. **managkunniber.** *a.* prone to cheating; corrupt; *n.* cheat; crook. **Intayab ti kunniber.** The *kunniber* monster flew away with it (said of losses). [Tag. *dayà* (cheat)]

kunnót: agkunnot. v. to breastfeed (*agpasuso*); suck (the thumb). **kunnoten.** *v.* to suck. **Ditoy ti pagkunnotan ti amin a talon ti purok.** Here is where all of the rice fields of the village get their nourishment (water supply). [Tag. *sipsíp*]

kóno: (Sp. *cono*: cone; hopper; Eng. *cone*) n. kind of rice mill.

kunúkon: n. pile. **kunukunan.** v. to pile; fill up with stones. **ikunukon.** v. to use to fill up a place with; to fill up a place with.

kúnol: agkunol, kumunolkunol. v. to squirm, wriggle. (*gulágol, galud-úd, kilíkil*) **Sumagmamano dagiti kumunolkunol iti kosina.** A few of them squirmed around in the kitchen. [Tag. *kiwal-kiwal*]

kunós: makunos. v. to be consumed completely. (*ibus*) **kunusen.** v. to consume completely.

kun-ós: var. of *kunos*: finish, consume completely. **Diak makun-os ti serbisiok.** I cannot finish my service.

konsagrádo: (Sp. *consagrado*) *a.* consecrated.

konsehál: (Sp. *consejal*: councilor) n. councilor. (*mamalakad*)

konsehála: (Sp. *consejala*: councilor) n. female councilor.

konského: (Sp. *consejo*: advice) n. advice; council. (*balakad, bagbaga*) **konsehero.** n. councilor. **ikonseho.** *v.* to council, advise.

konsekuénsia: (Sp. *consecuencia*) *n.* consequence. **Awatek dagiti konsekuensiana.** I will accept the consequences.

konsentidór: var. of *kunsintidor*.

konsentimiénto: (Sp. *consentimiento*: consent) n. consent; permission. (*palubos*)

konsentír: *var.* of *kunsintir*: consent.

konsépto: (Sp. *concepto*) n. concept.

konserbasión: (Sp. *conservación*) *n.* conservation.

konserbatório: (Sp. *conservatorio*) *n.* conservatory.

konserbatívo: (Sp. *conservativo*: conservative) a. conservative; old-fashioned.

konserbatório: (Sp. *conservatorio*: conservatory) n. conservatory, place for instruction in music.

konsertína: (Sp. *concertina*: concertina) n. concertina, accordion-type musical instrument.

konsi-: *prefix.* Denotes the action or referent expressed by the root is possessed or done insincerely or for inappropriate or negative reasons. Compare with the expression *kon de,* which is used only with nouns. **konsisapatos.** a. wearing shoes on an inappropriate occasion (to feel important, etc.). **konsi-Pranses.** a. speaking French incorrectly to boast intellectual prowess, etc. **konsibasa.** a. reading in front of others (to show off knowledge, although the reader may not understand what he is reading). **konsilugan.** riding unnecessarily in a car (a short distance, to boast wealth, etc.). **konsiardiod.** a. wearing excessive makeup, especially during an inappropriate occasion. Some of the terms using this prefix are used frequently and have lexicalized: **konsilamut.** n. party crasher, person who always accepts insincere invitations to eat, person who eats from house to house without feeling any shame.

konsibág: n. person who always carries around a purse, although it may be devoid of money.

konsiderár: (Sp. *considerar*: consider) **konsideraren.** v. to consider. (*usigen, panunoten*)

konsiderasión: (Sp. *consideración*: consideration) n. consideration.

konsiénsia: (Sp. *conciencia*: conscience) n. conscience. (*rikná, nákem*) **makakonsiensia, konsiensiaan.** v. to affect the conscience.

konsiérto: (Sp. *concierto*: concert) n. concert. **agkonsierto.** *v.* to give a concert. **agpakonsierto.** *v.* to go to a concert.

konsignatório: (Sp. *consignatorio*) n. consignee.

konsilámut: n. party crasher; person that accepts an insincere invitation to eat; person who freely eats from house to house with no shame.

konsílio: (Sp. *concilio*: council) n. council.

konsintidór: (Sp. *consentidor*: one who consents) n. consenter, person who consents with a bad deed, person of authority who allows someone to get away with something (i.e., parents letting their children go out late). **konsintidoren**. v. to consent to (a wrongdoing).

kunsintír: (Sp. *consentir*: consent) **kunsintiren**. v. to consent to. **Kinunsentir da papang ken mamang ti dakes nga aramidna**. Father and Mother consented to his bad act.

konsisinsál: n. reticular tissue under the skin of pigs, sheep, etc.

konsistório: (Sp. *consistorio*: consistory) n. consistory, high council.

kúnso: *conj.* even though; although; even with. (*uray no adda*) **kunso tsinelas, narugit ti sakana**. Even though she has slippers on, her feet are dirty.

kunsód: *a.* with a prominent posterior. (*duriri*)

konsuélo: (Sp. *consuelo*: consolation) n. consolation; comfort. **konsuelo de bobo**. n. consolation prize.

kónsul: (Sp. *consul*) n. consul.

konsuládo: (Sp. *consulado*: consulate) n. consulate.

konsolasión: (Sp. *consolación*: consolation) n. consolation. (*liwliwa*)

konsúlta: (Sp. *consulta*: consultation) n. consultation (with the doctor, etc.). **agpakonsulta**. v. to go for a consultation.

konsumído: (Sp. *consumido*: emaciated) a. worried, full of problems and anxiety, exasperated; consumed, used up.

konsumidór: (Sp. *consumidor*) n. consumer.

kunsumisión: (coll. Sp. *consumisión*: grievances) n. problems; cares; worries. [Tag. *kunsumisiyón*]

konsúmo: (Sp. *consumo*: consumption) n. consumption, rate of consumption.

konsonánte: (Sp. *consonante*: consonant) n. consonant; a. well suited, suitable, fit. **maikonsonante**. v. to go well with. (*maibagay*)

konsórte: (Sp. *consorte*: escort) n. escort.

konstabulário: (Eng.*) n. constabulary.

konstánte: (Sp. *constante*: constant) a. constant.

konstitusión: (Sp. *constitución*: constitution) n. constitution. [Tag. *saligang-batás*]

kónta: *var.* of *hunta*: junta, board, council.

kontadór: (Sp. *contador*: counter) n. gas meter; cashier; computer; accountant; teller; bookkeeper.

kontaduría: (Sp. *contaduría*: accountancy) n. accountancy.

kontaminádo: (Sp. *contaminado*) a. contaminated.

kuntár: (Sp. *contar*: count) n. count, numerical figure; estimate; estimation. **Eksakto manen ti kuntar dagiti sientista**. The scientists' figure is exact again.

konténto: (Sp. *contento*: happy) a. contented, happy. (*ragsak*)

kontestár: (Sp. *contestar*: answer) **kontestaren**. v. to protest against, contest.

kóntia: (Sp. *concha*: shell) n. mother-of-pearl shell.

kontinénte: (Sp. *continente*: continent) n. continent.

kontinuár: (Sp. *continuar*) **agkontinuar**. v. to continue (*tuloy*). **maikontinuar**. v. to be continued; extended (roads).

kuntíng: **kuntíng baláyang**. n. variety of yellow banana with many seeds.

kuntírad: n. steeple; tip of a pointed object. **nagkuntirad**. a. pointed. (*tirad*)

kontódo: (Sp. *con todo*: with all) with, complete with (having the quality or reference associated with the following word). **kontodo kumpas**. with perfect rhythm; with full enthusiasm. **kontodo bomba**. completely nude. **Kontodo bomba ti agdigdigos**. She bathes completely nude.

kóntra: (Sp. *contra*: against) something against or contrary to; against; vote against; negative side of the argument; counteracting; contrary; opposite; opposing. **kontrakontra**. n. quarrel, dissention. **kumontra**. v. to be against. **mangkontra**. v. to counteract; oppose. **kontraen**. v. to oppose; contradict. **kontra-kompas**. n. not following the rhythm.

kontrabándo: (Sp. *contrabando*: contraband) n. contraband, smuggled goods. (*puslit*) **kontrabandista**. n. smuggler of contraband.

kontrabída: (Sp. *contra* 'against' + *bida* 'protagonist') n. antagonist; villain in a movie or book; one who is always contradicting.

kontradiktár: (Eng.*) **kontradiktaren**. v. to contradict.

kontrapartído: (Sp. *contra* + *partido*: against party) n. political opposition, opposing political party.

kontrapéso: (Sp. *contrapeso*: counterpoise) n. counterpoise.

kontrário: (Sp. *contrario*: contrary) n. enemy. **al kontrario**. on the contrary.

kontrasénias: (Sp. *contraseña*: countersign) n. countersign; secret signal; password.

kontratár: (Sp. *contratar*) **kontrataren**. *v*. to contract.

kontratísta: (Sp. *contratista*: contractor) n. contractor.

kontráto: (Sp. *contrato*: contract) n. contract (*tulag*); deed. **kontratado**. a. contracted. **kontratista**. *n*. contractor.

kontrobérsia: (Sp. *controversia*) *n*. controversy.

kontroládo: (Sp. *controlado*: controlled) a. controlled.

kóntsa: (Sp. *concha*: shell) n. shell; conch; two-wheeled horse-drawn vehicle with a conch-shaped body.

kunwári: (Tag. *kunwari*) *a*. pretend (*agin-*, *aginkukuna*). **Agkunkunwariak laeng a naragsak**. I am just pretending to be happy.

kúnya: var. of *kúnia*.

kungkián: n. the *pangginggí* card game played by only two players.

kongkistadór: (Sp. *conquistador*) *n*. conqueror.

kungkóng: n. kind of small bird that cries at dusk; hollowed-out tree trunk used for sending messages. **kungkongen**. v. to pound; knock; hammer, make a hollow sound. **kungkongan**. v. to call by knocking; groove, hollow out. **kanungkong**. *n*. hollow sound, echo, reverberation (*áweng*). **Inul-ulida iti naikungkong iti bato a sinan-agdan**. They climbed the ladder made out of hollowed-out stone. [Tag. *alingawngáw* (echo); *hungkag* (hollow)]

kongkréto: (Sp. *concreto*) *n*. concrete. **nakongkreto**. *a*. paved with concrete.

kongréso: (Sp. *congreso*: congress) n. congress. (*pron*: *konggreso*) **kongresista**. n. congressman.

kúog: a. stupid; foolish. (*tabbed, nengneng, muno*) **kuogen**. v. to fool, trick, mislead, deceive. [Tag. *tangá, lokó*]

kooperár: (Sp. *cooperar*) **makikooperar**. *v*. to cooperate.

kooperasión: (Sp. *cooperación*: cooperation) n. cooperation.

kooperatíba: (Sp. *cooperativa*: cooperative enterprise) n. cooperative enterprise.

koordinádo: (Sp. *coordinado*) a. coordinated.

koordinasión: (Sp. *coordinación*: coordination) n. coordination.

kópa: (Sp. *copa*: glass, cup) n. glass (for drinking), tumbler. **kopíta**. n. small *kopa*, *kopón*. n. large *kopa*.

kúpa: **nakupa**. a. hollow, empty; thoughtless; brainless; stupid.

kúpag: n. copra, grated dry coconut meat; a. stupid. [Tag. *kalibkíb*]

kúpang: see *bagoén*: a kind of tall tree *Parkia* sp.

kópas: (Sp. *copa*: goblet, cup) n. the goblet suit of Spanish cards.

kúpas: **agkupas**. v. to fade; change color (*bakbak*). [Tag. *kupas*]

kup-áy: **ikup-ay**. v. to kick up dust. **maikup-ay**. v. to be kicked up (dust).

kópia: (Sp. *copiar*: copy) **kopiaen**. v. to copy something; xerox. **agkopia**. v. to copy (answers in a test, etc.). [Tag. *sipi*]

kupía: n. hat made by woven strips of the *buri* palm.

kopiár: (Sp. *copiar*: copy) **kopiaren**. v. to copy.

Kupído: (Sp. *cupido*) *n*. Cupid.

kupíes: **kopkopies**. n. *Flemingia strobilifera* shrub whose dry bracts, flowers, and fruits are used to stuff pillows.

kupiét: **nakupiet**. a. tight (clothes). (*ilét, kípet*)

kupíkop: a. thrifty. (*salimetmet*); n. possession; quality; characteristic. **kupikupan**. v. to keep; possess; hold in trust. **maikupikop**. v. to be blessed with; to be entrusted with. [Tag. *katangian* (characteristic)]

kupilán: **agkupilan**. v. to shoot up without yielding grain (said of rice).

kupiléng: a. flattened and distorted, folded (said of the ear). (*kuppileng*)

kupín: **kupinen**. v. to fold (*kapít, kulpi, píkon*); shut, close; fold in order to store away; forget; forgive and forget. **maikupin**. v. to be past and forgotten; to be folded. [Png. *topí, getget*, Tag. *lupî, tiklóp* (fold)]

kúpit₁: n. cheated money; cheated investment (*kusit*); pilfering. **kumupit, kupiten**. v. to filch money; flatten. **agkupit ti barukong**. *exp*. to suffer from hard breathing (i.e., during asthma). [Tag. *dayà, kupit*]

kúpit₂: *a*. flattened sideways. **kupiten**. *v*. to flatten (*kuppit*). **Kasla agkupit ti barukongko**. I could hardly breathe. [Knk. *kumsít*, Tag. *pipî*]

kopíta: (Sp. *copita*: small cup) n. small cup.

kupítre: (Sp. *pupitre*: desk) n. desk.

kupiyés: see under *kupies*: *Flemingia strobilifera* shrub.

kupkóp₁: **kupkupan**. v. to wrap, cover with the arms or wings. **kupkupen**. v. to take care of (mother hen and chicks). [Tag. *kupkúp*]

kupkóp₂: a. bald. (*kalbo, pultak*) **agkupkop**. *v*. to go bald. **kupkupan**. v. to make someone bald.

kópla: (Sp. *copla*) *n*. rhyming couplet in poetry.

kuplát: *n*. abrasion. **nakuplatan**. a. abraded, skinned. **kupkuplat**. a. skinned. **Saan a kuplakuplat ti pintana**. Its paint is not falling off. [Tag. *gasgás*]

kúpon: (Eng.) n. coupon; stub.

kúpong: kupong-kupong. n. a long time ago, the old days (*ugma*). **Saanen a kas idi tiempo ti kupongkupong.** It is no longer like it was in the old days.

kuppiléng: a. flat; twisted; distorted. **makuppileng.** v. to be flattened (*kuppit*). [Tag. *pipî*]

kuppít₁: n. kind of *upít* basket but twice as high.

kuppít₂: a. flat, flattened sideways. (*dapig, daplak, dulpak, dungpap*; *kuppileng, kupit*; *teppap*) **agkuppít.** v. to close, shut. **kuppiten.** v. to dent, misshape. **makuppit.** v. to be dented. [Tag. *pipî*]

kuppó: (*reg.*) kuppokuppo. *n.* crown of the head, fontanel of a baby (*lulonán*). **Kasla nadanog ti kuppokuppo ti lakay iti nangngegna.** The old man seems to have been hit in the head from what he heard.

kuppón: n. friend, person with similar interest. (*gayyém*)

kópra: (Sp. *copra*) n. copra, dried coconut meat. (*kúpag*)

kupsiát: *n.* abrasion, peeling of skin (*kuplat*); scar, scar tissue (*piglat*). **agkupsiat.** *v.* to peel (skin), scar (from scalding water or fire). **nakupsiat.** *a.* abraded, peeled; scarred. [Tag. *peklát* (scar)]

kupsít: *var.* of *kupsiát*: abrasion.

kúra: (Sp. *cura*: priest; plural is *kukura*) n. priest; curate, friar. **kura paroko.** n. parish priest. [Tag. *parì*]

kúrab: kuraben. v. to take a big bite; devour in a big bite (*kagat*). **Talaga a kukuraben dagiti luppona!** Her thighs are really devourable.

kúrad: n. kind of skin disease characterized by light blotches, like ringworm or eczema (when applied to dogs: *guríd*). **agkurad.** v. to have this skin disease. **kurad ti bólo.** n. *labaít* skin disease in the hands. **tudo ti kurad.** n. rain that falls when the sun is still shining. [Kal. *kuÿed*, Tag. *galís*]

kuraddóg: *n.* crook, wicked person; thief (*birkóg*). [Term used by the NPA]

kuradrád: *n.* strumming of a guitar. **kuradraden.** v. to strum (a guitar, etc.). (*kurengreng*)

kuragrág₁: n. variety of awned early rice; a. overused.

kuragrág₂: kuragragen. v. to strum (a guitar). (*kuradrád*)

kuráid: *var.* of *kiráid*: scratch; scrape.

kurákot: *n.* corruption, graft. **nakurakot.** a. corrupt (in politics); engaged in graft. **Ti la agkurkurakot ti aramidna.** He only does corrupt things.

korál: (Sp. *corral*: yard) n. cattle yard, corral. **ikoral.** v. to confine in a corral.

koráles: (Sp. *coral*: coral) n. corals; red gem.

kuramentádo: var. of *huramentado*: run amuck.

kurantóng: n. large container for wine; load, all things being carried on the body. **kurantongen.** v. to carry on the body. **Mailiklikanda met iti peggad gapu kadagiti rosario nga ikurkurantongda iti barukongda.** They avoid danger because of the rosaries they carry on their chests.

kurantrílio: (Sp. *culantrillo*: maidenhair plant) n. maidenhair plant.

kúrang: a. deficient, lacking; insufficient; in short supply. **agkurang.** v. to be short (in supply); to be in need. **kumurang.** v. to lessen, diminish. **kurangan.** v. to take away from, cause to diminish in supply. **kurkurang.** n. mental deficiency, stupidity. **sumurók kumurang.** approximately; more or less. **makurkurangan.** a. poor; destitute. **napakurang.** a. humble, lowly. **sipapakurang.** *a.* humbly. **agpakurang.** v. to humble oneself; apologize. **pagkurangan.** n. deficiency. **tagikurangen.** *v.* to consider something deficient. **sumurokkumurang.** adv. more or less; approximately. **Itay napan a tawen, nariknami ti pagkuranganmi.** Just last year we felt our deficit. **Agkurang ti torniliona.** He is missing a screw (said of a crazy person). **Pakawanennak iti adu a nagkurkurangak.** Forgive me for my many faults. [Bon. *kólang*, Ibg. *kurang*, Ivt. *napakarwan*, Kal. *kuÿang*, Kpm., Png., Tag. *kulang*]

kuránges: *a.* wretched, miserly; destitute. **agkuranges.** v. to live in misery; to be destitute. (*kalamaos*) **mangurkuranges.** a. destitute. [Tag. *darahóp*]

kurangráng: var. of *kurengreng*: strum a guitar.

kurápay: *a.* destitute, poor. **nakurapay.** v. poor, impoverished, indigent. (*panglaw*) **kinakurapay.** n. poverty, destitution.

kurapí: n. small variety of crab.

kurápis: a. thin, slender. (*kuttóng*)

kurapó: n. kind of speckled marine fish. (*lapulapu*)

kurappét: *a.* crumpled, wrinkled.

kurarábay: n. kind of freshwater mollusk with speckled shell.

kurárap: a. myopic, shortsighted; nearsighted; with defective vision (*arrap*). **agkurarap.** v. to be temporarily blinded by light. [Tag. *kuráp* (blink)]

kurarápit: nakurarapit. a. skinny (said of children). (*kuttong*)

kurarapnít: n. bat (flying rodent). (*panníki, kuraratnít*) [Kal. *pampalakÿong, pampalittan*, Knk. *kibkiblút*, Png. *kulalaknit, kaging*, Tag. *kalapnit, kabág*]

kuraratnít: var. of *kurarapnit*: bat. (*panníki*)
kurarato: n. pike eel, *Muraensox cinereus*.
kurarét: n. edible bracket fungi (*kuret*); *a.* shrunk; shriveled, wrinkled. **agkuraret**. v. to have a convulsion, cramp; shrink from cold; shrivel. **Kuraret dagiti imana uray no labuenna iti losion.** Her hands are shriveled although she smears them with lotion.
korasón: (Sp. *corazón*: heart) n. heart. (*puso*) **atake de korason**. n. heart attack. **dos korasones**. n. ring set with two gems. **aba de korason**. n. species of ornamental plant with heart-shaped leaves with reddish spots.
kurataáw: n. line of the *tabúkol* net. (*karataáw*)
kurátsa: (Sp. *cucaracha*: cockroach) n. folk music and dance especially popular in Samar.
kurattót: **kurkurattot**. a. spinning jerkily (top).
kúray₁: n. variety of awned rice.
kúray₂: **agkuray**. v. to scratch (like hens). (*karaykay*) **kurayan**. n. to scratch something toward someone. **ikuray**. v. to scratch away. [Tag. *kalmót, gasgás*]
kur-áy₁: **ikur-ay**. v. to scratch away; slide feet on the ground (as in kicking dirt).
kur-áy₂: **agkur-ay**. v. to cover. (*kalub*) **nakur-ay**. a. covered. [Tag. *takíp*]
kuráya: **kurkuraya**. n. kind of crab smaller than the *kappí*.
kurayappét: *a.* crumpled, wrinkled.
kúrba: (Sp. *curva*: curve) n. curve; turn; bend. **ikurba**. a. to curve; turn a curve. **nakurba**. a. curved. **kurbakurba**. zigzag. [Tag. *likô*]
kurbádo: (Sp. *curvado*: curved) a. curved; winding; turning.
korbáta: (Sp. *corbata*: necktie) n. necktie. **agkorbata**. v. to wear a necktie. **Agkorbata ti ubetna.** His buttocks wear a tie (said of unruly children, likened to mountain tribes that wear G-strings).
korbatín: (Sp. *corbatín*) *n.* small necktie; bow; knot.
kurbatúra: (Sp. *curvatura*) n. curvature.
kurbób: **agkurbob**. v. to wrinkle; crease; warp; rumple (sails with no wind); bend. [Tag. *pintál* (warp)]
kordápio: n. term of address used for servants; fem: *kordapia*.
kordéro: (Sp. *cordero*: lamb) n. lamb. (*karnéro*)
kúrdias: n. putting two cocks together to fight. **pakurdiasen**. v. to fight gamecocks.
kordiliéra: (Sp. *cordillera*: mountain chain) n. chain of mountains, specifically the mountain chain in northern Luzon.
kurdít: *n.* letter of the alphabet. **ikurdit**. v. to write; put in writing. (*surat*). **kurditan**. n. alphabet; literature. [Tag. *talâ*]

kordón: (Sp. *cordón*: cord) n. cord; shoestring; string. **kordonen**. v. to provide with a *kordón*. **ikordon**. v. to tie one's shoes. **kinordonan**. n. underwear of men with a waist string. **pangordonan**. *n.* hole for string to pass through, belt loop, shoelace hole. **nababa ti kordonna**. *exp.* denoting having no patience.
koréa: (Sp. *correa*: belt, leash) n. belt (for moving devices), machine belt.
Koreáno: (Sp. *coreano*: Korean) n. a. Korean.
koredór: (Sp. *corredor*: broker) n. broker (at customs or an exchange).
kuregrég: **agkuregreg**. v. to tremble, shake. (*tigerger*)
korehír: (Sp. *corregir*: correct) **korehiren**. v. to correct.
kuremrém: *var.* of *kiremrém*: with eyes half-closed. **agkuremrem**. *v.* to wink, partly close the eyes. [Knk. *kudimdím*, Tag. *kurát, kindát, kisáp*]
kurenrén: **agkurenren**. v. to wrinkle. (*kuretrét*)
korenténas: *reg. var.* of *kuarentenas*: quarantine.
kurengréng: *n.* sound of a guitar. **kurengrengen**. v. to strum a guitar (*kuritengteng, kutingting, kuradrad, kuragrag, kutengteng*). [Tag. *kalabít*]
koréo: (Sp. *correo*: mail) n. mail. (*tinnag*) **ipakoreo**. v. to mail.
kurét: n. kind of poisonous crab; kind of earthworm used as bait; bracket fungi. **agkukuret**. v. to huddle up; shrivel; shrink to cower. **makuret**. v. to be poisoned by bracket fungi; to be burned by lightning; to be electrocuted; to use up (all gambling money). **Kasla agkurkuret a pusa a mangsangsango iti dalikan.** He approached the stove like a cowering cat. [Tag. *kabuté*]
kuretrét: n. wrinkle. **agkuretret**. v. to wrinkle; crease; frown. [Png. *kumanét*, Tag. *kulubót, kunót, gusót*]
kurí: **kurkuri**. n. kitchen boy, scullery maid.
koriá: *var.* of *korea*: machine belt.
kuriáp: n. flock of chickens. (*kariap*)
kuriápi: n. tool used in superstitious practices.
kuriát: n. cricket, believed to be bad as they enter the ears and may cause hardship or death. **Napno kano ti kuriat ta ulom.** Your head is supposedly full of crickets. [Knk. *paltíngan, tíkan*, Png. *kóryat*, Tag. *kerwe, kuliglíg*]
kúrib: **kuriban**. v. to nibble, gnaw at. (*kibkib*) **makuriban**. v. to have a hole gnawed in it. **kurib-toktok**. n. nibbling sounds one often hears at night. [Tag. *ngatngát*]
kuribabéng: n. second growth of bittermelon leaves, small leaves of the bittermelon vine,

usually from a second growth after picking the original stem.

kuribabét: *var.* of *kuribetbét.*

kuribagsót: agkuribagsot. v. to jerk arms downward. [Tag. *dabóg*]

kuribatéd: n. shrunken leaves of Virginia tobacco.

kuribatég: agkuribateg. v. to shrink (in pain).

kuribatóng: n. plumb line (in construction of new houses); vertical laths along the walls of a house; kind of snare for birds.

kuribáw: n. kind of bamboo horn.

kuribetbét: n. *Tabernaemontana pandacaqui* shrub with white flowers used in medicine (boiled roots are used to cure stomach ulcers); a. wrinkled; withered; creased. **agkuribetbet.** v. to wrinkle; shrivel; shrink. **Immagepak iti kuribetbeten a bukot ti dakulapna.** I kissed the wrinkled back of his hand. [Tag. *kulubót* (wrinkle)]

kuribnás: agkuribnas. v. to gather (vegetables). **Paglinglingayanna ti agkuribnas kadagiti nateng iti turod.** He amuses himself by gathering vegetables on the hill.

kuríbot: n. large *alát* basket; hanging receptacle made of woven bamboo. **Kasla insaltek a kuribot ti pammagina.** Her physique is like a *kuribot* basket struck against the ground (slim). [Tag. *tiklís*]

korída: (Sp. *corrida:* bullfight; routine) n. routine course, route; bullfight.

kuridagdág: agkuridagdag. v. to writhe the body (in pain). (*kuripaspas*)

kuridasdás: n. scribbling. **ikuridasdas.** v. to scribble down; write sloppily.

kuridem: *a.* indistinct; faintly seen. **agkuridem.** *v.* to squint the eyes; see indistinctly. **Agkurkuridem a nangilukat iti ridaw.** He opened the door with his eyes half closed.

kuridemdém: agkuridemdem. v. to wink; glimmer; flicker. (*kirmed; kiray; kuyep; kirem*) **nakuridemdem.** a. flickering (light). [Tag. *kuráp*]

kuridóng: n. kind of dark insect-eating bird.

koriéndo: n. game marble. (*bulintík, hólen*) **agkoriendo.** v. to play marbles.

koriénte: (Sp. *corriente*) n. electricity. **makoriente.** v. to be shocked by electricity; to be electrocuted. **makakoriente.** *a.* electrocuting. **de-koriente.** *a.* running on electricity, electric (appliances).

kurikóng: n. kind of itchy skin disease. (*gudgod*)

kuríkor: n. kind of small eel-like fish; entering of a narrow passage; ear pick; toothpick. **agkurikor.** v. to clean the ears. **kumurikor.** v. to wriggle into a hole (especially the ear); enter

a narrow passage; be ear-splitting. **kumurikor nga aweng.** *n.* ear-splitting sound. **kurikuran.** v. to clean (ear or any narrow hole). **Kurikoranmi kuma ti kandadoyo?** *exp.* May we visit you (*lit:* turn your lock)? **Kumurkurikor iti panunotna ti singasing ti gayyemna.** The suggestion of her friend is wriggling in her thoughts. **Saan payen a kabaelan dagiti ayup a kutien ti lapayagda tapno mabugaw dagiti ngilaw a mangkurkurikor kadakuada.** The animals are not yet able to move their ears to shoo the flies getting into their ears.

kuriláw: n. sea catfish, *Arius sp.*

kurimangmáng: a. talkative (bad connotation).

kurimaóng: n. kind of fish similar to the *baraúngan*; thief, sometimes used as a mild curse word.

kurimát: (obs.) **kurimatan.** v. to loathe seeing.

kurimatmát: n. eyelash. [Bon. *kedem*, Ibg. *kimaq*, Ifg. *kodom*, Ivt. *cicimit*, Kal. *kimat*, Knk. *kedém*, Kpm. *irap*, Png. *sagumay(may)*, kolimatmát, Tag. *pilikmatá*]

kurimbáw: var. of *kuribaw.*

kurímed: ikurimed. v. to hide; to do stealthily. (*lemmeng*) **kurimeden.** v. to steal. **nakurimed.** *a.* secretive; stealthily; hidden, concealed. [Tag. *lihím*]

kurimés: agkurimes. v. to catch fish with the hands; gather with the hands (*kammél*); (*coll.*) steal. **kurimesen.** v. to catch something by groping in the dark. **Nalaingda nga agkurimes iti saba ken sandia.** They are good at gathering bananas and watermelon.

kurimínas: n. jellyfish. (*karominas*)

kurinday-óng: n. *Telosma procumbens* vine with greenish yellow flowers.

kurindinggís: n. variety of awned rice with a white kernel.

kurindírip: *n.* twinkling, flickering. **agkurkurindirip.** *v.* to flicker, twinkle. **Naraniag ti tangatang a nakaiburaisan dagiti agkurkurindirip a bituen.** The sky is scattered with twinkling stars. [Tag. *kutitap, kisláp*]

kuriníkon: *n.* curling up, coiling up (*kalunikon, kawikaw*). **agkurinikon.** *v.* to curl up, coil up.

kurinsabót: *a.* poor, wretched (*miráut*). **mangurinsabot.** *v.* to live in poverty or misery.

kuríng: kuring-kuring. a. illegible (handwriting).

kório: (Sp. *correo:* mail) n. mail. **korio de abut.** n. mailbox. (*buson*)

kurióso: (Sp. *curioso*) *a.* curious.

kuripagpág: var. of *kuripaspas, kulipagpag.*

kuripaspás: agkuripaspas. v. to writhe in agony or pain (slaughtered animal) (*bugsot; kulidagdag*); scatter (fish in a school); faint. **Napa-**

anang-ang a napalagto ti pusana sa nag-kurkuripaspas. Her cat jumped in pain and then writhed in agony.

kuripattóng: n. a kind of vine; var. of *kuridóng* bird.

kuripegpég: n. shivering. **agkuripegpeg.** v. to shiver, quiver; grasp. **kuripegpegen.** v. to grasp, grab.

kurípot: (Tag.) a. stingy, miserly. (*kirmet*)

kurírep: a. with upturned eyeballs (with eyes that cannot look down). **agkorirep.** v. to roll the eyeballs up.

kurirísi: n. variety of rice with small kernel.

kuríro: **makuriro.** v. to be bothered, disturbed. **kuriruen.** v. to bother, disturb. **Patinayonmo idi a kuriruen ni tatangmo.** You used to always bother your father.

korísta: (Sp. *corista*) n. member of a choir.

kur-ít: n. scratch; notch; nick; line drawn by a pencil. **kur-itan.** v. to scratch with one stroke (multiple strokes: *kiskis*). **kur-ikur-itan.** v. to scribble. **ikur-it.** v. to engrave; make a notch. **mangur-it iti posporo.** v. to strike a match. [Tag. *guhit*]

kuritá: n. octopus. **kimmurita.** a. like an octopus. **Kasla katay ti kurita ti nagiwes nga asuk.** The zigzagging smoke was like octopus saliva. [Ivt. *kuyta*, Png. *kolitá*, Tag. *pugità*]

kuritbóng: **agkuritbong.** v. to steal, take surreptitiously or illegally (*kibróng*). **maikuritbong.** v. to be stolen, plundered illegally, poached. [Tag. *nakaw*]

kuritangtáng: n. kind of marine fish. **kuritang-tangen.** v. to ring the bells. (*tangtang*)

kuríteg: **agkuríteg.** v. to shrivel (leaves with a plant disease); be stunted in growth. **nakuriteg.** a. stunted in growth. [Tag. *bansót* (stunted)]

kuríteng: **nakuriteng.** a. narrow minded; confined (space); scanty. **Nagkuriteng ti rikna ken kapanunotanda.** Their feelings and way of thinking were narrow minded.

kuriténg: n. kind of native guitar. (*kudiapi*)

kuritengténg: n. sound of a guitar. (*kurengreng*) **kuritengtengen.** v. to strum a guitar.

kurití: n. kind of native dance. **agkuriti.** v. to dance the *kuriti* dance.

kuriwakwák: n. species of bird similar to the *salaksák*.

kuriwáwet: n. tendril.

kuriwet: n. species of tree used in construction. [Knk. *kulíwet* = knotty wood]

kurkór: **agkurkor.** v. to call to feed chickens yelling *krrr*. **kurkuran.** v. to feed chickens (by scattering food). **Ipakanda ti kilabban iti aso wenno maikurkur iti manok.** They feed the cold rice to the dog or scatter it to the chickens.

kurmég: var. of *kulmég*: curl up; hide.

kurméng: **agkurmeng.** v. to be crushed, overburdened, weighed down; feel depressed.

kurná: (Sp. *cornal*: strap for hitching) **ikurna.** v. to tow; hitch (a yoke). (*pako*)

kornál: (Sp. *jornal*: daily) n. laborer; oxcart driver.

korného: (Sp. *cornejo*) n. dogwood tree.

kurnéta: (Sp. *corneta*: cornet) n. cornet; bugle.

kornetín: (Sp. *cornetín*: small bugle) n. cornet, trumpet.

kornísa: (Sp. *cornisa*) n. cornice, projecting part that crowns a wall.

kurnó: **agkurno.** v. to bow; genuflect, bend at the knees. **nakakurno.** a. bowing (*taméd*). **Nagkurno kalpasan ti panangideppelna iti tammudona iti pagbenditaan.** She genuflected after she dipped her finger in the holy water. [Tag. *yukô*]

kornukópia: (Sp. *cornucopia*) n. cornucopia.

kóro: (Sp. *coro*: choir) n. choir; chorus.

kuruás: n. small fishing net used to collect trapped fish.

kúrob: n. digging with the hands. **kuruban.** v. to clear of garbage, dirt, etc.; dig with the hands. **kumurob.** v. to dig into the ground, enter the earth. **pagkuruban.** n. mine. **kinurob.** v. kind of gold ore. **Nagranipak ken kimmurob dagiti buli iti baet dagiti sakada.** There was a loud sound and the lead (bullets) dug into the earth between their feet. [Tag. *hukay*]

kur-ób: var. of *kúrob*: dig with hands.

kúrod: n. mousetrap. (*saltok*)

kurudíkod₁: n. variety of sweet potato with white meat.

kurudíkod₂: **korodikudan.** v. to scrape the inside of a container.

kurúkor: n. erosion (*kurruoy*); landslide caused by water. **kurukuran.** v. to undermine banks (said of streams).

koróna: (Sp. *corona*: crown) n. crown. (*balangat*) **koronaan.** v. to crown. **koronado.** a. crowned. **nakakorona.** a. wearing a crown.

kuruníkon: n. coil, curl. **agkurunikon.** v. to curl up, coil; cuddle.

kuróng: n. jail, stockade; hell; animal cage.

kurúrot: **kurkururot.** n. word said when playing children's games, hiding the face with a cloth, playing hide-and-seek, etc. **agkororot.** v. to say the word *kororot* (while covering the head with a piece of cloth); cover the head with a piece of cloth. [Tag. *bulagâ*]

kúros: n. kind of freshwater shrimp.

kurús: (Sp. *cruz*: cross) n. cross. **kurkurus.** n. Ash Wednesday. **agkurus.** v. to cross oneself; make the sign of the cross; cross, intersect.

manguros. *v.* to make the sign of the cross.
agkikinnuros. *v.* to be intersecting. **kinuros.** *a.*
checkered. **ikuros.** *v.* to apply crosswise. **Kur-kurus.** n. Ash Wednesday.

korosáda: (Sp. *cruzada*: crossed) **nakorosada.**
a. intersected, crossed; crosswise.

kurót: **agkukurot.** v. to stand shrunk up when
body is ill (chickens); to be ill; depressed;
listless, weak. **Pagin-awaenna ti agkukurot a
rikna.** It relieves depressed feelings. **Kunam
no agkukurot a pato ta napuyatan idi rabii
iti pasala.** You would think he were a shrunk-
up duck because he stayed up all last night at
the dance.

korpiár: (Sp. *porfiar*: persist, argue) **agkorpiar.**
v. to wrangle. **korpiado.** a. disobedient; prone
to crying (children).

korpínio: (Sp. *corpiño*: bodice) n. bodice; embroidered silk undershirt.

korporasión: (Sp. *corporación*) n. corporation.

korrál: (Sp. *corral*: yard) n. cattle yard.

korráso: (Sp. *porrazo*: blow) **korrasuen.** v. to
knock down (with both fists).

kurráting: a. skinny (*kuttong*). [Tag. *patpatin*]

korre: *var.* of *kurrí*.

korréo: (Sp. *correo*: mail) n. mail. (*tinnag*,
karta)

kurrí: (Sp. *correr*: run; *ocurrir*: occur) **agkurri.**
v. to be in motion (vehicle); be in circulation
(money); occur; to be useful; apply; show up
(sickness); take effect (medicine). **ikurri.** *v.* to
use; apply. **pagkurrien.** v. to use, apply. **ikur-
rim ti ammom.** apply what you know.
pagkurrian. n. usage; use. [Tag. *gamit*]

kurruáy: *var.* of *kussuáy*: throw into the air.

kurrúoy: n. quicksand (*gayonggayong*); erosion.
agkurruoy. v. to erode; sink (*kurukor*). [Tag.
kuminóy (quicksand)]

kurrót: var. of *kurot*.

kursáda: (Sp. *cruzada*: crossroads) *n.* crossroad;
intersection. **kursadaen.** *v.* to cross, intersect.

kursapó: *var.* of *kusapó*: discolor, fade, become
dull.

korsé: (Sp. *corsé*) *n.* corset.

kursílio: (Sp. *cursillo*: short course) n. short
course of study, usually Christian; religious
retreat.

kursilísta: *n.* person who attends a *kursilio*;
Sunday school person; member of a religious
retreat.

kursíng: n. dead, peeling skin. (*kuyabyab*) **ag-
kursing.** v. to have blotches on skin from
peeling.

kúrso₁: (Sp. *curso*: course) n. course of study.

kúrso₂: (Sp. *corzo*: gazelle) n. gazelle, roebuck.
(*ugsa*)

kúrso₃: (Tag.) n. heavy diarrhea. (*buris*, *suyot*)
agkurso. v. to suffer from heavy diarrhea.

kursonáda: (Sp. *corazonada*: hunch; intuition)
n. interest in another person; crush on someone;
attraction to something; impulse of the heart;
inclination; *a.* eager, keen; infatuated, interested. **agkursonada.** v. to be interested in; to
have a crush on; to be infatuated with. **dayta ti
kursonadak.** I'm interested in that. **kur-
sonadadaka.** they are interested in you.

kursóng: **ikursong.** v. to thrust into a hole; put
legs in pants; put on clothes; lead astray.
maikursong. *v.* to be thrust in a hole; led
astray.

kórta: (Sp. *corta*: cutting) n. slab, piece; cut,
slice. **agkorta.** v. to clot; coagulate; curdle
(milk) (*balay*). **pagkorta.** *n.* cutter; instrument
used for plastering.

kórta-bísta: (Sp. *corta vista*: short sight) n. near-
sightedness (not being able to see far).

kortádo: (Sp. *cortado*: cut) a. cut; tanned
(leather); curdled (milk). **kortador.** n. big
scissors (*kartib*); cutter.

kortadúra: (Sp. *cortadura*: cuttings) n. cuttings;
rejected cuttings.

kortaplúma: (Sp. *cortaplumas*: pocketknife) n.
pocketknife.

kortár: (Sp. *cortar*: cut) **kortaren.** v. to cut.
(*puted*) **kortaran.** v. to cut the hair of someone
(*pukis*). [Tag. *gupit*]

kurtár: (Sp. *curtir*: tan leather) **kurtaren.** v. to
dye and cut leather.

kórte₁: (Sp. *corte*: court) n. court (*husgádo*,
pagsaklángan, *pagukomán*); cut, pattern; shape,
form. **korte supréma.** supreme court. **ikorte.** *v.*
to bring to court. **maikorte.** *v.* to be sent to
court. [Tag. *hukuman*]

kórte₂: (Sp. *fuerte*: strong) **nakorte.** a. hard (uncooked vegetables); too strong for chewing
(betel). **kumorte.** v. to burn the tongue with
betel nut.

kórte₃: (Sp. *curtir*: tan hides) *n.* tanned leather.
agkorte, mangorte. *v.* to tan hides. **agkor-
korte.** *n.* tanner.

kortésa: (Sp. *corteza*: bark) n. bark of a tree;
cortex.

kortésia: var. of *kortisia*.

kortína: (Sp. *cortina*: curtain) n. curtain (*bengbéng*). **Nakortinaan dagiti tawa iti ginansilio
a puraw.** The windows had white embroidered
curtains.

kortísia: (Sp. *cortesía*: courtesy) n. bow, courtesy. **mangortisia.** v. to invite someone to
dance. (*allop*)

kórto: (Sp. *corto*: short) a. short; narrow-minded;
n. shorts. **nakortuan.** *a.* closely cropped.

kórtos: (Sp. *cortos*) *n*. short Alhambra cigarette.
kortsétes: (Sp. *corchetes*: hook and eye) *n*. hook and eye, snap fastener.
kórtso: (Sp. *corcho*: cork) *n*. cork slippers.
kusaít: *n*. the *boktó* fish.
kusáng: *n*. kick (*kusáy, kup-áy*). ikusang. *v*. to kick up (dust).
kusapó: *n*. tanned; blonde. nakusapo. *a*. dull; tanned, scratched. kumusapo. *v*. to become dull; discolor, fade; tan. [Tag. *kupas* (fade)]
kusáy: *n*. kick (not as hard as *kugtar*). agkusay, kusayan. *v*. to kick (forward). ikusay. *v*. to kick away; kick off. agkusaykusay. *v*. to kick the feet while sitting. kusayan ti tugaw. *n*. space underneath a chair where feet are. Kimmusay iti isipna ti dina kuman panagtuloy. It kicked into his mind that he shouldn't continue. [Png. *sípa*, Tag. *sipà*]
kusaysáy: agkusaysay. *v*. to writhe, flutter, struggle in movement. (*kuripaspas*)
kusbó: makusbo. *v*. to collapse; to be bent (person). Napusek pay laeng iti pasahero, arigna makusbo a mangaw-awit kadagiti tampong. The passenger is still fully loaded, he seems about to collapse from the bundle he is carrying. [Tag. *bagsák*]
kúseg: kumuskuseg. *v*. to faint with hunger. [Tag. *liyó*]
kusél: nakusel. *a*. half-cooked (rice, etc.). (*lúdek*; *belbel*) No nakusel ti innapoy, saan a naimas nga ipauneg. If the rice is half-cooked, it is not delicious to put in the mouth.
kúsep: nakusep. *a*. burning badly (bad firewood, cigarettes hard to ignite). Adda kuskusepna daytoy kayo. This wood is hard to burn.
kúser: var. of *kusep*: burning badly.
kusgél: (obs.) *n*. coward (*takrót*). [Tag. *duwág*]
kusí: *n*. kind of wild fowl (*abuyo*). [Tag. *labuyò*]
kusiáw: *a*. pale, faded. nakusiaw. *a*. pale, faded (*kupas*). kumusiaw. *v*. to pale, fade. [Tag. *kupas*]
kusibéng: *n*. kind of small green and white bird; *Sapindus sp*. tree.
kusíbot: *n*. wrinkle, pleat, fold. ikusibot. *v*. to fold, pleat. Inkusibotna ti kamisetana a duyaw. He folded his yellow shirt. [Tag. *gusót*]
kusído: (Sp. *cocido*: stew) *n*. meat stew with vegetables.
kusíkos: *n*. coil; roll. kusikusen. *v*. to coil; wind thread; wrap up, envelop; make into a funnel. (*lukut*) agkusikos. *v*. to form a partnership in gambling; roll up; coil. sangakusikos. *n*. one roll, one coil. No nakakusikos ti alimatek iti tukot, napintas ti panawen. If the leech is coiled up deep at the bottom, the weather will be good. [Tag. *ikid*]

kus-íl: mangkus-il, kus-ilan. *v*. to remove an outer covering; peel off a shell (peanuts). Namrayanna ti nangkus-il iti mani. He impulsively shelled the peanuts.
kusílap: *n*. glare; sharp, angry side glance. kumusilap. *v*. to glare at. kusilapan. *v*. to glare at someone; throw a sharp look at someone. Panggepnak siguro a tulongan, ngem kinusilapak. He probably planned on helping, but I glared at him sharply. [Tag. *irap*]
kusíleng: kuskusileng. *n*. kind of small freshwater mollusk with round shell.
kusílit: agkusilit. *v*. to turn up the eyeballs as in mocking someone.
kúsim: nakusim. *a*. fastidious, dainty (in eating) (ant. *rawet*). kumusim. *v*. to become sparing in eating; to begin to eat very small portions. [Knk. *kuíl, kusim*, Tag. *tamilmíl*]
kusimáy: *n*. variety of awned late rice with red kernel.
kosína: (Sp. *cocina*: kitchen) *n*. kitchen (*paglutuan*); rear of a bus. mangusina. *v*. to cook, serve as a cook. [Kal. *byabyangaan, kusi*, Tag. *kusinà*]
kosináda: (f. *kosina*) *n*. kind of big, breakable pot.
kosinéro: (Sp. *cocinero*: cook) *n*. cook (fem. *kosinera*) (*paraluto*). [Tag. *tagapaglutò*]
kosinília: (Sp. *cocinilla*: kitchenette; camping stove) *n*. gas stove. (*gasonilia*)
kusipá: kuskusipa. see *kaláad*: Cissampelos pareira.
kusipét: *a*. having very small eyes; with slanted eyes (*singkít*); (*coll*.) term applied to the Japanese or Chinese. agkusipet. *v*. to close the eyes in slits. Agkusipet a kasla agpanunot. He squinted his eyes as in deep thought. [Knk. *kusípit*, Kpm. *kírat*, Png. *pinkít*, Tag. *singkít*]
kusísi: kusisien. *v*. to apply hot iron to, submerge burning iron into water; to tuft.
kúsit: *n*. cheat; cheater. nakusit. *a*. unreliable, untrustworthy. agkusit. *v*. to cheat (in a game of chance, politics, etc.). mangusit. *v*. to cheat, deceive. kusiten. *v*. to cheat someone (in a game of chance). managkusit. *n*. cheater. nakusit. *a*. cheated. [Bon. *tókong*, Ibg. *darógoq*, Ivt. *mangutap*, Kpm. *piráit*, Png. *saol*, Tag. *dayà, linláng*; Knk. *kúsit* = feel, be affected by]
kuskél: *n*. coward, craven (*takrót*). nakuskel. *a*. cowardly. kinakuskel. *n*. cowardice.
kuskús₁: *a*. bald (*kalbó, puridasdás, pulinangnáng*); bare. kuskusan. *v*. to shave off all hair. Kuskus ti pukisda ket kaaduan ti narapis, nalabit gapu iti dida pannangan iti rabii. Their hair is shaved off and most of them are

thin, probably because they go without dinner. [Png. *koskos*, Tag. *kalbó* (Sp.), *panot*]

kuskús₂: kuskusen. v. to scrape. (*kiskis*; *kirkir*; *karus*) **agkanuskus.** v. to rub the head with something rough; to make scratching noises. **kuskus balungos.** *exp.* (Tag.*)* potpourri of things; assortment of different, unnecessary things; many things to do; worthless talk. **Adu pay ti kuskus balungosna.** He still has a lot of things to do. [Kal. *gusgus*, Png. *kidkid*, *kadkad*, Tag. *kayod* (scrape)]

kosmétiko: (Sp. *cosmético*) *n.* cosmetics.

kusnáw: a. hazy; not completely visible. **kumusnaw.** v. to fade, discolor; turn pale. **nakusnaw.** a. faded, discolored. (*kupas*) **Inruarna ti daan ken agkuskusnaw a ladawan.** He took out the old and fading pictures. [Png. *paspás,pusisaw*, *pesyáw*, Tag. *kupas*, *labò*]

kusníg: *n.* yellow. **nakusnig.** a. yellow (*kiaw*, *kunig*). [Tag. *diláw* (yellow)]

kusó: nakusokuso. a. disorderly, messed up, disarranged (hair, etc.), tangled. **kusokusuen.** v. to disarray, dishevel, mess up. **kusuen.** v. to mess up; disarray; dishevel. [Tag. *gusót*]

kusúkos: kumusukos. v. to sink; descend. [Tag. *lubóg*]

kuspág: nakuspag. a. violent; cruel; arrogant, haughty. (*tangsit*; *dangkok*) **agkuspag.** v. to become cruel. **Ti balasang a nakuspag, awan kaniana ti agayat.** No one falls in love with a haughty woman. [Tag. *lupít*]

kuspíl: maikuspil. v. to lose; lose ground; be defeated. **ikuspil.** v. to prevent someone from advancing; inflict violence on; defeat, beat; make someone suffer. **maikuspil.** v. to be prevented from advancing, lose ground; to be defeated through weakness. **manangikuspil.** *a.* violent; cruel; vicious. **Apay ngarud nga itulokmo a maikuspil?** Then why do you give up and let yourself be defeated?

kuspiló: *a.* with one leg trailing behind. **agkuspilo.** v. to trail one leg in walking; bend; curve. **makuspilo.** v. to twist the ankle. **kuspiluen.** v. to bend; twist; give way.

kussuág: *var.* of *kudduág*: hurl, toss, fling, eject.

kussuáy: *n.* toss with the feet. **ikussuay.** v. to toss into the air with the feet; scatter. [Tag. *sikad*]

kostádo: (Sp. *costado*: side, flank) n. slab of lumber. (*kostaneda*)

kostál: (Sp. *costal*: sack) n. sack. **ikostal.** v. to place in the sack.

kostanéda: n. slab of lumber.

kostár: (Sp. *ajustar*) **makostar.** *v.* to adjust.

kóstas: (Sp. *costas*: expenses) n. expenses in a lawsuit.

kostiliádo: (Sp. *costilla*: rib + *-ado*) n. rib cage.

kostílias: (Sp. *costillas*: rib) n. rib, chop.

kústo: (Sp. *justo*: right, correct) a. right, correct. **kumusto.** v. to be enough, sufficient, fine. **apagkusto.** a. just right; just enough. **kustuen.** v. to make right. **kustokusto.** a. just right. [Tag. *husto*]

kustódia: (Sp. *custodia*) *n.* keeper; custodian.

kostúmbre: (Sp. *costumbre*: custom) n. custom. (*ugali*)

kostúra: (Sp. *costura*: stitching) n. sewing, stitching; needlework; surgical suture; seam.

kosturéra: (Sp. *costurera*: seamstress) n. seamstress, dressmaker. (*modista*)

kóta: n. fort, fortification; quota. [Tag. *kutà*]

kúta: Interjection used to call dogs.

kutabáw: n. kind of soap made from tree bark.

kuták: n. the cackling noise of a hen. (*kiak*; *kakak*) **agkutak.** v. to cackle (hen). **Ti agkutak, isu't nagitlog.** He who cackled laid the egg. **No kayat ti agsida iti itlog, anusan ti kutak ti manok.** If you want to eat eggs, bear the cackling of the hen. [Knk. *tagák*, Png. *koták*, Tag. *kakak*, *putak*]

kutálo: n. kind of winged insect destructive to rice plants. **kutaluen.** a. destroyed by the *kutalo* (said of rice harvests, etc.).

kutát: ikutat. v. to stop; cease.

kutatél: *n.* shriveling of plants. **nakutatel.** a. shriveled (plants). (*kuretret*)

kutáto: agkutato. v. to call dogs by yelling *kúta* or *tóto*.

kotého: (Sp. *cotejo*: comparison) n. comparison; (*dilíg*); canvassing. **Nakikotehoda iti kanginana.** They agreed on its price. They fixed its price.

kútel: n. leprosy; leper. (*kating*) **agkukutel.** n. leper. [Bon. *kolit*, Ivt. *dipad*, Knk. *kulít*, *katíng*, Png. *kating*, Tag. *ketong*]

kutengténg: n. sound of plucking strings; guitar. (*kutibeng*) **agkutengteng.** v. to strum, pluck the strings (of a guitar, harp, etc.). **kutengtengen.** v. to pluck (guitar strings) (*kurengreng*). **Diak inkaskaso ti kusilapna, kinutengtengko ketdi ti gitara nga intedna.** I did not pay attention to her glance, I just strummed the guitar she gave instead. [Tag. *kudyapí*]

kutép: ikutep. v. to insert. (*ligpit*)

kutertér: *n.* shivering (from cold). **agkuterter.** *v.* to shiver (from the cold). (*tigerger*, *pigerger*)

kutí: n. movement. **agkuti.** v. to move, stir. (*gunay*) **kutien.** v. to move, displace. **makapagkuti.** v. to be able to move. **nakutikuti.** a. restless, unquiet, always moving. **saan pay a nakutkuti.** never been touched; (*fig.*) still a virgin. [Png., Tag. *galáw*, Tag. *kilos*]

kútib: *n*. nibble, gnaw. **agkutibkutib**. v. to gnaw, nibble (*kibkib*, *kúrib*). **kutiban**. *v*. to nibble at. **Nakuttong dagiti kalding nga agkutkutib kadagiti kirriit a ruot**. The goats gnawing at the dry grass are thin. [Tag. *ngatngát*]

kutibéng: n. bamboo guitar; stringed instrument. (*kutengténg*)

kutíkut: n. punch used to enlarge holes. **kutikutan**. v. to widen a hole; clean the ear. **agkutikut**. v. to feel remorse; withdraw in shame. **kutikuten**. v. to wind.

kotilión: (Sp. *cotillón*) *n*. cotillion, quadrille dance. **agkotilion**. *v*. to dance the cotillion.

kutím: **agkutim**. v. to peel with the teeth; uproot with the teeth; remove the outer shell of (nuts, etc.) with the teeth; purse the lips. **Nakuttong dagiti kalding nga agkutkutib kadagiti kirriit a ruot**. The goats are thin uprooting the dry grass with their teeth. [Tag. *ngutngót*]

kut-ím: var. of *kutim*.

kutímek: **kutkutimek**. n. kind of marine fish.

kutimermér: *n*. shivering from the cold. **agkutimermer**. v. to shake from being cold and wet. (*tigerger*)

kutíng: n. kitten. **kutingen**. v. to check to see if an object is fixed in place; adjust; repair; handle; finger. [Png., Tag. *kotíng*]

kutingí: n. smallest of a litter; runt of a litter. (*kuttingi*)

kutingtíng: var. of *butingting*: toy with; finger with (in order to fix). **Kutkutingtingen ti agatasuk a pul-oy ti naingpis a puraw a kortina**. The smoke-scented breeze toyed with the thin white curtain.

kutipí: n. kind of tree with poor timber.

kútis: (Tag.*)* n. skin complexion.

kútit: n. rump, buttocks; tail end (*ubet*). [Tag. *puwít*]

kutít: n. a. the last in a row, last in number; last place team. **akinkutit**. a. last in a row, last in line; in last place. **maipakutit**. v. to be the last (*udi*). [Tag. *hulí*]

kutkót: n. grooving plane. **kutkuten**. v. to corrode; wear away (soil); erode; cut a groove in; dig; exhume. **agkutkot**. v. to curl up; huddle up; dig; scratch; exhume.

kúto: n. louse (pl. lice), when young and small called *kámay*, egg is called *lis-á*. **kutuan**. v. to delouse someone. **agkikinnuto**. v. to pick each other's lice. **kutokuto, kuto ti danúm**. n. water strider. **kutokuto**. a. always present; always attending (vagrant). **agikuto**. *v*. to delouse oneself. **ikutuan**. *v*. to delouse someone. **Ti laeng panagkikinnuto iti tukad ti agdan ti paglainganda**. They are only good at delousing each other on the rung of the staircase. [Ibg.,

Kpm. *kutu*, Ivt. *kutuq*, Kal. *tuma*, *kutu*, Png. *kotó*, Tag. *kuto*]

kutóg₁: *n*. shaking. **kutugen**. v. to shake the contents. (*kulog*) **agkutogkutog**. v. to shake repeatedly (contents in a jar, passengers in a car, etc.).

kutóg₂: *var*. of *gutók*: palpitation.

kutók: n. knock. (*toktók*) **agkutok**. v. to knock at the door. **agkutokkutok**. v. to rattle (contents).

kutúkot: **kumutukot**. v. to bore with the finger in the ground; to be piercing (pain); to be affected deeply. **kutukutan**. v. to pierce, bore a hole through.

kutukót: **kutukuten**. v. to shake up; rattle. **agkutukot**. v. to rattle and shake (knees). **Agkutukoten dagiti susuopna**. His joints are rattling. [Tag. *kiníg*]

kutón₁: n. ant; jacket. **kutonen**. v. to be attacked or eaten by ants. **kuton-kuton**. a. infested by ants; full of ants. **kakutunan**. n. nest of ants; army of ants. **ipakuton**. v. to place in an ant nest (as punishment); betray. **Kutonen kano ti tianmo no uminumka iti uray ania a nasam-it a pagpalamiis**. Supposedly your stomach will become ant infested if you drink any kind of sweet refreshment. **Ti kuton, uray ipataynan, agbatok idiay tagapulot**. The ant will dive into the molasses even though it knows it will kill him. [Ibg. *teggem*, Ifg. *gutul*, Ivt. *vuhawuq*, *vuhaw*, Kal. *igom*, Knk. *titínge*, Kpm. *pánas*, Png. *giláta*, Tag. *langgám*]

kutón₂: *n*. jacket.

kutór: **makuturan**. v. to shrink, shiver (with wet cold). **Kasla nakutoran a piek**. He is like a shivering chick. [Tag. *kilíg*]

kutribóng: **kutribongen**. v. to take advantage of someone's weaknesses (*gundaway*).

kutsába: **kakutsaba**. n. conniver; conspirator. **agkakutsaba**. v. to connive; conspire.

kutsára: (Sp. *cuchara*: spoon) n. spoon. (*idos*) **agkutsara**. v. to use a spoon in eating. **kutsaraen**. v. to pick up with a spoon; hit with a spoon. **ikutsaraan**. v. to spoon-feed. **kumutsara**. *v*. to take a spoonful of; dip a spoon in. [Bon. *kotdála*, Kal. *byakÿong*]

kutsaríta: (Sp. *cucharita*: teaspoon) n. teaspoon.

kutsarón: (Sp. *cucharón*: large spoon) n. tablespoon; large spoon. (*sidók*)

kutsáy: (Hok. *kʰû cʰàí*: green leek) n. small variety of garlic with edible scallions, leek.

kótse: (Sp. *coche*: car) n. car, automobile. (*lugan*) **dekotse**. a. owning an automobile. **nakakotse**. *a*. riding in a car. **kotse-kotse**. *n*. toy car.

kutséro: (Sp. *cochero*: coach man) n. driver of a *kalésa* (horse-drawn carriage). **mangutsero.** *v.* to drive a rig.

kutsiláda: (Sp. *cuchillada*: slash) n. acute angle. **kutsiladaan.** v. to cut slantwise.

kutsiliádo: (f. *kutsilio*) *a.* knifelike, knife-shaped.

kutsílio: (Sp. *cuchillo*: knife) n. table knife; knife (*imukó*). **agkutsilio.** v. to use a knife. [Kal. *gipan*]

kutsíno: (Sp. *cochino*: filthy) a. dirty, unkempt, untidy.

kutsínta: n. *puto* rice cake with food coloring.

kutsón: (Sp. *colchón*) *n.* cushion; mattress.

kuttapír: a. skinny, thin. (*kuttong*)

kuttingí: n. runt of the litter.

kuttóng: *n.* slenderness, thinness. **nakuttong.** a. slender, skinny, slim; poor; lean. (*pairpair*; *piit*; *ratiw*; *tariwatiw*) **kumuttong.** v. to become slender; lose weight. **agpakuttong.** v. to diet. [Ibg. *kebbel*, Ivt. *magulang*, Kal., Knk. *kuttung*, Knk. *nabígut*, Png. *ebéng*, *gápil*, Tag. *payát*]

kuttongí: n. very thin person. [Tag. *payát*]

kuttongít: var. of *kuttongi*.

kuwáw: n. typhoon signal.

kuy-ád: **agkuy-ad.** v. to kick the feet or swing the arms fast.

kuyabyáb: n. peeling of dry skin (*kursing*); var. of *payabyab*: kind of shady straw hat. **agkuyabyab.** v. to peel off, flake (dry skin). [Tag. *talup*]

kuyadyád: **agkuyadyad.** v. to struggle by kicking while seated.

kuyákoy: **agkuyakoy.** v. to wriggle, kick about the legs while suspended in mid air. **kuyakuyen.** v. to goad; spur a horse.

kúyam: **kuyamkúyam.** n. tapeworm. (*apatapat*) **agkuyamkuyam.** v. to crawl (*karayam*); slither; wriggle. **Kasla agkuyamkuyam nga igges ti pudot a rumasuk manipud iti rusok ti daga.** The heat flaring from the pit of the earth was like a slithering worm. [Png. *alombayar*, Tag. *ulyabid* (tapeworm)]

kúyap: **kuyapkuyap.** n. wrigglers. **agkuyapkuyap.** v. to feel dizzy. [Tag. *liyó* (dizzy)]

kuyás: *n.* steep slope; *a.* steep; sharp. **nakuyas.** a. steep; sharp (said of facial features); thin faced. **maikuyas.** *v.* to slide. **kuyasan.** n. kind of tree frog with clinging toes. **agpakuyas.** v. to slide down. **ipakuyas.** *v.* to throw something down a slope. [Tag. *tarík* (steep)]

kuyasyás: *n.* sliding. **agkuyasyas.** v. to slide (*galís*, *kuyás*). **mangipakuyasyas.** *v.* to slip; (*fig.*) to jot down, scribble down (notes). [Tag. *dulás*]

kuy-át: **ikuy-at.** v. to lift, raise the legs (*guy-ad*, *kay-at*); shove upward. **agkuy-at.** v. to kick the legs (as when swimming); push oneself forward. **Pinardasanna ti nagkuy-at.** He sped up his kicking (while swimming). [Tag. *sikad*]

kuyawyáw: (obs.) n. noose attached to a pole for catching chickens.

kuyayót: **agkuyayot.** v. to shrink (from cold, pain, etc.).

kuyegyég: **agkuyegyeg.** v. to jerk; tremble (*payegpég*). **nakuyegyeg.** a. jerky. [Tag. *katóg*]

kuyém: *n.* overcast sky. **nakuyem.** a. cloudy, overcast. (*ulep*; *alibuyong*; *daguyemyem*; *kunem*; *langeb*; *lulem*) **kumuyem.** v. to become overcast. **Bassit ti agtubo no nakuyem iti agmalem.** Very little will grow if it is overcast all day. **No masapa ti kuyemkuyem, init nga agmalmalem.** If it is cloudy early in the morning, it will be sunny the whole day. [Kal. *búlot*, Png. *lurém*, *udyem*, Tag. *kulimlím*]

kuyemyém: *n.* raincloud. **nakuyemyem.** *a.* cloudy, overcast (*kuyem*). [Kal. *búlot*]

kúyep: n. with half-shut eyes, blinking eyes; slit-eyed. **agkuyep.** v. to blink (*kimmay*; *kirmed*; *kiray*; *kuridemdem*; *kirem*; *kusipet*). [Tag. *singkít*]

kuykóy: **kuykuyen.** v. to gather together; scrape together with the fingers. (*akoy*) **Nakuykoy amin nga adda iti bolsak.** Everything in my pocket was gathered together. [Tag. *kuykóy*]

kúyog: **agkuyog.** v. to go together. (*kadua*) **kumuyog, kuyugen.** v. to go with, accompany; escort; attend. **kakuyog.** n. companion; escort. **makikuyog.** *v.* to accompany, go with. **kuyogkuyog, makipangkuyog.** n. companions **sangakakuyog.** n. party of people going together. **agpakuyog.** *v.* to look for a companion. **pakuyogen.** *v.* to make people go together. **ipakuyog.** v. to send along with; bid goodbye. **Dios ti kumuyog.** *exp.* May God go with you. **No adda papananna, ikuyognak latta.** If he is going someplace, he just brings me along. [Ibg. *vuluq*, Isg. *bulun*, Ivt. *rararay*, Kpm. *túki*, Png. *ibá*, Tag. *sama*]

kuyúkoy: **kuyukuyen.** v. to persuade; urge; convince. (*guyugoy*)

kuyúos: n. hunger pang. **agkuyuos, kumyuos.** v. to have hunger pangs, to feel hungry.

kuy-ós: **agkuy-os.** v. to feel hungry; feel like vomiting (*kuyuos*). **Kasla agkuy-os ti rusokna.** Her stomach is suffering from hunger pangs.

kuyót: **agkukuyot.** see *agkukurót*.

kuyóte: var. of *kióte*: light cinnamon color; light cinnamon-colored yarn.

kuyyákoy: *n.* swinging the legs when sitting. agkuyyakoy. *v.* to swing the legs while sitting (*kuyakuy*). [Tag. *kuyakoy*]

kuyyáng: *n.* sluggish feeling and slow moving of the body. nakuyyang. *a.* sluggish, slow moving. [Tag. *kuyad*]

kreádo: (Sp. *creado*) *a.* created; made.

kreatíbo: (Sp. *creativo*) *a.* creative.

krédito: (Sp. *crédito*: credit) *n.* credit. [Tag. *paniwalaan*]

kréma: (Sp. *crema*: cream) *n.* cream.

krímen: (Sp. *crimen*: crime) *n.* crime.

kriminál: (Sp. *criminal*: criminal) *n.* criminal (*managdakdakes*). [Tag. *salarín*]

kriminolohía: (Sp. *criminología*) *n.* criminology, scientific study of crime.

krísis: (Sp. *crisis*) *n.* crisis; famine; scarcity of food, money, harvest, etc.

kristál: (Sp. *cristal*) *n.* crystal. bola a kristal. crystal ball.

kristiáno: (Sp. *cristiano*: Christian) *n. a.* Christian. Doktrina Kristiana. Christian Doctrine. agkristiano. *v.* to be a Christian, convert to Christianity.

Krísto: (Sp. *cristo*: Christ) *n.* Christ; person responsible for keeping the bets at a cockfight. Hesukrísto. Jesus Christ. kristos. *n.* candle in the center of the candelabrum used during the *tinieblas* of holy week.

krístos: (f. *kristo*) *n.* candle in the center of the candelabrum used during the *tinieblas* ceremony of holy week.

kritikár: (Sp. *criticar*) kritikaren. *v.* to critique, criticize; analyze; evaluate.

krítiko: (Sp. *crítico*: critic) *n.* critic; *a.* critical.

kritikón: (Sp. *criticón*: critical person) *n.* destructive critic, unnecessarily habitual critic.

Kroáta: (Sp. *croata*) *n.*, *a.* Croat, Croatian.

krúdo: (Sp. *crudo*: crude) *n.* brown sugar; crude oil. *a.* crude.

krókis: (Sp. *croquis*: sketch) *n.* sketch; plan; outline; drawing.

krómo: (Sp. *cromo*) *n.* chrome, chromium.

krónikas: (Sp. *crónica*) *n.* chronicle.

krós: (Eng.*)* krosen. *v.* to cross out.

krús: (Sp. *cruz*: cross) *n.* cross.

krusáda: (Sp. *cruzada*) *n.* crusade.

krusipího: (Sp. *crucifijo*: crucifix) *n.* crucifix.

L

la: abridged form of *láeng*: only; just; merely; barely. **Nagamakak la idi damo.** I was just scared at first. **No adda la kuma mabalinko nga itulong.** If only I would just be able to help. **Nalaing la unay.** He is very intelligent. **Inkanto la agarado no bigaten!** Just go plow tomorrow. [Png. *labát*, Tag. *la(ma)ng*]

láad: nalaad. *a.* ugly, horrible; disgusting; hideous. (*alás*) **kinalaad.** *n.* ugliness. **Naglaaden!** How ugly! [Ibg. *fea, nakasisinnan*, Itg. *alas*, Ivt. *marahet*, Kpm. *matsura*, Png. *aliwá*, Tag. *pangit*]

láag: malaagan. *v.* to be uncultivated (rice fields); left idle, abandoned. (*laeg*) **aglaag.** *v.* to be useless; worthless; idle.

láaw: *n.* shouting; the cry of the hornbill. **aglaaw.** *v.* to shout. **ilaaw.** *v.* to shout something. [Tag. *sigáw, lahaw*]

láay: malaay. *v.* to grieve. **aglalaay.** *v.* (*obs.*) to languish. [Tag. *lungkót, tamláy*]

lába: (Sp. *lava*: lava) *n.* volcanic lava.

labá: (Sp. *lavar*: wash) *n.* act of washing the laundry. **aglaba.** *v.* to wash clothes. **linabaan.** *n.* washed clothes. **kallaba.** *a.* just washed (laundry). **paglabaan.** *n.* place where clothes are washed, Laundromat. **panaglaba.** *n.* laundering. [Ibg. *babbál*, Ivt. *mayvasavasaq*, Kal. *saksak*, Kpm. *pípi*, Png. *pesák*, Tag. *labá*]

lab-áb: *var.* of *lang-áb*: inhale, breathe in.

labábo: (Sp. *lavabo*: lavatory) *n.* washbowl; lavatory.

labáda: (Sp. *lavada*: wash) *n.* laundry.

labadúra: *var.* of *lebadura*: yeast.

lábag: *n.* a strand; single needleful of thread; line; passage (in literature). **labagen.** *v.* to separate strands from. **sangalabag.** *n.* one strand. **linabag.** *n.* threadlike strand.

labága: *n.* redness; (~ **ti itlog**) yolk of an egg. **nalabaga.** *a.* red (*labbásit*); one centavo. (*síping*) **lumabaga.** *v.* to color; turn red. **palabagaen.** *v.* to color something red. **Nadlawko a limmabaga.** I noticed that it turned red. [Ibg. *uzzin*, Itg. *maíngit*, Ivt. *vayaq*, Kal. *cheÿaeg*, Kpm. *malutuq*, Png. *balangá*, Tag. *pulá*]

labáha(s): (Sp. *navaja*: razor) *n.* razor. **labahasan.** *v.* to cut hair with a razor.

labahíta: *n.* blue-lined surgeon fish.

labahón: (Sp. *navajón*: large razor) *n.* kind of large knife.

labaít: *n.* an inflammatory disease of the face. (*kurad*), ringworm. **aglabait.** *v.* to be afflicted with *labait*. [Ibg. *vuni*, Ifg. *kupli*, Itg. *kúlad*, Ivt. *vuñiq*, Kpm. *búni*, Png. *kular*, Tag. *buni*]

labák: labaken. *v.* to maltreat; cut up an animal; abuse, beat; cut up. **Pinagsaggaysa ida ni Inangda iti labak.** Their mother beat them one by one.

labakára: (Sp. *lava*: wash, *cara*: face) *n.* washcloth.

lában: (Tag.) *n.* fight, quarrel; feud; competition. **lumaban.** *v.* to fight (*apa*); compete (*salisal*). **labanan.** *v.* to fight with someone. **aglaban.** *v.* to fight with one another; oppose; quarrel. **ilaban.** *v.* to fight for (a cause). **makilaban.** *v.* to join a fight, quarrel, brawl. **mannakilaban.** *n.* fighter. **ipalaban.** *v.* to have someone fight against someone else. **ipapalaban.** *n.* person or animal readied for a fight. **mannakilaban.** *n.* fighter.

labanág: aglabanag. *v.* to ripen (fruits). (*luom*, *darangidángan*)

labandéra: (Sp. *lavandera*: laundress) *n.* laundress; one who washes the clothes. **labandería.** *n.* laundromat.

labáng: *a.* spotted, specked; variegated; (*coll.*) without a political affiliation. **labangan.** *a.* spotted. **aglabanglabang.** *v.* to be spotted. **Ti la madaldalawat ta dilam a labang!** Your spotted tongue just chatters (gossip)!

labár: (Sp. *lavar*: wash) **labaren.** *v.* to sponge; wash (with a sponge or face towel).

lábas: *n.* passing; overlooking of something. **aglabas.** *v.* to pass by; skip, omit. **aglabaslabas.** *v.* to come and go, pass back and forth. **lumabas.** *v.* to pass by; pass on; pass through; get through. **labasan, labsan.** *v.* to overpass someone; skip; pass over, overlook. **malabasan.** *v.* to be passed by. **napalabas.** *a.* past. *n.* past. **ilabas.** *v.* to cause (a parade) to pass; pass by with something. **ipalabas.** *v.* to do in a superficial manner; dart a glance at. **palabsan.** *v.* to scan; skim. **palabsen.** *v.* to let go; not mind; let pass. **aglabaslabas.** *v.* to pass back and forth. **agpalabas.** *v.* to let pass; tolerate; be understanding. **makapagpalabas.** *v.* to be able to let something pass; tolerate. **kallabas.** *a.* just passed by. **awan labas.** all; without exception. **Nangpalabasan laeng iti oras ni Raul ti panangukradna iti pagiwarnak.** Raul just spent his time opening the newspaper. [Png. *labás*, Tag. *daán*]

labásit: nalabasit. *a.* red, reddish. (*labbasit*, *labbaga*)

labatíba: (Sp. *lavativa*: enema) *n.* enema. **aglabatiba.** *v.* to have an enema. **agpalabatiba.** *v.* to get an enema. **labatibaan.** *v.* to give someone an enema.

lábay: *n.* skein, measurement of yarn. **ilabay.** *v.* to reel cotton yarn. **lalabayan.** *n.* reel; bamboo roof supports.

labáy: *n.* rice porridge; tastelessness. **ilabay.** *v.* to mix the broth of something into rice. **labayen.** *v.* to make into porridge. [Tag. *labay*]

lab-áy: nalab-ay. *a.* tasteless, flat (food); lukewarm; uninterested. **lum-abay.** *v.* to become tasteless; to cool off (relationships).

labbá: *n.* basket, general term for handleless baskets. **linabba.** *a.* by the basket. **sangalabba.** *n.* one basketful. [Kal. *langaya*, Tag. *bakol*, *buslô*, *pangnán*]

labbága: *var.* of *labaga*: red. [Tag. *pulá*]

labbásit: *var.* of *labasit*: red. **Kasla nabartek ngamin ni Akong ta nakalablabbasit ti rupana.** Akong seemed to be drunk because his face was quite red. [Tag. *pulá*]

labbátis: *n.* red color, red tint (see *labbasit*).

labbég: aglabbeg. *v.* to beat the water when fishing with the hands (*kíbur*). **mailabbeg.** *v.* to be at a loss for words, to be left speechless.

labbét: aglabbet. *v.* to flock together (*aribungbong*); come to grips. **panglablabbetan.** *v.* to unite; overwhelm. **Naglabbet ti saem ken pungtot ti barukongna.** The pain and anger inside him mixed.

labbí: *n.* protruding lower lip in anger. see *libbi*.

labég: *n.* sign, omen. **malabgan.** *v.* to be confused; to lose one's bearings. **makalabeg.** *v.* to confuse, muddle. **labegen.** *v.* to frighten; startle. **mailabeg.** *v.* to be left speechless.

labentadór: *var.* of *rebentadór*: fireworks.

lábeng: labenglabeng. *n.* fishes caught in one netting; *a.* all without exception.

labéng: *a.* spotted, speckled. (*labang*)

labér: *n.* violin.

labés: *n.* any place beyond something; other side. **nalabes.** *a.* excessive; too much (*palalo*). **lumabes.** *v.* to go past or beyond; to have enough time. **ilabes.** *v.* to cause to go beyond; do just a little more than enough. **kallabes.** *a.* last; past. **kallabes a bulan.** this past month, last month. **labsan.** *v.* to overtake; overdo. **labsen.** *v.* to overdo; overtake; exaggerate. **aglablabes.** *v.* to be excessive. **apaglabes.** *adv.* just past; just across. **iti labes.** *prep.* beyond, across; nevertheless; despite. **iti mapalabes.** *prep.* after. **panaglalabes.** *n.* abusiveness; act of being excessive. **palabsen.** *v.* to let pass; be patient with someone. **Dakes ti ania man nga aglabes.** Anything done to excess is bad. **Nalabesen ti oras a nagtulaganmi a panagkita.** It's way past the time we agreed to see each other. **Aglablabeskan!** You are getting out of

hand! You're too much! [Png. *solók*, Tag. *higít* (excessive)]

lábi: (*obs.*) *n.* remnant. **labien.** *v.* to be overdue. **labilabi.** *n.* toad; obese person.

labiáng: aglabiang. *v.* to overflow (*lippias*; *pussuak*; *ragso*; *sayasay*; *silno*). [Tag. *apaw*]

labíd₁: *n.* a variety of palm. (*anaaw*)

labíd₂: *n.* gossipmonger. (*salawasaw*, *tarabitab*) **nalabid.** *a.* babbling, chattering, gossipy. **labiden.** *v.* to spread gossip or rumors. **Adu la unay ti lablabidem!** You really gossip a lot! [Tag. *daldál*]

labídaw: aglabidaw. *v.* to chatter, gab.

labíg: (*reg.* Cagayan) *n.* a farmer's raincoat. (*abbiang*; *anaaw*)

labílab: labilaban. *a.* with a thick edge or border; with thick lips (horses). **aglabilab.** *v.* to reveal a secret (*labláb*).

labindawáya: *n.* song sung while working. **aglabindawaya.** *v.* to sing while working.

labinduáya: (*obs.*) *n.* a variety of palm tree.

labinduayyá: *var.* of *labindawaya*: sing while working.

labintadór: (Sp. *rebentador*: explosive) *n.* firecracker.

lábit: *n.* possibility. **nalabit.** *a.* probable; likely. (*ngata*) **Adda lablabitna.** It is possible. **Nalabit agisangpetkanto iti sinupot a pirak.** It is likely that you will bring back a bagful of money. **Nalabit mangapkappo.** He is probably gathering clams. [Tag. *marahil*]

labitang: *var.* of *labitangtáng*: impertinent talk.

labitangtáng: *n.* idle talk, prattle. **labitangtangen.** *v.* to blab, prattle, speak idly; gossip. **Ania't labitangtangem?** What are you blabbing about?

labláb₁: *n.* scum from boiling; licking; bubbles from boiling. **aglablab.** *v.* to eat with a spoon something that is boiling; lick up. **lablaben.** *v.* to lick something.

labláb₂: nalablab. *a.* chattering, talkative. (*tarabitab*, *salawasaw*)

labnáw: (Tag.) **nalabnaw.** *a.* thin (said of liquids, soups, etc.); watery (*lasaw*). [Png. *lasaw*, Tag. *labnáw*]

labnég: lumabneg. *v.* to become black-and-blue (bruise). (*litem*)

labnéng: *n.* pond; dam. (*ban-aw*, *basáw*)

labnít: labniten. to pull off; to pull down.

lábo: labuen. *v.* to anoint; smear with oil. **nalabo.** *a.* covered in oil or grease. [Tag. *pahid*]

labuág: *n.* idol to a dead relative.

labudiáw: nalabudiaw. *a.* yellowish. (*duyaw*) **lumabudiaw.** *v.* to turn yellowish. [Tag. *diláw*]

labudóy: nalabudoy. *a.* smooth; fluffy; fat and weak (persons).

lábog: *n.* quicksand.

lab-úg: palab-ug. *n.* trap, pitfall. **agpalab-ug.** *v.* to trap an opponent. **maipalab-ug.** *v.* to fall into a trap. **ipalab-ug.** *v.* to trap; betray; lead into a trap. [Tag. *bitag*]

lab-ók: *n.* cornmeal.

labón: aglabon. *v.* to be in abundance. (*adu, ruay*) **aglablabon.** *v.* to have things in abundance. **napalabonan.** *a.* excessive. **nalabon.** *a.* abundant, plentiful. **kinalabon.** *n.* abundance. **Agmulakayo tapno aglablabonantayo iti taraon.** Plant so we will have abundant food. [Tag. *saganà, pasasà*]

lábong: labonglabong. *n.* jellyfish-like substance from the sea; clot of blood expelled during childbirth.

labóng: labonglabong. *a.* loose (clothes), ill-fitting. (*kalawkalaw*) **aglabonglabong.** *v.* to be ill fitting. [Tag. *luwáng*]

lab-óng: *n.* lasso used as a trap. **lab-ongan.** *v.* to lasso. (*silo, kay-ong*) **mailab-ong.** *v.* to be caught; to fall down a pit; to be ambushed.

labór: *n.* decoration, embellishment. **nalabor.** *a.* richly decorated, ornate, embellished.

laboratório: (Sp. *laboratorio*: laboratory) *n.* laboratory.

lábus: *a.* naked (from the waist down), naked from the waist up = *uksob.* **silalabus.** *a.* naked; nude. (*lamolamo*) **aglabus.** *v.* to take off one's clothes; strip. **labusan.** *v.* to remove the clothes of another person, strip someone. **nalabusan.** *a.* stripped (of one's clothing). [Ibg. *nevaruwasiyan,* Ifg. *numbolad,* Ivt. *dahwas, vahas,* Kal. *polas, patiwayway,* Knk. *lasúlas,* Kpm. *lubas,* Png. *lakseb,* Tag. *hubô, hubád*]

labútab: *n.* foam; spume; bubble. (*luag, tarabutab; burek*) **aglabutab.** *v.* to bubble, foam up. **Agwasangwasang, aglablabutab ti ngiwatna ken kasla ubing nga aganug-og.** He squirmed, dripped bubbles from his mouth, and whined like a baby. [Bon. *ósab,* Ibg. *vúgaq,* Ivt. *umhutab,* Kal. *tebuteb,* Knk. *lavúlab, luág,* Png. *burá, palwag,* Kpm., Tag. *bulâ*]

labúyak: see *yakuyak:* reproduce; diffuse; spread.

labúyo: (Tag. *labuyò:* wild chicken) *n.* wild chicken; cockfighting rooster.

labrá: (Sp. *labrar:* work; cut) **labraan.** *a.* to prune, trim (*taga*); cut wood.

labradór: (Sp. *labrador:* cutter, carver) *n.* one who cuts wood; carver.

labsín: lumabsin. *v.* to slip, slide out of place; stray.

labsíng: labsingen. *v.* to go against, disobey; violate. **lumabsing.** *v.* to slide out of place, deviate. **managlabsing.** *n.* violator. [Tag. *labág*]

labsíw: *syn.* of *labsin:* slip; slide out of place.

labsóng: *n.* muddy waterhole. (*libsong*)

labtáng: *n.* a kind of vine whose stems are used in ropes and whose roots have medicinal value.

labtík: *n.* beat, throb (of the heart); pant (out of breath).

ládak: *n.* (*obs.*) crag.

ládam: *n.* heat of the fire; radiation. **iladam.** *v.* to scorch over the fire. **maladaman.** *v.* to be scorched, burned. **ladaman.** *v.* scorch, burn something.

ládaw₁: *n.* a species of crab.

ládaw₂: naladaw. *a.* late. **managladladaw.** *n.* one who is usually late. **maladaw.** *v.* to be late. **ladladawen.** *v.* to do late. **iladaw.** *v.* to do something late. **Ania ngamin ti nakaladawam aya?** What made you so late (Why are you late)? **Masapol a maawat dagiti surat iti saan a naladladaw ngem intono umay a lawas.** The letters must be received no later than next week. [Ivt. *ahay, vayag,* Png. *ebés,* Tag. *hulí*]

ladáwan: *n.* image; picture; photo; painting. **iladawan.** *v.* to picture, imagine; depict. **inladawan ni.** illustrated by. **mailadawan.** *v.* to be portrayed. [Knk. *amínew,* Png. *lupa,* Tag. *larawan*]

ladawang: *n.* illegitimate child. (*anak ti ruar*)

laddák: mangladdak. *n.* occupants, inhabitants, dwellers.

laddég: (*reg.*) **naladdegan.** *a.* overpowered; outnumbered.

laddíng: see *lidding:* slight difference.

laddít: *n.* roller gin for cotton; scapegoat. **ladditen.** *v.* to crush; grind; gin cotton; (*fig.*) put the blame upon. **maladdit.** *v.* to be crushed; to be ground; to be blamed (for someone else's fault), be used as a scapegoat. **Siak ti ladditenna no makitanaka.** I will be the one he blames if he sees you. **Kabagian ken kabagian, aglinnaddit.** Relative against relative, they are blaming each other.

ladég: *var.* of *laddeg.*

ládek: *n.* coconut scum used to extract oil (by product of cooking *getta*).

ladét: *n.* rafters (in construction).

ladíno: (Sp. *ladino:* cunning, crafty; versed in languages) *a.* handy; skillful; clever. (*alibtak; sikap; tarem; alisto; saldet*)

ladíngit: *n.* sorrow; grief; distress. (*liday; leddaang*) **naladingit.** *a.* sorrowful, mournful. **nakaladladingit.** *a.* sorrowful, grievous. **agladingit.** *v.* to be sad, mournful. **ladingiten.** *v.*

to be sad about; to be sorry about; to mourn for. **pannakipagladingit.** *n.* condolence. **Makipagladingitkami.** We share in your sorrows (used in consoling bereaved people). **No pagladingitem ni amam wenno inam, addanto dakes nga inka malak-am.** If you hurt your father's or mother's feelings, you will be made to suffer for it. [Ibg. *reddem*, Ivt. *mangsah*, Kal. *langchu*, Kpm. *lungkót*, Png. *ermén*, Tag. *lungkót, lumbáy*]

ladírio: *var.* of *ladrilio*: brick.

ladlád: maladladan. *v.* to be smoothened after whetting; to increase; scrape the skin; saddled with duties. **ladladan.** *v.* to scrape the skin.

ládog: *n.* sediment of rivers; dregs. (*rinsaed*) **naladog.** *a.* full of sediments; turned to brown (said of feet that have been soaking in the rice fields for too long). **ladladogen.** *v.* (*fig.*) to wait for a long time doing nothing, be idle for quite some time (*lumot*). **No kanayon ngamin a mayuper iti taltalon, ladogenka iti kasta unay ken agbalin nga umamarilio dagiti sakam.** If you are always soaking in the fields, you will get infested with sediments and your feet will become yellow. [Tag. *latak*]

ladút: *a.* lean. poor; lean cotton balls and segments. **aglaladut** (*ti rikna*). *v.* to feel sluggish; dull (*mamayo*). **Aglaladut la ket ngarud a napan nagdiram-os.** He also went to wash his face sluggishly.

ladrílio: (Sp. *ladrillo*: brick) *n.* brick; tile.

ladrón: (Sp. *ladrón*: thief) *n.* thief, robber. (*mananakaw*)

laég: *a.* sterile; impotent (person); unproductive. **laegan.** *v.* to leave uncultivated; abandon. **aglaeg.** *v.* to become dull; (*obs.* to fit for operation); lie fallow. **agkalaegan.** *v.* to fallow; remain uncultivated. **lumaeg.** *v.* to spread inside the body (sickness). [Tag. *baóg*]

laém₁: *n.* inside of a house; principal part of a house. **lalaem.** *n.* viscera; entrails. **lumaem.** *v.* to go inside (into the living room). **makalaem.** *v.* to be able to enter; to get a foothold. **manglaem.** *v.* to reach the core; be affected deeply. **palaemen.** *v.* to have someone enter from outside; to have someone enter the living room. **agpalaem.** *v.* to enter a living room, go inside; (*fig.*) marry, go home together. [Knk. *leém*, Tag. *loób*]

laém₂: **ilaem.** *v.* to include in a meal. (*lak-am*) **nailaem.** *a.* included in a meal.

laén: (*obs.*) *n.* renting out rice fields.

láeng: *part.* only, just; ever (contrast *latta*). **met laeng.** though; nevertheless, anyway, however; also. **isu met laeng.** that is why, no wonder; it's the same. **laenglaengen.** *v.* to consider something much less important than what it actually is, belittle by using the word *laeng*. **Kadkaduaenta laeng ida.** Let's just accompany them. **Ti laengen nuangda a baket ti natda a tarakenda.** Only their old female water buffalo was left out of their animals. **Laenglaengem ti makabulan.** You think one month is nothing (are saying *laeng* to one month?) [Ibg. *láman*, Png. *bengát, labát, lambengát*, Tag. *lamang*]

laés: nalaes. *a.* tainted (meat); beginning to putrefy. **malaes.** *v.* to smell from being rotten; to lose color when rotting. [Tag. *bilasà*]

laét: laetan. *v.* to fortify; do more diligently. (*lagda*; *pigsa*; *saet*)

lága: *n.* a woven basket; basketwork. **aglaga.** *v.* to weave baskets. **paglaga.** *n.* material used in making baskets. **ilaga.** *v.* to put inside a woven basket. **linaga.** *a.* woven. **mailaga.** *v.* to be interwoven with. **Sinaklotna dagiti naglilinaga a ramayna.** He put his interwoven fingers in his lap. [Ibg. *manikol*, Ifg. *lagga*, Ivt. *mayapyapin*, Kpm., Tag. *lála*, Png. *laga*, Tag. *habi*]

lagáb: (*coll.*) **malagabán.** *v.* to be dominated by the wife (a henpecked husband). (*ander*)

lagában: (*obs.*) **malagabanan.** *v.* to get wet in a boat; be drenched with waves.

lagádan: *n.* a kind of speckled pigeon.

lágak: ilagak. *v.* to entrust with, put in charge. (*talek*)

lag-án: *n.* lightness; (*fig.*) easiness.. **nalag-an.** *a.* light (not heavy); nimble, active. **nalag-an a rikna.** compatible; easy disposition, free from tension. **laglag-anen.** *v.* to do something easily. **nalag-an a pannangan.** light meal. **lumag-an.** *v.* to become light, lighten up. **makapalag-an.** *a.* alleviating, giving relief. **palag-anen.** *v.* to lighten (a load). **Nalag-an ti rikna dagiti dadakkelna kaniak.** Her parents feel well toward me. **nalag-an a gasat.** *n.* good luck. **Limmag-an ti riknak iti nangegko.** My feelings eased up from what I heard. [Bon. *kilaw, yap-ew*, Ibg. *alappaw*, Ivt. *maqpaw*, Kal. *mallangpaw*, Knk. *yap-éw*, Kpm. *mayan*, Png. *leméw*, Tag. *gaán*]

laganáp: aglaganap. *v.* to spread over; spread.

lagandáya: (*obs.*) *n.* wide trousers.

lagangán: *n.* cloth upon which pots are placed.

lagárna: lagarna ti paltog. *n.* holster of a gun.

lágaw₁: malagawan. *v.* to be confused, stunned. **nalagaw.** *a.* impatient, restless. **aglagaw.** *v.* to be impatient, in a hurry; stunned. **Naglagaw itay kalikaguman ni Paula ti yuumayna kano ditoy ta sukonenna ni Carlos.** He was confused when Paula wanted him to come here because Carlos was fetching him. [Tag. *tarantá*]

lágaw₂: nalagaw. *a.* greedy, voracious (*rawet, antukab*). [Tag. *takaw*]

lagáy: (Tag.) *n.* tong; bribe. **aglagay.** *v.* to bribe; give tong money.

lagdá: nalagda. *a.* durable, strong; tough; reliable; trustworthy. **lagdaan.** *v.* to fortify, ensure; ratify; validate. **kinalagda.** *n.* durability. **palagdaen.** *v.* to make durable. **Mabalinta a paglagdaen ti ayat no ikkannak iti sabali a gundaway.** We can fortify our love if you give me another chance. [Png. *málet*, Tag. *tibay*]

lagdáw: *n.* a kind of small freshwater prawn; a variety of rice. **Kasla lagdaw a nabuyatan iti suka idi maamirisna ti inaramidna.** He was like a shrimp with vinegar poured on top when he found out what she did. [Kal. *lagchew, alamang, pangkok*, Tag. *hipon* (shrimp)]

lagép: lumagep. *v.* to dip in a river.

laggít: (*obs.*) *n.* lack of water. (*igaaw*)

lágid: ilagid. *v.* to whet, sharpen. (*asa*) **lumagid.** *v.* to wiggle about (dogs and cats), frolic about (*lagod*). **Lagid a lagid ti pusana iti sakana.** His cat just frolics about restlessly at his feet. [Tag. *lagís* (hone, whet)]

lagídaw: lagidawen. *v.* to feel sorry, sad; be insulted or hurt by something; be offended. (*babawi*)

lagílaw: *var.* of *lagidaw*: offended.

lagingána: *n.* variety of rice; variety of maize with red kernel.

lagíp: *n.* recollection; memory; remembrance. **malagip.** *v.* to remember. **makalagip.** *v.* to remember, be able to remember; be nostalgic. **lagipen.** *v.* to remember, recall. **palagip.** *n.* prayer in memory of the dead. **palagipan.** *v.* to remind; advise. **ipalagip.** *v.* to remind. **nakallalagip.** *a.* memorable. **pakalaglagipan.** *n.* remembrance, souvenir. **silalagip.** *a.* remembering, mindful. [Ibg. *deddemman*, Ivt. *katuvidan*, Kal. *masmasok*, Knk. *áka*, Kpm. *tandaq*, Png. *nónot*, Tag. *alaala*]

lágis: *n.* strips of bamboo in a bamboo fence.

lagisí: mailagisi. *v.* to slip off (a chair) (*ligasi*). [Tag. *dulás*]

lagkitán: *n.* variety of corn with white kernel; the seven stars variety of marijuana.

laglág: nalaglag. *a.* idiotic, dumb, stupid, asinine. (*tabbed, nengneng*)

lágud: aglagudlagud. *v.* to frolic about (*lagid*); caper; get in the way. **No lumagudlagod ti pusa kaniak no adda sangailik, makugtarak.** If the cat gets in my way when I have guests, I kick it.

laguérta: (Sp. *la huerta*: the garden) *n.* garden. (*bangkag; hardin; minuyongan; werta*)

lágum: ilagum. *v.* to bestow; include. (*raman*)

lagúna: (Sp. *laguna*: lagoon) *n.* lagoon.

lag-óy: aglag-oy. *v.* to walk cautiously; to skip; sway while walking; hop. **Napalalo ti panaglag-oy ti butiogna.** His fat stomach wiggled excessively. **Adu a balse ti kinantana a dinanggayan ti panaglaglag-oyna.** He sang a lot of waltzes accompanied by his skipping.

lagpít: *n.* closely woven basket. (*kalupi*) **nalagpit.** *a.* thin, emaciated. (*pipilay; pair; kuttong*)

lagsít₁: *var.* of *lagtit*: fast, swift.

lagsít₂: laglagsit. *n.* shrimps. (*kuros*)

lagtít: nalagtit. *a.* fast, swift, quick (*paspas, pardas*). **Saan! Uray napalagtit iti saretset ti bangos a naibbatanna iti pariok!** No! even if the milkfish he drops into the pot squirms as it sizzles!

lagtó: *n.* jump. **lumagto.** *v.* to jump. (*battoto; lokso; layaw*) **aglagto.** *v.* to jump over; jump rope. **lagtuen.** *v.* to leap over. **palagto.** *n.* a mudfish trap. **linnagtuan.** *n.* broad jump; jump; jumping competition. **no di lumagto.** *exp.* if it doesn't fail. **Limmagto ti pusok a nakasirpat iti ladawanna.** My heart jumped upon seeing the image of her. [Ivt. *hukso*, Png. *taboy*, Tag. *talón, lundág*]

láha: (Sp. *laja*: slab; flagstone) *n.* slab; flagstone.

lahár: (Eng.) *n.* running volcanic debris mixed with water, volcanic mudflow.

lahóta: (Sp. *la jota*: kind of dance) *n.* Spanish folk dance.

laí: *syn.* of *saluyot*.

láid: ilaid. *v.* to sharpen (knives); whet (*asa*). [Tag. *lagís*]

laíd: ilaid. *v.* to winnow; fan (rice). (*taep*)

láigo: (Sp. *laico*: layman) *n.* layman, person not associated with the clergy.

laílang: aglailang. *v.* to stroll. (*pasiar*)

laílo: *n.* caress. **aglailo.** *v.* to coax; cajole, caress, fondle. **aglinnailo.** *v.* to caress each other. **lailuen.** *v.* to touch tenderly, caress. **nalailo.** *a.* affectionate, loving, caressing. **kalailo.** *v.* to mutually caress. **ilalailo.** *v.* to do tenderly (speak, etc.). **silalailo.** *a.* affectionately, tenderly, lovingly. [Tag. *lamyâ, karinyo* (Sp.)]

láing: (Tag.) *n.* Bicolano dish of taro leaves cooked with dried fish, chili, and coconut milk.

laíng: *n.* intelligence; prowess; aptitude; beauty (encompasses many positive qualities). **nalaing.** *a.* smart, intelligent, good (at something), graceful, pretty; kind, friendly; competent; dexterous; well. **kinalaing.** *n.* intelligence; competence. **aglaing.** *v.* to be intelligent; to get better (sickness); to dominate in a field, do well. **laingen.** *v.* to do something well. **la-laingén.** *v.* to do to one's utmost. **aginlalaing.** *v.* to be presumptuous; pretend to be clever. **agpakpakalaing.** *v.* to make oneself sound better than others; to try to impress, put oneself in a good light. **lumaing.** *v.* to get well, improve; become intelligent. **kalainganna, kalkalaingánna.** just right; just the right amount. **kalálaingán.** *n.* the best time, to be at the height of (one's beauty, etc.). **kalalaingán.** *a.* wisest; most intelligent. **makapalaing.** *a.* comforting, able to relieve symptoms of a cold. **paglaingan.** *n.* field of specialty; skill. **agpápalaíng, agpalpalaing.** *v.* to recover from sickness, get well. **Aglalaingda manen.** They are on good terms again. **Kalalainganna laeng ti partak ti panagsalogko.** I went downhill at just the right speed. **Nalaing kadagiti nakaikamanganna.** He is on good terms with his in-laws. **Dikayo koma aginlalaing no awan met paglaingyo.** Don't pretend to be intelligent if you have no intelligence. **Nalaing a mangilut, nalaing pay a mangalbasia.** She is good at massaging, and she is also good at match-making. [Kal. *sam-ot, laing,* Png. *dunong,* Tag. *talino, galíng*]

láis: **laisen.** *v.* to despise (*uyaw*); scorn; discriminate. **makalais.** *a.* scornful; insulting. **mananglais.** *n.* one who despises; snob. **pananglais.** *n.* insult; snobbery. **Linalais ken kinatkatawaandaka dagiti am-ammotayo gapu kenkuana.** The people that we know despise you and laugh at you because of her. [Tag. *kutyâ*]

láit: **nalaitan.** *a.* trimmed; in good condition; orderly. (*urnos*)

láka: *n.* cotton yarn.

laká: **nalaka.** *a.* easy; cheap. **lumaka.** *v.* to become cheaper in price; easy. **ipalaka.** *v.* to sell at bottom prices. **laklakaen.** *v.* to do easily, without much effort; to sell at a cheap price. **panglakaan.** *n.* means of doing something easily. **ipalaka.** *v.* to sell at a low price (*taliwaga, sidor*). **Laklakaek laeng a tuktukkolen dagiti tultulangna.** I will easily break his bones. [Ibg. *neppoq* (cheap), Ivt. *mahumis* (cheap), *sunung* (easy), Kal. *laka,* Knk. *lak-á, oóto,* Png. *inomay* (easy), *múra* (cheap), Tag. *gaán* (easy), *murà* (cheap)]

lákad: **agpalakad.** *v.* to go by land; walk. (*pagna*) **lakadlakad.** *n.* walker; support for walking.

lakaddóg: *var.* of *lakaddóng*: very old.

lakaddóng: (*coll.*) **lakaddongan.** *a.* very old, decrepit; ancient.

lákag: **ikalakag.** *v.* to take under one's protection; defend.

lakág: **panglakagan.** *n.* means to do things easy; easy way; method; device. **Dagiti pagannurotan ken panglakagan iti panagsurat.** The rules and method of writing. [Tag. *pamamaraán*]

lakáid: **lakaiden.** *v.* to refuse, reject, discard.

lak-ám: **lak-amen.** *v.* to enjoy; comprehend; gain; include; share; *n.* suffering. **ilak-aman.** *v.* to take in; include. **aglak-am.** *v.* to benefit; bare; suffer undeserved punishment. **kalakaman.** *n.* luck, fate; misfortune. **Kakaasikami a naglak-am iti rigat.** We are pitiful in suffering hardships. [Tag. *sakop, sakláw*]

lakampána: (Sp. *la campana:* the bell) *n.* bell-shaped skirt.

lákan: (*obs.*) *n.* respected tribal leader.

lakángan: *n.* variety of awned rice.

lákas: **lalakasen.** *n.* sardinelike marine fish.

lakása: (Sp. *la casa:* the chest) *n.* truck; chest. **ilakasa.** *v.* to lock up in a chest. **lakasa ti tulag.** *n.* ark of testimony. **sangalakasa.** *n.* one trunkful; one chestful. [Kal. *kasun,* Tag. *kabán*]

lakatán: (Tagalog also) *n.* variety of sweet thick-skinned banana.

lakáy: *n.* old man; husband; colloquial term of address between males; *a.* old (males). **apo lakay.** *n.* parish priest; man in power. **panglakayén.** *n.* headman; chief. **linalakay.** *n.* something characteristic of old men. **lumakay.** *v.* to grow old (said of males). **aglakaylakay.** *v.* to act like an old man. **agallakay.** *n.* husband and wife. **agatlakay.** *n.* smell of old men. **laklakayan.** *a.* very old, ancient, antique. [Ibg. *lakalákay,* Ivt. *malkem,* Kal. *memeÿong-eg,* Knk. *alapó,* Kpm. *matwa,* Png. *sikén,* Tag. *matandâ*]

lakáyo: (Sp. *lacayo:* lackey) *n.* circus clown; stage jester, comic character.

lakép: *n.* a kind of flat marine fish; a kind of small songbird.

lakí1: *n.* full-grown cuttlefish (*bumagto*); squid, [Ivt. *kanañis*]

lakí2: see also *lalaki.* **lakién.** *a.* masculine; manly (woman) *n.* tomboy; lesbian. **kalakian.** *n.* male.

láking: *n.* endearing term of address for a grandfather.

lakkó: *n.* (*anat.*) ham. **lakko ti siko.** *n.* part of the arm opposite the elbow. [Kal. *kiyod,* Tag. *alakalakán*]

laklák: **malaklakan.** *v.* to be skinned; flayed.

lakmút: (*reg.*) **nalakmut.** *v.* caught by a storm.

laknáb: *var.* of *saknap*: spread, disseminate, become popular.

láko: *n.* merchandise for sale. **aglako.** *v.* to sell. **aglakolako.** *v.* to buy and sell. **ilako.** *v.* to sell something. **mailako.** *v.* to be sold. **malako.** *v.*

to be sold; (*coll.*) to be fooled. **tagilako.** *n.* merchandise. **paralako.** *n.* salesperson. **pagtagilakuan.** *n.* store; market. **paglakuan.** *n.* amount of sale. **pangilakuan.** *n.* selling price. **pannakilinnako.** *n.* trade, commerce. [Ibg. *máku*, Ivt. *dákaw*, Kal. *ngila*, Kpm. *tinda*, Png. *láko*, Tag. *lakò, bilí*]

lakuátsa: (Tag.) **aglakuatsa.** *v.* to spend time idly, go from place to place; to be truant. (*sorsor, baliudong, ballog*) **lakuatsero.** *n.* person who spends time idly.

lakúb: *n.* enclosure; encirclement. **lakuben.** *v.* to surround, encircle; block. **lalakuben.** *n.* variety of awned late rice. **malakub.** *v.* to be surrounded. **iti lakub.** *prep.* around. [Tag. *paligid*]

lakuét: **panaglilinnakuet.** *n.* negotiations, transactions.

lakúlap: (*obs.*) *n.* deteriorated, rotten rice.

lakón: *n.* enclosure. **malakon.** *v.* to be blocked; hindered; caught (by a storm); barred. **lakonen.** *v.* to isolate; enclose; surround. (*lawlaw*)

lakóniko: (Sp. *lacónico*: laconic) *a.* laconic, brief in speech, using few words.

lákong: **kalakóngan.** *n.* marshland.

lakutannáy: **nalakutannay** *a.* bent; stooping.

lákre: (Sp. *lacre*: sealing wax) *n.* sealing wax. **ilakre.** *v.* to apply sealing wax to.

laksá: (*obs.*) *n.* vermicelli. *num.* ten thousand **sangalaksa.** ten thousand. [Tag. *laksá*]

laksánte: (Sp. *laxante*: laxative) *n.* laxative. (*purga*) **aglaksante.** *v.* to take a laxative.

laksíd: *prep.* beyond, on the other side of. **i-laksid.** *v.* to set aside; get rid of; exclude; eliminate. **malaksid.** *prep.* except. **laksiden.** *v.* to disregard, forget; eliminate; exempt; put aside. **iti laksid.** *prep.* beyond, at the other side of, outside (of a fence); despite. **lumaksid.** *v.* to drop out, separate from a group. **iti laksid ti amin.** in spite of everything. **Saanna a nailaksid ti kabbibawna.** She did not get rid of her wry mouth. [Tag. *liban*]

laksíw: *var.* of *laksid*.

laktáw: *n.* jump; leap; stride. (*lagto*) **laktawen.** *v.* to leap over; skip; elude. **linnaktaw.** *n.* a girl's jumping game. **laktawan.** *v.* to skip, omit. **lalaktawan.** *n.* gate with a low bar to step over. [Knk. *lakdáw*, Tag. *talón, lagpás*]

lalabáyan: *n.* skein of thread; spinning instrument for thread.

laladút: *n.* bad feelings; (*ti ima*) *n.* hangnail. **aglaladut.** *v.* to feel bad.

lalaém: *n.* internal organs.

laláki: (pl. *lallaki*) *n.* boy; man; anything masculine; male. **napalalaki.** *v.* handy at men's work (women). **kalalaki.** *n.* the larger part of a pair of two things; male plant. **malalaki.** *a.* masculine; looking strong and responsible; daring; courageous; intelligent. **kinamalalaki.** *n.* masculinity, manhood, manliness. **lallaki.** *n.* boys (plural of *lalaki*). **aglallalaki.** *v.* to dominate over other men. **kalakian.** *n.* the male (of a pair of animals); masculine. **makilalaki.** *v.* to have an affair with a man. **pannakalalaki.** *n.* (woman) representing a man or taking a man's position. [Ibg., Kpm. *lalaki*, Kal. *leÿaki*, Ivt. *hakay*, Png. *lakí, bológ*, Tag. *lalake*]

lalán: *n.* deepening flood. **lumalan, aglalan.** *v.* to deepen and spread (rash, etc.).

lálat: *n.* leather; hide; skin. **lalaten.** *v.* to make into leather; flay; thrash. **lalatan.** *v.* to skin, remove the skin of. (*kulanit*) **palalat.** *n.* the leather band of a slingshot. **nakalalat.** *a.* wearing leather. **Uray no lalatem, saanen a maisubli ti tinakawna.** Even if you thrash him, what he stole will not be returned. [Knk. *kúdil*, Png. *katát*, Tag. *katad* (leather)]

laláw: **malalaw.** *v.* to wither (fruits); become soft through handling. **lalawen.** *v.* to cause to become soft by handling. [Tag. *lantá*]

lalawígan: *n.* a type of bird.

láli: *n.* dough. **lalien.** *v.* to roll in the hands; knead; squeeze in the hands. (*bulalo*)

lallakáy: Plural of *lakay*: old men; husbands.

lalláki: Plural of *lalaki*: boys; men.

lalláy: *n.* lullaby. **aglallay.** *v.* to sing a lullaby, to sing without words. [Tag. *uyayi*]

lallók: (*coll.*) *n.* hideaway (*lengleng*); *a.* remote, far, distant (*adayo*)

lálo: *adv.* especially; particularly. **aglalo.** *adv.* especially. **lallalo.** *adv.* the more. **nalalo.** *a.* serious, grave. **malalo.** *a.* too much. **napalalo.** *a.* excessive; overbearing; conceited. **agpalalo.** *v.* to be excessive, abuse; to be conceited. **palaluan.** *v.* to do something excessively. **mapalaluan.** *v.* to do in an exaggerated manner, too much. **napalaluan.** *adv.* too much, excessive. **lumalo.** *v.* to become worse (sickness, etc.) **lallaluen.** *v.* to arouse, excite; be obstinate; persist in doing something unnecessary. **Nasarakak laengen ti bagik a mangipatpategen kenkuana ngem lallaluak metten a nariribukan.** I just found myself treasuring her but the more trouble it caused. [Png, Tag. *lálo*]

lalótsa: *var.* of *nupsia*: marriage.

lámad: (*obs.*) **lamaden.** *v.* to hide (*lemmeng*); cover. **malamad.** *v.* to do slowly; softly. [Tag. *tagò* (hide)]

lámag: **palamag.** *n.* fish trap made out of bundles of *nipa* or coconut leaves and stems.

lámak: *n.* lavish party. **aglamak.** *v.* to picnic.

lamákan: (*obs.*) *n.* saucer. (*platito*)

lamáno: (Sp. *la mano*: the hand) *n.* handshake. **aglamano.** *v.* to shake hands. **kalamano.** *v.* to shake hands with someone.

lamáng: *n.* unfair division. **lamangan.** *v.* to cheat; get more than your share.

Lam-áng: *n.* Ilocano folk hero of the epic *Biag ni Lam-ang*.

lámat: *n.* crack in a glass or plate.

lámaw: *var.* of *ramaw*: load.

lamáw: *n.* boiled water used for scalding. **lamawen.** *v.* to scald. (*dilnak*; *loptoy*; *tapliak*) **linamaw.** *n.* animals skinned by pouring boiling water over them. **nalamaw.** *a.* scalded. **malamaw.** *v.* to be scalded. [Png. *lunák*, Tag. *pasò, banlî*]

lámay: *n.* wake for the dead; overtime work; *tebbeg*. **aglamay.** *v.* to work overtime. **makipaglamay.** *v.* to attend a wake for the dead. [Tag. *lamay*]

lambaán: *var.* of *nambaan*: stem of the banana plant.

lambána: *n.* fairy.

lambanóg: *n.* white wine made from coconut juice.

lambí: *n.* a kind of broad-mouthed jar; prepuce of the penis hanging from the shaft when circumcised. **lambilambi.** *n.* dewlap, wattle.

lambíke: (Sp. *alambique*: alembic) *n.* still, distilling apparatus.

lambíng: (Tag.) **aglamlambing.** *v.* to cuddle lovingly.

lambón: *n.* a kind of loose gown used by men in mourning.

lambóng: **nalambong.** *a.* boiled in water (*lingta*). **ilambong.** *v.* to boil in water (usually vegetables). [Tag. *lagà*]

lambutsíng: (*coll.*) **aglambutsing.** *v.* to neck, make out.

lamdók: *n.* gulp, swallow. **lamduken.** *v.* to swallow. (*tilmon*; *igup*; *alimon*; *arub-ub*) **sangalamdok.** *n.* one mouthful. [Tag. *lagók*]

lam-ék: *n.* cold; chill. **nalam-ek.** *a.* cold (weather). (*lammin*; *lamiis*) **lam-ekan.** *v.* to fool someone. **malam-ek.** *v.* to feel cold, chilly. **lamlam-eken.** *v.* (*reg.*) to fool. **panaglalam-ek.** *n.* cold season, winter. **lumam-ek.** *v.* to become cold; feel cold. **Lamlam-ekenak.** I feel cold. [Bon. *tengnen*, Ibg. *lemmin*, Ivt. *hanebneb*, Kal. *tungulin*, Knk. *tug-in*, *mentédek*, Kpm. *marimla*, Png. *betél*, Tag. *lamíg*, *gináw*]

lamentasión: (Sp. *lamentación*: lamentation) *n.* lament, lamentation. (*babawi*)

lámeng: **mailameng** (*obs.*) *v.* to penetrate the fingers into.

lamés: *n.* freshwater fish. **nalames.** *a.* fertile (soil, water with many fish, etc.) **manglames.**

v. to abound with fish. [Kal. *lamos*, Tag. *isdâ*; Knk. *lamés* = flesh, meat, muscle; fruit]

lamésa: (Sp. *la mesa*: the table, plateau) *n.* noon; twelve o'clock (*matuon*); summit; core. **manglamesa.** *v.* to get to the heart of the matter.

lamesíta: (Sp. *la mesita*: the small table) *n.* small table.

lamí: **nalami.** *a.* soft; flaccid; flabby; tender; flexible; easily injured,

lamígo: **aglamlamigo.** *v.* to be sensitive to cold (by disease).

lamígong: *var.* of *lamígo*.

lamíis: *n.* cold, chill. **nalamiis.** *a.* cool; chilly; cold; listless; spiritless; apathetic. (*lammin*; *lam-ek*) **lumamiis.** *v.* to become cold. **malamiisan.** *v.* to be affected by the cold. **palamiis.** *n.* refreshment (*pagpalamiis*). **agpalamiis.** *v.* to expose oneself to the cold; take refreshments. **palamiisan.** *v.* to cool off. **lamlamiisen.** *v.* to do calmly. **kinalamiis.** *n.* coldness, coolness; frigidity. [Ibg. *lemmin*, Ivt. *hanebneb*, Knk. *tug-in*, *mentedek*, Kpm. *marimla*, Png. *betél*, Tag. *lamíg, gináw*]

lámina: (Sp. *lámina*: picture) *n.* picture; photo. (*retrato*)

laminádo: (Sp.) *a.* laminated.

lamióng: **lamiongen.** *v.* to flatter; trick, deceive; make fun of. (*aliug, ayo, balatong*)

lamisáan: (Sp. *la mesa*: the table) *n.* table. **ilamisaan.** *v.* to place on the table; schedule for discussion. **manglamisaan.** *v.* to preside over a meeting. **paglamisaanan.** *v.* to use as a table. [Tag. *mesa* (Sp.)]

lamiséta: *n.* small table.

lamlám: *n.* smear (of dirt, food, grease, etc.). **palamlamen.** *v.* to give in small quantities; tolerate. **mapalamlaman.** *v.* to gather around to eat (dogs, chickens, etc.). [Tag. *kulapol*]

lammá: *n.* trace, mark, dent; welt. **aglamma.** *v.* to make a dent, mark, scar. **lamma ti ramay.** *n.* fingerprint.

lamméd: **nalammed.** *a.* wadeable, able to be crossed by walking (bodies of water).

lammín: *n.* cold, chill. **malammin.** *v.* to be cold. *a.* cold. (*lam-ek*; *lamiis*) **aglammin.** *v.* to feel cold; shiver with cold. **Lamminenak.** I feel cold. [Tag. *gináw*]

lámo₁: **lamolamo.** *a.* naked, nude. (*labus*) **aglamolamo.** *v.* to become nude. [Png. *lakseb*, Tag. *hubô, hubád*]

lámo₂: *n.* a kind of marine fish.

lamó: **lamuen.** *v.* to salt meat or fish for storing.

lamuéng: *a.* (*obs.*) undervaluing.

lam-óg: *n.* voracity. (*rawet*)

lamugáw: **lumamugaw.** *v.* to recover (from sickness). (*imbag*)

lamók: *n.* mosquito. **lamoken.** *v.* to be bitten by many mosquitoes. **nalamok, lamok-lamok.** *a.* full of mosquitoes. **linamok.** *a.* infested with mosquitoes. [Bon. *waswasayyan,* Ibg. *nemmuq, lemmuq,* Ifg. *wawwáne,* Ivt. *tamuneng,* Kal. *ilok,* Knk. *amillék, ibkán,* Kpm. *amuk,* Png. *ageyet,* Bon., Tag. *lamók*]

lámon: aglamon. *v.* to weed (grasses), clear land of weeds.

lámut: *n.* food, viands (*kaan; sida*). **lamuten.** *v.* to devour; eat; swallow; put up with. **ipalamut.** *v.* to feed (usually animals). **palpalamutan.** *v.* to care for as an added burden; to offer food and withdraw. **lalamutan.** *n.* uvula (of the throat). **konsilamut.** *n.* person who eats from place to place without shame, party crasher, person who always accepts insincere invitations to eat. **Di malamut ti aso ti saona.** *exp.* The dog can't eat his words. **Agtatakawka payen tapno adda ipalamutmo kenkuana.** You are still stealing so you have something to feed her. [Tag. *pagkain* (food)]

lamutéro: (f. *lamut*) *n.* glutton. (*rawet*)

lamuyó: nalamuyo. *a.* lax; flaccid, flabby; weak (body). **aglamuyo.** *v.* to feel weak (*kapsut*). [Tag. *lampá*]

lamúyot: nalamuyot. *a.* soft; smooth; velvety. **kinalamuyot.** *n.* softness, smoothness. **lumamuyot.** *v.* to become soft, soften. **lamlamuyuten.** *v.* to fondle; caress. **Nakalamlamuyot dagiti pamaskua a piesa a toktokaren ti pianista.** The Christmas pieces the pianist is playing are soothing. [Ibg. *finu,* Itg. *lamúyus,* Ivt. *mauhas,* Kal. *imuŷun, ayumamon,* Kpm. *kinis,* Png. *pulido, pino* (Sp.), Tag. *kinis, lambót; lamuyot* = seduce, persuade; squeeze]

lampá: (Eng.) *n.* calcium carbide light.

lampád: *n.* breadth of a log. **palampaden.** *v.* to strike with the flat of a sword. **lampadan.** *n.* a variety of awned early rice with red kernel.

lampadéro: (Sp. *lamparero:* lamplighter) *n.* lamplighter.

lampákan: *n.* kind of edible root crop.

lampángog: *n.* dunce, idiot, dupe. (*maag; tabbed; langgong; ang-ang; tungngang*)

lámpara: (Sp. *lámpara:* lamp) *n.* lamp. (*lamparaan*) **aglampara.** *v.* to use a lamp. **lamparaan.** *n.* small kerosene lamp with a wick. [Tag. *ilawan*]

lamparília: (Sp. *lamparilla:* small lamp) *n.* small kerosene lamp.

lampáso: (Sp. *lampazo:* mop) *n.* one-half coconut husk (used to polish a floor); mop. (*bunot*) **aglampaso.** *v.* to polish the floor with a *lampaso.* [Kal. *ablut*]

lampáy: *n.* sissy, crybaby; weakling. **nalampay.** *a.* one who easily falls; weak; crybaby; childish; sissy; brat. **aglampaylampay.** *n.* to throw a tantrum; to cry in order to get something wanted.

lampín: *n.* diaper. **lampinan.** *v.* to put a diaper on a baby. [Png. *lampíng,* Tag. *lampín*]

lampítaw: *n.* a kind of large sailing vessel with outriggers.

lampóng: *n.* barbarian; long-haired person; wild animal; a variety of awned late rice with very long awn; a mythological deer man; frequent absentee. **aglampong.** *v.* to cut class. **mananglampong.** *n.* one who is frequently absent.

lamsí: lamsien. *v.* to flatter for an ulterior motive; play tricks on. **turod ni lamsit, bantay ni kusit.** *exp.* denoting deception through flattery. [Tag. *lansí*]

lamsóy: nalamsoy. *a.* weak; having no courage or backbone. **kinalamsoy.** *n.* weakness. **Birngasanda iti lukmo gapu iti kinalamsoyna.** They nicknamed him *lukmo* because of his weakness.

lamtó: (*obs.*) *n.* dark beauty; glamour. (*pintas*)

lána₁: *n.* coconut oil; coconut butter. **paglanaan.** *n.* oil can. **lalanaan.** *n.* oil gland. **manglana.** *v.* to flatter; coax. **lanaan.** *v.* to add oil too; to flatter. **aglana.** *v.* to oil one's hair. [Kal. *lalog,* Png. *lárak,* Tag. *langís* (oil), *lana* = sesame oil]

lána₂: (Sp. *lana:* wool) *n.* wool. **de-lana.** *a.* woolen.

lánab: *n.* grease; ointment; oil. (*linab*) **lanaban.** *v.* to smear with oil or grease. [Png. *lárak,* Tag. *langís* (oil)]

lánad: ilanad. *v.* to inscribe; write; engrave. **mailanad.** *a.* written, inscribed. **Alaem daytoy kuentas a nakailanadan ti nagan daydi nanangmo.** Take this necklace on which is inscribed the name of your late mother. [Tag. *talâ*]

lanák: *n.* good soil; mire; mud. [Tag. *lusak*]

lan-ák: *n.* slime; mud; slush. **kalan-akan.** *n.* muddy place, mire. [Tag. *lusak*]

lánang₁: *n.* soldering material. **lanangen.** *v.* to patch up a quarrel; to solder. **aglanlanang.** *n.* welder.

lánang₂: *n.* devoid of feeling. **lanangen ti rikna.** to be devoid of feeling.

lanáp: aglanap. *v.* to spread over (*laganáp*). [Tag. *lanap* = inundated]

lanás: *n.* rising tide. **aglanas.** *v.* to rise (tide). **nalanas.** *a.* rising (tide).

lánat: ilanat. *v.* to scorch. (*ladam; lanet, lanáw; síram*)

lanáw: lanawen. *v.* to scorch in order to render flexible. **ilanaw.** *v.* to scorch; heat in a fire. **nalanaw.** *a.* scorched. (*síram*)

lánay: *n.* weakness of body reflected by eyes; slowness of gait. **nalanay.** *a.* affable; sociable; amiable; gentle; charming. **nalanay ti mata.** with drooping eyes. **lanayen.** *v.* to do gently, softly, etc. [Tag. *lumanay* (gentle; mild)]

lanáy: *n.* a kind of cylindrical marine fish. [Tag. *lanáy* = spread out]

landá: *n.* needlepoint; lace; overcasting stitches.

landág: landagan, paglandagan. *n.* cutting board (*langdet*); support to use when writing. [Tag. *katang*]

landás: *n.* fallow, uncultivated land. **aglandas.** *v.* to lie fallow. [Tag. *landás* = path, trail; pass; orbit; slipperiness]

landíng: (Eng. *coll.*) *n.* Filipino that has returned to the Philippines after having spent a long time abroad; term applied to long beans or the long *pallang* fruit. **mangilanding.** *v.* to return to the Philippines to marry (said of overseas Filipinos).

landióng: *syn.* of *lamiong*: deceive, make fun of.

landók₁: *n.* iron. **aglanlandok.** *v.* to have a sore throat. **limmandok.** *n.* a variety of awned late rice; *a.* hard as iron. [Kal. *kaga*, Tag. *bakal* (iron)]

landók₂: landokan. *v.* to weed around a plant; cultivate.

lanéd: aglaned. *v.* to fall down head first; dive. (*suek*)

lanét: nalanet. *a.* undercooked, rare on the inside; wilted, withered (*laylay*); half-boiled;. **ilanet.** *v.* to wilt over the fire; undercook; expose to the sun. **Kasla manglanlanet ti kudilna.** It seems to be burning his skin.

lánid: *n.* mountain-shaped evil spirit. **manglanlanid.** *n.* kidnapper. **nalanid.** *a.* clinging (said of children who cling to their mother). **lanidan.** *v.* to make excuses; disguise. **lanlanidan.** *v.* to dissimulate.

lanília: (Sp. *lanilla*: fine flannel) *n.* fine flannel. (*franela*)

lanípak: lumanipak. *v.* to make the sound of slippers on the floor; slap.

lánit: *n.* grease (*taba*; *sebo*; *grasa*; *kabut*); smear. **nalanit.** *a.* greasy, oily; fatty. **nalanitan.** *a.* smeared.

lanít: *n.* unbleached maguey fibers for making rope.

lanitóg: lumanitog. *v.* to produce an exploding sound.

lanlán: lumanlan. *v.* to increase; worsen. (*ran-rán*) **ilanlan.** *v.* to intensify; aggravate (sickness, etc.) **lanlanen.** *v.* to pester; do frequently

in order to disturb. **Limmanlan ti panaas ti barukongna idi nagpinnakadada.** The pain in her chest intensified when they said goodbye to each other. [Png. *alablabás*, Tag. *sidhî, lalâ*]

lannáy: nalannay. *a.* sad looking (*liday*; *leddaang*). [Tag. *tamláy*]

lanolína: (Sp.) *n.* lanolin, fatty substance obtained from sheep wool used in ointments.

lános: *n.* sterile plant.

lánot: *n.* vine. **lanotan.** *n.* a kind of tree, *Bombycidendron vidalianum.* **ilanotan.** *v.* to cut away vines. **agkalanotan.** *v.* to abound with vines. **kalanotan.** *n.* place abounding with vines. [Kal. *wakeÿ*, Knk. *lotáng*, Kpm. *bágin*, Tag. *baging*]

lanutí: *n.* a kind of tree with pink and white flowers and good wood for making furniture.

lansá₁: *n.* nail, peg. **ilansa.** *v.* to nail something. **lansaan.** *v.* to nail to. **silalansa.** *a.* nailed. [Knk. *paét*, Png. *pásak*, Tag. *pakò*]

lansá₂: lansalansa. *n.* ankle (*lipaylipay*; *pingil*). [Ibg. *alekkalekkuwag*, Itg. *lipaylipay*, Ivt. *bukeh*, Knk. *mukmukling*, Kpm., Tag. *búkung-búkung*, Png. *kálitkálit*]

lansád: *n.* base of a mountain; bottom of a well; ocean floor (*lansad ti baybay*). **lumansad.** *n.* to descend. **awan lansadna.** boundless, limitless, immeasurable. **lansaden.** *v.* to fathom; comprehend. **malansad.** *v.* to be able to reach the bottom.

lansángan: *n.* street. (*dalan*) **manglanlansangan.** *v.* to walk the street aimlessly.

lánse: *n.* climax of a story.

lanséro: (Sp. *lanceros*: lancers) *n.* lanciers, set of quadrilles; music for the quadrille dance.

lansí: aglansi. *v.* to fib; lie. (*ulbod*)

lansíta: (Sp. *lanceta*: lancet) *n.* pocketknife. **nakalansita.** *a.* with a pocketknife in one's possession. [Kal. *gipan*]

lansónes: (Tag. also) *n.* species of sweet, yellow, tropical fruit growing in grapelike clusters, *Larsium domesticum correa.*

lantág: nalantag. *a.* smooth, level; even, flat (*patad*). [Tag. *patag*]

lantáka: *n.* toy cannon made of bamboo.

lantána: (Sp.) *n.* species of plant.

lantíg: nalantig. *a.* fitting, proper. (*bagay*)

lantíp: aglantip. *v.* to come together; join; unite; marry. **paglantipen.** *v.* to join; unite in marriage. **ilantip.** *v.* to fit something with another thing. **Kayatko idi a makilantipak kenka.** I wanted to marry you before.

lantóng: *n.* young sweet potato shoot.

lántsa: (Sp. *lancha*: launch) *n.* boat; launch. **aglantsa.** *v.* to ride a launch.

lang: contraction of *laeng*: only; merely.

langá: *n.* face; features; looks. (*itsora*; *rupa*) **nalanga.** *a.* good-looking; with nice features. **aglanga.** *v.* to take shape; be like; put on makeup. **aglanglanga.** *v.* to put on airs. **Adda langana.** He is good looking. **ilangaan.** *v.* to distinguish; recognize. **mailangaan.** *v.* to be able to distinguish; recognize. **panaglanglanga.** *n.* features; characteristics; shape. **kalanglanga.** *n.* look-alike; *a.* similar, like. **agtagilanga.** *v.* to take shape (an apparition). **Nakubbuar ti danum sa nangin-inut a nagtagilanga a kas aso.** The water gushed out and then a doglike figure gradually took shape. **Saan nga agasug ngem mailangaanna.** He is not complaining, but it shows in his face. **Aglanglanga a kas ulila.** He looks like an orphan. **Diak mailangaan a nasayaat ta nakapsot ti matak.** I couldn't make him out well because my eyes are weak. [Png. *olágey* (appearance), Tag. *mukhâ* (face), *anyô* (form, appearance)]

lang-áb: **lumang-ab.** *v.* to inhale, breathe. **langaben.** *v.* to inhale (anything: smoke, etc). **Nalang-abna ti ayamuom ti malutluto a karne.** He breathed in the fragrance of the cooked meat. [Png. *sungap*, *ingás*, Tag. *langháp*]

langaláng: *n.* wilderness, uninhabited spot; deserted place, no-man's-land. **aglangalang.** *v.* to be deserted; to be left in ruins; to be idle (fields). **langlangalang.** *n.* open, unfrequented places. **mailangalang.** *v.* to wander in a deserted place. **paglangalangen.** *v.* to desert a place, leave barren. **Adu dagiti masaneb ken matakawan kadagiti langalang.** Many people are robbed and ambushed in the deserted place. [Tag. *iláng*]

lángan: *n.* absence; act of skipping something. **lumangan.** *v.* to be absent; to play hooky; skip, miss, fail to do something; miss a meal. **langanan.** *v.* to purposely miss a scheduled event. **lumanglangan.** *v.* to be periodic. [Tag. *liban*; Ibg. *langan* = celebrate]

lángas: *n.* the height of the wall. **nalangas.** *a.* high (walls).

lang-ás: *n.* appearance, shape (said of animals). **nalang-as.** *a.* pretentious. **aglang-as.** *v.* to pretend; brag. (*pangas*, *langat*)

langát: **nalangat.** *a.* boastful, bragging. **aglangat.** *v.* to boast; lie. [Tag. *yabang*]

langawén: *n.* a cock with red and white plumage.

langáy₁: **aglangay.** *v.* to frolic; run at fool speed; to joke; play; gallop. **aglanglangay.** *v.* to wander about (said of a crazy person); go in all directions.

langáy₂: **aglangay.** *v.* to shoot up fast (rice stalks). **nalangay.** *a.* with lustful growth.

lang-áy: **nalang-ay.** *a.* happy-go-lucky. (*langay*) **palang-ayan.** *n.* recreation; amusement. **aglang-ay.** *v.* to amuse oneself; frolic.

langbás: **aglangbas.** *v.* to disembark; to get out of bed (after having recovered from pregnancy).

langbáy: **lumangbay.** *v.* to overflow; to be overwhelmed by a certain emotion.

langdás: see *lengdas*: limit. (*beddeng*; *keddeng*)

langdét: *n.* chopping block; (*fig.*) scapegoat; whipping boy. **ilangdet.** *v.* to chop; dice. **langdeten.** *v.* to lay the blame on. **panglangdetan.** *v.* to reproach someone in the company of another person to whom the reproach is also intended; accuse, blame. [Ivt. *vagatu*, Kal. *totogtogen*, Knk. *damágan*, Kpm. *tagnán*, Png. *talagdanan*, Tag. *sangkalan*; Knk. *langdét* = complete, conclude]

langéb: *n.* dark cloud; overcast; gloom. **langeban.** *v.* to overwhelm. **manglangeb.** *v.* to cloud; be overcast; cloudy (*ulep*; *alibuyong*; *kuyem*; *kunem*). **Mangrugin nga agpukaw dagiti problema a nanglangeb kenka iti kallabes.** The problems that have overwhelmed you in your past are starting to disappear. [Tag. *kulimlím*]

langéd: **ilanged.** *v.* to tie, attach, fasten. (*parnged*)

langég: (*obs.*) adding a stimulant to boiling food.

langén₁: **makilangenlangen.** *v.* to live together, deal with, socialize with; get along with; associate with. **kalangenlangen.** *n.* associate; acquaintance; friend. **aglangenlangen.** *v.* to get along together, deal with one another. **mannakilangen.** *n.* friendly; active. **pannakilangen.** *n.* acquaintanceship; contact; relationship. **Saan a maliklikan ti pannakilangen dagiti mannalon ditoy kadagiti pestisidio.** The farmers here cannot avoid contact with pesticides. **Napintas ti langenlangenda a sangapamilia.** Their family relationships are good. [Tag. *salamuhà*]

langén₂: **malangenlangen.** *v.* to be dizzy.

lang-és: *n.* odor of fish. (*langsi*) **nalang-es.** *a.* smelling like fish. [Tag. *lansâ*]

langgágan: *n.* a kind of brown marine fish, eight inches long.

langgóng: *n.* idiot; fool; simpleton (*maag*; *tabbed*; *laglag*; *lampangog*; *tungngang*); a kind of bird whose cry is augural to mountain tribes; crybaby. **aglanggong.** *v.* to cry like a sissy.

langgótse: *n.* sack (usually for rice). **ilanggotse.** *v.* to place into a sack. **nakalanggotse.** *a.*

placed in a sack. **linanggotse a darat.** *n*. sand bag.

lángi: *n*. black sheep of the family, oddball sibling; *a*. overgrown; meager; decadent; depraved. **aglangi.** *v*. to deteriorate; decline; degenerate. **nalangi.** *a*. meager, not fruitful; depraved. **Inlangi ti panawen dagiti annak ti ling-et.** Time forsook the poor children (*lit*: children of sweat).

langilángan: *n*. old, hard, red bamboo; (*fig*.) old, sturdy person or animal.

langilangén: (*obs*.) *n*. disrelish. **aglangilangen.** *v*. to join, unite, associate.

langiód: *n*. liar; boastful person (*lastog*).

lángit: *n*. sky; heaven. **langitlangit.** *n*. canopy. **mananglangit.** *n*. astronomer; astrologer. **manglangit.** *v*. to daydream. **nailangitan.** *a*. heavenly; holy. **sangalangitan.** *n*. all heavenly powers. **agpalangit.** *v*. to go to heaven. **ilangit.** *v*. to raise to the sky; lift up toward heaven. [Bon. *dáya*, Ibg. *lángiq*, Ivt. *hañit*, Knk. *dáya*, Kpm. *banwa*, Png. *táwen*, Tag. *langit*]

lángka: *n*. jackfruit (*anangka*); variety of awned *diket* rice. **panglangkaen.** *n*. a kind of evergreen tree. [Ibg. *nangka*, Ifg. *kákaw*, Ivt. *nangkaq*, Kal. *sagakat*, Kpm. *yangkaw*, Png., Tag. *langkâ*]

langkápi: *n*. bamboo bench. (*papag*) **aglangkapi.** *v*. to sit with the legs dangling. **Nadanonna ti amana nga aglanglangkapi iti banko.** She found her father sitting on the bench with his legs dangling. [Tag. *papag*]

langkásan: *n*. a flat marine fish with a black dorsal fin and a yellow ventral fin.

langkuás: *n*. a kind of gingerlike herb, *Alpinia galanga*.

langkók: *n*. the lesser part of the thumb, which includes the first phalanx.

langkúban: *n*. variety of awned early rice with red kernel.

langláng: *n*. The space between the front of the hearth and the place of the fire; uninhabited place; first meal of the bride and groom together. **aglalanglang.** *v*. to sit together at a table. **paglanglangan.** *v*. to maltreat in the presence of bystanders; have a reason for getting together. **kalanglang.** *v*. to eat together. **Naglanglangda a nangan.** They ate together.

langó: *n*. distaste for something one is in contact with in excess. (*uma*) **malango.** *v*. to be tired of (after frequent use). [Tag. *suyà*]

lángob: **linangob.** *n*. awning; canopy, see *balawbaw*.

langóy: *n*. swim. **aglangoy, lumangoy.** *v*. to swim. **lumalangoy.** *n*. swimmer. **ilangoy.** *v*. to swim something over; carry by swimming.

langoy ti dila. *n*. mucous membrane of the mouth floor. **makalangoy.** *v*. to be able to swim. **paglangoyan.** *n*. place where one swims, swimming pool. **linnangoyan.** *n*. swimming competition. **paglalangoyan.** *n*. swimming pool. **langoy-aso.** *n*. the dog paddle (swimming with the head above the water). **bado a paglangoy.** *n*. bathing suit. [Ibg. *mettafug*, *mennunnug*, Ifg. *keke*, Ivt. *mayawat*, Kal. *kiyat*, Knk. *kiát*, *lánew*, Kpm. *káwe*, Png, Tag. *langóy*]

langpáw: **nalangpaw.** *a*. lush, robust; leafy; light (in weight); shallow; foolish, silly. **aglampaw.** *v*. to grow lush and thick (bearing less fruit).

langsáw: *n*. a kind of tree with poor timber. **nalangsaw.** *a*. boastful; braggart (*langsot*). [Tag. *yabang*]

langsí: (Tag. also) **nalangsi.** *a*. smelling fishy; smell of putrid blood. (*lang-es*). **Kasla napigsa a kugtar iti rusokna ti agal-allikubeng a langsi.** The fishy stench eddying about is like a strong kick in the stomach. [Ivt. *kelnaw*, Kal. *angsin*]

langsítan: (*obs*.) *n*. sudden happening.

langsót: **nalangsot.** *a*. bragging; always boasting; untrustworthy; unreliable; lying. (*lastog*) **aglangsot.** *v*. to lie; brag (exaggerate). [Png. *tilá*, *dúmsis*, Tag. *sinungaling* (lie)]

langtéd: *n*. a kind of vine used in curing wounds. **aglangted.** *v*. to stop bleeding. **malangted.** *v*. to staunch; cease bleeding. **pangpalangted.** *n*. something used to stop bleeding.

langtó: **nalangto, langtuen.** *a*. green (said of plants). **lumangto.** *v*. to grow lush and green. **Pinatay ti nagita ken makasabidong a balikasmo ti nalangto nga ayatko.** Your poisonous words killed my lush love. [Tag. *luntî*]

langúgan: *n*. kind of large, marine fish.

langyód: *var*. spelling of *langiod*: liar; boastful.

láud: (*Proto-Indonesian *laut*: sea) *n*. west. **agpalaud.** *v*. to go to the west. **makinlaud.** *adv*. on the west side. **laúden.** to the west of. **nalaud.** *a*. western; far to the west. **tagalaud.** *n*. westerner. [Ibg. *lalammeddan*, Ivt. *kavayatan*, Kal. *kapun abagatan*, Kpm. *albugan*, Png. *sagór*, Tag. *kanluran*]

láog: *n*. loop, hole (of a ring, a noose, etc.).

laóg: *var*. of *laég*.

laók: *n*. mixture. **ilaok.** *v*. to mix with something. **laokan.** *v*. to mix something. **makilaok.** *v*. to mix, mingle with. **aglalaok.** *v*. to intermingle; blend; fuse; amalgamate; mix up; muddle (thoughts). **kalaok.** *n*. element in a mixture. **paglaoken.** *v*. to mix; merge; mingle. **No kayatmo ti napapaut a biag, inaldaw nga**

uminom iti tubbog ti laya a nailaok iti diro. If you want to live longer, drink ginger juice mixed with honey everyday. [Png. *laók*, Tag. *halò* (mix)]

láon: *n.* capacity; contents. **malaon.** *v.* to hold; contain. **laonen.** *v.* to contain. **makalaon.** *v.* can contain. **mannakalaon.** *a.* having a large capacity. **Ginaw-at ti lakay ti nakasab-it a bayengyeng a naglaon iti tapuy.** The old man reached for the bamboo tube hanging from a hook containing the rice wine. [Png. *iyan*, Tag. *lamán* (contents)]

láong: *n.* the inner part. (*uneg*)

laureádo: (Sp.) *n.*, *a.* laureate.

laurél: (Sp. *laurel*: bay leaf) *n.* bay leaf.

laús: **nalaus, napalaus.** *a.* excessive (*palalo*); overmuch; extravagant. **(pa)lausan.** *v.* to do to excess (*labes*).

laús: *a.* outdated, out of style, old fashioned.

laót: **lauten.** *v.* to joint; fit together with rattan.

laóya: (Sp. *la olla*: the pot) *n.* food cooked in a jar; stewed meat in spices.

lápa: **mailapa.** *v.* to be deprived of the chance to do; to glance through the side of the eyes; bounce off obliquely. **lapaen.** *v.* to skin; flay. [Tag. *lapà* = butcher]

lapá: *n.* spadix of the betel palm. [Kal. *pasong*, Tag. *palapà*]

lápad: *n.* paddle (for boats). (*gaud*)

lápag: **ilapag.** *v.* to arm; set up; equip; set out; spread out.

lapaná: **nalapana.** *a.* slightly stout; healthfully stout; with broad shoulders.

lápat: *n.* a kind of intestinal worm. **nalapat.** *a.* slim, thin; subtle, tactful; strict, rigid. **malapat.** *n.* small *ipon* fish. **ilapat.** *v.* to set in place firmly. **agsao iti nalapat.** *exp.* to speak frankly.

lapáy: **lapayen.** *v.* to mash with salt in order to soften or get rid of the bitter taste (of *paria*); knead meat with salt to tenderize.

lapáyag: *n.* ear; ear conch. **lapayagan.** *n.* a kind of forest insect. **laplapayag ti bao** (*ti káyo*). *n.* tree ear; earlike fungi. **ipalapayag.** *v.* to announce, inform. **maipalapayag.** *v.* to overhear (unintentionally). **manglapayag.** *v.* to listen attentively (*pangag*). **ilapayagnan.** *v.* to cut off the ear of. **pagat-lapayag.** *a.* ear to ear (smile). **Dimmakel ti lapayagna.** *exp.* denoting eavesdropping (*lit*: his ears got bigger). **Naipalapayag kaniak ti panagus-usisa ti arsobispo maipapan kenka.** I heard about the archbishop's investigation of you. **Naingpis ti lapayagmo.** Your ear is thin (said to someone who has engaged in excessive sex. **Padpadakkelem la ti lapayagko.** You are kidding me

(enlarging my ear). **Pagatlapayag ti isemna.** Her smile was ear to ear. [Ibg. *talinga*, Ivt. *tadiñaq*, Kal. *inga*, Kpm. *balugbug*, Png. *layág*, Tag. *tainga, tenga*]

lapdóg: **malapdugan.** *a.* peeled, skinned from the heat. (*kuplat*)

lapés: *n.* a kind of ray or skate; Mullet fish, *Mugil sp.*

lapét: **linapet.** *a.* kind of snack made of *diket* rice wrapped in banana leaves.

lapgís: **lapgisen.** *v.* to tear, tear off, tear up. (*pigis*) **malapgis.** *v.* to be torn. **Adda met kasla nalapgis kenkuana iti pannakaipusingna iti ilina.** It seems like something is tearing him apart when he leaves his town. [Tag. *punit*]

lápi: *n.* thigh; ham; animal shoulder; beef round. (*luppo*)

lápida: (Sp. *lápida*) *n.* tombstone.

lapidário: (Sp.) *n.* gem collector, lapidary.

lapigáwen: *n.* a variety of awned rice with wavy upper leaf.

lapígos: *n.* wringing or pulling of the ear. **lapigusen.** *v.* to wring; pull or tweak the ear. **Lapigos met ti ganabek no diak agtungpal.** I get my ears tweaked if I don't obey. [Tag. *pingol*]

lapiók: see *lapiot*: bend; warp.

lapiúkot: **aglapiukot.** *v.* to bend, sag.

lapiót: **aglapiot.** *v.* to soften, bend; warp. **nalapiot.** *a.* soft; easily bent, pliant.

lápis: (Sp. *lápiz*: pencil) *n.* pencil. **ilapis.** *v.* to write down with a pencil. **lapisan.** *v.* to pencil in the eyebrows.

lap-ít: *n.* the flexible top part of a branch. **nalap-it.** *a.* flexible; fragile; frail. (*rasi*) **lap-iten.** *v.* to bend (a bow). **Nalap-it ti riknana no maipapan iti gubat.** He has weak feelings when it comes to war. [Tag. *lambót*]

lapítog: *n.* blister. (*kapuyo*) **aglapitog.** *v.* to blister. [Png. *lanók*, Tag. *paltós*]

laplap: **laplapen.** *v.* to cut thin (meat); cut nicely (hair); operate on; skin; (*coll.*) to pull one's leg **agpalaplap.** *v.* to get an operation. **Nasaysayaat no paikkatmon ti bukolmo, wenno palaplapmon dayta susom a nagtubuanna tapno saan nga agwaras.** It is better if you have the lump taken out or you have the breast operated on where it is growing so it doesn't spread. [Tag. *lapláp*]

lapnít: *n.* a tree whose bark is used to make ropes. **lapniten.** *v.* to make into thin strips; strip off. **Lapnitek ti nagango nga ubbak nga alupasi a paggalutkonto iti pagaladko.** I will strip off the dried bark of the *alupasi* to use to tie my fencing materials.

lápu: lapulapu. *n.* a kind of tree with bony nuts, *Gyrocarpus jacquini*; the grouper fish, *Epinephelus sp.*

lapóg: *n.* tobacco orchard; garden; upland unirrigated field. (*bangkag*) **lapugen.** *v.* to cultivate for planting.

lap-ók: *n.* sandy soil; dust; sand. **nalap-ok.** *a.* sandy (soil). **kalap-okan.** *n.* sandy place (*kadaratan*). [Tag. *buhangin* (sand)]

lapúlap: *n.* a kind of bird (*saksakulap*).

lapúnos: *n.* state of being totally covered; overflowing. **malapunos.** *v.* to be flooded; overflowing. **Kasla kankanayon a malapunos iti ragsak ti pusona.** The happiness of his heart seems to be always overflowing. [Tag. *apaw*]

lápus: *n.* state of being beyond the limit. **lumapus.** *v.* to exceed; protrude; go beyond. **aglapus.** *v.* to go beyond. **aglaplapusan.** *adv.* in excess of what's needed. **No aglaplapusananka iti ayat, mangibingayka iti pammateg.** If you have enjoyed excessive love, you will share your affection. [Tag. *lagpás*]

lapút: laputlaput. *n.* the pump drill; (*vulg.*) masturbator. (*salsal*)

lap-óy: *var.* of *lap-ók*: sandy place, dusty ground.

lapúyok: *syn.* of *kapuyo*: blister.

lappéd: *n.* obstacle, hindrance. (*tipéd*) **malappedan.** *v.* to be blocked; hindered; obstructed. **ilapped.** *v.* to use to block, hinder. **lappedan.** *v.* to block, obstruct, hinder. **Awan ti makalapped iti panggepko.** No one can hinder my plan. [Ivt. *apnet, valat,* Png. *makasbel,* Tag. *hadláng*]

lappiás: *var.* of *lippias*: overflow. [Kal. *lumayas,* Tag. *apaw*]

lappiót: nalappiot. *a.* easily bent, flexible. **aglappiot.** *v.* to bend.

lapsák: nalapsak. *a.* sturdy; robust.

lapsát: *var.* of *lapsak*: sturdy; robust; well-endowed; lush; sexy. [Tag. *lusóg*]

lapsí: lapsien. *v.* to tear off. **laplapsi.** *n.* hangnail. **malapsi.** *v.* to be torn off. [Knk. *sabongánay* (hangnail)]

lapsút: *n.* lining of the gizzard. **aglapsut.** *v.* to slip; escape the memory; escape unnoticed. **lapsuten.** *v.* to slip off, pull out. **lumapsut.** *v.* to free oneself. **lapsutan.** *v.* to skin a frog. (*kulanit*) **makalapsut.** *v.* to slip off, go free. **malapsut.** *v.* to slip off, to be drawn (sword). **laplapsut.** *n.* a vine whose bark easily slips off. **nalapsut** (*obs.*) *n.* shameless woman.

laptíng: nalapting. *a.* short (clothes, poles). (*kiting*)

laptóy: see *lapdug*: skinned; peeled; flayed.

lárba: (Sp. *larva*: larva) *n.* larva, the young of an insect.

lárga: (Sp. *largar*: set sail; send off; clear out) exclamation expressing approval, all right, go ahead; *n.* time of dismissal. **aglarga.** *v.* to leave, depart, set off. **ilarga.** *v.* to release, let go; open (a faucet). **lumarga.** *v.* to leave. **tagalarga.** *n.* umpire (at a cock fight). **Aglarga iti alas kuatro ti agsapa.** It leaves at four in the morning.

largabísta: (Sp. *larga*: long + *vista*: sight) *n.* binoculars. **largabistaan.** *v.* to look at someone through binoculars.

largamása: (Sp. *argamasa*: mortar) *n.* mortar (used in construction).

largár: *var.* of *larga*: set off; departure. **lalargaran, paglalargaran.** *n.* starter of a machine.

largaréte: (Sp.) *n.* kind of gill net used in fishing.

largéro: (Sp. *larguero*: jamb post) *n.* mullion.

lárgo: (Sp. *largo*: long) *a.* long (lumber) (*atiddog*); full-length; continuous; uninterrupted; nonstop. **aglargo.** *v.* to go directly to a place (*agdiretso*); go beyond the limit; go ahead with something. **paglarguan.** *n.* terminal for the bus. **ilargo.** *v.* to extend; enlarge; do straight.

lása: (Sp. *nasa*: bow net) *n.* a kind of bow net for sea fishing. [Tag. *lasa* = taste, flavor]

lasá: linalasa. *n.* rice pounded once with the pestle; half-milled rice.

laság: *n.* flesh, meat; muscle; sexual lust. **lumasag.** *v.* to affect deeply; bore into the flesh. **ilasagan.** *v.* to separate the meat from the fat. **agtagilasag.** *v.* to be full of flesh; to be realized (dream); come to fruition. **nalasag.** *a.* meaty, fleshy. **nainlasagan.** *a.* earthly, worldly; lustful. **narawet iti lasag.** *exp.* to be lustful. **Nailasagdan ti sugal.** They are addicted to gambling. [Ibg. *petteg,* Ivt. *asiq,* Kal. *bogas,* Knk. *begas, lamés; dáot,* Kpm., Png., Tag. *lamán*]

lásak: *n.* a black and white cock with white legs.

lásang: lasangen. *v.* to disjoin; separate; disconnect; tear apart; break off. **malasang.** *v.* to be torn apart, separated. **nalasang-lasang.** *a.* torn to pieces; completely dismantled; dilapidated. **balasang-a-nalasang.** *exp.* sexually experienced girl. **Nalasanglasang dagiti diding dagiti kamarote.** The walls of the cabin were dilapidated. [Tag. *gibâ*]

lásaro: (Sp. *Domingo de Lázaro*: Passion Sunday) *n.* Passion Sunday.

lásat: lumasat. *v.* to pass over; traverse. **aglasat.** *v.* to pass through; bear, endure; undergo. **malasat.** *v.* to pass through successfully; live through sickness; survive a catastrophe. **nakalasat.** *a.* able to pass through successfully; having survived a catastrophe. **lasaten.** *v.* to cross, go from one side to another. **ilasat.** *v.* to take across; carry through. **naglasatan.** *n.* what was passed, experienced. **paglasaten.** *v.* to let something pass, undergo. **Nagkinnatawakami ket saanen a nagsarday ti panagpinnadamagmi kadagiti naglasatanmi nga aldaw.** We laughed together and our inquiring about each other did not stop for the passing days. **Diak ipalubos nga aglasat iti rigat dagiti annakko.** I will not permit my children to undergo hardships. [Png. *balíw*, Tag. *tawíd*, *bagtás, daán*]

lásaw: nalasaw. *a.* thin, weak, watery (*labnáw*); sparse; scanty; easily consumed. [Tag. *labnáw*]

lasbáng: *n.* robustness; glamour; beauty; freshness. **nalasbang.** *a.* luxuriant, exuberant; beautiful; fresh; glamorous. **palasbangan.** *v.* to care for; recall; be nostalgic. **Matmatam ti lasbangna.** Look at how beautiful she is.

lasdóg: nalasdog. *a.* steep, elevated. (*rasdok*)

lasí: *n.* dandruff. [Bon. *laklak*, Knk. *laklakí*, Kpm. *balikúbak, kalikúbak*, Png., Tag. *balakubak*]

lasík: *n.* kind of edible freshwater shrimp.

lasílas₁: *n.* a kind of tree, *Terminalia comintana*.

lasílas₂: aglasilas. *v.* to skin, flay by rubbing. (*las-las*) **malasilas.** *v.* to be skinned, flayed by rubbing.

lásin: mailasin. *v.* to recognize, know; make out; distinguish (the difference). **ilasin.** *v.* to separate, set aside. **makilasin.** *v.* to keep clear of someone or something. **malasin.** *v.* to recognize; know; be able to distinguish the difference. **lumasin.** *v.* to separate from one's group. **pagilasinan.** *n.* mark by which something can be identified. **Dimo kadi annugoten a dayta nga ulep ket pagilasinan iti napigsa a tudo?** Don't you agree that that cloud is a clear sign of strong rain? [Ivt. *sincad*, Tag. *kilala*]

lasinggéro: *n.* drunkard. (*mammartek*)

lasíngo: *n.* drunkard. (*mammartek*)

lasíta: (Sp. *lazo*: ribbon) *n.* narrow *laso*.

laskóta: (Sp. *escota*: nautical sheet) *n.* sheet of sail.

laslás₁: (*coll.*) *a.* not true, in jest. **laslasen.** *v.* to skin; flay by rubbing (*lasilas*); to pull one's leg, deceive.

laslás₂: laslasan. *v.* to overtake someone (in racing, etc.). **makilinnaslas.** *v.* to compete in racing.

láso: (Sp. *lazo*: ribbon) *n.* ribbon, bow; tie; lasso; loop; lace. **nalasuan.** *a.* with ribbons.

las-úd: *n.* inside; within. (*uneg*) **aglas-ud.** *v.* to hold, contain. **las-uden.** *v.* to hold, contain. **ilas-ud.** *v.* to put into. **las-udan.** *v.* to occupy, step into. **pangilas-udan.** *n.* container. **lalasudan.** *n.* entrance; port, harbor. **Agkarasep-ak**

dagiti sanga iti ilalas-udko iti purok. The branches kept snapping as I entered into the village (through a forest path). **iti las-ud ti innem a tawen, unaannatayonton ti Vietnam.** Within six years, Vietnam will be ahead of us.

lásug: kalasúgan. *n.* gutter; channel; aqueduct; eaves. **agkalasugan.** *v.* to flow down the eaves' gutter.

láson: lasonan. (*obs.*) *v.* to add something to (add possessions of a dead man to his grave); to come upon an undecayed corpse when digging a grave. [Tag. *lason* = poison]

lasón: ilason. *v.* to put a plant in a flower pot.

lasoná: *n.* onion, *Allium cepa* (*sibuyas*). [Ivt. *bulyas*, Tag. *sibuyas* (Sp.)]

lásong: *n.* a big hole, pothole. **lasonglasong.** *a.* full of potholes. **manglasonglasong.** *v.* to walk along a rugged road. **mailasong.** *v.* to fall into a hole. [Tag. *lubák*]

lásos: *var.* of *laso*.

lasút: mailasutan. *v.* to be free, liberated, cleared from debt. **mailasut.** *v.* to escape (*libas, talaw*); *a.* free, relieved, liberated.

laspág: laspagen. *v.* to overuse. (*palaluen*)

laspár: manglaspar. *v.* to eat voraciously, gobble up (*rawet*)

lastá: *n.* a kind of lasso used by horse riders. (*silo*; *kay-ong*; *lab-ong*; *kaka*) **lastaan.** *v.* to lasso.

lastár: nalastaran. *a.* completed; paid for; covered.

láste: nalastean. *a.* filled. **ilaste.** *v.* to put in its place; invest (money). **aglaste.** *v.* to fill the stomach.

lastikó: *n.* rubber band. **aglastiko.** *v.* to withdraw a move (in chess).

lástima: (Sp. *lástima*: pity) *n.* pity, shame. (*sayang*)

lastóg: aglastog. *v.* to lie; fib. **nalastog.** *a.* dishonest; lying. **ilastog.** *v.* to boast of. **agpalpalastog.** *v.* to show off. [Png. *tilá, dúmsis*, Tag. *sinungaling* (lie), *yabang* (boast)]

láta₁: (Sp. *lata*: can) *n.* tin can; can. **delata.** *a.* canned. **ilata.** *v.* to preserve canned food, can, put in a can. **pagidelataan, pagilataan.** *n.* cannery.

láta₂: latalata. *n.* stupidity. (*tabbed*)

latá: lataen. *v.* to break up (ground). (*buga*; *guba*)

látak: *n.* very fine soil. [Tag. *latak* = dregs, residue]

laták: *n.* prominence. **nalatak.** *a.* plain, clear, obvious; well-known (*dayaw, tan-ok, damag*). **kinalatak.** *n.* fame, reputation. **ilatak.** *v.* to publicize, make known. **paglatakan.** *n.* field in which one excels. [Tag. *tanyág*]

latálat: (*obs.*) *n.* mudfish trap. (*bukatot*; *bangkat*)

látang: ilatang. *v.* to reserve; budget; make time for. **mailatangan.** *v.* to be reserved; to be budgeted. **mangilatang iti espasio.** to save space for.

latáw: aglataw. *v.* to float; drift.

latbáng: *var.* of *lasbang*.

láteg: *n.* testicles with scrotum. **nalatgan.** *a.* brave, bold, daring. **lat(e)gen.** *v.* to subdue, overpower; overcome (by hitting the groin). **lateglateg.** *n.* a kind of herb with yellow flowers, *Crotalaria quinquefolia*. **ilategan.** *v.* to castrate. **Adda lategna.** *exp.* He is daring. [Bon. *itlog, laglag-ey, laglag-ong*, Knk. *butlúg, kagkagléy, kutkutlúg*, Kpm. *báyag*, Png. *palták*, Tag. *bayág*]

latería: (Sp. *lata*: tin, can) *n.* tin or zinc parts of a building.

latéro: (Sp. *hojalatero*: tinsmith) *n.* metalworker, tinsmith. **kinalatero.** *n.* metallurgy.

latgén: see *láteg*.

láti: *n.* rust. **aglati.** *v.* to rust. [Png. *latí*, Tag. *kalawang*]

latík: (Tag.) *n.* scum of coconut milk after extracting oil by the fire. **sinuman latik.** see *suman*: kind of rice cake.

látiko: (Sp. *látigo*: whip) *n.* whip. (*baut*; *saplit*; *basnut*; *betbet*) **latikuen.** *v.* to whip someone or something.

Latín: (Sp. *latín*: Latin) *n.* Latin language. **ag-Latin.** *v.* to speak Latin.

latít: *n.* last in a row. (*údi*)

latlát: nalatlatan. *a.* frayed, sore from rubbing; lacerated. **aglatlat.** *v.* to peel.

látok: *n.* wooden plate for rice. **agkalatok.** *v.* to share the same plate. **nagan iti sirok ti latok.** *n.* name given to a sickly child (other than the baptismal name).

lat-óng: aglat-ong. *v.* to sit above a hole (toilet). **lat-ongan.** *v.* pit or hole used as a toilet; toilet bowl.

lattá: *adv.* only, just. (*laeng*) **Kastoy latta.** Just like this. **Bay-am latta ida.** Just let them be, Just leave them alone. **Ammok lattan a sutsutilendak.** I just know that they are joking with me. Contrast with *laeng*: **Manganka latta.** Just eat (don't mind them) vs. **Manganka laeng.** Just eat (don't do anything else). [Bon. *aped*, Tag. *lang*]

láwa: nalawa. *a.* wide; loose; roomy; broad. **aglawalawa.** *v.* to be loose fitting. **mailawa** (*obs.*) *a.* impaired (chicken). **lumawa.** *v.* to widen, become wide. **ilawa.** *v.* to widen. **ikalawa.** *v.* to widen, make wider. **palawaen.** *v.* to widen, extend, expand. **palawaen ti negosio.** to expand one's business. **Nalawa ti aang-sanna.** He is relaxed. **Buongenda aminen dagiti nalawa a daga.** They will break up all the large plots of land. [Kal. *eÿwa*, Knk. *anawá*, Png. *awáng, lagós, lápar*, Tag. *luwáng*]

láwag: pagpakalawagan. (*obs.*) *n.* something performed without difficulty; an easy thing to do, a cinch.

lawág: *n.* brightness; brilliance; light; glow; radiance; clarity. **nalawag.** *a.* clear; bright; shining; obvious; plain. **palawag.** *n.* explanation. **ipalawag.** *v.* to explain; expound; declare. **agpalawag.** *v.* to give an explanation; testify. **aglawag.** *v.* to brighten (the morning). **makilinnawag.** *v.* to discuss, reason with; settle a dispute; confront. **panaglinnawag.** *n.* confrontation. **apaglawag.** *n.* daybreak. **Adda kuma kayatmi a lawlawagan maipapan iti sueldom.** We would like to clear something up regarding your salary. **Nalawag pay laeng iti panunotna ti kababagas ti tagainepna.** The meaning of his dream is still clear in his thoughts. [Ivt. *sideng*, Kal. *mampadcha*, Png. *linéw*, Tag. *liwanag*]

lawán: *n.* species of tree used for lumber.

law-án: *n.* unplanned act. **mailaw-an.** *v.* to sin; err; go astray unintentionally, be mislead. **nailaw-an.** *a.* having done something bad unintentionally and repenting afterwards. **ilaw-an.** *v.* to fail; prove untrustworthy; cheat; disappoint. **pannakailaw-an.** *n.* regrettable action. **Pannakailaw-anko a nangpalagipen.** I regret having reminded her (of that). **Uray kasano nga ay-uan, adda latta mailaw-an.** No matter how much care is taken, someone will always be misled.

law-áng: *n.* universe; nature; world; (*lit.*) a kind of wide breeches. **mailaw-ang.** *v.* to fall into space. **sangalaw-angan.** *n.* the entire universe. **Sangkatangadna iti law-ang.** He keeps looking up at the sky. [Tag. *lawak*]

láwas₁: *n.* phalanx; internode of bamboo; internode of arm or leg. **nalawas, linawas.** *a.* long-limbed. **Nagdandanagkami ta makalawas a saan a simmangpet.** We were worrying because it has been a week and he hasn't arrived.

láwas₂: (*reg.*) *n.* week. (*lawasna*) **linawas.** *a.* weekly. **lawlawasna.** *n.* weekday. [Png. *simba*, Tag. *linggó*]

law-ás: *n.* braggart; boasting; boast; *a.* boastful. **nalaw-as.** *a.* boastful; exaggerating. **law-asan.** *v.* to overdo; exaggerate. **Pinalaw-asanna bas-sit ti magasto para iti madadael a materiales.** He exaggerated a bit about the cost for the damaged goods. [Tag. *hambóg*]

lawát: aglawat. *v.* to lie; fib (*ulbod*); spread rumors (*tarabitab*). **aglawatlawat.** *v.* to gossip.

lumawat. *v.* to talk out of turn. **Ania't lawlawatem?** What are you fibbing about?

láway: aglaway (*obs.*) *v.* to go naked. (*lamo-lamo, labus*)

láwer: aglawer. *v.* to wander for adventure.

láwi: *n.* food taboos in mourning. **aglawi.** *v.* to observe food taboos during mourning.

lawí: lawilawi. *n.* plume; showy feathers in a cock's tail.

láwig: lalawigan. *n.* a kind of bird with bright plumage. **kasla lalawigan.** *exp.* acting or moving sexily like the *lalawigan* bird (said of women).

láwin: *n.* fishhook; fishing gear (*banniit*). **aglawin.** *n.* to catch with the hook; to swallow halfway (fowls). **malawinan.** *v.* to be caught with a hook and line; *n.* catch of fish. [Tag. *bingwít*]

law-ít: nalaw-it. *a.* sharp pointed (*tirad*); nimble tongued.

lawláw: *n.* area around, circumference; a kind of small marine fish. **iti (ag)lawlaw.** *prep.* around. **aglawlaw.** *v.* to surround, encircle; wander, roam, go around. **malawlaw.** *v.* to be surrounded. **lawlawen.** *v.* to surround; go around. **palawlawan.** *v.* to encircle, surround a place. **napalawlawan.** *a.* surrounded by, enclosed with. **Di makalawlaw-kelleb.** *exp.* He has no patience; he is hot tempered. **Nagulimek ti aglawlaw.** It was silent all around. **Linawlawko ti purok.** I went around the village. [Png. *baríber*, Tag. *libot*]

lawlawígan: *n.* a kind of singing bird.

lawwá: lawwalawwa. *n.* spider. **bugi ti lawwalawwa.** *n.* cocoon of spider. **saput ti lawwalawwa, abel ti lawwalawwa.** *n.* spider web. **aglawwalawwa.** *v.* to raise spiders; to spider fight. **lawwalawwa ti aso.** *n.* daddy longlegs spider. **lawwalawwa ti Insik.** common house spider (not used in spider fighting). **Saan la nga ubing wenno babbarito itan ti aglawwalawwa, pati nataengan.** Not only children and the young spider fight today, even adults do. [Bon. *kawa*, Ibg. *alawalawa*, Itg. *kawwa*, Ivt. *kakamaw, hahawa*, Kal. *kawa*, Knk. *tiktikáwa*, Kpm. *bábagwaq*, Png. *gigang, genggeng*, Tag. *gagambá*, Tag. *lawálawá* = carabao grass]

lay: umlay. to become weakened. see *ellay*.

layá: *n.* ginger, *Zingiber officinale*, used in native medicine to cure rheumatism, wounds, cough, and stomachache. Ginger tea is called *salabát*. **agatlaya.** *a.* ginger smelling. **layaan.** *v.* to season with ginger. [Bon. *akbab*, Ibg. *laya*, Isg. *basang*, Ivt. *anahaq*, Knk. *layá*, Kpm. *láya*, Png. *agát*, Tag. *luyà*]

láyab: *var.* of *rayab*: flutter, drift to and fro.

láyag: *n.* sail (of a ship). **nalayagan.** *a.* left ashore; marooned. **aglayag.** *v.* to sail. [Ivt. *vidad*, Ibg., Kpm., Png., Tag. *layag*]

láyak: nalayak. *a.* wide, roomy; loose; ample. (*lawa*) **aglayaklayak.** *v.* to be extra loose.

layálay: *n.* a kind of long marine fish with a green backbone and pointed mouth; a kind of small striped bird. **aglayalay.** *v.* to subside; slow down.

layámay: see *mayamay*: quiet; calm; serene.

láyang: nalayang. *a.* high above the ground. [Tag. *taás*]

layáng: nalayang. *a.* open, clear (spaces). **Agpasgarak kuma ta nakalaylayang dagiti tanem iti kamposanto.** I should have been frightened because the graves in the cemetery were clear. [Tag. *lantád*]

lay-áng: *var.* of *layáng*.

layáp: *n.* shooting star; meteor; fireball. **lumayap.** *v.* to shine; be bright; fervent; ardent. [Png. *tai-bitewen*, Tag. *bululakaw* (meteor)]

láyas: *a.* sterile (females). (*lupes*) **aglayas.** *v.* to be sterile, barren; to work away from home (in a foreign country). **layasan.** *n.* place abroad where one finds work. [Tag. *baóg*]

layás: nalayasan. *a.* irrigated; flooded (*layos*). [Tag. *bahâ* (flood)]

lay-ás: manglay-as, lay-asan. *v.* to reduce the feed of; curtail privileges. [Tag. *bawas*]

láyat: *n.* weapon or hand raised in a threatening posture. **aglinnayat.** *v.* to threaten one another. **ilayat.** *v.* to threaten with physical violence. **layatan.** *v.* to raise the hand against, threaten. **sangapanglayat.** in a moment. **Linayatannak a keddelen.** He threatened to pinch me. [Tag. *akmâ*]

layáw: *n.* kind of *nipa* wine; height of a jump. **lumayaw.** *v.* to jump, leap. **layawen.** *v.* to leap over, skip (something in a series). **ilayaw.** *v.* to go across by jumping. **lumalayaw.** *n.* jumper. **aglinnayaw.** *v.* to have a jumping contest. **palayaw.** *n.* a type of freshwater fish trap. **palayawan.** *v.* to catch fish with the *palayaw*. **lalayawán.** *n.* jumpable area, part of a fence that is low to allow people to pass. [Tag. *talón*]

layét: nalayet. *a.* withered, wilted. (*layót; lanet*) **Aglayet ti ruot no dumteng ti kalgaw.** The grass withers when summer comes. [Tag. *lantá*]

layláy: nalaylay. *a.* withered; faded. **aglaylay.** *v.* to wilt, wither. **ipalaylay.** *v.* to expose to the heat in order to wilt; to put over a fire. [Ivt. *hayu*, Tag. *lantá; layláy* = droop]

láyog: nalayog. *a.* very tall; huge (said of vegetation only). [Tag. *tayog*]

lay-óg: aglay-og. *v.* to buckle under, give under the feet (bamboo flooring being trampled on); sag, droop.

layón: aglayon. *v.* to continue moving; continue to be in an office; remain, stay. **nalayon.** *a.* straightforward, direct. **ilayon.** *v.* to continue carrying up to a place, to take to a place; to vote an incumbent for reelection. **layon-layon.** *a.* stupid. **paglayonan.** *n.* place where one stays while on a trip. **Naglayonda iti pimmalasio a balay a pinaaramid ti ikitda.** They stayed in a palacelike home that their aunt had constructed. [Tag. *tulóy*]

layós: *n.* flood. (*diláp*) **aglayos.** *v.* to flood; overflow; be loaded with money. **layusen.** *v.* to inundate. **nalayos.** *a.* flooded. [Ibg. *malítuq*, Ifg. *dinlu*, Ivt. *ayuq*, Kal. *litap*, Knk. *lebéng*, Kpm. *álbug*, Png. *deláp*, Tag. *bahâ*]

layót: nalayot. *a.* withered; faded (*laylay*; *layet*; *malba*). **layoten.** *v.* to wilt. [Tag. *lantá*]

lebadúra: (Sp. *levadura*: yeast) *n.* leaven; baking powder; yeast. **lebaduraan.** *v.* to put yeast in.

lebbáang: nalbaang. *v.* to make a bursting, exploding noise. **palbaangen.** *v.* to explode (firecrackers, etc.).

lebbáw: lumbaw. *v.* to sink. (*lubo, lumlom*)

lebbáy: malbay. *v.* to be dismayed, distressed. [Tag. *lumbáy*]

lebbég: lumbeg. *v.* to become swollen (eyes after crying).

lebbék: *n.* cleaned, milled rice. **lebbeken.** *v.* to smash; pound. **malebbek.** *v.* to be pounded, smashed. **paglebbekan.** *n.* mortar. [Tag. *bayó*]

lebbén: *n.* stockpile; supply. **ilebben.** *v.* to stock. **lebbenen.** *v.* to keep in store; stockpile. [Tag. *tipon*]

lebbéng: *var.* of *lebbén*: stockpile; supply.

lebbuák: *n.* bubble. **lumbuak.** *v.* to boil (oil, lead) (*barekbek*). [Tag. *bulâ*]

lebléb: *n.* border (of a hat, basket, country, etc); rim of a basket. **lebleban.** *v.* to border; cover the rim.

leddá: *n.* a kind of tall, white flowering grass. **lumedda.** *n.* short slender sugarcane. **kaleddaan.** *n.* grasslands of *ledda* grass. [Tag. *talahib*]

leddáang: *n.* sorrow. (*liday*) **naleddang.** *a.* sorrowful, sad, gloomy. **lumdaang.** *v.* to grieve; mourn; be sad, sorrowful. **leddangen.** *v.* to be sad about; mourn for. **makapaldaang.** *a.* sad, causing sorrow. **nakalkaldaang.** *a.* sorrowful. **pagleddaangan.** *n.* cause for sorrow. [Ibg. *daddám*, Ivt. *angsah*, Png. *ermen*, Tag. *lungkót*]

leddág: lumdag. *v.* to start to ripen. **apagleddag.** *a.* slightly ripened. (*luom, darangidángan*)

leddangán: *n.* a species of snail. (*baran*; *duriken*; *kubbaong*)

leddég: *n.* a kind of small mollusk with a long, pointed shell. **nabaraniwan a leddeg.** dish made with the *leddeg* mollusk cooked with lemongrass.

leddúok: lumduok. *v.* to noisily swallow. **leledduokan.** *n.* depression at the inner ends of the two collar bones, sternal notch. (*ludduok*)

ledléd: ledleden. *v.* to rub the eyes; rub something itchy.

legál: (Sp. *legal*: legal) *a.* legal, proper.

legalidád: (Sp. *legalidad*: legality) *n.* legality.

leggák: *n.* rising (of celestial bodies). **lumgak.** *v.* to rise (stars, sun); to appear; be realized. **ipalgak.** *v.* to reveal, manifest. **leleggakan.** *n.* east; place of the sunrise. **nakalgaken ti bulan.** *n.* the moon is out tonight. [Kal. *sileÿ*, Tag. *sikat*]

leggéd: legden. *v.* to hide; conceal (*lemmeng*). [Tag. *tagò*]

leglég: *n.* a kind of small gnat or mosquito in a swarm.

lehión: (Sp. *legión*) *n.* legion.

lehislatúra: (Sp. *legislatura*) *n.* legislature.

lehítimo: (Sp. *legítimo*: legitimate) *a.* legitimate.

lek: umlek: *v.* to be speechless. see *ellek*.

lekbá: aglekba. *v.* to drop, slip (clothes, women's blouses). **ilekba.** *v.* to cause to flip.

lekbás: lekbasen. *v.* to diminish; reduce; (*obs.*) to tear off from the wall.

lekbén: see *palakay*: transplant.

lekkáb: lekkaben. *v.* to separate; sunder; remove; detach. **malekkab.** *v.* to be taken apart, torn off, severed, separated. **nalkab.** *a.* severed, separated; torn off; taken apart. **aglekkab.** *v.* to fall apart; disunite. **Dakkel a panglekkabam dayta.** That is very profitable for you. **Napanaas ti pannakalekkab ti kuko ti tangan ti labus a dapanna.** The tearing off of his toenail in his bare foot was excruciating. [Tag. *balták*]

lekkág: ipalkag. *v.* to reveal; spread. (*leggak*)

lekkáng: *a.* with glue removed. (*lekkab, palkang*) **lumkang ti pigket.** *a.* be lose stickiness (glue). **ipalkang.** *v.* to remove the stickiness (by soaking). **Limkang ti ukis ti kayo.** The bark of the tree peeled off. [Tag. *kiwal*]

lekkás: (*obs.*) temper of food. **lumkas.** *v.* to be removed by (dirt). **mapalkasan.** *v.* to be cleaned of dirt.

lekkéd: lekkeden. *v.* to skein (in weaving).

leksáb: leksaben. *v.* to disunite; separate. (*liksab, lekkab*)

leksión: (Sp. *lección*: lesson) *n.* lesson. (*paganninawan*) **agleksion.** *v.* to have or take lessons.

leksionen. *v.* to give lessons to; teach. **Masapol a maleksionan dagiti tao.** People need to learn a lesson.

lélang: *n.* grandmother (*lola*). [Png. *bái*, Tag. *lola*]

lellén: *var.* of *lenlén*.

lélong: *n.* grandfather (*lolo*). [Png. *láki*, Tag. *lolo*]

lemmá: *n.* dent; indentation; print; mark. **lemma ti ramay.** *n.* fingerprint. **aglemma.** *v.* to leave a mark. **agpalma.** *v.* to club into tightness; tighten. **Kaanonto a malipatak ti lemma ti sugat ti barukongko?** When will I forget the mark made by the wound in my heart? [Tag. *taták*]

lemméd: see *limed*: conceal.

lemméng: *n.* hideaway; hiding place; concealed area. **aglemmeng.** *v.* to hide oneself. **ilemmeng.** *v.* to conceal a thing; hide a thing. **aglinnemeng.** *v.* to hide from each other; play hide-and-seek. **linnemmengan.** *n.* hide-and-seek game. **palmeng.** *n.* secret; something concealed. **nalemmeng, nalmeng.** *a.* hidden. **Saandan nga agatling-et gapu iti pannakilinnemmengda.** They no longer smell like sweat from playing hide-and-seek. [Ibg. *isussuq, mettutuq*, Ivt. *tumayuq*, Kpm. *salikut*, Png. *amót*, Tag. *tagò*]

lemmés: malmes. *v.* to drown (in water, in sorrows, etc.). **ilemmes.** *v.* to drown (someone). **lemmesen.** *v.* to drown, put in water. **pannakalmes.** *n.* drowning incident. **malmes iti perreng.** *v.* to fall into a deep stare. **Malmes ti pusona iti ragsak.** Her heart drowned in happiness. [Ivt. *kamutan*, Png. *lenér*, Tag. *lunod*]

lemmúon: malmuonan. *v.* to be surprised; to be betrayed; to be misled.

lemón: (Sp. *limón*) *n.* lemon. **pan de lemon.** roll of bread.

lenlén: ilenlen. *v.* to wrinkle; ruffle (*karenken*); push to one side.

lennáad: ipalnaad. *v.* to reveal; foretell; disclose; give a warning.

lennáag: kalnaagan. *n.* outdoors. **ipakalnaagan.** *v.* to put outdoors (during the night). **malnaagan.** *v.* to be outdoors during the night.

lennéb: lenneben. *v.* to do the whole thing; to give to everyone; do without exception. [Tag. *lahát*]

lennéd: *n.* new moon. **lumned.** *v.* to sink; be flooded; engulfed. **palned.** *n.* a kind of net similar to the *sigay*. **palneden.** *v.* to sink; destroy; (*fig.*) spend unwisely. **ilenned.** *v.* to cause to sink. **pagpapalned.** *n.* curse, malediction. [Png. *lerég*, Tag. *lubóg* (sink)]

lennék: *n.* setting (of moon, sun); *a.* dented; compressed; concave; hollow. **lumnek.** *v.* to set (the sun); penetrate; to become deep set (eyes); sink in a hole. **lumnek diay init.** sunset. **nakalnek.** *a.* set (sun). **ipalnek.** *v.* to press down; put into a hole; put a hat on the head. **kaipalpalnek.** *a.* just plunged; just put in a hole. **Tagilnekánen ti init.** The sun is about to set. **Dandani lumneken ti init idi agpakadaak.** It was almost sunset when I said goodbye. [Tag. *lubóg*]

lennók: kalnokan. *n.* dense forest.

lénte: (Sp.) *n.* flashlight; lens. **aglente.** *v.* to use a flashlight; lighten; to ignite (a lighter). **lentean.** *v.* to lighten.

lentéhas: (Sp. *lentejas*) *n.* lentil.

lentihuélas: (Sp. *lentejuela*: spangle) *n.* spangle, small glittering object.

lengdás: *n.* unfinished job; extent of work at the time of interruption.

lengguáhe: (Sp. *lenguaje*: language) *n.* language. (*pagsasao*) **lengguahe ti kalkalsada.** *n.* slang; street talk. **lengguahe a maradaniw.** *n.* poetic, flowery language.

lengguéta: (Sp. *lengüeta*: small tongue) *n.* wire fastener; tongue of a buckle; belt holder; epiglottis.

lengléng: *n.* the ends of the earth, very far away; hidden place; *a.* remote (*lallok*). **Lengleng a lugar a di pay madanon ti elektrisidad.** It is a remote place where electricity hasn't reached yet.

lengngá: *n.* sesame seed; sesame plant, *Sesamum orientale*. **kalengngaan.** *n.* sesame field. [Ifg. *lungi*, Kal. *longa*, Knk. *lengá*, Png. *langís*, Tag. *lingá*]

lengngáag: *n.* voice, tone. (*timek; allingag*) **ilengngaagan.** *v.* to recognize by the voice.

lengngán: *n.* crack, crevice. **aglengngan.** *v.* to crack (*bettak*). [Tag. *biták*]

lengngáw: lengngawan. *v.* to skip over. (*labas*)

lengngés: *n.* nape, cervix; part that connects the culm with the ear of rice. **lelengngesan.** *n.* neck. **lengngesen.** *v.* to hold tight to the neck of; twist someone's neck; choke someone. [Png. *tenger*, Tag. *batok* (nape), *leég* (neck)]

lengsát: nalengsat. *a.* narrow (*lanes, akikid*). [Tag. *kipot*]

león: (Sp. *león*: lion) *n.* lion. **leon-taaw.** *n.* sea lion.

leopárdo: (Sp.) *n.* leopard.

lep-ák: *n.* stalk of banana or taro. **lep-aken.** *v.* to remove the layers of the stalk of a banana.

leplép: agleplep. *v.* to hush; keep silent. **leplepan.** *v.* to keep something silent; control one's emotions; prevent. **Adda met laeng**

pagnaan daytoy a dusa iti pannakaleplep ti yaadu dagiti krimen. There is a way this punishment can control the increase in crimes. [Tag. *tahimik*]

leppá: nalpaan. *a.* digested; properly rested after eating. **lumpa.** *v.* to digest; decrease, abate. **agpalpa.** *v.* to rest after eating.

leppáag: lumpaag. *v.* to subside (fire), abate. (*leppéng*)

leppák: *n.* taro stalk. (*lep-ák*) **leppaken.** *v.* to dislocate; separate at the joints.

leppáp: leppap, nalpap. *a.* compressed, flattened. **agleppap.** *v.* to become flattened. **Saan a leppap ti agongna.** His nose is not flat. [Tag. *pangó*]

leppás: leppasen. *v.* to finish, end, terminate, accomplish; perfect. **ileppas.** *v.* to finish, complete, do until the end. **ipalpas.** *v.* to have something finished. **kalkalpas, kalleppas, lepleppas.** *a.* just finished. **malpas.** *v.* to be able to finish. **malpasan.** *v.* to be able to finish; overdue. **Nalpasen.** It's over. It's finished already. **kalpasan.** *prep.* after. **kalpasanna.** *adv.* afterwards. **palpasen.** *v.* to await the conclusion of; wait one's turn. **pagleppasan.** *n.* final portion; finish line. **pannakalpas.** *n.* completion. **apagleppas.** *a.* just finished. [Ibg. *balín*, Knk. *anggéy*, Png. *sampot*, Tag. *tapos*]

leppáy: nalpay. *a.* drooping down. **malpay.** *v.* to droop; (*fig.*) in low spirits; to become flaccid (penis). [Png. *aluyluy*, Tag. *ukô, yukô, layláy*]

leppéd₁: see *lapped*: obstruction. (*tipéd*)

leppéd₂: *a.* flat (nose). (*leppap, lugpap*)

leppéng₁: malpeng. *v.* to be deafened by a shrill sound. (*tileng*) **nakalpeng.** *a.* deafening, earsplitting.

leppéng₂: lumpeng. *v.* to abate; decrease (*ati*). [Tag. *hupâ*]

leppés: lumpes. *v.* to droop (plants). **malpes.** *v.* to droop from moisture. [Tag. *luóy*]

leppét: *n.* cupule; operculum; head of an eggplant.

leppiád: *n.* blubber. *a.* reflected; bent back (feet).

leppúog₁: malpuog. *v.* to wither; dry; fade. (*laylay*). [Tag. *lantá*]

leppúog₂: malpuog. *v.* to go bald. (*kalbo, pultak*)

lépra: (Sp. *lepra*: leprosy) *n.* leper; leprosy (*kutel*). [Tag. *ketong*]

leprosário: (Sp. *leprosario*: leprosarium) *n.* leprosarium, hospital for lepers.

lepróso: (Sp. *leproso*: leprous; leper) *n.* leper. (*agkukutel*)

lésbia: (Sp. *lesbia*: lesbian) *n.* lesbian. (*lakien a babai*)

leslés: *n.* plait in clothing. (*tupi*)

lésna: (Sp. *lesna*: awl) *n.* awl; fishing spear.

lessá: lumsa. *v.* to settle (get smaller in cooking); to be properly digested (food) (*leppa; palpa*).

lessáad: see *lansad*: base (of a mountain, sea, etc.); level.

lesséb: *prep, adv.* inside; deep set (eyes). (*uneg*) **ilesseb.** *v.* to put inside; dig deep. **malseb.** *v.* to be deep set (eyes).

letanía: (Sp. *letanía*) *n.* litany.

let-áng: *n.* wasteland, desert; wilderness; outer space; midst. **malet-ang.** *v.* to stop; cease. **iti let-ang.** *prep.* in the midst of.

letlét₁: letleten. *a.* crowded, overloaded. **lumetlet.** *v.* to crowd oneself into; mix in a crowd. **aglilinnetlet.** *v.* to throng, hustle and bustle with a lot of people.

letlét₂: letleten. *v.* to have a plugged-up nose (in a cold).

letnég: (*obs.*) *a.* yielding to pressure. **lumetneg.** *v.* to yield to pressure.

létra: (Sp. *letra*: letter) *n.* letter of the alphabet. **letraan.** *v.* to put letters on. [Kal. *gili*]

letráto: *var.* of *retrato*: photograph, picture.

létse: (Sp. *leche*: milk) *n.* milk (*gatas*); dunce, idiot; ninth part of a ganta; mild curse word. **letse kondensada.** *n.* condensed milk. **letse ebaporada.** *n.* evaporated milk.

letseplán: (Sp. *leche flan*: custard) *n.* custard; flan.

létsuga: (Sp. *lechuga*: lettuce) *n.* lettuce.

letsón: (Sp. *lechón*: roast pig) *n.* roast pork. **agletson.** *v.* to prepare roasted pig. **letsonada.** *n.* party in which *letson* is served.

lettáak: lumtaak. *var.* of *lumtak*: crack; split; cleave.

lettáang: kaltaang (ti rabii). *n.* middle (of the night).

letták: *n.* crack; crevice. **lumtak.** *v.* to crack; split; be hot (sun). [Png. *leták*, Tag. *liták, putók*]

lettát: lettaten. *v.* to loosen; unfasten; undo; slacken, relax; release. **maltat.** *v.* to be released, unfastened, not ready for use; broken, damaged. **lelettatan.** *n.* screw or button used to unfasten. **maltatan.** *v.* to be out of the water (fish, dry rice field). **naltatan iti paragpag.** with broken ribs. **Dagus a linettatko ti imatangko kenkuana ket impasayagko iti baybay.** I immediately averted my attention from him and turned toward the ocean.

lettáw: *n.* an underwater demon. **lumtaw.** *v.* to appear suddenly and unexpectedly; to occur; present oneself; to surface (from under the water). **palettawen.** *v.* to raise; promote (in rank). **pinaltaw.** *n.* a kind of dessert made with rice and sugar. [Png. *letaw*]

lettég: *n.* boil; abscess. **lumteg.** *v.* to swell; become infected. **letteg a pakleb.** see *kelleb*.

agpalteg. *v.* to swell painfully. [Ibg. *baga*; *lappát*, Ifg. *pogha*, Itg. *busáli*, Ivt. *varut*, Kal. *busali*, Knk. *búyoy*, *pegsá* (boil), *lat-éd* (swell), Kpm. *tigsaq*, Png. *larág*, *pelsá*, Tag. *pigsá* (boil), *magâ* (swell)]

lettép: lumtep. *v.* to disappear; submerge.

lettíng: saggaltíng. *n.* small amount. **sumaggalting.** each a small amount.

lettuád: *n.* spring tide. **lumtuad.** *v.* to be new (the moon); to appear. **paltuaden.** *v.* to bring about, originate; be the author of; produce. **palpaltuad.** *n.* events, happenings (*pasamak*).

lettungáw: lumtungaw. *v.* to emerge, float; surface to the top (*lumtaw*). [Tag. *litáw*]

lettúong: (*obs.*) *n.* rough ground; trotting of a horse.

leyénda: (Sp. *leyenda*: legend) *n.* legend.

liáb: *n.* flame. **agliab.** *v.* to flare up (flames), blaze. (*seggiab*)

liábe: (Sp. *llave*: key) *n.* key; monkey wrench; pliers; key number in the *jueteng* gambling game; electric switch; key (*tulbek*). **liabe maestra.** *n.* master key. **liabe de tubo.** *n.* pipe wrench. **liabe inglesa.** *n.* monkey wrench.

liabéra: (Sp. *llavera*: key chain) *n.* key chain.

liád: *a.* bent or inclined backwards; with protruding abdomen and bent back. **maliad.** *v.* to be caused to fall backwards. **agliad.** *v.* to fall backwards. **iliad.** *v.* to cause to fall backwards. **Pagliadem ta tugawmo.** Put your seat down. [Tag. *liyád*]

liáli: agliali. *v.* to rock, sway. **iliali.** *v.* to rock gently. [Tag. *ugóy*]

liám: agliam (*obs.*) *v.* to steal underhandedly. (*takaw*)

liáma: (Sp. *llama*) *n.* llama.

liamáda: (Sp. *llamada*: call) *n.* doctor call or visit.

liamádo: (Sp. *llamado*: called) *n.* favorite (in betting, horse racing, etc.), favored team or competitor. (ant: *dehado*)

liamamiénto: (Sp. *llamamiento*) *n.* calling to arms, mobilization.

liána: (Sp. *llana*: trowel) *n.* plastering trowel.

lianéra: (Sp. *llano*: flat + *-era* nominal suffix) *n.* baking pan; dish for making molds in baking.

liáno: (Sp. *llano*: plain chant) *n.* calling bell; level field. **agliano.** *v.* to ring a calling bell.

liás₁: lumias. *v.* to shine; sparkle; gleam, glitter.

liás₂: lumias. *v.* to deviate, stray; swerve. **ilias.** *v.* to cause to leave without being noticed. [Tag. *lihís*]

libág: *n.* sound of a slamming door. **ilibag.** *v.* to slam a door. **manalbaag.** *v.* to fall with a slamming sound; slam. **kanalbaag.** *n.* continuous slamming sounds. **panalbaagen.** *v.* to slam.

libák: ilibak. *v.* to hide, conceal; suppress; leave undisclosed. **aglibak, paglibakan.** *v.* to tell a lie by concealing something. **libaken.** *v.* to deny. **malibak.** *v.* to be denied. **managlibak.** *n.* liar; person who is always in denial. **Kaano pay a naglibakak kenka?** When have I ever lied to you? [Kal. *puklitan*, Tag. *tatwâ* (deny)]

libáng: *n.* sound of gunfire.

líbas: *n.* unobserved escape. **aglibas.** *v.* to act secretly; to slip away without being noticed. **libasan.** *v.* to leave someone without being noticed. **libasen.** *v.* to take something without being noticed; do stealthily. **makalibas.** *v.* to be able to escape. **Ilibaslibasda ti sumusop iti marihuana.** They secretly puff marijuana. [Tag. *takas*]

libás: *n.* a kind of vine with white flowers and edible shoots, *Momordica ovata*.

lib-át: *n.* treacherous act. **lib-aten.** *v.* to strike treacherously; traduce; attack. [Tag. *taksíl*]

líbaw: aglibaw. *v.* to deviate; detour; go out of the way; to escape without being noticed. (*likaw*)

libáy: *n.* nap; dozing off. (*ridep*; *turog*; *tuglep*) **mailibay.** *v.* to doze unintentionally, take a nap. **Saanna nga ammo no kasano ti kapaut ti pannakailibayna.** He doesn't know how long he dozed off. [Png. *lirep*, Tag. *idlíp*, *hipíg*]

libbawáng: *n.* large opening. [Tag. *giwang*]

libbí: *a.* with drooping lower lip; pout. **aglibbi.** *v.* to protrude; pout the lips. **libbian.** *v.* to pout the lips at someone. **isem-libbi.** *n.* pouting, insincere smile. [Tag. *labì*, *ngusò*]

libbiáng: aglibbiang. *v.* to overflow; be filled to the top (*punno*, *lippias*). **Kinagiddan ti panaglibbiang ti danum ti namigerger a pukkawna.** Her trembling scream accompanied the overflowing of the water. [Kal. *lumay-as*, Tag. *apaw*]

libbúob: *n.* mist; fog. (*angep*) **aglibbuob.** *v.* to be misty. **nalibbuob.** *a.* misty, foggy. [Tag. *kulimlím*]

líbed: aglibed. *v.* to go around. [Tag. *ikot*]

libég: nalibeg. *a.* turbid, muddy; cloudy; dark; (*fig.*) sinister, wicked. **manglilibeg.** *v.* to make muddy (water). **aglibeg.** *v.* to become muddy. **panglibeg.** *n.* (*fig.*) politician who runs for an office in order to mislead and confuse the voters. [Bon. *bólek*, Kal. *gigibuk*, Tag. *labò*]

libélo: (Eng.) *n.* libel, defamatory statement.

líbeng: *n.* a kind of earthen jar placed at the entrance of the granary to block rats from entering. **manglibeng.** *v.* to be very fruitful; to be plentiful. **libenglibeng.** *n.* a kind of small marine fish. [Tag. *saganà* (abundant)]

liberasión: (Sp. *liberación*) *n.* liberation.

liberika: *n.* variety of coffee.

libertád: (Sp. *libertad*: liberty) *n.* liberty (*wayawaya*). [Tag. *kalayaan*]

libído: (Eng.) *n.* libido, sexual urge or desire.

libnáw: **libnawan.** *v.* to skip, omit; slip over. (*labas*)

libnós: *n.* beauty; glamour; grace. **nalibnos.** *a.* handsome; pretty; neat; clean; elegant; clear faced; shapely; first-class; (*coll.*) virgin. **lumibnos.** *v.* to become beautiful. **palibnusen.** *v.* to beautify. **idi kaliblibnosanna.** at the height of her beauty (*pintas*; *dayag*). [Tag. *gandá*]

libóg: **aglibog.** *v.* to fall down hard (with a thump). **kanalbuog.** *n.* continuous heavy sounds.

lib-ók: *n.* the third and last pounding of rice. **libuken.** *v.* to pound rice for the third time.

libukáy: *n.* the start of menstruation. (*sangaili*; *regla*) **malibukayan.** *v.* to begin menstruating.

libóng: *n.* sound of a gunshot. **aglibong, manalbuong.** *v.* to explode. **kanalbuong.** *n.* report of guns; explosions. **Nanalbuong ti paltogna.** His gun fired a shot.

líbut: *n.* procession, parade; traveling around (*libus*). **aglibut.** *v.* to go in procession. **aglibutlibut.** *v.* to promenade; go around. **libuten.** *v.* to travel around; tour. **sangkalibut.** *n.* one link of a chain. **ilibut.** *v.* to take around. [Png., Tag. *líbot*]

libuyóng: **nalibuyong.** *a.* clouded over; overcast (*naulpan*; *alibuyong*). [Tag. *kulimlím*]

líbra(s): (Sp. *libra*: pound) *n.* pound.

libránsa: (Sp. *libranza*: draft) *n.* bank draft; bill of exchange.

líbre: (Sp. *libre*: clear; free) *a.* free; clear (traffic). **ilibre.** *v.* to do something for free; treat others by paying their bill. **Ilibrenakami iti plete no agkakalugankami.** He pays our fare when we ride together.

libréta: (Sp. *libreta*: notebook; bankbook) *n.* pocketbook; notebook; book of tickets; bankbook.

libréto: (Sp. *librito*: small book) *n.* bankbook; account book. (*libreta*)

libríto: (Sp. *librito*: small book) *n.* booklet.

líbro: (Sp. *libro*: book) *n.* book. (*pagbasaan*) **ilibro.** *v.* to record in a book. **makilibro.** *v.* to share a book; share a textbook. **tenedor-de-libro.** *n.* accountant, bookkeeper. **Kasla silulukaten a libro ti biagko kenka.** My life is like an open book to you. [Kal. *liblu*, Tag. *aklát*]

libró: *n.* rumen, paunch. (*rakrakipa*) **liblibro.** *n.* tripe.

libsóng: *n.* puddle. (*lubnak*; *pilaw*) **mailibsong.** *v.* to step in a puddle. [Tag. *sanaw*]

libtá: *n.* negligence; carelessness; mistake; oversight. **aglibta.** *v.* to miss, omit; make a mistake.

libtáw: *n.* omission; miss; mistake. **aglibtaw.** *v.* to miss; oversee a mistake; skip class; be negligent. [Png. *lukso*, Tag. *laktáw*, *luktô*, *liban*]

libtó: **libtuan.** *v.* to disappoint; deceive. **aglibto.** *v.* to be negligent; fail to fulfill a promise.

libtók₁: **lumibtok.** *v.* to escape; break loose.

libtók₂: **palibtok.** *n.* a small net used to catch *ipon* fish; (*reg.*) marshy place.

libtóng: *n.* pond; reservoir (*basáw*); *var.* of *libsong*.

lídam: **nalidam.** *a.* forgetful; neglectful (*managlilipat*). **kinalidam.** *n.* forgetfulness, neglectfulness. [Tag. *limot*]

lidáy₁: *n.* sorrow; grief; melancholy; sadness. **naliday.** *a.* sad, grieving. (*leddaang*) **agliday.** *v.* to be sad; lonely. [Ibg. *reddem, daddám*, Ivt. *angsah*, Kal. *manchachauy*, Png. *ermen*, Kpm., Tag. *lungkót* (sad)]

lidáy₂: *n.* hillside (*bakras*; *barikir*; *ansad*).

liddá: *n.* a kind of hairy grass, *Saccharum spontaneum*. **lumidda.** *n.* a variety of short sugarcane.

liddangán: *n.* a kind of large, elongated brook mollusk.

liddáy: *var.* of *lodday*: deafening surf.

liddég: *n.* a kind of small edible snail with pointed shell.

liddíng: *n.* slight difference. **mailidding.** *v.* to be on the receiving end; to be blamed; to be put down. **ilidding.** *v.* to put down; blame.

liddó: **managliddo.** *a.* careless; thoughtless; negligent; inattentive. [Tag. *pabayà*]

lidduók: *n.* throat. **aglidduok.** *v.* to swallow vociferously; choke. **lidduokan.** *v.* to choke someone. **Linukayanna bassit ti siglot ti kurbatana ta mangrugin nga agapges ti lilidduokanna.** He loosened slightly the knot of his tie because it hurt his choking neck. [Tag. *lunók*]

lidduós: *n.* excessive perspiration. **agkalidduosan.** *v.* to sweat excessively (*daripespes*). [Tag. *pawis*]

lidém: **nalidem.** *a.* dim, not bright; gloomy; (*fig.*) evil (*ridem*). **manglidem iti dayaw.** disgrace one's honor. **Nalidem ti panagkitana.** His vision is dim. [Tag. *kulimlím, labò*]

lideráto: (Sp. *liderato*: leadership) *n.* leadership. (*panagdadaulo*)

lidílid: **ilidilid.** *v.* to press down gently with a slight rotary movement (pot on a stove).

líding: *n.* string; seal; ring; nose ring for the water buffalo. **lilidingan.** *n.* the hole pierced in the nose of the water buffalo. **lidingan.** *v.* to put a seal on. **palidingan.** *v.* to fix a nose ring into the nasal septum of (a water buffalo).

lidlíd: *n.* burnisher used to polish metals. **aglidlid.** *v.* to rub dirt off the body while bathing; rub the eyes. **lidliden.** *v.* to polish, burnish; smoothen; rub the eyes; flatter, **lidlidan.** *v.* to scrub someone. **palidlidan.** *v.* to run over someone. **Bumatokka ketdin ta lidlidem ti kabkab ta teltelmo.** Put your head in the water anyway to rub off the dirt from your nape. **Dina ibilang a nagdigos no saan a naglidlid iti pangersangen a bato.** He doesn't consider to have bathed without rubbing with a rough stone.

lidók: *n.* sound of gulping, swallowing. **lidoklidok.** *n.* sound of a gulping; palpitating chest. **lumidok.** *v.* to gulp; drink a little. **lidoken.** *v.* to swallow. **sangalidok.** *n.* one swig; one gulp. [Tag. *lunók*]

lídong: see *liddo*: careless; inattentive; thoughtless. [Tag. *pabayà*]

liébo: (Sp. *llevo*: carry over) *n.* carrying over a figure in mathematical computation, or the figure thus carried over.

liébre: (Sp. *liebre*: hare) *n.* hare, rabbitlike animal.

liém: **lumiem.** *v.* to crack; fissure; split. **mailiem.** *v.* to sink; to be embossed. **nailiem.** *a.* embossed. [Tag. *biták*]

liémpo: (Tag. via Hokkien *liám tô bàg*: stomach portion of pig) *n.* barbecued hunk of pork.

lienár: (Sp. *llenar*: fill) **lienaran.** *v.* to fill in (blanks).

liéno: (Sp. *lleno*: full) *a.* full (passenger vehicle). (*napno*)

liénso: (Sp. *lienzo*: linen, canvas) *n.* linen.

líes₁: *n.* nit, egg of the louse. (*lis-á*)

líes₂: **lumies.** *v.* to have gone by; to have passed.

líga: (Sp. *liga*: league) *n.* alliance; league.

ligálig: **ligaligen.** *v.* to strip a fruit of its skin while turning it.

ligaménto: (Sp. *ligamento*: ligament) *n.* ligament.

lígas: (Sp. *liga*: garter) *n.* garter, band or strap that holds up a sock.

ligasí: *n.* dislocation; dislocated bone. **agligasi.** *v.* to disjoint; deflect (*lagisi*); slip. **mailigasi.** *v.* to be dislocated, out of the proper position. **Agsublinsa ti ligasi ti pangak.** I think my jaw is broken again (the dislocation is returning).

ligasón₁: (Sp. *ligazón*: joining, linking) *n.* block (row of houses).

ligasón₂: (Sp. *ligazón*: linking) *n.* crack; large crevice. **agligason.** *v.* to crack. [Tag. *biták*]

lígaw: **maligaw.** *v.* to become weak, watered down. **agligaw** (*obs.*) *v.* to transit. [Tag. *ligaw* = court, woo]

lígay: *n.* wheel. (*rueda*) **maligayan.** *v.* to be run over. (*maatalan*) **ipaligay.** *v.* to roll down. [Tag. *gulóng*]

ligí: **mailigi.** *v.* to stumble.

ligiás: **lumigias.** *v.* to escape, get away from. (*talaw, libas*)

ligís: *var.* of *ligí*: stumble.

lig-ís: **lig-isen.** *v.* to crush (lice between fingernails); squeeze; (*obs.*) to accept whatever is offered. **ilig-is.** *v.* to crush a louse on the head. **agpalig-is.** *v.* (*fig.*) to have an abortion. **Inligisko la koman idi ubing pay!** I should have aborted him when he was still young. [Ibg. *iladdoq*, Ivt. *mandidisaq*, Kal. *gis-it*, Kpm. *dikdik*, Png. *lasik*, Tag. *tirís*]

ligkó: *var.* of *likkó*: curved, bent.

ligós: **maligos.** *v.* to be sprained. **paligusen.** *v.* to ring the ears of. **ligusen.** *v.* to disjoint. **naligos.** *a.* sprained. (*bullo*)

ligpít: **iligpit.** *v.* to enclose, insert. **nailigpit.** *a.* enclosed, inserted. (*sigpit, lúkon, ballaét*)

ligsáy: **maligsay.** *v.* to slip, slide out of place. **agligsay.** *v.* to sink (sun); decline. **ligsayen.** *v.* to remove from a list. **iligsay.** *v.* to get a tree branch out of the way. **apagligsay.** *n.* position of the sun and moon just after high noon or midnight. [Tag. *dulás*]

ligsí: **ligsien.** *v.* to excuse; exempt. **maligsi.** (*obs.*) *v.* to renounce.

ligtád: *var.* of *liktád*.

líha: (Sp. *lija*: sandpaper) *n.* sandpaper. **lihaen.** *v.* to sand with sandpaper. [Tag. *liha*]

lihía: (Sp. *lejía*: lye) *n.* lye, caustic soda.

líkaw: **nalikaw.** *a.* crooked, curved, meandering, roundabout. **aglikaw.** *v.* to go around. **aglikaw-likaw.** *v.* to go in circles, zigzag. **likawen.** *v.* to surround. **ilikaw.** *v.* to lead, take around; turn to left or right. **palikaw.** *n.* circumference. **agpalpalikaw.** *v.* to beat around the bush, not get straight to the point. **malikaw.** *v.* to be surrounded. **panglikawan.** *n.* circuitous route. **Diakon agpalpalikaw.** I am no longer beating around the bush. [Tag. *ligoy*]

likbá: *a.* slipping, sliding down (clothes); sagging; drooping. **aglikba.** *v.* to slip down, drop. **Nalikba dagiti abagana kenkuana.** Her shoulders dropped to him.

likbás: **linikbas.** *n.* superfluous twists of the *gan-ay*. **likbasen.** *v.* to trim; cut warp threads; tear from the wall; lessen.

likbát: **likbaten.** *v.* strike treacherously. (*lib-at*)

likídan: *n.* rolling pin used to roll metals into cords.

likidár: (Sp. *liquidar*: liquidate) **aglikidar.** *v.* to clear accounts (business); **likidaren.** *v.* to liquidate; (*coll.*) kill someone. **likidasion.** *n.* liquidation. [Tag. *todas*]

líkido: (Sp. *líquido*: liquid) *n.* liquid.

likíg: *a.* lopsided; sinking (sun); leaning to one side. **aglikig.** *v.* to lean on one's side; sink; decline. **likigen.** *v.* to cause to lean. [Tag. *kilíng*]

likkáb: *var.* of *lekkab*: sever; remove; pry open; take apart; take off (a mask).

likkakáng: *var.* of *likkukong*: concave, hollow. [Tag. *lukóng*]

likkaóng: *n.* hole, hollow. **nalikkaong.** *a.* hollow, uneven, rough (roads). **likkalikkaong.** *a.* potholed. [Tag. *lubák* (pothole; hollow), *lukóng* (hollow)]

likkiát: **likkiaten.** *v.* to disassemble; separate; open a can. **malikkiat.** *v.* to be disassembled; taken apart. [Tag. *tukláp*]

likkó: *a.* curved, bent. (*sikko*) **aglikko.** *v.* to turn (a corner). **ilikko.** *v.* to turn, curve. **lumikko.** *v.* to turn around. **paglikkuán.** *n.* turning point, bend. [Kal. *sikku*, Tag. *likô*]

likkúkong: see *likkaong*: hole; hollow. [Tag. *lukóng*]

liklík: *n.* detour. (*alliwit*; *liwliw*; *salikawkaw*) **liklikan.** *v.* to avoid; elude; slip away from; shun. **iliklik.** *v.* to keep someone from danger. **mangliklik.** *n.* diversion road; detour. **Kimmarab-as ti tappang tapno liklikanna dagiti alingo.** He jumped up and climbed the cliff in order to avoid the wild boar. [Tag. *iwas*]

likmút: *a.*, *prep.* around, on all sides of. **likmuten.** *v.* to surround; enclose; go around; encompass. **aglikmut.** *n.* environs, surrounding area. **palikmutan.** *v.* to encircle; surround. **napalikmutan.** *a.* surrounded by. **pagliklikmutan.** *n.* orbit. **Saan a makalikmot iti kelleb.** He cannot go around a pot lid (said of an impatient or temperamental person whose anger flares up before he has the chance to go around a lid). [Png. *liktob*, Tag. *sa likop*, *talikop*]

liknáw: *var.* of *litnaw*: clear; transparent.

likúd: *n.* back. (*bukot*) **iti likud.** *prep.* behind. **likudan.** *v.* to turn one's back; retract; reject; abandon; denounce; withdraw from. **iti malikudan.** *prep.* behind, in back of. **ipalikud.** *v.* to put at the back; put behind. **agpalpalikud.** *v.* to backbite; revile; deceive. **palikud.** *n.* substitute, proxy; the back door of a truck. **paglikudan.** *v.* to turn one's back on; renounce; retract. **malikudan.** *n.* those left behind in one's past. **iti likudan ti manibela.** behind the wheel. **Sika ti immuna a nanglikud ti**

karinkarita. You were the first to turn your back on our mutual promise. [Ibg. *likúg*, Kal. *ochog*, Png. *benég*, Tag. *likód*]

líkup: *n.* scooper; a kind of woodworm.

likúp: (*obs.*) *n.* a witch who changes into a deer.

liksáb: **liksaben.** *v.* to tear up; sever. **lumiksab.** *v.* to profit illegally; make a killing in business. [Tag. *tukláp*]

liktáb: **iliktab.** *v.* to conquer and control; put under one's custody.

liktád: *n.* bamboo ladder. **baliktad.** *a.* inside out. **liktadan.** *v.* to drain (a rice field). **liliktadan.** *n.* a rope used to hold a ladder in place. **iliktad.** *v.* to remove a ladder using a *liliktadan*; lift a ladder (used as an entrance to the house).

liktát: (*obs.*) *n.* drainage. (*paiyas*; *paaruyot*)

liktáw: *var.* of *laktaw*: omit, skip.

liktúb: *n.* enclosure; fence. **iliktub.** *v.* to confine, place in a restricted area. **liktuben.** *v.* to fence in; close up. (*likub*)

líla: *n.* grandmother (*lola*); (Sp. *lila*: lilac) *n.* lilac or violet color; lilac plant.

lílang: *n.* grandmother. (*lola*)

líli: **ilili.** *v.* to sway up (a flag); rock gently. **lilien.** *v.* to sway; rock (a child) (*indayon*). **Agpakpakadan ti kabus a bulan iti lulonan dagiti rumanitrit a pinuon ti kawayan nga ilillili ti nalamiis a pul-oy.** The full moon departed over the tops of the bamboo branches swaying from the cool breeze. [Tag. *ugóy*]

lilíg: *n.* pulpy segment (of a fruit); segment of an orange fruit. **liligen.** *v.* to separate the segments of an orange fruit (*lilit*). [Tag. *lihà*]

lílip: *n.* hem. **aglilip.** *v.* to hem garments. (*lupi*, *tupi*)

lilít: *n.* slice, segment; notch; slit. **malilit.** *v.* to blunt the edge of a weapon. **liliten.** *v.* to cut into small slices.

lílo: *n.* grandfather. (*lolo*)

lílong: *n.* grandfather. (*lolo*)

limá: *num.* five. **maikalima.** *ord. num.* fifth. **limalima.** *n.* starfish; *Dioscorea pentaphylla*, a type of yam with flower clusters in five. **apagkalima.** *num.* one-fifth. **pagkalimaen.** *v.* to divide into five parts. **saglilima.** *num.* five each. [Kal., Png, Tag. *limá*]

limáng: *var.* of *lemmeng*: hide.

limapúlo: *num.* fifty. [Knk. *bengngéy*, Tag. *limampû*]

limás: **limasan.** *v.* to bail out of water completely (*karas*). [Tag. *limás*]

limbáng: *n.* interval, space between. (*baet*) **aglimbang.** *v.* to plow in between rows. **limbangen.** *v.* to provide a space between. [Tag. *patláng*]

limbáyong: see *alimbayong*: slingshot.

límbo: (*myth.*) *n.* place for condemned souls.

limbóng: *n.* state of ease and comfort. **aglimbong.** *v.* to clear up; settle down; to go directly to; free from disturbance; go straight; to make up for lost time; turn a new leaf, doing something good after having done something bad. **nalimbong.** *a.* unanimous; clear (voices, sounds); straight; sincere; honest; peaceful. **paglimbongan.** *v.* to reform a child. **Dandani napukaw ti limbong ti panunotna.** He almost lost his clear thinking. [Tag. *tinô*]

limdó: *n.* sorrow; despair; grief; melancholy. **aglimdo.** *v.* to be cold, cross; to be touched, moved; doubt; to despair; feel sorry. [Tag. *lungkót*]

limdúos: **aglimduos.** *v.* to sweat excessively. (*daripespes*)

límed: *n.* concealed knowledge, secret. (*lemmeng*) **aglimed.** *v.* to do in secret; hide. **ilimed.** *v.* to hide, conceal. **managilimed.** *a.* secretive. **palimed.** *n.* secret; mystery. **nalimed.** *a.* secret; hidden; concealed. [Png. *amót*, Tag. *tagò, lihím*]

limitár: (Sp. *limitar*: limit) **limitaran.** *v.* to limit. **limitado.** *a.* limited.

limmúon: **malimmuonan.** *v.* to be misled; be taken unaware.

límo: **manglimo.** *v.* to disguise; to change oneself into; distinguish. **malimuan.** *a.* transformed; disguised. **malimo.** *v.* to forget; repudiate. **makalimo.** *n.* a variety of awned *diket* rice. **malimuan.** *v.* to forget, not be able to recognize a face; to be deceived. **limuen.** *v.* to deceive; cheat. [Tag. *balatkayô*]

limúg: **limugen.** *v.* to dilute, dissolve; blend, mix. **malimugan.** *v.* to be dissolved; diluted; mixed. **sangalimug.** *n.* one mixture. [Tag. *halò*]

limúkeng: see *alimukeng*.

limonáda: (Sp. *limonada*) *n.* lemonade.

limós: (Sp. *limosna*: alms) *n.* alms; stipend for mass; funeral fee. **agpalpalimos.** *n.* beggar, pauper. (*agpalpalama*) **limosan.** *v.* to give alms. **makilimos.** *v.* to beg for alms. **pananglimos.** *n.* almsgiving. [Tag. *limós*]

limosnéro: (Sp. *limosnero*: almoner) *n.* person who asks for alms on behalf of a worshipped saint (during a holy festival).

limpá: (Sp. *linfa*: lymph) *n.* lymph; (*obs.*) *n.* cooked vegetables (reduced after cooking).

limpák: **nalimpak.** *a.* compressed, flattened at the poles. (*daplat*)

limpátok: *n.* summit. (*patok; ngudo; murdong; sampa; aringgawis; alintotok; tapak; patok; toktok; alintotok; sapat*)

limpésa: *n.* smoother (piece of wood used by cement pourers). **aglimpesa.** *v.* to smoothen, level.

limpiá: (Sp. *limpia*: clean) **nalimpia.** *a.* clean (*dalos*); smooth (*lamuyot*); in order (*urnos*).

limpiabóta: (Sp. *limpiabotas*: shoeshiner) *n.* shoeshiner.

limpiésa: (Sp. *limpieza*: cleaning) *n.* cleaning (house). **limpiesaen.** *v.* to clean; scrub the floor.

limpiár: *var.* of *limpia*.

límpio: (Sp. *limpio*: clean) **nalimpio.** *a.* straight; stable; virtuous, righteous; sound; sane; healthy; accurate, correct. **aglimpio.** *v.* to improve, become better; be over (war). **limpiuen.** *v.* to give the finishing touches to. **manglimpio.** *v.* to make good. **aglimlimpio.** *v.* to have lucid intervals.

limténg: *n.* inability to hear.

lináay: **nalinaay.** *a.* gentle.

línab: *n.* grease; grease smear. (*lanit*) **nalinab.** *a.* smeared; soiled; daubed. **makilinab.** *v.* to attend a banquet; (*reg.* to crash a banquet without being invited.) **aglilinab.** *v.* to scum (said of boiled fat). [Tag. *langís*]

línak: **nalinak.** *a.* calm; tranquil; still; peaceful; clear. **luminak.** *v.* to become calm; to become tranquil (*talna*). [Ivt. *dinak*, Png. *linak*, Tag. *payapà, tahimik*]

línang: *n.* red clay used to glaze pottery. **palinang.** *n.* solid brown sugar shaped like the halves of a coconut shell.

lináon: (f. *laon*) *n.* contents; (*fig.*) essence, substance. **Agsisimparat ti linaon ti panunotko.** The meaning of my thoughts is cluttered.

linapdán: (f. *lapped*) *v.* having obstructed a person.

línas: *n.* string for binding. **malinasan.** *a.* overwhelmed with **agkalinas.** *v.* to be of the same mind; to be tied to the same string. **linasen.** *v.* to twine; tie with string. [Tag. *pisì*]

linása: (Sp. *linaza*: linseed) *n.* linseed.

línay: **nalinay.** *a.* cooked thoroughly (rice); perfectly done (work). **linayen.** *v.* to cook (rice) thoroughly; to do thoroughly. [Tag. *in-in*]

lináy: (*obs.*) *n.* morass. (*gayonggayong*)

lindéras: (Sp. *lindero*: boundary, limit) *n.* boundary, frontier. (*dulon*)

lindéros: (Sp. *lindero*: limit; boundary) *n.* boundary.

lindóng: (*obs.*) see *salinong*: shelter; shade. (*linong*)

línia: (Sp. *línea*: line) *n.* line; file; row. (*uged; batog*) **aglinia.** *v.* to stand in line. **makilinia.** *v.* to join in line. **pagliniaen.** *v.* to arrange in a row. **liniado.** *a.* ruled (paper).

línis: nalinis. *a.* smooth, even; clear; clean; pure; virgin. **malinis.** *n.* a variety of rice with a white kernel. **aglinis.** *v.* to clean, clean up. **ipalinis.** *v.* to have something cleaned. **linisan.** *v.* to clean out; clear away. **linisen.** *v.* to clean; clear away; clean out. **linis-kantores.** (*coll.*) *n.* choir girl's cleaning (referring to sloppy housework). [Kal. *kaglus, mampekas,* Png., Tag. *linis*]

linnáaw: *n.* dew. **malinnaawan.** *v.* to be exposed to the dew. **kalnaawan.** *n.* outdoors; open air (at night). **agkalnaawan.** *v.* to be outdoors (at night). **ipalnaaw.** *v.* to leave outside overnight. **nalnaawan.** *a.* left outside overnight; covered in dew. [Bon. *síngen,* Ibg. *engngoq, leppaq,* Ifg. *dulnu,* Ivt. *apun,* Kal. *chilú, chemimis,* Knk. *móngo, peg-ás,* Kpm. *ambon,* Png. *linaó,* Tag. *hamóg*]

linnáay: *var.* of *alinaay:* tranquil, calm. (*talna*)

líno: (Sp. *lino:* linen) *n.* flax; linen. **de-lino.** *a.* linen.

linód: kalkalnúodna. He just died.

linólio: (Sp. *linolio:* linoleum) *n.* linoleum.

línong: *n.* shade (from sun); shelter (from rain). **aglinong.** *v.* to take shelter, go to the shade. **luminong.** *v.* to shade oneself; siesta, take a nap. **ilinong.** *v.* to put under the shade. **linongan.** *v.* to shelter someone; shade from. **makilinong.** *v.* to take shelter under someone's roof, request to share the shade. **agkalinong.** *v.* to share the same shelter or shade. **nalinong.** *a.* shady. **paglinong.** *n.* something used as shade or shelter. [Bon. *álong,* Ivt. *avung,* Kal. *ichong, aÿong,* Knk. *alalangáw, lulóng,* Png. *siróm,* Tag. *lilim*]

linotípo: (Sp.) *n.* linotype machine.

linsaéd: *n.* dregs of muddy water. (*rinsaed*)

lintá: *n.* leech (*alimatek*); earthworm (*alinta; alumbayad*). [Png. *linta,* Tag. *lintâ*]

lintég: *n.* law; executive order. (*alagad; annurot*) **nalinteg.** *a.* straight; upright, honest; just; fair; unbiased; reasonable; to the point; legal; legitimate. **aglinteg.** *v.* to be straight; go straight. **agkalintegan.** *v.* to reason out; argue; defend oneself. **lintegen.** *v.* to make straight. **luminteg.** *v.* to become straight; straighten out; become upright. **ipalinteg.** *v.* to have something straightened, corrected. **panglintegan.** *n.* shortcut. **manglinteg.** *v.* to go by the short route; to go straight. **kalintegen.** *v.* to make something straight. **kalintegan.** *n.* privilege; right; *a.* straightest. **ikalintegan.** *v.* to justify; defend. **nainkalintegan.** *a.* righteous, lawful; reasonable. **pannakabagi ti linteg.** *n.* police officer. **Adda paglinteganda a dida maki-asawa iti dida kapammatian.** They have a law that they cannot marry outside their faith.

Linintegna ti takderna sana sinango ti abogado. He straightened his posture and then faced the lawyer. **Saan a naikkalintegan ti inaramidda.** What they did is not righteous. **Nalinteg ti asuk.** The smoke is straight (said when there's a party). [Ibg. *tunung,* Ivt. *matalineng,* Kal. *lintog,* Knk. *láwas, letég,* Kpm. *túlid,* Png. *peték,* Tag. *tuwíd* (straight); *batás* (law)]

lintók: lintokan. *v.* to knock out the top of a mollusk (to suck out the edible contents).

lingáling: *n.* a kind of screen to shade the sun while harvesting. **aglingaling.** *v.* to shake the head (*ngilangil, wang-il*); to stay under the *lingaling.* **mailingaling.** *v.* to be unnoticed; distracted. **lingalingen.** *v.* to disobey.

lingáy: linglingay. *n.* joy, entertainment. **lingayen.** *v.* to divert, amuse. *n.* a black and white cock. **makalinglingay.** *a.* amusing; entertaining. (*ray-aw*) **paglinglingayan.** *n.* entertainment; amusement. **Awan sabali a makalinglingay iti bagbagitayo no saan a datayo.** No one else can amuse ourselves but us. [Tag. *libang*]

lingéd: *n.* screen; concealed place. (*lemmeng*) **lingdan.** *v.* to screen, conceal, be in the way of one's view; hide. **panglinged.** *n.* shade, screen. **nalinged.** *a.* hidden. **aglinged.** *v.* to hide oneself. **makalinged.** *n.* something that obstructs (the view, etc.). **ilinged.** *v.* to hide, conceal something. [Tag. *tagò*]

ling-ét: *n.* sweat, perspiration (*limduos*); (*fig.*) toil, hard work. **agling-et.** *v.* to sweat. **agpaling-et.** *v.* to sweat intentionally (during a workout). **agkaling-etan.** *v.* to sweat profusely. **iling-et.** *v.* to sweat out. **bagas ling-et, balay ti ling-et.** *n.* prickly heat (sweat rash). **malingetan.** *a.* drenched with sweat. **agbagas ling-et.** *v.* to have prickly heat. **agtutukel a ling-et.** *n.* beads of sweat. **Saanen nga agatling-et gapu iti pannakilinnemmengna.** He no longer smells like sweat because of playing hide-and-seek. **Anaknak ti ling-et.** *exp.* I am poor (*lit:* the child of sweat). **Sayang dagiti paglingling-etanna ta sabali met ti mairanranud.** His toil is going to waste because another person is benefiting. [Bol. *saynget,* Ibg. *uggang,* Ivt. *inalengdeng,* Kal. *lingot,* Knk. *ágew, lingét,* Kpm. *páwas,* Png. *lingét,* Tag. *pawis*]

linggí: *n.* lathe of a loom. **agpalinggi.** *v.* to rock, sway. **aglinggilinggi.** *v.* to move the body in a graceful way (as when dancing). [Tag. *giray*]

lingguísta: (Sp. *lingüista:* linguist) *n.* linguist, polyglot, one fluent in several languages. [Tag. *dalubwikà*]

lingguístika: (Sp. *lingüística*: linguistics) *n.* linguistics, the science of language.

ling-í: iling-i. *v.* to turn away; to defend, back up (support); turn the head to the side. [Tag. *kilíng*]

lingién: *n.* a kind of bird.

língka: *n.* bamboo used inside a hat to fit the head. **lingkaan.** *v.* to provide a hat with a band. **lingkalingka.** *n.* interior of the curled upper part of the ear.

língkamas: *var.* of *singkamas*: jicama.

linglíng: *n.* entertainment; amusement; recreation. **aglingling.** *v.* to amuse oneself. **linglingen.** *v.* to amuse, cheer up; delay, procrastinate. **malingling.** *v.* to be frustrated, forgotten. [Tag. *libang*]

lingngá: *var.* of *lengngá*: sesame.

lingngán: (*obs.*) *n.* roll of a ship.

língo: (*obs.*) *a.* week. (*dominggo, lawas*)

lingó: **lingolingo.** *n.* a kind of tree used for lumber.

lingús: **aglingus.** *v.* to grimace while shaking the head.

lingsád: see *lansad*: base of mountain; ocean floor.

lingsát: **nalingsat.** *a.* narrow. (*akikid*)

lingtá: **lingtaen.** *v.* to boil (anything but meat). **malingta.** *v.* to be boiled (*anger, kelnat*). **lilingtaen.** *n.* vegetable good for boiling. [Kal. *lukmug*, Tag. *lagà*]

lión: (Sp. *león*: lion) *n.* lion.

lipág: **malpaag.** *v.* to collapse, cave in. **kanalpaag.** *n.* continuous crumbling sounds. **panalpaagen.** *v.* to crumble something down.

lipák: *n.* pounding clothes. **manalpaak.** *n.* sound of a slap. **lipaken.** *v.* to spank, slap. **kanalpaak.** *n.* slapping sounds. **ipanalpaak.** *v.* to slam; bang. **lumanipak.** *v.* to produce continuous slapping sounds.

lip-ák: *n.* taro stalk; banana stalk. (*leppak*) **mailip-ak.** *v.* to have the stalk detached; to be sprained by being pulled. **lip-aken.** *v.* to pull off the stalk. [Tag. *uhay* (stalk)]

lípat: *n.* forgetfulness. **malipatan.** *v.* to forget unintentionally. **lumipat.** *v.* to forget. **lipaten.** *v.* to forget something intentionally; disregard; neglect. **lipatan.** *v.* to forget someone. **managlilipat.** *v.* to be ungrateful; forgetful. **tagilipat.** *n.* forgetfulness. **aglinnipat.** *v.* to forget each other. **makalipat.** *v.* to forget; be able to forget. **di-kaliplipatan.** *a.* unforgettable. [Bon. *lídong*, Ibg. *mettaman*, Ivt. *wayak*, Kal. *liwat*, Knk. *abutawtáw*, *linglíng*, *leew*, *limattáw*, *sulimatmát*, Kpm. *kalingwan*, Png. *linguán, libáng*, Tag. *limot*]

lípaw: **aglipaw.** *v.* to leap out of the net. **lipawen.** *v.* to overpass, overtop; rise over. **malipaw.** *v.* to be submerged. [Tag. *talón*]

lípay: *n.* a kind of vine, *Mucuna sp.*, whose seeds children use as marbles. **lipaylipay.** *n.* ankle. (*pingil*) **aglipay.** *n.* a shooting game using *lipay* marbles. **Pitakpitak dagiti dapanda agingga iti ngatuen ti lipaylipay.** Their feet were covered with mud up to their ankles. [Kal. *tikling* (ankle), Png. *kalitkalit*, *batangan* (ankle), Tag. *bukung-bukong* (ankle)]

lipáyo: *n. nipa* fruit.

lípes: **lumipes.** *v.* to slip away without being seen. (*libas*)

lípi: **liplipi.** *n.* border of a hat. (*lebleb*)

lipíit: (f. *lipit*) **lumpiit.** *v.* to produce a slapping sound; snap the fingers. **manalpiit, lippiiten.** *v.* to slap. **agkanalpiit.** *n.* sound produced by a slap. **agilinnipiit.** *v.* to strike an opponent's hand with a card until he guesses what the card is.

lipít₁: *n.* narrow passage; beams used in floor construction. **lipiten.** *v.* to squeeze, press, compel, force. **malipit.** *v.* to be crushed; cornered. **aglipit.** *v.* to crowd. **aglilinnipit.** *v.* to throng, crowd. **lilipten.** *n.* armpit. **paglipit.** *n.* instrument used for squeezing. [Tag. *ipit*]

lipít₂: *n.* light slapping sound. **lipiiten.** *v.* to slap mildly. **lumpiit.** *v.* to produce a slapping sound; snap the fingers. **palpit.** *n.* ferule, whipping stick. **palpiten.** *v.* to whip with a *palpit*.

lipnók: *n.* deep part or pool of a river, large puddle (*ban-aw; libtong*). **nalipnok.** *a.* having a water puddle or small pool. **Bimmatok met iti lipnok ken nagpapaanud iti ayus.** He dived into the deep part and drifted with the current.

lipuéd: (*obs.*) *n.* obstruction (*tiped*); cover (*abung*).

lípong: *n.* crowd of people. **makilipong.** *v.* to join a crowd, get lost in a crowd. **Nakilipunglipong iti kaaduan ti tao.** He got lost in the crowd of people. [Tag. *lipon*]

lípus: **malipus.** *v.* to be submerged; to be shorter than the surface of the water. **lipusen.** *v.* to submerge; put underwater. **lipus-tao.** overhead, above the height of a man. **apaglipus ti danum.** The water has just reached the head.

líput: *n.* treachery, betrayal. **liputan.** *v.* to betray. **mangliliput.** *a.* treacherous; *n.* traitor. **aglinniput.** *v.* to betray one another (in a game, etc.). **Mangliliputda iti nakayanakan a daga.** They betray their native land. [Kal. *apsan*, Png. *paklap*, Tag. *taksíl*]

lipót: **aglipotlipot.** *v.* to repeatedly break wind. **agkanalpuot.** *n.* the repeated sound of breaking wind; boisterous farting. **manalpuot.** *v.* to fart; produce a flapping sound.

lippagó: *a.* having ears bent forward. (*sarang*)

lippáy: *var.* of *leppáy*: droop, bend down.

lippáyos: *a.* sloppy; unkempt.

lippiás: aglippias. *v.* to overflow (*bussuag*; *luppias*; *pusuak*); abound. **Naglippias ti dalemna.** He is suffering from jaundice. **Uray no adu ti makatubeng, aglippias ti waig agingga a makadanon iti baybay.** Although there are a lot of obstacles, the creek overflows until it reaches the sea. [Tag. *apaw*]

lippíit: lumpiit. *v.* to snap. **aglinniplipiit.** *v.* to strike each other.

liptó: *n.* abbreviation in writing. (*lokto*) **aglipto.** *v.* to miss; be negligent. (*libto*)

líra: (Sp. *lira*: lyre) *n.* lyre; lire (currency).

lírika: (Sp. *lírica*: lyric) *n.* lyric.

lírio: (Sp. *lirio*: iris, lily) *n.* iris; lily flower.

lis-á: *n.* nit, lice egg. (*itlog ti kuto*) **ilis-aan.** *v.* to clean the hair of nits. **lislis-a.** *n.* variety of seaweed. [Ibg. *lita*, Itg. *kílit*, Ivt. *disaq*, Kal. *ilit*, Kpm. *lias*, Png. *liyés*, Tag. *lisâ*, *kupí*, *kuyumád*]

lisád: aglisad. *v.* to hunt. **malisadan.** *n.* catch (in hunting).

lisáy: nalisayan. *v.* to have indigestion, stomach pain and diarrhea (*bullaaw*). [Tag. *impatso* (Sp.)]

lisbó: *n.* the perimeter of the base of a pile.

lisbóng: *n.* hole; pit. (*libsong*) **mailisbong.** *v.* to fall into a hole. **lisbo-lisbong.** *a.* full of holes (a potholed road). (*likkaong*)

lisdák: *n.* heap; quantity bought by; width, wide space. **aglisdak.** *v.* to spread (as with grains when a weight is applied to them). **nalisdak.** *a.* wide, spacious; high in quantity.

lisék: lumsek. *v.* to sink (ground, rice); become hollow and deep set (eyes). **lisken.** *v.* to slaughter an animal by piercing the heart. [Tag. *lubóg*]

lisénsia: (Sp. *licensia*: license) *n.* license. **lisensiaan.** *v.* to license. **lisensiado.** *a.* licensed.

lísi: aglisi. *v.* to move out of the way; keep away. **ilisi.** *v.* to get something out of the way; to keep something away from; avoid. **Aglisika wenno dungparenka.** Get out of the way or I'll crash into you. **Ti aglisi ti ammona a dalan, nalabit nga mayaw-awan.** He who strays from a known path is likely to lose his way. [Tag. *tabí*]

lisíit: (f. *lisit*) **palsiit.** *n.* catapult. **manalsiit.** *n.* the report of a gun. **pumalsiit.** *v.* to shoot with a catapult or slingshot.

lísing: *n.* a kind of large, greenish fly.

lisít: *n.* catapult for throwing stones (*lisiit*). **palsiit.** *n.* slingshot. **manalsiit.** *v.* to make the sound of a whip. **kanalsiit.** *n.* sound of continuous thunder.

liskabéng: *a.* having large eyelids that give the appearance of having small eyes. (*luskabéng*) **lumiskabeng.** *v.* to sink, become hollow (eyes). **naliskabeng.** *a.* pitted; potholed.

liskéb: see *liskabeng*: with large eyelids.

lislís: *n.* the rolling up of the sleeves or pant legs. **aglislis.** *v.* to roll up the sleeves. **sililislis.** *a.* with rolled-up sleeves. **lislisen.** *v.* to roll up a sleeve; pull up a dress. **malislis.** *v.* to be flayed. **Nakalislis dagiti pantalonda agingga iti baba ti tumeng.** Their pants were rolled up until under the knees. [Tag. *lilís*]

lisná: (Sp. *lesna*: awl) *n.* awl. [Tag. *punsón* (Sp.)]

lisnáy: aglisnay. *v.* to crouch; sit cross-legged; sit with legs to the side. (*lupisak*)

líso: (Sp. *liso*: smooth; flat) *a.* simple; plain; *n.* flat sheet of zinc.

lisút: *n.* popping sound. **kanalsuot.** *n.* continuous popping sounds. **palsuot.** *n.* bamboo popgun. **lumsuot, manalsuot.** *v.* to pop repeatedly.

lispók: malispok. *v.* to tumble; fall plump; crumble to the ground. [Tag. *guhò*]

lissáad: *n.* dregs, sediment. (*areb*; *rinsaed*; *intaer*; *ared-ed*; *aribudabud*) **aglissaad.** *v.* to sediment; settle. [Tag. *latak*]

lissáag: *n.* abyss, chasm. (*yuyeng*)

lissíit: (f. *lisit*) *n.* shrill, whistling sound. **manalsiit.** *v.* to produce a shrill sound.

lísta: (Sp. *lista*: list) *n.* list. (*listaan*) **ilista.** *v.* to put on a list. **agilista.** *v.* to list. **agpalista.** *v.* to enlist; enroll.

listáan: *var.* of *lista*: list.

listéros: (Sp.) *n.* timekeeper.

lísto: (Sp. *listo*: smart) *a.* clever. (*alisto*)

listón: (Sp. *listón*: ribbon) *n.* ribbon; shoelace; adornment on the brim of a hat.

listonádo: (Sp.) *n.* species of plant with long, narrow, multicolored leaves.

litáak: (f. *liták*) **lumtaak.** *n.* the sound of bamboos drying in the sun; *v.* to crack. **agkanaltaak.** *n.* the sound of rain on an iron roof.

liták: **litaklitak.** *n.* sound of repeated gunfire. **kanaltaak.** *n.* bursting or cracking sounds; gunfire. **manaltaak.** *v.* to burst open.

litálit: *n.* a kind of herb with light blue flowers, *Ageratum conyzoides*. **aglitalit.** *v.* to move to and fro; move up and down. (*allitalit*)

litanía: (Sp. *letanía*) *n.* litany, type of prayer.

litáw: *n.* mermaid. (*sirena*) **nalitaw.** *a.* clear (water).

lit-áw: *var.* of *litnaw*: clear.

lítek: *n.* noise made by finger joints; clicking noise (as when taking pictures); noise made by turning on or off a switch. **aglitek.** *v.* to crack; creak; register instantly in the mind; click; snap (a picture). **palitek.** *n.* handle, crank. **Agkaralitek dagiti kamera iti pumponna.** The cameras kept clicking at her funeral. [Tag. *lagitik*]

lítem: *n.* blackish color of a bruise. **nalitem.** *a.* livid, black-and-blue, bruised. (*luló*) **lumitem.** *v.* to become livid, black-and-blue. **panglitemen.** *a.* leaden. [Kal. *ladlum, galidgid,* Knk. *tudlém, dasiéng,* Tag. *pasâ*]

líteng: *n.* hard wood stuck together; sharp, acute sound (*liting*). **agliteng.** *v.* to resound (an acute sound); (*fig.*) to flash instantaneously (thought). **naliteng.** *a.* sharp, acute (ears). **nalitngan** (*obs.*) *a.* sultry. **Naspig ti isemna idi adda agliteng iti panunotna.** His smile broke when a thought occurred to him.

litép: **aglitep.** *v.* to submerge; to disappear under water. (*rareb*)

literatúra: (Sp. *literatura*: literature) *n.* literature. (*kurditán*)

litigasión: (Sp. *litigación*: litigation) *n.* litigation.

litíik: (f. *litik*) sound of gravel; dull sound of an earthen jar when hit. [Tag. *lagitik*]

litík: *n.* clicking sound. **aglitik.** *v.* to click; (*fig.*) register instantly in the mind. **paltik.** *n.* kind of homemade gun. **kanaltiik.** *n.* continuous ticking or clicking sounds.

litílit: **litilitan.** *v.* to trim the edges of; to bind rope fast and secure. **nalitilitan.** *a.* sewn with a buttonhole stitch. **ilitilit.** *v.* to use to trim the edges with.

líting: *n.* kind of shrub whose bark is made into rope, rope; twine.

litíng: *n.* shrill sound. **agliting, lumting.** *v.* to sound acutely (scream, cry, etc.); ring (in the ears). **kanaltiing.** *n.* shrill sounds. **maltiing.** *v.* to ring, sound (in the ears); *n.* faint sound.

lit-íng: **lit-ingan.** *v.* to remove the top of; cut end off; cut tail off. (*pit-ing*)

litlít: *n.* crumpling. (*gelgel; kuleng; kumon; kunes; lunes*) **nalitlit.** *a.* crumpled.

litnáw: *n.* clearness. **nalitnaw.** *a.* clear, pure, transparent. **palitnawen.** *v.* to clear things up; let things settle down. **Awan libeg a di aglitnaw.** There is no turbid water that does not clear up. [Png. *linéw,* Tag. *linaw*]

lítog: **lumitog.** *n.* a kind of marine fish.

lítog: **aglitog, agkanaltuog.** *n.* the sound of burning bamboos. **agpaltog, lumtuog.** *n.* report of a gun. **paltog.** *n.* gun. **pumaltog.** *v.* to fire a gun. **paltogan.** *v.* to shoot. **pinnaltogan.** *n.* shooting. **palpaltog.** *n. Physalis angulata.*

Nalabsanna dagiti ubbing nga agpalpalitog iti kuitis ken rebentador iti kanto. He passed the children shooting rockets and firecrackers in the corner. [Tag. *puták*]

litograpía: (Sp. *litografía*: lithography) *n.* lithography. **litógrapo.** *n.* lithographer.

litók: *n.* knocking sound. **aglitok.** *n.* to crack a joint; knock; click (heels); knocking sound. **kanaltuok.** *n.* the report of guns; continuous knocking sound. [Tag. *kalatok*]

litúp: **litupan.** *v.* to finish off; pay off; cover the bill of another person; answer for. **makalitup.** *v.* to be sufficient for. **malitupan.** *v.* to make up for; to be able to complete; to be able to cover for. **Adda giwang iti kaunggan toy pusok a saanna a malitupan.** There is a breach in the depth of my heart that she cannot compensate for.

liturhía: (Sp. *liturgía*: liturgy) *n.* liturgy.

lítro: (Sp. *litro*: liter) *n.* liter; one-third of a *salup.*

lítsi: *var.* of *letse*: mild curse word.

litsías: (Ch.) *n.* lychee fruit.

litsúgas: (Sp. *lechuga*: lettuce) *n.* lettuce.

litsón: (Sp. *lechón*: roast pig) *n.* roasted pig. **aglitson.** *v.* to have roasted pig; to roast a pig. **litsonen.** *v.* to roast a pig. **lilitsonen.** *a.* suitable for roasting (a pig).

littád: *var.* of *litkad.*

littíik: (f. *litik*) *n.* popping sound; sound of gravel falling down a slope; sound of an earthen jar when hit. **lumtiik.** *v.* to make a popping sound. **agkanaltiik.** *v.* to produce a succession of popping sounds. [Tag. *lagitik*]

littíing: (f. *liting*) *n.* sharp sound (as produced by a tight string. **maltiing.** *v.* to hear faintly. **paltiing.** *n.* revelation; inspiration. **ipaltiing.** *v.* to suggest, hint, imply. **paltiingan.** *v.* to inspire, persuade, influence.

littík: *n.* a small hole in jars. **littikán.** *v.* to perforate. **naltikán.** *a.* pierced. **paltik.** *n.* a kind of marking line. [Tag. *biták*]

littugáw: *n.* breeze. (*pul-oy*)

littukó: *n.* rattan fruit.

liwá: **palpaliwa.** *n.* amusement, recreation. **liwliwaen.** *v.* to comfort, console, cheer up. **liwliwa.** *n.* consolation, comfort; recompense; a variety of awned rice. **kaliwanliwa.** *n.* sweetheart, darling. **pagpalpaliwaan.** *n.* comfort, solace. **No awan trabahona, mapan iti pantalan a pagpalpaliwaanna.** When he has no work, he goes to the pier for amusement. [Tag. *aliw*]

líwag₁: **iliwliwag.** *v.* to put out of one's thoughts; to try to forget worries. **mailiwag.** *v.* to get rid of anxiety; forget; to be able to find solace. **Inliwliwagna ti sanaang babaen iti panag-**

gaggagetna a nangtrabaho iti dagana. He got rid of the pain through his hard efforts to work his land. [Tag. *waksí*]

líwag₂: liwagen. *v.* to postpone, put off, delay.

liw-án: naliw-an. *a.* special; unequaled, unparalleled. **liw-anan.** *v.* to miss; be absent.

liw-ás: lumiw-as. *v.* to exceed, go beyond what is necessary. **maliw-asan.** *v.* to exceed; overdue; exaggerate. (*law-as*)

líwat: *n.* absence (*langan*). **agliwat.** *v.* to be absent. **liwatan.** *v.* to interrupt, discontinue; neglect. **lumiwat.** *v.* to discontinue; neglect one's duty; suspend. **Saanda a liniwliwatan ti nangpakan kenkuana iti karne wenno ikan.** They do not neglect to feed him meat or fish. [Tag. *liban*]

liwáweng: paliwaweng. *n.* idleness. **agpaliwaweng.** *v.* to wander aimlessly, be idle (*ballog*); procrastinate.

líway: naliway. *a.* negligent, careless; forgetful. **liwayan.** *v.* to neglect; forget something. **kinaliway.** *n.* negligence. **Dina maliwayan ti mangipasiar kaniak kadagiti sardam.** He doesn't neglect to take me on evening walks. [Tag. *pabayà*]

líwed: *n.* a kind of green algae.

líweng: mangliwengliweng. *a.* deep; profound; without limits. **Mangliwengliweng ti ulimek.** There was profound silence. [Tag. *lalim*]

liwés: mangliwes. *v.* to go around; pass around. **iliwes.** *v.* to take around. **lumiwes.** *v.* to pass. [Tag. *ligid*]

liwlíw: *n.* sea fishing equipment, fishing tackle (*banniit*). **agliwliw, lumiwliw.** *n.* to fish with tackle. **iliwliw.** *v.* to move from side to side. **mangliwliw.** *v.* to go by a roundabout way; detour; fish. **liwliwen.** *v.* to go by a roundabout way. **liwliwan.** *v.* to trap; bait. **paliwliw.** *n.* fishing tackle, line and sinker. **Nasnasken ti pintas a pangliwliw iti abogado.** Beauty is more necessary to bait attorneys. **Pagap-apan dagiti lumiliwliw no panawen ti kalgaw.** The fishermen use it as bait in summertime. [Tag. *bingwít* (fishing tackle)]

liwliwá: (f. *liwa*) *n.* consolation; comfort. **liwliwan.** *v.* to comfort, console, raise the spirits of. **pagpalpaliwaan.** *n.* something that comforts.

loá: *n.* recitation to a saint.

luá: *n.* tear; interjection used to halt the water buffalo. **aglua.** *v.* to shed tears, cry. **aglulua.** *v.* to be tearful. (*makalulua*) **lua ti pawikan.** *n.* false tears. **lulua.** *n.* yellow weeds that grow on the surface of a pond. **luluan ti mata.** *n.* lachrymal gland in the eye. **makipaglua.** *v.* to sympathize with. **managlua.** *a.* oversensitive; prone to crying. **Nakaluaak iti ragsakko.** I

cried tears of joy. [Ibg. *luwa*, Ivt. *huwuq*, Kal. *luwa*, Knk. *ága*, *leéw*, *teéw*, Kpm. *luwaq*, Png. *luá*, Tag. *luhà*]

luáb: luaban. *v.* to top cooking rice; to remove the upper layer from the kettle. **agluab.** *v.* to be lifted away by the wind (thatch); to bubble, boil; rise. [Tag. *kulô* (boil)]

luág: *n.* foam; spume; cream. (by boiling or fermenting). **agluag.** *v.* to foam up, bubble. **paluagen.** *v.* to boil; make something foam up. [Tag. *bulâ*]

luák: maluak. (*obs.*) *v.* to be destroyed.

luáli: maluali. *v.* to start; loosen (teeth); move. (*wali*)

luálo: *n.* prayer. (*karárag*) **aglualo.** *v.* to pray. **lualuaen.** *v.* to say a prayer. **makilualo.** *v.* to join a prayer. **managlualo.** *a.* always praying; prone to pray. **ilualo.** *v.* to offer a prayer to. **ilualuan.** *v.* to utter a secret prayer against someone; pray for. **aginlulualo.** *v.* to pretend to pray. [Ivt. *hwahuk*, Knk. *sos-oá*, Png., Tag. *dasál*]

luáng: *n.* empty jar; wasteland. **naluang.** *a.* emptied (contents), lessened. **naluangan.** *a.* not full. **nangluang.** *n.* incubated egg without signs of young yet. [Tag. *luwáng* = loose; wide]

luás: *n.* starting time; departure. **agluas.** *v.* to set out; commence a (voyage). **lumuas.** *v.* to leave on a trip. **iluas.** *v.* to take on a trip; bring merchandise to the market. **pagluasan.** *n.* place of departure. **Kuna dagiti mangngagas a dandani naladawkami a nangiluas.** The doctor says that we were almost late on setting out (for the hospital). [Tag. *luwás*]

luásit: (*coll.*, *lua* + *pusitsít*) *n.* crybaby. **agluasit.** *v.* to shed tears. **pagluasiten.** *v.* to make someone cry. **Agluluasit ti lakay a mangasasa iti badangna.** The old man shed tears as he sharpened his machete.

lúba: naluba. *a.* weak; easily injured; frail (*kapsut*). [Tag. *hinà*]

lubá: lubaluba. *a.* covered with mud; splattered with blood.

lúbag: lubagen. *v.* to lower the sail of.

lúban: *n.* (*obs.*) blunt knife. (*ngudel*)

lúbang: see *laddit*.

lúbay: *n.* earring. (*aritos*) **paglubayan.** *v.* to turn around; *n.* turning point.

lubbó: malbo. *v.* to sink; be swallowed up (in an earthquake). [Tag. *lubóg*]

lubbuág: *n.* illegitimate child (*lubbuag ti daga*); first vegetation that appears; the tallest stalks of sugarcane in the fields. **aglubbuag.** *v.* to froth (waves).

lubbón: *n.* partnership. **aglubbon.** *v.* to associate together (in pairs); conquer; take over; live together; share a seat. **kalubbon.** *v.* to do something as a pair. **lubbonan.** *v.* to go with; ride with. **Naglulubbonda a nagsakay iti nuang.** They rode the water buffalo together.

lubbót: *n.* pit, hole. (*abut*) **lumbot.** *v.* to go, to be able to fit through or in (a narrow aperture); fall through. **agpalbot.** *v.* to bear, bring forth; give birth, deliver a baby. **ilubbot, ipalbot.** *v.* to put something through a hole. **mailubbot.** *v.* to fall into a hole. **lubbolubbot.** *a.* with many holes (floor). [Tag. *lusót* (go through narrow place)]

lúbed: nalubed. *a.* dim (lights); wet (firewood). **Uray isebbam ti nalubed, talaga a di sumged.** Even if you throw wet firewood in the fire, it doesn't ignite. [Tag. *labò* (dim); *basâ* (wet)]

lubí: linubian. *n.* a kind of dessert made of bananas, rice, coconut, and sugar. **aglubi.** *v.* to make this dessert.

lúbias: (Sp. *alubia*: French bean) *n.* a kind of green bean; snap bean.

lúbid: *n.* string, line; small eyes; roll of cigars. **aglubid.** *v.* to stay; stop (said of locusts). [Ibg. *keddeng*, Ivt. *huvid*, Kpm. *taliq*, *léting*, Png. *lobír*, Tag. *talì*]

lublób: lumublob. *v.* to get stuck in the mud.

lubnák: *n.* puddle (*libsong*; *pilaw*); mudhole. **aglubnak.** *v.* to wallow in (a puddle, mud, sin, etc.) **ilubnak.** *v.* to throw something into a puddle or in the mud. **mailubnak.** *v.* to fall in a puddle; get stuck in the mud. **ipalubnak.** *v.* to take animals to wallow. [Tag. *lublób* (wallow)]

lubnáy: (*obs.*) *n.* swarming.

lóbo₁: (Sp. *lobo*: wolf) *n.* wolf.

lóbo₂: (Sp. *globo*: balloon) *n.* balloon.

lubó: *n.* mud, mud hole; slough. (*pitak*) **mailubo.** *v.* to get stuck in the mud. **ilubo.** *v.* to cause to get stuck in the mud. **nalubo.** *a.* muddy. [Tag. *putikan*]

lúbok: *n.* bag of a fishing net. **limmubok.** *a.* bulging.

lóbulo: (Sp. *lóbulo*) *n.* lobe, lobule.

lúbong: *n.* world; universe; valley. **nailubongan.** *a.* worldly; lustful, lewd. **kinailubongan.** *n.* lust, sexual desire. **sangalubongan.** *n.* the whole world; universe. **nailubongan a rikna.** *n.* sexual desire, lust. [Bon. *batáwa*, *daga*, *lóbong*, Png. *talbá*, Tag. *daigdíg*]

lubóng: *n.* a variety of rice with soft kernel.

lúbos: palubos. *n.* permission. **ipalubos, palubosan.** *v.* to allow, permit; grant. **maipalubos.** *v.* to be allowed.

lúbut: see *lobok*: bag of a fishing net.

lubrikánte: (Sp. *lubricante*: lubricant) *n.* lubricant. **lubrikasión.** *n.* lubrication.

lubság: ilubsag. *v.* to place (on the floor) in a disorderly manner. **lubsagen.** *v.* to topple, dissolve (government). **nalubsag.** *a.* dissolved, abolished; rotten, decayed.

lubsák: *var.* of *lubsag.*

lubtág: aglubtag. *v.* to sleep on the floor without a mat.

ludáb: naludab. *a.* blunt, dull (*ngudel*); stupid.

lúdang: *n.* the second (penultimate) pounding of rice during the milling process; partially husked rice. **ludangen.** *v.* to partially pound rice. **ludangludang.** *n.* the motion of strong waves. **ludangludangen.** *v.* to overwhelm an opponent.

lúdap: *n.* worn out coins without markings. **naludap.** *a.* worn out.

ludás: makaludas. *v.* to be able to get free after having been caught. **lumudas.** *v.* to escape, free oneself; pass by; let go. **paludasen.** *v.* to let go; release, free; let pass by. **Namitlon a naludasan.** This is the third time he got away. [Tag. *makawalâ*]

ludáy: maluday (*obs.*) *v.* to be shaky.

luddáy: (*obs.*) *n.* deafening surf.

luddóg: naldog. *a.* overripe; rotten, decayed; deteriorated (wet wood).

luddúok: *n.* sound of a heavy swallow. **lumduok.** *v.* to swallow. **luludduokan.** *n.* sternal notch, the depression in the chest between the two collar bones. [Tag. *lunók*]

lúdek: maludek. *a.* to be partially cooked (rice) (*kusél*).

ludék: naludek. *a.* crushed, compressed (between two objects). **ludek-ludeken.** *v.* to trample and crush.

ludém: *n.* lead color.

ludiág: apagludiag. *n.* ripening fruit. (*labanag*) **lumdiag.** *v.* to start to ripen. (*lumdag*)

ludingás: *n.* half-bald; with bald forehead; with male-pattern baldness. (*kalbo, pultak*) **agludingas.** *v.* to be balding. [Tag. *kalbó* (Sp.)]

ludlúd₁: *n.* lip of fishes; cambium, first surface on the flesh of a coconut; the softest edible part of the coconut fruit. **ludludan.** *n.* a young deer without fully developed antlers.

ludlúd₂: agludlud. *v.* to remove grime off the skin, scrub off dirt. **agpaludlud.** *v.* to have one's skin scrubbed in order to remove dirt. **ludluden.** *v.* to scrub off dirt. **paludlud.** *n.* something used to scrub off dirt (towel, stone).

lúdok: naludokan. *a.* pricked; *n.* the instrument not sticking in the wound. (*puris*)

ludúlod: *n.* landslide, cave-in (*dudodos; duyos; kurukor*). **agludulod.** *v.* to cave in (*tebbag*). [Tag. *guhò*]

lúdon: **ludunen**. *v.* to huddle; to throw together without order; gather in a heap. **agludon**. *v.* to scramble, flounder. **agluludon**. *v.* to scramble for something. **ludonludunen**. *v.* to trample over; (*fig.*) overwhelm. **makiludon**. *v.* to board with a family.

lúdong: *n.* eye (of something), hole. **pangludong**. *n.* bolt, axle. **ludongan**. *v.* to bore a hole.

ludóng: *n.* fully grown *purong* fish.

luéd: *n.* dregs, sediment (*alibudabud*; *rinsaed*; *intaer*; *lissaad*; *basabas*; *ared-ed*; *lan-ak*)

luék: *n.* cove; sheltered bay. [Tag. *latak, loók*]

lugád: **lugaden**. *v.* to loosen by shaking. **agugadlugad**. *v.* to be loose; shake; wobble.

lug-ád: **palug-ad**. *n.* extension of a deadline (for payment, etc.). **palug-adan**. *v.* to allow someone to postpone a payment.

lúgam: **lugaman**. *v.* to weed out. (*lámon*)

lúgan: *n.* car, vehicle; (*reg.*) unborn child; small boat. **aglugan**. *v.* to ride; board a vehicle. **lumugan**. *v.* to board a vehicle. **kaluganan**. *n.* person one rides with, fellow passenger. **mailugan**. *v.* to be boarded; included, contained. **naluganan**. *a.* obsessed; possessed (by a spirit). **makilugan**. *v.* to ride with. **pagluganan**. *n.* means by which one travels. **ilugan**. *v.* to load in a vehicle; put on board. [Ibg. *takay*, Kal. *lugen*, Kpm. *sake*, Png. *lógan*, Tag. *sakáy*]

luganián: *n.* panicle (*alugangian*), straw of rice that is cut during the harvest.

lugangián: see *alugangian*: straw of rice.

lugár: (Sp. *lugar*: place) *n.* place, position, spot; room (for containment); opportunity, leisure; occasion; substitute. **lumugar**. *v.* to stay; *n.* resident. **ilugar**. *v.* to place something, put in the proper place; find space for; employ; do at the proper time. **palugaran**. *v.* to give someone a head start. **malugaran**. *v.* to have the chance to do; occupy a position. **lugaran**. *v.* to give a place to someone. **kalugaran**. *n.* townsman. **Awan ti lugar.** There is no space/time.

lúgaw: **linugaw**. *n.* rice porridge, gruel. **aglugaw**. *v.* to make gruel. **lugawen**. *v.* to make into gruel, rice porridge. [Ivt. *inavusang*, Png. *binolból*, Tag. *lugaw*]

lúgay: **aglugay**. *v.* to uncover; to salute, take off the hat to show respect. **lugayan**. *v.* to salute someone, give respect to. [Tag. *pugay*]

lugáyog: **aglugayog**. *v.* to move to and fro; to hop (on a trampoline); sway (on branch) (*yugayog*; *yugyog*). [Tag. *ugóy*]

lugés: **ilugesluges**. *v.* to press down, oppress; squash the feet (over an insect, etc.); trample. **nailuges**. *a.* pressed down; trampled; oppressed; defeated.

luggád: **agluggad**. *v.* to rock; sway.

luggáy: **agluggay**. *v.* to move when loose. (*wali*; *liali*)

luggód: **agluggod**. *v.* to be unsteady, shaky. (*wali, liali, luggay*)

luggók: (*obs.*) *syn.* of *lug-ob*.

lúgi: (Ch.) *n.* loss in business. **aglugi**. *v.* to suffer a business loss. **malugi**. *v.* to suffer a loss in business; to be shortchanged, become bankrupt. **lugien**. *v.* to shortchange; cheat. [Ibg. *perdision*, Ivt., Kpm., Tag. *lúgi*, Kal. *abyak*, Png. *alúgi*, *pirdi*]

lugít: *n.* guano; bird droppings. **aglugit**. *v.* to scatter dung. **malugitan**. *v.* to be defecated on by birds. **Inkayo sumalan a, amangan no lugitannakyo pay ti billit ditoy.** Go dance so the birds here don't defecate on you. [Knk. *tontoná* (hen dung)]

luglóg: **luglugen**. *v.* to make something mushy; knead, mix, beat; trample; manipulate. **agluglog**. *v.* to play in mud or water; (*fig.*) mess around in. **Nakitak ni Ompong a lugluglugenna ti talonmo.** I saw Ompong trampling in your field. [Tag. *luglóg*]

lugnák: *n.* soft part under the sides of the tongue. **aglugnak**. *v.* to splash around or play in the mud of a puddle. (*lubnak*) **mailugnak**. *v.* to fall into a puddle.

lugó: *n.* a kind of tree, the Malabar almond, *Terminalia catappa*. **nalogo**. *a.* musty; fetid.

lugób₁: **luguban**. *v.* to roast; abuse, maltreat; whip. **naluguban**. *a.* maltreated; mauled. **Ti ket kinaawan babainmo a manglugob iti tao a di met lumaban.** You have no shame, mauling people that are not even fighting. [Tag. *bugbóg*]

lugób₂: **luguban**. *v.* to huddle around; stay close to. (see lugób) **aglug-ob**. *v.* to cower, crouch down; take shelter. (*kulmég*)

lugúd: **malugudan**. *v.* to increase; multiply; worsen (ailments). **palpalugudan**. *n.* to give in to; yield to (*nuynuy*; *anámong*). **palugodan**. *v.* to permit; yield to. **ipalugod**. *v.* to provide. **napalugudan**. *a.* permitted. **Pinalugodanna ti nuang a naguper iti danum.** He permitted the water buffalo to soak in the water. [Tag. *lugód* = pleasure; enjoyment]

lugúlog: *n.* depressed or hollow part, concavity. **aglugulogan**. *v.* to form hollows. **pananglugulog**. *n.* criminal miscarriage. [Tag. *lukóng*]

lugpák: *a.* with a flat nose; flat (*kuppit*). **nalugpak**. *a.* flattened; collapsed (buildings). [Tag. *pangó*]

lugpáp: *var.* of *lugpák*: flat nose (*leppap*). [Tag. *pangó*]

lugpí: *a.* crippled, lame, paralyzed, invalid. **lugpien.** *v.* to cripple; cause someone to become crippled. **malugpi.** *v.* to become crippled. **Dua a lawasen a dina nasibugan manipud panaglugpina.** It has been two weeks that he hasn't watered the grass since he was crippled. [Png. *lupóy,* Tag. *lumpó, pilay*]

lógro: (Sp. *logro:* interest; profit) *n.* odds. **palogro.** *n.* odds; allowance; handicap; head start. **logro-dies.** odds of ten to eight.

lugsák: malugsak. *v.* to fall over.

lugsít: see *lusit:* crush.

lugsót: *n.* hemorrhoids (*almoranas, busigít*); protrusion of the rectum. **aglugsot.** *v.* with protruding rectum (children with dysentery); to suffer from hemorrhoids. [Tag. *almoranas* (Sp.)]

lóhika: (Sp. *lógica:* logic) *n.* logic, science of reasoning.

lohístiko: (Sp. *logístico*) *n.* logistics.

lúho: (Sp. *lujo:* luxury) *n.* luxury. (*ngayed*)

lúing: *a.* with uncovered genitals (said of men).

luít: *syn.* of *biit:* short interval of time. **maluit.** *n.* wild rice.

lóka: (Sp. *loca:* foolish) *n.* foolish woman.

lukáb: lukaben. *v.* to pry open (oyster, etc.); open from the bottom.

lúkad: lukaden. *v.* to compute; calculate; estimate (*patta*). [Tag. *tantiyá*]

lukadít: *n.* a kind of small, round mollusk.

lukág: *a.* early in getting up. **malukag.** *v.* to be awakened in one's sleep. **aglukag.** *v.* to awake in the middle of the night. **lukagen.** *v.* to awaken; develop; exploit. **Nalukagak iti pannakatapik ti abagak.** I was awakened by the tapping on my shoulder. [Tag. *gising*]

lukáis: see *lukas:* uncover; bare.

lokál: (Sp. *local*) *a.* local.

lukarét: *var.* of *lukarít:* insane, crazy.

lukarít: (slang) *a.* crazy; insane.

lúkas: *a.* uncovered, without cover; bare. **lukasan.** *v.* to uncover; unclothe. **aglukas.** *v.* to clear up (weather); shape; to pull up the dress. **malukasan.** *v.* to be uncovered; to be exposed. [Png. *lukás*]

lukát: *a.* open; exposed. **lukatan, luktan.** *v.* to open (*lukib, lukip, tukib*); free from obstruction; turn on (lights, television, etc.). **ilukat.** *v.* to open. **nakalukat, silulukat.** *a.* open. **aglukat-lukat.** *v.* to open and close. **paglukat.** *n.* something used to open; can opener. **ilukatan.** *v.* to open for someone; turn on for someone. **panglukatan ti silaw.** light switch. **Timmakder ken linukatanna ti radio.** He stood up and turned on the radio. [Ibg. *vukáq,* Ivt. *iwang,* Kal. *liwalit,* Png. *akalukás,* Tag. *bukás*]

luk-át: luk-atan. *v.* to release, liberate. **malukatan.** *v.* to be released, liberated.

lukáy: nalukay. *a.* loose, movable; shaky; insecure; mild, considerate, gentle. **lumukay.** *v.* to become loose. **lukayan.** *v.* to slacken; loosen. **Makaanges a nalukay.** He can breathe freely (is now relaxed). **Nalukay ti imana.** He has loose hands (denotes generosity). **Kinuddotnak iti nalukay sanak inarakup iti nakair-irut.** She pinched me gently and then embraced me tightly. **Limmukay ti pulipol ti beklat kenkuana.** The wrapping squeeze of the cobra on him loosened. [Knk. *keyáy,* Png. *lukák,* Tag. *luwág*]

lukbá: nalukba. *a.* sagging (said of clothes around neck).

lukbán: *n. Citrus decumana,* pomelo (*sua*). [Ivt. *dukban,* Kpm. *suaq,* Tag. *suhà*]

lukdít: *n.* glans penis (*lusí*); testicles (*ukel*). **nalukdit.** *a.* with glans penis exposed to view. **lukdit ni abalayan.** *n.* kind of esteemed *diket* rice. [Tag. *bayág*]

lúken: lukenen. *v.* to sleep due to numbness.

lukiáb: lukiaben. *v.* to open forcibly; detach. **nalukiab.** *a.* opened forcibly, detached.

lukíb: lukiben. *v.* to open slightly. (*lukip*)

lukíp: lukipen. *v.* to open slightly; to lift partly, leave ajar. **ilukip.** *v.* to open slightly. **apaglukip.** *a.* slightly opened.

lúkis: lulukisan. *n.* small, native orange fruit.

lukkáong: see *likkaong:* hollow; hole. [Tag. *lukóng*]

lukkiáp: lukkiapen. *v.* to pry loose; pry off. **malukkiap.** *v.* to be pried off, detached.

lukkuáb: lukkuaben. *v.* to separate, disunite; open by force.

lukkóg: lukkugen. *v.* to curve, bend (*bakkog*). [Tag. *baluktót*]

lukkúong: *n.:* hollow, hole. (*likkaong*) **lukkuong ti barukong.** *n.* chest crevice. [Tag. *lukóng*]

lukkót: palukkot. *n.* a kind of woven bamboo hat covered with leaves. [Tag. *salakót*]

luklók: luklokan. *v.* to slacken, loosen (*lukay*). **Agyamanak ta nawayway pay laeng ti kordon a paluklokam.** I am thankful that the rope you had loosened is still long.

lukmá: palukmaen. *v.* to tame; subdue. **lumukma.** *v.* to surrender; succumb to, submit (*rukma*).

lukmég: *n.* fat. (*bakag; taba*) **nalukmeg.** *a.* fat, obese, stout. **kinalukmeg.** *n.* obesity, fatness. **lumukmeg.** *v.* to become fat. **palukmegan.** *v.* to fatten up. **panglukmegén.** *a.* rather fat, chubby. [Ibg. *tava,* Ivt. *tavaq,* Kal. *lumpu,* Knk. *amusáde, atallég, loppokéy, peklán, tambúek,* Png. *tabá,* Kpm., Tag. *tabâ*]

lukmó: *n.* shellfish or crustacean without a shell; weakness; term applied to weak or timid people. **nalukmo.** *a.* weak, debilitated. **kallukmo.** *n.* crustacean deprived of its shell; animal that has just shed its skin. [Tag. *lampá*]

luknéng: *n.* softness; succulence. **nalukneng.** *a.* soft, tender; flexible; kind. **kinalukneng.** *n.* softness, tenderness. **pangluknengén.** *a.* rather soft. **lumukneng.** *v.* to become soft. **apagluknengʹ.** *a.* just became soft. **paluknengen.** *v.* to tenderize, soften. **lumukneng ti rikna.** to calm down, settle (feelings). **Nalukneng ti panagpuspusona.** He is kind hearted. [Ibg. *lapoq, lafoq,* Itg. *lumámek,* Ivt. *ahmaq,* Kal. *yum-os,* Png. *lemék,* Kpm., Tag. *lambót*]

luknís: *n.* cattle rustler. **luknisen.** *v.* to lift (a curtain); to steal and slaughter.

lóko₁: (Sp. *loco*: crazy) *n.* fool, idiot, airhead. **kinaloko.** *n.* foolishness; obstinacy. **linoloko.** *a.* foolish, absurd, idiotic, stupid. **lokuen.** *v.* to fool, trick, deceive (*bulatsíng*); play a joke on (*angaw*). **linoloko.** *a.* foolish; silly; stupid, idiotic. **Diak maako a nilokonata ni Delia.** I can't accept that Delia deceived us.

lóko₂: *n.* a kind of poisonous weed that causes insaneness of animals eating it.

luk-ób: **agluk-ob.** *v.* to lean the head on the hands, supported by the elbows, to lean the head on one's arms. [Tag. *tirapâ*]

lukúg: *n.* cheating at cards (*kusit*). **malukug.** *v.* to be paired off (fingernails). **lukugen.** *v.* to shuffle the cards in one's favor.

lokomotóra: (Sp. *locomotora*) *n.* locomotive engine.

lúkon: **ilukon.** *v.* to enclose; insert (money in a letter). **mailukon.** *v.* to be enclosed, inserted. (*ligpit*)

lúkong₁: *var.* of *lukon*: enclose, insert.

lúkong₂: *n.* hollow concavity, hollow of hand, hollow of the instep. **lukongen.** *v.* to make hollow; to cup the palm. [Tag. *lukóng*]

lukóp: *n.* kind of chisel used to make round holes.

lúkot: *n.* scroll. **lukuten.** *v.* to roll up. **ilukot.** *v.* to roll up. **lukotan.** *n.* pin used in rolling cotton. **lulukuten.** *n.* soft coconut meat between the stages of *karkaruyen* and *taramosian*. **mailukot.** *v.* to be rolled with. **Inyukradna ti nalukot nga ikamen a nakapasanggir iti adigi.** He opened the rolled-up mat leaning on the post. [Tag. *lukot*]

lúkoy: *n.* plowshare.

luksáb: *var.* of *leksab*: separate; sever.

luksáw: *n.* anger, disgust. (*gura, pungtot; sair*) **maluksaw.** *v.* to be angry, irritated, disgusted. **kaluksaw.** *v.* to be disgusted with. **pagluksa-**

wen. *v.* to enrage, make angry. **pakaluksawan.** *n.* cause for irritation. **Makaluksawakon a talaga kadagita nga agama.** I am just fed up with that father and son team. [Tag. *galit*]

luksiáw: *var.* of *lussiáw*: pale.

luksó: **aglukso.** *v.* to leap; sprint (horses), jump out of the water (fish); jump out of the net. [Tag. *luksó*]

luksób: **luksoban.** *v.* to skin, flay; remove a fingernail of someone. **naluksob.** *a.* skinned, flayed; removed (fingernail).

luktáp: **agluktap.** *v.* to cheat (*kúsit*); betray (*líput*). **aglukluktap.** *v.* to be deceitful, fraudulent; an impostor (*allilaw*). [Tag. *dayà*]

luktó: see *lipto*: abbreviation in writing. [Tag. *luktô* = omission; interval]

luktón: *n.* young wingless locust; young grasshopper (*dúdon* = locust, grasshopper). [Tag. *luktón*]

lóla: (Sp. *abuela*) *n.* grandmother. [Png. *bái,* Tag. *lola*]

lúlem: *n.* partial cloudiness; overcast sky. **nalulem.** *a.* overcast, cloudy, gloomy (*ulep; alibuyong; daguyemyem; kunem; kuyem; langeb*). **lumulem.** *v.* to become overcast. **Medio nasipngeten ta nalulem ti langit.** It is somewhat dark because the sky is overcast. [Tag. *kulimlím*]

lullón: *n.* curl; crease; wrinkle. **aglullon.** *v.* to hustle (in a crowd). **lullunen.** *v.* to crowd rudely, gather in confusion; crumple. [Tag. *kulubót*]

lólo: (Sp. *abuelo*) *n.* grandfather. [Tag. *lolo*]

luló₁: **luluen.** *v.* to beat until black-and-blue (*litem*); to cause a fruit to become soft by handling. **malulo.** *v.* to become soft by handling, beating, etc; to become badly bruised; spoiled by squeezing. [Tag. *lamóg*]

luló₂: **luluan.** *n.* a floating edible freshwater herb, water lettuce, *Pistia stratiodes*. [Tag. *kiyapò*]

luló₃: **luluán ti mata.** *n.* lachrymal gland in the eye.

lúlod: *n.* shin, front part of the calf of the leg; the back of the calf is called *butóy*. [Kal. *chunguÿ,* Tag. *lulód*]

luludduókan: *n.* depression in the front of the neck.

lúlok: *n.* looseness; weakness. **aglulok.** *v.* to weaken; become loose; (*fig.*) feel depressed. **nalulok.** *a.* loose; weak. **lulokan.** *v.* to loosen; release the tension. [Tag. *luwág*]

lulóken: *n.* numb state.

lulukísen: (f. *lukis*) *n.* mandarin, *Citrus nobilis*; (*lit. Limnanthemum cristatum*); lime.

lulumtóg: *n.* a kind of small ray or skate.

lulón: sangalulon. *n.* one small bundle of herbs.
lulonan. *n.* the soft part of a baby's head.
lulunen. *v.* to bundle. [Tag. *lulón* = roll of paper; swallow]
lulonán: *n.* fontanel, soft part of a baby's head.
lulót: *n.* dull blade (*ngudel*; *beddal*; *ngulngol*). [Tag. *puról*; *lulót* = overripe; withered]
lúma: maluma. *v.* to be worn out; tarnished, spoiled; incapacitated. [Tag. *lumà* = old]
lumános: *n.* a variety of awned *diket* rice.
lúmay: *n.* softness. **mailumay.** to sink, plunge, penetrate into soft substances.
lúmba: lumbalumba. *n.* kind of large marine animal; term applied to fat people.
lumbá: *n.* race (competition). **aglumba.** *v.* to race. **lumbalumba.** *n.* a kind of large marine fish. **kalumba.** *v.* to race with; compete with. **lumbaan.** *v.* to overtake. **malumbaan.** *v.* to be overtaken; to be passed by in a race. **makilumba.** *v.* to join a race, compete. **pinnalumbaan.** *n.* animal race. **No kayatmo, makipalumbakanto.** If you want, you can join in the competition. [Kal. *todtochak*, Knk. *lungbá*, Tag. *karera, takbuhan*; *lumbá* = continuous effort; drawing water from a well; *lumbâ* = gallop]
lumbágo: (Eng.) *n.* lumbago, rheumatic muscle pain in the groin.
lumbáw: (f. *lebbaw*) *v.* to sink. [Tag. *lubóg*]
lumbég: (f. *lebbeg*) *v.* to become swollen (eyes after crying).
lumbés: (f. *lebbes*) *v.* to be past; to exceed; be more; to go beyond; to have enough time.
lumbót: (f. *lubbot*) *v.* to go through or in (a hole, etc.).
lumbóy: *n.* Java plum (*lungboy*) **limmumboy.** *a.* like a Java plum (very dark complexion, etc.). [Tag. *duhat*]
lúmbre: (Sp.) *n.* skylight, window in a roof.
lumdáang: (f. *leddaang*) *v.* to be sad, sorrowful.
lumdág: (f. *leddag*) *n.* ripening fruit.
lumdás: malumdasan. *v.* to be skinned, flayed (*kuplat*). [Tag. *balát*]
lumdís: *var.* of *lumdas.*
lumdóg: *v.* to swell (eyes). (*lumteg*)
lumdúok: (f. *ledduok*) *v.* to swallow; produce the sound of swallowing.
lumén: *n.* a variety of thick-skinned, long banana. **aglumen.** *v.* to vanish; fade (*kupas*); disappear. **Ti ayat a napudno, di agmawmaw, di aglumen.** True love does not fade or perish. [Tag. *lahò* (vanish)]
lumgák: (f. *leggák*) *v.* to rise (said of the sun).
lómi: (Hok. *ló mi*) *n.* stew noodle) *n.* noodle dish of pork, beef, or chicken cooked in cream.

lomílio: (Sp. *lomo*: loin + *-illo* dim. suffix) *n.* small loin cut of meat.
luminário: (Sp. *luminario*: illumination show) *n.* illumination for a festival, sound and light show; luminary.
lumkáng: (f. *lekkang*) *v.* to come unpasted, unsoldered, undone.
lumlóm: *n.* ripening mature fruit in the dark. **mailumlom.** *v.* to sink, stick; to be placed in hot embers for roasting; be pushed through or under; get involved in (without control); to wallow in. **ilumlom.** *v.* to push through; force through or under. **lumumlom.** *v.* to sink in; go through. **nailumlom iti utang.** *v.* to be buried in debt. **Nailumlomak iti trabaho iti talon.** I got stuck with working in the rice fields. **Tunggal lumumlom dagiti ngipen ti nangisit iti lasag ti puraw, mariknana met ti saem ti pammales daytoy.** Every time the teeth of the black one sink into the flesh of the white one, the latter feels the pain of revenge. [Tag. *baón* (buried)]
lummánis: *a.* of unequal height (steps of a ladder).
lummuáy: (*obs.*) *n.* reopening of a wound; rejuvenating.
lumnéd: (f. *lennéd*) *v.* to sink. [Tag. *lubóg*]
lumnék: (f. *lennék*) *v.* to set (sun); penetrate. **lumnek 'diay init.** *n.* sunset. [Ivt. *suyib*, Png. *selék*, Tag. *lubóg*]
lómo: (Sp. *lomo*: loin) *n.* tenderloin of meat. [Knk. *alimás*]
lúmot: *n.* moss; a slippery river seaweed; fine freshwater alga. (*líwed*) **aglumot.** *v.* to grow moss. **lumuten.** *v.* to be covered with moss; (*fig.*) become very aged. **nalumot.** *a.* full of moss, mossy. **Linumot dagiti bato ken nakagalgalis pay ti daga.** The stones were covered in moss and the ground was even slippery. **Linumlumoten nga ugali.** *exp.* old-fashioned customs or traditions. [Bon. *bollagot*, Ibg. *lumuq*, Ifg., Kal., Knk. *bágiw*, Ivt. *humut*, Kpm. *lumut*, Png. *lamúyak*, Tag. *lumot*]
lumóy: nalumoy. *a.* soft, tender, smooth; weak, frail, delicate; flabby. **kinalulmoy.** *n.* softness; smoothness; delicateness; tenderness; frailness. **aglumoy.** *v.* to wriggle; float with the waves; become soft and flabby. [Tag. *luylóy*]
lumpá: (f. *leppá*) *v.* to digest food; decrease (sickness).
lumpáag: (f. *leppáag*) *v.* to subside, abate.
lúmpia: (Hok. *lûn pià*: spring cake) *n.* Philippine eggroll, spring roll, meat, vegetables, and/or shrimps wrapped in rice starch wrappers. [Tag. *lumpiyâ*]

lumsót: (f. *lusót*) *v.* to go through; burst through; pierce through; break through.

lumtáak: *n.* sound of bamboos drying in the sun and splitting.

lumtáw: (f. *lettaw*) *v.* to appear suddenly and unexpectedly; to occur; present oneself; to surface to the top of the water.

lumtég: (f. *lettég*) *v.* to swell; to develop boils on skin. [Ibg. *nebbaga*, Ivt. *umlatek*, Knk. *bumgeng*, *linmat-ed*, Kpm. *makalbag*, Png. *linmarag*, Tag. *mamagâ*]

lumténg: *v.* to intensify, be stunning (quietness); to be barely audible, to be half-heard. **Limteng ti napaut nga ulimek iti sala ti pagukoman.** The long silence in the courtroom was stunning.

lumtuád: (f. *lettuad*) *v.* to come out (spirits, moon, etc.).

lumtungáw: (f. *lettungáw*) *v.* to appear after a long absence. (*lumtáw*)

lumtúog: *v.* to make a loud bursting sound (guns, yelling voices).

lóna: *n.* canvas (*mantalona*); floor of a boxing ring. **Dandanida naggiddan a nanabtuog iti lona.** They almost fell to the floor of the boxing ring at the same time.

luna-de-miél: (Sp.) *n.* honeymoon. **agluna-de-miel.** *v.* to go on honeymoon; to spend a honeymoon. [Tag. *pulutgata*]

lúnag: **lunagen.** *v.* to melt, dissolve, liquefy. **malunag.** *v.* to be melted (*runaw*). [Tag. *tunaw*]

lúnak: *n.* remainder; balance left on a loan. (*udi*; *utang*)

lunákol: **aglunakol.** *v.* to be lazy. **nakalunakol.** *a.* lazy, idle, indolent (*sadut*). [Tag. *kupad*]

lunário: *n.* lunar calendar; zodiac calendar.

lúnas₁: *n.* worn out coin; blank board; an animal with no whorls of hair in the front. **malunas.** *v.* to be worn out. **nalunas.** *a.* flat breasted; plain. [Tag. *lunas* = cure; remedy; basin; bottom of a vase; keel of a boat; species of fern; species of bamboo]

lúnas₂: *n.* vertical line running from the navel downward. (*sintas*)

lunasión: (Sp. *lunación*) *n.* lunation, period of time between two successive new moons.

lunátiko: (Sp. *lunático*: lunatic) *n.* lunatic.

lunáy: **lunayen.** *v.* to have pain in the uterus after childbirth.

lunék: **luneken.** *v.* to squeeze, compress (in order to extract oil); crush. [Tag. *pigâ*]

Lúnes: (Sp. *lunes*: Monday) *n.* Monday. **lunesen.** *v.* to do on Monday. **linunes.** *a.* every Monday. **ipalunes.** *v.* to postpone until Monday. **Lunes Santo.** Monday of Holy Week. [Kal. *lulis*]

lunés: **malunes.** *v.* to tarnish; wear out; be crumpled; dishonored; (*fig.*) lose one's virginity. **lunesen.** *v.* to crumple; dishonor; (*obs.*) depreciate. **naluneslunes.** *a.* crumpled, wrinkled. (*kulengkuleng*) **Nalunes ti naingpis a badona ket aganninaw ti sukog ti pammagina.** Her thin dress is worn out, which reflected the form of her physique. [Tag. *kuyumós*]

Lunéta: (Sp.) *n.* moonlight park; seaside park in Manila.

lunéto: (Sp.) *n.* lunette.

lúnit: **aglunit.** *v.* to close, heal (wounds) (*púnit*). **luniten.** *v.* to close; fill up.

lunlón: **lunlunen.** *v.* to sweep aside (*kaykay*). **lunlonan.** *v.* to rinse (a bottle). **malunlonan.** *v.* to be rinsed.

lúnod₁: **malunod.** *v.* to sink; disappear, vanish; be lost at sea; lose all one's money; forget completely.

lúnod₂: **lunodan.** *v.* to remunerate, compensate; divide and distribute equally.

lunód: *n.* curse. **ilunod.** *v.* to curse. **mailunod.** *v.* to be cursed, damned. **Saanka kuma nga agilunod iti masakbayan ti maysa a tao.** You shouldn't curse a person's future. [Bon. *áwang*, Kal. *ewagen*, Png. *ayew*, Tag. *sumpâ*]

lúnos: **aglunos (ti anges).** *v.* to be breathless. **mailunos.** *v.* to be moved, touched, impressed; to soften.

lúnoy₁: (Tag.) **aglunoy.** *v.* to wallow in water; become addicted to drugs. **aglunoy iti ragsak iti sidong ti sabali.** *fig.* to commit adultery. (*kamalala*, *abig*)

lúnoy₂: **manglunoy-lunoy a buok.** *n.* wavy hair.

luntsá: *var.* of *lantsá*: launch.

lungáli: **aglungali.** *v.* to wobble, shake loose.

lungálong: *n.* shade, shelter. **aglungalong.** *v.* to guide. **ilungalong.** *v.* to propose a measure; start a campaign; spearhead a project. [Tag. *panukalà*]

lúngas: *a.* with glans penis nearly or partially uncovered (in a state of erection); *n.* glans penis. **aglunglungas.** *v.* to play with the glans penis. (*lungit*)

lúngat: *a.* exposed, bare glans penis (*lukdit*; *lusi*; *lungas*; *lungit*). [Tag. *burát*]

lung-áw: *n.* recovery from a difficult situation. **lumung-aw.** *v.* to emerge from drowning; escape, get clear from; be successful. **makalung-aw.** *v.* to be able to emerge; be free from hardships, sickness. **palung-awan.** *v.* to give room for; let a sunken object emerge. [Tag. *litáw*; *lungáw* = large hole in the ground]

lung-áy: *n.* graceful body movement; way; gait. **aglung-ay.** *v.* to lean the head sideways. **lunglung-ay.** *n.* gait; gestures; mannerisms. [Tag. *imbáy*]

lúngbos: malungbos. *v.* to be underwater; to be filled with water; to be overwhelmed with bad luck.

lungbóy: *n.* Java plum, *Eugenia jambolana*; blackberry. **lumungboy.** *v.* to become black-and-blue. **panglungbuyen.** *n.* a kind of tree with good timber and white flowers, *Eugenia bordenii*. [Tag. *duhat*]

lunggálong: *n.* hanging cradle with four strings.

longganísa: *n.* Chinese sausage, a kind of salty and sweet pork sausage.

lunggángan : *n.* bamboo that runs along the upper border of the *bangkay*; bar of the *lalabayan* reel.

lunggí: aglunggi-lunggi. *v.* to rock, totter, sway.

lúngit: *n.* foreskin of the penis. **lunglungiten.** *v.* to play with the foreskin of the penis (young children). [Knk. *lupsík*]

lunglóng: *n.* (*obs.*) harbor. **lunglongan.** *n.* brushwood used by hunters to shade them; kitchen utensils. **lulunglongan.** *n.* a kind of inedible marine fish without scales, but sharp fins.

lungngúop: *n.* heart of the forest. **kalnguopan.** *n.* hothouse; heart of forest; enclosed place. **lungnguopen.** *v.* to suffocate; choke; keep in a warm place to hasten the ripening process. **malnguopan.** *v.* to suffocate, choke, smother. [Tag. *kulob*]

lúngog: *n.* hole, cavity (hollow); depression. **aglungog.** *v.* to become hollow. **ipalungog.** *v.* to insert. **lungóngan.** *n.* kind of straight bamboo; hollow sound. [Tag. *lukóng*]

lungón: *n.* coffin; defect in the base of a house post the shape of a coffin believed to cause death of the inhabitants of the house. **ilungon.** *v.* to put in a coffin. **mailungon.** *v.* to be placed in a coffin. **agan-anud a lungon.** *n.* flying coffin. **sinan-lungon a kama.** *n.* trundle bed; enclosed bed. [Bon. *álob*, Knk. *álong*, Png. *longón*, Tag. *kabaóng*]

lungúop: *var.* spelling of *lungnguop*: heart of the forest. (*longngoop*) **malnguopan.** *v.* to suffocate; choke; smother.

lóngot: (*obs.*) *n.* aggregation.

lungpó: *n.* (*obs.*) young grass; robust growth; health. **lumongpo.** *v.* to become chubby, obese; become healthy. **nalungpo.** *a.* chubby; stout. (in good health). [Tag. *lusóg*]

lungpús: *n.* ninth night or day of mourning. **aglungpus.** *v.* to come to an end (mourning); end; terminate. **ilungpus.** *v.* to hold a feast and prayer during the ninth day of mourning.

malungpus. *v.* to be covered with; overwhelmed with grief. **nalungpus.** *a.* overwhelmed, worn down. **lungpusen.** *v.* to cover with something.

lungsít: (*reg.*) *n.* glans penis. **aglunglungsit.** *v.* to play with the glans penis.

lungsót: nalungsot. *a.* rotten; decomposed; spoiled; putrid. (*lungtot*; *dersay*; *rupso*; *tubeg*; *tumuy*; *dugmuy*; *duted*; *timming*) **lungsuten.** *v.* to rot. **Sapay kuma ta malungsotka iti pagbaludan.** I hope you rot in jail. [Ibg. *lebbeg*, Ivt. *nahtaq*, Kal. *lepos*, *byangÿos*, Knk. *dúnut*, *bangnges*, Png. *lupok*, *bulok*, *banget*, Kpm., Tag. *bulók*]

lungtót: *var.* of *lungsot*: rotten; spoiled; decomposed. [Tag. *bulók*]

luób: *n.* estuary; interior, inside. (*uneg*) **iti luob.** *prep.* inside. **agluob.** *v.* to live together. **lumuob.** *v.* to stay; live in someone else's house. **kaluob.** *v.* to live with; *n.* wife, husband. **agkaluob.** *v.* to live together as husband and wife. **makiluob.** *v.* to live in another man's house. [Tag. *loób* = inside]

lúod: *n.* loss of time. **iluod.** *v.* to destroy; overthrow. **mailuod.** *v.* to be destroyed; addicted to drugs. **Nailuoden iti apiang.** He is already addicted to opium. [Tag. *sugapà* (addicted)]

lúok: see *luek.*

luóm: *n.* ripeness (*darangidangan*). **naluom.** *a.* ripe, mature. **agluom.** *v.* to ripen. **Adu ti nagluoman ti panunotko bayat ti panangbasbasak kadagiti sinuratmo.** My thoughts matured a great deal as I read what you wrote. [Ibg. *nalutu*, Ivt. *navayaq*, Kal. *leum*, Knk. *ubág*, Kpm. *malulut*, Png. *alotó*, Tag. *hinóg*; *luóm* = enclosed with no access to fresh air]

lupá: *n.* warb, a kind of shrub with stinging hairs, *Laportea meyeniana.*

lúpak: mailupak. *v.* to sink in mud. **lumupak.** *v.* (*obs.*) to go barefoot. **ilupak.** *v.* to cause to sink. **ilupaklupak.** *v.* to trample; thrash an opponent. **kalupakan.** *n.* muddy place.

lupasáy: nakalupasay. *a.* exhausted and lying on the ground. [Tag. *lupasáy* = squatting, sitting on the haunches]

lúpaw: *n.* a large basket used to hold ropes.

lupáy: aglupay. *v.* to totter, stagger, wobble; shake.

lupaypáy: nakalupaypay. *a.* languid; droopy; dreary from lack of sleep; without energy. [Tag. *lupaypáy*]

lupdás: malupdasan. *v.* to be slightly skinned; abraded. [Tag. *galos*]

lupdís: see *kudis*: peeled; skinned (*lupniat*). [Tag. *galos*]

lupék: aglupeklupek. v. to stumble around on the ground. **lupeklupeken.** v. to mess around with something on the ground; trample on; degrade; enslave. **ilupek.** v. to oppress, crush down; trample down. **Inlupeklupekmo ti kinalalakik.** You crushed my masculinity.

lúpes: a. barren, sterile woman. (*baog* = sterile man) **aglupes.** v. to be infertile, unable to bear offspring. [Knk. *butíng, básig,* Tag. *baóg*]

lupí: n. fold. (*kupin*) **ilupi.** v. to fold; hem (*lílip*). [Tag. *lupí*]

lupiád: nalupiad. a. bent back (*balungiad*). **lupiaden.** v. to bend back something.

lupináy: aglupinay. v. to crouch; sit with the legs bent together to one side. (*dalumpinay*)

lupíng: n. drooping ears; crestfallen cock. **agluping.** v. to droop (said of the ears). [Tag. *layláy, lupíng*]

lúpis: n. pericarp of the cotton boll. **lupisan.** v. a small piglet with a short body.

lupisák: a. crippled, lame; paralyzed. **aglupisak.** v. to squat; sit on the ground; splash, splatter; slump down; sit improperly. **madalupisak.** v. to fall on the buttocks. [Png. *dopisák,* Tag. *lupasáy, tingkayád*]

lúpit: ilupitlupit. v. to persecute; punish; harass; insult one's reputation; discriminate; oppress (*rumen*). **mailupit-lupit.** v. to be persecuted; oppressed; abused; harassed; tortured. **No mailupitlupit ti kalintegan, biddut kadi no itakderan.** If your rights are oppressed, is it wrong to stand up for them? [Tag. *lupít*]

luplóp: (*obs.*) n. outfitting, making provisions for life; providing a bed with a curtain. **agluplop.** v. to make provisions for the future.

lupniát: malupniatan. v. to be skinned, flayed, abraded (*lupdís, kuplát*). [Tag. *galos*]

lúpog: n. a kind of coconut with soft meat; a kind of betel nut that never hardens; a kind of small fish with soft meat; soft wood.

lúpos: n. slough, sheddings of a serpent; cast-off shell of a mollusk. **aglupos.** v. to shed the outer skin; cast off the shell; (*fig.*) start a new life. **nagluposan.** n. the shed outer skin of a snake, slough; cast-off shell. [Tag. *hunos*]

lúpot: n. clothes; cloth; apparel; garments; garb; vestments. (*bado; kawes*) **ilupotan.** v. to provide with clothing. **agkalupot.** v. to be of the same dress material. [Kal. *silup,* Png. *kawés,* Tag. *damít*]

lupóy: nalupoy. a. weak; feeble; soft; smooth; flexible; clumsy. **kinalupoy.** n. weakness; clumsiness. **lumupoy.** v. to become clumsy; weak. **aglulupoy.** v. to feel weak. (*kapuy; kapsut*) **aglulupoy dagiti tumeng.** v. to be weak-kneed. **Taoak met a kas kenka a**

nalupoy. I am a man, weak like you. [Tag. *lampá*]

luppáaw: lupluppaaw. n. a kind of plant with yellow flowers, *Abutilon indicum.*

luppagít: a. with a broken heel (high-heeled shoes).

luppa-í: (*reg.*) **agluppa-i.** v. to totter, wobble; shake; be weak-kneed.

luppáy: a. bend down, folded down; drooping. **iluppay.** v. to bend down, fold down. **Inluppayna ti bulong ti payabyab iti rupana tapno saan a malasin.** He folded down the brim of his *payabyab* hat over his face so he couldn't be recognized.

luppí: luppien. v. to fold (*lupi; kupin*). [Tag. *lupí*]

luppiád: *var.* spelling of *lupiad*: bend back. **luppiaden.** v. to bend back something. **maluppiad.** v. to be bent back.

luppiás: agluppias. v. to overflow; *var.* of *lippias.* [Kal. *lumay-as,* Tag. *apaw*]

luppigát: naluppigat. a. dilapidated (furniture); crushed; collapsed to the ground.

luppíit: n. a kind of vine with white flowers and sap that hardens into rubber, *Parameria philippinensis.* **lumpiit.** v. to produce a shrill sound.

luppó: n. thigh (*lapi*). [Ibg. *pel, uffú,* Ivt. *páaq,* Kal. *epu,* Knk. *luplupióng,* Kpm. *puwad,* Bon., Png. *olpó,* Sbl. *too,* Tag. *hità*]

lupsák: see *lupisak*: crippled; lame.

lupsít₁: n. blister on the skin; sunburned skin; peelings. **aglupsit.** v. to peel off (sunburned skin). **malupsitan.** v. to be abraded; skinned. [Tag. *bakbák*]

lupsít₂: luplupsit. n. a kind of small, speckled marine fish similar to the *pallugsit.*

luptá: nalupta. a. tasteless (*lab-áy; amnaw; tamnay*). **kinalupta.** n. tastelessness. [Tag. *tabáng*]

lupták: n. crack, chap (of dry lips). **agluptak.** v. to chap (the lips); crack. [Bon. *lásib,* Tag. *biták*]

luptóy: maluptoyan. v. to be burnt, scalded (*dilnak*). [Tag. *banlî*]

lurdés: (French: *Lourdes*) n. blue sash worn by unmarried women in honor of our Lady of Lourdes. **aglurdes.** v. to wear the *lurdes* sash.

lorél: *var.* of *laurel*: laurel; bay leaf.

lória: n. a kind of thick-skinned yellow banana with a reddish stem.

lóro: (Sp. *loro*: parrot) n. parrot. [Bon. *ólis,* Kal. *kasi*]

lósa: (Sp. *loza*: china) n. chinaware; porcelain; tiled slab.

lúsa: nalusa. a. soft (said of rice).

lúsak: lusaken. *v.* to smash; crush. **nalusak.** *a.* crushed, smashed; flattened; flabby; not firm in consistency (*lúyak*). **malusak.** *v.* to fall to the ground and bruise (fruits); be smashed; crushed. [Tag. *lusak* = mud; slush]

lusálos: *n.* a kind of rifle. **aglusalos.** *v.* to move to and fro.

lósang: *var.* of *losa*: earthenware.

Los Bánios: (Sp. *los baños*) *n.* type of banana named after a town in Laguna.

lusbó: *a.* plenty; *var.* of *lisbo*. **nalusbo.** *a.* robust.

lusdák: malusdak. *v.* to collapse under a heavy load (*lusdáyak, lusdóy*); *var.* of *lusak*.

lusdáyak: aglusdayak. *v.* to sag, droop (flesh) (*lusdóy*); collapse under a heavy load.

lusdóy: *a.* drooping; weak, exhausted. **aglusdoy.** *v.* to droop, sag, hang down (fat); fall; collapse from fatigue; hang (part of one's clothing). **Simmardengda idi makitada a nalusdoy ni Kering.** They stopped when they saw that Kering was exhausted. [Tag. *lumó*]

luséro: (Sp. *lucero*: bright star) *n.* morning star, bright star; star on the forehead of some horses.

lúses: (Sp. *luces*: lights) *n.* sparkler firecracker; Roman candle firecracker.

lúsi: (*reg.*) *n.* exposed glans penis; opening of glans penis. (*lukdit*) **lusien.** *v.* to push back the foreskin to expose the glans penis. **malusi.** *a.* with exposed glans penis; *v.* to be drawn back (foreskin). [Tag. *burát*]

lusía: (Sp. *Lucía*) **Santa Lusia de mata.** *n.* kind of ornamental plant.

lusí: luslusi. *n.* a kind of small, edible, purple mollusk found in brackish water.

lusiáng: (*coll.*) *a.* unkempt; neglected (said of women). (*pindangga*)

lusiáw: nalusiaw. *a.* pale, pallid; faded. **aglusiaw.** *v.* to become pale. **Nagtaltalangkiaw ken inkagumaanna nga inlinged ti panaglusiawna kadagiti kaopisinaanna.** He looked around and tried to hide his paleness from his officemates. [Tag. *putlâ*]

lusilós: *n.* a primitive drill; *a.* blunt, dull (*ngudel*). [Tag. *buról* (dull)]

losión: (Sp. *loción*) *n.* lotion.

lúsit: lusiten. *v.* to squeeze; crush, smash (with heavy weight). **malusit.** *v.* to be crushed, smashed by heavy weight. [Tag. *pisâ*]

luskabéng: *a.* having very large eyelids that give the appearance of having small eyes. (*liskabeng*)

luslós: (Tag.) *n.* hernia. **agluslos.** *v.* to have a hernia; slip, slide backwards.

luslós: agluslos. *v.* to slip, slide; pull back and forth (uncircumcised penis); (*fig.*) masturbate.

iluslos. *v.* to slide down. [Tag. *luslós* = fallen; hanging down]

luslusí: (f. *lusi, lit.*) *n.* a kind of small, edible, purple mollusk.

lusngát: (*reg.*) *n.* glans penis. (*lusngi*)

lusngí: (*reg.*) *n.* glans penis; (*fig.*) fool; *a.* exposed (said of the glans penis). **lusngien.** *v.* to draw back the foreskin and show the glans penis. [Tag. *burát*, Bon *losngí* = torn fingernail]

lusngít: *n.* glans penis (*lusngi; buto*). [Tag. *burát*]

lúso: *a.* naked; exposed; bare. (*labus; uyos*; *lamolamo*) **agluso.** *v.* to strip naked. [Tag. *hubád, hubô*]

lusuát: lumsuat. *v.* to crack, break; burst. **malusuatan.** *v.* to burst, break by cracking.

lúsob: *n.* circular casing around a well. **nalusob.** *a.* concave, bowl shaped. **lusuban.** *v.* to line with a casing. [Tag. *lukóng*]

lusód: *n.* hole, pit. **mailusod.** *v.* to fall into a pit.

lusúlos: *n.* resignation. **aglusulos.** *v.* to excuse oneself; escape; slip away; resign from an office; withdraw candidacy; loosen. **lusulusen.** *v.* to renounce; resign an office; withdraw a proposal. **paglusulusen.** *v.* to ask someone to withdraw or resign. [Tag. *bitiw*]

lúsong: *n.* alluvial land. **ilusong.** *v.* to thrust in, insert, put in, put on (shoes). **mailusong.** *v.* to be inserted, put in (*úsok*); to fall into. [Tag. *suot*]

lusót: lumsot. *v.* to go through; break through; pass through; to protrude, spurt, break through; flow out; to escape (from danger). **ilusot.** *v.* to put through; thrust in. **palsuot.** *n.* popgun. **agpalsuot.** *v.* to use a popgun. **palusot.** *n.* rice planted with the hope it will survive the dry season; (*fig.*) scapegoat. **palsuten.** *v.* to cause something to pass through; break through. **Saggaysa a nalusotanna dagiti nangabbeng iti dalanna agingga a nakadanon iti pantok.** One by one, he broke through the obstacles in his path until he reached the summit. [Tag. *lusót* (go through)]

luspák: *a.* crippled; flat (*kuppit*). **agluspak.** *v.* to slump; flatten; sit on the ground. **maluspak.** *v.* to be flattened; crushed. **Maluspak ti tukak a mapayatanna.** *exp.* denoting a slow person (*lit:* the frog gets crushed when stepped on).

lussáyat: *a.* not firm, flabby (*luyak*); overripe (fruits). **Nalussayat ti luomna.** It is overripe (no longer firm).

lussiáw: *a.* pale. **nalussiaw.** *a.* pale; faded; discolored. **kinalussiaw.** *n.* paleness. **lumussiaw.** *v.* to become pale. [Tag. *putlâ*]

lussók: *a.* having a hole, perforated; (*fig.*) no longer a virgin. **lussuken.** *v.* to pierce, bore a hole in. **lulussokan.** *n.* the depression situated above the clavicles, apparent in thin people. **malussok.** *v.* to be pierced; perforated. **lussolussok.** *a.* full of holes. **paglussok.** *n.* hole puncher, perforating instrument. **lussoken ti langit ti ~.** *exp.* to do ~ to excess.

lútab: *n.* foam, spume, froth. (*labutab*) **aglutab.** *v.* to foam up; froth. [Png. *sabo*, Tag. *bulâ*]

lútak: *var.* of *lupak*: mud. **lutaklutak a kalsada.** *n.* muddy road.

lútang: aglutang. *v.* to float over water. (*lumtaw*)

lútay: aglulutay. *v.* to be weak, exhausted. **lutay-lutay.** *a.* with falling petals (flowers) or leaves. **Iti kalgaw, kasla malunag dagiti darat ken kasla malutay dagiti bulong ti niog.** In the summer, the sands seem to melt and the leaves of the coconut trees seem to fall.

lóte: (Sp. *lote*: lot) *n.* subdivision of real estate; lot, parcel of land.

Luteráno: (Sp.) *n.* Lutheran.

lotería: (Sp. *lotería*: lottery) *n.* lottery. (*agparipa*)

lútiam: *n.* a mold for the *damortis* earring.

lutlút: *n.* mud (*pitak*). **aglutlut.** *v.* to become muddy. **nalutlut.** *a.* muddy, miry. **lutluten.** *v.* to make muddy; to knead; smash; squeeze. **kalutlutan.** *n.* muddy place. **mailutlut.** *v.* to get stuck in the mud; sink in the mud. [Tag. *putik*]

lúto: *n.* culinary dish; manner of cooking; menu. **agluto.** *v.* to cook. **agpaluto.** *v.* to have someone cook. **naluto.** *a.* cooked. **lutuen.** *v.* to cook (food). **iluto.** *v.* to cook (an ingredient). **ipaluto.** *v.* to have something cooked. **paglutuan.** *n.* kitchen; cooking utensil. **paraluto.** *n.* cook, chef. **lulutuen.** *a.* suitable for cooking. **kaluluto.** *n.* kind of cooking (baking, frying, etc.). **kalutuan.** *v.* to be fond of cooking. **kalutluto, kalluto.** *a.* just cooked. **sangkalutuan.** *n.* one cooking. [Ibg. *lutu*, Ifg. *munháqang*, Ivt. *rutung, hutu*, Kal. *utu*, Knk. *óto*, Png. *lutó*, Kpm., Tag. *lutò*]

lutó: lumutoluto. *v.* to swarm, crowd (*pangen, aribungbong, bánga*).

lutúlot: *n.* marsh, swamp, bog; mud hole. **mailutulot.** *v.* to be stuck in the mud. (*lutlot*)

luttí: luttien. *v.* to turn while cooking; to turn while roasting (pig on a spit).

luttuád: *n.* bright new moon; spring tide; half-moon. **lumtuad.** *v.* to come out (moon, spirits, etc.); appear unexpectedly; come out for the first time. **paltuaden.** *v.* to create (*partuat*); originate; bring out. [Tag. *litáw*]

luttók: *n.* salivary fistula. **luttokan.** *v.* to cut a hole in; crack open an egg. **maluttok.** *v.* to be cracked open.

luttót: maltutan. *v.* to choke. **paltuten.** *v.* to squeeze out; to deliver a baby; force out matter from a hole. **mamaltot.** *v.* to deliver a baby. **mammaltot.** *n.* midwife. [Tag. *hirin* (choke)]

lúya: luyaan. *v.* to scold, berate, chide, rebuke. (*kariar; danengdeng; bir-it*) **maluyaan.** *v.* to be induced to cry, be affected by something sad; lose heart. **Naluyaan ket timrem ti luana.** He was induced to cry and the tears flowed.

lúyak: naluyak. *a.* sticky, gluey, adhesive (*pigket*); with too much water (said of rice); soft and flabby (*lúsak, lussáyat*).

lúyaw: luyawen. *v.* to stir, agitate (the water before fishing). (*kibor*)

luylóy: *n.* a kind of marine fish. **agluyloy.** *v.* to flow, have a running nose; slide down; become flabby (flesh). [Tag. *luylóy* (flabby)]

luyók: *n.* belly; bulging part of something. **agluyok.** *v.* to bulge downward.

luy-ók: *n.* bay, cove, inlet.

luyon: (*obs.*) *n.* cause of death.

luy-óng: *n.* pubic region, groin (*sellang*). **Kasla adda met alikuteg a kawitan iti luy-ongna.** It seems like there is a restless cock in his groin. [Bon. *sekang, lepyak*, Kal. *lapiák*, Tag. *pusón*; Kal. *luy-óng* = pocket]

lúyos: mailuyos. *v.* to be moved, influenced, affected (by the sorrow of others) (*luya*). [Tag. *bagbág*]

M

-m: Variant of *-mo* after vowels, or the suffixes *-an* and *-en*: **pusa + mo = pusam.** your cat. **basaen + mo = basaem.** you read it. [Png. *–m*, Tag. *mo*]

ma-: Potentive prefix indicating ability, non-volitional or accidental occurrence, passive possibility, or the coincidental nature of an action. Perfective form is *na-* **aramid.** action **maaramid.** to be able to do. **apuy.** fire. **maapuy.** to be burned, cooked (rice). **dungpar.** collide. **madungpar.** to accidentally collide. **Ammok a saannakto a mapakawan.** I know that you won't be able to forgive me. **Saan a madait dayta.** That can't be sewn. **Maapuy 'ta bagas.** That rice can be cooked.

máag: *n.* idiot, stupid person, dunce. (*tabbed*; *langgong*) **namaag.** *a.* dull, stupid; simple; dense (in intelligence). **Ania manen a minamaag ti pampanunotem?** What stupid thing are you thinking about again? [Png. *musmús*, *leglég*, *tangá*, Tag. *tangá*]

ma- -an: 1. Verbal prefix indicating the involuntary attainment of the state specified by the root. Perfective form is *na- -an*. **No agsida't sili, isu't magasangan.** He who eats chili pepper will get burned by the spice. **atal.** run over (root). **maatalan.** to be run over. **Adda met dagiti saludsod a masungbatan laeng babaen ti panagulimek.** There are also questions that get answered just through silence. 2. With certain roots, this prefix shows that the entity indicated in the root is suffered or endured by the subject of the verb (takes *-ak* pronouns, perfective form is *na- -an*): **mabisinan.** to be overcome by hunger; starve. **mapudotan.** to get very hot. **mainitan.** to be exposed to the sun. **matudoan.** to get caught in the rain. 3. With *–an* stems, may indicate ability (the potentive-abilitative form of an *–an* verb). **maawatan.** to (be able to) understand. **Uray ania ti sasawem, ket saanmo a masabidongan ti panunotko.** No matter what you say, you can't poison my thoughts.

máat: *a.* unwise; having no common sense; ignorant. [Tag. *maang*]

máay: *n.* usefulness; worth; value; importance. **pagmaayan, mamaay.** *n.* result, outcome; effect. **awan mamaayna.** *a.* useless; unnecessary; unimportant.

mabagbagí: (f. *bagí*) *n.* genitals.

mabalín: (f. *balín*) *a.* possible; perhaps, maybe; *v.* can, be able to. **Mabalin a matulongannaka.** He can help you. **Mabalinnak a suruan.** You can teach me.

mabkangán: (f. *bekkang*) *v.* to burst; crack; be overloaded with heavy objects; to carry heavy objects.

mabláaw: *a.* sudden; *v.* to be startled.

mabláy: (f. *bellay*) **mabmablay.** (*obs.*) *v.* to be extenuated.

mablég₁: *var.* of *madleg*: timid, shy, lacking self-confidence. **Suruam tapno saan a mableg.** Teach him so he is not timid.

mablég₂: (f. *bileg*) *v.* to become overpowering.

mabló: (f. *bullo*) *v.* to have a broken bone, sprain, etc.

mabúlo₁: *n. Diospyros discolor*, a tree with edible, brown, hairy fruits; variety of *diket* rice.

mabúlo₂: **pangmabuluen.** *n.* a species of tree used for timber.

mabséet: (f. *bisét*) *v.* to leave immediately; to go immediately. (*mababseet*)

mabsíl: *v.* to be sprained; dislocated.

mabták: (f. *bettak*) *v.* to crack; burst, explode.

mabtúor: *v.* to be overcooked and less grainy (rice cooked over a fire).

madagdagulít: (f. *dagulit*) *adv.* again and again.

madamá: (f. *damá*) *adv.* presently, going on now; *a.* current.

madamdamá: (f. *damá*) *adv.* later, later on. [Kal. *umooli*, Png. *naáni*, Tag. *mamayâ*]

madéha: (Sp. *madeja*: hank, skein) *n.* skein, small bundle of thread or wool.

madí: *v.* negative of *kayat*, takes the *-ko* pronoun suffixes, to refuse, not like, not want, be unwilling; reject; refuse; *a.* unsuitable; bad; incompatible: **Madina kayat.** He doesn't want it. **Madi ni Andy.** Andy refuses. **agmadi.** *v.* to refuse. **madmadi.** *a.* not feeling well; indisposed; refusing; reticent. **pagmadian.** *n.* refusal. **agimmamadi.** *v.* to pretend not to. **agmadimadi.** *v.* to vacillate; feel indisposed. **makamadmadi.** *v.* to be undecided. [Ivt. *askeh*, Tag. *ayaw*]

madióng: *n.* the Chinese game of mahjong. **agmadiong.** *v.* to play mah jong. **madiongero.** *n.* mahjong player. **pagmadiongan.** *n.* mahjong parlor.

madláw: (f. *dilláw*) *v.* to notice by chance; *a.* noticeable.

madlég: *a.* shy, timid. (*managbabain*)

Madóna: (Sp.) *n.* Madonna.

madpáag: (f. *deppáag*) *v.* to collapse; cave in.

madpér: (f. *deppér*) *v.* to become blunt (blade).

madrása: (Maranao) *n.* Roman script rendering of the Maranao Arabic script.

madrasta: (Sp.) *n.* stepmother.

mádre: (Sp. *madre*: mother, nun) *n.* nun; mother. **agmadre.** *v.* to become a nun. [Kal. *mache*, Tag. *mongha* (nun)]

madrekakáw: (Sp. *madrecacao*: mother cacao) *n.* species of tree, *Gliricidia sepium* (*madrid kakaw, kakawate*). [Tag. *kakawate*]

madríd: **madrid** (*kakáw*). *n.* kind of native tree with edible flowers, *Gliricidia sepium*. (*madrekakao, kakawate*)

madrína: (Sp. *madrina*: godmother) *n.* godmother; female sponsor at a wedding or baptism. (*ina ti bunyag*)

madrugáda: (Sp. *madrugada*: dawn) *n.* late riser.

maél: **pagmamael.** *n.* reliance. **agmael.** *v.* to boast one's prowess or importance. **pagmael.** *v.* to rely on; have confidence in.

maéstra: (Sp. *maestra*: female teacher) *n.* female teacher. (*manursuro a babai*) **kinamaestra.** *n.* master's degree of study; studying to be a teacher. **Saanna a natuloy ti agbasa iti kinamaestra gapu iti kinarigat ti panagbiagda.** She didn't continue her teaching course of study because of their hard life. [Tag. *gurò*]

maéstro: (Sp. *maestro*: male teacher) *n.* male teacher. (*manursuro*) **agmaestro.** *v.* to be a teacher; become a teacher. [Tag. *gurò*]

magá: **namaga.** *a.* dry; neat, tidy; correct in dress. **kinamaga.** *n.* dryness. **namagmagan.** *a.* very dry; well seasoned (wood). **mamagaan.** *v.* to dry up. **pagmagaan.** *n.* abomasum, the fourth compartment of the stomach of ruminants where food is digested; where something is dried. [Ibg. *nemmaga*, Ivt. *mavkuh, kulay*, Kal. *lameg-alan*, Kpm. *malangi*, Png. *magá*, Tag. *tuyô* (dry)]

Magaliánes: (Sp. *Magallanes*) *n.* Magellan.

magán- *pref.* interrogative prefix used with certain roots; see also *mag-án*. **magankapaut?** How long (in duration). **magankaadu?** How many? **magankadaras?** How often?

mag-án: How is he? How are you? **Mag-an ngay met ti biagmo idiay Manila?** So how is (your) life in Manila? **kamag-anen.** *v.* to inquire about one's health. **agkamag-an.** *v.* to greet each other inquiring about life (using *mag-an*).

magandáya: (*obs.*) *n.* earring; wide breeches.

maganó: *n.* variety of awned early rice with white kernel.

magasín: (Eng.) *n.* magazine. (*pagiwarnak*)

magéy: (Sp. *maguey*: American agave plant) *n.* fibrous *maguey* plant used in rope making; *a.* made from the *maguey* plant.

mágid: *n.* inflammatory disease of the eyes. **agmagid.** *v.* to have sore eyes. (*gidgid, kamatá*) **Kasla agmagid dagiti matana iti kurang ti turog.** His eyes seem to be sore from lack of sleep.

magitngá: **namagitnga.** *a.* central, middle; median. (*tengnga*) **mamagitnga.** *v.* to place oneself in the center. [Tag. *gitnâ*]

magmág: **namagmagan.** *a.* very dry; parched (*gango*; *maga*). [Tag. *tuyô*]

magná: *v.* to walk, takes the *-ak* series pronouns, see *pagna*; to take effect. **mannagna.** *n.* good walker, one who always walks. [Ibg. *lákag, lákeg*, Ivt. *mayam*, Png. *akár*, Kpm., Tag. *lakad*]

magnésia: (Sp.) *n.* magnesia.

mágo: (Sp. *mago*: wise man) *n.* one of the three wise men who paid homage to the infant Jesus; magician; necromancer.

maguprák: *n.* rice that is not *diket*.

magsát: (f. *gessát*) *v.* to snap; cut. **magsat ti anges.** *v.* to die, cut off breathing.

magsi-: (Tag.) *pref.* Indicates the action denoted in the root is performed by several persons individually (takes no pronouns); prefix of combined effort. **magsidalus.** everyone doing their own cleaning; people cleaning one by one; let's clean (everyone contributing). **magsigatang.** each one buying (on his own).

magténg: (f. *dateng*) *v.* to reach, arrive (*madanon*). **Di kad' tarigagayam unay a magteng ken makita ti lugarmi?** Don't you really want to come and see our place?

mahablánka: (Sp. *maja*: nice person + *blanco*: white) *n.* a kind of sweet.

mahestád: (Sp. *majestad*: majesty) *n.* majesty.

mahistrádo: (Sp. *magistrado*: magistrate) *n.* magistrate, judge, justice.

mahó: (*slang*) *n.* homosexual. (*baien*)

Mahóma: (Sp.) *n.* Mohammed. **mahometano.** *a.* Mohammedan.

mai-: Potentive prefix for theme focus *i-* verbs (Perfective is *nai-*, takes *-ko* pronouns, intransitive counterpart is *makai-*): **ilako.** to sell. **mailako.** to be able to sell something; to be sold. **maikorte.** *v.* to be brought to court.

mai- -an: Potentive affixation for theme focus verbs, (form of the *ma- -an* affix for *i-* verbs). Perfective form is *nai- -an*. **mayurnongan (ti gatad).** to be saved (the cost of something).

máig: **imaig.** *v.* to lead, conduct; direct. (*bagnos*)

maika-: *pref.* ordinal number prefix: **umuna.** first. **maikadua.** second. **maikatlo.** third. **maikapat.** fourth. **maikalima.** fifth. **maikanem.** sixth, etc. [Ibg. *meka-*, Tag. *ika-*]

maikamanó: 1. *a.* several, diverse; many. 2. Interrogative used to ask a question of succession, answered by an ordinal number. **Maikamanoak?** In what order am I? What is my rank? **Maikamanokan?** What level/grade are you in? **maikamano a daras.** How many times? (*mamin-ano*) [Tag. *pang-ilán* (in what order), *iláng beses* (how many times)]

maipa-: Potentive (abilitative or nonvolitional) affix for indirect theme *ipa-* verbs. Perfective form is *naipa-* **maipadamag.** to be revealed (let known). **maipakita.** to be revealed (let shown).

maipanggép: (f. *panggep*) *prep.* about, concerning, regarding; on behalf of.

maipapán: (f. *pan*) *prep.* about, concerning (*maipanggép*). [Tag. *tungkól*]

maipuón: (f. *puon*) *prep.* on account of, because of. [Tag. *dahil sa*]

maís: (Sp. *maíz*: corn) *n.* corn. **minaisan, kamaisan.** *n.* cornfield. **mamaisen.** *v.* to do without difficulty (*salsaluyoten*). [Ibg. *mangíq*, Kal. *gakaw*, Knk. *tígi*]

máit: *n.* insanity. **agmait.** *v.* to be insane, crazy (*bagtit*). **Adda mamaitna.** He is somewhat crazy.

maka-: 1. Intransitive potentive prefix, corresponding to the transitive *ma-* indicating potential, abilitative, accidental, or coincidental action. Perfective form is *naka-*, but no longer indicates possibility but rather completion of an action or an attained state: **Saanak a makaluto.** I can't cook. **Nakapanen.** He went already. **Awan ti makaagaw kenka kaniak.** No one can snatch you away from me. 2. With certain bodily functions, natural needs, or sentiments, the prefix *maka-* is used to indicate necessity or impending carrying out of the action expressed by the stem: **Makaturogak.** I feel like sleeping. **Makaisbo ti aso.** The dog feels like urinating. **Makakatawa.** She feels like laughing. **Makapungpungtot a makaik-ikkis ni Keanu iti nakitana ngem nagpatingga lattan iti nalamuyot a timekna.** Keanu felt like screaming in anger at what he saw, but just ended up (talking) in a soft voice; 3. With numbers, *maka-* indicates the desire to purchase the number of items implied by the stem: **Makalimakami.** We want to buy five. **Nakasiamda.** They bought nine. 4. With temporal roots, may indicate one unit: **makabulan.** one month. **makatawen.** one year. **Itay pay la a binaonko a mapan gumatang iti suka, makatawenna ketdin!** I had her buy some vinegar just a short while ago, and she takes a year!

makaCV(C)-: Intransitive prefix encoding the urge to perform the action denoted by the root. **makababaeng.** to feel like sneezing. **makaisisbu.** to feel like urinating. **Makababaengak iti ingel.** I feel like sneezing from the strong smell. **Makadigdigosak metten iti baybay.** I also feel like swimming in the ocean.

makabkáng: (f. *bekkang*) *v.* to crack; crack open; burst open.

makabúkaw: *n.* vine with very bitter bark. (see *makabukay*)

makabúkay: *n. Cois lachryma-jobi.* Job's tears, flowering grass. A vine with bitter bark whose infusion may be used to induce abortion. [Tag. *makabuhay*]

makai-: Potentive (abilitative or nonvolitional) prefix used with *i-* theme verbs (takes *-ak* pronouns, transitive counterpart is *mai-*). **ipan.** to bring. **makaipan.** to be able to bring with. **Awan ti makaiparit iti ania man a kayatko nga aramiden.** No one can forbid whatever I want to do.

makaipa-: Potentive prefix used with indirect theme *ipa-* verbs. It indicates the ability or accidental nature of an actor causing someone else to act. Perfective form is *nakaipa-*: **Makaipabassitka toy dayawko.** You are belittling my honor.

makakarangénget: *n.* a variety of sugarcane used for fodder.

makalpás: (f. *leppas*) *v.* finish; end.

makalsiában: *v.* to be dislocated; out of place.

makamanó: (f. *manó*) *interrog.* How many times? How many days (did you stay?) **makamanmano.** *n.* a long time. **Makamanoka nga mapan?** How many times did you go? [Tag. *makailán*]

makán: (f. *kaán*) *a.* edible, comestible, palatable; *v.* to be eatable; *n.* food (see *kaan*). [Tag. *makakain* (edible); *pagkain* (food)]

makaníning: *n.* a variety of awned late rice with a light-colored hull and white kernel.

makangég: (f. *dengngeg*) *v.* to hear; happen to hear; be able to hear.

makangkangngég: (f. *dengngeg*) *v.* to hear, be able to hear; usually hear. **Diak kayat ti makangkangngeg iti sao.** I don't want to hear a word.

makapa-: Potentive indirect prefix indicating involuntary (nonactive) causation of an action: **pintas.** beauty. **makapapintas.** able to improve the beauty. **makapakatawa.** humorous, causing laughter. **makapaldaang.** sad, causing sorrow. **Awan ti matda nga ariet a makapadangran iti salun-at ti tarakenyo.** There are no worms left that can hurt the health of your livestock.

makapag-: 1. Potentive verbalizing prefix used with *ag-* verbs to indicate potential ability, as opposed to innate ability. Perfective form is *nakapag-*. Notice the difference of meaning with *maka-*: **diak makasurat.** I can't write (I do not know how). **diak makapagsurat.** I can't write. (I do not have a pen at the moment.); 2. With instrumental roots, indicates efficiency: **makapagsurat toy lapisko.** This pencil of mine is good for writing. **Makapagkuyogta.** We can accompany one another **Saanda a makapagsao, nabatombalani dagiti bibigda.** They weren't able to speak, their lips magnetized to each other.

makapag- -inn-: Potentive reciprocal affixation for *makapag-* verbs, denoting reciprocity and potentiality (ability or nonvolitionality). Perfective form is *nakapag- -inn-.* **Makapagtinnulongda.** They are able to help each other. **Dida nakapagsinnurat.** They were not able to write each other.

makapagi-: Potentive abilitative prefix used with *i-* theme verbs. The perfective form is *nakapagi-.* **makapagiserrek.** to be able to put inside **makapagiruar.** to be able to put outside.

makapagpa-: Potentive prefix used with *agpa-* verbs. (see *agpa-*): **Makapagpa-Mindanaoda.** They are able to go to Mindanao. **makapagpalawag.** to be able to explain.

makapai-: Potentive causative prefix used with *i-* verbs. Perfective form is *nakapai-:* **makapailugan.** to happen to have someone ride.

makapaldáang: (f. *leddáang*) *a.* sad, causing sorrow.

makapamin-: *pref.* Denotes how many times an action takes place. **Dikam makapaminlima nga agraep.** We do not transplant rice five times.

makapunó: (Tag.) *n.* a variety of coconut commonly used in desserts and ice cream.

makasagmamanó: (f. *manó*) *interrog.* How many times each? **Makasagmamanokayo ti aldaw nga panagtrabahoyo idiay?** How many days (each) did (each of you) work there?

makastrék: (f. *serrek*) *v.* to be able to enter.

makatgéd: (f. *tegged*) *v.* to earn one's living; work. *n.* worker.

makatnág: (f. *tinnag*) *v.* to fall; make something fall. **Makatnag ti kali.** It makes the hawk fall (said of strong tobacco smoke).

maki-: 1. Participative (social), intransitive verbal prefix that takes the *-ak* series pronoun enclitics. Its transitive counterpart is *ka-*, and its perfective form is *naki-:* **Makisao ni Juan kaniak.** Juan talks with me. **Nakiapa ni Murphy ken Carol.** Murphy quarreled with Carol. 2. With certain items, the prefix *maki-* indicates the action of requesting: **Makinatengakto.** I will ask for vegetables.

maki- -inn-: Reciprocal participative affix that designates that the action denoted by the root is performed by a group of people together

(Nominalized by *paki- -inn-*): **pintas.** beauty. **makipinnintas.** participate in a beauty competition. **pakipinnintas.** means of competing in beauty. **makisinnurat.** to write to each other.

maki- -um-: *affix.* Expresses that the agent of the verb has the desire to perform the action expressed by the root (takes *-ak* pronouns): **sarita.** talk; converse. **Makisumaritaak.** I want to talk; have the desire to talk.

makika-: *pref.* companionship prefix (perfective form is *nakika-*). **Nakikaidda kaniak.** He lay down with me.

makimbági: (f. *bági*) *interrog.* whose. [Ivt. *dangu*, Tag. *kanino*]

makin-: Ownership prefix: see *akin-*; may also denote location. **makinkukua.** to own. **makimbalay.** whose house. **makindaya.** to the east. **makinlaud.** to the west. [Bon. *kan-*]

mákina: (Sp. *máquina*: machine) *n.* machine; sewing machine. **makinista.** *n.* operator of a machine; engine driver.

makinária: (Sp. *maquinaria*: machinery) *n.* machinery; mechanics.

makinília: (Sp. *máquina*: machine + dim. suffix *-illa*) *n.* typewriter. **agmakinilia.** *v.* to type. **makiniliado.** *a.* typewritten.

makinísta: (Sp. *maquinista*) *n.* machinist.

makipag-: *pref.* Social prefix used with *ag-* verbs that shows that the action implied by the root is done by the actor of the verb (shown with the *-ak* pronouns) in the company of others who similarly perform the same action. **Nakipagsala kadakami.** She danced with us (We danced too). **makipagnaed.** *v.* To board (live) with other people. **makipagrikna.** *v.* to sympathize.

makipagi-: *pref.* Intransitive comitative prefix used with *i-* verbs. The perfective form is *nakipagi-:* **makipagiruar.** to help bring outside.

makipaginCV-: *pref.* Social pretentative affix that indicates the feigned performance of an action with others. (Perfective form is *nakipaginCV-*). **Makipaginluluto.** He is pretending to cook with others. **Makipaginsusuratak.** I am pretending to write with others.

maklép: (f. *kellep*) *v.* to faint; fall down; black out from a blow. **maklepan.** *v.* to be surrounded by, to be entirely covered with.

makná: (f. *kenna*) *v.* to trap; catch.

makuntíng: *n.* a variety of awned early rice with light-colored hull and red kernel.

makúpa: *n.* the mountain apple, Malay apple, *Eugenia javanica.* [Ivt. *bayakbak*, Tag. *makopa*]

makuríro: *var.* of *makariro*: to be a disturbance, nuisance, bother.

makúto: (Sp. *macuto*: military knapsack) *n.* ruddersack (of a soldier).

makúy: agmakuy. *v.* to be weak, listless, feeble, inactive. (*kápuy*)

makrúod: *v.* to make a crashing of thumping sound (banging, lightning).

maksáy: (f. *kissay*) *v.* to subtract; reduce; lessen.

maktáng: (f. *kettang*) *v.* to tire being in the same position for a long time. (*nakettangan*). **Naktanganak nga agtugaw.** I'm tired of sitting.

ma-l: (Pil. slang, pronounced *maél*, from *malibog*) *a.* sexually aroused; lustful.

mála: malamala. *n.* filthiness.

malabáto: (*obs.*) *n.* one-fourth of a Spanish real.

malábi: *n.* a type of broad-mouthed jar. [Tag. *bangâ*]

malabitáng: *n.* gossiper. **agmalabitang.** *v.* to talk imprudently; to talk out of turn; to gossip. (*labitangtang*)

malabutít: *var.* of *marabutit*: small mouse.

maladága: *n.* infant under seven years. **kinamaladaga.** *n.* infancy. [Kal. *alak, mutlok,* Tag. *sanggól*]

malága: *n.* a marine fish with tasty meat, *Scatophagus argus.*

Malagénia: (Sp. *malagueña*) *n.* woman from Málaga, Spain.

malaikmó: *n. Celtis philippinensis* tree yielding good timber.

malakának: mangmalmalakanak. *v.* to encompass, be widespread; (*reg.*) to be soggy (rice).

Malakaniáng: (Tag. *Malacañang, Malakanyang*) *n.* the official residence of the president of the Philippines.

malákat: *n.* variety of late rice with a white kernel.

malaksíd: (f. *laksid*) *prep.* except. **Naglutokami amin malaksid ken ni Rocio.** We all cooked except Rocio. [Ivt. *veken,* Tag. *maiban sa*]

malámal: simamalamal. *a.* dirty, filthy, smeared (around mouth with food). **malamalan.** *v.* to dirty; smear. **mamalamalan.** *a.* splattered all over with dirt, mud, food, etc; to be attacked by a swarm of insects. [Tag. *kulapol* (smear)]

malangá: agmalanga. *v.* to be stunned, dazed, distracted; lost in thought; confused (*tikaw*). **Agmalmalanga ti babai a nangawat iti intedmo.** The girl was stupefied to receive what you gave. [Tag. *litó*]

malapáko: *n.* lacquer.

malária: (Sp.) *n.* malaria. **agmalaria.** *v.* to have malaria.

málas: (Tag. also, Sp. *mala*: bad) *n.* bad luck; jinx. (*daksanggasat*) **malasen.** *v.* to have bad luck; to reject, refuse. **namalas.** *v.* to be unlucky. **agdemalas.** *v.* to have bad luck.

malasádo: (Sp. *mal asado*: poorly roasted) *a.* half-cooked; parboiled (egg).

malasiáw: *n.* variety of rice with dark hull and white kernel.

maláwid: minamalawid. *n.* leaf hat.

maláwig: *n.* variety of rice with fragrant white kernel.

Maláy(o): (Sp.) *n., a.* Malay.

malbá: *v.* to wither away. (*laylay, layot*)

malbáang: (f. *lebbaang*) *v.* to explode; burst.

malbádo: (Sp. *malvado*: evil) *a.* wicked. (*damka*)

malbarósa: (Sp. *malva rosa*: pink mallow) *n.* species of hairy, woody plant with fragrant leaves.

malbó: *v.* to collapse; be destroyed by a bomb. (*marba*)

maldáang: (f. *leddaang*) *v.* to be sorrowful; pitiful; gloomy.

malday: (f. *liday*) **malmalday.** *v.* to be sad.

maldít: *n.* print; printing; imprint; mark; stamp. **imaldit.** *v.* to print, imprint; stamp, mark; fix in the mind (memory). **pagimalditan.** *n.* printing press. **simamaldit.** *a.* imprinted; fixed. [Png. *galót,* Tag. *limbág, taták*]

maldíto: (Sp. *maldito*: damn) **grano maldito.** *n.* a kind of ulcer.

malém: *n.* afternoon. **agmalem.** *n.* the whole day. **agmalmalem.** *v.* to do (happen, etc.) the whole day. **minalem.** *adv.* every afternoon. **agminalem.** *v.* to do every afternoon. **pangmalem.** *n.* afternoon meal. **pangmalemán.** *n.* dish; place where one eats supper. **agmalmalem.** *v.* to do the entire day. **malem kalman.** yesterday afternoon. **kamalman.** in the afternoon; the afternoon of. **imalmalem.** *v.* to do sometime late in the afternoon. **mamaleman.** *v.* to be overtaken by the afternoon. **imalmalem.** *v.* to do in the afternoon. **ipamalem.** *v.* to put off until the afternoon. **Agmalmalem, agpatpatnag a nagsangsangit agingga ti nagsakit ken nagistayan natay.** She wept all day and all night until she got sick and nearly died. [Bon. *sóyaw,* Ibg. *fúgeg,* Itg. *gídam,* Ivt. *makuyab,* Kal. *machema,* Kpm. *gatpanápun,* Png. *ngárem,* Tag. *hapon*]

maléta: (Sp. *maleta*: suitcase) *n.* suitcase. **agmaleta.** *v.* to pack. **maletero.** *n.* luggage carrier; maker of suitcases.

maletín: (Sp. *maletín*: small suitcase) *n.* small suitcase of valise.

maliéte: (Sp. *mallete*: gavel) *n.* gavel, mallet.

malígno: (Sp. *maligno*: malign) *n.* evil spirit.

malinsáad: agmalinsaad. *v.* to lean back in the chair with stretched legs.

málís: see *maris*: color; hue.

malísia: (Sp. *malicia*: malice) *n.* malice; spite; active ill will.

malisióso: (Sp. *malicioso*: malicious) *a.* malicious.

mallukóng$_1$: *n.* bowl. **imallukong.** *v.* to put into a bowl. **mallukongen.** *v.* to carry in a bowl. [Ivt. *madukung*, Kal. *chuÿong, ungot, chungchung*, Png. *yaóng*, Tag. *mangkók* (Ch.)]

mallukóng$_2$: **malmallukong.** *n. Nothopanax cochleatum* shrub with saucerlike leaves.

mallúto$_1$: **agmalluto.** *v.* to drip, trickle (*arubos*). [Tag. *tulò*]

mallúto$_2$: **malmalluto.** *n.* shrub with alternate leaves and red edible drupes.

malmés: (f. *lemmes*) *v.* to drown. [Ibg. *maleggebban*, Ivt. *kamutan*, Kpm. *lúmud*, Png., Tag. *lúnod*]

malnák: *v.* to die from excessive water (plants).

málo: *n.* stick used for beating clothes while washing. **maluen.** *v.* to club, hammer; pound, knock; badger. **malo-malo.** *n.* kind of cactus. [Tag. *palò*]

maluít: (f. *luit*) *n.* wild rice.

malukóng: *var.* of *mallukong*, bowl (*mallukóng*). [Tag. *pangkók*]

málong: *n.* loose clothes of the Muslims or Chinese; material used to make these clothes.

malús: **maimalusan.** *v.* to be justified; proved correct.

malutmút: *n.* investigation **agmalutmut.** *n.* investigator, interrogator. **malutmuten.** *v.* to investigate, see *palutput*. [Tag. *usisà*]

malpáag: *v.* to wane; die down (fire).

malpaán: (f. *palpa*) to rest after eating.

malpág: (f. *lipág*) *v.* to collapse.

malpás: (f. *leppas*) *v.* to be finished, over, concluded.

malpáy: (f. *leppay*) *v.* to droop.

malpés: (f. *leppes*) *v.* to droop; be discouraged.

malséb: (f. *lesseb*) *v.* to drop inside; be deep set (eyes).

malsiáb: *v.* to be dislocated, out of place (*mabsil*).

malsután: *var.* of *maltután*: to choke.

maltát: (f. *lettat*) *v.* to be unfastened; not ready for use.

maltéek: (f. *litek*) *v.* to make the sound of hanging up a phone.

maltíing: (f. *liting*) **awan mamaltiing.** *exp.* there is not a sound.

maltután: (f. *luttot*) *v.* to choke.

maltráto: (Sp. *maltrato*: mistreatment) *n.* mistreatment. **maltratuen.** *v.* to mistreat. **pannakamaltrato.** *n.* act of mistreating.

mam-: *var.* of *mang-* before *p, b,* and *m*.

mama-: Fused form of *mangpa-*. Perfective form is *nama-*. **mamadigo (mangpadigo).** *v.* to share one's food with another

mamá: *n.* concoction for chewing made of betel leaf, betel nut and lime; areca nut, tobacco, lime and betel leaves; (Sp. *mama*: mother) *n.* mother (*ina, nanay*). **agmama.** *v.* to chew betel. **pagmamaan.** *n.* container for *mama*. [Ibg. *maman, ngengngoq*, Ivt. *mamahen*, Kal. *loma*, Kpm. *mamaq*, Png. *gagalen*, Tag. *ngangà*]

mamaáy: (f. *ay*) *n.* result; effect.

mamadigó: (f. *padigo*) *v.* to share one's food with another.

mamadéra: (Sp. *mamadera*: breast pump) *n.* breast pump.

mamadór: (Sp. *mamador*: sucker) *n.* nursing bottle. (*biberon*)

mamag-: (*maN-* + *pag-*) Intransitive prefix denoting noncontrolled or incidental causative actions. **mamagsina.** to part, cause to separate. **Makaawatka iti damag a mamagliday kenka.** You understand the news that makes you sad. **Agbalin a taba a mangpalukmeg ken mamagbutiog kenka.** It will become fat that will make you fat and cause you to have a big stomach.

mamagbagá: (f. *baga*) *v.* to advise, counsel.

mamáka: (f. *baka*) *v.* to buy cows.

mamakawán: (f. *pakawan*) *v.* to forgive, be able to forgive.

mamákir: (f. *bakir*) *v.* to deforest.

mamalaybaláy: (f. *balay*) *v.* to go from house to house.

mamaléngke: (Tag., f. *palengke*) *v.* to shop, go to the market.

mamalmá: (*obs.*) *n.* fainting on the way.

mamálon: (f. *balon*) *v.* to carry food to.

mamamálad: (f. *palad*) *n.* palm reader. (*mammalad*)

mamamatáy: (f. *patay*) *n.* murderer.

mamaniwés: (*obs.*) *n.* speed.

Mamanuá: *n.* ethnic group of northeastern Mindanao; language of the *Mamanua* people.

mamáng: *n.* term of address for one's own mother.

mamaóng: *n.* the cardinal fish of the *Apogonidae* family.

mamaraángan: (f. *paraangan*) *v.* to go to one's gate or yard, visit a neighbor outside their house; go to the vicinity of a place. **Nakadominggo a di namaraangan iti kalapaw ti lakay.** It has been a week that he hasn't visited the hut of the old man.

mámasan: (Jap., *coll.*) *n.* woman in charge of a brothel.

mamaspás: (*obs.*) *n.* idolatry.

mamatá: *n. Scutengraulis hamiltoni* anchovy.

mámaw: (*coll.*) *n.* ghost, spook. (*al-alia*)

mamayó: (f. *mayo*) *n.* weak feeling of the body. (*annanayo; laladut*) **agmamayo.** *v.* to feel faint. [Tag. *tinatamád*]

mambég: *v.* to slip away unnoticed. (*takkias, libas*)

mambí: (f. *tibbi*) *v.* to spin cotton. (*manbi*)

mambóg: *n.* a variety of awned late rice with white kernel.

mambúnong: *n.* medicine man (from mountains).

mamég: imameg. *v.* to cram, force something into, drive in, stuff; press; oppress; crush; overburden. **maimameg.** *a.* overwhelmed, oppressed, crushed, to find oneself in a worse position (in court). **Kasla kimat a dumteng dayta a mangimameg ti biag.** That life crusher arrived like lightning. [Tag. *diín*]

mamék: (*obs.*) *var.* of *mameg.*

mámel: nakamamel. *a.* with mouth stuffed with food; stuffed. (*melmel, papel, pelpel*)

mamelóko: (Sp. *mameluco*: mameluke) *n.* children's drawers; bloomers.

mamgád: (f. *peggad*) *v.* to risk, venture into danger. **Dida namgad a nagnagna iti kasipngetan a langalang.** They didn't dare to go walking in dark, deserted places.

mami(n)-: Multiplicative prefix used with numeric roots. Perfective form is *namin-:* **maminsan.** once. **mamindua.** twice. **mamitlo.** three times. **mamimpat.** four times. **maminlima.** five times.

mámi: (Hok. *màq mi*: meat noodle) *n.* dish consisting of noodles cooked in a meat broth.

mamilúko: *var.* of *mameluko*: bloomers; women's drawers.

mamimpin-: Limitative multiplicative prefix used with numeric roots. **mamimpinsan.** only once; once and for all. **mamimpindua.** only twice. **mamimpitlo.** only three times. **Idi aklonek ni Maria, linipatkan a naminpinsan.** When I accepted Maria, I forgot you once and for all.

maminadó: *adv.* often; many times. **Naminadun a nangngegko kenka ti balikas a pakawan.** I have heard you say the word *forgive* many times.

mamin-anó: *interrog.* How often? How many times? (Perfective form is *namin-ano*). **Mamin-anoak?** How many times do I do it? **Namin-anoda?** How many times did they do it?

maminduá: (f. *dua*) *adv.* twice. [Tag. *dalawáng beses*]

maminsán: *adv.* once. (see *minsan*) **no maminsan.** in a way, from one aspect; sometimes. **sangsangkaminsan.** all at once; without exception. **paminsanen.** *v.* to do all at once. [Tag. *minsán*]

mamisók: (f. *pisok*) *v.* to rinse rice and put it in a pot before cooking.

mamísos: (f. *pisos*) *a.* worth one peso.

mamitló: (f. *tallo*) *adv.* three times. [Tag. *tatlóng beses*]

mamkí: (f. *bikki*) *v.* to make an impression, to be effective; affect; feel (cold). **di mamki.** *v.* to be ineffective; to not affect.

mamlés: (f. *pelles*) *v.* to get dressed, change clothing.

mamlíng: *n.* a superstitious practice of boiling oil in the outskirts of town; supernatural visit (usually harmful). (*amlíng*)

mamm-: *var.* of prefix *mang-* before labials (*p, b, m*) used when the initial labial consonant of the root is dropped.

mammábuy: *n.* a kind of black heron with a white neck.

mammadlés: (f. *padlés*) *n.* prophet.

mammadtó: (f. *padtó*) *n.* prophet.

mammabagá: (f. *pagbagá*) *n.* advisor. (*pagumanan*)

mammalitók: (f. *balitók*) *n.* a poisonous water spider.

mammallót: (f. *pallót*) *n.* cockfighting gamblers.

mammaltót: (f. *paltót*) *n.* midwife.

mamman-aw: (f. *pan-áw*) *n.* roof thatcher.

mammandáy: (f. *pandáy*) *n.* blacksmith, smith.

mammaniáng: (f. *paniáng*) *n.* witch doctor, one who practices superstitious rites to appease the spirits.

mammarték: (f. *barték*) *n.* drunkard.

mammasiár: (f. *pasiár*) *v.* to be fond of strolling, taking a walk; *n.* stroller, one who promenades often.

mammék: agimammek. *v.* to dissimulate, dissemble; offset.

mammendíta: (f. *bendíta*) *n.* a kind of hermit thrush.

mammerdí: (f. *perdí*) *n.* destroyer; one who spoils.

mammét: [*man* + *met*] also; too. **mammet laeng.** *exp.* after all. **Napanka mammet laeng.** So you went after all. **Saanmi mammet a rinanta ti nagkalugan.** Yes, we did plan to ride together (contrary to what you think). **Hoy, agsuratka mammet, a!** Hey, you better write, too!

mammigát: (f. *bigát*) *n.* breakfast.

mammílit: (f. *pílit*) *a.* forceful.

mamminggá: (f. *pinggá*) *v.* to end, stop. (*sardeng*)

mammúkis: (f. *púkis*) *v*. to cut the hair.
mammúling: (f. *púling*) *v*. to remove extraneous matter from the eye.
mammuló: (f. *bulló*) *n*. a bone setter, (an indigenous profession).
mammulót: (f. *pulót*) *n*. anointer, one who blesses in a ceremony that includes anointment; one who performs the last rites.
mammuslít: (f. *puslít*) *n*. smuggler.
mamnát: (f. *bennát*) *v*. to stretch, increase in size by stretching. **Iti rabii met, no nakaturogen ti tao, dumakkel dagiti tulang iti duri isu a mamnat bassit.** At night, when a person sleeps, the bones of the spine enlarge a bit so the person gets bigger.
mamngét: (f. *pangét*) *v*. to be stuck; get entangled.
mamón: *n*. sponge cake. **puspuso a mamon.** *exp*. soft, kind heart.
mamuniág: (f. *buniág*) *n*. priest officiating at the baptism.
mamrít: (f. *pamrít*) **mammamrit.** *v*. to snarl, talk angrily. [Tag. *lahaw*]
mamsék: (f. *messék*) *a*. full; *v*. to be fully developed.
man-: *var*. of the prefix *mang-* before alveolar consonants (*t, d, s*).
maN-: See under the prefix *mang-*
maNC-: *pref*. Used to form frequentative nouns or verbs. **mannurat.** author, writer (f. *surat*). **mammadles.** prophet (f. *padles*). **mammartek.** drunk (f. *bartek*). **mammati.** to believe (f. *pati*).
maNCV-: 1. Frequentative affixation for *maN*-verbs. **mannanao.** talkative (from *sao*); 2. With animals, it denotes stealing: **mamababoyda.** They steal pigs. **mangnunuang.** He steals water buffalo.
maNVC-: continuous aspect form of the *maN*-prefix: **dagiti mamutbuteng a ladawan.** the haunting images.
man: *part*. 1. particle of entreaty: please. **Iyawatnak man dayta.** Please hand me that. **Tulongannak man.** Please help me. 2. affirms a negative statement. **saan man.** affirmatively answers a negative question. 3. used with *wenno* coordination to express the alternates: **man wenno saan.** whether or not. **Nabaknang man wenno napanglaw, kumpayen ni patay.** Whether rich or poor, death will strike. 4. may express unexpected information. **Napudot man ita.** It is (surprisingly) hot today. 5. forms lexicalized expressions: **uray man.** so what. **umay man ta.** may it be so. **manen.** again. [Knk. *kad*, Tag. *ngâ*]
manaC- -V-: Prefix used with onomatopoetic roots to designate loud, continuous or repetitive

uncontrolled actions. **manabtuog.** fall down with a thump. **manabraang.** to explode. **manalpaak.** to slap. **manabsuok.** to fall down with a splash, make a splashing sound. [This prefix can be broken down into the potentive prefix *ma-* and the iterative infix *-an-*. For sounds in which there is more control, the prefix *agkana-* can be used]
manabáko: (f. *tabáko*) *v*. to smoke cigars.
manabráang: (f. *biráng*) *v*. to explode (gunfire).
manabséek: *v*. to leave immediately; go immediately.
manabsíit: *v*. to make the sound of a fired missile.
manabsúok: *v*. to make a splashing sound.
manabtúog: (f. *bitóg*) *v*. to thump; fall down with a thumping noise. **Agur-uray ti manabtuog.** He is waiting for something to drop (said of lazy people).
manáda: (Sp. *manada*: herd) *n*. stud (horse, etc.); cock used in breeding (*manador*); rooster. **agmanada.** *v*. to stud.
manadór: (f. *manada*) *n*. stud rooster. (*manada*)
manag-: (*ma(g)-* + *-an-*) *pref*. Adjectival prefix for frequentatives which attaches to *ag-* verbs, sometimes used with CV reduplication. No perfective form: **managsasao.** talkative. **managsakripisio.** *a*. always making sacrifices. **managpupudoten.** *a*. easily irritated. **managsasaduten.** *a*. quite lazy, always being lazy. **managbartek.** always drunk. **Managkasdiayda.** They always act that way. **Managlualo.** He is always praying.
managCV-: (see also *manag-*) Antiquated prefix formed by the combination of *mang-* and *sag-* used with numeric roots to specify that an action is performed in groups of the number indicated by the root (Vanoverbergh 1955: 106): **Managlilimada a napan.** They went five by five. Also denotes a characteristic quality: **managsasao.** loquacious, talkative
managCVC-: frequentative prefix which denotes a characteristic quality: **managpungpungtot.** *a*. irritable, easily angered, often angry.
manag- -inn-: *affix*. Frequentative reciprocal prefix: **Managtinnulongtulongda.** They are always helping each other. **Managinnapalda.** They always envy each other.
managíbi: (f. *tagíbi*) *n*. foster parent; *v*. to suckle.
managmamanó: (*obs*.) How many each? How frequently?
managúday: (f. *sagúday*) *v*. to triumph.
managpaN-: (*ma(g)-* + *-an-* + *paN-*) Frequentative verbalizing prefix for *paN-* nominal

roots. **panakkel.** pride. **managpanakkel.** proud, prone to conceit.

managsinan-: *pref.* Forms frequentative resemblance verbs from *sinan-* stems. **managsinanmadi.** to always act as if to refuse.

managtagi-: *pref.* frequentative form of *tagi-* verbs: **managtagibolo.** He is always carrying a *bolo.* **managtagibalay.** She is always taking care of the house.

manáing: (f. *sáing*) *v.* to put on the light.

manakalsákal: (f. *sakal*) *v.* to kick about in discomfort.

manakláang: (f. *kiláng*) *v.* to make a resonant sound (clanging metal pots).

manaklíing: (f. *kilíng*) *v.* to clink; make a clinking noise.

manakmán: (f. *nákem*) *n.* adult; *a.* judicious, prudent, with sound judgement.

manakráad: (f. *kirád*) *v.* to forcibly open a door or gate.

manakríis: (f. *kirís*) *v.* to make the sound of a rip or tear.

manakrúod: (f. *takruod*) *v.* to make the sound of lightning, banging tin cans, or a boisterous burp.

manaksí: (f. *saksí*) *n.* eyewitness; witness.

manakták: (f. *takták*) *v.* to delay.

manaktúol: (f. *kitól*) *v.* to knock noisily.

manal-áy: (f. *tal-áy*) *v.* to journey by land.

manalbáag: (f. *libág*) *v.* to slam the door.

manalapí: (f. *salapí*) *a.* worth half a peso.

manalbúong: (f. *libóng*) *v.* to explode (gunfire).

manalí: (f. *salí*) *n.* busybody; meddler.

manalpáak: (f. *lipák*) *v.* to slap loudly.

manalpiit: (f. *lipít*) *v.* to slap the face.

manalpúok: (f. *lipók*) *v.* to make a slight thumping sound (object landing after being thrown).

manalsíit: (f. *palsiit*) *v.* to spit, shoot out.

manaltáak: (f. *liták*) *v.* to make a clicking sound; sound of flipping a switch.

manaltalék: (f. *talék*) *v.* to inspire confidence.

manaltéek: (f. *liték*) *v.* to hang up the phone; make a clicking sound.

manaltúog: (f. *litóg*) *v.* to crackle; make a crackling sound.

manang-: *pref.* Frequentative prefix used with *mang-* verbs.

mánang: (Sp. *hermana*: sister) *n.* older sister, term used with name to designate a female elder of the same generation (*kaka*). [Bon. *iyon-a*, Knk. *yon-á*, Png. *atsí*, Tag. *áte*]

manangaási: (f. *(ka)ási*) *a.* merciful, charitable.

manapáya: (f. *tapáya*) *v.* to support (with the palm of the hand); sustain.

manapríing: *v.* to jingle (coins); rattle (cans).

manarábay: (f. *tarábay*) *v.* to guide, help.

manaraígid: (f. *taraígid*) *v.* to flow out (tears).

manárak: (f. *tárak*) *v.* to stop flowering (banana).

manarakén: (f. *taraken*) *v.* to look after, raise; attend to.

manaraón: (f. *taraón*) *v.* to nourish, feed, supply with food; sustain; foster.

manarawidwíd: (f. *tarawidwíd*) *n.* manager.

manarbúos: (f. *rebbuos*) *v.* to burst out one after the other (spilled contents, rapid defecation).

manarimaán: (f. *tarimáan*) *v.* to be going on; to be engaged in.

manaríta: (f. *sarita*) *a.* loquacious; talkative.

manarpáak: *n.* slap; sudden blow; door slam. **Panarpaakekto pay 'ta rupam.** I'll slap your face.

manarséet: *v.* to make the sound of biting into flesh.

manarsíbok: (f. *rissibók*) *v.* to fall down with a splash.

manartarús: (f. *tarús*) *v.* to immediately enter; go without delay.

mánas: *n.* beriberi.

manatbáag: (f. *tebbág*) *v.* to snap with a sound; fall with a thump; slam.

manáwang: (f. *sáwang*) *n.* kind of poisonous snake.

manayegtég: (f. *tayegtég*) *v.* to tremble; shake.

manáyon: (f. *náyon*) *adv.* eternal; everlasting.

manbí: (f. *tibbí*) *v.* to spin cotton; *n.* cotton spinner. (*mambi, mannibbi*)

mandadór: (Sp. *mandador*: one who orders) *n.* leader (in a play, etc.).

mandála: *n.* heap of bundles of harvested rice.

mandamiénto: (Sp. *mandamiento*: mandate) *n.* warrant, written order giving legal authority. **mandamiento de arresto.** *n.* warrant of arrest. **mandamiento de rekisa.** *n.* search warrant.

mandár: (Sp. *mandar*: command) **mandaren.** *v.* to command. **mandaran.** *v.* to order someone, give an order to someone. **Diak mapagkedkedan ti mandar ti pusok.** I cannot resist the order of my heart.

mandáto: (Sp. *mandato*: mandate) *n.* mandate, command. [Tag. *kautusán*]

mandiák: see *indiak.*

mandiguríng: *n.* a variety of awned late rice with speckled hull and white kernel.

manduduál: see *andudual.*

mandragóra: (Sp. *mandrágora*: mandrake) *n.* mandrake (*Mandragora officinarum*) herb imported from Europe with a forked root that was believed to facilitate conception.

mandríl: (Sp.) *n.* mandrill baboon; spindle of a lathe, mechanical chuck.

manehár: (Sp. *manejar*: direct, manage) **maneharen.** *v.* to direct; lead; manage (*turong; tara-*

widwid). **Sikanto ti mangmanehar kadagiti kinabaknangko.** You will be the one to manage my wealth.

maného: (Am. Sp. *manejo*: I drive) *n.* driver. **agmaneho.** *v.* to drive (a car); manage; direct.

manén: *(man + -en) adv.* again, once more. **Umayka manen.** Come again. [Bon. *kasi,* Png. *lamét,* Tag. *mulî, na namán*]

manengténg: (f. *tengténg*) *v.* to increase in price.

maní: (Sp. *maní*: peanut) *n.* peanut. **manimaní.** *n.* kind of common grass; clitoris; vagina. [Ibg., Ivt., Kpm., Png. *maní,* Ifg. *dikdikok,* Kal. *mali,* Tag. *maní*]

mánia: namaina. *a.* not trained, uncouth. **maniador.** *n.* untrained person.

maniáblo: (f. *diáblo*) *n.* pagan priest.

maniákis: (Eng., *slang*) *n.* maniac.

maníbas: *n.* a variety of awned early rice.

maníbela: (Sp.: *manivela*: crankshaft) *n.* steering wheel.

manibróng: (f. *sibróng*) *n.* thief; (*obs.*) person responsible for executing the *sibróng*, the executioner of the *sibróng*.

maniémpo: (f. *tiempo*) *v.* to observe the weather; take advantage of the most opportune time to do something.

manigéta: (Sp. *manigueta*: handle) *n.* handle; crank; haft.

maníkes: agmanikes. *v.* to stand with arms akimbo. (*bannikes*)

manikéta: (Sp. *manigueta*: crank; handle) *n.* crank (engine); haft; handle.

manikí: (Sp. *maniquí*) *n.* mannequin.

manikuá: *n.* doubt; uncertainty; indecision. **agmanikua.** *v.* to be undecided, unsure, undetermined (*duadua, ngatangata*). [Tag. *alinlangan*]

Maníla: *n.* Manila, Maynila, the capital of the Philippines. **kamanilaan.** *n.* metropolitan Manila, the vicinity of Manila. [Png. *Ibali*]

maní lang: (*reg.*) *n.* powder; dust. (*tapok*)

maní law: (f. *sílaw*) *v.* to light; fish with a light at night.

Manilénio: (Sp. *manileño*: Manilan) *n.* person from Manila; *a.* of or from Manila.

manimón: (f. *timón*) *n.* helmsman, person in charge of the rudder of the shift.

manindí: (f. *sindi*) *v.* to light, ignite.

manióbra: (Sp. *maniobra*: maneuver) *n.* maneuver. **imaniobra.** *v.* to maneuver; operate; proceed with work.

manipdól: *n.* ritual performed the day before the rice harvest in which the officiator of the ceremony gathers twenty stalks of rice to be blessed.

manipésto: (Sp. *manifesto*: manifest) *n.* manifest, public declaration by a ruler; list of a ship's cargo.

manípud: (f. *sipud*) *prep.* from; since. **nanipudan.** *n.* beginning (of), source, origin. **manipud rugi inggana't gibusna.** from start to finish. **Rimmuar manipud iti museo.** He exited from the museum. [Tag. *galing sa, mulâ sa*]

manipulár: (Sp.) **manipularen.** *v.* to manipulate. **Saan a mabalin a piliten wenno manipularen.** He cannot be forced or manipulated.

mankuérna: (Sp. *mancuerna*: pair tied together) *n.* pair of convicts tied together; cuff links.

Mankomunidád: (Sp. *mancomunidad*) *n.* Commonwealth.

manmanó: (f. *mano*) *a.* very few; seldom, infrequent.

mannábag: (f. *sábag*) *v.* to be dishonest, deceitful.

mannabáko: (f. *tabako*) *n.* tobacco farmer; cigar smoker.

mannabálo: (f. *balo*) *n.* frequent widow or widower; one who is destined to be a widow or widower (*managbabalo*).

mannabél: *n.* a long-necked wading bird that feeds on fish.

mannábong: (f. *sábong*) *n.* kind of black and red bumblebee.

mannagá: (f. *tagá*) *n.* woodpecker. [Kal. *takkikin*]

mannagná: (f. *pagna*) *n.* hiker; good walker.

mannaíding: *n.* sailboat made from a tree trunk; *v.* to catch fish on the rocks with a hook or net.

mannáit: (f. *dait*) *n.* seamstress, sewer.

mannaka-: *pref.* Frequentative prefix used with *maka-* verbs. It takes the *-ak* pronoun endings: **Mannakainum.** He always wants to drink. **Mannakaturogka.** You are always sleepy. **mannakaammo.** knowledgeable. **mannakaawat.** *a.* understanding.

mannákab: (f. *sákab*) *n.* wasplike insect.

mannákaw: (f. *takaw*) *n.* thief.

mannaki-: *pref.* Frequentative prefix used with social *maki-* verbs. It takes the *-ak* pronoun endings: **mannakibiang.** prone to meddle in another's affairs. **Mannakigubatda.** They are always waging war. **Mannakimanggaka.** You always ask for mangos.

mannaki- -inn-: Frequentative reciprocal affixation for social *maki-* verbs. **Mannakisinnuratda kaniak.** They always write to me (and vice-versa).

mannála: (f. *sála*) *n.* dancer. [Tag. *mananayáw*]

mannálaw: (f. *tálaw*) *n.* escapee; refugee.

mannálon: (f. *tálon*) *n.* farmer. [Tag. *magsasaká*]

mannámay: *n.* witch (*manggagamud*). [Tag. *mangkukulam, manggagaway*]

mannanákaw: (f. *tákaw*) *n.* thief. [Bon. *ngámel, omaákew*, Tag. *magnanakaw*]

mannániw: (f. *dániw*) *n.* poet. [Tag. *manunulà*]

mannangán: (f. *kaán*) *n.* eater; *a.* fond of eating. **Mannangan iti tsokolate.** He is fond of eating chocolate.

mannángit: (f. *sángit*) *n.* crybaby.

mannaúl: (f. *taúl*) *n.* small black bird that cries at night; *a.* prone to barking.

mannápaw: (f. *sápaw*) *n.* kind of nonpoisonous snake frequently found in thatched roofs.

mannaráy: (f. *taráy*) *n.* racer, one who runs in a competition.

mannarekdék: (f. *darekdék*) *n.* a slender vine used to cure boils.

mannaríta: (f. *saríta*) *a.* talkative. **Ti tao a mannarita, awan ti ania a magapuananna.** The talkative man accomplishes nothing. [Tag. *daldál*]

mannárog: (f. *tárog*) *n.* kind of black beetle.

mannengdéng: (f. *dengdéng*) *n.* small black and red insect.

mannibbí: (f. *tibbí*) *n.* cotton spinner.

manniblók: (f. *siblók*) *n.* thief, burglar.

mannibróng: (f. *sibróng*) *n.* thief; kidnapper; person responsible for executing the *sibróng*.

mannibsíbay: (f. *síbay*) *v.* to ramble around town.

mannipdót: (f. *sipdót*) *n.* snatcher; pickpocket.

mannírip: (f. *sírip*) *n.* peeper, peeping Tom.

mannubbót: (f. *subbót*) *n.* redeemer, savior.

mannugál: (f. *sugál*) *n.* gambler.

mannuká: (f. *suká*) *n.* vinegar fly.

mannukák: (f. *tukák*) *n.* kind of snake that feeds on frogs.

mannúkit: (f. *súkit*) *n.* mole (burrowing animal).

mannukmón: (f. *sukmón*) *n.* drinker of alcohol (usually natively brewed) at the local store, local alcoholic.

mannúlong: (f. *túlong*) *a.* helpful; *n.* helper.

mannúma: (f. *súma*) *n.* antidote specialist.

mannúmang: (f. *súmang*) *n.* antidote specialist.

mannúngpal: (f. *tungpál*) *a.* obedient.

mannuplóng: (f. *suplóng*) *n.* informer; tattletale.

mannuríken: (f. *duríken*) *n.* one who collects the *duriken* mollusk frequently or for livelihood.

mannúrog: (f. *túrog*) *n.* frequent sleeper.

mannursúro: (f. *súro*) *n.* teacher.

mannusó: (f. *susó*) *n.* another term for the *birút* fish.

máno: (Sp. *mano*: hand) *n.* act of kissing the hands of elders; right turn in traffic; person with the right to be first in a game; handful. *a.* first

in the order of playing. **agmano.** *v.* to flip a coin to determine order of play. **segúnda máno.** (Sp. *segunda mano*: secondhand) *a.* secondhand; previously used. **buéna mano.** (Sp. *buena mano*: good hand) *n.* first sale. **priméra mano.** (Sp. *primera mano*: firsthand) *a.* firsthand. **agmanomano.** *v.* to fight with bare hands. **manokan, manomon.** go ahead, start the game; you are first (in the game). **de-mano.** manual, with hand power. **a mano.** fitting; just enough; just on time.

manó: *interrog.* How many? How much? **manmano.** *a.* very few, seldom; rare; *adv.* occasionally; phenomenal; rarely. **makamano.** *v.* to do a number of times. **makamanmano.** *n.* a long time. **maikamano?** *interrog.* In what order (asking for a particular ordinal number of an entity or event); number of times. **sagmamano.** *interrog.* How much each? **agkamano.** *interrog.* into how many parts is something divided? **Agkamanoda?** Into how many parts are they divided? **pagkamanuen.** *v.* to divide. **Pagkalimaem ti sangapulo, dua.** Ten divided by five is two. **sumagmamano.** *a.* few; some. **Manoanka?** How many did you get? **mano met la dayta.** *exp.* no problem, it is easy. [Ivt. *papira*, Kal. *piga*, Kpm. *pilán*, Png. *pigá*, Tag. *ilán* (how many), *magkano* (how much)]

manubálit: (f. *subálit*) *v.* to reply.

manúbela: (Sp. *manivela*: crank) *n.* steering wheel. (*maníbela*)

Manóbo: *n.* Ethnic group from the island of Mindanao; language of the Manobo people, which can be classified according to at least the following varieties: Agusan, Ata, Bukidnon, Cinamiguin, Cotabato, Dibabawon, Ilianen, Matigsalug, Obo, Rajah Kabunsuwan, Sarangani, and Tagbanwa.

manubráng: *n.* herbal concoction of leaves.

manudénsia: *var.* of *menudensia*: internal organs.

manúdon: (f. *dúdon*) *v.* to catch locusts.

manúgang: (f. *túgang*) *n.* son-in-law; daughter-in-law. (*katugangan*) **manugangen.** *v.* to consider as one's prospective son/daughter-in-law. **Ipudnok kenka a kayatka a manugangen.** I will declare to you that I like you as a son-in-law. [Kal. *malugang*, Png., Tag. *manúgang*]

manóhos: (Sp. *manojo*: bundle, bunch) (*obs.*) *n.* big bundle of rice.

manók: *n.* chicken; poultry. **manmanok.** *n.* birds (general term). **agmamanok.** *n.* chicken thief. **agmanmanok.** *v.* to raise chickens. **manuken.** *v.* to vote for; to bet on; support. **panag-**

manukan. *n.* poultry raising. [Ibg. *manuq*, Isg. *anuq*, Ivt., Kpm., Kal. *malok*, Png., Tag. *manók*]

manukúnok: (f. *nukúnok*) *v.* to be concentrated (in one area); piled up.

manuláng: (f. *tulang*) *a.* reaching the bone (said of extreme cold).

manumbaláy: (f. *balay*) *v.* to go from house to house; to go to different houses. (*agbalam-balay*)

mánong: (Sp. *hermano*: brother) *n.* older brother; term of address used to designate male elders of the same generation, used before proper names. [Bon. *iyon-a*, Knk. *yon-á*, Tag. *kuya* (older brother)]

manúngay: (f. *dúngay*) *v.* to stagger; totter.

manungpál: (f. *tungpál*) *prep.* until; *v.* to be tired out; to be used up.

manursúro: (f. *súro*) *n.* teacher. [Tag. *gurò*]

manursurón: (f. *surón*) *n.* teaser.

mános: (Sp. *mano*: hand) *n.* bundling; bundle of tobacco leaves. **agmanos, makimanos.** *v.* to wrap or bundle tobacco leaves. **amanos.** *a.* even (in a game or bet).

manuskríto: (Sp. *manuscrito*: manuscript) *n.* manuscript.

manutsutíl: (f. *sutil*) *a.* always joking; fond of playing around.

mánsa: *var.* of *mantsa*: stain. **mansado.** *a.* stained; spotted.

mansánas: (Sp. *manzana*: apple) *n.* apple.

mansanília: (Sp. *manzanilla*: chamomile) *n.* the chamomile plant, used in native medicine against boils and stomachache; its oil is used against flatulence.

mansanítas: (Sp. *manzanitas*: little apple) *n.* *Zizyphus jujuba* plant.

mansáyag: *n.* the dead lying in state (at a wake). **nakamansayagen.** *a.* lying in state. (said of the dead) **imansayag.** *v.* to prepare a corpse to lie in state. **naimansayag.** *a.* lying in state. **pag-mansayagan.** *n.* funeral parlor; elevated platform where corpses lie in state. [Kpm. *burúl*, Tag. *burol*]

manséra: (Sp. *mancera*: plow handle) *n.* plow handle.

mansínang: *n.* variety of rice with a thin, long kernel.

mansión: (Sp. *mansión*) *n.* mansion.

mánso: *n.* club, hammer. (*pang-or*). **mansuen.** *v.* to beat, club.

mansó: (Sp. *manso*: meek) *a.* tame; domesticated. **agmanso.** *v.* to bronco bust, tame cattle. **mansuen.** *v.* to tame (cattle); punish an obstinate boy. **Buyaem laengen ti aramidek tapno ammomto met no sika ti agmanso.** Watch what I do so you'll know what to do when you are the one to bronco bust.

mánta: (Sp. *manta*: blanket) *n.* blanket. (*ules*)

mantalóna: (Sp. *manta*: blanket + *lona*: canvas) *n.* canvas.

mantáw: agmantaw. *v.* to go from one job to another; to live from place to place; roam. **Gapu iti ugalina a mantaw ken tawataw, saan a nagustuan dagiti kakabagianna.** Because of her habit of roaming around from place to place, her relatives do not like her.

mantéka: (Sp. *manteca*: lard) *n.* lard, fat. (*taba*) **agmanteka.** *v.* to produce cooking oil, lard. **namantekaan.** *a.* greased, larded. [Tag. *mantikà*]

mantekádo: (Sp. *mantecado*: vanilla ice cream) *n.* French vanilla ice cream.

mantekília: (Sp. *mantequilla*: butter) *n.* butter; margarine. **mantekiliera.** *n.* butter dish.

mantél: (Sp. *mantel*: tablecloth, altar cloth) *n.* tablecloth; altar cloth.

mantélis: (Sp. *mantel*: altar cloth) *n.* altar cloth.

mantenér: (Sp. *mantener*: maintain) **agmantener.** *v.* to stay a short time. **manteneren.** *v.* to maintain; support (financially); preserve.

mantília: (Sp. *mantilla*: mantle) *n.* mantle, cloak; veil for the head.

mánto: (Sp. *manto*: cloak) *n.* black veil used in mourning; mantle, cloak. **agmanto.** *v.* to wear black mourning clothes; to be cloudy, gloomy. **Nagmanto ti sibubukel nga ili gapo iti ipupusayna.** The whole town wore mourning clothes because of his death.

mantolína: *n.* black veil worn in church.

mantsá: (Sp. *mancha*: stain) *n.* stain. **agmantsa.** *v.* to stain. **mantsaan.** *v.* to stain something. **mantsado.** *a.* stained; spotted.

mang-: 1. Detransitivizing prefix (used to change transitive verbs (-*an* and -*en*) into an intransitive case frame. Perfective form is *nang-*. 2. It is also used: a) to indicate the action of gathering or collecting: **kayo.** wood. **mangayo.** to collect firewood. **ubas.** grapes. **mangubas.** to collect grapes; b) to form verbs expressing purchase: **baka.** cow. **mamaka.** to buy cows. **manok.** chicken. **mangmanok.** to buy chicken; c) to indicate movement with some roots: **mangasilias.** to go to the toilet. **mangarruba.** to visit the neighbors; d) in nominal frames, it indicates an actor: **salaknib.** protect. **mang-salaknib.** protector.

mangCV-: Prefix used to denote the taking of the entity denoted by the root: **Mamababoyda.** They steal pigs. **Mangnunuang ti lolom.** Your grandfather steals water buffalo.

mang: Contraction of *manong* and *manang*, term of address for an elder person of the same generation.

mangá: agmangamanga. *v.* to be uncertain, undecided.

mangalbásia: (f. *albásia*) *v.* to matchmake.

mangaldáw: (f. *aldáw*) *n.* lunch, midday meal; *v.* to have lunch, eat lunch.

mangán: (f. *kaán*) *v.* to eat. [Ibg., Ivt. *kuman*, Ifg. *kanon*, Kpm., Png. *mangan*, Tag. *kumain*]

mangápas: (f. *kápas*) *v.* to gather cotton.

mangappó: (f. *kappó*) *v.* to gather clams.

mangarabukób: (f. *karabukób*) *v.* to be over-satisfied with food; (*fig.*) filled to the throat.

mangarúba: (f. *kaarúba*) *v.* to visit the neighbors, go to the house of the neighbors.

mangasár: (f. *kasár*) *v.* to marry off; to marry (said of a priest).

mangasílias: (f. *kasílias*) *v.* to go to the toilet.

mangatúday: (f. *katúday*) *n. sawsaw-it* bird.

mangáyaw: (f. *káyaw*) *v.* to headhunt; captivate.

mangdá: (f. *tiddá*) *v.* to leave; cause to remain.

mangeddéng: (f. *keddéng*) *v.* to pass sentence on; decide; condemn.

manggá: *n.* the mango tree; mango fruit, (leaves used in native medicine against cough and fever).

manggagamá: *n.* scorpion. [Kpm., Tag. *alakdán*]

manggagámud: (f. *gámud*) *n.* witch; sorcerer. [Tag. *mangkukulam*, *manggagaway*]

manggás: (Sp. *manga*: sleeve) *n.* sleeve. **Imbabana ti agsumbangir a manggas ti kamisana.** He lowered both sleeves of his shirt.

manggásak: *n.* variety of awnless rice.

manggatsapóy: (Sp. *mangachapuy*) *n.* Mangachapuy tree with valuable timber.

manggéd: (f. *teggéd*) *v.* to work for wages. **mangmangged.** *n.* laborer in the fields, worker. **panggedan.** *n.* place of employment; business.

mánggo: (Sp. *mango*: handle) *n.* handle.

manggustín: (Sp.) *n.* mangosteen.

mangi-: Detransitive prefix for *i-* verbs. Perfective form is *nangi-*. **Napilitanda a nangilako kadagiti sanikuada idiay bantay.** They were forced to sell their property in the mountains. **Sino ti nangyospital kenka?** Who took you to the hospital? **Napilitan a nagikkat a mangisuro.** He was forced to quit teaching.

mangíbin: (f. *kibin*) *v.* to guide, escort.

mangika-: Detransitive affixation for *ika-* verbs indicating volitional increase of dimension. Perfective form is *nangika-* **Kasano ngaruden ti panggeptayo a mangikalawa ti kapilia.** What about our plan then to broaden the chapel?

mangipa-: Detransitive affixation for *ipa-* verbs. Perfective form is *nangipa-*: **mangipatungpal iti plano.** to carry out a plan.

mangkáw: *a.* wicked, atrocious; unruly, rebellious; headstrong. **agmangkaw.** *v.* to live in with a concubine. [Tag. *balakyót*]

mangkéd: see *talged.*

mangkiáw: mangmangkiaw. *var.* of *mangmangkik*: supernatural being, hobgoblin.

mangkík: mangmangkik. *n.* elf, small supernatural being; (*fig.*) crazy person. **No agararbis nga agin-init, agan-anak ti mangmangkik.** When it drizzles in the sunshine, an elf is giving birth.

mangkít: mangmangkit. *var.* of *mangkík*: elf.

mangló: (f. *ulló*) *v.* to work for wages. **mangmanglo.** *n.* ordinary laborer; daily wage earner. (*teggéd*)

mangmáng: *n.* itchy inflammation at the corners of the lips. **agmangmang.** *v.* to have inflammations on the corners of the mouth. **mamangmangan.** *n.* the corner of the mouth.

mangnáw: *n.* slender bamboo. *Schizostachyum sp.*

mangngá: mangngá-mangngá. *v.* doubt; indecision. **agmangngamangnga.** *v.* to be unsure, doubtful, uncertain (*duaduá*). [Tag. *alinlangan*]

mangngadilián: (f. *kadilián*) *n.* reef fisherman.

mangngágas: (f. *ágas*) *n.* doctor; faith healer. [Tag. *manggagamot*]

mangngálap: (f. *kálap*) *n.* fisherman. [Tag. *mangingisdâ*]

mangngamlíng: (f. *amlíng*) *n.* supernatural force that affects the health of someone; person who performs a supernatural rite.

mangnganúp: (f. *anúp*) *n.* hunter. [Tag. *mamamaril*, *mangangasó*]

mangngáput: (f. *káput*) *n.* kind of pelican.

mangngaráding: (f. *karáding*) *n.* sorcerer; witch (*manggagamud*). [Tag. *mangkukulam*, *manggagaway*]

mangngartíb: (f. *kartíb*) *n.* black and white destructive flying insect about 1½ inches long with two scissorlike jaws.

mangngég: (f. *dengngég*) *v.* to listen, hear; to be audible (*madengngeg*). **mangngegán.** *v.* to hear (*madengngegan*). [Tag. *makikíg*]

mangngílot: (f. *ílot*) *n.* masseur (male), masseuse (fem.); midwife; bone setter.

mangnginúm: (f. *inúm*) *n.* heavy drinker; alcoholic.

mangngúbet: (f. *úbet*) *n.* sodomite.

mangngúbog: (f. *úbog*) *n.* black bird that feeds on *ubog.*

mangngurnóng: (f. *urnóng*) *n*. collector; one who assembles; one who saves. **mangngurnong iti daan.** *n*. antique collector.

mangortísia: (f. *kortesia*) *v*. to invite someone to dance.

mang-ós: (f. *us*) *v*. to eat sugarcane.

mangutséro: (f. *kutséro*) *v*. to drive a coach.

mangpa-: Detransitivizing affix for *pa- -an* or *pa- -en* verbs. Perfective form is *nangpa-*. May also fuse to *mama-* **mangpapintas.** beautifying something **mangpasakit.** to make sick, hurt.

mangpag-: Detransitive affixation for causative *pag- -en* verbs. Perfective form is *nangpag-*. May also fuse to *mamag-* **mangpagtalna.** to tranquilize something, calm down something. **mangpagnakem.** to make somebody mature. **mangpagleddaang.** to make someone sorrowful.

mangrabií: (f. *rabií*) *v*. to eat dinner, evening meal. **pangrabii.** *n*. dinner, the evening meal.

mangrém: (f. *kerrém*) *v*. to pout the lips.

mangúbog: (f. *úbog*) *n*. a large, black bird that destroys coconuts.

mangtagi-: Detransitive affix for *tagi- -en* verbs. Perfective form is *nangtagi-*. **Ania ti pamkuatam a mangtagibassit kaniak?** What is your motive for belittling me?

mangy-: *var*. of *mangi-* before vowels. **ulog.** descent. **mangyulog.** to bring down.

maóng: (Tag. also) *n*. jeans; denim material.

mausoléo: (Sp. *mausoleo*) *n*. mausoleum.

mapa-: *pref*. 1. Indicates potential carrying out of a causative action. Perfective form is *napa-* **mapariaw.** he can be made to shout; 2. May also indicate instinctive (involuntary) actions that are done when prompted by an outside force. **mapanganga.** to open the mouth (in surprise). **mapaanang-ang.** to be made to whine (from a hit, etc.)

mapa- -an: *affix*. Abilitative causative prefix indicating that the action denoted by the root is performed on the subject by an external, unspecified force without control. **mapatulidan.** to be run over by something **No mapagasatanak.** If I have the luck. **Mapatulidanka dita.** You can be run over there.

mapaCpa: Continuous aspect form of *mapa-* verbs. **Awan ti mapaspasamak iti dalan.** Nothing is happening on the road.

mápa: (Sp. *mapa*: map) *n*. map. **imapa.** *v*. to chart out on a map; sketch on a map. **agmapamapa.** *v*. to appear in patches. **ipamapa.** *v*. to have something charted on a map.

mapag-: *pref*. Potentive (potential ability/non-volitionality) prefix used with *pag-* verbs. Perfective form is *napag-*: **mapagbaliw.** to be able to change something **mapagsingpet.** to be able to make someone behave. **Dakkel ti namnamana a mapagbaliw ti panunotko.** He had high hopes of being able to change my thoughts. **Dimo mapagbaliw ti pangngeddengko.** You cannot change my decision.

mapagpa-: *pref*. Potentive causative prefix. **pintas.** beauty. **mapagpapintas.** make others improve their beauty.

mapagténg: (f. *daténg*) *v*. to happen, occur; get; undergo. [Tag. *mangyari*]

mapán: (f. *pan*) *v*. to go; leave, depart; set forth; (with measurements) to be more or less, approximate. See also *in-*. **makapan.** *v*. to be able to go; to happen to go. [*Mapan* as an auxiliary verb takes the enclitic pronouns of the main verb: *Mapanko kumbidaen ida*. I'm going to invite them. Kal. *umoy*, Tag. *pumuntá*]

maparngít: *n*. variety of late awned rice with a speckled hull and white kernel.

mapdá: (f. *peddá*) *v*. to be tired; exhausted.

mapléng: (f. *pelléng*) *v*. to be stunned due to a blow on the head.

mapnék: (f. *pennék*) *v*. to be satisfied.

maprád: (f. *aprád*) *v*. to be affected by salt; have a dry mouth due to too much salt; have dry eyes.

mara-: *pref*. 1. Similarity prefix. **maraniog.** *a*. like a coconut. **mara-Hapon.** *a*. pro-Japanese; Japanese sympathizer (during the war). **marasagaysay.** *a*. like a comb. **Marmaratubbog dagiti matana.** His eyes are watery. 2. May indicate manner of impending nature of an action: **maraisem.** on the verge of smiling; likely to smile, about to smile. **marapukaw.** likely to disappear. **Marabettaken ti isemna.** His smile is about to break out. **Marmaratamnay a nangilukat iti ridaw.** He listlessly opened the door.

mára: **maramara.** *n*. reddish black marine fish.

mará: **agmara.** *v*. to stutter (*beddál*). [Tag. *utál*]

marabambán: *a*. milky; *n*. species of medicinal plant used to cure wounds.

marabangsít: (f. *bangsít*) *n*. kind of flowering plant with an unpleasant smell, sometimes used as a hedge.

marabília: (Sp. *maravilla*: marvel; marigold) *n*. kind of flower, marigold.

marabilís: (Sp. *maravedí*: old Spanish coin) *n*. farthing, old Spanish coin worth ¼ centavo (*marebilis*, *mirabilis*)

marabúteg: (f. *búteg*) *n*. young betel nut.

marabutít: (f. *butít*) *n*. newborn baby; small mouse. **Kaslakami maip-ipit a marabutit iti nagbaetan dagiti dadakkel a bato.** We are like clamped mice between the big rocks.

maradágum: (f. *dágum*) *n.* young cowpea; kind of slender grass.

maradapó: (f. *dapó*) *a.* ashen, ash-colored, gray.

maragátas: (f. *gátas*) *n.* species of tree with valuable timber and a central heart with many white spots.

maraínas: **agmarainas.** *v.* to be half dry. **pamarainasen.** *v.* to air a little, dry superficially.

marainúgas: *a.* of the color of dirty rice water (said of flood waters, etc.) **agmarainugas.** *v.* to be turbid and dirty (floodwaters). (*libeg*)

maraisá: **agmaraisa.** *v.* to be half dry. **pagmaraisaen.** *v.* to air to dry superficially. **Agmarmaraisa ti nangisit a daga gapu iti kinasapa ti ulep nga agkayab iti malem.** The black earth is almost dry because of the earliness of the clouds floating in the afternoon.

marakád: **agmarakad.** *v.* to sit on one's haunches (position of squatting without the buttocks touching the ground) (*marikadkad, marikadek*). [Tag. *lupasáy, tingkayád*]

marakalmán: (f. *kalmán*) *n.* kind of herb eaten by horses.

marakápas: (f. *kápas*) *n.* cotton tree; something resembling cotton; *a.* like cotton.

marákas: (Sp. *maracas*) *n.* maracas, a rattling percussion instrument made of dried gourds filled with seeds.

maralakién: (f. *laki*) *n.* tomboy girl; lesbian; masculine woman.

maramaís: (f. *maís*) *n.* species of plant used as cow fodder.

maran-: Prefix of resemblance. **marantiddog.** *a.* elongated.

Maranáo: *n.* an ethnic group of Mindanao; their language.

marantiddóg: *a.* elongated (*karantiddog*; see *atiddog*)

márang: *n.* species of tropical fruit with sweet white flesh around thick seeds and surrounded by a spiny covering.

maranghás: (Tag.) *n.* pomelo (*lukbán*). [Tag. *suhà*]

marangkás: *var.* of *maranghás*.

marangmáng: *n.* front; front row. **agmarangmang.** *v.* to be cloudy (when at sea); to go to the front during performances; to watch (a parade, etc.) as it passes by. **namarangmang.** *a.* remarkable; extraordinary, noticeable; wonderful; conspicuous. **Adda umarimbangaw a grupo a dimteng ket nabisngay dagiti nagmarangmang a babbai.** A noisy group of people arrived and the women onlookers made way.

marauggót: (f. *uggót*) *n.* young growth, shoot.

maraúgot: (f. *úgot*) *n.* medium tide, weak ebb tide of a river.

maraúmok: (f. *úmok*) *n.* hearth; comfortable home; nesting place.

maraunás: (f. *unás*) *n.* species of weed resembling sugarcane.

marapágay: (f. *págay*) *n.* species of grass.

marápay: *n.* a variety of awned late-maturing rice.

marapegpég: (f. *pegpég*) *n.* grain not fully developed.

marasabá: (f. *sabá*) *a.* ripe (said of the tamarind when yellow); almost ripe (said when a fruit is green and yellow). (*marsaba*)

marasámas: *n.* loose earth; soft fruit; roughness, coarseness. **namarasamas.** *a.* rough, coarse (not thoroughly cooked rice).

maraséda: *n.* species of banana.

marasiksík: (f. *siksík*) *a.* like scales. **marasiksikan.** *a.* scaly, covered with scales. **Agmarmarasiksik dagiti puraw nga ulep iti dayta a malem.** The clouds were scaly that afternoon.

marasinúkol: *a.* reaching puberty; inexperienced.

marasintók: (*slang*, f. *sintók*) *n.* virgin.

maratampóy: *n.* *Diospyros multiflora* tree.

maratangtáng: *n.* sea urchin, sea anemone.

maratáoka: *n.* *Albizzia saponaria* plant. (*marateka*)

maratéka: *var.* of *marataoka*.

maratekték: (f. *tektek*) *n.* variety of rice.

maratrígo: (Sp. *trigo*: wheat) *n.* darnel, species of weedy grass.

marayámay: **namarayamay.** *a.* dry (boiled things). (*parayapay*)

marbá: (f. *rebba*) *v.* to collapse.

marbibí: *n.* puckering, sour face (*musiig*). **marmarbibi.** *v.* to be on the verge of crying.

marbík: *n.* toasted dry corn (*maribik*).

marebilís: *var.* of *marabilis*: farthing.

maredméd: **agmaredmed.** *v.* to draw back; be hesitant; refrain from doing immediately, be reluctant (*tukkiad*). **namaredmed.** *a.* reluctant; hesitant. [see *medméd*]

maregmég: *n.* debris; ruins; crumbs; small change. **maregmeg ti tisa.** chalk dust.

maréhas: (Sp. *madeja*: skein) *n.* skein. **minarehas.** *a.* in skeins.

marekmék: *n.* bubbles coming from the bottom of a glass. **agmarekmek.** *v.* to simmer, start to boil. **Pagmarekmekenna ti darak.** He is making my blood boil (getting me angry).

máreng: *n.* vocative term of address for *komare*: fellow godmother.

margáay: (f. *reggáay*) *v.* to collapse, cave in; erode, slide down.

margáha: (Sp. *margajita*: white pyrites) *n.* volcanic ash; molding sand.

margarína: (Sp. *margarina*) *n.* margarine.

margaróta: *n.* kinky hair. [Tag. *kulót*]

margíd: see *magid*.

mari-: Similarity prefix. (see *mara-*).

mariaklára: (Sp. *María Clara*) *n.* kind of folk dance; woman's dress with a skirt and a *kamisa* with long embroidered sleeves; (*coll.*) chaste woman.

mariakusép: (f. *susmariosep, coll.*) *a.* exclamative adjective used to indicate something surprising or excessive, darned, damn. **Napamariakusepak iti kinunana.** I was really surprised by what she said.

mariasantísima: (Sp. *maría santísima*) *excl.* Holy Mary!

maribambán: (f. *bambam*) **maribamban a buok.** *n.* recently sprouted hair (pubic hair, unshaved beard).

maríbat: (*obs.*) *n.* abnormal obesity.

maribík: *n.* toasted dry corn (*marbik*).

marihuána: (Sp. *marijuana*) *n.* marijuana. **agatmarihuana.** *a.* smelling of marijuana.

marikádak: *n.* sitting on the haunches (*marikadek*). **agmarikadak.** *v.* to sit on the haunches.

marikadát: *n.* preparations. **agmarikadat.** *v.* to prepare. [Tag. *handâ*]

marikadék: *var.* of *marikadak*: to sit on the heels.

marikadkád: *var.* of *marikadek*: sit on the heels.

marikíta: (Sp. *mariquita*: ladybird) *n.* ladybird.

marímba: (Sp. *marimba*) *n.* marimba, wooden xylophone.

marína: (Sp. *marina*: navy) *n.* navy.

marinéro: (Sp. *marinero*: sailor) *n.* sailor.

marinéra: (Sp. *marinero*: sailor) *n.* dress cut like that of a sailor.

maríno: (Sp. *marino*: marine) *n.* marine; seaman.

marínde: (Sp. *rendir*: surrender) *v.* to be tired, fatigued (said of the body).

marinték, maririnktét: *n.* a variety of awned late rice with light-colored hull and white kernel.

marionéta: (Sp. *marioneta*: marionette) *n.* marionette, puppet pulled by strings.

mariósep: *var.* of *mariakusép*: darned. **Mariosepka a tao!** You darned man!

maripósa: (Sp. *mariposa*: butterfly) *n.* butterfly (*kulibangbang*); large nocturnal moth; butterfly orchid; bow tie.

máris: *n.* color. **marisan.** *v.* to color. **agmarismaris.** *v.* to be many colors, be iridescent. **kamarisan.** *a.* the best of the best (in a competition). [Kpm. *kule*, Png., Tag. *kulay*]

marisabá: *var.* of *marsaba*.

márit: *n.* culling of vegetables. **imaritan.** *v.* to cull vegetables (*muri*). **pagimaritan.** *n.* discarded peelings of vegetables.

maritangtáng: *var.* of *maratangtáng*: sea anemone, sea urchin.

márka: (Sp. *marca*: brand; mark) *n.* brand; mark; sign; trademark; grade (in school). **imarka.** *v.* to put a mark on. **marka ti saludsod.** *n.* question mark. **marka ti siddaaw.** *n.* exclamation mark. **marka demonio.** (*coll.*) *n.* gin.

markadór: (Sp. *marcador*) *n.* marker, anything used for marking; morpheme.

markás: (f. *rekkas*) *v.* to become unfastened, undone; freed from a trap; to be loosened; relaxed.

markés: (Sp. *marqués*) *n.* marquis.

márko: (Sp. *marco*: frame) *n.* frame or case (for pictures, doors, windows, etc.).

marmég: **imarmeg.** *v.* to press; crush; oppress. (*talmeg, pandag*)

mármol: (Sp. *mármol*: marble) *n.* marble.

marmoleriá: (f. *marmol*) *n.* marblework; marble factory.

marmolisádo: (f. *marmol*) *a.* made of marble, marbled; *n.* artificial marble.

marná: **marmarna.** *n.* supernatural event (see *karna*); ghost; hobgoblin, fairy, elf (*aliá*).

marnáak: *v.* to mutilate; gangrene; deteriorate by disease.

marnéb: (f. *renneb*) *v.* to sink. (*arinebneb*)

marnék: (f. *rennék*) *v.* to be satisfied.

marnuáy: (f. *rennuáy*) *v.* to be plentiful, abundant, abound.

máro: *n.* bartered goods. **agmaro.** *v.* to barter. **agmarmaro.** *n.* barter trader.

maró: *n.* variety of awned rice with light-colored hull and soft kernel.

marubaáy: *n.* variety of awned rice with light-colored hull and white kernel.

marunggáy: *n.* the horseradish tree, *Moringa oleifera*. Its leaves and fruits are eaten and used in native medicine for wounds and profuse bleeding. [Png. *marunggay*, Tag. *malunggay*]

marunggí: *var.* of *marunggay* in Abra.

marungpí: *n.* variety of awned late rice with dark hull and white kernel.

marupróp: *n.* Pleiades in the Taurus constellation.

marutmót: **agmarutmot.** *v.* to gather bit by bit.

marpí: (f. *rippí*) *v.* to crack; break in two, break due to fragility.

marpíis: (f. *rippís*) *v.* to make the sound of walking on dry leaves.

marpíl: (Sp. *márfil*: ivory) *n.* ivory (*gading*); very white teeth.

marpó: (f. *reppó*) *v.* to fall down; collapse. **marpuan.** *v.* to mature (trees ready for cutting); to become dry and hard (banana leaves ready for harvesting).

marpúog: (f. *reppúog*) *v.* to cave in; collapse, crumble down.

marsáak: (f. *ressáak*) *v.* to die (said of vegetables growing out of season); wither away; disintegrate. [Tag. *lantá*]

marsabá: *n.* ripe tamarind (*marasaba*). **agmarsaba.** *v.* to ripen; to be ripe and easy to peel. [Tag. *malasebo*]

marsialló: (Eng.) *n.* martial law. **marsialluen.** *v.* to declare martial law on the citizens.

marsíng: (f. *rissíng*) **marsingan.** *v.* to be removed; taken away; separated.

Márso: (Sp. *marzo*: March) *n.* March. [Kal. *lechew*]

marsúod: (f. *risúd*) *v.* to collapse, cave in; be destroyed; demolished; run down. (houses)

martabána: *n.* a kind of large jar.

Márte: (Sp.) *n.* Mars.

Mártes: (Sp. *martes*: Tuesday) *n.* Tuesday. [Kal. *kadwa*]

martíga: *n. Albizzia saponaria* plant whose bark is used as a fish poison.

martílio: (Sp. *martillo*: hammer) *n.* hammer. **agmartilio.** *v.* to hammer. **martilio karpintero.** *n.* claw hammer. **martilio de bolo.** *n.* ball peen hammer. **minartilio.** *a.* hammered. [Kal. *mantinyu*]

martínes: (Sp. *martínes*: kingfishers) *n.* kind of black and white talking bird. [Bon. *kéleng*]

martinéte: (Sp. *martinete*: drive hammer) *n.* pile driver, drop hammer.

martír: (Sp. *mártir*: martyr) *n.* martyr; (*fig.*) a person who suffers for others. **kinamartir.** *n.* martyrdom.

martírio: (Sp. *martirio*: martyrdom) *n.* martyrdom. (*kinamartir*)

mártsa: (Sp. *marcha*: march) *n.* march; music for marching. **agmartsa.** *v.* to march.

marwáy: (f. *ruay*, also *maruay*) *a.* abundant, plentiful. [Tag. *saganà*]

mas: (Sp. *mas*: more) *adv.* more (*pay*). **masmasto.** It will increase. **mas bien.** better. **mas bale.** the more. **mas de menos.** similar, resembling. **otsenta mas.** eighty more. **mas pay.** still more. [some of the Spanish uses are becoming archaic]

mása₁: (Sp. *masa*: dough) *n.* dough; mortar. **masaen.** *v.* to knead dough.

mása₂: (Sp. *masa*: masses) *n.* masses (of people).

masáhe: (Sp. *masaje*: massage) *n.* massage. (*ilut*) **masahien.** *v.* to give a massage to. **masahe ti buok.** *n.* shampoo.

masahísta: (f. *masáhe*) *n.* masseur, masseuse, one who gives massages.

masakbáyan: (f. *sakbáy*) *n.* future.

másang: mamasang. *v.* to fail to notice. **di pagmasangan.** to be attentive; not lose sight of.

masángad: *var.* of *masngáad*: squat. [Tag. *lupasáy, tingkayád*]

masansán: (f. *sansán*) *adv.* often; frequent. [Tag. *dalás*]

masbaálan: (f. *sebbáal*) *v.* to be able to endure; put up with; hold.

masdáaw: (f. *seddáaw*) *v.* to be amazed, surprised.

masdemán: (f. *seddém*) *v.* to be weighed down; oppressed.

masdó: (f. *seddó*) *v.* to feel faint, exhausted. **Masdo ti panggepna a mangasawa.** His plan to marry is faint.

masétas: (Sp. *macetas*: houseplant) *n.* houseplant, decorative plant; cultivated flower. **agmasetas.** *v.* to tend to houseplants; cultivate ornamental plants. [Tag. *halaman*]

masetéra: (Sp. *macetera*: flowerpot) *n.* flowerpot.

masgéd: (f. *seggéd*) *v.* to burn; (*fig.*) to be intense, passionate or fervent.

masi(n)-: Prefix used with *ma-* verbs with the connotation of concomitance of the action expressed in the root, not very productive: **Masitammel dayta babai.** That girl is struck dumb.

masiádo: (Tag., Sp. *demasiado*: too much) *adv.* too much, excessive (*napalalo*).

masiáw: (Ch.) *n.* kind of gambling.

masília: (Sp. *macilla*: putty) *n.* putty; mixture of whiting and linseed oil used for fastening glass panes, etc.

masínang: *n.* variety of rice with a thin, long kernel.

masinunuó: *a.* definitely sure.

masinggán: (Eng.) *n.* machine gun.

masíta: (Sp. *maceta*: hammer) *n.* mallet, maul.

maskáad: *var.* of *masngaad*: **agmaskaad.** *v.* to squat on the hams or heels. [Tag. *lupasáy, tingkayád*]

maskád: *n.* grouper fish of the *Serranidae* family; see under *sekkad*.

maskáda: (Sp. *mascada*: chewing tobacco) *n.* chewing tobacco.

máskara: (Sp. *máscara*: mask) *n.* mask.

maskír: (f. *sikkír*) *v.* to soften; overcome.

maskúlado: (Eng.) *a.* muscular. (*baneg, puner*)

maskóta: *n.* long, wide skirt.

maslég: *a.* shy, timid (*madlég, managbabain*); lacking self-confidence. **Saan a masleg a makipulapol.** He is not timid to socialize.

maslép: (f. *sellép*) *v.* to be drenched. (*sisesellep*)

masmá: (f. *semmá*) *v.* to take the wrong road; go astray.

masná: (f. *senná*) *a.* ordinary, common, habitual, customary, natural. (*kadawyan*) **di masna.** *a.* extraordinary; uncommon; unusual; atypical; unique (*naisalsalumina*). [Tag. *daniw*]

masnaáyan: (f. *sennáay*) *v.* to mourn; grieve; be sorrowful.

masnéng: (f. *saneng*) *v.* to languish; fade or faint from the heat.

masnóp: (f. *sunnóp*) *v.* to be selected; preferred; distinguished.

masngáad: **agmasngaad.** *v.* to squat. (*marikadek, lupisak*) **nakamasngaad.** *a.* squatting. [Tag. *lupasáy, tingkayád*]

máso: (Sp. *mazo*: mallet) *n.* mallet; sledge hammer. **masuen.** *v.* to hit with a mallet or sledgehammer.

masón: (Sp.) *n.* freemason; cement maker.

masonería: (Sp. *masonería*) *n.* freemasonry. **masóniko.** *a.* masonic.

masurka: (Sp. *mazurca*) *n.* mazurka, kind of folk dance.

maspák: (f. *sep-ak*) *v.* to break into two, producing a cracking sound (branches, etc.)

maspéd: (*obs.*) (f. *seppéd*) *v.* to decay (plants). (*laylay; lungsot*)

maspét: (f. *seppét*) *v.* to be choked, obstructed, clogged.

maspíg: (f. *sippíg*) *v.* to split (boards), crack. **Masmaspig ti isemna.** He broke into a smile.

maspók: (f. *sippok*) *n.* a white freshwater fish with tasty meat; *v.* to be torn off (branches).

massáyag: *var.* of *mansayag*: lying in state (said of the body of the deceased at a wake).

máta: **matamata.** *n.* a kind of marine fish; full-grown anchovy.

matá: *n.* eye; knot (of timber). (*duguldugul; bugkal*) **agmata.** *v.* to be watchful, alert; open one's eyes; bear fruit; result in, be the result of; be realized. **agimata.** *v.* to keep an eye on, watch; bear fruit; cut knots on wood or bamboo. **kamata.** *n.* sore eye; eye infection. **agkamata.** *v.* to have sore eyes. **agkamatmata.** *v.* to have the same eye features. **matamataan.** *v.* to stare at. **mataán.** *a.* large-eyed; variety of large-eyed fish. **mataen.** *v.* to observe keenly; belittle; despise. **mangmatamata.** *v.* to gaze at, stare at; look around surreptitiously. **minata.** *a.* open-worked (woven bamboo); *n.* open-worked basket. **namataan.** *n.* traditions, customs in which one is brought up. **nagmataan.** *n.* where one is born (*lit:* where one opened his eyes). **pamata.** *n.* spectacles. **pagimataan.** *n.* cut knots of wood, bamboo, etc. **simamata.** *a.* with

the eyes open wide, wide-eyed. **Kasla agpakpakaasi dagiti matana.** He seems to be looking for pity (his eyes seem pitiful). **Bulsekka a simamata.** You are blind even with your eyes open. **Agingga ita, di pay nagmata daydi a kari.** Until now that promise has yet to be realized. [Ibg., Ivt., Kpm., Png., Tag. *matá*, Kal. *ata*]

mataán: (f. *matá*) *n.* club mackerel fish, *Rastrelliger chrysozonus*.

matadéro: (Sp. *matadero*: butcher) *n.* butcher; slaughterhouse.

matadór: (Sp. *matador*: bullfighter) *n.* bullfighter.

matagi-: Nonproductive prefix used for forming unintentional or potentive verbs with *tagi*-stems: **matagikua.** to own. **mataginayon.** to last forever.

matánsa: (Sp. *matanza*: massacre) *n.* permit to slaughter.

matapóbre: (Sp. *mata* + *pobre*: kill poor) *n.* person who discriminates or belittles the poor; snooty person.

matár: (Sp. *matar*: kill) **mataren.** *v.* term used in card playing.

matáy: (f. *patay*) *v.* to die. **minatay.** *n.* the dead. **agpakamatay.** *v.* to commit suicide (*patayen ti bagi*). **minatayan.** *v.* funeral. [Ibg. *matay*, Ivt. *madiman*, Kal. *latoy*, Knk. *matéy*, Kpm. *mate*, Png. *onpatey*, Tag. *mamatáy*]

matbág: (f. *tebbág*) *v.* to crumble down, collapse, cave-in; fall in; erode (soil); **natbag a timek.** *a.* resonant voice, ringing voice.

matdá: (f. *tiddá*) *v.* to be remaining, left. (*mabati*)

máte: (Sp.) *n.* checkmate (in chess).

materiáles: (Sp. *materiales*: materials) *n.* materials.

matgéd: (f. *tegged*) *v.* to earn, work for wages. **matgedan.** *n.* wages, salary; income.

máti: **mangmatimati.** *v.* to struggle for breath when dying; to flicker (said of the fire, candle); to appear fleetingly in the distance.

matiádok: *a.* lazy; idle. (*sadut; kuliwengweng; ballog*) **agmatiadok.** *v.* to idle; waste time; hang around doing nothing. [Tag. *bulakból*]

matiág: **agmatiag.** *v.* to alter suddenly; awake aghast. [Tag. *balikwás*]

mátik: (*obs.*) *n.* moneybag girdle.

mátis: (Sp. *matiz*) *a.* many colored, variegated. **maimatis.** *v.* to be variegated. **Adda diperensia ti baram no maimatis ti dara iti tupram.** There is a problem in your lungs if the blood in your spit is variegated.

matisádo: (Sp. *matizado*: variegated) *a.* variegated.

mátit: *a*. slightly crazy. (*bagtit*) **Adda matmatitna.** *exp*. He has some screws loose, is slightly crazy. [Tag. *balíw*]

matitiléng: **matitileng payen.** Even.

matkád: *n*. grouper fish of the *Serranidae* family.

matláng: (f. *tellang*) *v*. to be caught in adultery.

matmát: *n*. stare; gaze. **matmatan.** *v*. to fix the eyes upon, stare; heed, observe. (*mingming, muttaleng*) **ipamatmat.** *v*. to show, display. **Minatmatanna dagiti padana a mangngalap iti asidegna.** He stared at his fellow fishermen near him. **Pangaasiyo ta ikkandak iti gundaway a mangipamatmat a talaga a nagbalbaliwakon.** Please give me the chance to show that I have truly changed. [Png. *linggis*, Tag. *titig*]

matmíng: (f. *timmíng*) *v*. to decay; rot through moisture.

matnág: (f. *tinnag*) *v*. to fall down.

matnéb: (f. *táneb*) *v*. to be partly covered with water.

matngél: (f. *tengngel*) *v*. to be controlled; restrained; repressed.

matón: *a*. brave, tough; *n*. bully. **agmaton.** *v*. to rule. **maimaton.** *v*. to notice; see; perceive.

matúon: **agmatuon.** *n*. noon, midday. [Ibg. *tengnga na aggaw*, Itg. *matuun*, Ivt. *máraw*, Kal. *mamatok*, Knk. *bengdá*, Kpm. *ugtungaldo*, Png. *ogtó*, Tag. *tanghalì*]

matpáng: (f. *teppáng*) *v*. to tumble down; collapse.

matráka: (Sp. *matraca*: rattle) *n*. wooden rattle used during holy week.

matréro: (Sp. *matrero*: tramp; sly person) *n*. meddler. (*biang*)

matríkula: (Sp. *matrícula*: tuition) *n*. tuition; registration for school. **agmatrikula.** *v*. to pay tuition.

matrimónio: (Sp. *matrimonio*: matrimony) *n*. marriage, matrimony.

matrís: (Sp. *matriz*: womb) *n*. womb. (*aanakan*)

matrogáda: (Sp. *madrugada*: dawn) *n*. species of cultivated flower.

matróna: (Eng.) *n*. matured married woman.

matsakaw: (Sp. *machacado*: crushed) *n*. pieces of bread toasted crisp.

matséte: (Sp. *machete*) *n*. saber worn by policemen during the Spanish regime.

matsúgi: (Pil., *slang*) *a*. finished off, ended; killed.

matsúrra: (Sp. *machorra*: barren female) *a*. full bodied (women, especially after bearing children); no longer fertile (female animals).

mattiádok: *var*. spelling of *matiadok*: **agmattiadok.** *v*. to be idle, lazy. (*sadut*)

mattídek: **agmattidek.** *v*. to stand up straight with the head held high.

mattíder: *n*. standing in an idle and relaxed manner. **agmattider.** *v*. to stand. (*takder*) **nakamattider.** *a*. standing in a relaxed manner. **Nagmattider iti balkonahe a makipinnereng iti lawag ti apagsingising nga init.** He stood on the balcony looking at the light of the rising sun. [Tag. *tayô* (stand)]

mattít: *a*. crazy, insane. (*bagtít*) **agmattit.** *v*. to go mad, become crazy. **matmattit.** *n*. lunatic tendency.

mattukóng: *n*. hat made of leaves. (*kattukóng*)

mawmáw: **agmawmaw.** *v*. to fade; abate; decrease; lose value. (*bawbáw*) **Nain-inut a nagmawmaw ti bileg ti tagiruotna.** The power of the potion gradually decreased.

may-: *var*. of *mai-* prefix before vowels.

máya: **mayamaya.** *n*. common red marine fish, *Lutianus sp*. snapper fish.

mayá: **agmaya.** *v*. to be in heat (sexually, said of female animals). (*kalkál*) **mayaan.** *v*. to copulate. **mangmaya.** *n*. boar (pig). [Bon. *onol*, Kpm. *landíq*, Png. *maya*, Tag. *kandî*]

mayáman: (Tag.) *a*. rich. (*baknang*)

mayámay: **agmayamay.** *v*. to slow down; abate, calm. **namayamay.** *a*. calm, peaceful, placid; withdrawn; shy. [Tag. *tahimik*]

mayána: *n*. a kind of shrub with reddish leaves used in medicine.

mayápis: *n*. *Shorea palosapis* tree.

mayát: *v*. to be willing; to want, desire. This verb, unlike *kayát*, is intransitive and takes series pronominal enclitics -*ak* forms. **agmayat.** *v*. to be willing; to consent; to agree. [Tag. *gustó* (want, Sp.); *payag* (agree)]

mayegmég: *n*. fever. (*gurigor*) **agmayegmeg.** *v*. to shake from a fever. [Tag. *lagnát*]

mayekmék: *n*. fine, powdery, or pulverized substance. **namayekmek.** *a*. finely powdered, pulverized. **mayekmekan.** *v*. to pulverize.

mayéng: *n*. perplexity; stunned condition. **agmayeng.** *v*. to be indifferent; apathetic; sluggish; hesitant; to be in suspense; stare at in an enraptured state. **maimayeng.** *a*. frustrated, bothered; perplexed. **Immapiring ni Joker ket inappupona ti kanawan nga ima ti maimaymayeng a balasang.** Joker approached the perplexed girl and held out his right hand.

mayengméng: **namayengmeng.** *a*. safe, secure; comfortable; protected; snug; cozy.

Máyo: (Sp. *mayo*: May) *n*. May. [Kal. *achawoy*]

mayó₁: *n*. a large marine fish.

mayó₂: **mamayo.** *n*. indisposition, weakness of the body. (*laladut*) **agmamayo.** *v*. to experience weakness of the body (with no apparent reason).

mayonésa: (Sp. *mayonesa*) *n.* mayonnaise.

mayór: (Sp. *mayor*: mayor) *n.* mayor; *a.* main (used in Spanish expressions). **altar mayor.** main altar. **misa mayor.** high mass. **mayor de edad.** person of age, no longer a minor.

mayóra: (Sp.) *n.* female mayor; wife of a mayor.

mayordómo: (Sp. *mayordomo*: steward) *n.* steward; second officer in a confraternity.

mayoría: (Sp. *mayoría*: majority) *n.* majority.

mayoridád: (Sp. *mayoridad*: majority) *n.* majority. (*kaaduán*)

máyot: mamayot. *n.* fatigue, lack of strength; languor (*muyót, mayó*). **agmamayot.** *v.* to feel sluggish, weak, with no strength; to be flabby. **pagmamayutan.** *v.* to weaken, cause to lose strength, exhaust.

maysá: 1. *num.* one. With certain prefixes, *maysa* shortens to *-ysa* or *-sa*: **saggaysa.** one each. **maminsan.** once; 2. *art.* a, an; *conj.* besides. **maysa pay.** one more; besides, moreover; furthermore. **makamaysa.** *v.* to be able to do in a certain span of time. **makaysa.** *v.* to stay one day. **santo maysa.** besides, in addition to; furthermore. **maysa unay.** especially. **kaniak a maysa.** I think, in my opinion. **maikamaysa.** *a.* first grade; number one. **agkaykaysa.** *v.* to unite; combine; do together. **panagkaykaysa.** *n.* unity; solidarity. **makikaykaysa.** *v.* to be in harmony; agree. **pagkaykaysaen.** *v.* to unite, put together. **pagkaykaysaan.** *v.* to do unanimously; agree to a common cause or action. **sangsangkamaysa.** *a.* united; joined. **ikaysa.** *v.* to unite with. **agmaymaysa.** *v.* to be alone, solitary. **maymaysa.** *a.* alone; only one. **ipamaysa.** *v.* to do sincerely; concentrate, focus on; devote oneself to. **agkaykaysa.** *v.* to unite, combine; agree. **tunggal maysa.** every one, each one. **maysa laeng.** only one. **maysa unay.** especially. **kaniak a maysa.** *exp.* in my opinion. **saggaysa.** *a.* one each. **saggaysaen.** *v.* to do one by one. **pagsasaggaysaen.** *v.* to give one each to. **managsaggaysa.** *a.* once in a while, intermittent; very slow. **nakaysa a biag.** *n.* life beyond. **maysaan.** *v.* to deceive someone; take advantage of someone. **mamaysaan.** *v.* to be able to deceive someone. **Pagsasaggaysáanyo.** Take one each. **kallaysa.** *n.* marriage. **agkallaysa.** *v.* to marry. **panagkallaysa.** *n.* wedding. **kallaysaen.** *v.* to solemnize a marriage. **mangallaysa.** *v.* to officiate at a wedding, wed two people. **makikallaysa.** *v.* to get married (said of women). **ikallaysa.** *v.* to marry (said of men), take as a wife.

(i)paikallaysa. *v.* to marry off one's daughter. **pangikallaysaen.** *v.* to marry off one's son. **maysa ken maysa.** everyone, each one. **maysa-maysa.** one by one; everyone, each one. **maysanmaysa.** one by one; one another; each one. **maminsan.** *adv.* once. **no maminsan.** once in a while, occasionally. **sagpaminsan.** *adv.* occasionally, once in a while, not too often. **sagpaminsanen.** *v.* to do once in a while. **agpinsan.** *v.* to be unanimous; do all at the same time. **ipaminsan.** *v.* to do all at once; do completely. **napinsan.** *a.* covered (with), full (of). **Kasla mabutengka ita iti kinamaymaysam.** It seems you are now afraid of being alone. **Data a talaga ti para iti maysanmaysa, awan duadua.** We are really for one another, there is no doubt. [There are various pronunciations of words with the stem *kaysá*, e.g., *pagkaykaysaen* will be pronounced as *pagkaykaysáen* by speakers who consider *maysá* to be the root as the stress will not shift after a closed syllable, while speakers who still maintain *isá* as the root will pronounce it *pagkaykaysaén*. Bon. *esa*, Png. *sakéy*, Kal., Tag. *isá*]

mayyáng: (*coll.*) *n.* girl.

mayyét: namayyet. *a.* slow, sluggish (*buntog*); inert, listless; languid. **agmayyemayyet.** *v.* to be sluggish. [Tag. *kupad*]

medália: (Sp. *medalla*: medal) *n.* medal. **mamedaliaan.** *v.* to be awarded a medal.

medalión: (Sp. *medallón*: medallion) *n.* medallion, large medal.

média: (Sp. *media*: half) *n.* one-half. (*kagudua*) **medianoche.** *n.* midnight; midnight mass. **pagmediaan.** *n.* square container for liquor or other liquids. **media-media.** *a.* half-half, fifty percent. **media botelia.** half a bottle. **media dia.** half-day.

mediágua: (Sp. *media*: half + *agua*: water) *n.* lean-to roof above a window; eaves; lower projecting edge of a roof.

mediabuélta: (Sp. *media vuelta*) *n.* half-turn (in military).

mediakuérpo: (Sp. *media*: half + *cuerpo*: body) *n.* half-length picture.

medialúna: (Sp. *media luna*) *n.* half-moon.

mediáno: (Sp.) *a.* medium sized; *n.* mean.

médias: (Sp. *media*: stocking) *n.* stockings; socks. **agmedias.** *v.* to wear socks. **mediasan.** *v.* to put socks on someone. **nakamedias.** *a.* with socks on.

medída: (Sp. *medida*: measurement) *n.* tape measure; measure.

medikílio: (Sp. *mediquillo*: quack) *n.* herbalist; herb doctor; quack doctor. (*erbulario*)

médiko: (Sp. *médico*: doctor) *n.* doctor (*mang-ngagas*); surgeon (*siruhano*). [Tag. *mang-gagamót*]

médio: (Sp. *medio*: half) *a.* somewhat, more or less; rather. **medio natayag.** somewhat tall. **por medio.** by means of.

medioáguas: (Sp. *medio*: half + *agua*: water) *n.* two-cornered roof on top with two slopes.

mediokuérpo: *var.* of *mediakuerpo*: half-length picture.

medisína: (Sp. *medicina*: medicine) *n.* medicine (*agas*). [Tag. *gamót*]

medméd: **medmedan.** *v.* to loosen, slacken; restrain, repress (anger, coughing, etc.); control; hold back. **namedmed.** *a.* saving, frugal; serious; earnest; sober; moderate, temperate; controlled. **Anian a nagsam-it ti namedmedmedan nga isemna!** What a sweet, repressed smile! **Medmedmedan ti ubing ti panagsangitana.** The child is holding back his crying. [Tag. *pigil*]

méek: *n.* the sound of a goat. (*mekmek*)

megmég: **imegmeg.** *v.* to press down hard (*gusúgus, mámeg*); oppress; overwhelm. **naimegmeg.** *v.* to be overwhelmed; oppressed; overburdened.

Méhiko: *n.* Mexico. **Mehikano.** *n.* & *a.* Mexican.

mehóras: (Sp. *mejoras*: improvements) *n.* improvements made on property.

mekániko: (Sp. *mecánico*: mechanic) *n.* mechanic.

mekanísmo: (Sp. *mecanismo*: mechanism) *n.* mechanism.

mekmék: *n.* sound of a goat. (*meek*) **mekmeken.** *v.* to pulverize; grind. **marekmek.** *n.* fine, powdery particles.

melásma: (Eng.) *n.* melasma, skin disorder characterized by a spotted rash of imperfect pigmentation.

melína: *n.* paper tree (*esmelina*).

mellét: *n.* large marine shell; variety of rice; earthen lamp using oil or wax.

melmél: *a.* having a full mouth; stupid; unable to speak because of a full mouth; *n.* poisonous, striped snake; variety of corn; variety of late rice with light-colored hull and white kernel. **agmelmel.** *v.* to eat greedily in large mouthfuls. **imelmel.** *v.* to cram the mouth with. (*mamel, pelpel*) **mamelmelan.** *v.* to be stuffed. **simemelmel.** *a.* stuffed (mouth).

melokotón: (Sp. *melocotón*: peach) *n.* peach.

memmém: *a.* stupid; foolish. **Nasaysayaat pay a dumakkelka a memmem ngem ti agbiagka iti lubong dagiti managinkukuna.** It is better

to grow up stupid than to live in a world of pretenders.

memória: (Sp. *memoria*: memory) *n.* memory. (*lagip*) **agmemoria.** *v.* to memorize. **imemoria.** *v.* to commit to memory, memorize something.

menmén: **namenmen.** *a.* slow, lingering; loitering (*ginad*). [Tag. *bagál*]

menná: **agmennamenna.** *v.* to be doubtful; undecided. [Tag. *alinlangan*]

menudénsia: (Sp. *menudencia*: giblets) *n.* dish consisting of entrails (*menudo*).

menúdo: (Sp. *por menudo*: in detail, retail; *menudo*: entrails dish) *n.* retail; entrails of an animal; dish consisting of cubes of pork and liver cooked with potato cubes, tomatoes, and spices.

menór: (Sp. *menor*: minor) *n.* minor. **agmenor.** *v.* to slow down; go into low gear. **menor de edad.** *n.* minor (in age).

menoriá: (Sp. *minoría*: minority) *n.* minority.

menós: (Sp. *menos*: less) **agmenos, menosen.** *v.* to lessen; underestimate (the ability). **makamenos.** *v.* to be able to lessen (expenditures).

mensáhe: (Sp. *mensaje*: message) *n.* message (*pablaak*). [Tag. *pasabi*]

mensahéro: (Sp. *mensajero*: messenger) *n.* messenger. (*agipadpadamag*)

mensuál: (Sp. *mensual*: monthly) *a.* monthly. (*binulan*)

ménta: (Sp. *menta*: mint) *n.* mint, peppermint.

mentí: (Sp. *mente*: mind) **mentien.** *v.* to say clearly.

mentís: *var.* of *mintis*: malfunction.

mentól: (Sp. *mentol*: menthol) *n.* menthol.

meriénda: (Sp. *merienda*: snack) *n.* snack between lunch and dinner. **agmerienda.** *v.* to snack between lunch and dinner. **Inawisnak nga agmerienda idiay balayna.** He invited me to have an afternoon snack at his house.

meríno: (Sp.) *n.* fine soft fabric resembling cashmere.

mérito: (Sp. *mérito*: merit) *n.* merit. (*kaikarian*)

merkádo: (Sp. *mercado*) *n.* market. (*paglakuan*) **merkado ti lubong.** *n.* world market. **supermerkado.** *n.* supermarket.

merkánsia: (Sp. *mercancia*: merchandise) *n.* merchandise, goods; freight.

merkúrio: (Sp. *mercurio*: mercury) *n.* mercury, quick silver. (*asóge*)

mermér: *n.* particle that gets into the eye. **namermeran.** *v.* to have a mote in the eye. **mermeran.** *v.* to throw something in the eyes of.

merráad: (f. *merrád*) *n.* sharp stare, gawk.

merrád: *n.* stare, gawk. **merradan.** *v.* to stare at. [Tag. *titig, dilat*]

merrét: *n.* anus. (*kimmót*; *muríit*; *kirrét*; *tatakkián*) **merretmo**. (*vulg.*) your ass. [Knk. *kimút*, Tag. *puwít*]

mersenário: (Sp. *mercenario*: mercenary) *n.* mercenary, hired assassin.

mesáda: (Sp. *mesada*: monthly wages) *n.* fee paid for a game.

mesías: (Sp. *mesías*) *n.* messiah.

mesíta: (Sp.) *n.* small table.

mesmés: *n.* grip; grasp; clutch; clench. **mesmesan.** *v.* to grasp, seize tightly, clutch, clasp; raise a fist at. **mangmesmes.** *v.* to make a fist in anger (*gemgem*, *iggam*). **Agmesmesmes iti pinagdugsudugsol iti bakrangna.** He is clenching his fists because of the stabbing pain at his side.

messék: namsek. *a.* fully developed (breasts, ears of corn, muscles), fully grown. (*bursók*, *benték*)

mestísa: (Sp. *mestiza*: female half-breed) *n.* female half-breed, of two races. **mestisa Pransesa.** *n.* kind of women's dress.

mestisília: (Sp. *mesticilla*) *n.* little female *mestisa*, can be used endearingly or pejoratively.

mestíso: (Sp. *mestizo*: male half-breed) *n.* male half-breed; hybrid; *a.* of two races; of native-born parentage.

met: *part.* also; though (particle used to show mild disapproval); besides; too. **Napan met ni Florence.** Florence also went. **unay metten.** expression that indicates surprise. **met laeng.** Nevertheless, though; after all. **Isu met laeng.** It's the same; That's why. **Adda met la tay pitakak.** My wallet was there after all. [See also *metten*. Bon. *ages*, Knk. *abé*, Png. *met*, Tag. *namán*]

metabolísmo: (Sp.) *n.* metabolism.

metér: (Sp. *meter*: put, meddle) **agmeter.** *v.* to meddle.

metmét: nametmet. *a.* avaricious, greedy (*ímut*); prudent, cautious; thrifty, frugal. **metmetan.** *v.* to hold tightly to (*iggám*).

método: (Sp. *método*: method) *n.* method. (*wagas*)

métro: (Sp. *metro*: meter) *n.* meter. **sangametro.** *n.* one meter. [Kal. *mitlu*]

métsa: *var.* of *mitsa*: wick; fuse.

metsádo: (Sp. *mechado*: stuffed) *n.* dish consisting of diced meat with garlic, onion, tomatoes, and potatoes.

metséro: (Sp. *mechero*: lighter, lamp burner) *n.* tube for a wick; carbide lamp burner.

mettén: Particle [*met* + *-en*] also; so (I see contrary to what I expected). **Nasingpet metten.** So he is well behaved (I expected

otherwise). **Ania metten.** *exp.* expresses disgust on the part of the speaker.

-mi: pronominal enclitic. First person plural exclusive in the ergative case (*-ko* series form): **Kayatmi dayta.** We (not you) want that. **balaymi.** our house (not yours). [Changes to *da* before the enclitics *ka* and *kayo*: *kayatdaka.* We want you. Png. *mi*, Tag. *namin*]

miatinís: *n.* Christmas ritual depicting Virgin Mary and Joseph asking for a room from house to house.

míding: miding, kinamiding, kinanamiding. *n.* small mole.

midíng: *n.* native wine made from coconut or sugarcane.

miémbro: (Sp. *miembro*: member) *n.* member. (*kameng*) **makimiembro.** *v.* to become a member.

miéntras: (Sp. *mientas*: while) *adv.* while (*kabayatan*); as long as; in case. **mientras tanto.** (*obs.*) if. (*no*)

Miérkoles: (Sp. *miércoles*: Wednesday) *n.* Wednesday. **Mierkoles de senisa.** Ash Wednesday. **minierkoles.** every Wednesday. [Kal. *katlu*]

mího: (Sp. *mijo*: millet) *n.* millet.

míka: (Sp. *mica*) *n.* mica.

míki: (Hok. *mi kî*: noodle + classifier) *n.* noodle (boiled, usually of wheat).

míkis: mikis-mikis. *n.* hocus-pocus.

mikítos: mikmikitos. *n.* hocus-pocus, made up words. (*mikismikis*)

mikkí: namikki. *a.* fastidious, finicky; prude, squeamish. **kinamikki.** *n.* fastidiousness; squeamishness; modesty; prudishness. **agmikkimikki.** *v.* to be fastidious; to be prudish; to walk sexily (*kinnikinni*). **Awan baimbain wenno mikkimikki ditoy, diretsaan.** There's no shyness or squeamishness here, go straight to the point. [Tag. *selang*]

mikmík: *n.* sound of a goat; goat (*kalding*).

míkol: *n.* five-centavo coin. **sagmimikol.** five centavos each.

mikróbio: (Sp. *microbio*: microbe) *n.* microbe, germ; virus.

mikrokósmo: (Sp. *microcosmo*) *n.* microcosm, miniature world.

mikrópono: (Sp. *micrófono*: microphone) *n.* microphone.

mikroskópio: (Sp. *microscopio*: microscope) *n.* microscope.

mil: (Sp. *mil*: thousand) *n.* one thousand (*ribo*). **dos mil.** two thousand.

milágro: (Sp. *milagro*: miracle) *n.* miracle. **agmilagro.** *v.* to perform a miracle.

milagrósa: (Sp. *milagrosa*: miraculous) *a.* miraculous; *n.* a high-yielding variety of rice.

milagróso: (Sp. *milagroso*: miraculous) *a.* miraculous.

milámil: *var.* of *malamal*: smeared or splattered (with dirt, food, etc.).

milát: *n.* dirty spot on face. (*pilkát*) **mamilatan.** *v.* to be stained, dirtied, soiled. **milatmilat.** *a.* dirty, grimy, soiled.

mília: (Sp. *milla*: mile) *n.* mile. **milia kuadrada.** square mile.

miliáhe: (Sp. *millaje*: mileage) *n.* mileage; milepost.

milión: (Sp. *millón*: million) *n.* million (*riwriw*). **milionario.** *n.* millionaire.

milísia: (Sp. *milicia*: militia) *n.* militia; military; science of war.

militár: (Sp.) *n.* military man.

milmíl: milmilan. *a.* mouth-stained with food or grease. **agmilmil.** *v.* to have a dirty mouth, mouth stains.

milplóres: (Sp. *mil* + *flores*: thousand flowers) *n.* Hydrangea plant. [Knk. *sugusug*]

mímis: *n.* young shoot of cogon grass; variety of rice. **mimisan.** *n.* a hardwood tree.

mína: (Sp. *mina*: mine) *n.* mine; mineral deposit.

minánga: *n.* mouth of the river at the ocean. (*sabangan*)

minár: (Sp. *minar*: mine) **agminar.** *v.* to be clearly evident; visible (*latak*). **Nagminar ti saway a kallidna iti yiisemna.** Her unique dimple was clearly visible from her smile.

mínas: (Sp. *mina*: mine) *n.* mine. **agminas.** *v.* to mine. **minasen.** *v.* to mine; dig for mines. **pagminasan.** *n.* mine; place of the mine.

minatá: (f. *matá*) *n.* open-worked bamboo basket.

minatáy: (f. *matáy*) *n.* corpse. **agminatay, makiminatay.** *v.* to watch over the dead.

mináy: agminayminay. *v.* to shake (said of the fat of obese people.)

mindóro: *n.* variety of *diket* rice.

minérba: (Sp. *minerva*) *n.* hand press. **minerbista.** *n.* operator of a hand press.

minéro: (Sp. *minero*: miner) *n.* miner.

míni: (Eng. many) **minimini.** *n.* rites, ceremonies, series of events; fuss, ado; (*coll.*) sexual act. **No nalpasen ti minimini, agkedked pay laeng.** When everything is done, will she still decline?

miniatúra: (Sp. *miniatura*: miniature) *n.* miniature.

ministério: (Sp. *ministerio*: ministry) *n.* ministry, cabinet in government.

minístro: (Sp. *ministro*: minister) *n.* minister; member of the cabinet.

minnaminná: *a.* doubting (*duadua*). [Tag. *alinlangan*]

minnóng: *n.* hat. (*kallugong*) **nakaminnong.** *a.* wearing a hat.

minór: (Sp. *menor*: minor; low) *n.* low gear; minor key in music. **agminor.** *v.* to shift to low gear. **minor de edad.** minor, underage person.

minoría: (Sp. *minoría*: minority) *n.* minority.

minoridád: (Sp. *minoridad*) *n.* minority.

mínus: (Sp. *menos*: less) *a.* lower; lacking to. **por lo minus.** at least. **maiminus.** *v.* to be deducted. **minusen.** *v.* to belittle, degrade; undervalue, underrate.

minúta: (Sp. *minuta*: memo, roll, list) *n.* list of church fees; book of accounts.

Minotauro: (Sp. *minotauro*) *n.* Minotaur, a mythological monster with the head of a bull and the body of a man.

minutéro: (Sp. *minutero*: minute hand) *n.* minute hand in a clock.

minúto: (Sp. *minuto*: minute) *n.* minute. **minutero.** *n.* minute hand.

minsán: maminsan. *adv.* once. **sagpaminsan.** *adv.* occasionally; once in a while (*no maminsan*). **ipaminsan, paminsanen.** *v.* to do all at once. **mamimpinsan.** once and for all, only once. **idi naminsan.** *adv.* the last time. **sangsangkaminsan.** *adv.* all at once without exception. **agpinsan.** *v.* to act as one; do all as one, be unanimous; go all in one direction. **napinsan.** full (of), covered (with). **pinsanen.** *v.* to do all at once. [Png., Tag. *minsan*]

mintakél: namintakel. *a.* hard (luck, heart, etc.).

mintálon: *n.* farmer (*mannalon*). [Tag. *magsasaká*]

mintís: (Sp. *mentís*: denial) *a.* false; not true; not to the point; error. **agmintis.** *v.* to miss; fail to explain; to be a dud (fail to explode); be incorrect, erroneous. [Tag. *mintis*]

minggá: mamingga. *v.* to stop; end. (*patingga*)

mingmíng: *a.* clairvoyant; psychic. **mingmingan.** *v.* to examine closely, scrutinize (*biling*); stare at (*matmát*); contemplate. [Tag. *masdán*]

mío: (Sp. *mío*: mine) **Diós mio!** My God!

míra₁: (Sp. *mirar*: look) **miraen.** *v.* to stare; gaze at (*matmat, mingming*). [Tag. *masdán, titig*]

míra₂: (Sp. *mirra*: myrrh) *n.* myrrh.

mirabilís: *var.* of *marabilis*: farthing.

mírag: pagmiragan. *v.* to pay attention to; notice. (*kaskaso*)

miráot: namiraot. *a.* tormented, tortured; living in hunger and misery. (*kuranges*) **agmiraot.** *v.* to be tormented. **Ania ti maganabko iti maysa a mamirmiraot a mangngalap?** What do I have to gain from a miserable fisherman?

mirasól: (Sp. *mirasol*: sunflower) *n.* sunflower. [Bon. *náwel, ag-ágob*]

miráy: **agimmimiray**. (*obs.*) *v*. to recover (from shock or unconsciousness).

mirdungét: *n*. frown; stern look. (*rupanget*)

mirdúot: *n*. sorrow; pout. **agmirduot**. *v*. to be sad, sorrowful; pout, look sullen. **nakamirduot**. *a*. sad; sorrowful; grieving (*rupanget*). **Nagimmimirduot ni Mayang**. Mayang pretended to be sad.

mirgád: *var*. of *magid*.

mirímir: *n*. edge, boundary. **mirimiran**. *v*. to begin something at the edge.

mirkát: *n*. mote in the eyes (*múkat*). [Png. *mukát*, Tag. *mutà*]

mirmír: *n*. dirt. (*pirpir*) **mirmiran**. *v*. to wipe off dirt. **kamirmirmir**. *a*. very dirty.

mirugróg: *n*. sour face. **nakamirugrog**. *a*. with a sour face.

mirón: (Sp. *mirón*: onlooker) *n*. onlooker; spectator; meddler; snoop. **namiron**. *a*. shameless; undisciplined; unrefined; meddling; snooping.

mísa: (Sp. *misa*: mass) *n*. mass (in church). **pamisa**. *n*. mass for the dead; death anniversary rites. **agpamisa**. *v*. to have mass (for the dead). **makimisa**. *v*. to attend mass. **agmisa**. *v*. to celebrate mass. **misa de gallo**. *n*. Christmas Eve mass. **misa resada**. *n*. low mass. **mannakimisa**. *n*. one who often attends mass.

misál: (Sp. *misal*) *n*. missal, mass book.

miserikórdia: (Sp. *misericordia*: pity) *n*. mercy, pity. (*asi*)

miskél: (f. *piskél*) **namiskel**. *a*. pulled (muscle); sprained.

misión: *n*. mission. **misionero, misionario**. *n*. missionary.

mismís: **namismis**. *a*. not eating due to lack of appetite; sparing in one's diet.

mísmo: (Sp. *mismo*: same) *a*. for sure; same; adverb that stresses the identity: very self: **siak a mismo**. I myself. **ti mismo a lakayna**. her very husband. **ora mismo**. right now. **kaaldawan mismo**. the very day.

mísua: (Hok. *mi suã*: noodle thread) *n*. kind of thin noodle.

misugsóg: *n*. sorrow. (*misuot, mirduot*). **agmisugsog**. *v*. to pout; brood; frown. **nakamisugsog**. *a*. frowning; pouting; brooding.

misúot: *n*. sorrow; pout. **agmisuot**. *v*. to show displeasure; pout. **misuotan**. *v*. to frown on (*murareg; rupanget; rungbed*). [Tag. *simangot*]

mistério: (Sp. *misterio*: mystery) *n*. mystery. (*palimed*) **misterioso**. *a*. mysterious.

místiko: (Sp. *místico*: mystic) *n*. mystic.

mistisísmo: (Sp. *misticismo*: mysticism) *n*. mysticism.

mitád: (Sp. *mitad*: half) *n*. one-half (*guddua*). **agmitad**. *v*. to divide in half; share equally.

mitímit: *a*. finicky, fastidious (*kúsim*); delicate.

mitír: (Sp. *meter*: put; insert) **agmitir, makimitmitir**. *v*. to meddle in someone else's affairs; interfere. (*makibiang*)

mitmít: see *kiddit*: with low yield.

míto: (Sp. *mito*: myth) *n*. myth.

mitolohía: (Sp. *mitología*) *n*. mythology.

mítra: (Sp. *mitra*: miter) *n*. diocese; miter.

mítsa: (Sp. *mecha*: spark) *n*. spark; dynamite wick; fuse. **mitsa ti riri**. *n*. the spark (trigger) of a fight or argument.

mitséro: (Sp. *mechero*: sparker, cigarette lighter) *n*. burner of a stove; tube for a wick; carbide lamp burner.

-mo: 1. possessive enclitic. Second person informal, singular genitive, attaching directly to noun roots. Its variant is *-m* after vowels and the suffixes *-an* and *-en*: **ti nuang*mo***. your water buffalo '**ta rupa*m*!** your face! (Shows displeasure.) '**diay kaanaka*m***. that niece of yours. 2. ergative (=*ko* series) pronoun indicating a second person actor of a transitive verb: **Lukta*m* man ti tawa**. Please open the window. **Basae*m* ti kayat*mo***. Read what you like. **Inaramid*mo* dayta?** You did that? [Changes to *na* before other fused enclitics: *Nakitanak?* Did you see me? Png. *–m, mo*, Tag. *mo*]

muák: *n*. antlerless deer. **namuak**. *a*. without antlers (deer).

mobilisár: (Sp. *movilizar*) **imobilisar**. *v*. to mobilize (an army).

móda: (Sp. *moda*: fashion) *n*. fashion, latest style. **de moda**. *a*. in fashion; of the latest style.

mudáag: **masimudaag**. *v*. to perceive clearly, discern. **ipasimudaag**. *v*. to show; display; make known; announce. **nasimudaag**. *a*. discerning; perceptive. [Tag. *hayag*]

múdel: **namudel**. *a*. dull, blunt. (*ngudel*) **paudelen**. *v*. to make blunt. [Tag. *puról*]

modélo: (Sp. *modelo*: model) *n*. model. (*pagtuladan; pagarigan; pagwadan*)

modérno: (Sp. *moderno*: modern) *a*. modern. (*rang-ay*)

múdia: (*obs.*) *n*. memory. (*lagip*)

múding: **kaimudingan**. *n*. worth; value; position. **pakaimudingan**. *n*. importance; value. **Awan kaimudinganna**. It is unimportant. [Tag. *halagá*]

múdis: **maimudis**. *v*. to be placed on the edge or border; placed edgewise.

modísta: (Sp. *modista*: dressmaker) *n*. dressmaker.

módo: (Sp. *modo*: manner) *n*. manner, way; (*wagas; ugali*); manners. **Kitaem ti modom**.

Mind your manners. **Awan ti modmodona.** He has no manners.

mudmúd: imudmud. v. to press down on a surface with the hands; keep down.

mudúmod: imudumod. v. to knock down and keep to the ground, strike down; to cry on someone's shoulder. **Immudumodko ti rupa iti baet dagiti takiagko.** I put my face between by arms. (*dumúdom, gusúgos, ngudangod*)

mudtóy: [*iyegmo ditoy*] bring it here.

muebleriá: (Sp. *mueblería*) n. furniture store; furniture factory.

muébles: (Sp. *muebles*: furniture) (*obs.*) n. furniture. (*alikamen*)

muél: (*obs.*) *var.* of *muak*: without antlers.

mueliáhe: (Sp. *muellaje*) n. wharfage dues.

muélie: (Sp. *muelle*: pier) n. metal spring; pier; wharf.

muéng: muengmueng. n. deformed vulva. **na-mueng.** a. deformed (said of the vulva).

muérto: (Sp. *muerto*: dead) **agmuerto.** v. to lease; give as interest. **nakamuerto.** a. leased; given as interest.

muéstra: (Sp. *muestra*: specimen) n. sample; specimen. **agmuestra.** v. to show. (*ipakita*)

muestrário: (f. *muestra*) n. sample book, collection of samples; catalog.

múging: n. forehead; brow; (*metaphorical*) mind. **mugingan.** a. having a large forehead, which denotes intelligence in Ilocano culture. **talimugingan.** n. cattle with a cowlick. **adda mugingna.** *exp.* denoting one's intelligence (*lit*: he has a forehead). **dagiti mamutbuteng a ladawan iti mugingna.** the haunting images in his mind (*lit*: forehead). **Nagkuretret ti mugingko a nangkita iti babai.** I wrinkled my forehead upon seeing the girl. [Bon. *kítong*, Ibg. *mukaq*, Ivt. *muyin*, Kal. *kichey, pulliliwas*, Knk. *kítung*, Kpm. *kánuan*, Png. *molíng*, Tag. *noó*]

mugmóg: mugmogan. v. to eat something that was stored and intended for other purposes.

mugná: n. pagan god.

muhersuéla: (Sp. *mujerzuela*: prostitute) n. prostitute. (*pampam*)

muhón: (Sp. *mojón*: boundary stone) n. concrete boundary post; boundary stones; landmark.

'mok: Contraction of *ammok*: I know. **'mok pay.** don't know.

móka: (Sp. *moca*: mocha) n. mocha coffee.

múkat: n. eye gum. **agmukat.** v. to discharge gum (eye). **agimukat.** v. to remove the *mukat*, clean the eyes. **mumukatan.** n. inner canthus, corner of the eyes where eye gum is discharged. **Ikkatek dagiti saput iti mumukatanda.** *exp.* I will wake them up so they can see the light (*lit*: take the web out of the corners of their eyes).

Ti makaturog, makamukat, ti nasalukag, agbiag. He who sleeps gathers eyebeams, he who is diligent lives. [Knk. *óki*, Png. *mukát*, Tag. *mutà*]

mukímok: mukimuken. v. to search for little things.

mukkúong: *var.* of *tukkuong*: to idle, stay in a place or state for a long period of time.

mukmók: n. remnants of food. (*murkát*)

mukó: agmuko. v. to doubt, hesitate; vacillate, be puzzled. [Tag. *alinlangan*]

múkod: n. heel. **mukodan.** a. with high heels; v. to provide with heels. **imukodan.** n. to tread on heels. [Ibg. *tumeng*, Ivt. *tuven*, Kal. *mukud*, Kpm. *sákung*, Png. *mukur*, Tag. *sakong*]

mukúmok: n. gold dust; rubble. **mukumuken.** v. to pulverize. **imukumok.** v. to broadcast; spread. [Tag. *kalat*]

múla₁: (Sp. *mula*: mule) n. mule.

múla₂: n. plant. **agmula.** v. to plant; cultivate. **agmulmula.** n. planter; farmer. **imula.** v. to plant; sow; implant; engrave; infix; instill (in the mind); inlay. **imumula.** n. seeds for planting. **makamula.** v. to be able to grow plants. **mumulaan.** n. field ready for planting. **Adda kayakto nga imulam iti panunotmo.** I would like to instill something in your brain. **Ti adda mulana, adda apitenna.** He who plants will have something to harvest. **Dimo imula dita pusom ti guram kenkuana.** Do not instill in your heart your anger toward him. [Ibg. *mula*, Ivt. *maymuhaq*, Kal. *muÿa*, Kpm. *tanam*, Png. *taném*, Tag. *halaman, taním*]

mulá: imulaan. v. to toast (in drinking); drink to the honor of (*tag-ay*). **mulaan.** v. to add meshes to a net. [Tag. *tagay* (toast)]

molábe: n. kind of tree, *Vitex arviflora* with valuable timber (*sagát*). [Tag. *mulawin*]

mulágat: a. wide-eyed; with large eyes; n. stare; look; wide open eyes; (*coll.*) a person who fails to see obvious things. **agmulagat.** v. to stare; open the eyes wide. **mulagatan.** v. to glare at; stare at with eyes opened wide. **namulagatan a kababalin.** customs in which one is brought up. [Kal. *chiyat*, Png. *murikat*, Tag. *dilát*]

múlat: n. stupidity; ignorance. **agmulat** (*obs.*) v. to grow cool; be frustrated.

mólde: (Sp. *molde*: mold) **imolde.** v. to imprint, impress on something, mark, stamp. (*sukogan*)

muldít: kamulmuldit. a. dirty, soiled, filthy. **kaimmuldit.** a. very small; inexperienced; newly born. [Tag. *dumi*]

moldúra: (Sp. *moldura*: molding) n. molding.

muldót: n. thin hair (growing on upper forehead or body); fine feathers. **muldótan.** a. with more *muldot* than usual.

mulengléng: *a.* wide-eyed; stupid; *n.* blank stare. **agmulengleng.** *v.* to stare (because of wonder or surprise) (*matmat*); have a blank stare. **mulenglengan.** *v.* to stare at, gaze at. **Mulmulenglengannak lattan.** She is just starring at me with a blank face.

molestár: (Sp. *molestar*: disturb) **molestaren.** *v.* to disturb, molest.

moléstia: (Sp. *molestia*: disturbance) *n.* bother, disturbance; favor asked.

muléta₁: (Sp. *muleta*: crutch) *n.* crutches. **agmuleta.** *v.* to walk with crutches. **nakamuleta.** *a.* using crutches, on crutches.

muléta₂: (Sp. *moleta*: muller; ink grinder) *n.* ink grinder; muller; polisher.

mulí₁: (Sp. *moler*: grind) **imuli.** to grind; mold (*giling*); put into effect. **namuli.** *a.* ground, crushed. **mulien.** *v.* to mold, shape. **Mulmuliek met ti bukodko a biag.** I will shape my own life. [Tag. *giling* (grind)]

mulí₂: **agmuli.** *v.* to mediate between two opposing sides.

múlie: (Sp. *muelle*: spring) *n.* spring. **demulie.** *a.* with springs.

mulihón: (Sp. *molijón*: grindstone) *n.* honing stone, grindstone.

mulímol: **mangmulmulimol.** *n.* retarded person, imbecile. **agmulimol.** *v.* to stare at stupidly.

molína: (Sp. *molino*: mill) *n.* thresher of a rice mill.

mulínaw: *a.* very hard; flintiness. **Pamulinawen.** Ilocano folk song; *a.* hard as a rock. **mulinaw a bato.** *n.* solid rock. **Mulinaw met ti ayatna.** His love is hard like a rock.

mulinílio: (Sp. *molinillo*) *n.* coffee grinder, cacao grinder.

molíno: (Sp. *molino*: mill) *n.* mill; windmill.

múlio: (*reg.*) *n.* blood pudding (*dinadaraan*).

mulít: *n.* dirt; dishonor, sin. (*rugit*) **namulitan.** *a.* dirty, filthy; defiled. **mulitan.** *v.* to dirty; soil; smear; blemish; dishonor; defile. **Impangtana ti nangmulit idi dayawda.** He plotted to defile their honor. [Tag. *dungis*]

mullúong: **mulmulluong.** *a.* stupid; mentally deficient. **Kasla mulmulluongen ti langada, nakulannayda.** Their faces seem to be stupid, they are slow. [Tag. *tangá*]

mulmól₁: *n.* red and yellow marine fish eaten whole, rainbow-colored parrot fish, *Scardiae* family.

mulmól₂: **agmulmol.** *v.* to keep something in the mouth without sucking (candy); to suck the thumb.

mulúmog: *n.* gargling. **agmulumog.** *v.* to gargle (*alimugmog*). [Png. *kumúkumo*, Tag. *mumog*]

mulóng: **imulongan.** *v.* to strip the leaves off. (*ibulongan*)

mulsí: **agimulsi.** *v.* to eject out; spit out; shoot out. (*pugso*)

mulsít: *n.* ejecting from the mouth, spitting out seeds. **agimulsit.** *v.* to eat fruit and spit out the seeds. **imulsit.** *v.* to eject from the mouth (seeds). **pagimulsitan.** *n.* fruit seeds that are stripped of meat and spit out.

múlta: (Sp. *multa*: fine) *n.* fine (penalty payment). **multaen.** *v.* to fine; penalize with a fine. [Kal. *muÿta, apas*]

multiplikádo: (Sp. *multiplicado*) *a.* multiplied.

multiplikadór: (Sp. *multiplicador*) *n.* multiplier; big wheel turning a smaller wheel.

multiplikár: (Sp. *multiplicar*) **multiplikaren.** *v.* to multiply. **multiplikasion.** *n.* multiplication.

multít: **kaimmultit.** *a.* newborn; very tiny.

mumalém: (f. *malem*) in the afternoon. **mumalemen.** It's already afternoon. **Iti mumalem, nagawid dagiti kakaseraanda.** In the afternoon, their boarders returned.

mómia: (Sp. *momia*: mummy) *n.* mummy.

múmo: *n.* a large, edible marine fish; a children's disease causing itching around the mouth. **mummumo.** *n.* (*obs.*) unaffected part; pyorrhea. [Tag. *mumo* = rice crumbs]

munámon: *n.* anchovy (used in *bogoong*). **daing a munamon.** *a.* sundried anchovy. [Tag. *dilis*]

monárka: (Sp. *monarca*: monarch) *n.* monarch. **monarkista.** *n.* monarchist.

monarkía: (Sp. *monarquía*) *n.* monarchy.

monasílio: (Sp. *monacillo*: acolyte) *n.* acolyte, assistant to a priest.

monastério: (Sp. *monasterio*: monastery) *n.* monastery.

múnaw₁: **agmunaw.** *v.* to decrease in effect. **mamunawen.** *v.* to sober up (said of a drunk person) (*maunawan, úsaw*). [Tag. *himasmás*]

múnaw₂: *var.* of *maguprak*: the generic term for rice which is not *diket*.

mundiál: (Sp. *mundial*: worldwide) *a.* worldwide. (*sangalubongan*)

monéda: (Sp. *moneda*: coin) *n.* coin used for clothes or jewelry decoration.

monehón: *var.* of *molihon*: grindstone.

múneng: **namuneng.** *a.* dull, thick headed. **munengmuneng.** *a.* senseless, brainless. [Tag. *tangá*]

muniéka: (Sp. *muñeca*: doll) *n.* doll (*tirtiris, bagawa*). [Tag. *manikà*]

munisílio: (Sp. *monacillo*: acolyte) *n.* altar boy.

munisiónes: (Sp. *munición*: ammunition) *n.* ammunition (*bala*). [Tag. *bala, munisiyón*]

múnit: *n.* chaff, refuse (of cotton), what is left after cleaning.

munmón: *n.* foundation; pillar; column; post. (*adigi*)

munnó: munnuen. *v.* to make something round. munnomunno. *a.* rounded out; stout; muscular; robust.

munnót: munnomunnot. *n.* kind of shrub with medicinal leaves, *J. populifolium.*

móno₁: (Sp. *mono*: monkey) *n.* monkey (*tsónggo, bakes*). [Tag. *matsíng*]

móno₂: monomono. *n.* animal fat.

múno: namuno. *a.* stupid. (*tabbed*)

monuménto: (Sp. *monumento*: monument) *n.* monument. (*batonlagip*)

monopólio: (Sp. *monopolio*: monopoly) *n.* monopoly.

montádo: (Sp. *montado*: set) *n.* set gem, gem adorning a ring or earring.

montadór: (Sp. *montador*) *n.* erector.

montadúra: (Sp. *montadura*: setting of jewels) *n.* setting of jewels.

montaniósa: (Sp. *montañosa*: mountainous) *n.* old name for the mountain province.

montár: (Sp. *montar*: set, mount) imontar. *v.* to assemble; mount; set a gem.

mónte: (Sp. *monte*: mountain) *n.* kind of card game.

montéro: (Sp. *montero*: mountaineer) *n.* mountaineer, forest ranger; player of *monte*.

muntón: (Sp. *montón*: heap) *n.* heap; pile; mass. (*penpen*)

muntúon: (f. *muntón*) *n.* heap; pile. (*bunton*) nakamuntuon. *a.* heaped up; piled up.

montúra: (Sp. *montura*: saddle) *n.* saddle.

muntúrod: *n.* small hill; heap; pile; hump (*bunton*). [Tag. *tambák*]

múnga: (*obs.*) *n.* orphanhood. (*ulila*)

múngay: *n.* nipple, teat; the edible banana flower; cone of a volcano; peak of a mountain. [Png. *musíng*, Tag. *utóng* (teat)]

mungél: (*obs.*) *n.* antler-less deer. (*muak*)

móngha: (Sp. *monja*: nun) *n.* nun.

mónghe: (Sp. *monje*: monk) *n.* monk.

mungíit: *n.* sneer; grin with the teeth showing. agmungiit. *v.* to grin with the teeth showing. Nagtungtung-ed a nagmungiit. She nodded while grinning.

mungmúngan: *n.* (*obs.*) a kind of Chinese bell.

múngot: naimungot. *a.* located at; situated at.

múog: (*coll.*) *a.* foolish, stupid. (*maag*)

moráda: (Sp.) *n.* variety of tobacco with short, broad leaves with oval-shaped tips.

morádo: (Sp. *morado*: purple) *n. a.* purple, violet-colored; *n.* variety of banana; mulberry.

murália: (Sp. *muralla*: wall) *n.* rampart, wall for a fortress.

moralidád: (Sp. *moralidad*: morality) *n.* morality. [Tag. *kalinisang-asal*]

murarég: *n.* frown. (*rungbed*; *rupanget*; *muregreg*; *misuot*) agmurareg. *v.* to frown. [Png. *sibangót, kulangét*, Tag. *simangot*]

móras: (Sp. *mora*: blueberry) *n.* mulberry.

murási: nakamurasi. *a.* bare, exposed; open; spread out.

murásit: *var.* of *mulsít*: eject, spit out; *var.* of *pullasit*; throw, hurl. agkaimurasit. *v.* to be strewn, thrown in various directions.

murát: imuratan. *v.* to pluck, pick; gather all (when harvesting vegetables).

muráy₁: agmurmuray. *v.* to wake up and stretch off sleepiness; take a while to get out of bed in the morning. mamurmurayan. *v.* to be fully awake. Nakamurmuray manen ti siudad. The city is once again waking up.

muráy₂: murmuray. *n.* variety of rice harvested in December.

murdíit: *n.* facial expression showing pain. agmurdiit. *v.* to contort the face in pain. Nagmurdiit ni Perla iti ut-ot. Perla contorted her face in pain.

murdóng: *n.* tip, apex. imurdongan. *v.* to cut the heads off; to cut off the ends. agmurdong. *v.* to end; finish. namurdong. *a.* too far out; too close to the tip. pagimurdongan. *n.* tip cuttings. ti murdong, umala iti puon. *exp.* like father, like son. iti agsimurdong. on both ends. [Png. *nguró*, Tag. *dulo*]

muregrég: *var.* of *murareg*: frown. Napamuregreg ta nasakit pay laeng ti ulona. He made a frown because he still had a headache. [Png. *sibangót, kulangét*, Tag. *simangot*]

moréno: (Sp. *moreno*: brown) *n. a.* dark brown (hair, skin, etc.).

muréng₁: *n.* dirty clothes to be washed; dirt that has collected on the skin (*kabkab, tikkab*). namureng. *a.* dirty, soiled. [Tag. *libág*]

muréng₂: *n.* variety of rice that is difficult to pound.

murí: imuri. *v.* to cull, take out extraneous matter in vegetables or grains; peel (beans); strip off leaves. pagimurian. *n.* peelings of vegetables. paimuri. *v.* to have something culled. Malagipko la unay daydi maysa nga aldaw a panangtulongko kenkuana nga agimuri iti balangeg. I really remember that day when I help her cull the water spinach. [Tag. *talup*]

muriáab: *n.* crying bitterly.

moriádo: *a.* crazy. (*samoriado*)

muriátiko: (Sp. *muriático*) *a.* muriatic. asido muriatiko. muriatic acid.

muríit: *n.* anus. (*kimmól, merret*; *kimmot*)

murímod: murimudan. v. to make a candle ready to light by lighting the wick and then blowing it out. mamurimudan. v. to become dirty (said of drinks with backwash of other people).

murímor: murimuren. v. to wear out, corrode; wear away; waste, consume. pangimurmurimuran. n. satisfaction offered by an innocent person. [Tag. bukbók]

murínit: n. variety of weed eaten by water buffalo. kamurinitan. n. grasslands of murinit weed.

muriót: a. insane, foolish; stupid. agmuriot. v. to go crazy about something; to feel lousy; to be irritated. pagmuriotan. n. cause of one's foolishness, irritation, or insanity. makapamuriot. a. causing one to be insane or irritated. Dayta ti pagmurmuriotak idi rabii. That's what drove me crazy last night. [Tag. tamláy]

moriskéta: (Sp. morisqueta: Moorish trick) n. boiled rice. morisketa-tostada. n. toasted rice (mixed with mean, eggs, and onions).

moriskí: n. harrow (sagad) agmoriski. v. to harrow. [Tag. suyod]

murít: var. of muri: to cull.

murkák: var.of murkat: crumb. [Tag. mumo]

murkát: n. crumb of food, variant of murkak. agmurkat. v. to drop crumbs (regreg). [Kal. bugta, mokmok, Kpm. mugmug, Png. mikmik, Tag. mumo]

murkít: agimurkit. v. to remove the ends of certain vegetables; remove worms from leaves.

morkón: (Sp. morcón: large sausage) n. dish consisting of beef, tomato sauce, karot yam, pepper, eggs and sausage, rolled-up, tied and fried, kind of local sausage.

Móro: (Sp. moro: Moor) n. Muslim; Moor. moro-moro. n. play which depicts the battles between the Christians and Muslims. kamoroan. n. territory of the Muslims.

muród: n. melon, Cucumis melo; (coll.) virgin.

murúmor: n. seedling; sowing of seeds. murumoran. v. to scatter seeds, sow. imumurumor. n. seeds ready for sowing. namurumoran. v. to be sown. Naimurumor dagiti minas idiay Cambodia. Mines were scattered in Cambodia. Iti labes dagiti narasay nga ulep, namurumoran ti tangatang iti rinibu a mata ti rabii. Beyond the sparse clouds, the sky was sown with thousands of night eyes.

muróng: n. loamy soil; unirrigated field.

murós: murusan (obs.) v. to clear up (of debris, weeds, etc.).

morósa: n. tondal banana.

moróso: var. of amoroso: behind in paying taxes.

murót: imurotan. v. to degrain.

morpína: (Sp. morfina: morphine) n. morphine.

morpolohía: (Sp. morfología) n. morphology.

murríit: n. anus. (kimmól, merret; kimmot)

mursádo: (Sp. forzado: forced) a. raped. (rames)

murséng₁: n. sprout of the loloan.

murséng₂: n. dirt; grease; dirty clothes. (rugit) namurseng. a. dirty; greasy; filthy. nakamurmurseng. a. really dirty, filthy (dugyot). [Tag. dumí]

mursíit: n. giggle. agmursiit. v. to giggle.

mortáha: (Sp. mortaja: shroud) n. shroud.

mortalidád: (Sp. mortalidad) n. mortality.

mortéro: (Sp. mortero: mortar) n. mortar for pounding (alsong). [Tag. lusong]

mortuário: (Sp. mortuario) n. mortuary.

murtógo: n. stupid person (tabbed). [Tag. gago]

músa: (Sp.) n. muse (baddi). [Tag. mutyâ]

músang: (Tag. also) n. wild cat, civet cat. Kasla musang a naglibas ni Peping. Peping secretly slipped away like a wild cat. [Knk. tánan]

muselína: (Sp.) n. muslin cloth.

muséo: (Sp. museo: museum) n. museum. agpamuseo. v. to go to the museum.

muséta: (Sp. muceta) n. academic cape worn over a graduation gown, hood; mozetta.

musíig: agmusiig. v. to grin; pucker up; contort the mouth; contort the mouth at someone. musiigan. v. to turn up one's nose at someone. Napamusiig ta kasla naukritan ti karabukobna. He grinned as his throat has been scratched (with good food). Napamusiig iti saniit. He contorted his mouth from the pain.

músika: (Sp. música: music) n. music (saniweng). [Tag. himig, tugtugin

musikéro: (f. musika) n. musician.

músiko: (Sp. músico: musician) n. musician.

moskáda: agmoskada, moskadaen. v. to chew tobacco leaves. mumoskadaen. n. high-grade tobacco for chewing. nues moskada. n. nutmeg.

moskatél: (Sp. moscatel) n. wine from Muscat grapes.

mosketéro: (Sp. mosquetero) n. musketeer.

moskitéro: (Sp. mosquitero: mosquito net) n. mosquito net.

moskubádo: (Sp.) n. raw, unrefined sugar.

muskuládo: (Eng.) a. muscular (nabaneg, napuner, maskulado). [Tag. tipunò]

muslád: agmuslad. v. to be weak sighted. nakamuslad. a. weak-sighted. (arrap)

musléng: var. of muslad: weak sighted.

musmós: n. dull person, dunce; coin minted with a defect; refuse of tobacco. namusmos. idiotic, dull. [Tag. tangá]

músong: n. core (of an apple, boil, etc.) imusungan. v. to pluck out the core of.

músot: *n*. small seedless Java plum; eye of an apple; half-developed ear of rice. **agmusot**. *v*. to be half-developed (rice).

mostása: (Sp. *mostaza*: mustard) *n*. mustard. **mustasa de Europa**. *n*. mustard plaster.

mustrá: *var*. of *muestra*: show; describe; specimen.

mostradór: (Sp. *mostrador*: showcase) *n*. showcase, display counter.

múta: *n*. stamen of a flower, anther.

mútal: *n*. bad pronunciation, not distinguishing between the consonants *k* and *t*. **agmutal**. *v*. to lisp; speak imperfectly.

mutekték: *n*. insight. **imutektekan**. *v*. to bear in mind, consider; observe; acquaint oneself with. **maimutektekan**. *v*. to be able to comprehend; get a grasp of; observe. **Kaanonto a maimutektekak manen ti disso a nakairuamak?** When can I observe again the place I was accustomed to? **Nasken a nalawlawa ti pannakaawat ken panagimutektekmo tapno naanayas ti panagbiagmo.** Your thoughts and understandings should be wide for your life to be smooth. [Tag. *unawà*]

mutiá: *n*. charm; gem; amulet; muse, goddess. [Tag. *mutyâ*]

motíbo: (Sp. *motivo*: motive) *n*. motive.

mutíl: see *ammutil*.

mutímot: **namutmutimot**. *a*. done gradually, little by little. **mutimuten**. *v*. to do little by little; inquire persistently.

mutíng: *n*. clitoris (*tamtampira*; *tildi*); budding shoot of *sayote*. [Tag. *tilin*]

mútit: *n*. Philippine squirrel; used as an insult.

mutittít: **namutittit**. *a*. full, satiated.

mutmút: **mutmuten**. *v*. to do carefully; inquire continuously. **mamutmut**. *v*. to understand totally; report in detail.

mútok: **imutokan**. *v*. to assign, designate; summon; cite (*dutok*). [Tag. *hirang*]

mutúmot: **namutumot**. *a*. curious, inquisitive. **mutumuten**. *v*. to inquire; quest. **mamutumot**. *v*. to understand thoroughly.

mutón: (Sp. *motón*: pulley) *n*. pulley.

motór: (Sp.) *n*. motor. **de-motor**. motorized.

motorsíklo: (Eng.) *n*. motorcycle.

mutsátsa: (Sp. *muchacha*: girl) *n*. house girl; errand girl; maid; servant. (*katulong a babai*)

mutsátso: (Sp. *muchacho*: boy) *n*. house boy; errand boy; servant. (*katulong a lalaki*)

mútso: (Sp. *mucho*: much) *a*. much, a lot (*adu*); wealthy (*baknang*).

muttálat: *n*. gaping stupidly, staring (*mulagat*; *muttaleng*). **maimuttalat**. *v*. to be exposed into view. **No ituloytayo ti agbasa kadagiti pagiwarnak, maimuttalat dagiti agsasamusam a didigra.** If we continue to read the newspapers, various disasters will be exposed.

muttaléng: *n*. staring at something open-mouthed (with awe) (*mulengleng*, *matmát*); gazing with vacant fixation; *a*. agape. **agmuttaleng**. *v*. to be agape, open-mouthed; to stare with wide eyes. **Napamuttaleng idi masirayanna ti dila ti apuy iti maikatlo a kadsaaran.** He was left open-mouthed looking at the mouth of the fire on the third story.

muyás: *a*. smooth and shiny. **mamuyasan**. *v*. to become smooth, shiny (by polishing). [Tag. *kinis*]

muyéng: *a*. depressed, downcast; *n*. mood swing, depression; gout, pain in the joints. **samsamuyeng**. *n*. mood swing, depressed feelings; anxiety; mental anguish.

muymúoy: **imuymuoyan** (*obs.*) *v*. to conform to the opinion of another person without hesitation.

muymóy: **muymuyen**. *v*. to gather every last piece (*kuyuskos*); (*obs.*) to drive away water buffaloes by shouting.

múyod: *n*. top of the ear of rice.

muyóng: *n*. garden plant; orchard; conformity of opinion. **kamuyongan**. *n*. garden, place full of cultivated vegetation; backyard. **minuyongan**. *n*. garden, orchard. [Tag. *halaman*, Bon. *muyóng* = seed of legume pods; Knk. *muyóng* = trees other than pine trees]

múyot₁: *a*. crazy; fool, stupid. (*bagtit*)

múyot₂: **maimuyot**. *v*. to be attracted to, allured to. **imuyot**. *v*. to entice; tempt.

muyót: *n*. languish, languidness. (*muriot*) **agmuyot**. *v*. to become languid, sluggish. [Tag. *tamád*]

N

-n: Variant of *-en* (now, already) after vowels: **Inka***n***!** Go now! **Pimmanawda***n***.** They left already.

na-: 1. Forms the perfective of the prefix *ma-*: **Nabatida idiay Vigan.** They remained in Vigan. **Nadaitmo 'ti badona.** Were you able to sew her dress? 2. An adjectivalizing prefix, forming adjectives from nominal roots: **na-pigsa.** strong. *na*baknang. rich.

naCVC-: Denotes the comparative quality of adjectives: **naimbag.** good. **naim-imbag.** better. **natayag.** tall. **nataytayag.** taller. **naemma.** nice. **naem-emma.** nicer.

-na: 1. Third person possessive enclitic: **ti sugat-na.** his/her wound. 2. Third person ergative (*-ko* series) enclitic pronoun, marks the actor of the transitive verbs: **Kayat***na* **ti tinapay.** He/she wants bread. **Binasa***na***.** He/she read it already. 3. In the case of the double pronouns (actor to patient), ergative to absolutive, the suffix *-na* may refer to the second person (taking the place of *-mo*), or third person actor: **Tulongan***na***k man.** Please help me. **Nakita***na***ka.** He/she saw you. [Png. *to*, Tag. *niyá*]

na- -an: *pref.* Forms perfective of *ma- -an*. **Natay kano a napaltogan.** He supposedly died by getting shot. **Napuoran ti sarusarda.** Their granary caught on fire.

Na!: Interjection expressing wonder.

náar: *n.* enjoyment. **agnaar.** *n.* to enjoy or benefit (from the fruit of one's labor). **Pang-gepna a rakraken ti ayatda tapno isu ti agnaar iti masapsapulan ni Ambong.** She plans to destroy their love so she will enjoy what Ambong needs.

Naay!: Interjection expressing sorrow.

naáy: **agnaay.** *v.* to result in; become. **agnanaay.** *v.* to pile up, accumulate, increase; to be various things. **pagnaayan.** *n.* result. **No makitlogen, agnaay a nakakutkuttongton.** After it has laid its eggs, it will become emaciated.

nabánab: **manabanab.** *v.* to be inundated; flooded; swamped; overwhelmed; worn down (with work); immersed. **nabanaben.** *v.* to flood, inundate; overwhelm. [Tag. *bahâ*]

nába: (Sp. *lava*: washing of metals) *n.* ore.

nabáhas: *var.* of *labahas*: razor.

nabánab: **manabanab.** *v.* to be inundated, flooded; swamped with; overwhelmed. **naba-naben.** *v.* to flood; overwhelm.

nábe: (Sp. *nave*: nave) *n.* nave, center part of a church or a cathedral between the side aisles.

nabéta: (Sp. *naveta*: incense boat) *n.* incense boat.

nabigadór: (Sp. *navegador*: navigator) *n.* navigator.

nabigasión: (Sp. *navegación*: navigation) *n.* navigation, science of finding the position of a ship or airplane.

nabló: (f. *bulló*) *a.* sprained, broken (bone, etc.).

nabnáb: **nabnaben.** *v.* to decorticate (bamboos, etc.). (*banut*)

nábo: (Sp. *nabo*: turnip) *n.* turnip.

nábo: **manabo.** *v.* to fall down; to drop (*tinnag*, *regreg*). [Tag. *hulog*]

nabsóg: (f. *bussóg*) *a.* full, satiated (with food). [Ibg. *bettug*, Ifg. *nabhug*, Ivt. *mabsuy*, Kpm. *mabsiq*, Png. *naksel*, Tag. *busóg*]

náda: (Sp.) *pron.* nothing. **por nada.** for nothing; in vain.

nadnád₁: *n.* massage (*ilot*). **nadnaden.** *v.* to massage well.

nadnád₂: **nadnadan.** *n.* outcome, consequence, result; conclusion, end **agnadnad.** *v.* to digest; settle; calm down; return to normal. **pag-nadnadan.** *n.* result; outcome. **Nagilad manen ket pinagnadnadna ti pannakaulawna.** He rubbed his body against the wall and calmed down his dizziness.

naéd: *n.* resident; residence, abode. (*balay*; *taeng*; *yan*) **agnaed.** *v.* to reside, live, dwell. **agkanaed.** *v.* to live together. **agpanaed.** *v.* to accept boarders in one's house. **pagnaedan.** *n.* residence. **makipagnaed.** *v.* to live with, board with. [Png. *manayan*, Tag. *tirá*]

nag-: Perfective form of the prefix *ag-*: *Nag*surat **ni Maria kaniak.** Maria wrote me. *Nag*kastoykami We acted this way. **Siak laeng ti** *nag*bakasion. Only I went on vacation. *Nag*-sardeng iti sango ti pasdek. He stopped in front of the building.

nag- -an: *circumfix.* Perfective form of the *pag-an*: *Nag*turoga*n*da? Where did they sleep?

nag- =(e)n: *affix.* Admirative adjectival affixation: *Nag*rugite*n*! How dirty! *Nag*lakan! How cheap!

nag- -inn-: Perfective form of the reciprocal form of *ag-* verbs. **Naglinnimedda.** They hid from each other. **Nagtinnulongda.** They helped one another.

nágan: *n.* name; term; appellation. **naganen.** *v.* to name, mention by name; designate. **inaganan.** *v.* to nominate, to name, call by name. **ipanagan.** *v.* name; give a name to. **kanagan, kanaganan.** *n.* namesake; birthday (*kasangay*). **agkanagan.** *v.* to have the same name. **agnagan, managanan.** *v.* to be called, named. **agkanaganan.** *v.* to have a birthday celebration. **mainagan.** *v.* to be named **sanka-nagan.** *n.* one thing, sort, class, category. **nagan iti sirok ti látok.** *exp.* name given to a sickly child in a pagan ritual to make him well. **Ti la maipampanaganna.** *exp.* sarcastically denoting a person who introduces himself by a fake name. [Ibg. *ngagan*, Ivt. *ngaran*, Kal. *ngachen*, Png. *ngarán*, Tag. *pangalan*]

nagánag: **managanag.** *v.* to fall to the ground (*regreg*). **agkanaganag.** *v.* to fall in great numbers (fruits during a storm, etc.). **Winag-wagna dagiti palatang ken nanaganagda.** He shook the midrib and (the fruits) fell down.

nagannák: (f. *anák*) *n.* parent; *v.* gave birth. [Kal. *sin-alak, langiyalak*, Tag. *magulang* (parents)]

nagastián: (f. *istáy*) *var.* of *nagistayan*: almost.

nagbaetán: (f. *baét*) *n.* interval.

nagbubugel: *n. Caranx sp.* Cavalla fish.

nagguduá: (f. *dua*) *v.* & *a.* divided into two parts.

naginCV-: Perfective form of the pretentative prefix *agin*CV-. **Naginkakatawada iti bainda.** They pretended to laugh out of their shame.

nagistáy: (f. *istáy*) **nagistay, nagistayan.** *adv.* almost, nearly. (*dandani*)

nagistayán: *var.* of *nagistáy*: almost.

nagka-: *pref.* fractional prefix used with cardinal numbers to express division into parts. Perfective form of *agka-*: **Nagkapat.** Divided into four parts. **Nagkalima.** Divided into five parts.

nagná: *v.* perfective form of *magna*, walked.

naguás: (Sp. *enaguas*: petticoat) *n.* underskirt, petticoat.

nagpa-: Perfective of *agpa-* verbs. **Nagpa-Bauangkami.** We went to Bauang. **Nagpa-pukisdan.** They already went to have a haircut.

nagpinna-: Perfective form of *agpinna-* **Nag-pipinnabasolda.** They were blaming each other.

nagsinan-: Perfective form of *agsinan-*

nagyán: *n.* content, substance. **awan nagyan.** *a.* empty.

nai-: Perfective form of the prefix *mai-*. **naipaw-it.** sent. **naited.** given. **naisurat.** written down.

nai(n)- -an: Affixation used to form abstract adjectives with a superlative quality. **nain-daklan.** very big. **naimpusuan.** sincere. **nain-kasigudan.** original. **naindaraan.** involving bloodshed, bloody. **naindramaan.** dramatic. **nainkappian.** peaceful.

naí: (*obs.*) *a.* joining, uniting.

náig₁: *n.* portion, piece of; a fold (in cloth, etc.) **sanganaig.** *n.* one fold. **duanaig.** *n.* two folds of fabric.

náig₂: **agkanaig.** *v.* to be related to; to have sexual relations with, sleep together. **mainaig.** *v.* to be related to; associated with; *prep.* besides, aside from. **inaig.** *v.* to relate to; correspond with. **kanaig.** *prep.* besides, aside from. **pannakainaigan.** *n.* link; relationship. **Adda kadi pakainaiganyo iti daytoy naka-angayantayo?** Do you have something to add to this meeting. **Nabayagen a dida nagkanaig.** They have not slept with each other for a long time already. [Tag. *ugnáy*]

naimpusuán: (f. *puso*) *a.* sincere, from the heart.

nain- -an: see *nai(n)- -an*.

naipa-: Perfective form of *maipa-* **naipadamag.** revealed, disclosed, let known.

naka-: 1. Perfective form of the potentive prefix *maka-* **Nakapanda.** They were able to go. 2. Indicates an attained state. **Nakatnagda.** They fell down. 3. With articles of clothing or portable items, the prefix indicates that the entity designated by the root is worn or carried: **nakapantalon.** wearing pants. **nakapalda.** wearing a skirt. **nakarelos.** with a watch.

nakaCVC-: Prefix used with adjectival roots to intensify the condition or state of the adjective: **naragsak.** happy. **nakaragragsak.** quite happy. **Nakaragragsak ti babai a nangagek ken-kuana iti panagpinnakadada.** The girl was quite happy to kiss him when they bid farewell to each other.

naka- -an: *pref.* Perfective form of *paka- -an*. **Nakasapulanna ditoy.** She found it here.

nakagténg: *v.* arrived (*simmangpet*).

nakai-: *pref.* perfective of *makai-* verbs. **nakai-parit.** to have been able to forbid, forbidden. **nakaipan.** to have happened to have brought along.

nakai- -an: Perfective form of *pakai- -an*. **Suki-matem ti gasatmo iti daga a nakayanakam.** Try your luck in the land where you were born.

nakaipa-: Perfective form of *makaipa-* verbs. **nakaipabassit.** to have belittled (unintentionally).

nakalgák: (f. *leggák*) *a.* risen (moon, sun, stars, etc.); appeared.

nakának: **agnakanak.** *v.* to drip; fall (tears). **manakanak.** *v.* to trickle, fall in drops (*arú-bos*). [Tag. *laglág*]

nakapag-: *pref.* Forms perfective of *makapag-* verbs. **Nakapagkuyogda.** They were able to accompany each other. **Dida nakapagsao.** They were not able to speak.

nakapag- -inn-: Perfective form of *makapag--inn-*, forming potentive reciprocal verbs. **Dida nakapagsinnurat.** They were not able to write each other. **Dikay pay nakapagwinnaswas**

ken Rosita? Weren't you able to divorce Rosita yet?

nakapagi-: Perfective form of *makapagi.* **nakapagiserrek.** to have managed to put inside.

nakapagpa-: Perfective form of *makapagpa-.* Potentive indirect or directional prefix. **Gapu iti baknangda, nalaka laeng a nakapagpa-Francia.** Because of their wealth, it was easy for them to be able to go to France.

nakapai-: *pref.* Forms the perfective of *makapai-* verbs: **nakapailugan.** to have had someone ride.

nakapamin-: Adverbial prefix indicating how many times an action occurred, perfective form of *makapamin-.* **Nakapaminliman a nagkiriring ti telepono.** The telephone had rung five times already.

nakapara-: combination of the stative prefix *naka-* and the Spanish loan prefix *para-:* **nakaparatimud.** wearing a chin strap. **nakaparasiket.** wearing a waistband.

nakasag-: Perfective distributive prefix used with numeric roots (with plural subjects only). **Nakasagpitodan.** They had seven each. **Nakasaggatlokamin (iti serbesa).** We had three (beers) each.

nakatnagán: (f. *tinnág*) *a.* fallen down.

nakatáyan: (f. *patáy*) *n.* place where someone died.

nákem: *n.* mind; will, free will; intellect, sense, reasoning, good mental capacity. **agnakem.** *v.* to be reasonable, to have sense. **manakem, nanakman.** *a.* wise, using good judgement, prudent. **kinamanakman.** *n.* prudence. **kananakem.** *n.* idea, opinion, thought; belief; intention. **pakinakem.** *n.* will, intention, thought; desire; feeling; conscience. **inak(e)man).** *v.* to influence; speak for. **agpakpakinamen.** *v.* to think seriously, mediate; contemplate, consider; ponder; deliberate. **pagnakeman.** *n.* something that will influence the behavior of somebody for the better (lecture, punishment, etc.). **agnaknakem, aginnanakem.** *v.* to do voluntarily. **agbaliw ti nakem.** *v.* to change one's mind. **nanakmán.** *a.* sensible; modest. **agnaknaken.** *v.* to do voluntarily. **sakit ti nakem.** *n.* hard feelings; ill will; regret. **manakman.** *n.* adult. **utang a naimbag a nakem.** *n.* debt of gratitude. **napigsa ti pakinakemna.** to be strong willed. **Ania ngata't adda iti nakemna?** What do you think is on his mind? **Ti utang, mabayadan, ngem ti naimbag a nakem saan.** Debts can be paid, but not piece of mind. [Ivt. *aktuktu*, Png., Tag. *isip*]

naki-: Perfective form of the social prefix *maki-* **Napan nakiani.** She went to participate in the harvest.

naki- -an: *pref.* forms perfective of *paki- -an.* *Naki*asawa*an*na ti ari. She married the king. **Sino ti *naki*saoam?** Who did you speak with?

nakika-: *pref.* forms perfective *makika-* verbs. **Nakikaidda kaniak.** He lay down with me.

nakimbági: (f. *bági*) *interrog.* whose? (in past sense) (*akinkua*)

nakin-: Perfective form of *akin-* and *pakin-* **Siak ti *nakin*kanawan.** I was on the right side.

nakipag-: Perfective form of *makipag-* **Maysaak kadagiti nakipagbagkat kadagiti kahon.** I was one of those who helped carry the boxes.

nakipag- -an: Perfective form of *pakipag- -an.*

nakipagi-: Perfective form of *makipagi-:* **nakipagiruar.** to have helped bring outside. **nakipagiserrek.** to have helped bring inside.

nakipaginCV-: Perfective form of *makipaginCV-:* **Nakipaginluluto.** He pretended to cook with others. **Nakipaginsusuratak.** I pretended to write with others.

nakkó: *var.* of *nakkóng:* term of address for young people.

nakkóng: (f. *anakko* + vocative *–ng*) *n.* term of address for young people, at least one generation younger than the speaker: my child.

nakmán: (f. *nakem*) *n.* modesty. **nanakman.** *a.* modest; sensible. **manakman.** *n.* adult. **kinamanakman.** *n.* sensibility; prudence.

naldóg: (f. *luddóg*) *a.* overripe.

nalnál: *var.* of *taltal.*

nalpás: (f. *leppás*) *v.* finished.

nalsók: (f. *lussók*) *a.* pierced, perforated.

naltát: (f. *lettát*) *a.* loose, unfastened; broken, not ready for use.

náma: namnama. *n.* hope, trust; confidence. **manginanama.** *v.* to hope, trust, rely on, confide in. **inanamaen.** *v.* to hope for. 'toy siiinanama. yours faithfully (used in closing letters). **Namnamaek a maawatannak.** I hope you understand me. **Saanko a ninamnama a mangabakak.** I didn't expect to win. [Kpm. *nasaq*, Png. *ilálo*, Tag. *asa*]

namag-: [*nang-* + *pag-*] Perfective prefix for potentive indirect verbs. **namagkulagtit.** startling, caused one to jerk. **Namagsikaw iti tianna.** It made his stomach grumble.

námak: particle used to form the absolute superlative or optative. **namak pay no.** what if, suppose; it would have been. **namak pay a gasatna.** what luck he has!

náman: naman ket no. so help me.

namarsuá: (f. *parsua*) *n.* creator; God.

nam-áy: *n.* comfort; contentment; wealth; ease; peace of mind. (*gin-awa*) **nanam-ay.** *a.* easy, not hard; free from responsibility of care; comfortable. **agnam-ay.** *v.* to become comfortable; benefit from. **pagnam-ayan.** *n.* source of comfort; welfare; benefit. [Tag. *ginhawà*]

namay-án: Perfective form of *pamay-an*: happened; done.

nambaán: *n.* banana tree. **Kaslaak la nambaan, awanan regta.** I am like a banana tree with no vigor.

nami-: *pref.* Perfective of *mami-*. **mamindua.** twice. *namin*dua. having been done twice.

namimpin-: Perfective form of *mamimpin-* multiplicatives taking numeric roots and indicating, to a limitative degree, the number of times an action takes place. **namimpinsan.** only once (happened), once and for all. **namimpindua.** only twice.

namin-: Perfective form of the multiplicative affix *mamin-*. **Namimpaten a nabaliwan ti panggepda.** Their intention has changed four times already.

namín: *n.* contribution.

namin-anó: *interrog.* Perfective form of *mamin-ano*, how many times?

naminsán: *adv.* perfective form of *maminsan*: having been done once.

namíng: *n.* resolution; proposal. **pagnana-mingan.** *v.* to resolve; pass a resolution.

namiskél: (f. *piskel*) *a.* muscular. (*baneg*)

namituén: (f. *bituen*) *a.* starry, with many stars. **namituen a langit.** *n.* starry sky.

namkí: (f. *bikkí*?) *v.* to feel; be affected by.

nammék: *n.* hardwood.

namná: (*obs.*) *prep.* among, amidst.

namnám: *n.* taste; flavor. (*raman, nanam*) **nam-namen.** *v.* to taste; to enjoy. [Tag. *lasa*]

namnáma: *n.* hope; expectation. see *nama*. **mangnamnama.** *v.* to be hopeful. **managnam-nama.** *a.* optimistic. **namnamaen.** *v* to hope; to expect. **ipanamnama.** *v.* to assure. **pangnam-namaan.** *a.* trustworthy. **panamnamaan.** *v.* to offer hope to. **makapanamnama.** *a.* encouraging, offering hope. **Diak ninamnama a makitaka ita.** I didn't expect to see you today. [Png. *ilálo*, Tag. *asa*]

namók: *n.* mosquito, variant of *lamók*.

namullaláyaw: (f. *bullalayaw*) *a.* with a rainbow.

Namongan: *n.* In Ilocano mythology, the mother of the epic hero, *Lam-ang*.

namungánay: (f. *pungánay*) *a.* began; started.

namrayán: Perfective form of *pamrayan*: to do what comes to mind in a particular situation; to act on the spur of the moment; do instinctively.

namsaákan: (f. *pamsaákan*) *v.* done to the utmost; done to the limit.

namsék: (f. *messék*) *a.* full (*napno*); fully developed; full grown. (*bursók, penték*)

nanaC- -V-: Perfective form of *manaC- -V-* onomatopoetic verbs. **nanabsuok.** fallen down with a splash. **nanabtuog.** fallen down with a thump.

nána₁: *n.* mother (*nanang, ina*); aunt.

nána₂: *n.* pus, pus matter (*ano*). **agnana.** *v.* to fester (wounds, boils). [Kal. *lola*, Png. *nenná*, Tag. *nanà*]

nánam: *n.* taste, flavor, savor. **nanamen.** *v.* to enjoy, relish (something). **nananam.** *a.* tasty, appetizing. **ipananam.** *v.* to shower with affection or anger. **pagnanam.** *n.* sense of taste. [Tag. *lasa*]

nánang: *n.* mother (*iná*). [Tag. *nanay*]

nánaw: **nanawan.** *v.* to look at something submerged. (*wanáwan*) **agnanaw.** *v.* to catch fish during the day.

náni: *n.* familiar term of address for one's daughter.

nang-: Perfective form of the detransitive prefix *mang-* **Nanganda ditoy idi kalman.** They ate here yesterday.

nang- -an: Perfective form of *pang- -an*. **Sadino ti nangaldawam?** Where did you eat lunch?

'nang: Contraction of *nanang*: mother.

nangi-: Perfective form of *mangi-* **Nangi-saangak iti danum a pagkapemi.** I put our coffee water over the stove. **Nangidasar iti sangamalukong nga agas-asuk nga adobo.** She set a bowl of smoking *adobo*.

nangika-: Perfective form of *mangika-* **nangika-dakkel.** having made bigger. **nangikalawa.** having made broader.

nangipa-: Perfective form of *nangipa-* **nangipa-tungpal iti plano.** carried out a plan. **nangipa-Manila.** having brought it to Manila.

nángka: *n.* jackfruit, *Artocarpus integrifolia*. [Tag. *langkâ*]

nángo: *n.* a large stinkbug (*dangaw*).

nangpa-: Perfective form of *mangpa-* **nang-pasakit.** having made someone hurt or sick. **nangpapintas.** having beautified something.

nangpag-: Perfective form of *mangpag-* **nangpagtalna.** having tranquilized someone. **nangpagleddaang.** having made somebody sad.

nangtagi-: Perfective form of *mangtagi-* **Nangtagibassitda kaniak.** They belittled me.

naulpán: (f. *ulép*) *a.* cloudy; overcast.

napa-: Perfective form of *mapa-* indicating nonvolitional or noncontrollable action. This prefix is often used with instinctive actions prompted by a force. **napanganga.** with mouth opened (no purpose, accidentally) **Napasennaayak.** I sighed (involuntarily let out a sigh). **Napaanges iti nauneg.** He breathed deeply. **Napaanang-ang a napalagto ti napanaan nga alingo.** The wild boar shot with an arrow jumped in pain. **Napamulagatda a nakaduktal iti natayen nga aso.** They were wide eyed upon discovering the dead dog.

napa- -an: Perfective form of *mapa- -an.* **napatulidan.** to have been run over by something.

nápa: agnapa. *v.* to be full, overflowing (*lippias*). [Tag. *apaw*]

napag-: *pref.* Perfective form of *mapag-* indicating potential ability with *pag-* verbs. **napagbaliw.** to have been able to change something. **napagsingpet.** to have been able to make someone behave. **Napagandar dagiti makina ti lantsa.** The engines of the launch were set in motion (turned on).

napagpa-: Perfective form of *mapagpa-* **napag-papintas.** to have been able to beautify something.

napeklán: (f. *pekkél*) *a.* devoted; excessively so; known for; real, genuine. **napeklán a bartek.** *n.* devoted drunk.

napnáp: inapnap. *v.* to scatter, spread. (*puser*) **agnapnap.** *v.* to spread (water).

napnó: (f. *punno*) *a.* filled, full. [Ibg. *mapnuq*, Ivt. *nafennu*, Kpm. *mitmuq*, Png. *napnu*, Tag. *punô*]

naptalína: (Sp. *naftalina*: naphthalene) *n.* mothball; naphthalene chemical used in moth repellants. (*alkampor*)

narán(g)ha: (Sp. *naranja*: orange) *n.* orange; orange color. **naranghado.** *a.* orange-colored.

naranghíta: (Sp. *naranjita*: small orange) *n.* mandarin orange.

narasión: (Sp. *narración*: narration) *n.* narration.

narbá: (f. *rebbá*) *a.* destroyed; demolished. (*narsúod*)

nárek: *n.* species of wood, *Balanocarpus cagayanensis.*

nargá: (f. *reggá*) *a.* deep; profound; heavy (sleep). **Nargaan ti turogna.** He slept soundly.

narkótiko: (Sp. *narcótico*: narcotic) *n.* narcotic.

narnár: *a.* crushed; broken. **narnaren.** *v.* to use to the limit or extreme, to wear clothes until they are worn out; separate the flesh of shellfish from the shells by boiling; pound in order to crush.

narnuáy: (f. *rennuay*) *a.* abundant, plentiful; numerous; exuberant.

narnúoy: *var.* of *narnuay*: plentiful.

narrá: *n. Pterocarpus sp.*, a kind of tree with yellow flowers whose wood is valuable in construction. **kanarraan.** *n.* grove of *narra* trees. [Kal. *taggey*]

nars: (Eng.) *n.* nurse. **agnars.** *v.* to study to be a nurse, to be a nurse.

narsúod: (f. *russúod*) *a.* demolished, destroyed. (*narba*)

narwáy: (f. *ruáy*) *a.* plentiful; abundant. [Tag. *saganà*]

nasakít: (f. *sakít*) *n.* sickness, illness; patient. *a.* sick, ill. [Tag. *may sakít*]

nasánas: manasanas. *v.* to be decimated. **nasanasen.** *v.* to decimate. [Tag. *bawas*]

nasangér: (f. *sangér*) *n.* strong wine; *a.* strong (said of wine).

nasgéd: (f. *seggéd*) *a.* burning; fervent, passionate; intense.

nasinan-: *pref.* forms statives of *sinan-* derived forms: **nasinan-letra L.** in the shape of the letter l.

nasión: (Sp. *nación*: nation) *n.* nation. (*pagilián*). **nasional.** *a.* national. (*nailian*)

nasionalísmo: (Sp.) *n.* nationalism.

nasionalísta: (Sp. *nacionalista*) *n.* nationalist.

nasisíta: (Sp. *necesita*: need) *a.* necessary. (*nasken*)

naskén: (f. *sekkén*) *a.* necessary; important. **Nasken a natibkerka.** You need to be tough.

nasnás: *n.* rag. (*nipis*) **nasnasan.** *v.* to rub with a cloth. **pagnasnasan.** *n.* scrubbing rag.

nataéngan: (f. *taéng*) *n.* adult, grown-up.

-nata: enclitic indicating third person actor on first person dual patient. **naawatannatan.** she already understood the two of us.

natáy: *n.* the dead; *v.* died. see *patay*. (*pusay*) **makinatay.** *v.* to watch over the dead. **Piesta dagiti Natay.** *n.* All Soul's Day. [Png. *inatéy*, *aleplép*, Tag. *patáy*]

natbág: (f. *tebbág*) *a.* loud; resonant. (*ringgor*)

naténg: *n.* vegetable. (*gulay*) **agnateng.** *v.* to pick vegetables. **agnanateng.** *n.* dealer of vegetables. **kanatengan.** *n.* vegetable garden. **mangnateng.** *v.* to harvest or gather vegetables. **natngen.** *v.* to gather vegetables. **ninatengan.** *n.* vegetable garden. **panagnanateng.** *n.* vegetable harvest season. **kannateng.** *a.* freshly picked (vegetables). **managnateng.** *a.* fond of eating vegetables; *n.* vegetarian. **Saankami a managnateng, ngem bin-ig a bulbulong ti linutona.** We are not vegetarians but she cooked only leaves. [Ibg. *ateng*, Ifg. *pihing*, Ivt. *rakanen*, Kal. *alimaỹay*, Knk. *madengdeng*, *lamtíng*, *ontó*, *dus-úyan*, Kpm. *gule*, Png. *pisíng*, Tag. *gulay*]

natibidád: (Sp. *natividad*) *n.* nativity, Christmas. **bihil ti natibidad.** *n.* vigil of Christmas.

natíbo: (Sp. *nativo*: native) *n.* native. (*patnéng*)

náto: *n.* bird ovary. (*iitlogán*)

natúra: (Sp. *natura*: nature) *a.* in kind (payment).

naturál: (Sp. *natural*: natural) *a.* natural.

naturalésa: (Sp. *naturaleza*: nature) *n.* physical nature; physiological constitution.

naturalisádo: (Sp. *naturalizado*: naturalized) *a.* naturalized (said of new citizens of a country).

naturalménte: (Sp.) *adv.* naturally.

náwi: **nawien.** *v.* to clean (rattan), clean reeds. **sanganawi.** *n.* one strip of rattan.

nawnáw: **nawnawen.** *v.* to dissolve; melt; to dilute in liquids. [Tag. *kanáw*]

nay: *adv.* informal adverb of place, here, there.

naymán: (*obs.*) Who knows?

naynáy: *adv.* continually; often, again and again. **agnaynay.** *v.* to continue; persevere, persist. **manaynaynay.** *v.* to die slowly and gradually. **manaynay.** *a.* everlasting, eternal, perpetual. [Png. *naynáy*, *betbét*, Tag. *parati*]

náyon: *n.* addition; part. **nayonan.** *v.* to increase; enlarge. **inayon.** *v.* to add to, affix, put with. **agnanayon.** *adv.* always. **kanayon.** *adv.* always. **patinayon.** *adv.* always. **manayon.** *v.* to last; live to a ripe old age; be durable. **taginayonen.** *v.* to use for a long time. **agtaginayon.** *v.* to persist, persevere. **sanganayon.** *n.* one entire piece. **sangsanganayon.** *a.* continuously, without stopping, uninterrupted. **Awan nayonna?** Isn't there free extra (used when asking for extra free food at the market during a purchase). **Diakto makabayad no nayonam pay ti utangko.** I won't be able to pay if you add more to my debt. [Ivt. *rapa*, Kal. *chuga*, Png. *náyon* (persist, last), Tag. *dagdág* (add; increase to)]

ne: exclamation: see; here. **Ne, alaemon.** Here, take it. [Pronounced *ni:*]

nebéra: (Sp. *nevera*: ice box) *n.* ice box, refrigerator. **ipanebera.** *v.* to put in the refrigerator.

neblína: (Sp. *neblina*: fog) *n.* fog; mist. (*ulep*)

nebnéb: **mainebneb.** *v.* to sink, founder. **inebneb.** *v.* to push in (deeper). **mainebneb.** *a.* driven in deeply; to be submerged. [Tag. *lubóg*]

negár: (Sp. *negar*: deny) *v.* to deny (*libaken*; *saanen*; *suppiaten*). [Tag. *tanggí*]

negatíbo: (Sp. *negativo*) *a.*, *n.* negative.

negosiadór: (Sp. *negociador*) *n.* negotiator; business agent.

negosiánte: (Sp. *negociante*: businessman) *n.* businessman; trader; merchant. [Tag. *manga-ngalakál*]

negósio: (Sp. *negocio*: business) *n.* business (*pagsapulan*; *aramid*); trade; transaction in business; business enterprise. [Kal. *amosanti*, Tag. *kalakal*]

Négra: (Sp. *negra*: black woman) *n.* black woman.

Negríto: (Sp. *negrito*: little black man) *n.* Negrito, the Philippine aborigine.

Négro: (Sp. *negro*: black) *n.* black male. (*nangisit*) **negra.** *n.* black female.

-nem: variant of *innem* with certain prefixes: **maikanem.** *num.* sixth. **sagnenem.** *num.* six each.

nemném: **agpanemnem.** *v.* to keep silent; dissimulate; have an emotional pain. **panemnemen.** *v.* to consider, think deeply about; hold a grudge on; have hard feelings toward.

néneng: (*reg.*) *n.* term of address for young girls.

nengnéng: *n.* slowness to learn; stupidity. (*tabbed*; *muno*, *bobo*) **nanengneng.** *a.* stupid, dimwitted, ignorant. **pangnengnengén.** *a.* rather stupid, rather dull. [Png. *nengneng* = see; Tag. *tangá*]

neumónia: (Sp. *neumonía*: pneumonia) *n.* pneumonia. (*pulmonia*)

nepnép: *n.* continuous rainfall; rainy season. **agnepnep.** *v.* to rain continuously. [Tag. *ulán*]

nepotísmo: (Sp. *nepotismo*: nepotism) *n.* nepotism, showing of favor or political power to one's relatives.

nérbios: (Sp. *nervios*: nerves) *n.* nerve. **agnerbios.** *v.* to be nervous. **kinamanagnerbios.** *n.* nervousness.

nerbióso: (Sp. *nervioso*: nervous) *a.* nervous. (*managkintayég*)

nesesidád: (Sp. *necesidad*: necessity) *n.* necessity. (*kasapulan*)

nesesíta: (Sp. *necesita*: need) *a.* necessary (*nasken*); urgent.

néto: (Eng.) *n.* net profit; net income. **maneto.** *v.* to be able to net. **Mano ti manetoda?** How much can they net?

ni: *art.* Singular of the personal article, used before names of people and intelligent animals (pets); possessive proper article; *interj.* An interjection expressing wonder, or to grab the attention of the hearer. **Ni Carmen ti nagsurat.** Carmen is the one who wrote. **ti aso ni Erlinda.** Erlinda's dog.

ni-: variant of the *-in-* infix or *in-* prefix before *l.*

'niá: Contracted form of *ania*: what.

nibél: (Sp. *nivel*: level) *n.* level. **nibelado.** *a.* leveled; exactly leveled. **nibelasion.** *n.* leveling; grading.

nibí: **mangnibinibi.** *a.* full, filled; thorough; excessive, extreme; deep, strong (emotions).

nído: (Sp. *nido*: nest) *n.* a bird's-nest soup; edible bird's nest used in soup.

niébe: (Sp. *nieve*: snow) *n.* snow. **agniebe.** *v.* to snow.

niéblas: *var.* of *tinieblas*: Lent; Tenebrae.

nigár: (Sp. *negar*: deny) **pagnigaran.** *v.* to deny.

nikel: (Sp. *niquel*) *n.* nickel; five-centavo coin. **nikelado.** *a.* nickel plated.

níket: *n.* a kind of hard timber.

nikotína: (Sp. *nicotina*: nicotine) *n.* nicotine, poison contained in tobacco leaves.

nímpa: (Sp. *ninfa*: nymph) *n.* nymph, lesser goddess of nature.

ninám: (*vulg.*) abbreviated attributive form of *ukinnam*. **Ninam nga ubing!** You damn child!

nináná: (*vulg.*) abbreviated attributive form of *ukinnana*. **Ninana ket daytoy nga salawasaw!** Damn this loudmouth!

ninanattóy: (*vulg.*) abbreviated attributive form of *ukinnana daytoy*. **ninanattoy nga ubing!** this damn child!

nínang: *n.* godmother (*iná ti buniág*); female sponsor at a baptism or wedding.

ninatengán: (f. *naténg*) *n.* vegetable garden.

nínin: *n.* cicada. (*andidit*; *kundidit*)

níning: **makanining.** *n.* variety of awned rice with soft white kernel.

nínio: (Sp. *niño*: child) *n.* child (used in certain religious terms). **Santo Ninio.** *n.* Holy Christ child.

niniogán: (f. *nióg*) *n.* glutinous rice cooked in coconut milk.

nínong: *n.* godfather (*amá ti buniág*); male sponsor at a baptism or wedding.

nióg: *n.* coconut (tree or fruit), *Cocos nucifera*. **niniog.** *n.* coconuts. **agnininniog.** *n.* a children's team game played with coconuts, consisting of hiding and finding them. **kaniugan.** *n.* coconut grove. [Bon. *inyog*, Bol. *úngut*, Ibg. *niyug*, *inyug*, Ivt. *nyuy*, Kal. *iyug*, Kpm. *ngúngut*, Png., Tag. *nióg*]

nípa: *n.* the *nipa* palm whose leaves are used for thatching; the alcoholic beverage distilled from this palm. [Ibg. *tata*, Ivt., Tag. *nipà*, Kal. *alaaw*, Knk. *atep*, Kpm. *sasa*, Png. *nipa*]

nípis: (Sp. *naipes*: cards) **innipis, nipis.** *n.* playing cards. **aginnipis.** *v.* to play cards.

nisí: *n.* a leaf used for manufacturing mats.

nisnís: *n.* a rag used to wipe dirty things (pots, etc.) **karuprupa't-nisnis.** *exp.* (*lit*: with the face of a rag) miserable and poor. **nisnisan.** *v.* to wipe with a rag. [Kal. *gitoy, geyon*, Tag. *basahan*]

níto: *n. Lygodium* sp. fern used in basket and hat making: *L. flexuosum*, *L. japonicum*; striped black and white, small, edible marine fish; black reed; catfish, *Plotosus anguillaris*.

nitróheno: (Sp. *nitrógeno*) *n.* nitrogen.

nítso: (Sp. *nicho*: niche) *n.* tomb, niche; vault; niche.

niwníw₁: **maniwniw.** *v.* to doze off, drowse; be faint, dizzy (*ulaw*). [Tag. *hiló*]

niwníw₂: **niwniwen.** *v.* to waste, spend unwisely.

no: **um-umno.** *v.* to be proper, correct.

no₁: *conj.* if; when (in the future). **no kasta.** thus. **no .. kuma.** introduces a conditional clause. **no ano man.** Never. **no dadduma.** Sometimes. **no la ketdi.** Provided that, if. **no di pay ket.** but also. **no di ket.** but rather. **no bilang ta.** in case. **no bilang adda.** in case of (+ N); just in case. **no kua.** then, later; afterwards. **uray no.** even though, although. **no kua ngay.** what if, suppose. **no maminsan.** sometimes. **no man no, no kas no.** if, in the case that. **Awanen ti maaramidna no di agulimek.** She couldn't do anything but remain quiet. **Adu dagiti kayatmi nga aramiden, no la ketdi kabaelan ti bagimi.** There are many things we would like to do, if only we were able to. [Bon. *mo*, Kpm. *nung*, Png. *no*, Tag. *kung, pag*]

no₂: subordinator may precede a clause denoting a mistaken impression. **Kunak no nagawidkan.** I thought you had already left.

no₃: subordinator that precedes interrogatives to form indefinite pronouns that head subordinate clauses (in main clauses *uray* is used for the same purpose): **Indiak ammo no ania ti kinayatna.** I don't know what he/she wanted. **Ammom kadi *no* apay a kanayon a kuykuyogenka?** Do you know why I always go with you? **Dina ammo *no* kasano ti kapaut ti pannakaipupokna.** She doesn't know how long he will be in jail.

nuágas: *var.* of *naguas*: underskirt, petticoat.

nuáng: *n.* water buffalo, carabao. **agnuang.** *v.* to win many times over in gambling. **kanuangán.** *n.* preferred, favorite carabao. **kanuángan.** *n.* place where there are many water buffalo. **saba ti nuang, sabatnuang.** *n.* variety of small, sweet yellow banana. **Kasla agdurduri a nuang.** *exp.* He has the backbone of a water buffalo (not sensitive to criticism or bad remarks). [Ibg. *nuwang* (generic); *abbáy* (female), Ivt. *pagad*, Kal. *luwang*, Knk. *nuáng*, Kpm. *damúlag*, Png. *duég*, Tag. *kalabáw*]

nobáto: (Sp. *novato*: novice) *n.* novice, greenhorn.

nobedád: (Sp. *novedad*) *n.* novelty; special news.

nobéla: (Sp. *novela*: novel) *n.* novel. **nobelista.** *n.* novelist.

nobéna: (Sp. *novena*: novena) *n.* novena, nine day prayer. **nobenario.** *n.* booklet containing a novena.

nobénta: (Sp. *noventa*: ninety) *num.* ninety (*siam a pulo*).

nobesiéntos: (Sp. *novecientos*: nine hundred) *n.* nine hundred. (*siam a gasut*)

nóbia: (Sp. *novia*: girlfriend) *n.* girlfriend, fiancée. (*kaayan-ayat*)

Nobiémbre: (Sp. *noviembre*: November) *n.* November. [Kal. *upok*]

nóbio: (Sp. *novio*: boyfriend) *n.* boyfriend, fiancé. **agnobio.** *n.* sweethearts. **Daydi la ti panagginnurami bayat ti panagnobiomi.** That was the only thing that we were mad at each other about when we were going steady.

nobisiádo: (Sp. *noviciado*: novitiate) *n.* novitiate, period of trial and preparation in a religious order; synonym for *nobisio*.

nóbisio: (Sp. *novicio*: novice) *n.* novice in a religious congregation.

nóble: (Sp.) *n.* nobleman; *a.* noble.

noblésa: (Sp. *nobleza*: nobility) *n.* nobility.

núbog: *a.* closed with gum (eyes).

nuébe: (Sp. *nueve*: nine) *num.* nine. (*siam*) **Alas nuebe.** Nine o'clock.

nués: (Sp. *nuez*: nut) *n.* nut. (*bukel a makan*) **nues moskáda.** *n.* nutmeg, spicy seed from the fruit of an East Indian tree. **nues de nogál.** *n.* walnut. [Tag. *nuwés*]

nogáles: (Sp. *nogal*: walnut) *n.* walnut. (*nués de nogál*)

nugúnog: *n.* internal decay. (*nunóg*)

nugót: inugot. *v.* to divide equally, apportion, allot, allocate. **mainugot.** *v.* to be in proportion; suitable, appropriate; in accordance with. **agkanugotan.** *v.* to agree, concur.

núka: *n.* defect in timber. **agnuka.** *v.* to be defective (timber only).

nuknók: nuknuken. *v.* to spool, wind into a ball.

nukúnok: *n.* heap, pile. (*penpen, gabsuon*) **agnukunok.** *v.* to heap up; pile up. [Tag. *buntón*]

noktúrno: (Sp. *nocturno*) *a.* nocturnal.

núman pay: *conj.* even if, even though. **Pagdaksanna kadakayo ta numan pay agasinusokayo iti biag ket nakatangtangkenen ti uloyo.** That's bad for you because although you are immature in life, you are still headstrong. (*nupay, uray no*)

númang: agnumang. *v.* to match, suit, form a pair; stand in front; stand in pairs. **agsinumang.** *v.* to stand on both sides.

numár: (Sp. *remunerar*: remunerate) **agnumar.** *v.* to gain, benefit. (*tubo*)

nombrádo: (Sp.) *a.* appointed; nominated.

nombramiénto: (Sp. *nombramiento*: nomination) *n.* nomination; appointment; commission.

nombrár: (Sp. *nombrar*: nominate) **inombrar.** *v.* to appoint; nominate.

nomenklatúra: (Sp. *nomenclatura*) *n.* nomenclature.

numerasión: (Sp. *numeración*) *n.* numbering; notation.

número: (Sp. *número*: number) *n.* number (*bilang*); figure. **numerado.** *a.* numbered.

nómina: (Sp. *nómina*: payroll) *n.* payroll.

nominár: (Sp. *nominar*: nominate) **inominar.** *v.* to nominate. **nominado.** *a.* nominated.

nominasión: (Sp. *nominación*) *n.* nomination.

numismátika: (Sp. *numismática*) *n.* numismatics.

numó: *n.* humility; smallness; poorness, inadequacy, inferiority, unimportance, insufficiency. **agnumo.** *v.* to enter into a contract (plural actor). **nanumo.** *a.* humble, poor, meager, inferior, unimportant, insignificant. (*pakumbaba*) **agnunumo.** *v.* to band together, league, combine plans; agree, come to terms. **mainumo.** *v.* to fit, suit, be appropriate for; be applicable. **agkanumo.** *v.* agree, concur; be compatible. **inumnumo.** *v.* to take into account. **kainumuan, pakainumuan.** *n.* worth; value; importance; appropriateness. **pagnumuan.** *v.* to agree upon. [Png. *mapaabeba*, Tag. *pakumbabâ*]

numóna: numona ta. *conj.* although; even though (*uray no*); since. **numnumóna:** *n.* aggravating circumstances to an already bad situation. **Sayang no di agbalin a macho numona ta guapo.** It's a shame if he doesn't become masculine because he is good looking. [Tag. *kahit na*]

numónia: (Sp. *neumonia*: pneumonia) *n.* pneumonia. **agnumonia.** *v.* to have pneumonia.

nónes: (Sp. *nones*: no) *a.* odd (in number). **nones ken pares.** *n.* odds and evens.

núnog: *n.* internal itch. (*obs.*) **agnunog.** *v.* to stay in water longer than necessary.

nunóg: *n.* internal decay under the skin (meat of animals). **agnunog.** *v.* to decay under the skin.

núnong: kanunong. *n.* fellow victim, sufferer. **kumanunong.** *v.* to agree, conform, comply. **kankanunong.** *n. Loranthus sp.* parasitic shrubs with leathery leaves.

núnot: nunutan. *v.* to bear, endure, tolerate; submit to, put up with. (*ibtur*)

núnsio: (Sp. *nuncio*: nuncio) *n.* nuncio, ecclesiastical representative.

nunton-anó: (*obs.*) *var.* of *inton-ano*.

núngka: (Sp. *nunca*: never) *adv.* never. **Nungka nga immayak.** I never came. (*uray inton kaano man*)

nungnóng: **nungnungan.** *v.* to favor, prefer. (*kaykayat*)

núo: **masinunuo.** *v.* to see be sure; have no doubts; see clearly, discern; completely understand. [Tag. *tiyák*]

nuó: **agnuo** (*obs.*) *v.* to touch the forehead. [Tag. *noó* = forehead]

núpay: *conj.* although, even though; granted that. (*uray no*) **nupay kasta.** *conj.* nevertheless, however, in spite of that, still, yet. **Medio naangtiten ti karne nupay naupran iti suka ken asin.** The meat has somewhat of a rotten smell although it was soaked in vinegar and salt. [Knk. *teté*, Png. *anggan*, Tag. *kahit*, *bagamát*]

núpsia: (Sp. *nupcia*: wedding) *n.* obedience.

nurnór: **nurnuren.** *v.* to do regularly and steadily, (a sailboat floating adrift, rain that doesn't change its intensity, etc.); to go straight ahead; to follow a path; follow a course. **Nakalaglag-an ti riknana idi pampanurnurendan ti puraw a kalsada.** He felt at ease as he went down the white road.

normál: (Sp.) *a.* normal. **normalidad.** *n.* normality.

nurúnor: **manurunor.** *v.* to erode from water contact.

nórte: (Sp. *norte*: north) *n.* north. (*amianan*)

Norwégo: (Sp. *noruego*) *n.*, *a.* Norwegian.

nusnús: **nusnusan.** *v.* to make thin; thin out the end of a thread before passing it through the needle.

nóta: (Sp. *nota*: note; grade) *n.* note; mark; grade; memorandum; bad reputation.

notário: (Sp. *notario*: notary) *n.* notary public. **agpanotario.** *v.* to go to a notary.

nótas: (Sp. *notas*: notes) *n.* comments; annotations.

notipikár: (Sp. *notificar*) **inotipikar.** *v.* to notify.

notísia: (Sp. *noticia*: notice) *n.* notice.

nutnót: **nutnuten.** *v.* to suck (the thumb) (*kunnot*). **Naregreg ti nutnutnutanna a tulang.** The bone he was sucking on dropped. [Tag. *nutnót*]

nótsebuéna: (Sp. *Nochebuena*: Christmas Eve) *n.* celebration after the midnight mass; Christmas eve.

nuynóy: **panuynuyan.** *v.* to tolerate; condescend; yield to, accommodate oneself to.

-nsa: suffix. variant of *-sa* after a vowel, also written *-n sa*: **Isuda***n* **sa.** I think it's them. **Agtagtagainepka***nsa***.** I think you are dreaming.

-nto: *enclitic.* variant of future enclitic *-to* after a vowel: **Tawaganka***nto***.** I *will* call you. **Mapanda***nto***.** They *will* go. **Iti***nto* **korte ti paglinnawaganta!** We will clear it up in court. [Bon. *esa*]

NG

-ng: suffix. Attaches to certain kin terms (in direct or indirect address). **Mamang.** Mother, Mommy. **Papang.** Father, Daddy. **Tatang.** Father, Daddy.

nga: *lig.* 1. a ligature that connects various parts of a sentence, its variant is sometimes *a* before consonants. This particle connects nouns and adjectives: **dakkel a balay.** large house. **bassit nga aso.** small dog; and is also used to introduce subordinate clauses (relative or complement): **Kayatko nga mapanka.** I want you to go; **Ti tao nga nagsardeng.** The man that stopped. [Png. *ya, -n, a,* Tag. *na, -ng*]

ngáaw: *var.* of *igaaw*: drought.

ngábit: agngangabit. *v.* to be on the verge of, to be just about to. **Agngangabit ti angesna.** He's on the verge of dying.

ngabngáb₁: *n.* width (of a hole); lip of a jar; someone who talks about something he doesn't understand. **mangabngaban.** *v.* to be blasted with a large hole. **Kimraang ti ittip iti ngabngab ti kaldero.** The rice crust around the mouth of the pot dried up. [Tag. *bungangà*]

ngabngáb₂: ngabngaben. *v.* to devour foods noisily (pigs).

ngábo: (*obs.*) **kangabuan.** *n.* descendant. **inngabo.** *a.* obtained by unlawful means.

ngabrás: (Sp. *hebra*?: fiber, thread) **nginabras.** *n.* strand. **tunggal nginabras ti pusok.** every strand of my heart.

ngad: see *ngarud.*

ngádal: agngadal. *v.* to experience difficulty in speaking (said of dying or drunk persons); to stammer (as drunks) (*beddál*). [Tag. *utál*]

ngádas: *n.* palate, roof of the mouth (*ngawngaw*); the rice that cleaves to the upper half of the jar in which it is cooked; the concave side of a jar or pot. **agngadas.** *v.* to have a sore palate; (*reg.*) to be unable to pronounce (said of dying people). **Kasla adda pay la iti ngadasko ti nanam ti igado.** The taste of liver seems to still be on my palate. [Bon. *tángen,* Png. *tawentawen,* Tag. *ngalangalá* (palate)]

ngakngák: *n.* cry of the water buffalo (*nguak*). **nangakngak.** *a.* (*fig.*) loquacious. [Tag. *ungâ*]

ngalángal: mangalangal. *v.* to be dislocated or open (said of wounds of bones, etc.).

ngalawngáw: *a.* talkative. **nangalawngaw.** *a.* talkative, loquacious; noisy, boisterous. (*salawasaw, tarabitab*)

ngálay: *n.* middle (time or space). **agngalay.** *v.* to be halfway. **iti ngalay ti dalan.** halfway iti

ngalay ti rabii. at midnight. [Png. *pegléy,* Tag. *gitnâ*]

ngalngál: ngalngalen. *v.* to masticate, chew on. **agngalngal.** *v.* to chew (*ngatíngat, karemkem, karut-óm, mamá*). **Kasla nakangalngal iti sili ti sairo iti panagdiwigna.** His crooked expression looks like he chewed on hot pepper. **Dika pay nangalngal, tilmonemon.** You still haven't chewed and you already are swallowing (said to a person who is too hasty). [Various Ilocano roots that deal with chewing are: *karit-óm, karut-óm, karemkém* (chewing crunchy foods), *atimálon* (chewing with both sides of the mouth), *kabúkab* (chewing with an empty mouth), *kabúl* (chewing with difficulty), *mamá, ngatíngat* (chewing for a prolonged time as when chewing on a cud or betel nut). Kal. *gùayon, kotkot,* Knk. *gamíw, gamíl,* Tag. *nguyâ*]

ngálug: *n.* purslane, *Portulaca oleracea,* which is cooked for hogfeed and used in native medicine against hepatitis. **ngalugngalug.** *n.* a kind of sea parsley.

ngáman: Interrogative particle; why. (literary) **ngaman no.** in that case.

ngamín: *part.* 1. particle that expresses reproof or emphasis. **apay ngamin?** Why (emphatic)? 2. may also indicate a causal relationship (because) or additional confirmation. **ngamin lalakida.** because they are boys. **Isu ngamin.** It was indeed him.

ngampáy: [*ngamin + pay*] why?

nganawngáw: (f. *ngawngáw*) **ngumanawngaw.** *v.* to mutter, grumble loudly.

nganemngém: (f. *ngemngém*) *n.* murmured complaints; mumbling (*dayamúdom*). **agnganemngem.** *v.* to murmur complaints; mumble. **ngumanemngem.** *v.* to mutter complaints under one's breath; mumble.

nganerngér: (f. *ngerngér*) *n.* sound of continuous growling or gnarling. **ngumangernger.** *v.* to continuously growl or grumble. [Tag. *angil*]

ngáni: nganngani. *adv.* nearly, almost, a little short of. (*dandani*) **ngangnani saan.** *adv.* scarcely, barely.

ngangá: *n.* pit of the stomach. **agnganga.** *v.* to open the mouth wide (*tungaab, tuyaab*). **nakananga.** *a.* agape; unshut. **napanganga.** *a.* amazed, astonished; perplexed. [Png. *nganga,* Tag. *higáb, ngangá* (agape)]

ngángaw: agngangaw. *v.* to be delirious; talk while sleeping; complain.

ngangáw: *n.* palate (*ngádas*). [Tag. *ngalangalá*]

ngángot: *a.* stupid; foolish (*tabbéd*). [Tag. *tangá*]

ngápit: agngangapit. *v.* to be on the verge of death.

ngárab₁: *n.* outline, border, edge; trim; rim. **Nakaiddaak iti ngarab ti maysa a waig.** I lay down at the edge of a creek. [Tag. *gilid*]

ngárab₂: *n.* lateral fins of the ray. (*pigar*)

ngaradángad: agngaradangad. *n.* the sound of a log being drawn over gravel. **mangaradangadan** (*obs.*) *v.* to be wounded (sole of foot).

ngaramngám: *n.* a small *daklis* seine.

ngarapngáp: *n.* *Calladium bicolor*, a multicolored herb; *n.* an edible mollusk, smaller that the *gosipeng.* **agngarapngap.** *v.* to spread, increase (skin diseases). (*ramram*)

ngarasángas: *var.* of *ngarasngas*: crunch.

ngarasngás: *n.* crunchy sound; sound of grating or scraping; sound of sandpaper. **nangarasngas.** *a.* brittle, fragile, frail; crunchy. **ngumarasngas.** *v.* to crunch while eating. (*sarangsang*)

ngarawngáw₁: ngumarawngaw. *v.* to make a crunching sound while eating. **ngarawngawen.** *v.* to crunch on, eat raw vegetables. **nangarawngaw.** *a.* crunchy.

ngarawngáw₂: nangarawngaw. *a.* noisy; talkative; (*obs.*) badly seasoned. **agngarawngaw.** *v.* to meow nosily (said of cats in heat).

ngarayngáy: ngarayngayen. *v.* to touch the edge of a knife to test its sharpness.

ngarebngéb: agngarebngeb. *v.* to gnash the teeth. (*ngariet, ngaretnget*)

ngaretngét: agngaretnget. *v.* to gnash the teeth repeatedly. **ngaretngeten.** *v.* to cut or gnash with the teeth. [Png. *ngayét, ngaletenget*, Tag. *ngalót*]

ngariét: agngariet. *v.* to gnash the teeth once. Compare with *ngaretnget*. **pagngarietan.** *v.* to do with so much effort that the teeth gnash. [Tag. *ngalit*]

ngarikngík: *n.* high-pitched, shrieking laughter. (said of females; *ungik* is used for pigs). **agngarikngik.** *v.* to laugh with high-pitched shrieking.

ngaríteb: *n.* sound of grinding teeth. **ngumariteb.** *v.* to chew extraneous matter in rice (small stones, etc.).

ngarubángib: *n.* the edge of a steep bank of a river.

ngarúd: *part.* then, so. **into ngarud no.** if, in case that. **anansa ngarud.** Therefore, wherefore. **No mapanka idiay ilik, agkaluganta la ngaruden.** If you are going to my town, let's ride together then. [Bon. *ngalod*, Png. *sírin*, Tag. *di, ngâ*]

ngarusángis: *n.* a wild herb full of milklike sap; a kind of speckled marine scallop.

ngarusíngis: *n.* the sound produced by dogs eating, rats gnawing. **agngarusingis.** *v.* to produce this sound.

ngarusngós: *a.* greedy. (*rawet*) **ngarusngusen.** *v.* to devour, eat raw vegetables (or other crunchy things) greedily. **Ngarusngusem pati ukisna no adda pay laeng ngipenmo.** Devour even the skin (of the vegetable), if you still have teeth. **Diak man ammo ta kasda la makangarusngos iti marasaba a salamagi nga agtilmotilmon a makakitkita kaniak.** I don't know why but it's like they are devouring a ripe tamarind and swallowing when they look at me.

ngaruyngóy: *n.* food craving. **agngaruyngoy.** *v.* to crave for a certain kind of food. **ngaruynguyen.** *v.* to eat voraciously.

ngarsáb: *a.* greedy in eating (animals); voracious. **ngarsaben.** *v.* to eat greedily, devour voraciously (*rawet*). [Tag. *ngasáb*]

ngarsíb: nginarsib. a kind of *wasig* cloth with alternating stripes of two colors. **agngarsib.** *v.* to chatter (teeth in cold). (*ngasib*)

ngasángas: agngasangas. *v.* to wear out (shoes); to suffer injury by use. **ngasangasen.** *v.* to break in tight shoes until they fit, loosen by wearing.

ngásib: agngasib. *v.* to chatter (jaws); (*reg.*) to be still, cease to move.

ngatá: *part.* perhaps, maybe (*siguro*); particle in questions that requests the opinion of the addressee. **agngatangata.** *v.* to be doubtful, hesitant, undecided. **ngatangataen.** *v.* to take lightly. **Ania ngata no inta pay mangrabii?** What if we go have dinner first? **Napintas ngata?** Do you think she's pretty? [Bon. *eleg, nganóya, ngen, ngata*, Tag. *yatà* (perhaps); *alinlangan* (doubt); Ibg. *ngattá* = why]

ngatíngat: agngatingat. *v.* to chew the cud, to chew betel. **mangatngatingat.** *v.* to be talked about (rumors). **maingatingat.** *v.* to spread rumors. **ngatingaten.** *v.* to chew on something for some time; to have a small snack. [Png. *gatgát*, Tag. *ngangà, nguyâ, ngatâ*]

ngatngát: *var.* of *ngetnget*: gnaw, tear with the teeth. **Nginatngatna ti naammolan ti tabakona sana intupra.** He gnawed on the cigar in his mouth then spit it out. [Tag. *ngatngát*]

ngáto: *n.* height; upstairs. **nangato.** *a.* high, (in position, location, social standing). **akinngato.** *a.* on top; high above. **agpangato.** *a.* to ascend; climb up; go up. **ngumato.** *v.* to rise; attain a better position; go up. **ingato, ipangato.** *v.* to raise, lift; promote; advance. **iti ngato.** *prep.* above, overhead. **aginngangato.** *v.* to be pretentious. **pangatuen.** *v.* to raise, increase. **singangato.** *a.* raised; uplifted. [Kal. *taklang*, Png. *tagéy*, Tag. *taás*]

ngawngáw: *n.* mouth (of a river), gorge; entrance to throat. **agngawngaw.** *v.* to meow (said of the cat), speak softly, under one's breath; gossip. **Uray anianton ti ngawngawen dagiti kaarubada kontra kenkuana, dida ammo nga isakit uray pay kaanakanna.** Whatever their neighbors gossip against him, they don't know that it also hurts his nephew.

ngay: Interrogative particle inciting response or affirmation from the hearer. **sika ngay?** what about you?

ngáya: ngumayangaya (*obs.*) *v.* chatterer.

ngayángay: *n.* plan, purpose (*gandat*; *gagara*; *gakat*; *sikat*; *panggep*; *ranta*). **agngayangay.** *v.* to plan; run for; apply for; make an attempt for. **ngayangayen.** *v.* to plan to do something; vie for a position; attempt. **ngumayangay.** *v.* to threaten rain. [Tag. *subok*]

ngayát: **agngangayat.** *v.* to desire, long for, wish (*iliw*; *kalikagum*; *tarigagay*). [Tag. *sabík*]

ngayéd: *n.* splendor, elegance. **nangayed.** *a.* graceful, grand, elegant, tasteful, refined, good-looking, charming; noble. **kinangayed.** *n.* elegance, charm, grace, beauty, splendor. **pangngayedén.** *a.* rather splendid, elegant, grand. [Png. *dakep*, Tag. *dikít*]

ngayemngém: **ingayemngem.** *v.* to mutter in disapproval. **ngayemngeman.** *v.* to mutter at someone.

ngayngáy: *adv.* repeatedly; often. **mangayngay.** *v.* to become frequent. **ngayngayen.** *v.* to do repeatedly. **inton mangayngay.** *exp.* in the end; as a result.

ngedngéd: **nangednged.** *a.* weak, feeble, simple minded; tightly roped; shortened. **ngedngedan.** *v.* to shorten, tighten (ropes, etc.); rein in, pull in; hold back. **Ngedngedak koma ti wingiwingko iti saludsodna ngem masapul a napudnoak iti sinapataak.** I should hold back shaking my head at his questions but I must be truthful to what I swore under oath.

ngeg: Contracted form of *dengngeg* after certain prefixes. **makangeg.** *v.* to be able to hear **mangngeg.** *v.* to listen, pay attention to; hear.

ngelngél: *a.* blunt, not sharp; stupid (*ngudel*). **No kasano ti kasikapna, kasta met ti kinangelngelna iti innarman.** Just as he is clever, he is stupid when it comes to courting.

ngem: *conj.* but. **ket saan ngem** (*obs.*) lest. *prep.* than. **Nataytayagka ngem siak.** You are taller than me. [Kpm. *inyang*, *onéng*, *dápot*, Png. *bálet*, *et*, Tag. *ngunit*]

ngemngém: *n.* mumbling when irritated. **ngumanemngem.** *v.* to mutter, murmur when annoyed, mumble.

ngenngén: ngumenngen. *v.* to increase, extend; spread; grow; augment; to worsen (sickness). (*samay*)

ngepngép: nangepngep. *a.* dark, narrow, strait. (*obs.*) disgusted **ngepngepen.** *v.* to cut the hair or trees close to the root (*punget*).

ngerngér: *n.* growling sound; sound of sawing. (*ngusungos*) **agngernger.** *v.* to gnarl, growl, snarl (dogs). **ngerngeran.** *v.* to growl at. **Dina nadlaw ti panangngernger kenkuana.** He didn't hear the growling at him. [Tag. *angil*]

ngesngés: ngesngesen. *v.* to have difficulty when breathing through the nose (as a person with sinusitis).

ngetngét: ngetngeten. *v.* to tear with the teeth; tear off. **Nangetnget ti pusok iti ilem.** *exp.* My heart was torn with suspicion. [Tag. *ngatngát*]

ngiáw: *n.* meow of a cat. **agngiaw.** *v.* to meow (said of the cat). [Knk. *ngaw*, Tag. *ngiyáw*; Knk. *ngiáw* = cat]

ngibngíb: *a.* having worn-out front teeth. (*ribrib*)

ngíit: *n.* muffled laughter, smile, grin. (*rungiit*) **ngiít**: agngiit. *v.* to crumple the face in anger.

ngíla: *n.* the indican of the indigo plant.

ngilángil: *n.* shaking of the head. **agngilangil.** *v.* to shake the head. (*lingaling*) **nangilangil.** *a.* partly threshed (rice). **Umis-isem nga agngilngilangil ni Soling a nangsipsiput kenkuana.** Soling smiled and shook her head as she watched him.

ngílaw: *n.* housefly. **ngilaw ti nuang.** *n.* horsefly. **nginilaw.** *a.* fly infested. **Maysa a ngilaw laengen ti di nakapagpirma.** *exp.* denoting that an event is soon to happen (*lit*: only one fly wasn't able to sign). [Bon. *láleg*, Ifg. *lálo*, Ivt. *naned*, Kal. *lingaw*, Knk. *laláeg*, Kpm. *lángo*, Png. *apángat*, Ibg., Tag. *langaw*]

ngílin: panagngilin. *n.* holy day; holiday. **agngilin.** *v.* to observe a holy day; holiday. [Png. *ngilín*]

ngína: *n.* price, cost; worth, value. (*gatad*; *pateg*; *presio*) **ngumina.** *v.* to go up in price. **nangina.** *a.* expensive, costly, dear; precious. **ipangina.** *v.* to increase the price of. **nginaan.** *v.* to pay. **panginaan.** *v.* to set a price on; to charge. **Dios ti agngina.** Thank you. **agpangina.** *v.* to be vain; conceited; to assume to be more important than one actually is. **tanginginaen.** *v.* to consider something expensive. **Nangina nga Aldaw.** *n.* Holy Week. **agimpapangina.** *v.* to play hard to get; to pretentiously show off material wealth although poor. [Ibg. *ngina*, Ivt. *mayñin*, Kal. *ngila*, Kpm. *mal*, Png. *bilí*, Tag. *mahál*, *halagá*]

ngínaw: *n.* first three months after conception. **agnginaw.** *v.* to be in the first three months after conception; to be pregnant; to ear (palay). **pagnginawen.** *v.* to impregnate. **pagnginawen.** *n.* something craved by a pregnant woman, something used to alleviate the cravings of a pregnant woman. (*ínaw*)

ngindarúpa: nangindarupa. *a.* evident, shown on one's face; blushing.

ngípen: *n.* tooth; cog. **agngipen.** *v.* to grow teeth. **ngipen ti bawang.** *n.* clove of garlic. **pangipen.** *n.* dentures, false teeth (*pustiso*). **pagpangipen.** *n.* money needed for dentures.[Bon. *bab-a*, Ibg. *ngifen*, Ivt. *ñipen*, Kal. *ngipon*, Knk. *bab-á*, Kpm. *ípan*, Png. *ngipén*, Tag. *ngipin*]

ngírad: *n.* hardwood used as a fuel for bakery ovens. [Tag. *bakawan*]

ngíraw: *var.* of *ngiaw*: to meow (said of cats). **Nagngirawngiraw a timmaray ti pusana.** His cat ran away meowing.

ngirét: agngirngiret. *v.* to gnash the teeth. (*ngariet*)

ngirngír: *n.* dirt; smear. **nangirngir.** *a.* dirty, soiled, smeared; greasy. **agngirngir.** *v.* to be dirtied, smeared, soiled. **tuél ngirngir.** *n.* croaker fish of the *Sciaenidae* family. **Kasla kalkali a kamote ti ubing iti kinangirngirna.** The child is like a freshly dug sweet potato because of his dirtiness. [Tag. *dungis*]

ngirsí: *n.* grin. **agngirsi, ngumirsi.** *v.* to make faces, grimace; grin (*rungiit*). **ngirsian.** *v.* to make a face at someone, grin at. [Png. *ngiriyet*, *pankobibit*, Tag. *ngibit*; *ngiwî*]

ngirsíit: *n.* giggle; smirk. **agngirsiit.** *v.* to giggle (with a smirk or grin).

ngísit: *n.* black. **nangisit.** *a.* black, dark-colored. **agmangisit.** *v.* to wear mourning clothes. **ngumisit.** *v.* to become dark (from the sun, etc.). **Nangisit ti darana.** *exp.* denoting a savage or evil person (*lit*: with black blood). [Bon. *ngítit*, Ibg. *ngisíq*, Ivt. *mavaheng*, Kal., Knk. *ngitit*, Kpm. *matuling*, Png. *asirég, dekét*, Tag. *itím*]

ngisngís: *reg.* variant of *ngiwngiw*: corner of the mouth.

ngitíngit: kangitingitan. *n.* middle, center; climax, height, the most impressionable part of a thing; seriousness. **agngitingit.** *v.* to reach the climax; come to the height of. [Tag. *sukdól*]

ngíwat: *n.* mouth. **agngiwat.** *v.* to talk loudly. **nangiwat.** *a.* talkative, loquacious; blatant, loudmouthed. **ngiwanngiwat.** *a.* mouth to mouth. **pannakangiwat.** *n.* spokesperson. **Saannak a ngiwngiwatan.** Don't badmouth me. [Ibg. *simuq*, Ivt. *viviq*, Kal. *sangi, tupok*, Knk. *tupék*, Kpm. *asbuk*, Png. *sangí, songót*, Tag. *bibíg*]

ngiwngíw: *n.* corner of the mouth; (*reg.*) upper lip, border of the lip; jaw.

nguák: *n.* the cry of the water buffalo. **agnguak.** *v.* to cry (said of the water buffalo). [Tag. *ungâ*]

ngubngób₁: *a.* having sunken lips due to toothlessness; neckless. **nangungob.** *a.* with a broken nose; with sunken lips (toothless person).

ngubngób₂: ingubngob. *v.* to slam the face of someone to the ground. **maingubngob.** *v.* to fall on one's face. **Ilayatna ti karaykay a ngubngubanna.** He raised the rake to hit him in the face with.

ngubngób₃: ngubnguban. *v.* to eat ravenously, devour. (*rawet*)

ngudángod: ingudangod. *v.* to knock down to the ground. (*mudumod*)

ngudél: *n.* dullness. **nangudel.** *a.* dull, not sharp, blunt; rude, unpolished, unrefined. **ngumudel.** *v.* to become dull (*ngelngel, dusber, mudél*). **Adda ngudngudelko nga agarem.** I am a bit dull at courting. [Ibg. *ngurel*, Itg. *katdul*, Ivt. *mangareh*, Kal. *pillot, palle*, Knk. *damúdam, dangmém, koplús, ngebngéb*, Kpm. *purul*, Png. *epél*, Tag. *puról, pulpól, pudpód*]

ngúdeng: agngudeng-ngudeng. *v.* to be hesitant, reluctant. (*sarimadeng*)

ngudíit: *n.* chuckle, snicker; soft laughter. **agngudiit.** *v.* to chuckle, snicker; laugh softly.

ngúdo: *n.* tip (of finger); top (of tree); cut bamboo; summit, peak, apex. **agngudo.** *v.* to end, reach the end. **nangudo.** *a.* too close to the tip. **panguduan.** *n.* the end of. [Png. *ngoró*, Tag. *dulo*]

ngugngóg: ngumugngog. *v.* to sob, weep convulsively (*anug-og*). [Tag. *nguynguy*]

ngulá: *n.* pulp, residue of crushed food. [Tag. *sapal*]

ngulángil: *var.* of *ngilángil*: shake the head.

ngúlay: ngulayngulay. *n.* wrist, carpus (*punguapungan*). [Tag. *galanggalangán*]

ngulngól₁: *a.* dull; not sharp. (*ngelngel, ngudel, dusber, lulot*) **ngumulngol.** *v.* to become dull. [Tag. *puról*]

ngulngól₂: ipangulngol. *v.* to give all; provide everything. **ngulngolan.** *v.* to strip the bone of all flesh.

ngúlo: (f. *ulo*) *n.* capital town.

ngóngo: *n.* person who speaks nasally.

ngurét: *n.* the base of the stalk of the sugarcane; a variety of sugarcane with short internodes. **nanguret.** *a.* very fibrous, with little juice or meat. [Tag. *himaymáy* (fibrous)]

nguríit: *var.* of *ngudiit*: chuckle.

nguríngis: *n.* cry of hungry piglets. **agnguringis.** *v.* to cry (said of hungry piglets).

ngurúngor: *a.* with the throat cut. **ngurunguren.** *v.* to behead, decapitate; cut the throat of (in slaughtering). **ngurungoran.** *n.* throat (of a hog). [Tag. *pugot*]

ngursíit: *n.* smirk, derisive smile; giggle. **agngursiit.** *v.* to smirk; giggle.

ngúsab: *n.* sound of voracious eating, chomping. **agngusab.** *v.* to clap, snap the jaws while eating (said of hogs). **Mayat ti ngusab ti lakay iti pinia a dinagas ti adingna.** The old man was devouring the pineapple his younger sibling brought over well. [Tag. *ngasáb*]

ngusángos: **agngusangos.** *v.* to show dislike by shaking the head (animal being fed something it doesn't like); put in the mouth. **Inngusangos ti takong ti pangalna.** The female pig shook her jaw in discontent.

ngusúngos: **agngusungos.** *v.* to growl (said of animals whose food is being taken away). [Tag. *angil*]

ngutáy: **maingutngutay** (*obs.*) *v.* to be very drunk. (*bartek*)

ngutngót: **ngutnguten.** *v.* to gnaw at something.

nguy-á: *n.* agony, death struggle. (*bugsot*) **agnguynguy-a.** *v.* to writhe in pain during a slaughter; to agonize before death. [Tag. *hingalô*]

nguyabbét: *var.* of *nguyapét*: starving; miserable; wretched.

nguyapét: **manguyapet.** *a.* wretched, miserable, indigent; starving. [Tag. *hikahós*]

nguyngóy: **agnguyngoy.** *v.* to whimper (said of children); pant (the last breath). [Tag. *nguyngoy*]

ngrúna: **nangruna.** *a.* especially, particularly, importantly **kangrunaan.** *a.* the most of all, most important; primary. **ipangruna.** *v.* to prefer, favor; to do with much care and attention. **naipangruna.** *a.* specially. **pangrunaen.** *v.* to prefer (*duma*); concentrate on, do with much care. **sumangkangruna.** *adv.* more especially. **Ania ti pangipangrunaam iti kastoy?** Why do you prefer this one? **Isuda ti mangliwliwa kaniak, nangruna pay dagiti makaparagsak a sursuratmo a mamatpatalged kaniak.** They are consoling me, especially the happy letters that advise me. **Sumangkangrunaka nga amada!** Especially you as their father. [Tag. *lalò na*]

O and *U*

In the pre-Hispanic phonemic syllabary of the Ilocanos, *o* and *u* were not distinguished, since they did not contrast meaning. Because of the influx of foreign loans, however, Ilocanos are able to distinguish the two sounds (recognize them as different). Some Ilocano writers choose to reflect the phonetic distinction in their writing, while others do not. In order to simplify the search for words with these letters, I am alphabetizing them together, since no official spelling conventions have been adopted. One convention in spelling is the use of the /o/ vowel when it occurs word-finally, i.e., *bulo, bolo* but not **bolu*, as in this position [o] is the nearest phonetic equivalent.

ubáas: *n.* discarded leaves; vegetable pulp, residue.

ubád: **ubadan**. *v.* to press down (with the fingernail); flatten a hem. **naubadan**. *a.* chafed, fretted (skin) (*kuplat*). **Kunam no mapugsat ti angesna iti pannakaubad ti karabukobna.** You would think he would die from his fretted throat.

óbalo: (Sp. *óvalo*: oval) *n.* oval. **obalado**. *a.* oval shaped, oval.

úban: *n.* gray hairs. **aguban**. *v.* to have gray hairs. **ubanan**. *v.* a variety of rice with white kernel; *a.* gray-haired. [Kal. *uben*, Png. *obán*, Tag. *putíng buhók*]

obário: (Sp. *ovario*: ovary) *n.* ovary.

úbas: (Sp. *uva*: grape) *n.* grapes. **kaubasan**. *n.* vineyard, area where grapes are grown.

ubát: (*obs.*) *n.* kind of coarse gunpowder.

ubbá: **ubbaen**. *v.* to carry on the hip (a baby). **agpaubba**. *v.* to let oneself be carried. **pagubbaan**. *n.* dowry for the parents of the bride (*sab-ong*). [Bon. *aba*, Knk. *abá*, Png. *ebá*, Tag. *kilik*]

ubbák: *n.* sheath of a banana leaf. (*alupási*) **ubbakan**. *v.* to remove the sheath of the banana. [Tag. *sahà*]

ubbáw: **nagubbaw**. *a.* vain, worthless, idle; hollow (words), empty; not mentally alert; *adv.* in vain. (*kawaw*) **kinaubbaw**. *n.* emptiness; falsehood. **agubbaw**. *v.* to become hollow; to become empty. **Ammonan a saan nga ubbaw ti pagbambannoganda.** She knows now that their toils were not in vain. [Tag. *hungkág*]

ubbíng: (pl. of *ubing*) *n.* children.

ubbó: *n.* birdling.

ubbóg: *n.* source, spring, fountain. **agubbog**. *v.* to spring from; gush out from (water). **pagubbogan**. *n.* source. **paubbogen**. *v.* to cause water to come down a well; (*fig.*) cause to produce. **ubbog ti kinaagtutubo.** fountain of youth. **Ubbog sa laengen ti pagsakduan dagiti tao.** I think that the people just get their water from the spring. [Kal. *uud*, Png. *suból*, Tag. *balong, batis, sibol*]

ubbúob: *var.* spelling of *ubuob*: vapor; steam; vapor bath.

obedénsia: (Sp. *obedencia*: obedience) *n.* obedience. (*panagtungpal*)

obéha: (Sp. *oveja*: sheep) *n.* sheep. (*karnéro*)

úber: (*obs.*) *var.* of *uper*.

obertúra: (Sp. *overtura*: overture) *n.* overture, musical introduction to an opera.

úbet: *n.* buttocks (*pátong, kútit*); rump, ass; anus (*merrét, kimmól, kimmót, murríit, purríit, tatakkián*); seat (of trousers). **agpaubet**. *v.* to slide down to the rear; stay at the rear. **mangngubet**. *n.* sodomite. **ubet-ubet**. *n.* kind of worm like the *solsolbot*. **pangubet**. *n.* a kind of small ant with a narrow section between the thorax and abdomen. **paubetan**. *v.* to do from behind; to whip the buttocks of. **ubet ti baso.** *n.* the bottom of the glass; (*fig.*) worthless gem. [Bon. *bágat, kóget, kóbet*, Ibg. *uvoq*, Itg. *pátong*, Ivt. *atang*, Kal. *ammot*, Knk. *kulángat, bulángag, balawét, kimút; tíli*, Kpm. *buldit*, Png. *ebét*, Tag. *puwít*; Knk. *úbet* = anus; Ivt. *uvet* = vagina]

obhetíbo: (Sp. *objectivo*: objective) *n.* objective. (*panggep; tarigagay; gandat*)

obhéto: (Sp. *objeto*: object) *n.* object. (*banag*)

úbi: *n.* purple yam used in many sweets, *Dioscorea alata*; *a.* purple. **ubien**. *n. Artocarpus sp.* timber or tree. [Ibg. *uvi*, Ivt. *uviq*, Knk. *túgi*, Png. *ubí*, Kpm., Tag. *ube*]

ubinnég: *n.* variety of rice.

ubíng: (pl. *ubbing*) *n.* child (*anák*); infant; servant. **agub-ubingan**. *v.* to act childish. **inuubingan**. *a.* childish. **nagubing**. *a.* immature; young. **ubing-ubing**. *a.* childish. **umubing**. *v.* to become younger; feel young; have a fresh outlook. **paubingen**. *v.* to make young. **ubingen**. *v.* to enslave. **paub-ubing**. *n.* servant; slave. **kaubingan**. *n.* contemporary; friend since childhood; *a.* youngest. **panagubing**. *n.* childhood. **agpaubing**. *v.* to undergo treatment to look younger; work as a servant (*agpabagen*). **Narigat ti paub-ubingen.** It is hard to work as a servant. **Pudno a nagkakaubingantayo a tallo.** It is true that the three of us grew up together. **Inkaubinganna ti panagayatna kenkuana.** He loved her since childhood. [Bon. *onga*, Ibg. *abbíng*, Ivt. *mutdeh*, Kal. *alak*, Knk. *banuág*, Kpm. *anak*, Png. *ogáw* (child), *languér* (young), Tag. *batà*]

obíspo: (Sp. *obispo*: bishop) *n.* bishop. **arso-bispo.** *n.* archbishop. **obispado.** *n.* diocese, episcopate. (*pagobispuan*)

obituário: (Sp. *obituario*: obituary) *n.* obituary.

ublág: *n.* discouragement. (*upay*) **maublag.** *v.* to be discouraged; to become weakened (affections). **ublagen.** *v.* to discourage; dissuade. **Talaga a kasta ti agayat, adda latta tubeng ken ublag.** That is really how love is, it has obstacles and discouragement. **No magna ti imbag, magna met ti ublag.** If there is goodness, there is also humiliation.

obligár: (Sp. *obligar*: oblige) **obligaren.** *v.* to oblige; force. (*pilit*) **obligado.** *a.* obliged.

obligatório: (Sp. *obligatorio*: obligatory) *n.* obligatory.

óbo: (Eng.) *n.* oboe. **agobo.** *v.* to play the oboe.

úbo: *n.* leak; leakage. (*tedted*) **agubo.** *v.* to leak (not by drops). [Ivt. *nahan*, Png. *terter, turo*, Tag. *tagas*]

ubó: ubuen. to carry something somewhere (*awit*). [Tag. *dalhín*]

ub-úb: ub-úban. *v.* to drink coconut water from the shell. (*ab-ab*)

úbod: *n.* pith of a young coconut tree, (soft, edible sweet heart of the young coconut tree).

úbog: *n.* unspread leaf of a palm; pith, heart of coco palm. **agubog.** *v.* to gather the unopened leaves of palm trees (to be eaten). **ubugen.** *v.* to get the pith of a palm tree; to study, think with care; analyze carefully; gloss yarn; wet thoroughly. **mangngubog.** *n.* a kind of large black bird that feeds on the *ubog*. [Ibg. *pára*, Itg. *pukul*, Ivt. *uvud*, Png. *apúngol*, Tag. *ubod*]

úbon: *n.* a string of beads. **maubon.** *v.* to be strung; pierced. **yubon.** *v.* to string, thread (a needle). **ubunen.** *v.* to thread (on a string). [Tag. *tuhog*]

úbong: *n.* pigpen, pigsty. (*apon*) **yubong.** *v.* to place in the pigpen; keep in the pigpen.

ubúob: *n.* vapor; steam. (*alingasaw*) **agubuob.** *v.* to tape a vapor bath. **ubuoben.** *v.* to burn herbal medicine for the benefit of a patient (*suob*); give a vapor bath to; fumigate fruit bearing trees. [Tag. *suób*]

úbor: agubor. *v.* to throw stones. **uburen.** *v.* to stone; throw stones at. (*ibato*) **innubor.** *n.* boy's stone-throwing war game. **aginnubor.** *v.* to throw stones at each other. **Ingawidko ti kasinsinko a mangubor iti balay.** I restrained my cousin from throwing stones at the house. [Tag. *bató*]

úbos: maubosan. *v.* to be emptied of all contents; drained; bled to death. (*adas*) **paubosan.** *v.* to drain, empty of all contents.

óbra: (Sp. *obra*: work) *n.* work (*teggéd, panggedán, trabáho*). **umobra.** *v.* to work; function. **agobra.** *v.* to work. **mangiobra.** *v.* to work for. **maobraan.** *n.* earnings, what can be achieved through work. **obra maestra.** *n.* masterpiece. **obras pias.** *n.* charity. **obra-demano.** *n.* handwork, handicraft. **obras-publikas.** *n.* public works. **pagobraan.** *n.* place of work. **Adu met ti agob-obra kadagiti pabrika.** Many people work in the factories. **No di umobra daytoy, agpatulongka iti padi.** If this doesn't work, get help from a priest.

obrántes: (Sp.) *n.* workers, workmen. (*obrero*)

obréro: (Sp. *obrero*: worker) *n.* worker. (*manggéd*)

obserbár: (Sp. *observar*: observe) **obserbaran.** *v.* to observe someone.

obserbatório: (Sp. *observatorio*: observatory) *n.* observatory.

obsesión: (Sp. *obsesión*: obsession) *n.* obsession. **obsesionado.** *a.* obsessed.

udáng: *n.* crayfish; lobster; variety of thick-skinned purple banana. **Kasla kinirog nga udang ti rupana.** *exp.* denoting a red, blushed face (like a fried lobster). **Iyanud ti danum ti matmaturog nga udang.** The water carries away sleeping crayfish. [Ibg. *payang, pasáyan*, Ivt. *payiq*, Kpm. *ulang*, Png. *kisingkísing, bingalo*, Tag. *sugpô, uláng*, Png. *oráng* = shrimp]

udáod: *n.* rope instrument used to frighten fish into a net. **udauden.** *v.* to pull to and fro (ropes, violin bow). **agudaod.** *v.* to ply a route (cars); go to and fro. **Lallakayen dagiti agud-udaod iti kinelleng iti asparagus.** The people going to and fro in the asparagus fields are all old men already. [Tag. *hilis*]

udátal: naudatal. *a.* lying dead. **Maudatalak iti bartekko.** *exp.* I am dead drunk.

úday: aguday-uday. *v.* to lean on something with the arms extended. (*sanggir*)

uddáy: naudday. *a.* straight (*kanátad*); loose; wide apart. **manguddakuddday.** *v.* to walk sluggishly (*kudday*). [Tag. *lugó*]

uddóg: aguddog. *v.* to spin; whirl. **nauddog.** *a.* whirling, spinning. (*alipuno, tayyek*) **pauddog.** *n.* spinning top (*kampuso, sunay*). **Gimluong manen ti timek a nailimog iti uddog ti angin.** The voice mixed with the spinning wind resounded again.[Tag. *ikot*]

údi: *n.* remainder; rear; balance of a debt or loan (*aptang*); tail end of a line. **naudi.** *a.* last; rear; latest. **agpaudi.** *v.* to stay at the rear; stay behind. **inaudi.** *n.* the younger of two, youngest. **inaudian.** *n.* youngest child. (*buridek*) **kamaudi.** *n.* the hind leg. **kamaudianan.**

a. last, final; in the end. **kamaudiannna.** *adv.* finally; at last. **kaudian.** *a.* latest; most recent; last. **maudi.** *a.* last; *v.* to be late; to remain. **ududien.** *v.* to consider last. **tartaraudi.** *n.* last part; last vestiges (of a memory). **Ti naudi, agapit.** The last one reaps. [Png. *otík*, Tag. *hulí*]

údip: udipen. *v.* to mend, patch (a basket). (*sukdip*; *takup*)

udír: udiren. *v.* to look after, take care of. (*awir*; *aywan*)

údit: *a.* barbecue spit. **uditen.** *v.* to put pieces of meat onto the spit.

udó: *n.* worm infestation. **kauduan.** *a.* affected with roundworms.

ud-ód: *n.* bargain. (*tawar*) **agud-od, ud-uden.** *v.* to haggle, bargain; to ask repeatedly, urgently. **umud-od.** *v.* to beg for, ask for repeatedly. **Lawas a panagud-od kadagiti banag nga inar-arapaapmo.** It's the week to ask for the things you dream of. [Tag. *tawad*]

údong: agudong. *v.* to go to town; to go to the market from the barrios. **paudongan.** *v.* to soothe (rough feelings); be more lenient (after scolding). **yudong.** *v.* to take to town (from the barrios). [Png. *luás*]

oéste: (Sp. *oeste*: west) *n.* west. (*laud*)

úga: *n.* sound of deer, cows. **aguga.** *v.* to moo (cows) (*emmak*). [Knk. *ugáa*, Tag. *atungal*]

ugáda: *n.* dish made with bamboo shoots, *boggong*, and coconut milk. **agugada.** *v.* to make a dish with coconut milk. [Tag. *ginataán*]

ugáli: *n.* habit, custom; nature, character; disposition; tradition. (*ruam*; *annawid*). **agugali.** *v.* to act (in a certain way). **kaugalian.** *n.* traditions; customs. **maipaugali.** *v.* to become customary, habitual. **ugalien.** *v.* to do habitually; make a habit of. **Iparit ti ugalimi ti panaginnayat ti tagapatad ken tagabantay.** Our traditions prohibit the love between lowlanders and mountain people. **Agug-ugali a diesiseis anios laeng.** He acts like he's only sixteen years old (like a sixteen-year-old). **Ugaliem a basaen.** Read it regularly. **Sabali nga ili, sabali nga ugali.** Different lands, different customs. [Ivt. *dadakay*, Knk. *kaippugáw*, lugádi, Png. *ogáli*, Kal., Tag. *ugali*]

úgam: maugam. *v.* to be ruined, destroyed, decimated. **ugamen.** *v.* to ruin, destroy, decimate; defame.

ugáog: agugaog. *v.* to moo (cows); to bawl (children). [Tag. *atungal* (moo); *ugaog* = shaking]

úgas: *n.* a kind of shrub; a rag; water used for rinsing rice. **agugas.** *v.* to rinse; wash (dishes).

ugasan. *v.* to wash, rinse (*bilnas*); do the dishes. **maugasan.** *v.* to be cleaned; rinsed; purified. **marainugas.** *a.* cream-colored. **Buybuyaenna kano ni Addong nga agug-ugas iti nanganan.** He is supposedly watching Addong rinsing dishes in their dining room. [Tag. *hugas*]

ugáw: *n.* (*myth.*) an elf; *a.* wasteful; meager. **naugaw.** *a.* liberal; costly, wasteful (food shrinking while cooked); empty (rice bin). [Png. *ogáw* = child; Tag. *ugáw* = stupid; large ape]

ogay-ayeng-éng: *n.* slight humming sound (church organ).

úged: *n.* line, stroke, dash; mark. (*ugis*) **ugedan.** *v.* to put a line on. **yuged.** *v.* to sketch; outline. **mayuged.** *v.* to be sketched; outlined; marked. **Kunada a nayugeden ti gasat ti tao iti pannakayanakna.** They say that the fate of man is determined (sketched) when he is born. [Tag. *guhit*]

úges: *n.* line; mark; wrinkle; stretch mark. (*ugis*)

oggayám: (Bon.) *n.* declamatory speech style, speech made in this style (*bitla*).

uggóp: nauggop. *a.* short (due to shrinkage). **mayuggop.** *v.* to fall short (of). **uggupen.** *v.* to cut short. [Tag. *iklî*]

uggór: *n.* (*reg.*) animal or baby entrusted to another's care. **ugguren.** *v.* to lead by a rope (*ugod*; *bagnos*); to bring along small children (*tugot*); take care of (*aywan, taripato*).

uggót: *n.* young banana leaf; small leaves of *utóng, kamóte, pariá,* etc; shoots of plants. (*sagibsib*) **aguggot.** *v.* to grow tops; grow leaves. **uggotan.** *v.* to take some leaves off (top). [Knk. *alinsayék*, Tag. *talbós*]

úging: *n.* charcoal; soot. (*úring*) **aguging.** *v.* to make charcoal. **ugingen.** *v.* to make something into charcoal. **umuging.** *v.* to smear with charcoal. **maugingan.** *v.* to be dirtied with charcoal or soot. **Immuging ti ulep iti surong.** The clouds were dark (*lit:* like charcoal) upstream. **Ti agsili magasangan, ket ti agiggem ti banga maugingan.** *exp.* He who eats chili pepper is affected by the spice, and he who handles the pot gets soot on his hands. [Ibg. *uking, beggang,* Ivt. *urin,* Knk. *úling,* Png. *oríng,* Kpm., Tag. *uling*]

úgis: *n.* line (*uged*; *uges*; *urit*; *ukrit*); the sign of the cross. **ugisan.** *v.* to line. **agugis.** *v.* to make the sign of the cross. **pagugis.** *n.* marker used for drawing lines. [Tag. *guhit*]

ugmá: *n.* ancient times. (*duog*) **idi ugma.** long ago, in the beginning. **inuugma.** *a.* pertaining to ancient practices. **sariugma.** *n.* ancient stories (coined term). [Bon. *kaysan*, Ibg. *gári*, Knk. *ges-ád*, Png. *úgma*, Tag. *noóng unáng panahón*; *ugmâ* = join, connect]

ugmál: **naugmal**. *a.* (*obs.*) gloomy, melancholy; overcast (*kuyem*). [Tag. *kulimlím*]

ugmók₁: *var.* of *umok*: nest, nesting place. [Tag. *pugad*]

ugmók₂: **ugmokan**. *v.* to do persistently. **Idi ammomon ti agbasa inugmokamon ti Bannawag.** When you knew how to read you persistently (read) *Bannawag* magazine. (*talinaéd*)

ugmón: *var.* of *dugmon*: nest of the wild boar.

ugnáy: *n.* flagpole; pickax helve.

ugúd: *n.* (*obs.*) drainage. **maugodan.** *v.* to run out of moisture (blood, sweat, tears, etc.).

ug-óg: *n.* weeping with closed mouth. **agug-og.** *v.* to weep with the mouth closed. **aganug-og.** *v.* to cry loudly with the mouth closed. [Tag. *ug-og* = violent shaking]

úgop: **maiyugop**. *v.* to be suitable; proper; fitting; reasonable. (*maibagay*)

úgot: **ugot, kaugot**. *n.* ebb tide. (ant. *atáb*) **umugot**. *v.* to ebb; subside (tide). **naugutan.** *a.* without blood, sweat or tears. (*naugodan*) **mangugut**. *v.* to fish in the ebb tide (with the hands); to fish with the hands in tide pools. (*labbeg*) **Nagsubli manen ti ugot ti baybay iti bigat.** The ebb tide returned again in the morning. [Ibg. *abbáq*, Png., Tag. *káti*]

úgoy: **sangkaugoy**. *n.* one bed of seeded grains used before transplanting.

ugsá: *n.* deer; deer meat (venison). [Ibg. *uttá*, Ifg. *makáwa*, Ivt. *agsaq*, Knk. *ugsá*, Png. *ulsá*, Kpm., Tag. *usá*]

ugtóp: *n.* joint. **ugtupen.** *v.* to join end to end. (*silpo*)

úha: (Sp. *hoja*: sheet of paper) *n.* old paper of ownership indicating location of land and size of plot, less formal than the deed; shape, form, resemblance. **kakauha.** *n.* of the same shape. **ohas de sim.** *n.* medicinal leaves used to treat the urinary tract; purgative.

ohál: (Sp. *ojal*: buttonhole) *n.* buttonhole. (*pagibotonesan*, *okalis*) **ohalan.** *v.* to do a buttonhole stitch; to make a buttonhole into a garment.

oháldres: (Sp. *hojaldre*: puff pastry) *n.* flattened kidney-shaped cookie.

uháles: (Sp. *ojal*: buttonhole) *n.* buttonhole.

óhas de sim: (Sp. *hoja*: leaf) *n.* medicinal leaves used to treat the urinary tract; purgative.

ohétes: (Sp. *ojete*: eyelet hole) *n.* round buttonhole (*uhales*); eyelet (in clothes).

ohiá: (Sp. *ojear*: cast the evil eye on) *n.* superstition of the evil eye.

ohíba: (Sp. *ojiva*) *n.* ogive, pointed arch.

oído: (Sp. *oído*: ear; hearing) *n.* ear for music, ability to judge harmony; musical talent.

úil: (*obs.*) **mawil**. *v.* to drop down from sleepiness.

ukág: **ukagen**. *v.* to rummage; ransack; open, spread out; leaf through. **ukag-ukagen.** *v.* to open one by one; to keep opening; leaf through. **Kayatmo kadi manen a maukag ti napalabas?** Do you want to open up the past again? [Tag. *buklát*]

ukakkák: **agukaakkak**. *v.* to take steps; take long strides. (*askaw*)

ukális: *var.* of *uhales*: buttonhole.

úkap: *n.* opening (from two sides). **agukap.** *v.* to open; de-leaf; open shellfish. (*ungap*) **ukapen.** *v.* to pry open. **Agtalna dayta ngiwatmo nga ukap nga ukap.** Shut your blabbering mouth (always open). [Tag. *buká*]

ukarkár: **agukarkar**. *v.* to bud, open (flowers); unfold, unfurl; unwrap; unroll; uncoil; unravel. (*ukrad*) **ukarkaren.** *v.* to unwrap something, to open. **Naukarkar ti nakabegkes a tualia iti bagina.** The towel wrapped around his body unraveled. [Png. *buskág*, Tag. *ladlád, kalás*]

úkas: **agukas, ukasen**. *v.* to loosen; unbind, untie; untangle; unbutton; untwist; cancel; repeal; annul. **maukas.** *v.* to be untied, loosened, unfastened. (*aliwaswas*; *warwar*) **Kasla adda naukas a siglot iti barukongna.** *exp.* denoting relief (It is like a knot untangled in his chest). **Inukasko ti sikkawilko sa inukapko bassit dagiti luppo.** I took my legs out of a crossed position and opened my thighs a little. [Tag. *kalás*]

okasión: (Sp. *ocasión*: occasion) *n.* occasion; opportunity; special event. **okasional.** *a.* occasional.

ukáy: *n.* loosening the earth of seedbeds. **ukayen.** *v.* to loosen the soil.

ukbós: **mayukbos**. *v.* to be spilled, poured out. [Tag. *bubô*]

ukbóy: **maukboy**. *v.* to be unthreaded, unstrung (*urboy*); to be spilled, scattered.

ukél: *n.* testicle. (*lateg, butillog*) **mauklan.** *v.* to give birth halfway. **ukel-ukel.** *n.* testicle; dish made from goat testicles. **uklan.** *a.* with testicles; with large testicles. [Png. *palták*, Tag. *bayág*]

úken: *n.* puppy, baby dog. [Kal. *ukon*, Kpm. *kwaq*, Png. *okén*, Tag. *tutà, bilót, kutyog*]

ukgáy: (*obs.*) *var.* of *ikgay*.

úki: *n.* vagina (*ambus*; *piting*); cave at the base of two adjoining hills. **ukinnam.** common profane phrase from [*uki ni inam*]. [Bon. *tékeng*, Ibg. *fuki*, Ifg. *piyat*, Ivt. *víviq, kerebet, uvet*, Knk. *tíli, sipít, itil, lawit*, Png. *baó*, Kpm. *pek, ántak*, Kpm., Tag. *puki*; Knk. *óki* = gum of the eyes]

ukiáng: *n.* kind of mollusk with a thin white shell.

ukík: *n.* cry of the fruit bat. **agukik.** *v.* to make the cry of the *panniki* fruit bat.

okilás: *var.* of *okra*: okra.

úkir: *n.* groove, furrow. **ukir ti suako.** *n.* filter for a pipe. **ukiran.** *v.* to engrave, carve; notch. [Tag. *ukit*]

ukís: *n.* eggshell; bark, skin of fruits, peel; membrane; rind; covering. **ukisan.** *v.* to peel off. **maukisan.** *v.* to be peeled; shelled; undressed. **nagukisan.** *n.* peelings; shell; bark. **pagukis.** *n.* peeler; instrument used for peeling. **Kasla naukisan a bawang ti pudaw ti bukotna.** The whiteness of his back was like peeled garlic. [Ibg. *tebbiq*, Ivt. *kudit*, Kal. *ukis*, Kpm. *balat*, Png. *obák* (bark), Tag. *banakal, balát*]

ukisnám: *n.* variety of rice; *var.* of *ukinnam*.

úkit: **aguk-ukit.** *n.* sculptor; *v.* to sculpt, sketch. **Umukit-ukit iti panunotna ti napuner a langana.** His brawny appearance was sketched in her mind.

ukkáng: **ukkangen.** *v.* to open (a tripod, pocket-knife, etc.). (*ungap*)

ukkuág: **ukkuagen.** *v.* to expose, reveal; divulge; push over a pile to see what is underneath.

ukkón: *n.* gathering. (*urnong, tipon, ummong, taripnong*) **ukkunen.** *v.* to join, unite; group together; throng; herd. **maukkon.** *v.* to be joined, united; throng; be herded. **Kasla adda mauk-ukkon a puris iti barukongko bayat ti yaadayona.** It seems as there were slivers thronging in my chest as she left. [Tag. *tipon*]

ukkór: *n.* necklace; collar; necktie. **yukkor.** *v.* to wear on one's shoulder; wear on one's neck; hang on the neck. **ukkoran.** *v.* to put a garment on somebody else's shoulder or neck.

ukláp: **uklapen.** *v.* to strip the leaves off (*bulong*). [Tag. *tukláp*]

uklóp: *n.* cap, head covering. (*uklot*) **uklopan.** *v.* to put a cap on. [Tag. *suklób*]

uklót: *n. var.* of *uklop*: cap.

uknóg: **uknugen.** *v.* to knock upside down in order to empty contents.

úkod: **ukuden.** *v.* to lead (animals or people); guide (*bagnos*). [Tag. *akay*]

uk-úk: *a.* foolish; crybaby; simpleton.

okulísta: (Sp. *oculista*: oculist) *n.* oculist, eye specialist.

okultísmo: (Sp. *ocultismo*: occultism) *n.* occultism.

ukóm: *n.* judge. **ukomen.** *v.* to judge; try someone; sentence. (*keddeng*) **maukom.** *v.* to be judged; to be tried (and punished). **pangukoman.** *n.* tribunal; court. **mangyukom.** *n.*

plaintiff. **nayukom.** *n.* defendant. **yukom.** *v.* to denounce; sue; accuse. **bomba a pangukom.** *n.* nuclear bomb. [Kal. *kuis*, Png. *okóm*, Tag. *hukóm*]

úkong: *n.* a kind of tailless bird; pony tail; hunched person. [Tag. *yukód* (hunched)]

ukúok: **umukuok.** *v.* to fester; smolder; worsen; affect deeply. [Tag. *timò*]

ukóp: *n.* hen sitting on its eggs. **mangukop.** *v.* to sit on eggs; *n.* brooder. **ukopan.** *v.* to sit on eggs. **nakaukopen.** *a.* with all eggs hatched (*nakapessán*). **Adda kadi maganabmo aya no agukopka?** Do you have anything to gain from brooding? [Tag. *halimhím*]

okupádo: (Sp. *ocupado*: occupied) *a.* busy; occupied.

okupánte: (Sp. *ocupante*: occupant) *n.* occupant.

okupár: (Sp. *ocupar*: occupy) **okuparen.** *v.* to occupy; be busy.

okupasión: (Sp. *ocupación*: occupation) *n.* occupation; employment.

úkoy: (Hok. *o kuè*: taro cake) *n.* a kind of fried shrimp cake. **ukoyen.** *v.* to clean rice, being washed with the fingers.

ókra: (Eng.) *n.* a type of vegetable popular in native dishes, okra. The two kinds of okra are *bilidan*, the reddish variety, and the green *dutdutan*.

ukrád: **ukradan.** *v.* to unfold, open (flowers); unroll. **yukrad.** *v.* to spread open. **apagukrad.** *a.* just opened; just reached puberty (girls). [Png. *buskág*, Tag. *bukád, buklát*]

ókre: (Sp. *ocre*: ochre) *n.* ochre, yellow, or orange-colored earth used as pigment.

ukrít: *n.* line; mark; slit; dash. **ukritan.** *v.* to mark with lines; scratch; slit. **ukriten.** *v.* to cut open; slit. **maukritan.** *v.* to get scratched; slit. **maukrit.** *v.* to be cut open. **Inibturanna ti pannakaukrit manen ti sugat ti riknana.** He endured opening again the wounds of his feelings. [Tag. *laslás*]

ukróy: *n.* string of objects. **naukroy.** *a.* strung together; strung up.

oksidénte: (Sp. *occidente*: occident) *n.* occident, west. (*laud*)

oksíheno: (Sp. *oxígeno*: oxygen) *n.* oxygen.

uksób: *a.* naked from the waist up (men); nude (women). **uksuben.** *v.* to put off; remove, take off shirt. **siuuksob.** *a.* nude; shirtless, half-naked. **aguksob.** *v.* to undress (women); take off one's shirt (men). **Inuksobna ti lupotna ta kimpeten iti bagina gapu iti pannakaslepna.** She took off her clothes because they stuck to her body due to being soaked. [See also *lamolámo* and *lábus*. Knk. *lúdis, way-ás*, Png. *lakseb*, Tag. *hubád*] uksút: uksuten. *v.* to pull out; unsheathe a sword; take off one's boots; withdraw penis in sexual intercourse; take off a knapsack. **Nakulipagpag ti papaget idi nauksot ti pana.** The *papaget* fish wiggled when the arrow was withdrawn. [Tag. *hugot*]

oktába: (Sp. *octava*: octave) *n.* octave. **oktabaen.** *v.* to postpone. (*igabay*)

oktabína: (Sp. *octavín*: piccolo) *n.* piccolo flute.

oktábo: (Sp. *octavo*: eighth) *num.* eighth. (*maikawalo*)

Oktúbre: (Sp. *octubre*: October) *n.* October. [Kal. *eÿachug*]

ulá: yula. *v.* to eject from the mouth, spit out (*mulsit*). [Tag. *bugá*]

úlak: ulaken. *v.* to split lengthwise, separate from end to end.

ulán: agul-ulan. *v.* (*obs.*) to roll oneself on the ground. (*tulid*)

Olánda: (Sp. *Holanda*: Holland) *n.* Holland, the Netherlands. **Olandés.** *n. a.* Dutch, feminine: *Olandésa.*

olandés: *n., a.* blond (*sapon*); see under *Olanda.*

ulantád: *var.* of *ulanták*: fall to the ground.

ulanták: maulantak. *v.* to be thrown flat on one's back; fall to the ground; (*fig.*) die. [Tag. *tihayà*]

ulántro: (f. *kulantro?*) *n.* medicinal seeds.

ólang: *n.* lady master, mistress, the feminine counterpart of *among.*

uláng: agulang-ulang. *v.* to roll oneself on the ground (*ulan*). [Tag. *uláng* = lobster; crayfish]

uláol: maulaulan. *a.* hurt, wounded, injured (*dunor*); scraped. **ulaulan.** *v.* to hurt; scrape; wound. [Tag. *galos*]

úlaw: *n.* dizziness; vertigo. (*talimpungaw*) **maulaw.** *v.* to feel dizzy; tipsy (when drinking). **makaulaw.** *a.* causing dizziness; confusing. **agulaw-ulaw.** *v.* to feel faint, dizzy. **ulawen.** *v.* to make dizzy; confuse. [Bon. *aliweng*, Kal. *uÿaw*, Knk. *úlaw, beséng*, Png. *eléw, iweng*, Tag. *hilo*]

úlay: *n.* neckerchief; wreath; neck hair of a different color. **agulay.** *v.* to wear a neckerchief. **yulay.** *v.* to throw (a scarf, etc.) over the shoulder. [Tag. *alampáy; ulay* = intestinal worm]

ulbód: *n.* lie. (*langsot*) **agulbod.** *v.* to deceive; convince. **ulboden.** *v.* to lie; deceive; persuade. **managulbod.** *n.* constant liar. **mangulbod.** *v.* to deceive; pretend not to know, break a promise. **kinaulbod.** *n.* deceit; deception. **yulbod ti kinapudno.** to deny the truth. [Ibg. *leddug, siri*, Itg. *utip*, Ivt. *dadaay*, Kal. *tuntulli, man-eelug*, Knk. *bontág, básed*, Kpm. *malaram*, Png. *tilá, báli, dúmsis*, Tag. *sinungaling*]

uldág: aguldag. *v.* to sit on the ground; lie around lazily; rest. **Nakauldag ni nanang iti papag iti lauden ti balaymi.** Mother is lying on the bamboo bench in the west side of our house. [Tag. *hilatà*]

uldás: aguldas (*obs.*) *v.* to writhe, squirm; recoil (snakes). (*kilíkil; gulágol*)

uldót: *n.* down (of plants); *a.* always asking for something; ask for something persistently; moocher. **mauldutan.** *v.* to decline, decrease in price. **uldotan.** *v.* to pester, bother; mooch. **Sada la ammo datao no adda mauldotda.** Then they just know me when they have to mooch.

uldóy: nauldoy. *a.* soft (*lamúyot*); languid. [Tag. *lambót*]

úleg: *n.* any kind of snake; (*fig.*) treacherous person; one who makes a vicious attack. **uleg tuleng.** *n.* a kind of small, poisonous snake. **mauleg.** (*obs.*) *v.* to fall asleep from soothing music. **ulegen.** *v.* to be bitten (or eaten) by a snake. **inuleg.** *a.* bitten by a snake; eaten by a snake; infested with snakes. **Saanak nga uleg a gayyem!** I am not a treacherous friend. **Kasla uleg nga agpampanunot.** *exp.* He thinks like a snake (treacherously and scheming). [Ibg. *iraw*, Itg. *uweg*, Ivt. *buday*, Knk. *úeg*, Kpm. *ubingan*, Png. *olég*, Tag. *ahas*]

óleo: *var.* of *olio*: oil (for painting); oil painting.

úlep: *n.* cloud. (*kuyem; alibuyong; daguyemyem; kunem; langeb; lulem*) **naulep, maulpan.** *a.* cloudy. **Naulpan ti panunotmo.** Your thoughts are unclear. **Kasla tumtumpaw iti ulep.** *exp.* like being on cloud nine (like floating on a cloud). **No nalabaga dagiti ulep no lumgak ti init, adda tudona iti sumuno nga aldaw.** If the clouds are red when the sun rises, there will be rain the following day. [Ibg. *kunem*, Ivt. *demdem*, Kal. *libuu*, Kpm. *lúlam*, Png. *lorém*, Tag. *ulap*]

ulés: *n.* blanket; bed sheet. **agules.** *v.* to cover oneself with a blanket. **ulsan.** *v.* to cover someone with a blanket. **yules.** *v.* to use as a blanket. **manangules.** *a.* fond of using a blanket. **kaules.** *n.* person with whom one shares a blanket. **agkaules.** *v.* to share a blanket. **pagules.** *v.* to relish; do with pleasure. **makikaules.** *v.* to share a blanket with someone. [Ibg. *uloq*, Ivt. *ayub*, Kal. *uÿos, kagoy*, Knk. *éwes, guyúgoy, laéy, galey*, Kpm. *ulas*, Png. *olés*, Tag. *kumot*]

úli₁: umuli. *v.* to go up, rise, to come in (a house), enter; climb (*kalay-at, kalabkab, kaladkad, kayutkot, sagpat, sápat, sang-at, kalamiat*). **agulian.** *v.* to recover, resuscitate oneself. **ulien.** *v.* to climb up, go up; to make arrangements for a marriage. **umuuli.** *n.* climber; lumberjack. **paulien.** *v.* to invite a guest in, ask someone to come up. **yuuli.** *n.* ascension; wedding custom where parents of the prospective groom meet the parents of the prospective bride to ask for her hand in marriage (*albasia*); ascending. **yuli.** *v.* to take something up (to the house); bring up; bring home a girl for a wife. **mauli.** *v.* to be scalable, climbable. **agpapauli.** *v.* to cause to ascend (kites). **Yulik ti darum kontra iti inana.** I will bring up the charge against his mother. [Bon. *káwat*, Ibg. *kalay*, Ivt. *kayat*, Kpm. *mukyat*, Png. *isapat, kalab*, Tag. *akyát* (climb)]

úli₂: *n.* a kind of white resin; oil cloth.

olíba: (Sp. *oliva*: olive tree; olive) *n.* a kind of small palm; olive.

olíbo: (Sp. *olivo*: olive tree) *n.* olive.

ulidán: *n.* example, model, pattern; lesson. (*pagwadan*) **pagulidanan.** *n.* example.

oligárka: (Sp. *oligarca*: oligarch) *n.* oligarch.

oligarkía: (Sp. *oligarquía*: oligarchy) *n.* oligarchy, form of government ruled by few.

ulikbá: (Tag. also) *n.* a hen with black meat.

ulíla: *n.* orphan. **naulila.** *a.* orphaned. **maulila.** *v.* to become an orphan. **ulilaen.** *v.* to make someone an orphan. **ulila a demmang.** *a.* twice orphaned. **Laglagipem, nasapatayo a naulila iti ama.** Remember, we were orphaned from father early. **Kasla ulila a baka.** He is like a motherless calf (said of a person with a gloomy face). [Bon. *ngóso*, Ivt. *nasbang*, Knk. *ngóso*, *ulila*, Png. *olilá*, Ibg., Kal., Kpm., Tag. *ulila*]

ulímaw: *n.* mythological dragon. [Tag. *halimaw*]

ulímek: *n.* silence. (*talná, línak; tangép*) **agulimek.** *v.* to be silent, still. **naulimek.** *a.* quiet, silent. **pagulimken.** *v.* to hush. **kaulimkan.** *n.* stillness; silence; serenity. **Adda karbengan a di agsao ken agulimek.** You have the right to remain silent. [Kal. *gigillok*, Png. *ulimék*, Tag. *tahimik*]

olimpiáda: (Sp. *olimpiada*: Olympics) *n.* Olympics.

ólio: (Sp. *oleo*: oil) *n.* oil (painting); oil painting. **santo-olio.** *n.* holy oil for anointing the sick.

úlit: uliten. *v.* to repeat; do for the second time. (*dúpag; sunot, surnad, dagullit*) **agulit.** *v.* to do again.. **maulit.** *v.* to be repeated, done again. **paulit-ulit.** *a.* repeated several times. **ulit-ulit.** *adv.* again and again. (*madagdagullit*) **Ulitem man ti kinunam.** Please repeat what you said. **Diak kayat a maulit pay daytoy.** I don't want this to be repeated. [Ibg. *uliyen*, Ivt. *pirwahen*, Kal. *ikasin*, Kpm. *pasibaywan*, Png., Tag. *ulit*]

ulitég: (pl. *uuliteg*) *n.* uncle. (*tío*) **aguliteg.** *n.* nephew and uncle. [Bon., Knk. *alitáo*, Ivt. *maraan*, Png. *pangamaén*, Tag. *amaín, tiyo* (Sp.)]

ulláw: *n.* kite. **agullaw.** *v.* to fly a kite; whirl, spin. **ullaullaw.** *n.* wheel of a spinning wheel; winder for cotton yarn. [Ivt. *kavadag*, Tag. *saringgola*]

ulláyak: *var.* of *ullayat*: do slowly.

ulláyat: *a.* slow and long winded (*buntog*), excessively long in duration (*bayag*). **ullayaten.** *v.* to do slowly (usually said of singing); to drag on for an excessive amount of time **naullayat.** *a.* slow; done intermittently; excessively long in duration. **Naullayat ti silbato dagiti bapor a pagkalap.** The whistle of the fishing boat dragged on.

ulló: agullo. *n.* the game of jacks; *v.* to work for a day's wages. **mangmanglo.** *n.* day laborer. **ulluen.** *v.* to earn by working. **mangullo, manglo.** *v.* to work for wages. (*teggéd*)

ulluák: umluak. *v.* to regain strength (after childbirth, after transplanting, etc.). (*úngar*)

ullók: agullok. *v.* to insist politely; bootlick; ingratiate oneself to someone's favor. [Tag. *sipsíp*]

ullóm: agullom. *v.* to stay indoors to avoid getting dark. **ullumen.** *v.* to pack, wrap tobacco carefully; pack and store to improve quality. **Nariknana ti angin-bakir a nangsuknor iti naullom a salimuot ti balay.** He felt the forest breeze enter the deep interior of the humid house. [Tag. *luóm*]

ulmóg: *n.* chicken tick. (*ayam*) **inulmog.** *a.* infested with chicken ticks. **ulmugen.** *v.* to be attacked by the chicken tick. [Ibg. *aliffúngoq*, Itg. *gayamu*, Ivt. *kayaw*, Knk. *tilalagá, atilalagá*, Kpm. *apsang*, Png. *ulmug*, Tag. *hánip*]

ulnás: *n.* sled. (*pasagad*) **agulnas.** *v.* to use a sled (for carrying a load). [Tag. *paragos*]

úlo: *n.* head; roof; roof frame; ruler. **uluanan.** *n.* head of a bed; headboard (*kabesera*). **pangulo.** *n.* head (of a corporation); president; chief; director; *a.* chief; official. **pannakaulo.** *n.* acting head. **naulo.** *a.* near the head; knocked on the head; with a large head. **uloulo.** *n.* source of water; heads, chiefs; *a.* bareheaded. **uluen.** *v.* to decapitate, cut off the head. **daulo.** *n.* ruler; leader; head of a company. **idaulo.** *v.* to lead. **paulo.** *n.* title; headline (news). **ipaulo.** *v.* to memorize, commit to memory. **umulo.** *v.* to surge to the head (in anger). **isaulo, yulo.** *v.* to memorize. **buong ti ulo, sakit ti ulo.** *n.* headache. **Umuluanka iti amianan.** Put your head toward the north (when lying down). [Ivt.

uhuq, Kal. *uÿu*, Kpm. *buntuk*, Png. *oló*, Ibg., Tag. *ulo*]

úlod: **uluden.** to drag, haul; pull. (*guyod*) **ma-ulod.** *v.* to be pulled, dragged. **Diak maulod dagiti sakak a sumrek iti ruangan.** I cannot drag my feet to enter the door. [Png. *gayugoy*, Tag. *kaladkád, hila*]

úlog: *n.* dormitory for marriageable girls among mountain tribes. **umulog.** *v.* to go down; leave a house; descend. **agulog.** *v.* to decline; decrease in value; fail; sink; lose in business. **ipaulog.** *v.* to translate; authorize. **yulog.** *v.* to bring down; translate; abduct. **ulugen.** *v.* to go down for; translate. **kaulog.** *n.* translation. (*tarus*) **kayulogan.** *n.* meaning. **Umul-ulogak a mapanko pakanen.** I am going down to feed him.

ul-ól: (*coll.*) *n.* barking of dogs. **agul-ol.** *v.* to bark. (*taúl*)

úloy: **uluyan.** *v.* to give the final death blow to. **mauluyan.** *v.* to die; breathe the last breath. **Ti buli a nangbisak ti ulona ti dagus a nanguloy iti biagna.** The bullet that cracked his head immediately ended his life.

ulpít: *n.* cruelty. (*dangkok, uyong*; *dawel*; *asing*; *ranggas*; *rungsot*) **naulpit.** *a.* cruel; fierce; ferocious; malicious. **kinaulpit.** *n.* cruelty. **ulpitan.** *v.* to cruelly inflict on someone. [Png. *dámsak, duksá, ongét*, Knk. *massó*, Tag. *lupít*]

ulsán: (f. *ulés*) *v.* to cover someone with a blanket.

úlsera: (Sp. *úlcera*: ulcer) *n.* ulcer.

último: (Sp. *último*: last) *a.* last, end; lowest (class of burial). **ultimo remedio.** *n.* the last resort, the last thing to do in order to alleviate a situation.

ultóg: *var.* of *uttog*: sexual lust; sexual desire.

-um₁-: *infix.* 1. Placed before the first vowel of the root, it forms intransitive, actor focus verbs that take the -*ak* series pronominal and signal the inchoative (attainment of a state): **dumakkel.** to become large. **sumayaat.** to get better. **kumapsut.** to become weak. **ngumisit.** to get dark, become black. 2. In opposition to the actor focus prefix *ag-*, the infix -*um*- implies the action denoted in the root is of less duration, usually a single action: **agtakderto.** stand. **tumakder.** to stand up. **agtugaw.** to sit. **tumugaw.** to sit down. 3. The infix -*um*- also implies the possibility of the action denoted by the root to take place, as opposed to the *ag*-actor focus verbs that imply that the action does take place: **Agkagat ti asom.** Your dog (actually) bites. **Kumagat ti asom.** Your dog threatens biting. 4. The perfective form of the infix -*um*- is -*imm*-: **umay.** he comes. **immay.**

he came. **uminomak.** I drink. **imminomak.** I drank. **tumulong.** he helps. **timmulong.** he helped. 5. Verbal paradigm of -*um*- verbs showing tense and aspect distinctions: **Tumulong.** He helps. **Tumultulong.** He is helping. **Timmulong.** He helped. (Perfective) **Timmulongen.** He has (already) helped. **Timmultulong.** He was helping. **Tumulongto.** He will help.

-um₂-: *infix.* With locative roots, indicates the residents or inhabitants of a place. **umili.** *n.* citizens, residents of the town or country. **bumalay.** *n.* residents of the house. **lumugar.** *n.* residents of the place.

úma: **makauma.** *a.* tiresome, boring, annoying. **mauma.** *v.* to tire, lose one's patience; to be fed up. **aguma.** *v.* to do until one loses interest. **No maumakan, mabalinnak a panawan.** If you are bored, you can leave me. **Nangrugin a pagbalayan ti lawwalawwa a di mauma a mangmangan kadagiti dadakkel a lamok.** The spider started to enwrap the large mosquitoes it did not tire of eating. [Ibg. *uláng*, Png. *sawá*, Tag. *yamót, sawà*]

umá: *n.* clearing of land for crops, swidden. (Tag. *kaingin*) **aguma.** *v.* to clear land in order to cultivate. **panaguma.** *n.* shifting cultivation. **mangnguma.** *n.* slash-and-burn farmer; *kaingin.* **Masapul nga umaenda ti kabakiran sakbay a makamulada.** They must clear the land before they can harvest. [Knk. *num-a, menda-us*, Kpm., Tag. *kaingin*, Png. *pinalápa*]

úmag: **maumag.** *v.* to become tasteless, flat (drinks), odorless (flowers), spiritless. **dinto maumag.** *exp.* will never lose its value, priceless. [Tag. *tabang*]

-uman-: Infix used with onomatopoetic roots to encode repetitive sounds occurring in rapid succession: **bitog.** *n.* sound of a thump. **bumanitog.** *n.* continuous, rapid thumping.

umán: *n.* advice; consultation. **makiuman.** *v.* to seek the advice of, consult. **pagumanan.** *n.* advisor. **kauman.** *v.* to interview. **kainnuman.** *v.* to confer with. [Tag. *payo, sanggunì*]

umanáy: *a.* enough; sufficient. (*umdas*)

úmang: *n.* hermit crab; anyone who continually moves (residence). **Kasla umang nga agakarakar.** He changes residence often like a hermit crab. [Tag. *umang* = snare bait, booby trap]

úmar: **umaren.** *v.* to do repeatedly; to crush; clear a rice field of stubble. **naumar.** *a.* perfect, without defects. (*darisay*) **nakaumar** (*obs.*) *a.* toothless. (*bungí; toppól*)

úmaw: *var.* of *kúmaw*: mythological kidnapper.

umáwa: *n.* excuse, pretext. (*pambar*) **agumawa.** *v.* to make excuses. [Tag. *dahilán*] umáy: (f. *ay*) *v.* to come. **Umayak man, apo.** May I come, sir (said when entering a house). [*Umay* may be considered a root of its own since certain derivatives take the *-um-* infix in their formation (maintaining a bisyllabic root), e.g., pretentative: *agin-aay* or *agin-uumay*; nominalization: *yaáy* or *yuumáy*; recent past formative: *kaay-áy* or *kaum-umáy*; potentive: *makaáy* or *makaumay*; social verb: *makiay* or *makiumáy*; frequentative: *agkaraay, agkara-umay*; indirect patient: *paayén, paumayén*; indirect potentive: *mapaay, mapaumay*. *Umay* also functions as an auxiliary verb which takes the enclitic pronouns of the main verb: *Umay-nak alaen.* Come get me. Tag. *dumatíng*]

umbáas: (f. *ebbáas*) *v.* to decrease; subside; abate (water level).

umbál: (f. *ebbál*) *v.* to swell (due to beriberi, etc.).

umbí: *n.* caress; affection. **agumbi.** *v.* to show affection; cajole. **naumbi.** *a.* affectionate; tender; passionate. **Pinaumbina ti timekna.** She spoke with an affectionate voice. [Tag. *lambíng*]

umbiát: (f. *biát*) *v.* to be swift; turn (a car, etc.). (*buelta*)

umbrás: *var.* of *umrás*: food sacrifice for dead spirits. (*atang*)

ómbre: (Sp. *hombre*: man) *n.* man (used as a term of address).

ombréra: (Sp. *hombrera*: neck of garment) *n.* yoke; neck of a garment.

umdás: *v.* to be enough, adequate. (*umanáy*) **Umdasen ti tawenmo tapno wayasem ti agpili.** You are old enough to be free to choose. [Tag. *sapát*]

umdét: (f. *eddét*) *v.* to grunt, groan while exerting one's strength.

umedád: (Sp. *humedad*: humidity) *n.* humidity. (*salimuot*)

úmedo: (Sp. *húmedo*: humid) *a.* humid. (*na-salimuot*)

úmel: *a.* unable to speak, mute, dumb; variety of rice with a small, red kernel. **nagumel.** *a.* dumb, unable to speak. **mapaumel.** *v.* to be speechless. **maraumel a katawa.** *n.* muttered laughter. [Ibg. *umal*, Kal. *ume*, Png. *emél*, Tag. *pipi*]

uménto: (Sp. *aumento*: increase) *n.* raise, increase in salary; bonus.

umíli: (f. *ili*) *n.* citizen; inhabitant.

umiliasión: (Sp. *humiliación*: humiliation) *n.* humiliation.

omisídio: (Sp. *homicidio*) *n.* homicide.

umisú: (f. *isu*) *a.* appropriate; proper; reasonable; right. [Tag. *nararapat*]

umit: **umiten.** *v.* to steal, pilfer (*takaw*). [Tag. *nakaw*]

umkís: (f. *ikkís*) *v.* to scream; yell. (*riaw*)

umláy: (f. *elláy*) to droop.

umlék: (f. *ellék*) to be stunned with high emotion, unable to speak due to extreme emotion; to laugh quietly to oneself.

ummó: *n.* pollen.

ummóng: *n.* heap, pile; crowd; gathering; group (*taripnong*). **ummongen.** *v.* to pile; to gather, assemble. **ummongan.** *n.* assembly; meeting. **maummong.** *v.* to be gathered, collected. **yummongan.** *v.* to place something into a pile. **paguummongan.** *n.* place of assembly. **Ditoy ti paguummongantayo.** This is our assembly place. [Png., Tag. *tipon*]

omnipoténsia: (Sp. *omnipotencia*) *n.* omnipotence.

omnipoténte: (Sp. *omnipotente*) *a.* omnipotent.

umnó: **umumno.** *v.* to be just right; to fit; be correct; be lawful; suitable; proper. [Tag. *tamà*]

úmok: *n.* nest of birds; entangled (hair, yarn, etc.) **agumok.** *v.* to build a nest. **pagumokan.** *n.* nesting place. [Kal. *sukbot*, Png. *obóng*, Kpm., Tag. *pugad*]

umuná: (f. *una*) *a.* first. [Tag. *una*]

umpáak: *v.* to simmer down; recede. **sumpaak.** *v.* to affect deeply. [Tag. *hupâ*]

umpáaw: (f. *eppáaw*) *v.* to abate, decrease (wind).

umpés: (f. *eppés*) to subside; unswell.

úmpot: *var.* of *ungpot*: finish, terminate.

úmrar: *v.* to loosen; slacken (*lukay*); relax; (*reg.*) discontinue. [Tag. *luwág*]

umrás: *n.* offering, food sacrifice for the dead. (*atang*) **agumras, yumras.** *v.* to offer the *umrás* to the dead.

umrés: (f. *errés*) to shrink. [Tag. *urong*]

umrí: (f. *íri*) *v.* to scream, cry with a shrill voice.

umsá: **umsáen.** *v.* to reprove; censure; find fault with (*basol, balaw*). [Tag. *sumbát*]

umsí: **umsién.** *v.* to despise; hate; neglect. (*uyaw*) **maum-umsi.** *a.* despised; ridiculed. **panag-umsi.** *n.* hatred; neglect; scorn. **isem-umsi.** *n.* insincere smile (*isem-libbi*). [Tag. *kutyâ*]

umsiág: *v.* to make a loud bursting noise; shout; make the sound of loud laughter.

-on: *var.* of *-en* after the enclitics *-ak*, *-k* or *-m*. **Nanganakon.** I already ate. **Nakitanakon.** He already saw me. [This is actually just the enclitic *-(e)n* after the original forms of the pronouns *-ko*, and *-mo*; *Nakitakon* is parsed as *na-kita-ko-n*]

un: (Sp. *un*: one) one (rare, used in certain expressions). **un metro.** one meter.

úna: (Sp. *una:* one) **umuna.** *num.* first; forefront; front line. *n.* front, forepart of something. **A la una, ala una.** One o'clock.

uná: *n.* first; front line; forefront. **umuna.** *a.* first; foremost. **inauna.** *n.* eldest child. **unaen.** *v.* to do first. **unaan.** *v.* to overtake. **apaguna.** *a.* a little ahead. **agunauna, aginnuna.** *v.* to compete with. **pakauna.** *n.* presage. **ipakauna.** *v.* to warn; foretell something. **agpakauna.** *n.* precursor, forerunner. **kamauna.** *n.* foreleg (of animals). **pauna.** *n.* down payment. **ipauna.** *v.* to give beforehand; offer a down payment. **paunaan.** *v.* to give a down payment to someone; order someone to overtake something, order someone to go ahead. **nagkauna.** *a.* ancient; aged. **aginnuna.** *v.* to go one after another. **yuna.** *v.* to do first; give priority to something. **idi un-unana.** once upon a time; long ago. **umuna ken kangrunaan.** first and foremost. **Mabalin nga iti saan a mabayag, unaannatayonton ti Tailandia.** It is possible that in a short time, Thailand will be ahead of us.

únab: **unaban.** *v.* to shake after soaking (maguey fibers). **yunab.** *v.* to put (yams) in a running stream. **agun-unab.** *v.* (*coll.*) to stay a long time in the water. **Mapanda agunab inton madamdama iti karayan.** They are going to soak in the river later. **No agpawaigda, kayakayanda ti yan ti pagun-unaban dagiti nakaar-ariwawa nga itik.** If they go to the creek, they will stay away from the place where the noisy ducks play in the water.

unabís: (Sp. *una vez:* once) *a.* all of one color; *adv.* at once, immediately.

unána: *n.* years of ancient days, long ago.

únas: **naunasan.** *a.* out of season; faded; no longer fresh; worthless; overripe and spoiling (fruits).

unás: *n.* sugarcane (to chew sugarcane: *mangus*). **kaunasan.** *n.* sugarcane field. **umunas.** *v.* to become hard (beans); to change flavor. **unas ti uleg.** *n.* a kind of reed. **bulong unas.** *n.* swordfish. [Ibg. *unaq*, Ifg. *una*, Ivt. *unas*, Kal. *ulás*, Kpm. *atbu*, Png. *onás*, Tag. *tubó*, *unas*]

únaw: **maunawan.** *v.* to abate, decrease; become sober. **agpaunaw.** *v.* to sober up. [Tag. *himasmas*]

únay: *adv.* very; very much; really; excessive (in exclamations). **yunay-unay.** *v.* to urge. (*gutúgut*) **yunay.** *v.* to urge. **unay-unay.** *adv.* absolutely. **ipaunay-unay.** *v.* to urge. **únayen, unay mettén, ayá únayen, aniá únayen, apayá únayen.** *interj.* expressions of mixed wonder and surprise. **Unaykan!** What's the matter with you? **Kasta unay.** Very much, surprisingly excessive. **Am-ammo unay dagiti tumbador daydi tatang.** The lumberjacks really knew (my) late father. **Dika unay agtangtangsit.** Don't be so haughty. **Kasta unay ti rawetna.** He was so voracious. **Seggaandakto unayen, diak pay simmangpet idiay balay.** They must really be expecting me, I still haven't arrived at the house. [Bon. *ig* (very)]

undá: *n.* interval (between steps, etc.) (*baét, ballaét*) **undaen.** *v.* to do little by little, intermittently. **maunda-unda.** *v.* to be arranged in rows. [Tag. *pagitan*]

undáy: *n.* length (of time, seasons, etc.). **naunday.** *a.* straight (*nalintég*); having a long life. **unday ti panawen.** past days. **undayen.** *v.* to lengthen. **Ikkannak kuma iti naunday a panawen a mangpanunot.** You should give me a while to think it over. [Tag. *habà*]

undáyas: *var.* of *undayat:* slope.

undáyat: *n.* slope. **agundayat.** *v.* to slope. **yundayat.** *v.* to hang lengthwise (wire, string, etc.); tie from post to post (sloping). **nakaundayat.** *a.* hanging lengthwise; tied from post to post; sloping.

undó: *n.* length. (*atiddog*) **ipaundo.** *v.* to join lengthwise.

undós: **paundosan.** *v.* to do lengthwise. (*undo*)

undóy: *var.* of *undo:* length. (*atiddog*)

unég: *prep.* (*iti uneg*) inside, in. (*laem; sakup*) **umuneg.** *v.* to go inside, enter. **naguneg.** *n.* contents. **nauneg.** *a.* profound, deep inside; remote. **ipauneg.** *v.* to put into, imprint in the mind, infix; take in, swallow. **nagunggan.** *a.* possessed. **yuneg.** *v.* to bring inside. **paunegen.** *v.* to invite a guest to come in. **kaunegen.** *v.* to dig deep; deepen. **kaunggan.** *n.* core; depth; subconscious. **agunggan.** *v.* to be possessed by evil spirits. **nauneg a sao.** *a.* word difficult to understand. **nakin-uneg.** *a.* inner. **Immanges iti nauneg.** He took a deep breath. **Awan ti kayatna nga ipauneg.** He doesn't want to put anything inside (food). **Nabayagen a nadlawko a nauneg ti pampanunotenna.** I have noticed for quite some time that he has been in deep thought. **Nakaun-uneg dagiti angesna a nagbasa.** His breaths were rather deep as he read. [Bon. *dálem*, Kal. *chayom*, Png. *dalém*, Png., Tag. *loób*]

onésto: (Sp. *honesto:* honest) *a.* honest. (*nadáyaw; nalintég, salindeg, regta*)

úni: *n.* sound, noise; voice. (*ringgor; timek*) **aguni.** *v.* to utter a sound. **pagpaguni.** *n.* whistle, an instrument blown to produce a loud sound. **agpagpaguni.** *v.* to blow an instrument. **unian.** *v.* to greet someone, hail a person. [Ibg. *guruq*, *gúni*, Itg. *aweng*, Ivt. *liak*, Kal. *ginga*, Kpm. *katniq*, Png. *tanól*, Tag. *tunog*]

uniás: (Sp. *agonía*) *n.* time of the angelus prayer. (*orasion*) **agunias**. *v.* to toll (angelus, at a death) (*rupiki*). [Tag. *orasiyón* (Sp.)]

unibersidád: (Sp. *universidad*: university) *n.* university. (*kangatuan a pagadalan*)

unibérso: (Sp. *universo*) *n.* universe. (*lúbong*)

unikórnio: (Sp. *unicornio*) *n.* unicorn.

uníneng: **magun-unineng**. *a.* transparent; ripe; profound; deep.

unión: (Sp. *unión*: union) *n.* union. **La Union**. *n.* La Unión, one of the three original Ilocos provinces created by the union of lands from the provinces of Ilocos Sur and Pangasinan.

unipórme: (Sp. *uniforme*: uniform) *n.* uniform. **aguniporme**. *v.* to wear a uniform.

unipormidád: (Sp. *uniformidad*) *n.* uniformity.

unnát: *a.* stretched; straight; sprawled. **unnaten**. *v.* to extend; stretch (*bennat*); strain; straighten out; lengthen. **agunnat**. *v.* to stretch oneself; lay out sprawled, at full length. **maunnat**. *v.* to be stretched, drawn tight; laid out at full length. **Kasla nagunnat nga uleg**. He is stretched out like a snake. [Tag. *unat*]

unnáy: (*obs.*) *a.* slowly (*buntóg*). [Tag. *bagal*]

unnód: **mangunnod**. *v.* to increase, augment. **umunnod**. *v.* to thrive; prosper; progress; improve (*dur-as, rang-ay*). [Tag. *unlád*]

unnók: *n.* a kind of black, freshwater mollusk.

unnót: **agunnounnot**. *v.* to pull, tug; strain in work (*gutád*). [Tag. *hila*]

unnóy: *n.* plead; request; lament. (*sainnék*; *rengréng*; *dáwat*; *kiddáw*; *ásug*; *karabá*) **agunnoy**. *v.* to moan; sigh; complain by moaning. **agun-unnoy**. *v.* to plead. **yunnoy**. *v.* to express with much affection. [Tag. *samò*]

úno: (Sp. *uno*: one) *n.* one (*maysá*). [Tag. *isá*]

únong: *n.* vengeance. (*pammáles, bales*) **yunong**. *n.* to report an injury or misconduct. **mangyunong**. *v.* to avenge; retaliate. [Tag. *higantí*]

unúon: **agunuon**. *n.* smudge fire (*temtem*); sound of rattled contents; bowel movement. *v.* to make the sound of a shaken coconut; to shake a coconut.

unuón: *n.* sound of a shaken coconut. **agunuon**. *v.* to be half-filled (coconut). **unuonen**. *v.* to shake a coconut; shake a bottle.

unór: **unuren**. *v.* to give to all; to give recognition; travel the full route, follow through.

únos₁: *n.* remuneration, share. (*bulnos*) **unosan**. *v.* to give a share to someone (who helped in harvesting, etc.). [Tag. *bahagi*]

únos₂: *prep.* during; *n.* duration. (*kabayatan*) **iti unos ti panagbiagmo**. during your lifetime. **Saan nga immaliwaksay iti lugar a naka-**

yanakanna iti unos ti panagbiagna. In his lifetime, he did not venture from the place of his birth. [Tag. *tagál*]

únos₃: **unusen**. *v.* to hoist; pull down.

unóy: *n.* a kind of broad bamboo raft; *var.* of *unnoy*. **ipaunoy**. *v.* to let float with the current. (*anud*)

ónsa: (Sp. *onza*: ounce) *n.* ounce.

ónse: (Sp. *once*: eleven) *num.* eleven. (*sangapulo ket maysa*) **Alas onse**. Eleven o'clock.

ónse: (*coll.*) **maonse**. *v.* to be cheated. **onsien**. *v.* to cheat. (*kusit*)

unsáy: **agunsay**. *v.* to dangle, hang straight down (*unsoy*). **maunsay**. *v.* to be injured, suffer pain due to dangling. **inunsay**. *n.* a kind of striped cloth. [Tag. *lawít*]

unsión: (Sp. *unción*: unction) *n.* unction; anointment.

onsíta: (Sp. *onza*: ounce + dim. suffix *-ita*) *n.* golden coin during the Spanish period.

unsóy₁: **maunsoy**. *v.* to be distended from having been dangling or stretched for so long. **agunsoy, unsuyen**. *v.* to dangle (*bitin, uyaoy*). [Tag. *lawít, bitin*]

unsóy₂: **inunsoy**. *n.* woven fabric with downward stripes of the same color.

untáy: **siuuntay**. *a.* suspended, dangling, hanging (*unsay*). [Tag. *bitin*]

ontología: (Sp. *ontología*) *n.* ontology.

ontólogo: (Sp. *ontólogo*) *n.* ontologist.

untón: *n.* inquisitive child. **agunton, untonan**. *v.* to examine, question closely, interrogate. **untonen**. *v.* to question (*saludsod*). **managunton**. *a.* inquisitive, curious; always asking questions. **Saanak nga immay ditoy tapno sungbatak amin a saludsod dagiti managunton**. I didn't come here to answer all the questions of the inquisitive people. [Tag. *tanóng*]

untóy: *n.* reaching one's destination little by little with rest breaks.

ungáb: **ungaban**. *v.* to notch, dent, chip. (*tipping*) **naungaban**. *a.* dented, nicked; cracked.

ungák: *n.* cry of the water buffalo (*nguak*). **agungak**. *v.* to cry (water buffalo). [Tag. *ungâ*]

ungáong₁: *a.* stupid (*unggáong*); useless.

ungáong₂: **nakaungaong**. *a.* suspended over a cliff.

úngap: *a.* open, forcibly opened. (*lukab, ukap, ungat, sukab*) **ungapen**. *v.* to open forcibly (shells). **agungap-ungap**. *v.* to open and close. **Naungap manen ti sugat iti mugingna**. The wound in his forehead opened again. **Mapilpilit a nangungap kadagiti bibigna**. She is forced to open her lips. [Tag. *buká*]

úngar: **agungar**. *v.* to revive, recover; be relieved, regain strength. (*bang-ar*) **agpaungar**.

v. to get better; convalesce. **panagpaungar.** *n.* convalescence. **umungar.** *v.* to become erect (penis). **panagungar.** *n.* resurrection. **maungaran.** *a.* to be revived; become erect (penis). **Guyodem ti itlogna tapno maungaran.** Pull his testis so he will become erect. **Agpapaungar itan iti pagtaenganda.** He is convalescing now in their home.

ungás: (Pil.) derogatory expression for males: stupid, rude; crude.

úngat: ungaten. *v.* to open (shellfish, a knife); to remove bumps. [Tag. *buká*]

úngaw: maungaw. *v.* to disappear; die out; become extinct, eradicated. (*pukaw*) **ungawen.** *v.* to kill; destroy; massacre; eradicate; squander away possessions. **Nasayaaten no maungaw tapno makabayaden ti kinaulpitna.** It will be nice if he is killed so he can pay for his cruelty.

ungbór: ungboran. *v.* to fill with water to remove the smell.

ungél: *n.* stub, stump (*pungdol*); bulb; tuber. [Tag. *tuód* (stump)]

ungét: *n.* anger. **naunget.** *a.* cranky, angry; touchy. **agunget.** *v.* to get angry. (*pungtot*) **ungtan.** *v.* to scold, chide. **kaunget.** *v.* to be angry with someone. **makapaunget.** *a.* irritating. **pagpaunget.** *n.* something that is used to make one upset or angry. **Arametenmi nga pagpaunget wenno pagpaakan iti taraken a lawwalawwa.** We use them as food or to goad the raised spiders. [Bon. *songet*, Ivt. *ipsuk, aket*, Kal. *mansasanga*, Png. *pasnók, aloboób*, Tag. *galit*]

unggán: (f. *uneg*) **naunggan.** *a.* deep; deep rooted (feeling). **agunggan.** *v.* to be possessed by evil spirits. **kaunggan.** *n.* core, deepest part; depth; subconscience.

unggáong: *a.* stupid (*tabbed*). [Tag. *tangá*]

ungguénto: (Sp. *ungüento*) *n.* ointment.

úngib: *a.* with black teeth; *n.* cavity; hole; hollowing; cave. **ungiban.** *v.* to bite in order to taste; bite off. **agungib.** *v.* to decay (teeth). [Tag. *yungíb* (cave)]

ungík: *n.* shrill cry of the pig. (*sarungikngik*) **agungik.** *v.* to shrill (said of pigs when caught).

ungít: ungitan. *v.* to avenge oneself on an innocent person. (*báles*)

ungkál: *n.* distaff. (*sukdáw*)

ungkáw: *var.* of *ungkós*: lose everything when gambling.

ungkáy: *n.* stem (*tangkáy*); handle; shaft; rod; stick; pole; umbrella pole. [Kal. *guktang*, Tag. *tangkáy*]

úngkel: (*coll.*) **maungkel.** *v.* to die; pass away. (*matay*) **ungkelen.** *v.* to kill. **makaungkel.** *a.* deadly. [Tag. *patay*]

úngkol: *var.* of *ungkel*: die. **maungkol.** *v.* to die. **innungkol.** *n.* killing each other, fight to the death. **Dayta ti nangrugian ti innungkol.** That started their fight to the finish.

úngkos: maungkosan. *v.* to lose everything in gambling (*anungos, ungkaw, pungak*). **Maungkosanto iti kuarta.** He will lose his money.

ungngák: *n.* bleating of a cow. **agungngak.** *v.* to bleat (said of a cow).

ungngó: ungngoan. *v.* to kiss. (*bisung, bisito, agek*) **agungngo.** *v.* to kiss each other. **Gandatennak a rakepen ken ungnguan iti uneg ti pagsinean.** He plans to embrace and kiss me inside the cinema. [Tag. *halík*]

ungngób: *a.* with a decayed nose (leper); noseless; with cleft palate. **ungnguben.** *v.* to decay (said of the nose). [Tag. *pudpód*]

ung-óng: nagung-ong. *a.* crazy; foolish; stupid. (*bagtit; nengneng*)

úngor: *n.* roaring sound (*daranudor*); growl; roar. **agungor.** *v.* to moan with closed mouth; roar; growl. **Naungor dagiti agsasallupang a lugan.** The meeting cars roared. [Tag. *ungol*]

úngos: agungos. *v.* to make blunt, taper.

úngot: *n.* scoop, made of a coconut shell. (*buyuboy; sabut; sudo*) **sangaungot.** *n.* one coconut scoopful. [Kal. *byakka*, Tag. *bao*]

ungpót: see *sungput*: conclude; complete; obey strictly; comply exactly. [Tag. *tapos*]

ungsáp: naungsapan. *v.* to be cut slantwise. **ungsapan.** *v.* to cut slantwise. (*tangraw*)

ungtó: *n.* tip, top; end; extremity. (*murdóng*) **agungto.** *v.* to end. **pagungtuan.** *n.* end; finish line. [Tag. *dulo*]

ungtób: maungtoban. *v.* to burn to ashes; become charred; scorched. **ungtoban.** *v.* to scorch, reduce to ashes. (*gungtob*)

uulitég: (pl. of *ulitég*) *n.* uncles.

úong: *n.* mushroom; (*obs.*) depths of a body of water. **uong ti kimat, uong ti mannagadu.** *n.* edible wild mushroom. **uong ti saba.** *n. vovariella* mushroom. **paguongan.** *n.* mushroom bed. **sinan-uong nga ulep.** *n.* mushroom cloud (nuclear explosion). **Kasla uong ti panagtuboda.** They grow like mushrooms. [Ivt. *tuputupu*, Knk. *damdamáyan*, Knk., Png. *óong*, Tag. *kabuté*]

uuyúsan: (f. *úyos*) *n.* drawer.

úpa₁: *n.* hen (*dumalaga*); (*fig.*) female. **Saanak met a nakapsut no upa ti pagsasaritaan.** I am not weak when it comes to females. [Knk. *mangák*, Tag. *inahín*]

úpa₂: upaan. *v.* to rent, lease. (*abang*) **ipaupa.** *v.* to lease out, rent out. **makiupa.** *v.* to work for daily wages. **upa-upa.** *n.* down (hair); undertail crissum of a bird; (*obs.*) rattan work. **mangupa.** *n.* renter. [Png. *abang*, Tag. *upa* (rent)]

úpal: **maupal.** *v.* to pant; be exhausted (*al-al*, *angsáb*, *tungláb*). **makaupal.** *a.* tiring, wearisome, exhausting. [Tag. *pagál*]

ópalo: (Sp. *ópalo*: opal) *n.* opal stone.

úpang: **umupang.** *v.* to become scarce; exhausted by wear; become obsolete. [Tag. *lipás*]

upáw: *n.* small leather money bag attached to the girdle. **yupaw.** *v.* to put into the *upaw*.

úpay: **upayen.** *v.* to disgust someone; discourage. (*ublag*) **maupay.** *v.* to be disgusted; discouraged; cool, weaken; be unsuccessful; lose interest. [Tag. *bigô*]

úped: **mauped.** *a.* to become dull, blunt; worn out (*ngudel*, *dusber*). [Tag. *puról*, *upód*]

úper: **aguper.** *v.* to stay immersed in water; (*fig.*) to spend too long a time doing something. **upran.** *v.* to soak in water. (*anta*) **yuper.** *v.* to dip in water; immerse. **nagupran.** *n.* water used in rinsing. **Adda kulasisina gapu iti panagup-upermo iti madiongan.** He has a mistress because you spend too much time in the mahjong parlor. [Ibg. *gattág*, Kal. *upaÿon*, Png. *lebléb*, *talém*, Tag. *babad*, *tigmák*]

ópera: (Sp. *ópera*: opera) *n.* opera.

operár: (Sp. *operar*: operate) **operaren, operaen.** *v.* to operate on. **operado.** *a.* operated on.

operasión: (Sp. *operación*: operation) *n.* operation. **agoperasion.** *v.* to have an operation.

operéta: (Sp. *opereta*: operetta) *n.* operetta, light opera.

opérta: (Sp. *oferta*: offer) *n.* offer, offering.

opertório: (Sp. *ofertorio*: offertory) *n.* offertory part of mass.

ópia: (*hopia*) *n.* a kind of *diket* rice cake. [Tag. *hopya*]

opiádo: (Sp.) *n.* opiate.

upíg: *n.* small basket. **upigán.** *n.* small basket to carry cooked rice; small rattan wallet.

ópio: (Sp. *opio*: opium) *n.* opium. (*apiang*)

opisiál: (Sp. *oficial*: official) *n.* official.

opisína: (Sp. *oficina*: office) *n.* office. (*takem*) **agopisina.** *v.* to work in an office; to go to the office. **kaopisinaan.** *n.* office mate.

opísio: (Sp. *oficio*: office; occupation) *n.* office; livelihood, employment; church service.

úpit: *n.* bamboo pouch. **upiten.** *v.* to compress; compact; harden; denounce, accuse.

upít: *n.* small basket with two parts, one smaller one fitting into the larger one.

uplák: *n.* bark; fresh sheath of the banana trunk. (*ubbák*)

uplás: *n.* a kind of tree, *Ficus sp.* whose coarse leaves are used for scouring. **panguplasen.** *n.* a kind of *Ficus* tree used for timber.

uplíg: *n.* a kind of tree of the *Ficus* species with flowers and worthless wood.

upúop: **upuopen.** *v.* to carry something on the shoulders. (*baklÃ¡y*)

oportunidád: (Sp. *oportunidad*: opportunity) *n.* opportunity. (*gundaway*).

oportunísta: (Sp. *oportunista*) *n.* opportunist. (*managgundaway*)

oposisión: (Sp. *oposición*: opposition) *n.* opposition. (*suppiat*) **oposisionista.** *n.* oppositionist.

uppápay: *n.* frowning countenance; distress. **nauppapay.** *a.* with a distressed countenance. **Aglalaok ti siddaaw ken uppapay iti rupana.** Amazement and distress were mixed in her face.

uppát: *num.* four. Sometimes this reduces to -*pat*. **maikapat.** *num.* fourth. **sagpapat.** *a.* four each. **uppaten.** *v.* to do in fours. **pamimpatén.** *v.* to do for a fourth time. **makauppat.** *v.* to be able to do four times; to be able to get four. **sinagpapat.** *a.* with four threads twisted together. [Bon. *epat*, Kal. *opat*, Knk., Png. *upát*, Tag. *apat*]

uppít: *a.* empty; hollow. (*awan nagyan*; *kawaw*) **aguppit.** *v.* to become hollow. [Tag. *hungkág*]

uppuél: *n.* a kind of suppository.

uppók: **uppokan.** *v.* to keep an eye on (*siim*); to guard; pay attention to; to live with someone.

upúop: **upuopen.** *v.* to carry something on the shoulder without a pole. (*baklay*)

oportunidád: (Sp. *oportunidad*: opportunity) *n.* opportunity. (*gundáway*)

oportunísta: (Sp. *oportunista*: opportunist) *n.* opportunist. (*managgundáway*)

oposisión: (Sp. *oposición*: opposition) *n.* opposition. (*diáya*)

opresér: (Sp. *ofrecer*: offer) **yopreser.** *v.* to offer. (*diáya*)

oprimír: (Sp. *oprimir*: oppress) **oprimiren.** *v.* to oppress.

opsión: (Sp. *opción*: option) *n.* option, choice. (*píli*)

optalmología: (Sp. *oftalmología*: ophthalmology) *n.* ophthalmology.

optalmólogo: (Sp. *oftalmólogo*: ophthalmologist) *n.* ophthalmologist. (*mangngagas ti mata*)

óptiko: (Sp. *óptico*: optician) *n.* optician, maker or seller of eyeglasses.

optimísta: (Sp. *optimista*: optimist) *n.* optimist.

optómetra: (Eng.) *n.* optometrist, eye doctor.

óra₁: (Sp. *hora*: hour) *n.* hour (used in certain situations). see *oras*. **ora santa.** *n.* holy hour. [Kal. *ulas*, Tag. *oras*]

óra₂: (Sp. *ahora*: now) **ora mismo.** right now.

úrad: *n.* ringworm, kind of skin disease. **uradan.** *v.* to scour. (*radrad*)

oradór: (Sp. *orador*: orator) *n.* orator. (*bumibitlá*)

urága: ipauraga. *v.* to retail (meat). **umuraga, uragaen.** *v.* to buy meat in retail. [Tag. *tingî*]

orákulo: (Sp. *oráculo*: oracle) *n.* oracle.

orál: (Sp. *oral*: oral) *a.* oral; spoken.

úram: *n.* fire; arson. (*apoy, puor*) **mauraman.** *v.* to be burned; be a victim of a fire. **uramen.** *v.* to set on fire. **umuuram.** *n.* a kind of small fish; arsonist. **uram-uram.** *n.* a kind of small bird; flathead fish of the *Platycephalidae* family. **panaguram.** *n.* arson. **Awan ti di mauram iti asideg ti apuy.** Nothing close to the fire escapes getting burned. **Nauram diay baybayen.** The sea has burned (referring to a late riser). [Png. *pool, angsit,* Tag. *sunog, siláb, sigá*]

urandóng: see *arandong*: a kind of shrub with small yellow flowers.

uránio: (Sp. *uranio*: uranium) *n.* uranium.

uráor: *n.* a kind of slender fish. **nauraor.** *a.* slim, slender, skinny. [Tag. *manipis*]

urárit: *n.* vein; grain; streak; fiber **naurarit.** *a.* streaked (wood); veined. **urariten.** *v.* to spin cotton finely.

uráro: *n.* hail (stones). [Knk. *dalálo*]

óras: (Sp. *horas*: hours) *n.* time; hour. **pagorasan.** *n.* clock; watch. **maorasan.** *v.* to be timed. **Ania ti orasen?** What time is it? **Tinangadna ti dakkel a pagorasan iti ngato ti ridaw.** He looked up at the big clock above the door.

orasión: (Sp. *oración*: prayer) *n.* the Angelus prayer (*lualo*); magic words; mantra. **agorasion.** *v.* to pray the Angelus; ring the bell for the Angelus.

urát: *n.* vein (*urarit*); artery; root; nerve; tendon; penis (of quadrupeds). **naurat.** *a.* veined; crafty; ingenious. **agurat.** *v.* to develop roots or veins. **kaur-urat.** *a.* with many veins. **yuratan.** *v.* to clean of fibers. **urat-uratan.** *a.* full of veins. **Uray la nangurat a nagpukkaw.** He shouted at the top of his voice. **Impayapayna dagiti urat-uratan a takiagna.** He waved his veiny arms. [Ibg. *ugaq, kelloq,* Ivt., Kpm. *uyat,* Kal. *uÿat,* Png. *olát,* Tag. *ugát*]

oratório: (Sp. *oratorio*: oratory) *n.* oratory, small chapel.

úray₁: *n.* thread; warp; *adv.* even, also, whatever. *conj.* even though (*uray no*); although; nevertheless. **uray no sadino.** wherever. **uray no ania.** whatever, no matter what. **uray no siasino.** whoever, no matter who. **uray no kaano.** whenever, no matter when. **uray no kasano.** however; no matter how. **uray . . . uray . . .** Either . . . or . . . **uray pay no; uray man no.** although, even though (*uray no*) **uray**

ania. whatever, anything. **Uray ania ti mapasamak, ileppasko ti banag a narugiak.** Whatever happens, I will finish the thing I started. **Maawatanka uray dimon baliksen.** I understand you even though you don't verbalize it. **Uray kasano ti kasakitna, madadaanak a paikallaysa kaniam.** No matter how sick she is, I am ready to marry her off to you. [Png. *anggan,* Tag *kahit* (although)]

úray₂: aguray. *v.* to wait. **urayen.** *v.* to wait for; await. **makauray.** *v.* to be able to wait for. **mauray.** *v.* to get, obtain; it can be waited for. **pagurayan.** *n.* waiting room; waiting place. **ur-uray.** *a.* hopeless, useless; empty; idle; trifling. **yuray.** *v.* to keep something for someone who will come. [Ibg. *magideg, maginneg,* Ivt. *mananayaq,* Knk. *eséb,* Kpm. *manáya,* Png. *alagár,* Tag. *hintáy*]

ur-áy: *n.* warp; woof; filling; (regional) *n.* sewing thread. **Agkarapugsat dagiti ur-ay iti makina.** The threads keep breaking in the machine.

urbá: (*obs.*) *n.* red. (*labasit, labaga*)

urbanidád: (Sp. *urbanidad*: urbanity) *n.* urbanity; good manners, etiquette.

urbó: umurbo. *v.* to resprout (*saringit*). [Tag. *usbóng*]

urbón: *n.* young (of animals). [Kal. *ayyabu*]

urbóy: maurboy. *v.* to be unthreaded; to be unstrung (necklaces). (*ukboy*)

urdás: agurdas. *v.* to crawl, walk on all fours (*karayam, sarimbaboy*). [Tag. *gapang*]

ordén: (Sp. *orden*: order) *n.* priest's crown; order; decree; tonsure. **urdenan.** *v.* to put the *orden* on the head of someone; to ordain. **naipasdek nga orden.** *n.* established order.

ordenádo: (Sp. *ordenado*: ordered; ordained) *a.* ordered; ordained.

ordenánsa: (Sp. *ordenanza*: ordinance) *n.* ordinance; municipal law.

ordinário: (Sp. *ordinario*: ordinary) *a.* ordinary (*kadawyan*); common; *n.* variety of tobacco.

urdón: urdonen. *v.* to collect; gather; assemble; lead by the nose (*urnong, singir; ukod*). [Tag. *tipon*]

úreb: *n.* sediment (*rinsaed; arinsaed*); ashes of burnt straw that have been left after extracting the lye (used as shampoo when mixed with water).

orégano: (Sp. *orégano*: wild marjoram) *n.* the oregano herb, *Coleus amboinicus,* used in native medicine for burns, cough, and stomachache.

organdí: (Sp. *organdí*: organdy) *n.* organdy; fine, thin, stiff material used for dresses.

orgániko: (Sp. *orgánico*: organic) *a.* organic.

organisár: (Sp. *organizar*: organize) **organisaren.** *v.* to organize. **organisado.** *a.* organized. **organisasion.** *n.* organization.

organisasión: (Sp. *organización*: organization) *n.* organization. (*gunglo*)

organísta: (Sp. *organista*: organist) *n.* organist, one who plays the organ.

órgano: (Sp. *órgano*: organ) *n.* organ. **agorgano.** *v.* to play the organ.

orgúlio: (Sp. *orgullo*: pride, *obs.*) *n.* self-pride; boastfulness. (*pasindayag*)

oría: (Sp. *orilla*: shore, edge) *n.* selvage, selvedge, edge of a fabric finished off to prevent unraveling.

uriáb: (*coll.*, f. *barrio*, reversed) **ur-uriab.** *n.* place deep in the country, remote outskirts of town (*away*). **Awan la't panagtalekko kadagiti tattao ditoy ur-uriab.** I just don't have any trust for the people here in the country.

uriág: aguriag. *v.* to shriek, shout. (*riaw*) **uriagan.** *v.* to shout at.

urídaw: *n.* a bird with a blue breast and black back.

urídeng: *n.* swollen belly (from disease).

oriénte: (Sp. *oriente*: orient) *n.* the Orient; east. (*daya*) **oriental.** *a.* oriental.

uriés: *n.* litter of a sow. **uriesan.** *a.* with a litter. [Tag. *biík*]

oríhen: (Sp. *origen*: origin) *n.* origin. (*paggapuan*)

orihinál: (Sp. *original*) *a.*, *n.* original; script of the *Moro moro*.

uríis: *var.* of *uríris*: cry of the hungry hog.

oríles: *n.* yellowfin tuna-like fish, called *tulingan* when small.

orinóla: (Sp. *orinal*: chamber pot) *var.* of *arinola*: bedpan, urinal bowl.

úring: *n.* charcoal, soot. see *uging*. **uringen.** *v.* to make into charcoal. **mauringan.** *v.* to be dirtied by charcoal. [Tag. *uling*]

uríngeb: *n.* a brown and yellow bird.

uríris: *n.* cry of a hungry hog. **aguriris.** *v.* to make the cry of the hungry hog (*ungik*). [Tag. *atungal*]

urísay: *interj.* used in calling hogs. **urisayen.** *v.* to call hogs to eat.

urísit: *n.* a kind of small roundworm; eruption of pimples throughout the body,

úrit: *n.* pilot; helmsman (*manimon*). **mangyurit.** *n.* pilot. **pangyurit.** *n.* rudder, helm. **payurit.** *n.* ball pen. [Tag. *ugit*]

urít: *n.* line; stripe; streak; (*ugis*); stroke; wrinkle. **yurit.** *v.* to underline; write; mark (*uged*). **urituritán.** *a.* striped, marked, streaked. [Tag. *guhit*]

orkést(r)a: (Sp. *orquesta*: orchestra) *n.* orchestra; main floor of a theater.

orkidárium: (Eng.) *n.* orchidarium.

orkídia: (Sp. *orquídea*: orchid) *n.* orchid. [Ivt. *rahakut*]

orkília: (Sp. *horquilla*: hairpin) *n.* hairpin.

urmá: urmaen. *v.* to color; dye; stain; tint. [Tag. *kulay*]

úrmot: *n.* pubic hair. **agurmot.** *v.* to grow pubic hair. **kaur-urmot.** *n.* a kind of seaweed (*ragutirit*). [Bon. *gelem*, Ibg. *vuvvul*, Ivt. *yamit*, Kal. *geÿom*, Knk. *bagu*, *geem*, *gem*, Png. *buldót*, Kpm., Tag. *bulból* (armpit or pubic hair)]

úrna: (Sp. *urna*: urn) *n.* ballot box; glass case; urn.

urnáw: urnawan. *v.* to leave a trail in the water.

ornitólogo: (Sp. *ornitólogo*) *n.* ornithologist.

órno: (Sp. *horno*: oven) *n.* oven. (*paggebbaan*) **yurno.** *v.* to bake, put in the oven. **pagurnuan.** *n.* oven.

urnóng: *n.* savings; gathering; collecting. **agurnong.** *v.* to collect; save. **aguurnong.** *v.* to assemble, gather, congregate. **urnongen.** *v.* to collect, gather; assemble; congregate (*taripnong*); store up; hoard; save for. **pakaurnóngan.** *n.* meeting place. **mangngurnong iti daan.** antique collector. **Adda urnongko a pangrugianmi kenkuana.** I have saved up for us to start up together. [Tag. *impók*]

úrnos: *n.* neatness; harmony; order; system. **agurnos.** *v.* to follow a system or order; to lie with. **urnusen.** *v.* to arrange in order; regularize; systematize; classify; adjust; settle (an agreement); make up (after fighting). **naurnos.** *a.* neat, orderly (person). **panangurnos.** *n.* syntax. **umurnos.** *v.* to be placed lengthwise and parallel to each other. **ipaurnos.** *v.* to place together (logs). **paurnosan.** *v.* to cut something lengthwise. [Kpm. *ligpít*, Png. *kamaongan*, Tag. *ayos*, *husay*]

óro: (Sp. *oro*: gold) *n.* gold. (*balitok*) **boda de oro.** *n.* golden wedding anniversary.

úro: *n.* cleanser used to clean bottles or containers. **ur-uroan.** *v.* to rinse hollow vessels.

uró: *n.* the fruit of the *ariwat*, *Tetrastigma harmandii*.

úruk: aguruk. *v.* to share contributions; contribute. **uruken.** *v.* to buy together, jointly. **aguuruk.** *v.* to contribute. (*ur-or*)

urók: *n.* snore. **agurok.** *v.* to snore (*agir*; *gerrek*). [Bon. *bódek*, Kal. *angguÿok*, Knk. *bud-ék*, *ngéek*, Png. *sanggook*, Tag. *hilik*, *harok*]

uróng: *n.* shaft; staff of a spear. **agurong.** *v.* to return; renounce; abandon; change one's mind.

urúod: nauruod. *a.* unstable, shaky, tottering; deformed.

uro-úro: uro-uroan. *v.* to cleanse with water. (*balbal, barnas*)

oropél: (Sp. *oropel*: tinsel) *n.* tinsel, foil.

ur-ór: *n.* savings; earnings; contribution. **agur-or**. *v.* to solicit. **yur-or**. *v.* to contribute; to furnish part of something. **ur-uren**. *v.* to gather, collect contributions. **maur-or**. *v.* to be collected, gathered. **Timmulong a nagur-or iti pundo manipud kadagiti umili.** He helped solicit funds from the townsfolk. [Tag. *ilak*]

óros: (Sp. *oros*: golds (suit in cards)) *n.* the gold coin suit in a Spanish deck of cards.

úrot: *n.* a bat with a long snout. **agurot**. *v.* to drop, fall (leaves, flowers, etc.); to shed (hair). **uruten**. *v.* to pull the hair of someone while delousing; pull grass without uprooting (*párut*); pull out weeds. **Agur-urot iti lis-ana iti pasagad iti sirok ti manggada.** He is pulling nits out of her hair on the sled under the mango tree. [Tag. *lagas* (fall out)]

urriáw: *n.* the approach of the harvest season.

urrón: *n.* anus (*kimmot, merret, muriit, tatakkian*). [Tag. *puwít*]

ursá: *n.* bend of a river. (*tikor, pikor*) **ursáen**. *v.* to turn, bend (a river).

ursóng: *a.* upside down (*balinsuék*; *baluknog*; *tumba*). [Tag. *tiwarík*]

urtikária: (Sp. *urticaria*: nettle rash) *n.* urticaria, rash.

ortograpía: (Sp. *ortografía*: spelling) *n.* spelling, orthography.

urtók: *n.* variety of awnless rice; *var.* of *purtok*.

us: **mang-us**. *v.* to chew sugarcane. (*us-us*) **nangusan**. *n.* skinned stalk of the sugarcane. [Tag. *pangós*]

usádo: (Sp.) *a.* used.

úsak: *var.* of *usok*: tunnel, cavelike opening. [Bon. *ósok*]

usána: (Sp. *hosana*) *n.* hosanna.

úsang: *n.* bagasse of sugarcane (*ngula*). [Tag. *yamás*]

usáor: umusaor. *v.* to sail upstream; to ascend a hill along the riverbank.

usáos: *n.* a bowlike instrument used by smiths to clean rings, earrings, etc. **usausen**. *v.* to fret; abrade; wear away by friction; polish. [Tag. *hilis*]

usár: (Sp. *usar*: use) **usaren**. *v.* to use (*aramat*; *kurri*). [Tag. *gamit*]

úsat: mangusat. *v.* to clear a path in the jungle, to open a road; start a new project. **mausatan**. *a.* to be cleared, opened (path in jungle).

úsaw: agusaw. *v.* to fade, discolor. (*kusnaw*, *kupas*) **mausawan**. *v.* to be discolored (when washed with a garment that fades); sober up (*mawmaw, munaw*). [Tag. *kupas*]

úsay: usayen. *v.* to settle differences by talking. **yusay-usay**. *v.* to explain in detail.

usdóng: usdongan. *v.* to view; look at; inspect; observe from above; (*lit*: to look down upon). [Tag. *tanáw*]

úsed: *n.* stakes put in rivers to guide waders.

úser: *var.* of *úsed*.

úsi: *n.* kidney (*bekkél*). [Bon. *batin*, Tag. *bató*]

usiák: agusiak. *v.* to break (waves). (*tapliák*)

úsig: usigen. *v.* to investigate; probe, study; search; think about carefully. **agusig**. *v.* to investigate; search. **usigan**. *v.* pass sentence for a crime; (*reg.*) to correct; punish. **pannakausig**. *n.* trial. **mangngusig**. *n.* investigator, examiner. **pagusigan**. *n.* courtroom. **parausig**. *n.* prosecutor. **Ikkannakami kuma iti gundaway a mangusig iti nagbasol.** He should give us the chance to put the guilty on trial. [Png. *salaysáy*, *suri*, Tag. *surì*, *siyasat*; *usig* = persecute]

usioséro: (f. *usioso*) *n.* person who is unduly curious; person prone to pry in on others.

usióso: (f. *usisa*) *a.* curious. (*onton*) **usiosuen**. *v.* to snoop around curiously. **Timmarayak a napan met nagusioso.** I ran to go take a curious look also.

osipikádo: (Sp. *osificado*) *a.* ossified, formed into a bone.

usísa: *n.* inquiry. (*usig*) **usisaen**. *v.* to examine; inspect; interview.

usít: sangkausit. *n.* little bit; *a.* very small, minute; meager. (*bassiusit*). **Sangkausit ti teggedmi idiay.** We have very little work there.

óso: (Sp. *oso*: bear) *n.* bear. **dakkel nga oso**. *n.* big dipper constellation, *lit*: big bear; the little dipper is called *bassit nga oso*.

úso: (Sp. *uso*: use) *a.* in style, of the latest fashion (*móda*); *n.* style; fashion; vogue. **mauso**. *v.* to be in style; to be popular (in fashion). **usuen**. *v.* to make in style.

úsob: *n.* a short, fat eel. (*igat*)

úsok: *n.* break in a wall; cavelike opening; tunnel. **umusok**. *v.* to crouch (bow the head) when passing under something. **yusok**. *v.* to insert from below; insert through; thread a needle.

úsong: *n.* badge of membership; religious garment. **agusong**. *v.* to don; put on clothes over the head. **yusong**. *v.* to don (*usok*); put on over the head. [Tag. *suot*]

usúos: *n.* a small freshwater fish, *Sillago sihama*.

usúra: *var.* of *usuria*: usury.

usoréro: *n.* usurer, person who lends money at high interest.

usúria: (Sp. *usura*: usury) *n.* usury, the practice of lending money at high interest.

us-ós: (f. *us*) **agus-os**. *v.* to chew sugarcane. **nang-usan**. *n.* skinned section of the stalk of the sugarcane, the part of the sugarcane already chewed. [Tag. *pangós*]

uspák: *a.* faded; discolored. (*kupas, paguspos, usaw, kusnaw*) **aguspak.** *v.* to fade; discolor. [Tag. *kupas*]

ospísio: (Sp. *hospicio*: asylum) *n.* orphanage; asylum.

ospitál: (Sp. *hospital*: hospital) *n.* hospital. (*pagtaraknán dagití masakít*; *pagagásan*) **yospital.** *v.* to confine in a hospital; take to the hospital. **mayospital.** *v.* to be confined in a hospital. [Tag. *págamutan*]

ussuát: *n.* starting point. (*rugi*; *rukuas*; *aruat*, *russuat*) **umsuat.** *v.* to dart; spurt out; break away. **yussuat.** *v.* to begin. [Tag. *lunsád*]

ussób: *a.* naked; shirtless. (*uksob, lamo, labus*) **agussob.** *v.* to take off one's clothes. **ussoban.** *v.* to take the clothes off someone. **Inussobna ti nabasa nga uniporme.** He took off his wet uniform. [Png. *lakseb*, Tag. *hubád*]

osteólogo: (Sp. *osteólogo*) *n.* osteologist.

osteolohía: (Sp. *osteología*) *n.* osteology, study of bones and their structure.

ustél: (*coll.*) **maustel.** *v.* to die suddenly.

ostentasión: (Sp. *ostentación*) *n.* ostentation.

óstia: (Sp. *hostia*: host) *n.* host, unleavened bread taken at church.

ustísia: *var.* of *husticia.* *n.* justice.

ústo: *var.* of *husto*: enough, sufficient; right; correct; proper. **ustuen.** *v.* to do just right; increase up to. [Tag. *husto*]

úta: **aguta.** *v.* to vomit violently (*sarwa, bakuar*). [Tag. *suka*]

útal: **utal-utal.** *n.* person with difficulty pronouncing (*wáwak*). [Tag. *utál*]

útang: *n.* debt, obligation; loan; duty; business credit; trust (in a debt). **umutang.** *v.* to borrow money. **utangan.** *v.* to borrow from somebody. **ipautang.** *v.* to lend money. **agpapautang.** *v.* lender. **pautangan.** *v.* to lend money to someone. **mautang.** *v.* to be in debt; to owe. **nakautang.** *n.* debtor. **nakautangan.** *n.* creditor. **siuutang.** *a.* in debt. **utangan.** *n.* place where one can get a loan. **agkarautang.** *v.* to be constantly borrowing. **yutang.** *v.* to give as collateral. **utangen (ti biag).** *v.* to kill. **utang a naimbag a nakem.** *n.* debt of gratitude, (Tagalog *utang na loob*). **no adda utang, adda bayadan.** *exp.* one must pay his debts. **utang-baybay.** *n.* debt of the sea (debt one will not pay back). **utang-sariap.** *n.* debt of a running stream (debt that will never be paid back). **Nagbirok iti pakautanganna iti kuarta a pangituloy iti pannakakali ti bubon.** He looked for a place where he can borrow money to continue digging the well.

[Ibg. *gatuq*, Ivt. *gatus*, Knk. *baón*, Kpm., Png., Tag. *utang*]

útek: *n.* brain; mind; (*fig.*) intellect; sense. **ma-utek.** *a.* brainy; wise; intelligent; brilliant; astute; sage; clever. **nautek.** *a.* brainy. **Kasla agut-utek a paltat.** *exp.* denoting utter stupidity (*lit*: He has the mind of a catfish). [Ibg. *utoq*, Ivt. *utek*, Kal. *utok*, Png. *oték*, Knk. *útek*, Kpm., Tag. *útak*]

otél: (Sp. *hotel*: hotel) *n.* hotel. **yotel.** *v.* to put someone in a hotel. **agotel.** *v.* to stay in a hotel.

uténg: *n.* tang, tongue of a knife.

útero: (Sp. *útero*: uterus) *n.* uterus, womb. (*aan-akan, matris*)

utilidád: (Sp.) *n.* utility.

utilitarísta: (Sp.) *n.* utilitarian; pragmatist.

utimék: **nautimek.** *a.* closed texture (cloth); thick grained; closely woven. [Tag. *sinsín*]

utnóg: see *oknog*: to knock out; pound out.

óto: *n.* automobile. (*lugan, kotse*)

útob[1]: *n.* prick, puncture, hole. **utuben.** *v.* (*reg.*) to give to everyone; to invite all; include all (*pinda*). [Tag. *tulis*]

útob[2]: **utuben.** *v.* to consider; ponder; meditate on. **mautob.** *v.* to be reflected upon. **Ut-uto-benna dagiti pasamak.** He is pondering the things that happened. [Tag. *limì*]

útok: **utuken.** *v.* to equalize, balance out; substitute; compensate.

útol: **agutol.** *v.* to crawl; swarm (insects). (*banga*)

útol: *n.* sibling, brother, sister. (*kabsat*)

otomátiko: (Sp. *automático*) *a.* automatic.

otomóbil: (Sp. *automóvil*: auto) *n.* automobile. (*kotse, lugan*)

otónio: (Sp. *otoño*: autumn) *n.* autumn.

utóng: *n.* the cowpea, long green bean. **ka-utongan, inutongan.** *n.* cowpea field. [Kal. *ngoÿay*, Knk. *bátong*, Kpm. *kamangyáng*, Png. *agáyep*, Tag. *sitaw*]

otorgár: (Sp. *otorgar*: grant; execute [will]) **otorgaren.** *v.* to admit (guilt).

otorisár: (Sp. *autorisar*: authorize) **otorisaren.** *v.* to authorize. **otorisado.** *a.* authorized.

utót: *n.* mouse (*bao, marabutit*). [Tag. *dagâ*]

ut-út: *n.* physical pain. (*saem*: mental pain, anguish) **naut-ut.** *a.* sore, aching. (*sakit*) **agut-ut.** *v.* to ache. **agpaut-ut.** *v.* to be in pain. [Png. *otót*, Tag. *hapdî, sakít*]

utóy: *n.* fatigue; exhaustion. **nautoyan.** *a.* crushed; oppressed; exhausted, tired out. **makautoy.** *a.* tiring, exhausting. **Mautoyanen nga agid-idda.** He is tired of lying down. [Tag. *pagál*]

utró: (Sp. *otro*: other) *a.* other, another (*sabali*); again (*manen*); the same; (*coll.*) *a.* meddlesome; naughty, misbehaved. **sumangkaotro.** yet another.

otsénta: (Sp. *ochenta*: eighty) *num.* eighty. (*walopulo*)

ótso: (Sp. *ocho*: eight) *num.* eight. (*waló*) **alas otso.** Eight o'clock. **otsosientos.** *num.* eight hundred.

uttóg: *n.* lust; sexual desire. **aguttog.** *v.* to be sexually excited (with erection). **kinauttog.** *n.* sexuality; lustfulness. **makauttog.** *a.* stimulating sexually. **nauttog.** *a.* lewd; lustful. (*derrép*) **makapauttog.** *a.* sexually attractive; inducing sexual desire. **managuttog.** *a.* frequently aroused. [Bon. *áyot*, Kpm. *libí*, Png., Tag. *libóg*]

uttogéro: (*coll.*) *n.* one who is excessively sexually active or aroused.

uttóm: uttoman. *v.* to roast in ashes (while wrapped in leaves.)

uttót: *n.* fart, rectal release of gas. (*barutbot*; *bassuot*) **umuttot.** *v.* to fart, release rectal gas. **agkarauttot.** *v.* to have flatulence, to fart repeatedly. **managuttot.** *a.* flatulent, prone to farting. **Naim-imbag pay tay agnunuang ngem tay aguttot a balasang, naim-imbag pay ta agkakabalio ngem tay aguttot a baro.** *exp.* Better is the water buffalo thief than the farting bachelorette, better is the horse thief than the farting bachelor. **Bungbungtot sino ti immuttot, isurom ti nagkauttot.** Ilocano version of eenie meenie miney moe. [Bon. *lot-og*, *otot*, Ibg. *ettuq*, Ivt., Kal. *utút*, Kpm. *atut*, Png. *atót*, Tag. *utót*]

uwáb: *n.* yawn (*suyaab*, *wab*). **aguwab.** *v.* to yawn. [Ibg. *awwág*, Kal. *uweb*, Knk. *oáb*, Png. *egáb*, *oáb*, Tag. *higáb*, *hikáb*]

uwáo: *n.* node of rice culm used as a whistle. **aguwao.** *v.* to blow a rice culm in order to whistle.

uwáw: *var.* of *waw*: thirst. [Ibg. *uwwaw*, *napangal*, Itg. *nadápu*, Ivt. *mawaw*, Kpm. *maw*, Png. *nakgaan*, *apaet*, Tag. *uhaw*]

uwáy: *var.* of *way*: rattan. [Kal. *iwoy*, Tag. *uwáy*, *yantók*]

úwwak: *n.* crow (*wak*). [Bon., Knk. *gáyang*, Kal. *gayang*, Png., Tag. *uwák*]

oy: Interjection used to call someone.

óya: (Sp. *olla*: stewpot) *n.* earthen jar with a narrow mouth.

úyad: aguyad. *v.* to lie crookedly; to lie down. **aguyad-uyad.** *v.* to creep; squirm; crawl crookedly on stomach (deformed person). (*karayam*) **Inyuyadna ti nagpampanunot.** He lay down thinking. [Tag. *hilatà*]

uyák: *n.* neckline of a blouse; slit of a skirt (*riang*). [Tag. *bitas*]

úyam: *n.* stratagem, deceptive device.

úyang: *n.* a polite term of address given to a woman by an older woman. **uyangen.** *v.* to address a younger woman politely. [Tag. *ale*]

uyáoy: aguyaoy. *v.* to dangle. (*tillayon*, *uy-oy*) **aguyaoy ti buteg.** *v.* to flow (nasal mucus). [Tag. *lawít*]

úyas: *n.* path of a snake; path of a hauled object. **aguyas.** *v.* to creep, crawl; slither (snake). (*karayam*) **ipauyas.** *v.* to haul, drag. **agpapauyas.** *v.* to slide down a rope (*alus-os*). [Tag. *dausdós*; *gapang*]

úyat: *n.* flaw (in metals, ceramics, etc.); crack. **aguyat.** *v.* to flatten (cakes).

uyáw: uyawen. *v.* to criticize; jeer; ridicule; gibe; mock; scorn. (*balaw*) **managuyaw.** *a.* arrogant; vain. **nauyaw.** *a.* despising; critical. **Ti tao a nadayaw, adayo nga mauyaw.** Courteous persons are never despised. [Ivt. *paru*, *rahet*, Kal. *ikiteg*, Png. *baláw*, Tag. *pintás*, *pulà*]

uyék: *n.* cough. **aguyek.** *v.* to cough. **uyek a pugiit.** *n.* whooping cough. **makapauyek.** *a.* causing one to cough. **agkarauyek.** *v.* to be always coughing. [Bon. *oyek*, *ok-ok*, Ibg. *ikeg*, Itg. *aguk-uk*, Ivt. *guqguq*, Kal. *bukos*, Knk. *éga*, *essé*, Kpm. *kúkuq*, Png. *okók*, Tag. *ubó*]

uyúkan: *n.* honeybee; *var.* of *ayukan* rice. [Tag. *pukyutan*]

úyon: *n.* a measurement for palay, usually ten *baar* (100 bundles of rice).

úyong: aguyong, agmauyong. *v.* to go crazy, insane (*bagtít*). **nauyong.** *a.* mean, severe, harsh, sour, merciless. **uyongan.** *v.* to fool, deceive, make jokes of; enchant, bewitch. **umuyong.** *v.* to become angry. **minamauyong.** *a.* crazy; foolish; stupid. **kinamauyong.** *a.* insanity; lunacy. **aguuyong.** *n.* crazy person, mad dog. **Talaga a pagmauyongennak ti pintasmo.** Your beauty is really driving me wild. **Ania manen a kinamauyong ti pampanunotem nga aramiden?** What crazy thing are you thinking of doing again? [Png. *bágel*, *tiwél*, Tag. *ulól*, *balíw* (crazy)]

úyos: *a.* unsheathed; drawn; undressed, naked. **aguyos.** *v.* to undress. **uyusen.** *v.* to drag, haul, pull along; to unsheathe a sword, pull out a drawer; pull thread through the eye of a needle; *n.* drawer. **mauyos.** *v.* to fall down. **mauyos ti biag.** *v.* to die. **aguyos.** *v.* to take the shirt off. **makauyos iti anges.** *v.* to be breathtaking. **uuyosan.** *n.* drawer. [Tag. *hugot* (pull out)]

úyot: *n.* temptation. (*sulisog*) **uyotan.** *v.* to induce, entice; persuade by flattery; tempt. **Na-**

bayagen nga uy-uyotandakami a kumappon kadakuada. They have been tempting us to join them for a long time. [Png., Tag. *tuksó*]

uy-óy: **aguy-oy.** *v.* to dangle, hang. (*tillayon*, *uyauy*) **yuy-oy.** *v.* to suspend from a rope. **pauy-oy.** *a.* hanging disorderly (a tablecloth hanging lower on one side, etc.). **Kanayon nga agpatinnag nga aguy-oy iti saputna, lalo no umaplaw ti angin.** It always drops, dangling from its web, especially when the wind blows. [Tag. *lawít*]

uyyáuy: *var.* of *uyauy*: dangle. (*tillayon*)

P

pa-: *pref.* 1. Causative/indirect prefix. Used to indicate various degrees of causation, indirect action, or transference of item to the place denoted by the stem; perfective is *pina-*: **ruar.** outside. **paruaren.** to make someone go outside. **serrek.** enter. **pastreken.** to allow someone to enter. **kanen.** food. **pakanen.** to feed. **tugaw.** chair. **patugawen.** to let someone sit down. **dakkel.** big. **mangpadakkel.** to enlarge, make bigger. **idaitan.** to sew for. **paidaitan.** to have something sewn for. **turog.** sleep. **paturogan.** to put someone to sleep. **No aramidem pay dayta kaniak ket papoliska.** If you still do that to me I will send you to the police. 2. Prefix of direction. **agpa-Manila.** *v.* to go to Manila. **panagpalaud.** *n.* the act of going to the west. **ipalaud.** *v.* to send toward the west. [Grammatical note: This prefix forms stems (that are sometimes lexicalized) that participate in reduplicative patterns as single units: **rigat.** difficulty, hardship. **parigaten.** to make something difficult. **parparigaten.** making matters difficult, continuative form of *parigaten.*]

pa- -an: Causative form of -an verbs. Perfective form is *pina- -an.* **Paturogam diay ubing.** Put that child to sleep.

pa- -en: 1. Verbalizing circumfix expressing active (instigated, volitional) causation or indirect action when attached to verbal stems. (Perfective is *pina-*): **turog.** sleep. **paturugen.** to put someone to sleep. **Pasimbengem ta nakemmo.** Calm down; 2. When attached to adjectival stems, it indicates a quality is being improved or intensified. **pintas.** beauty. **papintasen.** to improve the beauty of something.

páad: *n.* pruning trees. (*atud*) **paadan, paaden.** *v.* to trim, prune.

páag: kapaagan. *v.* to become tasteless; lose flavor. (*lab-ay*) **napaagan.** *a.* dry (said of bones). [Tag. *tabáng* (tasteless)]

paanó: (f. *anó*) **agpaano.** *interrog. adv.* asking direction of movement. **Agpaanokayo?** What direction are you going? **Ipaanoyo ti ubing?** Where are you bringing the child? [Tag. *paano* = how]

paardám: (*obs.*) *n.* calumny.

paarúyot: (f. *aruyot*) **paaruyutan.** *v.* to drain.

paatián: paatianan. (f. *ati*) *v.* to dry out. *var.* *patian, atian.* **maatianan.** *v.* to be dried out. [Tag. *tuyô*]

paawán: (f. *awán*) **paawanan.** *v.* to cause to disappear; cause to vanish.

páay: *n.* rejection of a proposal; refusal. **ipaay.** *v.* to grant, give to. **napaay.** *a.* disappointed; refused; rejected; frustrated. **papaayen.** *v.* to refuse, reject; thwart; slight; disappoint. **Ania't pakapaayanna?** Why is he frustrated? **No paayennak, agpakamatayak.** If you reject me, I will kill myself. **Pasig a panagrigat ken pannakapaay.** It is pure hardship and frustration. [Tag. *bigô*]

paáy: (f. *ay*) **agpaay.** *v.* to be intended for, to go to; *prep.* for. **maipaay.** *v.* to be for, to be intended for. **Pangipaayam ta burnay?** Who are you intending that jar to be for? **Ania ti maipaayko kadakayo?** What can I do for you?

paayáp: paayapan. *v.* to threaten by raising the hand. (*kayap; layat*)

pabábaw: agpababaw. *v.* to trip in wrestling.

pabánto: *n.* device for hurling stones; cannon. **napabantuan.** *v.* to be hit by a slung object. **pabanto a sao.** *n.* harsh language.

pabangló: (f. *banglo*) *n.* perfume, fragrance. [Tag. *pabangó*]

pabáreng: (f. *bareng*) **ipabpabareng.** *v.* to make an effort to do.

pabásol: (f. *basol*) **pabasolen.** *v.* to blame, accuse. [Tag. *sisi, salà*]

pabawér: *n.* flexible bamboo stick to which a lasso is attached in automatic snares.

pabilgén: (f. *bileg*) *v.* to strengthen, fortify.

pabílo: (Sp. *pabilo*: wick) *n.* wick of a candle, in old times made from the *balanggot* reed; (*fig.*) cause, instigator. **Isu ti pabilo ti amin.** *exp.* He is the cause of everything. [Tag. *mitsá* (Sp.)]

pabláak: (f. *bellaak*) *n.* news, message, announcement. (*pakdaar*) **ipablaak.** *v.* to publish, proclaim. **maipablaak.** *v.* to be published. **Pudno a naipablaak kadagiti pagiwarnak ngem maawatan met la ngata dagiti nakabasa?** It is true that it is published in the papers, but do you think the readers understand it? [Tag. *lathalà*]

pablád: (f. *bellad*) **pinablad.** *n.* cooked cereals. **pabladen.** *v.* to cook cereals in water until they puff up; (*fig.*) to expose; insinuate.

pábo: (Sp. *pavo*: turkey) *n.* turkey. (*burayuán*)

pábula: (Sp. *fábula*: fable) *n.* fable.

pabúlod: (f. *búlod*) **ipabulod.** *v.* to lend. [Tag. *pahirám*]

pabunár: (f. *bunár*) *n.* festivity, celebration; blowout for the winner of an election; going away party (*despedida*); campaign for a party. **agpabunar.** *v.* to host a festivity. **makipabunar.** *v.* to attend a festivity.

pabuniág: (f. *buniág*) *n.* baptismal party. **agpabuniag.** *v.* to have a child baptized.

pabór: (Sp. *favor*: favor) *n.* favor; bias, favoritism. **paboran.** *v.* to favor; side with.

paboráble: (Eng.) *a.* favorable; agreeable; conforming to.

paboreál: (Sp. *pavo real*: peacock) *n.* peacock.

paburék: (f. *burek*) **ipaburek, agpaburek.** *v.* to boil. [Tag. *lagà*]

pabur-í: (f. *bur-i*) **ipabur-i.** *v.* to give scarcely what one has in abundance.

paborítísmo: (Sp. *favoritismo*) *n.* favoritism.

paboríto: (Sp. *favorito*: favorite) *a.* favorite. **paboritismo.** *n.* favoritism. [Tag. *pinakatangì*]

pabúya: (f. *buya*) *n.* show, performance. **ipabuya.** *v.* to show to the public. [Tag. *palabás*]

pábrika: (Sp. *fábrica*: factory) *n.* factory (*pagpartuatan*). **pabrikante.** *n.* manufacturer; factory owner; producer of a good. **pabrikasion.** *n.* fabrication; manufacture; production. [Tag. *págawaan*]

páda: *n., a.* same, equal; *n.* peer. **agpada.** *v.* to be the same, equal; to match. (*pareho; padpad; patak; arked*) **pumada.** *v.* to be unequalled; supreme; unsurpassed. **padaen.** *v.* to equal, match; copy, imitate. **ipada.** *v.* to compare; make something the same or similar to something else. **paipada.** *v.* to compare, liken to. **kapada.** *n.* peer; equal, match. **pada a tao.** *n.* fellow man; neighbor. **padapada.** *a.* same, equal; everyone without exception or favoritism. **padapadaen.** *v.* to treat equally; to share alike. **makipada.** *v.* to be almost the same; be similar to. **pamadáen.** *a.* rather alike. **pagpadaen.** *v.* to treat equally; equate; balance out. **Ania ti pagpadaan ti kamote ken karabasa.** What do sweet potatoes and pumpkins have in common? **Agpadakami iti katayag ken kadakkel ti bagi.** We are the same in height and size. [Png. *para*, Tag. *pantáy, pareho*]

padáan: (f. *daan*) **padaanan.** *v.* to wait for results; wait for; be on the lookout for.

padágan: **ipadagan.** *v.* to preannounce; preinform (about a future contract). (*padamagan*)

padágir: (f. *dagir*) **padagiran.** *v.* to hurt the feelings of (*pasagid*); offend; *var.* of *padakir*: accuse indirectly.

padák: *n.* sound of a heavy footstep; hoofbeat. **agpadakpadak.** *v.* to make the sound of galloping horses. [Tag. *yabág*]

padákes: (f. *dakes*) *n.* slander. [Tag. *paninirangpuri*]

padákir: (f. *dákir*) *n.* indirect accusation. **agpadakir.** *v.* to make an indirect accusation; hurt the feelings of. **mapadakiran.** *a.* indirectly accused.

padálan: **padalanan.** *v.* to iron (*plantsa*); sew (*dait*).

padalaydáy: *n.* pole of a cart to which the yoke is attached. (*pallatiwan*)

padámag: (f. *dámag*) *n.* news. **ipadamag.** *v.* to tell news. **agipadamag.** *v.* to spread the news. [Tag. *balità*]

padápad: **padapaden.** *v.* to ravage; strip (a forest), lay waste; lay bare.

padapán: (f. *dapán*: sole of foot) *n.* runners of a sledge.

padára: (f. *dára*) **agpadara.** *v.* to hemorrhage; vomit blood.

pádas₁: *n.* a kind of marine fish used in *bugúong*; the *bugúong* made of *padas*. [Tag. *pagdurugô*]

pádas₂: *n.* experience; skill; wisdom gained by experience; trial, attempt; knowledge. **agpadas.** *v.* to try at a competition. **pumadas.** *v.* to try one's hand at. **Agpadasta.** Let's compete. **ipadas.** *v.* to try on (clothes), test. **kapadasan.** *n.* experience; adventure. **padasen.** *v.* to try, attempt; test; experiment. **mapadas.** *v.* to be able to try, test, experiment, experience. **pamadasan.** *a.* experimental; *n.* test; trial. **adda padas.** *a.* experienced. **padpadas.** *n.* experiences. **Nagpinnadasda iti pigsa.** They competed with each other in strength. **Di ammo nga agas no di napadas.** It will not be known to be medicine if it is not tried. **Iti edadna a tallopulo awan pay padasna iti babai.** At his age of thirty, he still has no experience with women. [Png., Tag. *subok*]

padatár: (f. *datár*) *n.* piece of woven bamboo used for fishing purposes.

padáw: *n.* a kind of small marine lobster. [Ibg. *pasáyan, payang*, Ivt. *payiq*, Kpm. *ulang*, Png. *kisingkísing*, Tag. *sugpô*]

padayá: (f. *dayá*) *n.* party, feast, celebration. **agpadaya.** *v.* to have a party, celebration. [Tag. *handaan*]

paddágan: *n.* grasshopper.

paddák₁: *n.* footprint; track; sole of an animal foot; heavy footstep. **pumaddak, agpaddak.** *v.* to stomp the feet. **mangipaddak.** *v.* to step on heavily. [Tag. *dabóg*]

paddák₂: **paddapaddak.** *n. Dactyloctenium aegyptium* coarse, spiky grass.

paddék: *var.* of *paddak*: stomp, step on heavily (*padek*). **Kadagiti tattao a managayat iti wayawaya, iwallagesda dagiti agdursok a mangipaddek iti patpatgenda a nakayanakanda a daga.** People that love liberty throw down those who dare to trample the beloved land of their birth. [Tag. *dabóg*]

paddúdon: *n.* grasshopper. **pagpaddudon.** *n.* circular net used to catch grasshoppers. [Tag. *tipaklóng*]

paddukól: **napaddukol.** *a.* rough, rugged (land); lumped.

padég: *var.* of *pidég*: pin down; push against; corner; *var* of *padér*: push against a wall.

padék: padekpadek. *n.* sound of footsteps.

pad-éng: ipadpad-eng. *v.* to suspend, postpone (*tantan*); delay; put off, stop temporarily (an action); kill time; wait for something to happen. **Nupay kasta unay ti gagarko, ipadpad-engko ta paglek a mayasidegak unay kenkuana.** Although I really want to, I put it off because I forbid myself to get too close to her. [Tag. *antala*]

padeppá: *n.* crosspiece of the cross.

padér: (Tag., via Sp. *pared*: wall) *n.* wall (*diding*); thorny fence. (*alad*; *bakud*) (*obs.*) **agpader.** *v.* to waddle.

pádes: *var.* of *pádis*: similar, same; compare.

padés: kapades. *n.* the height of a season (harvest, etc.) (*tibok*)

pádi: (Sp. *padre*: father; priest, plural: *papadi*) *n.* priest. (*kura*) **agpadi.** *v.* to become a priest. **napadian.** *a.* priestly. **agimpapadi.** *v.* to pretend to be a priest. **agpadipadi.** *v.* to play the priest (said of a layman). [Ivt. *pali*, Kal. *pachi*, Tag. *parì*]

padiáma: (Eng.) *n.* pajamas. **nakapadiama.** *a.* wearing pajamas.

padíkal: napadikal. *a.* bulky, with a big load. (*padiwákal*) **pimmadpadikal a bantay.** *n.* small hill.

pádil: padilen. *v.* to rub off with the hand (*pigad*). [Tag. *palís*]

padíla: (f. *dila*: tongue) *n.* tang of a knife.

páding: padingpading. *n.* hip; hip bone; haunch. [Tag. *balakáng*]

padíng: padingan. *n.* (construction) a disconnected piece of wall; *v.* to put a wall into; wall.

padingalngál: *n.* bridle, bit; mortise; wedge. (*tingal*) **ipadingalngal.** *v.* to wedge something between, put between; to throw in one's teeth (rebuking). **maipadingalngal.** *v.* to be wedged into; stuck against a hump, etc. **Napadingalngalan ti paragpag.** He has a rib stuffed (in his mouth).

padinggér: agpadpadingger. *v.* to imitate, mimic someone's gait. (*tulad*)

padípad: agpadipad. *v.* to cut down (trees). (*pukan*)

pádis₁: agpadis. *v.* to be similar, equal; match. **pagpadisen.** *v.* to equalize; balance out; compare. **ipadis.** *v.* to compare. **pagpapadísan.** *n.* similarities (*pada*). **kapadis.** *n.* equal; match; equivalent. [Tag. *pareho, paris*]

pádis₂: pinadis. *n.* cigar. (*tabako*)

padísi: padisién. *v.* to drive away; eject, cast out; defeat.

padiwádiw: *n.* extra length. **agpadiwadiw.** *v.* to be too long.

padiwákal: napadiwakal. *a.* too large to be packaged; bulky. (*bungkóng, padikal, ragkáng*)

padláw: (f. *dillaw*) **ipadlaw.** *v.* to cause someone to notice; reveal, display. **Awan ti mangngegna a mangipadlaw a siririing pay dagiti kabbalayna.** He didn't hear anything revealing that his housemates were still awake. [Tag. *hayág, bunyág*]

padlés: *n.* prophecy; prediction. (*padto*) **ipadles.** *v.* to foretell, prophesy, predict. **padlesan.** *v.* to solve (a riddle), guess. **agpadpadles.** *v.* to guess. **mammadles.** *n.* prophet. **panagpadles.** *n.* fortune-telling, prophesizing. [Png. *parlés*, Tag. *hulà*]

pádna: *n.* yard of rope attached to the *liding*.

paduál: (*reg.*) *n.* mound, heap, hill.

padúl: *n.* peg to which animals are tied. **padulan.** *v.* to provide with a peg.

padúlang: (f. *dulang*: table) *n.* device for pulverizing the soil.

padumná: *var.* of *padna*.

pádun: *n.* muzzle; stick on the leash of a dog that prevents it from biting. (*busal*) **padunan.** *v.* to muzzle. [Tag. *busál* (Sp.)]

padúng: ipadung. *v.* to designate, appoint to a certain duty. **maipadung.** *v.* to be designated, appointed to a certain duty (*patudon*). [Tag. *hirang*]

padungalngál: *var.* of *padingalngal*: wedge. **napadungalngal.** *a.* wedged into, stuffed into (one's mouth). **ipadungalngal.** *v.* to wedge into, put between.

paduyakyák: *n.* exhibition. **ipaduyakyak.** *v.* to reveal, disclose; openly declare. **maipaduyakyak.** *v.* to be revealed; disclosed; declared. **Nakitana ti nakapurpuraw a barbasna a mangipaduyakyak iti kinaduognan.** She saw his white beard that revealed his old age. [Tag. *lantád*]

padpád₁: agpadpad. *v.* to be like, equivalent; to match (*pareho*; *patad, pada*). **kapadpad.** *n.* equal; equivalent; match; peer. [Tag. *pareho*]

padpád₂: maipadpad. *v.* to land, reach the shore after having been gone a while; set foot on; drift; reach a destination. (*sadsad*) **Nagtalaw ket awanen ti makaammo iti nakaipadpadanna.** He escaped and no one knows where he landed.

padrást(r)o: (Sp. *padrastro*: stepfather) *n.* stepfather. [Tag. *amáin*]

pádre: (Sp. *padre*: father; priest) *n.* priest, father; short for *kumpadre* (*padi*). **padrenuestro.** *n.* our father (said in prayers). [Tag. *parì*]

padríno: (Sp. *padrino*: patron, male sponsor) *n.* sponsor at wedding (male); female is *padrina*.

padrón₁: (Sp. *padrón*: census) *n.* church register.

padrón₂: (Sp. *patrón*: pattern) *n.* pattern (for embroidery, etc.).

padsíng: napadsingan. *v.* to drive someone away from where he is seated; to feel chills and pallor due to meeting a ghost. **mapadsing.** *v.* to be fired from one's job.

padsó: (f. *dissó*) *n.* overthrow. **napadso.** *a.* overthrown; fallen over, toppled over; stunned; fatigued. **ipadso.** *v.* to knock over, topple down; defeat; (*fig.*) to put down. **padsuen.** *v.* to stun. [Tag. *lugmók*; *tulíg*]

padsók: napadsok. *a.* steep; sharp; with a peak. [Tag. *tarík* (steep)]

padtó: *n.* prophecy. (*padlés*). **padtuan.** *v.* to foretell an event; predict; prophesy. **mammadto.** *n.* prophet; fortune-eller. **Padpadtuanna no asino kadakuada ti nawelwel.** He is foretelling who among them is naughty. [Png. *parlés*, Tag. *hulà*]

paéd: *n.* a kind of fish trap similar to the *pasabing*.

paélia: (Sp. *paella*) *n.* rice stew with seafood, vegetables, chicken and saffron.

paéng: napaeng. *a.* short (nails, ears of rice); weak; simple minded.

paér: see *paed*: kind of fish trap.

paét: *n.* chisel. **paetan.** *v.* to chisel. **ipaet.** *v.* to wedge (a chisel or ax). **maipaet.** *v.* to be wedged; to stick into. **Kakasla paet dagiti ngipenna.** His teeth are like chisels. [Kal. *lusok*, Knk. *talíling*, Tag. *paít, panukól*]

pag-: Instrumental prefix, takes ergative *-ko* series pronouns. It is usually used for nominals. Perfective form is *pinag-* **pagkape.** to use for coffee; that which is used for coffee. **pagwasay.** to use as an ax; that which is used as an ax **Nangisaangak iti danum a pagkapemi.** I put our coffee water over the fire. **Pagpunasmo daytoy.** Use this to wipe. **Paglastogna unay ti kinaguapona.** He really boasts about his handsomeness (*lit*: uses his handsomeness to boast).

pag- -an: 1. Locative circumfix, indicating where an action takes place; perfective form is *nag- -an*. **ay-ayam.** play. **pagay-ayaman.** playground. **trabaho.** work. **pagtrabahuan.** workplace. 2. May also indicate reason, cause, or origin of an action. **Awan ti rumbeng a pagdanagam.** You should not worry about anything. **Awan ti pagalaanmi ti pagbiagmi.** We have nothing from which to get our livelihood. 3. Nominalization of *ag-* reciprocal verbs.

pagtulagan. making a contract with each other. **pagbibingayan.** sharing with each other.

pag- -en: circumfix. Used to form the causative of *ag-* verbs in patient focus (taking the *-ko* series pronouns): **agsurat.** to write. **pagsuraten.** to make someone write something. **Pagsuratem ni Earl.** Make Earl write something. **Masapul a pagnakemem dayta a lalaki.** You need to make that boy grow up (mature). **Pagtalnaem kuma ti konsensiana.** You should calm down his conscience. This affix denotes stronger causation than *pa- -en*. Notice the difference between this affix and *pa- -en*: **patugawen.** *v.* to allow (let) someone to sit down. **pagtugawen.** *v.* to force someone to sit down. **paurayen.** *v.* to make someone wait a while. **pagurayen.** *v.* to make someone wait.

pag- -inn- -an: Reciprocal form of *pag- -an* stems. **pagsinnungbatan.** cause, reason of arguing with each other

pag- -inn- -en: Causative affixation for reciprocal *ag- -inn-* verbs. Perfective form is *pinag--inn-*. **pagtinnulongen.** to have people help each other.

pagaC-, pagat-: Prefix indicating extent (in terms of the entity denoted by the root). Usually in the form *pagat* or with initial root consonant gemination: **Pagat-abaga ti buokna.** Her hair goes down to her shoulders. (reaches her shoulders) **Pagabbarukongnak.** She comes up to my chest. **pagattao a sarming.** full-length mirror (size of a man).

pága₁: ipaga, pagaan. *v.* to take special care of. (*ilalaen, ikutan*)

pága₂: napaga. *a.* finicky, fastidious. (*napili*) **ipaga.** *v.* to bet all. [Tag. *selang*]

pága₃: pagapaga. *n.* kite. (*bagabaga*)

pagádo: (Sp. *pagado*: paid) *a.* paid. (*nabayadan*)

pagadór: (Sp. *pagador*: payer) *n.* payer; paymaster.

pagalagádan: (f. *alagad*) *n.* rules, regulations; constitution. [Tag. *saligang-batás*]

pagalsém: (f. *alsem*) *n.* anything used to make food sour.

pagammuán: (f. *ammó*) *a.* suddenly, unexpectedly, all of a sudden, at once (*bigla*). *n.* source of information. **Pagam-ammuan, bimtak ti riaw dagiti agbuybuya.** All of a sudden the shouts of the spectators erupted. [Tag. *biglâ*]

pagan-anáy: *n.* wardrobe, clothing, garments, apparel. (*bado*; *kawes*; *aruat*; *lupot*) **agpagan-anay.** *v.* to wear thick clothes. [Tag. *lupot*]

pagan-anó: (f. *anó*) *interrog.* to be of what use; to be of what interest to. **Pagan-anom ti pirak**

no awan met ti ragsakmo? Of what use is money to you if you are not happy?

pagánat: (*obs.*) *n.* dogvane, telltale, a light windvane consisting of a strip of cloth mounted on a vessel used to ascertain wind direction.

pagannayásan: (f. *annayas*) *n.* situation, progress, state of affairs. (*kasasaad*)

pagannináwan: (f. *anninaw*) *n.* lesson. [Tag. *aralín*]

paganísmo: (Sp. *paganismo*: paganism) *n.* paganism.

pagáno: (Sp. *pagano*: pagan) *n.* pagan. **paganismo.** *n.* paganism.

pagapó: ipagpagapo. *v.* to reconcile; make friends out of former enemies. (*amo*)

pagapúgan: (f. *apog*) *n.* small earthen jar used by betel chewers to hold lime, resembling an ashtray.

pagár: (Sp. *pagar*: pay) **pagaran.** *v.* to pay someone (*bayadan*). [Tag. *bayad*]

pagarián: (f. *ari*) *n.* kingdom. **agkapagarian.** *v.* to be from the same kingdom. [Tag. *kaharian*]

pagarígan: (f. *arig*) *n.* example. **kas pagarigan.** for example. [Tag. *halimbawà*]

pagarún: (f. *arun*) *n.* inflammable material used to kindle a fire.

pagarúp: *n.* guess, supposition. **ipagarup, pagarupen.** *v.* to think; believe; presume; guess, suppose; suspect. **maipagarup.** *v.* to be presumed; assumed. **panangipagarup.** *n.* assumption; expectation. **Asino kuma ti mangipagarup nga adda kuarta idiay.** Who would have assumed that there is money there. **Pagarupek a saantanton nga agkita.** I guess we won't be seeing each other. [Knk. *kapkáp*, Png. *abaloan*, Tag. *palagáy, akalà*]

págas: (*obs.*) **mapagas.** *v.* to be blown or driven by the air.

pagasimbuyókan: (f. *asimbuyok*) *n.* chimney.

pagat-: Prefix used to indicate how far something reaches, see *paga(-RC)*: **Pagat-lapayag ti isemna.** His smile is from ear to ear. (reaches the ear). **Pagat-sipáng ti badona.** Her dress is up to her bikini line (i.e., is extremely short). **pagattao a sarming.** full-length mirror (human height).

págat: (*reg.*) *n.* cane, reed. **mapagat.** *v.* to collide with, strike against. (*dalapon*; *dungpar*; *dungso*)

pagatíng: *n.* old Ilocano practice of celebrating the first meal at the bride's house after the wedding. **agpagating.** *v.* to celebrate the first meal at the bride's house after the wedding. [Png. *pagatin*]

págaw: *n.* a kind of turtledove; variety of rice. **agpagpagaw.** *v.* to be always together (like

doves). **marapagaw.** *n.* young chicken the size of a *pagaw*. **agpagaw.** (*obs.*) *v.* to dawn. [Kal. *ut-ut*, Tag. *batubató*]

pagáw: *n.* small coconut shell used as a drinking vessel.

pagawápaw: *n.* sound of wind passing through crevices. **agpagawapaw.** *v.* to hiss (said of the wind). **Iti baet ti panagpagawapaw ti lapayagna, nakatimud iti wanerwer.** Among the passing sounds in his ear, he heard the sound of the engine.

pagawpáw: pagawpawen. *v.* to overfill; overload.

págay: *n.* rice (unhusked), *Oryza sativa.* **kapagayan.** *n.* rice field. **ipagayan.** *v.* to hire a worker for rice wages. **pagayan.** *n.* place where rice is grown; *v.* to plant with rice. **marapagay.** *n.* kind of grass that resembles *pagay.* **pagaybakir.** *n.* wild rice (*maluit*). **pagay-Iloko.** *n.* kind of fragrant upland rice with dark-colored hull and red kernel. **pagay-imbantay.** *n.* mountain rice, upland rice. **pimmagay.** *n.* slender bolo; venomous snake. [Bon. *págey*, Ibg. *emmay, irik*, Ifg. *páge*, Kpm. *pale*, Png. *pagéy*, Tag. *palay*]

pagáyam: *n.* friend (plural: *papagayam*). **agpagayam.** *n.* relationship between friends. **makipagayam.** *v.* to make friends; befriend. **mannakipagayam.** *a.* friendly (*gayyem*). [Tag. *kaibigan*]

pagayatán: (f. *ayát*) *n.* wish, desire. [Tag. *nais*]

pagayúpay: *n.* young locust larger than the *lukton.*

pagayúpoy: *n.* breeze (stronger than the *pul-oy*). **agpagayupoy.** *v.* to blow softly (breeze). [Tag. *simoy*]

pagbabasaán: (f. *basá*) *n.* wet, muddy place near the *bangsal.*

pagbagasán: (f. *bagás*) *n.* receptacle for uncooked rice.

pagbalúdan: (f. *bálud*) *n.* jail, prison. [Kal. *bebeÿÿuchen*, Tag. *bilangguan*]

pagbedngán: (f. *beddéng*) *n.* boundary, border; limit. [Tag. *hangganan*]

pagbuklén: (f. *bukél*) *v.* to complete; make round or circular. [Tag. *bilóg* (round)]

pagbunubónan: (f. *bunúbon*) *n.* seedbed.

pagdaksán: (f. *dákes*) *n.* the bad thing about it.

pagél: *n.* suffering; hardship. **ipagel.** *v.* to prohibit, forbid; hinder, impede; restrain. **napagel.** *a.* arduous, rigorous, hard; impatient; restless. **agpagel.** *v.* to disagree; to be unsuitable; to be annoying; offend; displease. **paglan.** *v.* to forbid, prohibit; hinder, prevent; **paglen.** *v.* to prohibit; disagree; dislike. **Paglek a mayasidegak unay kenkuana.** I forbid myself from getting too close to him. [Tag. *bawal* (forbid); *kahirapan* (hardship)]

pag-éng: *var.* of *pas-eng*: smell of leftover vegetables.

páger: *n.* thorny fence (*pader*).

pagér: *n.* palisade, paling, line used in leveling.

pagét: **papaget**. *n.* a kind of long marine fish.

pagetpét: *n.* *Eriochloa ramosa.* a kind of grass with green or purplish spikelets.

paggá: (*obs.*) *n.* unit of grain weight.

paggáak: *n.* loud laughter. (*garakgak*) **agpaggaak, pumgaak.** *v.* to laugh loudly. **pagga-akan.** *v.* to laugh at someone. **Kukuak met ti maudi a paggaak.** Mine will be the last laugh. [Tag. *halakhák*]

paggalsém: (f. *alsem*) *n.* guava fruit that is not yet ripe; (*coll.*) virgin.

paggáng: *n.* act of regretting wrongful deeds. **mapaggang.** *v.* to regret a wrongdoing (and reform). [Tag. *sisi*]

pagguadán: *n.* example, model. (*pagarigan*)

pagi-: Instrumental prefix for *i-* verbs. **Aginanatayo pay tapno adda pagituredtayo no rabii.** Let's rest so we will have (enough strength) to be courageous tonight.

pagi- -an: Nominalizing locative affixation for theme focus *i-* verbs: **ibelleng.** to throw away, **pagibellengán.** garbage can; **itarús.** to translate. **pagitarusán.** bilingual dictionary.

pagi- -en: Causative applicative circumfix used for *i-* theme focus verbs. **Pagikeddengenta ni Au no asino kadata ti natimtimbang.** Let's have Au choose which one of us is more dear to her.

pági: *n.* stingray, kind of edible ray. [Ivt. *napanici*, Tag. *pagi*]

pagilián: (f. *ili*) *n.* country. **sangapagilian.** *n.* the entire nation; one country. [Tag. *bansâ*]

paginCV- -en: Causative affixation used with *aginCV-* pretentative verbs. **pagimpipilayen.** to make someone pretend to limp. **pagimbabaknangen.** to have someone pretend to be poor. **pagintuturogen.** to make someone pretend to be asleep.

pagingetngét: *n.* hiding place; hideaway. (*lemmeng*) **ipagingetnget.** *v.* to hide, conceal; hoard.

pagípag: **pagipagan.** *v.* to stimulate, encourage, excite, animate (*regta*). [Tag. *pasiglá*]

pagitngá: *n.* centerpiece. **agpagitnga.** *v.* to stay in the center. (*patengnga*) **ipagitnga.** *v.* to place in the center. [Tag. *gitnâ*]

pagíwa: (f. *íwa*) *n.* knife, instrument for slicing.

pagiwárnak: (f. *warnák*) *n.* newspaper. **aginaldaw a pagiwarnak.** *n.* daily paper. [Tag. *diaryo* (Sp.), *pahayagán*]

pagka-: Prefix used to express fractional division. **uppat.** four. **maysa a pagkapat.** one-fourth. **pagkalima.** one-fifth.

pagka- -en: *circumfix.* with numeral roots, this transitivizing affix indicates division: **Pagkalimaenda.** They divide it into five parts. **Pagkawaluenta.** Let's divide it into eight parts. **pagkamanuen.** to divide (into so many parts).

pagkamanoén: (f. *manó*) *v.* to divide into so many parts. **Pagkalimaem ti tallopulo, innem.** Thirty divided by five is six.

pagkét: *n.* glue; paste. (*pigket; kola*) **ipagket.** *v.* to glue, paste. **pagketán.** *v.* to apply glue to. [Tag. *pagkít*]

pagmanoán: (f. *manó*) *interrog.* How many are needed for it?

pagná: (*pagná* is not the original root, as evidenced from the stress patters of suffixed derivatives: *pagnaán, pagnaén,* etc.) *n.* walk; gait. **agpagna** *a.* current, present. *v.* to walk **agpagnapagna.** *v.* to walk to and fro; stroll about. **magna.** *v.* to walk, go on foot. **magmagna.** *a.* walking; *n.* current fad; current happening. **pagnaán.** *n.* road, path, thoroughfare; result; outcome. **mapagnaán.** *a.* passable; to be able to pass. **ipagna.** *v.* to step; walk with; manage, operate; hand carry papers for approval. **pannagna.** *n.* manner of walking. **mannagna.** *n.* hiker, good walker; *a.* fond of walking. **makapagná.** *v.* to be able to walk. **mapagna.** *v.* to be able to walk a distance. **makapagpagna.** *n.* present occurrences. **'toy agpagna a bulan.** *n.* this current month. **pagnaen.** *v.* to walk the distance (instead of driving), to go to on foot. **pagpagnaén.** *v.* to give way, let pass. [Ibg. *lákag*, Ivt. *ayam*, Png. *akár, saráng, koráng*, Tag. *lakad*]

pagnaedán: (f. *naed*) *n.* address. (*pagtaengan*)

págo: (Sp. *pago*: payment) *n.* amount bet on a cockfight; payment of a debt. **pumago.** *v.* to bet in a cockfight. **ipago.** *v.* to put down money in a bet.

págua: (*obs.*) *n.* the *abaka* plant (*Musa textilis*).

págod: *n.* a kind of open hut. **napagod.** (*obs.*) *a.* slow in walking.

pagód: **ipagod.** *v.* to tie something with a long line (animal, ship, etc.); tether an animal, vessel, etc. [Tag. *talì; pagód* = tired]

pagóda: (Sp., Eng.) *n.* pagoda, towerlike Buddhist temple.

pagudpúd: *n.* *Cynodon dactylon.* Bermuda grass, green variety. (*galotgálot*)

pag-óng: *n.* tortoise, turtle. **pinag-ong.** *n.* a house with a hip roof. **pimmag-ong.** *a.* shaped like a turtle (native roofs), resembling a turtle. **Kasla pag-ong a sisasagana nga agkumeg.** She is like a turtle ready to hide in its shell. [Ibg. *degga*, Ivt. *irang*, Kpm. *pauq*, Png. *bakokól*, Tag. *pagóng*]

pagunggán: (f. *unég*) **agpagunggan**. *v.* to run amuck; run wild. (*úyong, huramentádo*)

pagurúpor: *n.* sound produced by diarrhea, a raspy voice. fluttering leaves, etc. **agpagurupor**. *v.* to make a whirring or purring sound.

págus: *n.* craving, eager desire. (*karayo*; *kalikagum*; *pikat*; *ragut*; *tarigagay*) **agpagus**. *v.* to crave. **napagus**. *a.* determined; ardent; craving; persistent. [Tag. *dubdób*]

paguspús: **mapaguspus**. *v.* to change, alter; fade (color); shift position. [Tag. *kupas* (fade)]

pag-út: **pag-uten**. *v.* to uproot, pull out from the roots. (*gabut*; *ganot*; *parut*) **agpapag-ut**. *v.* to have one's tooth extracted. [Bon. *gábot*, Png. *bagot*, Tag. *bunot*]

pagutpút: *n.* thin strips of bamboo used to fill in basket weaving. **pagutputen**. *v.* to fill in with more strips.

pagpa-: Nominalizing causative prefix. Indicates the means in which an action is caused to be done. **pagpabalay**. means of having a house built. **pagpapintas**. means of improving one's beauty.

pagpa- -an: Nominalizing circumfix indicating the location of an indirect or causative action: **pagpalutuan**. place where one has something cooked.

pagpág: *n.* rice with many empty spikes. **pumagpag**. *v.* to flutter, float, wave. **pinagpagan**. *n.* cloth woven without a loom. **ipagpag**. *v.* to shake off. **pagpagen**. *v.* to shake (and beat off dust, etc.). [Tag. *pagpág*]

pagpakán: (f. *kaan*) *n.* food; nourishment. (*taraon*)

pagpinna- -an: Nominalizing affixation for reciprocal *agpinna-* verbs. **pagpinnadamagan**. act of exchanging news. **Umayka pasiaren ita met laeng; ditanto ti pagpinnadamaganta**. I will come drop by there now anyway, we will exchange news at your place.

pagsá: (f. *segga*) *a.* kind of white, elongated fish.

pagsagátan: (f. *sagat*) *n.* strainer. [Tag. *panalà*]

pagsalapayán: (f. *salapáy*) *n.* clothesline. [Tag. *sampayan*]

pagsasaó: (f. *saó*) *n.* language. **nakayanakan a pagsasao**. *n.* native language. [Tag. *wikà*]

pagsép: **ipagsep, pagsepan**. *v.* to soak, saturate in; drench (*rúsep*). **maipagsep**. *v.* to be soaked, drenched. [Tag. *babad*]

pagsó: **agpagso**. *v.* to stumble.

pagsugálan: (f. *sugál*) *n.* casino, gambling place.

pagtaengán: (f. *taéng*) *n.* residence; home.

pagtagi- -an: Locative circumfix for *tagi-* stems. **pagtagilakuan**. market, place designated for the sale of merchandise.

pagtagitagiammoán: (f. *ammó*) *n.* something not known for sure; something doubtful.

pagtamdán: (f. *taméd*) *v.* to respect, revere; admire.

pagtaraknán: (f. *tarakén*) *n.* place of breeding, raising (animals).

pagténg: *n.* event, happening. (*pasamak*) **mapagteng**. *v.* to happen. **ipagteng**. *v.* to cause to happen. **ipapagteng**. *n.* arrival. **nakagteng**. *v.* to arrive; reach a destination. **Imbagada ti napagtengna**. They told what happened to her. **Ita ken dika pay laeng, di ammo ti mapagpagteng**. Between now and later, you do not know what will happen. [Tag. *pangyayari*]

pagtó: *var.* of *padto*.

pagwadán: (f. *wad*) *n.* example, model; prototype (*syn.* of *wadan*).

páha₁: (Sp. *paja*: straw) *n.* straw.

páha₂: (Sp. *faja*: band, strap) *n.* girdle, band; band used to wrap newspapers.

páhe: (Sp. *paje*: page) *n.* page, armor bearer.

páhina: (Sp. *página*: page) *n.* page. (*panid*)

pahinánte: (f. *pahe*) *n.* page; truck helper (one who helps to unload trucks). (*katulong*; *pahe*)

pahinasión: (Sp. *paginación*) *n.* pagination.

pai-: Causative prefix for theme focus *i-* verbs indicating causation of transference: **ipan**. to send. **paipan**. to have something sent. **ruar**. outside. **pairuar**. to have something taken out. **kasta**. like that. **paikasta**. to have something done that way.

pái: *n.* skin on the tail of a ray used for scouring.

páid: *n.* rejection. **paiden**. *v.* to reject, refuse. **napaid**. *a.* rejected; condemned, doomed. [Tag. *tanggí*]

paíd: *n.* fan (usually made of woven bamboo). **agpaid**. *v.* to fan oneself. **ipaid**. *v.* to fan with. **paidan**. *v.* to fan someone. [Png., Tag. *paypáy*]

paídam: *n.* disease infected through black magic. **ipaidam** *v.* to refuse, reject, deny; to deprive of. **napaidam**. *a.* stingy, avaricious; selfish. **mapaidaman**. *v.* to be refused, denied, rejected; deprived. **paidaman**. *v.* to refuse, deny; be stingy toward someone. **Napaidámanka iti ayat idi ubingka**. You were deprived of love as a child. [Png. *pulisay*, Tag. *tanggí, pagkaitán*]

paikapin-: Transitive verbalizing prefix indicating the number of times an action is caused to be done. Perfective form is *pinaikapin-* **Pinaikapinlimak**. I had it done for the fifth time.

páing: *n.* rest. (*inaná*) **agpaing**. *v.* to rest; run away from people, be a hermit; cower. **pagpaingan**. *n.* resting place.

paíng: **agpaing**. *v.* to take refuge; evacuate. **nagpaing**. *n.* refugee; evacuee. **pagpaingan**. *n.* evacuation center; refugee camp. **Uray sadino man a sulinek ti pagpaingam, siguradoak a diakto marigatan a mangbirok kenka.** No matter what remote place you take refuge in, I will probably not have any trouble finding you. [Tag. *likas*]

paipa-: Prefix indicating causation of transference: (*pa-* causative added to *ipa-* verbs:) **ipadaya**. to put something toward the east. **paipadaya**. to have someone put something to the east. **ipababa**. to lower something. **paipababa**. to have someone lower something.

paipi(n)-: Prefix used with numeric roots to indicate how many times a causative (indirect action, theme focus) is done, this prefix takes the *-ko* pronouns and its perfective form is *pinaipi(n)-*: **Pinaipitlomi.** We had it done three times. **Paipimpitom.** Have it done seven times.

páir: **pairpair**. *a.* skinny, emaciated (*lagpit*; *pipilay*; *kuttong*). [Tag. *payát*]

páis: **pinais**. *n.* thin, colored rice biscuits.

paisáhe: (Sp. *paisaje*: landscape) *n.* landscape painting; quoted excerpt from a literary work.

paisáno: (Sp. *paisano*: countryman) *n.* civilian; person in civilian clothes (although usually in uniform). **agpaisano**. *v.* to wear civilian clothes.

páit: **papáit**. *n.* bile, used in cooking (*apro*); *Mollugo oppositifolia* herb with white flowers used for salad. **pinapaítan**. *n.* dish made with meat seasoned in bile. **paítan**. *n.* *Lunasia amara* plant (*dayangdang*). [From the root *paít*. Tag. *apdô* (bile)]

paít: *n.* bitterness; bitter taste. **ipapait, ikapait**. *v.* to make something bitter (usually with bile or *paria*). **kinapait**. *n.* bitterness. **agkakapaít a luluá**. *n.* bitter tears. **paiten, kapaiten**. *v.* to make bitter. **pinapaitan**. *n.* a dish consisting of beef, onions, and intestines cooked with ginger, chili and bile. **Nagpaiten a lagipen.** It is so bitter to remember. [Ibg. *nafeq, napeq*, Ivt. *akpad*, Kal. *sampot*, Kpm. *payit*, Kal., Knk., Png., Tag. *paít*]

pak: **pakpáken**. *v.* to beat (a container to remove dirt or all contents); to hammer.

paka-: Nominalizing instrumental affix for potentive *maka-* verbs: **makasurat**. to be able to write. **pakasurat**. something with which one is able to write.

paka- -an: Nominalizing affix for *maka-* verbs; reason, source, or place of ability or chance to perform an action: **makasurat**. to be able to write. **pakasuratan**. place where someone can write; reason why someone can write. **maka-**

turog. to be able to sleep. **pakaturogan**. place where someone can sleep; reason why someone is able to sleep. **pakapilian**. selection. **pakasaritaan**. history, story. **Ania ti pakasapulam?** Why do you need it?

paka- -en: Causative affix of potentive *maka-* verbs: **makangeg**. to hear; be able to hear. **pakangegan**. to force someone to hear.

pakaammó: (f. *ammó*) **ipakaammo**. *v.* to inform, give notice of.

pakabuklán: (f. *bukél*) *n.* shape; complete form; summary; outcome, results; contents.

pákad: *n.* foot of a basket (bamboo strip at the basket base).

pakáda: *n.* goodbye; farewell; embassy; message. **agpakada**. *v.* to say goodbye; bid farewell; take leave. **ipakada**. *v.* to ask permission for someone to leave. **panagpakada**. *n.* adieu, farewell, formal departure. **pammakada a bitla**. *n.* farewell address. **Nagpipinnakadada.** They bid farewell to each other. **Rumabiin, agpakadata metten.** It's getting dark, let's say our good-byes. [Tag. *paalam*]

pakai- -an: Nominalizing affixation for potentive theme *makai-* verbs **pakairamanan**. inclusion.

pakák: *n.* *Artocarpus communis* breadfruit (*rimas*). **Kasla bulong ti pakak dagiti lapayag ti ipagko.** My sister-in-law's ears are like the leaves of the *pakak* tree (big). [Tag. *rimas*]

pakákak: (*coll.*) *n.* prostitute (*pampam*). [Tag. *puta* (Sp.)]

pakán: [*pa-* + *kaan* + *-an*] *v.* to feed. (*pakanen*) **agpakan**. *v.* to host a feast. **No pakanka a pakan, bumutiog a bumutiog.** If you keep feeding him, his stomach will keep expanding. [Tag. *pakanin*]

pakáok: *n.* young boys game consisting of spinning around on one's foot with the other foot entwined saying *pakpakaok sudo, lawwalawwa al-o*.

pakauná: *n.* advance news or information. **ipakauna**. *v.* to announce beforehand. **Agrambaktayo iti pakpakauna ti balligimi.** Let's celebrate in advance our victory.

pakápak: *n.* fallen leaves; branches in a river where fish and frogs live, smaller than *ramá*.

pakapamin-: *pref.* nominalizing prefix applied to *makapamin-* stems. **inton pakapaminduada.** at their second time.

pakarí: *n.* something to be proud of. **ipakari**. *v.* to boast.

pakárso: *n.* temporary country residence; resthouse. **agpapakarso**. *v.* to go to the resthouse.

pakasaritáan: (f. *sarita*) *n.* history.

pakasiét: *n.* a kind of syrup made from the *silag* palm sap.

pákat: *n.* yarn; kind of trap, snare. **ipakat.** *v.* to harness; set a trap; put into effect, implement (a plan); use a certain method, try a certain measure; try to the utmost. **maipakat.** *v.* to be implemented. **kapakatan.** (*obs.*) *n.* dry throat. **pakatan.** *v.* to trap a place, set a trap at a particular location. **pagpakatan.** *n.* place where a trap is set. **Impakatna ti sigay idi makitana ti pangen dagiti mataan.** He set the mesh net when he saw the school of *mataan* fish. **Rimmuarak ta kayatkon nga ipakat ti panggepko.** I went out because I want to implement my plan. **Pakatantayo iti sabali a pamuspusan.** Let's try to implement another means. [Tag. *sagawâ* (implement)]

pakát: **napakat.** *a.* tight fitting (*kipet*, *ilet*). [Tag. *sikíp*]

pakatáo: (f. *tao*) **agpakatao.** *v.* to usurp the place of another person, impose upon another; ask for admittance to a house; be impatient; to have good manners; be humane. [Tag. *pakatao*]

pakáti: **pinakati.** *n.* medicinal infusion.

pakatíng: *n.* postwedding ritual of receiving the dowry. **agpakating.** *v.* to carry out the *pakating* ritual.

pákaw: (*obs.*) *n.* surpassing.

pakáw: *a.* bowlegged; term used for Japanese soldiers during occupation; (*obs.*) surpassing. **pakpakaw.** *n.* large *talakitok* fish.

pakawáda: **agpakawada.** *v.* to divide, share something.

pakáwan: *n.* outrigger; handle; V-shaped handle of a *palsiit*. **pakawanan.** *v.* to provide with a forked handle.

pakawán: *n.* pardon; forgiveness. **agpakawan.** *v.* to ask for forgiveness. **pakawanen.** *v.* to pardon, forgive. **mapakawan.** *v.* to be forgiven; to be able to forgive something or someone. **pammakawan.** *n.* forgiveness; pardon. **pakpakawan.** no way. **Pikutenka ketdi, pakpakawan duri.** *exp.* I will never elope with you. **Immayak laeng ditoy tapno makapagpakawanak kenka.** I just came here so I can forgive you. [Kal. *pakawalon, liwatan*, Knk. *dágok*, Kpm. *panupáya, tawad*, Png. *pirdona* (Sp.), Tag. *patawad*]

pakbét: (f. *kebbet*) *n.* Ilocano vegetable dish. (*pinakbet*) **agpakbet.** *v.* to cook *pakbet*.

pakbó₁: (f. *kebbo*) **ipakbo.** *v.* to pour the contents out. (*bokbok*) **maipakbo.** *v.* to have the contents poured out. **mapakbo.** *v.* to capsize, overturn. **Nakitada dagiti sayot nga agsasaruno a maipakpakbo kadagiti bangka.** They saw the scoop nets being emptied one by one from the outriggers. [Tag. *buhos*]

pakbó₂: **pumakbo.** *n.* a kind of flattened, triangular marine fish.

pakdáar: *n.* introduction, preface; a kind of scarecrow made by two bamboo poles moved by a rope to scare animals away; notice; warning; announcement. **ipakdaar.** *v.* to announce, declare, reveal (beforehand). **maipakdaar.** *v.* to be announced, proclaimed. **mangipakdaar.** *v.* announce, inform; *n.* informer. **mapakdaaran.** *v.* to be given notice, to be informed. **pakdaaran.** *v.* to notify; warn. **mapakdaaran.** *v.* to be given due warning. **Naguni ti kampanilia a nangipakdaar ti panaggibus ti ranget.** The bell rang announcing the end of the fight. [Tag. *balà*]

pakdék: **pumakdek.** *n.* young *padaw* fish.

pakéte: (Sp. *paquete*: package) *n.* package; parcel. **ipakete.** *v.* to put into a package. **sangapakete.** *n.* one pack, one package.

paki-: 1. Nominalizing prefix for *maki-* verbs serving an instrumental purpose. **pakikuyog.** companion. 2. (Tag.) polite verbalizer, forming transitive social verbs or verbs of request. **Pakibagayo man laengen a madmadi ti riknak.** Can you please just tell him that I'm not feeling well. **Pakiitedmonto man laengen.** Please just give it to him.

paki- -an: Nominalizing affix for *maki-* social verbs indicating the place, reason, or person on whose behalf an action is done with others. Nominalization for collective acts. (Perfective is *naki- -an*): **makisao.** to speak with. **pakisaoan.** person with whom one speaks. **makimisa.** to attend mass. **pakimisaan.** place where one can attend mass. **Sino ti nakisaom?** With whom did you speak? **Awan ti pakibiangak kenka.** I have no concern for you.

pakiás: *n.* small creek, canal; irrigation canal (*banáwang*).

pakiáw: (Hok. *pák kiaù*: bundle submit) *n.* wholesale selling or buying. **pakiawen.** *v.* to do by the job (not by time). **pinapakiaw.** *a.* haphazard (work). **pumapakiaw.** *n.* wholesaler. [Kal. *geÿpi*, Tag. *pakyáw*; Knk. *pakpakiáw* = butterfly]

pákid: **sangapakid.** *n.* highland bamboos tied together. (*tig-ad*)

pakika- -an: Nominalizing affixation for *maki-ka-* comitative verbs. **Nagsisinada nga agbirok iti pakikatugawanda.** They all separated to look for girls to sit with.

pakikít: (f. *kikít*: middle finger) *n.* jack rafter.

pakíl: *n.* fatigue; exhaustion. (*bannog*; *paksoy*; *uloy*) **mapakil.** *v.* to be exhausted; tired. **ag-**

pakil. *v.* to get tired easily. **pakilen.** *v.* to overwork, cause one to become exhausted.

pak-íl: *n.* slight tap (*tapík*). **pak-ilen.** *v.* to tap slightly.

pakílo: apakpakilo. *v.* to be infected, spread (infection).

pakinákem: (f. *nakem*) *n.* opinion, mind, will; decision; judgment; conscience. **agpakpakinakem.** *v.* to reflect; mediate; ponder. **nangatngato a pakinakem.** *n.* subconscious mind.

pakiót: pakioten. *v.* to defeat; overthrow. (*parmek, abak*)

pakipag- -an: Nominalizing affix for *makipag*-verbs that indicates the place or reason for performing an action in the company of other people.

pakípot: (Tag.) *n.* playing hard to get, holding back desire. **agpakipot.** *v.* to hold back desire; to pretend not to like or want something desired; play hard to get.

pakíta: (f. *kita*) **ipakíta.** *v.* to show, display.

pakíto: *n.* kind of four-player card game played with the Spanish deck.

pakkáng: *a.* bowlegged. (*sakkang; akkang; kayang*) **agpakkang.** *v.* to straddle, walk bowleggedly. **Agarup pakkang a magna.** He walks like a bowlegged person. [Tag. *sakáng*]

pakkáw: agpakkapakkaw. *v.* to toddle.

pakkiás: *var.* of *pakias*: small canal.

pakkiáw: *var.* of *pakiaw:* buying wholesale.

pakkó: papakkuan. *n.* nape of an animal.

pakkóg: *a.* curved, bent, arched. (*bakkog*)

pakkúong: agpakkuong. *v.* to gather in a group.

paklát: *a.* slow in moving; sluggish (*pallat*). [Tag. *kupad*]

pakléb: *a.* prone, prostrate; inverted; overturned. **agpakleb.** *v.* to lie prostrate. (*tikleb; sakoba; rugma; daleb; daramudum*) **ipakleb.** *v.* to cause to fall prostrate. **maipakleb.** *v.* to fall prone accidentally; to be inverted; to be turned upside down. **paklebén.** *v.* to invert; turn over. **napakleb.** *a.* prostrate. **pagpaklebén.** *v.* to cause someone to lay on his stomach. **Iti paksuyna, nagpakleb iti rabaw ti luganna.** Out of weakness, he fell prone on top of his vehicle. [Png. *tikléb*, Tag. *dapâ*]

pakmér: see *parmek*: defeat; vanquish; outdo.

paknár: *n.* levee (*tambak*). [Tag. *pilapil*]

pakní: *n.* out of the way place; hiding place; storage. **agpakni.** *v.* to withdraw, retreat, retire. **ipakni.** *v.* to put out of the way, to put away; store; kill; exile. **napakni.** *a.* orderly, neat; secluded, private, retired; hidden; safe. **pagpaknian.** *n.* bathroom; toilet. [Tag. *libas; tagò*]

páko: *n.* yoke for beasts of burden. **ipako.** *v.* to hitch to a cart. [Tag. *pamatok*]

pakó₁: *n. Athurium esculentum*, an edible fern. **pakpako.** *n.* ferns resembling the *pako*.

pakó₂: agpako. *v.* to worsen. (*karo*)

pakúbas: agpakubas. *v.* to pretend, make believe, feign (to be poor, sad, etc.). **napakubas.** *a.* lazy; disobedient. [Tag. *kunwarì*]

pakól: *a.* clubfooted. **agpakol.** *v.* to walk like a clubfooted person.

pakúl₁: *n.* ladle (*aklo*). [Tag. *kutsarón* (Sp.), *sandók*]

pakúl₂: *n.* variety of awned rice with light-colored hull and large, broad white kernel.

pak-ól: *n.* harrow (*sagad*); club (*pang-or*); noise of a hammer, striking noise. **ipak-ol.** *v.* to strike, tap. **pak-olan.** *v.* to tap slightly (with a cane, etc.); knock on the head. [Tag. *bambó, batutà*]

pakólan: see *sallabáwan*: ridgepole.

pakulót: agpakulot. *v.* to have a perm; have the hair curled. **ipakulot.** *v.* to have curled (the hair) (f. *kulot*)

pakultád: (Sp. *facultad:* faculty) *n.* faculty (of a school).

pakumbabá: (Tagalog also) **napakumbaba.** *a.* humble; modest. (*numo*) **agpakumbaba.** *v.* to humble oneself, abase oneself. **kinapakumbaba.** *n.* humility; modesty.

pakúpak: *n.* rattle made of iron and a board. **agpakupak.** *v.* to use the *pakupak*, to make the sound of iron knocking against wood.

pakortár: (Sp. *cortar:* cut) **agpakortar.** *v.* to have a haircut (*papúkis*). [Tag. *gupít*]

pakutíbeg: *var.* of *pakutibeng*.

pakutíbeng: agpakutibeng. *v.* to be immovable; to be stubborn. **ipakutibeng.** *v.* to refuse to move; stand pat.

pakpák: *n.* bamboo rattle. **pakpaken.** *v.* to slap with the open hand; spank; clap; hammer. **agpanakpak.** *v.* to make the sound of the wooden club used in washing. [Tag. *sampál*]

pakríb: ipakrib. *v.* to sharpen, whet; hone (*asa*). [Tag. *hasà*]

pakrís: *n.* a kind of bamboo fence; barbed wire. **pakrisan.** *v.* to barb wire a fence.

paksá: *n.* theme of a meeting; agenda (*tíma*) **agpaksa.** *v.* to do with all one's effort or strength; exert. (*gaed*)

paksáy: (f. *kissáy*) **agpaksay.** *v.* to move the bowels (*umibléng*). [Tag. *tae*]

paksí: ipaksi. *v.* to throw out of the way; to be defeated at the polls, lose a contest; disappoint; frustrate.

paksiát: (f. *kissiát*) *n.* forcing someone out of his job; firing. **napaksiat.** *a.* laid off; driven away; fired; persecuted. **paksiaten.** *v.* to lay off; drive away; persecute; get rid of. **Panaginana**

laengen ti makapaksiat iti sakitna. Only rest can drive away his illness.

paksión: (Sp. *facción*) *n.* faction.

paksíw: (Tag. also) *n.* dish made with meat or fish seasoned with vinegar and salt. agpaksiw. *v.* to cook *paksiw*. ipaksiw. *v.* to make into *paksiw*. Gimmatangak pay iti bulilit ta naimas a paksiwen. I also bought *bililit* fish because it is delicious to pickle.

paksó: paksuen. *v.* to disunite, disjoint; pull out a nail. pamakso. *n.* anvil. [Tag. *bunot*]

paksóy: *n.* fatigue; exhaustion. (*kettang*; *bannog*) napaksuyan. *a.* worn down, tired to death, fatigued. Makainananto metten ti napaksuyanen a nuangna. His exhausted water buffalo will be able to rest. [Tag. *antók*, *hapò*]

pákta: *n.* framework of a house; foretelling of the weather at Christmas.

paktáal: *n.* a kind of hard and sticky candy. pumaktaal. *v.* to become hard. (*tangken*) Di met ngaminen lumukneng ta pimmaktaal a pusom. Your hard heart just won't soften. [Tag. *tigás*]

paktát: pinaktat. *n.* kind of boys' coin-throwing game.

pákto: napakto. *a.* confiscated; foreclosed.

paktór: (Sp. *factor*: factor; luggage clerk) *n.* factor, element; railway station baggage master, luggage clerk.

paktória: (Sp. *factoría*) *n.* baggage master's office at a railway station.

paktúra: (Sp. *factura*: bill) *n.* invoice; price list.

pakwán: (Tag.) *n.* watermelon. (*sandia*)

pála1: (Sp. *pala*: shovel) *n.* spade, shovel. (*soklad*) palaan. *v.* to shovel; hit with a shovel; tire down, do persistently; chase (game) until it is exhausted.

pála2: palapala. *n.* scaffold; framework for a temporary shelter. [Tag. *andamyo* (Sp.)]

palábas: (f. *labas*) *n.* watching; viewing (something pass). agpalabas. *v.* to watch (something pass). napalabas. *n.* past, *a.* last, past. Nasken a lipatem ti napalabas ta adda napatpateg nga agur-uray kenka iti masakbayam. You need to forget the past because there is something more precious waiting for you in your future.

palab-úg: (f. *lab-og*) *n.* trap for birds. [Tag. *umang*]

palab-óng: (f. *lab-ong*) *n.* trap for animals (camouflaged pit) palab-ongan. *v.* to trap in a *palab-ong*; entrap; trick. [Tag. *umang*, *panghuli*]

palabút: palabutan. *n.* to patch wood.

palábra: (Sp. *palabra*: word) palabra-de-honor. *n.* word of honor. palabraan. *v.* to talk something over.

palábras: (Sp. *palabras*: words) *n.* word. (*sao*, *pannao*)

pálad: (Tag. *palad* = palm; luck) *n.* line in the palm of hand, sole of foot; luck (*gasat*); destiny. mammalad. *n.* palm reader, palmist. agpapalad, paipaladan. *v.* to have one's palm read. paladpalad. *n.* three black veins of a coconut shell. ipaladan. *v.* to foretell one's destiny. (*padles*; *padto*) panangipalad. *n.* palmistry. Ipaladannak man. Please tell my fortune. [Ibg. *pálak*, Ifg. *tapayaan*, Ivt. *rapan*, Kal. *paÿed*, Kpm., Png., Tag. *palad*]

paláda: *a.* gold plated; silver plated; overlaid. papaladaan. *v.* to have something plated or overlaid. [Tag. *tubóg*]

paladpád: *n.* windowsill; fence around playpen. [Tag. *pasamano* (Sp.)]

pálag: *n.* small fishes dried in the sun (*pindang*); dried meat.

palagád: *var.* of *puruák*.

palagapág: *n.* fluttering (*payakpak*); floundering. agpalagapag. *v.* to flutter; flounder (fish); stomp the feet repeatedly; sing out of tune (*silang*). Pinagpalagapagna dagiti dapan dapan iti datar. He stomped his soles on the floor.

palagáy: (f. Tag. *lagay*: bet in gambling) agpalagay. *v.* to wager, bet (*posta*). [Tag. *tayâ*]

palagipíg1: agpalagipig. *v.* to break (fish).

palagipíg2: *n.* rustling noise of leaves in the wind. agpalagipig. *v.* to stir in the wind. [Tag. *palág*]

palagúpog: pumalagupog. *v.* to come one after another in quick succession. (words, steps, etc.)

paláis: ipalais. *v.* to sweep away (the wind). maipalais. *v.* to be carried off by the wind, be swept away; migrate, settle in another place. maipalpalais. *v.* to be naturalized into citizenship. Dina pay napadasan nga impalais ti ayatna. He still hasn't tried to offer his love. [Tag. *padpád*]

palakapák: *n.* springless *kareton* (cart); sound of pouring water; sound of walking on water. agpalakapak. *v.* to make the sound of a *palakpak*.

palákay: *n.* seedling. (*bunubon*) ipalakay. *v.* to transplant from one seedbed to another. [Tag. *punlâ*]

palakó: *n.* bundle of rattan poles.

palakól: (Tag.) *n.* ax. (*wasay*)

palakúpok: *var.* of *parakupok*: spill out, pour out all contents.

palakpák: *n.* clapping of hands; cutoff palm or banana leaf. **palakpákan.** *n.* applause. (*sipat*) **agpalakpak.** *v.* to applaud; clap the hands. [Tag. *palakpák* = applaud]

palaksáw: *n.* small ax (*wasay*). [Tag. *palakól*]

palál: *n.* a kind of hermit crab.

palalián: *n.* bracelets or anklets; fiancée pledge.

palálo: napalalo. *a.* excessive, overmuch. **napalaluan.** *a.* overused, overworked. **palaluan.** *v.* to do something excessively; use something excessively. [Png. *alabas,* Tag. *higít, masiado* (Sp.); Tag. *palalò* = conceit]

palamá: agpalama. *v.* to beg. **agpalpalama.** *v.* to beg; *n.* beggar. **makipalama.** *v.* to beg (*limós*). [Tag. *palimós*]

palámag: *n.* bundles of brush used to trap fish. (*bunuan; puluan*)

palámeng: agpalpalameng. *v.* to beat around the bush; speak approximately. **ipalameng.** (*obs.*) *v.* to give as a present.

palamíngko₁: *n.* variety of flat bean, lima bean.

palamíngko₂: (Sp. *flamenco:* flamingo) *n.* flamingo.

palánas: napalanas. *a.* smooth, even.

palános: (Kalinga) *n.* Kalinga harvest feast.

palantón: *a.* free (ranch cattle). [Tag. *pakawalâ*]

paláng: *n.* bolo, machete. (*badang; buneng*) **nakapalang.** *a.* with a machete in one's possession. [Tag. *iták*]

palanggána: (Sp. *palangana:* basin) *n.* basin, small tub for washing.

palanggapáng₁: agpalanggapang. *v.* to make the sound of cans rattling together.

palanggapáng₂: *a.* carefree and coquettish (said of girls only).

palangguád: *n.* pride. (*pannakel*) **napalangguad.** *a.* boastful. **agpalpalangguad.** *v.* to boast; spend time idly. [Tag. *pagmataás*]

palángka: (Sp. *palanca:* crow bar) *n.* chair, swivel chair. **agpalangka.** *v.* to sit down in a chair. **palangkaen.** *v.* to carry (the sick) in a chair. [Tag. *upuan*]

palaupó: *n.* door hinge (*bisagra*); tendon; hub of a wheel.

palaús: napalaus. *a.* extreme; excessive. (*laus; palalo*) **palausan.** *v.* to do to the extreme; overdo. [Tag. *sukdól*]

palápa: *n.* strips of bamboo used in making Venetian blinds. [Tag. *palapà* = pulpy leaves or joint of palms and banana plants]

palápal: *n.* missile, nonround object thrown at something; a kind of nonpoisonous snake famous for throwing itself; dragon; kind of silver marine fish called *bulilít* when young. **ipalapal.** *v.* to throw away. **palapalen.** *v.* to throw a missile (*palapal*) at (*basibas*). [Tag. *hagis*]

palapála: (f. *pála*) *n.* scaffold; framework for support; plan of building; makeshift shelter for a big crowd. **palapalaen.** *v.* to lay down the building plan before constructing the building.

palapáyag: (f. *lapáyag*) **maipalpalapayag.** *v.* to overhear.

paláran: (f. Tag. *pálad* + *-an*) *n.* luck; chance. (*gasat*) **palaranan.** *v.* to do through luck; do by groping; venture.

palásan: *n.* a kind of rattan used to make canes. (*way*)

palásio: (Sp. *palacio:* palace) *n.* palace; mansion. **pimmalasio.** *a.* palatial.

palasióta: *n.* small *nipa* hut.

palaspás₁: *n.* tobacco leaves harvested first (before the *káwad*); Palm Sunday (*Domingo de Ramos*); (*obs.*) spoon made of palm leaves. **agpalaspas.** *v.* to perform the first tobacco harvest. **palaspasen.** *v.* to remove tobacco leaves. [Tag. *palaspás* = Palm Sunday leaves]

palaspás₂: *adv.* entire, all, whole; without exception. **palaspasen.** *v.* lay off workers; give to everyone; do to everyone.

palátang: *n.* midrib of banana leaves; stem of palm leaves. **palatangan.** *n. Albizzia procera* plant (*adaan*). [Png. *nisnís, panís,* Tag. *tingtíng*]

palat-ángan: *n.* palm leaf; banana leaf. **pamalat-angan, palat-angan.** *n. Amoora sp.* tree.

paláting: *n.* male fruit of the papaya; male papaya tree that cannot bear fruit.

palatípot: *n.* soft honey candy. **pumalatipot.** *v.* to become soft and sticky.

palatpát: *n.* guess, conjecture. (*pagarup*) **palatpatan.** *v.* to guess; surmise. **Awan pamalpalatpatanna.** He has no idea. **Sinaludsodko no adda pamalpalatpatanna iti nanipudan ti marmarna a sirena iti waig.** I asked him if he had any conjecture as to the phenomenon of the mermaid in the creek. [Tag. *sapantahà, hulà; palatpát* = long strip of bamboo]

palawág : (f. *lawag*) **ipalawag.** *v.* to explain, make clearer. [Tag. *paliwanag*]

palawápaw: *a.* dull, empty; meaningless. **agpalawapaw.** *v.* to wander around without direction.

Palawénio: (f. *Palawan*) *n.* native of Palawan Island. (*taga-Palawan*)

palaw-ing: *n.* fluttering, low flight. **agpalaw-ing.** *v.* to flutter.

palawláw: (f. *lawláw*) *n.* border. **palawlawan.** *v.* to make a border of; to fence.

palawpáw: *a.* silly; stupid; foolish; empty. (*palawapaw*) **palpalawpaw**. *a.* haphazard; empty (words).

palaw-íng: *n.* low, fluttering flight. **agpalaw-ing**. *v.* to flutter.

paláwit: *n.* necklace; bracelet.

pálay: *n.* peg. **maipalay**. *v.* to be pierced (*salpot*); stuck; imbedded; firmly set. **palaypalay**. *n.* ankle. **ipalay**. *v.* to pierce; stab (*bagkong*). **pagatpalaypalay**. reaching the ankles. **Pagatpalaypalay ti kaunegna**. It is ankle deep. [Tag. *tarak* (pierce); *palay* = rice]

paláy: **palaypalay**. *a.* slight; not strong or serious (wind, fever, etc.); careless, haphazard.

paláyas: *n.* irrigation. **palayasan**. *v.* to irrigate.

paláyaw: *n.* nickname (*birngas*). [Png. *pananawag, banbansag*, Tag. *palayaw*]

palayáw: *n.* bamboo fish trap fence.

palayúpoy: *n.* cool breeze. (*pul-oy*) **agpalayupoy**. *v.* to blow gently. **mapalayupuyan**. *v.* to be refreshed from the breeze. **Pumalpalayupoy dagiti nginabras ti atiddog a buokna iti apros ti angin**. The strands of her long hair are blowing gently by the touch of the wind. [Tag. *simoy*]

palaypáy: *n.* dogvane, telltale (strip tied to a vessel to ascertain wind direction); butterfly sleeves (on women's garments).

palbáag: (f. *libág*) **palbaagen**. *v.* to slam the door. **pumanalbaag**. *v.* to slam loudly. [Tag. *kalabóg*]

palbuák: (f. *lebbuak*) **ipalbuak**. *v.* to boil. [Tag. *lagà*]

palbugén: (f. *lubbuág?*) *v.* to show, prove; bring out. (*paruaren, pagparangen*)

pálda: (Sp. *falda*: skirt) *n.* skirt. (*saya, kain*) **agpalda**. *v.* to wear a skirt. **nakapalda**. *a.* wearing a skirt. [Kal. *kain*]

paldág: **agpaldag**. *v.* to rest in bed (*idda, inana*); stay in the bed without doing anything; lie down lazily. **Bimmaringkuas iti papag a pagpalpaldaganna iti sirok ti salamagi**. She got up startled from the bench under the tamarind tree on which she was lying idly.

paldiáp: *n.* sideways glance. [Tag. *sulyáp*]

pal-ég: *n.* trap. (*pakat; palab-og*) **ipal-eg**. *v.* to set a trap in place. [Tag. *umong*]

palék: **ipalek**. *v.* to hammer nails. (*martilio*) **maipalek**. *v.* to be driven through by a hammer. **paleken**. *v.* to hit on the head or nape. **Kasla napalek a piek**. Like a chicken hit on the head (said of someone too shy to speak or move). [Tag. *bayó*]

pal-ék: *var.* of *palek*.

pal-éng: *a.* disobedient; stubborn. (*bangad*)

palengléng: *n.* staring. (*mulengleng, muttaleng, perreng*) **agpalengleng**. *v.* to stare.

palengpéng: **palengpengen**. *v.* to dissuade, persuade against.

paléro: (f. *palo*) *n.* shoveler, garbageman.

palét: *n.* thickness of liquids or dough. **napalet**. *a.* thick (said of food), as opposed to *labnáw*; sticky. **pumalet**. *v.* to become thick (without broth); to become sticky. **paleten**. *v.* to make something thick. **Napalpalet ti dara ngem ti danum**. Blood is thicker than water. [Knk. *sípek*, Tag. *lapot*]

pal-ét₁: *n.* kind of bee, *syn.* of *tegtég*.

pal-ét₂: **ipal-et**. *v.* to stick in between. **maipal-et**. *v.* to be stuck.

paléta: (Sp. *paleta*: palette) *n.* palette (used by artists); butter knife; little shovel; blade of a paddle.

palgák: (f. *leggak*) *n.* revelation. **ipalgak**. *v.* to reveal; predict. **Diak impalgak a diak ammo ti aglangoy**. I didn't reveal that I don't know how to swim. **Kitkitaennak laeng bayat ti panagipalgakko iti karíriknak**. She just looked at me while I revealed my feelings.

páli: *n.* pancreas; spleen; sweetbread. [Ivt. *ridas*, Knk. *láwey*, Png. *palí*, Tag. *palî, lapáy*, Bon. *páli* = spleen of the water buffalo]

pália: (Sp. *falla*: dud; omission) *n.* omission; absence; skipping of something; dud, defective bullet or firecracker. **agpalia**. *v.* to fail, not work (engine); to be a dud (firework).

paliádo: (Sp. *fallado*: failed) *n.* dud, defective bullet or firecracker; stubborn, old animal; defective match; weak lightbulb.

paliáw: *n.* kind of white-haired dog.

pal-íd: *n.* fan. (*paíd*) **pal-idan**. *v.* to fan, (to keep away flies, clean or to keep a fire burning); flap. **ipal-id**. *v.* to fan with. **napal-idan ti angin**. *a.* struck by the draft. **Pagpal-idna ti kallugongna**. He is using his hat as a fan. [Png., Tag. *paypay*]

palidpíd: *n.* border of a woven basket. **palidpidan**. *v.* to adorn with a border.

pálig: **ipalig**. *v.* to blow away; sweep off. **maipalig**. *v.* to be swept away by the wind (*palais*). **paligpalig**. *n.* weather vane (*pirápir*); name applied to anything that whirls; propeller; (*coll.*) mind that is always changing, fickle person; restless person.

palíg: **agpalig**. *v.* to be askew; go awry.

paligét: *n.* gold necklace. (*kuentas a balitok*)

paligGéd: **agpaligged**. *v.* to lean for support. (*sanggir*)

palígos: *var.* of *lapigos*: wring the ear. [Tag. *pigâ*]

palíiw: *n.* observation; attention; opinion. **agpaliiw.** *v.* to observe, keep an eye on. **agpinnaliiw.** *v.* to observe each other. **palíiwen.** *v.* to watch, observe; notice; pay attention. **pammaliiw.** *n.* observation; remark; comment. **managpaliiw.** *a.* observant; keen. **Pinatademko ti panagpaliiwko iti aglawlaw.** I sharpened my observation around me. [Tag. *pansín*]

palíkaw: (f. *likaw*) *n.* circumference. **agpalpalikaw.** *v.* to go around; (*fig.*) beat around the bush. **Saanakon nga agpalpalikaw.** I'm not going to beat around the bush.

palikawkáw: (notice resemblance to *pa-likaw*: circumference) **agpalikawkaw.** *v.* to beat around the bush. (*salikawkaw*)

palikéro: (Tag. also, *coll.*) *n.* playboy; man who is insincere with women.

palikúd: (f. *likud*) *n.* helper; substitute; proxy.

palikpík₁: *n.* fish fin (*pigar*). [Tag. *palikpík*]

palikpík₂: ipalikpik. *v.* to mention in a roundabout way (*palikawkaw, salikawkaw*). [Tag. *paligoy-ligoy*]

palíleng: *n.* the *ipon* fish when four inches long.

palílit: *var.* of *pallilit*: sideways glance.

paliméd: (f. *limed*) *n.* secret. **agpalimed.** *v.* to keep a secret. **palimedan.** *v.* to keep information from someone.

palimós: (Tag.) **agpalimos.** *v.* to beg. (*palama*)

palináak: see *pennaak*: middle. (*tengnga*)

palínang: *n.* kind of sticky candy made of hardened brown sugar.

palindayág: see *pasindayag*: boastful; vain; conceited. (*pangás; tangsít*)

palinsúsok: palinsusukan. *v.* to heap; fill to the brim.

palintúod: agpalintuod. *v.* to sit down on the heels. (*parintuod*)

páling: *n.* pintle of a rudder.

palingatngát: *n.* wedge. (*panget, tingal*) **maipalingatngat.** *v.* to be wedged into; stuck into. [Tag. *kalso* (Sp.)]

palíngay: *n.* shawl; cloth worn around women at the beach; Igorot headband.

palingét: napalinget. *a.* delayed (mail). (*tantan*)

palingpíng: *n.* weir placed on a fishing net to force the fish to enter the net. **palingpingan.** *v.* to attach a weir to the sides of a fishing net.

pálio₁: (Sp. *palio*: canopy) *n.* portable canopy in a procession; pall, heavy cloth of black, purple, or white velvet spread over a coffin, hearse, or tomb.

pálio₂: (Sp. *fallo*: judgment) *n.* decision or judgment of a board of judges; omission of print in textile.

palípad: palipaden. *v.* to move a log pulling both ends alternately.

palípal: *n.* witchcraft. (*gamud*) **palipalen.** *v.* to perform black magic on.

palíseg: (*obs.*) **papaliseg.** *n.* being ashamed of another's indecent behavior.

palispís: maipalispis. *v.* to miss the target. **ipalispis.** *v.* to palliate coarse language; use euphemisms; insinuate coarsely.

pal-ít₁: *var.* of *pait*: bitter. **pumal-it.** *v.* to turn bitter. [Tag. *paít*]

pal-ít₂: *n.* flipping of the tail (cows). **agpal-it.** *v.* to flip the tail (cows).

palitáda: (Sp. *paletada*: trowelful of mortar) *n.* pavement; cement mortar. **agpalitada.** *v.* to apply finishing touches to (cement, construction, etc.), plaster. **palitadaan.** *v.* to pave.

palíto: (Sp. *palito*: small stick) *n.* toothpick; matchstick. (*ingat*)

paliwá: (f. *liwa*) *n.* enjoyment, entertainment. **agpaliwa.** *v.* to enjoy. **agpalpaliwa.** *v.* to entertain oneself; comfort oneself. **Nasken nga agpalpaliwaka tapno madalusan ta nakemmo.** You need to amuse yourself so you can clear your thoughts.

paliwáweng: *var.* of *paliwengweng*: to idle. **agpaliwaweng.** *v.* to idle, loaf around (*ballog, baliudong*); be absent without leave. **ipaliwaweng.** *v.* to put off, procrastinate; avoid responsibility. **Naginkukunaanna laeng ti panagpaliwawengko idi kallabes a sardam.** He pretended about my loafing around last evening. [Tag. *lakwatsa*]

paliwengwéng: agpaliwengweng. *v.* to wander idly. **ipaliwengweng.** *v.* to evade, avoid; escape, flee; procrastinate.

palíwliw: (f. *liwliw*) *n.* fishing tackle.

palká: ipalka. *v.* to utter.

palkás: (f. *lekkas*) **mapalkasan.** *a.* cleaned of dirt (by soaking or sun).

palkáng: ipalkang. *v.* to lightly roast over the fire (goat meat); cook shellfish slightly until the shell opens and the animal is still soft. **apagpalkang.** *a.* light roasted (goat meat); slightly cooked (shellfish).

palkát: agpalkat. *v.* to steady; steadily fix (the eyes). **nakapalkat.** *a.* steady; steadily fixed. (*pilkat*)

pálko: (Sp. *palco*: theater box) *n.* elevated platform, scaffold, grandstand; balcony seat.

palládaw: *n.* kind of boomerang; species of snake that thrusts itself when attacking. **ipalladaw.** *v.* to throw; hurl; fling. **maipalladaw.** *v.* to be thrown; hurled; banished.

pallagtó: (f. *lagto*) *n.* mudfish trap made of bamboo.

pallaílang: *n.* strolling, roaming. **agpallailang**. *v.* to roam around; go for a stroll. **panagpallailang**. *n.* recreation; park. **Masansan nga agpalpallailang iti igid ti baybay.** He frequently strolls around the beach.

palláis: **maipalpallais**. *v.* to be carried off by the wind.

pallák: *n.* G-string that is black on the sides and white in the middle. **nakapallak**. *a.* wearing a *pallak* G-string.

pallakáw: **agpallakaw**. *v.* to drone.

pallákong: *a.* bowlegged. (*sakkang*)

palláng: *n. Psophocarpus tetragonolobus*, asparagus bean, a leguminous vine with light blue flowers and long, edible pods longitudinally winged along each angle; (*fig.*) term applied to excessively slender persons. **Kasla kimriit a bunga ti atap a pallang ti kuttongna.** His slenderness is like a wild asparagus bean fruit dried in the sun. **Kasla kullapit a bunga ti atap a pallang ti kinarapisna.** He is as skinny as the young pod of a wild asparagus bean. [Knk. *bulígan, beyéd*, Tag. *sigarilyas*]

pallangátok: **ipallangatok**. *v.* to throw upward. **maipallangatok**. *v.* to be thrown upward. **agpinnallangatok**. *v.* to toss upward in competition. (*pallatok*)

pallát: *var.* of *paklat*: slow footed; sluggish; lazy. [Tag. *kupad*]

pallatíbong: *n.* sling for herdsman. **agpallatibong**. *v.* to sling. (*alimbayong*)

pallatík: **agpallatik**. *v.* to swing; sway. (*kallatik*) **mapallatikan**. *v.* to be hit by something swinging.

palláting: **agpallating**. *v.* to sway to and fro. (*kallating*)

pallatíwan: *n.* shaft of a cart to which an animal is hitched. (*padalayday*)

pallátok: **ipallatok**. *v.* to throw upward. (*pallangatok*) **pinnallatok**. *n.* a game consisting of tossing coins upward. **palpallatok**. *n.* morning star, Venus, Lucifer. **pumpumlatok**. *v.* to run fast (with stones flying under feet); to echo resoundingly. [Tag. *hagis*]

palláw: (*coll.*) *a.* crazy, insane (*bagtit*). [Tag. *balíw, ulól*]

palláyaw: **ipallayaw**. *v.* to hint; allude to; suggest indirectly. **maipallayaw**. *v.* to be noticed incidentally. **pallayawan**. *v.* to probe deep into (one's thoughts).

palláyog: **pallayugen**. *v.* to rock (a baby) in a careless manner. **agpallayugan**. *v.* to swing, vibrate, oscillate. **napallayog**. *a.* rocking in a careless manner. [Tag. *ugóy*]

pallayúpay: **agpallayupay**. *v.* to sway, totter; waver. [Tag. *suray*]

pallikós: **pallikos ti biag**. way of life. **agpallikos**. *v.* to beat around the bush; do in a roundabout way (*palikawkaw*). [Tag. *paligoyligoy*]

pallílit: *n.* sideways glance. (*kusilap*) **pallilitan**. *v.* to glance at sideways. [Tag. *sulyáp*]

pallugsít: *n.* a kind of speckled marine fish.

palluká: *n.* leather sandal with a strap around the big toe. **nakapalluka**. *a.* wearing sandals.

pallokí: *n.* a kind of small, spherical mollusk.

pallungáy: *n.* catapult like the *palsiit*.

pallupágay: *n. Sceleria sp.* plants with toothed leaves.

pallót₁: *n.* cockfighting; cockfight (*bulang*). **pallotan**. *n.* cockfighting arena. **mammallot**. *n.* cockfighting aficionado. **agpallot**. *v.* to have a cockfight; match gamecocks. **pagpallotan**. *n.* cockpit. **ipallot**. *v.* to match a gamecock with another. **makipallot**. *v.* to bet on a cockfight. **pakipallot**. *n.* gamecock; money for betting on the *pallot*. **palloten**. (*coll.*) *v.* to woo a girl. (*armen*) **pallot ti lawwalawwa**. *n.* spider fight. [Ibg. *pelluq*, Itg. *tádi*, Ivt. *payarap su manok*, Png. *bulang*, Kpm., Tag. *sabong*]

pallót₂: **pallopallot**. *n. Teramnus labialis* vine with purple flowers and flat pods.

pallotéro: (f. *pallót*) *n.* cockfighting enthusiast; cockfighter.

pallúyan: see *paluyan*.

palmá: (Sp. *palma*: palm) *n.* palm tree; artificial flowers put in the hands of a dead child. (*obs.*) **pinalma**. *n.* round gold bracelet.

palméng: (f. *lemméng*) *n.* secret; something hidden.

palméra: (Sp. *palmera*: palm) *n.* ornamental palm.

palméta: (Sp. *palmeta*: ferule paddle) *n.* ferule paddle. **palmetaen**. *v.* to beat somebody with a ferule.

palnáad: (f. *lennáad*) **ipalnaad**. *v.* to reveal; prophesize. **maipalnaad**. *v.* to be revealed; prophesized. **Parbangonen kas ipalnaad ti taraok dagiti kawitan.** It was already dawn as the crows of the roosters revealed.

palnéd: (f. *lennéd*) *n.* kind of bamboo net similar to the *sigay*. **palneden**. *v.* to sink (a ship); (*fig.*) waste time. **pagpapalned**. *n.* curse, malediction. **agpalpalned iti oras**. *v.* to waste time.

pálo: (Sp. *palo*: stick) *n.* mast of a ship; flagpole. **agpalo**. *v.* to deposit eggs (said of locusts). **paluen**. *v.* to beat somebody with a stick. [Tag. *tagdán* (pole; staff); *palò* (beat, whip)]

paló: *n.* Conger eel of the *Congridae* family.

palúbos: *n.* permission; consent; authorization. **ipalubos.** *v.* to permit, allow. **palubusan.** *v.* to permit; authorize; grant permission; accompany a departing guest; dispatch, send away. **maipalubos.** *v.* to be allowed, granted, permitted. **pammalubos.** *n.* permission, consent; authority; farewell. **pasken a pammalubos.** *n.* farewell party *(despedida)*. **mamalubos.** *v.* to say goodbye *(pakada)*. **Palubosandak a rummuar!** Let me go out! **Dimo ipalubos a maadaywannaka.** Don't let her get away from you. [Kal. *iteun*, Png. *abuloy, patanir*, Tag. *pahintulot*]

palúdip: *n.* sideways glance. *(kusilap)* **paludipan.** *v.* to glance at sideways. [Tag. *sulyáp*]

palugápig: see *parunapin*: a kind of tree, *Tarrietia sylvatica*.

palugúd: palugudan. *v.* to grant the wishes of; give in to the wishes of.

pálok: ipalok. *v.* to drive nails into. [Tag. *baón*]

palomár: (Sp. *palomar*: pigeon house) *n.* *(obs.)* pigeon house.

palumária: (Sp. *palomar*) *n.* species of tree with a soft wood used to make shipping boxes.

palumpós: *var.* of *palungpós*: ceremony on the ninth day of mourning.

palunápin: *n.* layer; lining. **agpalunapin.** *v.* to pile up, heap up; arrange in a pile. **ipalunapin.** *v.* to insert, enclose. [Tag. *salansán*]

palunípin: ipalunipin. *v.* to put aside, arrange by putting aside; *var.* of *palonapin*. *(ipaigid)*

palóng: *n.* wave, not a breaker, which is a *dalluyon*. **napalong.** *a.* wavy. **agpalong.** *v.* to create waves, undulate.

palungáping: *n.* pectoral fin; small tobacco leaves. **agpalpalungaping.** *v.* to hang or dangle at one's side.

palungdó: *n.* perfection, excellence. *(aririt; saririt; pardanon; payos; sungdo)* **napalungduan.** *a.* excellent, perfect, first rate. [Tag. *gandá*]

palunggáping: agpalunggaping. *v.* to sway, rock back and forth (hanging object); dangle at one's side. *(palungaping)* **Agpalpalunggaping ti talunasan iti siketna.** His machete is dangling at his waist.

palungkít: *n.* advantage; grace period. **palungkitan.** *v.* to give a second chance; give a handicap; offer an advantage or grace period to. [Tag. *palugit*]

palóngo: see *pangulo*: chief; president; head (of company, etc.).

palungpóng: *n.* shoot, sprout growing out of a stump. **agpalungpong.** *v.* to sprout up. [Tag. *usbóng*]

palungpós: (f. *lungpós*) *n.* ceremony on the ninth day of mourning. **nakapalumpos.** *a.* celebrated the ninth day of mourning.

palopagí: *n.* a kind of white cowry.

palór: *var.* of *parol*: lantern; street lamp.

palóra: *var.* of *parola*: lighthouse.

palusápis: *n.* involucrum of cotton; tree with white timber.

palosébo: (Sp. *palo* 'stick' *cebo* 'grease') *n.* game in which contestants must climb a greased pole to claim the prize at the top.

paluspús: paluspusan. *v.* to let go; release; give leave; authorize. **Ad-adu ti mapaluspusam a gundaway no mangpatakderka iti alad a sisasagana a paglemmengan.** You will let go of many opportunities if you build a fence ready to hide from (others). [Tag. *hayà*]

pálot: *n.* variety of awnless rice.

palótis: (Sp. *palote*: stick, drumstick) *(obs.)* *n.* police baton. *(batuta)*

palutpút: palutputen. *v.* to investigate, examine; find out. **agpalutput.** *v.* to look into; investigate; question. [Tag. *usisà*]

palúyan: *n.* a kind of shrub; animal gut with a milky substance.

paluyúpoy: *var.* of *palayúpoy*.

pálpa: (f. *leppa*) **agpalpa.** *v.* to rest after eating. **malpaan.** *v.* to be rested after eating. **nakapalpa.** *a.* rested after eating. **Nagawidda apaman a nakapalpada.** They went home as soon as they have rested after eating.

palpáak: (f. *lipák*) **panalpaaken.** *v.* to slam; slap. **Pinanalpaakna nga inrikep ti ruangan iti likudanna.** She closed the door behind her with a slam.

palpál: *n.* bamboo harrow used to pulverize the soil. *(moriski; suyod)* **agpalpal.** *v.* to pulverize the soil after plowing. **ipalpal.** *v.* to drive a peg or stake into the ground. **Ania ti pagpalpal dagiti mannalon?** What do the farmers use to pulverize the soil?

palpás: (f. *leppas*) **ipalpas.** *v.* to have something finished. **palpasen.** *v.* to wait until something is finished; finish off.

palpék: *n.* punishment, penalty in a game, usually consisting of flicking the loser with a stick. *(bawél)*

palpí: *n.* knock, tap. **maipalpi.** *v.* to knock the head, fish, etc. **palpian.** *v.* to hit (with fingers or toes); knock. **maipalpipalpi.** *v.* to hit repeatedly (a bucket hitting the sides of the well upon its ascent).

palpít: (f. *lipít*) *n.* whipping stick. **palpiten.** *v.* to whip with a stick. [Tag. *pilantík*]

palpitasión: (Sp. *palpitación*: palpitation) *n.* palpitation.

pálsa: (Sp. *falsa*: false) *n.* suits that are not trumps (in cards).

palséb: (f. *lesséb*) **palseban.** *v.* to bury (someone) deep in the ground, submerge.

palséng: *n.* peg.

palsí₁: *n.* chink; crack; break; sprain; abraded edge. **napalsian.** *a.* sprained; abraded (wires, cords, etc.). **mapalsian.** *v.* to suffer a sprain; have a chink, abraded edge. [Tag. *biták*]

palsí₂: **napalsian.** *a.* tired, exhausted (said of work animals).

palsiit: (f. *lisít*) *n.* slingshot. **agpalsiit.** *v.* to shoot with a slingshot. **palsiitan.** *v.* to hit someone with a projectile from a slingshot. [Ivt. *padtin*, Tag. *tiradór* (Sp.)]

palsipíka: (Sp. *falsificar*: falsify) **palsipikaen.** *v.* to forge; falsify. **palsipikasion.** *n.* falsification.

pálso: (Sp. *falso*: false) *a.* false; fake; bogus.

palsukít: *n.* projection of a broken bone. **pinalsukit.** *n.* chignon at the back of the head. **agpalsukit.** *v.* to protrude; project. [Tag. *uslí*]

palsúot: (f. *lusót*) *n.* popgun. **palsuotan.** *v.* to shoot at someone with a popgun.

pálta: **ipalta.** *v.* to postpone. **agpalta.** *v.* to malfunction; be absent; miscarry; miss a mark. [Tag. *palya* (Sp.)]

paltát: *n.* catfish, appellation given to stupid people as catfish are said to have a small brain; see also [*pa-* + *lettát*]. **Pimmaltat ti ulona.** *exp.* He has the brain of a catfish. [Png. *tabangongo*, *íto*, Tag. *hitò*]

paltáw: *n.* deep-fried rice cake.

paltég: (f. *letteg*) **agpalteg.** *v.* to bulge; swell (frogs' throats).

palték: (f. *litek*) **palteken.** *v.* to hit with a stick (*paltíng*, *palék*)

paltiák: (*obs.*) *n.* rumor. (*sayanggoseng*; *rakurak*)

paltíing: (f. *litíing*) *n.* revelation; forewarning; omen; premonition. **ipaltiing.** *v.* to infer; imply. **paltiingan.** *v.* to warn; insinuate. [Tag. *salagimsim* (premonition); *pahiwatig* (imply)]

paltík: (f. *littík*) *n.* small homemade gun. **paltikan.** *v.* to shoot with a *paltík*. **agpaltik.** *v.* to make clicking sounds. **No dadduma agpalpaltik ti tianko aglalo no kalkalpasko a nangan.** My stomach sometimes makes clicking sounds, especially when I have just finished eating.

paltíng: **paltingen.** *v.* to tap lightly (*tapík*); hit with a stick.

paltít₁: *n.* small catfish. (*paltát*)

paltít₂: (*obs.*) **mapaltitan.** *v.* to have the genitals bared unintentionally.

paltuád: (f. *luttuád*) *n.* product; production; creation. **paltuaden.** *v.* to produce; create.

paltóg: *n.* gun. **agpaltog.** *v.* to shoot. **agpinnaltog.** *v.* to shoot at each other. **pumaltog.** *v.* to fire a gun; capable of firing or bursting. **paltógen.** *v.* to shoot something. **agpaltopaltog.** *v.* to fire into the air, shoot continuously. **mapaltógan.** *v.* to be shot. **palpaltog.** *n.* species of plant with pods that burst when pressed. [Root may have originally been *litóg*, but because of stress patterns with suffixation (*paltógan* instead of *paltogán*), *paltóg* should now be considered a simple root. Kal. *peÿtug*, Knk. *paltóg*, Png. *paltog*, Tag. *baríl*]

paltók: *n.* tip, apex, top. (*toktok*)

paltóng: *n.* edible leaves of the *utóng*; tops of vegetables (*uggót*). **agpaltong.** *v.* to top off. **paltongan.** *v.* to cut off the top of, pollard. **Mabalinen a paltongan dagiti utong.** It is possible to pollard the beans now. [Tag. *talbós*]

paltúog: (f. *litóg*) **paltuogen.** *v.* to shoot, kill. (*patayen*)

paltós: *n.* mistake. (*kammali*) **pumaltos.** *v.* to err.

paltót: (f. *luttót*) **paltuten.** *v.* to deliver a child. **maltutan.** *v.* to choke. **mammaltot.** *n.* midwife.

palwágan: *v.* to contribute money to a common cause and share among contributors.

pam-: *var.* of *pang-* prefix before *m*, *b*, and *p*. The *m* often reduplicates and replaces the initial labial consonant: **pammati.** belief, from *pati*. **pammagi.** body type, from *bagi*. **pammakawan.** forgiveness, from *pakawan*.

páma: (Sp. *fama*: fame) *n.* fame; reputation.

pamáang: *n.* breadwinner in a household. **agpamaang.** *v.* to rely on someone, depend on. **ipamaang.** *v.* to entrust work to someone. **napamaang.** *a.* dependent. **managpamaang.** *a.* very dependent.

pamáding: *n.* spring of a lock.

pamádo: (*reg.*) *n.* a person good with raising livestock; skill.

pamag-: (*paN-pag-*) Nominalizing prefix expressing the instrument or result of an action. **baga.** say, tell **pamagbaga.** advice.

pamaknángen: (f. *baknáng*) *n.* rich, influential man.

pamalatpátan: (f. *palatpát*) *n.* conjecture; idea. **Awan pamalatpatanna.** He has no idea.

pamalitién: (f. *baliti*) *n.* kind of tree similar to the *balíti*, *Ficus sp.*

pamalláag: (f. *balláag*) *n.* warning; notification.

pamandekán: (f. *pandék*) *a.* rather short.

pamanunótan: (f. *panúnot*) *n.* opinion; idea; way of thinking; realm.

pamantót: (f. *bantót*) *n.* heaviness (*dagsen*). [Tag. *bigát*]

pamaráng: *n.* façade; pretense; front tooth, incisor; *a.* pretend; fake. **agpampamarang.** *v.* to pretend (*agin-*).

pamardáya: (f. *pardaya*) *n.* slander, false testimony, false witness. [Tag. *paninirang-puri*]

pamárut: (f. *páut*) **agpamarut.** *v.* to shed feathers or hair. (*úrot*)

pamaksó: (f. *paksó*) *n.* anvil.

pamasgéd: (f. *seggéd*) *n.* fuel; kindling.

pamasmás: *n.* advantage (given to the underdog opponent). **pamasmasan.** *v.* to give an advantage to an opponent.

pamastrekán: (f. *serrek*) *n.* business, industry.

pamatá: (f. *matá*) *n.* spectacles. (*anteohos*)

pamatáy: (f. *patá*) *n.* instrument for killing.

pamatmát: (f. *matmá*) **ipamatmat.** *v.* to exhibit, display, show.

památo: (f. *bato*) *n.* quoit; something thrown for play. [Png. *pamatok*, Tag. *pamatò*, *batò*]

pamayán: **agpampamayan.** *v.* to do indifferently without enthusiasm or interest; happen to do out of instinct. **napamayán.** *a.* careless; negligent, neglectful; without heeding. **Saan a nagpamayan.** He didn't hesitate to do it, he did it with enthusiasm. **pampamayanen.** *v.* to do carelessly or recklessly, do without enthusiasm, nonchalantly (*guppapaw*).

pamay-án: (f. *ay*) *n.* what one wants to do; manner of doing, means, ways, procedure; *v.* to act in a certain way; treat (people). **Ania ti pamay-am?** What do you want to do (and how are you going to do it)?

pambár: (not original root, notice stress pattern of *pambarán*, the original root is perhaps **tebaR*, Bontok *tebal* = answer, Reid, p.c.) *n.* excuse; reason, motive; alibi. **agpambár.** *v.* to give an excuse, alibi. **agpampambár.** *v.* to pretend; use excuses. **ipambár.** *v.* to use as an excuse, alibi. **pagpambár.** *n.* excuse.

pambarán. *v.* to do something aside from what one planned to do, i.e., visit a friend on the way to the doctor's etc. **Pambarák a mapan?** Why should I go? **Impambárko a mapának manen agtrabaho idiay Manila.** I used the excuse that I was going to work in Manila again. **Pambaránna metten nga agkammel ken aguper iti karayan.** He went to hand-fish and soak in the river (contrary to what was originally planned). [Knk. *pamláy*, Tag. *dahilán*]

pambarítis: (*slang*, f. *pambar* 'excuse' + Eng. suffix *-itis*) *n.* tendency to make excuses.

pambáto: (Tag. *pambatò*) *n.* star player in a game. (*pammato*)

pamborár: (Sp. *borrar*: erase + instrumental prefix *paN-*) *n.* eraser.

pamedpéd: (f. *pedpéd*) *n.* small amount of food eaten to assuage hunger.

pameggés: (f. *peggés*) *n.* rapidness (of flow, running, etc.)

pami-: Multiplicative prefix used with numeric roots. **tallo.** three. **pamitluen.** to do three times. **ipamitlo.** to do a third time.

pami(n)- en: 1. Circumfix used with numeric roots indicating how many times something is done, perfective form *pinamin*. **No kasaomi, masapul a paminduaenmi ti saludsodmi sananto sungbatan.** If we speak to him, we have to repeat our questions twice then he'll answer. 2. May be also used to multiply cardinal numbers: **Paminduaem ti tallo, innem.** Three times two is six.

pamiénta: (Sp. *pimienta*: pepper) *n.* ground black pepper.

pamigát: (f. *bigát*) *n.* breakfast. **mamigat.** *v.* to eat breakfast. **makipamigat.** *v.* to have breakfast with others. **pamigatan.** *v.* to have for breakfast. [Ibg. *peggug*, Ivt. *riagen*, Knk. *kakan*, Kpm., Png., Tag. *almusál*]

pamigbígan: (f. *bigbíg*) *n.* mark of identity, something that facilitates identification; sign, clue; characteristic.

pamigsá: (f. *pigsá*) *n.* fortifying substance; source of strength. **pamigsaén.** *a.* rather strong.

pamília: (Sp. *familia*: family) *n.* family. (*kaman*) **agpamilia.** *v.* to have a family. [Png. *bolég*]

pamílawan: (f. *pílaw*) *n.* criticism; complaint. **Awan ti pamilawak kenka.** I have no criticism for you.

pamiláyen: (f. *pílay*) *a.* limping a little, slightly lame.

pamin-adwen: (f. *adú*) *v.* to multiply.

pamin-anó: (f. *anó*) **mamin-ano.** *interrog.* how many times? **pamin-anuen.** *interrog.* for how many times? **sagpamin-ano.** *interrog.* how many times each?

paminsán: **maminsan.** *v.* to do one time; *adv.* once. **paminsanen.** *v.* to do at one time. **sagpaminsan.** *adv.* occasionally, now and then.

pamínta: (Sp. *pimienta*: pepper) *n.* powdered black pepper.

pamintón: (Sp. *pimentón*: paprika) *n.* paprika.

pamipiaén: (f. *piá*) *a.* healthy; in good condition (clothes, body, etc.).

pamísa: (f. *misa*) *n.* mass; death anniversary; series of prayers (church). **agpamisa.** *v.* to have mass; celebrate a death anniversary.

pamitbítan: (f. *bitbít*) *n.* handle for carrying something.

pamitík: *n.* long supplementary rope tied to the head of a water buffalo, used to direct the movements.

pamittaúgen: (f. *bittáug*) *n.* a kind of tree, *Calophyllum sp.* similar to the *bittaug*: *Calophyllum inophyllum.*

pamkedán: *n.* reason; cause; motive. (*pamkuatan*)

pamkuátan: (f. *pekkuát*) *n.* motive, reason; excuse. **Ania ti namkuatan a nagsao a manggagamud ti ikitko.** What is the motive for saying that my aunt is a witch?

pamláy: **pagpamlayen.** *v.* to pretend not to know; to pretend to be surprised. [Tag. *kunwâ*]

pamlés: (f. *pellés*) **agpamles.** *v.* to get dressed. **nakapamles.** *a.* dressed. (*sibabádo*) **pamlesán.** *n.* clothes, attire intended for changing into; dressing room; *v.* to dress someone.

pamma-: *pref.* consisting of *pang-* and *pa-*, forms nominalizations of causative (indirect) stems (see *pammabain, pammabalaw, pammabasol, pammadayaw,* etc.).

pammabaín: (f. *baín*) embarrassment, humiliation, insult.

pammabaláw: (f. *babaláw*) *n.* criticism. (*pamilawan*)

pammabásol: (f. *básol*) *n.* accusation, charge. **Gundaway ngarud kaniak a sanguen ti pammabasol.** So it is it a chance for me to confront the accusation.

pammádas: (f. *pádas*) *n.* experiment, test, trial.

pammadáyaw: (f. *dayaw*) *n.* distinction; acknowledgments; honor.

pammag- [*paN-* + *pag-*] *pref.* Causative nominalizing affix used with *pag- -en* stems. **pammagtalaw.** *n.* exile, banishment.

pammagbagá: (f. *bagá*) *n.* advice. [Tag. *payo*]

pammagí: (f. *bagí*) *n.* condition of the body; body type; physique. [Tag. *pangangatawán*]

pammagkóng: (f. *bagkóng*) *n.* stabbing. [Tag. *saksák*]

pammagtálaw: (f. *tálaw*) *n.* exile, banishment. [Tag. *pagtatapon*]

pammalíiw: (f. *palíiw*) *n.* observation. [Tag. *masíd, matyág*]

pammakáda: (f. *pakáda*) *n.* farewell; the act of bidding leave. [Tag. *paalam*]

pammakawán: (f. *pakawán*) *n.* forgiveness. [Tag. *patawad*]

pammalákad: (f. *balákad*) *n.* advice. [Tag. *payo*]

pammáles: (f. *báles*) *n.* revenge; vengeance. [Tag. *higantí*]

pammalúbos: (f. *palubos*) *n.* permission, consent; farewell. **pasken a pammalubos.** *n.* farewell party. [Tag. *pahintulot*]

pammaneknék: (f. *paneknek*) *n.* proof. [Tag. *patibay*]

pammaráng: (f. *parang*) *a.* pretended; front (surface of cloth); *n.* front teeth; incisor. **agpammarang.** *v.* to show oneself off; disguise; pretend. **managpammarang.** *a.* pretentious. **pagpammarangen.** *v.* to let someone pretend. [Tag. *kunwâ*]

pammarpardáya: (f. *pardaya*) *n.* slander, false accusation. [Tag. *paninirang-puri*]

pammatég: (f. *pateg*) *n.* love; affection; care; value; interest. [Tag. *halagá*]

pammáti: (f. *páti*) *n.* belief; faith. **mammati.** *a.* easily convinced; gullible; *v.* to believe. **kapammatian.** *n.* person sharing the same faith, of the same religion. [Tag. *paniniwalà*]

pammatigmáan: (f. *tigmáan*) *n.* counsel; advice; admonition, warning. (*balákad*)

pammáto: *n.* star player. [Tag. *pambatò, pamatò*]

pammigát: *var.* of *pamigát*; breakfast.

pammigbíg: (f. *bigbig*) *n.* recognition. [Tag. *pagtanggáp; pagkilala*]

pammílin: (f. *bílin*) *n.* order; command. **iti pammilin ti Pangulo.** by order of the president. [Tag. *utos*]

pammílit: (f. *pílit*) *n.* force; violence.

pammuggó: (f. *buggó*) *n.* baptism (*buniag*). [Tag. *binyág*]

pammukél: (f. *bukél*) **agpammukel.** *v.* to become pregnant; to start to enlarge (breasts at puberty); to form fruits.

pammulót: (f. *pulót*) *n.* anointment; last rites.

pammuniág: (f. *buniág*) *n.* baptismal rites, things used for a baptism.

pammutbuténg: (f. *buténg*) *n.* fear. [Tag. *takot*]

pamnáak: (f. *pennáak*) *n.* middle (of something).

pamnekán: (f. *pennék*) *n.* reason or cause for satisfying; proof, evidence, that which ensures; *v.* to satisfy; ensure.

pamníit: *n.* indisposition; slight fever. (*gurigor*) **pamniiten.** *v.* to feel slightly sick. **Pampamniitenak.** I have a slight fever. [Tag. *sinat*]

pamnuósan: **pampamnuosan.** *v.* to be contented with the little things. (*páos*)

pamnúot: **pamnuotan.** *n.* means of knowing; way of knowing. (*pamuspúsan*)

pamudáwen: (f. *púdaw*) *a.* rather light in complexion. [Tag. *maputí*]

pamugbúgan: (f. *bugbog*) *n.* container for leftover food; Tupperware; trough, receptacle for pigs to eat.

pamugotén: (f. *bugót*) *a.* very dark complexioned.

pamuídan: *n.* reason, motive; cause; *v.* to do because of.

pamulináwen: *n.* hard rock; *a.* hard; iron-willed; difficult to convince.

pamullisíngen: *var.* of *pamullilisingen*: a kind of tree.

pamullilisíngen: (f. *bullilísing*) *n.* a kind of tree.

pamunpón: (f. *punpon*) *n.* funeral, funeral procession. **makipamunpon.** *v.* to attend a funeral.

pamuón: (f. *puón*) *n.* foundation. **pamuonán.** *n.* something used as capital.

pamuótan: (f. *púot*) *n.* reason for being alert.

pamuraddawén: (f. *puraddáw*) *a.* rather pale.

pamusián: *n.* egg-laying hen. [Kal. *upa*, Tag. *mangingitlóg*]

pamusnágen: (f. *busnag*) *a.* rather light in complexion.

pamóso: (Sp. *famoso*) *a.* famous.

pamuspúsan: *n.* way, means; remedy; accommodations. **ipamuspusan.** *v.* to find a way to remedy something or to accomplish a task; resolve; straighten out. **Inggana't adda pay angesko, aramidek amin a pamuspusan tapno agbiagak.** As long as I am still alive, I will do all I can to survive.

pamuttiogén: (f. *buttiog*) *a.* with a rather large belly (said of men).

pamuyáan: (f. *buya*) *n.* the way someone looks. **Adda met pamuyaanna.** She is good looking.

pampág: **pampagen.** *v.* to strike repeatedly, beat. **agpampag.** *v.* to beat against something. **ipampag.** *v.* to shake off (dirt); beat against a wall in order to clean.

pampám: *n.* prostitute; whore; easy girl. (*puta*)

pampáno: (Sp. *pompano*: pompano) *n.* species of marine fish, pompano.

Pampánga: *n.* Province of central Luzon. **Kapampángan.** *n.* the language of Pampanga and Tarlac Provinces; a native of these provinces. **Pampanggenio.** *n.* native of Pampanga.

pampás: *n.* *Kleinhovia sp.* tree.

pamráy: *n.* to act impulsively, to do instinctively on the spur of the moment something that suits the given occasion; solace; milking cow; wailing wall. **pamrayán.** *v.* to act on the spur of the moment; to do what comes to mind under a particular situation; do instinctively. **managpamray.** *v.* to offer excuses; be dependent on. **Namrayan laeng ni Kristobal ti immanges iti dakkel.** Kristobal just instinctively took a deep breath. [*Pamray* is not an original root as can be seen by the accentuation pattern *pamrayán*. Knk. *pamláy* = excuse, pretext]

pamrít: **agpampamrit.** *v.* to snarl, talk angrily. (*mamrit*)

pamsaákan: (f. *pessáak*) *n.* desire to satisfy one's hunger by voraciously eating; *v.* to do to the limit, do to the utmost, do as much as possible.

pan(n)-: Variant of the prefix *pang-* before *t*, *d*, and *s*: **dait.** sew. **panait.** thread.

paN-: Instrumental prefix that depicts a nominal quality or instrumental use of the entity denoted by the root. Its allomorphs are *pam-* before labial consonants *p*, *b*, and *m* and *pang-* before *k*, *g*, *ng*, *l*, *r* and vowels. In some cases the initial consonant of the root will assimilate to the nasal and geminate: **bigat.** morning: **pamigat.** breakfast. **dait.** sew. **panait.** thread. **tawen.** year **panawen.** time. **malem.** afternoon. **pangmalem.** afternoon meal, lunch. **dakkel.** big. **pannakkel.** pride.

paN- -en: Affix used with stative roots to specify moderate degree. The nasal of the prefix is assimilatory; it is realized as *ng* before liquid and velar consonants *ng*, *k*, *g*, *r*, and *l* and to *m* before labial consonants *m*, *b*, and *p*. The first consonant of the root drops when in contact with *paN-* (except for the liquids *r* and *l*): **tayag.** tall. **panayagen.** rather tall, somewhat tall. **timbukel.** round. **panimbuklen.** somewhat round. **lukmeg.** fat. **panglukmegen.** somewhat fat, rather fat. **rapis.** thin. **pangrapisen.** somewhat thin, rather thin. **singkit.** squint. **paningkiten.** with somewhat squinty or slanted eyes.

pan₁: **mapan.** *v.* to go, depart; leave; (*with amounts*) be approximately. **ipan.** *v.* to take along, carry, take with; convey. **ipapan.** *v.* to think, believe; assume; suppose; regard; make a trip to; *n.* going; departing; leaving. **kaipapanan.** *n.* meaning, signification; significance. **maipapan.** *prep.* concerning, regarding, about. **paipan.** *v.* to have something brought. **papanan.** *n.* place where one is going. **papanen.** *v.* to allow to go. **agpapan.** *n.* one way; *a.* going; *prep.* until; up to a point. **agpapan pay.** *prep.* nevertheless; despite; however. **maipapan.** *prep.* about; concerning; regarding. **kaipapanan.** *n.* meaning; importance; significance. **mangipapan.** *v.* to suspect; have doubts. **manangipapan, managipapan.** *a.* suspicious. **panangipapan.** *n.* suspicion. **kapkapan, kaap-apán.** *v.* just left. **Papanam?** Where are you going? **managapan.** *v.* to go frequently; to frequent. **apag-apan.** *a.* as soon as gone. **Ania ti pagay-ayaman ti nangipananda?** What playground did they go to? **Awan panangipapanna.** He has no idea. **No saan nga makaammo nga mangtaliaw ti naggapuanna, saan a makadanon iti papananna.** *exp.* If one does not know how to look back from where he came, he will not be able to arrive at where he is going. **Pappapanennakami iti siudad.** They are sending us to the city. [Bon. *ey*, Png. *la*, Tag. *puntá*]

pan₂: (Sp. *pan*: bread) **pan de bara.** *n.* loaf bread. **pan de kakaw, pan de sal.** *n.* roll of sweetbread. **pan Amerikano.** *n.* loaf bread.

pánа₁: *n.* arrow; dart; speargun. **mapana.** *v.* to be hit by an arrow. **panaen.** *v.* to hit with an arrow by use of a bow. **pumapana.** *n.* hunter; scuba diver. **pimmanapana a buok.** *n.* very straight hair. **sinampana.** *n.* arrowlike thing; pointing arrow. **mammana.** *n.* hunter. [Ibg. *pana*, Kal. *pesuk*, Png. *paná*, Ivt., Kpm., Tag. *panà*, Tag. *tunod*]

pánа₂: panapana, pumapana. *n.* *Echinotrix calamaris*, a kind of reddish sea urchin larger than the *maratangtang*.

panáas: *n.* stinging pain. (*ut-ot, sanáang*) **napanaas.** *a.* having a stinging pain. (*apgés*) **Adda panaas nga agkarkarayam iti barukongko.** I have a stinging pain crawling in my chest.

panabá: (f. *tabá*) *n.* manure.

panabás: (f. *tabás*) *n.* kind of bolo.

panab-úng: (f. *sab-ung*) *n.* dowry, what is given as a dowry.

panabráag: (f. *birág*) **panabraag.** *v.* to slam (the door).

panabráang: (f. *biráng*) **panabraangen.** *v.* to slam; explode; make a loud noise.

panabsíit: (f. *bisít*) *n.* **panabsiiten.** *v.* to whip loudly.

panabsúok: (f. *bisók*) **ipanabsuok.** *v.* to throw something in the water with a splash.

panabtán: (f. *sabét*) *n.* place where people meet or run across one another; rendezvous.

panabtúog: (f. *bitóg*) *n.* thumping sound.

panadéro: (Sp. *panadero*: baker) *n.* baker.

panadéria: (Sp. *panadería*: bakery) *n.* bakery.

pánag-: Nominalizing prefix for *ag-* verbs: **panagbasa.** reading. **panaglangoy.** swimming. **panagsangit.** crying. **panaglastog.** boasting. **Panagkaduata.** Since the time we were together.

panagCV-: Nominalizing prefix for *agCV-* stems. It is used with various roots to indicate appropriate time or season: **panagreregreg.** fall (time of falling leaves). **panaglalam-ek.** winter (time of cold). **panagtatabako.** tobacco season. **panagsasabong.** flowering season. **panagaapit.** harvest season. **panaguukrad.** budding season. **panagsusulbod.** spring (time of shooting). **panagkakappia.** time of peace.

panag- -inn-: Nominalizing reciprocal affixation for *ag- -inn-* verbs. **panaginniliw.** *n.* act of missing (with nostalgia) one another. **panagpinnakada.** *n.* act of saying goodbye to each other. **Maawatanna met ti panaginniliwto dagiti dua.** He understands that the two will miss each other.

panagCV- -inn-: Nominalizing reciprocal affixation for *ag-* verbs with the plural actor specified by the CV reduplication: **panagiinnapal.** *n.* act of envying one another, mutual envy.

pánag: *n.* outdoors at night; (*reg.*) shore; shoreline. **kapanagan.** *n.* treeless plain; shore; land bordering a stream. **agkapanagan.** (*reg.*) *v.* to sleep out in the open; to become treeless.

panagém: *n.* intention, purpose; ulterior motive. **panagemen.** *v.* to plan with an ulterior motive. [Tag. *masamáng balak*]

panaginCV-: Nominalizing prefix used to form pretense nominals. **singpet.** virtue, good behavior. **panaginsisingpet.** the act of pretending to be virtuous. **panagimbubulsek.** the act of pretending to be blind. **panagintutuleng.** the act of pretending not to hear.

panagkaykaysá: (f. *maysa*) *n.* cooperation, unity. [Tag. *pagkakaisá*]

panagpa-: *pref.* 1. Nominalizing causative (indirect action) prefix: **panagpabalay.** act of having a house built. **panagpapintas.** act of beautifying one's self. 2. Nominalizing directional prefix. **panagpa-Laoag.** act of going to *Laoag.*

panáit: (f. *dait*) *n.* thread for sewing.

panakkél: (f. *dakkel*) *n.* pride. **agpanakkel.** *v.* to become arrogant, haughty. **managpannakkel.** *a.* arrogant; conceited; boastful. **maipagnakkel.** *v.* to be worthy; deserving of honor. **kinamanagpannakel.** *n.* arrogance. [Png. *kimon*, Tag. *pagmamataás*]

panakpák: *n.* sound of clapping, sound of wooden objects striking. **agpanakpak.** *v.* to produce clapping or slapping sounds.

panakrúd: (f. *sakrud*) *n.* inguinal region of the abdomen.

panakrúod: panakruoden. *v.* to crash into something; make a crashing sound by hitting something.

panakteél: panakteelen. *v.* to hit on the nape; to hit on the head or skull.

panál: *n.* a kind of blue/gray sparrow-type bird. [Tag. *tarát*]

panalayápen: (f. *daláyap*: lemon) *n.* kind of tree, *Champereia manillana*, similar to the *dalayap.*

panalbáag: (f. *libág*) **panalbaagen**. *v.* to slam the door.

panalbán: (f. *taléb*) *n.* something used as a partition (bamboo wall); (*fig.*) shield.

panalpáak: (f. *lipák*) *n.* slap in the face. **panalpaaken**. *v.* to slap in the face.

panaltágan: (f. *taltág*) *n.* cemented area where rice is pounded.

panamag-: Complex prefix consisting of the nominalizing prefix *panaN-* and the instrumental prefix *pag-*: **panamagdiligmi**. our comparison.

panamáti: (f. *pati*) *var.* of *pammati*: belief; faith; credibility.

panamdán: (f. *taméd*) *n.* reason for praising or respecting; *v.* respect. **Ania ti panamdam kenkuana?** Why do you respect him?

panamulót: (f. *pulót*) *n.* anointment; last rites. (*pammulót*)

panantólen: (f. *santol*) *n.* a kind of tree similar to the *santol*.

panang-: Nominalizing prefix used with *mang*-verbs indicating how or when an action is done. **mangsurat.** to write something. **panangsurat.** how one writes something, manner of writing something.

panang- -inn-: Nominalizing reciprocal affixation for *maN-* verbs. **panangbinnaut.** beating one another. May occur with CV reduplication of the stem to further express plurality: **panangpipinnadakes.** act of slandering one another.

panangdán: (f. *tangdan*) *n.* salary; payment for services rendered.

panangi-: Nominalized form of *manangi-* **Adda kadi met panangipategmo kenkuana.** You still have feelings for her.

panangipa-: Nominalizing affixation for *ipa*-verbs, denoting the act of transferring an object to the place denoted by the root (with locative stems) or the act of causing the transference of an object by means of the action specified in the root (with theme stems). **panangipagarup.** *n.* act of assuming or expecting. **panangiparuar.** *n.* act of taking something outside. **Kaano ti panangipa-Manilayo?** When are you going to bring it to Manila? **Naranraniag ti aglawlaw ngem ti panangipagarupmo.** The outside is brighter than you imagine.

panangpa-: Nominalizing prefix for *mangpa*-causative verbs. **pintas.** beauty. **mangpapintas.** to beautify, make beautiful. **panangpapintas.** act of beautifying.

panangpinna-: Nominalizing reciprocal prefix used with *mangpa-* stems. **panangpinnadakes.** mutual slandering. May be pluralized with

initial CV reduplication of the stem: *panangpipinna-*.

panangpipinna-: Plural nominalizing reciprocal prefix of *mangpa-* stems: **panangpipinnadakes.** slandering one another.

pánap: **panapan.** *v.* to increase, augment to something. (*nayon*)

panapán: **agpanpanapan.** *v.* to linger, loiter, delay in action. **agpanapan.** *v.* to wander idly.

panaplák: (f. *saplak*) *n.* northwest wind.

panaplíd: (f. *saplid*) *n.* duster.

panaputién: *n.* species of hardwood tree, *Ormosia orbiculata*.

panarápar: **agpanarapar.** *v.* to become hoarse (voice) (*páraw*). [Tag. *paos, malát*]

panarasán: (f. *darás*) *n.* reason for visiting; *v.* to visit a place with an intention.

panaráten: (f. *dárat*) *n.* sandy soil. [Tag. *buhangin*]

panarpár: (f. *parpár*) **napanarpar.** *a.* splintering; smashed to pieces; ear-splitting (sound).

panarpúog: (f. *ripóg*) **panarpuogen.** *v.* to topple down, cause to collapse, destroy.

panarpúok: (f. *ripók*) **panarpuoken.** *v.* to smash, break to pieces (*burak*).

panarsáak: (f. *rissák*) **panarsaaken.** *v.* to step on dry leaves (and make a crunching sound).

panarsibók: (f. *rissibók*) **ipanarsibok.** *v.* to throw something in the water making a splash. **naipanarsibok.** *v.* to be thrown in the water.

panarsíit: (f. *rissít*) **panarsiiten.** *v.* to roast, cause to make a crackling sound from intense heat.

panarsúod: (f. *risód*) **panarsuoden.** *v.* to crumble down things, make collapse.

panartúok: (f. *rittók*) **panartuóken.** *v.* to cause to make a crackling sound, make the joints crackle.

panatawén: (f. *napán a tawén*) last year.

panaténg: *n.* cold, flu. **agpanateng.** *v.* to have a cold. **managpanateng.** *v.* to frequently catch colds. [Ibg. *sifun*, Ivt. *nguhey*, Kal. *lapalating*, Png. *panateng*, Kpm., Tag. *sipón*]

panátiko: (Sp. *fanático*: fanatic) *n.* fanatic.

panatísmo: (Sp. *fanatismo*: fanaticism) *n.* fanaticism, unreasonable zeal.

pánaw: **pumanaw.** *v.* to leave, go away, set out; die; withdraw; die. **panawan.** *v.* to leave, abandon; give up; forsake. **ipanaw.** *v.* to take away. **ipapanaw.** *n.* departure. **agpanaw.** *v.* to leave for good; evacuate. **makapanaw.** *v.* to be able to depart. **nagpanaw.** *a.* deserted; bare; abandoned. **papanawen.** *v.* to drive away, send away. **pagpanawan, pamanawan.** *n.* reason for leaving; someone to take care of someone left alone; provisions for someone left behind.

dagiti napanawan. the bereaved. kapanpanaw. *v.* just left. kaipanpanaw. *v.* just brought away. kapapaipanaw. *v.* just ordered something to be sent away. kapanawan. *n.* departure. Ipanawmo ti kotsek ditoy. Get my car out of here. Pagpanawendakami nga awan gapgapuna kalpasan ti panangpasayaatmi iti daga? Are you driving us away for no reason after we improved the land? [Ibg. *pánaw*, Ivt. *karuq, angay*, Knk. *káan*, Kpm. *mako*, Png. *patánir, taynán*, Tag. *alís*]

pan-áw: *n. Imperata cylindrica*, cogon grass, used in native medicine to lower blood pressure. kapan-awan. *n.* place filled with cogon grass. pinan-aw. *a.* thatched with *pan-aw* grass. Idi damo, pan-aw ti atepda. In the beginning, their roof was made of cogon grass. [Kal. *guÿun*, Tag. *kugon*]

panawén: (f. *tawen*) *n.* time; weather; season; epoch. kapanawenan. *n.* contemporary (*sadar*); the height of one's time, epoch. Awanan panawen. He has no time. Panawen ita ti agtalon. It is now time to farm. Panawen ti kinaagtutubo, panawen ti panagsursuro. The time of youth is the time of learning. [Bon. *láwag*, Ivt. *kawaan*, Png. *panaon*, Tag. *panahón*]

panáy: (Tag.) *a.* purely, all; always. panaypanay. *a.* always done; habitual; excessively frequent. panayen. *v.* to do continuously, successively.

panáyag: napanayag. *a.* spacious, wide. (*lawa*) ipanayag. *v.* to put in full view.

panayág: *n.* coolness; pleasantness. napanayag. *a.* cool; pleasant.

panayágen: (f. *tayag*) *a.* rather tall.

pandá: pandaen. *v.* to do consecutively, one by one without skipping. maipandaan. *v.* to be one's turn to do something. (*pinda*)

pandág: *n.* bamboo roof framework; ridge (*talangkub*); exterior layer of the *balawbáw*; lining of clothes; paper weight. ipandag. *v.* to use something as a weight to press down. pandagan. *v.* to press down; overrun; surpass. pangpandag. *n.* heavy thing used as a weight. maipandagan. *v.* to be weighed down. [Tag. *dagán*]

pandák: *n.* dwarf; dwarfish. (*pandaka*)

pandáka₁: *n.* dwarf; *a.* dwarfish. (*pandek*)

pandáka₂: pinandaka. *n.* variety of awned rice.

pándan: *n. Pandanus tectorius*, screw pine.

pandansí: *n.* kind of fragrant plant used in salads and boiling rice, (*pandan*)

pandángo: (Sp. *fandango*) *n.* fandango dance.

pandangg-éro/-éra: (Sp. *fandanguero*) *n.* fandango dancer. Uray no baketen kasla pan-

danggera latta ti pannagnana. Although she is already an old lady, she walks like a fandango dancer.

pandár: (Sp. *andar*: go) mapandar (mapaandar). *v.* to start the engine.

pandarás: *n.* carpenter's adz.

pandáy: *n.* blacksmith. agpanday. *v.* to make iron tools; legislate (laws). pandayen. *v.* to forge metals; make metal things; play pranks; forge a relationship. mammanday. *n.* blacksmith. dagiti agpampanday-linteg. *n.* lawmakers, members of the legislative body. [Tag. *pandáy*]

pandék: *a.* short in stature; *n.* short person; dwarf, pygmy. [Bon. *petnel*, Ibg. *alinnoq*, Itg. *atúpak*, Ivt. *vudis*, Kal. *soklog*, Knk. *alitáit, sulítik*, Kpm., Png., Tag. *pandák*]

pandekékok: (*coll.*) *n.* short person.

pandéng: *n.* vertical piece of wood that sustains the *tangbaw* of a plow.

panderéta: (Sp. *pandereta*: tambourine) *n.* tambourine.

pandesál: (Sp. *pan de sal*: salt bread) *n.* kind of round, soft biscuit.

pandesétas: *n.* sweetbread roll.

pandilíng: *n.* long skirt. (*káin*) nakapandiling. *a.* wearing a long skirt; (*fig.*) henpecked. [Kal. *kain*]

pandinggá: *n.* type of chignon formed by rolling both halves of the tresses. (*pinggol*)

pandisál: *var.* of pandesal.

pandóng: *n.* mantilla, women's scarf. agpandong. *v.* to wear a mantilla.

paneknék: *n.* proof; facts; evidence. ipaneknek. *v.* to vouch for someone; confirm. mapaneknekan. *a.* able to be proven or verified. paneknekan. *v.* to prove, confirm, verify; corroborate; validate; demonstrate one's love. Napaneknekakon nga ay-ayatenka. I already proved that I love you. [Png. *pamatnagan*, Tag. *patibay*]

panekpék₁: *n.* variety of awned *diket* rice with a light-colored hull.

panekpék₂: napanekpek. *a.* well built (body), fully developed.

panekpék₃: *n.* the sound of wood being beaten. pumanekpek. *v.* to resound (wood being beaten). Nangngegda dagiti panekpek dagiti allawagi a mangilepleppasen iti pagpartuatan. They heard the hammering sounds of the carpenters finishing up the factory.

panenglán: (f. *tengngel*) *n.* collateral.

panerpér: panerperen. *v.* to do one after the other. (*agsasaruno*)

pánes: napanes. *a.* strong, violent (wind). napanes nga angin. *n.* gale; squall; storm. [Tag. *lakás*]

panés: *n.* black mourning clothes. (*manto*) **agpanes**. *v.* to mourn, be in mourning (by wearing black). (*agmangisit*) **ipansan**. *v.* to wear black clothes in mourning. **sipapanes**. *a.* in mourning. **Nagpanes ti aldawko.** My day got gloomy. [Tag. *luksâ* (mourning)]

paniáng: *n.* ritual of leaving out food to appease spirits so an ill person can recover (*atang*). **agpaniang**. *v.* to leave food sacrifices outside the house for spirits.

pánid: *n.* page (of a book). **ipanid**. *v.* to page. **sangkapanid**. *n.* one segment, page, petal, leaf (unit for leaflike objects). [Tag. *páhina* (Sp.)]

paniéro: (Sp. *compañero*: companion) *n.* term used between lawyers to address fellow colleagues, fem: *paniéra*.

panígan: *n.* prophylactic infusion. (*tig-an*)

panigergerén: (f. *tigerger*) *a.* somewhat shaky; rather wobbly.

panígo: (Png.) *n.* first sale of the day. (*buena mano*)

panigurádo: (f. *sigurado*) *a.* sure.

panílaw: (f. *silaw*) *n.* torchlight; lantern; something used as a light (for catching fish or frogs at night, etc.).

panílpo: (f. *silpo*) *n.* connection.

panimbéng: (f. *timbeng*) *n.* balancing weight.

panimbuklén: (f. *timbukel*) *a.* somewhat round shaped; roundish (eyes).

panímid: (f. *timid*) **agpanimid**. *v.* to rest one's chin on one's hands.

paningkít: (f. *singkit*) *n.* state of having beady or slanted eyes. (*pangusipet*)

pánio: (Sp. *pañuelo*: handkerchief) *n.* handkerchief. **nakapanio**. *a.* with a handkerchief; carrying a handkerchief. [Ivt. *valungut*, Knk. *pangió*, Tag. *panyo*]

pàniodemáno: (Sp. *paño de mano*: handcloth) *n.* handcloth, cloth for wiping one's hands.

panioléta: (Sp. *pañoleta*: triangular shawl) *n.* triangular shawl.

paniolíto: (Sp. *pañuelito*) *n.* small handkerchief.

paniolón: (Sp. *pañolón*) *n.* large square shawl.

panípit: (f. *sipit*) *n.* device used as tongs.

panippíp: **agpanippip**. *v.* to make the sound of a gun. (*banagbag*)

panirigán: (f. *siríg*) *n.* outlook; opinion; point of view.

panirpír: *n.* fluttering sound; buzzing sound; fluttering sound; snoring sound. **agpanirpir**. *v.* to make a buzzing sound in one's ear; flutter in the air. **pumanirpir**. *v.* to tremble; flutter. **Immapras ti nasalemsem a pul-oy-sardam a namagpanirpir kadagiti bulong iti aglawlaw.** The fresh evening breeze whipped by, fluttering the leaves all around.

pánit: **panitan**. *v.* to skin; scalp. **napanit**. (*obs.*) chalky.

paNN-: Nominalizing prefix that usually associates with an instrument or theme (see also *paN-*): **pammati**. belief. **pangngeddeng**. decision. **pannursuro**. teachings. **pannagibi**. nurture, tender care.

pannagíbi: (f. *tagíbi*) *n.* care, attention; nurture; suckling. **Adda iti pannagibik.** He is under my care. [Tag. *arugâ*]

pannagná: (f. *pagná*) *n.* manner of walking. [Tag. *lakad*]

pannaguén: (f. *ságo*) *n.* gray-plumaged cock.

pannaka-: 1. Nominalizing prefix for potentive *maka-* verbs. **makadait.** to be able to sew. **pannakadait.** the act of being able to sew. 2. Also indicates a state of being with stative stems: **pannakapanglaw.** the state of being poor. 3. With some nominal roots, *pannaka-* indicates substitution or representation: **pannakaama.** person acting as father. **pannakaulo.** acting head. **pannakangiwat.** spokesperson. **pannakabagi.** representative. **pannakakanawan.** right hand man.

pannakai-: Nominalizing affixation for potentive theme focus *makai-* verbs. **pannakaitabon.** manner or time of being buried. **pannakaiwaksi.** removal; abolition. **pannakaingato.** raise, increment. **Nasayaat kano ti pannakaisagana ti plano ti ili.** The preparations for the city plan are supposedly good.

pannakadláw: (f. *dilláw*) *n.* notice, noticing.

pannakálen: *n.* bubo, swelling of the lymph gland at groin. **agpannakalen.** *v.* to have this swelling (*babara*). [Tag. *kulani*]

pannakáleng: *n.* var. of *pannakalen*.

pannakalmés: (f. *lemmes*) *n.* drowning.

pannakalnéd: (f. *lenned*) *n.* sinking.

pannakalpás: (f. *leppas*) *n.* completion.

pannakapa-: Nominalizing affix for potentive causative *makapa-* verbs. **pannakapapintas.** act of being beautified. **pannakapasalun-at.** being healthy (having nutritional value, etc.). **pannakapaadda.** creation.

pannakapai-: Nominalizing affix for potentive *makapai-* verbs. **Idi kalman ti pannakapaidamag a nagpukaw ti balasang.** Yesterday was when the news was revealed that the lady was lost.

pannakatnág: (f. *tinnág*) *n.* act of falling. **pannakatnag ti rikna.** *n.* falling in love.

pannakayanák: (f. *anak*) *n.* birthday. (*kasangay*)

pannakkél: (f. *dakkél*) *n.* pride. **managpannakkel.** *a.* proud, arrogant. **kinamanagpannakkel.** *n.* pride; arrogance. **maipagpan-**

nakkel. *v.* to be worthy, deserving. **sipapannakkel.** *a.* with pride; honorably. **Dinak kadin ipagpapannakkel?** Aren't you proud of me?

pannaki-: Nominalizing prefix for social *maki*-verbs. Indicates the act of participating in an action with other people. **makimisa.** to go to mass **pannakimisa.** act of participating in the mass. **makikuyog.** to accompany, go with. **pannakikuyog.** the act of accompanying.

pannakipag-: Nominalizing affixation for *maki-pag-* social stems. **pannakipagladingit.** act of sharing in one's sorrow. **pannakipagrikna.** act of sharing feelings, sympathizing. **Ulitek ti pannakipagladingitmi.** Once again, I will express our sympathy (sharing in your sorrow).

pannanaó: (f. *saó*) *n.* language. (*pagsasao*)

pannangán: (f. *kaán*) *n.* meal. [Tag. *pagkain*]

pannanggéd: (f. *tegged*) *n.* labor; work. (*trabaho*)

pannaó: (f. *saó*) *n.* word. **iti sabali a pannao.** in other words. **iti daan a pannao.** for a long time; from the beginning.

pannaplít: (f. *saplít*) *n.* whipping, thrashing.

pannarábay: (f. *tarábay*) *n.* guidance and help; direction (of a performance, etc.).

pannarakén: (f. *tarakén*) *n.* care; protection; support. (*pannagibi, pannaripato*)

pannarién: *n. Tacca pinnatifida.* Polynesian arrowroot.

pannaripáto: (f. *taripato*) *n.* care. (*pannagibi, pannaraken*)

pannáyag: *var.* of *panáyag:* **napannayag.** *a.* spacious; open, free from obstructions to block the view.

pannig-án: (f. *tig-án*) *n.* prophylactic infusion.

panníki: *n.* bat, fruit bat. (flying rodent) (*kurarapnit*). **dara ti panniki.** *n. basi,* sugarcane wine (*lit:* blood of the bat). [Ibg., Kpm. *paníki,* Ivt. *paniciq,* Kal. *paliki,* Png. *panikí, káging,* Tag. *paniki*]

pannílud: (f. *silud*) *n.* sting, stinger. **Nariknana ti pannilud ti kinamaymaysa.** He felt the sting of loneliness.

pannímid: (f. *tímid*) **agpannimid.** *v.* to rest the face on the palm of the hand (*kalumbaba*).

pannirién: *var.* of *pannarien:* Polynesian arrowroot.

pannúbek: *n.* one of the four vertical bamboos that connect the runners of a sledge with its body at each corner.

pannúbok: (f. *súbok*) *n.* trial; means of testing one's aptitude; weight. **pannubok ti biag.** trial of life.

pannúgot: *n.* permission (*palubos*); acceptance. [Tag. *hintulot*]

pannugsóg: (f. *sugsóg*) *n.* encouragement; influence; that which incites.

pannulígsog: (f. *sulísog*) *n.* temptation; seduction; attraction. [Tag. *panuksó*]

pannúlong: (f. *túlong*) *n.* help.

pannuráy: (f. *turáy*) **agpannuray.** *v.* to depend on. **pagpampannurayan.** *n.* something or someone one on which/whom one is dependent. **Ammona nga agpannuray ti kabaelanna ti pannakilangenna kadagiti tao.** He knows that his power depends on being able to associate with people. [Tag. *tiwalà*]

pannurón: (f. *surón*) *n.* teasing.

pannursúro: (f. *súro*) *n.* education; teaching.

pannúsa: (f. *dúsa*) *n.* punishment; method of punishment. **Puro pannusa ken panangirurumen.** It is pure punishment and torment. [Tag. *parusa*]

panó: panpano, pampano. *n.* a kind of marine fish similar to the *barambán.*

panuéldo: (f. *suéldo*) *n.* wages, salary.

panugyóten: (f. *dugyót*) *a.* rather filthy.

panúkod: (f. *túkod*) *n.* pole used for sounding the depths of water.

panokpók: *n.* sound of repeated knocking or hammering. **pumanokpok.** *v.* to knock or hammer repeatedly.

panoktók: (f. *toktók*) *n.* small iron hook used to open mollusks.

panúli: (f. *súli*) *n.* corner post. **Tapno masumang, kagatem ti panuli nga adigi ti balayyo apaman a makariingka.** In order to get better (from the spell or poison), bite the corner post of your house as soon as you get up.

panulpáken₁: (f. *dulpák*) *a.* rather flat (nose).

panulpáken₂: (f. *tulpák*) *a.* rather deaf, hard of hearing.

panundirísen: (f. *tundíris*) *a.* with a rather long nose, having a pointed nose.

panúnot: *n.* thought, reflection; attention, consideration; opinion; intention; judgment. **panunuten.** *v.* to think, believe, suppose; plan; consider; regard; recall. **agpanunot.** *v.* to think; meditate; deliberate. **pumanunot.** *v.* to think, reflect. **pampanunot.** *n. Viola odorata,* violet; thoughts. **pamanunutan.** *n.* opinion; idea; way of thinking. **kapanunutan.** *n.* opinion; way of thinking; idea. **agkapanunutan.** *v.* to think the same way, have the same idea. **makapanunot.** *v.* to be able to think; to be able to find a way. **managpanunot.** *a.* contemplative. **Kasla agpampanunot a paltat 'diay anakna.** *exp.* Her child thinks like a catfish (is not intelligent). **No ania man ti pampanunotem, agsardengka kuman.** Whatever you are thinking (about doing), you should stop. [Ibg. *nónoq, panonoq,*

Ivt. *aktuktuq*, Kal. *somsomok*, Knk. *nemnem*, Png. *nónot*, Kpm., Png., Tag. *isip*]

panúngad: (f. *súngad*) *n*. front teeth.

panurayén: (f. *turáy*) *n*. authority figure; person in authority.

panúos: *n*. the smell of smoke or burnt food. **napanuos.** *a*. smelling smoky or burnt (said of food). [Tag. *maasó*]

panurók: (f. *surók*) **maipanurok.** *v*. to be more than normal; to be in excess; to exceed (*sobra*; *palalo*). **Napampanurok payen ti kasasaadna ita ngem idi balasang no maipapan iti kawes ken pagpapintas ti bagi.** Her condition now concerning clothes and self-beautification is more excessive now than when she was a bachelorette.

panút: *n*. loose hair of old people that is easily uprooted. **agpanut.** *v*. to fall out (loose hair).

panutpót: *n*. sound of a horn; sound of wind; sound of farting. **pumanutpot.** *v*. to break wind repeatedly.

panutsá: (Sp. *panocha*: ear of maize; panicle) *n*. loose brown sugar that fails to harden in the coconut shell mold; molasses cooked with peanuts in small cakes. (*bulisangsang*)

panpán: (*obs*.) *n*. surplus.

panpáno: *n*. kind of deep-sea fish. (*pampano*)

pansít: (Hok. *pian sít*: ready food) *n*. generic name for noodles usually, rice noodle; dish made using noodles. **agpansit.** *v*. to make a noodle dish. **pansit kanton.** *n*. wheat noodles. **pansit bihon.** *n*. rice noodles. **pansit sotanghon.** *n*. mung bean noodles.

pansitería: (f. *pansit*) *n*. noodle restaurant.

pantág: **pantagen.** *v*. to set in order, put in order; set the table. (*dasar*)

pantalán: (PSp. *pantalán*: pier) *n*. wharf; pier. (*muelie*; *wayáng*)

pantália: (Sp. *pantalla*: screen) *n*. lampshade; screen; giving a false appearance of something; dummy (acting in business).

pantalón: (Sp. *pantalón*: pants) *n*. pants, trousers. **agpantalon.** *v*. to wear pants. **papantalonen.** *n*. clothing material for pants. [Ivt. *salaviñi*, Kal. *panteÿun*, Kpm. *salól*]

pantár: *n*. treeless plain; (*reg*.) shore, land bordering a stream; treatment of one person to another (*tratar*). **napantar.** *a*. treeless. **Nakalawlawag dagiti napantar a paset ti kabakiran.** The treeless parts of the forest are quite bright. [Tag. *pantáy* (plain)]

pantáy: (Tag.) *a*. same (*pareho*); even; equal.

panténg: *n*. a kind of hardwood used in construction.

panteóng: (Sp. *panteón*: pantheon) *n*. tomb. (*tanem*)

pantíng: **agpanting.** *v*. to fade; discolor (*uspak*); to have negative thought of. **agpanting dagiti lapayag.** *exp*. to react negatively upon hearing bad news, cringing ears. [Tag. *kupas*]

pantók: *n*. top, summit, peak; ridge; tip of long nose. **napantok.** *a*. long (said of the nose); high (mountain). [Tag. *tuktók*]

pantúkos: see *kammadáng*: kind of thick wooden shoe used in rainy weather.

pányo: *var*. of *panio*: handkerchief.

panyoléta: *var*. of *panioleta*: triangular shawl.

panyolíto: *var*. of *paniolito*: small handkerchief.

panyolón: *var*. of *paniolon*: large square shawl.

pang-: *var*. of the *paN-* prefix before velar consonants, *ng*, *k*, and *g*; *r*, *l* and vowels.

pang-: Nominalizing instrumental prefix used for *mang-* verbs (perfective *pinang-*): **mangsurat.** to write something. **pangsurat.** something used to write something with. **mangdalus.** to clean something. **pangdalus.** means of cleaning.

pang- -an: *circumfix*. Locative affixation for *mang-* verbs indicating the place where an action occurs (with *sadino* questions), the reason for the occurrence of an action (with *ania* questions), or the person on whose behalf an action is done (perfective form is *nang- -an*): **mangala.** to take. **pangalaan.** place to where someone takes something. **tarimaan.** repair. **pangtarimaanan.** place where something is repaired; reason why something is repaired. **Sadino ti nangalaam iti ubing?** Where did you take the child? **Ania ti nangalaam iti ubing?** Why did you take the child?

pang- -en: *var*. of *paN- -en* before velar consonants *ng*, *k*, and *g* and before liquids *l* and *r*. Before the velar consonants the initial velar consonant drops, but before liquids the consonant is preserved. Used with adjectival stems to denote considerable degree: **pangalbuen.** somewhat bald (f. *kalbo*). **panguloten.** somewhat curly; wavy (f. *kulot*). **pangrapisen.** skinny, a bit thin (f. *rapis*).

páng: *n*. term of address for one's father. (*papang*)

pang: **pangpángen.** *v*. to beat; hammer.

pangá: *n*. jawbone. [Tag. *pangá*]

pangaási: (f. *ási*) *v*. to have mercy; please. **Pangaasim ta isardengmo kuman ti panggepmo.** Please stop your plan. [Tag. *awà*]

pangabeseráan: (f. *kabesa*) *n*. head of the table.

pangábil: (f. *kábil*) *n*. temper, violent disposition; means of defeating someone in a fight. **Adda pangabilna.** He has a temper.

pangabláaw: (f. *kabláaw*) *n*. greeting.

pángag: **ipangag.** *v.* to pay attention to, heed; consider; observe; notice. (*taripato*) **di napangag.** *a.* obstinate; stubborn.

pangagdán: (*obs.*) *n.* west wind.

pángal: *n.* transom, crosspiece; step of a ladder; grade in school; crossbar. **ipangal.** *v.* to heave with the feet planted on the crossbar. **papangalan.** *n.* step of a vehicle; foothold; hook. **pangalen.** *v.* to step on the *pangal*; use a crossbar. [Tag. *trabisanyo* (Sp.)]

pangál₁: *n.* mumps; jaw. **papangalan.** *n.* angle of the lower jaw. **ipangal.** *v.* to bite with the jaw. **napangal.** *a.* with large square jaws. **awan pangalna.** *exp.* to be cowardly. [Kal. *sapichin*, Png. *pangál*, Tag. *pangá* (jaw)]

pangál₂: *n.* variety of awned rice with a dark kernel and light-colored hull.

pang-ál: **ipang-al.** *v.* to impose the hardest task or burden on.

pangaldáw: (f. *aldáw*) *n.* lunch, noon meal. **mangaldaw.** *v.* to have lunch. [Tag. *tanghalian*]

pangamaén: (f. *amá*) *n.* uncle. (*uliteg*)

pangán: (f. *káan*) **mangan.** *v.* to eat. **panganan.** *n.* dining room. **makipangan.** *v.* to eat with someone. **ipangan.** *v.* to eat with rice. **makapangpangan.** *v.* to feel like eating. **Dida makapangpangan.** They don't feel like eating. [Png. *kan*, Tag. *kain*]

pangantíngen: *n.* a kind of tree similar to the *kantíngen*, *Cedrela sp*.

pangapátan: (f. *ápat*) *n.* shortcut.

pangaplásin: *n. Mallotus philippensis* plant used for dyes.

pangarásan: *n.* strips of bamboo used to connect different parts of the *basar*.

pangardísen: (f. *kardís*) *n.* a kind of tree, *Dipterocarpus grandiflorus*, similar to the *kardis*.

pangárit: *n.* tusk of swine. (*saong*)

pangás: *n.* braggart, boaster. **napangas.** *a.* conceited, boastful, haughty, proud, braggart, self-centered. **agpangas.** *v.* to brag. [Knk. *baonggék*, Tag. *yabang*]

pang-ás: *var.* of *pangas*.

pangasáan: (f. *asa*) *n.* whetstone. [Tag. *hasà*]

Pangasinán: *n.* Province of central Luzon south of La Union; the language or a native of Pangasinan. **ag-Pangasinan.** *v.* to speak Pangasinan. **taga-Pangasinan.** *v.* to be from the province of Pangasinan.

Pangasinénse: *a.* coming from or related to Pangasinan.

pángat: *n.* jaws; uvula of palate. (*pangal*)

pangát: (Pil.) **ipangat.** *v.* to cook fish with sour tamarind seasoning. [Tag. *pangát*]

pangáw: *n.* loud, teasing laughter. **agpangaw.** *v.* to tease by laughing aloud. **ipangaw.** *v.* to put in the stocks or pillory; to tie to the whipping post.

pang-áw: *n.* boasting, bragging. (*pangás*)

pangawwengén: (f. *kawwéng*) *a.* rather hooked, bent, curved; arched; crooked; deformed. **Tapoktapok ken pangawwengen ti dapanna.** His soles are dusty and somewhat arched.

pangay-áyo: (f. *áyo*) *n.* consolation.

pangayyá: *n.* beauty mark.

pangdán: *n. Pandanus tectorius*. The screw pine plant whose leaves are used to make hats and mats. (*pandan*)

pangdás: *n.* guess (*pugtó*); prediction (*padlés*); outlook; *var.* of *pápas*.

pangén: *n.* large number, crowd, multitude; flock; group; platoon, squad; herd; school (of fish). **agpangen.** *v.* to group together in a flock or crowd. **sangapangen.** *n.* one herd of; flock of. [Tag. *kawan*]

pang-és: **agpang-es.** *v.* to blow the nose (*pangres*). [Tag. *singá*]

pangét: *n.* entanglement. **maipanget, namnget.** *v.* to stick, get stuck in, entangled. [Tag. *salabíd*]

panggál: *n.* triangular device tied to the neck of an animal to keep the animal from passing bamboo fences.

panggalatít: *var.* of *panggalatot*: Pangasinan.

panggalatót: *n.* derogatory term applied to the Pangasinan people and language.

panggedán: (f. *teggéd*) *n.* employment; work. **No kayatmo ti bumaknang, dika pilien ti panggedan.** If you want to be rich, don't be choosy about jobs. [Tag. *paggawâ*; *hanapbuhay*]

panggép: *n.* aim, purpose, intention; plan. (*gagara*) **agpanggep.** *v.* to plan; to have an ulterior motive. **maipanggep.** *prep.* concerning, regarding, about, with regard to, in the interest of. (*maipapan*) **panggepen.** *v.* to intend, plan; study; marry. **Saanko a panggep a saktan.** I didn't mean to hurt him. [Png. *gagala*, *getmá*, Tag. *balak*, *tangkâ*]

panggí: see *pinggi*: shake; agitate; move to and fro.

pangginggí: (Tag. also) *n.* a card game consisting of matching pairs with the object being to get rid of all your cards by putting down pairs. (*kungkian*)

panggó₁: *n.* using beasts of burden to pull a load. **pangguen.** *v.* to drag, haul a heavy load using beasts of burden.

panggó₂: **panggopanggo.** *n.* stew made of innards boiled with bile and *pias*.

panggót: *n.* a species of tree.

pangi-: Nominalizing instrumental affix for *mangi-* verbs. **pangiduron**. means of helping push an object. **pangilung-aw**. setting free; instrument used for clearing.

pangi- -an: Nominalizing locative affixation for *mangi-* verbs, indicating the means, place, or direction an action takes place. **pangidurunan**. *n.* place or direction where an object is pushed (f. *duron* 'push'). **pangikabilan**. *n.* container, place where something is put. **pangiluganan**. *n.* means of transportation (f. *lugan* 'car'). **pangidaliasatan**. means of transporting. **Alaem ti dyipna, isu ti pangiluganantayo kadakuada nga ipaili**. Get his jeep, it will be what we use to take them to town.

pangiapuán: *n.* frame or mold of an arch.

pángil: (*obs.*) *n.* side, edge, border (*igid*). [Tag. *tabí*]

pangína: (f. *ngína*) **agimpapangina**. *v.* to play hard to get. (*lit*: to make oneself look more valuable than one actually is).

panginaén: (f. *iná*) *n.* aunt; stepmother.

pangindaráen: (f. *dára*) *n.* light red, pink. **mangindaraen**. *v.* to blush. [Tag. *mamulá*]

pangipeten: (f. *kípet*) *a.* rather tight.

pángis: *a.* odd, unpaired. **agpangis**. *v.* to have its pair missing. **pangisen**. *v.* to remove the match of a pair; hold (a table, etc.) by its side. [Tag. *kabiyák*]

pang-ít: **agpang-it**. *v.* to butt with the side of the head (using only one horn). **pang-itan**. *v.* to butt someone with the side of the head (using one horn).

pangkiá: *n.* basket similar to the *kuribot* used to hold rice to be pounded.

pangkiáw: *var.* of *pangkis*: cross-eyed.

pangkís₁: *a.* cross-eyed; squinting. (*kusipet; ballag, duling, gilab*) **agpangkis**. *v.* to cross the eyes. [Ibg. *ligád*, Ivt. *babat*, Kal. *laligi*, Tag. *duling*; Knk. *pangkís* = strike, hit, slap]

pangkís₂: **pinangkis**. *n.* crossbarred pattern of striping.

panglangkáen: (f. *lángka*) *n.* a kind of tree, *Gelonium glomerulatum,* that is similar to the *lángka.*

pangláw: **napanglaw**. *a.* poor, impoverished, indigent; thickheaded. **ipanglaw**. *v.* to cause to become poor. **kinapanglaw**. *n.* poverty. [Knk. *amingáwan,* Png. *írap,* Tag. *hirap*]

panglungbóyen: (f. *lungboy*) *n.* a kind of tree, *Memecylon ovatum,* similar to the *lungboy.*

pangmalém: (f. *malém*) *n.* early supper; afternoon meal. **mangmalem**. *v.* to have an early supper; eat the afternoon meal.

pangná: see *pagná*: walk.

pangnó: *n.* responsibility, duty, obligation; concern (*rebbéng*). [Tag. *tungkulin*]

pangngabúyo: *n.* large striped bird with a big bill.

pangngaduá: (f. *dua*) **agpangngadua**. *v.* to be unsure; to doubt. [Tag. *alinlangan*]

pangngárig: (f. *árig*) *n.* comparison. [Tag. *pagtutulad*]

pangngáti: *n.* decoy; domesticated cock used to trap wild fowl. **pumapangngati**. *n.* person who hunts jungle fowl. [Tag. *pangatí*]

pangngeddéng: (f. *keddéng*) *n.* decision; determination. [Tag. *pasiyá*]

pango: **ipango**. *v.* to coax into doing something. [Tag. *suyò, samò*]

panguángen: (*obs.*) *n.* simulating, pretending.

panguartáan: (f. *kuartá*) *n.* use for money; source of money; income.

pangudó: *n.* beaded bracelet.

pangudrepén: (f. *kudrép*) *a.* rather dim.

pangók: *n.* plague, pestilence, epidemic disease. **agpangok**. *v.* to die in an epidemic (animals). [Tag. *peste* (Sp.)]

pangulandísen: (f. *olandés*) *a.* rather blond.

pangulngól: *n.* something given for free. **ipangulngol**. *v.* to give for free. **pangulngulen**. *v.* to strip the flesh off the bone.

pangúlo: (f. *úlo*) *n.* president; chief; leader, head. **agpangulo**. *v.* to act as president; become the leader. **ipanguluan**. *v.* to lead. [Knk. *bawéd, pakáo,* Tag. *pangulo*]

pangulotén: (f. *kulót*) *a.* wavy; curly.

pang-ór: *n.* club, cudgel. **pang-oren**. *v.* to beat with a club, club. **ipang-or**. *v.* to use as a club. **Pangpang-orenkayo no maduktalak nga inlemmengyo**. I will club you if I find out that you hid it. [Knk. *pat-ó,* Tag. *bambó*]

pangurandóngen: *n.* a kind of tree, *Trema orientalis* similar to the *urandóng: Wikstroemia ovata.*

panguritá: (f. *kurita*) *n.* fish spear for catching octopus.

pang-ós: **pang-usen**. *v.* to chew sugarcane. (*usos*)

pangusnáwen: (f. *kusnáw*) *a.* rather faded.

pangót: *n.* species of tree with edible fruits.

panguttongén: (f. *kuttóng*) *a.* rather thin, somewhat slender.

pangpa-: *pref.* indicates the means of intensifying an action, or the instrument of causative (indirect) action: **imas**. deliciousness; enjoyment. **pangpaimas**. means of intensifying enjoyment; something added to make food taste better. **pangpapigsa**. something used to fortify.

pangpáng: *n.* furrow made by a plow; stone set beside river banks to break water from a flood.

pangrabií: (f. *rabií*) *n.* dinner, evening meal. **mangrabii.** *v.* to eat dinner.

pangrága: *n.* (*obs.*) incertitude. [Tag. *alinlangan*]

pangrém: *n.* pouting look; frown. **agpangrem.** *v.* to close the lips and sharpen the eyes in disgust. **pangreman.** *v.* to pout at. [Tag. *mungot*]

pangrés: *n.* nasal mucus; snot. (*buteg*) **agpangres.** *v.* to blow the nose. **ipangres.** *v.* to blow nasal mucus out of the nose. **papangresan.** *n.* nostril. [Bon. *sang-et*, Tag. *singá* (blow the nose)]

pangrúna: (f. *ngrúna*) **ipangruna.** *v.* to favor; be biased toward; specialize in; concentrate on. [Tag. *kiling*]

pangsó: *n.* stench of trousers.

pangtá₁: *n.* threat, challenge; plot, conspiracy. **ipangta.** *v.* to conspire against, plot. **pangtaan.** *v.* to threaten. **mangipangpangta.** *a.* threatening. **napangtaan.** *a.* threatened; warned. [Tag. *bantâ*]

pangtá₂: **agpangta.** *v.* to brag, boast.

pangtéd: *n.* interruption, leaving something unfinished; unfinished, interrupted work. **pangteden.** *v.* to do in an orderly way; do systematically. **kapangtedan.** *n.* turn, opportunity. (*lengdas*; *batang*)

páo: *n.* variety of small mango; kind of large marine fish.

paúd: *n.* strings that attach the warp to the weaver, when weaving without a loom. **paudan.** *v.* to tie the base of a post in order to move it with a lever. **pinaud.** *n.* lowermost layers of *nipa* leaves making the eaves of thatching, thatched nipa leaves.

paóg: **papaog.** *n.* limping of persons with uneven leg length.

paúlo: (f. *ulo*) *n.* title; heading. **pauluan.** *v.* to entitle; give a title to. **mapauluan.** *v.* to be entitled.

páor: *a.* dry, completely ripe (coconut).

páos: *n.* overuse of a desired thing. **napausan.** *v.* to long for, crave; change old clothes; overacting; going beyond one's power. **agpapaos.** *v.* to be whimsical, capricious; to go beyond one's power.

páut₁: **napaut.** *a.* lasting, continuing, persistent, enduring. **agpaut.** *v.* to last long; to stay long. **makapagpaut.** *a.* enduring; durable; lasting. **kapaut.** *n.* duration. **ipaut.** *v.* to do for a long time, prolong. **magánkapaut?** for how long will it last? **Kasano ti kapautmo ditoy?** How long will you stay here? **Dida makapagpaut iti poder no guraen ida ti publiko.** They cannot stay in power long if the public becomes angry with them. [Png. *paot*, Tag. *tagál*]

páut₂: **pautan.** *n.* *Satiria sp.* tree.

paúy: **pauypaoy.** *a.* empty handed. (*ima-íma*)

paúyo: **agpapauyo.** *v.* to be sensitive; mildly jealous; be resentful; seduce; attract (*awis*). **managpauyo.** *a.* sensitive; jealous; resentful. **Arimpauyuen ni Chona ngem adda rimat kadagiti matana.** Chona was a bit resentful but there was a sparkle in her eyes.

paoyó: **agpaoyo.** *v.* to tire, weary; be bored, impatient; sulk. [Tag. *tampó* (sulk); *antók* (weary)]

pápa: *n.* Pope; wild duck, mallard. **susó papa.** *n.* kind of edible *suso* with a soft, round shell.

papá: (Sp. *papa*: father) *n.* father. (*tatang*)

papaáweng: (f. *aweng*) *n.* small bamboo bow attached to a kite to make a shrill sound.

papádi: Plural of *padi*: priests.

pápag: *n.* bamboo bench; bamboo or wood bed (with no mattress). (*langkapi*) **agpapag.** *v.* to sleep on a bamboo bed. [Png., Tag. *papag*]

papagáyo: (Sp.) *n.* papagayo, variety of parrot; kite shaped like a bird.

papáit: (f. *paít*) *n.* bile, bitter intestinal juice used in cooking (*apró*); *Mollugo oppositifolia* herb used in salads. **pinapaitan.** *n.* dish made using *papait*.

papanán: (f. *pan*) *n.* destination. **Papanam?** Where are you going? **Papanantayo?** Where are we going? **No saan nga makaammo nga mangtaliaw ti naggapuanna, saan a makadanon iti papananna.** *exp.* If one does not know how to look back from where he came, he will not be able to reach his destination. [Tag. *puntá*]

papánda: (Sp. *bufanda*: scarf) *n.* scarf, muffler. (*bupánda*)

papáng: (Sp. *papa*: father) *n.* term of address used for fathers. (*tata*; *tatang*)

pápas: **agpapas.** *v.* to enjoy. **ipapas.** *v.* to enjoy; do to the limit of one's capacity; to do thoroughly; to do excessively. **papasan.** *v.* to molest, harass; make sure one receives punishment for bad deeds; ostracize. **maipapas.** *v.* to be able to do thoroughly. **mapapasan.** *v.* to be bothered, molested, harassed; ostracized. **pagpapasen.** *v.* to let somebody enjoy.

pápay: **agpapay.** *v.* to wet one's clothes; to bed wet; to urinate in an improper place; have wet dreams. [Tag. *maihì*]

papáya: (Sp. *papaya*: papaya) *n.* papaya. [Kal. *apaya*, Kpm. *kapáyaq*, Tag. *papaya*]

papáyo: *n.* a kind of songbird that sings at dawn.

pápel: **ipapel**. *v.* to push, force, cram, press into. **nakapapel**. *a.* crammed; having mouth full of food. [Tag. *muwál* (with full mouth)]

papél: (Sp. *papel*: paper; role) *n.* paper; role (in a film). **papel de banko**. *n.* check. **papel de liha**. *n.* sandpaper. **papel hapon**. *n.* thin paper used in kite making. **papeles**. *n.* official documents; papers. **papeleta**. *n.* slip of paper; pass, permit; certificate. **agkapapelan**. *v.* to have the same characteristics. [Knk. *súlat*]

papelíto: (Sp. *papelito*: small piece of paper) *n.* small piece of paper, slip of paper; curl paper; paper folded containing a drug.

pápeng: *n.* young coconut. **pimmapeng**. *n.* species of large red chili pepper.

papetpét: (f. *petpet*) *n.* cash gift; bribe money.

papi(n)-: *pref.* used with numbers to form verbs (taking the *-ko* pronouns indicating how many times the actor of the verb has something done; perfective form is *pinapi(n)-*. **Papiduam**. Have it done twice.

papíro: (Sp. *papiro*) *n.* papyrus.

papuá: *n.* *Nothopanax fruticosum* shrub used for ornamentation.

paputók: (f. *putók*) *n.* firecracker.

pappáp: *a.* short, flat (said of the nose) (*lugpak*); *n.* honking sound. **Pagpappapen**. *v.* to honk. **Pinagpappapna ti lugan**. He honked the car. [Tag. *pangô* (flat nose)]

pappáw: **ipappaw**. *v.* to dip, plunge into water. (*rareb*)

para-: *pref.* from the Spanish preposition *para* 'for', indicates suitability, the person responsible or instrument used. **paraluto**. cook, person responsible for cooking. **parabomba**. pumper at a well. **paratrabaho**. work clothes. **paratimid**. chin strap. **paramanada**. fighting cock (as opposed to a rooster).

Pára!₁: (Sp. *para*: stop) *interj.* Stop! (*agsardengka!*) **ipara**. *v.* to stop; park. **agpara**. *v.* to stop (driving).

pára₂: (Sp. *para*: for) *prep.* for, on behalf of. **Para kadakayo**. It's for you.

pára₃: *n.* sprouting coconut. **agpara**. *v.* to bubble (water when it rains).

pára₄: **agparapara** (*obs.*) *v.* to scatter.

paraakkúb: (f. *akkub*) *n.* cover model (in a magazine).

paraángan: *n.* porch, front yard, lawn; upper lip under the nose. **mamarparaangan**. *v.* to loiter around. **agkaparaangan**. *v.* to have adjoining front yards. [Tag. *bakuran*]

parabitbít: (f. *bitbít*) *n.* porter.

parábola: (Sp. *parábola*: parable) *n.* parable.

parabómba: (f. *bómba*) *n.* person responsible for pumping a well (while another takes a bath, etc.).

parábur: *n.* gift; generosity. **naparabur**. *a.* generous. **iparabur**. *v.* to give, bestow. **kinamanagparabur**. *n.* benevolence; generosity. **paraburan**. *v.* to gift; bestow blessings on someone; be generous with someone. [Ivt. *dadaam*, Tag. *biyayà*]

paráda: (Sp. *parada*: parade) *n.* parade. **iparada**. *v.* to display in a parade, parade; to stake. **makiparada**. *v.* to join a parade. **pumarada**. *v.* to park.

paradípad: *n.* small enclosing wall; horizontal layer of *taléb* placed between the wall and the *bayangbayang* in *tinubeng* type houses; person who is always colliding into things; busybody; sound produced by scraping a bamboo wall.

paradór: (Sp. *aparador*: sideboard) *n.* cupboard, cabinet.

paradusdós: *var.* of *padarusdos*: kind of homemade dessert.

paragapág₁: *var.* of *paragpág*: rib. [Tag. *tadyáng*]

paragapág₂: **agparagapag**. *v.* to flounder (fish) (*palagapag*). [Tag. *palág*]

paragátas: *var.* of *alpargátas*: hemp sandals.

paraggalsém: *adj.* somewhat sour, slightly sour (*alsém*). [Tag. *asim*]

paragípang: *var.* of *parangipang*: olive.

paragipíg: **pumaragipig**. *v.* to shake the body; shake off water when wet. (*waragiwig*)

paragupóg: (*obs.*) *a.* old, stale. **iparagupog**. *v.* to drop suddenly and heavily. **maiparagupog**. *v.* to fall suddenly and straight down. [Tag. *hulog*]

parágos: *n.* sled pulled by the carabao used for plowing; Casanova, playboy (*parágot*).

parágot: *n.* harrow; (*fig.*) playboy. **paragutan**. *v.* to harrow. (*sagad*, *moriski*)

paragpág: *n.* rib; skeleton of a building; spokes of a kite; framework. **nakaparparagpag**. *a.* skinny, with the ribs showing. [Bon., Knk. *tadláng*, Ibg. *pareppeg*, *baraq*, Itg. *palagpag*, Ivt., Kal. *butik*, Ivt. *taglang*, Png. *taglÃ¡ng*, Kpm. *tagyang*, Tag. *tadyáng* (rib)]

paragsít: *n.* agility, nimbleness; vigor; alertness (*siglat*). **naparagsit**. *a.* agile, nimble; alert. **pumaragsit**. *v.* to become alert; be lively (*kulanggit*; *siglat*). **sipaparagsit**. *a.* fast, quickly, briskly. **Nakaparparagsiten nga immuli tapno mamles**. She went up briskly to dress. [Tag. *siglá*]

parainnáw: (f. *innáw*) *n.* dishwasher, someone responsible for doing the dishes.

paraípus: (f. *ípus*) *n.* tail end of something; train-bearer. **parparaipus.** *n.* person or animal who continually follows someone; uneven strand of hair or string in a haircut or rug respectively. **paraipusan.** *v.* to add to the end of; suffix.

paráis: *n.* shower of rain. **agparais.** *v.* to shower. **paraisan.** *v.* to shower someone (with love, gifts, etc.). [Tag. *ambón*]

paraíso: (Sp. *paraíso*: paradise) *n.* paradise.

parákad: *n. Rhizophora mucronata.* Tree of mangrove swamps whose bark is used to dye fish nets.

parakaída: (Sp. *paracaída*: parachute) *n.* parachute. **agparakaida.** *v.* to parachute.

parakaidísta, parakaidéro: (f. *parakaída*) *n.* parachutist, paratrooper.

parakapák: *n.* sound of artillery; sound of crashing water. **pumarakapak.** *v.* to chatter endlessly; fire (ammunition); crash (waves).

paraké: (Sp. *para qué*: why, for what) why? (used rebukingly).

parakéd: *n.* outrigger of a canoe.

parakúpok: **iparakupok.** *v.* to pour out all contents, spill out all.

parakpák: *n.* sound of gunfire. **parakpaken.** *v.* to shoot something repeatedly.

paraláko: (f. *lako*) *n.* salesperson.

paralélo: (Sp. *paralelo*: parallel) *a.* parallel.

paralisádo: (Sp. *paralizado*: paralyzed) *a.* paralyzed. **Naparalisado ti kaggudua't bagina.** He is paralyzed in half his body.

parálisis: (Sp. *parálisis*: paralysis) *n.* paralysis; immobility.

paralítiko: (Sp. *paralítico*: paralyzed person) *n.* paralyzed person; *a.* paralyzed.

paramanáda: (f. *manada*) *n.* fighting cock, as opposed to a rooster.

parammág: *n.* bluff; boaster. (*lastóg*) **agparammag.** *v.* to boast; be haughty, arrogant. **naparammag.** *a.* conceited, vain, boastful. **pagparammagán.** *v.* to act arrogantly toward someone. [Tag. *yabang*]

paránas: **naparanas.** *a.* smooth, level, even. (*patad*) **paranasen.** *v.* to smoothen, level, make even. [Tag. *patag*]

paranóya: (Eng.) *n.* paranoia, delusions of persecution.

paransúgay: *n.* vertical beam of the granary (*agamang*).

párang: **parangen.** *v.* to subdue; secure a person or vessel.

paráng: *n.* scene of a play; appearance. **agparang.** *v.* to appear, show up; become visible. **iparang.** *v.* to show, present, exhibit; disclose; publish. **pammarang.** *n.* incisor, front teeth;

back side of something; hypocrisy; make-believe thing. **naparang.** *a.* exposed; protruding (teeth). **agpammarang.** *v.* to make pretenses; pretend. **managpammarang.** *a.* pretentious. **mapagparang.** *v.* to be able to show, prove. **pagparangen.** *v.* to make something visible. **No nakitadak, agparammangak nga agkamkammel.** If they see me, I pretend to be fishing by hand. [Png. *parongtál*, Tag. *labás* (appear)]

parangárang: *n.* implication; manifestations of intent. **iparangarang.** *v.* to reveal, disclose; show off; manifest. [Tag. *pakita*]

parangáw: *n.* open mortise of concave cut at the upper end of a post that supports the tiebeams. **parangawan.** *v.* to make a concave cut at the upper end of a post.

parangét: **kaparanget.** *a.* adjacent, neighboring (*bangibang*). **agkakaparanget.** *v.* to be neighboring, next to (said of towns). **Daydaywen dagiti umili manipud kadagiti kaparanget a lugar.** The townspeople from the neighboring places praised him. [Tag. *karatig*]

parangípang: *n.* olive tree; olive fruit.

parangkáp: **iparangkap.** *v.* to donate; give away. **kinamanagparangkap.** *n.* charitableness. [Tag. *pamigáy*]

paraón: (Sp. *faraón*: pharaoh) *n.* pharaoh.

paraupó: *n.* sound or rapids, a noisy current. **agparaupo.** *v.* to make the sound of white water (noisy currents). [Tag. *lagaslás*]

paraúsig: (f. *usig*) *n.* prosecutor.

paráut: *n.* string, rope (for binding). **iparaut.** *v.* to use to tie or bind. (*galut*) **parautan.** *v.* to bind fast and secure; thrash to a tree. [Tag. *bigkís*]

parápar: **agpanarapar.** *v.* to be hoarse (*paraw*). [Kal. *lapaok*, Tag. *paos, malát*]

parapernál: (Sp. *parafernal*) *a.* paraphernal, under the control of the wife.

parapernália: (Sp. *parafernalia*) *n.* paraphernalia; articles of equipment.

parapína: (Sp. *parafina*: paraffin) *n.* paraffin.

párapo: (Sp. *párrafo*: paragraph) *n.* paragraph.

paráris: *n.* roller for moving heavy objects. **paririsan.** *v.* to move heavy objects using a roller.

páras: **naparas.** *a.* exposed to the wind (*paríir*). [Tag. *lantád*]

parasápas: *n.* sound of fast walking with light steps; sound of splashing water. **agparparasapas.** *v.* to splash around.

parasiáw: **agparasiaw.** *v.* to swim on the surface (fish), splash on the surface of the water.

parasíket: (f. *síket*) *n.* waistband, belt. **nakaparasiket.** *a.* wearing a waistband.

parasipís: *n.* sound produced by fish floundering in the water; sound of a shower. **agparasipis.** *v.* to wriggle, writhe; swim in shallow water.

parasíto: (Sp. *parásito*: parasite) *n.* parasite. **parasitiko.** *a.* parasitic.

paraspás: paraspasen. *v.* to cut the grass.

parassiáw: agparassiaw. *v.* to splash, splatter.

paratignáy: (f. *tignáy*) *n.* wheel, spring, balance, rack; motivation; agitator, stimulant.

parátik: *n.* variety of tobacco with short leaves with red scales and spots.

paratímid: (f. *timid*) *n.* chin strap for helmets or the *kattoukong* hat.

paratipít₁: *n. Scirups erectus* sedge.

paratipít₂: **agparatipit.** *v.* to make a very shrill sound (shriller than *paratopot*).

paratípus: (Sp. *paratifus*) *n.* paratyphoid.

parató: *n.* humor; joke; pun. (*angaw*; *rabak*) **naparato.** *a.* funny, humorous. **agparato.** *v.* to tease, kid. **parparato.** *n.* joke, witticism, fun. [Tag. *birô*]

paratudó: (f. *tudó*) *n.* pointer. [Tag. *panurò*]

parátok: *n.* silver ornament covering the *kattokong* hat.

paratóng: *n.* sandy soil on riverbanks or ocean. (*panaraten*)

paratupót: *n.* sound of rapid ammunition; (*fig.*) diarrhea. **agparatupot.** *v.* to produce the sound of diarrhea or rapid ammunition fire; to have diarrhea. **Pimmaratupot ti paltogna.** His gun fired rapid, successive shots. [Tag. *putók*]

páraw: *a.* hoarse. **agpaparaw.** *v.* to be hoarse. (*panarapar*) **paparaw.** *n.* hoarse voice. [Ibg. *pagag*, Itg. *palaw*, Ivt. *payaw*, Kal. *lapaok*, Kpm. *payus*, Png. *pagas*, Tag. *paos*, *malát*]

paráw: *n.* sailing vessel larger than the *biray*. **Yarigka 'tay paraw nga agkatangkatang.** *exp.* You are always on the go (like the drifting ship).

paráwad: *n.* contribution (to a wedding, i.e., money pinned on couple while dancing); in old days, the *parawad* was given in exchange for a drink offered by the married couple. **agparawad.** *v.* to give money to newlyweds following the *parawad* ritual. **iparawad.** *v.* to give as a gift to the newlyweds.

parawpáw: *a.* fake; exaggerated; untrue; false; insincere. **parawpáwan.** *v.* to exaggerate; camouflage; disguise. **parawpawen.** *v.* to do something carelessly or half-heartedly. **parawpawan ti sao.** *v.* to exaggerate. **inparawpaw.** *n.* a kind of blanket with a *pinilian* face. **Parawpaw ti tinnung-ed ken innisemda, awanan singed.** Their nodding and smiling to each other is fake, there is no friendliness. [Tag. *hungkág*]

parayág: *n.* boastful person (*lastóg*). **agparayag.** *v.* to boast; show off one's possessions. **managparayag.** *a.* prone to boasting.

parayápay: naparayapay. *a.* dry (cooked rice). (*marayamay*)

paray-ók: *var.* of *tiray-ok*: flattery.

parayúpay: see *barayubay*: fringe, decorated border; decoration.

paraypáy: see *barayubay*: fringe; decorated border; decoration.

parbángon: *n.* dawn, daybreak, early morning. (*bannawag*) **agparbangon.** *v.* to wake up at dawn. **parbangon nga apagsipasip.** *n.* break of dawn. **parbangonen.** *v.* to do at daybreak. **Pinarbangonda nga inyudong ti karosa.** They took the float to town at dawn. [Kal. *wiswisngit*, Png. *palbangon*, Tag. *liwaywáy*]

parbéng: (f. *rebbeng*) *n.* temperance; abstinence; self-restraint; self-control. **kaparbengan.** *n.* mean, middle. **maiparbeng.** *a.* suitable, appropriate, proper; reasonable. **naparbeng.** *a.* considerate, fair. **agparbeng.** *v.* to exercise self-control, refrain from doing something bad; to behave properly; be considerate, fair. **managparbeng.** *a.* respectful; modest; restrained. **kinamanagparbeng.** *n.* temperance; moderation. **panagparbeng.** *n.* self-control, self-restraint. **Agpayso nga adda idi di maiparbeng a relasionmi kenkuana.** It is true that I had an inappropriate relationship with her. [Tag. *timpî*]

parbó: *a.* fake, false; fabricated; invented; *n.* roof rafter; a house constructed by the owner and not inherited. **managparbo.** *n.* liar. (*ulbod*) **parbuen.** *v.* to tell lies; make up (stories). **parbo a nagan.** *n.* pen name; alias. **agparbo.** *v.* to cheat; lie; be fake. [Ivt. *dadaay*, Png. *inalig*, *bulaw*, Tag. *huwád*]

pardá: *n. Dolichos lablab.* Vine with pink-purple flowers and edible beans; the pod of this vine. [Tag. *bataw*]

pardánon: *n.* completed work. **pardanonen.** *v.* to do completely and perfectly. (*sungdo*) **intono mapardanonan ti luomna.** when it is perfectly ripe.

pardás: *n.* speed. (*paspas*) **napardas.** *a.* quick, fast, rapid, swift. **papardasen.** *v.* to urge to do faster. **pumardas.** *v.* to speed up, become faster. **Pimmardas ti bitek ti barukongna.** The heartbeat in his chest sped up. [Png. *kuyát*, *pelés*, *siglát*, Tag. *bilís*]

pardáw: *reg. var.* of *tardaw*.

pardáya: *n.* false accusation, slander. **mamardaya, pardayaen.** *v.* to bear false witness against; slander. **pamardaya, pangpardaya, pammarpardaya.** *n.* false testimony; slander. **Diak ugali ti mamarpardaya iti padak a tao.** It is not my habit to slander my fellow man. [Tag. *paninirang-puri*]

párdo: (Sp. *fardo*: bundle) *n.* bundle of tobacco leaves; bale. **sangapardo.** *n.* one bundle of tobacco leaves. **parduen.** *v.* to bundle. **pinardo.** in bundles.

pardúd: **parduden.** *v.* to fatten, feed in order to fatten (*palukmeg, seksek*). [Tag. *patabâ*]

páre: (Tag. also) term of address for one's friend or *kumpare*.

paréha: (Sp. *pareja*: pair, couple) *n.* pair; couple.

parého: (Sp. *parejo*: equal) *a.* same, similar, equal; *n.* partner in a dance. **agpareho.** *v.* to be equal, similar. **ipareho.** *v.* to equate. **kapareho.** *n.* something equivalent. **parparehuen.** *v.* to do equally; treat equally. [Ivt. *alit*, Tag. *pareho*]

párek: *n.* dregs of liquors (*ared-ed*; *alibudabod*). [Tag. *latak*]

paréntesis: (Sp. *paréntesis*) *n.* parenthesis. [Tag. *saklóng*]

pargáy: *n.* variety of awned *diket* rice.

pargí: **agpargi.** *v.* to dress up (women). **napargi.** *a.* agile, lively, nimble. **pargien.** *v.* to do with care and consideration; to do to the best of one's ability. [Tag. *gayák*]

pargód: *var.* of *pagúd*: hitch, fasten, tie.

pári: *n.* term of address for a friend or *kumpari*.

pariá: *n. Momordica charantia.* The bitter melon; variety of awned *diket* rice; (*coll.*) impotent sex organ. **kapariaan.** *n.* bittermelon vineyard. **parparia.** *n.* species of wild vine that resembles the bitter melon; (*coll.*) impotent genitalia. **Makapasalun-at kano ti bulong ti paria.** They say that *paria* leaves are healthy. **Di pay naluto ni paria, simmagpaw ni karabasa.** The bittermelon was not yet cooked and the squash jumped in (said after an unwelcome interruption). [Kal. *peya, apaget*, Kpm. *apalyaq, alpág*, Png. *palyá*, Tag. *ampalayá*, PSp. *amargóso*]

parián: *n.* (*reg.*) marketplace. (*tiendáan*)

parída: (Sp. *parida*: woman who just delivered a child) *n.* woman who attends church soon after delivering a baby.

parigipíg: *var.* of *paragipig*: shake the body.

paríir: *n.* fresh air. **napariir.** *a.* cool, fresh, breezy; ventilated. **ipariir.** *v.* to expose to the fresh air. **pagpariiran.** *n.* breezeway. [Tag. *lamíg*]

parikadkád: **agparikadkad.** *v.* to start to fight, approach one another belligerently; attack one

another (*sarigsíg*); strut (*sikad*). **Agparparikadkaden da tatang ken ni uliteg idi sumangpetkami.** Father and Uncle were attacking one another when we arrived.

parikút: (f. *rikút*) *n.* problem; trouble; worry. (*pakadanagan*) **agparikut.** *v.* to have a problem; worry. **pagparikutan.** *n.* cause of problems or trouble. **Nasken a maibagay ti plano kadagiti kasapulan ken parikut ti ili.** The plan must fit the needs and problems of the city.

pariksá: *n.* reinforcements. **pariksaen.** *v.* to strengthen; reinforce.

parília: (Sp. *parrilla*: grill) *n.* grill; metal framework attached to a car or bus to hold luggage.

pariliéra: (Sp. *parrillera*: grill) *n.* grill. (*parilia*)

parimrím: *n.* side glance. (*kusílap*) **agparimrim.** *v.* to pucker up when about to cry (children) (*musíig*); make a flirting countenance, give a side glance to. **parimriman.** *v.* to glance at; pucker up. [Tag. *sulyáp*]

parinsúsok: see *palinsusok*: to fill to the brim; heap up.

parintúmeng: **agparintumeng.** *v.* to kneel. (*parintuod*) **maiparintumeng.** *v.* to fall on the knees. **sipaparintumeng.** *a.* kneeling. **pimmarintumeng a kurimatmat.** *n.* curly eyelashes. **Pinagparintumengdak iti sango ti ari.** They had me kneel before the king. [Bon. *balintomeng*, Ibg. *palittúkeg*, Ifg. *mundukkun*, Ivt. *dumugud*, Kpm. *siklud*, Png. *talimúkol*, Tag. *luhod*]

parintúod: **agparintuod.** *v.* to kneel on one knee. (*parintumeng*) **nakaparintuod.** *a.* kneeling on one knee. [Tag. *luhod*]

paringgúyod: **paringguyuden.** *v.* to drag, haul. (*gúyod*)

paríngit: **parparingit.** *a.* stony (roads); cobbled. [Tag. *mabató*]

pariók: *n.* frying pan; skillet. (*sartin*) **agpariok.** *v.* to rotate, revolve, spin. **parioken.** *v.* to spin something, turn something around. **pinnariok.** *n.* a children's whirling game. **pimmariok.** *a.* in the shape of a pan. **Kasla agruprupa iti ubet ti pariok.** His face is like the bottom of a pot. [Ibg. *paryuq*, Ivt. *palyuk*, Kal. *pallangÿan*, Kpm. *kuwáli*, Png. *kawáli*, Tag. *kawalì*, Tag. *palyók* = clay pot]

parípa: (Sp. *rifa*: raffle + prefix *pa-*) *n.* raffle; lottery. **agparipa.** *n.* to raffle; have a lottery.

páris: (Sp. *par*: pair) *a.* even (not odd), paired up. **sangaparis.** *n.* one pair. (*asmang*) **pagparisen.** *v.* to match; make equal; compare. **paris-paris.** *a.* paired up. **pumaris.** *v.* to be the same, equal. **iparis.** *v.* to do the same way.

Agparis ti kinamalalakiyo. Your masculinity is equal. [Tag. *pares*]

parisídio: (Sp. *parricidio*: parricide) *n.* parricide, the act of killing one's parents.

párit: *n.* prohibition. iparit. *v.* to prohibit, forbid. maiparit. *a.* forbidden, prohibited; illegal. paritan. *v.* to forbid, prohibit. Awan ti mangiparparit kenka a makisarita kadakami. Nobody is forbidding you to speak with us. Panggepna ti makiay-ayam iti sungka nupay iparit ti amana. He plans to play *sungka* although his father forbids it. [Bon. *páwa*, Knk. *sága*, Png. *sebél*, Tag. *bawal*]

par-íw: maipar-iw. *v.* to be blown by the wind. (*palais*) agparpar-iw. *v.* to stagger (drunks).

parkág: naparkagan. *a.* very dry (*maga*, *ati*). [Tag. *tuyô*]

parkás: (f. *rekkás*) parkasen. *v.* to loosen; unfasten; liberate; set free; give slack to.

párke: (Sp. *parque*: park) *n.* park. agpaparke. *v.* to go to the park.

parlaménto: (Sp. *parlamento*: parliament) *n.* parliament. parlamentario. *a.* parliamentary; parliamentarian.

parmáag: iparmaag. *v.* to disclose, reveal. (*paduyakyák*, *waragáwag*)

parmák: parparmak. *n.* empty, futile reasoning not based on facts. agparparmak. *v.* to venture, risk, try one's luck.

parmaséutiko: (Sp. *farmaceutico*: pharmacist) *n.* pharmacist. (*botikario*)

parmásia: (Sp. *farmacia*: drugstore) *n.* pharmacy, drugstore. (*botika*)

parmatá: *n.* vision (in one's dreams). agparmata. *v.* to dream, envision. agparparmata.b *v.* to daydream. managparmata. *n.* visionary; *a.* imaginative. [Tag. *pangarap*]

parmék: (f. *rumék*) parmekén. *v.* to defeat, vanquish; outdo; surpass; subdue. (*atiw*; *abak*; *parukma*) maparmek. *v.* to be subdued, conquered. pannakaparmek. *n.* defeat; subjugation. panangparmek. *n.* conquest. Immanges iti nauneg tapno maparmekna ti saibbekna. He took a deep breath to subdue his sobbing. [Tag. *talo*]

parmúon: agparmuon. *v.* to play the spy; to try to get information under false pretenses; try one's luck; give an anticipatory sign.

parmút: *var.* of *ramut*.

párna: maiparna. *v.* to do concurrently; to happen at the same time (*naranaan*). iparna. *v.* to set to coincide with, do at a determined time. marmarna. *n.* ghost, spook. Naiparna nga mangmangankayon idi immayak. It happened that you were eating at the time that I came.

parnéb: (f. *rennéb*) iparneb. *v.* to sink something, plunge something in the water, submerge. [Tag. *lubóg*]

parnuáy: *n.* invention, creation. (*partuat*) agparnuay. *v.* to create; invent. managparnuay. *a.* creative; imaginative. parnuayen. *v.* to bring about; produce; cause to be; be the author of. parparnuay. *a.* imaginary; *n.* fiction; fantasy. Naparnuay ti sayangguseng idi agangay. Rumors were created as a result. [Tag. *likhâ*]

parngéd: iparnged. *v.* to tie (an animal). (*galut*) nakaparnged. *a.* tied. [Tag. *talì*]

paró: paroparo, paparo. *n.* a kind of butterfly (*kulibangbang*). [Tag. *paroparó* = butterfly]

paruá: *n. Pinus insularis.* a kind of pine with white timber.

paruád: see *parawad*: contribution (to a wedding, etc.); in old times, the gift was given in exchange for a drink offered by the newlyweds. iparuad. *v.* to give as a gift in a wedding. paruadan. *v.* to give a gift to a married couple.

parudípad: *n.* ledge of a table; *var.* of *paradipad*. agparudipad. *v.* to walk without direction.

paródia: (Sp. *parodia*: parody) *n.* parody, humorous imitation or a play or writing.

párog: parogparog. *n.* fruit of the *libas* (*Momordica ovata*).

parugróg: (*obs.*) *n.* cornering with questions. parugrugen. *v.* to question relentlessly; drill with questions. [Tag. *usisà*]

parókia: (Sp. *parroquía*: parish) *n.* church parish.

parokiáno: (Sp. *parroquiano*: regular customer) *n.* customer; client; parishioner.

paróko: (Sp. *párroco*: parish priest) *n.* parishioner; parish priest.

parukmá: (f. *rukmá*) parukmáen. *v.* to defeat, overcome, vanquish. (*parmek*) maparukma. *v.* to be defeated; vanquished; subjugated. [Tag. *talo*]

parukpók: *n.* rapids. agparukpok. *v.* to spill out; issue forth. iparukpok. *v.* to spill (blood for one's country). maiparukpok. *v.* to be spilled (blood). pumarukpok. *v.* to bubble (liquids squirting out of source). Addanto latta dara a maiparukpok. Blood will flow. [Tag. *agos*]

paról₁: (Sp. *farol*: lantern) *n.* lantern; street lamp.

paról₂: (Eng.) *n.* parole. naparolan. *a.* granted parole.

paróla: (Sp. *farola*: street lamp) *n.* lighthouse; large street lamp. parolero. *n.* lighthouse keeper; maker or seller of lanterns.

parunápin: *n. Tarrietia sylvatica.* A tree with hard timber used to make cart wheels.

paronápon: *a.* sterile, barren; unproductive. [Tag. *tigáng*]

paronápor: see *paronapon*: sterile, barren.

parungbó₁: **naiparungbo.** *a.* first class, prime, excellent, choice; elegant; beautiful. (*darisay*) **naimparungbuan.** *a.* blessed; favored. [Tag. *gandá*]

parungbó₂: **agparungbo.** *v.* to make a forced landing (due to bad weather).

parós: (*obs.*) *n.* sudden consumption.

parusápis: *n.* sound of splashing. (*rissibok*)

parusísi: **agparusisi.** *v.* to sway, totter; scatter everywhere. **maiparusisi.** *v.* to sway; be scattered in all directions. **naparusisi.** *a.* fallen down by a blow, staggering. [Tag. *suray*]

párut: **agparut.** *v.* to shed hair or feathers. **paruten.** *v.* to pull up; uproot (*pag-ut*); pluck (feathers); extract; pull out gray hairs. **ag-paparut.** *v.* to have one's tooth extracted. **Nagrupanget a nangil-ilut iti patongna ken nagparut kadagiti siit.** He contorted his face as he massaged his hip and extracted the thorns. [Png. *bagot*, Tag. *bunot*]

parutpót: *n.* sound of ammunition, report of a gun. **parutputen.** *v.* to shoot.

pároy₁: **naparoy.** *a.* inclined, lopsided.

pároy₂: *n.* haggler. (*tawar*) **paruyen.** *v.* to buy at a bargain. [Tag. *barát* (Sp.)]

par-úyog: **agpar-uyog.** *v.* to bend; lean, incline. (*tingíg*)

parpár: *a.* smashed, crushed, splintered. **na-parpar.** *a.* smashed, crushed; splintered; split. **parparen.** *v.* to smash, crush. **maparparan.** *v.* to be smashed, crushed. **naparpar a kara-bukob.** *n.* sore throat. [Tag. *sipák*]

parpó: (*obs.*) *n.* abandoned field.

parsá: *n.* a kind of bamboo scaffold used to support vines, trellis. [Tag. *balag*]

parsát: *n.* measure of ten days. **sangaparsat.** *n.* ten days. **parsatan.** *v.* to give the allowance of ten days.

parséd: *a.* vertical, perpendicular; steep. **pu-marsed.** *v.* to become steep. [Tag. *taník*]

parsék: **agparsek, parsekan.** *v.* to bore holes in the ground for planting seeds.

parséla: (Sp. *parcela*: parcel) *n.* parcel of land. (*lote*)

parsiák: **parsiákan.** *v.* to sprinkle, splatter; spray, splash. **maparsiákan.** *v.* to be sprinkled, splattered, sprayed. **iparsiak.** *v.* to sprinkle, splash, splatter on. [Png. *polasí*, Tag. *tilamsík*]

parsiál: (Sp. *parcial*: partial) *a.* partial; favoring one side.

parsiát: **agparsiat.** *v.* to break; splinter; chip (*barsiák*). [Tag. *pingas*]

parsibók: (f. *rissibok*) **agparsibok.** *v.* to splash in the water; jump in the water with a splash. **Nagparsibok dagiti poka manipud kadagiti pagdungdungsaanda nga agtatapaw a yelo.** The seals jumped in the water from the peaks of ice they were resting on.

parsík: (originally f. *rissik*, but may be analyzed as a simple root now, because of the pronunciation *parsíken* by certain speakers) *n.* over-measure of gratuity. **agparparsik.** *v.* to stir; move to and fro (fish). **parsíken** (or **parsikén**). *v.* to fry quickly in lard; till soil. **maparsik.** *v.* to puff up (fried corn).

parsuá: (f. *russua*) *n.* creation. (*lettuat*) **mamar-sua.** *n.* creator; God. **parsuáen.** *v.* to create. **nakaparsuáan.** *n.* nature; creation; *a.* natural. **pinaparsua.** *a.* created by the imagination. [Kpm. *lálang*, Png. *palsá*, Tag. *likhâ*]

partáan₁: *n.* inspiration; omen; premonition. **agpartaan.** *v.* to manifest in the form of a ghost. **ipartaan.** *v.* to inspire; advise, counsel; communicate with the spirit; forebode. **mai-partaan.** *v.* to be revealed in a mysterious way. [Kal. *abig*, *paliyaw*, Tag. *salagimsím*]

partáan₂: *n.* kind of vine with medicinal bark.

partáang: *var.* of *partaan*.

parták: *n.* speed. **napartak.** *a.* fast; nimble, quick, active, agile; beautiful. (*pardas*, *paspas*) **pumartak.** *v.* to gather speed; hurry up. **maipartak.** *v.* to be startled when awakening. **papartáken.** *v.* to make something faster, speed up something or someone. [Ibg. *mábiq*, Png. *pelés*, *siglát*, Tag. *bilís*]

párte: (Sp. *parte*: part) *n.* part, portion (*paset*); share; zone. **partek.** my turn. **partes.** (*legal*) relatives. **de-parte.** *n.* tract of land.

parténg: *n.* line of string, cord, etc. used to make straight roads, fences, etc. **partengan.** *v.* to put a line or cord on. (*banténg*)

partéra: (Sp. *partera*: midwife) *n.* unlicensed midwife.

partí: **agparti, partien.** *v.* to slaughter an animal. **mammarti.** *n.* butcher. **pagpartian.** *n.* slaughter house. **makiparti.** *v.* to help in slaughtering an animal. **Nagpartiak iti manok a nagsag-pawan iti bulong ti marunggay.** I slaughtered a chicken to use as broth with horseradish leaves. [Png. *labák*, Tag. *lapà*, *katay*]

partída: (Sp. *partida*: departure; certificate; shipment; lot) *n.* group of things taken at once, lot; certificate; margin, edge or advantage given at a race; advantage in sports; departure. **agpartida.** *v.* to buy something regardless of number, size, or quality. **pumartida.** *v.* to give or have an advantage.

partidário: (Sp.) *n.* partisan.

partidísta: (Sp. *partidista*: party member) *n.* Party member (of a political party) **Patgek a kapartiduak.** My dear fellow party member.

partído: (Sp. *partido*: political party) *n.* political party; relative (*kabagian*); *a.* parted; divided. **panagpartido.** *n.* relationship. **agkakapartido.** *v.* to belong to the same political party; to be relatives. **sangapartiduan.** *n.* the whole party; the whole group of relatives.

partidór: (f. *parti*) *n.* butcher; divider; cleaver; divisor.

partisáno: (Eng.; Sp. = *partidista*) *n.* partisan.

partisipár: (Sp. *participar*) **makipartisipar.** *v.* to participate.

partisípio: (Sp. *participio*) *n.* participle.

partuát₁: *n.* invention; product. (*parnuay, russua, taud; lettuad*) **mammartuat.** *n.* inventor; manufacturer; creator. **partuaten.** *v.* to invent; create; produce. **panagpartuat.** *n.* manufacture; creation; invention. **pagpartuatan.** *n.* factory, place of manufacturing. [Tag. *gawâ*]

partuát₂: *n.* spool; bobbin.

partúok: (f. *rittók*) **partuóken.** *v.* to cause to make a crackling sound, crack the joints.

parwád: *var.* of *parawad*: wedding ritual in which money is given to the newlyweds.

paryá: *var.* Tagalicized spelling of *paria*: bittermelon.

pása: (Sp. *pasa*: pass) *n.* quoit. **ipasa.** *v.* to pass the ball; pass on, transmit. **makapasa.** *v.* to be able to pass. **pasa-pasa.** *n.* relay. **pinnasa.** *n.* mutual settlement of debts.

pasabéng: *n.* cloth fence at sea used to catch fish.

pasablóg: (f. *sablóg*) *n.* trap; flattery (*lamióng*). **pasablugan.** *v.* to trap; catch fish with poison; irrigate for a short time or with a small quantity of water. **Didak man paspasablogan.** Please don't flatter me. [Tag. *hibok, hibò* (flattery)]

pasáda: (Sp. *pasada*: passage) *n.* rehearsal, practice run; reviewing of a paper or manuscript; regular route of a passenger vehicle. **agpasada.** *v.* to run a routine trip; review a manuscript, go over a piece of work. **nakapasada.** *a.* in operation (passenger vehicle).

pasadáan: (f. *pasáda*) *n.* earnings for a specific length of time. **mapasadasan.** *n.* what one earned for a specific length of time.

pasádo: (Sp. *pasado*: past; passed) *a.* former; past; qualified; approved, passed.

pasadóble: (Sp. *pasa*: pass + *doble*: double) **pasadoblean.** *v.* to tie around for the second time.

pasadór: (Sp. *pasador*: brooch; fastener) *n.* sanitary napkin; moistening rug used for ironing. **pasaduran.** *v.* to moisten clothes while ironing. **agpasador.** *v.* to use a sanitary napkin.

pásag: *n.* (*reg.*) ridgepole, rafter. **ipasag.** *v.* to throw down; tumble; precipitate; knock down. **pasagen.** *v.* to through someone down; (*fig.*) kill. **mapasag.** *v.* to fall suddenly, tumble down. **pagpasagan.** *v.* to fall on, to drop on; *n.* something that one will give their life for. **napasag.** *a.* thrown down. [Tag. *hulog, lugmók*]

pasagád: *n.* sled, sledge (*ulnas*). **ipasagad.** *v.* to transport a load on a sled. [Ivt. *tangkal*, Tag. *paragos, dagos*]

pasági: *n.* square.

paságid: (f. *ságid*) *n.* insinuation; implication; indirect talking; *a.* square.

pasáhe: (Sp. *pasaje*: fare) *n.* passage; fare. (*plete*)

pasahéro: (Sp. *pasajero*: passenger) *n.* passenger. **pangpasahero nga eroplano.** *n.* passenger airplane, commercial aircraft.

pasakálie: (Sp. *pasacalle*: lively march) *n.* musical accompaniment. **agpasakalie.** *v.* to sing backup vocals, accompany with music. **Pinasakaliannak.** He backed me up singing. **Mapaspasakalyen ti gitara dagiti babbaro iti laem.** The young boys inside accompanied the guitar.

pasakí: *n.* lap dog.

pasakuáti: *var.* of *kakawate*: the *madre cacao* tree.

pasaktán: (f. *sakit*) *v.* to hurt someone, to hurt one's feelings. **Saanmo a paspasaktan ti inak.** Do not hurt my mother's feelings.

pasálap: *n.* (*obs.*) bride price. (*sab-ung*)

pasalí: **agpaspasali.** *v.* to walk to and fro.

pasalíso: *n.* principal part of a native house, living room. (*laem; salas*)

pasámak: (f. *sámak*) *n.* event, happening; incident. (*pagteng*) **mapasamak.** *v.* to happen; occur. **Ania ti mapaspasamakmon?** What is happening to you? [Tag. *yari*]

pasámáno: (Sp. *pasamano*: handrail) *n.* handshake; handrail; windowsill. **agpasamano.** *v.* to shake hands. (*alamano*)

pasámános: (Sp. *pasamanar*: trim with lace) *obs. n.* lace.

pásang: *n.* counterpart, match. (*asmang, pada*) **agkapasang.** *v.* to form a pair, to match. **ipasang.** *v.* to substitute, give in exchange; transfer; endorse. **kaipasangan ti.** *prep.* in exchange for. [Tag. *palít* (exchange)]

pasangá: *n.* forked handle of the slingshot. [Tag. *hawakan*]

pasángan: (*obs.*) *n.* leaving out of sight what one is guarding.

pasápas: *n.* grass cuttings. pasapasen. *v.* to clear the land, cut down trees (*púkan*). mamaspasapas. *v.* to gesticulate (in anger).

pasaplák: (f. *saplák*) *n.* outrigger. [Kpm. *katig*, Png. *kasig*, Tag. *katig, batangan*]

pasapórte: (Sp. *pasaporte*: passport) *n.* passport.

pasár: (Sp. *pasar*: pass) agpasar. *v.* to undergo, experience; pass; eat. paspasaran. *v.* to do by chance. mapasaran. *v.* to undergo; experience. ipasar. *v.* to consider; think. Ipasarko nga awan patpategna. I think it has no value. Paspasarak ti immay. I came by chance.

pasaráy: *adv.* occasionally, sometimes, now and then, from time to time. paspasaray. *adv.* seldom. Pasaray agik-ikkis dagiti agbuybuya a pangipakitada iti panagdayawda kadagiti kandidata. Now and then the spectators screamed to show their support of the candidates. [Tag. *paminsan-minsán*]

pasariw-át: *var.* of *pasiraw-át*: ring finger. [Png. *pangánsi*, Tag. *palasingsingan*]

pasarunsón: *n.* something eaten after something else.

pasar-tiémpo: (Sp. *pasar* 'spend' + *tiempo* 'time') *n.* pastime, means of spending one's time. (*pasatiémpo*)

pásas: (Sp. *pasa*: raisin) *n.* raisin.

pásat: *n.* permanent injury. napasatan. *a.* injured permanently.

pásat: *n.* wedge. (*sanat, tingal*) pasatan. *v.* to wedge. [Tag. *kalang*]

pasatiémpo: (Sp. *pasatiempo*: pastime) *n.* pastime; amusement, diversion.

pásaw: *n.* braggart. agpaspasaw. *v.* to boast, brag; exaggerate; fib. napasaw. *a.* vain, boastful. pinapasaw. *n.* exaggeration. Ti sao ti pasaw, uray pudno ubbaw. *exp.* A liar is not believed even if he speaks the truth. [Tag. *yabang*]

pasayák: *n.* irrigation; drainage ditch. mapasayakan. *v.* to be irrigated. No malpas ti penned, rinibu nga ektaria a kataltalonan ti mapasayakan. When the dike is finished, one thousand hectares of fields will be irrigated. [Tag. *patubig*]

pasáyan₁: *n.* shrimp; prawn. pimmasayan. *a.* like a shrimp. [Ibg. *lasiq*, Itg. *udang*, Ivt. *ipun*, *ipitpit*, Kpm. *páro*, Png. *oráng*, Tag. *hipon*]

pasáyan₂: paspasayan. *n.* a kind of small aquatic stinging bug; the top of young shoots (*uggot*).

pasáyan₃: pimmasayan. *n.* species of long green pepper.

pasbáng: (f. *sebbáng*) *n.* a kind of snare for quails.

pasdék: *n.* building; institution. maipasdek. *v.* to stick in the ground; to be built; to be organized. ipasdek. *v.* to fix something in the ground; erect a building. pangipasdekan. *n.* site for a new building; organization. naipasdek nga orden. *n.* established order. [Tag. *gusalì* (building)]

pasdíl: ipasdil. *v.* to substitute, to put in the place of another; to work in place of another (*talali, sandi*). [Tag. *halili*]

pasdók: napasdok. *a.* steep, tall, elevated (*rasdák, táyag*). [Tag. *tarík*]

pasék: *n.* a kind of hearth or stove enclosed in boards and raised on legs (*dalikan*). ipasek. *v.* to put into the *pasek* stove. [Tag. *kalán*]

pásen: *n.* share, lot, portion. pasenen. *v.* to divide in portions. pasenan. *v.* to give a share or portion to. mapasenan. *v.* to be given a share. maipasen. *v.* to be apportioned. mapasenpasen. *v.* to be apportioned, divided. [Tag. *bahagi*]

pasénsia: (Sp. *paciencia*: patience) *n.* patience (*ánus*). pasiensiaan. *v.* to be patient with someone. napasensia. *a.* patient. [Tag. *pasensiya* (sorry; patience)]

pas-éng: *n.* smell of leftover vegetable dish or urine stains. napas-eng. *v.* to smell like leftover vegetables or urine-stained clothes.

paséo: (Sp. *paseo*: stroll) *n.* walk, promenade; drive.

páses: (Sp. *pase*: pass) *n.* pass; ticket; permit.

pasét: *n.* part; division; section; chapter; company; group. ipaset. *v.* to include. kapaset. *n.* part, division; chapter. pasempaseten. *v.* to divide in parts. (*bingay*) Paset dagita ti panagbiag. That's a part of life. Paset ti panggepko. It's a part of my plan. [Kal. *buli, bissak*, Png. *gáton, apág*, Tag. *bahagi*]

pasgá: *n.* young of the mullet fish, *Mugil sp.*

pasgár: (f. *seggár*) nakapasgar. *a.* terrified (with hair standing on end).

pasiá: pasiaen. *v.* to defeat, vanquish, overcome. (*ábak; átiw; parukmá; parmék; paksiát*)

pasiándo: (Sp. *paseando*: strolling) *n.* vagabond. (*ballóg, baliúdong*)

pasiár: (Sp. *pasear*: stroll) agpasiar. *v.* to take a walk. pagpasiaran. *n.* place to stroll, park, sights to see and enjoy. ipasiar. *v.* to take for a walk; take someone around. managpasiar, mammasiar. *v.* to be fond of strolling. [Tag. *pasyál*]

pasíbo: (Sp. *pasivo*: passive) *a.* passive; *n.* passive voice.

pasidák: pasidaken. *v.* (*obs.*) to drive away by force of arms.

pasiénsia: *var.* of *pasensia*: patience.

pasiénte: (Sp. *paciente*: patient) *n.* patient (in a hospital).

pásig₁: *a.* all; exclusively; solely; pure. **paspasig.** *a.* pure, of the same kind. **pasigen.** *v.* to do exclusively, only, purely. **Pasig a barusngi ti ammom.** What you know is all messed up. [Tag. *busilak*; *puro*]

pásig₂: agpaspasig. *v.* treat someone as a brother; to be friendly. **napasig.** *a.* friendly; close, intimate. **papasig.** *n.* familiarity, pertinacity. **pagpasigan.** *v.* to express friendship; urge persistently; *n.* person with whom one is friendly. **kapasigan.** *n.* person with whom one is friendly or affectionate.

pasíkal: *n.* labor in childbirth; labor pains. **agpaspasikal.** *v.* to be in labor, about to bear a child.

pasíkat: (Tag.) *n.* something to be proud of; boastful. **agpasikat.** *v.* to be proud of; boast.

pasikíng: *n.* knapsack, backpack. (*kaday*; *bako*) **ipasiking.** *v.* to carry in the backpack. [Kal. *pasiking, táyay*, Tag. *takuyan*]

pásil: agpasil. *v.* to compete with, contend, vie (*salísal*); persist.

pasílaw: agpasilaw. *v.* to ask a sorceress to help find a lost object through sorcery. **pasilawen.** *v.* to locate an object through sorcery.

pasilidád: (Sp. *facilidad*: facility) *n.* facility.

pasílio: (Sp. *pasillo*: hallway) *n.* hallway, hall, corridor; aisle.

pasiluág: *var.* of *basiluag*, kind of poisonous plant.

pasímad: pasimadan. *v.* to see, notice (*kita, madlaw*). **mapasimadan.** *v.* to be aware of, happen to notice, observe. **Diak napasimadan ti panagpurrasona kaniak ket naiparusisiak iti suli.** I didn't notice his striking me and I stumbled in the corner. [Tag. *pansín*]

pasimbáliw: see *pasumbaliw*: to vary; diversify.

pasimudáag: ipasimudaag. *v.* to show; reveal (one's true character); announce; declare. [Tag. *pahayag*]

pasinatnát: pasinatnatan. *v.* to follow up.

pasindámag: (*obs.*) *a.* proudly disrespectful.

pasindayág: *a.* boastful, vain, conceited. **agpasindayag.** *v.* to boast, brag; be vain, boastful, pretentious (*pasindayaw, lastog*). **napasindayag.** *a.* vain, conceited, boastful. **kinapasindayag.** *n.* vanity; conceit. **ipasindayag.** *v.* to be proud of. **Sipapasindayag ni Pipay a nangipakita iti singsingna.** Pipay proudly showed her ring. [Tag. *yabang, palalò*]

pasindáyaw: agpasindayaw. *v.* to boast, brag; be vain; conceited; wanting admiration (*pasindayag, lastog*). **napasindayaw.** *a.* vain, conceited, boastful. **ipasindayaw.** *v.* to be proud of. [Tag. *palalò*]

pasinúnod: ipasinunod. *v.* to submit to, yield; comply with; consent to, agree (*anamong*); permit (*palubos*); prove (*paneknek*); establish (by testimony). **napasinunod.** *a.* complying; yielding, submitting. [Tag. *sang-ayon*]

pasíngil: *n.* swelling in the neck; scrofula. **agpasingil.** *v.* to have a swelling in the neck.

pasingkéd: *n.* trust; assurance of protection; receipt for a debt. **ipasingked.** *v.* to ensure that a promise will be fulfilled. **pasingkedan.** *v.* to give property as collateral for a debt. **papasingkedan.** *v.* to require collateral for a debt. [Tag. *patiyák*]

pasión: (Sp.) *n.* passion; a kind of flower.

pasípi: *n.* room (*siled*; *kuarto*). [Tag. *silíd*]

Pasípiko: (Sp. *Pacífico*: Pacific) *n.* Pacific Ocean.

pásir: pasiren. *v.* to look at by shading the eyes. **ipasir.** *v.* to put up to the light; change the position of something to avoid reflecting too much light. **maipasir.** *v.* to be able to distinguish, discern, see at a distance; to be put up to the light. **mapasir.** *v.* to be dazzled; to be able to discern. **maipaspasir.** *v.* to become visible; to be seen through (gauzy material). **Maipaspasir ti luppona idiay seda a pandilingna.** Her thigh is visible through her silk skirt.

pas-íraw: maipaspas-iraw. *v.* to sway; totter when walking. (*basíng*) **Maipaspas-iraw a bimmangon.** He woke up tottering. [Tag. *suray*]

pasiraw-át: *n.* ring finger. [Png. *pangánsi*, Tag. *palasingsingan*]

pasirót: (f. *sirot*) **pasirutan.** *v.* to fasten, tie a knot.

pasísta: (Sp. *fascista*) *n.*, *a.* fascist.

paskád: see *sekkad*.

paskén: *n.* party; event; occasion; anniversary. (*padaya*) **agpasken.** *v.* to host a party; *n.* host of a party.

paskíl: (Sp. *pasquín*: lampoon) *n.* notice; poster; advertisement. **agpaskil.** *v.* to advertise; post up. **nakapaskil.** *a.* advertised, posted. [Tag. *patalastás*]

paskín: *var.* of *paskil*: post up.

Páskua: (Sp. *pascua*: Easter) *n.* Christmas; Easter; feast; Epiphany. **ag-Paskua.** *v.* to celebrate Christmas or Easter. **ipapaskua.** *v.* to give a Christmas gift. **makipaskua.** *v.* to spend Christmas at a place. **makipaspaskua.** *v.* to go

Christmas caroling. **pagpaskuaan.** *n.* Christmas things. **ayug-Paskua.** *n.* Christmas cheer. [Png., Tag. *Paskó*]

paskuás: (Sp. *pascuas*: Christmas) *n.* poinsettia. [Kpm. *depáskua*]

paslád: (f. *sellád*) **agpaslad.** *v.* to pull at the finished part of a basket while weaving to make it tighter and wider at the bottom.

pasláng: **ipaslang.** *v.* to display, serve, lay out; receive a guest. **Naipakni dagiti lamisaan a pakaipaslangan ti merienda.** The tables where the snacks were served were put aside.

paslép: *n.* steel. **pimmaslep.** *a.* hard as steel. **Pimmaslep ti nakemna.** He has a mind as hard as steel. [Png. *balátyang*, Tag. *bakal*]

paslóng: (var. of *pasláng*) **ipaslong.** *v.* to put in, insert; (*obs.*) receive a guest. **Paipaslongna dagiti ugsa iti desdes.** He had the deer fall in a trench in the path.

pasmá: (Sp. *pasmo*: spasm) **mapasma.** *v.* to relapse (a sickness); catch a cold (usually by exposure to a cold temperature).

pasmádo: (f. *pasma*) *a.* sick due to the cold, rain, or intense activity.

pasmók: *n.* something hidden to be used later, cache.

pasnáan: *n.* anvil (*paksó*). [Tag. *palihán*]

pásnek: (f. *sennék*) **napasnek.** *a.* fervent; passionate; intense; willing; dedicated, ardent; serious. **kinapasnek.** *n.* sincerity; devotion; dedication; seriousness. **ipasnek.** *v.* to do fervently, passionately. **naimpasnekan.** *a.* sincere; ardent. **sipapasnek.** *a.* sincerely; devotedly, attentively. **ipasnekmo ti agadal.** Study all you can. **Sipapasnekda a dumdumngeg.** They listened attentively. **Kellaat a pimmasnek ti timekna.** His voice suddenly became passionate. [Tag. *dubdób*]

pasníir: **ipasniir.** *v.* to air, air out; dry in the shade.

pasnít: *n.* alternative name for the *kagpaayan* tree.

pasngát: (f. *sengngát*) **pasngatan.** *v.* to place in between.

pasngáw: (f. *sengngáw*) *n.* drainage, sluice gate, emitted vapor. **pasngawan.** *v.* to cook by steam; vaporize.

pasngáy: (f. *sengngáy*, should be considered a simple root because of stress patterns of derivatives such as *pakaipasngáyan* and *nangipasngáyan*) *n.* creation, product, invention. **agpasngay.** *v.* to give birth. **ipasngay.** *v.* to give birth to; create; bring forth. **maipasngay.** *v.* to be born. **mamasngay.** *v.* to deliver a baby. **pannakaipasngay.** *n.* birth; birthdate. **pakaipasngáyan.** *n.* place of birth. **kaippasngay.** *n.*

newborn. **agkarapasngay.** *v.* to give birth often. **Adda latta kasingin a saem ti tunggal pannakaipasngay.** Every birth is accompanied by pain. [Tag. *silang*, *anák*]

páso₁: *n.* kind of large earthen pan. [Tag. *pasô* = flowerpot]

páso₂: **mapaso.** *v.* to be scalded, burnt. **pasuen.** *v.* to singe wounds (to disinfect). [Tag. *pasò*]

páso₃: (Sp. *paso*: pace) *n.* pace; horse trot. **napaso, de-paso.** *n.* ambler.

pasó₁: (Tag.) *n.* kind of large earthen jar. [Tag. *pasô* = flowerpot]

pasó₂: (Sp. *pasó*: passed) **agpaso.** *v.* to mature; expire, reach a deadline; become useless. **ipaso.** *v.* to drive into a corner. **pasuan.** *n.* deadline; finish line (in a race). **Nagpason ti pasaportena ket pabaruenna.** His passport expired, so he will renew it.

pasó₃: **pasopaso.** *n.* protuberance at the base of the neck of fat people.

pasugki: **napasugkian.** *a.* sulk, withdrawn in disgust (*pasugnod*). [Tag. *tampó*]

pasugnód: *n.* grudge; resentment; emotional hurt. **agpasugnod.** *v.* to show resentment or displeasure; sulk. **managpasugnod.** *a.* always sulking; overly sensitive. **napasugnodan.** *a.* disappointed; disgusted, displeased. **Nagpinnasugnodkami.** We resented each other. [Tag. *tampó, hinanakít*]

pások₁: *n.* stake. **ipasok.** *v.* to drive into the ground; stake. [Tag. *tulos*]

pások₂: *n.* baby's ability to stand by himself. **agpasok.** *v.* to take the first steps (babies).

pasuksók: *n.* bribe. (*soborno*) **agpasuksok.** *v.* to bribe. **ipasuksok.** *v.* to use to bribe someone. [Kpm. *suhul*, Png. *pakep, pakepkep*, Tag. *suhol, lagáy, pabagsak*]

pasúli: (f. *súli*: corner) *n.* triangular piece of timber used instead of the *pokló* as an angle brace.

pasumbáliw: **ipasumbaliw.** *v.* to vary, diversify. **paspasumbaliwan.** *v.* to affect with various things (diseases, etc.)

pasúngad: *n.* act of waiting for someone. **agpasungad.** *v.* to wait for someone's arrival.

pasóngo: (f. *songo*: snout) *n.* short piece of rope attached to the nose of a *nuang*.

pasúot: (f. *suot*) **mapasuot.** *v.* to consent, agree, yield to; hide in bed. **maipasuot.** *v.* (Pil.) to find oneself in a very embarrassing situation; to be caught in a predicament.

pasúrot: (f. *surot*) *n.* follower; supporter. [Png. *alagar*, Tag. *alagád, kampón*]

pásot₁: **agpasot, pasuten.** *v.* to take off one's clothes or shoes.

pásot₂: **papasuten.** *n.* the *gagabuten* grass.

paspás₁: (Tag. also) **paspasan**. *v*. to do quickly. (*pardas*; *partak*) **napaspas**. *a*. quick. [Kal. *kakma*, *cheÿson*, *uway*]

paspás₂: **ipaspasan**. *v*. to avenge on an innocent person. (*bales*)

paspás₃: **agpaspas**. *v*. to fade, discolor. (*kúpas*; *uspák*)

passiáw: see *parassiaw*: splatter; splash.

pásta: (Sp. *pasta*: paste; plaster) *n*. paste; tooth filling; plaster. **pastaan**. *v*. to paste; cover with plaster.

pastél: (Sp. *pastel*: pie; pastry) *n*. pie; pastry; pastel; (*printing*) disarranged types out of case.

pastelería: (Sp. *pastelería*: pastry shop) *n*. pastry shop.

pasterisádo: (Sp.) *a*. pasteurized.

pastidiár: (Sp. *fastidiar*: annoy, irritate) **pastidiaren**. *v*. to downgrade; annoy; do to excess (usually resulting in hardship).

pastílias: (Sp. *pastilla*: tablet, pill) *n*. tablet; kind of pastry, pastille. **pastilias de leche**. kind of powdery candy made of eggs, milk, margarine, and sugar.

pásto: (Sp. *pasto*: pasture) *n*. pasture; ranch; homestead; grazing land. **pagpastuan**. *n*. ranch; grazing land.

pastoléro: *var*. of *pastorero*: shepherd.

pastudiár: *var*. of *pastidiar*.

pastór: (Sp. *pastor*: pastor) *n*. shepherd; Protestant minister. **agpastor**. *v*. to take pasture sheep. **agpastor**. *v*. to study to be a minister. **pastoren**. *v*. to pasture an animal. **pagpasturan**. *n*. grazing field. **pumapastor**. *n*. sheep herder. [Tag. *pastól*]

pastoréro: (f. *pastór*) *n*. shepherd.

pastrék: (f. *serrék*) **ipastrek**. *v*. to have (someone) enter. **mapastrek**. *n*. income; earnings. **pastreken**. *v*. to invite someone in. **pamastrekan**. *n*. business; source of income. [Tag. *pasok*]

paswít: (Tagalog also) **agpaswit**. *v*. to whistle (*sultip*, *silbato*). [Kal. *maletip*]

pasyár: see *pasiár*: to go for a walk; stroll.

-pat: *var*. of *uppat* after certain prefixes: four. **maikapat**. *num*. fourth. **saggapat**. four each. **sinagpapat**. *n*. consisting of four strands twisted together. **mamimpat**. four times. **sagpamimpat**. four times each.

páta: *n*. light wood. [Tag. *pata* = kind of game played with wooden blocks]

patá: *n*. bone marrow. [Ibg. *uráng*, Knk. *bútag*, Tag. *utak sa butó*, Tag. *patâ* = fatigued]

patáan: *n*. allowance; extension. (*pawayway*) **pataanan**. *v*. to give an allowance or extension. [Tag. *pataán*]

pátad₁: *n*. plain; lowland; level land. **pataden**. *v*. to level ground. **tagapatad**. *n*. lowlander. [Kal. *talap*, Tag. *patag*]

pátad₂: **kapatadan**. *n*. peer, equal (*páda*); contemporary. **agkakapatad**. *v*. to be equal; to be the same (in height, etc.).

pátag: *n*. plain, level ground. **patagen**. *v*. to level (*patad*). **No medio patag ti dagayo, agmulakayo iti papaya**. If your land is somewhat level, plant papaya trees. [Tag. *patag*]

patagguáb: *n*. appendage to a house; extension of a roof. [Tag. *sibi*]

paták₁: *n*. raindrop. **agpatak**. *v*. to become obvious; to be evident. **napatak**. *a*. plain, clear, evident, obvious. **Inagawak ti simmang-at ta napatak ti paglinlingedanmi**. I tried hard to climb up because the place were we were hiding was easily visible. [Tag. *liwanag* (clear)]

paták₂: **patakpatak** (*obs*.) *n*. writhing when whipped.

patákad: *n*. conjugal property.

patál: (Eng.) *a*. fatal, deadly. (*makapatay*)

pataluntón: *n*. children's running and catching game. (*sampedro*) **agpalunton**. *v*. to take to the center line in the game of *patalunton*.

patáni: *n*. *Phaseolus lunatus*, lima bean. **Nangrugi ti gerra ti patani ken marunggay**. The fight broke out (the war between the lima bean and horseradish started). [Png. *pagdá*, Tag. *patanì*]

patánor: *n*. invention; design for a stained-glass window; native; someone brought up by foster parents.

patáng₁: *n*. conversation. (*tungtung*) **agpatang**. *v*. to talk idly; converse. **makipatang**. *v*. to converse. **pagpapatangan**. *n*. subject of a conversation. **Masapol a makapatangna dagiti annakna maipapan iti pangngeddengna**. He needs to talk to his children about his decisions. [Tag. *usap*]

patáng₂: **patpatangen**. *v*. to calculate, estimate, compute; guess. **patangan**. *v*. to guess, surmise.

patáng₃: **maipatang**. *v*. to happen occur, come to pass. **Naipatang nga . . .** It happened that . . .

patápat: *n*. bind, binding; binding strip wrapped around women who have just given birth to help them control their gait and to restore the pelvic bones. **patapaten**. *v*. to place a bandage; tie around. **pangpatapat**. *n*. something that binds together. **Masapol met ti anak a mangpatapat iti patempateg**. A child is necessary to bind together mutual affection (is the link to a loving family). [Tag. *gapos*]

patapáw: *n*. floater; buoy. [Tag. *palutang*]

patapáya: *n*. outermost of the two major beams that support the walls of the house.

pátar: *n.* starting point for a race; level. **patar ti baybay.** *n.* sea level. **pataren.** *v.* to level; flatten. **napatar.** *a.* flat; level. **saan a makapatar.** *v.* to be able to equal. (*saan a makapada*)

pataránta: (*coll.*) **agua pataranta.** *n.* liquor.

patarék: **pinatarék.** *n.* delicacy made of molded *diket*, banana, *tugí, sagó,* sugar, and coconut milk. (*padarusdós*)

patároy: see *tagapulot*: molasses; sugar syrup. **pumapataroy.** *v.* to become syrupy. [Tag. *pulót*]

pátas: (Sp. *pata*: leg) *n.* the same, equal. (*pareho, páda*) **agpatas.** *v.* to be the same, equal, equivalent. **panagpapatas.** *n.* equality. **Dandani agpatas ti timbangda iti pusok.** They are almost of equal weight in my heart. [Tag. *patas* = tie, draw (in a game)]

patátas: (Sp. *patata*: potato) *n.* potato.

pátaw₁: *n.* buoy; float; anchor; (*fig.*) anything used for support in times of danger; the person held responsible for a mistake made while someone else is in charge. **pataw-lakí.** *n.* cuttlebone. **agpataw.** *v.* to swim by using a flotation device. **pagpatawan.** *n.* buoy, something used to keep afloat. [Tag. *palutong* (buoy)]

pátaw₂: **ipataw.** *v.* to announce judicially, pass a sentence; levy (a fine); impose (a command). **No patawanyo ni Nikolaus iti pannusa a kasdiay, ania ti maganabyo?** If you impose on Nikolaus a punishment like that, what do you have to gain? [Tag. *pataw*]

pátay: *n.* stand, support. **ipatay.** *v.* to set on a support; to place on; pronounce sentence, decree; convict. **patayan.** *v.* to support with something. **pangipatayan.** *n.* support; rest. [Tag. *tukod*]

patáy: *n.* death. (*púsay*) **patayen.** *v.* to kill; turn of, extinguish (*iddép*). **ipatay.** *v.* to die of (cause). **kapatpatay.** *v.* to have just died. **matay.** *v.* to die; become extinct (*pumúsay*); stop (functioning) **natay.** *a.* dead, defunct. *n.* the dead. **natayán.** *n.* place where a dead person is; (*reg.*) bereaved family. **minatay.** *n.* corpse. **mammapatay.** *v.* to kill, slaughter. **mapapátay.** *v.* to be put to death. **agimpapatay.** *v.* to pretend to be dead. **agpatay.** *v.* to die; work to death, faint. **agpakamatay.** *v.* to commit suicide. **arimpatayén.** *v.* to be on the verge of death. **agpapatay.** *v.* to commit suicide. **pakatayán.** *n.* place where one dies; cause of one's death. **panagpatáy.** *n.* mortality. **pannakapatay, pannakakatay.** *n.* death. **ipapatay.** *n.* death. **panagpapatay.** *n.* suicide. **pannakapapatay.**

n. murderer. **pammapátay.** *n.* massacre; murder. **pamatay.** *n.* instrument for killing. **papatáy.** *n.* hiring someone to kill another; *v.* to have a person killed. **pinnatayan.** *n.* killing each other; violence. **papapátay.** *v.* to have someone killed. **pataypatay.** *a.* slowfoot; weak; moribund; slow in courting. **apagpatay.** *v.* just died; *a.* lukewarm (water). **Kapappapátayna.** He just killed someone. **Patay a patay kenkuana.** He is really in love with her. **Napigsa ti pakinakemko a makalasatak iti ania man a pakatayan ti gubat.** I had a strong will to survive any confrontations with death in the war. [Bon. *patey*, Ibg. *patay*, Ivt. *diman*, Kpm. *paten*, Png. *patey, doót* (kill), Tag. *patáy*]

patduyuán: *n.* to blame, accuse (*pabasolan*). [Tag. *isisi*]

patég: *n.* price, worth, value; (*reg.*) relative. **napateg.** *a.* precious, dear. **agkapateg.** *v.* to be equally valuable, important. **ipateg.** *v.* to value; cherish; appreciate. **patgan.** *v.* to appraise, estimate the value of; esteem, prize; consider; heed, mind. **patgen.** *v.* to treasure, esteem; prize; cherish. **agpinnateg.** *v.* to love one another. **manangipateg.** *a.* loving; generous; affectionate; thoughtful. **tagipatgen.** *v.* to esteem, value. **magankapatég?** What is the value? **pammateg.** *n.* love; affection; care; value; interest. **patempateg.** *n.* affection, mutual love. **Adda napateg unay a pagsaritaanta.** You and I have a very important matter to discuss. [Png. *kakanaan*, Tag. *mahál, halagá*]

paték: **patpatek.** (*obs.*) *n.* gilding of teeth.

paténa: (Sp.) *n.* paten, patina.

paténte: (Sp. *patente*: patent) *n.* patent; recorded right of ownership. **patentado.** *a.* patented.

patentéro: *var.* of *patintero*: children's tag game consisting of four squares. (*serbéb*)

patgén: (f. *pateg*) *v.* to treasure; value; prize; cherish. [Tag. *halagá*]

páti: **patien.** *v.* to believe; mind. **mamati.** *v.* to believe. **mammati, manamati.** *n.* believer. **managpati.** *a.* gullible, believing everything. **pammati.** *n.* faith; belief; superstition. **ipapati.** *v.* to convince of; to believe without reservations. **pamatian.** *n.* reason for believing. **pamatien.** *v.* to convince; persuade. [Ivt. *anuhed*, Kal. *pati*, Png. *sísia*, Tag. *paniwalà, tiwalà*]

páti: **ipapati.** *v.* to do seriously; do to one's utmost.

patí: (Tag. also) *prep.* together with, and also. (*ken; agraman*)

patiám: *n.* pledge of betrothal. **agpatiam.** *v.* to plan out the wedding.

pátid: patiden. v. to kick sideways; trip someone with the foot (*piddawil*). [Tag. *patid* (stumble)]

patíg: (Eng. fatigue) n. olive green color of soldier's uniforms; n. fatigues.

patigmáan: n. advice, counsel (*balakáden*); exhortation. **pammatigmaan.** n. counsel; advice. **patigmaanan.** v. to advise. **Timmibker ti riknak kadagiti patigmaanna.** My feelings strengthened from his advice. [Tag. *payo*]

patík: agpatik. v. to make the sound of the heel knocking the slipper when walking; sound of a bell.

patikawkáw: n. sluggard; loafer; idler (*ballog*). **agpatpatikawkaw.** v. to talk in a roundabout way. **napatikawkaw.** a. roundabout, circuitous. [Tag. *paligoy-ligoy* (roundabout talking)]

patíl: var. of *pat-il.*

pat-íl: n. light blow; tap. **pat-ilan.** v. to tap; strike gently with a stick (*tapik*). [Tag. *pilantík*]

patilambó: n. platter. (*bandehado*) **pinnatilambo.** n. carrying someone, by having them sit on enlaced arms of two other people.

patília: (Sp. *patilla*: sideburn) n. sideburns. [Kal. *saggi*]

patillág: n. kind of insect similar to the *sílam.* **agpatillag.** v. to hop; jump. **patillagen.** v. to cause to jump.

patín: (Sp. *patín*: skate) n. skate, roller skate.

patináyon: adv. always; very often. (*kanayon*) **patinayon no.** prep. whenever.

patinuynóy: patinuynuyan. v. to condescend to, yield to the wishes of. **pampanuynuyan.** v. to spoil (a child) **mapatinuynuyan.** v. to be given all one's wishes.

patintéro: (var. of *patentéro*) n. children's tag game consisting of four squares. (*serbeb*)

patíng: n. young shark (*yo*). [Kal. *iyo*, Png., Tag. *patíng*]

patínga: n. downpayment. **patingaan.** v. to pay in advance. [Tag. *unang hulog* (downpayment)]

patinggá: n. end, conclusion (*gibus*); limit. **agpatingga.** v. to end, terminate; end up as; reach the limit. **pagpatinggaan.** n. finish line; limit; last part. **patingaan.** v. to finish; put an end to. **Awan a pulos ti panagpatpatinggayo.** You just don't know when to stop (*lit*: there is no end to your behavior). **Agpatingganto laeng a basurero ditoy.** He will just end up as a garbage collector here. [Png. *anggá*, Tag. *wakás, tapos*]

patinggí: (f. *tinggí*) var. of *patinglag, patillág*: kind of insect resembling the *silam.*

patinglág: see *patillag*: kind of grasshopper-like insect.

patingnán: n. permanent firebrand. (*atong*)

pátio: (Sp. *patio*: patio) n. patio, inner courtyard; churchyard. **agpapatio.** v. to go to the patio.

patípat: patipaten. v. to seek eagerly; solicit. (*ur-or*)

patiray-ók: n. flattery. **agpatiray-ok.** v. to urinate high and far. **agpinnatiray-ok.** v. to compete in urinating the highest and farthest. (*payod*) **patpatiray-okan.** v. to second the motion. [Tag. *hibò*]

patís: (Tag. also) n. fish sauce used in cooking. **patisen.** v. to sprinkle with fish sauce. **agpatpatis.** v. to turn into *patis*, ferment; (*fig*.) to take a long time in doing something; grow old.

pátit: n. ringing of (church, school) bells. **patiten.** v. to ring bells, sound gongs. **patitan.** v. to ring the bells for someone. **Napatit ti relo iti maysa a siled iti kanawanna a kaabay ti beranda.** The clock struck from a room to the right side of the veranda.

patiwerwér: patiwerweren. v. to sound the engine by stepping on the gas pedal. **Maayatanak nga aglang-ay, pinatiwerwerko ti inarkilami a dyip.** Enjoying amusement, I stepped on the gas pedal of our rented jeep.

patlí: n. sacrifice. **agpatli.** v. to sacrifice one's life. **ipatli.** v. to punish the innocent for; to charge the innocent with a crime.

patnág: agpatnag. v. to do the whole night. **patnagan.** v. to do something all night long. **agpatpatnag.** n. the whole night. **Nagpatnagda a naturog.** They slept the whole night. [Tag. *magdamág*]

patnéng: n. native. [Tag. *taál*]

patngá: (f. *tengnga*) **agpatnga.** v. to go to the middle.

páto₁: (Sp. *pato*: duck) n. duck. [Kal. *kamit*, Knk. *pepá*, Tag. *pato*]

páto₂: ipato. v. to pronounce (sentence); announce judicially; make known; determine; suspect; believe; suppose, assume. **agipapato.** v. to judge rashly. **managipato.** a. suspicious; presumptuous. **pangipatuan.** n. suspicion; assumption. **Bay-am ti agipato no napudot pay ta ulo.** Avoid suspecting others if you are still in a bad mood. [Tag. *akalà* (assume, believe); *hinalà, sapantahà* (suspicion)]

pátod: agpatod. v. to swim with the legs protruding from the water.

patudón: agpatudon. v. to shift the blame or burden; have someone else do one's work. (*padung*) **patudunan.** v. to designate, appoint, assign. **patudunen.** v. to have someone else do one's work for them; appoint someone to do the job. **Saanak a napatudon ken napartakak kano nga aggunggunay.** I do not have other people do my job and they say I move fast.

pátok: patokpatok. *n.* summit, top, crest; *a.* chief, principal. [Tag. *tuktók*]

patúkad: *n.* rootstocks of tubers left underground to bear fruit or beans the next season.

pátul: patulan. *v.* to dare; challenge.

patúl: *n.* person slow in doing work.

pátong: *n.* hip; side of the buttock. **nakapatpatong.** *a.* with wide buttocks. [Ivt. *sapad*, Kal. *patong*, Knk. *tiwéd*, Png. *balambáng*, Tag. *balakáng*]

patóng: patongpatong. *n.* kind of native instrument made of bamboo. [Bon. *patóng* = sit; perch]

patungánay: *n.* middle-stem tobacco leaves harvested one week after the *palaspas* leaves.

patúpat: patupat ti sinublan. *n.* a kind of rice pudding (wrapped in palm leaves). **pagpatupatan.** *n.* palm leaves used to wrap the *patupat ti sinublam.*

pátor: see *kapator.*

patútot: *n.* idleness; position of a woman in coitus; prostitute; *a.* vagrant; idle and immoral. **agpatutot.** *v.* to be a tramp. [Png, Tag. *patútot*]

patpát: *n.* parings of rattan. **patpaten.** *v.* to cut down, clear the land of trees (*pukan*). **Malpas ti ani, patpat garami.** The harvest is finished, even the hay is cut (said when nothing is left). **Patpatenka a kasla lambaan!** I'll cut you down like a banana tree!

pátria: (Sp.) *n.* fatherland. (*nakayanakan a daga*)

patriárka: (Sp. *patriarca*: patriarch) *n.* patriarch, male ruler of a family, clan, or tribe.

patrióta: (Sp. *patriota*: patriot) *n.* patriot. **patriotismo.** *n.* patriotism.

patrúlia: (Sp. *patrulla*: patrol) *n.* police patrol. **agpatrulia.** *v.* to be on patrol.

patrón: (Sp. *patrón*: patron) *n.* patron saint; patron. **patrona.** *n.* patroness. **patronato.** *n.* patronage.

patsáda: (Sp. *fachada*: façade) *n.* façade, front of a building; title page of a book; frontispiece.

patsára: (f. *sara*) *n.* a kind of locust with 'horns'. [Perhaps from *uppát a sára*: four horns]

pattá₁: *n.* skeleton or framework of a building.

pattá₂: pattapattaen. *v.* to estimate, calculate. **pammattapatta.** *n.* calculation; estimation. **Pattapattaenna a sardamton no makadanon idiay balayda.** He estimates it will be evening when he arrives at their house. [Tag. *tantiyá*]

pattáli: *n.* exchange in marriage of brothers and sisters (marriage between at least two siblings between two households); waiting for a debt of a third party to be paid before paying debt to a second party.

pattayúgan: *n.* bamboo tube used to carry water.

pattikí: *n.* a kind of bird that feeds on fish.

pattinggí: *n.* a small locust; leafhopper.

pattítek: (*obs.*) *a.* satiated. (*pennek*) **mamattitek.** *v.* to be satiated. [Tag. *bundát*]

pattíway: maipattiway. *v.* to be alone. (*bugbugtong*)

pattó: (*obs.*) **pattuen.** *v.* to castrate animals (*kapon*). [Tag. *kapón* (Sp.)]

pattóg: mapattog. *v.* to capsize, overturn, turn over. **pattugen.** *v.* to overturn; spill over; win all. **ipattog.** *v.* to pour out; empty contents by turning over. **maipattog.** *v.* to be spilled; capsized; overturned. **Napattog ti kaldero.** expression denoting having lost everything (*lit:* the pot turned over). **Saanna nga ibagbaga a nayanudda iti taaw sada napattog.** He didn't say that they drifted away at sea and then capsized. [Tag. *taób*]

pattók: napattukan. *a.* enameled, enchased; intercropped; spotted; dotted. **maipattok.** *v.* to be spotted, dotted; intercropped, interlaced, enameled, enchased. **pattukan.** *v.* to ornament with spots, etc. **pattopattukan.** *v.* to take objects from various places. [Tag. *batik* (spot)]

pattukí: *n.* kind of sled whose two shafts can be extended to serve as runners. (*pasagad*)

pattukó: see *appuko:* to straighten; corner.

pattungágan: *n.* middle finger. [Png. *pangándo*, Tag. *datò, hinlalatò*]

páwad: *a.* fingerless; (shirts) collarless, sleeveless; with only one hand. **pawaden.** (*obs.*) *v.* to lop plants; to cut off one hand; to take away one of a pair. **pawad a kamiseta.** *n.* sleeveless shirt. **pawadan.** *v.* to cut off the hand or fingers of.

páwak: *n.* dorsal fin.

páway: agpaway. *v.* to go out of the town; to be alone. **pawpaway.** *a.* solitary; alone. **pawayen.** *v.* to do all alone. [Tag. *isá*]

pawaywáy: *n.* second chance; extension; allowance. **pawaywayan.** *v.* to give another opportunity to (*pataan*). [Tag. *palugit*]

pawíkan: (Tag. also) *n.* sea turtle. [Ivt. *irang*]

páwil: ipawil. *v.* to prohibit, forbid; inhibit. (*párit*) **pawilan.** *v.* to prohibit a person; reduce, abate; restrain, hold back; underfeed. [Knk. *túbab*, atompák, Tag. *bawal*]

páwis: *n.* pinion of a bird's wing; knee of quadrupeds. [Tag. *bagwís; pawis* = sweat]

paw-ít: *n.* something sent in care of another (sent via travelers). **agpaw-it.** *v.* to request something to be sent. **ipaw-it.** *v.* to send, forward (mail); transmit. **pagpaw-itan.** *n.* messenger; one who carries *paw-it.* **Nakapanunot iti pamuspusan tapno saanen a patuloyen ti dadduma pay a kaarubada ti**

agpaw-it. I thought of a way so some other neighbors won't send things to be delivered through me. [Png. *báki*, Tag. *padalá*]

pawpáw: *n.* nest of fish or frogs in shallow water. **agpawpaw.** *v.* to wash oneself; (*orig.*) to wash the vagina by splashing (while squatting) (*kawkaw*) **pawpawan.** *v.* to wash someone.

pay: *part.* still; yet; more; also; first. **maysa pay.** one more. **Ubingka pay.** You're still young. **Awan pay.** None yet. **Ania pay?** What else? **Adda pay.** There is still some; He is still here. **Diak pay nangan.** I haven't eaten yet. **No dimo ay-ayaten, apay pay laeng a makikabbalayka kenkuana?** If you don't love him, why are you still living with him? [Bon. *daan*, Ibg. *pagá*, Knk. *abé*, Png. *ni*, Tag. *pa*]

payabyáb: (f. *yabyáb*) *n.* wide-brimmed palm hat. **nakapayabyab.** *a.* wearing a wide-brimmed palm hat. **Impalpal-idna ti payabyabna iti rupa ken barukongna.** She fanned her palm hat on her face and chest.

payák: *n.* wing. **agpayak.** *v.* to grow wings. **payakán.** *a.* winged. **nagtagipayak ti damag.** *exp.* the news grew wings and flew. [Ibg. *payaq*, Ivt. *pañid*, Kpm. *pakpak*, Kal., Png. *payák*, Tag. *pakpák*, *bagwís*]

payakpák: *n.* the sound of flapping wings (*kayabkab*, *palagapag*, *yabayag*, *wayakwak*). **agpayakpak.** *v.* to make the sound of fluttering wings; to swing the arms or wings as in flight. [Tag. *payakpák*]

pay-án: (f. *ay*) **pamay-an.** *n.* manner of doing things; *v.* to do; make into something; treat in a certain way. **pakapay-an.** *n.* result; outcome; situation, condition. **mamay-an.** *v.* to do. **kapapay-an.** *n.* event, happening; something done. **nakapapay-an.** *a.* done. [Tag. *gawâ*]

payáp: (*obs.*) **payapan.** *v.* to thrust a finger in the eye. (*sulek*)

payápa: (Tag. *payapà*) **napayapa.** *a.* peaceful, quiet, tranquil, calm; gentle. (*talna*)

payápay: *n.* kind of crab with one claw bigger than the other; waving hand. **agpayapay.** *v.* to wave the hand. **payapayan.** *v.* to summon by hand signal; call using the hand. **agpinnayapay.** *v.* to wave to each other. [Tag. *kawáy*]

pay-ás: *n.* drainage; irrigation ditch (*banawang*). **Iti kano pay-as ti naggapuan ti ansisit.** The dwarf supposedly came from the irrigation ditch. [Tag. *patubig*]

payáso: (Sp. *payaso*: clown) *n.* clown, buffoon.

páyat: *n.* footprint; step. **payaten.** *v.* to trample, tread. (*baddek*) **payatan.** *n.* footstep, step of a vehicle. **papayatan.** *n.* treadle attached to the lower part of the *gur-on*. **payatpayaten.** *v.* to step on something repeatedly. **Maluspak ti tukak a mapayatanna.** *exp.* denoting a slow person (*lit*: the frog gets squashed when stepped on). **Nagranetret dagiti tukad ti agdanmi a kawayan a napayatak.** The steps of our bamboo ladder creaked as I stepped on them. [Png. *tapak*, *talpak*, Tag. *tapak*, *payak*]

pay-áw: *n.* the wind in the wake of a running vehicle. **mapay-awan.** *v.* to be in the wake of (fumes from the exhaust, etc.)

payég: *abbr.* of *ipaiyeg*: to bring something to someone.

payegpég: *n.* chill (in sickness). **agpayegpeg.** *v.* to shiver, tremble, have chills. (used for when referring to sickness). **Pasaray agpanateng ken agpayegpeg.** He often gets sick and has the chills. [Tag. *kaligkíg*]

payó: *n.* a kind of eel-like marine fish, Conger eel.

payubyób: **agpayubyob.** *v.* to smoke vigorously, puff away. **payubyuban.** *v.* to blow smoke at. **Adda isem kadagiti kuribetbeten a bibig ti baket a mangam-ammal iti tabako a paypayubyobenna.** There was a smile on the old lady's wrinkled lips holding the cigar she was puffing away at.

páyud: **pumayud.** *v.* to urinate at a great distance. (*patiray-ok*)

pay-ód: *n.* odor (usually blown by the wind). **napay-od.** *a.* with strong body odor (good or bad). **Nagadiwara ti pay-odna.** His odor diffused.

payugpóg: *n.* dust blown by the wind; strong wind. **ipayugpog.** *v.* to lift and carry along (wind). **maipayugpog.** *v.* to be carried off by the wind. **payugpugan.** *v.* to spray with dust. **mapayugpugan.** *v.* to be exposed to blowing dust; to be the object of a witch's anger.

pay-ók: *n.* flattery, adulation, sycophancy (*patiray-ok*). [Tag. *hibò*]

payukó: **agpayuko.** *v.* to stoop; to be round shouldered.

payukpók: *n.* a kind of small herb; *var.* of *payugpog*.

páyong: *n.* umbrella, parasol. **agpayong.** *v.* to use an umbrella. **agkapayong.** *v.* to share an umbrella. **payongan.** *v.* to shade using an umbrella. **ipayong.** *v.* to put an umbrella over someone. **payongpayong.** *n.* head of a nail, cap, head of mushroom. **makikapayong, makipayong.** *v.* to share an umbrella. **Mapaypayongan a mangan.** He eats under the shade of an umbrella (referring to someone born wealthy). [Kal., Knk., Png., Tag. *payong*]

payós: **napayos.** *a.* excellent, perfect. (*darisay*)

pay-ús: *n.* a variety of late rice with pink hull and thin kernel.

paypáy: *n.* fan. (*abaniko*) **agpaypay.** *v.* to fan oneself. **paypayan.** *v.* to fan someone. [Ivt. *papayid*, Png., Tag. *paypáy*]

paysó: **agpayso.** *a.* true. (*pudno*) **napaypayso.** *a.* true. **ipayso.** *v.* to do truly, sincerely. **paysuen.** *v.* to do truly, sincerely. **mapaysuan.** *v.* to be convinced, sure; come true; be lucky. **pumayso.** *v.* to come true; be fulfilled; turn out to be real. [Kal. *tuttuwa*, Png. *tuá*, Tag. *totoó*]

payyák: *var.* of *payak*: wing.

pe: (Sp. *fe*: faith) **pe de bautismo.** *n.* baptismal certificate.

Pebréro: (Sp. *Febrero*: February) *n.* February. [Kal. *malaba*, Knk. *ledéw*]

pedál: (Eng.) *n.* pedal. **pedalan.** *v.* to pedal.

pedáso: (Sp. *pedazo*: piece) *n.* piece (of cloth), fragment; portion; one fingerling. **pedasuen.** *v.* to cut into pieces of loaves. **sangapedaso.** *n.* one piece, one sheet.

peddá: **mapda.** *v.* to be fatigued, tired and worn out; to be satiated; to have had more than enough. [Tag. *busóg* (satiated); *antók* (tired)]

pedestál: (Sp. *pedestal*: pedestal) *n.* pedestal, base on which a statue stands.

pedído: (Sp. *pedido*: ordered) *a.* ordered (goods); *n.* order for goods, requisition.

pedopília: (Eng.) *n.* pedophile.

pedpéd₁: *n.* *Casearia sp.* trees whose leaves are smoked.

pedpéd₂: **pedpeden.** *v.* to lessen, reduce, diminish, alleviate; restrain, control; alleviate. **mapedped.** *v.* to be abated, lessened. **pamedped.** *n.* small amount of food that assuages hunger. **Mamedpedak laengen iti tinapay ken danum.** I am just snacking on bread and water.

pédro: (*coll.*) *n.* penis (*búto*). [Tag. *titi*]

peggád: *n.* danger, hazard, risk. **agpeggad.** *v.* to be in danger; to be risky. **ipeggad.** *v.* to endanger, jeopardize. **napeggad.** *a.* dangerous. **pagpeggadan.** *n.* danger. **mamgad.** *v.* to dare to do something dangerous, risk, venture. **Nalabsannan ti kapeggadan a paset ti sabangan.** He passed the most dangerous part of the mouth of the river. [Tag. *panganib*]

peggés: *n.* rapid flow of water in river; strong wind. **napges.** *a.* strong; swift running; violent (currents, wind, etc.) **agpegges.** *v.* to become violent (wind). **pumegges.** *v.* to gather speed. **Napegges ti bilog a nagpasabangan.** The canoe went swiftly to the mouth of the river. [Tag. *bilís*]

pegkét: *var.* of *pigkét*: stick; adhesive.

pegpég: *n.* beaten rice kernels. **marapegpeg.** *n.* small, newly formed fruit; small kernel not fully developed. **pumegpeg.** *v.* to break into small pieces. **Kasla pegpeg ti ling-etna.** His sweat is like rice kernels.

peinéta: (Sp. *peineta*: small comb) *n.* ornamental comb worn in the hair. [Ivt. *pantuci*, Tag. *payneta*]

pékas: (Sp. *peca*: freckle) *n.* freckle.

pekdá: **ipekda.** *v.* to say in brief, concisely. (*peksa*)

péke: (Eng.) *a.* fake, counterfeit, imitation; forged.

pekká₁: *n.* one grain of rice.

pekká₂: *n.* crack. **pekkaen.** *v.* to shatter, smash; break; open someone's fist forcefully; break free from bondage; disjoint. **napekka.** *a.* cracked; shattered; disjointed.

pekkéd: **pamkedán.** *n.* reason, cause. (*gapú*)

pekkél: *n.* squeezing; massage. **pekkelen.** *v.* to knead; massage; squeeze; ball-cooked rice. **pekkelan.** *v.* to wring clothes; wring neck. **kinapeklan.** *n.* devotion. **napeklan.** *a.* real, genuine; devoted; habitual; reputed for; known for. **namimpeklan.** *a.* very devoted to. **napeklan a bartek.** *n.* devoted drunk. **mapekkelan.** *v.* to be wrung. **pinekkel.** *n.* handful of rice; handful of *diket* rice with melted sugar. [Png. *mesmes*, *pisél*, Tag. *pisíl* (squeeze), *himas* (massage; squeeze), *pigâ* (wring); Knk. *peklán* = stout]

pekkuát: **pamkuatán.** *n.* reason, cause. (*gapú*)

pekpék₁: *n.* variety of short-eared maize; (baby talk) vagina. **pinekpek, panekpek.** *n.* variety of awned *diket* rice.

pekpék₂: **napekpek.** *a.* stuffed, crammed, filled up. **pekpeken.** *v.* to stuff, cram, overload. [Tag. *siksík*]

pekpék₃: **pumanekpek.** *v.* to produce the sound of wood when beaten.

peksá: **maipeksa.** *v.* to voice out; speak out one's feelings; do with all one's strength. (*paksa*) **Kayatko metten nga ipeksa dagiti nakapempem ditoy barukongko.** I want to voice out what is heaping on my chest. [Tag. *sabi*]

pelígro: (Sp. *peligro*: danger) *n.* danger. (*peggad*) **peligroso.** *a.* dangerous, hazardous. [Tag. *panganib*]

pelíkula: (Sp. *película*: film) *n.* film, movie. (*sine*)

pellá: **pellaen.** *v.* to cut up; split. **mapellapella.** *v.* to clot, coagulate. (*balay*)

pellás: **pellasen.** *v.* to sever; cut off (*puted*). [Tag. *putol*]

pelléng: **mapleng.** *v.* to be stunned (by a blow) (*ariweng*); irritated by a sound. **Napleng ni Myra ngem pinasimbengna ti rikna.** Myra was stunned but collected her feelings. [Tag. *tulíg*]

pellés: *n*. change of clothes; style of attire. **agpelles**. *v*. to change, dress. **mamles**. *v*. to change one's clothes. (*sukat*) **pelsan**. *v*. to change the clothes, dress up. **pamlesan**. *n*. dressing room; clothes which will be changed into. **inpelles**. *a*. hand spun. **nakaples**. *a*. dressed. **pagpellesan**. *n*. fitting room. [Png. *palés*, Tag. *bihis*]

pellós: **maplos**. *v*. to double, curve, bend. (*killó*)

pelnék: (*obs.*) **agpelnek**. *v*. to set (sun).

pelúka: (Sp. *peluca*: wig) *n*. wig. **agpeluka**. *v*. to wear a wig. **pelukero**. *n*. seller of wigs; wig maker.

pelúsa: (Sp. *pelusa*: fluff) *n*. kind of fine leather.

pelóta: (Sp. *pelota*: ball) *n*. the game of jai alai; the ball used in jai alai. **agpelota**. *v*. to play jai alai.

pelotári: (Sp.) *n*. *pelota* player.

pelpég: **pelpegan**. *v*. to even, smooth, level; cut off the top.

pelpél: **ipelpel**. *v*. to press down (through an opening); put on a wheel; thrust into (hole; mouth). **maipelpel**. *v*. to get stuck in an opening or hole. **nakapelpel**. *a*. crammed; having mouth full of food. **Naipelpel ti pana iti makakanigid a bakrang ti alingo.** The arrow got stuck in the left side of the wild boar. [Tag. *muwál*]

peltáng: **peltangen**. *v*. to dislocate (bones). **mapeltang**. *v*. to be dislocated. (*bullo*; *ligasi*)

pempén: see *penpen*: stock; pile; heap. [Tag. *salansá*; *mandalâ*]

pendého: (Sp. *pendejo*: good for nothing) *n*. husband whose wife is cheating on him.

pendiénte: (Sp. *pendiente*: pending) *a*. pending (lawsuit).

péndulo: (Sp. *péndola*: pendulum + English) *n*. pendulum, swinging weight.

península: (Sp. *península*: peninsula) *n*. peninsula, land bordered by water on three sides.

peniténsia: (Sp. *penitencia*: penance) *n*. penance, penitence; purgatory. **agpenitensia**. *v*. to do penance.

pennáak: *n*. middle (of temporal period: Lent, the rainy season, etc. or of a certain length: road). **pamnaak**. *n*. middle. **agpennaak**. *v*. to reach the height of a season; climax.

pennás: **mapennasan, kapnasan**. *a*. stripped of fruits. **pennasen**. *v*. to strip completely.

pennéd: *n*. *Andropogon zizanoides*, vetiver grass; dike, levee; dam. **penneden**. *v*. to dam. [Tag. *saplád*]

pennék: **agpennek**. *v*. to eat until satisfied; to work until tired. **ipennek**. *v*. to do to the utmost. **mapnek**. *a*. to be satisfied, satiated. **makapnek**. *a*. satisfying; gratifying. **napnekan**. *a*. mature, ripe; in season. **penneken**. *v*. to satisfy; make sure; give enough to. **kapnekan**. *n*. proof, evidence, verification. **kapkapnekan**. *v*. to be fully satisfied; without a doubt; sure; with sufficient proof. **pakap(en)nekán**. *n*. something that satisfies; proof, evidence. **pamnekán**. *v*. reason or cause for satisfaction. **pannakapnek**. *n*. satisfaction. **iti amin a pennekna**. with all his might. **Agpennek ita dagiti kalding nga agarab.** The grazing goats are now satisfied eating. [Tag. *siyá (kasiyahán)*]

pennét: *n*. tough meat; elastic tissue of quadrupeds; ligament of meat (*anut*). [Tag. *litid*]

penúltima: (Sp. *penúltima*: penultimate) *n*. penultimate syllable, second to the last syllable; *a*. stressed on the penultimate syllable.

penómeno: (Sp. *fenómeno*: phenomenon) *n*. phenomenon.

pénoy: (Tag.) *n*. hard-boiled duck egg.

penpén: *n*. heap, pile; rice stored away. **ipenpen**. *v*. to store, keep in reserve; accumulate, pile up; keep, conceal; hide. **naipenpen**. *a*. piled up; stored. [Tag. *mandalâ* (stack of rice)]

pensár: (Sp. *pensar*: think) *n*. aim, purpose; plan. (*panggep*) **pensaren**. *v*. to plain. propose, intend.

pensión: (Sp. *pensión*: pension) *n*. pension; scholarship. **agpension**. *v*. to receive a pension. **pensionan**. *v*. to give a pension to.

pensionádo: (Sp. *pensionado*: pensioner) *n*. pensioner, one who receives a pension; scholar, one awarded a scholarship.

pentáy: **agpentay**. *v*. to separate for good, bid farewell for good (*sina*). [Tag. *hiwaláy*]

penték: **napentek**. *a*. properly developed (said of grains). (*messék*)

pengéd: **pengdan**. *v*. to moderate, control, inhibit; restrain (*medméd*). **mapengdan**. *v*. to be controlled, restrained, inhibited. **Ginatangna tapno mapengdan ti masapa a panagkabaw.** He bought it to inhibit early senility.

pengngá: *n*. a kind of grass. **pengngapengnga**. *n*. *Heliotropium indicum*, weed, the *ar-aritos*.

pengngél: **penglan**. *v*. to attack (many against one); assault (*duklós*; *ambón*). [Tag. *lusob*, *salakay*]

pengngét: **agpengnget**. *v*. to grapple, come to blows. **pengngeten**. *v*. to grapple; seize.

peudál: (Sp. *feudal*: feudal) *a*. feudal. **peudalismo**. *n*. feudalism.

peón: (Sp. *peón*: peon; pawn) *n*. peon; pawn (in chess).

pépet: (*coll.*) *n*. vulva, female genitalia.

pepíto: *n*. kind of gambling card game.

per-ák: **naper-ak**. *a*. shattered, smashed, broken. (pottery). **per-aken**. *v*. to shatter; to shatter by throwing. **iper-ak**. *v*. to smash, shatter; utter angrily. [Tag. *basag*]

péras: (Sp. *pera*: pear) *n*. pear.

perdí: (Sp. *perder*: lose) *a*. wasted, lost; *n*. loss. **agperdi**. *v*. to destroy, damage; ruin. **maperdi**. *v*. to be destroyed, ruined. **mammerdi**. *n*. destroyer. **naperdian**. *a*. suffered a loss. **makaperdi**. *v*. can destroy; affect in a negative way. **pagperdian iti oras**. *n*. waste of time.

perdíble: (Sp. *imperdible*: safety pin) *n*. safety pin.

perdigónes: (Sp. *perdigones*: small shot) *n*. bird shot; pellets of a gun.

peregríno: (Sp. *peregrino*: pilgrim) *n*. pilgrim. **peregrinasion**. *n*. pilgrimage.

perehíl: (Sp. *perejil*: parsley) *n*. parsley.

pergamíno: (Sp. *pergamino*: parchment) *n*. parchment; scroll; vellum.

pergóla: (Sp. *pérgola*: roof garden) *n*. raised platform with a roof.

perhuísio: (Sp. *perjuicio*: damage, harm) *n*. nuisance, trouble; hardship; damage, injury; annoying person.

péria: (Sp. *feria*: fair) *n*. fair; exhibition. **iperia**. *v*. to bring to the fair, display at an exhibition.

periante: (Sp. *feriante*) *n*. fair maintainer or attendant.

periódiko: (Sp. *periódico*: newspaper) *n*. newspaper. (*pagiwarnak*)

periodísmo: (Sp. *periodismo*) *n*. journalism.

periodísta: (Sp. *periodista*: journalist) *n*. newspaperman; journalist. (*agiwarwarnak*)

pérlas: (Sp. *perla*: pearl) *n*. pearl. **pimmerlas**. *a*. like a pearl, pearly.

permanénte: (Sp. *permanente*: permanent) *a*. permanent. (*agnanayon*, *agpaut*) **agpermanente**. *v*. to stay in a place permanently. **ipermanente**. *v*. to make something permanent.

permí: *var*. of *pirmi*: permanent; usually, often; altogether; entirely; firm; pure.

permíso: (Sp. *permiso*: permission) *n*. permission (*palubos*); permit, license.

pérno: (Sp. *perno*: spike; bolt) *n*. bolt; spike; joint.

péro: (Sp.) *prep*. but (*ngem*); except. [Tag. *pero*]

peróka: *var*. of *pirruka*: species of bird.

perokaríl: (Sp. *ferrocarril*: railroad) *n*. railroad.

perpékto: (Sp. *perfecto*: perfect) *a*. perfect. **perpektuen**. *v*. to perfect.

perpér₁: (*obs*.) *n*. smegma. (*kaper*)

perpér₂: **sangaperper**. *a*. abundant. **iperper**. *v*. to sow, scatter (seeds) densely. (*pupog*)

perpétuo: (Sp. *perpétuo*: perpetual) *a*. perpetual, forever. (*agnanayon*)

perpúme: (Sp. *perfume*: perfume) *n*. perfume (*pabanglo*). [Tag. *pabangó*]

perréng: *n*. stare; glaze. (*matmat*) **iperreng**. *v*. to secure from wandering, fix; hold steadily; fix the eyes upon. **perrengen**. *v*. to look at someone eye to eye; fix the eyes at, stare. **pumerreng**. *v*. to stare. **agpinnereng**. *v*. to stare at one another. **malmes iti perreng**. *v*. to fall into a deep stare. **Nagpinnerengkami iti kapiduak a mannalon**. My second-cousin farmer and I stared at each other. [Png. *linggis*, Tag. *titig*]

perrés: *n*. the *daláyap* lemon; generic name for citrus fruits. **pumres**. *v*. to shoot out, gush out, jet. **persen**. *v*. to press, crush, squeeze. **persan**. *v*. to squeeze juice over. [Tag. *pigâ*]

perroká: **perperroka**. *n*. species of small, brown-plumaged bird. (*pirpirroka*)

persén: (f. *perrés*) *v*. to squeeze, press (in order to extract juice). **persan**. *v*. to squeeze juice from.

persáy: **napersayan**. *a*. torn, lacerated (body). **persayen**. *v*. to tear off. **persaypersay**. *a*. ragged, torn.

persiána: (Sp. *persiana*: Venetian blind) *n*. Venetian blind, shutter.

Persiáno: (Sp. *persiano*: Persian) *n*. *a*. Persian.

personáhe: (Sp. *personaje*: personage) *n*. personage, character in a book.

personál: (Sp.) *a*. personal; *n*. personality; character.

personalidád: (Sp. *personalidad*: personality) *n*. personality; character.

pertinénsia: (Sp. *pertenencia*: domain, property) *n*. superficial measure in mining.

perwísio: *var*. of *perhuisio*: hardship; trouble; harm; injury; damage (in a lawsuit).

pes₁: *n*. joke, sneer (contracted form of *eppes* with certain affixes.) **umpes**. *v*. to flatten (swellings).

pes₂: interjection that expresses disgust.

pesáda: (Sp. *pesada*: quantity weighed at one time) (*obs*.) **sangapesada**. *n*. one bundle of grass.

pesadór: (Sp., *obs*.) *n*. steelyard.

pes-ák₁: **pes-akan**. *v*. to wash (fibers); break plates.

pes-ák₂: **maipes-ak**. *v*. to fall into water or mud.

pésas: (Sp. *pesas*: weights) *n*. weights; barbell.

peséta: (Sp. *peseta*: peseta) *n*. twenty centavos.

pesimísmo: (Sp. *pesimismo*: pessimism) *n*. pessimism. **pesimista**. *n*. pessimist.

peskádo: (Sp. *pescado*: fish) *n*. fish (used in the names of certain recipes). **sinigang a peskado**. fish stew.

peskánte: (Sp. *pescante*: driving seat; coach box) *n.* coach box. **mangpeskante.** *v.* to drive (a bullcart).

peskería: *var.* of *piskiria*: fishery.

pespés: *n.* juice extracted from the stomach of ruminants used as sour seasoning to make *pinespesan*, also called *pinespes*. **pespesen.** *v.* to press, squeeze; harass. **pinespes.** *n.* juice extracted from ruminants containing half-digested food. **pinespesan.** *v.* dish made of raw beef with *pinespes*. **madaripespes.** *v.* to be drenched with sweat. [Ibg. *peggel*, Ivt. *pitus*, *písan*, Kpm. *paslan*, Png. *pespes*, Tag. *pigâ* (squeeze)]

pessá: agpessa. *v.* to hatch from the egg. **napsa.** *a.* unsocketed (eyes). **kapespessa.** *a.* newly hatched. **mapessaan.** *v.* to be hatched. **papessaan.** *v.* to hatch. **makapespessa.** *a.* broody. **Nagbilangka manen ti piek a saan pay a napessaan.** You counted the chickens again before they are hatched. [Tag. *pisâ*]

pessáaw: *n.* splashing sound when passing a river. (*pisáw*)

pessát: *n.* piece of cloth woven at one time; sufficient cloth for a garment. **sangapessat.** *n.* one piece of clothing material. **napessat.** *a.* torn, cut off. **pessaten.** *v.* to cut cloth; tear.

pessáw₁: agpessaw. *v.* to bother (by talking loudly). **makapsaw.** *v.* to bother, cause disgust. (*suya*)

pessáw₂: agpessaw. *v.* splash in the water.

péste: (Sp. *peste*: pest) *n.* pest, pestilence. (*angol*) **mapeste.** *v.* to die due to a plague, pest. [Bon. *móteg*, Png. *sálot*]

pestého: (Sp. *festejo*: festivity) *n.* festivity.

pestehádo: (Sp. *festejado*: person honored at feast) *n.* person honored at a feast.

pestého: (Sp. *festejo*: festivity) *n.* festival, festivity.

pestisídio: (Eng.) *n.* pesticide.

petáka: (Sp. *petaca*: tobacco pouch) *n.* wallet. **ipetaka.** *v.* to put in one's wallet. **nakapetaka.** *a.* carrying a wallet. [Tag. *pitakà*]

pétalo: (Sp. *pétalo*: petal) *n.* petal of a flower.

petpét: *n.* fist; grip; clench. (*gemgem*) **agpetpet.** *v.* to clench the fist; clutch, grab. **nakapetpet.** *a.* with a closed fist. **petpetan.** *v.* to grasp firmly, clutch. **pumetpet.** *v.* to hold. **sangkapetpet.** *n.* one handful. **papetpet.** *n.* cash gift; bribe money. **ipapetpet, papetpetan.** *v.* to give cash to children; to grease the palm with bribe money. **Ginutadna ti dakulapna iti petpetko ngem diak pinaluspusan.** He pulled his palm away from my grip, but I didn't let go. **Umis-isem ti butiog a nangipapetpet kenkuana iti dua ribo.** The large-bellied man

handed over two thousand (pesos) smiling. [Png. *kemkem*, Tag. *kimkím*, *kuyóm*, *hawak*]

petrólio: (Sp. *petroleo*: petroleum) *n.* petroleum, kerosene.

pétsa: (Sp. *fecha*: date) *n.* date. **mapetsaan.** *v.* to be dated. **petsado.** *a.* dated.

petsadór: (f. *petsa*) *n.* date stamp.

pétsas: (Sp. *ficha*: chip; piece in a game) *n.* mahjong tile; object ball in pool.

petsáy: (Hok. *péq cʰaí*: white vegetable) *n.* pechay plant, Chinese cabbage.

petsído: *a.* narrow (road), not wide enough; overloaded (schedule).

petsíng: *n.* female genitalia (*uki*). [Tag. *puki*]

pétso: (Sp. *pecho*: breast) *n.* breast (of chicken). [Bon. *gámoy*, *sekna*, Knk. *túmey*]

petták: *a.* broken; cracked. **pettaken.** *v.* to break, shatter, smash; crack. [Tag. *basag*]

pettát: napettat. *a.* unexpected, sudden, unprepared for. (*kellaat*) **Pettat ti papatayna.** He died a sudden death. **Adda pettat a gimmilayab iti unegna.** Something suddenly flared inside him. [Tag. *biglâ*]

petténg₁: *n.* emphasis. **ipetteng.** *v.* to emphasize; insist. **napetteng.** *a.* insistent. **Impetteng dagiti am-ammomi a bukbukodna a nagmaneho.** Our acquaintances insisted that he was driving alone. [Tag. *giít*]

petténg₂: mapteng. *v.* to rot, decay due to rain. (*rupsa*)

pi(n)-: *pref.* used with numbers in various combinations of affixation to indicate how many times something is done: *Pi*duaem ti agadal. Study twice. **Siak ti nag*pin*pat.** I am the one who did it four times. *Pimmi*tlokami. We did it three times.

pi(n)- -en: Transitive affixation used with numeric roots to indicate how many times an action is done. *Pi*duaem ti agraep. Transplant the seedlings twice.

piá: *n.* health, well-being. (*salun-at*) **kappia.** *n.* peace. **napia.** *a.* well, healthy. **pumipia.** *v.* to improve, get better, recover, ameliorate. **agpapia.** *v.* to regain strength after sickness, get better, improve. **pagpiaen.** *v.* to reconcile, restore friendship. **pipiaen.** *v.* to do well, better. **napapia, nappia.** *a.* mediocre, medium, fair, average. **napipia pay.** there is still enough. **napia kuma no.** optative expression: it would be good if. **napia pay ta.** it is fortunate that. **pagpiaan.** *n.* welfare; advantage; opportunity. **papiaen.** *v.* to do with ease; be idle. **Awan latta ti pimmiaanna.** He just didn't get any better. [Note: stress shift with suffixation is regional: *pagpiáen* = *pagpiaén*, etc. Ivt. *wawa*, Tag. *galíng*]

piadór: (Sp. *fiador*: guarantor) *n*. guarantor.

piák: *n*. sound of chickens. **agpipiak.** *v*. to make the sound of chickens.

piálo: inpialo. *n*. a sweet made of rice, water, and sugar.

piámbre: (Sp. *fiambre*: cold food) *n*. food in a tiered container.

piambréra: (Sp. *fiambrera*: lunch basket) *n*. tiered food container.

piáno: (Sp. *piano*: piano) *n*. piano. **agpiano.** *v*. to play the piano. **pianuen.** *v*. to play a piece on the piano. **pianista, pumipiano.** *n*. pianist.

piánsa: (Sp. *fianza*: bail) *n*. bail; bail bond. **agpiansa.** *v*. to post bail. **piansaan.** *v*. to bail out someone. **pagpiansaen.** *v*. to impose a bail.

piáng: **piangpiang.** *n*. cymbal. **agpiangpiang.** *v*. to clash, clang.

piángok: *n*. variety of awned rice; *a*. crazy. **agpiangok.** *v*. to become crazy. (*bagtit*)

piápi: **agpiapi.** *v*. to ride a horse with both feet to one side; to sit on a ledge with both feet dangling.

piár: (Sp. *confiar*: trust) *n*. trust, confidence (*talék*). **piaren.** *v*. to trust; have confidence in. **agpiar.** *v*. to have confidence in. **ipiar.** *v*. to entrust. **managpiaran.** *a*. trustworthy. **Piarek met ketdi ngem awan kas iti agannad.** I do trust him but there's nothing like being cautious. [Tag. *pagkatiwalà*]

piás: *n*. *Averrhoa bilimbi*. tree whose fruits are used to sour native dishes; variety of awned *diket* rice. [Ibg. *addúlu*, Png. *piyás*, Tag. *kalamyás, kamyás*]

piátan: *n*. variety of thin, hard sugarcane good for *basi*.

pidál: **pidalen.** *v*. to work gold.

pídas₁: **pidasen.** *v*. to teasel, scratch cloth to raise a nap.

pídas₂: **pidasen.** *v*. spread evenly (jelly on bread). [Tag. *pahid*]

piddawíl: **agpiddawil.** *v*. to stagger while walking (drunks). **piddawilen.** *v*. to trip someone. **napiddawil.** *a*. tripped (*sappídong, tippádong, simpálong*). [Tag. *suray*]

piddawít: *a*. bandy-legged (*sakáng*); striking one's leg against another's; implicate for a crime. [Tag. *sakáng*]

piddúkol: (coined from name of comic strip character, *Pedro + dukol*) *n*. nickname for hunchbacks.

pidég: *n*. highest point, top; culmination; pushing; dead end; corner. **ipideg.** *v*. to corner; place against the wall; put in contact with; pin down; push; affix, attach. **naipideg.** *v*. to be attached to; to be pinned to; pinned down, cornered; have one's back against the wall.

Pimmideg iti paladpad. He pinned himself against the windowsill. [Tag. *gipít*]

pidéos: (Sp. *fideo*: noodle) *n*. vermicelli.

pídil: **pidilen.** *v*. to nip, pinch lightly (*keddel; kuddot*). [Tag. *kurót*]

pidipíd: *a*. closely set together. **pidipiden.** *v*. to join, unite; stack up. (*silpo*) **napidipid.** *a*. closely set together; covered with sores, wounds, etc. [Note: *pidipidén* has a variant pronunciation of *pidipíden*. Tag. *salansán*]

pídis: **napidis.** *a*. sparse, scarce; nice, delicate; finicky. **ipidis.** *v*. to make sparse (remove rice plants from the field, etc.). **pidisen.** *v*. to do delicately. [Tag. *kakatiting* (scarce)]

pídit₁: **piditpidit.** *n*. earlobe. (*tetebbengan, pipiritan*)

pídit₂: **piditen.** *v*. to pinch without using the nails. [Tag. *kurót*]

piduá: (f. *duá*) *n*. second crop of palay. **piduaen.** *v*. to do a second time. **mamindua.** *a*. twice. **kapidua.** *n*. second cousin. **agkapidua.** *n*. relationship between second cousins.

pidóng: *n*. pond. (*basáw*)

pídut: *n*. pilfering; kleptomania. **agpidut, pumidut.** *v*. to pick up; pilfer; steal little by little. **piduten.** *v*. to pick up; pilfer. **pinnidut.** *n*. picking up objects in a race. **mapidut.** *v*. to be picked up; to happen to pick up, coincidentally pick up. **pamidutan.** *n*. something stored away for emergency use. **pinidpidut.** *a*. worthless. [Bon. *góyod*, Png. *dokdok*, Tag. *pulot*]

pié: (Sp. *pie*: foot) *n*. foot (in measuring). **pie kuadrado.** *n*. square foot. **de-pie.** *a*. powered by the foot (sewing machine).

piék: *n*. chick. **agpípiek.** *n*. the cry of the chick; *v*. to cry (said of chicks). **agpipiék.** *v*. to hunt (said of chicks). **Kaslada piek nga ul-ulila.** *exp*. denoting pitifulness (*lit*: like an orphaned chick). **Saankayo kuma nga agbilang ti piek a saan pay a napissaan.** You shouldn't count chickens before they are hatched. [Bon. *kinyog, bingki*, Kal. *isiw*, Knk. *pesá*, Png. *siwsíw*, Tag. *sisiw*]

piéltro: (Sp. *fieltro*: felt) *n*. felt.

piésa: (Sp. *pieza*: piece) *n*. piece; music piece; spare part. [Tag. *piyesa*]

piésta: (Sp. *fiesta*: feast) *n*. feast, party, banquet (*padaya*); holiday. **agpiesta.** *v*. to hold a feast, party, banquet. **ipiestaan.** *v*. to celebrate in honor of someone. [Tag. *pista*]

píet: *n*. fiber of palm leaves, which is made into ropes.

píga: **pigapiga.** *n*. kind of marine fish similar to the *pingpinggan*.

pígad: *n*. door mat; rag, mat, cloth or coconut shell placed by the door to rub dirt off the feet or shoes. **agpigad.** *v.* to rub the feet on a doormat. **ipigad.** *v.* to rub the dirt off one's feet on a doormat. **pagpigadan.** *n.* doormat. [Tag. *kuskós (ng paá)*]

pigadór: *n.* pincers.

pígar: *n.* fin (*sigar*); mane. [Kal. *ipay*, Tag. *kaluskós* (fin)]

pigergér: *n.* trembling. **agpigerger.** *v.* to tremble; shiver, quake. (*tigerger*) **Agpigpigerger dagiti tumengna iti butengna.** His knees are trembling in fear.

pígis: *n.* tear. (*pirgis*) **pigisen.** *v.* to tear, shred. **napigis.** *a.* torn. **sangkapigis.** *n.* one shred, rap, scrap. [Ibg. *pisil, geggep,* Ivt. *pirit,* Kpm. *pírat,* Png. *pilát, gayák,* Tag. *punit*]

pigít: **pigiten.** *v.* to touch, handle. **agpipinnigit.** *n.* a boys' chasing game. **agpigit.** *v.* to cheat in a card game.

pigkét: *n.* gum; glutinous substance from certain trees; glue. **napigket.** *a.* sticky, adhesive. (*dumket; kidkid; luyak; kumpet; kulamat*) **ipigket.** *v.* to stick on; paste. **pigketan.** *v.* to paste something on. **mapigketan.** *v.* to have something stuck on. [Bon. *páket,* Ibg. *dekkoq, zikkoq,* Ivt. *dumket,* Knk. *bukanít,* Kpm. *pakat,* Png. *kolnét,* Tag. *dikít*]

piglát: *n.* scar; blemish; birthmark. **agpiglat.** *v.* to scar. **piglatan.** *a.* full of scars. [Ibg. *pilaq,* Ivt. *kulad,* Kal. *pilat,* Knk. *báyang, kiblat,* Png. *piglát,* Kpm., Tag. *peklát*]

piglús: *a.* crippled, lame in one leg (*kuspilo*). [Tag. *pilay*]

pigúra: (Sp. *figura*: figure) *n.* figure; appearance; form (*itsura*); posture; face card (jack, queen, king).

pigsá: *n.* power, strength; force. **agpigsa.** *v.* to have the power; have a strong desire. **napigsa.** *a.* strong, powerful, vigorous, healthy, sturdy, potent. **kapigsa.** *n.* strength. **kinapigsa.** *n.* strength, power; intensity; powerfulness. **pamigsáen.** *a.* rather strong. **pigsáan.** *v.* to exert strength on; apply more power to; to make an appliance (TV) louder. **papigsáen.** *v.* to strengthen, make stronger, louder. **agpapigsa.** *v.* to convalesce; recuperate; recover. **Pattapatta nga iti kabikolan ti pagpigsaan ti bagio.** It is estimated that the storm will be strongest in the Bikol region. **Saanmo a pagpigsaan, a, ket mangngegda.** Don't make it louder, they can hear (it). [Ibg. *siken,* Ifg. *nalot,* Ivt. *ayet,* Kal. *koscheÿ,* Knk. *kílud, kisíl, lamnét, wáding,* Kpm. *sikan,* Png. *biskég, kasíl, pelés,* Tag. *lakás;* Tag. *pigsá* = boil; tumor]

pigsól: *n.* walking with a slight hop or limp. **agpigsol.** *v.* to walk with a slight limp; to be lame in one leg. **Nadlawko nga agpigsopigsol**

ti adingna. I noticed his younger brother was limping. [Tag. *pilay*]

pigtáw: *a.* half-session; half-day. **agpigtaw.** *v.* to work half the expected time.

pího: (Sp. *fijo*: fixed) *a.* fixed (price); firm; sure, certain.

píing: *n.* pliers used to straighten the teeth of a saw.

píit: *n.* skinny person. (*kuttong; pair; ratiw; tarawatiw*) **pipiit.** *n.* kind of small bird similar to the *sawsaw-it.* [Tag. *pipit*]

píka: *n.* spear, arrow. (*gusud; gayáng; turag; durus*) **mapika.** *v.* to be speared. **pikaen.** *v.* to spear.

pikáda: (Sp. *picada*: minced) **karne pikada.** *n.* minced meat.

pikadílio: (Sp. *picadillo*: fried ground meat) *n.* hash, recipe of fried ground meat with onions, garlic, peas, salt, tomatoes, and potatoes.

pikádo: (Sp. *picado*) *a.* provoked, piqued.

pikadúra: (Sp. *picadura*: cut tobacco) *n.* ready-cut pipe tobacco, trademark of tobacco.

pikánte: (Sp. *picante*: spicy) *n.* recipe of minced bacon and red pepper; *a.* pungent (*gasang*).

pikápik: *n.* trembling; unease; palpitation, throbbing. **agpikapik.** *v.* to throb, palpitate; tremble; be uneasy (*pitik; gutok*). **makapikapik.** *a.* inspiring; persuading; alluring, attracting, seducing; dramatic. [Tag. *pitík*]

pikár: (Sp. *picar*: goad, harass) **mapikar.** *v.* to be fed up; irritated. **pikaren.** *v.* to nettle; irritate, annoy (*sair*); incite; provoke. **Napikar sa ni Conching iti naudi nga imbagana.** I think Conching got irritated from the last thing he said. [Tag. *pikón* (Sp.)]

píkas: *var.* of *pékas*: freckles.

píkat: **agpikat.** *v.* to suddenly long for something or crave. (*rágut; págus*)

píkbong: *n.* kind of gun used by the Japanese in World War II.

píkek: **pikpikek.** *n.* a kind of small bird with a white breast and black back.

píkel: **pipikel.** *n.* numbness; cramp. **agpipikel.** *v.* to be prickly, numb, tingle, (sensation of a numb part of the body). (*bineg*) **agpipikel, pangpipikel.** *n.* anaesthetic. **Kasla napipikel ti dilana.** He is tongue tied. [Ibg. *bannég,* Kal. *labogbog,* Png. *alibegbég,* Tag. *manhíd*]

píket: *n.* glue, paste, birdlime. (*pigket*) **ipiket.** *v.* to paste on. **napiket.** *a.* sticky, adhesive. **piketan.** *v.* to paste together. [Tag. *dikít*]

pikí: *n.* a kind of white cotton cloth for men's attire.

pikíd: **pumikid.** *v.* to vanish, disappear (clouds). (*pukaw*)

pikípik: *n*. bubbling sound of water. **pumikipik.** *v*. to bubble, pour out noisily.

pikít: **agpikit.** *v*. to cheat at cards by manipulating the deck (*kúsit*). [Tag. *dayà*]

pikkóg: see *pellos*: bend; curve; double.

pikník: (Eng.) *n*. picnic. **agpiknik.** *v*. to have a picnic. **makipiknik.** *v*. to join a picnic. [Kal. *pitlik*]

píko: (Sp. *pico*: pickax) *n*. pickax; spout. **agpiko-piko.** *n*. variety of girls' hide-and-seek, in order to determine who will be 'it', each girl puts one finger in the palm of one's hand and when the hand closes, the caught finger is obliged to be the *sirút appót*, 'it'. [Tag. *piko*; *pikô* = hopscotch]

pikoléte: (Sp. *picolete*: bolt staple) *n*. staple.

píkon: **pikunen.** *v*. to wind around the arm; fold; roll up. **pinikon.** *n*. small intestine of chickens. **kapikon.** *n*. coil of a rope. **mapikon.** *v*. to be folded; doubled up. **tallo-kapikon.** *exp*. three coils of a rope (referring to someone tall). [Tag. *lukot*]

píkor: *n*. curve, bend (of a river, road, etc.). (*tikor*) **pagpikuran.** *n*. bend of a river; where the road curves; curvature. **Nagpikor ti dalan iti kanigid.** The road curved to the left.

píkut: (Tag. *pikot* = corner; surround) *n*. forced marriage. **pikuten.** *v*. to force a marriage. **Pikutenka ketdi, pakpakawan duri.** *exp*. I will never elope with you.

pikóta: (*obs.*) *n*. a kind of rack for torture.

pikpík₁: *n*. light tap, pat. **pikpiken.** *v*. to pat with the palm of fingers (*tapik*). [Tag. *pikpík*]

pikpík₂: (Pil.) **pinikpikan.** *n*. dish made with fresh slices of a slowly slaughtered animal.

pikpók: *n*. kind of gun.

piktagáaw: *n*. a kind of owl.

píla₁: (Sp. *pila*: battery; clay) *n*. clay; very hard soil converted to stone; battery. [Kal. *chiÿulit* (clay)]

píla₂: (Sp. *fila*: line; row) *n*. line (for waiting); row. **agpila, pumila.** *v*. to stand in line. **agpipila.** *v*. to line up. **pila-pila.** *n*. lineup. **pumila.** *v*. to stand in line.

pílak: *n*. stony soil.

pilaménto: (Sp. *filamento*) *n*. filament; thread.

pilántropo: (Sp. *filántropo*) *n*. philanthropist. **pilantropía.** *n*. philanthropy, love of mankind.

piláog: *n*. warp. **agpilaog.** *v*. to warp, twist.

pilaréte: (Sp. *pilarito*: small pillar) *n*. stud, studding, scantling (*marko*); tie beam supporting a roof.

pilát: *n*. a kind of big-bellied nocturnal toad; term applied to obese people. (*kengkeng*)

piláto: *n*. term applied to a mean person.

pílaw: *n*. flaw, blemish, imperfection; stigma; transgression; guilt. **pilawen.** *v*. to find fault; castigate; censure. **pakapilawan.** *n*. defects, flaws, imperfections, reasons to be criticized. **napilaw.** *a*. critical. **managpilaw.** *a*. critical, fond of criticizing. **pamilawan.** *n*. complaints, criticism. **di mapilaw.** cannot be criticized; (*coll.*) no wonder, not surprising. **Nasaysayaat no ibagayo met dagiti pakapilawanna.** It would be nice if you also tell his faults. [Tag. *puná*]

piláw: *n*. puddle, small pool of water. (*libsong*; *lubnak*) **agpilaw.** *v*. to form a puddle of water. **maipilaw.** *v*. to fall into a puddle. [Tag. *lusak*, *sanaw*]

pílay: *n*. limping; lame. **agpilpilay.** *v*. to walk with a limp. **pipilay.** *a*. with emaciated limbs. **pilayen.** *v*. to cause to be lame; cripple. **napilayan.** *a*. sprained; crippled. **pilay-ngato.** *a*. blind in one eye. **pamiláyen.** *a*. somewhat crippled, lame. [Ivt. *piday*, Knk. *akillá*, Png. *piléy*, Tag. *pilay*]

píldoras: (Sp. *píldora*: pill) *n*. pill. **agpildoras.** *v*. to take a pill. **agpilpildoras.** *v*. to take pills (repeatedly for a certain cause)

piléges: *var*. of *pleges*: fold, pleat.

pilét₁: *n*. variety of awned rice with red kernel.

pilét₂: *n*. sticky matter, adhesive. **ipilet.** *v*. to stick into. **agpilet.** *v*. to clot; stick. **mapiletan.** *v*. to stick; clot. [Tag. *dikít*]

píli₁: . **agpili., pumili.** *v*. to choose; select. **pilien.** *v*. to choose, select, pick out. **pilian.** *v*. to clean rice of dirt and extraneous matters. **napili.** *a*. fastidious, finicky, very selective; choice, select, high quality. **managpipili.** *a*. choosy, finicky. **pakapilian.** *n*. selection. **panagpili.** *n*. act of choosing; election. **panagpipili.** *n*. election, time for choosing. **pagpilian.** *n*. selection, things to choose from. **pagpilien.** *v*. to make someone choose. [Bon. *ontol*, Ibg. *píli*, Ivt. *mamidiq*, Png. *pilí, demét*, Kpm., Tag. *pilì*]

píli₂: **pinili.** *n*. variety of awned late rice.

píli₃: **pinilian.** *n*. a kind of cotton blanket with designs.

pília: (Sp. *pilla*: sly woman) *n*. naughty girl, see *pílio*.

pilíbot: *n*. large sailing vessel.

pílid: *n*. wheel (*rueda*); cart wheel; tire; flat roots of certain trees. **mapilidan.** *v*. to be run over by a vehicle. (*atal*) **pilidan.** *v*. to run the wheels over; run over; *a*. wheeled. **pilidpilid.** *n*. bamboo device for carrying water. **nagtagipilid a maleta.** *n*. suitcase with wheels. [Png. *dalíg*, Tag. *gulóng*]

pilíng: *n*. shrill sound. **pilliing.** *n*. whistle made from a rice culm. **pumliing.** *v*. to produce a shrill sound. **kanapliing.** *n.* succession of shrill sounds. **mapliing.** *v.* to produce a shrill sound.

pílio: (Sp. *pillo:* sly) *a.* naughty, wayward, wanton; mischievous. **agpilio.** *v.* to behave badly, be naughty. **pamiliuen.** *a.* rather naughty.

pilípig: *n.* a kind of gray larva that destroys rice plants; toasted and pounded rice grains. **agpilipig.** *v.* to roast immature rice.

Pilipínas: (Sp. *Filipinas*) *n.* The Philippines.

Pilipinísta: (Sp. *filipinista*) *n.* Philippinist, person who specializes in the Philippines.

Pilipíno: (Sp. *filipino*) *n. a.* Filipino, *fem: Pilipina.*

pílis: *n.* fruit of the *anangki* tree.

pílit: agpilit. *v.* to insist. **piliten.** *v.* to force, oblige; violate, rape. **ipapilit.** *v.* to force, insist upon. **kapilitan.** *v.* to do without the will; be forced to do; *a.* necessary, obligatory. **inkapilitan.** *a.* under compulsion. **mammilit.** *a.* forceful; *n.* rapist. **napilitan.** *a.* to be forced. **Napilitankami a nagkatangkatang kada ama ken ina.** We were forced to drift from house to house with our father and mother. [Png., Tag. *pilit*]

pilkát: *n.* stain (from soil), smudge, smear, blot. **napilkatan.** *a.* blotted, smeared, etc. **pilkatan.** *v.* to stain; smear, smudge. [Tag. *kulapol*]

pilkó: *a.* bent; folded. **agpilko.** *v.* to fold oneself, put oneself in a bent position. **pilkuen.** *v.* to fold; bend; double up. **pilko-pilkuen.** *v.* to infold. **napilko.** *a.* bent; crooked; folded. **napilko-pilko a bulong.** *a.* folded leaves. **Ti pamuspusan a maliklikam ket agpakleb wenno agiddaka saka agpilko a kasla bato.** The way to avoid (the bullets) is to fall prone or lie down then fold yourself like a rock. [Tag. *tiklóp*]

pilkóg: *a.* curved, crooked, bent. **napilkog.** *a.* curved, crooked, bent. (*nakillo*) **pilkugen.** *v.* to curve; bend. [Tag. *baluktót, tiklóp*]

pillakús: *a.* weak kneed, tottering, walking clumsily. **agpillakus.** *v.* to walk clumsily; to be weak kneed. [Tag. *lampá*]

pillás: *var.* of *pellás:* slice, cut. **pillasen.** *v.* to cut, slice (paper, cloth). **sangkapillas.** *n.* one cut of paper or cloth.

pillayód: *var.* of *pillayos.*

pillay-ós: *a.* with paralyzed legs.

pillíing: (f. *pilíng*) *n.* kind of flute made from rice hay. **pum(il)liing.** *v.* to sound shrilly. [Tag. *tagintíng*]

pillíng₁: *n.* (*obs.*) felling aromatic trees for fumigation.

pillíng₂: mapilling. *v.* to be stunned (*pelleng*). [Tag. *tulíg*]

pillós: *a.* lame, crippled. (*pilay*)

pil-ók: *n.* limping, walking with a hop having one leg shorter than the other. **agpil-ok.** *v.* to limp due to having uneven leg lengths. [Tag. *pilay*]

pilón: (Sp. *pilón:* heap) *n.* cube of sugar.

pílos: (Sp. *terciopelo:* velvet) *n.* velvet.

pilósopo: (Sp. *filósofo:* philosopher) *n.* philosopher; (*coll.*) person who thinks too much; smart aleck. **pilosopuen.** *v.* to talk back to in disrespect, be a smart aleck toward. **Dinak pilpilosopuen.** Don't be a smart aleck with me.

pilosopía: (Sp. *filosofía*) *n.* philosophy.

pílut: ipilut. *v.* to stick by pressing; apply grease to hair; spread (jelly, etc.) on bread. **maipilut.** *v.* to have glue stuck to; to be spread, smeared. **ipilutpilut.** *v.* to crush a bug under one's feet. **mapilutan.** *v.* to be smeared. **pilutan.** *v.* to smear on. [Tag. *pahid, kulapol*]

pilóto: (Sp. *piloto:* pilot) *n.* pilot. (*mangyurit*)

pilútok: pilpilutok. *n.* skin blister (*kapuyo*). [Tag. *paltós*]

pilpíl: *a.* crushed, flat. **pilpilen.** *v.* to crush, flatten. **napilpil nga isem.** *n.* shy smile. **napilpil a lugan.** *n.* crushed car. [Tag. *pipí*]

pilpilmí: *n.* term given to Filipino mountain guerillas during World War II.

pilták: *n.* blot of ink; stain, smudge, smear, blot larger than the *pilkát.* **ipiltak.** *v.* to stain. **mapiltakan.** *a.* stained; smeared. [Tag. *kulapol*]

piltík: piltiken. *v.* to flick something with the forefinger (by use of the thumb).

píltro: (Sp. *filtro:* filter) *n.* filter.

píman: *adv.* confirmatory adverb. What a pity. (*sayang*) **nakapimpiman.** *a.* pitiful.

pimbréra: (Sp. *fiambrera:* lunch box) *n.* dinner or lunch pail.

pimiénta: (Sp. *pimienta:* pepper) *n.* black pepper. [Tag. *pamintá*]

pimmi(n)-: Perfective form of *pumi-.* **Pimmitlokami.** We did it three times. **Pimmimpatda.** They did it four times.

pimpóng: (Mindanao Ilocano) *n.* snare for wild animals.

pinablád: (f. *bellád*) *n.* salted, boiled corn kernels to which coconut is added.

pin-: see under *pi(n)-*

pina-: Perfective form of *pa- -en* verbs. **Pinadakkelmo manen ti ulok.** You made my head big again (complimented me).

pinaCpa-: *pref.* perfective progressive form of *pa- -en* verb stems. **Siak ti pinalpaldaangam.** I am the one you saddened.

pína₁: *n.* slight hit or touch. **napinaan.** *a.* slightly hurt, slightly offended.

pína₂: (Eng.) *n.* fine. (*multa*)

pinádis: (f. *pádis*) *n*. big homemade cigar. [Tag. *tabako* (Sp.)]

pinag-: Perfective form of the instrumental prefix *pag-* or the causative affix *pag- -en*; also *var.* of *panag-* prefix. **pinagtipon.** assembled. **pinagulimek.** assembled. **pinagdakkel.** made larger. **Pinagdaitna ti tali.** She used the rope to sew it.

pinag- -inn-: Perfective form of *pag- -inn- -en* verbs, indicating perfective, causative, reciprocal action. **pinagkikinnayetket.** caused people to hold on to each other. **pinaginnarakup.** caused people to embrace each other.

pinaginCV-: Perfective of *paginCV-* causative pretentatives: **Apay a pinagintuturognak?** Why did you make me pretend to be asleep?

pinag-óng: (f. *pag-ong*: turtle) *n*. hip roof.

pinaikapi(n)-: Perfective form of the *paikapi(n)-* prefix. **pinaikapinlimak.** I had it done for the fifth time.

pinaipi(n)-: Perfective form of the *paipi(n)-* prefix. **Pinaipiduada.** They did it for the second time.

pinakbét: (p{in}a-kebbet) *n*. Ilocano vegetable dish.

pinaikapi(n)-: Perfective form of *paikapi(n)-* verbs. **Pinaikapinlimak.** I had it done for the fifth time.

pinaipa-: Perfective form of *paipa-* **pinaipababa.** to have had something lowered. **pinaipalaud.** to have had something put to the west.

pinál: (Sp. *final*: final) *a*. end, final. [Tag. *wakás*]

pinang-: *var.* of the *panang-* prefix.

pinangabákan: (f. *abak*) *n*. winnings from gambling.

pinapi(n)-: Perfective form of the *pinapi(n)-* prefix. **lima.** five. **pinapilimana.** She had it done five times.

pínas: *a*. level. (*patad*) **pinasen.** *v*. to smooth, level, even. **mapinas.** *v*. to be leveled; made smooth. **ipinas.** *v*. to spread evenly. [Tag. *patag*]

pinasín: *n*. brown sugar.

pínay: **napinay.** *a*. not excessive; moderate.

pináy: *a*. unable to move. **ipinay.** *v*. to post against a wall.

Pináy: (Tag.) *n*. a Filipino female, *Pilipina*.

pindá: **pindaen.** *v*. to do one by one consecutively without skipping; to examine consecutively without skipping. **-mamindapinda.** *v*. to go from house to house without exception.

pindáng: *n*. jerked meat; beef jerky. **mapindang.** *v*. to be dried in the sun. **pindangen.** *n*. to make beef jerky by drying in the sun; (*coll.*) to skin an enemy. **Nagadiwara ti bang-i ti**

sumarsarebseb a pindang. The smell of the frying jerked meat diffused.

pindanggá: *n*. unkempt woman. (*losiang*)

pinéras: *n*. sapodilla fruit (imported from Mexico).

pinésa: (Sp. *fineza*: finesse) *n*. finesse; fineness in structure.

pini-: *see pini(n)-*.

píni: *n*. *Canarium* sp. tree with fragrant resin and small flowers. **kapinian.** *n*. a grove of *pini* trees.

pínia: (Sp. *piña*: pineapple) *n*. pineapple; *piña* cloth. **kapiniaan.** *n*. pineapple plantation. [Ivt. *payñaw*, Kal. *pingyan*, Tag. *pinyá*]

pinión: (Sp. *piñon*) *n*. nut pine; pine nut.

pini(n)-: Perfective form of *pi(n)-* prefix. **Pininlimada.** They did it five times.

pinípig: *n*. roasted young *diket* rice. **agpinipig.** *v*. to roast immature *diket* rice.

pinípin: **ipinipin.** *v*. to find room for; arrange, set in order. **maipinipin.** *v*. to be given room; arranged neatly; stored properly. **pinipinan.** *v*. to dam a stream in order to scatter the flow. [Tag. *ayos*]

pinnaka-: *var.* of the *pannaka-* prefix.

pinnaki-: *var.* of the *pannaki-* prefix.

pinnó: **sangkapinno.** *var.* of *sangkapunno*.

píno₁: (Sp. *fino*: fine) **napino.** *a*. refined, fine. **papinuen.** *v*. to pulverize. [Kal. *pilu*]

píno₂: (Sp. *pino*: pine) *n*. pine tree.

pínoy: *n*. duck egg without the embryo formed (with the embryo formed it is called *balút*).

Pinóy: (Tag.) *n*. a Filipino male.

pinsán: **pinsanen.** *v*. to do at one time, at one stroke. **agpinsan.** *v*. to come simultaneously, all at once; be unanimous. **napinsan.** *a*. full of, covered with. **paminsanen.** *v*. to do once.

pinsár: (Sp. *pensar*: think) *n*. plan (*gandat*). [Tag. *balak*]

pinsél: (Sp. *pincel*: paintbrush) *n*. small brush.

pínsing: *n*. verbal joust (performed when walking to the *pagating* in a wedding ceremony). **agpipinsing.** *v*. to perform a verbal joust. (see *bukanegan*)

pinsíw: *n*. kissing or taking the hand of an elder to the forehead as a sign of respect. **agpinsiw.** *v*. to take the hand of an elder to the forehead to show respect; to kiss the hand. [Tag. *mano* (Sp.)]

pintá: (Sp. *pinta*: paint) *n*. paint. **agpinta.** *v*. to paint. **mapintaan.** *v*. to be painted. **pintado.** *a*. painted; printed (cloth).

pintakási: (Tagalog also) *n*. patron saint; cockfighting feast (usually associated with a patron saint).

pintál: pintalen. *v.* to soak thread or string before putting it on the netting needle.

pintás: *n.* beauty; elegance; attractiveness. (*libnos*; *dayag*) **napintas.** *n.* beautiful, good-looking, pretty, attractive, charming. **tagipintasen.** *v.* to consider something beautiful. **agpapintas.** *v.* to beautify oneself; wear makeup. **makapapintas.** *a.* beautifying. **papintasen.** *v.* to beautify. **kapintasan.** *a.* most beautiful. **kapintasen.** *v.* to beautify; do one's best. **pinnintasan.** *n.* beauty competition. **pumintas.** *v.* to become beautiful. **Agkakapintasda.** They are equally beautiful. [Bon. *begew*, Ibg. *kasta*, Itg. *básang*, Ivt. *mávid*, Kal. *bibiẏu, laleman*, Knk. *agiúd, alimáy, déngey, sagaytók*, Kpm. *malagu*, Png. *gána*, Tag. *gandá*]

pintaséro: (*coll.*) *n.* critical person.

pinték: napintek. *a.* muscular, robust; vigorous. (*baneg*; *puner*) **pumintek.** *v.* to become muscular. [Tag. *tipunò*]

pintók: see *pattók*: adorn; dot.

pintór: (Sp. *pintor*: painter) *n.* painter.

pintúra: (Sp. *pintura*: painting) *n.* painting; paint.

pínya: (Sp. *piña*: pineapple) *n.* pineapple. (*pinia*)

píngar: *n.* fish fin; comb of a cock (*tapingar*). [Tag. *palikpík* (fin)]

píngas: *a.* with cut-off ears; *n.* rooster without a comb. **pingasan.** *v.* to crop, cut off the ear; cut off the comb of a cock; to clip off.

pingáw₁: *n.* a kind of meter-long marine fish.

pingáw₂: *n.* cut garment. **napingawan.** *a.* chipped, notched, indented, nicked; torn (*tipping*). [Tag. *bungì*]

pingét: *n.* dedication to a job; perseverance; persistence; tenacity. **ipinget.** *v.* to persist; put all one's effort into a job. **napinget.** *a.* pertinacious, tenacious, persistent; fervent. **kinapinget.** *n.* persistence, tenacity. **maipinget.** *v.* to get caught in; stick to. **kapingetan a karibal.** the most persistent rival. [Tag. *sigasig*]

pinggá: *n.* menopause. **agpingga.** *v.* to reach menopause. **di-mamingga.** *a.* without end. [Tag. *pinggá* = lever; carrying pole]

pinggán₁: *n.* plate. **agpinggan.** *v.* to use a plate. **ipinggan.** *v.* to put on a plate. **agkapinggan.** *v.* to share a plate. **pagpingganan.** *v.* to use as a plate. **sangapingan.** *n.* one plateful. [Kal. *peẏatu*, Png. *lipong*, Tag. *pinggán*]

pinggán₂: pingpinggan. *n. pumakbó* fish; round, white, edible marine mollusk.

pinggí: pinggien. *v.* to shake; move from side to side. **agpingipinggi.** *v.* to stumble; shake repeatedly. **pinggi-pinggien.** *v.* to rock, shake repeatedly. [Tag. *ugà*]

pinggít: *n.* toying, touching, groping, fingering. **puminggit.** *v.* to finger, grope.

pinggúd: (*obs.*) see *píngud*: one eared.

pinggól: *n.* chignon, ponytail, also *pininggól*. **agpinggol.** *v.* to knot one's hair. **napinggol.** *a.* gathered in a knot (said of the hair); with a ponytail. **sangkapinggol.** *n.* one bunch. **Atiddog ti buokna a napinggol sa adda pay aritosna.** He has long hair with a ponytail and even has earrings. [Tag. *pusód*]

pingi: *n.* river fish trap.

pingíl: *n.* ankle; edge; corner. **mapingilpingil.** *v.* to do cornered, do something when being confronted on all sides (a mother with seven complaining children). [Tag. *bukung-bukóng* (ankle)]

píngir: *n.* tip; edge, margin; corner. (*igid*; *suli*) **mapingir.** *v.* to be on the edge. of. **iti pingir ti isip.** in the corner of one's mind. [Tag. *gilid*, *bingit*]

pingír: *n. var.* of *pingíl*, ankle.

ping-ír: *n.* small part, portion. **iping-ir.** *v.* to give a little piece of something, share. **sangaping-ir.** *n.* a little piece, portion.

píngit: *n.* indigo band of a *bandála* blanket.

píngka: *n.* swordfish.

píngkas: (Sp. *finca*: farm) *n.* real estate.

pingkí: *n.* flint and steel used to make fires. **agpingki.** *v.* to start a fire with flint; flash in one's mind; flare up (anger). **agpingki ti panagkitana.** *exp.* to flare up (anger). **agpingkipingki.** *v.* to flicker. [Tag. *pingkî*]

pingkít: *a.* with small eyes, almond eyed; small (*singkit, kusipét*). [Tag. *singkít*]

pingngá: *n.* species of medicinal plant.

ping-ó: *n.* sprain, strain. (*ligos*) **ping-uen.** *v.* to twist or sprain the arm or finger. **maping-o.** *v.* to be sprained. [Tag. *linsád*]

píngud: *a.* one eared. **pipingudan.** *n.* area around the ear. **pingudan.** *v.* to twist the ear of. [Tag. *pingód* (one eared); *pingól* (without ears)]

ping-ól: *n.* disabled hand; sprain. (*bullo*) [Png. *pingól*]

píngot: pinguten. *v.* to wring (the ear). (*lapigos*)

pingpíng: *n.* cheek. **pingping ti ubet.** *n.* buttock. (*kubongkubong*) **pingping ti uki.** *n.* labia majora of the vulva. **pingping ti sabangan.** *n.* sides of a bar at the mouth of a river. **pingping ti bulan.** *n.* the side of the moon. [Bon. *tamong*, Ibg. *pángal, mutung*, Ifg. *pahong*, Itg. *samping*, Ivt. *pisñiq*, Kal. *aping*, Knk. *tamíl, tamóng*, Png. *apíng*, Kpm., Tag. *pisngî*]

pingpinggán: *n.* windowpane oyster, sea animal similar to *Placuna placenta*.

piúka: *n.* contrivance of two sticks used by farmers to thresh bundles of rice.

piúkot: *a*. hunchbacked. (*kubbo*) **agpiukot**. *v*. to stoop. [Tag. *kubà*]

pioréa: (Sp. *piorrea*: pyorrhea) *n*. pyorrhea, disease of the gums.

piús: *n*. a kind of small, red-eyed, black bird; (*lit*.) native ceremonial dance.

piúte: *n*. kind of card game.

pípa: (Sp. *pipa*: pipe) *n*. pipe.

pipíit: *n*. very small bird.

pipíno: (Sp. *pepino*: cucumber) *n*. cucumber. [Knk. *kasímun*]

pípit: (*fam*.) *n*. vagina. (*piting*; *uki*)

pippí: **pippian**. *n*. a dish of meat and rice cooked in banana leaves and seasoned with *piás*.

pirák: *n*. money (*kuarta*); silver. **napirak**. *a*. rich, wealthy. **pirakan**. *v*. to finance; bribe. **pamirakan**. *n*. source of income. **pumirak**. *v*. to become silver-colored (hair). [Knk. *pilák*, Png. *pilák*, Tag. *pera* (money), *pilak* (silver)]

pir-ák: **pir-aken**. *v*. to break into pieces.

pirámida: (Sp. *pirámide*: pyramid) *n*. pyramid.

pirápid: *n*. line, row, file. (*batug*; *intar*)

pirapír: *n*. weather vane; strip, band. **agpirapir**. *v*. to flutter when hanging loose.

piráta: (Sp. *pirata*: pirate) *n*. pirate.

pirgís: *n*. scrap, shred, small bit of something. (*pisang*) **mapirgis**. *v*. to be torn, shredded. **pirgisen**. *v*. to tear. **pirgisan**. *v*. to tear off. **sangkapirgis**. *n*. one small piece of; one scrap of. **Nangpirgis iti napudot pay a pandesal ket insakmolna**. He tore off a piece of the still warm bread and put it in his mouth. [Png. *pilát*, *pinglis*, Tag. *pilas*, *punit*]

pirínsa: *n*. flatiron. (*plansa*) **agpirinsa**. *v*. to iron.

píring: **apagpiring**. (*reg*.) *a*. slightly different. (*supadi*, *sabali*)

pir-íng: *var*. of *ping-ir*: small piece or portion. **Uray no sangkapir-ing la koma, awan tinaktakawmi nga impapaunegyo**. We didn't steal anything to feed you with, not even a little morsel.

pírit₁: **piriten**. *v*. to crumble or roll between the fingers; pinch. **agpiritpirit**. *v*. to toy with, finger (said of babies fondling the mother's breasts). **ipirit**. *v*. to heed, consider; give importance to. **maipirit**. *v*. to be harassed; persecuted. **kas la sangsangkapirit**. *a*. shy. **sangkapirit**. *n*. one pinchful. **di-mangipirpirit**. to refuse to respect one's elders; be stubborn. **Nagaaribungbong dagiti babbai nga agpirpirit iti innipis**. The women crowded around fingering the cards. [Tag. *kurót*]

pírit₂: **pipiritan**. *n*. earlobe. (*tetebbengan*, *piditpidit*) **Naingpis ti pipiritanna**. *exp*. denoting excessive copulation (*lit*: thin earlobe). [Knk. *lapáy*, *liplipáy*]

piríw: **pirpiriw**. *n*. kind of small greenish black bird, green-tailed parrot.

pírma: (Sp. *firma*: signature) *n*. signature. **agpirma, pirmaan**. *v*. to sign. **ipirma**. *v*. to affix one's signature on something. **Maysa a ngilaw laengen ti di nakapagpirma**. *exp*. denoting recency of event (*lit*: only one fly hasn't signed).

pirmádo: (Sp. *firmado*: signed) *a*. signed.

pírmes: (Sp. *firmes*: firm) **agpirmes**. *v*. to stand at attention.

pírme, pirmí: (Sp. *firme*: firm; steady) *a*, *adv*. permanent; firm; pure; steady; *adv*. very; well; entirely; often, constantly; altogether; usually; utterly. **agpirmi**. *v*. to stay permanently. **ipirmi**. *v*. to put in place; position permanently. **Pirmi ti kuartana**. He has a lot of money. **Pirmi nga adda kuartana**. He always has money. **Pirmi ti pudot**. It is very hot. **Ammok a pirmi**. I know it well. **Pirmi ti panagkinnayammet ken panagkinnagatda no mapupokda iti baso**. They are constantly entangling and biting each other if they are confined in a glass.

pirméro: *var*. of *primero*: first.

pírmes: (Sp. *firmes!*: stand at attention!) **agpirmes**. *v*. to stand at attention.

pirngát: *a*. torn. (*pigis*) **pirngatan**. *v*. to tear, pull apart. **napirngat**. *a*. torn. [Tag. *punit*]

pirúkong₁: *n*. hollow part, concavity; *a*. hollow.

pirúkong₂: *a*. bent, hunched. **agpirukong**. *v*. to bend, hunch (*kubbo*). [Tag. *lukóng*]

pirútong: *n*. crowd, throng. **agpirutong**. *v*. to crowd, throng. **agpipirutong**. *v*. to cluster; group; (*coll*.) crowd about lazily.

pirpír₁: *n*. weather vane, vane.

pirpír₂: *n*. sound of fluttering. **agpirpir**. *v*. to flutter (when hanging); shake; quiver. **mamirpir**. *v*. to shiver, shake, tremble.

pirpír₃: **mapirpirpir**, **pirpir-pirpir**. *a*. raveled; worn out.

pirpír₄: *n*. food crumbs that stick around the mouth when eating. **agpirpir**. *v*. have food crumbs hanging around the mouth. [Tag. *dusing*]

pirroká: **pirpirroka**. *n*. kind of small brown bird.

pirsáy: *n*. shred, small piece; *a*. torn, shredded. **pirsayen**. *v*. to sever; shred. **mapirsay**. *v*. to be shredded; torn. **napirsaypirsay**. *a*. torn to shreds. **Pirsay ti dulpet a supot ti pungan**. The dank pillowcase was torn. [Tag. *punit*]

pirsík: *n*. small amount.

pirtáng: see *pirténg*: to stretch; strain.

pirténg: **pirtengen**. *v*. to stretch; strain. (*irteng*, *bennat*)

písang: *a.* torn; shredded. (*pigis*) **pisangen.** *v.* to tear to bits, shred. **mapisang.** *a.* to be torn to shreds; to be shredded. **Sintagari ni Macario a nangpisang iti surat.** Macario ripped up the letter without a word. **Linekkabna ti naipaskil a kartolina sana pinisangpisang.** He removed the posted placard (off the wall) and tore it up. [Kal. *pissay*, Tag. *punit*]

pisára: (Sp. *pizarra*: chalkboard) *n.* blackboard; chalkboard. **ipisarra.** *v.* to put on the blackboard. [Kal. *gigilliyan*]

pisát: *n.* piece of cloth, rope, etc. **agpisat.** *v.* to cut a piece of cloth.

pisáw₁: *n.* splashing sound; puddle of water. **agpisaw.** *v.* to make a splattering sound. **agpisawpisaw.** *v.* the splashing sound made when crossing bodies of water. **Pumisawpisaw dagiti dapanna a magna iti waig.** The soles of his feet splashed about as he walked in the creek. [Tag. *tilamsík*]

pisáw₂: *n.* kind of *buneng*.

pisél: **pislen.** *v.* to squeeze (*pespes*); press; knead. **Binay-ak a pinispiselna dagiti ramayko.** I let him squeeze my fingers. [Tag. *pisíl*]

pisgá: *n.* hunting spear (*gayang*). [Tag. *sibát*]

pisgár: *n.* neck feather of a fowl; hackle.

písi: *n.* part, fragment, piece (cut of a round object or lengthwise cut of a long object, a widthwise cut of a long object is called *puted*); (*coll.*) female genitalia. **agpisi.** *v.* to cut up, divide. **kapispisi, kappisi.** *a.* just cut, just divided. **ipapisi.** *v.* to have something divided, cut up. **ipisian.** *v.* to give a share to someone. **pisien.** *v.* to divide, separate; halve. **pisien ti bagik.** *n.* my spouse. **kapisi ti puso.** *n.* spouse, sweetheart. **pisi ti bulan.** *n.* crescent moon. [Kal. *bissak*, Tag. *kabiyák*]

písika: (Sp. *física*: physics) *n.* physics.

písiko: (Sp. *físico*: physicist) *n.* physicist.

pisiolohía: (Sp. *fisiología*: physiology) *n.* physiology. **pisiolóhiko.** *a.* physiological.

pisioterapía: (Sp. *fisioterapia*: physiotherapy, Ilocano accentuation) *n.* physiotherapy.

pisípis: *n.* movement of a trapped person or animal confined to a small place. **awan pagpisipisan.** *exp.* packed like sardines, not being able to move. **agpisipis.** *v.* to move restrainedly.

pis-ít: **pis-iten.** *v.* to crush between two things (*lig-ís*); compress; push a button; abort an embryo. **mapis-it.** *v.* to be crushed. **agpapis-it.** *v.* (*fig.*) to have an abortion. **Pinis-itna ti maikatlo a kadsaaran.** He pushed (the elevator button) for the third floor. [Tag. *pisâ*]

piskál: (Sp. *fiscal*: fiscal) *n.* fiscal attorney.

piskália: (f. *piskal*) *n.* fiscal's office.

piskánte: (Sp. *pescante*: driver's seat) *n.* driver's seat.

piskária: (Sp. *pesca*: fishing + *-ia*) *n.* fishponds. (*pukpukan, piskiria*)

piskél: *n.* large muscle of the arm or leg. **napiskelan.** *a.* pulled (said of a muscle); sprained. **namiskel.** *a.* muscular. [Kal. *kuÿat*, Tag. *kalamnán*]

piskiriá: *var.* of *piskaria*: fishery.

piskót: *n.* enclosed territory. **ipiskot.** *v.* to corner; enclose. **maipiskot.** *v.* to be cornered; to be enclosed. [Tag. *pikot*]

pisláng: *n.* half of something cut lengthwise; (*obs.*) fifty percent.

pisngát: *a.* open; dilated. **pisngaten.** *v.* to open; dilate. **napisngat.** *a.* open, dilated. [Tag. *buká*]

pisók: *n.* contents put into a container. **ipisok.** *v.* to throw or pour into a hole or a container. **naipisok.** *a.* flung into a hole, a container, etc. **mamisok.** *v.* to rinse rice and put it into a pot to cook. [Tag. *lagáy*]

písol: *n.* unevenness; having lumps. (*pissúol*)

pisón: (Sp. *pisón*: rammer) *n.* steamroller; paver's beetle. **pisunen.** *v.* to flatten with a steamroller; pave a road with a *pison*.

pisóng: **maipisong.** *v.* to slip into a hole (said of the feet).

písos: (Sp. *peso*: peso) *n.* peso; one hundred centavos. **mamisos.** *a.* worth one peso. **sagpipipos.** *a.* one peso each.

pispís: *n.* temple of the head. **pispísen.** *v.* to deseed cotton by hand. **pinispis.** (*obs.*) *n.* removing the jawbone. **mapispisan.** *v.* to be hit on the temple of the head. **papispisan.** *v.* to slap in the face. [Kal. *pispis*, Tag. *sentido* (temple, Sp.); *sampál* (slap)]

pissá: *var.* of *pessa*: hatch eggs. [Tag. *pisâ*]

pissáag: (*obs.*) **agpissaag.** *v.* to writhe in pain.

pissát: *see pessát*: cut.

pissí: (*obs.*) *n.* rope made of coconut husk fiber.

pissúol: *n.* bulge; mound; lump. **pissuolan.** *a.* heaping, filled to the top. **mamissuol.** *v.* to bulge; lump. **pissuolan.** *v.* to overfill. **Dalem ken battikuleng ti manok ken agpispissuol nga innapuy ti kinnanda.** They ate liver, chicken gizzards, and heaping amounts of rice. [Tag. *umbók*]

pistí: (*slang*) **pistien.** *v.* to kill. **napisti.** *a.* dead. [Tag. *patáy*]

pistóla: (Sp. *pistola*: pistol) *n.* pistol. **nakapistola.** *a.* carrying a pistol.

pístula: (Sp. *fístula*: fistula) *n.* fistula, long tube-like sore.

pistón: (Sp. *pistón*) *n.* piston.

pítak: *n.* mud, mire. (*lutlót*) **pinnitakan.** *n.* mud fight. **pitakpitak.** *a.* smattered with mud.

sipipitak. *a.* covered with mud. **agkapitakan.** *v.* to wallow in mud. **agpinnitak.** *v.* to throw mud at each other. **kapitakan.** *n.* mire; muddy place. [Ibg. *lufeq*, *fuyoq*, Itg. *lutúlot*, Ivt. *hutaq*, Kal. *pitok*, Knk. *pítek*, Kpm. *búrak*, Png. *piték*, Tag. *putik*]

piták: pitaken. *v.* to break circular objects. (eggs, *kalamansi*, etc.)

pitáka: (Sp. *petaca*: tobacco pouch) *n.* wallet, money bag; bag. **ipitaka.** *v.* to put in one's wallet. **nakapitaka.** *a.* carrying a wallet.

pitangkók: *n.* occiput, back part of the head or skull.

pitbóng: *n. var.* of *pikbong*: rifle used by the Japanese in World War II.

pítik: *n.* corporal punishment; flicking with the finger; flip. **pitiken.** *v.* to punish physically. **pitiken.** *v.* to flip with the finger; flick the ear in punishment. **pinnitik.** *n.* a children's game consisting of imitating motions of others after briefly uncovering the covered faces when motioned to do so; game consisting of the *pitik* as punishment for the loser. [Tag. *pitík*]

pitík₁: *n.* beat; throb; pulsation. (*bitek*; *giteb*; *gutok*) **agpitikpitik.** *v.* to beat, throb, pulsate. (heart) **Addakan iti pitik ti sabali a panawen, iti sabali a disso.** You are in the beat of a different time and place. [Tag. *tibók*, *pintíg*]

pitík₂: pitpitik. *n.* a kind of small insect.

pitíng₁: (*coll.*) *n.* female genitalia. [Tag. *puki*]

pitíng₂: agpiting. *v.* to move slightly, stir; flick. **pitingen.** *v.* to stir; move slightly; flick with the finger. **Kasla adda nagpiting iti kaunggak.** Something stirred inside me.

pitíng₃: pitpiting. *n.* a kind of small gray singing bird.

pit-íng: *n.* chip, nick. **pit-íngan.** *v.* to chip, notch, nick (*tipping*). **pit-ingen.** *v.* to break into pieces. **sangapit-ing.** *n.* small piece. [Tag. *pingas*]

pitípit: pitipitan. *v.* to fasten, tie, bind (*patapat*); (*obs.*) *n.* small handle. [Tag. *gapos*]

pitís: *a.* tight fitting (*ilet*, *kipet*). [Tag. *sikíp*]

pitlagáw: *var.* of *pittagáw*: **pitpitlagaw.** *n.* a kind of small black and white bird.

pitló: (f. *talló*) *adv.* three times (*mamitló*). **pitluen.** *v.* to do three times. **Ngem narumek ti buttiki idi pitluenna nga akkalen.** But the cowry shell was crushed when he forced it open for the third time.

píto: (Sp. *pito*: whistle) *n.* bamboo flute; whistle. **agpito.** *v.* to play the bamboo flute. **pituan.** *v.* to whistle at someone; play the flute at.

pitó: *num.* seven. **maikapito.** *num.* seventh. **pitpito.** only seven. **pagkapituen.** *v.* to divide into seven parts. **mamimpito.** *adv.* seven times.

sagpipito. *num.* seven each. [Kal., Png., Tag. *pitó*]

pítong: *var.* of *patong*: hip.

pitúpit: *n.* a kind of small grayish brown bird named after its cry.

pitpít₁: *n.* a variety of awned rice with depressed red kernel.

pitpít₂: *a.* flat, flattened, crushed. **pitpiten.** *v.* to forge crush; flatten; hammer metals. **mapitpit.** *v.* to be crushed (fruits); flattened. [Tag. *pipí*]

pítsa: (Sp. *ficha*: chip) *n.* chip used in gambling.

pitsíng: (*fam.*) *n.* young girls' vagina. (*piting*)

pítso: (Sp. *pecho*: breast) *n.* breast of chicken (*petso*). [Knk. *túmey*]

pitsóg: pipitsugen. *a.* not really delicious; tasteless.

pitsón: (Sp. *pichón*: young pigeon) *n.* squab, young pigeon.

pittagáw: *n.* species of songbird named for its song, also called *pitlagáw*. **No aguni ti pittagaw, aw-awaganna ti tudo.** When the *pittagaw* sings, it calls for the rain.

pittárok: *n.* conical-shaped woman's hat.

pittóki: *n.* kind of small, black round mollusk.

píwak: *a.* large (said of the mouth); deformed (brim of baskets). **agpiwak.** *v.* to deform; warp out of shape (baskets). **piwaken.** *v.* to widen.

píwir₁: piniwir. *n.* old-fashioned solid ring earring.

píwir₂: *n.* the position of the teeth of a saw; *a.* unaligned, not centered (as the teeth of a saw). **piwiren.** *v.* to set the teeth of a saw in proper position, making them unaligned to ease in cutting. **pagpiwir.** *n.* tool used to set the teeth of a saw in their proper position.

píwir₃: *var.* of *píwis*: awry, crooked, contorted, deformed; unsymmetrical. **Nabang-arankami idi saanen nga agpiwirpiwir ti balay.** We were relieved when the house was no longer awry.

píwis: *a.* crooked, twisted, awry, contorted; curved; deformed; *n.* scapular feathers. **agpiwis.** *v.* to have twisted lips. **piniwis.** *a.* unsymmetrical, irregular (in shape). **Agpiwpiwis ti isemna.** His smile is crooked. [Tag. *ngiwî*]

plahelánte: (Sp. *flagelante*: flagellant) *n.* flagellant. **plahelasion.** *n.* (self-)flagellation.

plahiadór: (Sp. *plagiario*: plagiarist + English) *n.* plagiarist, person who plagiarizes.

pláhio: (Sp. *plagio*: plagiarism) *n.* plagiarism.

pláka: (Sp. *placa*: disc) *n.* disc, record; license plate; plaque; photographic plate. **iplaka.** *v.* to record.

planáda: (Sp.) **maplanada.** *v.* can be leveled.

pláneta: (Sp. *planeta*: planet) *n.* planet.

planetário: (Sp. *planetario*: planetarium) *n.* planetarium.

pláno: (Sp. *plano*: plan) *n.* plan, project (*panggep*); layout; sketch. **agplano.** *v.* to plan. **maplano.** *v.* to be planned. **planuen.** *v.* to plan something. [Tag. *balak*]

plánsa: *var.* of *plantsa*: iron. **plansador.** *n.* ironing board. **plansado.** *a.* ironed. [Kal. *pulinsa*]

plánta: (Sp. *planta*: plant) *n.* physical plant (buildings); power plant. **Naammuanmi a mangipatakderka iti planta.** We knew that you are putting up a power plant.

plantár: (Sp. *plantar*: set up, plant) **iplantar.** *v.* to map out.

plantasión: (Sp. *plantación*) *n.* plantation.

plantília: (Sp. *plantilla*) *n.* plantilla, list of employees, positions, and salaries; mechanical template.

plantsá: (Sp. *plancha*: iron) *n.* iron (used for pressing clothes) **agplantsa, plantsaen.** *v.* to iron. **maplantsa.** *v.* to be ironed. **plantsado.** *a.* ironed.

plása: (Sp. *plaza*: plaza) *n.* town square, plaza. **agpaplasa.** *v.* to go to the plaza.

plasénta: (Sp. *placenta*: placenta) *n.* placenta, afterbirth.

plásma: (Sp. *plasma*: plasma) *n.* plasma.

pláso: (Sp. *plazo*: space of time; installment) *n.* handicap in a race or game; allowance; limit; deadline; installment payment; period allowed for installment payments; conditions of a contract. **Naikkanda iti lima nga aldaw a plaso a manyakar kadagiti natda a bakada.** They gave a five-day period for them to move their remaining cows.

plastádo: (Sp. *aplastado*: crushed) *a.* lying flat, prone; crushed; vanquished; bedridden; tight-fitting.

plastadór: (Sp. *aplastador*: crusher, flattener) *n.* kind of pliers used by cobblers to pull off soles.

plastár: (Sp. *aplastar*: crush, flatten) *n.* position; fitting, fit. **agplastar.** *v.* to sit up straight; be ready; position oneself; present oneself; fit (clothes). **iplastar.** *v.* to put on correctly; fix; adjust clothes; set in place; iron. **nakaplastar.** *a.* dressed up; adjusted, fixed in position. **plastaren.** *v.* to press (clothes). **naplastaran.** *a.* patched (tire). **Baliwannanto manen ti pag-plastaranna.** He will change his position again. **Saan a nasayaat ti plastar ti badona.** The fit of his suit is not good.

plastík: (Eng.) *n.* plastic; *a.* plastic, artificial; fake; (*coll.*) insincere.

pláta: (Sp. *plata*: silver) *n.* silver (*pirak*). **boda de plata.** *n.* silver wedding anniversary.

platapórma: (Sp. *plataforma*: platform) *n.* platform; rostrum; dais; bridge of a ship.

platéra: (f. *pláto*) *n.* shelf for plates; cabinet for plates, China cabinet.

platería: (Sp. *platería*: silversmith's workshop) *n.* workshop of a silversmith.

platéro: (Sp. *platero*: silversmith) *n.* silversmith.

platiádo: (f. *plateado*: silver plated) *a.* silver plated.

platíka: (Sp. *plática*: talk) *n.* sermon. **agplatika.** *v.* to preach.

platílio: (Sp. *platillo*: small plate) *n.* saucer; small plate; pan of a weighing scale.

platína: (Sp. *platina*: platen) *n.* platen; bedplate in printing; slide of a microscope.

platíno: (Sp. *platino*: platinum) *n.* platinum.

platíto: (Sp. *platito*: small plate) *n.* small plate, saucer. [Kal. *kisling*]

pláto: (Sp. *plato*: plate) *n.* plate. (*pinggán*) **agkaplato.** *v.* to share a plate.

pláya: (Sp. *playa*: beach) *n.* beach. (*apláya*) **agpaplaya.** *v.* to go to the beach.

plebesíto: (Sp. *plebiscito*) *n.* plebiscite.

plegadúra: (Sp.) *n.* folding; plaiting.

plegária: (Sp. *plegaria*: prayer) *n.* tolling of church bells for the dead; prayer.

pléges: (Sp. *pliegue*: pleat) *n.* pleat, fold in clothes.

plémas: (Sp. *flema*: phlegm) *n.* phlegm.

pléte: (Sp. *flete*: freight) *n.* fare for passengers. **agplete.** *v.* to pay the fare. **pagplete.** *n.* money for the fare. **iplete.** *v.* to spend on one's fare. [Kal. *puliti*]

plétsa: (Sp. *flecha*: arrow) *n.* arrow; dart. (*pana*)

pliégo: (Sp. *pliego*: sheet of paper) *n.* sheet of paper.

plúma: (Sp. *pluma*: pen) *n.* pen. (*pagsúrat*)

plumáhe: (Sp. *plumaje*: plumage) *n.* plumage; feathers.

ploméro: (Sp. *plomero*: plumber) *n.* plumber. (*tubéro*)

pluméro: (Sp. *plumero*: feather duster) *n.* feather duster.

ploréra: (Sp. *florera*: flower vase) *n.* flower vase; female florist.

ploréro: (Sp. *florero*: florist) *n.* florist.

plorída: (Sp. *florida*) **plorida blangka.** *n.* a kind of perfume.

plóta: (Sp. *flota*: fleet) *n.* fleet of ships.

plotadór: (Sp. *flotador*) *n.* floater (carburetor).

plotéra: (Sp.) *n.* earthenware tray.

plúta: (Sp. *fluta*: flute) *n.* flute. **agpluta.** *v.* to play the flute. [Kal. *tilupok, tungali*]

plotília: (Sp. *flotilla*: small fleet) *n.* small fleet of ships.

puá: (Sp. *poa*: bowline bridle) *n*. plectrum used in playing stringed instruments.

puágit: agpuagit. *v*. to leap, run wild (*buatit*). **Nakitana ti nalukmeg a kuneho a nagpuagit a kimmamang iti nalayang a tanap.** He saw the fat rabbit leap to take shelter in the clear field.

puák₁: *n*. caudal fin, tail fin. (*pigar*)

puák₂: mapuak. *v*. to break off at the root (horns).

puáli: *var*. of *bual*: fall down; knock down.

poblasión: (Sp. *población*: population) *n*. town proper.

publikáno: (Sp. *publicano*) *n*. tax collector.

publikár: (Sp. *publicar*) **ipublikar.** *v*. to publish. (*pabláak*)

publikasión: (Sp. *publicación*) *n*. publication.

públiko: (Sp. *público*: public) *n*, *a*. public; audience. **pampubliko a lugar.** *n*. place designated for public use.

publisidád: (Sp. *publicidad*: publicity) *n*. publicity; public notice.

publisísta: (Sp. *publicista*) *n*. publisher.

póbre: (Sp. *pobre*: poor) *a*. poor, indigent. (*napanglaw*) **matapobre.** *n*. person who belittles the poor. **pobresito.** *n*. poor boy.

pudagdág: *n*. pale, dull, with no gloss or shine; color of a dead person. (*lusiaw*) **pumudagdag.** *v*. to turn pale. [Tag. *putlâ*]

pudánir: agpudanir. *v*. to accuse an innocent person; throw the blame at someone else. (*pabasol*)

púdaw: *n*. whiteness. **napudaw.** *a*. light complexioned, white, whitish. **pumudaw.** *v*. to become lighter in complexion. **papudawen.** *v*. to make white; bleach. **pamudpudawen.** *a*. a little bit white. **pudaw-linong (ti kudil).** *a*. very white from keeping in the shade (said of skin). [Tag. *putî*]

podér: (Sp. *poder*: power) *n*. power (*pigsa*; *bileg*); authority. **ipoder.** *v*. to authorize.

pudnó: *n*. truth. *a*. true, real, actual, sure. (*payso*) **agpudno.** *v*. to tell the truth; confess. **napudno.** *a*. true; sincere; fervent. **pumudno.** *v*. to be realized, to materialize; come to pass. **makapudno, pumudno.** *v*. to do the right way; to accomplish; succeed. **mapudnuan.** *v*. to be able to tell the truth. **pagpudnuen.** *v*. to force someone to tell the truth. **ipudno.** *v*. to say; express; tell the truth; confess. **sipupudno.** *adv*. truly, sincerely. **Adda kuma ipudnok kadakayo.** I have something to confess to you. [Ibg. *kurug*, Ivt. *uyud*, Kal. *tuttuwa*, Kpm. *tutu*, Png. *tuá*, Tag. *totoó*]

pudó: *n*. fruit of the betel pepper.

púdon₁: *n*. bobbin, spool used to hole thread for the warp. **pagpudunan.** *n*. spool; winder for spooling thread.

púdon₂: pudunen. *v*. to gather without order; throw together in a disorderly way; crumple.

pudónan: *n*. peace pact among the mountain tribes. **agpudunan.** *v*. to make a peace pact.

púdos: *n*. physiognomy: appearance, aspect, look (*langa*) as used in fortune-telling. **ipudusan.** *v*. to tell a fortune by reading the palm or other features.

pudós: *n*. false hair worn in the chignon; wig.

púdot: *n*. heat, warmth; fever. (*bara*) **agpudot.** *v*. to be cranky, irritable. **agpapudot.** *v*. to warm oneself. **agpinnudot.** *v*. to fight with each other, argue. **napudot.** *a*. hot, warm; feverish. **pudot ti ulo.** *n*. anger. **napudot ti ulo.** *a*. angry. **pumudot.** *v*. to become hot; become feverish. **puduten.** *v*. to feel warm, hot. **kapudot.** *n*. temperature. **kapudutan.** *n*. outdoors under the sun. **agkapudutan.** *v*. to stay under the sun. **apagpudot.** *a*. lukewarm. **pamudpuduten.** *a*. lukewarm, slightly hot, tepid. **kinapudot.** *n*. heat; warmness; anger; irritability. **ipapudot.** *v*. to heat up, reheat. **managpudpudot.** *a*. irritable; easily angered. **pagpupudutan.** *v*. to be angry for no reason. **mapagpupudutan.** *v*. to be the object of someone's anger; to be the butt of jokes. **pudóten.** *v*. to feel hot, uneasy. **No agpadada ngata a managpudpudot, tumayab amin a plato.** If they are the same in their hot tempers, all the plates will fly. **Napudot ti kosina.** The kitchen is hot (said when there's a party). [Ibg. *fátu, pátu*, Ivt. *kuhat*, Kal. *attob*, Kpm. *mapáliq*, Png. *petáng*, Tag. *init*]

pudpód: pumudpod. *v*. to wear out (shoes, etc.).

pudtó: *n*. guess (*pugtó*). **pudtuan.** *v*. to guess. [Png. *parlés*, Tag. *hulà*]

pué(g): Interjection expressing disgust.

puéblo: (Sp. *pueblo*: town) *n*. municipality; township.

puéde: (Sp. *puede*: can) It is allowed, permitted. [Tag. *puwede* = be able to; allowed]

puég: *var*. of *pué*: interjection expressing disgust.

puégo: (Sp. *fuego*: fire) **albor de puego.** *n*. fire tree.

púek: *n*. owl (*kullaaw*). [Png. *kulayot*, Tag. *baháw, kuwago* (Sp.)]

puennát: kapuennat. *n*. side of a river.

puéra: (Sp. *fuera*: out) *prep*. except; excluding; besides; *interj*. Get out! Go away! **ipuera.** *v*. to exclude; get rid of. **agpuera.** *v*. to go away. **puera angaw.** joking aside. **puera de los buenos.** excluding the good ones (present company excluded). **puera usog.** knock on wood (expression said to rid oneself of bad luck). **Dagiti Ilokano ditoy puera de los buenos a mabaindan nga agsao iti Ilokano.** The Ilocanos here, excluding the good ones, are ashamed to speak Ilocano.

puérsa: (Sp. *fuerza*: strength, force) *n.* force, strength (*pigsa*); effort. **agpuersa.** *v.* to make an effort. **napuersa.** *a.* strong. **ipuersa.** *v.* to insist, enforce. **puersaen.** *v.* to force. **puersaan.** *v.* to force someone (*piliten*). **puersado.** *a.* forced.

puérta: (Sp. *puerta*: door) *n.* door, gate; vaginal opening. **Nadlawna a saanen nga iti ubetna ti rummuaran ti rugitna no di ket iti puertana.** She noticed that it was no longer from her anus that the excreta came out, but rather from her vagina.

puérte: (Sp. *fuerte*: strong) *a.* strong. (*pigsá*)

puérto: (Sp. *puerto*: port) *n.* port; harbor.

pués: (Sp. *pues*: well) transitional word: well; so.

poesía: (Sp. *poesía*: poetry) *n.* poetry. (*daniw*)

puésto: (Sp. *puesto*: post) *n.* post; job; position. **agpuesto.** *v.* to establish oneself in a place; place oneself; (*military*) take one's positions. **ipuesto.** *v.* to place a person in an office. **Binilin ti teniente dagiti buyotna nga agpuestoda iti kapiniaan.** The lieutenant ordered his troops to position themselves in the pineapple field.

poéta: (Sp. *poeta*: poet) *n.* poet. (*mannániw*)

puéy: *var.* of *pué*: interjection expressing disgust.

púga: (Sp. *fuga*) *n.* flight, escape; elopement. **agpuga.** *v.* to escape, flee; elope; leak.

púgad: *n.* *syn.* of *daná*: path. [Tag. *pugad* = nest]

pugagáw: *n.* see *pudagdag*: pale; dull; dead; not shiny.

pugánti: (Sp. *fugante*: fugitive; *gigante*: giant) *n.* fugitive; giant.

pugartít: *n.* jerk, quick move. **agpugartit.** *v.* to jerk, move fast.

púgas: **pugasen.** *v.* to wipe out; erase. **mapugas.** *v.* to be wiped out; erased.

pug-áw: *n.* puff of breath. **agpug-aw.** *v.* to blow out (from the mouth); snore blowingly. **pugawan.** *v.* to breathe upon; blow out a candle. **ipug-aw.** *v.* to puff; emit; (*fig.*) whisper a secret to. **agpipinnung-aw ti problema.** *v.* to share each other's problems. **Awan ti agipug-aw.** *exp.* No one will breathe a word. [Png. *bugá*, *yulá*, Tag. *bugá*]

púgay: *n.* discount. **pugayen.** *v.* to discount; deduct from. [Tag. *pugay* = take off hat]

pug-áy: *n.* groan. **pumug-ay.** *v.* to groan; grunt. **pumugpug-ay.** *v.* to blow gusts. [Tag. *igík*, *ungol*]

púged: *n.* corner; dead end; hiding place. **ipuged.** *v.* to pull together; rouse; abduct a woman; rape. [Tag. *gahasà*]

puggáak: *var.* of *paggáak*: unrestrained laughter.

pógi: (Tag.) *a.* handsome. (*taraki*; *guapo*; *taer*; *bisked*; *saldit*)

púgi: **pugien.** *v.* to start weaving. **pamugian.** *n.* first threads of the woof.

pugíit: *a.* with protruding buttocks. (*buriri*) **agpugiit.** *v.* to bend over with the buttocks up; (*fig.*) run like hell. **pugiitan.** *v.* to protrude the buttocks toward someone; (*coll.*) to moon. [Tag. *tuwád*]

pugípog: **pugipugen.** *v.* to cut down all; eliminate all; wipe out completely; annihilate. **napugipog.** *a.* eliminated; exterminated. **Agpinnugipog koma manen dagiti boksingero ngem naguni ti kampana.** The boxers should have exterminated each other, but the bell rang. **Napugipogmo met laengen dagiti arbengna.** You eliminated the obstacles.

pugít: *adv.* nearly; almost.

pugláy: **mapuglay.** *v.* to be cut off; to be stopped; slide down, fall down. **puglayen.** *v.* to cut off; cut down; control; stop. [Tag. *tigil* (control)]

puglít: *n.* small portion of stool. (*pultit*) **makapuglit.** *n.* sound produced by a small evacuation of feces. [Tag. *ipot*]

púgnas: **mapugnas.** *v.* to lose essence; lose spirit (alcohol); lose value; (*reg.*) to be cleansed of sin.

púgo: *n.* quail. **Kasla nadugsak a pugo.** *exp.* denoting excitability (*lit*: like a scared quail). [Ibg. *ammóq*, Png. *púgo*, Tag. *pugò*]

pugód: *n.* bobtail; *a.* tailless.

pugón: (Sp. *fogón*: oven) *n.* oven (*orno*); kitchen range. **makipugon.** *v.* to use someone else's oven. **ipugon.** *v.* to put into the oven. **napugon.** *a.* dried in an oven; baked in an oven. **pinugon.** *a.* baked; *n.* dried tobacco.

pugonéro: (Sp. *fogonero*: furnace tender) *n.* locomotive stoker, furnace tender; manufacturer of stoves or furnaces.

pug-óng: *n.* bundle (*reppet*); tie. **mapug-ong.** *v.* to be bundled; bound. **pug-ongen.** *v.* to bundle; bind together. **sangapug-ong.** *n.* one bundle, bunch. [Tag. *bungkós*]

pugóngan: *n.* small piece of network used to facilitate the start of a net that is later removed.

pugúpog: *n.* short piece of wood. **pugupugen.** *v.* to cut wood into short pieces. [Tag. *putol*]

púgus: *a.* short-haired; short-tailed; short-limbed. **pugusen.** *v.* to cut the web from the loom; to cut testicles off an animal.

pugót₁: *a.* headless. **pugutan.** *v.* to decapitate; cut the head off someone (*putol*). [Tag. *pugot*]

pugót₂: *n.* Negrito; spirit, nocturnal ghost; variety of tobacco with dark leaves; *a.* dark, dark complexioned; blackish. **napugot.** *a.* dark complexioned. **sinanpugot.** (*myth.*) *n.* a horrible monster having no head and fire for blood. **agappugot.** *v.* to have offensive body odor (*lit*: to smell like a *pugot*).

pugpóg₁: **inpugpug.** *n.* meat roasted over the fire. (*tuno*; *pulpog*) **pugpugan.** *v.* to broil; roast; barbecue. **mapugpugan.** *v.* to be broiled, roasted. [Tag. *ihaw*]

pugpóg₂: **pugpugen.** *v.* to spend one's wealth unwisely.

pugpóg₃: *n.* soil pulverizer. (*kuliglíg*)

pugrót: *excl.* showing mild displeasure (*aniá mettén*); *a.* poor, destitute (*panglaw*).

pugsát: *a.* cut in two, snapped. **mapugsat.** *v.* to snap in two. **pugsaten.** *v.* to cut shorter. **pugsapugsat.** *a.* in pieces; not fluent (language). **mapugsatan.** *v.* to die. **di agpugsat.** unending, continuous. **Nagpugsaten ti kanenmi.** We are already out of food. [Tag. *putol*]

pugsáy: see *pusay*: pass away; die.

pugsít: *n.* squirt. **agpugsit.** *v.* to gush out, squirt out. **agpugsipugsit.** *v.* to squirt out little by little. **pumugsit.** *v.* to squirt out (*kubbuar*). **pugsitan.** *v.* to squirt at. **pagpugsit.** *n.* spray can. **Pinugsitan ni Panchito iti bangbanglo ti puraw a pawadna.** Panchito squirted perfume on his white sleeveless shirt. [Tag. *pulandít, puslít*]

pugsó: **ipugso.** *v.* to vomit; belch out; shoot out (volcanoes); eject violently. **pugsuan.** *v.* to spew at; eject at. **sangapugso nga angin.** a gust of wind. [Tag. *bugá*]

pugsót: see *pugsat*: snap in two; cut shorter. **kapugso ti bágis.** (*reg.*) *n.* born of the same mother. **agpugsot.** *v.* to break off easily. **mapugsot ti anges.** *v.* to lose one's breath (die). [Tag. *putol*]

pugtít₁: *n.* small piece of excrement. (*puglit*) **makapugtit.** *v.* to involuntarily excrete a piece of excrement.

pugtít₂: *n.* hissing sound (as one spitting in disgust). **agpugtit.** *v.* to make a hissing sound.

pugtó: *n.* guess. **pugtuan.** *v.* to guess. **mammugto.** *n.* one who practices divination. **pinnugtuan.** *n.* riddle, guessing game. [Bon. *tenek*, Kal. *pugtuwan*, Kpm. *aúl, úla*, Png. *parlés*, Tag. *hulà*]

puhár: (Sp. *pujar*: push, bid up) **puharen.** *v.* to rent (fishpond, rice field, etc.).

póhas: (Sp. *foja*: leaf; folio) *n.* sheet of paper; panel.

puíd: **pamuídan.** *n.* reason, motive; cause.

púil: **mapuil.** *v.* to be knocked down by the wind. **puilen.** *v.* to knock down. [Tag. *tumbá* (Sp.)]

póka: (Sp. *foca*: seal) *n.* seal, a furry marine mammal.

púkal: *n.* breast (of cows); udder (*suso*). **nakapukpukal.** *a.* with rather large breasts or udders. **pukalan.** *a.* endowed with breasts or udders.

pukakkák: (*coll.*) *n.* female genitalia.

púkan₁: *n.* cut down bamboo or wood. **pukanen.** *v.* to cut down trees, fell; prune. **kappukan.** *a.* newly cut. **Kayatko a materred ti panagpukan dagiti kapurokantayo kadagiti kayo.** I would like to control our fellow villager's cutting down of the trees.

púkan₂: **kappukan.** *n.* meat eaten raw or rinsed in hot water.

púkaw: *n.* loss; losses. **agpukaw.** *v.* to disappear, vanish. **pukawen.** *v.* to lose; waste; annihilate; destroy, ruin. **mapukaw.** *v.* to lose, be lost; be destroyed, wasted; confused. **mapukawan.** *v.* to suffer a loss. **papukaw.** *v.* to rape. **mapukpukaw ti panunot.** *exp.* to be confused. **pannakapukaw.** *n.* loss. **panagpukaw.** *n.* disappearance. **panangpukaw.** *n.* destruction, manner of destroying, annihilation. **pangpukaw ti ut-ot.** pain reliever. **Awan ti mapukawko no agurayak.** I have nothing to lose if I wait. **Pagam-ammuan, nagpukawen a naminpinsan.** All of a sudden it disappeared once and for all. [Ibg. *nevuttu, nawawan*, Ifg. *tálak*, Ivt. *navuq*, Knk. *éngew*, Kpm. *mewalaq, mebáting*, Png. *bálang, tawtáw, ugál*, Tag. *mawalán*]

puk-áw: *var.* of *pug-áw*: puff of air. **agpuk-áw.** *v.* to release air from an open mouth when sleeping.

pukekék: *a.* stubby; short; with short legs.

pukipók: *n.* kind of tree with a round fruit used to cure itch.

púkis: *n.* haircut (*purtok, urtok, pulkit*). **agpapukis.** *v.* to have a haircut. **ipapukis.** *v.* to have the hair cut. **mamukis.** *v.* to cut the hair. **mammukis.** *n.* one who cuts hair, barber. **pagpapukisan, pagpukisan.** *n.* barber shop. **kappukis.** *a.* newly cut (hair). [Ibg. *usíp*, Kpm. *urúd*, Tag. *gupít*]

pukkáw: *n.* announcement; shout, cry. (*laaw*) **agpukkaw.** *v.* to shout when calling someone. **ipukkaw.** *v.* to tell by shouting. **Agal-aludoyak metten a pumanaw idi pukkawannak ti ulitegko.** I was just leaving unnoticed when my uncle shouted at me. [Kal. *pakoy*, Png. *belyág*, Tag. *sigáw*]

pukkúok: **ipukkuok.** *v.* to drop down, fling down; throw down.

pukkúol: **maipukkuol**. *v.* to bump against, collide (*dungpar*; *dalapon*; *dugpa*). [Tag. *bunggô*]

pokló₁: *n.* angle brace.

pokló₂: **pokpoklo**. *n.* kind of green seaweed with fingerlike leaves.

pokló₃: *n.* lower portion of a man or woman's brief. [Tag. *pundiya* (Sp.)]

póko: (Sp. *poco*: little) **poko-poko**. little by little (*in-nut*). **poko tiempo**. a while. **Masapul a poko-poko ti garaw**. The movement needs to be little by little.

pukól: *n.* one handed; one armed; one legged. **pukulan**. *v.* to cut off one hand or one leg. **mapukulan**. *v.* to lose one's hand; to have one's hand severed; (*fig.*) to lose one's line of defense (right hand).

pukpók₁: *n.* sum; summary (*dagup*). **pukpoken**. *v.* to sum up; summarize. **agpukpok**. *v.* to stand in the way, obstruct.

pukpók₂: *n.* sound or use of a hammer. **pukpuken**. *v.* to hammer, hit. **agpanukpok**. *n.* sound of things hitting each other. **mapukpok**. *v.* to knock against. **panukpok**. *n.* sound of hammering or knocking. [Tag. *pukpók*]

pukrán: **susó a pukran**. *n.* kind of snail with a white, round shell.

pukráy: **napukray**. *a.* easily crumbled, friable (squash); to be at the best ripening period (vegetables); to be at the time of the best taste. [Tag. *ligat*]

pulá: *n.* yellow or red central part of a crab; crab roe (*búgi*); fat of crabs of shrimp. **pulaan**. (*obs.*) *v.* to color. **napula**. *a.* full of roe (crabs). [Tag. *pulá* = red; eggs of a crab]

púlad: *n.* feather of an arrow; vane.

pulágid: **pulagidan**. *v.* to anoint, smear with; spread (butter). **ipulagid**. *v.* to wipe on something; smear on. **ipulagid ti ugali**. *exp.* to taint one's ways, do without honor. [Tag. *pahid, kulapol*]

pulaígad: **agpulaigad**. *v.* to wipe dirt off the hands of feet; smudge (*pígad, puligad*). [Tag. *pahid*]

polaínas: (Sp. *polaina*: legging) *n.* leggings.

pulákak: **pulpulakak**. *n.* spot on the skin; skin discoloration. (*kamánaw*)

pulákan: *n.* variety of awned *diket* rice with a light-colored hull and white kernel.

pulána: (Sp. *fulana*: female so-and-so) colloquial term of address for an unspecified woman.

puláno: (Sp. *fulano*: fellow) *n.* guy; fellow.

púlang: **ipulang**. *v.* to return (what has been borrowed) (*subli*); carry; give back; bring; replace; atone; satisfy. **pulangan**. *v.* to compensate, reimburse, pay a debt. **mapulangan**. *v.* to

recover to normal condition. (health, finances, etc.) **agpulang**. *v.* to return to one's original position; come to life; regain consciousness. **agpinnulang**. *v.* to make amends to each other (*litúp*); return mutually borrowed things. **No iti sao naibbatanen, saan a maipulangen**. If a word is released, it will never be recovered. **Saan pay a nagpulang ti puot ti balasang**. The young woman still hasn't regained consciousness. [Tag. *saulì*]

pulanggít: **ipulanggit**. *v.* to throw off; throw away; throw about. **maipulanggit**. *v.* to be thrown off (a bus); knocked down.

pulápol: **makipulapol**. *v.* to consort, keep company; deal with; socialize, mingle with. **mannakipulapol**. *a.* sociable; *n.* socialite. **pannakipulapol**. *n.* sociability. **kapulpulapol**. *n.* associates; companions. **Nawaya dagiti Ilokano a makipulpulapol uray sadino a disso**. Ilocanos are free to socialize in any place. [Tag. *salamuhà*]

pulár: **agpular**. *v.* to solicit help or contribution.

púlat: **mamulpulat**. *v.* to make something do or serve the purpose. **pulaten**. *v.* to make do.

pólbera: (Sp. *polvera*: powder box) *n.* powder box.

pólbo: (Sp. *polvo*: powder) *n.* powder; dust. **polboen**. *v.* to pulverize. **pimmulbo**. *a.* fine, powdery.

polborá: (Sp. *pólvora*: gunpowder) *n.* gunpowder.

polborón: (Sp. *polvorón*: powder cake) *n.* a kind of sweet made of coconut powder.

púlbos: (Sp. *polvo*: powder) *n.* face powder. **agpulbos**. *v.* to powder oneself.

poléa: (Sp. *polea*: pulley) *n.* pulley.

pulgáda: (Sp. *pulgada*: inch) *n.* inch. **pulgadera**. *n.* meter stick.

púlgas: (Sp. *pulga*: flea) *n.* flea (*tímel*). [Tag. *garapata*]

pulgít: **sangkapulgit**. *n.* a very tiny thing.

póli: (Sp.) *n.* in the card game *monte*, the dealer's assistant who is in charge of collecting the losing bets and paying the winner.

púli: **pulian**. *v.* to succeed (filling the vacancy).

pulí: *n.* race; breed; bloodline. **kapulpuli**. *n.* person of the same race; of the same breed. **agkapuli**. *v.* to be of the same breed, race. **puli ti tao**. mankind. [Kal. *gagat*, Png. *polí*, Tag. *lahì*]

pulído: (Sp.) *a.* neat; polished; with finesse.

poliéto: (Sp. *folleto*: pamphlet) *n.* pamphlet.

pulígad: **agipuligad**. *v.* to wipe dirt off; to project the blame on someone else (said of the guilty party). **Impuligadna ti tammudona iti agsumbangir a mumukatanna**. He wiped the corners of his eyes with his forefingers (to remove the *mukat*). (*pulagid*)

poligamía: (Sp. *poligamía*: polygamy) *n.* polygamy, practice of having more than one wife at the same time.

pulígos: **agpuligos**. *v.* to revolve, turn around. **puligusen**. *v.* to spin; rotate; turn the body. (*pusipus*) **Nagpuligos iti namitlo iti sango ti sarming sa rimmuar.** She turned around three times in front of the mirror, then went out. **Kasano ngamin ti panangpulpuligosmo iti utekna ta namati kenka?** How did you change his mind (turn his mind around) so he would believe you? [Tag. *ikot*]

pulikáaw: *n.* scream, shout. **pumulikaaw**. *v.* to scream, shout, yell.

pulíkat: *n.* cramps; *a.* stiff, rigid; cramped. (said of the legs). **agpulikat**. *v.* to become stiff (legs, etc.); suffer cramps. [Tag. *pulikat* (cramps)]

polília: (Sp. *polilla*: moth) *n.* clothes moth.

pulinangnáng: *a.* bald. (*pulták, kalbo, ludingas*)

polínas: (Sp. *polaina*: legging) *n.* leggings.

púling: *n.* mote in the eye (*mermér*). **ipulingan**. *v.* to remove a mote from the eye. **mapulingan**. *v.* to have a mote in the eye. [Ibg. *afuling*, *navuling*, Itg., Ifg., Knk. *búta*, Ivt. *pudin*, Kal. *beÿaw*, Kpm. *púling*, Tag. *puwing*]

puling-í: **mapuling-i**. *v.* to be twisted in an awkward position (neck, finger, etc.). **puling-ien**. *v.* to wring, twist.

pulinglíng: **pulinglingen**. *v.* to have in hand, at one's disposal; finger, toy with. **awan pagpulinglingan**. *exp.* to have little room to move or do things. **di makapulingling**. *exp.* to be very busy; to much work to do. **Bayat ti pannanganko, pinulpulinglingko ti botelia ti agas.** While I was eating, I toyed with the medicine bottle. [Tag. *butingtíng*]

pólio: (Sp. *folio*: folio) *n.* leaf of a register.

pulípol: **ipulipol**. *v.* to coil; wind. **pagpulipulan ti abél.** *n.* cloth beam. **pulipulan**. *v.* to coil, twist around; wrap around; bind with repeated windings. **agpulipol**. *v.* to wind, coil (ropes, yarn). **pumulipol**. *v.* to wind, coil (snakes). **mapulipol**. *v.* to be wound around (a post, etc.). **Pimmulipol ti panagkita ni Keanu iti lakko ken butoyna.** Keanu turned his gaze at her thighs and calves. [Tag. *pulupot*]

púlis: **makipulis**. *v.* to test a gamecock against another. **ipulis**. *v.* to wind around (rope, etc.); test (gamecocks) without using spurs.

pulís: (Eng.) *n.* police; policeman.

pólisa: (Sp. *póliza*: policy) *n.* insurance policy.

polisía: (Sp. *policía*: police force) *n.* police, police force; policeman.

polísta: (Sp. *polista*: polo player) *n.* polo player; (*obs.*) native serving in communal works.

politána: (Sp.) *n.* having three consecutive cards of the same suit beginning with an ace.

politeísmo: (Sp. *politeísmo*: polytheism) *n.* polytheism, belief in many gods. **politeista**. *n.* polytheist.

Pulitiágan: (abbreviated from *Puli ti Tiagan*, race from *Tiagan*) *n.* ethnic group from the interior mountains of La Union Province; member of the ethnic group.

política: (Sp. *política*: politics) *n.* politics. **pinnolitika**. *n.* politics (at work, in sports).

polítiko: (Sp. *político*: politician) *n.* politician; (*coll.*) politics.

pulitípot: *n.* thick syrup made of brown sugar.

pulkít: **pulkitan**. *v.* to cut the hair short.

pulkók: *n.* anxiety; worry. (*danag*) **agpulkok, mapulkukan**. *v.* to be worried, anxious. **Mapukaw amin a pulkokko no addaka.** I lose all my worries when you are here. [Tag. *aburido* (Sp.), *alaala*]

pullangí: *a.* dislocated, out of joint; twisted. **maipullangi**. *v.* to be dislocated, out of joint (*puling-í*). **Nagriaw dagiti agbuybuya ta naipullangi ti ulo ti dehado.** The spectators screamed because the underdog's head was twisted.

pullásit: **agpullasit**. *v.* to roll over (in an automobile accident, etc.). **ipullasit**. *v.* to hurl. **maipullasit**. *v.* to be hurled, thrown away.

pullát: *n.* cork; plug; stopper. **pullatan**. *v.* to plug, cork, stop. **ipullat**. *v.* to use to plug or stop flow. **maipullat**. *v.* to be plugged, stopped, plugged up (nose). **apagpullat**. *a.* just passing (said of grades) (*apaglussot*). **pagpullat**. *n.* something used as a plug; (*coll.*) person used as a stand-in. [Png. *polét*, Tag. *pasak*]

pulló₁: *num.* ten (*pulo*). **pinullo**. by tens, by decades, in groups of ten. **maminpullo**. around ten times (dozens of times). [Knk. *po*, Tag. *sampû*]

pulló₂: **agpullo**. *v.* to reach the limit of one's endurance; to reach the breaking point; to meet one's end; be caught and punished. **pagpulluen**. *v.* to bring to an end; punish.

pullúoy: (*obs.*, f. *pul-óy*) *n.* boisterous farting.

pulmónia: (Sp. *pulmonía*: pneumonia) *n.* pneumonia.

pólo₁: (Sp. *polo*: polo) *n.* polo, horse hockey; pole; polo shirt.

pólo₂: (Sp. *polo de desarrollo*: regional development center, *obs.*) *n.* forty-day period of personal service to the community during the Spanish regime.

púlo: **sangapulo.** *num.* ten. **maikasangapulo.** *num.* tenth. [Knk. *po*, Png. *poló*, Tag. *pû*]

puló: **pulpuluan.** *v.* to baste; smear; daub. **napuluan.** *a.* basted; smeared; daubed. **Pinuluapuluanna ti bukotko iti lugit.** She smeared my back with guano. [Tag. *kulapol*]

polomíngko: *n.* kind of vine vegetable with edible seeded fruit; lima bean.

púlong₁: *n.* report of bad conduct. **ipulong.** *v.* to tattle, tell on, report, inform against. **pagipulongan.** *n.* one who receives complaints. **Ipulongkanto ken baketmo!** I will tell your wife on you! [Knk. *sogbó*, Tag. *suplóng*]

púlong₂: **agpulong.** *v.* to gather together; assemble. [Tag. *pulong* (meeting)]

púlong₃: (*obs.*) *n.* forced labor by the Spaniards.

pulós: *a.* pure, all, entirely; *n.* beaded necklace. **agpulos.** (*obs.*) *v.* to be at variance. **ipulos.** *v.* to concentrate on one thing; give everything to one person. **nakapulpulos.** *a.* hardly any; with nothing at all. **pulusen.** *v.* to do solely; to do exclusively. **pulpulos.** *adv.* all the same. **awan a pulos.** nothing at all. [Tag. *lantáy*, *puro* (Sp.)]

polusión: (Sp. *polución*) *n.* pollution.

pulósis: (*slang*) *n.* none at all; entirely. (see *pulos*)

pulót: *n.* thick syrup made of sugarcane; molasses. **pulutan.** *v.* to anoint (priest, etc.). **mammulot.** *n.* priest who performs an anointment, anointer. **papulutan.** *v.* to have someone blessed by a priest. **pangipulutan.** *n.* scapegoat; whipping boy. **tagapulot.** *n.* syrupy sugar.

pulútan: (Tag.) *n.* finger food, food eaten (not including rice) while drinking alcohol. **pagpulutan.** *n.* things eaten with beer or liquor. **agpulutan.** *v.* to eat appetizers while drinking. **Imun-una a naibus ti lambanog ngem ti pulutan.** The coconut liquor was finished first before the *pulutan*. [Tag. *pulot* = pick up]

pulutípot: *n.* native dessert made of *diket* rice and molasses and coconut milk.

pul-óy: *n.* breeze. (*puyupoy*) **agpul-oy.** *v.* to have a breeze. **napul-oyan.** *v.* hit by a breeze. **ipuloy.** *v.* to carry away (said of a breeze). [Tag. *simoy*]

puluyúpoy: *n.* breeze. (*pul-oy*)

púlpito: (Sp. *púlpito*: pulpit) *n.* pulpit.

pulpúg₁: **agpulpog.** *v.* to burn an animal in an open fire until the hair is off; roast; barbecue. **mapulpug.** *v.* to be burned in an open fire. **Ania ti pulpugantayo?** What are we barbecuing? [Tag. *ihaw*]

pulpúg₂: **mapulpug.** *v.* to do continually.

pulpól: *a.* dull, blunt, without a point (person or knife) (*ngudel*). **pulpol a mannurat.** dull writer. [Tag. *pudpód*]

pulpúlto: *n.* a kind of shrub.

pulséras: (Sp. *pulceras*: bracelet) *n.* bracelet. **agpulseras.** *v.* to wear a bracelet. **nakapulseras.** *a.* wearing a bracelet.

púlso: (Sp. *pulso*: pulse) *n.* pulse. **ipulsuan.** *v.* to feel the pulse of.

pulsót₁: *n.* a kind of game where the object is to be the first to pull the head off a hanging cock.

pulsót₂: **agpulsot.** *v.* to snap off; miss a beat or tune. **pulsutan.** *v.* to cut off. **mapulsot.** *v.* to be cut off. **mapulsotan ti anges.** to be about to die. **pulsopulsot.** *a.* in pieces. **kapulso't-bagis.** *n.* born of the same mother. **awan pulsotna.** *exp.* endless, continual. **Pulsopulsot ti urokna.** His snoring was steady but in spurts. [Tag. *lagót*, *patíd*]

pulták: *n.* bald spot of head. *a.* bald; having the hair unevenly cut. **pultakan.** *v.* to cut the hair unevenly. **mapultakan.** *v.* to bald. [Tag. *kalbó* (Sp.)]

pultíng: **pultingen.** *v.* to reap, gather by cutting the stem; pluck off (*kettel*); top off. **sangapulting.** *n.* a small piece, small cut.

pultít: *n.* small piece of feces, usually the last to be expelled. (*puglit*) **kaippultit.** *a.* just moved (bowels); newly born. **makapultit.** *v.* to defecate a small piece of feces accidentally. [Tag. *ipot*]

pultó₁: *n.* protruding the tongue while talking. **agpulto.** *v.* to stick out the tongue while talking. [Tag. *dilà*]

pultó₂: **polpolto.** *Pseuderanthemum pulchellum.* *n.* a shrub with white flowers having a purple spot at the base.

pultóng: *var.* of *pulting*.

puma-: Intransitive directional affixation, consisting of the directional prefix *pa-* and the verbalizing infix *-um-*. See *agpa-* **pumadayo.** to go far away. **pumalalaem.** to go inside. **pumaili.** to go to town.

pomáda: (Sp. *pomada*: pomade) *n.* pomade, hair grease (used by men).

pumadéro: (Sp. *fumadero*, *obs.*) *n.* opium den.

pumakbó: (f. *kebbó*) *n.* a kind of small, flat, triangular marine fish.

pombréra: *var.* of *pimbrera*: lunch pail.

poménto: (Sp. *fomento*: fomentation) *n.* fomentation; compress, wet cloth applied to the body.

pomés: (Sp. *pomez*: pumice) *n.* pumice.

pumgaák: (f. *paggáak*) *v.* to laugh loudly.

pumi-: Prefix taking numeric roots to indicate how many times something is done. Perfective form is *pimmi-* **Pumiduaka a tumaray.** Run twice. **Pimmitlokami.** We did it three times.

pumlátok: (f. *pallátok*) *v.* to be thrown upward, be tossed; (*fig.*) echo.

pumlíing: (f. *pilíng*) *v.* to produce a shrill sound.

pumpón: see *punpón*: funeral.

pumsuák: (f. *pussuák*) *v.* to bubble; gush out; overflow.

punangnáng: *a.* bald. (*kalbo, pulták*)

púnas: *n.* rag; dust cloth. **agpunas.** *v.* to dust furniture; wipe. **punasan.** *v.* to wipe clean or dry. **ipapunas.** *v.* to have something wiped or erased. **mapunas.** *v.* to be wiped; to be erased. **punasen.** *v.* to wipe off. **pagpunas.** *n.* towel, rag, anything used to wipe. **pagpunasan.** *n.* napkin. [Ibg. *funát,* Ifg. *dan-iyan,* Kal. *pulas,* Kpm. *kuskus,* Png. *ponás,* Ivt., Tag. *punas*]

púnaw: *n.* fading (*kupas*). **agpunaw.** *v.* to fade; erase. **napunaw.** *a.* faded; erased.

púnay: *n.* a kind of large turtledove with dirty green plumage.

púnda(s): (Sp. *funda*: sheath, covering) *n.* inner pillowcase.

pundadór: (Sp. *fundador*: founder) *n.* founder.

pundár: (Sp. *fundar*: found) **agpundar.** *v.* to provide; found, start. **pundasion.** *n.* foundation. **ipundar.** *v.* to found; establish.

ponderósa: *n.* variety of *chico* fruit imported from Sulawesi, Indonesia.

pundí: (Sp. *fundir*: melt) **mapundi.** *v.* to burn out (said of lightbulbs).

pundído: (Sp. *fundido*: melted) *a.* burnt out (lightbulb); melted; cast (iron).

púndo: (Sp. *fondo*: fund) *n.* funds (in a bank account). **agpundo.** *v.* to dock a ship. **ipundo.** *v.* to deposit money; anchor a boat; dump.

punebre: *var.* of *puniébre*: funeral procession.

punér: **napuner.** *a.* muscular, brawny, fleshy; well-built (body); macho (*baneg*). **pumuner.** *v.* to become muscular. [Tag. *tipunò*]

punerária: (Sp. *funeraria*: funeral home) *n.* funeral home, funeral parlor; mortuary; hearse.

puní: *n.* things set on the table. **agipuni.** *v.* to set the table. (*dasár*) **punian.** *v.* to set the table; (*reg.*) decorate, adorn. [Png. *póni,* Tag. *hain*]

puniál: (Sp. *puñal*: dagger) *n.* dagger.

puniébre: (Sp. *fúnebre*: funeral) *n.* funeral; funeral march; funeral dirge. (*pumpon*) **makipuniebre.** *v.* to join a funeral march.

puniéta: (Sp. *puñetazo*: punch) *n.* mild curse word. [Tag. *punyeta*]

púnios: (Sp. *puño*: fist) *n.* cuff, wrist of a garment; wrist. **agpunios.** *v.* to Indian wrestle; arm wrestle.

punípon: *n.* gathering (*ummong*); bringing together of objects. **pagpunipunan.** *n.* gather-

ing place; watering hole; melting pot; *v.* to be blessed with many good qualities. **punipunen.** *v.* to bring together, assemble, gather; collect. [Png. *begtá, mokmok,* Tag. *tipon, kalipumpón*]

púnit: *n.* small hole or rip. **agpunit.** *v.* to close, shut (*rikép*); heal (wounds) (*lúnit*). **ipunit.** *v.* to shut, close. **punitan.** *v.* to shut in, confine, lock up; sew closed; cover a hole. **namunit.** *a.* closed by a bar. [Tag. *sará* (close, Sp.)]

punktualidád: (Sp. *punctualidad*: punctuality) *n.* punctuality. **punktualidad pilipina.** Philippine punctuality, applied to one who is customarily late (*oras pilipina*).

punnó: **agpunno.** *v.* to make up for what is lacking. **punnuen.** *v.* to fill up something. **punnuan.** *v.* to add what is lacking; to overlook one's faults; tolerate. **ipunno.** *v.* to add. **mapunnuan.** *v.* to be filled; fed up. **mapno.** *v.* to be filled. **napno.** *a.* full. **punnuan.** *v.* to fill up; overlook; tolerate. **sangapunno.** *n.* one quantity of yarn wound on the spindle (*takbían*). **makapno.** *n.* variety of awned early rice. **panagpunno.** *n.* filling of a position. **tagipunnuan.** *a.* almost full. **pamunnuén.** *a.* somewhat full. [Kal. *laplu,* Knk. *angbá,* Png. *panó, kerél,* Tag. *punô*]

punnók: **nagpunnukan.** *n.* center of (civilization, business).

punnúok: *n.* stump, stub (of plants) (*pungdól; tuod*). [Tag. *tuód*]

púno: **napuno.** *a.* dull, blunt; worn out (*ngudel*). **makapuno.** *n.* a variety of coconut. [Tag. *puról* (blunt)]

ponógrapo: (Sp. *fonógrafo*) *n.* phonograph.

púnot₁: *n.* aspect, appearance. (*pudas; langá*)

púnot₂: **punuten.** *v.* to absorb, sponge. **punutan.** *v.* to cleanse, wipe.

punpón: *n.* funeral, burial. (*pumpón*) **mamunpon.** *v.* to conduct a funeral. **ipunpon.** *v.* to bury (with rites). **ipapunpon.** *v.* to have someone buried with funeral rites. **makipamunpon.** *v.* to attend a funeral. **mamunpon.** *v.* to conduct a funeral. **pamunpon.** *n.* funeral procession. **punpunuen.** *v.* to bury, perform funeral rites on someone. [Ibg. *mananem, itanem,* Ivt. *ivuvun,* Kal. *ilubun,* Knk. *iká-ub,* Kpm. *kutkut,* Png. *ponpón,* Tag. *libíng*]

pónse: (Sp. *ponche*: punch) *n.* punch (liquor).

punsión: (Sp. *función*: function) *n.* social gathering; party. **agpunsion.** *v.* to have a party.

ponsionár: (Sp. *funcionar*) **agpunsionar.** *v.* to function.

punsuát: (*obs.*) *n.* commotion of the intestines.

punsón: (Sp. *punzón*: punch) *n.* wedge; driving punch.

púnta: (Sp. *punta*: point) *n.* point; (*coll.*) point, purpose. **ipunta.** *v.* to aim. **puntaan.** *v.* to shoot someone. **napuntaan.** *a.* hit (by a bullet). **narigat a punpuntaan.** hard to hit; hard to please.

puntablángko: (Sp. *punta blanco*: target practice) *n.* target practice; *a.* direct (hit). **agpuntablangko.** *v.* to practice target shooting.

punteria: *var.* of *puntiria*: aim, target.

puntéro: (f. *punta*) *n.* pointer; indicator (of a gauge); hand (of a watch or clock). [Tag. *panturò*]

puntília: (Sp. *puntilla*) *n.* narrow lace edging.

puntíng₁: **puntingen.** *v.* to shoot something (with a gun, etc.). **mapunting.** *v.* to be hit (by a bullet). [Tag. *tamà*]

puntíng₂: *n.* outrigger of the Ibanags. (*bilóg*)

pontísipe: (Sp. *pontífice*) *n.* pontiff.

puntíria: (Sp. *puntería*: aim) *n.* target; aim. **puntiriaen.** *v.* to aim.

Pontísipe: (Sp. *pontífice*: pontiff) *n.* pontiff; pope.

púnto: (Sp. *punto*: point) *n.* point; tone; intonation; mark; dot, period. **agpunto.** *v.* to be obstinate (spoiled children); to thicken (syrup). **alas siete en punto.** seven o'clock sharp.

puntuál: (Sp. *puntual*: punctual) *a.* punctual, on time.

puntóng: *n.* display of lunacy. **puntopuntongan.** *n.* person with unpredictable temper.

póntse: (Sp. *ponche*: punch) *n.* eggnog; liquor punch; milk punch.

punyéta: *var.* spelling of *puniéta*: curse word.

punyál: *var.* spelling of *puniál*: dagger.

púnyos: *var.* spelling of *puniós*: cuff.

pungák: **mapungak.** *v.* to have lost everything in gambling. (*ungkós*)

pungál: *a.* with decayed teeth. (*tuppól*)

pungán₁: *n.* pillow; cushion. **makipungan.** *v.* to share a pillow. **punganan.** *v.* to supply someone with a pillow; use someone as a pillow. **pagpunganan.** *v.* to use as a pillow. **kaaruba't pungan.** *exp.* spouse (pillow mate). **Ti kinatalna ti panunot ti kaluknengan a pungan.** *exp.* Peace of mind is the softest pillow. **Maymaysan ti awan kapunganna.** Only one does not have a spouse. [Ibg. *fungan*, Ivt. *hangnan*, Kal. *pungan*, Kpm. *ulunan*, Png. *danganán*, Tag. *unan*]

pungán₂: *n.* two bamboo slats tied together at both ends that keep the cogon grass *agsit* in place.

pungánay: *n.* beginning, commencement; initial stage; origin, source (*puon*); first fruit; first crop; third harvest of tobacco leaves following the *káwad*; parentage; ancestry. **apagpunga-**

nay. *a.* just begun. **ipunganay.** *v.* to trace one's ancestry; start from the beginning. **mamunganay.** *v.* to start from; originate from. **pamunganayan.** *n.* origin; source; starting point. [Png. *gapó*, *buat*, Tag. *simulâ*, *galing*]

púngat: *a.* with glans penis completely uncovered (circumcised persons). [Tag. *lungat*]

púngay: **napungay.** *a.* attractive (eyes); with a sentimental look in the eyes; about to fall asleep (eyes); radiant. **papungayen.** *v.* to make radiant (eyes). **pumungay.** *v.* to become radiant. **Kasla pimmungay dagiti matana.** Her eyes became radiant.

pungdól: *n.* tree stump; (*coll.*) short person; unresponsive person. **ipungdulan.** *v.* to remove the stump. **kasla pungdol.** like a tree stump (said of a frigid person, person not in the mood). [Kal. *lampokpokan*, Knk. *tungéd*, *lungéd*, Tag. *tuód*]

púnged: **napunged.** *a.* stubborn, obstinate; wayward; rebellious (*galasugas*; *sukir*; *suweng*; *subeg*; *bengngeg*). [Tag. *sutíl*]

púngeg: *n.* famine, plague, calamity; epidemic.

púnger: **agpunger.** *v.* to have bad feelings (crying babies, etc.); to be easily irritated.

pungét: *n.* stump, stubble, stub of plants. **ipunget.** *v.* to cut off, crop; cut at the base or root. **agpunget.** *v.* to pull the hair. **inggátpungét.** until death.

punggá₁: *n.* second helping, additional food; leftover rice. **agpungga.** *v.* to have a second helping. **pagpunggaann.** *n.* main container.

punggá₂: *n.* sexy person. **napungga.** *a.* sexy; voluptuous. **Dimo palusposanen dayta a pungga.** Don't let go of that attractive person.

punggá₃: **napungga ti anges.** *v.* to die.

punggés: *a.* having little hair (said of females).

punggó: *a.* tailless (bird).

punggáok: *n.* overweight person.

punggók: *a.* tailless (birds); with a short rear (cars). (*kibol*)

punggós: *n.* ponytail; bundle; bunch. **punggusen.** *v.* to pucker; take up four corners of a handkerchief or the mouth of a sack; bundle up (hair); tie in a bundle; clutch the collar of another in anger. **sangapunggos.** *n.* one bundle; one bunch. **Imbilinna a punggosenmi dagiti imana sami ipatulod idiay Santa Barbara.** He ordered us to tie up his hands and then we led him to Santa Barbara. [Tag. *bungkós*]

pungíl: *a.* without antlers; hornless. **mapungil.** *v.* to break off at the base. **pungilen.** *v.* to break, snap. [Tag. *baklî* (break off)]

pung-íl: *var.* of *pungil*.

pungló: *n.* bullet of a gun. (*bala*)

pungó₁: *n.* bundle; large bundle of *palay* made of four bundles tied together. **punguen.** *v.* to bind together the four limbs of; tie the hands of (a prisoner). **sangapungo.** *n.* one bundle of rice. **sipupungo.** *a.* tied, bound (hands or feet). [Ibg. *galuq*, Ivt. *pakedkeren*, Kpm, Tag. *gápos*, Png. *taker*]

pungó₂: **pungupunguán, punguaponguán.** *n.* wrist (*ngulay*). [Kal. *pangngunguway*, Png. *ngalongaloan*, Tag. *galánggalangán*]

púngot: **punguten.** *v.* to pull the hair of; lift by the hair. **mapungot.** *v.* to have one's hair pulled. [Tag. *sabunot*]

pungpóng: *n.* stump, stub of bamboos. (*pungdol*) **pungpongen.** *v.* to play with a baby by moving about his arms and legs.

pungsáy: **ipungsay, pungsayen.** *v.* to remove by tearing or cutting. **maipungsay.** *v.* to be cut, torn, severed. **Pangpidpidutanda ngata iti maipungsay nga ulo?** Where do you think they will pick up the severed heads? [Tag. *tigpás*]

pungtíl: *a.* without antlers, horns. **ipungtil, pungtilen.** *v.* to remove the top of.

púngto: *n.* end; tip; last part. **agpungto.** *v.* to end; conclude; finish; terminate. **agpapungto.** *v.* to move toward the end. **agsipungto.** *v.* to stand at both ends; to stand one end to another; to do one thing after another in quick succession (doing a job before another is done, having another child although the preceding one is still young). **iti agsipungto.** *prep.* at both ends. **agsisipungto a sikog.** frequent pregnancies (one after the other). **Nagsipungto a naganak.** She gave birth one after another (*lit*: from end to end). [Tag. *dulo*]

pungtót: *n.* anger; hatred. (*gura; rurod; luksaw*) **agpungtot.** *v.* to get angry. **makapungtot.** *v.* to be angry, irate. **kapungtot.** *v.* to be angry with someone. **managpungpungtot.** *a.* irritable. **Nagpupupungtotanna a pinuted ti ulo ti uleg.** He cut off the head of the snake in a rage. **Rimmubrob ti pungtotna.** His anger flared up. **Asino aya ti kapungpungtotmo?** Who are you angry with? [Knk. *búnget*, Png. *pasnók, aloboób, sanók*, Tag. *galit*]

puón₁: *n.* beginning; origin; source; base; root; trunk; lower part; parentage; ancestry; unit for counting trees; cause, reason. **puonan.** *n.* capital (in business), stock. **pamuon.** *n.* foundation. **pamuonan.** *v.* to use as capital. **agpuonan.** *v.* to have capital. **makikapuonan.** *v.* to contribute to the capital. **puonen.** *v.* to begin. **kapuon, pinuon.** *n.* number of trees in a given area. **kapuonan.** *n.* lineage, pedigree, genealogy; line of descent; stock. **ipuon.** *v.* to sever at the bottom; do out of consideration for.

pumuon. *v.* to produce; grow. **marapuon.** (*obs.*) *n.* dense jungle. **ti murdong, umala iti puon.** *exp.* like father, like son. [Ibg. *fun*, Png. *gapó, buat*, Tag. *simulâ*]

puón₂: *n.* cause, reason. **pakaipuonan.** *n.* person for whose sake something is done. **pangipuonan.** *n.* reason why somebody does something; person for whose sake one does something. **puon ti nakatayanna.** *n.* cause of his death. **puon ti biag.** *n.* reason for living (said of loved one). **maipuon.** *prep.* on account of, because of, for. [Tag. *dahil*]

puónay: Contraction of *apounayen*: exclamation denoting surprise.

púor: *n.* fire; blaze. (*uram; apoy*) **puoran.** *v.* to blaze, burn, char. **agpuor.** *v.* to start a fire, make a bonfire. **ipuor.** *v.* to throw into the fire. **mapuoran.** *v.* to be burned. **puor ti kararua.** *n.* mortal enemy. **Pinuoranen ni Josie dagiti amin a rangtay iti nagbaetanmi.** Josie burned all the bridges between us. [Ibg. *tuggi*, Ivt. *susuhan*, Kpm. *silab*, Png. *pool*, Tag. *sunog*]

púot: *n.* perception, awareness, consciousness; sense; mind. **agpuot.** *v.* to wake up; sleep light. **agpupuot.** *v.* to be alert; sleep light. **makapuot.** *v.* to be awaken; be aware; regain consciousness. **mapuotan.** *v.* to perceive, notice; experience; be aware. **puoten.** *v.* to be on the lookout; be watchful; experiment, test; try. **mannakapuot.** *a.* easy to wake up. **pamuotan.** *n.* reason for being alert. **manipud adda puotko.** *exp.* from the time I can remember. **awanan-puot.** *a.* unconscious. **maawan iti puot.** *v.* to lose consciousness. **Aldawen idi makapuotda iti kabigatanna.** It was late in the day when they woke up the next morning. [Png. *pakaliknát, pakalikas*, Tag. *malay*]

pópa: (Sp. *popa*: poop) *n.* poop; stern, hind part of a ship.

pupítre: (Sp. *pupitre*: desk) *n.* student's desk.

púpog: *a.* densely sown. **napupog.** *a.* dense; densely sown. **pupugen.** *v.* to sow densely; plant seeds very close together; shower with kisses. [Tag. *pupog* = pecking; repeated kissing]

púpok: *n.* prison; prisoner (*balud*); animal kept for eating. **ipupok.** *v.* to lock up, confine, imprison, enclose. **napupok.** *a.* imprisoned; isolated; enclosed; stranded. **pupoken.** *v.* to imprison, confine. **nakapupokan.** *n.* reason why someone is confined. **pagpupukan.** *n.* jail; prison; fish pond. **Kanayon a nakapupok iti kuartona.** He is always confined in his room. [Png., Tag. *kulóng*]

pópor: *n.* flower head of the safflower.

populár: (Sp. *popular*: popular) *a.* popular.

populasión: (Eng.) *n.* population.

por: (Sp. *por*: for) Preposition used in certain expressions inherited from Spanish (some expressions are written as one word in modern Ilocano): for; by. **Por Dios.** Good God! **por menudo.** by retail. **por nada.** for nothing. **por lo menos.** at least. **por mayor.** wholesale. **por turno.** by turns. **por interes.** at interest. **por lata.** by the can. **uno por uno.** one by one.

puraddáw: *a.* faded white. **agpuraddaw.** *v.* to turn white, become pale.

purakrák: *n.* brilliance of white things. **napurakrak.** *a.* brilliant (said of white things).

purár: mapurar. *v.* to dazzle (*sirap*); to be blinded by light. **makapurar.** *a.* dazzling. **puraren.** *v.* to dazzle; blind by a bright light; (*fig.*) mislead. [Has a regional variant *púrar*. Tag. *silaw*]

puráw: *a. n.* white. **pumuraw.** *v.* to whiten; become white. **pamurpuraw.** *v.* to become pale; faint. **papurawen.** *v.* to whiten. **puraw ti itlog.** *n.* albumen. **Pimmuraw dagiti matana iti panagur-urayna.** He waited a very long time (*lit*: his eyes whitened from his waiting). **Purawto ti waken, nangisitto diay kannawayen.** The crow will turn white and the *kannaway* bird black (expressing impossibility). [Ibg. *furáw*, Itg. *pulaw*, Ivt. *idak, relak*, Kal. *putilak*, Knk. *múngaw*, Png. *putí*, Kpm., Tag. *putí*]

purawráw: napurawraw. *a.* very pale (from sickness). [Tag. *putlâ*]

pordiós: (Sp. *Por Dios!* By God!) *excl.* By God! for heavens sake. **ipordios.** *v.* to implore; beseech. (*araraw*)

pordó: (*obs.*) *n.* gold earlap.

púrdot: purduten. *v.* to snatch (leaves from the stem).

porestál: (Sp. *forestal*) *a.* forest; *n.* forestry. **zona porestal.** forest zone.

púrga: (Sp. *purga*: purgative) *n.* purgative, medicine taken to kill intestinal worms. **agpurga.** *v.* to take a purgative. **agpapurga.** *v.* to get a purgative. **mapurga.** *v.* to be purged. **purgaen.** *v.* to give a purgative to.

porgáda: (Sp. *pulgada*: inch) *n.* inch.

purgánte: *n.* purgative. (*pagpurga*)

purgatório: (Sp. *purgatorio*) *n.* purgatory.

Purgí: (Hawaii) *n.*, *a.* (*coll.*) Portuguese, more formal term is *portuges*.

púri: mapuri. *v.* to fall down, fall off; fall out (teeth). **purien.** *v.* to drop from the base; throw down; uproot a tree. [Tag. *buwál*]

puridasdás: napuridasdas. *a.* bald (*pulták*); bare (ground).

puríket: *n. Bidens pilosa*, beggar ticks (grass with thorny appendages that stick to clothing); oil of orange peel or orange bark. [Knk. *dalukdúk*]

purintíteng: mapurintiteng. *v.* to be tense, tight, taut (*irténg*).

puringí: see *purngi*: grin and laugh (showing the teeth).

puripikadór: (Sp. *purificador*: purifier) *n.* water purifier. **puripikasión.** *n.* purification. **puripikado.** *a.* purified.

púris: *n.* sliver (usually sticking to the sole of a foot). (*rud-ák*; *siít*; *salugsóg*) **mapurisan.** *a.* pricked with the splinter or thorn remaining in the wound. **makapuris.** *v.* to pierce, stab. **puris ti barukong.** heartache.

pur-ís: *n.* feces, excrement. (*takkí*)

purísta: (Sp. *purista*: purist) *n.* purist.

purítak: *n.* plant grown from a seed dropped inadvertently; (*fig.*) illegitimate child; mire. **ipurikak.** *v.* to smear, spatter. **napuritak.** *a.* smeared, spattered (*pulágid*). **puritakan.** *v.* to smear, spatter with. **sangapuritak.** *n.* a small group of plants growing in a field of a different crop.

puritáno: (Sp. *puritano*: puritan) *n.* puritan; very strict person.

pórke: (Sp. *porque*: because) *conj.* because. (*gapu ta*)

purkéd: *a.* short and stubby. **napurked.** *a.* short and robust.

purkíd: *n.* variety of maize with red and yellow kernels.

purláta: (Sp. *por lata*: by can) *a.* by the can. **Napurlatan ti gasatna.** *exp.* His luck ran out.

porlóko: agporloko. *v.* to do bad; to do something that is socially unacceptable.

pórma: (Sp. *forma*: form) *n.* form; penmanship; ways of a person; unconsecrated host. **pormaan.** *v.* to react angrily.

pormadór: (Sp. *formador*: one that forms) *n.* form; mold.

pormál: (Sp. *formal*: formal) *a.* formal; stuffy, stiff; prim; serious, grave, solemn. **agpormal.** *v.* to act in a formal manner.

pormalidád: (Sp. *formalidad*) *n.* formality.

pormár: (Sp. *formar*) **pormaren.** *v.* to organize, form (an association).

pórmas: (Sp. *formas*: small host) *n.* unconsecrated host.

pormasión: (Sp. *formación*) *n.* formation.

pórmula: (Sp. *fórmula*: formula) *n.* formula.

pormulário: (Sp. *formulario*: formulary) *n.* formulary; formulas; prescriptions; application blank.

pormósa: (Sp. *formosa*: Taiwan) *n.* Chinese bamboo.

purmót: awan pamurpurmotan. to have no idea, be clueless. **Awan pamurpurmotak.** I have no idea.

pornáda: (Sp. *por nada*: for nothing) **napurnada.** *a.* not followed through (plans); done to excess (spending money, eating). **Napurnadan a namimpinsan ti panggepda.** Their plan failed once and for all.

purngí: *n.* grin with the teeth exposed. **agpurngi.** *v.* to grin, to laugh with the teeth exposed.

purngíit: napurngiit. *a.* grinning. (*porngí*)

purngíngit: *var.* of *purngiit*: grin.

purngót: *n.* tug-of-war game. **purnguten.** *v.* to tear off by handfuls.

púro₁: *n.* island. *a.* **purpuro.** *n.* archipelago. [Ibg. *fugu*, Ifg. *bable*, Ivt. *tanaq*, Kpm. *isla*, Png. *pólo*, Tag. *pulô*]

púro₂: (Sp. *puro*: pure) pure; genuine; all. **nakapurpuro.** *a.* only of one kind. **napuroan.** *a.* excessively. **agpuro.** *v.* to have a good hand; to roll a good game of dice.

puruá: (Sp. *proa*: prow) *n.* prow of a boat; (*fig.*) pride. **Nangato ti puruana.** *exp.* denoting arrogance (*lit*: with a high prow).

purók: *n.* village; community; group, cluster, assembly, company, meeting, gathering. (*um-mong*) **agpurok.** *v.* to gather; assemble; meet in session. **kapurokan.** *n.* groupmate; village mate. **agkapurukan.** *v.* to be from the same village. **pumurok.** *v.* to attack, assault; *n.* villager. **mapurokpurok ti tudo.** to rain intermittently. **sangapurokan.** *n.* the whole community. **naisangsangayan a panagpurok.** *n.* special session. **Paset ti panggepko a mangkellaat kadagiti kapurokak.** It is a part of my plan to surprise my fellow villagers. [Png. *úma*, Tag. *nayon* (village); *poók* (place); [Tag. *lusob, salakay* (attack)]

puruntóng: (*slang*, coined from last name of television sitcom character) *a.* awkwardly dressed, wearing unsuitable clothing that doesn't match. **kurbata ti puruntong.** loud, ugly tie.

puróng: *n.* a kind of white elongated fish called *sisiaw* when small and *ludóng* when more than a foot long.

porónggo: *n.* long-necked bottle.

purós: purusen. *v.* to gather; pluck, pick. (fruits) **mapuros.** *v.* to be picked (fruits); to be freed, released. **pupurusan.** *n.* part of the plant torn off with the fruit when picked. **kappurus.** *a.* recently picked; just gathered. **pupurosan.** *a.* pickable (having lots of fruit); *n.* part of a tree

with fruit that is picked off. **agpapuros.** *v.* (*fig.*) to have an abortion. [Tag. *pitás*]

purót: **mapurutan.** *v.* to be sprinkled, splattered (*parsiak*). [Tag. *pilansík, tilamsík*]

porpólio: (Eng. portfolio) *n.* briefcase. **naka-porpolio.** *a.* with a briefcase.

purpór: *n.* split ends of hair. **agpurpor.** *v.* to have split ends in hair; to have ripped ends of garments; fade; shed (feathers); not develop (rice).

púrpura: (Sp. *púrpura*: purple) *n.* purple.

pórra: (Sp. *porra*: damn; bludgeon) *a.* naughty; shameless (used in derogative address).

purráso: (Sp. *porrazo*: knock, blow) *n.* knock, blow; beating. **agpurraso.** *v.* to strike, hit; beat.

purriít: *n.* anus (*ubet*). **Kas met la masilsilian ti purriitna.** His anus seems to be affected by chili pepper (said of an anxious person). [Tag. *puwít*]

purruák: *n.* upland rice planted by broadcasting. **ipurruak.** *v.* to scatter, spread around. **purruakan.** *v.* to throw something to; scatter food to (animals); share the benefits of. **maipurruak.** *v.* to be scattered; to be broadcast. **impurruak.** *n.* upland rice that is planted by broadcasting. [Tag. *sabog*]

purrúok: *n.* dash, violent effort; profuse sprinkling. **ipurruok.** *v.* to sprinkle profusely; heap upon; exert effort; put everything into doing something. **purruokan.** *v.* to sprinkle on generously.

purrór: agpurror. *v.* to fall out (hair, feathers). (*urot*)

porsádo: (Sp. *forzado*: forced) *a.* forced. (*pilit*)

porsár: (Sp. *forzar*: enforce) **iporsar.** *v.* to enforce. **babaen ti panangpursarda.** through their enforcement.

porsegí: *var.* of *pursigi*: persevere.

porselána: (Sp. *porcelana*: porcelain) *n.* porcelain; chinaware.

pursélas: (Sp. *pulsera*: bracelet) *n.* bracelet; armlet. [Kal. *gaching*, Tag. *pulseras*]

porsiénto: (Sp. *porciento*: percent) *n.* percent, percentage. **makiporsiento.** *v.* to have a percentage.

pursigí: (Sp. *perseguir*: chase) **agpursigi.** *v.* to pursue; persevere. **ipursigi.** *v.* to enforce; insist. (*dagadag; deldel; ullok; ipapilit*). **pursigido.** *a.* persevering; insistent.

porsilána: *var.* of *porselana*.

pursíng: mapursing. *v.* to break off, snap. (*lapsi; sep-ak*) **papursingan.** *n.* the part of a branch where it is torn off. **Impursingannak iti tallo a saba.** She broke off for me three bananas. [Tag. *pilas* (tear)]

porsisiáw: *n.* silversmith's solder.

pórta: (Sp. *porta*: porthole) **agporta.** *v.* to block (passage).

portáda: (Sp. *portada*: portal) *n.* front door; façade; portal.

purták: **mapurtak.** (*obs.*) *v.* to be carried away by the wind or current.

portál: (Sp. *portal*: doorway) *n.* entrance (of a tunnel).

portamonéda: (Sp. *portamoneda*: coin purse, *obs.*) *n.* wallet. (*pitaka*)

portéro: (Sp. *portero*: porter) *n.* gatekeeper; cemetery keeper; porter, doorkeeper.

purtís: *n.* Protestant. (*protestante*)

Portugés: (Sp. *portugués*) *n. a.* Portuguese. **ag-Portuges.** *v.* to speak Portuguese. **iportuges.** *v.* to translate into Portuguese.

purtók₁: **purtukan.** *v.* to cut (the hair of someone). **agpapurtok.** *v.* to get a haircut (*pukis*). [Tag. *gupít* (haircut)]

purtók₂: *n.* variety of awnless rice.

portúna: (Sp. *fortuna*: fortune) *n.* fortune. (*gasat*)

purwák: *var.* of *purruak*: scatter, spread, throw.

púsa: *n.* cat. **pusapusa.** *n.* larva of the rhinoceros beetle. (*alimpupusa*) **pusambao.** *n.* (*lit.*) cat and mouse, hide-and-seek game played by girls. **agpinnusambao.** *v.* to play hide-and-seek (girls). **Kasla di makaanak a pusa.** *exp.* denoting a restless person (*lit*: like a cat unable to give birth). **Pinusa ngata.** It was probably eaten by a cat. **Saan a makaruar ti pusa.** *exp.* denoting heavy rain (the cat can't go outside). [Bon. *kósa*, Ibg. *kusa*, *kitaw*, Ivt. *pusak*, Knk. *dúnia*, *ngiáw*, *púsa*, Png. *pusá*, Kpm., Tag. *pusà*]

posakomún: (Sp. *fosa común*: common grave) *n.* container for scattered cemetery bones.

pusaksák: *n.* immaculateness; grace, beauty; charm. **napusaksak.** *a.* immaculate; very white, pure white; exquisite. **Agkakaingaskayo, agpadakayo a napusaksak.** You look the same, you are the same in immaculateness. [Png. *kirlap*, Tag. *busilak*]

pusanbaó: (f. *pusa* 'cat' and *baó* 'mouse') **agpinnusanbao.** *v.* to play hide-and-seek (girls' game).

pósas₁: (Sp. *esposas*: handcuffs) *n.* handcuff. (*putáw*) **nakaposas, sipoposas.** *a.* handcuffed. **posasan.** *v.* to put handcuffs on.

pósas₂: (Sp. *posa*: halt to sing a response; passing bell) *n.* stop made by the clergy during a funeral procession. **agposas.** *v.* to sing a response; make a stop during a procession.

pusasáw: *a.* faded; pale; blurred. **pumusasaw.** *v.* to fade, change color; blur. **nagpusasaw.** *a.* faded, discolored. **Napusasaw a maris-berde ti makitam iti kasipngetan.** A pale green is what you see in the dark. [Tag. *kupas*]

pusawán: *n.* puddle; pond; fishpond. [Tag. *lawà* (pond)]

púsay: **ipupusay.** *n.* death. (*patáy*) **ipusay.** *v.* to take away; separate; wean a child. **maipusay.** *v.* to be separated; to be gone. **pumusay.** *v.* to pass away, die. **pumuspusay.** *v.* to separate, part company. **pusayen.** *v.* to part, separate, disconnect; remove, disown, banish; wean a child (*pusót*). [Tag. *patay* (death); *walay*, *hiwaláy* (separate)]

púseg: *n.* bellybutton, navel; umbilical cord; eye of an apple; innermost part of a cave. **napusgan.** *a.* sincere, ardent, passionate. **puseg ti ili.** *n.* heart of town; downtown. [Ibg. *fúteg*, Ivt. *pused*, Kal. *pusog*, Kpm. *púsad*, Png. *puség*, Tag. *pusod*]

puség: **pusgan.** *v.* to designate, appoint, assign. **mamuseg.** *v.* to be appointed, designated (*dútok*). **mapusgan.** *v.* to know, be aware of; be appointed. **Pinusgan ti tatangna a mangmanehar iti dagdagada.** His father appointed him to manage their lands. [Tag. *hirang*]

pusék: **napusek.** *a.* dense, crowed together, compact, tightly packed. **puseken, ipusek.** *v.* to pack tightly, fill up; overload. **Napusek ti teatro iti kaadu ti nagatendar.** The theater was packed from the large number attending. [Tag. *siksík*]

púser: *n.* Schizostachyum fenixii bamboo with thick-walled stems; device used to remove the cuticle of a nail.

pusgán: (f. *puség*) *v.* to designate, appoint, assign. **mapusgan.** *v.* to be designated, appointed, assigned.

púsi: *n.* shelled corn; (*fig.*) broken teeth. **pusien.** *v.* to shell (corn); knock off a tooth. **napusi.** *a.* shelled; fallen out (teeth) **Agpuspusi iti mais iti balitang.** He is shelling corn in the bamboo bench. [Tag. *himay* (shelling of grains)]

pusiáw: **napusiaw.** *a.* faded to yellow (clothes, paper, etc.).

posibilidád: (Sp. *posibilidad*: possibility) *n.* possibility (*kabalinan*). [Tag. *pagkamaaarì*]

posíble: (Sp. *posible*: possible) *a.* possible (*mabalin*). [Tag. *naaarì*, *marahil*]

pusíl: (Sp. *fusil*: rifle) *n.* gun, rifle. (*paltog*)

pusíng₁: **ipusing.** *v.* to separate, detach; disconnect. **kappusing.** *n.* baby who just stopped breast-feeding (*kappusot*). [Tag. *walay*]

pusíng₂: **pusingen.** *v.* to explain distinctly.

pusípos: *n*. revolving, rotating. **agpusipos**. *v*. to revolve, rotate, turn around; do house chores. **pusipusen**. *v*. to rotate, revolve, turn around something. **pusipusan**. *n*. pin of a spinning wheel; lock handle; doorknob. **pamusiposan ti ridaw**. *n*. doorknob. **awan pagpusipusan**. *exp*. to not have enough space to move around. **mangpusipos iti kambio**. *v*. to change gears. **Pinusiposna ti as-asarenna ket nagsaretret ti apuy**. He turned what he was roasting and the fire sizzled. [Ibg. *levvuwan*, Ivt. *maycadisuhed*, Kpm. *dúrut*, Png. *telek*, *peyes*, Tag. *ikot*]

pusísak: **ipusisak**. *v*. to separate, remove, detach; dispose of, get rid of; sell. [Tag. *walay*]

posisión: (Sp. *posición*: position) *n*. position (*kasasaad*); rank, status; standpoint, viewpoint.

pusísit: **agpusisit**. *v*. to squirt, spurt water. [Tag. *puslít*, *pulandít*]

pusít: *n*. squid (*laki*). [Ivt. *anus*, Png., Tag. *pusít*]

positíbo: (Sp. *positivo*: positive) *a*. positive; sure.

pusítsit: **agpusitsit**. *v*. to squirt (blood, water) (*pusisit*; *pugsit*). [Tag. *puslít*, *pulandít*]

puskól: *n*. thickness. **napuskol**. *a*. thick; dense (clouds, forest) **pinuskol**. *n*. upper part of the rumen after the esophagus. **papuskolen**. *v*. to make thick; sow densely; to set aside one's self-respect, act without dignity. **pumuskol**. *v*. to thicken; become thick. **pamuskolén**. *a*. rather thick. **napuskol ti rupana**. *exp*. thick headed, with no shame. [Ibg. *kannég*, Ifg. *mandol*, Ivt. *tukpuh*, Kal. *mampoong*, Knk. *ip-íp*, Kpm., Png., Tag. *kapál*]

puslít: *a*. smuggled; *n*. smuggled items; contraband. **ipuslit**. *v*. to smuggle. **agpuslit**. *v*. to escape; slip away unnoticed. **ipapuslit**. *v*. to have something smuggled. **mammuslít**. *n*. smuggler. [Png., Tag. *puslít*]

póso: (Sp. *pozo*: well) *n*. (pumping) well. **poso negro**. *n*. septic tank.

púso: *n*. heart. **nakapuspuso**. *a*. kind hearted, loving. **naimpusuan**. *a*. sincere. **ipapuso**. *v*. to take sincerely. **kapisi ti puso**. *n*. better half; spouse. **kapuspuso**. *a*. of similar feelings, desires. **sipupuso**. *adv*. sincerely, heartily. **puspuso a mamon**. *n*. soft heart, kind heart. **puspuso a bato**. *n*. heart of stone. **sinampuso**. like a heart; heart shaped. **Awan ti sabali nga agas ti sakit ti puso no saan met la tay kapuspusona**. There is no cure for a heartache but the one who caused it. **Mapaluknengko laeng ti natangken a panagpuspusona**. I will soften up his hard heart. [Ibg. *futu*, Ivt. *tawul*, Knk. *balitináw*, *púso*, Kal., Png. *póso*, Kpm., Tag. *pusò*]

pusuák: **agpusuak**. *v*. to overflow (*lippias*; *rogso*; *labiang*; *sayasay*; *silno*). [Tag. *apaw*]

pusuélo: (Sp. *pozuelo*: small well) *n*. small bowl; saucer.

púsol: *n*. anthill; hill made by animals. **pumusol**. *v*. to grow into a mound. [Png. *pungól*, Tag. *punsó* (anthill)]

pusóng: **napusong**. *a*. haughty, proud, arrogant. (*pangas*; *tangsit*) **agpusong**. *v*. to be arrogant. [Tag. *palalò*]

pus-óng: *n*. hypogastrium, lower, front-central region of the abdomen below the navel. [Kal. *pus-on*, Tag. *pusón* (abdomen)]

pusót: **pusuten**. *v*. to wean a child (*pusing*); deprive of; debar; bereave; hinder from possessing. **agpusot**. *v*. to stop breast-feeding; sit down heavily, slump on the ground or chair. **kappusot**. *n*. child who has just stopped breast-feeding. **Nadagsen ti panangipusotna iti bagina iti tugaw**. He slumped his body heavily on the chair. **Naipusoten iti witiwit**. He stopped breast-feeding at the plow (farmed at a very young age). [Tag. *awat* (wean)]

pósporo: (Sp. *fósforo*: match) *n*. match. (*gurabis*) **posporera**. *n*. lighter.

puspós₁: **puspusen**. *v*. to rotate (*pusípos*). [Tag. *ikot*]

puspós₂: *n*. a kind a tree, *Ficus payapa*, whose powdered roots are used to apply to wounds.

pussó: **napusso ti anges**. *v*. to die. **pussuen ti anges**. *v*. to kill. [Tag. *patay*]

pussuák: *n*. bubble; spout; fountain. **pumsuak**. *v*. to bubble; gush out; overflow. [Tag. *bukál* (Sp.)]

pussók: *var*. of *pussót*: to break off from the stem; tear off. (*tukkol*)

pussót: **pussuten**. *v*. to tear off; break off.

pústa: (Sp. *apostar*: bet) *n*. bet, wager, pool; stakes. (*palagay*) **ipusta, pumusta**. *v*. to bet, wager. **pustaan**. *v*. to bet on; *n*. betting. **agpinnusta**. *v*. to wager against one another. **parapusta**. *n*. person responsible for betting. **Sipupusta ti biagko no adda sabali a makaammo**. My life is at stake if someone else knows. [Ibg. *attán*, Tag. *tayâ*]

póste: (Sp. *poste*: post) *n*. post; pillar. (*adigi*) **Inaldaw nga agbilbilang iti poste**. *exp*. denoting an idle person (*lit*: counting posts everyday). [Tag. *haligi*]

posteridád: (Sp. *posteridad*: posterity) *n*. posterity.

postíso: (Sp. *postizo*: artificial, fake) *n*. false teeth, dentures.

postór: (Sp. *postor*: bidder) *n*. bid; bidder. **postoran**. *v*. to bid.

postóra: (Sp. *postura*: posture) *n*. posture. (*takder*) **agpostora**. *v*. to pose. **napostora**. *a*.

beautiful; nice. **nakapostura.** *a.* dressed up, dressed elegantly.

póstre: (Sp. *postre*: dessert) *n.* dessert, sweets. (*sam-ít*)

púta: (Sp. *puta*: whore) *n.* prostitute, whore, slut. (*pampam*) **agimpuputa.** *v.* to pretend to be a prostitute.

potáble: (Sp. *potable*: potable) **agua potable.** *n.* drinking water.

potáhe: (Sp. *potage*: stew) *n.* dish; dishes; stew; viand.

putín: *n.* handle; shaft of a spear. **iputan.** *v.* to fix a handle. **agiputan.** (*obs.*) *v.* to avail oneself of another's words. [Tag. *manggó*]

pútar: *n.* product, creation; invention; foundation of a building; building under construction. *a.* not completely made. **agputar.** *v.* to build, produce, manufacture; construct; frame. **putaren.** *v.* to create; author, invent; construct, build. **mammutar.** *n.* inventor; creator; manufacturer. [Tag. *likhâ*]

putatsíng: (*slang*) *n.* whore, prostitute. (*puta*)

putáw: *n.* fetters, handcuffs, shackles. (*posas*) **putawan.** *v.* to handcuff. [Tag. *kadena* (Sp.); *putháw* = hatchet]

putdól: putdulan. *v.* to cut off the upper part.

púted: *n.* piece, fragment cut off. **putden.** *v.* to cut; shorten by cutting. **putdan.** *v.* to cut off, shorten. **putde-putden.** *v.* to cut into short pieces. **maputed.** *v.* to be cut off. **pamutdan.** *n.* part from which to cut. **sangkaputed.** *n.* a cut, fragment. **Putedputed a pinagsisilpok daytoy tali.** I connected this string by pieces. [Bon. *pótot*, Ibg. *geppoq, gedduwa*, Ivt. *aktiven*, Kpm. *pútut*, Png. *potér, pegpég*, Tag. *hiwà, putól*]

pútek: *n.* stub of bamboo. **Nakagalut ti bolsa iti maysa a putek iti kadaratan.** The raft was tied to a bamboo stub in the sand. [Tag. *putik* = mud]

poténsia: (Sp. *potencia*: power) *n.* power; halo.

putík₁: *n.* a kind of small *burnáy.* **sangaputik.** *n.* a jarful, one jar. [Tag. *putík*]

putík₂: pinutikan. *n.* kind of stitch used in mending.

putingtíng: *var.* of *butingting*: toy with, finger with in order to fix.

putípot: *n.* binding, bandage; coil. **putipot ti takiag.** *n.* armlet. **iputipot.** *v.* to bind; coil. **putiputan.** *v.* to bandage; wind something around. **Ginaw-atna ti nakasalapay nga ules sana imputipot iti bagina.** She reached for the blanket hanging on the clothesline and then wrapped it around her body. [Tag. *pulupot*]

putló: putputlo. *n.* kind of edible seaweed. (*puklo*)

púto: (Tagalog also) *n.* rice cake made with eggs, grounded rice, sugar, water, and coconut.

potló: popotlo, potpotlo. *n.* kind of rough, edible seaweed.

pútok₁: putuken. *v.* to pick out, select, choose. [Tag. *pilì*]

pútok₂: naputputok. *a.* alone, solitary (*putong; bugtong*). **maiputputok.** *v.* to be isolated, alone. [Tag. *nag-iisá*]

putók: *n.* blast; bursting sound. **agputok.** *v.* to make a bursting sound. (bullet) **iputok.** *v.* to launch in the air; fire a gun; ejaculate. **paputok.** *n.* firecracker. **paputokan.** *v.* to fire at. **paputoken.** *v.* to explode, fire. **Naglingedak ngem nasiputanna ti naggapuan ti putokko.** I hid but she was able to discern where my gunshot came from. [Tag. *putók*]

pútol: *a.* beheaded, decapitated; manner in which a woman's dress, neckline, or hair is cut. **putulan.** *v.* to decapitate, behead. **naputulan.** *a.* beheaded, decapitated; low necked. **puputulan.** *n.* upper part of the bust uncovered in women. [Tag. *putol* = cut]

putól: (Pil.) *a.* cut, with a part cut off. (*pútol*)

pútong: *a.* separate, solitary. **putputong.** *a.* desolate; isolated. **iputong.** *v.* to separate; isolate. **maiputputong.** *v.* to be isolated, desolate. **naiputputong.** *a.* isolated. **Putputong dagiti manmano a balbalay ngem nabaknang ti aglawlaw iti narurukbos a kaykayo a mangipalpal-id iti nalamiis a puloy.** The few houses are isolated, but the surroundings are rich from the leafy trees fanning in the cool breeze. [Tag. *putong* = turban; crown]

putóng: *n.* internode of bamboo used to hold water. **naputong.** *a.* short; narrow; tight. [Tag. *sikíp* (tight)]

putúro: (Sp. *futuro*: future) *n.* future tense. [Tag. *panghinaharáp*]

pútot: *n.* child, descendant, offspring (of men). **agputot.** *v.* to procreate; father a child. **kaputotan.** *n.* generation. **sangaputotan.** *n.* one family, one generation. **pututen.** *v.* to father a child. **makaputot.** *a.* fertile (said of men); able to father a child. **Nagadu a putotmon ngem mapanunotmo pay lat' agbabai.** You already have a lot of children but you are still thinking of keeping a mistress. [Note: offspring of both men and women: *anák.* Tag. *anák*]

putót: *n.* shorts; short-sleeved coat; bobtail. **pututan.** *v.* to shorten (parts of garments). [Tag. *putót* (cut short)]

putpót₁: putpoten. *v.* to do entirely; finish. **maputpot.** *v.* to be able to do entirely; able to finish.

putpót₂: agputpot. *v.* the sound of a car horn. **panutpot.** *n.* sound of a car horn, or repeated farting.

putragís: (Pil.) *excl.* expressing mild frustration.

putrído: (Sp. *pútrido:* putrid) *n.* grassland.

putrís: *var.* of *putragís.*

putrítos: *n.* kind of folk dance.

pótro: (Sp. *potro:* colt) *n.* colt, young horse or donkey.

potséro: (Sp. *puchero:* earthenware cooking pot; stew) *n.* dish made with meat, vegetables, and broth.

puttáw: *n.* (*obs.*) desert. **kaptawán.** *n.* cage.

puttúok: maiputtuok. *v.* to see or find accidentally; be opportune.

puttót: *n.* dam used in irrigation; fishpond; dike. **agputtot.** *v.* to build a dam or dike. (*tanggal*) **puttutén.** *v.* to dam up. [Tag. *saplád*]

puwís: *var.* of *piwis:* contorted, awry, twisted.

puyápoy₁: napuyapoy. *a.* slow, sluggish (*bontog*). [Tag. *kupad*]

puyápoy₂: puyapuyan. *n.* lowest part of a sloping field where drainage collects; drain, sewer; sink; (*obs.*) cascade.

púyat: *n.* sleeplessness. **agpuyat.** *v.* to stay up all night; to refrain from sleeping. **puyaten.** *v.* to cause someone to stay up all night. **mapuyat.** *v.* to feel sleepy. **mapuyatan.** *v.* to lose sleep; happen to stay up all night. **napuyatan.** *a.* drowsy due to lack of sleep. **Nabannog ket napuyatan iti biahe.** He was tired for lost sleep from the trip. [Png., Tag. *púyat*]

púyaw: *n.* thin, kite paper.

puyó: pumuyo. *v.* to swell, puff up. **pinuyo.** *n.* a kind of fried flat cake made of rice. [Tag. *bintóg*]

puyód: *n.* sliver of beaten cotton. **puyuden.** *v.* to prepare cotton for spinning.

puyóng: *n.* improvised purse or bag; contents of an improvised purse or bag. **puyongen.** *v.* to form into a purse of bag (joining together four corners of a cloth, etc.) (*punggós*). **ipuyong.** *v.* to put into an improvised purse. **Malagipko ita ti buy-ong ni Rowena a pinuyong ti trahe-de-bodana.** I remember the large belly of Rowena bagged by her wedding gown.

puyúpoy: *n.* breeze; southwest wind. (*pul-óy*) **mapuyupoy.** *v.* to spray water; flicker (flames); fly (dust). **napuyupoy.** *a.* breezy. **Nalamiis ti puyupoy ti aglawlaw nga aggapu kadagiti katurodan.** The surrounding breeze coming from the hills was cool. [Tag. *simoy; puyupoy* = wagging of the tail]

puyót: puyuten. *v.* to blow (the fire). **puyutan.** *v.* to blow at, inflate; puff. **mapuyotan.** *v.* to be blown; blown out. **pupuyotan, pangpuypu-**

yutan. *n.* lower part of the trachea of animals. **agpipinnuyot.** *v.* to blow out a candle (in competition). **puypuyot.** *n.* inflatable toy. **Nasken ti panangpuyotmo iti bukodmo a tangguyob.** You must blow your own horn. [Ibg. *suq*, Ivt. *alupan*, Kal. *sap-uy*, Knk. *sip-uy, águ,* Kpm. *labul,* Tag. *híhip*]

puypúy: *n.* caudal fin; fish tail.

pragátas: *var.* of *alpargátas:* hemp sandals.

práile: (Sp. *fraile:* friar) *n.* friar.

práktika: (Sp. *práctica:* practice; training) *n.* practice (of physician); training; experience.

prankísa: (Sp. *franquicia:* franchise) *n.* franchise, privilege granted by the government.

pranéla: (Sp. *franela:* flannel) *n.* flannel.

Pransés: (Sp. *francés:* French) *n. a.* French. (fem: *Pransesa*) **agpranses.** *v.* to speak French. **konsi-Pranses.** *n.* person who speaks French for an ulterior motive (to impress, although he may have a heavy accent or bad grammar).

prangkísia: (Sp. *franquicia:* franchise) *n.* franchise.

prángko: (Sp. *franco:* frank) *a.* frank (fem: *prangka*). **iprangko.** *v.* to say frankly. [Tag. *tapát, tahás*]

praskéra: (Sp. *frasquera:* small bottle) *n.* small bottle.

praskíta: (f. *prasko*) *n.* small bottle.

prásko: (Sp. *frasco:* bottle) *n.* large bottle. **sangaprasko.** *n.* one bottle.

práyle: (Sp. *fraile:* friar) *n.* friar, monk.

prebénda: (Sp. *prebenda*) *n.* prebend.

preguntá(r): (Sp. *preguntar:* ask) **preguntaran** *v.* to interrogate.

premiádo: (f. *premio*) *a.* awarded a prize.

prémio: (Sp. *premio:* prize) *n.* prize, award. (*gunggona*) **mapremiuan.** *v.* to be given a prize. **premiuan.** *v.* to give a prize to. [Tag. *gatimpalà*]

prénda: *n.* mortgage; engagement ring (symbol of mutual agreement); pledge; hostage. **iprenda.** *v.* to mortgage; pawn. **nakaprenda.** *a.* engaged; mortgaged, pawned off. [Tag. *sanglâ*]

préno: (Sp. *freno:* brake) *n.* brake. **agpreno.** *v.* to step on the brakes.

prénsa: (Sp. *prensa:* press) *n.* (media) press (*imprenta; pagmalditan*); printed material.

prénta: (Sp. *imprenta:* print) *n.* print (*maldit*). [Tag. *lathalà, taták*]

preparádo: (Sp. *preparado:* prepared) *a.* prepared (*sagana*). [Tag. *handâ*]

preparatória: (Sp.) *n.* preparatory course.

prepásio: (Sp. *prefacio:* preface) *n.* preface. [Tag. *paunáng salitâ*]

preperénsia: (Sp. *preferencia*) *n.* preference.

preposisión: (Sp. *preposición*) *n.* preposition. [Tag. *pang-ukol*]

présa(s): (Sp. *fresa*: strawberry) *n.* strawberry.

presentá(r): (Sp. *presentar*: introduce; present) **ipresentar**. *v.* to present; introduce. **presentaren**. *v.* to introduce. (*pakaammo*) **presentado**. *a.* presented; submitted; introduced.

presénte: (Sp.) *a.* present.

preserbádo: (Sp. *preservado*) *a.* preserved.

preserbatíbo: (Sp. *preservativo*: preservative) *n.* preservative.

presidénsia: (Sp. *presidencia*) *n.* municipal hall.

presidénte: (Sp. *presidente*: president) *n.* president. (*pangulo*) **Presidente elekto**. *n.* president-elect. [Tag. *pangulo*]

presínto: (Sp. *precinto*: precinct) *n.* precinct; voting place; district of a city.

présio: (Sp. *precio*: price) *n.* price, cost. (*bayad*) **presiuan**. *v.* to estimate the cost of. **napresio**. *a.* able to sell, in demand; expensive, costly.

presión: (Sp. *presión*: pressure) *n.* pressure. **alta-presion**. *n.* high blood pressure.

presióso: (Sp. *precioso*: precious) *a.* precious (*ngina, pateg*). [Tag. *halagá*]

présko: (Sp. *fresco*: fresh) **napresko**. *a.* fresh; cool, breezy. [Tag. *sariwà*]

préso: (Sp. *preso*: prisoner) *n.* jail, prison. (*pagbaludan*); prisoner (*balud*). **ipreso**. *v.* to imprison; confine. **preso a soldado**. *n.* prisoner of war. [Tag. *bilanggô*]

presupuésto: (Sp. *presupuesto*: supposition; estimate; budget) *n.* budget; amount set aside; fixed price; appropriation.

prestíhio: (Sp. *prestigio*: prestige) *n.* prestige. **prestihioso**. *a.* prestigious. [Tag. *katanyagán*]

pribádo: (Sp. *privado*: private) *a.* private (*napakní; pótong*). [Tag. *palihím; pansarili*]

pribiléhio: (Sp. *privilegio*: privilege) *n.* privilege (*kalintegan*). [Tag. *tanging karapatán*]

príma: (Sp. *prima*: first) *n.* first ringing of the church bells in the morning; insurance premium. **agprima**. *v.* to ring the bells in the early morning.

primabéra: (Sp. *primavera*: spring) *n.* spring, season between winter and summer. [Tag. *tagsibol*]

primádo: (Sp. *primado*: primate) *n.* primate.

primadóna: (Eng.) *n.* prima donna.

primária: (Sp. *primaria*: primary) *a.* primary; *n.* primary school.

priméra, priméro: (Sp. *primera*: first) *a.* first (*umuná*); of finest quality; first gear. **primera klase**. first class. **imprimerak**. I put it in first gear. [Tag. *uná*]

primitíbo: (Sp. *primitivo*: primitive) *a.* primitive.

prínsa: (Sp. *prensa*: press) **prinsaen**. *v.* to iron clothes (*plantsa*).

prinsésa: (Sp. *princesa*: princess) *n.* princess. **prinsesita**. *n.* young princess; (*coll.*) spoiled girl.

prinsipál: (Sp. *principal*) *n.* principal (in school).

prínsipe: (Sp. *príncipe*: prince) *n.* prince. (*anak ti ari*)

prinsípio: (Sp. *principio*: principle) *n.* principle. **prinsipiado**. *a.* having principles; of moral character.

prínti: (Sp. *frente*: front) **agprinti**. *v.* to stand at attention.

prioridád: (Sp. *prioridad*: priority) *n.* priority. [Tag. *kaunahan*]

prisínta: **agprisinta**. *v.* to apply; apply for a job.

prisión: (Sp. *prisión*: capture, imprisonment) *n.* seizure, capture; prison; shackle.

príto: (Sp. *frito*: fried) *a.* fried. (*gisá*) **agprito, prituen**. *v.* to fry. [Kal. *sangliwon*, Tag. *sangág*]

próa: *var.* of *purrua*: prow of a ship.

probabilidád: (Sp. *probabilidad*: probability) *n.* probability, chance.

probádo: (Sp. *probado*: proved) *a.* proved.

probasión: (Sp. *probación*: probation) *n.* probation; conditional liberty.

probérbio: (Sp. *proverbio*: proverb) *n.* proverb. [Png. *sanaysáy*, Tag. *salawikain*]

probetsár: (Sp. *aprovechar*: take advantage) **probetsaran**. *v.* to profit with something, take advantage of. (*gundáway*)

probétso: (Sp. *provecho*: advantage) *n.* profit; benefit; advantage; gain. [Tag. *pakinabang*]

probínsia: (Sp. *provincia*: province) *n.* province; country (rural part) **probinsiana**. *n.* country girl. (*taga-áway*) **probinsiano** *n.* country boy; person from the province. [Png. *lúyag*, Tag. *lalawigan*]

probinsiál: (Sp. *provincial*) *a.* provincial.

probléma: (Sp. *problema*: problem) *n.* problem. (*parikút*) **problemátiko**. *a.* problematic.

probokár: (Sp. *provocar*: provoke) **probokaren**. *v.* to provoke. **Kayatmo a probokarennaka manen ti anakmo.** Do you want your child to provoke you again?

prodúkto: (Sp. *producto*: product) *n.* product; produce. (*paltuád, patáud*)

pruéba: (Sp. *prueba*: proof) *n.* proof (*paneknék*); proof sheet in printing.

prográma: (Sp. *programa*: program) *n.* program. (*pamwidán*)

progréso: (Sp. *progreso*: progress) *n.* progress. (*rang-áy*)

proklamádo: (Sp. *proclamado*: proclaimed) *a.* proclaimed. **proklamasión**. *n.* proclamation. (*balláag*)

prokuradór: (Sp. *procurador*) *n.* proctor; procurator; law of judicial solicitor.

proletário: (Sp. *proletario*) *n.* proletarian.

prólogo: (Sp. *prólogo*) *n.* prologue.

promédio: (Sp. *promedio*: grade) *n.* grade (mark) in school; general score in a test.

prominénte: (Sp.) *a.* prominent.

promosión: (Sp. *promoción*) *n.* promotion.

promotór: (Sp.) *n.* instigator.

pronómbre: (Sp. *pronombre*: pronoun) *n.* pronoun. (*sao a maisandi iti nagan*)

prónto: (Sp.) *a.* quick; on time.

propagánda: (Sp. *propaganda*: propaganda) *n.* propaganda. **propagandista**. *n.* propagandist, person who spreads propaganda.

propesión: (Sp. *profesión*: profession) *n.* profession. (*pagsapulan*)

propesionál: (Sp. *profesional*) *n.* professional.

propéso: (Sp. *profeso*: professed) *a.* professed; having taken the vows of a religious order.

propesór: (Sp. *profesor*: professor) *n.* professor; instructor (*manursuro*). [Tag. *gurò*]

propéta: (Sp. *profeta*: prophet) *n.* prophet (*mammadles*). [Tag. *manghuhulà*]

propetário: *var.* of *propietario*: proprietor.

propiedád: (Sp. *propiedad*: property) *n.* property. [Tag. *ari-arian*]

propietário: (Sp. *propietario*: owner) *n.* owner, proprietor; landlord; ownership; pure by birth; aborigine (referring to peoples who preceded Ilocano settlers). [Tag. *may-arì*]

própugo: (Sp. *prófugo*: refugee) *n.* refugee; homeless person. **kinto propugo**. *n.* deserter (in an army); person who refuses to sign up for military service. [Tag. *takas*]

prósa: (Sp. *prosa*: prose) *n.* prose.

prosekusión: (Sp. *prosecución*) *n.* prosecution (in court).

prosesión: (Sp. *procesión*) *n.* procession.

prospékto: (Sp. *prospecto*: prospect) *n.* prospect.

prosperidád: (Sp. *prosperidad*) *n.* prosperity. [Tag. *tagumpáy*]

prostitúta: (Sp. *prostituta*: prostitute) *n.* prostitute. (*puta, pampam*)

prútas: (Sp. *frutas*: fruit) *n.* fruit. [Tag. *bunga*]

protehér: (Sp. *proteger*) **proteheran.** *v.* to protect.

protehído: (Sp. *protegido*: protected) *a.* protected. (*salakan*)

proteksión: (Sp. *protección*: protection) *n.* protection. (*pagsalakan, salakníb*)

prutéra: (f. *prutas*) *n.* basket or bowl of fruit; female fruit vendor.

prutéro: (f. *prutas*) *n.* male fruit vendor.

prutería: (f. *prutas*) *n.* fruit store; fruit stall.

protésta: (Sp. *protesta*: protest) *n.* protest. [Tag. *pagtutol*]

Protestánte: (Sp. *protestante*: Protestant) *n. a.* Protestant. (*purtis*) **Protestantismo.** *n.* Protestantism.

protína: (Sp. *proteína*: protein) *n.* protein.

protoplásma: (Sp. *protoplasma*) *n.* protoplasm.

prototípo: (Sp. *prototipo*: prototype) *n.* prototype.

proyékto: (Sp. *proyecto*: project) *n.* project. (*gandát, síkat*)

psé: interjection of disapproval or contempt.

psikiátra: (Sp. *psiquiatra*) *n.* psychiatrist. (*sikiatra*)

psikiatría: (Sp. *psiquiatría*) *n.* psychiatry. (*sikiatria*)

psíkiko: (Sp. *psíquico*: psychic) *a.* psychic. (*sikiko*)

psikoanálisis: (Sp. *psicoanálisis*: psychoanalysis) *n.* psychoanalysis. (*sikoanalisis*)

psikolóhiko: (Sp. *psicológico*: psychological) *a.* psychological. (*sikolohiko*)

psikolohía: (Sp. *psicología*: psychology) *n.* psychology. (*sikolohia*)

psikólogo: (Sp. *psicólogo*: psychologist) *n.* psychologist. (*sikologo*)

psikópata: (Sp. *psicópata*: psychopath) *n.* psychopath. (*sikopata*)

psikopatía: (Sp. *psicopatía*: psychopathy) *n.* psychopathy. (*sikopatia*)

psikosomátiko: (Sp. *psicosomático*: psychosomatic) *a.* psychosomatic. (*sikosomatiko*)

psikoterapía: (Sp. *psicoterapia*: psychotherapy) *n.* psychotherapy. (*sikoterapia*)

R

ráang: see *paraángan*: yard.

ráar: **naraar**. *a.* sensual, voluptuous; lewd (*uttog*). [Tag. *libóg*]

ráas: (*reg.*) *n.* scarcity of food or money. **agraraas**. *v.* to be in scarce supply.

raás: **agraas**. *v.* to pretend, feign.

ráat: **agraat**. *v.* to clear away shrubs, undergrowth, branches, etc. (*agtás*) **panagraat**. *n.* cutting away weeds. **raatan**. *v.* to cut away weeds, shrubs. **raaten**. *v.* to clear a forest path by hacking away through a thicket. **maraatan**. *v.* to be hacked, cut away (weeds), cleared (jungle road).

raáy: *n.* bunch, cluster (of fruits other than bananas). **agraraay**. *a.* in clusters, in bunches. **sangaraay**. *n.* one bunch; one cluster. [Tag. *kumpól*]

rába: **rumaba**. *v.* to increase, worsen (sickness); become heated. (*karo*) **parabaen**. *v.* to intensify. **karabaanna**. *n.* height; climax. **Rimmaba ti ragutok ti barukongna**. The pulse in his chest intensified. [Tag. *tindí, lalà*]

rábak₁: *n.* joke; fun. (*angaw*) **makirabak**. *v.* to joke with. **manangrabak**. *n.* joker. **narabak**. *a.* joking, full of jokes. **rabaken**. *v.* to banter; ridicule; say in jest. **Ti dua nga naimbag nga aggayyem, dika rabrabaken.** Don't create trouble between two good friends. **No awan rabak, awan met ragsak.** Where there are no jokes, there is no joy. **Ayna, rabrabakko laeng.** Oh my, I'm just joking. [Png. *sulon, labay, galaw*, Tag. *birò*]

rábak₂: **rumarabak**. *n.* kind of small, black ant.

rabanós: (Sp. *rábano*: radish) *n.* radish. [Tag. *labanós*]

rabárab: *n.* edge; brim; rim. (*ígid*) **rabaraban**. *n.* to trim the ends (*tabtáb*). **Siuuksob ti badona kabayatan ti panangrabarabna iti panakkelen a puon ti kayo.** He had his shirt off as he trimmed the large tree trunk. [Tag. *gilid*]

rabáng: *n.* species of freshwater plant common in rivers.

rabása: *n.* a kind of grass.

rabáw: *n.* upper side; top of, highest point on something. **iparabaw**. *v.* to place something on top. **iti rabaw**. *prep.* on top of, on, upon, above. **narabaw**. *a.* shallow; superficial; easy to understand. **kinarabaw**. *n.* shallowness, superficiality. **naparabawan**. *a.* covered, with something on top. **rumabaw**. *v.* to climb to the top of, go to the top. **pakinrabawén**. *v.* to place on the top. **parabawán**. *v.* to place on top of. **parabawén**. *v.* to make something shallow. **Imparabawna dagiti sakana iti lamisaan.** He put his feet on the table. [Kal. *lap-at*, Png. *tapéw*, Tag. *ibabaw*]

ráber: *n.* thick vegetation. (*samék*) **naraber**. *a.* lush (vegetation); green, verdant. **kinaraber**. *n.* lushness, thickness of vegetation. **rumaber**. *v.* to grow lush. **Mapanda agsapul iti narabraber a pagarabanda iti ganggannaet.** They are looking for greener pastures in foreign lands. [Png. *buná*, Tag. *lagô, labay, luntî*]

rabií: *n.* night, evening. (*sardam*) **agkarabii, agparabii**. *v.* to stay out late at night. **rinabii**. *adv.* every night. **rumabii**. *n.* nightfall. *v.* to turn into night. **marabiian**. *v.* to be overtaken by the night, to be late at night (in arriving, etc.). **mangrabii**. *v.* to eat dinner. **pangrabii**. *n.* dinner. **nakapangrabii**. *a.* having eaten dinner. **idi rabii**. last night. **iti karabiian**. the night of. **mangrabrabii**. *n.* kind of winged green cricket; thieves; (*reg.*) near childbirth. **karabiyanna**. last night. **iparabii**. *v.* to wait until night; do at night, postpone until night. **apagrabii**. *a.* just beginning to get dark. **Dika agparparabii.** Don't stay out late. **Kayatko kuma nga ikkaten ti ugali ti agkarabii.** I want to break the habit of staying out late at night. [Bon., Knk. *labí*, Ibg. *gavi, gabi*, Ifg. *hilo*, Itg. *labi*, Ivt. *ahep*, Kal. *labi*, Kpm. *béngi*, Png. *lábi*, Tag. *gabí*]

rabírab: *n.* lip of a container, lip of a jar; clamorous speech, tirade. [Knk. *labílab* (clamorous speech)]

rabnís: **rabnisen**. *v.* to tear off; snatch. [Tag. *sambilat, saklót*]

rabnós: see *rabnót*: snatch.

rabnót: **rabnuten**. *v.* to snatch; remove forcibly and suddenly. [Tag. *sambilat, saklót*]

rabngís: **rabrabngisen**. *v.* to address familiarly; to address disrespectfully (*rasáw*); insult; act imprudently. **pannakarabngis**. *n.* violation. **Diyo rabngisen ti pangngeddengko.** Do not go against my will. **Naginsisintunado tapno rabngisennak.** He is pretending to sing out of tune to insult me.

rábok: **mairabok**. *v.* to come upon by chance; arrive in time for an unexpected event. **rumabok**. *v.* to eat without invitation; participate without being asked.

rabók: *n.* species of taro with lots of shoots.

rábon: **irabon**. *v.* to start, begin (rain).

rabóng: *n.* bamboo shoot; variety of awned late rice. [Png., Tag. *labóng*]

rábor: **rinabor, nirabor**. *n.* wine made from molasses.

rabúray: *n.* kind of Borneo jar.

rabóy: **naraboy**. *a.* lush; healthy (plants); robust. **kinaraboy**. *n.* lush grown, robustness; (*fig.*) opulence. **rumaboy**. *v.* to become lush (vegetation) (*raber, samek*). [Png. *buná*, Tag. *lagô*, *labay*]

rabráb₁: nagrabrab. *a.* greedy, avaricious; talkative; taking a lot of food with no shame; eating continuously. [Tag. *takaw*]

rabráb₂: *var.* of *rabárab*: edge, rim. [Tag. *gilid*]

rabsút: rabsuten. *v.* to snatch away (*rabnot*). **Dina marabsut ni liday a naipilot iti kararuana.** He cannot snatch away the sadness smeared on his soul. [Tag. *agaw*]

rádam: *n.* night blindness, nyctalopia. **agradam.** *v.* to be night-blind, suffer from nyctalopia.

radárad: *var.* of *radrád*: grate; scrape; scour.

radáw: radawan. *v.* to cut trees high off the ground. **iradaw.** *v.* to prune; cut sparingly. **naradaw.** *a.* sparing; superficial.

radéla: *var.* of *rodela*: wooden plastering trowel.

radiadór: (Sp. *radiador*: radiator) *n.* radiator.

rádio: (Sp. *radio*: radio) *n.* radio. **iparadio.** *v.* to broadcast over the radio, transmit over the radio. [Tag. *radyo*]

radioaktíbo: (Sp. *radioactivo*) *a.* radioactive.

radrád: radradan. *v.* to rub hard, scour; scrape. **iradrad.** *v.* to rub hard on something, scour; scrape (*kaskas, radárad, rasrás*). [Tag. *kaskás*]

radrílio: *var.* of *ladrilio*: brick.

raéb: *n.* a kind of large net for marine fishing, larger than the *tabúkol*. **agraeb.** *v.* to catch with the *raeb* net. **rumaeb.** *v.* to go deep inside; to go to the interior.

raéd: agraed. *v.* to rasp while talking, talk with a hoarse voice (*barbár*); to bow. **iraed.** *v.* to say in a hoarse voice. [Tag. *paos, malát* (hoarse)]

raém: agraem. *v.* to be polite, respectful. **pagraeman.** *v.* to respect, revere. **raemen.** *v.* to appreciate; admire. **managraem.** *a.* respectful. **maráraem.** *a.* respectable, dignified; upright. **Rinaemko ti sukog ti pammagina.** I admired the form of her body. **Raementayo kuma ti pammatida a kas met ti panagraemda ti pammatitayo.** We should respect their beliefs as they respect ours. [Png., Tag. *galang*]

raép: *n.* newly transplanted rice seedlings. **agraep, iraep.** *v.* to transplant seedlings of rice (*tulméng*). **agraraep, rumaraep.** *n.* rice planter, transplanter; farmer in charge of transplanting. **manangraep.** *n.* one who is a good transplanter. **maraepan.** *v.* to be planted with rice. **raepan.** *v.* to transplant rice to a particular field. **No nakisang ti tudo, maabbatan dagiti raepda.** If the rain is scarce, their seedlings will dry up. [Tag. *punlâ* (seedling), *lipat* (transplant)]

ragadéra: *var.* of *regadera*: water sprinkler.

ragadéro: (f. *ragadi*) *n.* sawyer.

ragádi: *n.* carpenter's saw; prickles on the stems of buri palm leaves. **agragadi.** *v.* to saw; to be

two faced, hypocritical. **iragadi.** *v.* to saw with. **ragadien.** *v.* to saw something, cut by sawing. **manangragadi.** *a.* expert in sawing. **nagragadian.** *n.* sawdust. **ragragadi.** *n.* Achyranthes aspera spiky sawlike herb. **rimmagadi.** *a.* like a saw; serrated. **Rimmagadi dagiti iking ti bulong.** The edges of the leaves are serrated. [Bon. *lagádi, kompol*, Ibg. *geggél*, Itg., Knk. *lagádi*, Ivt. *galagal*, Png. *lagári*, Kal. *lagachi*, Kpm., Tag. *lagarì*]

ragánag: agkaranaganag. *v.* to drop, fall profusely. **naraganag.** *a.* falling profusely.

ragangírang: (*obs.*) *n.* threshold (of a jungle); dry, parched land. **agragangirang.** *v.* to become dry, parched. **Awan mamaay ti ragangirang a daga nga ipatawidmo kenkuana.** There is no use for the parched land that you are giving him as an inheritance.

ragárag: *var.* of *ragánag*: fall profusely.

rágas: *n.* cut piece. **ragasen.** *v.* to cut, cut out; trim (ends). **ragasan.** *v.* to shorten (clothes). **agkaragas.** *v.* to be cut out of the same piece. **pagragasan.** *n.* cuttings.

ragatúnok: *n.* blister on the skin (*ratúnok*). **agraragatunok.** *v.* to have imperfections on the skin (rashes, blisters, bites, etc.).

ragáw: ragawan. *v.* to trim, prune trees. (*paad*)

rágay: iragay. *v.* to brandish a weapon.

ráging: *n.* ridge of mountains; rough (not smooth) surface. **ragingan.** *a.* rough (said of the surface or edges).

ragingírang: *var.* of *ragangírang*: dry, parched land. (*ragírang*)

ragírang: *n.* dry, parched land. **agragirang.** *v.* to become dry and parched.

ragkáng: *n.* crack. (*regkáng*) **naragkang.** *a.* bulky, cumbersome; cracked.

rag-ó: *n.* joy, jubilation, exultation, delight. (*ragsák*) **agragrag-o.** *v.* to be glad, rejoice; skip, jump. **narago.** *a.* joyful, very glad. **makaparag-o.** *a.* joyous, causing joy. **pagrag-uan.** *n.* cause of rejoicing. [Knk. *damiág*, Png. *likét*, *gayaga*, Tag. *galák*]

ragunót: ragunuten. *v.* to pull (hair, strings). **rumagunot.** *v.* to make a crackling, creaking sound. [Tag. *hagunót*]

ragúp: *n.* date set for a meeting; assembly of people; crowd; flock; herd. **makiragup, agraragup.** *v.* to be together, join someone in doing. **iragup.** *v.* to join, connect two things; include in a group. **pagraragupán.** *n.* meeting place, place of assembly; melting pot. **No adu ti ammom, uray ania nga ummong ti pakairagupam, adda latta masaom.** If you know a lot, no matter what group you join you will have something to say. [Tag. *pangkát* (crowd)]

rágut: *n.* craving; strong desire. **agragut**. *v.* to crave, long for strongly. **agragut ti puso**. *exp.* to crave for strongly from the heart. **naragut**. *a.* eager; aggressive. **pagragutan**. *n.* craving, desire. [Tag. *sabík*]

ragút: *n.* ugliness (*alás*, *láad*); awkwardness. **naragut**. *a.* ugly; awkward; clumsy. [Tag. *pangit* (ugly)]

ragutínit: *var.* of *ragutirit*: kind of seaweed.

ragutírit: **ragragutirit**. *n.* a brown, edible seaweed with round sporocarps.

ragutók: *n.* rapid beating of the heart; pulsation; rapid firing of gun. **agragutok**. *v.* to make a cracking sound (like burning reed); to rapidly beat (said of heart) (*kibbakibbá*, *pitík*). **Pimmardas ti ragutok ti barukongna**. The beating of his heart (*lit*: chest) sped up. [Tag. *pintíg*]

ragpát: *n.* attainment; achievement. **maragpat**. *v.* to attain, achieve; reach one's goal. **naragpat**. *a.* having achieved honors; attained, achieved. **ragpaten**. *v.* to obtain, acquire; achieve; earn, gain. **iragpat**. *v.* to honor, exalt; promote. **makaragpat**. *v.* to be able to achieve, reach one's goal. **Namnamaem ti pannakaragpatmo iti tartarigagayam**. Expect to achieve what you desire. [Png. *pakala*, *gamór*, Tag. *kamít*, *tamó*]

ragpín: *n.* enclosure. **ragpinen**. *v.* to enclose; insert in. (*rapin*) **iragpin**. *v.* to enclose; include. **mairagpin**. *v.* to be enclosed; included; inserted. [Png. *tekép*; *sulong*, *surob*, *sipit*, Tag. *lakíp*; *sakop*, *sakláw*; *ipasok*, *ipaloób*]

ragpúyo: **agragpuyo**. *v.* to incline, lean, be lopsided (*irig*, *tingíg*). [Tag. *kiling*]

ragrág: *a.* old and worn out; shaky, tottering, rickety; about to collapse.

ragsák: *n.* happiness, joy, pleasure (*rag-ó*). **ragragsak**. *n.* happy occasion; feast; recreation. **naragsak**. *a.* happy, joyous. **kinaragsak**. *n.* happiness, joy. **paragsaken**. *v.* to make happy; comfort. **pagragsaken**. *v.* to make someone happy, comfort. **rumagsak**. *v.* to skip for joy, gambol. **ragsaken**. *v.* to take pleasure in; do happily. **pagraragsakan**. *n.* party, feast, fiesta, place of fun. **Ragsakek ti matay gapu kaniam**. I am happy to die for you. **balay a pagraragsakan**. *n.* whorehouse; fun house. [Ibg. *magayáyaq*, Itg. *lagsak*, Ivt. *máyak*, *saray*, *suyut*, Kal. *lat-op*, *lagalas*, Knk. *alsík*, Png. *gayága*, *likét*, *sayaksák*, Kpm., Tag. *sayá*]

ráha: (Sp. *raja*) *n.* rajah.

ráip: **iraip**. *v.* to join; include. **karaip**. *a.* adjacent; near; adjoining. **pagraipen**. *v.* to put adjacent to. **Idi agsina dagiti bibigmi, ammokon a didanton agraip uray kaano man**. When our lips separated I knew that they would

never join again. [Png. *rasig*, *abay*, Tag. *karatig*, *sanib*, *tabí*]

ráir: see *irair*: cry of hogs or babies.

raíra: **agraira**. *v.* to come out (ghosts; criminals); to be the time to appear. (supernatural things.); to spread; have a resurgence of. **Agraira manen dagiti ansisit**. The dwarfs are on the loose again.

ráire: *n.* smooth speech. **naraire**. *a.* speaking easily, articulate.

ráit₁: *n.* cold sore or blister (*kapúyo*). **agrait**. *v.* to have a cold sore. [Tag. *singáw*]

ráit₂: *var.* of *ráip*: **agkarait**. *v.* to be contiguous (fields). **irait**. *v.* to put alongside, to put to the side of.

rákab₁: *n.* strip of rattan used to bind bamboo to posts; width; breadth. **irakab**. *v.* to fasten, tie; bind. **narakab**. *a.* broad, wide. **rumakab**. *v.* to broaden. **narakrakab a rupa**. broad, round face. **Narakab ti patongna**. She has broad hips. [Tag. *lapad* (breadth)]

rákab₂: **agrakab**. *v.* to fight closely with, grapple.

rákad: **irakad**. *v.* to carry many things, be overloaded (people).

rakaták: *n.* sound of typing or continuous tapping.

rakáya: **agrakaya**. *v.* to deteriorate (the body); wear out, decay; be dilapidated. **Kayatna a pabaruen ti agrakrakayan a taengda**. He wants to renovate their deteriorating home.

rakéd: *n.* hitching post. (*rakos*; *pangaw*) **iraked**. *v.* to tie; tie an animal to a tree or post. **paraked**. *n.* outrigger of a canoe. [Knk. *takéd*]

rakém: *n.* sickle; scythe, reaper's knife for cutting rice; handful. **agrakem**. *v.* to harvest palay with a sickle. **sangkarakem**. *n.* one handful. **rakmen**. *v.* to harvest palay with a sickle; to grasp; have in one's hand or under one's control; grab by the handful; scoop a handful of. **mangrakem**. *v.* to take a handful. [Png. *kamet*, *sangkaakop*, Tag. *dakot* (handful)]

rakép: *n.* embrace; hug. (*arakup*) **agrakep**, **rumakep**. *v.* to embrace; clasp. **sangarakep**. *n.* measurement reached by wrapping both arms around a tree, post. **agrinnakep**. *v.* to embrace each other. **Nairut ti panagrinnakepda**. Their embrace was tight. [Png. *lakáp*, Tag. *yakap*]

rakéta: (Sp. *raqueta*: racket) *n.* tennis racket.

rakípa: **rakrakipa**. *n.* pancreas; rumen, paunch (*liblibro*). [Tag. *lapáy*]

rákit₁: *n.* bamboo raft. **agrakit**. *v.* to ride in a *rakit*. [Png. *lámo*, Ibg., Kpm., Tag. *balsa* (Sp.)]

rákit₂: **parakit**. *n.* bamboo or wood that covers the rafters; scaffolding, the part of a scaffold workmen stand on.

rakít: narakrakit. *a.* well versed in storytelling; articulate in conversation; talkative. **rakrakit.** *n.* kind of black bird with a white breast. **rakitrakit.** *a.* talkative.

rakká: *var.* of *rekká:* fissure, crack in glass, a mirror, etc.

rakkáng: narakkang. *a.* bulky (*padiwákal*). **mairakkang.** *v.* to occupy a lot of space; to be bulky.

rákur: rakuren. *v.* to gather all, collect all; win all, sweep. (*kayuskós*)

rakúrak: *n.* divulged news. **agrakurak.** *v.* to become popular, well known. **irakurak.** *v.* to spread the news, publicize; announce. **mairakurak.** *v.* to be publicized; spread (news); be rumored. **agirakurak.** *n.* announcer; master of ceremonies. **Tiemponan tapno pabiskedem ti panangirakurakmo iti bagim.** It is time for you to advertise yourself more powerfully. [Tag. *pahayag*]

rákos: rakusan. *v.* to bind, tie. (*rakéd, gálut*) **nairakos.** *a.* strongly tied to. **irakos.** *v.* to tie, attach to a post. **Inrakosna dagiti takiagna iti tengngedko.** She tied her arms around my neck. [Tag. *tali*]

rakrák: *a.* demolished, destroyed, ruined. **rakraken.** *v.* to demolish, destroy, break; undo; annihilate; abolish. **Saanko a gandat a rakraken ti pamiliam.** It is not my intention to destroy your family. [Tag. *sirâ*]

rakrakípa: (f. *rakípa*) *n.* pancreas. [Tag. *lapáy*]

ramá: *n.* branch of tree placed in water for a long time to catch fish that decide to dwell in it; brushwood used to obstruct passage in rivers. **ramaan.** *v.* to trap fish by means of the *rama*. (*puluan*)

ramáda: *n.* improvised shelter or shed used in a wedding or feast. (*damara*)

Ramadán: (Sp.) *n.* Ramadan, the Muslim rites celebrating the ninth month of the Mohammedan year, which are observed for a month with daily fasting from sunrise to sunset.

ram-ág: agparam-ag. *v.* to show off one's possessions; boast. **naparam-ag.** *a.* pretentious, boastful.

ram-ák: mairam-ak. *v.* to fall prone or prostrate on something; fall on all fours. **maram-akan.** *v.* be trampled on; fall under a heavy load. [Tag. *dapâ*]

ráman: *n.* addition. **iraman.** *v.* to count, include; reach; extend one's influence over; penetrate; implicate. **mai(ram)raman.** *v.* to be included with; to be implicated. **makiraman.** *v.* to take part in, participate; include oneself in. **rumaman.** *v.* to participate, partake in, share. **pagraramanan.** *n.* something open to the public, for general use. **agparaman.** *v.* to share. **iparaman.** *v.* to share something. **paramanan.** *v.* to give a share to someone. **agraman.** *prep.* with, including. *v.* to be added, included. **pakairamanan.** *n.* inclusion; reason for being involved. **pagraramanan.** *a.* public; for general use. **pannakairaman.** *n.* involvement. **Gapo ta masapulda ti dadduma pay a kaduada, maysaak kadagiti nairaman nga innalada.** Because they need a few more companions, I was included in those that they got. [Tag. *sali* (participate); *damay* (implicate), *lakíp* (include)]

ramán: *n.* flavor, taste. **naraman.** *a.* flavorful, tasty. **ramanan.** *v.* to taste; experience; undergo. **maranaman.** *v.* to be able to experience or taste. **makaraman.** *v.* to be able to taste; (*fig.*) be punished. **paramanan.** *v.* to offer to be tasted; (*fig.*) give a taste of, inflict (pain). **iraman.** *v.* to test, try. **iparaman.** *v.* to give something to be tasted. **agraraman.** *v.* to learn as an apprentice; go beyond one's power; *n.* novice, inexperienced person. [Bon. *laman*, Ivt. *taham*, Kal. *simsim*, Knk. *sílam, simsím*, Png. *nanám, símsim, tawáy*, Tag. *lasa* (flavor); *tikmán* (to taste)]

ramáram: *n.* spreading (of skin diseases); transfer of fire from house to house. **agramaram.** *v.* to spread further. **ramaramen.** *v.* to affect; spread to. **mairamaram.** *v.* to abound, be more plentiful than imagined. **Saanen a madaeran ti panagramaram ti birus.** They can no longer withstand the spread of the virus. [Tag. *kalat*]

rámas: *n.* mixing ingredients well; hand-to-hand combat. **iramas.** *v.* to mash, knead into. **ramasen.** *v.* to knead. **agraramas.** *v.* to fight, battle hand-to-hand. **agparamas.** (*fig.*) *v.* to have an abortion. [Tag. *lamas* (mash)]

ramasámas: naramasamas. *a.* coarse; hard, not thoroughly cooked rice.

rámat: *n.* crack, fissure, chink (*bettak*). [Tag. *lamat, biták*]

rámaw: *n.* overload; additional burden. **iramaw.** *v.* to overload. **agramaw.** *v.* to ride on one's shoulders (when crossing a river). [Tag. *dagdág*]

rámay: *n.* finger; (~ **ti saka**) toe. The lexicalized fingers are: **tammudó.** *n.* forefinger. **pattungagan.** *n.* middle finger. **sisingsingan.** *n.* fourth finger. **kikít.** *n.* little finger. **tangan.** *n.* thumb. **ramayan.** *n.* a kind of shrimp with long feet; measurement of a finger. **ramayramayan.** *a.* with long fingers; with large claws; with many fingers. [Bon. *ledeng*, Ibg. *kurameng*, *kurámay*, Ifg. *gumut*, Ivt. *kakamay*, Kal. *gammat*, Knk. *ledéng*, Kpm. *talíriq*, Png. *gamét*, Tag. *dalirì*]

rambák: *n.* feast; celebration; festival; pomp. (*padaya*) **agrambak.** *v.* to feast, celebrate revel; be happy. **parambak.** *n.* feast, celebration, festivity. **agparambak.** *v.* to hold a celebration, feast. **makipagrambak.** *v.* to attend a feast, participate in a celebration. **narambak.** *a.* joyous; pompous. **rambakan.** *v.* to feast; solemnize, celebrate in honor of. **ramrambak.** *n.* festivities. [Tag. *sayá*]

rambáng: *n.* a type of thin casting net.

rámbol: (Eng. rumble) *n.* brawl, scuffle, street fight; uproar. **makirambol.** *v.* to join in a brawl. **rambulan.** *n.* fight (many people against one).

rambután: *n.* species of tropical fruit with a red spiny covering and white flesh.

raméd: agramed. *v.* to bend; be weighted with seed (plants); to bend under weight. **pagramedan.** *v.* to bend and lean one's weight upon; put one's weight on. [Tag. *yukô*]

ram-éd: *var.* of *raméd*: bending due to weight, pressure caused by weight.

ramék: *var.* of *tam-ék*: obstruction; impalement.

ramén₁: *n.* showy garments or jewels. **naramen.** *a.* luxurious, sumptuous.

ramén₂: *n.* seasoning; ingredients; flavor; different parts of a work of literature. **iramen.** *v.* to season with, flavor with. **ramenan.** *v.* to add seasoning or ingredients to. [Tag. *timplá*]

ramés: *n.* rape (*panangramés, aradas*). **marames.** *v.* to be raped. **narames.** *a.* raped; cruel; impolite, disrespectful; arrogant; rude. **ramesan.** *v.* to rape; (*fig.*) take advantage of one's weakness. [Tag. *gahasà*]

ramí: (Eng.) *n.* ramie plant; fiber from the ramie plant.

ramídat: (*obs.*) **rumamidat.** *v.* to raise the head to look over other people's heads.

ramiénta: *var.* of *rimienta, eramienta*: tools. (*ramít, alikámen*)

raminád: *n.* awned late-maturing rice.

rámir: (*obs.*) *n.* crack; flaw. [Tag. *biták*]

ramít: ramramit. *n.* tools; items; facts; circumstances; components; ingredients; elements; constituents. **ramitramit.** *n.* unnecessary additions. [Tag. *kagamitán*]

rammág: *var.* of *ram-ag*: boastful, pretentious.

rammáw: rammawan. *v.* to topple over (said of waves).

ramók: naramok. *a.* plentiful, abundant; pompous, showy; lush; verdant. [Tag. *saganà*]

rámos: (abbreviated from *Domingo de Ramos*: Palm Sunday.) *n.* Palm Sunday; palm leaves used during Palm Sunday. **makiramos.** *v.* to attend mass on Palm Sunday (*palaspas*). [Tag. *palaspás*]

ramót: *n.* root. **agramot.** *v.* to grow roots. **iramutan.** *v.* to cut off the roots. **ramramot.** *n.* tendon, sinew (of hand or foot). **karamramut.** *a.* full of roots. **makaramut.** *v.* to be able to grow roots, take root; (*fig.*) to be financially stable. **ramuten.** *v.* to uproot. [Ibg. *gamuq*, Ivt., Kpm. *yamut*, Kal. *lamot*, Knk. *lamót*, Png. *lamót, sengég*, Tag. *ugát*]

ram-óy: ram-uyen. *v.* to buy at a price lower than the value; undervalue. **makiram-oy.** *v.* to engage in haggling, bargain. **Kasla makiram-oy nga agpalpalama no gumatang iti lames.** She is like a bargaining beggar when she buys fish. [Tag. *barát* (Sp.)]

ramparaán: (Sp. *lámpara*: lamp) *n.* kerosene lamp.

rampáya: *var.* of *rangpaya*.

ramrám: agramram. *v.* to spread (skin diseases, fire, etc.).

raná: *n.* two events happening coincidentally, chance happening. **agrana.** *v.* to meet by chance (accidentally); coincide. **agrarana.** *n.* several simultaneous events; *v.* to happen all at once. **irana.** *v.* to do an action at the same time as another. **mairana.** *v.* to happen by chance. **maranaan.** *v.* to meet unexpectedly; to be on time for; to be caught in the act. **ranaen.** *v.* to do at the time something else happens; meet by agreement. **rumana.** *n.* to attend a meeting, meet several people. **panagrana.** *n.* meeting of two people by chance. **maranrana.** *n.* evil spirits. **Nairana a nagsakit ti pututko idi rabii.** It happened that my child got sick last night. **Ammoda nga irana iti kapigsa ti tudo wenno agbagbagio ti panaggunay dagiti agaagab.** They know that the movements of the cattle hustlers coincide with a strong wind or storm. **Agtitinnung-ed ken agiinnisem met no agraranada iti sango ti balay.** They nod and smile at each other if they catch each other in the front of the house. **Nairanrana laeng siguro.** It is probably just coincidental. [Kal. *liyaspuÿ*, Tag. *mataón*]

ránad: ranadan. *v.* to replace the bord of (a net).

ranadnád: (f. *radrád*) *n.* grating sound of a file.

ranagutók: (f. *ragutók*) *n.* sound of continuous pulsation or heartbeats. **agranagutok.** *v.* to throb continuously. [Tag. *pintíg*]

ránap: maranapan. *v.* to be covered evenly (with locusts, blisters, etc.).

ráneb: *var.* of *rennéb, táneb*: submerge in water.

ranekrék: *var.* of *ranetret*: rustling sound.

ranetrét: (f. *retret*) *n.* sound of rustling trees; creaking floor; sound of boiling water. **agranetret.** *v.* to make a rustling or light creaking sound. [Png. *larateret,* Tag. *dagaldál, garalgál*]

ránia: *var.* of *arania*: chandelier.

raniág: *n.* brightness, brilliance, radiance; luster. **naraniag.** *a.* bright, brilliant; glittering, sparkling, radiant. **makaraniag.** *n.* variety of awned early rice. [Ibg. *nanáwag,* Ivt. *sehdang,* Kpm. *masálaq,* Png. *liwáwa,* Tag. *liwanag*]

raníkab: (f. *rikáb*) *n.* sound of continuous beating of the heart; sound of grating.

raníkad: (f. *rikád*) *n.* continuous grating sound (*kanarkáad*), sound of shutters slamming in a strong wind.

ranípak: (f. *ripák*) *n.* noise made by cutting trees and wood; crackling noise. **agranipak.** *v.* to crackle.

ranitrít: (f. *ritrít*) *n.* noise of branches rubbing against one another; creaky sound. **agranitrit.** *v.* to creak; rub against one another (branches). **Nagranitrit ti inakilis a datar.** The wickerwork rattan floor creaked. [Tag. *laginít*]

ránud: agraranud, makiranud. *v.* to participate; share; partake. **agparanud.** *v.* to share, give a share to; give away. **mairanud.** *v.* to hear mass. **pagraranudan.** *n.* communion, participation. **iparanud.** *v.* to give away; donate. **rumanud.** *v.* to partake in, get a share of. **ranuden.** *v.* to benefit from; partake in. **pakairanudan.** *n.* something beneficial; worthwhile. [Tag. *bahagi*]

ranudród: rumanudrod. *v.* to make a roaring sound (vehicles). [Tag. *ungal, ugong*]

ránso: (Sp. *rancho*: ranch) *n.* ranch. **ransero.** *n.* ranch man; rancher.

ránta: *n.* plan; aim; goal. (*gagára*) **agranta.** *v.* to plan. **rantaen.** *v.* to plan; do on purpose; look for a convenient or suitable occasion to do. **iranta.** *v.* to do at an opportune time. **nairanta.** *v.* done on purpose, done at an opportune time. **nakairantaan.** *n.* intention, purpose. **Adda kalapaw a nairanta a kosina ken pangananda.** There is a hut used as their kitchen and dining room. [Png. *kanonotan,* Tag. *balak*]

rántso: (Sp. *rancho*: ranch) *n.* rest stop; *var.* of *ranso*: ranch. **agrantso.** *v.* to stop somewhere to eat or rest.

ránga: *n.* a kind of large jar. **Imbuyátna ti danum iti ranga.** He poured the water in the jar.

rangá: *n.* dignified appearance. **naranga.** *a.* worthy of respect; honorable; glamorous; splendid. **karanga.** *v.* to respect, esteem. **rangaen.** *v.* to respect a person. **agparanga** (*obs.*) *v.* to blossom (rice). [Tag. *dangál*]

rangárang: narangarang. *a.* clear; manifest. **iparangarang.** *v.* to show; manifest. [Tag. *liwanag*]

rángas: *n.* fistfight; fight with tooth and nail. **agrangas.** *v.* to fight with the fists; fight with tooth and fingernails. **rangasen.** *v.* to carry off out of a crowd; take away by force. **rangrangasen.** *v.* to be assailed on all sides or by many at the same time. [Tag. *suntukan*]

rángat₁: *n.* edge; margin, border; rim. [Tag. *gilid*]

rángat₂: rumarangat. *n.* a kind of marine fish. **rinangat.** *n.* kind of *kappi* crab with warts.

rángat₃: *n.* variety of awned late rice.

rangáw₁: *n.* edible branches or vines (*uggót*). **agrangaw.** *v.* to gather the tops of vines. **rangawan.** *v.* to cut the tops of vines. [Tag. *talbós*]

rangáw₂: parangaw. *n.* mortise at the top of a post to which a tiebeam is fitted. **parangawan.** *v.* to mortise.

rang-áy: *n.* prosperity; economic progress; wealth. **rumang-ay.** *v.* to grow; thrive, flourish; prosper; increase. **narang-ay.** *a.* prosperous. **kinarang-ay.** *n.* prosperity. **parang-ayen.** *v.* to develop, cause to grow economically. **panagrang-ay.** *n.* development; economic growth. **Nagbangon ti laboratorio tapno parangayenna ti industria ti panagpatubo iti uong.** The laboratory was erected to further develop the mushroom-growing industry. [Png. *aligwas,* Tag. *unlád, sulong*]

rangáya: *n.* a basket with a round rim and square bottom, twice the size of a *labba*. (*apirang*)

rangbáw: agrangbaw. *v.* to be on top (people). (*rabaw*)

rangbó: narangbo. *a.* opulent; rich; wealthy (*baknang*). **Saannan a maaramid dagiti narangbo a biagna iti Malacañang.** She can no longer lead her opulent lifestyle in the *Malacañang.*

rangéd: see *parngéd*: hitch to a tree (*langéd*).

rangén: *n.* glow of live coals or burning embers. (*gil-ayab*) **narangen.** *a.* blazing (fire); glittering; flourishing. **rumangen.** *v.* to inflame; kindle; grow, thrive; glitter. [Png. *ngaláb,* Tag. *baga, dupong* (ember); *yabong* (flourish)]

rangép₁: agrangep. *v.* fit exactly, join neatly. **pagrangepen.** *v.* to join together.

rangép₂: agrangep. *v.* to fight, combat (*apa*). [Tag. *laban*]

rangét: *n.* garbage floating in a river; fight, combat. **agranget.** *v.* to fight each other, battle. **rumanget.** *v.* to attack head on. **karangranget.** *a.* engaged in war. [Tag. *laban* (fight); [Tag. *lusob, salakay* (attack)]

ranggá: makirangga. *v.* to carry somebody off precipitately out of a crowd; carry off by force.

ranggás: *n.* cruelty. (*dawél, ulpít, damká, dangkés*) **naranggas.** *a.* cruel, brutal, harmful, destructive. **kinaranggas.** *n.* cruelty, brutality, destructiveness. **ranggasan.** *a.* to harm, damage, hurt, injure, mar (*dangrán*). **maranggasan.** *v.* to be harmed (through black magic). **Ti tao a masugat, isu ti inna panagranggas.** The hero when wounded becomes even braver. [Tag. *lupít*]

ranggáw: agraranggaw. *v.* to mob, gang up. (*ambón*)

ranggó: (Sp. *rango*: rank) *n.* rank; status. (*sáad*) **iranggo.** *v.* to rank, put in order according to status. **naranggo.** *a.* ranked. [Tag. *katungkulan*]

ranggúd: rangguden. *v.* to obtain by coercion or constraint.

rangiá: narangia. *a.* leaden, dull gray; overcast (*lidem*). [Tag. *kulimlím*]

rangiád: *n.* crack on the heel. **agrangiad.** *v.* to crack, chap (sole of the foot).

rangírang: *n.* entrance into a jungle.

rángis: rangisen. *v.* to handle clumsily with one hand. **rinangis.** *a.* unsymmetrical; irregular. **narangis.** *a.* abrupt; steep; unsymmetrical.

rangkáng: (*obs.*) *a.* disjointing.

rangkáp: *n.* present, gift; donation; tip; alms. **irangkap, iparangkap.** *v.* to give, bestow. **makirangkap, rangkapen.** *v.* gain, profit from; to request, ask for, petition; beg for (*gawáwa*). **managparangkap.** *a.* generous. **kinamanagparangkap.** *n.* generosity. **parangkapan.** *v.* to give to someone, bestow. [Tag. *pamigáy*; *pakinabang*]

rangkáy: *n.* cut body parts; cut (of meat). **rangkayen.** *v.* to cut up, chop; dismember; butcher; carve. **sangkarangkay.** *n.* one cut (of meat). **Rinangrangkaydakan.** They would tear you to bits. [Tag. *katáy*]

rangkiár: var. of *rikiár*: argue, dispute.

rángkis: *n.* cliff, precipice. (*derraas*; *kayas*; *teppang*) **mairangkis.** *v.* to fall off a cliff. **Napan met nagintatannawag iti rangkis.** He went to pretend to look down the cliff. [Png. *alosarsar*, Tag. *talampás*]

rángko: var. of *ranggo*: rank.

rangkór: *n.* armful. **sangarangkor.** *n.* one armful. **rangkuren.** *v.* to carry by the armful.

rangpáya: *n.* wide spreading growth of a bush. **agrangpaya.** *v.* to grow wide spreading with branching off in full. **narangpaya.** *a.* branching out; wide spreading. **parangpayen.** *v.* to allow to grow wide spreading. **rumangpaya.** *a.* to develop fully; grow with many branches; become progressive. [Tag. *lagô*]

rangráng: *n.* heat from a blazing fire. (*seggéd*; *daráng*; *gil-áyab*) **narangrang.** *a.* very hot. **rumangrang.** *v.* to flame, glare, glow. **parangrangen.** *v.* to brighten. [Tag. *liwanag*]

rangtáy: *n.* bridge. (*taytáy*; *talaytáy*) **agrangtay.** *v.* to build a bridge; cross a bridge; walk a tightrope. **rangtayan.** *v.* to build a bridge over (a body of water). **marangtayan.** *v.* to be able to build a bridge over. **mangrangtay.** *v.* to bridge; connect. [Ibg. *balátay*, Ivt. *barátay*, Kal. *langtay*, Knk. *talaytáy*, Kpm. *téte*, Png. *taytáy*, Tag. *tuláy*]

ráok: raukan. *v.* to cut out in order to make fit, (collar)

raóng: *n.* cry of the hungry hog. **agraong.** *v.* to make the cry of a hungry hog. [Tag. *ungol*]

raót₁: *n.* raid, unexpected attack. **rumaot, rauten.** *v.* to attack, raid; invade. **rarrauten.** *v.* to raze; abuse; insult; upset. **iraraot.** *n.* invasion, attack. **Ti Amerika ti mangsalaknib ti pagilian no maraot.** America will save the country if it is invaded. [Tag. *lusob*]

raót₂: *n.* drawing out rice from the granary. **rauten.** *v.* to draw out rice from the granary.

rapá: *n.* small wound in the palm of the hand or foot. **narapa.** *a.* wounded in the hand or foot. **rapaen.** *v.* to wound in the palm of the hand or foot. **raprapa.** *n.* a kind of small herb with long fruits full of bristles used to cure boils. [Tag. *galos*]

rápad: *n.* machete with a straight-edged tip on top; machetes with a curved top are called *rupáan*. **irapad.** *v.* to fit together (rocks in a wall, etc.).

rápang: *n.* branches of ginger root; variety of banana whose fruits stick together. **agrarapang.** *v.* having fingers or toes grown together (*agririping*); having many branches; to stick together.

rápas: *a.* having one continuous line in the palm of the hand; such people are said to be good with knives or in business, but are also prone to have a temper. **rapasen.** *v.* to cut at one stroke. **rapas ti tian.** *n.* glutton. [Tag. *haláng*]

rapéd: rapden. *v.* to break in two, snap (*maspak*, *tukkol*). [Tag. *baklî*]

rapét: kumarapet. *v.* to cling on to. [Tag. *kapít*]

rápido: (Sp. *rápido*: fast) *a.* fast. (*paspas*, *partak*) **rapiduen.** *v.* to do something fast. **de-rapido.** *n.* automatic firearm. [Tag. *paspás*, *bilís*]

rapikí: var. of *rupiki*: ringing of church bells.

rapín: agrapin. *v.* to be side by side with each other; to be stuck to each other; carry one in each hand; to do several things simultaneously. **irapin.** *v.* to insert, put between; include; mix up (*ragpin*). [Png. *tekép*; *sulong*, *surob*, *sipit*, Tag. *lakíp*; *sakop*, *sakláw*; *ipasok*, *ipaloób*]

rápis: *n.* slenderness. (*kuttong*) **narapis.** *a.* slender, thin. **rumapis.** *v.* to become slender. [Tag. *payát*]

rapít: rapiten. *v.* to take two or more with one hand, take more than one; to do something in addition to something else. **irapit.** *v.* to include; enclose (*ragpin*). [Tag. *lakíp*]

rápok: *n.* commotion; crowd; scuffle. **agrarapok.** *v.* to act together, do something jointly. **rapokrapok.** *a.* with much commotion; *n.* commotion; free for all fight, scuffle. **makirapok.** *v.* to join a crowd; join in a scuffle. **Idi kuan, nagtungpal a rapokrapok ti dinnil-ag.** Then, the shouting match turned into a major commotion.

rápon: marapon. *v.* to lose all (everybody dying in a plane crash, all fruits falling down, etc.). **rapunen.** *v.* to take all.

rappípi: maraprappipi. *v.* to be overburdened, overloaded.

rára: *n.* honeycomb. **nirara.** *n.* honeycomb. **agrara.** *v.* to do excessively (to eat a lot, to overspend). **Agraraka nga mangan ti saba.** You eat bananas too much. [Tag. *panilán, saray* (honeycomb)]

raráng: *n.* kind of large, elongated mollusk with a pointed shell; mother-of-pearl. [Tag. *kabibe*]

rarasá: (f. *rasá*) *n.* ovary (*iitlogán*); athlete's foot, rash between toes. **agrarasa.** *v.* to have skin rashes between the toes. **Saanen nga agtarindanum ken agrarasa.** He no longer has skin blisters or rashes. [Tag. *buni*]

ráreb: *var.* of *rárem*: immerse. [Tag. *lubóg*]

rárek: *n.* rhonchus, rale, creaky voice, abnormal sound from the lungs or trachea. **agrarek.** *v.* to have rhonchus; have the death rattle; to make a creaking sound (radio). **irarek.** *v.* to say in a creaky or rattling voice. [Tag. *garalgál*]

rárem: irarem. *v.* to immerse, dip in water; to get involved deeply. **mairarem.** *v.* to be immersed; (*fig.*) to get involved deeply. **Ti kinadakes ti politika ti kadakkelan a mangirarrarem ken mangwarwara iti talnami.** The badness of politics is the biggest thing that involves us and breaks our peace. [Tag. *lubóg*]

rárit: rariten. *v.* to ruin, devastate (*rakrak*); diminish by constant loss; waste. **nararit.** *a.* devastated; ruined. **Nasayaat met ta nagasawa, no saan, rinibu koma pay laeng ti rarraritenna.** It's good that he got married, if he didn't he would still be wasting thousands. [Tag. *sirâ*]

rarrán: (*obs.*) *n.* increasing loss, worsening (*lanlan*). [Tag. *lalà*]

rartáya: (*obs.*) *n.* sail ropes of the bow.

rása: (Sp. *raza*: race) *n.* race of people; breed (of animals). (*pulí*)

rasá₁: *n.* a kind of large crab. **Kasla nakirog a rasa ti rupana.** *exp.* He has a face as red as a fried crab. [Tag. *alimango*]

rasá₂: agrarasa. *v.* to have a skin eruption caused by sitting on a water buffalo.

rasá₃: rarasa. *n.* ovary. [Tag. *bahay-itlóg*]

rásak: *a.* brittle, fragile (*rasi*). [Tag. *dupók*]

rásang: narasang. *a.* short, brief (in time) (*biit*). [Tag. *igsî*]

rasáw: narasaw. *a.* insolent, impudent, brazen; boisterous; noisy; vulgar. **kinarasaw.** *n.* insolence; vulgarity; boisterousness. **rumasaw.** *v.* to be insolent; to talk impudently (as when drunk). [Tag. *ingay* (noisy)]

rásay: *n.* scarcity (in growth). (*salaysay*) **narasay.** *a.* scarce, rare; infrequent; uncommon; sparse (growth); thin; transparent (cloth). **rumasay.** *v.* to become scarce, uncommon, infrequent. **Rimmasayen dagiti lames kadagiti basay.** The fish became more scarce in the ponds. [Tag. *dalang* (sparse)]

rasbóy: *n.* lush growth (*rukbós*). **narasboy.** *a.* robust; lush; with many branches; growing vigorously. [Tag. *lagô*]

rasdók: *a.* steep, ascending (said of a roof). [Tag. *tarík*]

rasí: *n.* fragility; weakness in character. **narasi.** *a.* fragile; brittle; delicate. **kinarasi.** *n.* fragility, brittleness. **rumasi.** *v.* to become brittle, fragile. [Knk. *gápo*, Tag. *dupók*]

rasión: (Sp. *ración*: ration) *n.* supply; ration (*abasto*). **rasionan.** *v.* to give a ration to.

rasionalísmo: (Sp. *racionalismo*) *n.* rationalism.

rásir: marasir. *v.* to be fragile, brittle (for having been exposed to the sun).

raskadór: (Sp. *rascador*: scraper) *n.* scraper; back scratcher.

raskíta: (Sp. *rasqueta*: scraper) *n.* three-edged instrument for removing dirt.

ráso: (Sp. *raso*: satin) *n.* satin.

rások: *a.* hot; passionate, aggressive; *n.* passion; kindling; flaring up. **agrasok.** *v.* to steam up. **rumasok.** *v.* to flame, flare up; burn, kindle; become passionate. **narasok.** *a.* hot; aggressive; passionate. **kinarasok.** *n.* aggressiveness; passionateness. **parasuken.** *v.* to make someone aggressive, passionate. **Kasla bulkan ti irarasok ti barukongna.** His chest was flaring up like a volcano. [Tag. *pusók*]

rasón: (Sp. *razón*: reason) *n.* reason; cause, motive (*pagrasonan*). [Tag. *dahílán*]

rasonáble: (Sp. *razonable*: reasonable) *a.* reasonable; moderate.

rasúon: see *túon*.

ráspa: (Sp. *raspa*: scrape) *n.* scraper; curettage; (*fig.*) induced abortion (*paregreg*). **raspaen.** *v.* to scrape, curette.

raspár: rasparen. *v.* to eat greedily; to scrape something with a coarse file. [Tag. *lamon*]

rasrás: *n.* scratching sound. **agrasras.** *v.* to scratch, rub oneself. **rasrasan.** *v.* to rub, scratch. **narasrasan.** *a.* frayed, fretted, chafed. **Dagita a balikas ti kasla asin nga inrasrasmo iti sugatko.** Those words are like the salt that you rubbed on my wound. [Tag. *gasgás*]

rasyón: *var.* spelling of *rasión:* ration. **irasyon.** *v.* to ration, distribute as a ration. **rasyonan.** *v.* to ration to.

ráta: *n.* crack, chink; broken pieces of glass (*rekká*). [Tag. *bubog* (broken glass)]

rátab: *n.* overhanging branch, length of bushes of plants. **rataban.** *v.* to trim (overhanging branches). **Rimmaber dagiti ratab kalpasan ti tudo.** The ends of the bushes grew lush after the rain.

ratík: *n.* spot of mold or mildew. **agratik.** *v.* to become moldy. **ratikratik.** *a.* mildewed; spotty (said of clothes) (*búot*). **Agratik ngamin ti way uray malinnaawan laeng iti agpatnag.** Rattan gets mildew spots even if it is just affected overnight by dew. [Tag. *amag* (mildew)]

ratiles: (Sp. *dátiles:* dates) *n.* kind of plant eaten by goats.

ratíp: iratip. *v.* to insert; put in between. (*rutáp, bal-ét*) **mairatip.** *v.* to be inserted between.

ratípan: *n.* gomuti palm.

ratipikár: (Sp. *ratificar:* ratify) **ratipikaren.** *v.* to ratify. **ratipikasion.** *n.* ratification.

rátiw: *n.* slenderness. **naratiw.** *a.* very slender, very thin, skinny (*kuttong; pair; piit; tariwatiw*). [Tag. *patpát*]

ratók: iratok. *v.* to tether, tie animals. (*rakéd, parngéd*)

ratúnok: *n.* blister (*kapúyo*). [Tag. *lintóg*]

ratunók: *n.* cluster. **Nalabsanmi ti ratunok dagiti balay iti purok.** We passed the cluster of houses in the village.

rattót: nakarattot. *a.* in a hurry.

ráwad: narawad. *a.* long legged (*bangkawás*), lanky.

raw-ák: raw-aken. *v.* to crumble, pulverize; destroy; slash and spill guts (when slaughtering). **maraw-ak.** *v.* to be crashed; slashed; pulverized. **raw-araw-ak.** *a.* slashed up, jagged (wounds). [Tag. *durog, laslás*]

rawáng: *n.* hollow between rocks.

ráway: agraraway. *v.* to be new to the job; to be inexperienced; novice. **rawayraway.** *n.* the part of the hand between the thumb and index finger; coils of a vine. **rawayrawayan.** *a.* branchy, covered with branches. [Tag. *baguhan* (novice)]

ráwet: *n.* gluttony. **narawet.** *a.* gluttonous, ravenous; lustful; with a healthy appetite (*ant:*

kúsim). **agrarawet.** *v.* to have a strong desire to eat something. **kinarawet.** *n.* gluttony. [Bon. *okab, kaklab,* Knk. *akgíd, aklóng, angngáw, akmúd,* Png. *labláb, sibá,* Tag. *takaw, sibà*]

rawírak: (*obs.*) *n.* breaker wave away from the shore.

ráwis: *n.* cape jutting into the sea; part of the hypochondriac and epigastric regions that border on the eighth, ninth, and tenth ribs; tip (of a branch). **narawis.** *a.* too far out at the tip; hanging near the edge of a branch (fruits). [Tag. *lungos* (cape); *dulo* (tip)]

rawráw: rawrawen. *v.* to agitate; disturb (still water).

ráya: (Sp. *raya:* stroke, dash, line) *n.* ray of the sun; ray; stroke, dash; stripe; boundary, frontier; score; parting of the hair (*bisngáy*). **rinaraya.** *n.* women's hat.

rayá₁: rayaraya. *n.* kind of moraceous tree (*Ficus sp.*).

rayá₂: rayaraya. *a.* branching in all directions.

ráyab: agrayabrayab. *v.* to flutter, sway in the wind; drift to and fro. [Tag. *pagaypáy, wagaywáy*]

ray-áb: *var.* of *gay-ab:* tear; rip; *pisang.* [Tag. *punit*]

rayadílio: (Sp. *rayadillo:* striped) *n.* striped cloth; revolutionary uniform. **nakarayadilio.** *a.* wearing a striped vestment; wearing the attire of a revolutionary.

ráyag: agparayag. *v.* to show off one's possessions.

ray-áw: *n.* joker; amusement. **naray-aw.** *a.* amused, diverted. **makaray-aw.** *n.* a variety of awned early rice; *a.* amusing. **mangrayray-aw.** *v.* to joke, make laugh. **rayawen.** *v.* to make (a baby) laugh; amuse. [Tag. *libang*]

ráyo: agrayo. *v.* to have a date with; court; fall in love (*árem; dáton*). **Agrayoak iti aso.** I'm in love with a dog. [Tag. *ligaw*]

rayó: agrayo. *v.* to be pleased with; be fond of; love; like; be attracted to. **agrarayo.** *v.* to take delight in. **irayo.** *v.* to influence someone to do. **mairayo.** *v.* to be influenced to do.

rayód: *a.* arrogant usually because of a special trait. **kinarayod.** *n.* arrogance.

ráyok₁: *n.* smell of salted fish (*buggúong*). **narayok.** *a.* having the smell of *buggúong.* **Sika't kadadaksan ta agsilamotka't bugguong a karayokan.** You are the worst, for you lick the stinkiest *bugguong.*

ráyok₂: narayok. *a.* very high (mountains, houses, etc.).

rayók: irayok. *v.* to broadcast, spread (news); circulate. **Nagrinnayoken ti dung-awda.** Their laments circulated amongst themselves.

rayúma: (Sp. *reuma*: rheumatism) *n*. rheumatism. **agrayuma**. *v*. to have rheumatism.

rayumátiko: (f. *rayuma*) *a*. rheumatic; *n*. a person suffering from rheumatism.

ráyos: (Sp. *rayo*: ray; spoke) *n*. spoke of a wheel; ray (*raya*).

rayráy: *n*. flare of fire. **narayray**. *a*. fervent, ardent, burning; shining. **parayrayen**. *v*. to enhance, to make the fire burn brighter. **rumayray**. *v*. to flare, sparkle, flash. **Narayray ti init ti bigbigat**. The morning heat was burning. [Tag. *dubdób*]

rayyarayyá: *n. Ficus sp.* tall moraceous tree.

re: (Sp. *rey*: king) *n*. king (in cards). (*ári*)

reaksión: (Sp. *reacción*) *n*. reaction.

reál: (Sp. *real*: royal) *a*. royal. **palasio real**. royal palace. **pabo real**. peacock.

rebáha: (Sp. *rebaja*: discount) *n*. discount, reduction. **agrebaha**. *v*. to go down (prices), have a sale.

rebahár: (Sp. *rebajar*: lower, reduce; (carp.) shave down) **mangrebahar**. *v*. to remodel (a house).

rebálida: (Sp. *reválida*: university exam) *n*. oral examination for postgraduate students.

rebbá₁: *n*. ruins. **agrebba**. *v*. to break down, collapse, crumble down. **marba**. *v*. to be shipwrecked; wrecked; crumble down, collapse; to fall down; decay. **rebbaen**. *v*. to demolish, run, destroy (*reggaay*). **kasla narba nga Insik**. *exp*. like a Chinese whose house has been demolished (referring to noisy, disagreeable talk). **Narba diay bantayen**. The mountain has tumbled down (referring to a sleepyhead). [Ibg. *rebba*, Ivt. *nalduy*, Kpm. *siraq*, Png. *kusbu*, Tag. *gibâ*]

rebbá₂: *n*. piece of land tilled for the first time. **rebbaen**. *v*. to break ground for planting rice.

rebbáag: (f. *ribág*) *n*. continuous sound of falling heavy objects. **manarbaag**. *v*. to crumble down, fall, collapse. **pananarbaagen**. *v*. to cause to collapse, topple over.

rebbáas: *n*. period of time following a flood; aftermath. **agrebbaas**. *v*. to quiet down and return to normal.

rebbák: *n*. first plowing of a field (*buga, guba*) **rebbaken**. *v*. to plow for the first time.

rebbék: *n*. ruins (*rebbá*); waste; destruction; demolition. **rebbeken**. *v*. to demolish, ruin, devastate, ravage. **narebbek**. *a*. demolished; ruined; devastated. **Ni Ari Agamemnon ti nangrebbek iti siudad ti Troy**. King Agamemnon demolished the city of Troy. [Tag. *guhò*]

rebbéng: *n*. duty, obligation, responsibility. **agrebbeng**. *n*. person responsible for; legal heir; authority. **rumbeng**. *v*. to be reasonable, neces-sary, essential; should. **rebbengen**. *v*. to be responsible for; be obliged to do. **karbengan**. *n*. duty; responsibility; obligation; right. **a kas karbenganna**. as it should be. **maiparbeng**. *v*. to be proper, right; fit. **agparbeng**. *v*. to show regard; give due respect. **pagrebbengan**. *n*. position; office; authority. **iparbeng**. *v*. to act in good taste. **managparbeng**. *a*. respectful; considerate; honorable. **kinamanagparbeng**. *n*. respectfulness; consideration. **akinrebbeng**. *n*. person in charge; person responsible. **Dimo kuma aramiden ti saan a rumbeng**. You shouldn't do what is not proper. [Knk. *túmu*, Png. *nepeg*, Tag. *dapat*]

rebbúos: (f. *ribós*) **kanarbuos**. *n*. hustle and bustle; successive thumping or bursting sounds. **manarbuos**. *v*. to hustle and bustle; make quick, successive slight thumping or bursting sounds (rapid defecation, spilled contents, etc.).

rebélde: (Sp. *rebelde*: rebel) *n*. rebel; *a*. rebellious.

rebelína: *n*. a kind of dance.

rebentadór: (Sp. *reventar*: burst) *n*. firecracker (*paputok*). [Tag. *labintadór*]

rebisár: (Sp. *revisar*: revise) **agrebisar**. *v*. to revise; change one's mind. **rebisádo**. *a*. revised. **rebisión**. *n*. revision.

rebísta: (Sp. *revista*: magazine) *n*. magazine.

rebkás: **rebkasen**. *v*. to damage, destroy (*rakrák*); injure; mutilate; vandalize a house during a burglary.

rebuláso: *var*. of *remulaso*: tantrum.

rebólber: (Eng.) *n*. revolver (gun).

rebolusión: (Sp. *revolución*) *n*. revolution. (*yaalsa*)

rebolusionário: (Sp. *revolucionario*: revolutionary) *a*. revolutionary.

rebúlto: (Sp. *rebulto*: religious image) *n*. image of a saint or God; Holy statue.

rebosádo: (Sp. *rebosado*: brimmed over) *a*. dipped in batter before frying, breaded. **kamaron rebosado**. breaded shrimps.

rebréb: **irebreb**. *v*. to damage; injure; immerse; plunge into; sink; submerge (*rareb*). **agrebreb**. *v*. to drink to excess. **marebreb**. (*obs.*) *v*. to fall apart. [Knk. *sugbá*, Tag. *lubóg, lunod*]

reddék: *n*. sparerib; share, portion. **reddeken**. *v*. to cut up into parts; divide. **reddekan**. *v*. to give a piece to someone. [Tag. *bahagi*]

redóma: (Sp. *redoma*: flask) *n*. flask; vial.

redóndo: (Sp. *redondo*: round) *a*. round. (*timbukel*)

regadéra: (Sp. *regadera*: sprinkler; watering can) *n*. water sprinkler. (*ragadera*)

regadéro: (Sp. *regadero*: irrigation ditch) *n*. irrigation ditch.

regálo: (Sp. *regalo*: gift) *n*. gift, present. (*sagut*) **regaluan.** *v*. to present a gift to someone.

reggá: narga. *a*. deep, profound; heavy (sleep); wallowing. **margaan.** *v*. to be sound asleep (*rennék*). **Nargaan ti turogna.** He is in deep sleep.

reggáay: *n*. landslide; ruins. **margaay.** *v*. to slide down; cave in; collapse (*dadpuor, dappuor, dipag, rebba, rissuod, rugnay, tebbag, tippuog, teppaag*). **regaayen.** *v*. to cause to collapse. **agpargaay.** *v*. to shed pollen; be about to ear (rice). [Tag. *guhò*]

reggés: *n*. slice of fish. **regsen.** *v*. to cut up; decapitate; tear off by twisting. [Tag. *gilít*]

reggét: *n*. diligence; industry; perseverance. (*gaget*; *saldet*) **narget.** *a*. diligent, laborious, hard-working, persevering (*gagét*; *siseg*; *anep*). **kinaregget.** *n*. industry, diligence. **iregget.** *v*. to do seriously, diligently. **regtan.** *v*. to do diligently, assiduously. **Agregget a makasuro iti Iluko.** He persists diligently in studying Ilocano. [Tag. *sipag*]

regkáng: *n*. crevice, crack, fissure (*betták*). [Tag. *biták*]

régla: (Sp. *regla*: menstruation; rule) *n*. menses; menstrual blood (*kadawyán, sangaíli, libukáy*); ruler. **agregla.** *v*. to menstruate. **panagregla.** *n*. menstrual flow. [*Libukáy* = beginning of menstruation. Tag. *sapanahón*]

regladór: (Sp. *reglador*: one who rules) *n*. ruler (instrument for drawing straight lines).

reglaménto: (Sp. *reglamento*: regulation) *n*. regulation. **maisuppiat iti reglamento.** against regulations. [Tag. *alituntunin*]

regléta: (Sp. *regleta*) *n*. reglet.

reguladór: (Sp. *regulador*) *n*. regulator

regmég: *n*. crumbs, pulverized material (*regrég*). **agregmeg, regmegan.** *v*. to pound, pulverize. **maregmeg.** *v*. to be pulverized; broken into particles. [Tag. *ligís*]

regnás: *n*. kernels, spikelets, and ears of rice detached from one or more bundles. **maregnas.** *v*. to fall from spikes (grains of rice).

regrég: *n*. droppings; particles of food falling off a plate; crumbs. **maregreg.** *v*. to drop, fall down; slip, slid out of one's grasp; drop; fall out of one's pocket; (*fig*.) to have an abortion. **makaregreg.** *v*. to lose stupor by a disease (myth: by having 'dropped' one's spirit); to lose something. **regregan.** *v*. to drop; intentionally drop food under the table for the dog. **regregen.** *v*. to abort; drop. **agparegreg.** *v*. to have an abortion. **iregreg.** *v*. to drop something into. **agparegreg.** *v*. to induce abortion. **panangparegreg.** *n*. act of intentional dropping; abortion. **panagreregreg.**

n. fall (season). **Nalaingka nga uminom ngem dika met mangregreg uray sentimo.** You are a good drinker, but you don't even drop a penny (to pay). [Png. *pelág, tedted*, Tag. *laglág*]

regtá: *n*. honesty; diligence. (*lintég; gagét, reggét, salindég*) **naregta.** *a*. straight; upright, virtuous, faithful, honest; diligent. **regtaan.** *v*. to keep straight, honest; watch to make sure one fulfills his obligations, work diligently; be active. **pagparegta.** *n*. stimulant. **pangparegta.** *n*. encouragement; inspiration. **paregtaen.** *v*. to encourage; inspire; make someone diligent, active, etc. [Tag. *sipag*]

réhas: (Sp. *rejas*: bars) *n*. window bars, grille; railing. **agrehas.** *v*. to bar a window. **narehasan.** *a*. barred (windows).

rehimen: (Sp. *régimen*: regime; system; government) *n*. regime; government; regimen; policy; system; management.

rehim(i)énto: (Sp. *regimiento*) *n*. regiment.

rehión: (Sp. *región*: region) *n*. region.

rehionalísmo: (Sp. *regionalismo*) *n*. regionalism.

rehistrádo: (Sp. *registrado*: registered; recorded + English) *n*. registered.

rehistradór: (Sp. *registrador*: recorder) *n*. recorder; registrar; cash register; taxi meter.

rehístro: (Sp. *registro*: check; registry) *n*. register; registry; record; entry.

réina: (Sp. *reina*: queen) *n*. queen. (*aribái*)

réino: (Sp. *reino*: kingdom) *n*. kingdom. (*pagarian*)

rekádo: (Sp. *recado*: outfit; compliments) *n*. spice, seasoning, marinade, condiment. (*templa*) **narekado.** *a*. marinated, spiced. **rekaduan.** *v*. to add spice to, marinate. **rumerekado.** *n*. preservatives (for tobacco); one who likes spices. [Tag. *timplá*]

rekárgo: (Sp. *recargo*: additional charge) *n*. additional tax; fine; additional charge; increase of a sentence or jail term.

reketítos: *var*. of *rekisitos*: requirements, requisites, formalities.

rekísa: (Sp. *requisa*: confiscation; inspection) *n*. thorough inspection. **rekisaen.** *v*. to search thoroughly, frisk. **mandamiento de rekisa.** *n*. search warrant.

rekisítos: (Sp. *requisito*: requisite) *n*. requirements, requisites.

rekká: *n*. fissure; crack. (*regkang*) **agrekka.** *v*. to crack. [Tag. *biták*]

rekkáad: (f. *rikád*) *n*. sound of a crumbling building. **rumkaad.** *v*. to crumble down.

rekkáng: *n*. scab (dry skin around wound); (*keggang*); slit. **agrekkang.** *v*. to develop a scab. [Tag. *langíb*]

rekkás: rekkasen. *v.* to loosen, untie, undo, slacken; unset a trap; break down. **narkas.** *a.* untied; broken down; undone. **rumekkas.** *v.* to be unfastened; get out of a trap. [Tag. *alpás*]

rekkét: *n.* rice weevil. **agrekket.** *v.* to stick together (rice kernels; eyelids). [Tag. *dikít*]

reklamadór: (Sp. *reclamador*: complainer) *n.* complainer.

reklamánte: (Sp. *reclamante*) *n.* complainant; accuser.

reklámo: (Sp. *reclamo*: complaint) *n.* complaint; claim; objection. **agreklamo.** *v.* to complain; object to. [Kal. *lili*, Tag. *daíng, sumbóng*]

reklusión: (Sp. *reclusión*) *n.* imprisonment. **reklusion perpetua.** life imprisonment.

rekuérdo: (Sp. *recuerdo*: memory) *n.* souvenir; remembrance. [Tag. *tagapagpaalaala*]

rekolóta: (Sp. *recluta*) *n.* recruit; apprentice.

rekomendár: (Sp. *recomendar*: recommend) **irekomendar.** *v.* to recommend something. **rekomendádo.** *a.* recommended. [Tag. *tagubilin*]

rekonosí: *var.* of *rikonosi*: diagnose, examine.

rekomendasión: (Sp. *recomendación*: recommendation) *n.* recommendation.

rekonisí: *var.* of *rikonosi*: diagnose, examine.

rekonsiliasión: (Sp. *reconciliación*: reconciliation) *n.* reconciliation.

rekórd: (Eng.) *n.* record. **irekord.** *v.* to record.

rekorída: (Sp. *recorrido*: course; round) *n.* patrol, round of police. **agrekorida.** *v.* to patrol.

rekúrso: (Sp. *recurso*: resource) *n.* resource. **rekursos naturales.** *n.* natural resources.

rekrék: *n.* cluster, thicket; dense growth; bubbling sound of cooking rice; sound of sniffling snot. **agrekrek.** *v.* to make the sound of sniffling snot or cooking rice; to have difficulty breathing due to a running nose. **Idi agsubli ti puotko, addaak metten iti rekrek ti kawayan iti turod.** When I regained consciousness, I was in the bamboo thicket on the hill.

rekréo: (Sp. *recreo*: recreation) *n.* recreation; amusement. (*liwliwa*)

rektánggulo: (Sp. *rectángulo*: rectangle) *n.* rectangle, four-sided figure with four right angles.

rektipikár: (Sp. *rectificar*: rectify) **rektipikaren.** *v.* to rectify; correct. **rektipikasion.** *n.* rectification; correction.

relasión: (Sp. *relación*: relation) *n.* relationship, relation; connection.

relébo: (Sp. *relevo*: relief) *n.* relief; substitute. **relebuan.** *v.* to relieve someone.

réles: *var.* of *ríles*: rail, railroad.

reliébe: (Sp. *relieve*: relief work) *n.* embossing, raised work, relief work.

reliébo: (Sp. *relevo*: relief; change) *n.* relief, substitute in work. **mangreliebo.** *v.* to relieve.

reliéno: (Sp. *relleno*: stuffed) *a.* stuffed; *n.* stuffed (fish, chicken, etc.).

relihión: (Sp. *religión*: religion) *n.* religion. (*pammati*) **religioso.** *a.* religious, devout, pious.

relíkia: (Sp. *reliquia*) *n.* relic.

reló(s): (Sp. *reloj*: watch, clock) *n.* clock; watch; chronometer. **nakarelos.** *a.* wearing a watch. **relohéro.** *n.* watchmaker; dealer in watches. **relohería.** *n.* watch shop. [Kal. *lilus*]

remáta: (Sp. *remata*: knock down (at an auction) *n.* foreclosure; public sale of mortgaged property.

rematádo: (Sp. *rematado*: finished off) *n.* foreclosed; forfeited; auctioned off.

remáte: (Sp. *remate*: end, finish; auction) *n.* deadline. **remremates.** *n.* preparations for marriage; spare parts. **agremate.** *v.* to draw to a close.

remátse: (Sp. *remache*: rivet) *n.* rivet. **rematsado.** *a.* riveted.

remédio: (Sp. *remedio*: remedy) *n.* remedy; means. **agremedio.** *v.* to remedy; make the best out of a difficult situation. **último remedio.** *n.* last resort.

rem-ék: *var.* of *rumék*: pulverize, smash, crush.

remésa: (Sp. *remesa*: shipment; delivery; remittance) *n.* remittance of payment; shipment of merchandise.

remiénta: (Sp. *herramienta*: tool) *n.* tools. (*gamígan*)

remmáy: remmayen. *v.* to crumble; break into pieces. **marmay.** *a.* crumbled; tattered; rotting, decaying (*rupsá*).

remmék: *n.* a kind of spherical white marine mollusk.

remméng: *n.* branches placed by fences or over seedbeds to keep animals away; barbed wire. **remmengan.** *v.* to obstruct a place with branches or barbed wire. **Inlemmengna iti karemremmengan.** He hid it in the scattered branches.

remóda: (Sp. *remuda*: change of clothes) *n.* spare. **agremoda.** *v.* to store for an emergency.

remuláso: *n.* tantrum; fierce complaint.

remolátsa: (Sp. *remolacha*: beet) *n.* red beet.

remólke: (Sp. *remolcar*: tow) *n.* towing. **iremolke.** *v.* to tow.

remunerasión: (Sp. *remuneración*: remuneration) *n.* remuneration, act of compensation; reward.

remontádo: (Sp. *remontado*: frightened away) *n.* native who has abandoned civilization and fled to the mountains.

remordimiénto: (Sp. *remordimiento*: remorse) *n.* remorse.

remrém: **iremrem**. *v.* to drown; submerge; immerse (*rareb*); destroy one's honor. **Adu dagiti mabalinna a pagtangsit a ditay kabaelan ngem iremremyo met ti kinataona.** He has a lot of things to be proud of that we can't do, but you destroyed his identity. [Tag. *lubóg*]

réna: *var.* of *reina*: queen.

rénda: (Sp. *rienda*: rein) *n.* reins.

rendído: (Sp. *rendirse*: become exhausted) *a.* fatigued, exhausted, worn out.

rendír: (Sp. *rendir*: yield, brought to submission; worn out) **narendir**. *a.* tired, exhausted.

renikário: (Sp. *relicario*: reliquary, locket) *n.* pyx, metal container used to carry the eucharist to the sick; reliquary.

rennéb: **marneb, makarneb**. *v.* to sink. **iparneb**. *v.* to sink something; plunge something into the water (*arinebneb*).

rennék: *n.* satisfaction; satiation. **agrennek**. *v.* to enjoy, be satisfied. **marnek**. *v.* to be satisfied (food or sleep). **renneken**. *v.* to satiate. **Inrennekna ti bagina iti adal.** He satiated himself with his studies.

rennuáy: **narnuay**. *a.* plentiful, many, numerous, abundant. (*ruay*)

rennúoy: **narnuoy**. *a.* plenty, many. **narnuoyan**. *a.* plentiful (harvest).

réno₁: (Sp. *reno*) *n.* reindeer.

réno₂: (Sp. *reino*) *n.* kingdom (*pagarián*).

renúnsia(r): (Sp. *renunciar*: renounce) **agrenunsia**. *v.* to renounce; resign.

renrén₁: *n.* accumulation of flotsam. [Tag. *yagít*]

renrén₂: *n.* wrinkles; pleats. **agrenren**. *v.* to crease, wrinkle. (*karenkén*) **renrenen**. *v.* to ruffle, plait, pucker.

réntas: (Sp. *renta*: rent; state revenues, *obs.*) *n.* taxes (*buis*). [Tag. *buwís*]

reng-ád: *var.* of *rung-ád*: wring; twist; distort. [Tag. *pigâ*]

rengdá: (*obs.*) **mangirengda**. *v.* to rest on the way.

rengkék: *a.* having a strong neck; bull-necked.

rengngáad: **agrengngaad**. *v.* to produce a sound similar to logs breaking in two. (*reppaak*)

rengngát: *n.* crack (in dry earth); parched earth. **agrengngat**. *v.* to crack, split, cleave, part. [Kal. *ladngak*, Tag. *biták*]

rengngép: *var.* of *rangép*: fight, scuffle.

rengréng: *n.* plead; disturbing insistence, nagging. **marengreng**. *v.* to be confused, perplexed; agitated, annoyed, irritated; disturbed. **irengreng**. *v.* to insist; nag. **mangrengreng**. *v.* to insist, plead, ask for something in a crying manner. **rengrengen**. *v.* to nag, disturb, bother; request repeatedly. **Makalawasen a mangrengrengreng ni Agong iti igagatang ni Nang Karming iti telepono kas inkarina.** Agong has been nagging Aunt Karming for a week already to buy the telephone as she promised. [Tag. *kulít*]

rengsáy: **rengsayen**. *v.* to cut up, chop; dismember.

reúma: (Sp.) *n.* rheumatism. (*rayúma*)

reorganisár: (Sp. *reorganizar*: reorganize) **reorganisaren**. *v.* to reorganize. **reorganisado**. *a.* reorganized. **reorganisasion**. *n.* reorganization.

rep-ák: *var.* of *reppak*: snap in two.

reparasión: (Sp. *reparación*) *n.* reparation.

repáso: (Sp. *repaso*: review) *n.* review (for a test, etc.); rehearsal. **repasuen**. *v.* to review; go over again; rehearse.

repénte: (Sp. *repente*: suddenly) **de repente**. *adv.* suddenly.

reperéndum: (Sp. *referendum*) *n.* referendum.

reperénsia: (Sp. *referencia*: reference) *n.* reference.

repertório: (Sp. *repertorio*: repertoire) *n.* repertoire.

repikár: (Sp. *repicar*: chime) *n.* chimes, ringing of bells. **agrepikar**. *v.* to ring the bells. **repikaran**. *v.* to ring the bells in honor of someone.

repíke: (Sp. *repique*: chime) *n.* chime, peal of bells. **agrepike**. *v.* to toll, peal (said of bells).

repinádo: (Sp. *refinado*: refined) *a.* refined; ground fine; *n.* a variety of *diket* rice.

repinería: (Sp. *refinería*: refinery) *n.* refinery.

repíte: (Sp. *repite*: repeat) *n.* encore. **agrepite**. *v.* to repeat (a class, a word, etc.).

replika: (Sp. *réplica*: reply, retort; replica) *n.* reply, retort, answer (*sungbát*); image, likeness; portrait; reflection.

repúblika: (Sp. *república*: republic) *n.* republic.

repuérso: (Sp. *refuerzo*) *n.* reinforcement.

repúhio: (Sp. *refugio*: refuge) *n.* refuge, asylum.

repólio: (Sp. *repollo*: cabbage) *n.* cabbage. [Kal. *llipunyo*]

repórma: (Sp. *reforma*: reform) *n.* reform; improvement. **repormado**. *a.* reformed. **repormasion**. *n.* reformation. **repormista**. *n.* reformer, reformist. [Tag. *pagbabago*]

repormatório: (Sp. *reformatorio*: reformatory) *n.* reformatory, institution for young juvenile delinquents.

report: (Eng.) *n.* report. **ireport**. *v.* to report. [Tag. *ulat*]

repositório: (Sp. *repositorio*) *n.* repository.

reputasión: (Sp. *reputación*) *n.* reputation.

reppáak: *n.* large feast or banquet; sound of breaking branches or falling bamboo. **agreppaak.** *v.* to make the sound of falling bamboos; resound from a fall.

reppák: **marpak.** *v.* to snap, break in two. **mairpak.** *v.* to snap off. **nairpakan.** *a.* hit by a falling branch.

reppék: **marpek.** *v.* to drop, fall; be smashed, crushed; shattered; overripe. **marpekan.** *a.* burdened, loaded. *v.* to be mute, speechless. [Tag. *basag*]

reppéng₁: *a.* with paralyzed fingers; with fingers grown together (*ríping*); *n.* variety of banana whose fruits stick together. **agreppeng.** *v.* to stick together.

reppéng₂: *n.* a variety of early rice.

reppéng₃: **agreppeng.** *v.* to be equal in measure or magnitude. **ireppeng.** *v.* to incorporate; integrate; make a part of; compare.

reppét: *n.* tie for binding. (*barakus*; *kerker*) **ireppet.** *v.* to include in the bundle. **reppeten.** *v.* to tie up, bind; wrap up. **sangarpet, sangkareppet.** *n.* one bundle, bunch. [Tag. *panalí*]

reppó: **marpo, rumpo.** *v.* to collapse; fall down (trees). **marpuan.** *v.* to fully mature (trees ready to be cut down). [Tag. *bagsák, hulog*]

reppúog: **marpuog.** *v.* to fall down, fall and break; cave in, collapse. **Narpuogen ti namnamana.** His hopes collapsed. [Tag. *bagsák*]

reppúok: **marpúok.** *v.* to be shattered, smashed, crushed.

reprán: (Sp. *refrán*: refrain) *n.* refrain; proverb.

reprép: *n.* crowd, multitude; large number of; flotsam. **sangareprep.** *a.* many. [Tag. *kalipumpón*]

representánte: (Sp. *representante*: representative) *n.* representative; deputy; congressman. [Tag. *kinatawán*]

representár: (Sp. *representar*) **irepresentar.** *v.* to represent.

représko: (Sp. *refresco*: refreshment) *n.* refreshment (*palamiis*). [Tag. *pampalamíg*]

reprihadóra: (Eng.) *n.* refrigerator. **ireprihadora.** *v.* to place in the refrigerator.

reptília: (Sp. *reptilia*: plural of *reptil:* reptile) *n.* reptile.

rerrén: see *renren*: wrinkle; pucker.

resáda: (Sp. *rezar*: pray) *n.* low mass; burial that is not sung.

resáta: *n.* withdrawal of intention to marry. **agresata.** *v.* to withdraw from a marriage.

resérba: (Sp. *reserva*: reserve) *n.* reserve; spare; spare tire; military reserves. **reserbaen.** *v.* to reserve; save for future use. **reserbasion.** *n.* reservation.

reserbár: *var.* of *reserba*: reserve.

reserbádo: (Sp. *reservado*: reserved) *a.* reserved. (*latang*)

reséta: (Sp. *receta*: prescription) *n.* doctor's prescription. **ireseta.** *v.* to prescribe medicine.

resetário: (f. *reseta*) *n.* doctor's prescription pad.

résga: *n.* homesickness; feeling of compassion with slight anger.

résgo: (Sp. *riesgo*: risk) *n.* risk. **naresgo.** *a.* risky. (*delikádo*)

resgádo: (f. *resgo*) *a.* risky, dangerous.

resguárdo: (Sp. *resguardo*) *n.* protection (weapon).

resibário: (Sp. *recibario*: receipt book) *n.* stub book, pad of receipt blanks.

resibí: (Sp. *recibir*: receive) **resibien.** *v.* to receive (*áwat*). **agparesibi.** *v.* to submit.

resíbo: (Sp. *recibo*: receipt) *n.* receipt. **resibuan.** *v.* to issue a receipt.

residénsia: (Sp. *residencia*: residence) *n.* residence. (*pagtaengan*)

residénte: (Sp. *residente*: resident) *n.* resident. (*umili*)

resignár: (Sp. *resignar*: resign) **agresignar.** *v.* to resign. **resignasion.** *n.* resignation.

resíko: (Sp. *reseco*: dried out; spare, lean) *n.* lack of weight of sold contents.

resína: (Sp. *resina*) *n.* resin.

resintomádo: (Sp. *resentido*: resentful) *a.* resentful.

resipiénte: (Sp. *recipiente*: recipient) *n.* recipient. [Tag. *tumanggáp*]

resisténsia: (Sp. *resistencia*) *n.* resistance.

resitasión: (Sp. *recitación*: recitation) *n.* recitation. [Tag. *pagsasalaysáy*]

resolbér: (Sp. *resolver*) **resolberen.** *v.* to solve.

resolusión: (Sp. *resolución*) *n.* resolution.

resúlta: (Sp. *resulta*) *n.* result; consequence (*nagbanágan*). [Tag. *bunga*]

respetáble: (Sp. *respetable*) *a.* respectable.

respéto: (Sp. *respeto*: respect) *n.* respect. (*dayaw*; *raem*; *pagtamdan*) **respetuen.** *v.* to respect. [Tag. *galang*]

respiniádo: *a.* twisted together (strands of a rope).

respiradór: (Sp. *respirador*) *n.* respirator.

respiratório: (Sp. *respiratorio*) *a.* respiratory.

respitáble: (Sp. *respetable*) *a.* respectable.

respitár: (Sp. *respetar*: respect) **respitaren.** *v.* to respect. **narespitar.** *a.* respectful.

respónde, respondér: (Sp. *responder*: respond) *n.* charge. **agresponde.** *v.* to be responsible for, to answer for. **responderan.** *v.* to be responsible for.

responsabilidád: (Sp. *responsabilidad*: responsibility) *n.* responsibility; obligation, duty. [Tag. *tungkulin, pananagutin*]

responsáble: (Sp. *responsable*: responsible) *a.* responsible. (*makaammo*). [Tag. *nananagót, mapagkakatiwalaan*]

respónso: (Sp. *responso*) *n.* responsory for the deceased.

responsorio: (Sp. *responsorio*: responsory) *n.* responsory, liturgical response.

resrés: resresen. *v.* to pucker, ruffle, plait.

ressá: *reg. var.* of *ressát*: cease. [Tag. *pigil*]

ressáak: *n.* sound of crushed dry leaves. **marsaak.** *v.* to waste away, decay, disintegrate; age; be overripe (cereals).

ressáng: *a.* chipped. **marsang.** *v.* to be chipped. **narsangan a lapayag.** *n.* split pierced ear due to wearing heavy earrings. **ressangen.** *v.* to chip off. [Tag. *pingas*]

ressát: *n.* cessation. **agressat, rumsat.** *v.* to stop, cease; be interrupted. **ressaten.** *v.* to bring to an end, stop. **parsaten.** *v.* to stanch wounds, stop the flow of blood from a wound. **Di agressat ti panagdaydayawda kenkuana.** Their honoring him does not end. [Tag. *pigil*]

ressék: *var.* of *rissík*: spark.

restánte: (Sp. *restante*: remaining) *n.* remainder.

restár: (Sp. *restar*: subtract) **agrestar.** *v.* to subtract.

réstos: (Sp. *restos*: remains) *n.* remains (of a corpse).

retáso: (Sp. *retazo*: remnant) *n.* remnant; scrap of cloth; (*fig.* offspring). **Mano ti retasom?** How many children do you have?

retenído: (Sp. *retenido*: retained) *a.* detained, confined.

retenír: (Sp. *retener*: retain) **naretenir.** *a.* detained, confined.

rétina: (Sp. *retina*: retina) *n.* retina of the eye.

retíra: (Sp. *retirar*: withdraw, dismiss) *n.* dismissal. **agretira.** *v.* to be dismissed.

retirádo: (Eng.) *a.* retired.

retíro: (Sp. *retiro*: retirement) *n.* retreat; retirement. **iretiro.** *v.* to retract. **agretiro.** *v.* to retreat; retire.

réto: (Sp. *reto*: challenge) *n.* challenge. [Tag. *hamon*]

retokádo: (Sp. *retocado*) *a.* retouched.

retóke: (Sp. *retoque*: retouching) *n.* retouching job.

retratísta: (f. *retrato*) *n.* photographer.

retráto: (Sp. *retrato*: portrait, picture) *n.* photograph; picture. (*ladawan*) **agparetrato.** *v.* to have one's photo taken. **makipagretrato.** *v.* to take one's photo with. **naretrato.** *a.* photographed. [Tag. *larawan*]

retroaktíbo: (Sp. *retroactivo*: retroactive) *a.* retroactive.

retrét: agretret. *n.* sound of the spinning wheel. **agranetret.** *n.* sound of shaking bamboo, grating door. [Tag. *langitngít*]

retsasádo: (Sp. *rechazado*: rejected) *a.* rejected. [Tag. *tanggí*]

rettáb: *n.* start of the rainy season when vegetation starts to thicken. **rumettab, rumtab.** *v.* to grow shoots, develop (plants, skin diseases); fester (wounds). [Tag. *usbóng* (bud)]

réyna: (Sp. *reina*: queen) *n.* queen (*aribái*). **pannakareyna.** *n.* substitute queen, proxy queen.

riák: *n.* clamor; noisy talking. **rumiak.** *v.* to swagger; talk with noisy violence. [Tag. *ingay*]

riáng: *n.* perforated bamboo used in roofing; mortise for a tiebeam; slit in woman's skirt; slit. **riangan.** *v.* to put a slit in. [Tag. *punit, laslás, bitas* (slit)]

riári: *n.* male cicada; cry of the cricket. (*andidit*) **agriari.** *v.* to cry (said of the cricket).

riáw: *n.* shout, loud noise, yell. (*ikkís; pukkáw*) **agriaw.** *v.* to yell, shout, cry out. **riawan.** *v.* to yell at someone. **iriaw.** *v.* to say in a shouting manner. **Intudona ti ridaw sana inriaw ti panagawidko.** She showed me the door and then yelled for me to go home. [Png. *bélyag*, Tag. *hiyáw, sigáw*]

ribág: *n.* sound of heavy falling objects. **kanarbaag.** *n.* continuous falling heavy objects. **manarbaag.** *v.* to fall down heavily.

ríbak: *n.* potsherd; fragment of broken pottery. [A *ríbak* is smaller than a *gíbak*]

ribál: *n.* rival. (*busor*) **agribal.** *v.* to be rivals. **karibal.** *n.* rival (two men competing for the same woman). **Awan ti magangganabta no pagribalanta ni Perla.** We have nothing to gain if we compete with each other for Perla.

ribbúot: ribbuoten. *v.* to raid, attack; invade (*rubbuot*). [Tag. *lusob, salakay*]

ribéte: (Sp. *ribete*: edge, trimming) *n.* trimming (for a dress); welt; strip of leather over shoe; embellishment.

ríbin: iribin. *v.* to include, insert. [Png. *tekép; sulong, surob, sipit*, Tag. *lakíp; sakop, sakláw; ipasok, ipaloób*]

ríbing: *var.* of *ríting*: abnormal growth.

ríbo: *num.* thousand. **sagriribo.** one thousand each. **sangaribo.** one thousand. **rinibo.** thousands. **Rinibribon a daras a pinagnana dayta nga inaladan.** He walked around the fenced-in area thousands of times. [Ibg. *zivú*, Kal. *libo*, Bon., Knk., Png., Tag. *líbo*]

ríbuk: (*riríbuk* has a regional variant *riribók*) **riribuk.** *n.* trouble, unrest, disorder, riot, turmoil. **riribuken.** *v.* to trouble, disturb; upset; confuse; molest, bother; annoy, irritate; tease. **ikaribúk.** *v.* to profit from a turmoil; take advantage of a situation. **manangriribuk.** *n.* troublemaker. **Saanka a mangiribuk iti uneg ti balayko.** Do not create trouble in my house. **Addan sa pakariribukan dayta pusom.** I think something is troubling your heart. **Ginundawayanda ti pannakariribuktayo itay.** They took advantage of our trouble a short while ago [Tag. *guló*]

ribúk: karibuk. *n.* height of a season (*tibúk*); *v.* to take advantage of a situation (with negative overtones). **ikaribuk.** *v.* to do a certain advantageous act; to profit from a turmoil.

ribós: kanarbúos. *n.* hustle and bustle. **agkanarbuos.** *v.* to hustle and bustle.

ribusádo: *var.* of *rebusado*: dipped in batter.

ribríb: *n.* decayed, black teeth of children. **agribrib.** *v.* to decay (said of milk teeth).

rídam: *n.* habit of early rising; vigilance; sleeplessness. **agridam.** *v.* to be vigilant; to sleep lightly. **naridam.** *a.* vigilant, alert, sleepless; early riser; (*fig.*) industrious (*gaget*). **Masapol nga agridamka no kayatmo ti umasenso.** You need to be vigilant if you want to increase your wealth. **Agridamka nga agkalap!** Wake up early to fish! [Tag. *alisto* (Sp.)]

rídaw: *n.* doorway, door, entrance of a house (*ruangan*). **iridaw.** *v.* to bring to the door. **rumidaw.** *v.* to go to the door. **Kasla ridaw ti simbaan.** Like a church door (referring to noisy, disagreeable talk). **Saan a makaridaw ti pusa.** The cat cannot reach the door (said during strong rain). [Ivt. *pantaw*, Kal. *olob*, Png. *pínto*, Tag. *pintô*]

ridéla: *var.* of *rodela*: wooden plastering trowel.

ridém: naridem. *a.* dim; overcast (*kuyem*; *lidem*). [Tag. *kulimlím*]

ridép: *n.* nap, short sleep. (*libay*; *inana*) **rumidep.** *v.* to start sleeping. **mairidep.** *v.* to doze off. **apagridep.** *v.* to start up from the first sleep. [Png. *lirep*, Tag. *idlíp*, *hipíg*, *himláy*]

ridírid: iridirid. *v.* to scrape; grind (with a roller like device). **Kasla naridirid a balatong ti balikas ti babai.** The girl's speech was like ground mung beans. [Tag. *kiskís*]

ridís: iridis. *v.* to step on a cigarette to put out the fire; to crush certain spices to get the flavor out; to overemphasize the stress of a word; squash an insect on the ground. **agparidis.** (*fig.*) *v.* to have an abortion (*paregrég*).

ridúma: *n.* bits, fragments.

ridón: sangaridon. *n.* one bundle.

ridríd: *var.* of *ridirid*: grind.

riéb: (*obs.*) *n.* hubbub. (*arimbangaw*)

riéd: riried. *n.* a kind of small, brown grasshopper.

riénda: (Sp. *rienda*: reins) *n.* reins. **riendaan.** *v.* to control with reins.

riésgo: (Sp. *riesgo*: risk) *n.* risk.

riét: *n.* bamboo thicket. **rumiet.** *v.* to be abundant, plentiful. [Tag. *kasukalan* (thicket)]

riga: *n.* omen, portend; intuition. **mangriga.** *v.* to have an intuition, foretell. **Kayatdan ti agawid ta adda nangriga nga adda napasamak iti amada.** They want to go home because someone had an intuition that something happened to their father.

rigadéra: (Sp. *regadera*: watering can, sprinkler) *n.* water sprinkler.

rígat: *n.* difficulty, hardship; suffering. **narigat.** *a.* difficult, hard, wearisome, fatiguing; painful. **agrigat.** *v.* to suffer hardships; become worse. **parigaten.** *v.* to make harder; make matters difficult; make hard; mortify; torture. **rigaten.** *v.* to suffer from; be hurt. **marigatan.** *v.* to be in a difficult position; to be difficult. **rumigat.** *v.* to become poor; to encounter difficulties, be confusing. **ikarigatan.** *v.* to punish; to try, to do to one's utmost; bear, suffer. **marigrigat.** *a.* poor, destitute. **kinamarigrigat.** *n.* state of being destitute. **pakarigatan.** *n.* difficulties. **pangrigáten.** *a.* a bit difficult, somewhat difficult. **naparigat.** *a.* mistreated; tortured. **tagirigaten.** *v.* to feel hurt; lack effort. **aglakam iti rigat.** suffer hardships. **Narigatna a patien ti nakitana.** It is hard for him to believe what he saw. **Apay a parparigatem pay la 'ta bagim.** Why are you still making things hard on yourself? **Parigatenda ida sadanto paltogan.** They will torture them and then shoot them. [Bon. *seláeg*, *lígat*, *sígab*, Ibg. *zigáq*, Itg. *lígat*, Ivt. *sadit*, Kal. *mansukun*, Knk. *sulít*, Png. *írap*, Tag. *hirap*]

rígay: *n.* comb of a fowl (*tapingar*). (*obs.*) **rigrigáyan.** *n.* dentate leaf.

rigírig: agrigirig. *v.* to crumble. **rigirigen.** *v.* to grind into bits. (*ridírid*)

rígis: *n.* rag, tattered cloth. **rigisrigis.** *n.* tattered, ragged clothes. **rigisen.** *v.* to tear; shred. [Tag. *punit*]

rigodón: (Sp. *rigodón*: rigodon) *n.* kind of dance, rigodon; quadrille.

rigpón: see *riput*: to kill many at once; to tie several things into one.

ríd: riiden. *v.* to grind cereals. **riniid.** *n.* ground cereals such as mung beans. [Tag. *durog*]

ríing: makariing, agriing. *v.* to awake. **nakariing.** *a.* awake. **riingen.** *v.* to wake up someone. **siririing.** *a.* awake. **iriing.** *v.* to remind. **nariingan.** *n.* skills or customs in which one is brought up; traditions. **Nariingak iti pannakaiggem ti punguapunguak.** I was awakened by his grasp of my wrist. [Ibg. *lukagen*, *sikkagen*, Itg. *liin*, Ivt. *yukay*, Png. *leíng*, Kpm., Tag. *gising*]

rikáb: *n.* grating sound; pounding of the chest when out of breath. **agrikab.** *n.* grating sound of a door being opened; wobbling motion of breast when running. **agrikabrikab.** *v.* to pant; be out of breath; gasp; catch one's breath. **rumanikab.** *v.* to pound continuously (heart). **Adda agrikabrikab a gagar iti kaungganna.** He has pounding eagerness inside him. [Tag. *kibá*]

rikád: rumanikad. *n.* sound of animals crashing through bamboo fences. **agrikadrikad.** *n.* grating sound of shutters in the wind.

ríkat: (*obs.*) **irikat.** *v.* to regard with desire.

rikbás: *var.* of *rebkás*: damage; injure.

rikép: *n.* shutter; panel of door. **rikpan.** *v.* to close, shut. **irikep.** *v.* to close. **marikpan.** *v.* to be closed. **mangrikep.** *n.* doorkeeper. **irikepan.** *v.* to close for someone. [Kal. *liyolob*, Tag. *sará* (Sp., close)]

rikét: nariket. *a.* difficult, laborious, hard (*rígat*); dense, thick. **agriket.** *n.* the sound of a moving, thumping table. **agriketriket.** *n.* sound of bamboos hitting each other.

rikiár: (Sp.? *quejar:* complain) *n.* quarrel. **agrikiar.** *v.* to quarrel verbally, argue (*apa*). **agrinnikiar.** *v.* to quarrel with each other, argue. **makirinnikiar.** *v.* to engage in a quarrel. **Agrinrinnikiarda a kasla mangukop a pamusian.** They argue with each other like brooding hens. [Tag. *away*]

rikísa: (Sp. *requisa*: inspection) *n.* thorough inspection, frisking. **rikisaen.** *v.* to frisk; search thoroughly. [Tag. *kapkáp*]

rikitítos: *n.* assorted collections of things; junk; course requirements.

rikkí: *n.* crack; crevice; chink; fissure. **agrikki.** *v.* to crack; chink. **Saan nga aglunit ti rikki ti pannakasugatko.** The crack in my wound won't heal. [Tag. *biták*]

rikkiár: *var.* spelling of *rikiar*: quarrel. **Kasla addansa karikrikkiarmo itay.** It seems you have just quarreled. [Tag. *away*]

rikná: *n.* feeling, sense, sensation, perception; emotion. **marikna.** *v.* to feel; perceive; be aware of; sense. **agparikna.** *v.* to hint, make suggestions; have an apparition. **riknaen.** *v.* to feel, touch; test. **rumikna.** *v.* to have a feeling, impression. **mangrikna.** *v.* to resent. **manangrikna.** *v.* to be sensitive, delicate. **iparikna.** *v.* to hint; suggest. **pagrikna.** *n.* sense of touch. **makipagrikna.** *v.* to sympathize. **pannakipagrikna.** *n.* sympathy; overall sentiment. **Makipagriknaak.** I sympathize. **Adda rikriknaenna.** He is not feeling well. **Kasla agparparikna kaniak nga agpampammarang nga agsakit.** He seems to be hinting to me that he is feigning

his sickness. [Bon. *gikna*, Ivt. *didyew*, Kal. *gikla*, Png. *likná*, Tag. *damdamin*]

rikó: agriko. *v.* to keep something in sight; be on the lookout.

rikúb₁: irikub. *v.* to excavate, dig slantwise, leaving a narrow opening. (*lakúb*)

rikúb₂: rikuben. *v.* to surround (*lawláw*, *lakúb*). [Tag. *paligid*, *pikot*]

rikódo: (Sp. *recodo*: elbow twist, turn) **pagrikuduan.** *n.* place to turn when plowing (*paglubáyan*).

rikonosí: (Sp. *reconocer*: recognize) **panagrikonosi.** *n.* diagnosis. **rikonosien.** *v.* to diagnose an illness.

ríkos: *n.* lap; full circle; cycle, one complete revolution. **agrikos.** *v.* to revolve a full circle; complete a lap or round. **rikusen.** *v.* to pass completely around; to do frequently. **rikosrikos.** *a.* circuitous, meandering, zigzagged. **agrikosrikos.** *v.* to go around. **Uray rikusem ti sibubukel a tiendaan, awan ti mabirokam.** Even if you go around the entire market, you won't find anything. [Tag. *ikot*]

rikút: narikut. *a.* difficult, hard, complicated. **parikutan.** *v.* to compel, force; press. **parikut.** *n.* trouble. **agparikut.** *v.* to have problems. **maparikutan.** *v.* to be worried. **rumikut.** *v.* to become difficult. **Rumikut a rumikut ti biag.** Life has many hardships. [Tag. *hirap* (difficult)]

rikpán: (*rikep* + *-an*) *v.* to close. [Tag. *sará*, (Sp.)]

riktáb: *n.* dry season (*kalgáw*). [Tag. *tag-tuyót*]

ríles: (Sp. *carriles*: rails) *n.* rails for trains; railroad track.

ríma: (Sp. *rima*: rhyme) *n.* rhyme. [Tag. *tugmâ*]

rimárim: nakarimrimarim. *a.* dreadful, horrible; wretched, woeful.

rímas: *n. Artocarpus communis*, breadfruit. [Tag. *rimas*]

rimás: rinimasan. *a.* of two alternating colors.

rimát: *n.* glitter; sparkle; flash. **agrimat.** *v.* to flash, sparkle. **marimat.** *v.* to perceive from afar; detect indistinctly. **parimaten.** *v.* to brighten, make flash; dazzle. **rumimat, agrimatrimat.** *v.* to flash, sparkle, glimmer. **Agrimatto ti naganna.** His name will flash (he will become famous). [Tag. *kisláp*]

rimatsí: (Sp. *remache*: rivet) *n.* repair; rivet. (*rematse*)

rimbáw: *n.* top; peak; summit. **narimbaw.** *a.* exceeding in height, overtowering; eminent, illustrious; dignified. **rimbawan.** *v.* to excel, surpass. **agririnnimbaw.** *v.* to compete with others for first place. **marimbawan.** *v.* to be surpassed. [Tag. *higít* (excel)]

rimensór: see *agrimensor*: land surveyor.

rímer: *n.* dense growth of plant; dimness; obstacle, obstruction. **narimer.** *a.* doubtful; diluted; unclear. **marimeran.** *v.* to be doubtful, suspicious. **Nagrukob a nangyasideg iti rupa- na iti narimer a sarming.** He stooped as he approached his face in the hazy mirror.

rimiénta: *n.* implements; equipment (*ramít*). [Tag. *kagamitán*]

rim-ík: *var.* of *rim-it*: break into fragments; crush; smash. [Tag. *durog*]

rimírim₁: *n.* edge (*ígid*). **rimiriman.** *v.* to trim. **Sumagmamano laeng a bukel ti timmangken nga innapuy ti dimket iti rimirim ti sabút.** A few seeds of hardened rice stuck to the edge of the coconut shell. [Tag. *gilid*]

rimírim₂: **iparimirim.** *v.* to insinuate (*ripírip*). [Tag. *hiwatig*]

rim-ít: **rim-iten.** *v.* to break into fragments (*rim- ik*). **marim-it.** *v.* to be crushed; break into pieces. **Narim-itda iti napilpil a lugan.** They were crushed in the smashed car. [Tag. *durog*]

rimmúok: *n.* clump; cluster. **agririmmuok.** *v.* to gather in clusters. [Tag. *kumpól*]

rimmúong: *var.* of *rimmuok*: cluster.

rimón: *n.* strong dislike. **nakarimrimon.** *a.* dis- gusting, nauseating, revolting. **marimon.** *v.* to hate, be disgusted with. **karimon.** *v.* to hate; loathe. [Tag. *rimarim*]

rímong: (*obs.*) *n.* heap of fuel or fodder.

rimpunók: *var.* of *arimpunók*: gathering, assem- bly. (*aripunó*)

rimpóng: *n.* bonds; binding the four limbs together or animals; tying elbow to elbow. **rim- pongen.** *v.* to bind the four legs of an animal. (*pungo*) **Rimpongenda dagiti kabusorda sada ibitin ida idiay kampoda.** They bind the four legs of their enemies together and then hang them in their camp.

rimrím: see *parimrim*.

rinanhádo: (Sp. *anaranjado*: orange) *n.* salmon color.

rinét: *n.* extraneous matter (small stones in rice). **narinet.** *a.* full of small stones (rice). **Saan a naikaskaso idi ta imbilangda laeng a kas bassit-usit a rinet a mabaddebaddekan.** He wasn't acknowledged before because they considered him a small particle to step on. [Tag. *bató*]

rinníit: see *ritrit*: tear down; saw down.

rinsaéd: *n.* sediment, dregs, settlings (*aribu- dabod*; *areb-eb*; *intaer*; *lissaad*; *lued*; *basabas*). [Png. *gaér*, Tag. *latak*, *tining*]

rinsók: *n.* ellipse; *a.* elliptical. **narinsok.** *a.* elliptical.

ringaringét: (*obs.*) rootlets of bamboos.

ríngas: *a.* with partly clipped ear or ears. (*ríngud*, *píngas*)

ringbáw: **rumingbaw.** *adv.* over, above. **ring- bawan.** *v.* to ascend.

ringgawís: *var.* of *aringgawis*: very tip (of a branch).

ringgília: *var.* of *heringgilia*: syringe.

ringgór: *n.* noise; lawsuit, court case; fight; quarrel. **agringgor.** *v.* to quarrel; fight; bring to court, litigate. **ringgoren.** *v.* to bother; pester; make trouble for. **maringgoran.** *v.* to be confused; irritated, annoyed; confused; to be busy; to have one's hands full. **makiringgor.** *v.* to quarrel with. **naringgor.** *a.* troublesome; boisterous, noisy. [Tag. *away*]

ringiád: *n.* crack in the sole of the foot. **agringiad.** *v.* to have cracks in the sole of the foot.

ringkék: *a.* short necked; bull-necked (*rengkek*). [Knk. *tiptípew*]

ríngkon: *n.* hill of plants. (*reppet*, *bangbang*) **ringkunen.** *v.* to make a hill around plants.

ringlít: *a.* curly hair. (*kulot*) **agparinglit.** *v.* to get a perm; to have the hair curled.

ríngud: *a.* having only one ear. (*pingod*) **ringu- den.** *v.* to cut off an ear. [Tag. *pingas*]

ringpás: **ringpasen.** *v.* to finish, terminate, end, conclude; accomplish; kill. **mairingpas.** *v.* to be done fully; to be accomplished; killed. **Masapul a ringpasenna dagiti aruatna a gansiluen.** She needs to finish her clothes she is crocheting. **Kunada a nasken nga iringpasna iti dua a panangtakemna.** They say he needs to accomplish his two duties. [Tag. *tapos*]

ringtá: (*obs.*) *a.* with might and main.

riubárbo: (Sp. *ruibarbo*) *n.* rhubarb.

rípa₁: (*obs.*) *a.* fully determined.

rípa₂: (Sp. *rifa*: raffle) **paripa.** *n.* raffle. **ripaen.** *v.* to draw numbers; to draw lots. **agparipa.** *v.* to have a raffle.

ripák: **agripak, rumanipak, agkanarpaak.** *n.* the sound of a plate breaking, a door slamming, etc. **panarpaaken.** *v.* to fire a gun.

rípar: **mangripar.** *v.* to perceive; observe; **ma- ripar.** *v.* to notice; perceive. **Nariparna itayen ti lalaki a nagkabalio a kasla agap-apo iti paraanganda.** He noticed the man on horse- back calling *apo* in their yard. [Tag. *hiwatig*; *halatâ*]

ripárip: **riparipan.** *v.* to trim (*ratab*; *rimirim*). [Tag. *tabas*]

rípas: *n.* yarn waste; thread of a fringe. **ripas ti timek.** *n.* vocal cords.

rípat₁: **ripaten.** *v.* to sever at the root.

rípat₂: **apagripat.** *a.* transient, fugitive; momen- tary. [Tag. *kagyát*]

ríper: *n.* small extraneous matter in liquids. **nariper**. *a.* slightly turbid (water).
ríping: *a.* grown together, double (fruits, fingers, bodies, etc.) **agripingriping**. *v.* to carry two babies at the same time. **riping a singin**. Siamese twins. [Tag. *kambál* (twin)]
ripírip: **maripirip**. *v.* to deduce, infer, conclude form the facts. **rumipripirip**. (*obs.*) *v.* to peep out from afar. **iparipirip**. *v.* to hint, imply, insinuate. **maripirip**. *v.* to deduce; be able to sense. **pangripiripan**. *n.* hint. [Tag. *hiwatig*]
ripís: **manarpiis**. *n.* the sound of snapping twigs.
ríple: (Sp. *rifle*: rifle) *n.* rifle.
ripóg: *n.* sound of crumbling. **rumpuog**. *v.* to crumble down loudly. **kanarpuog**. *n.* continuous crumbling, crashing down. **marpuog**. *v.* to crumble down; collapse, cave in. **panarpuogen**. *v.* to tumble down.
ripók: **rumpuok**. *v.* to break with a smashing sound. **marpuok**. *v.* to shatter, break to pieces. **kanarpuok**. *n.* continuous shattering sounds.
rip-óng: **agririp-ong**. *v.* to grow in clusters or bunches. (*raay*)
ripút: **riputen**. *v.* to catch red handed; catch all, take two or more things with one hand; to kill many at once. **mariput**. *v.* to be caught red handed; caught in the act. **Pinaltoganna ida ta nariputna kano idi rabii dagiti dua**. He shot them because he supposedly caught the two red handed last night. **Riputentayo ti estranghero a padi!** Let's catch that foreign priest (in the act).
rippí: *n.* crease. **marpi, rippien**. *v.* to break in two after doubling; fold, crease.
rippíing: *n.* sound of twanging; sound-breaking silence. **marpiing**. *v.* to resound.
rippíis: *n.* noise made by walking on a bamboo floor; sound of dry leaves. **rumpiis, agrippiis**. *v.* to make this sound.
rippíit: *n.* sound of dry things breaking. **marpiit**. *v.* to break (said of dry things).
rippúog: (f. *ripóg*) *n.* ruins; rubble. **marpuog**. *v.* to crumble; be demolished; cave in. **rippuogen**. *v.* to destroy; demolish; ruin; overthrow. [Tag. *guhò*]
rippúok: (f. *ripók*) **marpuok**. *v.* to be crushed; smashed. **rippuoken**. *v.* to crush; smash. [Tag. *durog*]
ríreng: **rumireng**. *v.* stick, stay; hide; turn a deaf ear. **agrireng**. *v.* to safely hide. **marireng**. *v.* to be safely hidden; be dumbfounded. [Tag. *tulalâ* (dumbfounded)]
ríri: *n.* trouble, disturbance; misunderstanding. **agriri**. *n.* to make trouble, dispute. **iriri**. *v.* to insist on being right even when wrong. **nariri**. *a.* noisy (*ringgor*); complaining; demanding;

making trouble. **makiriri**. *v.* to argue, quarrel.
mannakariri. *n.* troublemaker. **nariri**. *a.* troublesome, noisy; complaining. [Tag. *away* (quarrel)]
riríbuk: (f. *ríbuk*) *n.* trouble; turmoil; fighting; scandal; disturbance. **riribuken**. *v.* to disturb, upset, trouble, irritate; worry; nag. **mariribuk**. *v.* to be worried; troubled. **mangriribuk**. *n.* one who disturbs. **nariribuk**. *a.* worried, troubled; chaotic. **Mariribuken ti agtutubo a mangbirok iti kinataonaken iti kayatna a biag**. Young people have trouble finding themselves and what they want out of life. [Tag. *guló*]
rirít: *n.* strip of wood. **ririten**. *v.* to divide into strips.
ríro: *n.* mistake. (*biddut*) **mariro**. *v.* to be distracted; confused; make a mistake. **mariruan**. *v.* to be distracted by many things at once. **riruen**. *v.* to distract, confuse. **No diak agriro**. If I'm not mistaken. [Png. *alingó*, Tag. *kamalî*]
risák: **rumisak**. *v.* to bound; leap; spout out; gush out; spurt; to start to gossip. **Narisak ti iliw iti barukongko**. Homesickness struck my chest.
rísang₁: **narisang**. *a.* short, brief (in duration). (*biít*)
rísang₂: **nairisang**. *a.* separated, parted; retired. **marisangrisang**. (*obs.*) to be set upon on all sides. **risangrisangen**. *v.* to tear up, mangle; lacerate. **risangen**. *v.* to separate; tear off. [Tag. *putol*]
rísay: *a.* torn (ear) (*marisayan*); *interj.* used to call pigs. **marisayrisay**. *a.* torn up, mangled, shredded, lacerated. [Tag. *punit* (torn)]
rísek: *n.* a kind of small skate or ray.
risgó: (Sp. *riesgo*: risky) **narisgo**. *a.* risky. [Tag. *mapanganib*]
risíris: *n.* conflict; friction; rivalry. **agrisiris**. *v.* to rub, fray, scrape against one another; strive for, vie; contend, compete. **agrinnisiris**. *v.* to argue with one another; compete. **irisiris**. *v.* to ground an opponent. [Tag. *pagtatalo* (competition); *kiskís* (scrape)]
risngí: *var.* of *ngirsi*: grimace. **agrisngi**. *v.* to grimace. [Tag. *ngibit, ngiwî*]
risúd: **marsuod**. *v.* to collapse, cave in. **agrissuod**. *v.* to collapse. **manarsuod**. *v.* to crumble down. **kanarsuod**. *n.* continuous crumbling, collapsing. **rumsuod**. *v.* to go in and out of a house; fall through. (*rebbá, reggáay*)
risút: *n.* conclusion. (*gíbus*) **risuten**. *v.* to conclude (a discussion); solve. **makirinnisut**. *v.* to settle a dispute. **pakarisutan**. *n.* solution; way of settling of a dispute.
risrís: *n.* rubbing against each other; fluttering of the *abal-abal* beetle. **agrisiris**. *v.* to contest in a

basketball game. **agparisris**. *n.* sound of fluttering June bugs when holding them by their outer wings. **parispis**. *n.* taking hold of the outer wings of June bugs so they flutter and attract other June bugs.

rissáak: *var.* of *ressáak*: disintegrate, waste away; collapse.

rissák: *n.* sound of leaves being crushed. **kanarsaak**. *n.* continuous crushing sound.

rissát: **narissat**. *a.* broken; torn (corner of a box). **Nagrissaten ti kanenmi tattan.** We no longer have any food (food supply is consumed).

rissibók: *n.* sound of splashing in water. **kanarsibok**. *n.* continuous splashing. **ipanarsibok**. *v.* to throw something in with a splash. **manarsibok**. *v.* to fall in the water with a splash.

rissíit: *n.* the hissing sound of something being burned. **narsiit**. *a.* burning hot (sun). **rumsiit**. *v.* to hiss when burning.

rissík: *n.* spark; sound of frying lard. **rumsik**. *v.* to spark, sparkle; crack when breaking. **maparsik**. *v.* to soften in cooking. **agparparsik**. *v.* to move to and fro. (schools of fish) **parsik**. *n.* overmeasure of gratuity. **kanarsiik**. *n.* continuous cracking sounds. **Panawen ti panagrissik ti bunga ti kakawate.** It is the season of the crackling of the fruits of the *madre cacao* trees.

rissíng: *n.* fragment; part. **rissingen**. *v.* to separate, sever, remove, take away. **marsingan**. *a.* separated; severed; removed. **narsing a biag**. dead.

rissít: *n.* sound of burning flesh; intense heat of the sun (*sanetsét*). **kanarsiit**. *n.* roasting sound. **rumsiit**. *v.* to be very hot, scorching; to roast. **manarsiit**. *v.* to produce a crackling sound (as when burning).

rissúod: (f. *risúd*) *n.* collapse, cave-in. **agrisuod, marsuod**. *v.* to collapse, cave in. **manarsuod**. *v.* to crumble down. **kanarsuod**. *n.* continuous crumbling down. **Pinanarsuodna dagiti pasdek.** He toppled down the buildings. **Rumsuodka dita!** You might fall (through the floor) there!

ritárit: *n.* kind of bamboo toy that snaps when twirled.

rítem: (*obs.*) *n.* crowd of people. (*ummóng; pangén; gímong*)

ríting: *n.* abnormal growth (double thumb, etc.); small skin tumor. **ritingan**. *a.* with protuberances.

rítmo: (Sp. *ritmo*: rhythm) *n.* rhythm.

ríto: (Sp. *rito*: rite) *n.* rite, ceremony.

rituál: (Eng.) *n.* ritual.

ritubár: *n.* change, alteration. **ritubaren**. *v.* to change; remodel, repair; make amends for a bad deed. **agparitubar**. *v.* to have something

repaired. **Kayatna a ritubaren ti kammalina.** He wants to fix his mistake.

rituér: *a.* very malignant; *n.* kind of small, wrinkly, poisonous crab; stain; turbidity. **narituer**. *a.* a little turbid; tainted; dim; dirtied; malignant; (*reg.*) full of wrinkles. **agrituer**. *v.* to have the eyesight become weak; to become turbid. **Nalabsanna dagiti ubbing nga agbambanniit iti narituer a waig.** He passed the children baiting their poles in the turbid stream.

ritunó: **agrirituno**. *v.* to gather; assemble; congregate. (*tipon*)

ritúok: *n.* sound of cracking joints. (*rittók*) **agrituok**. *v.* to crack joints (in fingers, etc.)

rítor: *n.* fatigue. **naritor**. *a.* exhausted; tired. **rituren**. *v.* to tire, exhaust. **Nasurok a sangapulo a tawen ti bimmaketan ni Alsing iti tawenna a tallopulo ket uppat gapu iti pannakariturna iti panagteggedna.** Alsing aged over ten years at her age of thirty-four because of her exhausting work.

ritrít: *n.* the sound of tearing. **agritrit**. *v.* to make the sound of paper being torn. **rumanitrit**. *n.* sound of paper being torn, wheel of a cart. **ritriten**. *v.* to tear; saw (logs). [Tag. *laginít*]

rittík: *n.* crackling sound. **agrittik**. *n.* sound of crackling wood in the fire; sound of beans bursting in the sun. [Tag. *kaluskós*]

rittók: **agrittok**. *v.* to crackle (finger joints).

rittúok: (f. *ritók*) **agrittuok, rumtuok**. *v.* to crackle (joints), produce a crackling sound. **rittuoken**. *v.* to crack the joints. **ritrittuok**. *n.* a kind of bush whose flowers crackle when squeezed. **marittuok**. (*obs.*) *v.* to have a wounded sole of the foot. **panartuoken**. *v.* to cause to crackle.

ríweng: **mariweng**. *v.* to be stunned (by fainting, a blow to the head, etc.) (*alimpayéng; aríweng; síleng*). [Tag. *tulíg*]

riwét: *n.* darkness at dawn. **apagriwet**. *n.* twilight. (*sarsardam; suripet*) **nariwet nga agsapa**. the twilight of the morning. **rumiwet**. *v.* to become dark. [Tag. *dilím*]

ríwis: *n.* oblique cut. (*tangraw*) **riwisen**. *v.* to cut slantwise (*tangraw*). **nagriwisriwis**. *a.* deformed (baskets).

riwríw: *num.* million. **sangariwriw**. *num.* one million. **riniwriw**. millions. **Nagbalin a sangariwriw ti rupak.** My face became a million (dollars). [Png. *laksá*, Tag. *angaw*]

riyáw: (*obs.*) **rumiyaw**. *v.* to be ready for reaping (rice).

ruák: *var.* of *buák*: shoo; quiver.

ruám: *n.* habit, custom. (*inam; ugali*) **ruamen**. *v.* to familiarize, accustom to; train; tame; acclimate. **iruam**. *v.* to establish a habit;

accustom to something. **mairuam**. *v.* to be accustomed to. **naruam**. *a.* accustomed to. **panangruam**. *n.* taming of animals. **pakairuaman**. *n.* habit. **Naruamkami a makakita kenka a nauyong**. We are used to seeing you mean. **Pinaruamam ida**. *exp.* You spoiled them (made them accustomed). **Sadino man a papanan, sumursurot ti nakairuaman**. Wherever one goes, his habits follow. [Png. *ilwán*, Tag. *daniw*]

ruángan: *n.* entrance (*daramuangan, darimangan, serrek*); passage; gate; door (*ridaw*). **iruangan**. *v.* to anticipate; start, open a discussion. **ruangan ti langit**. *n.* the gate of heaven. [Bon. *eneb, liwangan*, Kal. *sawang*, Knk. *dasángan, pangtéw*, Png. *pinto*, Tag. *pintô*]

ruár: *n.* outside; date of issue. **agruar**. *v.* to issue forth; (*fig.*) come out, become fashionable. **ru(m)muar**. *v.* to go outdoors, go outside; exit. **iruar**. *v.* to put outside; issue; expel, emit. **iti ruar**. *prep.* outside. **paruarén**. *v.* to let go outside, take outside; wait until something appears (moon). **makaruar**. *v.* to be able to get out; to pass (a test). **naruar**. *a.* popular; fashionable. **pagruarán**. *n.* exit. **managruar**. *a.* always going out. **akinruar**. *a.* outer. **agparuar**. *v.* to bring out; go outside; (*coll.*) masturbate, ejaculate (*kissit, salsal*). **pagruarán**. *n.* exit, outlet; vent. [Bon. *dela*, Ivt. *ahbet*, Kal. *lasin*, Png. *pawáy*, Tag. *labás* (out, exit)]

ruáy: *n.* amount, number; (*obs.*) blackberry. **naruay**. plentiful, numerous, abundant (*narwáy; adu*). [Tag. *marami* (numerous)]

rúbang₁: **rumubang**. *v.* to sprout, germinate, shoot up (*rusing*). [Tag. *tubò*]

rúbang₂: **agparubang**. *v.* to suffer the pangs of childbirth, be in labor. (*sikal*)

rubár: (Sp. *robar*: rob) **agrubar**. *v.* to draw cards that are not trump in exchange for cards that do not follow suit.

rubbuát: *n.* preparations; manner of growing up or starting something; style. **agrubbuat**. *v.* to make oneself ready to go; start a journey; commence. **irubbuat**. *v.* to make ready, prepare; arrange beforehand. **pagrubbuatan**. *n.* place of departure. **makarubbuat**. *v.* to be ready to go. **parubbuatan**. *v.* to send off someone; help someone prepare to go. **rubbuatan**. *v.* to dress someone up; prepare someone for a special occasion (*luás, gabbuát*). **Inikkandakami iti maysa nga oras nga agirubbuat kadagiti gamigammi**. They gave us one hour to prepare our weapons. [Tag. *handâ*]

rubbók: **agparubbok**. *v.* to appear from the ground, break through the surface (as a shoot coming up).

rubbúot: *n.* surprise attack; conquest. **rubuoten**. *v.* to attack by surprise; conquer. **Kellaat a rinubbuot dagiti gerilia ti simbaan**. The guerillas suddenly attacked the church. [Tag. *lusob, salakay*]

rubí: (Sp. *rubí*: ruby) *n.* ruby.

rubíngki: **rinubingki**. *n.* rope made of several cords twisted together.

rubírob: *a.* pug-nosed; flat nosed. (*leppap*; *lugpak*; *pappap*) **rubiruben**. *v.* to chop off. [Tag. *pangó*]

rubkás: **marubrubkas**. *v.* to deteriorate; degenerate. **narubkas**. *a.* dilapidated, deteriorated. **Marubrubkasen ti dadduma a paset ti tinidtid a kawayan a diding**. A few parts of the close-woven bamboo wall were deteriorating.

rubkí: **rubkien**. *v.* to penetrate, go to the interior of. **narubki**. (*obs.*) *a.* dense (forest).

rubnáy: *var.* of *rugnay*: collapse, crumble down.

rúbo₁: *n.* ear of Indian corn.

rúbo₂: **irubo**. *v.* to betray; mislead. **mairubo**. *v.* to be mislead; bankrupt; ruined financially. **pakairubuan**. *n.* betrayal; temptation. **manangirubo**. *n.* one who betrays. [Tag. *taksíl*]

rúbong: (*obs.*) *n.* young leaf. [Tag. *dahon*]

rubúrob: *a.* steep; pug-nosed; dull pointed; sandy pathway down to a riverbank. **karuburuban**. *n.* sand dune, sandy ground. **naruburob**. *a.* sandy. (*darat; paratong*) **mairuburob**. *v.* to get stuck in sandy soil. **Ruburob ken natapok ti dalan no kalgaw**. The road is sandy and dusty in the summer.

rub-ós: **marub-os**. *v.* to suddenly burst open with contents spilling (*bekkes*). [Tag. *sambulat*]

robústa: (Sp.) *n.* variety of coffee.

rubrúb: **rumubrub**. *v.* to flame up, flare up (said of anger, fire, etc.); change into a deer (witches). **rubruban**. *v.* to blaze, inflame (fire); inflame; excite (feelings). **Ad-addanto la a marubroban ti gurana kaniak**. It is most probable that his anger toward me will flare up. [Tag. *dubdób; liyáb*]

rubsáy: **rubsayen**. *v.* to open; force one's way into. **mairubsay**. *v.* to fall in seemingly solid ground.

rubsí: **rubsien**. *v.* to alter; annul; void; nullify. **di marubsi**. *a.* unchangeable; uncompromising. [Tag. *pawaláng-bisà* (void)]

róda: (Sp. *roda*: nautical stem) *n.* figurehead; figure placed on the front of a ship as an ornament.

rúda: (Sp. *ruda*: rue) *n.* rue plant.

rud-ák: *n.* large thorn or splinter that gets stuck in the sole of the foot; smaller splinters are called *puris*. **marud-akan**. *v*. to get a splinter in the foot. [Tag. *tibò*]

rudárod: **rudarudan**. *v*. to scrape, scour.

rudék: *var*. of *ludék*: crush; step heavily on; *rumék*: pulverize.

rodéla: (Sp. *rodela*: round shield, buckler) *n*. wooden plastering trowel. (*ridela*)

rodílio: (Sp. *rodillo*: roller) *n*. roller used in leveling.

ruéda: (Sp. *rueda*: wheel) *n*. Ferris wheel; wheel (*lígay*); cockpit ring; boxing ring.

ruédo: (Sp. *ruedo*: turn) *n*. spinning wheel. **agruedo**. *v*. to spin. **de-ruedo**. with a wheel; turning.

ruék: (*obs*.) see *ariwekwek*: plentiful; numerous. (*ruáy*)

rugák: *a*. worn out, shabby, threadbare (*rugak-rugak*); rickety, dilapidated. **rumugak**. *v*. to become worn out. **Patarimaanna kano ti rugak a rangtay**. He supposedly will have the rickety bridge fixed. [Tag. *sirâ*]

rugárog: *n*. grunt of the hog; sniveling disease of the water buffalo. **agrugarog**. *v*. to grunt; to be affected with a sniveling disease (said of the *nuáng*). [Tag. *igík*]

rogasión: (Sp. *rogación*: rogation, request, petition) *n*. public supplication during a calamity.

rogatíba: (Sp. *rogativa*: supplicatory) *n*. ringing of bells for someone who is dying.

rugí: *n*. beginning. (*damo*; *aruat*; *ussuat*; *dulno*; *rusat*) **rugian**. *v*. to begin, start, commence; set about; initiate; inaugurate. **makarugi**. *v*. to be able to start. **mangrugi**. *v*. to begin from (time specified); start. **irugi**. *v*. to begin (work). **karugrugi**. just started. **iti rugina pay laeng**. from the very start. **pangrugian**. *n*. starting point. **manipud rugi inggana't gibusna**. from start to finish. [Bon. *ligwat*, *logi*, Ivt. *sitnan*, Knk. *itém*, Kpm. *umpisá*, Png. *buát*, *gapó*, Tag. *mulâ*]

rugít: *n*. dirt, filth; excreta. **narugit**. *a*. dirty, filthy; nasty, obscene; defective; faulty; imperfect. **rugitan**. *v*. to dirty, soil, stain; defile. **karugit**. *v*. to have an intense dislike toward. **marugitan**. *v*. to become soiled. **rugit ti tao**. *n*. human excrement. [Ibg. *daping*, Ifg. *lugit*, Itg. *naiseg*, Ivt. *rudit*, *kuris*, Kal. *kaisaw*, Knk. *bidák*, *kílut*, *síbud*, Kpm. *marinat*, Png. *duták*, *dingót*, Tag. *dumí*]

rugmá₁: *n*. attack of many dogs. **rugmaan**. *v*. to attack as of many dogs. [Tag. *lusob*, *salakay*]

rugmá₂: **mairugma**. *v*. to fall prone (on something that hurts). **rugmaan**. *v*. to prostrate; fall prone on someone; throw one's body on someone. **Makitana dagiti pakabuklan dagiti nataytayag a kaykayo a kasla mangur-uray**

a mangrugma kadakuada. He saw the shapes of the tall trees appearing as if they were waiting to fall on them. [Tag. *dambá*]

rugnáy: **agrugnay**. *v*. to collapse, break down.

rugnayen. *v*. to eliminate, erode away, remove by erosion; erode. **Talaga nga agsagsagaba ti Australia iti panagrugnay ti ekonomia**. Australia is really suffering from the collapse of the economy.

rúgos: *a*. cut off, severed. **rugusen**. *v*. to cut off (for sewing). **rugosan**. *v*. to cut the tops off. **narugos**. *a*. cut off. **Narugos ti gurongna iti disgrasia**. His leg was cut off in the accident. [Tag. *putol*]

rugpá₁: **rugpaen**. *v*. to break down (buildings); crush. **marugpa**. *v*. to collapse, break down, be crushed. [Tag. *gibâ*]

rugpá₂: *var*. of *dugpá*: butt.

rugpó: **narugpo**. *a*. destroyed, collapsed. **rugpuen**. *v*. to destroy. [Tag. *gibâ*]

rugrúg: **narugrug**. *a*. large and blazing (said of a fire).

rugsó: *n*. passion; ardent desire; lust. **narugso**. *a*. overflowing, intense, ardent, burning; enthusiastic. **agrugso, rumugso**. *v*. to be passionate; be sexually aroused. **kinarugso**. *n*. passionateness. **parugsuen**. *v*. to incite; inflame. **sirurugso**. *a*. passionately. **Nabayag a nagur-urayda iti gundaway tapno maep-ep ti rugsoda**. They have been waiting a long time for the chance to quench their passion. **Inagkak a sirurugso**. I kissed her passionately. [Tag. *dubdób*, *pusók*; *silakbó*]

róha: (Sp. *roja*: red) **krus róha**. *n*. Red Cross.

ruídaw: **ruruidaw**. *n*. a kind of small, dark bird with a blue breast.

ruína: (Sp. *ruina*: ruins) *n*. ruins.

ruiseniór: (Sp. *ruiseñor*) *n*. lark, nightingale.

ruká: *n*. soft state of the soil. **naruka**. *a*. soft, loose (soil); easy to cultivate. **mamagruka iti salun-at**. to weaken the health. [Tag. *buhaghág* (spongy soil)]

rúkab: *n*. cavity of a tooth. (*binokbók*) **agrukab**. *v*. to develop a hole; to have tooth decay. **marukaban**. *v*. to be damaged, injured; having a hole or cavity. **rukaban**. *v*. to open, remove a board form. **Iselselmo iti rukab ti ngipenmo**. Fill in the decay in your tooth. [Tag. *sirâ*]

rukapí: *a*. with uneven teeth, coupled teeth. **agrukapi**. *v*. to have uneven teeth. [Tag. *sungkî*]

ruk-át: **ruk-atan**. *v*. to free; liberate. **rumuk-at**. *v*. to get free. **maruk-atan**. *v*. to be released; to be liberated. **pannakaruk-at**. *n*. liberation, independence. [Tag. *kawalâ*]

rukáy: **agrukay**. *v*. to cultivate (*sukay*). **rukayen**. *v*. to dig, cultivate.

rukbáb: *n.* worship. **agrukbab**. *v.* to worship; bow deeply, bend low. **pagrukbaban.** *v.* to honor someone. **pagrukbab.** *n.* commemorative. **Kas pagrukbab, ramrambakantayo iti Disiembre 30 iti tinawen a panglagip ken ni Jose Rizal.** In reverence, we celebrate December 30 yearly to remember José Rizal. [Tag. *yukód*]

rukbós: **narukbos.** *a.* leafy; full of branches. (*barusbos*) **rumukbos.** *v.* to become leafy. [Tag. *yabong*]

rukbót₁: **narukbot.** *a.* magnificent; pompous; robust. **kinarukbot.** *n.* magnificence; pomposity; robustness. [Tag. *dingal*]

rukbót₂: *var.* of *rukbós*: lush, leafy.

rukbóy: *var.* of *rukbáb*: honor, pay respect.

rúker: *n.* larva. **agruker.** *v.* to decay; deteriorate. **rinuker.** *a.* decaying; bug-eaten; corrupt; unscrupulous. [Tag. *bulók* (decay)]

rukiáb: *n.* crevice, fissure; gap. (*rúkib*)

rúkib: *n.* cave, grotto, cavern. (*gukáyab*) **timid ti rukib.** *n.* mouth of the cave. [Png. *ongib*, Tag. *yungíb*]

rukíb: **parukibán.** *v.* to glance out of the corners of the eyes (*kusílap*). [Tag. *sulyáp*]

rukiéb: **agrukieb.** *v.* to be situated underground; to enter the ground.

rukít: **rukiten.** *v.* to dig; make a hill for planting (*ringkon*). **irukit.** *v.* to dig up. **Diak koma kayat ti mangirukit manen kadagiti ngatangatak kenka.** I don't want to dig out again my doubts toward you.

ruk-ít: *var.* of *rukit*: dig; cultivate.

rukkúas: *var.* of *rukuás*.

rúkma: **rumukma.** *v.* to surrender; submit to. **irukma.** *v.* to give up, surrender. **parukmaen.** *v.* to conquer; vanquish. **maparukma.** *v.* to be conquered; to be defeated. **Pinarukma ti maingel a dadaulo dagiti kabusor.** The valiant leaders vanquished the enemies. [Tag. *sukò*]

ruknís: *n.* opening (*lukáis*); work shift, turn. **ruknisen.** *v.* to open, lay bare, uncover. **Rinuknisna ti pandiling ti baket.** He lifted the skirt of the old lady.

ruknóy: *n.* bowing low, obeisance. (*rukob; kulob*) **agruknoy.** *v.* to bow, stoop, bend; court, offer one's love. **iruknoy.** *v.* to bend, stoop, lower the body to avoid hitting branches; offer respectfully; offer to; dedicate to. **mairuknoy.** *v.* to be dedicated to; offered in honor of. **Iruknoyko kenka ti kinapudnok.** I offer you the truth. [Tag. *yukód* (bow); *ligaw* (court)]

rukuás: **irukuas.** *v.* to break the bindings; force oneself from under a heavy weight; commence, start, begin (*rugi, ussuat*). **rumkuas.** *v.* to get set and go; burst out suddenly; emerge from the water. **Rimkuas ti apuy iti barukongna.** The fire (of passion) burst from his chest. **Awan ti rumkuas a dutdotko kenka.** *exp.* You do not excite me (*lit*: none of my body hairs emerge because of you). [Tag. *luksó* (leap)]

rúkob: *n.* bending, stooping. (*dumog*) **agrukob.** *v.* to bow, bend, stoop. **parukuben.** *v.* to subdue, vanquish; store away. [Tag. *hukót*]

rukód: *n.* line, rod; yardstick, tape measure, strip used in measuring. **rukuden.** *v.* to measure. **agparukod.** *v.* to have one's measurements taken. **marukrukod.** *v.* to walk with measured steps; to speak very carefully. **marukodrukod.** *v.* to arrange according to size. **pakarukudan.** *n.* measurement; dimension. **Kon-rukod dagiti annakna.** She gives birth regularly. **Kasano't kalawa ti pattapattam 'toy rukrukodentayo?** What is your estimate of the width of what we are measuring? [Ivt. *adpang*, Png., Tag. *sukat*]

rukóp₁: *n.* a kind of small freshwater fish; variety of awned *diket* rice.

rukóp₂: **narukop.** *a.* brittle, weak, flimsy, fragile; rotten, decayed. **agrukop.** *v.* to wear out; rot; decay; weaken. **Panawen ti manglitup ti kinarukop ken kinaliday.** It is time to get rid of decadence and sadness. [Png. *lupók*, Tag. *hunâ, dupók*]

rukúrok: *var.* of *kurokur*: undermine (said of streams, etc.), erode.

rukrók: **irukrok.** *v.* to sink a weapon in an animal's body. **rukruken.** *v.* to slaughter by sticking a knife in the neck. **marukrok.** *v.* to be killed by a piercing knife. [Tag. *ulos*]

ruksó: *var.* of *rugso*: passion.

ruktót: **ruktuten.** *v.* to choke, suffocate under one's weight. **agruktot.** *v.* to give way; sink under weight. [Tag. *lugmók*]

ruléta: (Sp. *ruleta*: roulette) *n.* roulette.

rólio: (Sp. *rollo*: roll) *n.* roll; roller; reel. **rolio dagiti bala.** *n.* round of bullets. **rinolio.** in rolls.

romána: (Sp. *romanar*: weigh with a steelyard) *n.* steelyard.

romanísta: (Sp. *romano*: Roman) *n.* Roman Catholic.

románo: (Sp.) *n., a.* Roman; Roman Catholic.

románsa: (Eng.) *n.* romance; (*fig.*) sexual intercourse. **agromansa.** *v.* to have love affairs.

románse: (Sp. *romance*) *n.* romance novel.

romántiko: (Sp. *romántico*: romantic) *a.* romantic.

rúmas: *n.* kind of tree with thorny branches common at the beach.

rumbéb: *a.* blunt; with sunken lips (*rungbéd*); a type of gobi.

rumbéng: (f. *rebbéng*) *n.* lawful heirs; *a.* proper; right; correct; appropriate; *v.* should; ought. **ru-**

mumbeng. (*obs.*) *v.* to sprout again. **Saan a rumbeng a pinuoram ti basura.** You should not have burned the garbage. [Tag. *tumpák* (proper); *dapat* (should)]

rúmbo: (Sp. *rumbo*: course) *n.* direction; course.

rumék: rumeken. *v.* to smash, break, shatter; pulverize; pound. **Adda sangagpa a sanga a pinangrumekna iti lateg ti nuang.** He has a branch the size of one armspan he used to pound the water buffalo's testicle. [Tag. *durog*]

rumén: irurumen. *v.* to despise; harm, injure, hurt; molest, tease, pester, torment; annoy, tire. **manangirurumen.** *a.* vicious; cruel. **marumen.** *v.* to feel disgusted; be nauseated. **makarumen.** *a.* nauseous. **panangirurumen.** *n.* persecution; slavery. **Nasaysayaat ti naimbag a gayyem ngem ti kabsat a mangirurumen.** A good friend is better than a sibling who will put you down. [Tag. *lupít*]

rumensór: see *agrumensor*: land surveyor.

rúmer: irumer. *v.* to immerse, plunge, dip into water. [Tag. *lubóg*]

roméro: (Sp. *romero*: rosemary) *n.* rosemary, kind of medicinal plant with small leaves.

rumiád: *var.* of *garumiad*: scratch. [Kal. *lagalidgichen*]

rumkuás: (f. *rukuás*) *v.* to emerge; burst out; get set and go.

rummók: narummok. *a.* dense (forest). (*samek*)

rumnéb: (f. *rennéb*) *v.* to sink (*arinebneb*). [Tag. *lubóg*]

rumúrom: mairumirom. *v.* to pitch (ships at sea).

rumpáak: (f. *ripák*) *n.* noise of breaking bamboo.

rumpég: *n.* a kind of small flattened marine fish.

rumpék: narumpek. *a.* chubby; short and stout.

rómpekabésa: (Sp. *rompecabezas*: riddle, puzzle) *n.* riddle; conundrum.

rompeólas: (Sp. *rompeolas*) *n.* breakwater.

rumpí: narumpi. *a.* red (said of the lips). (*rungpi*) **agparumpi.** *v.* to make the lips red.

rumpíis: (f. *ripíis*) *v.* to make the sound of walking on a bamboo floor with light footsteps.

rumpíteg: narumpiteg. *a.* flattened, depressed.

rumpó: see *reppó*.

rumpúog: (f. *reppúog*) *v.* to fall down; collapse; cave in.

rumsá: *n.* grasshopper; barrenness in animals. [Tag. *tipaklóng* (grasshopper)]

rumsáak: (f. *ressáak*) *v.* to waste away; wither; dry out and fall (leaves); disintegrate.

rumsík: (f. *rissík*) *v.* to sparkle; crack when breaking.

rumsuá: (f. *russuá*) *n.* new development arising from the analysis of a problem; *v.* to arise (new

growth); appear (in growth) **No dika agannad, rumsua ti di panagkikinnaawatan iti pagtaengam.** If you are not careful, misunderstandings will arise in your home.

rumtáb: (f. *rettáb*) *v.* to grow; develop (plants; skin diseases, etc.).

rúna: *see ngrúna*: important; special; especially.

rúnaw: marunaw. *v.* to melt; dissolve; waste away; be digested. **makarunaw-puso.** *a.* heartthrob; able to melt the heart. **runawen.** *v.* to melt, dissolve. **irunaw.** *v.* to dissolve in (a liquid). [Png. *tonáw*, Tag. *tunaw*]

rónda: (Sp. *ronda*: patrol, round) *n.* village guard; night patrol; round (of drinks, etc.).

rondália: (Sp. *rondalla*: fable, story) *n.* round guitar, banjo-type instrument with double strings; guitar ensemble; string orchestra.

rondílio: (Sp. *rondillo*) *n.* roller; rolling pin.

rúno: *n. Miscanthus sinensis*, bamboo grass; reed. **rimmuno.** *n.* variety of thin sugarcane with long internodes. **Baybay a Karunuan.** Red Sea (Reed Sea).

rúnot: agrunot. *v.* to rot, decay; wear out. **narunot.** *a.* worn out, worn down, decayed; rotten. **runuten.** *v.* to consume; wear out through constant use. **rumunot.** (*obs.*) *v.* to suck greedily. [Tag. *bulók*]

rúnoy: marunuyan. *v.* to be abundant. (*ruay*; *adu*)

runrón: *n.* fold, pleat. **runrunen.** *v.* to fold, pleat. [Tag. *tiklóp*, *lupí*]

rungáab: *n.* loud crying; shapeless opening. **agrungaab.** *v.* to cry loudly. **nakarungaab.** *a.* opened wide; yawning. **tuel-rungaab.** *n.* croaker fish of the *Sciaenidae* family. **Nagrungaab a nagkusaykusay.** He cried kicking. **No matay, awan a pulos ti agrungaab.** If he dies, nobody at all will cry. [Tag. *atungal*]

rung-ád: *a.* bent backward. **rung-áden.** *v.* to wring; twist violently; distort. **marung-ad.** *v.* to be twisted backward. [Tag. *pigâ*]

rungáong: *n.* cry of a hungry pig. (*nguringis*) **agrungaong.** *v.* to cry (said of a hungry pig).

rungári: (*obs.*) **rungarien.** *v.* to set afloat.

rungárong: *a.* protruding; sticking out. **rumungarong.** *v.* to stick out the head. **agrungarong.** *v.* to protrude. **Nagtugaw iti agrungrungarong a ramut.** He sat on the roots protruding from the ground. [Tag. *uslî*]

rungarungéb: (*obs.*) *n.* bodily dirt (*kabkab*). [Tag. *libág*]

rungbáb: *var.* of *rungbeb*: blunt, dull; pugnosed.

rungbéb: *a.* blunt; short; with sunken lips; pugnosed. **rumungbeb.** *v.* to become dull (*ngudel*). [Tag. *puról* (blunt)] rungbéd: narungbed. *a.* dull, blunt; with sunken lips. (*rumbed*) rumungbed. *v.* to frown. [Tag. *puról* (blunt)]

rungbó: narungbo. *a.* lavish; grand. (*garbó*; *ngayéd*)

rungdáw: *n.* sharp stub, pointed stub. (*rud-ak*) marungdaw. *v.* to be wounded or hurt by a stub. rungdawan. *a.* stubby, full of stubs.

rungdó: marungdo. *v.* to break in two by snapping (*rung-o*). rungduen. *v.* to break the bones. Narungdo ti tulang dagiti sakak gapu iti aksidente. The bones in my feet broke because of the accident. [Tag. *bali*]

rungéb: *n.* bodily dirt (*kabkáb*).

runggó: agrunggo. *v.* to gather around noisily. agrurunggo. *n.* confusion of many voices talking at once. Sapsapulem ti rungrunggo. You need some live entertainment (fun noise). Manmano met no uminomkami ta sagpaminsan met la ti kakastoy a panagrurunggomi. It is rare that we drink and we only get together noisily like this every once in a while.

rung-í: rung-ien. *v.* to wrench off, break off by twisting (*rung-o*). [Tag. *baklí*]

rungiád: *var.* of rangiád: chap, crack. [Tag. *biták*]

rungíit: *n.* grimace, grin (*ngirsi*). makarungiit. *v.* to laugh; grin. agrungiit. *v.* to grimace. Pagatlapayag ti rungiitna. His grin is from ear to ear. [Tag. *ngisi*]

rungírong: narungirong. *a.* dense (forest).

rúngo: *n.* barb (of fish); antenna (shrimps); rungorungo. *n.* kind of herb used to cure throat sicknesses; kind of small marine fish with long barbells.

rung-ó: rung-uen. *v.* to wring the neck of. (*rungdó*) marung-o. *v.* to have the neck broken. [Tag. *pigâ* (wring)]

rúngos: *n.* part of the rice stalk closest to the grains. rungusen. *v.* to cut off the ears of rice. rurungos. (*obs.*) *n.* lasting humidity.

rungpí: narungpi. *a.* red (lips). agparungpi. *v.* to apply rouge to the lips. (*rumpí*)

rungróng: *n.* stump, stub; stub of a cigarette. agrungrong. *v.* to be reduced to a stump; decay gradually (*runot*). [Tag. *upós* (cigar butt)]

rungsíit: see *rungiit*: grimace; laugh.

rungsót: *n.* fierceness, violence; cruelty. (*asing*; *dawel*; *ulpit*; *ranggas*) narungsot. *a.* cruel, quick tempered, fierce, violent. agrungsot. *v.* to be furious, raging mad, angry. [Tag. *galit*, *bagsík*]

rúok: rimmuok. *n.* pile; cluster. rumuok. *v.* to pile up (trash, flotsam, etc.). agririmmuok. *v.* to cluster together, clump together. Kasla

nagririmmuokanda nga uong. They are like clustered mushrooms. [Tag. *buntón, salansán*]

rúong: rumuong. *v.* to pile up; group together.

rúos: mangiruos. *v.* to put someone in a difficult financial position.

rúot₁: *n.* grass; weeds; litter (garbage). mangruot. *v.* to cut grass. agruot. *v.* to scatter garbage. agiruot. *v.* to cut the grass. iruotan. *v.* to pasture animals. karuotan. *n.* grassland, grassy place, weedy place. agkaruotan. *v.* to become overgrown with grass. ruot ti kalsada. *n.* vagabonds; loafers. ruot-taaw. *n.* seaweed. Iruotam dagiti nuang tapno adda kanenda no manglayus. Pasture the water buffalo on the grass so they will have food when it floods. Awan ti serserbi ti ruot no matayen ti kabalio. *exp.* Grass is of no use when the horse is dead (money can't be taken to the grave). [Ibg. *keddoq*, Itg. *luut*, Ivt. *dibubut*, Kal. *luut, sagamsam*, Knk. *lóot*, Kpm. *dikut*, Png. *diká*, Tag. *damó*]

rúot₂: tagiruot. *n.* charm; talisman. tagiruoten. *v.* to cast a spell on using a charm; seduce, entice. [Tag. *agimat*]

rúpa: *n.* face; façade; front; title page. rupa ti dapan. *n.* side of the foot. irupaan. *v.* to recognize by the face. mairupaan. *v.* to be able to recognize by one's face. iparupa. *v.* to speak against a person to his face; position in the front. mairupa. *v.* to show in one's face. rupanrupa. *a.* face-to-face. agkaruprupa. *v.* to resemble each other. karuprupan. *n.* one that has a similar face to. parupa. *n.* façade; front room; showpiece; headline news. parupa a damdamag. *n.* headline news. parupa a silaw. *n.* headlight. ta rupam! Exclamation expressing shame against boldness of the person it is addressed to. mairupaan. *a.* able to be recognized by the face. rupaan a buneng. *n.* curved-edge bolo; straight edged is called *rapad*. agrupa. *v.* to show in one's face. pagkarkarupaan. *n.* features, facial similarities. mangindarupa. *v.* to show the emotion's in one's face. Adda pay la gayam rupayo nga agpakita ditoy kalpasan ti panangliputyo kaniak. You really have the nerve to show yourself here after your treachery toward me. Kasla agruprupa a kuarta. He has the face of money (describing a grasping person). [Ibg. *mutung*, Itg. *tamel*, Ivt. *danguy, muyin*, Kal. *lupa, buseÿ*, Kpm., Png. *lúpa*, Tag. *mukhâ*]

rúpak: *n.* battle. (*gubat*) agrupak. *v.* to clash, collide. (*dalapon*; *dungpar*) makirupak. *v.* to go to battle with; fight with. Sika laeng ti makatulong kaniak iti umay a rupakko. Only you can help me in my next battle. [Tag. *sagupà, digmâ*]

rupangét: *n.* frowning. (*murareg*; *misuot*; *rungbed*) **agrupanget.** *v.* to scowl, frown. **narupanget.** *a.* frowning; stern. **rupangetan.** *v.* to frown at. [Tag. *simangot*]

rupanggá: **agrupangga.** *v.* to argue. **rupanggaen.** *v.* to resist, oppose; contradict; disobey; violate. **mairupangga.** *v.* to oppose, contradict; be in disagreement. **Sakbay a makapagrinnupanggada, kinayetketan ni Lelong ni Lelang.** Before they were able to argue with each other, Grandfather embraced Grandmother. [Tag. *away*]

rúped: see *raped*: snap; break in two.

rúpeng: *a.* flat (nose) (*lugpák*). [Tag. *pangó*]

ropéro: (Sp. *ropero*: hamper) *n.* hamper; hat rack.

rúpid: *var.* of *rúped*: snap, break in two.

rúpig: **narupig.** *a.* destroyed, wrecked (car). [Tag. *sirâ*]

rupikár: (Sp. *repique*: chime) *var.* of *rupiki*: tolling of bells, chime.

rupíki: (Sp. *repique*: chime) *n.* chime, peal of bells. (*repike*) **agrupiki.** *v.* to ring (church bells, etc.).

rúpir: *n.* debate; discussion. (*debate*; *subang*) **i-rupir.** *v.* to defend, fight for one's right; maintain a point; insist; demand. **makirupir.** *v.* to debate, discuss. **rupiren.** *v.* to strive to do; exert one's efforts to do; surpass; outdo; threaten. **Pinalabasna ti limapulo a tawen iti biagna a nangirupir ti pannakawayawaya ti daga a tinubuanna.** He spent fifty years of his life defending freedom in the land where he grew up.

rúpis: *n.* number, count; counter (something that aids in counting). (*bilang*) **agrupis.** *v.* to count using counters. **rupisan.** *v.* to count carefully.

rupúrop: **rupurupen.** *v.* to cut straight without chips; cut across.

ruppók: **ruppuken.** *v.* to snap, break in two (*tukkól*). [Tag. *baklî*]

rupsá: **agrupsa.** *v.* to decay (*rupsó*). [Tag. *bulók*]

rupsó: **marupso.** *v.* to decay, rot, spoil (*lungsot*; *tubeg*; *dugmuy*; *duted*; *dersay*; *dor-oy*). [Tag. *bulók*]

ruród: *n.* anger; disgust; resentment. (*pungtot*, *gura*) **marurod.** *a.* angry, enraged, furious. **makarurod.** *v.* to be angry. **makaparurod.** *a.* disgusting, causing anger, annoying. **karurod.** *v.* to resent, be angry at. **ruruden.** *v.* to mock, ridicule, taunt, sneer at; irritate. **Maruroden iti kanayon a panangipalagipda ti panangasawada.** He is angry about them constantly reminding him about their wedding. [Png. *pasnók*, *aloboob*, Tag. *galit*]

ruróg: *n.* skeleton; (*reg.*) skull. **rumurog.** *v.* to become a skeleton. [Tag. *kalansáy*]

ruróng: *n.* large variety of poisonous land snail.

rurós: **rurusen.** *v.* to pick, gather; pluck, pull off with the fingers (*puros*); husk corn; to fall down one after the other. **Naruros dagiti nagango a bulong.** The dried leaves fell down one after another. [Tag. *pitás*, *labnót* (pick); *hulog* (fall)]

rurrón: *n.* cords connecting the heddles and the treadles in the harness of a hand loom; pleats of a shirt collar. **rurrunen.** *v.* to plait.

rósa: (Sp. *rosa*) *n.* rose (general term is *rosas*). **rosa de Hapon.** pink rose. **rosa amarilia.** yellow rose.

rosál: (Sp. *rosal*: rose bush) *n.* gardenia flower.

rusangér: *n.* coarseness, roughness. **narusanger.** *a.* rough (not smooth); coarse. **rumusanger.** *v.* to become coarse, rough. [Tag. *gaspáng*, *gasláw*]

rosário: (Sp. *rosario*: rosary) *n.* rosary. **agrosario.** *v.* to pray the rosary. **santo rosario.** *n.* holy rosary.

rósas: (Sp. *rosa*: rose) *n.* rose; the color pink. **derosas.** *a.* pink. **dumerosas.** *v.* to become pink; blush. **rosas de Hapón.** *n.* chrysanthemum.

rúsat: *n.* something started. **irusat.** *v.* to begin, set about, start, commence (*rukuás*; *rugí*; *dulnó*; *wáyat*). [Tag. *simulâ*]

rusbáw: **mairusbaw.** *v.* to sink, fall into the ground (*rusbóng*). **irusbaw.** *v.* to plunge into the ground, dig the earth.

rusbóng: **mairusbong.** *v.* to fall into a hole, sink into the ground (*rusbáw*); (*fig.*) to be tricked (*libsóng*); trapped. **Ita agbabawikan ngem dita abut nairusbongkan.** Now you repent but you're already trapped in that hole.

rusbóy: **marusboy.** *a.* robust; healthy (*rukbós*). [Tag. *lagô*]

rusdangí: *n.* grin, grimace (*ngirsí*). **agrusdangi.** *v.* to grimace, grin. [Tag. *ngisi*]

rusdingí: *var.* of *rusdangí*: grin, grimace.

rusdók: *n.* high, pointed roof.

rúsep: **narusep.** *a.* drenched, soaked. **rusepen.** *v.* to soak, drench, saturate. **Marusep dagiti ubbing iti ling-et iti agpatnag.** The children are drenched in sweat from (playing) all night. [Png. *talem*, Tag. *tigmák*, *babad*, *pigtâ*]

rúsing: *n.* seedling; shoot; new growth. **agrusing.** *v.* to germinate, shoot up. **pagrusingen.** *v.* to cause to germinate. **rumusing.** *v.* to bud, germinate; have the first feelings for. **karusrusing.** *a.* newly sprouted; newly felt. **Adda imon a rimmusing iti kaungganna.** Jealousy arose inside him. **Ikarkararagko a rumusingto ti panagayatmo kaniak.** I pray that your love for me will germinate. [Kal. *simit*, Png. *palakay*, Tag. *punlâ* (seedling)]

rusísi: see *parusisi*: stumble; totter.

roskáldo: *var.* of *aroskaldo*: rice porridge.

róskas: (Sp. *roscas*: thread of a screw) *n.* thread of a screw. **roskasen.** *v.* to thread a screw. [Tag. *roskas*, Kpm. *roskas* = screw]

rusngí: *a.* reverse; contradictory. **irusngi, rusngien.** *v.* to invert the position of; move to the original position; slightly move out of place, compare with *barusngi*; oppose, contradict. **narusngi.** *a.* out of position. [Tag. *tiwarík*]

rusngíit: *n.* grimace. *(ngirsi)* **irusngiit.** *v.* to grimace. [Tag. *ngisi*]

Rúso: (Sp. *ruso*: Russian) *n.* Russian. **ag-Ruso.** *v.* to speak Russian.

rusód₁: *n.* steep bank; cliff; precipice. **agrusod.** *v.* to fall; drop. **irusod.** *v.* to drop, throw down. **rusod ti tudo.** *n.* rainfall. **marusudan.** *v.* to be hit by a falling log. **rusodanan ti agdan.** *n.* foot of a staircase. [Tag. *hulog* (fall)]

rusód₂: **rusudan.** *v.* to mix, alloy.

rúsok: *n.* epigastrium, pit of the stomach; abdomen; concavity. **rurusuken.** *v.* to eructate fetidly. **makarurusok.** *a.* nauseating. **di mairusok.** cannot stomach it, cannot stand it. **marurusok.** *v.* to feel like vomiting. **rusok ti dapan.** *n.* lower part of the instep. **rusok ti ubet.** *n.* depression at the side of the buttocks. **Pagatrusok ti bussogda.** They are very satisfied (from eating).

rusúros: **agrusuros.** *v.* to rub, chafe, gall. *(gidígid)*

rúsot: *n.* a kind of small white mollusk that burrows in sunken wood; shipworm.

ruspinggí: **ruspinggien.** *v.* to wrench violently.

rusrús: **rusrusen.** *v.* to slip down, lower a garment in a hurry without unfastening or unbuttoning.

russuá: **rumsua.** *v.* to happen; come to pass; come in sight; become visible; reveal or show oneself. **parsua.** *n.* creature; creation. **parsuaen.** *v.* to create, cause to exist. **mamarsua.** *n.* creator; inventor. **nakaparsuaan.** *n.* nature; *a.* natural. [Png. *lesá*, Tag. *likhâ*]

russuát: *n.* project; objective, aim. *(panggep)* **irussuat.** *v.* to begin, commence, initiate; get set.

russúod: (f. *risód*) *n.* base of a steep cliff; *var.* of *rissuod*: collapse. **marsuod.** *v.* to collapse, fall in. **rumsuod.** *v.* to enter and leave the house

repeatedly; to make a thundering sound when crumbling. [Tag. *guhò*]

rústika: (Sp. *rústica*: paperbacked) *n.* paperback, paper cover of a book; *a.* paperback bound (said of books).

róta: (Sp. *ruta*: route) *n.* route; itinerary.

rutáp: *n.* fold, layer; lining of a garment. **rutapan.** *v.* to line a garment. **rutapen.** *v.* to fold; patch up. **agrurutap.** *v.* to lie one above another, to stand in rows or lines; to layer. **nagrutap.** *a.* doubled, folded. (garment) **agrurutap a mapampanunotna.** his thoughts are muddled. [Tag. *sapín* (layer)]

rútay: **agrutay.** *v.* to become tattered. **rutayrutay.** *a.* shabby, ragged, tattered, shredded. **rutayrutayan.** *a.* wearing shabby, ragged clothes. *(pisangpisang)* **marutay.** *v.* to be torn to shreds. [Tag. *gutáy, gulanít*]

rutína: (Sp. *rutina*: routine) *n.* routine.

rúting: *n.* bud; splinter, sliver; strip of wood. **rumuting.** *v.* to germinate, shoot. **Kinaykayna dagiti nagango a ruot ken ruting sana sineggedan.** He swept the dried grasses and shoots and then set them afire. [Tag. *siból*]

rutók: **rumutok.** *v.* to swarm; school (fish); teem with (ants, worms, bees, etc.) *(pangen; taklong; gateb; dalaidi)*. [Tag. *kawan*]

rótulo: (Sp. *rótulo*: lettering, label, tag) *n.* inscription on the cross or a grave.

rotúnda: (Sp.) *n.* rotunda; circular building; circular road.

rútong: *n.* protuberance on some fruits. **rumutong.** *v.* to protrude. **rutongrutongan.** *a.* with many protuberances. **Agrurutong 'ta kamuro 'ta rupam.** Your face is filled with pimples (protruding). [Tag. *bukol*]

rutrót: *a.* threadbare, tattered, ragged. *(rutayrutay)* **marutrutan.** *v.* to become worn out. [Tag. *punít-punít*]

ruttók: *var.* of *rittók*: sound of cracking joints.

ruttúok: (f. *ruttók*) *n.* cracking of a joint *(rittók, ruttók)*. [Tag. *putók*]

ruyág: *n.* wide spreading growth of branches. *(rangpaya)* **agruyag.** *v.* to spread out (branches), spread out and overhang; droop downward.

rúyot: **maruyot.** *v.* to be burdened with, loaded with; bear a lot of fruit in one season.

ruyrúy: **agruyruy.** *v.* to be frayed, worn out at the edges. *(suysóy)*

S

sa₁: *adv.* so; then; probably; I think so; **Nagpalpa pay** *sa* **nagawid.** He rested after eating first, then went home; Interjection used to drive away a cat. **santo maysa.** *adv.* in addition to; besides. [Tag. *tapos*]

sa₂: *encl.* (*-nsa* after vowels). probably; I think so. **We***n* **sa.** Yes I think so. **Mapanda***n* **sa.** I think they'll go. **Kayatdatay** *sa***n a patayen.** I think they want to kill us. [Tag. *akalà ko, yatà*]

sáad: *n.* condition; position; status. **agsaad.** *v.* to be in the position to. **kasasaad.** *n.* condition, position, employment, status; situation. **isaad.** *v.* to put, locate, set; appoint; assign. **saad ti mata.** *n.* eye socket. **pagsaadan.** *n.* location, spot, site where something happened. **maisaad.** *v.* to be appointed; to be assigned; set. **Saanmo a basol ti kasasaadmo.** You are not to blame for your condition. **Dumtengto ti panawen a nangatngato ti danum ti karayan ngem iti daga a nakaisaadan ti ili a Palanan.** The time will come when the water from the river is higher than the land where the town of Palanan is. [Knk. *tée*, Png. *kipapasen*, Tag. *lagáy, tungkulin*]

sáal: *n.* sandbank; protuberance. **maisaal.** *v.* to ground; strand. **masaal.** *v.* to be inconvenienced or obstructed by a protuberance; to be stranded. [Tag. *bukol* (protuberance)]

saán: *neg.* no (see also negative *di-* prefix); clause negator. **saan man.** Yes. (in answer to a negative question) **agsaan.** *v.* to answer negatively. **aginsasaan.** *v.* to pretend to deny. **Saansa.** I don't think so. **saanen.** no more; not now; never mind; not any longer. **aginsasaan.** *v.* to pretend to say no. **saan ketdi + N.** rather than; instead of. **Saanak a kasdiay.** I am not like that. **Saanka nga agsangit!** Don't cry. [Bon. *baked* (nouns), *adi*, Knk. *adí*, Png. *andí*, Tag. *hindî* (non-command), *huwág* (command)]

saáni: *n.* irony.

saanmán: (also *saan man*). Answers affirmatively to a negative question: Yes I will (on the contrary to what you said).

sáang: *n.* pot of food cooked over the heat of the stove; one quantity of food to be cooked. **isaang.** *v.* to put something on the fire. **pagsaangan.** *n.* support for a jar or pan put over fire. **sangasaangan.** *n.* period of time required to cook rice; one serving of cooked rice enough for a meal. **Nangisaangak iti danum a pagkapemi.** I put the water on the fire for our coffee. [Ibg. *magafi, tallág* Ivt.

mangapuy, Kpm. *manese*, Png. *ilar*, Tag. *saing, salang*]

sáaw: **agsaaw.** *v.* to act inconsiderately or haphazardly. **masaaw.** *v.* to fail, miss; miscarry; be frustrated. **saawen.** *v.* to do haphazardly. [Tag. *bigô*]

sába: **masaba.** *v.* to restrain, repress; avoid; be able to bear (hardship); able to take it. [Tag. *tiís* (bear)]

sabá: *n.* banana; (cooking banana = *dippig*). **sabaan.** *v.* to use bananas in cooking. **sinabaan.** *n.* banana grove. **kasabaan.** *n.* banana grove. **mar(a)saba.** *n.* ripe tamarind. **sabatnuang, saba ti nuang.** *n.* variety of small sweet banana. [Bol. *batag*, Ibg. *dupoq*, Itg. *suba*, Ivt. *viñiveh*, Kal. *byaÿat*, Knk. *báat*, Kpm. *sagin*, Png. *pónti*, Tag. *saging*, Tag. *sabá* = species of cooking banana]

sábad: **nasabad.** *a.* restless. (*kutikuti*)

sábado: (Sp. *sábado*: Saturday) *n.* Saturday. **Sabado de Gloria.** The Saturday before Easter. **sinabado, kada sabado.** every Saturday. [Kal. *sabechu*]

sábag: **mannabag.** *v.* to be deceitful, dishonest. **sinabagan.** *a.* acquired fraudulently. **sabagen.** *v.* to cheat; deceive; do dishonestly. (*kusit*)

sabágay: (Tag.) *conj.* anyway; therefore.

sabák: **sinabak.** *a.* false, deceptive. **sabaken.** *n.* pattern, preliminary sketch. [Tag. *huwád*]

sabákir: **makasabakir.** *v.* to be unpleasant smelling.

sábal: **sabalen.** *v.* to dig (*kali*); dig out of the soil; loosen the soil.

sabáli: *a.* other, another; separate; diverse, different; someone else, something else. (*supadi; salumina; giddiat; baliw*) **agsabali.** *v.* to become different; to change. **agsasabali.** *v.* to be changing; messy; confused. **agsabasabali.** *v.* to be changing; to be unsystematic. **sabalian.** *v.* to change something; do again. **sabali nga ili, sabali nga ugali.** Different nations have different customs. **sangkasabali.** *n.* different group; different part; *a.* changing often. **sabali laeng + N.** apart from. [Ibg. *tanakuwan*, Ivt. *tarek*, Kal. *sabyali*, Knk. *tekén*, Kpm. *aliwa*, Png. *sananéy, duma*, Tag. *ibá*]

sabanás: (Sp. *sábana*: sheet) *n.* bed sheet.

sabanión: (Sp. *sabañón*: chilblain) *n.* chilblain.

sábang: *n.* broadness; width; corpulence. **nasabang.** *a.* corpulent, husky; massive; stout. **Sinaltaanna ti nasabang a bukot ti nuang.** He hopped on the husky back of the water buffalo. [Tag. *lapad*]

sabángan: *n.* mouth of a river, harbor, etc. (*minanga*) **sumabangan.** *v.* to go to the mouth of a river. [Png. *sabáng*]

sábar: sabarsabar. *n.* kind of shrub similar to the *basarbásar.*

sábat: *n.* welcome; greeting; meeting of a person. **sumabat, sabten.** *v.* to meet (or greet) a friend. (*sabet*) **agsabat.** *v.* to meet; agree. **agsinnabat.** *v.* to meet each other; agree with each other (*nagsinnabat ti panagkinnita*). **pagsabaten.** *v.* to negotiate on behalf of; to make both ends meet. **pagsabatan.** *n.* meeting place. **kasabat.** *n.* person one meets. **pannakasabat.** *n.* welcome. **Simmabat ti anaw-aw dagiti aso idi lumaemak iti purok.** The howls of the dogs greeted me when I entered the village. [Bon. *abat, abet,* Knk. *sib-át,* Tag. *salubong*]

sabát: *n.* spear, harpoon (*gayang; pika; gusud; dúrus; turág*). [Tag. *sibát*]

sab-át: isab-at. *v.* to carry on the shoulder.

Sabatísta: (Sp.) *n.* Sabbatist.

sabatnuáng: [*saba ti nuang*] *n.* variety of small sweet banana.

sabáwil: *n. Mucuna pruriens* vine with hairy pods and dark purple flowers; *Mucuna lyonii* vine with edible beans. **makasabawil.** *v.* to cause itching (*gatel*). **sabawilan.** *v.* to cause itching by inflicting someone with *sabawil.* **Armenda ken sabawilanda kano pay ti tugawna.** They courted her and they also supposedly put *sabawil* vines on her chair to cause itching.

sábay: *n.* lace, fringe; *Paspalum sp.* grasses.

sabáy: agsabay. *v.* to act simultaneously; to go, do, etc. together. (*giddan*) **sabayan.** *v.* to accompany; go together. [Tag. *sabáy*]

sabbádaw: agsabbadaw. *v.* to stumble, stagger, totter (*bariring; dawiris; duir; basíng*). [Tag. *suray*]

sabbikél: isabbikel. *v.* to insert something in one's waistband. [Png., Tag. *sukbít*]

sabbuág: isabbuag. *v.* to cast; throw; cast a gamecock at the opponent.

sabbúkay: sabbukayen. *v.* to revive; reanimate; recall, bring back to the memory. **masabbukay.** *v.* to revive; flare up (anger).

sábeng: sinabeng. *n.* shutter used to close the *balawbáw.*

sabéng: nasabeng. *n.* having the stench of certain fruits. **nasabeng nga isem.** *n.* sour smile.

sabét: *n.* religious ritual portraying the meeting of Christ and the Virgin Mary after resurrection. **sumabet.** *v.* to meet someone arriving. **sabten.** *v.* to meet someone. **agsabet.** *v.* to meet (each other), approach from different directions. **isabet.** *v.* to present something to someone upon arrival. **masabet.** *v.* to meet with, encounter, find. **panabtan.** *n.* meeting place;

rendezvous. **apagsabet (ti luto).** half-cooked. [Bon. *abet,* Tag. *salubong*]

sábi: sumabi. *v.* to reach the top (in order to carry the day). [Tag. *sabi* = say]

sabidóko: sabsabidoko. *n.* variety of small, white edible flower.

sabidúkong: *n.* kind of edible herb, see *sabiduko.*

sabídong: *n.* poison; venom. (*gamut; samal*) **nasabidongan.** *a.* poisoned. **makasabidong.** *a.* poisonous; malignant. **sabidongan.** *v.* to poison someone; (*fig.*) pollute the mind. **Saanmo kuma a sabidongan ti riknak.** You shouldn't poison my feelings. [Knk. *giwáday, kadét,* Png. *samál,* Tag. *lason*]

sabikél: isabikel. *v.* to girdle; insert something in one's waistband. (*salikád; sabbikel*) [Png., Tag. *sukbít*]

sabilá: *n.* the aloe vera plant, used in traditional medicine to treat burns, wounds, and shedding hair.

sabilúkok: *n.* kind of small herb.

sábing: pasabing. *n.* kind of wickerwork trap for fish.

sábir: maisabir. *v.* to be caught while falling down. (*salat*)

sábit: sabitan. *v.* to pin a medal on.

sab-ít: *n.* hook; hanger. **isab-it.** *v.* to hang from a hook, hook. **maisab-it.** *v.* to be hooked; to be delayed on the way due to meeting friends. **sasab-itan.** *n.* peg, hanger, hook, rack (of hooks); ritual dance at a wedding consisting of pinning money on the married couple in exchange for a dance. **Naisab-it ti ladawanna iti diding.** His picture was hooked on the wall. [Png. *sagór,* Tag. *kawit, sabitán*]

sabláy: sabsablay. *n.* kind of sea urchin whose spines are used as a diuretic. **agsablay.** *v.* to miss; miss the mark.

sablí: (Sp. *sable:* sable) *n.* sword. (*kampilan*)

sablóg: pasablogan. *v.* to catch fish with a small amount of poison; to irrigate with a small amount of water; to coax, cajole. **pasablog.** *n.* flattery; the act of catching fish with poison.

sablót: *n. Litsea glutinosa* tree with small, yellowish flowers whose leaves are used for mortar.

sabó: sabuan. *v.* to sprinkle with water. (*sayo*) **masabuan.** *v.* to be sprinkled with water. [Tag. *saboy*]

sabuág: isabuag. *v.* to cast something at one's opponent; to cast earth out of a hole in the ground. **masabuagan.** *v.* to be splashed by a breaking wave; to be sprinkled with dirt. **sabuagan.** *n.* breakwater; *v.* to throw (water, dirt) at someone. [Kal. *passak,* Tag. *saboy*]

sabuáng: *var.* of *sabuag*.

sabuét: see *sabét*: meet.

sábog: *n. Setaria italica*, Italian millet.

sabúg: *a.* (slang) high on drugs. **desabog**. *(fam.)* *n.* machine gun; shotgun.

sabók: **agsabsabok**. *v.* to splash water at one another; scatter. *(sayo)*

sab-ók: *n.* tucked up skirt or shirt used to carry items; lap (for carrying). **sab-uken**. *v.* to carry, catch, etc. in one's lap, apron. **isab-ok**. *v.* to put in one's lap, apron, etc. **sisasab-ok**. *a.* pregnant; tucked in one's skirt, apron, etc. **sinab-ok**. *n.* fetus; that which is tucked up one's skirt, shirt, etc. **Sisasab-ok ti babai kadagiti nadumaduma a kita ti sabong.** The girl had several kinds of flowers tucked in her skirt.

sabúlod: *(obs.)* *n.* rattan ring.

sabón: (Sp. *jabón*: soap) *n.* soap. *(kotabáw)* **agsabon**. *v.* to wash with soap; to make soap. **sabonen**. *v.* to soap something; *(fig.)* to scold for a fault, to chastise verbally. **sabonan**. *v.* to soap someone, apply soap to; *n.* soap container; soap factory. **sabonsabon**. *a.* thoroughly lathered in soap.

sábong: *n.* flower; petals; blossom; *(fig.)* female genitalia. **agsabong**. *v.* to blossom; bear flowers. **mannabung**. *n.* kind of black and red bumblebee. **sabongen**. *v.* to pay court to. **sabung ti kukó**. *n.* lunula of the nail. **sabsabongen**. *n.* maiden being courted. **sabong-sabongan**. *a.* flowered. **sinabongan**. *n.* filigree. **nasabsabongan**. *a.* flowery. **No adda sabsabong, agaarak dagiti kulibangbang.** Where there are flowers, there are butterflies. [Ibg. *lappáw*, Ifg. *lappaw*, Ivt. *savusavung*, Kal. *sabong*, Knk. *bengá*, Kpm. *sampaga*, Png. *rosas*, Png., Tag. *bulaklák*]

sab-óng: *n.* dowry (given by man to bride). *(panab-ong)* **isab-ong**. *v.* to give as a dowry. **sabongan**. *v.* to give a dowry to someone. [Png. *dasél*, Tag. *bigáy-kaya*, *dote* (Sp.)]

sabóngan: *n.* cockpit. *(pallotan)*

sabungánay: *n.* edible unopened flower cluster of banana; end of G-string. **agsabunganay**. *v.* to have an unopened flower cluster (said of the banana) **sabsabunganay**. *n.* riblike parts under crab shell. **simmabunganay**. *a.* shaped like an unopened flower cluster of the banana plant (referring to muscular legs or arms). **simmabunganay a gurong**. *n.* attractive legs (like a banana cluster). [Tag. *pusò ng saging*; Knk. *sabongánay* = hangnail]

sabór: (Sp. *sabor*: taste) **nasabor**. *a.* tasty, delicious. *(imas)*

sabóray: *(obs.)* *n.* kind of jar imported from Borneo.

sabót: *n.* half a coconut shell used as a container *(abaab)*; coconut shell. **sabotsabot**. *n.* cranium, brain case. **sabsabot**. *n.* coconut shell. **sabsabot ti ulo**. *n.* skull. **sabotan**, see *pangdán*: the screw pine. **sinnabot**. *n.* girl's game played with pebbles and coconut shell. **bantay-sabot**. *n.* "it" in a game *(lit:* guarder of the coconut shell).

sabotáhe: (Sp. *sabotaje*: sabotage) *n.* sabotage.

sabrák: **agsabrak**. *v.* to swear (saying bad words); be impolite. **nasabrak**. *a.* rude, impolite; vulgar; swearing; violent. **kinasabrak**. *n.* insolence; rudeness; violence; cruelty. [Tag. *dahás*]

sabróng: **sabsabrong**. *n. Asclepias sp.* weed used for medicinal purposes.

sabrót: *n.* profit; redemption. **sabruten**. *v.* to recover (a loss); make up for; compensate for; retrieve; redeem. [Tag. *bawì*]

sabsáb: (Hok. *sàp sàp*: eat like hog) **sumabsab**. *v.* to gulp down, guzzle; munch down; eat voraciously. **sabsaben**. *v.* to guzzle; gulp down food. **agsabsab**. *v.* to eat noisily (as a pig). [Tag. *sabsáb*]

sáda₁: *n.* ambuscade; meeting people coming from the farms in order to buy produce at wholesale. **agsada**. *v.* to buy farm produce wholesale by meeting farmers on the way to market; to wait for a passenger bus on the highway. **sadaen**. *v.* to ambush *(abang; saed)*; halt, stop.

sáda₂: *(obs.)* *n.* seal; mark.

sádag: *n.* support; back rest, **agsadag**. *v.* to lean, incline; rest. **isadag**. *v.* to lean on a support. *(sanggir)* **marasinadag**. *a.* leaning, sloping, not erect. **Masapul nga agsadagak iti pangngeddengko.** I must support my decision. [Tag. *sandál*]

sadág: **sumadag**. *v.* to be suitable, right, fit, just, fair (used in negative constructions). *(bagay)*

sádak: *n. Ichnocarpus ovatifolius* vine with white flowers used for binding. **sinádak**. *(obs.)* *n.* sprout, young branch.

sadák: **sadaken**. *v.* to trample; step on. *(baddek; páyat)*

sádap: *n.* suspicion. *(atap)* **sadapen**. *v.* to suspect. [Tag. *alinlangan*]

sádar: **agkasadar**. *v.* to be of the same age. *(agkatawen; taeb)* **Agkasadarda.** They are contemporaries. [Tag. *kapanahón*]

sádaw: **masadaw**. *v.* to be foiled, frustrated; thwarted; to fail. [Tag. *tuliró*]

sad-áy: **sad-ayen**. *v.* to hang. **nakasad-ay**. *a.* hanging.

sádeng: *n.* kind of net used for catching marine fish. **agsadeng**. *v.* to catch fish (sardines) using the *sadeng* net.

sadéng: *n.* fence used to prevent heap of fuel from breaking down; kind of four-legged stand for storing pillows, etc.

sadér: sumader. (*obs.*) *v.* to be higher, taller. (*tayag*)

sadí: *prep.* (used with locatives) to, at, in (*sadiay, idiay*). [Png. *ed sa*, Tag. *sa*]

sadiá₁: *n.* charm; elegance; well-being; freshness; gentleness. **nasadia.** *a.* kind; gentle; meek; suave; bland; fine; elegant; soft (color). [Tag. *galíng, buti*]

sadiá₂: (*coll.*, Tag. *sadyâ*) **sadiaen.** *v.* to do on purpose. (*gagara*) **Siguro sinadiam daytoy nga inaramid tapno agap-apakami.** You probably did this on purpose so we would fight.

sadiáy: distal locative; there, far from both speaker and hearer (*idiay*). [Tag. *doón*]

sadimpainék: *a.* remote, distant (*adayo*). [Tag. *layó*]

sadína: (*obs.*) *a.* finished (*nalpas*). [Tag. *tapós*]

sadíno: *interrog.* where? (*adino*) **Sadino ti nagturogam idi kalman?** Where did you sleep yesterday? [Ibg. *sitáw*, Ivt. *dinu*, Png. *inér*, Tag. *saán*]

sadíri: pagsadirian, sadiri. *n.* prop, support; guard; moral support; shelter, refuge. **isadiri.** *v.* to use as a support, protection, etc. (*kamang*) [Tag. *tanggól; sarili* = self]

sadírit: *n.* variety of awned late rice with dark hull and white kernel.

sadísmo: (Sp.) *n.* sadism.

sadísta: (Sp.) *n.* sadist.

sadíwa: nasadiwa. *a.* fresh (meat or fish); raw (wound). **sumadiwa.** *v.* to become fresh. **kinasadiwa.** *n.* freshness. [Png. *taríwa*, Tag. *sariwà*]

sadukáng: see *dukáng*: bulky.

sadúl: *n.* line from which several nooses hang used to catch birds; kind of tool used to till the soil.

sadút: *n.* lazy person (*bantot; dugmel; ginad; kudad; betbet; kamol; kuliwengweng; kulengleng; lunákol; mattiadok; tamlag*) **nasadut.** lazy, slothful, idle. **masadut.** *v.* to have no appetite of will. **sasadut.** *n.* hangnail. **agsasadut.** *v.* to become languid; lose strength. [Ibg. *talakag, tammag*, Ifg. *híga, mangidlu*, Ivt. *talakak*, Kal. *sachut*, Knk. *bidús, tángad, sadút, tanglá, sokpút, tuttút*, Png. *soyát, ngíras, kémeg*, Kpm., Tag. *tamád*]

sadsád: maisadsad. *v.* to strand, ground. **sadsadan.** *v.* safe place to strand oneself in a swift river. **Nakagin-awa idi maisadsad ti murdong ti rakit iti kabatuan.** *n.* He was relieved when the tip of the raft stranded on the rocky coastline. [Ibg. *dakká*, Tag. *sadsád*]

saéd: agsaed. *v.* to ambush, lie in wait for. (*saneb; abang; sada*) **saeden.** *v.* to waylay, ambush; block. [Tag. *abáng*]

saél: masael. *v.* to be bored; annoyed (*uma*) **makasael.** *a.* tedious, boring; annoying.

saém: nasaem. *a.* sharp, acute, pungent; deep (wound); stinging, biting; abusive. **kinasaem.** *n.* painfulness. **Masapul a mangwaksi iti saem.** It is necessary to forget the pain. [Tag. *hapdî, kirót*]

saéng: *a.* feebleminded; slow (retarded).

saép: sumaep. *v.* to smell (dogs); sniff. **saepan.** *v.* to fumigate; sniff; snoop. **Agsaepsaep dagiti aso a kimmamang iti kasamekan.** The dogs sniffed around, taking shelter in the dense undergrowth. [Tag. *amóy*]

saét: *n.* industry, hard work. (*gagét*) **nasaet.** *a.* industrious, hard-working. **saetan.** *v.* to do diligently. **Isu idi ti kasaetan kadagiti nagrayo kenkuana.** He was the most diligent of her courters.[Tag. *sipag*]

sagCV-: *pref.* used to form distributives. **saggaysa.** one each. **sagdudua.** two each. [Png. *san(CV)-*, Tag. *tig-*]

sag- -en: Affix used with numeric roots to indicate how many things are to be done at one time. **saggaysaen.** *v.* to do one at a time. **saglilimaen.** to do five at a time.

sagá: nasagasaga. *a.* disarranged; confused. (*kuso*) **sagaen.** *v.* to throw in disorder.

sagába₁: *n.* suffering. (*tuok*) **agsagaba.** *v.* to suffer. **sagabaen.** *v.* to undergo, suffer; endure, experience; sustain. **panagsagaba.** *n.* suffering **Kayatmo kadi nga agsagsagabaka agingga iti tungpal biagmo?** Do you want to suffer your whole life? [Tag. *dusa*]

sagába₂: *n.* large dike or dam used to divert the flow of water (larger than a *tambak*). **sagabaan.** *v.* to provide with a dike.

sagabásab: *n.* mild fever; rise in body temperature. (*gurigor*) **agsagabasab, sagabasaben.** *v.* to suffer a fever; undergo a slight rise in body temperature. [Tag. *sinat*]

ságad: *n.* broom, sweeping implement; harrow; *molave* tree. **sagaden.** *v.* to sweep dirt. **sagadan.** *v.* to sweep floors, etc. **parasagad.** *n.* sweeper; person whose responsibility is to sweep. **isagadko ti presiok kenka.** I will sell it to you at a low price (with no profit). [Ibg. *kagég*, Ivt. *vuyas*, Kal. *saged*, Knk. *sígid*, Kpm. *palis*, Png. *pánis*, Tag. *walís*]

sagád: *n.* harrow. (*moriski; suyod; palpal*) **pasagad.** *n.* sled, sledge pulled by the *guyódan* rope. [Tag. *paragos*]

sagadák: *n.* offspring; *a.* pure.

sagadsád: sumagadsad. *v.* to run aground. (*sadsad*) **agsagadsad.** *v.* to act, do, etc. in succession. **sagadsaden.** *v.* to do in succession. **Palugodannak kuma nga agpalawag ti panagsasagadsad dagiti pasamak manipud pinanawannak.** Please allow me to explain the succession of events since you left me. [Tag. *sadsád*]

sagága: *n.* kind of edible sea urchin; kind of elongated marine fish with dark coloring. **isagaga.** (*obs.*) *v.* to protect a sore part of the body.

sagagéng: agsagageng. *v.* to turn the eyes away from something offensive or painful (*baw-ing*). [Tag. *baling*]

sag-ák: isag-ak. *v.* to clear the throat (with phlegm, stuck food, etc.). [Kpm. *tigím*, Tag. *tikhím, dahak* (phlegm)]

sagála: (Sp. *zagala*: young shepherdess) *n.* maiden in festive costume in religious processions.

sagalério: *var.* of *sigarilio*: cigarette.

sagamantíka: *n.* ancient wedding dance of Pangasinan.

sagána: *n.* preparations. **agsagana.** *v.* to prepare; put things in order. **isagana.** *v.* to prepare, make something ready. **saganaen.** *v.* to prepare, arrange, make ready. **nakasagana.** *a.* ready. **managsagana.** *a.* always prepared. **Diak kayat ti maigalut a di nakasagana.** I do not like to tie up what is not prepared. [Kal. *iyala, lapeÿti*, Png. *sagána*, Tag. *handâ*]

saganád: sumaganad. *v.* to follow, succeed. **agsasaganad.** *v.* to follow one after the other. **isaganad.** *v.* to cause to follow. **sagsaganaden.** *v.* to do in order. **pagsaganaden.** *v.* to arrange in a series, put in order. [Tag. *sunód*]

ságang: *n.* kind of animal resembling the wild cat; kind of large black and white bird the size of a pigeon.

sagáng: masagang. *v.* to meet with; encounter (something bad); suffer; undergo; meet with a fatal end. **Adu dagiti nasagangna a baliwegweg iti dalan.** He encountered many bad people on the road. [Tag. *salubong*]

sagangasáng: nasagangasang. *v.* pungent, piquant (horseradishes). (*gasang*) **sumagangasang.** *v.* to be pungent to the taste. [Tag. *angháng*]

ságap: *n.* large *baringríng* net. **agsagap.** *v.* to collect. **agsagap ti damag.** *v.* to catch the news. **agsagap ti tapok.** *v.* to collect dust. **masagap.** *v.* to catch with the *sagap* net.

sagapá: *n.* cloth pad on which jars are placed (*dikén*); base of a pot. **agsinan-sagapa.** *v.* to be ringlike (posture of flattened buttocks when sitting, coiled snake, etc.). **simmagapa nga ubet.** *n.* flattened, rounded buttocks when sitting (said of large rumps).

sagápon: agsagapon. *v.* to meet, join; intersect (people, rivers, etc.). (*sabat*)

ságat: *n.* filter; strainer. (*sagatan*) **sagaten.** *v.* to filter, strain; sieve; pick the best. **pagsagatan.** *n.* strainer, colander; sieve. [Png. *sapit*, Tag. *salà, panalà*]

sagát: *n. Vitex parviflora* tree with blue flowers, and hard wood, *molave.* **sinagat.** *n.* variety of awned early rice.

sagátan: (f. *sagat*) *n.* sieve; strainer; filter.

sagawísiw: *n.* whistling. **agsagawisiw.** *v.* to whistle. (*sultíp*) **sagawisiwan.** *v.* to whistle at someone. **sagawisiwen.** *v.* to whistle a tune. **Insagawisiwko ti danagko kabayatan ti panagsukatko.** I whistled my worries while I changed. [Kal. *mangisiw*, Png. *ngísiw*, Tag. *sipol*]

sagawsáw: (Bag-o) *n.* ritual exorcism from evil spirits. [Tag. *sagawsáw* = gurgling sound of poured liquids]

sagáyad: *n.* cable, strong rope; train of a gown; bottom of a dress. **agsagayad.** *v.* to drag, trail behind (dresses, etc.) (*saringgayad*). [Tag. *sayad, sagayad*]

sagaysáy: *n.* comb. **agsagaysay.** *v.* to comb one's hair. **sagaysayen.** *v.* to comb someone. **marasagaysay(an).** *n.* down, fine hair; bird hair; young pubic hair. [Ibg. *tagétay*, Ivt. *surud*, Kpm. *sukle*, Knk. *sag-áy, sig-áy*, Kal., Png. *sagaysáy*, Tag. *sukláy*]

sagbén: *n.* barricade; dam; obstruction; blockade; obstacle. **maisagben.** *v.* to be blocked, closed; to ground, strand. **sagbenan.** *v.* to block; obstruct; barricade (*bangen, lapped*). [Tag. *hadláng*]

sagedséd: sagedseden. *v.* to put things closely together.

sagepsép: sumagepsep. *v.* to absorb; soak, become saturated or pregnant; seep. **sagepsepen.** *v.* to absorb; imbibe knowledge. **napasagepsepan.** *a.* brainwashed; trained. **ipasagepsep.** *v.* to imbibe knowledge; let something be absorbed. **Kayatna nga ipasagepsep kadakuada ti maipagpannakkel a kultura ken kannawidantayo a kas puli.** He wants to imbibe in them the knowledge of our proud culture and customs as a race. [Tag. *sipsíp*]

sagersér: (*obs.*) see *sagorsór*: entangled; full of knots. [Tag. *buhól*]

sagga-: *var.* of *sag-*, distributive prefix: **saggaysa.** one each. **saggapat.** four each. **saggadu.** many each. [Tag. *tig-*]

saggáak: (*obs.*) **agsagaak.** *v.* to shriek.

saggabassít: (f. *bassít*) *adv.* little by little; *n.* small amount. **Saggabassit lat' it-itedna.** He is giving only a small amount.

saggaltíng: (f. *letting*) *n.* a little bit, a small share. **sumaggalting.** each a little.

saggatló: (f. *tallo*) *num.* three each. **saggatluen.** *v.* to do three at a time.

saggaysá: (f. *maysa*) *num.* one each. **saggaysaen.** *v.* to do one at a time. **pagsasaggaysaen.** *v.* to give one each. **managsaggaysa.** once in a while; very slow (breathing). **Sinaggaysa nga inisipna dagiti kakabagianna.** He thought about his relatives one at a time. **No kasaoda, managsaggaysa ti panagsungbatda.** When they talk, they usually answer one at a time. **Masapul nga ibagam a saggaysaen.** You must tell it in full detail (one by one).

saggaysí: *var.* of *sagisí*: species of palm.

saggéd: **sinagged.** *n.* flotsam, driftwood. (*gabat*)

sagiáb: **sumagiab.** *v.* to be overabundant.

sagiangít: (*obs.*) **nasagiangit.** *a.* heavy bearded.

sagiát: *n. Goniothalamus amuyon* tree whose fruits are used to cure swellings.

sagíban: **nasagiban.** *a.* possessed by an evil spirit.

sagíbar: *n.* irritation; sarcasm. **nasagibar.** *a.* biting, caustic, sharp; satirical, ironic. **makasagibar.** *a.* irritating. **sumagibar.** *v.* to be sarcastic; to be lodged in the throat when swallowing. **Adda nariknak a sagibar iti ayugda.** I felt sarcasm in their tone. [Tag. *hirin* (choke)]

sagíbat: **sumagibat.** *v.* to meddle, interfere; intervene. [Tag. *himasok*]

sagibát: **maisagibat.** *v.* to graze, scrape; touch in passing; miss by an inch. **sumagibat.** *v.* to miss by an inch. [Tag. *daplís*]

sagíbo: *n.* aftergrowth of rice; (*reg.*) offspring. **agsagibo.** *v.* to develop a second growth. [Tag. *usbóng*]

sagibsíb: *n.* young shoot of a plant, (taro, banana, etc.) (*subbual*); illegitimate children. **agsagibsib.** *v.* to develop a young shoot.

ságid: *n.* touch. (*apros; kalbit; kulding*) **agsagid, maisagid.** *v.* to collide; brush up against; touch accidentally or incidentally. **agpasagid.** *v.* to coxcomb. **agpaspasagid.** *v.* to hang about the girls; haunt; (*fig.*) allude, insinuate. **ipasagid.** *v.* to imply, insinuate. **sagiden.** *v.* to touch; lay hands upon; hint to, tell casually. **sumagid.** *v.* to meet casually, touch in passing; brush up against; (*fig.*) to be partly correct. **pasagidan.** *v.* to hurt the feelings of; offend, wound. **pamasagid, pangpasagid.** *n.* insinuation, hint, allusion. **pammasagid, panangpasagid.** *n.* indirectly hurting one's feelings. [Kal. *tikchin*, *sagichon*, Tag. *hipò* (touch)]

sagiksík: *n.* lively; briskness. (*siglat*) **nasagiksik.** *a.* brisk; nimble; agile; active; quick. **sagiksiken.** *v.* to do briskly. [Tag. *siglá*]

saginnét: **sagsaginnet.** *a.* piecemeal; little by little. **sagsaginneten.** *v.* to do little by little (*inut*). [Tag. *untí-untí*]

saginúnod: **isaginunod.** *v.* to leave for last; place at the end; save for last; do after everything else is finished. [Tag. *hulí*]

sagingsíng: *n.* distinctive feature; peculiarity. **nasagingsing.** *a.* with good qualities, distinctive. (*pudos*)

sagíp: **agsagip, sagipen.** *v.* to save.

sagipéd: *n.* crossbar. (*alaped*) **sagipedan.** *v.* to provide with a crossbar. [Tag. *halang*]

sagiperpér: **sumagiperper.** *v.* to shiver, tremble, shake (*pigerger; tigerger*). [Tag. *kiníg*]

sagírad: **agsagirad.** *v.* to trail, drag (*saringgayad*); brush against. **nasagirad.** (*obs.*) *a.* with the body covered with protuberances. **Nagpuligos ti kallugongko a sinagirad ti bala.** My hat spun as it was brushed by the bullet.

sagisápat: **sagisapatan.** *n.* forenoon; noontide.

sagisí: *n. Heterospathe elata*, species of slender, wild palm.

sagitsít₁: *n.* hissing sound, sound of frying lard. **agsagitsit.** *v.* to make a hissing sound.

sagitsít₂: *n.* scorching heat, the burning heat of the sun. (*sanetset*) **Sumagsitsit nga init.** The scorching sun.

sagiwálay: see *dagótay*: run, flow (saliva, mucus).

sagiwísiw: *var.* sagawísiw: whistle. (*sultip; silbato*)

sagkák: *n.* phlegm; the sound of discharging phlegm. (*turak*) **agsagkak.** *v.* to clear one's throat of phlegm. [Tag. *kalaghalâ*]

sagkíng: *a.* unstable, unbalanced. (*sigking*) **agsagking.** *v.* to limp; hobble. **Agsagsagking nga immadayo.** He left limping.

sagmák: *n.* danger. (*peggad; rubo*) **isagmak.** *v.* to jeopardize, endanger; imperil. **maisagmak.** *v.* to be in danger; to be jeopardized. **Dandanikay' ketdi naisagmak iti riribuk gapu kaniak.** You almost fell into danger because of me. [Tag. *panganib*]

sagmamanó: *interrog. part.* How many each? How much each? [Kal. *simpipiga*, Tag. *tigilán*]

sagmáy: *n.* innermost feelings; concern.

sagmúy: **agsagmuy.** *v.* to fall down the forehead (bangs); bend (tall grass). (*agmuy*)

sagnéb: *n.* marshy land. (*aloyóoy; gayong-gayong*) **agsagneb.** *v.* to get wet. **isagneb.** *v.* to instill (fear, hope, etc.). [Tag. *latî*]

sagní: *n.* original part of; pair, companion; *a.* inborn; innate. **agsagni.** *v.* to form a pair in dancing (*asmang*), pair up; do together. **Kasla agsagni ti pusona iti panangmatmatna iti**

anak. Her heart seemed to join his upon staring at the child. [Tag. *katutubò*]

sagníw: *var.* of *sagní*: pair up (in dancing, etc.). **Magnada nga agsagsagniw nga agkankanta.** They walked along singing together.

sagniném: (f. *innem*) *num.* six each.

ságo: *n.* pus, watery matter in wounds. (*nana*) **pannaguen.** *n.* cock with gray plumage. [Tag. *nanà* (pus)]

sagó: *n. Maranta arundinacea*, arrowroot; tapioca. [Tag. *sagó*]

saguáro: *n.* species of cactuslike plant.

sagubánit: *n.* temporary illness; indisposition; languor. (*sagabásab*; *sakit*) **agsagubanit.** *v.* to be sick; have a temporary illness. **kinamanagsagubanit.** *n.* the state of being sickly. [Tag. *sinat*]

sagubáreng: (*obs.*) *var.* of *sagubanit*, *sagureng*: temporary illness.

sagubél: **nasagubel.** *a.* walking with difficulty due to heavy or awkward clothes. **agsagubel.** *v.* to walk with difficulty due to uncomfortable clothes.

sagúd: **maisagud.** *v.* to be entangled, hooked, caught; delayed on the way. **agsagud.** *v.* to stay, cumber; falter. **pinnasagud.** *n.* game composed of fighting kites. **agpinnasagud.** *v.* to cause two kites to hit each other. **Adu ti pakaisagsagudanna.** Many things delayed him on his way.

sagúday: *n.* privilege, prerogative; gift, talent, superiority, merit. **sagudayen.** *v.* to surpass, exceed; explain; make clear; excel, outdo, outrun; *n.* provisions of a contract. **sagudayan.** *v.* to surpass, excel. **isaguday.** *v.* to favor, prefer, advantage. **Ti umuna managuday, ti maudi magabay.** The first triumphs, the last is late. [Tag. *tangì*]

sagudsód: *n.* reinforcements.

sagulayláy₁: *n. saguyepyép* plant.

sagulayláy₂: *n.* kind of mournful song.

sagumaymáy: *n.* eaves, awning. [Tag. *sulambí*]

sagumbí: *n.* penthouse, annex; wing of a building; room opening to the *lálem* (main part of house) with no door connecting it to the outside.

sagumísim: (*obs.*) **sagumisimen.** *v.* to become black; discolor.

sagunnót: **isagunnot.** *v.* to thrash someone to the ground (and keep him there). (*mudumod*)

sagunód: see *saganád*: succeed; follow.

sagupít: (*reg.*) conversational song (*suayan*); rattan backpack, rattan waist pack.

sagurán: (*reg.*) *n.* rice sack. (*langgotse*)

sagúreng: see *sagubanít*, *sagubareng*: indisposition; slight disorder.

sagurnók: **sagsagurnok.** *a.* sporadic, random; at irregular intervals; occurring in scattered cases.

Nagdawa ti pagayko ngem sagsagurnok laeng. My rice plants bore fruits, but in patches.

sagursúr: *n.* chicken with feathers that stand on end; loose ends of thread at the end of cloth. **nasagursur.** *a.* entangled, coarse, burly; full of knots. **agsagursur.** *v.* to be full of fibers due to a badly spun fabric.

págut: *n.* donation; gift; tip; grant; fee. (*sarabo*; *diaya*; *regalo*; *parabur*) **isagut.** *v.* to give, bestow; grant; present. **mannangisagut.** *n.* habitual gift giver. **maisagut.** *v.* to be given a gift. [Kal. *atod*, Png. *lángkap*, Tag. *handóg*]

sag-út: *n.* cotton yarn for weaving (*singdán*). **sag-uten.** *v.* to make into yarn or thread. **Sinagotna ti sadak sana impamaga.** He made the *sadak* vine into thread and then dried it.

saguyemyém: **nasaguyemyem.** *a.* cloudy, overcast. (*kuyem*)

saguyepyép₁: *n. Mussaenda philippica* shrub with yellow flowers.

saguyepyép₂: *n.* drowsiness. (*dungsa*) **saguyepyepen.** *v.* to become drowsy; be half asleep. **makasaguyepyep.** *a.* to cause drowsiness. **Winagwagna ti ulona ta saguyepyepen.** He shook her head because she was falling asleep.

sagpami(n)-: Prefix used to form distributive multiplicative numbers: **sagpamindua.** each two times. **sagpamitlo.** each three times. **Sagpaminpitoda nga napan.** They each went seven times.

sagpamin-anó: *interrog.* How often each? How many times each? (*sagtumunggál mano*)

sagpaminsán: *adv.* once in a while, from time to time, now and then, occasionally. **sagpaminsanen.** *v.* to do occasionally.

sagpapát: (f. *uppat*) *num.* four each. (*saggapat*) **sagpapaten.** *v.* to do four at a time.

sagpát: *n.* hanging woven bamboo receptacle used to hold clothes; upstairs; higher level; *a.* upland. **isagpat.** *v.* to place on a higher level. **nasagpat.** *a.* steep; high above the ground. **sumagpat.** *v.* to go up, ascend, climb. **masagpat.** *v.* to reach, get as far as, come to; be able to attain. **sasagpatan.** *n.* elevated place; landing of the stairs. **pagay ti sagpat.** *n.* upland rice. **Sumagpatto pay dagiti nalulukmeg nga igat kadagiti bato.** The fat eels will ascend the rocks first. **Duan ti annakda iti apagsagpat a tallopuloda.** They had two children upon reaching thirty. **Nakasagpatakon a tallopulo idi agpalaemkami ken ni baketko.** I reached thirty when my wife and I married. [Tag. *taás*]

sagpáw: *n.* meat or fish added to flavor broth; dish made with fish and vegetables. **sumagpaw.** *v.* to intrude, intermeddle, poke into someone else's affairs. **isagpaw.** *v.* to put between, join one thing to another, interpose.

Saanka a makisagsagpaw! Don't interfere! **Di pay naluto ti paria, simmagpaw ti karabasa.** The bittermelon was not cooked yet and the squash jumped in (said after an unwelcome interruption). [Tag. *himasok*]

sagpít: (*obs.*) *n.* vulva. (*uki*); parts of walls where things are tucked into. **isagpit.** *v.* to include in a bundle; to carry as an added load.

sagrádo: (Sp. *sagrado:* sacred) *a.* sacred, holy; religious, devout. **nasagraduan.** *a.* anointed; made sacred. **sagrada pamilia.** holy family.

sagrák: nasagrak. *a.* lonely.

sagráp: *n.* act of receiving (from natural circumstances); gain. (*awat; ragpat*) **agsagrap.** *v.* to receive whatever comes; enjoy (good things that come); suffer (bad things that come). **sagrapen.** *v.* to receive; benefit from; suffer from. **Diak kayaten ti agsagrap iti pait ken leddaang.** I don't want to receive bitterness or sadness anymore. [Tag. *tamó*]

sagrário: (Sp.) *n.* tabernacle.

sagság: masagsag. *v.* to become destroyed by beating or shaking. **sagsagen.** *v.* to wear out. (*ragrag*) **Tunggal agbagio, masagsag ti atepda.** Every storm, their roof is destroyed.

sagt(um)unggál: adverb used to form distributive cardinal numbers. **sagtunggal maysa.** each one.

sahitário: (Sp. *sagitario:* Sagittarius) *n.* Sagittarius (sign in the zodiac). [Knk. *tikém*]

saibbék: agsaibbek. *v.* to sob. (*sainnék*) **Agsasaibbek a pimmanaw.** He left sobbing. [Knk. *sibék*, Png. *sibek*, Tag. *hibík, hikbî*]

saiddék: *n.* hiccup. **agsaiddek.** *v.* to hiccup. **managsasaiddek.** *a.* prone to hiccup (said of babies). [Bon. *alindadek*, Kal. *sigsig-ok*, Knk. *alinsadók, saindék*, Kpm. *sigúk*, Png. *sinék*, Tag. *sinók*]

saíding: *n.* kind of fishhook. (*lawin; banniit*)

saigórot: *n.* kind of native red rice.

sáil: sailen. *v.* to trip an opponent (in wrestling, etc.). [Tag. *patid*]

sailúko: *n.* kind of Ilocano cloth; Ilocano translation. **isailuko.** *v.* to translate into the Ilocano language.

sainéte: (Sp. *sainete:* burlesque; one-act farce) *n.* one-act farce.

sainnék: agsainnek. *v.* to sob; plead. (*unnoy; rengreng; asug; ikakaasi; saibbek*) **sasainnek.** *n.* pleadings. **Awan lalaki nga natured wenno nabaneg no ti babai ti sanguanan agsainnek.** There is no brave or strong man in the presence of a sobbing woman. [Png. *sibok*, Tag. *hibík, hikbî*]

sainó: (*obs.*) **agsaino.** *v.* to meditate, reflect (*panunot; isip*). [Tag. *isip*]

sáing: *n.* old-fashioned oil lamp; light. **manaing, saingan.** *v.* to put on the light. **lawag-pagsaingan.** *n.* lamp light, artificial light.

sáip: *n.* additional piece added to something (tight-fitting garment); joint. **saipan.** *v.* to widen, broaden; patch. [Tag. *sugpóng*]

sáir: *n.* feeling something foreign on the surface of the skin; irritation. **isasair.** *v.* to attempt, try, risk. **sairen.** *v.* to irritate; touch the gums with the tongue; hurt one's feelings; annoy. **masair.** *v.* to have one's feelings hurt; to be irritated, annoyed. **Nasair ti riknana iti nangngegna.** He had his feelings hurt from what he had heard. **No masair tay puris sumakit a sumakit.** When a thorn in the flesh is touched, it hurts (people are hurt when a sore spot is touched). **Diak ranta a sairenka.** It wasn't my plan to hurt your feelings. [Tag. *saktán*]

saíro: *n.* evil, temptation, seduction; enticer to evil, devil. **sairuen.** *v.* to tempt, seduce, lure; decoy. **nainsairuan.** *a.* devilish, satanic, hellish, wicked. **sili't-sairo.** *n.* species of hot red pepper. **sairo't-bangkag.** *n.* nuisance. [Tag. *diyablo* (Sp.)]

saís: (Sp. *seis:* six) *num.* six. (*innem*)

sáit₁: isait. *v.* to sharpen, whet (*asa*). [Tag. *hasà*]

sáit₂: *n.* test for sharpness; enter a contest. **agsinnait.** *v.* to try to outdo one another (song competition, contest). **Kasla agsisinnait nga agkanta dagiti aglaklako iti bangus.** The milkfish vendors seem to be competing in singing.

saittíl: *n.* kind of small mollusk with hairy shell.

sáka: *n.* foot; leg. **pasaka.** *n.* string of rattan, string used to tie fowl. **pasakaan.** *v.* to tie at the leg; beat the leg. **sakasaka.** *a.* barefoot, *n.* Adenia coccinea vine with red fruits. **agsakasaka.** *v.* to walk around barefoot. **sakaanan.** *n.* part of the bed where the feet are; foot of the stairs; foot of a mountain. **sisasaka.** *a.* barefoot. **Addadan iti sakaanan ti kakaywan a turod.** They are at the foot of the forested hill. [Ibg. *tekki*, Ifg. *dapan*, Ivt. *kukud*, Kal. *iki*, Knk. *sikí*, Kpm. *bitis*, Png. *salí*, Tag. *paá*]

saká: (Sp. *sacar:* get; take) *n.* ransom; cash used to redeem a mortgage; interjection used to drive away cats. **sakaen.** *v.* to redeem; ransom. **pangsakaan.** *n.* pawnshop. [Ibg. *apen, tevvutan*, Ivt. *pavidien*, Kpm. *nitbus*, Png. *dundun*, Tag. *tubós* (redeem)]

sakaánan: *n.* foot (of a mountain, stairs, etc.). [Tag. *paanán*]

sákab: *n.* paper covering the lantern framework; cover. **sakaban.** *v.* to mend; cover; repair; frame. **mannakab.** *n.* kind of wasplike insect. **isakab.** *v.* to stretch skin over a drum; stretch out on a bench (to be whipped). **maisakab.** *v.* to be framed; to be stretched on one's stomach. **sumakab.** *v.* to stretch; lie down on a bench to be whipped. [Tag. *takíp* (cover)]

sakabútse: (Sp. *sacabuche*: sackbut) *n.* zither.

sákad: **masakad.** *v.* to be wadeable; able to carry, bear. **isakad.** *v.* to bear (the responsibilities); support (a family). **Adu a rigat datao a mangisaksakad iti panagadalmo.** I faced many hardships supporting your studies. **Ngem no makitak ti rigatda a mangisakad kadagiti annakda, bumalesak a mangantiaw kadakuada.** But when I see their troubles in supporting their children, I joke in return.

sakáda₁: (Sp. *sacada*: district separated from a province, Tagalog also) *n.* out of town laborers hired at a lower price.

sakáda₂: (Sp. *sacada*: getting) **agsakada, sakadaen.** *v.* withdraw, remove from a warehouse. **Tulonganka a mangawit ti sakadaem.** I will help you carry what you are taking out of the warehouse.

sakáda₃: *n.* the first part of a solemn burial, which consists of sprinkling the coffin with holy water. **isakada.** *v.* to perform the *sakada* ceremony on a recently deceased person.

sákal: **maisakal.** *v.* to enjoy, profit by. **isakal.** *v.* to stir in a ladlelike fashion. **agsakalsakal, manakalsakal.** *v.* to kick about in discomfort.

sakál: (Tagalog) **sakalen.** *v.* to squeeze the neck (of another).

sakáng: (Tag. also) *a.* bow-legged. (*sakkang*; *akkang*)

sakapuégo: (Sp. *sacar fuego*: get fire) *n.* matchbox, matches. [Knk. *andúlus*]

sakár: **agsakar.** *v.* to plagiarize; cheat by copying; copy an exam. **agpasakar.** *v.* to allow someone to copy one's answer.

sakarína: (Sp. *sacarina*: saccharin) *n.* saccharin.

sakásak: **sumakasak.** *v.* to hustle; force one's way through (*sarakusok*).

sakat: *a.* with glans penis completely uncovered. (*pungat*)

sakáte: (AmSp. *zacate*: hay, fodder) *n.* animal fodder (usually grass). **sakatero.** *n.* hay man, one whose responsibility is to collect *sakate*.

sakáw: **nasakaw.** *a.* included; embraced; stepped over; encircled. **masakawán.** *v.* to be comprised, included in, counted in; contained; meet by chance. **sakawen.** *v.* to include; step over. **nasakawan.** *a.* stepped over; included; embraced. **pasakawan.** *v.* to use in order to gain or profit; use as a trap. **Idi Biernes, maysa a kinaturposanmi ken Meding ti nasakawko idiay Parawir.** Last Friday I ran into one of Meding's and my fellow graduates in Parawir.

sakáy: (Tag. also) *n.* passenger. **agsakay.** *v.* to ride (an animal) **isakay.** *v.* to load in, load on. **makisakay.** *v.* to ride with someone; hitch a ride (lugan). **sasakayán.** *n.* steamships, horses carrying passengers; sailing vessel. **sumakay.** *v.* to ride; embark on a ship. [Kal. *sakyat, lugen*]

sakáyap: **sumakayap.** *v.* to encompass, go over and enclose (waves).

sakbáb: *n.* the way a pig eats, snapping of the mouth when eating. **agsakbab.** *v.* to snap at food; seize with the teeth (*sakrab*). [Tag. *sagpáng*]

sakbát: **sakbaten.** *v.* to carry on the shoulder (*baklay*). **nakasakbat.** *a.* carried on the shoulder.

sakbáy: *prep.* before. **kasakbayan.** *prep.* before. **masakbayan.** *n.* future. **agsakbay.** *v.* to foresee; overtake by using a shortcut; to be prepared for the future. **managsakbay.** *a.* always preparing for the future. **isakbay.** *v.* to set a net to intercept the quarry; make preparations well in advance; give notice ahead of time. **sakbáyan.** *v.* to overtake someone by use of a shortcut. **pasakbáyen.** *v.* to have (the wind, etc.) carry away odors. **sumakbay.** *v.* to stand in the way, blocking passage. **Ti agsakbay, agsaguday.** He who has foresight will triumph. [Png. *sakbáy*, Tag. *bago*]

sakbít: **sakbiten.** *v.* to carry on or under the arm (*igpil*). [Tag. *kipkíp*]

sakbúet: see *sarobósob*: fall into the water.

sákbot: *n.* pillowcase; long bag used for catching fish and frogs. [Tag. *pundá* (pillowcase)]

sakdó: *n.* water drawn from a well. **sumakdo.** *v.* to draw water from a well. (*saréb*). **sakduen.** *v.* to draw water; imbibe knowledge. **Pinaruam ida, ita sikan ti umayda pagsakduan.** *exp.* You spoiled them, now they come to you when they need something (*lit:* you're the one they come to to draw water). [Ibg. *tágag*, Ivt. *muranum*, Kal. *malakchu*, Kpm. *saklu*, Png. *asól*, Tag. *igíb, salok*]

sakém: **sakmen.** *v.* to gather everything in reach; take all one can; (*reg*). *v.* to include in one's jurisdiction; take everything in reach. [Tag. *sahóg*]

sáket: *n.* kind of tree with good building timber and whose bark is used to dye nets black.

sáki: **sakien.** *v.* to gather, collect (rice plants), scoop up rice after it has been threshed.

sakíbot: *n.* place in clothing where something can be hidden; pocket. **isakibot.** *v.* to tuck in (clothes); tuck something in the clothes (usually in the waist area).

sakídol: *n.* sickly disposition. **saksakidol, sinakidol.** *a.* sickly, prone to catching disease (*ma-*

nagsakit). **Saksakidolenak manen.** I am sick again (as usual). **Kellaat a nagpukaw ti aso ti sakidulna.** The dog suddenly lost his sickly disposition.

sakíng: *(obs.)* **sumaking.** *v.* to brush against someone in passing. *(kalbit)*

sakísak: *a.* ordinary; common; widespread. [Tag. *laganap*]

sakít: *n.* sickness, disease, ailment *(sagubánit);* pain, ache *(ut-ót).* **agsakit.** *v.* to be sick, to hurt, ail. **agsinnakit.** *v.* to help one another. **masakit.** *n.* patient, *v.* to be sick. **nasakit.** *a.* sick; aching, hurt, sore. **Nasakit ti ulok.** I have a headache. **Nasakit ti matana.** He has a sore eye. **Nasakit ti nakem.** *v.* regret, grieve, be sorry; to have hard feelings for; ill will. **isakit.** *v.* to defend, protect, aid; help, support; uphold. **manangisakit.** *a.* helpful, thoughtful, generous; defensive, supporting, prone protective. **sakiten.** *v.* to hurt, ache. **sakit ti nakem.** *n.* hard feeling; hurt feeling; remorse; sorrow, regret. **sakiten ti nakem.** *v.* to feel sorry for, regret, repent. **pasakitan.** *v.* to pain, afflict; distress; hurt; trouble; torment. **Dika agpanggep iti dakes no dimo kayat ti masakitan.** Do not plot evil if you do not want to be hurt. [Ibg. *takíq,* Itg. *sígab,* Ivt. *maynen* (pain), *magañit, iñen* (sick), Kpm., Png., Tag. *sakít*]

sakkáb: nasakkab. *a.* separated, disunited, severed; *var.* of *sagkak.*

sakkáng: see *akkáng:* straddle; walk with the legs apart *(pakkang; kayang).* [Ivt. *kawal,* Tag. *sakáng*]

sakkiáb: sumakkiab. *v.* to fly away.

sakkúb: *n.* kind of basket put over the mother hen to keep her in place with small openings for the chicks to run in and out *(batulang; kagab);* cover. **sinakkub.** *n.* cover; sugar in shape of half a bowl and joined together with the other half.

saklá: pasakla. *n. Ficus sp.* tree resembling the *balíte.*

saklóng: *n.* presence (of an authority); legal proceedings. **iti saklang.** *prep.* in front of; facing; face-to-face with; before. **sumaklang.** *v.* to stand in front of; to sue; prosecute. **isaklang.** *v.* to bring to court; sue. *(darum)* **maisaklang.** *v.* to be brought to court. [Tag. *haráp*]

sakláp: isaklap. *v.* to spread out; lay out (to dry, etc.). *(aplag)*

sakláw: masakláwan, sakláwan. *v.* to overtake by a shortcut. **saklawen.** *v.* to include, comprise, contain. *(saguday)*

saklíli: see *aklíli:* to carry under the armpit.

saklít: *n.* term used for when one number comes out in the *hueteng* lottery game.

saklúb: *var.* of *saklup:* cover (with cloth) for protection or concealment. **sinaklub.** *n.* kind of sweet made from sugarcane.

saklúlo: *n.* lap; protection; womb; care; guidance. *(aklulo)* **sakluluen.** *v.* to take under one's care. **Addan agpitpitik a bunga iti saklulok.** There is a fruit beating in my womb (said by a pregnant woman).

saklóp: *n.* inside, interior. *(uneg)* **saklopan.** *v.* to cover; spread over. **isaklop.** *v.* to put something under something to hide or protect it. [Tag. *loób*]

saklót: *n.* lap. **sakloten.** *v.* to hold in the lap; cuddle. **sinaklot.** *n.* baby in the womb. **Sinaklotna dagiti naglilinaga a ramayna.** He put his interwoven fingers in his lap. **Ti mangsaklot iti imana, narigat ti panagbiagna.** He who puts his hands in his lap will have a hard life. **Saksaklotenna ti dalikan.** He carries a stove in his lap (refers to an industrious chef). [Png. *akwál,* Tag. *kandóng*]

sakmál: sakmalen. *v.* to snatch and run; run away with; grab with the mouth; bite (dogs). **nasakmal.** *a.* snatched by a mouth; bitten (by dogs). **Naglaing nga agsakmal kadagiti babasit a kas kadatayo.** It is good at snatching small ones like us. [Tag. *sakmál*]

sakmól: isakmol, sakmolen. *v.* to put in the mouth. **makasakmol.** *v.* to be able to put in the mouth. **sangkasakmol.** *n.* one mouthful. **Insakmolna ti sappupona a kasuy.** He put the handful of cashew nuts in his mouth. [Knk. *sakmíl, seng-á,* Png. *subó, sanka,* Tag. *subò*]

saknáp: agsaknap, maisaknap. *v.* to spread (news, diseases, liquids, etc.); become popular. *(sapnák).* **naisaknap a saó.** *n.* current usual term. **nainsaknapan a welga.** *n.* general strike. **maisaknap.** *a.* widespread. **nasaknapan.** *a.* covered with, full of. **Idi sumangpetkami idiay away, napintas ti panagsaknap ti init kadagiti kataltalonan.** When we arrived at the hinterlands, the sun spreading over the rice fields was beautiful. [Tag. *laganap*]

saknár: sumaknar. *v.* to enter the mouth of a river (tide). *(suknor)* **masaknar.** *v.* to be weary, exhausted; be affected deeply; overwhelmed. **masaknaran.** *v.* to be affected. **saknaren.** *v.* to affect deeply; enter the mouth of a river.

sakníb: *n.* overlapping. *(salip; takip; átip)* **agsaknib, sakniben.** *v.* to lap over, overlap, lap. **Awan sardayna a panangdungpar dagiti ikan iti inut-inut a panagsaknib ti iket.** He continually collided into the fish as the net was gradually folded over. [Tag. *taklób*]

saknóng: *(obs.)* **masaknong.** *v.* to be enclosed, be added to. [Tag. *dagdág*]

sáko: (Sp. *saco*: sack) *n*. sack. (*kados*) isako. *v*. to put in a sack. sangasako. *n*. one sack of. [Tag. *kostál*]

sakúb: sinakub. *n*. hardened brown sugar molded in a half coconut shell. pagsakuben. *v*. to join (two things facing each other).

sakobá: agsakoba. *v*. to bow; lie prone. (*pakleb*; *tikleb*; *dugmam*; *rugma*; *daleb*; *dapla*; *sakab*) maisakoba. *v*. to fall prone. [Tag. *dapâ*]

sakóbo: *n*. angle brace connecting two tiebeams (the *awanán* and *sekkég*). (*poklo*)

sákol: agsakol. *v*. to limp by walking with one of the soles of the feet turned inward.

sakúlap: saksakulap. *n*. kind of large bird; kind of small, black freshwater fish resembling a cockroach.

sakulí: *reg. var*. of *takolí*: canoe.

sakúlob: sakuluban. *v*. to cover; place over; screen; guard; secure; shelter, protect; conceal. [Tag. *takíp*]

sakuntáp: *n*. smacking noise. (*sakuntip*) agsakuntap. *v*. to smack; to make noise when eating (hogs). [Tag. *palaták*]

sakuntíp: *n*. smacking of the lips. agsakuntip. *v*. to lightly smack the lips (connotes displeasure as in scolding, etc.) (*sanamtek*, *sakuntap*). [Knk. *sayamták*, *semták*]

sákup: sakup, kasakupan. *n*. jurisdiction; territory; sphere of authority. (*beddeng*) sakupen. *v*. to include, contain, comprise; invade, take over. masakup. *v*. to be included, contained. masakupan. *v*. to rule; have under one's jurisdiction; be included. sumakup. *v*. to invade. panangsakup. *n*. invasion. |Bayat ti kaaddam dita, agsukisokka no mabalin a sakupentayo ti daga. While you are there, investigate as to whether we can take over the land. [Png., Tag. *sakop*]

sakúp: *n*. common, public; for general use.

sakupít: *n*. woven rattan pack, usually used for carrying betel nut and tied to the waist. isakupit. *v*. to place in the pack. maisakupit. *v*. to be placed in a pack. Nawadwad ti maisakupitmo ita. Now you can carry much in your pack.

sakúray: (*obs*.) agsakuray. *v*. to prepare charcoal from different kinds of wood.

sakóte: masakote. *v*. to be caught in the act. (*tiliw*)

sakrá: (Sp. *sacra*) *n*. each of the three tablets on the altar that the priest may read upon saying mass.

sakráb: sakraben. *v*. to seize with the teeth. sumakrab. *v*. to take bait; bite (fish on a line). [Tag. *sakmál*]

sakraménto: (Sp. *sacramento*: sacrament) *n*. sacrament.

sakrár: agsakrar. *v*. to be fickle, capricious, wishy-washy. masakrar. *v*. to be confused, perplexed; embarrassed.

sakriléhio: (Sp. *sacrilegio*) *n*. sacrilege.

sakripísio: (Sp. *sacrificio*: sacrifice) *n*. sacrifice; hardship. (*patli*) agsakripision. *v*. to sacrifice; undergo hardship. isakripision. *v*. to offer something in sacrifice.

sakristán: (Sp. *sacristán*: sexton) *n*. altar boy; sexton.

sakrúd: *n*. small net used to catch birds and locusts. sakruden. *v*. to catch with the *sakrud* net. panakrud. *n*. inguinal region of the abdomen.

sakrosánto: (Sp. *sacrosanto*) *a*. sacrosanct, most holy.

sakróy: *n*. arms for carrying. sakruyen. *v*. to carry in the arms (babies). agpasakroy. *v*. to allow oneself to be carried; get carried in the arms of someone else. sangasakroy. *n*. one armful. Nagimpupukaw iti puot tapno sakruyenna. She pretended to lose consciousness so he would carry her in his arms. [Tag. *pangkô*]

saksák₁: agsaksak. *v*. to clear one's throat. saksaken. *v*. to flog, thrash; (*Tag*.) stab with a knife. (*bagkong*) Saanakon a matmaturog iti balaymi ta agamakak a pasaksakandak dagiti kabusorko. I can't sleep at our house out of fear that my enemies will stab me.

saksák₂: saksaken. *v*. thresh dry pods of beans; stomp on rice to remove the grains (*irik*). [Tag. *lugás*]

saksák₃: isaksak. *v*. to insert; put in; plug in. pagsaksakan. *n*. electric outlet. [Tag. *saksák* (stuff, pack tightly); stab]

saksák₄: ipasaksak. *v*. to blame someone publicly; to divulge, say in public (what should have been said in private); to tell someone to his face. Isaksakmo latta ti kayatmo a sawen. just say clearly what you really mean. [Tag. *saksák* = stab]

saksakitén: (f. *sakit*) *n*. disease.

saksí: (f. Sanskrit *sâkshin*) *n*. witness. saksian. *v*. to witness; testify; give evidence or testimony. manaksi. *n*. eyewitness; witness a marriage. agsaksi. *v*. to appear before the priest before marriage; appear as a witness. Daksanggasat ta saanna a masaksian ti bunga ti nagrigrigatanna. It is just bad luck that he couldn't witness the fruits of his labor. [Png. *takúbuno*, Tag. *saksí*]

saksopón: (Sp. *saxofón*) *n*. saxophone. agsaksopon. *v*. to play the saxophone.

sála: (Sp. *sala*: parlor; living room) *n.* parlor; living room (*salas*); courtroom.

sála: *n.* dance. agsala. *v.* to dance. agkasala. *n.* partners in a dance. isala. *v.* to dance with someone. kasala. *v.* to dance with; *n.* dance partner. pasala. *n.* ball, ballroom. mannala. *n.* dancer; good dancer. pagsasalaan. *n.* dance hall. [Ibg. *tála*, Ivt. *tumádaq*, Kal. *sagli*, Kpm. *térak*, Png., Tag. *sayáw*]

salábat: salabaten. *v.* to intercept; stop on the way. [Tag. *salabad*]

salabát: (Tag. also) *n.* boiled ginger with sugar, said to improve the voice. agsalabat. *v.* to drink ginger tea (supposedly beneficial to the voice); to make ginger tea.

salábay: *var.* of *sallabay*: put arm around; ride on back.

salabídang: (*obs.*) *n.* collision of persons. agsalabidang. *v.* to bump into.

salábug: masalabugan. *v.* to get wet from leakage.

salabúsab: nasalabusab. *a.* inconsiderate, careless, thoughtless; voracious; hasty; rash.

salad-áy: salad-ayan. *n.* something used to hang clothes to dry on. (*banténg*) isalad-ay. *v.* to hang on; drape. [Tag. *sampáy*]

saládo: (Sp. *salado*: salty) *n.* undrinkable tap water, salty.

sálag: salagan. *v.* to redeem; to liberate from an obligation by paying a debt. (*saká*) salagen. *v.* to pay a debt of someone else. [Tag. *tubós*]

salagásag: see *saragásag*: thin; transparent; gauzy.

salagbít: (*obs.*) *n.* girdle; examination.

salagínto: (*obs.*) *n.* director (of processions, etc.). [Tag. *salagintô* = goldbug]

salagság: agsalagsag. *v.* to be transparent, gauzy. (*saragasag*)

salákan: *n.* protector, savior. isalakan. *v.* to rescue, save; defend, protect; relieve. manangisalakan. *n.* savior; redeemer. Nagyaman manen iti pannakaisalakanna iti dandani pannakatayna. He thanked again the person who saved him from almost dying. [Knk. *benglít*, Png. *adondón*, Tag. *ligtás*]

salakdáy: isalakday. *v.* to hang in order to dry.

salakéb: *n.* bamboo fish trap. [Kal. *kupkup-ung*, *ugat*, Tag. *salakáb*]

salakí: (Sp. *sal de aquí*: to go away from here) Interjection used to drive away dogs.

salakníb: *n.* protection. (*salakan*) mannalaknib. *n.* protector; guardian. salakniban. *v.* to cover, guard, protect, screen, secure. [Tag. *tanggól*]

salakúb: *n.* straw hat.

salakót: (Tag. also) *n.* native woven hat. (*kattukong*)

salaksák: *n.* kind of kingfisher bird with blue and black plumage, larger than the *bíding*, named for its sound that is thought to bring about bad luck. agsalaksak. *v.* to cry (said of the kingfisher). [Kal. *sayaksak*, Tag. *sulsulbót*]

salamá₁: salamaan. *v.* to catch in the act. masalamaan. *v.* to be caught in the act; to meet by chance along the way. [Tag. *makasalubong*]

salamá₂: *n.* a kind of fishing net.

salamági: *n. Tamarindus indica*, the tamarind, used in native medicine for asthma, fever, and cough. salamagien. *v.* to season with tamarind. salsalamagi. *n.* tonsil, amygdala. [Png. *salomági*, Tag. *sampalok* (tamarind)]

salamantéka: *n.* kind of slow dance. agsalamanteka. *v.* to dance the *salamanteka* dance.

salamángka: *n.* magic; magic trick; juggling; prestidigitation. agsalamangka. *v.* to perform magic; to juggle.

salamangkéro: *n.* magician; sorcerer; juggler.

salambáw: *n.* kind of large fishing net. (*ikét*) salambawen. *v.* to draw the *daklís* seine inside the canoe.

salampingát: *n.* wanton or flirtatious girl. (*sarampingat*)

salampugít: *n.* nickname given to ridicule personal defects. masalampugit. *v.* to fall on all fours.

sal-án: *var.* of *sal-ang*: put between; thrust in.

salándra: (Sp. *coladera*: sieve) *n.* sieve, screen for straining sand. (*yakayak*) agsalandra. *v.* to screen, sift, filter (sand). [Tag. *salà*]

salánsan: *n.* heap; pile. (*buntuon*; *dagumpo*) salansanen. *v.* to heap up; pile. [Tag. *salansán*]

sal-áng: isal-ang. *v.* to intrude, put between, interpose (different objects).

salangá: nasalanga. *a.* stupid; silly. [Tag. *tangá*]

salángad: salangaden. *v.* to accuse, charge with, reprimand, rebuke for damage done to a third person; to accuse an innocent person; argue with; disagree with; confront a wrongdoing (*sungat*) Salangadek kuma iti panagpukawna. I should charge her for his loss.

salangád: nasalangad. *a.* careless, unobservant, always dropping things.

salangguítis: *n.* gossiper. (*tsismoso*; *tarabit*; *salawasaw*)

salanggúsong: isalanggusong. *v.* to fit the end of a tube in a socket, adjust.

salangsáng: *var.* of *salansán*: pile, heap.

salapáng: (Tagalog also) *n.* trident for a sling shot; harpoon.

salapásan: (*obs.*) agsalapasan. *v.* to be flooded. (*layos, malípus*)

salapásap: *n.* water cover over the ground, partial flooding (not as serious as *layos*). maisalapasap.

v. to spread (water from a pool when raining) (*salnap*). **masalapasapan.** *v.* to be flooded with pool water, to be partially flooded. **salapasapen.** *v.* to inundate, flood (milder than *layos*). **salsalapasap.** *n.* reefs, shallows. **apagsalapasap.** *v.* to have just enough water to cover the surface.

salapáy: isalapay. *v.* to hang (to dry); wear a shawl over shoulders. **salapayan, maisalapay.** *v.* to hang, dangle; overflow. **salapayan.** *n.* clothesline. (*banteng*) **Ginaw-atna ti nakasalapay a tualia sana imputipot iti bagina.** He reached for the towel hanging on the clothesline and then wrapped it around his body. [Png. *sampáy*, *balaybay*, Tag. *sampáy*]

salapdáy: see *salapáy*: hang; suspend.

salapgí: *n.* second and fifth toe or digit of the *Artiodactyla*.

salápi: *n.* young ear of Indian corn; (*obs.*) cutlass, sword. **agsalapi.** *v.* to begin to ear (corn).

salapí: *n.* half peso, fifty centavos; (*fig.*) round physical blemish on the skin. **agsalapi.** *v.* to begin to ear (corn). **manalapi.** *a.* worth half a peso. **Awan ti salapi kadagiti gurongna.** She has no blemishes on her legs. [Tag. *salapî* = fifty centavos; money]

salápon: sumalapon. *v.* to collide; push someone ahead. (*dalapos*) **masalapon.** *v.* to accidentally bump into. [Tag. *bunggô*]

salapúsop: *n.* vapor bath; steam cooker. **masalapusupan.** *v.* to fume, smoke; spray. **salapusupan.** *v.* to cook by steam. **sinalapusop.** *n.* kind of pudding made of rice, water, sugar, and coconut meat cooked in a section of bamboo. **pagsasalapusupan.** *n.* steamer. [Tag. *singáw* (steam)]

salapsáp: *n. bulóng unás* fish when larger than the *ballawítan*. **salapsapen.** *v.* to pick, pluck (bulky fruits, corn).

sálas: (Sp. *sala*: hall) *n.* hall; living room. (*tengngá*) **agpasalas.** *v.* to go to the living room.

salát: isalat. *v.* to cast; throw down someone in wrestling. **naisalat.** *a.* cast down; thrown down in wrestling; caught by branches when falling from a tree (*sabir*, *salumbinit*). **Iti panagdumogna, naisalat dagiti matana iti riang ti bestidana.** As he bowed, his eyes looked down into the slit of her dress. **Naisalat lattan dagiti matak iti nabaknang a barukongna.** My eyes were cast on her rich chest. [Tag. *salát* = scarce; touch; palpitation]

sal-át: *n.* lightning; a curse word. (*sal-ít*) **sumanal-at.** *a.* cursing; swearing. **masal-at.** *v.* to be damned. [Tag. *lintík*]

salátong: (*coll.*) *var.* of *balátong*: salatongen. *v.* to deceive; joke around with. **Salsalatongennak ketdi!** You must be pulling my leg!

sálaw: (*obs.*) *n.* kind of very large jar.

saláw: masalaw. *v.* to meet, see a person. (*salama*) **masalsalaw.** *n.* unseen spirits met on the way. **Awan nasalawko nga am-ammok ket awan met nakabigbig kaniak.** I didn't see anyone I know and nobody recognized me either. [Tag. *salubong*]

saláwad: agsalawad. *v.* to stay somewhere in expectation of something; wait anxiously.

salawásaw: *n.* tattler, one who cannot keep a secret. (*tarabítab*; *gasagas*; *tar-ap*) **agsalawasaw.** *v.* to boast, brag, swagger, swear (use bad language). **Agpayso kadi ti salsalawasawen daytoy a bruha?** Is it true, what this witch is gabbing about?

salawitwít₁: *n.* wit; agility; intelligence; sharpness of tongue. **nasalawitwit.** *a.* loquacious, talkative; sarcastic, biting (speech); agreeable, accommodating; nimble, brisk, active; witty.

salawitwít₂: agsalawitwit. *v.* to conform, adapt oneself. **nasalwitwit.**

sálay: salayan. *v.* to peel (*ukis*). [Tag. *talop*]

sal-áy: agsal-ay. *v.* to travel by land (walking). (*baniaga*)

salayásay: nasalayasay. *a.* thin, sparse. (forest, woven fabrics, etc.) (*naingpis*, *nasaragasag*; *narasay*) **sumalayasay.** *v.* to become sparse. [Tag. *dalang*]

salayúsoy: *n.* evening breeze at sea; sound of wind and water by the sea. **agsalayusoy.** *v.* to pass through; penetrate; pass between the legs (fish); to sound (said of the sea). (*agtedted*)

salaysáy₁: (Tag. also) *n.* story; narration. **pakasalaysayan.** *n.* story; epic. **salaysayen.** *v.* to narrate, tell, relate a story.

salaysáy₂ *n.* Malabar almond. (*logó*).

salaysáy₃: salaysayen. *v.* to investigate, examine into, inquire upon, interrogate; probe into; find out. (*usig*)

salaysáy₄: pasalaysay. *n.* leash rod inserted in the warp to prevent yarns from becoming entangled.

sálba: (Sp. *salva*) *n.* salvo, gun salute. **agsalba.** *v.* to fire guns in the air to salute.

salbabída: (Sp. *salvavidas*: life preserver) *n.* life preserver, life buoy.

salbadór: (Sp. *salvador*) *n.* savior; rescuer.

salbág₁: *n.* expression used in cursing. **Salbagkan ubing!, Sinalbag nga ubing!** Damn child! [Tag. *lintík*]

salbág₂: salbagen. *v.* to transfix, transpierce; pierce. **nasalbag.** *a.* transpierced; penetrated, affected (by pain, grief, etc.).

salbáhe: (Sp. *salvaje*: savage) *n.* savage. (*naatap a tao*)

salbár: (Sp. *salvar*: save) **salbaren**. *v*. to save; redeem (*salakan*; *salaknib*). [Tag. *ligtás*]

salbasión: (Sp. *salvación*) *n*. salvation.

salbát: **salbaten**. *v*. to intercept along the way. [Tag. *harang*]

salbatána: *var*. of *sarbatana*: blowgun. [Tag. *sumpít*; *salbatana* = species of banded sea snake]

sálbe: (Sp. *salve*) *n*. hail (of a prayer); God bless!

saldá: *n*. mortgage; security; something dearly loved; security for a debt. **isalda**. *v*. to mortgage; pawn. **saldaan**. *v*. to hold in mortgage. **salda ti biag**. *n*. love of one's life. **salda-patay**. *n*. unredeemed mortgaged property after the redeemable period has elapsed. [Tag. *sanlâ*]

saldegéra: (Sp. *sal de higuera*) *n*. Epsom salts.

saldét: **nasaldet**. *a*. faithful; clever, smart, shrewd; diligent; (*obs*.) happy. **saldetan**. *v*. to do with perseverance. [Tag. *sigasig*]

saldiáp: see *taldiáp*: glance; glimpse.

saldít: **nasaldit**. *a*. handsome, pretty, good-looking (*taer*; *guapo*; *taraki*; *pogi*; *pintas*). [Tag. *gandá*]

sáldo: (Sp. *saldo*: balance) *n*. balance in an account. **saldo-a-pabor**. *n*. balance in hand of an account.

salegség: **salegsegen**. *v*. to cram, stuff, fatten. **nasalegseg**. *a*. fat, fattened. [Tag. *siksík*]

saléko: *var*. of *tsaleko*: vest; sleeveless pullover.

saleksék₁: *n*. package stuffing. **isaleksek**. *v*. to cram, crowd, stuff. **nasaleksek**. *a*. crammed, stuffed; hidden; secret; withdrawn. **saleksekan**. *v*. to cram, stuff; fatten. [Tag. *siksík*]

saleksék₂: *n*. hideaway place; secret corner. **sumaleksek**. *v*. to snuggle, curl oneself up, cuddle. **nasaleksek**. *a*. hidden; deep; secret; withdrawn. [Tag. *tagò*]

salém: **nasalem**. *a*. sour; tart. (*alsém*) **Immapiras ti nasalem nga angot ti nabuntuon a basura iti igid ti kalsada**. He sensed the tart smell of the piled garbage at the edge of the street. [Tag. *asim*]

salemsém: **nasalemsem**. *a*. fresh, cool, invigorating, brisk. **sumalemsem**. *v*. to become cool; freshen up. **Nasalemsem ti amian nga aggapo iti akinlaud a bakrang ti Cordillera**. The northern wind coming from the western side of the Cordillera mountains was invigorating. [Tag. *lamíg*]

salensén: **salensenan**. *v*. to overburden; oppress, weigh down; (*reg*.) pile up.

sáleng: *n*. *Pinus insularis* pine, pitch pine, timber of this pine. (*aruo*; *parua*) **sumaleng**. *v*. to become stiff from fatigue (feet) **salngen**. *v*. to cut into firewood; *n*. *Vatica mangachapoi* tree (*narig*). **salengsáleng**. *n*. kind of bony fish,

leather jacket fish, *Scomberoides sp*; kind of brown mantislike insect. [Kal. *saÿong*, Knk. *lawían*, *nána*, *sáleng*, Tag. *sahing* (pine)]

salepsép: **sumalepsep**. *v*. to penetrate (cold, etc.); absorb (*sagepsep*). [Tag. *sipsíp*]

saléro: (Sp. *salero*) *n*. salt shaker; salt pan.

sálet: *n*. plant resembling taro used to cure boils.

salét: (*obs*.) *n*. kind of necklace.

sal-ét: **masal-etan**. *v*. to be intercropped; to be careful.

salgíd: **salgíden**. *v*. to touch. (*sagid*, *kulding*)

sáli: **sumali**. *v*. to join a game, contest, etc.

salí: **sumali**. *v*. to get in the way; anticipate, to take prior action to avoid something from happening; place oneself in the way. **manali**. *n*. busybody, meddler, obtruder. **pasalsali**. *n*. busybody; substitute. **Makasalika!** Go away, you're not needed!

saliá: **isalia**. *v*. to hurl something with force.

saliási: see *siliási*: kind of large iron pot with round bottom.

saliát: (*obs*.) *n*. looking around wildly. **agsaliat**. *v*. to look around wildly or suspiciously. [Tag. *lingâ*]

salibadiókers: (*slang*) *n*. illegal loggers.

salibúkag₁: *n*. feeling of freshness (after bathing). **agsalibukag**. *v*. to feel fresh, cool. **Pasalibukagenna ti rikna**. He freshens up his feelings (to a state of joy). **Nakarikna ti bang-ar ken salibukag**. He felt relief and freshness.

salibúkag₂: **agsalibukag**, **sumalibukag**. *v*. to puff up, inflate; to be hardworking. **sumalibukag ti bagi**. *v*. to become fat, obese. (*bellad*)

salída: (Sp. *salida*: exit) *n*. exit; going on call (doctor); response to an emergency call; appearance (of an actor on stage). **agsalida**. *v*. to appear. **sumalida**. *v*. to leave; exit. **salidaan**. *v*. to take precautions.

salidum-áy: (Igorot) *n*. species of wild herb with white flowers.

sálig: **sinaligan**. *Cordia myxa* tree; variety of awned early rice.

salíg: *n*. obstruction. (*lapped*; *tiped*; *tubeng*) **sumalig**. *v*. to be in the way, obstruct passage. **saligen**. *v*. to obstruct, hinder from passing; intercept. **Sarunuek kuma a litaken ti pispisna ngem nadlawsa ni Manong ti panggepko ken sinalignak**. I should have been the next to hit his temple, but I think my older brother noticed my intention and stopped me.

salígaw: *n*. *Croton tiglium* tree from which croton oil is extracted and whose fruit is used as a fish poison.

saligemgém: *n*. chill, cold; paroxysm. **sumaligemgem**. *v*. to suffer from fever, beginning of a paroxysm; shiver from the cold. (*kutimermer*)

nasaligemgem nga angin-baybay. *n.* cold ocean wind. **Makapasaligemgem ti angin nga immarakup kenkuana.** The wind embracing him was shivering.

saligsíg: saligsigen. *v.* to tighten, cram. (*salegseg*)

salikád: *n.* waistband. **isalikad.** *v.* to insert in one's waistband. **nakasalikad.** *a.* inserted in one's waistband.

salikadáng: *n.* stilt. (*kadangkadáng*)

salikawkáw: agsalikawkaw. *v.* to detour; walk or talk in a roundabout manner; surround. [Tag. *likô*]

salikbáw: salikbawan. *v.* to overtake by use of a shortcut. (*salikbay*)

salikbáy: salikbayan. *v.* to overtake by use of a shortcut; block a fleeing prisoner.

salikepkép: agsalikepkep. *v.* to fold arms toward the chest. (*kepkép*) **salikepkepan.** *v.* to guard someone with one's arms. [Tag. *halukipkíp*]

salikubkób: salikubkuben. *v.* to surround. (*lawlaw*)

salíling: sumaliling. *v.* to seek shelter temporarily (in the shade) (*linong*). [Tag. *silong*]

salímat: agsamlimat. *v.* to lick the lips, fingers, etc.

salimbábuy: sinnalimbabuy. *n.* children's race where they run on hands and feet. (*sarimbaboy*)

salimetmét: *a.* thrifty with money; economy. (*imut*) **salimetmetan.** *v.* to save; protect, defend; preserve; consider; reflect upon; keep in mind. **mannalimetmet.** *n.* keeper of treasured things; packrat. **managsalimetmet.** *a.* thrifty; frugal; stingy. **No kayatmo ti bumaknang, salimetmetam ti kuarta a masapulam.** If you want to get rich, save the money that you earn. **Iti kinasalimetmetna, nakaurnong iti pagpuonan nga agnegosio.** From his thriftiness, he was able to save the capital for his business. [Png. *pangimper*, Tag. *tipíd*]

salimúkok: *n.* depressed feelings; anxieties, worries. **agsalimukok.** *v.* to be sad, depressed; to stay in the corner in self-pity. [Tag. *alalahanin*]

salimúot: *n.* warm, sultry weather; warm air caused by low, dark clouds; humidity. **nasalimuot.** *a.* with warm air conditions, sultry, humid. **agsalimuot.** *v.* to feel restless during hot weather; to swelter. [Tag. *alinsangan* (sultry weather)]

salimúyaw₁: *n.* variety of awned late rice.

salimúyaw₂ *a.* fed up (with eating a certain food). **masalimuyaw.** *v.* to cause disgust; nauseate. (*ariek, suya*) **Masalimuyawak san iti sardinas.** I'm tired of eating sardines.

salimpúpok: salimpupuken. *v.* to encircle, surround. (*lawlaw*)

salindég: *n.* refuge; protection; trust. (*kamang*) **agsalindeg.** *v.* to trust; take shelter, seek protection. **nasalindeg.** *a.* righteous, upright, unbiased, honest; cozy.

salíndro: *n.* harmonica. **agsalindro.** *v.* to play the harmonica. (*silindro*)

salinkayát: (*obs.*) *var.* of *salingkayat*: glad; overjoyed.

salinkób: sumalinkob. *v.* to revolve, circle; hover in flight.

salínong: *n.* shade from sun; shelter from rain; place of refuge. **nasalinong.** *a.* shady, sheltered. (*linong*) **agsalinong, sumalinong.** *v.* to shelter, seek shelter. [Tag. *lilim, silong*]

salínga: (*obs.*) *n.* kind of tissuelike fabric.

salingát: *n.* wedge. (*tingal*) **isalingat.** *v.* to wedge in. **sumalingat.** *v.* to strike in the mind; to get an instant thought; interfere; intrude. [Tag. *singit*]

salingbát: *n.* interruption. **isalingbat.** *v.* to answer in an interruption; interpose; interject (*sampitaw*). **Mabalin ti sumalingbat?** May I interrupt? [Tag. *singit*]

salingéd: *n.* screen; cover; divider; hiding place. **agsalinged, sumalinged.** *v.* to hide, seek shelter. **nasalinged.** *a.* sheltered, safe, secure. **salingden.** (*obs.*) *v.* to turn upside down. [Tag. *tabing*]

salingét: *var.* of *salingat*.

salingetngét: *n.* crevice; narrow space between. **agsalingetnget, sumalingetnget.** *v.* to hide, take cover (in a narrow space); get stuck in a narrow space. **maisalingetnget.** *v.* to lodge between the teeth; to be wedged between. [Tag. *salabit, siwang, biták*]

salinggáyad: *n.* trail of a gown; cloak for women. (*saringgayad*)

salinggúyod: *n.* trail of a gown, mourning cloak. (*saringguyod*)

salingkayát: agsalingkayat. *v.* to be overjoyed; glad. **makasalingkayat.** *a.* overjoyed, glad.

salíngkob: *n.* whirlwind. **agsalingkob.** *v.* to whirl; hover above; encircle. [Tag. *buhawì*]

salingsíng: salingsingan. *v.* to trim branches; clear branches.

salióna: *n.* coin-tossing game consisting of pitching coins toward a stack of coins placed over a *butil* (lowermost coin). Upon hitting the stack, all coins falling off the *butil* become property of the pitcher. **agsaliona.** *v.* to play the *saliona* game.

sálip: *n.* solar eclipse. **agsalip.** *v.* to overlap; eclipse; applaud, clap; clash. **pagsalipen.** *v.* to overlap; fence with swords.

salíp: *n.* contest, competition; coming together of two armies. (*salísal*; *artak*; *dayó*) **maisalip.** *v.* to contend; be in a contest.

salipengpéng: **pasalipengpengan.** *n.* port; waiting shed for passengers. **sumalipengpeng.** *v.* to seek shelter from the heat; lie close to the ground; crouch; take shelter (*kulmeg*). **Simmalipengpeng iti suli idi asitgan ti berdugo.** He cowered in the corner when the executioner approached.

salipúpus: (*obs.*) see *talipúpus*: to do entirely; completely do.

salipsíp: *n.* trimmings. (*salingsing*) **salipsipen.** *v.* to peel bamboo; trim bamboo; cut corn off the cob.

salír: (Sp. *salir*: leave) **agsalir.** *v.* to appear (star).

salísal: *n.* contest; competition. (*salip*) **agsasalisal.** *v.* to compete, contend. (*salíp*; *batara*; *artak*; *balubal*; *dayó*) **makisalisal.** *v.* to participate in a competition. [Tag. *ligsá*]

salísta: (Sp. *alistar*: enroll) **agpasalista.** *v.* to enroll in school. **panagpasalista.** *n.* enrollment.

sal-ít: Interjection expressing disgust; *n.* flash of lightning. **sal-iten.** *v.* to be struck by lightning; damn; beat up. **sal-it nga lakayen.** damn old man. **No diyo ibaga ti yanna, sal-itenkayo amin ita.** If you don't tell where he is, I will curse all of you now. [Tag. *lintík*]

salítre: (Sp. *salitre*: saltpeter) *n.* saltpeter.

salíw: (*obs.*) **saliwen.** *v.* to buy slaves; traffic in slaves or prostitutes.

saliwagkíng: *a.* clumsy; snooping; restless. **Saliwagking ti panagim-imana.** His hands are restless (touching everything).

saliw-án: **saliw-anan.** *v.* to surpass, outdo; take advantage of. **isaliw-an.** *v.* to add to; overwork. **masaliw-anan.** *v.* to take in excess. **nasaliwan.** *a.* impertinent; meddlesome.

saliwanáy: *n.* hook of an earring; rope of a seine fishing net.

saliwanwán: *n.* wealth; affluence. (*baknang*) **nasaliwanwan.** *a.* wealthy; affluent; free, unencumbered; agile, nimble; brisk; loose. **Diak met kalikaguman ti kinasaliwanwantanto kas agassawa.** I didn't want affluence in our marriage. [Tag. *yaman*]

saliwangkíng: *a.* always moving, unquiet, restless; naughty. **saliwangking ti panagim-imana.** He is always touching everything.

saliwásiw: **agsaliwasiw.** *v.* to meet each other when coming from different directions. (*salliwasiw*) **agsinnaliwasiw.** *v.* to separate and meet each other again. **sumaliwasiw.** *v.* to disobey, transgress, sin.

saliwawá: **nasaliwawa.** *a.* imprudent, indiscreet; stupid, foolish.

saliwetwét: *var.* of *salawitwit*.

sallábat: *var.* of *salábat*: intercept on the way.

sallabáwan: *n.* ridgepole; tiebeam pole; lower beam of the *bobongán*. [Tag. *palupo*]

sallábay: **agsallabay.** *v.* to ride on the back of someone. **sallabayen.** *v.* to carry on the back, piggyback style; to put one's arm around another's shoulder. **agsinnalabay.** *v.* to put the arms around each other's shoulders. **pasallabay.** *n.* upper leaves of topped tobacco plants. **Nagsinnallabaykami a nagparetrato.** We had our pictures taken with our arms around each other. [Tag. *akbáy*]

salláday₁: *n.* something to lean on when lying down; pillow used for resting the legs. **salsalladayan.** *v.* to place something over something else; rest arms or legs for support. **agsalladay.** *v.* to sit down with feet resting on support; (*obs.*) to hit someone with a stone.

salláday₂: *n. Cnestis diffusa*, vine whose leaves are poisonous to dogs.

sallaét: **isallaet.** *v.* to insert between two things; to attend to something for the time being, temporarily putting the original task aside.

sallagádaw: (*obs.*) **agsallagadaw.** *v.* to jump out of the mortar (rice kernels being pounded).

sallaguáng: *n.* kind of large funnel-shaped wickerwork bow net used to catch freshwater eels, lobsters, etc. (*barekbek*; *bubo*)

sallaíbad: see *allitálit*: moving multitude; bustling crowd; throng.

sallakápo: **salsallakapo.** *n. Tournefortia sarmentosa* vine with oblong shine leaves and pale green flowers.

sallakét: *n.* embrace (*salikepkep*); clasp. **Nairut ti sallaketda iti luppona.** They are tightly clasped to his thigh.

sallakuáp: *n.* kind of snare with four nooses for herons.

sallakúb: *n.* blanket; enwrapping oneself with a blanket. (*kumot*)

sallákung: *a.* knock-kneed.

sallákup: *a.* bandy-legged. (*akkáng*) **sallakupan.** *v.* to include; encompass; embrace. [Tag. *sakáng*]

sallakót: *var.* of *salakót*: wide-brimmed hat.

sallángad: **nasallangad.** *a.* equidistant.

sallángat: see *sallangad*.

sallapíd₁: *n.* braid, plait of hair. **nakasallapid.** *a.* braided (hair); crossed (legs) **sinallapid.** *a.* consisting of four strands (ropes.) **isallapid.** *v.* to insert in a braid or plait. **sallapiden.** *v.* to braid. [Tag. *tirintás* (Sp.)]

sallapíd₂: **agsallapid.** *v.* to trip when walking, walk crossing the legs as drunks do; fling into each other. **sallapiden.** *v.* to trip someone.

sallapíding: *n.* mole, beauty mark. (*siding*) **sallapidingan.** *a.* with many moles. [Tag. *taling*]

sallapíngaw: *n.* kind of swallow (bird). **Nakitana dagiti gikgik ken sallapingaw nga agaayam iti law-ang.** He saw the falcons and swallows playing in the sky. [Tag. *langaylangayan*]

sallapít: *n.* kind of small bird.

salláwat: *var.* of *allawat*.

salláwid: *n.* ring made of rope, wire or rattan to keep the gate closed. **isallawid.** *v.* to close the gate with a *sallawid.* **masallawidan.** *v.* to get caught in a noose.

sallayúsay: *n.* variety of late awned rice with white kernel; variety of long bean.

sallí: (*obs.*) **maisalli.** *v.* to turn (luck). **agsalli.** *v.* to be out of place, not fit in with the group. **isalli.** *v.* to shift the blame. **sallien.** *v.* to cut off an entire leg. [Tag. *bago*]

salliásid: **agsalliasid.** *v.* to meet; cross.

salliásig: **agsalliasig.** *v.* to miss each other along the way coming from opposite directions. (*salliwasiw*)

sallíket: **agsalliket.** *v.* to get tangled together (bodies, snakes, crabs, etc.).

sallikúbeng: **agsallikubeng.** *v.* to move back and forth (said of fires).

sallín: **sumallin.** *v.* to usurp someone's place; get in the way; intrude. **isallin.** *v.* to intrude; use cosmetics (deodorants, perfumes, makeup); change clothes; drive away someone. [Tag. *singit*]

sallipút: **salliputan.** *v.* to escape from a pursuer. **isalliput.** *v.* to lead a pursuer astray, allowing oneself to escape. **Saanen a maitudo ti kutitmo a simmalisalliput kadagiti tao.** Your tail no longer shows as you run away from the people.

salliwásiw: **agsalliwasiw.** *v.* to miss each other when coming from opposite directions. (*salliasig; allabat*)

sallúkob: **sallukuban.** *v.* to cover; spread over; protect. [Tag. *takíp* (cover)]

sallúpang: **agsallupang.** *v.* to dance vis-à-vis; to be going in different directions. **agsasallupang.** *v.* to face one another, meet face-to-face; confront. **Naungor dagiti agsasallupang a lugan ti agsumbangir a kalsada.** The cars meeting each other face-to-face on both sides of the street were noisy.

sallóy₁: *a.* loose fitting; baggy (*kalawkaláw*); falling sloppily over the shoulder (large shirts). **agsalloy nga agong.** *n.* running nose.

sallóy₂: *n.* weak; unable to decide for oneself; unable to take initiative; (*fig.*) impotent. **agsalloy.** *v.* to be tired, fatigued; weakened (*kapuy, kapsut, lupoy*); to be impotent. **Agsalsalloy a nagpakosina.** He went to the kitchen listlessly. [Tag. *hinà*]

sallóy₃: *n.* dip net, scoop net.

sallúyan: *n.* rope used to support and drag heavy objects on ground.

salmísta: (Sp.) *n.* psalmist.

sálmo: (Sp. *salmo*: psalm) *n.* psalm.

salmuéra: (Sp. *salmuera*: brine) *n.* brine, salty liquid used in pickling.

salmón: (Sp. *salmón*: salmon) *n.* salmon; salmon color.

salnáp: **sumalnap.** *v.* to spread; diffuse. (*kayamkam*) **salnapen.** *v.* to cover entirely; spread over. [Tag. *kalat*]

salngén: *n.* tree similar to the *saleng*.

saluád: *n.* carefulness; protector; guardian. (*salaknib; salakan*) **saluadan.** *v.* to protect, guard; provide for. [Tag. *sanggalang*]

saluáp: *n.* portion of cooked rice under the *ápin*.

salubásib: **salubasiban.** *v.* to weed out the edges of (dikes); (*obs.*) exceed.

salúbung: *n.* welcome party. **salubungan.** *v.* to penetrate, permeate, enter (water, wind); welcome. [Tag. *salubong* = meet]

salubsób: *n.* small splinter or thorn that gets caught in the skin. **masalubsoban.** *v.* to be pricked by a thorn or splinter.

sálud: **sinalud.** *a.* double (garments, fences, etc.).

saludár: (Sp. *saludar*: greet) **saludaran.** *v.* to greet someone.

salúdo: (Sp. *saludo*: greeting) *n.* greeting. **agsaludo.** *v.* to greet, salute.

saludsód: *n.* question, inquiry. **agsaludsod.** *v.* to ask, question; investigate. **saludsuden.** *v.* to ask about, interrogate; question. **managsaludsod.** *a.* always asking questions. **pagsaludsudan.** *v.* to ask someone. [Ibg. *patebbag, ivutan*, Ifg. *baga*, Ivt. *yahes, nahes*, Kal. *imuson*, Kpm. *kutang*, Png. *tepét*, Tag. *tanóng*, Tag. *saludsód* = trowel; uproot; basting; loose stitch]

sálog: **sumalog.** *v.* to go down, come down, descend; decline. **agsalog.** *v.* to slope downward. **sasalogan.** *n.* sloping footpath. [Tag. *babâ*]

salóg: *n.* cuttings of sugarcane used for propagation. [Tag. *tibtíb*]

salugásig: (*obs.*) *n.* bird's song at dawn.

salugsóg: *n.* sliver, bigger than the *puris* but smaller than the *rud-ak.* **salugsugan.** *v.* to get a sliver; pierce sideways, stab sideways. **masalugsugan.** *v.* to be pricked, pierced. **makasalugsog a paggaak.** piercing laughter. **Nagsardeng ta adda nangsalugsog iti isipna.**

He stopped because something struck (*lit:* pierced) his mind. [Tag. *salubsób*]

salúkag: *n.* waking up early; diligence, caution, punctuality; early riser. **agsalukag.** *v.* to be alert, diligent. (*saet; gaget*) **pasalukagen.** *v.* to warn, caution, make aware. **isalukag.** *v.* to warn of. **Ti makaturog makamukat, ti nasalukag, isu't agbiag.** The sleepyhead gathers eyebeams, the diligent person lives. [Tag. *sikap, sipag*]

salukdóy: agsalukdoy. *v.* to droop (limbs or wings) due to weakness.

salukét: *n.* place in a bamboo wall where something can be hung or tucked in. **sasaluketan.** *n.* part of wall where something can be hung. **isaluket.** *v.* to stick, hang on a wall; affix; stick a pencil over the ear. **maisaluket.** *v.* to be hung; affixed; inserted; placed on a wall. **Nakasaluket ti sagaysayna iti bibisngayanna.** Her comb was affixed to the part of her hair. [Tag. *saluksók*]

saluknángan: (*obs.*) *n.* flank of an animal.

salúkob: salukuban. *v.* to cover (in order to protect); defend, shelter; conceal. **isalukob.** *v.* to shield; guard; conceal.

saluksók: *n.* strip inserted at each of the four corners of a woven basket that serve to shape the basket. **isaluksok.** *v.* to insert, put between; put under a pillow; tuck in. **saluksukan.** *v.* to put something underneath; wedge from underneath; change the bedding of a bedridden person. **Insaluksokna ti tinudok a dalag iti ngatuen ti balatbat.** He inserted the speared mudfish on top of the bamboo rafters.

salúlog: *n.* gutter; water pipe (*kalasugan; sayugan*). [Tag. *alulód*]

salomági: see *salamági:* tamarind; tonsil.

salumbát: (*obs.*) **masalumbat.** *v.* to intrude (*salingbat*). [Tag. *singat*]

salumbínit: maisalumbinit. *v.* to get caught on a branch or wire and hang. **agkarasalumbinit.** *v.* to hang in disarray; to hang from branches. [Tag. *lambitin*]

salumína: agsalumina. *v.* to be different from each other. **maisalumina.** *v.* to differ; be different. **naisalsalumina.** *a.* unique; outstanding; very different than usual. **sumalumina.** *v.* to differ. [Tag. *ibá*]

salumpagí: see *samsampíng:* a kind of vine, *Clitorea ternatea.*

salumpáyak: *n.* wide-spreading branches. **agsalumpayak.** *v.* to bend under the weight of fruits or leaves. **nasalumpayak.** *a.* leafy; with many widespreading branches. **nakasalumpayak.** *a.* sitting cross-legged. [Tag. *lagô*]

salumpingáwan: (*obs.*) *n.* young bamboo shoot.

salun-át: *n.* health. (*pia*) **nasalun-at.** *a.* healthy. **salun-atan.** (*obs.*) *v.* to relieve. (*bang-ar*) **masalun-át.** (*obs.*) *v.* to recover. **makapasalunat.** *a.* healthy; nourishing; nutritious. **pasalunaten.** *v.* to make healthy; nourish. [Ivt. *wawa*, Knk. *tédek*, Png. *lagó, tabá*, Tag. *lusóg*]

salunsún: salunsunen. *v.* to stack up. (*sarunsún*).

salungásing: agsalungasing. *v.* to stand apart; separate from a group; be different; disobey. **salungasingen.** *v.* to disobey, violate; transgress. **managsalungasing.** *a.* disobedient; always violating rules or transgressing. **Diak impagarup a salungasingennakami ken Nanangmo.** I didn't figure that you would disobey your mother and me. [Tag. *labág*]

salungát: *a.* opposing; contrary. (*suppiat*) **salungaten.** *v.* to oppose; resist.

salúngay: *var.* of *salungayngay.*

salungayngáy: *a.* lame; paralyzed; losing strength as when becoming unconscious. **agsalungayngay.** *v.* to become paralyzed, unconscious. [Tag. *lungayngáy*]

salungkít: *n.* prong; long stick with a hook at one end to pick fruits, etc. (*sukdal; sarukang*); large clip; bar of a door. **salungkitan.** *v.* to catch something dangling with a prong; pick with a long hooked stick (fruits, etc.). [Tag. *sungkít*]

salungsóng: *n.* kind of rattan; leaves twirled into funnel-shaped cones used for wrapping (rice cake, fish roe, etc.). **agsalungsong.** *v.* to prepare betel nut for chewing. **salungsungen.** *v.* to fold into a funnel-shaped cone (leafs, paper). **salungsungan.** (*obs.*) *v.* to keep all the winnings.

salúp: *n.* measure equivalent to three liters, used for dry goods. (*ganta*) **sumalup, salupen.** *v.* to measure by the *salup*. **Sayang ti bannogda no sumagmamano laeng a salup ti maalada.** Their fatigue went to waste if they were only able to get a few *salup*-fuls.

salup-áyak: agsalup-ayak. *v.* to bend (branches); lower (shoulders).

salupaypáy: *a.* hanging imperfectly (clothes draped crookedly on the body).

salupingpíng: *n.* pectoral fin. **isalupingping.** *v.* to tuck in, tuck up the shirt. [Tag. *suksók* (tuck)]

salupúsop: see *salapósop:* vapor bath; *v.* smoke; fume.

salusón: isaluson. *v.* to lay something down (rug on the floor, etc.).

sal-ót: *var.* of *sal-it:* mild curse word.

saluyabyáb: *a.* torn and hanging (skin, clothes, etc.). **agsaluyabyab.** *v.* to hang (torn clothes, etc.). **Linekkabna ti nagsaluyabyab nga ukis ti kayo.** He tore off the detached and hanging bark of the tree.

salúyaw: *n.* variety of awnless *diket* rice with striped hull and dark kernel.

saluyúsoy: see *salayúsoy*: pass through; penetrate.

salúyot: *n. Corchorus olitorium*, Jews' mallow with edible spinachlike leaves famous in Ilocano cuisine; appellation given to the Ilocano people. **salsaluyot.** *n. Trimfetta sp.* herbs with toothed leaves and yellow flowers. **saluyoten.** *v.* to do with ease. **saluyot-Amerikano.** *n.* okra plant. **kinasaluyot.** *n. (coll.)* Ilocanoness. **Napalalo ti kinasaluyotna.** He is excessively Ilocano. **Kalpasan ti sumagmamano laeng nga aldaw, salsaluyotekon ti mangwarwar ken mangisubli iti daan a makita ti lugan.** After just a few days I was able to disassemble and put together old car engines with ease.

salúysoy: *var.* of *salayusoy*.

sálpa: *n.* platform. **sumalpa.** *v.* to jump on; overflow (river). **isalpa.** *v.* to place on a platform. **Sumalsalpan iti rakit idi kellaat a madungpar ti kanawan a sakana.** He was already on the platform of the raft when suddenly he bumped his right foot.

salpád: *a.* plain, level. (*patad*) **isalpad.** *v.* to load (in a cart).

salpakáya: *n.* easy girl; girl who sits in an easy fashion showing crotch. **agsalpakaya.** *v.* to sit in an unsightly way showing crotch (said of women).

salpáw: *n.* stand for drying.

salpéng: *var.* of *sulpeng*: slow; stubborn.

salpíka: (Sp. *replica*: reply) *n.* reply, answer; entirely new subject introduced in a conversation. **isalpika.** *v.* reply, answer.

salpót: **salputen.** *v.* to pierce through; cross; pass through. **nasalpoan.** *a.* pierced, transfixed; **masalpot.** *v.* to reach (the main road by a bypath). **salsalpot.** *n.* rambling talk; *Andropogon aciculatus* grass with spikelets that adhere to clothing; kind of fish; one who pops in and out at will. **sumalpot.** *v.* to permeate; soak through; go through. **Adda nailet a dalan ditoy a sumalpot iti simbaan.** There is a narrow road here that goes through to the church.

sálsa: *var.* of *sarsa*: sauce, gravy.

salsál₁: **agsalsal.** *v.* to rebound; dribble; beat repeatedly. (*ballatek*)

salsál₂: *n.* masturbation. **agsalsal.** *v.* masturbate (*kalkal, gutad, tultog, laput*). **salsalen.** *v.* to masturbate a part of the body. [Bon. *salsal,* setset, Tag. *salsál*]

salsalamági: (f. *salamagi*) *n.* tonsil.

sálta: (Sp. *saltar*: jump) **saltaen.** *v.* to invade; get on (horse); get in (vehicle). **Sinaltaanna ti nasabang a bukot ti ayup.** He got on the husky back of the animal.

salték: *n.* house lizard. **agsaltek.** *v.* cry of the *salték* (to announce visitors); focus one's eyes or attention. **agsaltek ti mata.** *v.* to focus the eyes. **isaltek.** *v.* to strike against the ground. **maisaltek.** *v.* hit the ground, fall on one's buttocks. **Kasla insaltek a bay-on.** Like a sack whose contents were shaken to the bottom (referring to short persons). **Nagsaltek ti imatangna kadagiti pumurok a sumangsangat nga agturong iti kapilia.** He focused his attention on the villagers ascending toward the church. [Tag. *butikî*]

sálto: (Sp. *salto*: jump) **agsalto.** *v.* to slip (transmission); give way. **saltuen.** *v.* to bring something up with force, raise, lift. **isalto.** *v.* to promote to a higher position (while skipping an intermediary one). **Aguy-uyaoy ti dilana ken simmalto ti bukel dagiti matana.** His tongue tangled and the whites of his eyes appeared.

saltód: **masaltod.** *a.* consumed.

saltók: *n.* bamboo crab trap; slingshot; mousetrap. (*kúrod*)

saltsitsón: (Sp. *salchichón*: sausage) *n.* sausage. (*longganísa, binatútay*)

sáma: **masama.** *v.* to miss, not hit (*tawás*); stray. **masmaan.** *v.* to miss, error; choose incorrectly. **sinama.** *n.* small jack; young branches of vines. **awán ti sámana, di sumáma.** without fail, without doubt; surely, certainly. [Tag. *kamalî*]

samáda: *n.* collar (of a shirt).

sámak₁: *n. Macaranga tanarius* tree whose bark and bitter leaves are used to brew *bási* and give it a brown color.

sámak₂: **mapasamak.** *v.* to happen, occur; take place; experience; endure, undergo; suffer. **pasamak.** *n.* event, occurrence; outcome; consequence. **pasamáken.** *n.* event yet to occur. **Ania ti napasamak?** What happened? [Tag. *yari*]

samák: **kasamak.** *n.* tenant. **makikasamak.** *v.* to work as a tenant farmer. [Tag. *kasama*]

Sámal: *n.* Muslim ethnic group from Sulu and Zamboanga City; language of the *Samals*.

samál: *n.* a kind of potent poison. (*sabidong*) **Adadda a dumakes ti pagilian no agbalin a samal ti rikna a di mayebkas.** The country would most likely worsen if the unexpressed feelings turn to poison. [Png. *samál*]

sáman: *conj.* as if.

samántong: samsamantong. *a.* crazy; insane; moronic. (*mulluong*; *bagtit*)

sámang: *n.* kind of shelf made of woven bamboo. isamang. *v.* to place on a shelf.

sámar: sinamar. *n.* ray of light; trail of a comet; sap of coco palm. agsinamar. *v.* to brighten up; become well known. [Tag. *silahis*]

samára: (*obs.*) *n.* kind of black, fragrant paste.

samaritáno: (Sp. *samaritano*: Samaritan) *n.* Samaritan.

sámay: sumamay. *v.* to penetrate, permeate; diffuse, spread; take affect (medicine); be affected; influence the feelings of. samayen. *v.* to permeate, penetrate; diffuse; affect. nasamay. *a.* effective; strong; influential. kinasamay. *n.* effectiveness. Kasla bumtak ti darangidong ken lapayagna idi sumamay ti ingel ti pagisawsawan nga insubona. His nose and ears seemed to explode when the strong spice of the dip he put in his mouth took effect. [Tag. *bisà*]

Sambál: *n.* native of Zambales Province; Zambal language.

sambaldóke: *n.* cashew tree. (*kasuy*)

sambílak: *n.* variety of awned rice.

sambirgá: *n.* removable basket placed on a sled to carry transported items. isambirga. *v.* to load something into the *sambirga*.

sambirí: *n.* waved edging (crochet or lacework); homemade helmet (*barayubay*). [Tag. *palamuti*]

sambírit: agkarasambirit. *v.* to be hung indiscriminately (clothes) (*salumbinit*). [Tag. *lambitin*]

sámbong: isambong, sambongen. *v.* to cook slightly (*kilnat*). sinambong. *n.* slightly cooked dish.

samborión: *n.* chimney of the *anáwang* furnace. (*simburion*)

sambút: agsambut. *v.* to rush, hurry. (*kamakam*) Sambutem! Hurry up! (*darasem!*) maisambut. *v.* to be in time for. sambutan. *v.* to recover; compensate; redeem; satisfy; repay. isambut. *v.* to finish, get ready in time; prepare. maisambut. *v.* to be ready in time for. pagsasambut. *a.* prepared, easy to make (instant coffee). [Tag. *habol* (chase; hurry); *sambót* (catch; recover)]

samék: nasamek. *a.* dense (undergrowth). samsamek. *n.* earless maize (used for fodder). sumamek. *v.* to grow lush. kasamekan. *n.* thick underbrush; lush area of vegetation. kinasamek. *n.* lushness of vegetation. [Png. *buná*, Tag. *lagô*, *labay*]

sámer: sameren. *v.* to regulate the flow of water. pagsamer. *n.* contrivance used to regulate the flow of water.

samét: samsamet. *a.* interrupted (sleep).

samíding: *n.* dire consequences of a bad deed; wrong move.

saminár: (Sp. *examinar*: examine) saminaren. *v.* to scrutinize, examine, look at carefully.

sámir: samiren. *v.* to shun, shrink from. sinamir. *n.* shade made from woven coconut palm leaves. (*lingaling*) di samiren. *v.* to do without complaints. Saan a sinamir ni Gracia iti rigat. Gracia did not shun hardships. [Tag. *iwas*]

samirá: *n.* spare time. agsamira. *v.* to keep time; take time. isamira. *v.* to insert; to take time; do during one's spare hours. awan samira. *exp.* to be always busy with no free time. Isamirana a taliwaen dagiti pasdek. He took the time to look back at the buildings.

samírad: *n.* mat of palm leaves for covering.

sam-ít: nasam-it. *a.* sweet. pasam-itan, pasamiten. *v.* to sweeten. masam-itan. *v.* to be surfeited; enjoy. pagsinam-it. *v.* to serve sweets after meals. samsam-it. *n.* kind of small freshwater crab. sinam-it. *n.* sweets. managsinam-it. *a.* fond of sweets, sweet-toothed. napasam-it. *a.* sweetened. Nasamsam-it ti ayat iti maikadua a gundaway. Love is sweeter during the second chance. [Ibg. *ammíq*, *nemmieq*, Ivt. *unawnas*, *masdep*, Kal. *mammiis*, Knk. *sum-út*, Kpm. *mayúmu*, Png. *samít*, Tag. *tamís*]

samíweng: *n.* music (*tokar*); melody.

sammakéd: *n.* prop, support; trust. pagsammakedan. *n.* fort; garrison. agsammaked. *v.* to support; lean on; rely on. Nagsammaked iti tawa iti panangtannawagna iti baybay. He leaned against the window as he looked down at the sea. [Tag. *tukod*, *suhay*]

sammaltó: *n.* species of jumping fish.

sammán: Contraction of *saan man*: affirmative declaration countering a negative one.

sammát: *n.* unjust acquisition; grabber, opportunist. agsammat. *v.* to act incoherently; mix up actions (drink from two cups, etc.); grab.

sammí: sammisammí. *n.* kind of small, green, glossy beetle. sumammisammi. *v.* to shine, be glossy. simmammisammi. *v.* to be very black. [Tag. *salagubang*]

sammímit: sammimitan. *v.* to hold with the lips. (*ammi*) nakasammimit. *a.* held in the lips (cigars).

sammúkak: agsamsammukak. *v.* to eat gluttonously.

sammúkat: *n.* eating between meals. agsammukat. *v.* to eat between meals. (*taknang*)

sammukól: masammukol. *v.* to be clumsy, awkward; bulky; uncomfortable.

sammúsam: *n.* mixed variety, many kinds of rice.

samukól: *var.* of *sammukol*: clumsy, awkward; bulky; uncomfortable.

sam-ól: *var.* of *sakmol*: put in the mouth.

samón: *n.* spider commonly found in *samsamon* grass. **samsamon.** *n.* *Themeda triandra* grass with leafy stalks.

samóng: *var.* of *samon*.

samór: **masamoran.** *v.* to infect (disease); mix; pollute. (*gamer; kapet; laok*)

samoriádo: *var.* of *moriado*: crazy, out of one's mind. (*bagtit*)

samúsam: *n.* medley, mixture; kind of rice field weed; *a.* common, usual. **agsasamusam.** *v.* to be saddled with too many problems. **Nakullaapan ti panunotna gapu kadagiti agsasamusam a nalidem a pagteng.** His mind cleared up from many gloomy events. [Tag. *patung-patong*]

sámot: **samotsamot.** *n.* frazzle, frayings; cobwebs. [Tag. *samut-samot*]

samuyéng: *n.* sorrow, grief, anguish, distress; indisposition; general weak feeling of sickness. **agsamuyeng.** *v.* to feel ill. **Pasaray malipatakon ti bagik gapu iti samuyeng a diak mabalin a liklikan.** Often I forget myself because of the anguish I cannot vanquish. [Tag. *balisa*]

sampá: *n.* top, peak, summit of a mountain. (*sápat; pantok; murdong; aringgawis; alintotok; toktok; tapaw*) **sumampa.** *v.* to reach the top. **isampa.** *v.* to carry to the top; file a court case.

sampága₁: *n.* *Jasminium sambac*, Arabian jasmine.

sampága₂: **agsampaga.** *v.* to bloom. **nasampaga.** *a.* robust (trees) (*rukbos*). [Tag. *bukadkád*]

sampagíta: (Sp. *sampaguita*: native species of flower, see *sampága*) *n.* small jasmine flower, national flower of the Philippines.

sampán: (Eng.) *n.* champagne. (*obs.*) **sam-sampan.** *n.* sampan.

sampátaw: *n.* interruption. (*sagpaw, sampítaw*).

sampáy: Contraction of *saan* and *pay*: not yet.

sampáyaw: (*obs.*) *n.* bracelets (*binallad; galang; gapak; pangodo*)

sampédro: (Sp. *San Pedro*) see *patalunton*: Filipino assistant priest during Spanish colonial days.

sampíla: **agsampila.** *v.* to sit on the ground with both legs on the same side; to sit cross-legged.

sampílok: *n.* kind of native machete.

sampílot: *n.* variety of awned *diket* rice with speckled hull and red kernel.

sampíng: **isamping.** *v.* to tuck in. (*sab-it*) **sam-samping.** *n.* *Clitorea ternatea* vine with edible

pods, blue pea vine. [Png. *samsampíng*, Tag. *pukinggán*]

sampítaw: **sumapitaw.** *v.* to meddle; interfere officiously; interrupt. (*biang; salingbat*) **isampitaw.** *v.* to interpose. [Tag. *singit, himasok*]

sampór: **agsampor.** *v.* to reel twine for netting on the *sikuán*. **sampuren.** *v.* to reel twine of two different kinds.

samporádo: *var.* of *tsampurádo*: rice porridge with chocolate.

sampóy: *var.* of *tsampóy*: salted or sweetened dried fruit.

samrá: *n.* blouse with long sleeves and no collar. **nakasamra.** *a.* wearing a blouse with long sleeves and no collar.

samráw: *n.* indigo dye. **samrawen.** *v.* to dye cotton yarn with indigo. **sumamraw.** *v.* to interpose impertinently.

samríd: *n.* kind of black hairy stinging caterpillar whose stings itch. **samriden.** *v.* to be affected with the rash of the *samrid*; to die by eating the *samrid*. **masamrid.** *v.* to be stung by a caterpillar. **masamridan.** *v.* to be affected by the caterpillar sting.

samróy: (*obs.*) *n.* clean, shady lane.

samsám: *n.* loot, pillage, booty, spoils in war. **nasamsam.** (*obs.*) *a.* facetious. **samsamen.** *v.* to loot; steal everything. [Png., Tag. *samsám*]

samtiék: *var.* of *samtík*: clicking sound in throat.

samtík: **agsamtik.** *v.* to make a clicking sound in the throat. (*sanamtek*)

samtóy: [*saomi 'toy*] *n.* native language (of the Ilocanos). **agsinasamtoy.** *v.* to talk in one's native language; to speak Ilokano.

San: (Sp.) Saint (used before male names of saints). **San Marcos.** Saint Mark; ringing of churchbells for the dead. **San Miguel, sammigel.** *n.* trademark of a popular beer and gin. **San Bisente.** *n.* type of bush with white or violet flowers with five petals. **San Ramon.** *n.* variety of coffee. **San Francisco.** *n.* species of ornamental shrub with white or violet flowers. **San Antonio.** *n.* frock similar to that of Saint Anthony.

saná: *n.* salt made from seawater. (*asin*) **agsana.** *v.* to make salt by cooking seawater. **agsansana.** *n.* salt maker. **pagsanaan.** *n.* place where salt is made from seawater.

sanáang: **nasanaang.** *a.* painful, poignant, stinging, biting. (*ut-ot*) **agsanaang.** *v.* to suffer a biting pain. **pagsanaangen.** *v.* to cause someone to suffer pain. **Padpadasek payen a lipaten ni Maria ngem agsanaang met 'toy barukongko.** I am still trying to forget Maria, but my chest still is filled with pain. [Tag. *hapdî*]

sanabsáb: (f. *sabsáb*) *n*. sound of noisy chewing.

sanagawísiw: (f. *sagawisiw*) *n*. loud or intense whistling. **sumanagawisiw.** *v*. to whistle; whoosh.

sanakuntíp: (f. *sakuntip*) **sumanakuntíp.** *v*. to smack the lips; make the sound of smacking lips.

sanalték: *var*. of *sanaltep*: smacking the lips.

sanaltép: (f. *salltep*) **agsanaltep.** *v*. to smack the lips; say *tsk!* (*sakuntip*)

sanamték: (f. *samték*) **sumanamtek.** *v*. to smack the lips. [Tag. *palaták*]

sanang-í: (f. *sang-i*) **agsanang-i.** *v*. to sob continuously (children).

sanaó: (f. *sao*) **sumanao.** *v*. to speak vociferously; to gossip, speak idly. (*tababbaaw*)

sánap: *n*. suspicion; doubt. (*atap*; *sadap*) **sanapen.** *v*. to include all. [Tag. *hinalà*]

sanapsáp: (f. *sapsap*) *n*. sound produced by voracious eating of food. **agsanapsap.** *v*. to chomp on one's food (as pigs eating).

sánat: *n*. prop, wedge; support. (*basil*; *pasat*) **sanatan.** *v*. to put a wedge in (to make something steady). [Tag. *kalang* (Sp.)]

sanatório: (Sp. *sanatorio*: sanatorium) *n*. sanatorium.

sanatsát: (f. *satsat*) *n*. the sound of repeated whipping.

sánay: **sanayen.** *v*. to exercise oneself, practice; train; get used to. **nasanay.** *a*. in practice. **pagsanayan.** *n*. training center. [Tag. *sanay*]

sanáyas: *n*. impression, track (in water).

sanayyét: (f. *sayyét*) **sumanayyet.** *v*. to flirt immodestly.

sandálias: (Sp. *sandalia*: sandal) *n*. sandals.

sandí: *n*. substitute; replacement. **sandian.** *v*. to substitute, replace; take place of. **Isu ti mangisandi kaniak kadagiti klasek no adda samuyengko.** He is the one who substitutes for me in my classes when I'm ill. [Tag. *palít*]

sandía: (Sp. *sandía*: watermelon) *n*. watermelon. [Ivt. *simun*, Png., Tag. *pakwán*]

sandír: **agsandir.** *v*. to lean on one's back; *var*. of *sindir*: to keep in order.

sandó: (f. Japanese) *n*. sleeveless undershirt, muscle shirt (*pawad*). **nakasando.** *a*. wearing a sleeveless undershirt.

sandugó: *n*. blood pact. **agsandugo.** *v*. to be intimate friends (used by mountain people). [Tag. *sandugô*]

sanéb: *n*. ambuscade. (*saed*; *abang*) **sanben.** *v*. to waylay, ambush; entrap, mislead. **Iti panagisalogda iti troso, adda nagsaneb kadakuada a nagtagiarmas.** When they brought down the log, armed men ambushed them. [Tag. *haráng*]

san-ék: *var*. of *saltek*, *sen-al*.

sanéng: **masneng.** *v*. to languish, fade (through excessive moisture) (plants); to faint from the heat; to be withered; to be overcooked. [Tag. *luóy*]

sanengséng: (f. *sengséng*) *n*. sound of bullets whizzing. **agkasanengseng.** *n*. rapid firing of bullets. **Simmanengseng ti bala iti ngatuen ti ulona.** The bullets whizzed over his head.

sanersér: (f. *serser*) *n*. sound of an ascending kite. **agsanerser.** *v*. to ascend (kite).

sanetsét₁: (f. *setset*) **sumanetset.** *v*. to be burning hot. (*sayetset*, *rissit*)

sanetsét₂: (f. *setset*) *n*. hissing sound of frying lard. **sumanetset.** *v*. to hiss (said of frying lard).

saniáta: *n*. jewel, gem (*alahas*); commodities; goods. **agsaniata.** *v*. to dress in splendid attire. **nasaniata.** *a*. affluent; rich (*baknang*). [Tag. *mutyâ*]

sánib₁: saniben. *v*. to check, restrain, hold back; stop a boat with the oars (*sardeng*). [Tag. *pigil*]

sánib₂: **sumanib.** *v*. to mix; be possessed by an evil spirit. **saniban.** *v*. to possess (said of an evil spirit). (*annong*, *kablaaw*)

sanidád: (Sp. *sanidad*: sanity) *n*. sanity; sanitation, cleanliness; sanitary inspector.

sanigkí: **sumanigki.** *v*. to start up from sleep with heavy breathing.

saniít: **nasaniit.** *a*. scorching (heat, pain). **sumaniit.** *v*. to feel pain. **sansaniiten.** *v*. to have a severe fever. **Napamusiigda iti saniit.** They contorted their mouths in pain.

saníkar: *n*. agility; activeness (*siglat*). **nasanikar.** *a*. active; agile; brisk; lively. **Nasanikar ti panagsasaoda.** Their speech is lively. [Tag. *siglá*]

sanikuá: *n*. property, goods, possessions. **nasanikua.** *a*. opulent, wealthy. (*baknang*) **masanikua.** *v*. to have leisure time; to be ready. [Kal. *kukkuwa*, Tag. *arì*]

sanil-í: *var*. of *sanang-i*.

saning-í: *n*. whining; sob. (*sang-i*; *sainnek*; *saibbek*) **agsaning-i.** *v*. to sob; whine. [Tag. *hikbî*]

saninglót: (f. *singlót*) **agsaninglot.** *v*. to suck up nasal mucus; sob while sucking up nasal mucus.

saníp: *n*. cluster of palm flowers; variety of awned early rice with red kernel.

sanípa: *n*. patchwork on a thatched roof; thatchwork; venetian blind.

sanírip: (f. *sirip*) **sumanirip, sumanarinip.** *v*. to peep about, poke one's nose around.

sanitário: (Sp. *sanitario*: sanitary) *n*. sanitary inspector, health inspector.

saniwéng: *var*. of *samiweng*: *n*. music.

sanníket: **sansanniket.** *n*. kind of herb resembling the *kúnig*.

sanúd: agsanud. v. to go backward, recant; withdraw; recede; retrograde; change one's mind; postpone; retreat; surrender. panagsanud. n. stepping backward; going backward. isanud. v. to move back; postpone; change one's mind. Isanudmo laengen ti kaso. Just postpone the case. Ti pudno a lalaki, saanna nga ammo ti agsanud uray iti wangawangan ti patay. A real man doesn't know how to surrender even on the verge of death. [Tag. *urong*]

sanúod: var. of sanud.

sanúong: sansanuong. n. idiot; crazy person. agsanuong. v. to go crazy (*bagtit; balla*). Agsansanuong. He is going crazy; (*coll.*) he is penniless.

sanúp: sanupan. v. to cover, wrap up (fruits when protecting from birds). [Tag. *balot*]

sanursór₁: agsanursor. v. to slurp up.

sanursór₂: agsanursor. v. to wander from place to place (*sorsor*).

sánut: sumanut. v. to reach; be sufficient; be as long as necessary; to be patient, tolerant. pasanuten. v. to suckle, curse; nourish; teach, instruct; discipline; rear, foster.

sanút: sanutan. v. to whip; lash; destroy; damage. nasanut. a. straight and level (roads); worn out, ruined, damaged; beaten. [Tag. *hagupít*]

sanpédro: (Sp. *San Pedro*) sinnanpedro. kind of girl's game in which a blindfolded player is whirled and must point at another player. (*binnigkét*). nasanpedro. a. confused; blindfolded.

sanráy: n. small tobacco leaves surrounding the flower of Virginia tobacco.

sansán: masansan. adv. often, frequently. sansanen. v. to do frequently, many times. kinamasansan. n. frequency. Ti la kadandanagko, isu ti masansan a panagmaymaysak. The thing I worry about is my frequently being alone. [Kal. *kookoon*, Knk. *wan-í*, Png. *betbet*, Tag. *dalás*]

sansílmo: n. Saint Elmo's fire, supernatural force that makes people lose their way; traveling fireball.

sánta: (Sp. *santa*: holy; female saint) n. female saint; a. holy. Santa Biblia. n. Holy Bible.

santák: n. layer; offshoot. sumantak. v. to grow lush. nasantak. a. lush; verdant (*samek*). [Tag. *lagô*]

santán: n. species of ornamental flower, *Ixora chinensis*.

santáng: n. *Ixora chinensis* shrub with pinkish flowers.

santiguár: (Sp. *santiguar*: make the sign of the cross) manantiguar. n. pagan rites; v. to perform pagan rituals; bless; anoint.

santílmo: var. of *sansilmo*: St. Elmo's fire, supernatural force that makes people lose their way.

santipikár: (Sp. *santificar*) santipikaren. v. to sanctify.

santísima: (Sp. *santísima*: most holy) santisima kurus. exp. denoting mild surprise (*lit*: most holy cross).

santísimo: (Sp. *santísimo*: most holy) a. most holy.

santíta, santíto: (Sp. *santito*: little saint) simmantito. a. saintly. aginsasantito. v. to pretend to be very good. simmantita a rupa. saintly face.

sánto: (Sp. *santo*: saint; holy) n. saint; *sa + nto*: then he will. nasantuan. a. holy. kinasanto. n. sainthood; holiness. santo rosario. n. holy rosary. mamasanto. v. to sanctify.

santuário: (Sp. *santuario*: sanctuary) n. sanctuary, sacred place.

santól: n. *Sandoricum koetjape* tree with yellowish acidic fruits, eaten salted and dried. panantolen. n. kind of tall tree valuable for its timber. Kasla adda met naisullat a santol iti lilidduokanna. There seems to be a plugged *santol* in his throat. [Tag. *santól*]

santorosário: (Sp. *santo rosario*: holy rosary) n. rosary. agsantorosario. v. to pray the rosary.

sanga-: (f. *maysa nga*) prefix used to form units of length, capacity, time, etc. meaning one unit of: sangapulo. ten (one group of ten). sangaraay. one bunch, cluster. [Ibg. *tanga-*, Tag. *isáng, san-*]

sanga- -an: circumfix denoting entirety: sangalubongan. the whole world. sangalaw-angan. the entire universe. sangalangitan. all the powers of heaven. sangagungluan. the whole society; the whole organization.

sánga: n. larva of the clothes moth; silverfish; mothball. sinanga. a. eaten by silverfish. [Tag. *tangà*]

sangá: n. branch, point; offshoot; division, section. agsanga. v. to branch out; diversify. pasanga. n. packsaddle; kind of bird snare with a noose (*baór*) and a catch (*baklíng*). agsangasanga ti saritaanda. Their stories do not concur. sangaan. a. with many branches. nagsangaan ti dalan. n. intersection. Nagsasanga dagiti dalan a mabalin a suroten. The road you may follow has many offshoots. [Kal. *panga*, Knk. *ánga*, Png., Tag. *sangá*]

sangaanó: nagsangaano ta. maybe, perhaps (*siguro, ngata*). [Tag. *maaari*]

sangabték: (f. *bették*) n. one bundle of palay.

sangadpá: (f. *deppá*) n. one armspan.

sangaíli: (f. *ili*) n. menses; guest. agsangaili. v. to menstruate; to entertain guests. pagsangaili.

n. something to be used for guests; something to serve to guests. **sangailien.** *v.* to receive as a guest. **managsangaili.** *a.* hospitable. **kinamanagsangaili.** *n.* hospitality; act of frequently entertaining guests. **sangsangaili.** *n.* stranger. **Baradibod laeng ti kabaelanda a pagsangaili.** Sweet potato porridge is all they have to give their guests. **Saandak a sangailien no bisitaenkayo.** Do not receive me as a guest when I visit you. [Bon. *ebes* (menses), *lang-ay* (guest), Kal. *mangili*, Png. *sankaili*, Tag. *dalaw* (guest, visitor)]

sángal: *n.* kind of tree that yields valuable timber; project; knots to which ropes are joined; joint; scarf joint in a post. **isangal.** *v.* to join (a contest, debate, etc.). **pagsangalan.** *n.* joint, where two parts join. **sangalen.** *v.* to join, unite, connect; put together; compose. **Nalaingda nga agsangal iti daniw.** They are good at composing poetry. **Sinangona ti makinilia tapno sangalenna ti bitlana.** He got in front of his typewriter so he could put together his speech. **Naisangsangal iti bukanegan idi agtutubo.** He joined poetry jousts when he was young. [Tag. *sangál* = cut branches of trees]

sangalubóngan: (f. *lubong*) *a.* worldwide.

sangapúlo: (f. *pulo*) *num.* ten. [Kal. *simpuÿu*, Png. *sampolo*, Tag. *sampû*]

sángar: **isangar, sangaren.** *v.* to disobey authority (*sukir*); to butt with horns (water buffalo).

sángat: **sangaten.** *v.* to inspect; demand explanation of; demand apology. **isangat.** *v.* to accuse, charge with. **masangatan a natay.** *v.* to be found dead. **agsangat.** *v.* to inspect (a fish trap) to see if it is ready to collect the catch.

sang-át: *n.* land (distinguished from water) (*daga*); upland region; bank; ledge. **isang-at.** *v.* to carry up to a place; land; take to the mountains (a captive). **nasang-at.** *a.* high; steep. **sang-aten.** *v.* to climb a mountain. **sumang-at.** *v.* to ascend, climb; disembark; land. **sasangatan.** *n.* disembarking area; footpath on a river.

sang-áw: *n.* breath (*ánges*). **isang-aw.** *v.* to exhale. **sumang-aw.** *v.* to breathe, exhale. **sang-awan.** *v.* to breathe upon, blow upon. **makasang-aw.** *v.* to be able to breathe. **masang-awan.** *v.* to be affected by the breath of someone (smell the foul breath of someone). **agassang-aw ti gatas.** *v.* to have milk breath (said of babies or immature youngsters). [Tag. *hiningá*]

sángay: *n. Pahudia rhomboidea* tree with yellowish red flowers yielding a valuable timber.

sangáy: *n.* matter on hand; branch (of an office). **naisangayan.** *n.* something different from all matters.

sangayán: **naisangayan.** *a.* exceptional, extradinary, outstanding; different (*salumina*; *duma*); superior; rare. **isangsangayan.** *v.* to do especially for. **Kasla adda naisangsangayan a pigsa a nagpussuak iti kaungganna.** It's like exceptional strength spouted in him. [Tag. *pambihirà*]

sangay-án: (*obs.*) *n.* changing one's opinion.

sangbár: **maisangbar.** *v.* to be affected by negative elements, experience a calamity; to be destroyed by a calamity. **Nagparikna ngata kenkuana daytoy nakaisangbaranda a peggad?** Do you think he was forewarned about the danger they experienced?

sangbáy: **pasangbayen.** *v.* to lodge, receive a guest. **mamasangbay.** *n.* host. **maisangbay.** *v.* to jam, become obstructed. **sumangbay.** *v.* to lodge; stay for the night; to happen when least expected; obstruct. **sangbayan.** *n.* lodging for the night. **Situturedak a nangsango kadagiti parikut a simmangbay iti biagko.** I have the courage to confront the problems that obstruct my life. [Tag. *tuloy*]

sangdó: **sumangdo, sangduen.** *v.* to butt, strike with the head or horns; attack. **maisangdo.** *v.* to strike the head against; bump (*dungpar, dupong, sang-il, saw-ing, bangdol, bungdol*). **agsinnangdo.** *v.* to butt each other with the horns or head. **agpinnasangdo.** *v.* to cause two animals to bump in a game; to fight two June bugs. **Nasangdoak iti nuang.** I was butted by a water buffalo. **Saanka a pinagadal tapno sangduennak laeng.** I didn't put you through school just so you can attack me. [Tag. *suwág*]

sangér: *n.* strong smell of liquors or tobacco. **nasanger.** *a.* strong smelling (said of alcohol); brave. **sumanger.** *v.* to become strong (alcohol); ferment. **Nagiwarasda iti tinapay ket pagpalamiis kadagiti immay a saan nga umin-inum iti nasanger.** They put out bread and refreshments for the guests who came that do not drink alcohol. [Tag. *tapang*]

sangét: *n.* central part of the unopened spade of a betel palm; splint (for broken bones); graft of plants. **sangetan.** *v.* to apply splints on. [Tag. *balangkát*]

sanggá: *n.* collar around the blade of a *bolo*; saucer. **pagsanggaan.** *n.* saucer. **masangga.** *v.* to strike against, collide with. **sanggaen.** *v.* to fend off; turn aside (with a sword); shield; deflect. **kasangga.** *n.* teammate. **agkasangga.** *v.* to be teammates. **sangga-sangga.** *a.* divided into teams. **Tunggal rengrengenna idi ni Meding, isangga met daytoy.** Every time he disturbed Meding before, she warded him off. [Tag. *sanggá*]

sanggál: *n.* saddle.

sanggalá: sanggalaen. *v.* to place crosswise. **pagsasanggalaen.** *v.* to stack (arms). **agsasanggala.** *v.* to crisscross one another. [Tag. *sala-salabát*]

sanggáw: *n.* heavy upper beam of the *linggí* in a loom.

sanggír: agsanggir. *v.* to lean, incline (rest on for support). **isanggir.** *v.* to lean, incline. **pasanggir.** *n.* rafter; sawhorse. **Pinadatana ti rakit a naipasanggir iti niog.** He put the raft on its back, leaning against the coconut tree. **Kayatko a nasalun-atta nga agpadpada tapno nabilegto ti sanggir dagiti anakta.** I want us both to be healthy so our children will have strong support. [Ibg. *mamérig*, Ifg. *midangkig*, Ivt. *manáreng*, Kpm. *sandal*, Png. *saral*, Tag. *sandál*]

sangguét: (*obs.*) *n.* foreigner. (*ganggannaet*)

sanggól: *n.* arm wrestling; contrivance used to raise posts. **agsanggol.** *v.* to wrestle to the ground with the arms; arm wrestle. **pagsanggolen.** *v.* to couple, connect. **sanggolen.** *v.* to hook the arm around the neck or under the arm of; put the arm around the neck or back of; to link elbows. [Tag. *bunóng braso* (arm wrestling); *sanggól* = infant]

sanggúyop: agsangguyop, sangguyupen. *v.* to blow tobacco smoke into the ear (in order to remove ants, etc.). **masangguyopan ti lapayag.** *v.* to be able to be smoked (said of the ears) in order to remove ants.

sángi: *n.* molar tooth; pinna at base of palm blade. **agsangi.** *v.* to have a toothache. **sumangi.** *v.* to be bullheaded. **Magustuak ti tangken ti sangina.** I like how hard his molar tooth is (referring to a stubborn person). [Ibg. *bagang, kamáloq*, Ifg. *worwor*, Isg. *wangli*, Ivt. *kamansasangah*, Knk. *wéwe, ngot-ó*, Kpm., Tag. *bagang*, Png. *pangal* (molar)]

sang-í: agsang-i. *v.* to sob. (*saiddek*) **agsanang-i.** *v.* to make continuous sobbing noises. [Tag. *hikbí*]

sang-íl: sumang-il. *v.* to butt sideways (*sangdo*). [Tag. *suwág*]

sangílo: *n.* species of small tree with yellowing green wood, *Pistacia chinensis bunge.*

sangió: *n.* shrew with a long nose, mole (rodent).

sángit: *n.* crying; cry. **agsangit.** *v.* to cry, weep. **agsangit ti ubet.** (*fig.*) *v.* to have diarrhea. (*buris*) **managsangit.** *n.* crybaby; sissy. **sangitan.** *v.* to lament. **arinsangíten.** *a.* on the verge of tears. **makasangsangit.** *v.* to feel like crying. [Bon. *ágal*, Ibg. *kuleq, tángiq*, Ivt. *tañis*, Kal. *ibin*, Knk. *úga, ága, eá, kulágaw, kosnó*, Kpm. *kiyak*, Png. *akís*, Tag. *iyák*]

sang-íw: see *sang-íl*: butt sideways; strike with the horns sideways.

sangka-: see *sanga-* prefix, frequentative prefix that takes the ergative *-ko* series pronouns. **sangkadamagnaka.** He's always asking for you. **sangkasaonaka.** He's always talking about you. **Segseggaak ti sangkakunana nga isasarungkarna iti balaymi.** I am anxious he constantly says that he will visit our house. **Apay a sangkadamagmo lat' oras ti isasangpetko?** Why do you keep asking about the time of my arrival? **Amin a papananna, sangkasaludsodda no agpayso ti damag.** Wherever he goes, they keep asking if the news is true.

sangka-: *var.* of *sanga-*. **sangkasakmol.** one mouthful. **sangkasingay.** one bundle of rice. **sangkareppet.** one bunch, one bundle. [Tag. *isáng*]

sangkā- -ān: circumfix that denotes entirety, completeness of one. **sangkaamaan.** the whole family. **sangkabarkadaan.** the whole group of friends. **Para iti pagimbagan iti sangkaaduan.** It's for the good of the majority. **Sangkakirogan ti naurnongda nga abal-abal.** They gathered enough June bugs for one whole roast.

sangkai-: *var.* of *sangka-*.

sangkáp: *n.* chip of wood; variety of *díket* rice. **Narusanger ti sangkap a nalikab iti kayo.** The chip of wood removed from the tree was coarse.

sangkít: *n. Illicium sp.* star anise.

sangklétas: (Sp. *chancleta*: slipper) *n.* slipper.

sangkutsár: *n.* native dish made of goat intestines, blood, lungs, and tripe seasoned with onions, pepper, garlic, salt, and vinegar.

sanglád: sumanglad. *v.* to anchor; reach the shore; land (planes). **maisanglad.** *v.* to strand, hit the bottom, ground. **sangladan.** *n.* airport; docking area. [Tag. *lunsád*]

sangláw₁: *n.* species of tree whose roots are used to cure wounds, *Ficus stipulosa.*

sangláw₂ *a.* imperfect, defective; incomplete; tasteless cooking. **sinanglaw.** *n.* dish made of pieces of beef boiled in vinegar and water; defective, imperfect thing. **Sinanglawenna ti sangkakilo a karne ti baka.** He is making one kilo of beef into *sinanglaw*.

sangláy₁: (Hok. *sang lai*: deliver goods) *n.* Chinese; Chinese merchant. (*Insik*)

sangláy₂: sangsanglay. *n.* kind of thin, elongated dragonfly.

sangláy₃: agsanglay. *v.* to weaken from fatigue. (*kapuy*)

sanglét: sumanglet. *v.* to reach the shore.

sángo: *n.* fore part; front; façade; genitals; *prep.* before. **kasanguanan.** *prep.* before. **masanguanan.** *n.* future; before; next (in time) **nagsanguanan.** *a.* having two; having doubly; with both parents living. **sumango.** *v.* to face; front. **sanguen.** *v.* to confront. **masango.** *v.* to have time to do. **makisango.** *v.* to confront; engage in serious talk. **kasango.** *n.* person one faces, opponent. **nagsango.** *a.* faced; confronted; (cloth) with symmetrical striped coloring. **pasanguan.** *v.* to put something in front of somebody. **ipasango.** *v.* to put in front. **agsango-sango.** *v.* to face each other; confront. **akinsango.** *a.* in front. **iti sangosango.** face-to-face. **Masapol a sanguem ti kinapudno.** You need to face the truth. **Nasayaat ta makapagsasangotayo met laeng.** It is good that we were nevertheless able to see each other face-to-face again. **Idi, nganngani saami a masango a kudkuden ti nagatel iti kaadu ti trabaho.** Before, we barely had time to scratch our itches because of the abundance of work. [Png. *aráp*, Tag. *haráp*]

sanguánan: (f. *sango*) *n.* front; façade.

sangól: *n.* see *páko* (yoke); kind of hook used to pull up grasses. **isangol.** *v.* to hitch. **kaissangol.** *n.* apprentice; newly trained person or animal. **pasangol.** *n.* yoke. [Tag. *pamatok*]

sang-ór: **pagsang-uran.** *n.* hematemesis, coughing up or vomiting of blood. (*agpadara*) **agsang-or.** *v.* to have a nosebleed (*daringungo*). [Tag. *balinguyngóy*]

sang-ót: **sumang-ot.** *v.* to smell an odor; smell (dogs) on the hunt. (*saep; angot*)

sangpét: *n.* arrival. **sumangpet.** *v.* to arrive; come home. **isangpet.** *v.* to bring in; bring home; import. **makasangpet.** *v.* to find upon arriving at one's house. **pasangpeten.** *v.* to encourage citizens living abroad to return home; to await for someone's arrival. **agsangpet.** *v.* to be arriving one after the other (guests at a party, etc.) **naimbág nga isangpet.** *exp.* welcome. **Rumbeng a naragsak ti isasangpetna.** His arrival must be happy. [Ibg. *labbéq*, *dettál*, Ivt. *waraq*, Knk. *áli*, *sáa*, Kpm. *dátang*, Png. *sabí*, *sempét*, Tag. *datíng*]

sangrá: (Sp. *sangrar*: bleed) *v.* to bleed; overcharge.

sangráb: **sumangrab.** *v.* to inhale. (*lang-ab*) **sangraben.** *v.* to inhale odors.

sangrád: see *sanglád*: to anchor; hit bottom.

sangrát: *n.* intention; aim; plan. **maisangrat.** *v.* to be intended. **nakaisangratan.** *n.* intention, purpose, aim; objective. **Isu ti natiruan iti bala a naisangrat kuma iti adingna.** He was hit by the bullet that was intended for his younger brother. **Diak ilako, adda nakaisang-**

ratanna. I'm not going to sell it, it is intended for someone.

sangsáng: **sangsangen.** *v.* to pluck (leaves); wear out (clothes). **nasangsang.** *a.* worn out; tattered; with a strong, potent smell (perfumes).

sangsanga-: Prefix indicating having only one group of the entity denoted by the stem. **sangsangapulo.** only ten. **sangsangabakig.** only one group of ten. **sangsangabaki.** only one nestful. **sangsangabaar.** only one group of ten bundles of rice.

sangsangka-: *var.* of *sangsanga-* prefix. **sangsangkasakmol.** only one mouthful. **sangsangkareppet.** only one bundle, bunch. **sangsangkasingay.** only one bundle of rice.

sangsangayan: **maisangsangayan.** *v.* to be extraordinary, exceptional.

saó: *n.* word (*balikas*); speech, talk; conversation; language; statement; saying; conversation; terminology; expression; proverb. **agsao.** *v.* to speak, talk; converse. **saoen, sawen.** *v.* to say, utter; state. **kayatna a sawen.** *v.* it means; it signifies. **isao.** *v.* to say; express. **pagsasao, pannanao.** *v.* language; saying. **mannanao.** *n.* good talker; gossiper; *a.* loquacious. **masasao.** *v.* to be known. **pagsasaoan.** *v.* to speak harshly at; give someone a piece of one's mind. **pannao.** *n.* word. **iti sabali a pannao.** in other words. **panagsasaó.** *n.* conversation. **panagsásao.** *n.* manner of speech. **sumanaosao.** *v.* to talk idly; chatter. **makisao.** *v.* to speak with, converse. **minamannao.** (*obs.*) *n.* respectful speaking. **sumao.** *v.* to speak up. **saosao.** *n.* rumor; idle talk. **Nasaomon!** *exp.* You said it! **agpakasao.** *v.* to give others a chance to talk. **mapagsao.** *v.* to be made to speak. **nakayanakan a pagsasao.** *n.* native language. **pasaoen.** *v.* to let someone talk. **pagsaoen.** *v.* to make someone talk. **Diak kayat nga addanto pakasasawanda kaniak.** I don't want to give them a reason to be saying things about me. **Adda pagsasao a napigpigsa ti bales ti bagio.** There is language that is stronger than the strength of a storm. [Bon. *apat*, *kali*, Ibg. *uvóvug*, Ivt. *mayliliak*, *cirin*, Kal. *ugud*, Kpm. *manyábi*, Png. *salíta*, Tag. *salitâ*; *usap*]

saúd: **isaud.** *v.* to hitch to a post. **saudan.** *n.* yoke tied to the *tangbáw* pole. **agsaud.** (*obs.*) *v.* to screen oneself. [Tag. *talì*]

saóng: *n.* canine tooth; tusk; ivory. **agsaong.** *v.* to grow a tusk. **saongan.** *a.* with tusks. [Kal. *ngangaw*, Png. *pasingil*, Tag. *pangil*]

saúp₁: *n.* joint. **pagsaupen.** *v.* to join; fit together. **saupen.** *v.* to join together; sew together. **saupan.** *v.* to widen in sewing; enlarge by joining. [Tag. *sugpóng*]

saúp₂: *n.* substitute, proxy. (*sandi*) **isaup.** *v.* to substitute; proxy; join. **mangisaup.** *n.* substitute, proxy; deputy. [Tag. *katawanin*]

sáur: *n.* deceitful person, liar; cheating. (*kusit*; *ulbod*) **agsaur.** *v.* to cheat, swindle; lie. **sauren.** *v.* to swindle; commit fraud; cheat. **masaur.** *v.* to be cheated, swindled; to be able to do, carry. **sasaur.** in vain; without success. **Sasaur bambannog no sabali ti aglamlamut.** It is useless effort if somebody else eats (the fruits of one's labor). [Tag. *dayà*]

sápa: **nasapa.** *a.* early; seasonably. **sapaen.** *v.* to do something early. **kinasapa.** *n.* act of being early. **agsapa.** *n.* morning (*bigat*). **kaagsapanna.** *n.* the next morning. **isapa.** *v.* to do something early. **pangsapa.** *n.* morning meal. **iti kasapaan a panawen.** as soon as possible. **Sapaentayo ti aggunay, amangan no maipustayo.** We must move early so we don't lag behind. [Ivt. *kalu*, Kal. *sapa*, Png. *sakbáy*, Tag. *aga*]

sapá: *n.* residue of chewed betel. **sapaen.** *v.* to spit out chewed betel.

sápad: *n.* hand of bananas (holding the *bulig*, or bunch). **sapaden.** *v.* to detach by hand (bananas). [Kal. *bulig*, *saped*, Tag. *piling*]

sapád: *n.* crewcut; flat on one side (heads). **agpasapad.** *v.* to get a crewcut.

sapádo: (*coll.*) *a.* sufficient, enough. (*umanay*)

sapák: Interjection implying wonder.

sápal: *n.* fork of a tree, etc. **agsapal.** *v.* to intersect; cross. **sapalan.** *v.* to decorticate coconuts, leaving a strip to tie them into a bunch. **nagsapalan.** *n.* crossing junction; intersection. [Tag. *sangandaán* (intersection)]

sap-ál: *n.* Dutch wife; someone or something put between the legs for comfort. **isap-al.** *v.* to rest; use a Dutch wife; embrace with the legs (*kawil*, *salladay*, *kaladay*); put pillow under one's side. **agsinnap-al.** *v.* to entwine the legs around each other. **pasap-al.** *n.* bamboo poles used for weighing down thatched roofs. **sap-alan.** *v.* to rest the legs on. **Addaytan ti purok a naibarikir kadagiti nagsisinnap-al a turod.** There's the village nestled between the entwined hills.

sapáng: *n. Caesalpinia sappan* tree with yellow flowers and red bark. **sapangan.** *v.* to color nets; poison fish.

sapár: (Sp. *zafar*: clear; dodge) *n.* work to accomplish (in one's spare time); leisure time, free time. **isapar.** *v.* to do in one's spare time; make time to do something. **masaparan.** *v.* to have leisure time; find time to do. **No adda saparmo, sarungkarannak.** If you have spare time, visit me.

sapásap: *a.* common, usual; current; universal; general; familiar; public; ordinary. **maisapasap.** *v.* to become general, ordinary. **sapasapen.** *v.* to include all; treat everyone equal. **isapasap.** *v.* to level something. [Png. *lápag, gendát*, Tag. *laganap, palasák*]

sápat: *n.* top, summit, peak. (*ngudo*; *pantok*; *limpatok*; *sampa*; *murdong*; *aringgawis*; *alintotok*; *alimpapatok*; *tapaw*; *patok*; *toktok*) **sumapat.** *v.* to go to the top, ascend; reach the second half; pass the meridian (sun). [Tag. *tuktók*]

sapatá: *n.* oath. (*huramento*) **agsapata.** *v.* to take an oath; swear in. **sapataan.** *v.* to swear; declare under oath. **isapata.** *v.* to promise or swear to do something. **pagsapataen.** *v.* to bind to an oath. **panagsapata.** *n.* oath taking. [Png. *sambá*, Tag. *sumpâ*]

sapatería: (Sp. *zapatería*: shoe store) *n.* shoe store; shoemaker's shop.

sapatéro: (Sp. *zapatero*: cobbler) *n.* shoemaker (feminine: *sapatera*).

sapatília: (Sp. *zapatilla*: slipper) *n.* slipper (*tsinelas*); washer (in a faucet).

sapatón: (Sp. *zapatón*: large shoe) *n.* slipper with a closed front decorated with beads.

sapátos: (Sp. *zapato*: shoe) *n.* shoe; horseshoe. **agsapatos.** *v.* to wear shoes. **sapatosan.** *v.* to shoe; put shoes on someone's feet. **nakasapatos.** *a.* with shoes on. [Ivt. *tukap*, Kal. *kapatos*]

sápaw: *n.* shade, shelter; screen. **sapawan.** *v.* to shelter; screen; shade. **mannapaw.** *n.* kind of nonpoisonous snake found in thatched roofs. [Tag. *palapala*]

sapáw: *a.* with scattered gray hairs. **agsapaw.** *v.* to ear (rice); gray (hair).

sápay: Optative particle, used with *kuma*. **sapay kuma.** I hope so. **Sapay kuma ta kasta.** So be it. **Sapay kuma ta makatulogda.** I hope they can help. [Tag. *sana, harinawâ*]

sapayán: *n.* bar between the yarnbeam and upper tiebeam (*sekkég*) of a loom. (*síkang*).

sapdá: **isapda.** *v.* to drift ashore; drive to land; cast ashore. **maisapda.** *v.* to be cast ashore; to drift ashore. [Tag. *sadsád*]

sapgíd: *var.* of *sapgud*.

sapgúd: **nasapgudan.** *a.* smeared (with mud). **isapgud.** *v.* to smear mud on.

sápi: **sapisápi.** *n.* a kind of bird; kind of triangular kite.

sapiáw: *n.* kind of fish net. **Saan a nagbiddut a yo ti nalakubda iti sapiaw.** He was not mistaken that a shark is what they caught in the net.

sapidéng: **sumapideng.** *v.* to shelter, take refuge in a corner; harbor. **sapidengan.** *v.* to protect.

maisapideng. *v.* to be cornered. **pagsapidengan.** *n.* place to take shelter or refuge. **Nagsigam a kas man adda simmapideng iti panunotna.** He cleared his throat as if something harbored in his thoughts. [Tag. *kublí*]

sap-íl: *n.* digging stick. **sap-ilen.** *v.* to dig with a *sap-íl.*

sapilatlát: *n.* long-limbed freshwater crayfish.

sapíloy: *a.* lame, paralyzed in the legs, not paralyzed by birth. (*lugpí*: paralyzed at birth). [Tag. *lumpó*]

sapín: *n.* drawers; underpants; panties; trousers. **sapinan.** *v.* to cover for protection from wetness; to put *sapin* on someone. **nakasapin.** *a.* wearing underpants. [Kal. *agibey*, Tag. *sapín* = lining; pad; layer; cushion, *sasapnán* = upper part of the buttocks]

sapín-sapín: (f. *sapín*) *n.* native Philippine plant; native delicacy made with rice cake cooked in coconut milk and arranged in various layers with different colors.

sapingan: *n.* *Gymnocranius griseus* snapper fish.

sapíro: (Sp. *zafiro*: sapphire) *n.* sapphire.

sapísap: *n.* kind of plate made from the shell of a *tabúngaw.*

sapisápi: *n.* kind of triangular kite; kind of bird.

sápit: *n.* mat made from strips of bark and leaves placed in a canoe to keep water out.

sapít: isapit. *v.* to enclose, insert; insert (in an envelope). **Adda naisapit a ladawan iti suratna.** There is a picture enclosed in his letter. [Tag. *lakíp*]

sapíta: (Sp. *zapatilla*) *n.* plunger of a pump.

saplák: agsaplak. *v.* to creep; spread (vines). **isaplak.** *v.* to spread, unfurl. **pasaplak.** *n.* outrigger; layer of *daplát* or *minatá* covering the rafters of some house to support the thatch; interior layer of *balawbáw.* **panaplák.** *n.* northwest wind. [Tag. *gapang*]

saplíd: agsaplid. *v.* to remove dust. **sapliden, saplidan.** *v.* to remove dust from; dust. **panaplid.** *n.* duster. [Tag. *palís*]

saplít: *n.* thrashing; *mortiga* plant. **sapliten.** *v.* to whip, thrash, lash, flog. (*basnut*; *baut*; *aplit*; *latiko*; *betbet*) **agsaplisaplit.** *v.* to thrash the tail at flies. [Knk. *saplít*, Png. *bakbák*, Tag. *hagupít, bugbóg*]

sapó: *n.* ointment. **sapuan.** *v.* to anoint; smear with grease. **agsapo, sapuen.** *v.* to dye. **sapsapo.** *a.* incomplete; defective; imperfect. **pagsapsapo.** *n.* ointment.

sapuéd: (*obs.*) *n.* entering abruptly; launching a boat with one shove. **agsapued.** *v.* to do in an abrupt manner; do in one sweep.

sápul: *n.* job; property acquired; earning; income; catch. **agsapul.** *v.* to look for; earn; want. **apagsapul.** *a.* just found. **masapul.** *v.* to need; be necessary, essential; want. **masapsapul.** *n.* needs, necessities. **kasapulan.** *v.* to need; *n.* needs; requirements. **pagsapulan.** *n.* job; work; task; means of making one's living, livelihood. **pangsapulan.** *n.* the place to find something. **sapulen.** *v.* to look for; seek; long for, crave. **masapulan.** *v.* to find, discover; earn; fall in love with. **nasapulan.** *a.* found; illegitimate (child). **isapul.** *v.* to look for; remedy. **isapulan.** *v.* to find something for somebody. **ipasapul.** *v.* to have something found. **sapsapulen.** *v.* to long for; crave. **sangkasapulan.** *n.* earnings for the day. **sumapul.** *v.* to look for work. **Pakasapulam?** Why do you need it? **agkasapulan.** *v.* to need badly. **Ti nalaka ti pannakasapulna, nalaka met ti pannakapukawna.** *exp.* What is easily found is easily lost. **No intuloy kuma ni Raul ti nagsapul, nakitana kuma ti kotse idiay.** If Raul would have continued to search, he would have seen the car there. **Panagkalap ti kangrunaan a pagsapulanda.** Fishing is their primary means of livelihood. [Ibg. *áwag*, Png. *anáp*, Tag. *hanap*]

sapón: *n.* blonde. (*olandes*)

saporíding: (*obs.*) *n.* clitoris. (*tuldi*; *mutíng*; *tamtampira*)

sapuríket: agsapuriket. *v.* to steal at night.

sáput: *n.* spider web; membrane. **saputan.** *v.* to involve; wrap; envelop. **agsaput.** *v.* to weave a web. **nasaputan.** *a.* covered with cobwebs. **sangalubongan a saput.** *n.* worldwide web. [Kal. *beÿoy*, Tag. *sapot*]

sapút: saputan. *v.* to answer for, to be responsible for someone.

sapóte: (Sp. *zapote*: sapodilla) *n. Diospyros ebenaster, sapote* date plum; cheat at cards (*pikit*).

sappá: nasappa. *a.* flat (roofs); thick and wide (lips).

sappág: *n.* boundary; territory; limits. (*dulon*) **sappagen.** *v.* to include within one's jurisdiction (*sakup*). [Tag. *hangganan*]

sappán: *var.* of *sapáng*: species of tree.

sappéd: *n.* blockade; hindrance, obstruction. (*lapped*)

sappúpo: *n.* clasped handful, cupped handful. **sappupuen.** *v.* to put contents into two clasped hands. **Insakmolda ti sappupoda a mani.** They put their cupped handful of peanuts in their mouth.

sappúyot: *n.* loving care; gentle touch. **sappuyuten.** *v.* to cuddle, snuggle (a baby); touch gently. **marasappuyot.** *n.* kind of green nonedible freshwater alga. **Sinappuyotna ti**

bakrangna ta kasla adda dimmuyok. She gently touched his back as if something were hurting him. [Tag. *haplós*]

sappríd: agsapprid, sappridan. *v.* to flick away dust.

saprák: *var.* of *suprák.*

saprí: *n.* sprinkling; rain blown through a door. **agsapri, sumapri.** *v.* to sprinkle; scatter in small drops; to spray (said of rain blown by air). **masaprian.** *v.* to be sprinkled. [Tag. *anggí*]

sapríd: *var.* of *saplíd:* remove dust, dust off.

sapsáp: *n. gumabbék* fish in fresh water. **sapsapan.** *v.* to trim the joints. **sapsapen.** *v.* to rasp, scrape. **agsanapsap.** see *sakuntáp:* to make a smacking noise when eating. [Tag. *kayas* (scrape)]

sapsaparília: (Sp. *zarzaparilla*) *n.* sarsaparilla; root beer.

sára: *n.* horn, antler. **agsara.** *v.* to grow horns; to become stubborn. **sasaraan.** *n.* region of the parietal bone. **nagsara.** *a.* with horns, horny. **sarasara.** *n. Strophanthus sp.* plant with poisonous bark. **sara-saraan.** *n.* kind of edible mollusk similar to the *kusíling.* **agsarasara.** (*obs.*) *v.* to have the head bent and wrinkly. [Ibg. *taggug*, Itg. *saklud*, Ivt. *ulung*, Knk. *sakgangá, sakgúd*, Kpm. *sagu*, Png. *saklór*, Tag. *sungay*]

sará: sinara. *n.* checker weaving.

saráaw: *n.* craving for food (in stomach); hunger pang. **agsaraaw (ti tian).** *v.* to crave for food; have a hunger pang in the stomach. **Makapasaraaw ti alingasaw ti adobona.** The fumes from her *adobo* are mouthwatering. **Agsarsaraaw ti pitakak.** My wallet is hungry. [Tag. *hilab*]

sárab: saraban. *v.* to singe, scorch; put into direct heat. (*sarabasab*) **insarab.** *n.* slightly roasted meat or fish. [Tag. *salab*]

sarabagtít: *n.* flirtatious girl.

sarabásab: isarabasab. *v.* to roast over the fire; dry in the shade; warm.

sarábay: (*obs.*) *n.* lint, raveling.

sarábo: *n.* gift, present brought by a traveler coming home. **agpasarabo.** *v.* to distribute gifts. **sumarabo.** *v.* to visit a person recently returned from a trip; to ask or receive a *sarábo.* **sarabuen.** *v.* to welcome; receive gladly. **Kasla ubing nga agsapul iti sarabo ti alisto ni Kundring a nangsabat kenkuana.** Kundring greeted her as quick as a child searches for his present. [Png. *sarábo*, Tag. *pasalubong; dalaw*]

sarabúsab: see *salabúsab:* thoughtless; inconsiderate; *n.* greedy eater.

saróg: saragen. *v.* to be able to do; to outdo.

saragásag: nasaragasag. *a.* thin, transparent; gauzy; able to see through (*aragaag*). [Tag. *aninag*]

saragáte: (AmSp. *zaragate:* despicable person) *n.* careless person; rascal.

saragattít: *a.* restless, fidgety (said only of girls).

saraguáb: isaraguab. *v.* to remove by force. **maisaraguab.** *v.* to be removed or thrown off forcefully.

saragság: *a.* restless, fidgety (said only of girls).

saraínad: agsarainad. *v.* to trail, drag (clothes) (*saringgayad*). [Tag. *sayad*]

saraísa: *n.* small plumlike tree.

saraisí: *n.* stream. **agsaraisi.** *v.* to ripple (said of a stream); flow. [Tag. *sapà*]

saráit: *n.* patch; stitch. (*aludab; dalubdob*) **saraiten.** *v.* to overstitch, overseam; sew. **agsarait.** *v.* to stitch, sew with the hand. **nasarait.** *a.* stitched, sewn. **Kasla nasarait ti bibigna.** Her lips seem to be stitched shut. [Tag. *tahì*]

saraittíg: *n.* flirtatious girl. (*sarampingat; garatigit; garampang*)

sárak: masarakan. *v.* to meet; discover; find; encounter. **agsarak.** *v.* to meet. **isarak.** *v.* to put in jeopardy, imperil. **maisarak.** *v.* to be jeopardized. **saraken.** *v.* to look for; find. **ipaspasarak.** *v.* to do without a system; to do blindly. **maipaspasarak.** *v.* to be done by accident or chance. **pagsasarakan, pagsisinnarakan.** *n.* rendezvous; meeting place. **Dayta a dilayo, isu ti nabileg a pakaisarsarakanyo.** Your tongue is what gets you into trouble most. [Tag. *tagpô*]

sarakúsok: *a.* reckless, rash. **sumarakusok.** *v.* to hustle; intermeddle; hurry; to do rashly, do impudently (go out during a storm, attack a stronger opponent, etc.). **sarakusuken.** *v.* to go headlong into the thick of things; do something rashly without thinking first; to venture into, brave. [Tag. *dahás*]

sarakusúkos: *var.* of *sarakusok:* venture, dare, risk. **Di mabayag, sarsarakusukusennan ti kasipngetan.** After a while, he ventured into the darkness.

sarákoy: *n.* support; brace; prop. (*tukal*) **sarakuyen.** *v.* to prop; support; aid; harbor someone temporarily. **pagsarakoyen.** *v.* to buy in bulk without choosing; mix up; put together unsuitably; make a pair. [Tag. *suhay*]

saraksák: (*obs.*) **isaraksak.** *v.* to drive a boat across an arm of the sea.

saramísam: saramisaman. *v.* to drive away insects at night by torchlights. **isaramisam.** *var.* of *isarabasab:* roast over the fire.

sarámok: sumaramok. *v.* to come near, close; rush through the rain; calm an angry person.

saramuken. *v.* to approach, come close to. [Tag. *payapà* (calm down)]

saramuliéte: (Tag.) *n.* goatfish. [Ivt. *tivuyin*]

saramúlio: *n.* person without manners (*mirón, garamúgas*); obstinate; conceited. **agsaramulio.** *v.* to be ill-mannered; have a tantrum.

saramusián: *n.* hard coconut meat. (*taramusián*)

saramúsom₁: **sumaramusom.** *v.* to push ahead, hustle. (*sarakusok*) **saramusuman.** *v.* to elbow, push rudely; force out of place. **saramusumen.** *v.* to dare to do, venture.

saramúsom₂: **agassaramusom.** *v.* to smell like smoke.

sarampiáng: *syn.* of *sarampingát*: flirtatious girl, immodest girl.

sarampingát: *syn.* of *ampáng*: easy girl; flirtatious girl. (*garampingat*; *sayet*)

sarampitíng: *n.* restless, fidgety girl (*saragsag*); immodest, unchaste.

saramsám: *n.* small snack; junk food; gift for newlyweds. **agsaramsam.** *v.* to snack. **nasaramsam.** *a.* funny, humorous. **Ania ti masaramsam iti balayyo?** What do you have to eat at your house? [Tag. *meryenda* (Sp.)]

saránay₁: *n.* protection; support; help, aid, assistance. **saranayen.** *v.* to look after, take care of; protect; help, assist; defend; support. **panagsisinnaranay.** *n.* solidarity; mutual defense. **No adda parikutko, awan ti mayat a sumaranay kaniak.** When I have a problem, no one is willing to help me. [Tag. *tulong*]

saránay₂: *n.* variety of awned early rice.

saránip: **saranipen.** *v.* to look at while shading the eyes from the sun; catch sight of; see from afar.

sarantá: **nasaranta.** *a.* active; lively, with spirit; often, frequently. (*masansán*) **sumaranta.** *v.* to become active. **Nakasarsarantaakon a bimmangon iti kabigatanna.** I woke up enthusiastically the next morning. [Tag. *siglá*]

saráng: *a.* having extremely large, bending ears. **agsarang.** *v.* to confront; come face-to-face. **isarang.** *v.* to turn toward the sun; put under sun. **agsarang ti lapayag.** with big ears that turn outward. **sumarang.** *n.* frisbee; *v.* to turn toward the sun. **pasarangan.** *v.* to point a gun at. **agsinnarang.** *v.* to meet face-to-face. **sarangen.** *v.* to face somebody. [Tag. *haráp*]

sarangásang: *var.* of *sarangsang*.

sarangét: **sumaranget.** *v.* to face an enemy; confront. **sarangten.** *v.* to confront; attack; withstand. **Naanus ni Pilipino nga aglak-am iti uray ania a rigat ken natured a mangsaranget iti uray ania a peggad.** Filipinos are patient to stand any kind of hardship and brave to confront any type of danger. [Tag. *laban*]

saranggáyad: *var.* of *saringgayad*.

sarangkínod: *n.* walking with curved knees and protruded abdomen. (see *kiád, talongkiád*). **agsarangkinod.** *v.* to walk with curved knees and a protruding abdomen; to walk with a slight jerking of the knees.

sarangúsong: *n.* funnel (*imbudo*); upper half of coconut; (*coll.*) heavy alcoholic drinker (*mammartek*). [Tag. *imbudo* (Sp.)]

sarangsáng: *n.* snack; dessert; something crispy or humorous. **nasarangsang.** *a.* easily chewed; crunchy; crispy; funny, humorous; brittle; (~ *a ngiwat*) *a.* talkative; loud; (*fig.*) sarcastic. **sumarangsang.** *v.* to crackle in the fire; become crispy. **Nakasarsarangsang ti uni ti saltek.** The noise of the lizard was crackling. [Tag. *lutóng* (crispy)]

sarausó: **sumarauso.** *v.* to come in a big crowd all at once; to do simultaneously as a whole crowd.

saráot: (*obs.*) **sarauten.** *v.* to tie up in strips of bamboo.

sarápa: **sarapaen.** *v.* to support from the bottom; ward off; turn aside; catch. **isarapa.** *v.* to use as a shield; shield oneself with. [Tag. *sanggá*]

sarapnút: **sarapnuten.** *v.* to outdo; surpass, excel; prevent; thwart.

sarápong: (*obs.*) **sarapongan.** *v.* to strengthen (with lining).

sarára: *n.* kind of small, brown, hairy caterpillar.

sarásar: **sarasaren.** *v.* to pick out, choose, select (*pili*). [Tag. *pilì*]

saratsát: **saratsaten.** *v.* to weed; disembowel; gut; unseam. **pasaratsat.** *n.* tool used to cut tall weeds before plowing. [Tag. *tastás*]

sáraw: **masarsaraw.** *v.* to appear suddenly and unexpectedly (a person who is being talked about, etc.).

sarawagkíng₁: *a.* staggering, tottering. [Tag. *suray*]

sarawagkíng₂: *a.* extravagant; excessive in one's behavior.

sarawínis: (Sp. *zaragüelles*: breeches) *n.* breeches; underwear. **nakasarawinis.** *a.* wearing breeches.

sarawsáw: **sarawsawan.** *v.* to botch, cut unevenly; know disconnectedly; do unsystematically. [Tag. *hapaw*]

sar-áy: *n.* spadix of the coco palm, cluster fruits or coconuts. (*lapá*) **isar-ay.** *v.* to hang in clusters or bunches.

saray-éng: (*obs.*) *n.* cry of children when cutting their teeth.

saray-6b: **sumaray-ob.** *v.* to be sultry. [Tag. *alis-ís*]

sarbatána: (Sp. *cerbatana*: popgun) *n.* blowgun (*salbatana*). [Tag. *sumpít*]

sardám: *n.* evening. (*rabii*) **kasardaman.** *n.* the evening of. **sarsardamen.** *v.* to do early in the evening. **ipaspasardam.** *v.* to wait until evening. **ipasardam.** *v.* to postpone until evening. [Bon. *sedem*, Knk. *madsém*, Png. *lábi*, Tag. *gabí*]

sardáy: **agsarday.** *v.* to stop; cease. (*sardéng*) **Dina sinardayan ti naggaud.** He didn't stop rowing. **Saan a nagsarday ni Melching a nagbayad iti buis iti akindaga.** Melching did not stop paying taxes to the landowner. [Ivt. *abhes*, Kal. *illong*, Tag. *tigil*]

sardéng: *n.* stop (*sarday*). **agsardeng, sumardeng.** *v.* to stop, cease, terminate; quit; pause; finish; end. **isardeng.** *v.* to suppress, stop, discontinue, interrupt; terminate; suspend. **pangisardengan.** *n.* stop zone; loading zone. **sardengan.** *v.* to stop for someone. **agsardesardeng.** *v.* to be stopping and going. **Nagsardesardeng nga ageskuela tapno tulonganna dagiti dadakkelna nga aglapog iti lasona.** He went to school on and off so he could help his parents plant onions. [Ivt. *abhes*, Kal. *illong*, Png. *tondá, teldán*, Tag. *hintô*]

sardínas: (Sp. *sardina*: sardine) *n.* sardine.

saréb: *n.* water drawn from a well; water used for washing clothes or dishes. **sumareb.** *v.* to draw water (not drinking water). (*sakdó*) **pagsarban.** *n.* water container. [Tag. *igíb*]

sarebséb₁: *a.* marshy soil; hissing sound. **sumarebseb.** *v.* to hiss (said of frying lard); crackle. **Nagadiwara ti bang-i ti sumarsarebseb a pindang.** The smell of the frying jerked meat diffused. [Tag. *latì* (marsh)]

sarebséb₂: *n.* twilight. (*suripet*)

sarebséb₃: *n.* marshy soil; bog.

sarég: (*obs.*) **agsarég.** *v.* to glean after the harvest. (*tudtod*)

saregrég: *n.* strutting of a cock around a hen (walking in an affective manner). [Png. *kalirkír*, Tag. *girì*]

sárep: **sarpen.** *v.* to dam a stream in order to catch fish. **agsarep.** *v.* to catch fish floundering in a stream.

saretsét: **sumaretset.** *v.* to sizzle (frying lard); (*fig.*) to be scorching hot. (*sarepsep*) **Simgiab ken nagsaretset ti umasul nga apoy.** The blue fire flared and sizzled. [Png. *sanitsít*, Tag. *sagitsít*]

sargá: **pasarga.** *n.* puffed sleeves (of a lady's dress).

sarguélas: *n.* Spanish plum, a kind of tropical fruit. [Tag. *siniguwelas*]

sarhénto: (Sp. *sargento*: sergeant) *n.* sergeant.

sári₁: **sumari.** *v.* to break through, break into; burst in or out.

sári₂: (Pil.) **sarisári.** *n.* small store selling general merchandise.

sariána: *n.* rapids. (*obs.*) **agsariana.** *v.* to cast or draw lots.

saridan(g)dán: (*lit.*) *n.* a woman who never takes life seriously.

sariáp: *n.* cascade; current, rapids, running stream. **utang-sariap.** (*coll.*) a debt that the debtor does not intend to pay. [Tag. *agos*]

saribsíb: *n.* shoot (of taro or banana) (*sagibsib*). **In-inutenen a saribsiben ti sipnget ti lawag.** The darkness gradually overtook the light.

saridát: **sumaridat.** *v.* to follow, succeed in order; write the body of a letter; explain what has been said before. [Tag. *sabi*]

sarigsíg: **agsarigsig, sumarigsig.** *v.* to move in a half circle; strut; attack from the side (cocks). **sarigsigan.** *v.* to incite (cocks); circle around a hen (said of a cock), attack from the side; (*fig.*) court a girl. **agsinnarigsig.** *v.* to move around each other (as in boxing, etc.). **Saan met ngata a dillawen dagiti kaarrubana no ni Meding ti sarigsiganna.** His neighbors probably won't criticize him if he goes for Meding. [Tag. *girì*]

sarikadkád: **sumarikadkad.** *v.* to brace oneself before attacking. [Tag. *handâ*]

saríkaw: *n.* woven rattan band used as a frame for hats. (*lingka*) **isarikaw.** *v.* to insert a band in a hat.

sarikbúbo: **sarikbubuen.** *v.* to spread out with the ears uppermost; to invert and spread in the sun to dry. **nasarikbubo.** *a.* bulging (clothes); upside down (clothes when one is upside down).

sarikedkéd₁: *n.* foundation; prop; support; strength; endurance; refuge; help; courage. **agsarikedked, sumarikedked.** *v.* to rest for support; rely on, depend on; trust, count on; have faith in. **sarikedkedan.** *v.* to endure, support without breaking. [Tag. *tanggól*]

sarikedkéd₂: *n.* variety of awned early rice with a light-colored hull and white kernel.

sarimadéng₁: *n.* hesitation to do something. (*arimadéng*) **agsarimadeng.** *v.* to hesitate to do; pause. **Agsarsarimadeng nga immuli.** They hesitated to go up. [Tag. *atubilí*]

sarimadéng₂: *n.* semicolon (;) punctuation mark.

sarimatmát: **sarimatmatan.** *v.* to notice, see.

sarimbáboy: **agsarimbaboy.** *v.* to walk on all fours (*urdas*). **simmarimbaboy.** *a.* shaped like a quadruped. [Tag. *gapang*]

sarimbángon: *var.* of *tarimbangon*.

sarimedméd: **agsarimedmed.** *v.* to hesitate, vacillate. (*bumdeng*)

sartín: (Sp. *sartén*: frying pan) *n*. frying pan (*pariok*); tin cup.

sása: *n*. odd number; leftover, remainder. (*gansal, tidda*)

sasá: **masasa**. *v*. to be damaged (said of plants).

saserdóte: (Sp. *sacerdote*: priest) *n*. priest. (*padi*)

sásik: (*obs*.) **agsasik**. *v*. to make salt from salt water. (*sána*)

sasús: *n*. kind of large black crustacean.

sástre: (Sp. *sastre*: tailor) *n*. tailor. **sastreria**. *n*. tailor's shop.

sáta: **masata**. *v*. to not be completed or carried out; to fail to undergo. **sataen**. *v*. to not go through with; fail to realize an event.

satanás: (Sp. *satanás*: Satan) *n*. devil, Satan. (*sairo*)

satín: (Sp. *satín, satén*) *n*. satin.

satúrno: (Sp. *saturno*: Saturn) *n*. Saturn.

satsát: **satsaten**. *v*. to unravel; tear, rip garments; demolish; undo crochet work by pulling the string. **satsatan**. *v*. to thrash, maul. **agsanatsat**. *v*. to make a thrashing sound. [Tag. *tastás*]

satsatéra: *n*. babbler, gossipy woman.

sawá: see *simmawá*.

sáwak: **sawakan**. *n*. kind of large marine fish with large mouth.

sawák: *a*. crooked, distorted (horns of the water buffalo).

sáwat: **isawat**. *v*. to insert into another's conversation.

sawáli: *n*. interwoven splits of bamboo used in walls.

sáwang: *n*. breach, opening; sluice. **isawang**. *v*. to manifest; declare; express; utter. **manawang**. *n*. kind of poisonous snake. **sawangen**. *n*. to open, breach (a dam, etc.). **Dika kuma agisawang iti kasta**. You shouldn't say things like that. [Tag. *sabi, pahayag*]

áwar: **sawaren**. *v*. to search, look for by groping. **agsawar**. *v*. to search around; patrol an area; break in (robbers). **Sinawarda dagiti kamarote**. They searched the cabins. **Immaynakam inayaban ni nanangmo ta umaydaka ulongan nga agsawar**. Your mother came to call us so we could come help you search. [Tag. *anap*]

ásaw: *n*. excess; overlength; part of undergarment that protrudes over the edge of upper othing. **sumawasaw**. *v*. to be in excess; overow; (*obs*.) to sprout.

áw: *a*. hoarse. **agsawaw**. *v*. to vent; issue ough a vent; utter in a hoarse voice; breathe ough. **sawaw a timek**. *n*. dry, hoarse voice.

y: *a*. odd; unmatched (*pangis*); excess; lus in distribution. **nagsaway**. *a*. uniched, unparalleled. **kinasaway**. *n*. distinc-

tion; act of having an unparalleled characteristic; oddness.

saw-áy: (*reg*.) **isaw-ay**. *v*. to express verbally. **Diak maisaw-ay kadakayo ti adda a riknak**. I cannot express my feelings to you.

sawéd: **nasawed**. *a*. easy due to knowledge or experience. **saweden**. *v*. to continue something already begun; do with ease. [Tag. *dalî*]

saw-éd: **naisaw-ed**. *a*. focused on one point (the eyes).

sawét: (*reg*.) *var*. of *siwet*: do swiftly.

sáwi: *n*. kind of hawk; (*obs*.) poor-quality gold.

sáwil: **sawilen**. *v*. to raise with a lever. (*suil*)

saw-íng: *n*. tusk of a wild boar. (*saóng*) **sawíngen**. *v*. to gore with a tusk or horn. **sawingan**. *a*. having a tusk (said of the wild boar). [Tag. *pangil*]

sawír: *n*. roving hog; house chores; problems; difficulties; vagrant. **nasawir**. *a*. tolerable; vagabond, vagrant. **masawir**. *v*. to be tolerable, bearable, supportable. **Adda sawsawirko**. I have things to do; someone to take care of. **Awan sawsawirna a nakalasat dagiti nagtipon a resolusion**. He has no difficulties passing the combined resolutions.

sawirí: (*reg*.) *a*. crooked; twisted; (*fig*.) deceptive, fooling. **Immisem iti sawiri**. He smiled crookedly.

sáwit: *n*. barb of an arrow, spear, hook, etc. (*sima*). [Tag. *kawit*]

saw-ít: *n*. very small cup without handle used to measure *boggóong*. **sawsaw-ít**. *n*. kind of tailor bird.

sawsáw: **isawsaw**. *v*. to dip, dunk. **sawsawan**. *n*. dipping sauce. **maisawsaw**. *v*. to be dipped into. **pagsawsaw**. *n*. ingredients used for dipping. **pagisawsawan**. *n*. dipping sauce. **Naisawsaw iti eskandalo**. He was immersed in scandal. [Png., Tag. *sawsáw*]

sáya: (Sp. *saya*: skirt) *n*. skirt. **nakasaya**. *a*. wearing a skirt. **sayasaya**. *n*. common bird in the Bicol region whose song is said to bring bad luck. [Png. *sapey*]

say-á: *n*. clearing of the throat, sound produced by clearing the throat. **agsay-a**. *v*. to clear the throat (*sig-ám*). **isay-a**. *v*. to eject out while clearing the throat. **Nagsay-a tapno ipangngegna ti kaaddana**. He cleared his throat to show his presence. [Bon. *seláak*, Kpm. *tigím*, Tag. *tikhím, dahak*]

sayáat₁: [also spelled *siaat*] *n*. goodness; virtue. (*imbag*) **nasayaat**. *a*. good; pretty; handsome; elegant; fit; suitable; appropriate; charming. **sayaaten**. *v*. to do well. **pagsayaatan**. *n*. welfare; well-being; improvement; benefit. **saysayaaten**. *v*. to do well; to do carefully; to im-

sarímok: (*obs*.) **sumarimok**. *v*. to take stands below shots of the enemy (said of boats); to be within range.

sarimúlio: *var*. of *saramulio*: rude, ill mannered (*bastos*); conceited.

sarimutmót: **sarimutmuten**. *v*. to glean (what was missed by harvesters). **nasarimutmutan**. *n*. earnings from gleaning. (*tudtod*)

sarinagnág: **masarinagnagan**. *v*. to be half-dry.

sarinatnát: **pasarinatnatan**. *v*. to follow right after; second the motion.

sarindániw: [*sarita + daniw*] *n*. narrative poetry.

sarínip: **sarinipen**. *v*. to peep through a small opening; to scan (with the eyes).

sarínok: (*obs*.) **sumarinok**. *v*. to join the crowd; mingle.

sarinúnud: see *sanúd*: go backward; recant. (*sanut*)

sáring: **sarisaring**. *n*. kind of foot-high herb.

saringgáyad: **agsaringgayad**. *v*. to drag, trail on the ground. **isaringgayad**. *v*. to cause to trail or drag (*sagayad*). [Tag. *sayad*]

saringgayáman: (f. *gayáman*) **agsaringgayaman**. *v*. to creep, crawl on the ground like a centipede.

saringgúyod: **agsaringguyod**. *v*. to drag, trail on the ground. [Tag. *hila*]

saríngit: *n*. shoot (of bamboo, etc.); bud; offspring. **agsaringit**. *v*. to develop a shoot or bud. [Kal. *simit*, Tag. *usbóng*]

sariugmá: [*sarita idi ugma*] *n*. ancient legend. [Tag. *alamát*]

saripakpák: **agsaripakpak**. *v*. to expand, extend, swell, spread; spread and flutter (wings). **masaripakpakan**. *v*. to expand, dilate; swell. [Tag. *pagaspás* (flap wings)]

saripatpát: **masaripatpatan**. *v*. to catch a glimpse of; to recognize someone from afar. **apagsaripatpat**. *a*. just enough to recognize. **Adda nasaripatpatanna a lalaki a nakasakay iti nuang iti ruar ti inaladanda**. He caught a glimpse of a man riding a water buffalo outside their yard.

saripdá: *n*. ivory button; doorstop; shield; screen; bar; anything used to prevent air of water from entering the house (*sagiped*; *balunet*). **saripdaen**. *v*. to fend off, ward off; defend. (*sarapa*) **saripdaan**. *v*. to bar a door; shield; screen a window. **Di nagkutkuti iti sirok ti inyulesna a kamiseta a saripdana iti tumaytayok a darat**. He didn't move from under the shirt he used as a blanket to fend off the flying sand. [Tag. *sanggá*]

saripéd: (*obs*.) *n*. doorstop. (*sagiped*)

saríping: *n*. new growth of plants (where plants were trimmed). (*saringit*) **sumariping**. *v*. to

approach, come closer. **isariping**. *v*. to place near; do something adjacent to. **naisariping**. *a*. adjacent. **Nagdigos iti banio a naisariping iti kuartona**. She bathed in the bath next to her room.

sarípit: *n*. hair clip; device in the form of an X used to raise logs. **sarsaripit**. *n*. painful urination. **sarsaripiten**. *v*. to suffer from irregular small discharges of urine; suffer from gonorrhea; not be able to urinate; to urinate painfully. [Bon. *alotiptip*, Tag. *balisawsáw*]

sarípot: *n*. kind of bow net used to catch *ípon*. (*bubo*) **sariputen**. *v*. to catch in a bow net.

saripsíp: **saripsipen**. *v*. to cut grass to the roots.

sarírit: *n*. intelligence; wisdom; wit; talent; knowledge. (*aliwatek*; *sirib*; *ammo*; *laing*) **nasaririt**. *a*. bright, shrewd, intelligent; keen; clever; skillful. [Png. *dunong*, Tag. *dunong*, *talino*]

sarísa: *reg*. *var*. of *seresa*: cherry.

saríta: *n*. story; tale; legend; fable; recital; conversation, talk. **agsarita**. *v*. to converse; tell a story. **sumarita**. *v*. to talk. **sumanarita**. *v*. to talk nonstop; gossip. **isarita**. *v*. to reveal, disclose. **kasarita**. *v*. to converse with; speak with. **makisarita**. *v*. to speak with. **mannarita**. *a*. talkative; *n*. loquacious person. **saritaan**. *v*. to talk to someone; entertain. **saritaen**. *v*. to tell, relate; communicate; reveal. **sarsarita**. *n*. legend; fable; rumor. **pagsaritaan**. *n*. topic of conversation; reason for talking; *v*. to talk about. **pakasaritaan**. *n*. history; biography. **Ti tao a mannarita, awan ti ania nga magapuananna**. The man who talks much accomplishes little. **Dayta ti kayatko kenka ta saanka a narigat a kasarsarita**. That's what I like about you because you are not difficult to talk to. **Diak kayat a pagsaritaan dayta**. I don't want to talk about that. [Bon. *ógod*, Png. *salíta*, Tag. *salaysáy, salitâ*]

sariwagká: *var*. of *sariwakka*: untidy; clumsy.

sariwagténg: **agsariwagteng**. *v*. to walk away pouting and kicking.

sariwagwág: **sariwagwagen**. *v*. to shake in order to dry (hair, etc.); fluff cotton with sticks. **agsariwagwag**. *v*. to shake oneself to clean or dry. [Tag. *pagpág*]

sariwakká: *a*. untidy; clumsy; not careful (used for women). [Tag. *burarâ*]

sariw-át: **sumariw-at**. *v*. to protrude, jut out. **nagsariw-at**. *v*. uneven; protruding. **pasariw-at**. *n*. ring finger. [Tag. *uslî*]

sariwáwek: *var*. of *sariwawet*: roaming to a far place.

sariwáwet: *n*. bad manners; greediness. **nasariwawet**. *a*. having roamed around to a far place (chickens); having bad manners (at the table). **agsariwawet.** *v.* to roam to a far place (chickens, pigs, etc.). **Sariwawet metten dagiti matana.** His eyes are roaming.

sárkak: *n.* phlegm. (*sagkak; daak*) **agsarkak.** *v.* to discharge phlegm. [Tag. *kalaghalâ, dahak*]

sarkéd: sarkeden. *v.* to withstand, oppose, resist. **sumarked.** *v.* to resist, oppose. **masarkedan.** *v.* to be able to endure, oppose, resist. **Kanayonna nga ipukkaw no kasta a dinan masarkedan ti apges ti kinaagmaymaysana.** He always shouts like that when he can't endure the pain of his loneliness.

sarmáy: (*obs.*) **agsarmay.** *v.* to reshoot. (*saringit; sulbod*)

sarmíng: *n.* mirror; glass; eyeglasses; window (of a car); windshield. **agsarming.** *v.* to look at oneself in a mirror (*espeho*); wear glasses, use glasses. **sarming ti mata.** *n.* eyeglasses; iris. **pagsarmingan.** *n.* model, example, pattern. **manarming.** *v.* to look in/use a mirror. **sarmingan.** *v.* to put eyeglasses on someone. **sarmi-sarming ti lapayag.** *n.* eardrum. **pagattao a sarming.** *n.* full body mirror. **Maiwayat kuman ti pannakabitayna tapno adda pagsarmingan dagiti managdakdakes.** They should carry out his hanging to set an example for the criminals. [Bon. *lid-ang, pang-aw*, Png. *salming*, Tag. *salamín*]

sarnáed: agsarnaed. *v.* to hesitate, advance in a hesitating manner.

sarnáy: nasarnay. *a.* frequent. (*masansan, kanayon*) **kinasarnay.** *n.* frequency. [Knk. *wan-í*, Tag. *dalás, limit*]

sarní: sarnien. *v.* to weed. (*lamon*)

saruá: *n.* vomit. (*bakuár; dul-ók, balinawnáw, alidukdúk, alildabdáb, bel-á, úta, rúsok*) **agsarua.** *v.* to vomit, throw up. **isarua.** *v.* to vomit out. **saruaan.** *v.* to vomit on someone. **arinsaruáen.** *v.* to be on the verge of vomiting. **makasarsarua.** *v.* to feel like vomiting. [Bon. *óta, otbo*, Ibg. *maguta*, Ivt. *mutaq*, Kal., Knk. *uta*, Png. *otá*, Kpm., Tag. *suka*]

saruág: isaruag. *v.* to cast (nets) (*puruak*). [Tag. *hagis*]

sarubabéng: agsarubabeng. *v.* to hesitate; be afraid. (*sarugaddeng, sarimadeng*)

sarubaybáy: *n.* fringe; anything hanging loose. **agsarubaybay.** *v.* to hang loose, flutter; flap.

sarubúsob: *a.* steep. **masarubusob.** *v.* to stumble into the water; to fall head first. [Tag. *tarik* (steep)]

sarubsúb₁: pinnasarubsub. *n.* boy's game played with sticks in the ground.

sarubsúb₂: sarsarubsúb. *n.* kind of small black beetle.

sarubsúb₃: isarubsub. *v.* to push forward with the snout. **sarubsuben.** *v.* to turn up the earth (with the snout); bulldoze. **maisarubsub.** *v.* to be stranded; to be upturned (earth).

sar-úd: *n.* strike, punch. (*danog*)

sarugaddéng: agsarugaddeng. *v.* to hesitate; pause; be indecisive. [Tag. *atubilí*]

sarúkag: sarukagen. *v.* to fluff pillows or mattresses by beating. (*tarukanag*)

sarúkan: *var.* of *sarúkang*.

sarúkang₁: *n.* bamboo device used to pluck mangos resembling a scoop net; pole used to pick fruits out of reach (*salungkit*). **agsarukang.** *v.* to use a pole to collect fruits. **isarukang.** *v.* to gather fruits with the *sarúkang*. **Agsarsarukang ti balasang iti bunga ti sayote.** The young lady is picking *sayote* fruits with a *sarukang*.

sarúkang₂: *n.* place where the dead are kept temporarily before burial.

sarúkang₃: *n.* a kind of bell-shaped, open-worked basket used to house a mother hen.

sarukigkíg: *var.* of *sarukikkik*: stagger.

sarukikkík: agsarukikkik. *v.* to stagger; trip; stumble; walk as a cripple; limp.

sarukísok: *n.* place overgrown with weeds.

sarukód: *n.* cane, walking stick; crook. **agsarukod.** *v.* to use a cane. **sarukudan.** *v.* to prop, support. **sarsarukod.** *n.* plant with green and brown leaves. [Png. *tukog*, Tag. *tungkód*]

sarukúsok: *var.* of *sarakusok*: venture, dare.

saroksók: see *saluksúk*: insert between or underneath.

saról: *var.* of *tsaról*: patent leather.

saromámit: nasaromamit. *a.* pointed, sharp, acute (*tarumamis*). [Tag. *tulis*]

sarumbínit: *var.* of *sarumbingit*.

sarumbíngit: agkaisarumbingit. *v.* to lie scattered; lie around; be all over the floor.

sarumbítin: *a.* adornment. **agkarasarumbitin.** *v.* to hang in disarray.

sarunó: *n.* line. **agsaruno.** *v.* to stand in line. **agsasaruno.** *v.* to come one after the other. **isaruno.** *v.* to do after something has been finished. **napasarunuan.** *a.* followed by. **sumaruno.** *prep.* next, *v.* to follow. **sarunuen.** *v.* to follow, go behind, succeed. **pagsarunuan.** *n.* long rope of a carabao used in plowing. **agpasaruno.** *v.* to sow additional seedlings. **Kasarunuanna ti kabalio.** He can easily manage (handle) the horse. **Pinagsasaruno manen ni Inangda ti tsinelas iti ubetda.** Their mother beat them again on their buttocks one after the other with a slipper. **Sarsarunuenna ti tianna.** He is walking behind his stomach (said of a hungry person). [Png. *tombok*, Tag. *sunód*]

sarunsún: sarunsunan. *v.* to add to, increase; cause one to follow closely; advance to fight, attack. **pasarunsunan.** *v.* to drink a chaser. **pasarunsonen.** *v.* to add water to a pumping well to get it to pump again. **ipasarunsun.** *v.* to add to what has been said; to second the motion.

sar-óng: *n.* chance visit. **maisar-ong.** *v.* to go to a place rarely visited; happen to arrive at. **Uppatton a tawenna ditoy Bauang ngem ita laeng a maisar-ong itoy a disso.** It will be four years that he has been here in Bauang, but it is just now that he has arrived at this place. [Tag. *dalaw* (visit)]

sarungaddéng: *n.* pause (*sarugaddeng*). **agsarungaddeng.** *v.* to pause, stop before entering; make a stop before proceeding on. **Nagsarungaddeng a nangtaliaw kenkuana.** He paused to look back at her.

sarungáni: sumarungani. *v.* to deviate, swerve; differ; argue; contradict (*sungani; siasi*). [Tag. *salungát*]

sarunggángat: *n.* small section of bamboo that pricks the nasal septum of a carabao upon pulling. **agkaisarunggangat.** *v.* to lie around; be scattered all over, be strewn. [Tag. *pakalatkalat*]

sarunggáyad: *n.* trail of a dress; extra length of a dress.

sarungguáb: isarungguab. *v.* to move with the snout (dogs, pigs, etc.) (*tangguab*). [Tag. *ngusò* (snout)]

sarungikngík: *n.* the cry of hungry pigs; crybaby. **agsarungikngik.** *v.* to cry (said of hungry pigs); to whine. **Ad-addan ti sarungikngik ti tallo a baboy idi madlaw dagitoy ti mangpakan kadakuada.** There were loud cries from three pigs when they noticed the people feeding them.

sarungkád: agsarungkad, sumarungkad. *v.* to prop; plant feet firmly on the ground. (*sekkad*) **maisarungkad.** *v.* to fall on one's feet. **Naimbag ta naisarungkad iti imana.** It's good that he fell on his hands. [Tag. *sikad*]

sarungkár: *n.* kind of herb used in infusion. **agsarungkar.** *v.* to visit; call upon as a guest. **sarungkaran.** *v.* to pay a visit to. **Sarungkarannak iti kabiitan a panawen.** Visit me as soon as possible. [Tag. *dalaw*]

sarúrong₁: *n.* see *sarípit*. **sumarurong.** *v.* to nauseate, be nauseous from hunger. **makasarurong.** *a.* nauseous (*ariek*).

sarúrong₂: sarurongan. *v.* to confirm; agree; second the motion (*anamong*). [Tag. *payag*]

sarusakít: (*obs.*) **agsarusakit.** *v.* to nurse the sick (*taripato*). [Tag. *alagà*]

sarúsar: *n.* granary, warehouse. (*agamang, kamalig*) **isarusar.** *v.* to store in the warehouse. [Tag. *kamalig*]

sarusíng: *n.* kind of oval mollusk with wart-covered shell.

sárut: *n.* tuberculosis; consumption. (*daig*) **agsarut.** *v.* to have tuberculosis. [Knk. *síok*, Tag. *tuyô*]

sarót: *n.* liquid that has seeped through. **nasarot.** *a.* keen; bright; intelligent. (*sarírit*) **sumarot.** *v.* to penetrate (said of moisture or light); (~ *ti mata*) be keen, sharp-eyed. **Simmarot dayta a balikasna iti katangkenan a paset ti pusok.** That word (he said) penetrated the deepest part of my heart. [Tag. *timò* (penetrate)]

sarutsó: (Sp. *serrucho*: handsaw) *n.* crosscut saw, ripsaw.

sarutsót: *n.* close succession; *adv.* coming one after another, in close succession. **agsarutso** *v.* to follow in quick succession. **sarotsuten** to loosen, untie, unfasten; remove thread fro (*tastas; satsat*) **nasarutsot.** *a.* easily unt loosened. **masarutsot.** *v.* to be unfaste loosened; run. **Agsasarutsot ti pabanto d kabusor.** The enemies' missiles came in succession. **Binuybuyana dagiti naruay estudiante a nasarsarutsot a bimmalasi watched the many students cross the stre after the other. [Tag. *tastás* (untie)]

sároy: saroysaroy. *n.* loose thread of a g frayings.

sarúyaw: see *tarúyaw*: rice with red kern

saruysóy: *n.* loose thread.

sárpaw: *n.* temporary shelter for outdo (*arpaw*). **masarpawan.** *v.* to just mark; to just make the cutoff point; to passing grade by a narrow margin.

sarraisí: *n.* rivulet. [Tag. *sapà*]

sarráy: (*obs.*) see *serráy*: push throug

sarruád: *n.* band, group, company; throng; swarm (of insects); scho etc.

sarruág: isarruag. *v.* to cast (nets,

sarruáp: see *sarruád*: band; co flock; swarm.

sarsá: (Sp. *salsa*: sauce) *n.* grav sauce. **sarsaan.** *v.* to apply sauce

sarsár: masarsaran. *a.* with s corn.

sarsardám: (f. *sardam*) *n.* twi ning.

sarsiádo: (f. *sarsa*) *n.* native re fish in a sweet sauce.

sarsuéla: (Sp. *zarzuela*: op native operetta; musical dra stage player of a *sarsuela*.

prove. **nasay-sayaat**. *a*. better. **kasayaatan**. *a*. best. **Impamaysa ken sinaysayaatko ti panagtrabahok iti ipatpatakdermi a bodega.** I concentrated on and improved my work in our building of the warehouse. [Ibg. *piya*, Itg. *nabalu*, Ivt. *mapyaq*, Kpm. *santing*, Png. *maóng*, Tag. *buti*]

sayáat₂: *n*. variety of awned early rice with dark hull and red kernel.

sayábat: **nasayabat**. *a*. bold; shameless; disrespectful; impudent; rude; impertinent. [Tag. *dahás*]

sayabsáb: **napasayabsaban**. *v*. to be almost hit (by thrown objects or bullets). **pasayabsaban**. *v*. to shoot at (but not hit), to shoot away; hurl away.

sáyad: see *sadsad*: to ground; strand.

sayád: **nasayad**. *a*. shallow (plates, etc.); flat.

sayág₁: **sum(a)yag**. *v*. to deflect; deflect; swerve; move with the wind; drift along; throw in the air (*ampayag*). **Impasayagna ti imatangna iti baybay.** He turned his attention toward the sea. [Tag. *lihís*]

sayág₂: **agpasayag**. *v*. to urinate. (*isbo*) **pasayagan**. *v*. to urinate at.

sayák: **pasayak**. *n*. irrigation canal. (*banawang*) **pasayakan**. *v*. to irrigate; flood with water.

sayaksák₁: **agsayaksak**. *v*. to be glad, happy, cheerful, merry; lively; active; enjoy life outside.

sayaksák₂: **pasayaksakan**. *v*. to hit at random; shoot at random. (*saksak*)

sayamúsom: *n*. fragrance. (*banglo*, *ayamuom*) **agsayamusom**. *v*. to be fragrant, sweet-smelling. [Tag. *bangó*, *samyô*]

sáyang: (Pil.) What a waste! What a pity! What a shame! (*piman*, *ilala*) **sayangen**. *v*. to waste; miss an opportunity. **masayang**. *v*. to be wasted. **Saanmo a sayangen ti kinaagtutubom.** Do not waste your youth. [Png., Tag. *sáyang*]

sayanggóng: *n*. kind of seine resembling a *daklís*.

sayanggúseng: *n*. gossip; rumor; buzzing sound. **agsayangguseng**. *v*. to buzz. **Nagwarasen ti sayangguseng nga adda anting-antingna.** The gossip that he has magical charms spread. [Tag. *bali-balità* (gossip); *hugong* (buzz)]

sayangkát: **isayangkat**. *v*. to implement a project; carry out (a project); apply; plan, plot; prepare; provide for. **Isayangkatmi ken Nanangmo ti panagbasam.** Your studies are provided for by your mother and me. [Tag. *sagawâ*]

sayápad: *n*. cable of a vessel.

sayásay: **agsayasay**. *v*. to flow out, run out; overflow. (*pussuak*; *lippias*; *labiang*; *silno*; *paruk-*

pok) **Diakon maibturan a buyaen ti panagsayasay pay ti ad-adu a dara.** I cannot stand to watch more bloodshed. [Tag. *danak*]

sáyaw₁: *n*. martial dance. [Tag. *sayáw* = dance]

sáyaw₂: **sayawen**. *v*. to wish slightly; wish without hope.

sáyaw₃: **pasayaw**. *n*. kind of edible marine fish.

sayáw: **nasayaw**. *a*. thin, watery (soup). [Tag. *labnáw*]

sayemsém: *n*. cool breeze (*salemsem*); cool moisture in the air. **No agpukawen ti sayemsem ti abagatan, agtubo kadagiti bato ti kadilian dagiti ruot ti baybay.** When the cool breeze of the south is gone, seaweed grows on the rocks of the reef.

sayengséng: *n*. rumors; buzzing sound. **agsayengseng**. *v*. to make a buzzing sound. **sayengsengan**. *v*. to importune with advice, requests, etc. **Simmayengseng dagiti bala iti ngatuen ti ulomi.** The bullets buzzed over our heads. [Tag. *haging*]

sayét: **nasayet**. *a*. flirtatious; lewd. (*garampang*) **sumayet**. *v*. to act immodestly (said of women).

sayetsét: *n*. hissing sound (*saretset*); (*fig.*) burning heat of the summer sun. **sumayetset**. *v*. to make a hissing sound (when frying). [Tag. *sagitsít*]

sayó: **sayuan**. *v*. to splash water against; wash gold. **agsasayo**. *v*. to splash when bathing. **sinnayo**. *n*. splashing game. **masaywan**. *v*. to be splashed. [Tag. *saboy*]

sayód₁: **nasayod**. *a*. handy; adroit; dexterous; orderly; neat; fluent. **pasayuden**. *v*. to make neat; facilitate. **Nasayod ti panagsaona iti Inggles.** His English speech was fluent. [Tag. *ayos*]

sayód₂: **masayod**. *n*. rice field that relies on rainfall; rice from a *masayod* field. [Tag. *sayód* = dried up]

sáyog: **sayugan**. *n*. bamboo water pipe; bamboo urinal for women. **isayugan**. *v*. to make something flow through the *sayugan*.

sayukmó: **nasayukmo**. *a*. weak, dull, languid, spiritless (*ginad*). [Tag. *kupad*]

say-óp: **masay-op**, **say-upen**. *v*. to perceive the smell of; smell (*angot*). **say-upen**. *v*. to sniff. [Tag. *langháp*]

sayúsay: **agsayusay**. *v*. to pass between legs (liquids).

sáyot: *n*. kind of scoop net with thin cloth for netting. **sayuten**. *v*. to catch in a scoop net. [Kal. *saklong*, Tag. *salok*]

say-út: **saysay-ut**. *n*. kind of small flying fish resembling the *bulóng unás*.

sayóte: (Sp. *chayote*: chayote) *n*. the *chayote* vine and its pear-shaped vegetable (Aus.), chokoes. [Tag. *sayuti*]

saysayót: *n.* tender tops of *sayote*.

sayyá: **agsayyasayya**. *v.* to scatter, disperse; break; disband. **masayyasayya**. *v.* to break up; separate. [Tag. *kalat*; *buwág*]

sayyág: **sumyag**. *v.* to swerve, deviate (*siasi*); fly off, dash off.

sayyét: *var.* of *sayet*: immodest girl. **Tengnga ti bangbangkag ti pakisaysayyetam!** You are acting immodestly right in the middle of the fields!

sayyó: *var.* of *sayo*.

seál: see *síwal*: large notch, nick.

sebáda: (Sp. *cebada*: barley) *n.* barley.

sebátse: (Sp. *azabache*: jet) var. of *asabatse*: jet black, black and shiny (horse).

sebbá: **agsebba**. *v.* to throw oneself into the fire. (insects); to endanger oneself. **maisebba**. *v.* to be exposed to danger, attack, etc. **isebba**. *v.* to throw into the fire. **Agsebba a kasla simut-simot**. He jumps into the fire like a winged ant.

sebbáal: **masbaalan**. *v.* to be able to endure, put up with; hold, contain. **Ammo lattan ti baro ti dagensen a di masbaalan ni Krista.** The young man knows the grief that Krista cannot endure. [Tag. *batá*]

sebbák: *n.* stock of sugarcane.

sebbáng: *n.* trail, path (followed by wild animals); track; rites, ceremonies; danger; temptation. **isebbang**. *v.* to lead into danger, sin, etc. **sebbangan**. *n.* kind, sort, species (*kita*); *v.* make a track. **pasbang**. *n.* quail snare with a noose. [Tag. *landás*]

sebbát: **agsebbát**. *v.* to deviate, give place for, make room for; give allowance for. (*lisi, siasi*)

sebbét: *n.* recovering losses in gambling. **agsebbet**. *v.* to recover losses in gambling. **sebbeten**. *v.* to defeat an opponent.

sebbuég: (*obs.*) *n.* panting. (*angsab*)

sebília: *var.* of *hebilla*: buckle.

sebo: *n.* grease; fat. (*taba; lanit; kábut*)

Sebuáno: *n.*, *a.* Cebuano, person from Cebu; Visayan language of the Cebuano people.

sébra: (Eng.) *n.* zebra.

sebséb: **sebseban**. *v.* to extinguish with water. **masebseban**. *v.* to be extinguished with water. **Nasebseban ti umap-apoy itay a riknana.** His fiery feeling a while ago calmed down (was extinguished).

séda: (Sp. *seda*: silk) *n.* silk. **de seda**. made of silk. **maraseda**. *a.* like silk; silky.

sedalína: (Sp. *seda lina*) *n.* silk mixed with linen

sedatíba: (Sp. *sedativa*: sedative) *n.* sedative. (*pangpatalna*)

seddáal: *var.* of *siddaal*.

seddém: **masdemán**. *v.* to be weighed down, oppressed; depressed; downcast (*leddaang*). [Tag. *lungkót*]

seddén: *n.* petroleum gas. (*segden*)

seddó: *n.* concern; lockjaw. **masdo**. *v.* to be faint headed; suffer heatstroke. **sedduen**. *v.* to strike home (threads of woof). **pannakasdo**. *n.* cause of exhaustion. [Tag. *pag-alaala* (concern)]

Séde: (Sp. *Sede*) **Santa Sede**. Holy See.

sédula: (Sp. *cédula*: slip) *n.* residence certificate; confirmation slip; residence tax.

sédro: (Sp. *cedro*: cedar) *n.* cedar; Spanish juniper.

sedséd: *n.* heap of brushwood. **sedseden**. *v.* to compress, ram. **masedsed**. *v.* to settle, sink (soil over tomb). [Tag. *siksík* (compress)]

seg-ám: see *say-á*: to clear one's throat.

segdén: (f. *segged*) *n.* oil, gas; *v.* to ignite; feed a flame.

seggá₁: *n.* eagerly awaiting someone's arrival. **sumga**. *v.* to be anxious; concerned, uneasy; worried for someone's arrival. **Adtoyen ti asawana a segseggaanna.** His wife, who was eagerly awaiting him, is here already. [Tag. *sabík*]

seggá₂: **pasga**. *n.* kind of white elongated fish.

seggáng: **nasgang**. *a.* noble; aristocratic; shining, radiant (*deggang*). [Tag. *dakilà*]

seggángat: (*obs.*) *n.* kind of feathered arrow.

seggár: *n.* bristling of hair. **sumgar**. *v.* to stand on end (hair). **nakapaspasgar**. *a.* horrible, dreadful. **pasgaren**. *n.* feathers that stand on end. **Adda simgar iti kaungganna.** *exp.* denoting excitement and mild fear (something bristled inside him). [Knk. *sengág*, Tag. *mangalisag*]

seggáy: *n.* kind of tree that yields valuable timber.

seggéd: *n.* flame. (*gil-ayab*; *rasok*; *apuy*; *darang*) **sumged**. *v.* to burn; (*fig.*) flare up (anger). **ipasged**. *v.* to burn; throw into the fire. **isegged**. *v.* to light from. **nasged**. *a.* fervent, passionate, intense, burning. **segden**. *n.* oil for lamps, petroleum. **pasgeden**. *v.* to kindle, ignite, light. **pasgedan**. *v.* to set fire to; inflame. **pammasged**. *n.* manner of lighting. **sisesegged**. *a.* burning, alight. [Tag. *ningas*]

seggép: *n.* scheme; plot; career; profession, occupation, business. **segpén**. *v.* to intend, propose, plan. **agseggep**. *v.* to frame the roof of a house. [Tag. *balak*]

seggét: *n.* water in which rice is boiled. **iseggetan**. *v.* to draw milky liquid from boiling rice. [Tag. *am*]

seggiáb: **sumgiab**. *v.* to ignite; flare up; be irritated. **sumgiab ti pungtot**. *v.* to flare up

sarímok: (*obs.*) **sumarimok**. *v*. to take stands below shots of the enemy (said of boats); to be within range.

sarimúlio: *var*. of *saramulio*: rude, ill mannered (*bastos*); conceited.

sarimutmót: **sarimutmuten**. *v*. to glean (what was missed by harvesters). **nasarimutmutan**. *n*. earnings from gleaning. (*tudtod*)

sarinagnág: **masarinagnagan**. *v*. to be half-dry.

sarinatnát: **pasarinatnatan**. *v*. to follow right after; second the motion.

sarindániw: [*sarita* + *daniw*] *n*. narrative poetry.

sarínip: **sarinipen**. *v*. to peep through a small opening; to scan (with the eyes).

sarínok: (*obs.*) **sumarinok**. *v*. to join the crowd; mingle.

sarinúnud: see *sanúd*: go backward; recant. (*sanut*)

sáring: **sarisaring**. *n*. kind of foot-high herb.

saringgáyad: **agsaringgayad**. *v*. to drag, trail on the ground. **isaringgayad**. *v*. to cause to trail or drag (*sagayad*). [Tag. *sayad*]

saringgayáman: (f. *gayáman*) **agsaringgayaman**. *v*. to creep, crawl on the ground like a centipede.

saringgúyod: **agsaringguyod**. *v*. to drag, trail on the ground. [Tag. *hila*]

saríngit: *n*. shoot (of bamboo, etc.); bud; offspring. **agsaringit**. *v*. to develop a shoot or bud. [Kal. *simit*, Tag. *usbóng*]

sariugmá: [*sarita idi ugma*] *n*. ancient legend. [Tag. *alamát*]

saripakpák: **agsaripakpak**. *v*. to expand, extend, swell, spread; spread and flutter (wings). **masaripakpakan**. *v*. to expand, dilate; swell. [Tag. *pagaspás* (flap wings)]

saripatpát: **masaripatpatan**. *v*. to catch a glimpse of; to recognize someone from afar. **apagsaripatpat**. *a*. just enough to recognize. **Adda nasaripatpatanna a lalaki a nakasakay iti nuang iti ruar ti inaladanda**. He caught a glimpse of a man riding a water buffalo outside their yard.

saripdá: *n*. ivory button; doorstop; shield; screen; bar; anything used to prevent air of water from entering the house (*sagiped*; *balunet*). **saripdaen**. *v*. to fend off, ward off; defend. (*sarapa*) **saripdaan**. *v*. to bar a door; shield; screen a window. **Di nagkutkuti iti sirok ti inyulesna a kamiseta a saripdana iti tumaytayok a darat**. He didn't move from under the shirt he used as a blanket to fend off the flying sand. [Tag. *sanggá*]

saripéd: (*obs.*) *n*. doorstop. (*sagiped*)

saríping: *n*. new growth of plants (where plants were trimmed). (*saringit*) **sumariping**. *v*. to

approach, come closer. **isariping**. *v*. to place near; do something adjacent to. **naisariping**. *a*. adjacent. **Nagdigos iti banio a naisariping iti kuartona**. She bathed in the bath next to her room.

sarípit: *n*. hair clip; device in the form of an X used to raise logs. **sarsaripit**. *n*. painful urination. **sarsaripiten**. *v*. to suffer from irregular small discharges of urine; suffer from gonorrhea; not be able to urinate; to urinate painfully. [Bon. *alotiptip*, Tag. *balisawsáw*]

sarípot: *n*. kind of bow net used to catch *ípon*. (*bubo*) **sariputen**. *v*. to catch in a bow net.

saripsíp: **saripsipen**. *v*. to cut grass to the roots.

sarírit: *n*. intelligence; wisdom; wit; talent; knowledge. (*aliwatek*; *sirib*; *ammo*; *laing*) **nasaririt**. *a*. bright, shrewd, intelligent; keen; clever; skillful. [Png. *dunong*, Tag. *dunong*, *talino*]

sarísa: *reg. var*. of *seresa*: cherry.

saríta: *n*. story; tale; legend; fable; recital; conversation, talk. **agsarita**. *v*. to converse; tell a story. **sumarita**. *v*. to talk. **sumanarita**. *v*. to talk nonstop; gossip. **isarita**. *v*. to reveal, disclose. **kasarita**. *v*. to converse with; speak with. **makisarita**. *v*. to speak with. **mannarita**. *a*. talkative; *n*. loquacious person. **saritaan**. *v*. to talk to someone; entertain. **saritaen**. *v*. to tell, relate; communicate; reveal. **sarsarita**. *n*. legend; fable; rumor. **pagsaritaan**. *n*. topic of conversation; reason for talking; *v*. to talk about. **pakasaritaan**. *n*. history; biography. **Ti tao a mannarita, awan ti ania nga magapuananna**. The man who talks much accomplishes little. **Dayta ti kayatko kenka ta saanka a narigat a kasarsarita**. That's what I like about you because you are not difficult to talk to. **Diak kayat a pagsaritaan dayta**. I don't want to talk about that. [Bon. *ógod*, Png. *salíta*, Tag. *salaysáy*, *salitâ*]

sariwagká: *var*. of *sariwakka*: untidy; clumsy.

sariwagténg: **agsariwagteng**. *v*. to walk away pouting and kicking.

sariwagwág: **sariwagwagen**. *v*. to shake in order to dry (hair, etc.); fluff cotton with sticks. **agsariwagwag**. *v*. to shake oneself to clean or dry. [Tag. *pagpág*]

sariwakká: *a*. untidy; clumsy; not careful (used for women). [Tag. *burarâ*]

sariw-át: **sumariw-at**. *v*. to protrude, jut out. **nagsariw-at**. *v*. uneven; protruding. **pasariw-at**. *n*. ring finger. [Tag. *uslî*]

sariwáwek: *var*. of *sariwawet*: roaming to a far place.

sariwáwet: *n*. bad manners; greediness. **nasariwawet**. *a*. having roamed around to a far place (chickens); having bad manners (at the table). **agsariwawet.** *v.* to roam to a far place (chickens, pigs, etc.). **Sariwawet metten dagiti matana.** His eyes are roaming.

sárkak: *n.* phlegm. (*sagkak; daak*) **agsarkak.** *v.* to discharge phlegm. [Tag. *kalaghalâ, dahak*]

sarkéd: sarkeden. *v.* to withstand, oppose, resist. **sumarked.** *v.* to resist, oppose. **masarkedan.** *v.* to be able to endure, oppose, resist. **Kanayonna nga ipukkaw no kasta a dinan masarkedan ti apges ti kinaagmaymaysana.** He always shouts like that when he can't endure the pain of his loneliness.

sarmáy: (*obs.*) **agsarmay.** *v.* to reshoot. (*saringit; sulbod*)

sarmíng: *n.* mirror; glass; eyeglasses; window (of a car); windshield. **agsarming.** *v.* to look at oneself in a mirror (*espeho*); wear glasses, use glasses. **sarming ti mata.** *n.* eyeglasses; iris. **pagsarmingan.** *n.* model, example, pattern. **manarming.** *v.* to look in/use a mirror. **sarmingan.** *v.* to put eyeglasses on someone. **sarmi-sarming ti lapayag.** *n.* eardrum. **pagattao a sarming.** *n.* full body mirror. **Maiwayat kuman ti pannakabitayna tapno adda pagsarmingan dagiti managdakdakes.** They should carry out his hanging to set an example for the criminals. [Bon. *lid-ang, pang-aw,* Png. *salmíng,* Tag. *salamín*]

sarnáed: agsarnaed. *v.* to hesitate, advance in a hesitating manner.

sarnáy: nasarnay. *a.* frequent. (*masansan, kanayon*) **kinasarnay.** *n.* frequency. [Knk. *wan-í,* Tag. *dalás, limit*]

sarní: sarnien. *v.* to weed. (*lamon*)

saruá: *n.* vomit. (*bakuár; dul-ók, balinawnáw, alidukdúk, alildabdáb, bel-á, úta, rúsok*) **agsarua.** *v.* to vomit, throw up. **isarua.** *v.* to vomit out. **saruaan.** *v.* to vomit on someone. **arinsaruáen.** *v.* to be on the verge of vomiting. **makasarsarua.** *v.* to feel like vomiting. [Bon. *óta, otbo,* Ibg. *maguta,* Ivt. *mutaq,* Kal., Knk. *uta,* Png. *otá,* Kpm., Tag. *suka*]

saruág: isaruag. *v.* to cast (nets) (*puruak*). [Tag. *hagis*]

sarubabéng: agsarubabeng. *v.* to hesitate; be afraid. (*sarugaddeng, sarimadeng*)

sarubaybáy: *n.* fringe; anything hanging loose. **agsarubaybay.** *v.* to hang loose, flutter; flap.

sarubúsob: *a.* steep. **masarubusob.** *v.* to stumble into the water; to fall head first. [Tag. *tarik* (steep)]

sarubsúb₁: pinnasarubsub. *n.* boy's game played with sticks in the ground.

sarubsúb₂: sarsarubsúb. *n.* kind of small black beetle.

sarubsúb₃: isarubsub. *v.* to push forward with the snout. **sarubsuben.** *v.* to turn up the earth (with the snout); bulldoze. **maisarubsub.** *v.* to be stranded; to be upturned (earth).

sar-úd: *n.* strike, punch. (*danog*)

sarugaddéng: agsarugaddeng. *v.* to hesitate; pause; be indecisive. [Tag. *atubilí*]

sarúkag: sarukagen. *v.* to fluff pillows or mattresses by beating. (*tarukanag*)

sarúkan: *var.* of *sarúkang.*

sarúkang₁: *n.* bamboo device used to pluck mangos resembling a scoop net; pole used to pick fruits out of reach (*salungkit*). **agsarukang.** *v.* to use a pole to collect fruits. **isarukang.** *v.* to gather fruits with the *sarúkang.* **Agsarsarukang ti balasang iti bunga ti sayote.** The young lady is picking *sayote* fruits with a *sarukang.*

sarúkang₂: *n.* place where the dead are kept temporarily before burial.

sarúkang₃: *n.* a kind of bell-shaped, open-worked basket used to house a mother hen.

sarukigkíg: *var.* of *sarukikkik:* stagger.

sarukikkík: agsarukikkik. *v.* to stagger; trip; stumble; walk as a cripple; limp.

sarukísok: *n.* place overgrown with weeds.

sarukód: *n.* cane, walking stick; crook. **agsarukod.** *v.* to use a cane. **sarukudan.** *v.* to prop, support. **sarsarukod.** *n.* plant with green and brown leaves. [Png. *tukog,* Tag. *tungkód*]

sarukúsok: *var.* of *sarakusok:* venture, dare.

saroksók: see *saluksúk:* insert between or underneath.

saról: *var.* of *tsaról:* patent leather.

saromámit: nasaromamit. *a.* pointed, sharp, acute (*tarumamis*). [Tag. *tulis*]

sarumbínit: *var.* of *sarumbingit.*

sarumbíngit: agkaisarumbingit. *v.* to lie scattered; lie around; be all over the floor.

sarumbítin: *a.* adornment. **agkarasarumbitin.** *v.* to hang in disarray.

sarunó: *n.* line. **agsaruno.** *v.* to stand in line. **agsasaruno.** *v.* to come one after the other. **isaruno.** *v.* to do after something has been finished. **napasarunuan.** *a.* followed by. **sumaruno.** *prep.* next, *v.* to follow. **sarunuen.** *v.* to follow, go behind, succeed. **pagsarunuan.** *n.* long rope of a carabao used in plowing. **agpasaruno.** *v.* to sow additional seedlings. **Kasarunuanna ti kabalio.** He can easily manage (handle) the horse. **Pinagsasaruno manen ni Inangda ti tsinelas iti ubetda.** Their mother beat them again on their buttocks one after the other with a slipper. **Sarsarunuenna ti tianna.** He is walking behind his stomach (said of a hungry person). [Png. *tombok,* Tag. *sunód*]

sarunsún: sarunsunan. *v.* to add to, increase; cause one to follow closely; advance to fight, attack. **pasarunsunan.** *v.* to drink a chaser. **pasarunsonen.** *v.* to add water to a pumping well to get it to pump again. **ipasarunsun.** *v.* to add to what has been said; to second the motion.

sar-óng: *n.* chance visit. **maisar-ong.** *v.* to go to a place rarely visited; happen to arrive at. **Uppatton a tawenna ditoy Bauang ngem ita laeng a maisar-ong itoy a disso.** It will be four years that he has been here in Bauang, but it is just now that he has arrived at this place. [Tag. *dalaw* (visit)]

sarungaddéng: *n.* pause (*sarugaddeng*). **agsarungaddeng.** *v.* to pause, stop before entering; make a stop before proceeding on. **Nagsarungaddeng a nangtaliaw kenkuana.** He paused to look back at her.

sarungáni: sumarungani. *v.* to deviate, swerve; differ; argue; contradict (*sungani; siasi*). [Tag. *salungát*]

sarunggángat: *n.* small section of bamboo that pricks the nasal septum of a carabao upon pulling. **agkaisarunggangat.** *v.* to lie around; be scattered all over, be strewn. [Tag. *pakalatkalat*]

sarunggáyad: *n.* trail of a dress; extra length of a dress.

sarungguáb: isarungguab. *v.* to move with the snout (dogs, pigs, etc.) (*tangguab*). [Tag. *ngusò* (snout)]

sarungikngík: *n.* the cry of hungry pigs; crybaby. **agsarungikngik.** *v.* to cry (said of hungry pigs); to whine. **Ad-addan ti sarungikngik ti tallo a baboy idi madlaw dagitoy ti mangpakan kadakuada.** There were loud cries from three pigs when they noticed the people feeding them.

sarungkád: agsarungkad, sumarungkad. *v.* to prop; plant feet firmly on the ground. (*sekkad*) **maisarungkad.** *v.* to fall on one's feet. **Naimbag ta naisarungkad iti imana.** It's good that he fell on his hands. [Tag. *sikad*]

sarungkár: *n.* kind of herb used in infusion. **agsarungkar.** *v.* to visit; call upon as a guest. **sarungkaran.** *v.* to pay a visit to. **Sarungkarannak iti kabiitan a panawen.** Visit me as soon as possible. [Tag. *dalaw*]

sarúrong₁: *n.* see *sarípit.* **sumarurong.** *v.* to nauseate, be nauseous from hunger. **makasarurong.** *a.* nauseous (*ariek*).

sarúrong₂: sarurongan. *v.* to confirm; agree; second the motion (*anamong*). [Tag. *payag*]

sarusakít: (*obs.*) **agsarusakit.** *v.* to nurse the sick (*taripato*). [Tag. *alagà*]

sarúsar: *n.* granary, warehouse. (*agamang, kamalig*) **isarusar.** *v.* to store in the warehouse. [Tag. *kamalig*]

sarusíng: *n.* kind of oval mollusk with wart-covered shell.

sárut: *n.* tuberculosis; consumption. (*daig*) **agsarut.** *v.* to have tuberculosis. [Knk. *síok*, Tag. *tuyô*]

sarót: *n.* liquid that has seeped through. **nasarot.** *a.* keen; bright; intelligent. (*sarírit*) **sumarot.** *v.* to penetrate (said of moisture or light); (~ *ti mata*) be keen, sharp-eyed. **Simmarot dayta a balikasna iti katangkenan a paset ti pusok.** That word (he said) penetrated the deepest part of my heart. [Tag. *timò* (penetrate)]

sarutsó: (Sp. *serrucho*: handsaw) *n.* crosscut saw, ripsaw.

sarutsót: *n.* close succession; *adv.* coming one after another, in close succession. **agsarutsot.** *v.* to follow in quick succession. **sarotsuten.** *v.* to loosen, untie, unfasten; remove thread from. (*tastas; satsat*) **nasarutsot.** *a.* easily untied, loosened. **masarutsot.** *v.* to be unfastened, loosened; run. **Agsasarutsot ti pabanto dagiti kabusor.** The enemies' missiles came in quick succession. **Binuybuyana dagiti naruay nga estudiante a nasarsarutsot a bimmalasiw.** He watched the many students cross the street one after the other. [Tag. *tastás* (untie)]

sároy: saroysaroy. *n.* loose thread of a garment; frayings.

sarúyaw: see *tarúyaw:* rice with red kernel.

saruysóy: *n.* loose thread.

sárpaw: *n.* temporary shelter for outdoor parties (*arpaw*). **masarpawan.** *v.* to just make the mark; to just make the cutoff point; to achieve a passing grade by a narrow margin.

sarraisí: *n.* rivulet. [Tag. *sapà*]

sarráy: (*obs.*) see *serráy:* push through a crowd.

sarruád: *n.* band, group, company; flock; herd; throng; swarm (of insects); school (of fish); etc.

sarruág: isarruag. *v.* to cast (nets, etc.).

sarruáp: see *sarruád:* band; company; herd; flock; swarm.

sarsá: (Sp. *salsa*: sauce) *n.* gravy (for *lechón*); sauce. **sarsaan.** *v.* to apply sauce to.

sarsár: masarsaran. *a.* with scattered ears of corn.

sarsardám: (f. *sardam*) *n.* twilight, early evening.

sarsiádo: (f. *sarsa*) *n.* native recipe consisting of fish in a sweet sauce.

sarsuéla: (Sp. *zarzuela*: operetta) *n.* kind of native operetta; musical drama. **sarsuelista.** *n.* stage player of a *sarsuela.*

sartín: (Sp. *sartén*: frying pan) *n.* frying pan (*pariok*); tin cup.

sása: *n.* odd number; leftover, remainder. (*gansal, tidda*)

sasá: masasa. *v.* to be damaged (said of plants).

saserdóte: (Sp. *sacerdote*: priest) *n.* priest. (*padi*)

sásik: (*obs.*) **agsasik.** *v.* to make salt from salt water. (*sána*)

sasús: *n.* kind of large black crustacean.

sástre: (Sp. *sastre*: tailor) *n.* tailor. **sastreria.** *n.* tailor's shop.

sáta: masata. *v.* to not be completed or carried out; to fail to undergo. **sataen.** *v.* to not go through with; fail to realize an event.

satanás: (Sp. *satanás*: Satan) *n.* devil, Satan. (*sairo*)

satín: (Sp. *satín, satén*) *n.* satin.

satúrno: (Sp. *saturno*: Saturn) *n.* Saturn.

satsát: satsaten. *v.* to unravel; tear, rip garments; demolish; undo crochet work by pulling the string. **satsatan.** *v.* to thrash, maul. **agsanatsat.** *v.* to make a thrashing sound. [Tag. *tastás*]

satsatéra: *n.* babbler, gossipy woman.

sawá: see *simmawá*.

sáwak: sawakan. *n.* kind of large marine fish with large mouth.

sawák: *a.* crooked, distorted (horns of the water buffalo).

sáwat: isawat. *v.* to insert into another's conversation.

sawáli: *n.* interwoven splits of bamboo used in walls.

sáwang: *n.* breach, opening; sluice. **isawang.** *v.* to manifest; declare; express; utter. **manawang.** *n.* kind of poisonous snake. **sawangen.** *n.* to open, breach (a dam, etc.). **Dika kuma agisawang iti kasta.** You shouldn't say things like that. [Tag. *sabi, pahayag*]

sáwar: sawaren. *v.* to search, look for by groping. **agsawar.** *v.* to search around; patrol an area; break in (robbers). **Sinawarda dagiti kamarote.** They searched the cabins. **Immaynakam inayaban ni nanangmo ta umaydaka tulongan nga agsawar.** Your mother came to call us so we could come help you search. [Tag. *hanap*]

sawásaw: *n.* excess; overlength; part of undergarment that protrudes over the edge of upper clothing. **sumawasaw.** *v.* to be in excess; overflow; (*obs.*) to sprout.

sawáw: *a.* hoarse. **agsawaw.** *v.* to vent; issue through a vent; utter in a hoarse voice; breathe through. **sawaw a timek.** *n.* dry, hoarse voice.

sáway: *a.* odd; unmatched (*pangis*); excess; surplus in distribution. **nagsaway.** *a.* unmatched, unparalleled. **kinasaway.** *n.* distinction; act of having an unparalleled characteristic; oddness.

saw-áy: (*reg.*) **isaw-ay.** *v.* to express verbally. **Diak maisaw-ay kadakayo ti adda a riknak.** I cannot express my feelings to you.

sawéd: nasawed. *a.* easy due to knowledge or experience. **saweden.** *v.* to continue something already begun; do with ease. [Tag. *dalî*]

saw-éd: naisaw-ed. *a.* focused on one point (the eyes).

sawét: (*reg.*) *var.* of *siwet*: do swiftly.

sáwi: *n.* kind of hawk; (*obs.*) poor-quality gold.

sáwil: sawilen. *v.* to raise with a lever. (*suil*)

saw-íng: *n.* tusk of a wild boar. (*saóng*) **sawíngen.** *v.* to gore with a tusk or horn. **sawingan.** *a.* having a tusk (said of the wild boar). [Tag. *pangil*]

sawír: *n.* roving hog; house chores; problems; difficulties; vagrant. **nasawir.** *a.* tolerable; vagabond, vagrant. **masawir.** *v.* to be tolerable, bearable, supportable. **Adda sawsawirko.** I have things to do; someone to take care of. **Awan sawsawirna a nakalasat dagiti nagtipon a resolusion.** He has no difficulties passing the combined resolutions.

sawirí: (*reg.*) *a.* crooked; twisted; (*fig.*) deceptive, fooling. **Immisem iti sawiri.** He smiled crookedly.

sáwit: *n.* barb of an arrow, spear, hook, etc. (*sima*). [Tag. *kawit*]

saw-ít: *n.* very small cup without handle used to measure *boggóong*. **sawsaw-ít.** *n.* kind of tailor bird.

sawsáw: isawsaw. *v.* to dip, dunk. **sawsawan.** *n.* dipping sauce. **maisawsaw.** *v.* to be dipped into. **pagsawsaw.** *n.* ingredients used for dipping. **pagisawsawan.** *n.* dipping sauce. **Naisawsaw iti eskandalo.** He was immersed in scandal. [Png., Tag. *sawsáw*]

sáya: (Sp. *saya*: skirt) *n.* skirt. **nakasaya.** *a.* wearing a skirt. **sayasaya.** *n.* common bird in the Bicol region whose song is said to bring bad luck. [Png. *sapey*]

say-á: *n.* clearing of the throat, sound produced by clearing the throat. **agsay-a.** *v.* to clear the throat (*sig-ám*). **isay-a.** *v.* to eject out while clearing the throat. **Nagsay-a tapno ipangngegna ti kaaddana.** He cleared his throat to show his presence. [Bon. *seláak*, Kpm. *tigím*, Tag. *tikhím, dahak*]

sayáat₁: [also spelled *siaat*] *n.* goodness; virtue. (*imbag*) **nasayaat.** *a.* good; pretty; handsome; elegant; fit; suitable; appropriate; charming. **sayaaten.** *v.* to do well. **pagsayaatan.** *n.* welfare; well-being; improvement; benefit. **saysayaaten.** *v.* to do well; to do carefully; to im-

prove. **nasay-sayaat.** *a.* better. **kasayaatan.** *a.*
best. **Impamaysa ken sinaysayaatko ti panagtrabahok iti ipatpatakdermi a bodega.** I concentrated on and improved my work in our
building of the warehouse. [Ibg. *piya*, Itg. *nabalu*, Ivt. *mapyaq*, Kpm. *santing*, Png. *maóng*,
Tag. *buti*]
sayáat₂: *n.* variety of awned early rice with dark
hull and red kernel.
sayábat: nasayabat. *a.* bold; shameless; disrespectful; impudent; rude; impertinent. [Tag.
dahás]
sayabsáb: napasayabsaban. *v.* to be almost hit
(by thrown objects or bullets). **pasayabsaban.**
v. to shoot at (but not hit), to shoot away; hurl
away.
sáyad: see *sadsad*: to ground; strand.
sayád: nasayad. *a.* shallow (plates, etc.); flat.
sayág₁: sum(a)yag. *v.* to deflect; deflect; swerve;
move with the wind; drift along; throw in the
air (*ampayag*). **Impasayagna ti imatangna iti
baybay.** He turned his attention toward the sea.
[Tag. *lihís*]
sayág₂: agpasayag. *v.* to urinate. (*isbo*) **pasayagan.** *v.* to urinate at.
sayák: pasayak. *n.* irrigation canal. (*banawang*)
pasayakan. *v.* to irrigate; flood with water.
sayaksák₁: agsayaksak. *v.* to be glad, happy,
cheerful, merry; lively; active; enjoy life
outside.
sayaksák₂: pasayaksakan. *v.* to hit at random;
shoot at random. (*saksak*)
sayamúsom: *n.* fragrance. (*banglo*, *ayamuom*)
agsayamusom. *v.* to be fragrant, sweet-smelling. [Tag. *bangó*, *samyô*]
sáyang: (Pil.) What a waste! What a pity! What a
shame! (*piman*, *ilala*) **sayangen.** *v.* to waste;
miss an opportunity. **masayang.** *v.* to be wasted.
Saanmo a sayangen ti kinaagtutubom. Do not
waste your youth. [Png., Tag. *sáyang*]
sayanggóng: *n.* kind of seine resembling a
daklís.
sayanggúseng: *n.* gossip; rumor; buzzing sound.
agsayangguseng. *v.* to buzz. **Nagwarasen ti
sayangguseng nga adda anting-antingna.** The
gossip that he has magical charms spread. [Tag.
bali-balità (gossip); *hugong* (buzz)]
sayangkát: isayangkat. *v.* to implement a project; carry out (a project); apply; plan, plot;
prepare; provide for. **Isayangkatmi ken Nanangmo ti panagbasam.** Your studies are
provided for by your mother and me. [Tag.
sagawâ]
sayápad: *n.* cable of a vessel.
sayásay: agsayasay. *v.* to flow out, run out; overflow. (*pussuak*; *lippias*; *labiang*; *silno*; *paruk-*

pok) **Diakon maibturan a buyaen ti panagsayasay pay ti ad-adu a dara.** I cannot stand to
watch more bloodshed. [Tag. *danak*]
sáyaw₁: *n.* martial dance. [Tag. *sayáw* = dance]
sáyaw₂: sayawen. *v.* to wish slightly; wish without hope.
sáyaw₃: pasayaw. *n.* kind of edible marine fish.
sayáw: nasayaw. *a.* thin, watery (soup). [Tag.
labnáw]
sayemsém: *n.* cool breeze (*salemsem*); cool
moisture in the air. **No agpukawen ti
sayemsem ti abagatan, agtubo kadagiti bato
ti kadilian dagiti ruot ti baybay.** When the
cool breeze of the south is gone, seaweed grows
on the rocks of the reef.
sayengséng: *n.* rumors; buzzing sound. **agsayengseng.** *v.* to make a buzzing sound. **sayengsengan.** *v.* to importune with advice,
requests, etc. **Simmayengseng dagiti bala iti
ngatuen ti ulomi.** The bullets buzzed over our
heads. [Tag. *haging*]
sayét: nasayet. *a.* flirtatious; lewd. (*garampang*)
sumayet. *v.* to act immodestly (said of women).
sayetsét: *n.* hissing sound (*saretset*); (*fig.*) burning heat of the summer sun. **sumayetset.** *v.* to
make a hissing sound (when frying). [Tag.
sagitsít]
sayó: sayuan. *v.* to splash water against; wash
gold. **agsasayo.** *v.* to splash when bathing. **sinnayo.** *n.* splashing game. **masaywan.** *v.* to be
splashed. [Tag. *saboy*]
sayód₁: nasayod. *a.* handy; adroit; dexterous; orderly; neat; fluent. **pasayuden.** *v.* to make neat;
facilitate. **Nasayod ti panagsaona iti Inggles.**
His English speech was fluent. [Tag. *ayos*]
sayód₂: masayod. *n.* rice field that relies on rainfall; rice from a *masayod* field. [Tag. *sayód* =
dried up]
sáyog: sayugan. *n.* bamboo water pipe; bamboo
urinal for women. **isayugan.** *v.* to make
something flow through the *sayugan*.
sayukmó: nasayukmo. *a.* weak, dull, languid,
spiritless (*ginad*). [Tag. *kupad*]
say-óp: masay-op, say-upen. *v.* to perceive the
smell of; smell (*angot*). **say-upen.** *v.* to sniff.
[Tag. *langháp*]
sayúsay: agsayusay. *v.* to pass between legs
(liquids).
sáyot: *n.* kind of scoop net with thin cloth for
netting. **sayuten.** *v.* to catch in a scoop net.
[Kal. *saklong*, Tag. *salok*]
say-út: saysay-ut. *n.* kind of small flying fish
resembling the *bulóng unás*.
sayóte: (Sp. *chayote*: chayote) *n.* the *chayote*
vine and its pear-shaped vegetable (Aus.),
chokoes. [Tag. *sayuti*]

saysayót: *n.* tender tops of *sayote*.

sayyá: agsayyasayya. *v.* to scatter, disperse; break; disband. **masayyasayya.** *v.* to break up; separate. [Tag. *kalat*; *buwág*]

sayyág: sumyag. *v.* to swerve, deviate (*siasi*); fly off, dash off.

sayyét: *var.* of *sayet*: immodest girl. **Tengnga ti bangbangkag ti pakisaysayyetam!** You are acting immodestly right in the middle of the fields!

sayyó: *var.* of *sayo*.

seál: see *síwal*: large notch, nick.

sebáda: (Sp. *cebada*: barley) *n.* barley.

sebátse: (Sp. *azabache*: jet) var. of *asabatse*: jet black, black and shiny (horse).

sebbá: agsebba. *v.* to throw oneself into the fire. (insects); to endanger oneself. **maisebba.** *v.* to be exposed to danger, attack, etc. **isebba.** *v.* to throw into the fire. **Agsebba a kasla simut-simot.** He jumps into the fire like a winged ant.

sebbáal: masbaalan. *v.* to be able to endure, put up with; hold, contain. **Ammo lattan ti baro ti dagensen a di masbaalan ni Krista.** The young man knows the grief that Krista cannot endure. [Tag. *batá*]

sebbák: *n.* stock of sugarcane.

sebbáng: *n.* trail, path (followed by wild animals); track; rites, ceremonies; danger; temptation. **isebbang.** *v.* to lead into danger, sin, etc. **sebbangan.** *n.* kind, sort, species (*kita*); *v.* make a track. **pasbang.** *n.* quail snare with a noose. [Tag. *landás*]

sebbát: agsebbát. *v.* to deviate, give place for, make room for; give allowance for. (*lisi, siasi*)

sebbét: *n.* recovering losses in gambling. **agsebbet.** *v.* to recover losses in gambling. **sebbeten.** *v.* to defeat an opponent.

sebbuég: (*obs.*) *n.* panting. (*angsab*)

sebília: *var.* of *hebilla*: buckle.

sebo: *n.* grease; fat. (*taba*; *lanit*; *kábut*)

Sebuáno: *n.*, *a.* Cebuano, person from Cebu; Visayan language of the Cebuano people.

sébra: (Eng.) *n.* zebra.

sebséb: sebseban. *v.* to extinguish with water. **masebseban.** *v.* to be extinguished with water. **Nasebseban ti umap-apoy itay a riknana.** His fiery feeling a while ago calmed down (was extinguished).

séda: (Sp. *seda*: silk) *n.* silk. **de seda.** made of silk. **maraseda.** *a.* like silk; silky.

sedalína: (Sp. *seda lina*) *n.* silk mixed with linen

sedatíba: (Sp. *sedativa*: sedative) *n.* sedative. (*pangpatalna*)

seddáal: *var.* of *siddaal*.

seddém: masdemán. *v.* to be weighed down, oppressed; depressed; downcast (*leddaang*). [Tag. *lungkót*]

seddén: *n.* petroleum gas. (*segden*)

seddó: *n.* concern; lockjaw. **masdo.** *v.* to be faint headed; suffer heatstroke. **sedduen.** *v.* to strike home (threads of woof). **pannakasdo.** *n.* cause of exhaustion. [Tag. *pag-alaala* (concern)]

Séde: (Sp. *Sede*) **Santa Sede.** Holy See.

sédula: (Sp. *cédula*: slip) *n.* residence certificate; confirmation slip; residence tax.

sédro: (Sp. *cedro*: cedar) *n.* cedar; Spanish juniper.

sedséd: *n.* heap of brushwood. **sedseden.** *v.* to compress, ram. **masedsed.** *v.* to settle, sink (soil over tomb). [Tag. *siksík* (compress)]

seg-ám: see *say-á*: to clear one's throat.

segdén: (f. *segged*) *n.* oil, gas; *v.* to ignite; feed a flame.

seggá₁: *n.* eagerly awaiting someone's arrival. **sumga.** *v.* to be anxious; concerned, uneasy; worried for someone's arrival. **Adtoyen ti asawana a segseggaanna.** His wife, who was eagerly awaiting him, is here already. [Tag. *sabík*]

seggá₂: pasga. *n.* kind of white elongated fish.

seggáng: nasgang. *a.* noble; aristocratic; shining, radiant (*deggang*). [Tag. *dakilà*]

seggángat: (*obs.*) *n.* kind of feathered arrow.

seggár: *n.* bristling of hair. **sumgar.** *v.* to stand on end (hair). **nakapaspasgar.** *a.* horrible, dreadful. **pasgaren.** *n.* feathers that stand on end. **Adda simgar iti kaungganna.** *exp.* denoting excitement and mild fear (something bristled inside him). [Knk. *sengág*, Tag. *mangalisag*]

seggáy: *n.* kind of tree that yields valuable timber.

seggéd: *n.* flame. (*gil-ayab*; *rasok*; *apuy*; *darang*) **sumged.** *v.* to burn; (*fig.*) flare up (anger). **ipasged.** *v.* to burn; throw into the fire. **isegged.** *v.* to light from. **nasged.** *a.* fervent, passionate, intense, burning. **segden.** *n.* oil for lamps, petroleum. **pasgeden.** *v.* to kindle, ignite, light. **pasgedan.** *v.* to set fire to; inflame. **pammasged.** *n.* manner of lighting. **sisesegged.** *a.* burning, alight. [Tag. *ningas*]

seggép: *n.* scheme; plot; career; profession, occupation, business. **segpén.** *v.* to intend, propose, plan. **agseggep.** *v.* to frame the roof of a house. [Tag. *balak*]

seggét: *n.* water in which rice is boiled. **iseggetan.** *v.* to draw milky liquid from boiling rice. [Tag. *am*]

seggiáb: sumgiab. *v.* to ignite; flare up; be irritated. **sumgiab ti pungtot.** *v.* to flare up (anger). **sumgiab ti rikna.** *v.* to intensify (feelings).

segída: (Sp. *seguida*: immediate) *adv.* immediately. (*ensegida*)

segidília: (Sp. *seguidilla*: diarrhea) *n.* asparagus bean. (*palláng*)

seglár: (Sp.) *a.* secular; worldly; *n.* lay person.

segménto: (Sp. *segmento*: segment) *n.* segment. (*paset*)

según: (Sp. *según*: according to) *prep.* according to, in accordance with; (*coll.*) it depends.

segúnda: (Sp. *segunda*: second) *num.*, *a.* second (*maikadua*) **sumegunda.** *v.* to be second. **segunda mano.** *a.* secondhand; previously used. **segunda klase.** *a.* second class. **manegunda.** *v.* to be second to. **masegundaan.** *v.* to be given a second coating of paint; to be seconded.

segundário: (Sp. *segundario*: second hand) *n.* second hand of a timepiece; *a.* secondary.

segúndo: (Sp. *segundo*: second) *n.* second (of time). [Kal. *kumadwa*]

segoniál: (Sp. *cigoñal*: swape-well; beam for raising a drawbridge) *n.* crankshaft.

segurádo: *var.* of *sigurado*: sure.

seguridád: (Sp. *seguridad*: safety) *n.* safety, security; certainty; assurance.

segúro: (Sp. *seguro*: certain) *adv.* probably. (*ngata*); *n.* insurance. **agpaiseguro.** *v.* to apply for insurance. **iseguro.** *v.* to insure. **seguruen.** *v.* to make sure. **maseguro.** *v.* to make certain; make sure something happens. **segurista.** *n.* one who always makes sure of a successful outcome before continuing, one who does not take risks.

segség: see *tegtég*: chop; mince.

séis: (Sp. *seis*: six) six. (*innem*) **alas seis.** (**alas sais**) six o'clock.

seisiéntos: (Sp. *seiscientos*: six hundred) *n.* six hundred. (*innem a gasut*)

sekánte: (Sp. *secante*: secant, blotting) *n.* blotting paper; blotter. **sekantien.** *v.* to dry with blotting paper.

sekká: *n.* clay for pottery; uprooted rice seedlings ready for replanting. **sekkaen.** *v.* to pull up seedlings of palay. [Tag. *bunot*]

sekkád: **sumkad.** *v.* to prop; resist; make a stand against; set feet firmly in the ground; not be able to swallow. **agpaskad.** *v.* to resist (with feet firmly on the ground). **Sumkad kaniak ti raman ti serbesa.** I dislike the taste of beer. **Nupay sumkad ti riknana, binay-an lattan ni Bong a sumurot ni Elsing iti ili.** Even though he didn't feel like it, Bong let Elsing follow him into town. [Tag. *sikad*]

sekkár: *n.* ring of bamboo used to bind together parts of a broom; hair clip. (*kalúlot*) **sekkaran.** *v.* to bind together a broom with a bamboo ring.

sekkéd: **sekden.** *v.* to reach, top, arrive at. **sekdan.** *v.* to reserve for future use (*latang*, *lebbén*); join; (*obs.*) minimize (expenses).

sekkég: *n.* tiebeam running from the *dógo* (corner post) to the other. (*awanán*)

sekkén: **seknan.** *v.* to touch, affect; influence. **sumken.** *v.* to affect someone; attack (said of headache); come to mind. **maseknan.** *v.* to be affected; to be involved. **nasken.** *a.* necessary; important. **pakaseknan.** *n.* things in which one is concerned. **Simken ti dadanagak.** My worries came back. **Seknanna kadi a talaga ti ayan-ayatda?** Does he really have an affect on their love? [Tag. *alaala*]

sekkér: *var.* of *sekkar*.

séko: (Sp. *seco*: dry) **puto seko.** *n.* kind of hard rice cake; kind of dry cookie.

sekulár: (Sp. *secular*) *a.* secular, lay; *n.* centennial, centenary.

sekularísmo: (Sp. *secularismo*: secularism) *n.* secularism.

sekundária: (Sp. (*escuela*) *secundaria*: secondary school) *n.* high school.

sekundário: (Sp. *secundario*: secondary) *a.* secondary; *n.* second hand of a watch.

sekréta: (Sp. *secreta*: secret investigation) *n.* detective; secret service; private investigator.

sekretário: (Sp. *secretario*: secretary) *n.* secretary, *fem.* sekretaria.

sekréto: (Sp. *secreto*: secret) *n.* secret (*palimed*). **sekreto-de-amor.** *n.* bleeding heart vine.

seksahésima: (Sp. *sexagésima*) *n.* sexagesima, second Sunday before lent.

seksék: *n.* innermost part; thicket; sound of the *maya* bird, the *maya* bird itself (*billit-tuleng*). **agseksek.** *v.* to shuffle cards. **sumeksek.** *v.* to penetrate to the innermost part. **iseksek.** *v.* to cram, force into, stuff, crowd. **sekseken.** *v.* to cram; shuffle cards. **seksekan.** *v.* to stuff; fill up with. **paseksekan.** *v.* to fatten up livestock. **maneksek.** *v.* to rise high (tide). **naseksek.** *a.* crammed, packed full; remote; far flung. [Ibg. *tattág*, Tag. *siksík*]

seksí: (Eng.) *a.* sexy. (*sippukel*)

sékta: (Sp. *secta*: sect) *n.* sect, denomination of people.

seladór: (Sp. *celador*: attendant; supervisor) *n.* promoter of a religious organization.

sélda: (Sp. *celda*: cell) *n.* prison cell; small room in a convent.

seldán: pagseldanan. *n.* water container (not for drinking water). **sumeldan.** *v.* to draw water (not for drinking). (*sakdo*)

selebrár: (Sp. *celebrar*: celebrate) **agselebrar.** *v.* to celebrate. **selebrasion.** *n.* celebration.

séleri: (Eng.) *n.* celery.

seliár: (Sp. *sillar*: square-hewn slab of stone; back of a horse) *n.* square-hewn stone.

sélio: (Sp. *sello*: stamp; seal) *n.* stamp; seal. **seliado.** *a.* stamped (envelope). **sobre-seliado.** *n.* stamped envelope.

sellá: sinla. *n.* variety of soft-kerneled rice.

sellád: agpaslad. *v.* to pull at a basket to make it wider during the weaving process.

sellág: *n.* moonlight. **naslag.** *a.* bright; beautiful; handsome; shining. (*kanagkag*) **kinasellag.** *n.* the brightness of the moon. [Kpm. *aslag*]

selláng: *n.* groin. (*luy-ong*) **sellangen.** *v.* to hit at the groin. **pagatsellang.** *a.* reaching the groin. [Tag. *singit*]

sellég: masleg. *a.* timid, shy (*bain*); with an inferiority complex.

sellém: *n.* round shallow net to catch fish and crabs. **masellem.** *v.* to turn sour (honey).

sellép: isellep. *v.* to dip in water. **naslep.** *a.* soaked, drenched. (*sisesellep, rúsep*) **sumlep.** *v.* to absorb moisture; penetrate; imbibe knowledge. **paslep.** *n.* steel. **ipaslep.** *v.* (*fig.*) to let something be absorbed, imbibed, assimilated. [Tag. *babad*]

sellét: sumlet. *v.* to barter, exchange. **islet.** *v.* to exchange (food). **selten.** *v.* to receive (food) in exchange.

sélula: (Sp. *célula*: cell) *n.* cell.

selóso: (Sp. *celoso*: jealous) *a.* jealous. (*apal*)

selsél: *n.* filling, stuffing (*seksek*); far corner; deepest part of a box; midst of a crowd. **iselsel.** *v.* to cram, stuff. **selselan.** *v.* to cram, stuff. **sumelsel.** *v.* to penetrate, crowd. **pagselsel.** *n.* stuffing; fillings. **naselsel.** *a.* crammed, stuffed; (*fig.*) faraway, distant (place), remote. [Tag. *siksík*]

selsíit: (*obs.*) **manelsiit.** *v.* to burn (sun).

sélyo: (Sp. *sello*: stamp) *n.* postage stamp. **selyuan.** *v.* to put a stamp on.

semáda: *var.* of *ensaymada*: sweet wheat flour bun.

semána: (Sp. *semana*: week) *n.* week. (*domingo, lawas*) **Semana santa.** Holy week, Easter.

semanéro: (Sp.) *n.* weekly duty person. **agsinnamanero.** *v.* to alternate on a weekly basis with one another.

semántika: (Sp. *semántica*: semantics) *n.* semantics, meaning.

seménto: (Sp. *cemento*: cement) *n.* cement (*galém*; *galagála*); plaster cast; filling for teeth.

sementado. *a.* cemented. **nasementuan.** *a.* cemented; in a plaster cast. **ipasemento ti ngipen.** *v.* to have the teeth filled.

seméstre: (Sp. *semestre*: semester) *n.* semester.

semiliá: (Sp. *semilla*: seed) *n.* seedlings (*bunubon*); ~ **ti lalaki.** *n.* sperm (*kissit*). **pagsemiliaan.** *n.* seedbed. [Tag. *tamód* (sperm)]

seminár: (Eng.) *n.* seminar; workshop. **makiseminar.** *v.* to attend a seminar.

seminário: (Sp. *seminario*: seminary) *n.* seminary. **seminarista.** *n.* seminarian, student in a seminary.

semítiko: (Sp. *semítico*) *n.*, *a.* Semite; Semitic.

semmá: masmá. *v.* to take the wrong road; go astray (*wawa*; *pukaw*). [Tag. *ligáw*]

semmáay: *var.* of *sennaay*: sigh.

semsém: *n.* disturbance; inconvenience. **semsemen.** *v.* to molest; disturb, inconvenience; annoy. **makasemsem.** *a.* annoying; disturbing; controversial; problematic.

séna: (Sp. *cena*: supper) **Santa Sena.** Last Supper.

senádo: (Sp. *senado*: senate) *n.* senate.

senadór: (Sp. *senador*: senator) *n.* senator.

senákulo: (Sp. *cenáculo*) *n.* Cenacle, place of the last supper; rites honoring the Cenacle.

sen-ál: isen-al. *v.* to knock contents of a basket to make them settle. (*san-ek*) **maisen-al.** *v.* to be knocked down.

senário: (Eng.) *n.* scenario; outline of a play; scenery.

senépa: (Sp. *cenefa*: border, edge; trimming; hem) *n.* decorative border or edging.

seniál: (Sp. *señal*: sign; signal) *n.* sign; mark (*tanda*); omen. **agsenial.** *v.* to signal; mark; foreshow. **senialan.** *v.* to put a sign on, mark.

sénias: (Sp. *seña*: sign) *n.* signal; sign. (*tanda*) **isenias.** *v.* to signal; flash blinkers on a car. **Adda agsasagawisiw ken agsisinnenias.** There were people whistling and making signs at each other.

senniór: (Sp. *señor*: sir) *n.* sir, gentleman (*ápo*); master (*ámo*).

senióra: (Sp. *señora*: lady) *n.* (used for the upper classes) married lady; madam; matron; mistress.

senioríta: (Sp. *señorita*: miss) *n.* young lady, miss; (*fig.*) rich lady who does not work. **agsenseniorita.** *v.* to behave like a rich young lady. **aginseseniorita.** *v.* to pretend to be a rich young lady.

senioríto: (Sp. *señorito*: master) *n.* young gentleman; (*fig.*) rich young man who doesn't work. **agsenseniorito.** *v.* to act like a rich young man who doesn't work. **aginseseniorito.** *v.* to pretend to be a rich young man.

senísa: (Sp. *ceniza*: ash) *var.* of *sinisa*: ashes. (*dapo*) **Mierkoles de Senisa**. *n.* Ash Wednesday. **senisado**. *a.* gray, ash-colored.

senná: **masna**. *a.* usual, ordinary, customary. (*kadawyan*)

sennáay: *n.* sigh. (*sainnek*) **agsennaay**. *v.* to sigh. **masnaayan**. *v.* to mourn, sorrow; be sad; grieve. **pagsennaayan**. *n.* cause for depression. [Kpm. *singal*, Png. *dageyen*, Tag. *buntónghiningá, himutók, hinagpís*]

sennéb: **agsenneb**. *v.* to take charge of everything (many duties at one time); do many things at once. **masneban**. *v.* to be saturated; soaked in; grieve. **senneben**. *v.* to penetrate; overwhelm (with sadness). **Nasneban iti liday**. He is overwhelmed with sadness.

sennék: **sumnek**. *v.* to move; affect, touch; penetrate. **sumnek ti asi**. *v.* to be moved by compassion. **isnek**. *v.* to cause to move, penetrate; feel pity for. **isnek ti ási**. *v.* to take pity upon. **ipasnek**. *v.* to do earnestly; feel deeply for; to do fervently. **napasnek**. *a.* fervent, ardent, earnest; sincere (*tennek, puso*); dedicated; serious. **kinapasnek**. *n.* dedication. **naimpasnekán**. *a.* with dedication, sincere. **pumasnek**. *v.* to become sincere, dedicated. [In suffixed forms, *pasnék* is the root; Tag. *antíg*]

senóda: (*obs.*) *n.* kind of big white sweet potato.

sensén: **sensenen**. *v.* to compress, squeeze, condense. **ipasensen**. *v.* to close, unite. [Tag. *sinsín*]

sensílio: (Sp. *sencillo*: simple) *n.* spare change; coins (as opposed to paper money) *a.* simple. **agpasensilio**. *v.* to change bills for paper money. [Tag. *baryá*]

sénso: (Sp. *censo*: census) *n.* census. **isenso**. *v.* to register in a census. **agsenso**. *v.* to take a census.

sensór: (Sp. *censor*: censor) *n.* censor. **sensoren**. *v.* to censor.

sensúra: (Sp. *censura*: censorship) *n.* censorship.

sentábo: (Sp. *centavo*: centavo) *n.* centavo, cent.

sentenário: (Sp. *centenario*: centennial) *n.* centennial, one hundredth anniversary.

senténo: (Sp. *centeno*) *n.* rye.

senténsia: (Eng.) *n.* sentence, conviction. **sentensiaan**. *v.* to sentence (a criminal). **sentensiado, nasentensiaan**. *a.* sentenced. [Tag. *hatol*]

sentensiadór: *n.* referee in a cockfight; judge (in a contest).

sentído: (Sp. *sentido*: sense) *n.* sense (*rikná; nákem; púot*); meaning; temple of the head. **sentido-komún**. *n.* common sense.

sentigrádo: (Sp. *centigrado*: centigrade) *n.* centigrade.

sentimétro: (Sp. *centimetro*: centimeter) *n.* centimeter.

sentimiénto: (Sp. *sentimiento*: feeling) *n.* feelings (*rikná*). **agsensentimiento**. *v.* to be sentimental.

séntimos: (Sp. *centimo*: cent) *n.* cent; centavo, one-hundredth of a peso.

sentinéla: (Sp. *centinela*: sentinel) *n.* sentry, sentinel.

senturéra: (Sp. *cintura*: waist) *n.* belt holder.

sentrál: (Sp. *central*) *a.* central; *n.* center; town center; sugar refinery; telephone exchange. **sentralisado**. *a.* centralized.

séntro: (Sp. *centro*: center) *a. n.* center, middle. (*tengnga*)

sényas: *var.* of *senias*: sign, signal.

senyór: *var.* of *senior*: sir (see *seniór* for various forms).

sengngáay: (*obs.*) **agsengngaay**. *v.* to separate. [Tag. *hiwaláy*]

sengngát: *n.* space in between (*baet*); *prep.* in between. **makasngat**. *v.* to be able to interpose. **sumngat**. *v.* to stand between; to do between. **isengngat, ipasngat**. *v.* to put in between; insert. **iti sengngat**. in between. **iti nagsengngatan**. *prep.* between. **Maipasngat iti trabaho**. He is deeply engaged in work. [Tag. *pagitan, singit*]

sengngáw: *n.* vapor, steam (*alingasaw*); mist; breath. **sumngaw**. *v.* to evaporate, breathe out; fume; emit vapor; appear unexpectedly. **yesngaw, isngaw**. *v.* to reveal, declare; express one's thoughts. **sengngawán**. *v.* to originate, effect. **pasngaw**. *n.* drainage; sluice gate. **pasngawán**. *v.* to steam cook. **makasngaw**. *v.* to be able to steam; to be able to express oneself. **Awan ti simngaw a timekna**. He didn't breathe a word. **sengngawan**. *v.* (*obs.*) to originate, produce. [Kal. *os-aw*, Tag. *singáw* (steam)]

sengngáy: **sumngay**. *v.* to be born (*pasngay*); emerge, issue forth. **ipasngay**. *v.* to bring forth, give birth to; deliver; create. **kaipasngay**. *a.* newly born. **kasangay**. *n.* birthday. **mamasngay**. *v.* to deliver a baby. **agpasngay**. *v.* give birth to a baby. **agkarapasngay**. *v.* to frequently give birth. **maipasngay**. *v.* to be born. **pasngay**. *n.* creation; product; invention (*partuat*); production. **pakaipasngáyan**. *n.* place of birth. **Kaipaspasngáyanna iti singin**. She just gave birth to twins. [Grammatical note: *pasngay* is considered a root, so there is no stress shift to the suffix; compare it with *sengngáw*. Bon. *sádal*, Ivt. *suvek* (livestock birth), *anak* (generic giving birth), Tag. *silang* (born); *litáw* (emerge); *kaarawán* (birthday)]

sengngél: (*obs.*) *n.* annoyance. (*semsem*) **sengngelen.** *v.* to annoy; vex.

sengséng: isengseng. *v.* to cram, stuff, force contents into. (*selsel*) **sumanengseng.** *v.* to whiz; hiss. [Tag. *saksák*]

sep-ák: *var.* of *seppák:* break in two. [Tag. *baklî*]

sep-áng: *n.* upper part of the thigh at the inside. **sep-angan.** *v.* to twist off. (*sip-ak*)

separádo: (Sp.) *a.* separated; ready to go (*sagana*); set aside (money).

sépia: (Sp. *sepia:* brown photograph) *n.* brown photograph, sepia.

sepílio: *var.* of *sipilio:* toothbrush.

seplíng: *n.* banana shoot. (*subbual*)

sépo: (Sp. *cepo:* block) *n.* truss; beam for architectural support.

sepulturéro: *var.* of *sipulturero:* keeper of a cemetery; cemetery guard.

seppáat: sumpaat. *v.* to penetrate; (*obs.*) come immediately; happen in a flash.

seppák: maspak. *v.* to break by snapping; break in two. (*sip-ak*) **seppaken.** *v.* to break the jaws of an animal. [Tag. *baklî*]

seppál: (*obs.*) **agseppal.** *v.* to swallow. (said of animals) (*alimon*)

seppéd: (*obs.*) **masped.** *v.* to decay (plants) (*rupsa*). [Tag. *bulók*]

seppég: *n.* kind of large speckled bird. **sumpeg.** *v.* to swoop down and pounce upon prey (*sippayot*); (*fig.*) overcome. **Kasla adda nangseppeg kenkuana.** *exp.* denoting fear or nervousness (like something swooped down upon him). **Dagusda nga agsinnepeg no agsabatda.** They immediately pounce on each other when they meet. [Png. *singkát*, Tag. *sibád, dagit*]

seppét: maspet. *v.* to be choked, obstructed, clogged. [Tag. *sakál*]

seppók₁: sumpukan. *v.* to place where one enters the bushes.

seppók₂: maspok. *a.* abundant, much, many, plenty; (*coll.*) dead. [Tag. *dami*]

sepsép: *n.* kind of small gnat; (Tag. *sipsip*) bootlicker. **sepsepan.** *v.* to suck blood; drain; exhaust financially. **sumepsep.** *v.* to absorb moisture; bootlick. [Tag. *nikník* (gnat)]

Septiémbre: (Sp. *septiembre:* September) *n.* September. [Kal. *sechang,* Knk. *tíway*]

séptimo: (Sp.) *a.* seventh. (*maikapito*)

séra: (Sp. *cera:* wax) *n.* wax.

seradúra: (Sp. *cerradura:* lock) *n.* lock. (*kandado*) **Pinuligosna ti seradura ket induronna ti rikep.** He turned the lock and pushed open the door.

serámika: (Sp. *cerámica*) *n.* ceramics.

seray-ób: see *saray-ób:* sultry; very hot.

serbéb: (*reg.*) *var.* of the *patintéro* game.

serbésa: (Sp. *cerveza:* beer) *n.* beer. **agserbesa.** *v.* to drink beer. **agatserbesa.** *v.* to smell like beer.

serbí: (Sp. *servir:* serve) *n.* service; use. (*kaeseskan*) **agserbi.** *v.* to serve; be of use. **awan serbina.** it is of no use. **serbian.** *v.* to serve someone. **iserbi.** *v.* to use, apply; make use of; spend on (money); put into service. **agserserbi.** *n.* servant; minister. **naserbi.** *a.* useful. **kinaserbi.** *n.* utility, use. **pagiserbian.** *n.* use; purpose; validity. **Ania kuma ti pangiserbiam iti bubon?** What could your use be for the well? **Ania' serbi ti kinabaknang no mapukaw met ti salun-at.** Of what use is being rich if the health is gone? [Tag. *silbí*]

serbidór: (Sp. *servidor:* waiter) *n.* waiter; server.

serbidóra: (Sp. *servidora:* waitress) *n.* waitress.

serbiliéta: (Sp. *servilleta:* napkin) *n.* napkin.

serbísio: (Sp. *servicio:* service) *n.* service. **serbisio sibil.** civil service. **serbisio publiko.** public service. **serbisio militar.** military service.

serbó: serbuan. *v.* to hydrate (lime).

sereál: (Sp. *cereal*) *n.* cereal.

seremónia: (Sp. *ceremonia:* ceremony) *n.* ceremony.

serenáta: (Sp. *serenata:* serenade) *n.* serenade. (*tapat*)

seréno: (Sp. *sereno:* night watchman; serene) *n.* security guard for buildings, night watchman (*bantay*); *a.* serene, calm. (*talna*)

serésa: (Sp. *cereza:* cherry) *n.* cherry.

seriáles: (Sp. *cirial:* processional candlestick) *n.* crucifix and two candlesticks used for religious processions.

série: (Sp. *serie:* series) *n.* series. (*urnos, intar*)

seringgília: (Sp. *jeringilla:* small syringe) *n.* syringe. (*heringgilia*)

serióso: (Sp. *serio:* serious + -*oso*) *a.* serious. (*nakaro*)

serkák: agserkak. *v.* to clear one's throat. (*sigam; say-a*) **sumerkak.** (*obs.*) *v.* to ruminate.

serkán: (f. *serrék*) *n.* entrance; gate; *v.* to enter; pass into; join a club; begin.

serkég: serkegan. *v.* to keep closed (the mouth).

sermón: (Sp. *sermón:* sermon) *n.* sermon; lecture. (*kasaba*) **agsermon.** *v.* to deliver a sermon. **isermon.** *v.* to preach to.

séro: (Sp. *cero:* zero) *n.* zero. (*awan*)

serpentína: (Sp. *serpentina:* streamer) *n.* balloon dress, kind of wide skirt; streamers.

serpiénte: (Sp. *serpiente:* serpent) *n.* serpent. (*uleg*)

serpílio: (Sp.) *n.* clown.

serrá: (Sp. *cerrar:* to close) *n.* that which closes or blocks. **serraan.** *v.* to close; bar, barricade, clog; adjourn. **makaserra.** *v.* to settle accounts, liquidate. **nakaserra**. *a.* closed. (*rikep*) **Naserraanen ti barukongko iti asinoman a lalaki.** My heart is already closed to any man. [Tag. *sará*]

serrádo: (Sp. *cerrado*: closed) *a.* closed (*nakarikep*). [Tag. *sarado*]

serradúra: (Sp. *cerradura*: lock) *n.* door lock; keyhole. [Tag. *seradura*]

serráy: **sumray**. *v.* to crowd, push one's way through. (*letlet*)

serréb: *var.* of *sareb*: drawn water used for washing dishes or clothes. **sumreb**. *v.* to draw out water (to wash dishes or clothes).

serrég: *n.* sharp points at the funnel-shaped entrance of a bow net. **serregan**. *v.* to block; barricade. [Tag. *harang* (block)]

serrék: *n.* time of work; time of classes. **sumrek**. *v.* to enter, come in; be admitted (to school). **serkan**. *n.* entrance; gate, *v.* to enter, pass into; begin; join a club, become a member of. **ipas-(t)rek, pasreken**. *v.* to make someone enter; introduce; usher; record. **makastrek**. *v.* to be able to enter. **mastrek**. *v.* able to be entered; to be able to enter something. **mapastrek**. *n.* profit; gain; interest. **makapastrek**. *v.* to be able to let someone enter; to be able to gain from, profit. **pamastrekan**. *n.* business; source of income. **panagseserrek**. *v.* time of classes or work. **pagserkan**. *n.* entrance; place of business; office. **adda serrek**. *v.* to have school; to have work. **No bassit ti maapitda, awan manen ti namnamana a sumrek iti pagadalan inton panagseserrek.** It they have a small harvest, he has no hope again to enter school when it is class time. **Saan ngarud a sumrek ti kaan kaniak.** I don't feel like eating (eating doesn't enter me). [Bon. *segep*, Ibg. *tallung*, Ivt. *asdep*, Knk. *sil-ók*, Png. *loób*, *tobóng*, Tag. *pasok*]

sersér: **agsanerser**. *v.* to make the sound of an ascending kite; whiz in the air. (*banerber*)

sertipikádo: (Sp. *certificado*: certified) *a.* certified.

sertípiko: (Sp. *certificado* - *-ado*) *n.* certificate.

sesánte: (Sp. *cesante*: suspended from office) **nasesante**. *a.* fired, dismissed; suspended from office; unemployed.

sesénta: (Sp. *sesenta*: sixty) *n.* sixty. (*innem a pulo*)

sesión: (Sp. *sesión*: session) *n.* session.

sesúra: (Sp. *cesura*: cæsura) *n.* cæsura, break or pause in a line of verse.

seténta: (Sp. *setenta*: seventy) *num.* seventy. (*pito a pulo*)

setesiéntos: (Sp. *setecientos*: seven hundred) *n.* seven hundred. (*pito a gasut*)

sétro: (Sp. *cetro*: scepter) *n.* scepter; symbol of royal power or authority.

setsét: **sumanetset**. *v.* to make the sound of a whip; hiss (when being roasted, from the scorching heat of the sun). [Tag. *sagitsít*]

si: *obs. var.* of *ni*: singular of personal article. **Siasino?** Who? The ancient article appears in the independent personal pronouns: *siak, siká, sitá, sikamí, sitayó, sikayó*]

siCV-: Prefix that forms stative lexemes and adverbs. **anos**. gentle, nice. **siaanos**. gently, nicely. **Iti kasta maammuanna a silalagipka pay laeng kenkuana.** That way he will know that you still are thinking about him. **Bulsekka a simamata.** You are blind with your eyes open.

siá: Interjection used to drive away chickens.

siáat: spelling variant of *sayáat*: good; kind; well.

siáb: **sumiab**. *v.* to burn in a blaze; to flare up. (*giab*)

siág: **sumiag**. *v.* to deflect, swerve, deviate; dive; dart (fish); drift along, move with the wind.

siák: [historically *si-* + *ako*, before the enclitic =*n*, the old form *ako* is retained] *pron.* Independent first person singular pronoun: I. **sisiak**. *pron.* only I, I alone. **Siak la a siakon.** It's always me. **Siak ti napan idiay.** I was the one who went there. **No siak ti sika.** If I were you. [Bon. *sak-en*, Knk. *sak-én*, Png. *siák*, Tag. *akó*]

siakók: see *kakók*: a kind of cuckoo; kind of spiny fish.

siálak: (Eng.) *n.* shellac, varnish.

siám: *num.* nine. **agsiam**. *v.* to reach the ninth day (of a *novena*, etc.) **maikasiam**. *num.* ninth. **sagsisiam**. *num.* nine each. **isiam**. *v.* to hold a novena prayer for the deceased. **agsiamsiam**. *v.* to be dizzy; to be stunned (when hit); (*coll.*) to see the stars (when hit). **Nakaraman iti siamsiam; Nagsiamsiam ti kinitana.** *exp.* He saw different colors (when hungry, exhausted); to see stars (when hit). [Png. *siám*, Kal., Tag. *siyám*]

siámpo: (Eng.) *n.* shampoo. **agatsiampo**. *v.* to smell like shampoo.

sianay: *adv.* utterly.

siánsi: *var.* of *tiani*: kitchen turner; cooking tweezers.

siáp: *n.* coffee color; bark of a tree yielding a brown/red dye.

siáping: (Eng. shopping) *n.* shopping **agsiaping**. *v.* to go shopping. **pagsisiapingan**. *n.* shopping place, mall.

siár: **masiar**. *v.* to be splintered. [Tag. *sipák*]

siási: *n.* out of the way road. **sumiasi**. *v.* to deviate, stray, wander away. **isiasi**. *v.* to mislead. **Mabalintayo nga isiasi ti tao iti kina-daksanggasat.** We are able to mislead people into evil ways. [Tag. *lihís*]

siasíno: *interrog.* who? **siasino man.** whosoever; whoever. **kinasiasino.** *n.* identity. **Diak paka-wanen ti siasino man nga agtraidor iti partido.** I will not forgive anyone who betrays the party. [Png. *siopá*, Tag. *sino*]

siát: siaten. *v.* to indent, notch. (*tipping*)

siáw: sisiaw. *n. puróng* fish when small.

siáy: *n.* kind of snare for jungle fowls consisting of nooses and pegs and a *pangngáti* (tame cock) put in the middle used as a decoy.

síba: *n.* danger; temptation; (*reg.*) path of jungle animals; (*reg.*) rice pests. **nasiba.** *a.* damaged, spoiled, ravaged (*kerraay*); ruined, injured, impaired. **sibaen.** *v.* to damage by eating (said of animals eating plants); spoil, ruin. **agsiba.** *v.* to destroy crops (animals). **pagsibaan.** *n.* temptations. [Tag. *landás* (path); *panganib* (danger); *hibò* (temptation); *sibà* = gluttony; greed]

sibakóng: *n.* bamboo band; internodes of bamboo used to make music.

síbalos: *n.* milkfish fingerlings.

síbang: isibang. *v.* to do one's best; make an effort to do (*saet*); exert oneself. **maisibang.** *v.* to take the time to do; be able to carry out. **Manmano ngamin a maisibangmi ti agdalus.** It's because it's very rarely that we take the time to clean.

síbar: (*obs.*) suddenly. (*bigla*; *apagdarikmat*; *alibadbad*) **nasibar.** *a.* sunburnt.

sibár: isibar. *v.* to scatter (rice seedlings in bundle in a paddy).

sibát: pasibat-sibát. *n.* beating around the bush; faltering, wavering.

síbay: *n.* neighborhood, vicinity. **iti sibay.** *prep.* at the side of, in the company of. **mannibsibay.** *v.* to ramble around town; roam the streets. **sibayen.** *v.* to catch someone fainting or falling. [Tag. *kapaligiran* (vicinity)]

sibbá: see *sebba*: put in fire; (*fig.*) endanger.

sibbáng: see *sebbang*.

sibbarót: sibbaruten. *v.* to snatch; grab; seize. (*rabnót*; *rabsot*) **Sinibbarot dagiti polis ti igamna sada pinosasan.** The police seized his weapon, then handcuffed him. [Tag. *agaw*]

sibbawéng: *n.* the *abal-ábal* beetle when just out of larval stage. [Tag. *salagubang*]

sibbó: isibbo. *v.* to do or use for the first time (new clothes, etc.). **agsisibbo.** (*obs.*) *v.* to fall in a cataract. **pangisibbuan.** *n.* occasion for wearing new clothes for the first time. [Tag. *bago* (new)]

sibbuán: *n.* jumping down. (*tappuak*) **agsib-buan.** *v.* to jump down.

sibból: *n.* bamboo cane with a hook at one end. (*sukdal*) **sibbulen.** *v.* to catch with a *sibbúl*. **kassibol.** *a.* freshly picked with a *sibból*. [Tag. *sungkít*]

sibbunót: (*obs.*) *n.* single-pointed arrow.

síbed₁: *n.* kind of small-shelled mussel used to sweeten broth.

síbed₂: *n.* a kind of bird with reddish eyes. **sim-mibed a mata.** *n.* eyes like the *sibed* bird, sharp eyes.

síbeg: *n.* kind of red quaillike bird. **simmibeg.** *a.* like a quail (fast moving).

síbet: *n.* waist. (*síket*) **pagatsibet.** *a.* up to the waist; reaching the waist. [Tag. *baywáng*]

sibét: sumibet. *v.* to depart, leave; go to fresh water to breed (said of *ípon* fish). **masibet.** *v.* to be away only for a short while. **kasibsibet.** just left, just gone. **pasibten.** *v.* to wait until the end (of party, rain, etc.). **Idi nasibet dagiti agka-pidua ken natungpalko ti imbaon ni Inang, nagbasaak.** When the second cousins left and I carried out what mother ordered, I read.

síbiko: (Sp. *cívico*: civic) *a.* civic.

sibíl: (Sp. *civil*: civil) *n.* civilian. (*sibiliano*) **guardia sibil.** *n.* civil guard.

sibiliáno: (Eng.) *n.* civilian.

sibilisádo: (Sp. *civilizado*: civilized) *a.* civilized. **sibilisasion.** *n.* civilization.

siblók: siblukan. *v.* to rush; assail, assault; go after; intrude; fool; victimize. **agsiblok.** *v.* to steal; cheat; deceive. **masiblokan.** *a.* robbed; cheated. **paniblók.** *a.* held in leash. **manniblok.** *n.* robbers. **Agpuspusi ni Pating iti mais a siniblokan a pinidut iti bilag ni Maning.** Pating is popping corn she took from Maning's things left under the sun to dry. [Knk. *siblók* = rape, kidnap a woman]

síbo: *n.* bubble. **agsibo, sumibo.** *v.* to bubble (water); boil. (*burek*)

sibúg: *n.* water used for watering plants. **si-bugan.** *v.* to water plants (*bisibis*); baptize. [Ivt. *dilig*, Png. *salóg*, Tag. *dilíg*]

sibúkaw: *n.* species of small tree, *Caesalpinia sp.*

sibón: sinnibon. *n.* kind of children's game in which players must pass through a space without being touched.

síbong: *n.* the young of birds. [Tag. *inakáy*]

sibúr: kasiburán. *n.* height of a season, time of plenty. **agkasiburan.** *v.* to be a time of plenty.

sibúyas: (Sp. *cebolla*: onion) *n.* onion (*lasoná*). **sibuyas bumbay.** *n.* kind of large onion.

sibró: isibro. *v.* to use for the first time.

sibróng: *n.* old custom in which a dying person holds up his fingers to tell how many people must be executed upon his death. **mannibrong.** *n.* person responsible for executing the *sibróng*; kind of small bird; thief, robber.

sidá: *n.* viand, anything eaten with rice; (*southern regions*) fish; food; **sida(en).** *v.* to eat (perfective form is *sinda*). **sinda.** *v.* ate (with rice); *n.* viand. **makasidsida.** *v.* to feel like eating (a particular dish); crave a certain food. **makisida.** *v.* to share someone's dish. **nagsidaan.** *n.* droppings, crumbs after a meal. **masida.** *n.* food eaten with rice; *a.* edible. **ipasida.** *v.* to feed. (*pakanen*) **Ania ti sidatayo?** What are we having to eat? **Makasidsidaak la unay ti pasayan.** I really feel like eating shrimp. [Bon. *ígop* (viand), Ibg. *iyyíkan*, Ivt. *ican* (viand), *amung* (fish), Kal. *tipoy* (viand), Knk. *sibu, sida, pangán*, Kpm. *asan*, Png. *sirá*, Tag. *isdâ* (fish), *ulam* (viand)]

sídap: **nasidap.** *a.* sharp (knife, intellect); keen. **Nasidap ti matana iti sirok ti nabengbeng a kidayna.** His eyes under his thick eyebrows are keen.

sidáw: **sumidaw.** *v.* to make a brief visit. (*dawas*) **sidawsidawen.** *v.* to do stealthily, secretly. [Tag. *dalaw* (visit)]

siddáal: **sumdaal.** *v.* to sympathize with, pity, be touched; moved by compassion.

siddáaw: **masdaaw.** *v.* to wonder, be astonished, amazed. **agsidsidaaw.** *v.* to be startled at every moment for no reason. **nakakaskasdaaw.** *a.* surprising, astonishing, amazing. **siddaawen.** *v.* to startle, surprise, astonish. **pagsidsiddaawan.** *n.* object of surprise or wonder. **Nakalua ta nagsiddaawanna ti kinamanangngaasi ken kinamanagparabur ti lolona kenkuana.** She was tearful because she was surprised about the kindness and generosity of her grandfather toward her. [Ibg. *karáring, keddég*, Ivt. *makñen*, Kpm. *misdan*, Png. *keláw*, Tag. *taká, hangà*]

siddát: **siddaten.** *v.* to detach, break away.

siddít: see *kiddít*: with a low yield (wells, cows, etc.).

siddúker₁: *n.* expression of the face of someone unwilling to go; shuddering during fear. **agsidduker, sumidduker.** *v.* to shudder (from fright). **makapasidduker.** *a.* frightening. [Tag. *kabá*]

siddúker₂: **agsidduker.** *v.* to be clogged, obstructed, blocked; choked.

siddóng: **kasiddongan.** *prep.* following, next, subsequent.

siddúor: **masduor.** *v.* to be agitated, disturbed.

sidég: *var.* of *asidég*: near.

sidét: **nasidet.** *a.* thick, dense, crowded; compact. **sumidet.** *v.* to become dense, thick.

síding: *n.* imperfection of the skin: mole, beauty mark, birthmark (believed to reveal certain qualities of a person depending upon what part of the body it appears). **simmiding.** *v.* to resemble; imitate; be similar in habits; inherit a trait. **sidingan.** *a.* with a mole or beauty mark. **Nagsiding ti dilana, Adda siding ti dilana; Adda siding ti bibigna.** He has a mole on his mouth; lip (is very talkative). (*tarawitiw*) **Adda siding ti butona.** (*coll.*) *exp.* He has a mole on his penis (said of men who frequently have sexual intercourse. [Kal. *tuching*, Knk. *síding*, Kpm. *alimpúyug*, Png. *kakampoyo*, Tag. *taling, lunár, nunál* (Sp. *lunar*)]

sidíngan: *n.* species of marine fish.

sid-íng: **sid-ingan.** *v.* to tip, touch, tap (*pikpik*). [Tag. *tapík*]

sidír: **sidiren.** *v.* to test; blame; bother. **Manidsidir ti tono ti baket.** The tone of the old lady is bothersome.

sidíran: *a.* near, adjacent, at the side of (*bangibang; asideg; tapil*). [Tag. *sa tabí*]

sídok₁: *n.* spoon. (*kutsara*) **siduken.** *v.* to scoop with a spoon.

sídok₂: **sidoksidok.** depression at the lower part of the breastbone. (*luludduokan*)

sidól: **sidulen.** *v.* to touch lightly; elbow. (*siko*) **masidol.** *v.* to elbow accidentally. **agsinnidol.** *v.* to elbow one another. [Tag. *siko*]

sidúmbre: *n.* sulking, hurt feelings. **agpasidumbre.** *v.* to die of exhaustion, thirst (animals); to sulk.

sidón: **masidunan.** *v.* to be worn down, harddriven. **pakasidunan.** *n.* pressure (from work); something that causes exhaustion.

sídong: *n.* communion, membership; vigilance; charge. **agsidong.** *v.* to belong to a particular family, place, club, etc. **iti sidong.** *prep.* under the care of; within; beside; near. **Adda amin kalintegantayo iti sidong ti maysa a pammati.** We have all the rights to belong to a particular faith.

sidungét: *n.* frown. (*murareg; rupanget*) **nasidunget.** *a.* serious, grave; solemn, sober. **agsidunget.** *v.* to show a solemn face; frown. **Nakasidunget ngem immisem met laeng idi makitanak.** He was solemn but smiled anyway when he saw me. [Tag. *simangot*]

sídor: **agpasidur.** (*reg.*) *v.* to sell cheap. (*laka*)

sidór: (Sp. *sudor*: sweat?) *n.* treatment for women who have just delivered, consisting of having them sit above a pot of burning charcoal in order to fumigate the vagina.

sidúrmang: **agsidurmang.** *v.* to stay in the front row.

sídra: (Sp. *cidra*: cider) *n.* cider.

sidronéla: (Sp. *cidronela*: common balm) *n.* citronella, fragrant grass from southern Asia used in perfumery.

siék: *n.* kind of freshwater mollusk.

siémpre: (Sp. *siempre*: always) *adv.* always; of course.

siénsia: (Sp. *ciencia*: science) *n.* science. [Tag. *aghám*]

sientípiko: (Sp. *científico*: scientific) *a.* scientific.

siénto: (Sp. *ciento*: hundred) *n.* one hundred (*gasut*). [Tag. *daán*]

siérto: (Sp. *cierto*: sure) *a.* sure, certain. (*pudno*; *mapaysuan*; *sinunuo*) **siertuen.** *v.* to make sure. [Tag. *tiyák*]

siésta: (Sp. *siesta*: nap) *n.* nap; rest (*libáy*; *inaná*). [Tag. *pahingá*]

siéte: (Sp. *siete*: seven) *num.* seven. (*pito*) **alas siete.** seven o'clock. **makisiete.** (*coll.*) *v.* to gossip, gab (coined from the *jueteng* game in which the number seven corresponds to *tsismis*).

síga: (Tag.) **sigasiga.** *n.* bully.

sigá: **sigaan.** *v.* to ignite (a match). (*silmut*)

sig-áb: *n.* hiccup (*saiddek*); burp (*tig-ab*). **agsigab.** *v.* to hiccup; burp.

sig-ám: **agsig-am.** *v.* to clear the throat (*say-a*). [Kpm. *tigím*, Tag. *tikhím*, *dahak*]

sigáng: (Tag. also) **sinigang.** *n.* dish made with fish cooked in a sour broth (tamarind, *piás*, etc.) **pagsigang.** *n.* sour ingredients used to make a *sinigang*.

sígar: *n.* fish fin. (*pigar*) **masigar.** *v.* to be hurt by a fin of a fish. [Tag. *palikpík*]

sigargár: *n.* chicken whose feathers stand on end. (*seggar*) **agsigargar.** *v.* to stand on end.

sigarílias: (Tag.) *n.* seguidillas, asparagus bean. (*pallang*)

sigarílio: (Sp. *cigarillo*: cigarette) *n.* cigarette. **agsigarilio.** *v.* to smoke. **makisigarilio.** *v.* to ask for a cigarette. **pagsigarilyuan.** *n.* smoking area. **agatsigarilio.** *v.* to smell like cigarette smoke.

sigáro: (Sp. *cigarro*: cigar) *n.* cigar. (*abano*)

sig-át: **sig-atan.** *v.* to cure meat or fish; cook thoroughly; dry up. **masig-atan.** *v.* to be dried up (rice fields). **masig-atan ti salun-at.** *v.* to lose one's health.

sígay: *n.* kind of fine mesh net used to catch fish at sea or in slow streams. [Tag. *sigay* = small cowrie shell]

sigay-ót: *n.* knot. (*siglot*) **sigay-utan.** *v.* to knot the G-string or *baag*. **sigay-uten.** *v.* to hook or button at the back. [Tag. *buhól*]

sigé: (Sp. *seguir*: follow) expression indicating departure by either speaker or hearer: go ahead, carry on (*aria*, *bira*); word used to express consent: OK. **isige.** *v.* to go ahead with; do in spite of impediments. **Sige, agpinnataykayon!** Go ahead, kill one another! [Png., Tag. *sige*]

siggawá: **sigsiggawa.** *n.* vine with edible shoots.

siggáwat: **siggawaten.** *v.* to snatch away (*ágaw*). **Insiggawat ni Melang ti imana.** Melang snatched his hand. [Tag. *sunggáb*]

siggawíng: *n.* person whose line between the navel and groin is not straight. It is considered bad luck, so babies with this condition must undergo the *sumang* ritual.

siggép: **sigpen.** *v.* to observe with a watchful eye. (*seggep*)

siggiáb: *var.* of *seggiab*: blaze, flame, burn.

sígi: *n.* sieve; strainer. (*gasagas*; *tar-ap*; *yakayak*; *sagat*) **isigi.** *v.* to sift, sieve (rice). [Tag. *salà*]

sígit: **agsigit, sumigit.** *v.* to transfer liquids from a large container to a smaller one.

sigít: *n.* cut piece (*pisi*); fragment. **sigiten.** *v.* to cut lengthwise; to cut a circular object. **Aladanda ti pallotan iti nasigit a kawayan.** They fenced the cockfighting arena with cut bamboo. [Tag. *hiwà* (slice)]

sigká: **sigkaan.** *n.* bamboo needle for a net.

sigkál: *n.* stumbling. **sigkalen.** *v.* to tumble down, cause to stumble, topple over. **masigkal.** *v.* to stumble, fall. **Nasigkalna ti nakarungarong a ramut ngem natimbengna ti bagina.** The protruding roots toppled her but she balanced herself.

sigkár: *n.* bamboo fish trap.

sigkát: **panigkat.** *n.* prop. **sigkaten.** *v.* to raise, prop up, lift. **masigkat.** *v.* to feel pain in the body due to lifting. **Insigkatna dagiti sikona iti tumengna sa nagtapaya.** He propped his elbow on his knee and supported himself up. [Tag. *tukod*]

sigkáy: *n.* share, allotment (*bingay*); boundary (*beddeng*). **sigkayen.** *v.* to divide, allot, distribute. **kasigkay.** *a.* contiguous, adjacent. [Tag. *bahagi*]

sigkí: **agsigki.** *v.* to be startled from sleep. **sumanigki.** *v.* to start up from sleep with a sudden jerk; sob, sigh.

sigkíng₁: *n.* hopscotch; mistress. **agsigking.** *v.* to limp, hobble; play hopscotch. **sigkingen.** *v.* to jump with one leg aside; do in a moment. [Png. *kitkit*, Tag. *pikô* (hopscotch)]

sigkíng₂: *n.* mistress, concubine. (*babai*, *kamalala*)

sigkingbádo: *var.* of *sigking*: hopscotch.

sigkír: see *sikkír*.

sigkúko: (*obs.*) **sigkukuén.** *v.* to sin frequently.

sigkól: *var.* of *singkól*: paralysis of the hand or hands.

siglát: kinasiglat. *n.* daring, nerve; agility; rapidity; alertness; sharpness (of the mind). nasiglat. *a.* fast, swift, quick, rapid; daring; clever; alert. Nasiglat ti ulona. He has an alert mind. Ti tao a nasiglat, uray kasano't rigat sumaranget a siraragsak. A brave man will happily face a situation no matter how dreadful it seems (*ganaygay, paragsit, karantíng*; *saliwanwan, sarantá, saliwitwit, sigrát*). [Knk. *galát*, Tag. *bilís* (fast); *siglá* = lively; enthusiasm]

sigláw: masiglaw. *v.* to die suddenly and unexpectedly; to be taken by surprise. (*kellaat*)

síglo: (Sp. *siglo*: century) *n.* century. (*sangagasut a tawen*)

siglót: *n.* knot. sigluten. *v.* to knot; close a contract. pagsigluten. *v.* to close, conclude. siglutan ti panio. *exp.* to knot the handkerchief upon seeing a shooting star (in order for a wish to come true). Awan anakmi a mangsiglot koma iti kasamientomi. We have no children to tie the knot of our marriage. [Png. *búknol*, Tag. *buhól*]

sigmát: (*obs.*) sigsigmaten. *v.* to change clothes.

sígmaw: sumigmaw. *v.* to pay a short visit (*dawas, sidaw*). [Tag. *dalaw* (visit)]

signár: (Sp. *asignar*: assign) signaran. *v.* to designate; assign.

sígno: (Sp. *signo*: sign) *n.* sign, signal (*tanda*); fate, destiny.

sígo₁: isigo. *v.* to joint, unite by a joint.

sígo₂: kasisigo. *a.* ready to use; easy to fit; fluent; expert. kasiguan. *v.* to be accustomed to, used to. nasigo. *a.* expert; trained; accustomed, used to. inkasiguan, nakaisiguan. *n.* customs, traditions. Kasiguanna ti agmaneho idiay Manila. He is used to driving in Manila.

sigubánet: (*obs.*) see *sagubanít*: slight fever or cold.

sígud: *adv.* originally, from the beginning; essentially; *a.* intrinsic; inborn; inherent; innate. kasigud. *n.* something that one has from the beginning; first spouse; guardian angel. kasisigud. *n.* habit, custom. (*ugali*) kasigudan. *v.* to inherit. naikasigud. *a.* original, innate, natural, inherent. nakaisigudan. *n.* customs; tradition; *a.* original; traditional; inborn. siguden. *v.* to do from the beginning; do right away. isigud. *v.* to pay in part, pay in advance; do early. maisigud. (*obs.*) *v.* to sink to a level. naisigud. *a.* innate, inborn; native; inherent; natural. nainkasigudan. *a.* native; inherent; inborn. Isu ti nakaisigudanmi. That's what we are used to. Sigud a maris-gatas ti kudilda. They had milk-colored skin since birth. Sigudek nga

ilaba ti murengmi. I will wash our dirty clothes right away. [Png. *tubó*, Tag. *tubò*; *dati*]

siguída: (Sp. *seguida*: immediate) *adv.* at once, immediately.

sigurádo: (Sp. *segurado*: sure) *a.* sure. siguraduen. *v.* to make sure. Masiguradom? Can you be sure of it?

sigurísta: (Sp. *seguro*: sure + -*ista*) *n.* person who will undertake things only if he is certain he will succeed.

sigúro: (Sp. *seguro*: sure; insurance) *adv.* perhaps, maybe (*ngata*); *n.* insurance. siguruen. *v.* to make sure (*segurado*; *sierto*). Siguruenyo nga agtomar a kanayon iti agasna. Make sure he always takes his medicine. [Tag. *marahil*]

sigpát: sigpaten. *v.* to cut in one slantwise stroke; trim overhanging branches. Sinigpat dagiti bala dagiti rinaay a bunga dagiti niog. The bullets cut up the clustered coconut fruits. [Tag. *tagpás*]

sigpáw: sigpawen. *v.* to catch.

sigpén: (f. *seggep*) *v.* to plan to do, intend; scheme; eye something cunningly.

sigpít: *n.* clip, clasp; border of a basket; strip of bamboo that run across a layer of *taléb*. sigpiten. *v.* to pinch, grip, grasp; put a clip on. isigpit. *v.* to insert between, intercalate. sinigpit. *n.* part of the brisket between the forelegs; thatched *cogon* grass for roofing. [Tag. *sipit*]

sigrát: *var.* of *siglat*: agility, activeness.

síib: *n.* trap for mudfish made of wickerwork. (*kalubkub*)

siíd: *n.* wickerwork mudfish trap.

siím: agsiim. *v.* to spy on, peep, peer. No adda wayak, agsiimak. If I'm free, I'll have a look. Sisiimennak gayam, aya? So you are spying on me, aren't you? [Knk. *siím, tídum*, Png. *siím, sikáp*, Tag. *tiktík, manmán*]

siít: *n.* fish bone; thorn; spine. (*tiník*) nasiit. *a.* spiny, full of fishbones. isiitan. *v.* to remove fish bones. siitan. *n.* Bambusa blumeana bamboo with spiny branches; generic name for spiny, thorny plants. masiitan. *v.* to be pricked by a thorn. siitan a barut. *n.* barbed wire. sisiitan. *n.* generic term for thorny plants. [Bon. *sibit*, Ibg. *siq, síten*, Ifg. *pagit*, Itg. *sait*, Ivt. *kamanuluk*, Kal. *chuli, tong-e, lasi*, Knk. *sibít, pagát* (thorn), *íga* (fishbone), Kpm. *suksuk*, Png. *siít*, Tag. *tiník, simì*; Tag. *siít* = twig, thorny branch of bamboo]

sika-: *pref.* old variant of *apagka-, pagka-* fractional prefixes: sikatlo. one-third. sikapát. one-fourth. sikaném. one-sixth.

síka: *n.* dysentery; diarrhea (*buris*). agsika. *v.* to have dysentery. [Png. *pantál*, Tag. *iti*; Knk. *síka* = swell, incease, said of cooked rice]

siká: *pron.* you (singular, informal). **siksika.** just you, only you, you alone. [Knk. *sik-á*, Png. *siká*, Tag. *ikáw*]

síkad: agsikad. *v.* to strut, walk with the head erect and body bent backward; pedal a paddleboat. **pagsikaden.** *v.* to practice game-cocks. [Tag. *sikad* = kick; energy, potency]

síkal₁: *n.* contraction (of pregnant woman); pain in the abdomen; grumbling of an empty stomach. **agsikal.** *v.* to feel pain in the abdomen; to be in labor. **agpasikal.** *v.* to be in labor, suffer pains of childbirth. **Agsikal manen ti tianna.** She is having abdominal pains again. [Tag. *kalám* (abdomen pain)]

síkal₂: *n.* reed grass. (*ledda*)

sikám: *var.* of *sikamí:* we (exclusive)

sikamí: *var.* of *dakamí:* we (exclusive. **siksikami.** only us (exclusive).

síkang: *n. bekkér* tiebeam; bar of the loom (*sapayán*).

síkap: nasikap. *a.* sly, cunning, prudent, cautious. (*alibtok; alisto; tarem; saldet*) **agsikap.** *v.* to be shrewd, clever; deceive. **sikapan.** *v.* to fool, cheat; swindle; mislead; overreach. **Mataykami ditoy no dikami agsiglat ken makisinnikap.** We will die here if we are not swift and cautious with each other. **Ti tao a managsikap, dinto agbiag a nasayaat.** He who cheats will not lead a good life. [Tag. *tuso*]

sikapát: *n.* half a *binting*, twelve and one-half centavos; one-fourth (*apagkapat*).

síkat: *n.* plan; plot; conspiracy (*ranta; balala; daremdem; gakat; ngayangay; panggep; gandat*) **isikat.** *v.* to intend, plan; determine upon; conspire. **pasikat.** (Tag.) *n.* spoiled brat; *a.* spoiled (child). [Tag. *tangkâ*]

sikát: *n.* celebrity; popular guy.

sikatló: old variant of *apagkatló:* one-third.

síkaw: agsikaw. *v.* to grumble (said of the stomach); feel pain in the abdomen. (*sikal; saraaw*) **agsikassikaw.** *v.* to ramble around the streets. **isikawsikaw.** *v.* to beat around the bush. **mamagsikaw.** *v.* to cause the stomach to grumble. **Dina ammo no siddaaw wenno pannakaklaat ti nagsikaw iti barukongna idi mangngegna ti pakaammo ni Charito.** He doesn't know if it was wonder or surprise that made his abdomen rumble when he heard Charito's report. [Tag. *kulô*]

sikawaló: *n.* half a *sikápat*, one-fourth of a *bintíng*, six and one-fourth centavos; one-eighth (*apagkawalo*).

sikayó: *var.* of *dakayó:* you plural; you polite. **siksikayo.** only you.

sikbáb: agsikbab, sikbaben. *v.* to seize with the mouth. **Sinikbabna ti appanda.** It seized their

bait. **Maidumaak a klase a pating, piliek laeng dagiti kayatko a sikbaben.** I'm a different kind of shark, I just choose what I want to bite. [Tag. *sakmál*]

sikbáway: (*obs.*) *n.* kind of monotonous singing performed when pounding rice.

sikból: *n.* pole with a hook used to reach for far-away objects. (*sukdal*)

sikdáp: *var.* of *sikap.*

sikdót: *n.* snatching; pickpocketing. **sikduten.** *v.* to snatch, take from. **Iti panagsinnukatmi iti sida, kautek ti pingganna ken sikdutenna ti sidak.** In our exchanging of food, I grab from her plate and she snatches my food.

síke: (Sp. *cheque*) *n.* bank check.

síken: sumiken. *v.* to increase, augment; to become compact. **nasiken.** *a.* compact; solid; concise. [Tag. *siksík* (compact)]

síket: *n.* waist; waistband. (*sibet*) **siketen.** *v.* to feel pain in the waist. **agsinniket.** *v.* to hold each other by the waist. **pagassiket.** *a.* waist high. **sumiket.** *v.* to curtsy. [Ibg. *áwaq*, Ivt. *katinghan*, Kal. *awak*, Kpm. *awákan*, Png. *balangbáng*, Tag. *baywáng*]

sikét: *n.* kind of two-edged knife.

sikí: agsiki. *v.* to toss something and catch it on the back of the hand. **isiki.** *v.* to do as an additional job in one's spare time. (*samira; sapar*) **masiki.** *v.* to have spare time for something else. **isiksiki.** *v.* to get closer (while walking).

sikiátra: (Sp. *psiquiatra:* psychiatrist) *n.* psychiatrist. (*psikiatra*)

sikiatría: (Sp. *psiquiatría:* psychiatry) *n.* psychiatry. (*psikiatria*)

sikíg: *n.* side; *a.* sideways. **sikigan.** *n.* side of a mountain (*kirbay*); side of a body. **agsikig.** *v.* to lie on the side; move sideways, turn on the side. **pasikigen.** *v.* to place on the side, sideways. **Sangkataliawna dagiti malabasanna a siriri-kep a kuarto iti agsumbangir a sikiganna.** He kept looking back at the open rooms he passed on each side. [Png. *gilig, tambib,* Tag. *tabí, tagiliran*]

síkiko: (Sp. *psíquico:* psychic) *a.* psychic. (*psikiko*)

síkil: *n.* barbel of fishes. **agisikil, sikilen.** *v.* to elbow; attack with the *sikil* (fish). **sumikilsikil.** *v.* to elbow one's way through. **sisikilan.** *n.* axilla of animals. [Tag. *sikil* = push of a paddle]

síkka: agsikka, sumikka. *v.* to uproot rice seedlings.

sikkárod: sikkaruden. *v.* to hit with the toes when walking (*sipparod*). **makasikkarud.** *v.* to accidentally hit when walking. **sisikkaruden.** *a.* easy to get (prostitutes). **Nasikkarudna ti**

nagrungarong a ramut. He stumbled upon the protruding roots. **Diak mabilang ti karuay ti babassit a templo ken pagoda a masikkarud dagiti matak.** I can't count the numerous small temples and pagodas that catch my eye. [Tag. *tisod*]

sikkawíl: agsikkawil. *v.* to cross the legs. (*kawíl*). **sikkawilen.** *v.* to lock a leg with another. **nakasikkawil.** *a.* with the legs crossed. **Nakasikkawilda nga agsigsigarilio iti papag.** They crossed their legs while smoking on the bamboo bench. [Tag. *dekuwatro* (Sp.)]

sikkáyod: agsikkayod. *v.* to drag the legs. (*sikkarod*) **masikkayod.** *v.* to tilt and lift. **sikkayuden.** *v.* to trip; cause to stumble.

sikkí: *n.* kind of game played by tossing pebbles and catching them; those that fall to the floor are made to hit each other. **agsikki.** *v.* to play this game together. (*kudo*)

sikkíl: agsisikkil. *v.* to be stiff; to stiffen. **nasikkil.** *a.* stiff, stark, solid, robust, tough; rigid. **sumkil.** *v.* to stiffen; harden. **pasikkil.** *n.* rod, support. **agpasikkil.** *v.* to stiffen up; stiffen (near death). [Png. *kigtel*, Tag. *tigás*]

sikkír: maskir. *v.* to overcome; soften, eliminate. **sumkir.** *v.* to force one's way through; steal.

sikkó: agsikko. *v.* to turn a corner. **agsikkosikko.** *v.* to zigzag. **pagsikkuan.** *n.* juncture; place where one turns; corner. **Nagsikkoda sada manen inibbatan.** They turned and let go of him again. [Ibg. *bira*, *lekku*, Ivt. *mayweswes*, Kpm. *korba*, Png. *liku*, Tag. *likô*]

sikkúbeng: *a.* twisted, curved, contorted, crooked (said of horns).

sikkúko: *var.* of *sikuko*.

sikkúkong: *n.* the rare condition of having forward-facing horns or antlers (carabao, deer).

siklísta: (Sp. *ciclista*: cyclist) *n.* cyclist.

síklo: (Sp. *ciclo*: cycle) *n.* cycle.

sikmáw: sikmawen. *v.* to catch (snatch) with the mouth. (*sakráb*).

siknár: masisiknaran. *v.* to be affected by; hurt by. (*saknar*)

siknó: *n.* flaw; injury; disfigurement; chronic illness.

síko: *n.* elbow. **agsinniko.** *v.* to elbow one another. **sikuen.** *v.* to elbow; hit with the elbow. [Kal. *siku*, Png. *sikó*, Tag. *siko*]

sikó: (*obs.*) **nasiko.** *a.* difficult (*narígat*). [Tag. *hirap*, *salimuót*]

sikuán: *n.* wooden tablet with notches in which twine is wound. **marasikuan.** *n.* kind of marine mollusk, smaller than the *raráng*.

sikoanálisis: (Sp. *psicoanálisis*: psychoanalysis) *n.* psychoanalysis. (*psikoanalisis*)

sikuát: sikuáten. *v.* to snatch (*agaw*). **masikuat.** *v.* to be snatched, grabbed.

sikóg: *n.* pregnancy; fetus in the womb. **masikog.** *v.* to be pregnant (*sisasab-ok*). **agsikog.** *v.* to get pregnant, impregnate. **masikogan.** *v.* to become impregnated. **sikugen.** *v.* to impregnate. **panagsikog.** *n.* pregnancy. [Grammatical note: *Masikóg* is not used perfectively or as a *na*- stative adjective. Ibg. *vussiq*, Itg., Kal. *búgi*, Knk. *listúg*, *sónga*, *ten-án*, Ivt. *walaq*, Png. *luken*, Tag. *buntís*]

sikúko: *n.* a large mountain bird.

sikukó: *n.* ladle for vegetable dishes. (*aklo*)

síkol: *n.* arm disabled at the elbow. **sikulen.** *v.* to embarrass; straighten, hem in; impede. **masikol.** *v.* to be straightened; to be pestered; to be encumbered.

sikól: sikulen. *v.* to elbow. (*kidag*)

sikolóhiko: (Sp. *psicológico*: psychological) *a.* psychological. (*psikolohiko*)

sikolohía: (Sp. *psicología*: psychology) *n.* psychology. (*psikolohia*)

sikólogo: (Sp. *psicólogo*: psychologist) *n.* psychologist. (*psikologo*)

sikimóro: (Sp. *sicomoro*) *n.* sycamore.

síkon: *n.* block of wood under the *tumbalí* lever that keeps the *tumbalí* from sliding.

sikópata: (Sp. *psicópata*: psychopath) *n.* psychopath. (*psikopata*)

sikopatía: (Sp. *psicopatía*: psychopathy) *n.* psychopathy. (*psikopatia*)

sikór: *n.* worry; anxiety. (*danag*; *pulkok*) **nasikor.** *a.* difficult, complicate, intricate. **masikuran.** *a.* troubled; anxious; depressed, low-spirited. **masiksikuran.** *a.* anxious for someone to come; anxious. **pakasikuran.** *n.* problems, troubles; difficulties. **Dinak pakasikoran, agawidakon.** Don't trouble me, I'm going home already. [Tag. *balisa*]

sikosomátiko: (Sp. *psicosomático*: psychosomatic) *a.* psychosomatic. (*psikosomatiko*)

síkot: (Tag. *sikot*: doing in a roundabout way) **pasikotsikot.** *n.* details; daily activities; red tape, excessive bureaucracy; (*coll.*) the ropes; *a.* roundabout, not direct. **Ipakitaka ti pasikotsikotna.** I will show you the ropes, I will teach you all the details about it.

sikoterapía: (Sp. *psicoterapia*: psychotherapy) *n.* psychotherapy. (*psikoterapia*)

sikpát: (*obs.*) **agsikpat.** *v.* to lop, top trees. (*sigpat*)

sikraóng: *n.* halter; hitch; kind of large bamboo bag used to carry *burnáy* jars of *bási*.

siksík₁: *n.* scale (of fish, etc.). **marasiksikan.** *a.* scaly. **siksikan.** *v.* to remove the scales of. [Kal., Png. *siksík*, Tag. *kaliskís*]

siksík₂: siksik. *n. Adianthum sp.* ferns.

sílaba: (Sp. *sílaba*: syllable) *n.* syllable. [Tag. *pantíg*]

silabário: (Sp. *silabario*: spelling book) *n.* spelling book.

sílabo: (Sp. *sílabo*: syllabus) *n.* syllabus.

sílag: *n. Corypha elata, buri* palm used to make mats. **kasilagan.** *n.* grove of *buri* palms. [Tag. *buri*]

sílam: *n.* kind of grasshopper with sharp jaws.

silámot: *n.* improper eating; licking the fingers when eating. **agsilamot, sumilamot.** *v.* to lick the lips, fingers. **natda nga agsilsilamot.** *exp.* to be left licking the fingers (to be at the losing end of a situation). **konsilamot.** *n.* person who eats at an inopportune time (as when uninvited); party crasher. [Knk. *silámot*, Tag. *himod*]

Siláni: *n., a.* Sri Lankan.

siláng: agsilang. *v.* to sing out of tune. (*sintunado*) **silangsilang.** *a.* out of tune. [Tag. *sintunado; siláng* = mountain pass]

siláp: *n.* plow with moldboard; glitter; gloss; sparkle. (*sileng*) **sumiláp.** *v.* to sparkle, glitter, flash. [Tag. *kináng*]

sílaw: *n.* light. **silawan.** *v.* to light; illuminate; seek with a light. **manilaw.** *v.* to light; fish with a light. **pagsilawan.** *n.* lamp. **panilaw.** *n.* light used for catching mudfish at night. **silaw-taaw.** *n.* lighthouse (*parola*). **silaw-trapiko.** *n.* traffic light. [Ivt. *ryal* (natural light), *ralaken* (artificial light), Knk., Png. *siléw*, Tag. *ilaw*, Tag. *silaw* = dazzling glare of light]

silaw-ít: (coined from *silaw* 'light' + *sal-it* 'thunder') *n.* electricity. (*koriente*)

silbáto: (Sp. *silbato*: whistle) *n.* whistle. (*sultip, sagawisiw*) **silbatuan.** *v.* to whistle at someone.

silbáy: *n.* reed flute.

siléd: *n.* room, sleeping room. (*silid, kuarto*) **agkasiled.** *n.* roommate; *v.* to share a room. **gurabis a nasiledsiled.** boxed matches. **Mabutengko nga agmaymaysa idiay siledko.** I am afraid of being alone in my room. [Png. *sipí*, Tag. *silíd*]

silég: masleg. *v.* to be timid; shy. (*dileg; bain*)

silensiadór: (Sp. *silenciador*) *n.* silencer.

silénsio: (Sp. *silencio*) *n.* silence. (*ulimek*)

síleng: makasisileng. *n.* strong sound; *v.* stunning; deafening (*tileng*). **sisilengen.** *v.* to annoy by use of sounds; deafen. [Tag. *tulíg*]

siléng: nasileng. *a.* bright, glittering, flashing, brilliant, splendid; radiant. (*silap*) **masileng.** *v.* to be dazzled, shine. **pasilengen.** *v.* to make shiny, polish. **Simmileng ti suli dagiti matana.** The corners of his eyes dazzled. [Tag. *kináng, kintáb*]

silét: *n.* small intestine (of chickens).

síli: *n.* hot chili pepper (generic name), *Capsicum sp.* sili ti diáblo. *n. Capsicum frutescens,* very pungent chili pepper. (*sili ti sairo*) **agsili.** *v.* to use chili, season with chili pepper; (*obs.*) *n.* to barter. **managsili.** *a.* fond of spicy foods. **silian.** *v.* to season with pepper. **masilian.** *v.* to be affected by spice; (*fig.*) to be affected by stinging words. **Ania't pakasiliam?** What's hurting you? **Ti agsili, magasangan.** He who eats chili will get burned. [Kal. *sichut*, Tag. *sili*]

sil-í: agsanil-i. *v.* see *sang-i*: to make continuous sobbing noises.

sília: (Sp. *silla*: chair) *n.* saddle; (*obs.*) chair. **silia elektrika.** *n.* electric chair. **nasiliaan.** *a.* saddled. **nakasilia.** *n.* left turn; ridge of mountains with cliffs on both sides; *a.* seated; saddled.

silián: see *siliási*: large, round iron pot.

siliási: *n.* kind of large, round iron pot with no handle, around two to three feet at the rim; when smaller it is called a *pariók*. **isiliasi.** *v.* to place in the *siliasi* pot.

siliásig: agsiliasig. *v.* to miss each other when coming from different directions (*siliwasiw*). **sumiliasig.** *v.* to oppose, violate; contradict; deny; transgress.

silíd: (Tag.) *n.* room; sleeping room. (*kuarto; siled*) **kasilid.** *n.* roommate. **pakasilidan.** *n.* box or room where something can be stored.

siliéta: (Sp. *silleta*: seat) *n.* bicycle seat.

silíndro: (Sp. *cilindro*: cylinder) *n.* harmonica; cylinder. **agsilindro.** *v.* to play the harmonica. **silindruen.** *v.* to play a tune on the harmonica.

siliniadór: (f. *silindro*) *n.* cylinder (of a car).

silión: (Sp. *sillón*: large seat) *n.* large chair (*dakkel a tugaw*); sofa.

siliwásiw: *var.* of *silliwasiw*.

sillákong: *a.* bowlegged. (*sakang*)

sillalábas: (*obs.*) **agsillalabas.** *v.* to pass stealthily. **sumillalabas.** *v.* to roam the streets.

sillaúd: sillaudan. *v.* to wind a rope around to bind. (*paraut*)

sillásig: agsillasig. *v.* to miss each other when coming from opposite directions. **sumillasig.** *v.* to oppose, contradict; violate.

silláwat₁: sillawaten. *v.* to catch (*sippaw*); grasp. **silsillawaten.** *v.* to toss upward. **Nasillawatna ti ngulayngulayna, rinung-ona, sana tinaso ti teltel.** She grasped his wrist, broke it, then she beat his nape. [Tag. *saló*]

silláwat₂: *n.* hyphen.

sillawíd: agsillawid. *v.* to cross the legs in running; to stumble over one's own feet.

silléng: sumleng. *v.* to have a fit (paroxysm); get very hot in the body and have a convulsion.

sillín: see *sallín*: intrude; usurp.
silliwásiw: **agsilliwasiw**. *v*. to miss one another when coming or going (*salliwasiw*); to separate and meet again (in dances). **sumilliwasiw**. *v*. to violate; transgress; disobey.
sillók: **nasillok**. *a*. arched. (*nagarko*)
sillóng: **sillongen**. *v*. to assault (*duklos*; *raot*). [Tag. *lusob*]
silmút: **silmutan**. *v*. to set fire to, ignite; kindle. (*sinit*) **masilmutan**. *v*. to be burned, singed. **Pudot nga awanan saem ngem kasla in-inut a nangsilmot kadagiti amin a nginabras ti lasagna**. It was a painless heat but it seemed to slowly burn away all the strands of his flesh. [Tag. *sindí*]
silnág: *n*. shine from the moon. (*sellag*) **makasilnag**. *v*. to sparkle; twinkle; shine; glitter; gleam. **sumilnag**. *v*. to lighten up; brighten. **silnagan**. *v*. to shine on, illuminate; gleam. **nasilnag**. *a*. bright, illuminated, radiant (*raniag*). **Sinarut dagiti matana ti nagbabaetan dagiti kaykayo iti arubayan a silsilnagan ti lumlumneken a bulan**. His eyes penetrated between the trees around him that were illuminated by the setting moon. [Tag. *liwanag*]
silnó: **agsilno**. *v*. to undulate, wave. **maisilno**. *v*. to overflow; spill. [Tag. *ligwák*]
silnóg: **sumilnog**. *v*. to shine, sparkle, flash, glitter. **nasilnog**. *a*. clear; shiny; clean. [Tag. *liwanag*, *kináng*]
silnók: **sumilnok**. *v*. to influence the feelings; come to mind. (*sekken*; *siplot*)
sílo: *n*. lasso, noose, snare. (*kay-ong*; *lab-ong*; *kaka*; *lasta*) **siluan**. *v*. to lasso; to ensnare. **masiluan**. *v*. to be ensnared; caught in a trap. **Mabalin a siluan ti subsubna**. *exp*. you can lasso his snout (said of snobby people). [Kal. *bitu*, Png. *silót*, Tag. *silò*]
sílud: *n*. sting (of bees, wasps, an alcoholic beverage etc.). (*dugayong*) **makasilud**. *a*. stinging; biting. **siluden**. *v*. to sting (bees, etc.). **sumilud**. *v*. to be a stinging creature. **Kasla sinilud ti alumpipinig ti lapayagna iti nangngegna**. *exp*. It seemed he was hurt by what he heard (like his ears were stung by a wasp). [Tag. *durò*]
siluéta: (Sp. *silueta*: silhouette) *n*. silhouette.
sílug: **agsilug**. *v*. to roam the streets at night.
silúg: *n*. sting. (*var*. of *silúd*)
silohísmo: (Sp. *silogismo*: syllogism) *n*. syllogism.
silók: **siloksilok**. *n*. an affliction in which the victim imitates or mimics what he sees or hears others are doing.
silóng₁: *n*. rice paddy, rice plot. **sinilong**. *n*. plots in a rice field. **sangkasilong**. *n*. one plot (of a field).

silóng₂: *n*. twisted rattan device used to lift objects from the fire. **silongen**. *v*. to lift a pot from the fire using the *silóng* device.
silópono: (Sp. *xilófono*) *n*. xylophone.
silpó: *n*. continuation; continuity; part. **silpuen**. *v*. to unite, connect, fit together. **agsilpo**. *v*. to be linked together; connect. **agsisilpo**. *n*. cursive writing. **kasilpo**. *n*. continuation; part of. **isilpo**. *v*. to link; add to increase something too short. **silpuan**. *v*. to lengthen. **pagsilpuan**. see *pagsangalan*. **panilpo**. *n*. connection. **makapagsilpo**. *v*. to be able to connect. **kasilpo ti biag, kasilpo ti anges**. *n*. spouse. **kasilpo ti bagis**. *n*. sibling. **silposilpo**. *a*. with many links or connections. **sumilpo**. *v*. to join the end of; stand at the end of a line. **Agsisilpo ti angesna**. He has rapid breathing. (*tug-op, tangep, tugmok*; *saip, raip, sipol, suop*). [Knk. *solpó*, Png. *peket*, Tag. *kabít, dugtóng*]
silsíit: (*obs*.) *n*. kind of thorny tree; (*reg*.) popgun.
siltík: *n*. small improvised blowgun (like a straw). **agsiltik**. *v*. to blow something through a *siltik*.
sílya: (Sp. *silla*: chair) *n*. chair. (*tugaw*; *silia*)
silyéta: (Sp. *silleta*: seat) *n*. bicycle seat. (*silieta*)
silyón: (Sp. *sillón*: large seat; armchair) *n*. large chair. (*silion*)
sim: *n*. galvanized iron sheet used for roofing. (*galba*)
síma: *n*. barb (of a hook, arrow, etc.). (*saw-it*) **simaan**. *a*. barbed. **tagisima**. *n*. hook and sinker.
simáay: *n*. branch, arm (of a river, etc.). **simaayen**. *v*. to divert water from a river.
simaáy: *n*. variety of rice.
símad: see *pasimad*: observe, notice.
símang: *n*. branch; arm; offshoot; division; ramification. **sumimang a dalan, nasimangan ti dalan**. *n*. crossroads. **mansimang, simangan**. *a*. ambiguous. [Tag. *sangáy*]
simarón: (Sp. *cimarrón*: unruly) *n*. stud (for breeding).
simáw: **masimawan**. *v*. to be able to go after; to be able to follow through. **di masimawan**. *v*. to lose track of.
simbáan: *n*. church; chapel. **agpasimbaan**. *v*. to go to the church (*misa*). [Ibg. *sibbán*, Ivt. *timbaan*, Png. *simbaán*, Tag. *simbahan*]
simbábuy: *n*. kind of black pillbug.
simbáliw: *var*. of *sumbaliw*.
simbalúd: **masimbalud**. *v*. to trip (over a rope); have the feet entangled. **Nasimbalud ti dilana**. He is tongue-tied. [Tag. *salabíd*]
simbángir: see *sumbangir*: on both sides.
simbará: *n*. game consisting of throwing stones in the air, catching them and sending them

'home' (in one's bank of stones) while bouncing a ball.

simbéng: nasimbeng. *a.* calm; tranquil; peaceful; with same rate of growth; steady (voice); stable (conditions, life); comfortable. **sumimbeng.** *v.* to calm down; become peaceful. **kinasimbeng.** *n.* stability. **Simmimbeng ti riknak iti kinunana.** My feelings calmed down from what he said. **Pasimbengem ta panunotmo.** Calm your thoughts. [Tag. *tatag*]

simbér: sinnimber. see *sinnibón*.

simberguénsa: (Sp. *sinvergüenza*: shameless) *n.* shameless person.

símbolo: (Sp. *símbolo*: symbol) *n.* symbol. (*tanda*) **simboliko.** *a.* symbolic.

simbório: (Sp. *cimborio*: dome) *n.* church dome, cupola.

simburión: (f. *simborio*) *n.* chimney (*tibaw*; *tambutso*); dome.

simbrón: *n.* anger; frustration; anxiety. (*rurod*) **makasimbron.** *v.* to be bothersome; frustrating. **masimbron.** *v.* to be angry.

siméd: (*obs.*) **isimed.** *v.* to do with caution.

simék: *n.* speech; noisy conversation; hubbub; saying. **simken.** *v.* to pulverize; grind; perfective form of *sumken.* **agsimek.** *v.* to talk (*timek*). [Tag. *ingay*]

simetría: (Sp. *simetría*: symmetry) *n.* symmetry, well balanced arrangement on both sides.

simgát: see *singgát*.

simísim: agsimisim. *v.* to spy on. (*siim*; *tiktik*)

simkíl: (f. *sikkil*) *v.* stiffened.

simmampabián: (f. *San Fabian*) *n.* variety of rice.

simmangka-: *pref.* Perfective form of *sumangka-* expressing frequentative actions in the past. **Simmangkalaglag daydi amam ta nagbalinka a kasta!** Your deceased father was so foolish, so you became like that.

simmawá: *n.* June bug. (*abal-abal*)

simó: simuen. *v.* to knot, tie (*siglút*). **Dinagdagus ni Peping a sinimo ti napugsat nga uray.** Peping immediately tied the snapped warp thread. [Tag. *buhól*]

simudáag: see *mudaag*.

símut: simutsimut. *n.* winged ant; insect that flies around lights at night; moth. **No adda apuy wenno silaw, agaarak dagiti simutsimot.** Where there is fire or light, winged ants are attracted. [Kal. *likging, liyok*, Tag. *gamugamó* (moth)]

simút₁: isimut. *v.* to dip. **agsimut.** *v.* to eat by dipping in sauce. **agsimsimut.** *v.* to eat rice with salt. [Tag. *sawsáw*]

simút₂: (Tag.) **masimut.** *v.* to have nothing left. **simuten.** *v.* to take all; finish off (leftovers,

etc.). **simutém!** finish the leftovers! [Tag. *simot* = consume completely]

simpá: *n.* well-balanced state, stability. **nasimpa.** *a.* level, flat, smooth. **agsimpa.** *v.* to stand firm and steady; start using judgment; have everything in order; establish oneself; settle down and wed. **simpaen, isimpa.** *v.* to level, make flat; put in order; stabilize; fix well; arrange. **pagsimpaen ti nákem.** *v.* to come to a decision; put one's mind at ease. **Simmirip iti sarming iti panangisimpana iti kueliona.** He peeped in the mirror to adjust his collar. **Sisasaganaakto met ngatan nga agsimpa no makasarakak iti babai a pudno nga ayayatek.** I probably will be ready to settle down if I find the girl I really love. **Tinulagda ti panagsimpada.** They arranged their marriage. [Png. *palanas*, Tag. *patag, tatág*]

simpalóng: *n.* hobbles; clog. **agsimpalong.** *v.* to trot. **simpalongán.** *v.* to hobble (horse); bind for provisions; surprise, come upon without warning. **simpalongen.** *v.* to kick with the side of the foot; to trip someone.

simpán: simpanen. *v.* to put in order. (*urnos*; *simpa*)

simpangála: agsimpangala. *v.* to be uncertain, undecided; (*obs.*) to be nephews or nieces of the same person. (*duadua*; *ngatangata*)

simparát: *a.* differing (opinions). **simparaten.** *v.* to differ (in opinions). **agsisimparat.** *a.* cluttered (thoughts). **Agsisimparat ti mapampanunotna bayat ti panaginumna.** He had cluttered thoughts while drinking.

simpatía: (Sp. *simpatía*: kindness; sympathy) *n.* sympathy; friendly feeling; kindness; liking.

simpátiko: (Sp. *simpático*: kind) *n.* kind; nice; pleasant. (*anus*)

símple: (Sp.) *a.* simple. **papel simple.** *n.* a kind of thin paper.

simplipikár: (Sp. *simplificar*: simplify) **simplipikaren.** *v.* to simplify.

simpó: simpuan. *v.* to devise; plan a strategy. **nasimpo.** *a.* ingenious. [Tag. *tuso* (clever)]

simpukél: *var.* of *sippukel*: sexy, with a good body figure. **Nasimpukel ti bagina.** She has a sexy body.

simponía: (Sp. *sinfonía*: symphony) *n.* symphony.

simpungálan: kasimpungalan. *n.* spouse; dearly loved one. **agkasimpungalan.** *v.* to be husband and wife (*asawa*; *kaingugnot*). [Tag. *kasi*]

simpúon: *n.* beginning of a story. **simpuonen.** *v.* to question from the beginning; start telling from the beginning. **pakasimpuonan.** *n.* gist; outline; summary (*pukpok*). **No simpuonen,**

nainaw ti bomba atomika iti nalaus nga amak. In the beginning the atomic bomb was conceived out of extreme fear. [Tag. *buód*]

simrón: *n.* worry; anxiety; anger; frustration; bother. **nasimron.** *a.* sad; downcast; depressed; heartsick. **masimronan.** *v.* to be worried; depressed. **makasimron.** *v.* to be angered; bothersome. [Tag. *balisa*]

simsím: simsiman. *v.* to taste; test the quality; eat just a little. **apagsimsim, kasimsim.** *a.* just weaned (animals). **makasimsim.** *v.* to have a taste of. **Simmimsim iti indiaya dagiti babbaro.** He tasted what the young men offered.

sin-: (Sp. *sin*: without) (*reg.*) prefix meaning without. **sinsao, sintagari.** *adv.* without saying a word, without talking. **sintaliaw.** *adv.* without looking back. **Sintimekkami met ken ni mamang a nanguray iti pangngeddengna.** Mother and I waited for his decision without speaking.

sína: sumina. *v.* to separate; abandon; die. **agsina.** *v.* to separate; withdraw; divorce. **agsisina.** *v.* to scatter, disperse; break up. **isina.** *v.* to abandon, forsake; quit. **naisina.** *a.* separate. **nasinaak.** *a.* my deceased spouse. **pagsinaen.** *v.* to separate; disconnect; scatter. **pagsisinaen.** *v.* to break up, disintegrate, disjoint. **pagsinaan ti dalan.** *n.* crossroad. **agpasina.** *v.* to grieve over the death of someone. **pinasina.** *n.* deceased person. **simmina.** *a.* deceased. **sinasina.** *a.* separated; broken into parts; scattered; disassembled. **Diak insina ti panagkitak iti babai.** I didn't take my eyes off the girl. [Ivt. *savwal*, Knk. *desiáng, ídang, sían*, Png. *bíg*, Tag. *hiwaláy*]

sinag-: *pref.* perfective form of *sag-*.

sinagCV-: Prefix used with ordinal number roots to indicate how many strands are twisted together. **sinagdudua.** *n.* rope consisting of two strands twisted together. **sinagpapat.** *n.* four strands twisted together.

sinága: *n. tres en raya*, a boys' game. **agsinaga.** *v.* to play *tres en raya.*

sinagóga: (Sp. *sinagoga*: synagogue) *n.* synagogue.

sinam-: *var.* of the prefix *sinan-* before *m, p,* or *b.* **sinambituen.** *a.* starry, like a star.

sinámar: *n.* ray of light; tail of a comet. **agsinamar.** *v.* to radiate; light up; become well known. [Tag. *silahis*]

sinámay: *a.* soft; smooth; caressing. [Tag. *lamyós*]

sinamáy: *n.* transparent woven cloth from *abaká* fiber.

sinampádi: (myth.) *n.* kind of ghost that resembles a priest.

sinan-: *pref.* like, resembling; also expresses imitation; *n.* something resembling it. **sinantao.** like the figure of a man. **sinambalay.** resembling a house. **sinambilog.** toy *bilog* boat. **sinambituen.** starry thing, like a star. **sinanlungon a kama.** *n.* trundle bed, enclosed bed. **sinanpaltog a pagbakuna.** vaccination that is given as a gunshot.

sinán: sinansinan. *a.* not well made; haphazardly done. **sinsinan.** *a.* fake; make-believe.

sinánap: sinanapen. *v.* to take all things from one place (in an orderly manner); take fruits all from one tree in an orchard. (compare with antonym *pattopattokan*)

sinantá: *n.* unit of weight. (6.32629 kg.)

sinatnát: sinatnatan. *v.* to follow up. **pasinatnat.** *n.* follow up.

sin-áw: nasin-aw. *a.* clear, transparent; of noble blood. **sumin-aw.** *v.* to clear up. **pasin-awen.** *v.* to purify; clean. **kinasin-aw.** *n.* purity; chastity. **Nangin-inut a simmin-aw ti panagkitak.** My vision gradually cleared.

sináy: *n. Phaseolus calcaratus* vine with yellow flowers and edible beans.

sindá: Perfective form of *sida* or *sidaen*: ate, had as a viand. **Ania't sindana?** What did he have to eat? **Agriingkan, Ramon, sindada tay sidamon!** Wake up Ramon, they have eaten your viand! (said to a man whose sweetheart is being stolen by someone else).

sindáyag: agpasindayag. *v.* to be vain, conceited; to boast.

sindég: isindeg. *v.* to keep in place; keep in order.

sinderéla de notse: *n.* kind of flower.

sindí: (Sp. *encender*: to light) *n.* flame; light. **agsindi.** *v.* to catch on fire. **sindian.** *v.* to ignite; set on fire; light a match. **makisindi.** *v.* to borrow fire from someone in order to light. [Tag. *sindí*]

sindikáto: (Sp. *sindicato*: syndicate) *n.* syndicate; organized gang.

sindír: isindir. *v.* to keep in order; keep in place.

sindó: (*coll.*) *a.* with everybody saying or doing; each, every. **sindo kuna.** everybody is saying.

sinduyóngen: *n.* cock with dark reddish plumage.

síne: (Sp. *cine*: movie) *n.* movie; cinema; film. **agsine.** *v.* to see a movie. **isine.** *v.* to take to a movie; make into a movie. **ipasine.** *v.* to put into a movie; show in a movie. **agpasine.** *v.* to give a show. [Tag. *sine*]

sinélas: *var.* of *tsinelas*: slippers.

sinigáng: *n.* fish chowder.

siniguélas: (Sp. *ciruela*: plum) *n.* plum. (*sarguelas*)

sinin-: *pref. var.* of *sinan-*: similarity or imitation prefix.

sinínába: *n. Alocasia sp.* plant.

sinipéte: *n.* anchor. (*angkla*) **agsinipete.** *v.* to anchor. [Tag. *angklâ*]

sinísa: (Sp. *ceniza*: ash) *n.* ash. **Mierkoles de Sinisa.** *n.* Ash Wednesday.

sinisádo: (Sp. *cenizado*: ashen) *a.* ash-colored, gray.

siniséra: (Sp. *cenicero*: ashtray) *n.* ashtray.

sinít: **nasinit.** *a.* brunt, scorched; (*coll.*) tipsy. **siniten.** *v.* to set fire to; burn; light a fuse. **Apay nga masinsinit ditoy?** *exp.* Why is she staying such a short while here? [Kal. *atung*, Tag. *pasò*]

sinkamás: *n. Pachyrhizus erosus*, jícama.

sínko: (Sp. *cinco*: five) *num.* five. (*limá*) **alas sinko.** five o'clock.

sínkopa: (Sp. *síncopa*: syncope) *n.* syncope, elision of sounds, deletion of root vowels during affixation; shifting of metrical accent in music.

sinkópata: *var.* of *sinkopa.*

sinnábug: *n.* gold filings. **sininnabugan.** *n.* filigree.

sinnó$_1$: *interrog.* who (*asino, siasino*). [Ibg. *sinni*, Png. *siopá*, Tag. *sino*]

sinnó$_2$: *var.* of *silnó*: undulate; spill. **sinnosinno.** *n.* movement of water in a jar.

sinnukél: *n.* pustules (on intestines, neck of pigs).

síno: *var.* of *sinno*: who. (*asino; siasino*) **Sino-katta?** Who are you there? [Png. *siopa*, Tag. *sino*]

sinublán: *n.* very large *siliási* pot for cooking sugarcane juice. **simminublan.** *n.* resembling a *sinublán.*

sinúlid: *n.* sewing thread. [Kal. *kapós*, Tag. *sinulid*]

sinunuó: *adv.* almost sure of fulfillment; certain; determined. **masinunuo.** *v.* to be possibly approved; to be certain; sure. **Masinunuom?** Are you sure? **Saanna a masinunuo ti arami-denna.** He is not sure of what he is doing. [Tag. *tiyák*]

sinóng: (*obs.*) see *urnóng*: arrange; put in order.

sinúp: **agsinup.** *v.* to fix, arrange, put in order. **isinup.** *v.* to put something in the proper place. **sinupen.** *v.* to arrange, put in order.

sínsa: (Sp. *cincha*: girth) *n.* girth for a saddle or harness. **sinsaen.** *v.* to tighten the girth.

sinsaó: (f. *sao*) *adv.* without talking.

sinsél: (Sp. *cincel*: chisel) *n.* chisel.

sinseridád: (Sp. *sinceridad*: sincerity) *n.* sincerity.

sinséro: (Sp. *sincero*: sincere) *a.* sincere. (*naimpusuán*)

sinsília: (Sp. *sencilla*: simple) *a.* simple (not double).

sinsílio: *var.* of *sensilio*: loose change, small change.

sinsín: *adv.* one for each. (see *sag-* prefix) **agsinsin.** *v.* to take one by one; take one each. **kasinsin.** *n.* cousin. [Tag. *tig-isá*]

sinsinán: *a.* fake, imitation; make-believe. **sinsinan a kasar.** *n.* fake wedding; paper marriage.

sinsóro: (Sp. *chinchorro*: fishing net) *n.* dragnet in fishing (general term).

sínta$_1$: (Sp. *cinta*: ribbon) *n.* ribbon (*laso*); rope used to fasten the yoke; felly, a curved piece of wood that forms the circular rim of a wheel. [Tag. *sintá* = love]

sínta$_2$: (Sp. *sienta*: sit) **agsinta.** *v.* to raise the forelegs (mad horse), prance when irritated. [Tag. *dambá*]

sintagarí: (f. *tagari*) **awan sintagari.** no one said a word.

sinták: **nasintak.** *a.* leafy (plants). (*rukbos*)

sintás: (Sp. *cinta*: ribbon) *n.* leather strap. **sintasan.** *v.* to strap.

sintáw: **sintawen.** *v.* to divide by one stroke; behead. [Tag. *tigpás*]

sínti: Contraction of *sino ti*: who.

sintík: **agsintik.** *v.* to flick marbles. (*bulintik*)

sintír: (Sp. *sentir*: feel; regret) **sintiren.** *v.* to resent; charge someone on account of his actions. **nasintir.** *a.* resentful.

sintók: *n.* knuckles. **sintuken.** *v.* to knock on the head with the knuckles. **marasintok.** (*coll.*) *n.* virgin (having breasts like knuckles). **Kasla nasintokan iti nangngegna.** *exp.* He was hurt by what he heard (*lit:* was hit by what he heard). [Tag. *sintô* = mental weakness]

sintóma: (Sp. *síntoma*: symptom) *n.* symptom.

sintunádo: (Sp. *sin*: without + *tunado*: tuned) *a.* out of tune. (*beddáng, siláng*)

sintúra: (Sp. *cintura*: waist) *n.* waistline measurement.

sinturón: (Sp. *cinturón*: belt) *n.* belt. (*baríkes, birko*) **nakasinturon.** *a.* wearing a belt. **sinturonen.** *v.* to whip with a belt. **sinturon ni Hudas.** *n.* kind of firecracker that emits multiple explosions.

singá: **masingsinga.** *v.* to be confused, perplexed; bothered; always stopping. **singaen.** *v.* to bother, disturb, annoy, irritate. **singsingaka met.** you're bothering me. **makasinga.** *a.* disturbing; bothering. **Saannak a singaen, pangaasim!** Please don't disturb me! [Tag. *abala*]

síngal: **isingal.** *v.* to insert (a wedge, etc.) (*tingál*). [Tag. *singit*]

singángar: **masingangar.** *v.* to be busy; work competitively. **singangaran.** *v.* to keep busy;

overtax; ask too much from (in terms of work). [Tag. *abala*]

síngar: *var*. of *íngar*.

singásing: *n*. suggestion; recommendation; proposal. **singasingen**. *v*. to suggest; recommend; interrupt; interfere. **isingasing**. *v*. to suggest; recommend; leave; withdraw oneself; interrupt; propose. [Tag. *mungkahì* (suggest); *himasok* (interfere)]

singát: *n*. instrument used to forcibly open something. **singaten**. *v*. to open forcibly. **pagsingat**. *v*. to use to pry something open.

síngay: *n*. small bundle of rice; strips of bamboo used for tying rice stalks into small bundles. **agsingay, singayen**. *v*. to tie in small bundles. [Tag. *panalì*]

singdán: *n*. string, strip; shoestring (differentiated from the *gálut* by length, the *singdan* leaves more room between objects; when thick it is called *talí*, when small *línas* or *lúbid*, *sinúlit* (thread)) Type of strings in Ilocano: *singdan*. *n*. used to attach objects (not immediately connected to one another). *gálut*. *n*. used to bind objects together. *talí*. *n*. used to bind, thicker than a *singdán*. *línas*. *n*. string, stronger than the *lúbid*. *lúbid*. *n*. fine string. *sinúlit*. *n*. sewing thread. *sag-út*. *n*. cotton yarn. **singdanan**. *v*. to tie, bundle. [Tag. *talì*]

singdát: *adv*. at once. (*dagus*) **isingdat, singdaten**. *v*. to do immediately. **nasingdat**. *a*. immediate; quick; fast; straightforward. [Tag. *agad*]

singéd₁: **singden**. *v*. to attach the leash of an animal to a stick to prevent the animal from escaping or biting.

singéd₂: **singensinged**. *n*. closeness (in friendship). **nasinged**. *a*. close, intimate. **Tanda ti singen-singed**. It is a sign of close friendship. **Dida madlaw dagiti adda iti aglawlawda, uray pay dagiti kasingedda**. They don't notice what's around them, not even what is close. [Tag. *lapit*]

singgalút: *n*. tie; bond. (*siglot*) **agsinggalut**. *v*. to join in marriage; tie the knot. **masinggalut**. *v*. to be knotted. [Tag. *buhól, buklód*]

singgapó: *n*. ancestor; ancestry. (*puon*) **agsinggapo**. *v*. to trace one's ancestry. **singgapuen**. *v*. to get to the bottom of things. [Tag. *angkán*]

singgapól: **singgapulen**. *v*. to leash; tie, bind; shackle.

singgápong: *n*. square net used to catch birds. **singgapongen**. *v*. to catch in the *singgapong*.

singgát: **nasinggat**. *a*. unbruised, whole (grains of pounded rice); fair, clear (weather); resonant (voice).

singgí: **singgien**. *v*. to melt down lard. (*lunág*)

singgít: *n*. high pitch. **nasinggit**. *a*. high in pitch; shrill. **Naduaya iti singgit dagiti agsisinnungbat a kundidit**. He was lulled to sleep by the shrills of the conversing cicadas. [Tag. *tinís*]

sing-í: see *sang-í*: sob.

síngil: *n*. barbel of fish. **masingil**. *v*. to be pricked with the barbel of a fish. **pasingil**. *n*. scrofula. **paspasingil**. *n*. scrofulous inflammations on the skin. **sisingílan**. *n*. part of the body between the humerus and shoulder blade.

síngin: *n*. twins. (*kambal*) **agkasingin**. *v*. to be twins. [Png. *singín, sipíng*, Tag. *kambál*]

singíng: *n*. kind of edible marine fish.

singír₁: **agsingir**. *v*. to collect debts; claim. **singiren**. *v*. to collect debts. **parasingir**. *n*. collector of debts. **sisingiren**. *n*. collectibles. **isingir**. *v*. to make someone account for his words or actions. **managisingir**. *n*. person who is prone to recriminate. [Png., Tag. *singíl*]

singír₂: **sumingir**. *v*. to reappear (ailments).

singísing: *n*. rising of the sun. (*leggak*) **sumingising**. *v*. to rise (the sun). **sumingsingising a bituen**. *n*. rising star (in show business). **Mariknanan ti bara ti dandanin sumingising nga init**. He feels the heat of the just-rising sun.

síngit: *n*. posts of a granary or house used to support the *busóran* girders; (*obs*.) little fork. **isingit**. *v*. to insert; include; interpose (*sengngat*). [Tag. *singit* = slit; groin]

sing-ít: *n*. part of a bundle (*síngay*). **sing-iten**. *v*. to take from a bundle.

singítan: *n*. *Sida retusa* shrub with yellow flowers; kind of scallop.

síngkamas: (Sp. *jícama*) *n*. jícama root (*Pachyrhizus erosus*). (*kamás*)

síngkaw: *n*. yoke. **isingkaw**. *v*. to hitch. (*pako*) **Kalpasan ti panangisingkawna iti nuang, simmalpa sa nagtugaw iti abay ti baketna**. After he yoked the water buffalo, he jumped down and sat next to his wife. [Png. *pako*, Tag. *pamatok, yugo, paód*]

singkéd: *n*. trust. (*talék; salindég*) **pasingkedán**. *v*. to confirm; authorize; verify; ratify. **agpasingked**. *v*. to ratify; confirm; make sure. **pasingked**. *n*. legal document; promissory note; confirmation. **makipasingked**. *v*. to have something verified or confirmed. **nasingked**. *a*. trustworthy. [Tag. *patunay*]

singkíl: *n*. bamboo tube with a handle used to draw liquids or drink; a native dance from Mindanao. **isingkil**. *v*. to feed an animal from a *singkil*.

singkít: (Ch.) *a*. slit-eyed; almond-eyed. (*pingkit; kusipet*) **agsingkit**. *v*. to close the eyes in slits. [Tag. *singkít*]

singklétas: *n.* native slippers. (*tsinelas*) **naka-singkletas**. *a.* wearing slippers.

síngko: (Sp. *cinco*: five) *num.* five. (*lima*) **alas singko**. five o'clock. **sagsisingko**. five each.

sìngkopá: (Sp. *síncopa*) *n.* syncope, loss of sounds in a word.

singkopátit: (*slang*) *n.* psychopath.

sinkuénta: (Sp. *cincuenta*: fifty) *n.* fifty. (*limapulo*) **sagsisinkuenta**. fifty each.

singkól: *a.* paralyzed in one or both hands; deformed in the arm. [Knk. *sagakoéng*, Png. *sikwél*, Tag. *pingkól, kimáw*]

singkutsár: *var.* of *sangkutsar*: native dish made of goat, tripe, intestines, lungs, *dinadaraan*, salt, pepper, onions, garlic, and vinegar. **singkutsaren**. *v.* to prepare meat in this way.

singlág: **agsinglag**. *v.* to extract oil from coconut milk by cooking. **sininglag**. *n.* coconut oil. (*lana*) **singlagen**. *v.* to cook coconut until only the oil remains. **kassinglag**. *a.* freshly extracted (coconut oil).

singlót: **agsinglot**. *v.* to suck up nasal mucus, sniff in. **agkarasinglot**. *v.* to sniff in continuously. **singluten**. *v.* to suck up through the nose. **agsaninglot**. *v.* to sob. **sisingloten**. *n.* inhalant. **Agkarasinglot nupay di met agpanateng wenno agbutbuteg.** He keeps sniffing in although he doesn't have a cold or running nose. [Kal. *sing-uy*, Tag. *singhót*]

singngí: (*obs.*) **singngien**. *v.* to cut off a leg.

singudúos: (*obs.*) **agsinguduos**. *v.* to perspire profusely. (*ling-et, lidduos; kalimduos*)

singúngo: **sumingungo**. *v.* to smell (said of dogs). (*saep*)

singpáw: *n.* edge of a wall; border of a canoe.

singpét: **nasingpet**. *a.* well-behaved; virtuous; sinless; innocent; mile; gentle. **agsingpet**. *v.* to behave well. **aginsisingpet**. *v.* to pretend to be virtuous. **kinasingpet**. *a.* goodness; virtue; virginity. **singpet ti kiteb**. *n.* the virtue of a bedbug (said of people who exhibit good behavior but are actually bad on the inside). **Agsingsingpetka ken agkararagka.** Behave yourself and pray. [Ivt. *kapsek*, Knk. *balikáug*, *bulikáug*, Png. *kalákal*, Tag. *banál, baít*]

singrúob: **masingruoban**. *v.* to be fumigated, filled with smoke. (*masuuban*) **singruoban**. *v.* to fumigate; smoke (meat).

singsíng: (Ch., Tagalog also) *n.* ring. **singsingan**. *a.* wearing a ring; *v.* to put a ring on someone. **paningsingan**. *n.* ring finger. **pasingsing**. *n.* the ring on the handle of a machete. [Ibg. *sakkalang, seklang*, Ifg. *takkalang*, Ivt. *gadang*, Kpm., Png., Tag. *singsíng*]

singsingá: *n.* someone who prevents the progress of work. **sinsingaen**. *v.* to bother.

singtáw: *n.* slash, diagonal cut. **singtawen**. *v.* to slash, lop off with one stroke. **kassingtaw**. *a.* freshly slashed. (*sintáw*)

sió: Interjection used to drive away animals.

siudád: (Sp. *ciudad*: city) *n.* city. (*ili*) **Dimi kayaten a makita ti rupam ditoy siudad.** We don't want to see your face any longer in this city.

siudadáno: (Sp. *ciudadano*: citizen) *n.* citizen. (*umili*)

siúdot: (*coll.*) *n.* anger. **agsiudot**. *v.* to get angry. (*pungtot, ruród*) **makapasiudot**. *a.* irritating, annoying. **Ania't pagsiudotam?** What are you getting upset about? **Naabbukay ti siudotna.** His anger was revived.

siók: *var.* of *ipdok*.

siókaw: *n.* species of tasty marine fish.

siúkoy: (Tag. via Hok. *cuí kuì*: water ghost) *n.* mermaid; merman. (*sirena*)

sioktóng: (Tag. via Ch.) *n.* rice wine. (*basi*)

siómai: (Hok. *sio mai*: hot sell, pronounced: *siómay*) *n.* steamed noodle dumpling filled with meat.

siúman: [*pl. sisiuman*] *n.* stepchild. **agsiuman**. *n.* stepparent. **agkasiuman**. *n.* stepbrothers, stepsisters. **siumanen**. *v.* to enslave, deal with harshly.

siónga: (*coll.*) *n. a.* Chinese. (*insik*)

siópao: (Hok. *sio pau*: hot dumpling, pronounced: *siopaw*) *n.* steamed bun filled with meat.

siót: (Eng. shot) *n.* basketball shot. **agsiot**. *v.* to take a shot in basketball.

sióta: (Tag. *syota*) *n.* girlfriend. (*kaayan-ayat*)

siúting: (Eng.) *n.* shooting of a movie.

siutíng: (f. *siota*) (*coll.*) *n.* endearing term of address for a girlfriend.

sípa: (Tag. *sipà* 'kick') *n.* hacky sack. A kind of boys' game that consists of standing in a circle and kicking up a small light ball, keeping it in the air as long as possible. **agsipa**. *v.* to play this game. **sipaen**. *v.* to kick.

sípad: **sipaden**. *v.* to lop of. (*sep-ak; sep-ang*) **nasipad**. *a.* lopped off.

sip-ák: **maspak**. *v.* to be broken (branch of tree); to snap. **sumip-ak**. *v.* to break (off). **sip-aken**. *v.* to break off, snap off, dislocate, detach. [Tag. *baklî*]

sipáng: *n.* chip; broken off fragment. **masipang**. *v.* to chip. **sipangan**. *v.* to chip; break off in small pieces. **sipangen**. *v.* to chop off; separate. [Tag. *tatal*]

sip-áng: *n.* upper part of legs, bikini line.

sipár: **agsipar**. *v.* to hinder; impede. **makasipar**. *v.* to obstruct, hinder. **manipsipar**. *v.* to hamper, impede. [Tag. *sagabal*]

sipásip: sipasipen. *v.* to discover; catch sight of. **sumipasip.** *v.* to jut out, protrude. **apagsipasip.** *a.* barely visible; just coming into view; emerging. **pagsipasip nga lawag.** *n.* daybreak, dawn. [Tag. *litáw* (emerge)]

sípat: agsipat. *v.* to reap sorghum or sesame. **sipaten.** *v.* to reap, gather; cut at a harvest.

sipát: *n.* slap, spank; applause. **sipaten.** *v.* to spank (*arrabis*); slap (*tungpa*). **agsipat.** *v.* to spank; slap; clap, applaud (*palakpak*). **sipsipat.** *n.* drum beats, rhythm. [Tag. *tampál* (slap); *palakpák* (applaud), Bon *sipát* = slashing cut]

sipdóng: sipdongen. *v.* to hit with the elbow or shoulder to call one's attention.

sipdót: sipduten. *v.* to tear off; pull apart; pull up (weeds); abruptly take away; snatch, rob. **masipdutan.** *v.* to be robbed, victimized. **agsisipdot, mannipdut.** *n.* snatcher; pickpocket. [Tag. *dukot*]

sípet: *n.* cockroach. (*ípes*) **sinipet.** *a.* infested with cockroaches. [Png. *asípet, bulák,* Tag. *ipis*]

sipí: *n.* small storeroom (smaller than a *bodéga*); closet (*sagumbi*). [Tag. *sibi; sipì* = copy]

sipiá: (Sp. *sepia,* Tag. *sipi:* copy) *n.* brownish copy of a photograph.

sipílio: (Sp. *cepillo:* toothbrush) *n.* toothbrush. **agsipilyo.** *v.* to brush one's teeth.

sípilís: (Sp. *sífilis*) *n.* syphilis.

síping: *a.* grown together (fruits, parts of bodies, etc.); one centavo piece; inseparable. (*riping*) **nagsiping.** *a.* twinned; with two branching out; grown together. **agsiping.** *v.* to grow together. **agsiping ti dilana.** *exp.* denoting a loquacious person. **Idi ubingak, sagsisiping ti kendi.** When I was a child, candy was one centavo each. **Saandakon nga ikkan iti uray siping.** They don't give me even a penny any more. **Napatpateg ta siping a nasapulan ngem ti pisos a tinakawan.** Fifty centavos earned is more valuable than a stolen peso. [Tag. *kambál*]

sipísip: (*obs.*) *n.* a little fork.

sípit: *n.* tongs, forceps; chopsticks. **agsipit.** *v.* to use tongs, forceps, chopsticks. **sipiten.** *v.* to pick up with tongs. **panipit.** *n.* device used as tongs. [Png. *angkop,* Tag. *sipit*]

siplág: *n.* sudden attack of a rooster or person. **sumiplag.** *v.* to fling, launch toward (chickens defending young); flash (in one's mind) (*agibas*). **siplagan.** *v.* to fling toward; attack. **Simmiplag ti napalabas iti panunotko.** The past flashed in my mind. **Siniplagan ti dalluyon ket ingguyudna iti kaadalman.** The waves flung toward him and dragged him into the deep.

siplóg: nasiplog. *v.* to be affected badly by a current of air. **siplogen ti angin.** the wind is extremely strong.

siplót: sumiplot. *v.* to attack; have an attack (of anger, etc.); come to mind. **sumiplot iti mugingna.** *exp.* to come to mind; instantly recall.

sipngét: *n.* darkness; dusk. **nasipnget.** *a.* dark; gloomy; obscure. **sumipnget.** *n.* twilight, dusk (*suripet*); sunset; *v.* to get dark. **agsipnget ti panagkita.** *exp.* to black out; lose consciousness; be blinded by anger. **panipngeten.** *a.* somewhat dark. [Ibg. *ribboq, zibboq, zilám,* Itg. *pánget,* Ivt. *sariq,* Kal. *gikbot,* Kpm. *dalumdom,* Png. *selongét, bilongét,* Tag. *dilím*]

sipo: agsipo. *v.* to hold the genitals.

sípud: *n.* origin; beginning; cause. (*punganay; gapo*) **manipud, sipud.** *prep.* from. **sipud idi, manipud idi.** since. **agsipud (ta).** because; since. **nanipudan.** *n.* origin, beginning of everything. **sipuden.** *v.* to do from the beginning. **isipud.** *v.* to commence, start, begin. **Daydin ti sipud ti nagsasaruno a malasko.** That was the start of my continual bad luck. [Png. *sípor,* Tag. *mulâ*]

sipuéd: (*obs.*) *n.* gold or ivory buttons on the girdle.

sípok₁: *n.* small heap of harvested rice.

sípok₂: sipuken. *v.* to cut at the base (trees). (*pukan*)

sipók: masipok. *v.* to be broken.

sípul: sipulen. *v.* to cut up, sever; (*obs.*) do from the beginning. (*sipok*)

sipól: *a.* joined; linked together. **agsisipol.** *v.* to come one after another, as when linked (ants in a trail); (~ **ti sigarilio**) *n.* chain smoker. **nagsipul.** *a.* joined. **makisinsinnipol.** (*coll.*) *v.* to copulate. **pagsipulen.** *v.* to join; attach. **Lisiak kuma idi ni Alex ngem ad-adda a sinipulannak.** I should have got away from Alex but he probably would have come after me. [Tag. *kabít*]

sip-ól: agsip-ol. *v.* to be leashed, tied; fettered.

sipón₁: (Sp. *sifón:* siphon) *n.* sneezing during a cold.

sipón₂: (Sp. *sifón:* siphon) *n.* siphon.

sipulturéro: (Sp. *sepulturero:* grave digger) *n.* cemetery guard; grave digger. (*bantay ti kamposanto*)

sip-ón: agsip-on. *v.* to take, buy everything. **sipunen.** *v.* to clear land of stumps.

síput: siputan. *v.* to keep an eye on; observe; observe; watch over. **masiputan.** *v.* to notice; perceive; observe. **nasiput.** *a.* vigilant; attentive; observant. **Sinipsiputan ni Melay ti masarsarutsot a panagsangpet dagiti sangaili.**

Melay observed the continuous arriving of the guests. [Tag. *manmán*]

sippádaw: *var.* of *sippadong*: stumble, trip.

sippádong: masippadong. *v.* to stumble, trip. (*piddawíl*) **sippadongen.** *v.* to stumble; hit the foot against; trip someone. **Sinippadongnak ket iti pannakaidarumko, natiro iti iking ti tugaw ti mugingko.** He tripped me and as I fell, my forehead hit the edge of the chair. [Tag. *patid*]

sippág: sumippag. *v.* to spread the wings and attack (said of the mother hen defending her young).

sippakól: *a.* bowlegged. (*sakáng, akkáng*) **agsippakol.** *v.* to entangle the legs and fall.

sippángol: sippangulen. *v.* to strike in the nape. (*sippápo*)

sippápo: *n.* strike on the nape. **sippapuen.** *v.* to strike someone in the nape (*sippangol*). **Kellaat a sinippapo ni Beng ni Uriki.** Beng suddenly struck Uriki (on the nape).

sippárud: *n.* kind of spiny vine. **agsipparud.** *v.* to catch another person's foot; to walk abnormally and noisily; stagger. [Tag. *tisod* (trip)]

sippáw: sippawen. *v.* to catch. **manangsippaw.** *n.* good ball catcher. [Knk. *sikpáw*, Tag. *saló*]

sippáyot: *n.* kind of small bird with brown plumage. **sippayuten.** *v.* to catch objects in the air (birds), dive to in order to catch, prance, swoop. (*seppeg*) **nasippayot.** *a.* seized by a hawk, seized by a swooping animal.

sippíg: *n.* crack (in wood). **maspig.** *v.* to split; crack (boards). (*bettak*)

sippít: *n.* beak, bill. **sippiten.** *v.* to peck; bite (birds). **sumsumpiit.** *v.* to sting. **makisinnippit.** *v.* to be beak to be; (*fig.*) mouth to mouth. **Pasaray sippiten ti billit ti rehas ti tangkal.** The bird often pecks at the bars of the cage. [Kal. *tukkay*, Png. *topék*, Tag. *tukâ*]

sippók: maspok. *v.* to be broken off (tree branches).

sippukél: nasippukel. *a.* having a shapely body; sexy; voluptuous. **agsippukel.** *v.* to have a curvaceous body.

siprád₁: pagsipradan. *n.* obstruction (from view). **agsiprad.** *v.* to obstruct; malfunction.

siprád₂: agsiprad. *v.* to become coarse (voice); miss when writing.

sipráw: siprawan. *v.* to trim (branches). (*arbas*)

siprés: (Sp. *cipres*: cypress) *n.* cypress.

sipróng: *var.* of *tiprong*.

sipsíp: *a.* sucking; brown-nosing; sycophantic; mooching. **sipsipan.** *v.* to weed (*lamon*). [Knk. *supsúp*, Tag. *sipsíp*]

sírab: *var.* of *sarab*.

síram₁: siraman. *v.* to scorch; kindle wood in order to clean or eradicate. [Tag. *siláb*]

síram₂: siramsiram. *n.* kind of small flying insect.

sírap: masirap. *v.* to be blinded by the light. **masisirap.** *v.* to dazzle (*purar*); shade eyes from the sun. **Makasisirap ti sumirsirip a lawag ti init.** The peeping light of the sun is dazzling. [Tag. *silaw*]

sirárak: *var.* of *sirarat*: discern; observe.

sirárat: siraraten. *v.* to discern; observe carefully in the distance; try to make out a figure in the dark. (*sipasip*) **Kinaykayatmo ti nagsisirarat idinto nga adda kuma met pagsilawmo.** You preferred to (read) in the dark when you should have had a light. **Sinirsiraratko no sadino a paset ngata sadiay ti nagdissuan dagiti immuna a tao a napan iti bulan.** I tried to discern in what part (of the moon) the first people who went to the moon landed. [Tag. *aninag*]

síraw₁: sumiraw. *v.* to rise (sun, moon, etc.). (*leggak*) **mapaspasiraw.** *v.* to stagger, totter (*basing*). [Tag. *sikat* (rising of celestial bodies)]

síraw₂: sirawsiraw. *n.* kind of herb growing in rice fields.

siraw-át: pasiraw-at. *n.* ring finger (*sising-singan*). **Nakidemak tapno mateppelak ti lua ni ragsak idi yusongna ti singsing iti pasiraw-atko.** I blinked to control the tears of happiness when he put the ring on my ring finger. [Png. *pangánsi*]

síray₁: *n.* glance (*taldiap*). **isiray.** *v.* to turn the eyes to; force eyes to open when hard to open. **sumiray.** *v.* to emerge, rise. **nasirayan.** *a.* illuminated. **Napamuttaleng idi masirayanna ti dila ti apuy iti maikadua a kadsaaran.** He was left agape when he gazed at the tongue of the fire on the second story. [Tag. *sikat* (rising of the sun or stars)]

síray₂: (*obs.*) *n.* famine. [Tag. *tagsalát*]

siráyap: sumirayap. *v.* to set (sun) (*lumnek*). [Tag. *lubóg*]

siráyat: sumirayat. *v.* to rise (sun or moon). [Tag. *sikat*]

siréna: (Sp. *sirena*: mermaid) *n.* mermaid. (*kuwaw; abada; litáw*) **simmirena.** *a.* like a mermaid.

sirháno: *var.* of *siruhano*: surgeon.

síri: nasiri. *a.* strong (wind, current); rapid (current).

siriál: *var.* of *siriales*.

siriáles: (Sp. *cirial*: processional candlestick) *n.* candlestick on a pole (for a procession).

sírib: *n.* wisdom; knowledge; cunning; intelligence. **masirib.** *a.* wise; learned; astute; intelligent. **siriban.** *v.* to scrutinize. **sinniriban.** *n.* tricky game. **pagsiriban.** *n.* field of expertise; profession; wisdom; technology. **Dagiti masirib itayen?** Where are the wise men now? (said by a person who has been reading a lot and wants to impress others, the response is: **Nasultop ti bisukolen.** The snails are already sucked out). [Ivt. *sulib*, Kal. *lasomsomkan*, Png. *sílib*, *kabat*, Tag. *dunong*, *talino*]

siríg: *n.* posture; aim. **sirigen.** *v.* to aim; test an object for its straightness (by sight). **agsirig.** *v.* to scan; peer; peep. **agpasirig.** *v.* to expose oneself in public to attract the opposite sex. **sumirig.** *v.* to aim. **panirigán.** *n.* opinion. **Sinirigna ti dakkel.** He aimed for the big one. **Dua a billit a mapuntaan iti maysa la a sirig.** Two birds shot in only one aim. **Masapol laeng a mabaliwan ti panirigantayo iti panagtalon tapno ayatentayo daytoy a trabaho.** We just have to change our opinions about farming so we like this kind of work. [Tag. *sipat* (aim)]

sirimbaknáng: *n.* person who pretends to be rich. (*agimbabaknang*)

sírip: agsirip. *v.* to peep, peer. **sumirip.** *v.* peep through a crevice; peer in (said of light through small hole); look through a microscope. **mannirip.** *n.* Peeping Tom. **No tumangadka, masirsiripmo laengen ti tangatang iti baet dagiti bulong.** If you look up you can just peep at the sky between the leaves. [Bon. *diil*, Png., Tag. *sílip*]

sírit: siríten. *v.* to give up (when trying to solve a riddle or a solution to a problem, one utters *sirit*).

siríw: *n.* kind of marine fish with long jaws, a blue back, and a white belly, *Tylosurus sp.* **sir- siriw.** *n.* species of small bird.

sirkéro: (Sp. *cirquero*: circus man) *n.* stuntman; circus man; acrobat.

sírko: (Sp. *circo*: circus) *n.* circus. **agsirko.** *v.* to somersault; roll over. **agsirkosirko.** *v.* to walk by tumbling and getting up; fly up and down along a path.

sírkulo: (Sp. *círculo*: circle) *n.* circle. (*bukel*) **sirkuluen.** *v.* to encircle. **sinirkulo.** *n.* company, division of society; *a.* encircled.

sirmatá: *n.* vision; insight. (*parmata*) **masir- mataan.** *v.* to appear; be obvious; discern; perceive; come into view. **ipasirmata.** *v.* to display, appear distinctly, manifest. **sirmataen.** *v.* to perceive; visualize. [Tag. *pananáw*]

sirnáat: sumirnaat. *v.* to clear up (clouds). (*waknit*) **agsirnaat.** *v.* to stop raining; clear up (weather). **nasirnaat.** *a.* clear, free from rain. **Nasaon ni ulitegna a nasayaat ti tubo dagiti sabong no sumirnaat ti init.** His uncle said that the growth of the flowers will be good if the sun comes out. [Tag. *tilà*]

sirnáaw: *n.* cessation of continuous rainfall (*sirnaat*). **sumirnaaw.** *v.* to clear up (said of the weather). [Tag. *tilà*]

síro: *n.* first palay harvested in a rice field.

sírob: *var.* of *sirab*.

siruháno: (Sp. *cirujano*: surgeon) *n.* surgeon.

siruhía: (Sp. *cirugía*: surgery) *n.* surgery.

sírok: *n.* crawl space of a house; space under something. **iti sirok.** *prep.* under; beneath; below; *adv.* downstairs, below. **masirok.** *v.* to be able to discover or decipher. **pasirok.** *n.* successor. **pasirokan.** *v.* to cheat, deceive; grow crops between trees. **sumirok.** *v.* to go under; go in the shade. **agsisirok.** *n.* chicken thief (stealing chickens kept under the house). **Inan-anatko nga indisso ti inassiwak a sako ti mani iti sirok ti kakawati.** I carefully placed the bag of peanuts I carried on a pole over my shoulder under the *madre cacao* tree. [Ibg. *arug*, *silárun*, *góweng*, Ivt. *ahbuq*, Kal. *guweb*, *cheÿa*, Kpm. *lálam*, Png. *sílong*, Tag. *ilalim*]

sirót: *a.* knotted; tied. (*siglut*; *simo*) **siruten.** *v.* to lace garments; tie; knot; clench a deal. **pasirot.** *n.* end of the rope in a slipknot. **sirot a baláy.** *n.* house in the form of a truncated pyramid. **pasirutan.** *v.* to fasten with a slipknot. **sirut- appút.** *n.* game consisting of each player putting one finger in the palm of another's hand; when the hand closes the loser is the one whose finger is caught. It is often played to determine who will be 'it' in hide-and-seek games. [Tag. *buhól*]

sirpát: masirpat. *v.* to see at a distance. **agpa- sirpat.** *v.* to show oneself; to flirt. **sumirpat.** *v.* to window shop; flirt with girls. **ipasirpat.** *v.* to show; display. **sirpaten.** *v.* to look; view; see. **Nagdalagudog ti barukongna idi masirpat- nan ti likudan ti ayup.** His chest pounded heavily when he sighted the back of the animal. **Dagiti babbaro, pamrayanda ti umay sumir- pat ken pasirpat.** The young boys usually come to flirt and be flirted with. [Tag. *masdán*]

sirpít: *n.* kind of leash rod used in weaving; hair clip. **sirpitan.** *v.* to fasten the hair with a clip.

sirrárat: *var.* of *sirarat*: do in the dark.

sirríid: sirriiden. *n.* to shell (mung beans) (*riid*). [Tag. *himay*]

sirrít: *n.* nickname used to ridicule flatterers.

sisál: *n.* species of maguey with fine fiber.

sisasáka: (f. *saka*) *a.* barefoot.

síseg: nasiseg. *a.* diligent; laborious; attentive. (*anep*; *gaget*; *regget*) **sisegen.** *v.* to do diligently. [Tag. *sipag*]

sísi: sisien. *v.* to extract lard by frying. **sinisi.** *n.* lard. (*mantéka*)

sisiáw: (f. *siaw*) *n.* grunt fish, *Datnia plumbea*.

sisikkarúdin: (f. *sikkarud*) **babai nga sisikka-rudin**. *n*. prostitute. (*pampam*; *puta*)

sisiléng: (f. *sileng*) **masisileng**. *v*. to be deafened by a loud sound.

sisingsíngan: (f. *singsing*) *n*. fourth finger, ring finger. (*pasiraw-at*)

sísip: **sisipen**. *v*. to sip with closed teeth (*igup*). [Knk. *suy-up*, *singíp*]

sísir: **masisir**. *v*. to curve, bend; turn; become rough; be twisted.

sisíwa: **sisiwaen**. *v*. to nurse an orphan. [Tag. *alagà*]

sismís: *var*. of *tsismis*: gossip. **sismoso**. *a*. gossiping.

sismógrapo: (Sp. *sismógrafo*: seismograph) *n*. seismograph.

sismolohía: (Sp. *sismología*: seismology) *n*. seismology.

sistéma: (Sp. *sistema*: system) *n*. system; method (*pamuspusan*; *wagas*). [Tag. *paraán*]

sistemátiko: (Sp. *sistemático*: systematic) *a*. systematic.

sistérna: (Sp. *cisterna*: cistern) *n*. cistern, water tank.

sísto: (Sp. *sexto*) *a*. sixth (*maikanem*). **sisto grado**. sixth grade.

síta: (Sp. *cita*: cite) *n*. cite, quote; summoning, calling up; convoking a meeting. **sitaen**. *v*. to confiscate; summon; cite, quote.

sitá: *var*. of *data*: you and I. **sitsita**. only you and I. [Png. *sikatá*]

sítak: **agkanalsitak**. *v*. to make the sound of clashing swords. **sitaken**. *v*. to divide into groups; to disperse. **masitaksitak**. *v*. to be scattered, dispersed, divided into groups. **Adu ti nasitaksitak a puli idiay Luzon.** There are a lot of scattered ethnic groups in Luzon.

sitár: **agsitar**. *v*. to inquire about; investigate. **panangsitar**. *n*. investigation. **Nagdumog idi sitarek iti dina panagsurat kaniak iti las-ud ti uppat a bulan.** She drooped her head when I asked why she hasn't written me for four months.

sitasión: (Sp. *citación*: citation) *n*. citation.

sítaw: (Tag. via Hok. *c^{h}î tau*: green bean) *n*. species of green string bean. (*utong*) [Png. *agáyep*, Tag. *sitaw*]

sitáy: *var*. of *sitayo*: we (inclusive).

sitayó: *var*. of *datayo*: we (inclusive).

sitbóng: **sinnitbongan**. *n*. hide-and-seek. **ag-sinnitbongan**. *v*. to play hide-and-seek. [Tag. *taguan*]

sitík: **sitsitik**. *n*. kind of small black bird.

sítio: (Sp. *sitio*: site) *n*. sitio, hamlet; site.

sitíw: **sitsitiw**. *n*. kind of small black bird. (*sitsitik*)

situasión: (Sp. *situación*: situation) *n*. situation.

sitráong: *n*. string used for wrapping jars to be carried. **sitraongen**. *v*. to wrap (a jar) with string to be carried, string a *burnay*.

sitráto: (Sp. *citrato*: citrate) *n*. citrate.

sítriko: (Sp. *cítrico*: citric) *a*. citric.

sitsaró: (Sp. *chicarro*: crackling) *n*. green peas.

sitsarón: (Sp. *chicharrón*: bacon rind) *n*. bacon rind cooked until puffy.

sitsiriá: (Pil., f. *sitsarón*) *n*. crunchy snack foods.

sitsít₁: **sitsítan**. *v*. to drain; take broth out of a dish; to incite a dog to attack; call using a hand signal. **agpasitsit**. *v*. to incite a dog to attack people. **nasitsitan**. *a*. drained, with no broth left. (*aruyot*)

sitsít₂: *n*. hissing sound (used to call attention); sizzling sound. **agsitsit**. *v*. to hiss, sizzle. **sitsitan**. *v*. to hiss at someone to call their attention. **Sinitsitan ti tallo a lallaki ni Dexina.** Three men hissed at Dexina (to call her attention).

sitsitbúng: *n*. hide-and-seek game. (*girit*, *kirikit*) **agsitsitbung**. *v*. to play this game.

sittíl: *n*. variety of small seashell with edible meat.

síwak: **masiwak**. *v*. to be cracked at the brim, split at top. **siwaken**. *v*. to crack at the top; widen; divide in two. [Tag. *bungì*]

síwal: *n*. manmade opening: large notch in a tool, gap made in a dam; restlessness. **nasiwal**. *a*. large-chested; prone to changing positions when sleeping. restless; always moving about. **agsiwal**. *v*. to be restless in bed (*alinsawad*, *tíweng*); hustle and bustle; to grumble (famished stomach). **Sukainam nga in-inayad ta no nasiwalka, masidolmo no kua ti matmaturog a lawwalawwa.** Look around very slowly and carefully because if you move about too much, you will accidentally hit a sleeping spider.

síwan: (*obs.*) **nasiwan**. *a*. indisposed through heat or fatigue.

siwáng: *n*. notch; gap; opening. **masiwang**. *v*. to be breached (*sawang*). [Tag. *siwang*, *gihà*]

siwárak: **agsiwarak**. *v*. to wander; stroll; spread. **Nagsiwarak ti damag a panangpadisi dagiti Ingles kadagiti Kastila iti Manila.** The news of the English ejecting the Spanish from Manila spread. [Tag. *galà*]

siwáwir: *var*. of *diwerdiwer*: moving sideways.

siwét: **isiwet**. *v*. to do fast; do instantly. **apagsiwet**. *adv*. in a brief instant. (*apagbiit*) **Kalpasan a nakapagpakada ni Keanu, pinasiwetnan ti luganna.** After Keanu said his goodbyes, he dashed off in his car. [Tag. *bilís*]

siwsíw: *var*. of *sawsaw*: dip. **Insiwsiwna ti tinuno nga okra iti bugguong a nakalamansian.**

He dipped the broiled okra in fish paste with lime.

suá: *n. Citrus decumana*, pomelo, used in native medicine against fever (*lukban*); interjection used to drive away animals. [Png. *lukbán*, Tag. *suhà*]

suáb: *n.* long, ugly mouth.

suábe: (Sp. *suave*: smooth) *a.* smooth. (*lamuyot*)

suág: **suágen**. *v.* to pry with a lever. (*aspiki*; *battuil*)

suágaw: **masuagaw**. *v.* to trip and fall, stumble. (*daramudom*)

suáko: *n.* pipe for smoking. **agsuako**. *v.* to smoke a pipe. [Tag. *kuwako*]

suál: *n.* kind of small spade for digging. **sualen**. *v.* to dig up. [Tag. *sudsód*; *suál* = pushing with the tip of the tongue]

suálit: **masualit**. *v.* to fall; drop; be scattered. **isualit**. *v.* to drop something; to uproot and throw down; scatter around; overturn. **Agkara-isualit dagiti sirawsiraw.** The *sirawsiraw* weed often scatters.

suápang: (Tag.) *a.* greedy. (*agum*)

suát: **suaten**. *v.* to prick; gouge; take out a sliver with a pointed instrument. **Kasla adda nasuat a puris iti barukongna.** *exp.* It seems there is a thorn pricking his chest (he is deeply troubled).

suáw: **agsuaw**. *v.* to talk indistinctly (one who has lost their teeth).

suáwi: (*obs.*) **sumuawi**. *v.* to disobey. (*sukir*; *supring*)

suáyan(g): *n.* kind of song sung in a conversational duet, singing joust. **agsuayan**. *v.* to engage in a singing joust.

súba: *n.* sloping end of roof (hip roof) of *pinagóng* houses; width. **sumuba**. *v.* to go against the current or wind; oppose. **agsuba**. *v.* to be on the verge of death. **subaen**. *v.* to go against (current, wind, etc.); to refuse to pay a debt. **Ti laengen pegges ti karayan ti subaenna.** He is only going against the strong current of the river. [Tag. *subà* = cheat; swindle]

subád: *n.* payment; compensation. (*bayad*) **subadan**. *v.* to reciprocate; repay; recompense; reward. **Kasanokaminto ngata a makasubad kenka?** How will we ever be able to repay you? How can we make it up to you? [Knk. *ugáli*, Png. *bales*, Tag. *gantí*]

subákal: *n.* group of *barakílan* at one side of the roof. (*kílo*).

subálit: *n.* reward; answer of a letter; recompense; revenge. **agsubalit, subalitan**. *v.* to reciprocate; repay; answer a letter. **mannubalit.** *v.* to reply. [Tag. *sagót*; *subalit* = but]

Subánon: *n.* ethnic group living along Singdangan Bay and the mountains of Misamis in Mindanao; language of the Subanon people.

subáng: *n.* misunderstanding; heated debate. (*susik*; *tubar*; *baranget*; *apa*) **agsubang, makisubang.** *v.* to quarrel, argue, brawl. **Iti aguppaten a tawen a pangdennada, awan pay nagsubanganda.** In their four years at each other's side, they still had nothing they quarreled over. **Pudno gayam tay kunada a manmano kano ti agiipag a di latta agsubang.** So it's true what they say that few sisters-in-law just don't argue. [Tag. *salungát*]

subásub: **maisubasub.** *v.* to fall prostrate; fall on the face (*daramudom*). [Tag. *subasob*]

subásta: (Sp. *subasta*: auction) *n.* auction. **agsubasta.** *v.* to have an auction; bid. **makisubasta.** *v.* to attend an auction. [Kal. *ipÿak*]

subaybáy: (Tag.) **agsubaybay, subaybayan**. *v.* to do a certain thing regularly; keep tab with, keep up with; to be an avid fan of. **Subaybayak ti damag idiay Malaysia.** I am keeping up with the news in Malaysia.

subbá: see *sebbá*.

subbó: **sumbo.** *v.* to break out (sweat) (*sibo*); issue forth (tears). [Tag. *gitiw*]

subbuál: *n.* shoot (banana, sugarcane, etc.). (*sagibsib*) **agsubbual.** *v.* to grow shoots. [Tag. *siból*]

subbók: *n.* snout (of swine). (*subil*; *subsub*) **subbuken.** *v.* to dig and sniff with a snout. [Tag. *ngusò* (snout)]

subbót: **subbuten.** *v.* to redeem; deliver; save. (*sabrut*; *salakan*) **masubbot.** *v.* to be able to redeem (losses in gambling, etc.) **pannaka-subbot.** *n.* redemption. **agsubbot.** *v.* to give the lose a chance to win back his losses. **pasubbot.** *v.* to demand ransom. [Png. *panundon*, Tag. *tubós*]

súbed: *n.* slowness to learn.

súbeg: **agsubeg.** *v.* to disobey. (*sungit*, *sukir*) **nasubeg.** *a.* disobedient, obstinate, stubborn; wet and difficult to kindle (firewood). [Bon. *tókaw*, Png. *seláng*, Tag. *suwáy*, *labág*]

súbeng: *var.* of *sueng*: disobedience.

soberánia: (Sp. *soberanía*) *n.* sovereignty.

soberáno: (Sp. *soberano*) *a.* sovereign.

sobérbia: (Sp. *soberbia*: self pride) *n.* loquacity, prone to spread bad gossip. **nasoberbia.** *a.* spreading injurious gossip.

subersíbo: (Sp. *suversivo*) *a.* subversive.

súbi: **subisubi**. *n.* beriberi. **agsubisubi.** *v.* to be afflicted with beriberi (*ebbal*). [Tag. *manás*, *panás*]

subí: (Sp.? *subir*: ascend) **agisubi.** *v.* to deposit shells in one's 'house' in *sungka*.

subída: (Sp. *subida*: raise; going up) *n.* boarder of a bus; ceremonies performed at home by a priest in honor of a recently deceased person; ascent, rise; doctor's call; fee for a doctor's visit.

súbil: *n.* snout (*subbok*; *sungo*; *subsub*). [Tag. *ngusò*]

subkár: *n.* repelling taste or character. **sumubkar.** *v.* to resist; oppose. **makasubkar.** *a.* repelling. **Nalipatannan ti makasubkar nga angot.** He forgot the repelling smell.

subkontratísta: (Sp. *subcontratista*) *n.* subcontractor.

sublát: **agsublat, sumublat.** *v.* to take one's turn in doing; borrow money for a short term. **agsusublat.** *v.* to alternate, do by turns (one after another). **ipasublat.** *v.* to lend something. **pasublatan.** *v.* to lend to someone. **sublatan.** *v.* to take the place of (someone's turn). **sublaten.** *v.* to borrow something. **agsinnublat.** *v.* to alternate; take turns. **Ti kukua, pagsusublatan.** Wealth passes from one person to another. **Nagsisinnublatandak nga inarakup dagiti kakabsatko.** My siblings took turns embracing me. [Tag. *halili, palit-palít*]

sublí: **agsubli.** *v.* to return, come back. **agsublisubli.** *v.* to go back and forth. **isubli.** *v.* to return, give back. **maisubli.** *v.* to return; be reset (broken bones). **pagsublian.** *n.* turning point. **sublien.** *v.* to return for, turn back for. **sublian.** *v.* to do again; return to an old habit. **agkarasubli.** *v.* to always return; frequently come back. **panublian.** *n.* reason for returning. **mapasublian.** *v.* to relapse. **agsinnublian.** *v.* to reconcile, return to each other. **pagsinnublianen.** *v.* to make people reconcile with each other. [Bon. *awid*, Ibg. *tóli*, Knk. *taúli*, Png. *pawíl*, Tag. *balík*]

sublimidád: (Sp. *sublimidad*: sublimity) *n.* sublimity.

submaríno: (Eng.) *n.* submarine.

subnád: **nasubnad.** *a.* disobedient. (*sukir*)

subnét: *var.* of supnét: grating; rasping.

súbo: (Tag. also) *n.* amount of food put in the mouth. **subuen.** *v.* to feed. **isubo.** *v.* feed; supply; to pass warp threads through the reed in weaving. **subuan.** *v.* to replace; substitute; take over someone else's responsibility. **naisubo.** *a.* passed through the reed (warp threads). **sumubo.** *v.* to attack; put something in the mouth. **ipasubo.** *v.* to endanger; put in an embarrassing position; force someone to do something. **agpakasubo.** *v.* to be forced to do an activity against one's will. **Dimo kagaten ti ima a mangsubsubo kenka.** Do not bite the hand that feeds you. [Tag. *subò*]

súbok: *n.* weight. (*pannubok*) **subuken.** *v.* to weigh; test; try. **isubok.** *v.* to try (*padas*). **pagsubuken.** *v.* to compare in weight. **pannubok.** *n.* trial; weight; endurance. **agkasubok.** *v.* to be equivalent in weight; agree. **masubukan.** *v.* to be proven otherwise. **subukan.** *v.* iron bar used for shaping the *kalúlot* collar. [Tag. *bigát* (weight); *subok* (try)]

subók: **subuken.** *v.* to turn up the earth with the snout (*subsub*). [Tag. *ngusò* (snout)]

sub-ók: *n.* hole in the nasal septum of beasts of burden (*taldéng*)

sóbol: *n.* kind of mollusk.

súbor: **agkasubor.** *v.* to alternate; be on a friendly footing. **suburan.** *v.* to trade for, barter. **isubor.** *v.* to trade something for; barter. **pagsuburen.** *v.* to compare (in physical attributes) **agsinnubor.** *v.* to argue; debate. [Tag. *hambíng* (compare)]

sobórno: (Sp. *soborno*: bribe) *n.* bribe. (*pasuksok*) **sobornuan.** *v.* to bribe; to add. [Tag. *suhol*]

subúsub: *n. Blumea balsamifera* herb with yellow flowers. **maisubusub.** *v.* to fall face down. [Tag. *subasob*]

subpéna: (Eng.) *n.* subpoena, order to appear in court.

sóbra: (Sp. *sobra*: excess) *n.* leftover; in excess. **agsobra.** *v.* to be in excess. **sobraan.** *v.* to put more that necessary. **sobrado.** *a.* too much, excessive. (*palalo*) **Sobran ti pannakibiangna.** His interference is in excess. [Tag. *labis*]

sóbre: (Sp. *sobre*: envelope) *n.* envelope. **ipasobre.** *v.* to insert in an envelope. **maisobre.** *v.* to be enclosed in an envelope. **sobre-seliado.** *a.* stamped envelope. **sinobre.** *a.* enclosed in an envelope.

sobreadígi: (Sp. *sobre*: on + *adigi*) *n.* guidepost.

sobrekáma: (Sp. *sobrecama*: bedspread) *n.* bedspread.

sobrekárga: (Sp. *sobrecarga*: overload) *n.* overload.

sobrekílo: (Sp. *sobrequilla*: keelson) *n.* rafter in construction. (*ladét*)

sobrenaturál: (Sp. *sobrenatural*: supernatural) *a.* supernatural.

sobrepága: (Sp. *sobrepaga*: overpay) *n.* extra pay.

sobrepelyís: (Sp. *sobrepelliz*: surplice) *n.* surplice, loose, white, knee-length vestment worn by priests.

sobrepuéra: (Sp. *sobre*: on + *fuera*: out) *n.* outside ceiling (ceiling of a balcony).

sobresaído: (Sp. *sobresalido*: outstanding) *n.* one acquitted of a charge in court but still accusable of the same offense if the prosecutor finds new evidence.

sobresaliénte: (Sp.) *a.* excellent, outstanding.

sobretílyis: *var.* of *sobrepelyis*: surplice.

subró: *var.* of *surro*.

subsúb$_1$: *n.* snout; plowshare. **agsubsub.** *v.* to turn up earth with the snout; eat (said of pigs only). **Kasla subsob ti takong ti kaatiddog a misuotna.** His pout is as long as the snout of a sow. [Knk. *ngúlab*, Tag. *ngusò* (snout)]

subsúb$_2$: **sumusubsub.** *n.* kind of rhinoceros beetle. **pannubsub.** *n.* kind of dark brown dung fly.

subsúb$_3$: *n. Blumea balsamifera* plant.

sudák: *n.* instrument used for scraping or prying out substances. **isudak, sudaken.** *v.* to pry, scrape out (coconut meat). (*igad*) **pagsudak.** *n.* instrument used for scraping out (coconut meat, etc.). **nasudak ti rikna.** *exp.* hurt feelings. **Asaenda dagiti barusokda tapno naalalibtak ti panagsudakda.** They sharpened their knifes so they could scrape out the coconut meat faster. **Adda rikna a nangsudak iti puso ken kararuana.** The feeling scraped at his heart and soul. [Tag. *sikwát*]

sud-ák: *var.* of *sudak*: scrape out (coconut meat).

sudál: **agsisinnudal.** *v.* to elbow one another. (*kidag*)

suddúor: **masduor.** *v.* to be agitated; disturbed. (*siddóor*)

súdi: *n.* noble worth; purity; chastity. **nasudi.** *a.* noble, illustrious, famous, well known; brilliant; distinguished. **isudi.** *v.* to assay gold. **susudian.** *n.* Lydian stone, touchstone. [Png. *bantóg*, Tag. *bunyî, lantáy*; Knk. *súdi* = matured fetus]

súdip: *n.* patching in carpentry. **sudipen.** *v.* to patch up, mend, repair (in carpentry). (*údip, sukdíp*)

súdo: *n.* kind of ladle or cup made with a coconut shell. (*pagtáko; buyuboy; sabut; ungot*).

sudór: (Sp. *sudor*: sweat) **agsudor.** *v.* to cure through perspiration; sit on a pail of warm water to soothe the womb (done by women after the *tanggad* period of their childbirth). **suduren.** *v.* to have someone sit on a pail of warm water; to cure someone through perspiration.

sudsúd: *n.* sticks thrown in a brook to drive fish toward the net; dibble used for transplanting rice. **sudsudan.** *v.* to throw *sudsúd* in water; to push sticks through to find snakes, rats, etc; plunge a pole into the hole; dibble.

suék: *n.* nosedive. **agsuek.** *v.* to fall (leaves) in the wind; to flutter down (birds, leaves, etc.);

dive; to go bankrupt; plummet; take a nosedive. **Nagsuek ti ekonomiami.** Our economy plummeted. [Tag. *bulusok*]

Suéko: (Sp. *sueco*: Swedish) *n. a.* Swedish; *n.* Swede. **ag-Sueko.** *v.* to speak Swedish.

suékos: *n.* wooden shoe, clogs. (*kammadang; bakia*) **agsuekos.** *v.* to wear wooden shoes. [Tag. *bakyâ*]

suél: (*obs.*) **susuel.** see *lumbalumbá*.

suélas: (Sp. *suela*: sole) *n.* sole of a shoe. **agpasuelas.** *v.* to have one's shoes soled.

suéldo: (Sp. *sueldo*: salary) *n.* salary, wages, pay. (*kita; tegden; tangdan*) **agsueldo.** *v.* to earn as salary. **suelduan.** *v.* to pay salaries; give out wages to. **susueldo.** see *karimbubuáya*: kind of cactuslike plant. **desueldan.** *a.* salaried. **Saanda a lugi iti panangsusueldoda kaniak.** They are not losing money from paying my salary.

suéldo't-baybay: *n.* species of edible seaweed, *Gracilaria crassa*.

suélo: (Sp. *suelo*: floor) *n.* floor (*datár*). [Tag. *sahíg*]

suélto: (Sp. *suelto*: separate, loose; disconnected) *a.* disconnected; loose; single; separate.

suéng: *abbr.* of *barasuweng*: obstinate; stubborn; not well behaved.

suér: *n.* bronze; brass. **suer a binárut.** *n.* brass wire. **nasuer.** *a.* obstinate; stubborn. [Png. *tansó*, Tag. *tansô* (bronze, brass)]

suéro: (Sp. *suero*: serum) *n.* dextrose; serum. (*asuero*)

suérte: (Sp. *suerte*: luck) *n.* luck (*gasat*). **masuertean.** *v.* to be lucky, fortunate. [Tag. *palad*]

suérto: (Sp. *cierto*) **nasuerto.** sure. **isuerto ti oras.** to fix the time.

suéter: (Eng.) *n.* sweater. **nakasueter.** *a.* wearing a sweater.

súga: *n.* stake, pointed sticks placed in the ground to prevent people or animals from entering. **sugaan.** *v.* to provide with pointed sticks. [Tag. *tulos*]

sugabbá: *n.* disheveled, untidy (hair). **nakasugabba.** *a.* with disheveled, uncombed hair; untidy. **Nakasugabba ken naalunapet ti badona.** Her clothes were disheveled and dank.

sugadór: (Sp. *jugador*: gambler; player) *n.* impulsive gambler. (*mannugal*)

sugakgák: *a.* dilapidated; old, worn out, shabby; rickety; threadbare (*rugák*)

sugál: (Sp. *jugar*: play; gamble) **agsugal.** *v.* to gamble. **makisugal.** *v.* to gamble with someone. **pagsugalan.** *n.* casino. **mannugal.** *n.* gambler. **isugal.** *v.* to gamble one's possessions. **Isugalko kenka ti panagtalekko.** I'm gambling my trust on you. [Kal. *bangking*]

sugaléro: (f. *sugal*) *n.* gambler.

sugápa: (Tag. also) *n.* dope addict; drug abuser; junkie.

sugargár: *a.* unkempt (hair); bristling. **nasugargar**. *a.* erect, bristling (hair) (*seggar, sigargar*). **agsugargar**. *v.* to bristle (uncombed hair).

sugásug: **sugasugen**. *v.* to pump water from a well; to thrust in and out of a tube.

súgat: *n.* wound. (*dunor*) **masugat**. *v.* to be wounded. **makasugat**. *v.* to be stinging, wound. **sugaten**. (*obs.*) *v.* to call by its specified name. **isugat**. *v.* to inflict a wound with. **Ti sugat a gapuanan ti ayat ti kasam-itan a saem.** The wound of love is the sweetest pain. [Ibg. *bigag*, Ifg. *nag-od*, Ivt. *rawaq*, Png. *sugát*, Kpm., Tag. *sugat*]

súgay: *n.* bamboo fish trap. (*palayáw*)

Sugbuánon: (Cebuano) *n.* Cebuano, native of Cebu; language of the Cebuano people.

sugél: *n.* sleepiness. **agsugel**. *v.* to nod while dozing off (*tuglep*). **isugel**. *v.* to knock the face of somebody against the ground; to shake or rub the head of someone else against a wall; squeeze a cigarette butt out. [Tag. *idlíp*]

suggóng: **nasuggong**. *a.* charming, graceful. (children)

sugígi: *n.* toothbrush. **agsugigi**. *v.* to clean the teeth (*sipilio*). **isugigi**. *v.* to sweep with the tip of a broom; insist. [Png. *sugígi*]

sugkár: **makasugkar**. *v.* to cause to vomit because of bad taste or manners; to feel nauseous after having drunk too much alcohol.

sugkí: **napasugkian**. *a.* sulked, withdrawn in disgust (*sugnud*); hurt emotionally.

sugkíl: *n.* cultivating plants.

sugkít: **maisugkit**. *v.* to stumble. **sugkiten**. *v.* to till, cultivate (soil). [Tag. *linâng* (cultivate)]

sugmék: **maisugmek**. *v.* to nod when dozing. (*sugél*; *tuglep*) **agsusugmek**. *v.* to doze off.

sugmók: **masugmok**. *v.* to find oneself in a predicament (*súmok*).

sugnád: **agsugnad**. *v.* to resist; refuse. **nasugnad**. *a.* tough, coarse (timber); reluctant.

sugnét: *var.* of *supnét*: harsh, rough; grating, scraping.

sugnó: **sugsugno**. *n.* flattery. **sugsugnuen**. *v.* to flatter (*ay-aywen*). **Mabayag a sugsugnuen santo masukdal ti ayatna.** He will flatter her for a long time and then capture her love. [Tag. *himok*]

sugnúd: **agpasugnud**. *v.* to withdraw in disgust; sulk.

súgod: *n.* reed of a loom; comb with a row of thick teeth on both sides; lice comb. **sugudsugod**. *n.* fruit of the *libás*. (*parogpárog*). **suguden**. *v.* to comb nits with a lice comb;

(*fig.*) to scrutinize something very carefully. [Kal. *sugud*, Tag. *suyod*; *sugod* = sudden advance, rush, attack]

sug-óp: **sug-upen**. *v.* to sew together; join; interlock (*tug-óp*, *silpo*). [Tag. *sugpóng*]

súgot₁: **sugutan**. *v.* to fill up (*punno*). [Tag. *punô*]

súgot₂: *n.* tobacco harvesting; seedlings used for replacing decaying rice. **sugutan**. *v.* to remove dead rice plants and replace them with new seedlings.

sugpél: *n.* kind of small gastropodous mollusk. **nasugpel**. *a.* blunt, dull. **landók a sugpél**. *n.* surgical probe. [Tag. *puról*]

sugpét₁: **nasugpet**. *a.* sour, tart; not ripe (said of bananas). **nasugpet nga ayat**. *n.* lost love, love affair that turns sour. **sumugpet**. *v.* to turn sour. [Tag. *paklá* (tart)]

sugpét₂: **nasugpet**. *a.* with bluish circle under lower eyelid. **Nasugpeten dagiti matam.** Your eyes are already tired looking.

sugpón: *n.* partnership; share; stock. **agsugpon**. *v.* to associate, form a company; to put capital together. **isugpon**. *v.* to put capital toward a business, add to a mutual investment. **kasugpon**. *n.* junior partner as in farming. **makikasugpon**. *v.* to work as a tenant. **Inkeddengna nga agsugponda iti bangonen a panganan.** He decided that they would form a partnership in putting up a restaurant. **Kayatmi nga isugpon ti dadduma a kuartatayo iti negosiona.** We would like to put some of our money toward his business.

sugsóg: *n.* provocation. (*aliug*) (*obs.*) *n.* crossing (meeting and passing) **sugsugan**. *v.* to provoke; urge. **sugsugen**. *v.* to burn (what is left after the wind turns). **mannugsog**. *n.* inciter, agitator, provoker. **Kagurak dagiti dadakkelko iti panangisugsugda kenkuana.** I am angry with my parents for provoking her. [Tag. *sulsól*]

suherír: (Sp. *sugerir*: suggest) **isuherir**. *v.* to suggest. (*singasing*)

suhéto: (Sp. *sujeto*: subject) *n.* subject, topic.

su-í: **agsu-i**. *v.* to get angry. (*pungtot*)

suíd: (*obs.*) **masuid**. *v.* to be robbed (said of a guard).

suíki: *n.* fish basket.

súil: *n.* kind of hoe. **suilen**. *v.* to pry open; lever. [Tag. *sikwát*]

suír: *var.* of *suil*: hoe.

suisídio: (Sp. *suicidio*: suicide) *n.* suicide.

súit: *n.* small cup.

suítik: (Pil.) *n.* cheat; rascal. **agsuitik**. *v.* to cheat. (*kusit*; *saur*) **suitiken**. *v.* to deceive someone.

suká: *n.* vinegar. **agsuka**. *v.* to ferment. **mannuká**. *n.* vinegar fly. **sukasuka**. *n.* adipose tissue at end of rumen of cows. **sukaen**. *v.* to make into vinegar. **sukaan**. *v.* to season with vinegar. **suka't Tagalog**. *n.* white coconut vinegar (Ilocano vinegar is usually made of sugarcane and is brown). [Ibg. *silám*, Ivt. *silam*, Knk. *tengbá* (camote vinegar), Kpm. *aslam*, Png. *tuká*, Tag. *sukà*, Tag. *suka* = vomit]

sukáb: see *lukáb*: to open from the bottom; open from below.

sukáin: **masukainan**. *v.* to be found out, discovered. **sukainan**. *v.* to search; scrutinize; scan; explore. [Tag. *halungkát*]

súkal: *n.* antidote. **sukalen**. *v.* to restrain, hold back; prevent; to take an antidote for poisoning. **masukal**. *v.* to hold back; keep a secret. **Umínomka manen tapno sukalenna ti sakit ti ulom**. Drink again to relieve your headache. [Tag. *sukal* = rubbish, flotsam; thicket]

sukál: **sukalan**. *v.* to detect; examine; inspect; investigate; find out. **sukalen**. *v.* to offset the wrath of spirits by a certain ritual (food offering, praying, etc.). **masukalan**. *v.* to be discovered; caught in the act.

súkat: *n.* measure (*rukód*); size, measurement. **sukaten**. *v.* to measure. **agpasukat**. *v.* to have one's measurements taken. [Kal. *isong*, Png. *tákal*, Tag. *sukat*]

sukát: *n.* change; substitute; replacement. **sukatan**. *v.* to change; succeed; relieve; replace, take the place of; remove. **agsukat**. *v.* to change one's clothes; change. **agpasukat**. *v.* to get change (break a large bill into smaller denominations); to get dressed. **isukat**. *v.* to exchange. **sumukat**. *v.* to succeed, fill a vacancy in an office. **masukansukat**. *v.* always changing (times, etc.). **mangsukat**. *n.* heir; successor. **pagsinnukaten**. *n.* to change places with one another. **pagpasukatan**. *n.* money changer. **Agsukatkayon ta adda papanantayo**. Get dressed because we are going somewhere. **Nasukansukat met ti kaatagna iti agpatnag**. Her bed partners continually change all night. [Ibg. *lili*, *táli*, Ifg. *hannot*, Ivt. *manádi*, Kal. *salot*, Kpm. *balas*, Png. *salát*, Tag. *palít* (exchange), *bíhis* (dress)]

súkaw: *n.* kind of water lily; kind of poisonous snake. **marasinukaw, marasinukawan**. *n.* becoming sour (*bási*, etc.); *n.* native drink made from sugarcane.

sukáy₁: **sukayan**. *v.* to search, explore, inspect (for lice, etc.); overturn (when looking for something). **masukayan**. *v.* to be discovered, found out, detected (*duktal*) [Tag. *tuklás* (discover)]

sukáy₂: **sukayen**. *v.* to loosen, make less dense (earth, etc.); till. (*sukil, sugkil, rukáy*) **Mayatak a sukayenyo ti daga ngem rumbeng nga ag-**

buiskayo iti apagkatlo nga apitenyo a nateng. I am happy that you will till the land, but you must pay a tax with one-third of your vegetable harvest. [Tag. *lináng* (farm soil)]

sukdál: *n.* long pole with a hook at one end used to grasp objects out of reach. **sukdalen**. *v.* to grasp high fruits with a pole. [Kpm. *sundul*, *sungkit*, Tag. *sungkít*]

sukdáw: *n.* distaff.

sukdíp: *n.* thatch used to mend a leaking roof. **sukdipan**. *v.* to patch up, mend (roof).

súki: (Hok. *cù k^{h}èq*: important customer) *n.* frequent, faithful customer. [Tag. *sukì*]

sukíb₁: **sumukib**. *v.* to seek cover. **isukib**. *v.* to put under the cover. **Pinasukibanna a kinita ti maestra**. He stole a glance at the teacher.

sukíb₂: **pasukib**. *n.* bribe. (*pasoksok*) **pasukiban**. *v.* to bribe. [Tag. *suhol*]

sukíl: **sukilen**. *v.* to wedge (open an oyster); remove a nail with a screwdriver as a wedge; loosen the earth; dig; cultivate. **Dida met makuna nga awan a pulos maitultulongko kadakuada ta masukilko met amin a mulada a nateng iti likud ti balayda**. They can't think that I don't help them at all because I dug all their vegetables in the back of their house.

sukímat: *n.* research; investigation. (*sukisok*) **sukimaten**. *v.* to examine thoroughly; search; explore; get to the bottom of; scan. **Sukimatem ti gasatmo iti daga a nakayanakam**. Try your luck in the place of your birth. [Knk. *sukísik*, Tag. *saliksík*]

súkir: **agsukir**. *v.* to disobey. (*sangar*) **nasukir**. *a.* stubborn; disobedient. **isukir**. (*reg.*) *v.* to insist; persist. [Tag. *suwaíl*]

sukísok: **sukisuken**. *v.* to examine, investigate, search. (*sukimat*) **managsukisok**. *a.* inquisitive; investigative. **Bayat ti kaaddam dita, agsukisokka no mabalin a sakupentayo ti daga**. While you are there, investigate whether we can take over the land. [Knk. *sukísik*, Tag. *saliksík*]

súkit: *n.* pole with hook used to pick fruits. **agsukit**. *n.* kind of children's game. **mannukit**. *n.* mole (burrowing animal). **sukiten**. *v.* to lift, raise; prick; get something out of a crack by used of a wedge, pry out. [Tag. *sungkít*]

suk-ít: **sinuk-it**. *n.* variety of awned *diket* rice.

sukkít: **sukkiten**. *v.* to loosen (the soil). [Tag. *lináng*]

suklád: *n.* spade; shovel (*pala*); flat horn of a cow. **sukladen**. *v.* to shovel out. [Tag. *palà* (Sp.)]

sukláy: **suklayen**. *v.* to reach with a stick; stir rice in mortar.

sukmón: *n.* wine. (*arak*) **agpasukmon**. *v.* to sell liquors in detail. **sumukmon**. *v.* to buy liquors in detail; drink wine at the local store. **pagpasukmonan.** *n.* liquor store. **Dumawat ti lakay iti isukmonna.** The old man is asking for liquor money. [Bon. *sukmon* = buy rice]

suknál: sumuknal. *v.* to visit. (*sarungkar*) **agsuknal.** *v.* to visit church; go on a pilgrimage, pay homage to. **suknalan.** *v.* pay a visit to. [Tag. *dalaw*]

suknét: see *supnét*: rasping; grating; rough; scraping.

suknób: *n.* trench, dugout covered with weeds for hiding.

suknór: sumuknor. *v.* to enter the mouth of a river (tide); to affect deeply. **sumuknor iti ulona.** to enter one's mind; affect one's thoughts. **sumuknor iti agong.** to penetrate the nose (smell). **Adda pay laeng ti sumuknor iti pus-ongmo?** Do you still feel something in your abdomen? **Mariknana ti idadayas ti angin-bakir a nangsuknor iti naullom a salimuot ti baybay.** He felt the cleansing of the forest air that entered the indoor humidity of the house. [Tag. *timò*]

súko₁: *n.* unit of weight equivalent to 316.36 grams.

súko₂: (Tag. also) *n.* surrender. **sumuko.** *v.* to surrender. **pasukuen.** *v.* to convince a fugitive to surrender; subjugate. **mamasuko.** *v.* to let someone surrender. [Png. *suko*, Tag. *sukò*]

súkob: (Tag. also) **sumukob.** *v.* to seek protection, shield oneself from; live together under one roof. **agkasukob.** *v.* to be related by blood or alliance. **kasukob.** *n.* relative. [Tag. *sukob* (shelter)]

sukóg: *n.* shape; arch of shoes; frame of a roof; pattern; mold; *a.* arched. **agsukog.** *v.* to take shape, have the form or shape of. **pagsukogán.** *n.* mold; arch mold of a window or doorway. **isukog.** *v.* to pour into a mold. **sukogan.** *n.* mold. **agkasukog.** *v.* to be of a similar shape, have the same form. **pakasukogan.** *n.* the finished form. **Aganninaw ti sukog ti pammagina ta naingpis ti badona.** The form of his body was reflected due to his thin clothing. [Tag. *hugis, hulmá*]

súkon: *n.* invitation to gamble. **sukunen.** *v.* to convene, summon, meet, assemble; invite; fetch. **Idi agturposkami, inkarik a sukonek tapno agkasarkami.** When we graduate, I promise to fetch her so we can get married. [Tag. *kaón* (fetch)]

súkong: nasukong. *a.* deep; concave (plates). [Tag. *lukóng*]

sokóro: (Sp. *socorro*: help) *n.* succor, help, aid. (*tulong*)

sukót: *n.* double flowers. **agsukot.** *v.* to be superimposed on each other (bowls, plates); to be alternately arranged. **agsusukot.** *v.* saddled; with too many chores. **suksukot.** *n.* kind of vine. **Agsusukot dagiti kulibangbang nga umarak kenkuana.** The butterflies are coming to him one on top of the other. **Ita, agsusukot ti parikutko.** Now I am saddled with many troubles.

sukrób: *n.* sip. **sukruben.** *v.* to sip liquids (*igup, sul-oy, sur-ob*).

sukrót: (*obs.*) **sukroten.** *v.* to wound upward; to approach shyly (animals asking for food).

suksók: isuksok. *v.* to hide; conceal (in one's lap). **sumuksok.** *v.* to hide; take refuge. **suksukan.** *v.* to instigate; bribe. **pasuksok.** *n.* bribe. **nasuksok.** *a.* hidden, concealed. [Tag. *suhol* (bribe)]

suktó: *a.* detached, severed; dismantled, taken apart. **suktuen.** *v.* to separate, sever; dismantle; take apart. **susuktuen.** *n.* kind of small mollusk. **Sinuktona ti balunet ti tawa.** He took off the bar of the window. **Linislisko ti pantalonko ken sinuktok ti sapatosko.** I rolled up my pants and took off my shoes. [Tag. *hugot*]

sol: (Sp. *sol*: sun) *n.* the sun in a *lunario* calendar; string of a banjo; sol (music).

sulá: *n.* first sugarcane to be pressed. **agsula.** *v.* to harvest for the first time. **sulaan.** *v.* to sample the first fruits of the harvest.

súlam: agsulam. *v.* to embroider with untwisted silk. **masulam.** *v.* to be blinded by a bright light. [Tag. *silaw* (dazzle by bright light)]

solaménte: (Sp. *solamente*: only) *adv.* only (*laeng*). [Tag. *lamang*]

suláng: *var.* of *suléng*: very bright, blinding. **makasulang.** *a.* glaring, blinding (light). **Makasulang ta kalbo nga ulom!** Your bald head is blinding! [Tag. *silaw*]

suláp: *n.* sliver or splinter of wood partly detached. (*tikap*) **masulap.** *v.* to be chipped; to be splintered. [Tag. *tatal*]

solápa: (Sp. *solapa*: flap) *n.* lapel.

solár: (Sp. *solar*: lawn) *n.* lot; lawn; yard.

sólas: (Sp. *solas*: alone) *a.* alone, solo. (*agmaymaysa*; *bugbugtong*) **agsolsolas.** *v.* to live alone. **solasen.** *v.* to do something alone.

solbár: (Eng.) **solbaren.** *v.* to solve. [Tag. *lutás*]

solbér: (Sp. *solver*) **solberen.** *v.* to solve.

solbatána: *n.* blowgun; small improvised blowguns are called *sultik*.

sulbód: *n.* second shoot after the first shoot has been cut. **agsulbod.** *v.* to grow shoots (bananas, palay). **kassulbod.** *n.* plant that has just grown a second shoot. **panagsusulbod.** *n.* spring (season). [Tag. *usbóng*]

sulbóg: *n.* shooting core of the stalk of a sugarcane; temptation. **sulbogen.** *v.* to seduce; entice; tempt. (*sulisog*) **sulbogero.** *n.* one who seduces or tempts. **Dida kuma agriri no dimo sinulbogan ida.** They should not have breathed a word if you didn't tempt them. [Tag. *sulsól* (entice)]

sulbóng₁: *n.* fitting tube. **isulbong.** *v.* to fit into a hole, insert in a tube; insert in a long hole. **naisulbong.** *a.* joined (*silpo*); inserted. **Insulbongna ti tulbek iti seradura.** He inserted the key in the lock.

sulbóng₂: *a.* two-colored. **sulbóngan.** *a.* two-colored. **agisulbong.** *v.* to tell on someone without his knowledge.

sulbót₁: sulsulbot. *n.* kind of larva resembling the *ubet-úbet*.

sulbót₂: sumulbot. *v.* to appear from a hiding place or hole. [Tag. *sulpót*]

soldádo: (Sp. *soldado*: soldier) *n.* soldier. (*búyot*) **agsoldado.** *v.* to be a soldier. [Kal. *suÿchachu*, Png. *sondálo*, Tag. *sundalo*]

soldadór: (Sp. *soldador*: soldering rod) *n.* soldering rod, soldering iron.

soldadúra: (Sp. *soldadura*: soldering) *n.* soldering.

soldákes: [*soldado* + *dakes*] (*coll.*) *n.* training soldier.

suldít: *n.* poker type gambling game. **makisuldit.** *v.* to participate in a game of *suldit*.

suldóng: isuldong. *v.* to connect; join. (*silpo*)

soledád: (Sp. *soledad*) *n.* solitude.

sulék: masulek. *v.* to be hit on the eyes; to be pricked in the eyes. (*payap*) **suleken.** *v.* to poke the eyes with a pointed object. **Nasulek dagiti matana iti nakitana.** *exp.* He was hurt by what he saw (*lit*: his eyes were pricked by what he saw). [Tag. *sundót*]

solémne: (Sp. *solemne*: solemn) *a.* solemn.

suléng: nasuleng. *a.* half blind. **masuleng.** *v.* to be blinded by bright light. **makasuleng a lawag.** *n.* blinding light (*sirap*; *sulam*). [Tag. *silaw*]

soléras: (Sp. *soleras*: cross beam) *n.* floor joist (*dellég*). [Kal. *sulilas, pisipis*, Tag. *suliras*]

solféo: (Sp. *solfeo*: solfa) *n.* musicology, the study of reading notes in music; written music. **agsolfeo.** *v.* to read music.

súli: *n.* corner; angle. **pasuli.** *n.* angle brace. **panuli.** *n.* corner post. **maipaspasuli.** *v.* to be neglected. **naipasuli.** *a.* cornered. **sinnulisuli.** *n.* girl's game. **ipasuli.** *v.* to place in the corner. **Sadino a suli ti lubong ti naggapuam?** From what corner of the world did you come from? [Kal. *igid, pat-ing*, Knk. *sagúpit*, Png. *sokóng*, Tag. *sulok*]

súlid: *n.* thread. (*sinulid*; *panait*)

sólido: (Sp. *sólido*: solid) *a.* solid.

sulinék: sulsulinek. *n.* remote place. (*adayo*)

sulíras: (Sp. *solera*: crossbeam) *n.* floor joist (*delleg*). [Tag. *suleras*]

solisitár: (Sp. *solicitar*) **solisitaren.** *v.* to solicit.

sulísog: *n.* temptation. **sulisugen.** *v.* to tempt, attract; seduce, lure. **masulisog.** *v.* to be tempted, seduced, attracted. **makasulisog.** *a.* tempting, seductive. **pannakasulisog.** *n.* temptation (*sulbog*). **Manulsulisog ti lam-ek iti dayta a rabii.** The coolness of that night was enticing. [Tag. *tuksó*]

súlit₁: *n.* substitute; replacement. **sulitan.** *v.* to substitute, replace. **suliten.** *v.* to win back one's losses in gambling, regain what one has lost. [Tag. *palít*]

súlit₂: sinulit. *n.* thread (*sinulid*). [Tag. *sinulit*]

sulít: *n.* impatience. **nasulit.** *a.* complicated, difficult, hard; lacking in persistency. **suliten.** *v.* to consider an easy job hard. **masulit.** *v.* to be adamant about doing something difficult. [Tag. *hirap*]

solitária: (Sp. *solitaria*: tapeworm) *n.* tapeworm.

solitário: (Sp. *solitario*: solitary) *a.* solitary; *n.* solitaire.

sullát: *n.* plug. (*tapón*) **sullatan.** *v.* to plug, clog, obstruct. **apagsullat.** *a.* barely passing (in a test); just enough. **Kasla agsullat ti karabukobna tunggal gandatenna nga ibaga.** His throat seems to clog every time he plans to tell it (he is unable to tell it). [Knk. *supút*, Png. *polét*, Tag. *pasak*]

sullogát: *n.* kind of fish.

sulluóp: sulluopán. *v.* to join, fit together; set; plug up; dovetail; plug up. **Sakbay nga insulluopna manen ti earphone iti lapayagna, tinupraannak.** Before she set the earphone on her ear again, she spit at me. [Tag. *tugmâ*]

sulnít: *n.* replacement; payment in kind. **sulnitan.** *v.* to replace; pay in kind; make amends, make up for something. **Inkarina a paragsakennak ket sulnitanna ti nataktakneng pay nga ayat.** He promised to make me happy and to make amends with more comforting love. [Tag. *palít*]

sulnót: sulnóten. *v.* to tug at; strain at; draw out (breath). **nasulnot ti anges.** breathless. **Kasla masulnot ti riknana.** It seemed something was tugging at his feelings. **Kasla uggot ti saba a kassulnot.** He is (clean and fresh) like freshly dug banana tops. [Tag. *hugot*]

sólo: (Sp.) *a.* single, solo; only; pure, unadulterated; alone. **masolo.** *v.* to be able to do on one's own; to handle alone. (*mabukodan*)

soloista. *n.* soloist. **solsolona.** only child.
agsolo. *v.* to do alone; sing a solo.
sul-ób: *var.* of *sul-óy:* slurp, sip.
súlok: sulukan. *n.* rafter (connecting the *dógo*, corner post, with the ridgepole; hip rafter. **agpaspasulok.** *v.* to be arrogant; excessively proud.
solomílio: (Sp. *solomillo:* sirloin) *n.* loin, sirloin.
súlong: *n.* boxing match; fist blow. **sulongen.** *v.* to box; strike; slap. **sumulong.** *v.* to depart, set out on a trip; attack, strike. **agsinnulong.** *v.* to box with each other. [Tag. *suntók; sulong* = turn in a game; forward motion; installment]
súlot: (*obs.*) *n.* kind of ring used as a souvenir.
sulót: suluten. *v.* to do in an underhanded manner. [Tag. *sulot*]
sul-ót: (*reg.*) *a.* deaf (*tuleng*). [Tag. *bingí*]
sul-óy: sul-óyen. *v.* to sip; inhale (slippery substances). **sulsul-oyen.** *v.* to appease; calm; pacify. **mapaspasul-oy.** *v.* to inhale (in excitement). **mapasul-oy-a-mapataliaw.** (*exp.*) *a.* causing one to take a deep breath and turn around, a turn on. [Png. *ilóp,* Tag. *higop*]
sulpáp: *a.* with a flat nose (*pappap; lugpap*). [Tag. *pangó*]
sulpáto: (Sp. *sulfato:* sulfate) *n.* sulfate.
sulpáy: *a.* paralyzed in one or both hands.
sulpéng: *a.* clumsy; awkward; silly; stubborn; obstinate. **agsulpeng.** *v.* to be slow; sluggard; obstinate (*sukir*). **kinasulpeng.** *n.* disobedience, insolence; obstinacy. [Tag. *suwaíl*]
sulpéo: *var.* of *solfeo:* written music notes.
sulsól₁: agsulsol. *v.* to pull one's ears crossing the arms; pound. **sulsulan.** *v.* to kindle, ignite; incite. **sulsulen.** *v.* to pull the ears of; to shell rice or beans. **masulsol.** *v.* to be flattened out (nails, etc.). [Tag. *himay* (shelling of grains)]
sulsól₂: sulsolan. *v.* to incite. **masulsulan.** *v.* to be incited, inflamed. [Tag. *sulsól*]
soltáda: (Sp. *soltada:* release) *n.* round in a cockfight. (*pallot*) **soltador.** *n.* cockfighter.
sultág: pasultagen. *v.* to insist, urge; force. (*pilit*)
sulták: sultaken. *v.* to kill. (*patayen*)
sultán: (Sp. *sultán:* sultan) *n.* sultan, ruler of an Islamic country.
soltár: (Sp. *soltar:* release) **nasoltaran.** *a.* released (prisoner).
soltéro: (Sp. *soltero:* single) *a.* single, unmarried. (*baro, balasang*)
sultí: *n.* thick yellow and green tobacco leaves unable to be used for commercial purposes. (*limmalat a bulong*)
sultíp: *n.* kind of small snake; whistle. **agsultip.** *v.* to whistle (*pito, sagawisiw; silbato*). **sultipan.** *v.* to whistle at. [Knk. *sultíp,* Tag. *pito*]
sultóp: sultupen. *v.* to suck. **nasultop.** *a.* sucked. **Nasultop ti bisukolen.** The snails are already

sucked out (said to someone who has done too much reading). [Tag. *ut-ót*]
súma₁: (Sp. *suma:* sum) *n.* sum. **sumaen.** *v.* to sum up, total, add up.
súma₂: *n.* antidote; *Anamirta cocculus* antidote for snake bites. **agpasuma.** *v.* to get treated with an antidote. **mannuma.** *n.* antidote specialist, maker of antidotes. **sumaen.** *v.* to counteract with an antidote; foretell; obstruct; resist; hinder; withstand; prevent.
sumagCV-: Prefix used to form indefinite numbers. **sumagmamanó.** *a.* a few, some; several; *interrog.* about how many? **sumaggatlo a balay.** some three houses. **Sumagpipito pay nga addang ti nagbaetanda.** There are still about seven steps between them. [Tag. *mga*]
súmag: *n.* joint (meeting place of two boards, bamboos, etc.). **agsumag.** *v.* to unite end to end. **isumag.** *v.* to join, connect. [Tag. *sugpóng*]
sumagmamanó: *adv.* some; *interrog.* of indefinite numbers, about how many? **Nagkinnaawatankami kalpasan ti sumagmamano nga aldaw.** We understood each other after a few days. [Tag. *mga ilán*]
sumalasó: [*isu met laeng nga isu*] *exp.* it's just the same.
súman: *n.* native rice cake made with *díket* and *gettá.* **sinúman ípus.** *n.* kind of soft rice pudding rolled up in a cone. **sinúman latík.** *n.* rice pudding in the form of a flat cone. [Png., Tag. *suman*]
súmang: *n.* antidote (*suma*); ritual that counteracts evil spirits. **sumangen.** *v.* to cure someone supernaturally sick by performing a certain rite. [Knk. *súmang* = medicine]
sumangka-: *pref.* used to form additional or conditional imperative: still more. **sumangkapintas.** *a.* more beautiful than. **No tabbed ti anakko, sumangkatabbed ti anakmo.** If my child is stupid, your child is even more stupid.
sumár: (Eng.) **sumaren.** *v.* to sum things up. **mannumar.** *n.* fortune-teller. (*mammadles*) **agpasumar.** *v.* to go to a fortune-teller.
sumariá: (Sp. *sumaria:* summary; indictment) *n.* court session. **sumariaen.** *v.* to question; interrogate.
sumbáboy: *n.* species of clam with a heart-shaped shell.
sumbáliw: agpasumbaliw. *v.* to diversify. **ipasumbaliw.** *v.* to diversify, vary.
sumbángir: agsumbangir. *v.* to be on both sides or on either side. **pagsumbangiren.** *v.* to place on both sides. **isumbangir.** *v.* to place on the other side. **agsinnumbangir.** *v.* to be on both sides of each other. **Makakayaw ti agsum-**

bangir a kallidna. His dimples on both cheeks are charming. [Knk. *mentinupák*, Tag. *magkabilâ*]

sumbát: *var.* of *sungbat*: answer.

sumbó: (f. *subbo*) *v.* to issue forth (tears).

sómbra: (Sp. *sombra*: shade) *n.* shade or shading (used in painting). (*linong*)

sombréro: (Sp. *sombrero*: hat) *n.* hat. **No agsombrero ti lalaki, lalaki manen.** When a man dons a hat, he's a man again (a moral fall doesn't hurt a man). (*kalugong*)

sumbró: *var.* of *sumro*.

sumdí: sumdian. *v.* to stuff, fill up. [Tag. *saksák*]

sumél: isumel. *v.* to cram, stuff. (*selsel, pelpel*)

sumiág: *v.* to do fast; do quickly.

sumgá: (f. *segga*) *v.* to anxiously await. **Matdaak a sumsumga iti idadatengna.** I just stayed, anxiously awaiting his arrival.

sumgár: (f. *seggar*) *v.* to stand on end; bristle.

sumgiáb: (f. *seggiab*) *v.* to be provoked; to flare up; ignite. **sumgiab ti rikna.** *v.* to flare up (emotions).

sumkád: (f. *sekkad*) *v.* to prop; resist, make a stand against; set feet firmly on the ground.

sumkén: (f. *sekken*) *v.* to affect; return again. **Simken ti danagna.** His worries came back.

sumkíl: (f. *sikkil*) *v.* to harden, stiffen; toughen. [Tag. *tigás*]

sumléng: *v.* to get hot inside the body; to have convulsions due to the heat.

sumlép: (f. *sellep*) *v.* to absorb moisture; become drenched. [Tag. *babad*]

sumnék: (f. *sennek*) *v.* to move; penetrate; affect; touch.

sumnét: *var.* of *supnet*.

sumngát: (f. *sengngat*) *v.* to stand between; go between; intervene; interpose; interrupt. [Tag. *singit*]

sumngáw: (f. *sengngaw*) *v.* to emit, breathe out; evaporate; appear unexpectedly; leak out. **Nakapsut a saibbek ti simngaw iti karabukobna.** A weak sigh was emitted from his throat. [Tag. *litáw*]

sumngáy: (f. *sengngáy*) *v.* to be born; originate; issue forth. [Tag. *silang*]

súmok: *n.* accidental meeting; direction. **masumok.** *v.* to find oneself in a certain position or predicament (*sugmok*). **Sipud pay idi 1976 a pannakasumokko nga agbasa iti** *Bannawag.* Ever since 1976, I found myself reading *Bannawag.* **Nasumoken iti droga.** He ended up taking drugs. [Tag. *lulóng*]

súmon: nasumonsumon. *a.* entangled, intertwined; complicated. **sumon-sumonen.** *v.* to gather in a disarray. **sumonsumon.** *n.* kind of thin, rough, edible seaweed.

sumúsum: *a.* fragrant, sweet smelling; smell of the exhalations of the soil after the rain. (*sayamósom*)

sumpáat: (f. *seppaat*) *v.* to penetrate; to prick the skin; happen in a flash.

sumpég: (f. *seppeg*) *v.* to swoop down and pounce upon prey.

sumpít: (Tag. also) *n.* injection; syringe; enema; blowgun; small glass used by *erbularios* to draw out venom from snakebite victims. **agsumpit.** *v.* to use a syringe; play with a syringe. **sumpiten.** *v.* to hit with a popgun; to draw out poisoned blood from a snakebite victim.

sumpók: (f. *seppok*) *n.* hiding in the forest from the authorities; uneasy feeling. *v.* enter a crowd; enter the bushes; go through to; **sumpókan.** *v.* to place where one enters the bushes. **Nagpakanawan iti kalsada a sumpok iti kabalbalayan.** He turned right at the street that led to the houses.

sumrá: sumraen. *v.* to contradict; counteract.

sumrék: (f. *serrek*) *v.* to enter.

sumriá: agsumria. *v.* to bother; disturb.

sumriám: sumriam. *v.* to flare up (in anger); warm up (heat); bristle (hair). **Simriam ti bara ti agmatuon iti rupam.** The noon heat warmed your face. **Sumsumriam dagiti dutdotko.** My body hair flared up. **Sumrumriam dagiti matana iti pungtotna.** His eyes flared up in anger.

sumró: (f. *surró*) *v.* to have a fit of anger or sickness.

sumyág: see *sumiag*.

sóna: (Sp. *zona*: zone) *n.* zone. (*sákup, las-úd*)

sonákas: (Sp. *sonaja*: timbre; jingle) *n.* timbrel, tambourine.

sonambulísmo: (Sp. *sonambulismo*: sleepwalking) *n.* walking in one's sleep.

sonámbulo: (Sp. *sonámbulo*: sleepwalker) *n.* sleepwalker.

súnay: *n.* top; peg; cross; spindle. **agsunay.** *v.* to spin a top. (*kampuso*; *trumpo*) **pasunayen.** *v.* to keep on the go; deceive with false promises. **sunayen.** *v.* to twist yarn with a *súnay.* **sunaysunay.** *n.* edible innermost part of the banana cluster. [Tag. *linláng* (deceive); Knk. *súnay* = labor pains]

sundá: (Sp. *sonda*: probe) *n.* probing instrument; catheter. **pagsunda.** *n.* instrument used for probing. **agsunda.** *v.* to probe (the ground with a tube to search for water, etc.); insert a catheter.

súndo: *n.* breech child, baby born feet or hands first (*suni*). [Png. *suní*, Tag. *suhî*]

súndo: (Tag.) **agsundo, sunduen.** *v.* to pick up someone.

sunél: isunel. *v.* to squeeze a cigarette butt in the ashtray; to stab burning firewood into ashes.

sunét: *n.* small parts of rice husk that remain with the kernel after pounding.

sonéta: (Sp. *soneta*) *n.* sonnet, love poem.

súni: *a.* in the opposite direction, contrary; crazy; breech baby. **sunian.** *v.* to do the opposite way; invert. **agminamasuni.** *n.* kind of play talking in which the syllables are inverted (*baliktád*). [Png. *sunî*, Tag. *suhî* (breech baby); Knk. *súni* = turn over; upside down]

sunnók: see *sunnóp*: prefer; distinguish.

sunnóp: sunnupen. *v.* to prefer; distinguish; make separate, distinct, set apart. **masnop.** *v.* to be preferred; distinguished; apart from others. **Masmasnop ti tultulonganna.** He only helps the ones he likes (the chosen few). [Tag. *tangi*]

súno: *n.* representative; substitute; successor. (*sandi*) **sumuno.** *v.* to succeed; follow; substitute. **sunuan.** *v.* to succeed; replace; substitute for; relieve; remove; supply. **isuno.** *v.* to exchange; replace with a substitute. [Tag. *sunod* (follow); *sunò* = share a ride]

sunód: *n.* next person (in line). **agsusunod.** *v.* to stand in a row; walk behind; retreat. **sunodsunod.** *a.* one after the other (in a row). [Tag. *sunód* (next; follow)]

súnog: sunugen. *v.* to take the honeycombs away from the beehives by smoking out the bees. **agsunog.** *v.* to smoke out bees from their honeycombs. [Tag. *sunog* = fire]

súnot: sunutan. *v.* to repeat, do again. (*dubli*; *dupag*; *ulit*; *surnad*) **masunutan.** *v.* to happen again. **Diakon nasunotan ti nagpasiar iti balayda.** I didn't pass by their house again.

sunsíki: *n.* iron bar used by smiths for flattening.

sunsón₁: *n.* *ípon* fish before it has ascended the river.

sunsón₂: sunsunen. *v.* to convoke, assemble, congregate; drive animals into a corral; go after without hesitation. [Tag. *tabóy* (chase away)]

sunsón₃: agsunson. *v.* to gasp for breath (*tunglab*). [Tag. *singáp*]

súnta: suntaan. *v.* to connect two pieces of wood together. (*silpo*)

súngab: sungaban. *n.* mouth (of scoop nets); neck opening; entrance.

sung-áb: *n.* quick, heavy breathing; gasp (*al-al*); convulsion. **agsung-ab.** *v.* to gasp, pant; be out of breath. [Tag. *singáp*]

súngad: *n.* approach. (*asideg*) **sumungad.** *v.* to draw near, approach. **sungaden.** *v.* to come upon first. **ipasungad.** *n.* first song in caroling; introduction; greetings. **pasungaden.** *v.* to be waiting for, expecting. **masungad.** *n.* the first house to come across; future. **masungadan.** *v.*

to come upon. **agpaspasungad.** *v.* to wait for the arrival of someone. **pamasungad.** *n.* greetings; introduction. **mapasungad.** *n.* future. **mapasungadan.** *v.* to wait for someone. **mapasungadan.** *v.* to be seen arriving. **Agdaldalagudog ti barukongko bayat ti isusungadmi iti simbaan.** My chest heaved as we approached the church. [Tag. *bungad*]

sungalngál: *n.* gag. **ipasungalngal.** *v.* to put on a gag; to force something in someone's mouth; to put someone in an embarrassing or compromising situation. **naipasungalngal.** *a.* trapped in a predicament.

sungáni: *a.* opposite; different; contradictory. (*sarungani*; *suppiat*) **masungani.** *v.* to be reversed, repudiated. **kasungani.** *n.* opposite. **sunganien.** *v.* to reverse, turn around; repudiate. [Png. *sungpá*, *sumláng*, Tag. *salungát*]

sungáng: agsungang. *v.* to have the upper (or lower) teeth jutting out.

súngat: *n.* person with a cowlick. **sungaten.** *v.* to accost; remonstrate; go against the current, flow of traffic; orally confront a wrongdoing; try to alleviate a situation by oral confrontation. **agsungat.** *v.* to bristle, stand on end. [Tag. *sumbát*]

sung-áw: (*reg.*) *n.* last breath of a dying person; *var.* of *sang-áw*: emit; exhale.

súngay: kasunsungay. *v.* to be at the highest point. [Tag. *sungay* = horn]

sungáyan: *n.* species of fish similar to the *barangan* but larger.

sungbát: *n.* reply; answer. **sumungbat, agsungbat.** *v.* to answer; respond, reply. **sungbatan.** *v.* to reply to, answer. **isungbat.** *v.* to reply, return an answer. **agsinnungbat.** *v.* to argue heatedly. **panagsinnungbat.** *n.* argument, quarrel. **masungbatan.** *v.* to be answered. **Pangngasim ta dimo ulitenen ta diak kayat nga isu ti pagsinnungbatanta.** Please don't repeat it anymore because I don't want him to be the cause of our argument. [Bon. *sebat*, Ibg. *tebbag*, Ifg. *húmang*, Ivt. *atvay*, Kal. *songbyat*, Knk. *sibát*, Kpm. *pekibat*, Png. *ebát*, *esel*, Tag. *sagót*]

sungdó: agkasungdo. *v.* to agree. **nasungdo.** *a.* gentle, kind; considerate; patient. **sungduan.** *v.* to perfect; do perfectly. **kinasungdo.** *n.* gracefulness; graciousness. [Tag. *sundô* (agree)]

súngeg: masusungeg. *a.* sick and tired; bored (*uma*).

sungét: *n.* small parts of the husk of rice that remain attached to the kernel after beating. **nasunget.** *a.* stubborn; disobedient; full of small pieces of husk. [Tag. *sungot* (pointed ends of rice grains)] sunggáno: *n.* difficult person.

sunggángat: maisunggangat. *v.* to become wedged in, stuck, etc. (*panget*)

súnggo: (Pil.) *n.* monkey (*tsónggo, bakes*). [Tag. *tsonggo, unggóy, matsíng*]

sunggóng: see *suggóng*: graceful; charming.

súngit: (Tag. also) nasungit. *a.* disobedient; obstinate; unruly; rebellious (*sukir, bangad*).

sungká: *n.* kind of native game played with small *butíti* shells and a board with twelve holes. agsungka. *v.* to play this game together. kasla pagsungkaan. *a.* potholed. sungsungkaen iti isip. to sort out in one's mind; analyze. sungkaan a dalan. *n.* potholed road. Sungsungkaek iti panunotko no asinoka. I am trying to figure out who you are (sorting out in my mind). [Tag. *sungkâ*]

súngo: *n.* muzzle, snout; upper lip. agsungo. *v.* to have a prominent snout. isungo. *v.* to point out with the nose. pasungo. *n.* rope attaching the nasal septum of a carabao to the larger rope, shorter than the *padná*. agpinnasungo. *v.* to pierce the nose of a carabao in competition. agkasunguan. *v.* to understand each other; to be compatible. [Tag. *ngusò* (snout)]

sungúsong: *n.* funnel. (*balisongsong; sarongusong*) sungusungan. *v.* to burn a hole in; hollow out by burning. masungusungan. *v.* to be smoked, fumigated; to funnel.

sungpót: sungputen. *v.* to obey strictly; conclude; fulfill to the last detail; perfect; finish (*ungpot*). [Tag. *tapos* (finish)]

sungród: *n.* fuel (usually firewood). pagsungrod. *v.* to use as fuel or firewood. sungrodan. *v.* to add fuel to the fire. pagsungrodan. *n.* part of furnace where fuel is added. masungrodan. *v.* to add fuel to; nurse; encourage; promote the growth of. [Png. *itongó*, Tag. *gatong* (fuel)]

sungsóng: *n.* example. isungsong. *v.* to found, establish; organize; inaugurate; to do something forbidden; incite; lead on; instigate. maisungsong. *v.* to be involved in something bad; to be instigated. pasungsungen. *v.* to change with coins. sungsungen. *v.* to go against the wind or current; complete, terminate (a woven fabric). Kayatmo a sawen a siak ti akimbasol iti pannakaisungsungna iti bisio? Do you mean to say that I am the one responsible for his falling into vice? Naisungsong iti maiparit nga agas. He was involved in illegal drugs. [Tag. *sungsóng* = going against current]

sungtót: (*coll.*) nakasungsungtot. *a.* bad smelling; abominable (last name).

súob: *n.* incense. suuban. *v.* to smoke, fumigate; incense. [Knk. *súguy*, Png. *soób*, Tag. *súob*]

súol: suolan. *v.* to fill to the brim. (*punno*) agsuolan. *v.* to be filled to the brim. [Tag. *apaw*]

soolohía: (Sp. *zoología*: zoology) *n.* zoology, the study of animals.

suón: susuon. *n.* pad placed on the head for supporting carried objects; objects carried on the head. susuonen. *v.* to carry on the head.

súong: suóngan. (*obs.*) *n.* pipe of a sugar mill. [Tag. *suóng* = face danger]

súop: *n.* joint of the body. (*takig*) isuop. *v.* to join, connect. maisuop. *v.* to yield the capital without profit or loss. [Tag. *sugpóng*]

súor: isuor. *v.* to smoke. suoran. *v.* to smoke out; fumigate. kasuoran. *n.* part of roof over the stove covered with soot; shed used for temporary shelter. pagsuoran. *n.* bamboo tray put over fire to dry wood, rice, etc. Kasla narba a kasuoran ta rupam. Your face is like a collapsed *kasuoran* (sad). [Tag. *suób* (fumigate)]

súot₁: *n.* test; trial. (*subok*) suoten. *v.* to try, test; put to trial. nasuot. *a.* experienced. [Tag. *subok*]

súot₂: isuot. *v.* to put on (clothes, jewelry). nakasuot iti alahas. *a.* wearing jewelry. [Kal. *iyuseÿ*, Tag. *suót*]

súpa: (Sp. *chupa*: suck) *n.* one-eighth of a *ganta*, *chupa*. tallo supa, kanen ti dua, awan pay matda a kanen ti pusa. *exp.* three *chupas* of rice eaten by two, there is nothing left for the cat.

sopá: (Sp. *sofá*: sofa) *n.* couch, sofa.

supáang: masupaangan. *v.* to be tired of eating a certain food. (*suya*) Nasupaanganka iti itlog. You are tired of eating eggs.

supádi: agsupadi. *v.* to be different; opposite; traverse fluttering (locusts). maisupadi. *v.* to be opposed; to be dissimilar. maisupsupadi. *a.* unique, distinct. (*maisalsalumina*) sumupadi. *v.* to disagree. [Png. *sungpá, sumláng*, Tag. *salungát*]

supagét: *n.* pout; frown. agsupaget. *v.* to show anger, frown (*rupanget; murareg*). [Tag. *simangot*]

supalpál: agsupalpal. *v.* to counteract; block (a ball in sports). supalpalan. *v.* to block; stuff the mouth with.

súpang: *n.* second shoot of (banana, palay, grass, etc.) agsupang. *v.* to grow shoots for the second time.

supangét: nasupanget. *a.* opposing; rivaling. iti kasupanget a suli. in the opposite (opposing) corner.

supangíl: *a.* different, other; fight. agsupangil. *v.* to argue; fight. Ania ti pagsusupangilanda? Why are they fighting?

supápak: *n.* prize; reward. **supapakan**. *v.* to repay, return; deny; contradict; oppose; dispute; give as a reward. **agsupapak, makisupapak**. *v.* to repay in cash; dispute; argue; brawl. **Masupapakkan kadagiti narigrigatam.** You will be rewarded for your hardships. [Tag. *gantí, gantimpalà*]

sópas: (Sp. *sopa*: soup) *n.* soup.

sopéra: (Sp. *sopera*: soup bowl) *n.* soup bowl.

superióra: (Sp. *superiora*: mother superior) *n.* mother superior.

superioridád: (Sp. *superioridad*: superiority) *n.* superiority.

sopéro: (Sp. *sopero*: soup dish) *n.* soup bowl, soup dish.

supí: *n.* sleeping room. (*silíd* of small houses).

supiát: *var.* of *suppiat*: contradict; oppose.

supího: (Sp. *sufijo*) *n.* suffix.

súping: **kasuping.** *n.* opponent, enemy (*supangil, suppiat; búsor*).

suplá: *n.* soft, untwisted silk. (*sutla*) **suplaen.** *v.* to insult; ridicule.

suplád: *n.* kind of wooden shovel; peel used by bakers.

supládo: (Sp. *soplado*: blown (up)) *a.* snobbish; conceited; stuck-up; haughty. (*fem. suplada*)

sopladór: (Sp. *soplador*: blower) *n.* blowpipe.

supleménto: (Sp. *suplemento*: supplement) *n.* supplement.

sopléte: (Sp. *soplete*: blowpipe) *n.* blowtorch.

suplí: *n.* change (money). **pasuplian.** *v.* to break larger bills into smaller denominations. **suplian.** *v.* to give change. [Png. *pa-suplí*, Tag. *suklí*]

suplíka: (Sp. *suplicar*: appeal) **suplikaen.** *v.* to oppose, contradict; appeal.

suplíng: (*coll.*) *n.* child (*putot*). [Tag. *batà*]

suplóng: **agisuplong.** *v.* to tell on; report wrong doing. (*púlong*) **naisuplong.** *a.* reported.

supnét: **nasupnet.** *a.* scraping; tough; sticky; coarse. [Tag. *kunat*]

súpo: *n.* kind of boy's game.

supórta: (Sp. *soportar*) *n.* support. **suportaan.** *v.* to support. **suportado.** *a.* supported.

suportár: (Sp. *soportar*: support) **suportaran.** *v.* to support. (*tapáya; saránay*)

supositório: (Sp. *supositorio*: suppository) *n.* suppository.

supúsop: *n.* addition to inadequate funds; addition to a garment; *a.* joined; linked. **supusupan.** *v.* to lengthen a garment; enlarge; make up for another deficiency. [Tag. *susog*]

súpot: *n.* paper bag; bag; pouch; scrotum; afterbirth. **isupot.** *v.* to place in a bag. **isupotan.** *v.* to put in a bag for someone. **supotsupot.** *n.* hives, nettle rash. **agsupotsupot.** *v.* to have

hives. **Mabalino ti agsublisubli iti** *buffet*, **ngem di mabalin ti agisupot iti yawid.** You may go back and forth to the food at a buffet, but you cannot take food home in a bag. [Png., Tag. *súpot*]

supót: (Tag.) *n.* uncircumcised male (*ant: kugit*). **agsupot.** *v.* to be underdeveloped (said of grains attacked by pests). [Bon. *lokyop*, Knk. *lúyup*]

suppiát: **maisuppiat.** *v.* to be opposite, against; contradictory; *prep.* against. **suppiaten.** *v.* to contradict (*kaniwás, kaniwasiw, rusngí, súkir, subkár, tubngár, labsíng, barusngí, allábat, surngí, supríng*); resist; oppose; disobey. **agsinnuppiat.** *v.* to argue with each other. **pagsuppiatan.** *n.* argumentation; discussion. [Bon. *sókad*, Png. *sungpá, sumláng*, Tag. *salungát*]

suppók: *n.* undergrowth; thicket. **sumuppok.** *v.* to hide in the thick vegetation; go into a thicket.

suprád: **masuprádan.** *v.* to have an itchy throat caused by too much acidic or salty foods. (*aprad*)

suprák₁: **sumuprak.** *v.* to refuse; disobey (*supring; subeg, paay*). [Tag. *suwáy*]

suprák₂: **nasuprak.** *a.* coarse, rough (said of cooked rice). (*parayapay*)

suprémo: (Sp. *supremo*: supreme) *a.* supreme.

supríng: *n.* whirl in the front of the hair; opposition. *a.* rebellious. **nasupring.** *a.* with hair bristling; disobedient; rebellious. **supringen.** *v.* to violate, break; resist; disobey. **agsinnupring.** *v.* to oppose each other. **sumupsupring.** *n.* subversive elements. [Tag. *suwáy* (disobey)]

súpsop: *n.* small glass used by medicine men to suck venom from a victim's veins. **supsupen.** *v.* to suck venom out of. [Tag. *supsóp* (suck)]

Sor: (Sp. *sor*: sister) sister (of a convent).

sur: (Sp. *sur*: south) *n.* south. (*abagatan*)

súra: (*obs.*) **surasura.** *n.* calling domestic fowls.

surág: see *tókal; burág*.

súrak: **suraken.** *v.* to inspect at night. **sumurak.** *v.* to crowd; force one's way through.

surángi: (*obs.*) **sumurangi.** *v.* to refuse to enter; leave the herd; force a passage through a crowd.

surásid: **isurasid.** *v.* to plant around a fence. (*ipaig, taraikiden*)

súrat: *n.* letter; writing; note; anything written. **agsurat.** *v.* to write. **agsinnurat.** *v.* to write to each other. **isurat.** *v.* to inscribe. **suratan.** *v.* to write to someone. **susuraten.** *v.* something intended to be written. **makisinnurat.** *v.* to write to each other, exchange letters. **kasuratan.** *n.* contract, written agreement. **agsinuratan.** *v.* to have a written agreement. **kasinnurat.** *n.* pen pal. **sinurat.** *n.* article; essay;

document. **surat-ima.** *a.* handwritten. [Bon. *sólat*, Ibg. *túraq*, Ifg. *túdok*, Ivt. *tulas*, Kal. *gili*, Kpm., Png., Tag. *súlat*]

suráti: *n.* variety of awned early rice; variety of maize with mixed yellow and red kernels.

súray: *n.* prop, stay. (*túkal*; *singit*) **surayen.** *v.* to support with a prop. [Tag. *tukod*; *suray* = wobble]

suráya: *n.* prop of two pieces of crossed timber used to support houses, trees, etc; angle braces.

surbék: see *surong*.

sorbetéro: (f. *sorbetes*) *n.* ice-cream vendor; ice-cream maker.

sorbétes: (Sp. *sorbetes*: sherbet) *n.* ice cream.

surbók: sumurbok. *v.* to go upstream. (*súrong*) **nasurbok nga away.** *n.* upstream hinterlands.

surbót: *var.* of *surbok*.

surdíp: *n.* short-pointed strip used to help weave. (*balunok*) **surdipan.** *v.* to insert a strip by means of a *surdip*.

surdó: *n.* person without work; foolish. **surduen.** *v.* to bother; irritate, harass; make a fuss about; tease. **Ita, siak ti sangkasurdo dagiti padak a baro.** Now I am the one who is constantly teased by my fellow bachelors. [Tag. *yamót*]

surdóng: isurdong. *v.* to say in a very low voice.

sorélas: *var.* of *soleras*: floor joist.

surgíd: *n.* small pimple (*kamuro*). [Tag. *tagihawat*]

suriáb: *a.* with deformed upper lip (with lip bulging toward the nose). **agsuriab.** *v.* to deform (rim of baskets). [Tag. *ngiwî* (crooked mouth)]

suriál: sumurial. *a.* awry; twisted; crooked (said of cavities: caves, houses, mouths of jars, etc.).

surihír: *var.* of *suherír*: suggest.

súring: *n.* variety of banana. **suringen.** *v.* to go against the current or wind; to give in excess of what is required (food).

surión: *n.* leather strap used for whipping.

suripét: *n.* twilight (*apagriwet*; *sarsardam*). [Knk. *amíngaw*, Tag. *takíp-sílim*]

soríso: *var.* of *tsoriso*: pork sausage.

sur-ít: *n.* maggot. **sinur-it.** *a.* maggot infested. [Tag. *uod* (worm also)]

surkáno: *n.* herbal doctor; quack doctor. (*erbulario*)

surná: *n.* small additional teat of animals. **pasurnaan ti agsaó.** *v.* to exaggerate.

surnád: *n.* repeat; follow up. **surnadan.** *v.* to repeat; follow up. (*ulit*; *dupag*; *dubli*; *sunot*)

surníp₁: *n.* triangular piece of cloth.

surníp₂: *n.* scales of a fowl's leg.

surngí: *a.* inverted, reverse; contradictory. (*suppiat*) **surngien.** *v.* to do in the opposite way; reverse; invert; contradict. **sumurngi.** *v.* to be

contradictory. **Nasurngian iti panagellekna.** He was inverted from his laughter. [Tag. *taliwás*]

sóro: (Sp. *zorro*: fox) *n.* fox.

súro: sursuruan. *v.* to teach; tutor; educate. **sursuruen.** *v.* to learn; study. **isuro.** *v.* to teach; show; point out; reveal. **pangisuro.** *n.* instructional materials. **mannursuro.** *n.* teacher. **sursuro.** *n.* learning; education; upbringing. **agsursuro.** *v.* to learn, study. **paisuro.** *v.* to have something taught. **agpaisuro.** *v.* to have oneself taught. **pangisuro.** *n.* instructional materials. **makasursuro.** *v.* to be able to learn. **pannursuro.** *n.* teachings; instructions. **Gapo a saanakon a nakatuloy nga agadal, nagsursuroak a nagallawagi.** Because I was not able to finish my studies, I learned to be a carpenter. **Ti balasang nga awan surona, kas sabong nga awan banglona.** An uneducated maiden is like a flower without fragrance. [Bon. *sólo*, Ibg. *tudduwan*, Ivt. *sulib*, Kal. *tuchu*, *acheÿ*, Kpm. *byasa*, Png. *bangát*, Tag. *turò*]

suruág: *var.* of *saruag*: cast a net. [Tag. *hagis*]

sur-ób: *n.* sip, draught. **sur-oben.** *v.* to sip. (*suloy*, *sukrob*)

surók: *n.* surplus; excess; remainder. **agsurok.** *v.* to be in excess. **nasurok.** *a.* excessive, surplus. **suroken.** *v.* to do to excess. **isurok.** *v.* to add to. **surokan.** *v.* to increase; cause a surplus; make too big. **sumurók-kumúrang.** more or less, approximately, give or take. **Nasuroken a sangapulo a tawen nga agmulmulaak iti paria.** I have been planting bittermelon for over ten years. [Knk., Png. *solók*, Tag. *higít*]

surón: suronen. *v.* to tease; annoy; provoke; irritate. **agsusuron.** *n.* teaser. **isuron.** *v.* to tease; irritate. [Kpm. *sunúg*, Tag. *tuksó*, *tudyó*, *yamót*]

suronádo: (f. *suron*) *n.* teaser, tease. (*fem.* *suronada*)

súrong: *n.* church altar; *a.* upstream. **agpasurong, sumurong.** *v.* to go upstream; go to the main altar. **Nagpasurong pay tapno adda pawayway iti pannakayanudna.** They went farther upstream to give allowance for their drifting. [Tag. *salungát sa agos* (upstream)]

surúsor: *n.* coconut shell with a hole in it used for making *kelléb*. **masurusor.** *v.* to rot (trees).

súrot: suroten. *v.* to follow; pursue; obey; pledge allegiance to; yield; keep the mind upon; understand. **pasurot.** *n.* follower, disciple. **pasurotan.** *v.* to trace, copy; support a suggestion; condescend. **kasurotan.** *n.* one who is fond of following. **agkasurotan.** *v.* to be on good terms. **sumurot.** *v.* to follow; obey; understand. **isurot.**

v. to take along with. **maisurot.** *v.* to be affected (influenced) by the feelings of the majority, to be swayed by public opinion. **masurotan.** *v.* to be able to follow, understand; to discover a different meaning or route. **surotsurot.** *n.* tag-along, someone who continually follows along although uninvited. **pagsurotan.** *n.* model, example; guidelines. **Sisusurotkami iti pangngeddengmo.** We will follow your decision. [Bon. *onod*, Knk. *tauptúp*, Png. *tombok*, Tag. *sunód*, Tag. *surot* = bedbug]

sorprésa: (Sp. *sorpresa*: surprise) *n.* surprise (*masdaaw*). [Tag. *gulat*]

surrát: *a.* pug-nosed.

surró: sumró. *v.* to have a fit of anger or sickness, attack (illness). **sumsumro.** *n.* simpleton; crazy person.

surruág: see *sarruág:* casting nets.

surrúob: (*obs.*) **sumruob.** *v.* to sink (swimmers) (*lenned*). [Tag. *lubóg*]

sursí(r): agsursir. *v.* to mend a patch; sew together a hole.

sursopón: *var.* of *saksopón:* saxophone.

sursúr: agsursur. *v.* to go from house to house; place to place. **sursuren.** *v.* to look for everywhere; visit every place. **pasursur.** *n.* thatch covering the ridging.

sortído: (Sp. *surtido*: assorted) *n.* a kind of folk dance; *a.* assorted.

sortéo: (Sp. *sorteo*: drawing lots) *n.* act of drawing lots.

sus: exclamatory word, short for *Hesús!* Jesus!

sósa: (Sp.) *n.* soda (*bikarbonato*).

susapó: exclamatory word contracted from *Hesús* (Jesus) and *apo* (sir).

súsay: *n.* blue marlin fish.

susbúot: masusbuot. *v.* to be submerged, immersed (*rareb, renneb*). [Tag. *lublób*]

susí: (*obs.*) *n.* padlock (*tulbek; kandado*). [Tag. *susì* = key]

sosiál: (Sp. *social*: social) *a.* social; *n.* socialite. **pasosial.** *n.* social affair usually for fundraising.

sosialísmo: (Sp. *socialismo*: socialism) *n.* socialism. **sosialista.** *n.* socialist.

sosiedád: (Sp. *sociedad*: society) *n.* society. (*kagimongan*)

súsik: agsusik. *v.* to dispute, argue; squabble. (*apa; subang; tubar; baranget*) **susiken.** *v.* to contest; contend. [Tag. *away*]

sósio: (Sp. *socio*: partner) *n.* business partner; colleague. **agsosio.** *v.* to be partners; form a partnership. **sosio a negosio.** *n.* business partner. [Png. *samák*]

sosiolohía: (Sp. *sociología*: sociology) *n.* sociology. **sosiolohista.** *n.* sociologist.

suskribír: (Sp. *suscribir*) **agsuskribir.** *v.* to subscribe.

susmariósep: *interj.* expressing surprise.

súso: *n.* breast; teat; udder. **sumuso.** *v.* to suck at the breast. **manangsuso.** *a.* greedy. **agpasuso.** *v.* to nurse. **agassinuso.** *a.* inexperienced; very young; immature. **pasusuan.** *v.* to strike someone on the breast. **pasusuen.** *v.* to breastfeed, give the breast to. **pamasusuan.** *n.* dowry. [Ifg. *págo*, Ivt. *susuq*, Kal. *susu*, Png. *susó*, Ibg., Kpm., Tag. *suso*]

susó: *n.* freshwater snail with blackish shell. **susó a pukrán.** *n.* kind of *sosó* with a round, white shell. **susó pápa.** *n.* kind of *sosó* with soft, round shell. **mannusó.** *n.* the *birút* fish (which feeds on *sosó*). **pamasusuan.** *n.* dowry (*sabong*). [Knk. *bilolokó*, Png. *alireg, bisokól*, Tag. *susô*]

susuéldo: (f. *sueldo*) *n.* leafless plant whose sap is poisonous to the eyes.

susuón: (f. *suón*) *n.* objects carried on the head; headpad used for carrying objects. **agsusuon.** *v.* to carry on the head.

susúop: *n.* bone joint (elbow, knee, etc.)

súsop: *n.* banana blossom; an instrument used for sucking. **agsusop, sumusop.** *v.* to suck; puff at a pipe. **agisusop.** *v.* to ask someone smoking to light one's cigar. **makasusop.** *v.* to become infected (wounds). **makisusop.** *v.* to ask for a puff of another person's tobacco. **susupen.** *v.* to suck; puff at. [Ibg. *sussuq, sussup*, Ivt. *sepsep*, Kpm., Png., Tag. *sipsíp*; *hithít* (inhale smoke)]

suspendér: (Sp.) **suspenderen.** *v.* to suspend.

suspendído: (Eng.) *a.* suspended.

suspénso: (Sp. *suspenso*) *a.* suspended (from school). **suspensuen.** *v.* to suspend.

sospétsa: (Sp. *sospecha*: suspect) *n.* suspicion; suspect.

sospetsóso: (Sp. *sospechoso*: suspicious) *n.* suspicious (feminine: *sospetsosa*).

sustánsia: (Sp. *sustancia*: substance) *n.* substance; nutritional content; nutrient; nutrition. **nasustansia.** *a.* nutritious.

sustantíbo: (Sp. *sustantivo*: substantive) *n.* substantive, noun.

sostenér: (Sp. *sostener*: sustain) *n.* support; livelihood. **sosteneren.** *v.* to sustain; support; keep one's word.

sustentár: (Sp. *sustentar*) **sustentaren.** *v.* to sustain, support a family.

susténto: (Sp. *sostento*: sustenance) *n.* sustenance; financial support; maintenance. **sustentuan.** *v.* to support; supply. **sustentuen.** *v.* to fulfill one's promise. **Agsardengto metten ti sustentona iti baket.** His support to the old lady will end.

sóta: (Sp. *jota*: jack) *n*. jack (in cards).

sotána: (Sp. *sotana*: cassock) *n*. cassock.

sotanghón: (Hok. *sua tâng hùn*: Shantung flour) *n*. mung bean noodle.

sutíl: *n*. joker; teaser. **isutil**. *v*. to joke; tease; provoke. (*artiok*; *durog*; *angaw*; *suron*; *parato*) **nasutil**. *a*. joking, teasing. **manutsutil**. *a*. always joking, prone to tease. **Bulsekak no maipapan iti rugso ken sutil**. I am blind to passion and joking. [Png. *sutíl*, Tag. *birò*; *tuksó*; Tag. *sutíl* = undisciplined; stubborn]

sutíng: **apagsuting**. *a*. half-drunk. **sutingen**. *v*. to remind one of. (*palagip*)

sutlá: *n*. soft, untwisted silk (*suplá*); fine skin.

sutúra: (Sp. *sutura*: seam, suture) *n*. surgical thread; surgical stitch.

sutsút₁: *n*. hissing sound used to call attention; loose threads from a garment (*samot*, *saroy*). **sinutsut**. *n*. lint, raveling. **sutsutan**. *v*. to remove loose threads from a garment; call attention by whistling. **sutsuten**. *v*. to remove (loose threads). [Tag. *sitsít* (hiss)]

sutsút₂: **nasutsútan**. *a*. grown thin (a sick person).

sutsút₃: **sutsutan**. *v*. to squeeze, press intestines to extract the juice. **sutsuten**. *v*. to squeeze out, press out (juice from intestines).

suwánso: **agsuwanso**. *v*. to seesaw; rock in a rocking chair.

suwáw: **agsuwaw**. *v*. to leak. (*ubo*)

suwék: *var*. of suek.

suwéng: *a*. obstinate, stubborn. (*súngit*, *súkir*, *súbeg*; *galasugas*)

suwérte: (Sp. *suerte*: luck) *n*. luck. (*gasat*)

sóya: (Sp. *soya*: soy) *n*. soybeans.

súya: (Hok. *sué à*: loose luck) *n*. dislike; disgust. **makasuya**. *v*. to cause nausea; disgust; dislike.

masuya. *v*. to nauseate; feel disgust; tire; bore (*supaang*). [Png. *busol*, Tag. *suklám*, *sawà*, *adwâ*]

suyáab: *n*. yawn. **agsuyáab**. *v*. to yawn (*wab*). **Suysuyaabanna ti bussogna**. He is yawning off his full stomach. [Kal. *uweb*, Png. *wab*, Tag. *higáb*, *hikáb*]

súyat: *n*. delay (in construction, sale, etc.) (*tantan*); sluggishness in selling. [Tag. *tumal* (slow business)]

suyát: *n*. spout of a teapot. **isuyat**. *v*. to pour out. **maisuyat**. *v*. to spill (*buyat*). [Tag. *buhos*]

súyep: **agsuyep**. *v*. to feel sleepy; to blink. (*kúyep*)

súyo: **agsuyo**. *v*. to pitch pennies in a game. (*tanggá*). **isuyo**. *v*. to throw from under.

súyod: *n*. farmer's implement used to weed rice fields; harrow. **suyuden**. *v*. to harrow (*moriski*; *sagad*). [Kal. *aÿachu*, Tag. *suyod* = fine comb]

suy-ók: *n*. curvature or hollow between cliffs, pit (*rúsok*). [Knk. *suy-ók* = corner, angle]

suyúp: *n*. blister. (*kapuyo*) **sumuyup**. *v*. to blister. [Png. *lanók*, Tag. *paltós*]

suyót₁: *n*. extreme case of diarrhea, liquid feces. (*buris*) **agsuyot**. *v*. to have an extreme case of diarrhea; spout out; squirt out. [Tag. *kursó* (diarrhea)]

suyót₂: **sumuyot**. *v*. to shoot forth, spurt; squirt; spout; crackle; crepitate. **pasuyutan**. *v*. to spray, squirt out. **lata a pagpasuyot**. *n*. spray can. [Tag. *sagitsít*]

suysúy: **agsuysuy**. *v*. to ravel, fray. (*sutsut*) **suysuyen**. *v*. to pull loose threads of a garment. (*sutsot*) **suysuy a gayadan**. *n*. raveled hemline, as in cutoff jeans. [Png. *abarbár*, Tag. *kalás*, *tastás*]

Swíso: (Sp. *suizo*: Swiss) *n*., *a*. Swiss.

T

't: Abbreviation of *ti* or *iti* after a vowel: **Ania ti naganmo?** = **'Nia't naganmo?** What's your name?

-ta: *enclitic*. absolutive form of *data*: first person dual pronoun: You and I. **In***ta***n.** Let's go (dual). **Mangan***ta***n.** Let's eat. [Png. *ta*]

ta: Abbreviation of *dayta*: that (near speaker); *conj*. so, because; that (*gapo ta*); conjunction connecting causative or resultative clauses. **Gapo ta.** because. **anansa ta.** therefore. **ibagam ta umay.** tell him to come. **Agurayka ta sapulek.** Wait and I'll look for it. **Umayka ta kayatnaka kano met a makaam-ammo.** Come because he supposedly wants to get to know you too. **Urayennak ta umaykanto alaen.** Wait for me and I'll fetch you. **Pangngaasim ta saanmo a rakraken ti dayawko.** Please do not destroy my honor. [Png. *ta*]

taál: *n*. variety of small coconut with bitter meat. *v*. to make an extension; make allowance for. and a hard shell.

táan: **agtaan.** *v*. to bet; wager. (*pósta*, *taya*) **pataanan.** *v*. to make allowance for; make an extension.

táang: *n*. scarcity of fruits. **nataang.** *a*. scare (said of fruits). [Tag. *taáng* = appetizer]

taáw: *n*. ocean, sea. (*baybay*) **agpataaw.** *v*. to go to the deep sea. **Agpatpataaw pay laeng ti birayda.** Their boat is still going off to sea. [Ibg. *alarem a bévay*, Itg. *adáem*, Ivt. *marahem a taaw*, Kpm. *laúta*, Png. *pegley na dáyat*, *taéw*, Tag. *dagat*]

taáy: *n*. a kind of bird snare. **taayen.** *v*. to trap birds in a bird snare.

tabá₁: *n*. adipose tissue, fat; grease; bacon; cream. **nataba.** *a*. fatty; greasy; fertile (soil). **panaba.** *n*. manure (*ganagan*). [Ibg. *tava*, Itg. *tabeg*, *taba*, Ivt. *tavaq*, Kal. *tabya*, Knk. *laléb*, Png. *taba*, Kpm., Tag. *tabâ*]

tabá₂: **tabtaba.** *n*. spume or scum carried by rivers.

tabak: *n*. *Ternstroemia sp.* tree.

tabakaléra: (Sp. *tabacalera*: tobacco dealer) *n*. tobacco dealer.

tabakéra: (Sp. *tabaquera*: snuffbox) *n*. female cigar maker; snuffbox.

tabakería: (Sp. *tabaquería*: tobacco shop) *n*. cigar factory; tobacco shop.

tabakéro: (Sp. *tabaquero*: tobacconist) *n*. tobacconist; cigar maker.

tabáko: (Sp. *tabaco*: tobacco) *n*. tobacco (Ilocano varieties include: *antígo*, *pugot*, *paratik*, *morada*, *simmaba*); cigar (*abano*; *pinadis*). **agtabako.** *v*. to smoke tobacco. **agattabako.** *v*. to

smell like tobacco; smell like smoke. **mannabako.** *a*. prone to smoking cigars. **makitabako.** *v*. to ask for a cigar. **makatabako.** *v*. to feel like smoking, want to smoke. **katabakuan.** *n*. tobacco field, tobacco plantation. **patabakuan.** *v*. to give a cigar to. **tabtabako.** *n*. pl. of *tabako*; *Cynoglossum zeylanicum* plant. [Bon. *taleptep*]

tábal: **tabalan.** *v*. to cut the tops off overgrown palay.

tabála: (*obs*.) coffin (*lungon*); (*reg*.) crazy woman; nag.

taballá: **matabtaballa.** *v*. to speak nonsense (see *balla*: crazy).

tában: *n*. quality; superior choice (fruits). *a*. select, superior, choice.

tabáng: **natabang.** *a*. brackish, salty (water). [Kal. *lamsit*, Tag. *alat*, Tag. *tabáng* = insipid]

tabangúngo: *n*. a kind of marine fish.

tábas: *n*. style; cut; pattern; outline; form; look. **tabasen.** *v*. to cut a garment using a pattern. **matabas.** *v*. to be cut following a pattern (clothes). **nagtabasan.** *n*. cloth cuttings. **pagtabasan.** *n*. pattern (of clothes). [Tag. *tabas*]

tabás: *n*. kind of machete used to cut grass (*bolo*). **agtabas, tabasen.** *v*. to cut grass; trim. **tabasan.** *v*. to clear an area of grass. **panabas.** *n*. instrument used for cutting grass, machete.

tabaséro: (f. *tabás*) *n*. grass cutter.

tabátab: **tabataben.** *v*. to trim the brim of a hollow container; mark a line (before cutting). [Tag. *tabtáb*]

tabatsóy: (*coll.*, Tagalog also) *a*. very fat. (*lukmeg*)

tábaw: **tabawtabaw.** *n*. a kind of vine with bitter fruits, *Luffa* and *Momordica* sp. **tabawen.** *v*. (*obs.*) to pick off from the ground.

tabbáaw: *n*. swearing, cursing; blasphemy. **agtabtabbaaw.** *v*. to curse (*lunod*); swear; blaspheme (*bassawang*). **matabbaawan.** *v*. to be cursed. **agtanabbaaw.** *v*. to curse loudly and repeatedly; curse with bodily movements. **managtabbaaw.** *a*. prone to cursing, with a foul mouth. **panagtabbaaw.** *n*. blasphemy. **tabbaawan.** *v*. to swear at someone. **Tinabbaawannak iti di malamlamot ti aso.** He swore at me harshly (with words a dog wouldn't eat). [Tag. *manungayaw*]

tabbáyog: (*obs.*) *n*. mishmash of colors.

tabbéd: **natabbed.** *a*. stupid; slow (in learning); dull; rude; not running smoothly (machines). **agtabbed.** *v*. to be dull, stupid, etc; to stammer. [Png. *leglég*, Tag. *tangá*]

tabbél: *n*. hard bowels; constipation, hard evacuation of feces. **agtabbel.** *v*. to have difficulty in defecating. **makapatabbel.** *v*. to cause constipation (certain foods). [Kal. *tubye*, Png. *etél*]

tabbí: agtabbi. *v.* to fall down together (in wrestling, fighting, etc.).

tabbióg: *n.* heavy punch, hit (*danog*). **tabbiogen.** *v.* to punch, hit heavily. **Tinabbiogna ti bukotko.** He hit me on the back.

tabbíraw: *n.* meddler (*biang*). **tumabbiraw.** *v.* to intermeddle; intrude; interrupt; look behind over the shoulder. **tabbiráwan.** *v.* to meddle in someone's affairs. **pagtabbiráwan.** (*obs.*) *n.* prostitute. **agtabbiraw.** (*obs.*) *v.* to draw water from a public well. **No makatabbirawka iti politika, rugitam dagita imam.** If you meddle in politics, you will soil your hands. [Tag. *makialám*]

tabbóg: *n.* sound of falling in water; noisy immersion in water. **itabbog.** *v.* to immerse, put in water, splash in water. [Kpm., Png. *tabóg*]

tabbúga: *n.* sound of foot stamping. **agtabbuga.** *v.* to stamp; stomp (with the feet). [Tag. *dabóg*]

tabbúog: (f. *tabóg*) **agtabbuog.** *v.* to stamp the feet. (*tabbuga*)

tabbúor: *var.* of *tabbuga*.

tabbúyog: (*obs.*) *n.* competition of many against one.

tabérna: (Sp. *taverna*: tavern) *n.* tavern (for selling alcoholic drinks).

tabernákulo: (Sp. *tabernáculo*: tabernacle) *n.* tabernacle.

tabíd: tabiden. *v.* to twist (thread). [Tag. *palihin*]

tabidáw: *n.* kind of square woven bamboo basket.

tabiláng: natabilang. *a.* careless, negligent. (*nalíway*)

tábing: *n.* screen; curtain; wall cloth. (*balembem*) **tabingan.** *v.* to screen; provide with a divider.

tabingí: (Tag. *tabingî*) *a.* uneven; unsymmetrical; unbalanced. **tabi-tabingi.** *a.* quite askew; very unbalanced, unsymmetrical.

tabkáw: agtabkaw. *v.* to do (sweep, weed, etc.) omitting certain portions; miss (*labas*). [Tag. *laktáw*]

tábla: (Sp. *tabla*: plank, board, Tag. also) *n.* board, plank, thinned lumber; beam.

tablá: *n.* tie, draw (in a game). **agtabla.** *v.* to be tied (in score). **itabla.** *v.* to make into a draw (where there is no winner or loser). [Png. *nanpará*, Tag. *patas*]

tabléria: (Sp. *tablero*: board + -*ía*) *n.* lumberyard; timber yard.

tabléro: (Sp. *tablero*: board) *n.* checkerboard; chessboard.

tabléta: (Sp. *tableta*: tablet) *n.* tablet; pill. (*pildoras*) **agtableta.** *v.* to take a tablet. **tableta a pagpaturog.** *n.* sleeping pill.

tablón: (Sp. *tablón*: board) *n.* wooden board; *a.* wooden. (*káyo*)

tabnáw: tumabnaw. *v.* to dive; immerse oneself; step in, interfere; plunge. **itabnaw.** *v.* to throw into water; immerse something, plunge, dip in water. **Intabtabnawko dagiti ima ken sakak iti napudot a danum ngem awan met pianna.** I dipped my hands and feet in warm water but they didn't get any better.

tábo: *n.* scoop (originally made of bamboo). **tumabo, tabuen.** *v.* to scoop (*akluen, supladen*). [Tag. *tabò*]

tabú: (Eng.) *n.* taboo, something forbidden. (*parit*)

tabuéng: (*obs.*) *a.* illegitimate child (*anak ti ruar*); young of animals.

tabóg: *n.* kind of red mussel shell. **katabogan.** *n.* place with a lot of red mussels. [Tag. *tabóg* = feet stamping]

tabúga: *var.* of *tabbuga*: stamping of the feet.

tabúkol$_1$: *n.* round net with cord (*koratáw*) at the center and lead sinkers around the circumference. **tabukolan.** *v.* to cast a net. **matabukulan.** *v.* to be caught by a net (fish). **Innakto agtabukol no parbangon.** I am going to catch fish with a net at dawn. **Adu gayam ti natabukolam!** So you have caught a lot in the *tabukol!* [Kal. *saguy, sichuk*]

tabúkol$_2$: tabtabúkol. *n. Trianthema portulascastrum* herb with pink flowers used as swine food.

tábon$_1$: *n.* burial (*punpon*). **agtabon.** *v.* to be buried; set (sun). **itabon.** *v.* to bury, inter. **makitabon.** *v.* to attend a funeral. **tabonan.** *n.* to embank; fill with earth. [Png. *ponpón, tulór*, Tag. *libíng; tabon*]

tábon$_2$: *n.* a kind of bird.

tabunó: agtatabuno. *v.* to accumulate, crowd. (*arak, ummong*) **makitabuno.** *v.* to be in a group. **makatabuno.** *v.* to be able to attend. **tumabuno.** *v.* to join a large group. **tabunuen.** *v.* to heap up, amass, agglomerate. [Tag. *daló*]

tabúngaw: *n. Lagenaria leucantha*, the bottle gourd squash; a dish made with this squash; a hat made from this gourd; **(tangken)-tabungaw.** (*fig.*) a person who is hard on the outside but soft on the inside (*agintatangken*). [Kal., Knk., Png. *tabungaw*, Png. *gubuéy*, Tag. *upò*]

tabúray: tinnaburay. *n.* game consisting of throwing sand at one another.

taburéte: (Sp. *taburete*: stool) *n.* stool.

taburkík: *n.* kind of small, brown, schooling marine fish.

taburtít: *var.* of the *taburkik* fish.

tábuy: itabuy. *v.* to excite; encourage, urge. (*dagdágen, gutugóten; abuy*) **maitabuy.** *v.* to be excited, stimulated, encouraged, etc. [Tag. *udyók*]

tabrília: (Sp. *tablilla*: bar of soap) *n*. bar of soap.

tabsáw: *var*. of *tabnaw*.

tabtáb₁: **tabtaban**. *v*. to hollow out boards for putting rungs of stairs in them when making a ladder; (*reg*.) trim. **itabtab**. *v*. to remove from the edge; trim.

tabtáb₂: (*reg*.) *a*. talkative. (*tarabitab*) **tabtabera**. *a*. talkative (said of women).

tádaw: **tadawan**. *v*. to cut the top of; top off (trees). **agtadaw**. *v*. to harvest sugarcane. [Tag. *putul*]

taddó: *n*. round container for holding food to be dried in the sun. **sangataddo**. one container full. **sangataddo a bibingka**. one *taddo* of rice cake.

tadék: *n*. ritual dance among mountain tribes. (*alikenken*); wedding ceremonial dance of the Itneg and Bago. **agtadek**. *v*. to dance the *tadek* (Ilocano *taraddék* = move with quick steps).

tadém: *n*. edge (of a cutting instrument). (*tírad*) **katadman**. *a*. very sharp. **natadem**. *a*. sharp; shrewd; stinging, piercing. **patadem**. *n*. knife. **patadman**. *v*. to sharpen a knife. **tumadem**. *v*. to become sharp, keen. **tadmen**. *v*. to hack. **Pinatademna ti paliiw ken panagdengngegna**. He sharpened his observation and listening. [Ibg., Ivt., Png. *tarém*, Kal. *topok*, *tachom*, Kpm. *taram*, Tag. *talím*, *talas*]

tadéro: *n*. person responsible for placing the razor blade on the legs of gamecocks.

tádi: *n*. gaff (metal spur or razor blade tied to a gamecock). (*kawwet*) **itadi**. *v*. to match a gamecock with another. **makitadi**. *v*. to have gamecocks fight. **pagtadian**. *n*. pit for fighting gamecocks. **tatadien**. *n*. gamecock. [Ibg. *táriq*, Png. *tári*, Tag. *tarì*]

tádug: *n*. threshold. (*obs*.) **tadugen**. *v*. to protect. (*salakan*, *salaknib*) **itadug**. *v*. to deliver a prisoner to the authorities. **tumadug**. *v*. to enter a threshold; enter the *sala*; rise up. (*laem*; *serrek*) **Siraragsak a nangpatadog kadakami**. He is happy to take us in.

táduk: **agtaduk, tumaduk**. *v*. to begin earring (rice). (*bugi*, *dawa*); become erect.

tádul: *n*. protrusion. **tumadul**. *v*. to protrude; jut out. (*agdawádaw*, *dukol*, *tumungángaw*) **Natadul dagiti tulang ti rupana**. The bones of his face protrude. **Siuulimek a nagkarayam dagiti lua iti tadul ti pingpingna a kinisset ti init**. The tears quietly fell over her protruding cheeks burned by the sun.

tadtád: **tadtaden**. *v*. to chop up; mince. (*reddekén*) **tinadtad**. *n*. minced meat, chopped up fish, etc. **matadtad**. *v*. to be cut into pieces.

natadtad. *a*. chopped up, cut into pieces. **Ibagam no ania ti inaramid kenka dayta a lalaki ta innak tadtaden**. Tell what that guy did to you and I'll rough him up. [Png., Tag. *tadtád*]

taéb: **agkataeb**. *v*. to be of the same age (*taég*, *sadar*, *kapatadan*). [Tag. *kaedád* (Sp.)]

taég: **agkataeg**. *v*. to be of the same age. (*taéb*, *sadar*)

taél: (Sp. *tael*: Philippine unit of weight and old coin) *n*. unit of weight about 39 grams.

taén: (*reg*.) *n*. bet, wager. (*pósta*; *taman*) **itaen**. (*obs*.) *v*. to raise an armed hand; place a bet. [Tag. *tayâ*]

taéng: *n*. residence; dwelling place; (*reg*.) age; maturity. (*pagyanán*, *naéd*) **agtaeng**. *v*. to reside, dwell; abstain, hold back. **pagtaengan**. *n*. residence; to detain, abstain. **makipagtaeng**. *v*. to reside with; live with. **nataengan**. *a*. mature, in season (fruits); adult. **kataengan**. *n*. one who is the same age. (*kasádar*) **Inton siak ti mataengan, negosio ti serkek**. When I get older I will go into business. **Natataengankami ngem sika**. We are older and wiser than you. [Kpm. *tuknang*, Png. *manayan*, Tag. *tirá*]

taép: *n*. husk, hull; chaff. **agtaep, itaep, taepan**. *v*. to winnow (*laíd*, *tiktik*). [Ibg. *etta* (rice husk), *saq* (winnow), Ifg. *dugi*, Itg. *dulsu*, Ivt. *apdiq* (husk), *wakwak* (winnow), Kal. *topa*, Knk. *tegap*, Kpm. *apa* (husk), *tatap* (winnow), Png. *taép*, Tag. *ipá* (husk), *tahíp* (winnow)]

taér: *n*. good posture; elegant, confident way of carrying oneself. **nataer**. *a*. elegant, graceful; well-shaped; handsome.

tagá-: *pref*. indicating origin or citizenship. **taga-anoka?** Where are you from? **taga-Viganak**. I am from Vigan. **Umuna nga innagek ti taga-baba ken tagabantay**. It was the first kiss between a lowlander and a highlander. [Png., Tag. *tagá-*]

tága: *n*. trap; snare. **tagaen**. *v*. to await (*urayen*); catch (*sippawen*, *tiliwen*, *kemmegén*). [Tag. *saló*, *panghuli*]

tagá₁: **tagaen**. *v*. to trim, shape (by cutting). (*arbás*, *rimírim*) **tinaga, nagtagaan**. *n*. chips of wood, stone, etc. **mannaga**. *n*. woodpecker. **Nanakliing ti sampilok a naitaga iti bato**. The machete chipping the stone made a clanging sound. [Tag. *tagâ*]

tagá₂: **tagtaga**. *n*. dried cowpeas; kind of small gray bird that nests in tree holes it bores.

tagaammó: see *tagiammó*.

tagaanó: *interrog*. From where? **Tagaanoda?** Where are they from?

tagáang: *n*. kind of underground furnace; stone stove (*anáwang*; *karraang*) **itagaang**. *v*. to put into the *tagaang*.

tagaángay: (*obs.*) *a*. close to parturition.

tagabán: *n*. kind of fish trap of woven bamboo. **agtagaban**. *v*. to catch fish with the *tagaban* trap.

tagábo: *n*. servant (*katulong*); slave. (*adipen*) **agpatagabo.** *v*. to work as a servant. **tagabuen.** *v*. to enslave, cause to be a servant. **tinagabo.** (*obs.*) *n*. adopted child (*tagibi*). [Kal. *musassu* (Sp.), Png. *aripén*, Tag. *busabos, alipin*]

tagád: **itagad.** *v*. to invite to come along without prior notice.

tagadtóy: [*tagá-* + *ditóy*] *a*. from here. **Tagadtoyak**. I am from here. [Tag. *tagarito*]

tagadtád: *n*. line; row. (*batog*) **tagadtaden.** *v*. to put, say, etc. in an orderly way. [Tag. *ayos*]

tagainép: *n*. dream. (*arapaap*) **agtagainep.** *v*. to dream. **managtagainep.** *a*. always dreaming. **tagainepen, tagimpen.** *v*. to dream of. **tumatagainep.** *n*. dreamer. [Bon. *kídam, ítaw*, Ibg. *tatagénoq*, Ivt. *tayaynep*, Kal. *in-ilop*, Knk. *iítaw*, Kpm. *panínap*, Png. *kúgip*, Tag. *panaginip*]

Tagakaólo: *n*. ethnic group from south Cotabato, Mindanao.

Tagakogon: *n*. ethnic group living in the pasture plains between Davao and Cotabato in Mindanao.

Tagála: (Sp.) *n*. Tagalog woman.

Tagalísta: (Sp. *tagalista*: Tagalog specialist) *n*. Tagalog specialist; person who is proficient in Tagalog.

Tagálog: *n*. Ethnic group of central Luzon; language of this ethnic group, the basis of the Filipino language; *a*. of or relating to this ethnic group. **ag-Tagalog.** *v*. to speak Tagalog. **tagalogen.** *v*. to say in Tagalog. **barong Tagalog.** *n*. a kind of formal men's shirt made of pineapple fabric. [Bon. *tagálob*]

tagálok: *n*. scorpion. (*manggagama*). [Png., Tag. *alakdán*]

tagaltáw: (*obs.*) see *tanggaltaw*: buoy; float.

tagamál: **tagamalan.** *v*. to take up with both hands.

tagamtám: **tagamtámen.** *v*. to include (when making an accusation, defining a boundary, etc.); include things that are not supposed to be included. **Saanko a kayat a tagamtamen ti tulong ti sabali.** I do not want to include the help of others. [Tag. *sakup*]

tagangtáng: *n*. humor, joke; wit; sport. (*angaw, rabak*) **agtagangtang.** *v*. to speak humorously.

tagapangúlo: (f. *ulo*) *n*. president.

tagapét: **mannagapet.** *n*. someone that brings bad luck; person with bad luck. **matagaptan.** *v*. to be prevented from succeeding.

tagapníd: **tagapniden.** *v*. to implicate, involve (innocent persons) (*raman*). [Tag. *dawit*]

tagapulót: *n*. sugar; when syrupy (*patároy*), when powder (*burisangsáng*), when refined (*asúkar* or *repinádo*); variety of awned *díket* rice. **tagapuloten.** *v*. to make into sugar. **timmagapulot nga isem.** *n*. sweet smile (*lit*. like sugar). **No adda tagapulot, umarak dagiti kuton.** If there is sugar, the ants will convene. **Tagapulotam tapno sumam-it.** Put sugar on it so it is sweet. [Tag. *pulót* (honey; molasses)]

tagaptán: (f. *tagapét*) **matagaptan.** *v*. to be prevented from proceeding.

tagarí: **agtagari, tumagari.** *v*. to babble, chatter; talk; gossip. (*saríta, saó*) **tagarien.** *v*. to talk about, divulge. **natagari.** *a*. talkative, prattling. **baribari tagtagari.** magical words used to protect oneself against the spirits when passing a place. [Tag. *ingay*]

tagaslíng: *n*. *Loranthus confusus* plant.

tagátag: *n*. scattered stakes used as a provisional fence. [Tag. *tulos*]

tagawátaw: *var*. of *tawátaw*.

tágay: (Tag. also) *n*. toast (with drinks) **itagay.** *v*. to make a toast (to).

tag-áy: **itag-ay.** *v*. to raise, lift. (*ipangato*) **natagay.** *a*. high. [Knk. *túdag*, Tag. *taás*]

tagayán: *n*. cup. (*tasa*).

tagayatán: (*obs.*, f. *ayát*) **tagayatanan**. *v*. to charm into love. (*kayawan*)

Tagbanuá: *n*. ethnic group of Aborlan, Palawan; language of the Tagbanwa people.

tagbát: *n*. cut; slash. **tumagbat, tagbaten.** *v*. to slash, hack, cut. (*iwaen*) **Tinagbatnan ti tengngedna.** He slashed its neck. **Intagbatna ti naganna iti bato.** *exp*. He carved his name in stone (to legitimize an oath or pact). [Tag. *laslás*]

tagdá: (*obs.*) *n*. kind of large oar. (*dakkel a gáud*)

tagdáy: **itagday.** *v*. to spread, stretch; dry in rows (said of tobacco leaves). [Tag. *ladlád*]

tagéngot: (*slang*) *n*. derogatory term for Tagalog people or their language.

tagengténg: *n*. hardness of the soil. **natagengteng.** *a*. solid, firm (soil) (*natibkér; natangken*). [Tag. *tigás*]

tagertér: *var*. of *tigerger*: shake.

taggabán: *var*. of *tagaban*.

taggátan: *n*. money bag strapped around the waist. **itaggatan.** *v*. to place into the money belt.

taggáy: *n*. *Hopia plagata* plant.

tagguáb: see *patagguab*: penthouse, appendage to a building; *var*. of *tangguab*.

tagi-: 1. *pref*. used to form substantives, indicating a close relationship with the entity denoted by the root: **lipat.** forget. **tagilipat.** oblivion. **pateg.** worth, value. **tagipatgen.** values, cherished things or beliefs. 2. May also express possession (see *maki-*) or a subjective attitude toward the action denoted by a verb root. **balay.** house. **agtagibalay.** to keep house. **buneng.** machete. **agtagibuneng.** to be with a machete; carry around a machete. **dakes.** bad. **tagidaksen.** to consider as bad. **Tagiurayna kenkuana.** He seems to be waiting for her. **Tagipanunotenna ti napukaw a pitakana.** As if he were thinking of his lost wallet. **Kinsena pay laeng ngem tagibalasangen dagiti mangap-apura.** She is still fifteen but the quick (assailants) already consider her to be a young lady. 3. Like many of the less productive affixes of Ilocano, *tagi-* often becomes fossilized in lexicalized stems: **ruot.** grass. **tagiruot.** magical charm. **ammo.** know; knowledge. **tagtagiammuan.** doubtful.

tagi- -en: Affix used with adjectival roots meaning: to consider something to be the quality expressed by the root: **pintas.** beauty. **tagipintasen.** to consider an object beautiful although it isn't. **bassit.** small, little. **tagibassiten.** to belittle, consider unimportant.

tagiammó: (f. *ammó*) **tagtagiammuan.** *a.* doubtful, uncertain. (*duadua*) **Pagtagtagiammuan nga ipatayna ti kantiridas.** *n.* The cantharides probably will kill him.

tagibaláy: (f. *baláy*) **agtagibalay.** *n.* housewife; *v.* to keep house.

tagibás: (metathesized variant of *sagibat*) **agtagibas.** *v.* to graze; scrape; miss by a hair. (*tawás, sagibát*)

tagibassít: (f. *bassít*) **tagibassiten.** *v.* to belittle; underestimate; ignore. **Napalalo ti panangtagibassittayo kadagiti tagabantay a kakabsattayo.** We greatly underestimate our mountain brothers. [Bon. *layos*, Tag. *maliitín*]

tagibén: tagibenén. *v.* to maintain. **pannakatagiben iti aglawlaw.** maintenance of the environment or surroundings.

tagíbi: *n.* adopted child; suckling, foster child. **agtagibi.** *v.* to suckle, nurse. **tagibien.** *v.* to suckle, nurse, rear. **managibi.** *n.* foster parent, foster mother. *v.* to suckle; nurse. [Png. *tagibi*]

tagidpuán: (f. *duppo*) *n.* beginning of the rainy season.

tagikuá: *n.* property, possessions. (*kukua*) **agtagikua, tagikuaen.** *v.* to own, possess. **ipatagikua.** *v.* to bequeath; donate. **makapagtagikua.** *v.* to be able to cooperatively own. **Masapol a matagikuak.** It must be mine. [Knk. *uká*, Tag. *arì*]

tagiktík: *n.* heavy rain. (*tarakitik*) **tumagtagiktík.** *v.* to rain cats and dogs, rain heavily. [Tag. *tagakták*; *tagiktík* dripping liquids, sound of a clock]

tagilnekán: (f. *lennek*) *n.* sunset. (*lumnek 'diay init*)

tagimpén: (f. *tagainep*) *v.* to dream about.

tagintúdo: *n.* backstroke. **agtagintudo.** *v.* to swim the backstroke (on the back); to shower under the rain.

tagíng: *n.* two points of the crescent moon. **taging iti daya.** before the first quarter. **taging iti laud.** after the third quarter.

tagingtíng: *n.* young *bólo* bamboo.

tágip: (*obs.*) **natagip.** *a.* filled with, full of. (*napno*)

tagipíd: *n.* sideboards of a boat to prevent passengers from getting wet.

tagipuéd: (*obs.*) *n.* board added to sides of canoe to keep passengers dry.

tagipúro: *n.* small island. (*puro*)

tagiráyad: *n.* herb charm. (*ginginammol*; *tagiruot*) **tagirayaden.** *v.* to bewitch by use of a charm.

tagirgír: agtagirgir. *v.* to tremble, shake. (*tigerger*)

tagirúot: (f. *rúot*: grass) *n.* love charm. (*ánib*, *tagiráyad*) **tagiruoten.** *v.* to bewitch; charm. **matagiruot.** *v.* to be under the influence of the *tagiruot*. **Tinagiruotnaka ketdin ni Zorayda ket adipennakan ti anitoda?** Did Zorayda cast a spell on you for their spirits to enslave you? [Png. *panagayat, diká*, Tag. *gayumà*]

tagisíma: (f. *sima*) *n.* hook and sinker.

tagná: *n.* remainder, residue. (*tidda*; *ared-ed*)

tagnáwa: *n.* communal work. (*gamal*; *batara*; *ammuyo*) **makitagnawa.** *v.* to cooperate in doing a task; do a job communally. [Tag. *bayanihan*]

tagnép: (*obs.*) **matagnep.** *a.* continually; often (*masansan*). [Tag. *dalás*]

tagní: agtagni. *v.* to patch up (sewing). **tagnitagni.** *a.* patched-up. [Tag. *dugtóng*]

tagó: agitago. *v.* to keep (*idulin*); conceal underground; hide (*lemmeng*). [Tag. *tagò* = hide]

taguáb: pataguab. *v.* lean-to roof; penthouse (*duag*); *var.* of *tangguab*: move with the snout.

taguán₁: *n.* oar. (*gaud*).

taguán₂: *n.* kind of small bird similar to the *toldó*.

tagúban: *n.* quiver for carrying arrows.

tagubanáy: *n.* variety of rice.

tagubay-á: matagubay-aan. *v.* to pass unnoticed; to be skipped inadvertently. **managtagubay-a.** *a.* careless, thoughtless, inattentive. (*liway*) **tagubay-aan.** *v.* to neglect; overlook.

tágud: *n.* comb made of coconut shell to comb cotton yarn. **tagudan.** *v.* to comb cotton yarn. **matagudan.** *n.* combed cotton ready for weaving; *a.* combed (said of cotton). **pagtagudan.** *n.*

contrivance where cotton yarns are stretched to be combed, combing frame.

tagúdas: (*obs.*) **pagtagudasen**. *a.* crossed half-way.

tágul: *n.* operculum of the *raráng* mollusk. **tagultágul**. *n.* ankle (*pingí*); *n.* kneecap.

tagulayláy: *n.* kind of song.

tagumbáw: *n. Jatropha curcas*, physic nut.

tagumpáy: (Tag. *tagumpáy*: success; victory) *n.* kind of alcoholic drink. (*lambanog*)

tagúob: *n.* howl of a dog. (*taul, uga*) **agtaguob**. *v.* to howl. **managtaguob**. *a.* always howling, prone to howl. **agtinnaguob**. *v.* to howl at each other. **agkarataguob**. *v.* to howl repeatedly. **taguoban**. *v.* to howl at. **Idi damo, diak maawatan no apay nga agkarataguob ti asoda.** At first, I didn't understand why their dog would frequently howl. [Tag. *alulóng*]

taguráyaw: **tagtagurayaw**. *n.* kind of edible burrowing beetle.

taguyupyúp: *n. var.* of *igadigad*.

tagpaáyan: *n. Justicia gendarussa*, shrub with white or pink flowers with purple spots.

tagpás: *var.* of *tigpas*: chop, cut. [Tag. *tagpás*]

tagpáw: *n.* superior part of the buttocks where they inflect toward the back (*kibongkíbong*); region between waist and protuberant part of the umbilical region.

tagpaya: *n. Justicia gendarussa* shrub. (see *tagpaayan*)

tagpí: **tagpian**. *v.* to patch. (*takup*)

tagráng: *n.* kind of *kattokóng* (hat) made from the *anáaw* palm. (*palokkot*)

tagtág: **tumagtag**. *v.* to walk with a heavy, jerky gait; jerk. **matagtag**. *v.* to be shaken, jerked. **tagtagen**. *v.* to shake, jerk.

tagtagi-: *pref.* Progressive (incomplete) form of the *tagi-* prefix. **Isuna ti tagtagiurayna.** He is the one she seems to be waiting for.

taháda: (Sp. *tajada*: slice) *n.* slice. (*iwa*)

tahadéra: (Sp. *tajadera*: slicing knife) *n.* slicing knife.

tahár: (Sp. *tajar*: chop, cut) **agtahar, taharan**. *v.* to sharpen a pencil. (*itadman*)

tahú: (Hok. *tau hû*: bean curd) *n.* a kind of delicatessen made from soybean or mung bean meal and syrup. The Philippine version is served sweet, not salty as the original Chinese.

tahóng: (Tag.) *n.* mussel. (*kaong*)

tahór: *n.* excessive gambler. (*managsugsugal*)

taká: *n.* hesitation. (*arimadéng*) **agtaka**. *v.* to hesitate, vacillate. **managtaka**. *a.* unsure of oneself.

tákad: **takadan**. *v.* to give food to someone in a limited amount. **mataktakadan**. *a.* receiving food in a limited amount; malnourished.

takadáw: **itakadaw**. *v.* to do secretly. (*lemmeng*)

tákal: (Tag.) *n.* measurement of volume. **tumakal**. *v.* to pour; to take a measure (*sukat*). **takalen**. *v.* to measure. **pagtakalan**. *n.* measuring device.

takál: *n.* stud, animal used for breeding. **agtakal**. *v.* to copulate (animals). **takalen**. *v.* to breed animals (*dakep*). [Tag. *kastá, lahi*]

tákap: *n.* apportionment, allotment; area around transplanter of rice seedlings; area for planting. **natakap**. *a.* full of, covered with. **takapen**. *v.* to plant; harvest. [Tag. *takáp* = babble]

takará: *n.* shallow, round basket the size of a plate. **itakara**. *v.* to place in the *takara* basket.

takaták: *n.* sound of a typewriter. **agtakatak**. *v.* to type loudly.

tákaw: **agtakaw, tumakaw**. *v.* to steal, rob. (*samsamen, tikasen*) **takawen**. *v.* to steal; embezzle. **takawan**. *v.* to rob; loot. **mannanakaw**. *n.* thief; pirate; embezzler. **tinnakawan**. *n.* girl's game with a hen guarding her eggs (stones) while another steals and hides them. **patakawan**. *v.* to have someone robbed. **pagtakawen**. *v.* to order someone to steal. **maitakaw ti taldiap**. *v.* to steal a glance. **itakaw**. *v.* to do stealthily; do something when there is no time. **Agsasamusam ti trabaho, itaktakawko pay ti agsurat.** Work is piling up, I'm stealing time to write. **Agtaktakawka payen tapno adda ipalamutmo kenkuana.** You are still stealing so you can have something to feed her. [Ibg. *kókoq*, Ivt. *manakaw*, Kpm. *náko*, Png. *takéw*, Tag. *nakaw*, Tag. *takaw* = greed, voracity]

takbá₁: **tumakba**. *v.* to embrace from behind; hang on somebody's neck while being carried on the back; cover; copulate on the back.

takbá₂: **patakba**. *n.* kind of rectangular basket, sometimes carried on the back like a knapsack. (*kalupí; pasiking*)

takbián: *n.* spindle of a spinning wheel, slender rod of *belláng*.

takdáng₁: *n.* kind of net used to catch freshwater fish; stepping on dry ground after wading.

takdáng₂: **tumakdang**. *v.* to go ashore. **itakdang**. *v.* to strand to shore, beach, set ashore. **katakdangan**. *n.* surf in the shallows. [Tag. *katihan, pasigan*; *takdáng* = short length of skirts]

takdáy: *n.* net like the *takdáng*, but broader and longer; poles stuck in the ground near the shore to put fishing nets on to dry. **itakday**. *v.* to hang fishnets to dry.

takdér: *n.* figure; appearance; shape; posture; semblance. (*itsora; langa*) **agtakder**. *v.* to stand, remain standing. **tumakder.** *v.* to stand up. **itakder, takderan.** *v.* to set upright, cause to stand; stand by one's word. **itakderan.** *v.* to represent, stand for something. **makatakder.** *v.* to be able to stand; to withstand. **natakder.** *a.* upright; erect; straight-up. **patakder.** *a.* under construction (houses); in a standing position; *n.* building; structure; scaffold. **pagtakderan.** *n.* point of view; position. **pagpatakderan.** *n.* the place where something is constructed. **ipatakder.** *v.* to construct, build. **Itakdermo ti dayawko!** Stand up for my honor! **tumakder dagiti dutdut.** *exp.* to bristle (body hair when afraid). **lintegen ti takder.** *v.* to straighten one's posture. [Bon. *takdeg*, Ibg. *taddág*, Itg. *sikad*, Ivt. *tínek*, Kpm. *tikdo*, Png. *alagéy*, Tag. *tayô*]

takéb: *(obs.)* *n.* shoulder blade. *(akloaklo)*

takéd: *n.* cuticle, part of the skin that covers the base of the nail. **nataked.** *a.* strong, robust, sturdy. *(baked)*

takém: *n.* office, employment, rank; *(reg.)* marked, designated. **agtakem.** *v.* to hold an office or position. **mapatakman.** *v.* to appoint to an office. **takmen.** *v.* to choose for one's office. **panagtakem.** *n.* term of office. [Png. *kanepegan*, Tag. *tungkól*]

takiág: *(pron. takkiag)* *n.* arm. **itakiagan.** *v.* to do with the bare hands; to shoulder (expenses). **tinnakiagan.** *n.* bare-handed fight. **maitakiagan.** *v.* to defend oneself with the arms. **natakiag.** *a.* having strong arms. **tinnakiagan.** *n.* bare-handed fight. [Kal. *takÿay*, Knk. *takkáy*, Bon., Png. *takláy*, Tag. *bisig*]

takiás: *(pron. takkias)* **tumakias.** *v.* to slip out; run away secretly, escape without being noticed *(lasút; libas)*. [Png. *takiás*, Tag. *talilis*]

tákig: *n.* juncture; joint. *(suop)*

takigrapía: (Sp. *taquigrafía*: stenography) *n.* shorthand, stenography.

takígrapo: (Sp. *taquígrafo*: stenographer) *n.* stenographer.

takília: (Sp. *taquilla*: box office; ticket window) *n.* box office (at the cinema).

takiliéro: (Sp. *taquillero*: ticket booth clerk) *n.* ticket booth clerk, theater clerk; bank teller.

takín: **takintakin.** *n.* obstacle, hindrance *(lappéd, tipéd)*; *v.* to ramble, carry something for no purpose.

tákip₁: *n.* cover. *(kalúb, abbóng)* **pagtakipen.** *v.* to cover; unite, join; overlap.

tákip₂: **takipan.** *n.* Caryota sp. palm.

takís: **tumakis.** *v.* to escape. *(takías)* **takisan.** *n.* thief. *(tikas, takaw)* **agtakis, takisen.** *v.* to steal.

takkáb: *n.* cover, lid *(abbung, kalúb, kelléb)*; *var.* of *sakkúb*. **takkaban.** *v.* to cover something; trace. **itakkab.** *v.* to use as a cover

on; trace. **Intakkabna dagiti ramayna iti rupak nga agkatkatawa.** He covered my face with his fingers, laughing. [Tag. *taklób*]

takkí: *n.* excrement, feces, dung. *(pur-is; tabbel; pultit)* **itakki.** *v.* to excrete as excrement. **tumakki.** *v.* to defecate. **takkian.** *v.* to defecate on. **agtakki.** *v.* to have a loose bowel movement, have diarrhea *(buris)*. **makatakki.** *v.* to feel like defecating. **pagtakkian.** *n.* toilet. *(kasilias)* **tatakkian.** *n.* anus. *(moriit; merret; kimmut; busigit)* **takkin baka.** *n.* kind of medicinal plant, *Malva sp.* or *Sida sp.* [Bon. *tái*, Ibg. *ettay*, Ivt. *taciq*, Kal. *attay*, Knk. *takkí, tái*, Kpm. *takláq*, Png. *taí*, Tag. *tae*]

takkiág: *var.* spelling of *takiag*: arm.

takkiás: *var.* spelling of *takias*: slip away, escape.

takkín báka: (Sp. *vaca*: cow) *n.* kind of plant used in medicine, *Malva sp.* or *Sida sp.*

takkuáp: *n.* snare for herons using a frog for bait. **takkuapan.** *v.* to repatch, patch up.

takkuát: *n.* discovery. *(pannakasárak)* **matakkuatan.** *v.* to discover unexpectedly; find out by chance; take by surprise. **Natakkuatan metten ti lakay ti pannakapukaw ti dippigda.** The old man discovered his lost bananas. [Tag. *tuklás*]

takkúb: *n. var.* of *akkub* (cover).

takkón: **natakkon.** *a.* scanty, scarce; rare. *(rásay; kisang; kurang)* **pagtatakkonan.** *v.* to prefer something out of lack of choice.

takkúong: *var.* of *tukkuong* or *tikkuong*: idle sitting around in a group. **nakatakuong.** *a.* passing the time away in a group idly. **Kasla natuktokan a bisukol ti barkadana a nakatakkuong iti sirok ti kamantiris.** His group of friends idling under the *kamantsile* tress are like opened snails.

taklá₁: **agtakla.** *v.* to click the tongue. [Tag. *paláták*]

taklá₂: **taktakla.** *n.* kind of small freshwater crayfish only an inch long, named for the sound it makes.

takláb: **tumaklab.** *v.* to attack with the teeth (animals); to click repeatedly *(sakrak)*. [Tag. *sakmál*; *takláb* = granary]

taklád: *n. var.* of *tarik*.

taklín: *n.* refuge, asylum, shelter *(pagtaklinan)*. **agtaklin.** *v.* to seek protection, shelter; rely on, trust. [Tag. *pakupkóp*]

taklúbo: *(obs.)* *n.* rushing, attacking. *(duklós)* **taklubuen.** *v.* to attack by rushing. [Tag. *sugod*; Png., Tag. *taklubo* = species of large clam; Tag. *taklubo* = mother of pearl]

taklóng: *n.* school of fish. *(pangen ti sida, gateb; rotok)* **maitaklong.** *v.* to be caught in a net.

taknáng: **agtaktaknang.** *v.* to nibble. (*kittíb*, *sammukat*, *kibkib*)

taknéng: *n.* honor; dignity. (*dayaw*) **kina-takneng.** *n.* honesty; dignity. **natakneng.** *a.* suave, mild, peaceful; temperate; dignified; honorable. **pagtaknengen.** *v.* to quiet, pacify, appease, soothe; comfort, relieve. **Natakneng-da ken naanusda a nagsukisok.** They investigated nice and peacefully. [Tag. *dangál*]

táko₁: (Sp. *taco*: billiard cue) *n.* cue in billiards.

táko₂: *n.* dipper, scoop; section of a dry bottle gourd (*tabungaw*). **agtako, tumako.** *v.* to dip to draw liquids. **takuen.** *v.* to dip out, scoop. **pagtako.** *n.* dipper (*sodo*). [Tag. *tabò*]

takó: **agtaktako.** *v.* to slap one's head with the palm.

takuáp: *var.* of *takkuáp*: repatch.

takuát: *var.* of *takkuát*: discovery. [Tag. *tuklás*]

takudóg: *n.* kind of scaly larva that leaves a path when it moves.

takúdor: **maitakudor.** *v.* to be placed alongside. **itakudor.** *v.* to place alongside; arrange.

takúlaw: **takulaw-puraw.** *Saccopetalum longipes* plant.

takulí: *n.* kind of small boat made of a hollowed tree trunk with no outrigger. [Tag. *takurî* = teakettle]

tákon: (*obs.*) *n.* companion; one of a pair. (*kadua*; *pangis*)

takón: (Sp. *tacón*: heel) *n.* heel of a shoe; horseshoe. **patakonan.** *v.* to fix a heel; put on a horseshoe. [Tag. *takóng*]

takunaynáy: **katakunaynay.** *n.* helper, assistant, attendant. (*katulong*) **pannakitinnakunaynay.** *n.* cooperation. **Kaanonto met ngata a masarakak ti katunaynayko iti biag iti agnanayon?** And when will I find my lifetime companion? [Tag. *makiramay*]

takundá: *n.* items arranged according to length or size. **nagtakunda.** *v.* to be unequal in length. **agtakunda.** *v.* to dangle; to be graded, graduated (arranged in steps). **mataktakunda.** *v.* to be arranged accordingly. [Tag. *hanay*]

tákong: *n.* sole of shoe.

takóng: *n.* sow, female hog; (*fig.*) condition of having a stretched breast after childbirth (said of female animals). [Bon. *ogol*, Kal. *pidcheÿ*, Knk. *kalóng*; Tag. *takóng* = heel (Sp.)]

takúp₁: *n.* patch. (*sug-op*) **agtakup.** *v.* to patch; to marry a girl who is no longer a virgin. **takupan.** *v.* to patch. **natakup.** *a.* patched; (*fig.*) false, untrue, insincere, tricky. **pagtakup.** *n.* patching material. **Uy-uyawendak dagiti kaadalak gapu iti lupotko a takuptakop.** My classmates criticize me because of my patched-

up clothes. [Png. *sakáb*, Tag. *tagpî*, *tapal* (patch); *takíp* = cover]

takúp₂: **taktakup.** *n. Desmodium sp.* herbs with twisted pods.

takurí: *n.* teapot; water pot. [Ivt., Tag. *takurî*]

takpál: **itakpal.** *v.* to add something in order to secure. **pagtakpalen.** *v.* to join, unite, connect in order to secure (*tapkal*). [Tag. *taklób*]

takpíl₁: **agtakpil.** *v.* to patch; bind together; double. (*takpal*)

takpíl₂: **tinakpil.** *n.* kind of thick cloth used for sacks.

takráp: see *sakrár*: confused; fickle; inconsistent; unstable.

takrót: *n.* coward. (*managbutbuteng*) **natakrot.** *a.* cowardly, timid, craven. **mapatakrotan.** *v.* to be overwhelmed with fear. **tumakrot.** *v.* to be cowardly. **kinatakrot.** *n.* cowardice. [Bon. *koymot*, Ivt. *tahaw*, Knk. *kiltút*, Png. *payóte*, Tag. *duwág*]

taksáy: see *tatsáy*: kind of round casting net, larger than the *tabúkol*. [Tag. *taksáy* = slipmouth fish]

táksi: (Eng.) *n.* taxi, cab. **agtaksi.** *v.* to go by taxi; ride in a taxi.

taksíng: *var.* of *tatsing*.

takták: *n.* delay. (*gábay*; *imberna*, *tantan*) **agtaktak, manaktak.** *v.* to delay, linger, loiter. **taktaken.** *v.* to detain, delay, hold back; bother. **pakataktakan.** *n.* cause of delay. **No adda wayada a manglib-at dida agtaktak.** If they have the time to attack, they won't delay. [Tag. *antala*]

táktika: (Sp. *táctica*: tactics) *n.* tactics, strategy. (*sikap*, *pamuspusan*) **taktika militar.** *n.* military tactic.

tála: *n.* a kind of white bird. [Tag. *talà* = star, *tala* = species of herb used in flavoring]

tal-á: **ital-a.** *v.* to eject something from the throat. (*dul-o*)

talaágum: (*obs.*) *n.* a kind of large jar. (*burnay*)

taláan: *n.* hindrance. (*lappéd*) **talaanan.** *v.* to hinder, impede, obstruct, prevent. **matalaan.** *v.* to be hindered, impeded; delayed. **pakatalaanan.** *n.* cause of delay. [Tag. *pigil*]

taláb: (Tag.) **tumalab.** *v.* to take effect (*talubo*). **Awan met makitak nga itatalab ti tagi-ruotko.** I don't see my potion taking any effect.

talabá: (Tag.) *n.* kind of large oyster. (*tirem*)

talabóng: *n.* tilted hammock (*indayon*). [Tag. *duyan*]

talád: **taladan.** *v.* to compensate, pay, give what is due. [Tag. *gantimpalà*]

taládo: *n.* food offered to the dead (*atang*, *sumang*); divination. **agtalado.** *v.* to practice divination; offer to the spirits of the dead.

taladuen. *v.* to appease the spirits by offering food. **tumatalado.** *n.* witch doctor, one who practices divination.

taládro: (Sp. *taladro*: drill) *n.* drill; perforator, puncher; ticket puncher.

taladtád: **tumaladtad.** *v.* to move on rollers. **mataladtad.** *v.* to fall down the stairs. **pataladtad.** *n.* roller. **pataladtadan.** *v.* to spread, place under a roller. [Tag. *pamipis*]

tálag: **agtalag.** *v.* to be prudent; careful (*annad*). [Tag. *ingat*]

talagá: (Tagalog also) *adv.* really, truly. *a.* true, in fact. (*pudno, agpayso*) **Agmauyongka a talaga.** You are really crazy. **No talaga nga ayayatennak ket rebbengna ngarud a dayawennak.** If you really love me, you should honor me then. **Sabalika talaga kadagiti naam-ammokon.** You are really different from the people I know. [Bon. *dadlo, daglos*, Png., Tag. *talagá*]

talagálo: (*obs.*) *n.* toad. (*pilát*)

talagítag: *n.* bamboo joists to support roofing or flooring.

talagutóg: *var.* of *talugutog*.

talaín: **agtalain.** *v.* to blush, feel shame. (*aglabbasit*)

talakápo: *n.* *Tournefortia horsfieldii* tree. (*salakapo*)

talakbóng: *n.* shroud, covering over the body. **agtalakbong.** *v.* to shroud, cover the body (as a blanket). **Agkalimduosanak iti ling-et iti agpatnag a panagtalakbongko iti ules.** I was drenched in sweat from being covered all night by the blanket.

talakéb: *n.* kind of fish trap made of bamboo. (*asád*)

talakiás: **agtalakias.** *v.* to escape. (*libas, takiás*)

talákib: *n.* roof made of bamboo.

talákid: *var.* of *akilis*.

talakítok: *n.* kind of small, speckled marine fish with dark meat, called *tariptíp* or *taliboknó* when very small, *Caranx sp.*

talákub: *n.* reglets used to cover joints between boards, coverlets.

talakták: *n.* *Capparis horrida* plant.

találi: *n.* replacement; substitute. **talalian.** *v.* to change, substitute. (*sandí, pattáli*) **italali.** *v.* to substitute, exchange for.

talám: (*obs.*) **tatalam.** *n.* censure; blame.

talamít: *n.* coarse grass used as fodder. (*amgid*)

talamítim: **agtalamitim.** *v.* to move the lips without speaking, mumble; make a muffled sound (of falling water).

talamúging: **talamugingan.** *a.* with a blaze on the face, star on forehead.

talantán: *n.* kind of coarse cloth; attendance. **tumalantan.** *v.* to come from another town; attend. **italantan, talantanen.** *v.* to arrange in a row, align.

talanggutáng$_1$: *n.* a kind of large snail shell; vagabond. **agtalanggutang.** *v.* to wander, stray (*ballog*).

talanggutáng$_2$: *n.* a kind of noisy bird; gossiper. **mataltalanggutang.** *v.* to gossip (*sismis, tarabitab*); chatter. **Taltalanggutangem, aya?** Are you chattering?

talangkáw: *a.* having lost self-control (due to inebriation, etc.); *Plumbago zeylanica*.

talangkéd: **talangkeden.** *v.* to investigate, inquire; make sure. (*palutputen*)

talangkiáw: **agtalangkiaw, tumalangkiaw.** *v.* to gaze in various directions, look around. **Iti panagtaltalangkiawna, nakitana a nasamsamek iti bangir ti baresbes.** As he gazed around, he saw that on the other side of the stream it was more lush. [Tag. *palingonlingón*]

talangkíd: (*obs.*) *n.* naughtiness (*tangsit; pilio; welwel*). **natalangkid.** *a.* haughty.

talangkúb: *n.* sill, ridging, windowsill. (*dapián*)

talátal: **agtalatal, tumalatal.** *v.* to revolve on an axis, turn over and over. (*tayyék, pusípus*) **italatal.** *v.* to cause to spin; cause to revolve. [Tag. *ikot*]

tálaw: *n.* evacuation. (*libas*) **agtalaw.** *v.* to escape, run away; vanish. **agpatalaw.** *v.* to order someone to run away. **tumalaw.** *v.* to go away, run away. **talawan.** *v.* to run away from someone. **italaw.** *v.* to run away with; kidnap; ravish. **pagtalawen.** *v.* to drive away, expel, eject, exile; send away. **matalaw.** *v.* to suffer from heat or cold; succumb, grow faint. **agpatanpatalaw.** *v.* to fight it out. **pagpatalawan.** *n.* drainage. **pannakapagtalaw, pammagtalaw.** *n.* exile, banishment. **napagtalaw.** *a.* forced out; exiled, banished. **pangpagtalawan.** *n.* reason for exiling someone. **pakapagtalawan.** *n.* reason for being exiled. [Png., Tag. *takas*, Tag. *layas*]

taláw: *n.* dry shell of a bottle gourd used to carry water.

talawátaw: *n.* wanderer. (*sorsor, katang*) **agtalawataw.** *v.* to search by making inquiries all around; wander. **talawatawan.** *v.* to seek, search (in water). [Tag. *galà*]

talawtáw: **talawtawen.** *v.* to search in water.

tal-áy: **agtal-ay, manal-ay.** *v.* to journey by land. (*baniaga*)

talaytáy: *n.* bamboo or tree-trunk bridge. (*rangtay ti kawayan*) **agtalaytay.** *v.* to walk on a *talaytay*. **talaytayen.** *v.* to pass over a bridge.

patalaytay. *n.* shoulder part of a coat; tight-rope. [Tag. *tuláy; talaytáy* = flow]
talbég: patalbeg. *n.* kind of drum. (*tambór, bómbo*)
taldéng: *n.* hole (perforated in ear, nasal septum, etc.) (*sub-ok*) **taldengan.** *v.* to pierce, perforate, bore. **tataldengan.** *n.* hole perforated in animals. **kattaldeng.** *n.* novice, apprentice. **Na-rigat ti kallawitan ti di pay nataldengan.** *exp.* It is difficult to accomplish a monumental task without one foot in the door (*lit.* it is hard to hook what has not been perforated).
taldiáp: *n.* glance, glimpse. (*saripatpát, kissiát, kisláp, palúdip*) **tumaldiap.** *v.* to glimpse, glance. **mataldiapan.** *v.* to catch a glimpse of. **apagtaldiap.** *a.* fleeting; instantaneous. [Png. *pasikyap*, Tag. *sulyáp*]
taléb: *n.* wooden partition inside a house; overlapping bamboos (split lengthwise and lined up so the halves face one another and the convex part on both sides of the partition shows. Each split bamboo fits half in one opposite bamboo and half in the other). **panalban.** *n.* wall; partition; (*fig.*) shield. **natalban.** *a.* walled. **taleban.** *v.* to build a bamboo wall. **Inasutna ti badáng iti taleb.** He unsheathed the sword from the *taleb.* **Natalban ti banio iti nasigpit a bulong ti silag.** The bathroom was walled with *silag* leaves woven together. [Ibg. *zizzing*, Ivt. *gadagadaq*, Knk. *kubkub*, Knk., Kpm., Png., Tag. *dingdíng* (wall)]
talék: *n.* confidence; trust. (*pammáti, talgéd; salindeg; namnama; sammaked; singked; kammatalek*) **agtalek, agkammatalek.** *v.* to trust, rely on, have faith in. **pagtalkan.** *n.* somebody one has confidence in; faithful person. (*katalek*) **matalek.** *v.* to be reliable, trustworthy. **manaltalek.** *v.* to inspire confidence. **katalek.** *n.* overseer; keeper; majordomo; right-hand man. **managtalek.** *a.* excessively trusting; overconfident. **mapagtalkan.** *a.* trustworthy. **natalek.** *a.* trustworthy; close, intimate. **italek.** *v.* to attend, look after, mind; pay attention. **talken.** *v.* to trust, confide in. **talek pay.** Lucky! (*na-gasat*). [Png. *pánpia, talék*, Tag. *tiwalà*]
talentén₁: talentenen, matalenten. *v.* to crowd; press together.
talentén₂: talentenen. *v.* arrange in rows. **matalenten.** *v.* to be lined up. [Tag. *hanay*]
talénto: (Sp. *talento:* talent) *n.* talent. (*talu-gáding; sarirít*)
táleng: talengtaleng. see *kulangít:* young *bu-notán* fish.
talengténg: agtalengténg. *v.* to lose one's seat; lose one's position. **italengteng (iti igid).** *v.* to steal; take away.

talgéd: *n.* hope; prospect; safety. (*namnama*) **agtalged.** *v.* to lean, rely on, depend on; trust, confide in. (*talék*) **natalged.** *a.* hopeful, positive, sure, certain. **ipatalged.** *v.* to advise; recommend; guarantee. **patalgedan.** *v.* to verify, establish; approve; confirm. **pammatalged.** *n.* assurance; advice. **panangipatalgedna.** upon his assurance. **Mamatpatalged dagiti suratmo kaniak.** Your letters to me are hopeful (provide hope). **No pagtalgedem ti puso, abakem ti kabusormo.** If you assure your heart, you will beat your enemy. **No ti panagballigi ti sapsapulem, patalgedem ta nakem.** Victory is attained through courage. [Tag. *ligtás, tiyák, patunay*]
talí: *n.* rope, cord, string, cable. (*singdan*) **itali.** *v.* to tie (*galut*), bind, attach to something with a rope. **talian.** *v.* to rope, tie, bind; entwine; grip, grasp. **talien.** *v.* to bind; twist into a rope. **tumali.** *v.* to twist into a rope, rope. **tinali.** *n.* rope consisting of two or more strands. **nagtinnali.** *a.* entwined; interwoven; entangled. **nakatali.** *a.* tied; bound. **pagtalien.** *v.* to entwine. [Ibg. *luvig*, Ivt. *pinuspus, itan, kedked*, Kal. *tali*, Knk. *talí*, Kpm. *lúbid*, Png. *lobir, kulili*, Tag. *lubid, talì*]
tália: (Sp. *talla:* carving) *n.* wood carving; raised woodwork, fresco; sculpture.
taliáda: (Sp. *tallada:* engraved) *n.* engraved; cut; carved.
taliágum: *a.* common, ordinary, typical, usual (*kadawyan; gagangay*). [Tag. *karaniwan*]
taliáw: *n.* looking back. **tumaliaw, agtaliaw.** *v.* to look back; look behind; pay attention to, care about, mind. (*imatang*) **taliawen.** *v.* to look back at; regard; mind someone's requests. **italiaw.** *v.* to turn the eyes. **managtaliaw.** *v.* to look arrogantly. **No naumakan iti kasar-saritam, taliawen ti sabali a kaabaymo.** If you are bored with the person you are speaking with, turn back to someone else at your other side. [Tag. *lingón*]
talibágok: *n.* glamour; luck, fortune, chance (*gasat*); success, advantage; talisman that brings luck. **natalibagokan.** *a.* charming; charismatic.
talibágot: *var.* of *talibagok:* charm.
talibugnáy: *a.* secondhand (*segunda mano*); worn, used; worn down.
talibuknó: *n. talakítok* fish when larger than the *tariptíp*, of the *Leiognathidae* family.
tálie: (Sp. *talle:* figure; fit) *n.* proportion; form; shape. (*itsora*)
taliér: (Sp. *taller:* auto repair shop) *n.* auto repair shop; workshop; garage for repairing cars. **agpatalier.** *v.* to go to the auto shop.

talikalá: see *tanikalá*: gold chain. (*kawar a balitok*)

talikebkéb: **talikebkeben**. *v.* to fence; encircle, surround. (*lawlaw*)

talikúd: *var.* of *tallikud*.

talimago: **talimagúen**. *v.* to dye; change the color of something.

talímeng: **natalimeng**. *a.* hidden, concealed (*lemmeng*); mysterious; profound; obscure. **italimeng**. *v.* to keep; hide, conceal; hold dear, value.

talimúdaw: *n.* dizziness; vertigo; fainting. **agtalimudaw, matalimudaw**. *v.* to feel dizzy; to feel faint (*ulaw*). [Png. *alimuréng*, Tag. *himatáy, hilo*]

talimúdok: **agtalimudok**. *v.* to persevere; persist (*agtalinaéd*); to be affected deeply; to be concentrated on. **italimudok**. *v.* to concentrate on, focus on. **Dita ti nakaitalimudokan ti katawa, leddaang, ken ugalimi**. That is where our laughter, sadness, and customs are persistent [Tag. *timò*]

talimúging: *n.* birthmark on the forehead. **talimugingan**. *a.* with a birthmark on the forehead; to have a prominent forehead. **Dadaelen ti talimugingna ti tarakina**. The birthmark on his forehead destroys his handsomeness.

talimpúngaw: see *talipugnaw*.

tálin: (*obs.*) **taltalinen**. *v.* to breathe deeply while eating.

talináay: *n.* tranquility; peace; comfort. (*talna*) **natalinaay**. *a.* peaceful, tranquil, calm. **agtalinaay**. *v.* to calm down; abate (weather); subside (flood). **kinatalinaay**. *n.* calmness, tranquility. **patalinaayen**. *v.* to calm down. **Panalinaayen ti baybay, umas-asul ti danum**. The sea was rather calm, the waters were blue. [Tag. *payapà*]

talinaéd: **agtalinaed**. *v.* to dwell, abide (*naed, taeng*); persist, persevere (*agtalimúdok*); remain (*agbati*) **pagtalinaeden**. *v.* to maintain, keep on; detain. **pagtalinaedan**. *n.* place where one stays for a long time. **No la kuma agtalinaedakon a napintas**. If only I could remain beautiful. **Nagtalinaed a nakamulengleng iti ulep**. He kept staring into the clouds. [Tag. *manatili; magpatuloy*]

talinúm: *n.* species of plant eaten by goats.

talínga: *n.* ear (*lapayag*); pierced ear; handle. (*talingaan, bároy, tebbeng*)

talingáan: *n. Pterospermum obliquum* plant.

talingéd: (*obs.*) **natalinged**. *a.* negligent. (*talipanpán*)

talingenngén: **natalingenngen**. *a.* quiet, peaceful, tranquil; secure (*talna*). **Awan kuma ti talingenngenmo!** You should have no peace and quiet! [Tag. *tatag*]

talinggáwid: *n.* hindrance, obstacle, restraining force. **nakaitalinggawidan**. *n.* restraining force, cause of hindrance.

talipapá: (Tag. *talipapâ*) *n.* small market (usually temporary). **Gumatgatangkami idi iti ikan a lako ti baket iti talipapa**. We used to buy fish sold by the old woman in the small market.

talipanpán: **natalipanpan**. *a.* neglectful, negligent, thoughtless. (*líway*)

talipugóng: *n.* bangs of hair; crest of feathers; bun, chignon. **talipugongen**. *v.* to knot the hair; arrange into a bun. [Tag. *pusód*]

talipúngaw: *n.* confusion; dizziness; loneliness (*allilaw; ulaw*) **matalipungawan, talipungawen**. *v.* to be confused; feel lonely; feel faint; be unconscious. **Kasla mataltalipungaw a limmaem**. He went inside in a confused state.

talipúpos, talipuspús: *a.* complete, finished. **talipu(s)pusen**. *v.* to do completely; finish off (*salipupos, ungpot*). [Tag. *buó*]

talitugút: (*obs.*) *n.* compliance. **mangitalitugut**. *v.* to be compliant. (*tungpal*)

taliwaddáy: *n.* neckerchief. **agtaliwadday**. *v.* to wear a neckerchief over the chest; to put a towel around oneself after bathing.

taliwága: *a.* ordinary, average; poor quality (cloth, etc.).

talíwan: (*obs.*) *n.* payment of a debt by a third person to a creditor of lending agent. **nataliwan**. *a.* profligate.

taliwaywáy: *a.* negligent. (*liway*) **taliwaywayan**. *v.* to set free, let go; disregard; overlook.

talkéd: see *talgéd*: hope; prospect. (*namnama*)

tálko: (Sp. *talco*: talc) *n.* talc, talcum powder.

tallá: **tallaen**. *v.* to select; pick from a collection of things; choose at random. (*píli*) **tallatalla**. *n.* group of things arranged disorderly. **tallaan**. *v.* to meddle. **matallatalla**. *v.* to be in disarray; to be arranged unsystematically. [Tag. *guló*]

tallaán: **tumallaan**. *v.* to intrude, intermeddle. (*sumangpataw*)

tallábaw: (*obs.*) *var.* of *tallápaw*: transfer a load.

tallakéb: *n.* basketlike trap for catching fish in shallow water. **agtallakeb, tallakeban**. *v.* to catch fish with this trap.

tallakúb: *n.* woven contrivance used to keep the hen in place with small holes to allow chicks to go in and out. (*kagab; kalalaw*)

tallangáw: *n.* kind of bird snare with a noose over a ring. **tallangawan**. *v.* to ensnare; trap; surprise; ambush.

tallaúgod: **natallaugod**. *a.* gentle, docile. (*linaáy, alumámay*)

tallaóng: *n.* gathering, assembly, meeting, circle; crowd. (*ummong*) **tumallaong**. *v.* to join a gathering. **sitatallaong.** *a.* in attendance. **Piner-rengna ti tunggal naitallaong.** He stared at everyone in attendance. [Tag. *tagapakiníg*]

tallápaw: **itallapaw.** *v.* to transfer a load to the other shoulder; transfer a load from one place to another; pass over an object. **Imbes a mang-itallapaw, ad-adda ketdi a mangiremrem kaniak.** Instead of going over me, he will probably sink me.

tallápok: **tumallapok.** (*obs.*) to mix culprits with those that have been punished; to join a crowd; rally.

tallayútay: **agtallayutay.** *v.* to swing; dangle. (*tillayon*)

talliási: *n.* round kettle; large vat (*siliasi*).

tallíkaw: *n.* kind of tissue. **taltallikawan.** (*obs.*) *v.* to do intermittently; do during spare hours.

tallikúd₁: *a.* back to back; with the back turned. **itallikud.** *v.* to turn the face away; put at the back; turn the back. **matallikudan.** *v.* to be at the back of. **tallikudan.** *v.* to turn one's back on; abandon, desert; forsake; reject; refuse; ignore. **tumallikud.** *v.* to turn one's back on, desert; treat with contempt; renounce. **tinna-likud a taray.** *n.* backwards race. **Saanna a napanunot a tallikudan ti kinamannalonna gapu iti kinarigat ti agtalon.** He didn't think to forsake his farming because of the difficulty of working in the fields. [Tag. *talikód*]

tallikúd₂: **taltallikud.** *n.* kind of herb whose leaves are boiled and drunk to help menstruation.

tallínga: **tallingaen.** *v.* to decay (toenails, etc.). [Tag. *bulók*]

tallíngo: *n.* variety of awned *diket* rice. **ma-tallingo.** *v.* to make a mistake, err. (*biddut*)

talló: (contracts to -*tlo* after certain prefixes) *num.* three. **maikatlo.** *num.* third. **mamitlo.** *adv.* three times. **taltallo.** *num.* only three. **tallopullo.** *num.* thirty. **pamintalluen.** *v.* to do something three times. **saggatlo.** *a.* three each. **tinallo.** *n.* twilled work of three warp crossings. **sinaggatlo.** *a.* consisting of three strings twisted together. **tallotallo.** *n.* a kind of vine with trifoliate leaves. **talluen.** *v.* to do three times. **tallonsa ti matana.** *exp.* He must have three eyes (as he sees everything). [Kal. *teÿu*, Knk. *tuló*, Png. *taló*, Tag. *tatló*]

tallúgod: *n.* obedience (*tudio*); compliance. **ag-tallugod.** *v.* to obey; follow orders. **natallugod.** *a.* obedient. **sitatallugod.** *a.* willingly. **Sitatal-lugod dagiti kaaruba a mangiburay iti ka-asida.** The neighbors willingly bestowed their mercy. [Tag. *sunod*]

tallumbági: *num.* three *sikápat*, or one *bintíng* and one *sikápat*.

tallupágay: see *pallopágay*: *Sceleria sp.* leafy sedge.

talmég: *n.* pressure. **italmeg, talmegan.** *v.* to press down; detain; withhold; conceal; push a button; (*fig.*) put someone in a critical position. **intalmeg ti pugot.** *exp.* pressed down by a ghost (said of short people). **Tinalmeganna ti bosinana.** He honked his horn. [Tag. *diín*]

talná: *n.* peace; tranquility, serenity, calmness. (*pia*) **agtalna.** *v.* to keep calm, silent. **natalna.** *a.* peaceful, calm, tranquil, serene. **tumalna.** *v.* to become calm, silent, serene. **agintatalna.** *n.* hypocrite, deceiver. **Nakataltalna iti ruar.** It is calm outside. [Kal. *lin-awa*, Png. *maligén*, *mareén*, Tag. *payapà*]

tálo: **talotalo.** *n.* variety of awned rice with short awn.

tal-ó: **ital-o.** *v.* to deliver, reach by lifting or raising; praise, honor (*dayaw*); promote. **tumal-o.** *v.* to raise. **Intal-ona ti ulona sana inagkan dagiti bibigna.** He raised his head and kissed her lips. **Timmal-o ti patongna iti kigtot.** His hips raised in fright. [Tag. *taás*]

talúbo: **tumalubo.** *v.* to be early in development or growth. [Tag. *yabong*]

talugáding₁: *n.* virtue; charm; charisma; priv-ilege, distinction; special gift. **natalugading.** *a.* privileged; gifted; charismatic. **talugadingan.** *v.* to privilege, favor. **italugading.** *v.* to mention privately; whisper. [Png. *talongáring*, Tag. *katangian*]

talugáding₂: *n.* amulet, charm. (*anting-anting*)

talugutóg: **italugutóg.** *v.* to dribble; hurl down. **tumalugutog.** *v.* to make the sound of heavy thumping objects; stampede. [Tag. *kalabóg*]

talukab: *n.* eyelid (*kalúb ti mata*). [Png. *talókap*]

talukab: *n.* carapace of crabs.

talukátik: *n.* inspiration; premonition. **agtalu-katik.** *v.* to play a tune with the fingers; tap the fingers on something; resound. **talukatiken.** *v.* to touch, impress, inspire. [Tag. *alingawngáw*]

talukátok: *n.* hummock; ground over a flooded area.

talúki: (*obs.*) *n.* one piece of silk cloth.

talúlong: *n.* *Cudrania javanensis* shrub. **tina-lulong.** *a.* tawny.

talumítim: *n.* murmur. **agtaltalumitim.** *v.* to move the lips (murmuring).

talumpúnay: *n.* kind of medicinal plant used to cure boils.

tálon: *n.* rice field. **agtalon, talonen.** *v.* to work a rice field; farm. **ipatalon.** *v.* to have one's field farmed. **makitaltalon.** *n.* tenant; tenant farmer. **mannalon.** *n.* farmer. (*mintalon*) **matalon.** *v.* to be suitable for farming, arable. **katalonan.** *n.* tenant farmer. **kataltalonan.** *n.* wide rice field, area of large rice fields. **tatalonen.** *a.* arable, suitable for farming. **itatalon.** *a.* suitable for planting. **Kaaduan ti agtaltalon nga umili ngem bassit kano ti maapitda.** Most of the townsfolk are farmers, but their harvest is said to be little. [Ibg. *kuman*, Itg. *buba*, Ivt. *takey*, Kal. *payaw*, *uma*, Knk. *payéw*, Kpm. *asikan*, Png. *pásol*, Tag. *bukid*, *linang*, Bon. *tálon* = forest; sky; world]

talón: (Sp. *talón*: coupon, voucher) *n.* stub (of a checkbook or receipt book).

talonário: (Sp. *talonario*: coupon book) *n.* checkbook; stub book; register book.

talunásan: *n.* machete. (*buneng*; *bolo*) **nakatalunasan.** *a.* carrying a machete.

talun-ód: **talun-oden.** *v.* to inquire persistently. (*malutmot*)

taluntón₁: *n.* investigation. **taluntonen.** *v.* to study, investigate; follow a path. [Tag. *usisà*]

taluntón₂: **patalunton.** *n.* a kind of chasing game played by young children. **agtinnalunton.** *v.* to chase after each other (children playing). **Naarimbangaw dagiti ubbing a nagtitinnalunton iti kalsada.** The children chasing each other in the street were noisy.

talunggatíng: *n.* hobbles to control a horse's gait.

talungkiád: *n.* walking with the legs and chest protruding forward. [Tag. *liyád*]

talupák: *n.* sheath of the banana leaf.

talpiák: *var.* of *tapliak*.

taltá: **italta.** *v.* to stir something (when cooking) (*kiwar*); shake a winnow. **taltaen.** (*obs.*) *v.* to break the neck of.

taltág₁: **agtaltag.** *v.* to trot; dribble a ball. **tumaltag.** *v.* to trot; rebound.

taltág₂: **agtaltag.** *v.* to pound palay. **taltagen.** *v.* to shell palay (pound rice to remove the husk), pound palay. **panaltagan.** *n.* threshing vessel (made of a hollowed log).

taltál: **taltalen.** *v.* to crush; bray; pound in order to pulverize. (*lipitén*, *pespesén*, *pis-íten*) **taltallikúd.** *n. Paspalum longifolium.* **Timmaltalak iti bulong nga intapalko iti sugat.** I crushed the leaves I used to patch the wound. [Tag. *durog*]

taltég: **agtalteg.** *v.* to bounce. **matalteg.** *v.* to be jolted.

talyér: (Sp. *taller*: auto repair shop) *n.* auto repair shop. (*talier*)

táma: **tumama, tamaan.** *v.* to hit with a missile; hit a target. **maitama.** *v.* to happen at a convenient time; coincide. [Tag. *mataón*, *tamà*]

tamá: (*obs.*) *n.* careful inspection. (*sukímat*)

tamáles: (Sp. *tamal*: dumpling) *n.* dish made of fish seasoned with vinegar, salt, and ginger,

wrapped in banana leaves, and steamed. **agtamales.** *v.* to cook this dish. **tamalesen.** *v.* to make (fish) into this dish. [Tag. *tamalis*]

táman₁: *n.* bet; wager; stake; ordinary way to place floor joists. **itaman.** *v.* to place a bet on (*pusta*). [Tag. *tayâ*]

táman₂: **agtaman.** *v.* to lie on the edge; lie on the narrower side.

táman₃: **tamantaman.** *n.* labia minora of the vulva.

tamánio: (Sp. *tamaño*: size) *n.* measurement of lumber.

tamaráw: (Tag.) *n.* the Mindoro wild water buffalo, *Babalus mendorensis*.

tamaríndo: (Sp. *tamarindo*) *n.* tamarind. (*salamagi*)

tamátis: *var.* of *kamátis*, tomato.

tamáy: *n.* witchcraft. (*kulam*, *gamud*) **mannamay.** *n.* witch.

tambá: **natamba.** *a.* weak, thin (liquors, vinegar). **tambaan.** *v.* to dilute, thin. **Tambaam dayta ta napait.** Dilute that because it is bitter. [Tag. *bantô*]

tambák: (Tagalog also) *n.* dam, dike (*pennéd*, *puttót*); bank. **agtambak.** *v.* to build a dike. **tambakan.** *v.* to build a dike across or around. [Png. *pilapil*, Tag. *pilapil*, *palimpíng*]

tambán: *n.* kind of sardine larger than the *bilís*; weak brine used in preserving fish.

tambáng: (Tagalog also) **agtambang, tambangan.** *v.* to ambush; raid; attack; waylay; obstruct a voyage; hold up and rob; block one's way (*saed*). [Tag. *harang*]

tambiólo: (Sp. *tambor*: drum) *n.* lottery drum; box containing raffle entries.

tambúbung: *n. bulóng unás* fish at its largest; hood of a *kalesa*. **tambubongan.** *v.* to provide with an improvised roof or hood.

tambók: **natambok.** *a.* having a hump in clothes due to a protruding body part.

tambukógan: *n.* the fully grown *bulong-unás* fish; Japanese hairtail fish, *Trichiurus japonicus*.

tambúkor: *a.* uneven, bumpy; lumpy. **natambukor.** *a.* rough on the surface, not flat, bumpy. **agtambukor.** *v.* to protrude; have a lump. [Tag. *umbók*, *bukol*]

tamból₁: *a.* uneven (*tibbakól*); warped. [Tag. *pintád*]

tamból₂: **pagtambol.** *n.* stimulant; agent that augments thirst. [Tag. *pampasiglá*]

tambúli: *n.* musical horn made from a carabao horn.

tambóng: **tambu-tambóng.** *n.* sweet coconut soup dessert with rice balls, tapioca, and jackfruit. [Png. *tambotambóng*; *kiléd*, Tag. *ginataán*]

tambór: (Sp. *tambor*: drum) *n*. drum. (*bombo*) **agtambor.** *v*. to beat a drum. **tamboren.** *v*. to drum to; add percussion to a piece. **tamborero.** *n*. drummer. [Kal. *tambuÿ*, Knk. *solíbaw*, Tag. *tamból*]

tambúrog: *n*. hump; minor protrusion. **nagtamburog.** *a*. humped. **tumamburog.** *v*. to become a hump, swell in a hump; (*fig*.) grow breasts. **Napardas man ti itatamburog ti barukongna.** Her chest developed quickly.

tambútso: *n*. chimney; car exhaust pipe. (*pagasimbuyoken*)

tamdág: **agtamdag, tumamdag.** *v*. to look down. (*tan-áw*) **itamdag.** *v*. to bring (a light, etc.) to a window. **Tamdaganda ti alipuspusmo.** They are looking down at your whorl (belittling you). [Tag. *dungaw*]

taméd: **agtamed.** *v*. to nod forward; bend forward; yield, submit to; bow. (*tung-éd*) **itamed.** *v*. to bend the head downward, incline. **pagtamdan.** *v*. to respect; revere; *n*. one respected; *a*. respected; dignified. **panamdan.** *v*. to respect. [Png. *tanger, tuwék*, Tag. *yukód, yukô*]

tam-ék: **matam-ekan.** *v*. to fall on something sharp; to impale oneself; to have the throat clogged by food; gulp down. [Tag. *tiník*]

tamíng: **tumaming.** *v*. to care, mind, pay attention to. (*pangag, imátang*) **tamingen.** *v*. to consider, notice, think of; accept to do something. **mataming.** *v*. to be done; finished. **Kasla saanna a tamtamingen ti kaaddak iti yanda.** It seems he doesn't notice that I am at their place.

tamlág: **natamlag.** *a*. lazy, slothful (*sadut*). [Tag. *tamád*]

tamlég: *var*. of *tamlag*: lazy. (*sadut*)

tammá: **maitamma.** *v*. to find or see all of a sudden; to happen unexpectedly.

tammáked: *var*. of *sammaked*.

tammél: **masitammel.** *v*. to be dumbfounded, lose one's speech due to surprise or astonishment. (*kigtot, mayeng*)

tamméng: *var*. of *tammíng*: elope, run away.

tammí: *a*. with protruding underlip (giving the appearance of having a long chin; (ant. *soriáb*: with protruding upper lip). **agtammi.** *v*. to have a protruding underlip. [Png. *takéyeb*]

tammídaw: *n*. brief visit. **agtammidaw, tumammidaw.** *v*. to pay a complimentary visit (*ammingaw*); appear briefly. **Nagtammidaw manen ti isemna.** Her smile appeared briefly again.

tammíkil: **agtammikil.** *v*. to have something in the mouth while talking. **nakatammikil.** *a*. holding in the mouth.

tammími: **agtammimi.** *v*. to hold with the lips (cigars, etc.). **nakatammimi.** *a*. holding with the lips.

tammíng: **agtamming.** *v*. to run away with, elope. **itamming.** *v*. to elope with. (*taray*)

tammudó: *n*. index finger, forefinger. (*var*. of *tamudó*) **sangatammuduan.** *n*. distance between extended thumb and forefinger. [Kal. *pattutuchu*, Knk. *tedék*, Png. *tamuró*, Tag. *hintuturò*]

tammóg: **natammog.** *a*. bent, curved. (*killó*)

tamnáy: *n*. insipidity, tasteless state (*amnaw, lab-ay*); freshwater. **natamnay.** *a*. tasteless, without flavor; lacking salt; insipid; not interesting; uninterested. **agmarmaratamnay.** *v*. to be indifferent; lukewarm. **agtitinamnay.** *n*. ritual meal after marriage celebrated by close family and friends consisting of flavorless food. **ikan-tamnay.** *n*. freshwater fish. **Natamnay ti nakemna a sumurot.** He is not excited about going. **Natamnay dagiti simmaruno nga aldaw iti panagbiagda.** The following days of their lives were not interesting. [Ibg. *tabeng*, lallag, Ivt. *tavang*, Knk. *tammáy, líting*, tab-áng, tagabtáb, lagabúlab, tagulengléng, Kpm. *tábang*, Png., Tag. *tabáng*]

tamó: **tumamo.** *v*. to do inconsiderately, thoughtlessly, imprudently. **natamo.** *a*. rash; bold; indiscrete. [Tag. *pusók*; *tamó* = acquire]

tamuék: (*obs*.) see *taméd*: nod; bow; lean forward; yield.

tamúrog: *n*. protrusion; something jutting out. (*tádul, dawádaw, tungángaw*) **agtamurog.** *v*. to protrude; jut out.

tampá: *n*. security deposit; something given as a pledge to complete a transaction; reservation. **tampaan.** *v*. to make a down payment; make a reservation.

tampéra: *a*. talkative; chattering. (*tamtampera*)

tampípi: (Tag. *tampipì*) *n*. kind of rectangular light bamboo trunk with flat sides, used for traveling. **itampipi.** *v*. to place (provisions, etc.) in the *tampipi*.

tampíra: **tamtampira.** *n*. clitoris (*muting; tildi; manimani*). [Kpm. *turíl*, Tag. *manî*]

tampók: *n*. distinction: stone set in a ring; distinctive part of a person or object; center of attraction; crowning glory; culminating activity. **itampok.** *v*. to set something into a ring (jewel); to glamorize; put into the limelight; idolize; encase. **maitampok.** *v*. to be set; to be glamorized; to be idolized; to be encased; to be the life of the party. **tampokan.** *v*. to set; decorate; enchase, ornament. **natampokan.** *a*. decorated, ornamented; enchased. **bató a pagtampok.** *n*. stones for mosaic work. **Nag-**

balin a tampok ti Samtoy ti "Biag ni Lam-ang". The "Life (legend) of *Lam-ang*" became the crowning glory of the Ilocanos.

tampóng: *n.* bundle, package. **agtampong.** *v.* to pack in a bundle.

tampóy: (Tag. also) *n. Eugenia jambos* tree with pink or red edible fruits. (*barakbak*)

taná: maitana. *v.* to be fitting, appropriate. (*mainugót*) **agpatana.** *v.* to give a surplus, give allowance for; make a garment larger than needed for room to grow.

tanabbáaw: (f. *tabbaaw*) **tumanabbaaw.** *v.* to curse repeatedly or vociferously.

tanábug: *n.* young twig; (*fig.*) offspring.

tanabátab: *n.* sound of voices from afar. (*anabáab*) **agtanabatab.** *v.* to talk from afar.

tanabútob: *n.* mumbling; muttering. **agtanabutob.** *v.* to mutter, mumble in discontent. [Tag. *bulóng*]

tanádang: *n.* kind of herb used in popular medicine.

tának: agtanak. *v.* to settle (liquids); become calm (*talna*).

tanakaták: *n.* sound of a manual typewriter.

tanakták: *n.* sound of galloping horses.

tanamítim: agtanamitim. *v.* to move the lips without speaking (as in prayers); murmur. [Tag. *bulóng*]

tánang: natanang, sitatanang. *a.* calm, composed, nonchalant; sober; careful. (*talna; annad*) **agtanangka!** Calm down! [Tag. *ingat*]

tanang-áb: tumanang-ab. *v.* to gossip; be loquacious.

tanául: (f. *taul*) *n.* repeated barking of dogs. **tumanaul.** *v.* to bark repeatedly (dogs).

tanáp: *n.* level land, plain; mesa (flat top of a mountain). (*tay-ak*) **tanapen.** *v.* to level. [Tag. *patag*]

tanaráy: (f. *taráy*) **tumanaray.** *v.* to always be running, be rushing.

tanarpók: *n.* sound of branches in the wind.

tanattát: *n.* gabbing; gossip. **agtanattat.** *v.* to make the sound of continuous walking; to gab.

tan-áw: agtan-aw, tuman-aw. *v.* to look down. (*tamdág*) **itan-aw.** *v.* to bring something to a window. **tan-awen.** *v.* to look down at. **matan-awan.** *v.* to be visible from a distance. **Nagtan-aw iti desarming a tawa.** He looked down from the mirrored window. [Ibg. *ubbawan*, Ifg. *dung-o*, Ivt. *laláung*, Kpm. *dúngo*, Png. *dungaw, tandag*, Tag. *dungaw, tanáw* = view at a distance]

tanáwag: tumanawag, tanawagan. *v.* to look through a window. (see *tannáwag*)

tanawátaw: agtanawataw. *v.* to wander from place to place.

tanawtáw: agtanawtaw. *v.* to boast, brag (*agpasindayaw, agpangas*); gab; gossip. **Kalkalpas ti padayatayo itay lawasna, padaya manen ti tantanawtawem!** We just had a party last week and you're gabbing about another party again!

tanáy: *n.* bundles of *palay* bound into a *pongó.*

tan-áy₁: itan-ay. *v.* to lift; honor; promote. **maitan-ay.** *v.* to be lifted; promoted. **patanayan.** *v.* to increase; augment. [Tag. *unlád*]

tan-áy₂: tan-ayen. *v.* to manage; upgrade, increase production; develop. **matan-ayan.** *v.* to be upgraded; managed carefully; developed. **Adda tallo a gukayab idiay a mabalin a mapatan-ay a kas pagturistaan.** There are three caves there that can be developed as tourist spots. [Tag. *unlád, sulong*]

tánda: *n.* memory. (*lagip*) **tandaanan.** *v.* to remember; bear in mind. **managtandaan, natandaan.** *v.* to have a good memory.

tandá: *n.* sign, signal, quality, attribute, trait; guarantee. **tandaan.** *v.* to put a mark or sign on; *n.* sign, token, trait; symbol, emblem. **agtanda.** *v.* to make the sign of the cross. **pagtandaanan.** *n.* sign, emblem, badge, insignia. **tandaanan.** *v.* to stamp, mark, brand; notice; remember. **natandaanan.** *a.* observant, attentive, with a good memory. **agtandaan.** *v.* to make the sign of the cross. [Png. *tandá*, Tag. *tandâ*]

tandán: *var.* of *tangdan*: wages, pay.

tandandók: *n. Polanisia icosandra* weed. **tantandok a dadakkel.** *n. Gynandropsis gynandra* weed.

tandúdo: *n.* rise, ascent. **itandudo.** *v.* to honor (*raem*); extol; respect; applaud; rise in social standing; lift up; support. **No tumaud a nasayaat ti anak, ti ina ti umuna a maitandudo.** If the child turns out well, the mother is the first to be praised. [Png. *tandúro*, Tag. *puri*]

tandók₁: *n.* cup made of horn; method of removing poison or curing, dry cupping. **tanduken.** *v.* to remove poison by cutting the infected area to let the blood drain; dry cup (method of curing). **Uray natandok, matay met laeng.** Even though he was cupped, he will die anyway. **Sara ti nuang ken baka ti us-usaren dagiti lallakay nga agtandok.** The old cuppers use horns of water buffalo and cows. [Tag. *tandók*]

tandók₂: tantandok. *n. Gynandropsis pentaphylla* herb with white and purple flowers considered a caustic.

tanduyóng: *n.* color of mahogany; maroon. [Tag. *kamagóng*]

táneb: itaneb. *v.* to submerge partly. (*rareb*) **matneb.** *v.* to be partly covered with water, immersed. [Tag. *lubóg*]

tanéb: taneben. *v.* to ambush. (*tambang, sada*)
tanék: see *tintinnanek.*
tanekték: agtanektek. *v.* to tick; make the sound of a manual typewriter.
taném: *n.* tomb, grave. (*tumba, panteón*) **itanem.** *v.* to bury, entomb, inter. **agingga't tanem.** *exp.* until the end. **maitanem.** *v.* to be buried; to be forgotten. **Ikarik a pasiarek ti tanemmo iti inaldaw.** I promise to pass by your grave every day. [Ibg. *tanam,* Kal. *lobon,* Png. *lobók,* Tag. *libíng*]
taní: *n.* pledge, guarantee (in a contract); (*obs.*) agreement between parents that their unborn children will wed each other. **tanian.** *v.* to deposit for security; pledge; mark for a future purpose. **tumani.** *v.* to mark plots of ground. **Saanen a mabalin a waswasen ti tani.** It is no longer possible to cancel the pledge.
tánig₁: (*obs.*) **tanigan.** *v.* to monopolize.
tánig₂: tanigen, itanig. *v.* to keep secret.
taníg: (*obs.*) **tanigan.** *v.* to appropriate forcibly; usurp.
tanigansá: *n.* policy; rules and regulations.
tanikalá: (Tagalog also) *n.* gold chain. (*kawar a balitok*)
tanimítim: *var.* of *tanamitim:* murmur, move lips without speaking.
taníng: (Tag.) *n.* limit; deadline. **nataningan.** *a.* limited.
tannáwag: agtannawag, matannawagan. *v.* to be mutually visible from a distance; to direct words to the audience. **tannawagan.** *v.* to look down upon from an elevated point. **Agkirem-kirem a nangtannawag iti babaenna.** He repeatedly blinked as he looked down below. **Nagtugawda iti bangko iti ampir ti tawa a tumannawag iti paraangan.** They sat down next to the window looking at the yard. [Tag. *tanáw*]
tanúbong: *n. Phragmites vulgaris* grass with many flowered panicles.
tánod: *n.* guard. (*bantay*)
tánug: tatanugen. *n.* kind of poisonous snake.
tanugtóg: tumanugtog. *v.* to make a rumbling sound (crowd running).
tan-ók: *n.* glory. (*dayág, dáyaw*) **natan-ok.** *a.* elevated, exalted, noble, illustrious, honorable, distinguished. (*sudi*) **itan-ok.** *v.* to exalt; praise, applaud. [Tag. *galang*]
tanukó: tantanuko. *n.* kind of broad-leaved herb.
tánong: (*obs.*) **tanongen.** *v.* to collect, gather. (*urnongen, singiren*)
tanupék: (f. *tupek*) *n.* sound of chopping; light stomping sound.
tanupó: *n. Kolowratia elegans* herb with leafy rootstocks.

tanuprá: (f. *tupra*) **itanupra.** *v.* to eject spit while talking; interject while spitting.
tánor: *n.* sprout, shoot. **tumanor.** *v.* to increase; advance; grow; develop. **patanoren.** *v.* to grow; breed. [Tag. *unlád*]
tános: *n.* main branch of a tree. **natanos.** *a.* high and straight-limbed. (*balunay*)
tanutubó: (*obs.*) *n.* kind of reed grass.
tanuttót: *n.* sound of continuous talking; cry of rats. **tumanuttot.** *v.* to make the sound of rats or continuous talking; gossip.
tánoy: (*obs.*) *n.* rascality. **agtanoy.** *v.* to become habitual; *adv.* eventually; gradually.
tánsan: *n.* bottlecap. [Png. *polét,* Tag. *tansán*]
tantán: agtantan. *v.* to delay unnecessarily. **itantan, tantanen.** *v.* to postpone, put off. **maitantan.** *v.* to be delayed, deferred. [Tag. *antala*]
tántia: (Sp. *tantear:* try; test, estimate) **tantiaen.** *v.* to estimate; calculate. (*pattapatta*) **tantiado.** *a.* estimated; calculated. **Nagsarimadengda a kasla adda tantantiaenda.** They paused as if they were estimating something. [Tag. *tantiyá*]
-tanto: *enclitic.* [*-ta* + *-(n)to*] indicating dual, inclusive absolutive actor and future time. **Mapantanto.** We'll go. (dual)
tangá: (Tag.) **nagtangá.** *a.* stupid, ignorant. (*tab-béd*); *Pygeum glandulosum.*
tangáag: natangaag. *a.* stupid.
tang-áb: itang-ab. *v.* to reveal, make known. **tumanang-ab.** *v.* to gossip, be loquacious. **Dika ngata agang-angaw iti dayta a tang-tang-aben ta ngiwatmo.** You are probably not joking about what your mouth is revealing.
tangabaran: *n.* kind of large bird.
tángad₁: *n.* kind of brown waterbird; person who continually walks with head and eyes raised.
tángad₂: itangad. *v.* to turn upward. **tumangad.** *v.* to look up; raise the eyes. **agtangtangad.** *v.* to be walk with the head up; to be looking up. **manangadtangad.** *v.* to look for a nest (chickens); to look up at trees to see if the fruits are ready to harvest. **patangaden.** *v.* to raise, lift up, make erect. **tangaden.** *n.* elders, authorities; *v.* to look up at; accost someone in his own house. **Kayatmo ti agtangad ti barsanga?** *exp.* Do you want to die? (*lit.* look up at the barsanga). [Tag. *tingalâ*]
tangadá: see *tangayyá:* to offer; exhibit to sight.
tangál: itangal. *v.* to carry in the teeth. (*ammal, abbal*)
tangálay: itangalay, tangalayen. *v.* to lean, rest on for support.
tangalíb: agtangalib. *v.* to be out of order; to become dislocated.
tangaltáw: see *tanggaltáw:* buoy; float.

tangán: *n.* thumb, big toe. [Kal. *paama*, Knk. *pagpag-amá*, Png. *tangán*, Tag. *hinlalaki*]

tángar: (*obs.*) **itangar**. *v.* to keep in store; reserve (*latang*).

tangár: **tumangar**. *v.* to strut; become arrogant; become erect (penis); stiffen; bristle. **natangar**. *a.* erect; stiff; vain; haughty. **nakatangar**. *a.* erect; stiff (ears, etc.). **Nakatangtangar ni Luli nga immuli**. Luli strutted up (the stairs). [Tag. *bikas*]

tangátang₁: *n.* sky; heavens. (*langit*) **agpatangatang**. *v.* to soar into the sky. [Png. *táwen*, Tag. *himpapawid*]

tangátang₂: *n.* rice field that has remained uncultivated for over a year. **agtangatang**. *v.* to remain uncultivated for over a year. **nagtangatang**. *a.* uncultivated for one or more years.

tangátang₃: *n.* a kind of bamboo shelf. **itangatang**. *v.* to place shelves; rest something on two objects; hang, suspend.

tángaw: **tangawen**. *v.* to poll, prune the top off; shorten; condense; misquote. **tangaw-tangaw**. *a.* fickle, indecisive; vagabond.

tángay: *conj.* whereas; since; anyway; anyhow (*yáta*). **Uray patayennak itan tangay naipudnokon ti riknak**. Even if you kill me now, at least I expressed my feelings. **No ni la kuman Meding ti asawaem tangay napintas met ken ub-ubing pay**. If you would just marry Meding since she is beautiful and still young. **Inton mangrabiika, ibasbassitmon ti kanem tangay aginanakan ket saanmon a maaramat ti enerhia**. When you have dinner, eat less food since you'll rest and won't use the energy. [Tag. *yamang*]

tangayá: see *tanggayá*: offer; present; put in view; exhibit.

tangbáw: *n.* beam, shaft of a plow or sugar mill. **tangbaw ti bullalayaw**. *n.* beam of a rainbow. **Kukotenna a kasla tangbaw ti bagina**. He is bending his body like a beam.

tangdán: *n.* salary, wages; stipend; pay. (*sueldo*) **tangdanan**. *v.* to give salary to, pay for work done. **makitangdan**. *v.* to work for hire (*tegged*). **makitangtangdan**. *n.* laborer. **panangdan**. *n.* salary, payment for services rendered. [Png. *salod*, Tag. *sahod*]

tang-éd₁: *n.* nod. **tumang-ed**. *v.* to nod the head in assent. (*tung-éd*) **agtangtang-ed**. *v.* to continually nod the head (as old men) **tangedan**. *v.* to nod the head at. [Bon., Knk. *yang-ed*, Png. *tangér*, Tag. *tangô*]

tang-éd₂: **tangtang-ed**. *n.* click beetle that nods its head with a click. [Knk. *yangyang-éd*]

tangék₁: *a.* stupid, dull.

tangék₂: **tatangkan**. *n.* a large jar.

tangél: *n.* jellyfish (*karominas*); the itching associated with the sting of a jellyfish.

tangép: *n.* joint between two boards; twilight. **agtangep**. *v.* to remain closed; to become silent all of a sudden; to set (sun at dusk). **itangep**. *v.* to close. (*rikep; punit*) **agpatangep-sipnget**. *v.* to become dim when the sun sets. **Natangepen ti sipnget idi makadanon iti purokda**. The darkness cast over them when they reached their village.

tanggá: **agtangga**. *v.* to pitch pennies (in a game). (*tatsing*)

tanggád: *n.* period after childbirth. **agtanggad**. *v.* to be confined (after pregnancy); to be on a diet after childbirth; to abstain from something harmful. **tanggadan**. *v.* to abstain from anything that might cause an illness to get worse. **tanggaden**. *v.* to diet after childbirth; mistrust; suspect. **makatanggad**. *v.* to be able to regain one's strength after delivery. **patanggadan**. *v.* to take care of a woman who has just given birth. [Tag. *dimón*]

tanggaép: *var.* of *tangep*.

tanggál: *n.* dam (*puttot*); sluice; swamp or pond created by damming. **tanggalen**. *v.* to dam a river. [Tag. *saplád; tanggál* = detach, remove]

tanggaltáw: *n.* float, buoy. (*bóya*)

tanggár: *n.* funnel-shaped bag net used for catching fish in streams. **tanggaren**. *v.* to catch by holding out a container or net (rainwater, fish, etc.).

tanggáy: *var.* of *tanggar*.

tanggayá: **itanggaya**. *v.* to hold out, offer. (*diaya*) **sitatanggaya**. *v.* to be exhibited; be at one's disposal. [Tag. *alók*]

tanggí: *n.* malicious, sudden jerk of the head. **agtanggi**. *v.* to jerk the head as in refusal.

tanggígi: *n.* kind of marine fish, usually eaten raw in *kilawen*, Spanish mackerel.

tangguáb: **tumangguab**. *v.* to drink down. **i-tangguab**. *v.* to move with the snout (dogs, pigs); turn over a glass when drinking.

tangguáp: *var.* of *tangguab*.

tangguýob: *n.* horn made from a water buffalo horn. **agtangguyob**. *v.* to blow a horn. **Kellaat nga immaweng ti tangguyob**. The horn suddenly sounded. [Png. *tambuyog*, Tag. *tambuli*]

tangí₁: *n.* a meter-long elongated marine fish, bonito, of the *Thunnidae* family. [Tag. *tulingan*]

tangí₂: (*coll.*) *a.* stupid. (*tanga, nengneng*)

tangíg: **natangig**. *a.* arrogant, conceited (*tangsit, pangas*). **sitatangig**. *a.* arrogant, conceited. **Inkagumaanna latta ti agin-tatangig**. He just made an effort to pretend to be arrogant. [Tag. *yabang*]

tangíle: (*pron. tanggile*) *n.* species of native hardwood.

tangíngi: *n.* very fine black sand used as ink blotter; **pagtangingian.** *n.* sandbox; shaker for sprinkling sand on wet ink.

tangkál: *n.* birdcage. (*kulungan*) **itangkal.** *v.* to confine in a cage. **sitatangkal.** *a.* caged. **Masdaawak laeng ta agingga ita, saan pay a naitangkal ta pusom.** I am surprised because until now your heart was never caged. [Png. *tangkalang*, Tag. *tangkál*]

tangkárang: maitangkarang. *v.* to be exposed.

tangkáy: *n.* stem of a plant. (*ungkay*)

tangkáyag: tumangkayag. *v.* to ascend. (*agpangato*) **Kasla masinsinit iti beggang ti kudilko nupay apagtangkayag ti init.** My skin seems to be burnt in the coals although the sun has just risen. [Tag. *taás*]

tángke: (Sp. *tanque*: tank) *n.* tank; vat.

tangkén₁: natangken. *a.* hard, firm, solid; tough. (*natibkér*) **natangkenán.** *a.* completely hardened; mature, in season; full-grown. **ipatangken.** *v.* to stubbornly insist. **patangkenen.** *v.* to allow fruits to reach maturity; make firmer. **matangkenan.** *v.* to be in season; to be matured. **agintatangken.** *v.* to pretend to be strict, rigid. **tumangken.** *v.* to harden; mature, be in season. **Agpinnatangkenda.** They are stubborn with one another. **tangken-tabungaw.** *a.* hard like the bottle gourd (referring to a person who is hard on the outside but soft on the inside). [Ibg. *teggáq*, Itg. *kelsang*, Ivt. *kehnet*, Knk. *kentég*, Kpm. *masyas*, Png. *awét*, *bisél*, Tag. *tigás*]

tangkén₂: tangtangken. *n.* kind of marine fish; kind of vine used in medicine to cure boils.

tangkiáw: tangkiawan. *v.* to joke, tease.

tangkíg: *n.* high land that cannot be irrigated. [Tag. *bakood*]

tangkíran: *n.* sturdy old age; unripe fruit; maturity. **Saan a marungsot iti tao dagiti buaya, uray ti katangkiranan ken kabakedan.** Alligators are not infuriated by people, even the most mature and robust.

tangkírang: *a.* parched (land). **tumangkirang.** *v.* to become parched. **Awanen dagiti nalangto a mais ta timmangkirangen ti daga.** There are no more ripe corn plants because the land has dried up.

tangkúlong: *n.* kind of child's stroller; crib. **itangkulong.** *v.* to take some (food or drink); place in a stroller or crib.

tangkóng: *n. Ipomoea reptans* edible plant common in streams and pools.

tangkóy: *n. Benincasa hispida* vine with oval, edible fruits and white bristle. **timmangkóy.** *a.* like a *tangkoy* (referring to large breasts).

tanglág: *n.* elephant grass. [Knk. *tanglág* = bare; nude; bald]

tanglás: *n.* a species of tree.

tangnáwa: *n.* the act of a community getting together for communal farmwork or building houses. **agtangnawa.** *v.* to do communal work for the good of the community. [Ivt. *yaru*, Tag. *bayanihan*]

tangngaép: see *tangép.*

tanguáp: itanguap. *v.* to completely empty a load; drink up.

tángos: natangos. *a.* high-nosed. (*tundiris*)

tangrá: *n. var.* of *aladan* plant.

tangráb₁: tangraban. *v.* to cut slantwise (*tungiab, tangraw*).

tangráb₂: *n.* a kind of bird with black and yellow speckled plumage resembling the quail (*púgo*) but larger.

tangrág: natangrag. *a.* wrinkled and decrepit (old women).

tangrár: *n.* species of weed.

tangráw: tangrawan. *v.* to cut slantwise. (*tangráb, tikiáp*); *n.* a bird resembling a large quail.

tangríb: *n.* outer edge, brink (*ngárab, ígid*); rocky precipice near the shore. **katangriban.** *n.* rocky shoreline.

tangsít: *n.* arrogance. (*pangás, pasindayaw, pannakel, tangig*) **natangsit.** *a.* arrogant, proud, haughty, conceited, stuck up, vain. **tumangsit.** *v.* to become vain, arrogant. **itangsit.** *v.* to be proud of; take pride in. **Kaanonto a maikkat ti kinatangken ti ulom ken kinatangsitmo?** When will you get rid of your haughtiness and stubbornness? [Ivt. *daay*, Png. *pasáng*, Tag. *yabang*]

tangsó: natangso. *a.* arrogant. (*langsot; pangas; tangig*)

tangtáng₁: *n.* sound of metal being beaten (bells). **tangtangen.** *v.* to beat metals. [Tag. *tangtáng*]

tangtáng₂: matangtang. *v.* to be ruined, spoiled. **tangtangen.** *v.* to spoil, put out of order.

tangtáng₃: maratangtang. *n.* sea urchin.

tangwá: tumangwa. *v.* to look over; look up; look through a window.

táo₁: *n.* (pl. *tattao*) human, man, human being, person; people; individual. **agpakatao.** *v.* to treat as a human being; know how to deal with people, have good manners; to call for admittance at a house. **agpatao.** *v.* to help a woman deliver her baby. **agkatawan.** *v.* to be the same age. **taotao.** *n.* pupil of the eye. **katao.** *n.* number of persons. **kinatao.** *n.* humanity; individuality; character; identity. **katatao.** *n.* ancestry; lineage; human nature. **agkataoan.** *v.* to be of the same age. **maitao.** *v.* to be born; be delivered. **matagtagitao.** *v.* to be inhabited by people. **awan matagtagitao.** *exp.* there's no one around. **itao.** *v.* to deliver a baby. **itatao, pannakaitao.** *n.* incarnation; birth. **maitao.** *v.* to be delivered, born. **naintaoan.** *a.* human; humane. **taoan.** *n.* followers. **di katataoan.** *n.* demon, evil spirit (said to have no head). **sangatawan.** *n.* humanity; human race, mankind. **sinantatao.** *n.* mannequin; scarecrow. **agmarmaratao.** *v.* to conceive; be pregnant. **tumao.** *v.* to be born. **matatao.** *n.* inhabitants, dwellers. **pangitaoan.** *n.* place where a woman will deliver her child. **Dikayo pay agpakatao.** You still don't know the proper way to deal with your fellow men. [Bon. *ipogaw, tágo,* Ibg., Isg. *tólay,* Ivt. *tauq,* Kal. *tagu,* Knk. *ipugáw,* Png. *toó,* Kpm., Tag. *tao*]

táo₂: *var.* of *datao:* pronoun of indefinite reference. **Nadaras tao a lumakay no kastoy.** One gets old quickly like this.

táo₃: **taotao.** *n.* pupil of the eye. [Isg. *xintotólay,* Kal. *kalimattagu,* Knk. *bokbokká, bokbokkáeg,* Png. *ogawogaw,* Tag. *balintatáw*]

táob: *n.* small bowl made from a coconut shell.

táud: **agtaud.** *v.* to come from, originate. **tumaud.** *v.* to come into being, emerge, result; originate; grow up in. **taudan.** *n.* origin. **pagtaudan.** *n.* place where one was born; origin; beginning. **pagtataudan.** *n.* source. **patauden.** *v.* to bring into existence; create; produce; originate. **panagtaud ti peste.** *n.* pest succession, the emergence of a different pest after one has been eradicated (through pesticides). **Kas kenka, nagtaud met iti nakurapay a pamilia.** Like you, he came from a poor family. [Tag. *litáw; simulâ*]

táog: *n.* dipper. (*sudo*) **taugen.** *v.* to scoop, dip liquids from a ladle.

taúkan: *n.* a kind of small speckled wading bird.

taúl₁: **agtaul.** *v.* to bark (*taguob, ul-ol*). **mannaul, managtaul.** *a.* prone to barking. **taulan.** *v.* to bark at. **agtinnaul.** *v.* to bark at each other. **Ti aso a mannaul, adayo ti pakamatna.** The barking dog is far from his prey. [Bon. *ngongo, giyaw,* Knk. *ting-ók, atinggalók,* Kpm. *bitaúl, kaóng,* Png. *dangól, taól,* Tag. *kahól*]

taúl₂: **mannaul.** *n.* kind of small black bird that cries at night.

taupí: (Hok. *tau p^hé:* bean skin) *n.* thin bean wrapper for the *kikiam* sausage.

taurár: *n. Themesa gigantea.*

taúro: (Sp.) *n.* Taurus.

tausí: (Hok. *tau si:* bean preserved) *n.* salted, fermented beans; black bean paste.

tápa: (Tag. also) *n.* dried, thin slices of salted meat, jerked meat. **agtapa.** *v.* to make *tapa.* **tapaen.** *v.* to cure meat into *tapa.*

tapadéra: (Sp. *tapadera:* cover, lid) *n.* cover of a jar or bottle.

tápak: *n.* outrigger of a canoe. **tapaktapak.** *n.* occiput; top of the head.

tápal: (Tag. also) *n.* patch, plaster. (*takúp, sugóp*) **tapalan.** *v.* to patch, plaster. **itapal.** *v.* to patch on.

tapalúdo: *n.* bumper of a car, fender; mudguard over a wheel.

tapangár: *var.* of *tapingár:* comb of a fowl.

tapár: *n.* neckhole of a garment; patch; lining; cover; window lid (on airplanes). **taparan.** *v.* to line (a garment); patch, plaster; to cover; (*coll.*) lowest-scoring person on a test.

tapáro: *n.* small round box. (*kahón*)

tapát: *n.* serenade. (*harana, serenada*) **agtapat, tapaten.** *v.* to serenade. [Png. *arana,* Tag. *harana, tapát*]

tápaw: *n.* highest point, summit, crest. (*pantók, aringgawís, tuktók, murdóng*) **natapaw.** *a.* high; on top. **Nasipngeten idi makadanonda iti tapaw ti maudi a turod.** It was already dark when they reached the summit of the last hill.

tapáw: (*obs.*) *n.* beam. **tumpaw.** *v.* to float. (*lumtaw*) **natapaw.** *a.* buoyant. **itapaw.** *v.* to dip; put on the surface of the water. **ipatapaw.** *v.* to cause to float; (*fig.*) to ameliorate coarse language, using euphemisms. **Nagtaptapaw ti pusona iti ragsak.** His heart leaped for joy. [Bon. *tapew,* Ibg. *luttaq,* Ivt. *mehtaw,* Kpm. *gáto,* Png. *letaw,* Tag. *lutang* (float)]

tapáya: **tapayaen.** *v.* to hold, support on the palm of the hand. **agtaptapaya.** *v.* to lean the head on the hand. **patapaya.** *n.* beams serving as support for walling, connecting the corner posts. **sitaptapaya.** *a.* holding something in the hands. **mataptapaya nga itlog.** *n.* egg in the palm of one's hand (referring to a precious child). [Tag. *mangalumbaba*]

tapél: (*obs.*) *n.* garment collar; black teeth.

tapéte: (Sp. *tapete:* table cover) *n.* the green cloth of a billiard table; small rug.

tápey: *n.* kind of fermented drink made by the *Igorots.*

tapí: *n.* slab, flat piece of something, board, panel. **tapian.** *v.* to cover with a board. **tapi a bató.** *n.* tablets of the law, tablets of stone; flagstone. **Dimo nabasa ti nakatapi a pakaammo idiay balay?** Didn't you read the boarded notice on the house? [Png. *tápi; tapí* = hip bone]

tapiás: *n.* cutting off a small piece. **Natapiasan ti teritorioda.** Part of their territory was taken away.

tapidéng: **tumapideng.** *v.* to shrink; sneak away; cower. (*sapideng*)

tapík: tapiken, patapiktapik. *v.* to pat someone on the shoulder.

tapíl: *var.* of *tap-il.*

tap-íl: agtap-il. *v.* to be adjacent to each other; to touch each other. [Tag. *dikít*]

tapingár: *n.* comb of a fowl, cock's comb. **taptapingar.** *n. Celosia cirstata,* cockscomb. **tapingaran.** *a.* having a large comb (said of roosters). [Kal. *bengabing,* Png. *palóng,* Tag. *palong*]

tapióka: (Eng.) *n.* tapioca, granulated cassava starch.

tápis: (PSp *tapis*: sash) *n.* towel; large cloth; sash worn over and around the skirt of a *mestisa* dress. **itapis.** *v.* to wrap a towel around.

tapís: *n.* slap. (*sipat*)

tapisería: (Sp. *tapiz*: tapestry + English) *n.* tapestry.

tapkál: tapkalan. *v.* to plaster; smear with something sticky; patch. (*takpal; tapal*)

tapkíl₁: makitapkil. *v.* to mingle; mix; associate with. (*bunggoy*)

tapkíl₂: tinakpil. *n.* a kind of *wasíg* cloth.

tapliák: *n.* waves splashing at the shoreline. **agtapliak.** *v.* to splash; spill; lap at the shore (waves). **tapliakan.** *v.* (*reg.*) to scald (*delnákan, lamawén; luptoy*); splash. **itapliak.** *v.* to pour hot water on. **Agtapliatapliak ti dalluyon iti sakaananda.** The waves are breaking at their feet.

tapnó: *conj.* so that, in order that, so. **Agmulaka iti kayo itan tapno addanto paglinongam iti masanguanam.** Plant trees now so you will have shade in your future. [Bon. *tatno,* Ibg. *tapenu,* Knk. *ta siáy,* Png. *pián,* Tag. *upang*]

tapuág: tapuágan. *n.* variety of awned white rice.

tapuák: agtapuak. *v.* to plunge; jump down. **itapuak.** *v.* to hurl down.

tapóg: *n.* beginning (*punganay*); entrance of a course; diving. **agtapog.** *v.* to start, commence. **tumapog.** *v.* to jump into the water; enter college; get involved in politics; go into business. **itapog.** *v.* to throw something into the water; launch. **matapugan.** *v.* to be at the start of the season. **tapugan.** *v.* to make soup out of. **tumpoog, agkanalpoog.** *v.* to make a thumping sound. **apagtapog.** *a.* just started (season, month). **Isu ngarud a diak tumapogen ta ammok nga awan ti maala.** That's why I don't dive anymore because I know there's nothing to catch. **Awan pay met ti nakaabakan sipud timmapog iti politika.** He still has not lost (a race) from the time he entered politics. [Tag. *lusong; bunsód*]

tápok: *n.* dust. **tapukan.** *v.* to make dusty; dust. **tumapok.** *v.* to turn to dust; be pulverized; stir up dust. **agkatapukan.** *v.* to wallow in dust. **matapukan.** *v.* to be soiled in dust. [Ibg. *keffuq,* gavu, Itg. *dabuk,* Ivt. *gahbek,* Kal. *tapok,* Png. *dabók, sapok,* Kpm., Tag. *alikabók*]

tapón: (Sp. *tapón*: plug) *n.* cork, plug (for a hole). (*sullat*) **itapon.** *v.* to plug a hole.

tapóng: *n.* husked rice soaked in water before it is pounded into powder. **tapongen.** *v.* to pound into powder. (*butay*) **natapong.** *a.* pounded into powder; (*coll.*) used up (said of gambling money). [Tag. *galapóng*]

tapúngor: *n.* bandana for covering hair. **nakatapungor.** *a.* with hair covered (by cloth).

tápus: *n.* end, conclusion, termination. (*gíbus*) **agtapus, tapusen.** *v.* to end; finish. **matapus.** *v.* to conclude; finish; close. **patapus.** *n.* end of mourning; end of a *novena.* [Png. *sampot,* Tag. *tapos, wakas*]

tápuy: see *binubódan,* a kind of fermented native rice drink. (*tapey*)

tap-óy: *n.* sand (*darat*); loose earth.

tapúyaw: taptapuyaw. *n.* apex of an anthill; ant lion larva.

tapúyo: taptapuyo. *var.* of *taptapuyaw*: ant lion larva. **Kasla balay ti taptapuyo ti pusegna.** His navel is like the house of the ant lion larva.

tappáak: *n.* sound of breaking boards. **agtappaak.** *v.* to make the sound of breaking boards.

tappáal: see *tapkál*: plaster; soil; smear.

tappáw: *reg.* variant of *tapáw.*

tappí: tappian. *v.* to fill to the brim. **manappitappi.** *v.* to do something to the excess. [Tag. *punô*]

tappuág: tappuagen. *n.* variety of awned rice.

tappuák: tumappuak. *v.* to jump down. **itappuak.** *v.* to throw down. [Tag. *talón*]

taptáp₁: *n.* a species of fish.

taptáp₂: taptapan. *v.* to restrain, repress; hold back (the boil).

tapwák: see *tappuák*: jump down.

tára₁: taratara. *n. Limnophila sp.* aromatic marsh plant.

tára₂: (Sp.) *n.* tare, free additional weight added to a quantity bought. (*nayon*)

taráab: (*obs.*) **itaraab.** *v.* to open. (*lukat*)

tarabáko: (Sp. *trabajo*: work) *n.* work. (*tegged*)

tarabáng: *n. Ottelia alismoides* edible freshwater herb with white flowers; blush. **agtarabang, tumarabang.** *v.* to blush. **Timmarabang a nangibolsa iti sensilio.** He blushed as he put the coins in his pocket.

tarábay₁: *n.* guidance and help; tutor; guardian. **tarabayen.** *v.* to teach; tutor; guide; lead. **tarabayan.** *v.* to help, guide someone. **Tinarabay-**

nak a magna inggana iti ruangan. He guided me (walking) to the door. [Png. *tonton*, Tag. *patnubay*]

tarábay₂: (*reg.*) **tarabayen.** *v.* to faint, swoon.

tarabesánio: *var.* of *trabesanio*: transverse horizontal stud; sleeper of a railroad.

tarabesía: (Sp. *travesía*: traversing) **tarabesiaen.** *v.* to go straight to a place, not following the roads.

tarabiít: tarabiiten. *v.* to do immediately.

tarabít₁: natarabit. *a.* fast, rapid, speedy (*paspas, parták*); loquacious. **tarabitan.** *v.* to do quickly.

tarabít₂: natarabit. *a.* quick tongued, loquacious. **Timmarabit ti dilana.** *exp.* His tongue is fast (indicates loquacity).

tarabítab: natarabitab. *a.* idle talking, chatty. (*saosao, salangguitis, salawasaw*) **agtarabitab.** *v.* to gossip, chatter. **tarabitaben.** *v.* to gossip about.

tarabútab: *n.* foam, spume (*lutab, labutab*). [Tag. *bulâ*]

tarabútob: see *tanabútob*: to mumble in discontent.

tarabutób: *n.* bubble on melting metals; skin blister (*kapuyo*). [Tag. *paltós*]

tarabtáb₁: *n.* variety of awned late rice with red kernel; *Capparis micracantha* spiny shrub with white flowers and sour red fruits.

tarabtáb₂: tarabtaban. *n.* gossiper. (*tarabitab*)

taraddék: agtaraddek. *v.* to move with light, quick steps.

taradiéng: *n.* word used to stimulate youngsters to dance or play (*taradieng potpot*)

taradió: *n.* weight of a balance; level (instrument). **taradiuen.** *v.* to make level, make flat. [Tag. *nibil*]

taragátag: agtaragatag. *v.* to thump the fingers continuously.

tarágob: *n.* medley of different kinds of gold ore.

taragutóg: see *talogotóg*: throw down; sound of thumping.

taráha: *var.* of *traha*: thread of pipes or screws.

taraígid: *n.* border, edge. (*ígid*) **agtaraigid.** *v.* to walk along the edge; to flow out; burst out (tears). **manaraigid.** *v.* to flow out (tears). **taraigiden.** *v.* to walk along the edge or border. **naitaraigid.** *v.* to be along the edge. **naitaraigid ti baybay.** along the edge of the ocean (coast).

tárak: *n.* inheritance. (*táwid*) **taraken.** *v.* to take out of the nest (young birds); remove from a litter. **manarak.** *v.* to stop flowering (banana). **tumarak.** (*obs.*) *v.* to spread a fishing net. **taraken ti bumario.** *exp.* a person who eats all over town in other people's houses.

tarakaták: *n.* sound of rain beating down on an iron roof; sound of a dripping faucet. **agtarakatak.** *v.* to make the sound of heavy falling rain; to drip heavily (faucet).

tarakaták: *n.* kind of small gray bird; small drum.

tarakátok: (*obs.*) see *tarakátak*: sound of heavy rain.

tarakén: *n.* pet; ward. **taraknen.** *v.* to breed; raise, rear; educate; nurse; attend to; look after. **mataraken.** *v.* to be cared after (*taripato*); to be educated, raised properly. **pagtaraknan.** *n.* breeding, raising (animals). **Taraknem 'ta bagim.** Take care of yourself. [Tag. *alagà*]

taráki: *n.* handsomeness; posture. (*guápo, taér, pogi*; *libnas*; *saldit*; *dangas*; *bisked*) **nataraki.** *a.* handsome, beautiful, good looking; elegant; tasteful. **Saysayaatenyo ti umisem tapno natarakikayo iti kamera.** Smile better so you look handsome for the camera. [Knk. *gálat*, Png. *taríkin*, Tag. *guwapo* (Sp.), *bikas*]

tarakítik: agtarakitik. *v.* to make the sound of drizzling rain. [Tag. *ambón*]

tarakutók: *n.* kind of small marine fish striped blue and white. **agtarakutok.** *v.* to sing (said of the turtledove). **tarakutukan.** *n.* Cavalla fish of the *Carangidae* family.

taralalláy: *n.* humming. **agtaralallay.** *v.* to hum (a tune).

tarambán: tarambanan. *v.* to speak rapidly; to excel a person in speaking. (*tarangban*)

taramídong: *n.* pimple. (*kamuro*). **agtaramidong.** *v.* to develop pimples. [Png. *kamoro*, Tag. *tagihawat*]

taramítim: *n.* mold spot on clothing. **tinaramitim.** *a.* full of mold spots (clothing left damp for a long time).

taramnáy: matartaramnay. *v.* to do something without spirit or interest; to feel lousy.

taramusián: *n.* hard coconut meat. (*kakaruyen, lulukoten*)

taramúya: *n.* scaffolding used for angels on Easter Sunday.

tarampás: *n.* fast, skilled action. **tarampasen.** *v.* to do something fast.

tarámpo: *n.* top (spinning toy). (*kampuso, sunay, trampo*) **agtarampo.** *v.* to spin a top.

taránaw: *n.* horizon of the sea.

taránta: (Sp. *atarantar*: bewilder, stun) **matartaranta.** *v.* to be in a hurry. (*darás*)

tarantádo: (Sp. *atarantado*: stunned; bewildered) *a.* naughty; mischievous; shameless; disrespectful. (*súkir, aliwegwég*; *loko*)

tarangbán: tumarangban. *v.* to talk continuously, chatter. (*taramban*)

tarang-éd: **agtarang-ed, tumarang-ed.** *v.* to continually nod the head (horses galloping).

tarangútong: *n.* pile; heap. (*dagumpo*) **agkaitarangotong.** *v.* to be heaped up in a great quantity. **agtatarangutong.** *v.* to crowd, gather together doing nothing (*mattider*). [Tag. *tambák*]

taraúdi: (f. *udi*) *a.* ending; last part; additional, extra; postscript; epilogue. **itaraudi.** *v.* to place at the last; add at the end. **maitaraudi.** *a.* to be done last; to be placed last. **tartaraudi.** *n.* last parts of, vestiges of. **nataraudi.** *a.* last, final. **Awan umuna nga agbabawi no di ket agtartaraudi.** *exp.* Repentance always comes afterwards. **Natimudna dagiti taraudi a balikas.** He heard the last words. [Tag. *hulihán*]

taráok₁: *n.* crow of a rooster. **agtaraok.** *v.* to crow (rooster). **Agtaraokton ti bisokol.** The snail will crow (referring to an impossible event or situation). [Bon. *kóok*, Png. *kukaok*, Tag. *tilaok, talaok*]

taráok₂: **tartaraok.** *n. Quisqualis indica* shrub with fragrant flowers.

taraón: *n.* food; nourishment. (*kanen*) **manaraon.** *n.* supplier of food. **itaraon.** *v.* to five food; support. **taraonan.** *v.* to nurse, feed, foster; sustain (*pakanen*). [Bon. *talaon*, Knk. *taganó*, Tag. *pagkain*]

tar-áp: **itar-ap.** *v.* to sift, sieve; winnow; spread around. **matar-apan.** *v.* to be crowded, filled. **kasla intar-ap.** *a.* scattered; spread. [Ibg. *saq*, Ivt. *wakwak*, Knk. *teg-ap*, Kpm. *tatap*, Png. *taep*, Tag. *tahíp* (winnow)]

tarapáng: *n.* harpoon; trident. **tarapangen.** *v.* to hit with a harpoon. **matarapangan.** *a.* harpooned. **Kunam no naigayang a tarapang dagiti matana kadagiti babbai iti aplaya.** You would think his eyes were speared harpoons on the girls at the beach. [Png. *pika*, Tag. *salapáng*]

tarapók: **agtarapnok.** *v.* to crowd; hustle and bustle; gather. [Tag. *tipon*]

tarapnós: **agtarapnos.** *v.* to proceed to do another job. **tarapnusen.** *v.* to do all. **itarapnos.** *v.* to make time to do an additional job; proceed to another job. **Agimukmukat a simmango iti ridaw sa intarapnosna nga insagaysay dagiti dadakkel a ramayna iti apsay a buokna.** She cleaned her eyes facing the door and then proceeded to comb her straight hair with her fingers.

tarapók: **agtatarapok.** *v.* to gather, assemble; congregate; unite. (*ummong*) **tumarapok.** *v.* to join a gathering.

tarapóng: **agtarapong.** *v.* to come together, unite, gather. (*tarapok*)

taraptáp: **taraptapen.** *v.* to cut successively (stalks of rice).

tarás: *n.* a kind of small black bird with a white breast. [Tag. *tarás* = boldness, frankness in speech]

tarastás: **tarastasen.** *v.* to do completely without interruption; to do entirely.

tarat: **tartarat.** *n. Quisqualis sp.* plant with fragrant flowers. [Tag. *tarát* = long tailed sparrow]

tarátar: *n.* row; line. (*aray, talenten*) **itaratar.** *v.* to align, place in line. **nataratar.** *a.* lined up, in a row. **tarataren.** *v.* to place in a row, align (*ibátog*). **Nataratar dagiti pagkapean iti igid ti karayan.** The cafés were lined up along the edge of the river.

táraw₁: *n.* kind of tree with big leaves.

táraw₂: **tarawan.** *v.* to cut off the top (of plants). (*uggot*)

tarawidwíd: *n.* management of a business. (*taripáto, imaton*) **manarawidwid.** *v.* to defend; guard, protect; care for; guide, direct; manage; edit. **mangtarawidwid.** *n.* manager. **agtarawidwid.** *v.* to trust, rely on. **tartarawidwidan.** *v.* to be in charge of. [Tag. *patnugot*]

tarawítaw: **natarawitaw.** *a.* talkative, loquacious. (*managsasao*)

tarawítiw: *var.* of *tarawitaw*: talkative, loquacious.

tarawitwít: *a.* loquacious, loose-tongued.

taráy₁: *n.* run; speed; operation or functioning (of a machine); drift; elopement. **agtaray, tumaray.** *v.* to run; elope. **panagtaray.** *n.* elopement. **itaray.** *v.* to run away with, kidnap, abduct; elope with. **itarayan.** *v.* to run away from. **makitaray.** *v.* to elope with. **kataray.** *v.* to run away with; elope. **mannaray.** *n.* racer, one who runs a race. **nataray.** *n.* runner. *a.* sold quickly and easily. **tarayen.** *n.* distance to run in a race. *v.* to run to. **taray-taray.** *n.* evacuation. **tinnarayan.** *n.* running competition. **pagtarayan ti dara.** *n.* blood vessel. **arintarayén.** *a.* about to run. **Sangatarayan, sangaapuyan.** *exp.* denoting poverty (*lit.* cooking what is caught). **Napintas ti taray ti negosiona.** The operation of his business is good. [Bon. *tagtag*, Ibg. *paládiyu, karéra*, Ivt. *mayayuq*, Kpm. *mulayi*, Png. *batik*, Tag. *takbô*]

taráy₂: **tartaray.** *n. Spinifex littoreus* grass, boiled and used to wash infants so they will learn to walk and run fast.

taráy-kúgit: (*coll., reg.*) *n.* quitting while one is ahead (said of gamblers).

tarayútoy: *n.* squirt, gush, spurt of liquids. (*pussuák*) **agtarayutoy.** *v.* to gush out; squirt. [Tag. *tulò*]

tarbangáw: **tartarbangaw**. *n*. one who changes the subject of a conversation.

tarbéb: (*obs*.) see *patalbeg*: kind of native drum.

tardáw₁: **tardawan**. *v*. to poll, clear land for a new rice field. [Tag. *putól*]

tardáw₂: **natardaw**. *a*. tall; protruding.

tárde: (Sp. *tarde*: late) **natarde**. *a*. tardy, late to class.

taredtéd: *n*. drop; drip. **tumaredted**. *v*. to drip (*tedtád*). [Tag. *paták*]

tarekték: *n*. cry of rooster or hen. **agtarektek**. *v*. to make the cry of the rooster or hen. **tumarektek**. *v*. to change the voice (at puberty); to have the first impulses of sexual desire, run after girls.

tarém: *n*. preparation. **natarem**. *a*. smart, clever, bright, intelligent, astute (*alisto*; *sikap*; *alibtok*). [Tag. *talino*]

tarengténg: *n*. vagabond. (*baligawgaw*; *basingkawil*; *birkug*; *sawir*) **agtarengteng, tumarengteng**. *v*. to walk directly to a place; with light steps; to do something straight away; follow a straight course. **tarengtengen**. *v*. to follow a straight path. **Dimsaag ti maysa a baket sa timmarengteng a simrek iti salas a yanmi**. An old woman got off and directly went into the living room where we were. **Apagsaona, intarengtengnan ti nangpanaw kaniak**. As soon as he spoke, he immediately left me.

tarhéta: (Sp. *tarjeta*: business card) *n*. business card; card; label of a package.

tari(n)-: Fossilized prefix (lexicalized use): **tarikayo**. timber. **taributngen**. afraid.

tari- -an: Affix used with verbal stems to indicate impending action: **Tarianakán ni Claudia**. Claudia is about to give birth. **Taribautanak kenka**. I'm going to whip you.

tári: **taritari**. *n*. *Blechum brownei* plant.

taribáaw: *n*. the final part of a feast or celebration.

taribadiók: *n*. illegal logging.

tárid: *a*. long and pointed (said of nose). (*tundiris*)

tarigágay: *n*. wish, desire. (*kalikaguman*, *essem*) **tarigagayan**. *v*. to desire; wish; covet; crave, long for. **Tarigagayak ti panagbaliw ti biagko**. I wish to change my life. [Knk. *kagás*, Png. *pirawat*, Tag. *nasà*, *nais*]

tarigmó: see *tarapóng*: join; unite; assemble.

tárik: *n*. rectangular piece of wickerwork used to carry a dead person to the grave or for trapping fish. **tarikan**. *v*. to enclose with a *tarik*.

tarikáyo: (f. *kayo*) *n*. timber. **agtarikayo**. *v*. to gather timber. **pagtarikaywan**. *n*. lumberyard. (*tableria*)

tariktík: *n*. kind of small bird. (*tagiktik*, *tarakitik*)

tarilalláy: *n*. lullaby; song without words. **agtarilallay**. *v*. to sing *la la la* (without words). [Tag. *oyayi*]

tarimáan: **agtarimaan**. *v*. to fix, repair; revise. **tarimnen**. *v*. to fix, mend, arrange; adjust; prepare; heal. **matarimaan**. *v*. to arrange. **manarimaan**. *v*. to be going on; to be engaged in; to be current. **patarimaan**. *v*. to have something repaired. **Tinarimaanna ti bidangna a tualia ta nagparang dagiti luppona**. She fixed the towel wrapped around her because her thighs were showing. **Sangkasaona a patarimaanna ti rangtay**. He keeps saying he will have the bridge fixed. [Png. *apíger*, Tag. *ayos*, *husay*, Tag. *tarima* = movable platform]

tarimáyong: *n*. tip of a nose (not long). (*tundiris*)

tarimbán: *n*. crate; hamper; woven bamboo hurdle used to carry dead bodies to the cemetery; trash can.

tarimbángon₁: *n*. delirium (*ammangaw*); shock. **matarimbangon**. *v*. to be shocked; startled. **tarimbangonen**. *v*. to shock. [Tag. *pagkahibáng*, *kabiglaanan*]

tarimbángon₂: **tarimbangonen**. *v*. to lift a hypnotized person with the fingers, playing the "light as a feather stiff as a board" game.

tarin-: *var*. of the prefix *tari-*

tarínak: *n*. body of an outrigger boat.

tarindanúm: (f. *danúm*) *n*. skin eruption caused by prolonged immersion in water; fungal infection in the skin. **agtarindanum**. *v*. to have thick wrinkled skin due to prolonged soaking in water; to have an infection in the skin (due to prolonged moistness).

taringgáwid: (f. *gawid*) *n*. restraining force, something that causes someone to have second thoughts. **mataringgawid**. *v*. to be caused to have second thoughts, to be restrained by a force.

taringgúyod: (f. *guyod*) *n*. magnetism, magnetic force, something that attracts. **mangtaringguyod**. *v*. to attract. **Kasla adda batombalani a nangtaringguyod kadagiti matana**. It is as if there were a magnet attracting her eyes.

tarípa: (Sp. *tarifa*: tariff) *n*. tariff. **de-taripa**. *a*. flat (rates), fixed (price).

taripáto: **agtaripato**. *v*. to be in charge of; take care of; nurse the sick (*tarawidwíd*) **taripatuen**. *v*. to guard, take care of, read; look after; take charge of. **nataripato**. *a*. watchful; considerate, thoughtful. **managtaripato**. *v*. to be careful, vigilant. **Taripatuem ti bagim**. Take care of yourself. [Knk. *allá*, *ayáko*, Tag. *alagà*]

taripnóng: *n.* gathering, meeting; crowd. (*um-mong*) **tumaripnong, makitaripnong**. *v.* to gather, convene, meet. **pagtaripnongan**. *n.* place of a meeting; junction of two things meeting (roads, rivers, etc.). [Png., Tag. *tipon*]

tariptíp₁: *n.* kind of herpes or tetter. [Tag. *buni*]

tariptíp₂: *n. talakítok* fish when small.

tarísi: agtarisi. *v.* to escape secretly; avoid; shun responsibilities.

taritáw: (*obs.*) see *ínaw*: appetite of pregnant women.

tariwátiw: natarawatiw. *a.* very skinny. (*kuttongi*; *ratiw*; *pairpair*)

tarkók: *n.* coward. (*takrót*).

tarlák: *n.* kind of green and red bird.

tarlás: see *tarás*: kind of small bird with a white breast and black wings and tail.

tarlinggá: *n.* kind of tissue or woven fabric.

tarmídong: *n.* pimple. (*taramidong*, *kamuro*) **agtarmidong**. *v.* to have pimples. [Png. *kamoro*, Tag. *tagihawat*]

tarnáw: *n.* happy face. **natarnaw**. *a.* having a happy face, devoid of worries; clean; pure; clear. **tumarnaw**. *v.* to become clear, pure. **Natarnaw dagiti mata a naiturong kadagiti agayan-ayat**. His eyes were happy facing the lovers. [Tag. *linaw*]

táro: (*obs.*) *n.* competition in tolerance; stake; wager; bet. (*taman*, *pusta*, *taya*) **agtaro**. *v.* to place a bet. [Tag. *tayâ*]

tarubáay: tarubaayen. *v.* to be weak when waking up due to not eating the night before.

tarubák: agtatarubak. *v.* to act in haste; to happen simultaneously; to keep up with, not fall behind. **Saan a nakitarubak ni Leting iti panagsarsaritada**. Leting did not keep up with their conversation. [Tag. *magmadalî*]

tarubimbín: *n.* guide; guiding light. **tarubimbinen**. *v.* to lead; guide (*turong*). [Tag. *patnubay*]

tarúbo: *n.* shoot; growth; sprout. (*sagibsib*) **tumarubo**. *v.* to grow rapidly (plants). [Tag. *usbóng*]

tarubók: tumarubok. *v.* to be effective, bring on a good result (advice).

tarúbong: *n.* sprout, shoot of a root or tuber. (*sagibsib*) **tumarubong**. *v.* to sprout.

tarúday: *n.* candle droppings. **tarudayan**. *v.* to line; strengthen by adding something stronger. [Tag. *tibay*]

tárog₁: tarugen. *v.* to cool by stirring.

tárog₂: mannarog. *n.* a kind of black beetle.

tarúgo: (Sp. *tarugo*: wooden peg) *n.* wooden peg for fastening a door or window.

tarugtóg: tarugtugen. *v.* to knock (at the door). (*tuktok*)

tarukánag: patarukanagen. *v.* to fluff pillows (or mattresses) by beating them. (*sarúkag*)

tarukaték: *n.* the sound of quick light steps. **agtarukatek**. *v.* to move with quick light steps.

tarukítik: see *tarakítik*: sound of drizzling rain.

tarúkoy: *n.* kind of small crab with one claw larger than the other. **agtarukoy**. *v.* to walk or run in a crouching position. **Nagtarukoy sa nagdapla ti soldado**. The soldier crouched his way forward and then fell prone. **Kasla tarukoy a sipupungo**. He is like a bound crab (said of an idle person).

taroktók: *n. Bombax ceiba*.

tarumámis: *n.* sharp edge of a cutting instrument. (*sarumamit*) **natarumamis**. *a.* very sharp. (*natadem*, *natírad*) **patarumamisen**. *v.* to sharpen. [Tag. *talím*]

tarumátim: *n.* kind of shell animal that grows in colonies on bamboos.

tarumnáy: (*obs.*) see *taramnáy*: do something without interest.

tarumpíngay: *n.* grief; that which causes one to be upset; loneliness; nostalgia; sorrow. (*liday*; *iliw*) **agtarumpingay**. *v.* to be emotionally disturbed, upset; confused; lonely. **matarumpingay**. *v.* to be lonely; upset. **No dimo maibturan a matilmon ti apro ti tarumpingay, dimo met maipapas a manamnam ti diro ti ragsak**. If you cannot stand to swallow the bile of grief, you cannot enjoy trying the honey of joy. [Tag. *dalamhatì*]

tarumpís: matarumpis. *v.* to be hit, slapped. (*tapís*)

tarumpó: *n.* kind of young boy's hide-and-seek game. **makitartarumpo**. *v.* to play the *tarumpo* game.

taróng₁: *n. Solanum melongena*, eggplant, aubergine; term applied to a penis in certain expressions. **katarongan**. *n.* eggplant field. **tarong ti áso**. *n. Solanum cumingii* plant. [Ibg. *tarung*, *barenghénas*, Ifg. *balantína*, Ivt. *vahusaq*, Kal. *biyagsi*, *talong*, Kpm. *balasénas*, Png. *talón*, Bon., Knk., Tag. *talóng*, (Sp. = *berenjena*)]

taróng₂: tinarong. *n.* variety of awned early rice with elongated spike.

tarungúdong: (*obs.*) *n.* row, file; line. (*uged*, *úgis*, *batog*, *aray*)

tarupék: agtarupek. *v.* to make a busy sound (of several people working with tools or knocking, etc.); to make a chopping sound.

taruptúp: agtaruptup. *v.* to accumulate; multiply; pile up. **taruptupan**. *v.* to augment, increase; multiply (ailments, debts, crimes.). **Agtataruptup ti malaglagipna**. His memories are accumulating.

tarús: **agtarus.** *v.* to go straight to without delay, move on; pierce, penetrate. **itarus.** *v.* to do something after something else. **itarusan.** *v.* to guess, arrive at, get to the true meaning; come upon; comprehend. **natarus.** *a.* acute, sharp; bright, intelligent; clear; lucid; straightforward. **manartarus.** *v.* to immediately enter; go without delay. **matarusan.** *v.* to be able to understand. **pagtarusen.** *v.* to pierce through. **pagitarusán.** *n.* dictionary. **pakaipatarusan.** *n.* meaning; translation. **agtinnarusan.** *v.* to agree with each other; understand each other. **Mapanak idiay Goleta, ammok nga idiay ti pagtarusanna.** I am going to Goleta, I know that's where he is headed to. [Tag. *tuloy*; *liwanag*]

tarutukan: *n.* cavalla fish of the *Carangidae* family.

tároy: **pataroy.** see *tagapulot*: sugar; molasses, liquid sugar.

taróy: *syn.* of *daróy*: thin, weak (soup, etc.) (*labnaw*)

tarúyaw: *n.* rice with a red kernel.

taruyútoy: **tumaruyutoy.** *v.* to come one after another in swarms (people waiting for taxis, etc.). (*agsasaruno*)

taruytóy: **taruytuyen.** *v.* to lightly sprinkle (liquids) on something.

tarpúok: **tumanarpuok.** *v.* to make the sound of branches in the wind.

tartanília: (Sp. *tartanilla*: two-wheeled carriage) *n.* two-wheeled, horse-drawn carriage with a round top.

tartár: **agtatartar.** *v.* to happen at the same time or in quick succession. **maitartar.** *v.* to happen immediately. **itartar.** *v.* to do immediately; to do at one's leisure.

tártaro: (Sp. *tártaro*: tartar) *n.* cream of tartar.

tása: (Sp. *taza*: cup) *n.* cup. (*tagayán*) **sangatasa.** *n.* one cupful.

tasadór: (Sp. *tasador*: appraiser) *n.* assessor, appraiser.

tasár: (Sp. *tasar*: appraise) **tasaran.** *v.* to appraise, rate; regulate; tax.

tasí: (*obs.*) **natasi.** *a.* very fragile. (*rasí, rukop*)

táso: **tasuen.** *v.* to beat; maul (*lugos*). **Tinasona ti teltelna.** He mauled his nape. [Tag. *bugbóg*]

tastás: **tastasen.** *v.* to rip, tear up; unstitch; demolish (*satsat*). [Bon. *basbas*, Tag. *tastás* = unstitch]

táta: *n.* term of address used for a father or uncle, male one generation above speaker. (*tatang*) **agtata.** *v.* to float. (*alintuto*)

tatadién: (f. *tadi*) *n.* gamecock.

tátag: *n.* dry shell of the bottle gourd used for holding lime. [Tag. *tatag* = establish]

tátang: *n.* father, daddy. (*tata*) **tatang iti bunyag.** *n.* godfather (*ninong*). **dagiti tattatangenna.** his elders. [Png. *amá, tata*, Tag. *tatang*]

tatangkán: (f. *tangek*) *n.* kind of large jar.

tátay: (Tagalog also) *n.* endearing term of address for one's father, daddy.

táteg: **tattateg.** see *antatateg*: kind of white larva.

taték: *n.* small silver money. (*pirak*) **tatken.** *v.* to pulverize, crush; mangle; riddle with bullets. **matatek.** *v.* to be riddled with bullets. **mangtattatek.** *v.* to riddle with bullets. **Natatek iti bala ti bukotna.** His back was riddled with bullets.

tátel: **agtatel.** *v.* to stammer when speaking. (*bede, beddal*)

táting: *n.* form of native stitchwork, looped and knotted lace; shuttle for making lace.

tatú: (Eng.) *n.* tattoo. (*baték*) **agpatatu.** *v.* to get a tattoo. **itatu.** *v.* to tattoo something on the skin.

tatús: (*obs.*) see *sasús*: kind of large black crustacean.

tatot: *n.* gobi fish, *Chonophorus melanocephalus*.

tatsáy: *n.* round casting net larger than the *tabúkol*.

tatsíng: *n.* game of pitching pennies; game of marbles. **agtatsing.** *v.* to play at pitching pennies.

tattáo: *n.* Irregular plural of *tao*: people; men.

tattát: **agtanattat.** *v.* to make the sound of continuous walking; to chatter. [Tag. *daldál*]

táwa: *n.* window. (*bentána*) **tawa ti kararua.** *exp.* eyes (window of the soul). **tawatawa.** *n. Ricinus communis.* [Kal. *tagibyang*, Kpm. *áwang*, Png. *dorongáwen*, Tag. *dúrungawán*, Tag. *tawa* = laugh]

táwag₁: **itawag.** *v.* to publish, cry, proclaim. (*ayab, pukkáw, pakdaar*)

táwag₂: (Tag.) *n.* phone call (*awag*); calling on the phone. **tumawag.** *v.* to call on the phone. **tawagan.** *v.* to call someone on the phone. [Png., Tag. *tawag*]

tawáng: **maitawang.** *v.* to be clearly discerned at a distance.

taw-áng: **maitaw-ang.** *v.* to fall suddenly into a large opening from a high place. [Tag. *hulog*]

táwar: *n.* bargain, cheaper price. **tumawar.** *v.* to haggle, bargain. **tawaran.** *v.* to haggle for. **Awan tawarnan?** *exp.* Is there no better price? [Png. *táwal*, Tag. *tawad*]

táwas: (Tagalog also) *n.* alum; alum powder.

tawás: *a.* missed (target). **tumawas.** *v.* to miss a target. (*mintis, tagibas*)

tawátaw: **agtawataw.** *v.* to roam, wander. (*alla-allá*, *mantaw*) **maitawataw.** *v.* to stray, wander. **tumawataw.** *n.* bad word, ugly term, rude statement. **tanawataw.** *n.* chatter. **Kinaasianka idi agtawtawatawka.** I had pity on you when you were wandering. [Tag. *layas*]

táway: *n.* tasting the flavor of something. (*raman*) **tawayan.** *v.* to taste; savor. **agtawtaway.** (*obs.*) *v.* to live wild in the jungle. [Tag. *tikmán*]

tawén: *n.* year; age. (*idád*) **agtawen.** *v.* to be so many years old, to have as age. **agkatawen.** *v.* to be the same age. (*sadar*, *taeb*) **katawen.** *n.* person born the same year as someone else. **panawen.** *n.* time. **tumawen.** *n.* first-year anniversary. **makatawen.** *adv.* of the duration of one year. **matawenan.** *v.* to be one year old; to come of age. **idi napan a tawen.** last year. **tinawen.** *adv.* every year. **tawentawen.** *a.* yearly. **idi kasangatawen.** the year before last. **idi katimmawen.** three years ago. **intono sangatawen.** after two years. **Mano ti tawenmon?** How old are you? [Ibg. *dagun*, Ifg. *tóon*, Ivt. *awaan*, Kal. *tawon*, Knk. *tew-én*, Kpm. *banwa*, Png., Tag. *taón*]

táweng: *n.* (*reg.*) ladle. (*aklo*) **maitaweng.** *v.* to vanish from sight. [Tag. *walâ*]

táwid: *n.* inheritance. **agtawid, tumawid, tawiden.** *v.* to inherit; *n.* heir. **mangtawid.** *v.* to inherit. *n.* heir. **ipatawid.** *v.* to give as inheritance; pass on to the next generation. **patawidan.** *v.* to bequeath to someone. **kannawidan.** *n.* customs; culture; habit; tradition. **básol a tawid.** *n.* original sin. **Nagtitinnawidanmi a sangapuonan ti panagsuma.** We have passed on as a family from generation to generation the art of antidote making. **Ti sangit ti agtawid, katawa a nalimed.** The cries of the heirs are really suppressed smiles. [Ivt. *amuhun*, Knk. *táwid*, Png. *tawíd*, Tag. *mana*]

tawílis: (Tag.) *n.* species of freshwater sardine.

táwing: *n.* dipper for drawing water from a well. **tumawing.** *v.* to draw water from a well.

tawíng: **tumawing.** *v.* to cross; go to the other side. (*lumasat*)

tawtáw: **natanawtaw.** *a.* boasting, bragging. (*pangás*, *tangsít*). **matawtaw.** *v.* to be lost along the way; confused. **itawtaw.** *v.* to confuse, mislead, misguide; intentionally lose. **maitawtaw.** *v.* to be misguided, misled, confused; misplaced, lost. **Impabulod dagiti kabbalayko ket naitawtawen.** I lent it to my housemates and it got lost. [Tag. *ligáw*]

tawwá: **tawwatawwa.** *n. Ricinus communis*, the castor-oil plant. **No aglungsoten dagiti bunga ti tawwatawwa, umayen ti panagtudo.** When the fruits of the castor-oil plant rot, rain will come.

tawwáw: *a.* crazy. **kinatawwaw.** *n.* craziness. (*bagtit*, *balla*)

tawwék: **itawwek.** *v.* to insert, put a dagger in the wound; hurl. **maitawwek.** *v.* to be thrust, inserted; hurled.

-tay: abbreviation of *-tayo*: we (inclusive), our (inclusive).

tay: abbreviation of *daytay*; see *patay*.

táya: **agtaya, itaya.** *v.* to receive, catch (rain, a blow, etc.); catch dripping rain in a bucket. **pagtaya.** *n.* container used to catch falling liquids.

tayá: (Tagalog *tayâ*) *n.* stakes in gambling; person responsible for the bill. **itaya.** *v.* to place a bet. **sitataya.** *a.* at stake. **laglagipem a sitataya ti dayaw ti ilitayo.** Remember that the honor of our town is at stake. **Ni Pusing ti taya ta isu kano ti kabaknangan ken kalakayanmi amin.** Pusing took the bill because he is supposedly the richest and oldest of all of us.

táyab: *n.* clay pot similar to the *banga* but wider for cooking.

tayáb: *n.* flight. **tumayab.** *v.* to fly. **tumatayab.** *n.* bird. (flying creature.) **itayab.** *v.* to carry off (said of the wind.) **ipatayab.** *v.* to induce to fly; make fly; put on the air (through radio). **tayaben.** *v.* to fly to. **makatayab.** *v.* to be able to fly. **nababa ti tayabna.** *exp.* denoting an easy lady, prostitute. **patayaben.** *v.* to let loose (a bird); blow with a gun. **Patayabek ti bangabangam.** *exp.* I'll blow your brains out (*lit.* make your skull fly). [Bon. *táyaw* (flying of bird), *táyap* (flying of spear), Ibg. *kágag*, Ivt. *sumayap*, Kpm. *sulápo*, Png. *tikiáb*, Tag. *lipád*]

Tayábas: (Tag.) *n.* the former name of Quezon Province.

tayabútab: *n.* rambling talk, loquacity.

tayadór: (f. *tayá* + Sp. agentive suffix *-dor*) *n.* gambler, one who places a bet.

táyag₁: *n.* height (*ngato*). **natayag.** *a.* tall (people). **tumayag.** *v.* to become tall. **itayag.** *v.* to set up, put in an upright position. [Ibg. *atennag*, Itg. *anáwas*, Ivt. *karang*, Kal. *taklang*, Knk. *ulanguéy*, *yádew*, *dakdaké*, *dangáley*, Kpm. *mátas*, Png. *tagéy*, Tag. *taás*]

táyag₂: **sangkatayag.** *n.* one length of yarn between the *takbían* and the *puyúd*.

tay-ák: *n.* treeless plain, savanna, desert; open land; battlefield. **natay-ak.** *a.* on a high plain.

tayakták: *a.* open; bear. **tumayaktak.** *v.* to amuse oneself outside; begin to walk; leave the nest; to start a project after having procrastinated for a long time.

tayamútam: *n.* loquacity; *a.* loquacious, loose-tongued.

tayanggáw: **agtayanggaw.** *v.* to run away, flee (*talaw*); to wander off (*bayanggudaw*). **Agsangsangit ta nagtayanggaw ti amana.** She is crying because her father wandered off.

tay-ás: **tumay-as.** *v.* to slip away, leave secretly, escape unnoticed. (*takiás*)

tayegtég: **agtayegteg; manayegteg.** *v.* to shake, tremble. (*tigerger, payegpég*)

tayengténg: *n.* strongness of a color; sheltered place. **natayengteng.** very dark, strong (color); sheltered; hidden. **Nakataytayengteng ti atiddog a buokna a nagsalupayak iti barukongna.** Her long hair lowered over her chest was dark black.

-tayó: enclitic *pron.* we, us; our, inclusive (includes addressee). **In*tayon***. Let's go. (see also *–kamí*). [Knk. *takó*, Png. *(i)tayo*, Tag. *táyo*; *natin* (agentive, possessive)]

tayúdok: *n.* heavy rain. **tumayudok.** *v.* to fall heavily (said of the rain).

táyog: **natayog.** *a.* tall; hovering (*tayag*). [Tag. *tayog* = height, elevation]

tay-úg: *n.* bamboo wickerwork trap for mudfish.

táyok: **tumayok.** *v.* to soar, sail upward, ascend. **natayok.** *a.* high. **agpatayok.** *v.* to urinate at a great distance (said of men). [Tag. *tayog*]

táyum: *n. Indigofera suffruticosa*, the indigo plant (*anyíl*). **tayumtayum.** *n. Indigo hirsuta*, herb with reddish brown stems covered with purplish hairs. [Tag. *tayom*]

-tayonto: [*-tayo* + (*n*)*to*] Enclitic pronoun expressing first person plural inclusive actor and future time, dual form is *-tanto*. **Mapantayonto.** We (and you) will go. **Mapantanto.** You and I will go.

tayútay: **tayutayen.** *v.* to retail. (*tingí*) **itayutay.** *v.* to postpone; do slowly. **maitayutay.** *v.* to be postponed; delayed. [Tag. *tayong*]

tayútoy: **tumayutoy.** *v.* to drip (said of the nose). (*tuyutoy*)

taytáng: **maitaytang.** (*obs.*) *v.* to fall from a window, etc.

taytáy: *n.* bamboo bridge (*rangtay, kalantay, talaytay*). [Png., Tag. *taytáy*, Tag. *tuláy*]

-tayto: *var.* of *-tayonto*.

tayyék: **agtayyek.** *v.* to whirl, spin. (*alipuno*) **agpinnatayyek.** *v.* to spin a top in competition. **patayyeken.** *v.* to spin an object (top, etc.). **Nagtayyek ti panagkitana ket naawanan iti puot.** His vision whirled and he lost consciousness. [Bon. *yáyep*, Ivt. *valiweswes*, Knk. *únat*, Png. *telek, peyes*, Tag. *ikot*]

teatrál: (Sp. *teatral*: theatrical) *a.* theatrical.

teátro: (Sp. *teatro*: theater) *n.* theater. (*pagipabuyaan*)

tebbá: **agtebba, tebbaen.** *v.* to cut a stem of bananas. **nanbaan.** *n.* lower part of the banana stem.

tebbág₁: *n.* landslide; cave-in. **natbag.** *a.* collapsed; crumbled; caved in. **tebbagen.** *v.* to break down rocks; cave in. [Tag. *tibág*]

tebbág₂: *n.* intonation, pitch of the voice; accent. **natbag.** *a.* (~ *a timek*) sonorous, resonant, ringing; loud. **itebbag.** *v.* to say loudly.

tebbáng₁: *n.* cliff, precipice (*derráas, rangkis, garangúgong*); **maitebbang, matbang.** *v.* to fall headlong; slip down; erode; fall in. [Tag. *talampás*]

tebbáng₂: *n.* temptation; sin. (*sulisog*) **itebbang.** *v.* to lead into sin; tempt. **manangitebbang.** *n.* seducer, temptress. [Tag. *tuksó*]

tebbáy: *var.* of *tibbay*.

tebbég₁: *n. Ficus sp.* trees whose fruit yields a kind of oil.

tebbég₂: *n.* kind of gray bird.

tebbéng: *n.* hole in the earlobe. (*tuldo; tibbeng*) **agtebbeng.** *v.* to pierce a hole in the earlobe. **tebbengan.** *v.* to pierce a hole in the earlobe of. **tetebbengan.** *n.* earlobe (*piditpidit, pipiritan*). [Tag. *butas ng tainga*]

tébol: (Eng., *slang*) **itebol.** *v.* to hire an escort for the table (done in bars). **Dayta kadi laeng ti gapuna nga intebolnak?** Is that the only reason why you hired me to be at your table?

tebtéb: *n.* coconut shell used for drinking. **tebteben.** *v.* to destroy, demolish (*dadael*); break into pieces; fashion. [Tag. *durog; pantáy*]

ted: see *ited*: give.

teddá: see *tidda*.

teddák: **agteddak, teddaken.** *v.* to burst (abscesses, etc.) by pricking. [Tag. *tusok*]

teddék: *n.* pillar, post (*adigi*); chief. [Tag. *haligi*]

tedtéd: *n.* drop, leak. (*taredtéd*) **agtedted, tumedted.** *v.* to leak, drip. **ipatedted.** *v.* to drain. **mangipatedted.** *v.* to spill a drop of wine to appease the spirits; prepare a libation. **taredted.** *n.* droplets; drip; leak. **Pinattogak ti baso iti arak ken pinatedtedak iti sabidong.** I poured the glass with wine and put in a few drops of poison. [Ibg. *turu*, Ivt. *manayeteng*, Kal. *tudtud*, Png. *térter*, Kpm., Tag. *tulò*]

teggáak₁: *n.* kind of wading bird, heron. **teggaak a tengnged.** *n.* long neck (like a heron). **Kunam la no teggaak a mangal-alimon iti naisiblokanna a bunog iti panangbennatna iti tengngedna.** You would think he was a heron swallowing the *bunog* fish it stole the way he stretches his neck. [Tag. *tagák*]

teggáak₂: *n.* kind of jar with a long, cylindrical neck.

teggéd₁: *n.* work, job. (*trabáho*) **mangged.** *v.* to work by the day for wages. **mangmangged.** *n.* day laborer. **tegden.** *n.* wages, pay; *v.* to follow eagerly. **agpategged.** *v.* to employ. **matgedan.** *n.* income; salary; wages. **Ammona a saan nga umanay ti matgedanna sadiay no kuentaenna ti magastosna iti inaldaw.** He knows that his salary there is not enough when he counts his daily expenditures. [Ibg. *ikalángan*, Ifg. *ngunu*, Ivt. *trabahuq*, Knk. *lagbó*, Kpm. *obra* (Sp.), Tag. *trabaho*]

teggéd₂: **agtegged.** *v.* to defecate green stool (babies); to abide by certain restrictions (said of pregnant women).

tegtég₁: *n.* kind of honeycomb-making small bee.

tegtég₂: **tegtegen.** *v.* to mince, chop; jolt (*tagtag*). **tinegteg.** *n.* mincemeat. **sangkategteg.** *n.* one chop, cut (of meat); slice.

téha: (Sp. *teja*: roof) *n.* roof tile.

tehéras: (Sp. *tijeras*: scissors) *n.* folding cot, wooden display cot on which vendors sell their merchandise; small living quarters under a house.

tehéro: (Sp. *tejero*: tile maker) *n.* tile maker.

tehuélo: (Sp. *tejuelo*: small tile) *n.* small tile.

téka: (Sp. *teca*: teak) *n.* teak.

tékab: (*slang, baliktad* of *bakét*) *n.* elder woman; wife.

tekká₁: *n.* a kind of gecko. **Kasla tekkan a dumket kenkuana.** He sticks to her like a gecko. [Tag. *tukô*]

tekká₂: **maratekka.** *n.* kind of hardwood.

tekkén: *n.* bamboo pole used to propel a boat; tall, thin person. **tinnekkenan.** *n.* polling in competition, pole vault. [Ivt. *tukin*, Ivt. *anayasan*, Kpm. *atkan*, Png. *teken*, Tag. *tikin* (boat pole)]

tékla: (Sp. *tecla*: key) *n.* key (of a piano). **teklado.** *n.* keyboard (of a piano).

tekmá: **tektekma.** *n.* a kind of small spider.

téknika: (Sp. *técnica*: technique) *n.* technique.

tékniko: (Sp. *técnico*: technician) *n.* technician; *a.* technical.

teknólogo: (Sp.) *n.* technologist.

teknolohía: (Sp. *tecnología*) *n.* technology.

teknologísta: (Sp. *tecnologista*) *n.* technologist.

téksas: (Pil., f. Eng. *Texas*) *n.* high-quality fighting cock.

tekték₁: *n.* pin, peg of the warping frame; cry of the house lizard; sound of a clock. **agtektek.** *v.* to tick (clock); cry (lizard).

tekték₂: *n.* anxiety; uneasiness. **matektekan.** *v.* to be burdened; to be anxious, uneasy. **matektekan.** *v.* to be bent over a load, weighed down,

oppressed, burdened; anxious. **Natektekanak nga agtakder.** I'm tired of standing up. **Nariknana ti pannakatektek ni Sayra iti panagtakderna iti pantalan.** He noticed Sayra's uneasiness as she stood at the pier. **Darasem ket matektekan unayen dagiti mangur-uray kenka.** Hurry up because the people waiting for you are anxious (tired of waiting).

tekték₃: **maratektek.** *n.* variety of awned rice with striped kernel.

téla: (Sp. *tela*: fabric) *n.* cloth, fabric. **tela-alambre.** *n.* wire netting; wire screen.

tel-áy: **agtel-ay.** *v.* to walk on the tiptoes; limp (as someone walking on one's tiptoes). (*til-ay*)

telbáwa: (*obs.*) *n.* sound of the foot when thrust in a hole.

teldék: (*obs.*) see *tuldék*.

telebábad: (Pil., f. Tag. *tele* + *babad* 'soak') *n.* telephone conversation of a long duration, staying a long time on the telephone. **agtelebabad.** *v.* to talk on the telephone for a long time.

telebisión: (Sp. *televisión*: television) *n.* television. **agtelebision.** *v.* to watch television.

telegráma: (Sp. *telegrama*: telegram) *n.* telegram. **itelegrama.** *v.* to send a message by telegram.

telegrapía: (Sp. *telegrafía*: telegraphy) *n.* telegraphy.

telegrapísta: (Sp. *telegrafista*: telegraph operator) *n.* telegraph operator.

telégrapo: (Sp. *telégrafo*: telegraph) *n.* telegraph.

telenobéla: (Sp.) *n.* serialized show on television, soap opera.

telepatía: (Sp. *telepatía*: telepathy) *n.* telepathy.

teleponísta: (Sp. *telefonista*: operator) *n.* telephone operator.

telépono: (Sp. *teléfono*: telephone) *n.* telephone, phone. (*pagayaban*) **agtelepono, teleponuan.** *v.* to call of the phone.

teleskópio: (Sp. *telescopio*: telescope) *n.* telescope.

telkák: (*obs.*) see *turkák*: spit; phlegm.

telláay: *n.* short stop. **tumellaay.** *v.* to make a short stop.

telláng: **matlang.** *v.* to be caught in adultery.

telláy: **matellay.** *v.* to prevent (*lapdán, tubngén, pawílan*); be relieved (*ep-ep*). **tellayen.** *v.* to relieve, alleviate.

telléd: **telden.** *v.* to mock, imitate, mimic (*tuladen, silok*). [Tag. *gaya*]

telón: (Sp. *telón*: curtain) *n.* curtain (in a play or movie). **telon ti matá.** *n.* eyelid. (*kurimatmat*)

teltég: **teltegen.** *v.* to thump, knock, strike. **natelteg.** *a.* blunt, dull. (*ngudel, dusber, ngelngel*)

teltél: *n.* upper part of the nape covered with hair. **pateltelan.** *v.* to hit on the nape of the neck. **pagatteltel.** *a.* reaching the neck (hair). **No adda pay mangibaga nga ibbong ket banglesak, pateltelak!** If anyone else says that I am sterile and rotten, I will hit him on the nape! [Bon. *ípok*, Kal. *tongod*, Tag. *batok*]

téma: (Sp. *tema*: theme) *n.* theme.

temmáw: (*obs.*) *n.* sandbanks in a river, ridges in the sand.

temperatúra: (Sp. *temperatura*: temperature) *n.* temperature.

templá: (Sp. *templar*: temper; blend; moderate) *n.* correct mixture; seasoning, marinade. **na-templa.** *a.* marinated; mixed. **templaen.** *v.* to mix; put into correct proportions; marinate. **Templaam 'ta riknam.** Calm down, relax. **Mangtemplaka iti kapem.** Make your coffee (with the appropriate mixture).

templádo: *a.* mixed, marinated, with spices or salt added; temperate.

témplo: (Sp. *templo*: temple) *n.* temple.

temporário: (Sp. *temporario*: temporary) *a.* temporary.

temtém: *n.* bonfire; embers. **agtemtem.** *v.* to make a bonfire. **itemtem.** *v.* to bake something in ashes. **agtemtem.** *v.* to kindle over a slow fire. **tumemtem.** *v.* to burn slowly. [Png. *poól*, Tag. *sigâ*]

ténde: **itende.** *v.* to put in the proper position.

tendénsia: (Sp. *tendencia*: tendency) *n.* tendency.

tendéro: (Sp. *tendero*: shopkeeper) *n.* vendor, storekeeper.

tenedór: (Sp. *tenedor*: fork) *n.* fork. (*túdok*) **tentenedor.** *n. Quamoclit pennata.* **tenedor-de-libro.** *n.* bookkeeper, accountant. **tene-duren.** *v.* to take with a fork. [Kal. *tilachuÿ*]

teneduría: (Sp. *teneduría*: accounting) *n.* bookkeeping, accounting.

teniénte: (Sp. *teniente*: lieutenant; plural is *titeniente*) *n.* lieutenant; highest barrio official. **teniente-koronel.** *n.* lieutenant colonel. **tenien-te-heneral.** *n.* lieutenant general. **teniente-mayor.** *n.* vice-mayor.

tennáay: **agtennaay.** *v.* to abate, subside, calm down (*talná*). **Nabayagen a nagtennaay dagiti allon ngem awan pay ti aggargaraw kadagiti mangngalap.** The waves have subsided for a long time now but there is still no movement among the fishermen.

tennéb: *n.* tempering of metals; skill. **tenneben.** *v.* to temper by high heating and sudden cooling. **tennebán.** *n.* water receptacle used by smiths to temper blades. **matenneb.** *v.* to be tempered; to be experienced; purified. **paka-**

tenneban. *n.* trying experience, testing circumstance. [Tag. *subó*]

tennék: **tumnek.** *v.* to pierce, penetrate. **ipatnek.** *v.* to do with all one's heart (*ipasnek*). [Tag. *tiím*]

tenúg: (*obs.*) *a.* stupid. (*tabbed, nengneng*)

tentákulo: (Sp. *tentáculo*: tentacle) *n.* tentacle.

tentár: (Sp. *tentar*) **tentaren.** *v.* to tempt. **ten-tasion.** *n.* temptation.

tentasión: (Sp. *tentación*: temptation) *n.* temptation.

tengkén: (*reg.*) *var.* of *tekkén*: bamboo pole used to push boats.

tengngá: *n.* center; middle; sitting room (*salas*). **agtengnga.** *v.* to be in the midst, in the middle. **agpatengnga.** *v.* to go to the middle. **ipateng-nga.** *v.* to place in the center. **patengngaan.** *v.* to hit at the center. **iti tengnga.** *prep.* in the middle of, halfway, in the center of. **agtengtengnga.** *v.* to be neutral. **akintengnga a nagan.** *n.* middle name. **katengngaan.** *a.* centermost. **katengngaan ti ili.** *n.* downtown, centermost part of town. **Tumengnganto ti rabii no agawidda.** It will be midnight when they come home. [Bon. *gáwa*, Kal. *gawa*, Knk. *bet-áy, tengá*, Png. *pegléy, laém*, Tag. *gitnâ*]

tengngáag: (see also *tángad*: look up) **tumengngaag.** *v.* to stretch the neck in order to see. **napatengngaag.** *a.* with a stretched-out neck. **Adu dagiti napatengngaag.** Many stretched their necks (to see).

tengngéd: *n.* neck; collar of a garment. **teng-ngedan.** *a.* long-necked. **tengngeden.** *v.* to strangle; hold by the neck (*lengnges*). **para-tengnged.** *n.* short rope that holds the yoke of the water buffalo; neck strap of a bottle. **pa-tengngedan.** *v.* to hit someone in the neck. [Ibg. *vulláw*, Ivt. *lagaw*, Kal. *begang*, Knk. *bagang*, Kpm. *bátal*, Png. *bekléw*, Tag. *leég*]

tengngél: *n.* control. (*turay*) **agtengngel.** *v.* to control; *n.* controller. **tenglen.** *v.* to stop, hold back, detain; restrain (*medmed*); arrest; control; hold steady; manage. **matengngel, matngel.** *v.* to be able to control; to be able to stop, detain. **panenglan.** *n.* collateral. **Diakon matengngel ti riknak.** I can't control my feelings any longer. **Nagasat ketdi ta natengngelna ti panagsuek ti ekonomia.** It is lucky nevertheless that he was able to stop the collapse of the economy. [Tag. *pigil*]

tengpá: see *tungpá*: slap.

tengténg: *n.* (*obs.*) ounce. **tengtengen.** *v.* to stretch; strain; weigh. **manengteng.** *v.* to increase in price. **ipatengteng.** *v.* to raise the price to its utmost; persist; insist; to tighten an animal (cow).

teolohía: (Sp. *teología*: theology) *n.* theology.

teólogo: (Sp. *teólogo*: theologian) *n.* theologian.

teoréma: (Sp. *teorema*) *n.* theorem.

teoría: (Sp. *teoría*: theory) *n.* theory.

tepkál: *var.* of *tapkál*: smear; soil; plaster.

teppáag: *var.* of *deppáag*: collapse; cave in.

teppáal: *a.* pointless, blunt (*ngudel, ngelngel, dusber*). [Tag. *puról*]

teppáng: *n.* cliff, precipice (along the riverbank). (*derráas, tebbáng*) **matpang.** *v.* to tumble down, collapse. **manneppang.** *n.* kind of freshwater *tarókoy* crab. **teppangen.** *v.* to crumble; cause to collapse. [Png. *alosarsar*, Tag. *talampás* (cliff)]

teppáp: *a.* flat (object or nose). **tumpap.** *v.* to be flat. (*kuppit*; *leppap*)

teppáy: *var.* of *tippáy*.

teppél: *n.* restraint, self-control (*terred*); abstinence. **nateppel.** *a.* restrained; patient; pure; chaste; sober. **agteppel.** *v.* to be sober, abstemious; abstain; restrain oneself. **agitpel.** *v.* to restrain anger. **teppelan.** *v.* to abstain from, hold back; control. **makateppel.** *v.* to control oneself, be able to restrain from doing something bad. **Ti tao nga awan teppelna, kas sasakyan nga awan timonna.** A person without self-control is like a boat without a rudder. **Mariknak it sakit ti nakemna ken ti tepteppelanna a pungtot.** I can feel his bad feelings and his restrained anger. [Tag. *ngilin* (abstain)]

teppéng: *n.* kind of *dúyog* for measuring rice about three liters, approximately one-eighth of a *ganta*.

teptép: **teptepen.** *v.* to knock papers against something (such as a desk) to put them in order; to strike home the threads of a woof; to cut disorderly ends of bundled rice; pat (on the head).

terapeúta: (Sp. *terapeuta*: therapeutist) *n.* therapeutist.

terapeútika: (Sp. *terapéutica*: therapeutics) *n.* therapeutics.

terapeútiko: (Sp. *terapéutico*: therapeutic) *a.* therapeutic; curative.

terása: (Sp. *terraza*: terrace) *n.* terrace; balcony; porch. **agpaterasa.** *v.* to go to the terrace.

teréhas: *var.* of *teheras*: folding cot.

teribusón: *var.* of *tirabuson*: corkscrew.

teritório: (Sp. *territorio*: territory) *n.* territory.

terlínga: *n.* kind of woven fabric.

término: (Sp. *término*: term) *n.* term, word.

terminolohía: (Sp. *terminología*: terminology) *n.* terminology.

términos: (Sp. *términos*: terms) *n.* conditions of a contract.

termómetro: (Sp. *termometro*: thermometer) *n.* thermometer.

térna: (Sp. *terno*: suit) *n.* evening gown. **nakaterna.** *a.* wearing an evening gown.

ternário: (Sp.) *n.* three-day sacred devotion.

ternék: *n.* droplet (of urine). (*papay*) **agternek.** *v.* to urinate by droplets (usually after finished urinating). **nakaternek.** *a.* having urinated a few drops (in underwear, etc.); stained by urine drops. [Tag. *tulò*]

ternét: *var.* of *ternek*.

térno: (Sp. *terno*: suit) *n.* suit; formal dress. **agterno.** *v.* to wear a suit.

terorísmo: (Sp. *terrorismo*: terrorism) *n.* terrorism.

terorísta: (Sp. *terrorista* terrorist) *n.* terrorist.

terréd: *n.* self-control; flock of fowls. **agterred.** *v.* to have self-control; use frugally. **terden.** *v.* to economize; use frugally; slacken reins. **Kayatko a materred ti panagpukanda kadagiti kayo ditoy.** I want to control their cutting down trees here. [Tag. *pigil*]

terrém: **tumrem.** *v.* to flow slowly, ooze. (*sayásay*) **Naluyaan ket timrem ti luana.** He was scolded and his tears flowed. [Tag. *tulò*]

terrés: *n.* black widow spider.

terséna: (Sp. *tercena*: tobacco warehouse) *n.* shop, small store. (*tianggi, garreta*)

terséra: (Sp. *tercera*: third) *n.* third gear; third class. **itersera.** *v.* to put in third gear.

terséro: (Sp. *tercero*: third) *n.* third. (*maikatlo*)

térsia: (Sp. *tercia*: third) *n.* one-third. (*apagkatlo*)

térsio: (Sp. *tercio*: third) *n.* third, extra player of an already started game.

tersiopélo: (Sp. *terciopelo*: velvet) *n.* velvet.

tertér: **terteren.** *v.* to prepare twine. **agterter.** *v.* sound produced in the bowels. **naterter.** *a.* overwatered.

tesáuro: (Sp. *tesauro*: thesaurus) *n.* thesaurus.

tésis: (Sp. *tesis*: thesis) *n.* thesis.

tesorería: (Sp. *tesorería*: treasury) *n.* treasury.

tesoréro: (Sp. *tesorero*: treasurer) *n.* treasurer.

tesóro: (Sp. *tesoro*: treasure) *n.* treasure. (*gameng*)

testádo: (Sp. *testado*) *a.* having left a will; disposed of in a will (property).

testadór: (Sp. *testador*: testator) *n.* testator, one who makes a will.

testaménto: (Eng.) *n.* testament; last will. **agtestamento.** *v.* to make a will, will.

testár: (Sp.) **agtestar.** *v.* to make a testament or will.

testígo: (Sp. *testigo*: witness) *n.* witness. (*saksí*) **agtestigo.** *v.* to witness; testify. [Tag. *saksí*]

testimónia: (Sp. *testimonio*: testimony) *n.* testimony. (*paneknek*)

tésto: (Sp. *texto*: text) *n.* text; subject matter; textbook.

tétano: (Sp. *tétano*: tetanus) *n.* tetanus.

tetél: (*reg.* Pang.) **tetelén.** *v.* to blame. (*pabasolan*)

tetília: (Sp. *tetilla*: nipple) *n.* nipple of a bottle.

ti: *art.* singular common noun core *Iloko* article (may abbreviate to '*t* after vowels), plural *dagití*; spoken variant of *ití*. **Nagsangit ti ubing.** The child cried. **Sino ti amam?** Who is your father? **Ania't naganmo?** What is your name? [Png. *say*; *so*, *-y*, Tag. *ang*; *ng*]

tía: (Sp. *tía*: aunt) *n.* aunt. (*ikit*)

tiád: **agtiad.** *v.* to protrude the chest and abdomen. **tumiad.** *v.* to bend backward (*agkiad*, *agliad*). [Tag. *tiyád* = tiptoe]

tiág: **matiag.** *v.* to start up from sleep aghast; to scatter suddenly; to be startled. [Tag. *gulat*]

tialéko: (Sp. *chaleco*: vest) *n.* vest, sleeveless pullover.

tiámba: (Sp. *chamba*: fluke) *n.* fluke; luck, chance. (*gasat*) **tiambaan.** *v.* to do something by chance. **matiambaan.** *v.* to come upon by chance, meet by chance.

tián: *n.* belly, abdomen (*buksit*); womb, uterus (*aanakan*). [Ibg. *san*, Itg. *dagem*, Ivt. *vedek*, Kal. *botak*, *buwang*, Knk. *ludúy*, *tábo*, Kpm. *atyan*, Png. *egés*, Tag. *losók*; *tiyán*]

tianák: (Tagalog also) *n.* evil fiend. (*katataoan*)

tiáni: (Ch.) *n.* pliers, tweezers. (*tsáni*) **pagtiani.** *v.* to use as tweezers. [Ivt. *susupit*, Tag. *tiyani*]

tiánsing: (Eng. chancing) *n.* physical advances in courting. **agtiansing.** *v.* to make physical advances for the first time.

tiáng: (Sp. *tía*: aunt) *n.* term of address for one's aunt. (*ikit*)

tiánggi: *n.* small store (*tersena*, *garreta*)

tiára: (Sp. *tiara*: tiara) *n.* tiara, triple crown.

tiayá: *n.* being promptly at someone's service. **agtiaya.** *v.* to be promptly at someone's service.

tíba: (*obs.*) *a.* wounded in the head. (*kammuol*)

tibáb: *n.* knock. **tibaben.** *v.* to knock (under the chin, on the head, etc.) (*timam*, *dungbab*). **Nangtibab ti manibela iti ulona ken namagsipnget iti panagkitana.** The steering wheel knocked into his head and his vision went black.

tíbaw: (*obs.*) *n.* chimney. (*tambútso*, *simborio*)

tibáya: (*obs.*) *n.* a wood toy that makes noise when being whirled.

tibbáaw: *n.* unequal surface on roads.

tibbakól: **tibtibbakol, natibbakol.** *a.* rough, coarse; bumpy (*rusangér*; *kibbatol*); not even. (*tamból*) **agtibbakol.** *v.* to trip when walking; to falter when speaking. [Tag. *baku-bakô*]

tibbangí: *a.* not exactly in the right position.

tibbáy: **tibbayen.** *v.* to prepare twine for netting. (*terter*)

tibbáyo: *n.* irregular palpitation of the heart; shudder. **agtibbayo.** *v.* to startle; heave (chest) from fright, shudder. **tibbayuen.** *v.* to rock hard in one's arms. **Nagtibbayo idi insardeng ti tsuper ti taksi ket intudona ti balay.** His chest heaved when the taxi driver stopped the car and pointed at the house. [Tag. *kabá*]

tibbéng: *var.* of *tebbéng*: pierce a hole in the earlobe.

tibbí: **tibbien, manbi.** *v.* to spin cotton (on a spinning wheel). **mannibbi.** *n.* cotton spinner. **pagtibbian.** *n.* spinner. [Tag. *ikid*]

tíbek: *n.* the *ípon* fish at two inches.

tibítib: **tibitiben.** *v.* to arrange things as systematically as possible in order to take advantage of a small amount of space (as in packing). [Tag. *ayos*]

tibkér: **natibker.** *a.* firm, stiff, rigid. (*sikkíl*) **natibker ti nakemna.** He has a fighting spirit. **Natibker ken nakired pay laeng ti pammagina.** His body is still firm and strong. **Ipakitayo ti kinatibker ti ayan-ayatyo.** Show how strong your love is for each other. [Kal. *pakchot*, Png. *kígtel*, *awet*, *ligén*, *elét*, Tag. *tigás*]

tibkól: **maitibkol.** *v.* to trip, stumble; make a mistake (*agtinnag*). **pakaitibkolan.** *n.* stumbling block. **Naruam no agkaratibkolka!** You are used to it if you keep stumbling. [Png. *patir*, Tag. *tisod*, *takid*]

tibnág₁: **agtibnag.** *v.* to exercise lightly while convalescing. **tibnágen.** *v.* to exercise after illness or childbirth.

tibnág₂: **matibnág.** *v.* to repent (*babawi*).

tibnág₃: **tibnagen.** *v.* to hurry up someone, rush. (*dagdag*)

tibnág₄: **matibnag.** *v.* to fester (wounds).

tibnók: **tibnókan.** *v.* to add cold water to hot water to make it cooler; dilute. **itibnok.** *v.* to throw into hot water (to make it cooler). **agtibnok.** *v.* to blend, mix (*laok*). [Tag. *bantô*]

tibnól: **tumibnol.** *v.* to shoot up, emerge (plants).

tibngár: *n.* rough, broken ground. [Tag. *bakô*]

tibúk: **katibuk.** *n.* height of a season or time (*kapades*). **idi katibuk ti.** at the height of.

tibúlon: *n.* coconuts tied two by two and strung on a pole in the ground.

tíbong: *n.* vibration, resonance; deep quality of a sound. **natibong.** *a.* vibrating; resonating. [Tag. *tagintín*]

tibúng: *n.* deep mortar. **tibungan.** *v.* to add threads to the warp to widen the tissue.

tibúr: *n.* large jar used for storing wine or vinegar.

tibúyong: (*obs.*) *n.* gutter.

tiddá: *n.* remainder, residue; leftover. **itidda**. *v.* to leave as a leftover. **matda**. *v.* to be left, remain, be left over. **mangda, tiddaen**. *v.* to leave; cause to remain. **tiddaen**. *v.* to leave some for others. **tedtedda**. *n.* leftovers; crumbs. **Inruarna ti tiddana nga innapoy.** He took out the leftover rice. [Kal. *lasaweÿ, bula,* Png. *kerá,* Tag. *tirá*]

tidtíd: *n.* close-woven bamboo used for walls. **tidtiden**. *v.* to flatten halves of bamboo for walls. **Sumirsiripen ti init iti baet iti tinidtid a kawayan a diding ti kalapaw.** The sun peeped in through the woven bamboo wall of the hut. [Tag. *sawalì*]

tiémpo: (Sp. *tiempo*: time; weather) *n.* time; weather; leisure; timing, rhythm. **maniempo**. *v.* to observe the weather. **tiempuan**. *v.* to come upon by chance. **paniempo**. *n.* time; weather. **maitempuan**. *v.* to be able to do at the opportune time. **agkatiempuan**. *v.* to be contemporaneous; to happen at the same time. **itiempo**. *v.* to do something at the right time. **naitiempo**. *a.* in season (vegetables); at the right season. [Tag. *panahón*]

tiénda: (Sp. *tienda*: store) *n.* store, shop. (*terséna*) **makitienda**. *v.* to buy at a store; go shopping. **tiendaan**. *n.* market. [Tag. *tindahan*]

tiésa: *n.* kind of yellow fruit with a brown seed; carristel. [Tag. *tiyesa*]

tig-áb: *n.* burp, belch. **agtig-ab**. *v.* to eructate, burp. (*areb-eb*) **Ariggurruod ti tig-abna.** His burp is like thunder. [Bon. *teg-eb,* Kal. *talikgaog,* Knk. *seng-áb, teg-áb,* Png. *teláb,* Tag. *digháy; tigáb* = weak gasping for breath]

tig-ád: **manig-ad**. *v.* to cut highland bamboos, reeds, etc. (*bulo, pakid*)

tig-án: *n.* prophylactic drunk by women after delivery. **matig-anan**. *v.* to worsen; stunt, be arrested in development; to decay (teeth); have pain in the abdomen for lack of food. **pannigan**. *n.* concoction of wine and roots drunk by women after delivery. **agtig-an**. *v.* to drink a prophylactic regularly.

tigbakay: (*reg.* Mindanao) *n.* cockfight in the trees (held during fiestas).

tigergér: **agtigerger**. *v.* to tremble, shake (*kintayég, payegpég, pigerger*). [Tag. *kiníg, manginíg*]

tiggíd: *var.* of *tiggit*: small yield.

tiggít: see *kiddít*: with a small yield; meager; scarce. [Tag. *kakauntî*]

tígi: **tigitigi**. *n. Tacca palmata,* slender herb with purple and green flowers and round red fruits eaten by swine.

tig-í: *n.* the *kalí* bird; cry of the *kalí* bird.

tigkól: *var.* of *tibkol*.

tigmá: see *patigmaan*: advice.

tigmód: (*obs.*) *a.* with a flat forehead.

tigmók: **pagtigmoken**. *v.* to put together, arrange side by side; close the legs when sitting.

tignáy: *n.* movement; action. (*gunáy, garáw*) **agtignay, tignayen**. *v.* to stir, move; act. **matignay**. *v.* to be moved, touched, stirred, excited. **pannakatignay**. *n.* motivation to work. **paratignay**. *n.* stimulant; anything that motivates someone to act. [Png., Tag. *galáw,* Tag. *kilos;* Knk. *tignáy* = feel pains of childbirth]

tignók: *var.* of *tibnok*.

tignóp: see *tibnók*: mix; blend; temper hot and cold water.

tígpas: **tigpasen**. *v.* to chop off (*sigpat*). [Tag. *tagpás*]

tígre: (Sp. *tigre*: tiger) *n.* tiger. **timmigre**. *a.* like a tiger.

tií: *n.* silverside fish, *Atherina forskali*.

tíin: (*obs.*) **tiinen**. *v.* to fill with liquid.

tíing: **tiingen**. *v.* to decant, rack.

tíit: **titiit**. *n.* kind of small blue bird.

tikáb: *n.* kind of wovenwork basket that is carried on the back (*pasiking*).

tíkag: *n.* drought. (*igaaw*) **natikag**. *a.* arid, barren; parched; dry. [Tag. *tuyót*]

tíkal: (*obs.*) *a.* with bruised feet due to walking; strong on account of much heat.

tikám: *n.* species of small, freshwater mollusk.

tikáp: *n.* chip. **tikapen**. *v.* to chip off; cut superficially. [Tag. *tatal*]

tíkaw: **tikawen**. *v.* to confuse. **natikaw**. *a.* confused. **makatikaw**. *a.* confusing. (*sadaw*) **Maat-atianen ti pasensiak ket matiktikaw ti panunotko no ania ti rumbeng nga aramidek.** My patience has dried up and my thoughts are confused as to what I should do. [Tag. *litó*]

tikbábuy: *n.* kind of bird resembling a crane but smaller and with a white neck.

tikbálang: (Tag. also, *myth.*) *n.* long-legged supernatural being that takes human form and leads people down wrong paths; minotaur-like creature with a human body but the head of a horse and hooves.

tikbáway: (*obs.*) *n.* kind of monotonous rhyming song sung when pounding rice. **agtikbaway**. *v.* to sing a *tikbaway* while pounding rice.

tikék: *n.* kind of biting house lizard. (*alotiit*)

tíker: *n. Pycreus nitens,* small, slender, erect tufted sedge.

tíket: (Eng.) *n.* ticket; lottery ticket. **agtiket.** *v.* to get a ticket. **tiketan.** *v.* to give a ticket to.

tikiáp: tikiapan. *v.* to slash; cut slantwise.

tikítik: matikitik. *v.* to be spent little by little (*inut*). **tikitiken.** *v.* to spend little by little. [Tag. *tipíd*]

tikkáb: *n.* dirt (on skin) (*kabkab*). **natikkab.** *a.* dirty, filthy. **Burangen ti rupana ken natikkab pay.** His face was hideous and it was also dirty.

tikkó: see *sikkó*: turn a corner.

tikkúong: *n.* spending idle time in a group (*takkuong, tukkuong, mattider*) **agtitikkuong.** *v.* to hang around, spend time idly in groups.

tiklád: tiniklad. *n.* slices of tubers (sweet potatoes, taro, etc.) dried in the sun and cooked until mushy.

tikláy: tumiklay. *v.* to tiptoe. (*til-ay*)

tikléb: maitikleb. *v.* to fall prone on one's face.

tiklí: *var.* of *til-i*: infantile beriberi.

tikliáp: *var.* of *tikkiap*: chop off pieces.

tiklís: (Pil.) *n.* large vendor's basket with handles on both sides. **sangatiklis.** *n.* one basketful.

tikló: matiklo. *v.* to know. (*maammuan*)

tiknéng: agtikneng. *v.* to settle (liquids). (*arinsaed*)

tiknól: tiknulen. *v.* to tap; hit, strike. (*tik-ol*)

tikúb: *n.* enclosure. (*lakub*) **tikuben.** *v.* to fence in, enclose (*aladen*). [Tag. *kulong*]

tíkol: (*obs.*) **agtikol.** *v.* to work in company.

tik-ól: *n.* knock. **tik-olan.** *v.* to knock on the head. **agtik-ol.** *v.* to strike against each other. **itik-ol.** *v.* to knock on something. **Pinagtinnikolmi dagiti basomi sakami naggiddan a nangitangad.** We knocked our cups together then looked up at the same time.

tikóp: (*reg.*) *n.* kind of bird or fish net.

tíkor: *n.* bend, curve (of a river). (*pikor*) **agtikor.** *v.* to bend; curve (said of a river)

tikrúbong: tiktikrubong. *n.* variety of gray quaillike songbird.

tikróp: see *lakúb*: surround; encircle; block.

tiktík₁: (Tag. also) *n.* spy, informer. **agtiktik.** *v.* to inform; spy on. **matiktikan.** *v.* to be spied on. **tiktikan.** *v.* to spy on someone.

tiktík₂: tiktiken. *v.* to winnow.

tiktík₃: *n.* a kind of night bird.

tiktík₄: *n.* sound of knocking metal against stone. **agtiktik.** *v.* to make the sound of a cutting ax. **tiktikan.** *v.* to tap, give a light blow to ascertain the hardness of its shell.

tilár: *n.* native loom; textile mill.

til-áy: agtil-ay, tumil-ay. *v.* to tiptoe. (*danapisip; yatyat*) **Nagtil-ay a nagpakosina.** He tiptoed to the kitchen. [Knk. *tíad, lantíad,* Tag. *tiyád*]

tilbák: *n.* peelings. **matilbakan.** *v.* to lose the external coating; to be peeled. [Tag. *tukláp*]

tildé: (Sp. *tilde*: dash, tilde) *n.* period in punctuation.

tildí: *n.* clitoris (*tuldi; taman*). [Kpm. *turíl,* Tag. *maní*]

tíleng: matitileng. *v.* to be deafened by a loud sound. **titilengen.** *v.* to deafen. (*sileng*) **Makatitileng dagiti nagsasaruno a kanalbuong.** The continuous cannon fire was deafening. [Tag. *tulíg*]

til-í: til-ien. *v.* to have spasms, convulsions (said of dying children). [Tag. *suba*]

tiliadóra: (Sp. *trilladora*: thresher) *n.* rice thresher.

tiliár: (Sp. *trillar*: thresh) **agpatiliar.** *v.* to have one's rice threshed.

tilíw: tiliwen. *v.* to catch, capture; arrest. (*sippáw*) **agtiliw.** *v.* to catch. **agtinniliw.** *v.* to catch one another (game); to come to blows in arguing. **kattiliw.** *a.* just caught; just captured; *n.* novice; trainee; inexperienced person, beginner. **matiliw.** *v.* to arrest. **matiliwan.** *a.* to be caught, arrested; caught in the act. **pannakatiliw.** *n.* arrest. **ipatiliw.** *v.* to have an animal caught, a person arrested, etc. **tiliwen ti rikna.** *v.* to attempt to understand the feelings of another. **Nakatiliwam iti billit?** Where did you catch the bird? **Diyo kadin tiltiliwen dagita lawwalawwa dita balayyo ta isu pay dagita nga agkaan iti lamok.** Don't catch the spiders in your house because they are the ones who eat the mosquitoes. [Ibg. *alawen, afuten,* Ivt. *manalaq,* Kpm. *dakap,* Png. *narel, singkat,* Tag. *huli, dakíp*]

tiliwatíw: agtiliwatiw. *v.* to dangle; wobble; wag (tail).

tilkág: *a.* liable to dry up. (*tikag*)

tillág: patillag. *n.* kind of insect resembling the *silam*. **patillagen.** *v.* to cause to jump.

tilláyon: agtillayon. *v.* to swing, sway; dangle. [Tag. *indayog*]

tilmón: *n.* swallow of food or water. (*igup; lamdok; arub-ub*) **sangkatilmon.** *n.* one swallow of water. **tilmonen.** *v.* to swallow. [Bon. *okmon,* Ibg. *tellen,* Ivt. *hamunen,* Kal. *ukmol,* Knk. *amínok, igók,* Kpm. *akmul,* Png. *akmun,* Tag. *lunók*]

tilnóg: tilnogan. *v.* to mix cold and hot water.

tilpák: *var.* of *tiplak*: slap.

tiltíl: matiltil. *v.* to feel weak due to excessive handling; to be overworked; to be stunted in growth; weakened. **makatiltil.** *v.* to be exhausting; (*obs.*) to be slow in obeying orders. **tiltilen.** *v.* to cause stunted growth due to excessive handling. [Tag. *bansót*]

timakudúg: *n.* kind of hairy green caterpillar poisonous to animals. **matimakudugan.** *a.* poisoned by the *timakudug* caterpillar.

timaldéng: (*obs.*) *n.* being slow in obeying orders (*makatiltil, ginad*). [Tag. *kupad*]

timám: **timamen.** *v.* to knock on the chin or mouth. (*tibab*)

timára: (*obs.*) *n.* slow in obeying orders. (*makatiltil, timaldeng*).

timarmár: (*obs.*) see *atimarmár*: recover; smear oneself.

timáw: **timtimaw.** *n.* steep grade on road.

tímba: (Sp. *timbal*: kettledrum) *n.* pale, bucket. (*balde*) **timbaen.** *v.* to use a pail in getting something. **sangatimba.** *n.* one bucketful.

tímbang: (Tag.) *a.* equal in weight; balanced. (*timbeng*) **timbangan.** *n.* scale, balance; weight. **agtimbang.** *v.* to be of the same weight; to be balanced. **timbangen.** *v.* to weigh something. **natimtimbang.** *a.* heavier; worth more; (*fig.*) more dear to one's heart. **katimbang.** *n.* equal, equivalent; match. **Dandani agpatas ti timbangda iti pusok.** They are almost equally dear to me (to my heart). **Sakbay a matimbangko ti bagik, nanabsuokakon iti danum.** Before I could balance myself, I fell into the water with a splash. [Tag. *timbáng*]

timbéng: **agtimbeng.** *v.* to be balanced, equal, proportionate. **timbengan.** *n.* balance, scales; *v.* to balance, do temperately, sparingly; weigh; stop something from moving. **natimbeng.** *a.* calm, prudent; balanced; calm; restrained. **katitimbeng.** *a.* equivalent. **katimbeng.** *a.* equivalent; proportionate. **panimbeng.** *n.* weight, definite mass of something; balancing weight. **kinatimbeng.** *n.* reasonableness; judiciousness.

timbukél: *n.* sphere. **nagtimbukel.** *a.* round, spherical. **pagtimbukel.** *v.* to make round. **timbukelen.** *v.* to make round or spherical. **panimbuklen.** *a.* somewhat round, roundish (eyes, etc.). **kinatimbukel.** *n.* roundness. [Ibg. *dalimummun, alivvukeg*, Itg. *nagbukel*, Ivt. *madéded*, Kpm. *bílog*, Png. *limpak*, Tag. *bilóg* (round)]

timbúrog: *n.* bulge; hump. **agtimburog.** *v.* to bulge; to hump. **natimburog.** *a.* humped; bulging. [Tag. *umbók*]

tímbre: (Sp. *timbre*: seal; stamp; doorbell) *n.* seal of a notary public, stamp; doorbell. **agtimbre.** *v.* to ring a doorbell; affix a seal.

tímek: *n.* voice, sound. (*bóses*) **agtimek.** *v.* to speak out; to sound (bells). **itimkan.** *v.* to listen and recognize a voice; to speak for a group. **pagtimkan.** *v.* to talk to casually. **maitim(e)kan.** *v.* to be able to recognize the voice of

a person. **Nababa ti timekna a nangipakaammo iti gagarana.** His voice was soft in letting (them) know his purpose. **Nabayag a dida nakatimek.** They haven't uttered a word in a long time. **Ti saan a matimtimek, nauyong no makaunget.** Silent people are terrible when angered. [Ibg. *ngáral*, Itg. *tebag*, Ivt. *liak, iyak*, Kal. *ginga*, Kpm. *suála*, Png. *tanól*, Tag. *tinig*]

tímel: *n.* flea. **timelen.** *v.* to be attacked by fleas. **tinimel.** *a.* infested by fleas. **katimelan.** *n.* nest of fleas. [Bon., Knk. *tílang*, Ivt. *dipuan*, Kal. *tilang*, Kpm., *niknik*, Png. *timél*, Tag. *pulgás* (Sp.), *niknik*]

tímid: *n.* chin; (~ **ti rukib**) mouth of a cave. **timidan.** *a.* with a long or pointed chin. (*tammi*) **agpannimid.** *v.* to lean one's chin on the hand. **paratimid.** *n.* chinstrap for a hat. **Nangato ti timidna.** *exp.* denoting arrogance (*lit.* his chin is high). [Bon. *sángi*, Ibg. *símig*, Ivt. *tumid*, Kal. *sangi*, Knk. *padánga, pátang*, Png. *timír*, Kpm., Tag. *babà*]

timítim: **timitiman.** *v.* to remove (point, hair, etc.); blunt.

timmangol: (*lit.*) *n.* place strewn with unburied corpses. (*angol*)

timmáwa: *n.* common people; peasant; middle class. **timmawaen.** (*obs.*) *v.* to emancipate, liberate. [Tag. *tubús*]

timmíng: **matimming, matming.** *v.* to decay, rot through moisture (*tubeg; tumuy*). [Tag. *bulók*]

timmúl: see *kimmól*: coccyx. [Tag. *tabugí = coccyx*]

timmúno: **nagtimmuno.** *a.* round, spherical (*timbukel*). [Tag. *bilóg*]

timmútil: *n.* Adam's apple.

timuáy: (*obs.*) *n.* twisting ropes, etc. (*tiritir*)

tímud: **timuden.** *v.* to listen to, hear, pay attention to a faint sound. **matimud.** *v.* to hear. (*alingag, imdeg; dengngeg*) **Numan pay addaak iti sabali a lamisaan, matimudko pay laeng ti saritaanda.** Although I am at the next table, I can still hear what they are talking about. [Tag. *pakinggán*]

tim-óg: **agtim-og.** *v.* to collide against each other. (*bangdol; dalapus; salapon; kintol; dungpar; dunget; dugpa; dungpap*) **matim-og.** *v.* to knock, bump (the head). **maitim-og.** *v.* to accidentally bump the head. **pagtim-ogen.** *v.* to knock together; (*fig.*) match two people forcefully. **Pagtim-ogek da Tata Sinting ken Nana Pipay.** I am going to knock Father Sinting and Nana Pipay together. [Tag. *untóg*]

timók: **tinimok.** *n.* powder, dust. (*polbos; tapok*)

timón: (Sp. *timón*: rudder) *n.* helm, rudder; joystick. **timonan.** *v.* to guide by a rudder. **timonero.** *n.* helmsman. [Ivt. *agusan*, Tag. *ugit*]

tim-óng: (*obs.*) *n.* knocking someone's head with a stone. (*tim-og*)

timpág: see *pampág*: beat; strike repeatedly. [Tag. *pampág*]

timpalós: **timpalosen.** *v.* to slap someone on the occiput. (*sipat*)

timpáyug: **timpayugen.** *v.* to swing, dangle, rock with force (*tillayon, yugyog*). [Tag. *ugà*]

timpáyok: **agtimpayok.** *v.* to fly around in the wind. (*atipukpok*)

timplá: *var.* of *templa*: mix, marinate.

timpurók: *n.* cluster, group. **agtitimpurok.** *v.* to cluster in groups.

timpúyog: *n.* team; cooperation; club, association; harmony. **agtitimpuyog.** *v.* to agree; unite. **panagtimpuyog.** *n.* agreement; unity; act of teaming up. **Ti timpuyog ti agkakaddua, isu ti mangted iti pigsa.** Unity (teaming up) gives strength. [Png. *muyong, tugyop*, Tag. *pangkát*]

tímre: *var.* of *timbre*.

tímtim: **timitiman.** *v.* to sip; taste (*simsim*); remove the end of. **Ad-adda nga immuyong idi matimtimanna ti apgad ti dara ti bibigna.** He most likely got mad when he tasted the saltiness of the blood of his lips. [Tag. *tikmán*]

tína: *n.* dye; indigo. **tinaen.** *v.* to dye black. **agtina.** *v.* to dye the hair. **matina iti dara.** *v.* to be bloodstained. [Tag. *tinà*]

tinabbí: *n.* sewing thread (*panáit*).

tinagi-: *pref.* perfective form of *tagi- -en*.

tináha: (Sp. *tinaja*: large earthen jar) *n.* large water jug (used to store *basi*).

tinahón: (Sp. *tinajón*: large jar) *n.* large jar; small tank.

tinalló: (f. *talló*) *a.* threefold.

tinani: **tintinani.** *n. Ixora philippinensis* plant.

tinápa: (f. *tápa*) *n.* salted, smoked fish.

tinápay: *n.* bread. **agtinapay.** *v.* to have bread; to make bread. [Kal. *tilapay*, Png., Tag. *tinapay*]

tinása: (Sp. *tenaza*: pincer) *n.* tongs, pincers. (*sipit, tsani*)

tindék: **agtindek.** *v.* to be straight overhead (twelve o'clock sun). **natindek.** *a.* straight up, straight overhead.

tindéro: (Sp.) *n.* shopkeeper.

tin-ék: *n.* intermittent respiration of a dying person. **agtin-ek.** *v.* to gasp (said of a dying person); to simmer down; weigh down. [Tag. *hingalô*]

tíneng: **natineng.** *a.* whirling, spinning. (*tayyek*)

tínep: **itinep.** *v.* to immerse, plunge, submerge. (*ipabátok, lungbos*) **tinpen.** *v.* to plunge; love; enrich. [Tag. *lubóg*]

tiniéblas: (Sp. *tiniebla*: darkness) *n.* matins sung on the last three days of the Holy Week service, Tenebrae.

tiniklíng: (Pil.) *n.* national folk dance of the Philippines performed with two bamboo poles. **agtinikling.** *v.* to dance the *tinikling*.

tinnáay: **agtinnaay.** *v.* to subside.

tinnág: *n.* mail; plumb line; down payment, advance payment; installment. **agtinnag.** *v.* to fall down; drop; result in, end up with. **agpatinnag.** *v.* (*fig.*) to have an abortion. **matinnag, matnag.** *v.* to fall, drop; sin; (*reg.*) fail to pass a grade, flunk. **nakatnagán.** *a.* fallen down. **itinnag.** *v.* to drop something; deposit; drip; release; mail a letter. **tinnagan.** *v.* to drop something into; pay by installments; alloy gold. **tinninnagan iti panio.** *n.* chasing game played by girls using a handkerchief. **tinnagen.** *v.* to win a girl's love; cause to fall. **katkatnag.** *a.* just fallen. **pagtinnagan.** *n.* result, outcome. **pagtinnagen.** *v.* to cause something to fall. **tinninnagan iti panio.** *n.* girls' game of circle tag played with a handkerchief. **Ti Pannakatinnag ti Roma.** The Fall of Rome. **Intinnagnaka ti langit.** *exp.* You are heaven-sent (*lit.* heaven dropped you). **matnag ti rikna.** *exp.* to fall in love. **Agtinnagka iti dakulapko.** I have you in the palm of my hands. **Adda met dagiti mayat a makiasawa ngem nagtinnagda a nabaketan a balasang.** There are those that want to get married but end up as old maids. **Madmadlawna a matmatnagen ti riknana iti balasang.** He is noticing that he is falling in love with the young lady. [Ibg. *fennaq*, Ivt. *magagtus*, Kpm. *nábu, báldung*, Png. *potpót, pelág*, Tag. *hulog*]

tinukél: (f. *tukel*) *n.* bit; particle. (*tippíng*)

tinóla: *n.* dish made of chicken cooked with unripe papayas.

tínong: *n.* agreement, concord; smartness, intelligence. **matinong.** *v.* to be in agreement; to decide, resolve. **tinongen.** *v.* to agree upon; resolve; decide; determine. **mangtinong iti kasar.** *n.* wedding planner; go-between in a wedding. **Nasken a matinongta itan no kaano ti panagkasarta.** We need to decide now when our wedding will be.

tínta: (Sp. *tinta*: ink) *n.* ink. **matintaan.** *v.* to be smeared or stained with ink. **tintatinta.** *n. Eclipta alba.* (*tultulisan*)

tintéro: (Sp. *tintero*: inkstand) **pagtinteruan.** *n.* inkstand, inkwell.

tintinnanék: *n.* small bush with white flowers, similar to the *santan*.

tintúra: (Sp. *tintura*: tincture) *n.* tincture; solution of medicine.

tingá: **agtinga.** *v.* to separate again (something mended). **tingaen.** *v.* to shield (from blows); block. [Tag. *sirâ*]

tingál: *n.* prop, wedge. (*súray, túkol, túkal, síngit*) **itingal.** *v.* to use as a prop. **tingalan.** *v.* to prop or support something. **maitingal.** *v.* to be wedged.

tinggá: *n.* half-tribute; half of money. **tinggaen.** *v.* to ward off; prevent. (*sarapa*)

tinggál: *n.* solder to join gold; ambler whose hind legs change gait.

tinggár: **tinggaren.** *v.* to prevent; block; obstruct; stop from doing.

tinggáw: **natinggaw.** *a.* sonorous; clear (voice or eyes) (*aweng*). **tuminggaw.** *v.* to become loud; resonant. **Nabayagen a naibabana ti auditibo ti telepono ngem kasla nakatingtinggaw pay la ti timek ni Carlos a mangmangngegna.** She put down the receiver of the telephone a while ago but it seems like she was still hearing the clear voice of Carlos. **Natinggaw ti katkatawada iti nanumo a pagtaenganda.** Their laughter was loud in their humble abode. [Tag. *tagintíng*]

tinggayá: *n.* readiness. (*nakasagsagána*) **agtinggaya.** *v.* to be ready. **itinggaya.** *v.* to make ready. **sititinggaya.** *a.* always ready.

tinggí: **patinggí.** kind of insect resembling the *silam.*

Tinggián: *n.* ethnic group from Abra Province inhabiting the western side of the Central Cordillera mountains.

tingí: **agtingi.** *v.* to retail. (*tayútay*) **patingi.** *v.* to retail.

ting-í: **agting-iting-i.** *v.* to slightly lean from side to side.

tingíg: *a.* leaning sideways (head). **agtingig.** *v.* to lean sideways. **itingig.** *v.* to lean. **napatingig.** *a.* lopsided. **patingigen.** *v.* to place in an askew position. **Agsasagawisiw latta ket agtingigtingig.** He just whistles and leans from side to side. [Tag. *tagilíd*]

tingíting: **tingitingen.** *v.* to weigh; examine carefully; test; think something over. **agtingiting.** *v.* to be straight overhead (sun). **Adda kenka iti ti kabaelan a mangtingiting iti umno ken saan.** It's up to you now to be able to weigh the right from wrong.

tingkáb: **tingkaben.** *v.* to pry open (with a crowbar). [Tag. *tukláp*]

tingkál: see *tókal*: prop for a window. (*súray, túkal*)

tinglíw: **agtingliw.** *v.* to sleep intermittently. (*alimbasag*)

tingngayá: see *tanggayá*: offer; hold out.

tingngiáw: (*obs.*) *n.* fearful walking. (*talangkiaw*) **tingtingngiawen.** *v.* to expect. (*daánan*)

tingpá: *var.* of *tungpa*: slap, spank.

tingrá: **tumingra.** *v.* to tan (in the sun); regain color after an illness; prick up the ears or bangs (of animals); become erect after transplanting (seedlings). **natingra.** *a.* erect; bright, with strong colors. **Iti dandanin agmatuon nga init, kasla timmingra ti kayumanggi a kudil ti balasang.** In the almost noon sun, the brown skin of the lady seemed bright.

tingtíng: *n.* ringing of bells. **agtingting.** *v.* to make the sound of a small bell. **tingtingen.** *v.* to try, test, use for the first time; test the quality of. [Tag. *kulilíng*]

tío: (Sp. *tío*: uncle) *n.* uncle. (*uliteg*)

tiobíbo: (Sp. *tiovivo*: Ferris wheel) *n.* Ferris wheel. (*ruedo*)

tión: (*obs.*) *n.* cluster of coconuts. (*raay*)

tióng: *n.* vocative term of address for an uncle or an intimate male one generation above the speaker. (*uliteg*)

tipák: *n.* sound of a heavy fall. **tumpaak.** *v.* to fall down with a plump. **agkanatpaak.** *v.* to resound (waterfall, falling object). **matpaak.** *v.* to fall down with a plump. **panatpaaken.** *v.* to throw down something, causing a bang.

tipál: (*obs.*) *n.* urine. **agtipal.** *v.* to urinate (*umisbo*).

tipáp: **matipap.** *v.* to be full (containers). **tipapen.** *v.* to fill up; slap the forehead. [Tag. *tampál*]

típat: **agtipat.** *v.* to applaud, clap the hands (*sipat*). [Tag. *palakpák*]

tipáw: **tipawen.** *v.* to ward off with the hand, fend off a blow; slap someone's hand in order to make him drop something. **Tinipawna ti kape nga ig-iggaman ni Sita.** He knocked down the coffee in Sita's grasp (by slapping).

típay: *n.* a bar of iron. (*sagipéd*) **tinipay.** *n.* small piece of soap, sugar, wax, etc. **tipayen.** *v.* to break into smaller pieces of any shape. [Tag. *tipák*]

tipéd: *n.* obstruction. (*lapped*) **agtipiled.** *v.* to economize, be frugal. (*terréd, tipít, ínut*) **tipden.** *v.* to block; obstruct; conserve, use economically; impede. **makatiped.** *n.* impediment; obstruction. **mannakatiped.** *a.* always in the way. **paniped.** *n.* bar, something used to obstruct the way. **Tinipedko ti rumkuas a pungtotko.** I controlled my emerging anger. [Png. *makasbel*, Tag. *sagabal, hadláng*, Tag. *tipíd* = thrift]

tipít: (Tag. *tipíd*) **natipit.** *a.* economical, not wasteful. (*terréd, ínut*)

tipkél: *n.* lump of something, mass (of people). **agtitipkel.** *v.* to lump together. **pagtitipkelen, tipkelen.** *v.* to make into a lump. [Tag. *kimpál*]

tipkíl: **agtitipkíl.** *v.* to stick together.

tiplák: tiplaken. *v.* to slap with the open hand.

típle: (Sp. *tiple*: treble) *n.* treble or soprano voice.

típo: (Sp. *tipo*: type; style) *n.* type; style; class; kind. (*kita, klase*) **agkatipo.** *v.* to belong to the same class, of the same kind. **Ania ti tipom a lalaki?** What is your type of man?

tipóg: *var.* of *ripúg.* **agtippuog, tumpuog, matpuog.** *v.* to collapse, crumble down. **tippuogen.** *v.* to tumble down, cause to collapse. **agkanatpuog.** *v.* to tumble down loudly; crush down; cave in.

tipók: natipok. *a.* inverted (said of skirts, etc.). (*ballusong*) **matipok.** (*obs.*) *v.* to fall on one's knees.

típon: *n.* mixture; assembly, gathering. **tumipon.** *v.* to join; live with. **agtipon.** *v.* to assemble, unite, gather, convene, meet. **tipunen.** *v.* to gather; collect; assemble. **itipon.** *v.* to add, join, unite with. **pagtitiponan.** *n.* gathering of people; meeting place. **Nagtipon ti luksaw ken gura iti kaungganna.** The anger and frustration mixed inside him. [Tag. *tipon*]

típor: *n.* kind of large gray crane. [Png. *sípol*]

típus: (Sp.) *n.* typhoid fever. **agtipus.** *v.* to suffer from typhoid fever.

tippádong: *var.* of *sippadong*: stumble, trip.

tippáw: *var.* of *tipáw*: fend off, ward off.

tippáy: tumippay, tippayen. *v.* to knock out of someone's hand. **natippay.** *a.* frustrated, thwarted, foiled.

tippáyog: see *timpáyog*: swing; dangle; rock.

tippíng: *n.* chip; notch. **tumipping, tippingan.** *v.* to notch, indent, chip; break the neck of a bottle. **matipping.** *v.* to be chipped. **natping.** *n.* chip, broken off fragment. [Tag. *pingas, bubog*]

tippúog: (f. *tipog*) **agtippuog.** *v.* to knock over; crush. **mangtippuog.** *v.* to overthrow. **matippuog.** *v.* to accidentally knock over; be able to overthrow; happen to overcome. **Agpangpanggepda a mangtippuog iti turay.** They are planning to overthrow the government.

tipróng: *a.* walking with the knees meeting, knock-kneed; bowlegged. (*akkang, pakaw*)

tíra₁: (Sp. *tira*: shoot) *itira.* *v.* to use as an instrument in a crime. **tira latta.** *exp.* go ahead. (*sige, aria*). **tumira.** *v.* to shoot.

tíra₂: (Sp. *tira*: pull) **tiratira.** *n.* taffy; molasses candy.

tirabusón: (Sp. *tirabuzón*: corkscrew) *n.* drill, auger; corkscrew.

tírad: *n.* sharp point, sharp end. (*tadém*) **natirad.** *a.* sharp, pointed. **patiraden.** *v.* to sharpen a point. **tiraden.** *v.* to sharpen. **tiradan.** *v.* to furnish with a point. [Png. *tarém*, Tag. *talím, talas*]

tiráda: *n.* purpose (*panggep, gandat*); object ball in billiards; first-thrown card; issue, edition.

tiradór: (Sp. *tirador*: shooter) *n.* sharpshooter; slingshot.

tiranía: (Sp. *tiranía*: tyranny) *n.* tyranny.

tirániko: (Sp. *tiránico*: tyrannical) *a.* tyrannical.

tiráno: (Sp. *tirano*: tyrant) *n.* tyrant. **Abaho los tiranos!** Down with the tyrants!

tiránte: (Sp. *tirante*: suspenders) *n.* suspenders; bra strap; rein.

tirátir: tiratiren. *v.* to arrange, put in order (*urnosen*). [Tag. *isaayos*]

tiráyok: tumirayok. *v.* to gush out, squirt. (*pussuák*) **ipatirayok.** *v.* to urinate high and far (usually in competition). **tinnirayok.** *n.* young boy's game whose object is to see who can urinate the farthest. [Tag. *pulandít*]

tiray-ók: patiray-okan. *v.* to flatter; exaggerate. **papatiray-okan.** *a.* easily flattered. **panangpatiray-ok.** *n.* flattery; exaggeration.

tírem: *n.* oyster. **katireman.** *n.* oyster pond; place where oysters abound. **Iti kalgaw, pasaray umayda agbatok iti tirem.** In the summer, they often come to dive for oysters. [Png., Tag. *talabá*]

tírgas: (Eng.) *n.* tear gas. **tinirgas.** *a.* sprayed with tear gas.

tíri: agtiri. *v.* to lie, fib. (*aglastog, agulbod*) **natiri.** *a.* liar. [Tag. *sinungaling*]

tirí: tiniri. *n.* speckled cotton yarn.

tirígo: tirtirigo. *Setaria geniculata* millet.

tiríntas: (Sp. *trenzas*: braid) *n.* curly braid; pigtail; plaid. **agtirintas.** *v.* to plait; braid. **agpatirintas.** *v.* to have one's hair braided. **matirintas.** *v.* to be overwhelmed with too much work; to be braided (*kirikir*).

tirís: (Sp. *triza*: shred, *hacer trizas*: smash, crush; Tagalog also) *n.* crushing of lice between thumbnails. **tiristirisen.** *v.* to crush until pulped.

tirís: tirtiris. *n.* puppet; dummy; *Bulbostylis barbata.* **tirtirisen.** *v.* to make a fool of. [Tag. *tautauhan*]

tirítir₁: *a.* twisted. **agtiritir.** *v.* to become twisted; writhe; recoil; twist oneself. **tiritiren.** *v.* to wring, twist violently. **Nagtiritir iti ellekna.** He writhed from his laughter. **Pinadasna a ginutad dagiti natiritir a takiagna.** He tried to pull his twisted hands. [Tag. *pilipit*]

tirítir₂: *n.* variety of awned rice with a light-colored hull and white kernel.

tirittittít: *n.* singsong melody without words. **agtirittittit.** *v.* to sing without words, just with *tirittittit.*

tirmíd: *n.* sip, draught. **sangkatirmid.** *n.* one sip, one draught. **tumirmid.** *v.* to sip. **Tumirtirmid**

iti serbesa iti sirok ti dagidagi. He is sipping on beer under the hammock.

tirmúy: tirmuyan. *v.* to remove the point of; blunt the point. (*ngudel*; *ngelngel*; *dusber*)

tirnék: *var.* of *ternek*: droplet of urine.

tíro: (Sp. *tiro*: shoot) **itiro.** *v.* to shoot (with a gun) (*paltogan*); deliver a blow to, hit. **natiruan.** *a.* shot; struck by a bullet. **tiruan.** *v.* to shoot. **tiruen.** *v.* to hit; punch.

tirúbong: titirubong. *n.* kind of small brown bird with long tail. (*tiktikrubong*)

tírong: (Sp. *tiro*: theft) *n.* pirate. **agtirong.** *v.* to pillage as pirates do. **katirongan.** *n.* place with a lot of pirates, pirate infested place.

tiróng: *n.* kind of marine fish resembling the *siríw*, from the *Exocoetidae* family.

Tirúray: *n.* ethnic group from the coastal mountains of Maguindanao, Mindanao.

tirotéo: (Sp. exchange of gunfire) *n.* trumpeting.

tirtirís: *n.* doll; elf. **tirtirisen.** *v.* to make someone lose his mind. **Tirtirisendaka.** They will take away your mind (*lit.* make you into a doll).

tísa₁: (Sp. *tiza*: chalk) *n.* chalk.

tísa₂: (Sp. *teja*: tile) *n.* roof tile. **agpatisa.** *v.* to have one's roof tiled. **agtisa.** *v.* to tile (a roof).

tisáy: (Pil., *coll.*) *n.* woman with a light complexion. (*pudaw*)

tísert: (Eng.) *n.* T-shirt. (*kamiseta*)

tísiko: (Sp. *tísico*) *a.* consumptive.

tísis: (Sp. *tisis*: consumption) *n.* tuberculosis, consumption. (*sarut*)

tisóy: (Pil., *coll.*) *n.* man with a light complexion.

tistís: (Tag.) *n.* surgical operation. **agtistis.** *v.* to saw (*ragadi*); operate on.

títa: (Tagalog also) *n.* aunt, auntie. (*ikit*, *tia*)

títit: tititan. *v.* to call a puppy.

títser: (Eng.) *n.* teacher. (*maestro*, *maestra*)

título: (Sp. *título*: title) *n.* title; degree; rank; deed (of land) (*nagan*; *paulo*) **titulado, de-titulo.** *a.* having a title; having an academic degree.

tíwan: *n.* oar with a long handle. (*gaud*) **tiwan-tiwan.** *n.* kind of large swordfish. **kasla tiwan-tiwan.** *a.* tall and lean (person); long-legged.

tiwangwáng: (Tag.) **nakatiwangwang.** *a.* wide open; exposed.

tiwarík: nakatiwarik. *a.* listless, drooping from lack of energy.

tiwatíw: agtiwatiw. *v.* to dangle, hang (*tillayon*, *tiliwatiw*). [Tag. *lawít*]

tiwawég: *var.* of *kiwaweg*.

tíwed: agtiwed. *v.* to not bother paying a debt; to be hesitant to pay a debt. **natiwed.** *a.* not paying a debt. [Tag. *manunubà*]

tiwéd: agtiwedtiwed. *v.* to shake, stagger, sway (*tigergér*; *gudday*; *dawiris*; *ibar*; *bariring*). [Tag. *suray*, *hapay*, *giray*]

tíweng: agtiweng. *v.* to move from one side of the bed to another when sleeping; to be unsteady (spinning tops). **natiweng.** *a.* restless (in one's sleep), always moving; unsteady. **tini-tiweng nga aramid.** haphazard work. **Tapno mayaw-awanna ti panagtiweng ti panunotna, nagwatwat.** In order to rid himself of his restless thoughts, he exercised. [Tag. *likó*]

tiwerwér: patiwerweren. *v.* to drive a car at full speed.

tiwwatíw: *var.* of *tiwatiw*: dangle, hang. (*tillayon*)

-tlo: *var.* of *talló*: three after certain prefixes: **maikatlo.** third.

-to: (*-nto* after vowels) enclitic indicating future action of verbs. **Mapanakto.** I will go. **Mapankanto.** You will go. **Basaekto.** I will read it. **Basaennanto.** He/she will read it. [Bon. *esa*, Tag. CV reduplication]

tuád: *n.* large net used to catch *ípon* fish. **sangkatuadan.** *n.* the owners of the *tuad*.

tuáli: agtuali. *v.* to be loose, shaky (chairs, etc.). (*wali*)

tuália: (Sp. *toalla*: towel) *n.* towel. (*pagpunasan*) **agtualia.** *v.* to use a towel. [Kal. *tuweÿya*]

tualyíta: (Sp. *toallita*: small towel) *n.* small towel; face towel.

tuáng: matuang. *v.* to fall down, collapse. **tuangen.** *v.* to cause to fall down, knock over. **No sadino ti irig ti kayo, isu ti pakatuangannanto.** Where the tree is bent, so it will fall. [Tag. *tumbá*]

tuáp: (*obs.*) **agtuap.** *v.* to compete. (*agsasalísal*)

tuáto: *var.* of *tuwato*: dragonfly.

túba: *n.* fish poison, *Croton sp.* plant. **tubaen.** *v.* to poison fish in the water. [Tag. *lason*]

tubá: *n.* juice of the *buri* palm, drink made from this juice. **agtuba.** *v.* to get extract juice from the buri palm. [Tag. *tubâ*]

tubabék: *a.* flat headed; blunt pointed. **natubabek.** *a.* stocky, short and stout. [Png. *matampok*, Tag. *tandakíl*, *sapád*, *pudpód*]

túbag: *n.* middle rafter of a hip roof, rafter of the *sóba*. **tubagen.** *v.* to support; prop (*suráyen*); push a boat to avoid getting stranded (*sarapaen*). [Tag. *suhay*]

tubág: tubagen. *v.* to cause to crumble. [Tag. *gibâ*]

túbang: *n.* leaves of the *buri* palm used for walls. **matubang.** *v.* to rot from excessive soaking. (*tubeg*)

túbar: agtubar. *v.* to argue, dispute. (*apa*; *tubar*; *susit*; *baranget*; *subáng*, *riri*)

túbay: tinubay. *a.* rounded and erect; beautifully proportioned; well-shaped. **matubay.** *v.* to be shaped; to be molded. **kasla manubay.** *a.*

staring. **tubayen.** *v.* to mold; shape; bring up a child properly; form. [Tag. *likhâ*]

tubbáng: itubbang. *v.* to push; shove. (*durón, tebbang*)

tubbáw: *n.* large gaping hole. (*abut*) **natubbawan.** *a.* perforated; having lost its flavor (wine kept standing, etc.). **tubbawan.** *v.* to make a large hole. [Tag. *hukáy*]

tubbó: *n.* kind of small black and white bird; harvesting of sugarcane. **agtubbo.** *v.* to harvest sugarcane. **tubbuen.** *v.* to pull out (sugarcane). **Impakitana ti alibtakna nga agtubbo.** He showed how good he is at harvesting sugarcane.

tubbuák: tumbuak. *v.* to issue out; burst forth; break out (fire); appear; start, originate. [Tag. *sikláb*]

tubbóg: *n.* juice; sap. **agtubbog, tumbog.** *v.* to emit liquid; issue forth; water (mouth). **tubbog ti suso.** *n.* mother's milk. **natubbog.** *a.* juicy. **agmaratubbog.** *v.* to become watery; to become juicy. **patubbogen.** *v.* to allow to fester (wounds). **Marmaratubbog dagiti matana.** His eyes are watery. **Timbog ti darana.** His blood ran (issued forth). [Ibg. *anníq*, Ivt. *asi*, Png. *taból*, Tag. *katás*]

túbeg: matubeg. *v.* to decay; rot due to humidity (*lungsot; dersay; rupso; tumuy; dugmuy; duted; timming*). [Tag. *bulók*]

tubél: *n.* hemorrhoids. (*almoranas*) **natubel.** *a.* slow; behind; backward. **kaitublan.** *v.* to be harvested afterwards.

túbeng: *n.* first leaves of the tobacco plant. **tinubeng.** *n.* house with a gable roof (*bayangbayang*). [Tag. *sagabal*]

tubéng: *n.* obstacle, obstruction. (*lappéd; tiped*) **matubeng.** *v.* to be blocked; hindered, obstructed. **tubengen.** *v.* to block, hinder, obstruct; stop. [Png. *makasbel*, Tag. *hadláng*]

tubería: (Sp. *tubería*: plumbing) *n.* plumbing.

tubéro: (Sp. *tubero*: plumber) *n.* plumber.

túbing: tubingtubing. *n.* kind of large marine mollusk with a blackish shell.

tubkáng: matubkangan. *v.* to be disjointed. (*bekkang*)

tubkél: *var.* of *tugkél.*

tublák: itublak. *v.* to kick in order to knock down; cause to fall prone. **maitublak.** *v.* to tumble down, fall down; to be lead into temptation; fall prone.

tubngár: tubngaren. *v.* to contradict; rectify; block; prevent. **Saanko a tubngaren no dayta ti kayatmo.** I won't go against it if that is what you want. [Tag. *salangsáng, salungát; sansalà*]

túbo: *n.* shoot, sprout, bud; profit; gain; interest; lineage; origin; native, raised in a certain area.

tumubo. *v.* to germinate, sprout. **tubuen.** *v.* to gain; profit. **agtutubo.** *n.* youth, young person; rising generation. **agtubo.** *v.* to grow; germinate; gain; profit. **patubo.** *n.* seedlings; sprouts. **agpatubo.** *v.* to practice usury; to put a high interest in; cause to grow. **agkatubo.** *v.* to be of the same age, to be contemporaneous. **katutubo.** *n.* nature, character; native. **katubuan.** *n.* living together; living in concubinage. **kinaagtutubo.** *n.* youth; adolescence. **tinubuan.** *n.* native land; place where one grew up. **Tubo ti Isabela.** He grew up in Isabela. **Saanmo a sayangen ti kinagtutubom.** Do not waste your youth. **Napudot idiay daga a tinubuanna.** It is hot in the land where he grew up. [Ibg. *tuvu*, Ifg. *tummol*, Ivt. *tuvuq*, Kpm. *dágul*, Png. *tubó*, Tag. *tubò* (grow)]

túbo: (Sp. *tubo*: tube) *n.* tube; pipe; pipeline. (*tubong*)

tub-ók: *n.* blacksmith's punch used to make holes in iron. **tub-oken.** *v.* to pierce, perforate; nail something to. **tutub-okan.** *n.* nasal septum of animals.

túbong₁: *n.* tube of bamboo; wind instrument. **itubong.** *v.* to put in a tube. **tubongtubong.** *n.* base of the aorta. **matubongan.** *v.* to become filled with water (the ear). **maitubong.** *v.* to be heard indistinctly; to be contained in a tube; to be put in a tube. **Pinennekna nga inimtuod no agpayso ti naitubong itay iti lapayagna.** He asked inquisitively if what he just happened to hear was true. [Ibg. *angang*, Ifg. *alúwog*, Ivt. *tavuhen*, Png. *tubung*, Kpm., Tag. *bumbóng* (bamboo tube or container)]

túbong₂: tinubong. *n.* kind of rice cake made of ground *diket* rice, sugar, and coconut milk; (*slang*) diploma.

tubútub: tubutuben. *v.* to open from beneath; break from the bottom. **matubutub.** *v.* to open up at the bottom.

túboy: tubuyan. *v.* to agree, allow, consent to; approve. **patubuyan.** *v.* to give leeway; give consideration to. [Tag. *hayà*]

tubtób: tubtuben. *v.* to knock, pound, hammer, beat; demolish buildings. **agtubtob.** *v.* to break down a wall. (*reg.*) *var.* of *tubutob*: open from bottom. [Tag. *gibâ*]

túdan: (*obs.*) *n.* maturity (*luom*). [Tag. *hinog*]

tódas: (Sp. *todas*: all) *a.* winning all; state of having nothing left; liquidated, all killed; *n.* end, finish; all. **agtodas.** *v.* to win all (a match, hand of cards). **tumodtodas.** *v.* to be winning at a particular point in the game; to be ahead in the score. **todasen.** *v.* to murder a person, finish someone off; wipe out completely; consume everything.

tuddóng: tuddongen. *v.* to place something on a support to prevent it from getting wet; brace. [Tag. *katang*]

tudík: *var.* of *turík*: freckled; spotted. [Tag. *batik*]

túding: ituding. *v.* to assign; designate, determine; appoint; specify; set a price. (*dutok*) **maituding.** *v.* to be designated, appointed. **naituding.** *a.* designated, appointed, specified. **Adun dagiti naituding nga agkasar ngem saanda a matuloy.** There are many people designated to marry but they do not all follow through with it. [Png. *getár*, Tag. *takdâ*]

tudió: natudio. *a.* submissive, obedient, docile, dutiful. (*tungpal*; *annúgot*) **agtudio.** *v.* to be obedient, docile, meek, submissive. [Tag. *sunód*]

tudlép: *var.* of *tuglep*: drowsiness.

tódo: (Sp. *todo*: all) *n.* all. **todo-todo.** everything, all.

túdo: *n.* rain. **agtudo, tumudo.** *v.* to rain. **matuduan.** *v.* to be caught in the rain. **ipatudo.** *v.* to expose to the rain. **matutudo.** *a.* rainy; *n.* rainy season. **agkatuduan.** *v.* to play in the rain. **agkalintuduan.** *v.* to stay in the rain. **panagtutudo, matutudo.** *n.* rainy season. **pagtuduen.** *v.* to shower upon (with bullets). **tudo ti kurad.** rain and sun at the same time. **Agpukaw a kas asuk ket dumteng a kas ti tudo.** It disappears like smoke and appears like the rain. **No aguli dagiti kuton, agtudo.** When ants go up it's going to rain. **Makatudtudo.** It is about to rain. **Pinagtudoda ti kalapaw ti bala, pana ken gayang.** They showered the huts with bullets, arrows, and spears. [Ibg., Kpm. *urán*, Itg. *deges*, Ivt. *cimuy*, Kal. *uchen*, Knk. *udán*, Png. *orán*, Tag. *ulán*]

tudó: *n.* pointer, indicator; branchless antler. **itudo.** *v.* to point out, indicate; explain; designate; reveal. **paratudo.** *n.* pointer. **maitudo.** *v.* to be pointed out; to be singled out. [Ibg. *tuddu*, Ivt. *tungduhen*, Knk. *sílip*, Kpm. *tulduq*, Png. *toró*, Tag. *turò*]

túdok: *n.* spit for roasting meat over the fire; injection. **natudok.** *a.* pierced. **tudoken.** *v.* to pierce, stab; inject; thread meat on a spit. **tudoken ti urat.** *v.* to bleed. [Kal. *tobkon*, Kpm. *akbák*, Tag. *turók*]

tudón: agpatudon. *v.* to shift one's responsibility to another person. **patudonen.** *v.* to have someone else do one's own work, transfer a job to someone else. **pamatudonan.** *n.* person to whom one shifts responsibility. **agpipinnatudon.** *v.* to assign work to one another.

tódos: (Sp. *todos*: all) **Todos los Santos.** *n.* All Saint's Day.

túdtod: tudtuden. *v.* to glean (*sáreg*). [Tag. *himaláy*]

tudtúd: itudtud. *v.* to suggest. (*singasing*)

tuél: *n.* croaker fish, *Sciaenidae* family. (*tuel balat, tuel ngirngir, tuel rongaab*)

tuérka: (Sp. *tuerca*: nut) *n.* nut (for screwing).

tóga: (Sp. *toga*: toga) *n.* toga; academic gown; judicial robe. **agtoga.** *v.* to wear a *toga*.

túgang: *n.* distant relative; in-law. **manúgang.** *n.* son-in-law; daughter-in-law. **katugángan.** *n.* father-in-law; mother-in-law. **agkatugangan.** *n.* relationship between parent and child in-laws. [Knk. *túgang*, Tag. *biyenán*]

tugáw: *n.* seat, chair; (*obs.*) fever blister. **agtugaw.** *v.* to sit down; to be inaugurated, assume a political position. **ipatugaw.** *v.* to sit; install; place in a position or office; nominate. **itugaw.** *v.* to seat, cause to sit down. **katugaw.** *n.* seatmate. **maitugaw.** *v.* to do slowly. **maipatugaw.** *v.* to be appointed in a position. **makikatugaw.** *v.* to sit down together. **mapatugaw.** *v.* to fall on one's seat. **panagtugaw.** *n.* act of taking office. **makapagtugaw.** *v.* to be able to sit down; to assume a position or office. **tugawan.** *v.* to sit on. **dakkel ti natugawan.** *a.* presumptuous, arrogant. **natugawanna.** *a.* presumptuous; vain; overbearing; having big balls. **pagtugawan.** *n.* seat; place where one sits. **parabutbut ti tugaw.** *n.* wallflower, person who does not dance at a party (glued to the seat). **Dakkel ti natugawanna.** *exp.* He is excessively vain. **Pinastrekna ti baket sana pinagtugaw.** He had the old lady enter and then had her sit down. [Bon. *patong*, Ibg. *tuveng*, Itg. *tegaw*, Ivt. *sidnaq*, Kal. *tugew*, Kpm. *lukluk*, Png. *iróng*, Tag. *upô*]

tug-áw: (*obs.*) *n.* wonder. (*siddaaw*) **tug-awen.** *n.* to occasion scandal on the part of.

tugáy: *n.* wooden prop used to support posts (in construction). (*turarak*)

tuggád: agtuggad. *v.* to rock, sway to and fro. **manuggadtuggad.** *v.* to cradle back and forth (*indayon*). [Tag. *duyan, ugoy*]

tuggaréng: *n.* a kind of small blue bird; idiot. **natuggareng.** *a.* stupid, dense, dull. (*tabbed*)

tuggúd: ituggud. *v.* to persecute; treason; to influence into evil or bad. **maituggud.** *v.* to be influenced to do bad; fall into bad company. **tugguden.** *v.* to persecute, oppress. **manugtuggud.** *n.* persecutor. **mangituggud.** *n.* traitor. [Tag. *akit*]

tóge: (Hok. *tau gé*: bean sprout) *n.* mung bean sprouts.

tugí₁: (Tagalog *tugî*) *n. Dioscorea fasciculata*, yam with brown skin and white meat, goa yam. [Knk. *tugí* = sweet potato]

tugí₂: **tugtugi.** *n. Stephania japonica* vine. **marmaratugi.** *n.* a kind of herbaceous vine.

tugkák: *n.* phlegm (*sarkak*). [Tag. *kalaghalâ*]

tugkáw: (*obs.*) **matugtugkaw.** *v.* to be used up, finished. (*ibus*)

tugkél: *a.* sticking; having no toes. **itugkel.** *v.* to stick; drive into the ground; fix in, set upright, make stand; offer a lighted candle. **tinnugkel.** *n.* pointing to a group of numbers with a stick without looking at the numbers, and then reading the page of the number picked from a book of divination. **situtugkel.** *a.* stuck in the ground. **tugkelan.** *v.* to stake out (mark limits by stakes). **Intugkelna ti tinarimaanna a naperdi a krus.** He drove the broken cross he fixed into the ground. **Intugkelna ti imatangna iti baket.** He fixed his attention on the old woman. [Tag. *tusok*]

tugkík: *n.* stick for stabbing. **tugkiken.** *v.* to stab; prick. **matugkik.** *v.* to be stabbed; to be pricked. **Kasla natugkik ti kimmotna iti nangngegna.** *exp.* denoting displeasure with what was said, (*lit.* it seems his anus was pricked with what he heard). [Tag. *sundót*]

tugkíng: **agtugkituging.** *v.* to limp when walking.

tugkír: *var.* of *tugkik*: stab.

tuglép: **agtuglep.** *v.* to nod with the eyes closed when sleeping; to be drowsy, doze off (*saguyepyep, dungsa*). **makapatuglep.** *a.* tiring, causing drowsiness. **Makapatuglep dagita kanta a kasta.** Songs like that are tiresome. [Knk. *alimayéng*, Png. *toglép*, Tag. *antók*]

tugmók: **agtugmok.** *v.* to join end to end; meet; to be compatible. **pagtugmoken.** *v.* to put point to point (*silpo*); *n.* meeting point; joint. **Agsagabata nga agpadpada no saan nga agtugmok ti riknata.** We will suffer together if our feelings are not compatible. **Daytoy ti paset ti tawen a panagtugmok ti aldaw ken rabii.** This is the part of the year when day meets night. [Tag. *sugpóng*]

tug-ó: **tugtug-o.** *n.* turtledove (named for its call). (*págaw*)

túgud: **tuguden.** *v.* to sew together; join together; (*obs.*) to cut open an animal. [Tag. *sugpung*]

tugúgot: (*obs.*) **tuguguten.** *v.* to be occupied with.

tug-óp: **tug-upen.** *v.* to sew together. (*sug-op*; *silpo*)

túgut: **itugut.** *v.* to carry along; bring along. **katutugot.** *a.* ready to bring along. **maitugut.** *v.* to be able to bring along something. [Tag. *isama*]

tugút: *n.* footprint, trace left; footstep. **itugutan.** *v.* to track; follow the trail of. **maitugutan.** *v.* to

be able to understand; to be able to distinguish (tracks). **Inton dumakkelka, saammo a sursuroten dagiti tugotko.** When you grow up, do not follow in my footsteps. [Png. *bakát*, Tag. *bakás*]

túgpa: **tugpáan.** *v.* to patch up. (*takup*) **tugpatugpa.** *a.* patched up. **tugtugpa.** *a.* with many links or connections; coming one right after the other. **Nalamiis ti puyupoy nga aggapu iti abagatan a danggayan ti parais dagiti allon a mangtugtugpa iti rakit.** The southern breeze was cool, accompanied by the shower of waves continuously hitting the raft. [Tag. *tagpî*]

tugpó: (*obs.*) *n.* groin. (*luy-óng*, *pus-ong*) **tugpuen.** *v.* to butcher an animal for meat.

tugtóg₁: *n.* knock. (*tuktok*) **agtugtog.** *v.* to knock. **tugtogen.** *v.* to knock on something, beat on a drum. **tumanugtog.** *v.* to make a rumbling sound. [Png. *toktók*, Tag. *tuktók, katók*]

tugtóg₂: (Tag.) *n.* music. (*tokar, samiweng*) **patugtogen.** *v.* to have a band play at a party. **patugtogan.** *v.* to play a particular piece of music for someone. [Png. *tugtóg*, Tag. *tugtugin*]

tuí₁: *n. Dolichandrone spatacea*, tree with white flowers.

tuí₂: *n.* variety of awned early rice with short awn.

tuít: **tutuit.** *n.* kind of very small green and yellow bird.

tóka₁: (Sp. *toca*: headdress) *n.* bridal veil.

tóka₂: (Sp. *toca*: touch) **maitoka.** *v.* to fall on; bump against.

tóka!₃: (Sp. *toca*: play (instrument)) *interj.* asking one to play a musical instrument; *Wikstroemia lanceolata*.

tukáb: **nakatukab.** *v.* folded upward (brim of a hat). (*tukayab*)

túkad: **itukad.** *v.* to contrast; compare; offer. **pagtukaden.** *v.* to compare with the original. **agkatukad.** *v.* to be of the same quality; to be equal. [Tag. *patas*; *hambíng*]

tukád: *n.* rung, step of a ladder or staircase; grade (in education) **matukadtukad.** *v.* to be arranged from the lowest rung to the highest. **maikatlo a tukad.** *n.* third grade. **katukad.** *n.* grade; story (of a building); step of a ladder. [Tag. *baitang*]

tokádo: (Sp. *tocado*: touched) *a.* cramped, crowded.

tokadór: (Sp. *tocador*: dressing table; dressing room) *n.* dresser; dressing table.

túkak: **tukatukak.** *n.* wart. (*bittíg*) **agtukaktukak.** *v.* to have warts. **managtukaktukak.** *a.* prone to having warts. **No makabettakka ti**

itlog ti alutiit, agtukaktukakka. If you happen to break the eggs of a lizard, you will get warts. [Kal. *segeÿa*, Tag. *kulugó*]

tukák: *n.* frog. **mannukak.** *n.* a kind of snake that feeds on frogs. **ginettaan a tukak.** *n.* frog meat cooked in coconut milk. **Maluspak ti tukak a mapayatanna; Matay ti tukak a mabaddekanna.** expressions denoting one's slowness (*lit.* the frog gets crushed when stepped on). [Bon. *kotyang*, Ibg. *tukaya*, Ivt. *palakaq*, Knk. *bakbák, gudak*, Kal. *tukak*, Kpm. *tugak*, Png. *patáng*, Tag. *palakâ*]

tukákab: *n.* difficult breathing. (*tunglab*) **agtukakab.** *v.* to rasp while breathing. (*rarek*)

túkal: *n.* prop used to keep a window from being able to slide. (*súray, tukod*) **tukalan.** *v.* to prop.

tukáng: itukang. *v.* to leave half-open. **tukangan.** *v.* to prop in order to leave half-open. [Tag. *tukod*]

tokár$_1$: (Sp. *tocar*: play (music)) *n.* music. (*samiweng, tugtug*) **agtokar, tokaren.** *v.* to play a musical instrument. [Tag. *tugtóg*]

tokár$_2$: (Sp. *tocar*: touch) **agtokar ti sakit.** *v.* to relapse. (*begnat*)

túkat: (*obs.*) **itukat.** *v.* to cease. (*sardeng*)

tukáy: tukayen. *v.* to disrupt the sleep of; disturb a sleeping person; arouse, entice. **matukay.** *v.* to be disrupted (said of sleep); to be affected, touched (feelings). **Nalaka a matuktukay ti riknana.** His feelings are easily hurt. **Natukay ti panagpampanunotko idi agiwarasda iti pangmalemmi.** My thoughts were disrupted when they distributed our lunches.

tukáyab: agtukayab. *v.* to flap upward; fold up. **tukayaben.** *v.* to rip off (roof from wind). **Nakakallugong iti silag a napatukayab iti sango.** He was wearing a palm hat flapping in the front. [Tag. *laslás*]

tokáyo: (Sp. *tocayo*: namesake) *n.* person with the same name (*kanaganan*). [Bon., Knk. *abíik*]

tukbób: tukbuben. *v.* to push up, hammer from beneath. **patukbob.** *n.* king post. [Tag. *sundót*]

tóke: (Sp. *toque*: touch) *n.* touch, artistic touch.

tukél: *n.* bit; particle; seed; grain. **agtutukel.** *v.* to clot; curdle; form in drops. **tinukel ti tudo.** *n.* raindrop. **Agtigtigerger ken nalamiis ti bagina ken napigket dagiti agtutukel a ling-et iti mugingna.** His body was shaking and cold and the drops of sweat were sticky on his forehead.

tukén: *var.* of *tukéng*.

tukéng; agtukeng. *v.* to stop, quit, cease (*sardeng*); to pause briefly (*mayeng*). **maitukeng.** *v.* to pause. **naitukeng.** *a.* surprised; astonished. [Tag. *tigil*]

tukgó: *n.* kind of parrotlike bird. **agtuktukgo.** *v.* to coo.

tukí$_1$: *n.* defect, blemish. [Tag. *kasiraan*]

tukí$_2$: tinuki. *n.* variety of awned early rice.

tukiád: *var.* of *tukkiad*: to refuse; draw back.

tukíb: *var.* of *lukíb*.

tukín: *n.* pushing a canoe with a *tekken* (pole) in the ground. **tukinen.** *v.* to summon to meet, call together; push a boat sideways with a pole. [Tag. *tikin*]

túkit: tukiten. *v.* to excavate, dig out; mark a skein or hank. **matukit.** *v.* to grieve. **No ania ti intukitmo, isu ti apitem.** Whatever you dig, you will harvest.

tukít: itukit. *v.* to plant; teach; instill. **tukiten.** *v.* to make a hill around a plant. **maitukit.** *v.* to be reminded. (*dukit*) [Tag. *taním*]

tukkáw: tukkawan. *v.* to catch with a hook; peck (birds); attack (snakes). **tumukkaw.** *v.* to peck; bite. [Tag. *tukâ*]

tukkí: *var.* of *tukí*.

tukkiád: *n.* sudden stop; brief pause. **agtukkiad.** *v.* to change one's mind; make a sudden stop; give up; renounce; draw back; be hesitant to do. **Arintukkiaden sa nga aglugan iti Volks.** I think he is hesitant to ride a Volkswagen.

tukkík: tukkiken. *v.* to poke, prick.

tukkól$_1$: *n.* cut piece, broken pieces; *a.* broken. **tukkolen.** *v.* to snap in two. (*maspák*) **matukkol.** *v.* to be broken, snapped into two. **Natukkol ti al-o.** *exp.* denoting preparations are all consumed (*lit.* the pestle is broken). **Pampanunotek itayen a tukkolek ti tulangna.** I was just thinking a while ago of breaking his bones. [Ibg. *litang, teppang*, Ivt. *putut*, Kpm. *pakli*, Png. *puter*, Tag. *balì*]

tukkól$_2$: (*slang*) one, used in counting expressions: *sangatukkol ket innem*, sixteen.

tukkúong: *n.* passing the time idly in a group. **agtukkuong.** *v.* to assemble in a group, spending time idly (*mattider*). **nakatukkuong.** *a.* passing the time idly in a group.

tukláb: tumuklab. *v.* to attack (said of wild boars). (*sakrab*) **tumuktuklab.** *v.* to fight, be rushing and retreating. [Tag. *sakmál*]

tuklálo: tuklaluen. *v.* to roll into a ball. (*bulalo*)

tukláw$_1$: tuktuklaw. *n.* a kind of herb; kind of small gnat that enters the eyes at night.

tukláw$_2$: tumuklaw, tuklawen. *v.* to attack; bet; bite bait. **agtuklaw, tumuklaw.** *v.* to leap out of the water (fish). **Timmuklaw ti kakaisuna a panakkelen a paltat iti palibtok.** The sole, rather large catfish leapt from the bow net. [Tag. *tukláw* = snakebite]

tuklíng$_1$: *n.* kind of quail; chick is called *arbán*.

tuklíng$_2$: maratukling. *n.* variety of late rice with thin hull and elongated spike.

tukmá: **tumukma, tukmaan.** *v.* to seize, lay ones hands on (*iggem*). **natukmaan.** *a.* grabbed; captured. **Tinukmaak ti imana idi agtugaw iti sangok.** I grasped his hand when he sat in front of me. **Un-unaanna ni ulitegna a mangtukma iti bangos.** He grabbed the milkfish first before his uncle. [Tag. *dakmâ*]

tukmém: *n.* kind of scallop; (*fig.*) stupid person. **kasla tukmem.** *a.* stupid, dense; person who always hides in the corner. **Agbalintayo a tukmem no agsasarita dagiti kasangsangotayo ta awan met ti maibagatayo.** We become shy and dumb when the people in front of us talk and we have nothing to say. [Tag. *tangá*]

tuknád: tuknadan. *v.* to call; assemble; convoke. (*awag*)

tuknó: matukno. *v.* to be able to be reached by the head; to accidentally bump with the head. **pannakatukno.** *n.* reaching by the head. **tuknuen.** *v.* to reach with the head; summon (*súkon*); send for. **tumukno.** *v.* to reach up to. **makatukno iti atang.** *v.* to suffer a temporary loss of sanity due to spiritual influence. **Tumukno sadi langit ti pannakelna.** His pride went to his head.

tukó₁: *n.* chicken pox. (*batungol*) **agtuko.** *v.* to have chicken pox. [Png. *gulutóng*, Tag. *bulutung-tubig*, *tigdás*]

tukó₂: agituko. *v.* to arrange the border of a casting net by tying additional meshes.

tokuá: (Hok. *tau kuâ*: bean dried) *n.* bean curd, tofu.

túkod₁: *n.* prop; brace; *prep.* the bottom of. **tukoden.** *v.* to measure the depth of, fathom. **tukon-tukod.** *n.* brace used to support a roof. **agtukontukod.** *v.* to explore the bottom of a body of water with a stick, etc. **matukod.** *v.* to be fathomable, intelligible, conceivable. **panukod.** *n.* pole for sounding the depths of water. [Tag. *tukod*, *suhay*]

túkod₂: tukodtukod, tukontukod. *n. Marsilea crenata* plant with creeping rootstocks. **tukod lángit.** *n.* a kind of small herb with edible leaves.

túkok: *n.* bottom (of a pit, well, etc.); heart of the matter. **maitukokan.** *v.* to be able to fathom; to be able to comprehend. **tumukok.** *v.* to penetrate deeply. **Nabang-aran ti bagina iti lamiis ti danum iti tukot.** His body was relieved from the cold water at the bottom. [Tag. *ilalim*]

túkol₁: *n.* prop (*súray*). **tukolen.** *v.* to prop up. **Intukolna ti dakulapna iti timidna.** He propped his chin with the palm of his hand. **agtukol.** *v.* to protrude, stick out. **patukolan.** *v.* to let someone feel the stiffness of one's organ. [Tag. *tukod*, *suhay*]

túkol₂: *n.* variety of banana.

túkol₃: *n.* heated cotton wad with oil that is applied to a wound. **tukolen.** *v.* to apply a *tukol* to a wound in order to disinfect.

túkon: see *súkon*: convene; assemble. (*agummong*)

túkong: *n.* a tailless bird; *a.* short-tailed; tailless. [Tag. *punggók*]

tukót: *var.* of *tukok*.

tukráb: (*obs.*) **tuktukrab.** *n.* fighting in retreat.

tukréb₁: natukreb. *a.* sweet-toothed.

tukréb₂: tuktukreb. *n.* a kind of bird.

tuktók₁: *n.* top, summit; crown of the head. **agpatuktok.** *v.* to go to the summit. [Bon. *motlok*, Ibg. *porpitu*, Ivt. *tútuk*, Kal. *lap-at*, Kpm., Png., Tag. *tuktók*]

tuktók₂: *n.* sound of pecking; knocking. **tuktoken.** *v.* to peck. **tuktokan.** *v.* to knock at. **ituktok.** *v.* to knock a bone to get the marrow out; knock against. **agtuktok.** *v.* to knock eggs against each other; to make a knocking sound. [Tag. *tukâ*]

tuktók₃: pannuktok. *n.* kind of speckled woodpecker bird.

tuktók₄: *n.* kind of iron hook for roughening whetstones. **panuktok.** *n.* small iron hook used to open mollusks.

tókwa: *var.* of *tokua*: bean curd, tofu.

túla₁: tultulaen. *v.* to belittle, depreciate; to undervalue in order to discourage competitors.

tóla₂: (Tag.) **tinola.** *n.* dish consisting of chicken cooked with unripe papayas.

túlad: agtulad. *v.* to copy, imitate. **agtutulad.** *n.* imitator. **tuladen.** *v.* to copy, imitate, mock. **napatuladan iti dákes.** *a.* perverted, corrupted, debased. **pagtuladan.** *n.* model, example. (*pagwadan*) **pagpatulad.** *n.* example, pattern. **agpatulad.** *v.* to do by example. **itulad.** *v.* to copy after, pattern after; compare with something else. **ipatulad.** *v.* to have something copied, imitated. **agpatulad.** *v.* to have someone copy or imitate. **patuladan.** *v.* to show a bad example to someone. **agtinnulad.** *v.* to copy one another. **napatuladan iti dakes.** *v.* influenced badly. **tinultulad.** *a.* imitation, copy, fake. [Ivt. *tahataha*, Knk. *day-ón*, Png. *sakál*, *alig*, Tag. *tulad*]

tuladítid: *var.* of *túlid*: roll, roll over.

túlag: *n.* contract, agreement, treaty; bargain. **agtulag.** *v.* to make a contract, agree (plural subject). **katulagan.** *n.* document. **katulag.** *v.* to have a contract or agreement with. **makapagtulag.** *v.* to be able to draw up a contract, negotiate. **makitulag.** *v.* to negotiate with, make a contract. **itulag.** *v.* to agree on behalf of. **pagtulagan.** *v.* to make a contract with each other. **tulagen**. *v.* to discuss the details of a plan; plan a course of action. **Nagtulaganmi nga agkitakaminto idiay pagsinean.** We agreed to see each other at the movie theater. [Ivt. *papanmwan*, Png. *tonong*, Tag. *sundô*]

tulákak: **tumultulakak.** *v.* to choke; gasp. (*tungláb*)

tuláli: *n.* bamboo flute used to accompany the *dallot.* (*plauta*)

tulálo: **tulaluen**. *v.* to roll into a ball. (*bulalo*)

túlang: **tulangtulang**. *n. Ixora philippinensis.*

tuláng: *n.* bone; cartilage; skeleton (*rurog*). **itulangan.** *v.* to strip the bone of meat. **katultulang.** *a.* bony; skin-and-bones. **tumulang.** *v.* to penetrate deeply into the bones (cold). **manulang ti lamiis.** *exp.* it is freezing cold (the coolness reaches the bone). **pagitulangán.** *n.* discarded bones. **natulang.** *a.* bony. [Bon. *tong-al*, Ibg. *tulang*, Ifg. *gunit*, Itg. *tul-ang*, Ivt. *tu-hang*, Kal. *tong-e*, Knk. *ingit, tung-á*, Kpm. *bútul*, Png. *pokél*, Tag. *butó* (bone); Kpm. *tuláng* = dragonfly]

tularámid: (coined word) *n.* play, drama.

tulátid: **agtulatid.** *v.* to roll; revolve. (*tayyék*) **itulatid, tulatiden.** *v.* to cause to roll; turn over. **Nagtulatid a natnag ti tallo bukel a lua iti pitakpitak ken daradara a rupana.** Three full tears rolled down his dirty and bloody face. [Tag. *gulong*]

tuláw: *n.* stain, spot, blemish, smear. **matulawan.** *v.* to be stained, spotted, soiled; dishonored. **tulawan.** *v.* to smear, stain; (*fig.*) rob a maiden of her virginity, dishonor someone. [Tag. *batík*]

túlay: *reg. var.* of *pádun*: muzzle.

tulbék: *n.* key. **tulbekan.** *v.* to lock with a key; open with a key. **matulbekan.** *v.* to be locked; to be locked out. **mannulbek.** *v.* locksmith. [Kal. *teýbik*, Knk. *kulúkul, súsi*, Png. *tombók*, Kpm., Tag. *susì*; Knk. *tulbék* = nail, stud]

tulbó₁: *n.* using a punch to drive nails.

tulbó₂: **itulbo.** *v.* to insert the wick of a lamp.

tólda: (Sp. *toldo*: awning) *n.* tent; removable canvas hood of a convertible car. (*lingáling*)

tuldék: *n.* accent written over a letter; period (punctuation); point. **tuldekan.** *v.* to place an accent mark; mark with a dot; punctuate with a period. [Tag. *tuldók*]

tuldí: *n.* clitoris (*tildi, sapuriding, taman, muting*). [Kpm. *turíl*, Tag. *manî*]

tuldó₁: *n.* hole in the earlobe. [Tag. *butas ng tainga*]

tuldó₂: **agpatuldo.** *v.* to follow a model. **ipatuldo.** *v.* to teach; explain; point out; show; indicate. [Tag. *turò*]

tuldó₃: **patuldo.** *n.* a kind of tree.

tuldó₄: *n.* kind of small gray bird.

tuldók: *n.* variety of thick-skinned, very large, greenish banana.

tuldóng: **ituldong.** *v.* to do fervently; concentrate on one thing. (*ipamaysa, ipasnek*) **maituldong.** *v.* to be done fervently; to be concentrated on.

túleng₁: *a.* deaf. **agtuleng.** *v.* to be deaf, hard of hearing. **agintutuleng.** *v.* to pretend not to hear. **arintulengen.** *a.* somewhat deaf, a little bit deaf. **tutuleng.** *n.* groove in the back of the ear. **pagintutulngan.** *v.* to refuse to listen; turn a deaf ear. **ipatpatuleng.** *v.* to refuse to pay attention to. **tutuleng.** *n.* the groove at the back of the ear. **Kasla nakangeg a tuleng.** He's like a deaf person hearing for the first time. [Ibg. *kitul, bangngág*, Itg. *tulpak*, Ivt. *kuteng*, Kal. *tuÿong*, Knk. *túeng, paglék*, Kpm. *maklak*, Png. *benger, telek, tuweng*, Tag. *bingí*]

túleng₂: **billít tuleng**. *n.* a kind of sparrow that devastates rice fields, *maya* bird. **uleg tuleng.** *n.* kind of small black snake whose head is hard to differentiate from the body.

tuléng: **matuleng.** *v.* to be blinded from seeing light after being in the dark for a period of time. **tumuleng.** (*obs.*) *v.* to calm (the wind).

túlid₁: *n.* rotation. **agtulidtulid.** *v.* to turn over; revolve, wheel. **tuliden.** *v.* to roll. **patpatulid.** *n.* hoop used in playing. [Tag. *gulong*]

túlid₂: **patulid.** *v.* trap for fish with rectangular bamboo platform.

tulingán: *n.* kind of large marine fish with a red back resembling the *mataán.*

tulisán: (Tagalog also) *n.* thief, robber. (*mannakaw*); *Dussumieria sp.* sardine. **agtulisan.** *v.* to rob, steal.

tulláy: **agtullatullay.** *v.* to rock, sway. [Tag. *giray*]

tulláya: **tultullaya.** *n.* tree with good timber.

tulméng₁: **itulmeng.** *v.* to humiliate, humble, shame. **maitulmeng.** *v.* to be humbled; to be humiliated. [Tag. *pahiyâ*]

tulméng: **itulmeng.** *v.* to transplant using the fingers.

tulmíg: (*obs.*) see *túlad*: imitate.

tulnég: **itulneg.** *v.* to press; pull the trigger.

tulnék: *n.* period (*tuldek*). **tulne-tulnek.** *a.* full of spots, speckled.

tulnóg: **agtulnog.** *v.* to obey. (*tungpal; annugot; sungput*) **natulnog.** *a.* obedient, submissive; compliant. **kinatulnog.** *n.* obedience. **itulnog.** *v.* to lead, conduct; guide; lead; escort (*tulud*); introduce; accompany home. **agpaitulnog.** *v.* to ask for a companion when going somewhere, request an escort. **Situltulnogak a nagtung-ed.** I obediently shook my head in agreement. [Kal. *tuttuwaon*, Tag. *sunód; hatíd*]

tulúd₁: **itulud**. *v.* to conduct, escort; send. (*bagnos*; *kuyog*) **tuloden**. *v.* to escort someone to a place. **pangitulodan**. *n.* destination. **agpaitulud**. *v.* to request an escort. **mangitulud**. *v.* to escort; *n.* messenger. **patuludan**. *v.* to send (money) to someone. **Bayadam dagiti impatpatulodko a pinagbasam idiay Manila**. Pay for the money I sent for your studies in Manila. [Ibg. *tulug*, Itg. *bulunan*, Ivt. *yangay*, Kpm. *atad*, Png. *tulur*, Tag. *hatíd*]

tulúd₂: **itulud**. *v.* to rock, sway. (*indayon*) **itultulud**. *v.* to rock a hammock or swing, etc. [Tag. *giray*]

tulók: *n.* obedience. (*panagtungpal, tulnóg, annúgot, tudió*) **agtulok**. *v.* to be meek; obedient, submissive; go voluntarily. **itulok**. *v.* to give up; give in; let oneself undergo; permit, allow; tolerate; condone. **kinatulok**. *n.* meekness. **natulok**. *a.* obedient, submissive, obsequious; compliant. **patuloken**. *v.* to have someone else do what one is responsible for; to have an alternative under pressure. **tuloken**. *v.* to allow; permit; tolerate. (*palabus; bay-a*) **tumulok**. *v.* to give in, yield; obey, be obedient. **Itulokyo ngarud nga agkakallautangtayo**. Just let us drift aimlessly then. **Diak itulok a dadaelenda ti nabayagen nga arapaapko**. I will not permit them to destroy my longtime dream. [Ibg. *tulúq*, Png. *tolók*, Tag. *talima, sunód* (obey)]

tuluktók: *n. Kleinhovia sp.* tree.

túlong: *n.* help, assistance (*saranay, arayat, badang, dar-ay, ambag, abuloy, sarakoy; bataris*); support. **itulong**. *v.* to give as help or assistance. **katulongan**. *n.* helper; servant (*baon*). **tumulong**. *v.* to aid, assist, help. **tulongan**. *v.* to help someone, assist; support, back; favor. **makatulong**. *v.* to be able to help. **mannulong, mannakatulong**. *a.* always willing to help, helpful. **mannakitinnulong**. *a.* cooperative. **agpatulong**. *v.* to ask for help. **agtinnulong**. *v.* to help each other. **managtulong**. *a.* helpful. **kinamanagtulong**. *a.* helpfulness. [Ibg. *ebbag, uffún*, Ivt. *sidung*, Knk. *ugbó*, Kpm. *sáup*, Png., Tag. *tulong*]

tul-óng: *n.* pillory, stocks; mortise; two bamboos placed between the *sallabáwan* and *pakabáyo* of the ridge of the roof.

tulós: (Tagalog also) *n.* pole; stake. **tulusan**. *v.* to stake out.

túloy: *n.* continuation. **agtuloy, tumuloy**. *v.* to continue, proceed. **agpatpatuloy**. *v.* to continue, carry on (work, etc.). **tuluyen**. *v.* to end, complete, terminate, finish; continue. **patuluyen**. *v.* to continue, carry out; ask someone to come in. **maituloyto**. *v.* to be continued. **ituloy**. *v.* to continue; go through with. **ma-**

tuluyan. *v.* to expire, die. **makapagtuloy**. *v.* to be able to continue. **Dina intuloy a kinalbit ti gatilio**. He didn't go through with pulling the trigger. [Bon. *tóley*, Png., Tag. *tuloy*]

tulpák: *a.* hard of hearing, deaf (*tuleng*); *var.* of *tupak*. [Itg. *tulpak* = deaf]

tultóg: (*obs.*) *n.* masturbation (*salsal*); pollution.

tultól: **tultolen**. *v.* to follow; endeavor to overtake; go after somebody. **itultol**. *v.* to convey to, bring to following somebody. [Tag. *sundán*]

tóma: (Sp. *toma*: drink) *n.* drinking of liquor. **pangtoma**. *n.* money intended to buy liquor, pourboire. (*sukmon*)

túma: *n.* body louse. [Head louse is *kúto*. Knk. *túma*]

tumádeng: *n.* tree with valuable building timber.

tomár: (Sp. *tomar*: drink; take) **agtomar**. *v.* to take medicine orally. **Siguruem nga agtomar iti agasna**. Make sure he takes his medicine.

túmba: (Sp. *tumba*: tomb) *n.* tomb.

tumbá₁: (Sp. *tumbar*: knock down) *a.* upside down (*balinsuek; baluknog; ursong; baliktad*); fallen down; bankrupt. **agtumba**. *v.* to hang down; knock down. **matumba**. *v.* to fall down; to lose all, become bankrupt. **tumbaen**. *v.* to defeat; throw down. **itumba**. *v.* to drop.

tumbá₂: **tumbaen**. *v.* to drink up, gulp down all the contents of a glass. [Tag. *tunggâ*]

tumbadór: *n.* lumberjack (*atsero*). [Tag. *magtroso*]

tumbaláy: (f. *balay*) **manumtumbalay**. *v.* to go from house to house. **itumbalay**. *v.* to take from house to house, go from house to house.

tumbalí: *n.* lever of a loom.

tumbangí₁: *n.* anything inverted. **agtumbangi**. *v.* to be inverted; reversed. [Tag. *baliktád*]

tumbangí₂: *n.* kind of woven cloth.

tumbuék: (*obs.*) *n.* sound of the pestle in mortar.

tumbóg: (f. *tubbog*) *v.* to emit liquid; issue forth. **Adda tumbog iti pusom**. Something is flowing from your heart (you are falling in love).

tumbók: *n.* kind of iron pestle used for pounding metalwork into a mold or shaping.

tombútso: *var.* of *tambutso*: muffler.

tómboy: (Eng. tomboy) *n.* tomboy; masculine woman; lesbian. (*maralakien, lakien*)

tumég: **itumeg**. *v.* to knock the head. **maitumeg**. *v.* to knock against something (head); to be brief (said of time in which to do or prevent something.); to be pressed for time. [Tag. *untóg*]

tumék: *n.* powder. (*polbos*) **natumek**. *a.* crushed, pulverized. **tumeken**. *v.* to crush, pulverize. [Tag. *durog*]

túmel: *n.* variety of thin-skinned banana resembling the *dippíg*.

tumén: (*obs.*) see *ngangá*.

túmeng: *n.* knee. **agparintumeng.** *v.* to kneel. **maparintumeng.** *v.* to fall on one's knees. **sipaparintumeng.** *a.* kneeling down. **iparintumeng.** *v.* to plead on one's knees. **pagattumeng.** *a.* knee-high. **ápo ti tumeng.** *n.* great-grandparent. **tumengen.** *v.* to hit with the knees. **appo ti tumeng.** *n.* great-grandchildren. **Natangken ti tumengna.** He has hard knees (does not humble himself). [Bon. *poweg*, Ibg. *tulung, atug,* Ifg. *lúlug,* Ivt. *túud,* Kal. *mong-u* (knee), *byangabyanga* (kneecap), Knk. *pagólong, púeg,* Kpm. *tud,* Png. *poég,* Tag. *tuhod*]

tumkiás: (f. *takkias*) *v.* to leave for; escape; run away.

tumméeng: **agtummeeng.** *v.* to be in shock; to be deep in thought (while sitting). **Masansan a nakatummeeng dagiti pilosopo.** Philosophers are often in deep thought.

tummó: **agtummo.** *v.* to meet unexpectedly (*rana; askul; darudan*). [Tag. *magkita*]

tumngáag: (f. *tengngaag*) *v.* to stretch the neck (in order to see).

tumngáw: (*obs.*) *a.* crazy. (*bagtit, balla*)

tómo: (Sp. *tomo*: volume) *n.* volume (book in a series); tome, large book.

túmok: *n.* variety of thin-skinned, greenish banana, *var. suaveolens.* **tumok-bakes.** *n.* smaller variety of *tumok.*

tum-óng: see *tim-óg*: knock into; collide; bump into. (*dalapus; bangdol; dunget; dungpar; pukkuol; salapon; dugpa*)

tumunggál: (f. *tunggal*) *adv.* each; every.

tumór: (Sp.) *n.* tumor, abnormal growth.

túmuy: **natumuy.** *a.* rotten; putrefied, decayed through humidity (*lungsot; timming; tubeg*). **agtumuy.** *v.* to rot, putrefy. [Tag. *bulók*]

tumpáak: *n.* sound of soft objects falling, raindrops, etc.

tumpáp: *n.* flat end (bottom of glass); flatnose (*leppap*). [Tag. *pangô*]

tumpáw: (f. *tapaw*) *v.* to float. [Ibg. *luttaq,* Ivt. *mehtaw,* Kal. *malapÿak,* Kpm. *gáto,* Png. *letaw,* Tag. *lutang* (float)]

tumpiók: (*obs.*) **tumumpiok.** *v.* to curve, bend. (*bakkog; pikor*)

tumpuár: (f. *tuppuar*) *v.* to appear suddenly and unexpectedly.

tumpóng: **agtumpong.** *v.* to agree, be in harmony with. **tumpongan.** *v.* to hit upon; guess right, arrive at conclusion. **agtumpong dagiti matada.** Their eyes met. **maitumpong.** *v.* to be just right. **makatumpong.** *v.* to come across, come upon; find; meet. **matumpongan.** *v.* to hit right on the head; to have done something just right. **Apay ngamin a nakatumpongak iti**

sabali a puli. Why do I find myself in a different race? [Png. *tonong,* Tag. *sundô*]

tómpson: *n.* kind of long gun with rounded bullet canister.

tumrárong: *v.* to emit; come into sight, appear.

tumrék: (*obs.*) *n.* concealed hate.

tumrém: **agtumrem.** *v.* to start to water (said of they eyes); ooze out; flow out. **Nagsangit inga't awanen ti tumrem a luana.** She cried until there were no more tears to flow out.

ton: Contraction of future article *intono* or *intón.*

ton-anó: Contraction of *inton-anó*: when?

túnaw: (Tagalog also) **matunaw.** *v.* to melt, dissolve. (*runaw*) **tunawen.** *v.* to melt something; shape gold into bullion. **Kasla matuntunaw nga asin iti bainna.** He is melting like salt in his shame. [Knk. *lúnaw, lúnag,* Png., Tag. *túnaw*]

tundá: **itunda.** *v.* to lead, conduct; escort (*tulnog, tulud*). **maitunda.** *v.* to be led, escorted. **Ditoynak nga intunda ti tagainepko.** This is where my dreams led me. [Tag. *hatíd*]

tondál: (f. French name *Letondal*) *n.* variety of thin-skinned yellow banana. (*aritondál*)

tundíris: *n.* high point of the nose. **natundiris.** *a.* with a pointed nose (*tarimayon*). [Knk. *bengiéd*]

tónek: (*obs.*) *n.* beginning of a work.

tunék: *var.* of *sunék*: small parts of the husk that remain after rice has been pounded.

túnel: (Sp. *túnel*: tunnel) *n.* tunnel. **tunelan.** *v.* to make a tunnel through.

toneláda: (Sp. *tonelada*: ton) *n.* ton. **sangatonelada.** *n.* one ton.

toneláhe: (Sp. *tonelaje*: tonnage) *n.* tonnage; carrying capacity of a vehicle.

túnika: (Sp. *túnica*: tunic) *n.* tunic; gown; robe. **nakatunika.** *a.* wearing a tunic.

tuníka: **tuntunika.** *n.* doll; puppet.

tóniko: (Sp. *tónico*: tonic) *n.* tonic, medicine for strength.

tóning: **tumutoning.** *v.* to get drunk. (*bumartek; manginum*) **agtoning.** *v.* to drink liquor.

tunnál: *a.* protruding; running (from the nose); with tongue sticking out. **agtunnal.** *v.* to bulge; protrude. **nakatunnal.** *a.* protruding; bulging out. **Adda nakatunnal a takki iti ubet ti manok.** The chicken has excrement protruding from its anus.

tunnamí: **tuntunnamí.** *Gymnosporia spinosa* plant.

tóno: Contraction of the future article *intono.* **(in)tono bigat.** *adv.* tomorrow.

tóno: (Sp. *tono*: tone) *n.* tone; tune; pitch (of sound); inflection (of voice); intonation. [Tag. *himig*]

túno: **ituno, tunuen**. *v.* to roast, broil, singe; barbecue. **matuno**. *v.* to be roasted; barbecued. **tinuno**. *n.* anything broiled, roasted, etc. [Ibg. *tun(n)o*, Ivt. *pasuhen*, Kal. *ichawis*, Knk. *dáwis*, *mendákiw*, Kpm. *ningnang, nangnang*, Png. *kalót*, Tag. *ihaw*]

túnos: *n.* harmony; compatibility. **agtunos**. *v.* to agree; to be compatible. (*agtumpong*) **pagtunusen**. *v.* to mediate, make agree. **katunos**. *n.* partner. **makitunos**. *v.* to agree with. **maitunos**. *v.* to be able to agree or go along with. [Tag. *kaisá*]

túnoy: (*obs.*) **tuntunoyan**. *v.* to walk slowly. (*inayad, bontog*)

tun-óy: **katun-oyan**. *n.* capability, ability. (*kabaelan*) **pagtun-oyan**. *n.* effect, outcome, result. **tun-oyen**. *v.* to attain, strive to attain; reach; achieve. **Dina kayat a kinamannurat ti pagtun-oyam.** He doesn't want you to end up as a writer. **As-asideg ita ti tuntunoyem a gameng.** The treasure you are striving to attain is more within reach today. [Tag. *kamtín*]

tonsúra: (Sp. *tonsura*: tonsure, *obs.*) *n.* tonsure.

tuntón: *n.* searching for a lost object; compensation; claim for damages. **agtunton**. *v.* to find something out. **pagtunton**. *n.* metal detector. **managtunton**. *a.* inquisitive. **tuntonen**. *v.* to ask, inquire (for a lost object); make a claim; make demands. **matuntonan**. *v.* to find; discover. **Nakatuntunam iti gameng?** Where did you find the treasure?

tontoníka: *n.* doll; puppet.

tong: (Hok. *tông*: percentage cut of a gambling taken from winners) *n.* bribe money; grease money. (*pasukib*) **agtong**. *v.* to give bribe money. [Tag. *suhol*]

tungá: **agtunga**. *v.* to do (read, etc.) confusedly.

tungáab: *a.* agape. (*nganga, tuyaab*) **agtungaab**. *v.* to open the mouth wide. [Tag. *tungangà*]

túngab: *n.* tribal leader.

tungáil: **agtungail**. *v.* to rock, sway (something not fixed well into the ground).

tungaltóng: **tungaltongan**. *v.* to weigh down something to force it to drown.

tungangá: **nakatunganga**. *a.* caught by surprise.

tungángaw: **tumungangaw**. *v.* to peep out, peer; begin to emerge.

túngaw: *n.* mite. (*ayám, tuma*). **tinungaw**. *a.* infested with mites.

tungbó: **tinungbo**. *n.* kind of sweet made of rice and sugar cooked in bamboo over an open fire; rice cooked by steam. **tungbuen**. *v.* to cook in bamboo nodes.

tungból: **tumungbol**. *v.* to sprout. (*sagibsib*) **kattungbol**. *a.* just sprouted; newly germinated; just reaching puberty; novice. **natungbol**. *a.* new; novice (person). [Tag. *siból*]

tungdáy: *n.* miscarriage; failure; disappointment; *a.* rebellious, disobedient. **tungdayen**. *v.* to frustrate; disappoint. (*paay*) **Sinangitak ti panagsinami ta adu't arapaapko a natungday.** I cried about our separation because a lot of my dreams failed. [Tag. *bigô*]

tungéd: **tungden**. *v.* to shorten, abridge, cut a part of. **agtunged**. *v.* to end abruptly. **tunged a kalsada**. *n.* dead-end street. [Tag. *putol*]

tung-éd: *n.* nodding of the head. **agtung-ed**. *v.* to nod the head (*tang-éd*). [Bon., Knk. *yang-ed*, Png. *tangér*, Tag. *tangô*]

tunggál: *a.* each, every; *conj.* whenever. **tunggal maysa**. each one; every one. **Nagasat sa dagitoy nuangmi ta kanayon a nasayaat ti apitmi tunggal panagani.** Our water buffalo must be lucky because every time we harvest a lot every harvest season. [Kpm. *bálang*, Png. *tonggál*, Tag. *bawa't*]

tunggáli: *n.* barter, exchange. (*pattáli, pannakisinnukát, maró*)

tunggáya: **agtunggaya**. *v.* to swim the backstroke.

tunggíl: (*coll.*) *n.* clitoris (*tuldi*). [Kpm. *turíl*, Tag. *maní*]

tungguáb: **itungguab**. *v.* to drink up; *var.* of *tangguap*.

tungí: (*slang*) *a.* stupid, idiotic. **tungitungi**. *n.* species of freshwater fish.

túngil: **natungil**. *a.* very small, dwarfish; stunted (*tiltil*). [Tag. *bansót*]

tong-ít: *n.* poker-type gambling card game.

tungkál: *n.* pawl, catch of a loom; support for something falling. **tungkalan**. *v.* to prop up.

tungkír: *var.* of *tugkík*: stab.

tongkuá: **tongtongkuaen, i(tong)tongkua**. *v.* to delay, postpone (*igábay, ando, tantan*). [Tag. *hulí, antala*]

tungkód: (Tag.) *n.* cane, pole used as an implement. (*sarukod*)

tungláb: **agtungtunglab**. *v.* to gasp; pant violently (*tulálak, lunos*). [Png. *sungayat*, Tag. *singáp*]

tungngá: (*obs.*) **agtungnga-tungnga**. *v.* to shake the head continuously.

tungngáag: **agtungngaag**. *v.* to stretch the neck (in order to see). **nakatungngaag**. *a.* with the neck stretched.

tungngáang: *var.* of *tungngang*.

tungngáli: *a.* loose, shaky, wobbly. **agtungngali**. *v.* to be loose, shaky. (*tungail, wali*)

tungngáling: *var.* of *tungngali*: shaky, loose.

tungngáng: *n.* fool, idiot, imbecile; chink in a wall. **nagtungngang**. *a.* idiotic (*maag; tabbed*;

langgong; laglag; muno; ang-ang). [Tag. *tangá*]

tungngiáb: see *tangráb:* chop off slantwise.

tungngó: *n.* firewood, fuel. (*sungrod*) **itungngo.** *v.* to add fuel or firewood to; fuel. [Tag. *gatong*]

tungó: *n.* firewood; fuel. (*sungrod*)

tungpá: *n.* slap in the face. **matungpa.** *v.* to be slapped. **tungpaen.** *v.* to slap. **tungpatungpaen.** *v.* to slap left and right. [Png. *tampí,* Tag. *sampál, sampilóng*]

tungpál: *n.* end; conclusion; outcome; result; *prep.* until, to. **agtungpal.** *v.* to obey; complete; end up; result in. **tungpalen.** *v.* obey; to end, finish, conclude; complete; achieve; comply; carry out; perform; accomplish; fulfill. **ipatungpal.** *v.* to carry out; execute; implement. **makatungpal.** *v.* to be able to carry out; to be able to fulfill one's obligation. **manungpal.** *prep.* until; *v.* to be used up, tired out; killed; dead. **mannungpal.** *a.* obedient. **pagtungpalan.** *n.* end. **pagtungpalanna.** *n.* his final destination. **itungpal.** *v.* to complete; fulfill; marry after having had sexual relations (go through with the wedding). **matungpal ti kari.** *v.* to fulfill a promise. **panungpalan.** *n.* end. **paitungpal.** *v.* to let someone marry someone else, have someone marry. **tungpal biag.** until the end of life; as long as alive. **tungpal tanem.** until death. **awan tungpalna.** without end. **Tinungpalko ti balakadmo.** I carried out your advice. **panangipatungpal iti linteg.** law enforcement. **Adu ti saona a dina matungpal.** He says a lot of things he doesn't carry out. **Ti ubing a matungpal amin a kayatna, awan ti nasayaat a banagna.** A child who ends up with everything he wants will not succeed in life. **Nagtungpal idiay impierno.** He ended up in hell. **Ti ragsak a nalabes, pagtungpalanna't dakes.** Too much happiness ends in sorrow. [Png. *sompál,* Tag. *tupád; wakas*]

tungpáp: *var.* of *tumpáp.*

túngrab: **tungraban.** *v.* to chop off slantwise. [Tag. *tapyás*]

tungráraw: **tumungraraw.** *v.* to peep in; peer out; show oneself briefly; peer out of a window. (*tammidaw*) **Naitungraraw ti rupana iti apagbingngi a tawa.** His face peered out of the slightly open window. **Intungrarawna ti ulona iti narehasan a tawa.** He peered his head out of the railed window. [Tag. *sungaw*]

túngro: *n.* grasshopper; rice disease caused by the *tungro* grasshopper.

tungtúng₁: *n.* top of the *anáwang* furnace.

tungtúng₂: *n.* tribal peace assembly. **makitongtong, katongtong.** *v.* to converse with. (*maki*

sao, patang; sarita) **tungtungan.** *n.* conversation; reached agreement; *v.* converse with. **pagtungtungan.** *v.* to talk something over. **Katungtungannak.** He likes to talk to me. [Bon. *toya,* Png. *tongtong,* Tag. *usap* (converse)]

tungwá: *var.* of *tangwá:* look up; show one's face; look straight at.

tóo: Interjection used to call dogs.

túod: *n.* old age. **tuodan.** *a.* experienced, wise; aged. **apo iti tuod.** *n.* great-great-grandparent. **agparintuod.** *v.* to kneel on one knee. [Tag. *tandâ*]

túok: *n.* torture; suffering (*sagaba*); torment. **agtuok.** *v.* to suffer, be tormented. **tutuoken.** *v.* to torture. **matutuok.** *v.* to endure pain, suffer. **matuokan.** *a.* tortured; really suffering. **natuok.** *a.* difficult to endure. [Tag. *dusà, pahirap*]

tuók: *n.* kind of large red bird with blue breast.

tuólan: *n.* handle of an ax.

túon₁: *n.* pile; interest on money; layer; tier. (*buntón, gabsóon, penpén, montón*) **ituon.** *v.* to superimpose; place on top. **pagtutuonen.** *v.* to place in tiers. **tuonan.** *v.* to pile up; augment, add to, increase. **tumuon.** *v.* to go to the top of (*agparabaw; umili*); copulate. **agtuon.** *v.* to have one on top of other; copulate. **natutuon.** *a.* stacked. **pagtutuon.** *v.* to stack on top of one another. **katuon.** *n.* tier; layer. **agtinnuon.** *a.* one above the other. **Pinagsadagna ti bukotna iti napagtuon a pungan.** He supported his back against the stacked pillows. [Tag. *salansán*]

túon₂: **matuon.** *n.* mood, midday. **matmatuonen.** *v.* to do something at noon. **Agmatuonen.** It is already noon. [Tag. *tanghalì*]

túop: **tuopen.** *v.* to place end to end, point to point. [Tag. *dugtóng*]

túpa₁: (Tag.) *n.* sheep. (*karnero*)

túpa₂: (Sp. *topar:* bump, knock against) **agtupa.** *v.* to collide; bump into. **maitupa.** *v.* to hit the head accidentally; collide into. **itupa.** *v.* to knock against. **Iti pigsa ti kugtarna, naitupa ti pusa iti alad.** From the force of her kick, the cat collided into the fence. [Tag. *bunggô*]

tupáda: *n.* game consisting of one person rolling a coconut while another tries to throw another coconut to break it; illegal cockfighting. **agtupada.** *v.* to play the game of *tupada;* to practice illegal cockfighting.

tupák₁: *n.* violent fall; amount of money wagered. **itupak.** *v.* to throw down; hang up a phone. **tumpaak.** *v.* to make the sound of falling raindrops. **agtupak.** *v.* to fall down violently; throw down one's bet in gambling;

name the dowry price. **Intupakna ti bagina a timmugaw.** She threw down her body when she sat down.

tupák₂: *n.* money given to newlyweds.

tupár: (Sp. *topar*: strike, knock against) *n.* direction; approach; bumping, knocking against; chance meeting. **matupar.** *v.* to be just right ahead; to be in the line of; to see someone just before seeing someone else (visiting the secretary before visiting the doctor); run into. **tuparen.** *v.* to approach; knock, strike against. **itupar.** *v.* to direct, guide to a certain point. **Agin-iniin ti rakit a tuptuparen dagiti allon.** The raft rocked, bumped by the waves. [Tag. *bungad*]

topásio: (Sp. *topacio*: topaz) *n.* topaz.

tupátop: agtupatop. *v.* to assemble, convene, congregate. (*agummong*) **agtupatop ti rigat.** *v.* to pile up hardships. **pagtutupatopan.** *v.* place of assembly. [Tag. *sama-sama*]

túpay: (*obs.*) **matupay.** *v.* to change one's mind.

tup-áy: see *kusáy*: kick forward.

tupé: (Eng.) *n.* toupee, small wig. **agtupe.** *v.* to wear a toupee.

tupék₁: tupken. *v.* to crush; pound into pieces; ground. [Tag. *durog*]

tupék₂: maipatupek. *v.* to be cornered; surrounded. (*suli*) **mapatupek.** *v.* to be cornered, surround; to be overwhelmed. [Tag. *pikot*]

tupék₃: patupek. *n.* extremity of floor cut to give room for a post.

tupí: *n.* hem, fold; seam. **itupi, tupien.** *v.* to hem; seam (*luppi, ubadan*). [Png. *topí*, Tag. *tupí*]

tópia: *n.* feathered pestle of the bellow; start of a weaving pattern; sides of the *kulluong*. **topiaan.** *v.* to fill up; complete.

túpig: *n.* kind of rice cake baked in banana leaves.

túpil: matutupil. *v.* to be blunted (edges) (*ngudel, ngelngel*). [Tag. *pudpód*]

tupináy: (*obs.*) see *lupináy*: to crouch sitting.

túping: *n.* stones placed for damming water or for preventing erosion. **tupingan.** *v.* to provide with a stone wall to prevent erosion.

tupítop: natupitop. *a.* narrow, restricted; without much room; tight. **itupitup.** *v.* to make do. [Tag. *sikíp*]

tupngár: see *tubngar*: contradict; rectify.

túpo: itupo. *v.* to bet everything in gambling.

topografía: (Sp. *topografía*: topography) *n.* topography.

topográpo: (Sp. *topógrafo*: topographer) *n.* topographer.

tuppuár: tumpuar. *v.* to appear suddenly and unexpectedly; emerge out of hiding; rise (sun). [Tag. *labás*]

tuppól: *a.* having teeth missing. (*bungí*) **matuppolan.** *v.* to lose teeth; break (pencils, saws). [Ivt. *lipang*, Knk. *gib-áw*, Tag. *bungí*]

tuprá: *n.* saliva, spit. (*katay*) **agtupra, tumupra.** *v.* to spit. **ituptupra.** *v.* to reject, refuse. **pagtupraan.** *n.* cuspidor, spittoon. **tupraan.** *v.* to spit on. [Bon. *tobba*, Ibg. *lutag*, Ivt. *cípaq*, Kal. *angiw*, *tuppa*, Knk. *tubpa*, *tékak*, Kpm. *luraq*, Png. *lópda*, Tag. *laway*, *durâ*]

turág: *n.* kind of long, four-angled spear. (*pika*; *gayang*; *dúrus*; *sabat*) **kasla turag.** *a.* extremely skinny.

turángad: *var.* of *tangad*: to look up, raise the head.

turárak: *n.* device of two bamboos in the form of a St. Andrew's cross, used to raise posts, etc; prop for plants. **turarakan.** *v.* to support; prop.

turáy: *n.* rule; political administration; government; sovereignty. **agturay.** *v.* to rule, command, have authority; *n.* ruler, governor, authorities. **iturayan.** *n.* subject, vassal. **ipaturay.** *v.* to do to the utmost; to do thoroughly. **mannakaturay.** *a.* powerful; influential. **naturay.** *a.* authoritative, supreme. **mapaturay.** *v.* to have the authority to do. **paturay.** *v.* to commit to, refer it to; expect. **paturayen.** *v.* to do to one's utmost or worst. **agpannuray.** *v.* to depend on; be at the pleasure of; to await someone's command. **saan a makaturay.** *v.* to be obliged, forced; to be powerless. **pagturayan.** *n.* sovereign nation. **Linadpak ti agngayangay a luak ngem naturay ti iliw.** I blocked the flowing tears, but nostalgia took over. [Png. *oléy*, Tag. *ngasiwà, pangyari*]

turáyok₁: *var.* of *tiray-ok*: urination of men. **agpaturayok.** *v.* to urinate. **ipaturayok.** *v.* to direct the flow of urine (men). **Mapan agpaturayok iti puon iti suli ti paraangan.** He is going to urinate on the tree trunk in the corner of the yard.

turáyok₂: naturayok. *a.* high (*ngato*). [Tag. *taás*]

turbánte: (Sp.) *n.* turban.

turbína: (Sp. *turbina*: turbine) *n.* turbine.

toreadór: (Sp. *toreador*: bullfighter) *n.* bullfighter. (*torero*)

turebbét: *var.* of *tur-ing*: having a large protruding buttocks.

turéd: *n.* courage; bravery. **itured.** *v.* to endure, suffer, patiently; stand, bear with patience; have courage for. **natured.** *a.* bold, daring, courageous, valiant, brave, fearless; audacious. **kinatured.** *n.* courage, bravery. **turdan.** *v.* to endure, withstand. **itured.** *v.* to endure, bear, put up with; tolerate; dare, venture. **maitured.** *v.* to be able to do out of courage; to be able to endure, suffer, bear. **paturden.** *v.* to make brave; encourage; strengthen. **tured-sipit.** *a.* cowardly. **Adda metten sumagmamano a medaliak a mangipaneknek iti kinaturedko iti pagbabakalan.** I also have a few medals testifying to my courage in battle. **Naturtured ti tumaray ngem ti sumango ken patay.** It is braver to run than to face death. [Bon. *toled*, Ibg. *nagutuq, mangiyyangngoq*, Itg. *tuled*, Ivt. *angdet*, Kal. *lateÿud*, Knk. *sengé, tepé, pot-ó*, Png. *belér, makpél, sibeg*, Kpm., Tag. *tapang*]

turék: *var.* of *turík:* spot; freckle. **turekturekan.** *a.* spotted; freckled.

toréro: (Sp. *torero:* bullfighter) *n.* bullfighter. (*toreador*)

toréte: (Sp. *torete:* bullock) *n.* young bull.

toriadór: (Sp. *toreador:* bullfighter) *n.* bullfighter. (*toreador*)

turík₁: *n.* freckle (*pekas*); spots (*batek; tudek*). **turikan, turikturikan.** *a.* freckled; spotted; dotted. [Tag. *batík*]

turík₂: *n.* variety of rice.

túring₁: turingturing. *n.* the *gumabbék* fish when it is still living in the sea, with half an inch diameter.

túring₂: agturingturing. *v.* to have a plant disease characterized by leaves growing smaller than usual.

tur-íng: *n.* person with a large protruding buttocks.

turíri: see *buríri:* with protruding buttocks. (*turirit*)

turírit: *n.* walking with protruding buttocks; with large buttocks. **agturirit.** *v.* to walk with protruding buttocks.

turís: *n.* diarrhea; watery bowels. (*buris*) **agturis.** *v.* to have diarrhea.

turísmo: (Sp. *turismo:* tourism) *n.* tourism.

turísta: (Sp. *turista:* tourist) *n.* tourist.

turitrít: *var.* of *turirit:* protrude the buttocks.

turkák: *n.* phlegm, spit. (*tupra, sarkak*) **agturkak.** *v.* to spit phlegm. [Tag. *kalaghalâ*]

turkésa: (Sp. *turquesa:* turquoise) *n.* turquoise.

túrko: (Sp. *turco:* Turk) *n. a.* Turk; *n.* Turkish language. **kabesa turko.** *n.* variety of edible flower.

torménto: (Sp.) *n.* torment; affliction.

tornabiáhe: (Sp. *tornaviaje:* round-trip, *obs.*) *n.* round trip voyage, return trip.

tornasól: (Sp. *tornasol:* sunflower; litmus) *n.* litmus paper.

tornéo: (Sp. *torneo:* tournament) *n.* tournament.

tornéro: (Sp.) *n.* turner, latheman.

tornílio: (Sp. *tornillo:* screw; bolt) *n.* screw; bolt. **itornilio.** *v.* to screw. **pagtornilioan.** *n.* hole for a screw.

tórno₁: (Sp. *torno:* lathe) *n.* lathe (machine). **agtorno.** *v.* to operate a lathe; use a lathe when shaping something.

tórno₂: (Sp. *turno:* turn) *n.* work shift; alternating turn. **tornuen.** *v.* to make something round. **tinnorno.** *a.* by turns, alternating.

tóro: (Sp. *toro:* bull) *n.* bull; stud. (*bulóg; kalantangán*)

túro: *n.* lye; shampoo made from water poured over burnt rice straw. **agturo.** *v.* to shampoo (*gulgol, ureb*). [Tag. *gugò*]

túrod: *n.* hill. **naturod.** *a.* hilly. **munturod.** *n.* bump; protuberance. **Diak malipatan daydi nadara ngem naballigian a bakal idiay turod ti Kasamata.** I can't forget that bloody but victorious battle on Kasamata Hill. [Knk. *pulíli, wílig, wítig*, Png. *pugaro*, Tag. *buról*]

túrog: *n.* sleep. **maturog.** *v.* to sleep; coagulate. **makaturog.** *v.* to be able to sleep; to coagulate. **makapaturog.** *n.* something that causes someone to sleep, sleeping pill. **makiturog, katurog.** *v.* to sleep with (someone) **mannaturog.** *n.* good sleeper. **agpaturog.** *v.* to put to sleep, order someone to sleep. **paturogan.** *v.* to put someone to sleep; *n.* sleeping quarters; bed. **pagpaturog.** *n.* sleeping pill; that which induces one to sleep. **pannaturog.** *n.* manner of sleeping, time of sleeping. **maturogan.** *v.* to fall asleep while on watch. **tuturogan.** *n.* the desire to sleep. **Awan ti tuturogak.** I cannot sleep, have no desire to sleep. [Bon. *séyep*, Ibg. *turug*, Ivt. *kayceh, iceh*, Knk. *súyup, séyep, dayaét, engék*, Kpm. *tudtud*, Png. *ogíp*, Tag. *tulog*]

tur-óg: *n.* sleepyhead; lazy person who continually sleeps. (*mannurog, mannaturog*)

torokoták: agtorokotok. *v.* to coo (pigeons).

turón: (Sp. *turrón:* fritter) *n.* banana fritter, banana wrapped in a pastry wrapper then fried.

turóng: *n.* direction. **agturong.** *v.* to go toward a place; lead to. **iturong.** *v.* to guide, lead, direct. (*bagnos*) **ipaturong.** *v.* to point at (a gun); direct the flow of water. **mangiturong.** *n.* leader; director; master of ceremonies. **paturongan.** *v.* to point a gun at (*pasarangan*). **Awan ti turongen ti panagsasaritatayo.** Our discussion is not leading anywhere. **Naiturong amin a mata kenkuana.** All eyes were directed at him. [Kal. *suyop*, Png. *pasen*, Tag. *gawî*]

tururút: *n.* sound of the trumpet; trumpet. **agtururut.** *v.* to make this sound.

turútor: (*obs.*) **maturturutor.** *v.* to decrease slowly; to be slowed down. [Tag. *harurot*]

turútot₁: *a.* loquacious, talkative (*tarabitab*). [Tag. *daldál*]

turútot₂: *n.* (*coll.*) *n.* prostitute (*pampam*). [Tag. *puta*]

turutút: *n.* trumpet, sound of trumpet. (*tang-gúyob*)

tórpe: (Sp. *torpe*: stupid) *a.* stupid; rude (*tabbéd*). [Tag. *gago*]

túrpos: **maturpos.** *v.* to finish, end, conclude; achieve. **turposen.** *v.* to finish. **agturpos.** *v.* to graduate; end. **panagturpos.** *n.* graduation; commencement ceremony. **Katurturposna ti kinamaestra.** He has just finished his teaching degree. [Tag. *tapós*]

tórre: (Sp. *torre*: tower) *n.* tower; steeple.

túrsi: (Sp. *torcer*: twist, wrench) *n.* finger wrestling. **agtursi.** *v.* to finger wrestle; twist. **tursien.** *v.* to twist; wring out. **tursido.** *a.* twisted; crooked. **Awan ti makadaer ken-kuana iti sanggol ken tursi.** Nobody can beat him in arm wrestling or finger wrestling. [Arm wrestling = *sanggól*; Knk. *tulsí*, Tag. *sumpíng*]

torsiádo: *n.* third string of the banjo.

tursír: *var.* of *sursir*: mend clothes.

tórta: (Sp. *torta*: cake) *n.* dish made with eggs and meat, or eggs and eggplant.

tortília: (Sp. *tortilla*: omelet) *n.* small omelet.

turtób: *n.* kind of painful spasm of the chest; cramp.

turtóg: see *turtób*: kind of chest spasm.

tortúga: (Sp. *tortuga*: tortoise) *n.* tortoise. (*pag-ong*)

turtór: **maturtoran.** *v.* to be overworked, kept on the go. **turtoran.** *v.* to overload someone with work; to torment.

tosíno: (Sp. *tocino*: bacon) *n.* salted pork lard; bacon.

túso: *n.* rascal; daredevil.

tosperína: (Sp. *toz ferina*: whooping cough) *n.* whooping cough.

tostádo: (Sp. *tostado*: toasted) *a.* toasted, roasted. **tostaduen.** *v.* to toast, roast. [Kal. *chemchem*]

tustús: *n.* crust of rice that sticks to the bottom of the pot. (*ittip*) **natustusen** (*ti trabaho*). *a.* overworked.

tutáit: *n.* kind of small dragonfly.

totál: (Sp. *total*: total) *adv.* after all; anyhow; anyway; *n.* total, sum. **totalen.** *v.* to sum up, total. [Tag. *sa anú't anumán*]

tóto: An interjection used in calling dogs; regional variant of the *ayungín* fish.

tutó: **tutuen.** *v.* to crush, beat, pound.

tútok: **agtutok.** *v.* to aim; point; focus (eyes). **agitutok.** *v.* to point at. **Nakatutok ti imuko iti bakrangna.** The knife was pointed at his back.

tútung: *n.* breast (*suso*)

tutúp: **agtutup.** *v.* to agree; happen at the proper time. **itutup.** *v.* to do according to one's abil-ities; to do accordingly. **maitutup.** *v.* to be suitable, reasonable, proper; do appropriately. **natutup.** *a.* reasonable, fitting, suitable, proper. **tutupan.** *v.* to supply; compensate for; to finally give in after a period of self-restraint (fighting, sex, etc.); to come down to the level of; equal, match. **kaitutupan.** *n.* equivalent. **Amkenna a dina maikkan iti tumutop a sungbat.** He fears that he cannot give the appropriate answer. **Nasken nga ammuen dayta nga arte tapno maitutopka itoy nga ay-ayam.** It is necessary to know that art so you can play this game properly. [Tag. *akmâ*]

tútor: **agtutor.** *v.* to take one's time; be patient; **tutoren.** *v.* to do patiently and calmly. **patutoren.** *v.* to give time for. **makatutor.** *v.* to have time for; to be patient, calm. **Saan a makatuttutor.** He has no patience. **Tutorem amangan no mabegnatka.** Have patience so you don't have a relapse. [Tag. *dahan*]

tútot₁: *n.* resin; oil; sap; pus. **agtutut.** *v.* to secrete sap, pus; to putrefy (corpses). [Kal. *lota*, Tag. *dagtâ*]

tútot₂: *n.* kind of freshwater fish, eight inches long with a flattened body.

tutsáng: (Hok. *tʰaú cang*: pigtail) *n.* erect, spiky hair; bristle.

tutsukaw: *n. Sopubia trifida* plant.

tuttót: *n.* sound of a car horn. **tumanuttot.** *n.* cry of rats, sound of continuous talking. **Agtututtot-da iti nalimed.** They are talking in secret.

tuttotéra: (f. *tuttot*) *n.* gossiper. (said of women) (*tsismósa*)

tuwátit: *n.* kind of small gray bird.

tuwáto: *n.* dragonfly. **agtuwato.** *v.* to seesaw. **timmuwato.** *a.* like a dragonfly. **timmuwato a siket.** slim waist (like a dragonfly). [Bon. *kostíngaw*, Kal. *belliling*, Knk. *papáong*, *tákan*, Kpm. *tuláng*, Tag. *tutubí*]

tuwáw: *n.* kind of small black bird that cries at dusk.

'toy: *art.* abbreviation of *daytoy*: this.

tuyáab: **agtuyaab.** *v.* to gape, open the mouth; open wide (*nganga, tungaab*). **nakatuyaab.** *a.* agape, with the mouth open. [Tag. *tungangà*]

tuyág: **ituyag.** *v.* to pour; lean, incline in order to pour out the contents. **tuyagan.** *v.* to fill up (a glass). [Png. *bundak*, Tag. *buhos*, *salin*]

tuyáng: **ituyang.** *v.* to decree; declare; authorize; manifest, display, exhibit, reveal; prove; express; establish; disclose. **maituyang.** *v.* to be decreed, declared; ordered; imposed. **panangi-tuyang.** *n.* manifestation; institution; introduction, preface. [Tag. *atas*]

túyo₁: *n.* rice bran. [Bon. *óped, tóyo,* Ibg. *sissiq,* Ifg. *upok,* Ivt. *nápes,* Kal. *chug, opok,* Png. *bábang,* Kpm., Tag. *darák*]

túyo₂: (Tag. via Hok. *tau iú*: bean oil) *n.* soy sauce. [Tag. *toyò*]

tuyó: (Tag. *tuyô*: dry) *n.* dried fish (*daing, karing*). **panagtutuyo.** *n.* season for drying fish.

túyod: (*obs.*) **maituyutuyod.** *v.* to be weak; dizzy (*kapsut, kapoy, masdo*)

tuyók: **patuyukan.** *v.* to shift the burden upon another's shoulders.

túyot: *n.* period of drought when harvest is poor. (*kalgaw*)

tuyútoy: **tumuyutoy.** *v.* to pass along endlessly; go one after another; crowd; stampede; *n.* many people. [Tag. *siksík*]

tuytóy: *n.* kind of caster for holding wine, oil, etc. **ituytoy.** *v.* to place into the caster.

trabahadór: (Sp. *trabajador*: worker) *n.* worker. (*mangged*)

trabahadóra: (Sp. *trabajadora*: female worker) *n.* hardworking woman. (*gaget*)

trabáho: (Sp. *trabajo*: work) *n.* work; job; task; position; trade; employment. (*aramid; tegged*) **agtrabaho.** *v.* to work. **itrabaho.** *v.* to have papers approved. **agpatpatrabaho.** *n.* employers; management. **pagtrabahuan.** *n.* place of employment. [Ibg. *ikalángan,* Ifg. *ngunu,* Ivt. *trabahuq, anung, parin,* Kpm. *obra,* Png. *kímey,* Tag. *trabaho*]

trabiésa: (Sp. *traviesa*: cross tie, rafter) *n.* cross tie; sleeper in a railway track.

trabisánio: (Sp. *travesaño*: crossbar) *n.* transom, crosspiece; crossbar.

traduktór: (Sp. *traductor*: translator) *n.* translator.

tradusír: (Sp. *traducir*: translate) **itradusir.** *v.* to translate. (*patarus*)

tráha: *n.* thread of a screw. (*roskas*)

tráhe: (Sp. *traje*: suit) *n.* suit. (clothes) (*térno*) **agtrahe.** *v.* to wear a suit. **trahe de boda.** *n.* wedding gown.

trahédia: (Sp. *tragedia*: tragedy) *n.* tragedy. (*pasamak a nakalkaldaang*)

tráhiko: (Sp. *trágico*: tragic) *a.* tragic.

traidór: (Sp. *traidor*: traitor) *n.* traitor (*mangliliput*). [Tag. *taksíl*]

trak: (Eng.) *n.* bus, truck. **sangatrakan.** *n.* one busload; one truckload.

traktóra: (Sp. *tractor*: tractor) *n.* tractor.

trámbia: (Sp. *tranvía*: streetcar) *n.* kind of cotton cloth; streetcar.

trámo: (Sp. *tramo*: section; flight of stairs; stretch of road) *n.* railroad tracks; elevated dirt road; section of a bridge.

trámpo: (Sp. *trompo*: top) *n.* spinning top (*kampuso, sunay*). [Tag. *trumpo*]

transít: (Eng.) *n.* bus; transit.

trángka: (Sp. *tranca*: bar) *n.* bar used to lock a door. (*balunet*) **trangkaan.** *v.* to bar a door; bolt shut.

trangkáso: (Sp. *trancazo*: flu) *n.* cold; flu (*panateng; sakit*). [Kal. *boglat*]

trapikánte: (Sp. *traficante*: trafficker) *n.* drug trafficker; trader in smuggled goods. (*kontrabandista*)

trápiko: (Sp. *tráfico*: traffic) *n.* traffic. [Tag. *trapik*]

trapítse: (Sp. *trapiche*: sugar mill; olive press) *n.* sugar mill; sugarcane-grinding machine.

trápo: (Sp. *trapo*: rag) *n.* rag. (*nipis, pagpunas*) **agtrapo, trapuan.** *v.* to wipe with a rag.

tratár: (Sp. *tratar*: treat) **agtratar.** *v.* to treat.

tráto₁: (Sp. *trato*: agreement, treaty) *n.* contract; agreement. (*tulag*) **agtrato.** *v.* to make a contract; agree.

tráto₂: (Sp. *trato*: treat) *n.* treatment. **tratuen.** *v.* to treat someone in a certain way.

tréinta: (Sp. *treinta*: thirty) *num.* thirty. (*tallopulo*)

trementína: (Sp.) *n.* turpentine.

trémulo: (Sp. *trémolo*: tremolo) *n.* tremolo, tremor. **agtremulo.** *v.* to tremor, shake (said of a voice).

tren: (Sp. *tren*: train) *n.* train.

tres: (Sp. *tres*: three) *num.* three (*talló*). **Alas tres.** Three o'clock.

tróse: (Sp. *trece*: thirteen) *num.* thirteen (*sangapullo ket tallo*)

tresiéntos: (Sp. *trescientos*: three hundred) *num.* three hundred. (*tallo a gasut*)

tresiéte: *var.* of *entresiete*: game of cards played by several people divided in pairs with the highest cards being the ace (*alas*) and two and three (*politana*).

triánggulo: (Sp. *triángulo*: triangle) *n.* triangle. (*tallo ti sulina*)

tríbu: (Sp. *tribu*: tribe) *n.* tribe. (*kapoonán*)

tribulasión: (Sp. *tribulación*) *n.* tribulation, affliction.

tribúna: (Sp. *tribuna*: tribune; grandstand) *n.* board of judges; tribunal, court; dais; rostrum; grandstand.

tribunál: (Sp. *tribunal*: court) *n.* court; court room. (*pangukoman; pagsaklangan*)

tribusón: (Sp. *tirabuzón*: corkscrew) *n.* corkscrew. (*kulukol*)

tributário: (Sp.) *a.* tributary; *n.* taxpayer.

tríduo: (Sp. *triduano*: three-day, *obs.*) *n.* triduum, three days of prayer.

trígo: (Sp. *trigo*: wheat) *n.* wheat. **katriguan.** *n.* wheat field.

trigonometría: (Sp. *trigonometría*: trigonometry) *n.* trigonometry.

triliadóra: (Sp. *trilldora*: thresher) *n.* thresher.

triméstre: (Sp.) *n.* trimester.

trinidád: (Sp. *trinidad*: trinity) *n.* trinity.

trínsera: (Sp. *trinchera*: trench) *n.* trench; ditch. **agtrinsera.** *v.* to dig a trench. **matrinseraan.** *v.* to be entrenched.

tríntas: (Sp. *trenzas*: braid) *n.* pigtail; braid. (*tirintas*)

trío: (Sp. *trío*: trio) *n.* trio, group of three.

tripília: (Sp. *tripilla*: tripe) *n.* chicken innards. (*silet*)

tríple: (Sp.) *a.* triple. **triple kuatro.** three times four.

triplikádo: (Sp. *triplicado*: triplicate) *a.* triplicate.

tripulánte: (Sp. *tripulante*: crew) *n.* crew (of a ship, plane, etc.).

trisáhio: (Sp. *trisagio*) *n.* trisagion.

trubináis: (f. brand name) *n.* formal polo shirt with a stiff collar.

tróle: (Sp. *trole*: trolley) *n.* trolley.

trombón: (Sp.) *n.* trombone.

trúmpa: *n.* bell-shaped opening of wind instruments; *var.* of *trompeta*: *n.* trumpet (*trumpéta, tanggúyob, turorót*)

trompélo: *n.* kind of swirling firecracker.

trompéta: (Sp. *trompeta*: trumpet) *n.* trumpet. (*tanggúyob, turorót*)

trúmpo: *n.* spinning top. (*kampuso*)

tróno: (Sp. *trono*: throne) *n.* throne. **agpatrono.** *v.* to go to the throne.

trópa: (Sp. *tropa*: troop) *n.* troop. (*búyot ti soldádo*)

tropéo: (Sp. *trofeo*: trophy) *n.* trophy. (*tanda ti panagballigi*)

trópiko: (Sp. *trópico*) *n.* *a.* tropic. **pagtropikuan.** *n.* the tropics, tropical regions of the earth.

tróso: (Sp. *trozo*: log) *n.* log. **agtroso.** *v.* to cut trees into logs; go logging. **panagtroso.** *n.* logging.

tróte: (Sp. *trote*: trot) *n.* trot. (*buabo*) **agtrote.** *v.* to trot.

tsá, tsaá: (Ch.) *n.* tea. (*itsá*) **tsa ti bakir.** medicinal infused herbs used to treat diarrhea and upset stomachs.

tsakéta: (Sp. *chaqueta*: jacket) *n.* jacket. (*amerikána, sáko*)

tsaketília: (Sp. *chaquetilla*: short jacket) *n.* tuxedo.

tsaléko: (Sp. *chaleco*: vest) *n.* vest; sleeveless pullover.

tsalét: (Eng.) *n.* chalet. **agpatsalet.** *v.* to go to the chalet.

tsalmalukong: *n.* *Scaevola frutescens* plant growing chiefly along the seashore.

tsámba: *var.* of *tiamba*: fluke, luck, chance.

tsámbra: (Sp. *chambra*: blouse) *n.* old-fashioned blouse with long, wide sleeves.

tsampáka: *n.* *Michelia champaca* tree with fragrant flowers and white sapwood.

tsamporádo: (Sp. *champurrado*: chocolate gruel) *n.* chocolate gruel; adulterated coffee; mixture of gold and silver. **agtsamporado.** *v.* to make chocolate gruel.

tsampóy: (Tagalog also) *n.* bayberry, Chinese strawberry.

tsáni: *var.* of *tiani*: tweezers, pliers. [Ivt. *susupit*]

tsanggí: tsumanggi. *v.* to abruptly turn the head to the shoulder expressing sarcasm. (*tianggi*)

tsápa: (Sp. *chapa*: badge) *n.* metal badge (of a police officer, etc.)

tsaperón: (Eng.) *n.* chaperone. **agtsaperon.** *v.* to chaperone someone; to have a chaperone.

tsapsóy: (Eng.) *n.* chop suey, sautéed vegetables with meat.

tsaról: (Sp. *charol*: patent leather) *n.* patent leather.

tsásis: (Eng.) *n.* chassis (of an auto).

tsásko: (Sp. *chasco*: joke; trick) *n.* failure; disappointment.

tsáta: (Sp. *chata*: flat) *a.* flat, flattened. **arinolatsata.** *n.* flat metal bedpan.

tsedéng: (Pil., *slang*) *n.* Mercedez Benz.

tséke: (Sp. *cheque*: check) *n.* bank check.

tserimúyas: (Sp. *chirimoya*) *n.* cherimoya.

tsésa: *var.* spelling of *tiesa*: kind of yellow fruit with a brown seed; carristel.

tsétse burétse: (Pil. *tsetse baletse*) *n.* miscellaneous things.

tsibóg: (Pil., *slang*) *n.* eating; food. (*kaan*)

tsíka: (Sp. *chica*: girl) *n.* term of address for a close female friend. **agtsika-tsika.** (*coll.*) *v.* to gossip among females.

tsikíto: (Sp. *chiquito*: little boy) *n.* darling (said to a young boy).

tsíko[1]: *n.* kind of sweet tropical fruit; the tree bearing this fruit, sapodilla fruit. **agattsiko.** *v.* to have alcohol breath (*lit* to smell like sapodilla fruit).

tsíko[2]: (Sp. *chico*: boy) *n.* term of address for a close male friend.

tsimenéa: (Sp. *chimenea*: chimney) *n.* chimney; funnel of a ship.

Tsína: (Sp. *china*: China) *n.* China.

tsinélas: (Sp. *chinela*: slipper) *n.* slipper. (*singklétas*) **agtsinelas.** *v.* to wear slippers. **tsinelasen.** *v.* to beat with a slipper.

Tsiníta: (Sp. *chinita*: Chinese girl) *n*. Chinese girl; *a*. slit-eyed (*kusipet*).

Tsiníto: (Sp. *chinito*: Chinese boy) *n*. Chinese boy.

tsipipáy: (*coll*.) *n*. immodest, cheap girl; whore.

tsipón: (Eng.) *n*. chiffon fabric.

tsísmis: (Sp. *chisme*: gossip) *n*. gossip. (*busatsat*) **agtsismis.** *v*. to gossip; blab.

tsismóso: (Sp. *chismoso*: gossipy) *a*. gossipy. (*fem: tsismosa*) (*tarabitab*)

tsítsaro: (Sp. *chícharo*: pea) *n*. pea (*sitsaro*). [Tag. *sitsaró*]

tsitsarón: (Sp. *chicharrón*: pork rind) *n*. crispy, fried pork rind. [Tag. *sitsarón*]

tsitsiriá: (Pil., f. *tsitsaron*) *n*. crunchy snacks; junk food. [Tag. *sitsiriá*]

tsúgi: (Pil., slang) **matsugi.** *v*. to end; be killed, destroyed.

tsóke: (Sp. *choque*: crash) *n*. crash, collision; clash; conflict.

tsokoláte: (Sp. *chocolate*: chocolate) *n*. chocolate; cocoa. **agtsokolate.** *v*. to make chocolate; to have chocolate.

tsúletas: (Sp. *chuleta*: chop of meat) *n*. slice, cutlet; pork chop.

tsónga: (*slang*) derogative term applied to Chinese.

tsónggo: *n*. monkey (*bakes, sunggo*). [Png. *chónggo, bakés*, Tag. *tsunggo, unggóy*]

tsóngki: (*slang*) *n*. marijuana.

tsúper: (Sp. *chófer*: driver) *n*. chauffeur; driver. (*maneho*)

tsupéra: (Sp. *chupera*) *n*. pacifier.

tsupón: (Sp. *chupón*: nipple, sucker) *n*. nipple of a bottle; pacifier (for suckling).

tsoríso: (Sp. *chorizo*: sausage) *n*. spiced pork sausage.

W

wa: *var*. of *wen*: yes, yeah.

Wa!: *interj*. an interjection used in frightening a person; cry of an infant.

wab: *n*. yawn; yawning. **agwab**. *v*. to yawn (*suyáab*; *uwab*). [Ibg. *awwág*, Knk., Png. *oáb*, Tag. *higáb*, *hikáb*]

wabwáb: *a*. gaping (holes, wounds). **mawabwaban**. *a*. to be inflicted with a gaping hole (bombed earth, etc.) **wabwában**. *v*. to create a gaping hole into. [Tag. *ngangà*]

wad: **pagwadán**. *n*. example, model, pattern, prototype. **waden**. *v*. to copy, imitate; follow.

wadá₁: **nawada**. *a*. clear; open (spaces); distinct; plain; lucid; clearly visible; happy faced. **agpakawada**. *v*. to share by dividing in portions. **wadaan**. *v*. to clear a path in the forest; initiate negotiation; make a head start. **Limmas-ud iti nawada a tanap nga awanan balay wenno ruot.** He entered the wide plain that had no houses or grass. [Tag. *liwanag*]

wadá₂: *var*. of *adda* in some districts.

wádag: **agwadag**. *v*. to swing the arm backward. **wadagen**. *v*. to throw forcibly away, fling, cast off, also said of habits. **iwadag**. *v*. to fling or throw aside (an object), **agwadagwadag**. *v*. to shake off a grip. **No koma nasursurom nga iwadag ti mangidurduron kenka.** If only you learn how to cast off those who push you. [Tag. *tabig*]

wadán: *n*. rule; system; standard. **pagwadan**. *n*. pattern; model; example.

wadáwad: **iwadawad**. *v*. to strike right and left with the arm. **agwadawad**. *v*. to fling the arms left and right. [Tag. *palág*]

wadwád: **nawadwad**. *a*. much, many, abundant, plentiful; exuberant, profuse, lavish, ample. (*ruay*, *adu*) **agwadwad**. *v*. to grow in number. [Tag. *dami*]

wáeng: *a*. crazy, insane (*bagtit*, *balla*). [Tag. *ulól*]

waepék: (Pil, slang, from *waláng epékto*) *a*. with no effect, no use. **Pordios, waepek ti gimikko.** God, my gimmick had no effect (is of no use).

wágas: *n*. method, air, style, manner, look, appearance; attitude, demeanor; style; fashion. (*pamuspusan*) **wagas ti biag**. *n*. way of life (*pagbibiagan*). [Png. *pangawa*, Tag. *paraán*]

wágat: **maiwagat**. *v*. to be misplaced or mislaid. **iwagat**. *v*. to misplace; forget bad memories; drop bad habits. **Simmangpet ti pul-oy a nangiwagat iti agongna iti arak.** The breeze arrived that got rid of the smell of wine. [Tag. *walâ*]

wagaywáy: *n*. flag; banner; streamer. (*bandera*) **iwagayway**. *v*. to sway as a flag. [Png. *layláy*, Tag. *watawat*, Tag. *wagaywáy* = wave, flutter]

wáging: *n*. kind of small cart.

wágis: **agwagwagis**. *v*. to wave; to be noticed by someone. **wagisan**. *v*. to wave to someone, signal someone with the hand. **kasla kandidato iti kawagiswagisna**. *exp*. used to denote sycophancy (waving like a politician). **Nakiwinnagisen kadagiti kapurokanna.** He waved to his fellow villagers (and they waived back).

wagnés: (*obs*.) **wagnesen**. *v*. to leave a track through a paddy. **iwagnes**. *v*. to shake off an object by prancing.

wagnét: **nawagnet**. *a*. rough, blunt, brusque; rugged, rude; brutal, ferocious; savage (*sabrak*; *rasaw*). [Tag. *bastós*]

wagsák: **agiwagsak**. *v*. to shake (a cloth) holding it by two corners. **maiwagsak**. *v*. to be forgotten; to be shaken off. [Tag. *wagwág*]

wagsít: **iwagsit**. *v*. to shake off violently with the hand. [Tag. *wagwág*]

wagténg: **agwagteng**. *v*. to prance and flail. **iwagteng**. *v*. to shake off (someone's grasp, etc.) (*wagnét*) **Mabayagto metten a wagtewagtengannak.** He took a long while to shake off my grasp. [Tag. *palág*]

wagtít: *var*. of *wagténg*: to shake loose; shake off one's grip.

wagwág₁: *n*. variety of awned early rice with light-colored hull, few awns, and white kernel.

wagwág₂: **agwagwag**. *v*. to shake. **wagwagen**. *v*. to shake, make tremble. **mangwagwag**. *v*. to exercise the cramps away. **mawagwag**. *v*. to fade (colors); to be shaken. **Pinanakraadna a winagwawagwag.** He whipped it shaking. [Png. *pagpág*, Tag. *wagwág*]

wáig: *n*. small stream, brook, creek. **agpawaig**. *v*. to go to the creek. [Bon. *wáil*, Kal. *wain*, *ewagit*, *suÿong*, Knk. *ketáng*, *síngi*, *wengwéng*, Png. *kulós*, Tag. *sapà*]

wáis: **nawais**. *a*. free, open, clear (paths); unobstructed.

wak: *n*. crow; variety of awned *diket* rice with very dark hull. **no pumuraw ti wak**. *exp*. when the crow turns white, (*fig*.) never, no hope. **digos ti wak**. *n*. crow's bath (referring to a sloppy bath, bath wetting only the head). [Ibg., Knk. *gayang*, Kpm. *wak*, Png. *wawak*, Ivt., Tag. *uwák*]

wákas: **mangwakas**. *v*. to clear up (weather), free or disengage oneself (from debts, obligations, incertitude, etc.); settle a debt. [Tag. *liwanag*]

wakás: **iwakas, wakasen**. *v*. to get rid of, free oneself of; settle a debt or obligation; complete a task, finish work. **Parbangonto ngatan no makaiwakaskami.** It will probably be dawn already when we are done working. [Tag. *tapós*]

wákat: agwakatwakat. *v.* to sway, move back and forth; wiggle. [Tag. *ugà*]

wakáwak: **wakawakan**. *v.* to dust, powder; spray fertilizer; spray salt. (*warakiwak*) **iwakawak**. *v.* to sprinkle dust or powder on something. [Tag. *wakawak* = falling into disrepute]

wakdár: *var.* of *waknar*: spread out to dry.

wakírat: **wakwakirat**. *n.* gossiper; tattler.

wakíwak: **wakiwakan**. *v.* to sprinkle on; spread on. (*warakiwak*)

waklít: **iwaklit**. *v.* to shake off one's grasp; to move hair out of one's face; move out of the way; lower arm out of the way.

waknáng: see *watnag*: scatter; disperse; break apart.

waknár: **iwaknar**. *v.* to spread out (in order to dry).

waknís: **waknisan**. *v.* to clear, open for passage, lay bare, uncover. **mawaknisan**. *v.* to clear up (weather). **mangwaknis**. *v.* to clear up, become fair (weather), to free oneself from doubt. [Tag. *hawì*]

waknít: **mawaknitan**. *v.* to clear up (stormy weather, gloomy face) **waknitan**. *v.* to clear of obstructions; make way. **Nagwaknit ti nakuyem a lubong kaniak.** My gloomy world cleared up. [Tag. *liwanag*]

wakrá: see *wara*: scatter.

wakrás: **wakrasen**. *v.* to clear, open up; lay bare. (*waknis*)

wakrát: **mawakrat**. *v.* to be torn apart; to be bankrupt.

wakráy: *n.* loose, disheveled hair; variety of awned rice with light-colored hull and white kernel. **wakrayen**. *v.* to loosen; unbind; undo; dishevel. **agwakray**. *v.* to let the hair hang down. **Agkaiwara dagiti bilog, agsasarum-binit dagiti nakawakray nga iket ken tabukol.** The outriggers are scattered and the loose nets are strewn all over. [Tag. *lugáy*]

waksí: **iwaksi**. *v.* to shake (off); rid oneself of; reject, discard. **mangwaksi**. *v.* to remove the sign of mourning. **agwaksi**. *v.* to stop mourning (in dress). **maiwaksi**. *v.* to be forgotten. **pannakaiwaksi**. *n.* removal; abolition. **Inwaksina iti isipna dagita a napanunotna.** He cleared out of his mind those thoughts. [Png. *wagsil*, Tag. *waksí*]

wakwák: *n.* lateral appendages of the stem (leaves, etc.); crust, slough (of smallpox); quacking sound of a duck. **mawakwak**. *v.* to be injured with a gaping wound. **iwakwak**. *v.* to open wide (window). **agwakwak**. *v.* to quack (ducks). [Tag. *wakwák* = laceration, large tear]

walagwág₁: walagwagen. *v.* to dry clothes on a clothesline.

walagwág₂: walagwagen. *v.* to shake off; clean or dry by shaking. (*sariwagwag*)

wálang₁: *a.* loose, astray; without covering; *n.* loafer; vagabond. **iwalang**. *v.* to lay down something anywhere; abandon, desert; (*coll.*) to kill, salvage. **naiwalang**. *a.* deserted, forsaken, abandoned; killed. **agwalang**. *v.* to be vagrant; nomadic; wayward; capricious; wander. **walangwalang**. *a.* wandering. **Agkaraiwalang dagiti bangkay kadagiti karayan a pagipi-piestaan dagiti buaya.** The corpses on which the crocodiles feasted were strewn all over the rivers. [Tag. *iláp, laboy*]

wálang₂: (*reg.*) *n.* sign, token; indication.

wálat: nawalat. *a.* big; large (animals, smiles, etc.); long-limbed. **Nagwawalat ti askawna a simrek.** He took long strides as he entered.

waláwal: *n.* a dibble, instrument used to make holes in the ground. **iwalawal**. *v.* to dibble a hole in the ground (*sudsod*). [Kal. *saÿuwan*]

wálay: *n.* homeless wanderer (*ballog*). [Tag. *walay* = wean; separate]

waldás: (Tag., *coll.*) *n.* spendthrift, one who wastes or squanders money. (*gastador*)

wáli: agwali. *v.* to wobble. **agwaliwali**. *v.* to be loose and wobble (teeth, screws, etc.). **wali-walien**. *v.* to loosen (*luali*). **Kasla agwaliwali a darekdek ti pannagnana.** He walks like a wobbling stake. [Tag. *hapayhapay, ugà*]

wálin: *adv.* on the side. **iwalin**. *v.* to put aside, put out of the way; get rid of; free oneself from. **walinwalin**. *n.* a kind of small, edible marine fish. [Tag. *tabig*]

wáling: walingwaling. *n.* type of wild orchid. [Tag. *walingwaling*]

walís: (Tag.) *n.* dust broom (*buybuy*). **walistambo**. *n.* broom made out of reeds.

wallagés: iwallages. *v.* to throw down, throw to the side. **wallagesen** (*obs.*) *v.* to strike with the back of the hand. [Tag. *hagis*]

walnís: walnisan. *n.* artificial shade.

wálo: *n.* a kind of plant whose leaves are used to refresh the head.

waló: *num.* eight. (*otso* (Sp.)) **maikawalo**. *num.* eighth. **sagwawalo**. *a.* eight each. **maminwalo**. *a.* eight times. **walopulo**. *num.* eighty. [Kal. *waÿu*, Knk. *waó*, Png., Tag. *waló*]

walopúlo: *num.* eighty. (*otsenta* (Sp.))

wammét: Contraction of *awan met*: there is none; he is not here. [Tag. *walâ namán*]

wampáy: Contraction of *awan pay*: there isn't any more; he/she/it is no longer here. [Tag. *walâ pa*]

wanág: **agwanag**. *v.* to clear (a yard); be clear. **nawanag**. *a.* clear, open; distinct, plain, lucid, readily perceptible. [Tag. *liwanag*]

wanán: see *awanan*: tie beam used in construction.

wánar: (*obs.*) **iwanar**. *v.* to keep ready.

wánas: **wanasen**. *v.* to do from the beginning to end. **mawanas**. *v.* to finish doing something from the beginning to the end. [Tag. *simulâ*]

wanáwan: *n.* guard. (*bantay*) **agwanawan**. *v.* to spot lost animals from a high place; be on the lookout; look out for. **wanawanan**. *v.* to look at something from a high place; to watch, focus one's attention on; look out for (an unexpected visitor, etc.). [Tag. *bantáy*]

wanengwéng: *n.* buzzing sound; sound of a police siren. **wumanengweng**. *v.* to make a buzzing sound (breeze, airplane, etc.).

wanér: **nawaner**. long (expanses of land).

wanerwér: *n.* sound of a chainsaw or sewing machine; sound of flapping wings. **agwanerwer**. *v.* to make the sound of a sewing machine or flapping wings. [Tag. *pagaspás* (flapping wings)]

wanés: *n.* track, trail, path (through grass); direction of wind. **mawanesan**. *v.* to be along the path of (a storm, etc.). [Tag. *daán*]

waneswés: *n.* noise of windy leaves. **agwaneswes**. *v.* to make the sound of rustling leaves.

wanét: *n.* carabao leash, rope used to guide or pull the water buffalo; stretch of road; footpath.

wánit: **iwanit**. *v.* to open (doors, windows), remove the shutters. **wanitan**. *v.* to open; clear; be empty; free, rid.

wanwán: **iwanwan**. *v.* to instruct, teach (*suroan*); lead, guide (*bagnos*).

wangáwang: *a.* open. **wangawángan**. *n.* mouth of a river; orifice of the stomach; *v.* to open wide; clear a wide opening. **wangawangan ti patay**. the gate of death. [Tag. *bukás*]

wángay: **wangayen**. *v.* to designate (for duty, etc.); name. (*dutok*)

wanggín: *n.* a kind of glazed earthenware Chinese jar.

wangíl: **agwangilwangil**. *v.* to wobble; shake back and forth.

wang-íl: **agwang-il**. *v.* to shake one's head (said of animals to drive away flies, etc.). (*wang-it*)

wang-ít: **agwang-it**. *v.* to sway with the wind; butt sideways (with horns). **Nagwang-it ti nuang a kinagiddan ti panangyaplitna iti ipusna**. The water buffalo butted his horns as he whipped his tail. [Tag. *suwág*]

wangngá: **agwangnga**. *v.* to waddle, walk while swinging the hips and swaying the arms. (*kinnikinni*)

wangwáng: *n.* abyss; chasm; gulf. **mawangwangan**. *v.* to be dug up; breached wide open. **maiwangwang**. *v.* to be lost at sea; to be wide open.

wapwáp: *var.* of *wabwab*: gaping (hole).

wará: **nawara**. *a.* messy; scattered. **iwara**. *v.* to scatter, throw about; spread; sprinkle. **waraen**. *v.* to scatter; dismantle, take apart; loosen; untie. **nawarawara**. *a.* disheveled (hair); fallen into disorder. **agwara**. *v.* to spread out; break up (a crowd); disintegrate; become commonplace (news); exude. **agkaiwara**. *v.* to be scattered, strewn. [Png. *sibwag*, Tag. *sabog*]

waradíwad: see *wadawad*: fling or strike with the arms. **maradiwadan**. *v.* to be hit by a person's swinging arms. [Tag. *kawág*]

waragáwag: see *warragawag*: announce, inform; disseminate; divulge. [Tag. *pahayag*]

waragíwag: **agwaragiwag**. *v.* to shake the body (animals).

waragíwig: **agwaragiwig**. *v.* to shake oneself. (*paragipig, tigerger*)

waráis: **iwarais**. *v.* to scatter, strew.

waraíwi: *var.* of *waraiwis*: scatter; sprinkle.

waraíwis: *var.* of *warais*: scatter, strew.

warakáwak: *var.* of *warakiwak*. (*wakawak*)

warakíwak: **iwarakiwak**. *v.* to scatter; strew; spread; sprinkle. **warakiwakan**. *v.* to scatter on, sprinkle on. [Tag. *kalat*]

warakíwik: *var.* of *warakíwak*: sprinkle, scatter.

warakwák: **nawarakwak**. *a.* spongy, porous; elastic.

wárang: **naiwarang**. *a.* disregarded, neglected, abandoned (*panaw, bay-a*). **iwarang**. *v.* to abandon; neglect. **Warangwarang latta kadin dagiti kakastoy nga ubbing?** Do you think these children are just abandoned? [Tag. *pabayaan*]

wáras: **iwaras**. *v.* to distribute; deal out, allot, apportion; to cast the eyes around; to give thought to (one's conduct); to fly from one subject to another. **iwaraswaras**. *v.* to scatter, cast here and there, throw about (*wara*). **iwaras ti panagkita**. *v.* to look around. **makawaras**. *v.* to be sufficient; enough. **agwaras**. *v.* to spread out; permeate; diffuse (*salnap, ramram*). **nawarasan**. *a.* distributed; provided with. **warasan**. *v.* to distribute to everyone around.

warasíwas: see *warasiwis*: sprinkle, scatter.

warasíwis: **iwarasiwis**. *v.* to sprinkle, scatter. **warasiwisan**. *v.* to spray; sprinkle on. [Tag. *wilíg*]

warát: *var.* of *wakrat*: torn apart; bankrupt.

waráwar: *var.* of *warwar*: unfasten; untangle; undo.

Waraywaráy: *n.* Ethnic group of Samar and Leyte Islands; their language.

wardás: **agiwardas, iwardas.** *v.* to teach, instruct, give lessons in; explain, make known, inform of. [Tag. *paliwanag, surò*]

wardí: **agwardiwardi.** *v.* to move in all directions. **wardiwardi.** *a.* haphazardly done.

wáris: **agwaris.** *v.* to sprinkle, scatter liquids over in small drops; sow seeds (rice). **iwaris.** *v.* to scatter, strew. **pagwaris.** *n.* sprinkler. **warisan.** *v.* to sprinkle on, scatter on; throw rice at newlyweds. **Kasla uong dagiti kalapaw a naiwaris iti bantay.** The huts are scattered in the mountain like mushrooms. [Tag. *wilíg, sabog*]

waríwad: (*obs.*) see *ukarkar*: unwrap; uncoil; open.

warnák: **iwarnak.** *v.* to publish, bring before the public. **agi(war)warnak.** *n.* newspaperman, reporter. **agsiwarnak.** *v.* to publish the news. **pagiwarnak.** *n.* newspaper, magazine (*warnakan*). **warnakan.** *n.* media. **aginaldaw a pagiwarnak.** *n.* daily paper. [Png. *nigalot*, Tag. *lathalà, limbág, pahayag*]

warragáwag: *n.* announcement. **iwarragawag.** *v.* to disseminate; divulge; publish; proclaim; promulgate; announce; inform. **maiwarragawag.** *v.* to spread (news), to be made more known (rumors, news, etc.). **parawarragawag.** *n.* announcer. **Alas dos ti parbangon idi maiwarragawag ti nangabak.** The winner was announced at 2:00 AM.

warsí: **agwarsi.** *v.* to sprinkle with water; shake off water. **iwarsi.** *v.* to shake off, throw off; rid oneself of. **warsian.** *v.* to sprinkle clothes with water before ironing. **Apagwarsik ti buggok, napanko intuloy ti ar-araduek.** As soon as I shook off the water from my hands, I went to continue plowing. [Knk. *walsí*, Tag. *wisík*]

warwár: *a.* loose. **warwaren.** *v.* to unfold; spread out, lay out; unwrap, unbind; expand, extend; unfasten, untie; take apart, disassemble; dismount; untie animals (to be grazed). **ma-warwar.** *a.* unraveled, disentangled, unbound, unpacked, undone, untwisted, unfastened. [Png. *buskag*, Tag. *kalág*; *ladlád* (unfold)]

warwáriko: (*coll.*) *n.* lousy mechanic, one who knows how to disassemble, but cannot put things back together.

was: *n. Mallotus philippensis.* A euphorbiaceous tree with large, oblong-ovate leaves and capsules covered with a red powder. **ma-was.** *v.* to renounce; relinquish; withdraw from; take back, retract; give up; disavow; (*obs.*) forget.

wasen. *v.* to disavow; relinquish. **was nga puraw.** *n. Harpullia sp.* tree. **Na-was ti suyaabna.** He withdrew his yawn. [Tag. *urong*]

wasák: **agwasakwasak.** *v.* to speak extravagantly and out of order with no constraint; intrude; trespass (*basak*). [Tag. *wasak* = destroy]

wásang: **agwasangwasang.** *v.* to squirm, writhe, wriggle, contort oneself. **Agam-ammangaw ken wasang a wasang.** He is delirious and continually squirming. **Tunggal maisagid ti tali iti ulona, agwasang ket yablatna ti ipusna.** Each time the rope hits his head, he squirms and whips his tail. [Tag. *pilipit*]

wasáwas: *n.* movement of an attached object. **iwasawas.** *v.* to strike left and right; to shake, drag, pull to and fro; to cast a net; to whirl around; wave (a flag). **agwaswasawas.** *v.* to make derogatory remarks. **Nagkayang a nangiwasawas iti atiddog ti tengngedna a botelia.** He shook the long neck of the bottle back and forth while straddling. [Tag. *wasiwas*]

wásay₁: *n.* ax. **wasayen.** *v.* to ax something or someone (*balsíg*). [Ivt. *vavada*, Kal., Knk. *wásay*, Png. *wasay, palaksaw*, Tag. *palakól, palatháw, putháw*]

wásay₂: **wasaywasay.** *n.* praying mantis. **Kasla agassawa a wasaywasay.** *exp.* like a praying mantis couple. [Kal. *iwed*, Knk. *dangadángan*, Tag. *sasambá*]

wasdéng: (*slang*) *a.* very drunk; excessively inebriated. (*barték*)

wasíg: *n.* a kind of woven cotton cloth; generic name for more specific varieties: *inonsuy, nginarsib, inisa, dinur-us, tinapkil,* etc.

wasíwas: (Pil.) **iwasiwas.** *v.* to wave to and fro.

wasnák: see *warnak*: publish.

wasnáng: **nawasnang.** *a.* tall. (*tayag*)

wasnáy: **nawasnay.** *a.* straight-grained; long-legged; with long fingers. **Kasla susukaan a singkamas dagiti nawasnay a gurongna.** Her long legs are like jicama fruit ready for vinegar.

waswás: **agwaswas.** *v.* to shake (a tree, etc.), *n.* someone assigned to undo something. **maki-winnaswas.** *v.* to break up, end a relationship. **nawaswas.** *a.* terminated, concluded, ended, over; rescinded. **waswasen.** *v.* to undo what was poorly done; to nullify an agreement; rescind. **Nadamagko a mausigen ti kaso ti panagwinnaswasda.** I heard that their divorce case will be tried. **Ni Ramon ti nangdawat iti pannakawaswas ti tanida ken Viviana.** It was

Ramon who asked for the termination of his pledge with Viviana. [Tag. *kalás*; *waswás* = shaking of dust from clothes; movement of leaves in wind]

waták: maiwatak. *v.* to be divulged, made public, disclosed (secrets) **iwatak.** *v.* to reveal; divulge; disclose. **mawatakwatak.** *v.* to scatter; disband; disperse, spread out in different directions; torn to pieces. **Nakapagtitipon metten dagiti nawatakwatak a soldado.** The scattered soldiers assembled. [Tag. *waták, hayag*]

wátang: agwatangwatang. *v.* to roam around. [Tag. *galà*]

watíl: agwatilwatil. *v.* to wiggle (slender things). [Tag. *kawág, kislót*]

watís: watis la a watis. *exp.* restless.

watíwat: nawatiwat. *a.* long, extended (roads, etc.) **nagwatiwatan.** *n.* the long, straight part of the road. **watiwatem ti panunotmo.** *exp.* open your mind (to new ideas, etc.). **Nawatiwat a panagsagaba ken panaguray.** Suffering and waiting lasts a long time. [Tag. *habà*]

watnág: iwatnag. *v.* to scatter, disperse, break apart (*wara*). [Tag. *kalat*]

watwát: agwatwat, mangwatwat. *v.* to exercise. **iwatwat.** *v.* to exercise a certain part of the body to relieve pain. **pagwatwatan.** *n.* gym; place of exercising. **watwaten.** *v.* to exercise, train; practice; drill. **Kasapulan met ti bagi ti watwat.** The body also needs exercise. [Png. *pasál* (Sp.), Tag. *sanay*]

waw: *n.* thirst. (*alabaab*) **mawaw.** *a.* thirsty **pakawawan.** *n.* something that causes thirst. **pawawan.** *v.* to cause someone to be thirsty. **Mawaw iti pammateg dagiti dadakkelna isu a nagrebelde.** He hungered (*lit.* thirsted) for the affection of his parents, so he went astray. [Bon. *ewew*, Ibg. *uwwaw, napangal*, Itg. *nadápu*, Ivt. *mawaw*, Kal. *uwaw*, Kpm. *maw*, Png. *pegá*, Tag. *uhaw*]

wáwa: *n.* rice stem whistle. **agwawa.** *v.* to blow on a rice culm to produce a shrill sound; to utter sounds while slapping the mouth with a hand (Indian call). **iwawa.** *v.* to lead someone astray; mislead. **maiwawa.** *v.* to stray, wander; go astray. [Png. *leyengleyeng*, Tag. *layás, libót, galâ, lagalág* (wander)]

wáwak: *n.* person who has difficulty in correctly pronouncing. **nawawak.** *a.* having difficulty in pronouncing. (*útal*)

wawák: *n.* bogeyman.

wawék: see *tawwek*: insert, put dagger in wound.

wawwék: *n.* hidden, faraway place.

way: *n.* rattan, *Calamus sp.*; *C. mollis.* blanco (*bárek*). [Bon. *owey*, Ibg. *uway*, Ivt. *cibdas*,

Knk. *uéy*, Kpm. *yantuk*, Png. *babúyan*, Tag. *uwáy, yantók*]

wayá: *n.* leisure time, opportunity, freedom; chance. **agwaya.** *v.* to be free; stand clear, give way. **agwayawaya.** *v.* to have leisure time; to be free. **mawayaan.** *v.* to be able to have the time to do something (usually used in the negative). **nawaya.** *a.* spacious, roomy. (*nalawa*) **wayawaya.** *n.* liberty, independence, power to do as one pleases. **nawayawayaan.** *a.* liberated, emancipated, freed. **siwayawaya.** *a.* free. **wayaan.** *v.* to free; set free; let loose; give way; clean up. **wayaan.** *v.* to give way, clear some space. **Saan a bimmales nupay nawaya kuma a dinanog ti rupana.** He didn't take revenge although he was free to punch (the other person's) face. **Ti wayawaya ti ili, saan a magatang ti uray mano nga balitok.** A country's freedom cannot be bought with any amount of gold. **Agwayakayo man tapno maanginan.** Please give way so we can have air (to breathe). [Png. *kawayangán*, Tag. *layà*]

wayakwák: agwayakwak. *v.* to swing the arms like a bird in flight. (*payakpák*)

wayáng₁: *n.* mole, pier, jetty; wharf; bay; shore. **iwayang.** *v.* to indicate, point out, designate; announce, make known, promulgate; find time for.

wayáng₂: nawayang. *a.* spacious, roomy, open, clear, free (*lawa*). [Tag. *luwáng*]

wáyas: *n.* unmarried person, (male) bachelor, spinster. **agwayas.** *v.* to be alone, solitary, isolated; do alone; be independent from one's parents after marriage. **makawayas.** *v.* to be able to do by oneself. **managwayas.** *n.* loner; person frequently alone. **agwaywayas.** *v.* to be independent; sovereign. **Umdasen ti tawenna tapno wayasenna ti agpili.** He is old enough to choose on his own. [Tag. *mag-isá*]

wáyat: *n.* strategy; project; plan (*balabala, gakat*); proposal. **iwayat.** *v.* to begin, set about, start, commence; spread out, extend (a fishing net); lay out (duties, plans). **pannakaiwayat ti gubat.** *n.* proclamation of war; warfare. **Saan a mabalin a maiwayat ti pannakabitay dagiti sentensiado.** It is not possible to commence the hangings of the convicted. [Tag. *sagawâ*]

wayáway: *n.* outskirts of town (*áway*); east wind (*kasáor*). **agwayaway.** *v.* to go to the fields; to be attacked with evacuations; to emit offensive humors (the dead); to tend outward (to avoid crowding); sigh. **nawayaway.** *a.* outward; in the outskirts. **iwayaway.** (*obs.*) *v.* to take from what is the most distant. **pagwayawayen.** (*obs.*) *v.* to descry to adjacent objects.

wayawayá: (f. *wayá*) *n.* freedom; liberty. **wayawayaan.** *v.* to set free; release; grant liberty to. **mawayawayaan.** *v.* to be liberated, emancipated; released (from prison). [Tag. *kalayaan*]

waywáy: *n.* a large rope attached to the leashes of animals to allow more space for grazing. **iwayway.** *v.* to pasture, allow more space for pasturing. **mangpawayway.** *v.* to give room, space. **nawayway.** *a.* generous, liberal; lavish; profuse. **pawayway.** *n.* extension; allowance. **pawaywayan.** *v.* to give allowance to; extend a deadline. **waywayan.** *v.* to slacken, loosen, let out the rope. **ited ti pawayway.** *v.* to cut some slack. [Tag. *waywáy* = long piece, entire length]

webéra: (Sp. *huevera*: egg cup) *n.* egg cup.

wedwéd: **wedwedan.** *v.* to check, restrain, hold back, repress, curb (*medmed*). [Tag. *pigil*]

wégaw: **wegawen** (*obs.*) *v.* to devour (said of birds).

wegwég: *n.* dibble used in transplanting rice. (*asad*) **mawegweg.** *v.* to be jolted; dibbled. **wegwegen.** *v.* to jolt; shake. **iwegweg.** *v.* to press down with force. [Tag. *ugà*]

wekwék: **iwekwek.** *v.* to thrust deep into. **wekwekan.** *v.* to stab someone. [Tag. *baón*]

wélga: (Sp. *huelga*: strike) *n.* labor strike. **agwelga.** *v.* to go on strike. **welgaan.** *v.* to walk out on. **welgista.** *n.* striker.

welláwel: *n.* species of medicinal plant used to stop profuse bleeding.

welwég: see *wegweg*.

welwél: *a.* slow in obeying orders; naughty; uncontrollable (child); *n.* a kind of thin, edible eel. **iwelwel.** *v.* to wriggle into the ground.

wen: Affirmative particle. yes. **agwen.** *v.* to say yes; answer affirmatively. **iwen.** *v.* to approve. **Wen, a.** Yes, indeed. **wenen.** *v.* to say yes to something; agree to a proposal. [Bon. *ée, ey,* Ibg. *wan,* Knk. *aw, ées, ses, siá,* Png. *on,* Tag. *oo* (familiar); *opò* (polite)]

wennó: *conj.* or; **wenno X wenno Y.** Either X or Y. **wenno saan.** or not, or else. [Ibg., Png., Tag. *o* (Sp.)]

wenwén: see *welwel*: uncontrollable; naughty; disobedient.

wengwéng: *n.* buzzing sound. **agwengweng.** *v.* to buzz into the ears; make buzzing sound. [Png. *banengbeng,* Tag. *hugong, ugong, higing*]

werrét: *n.* noise of an electric fan. **agwerret.** *v.* to spin around, rotate; (*fig.*) centralize around a certain theme; stray (thoughts). **Saan a nagpatingga ti panagwerret ti panunotna.** His thoughts did not stop spinning.

wérta: (Sp. *huerta*: garden) *n.* garden (*laguerta, minuyongán, hardín*). [Tag. *hálamanán*]

werwér: *n.* the sound of the sewing machine or propellers. **agwanerwer.** *v.* to make this sound. **pawerweren.** *v.* to rev up (an engine). [Tag. *higing*]

wéste: (Sp. *oeste*: west) *n.* west (used in geographical names). (*laud*)

weswés: *n.* iron broach used in piercing holes and used while it is red hot; a child's whirling toy made from coconut shells that produces a hissing sound. **wumaneswes.** *v.* to produce a whirring, hissing sound. [Tag. *higing*]

wéteng: (Tag. *huéteng*) *n.* kind of lottery gambling game.

wetwét: **nawetwet.** *a.* tight; compact, solid, firm; dull, stupid. **pagwetwetan.** *n.* the last threads of the woof and the corresponding parts of the warp threads. **wetweten.** *v.* to finish, conclude weaving. **wetwetan.** *v.* to tighten. [Tag. *siksík*]

widáwid: **agwidawid.** *v.* to swing the arms while walking. **siwiwidawid.** *a.* empty handed, empty armed. **Pagam-ammuan, nagparangen iti desdes iti dua a lallaki a nagtagisilaw iti kawayan ken maysa ti nakawidawid.** All of a sudden, in the path appeared two boys carrying bamboo lanterns and one empty handed. [Tag. *imbáy*]

wído: (Sp. *oído*: ear) *n.* aptitude, natural ability (for music). **nawido.** *a.* intelligent; smart; wise (*sirib*); musically talented.

wiláwil: **agwilawil.** *v.* to wriggle in and out, to move to and fro. **wilawilen.** *v.* to wriggle something (to loosen). [Tag. *kiwal*]

wing-i: *n.* shaking of the head (*wingiwing*). **agwing-i.** *v.* to shake the head. **Di agsardeng ti panagwingwing-i ti ulona.** Her head doesn't stop shaking. [Png. *peyéng,* Tag. *ilíng*]

wingíwing: *n.* shaking of the head. **agwingiwing.** *v.* to dissent by shaking the head. **wingiwingan.** *v.* to shake the head at. [Png. *peyéng,* Tag. *ilíng*]

wingnasawás: **agwingnasawas.** *v.* to hit each other with something; to snap a towel.

wiráwir: (*reg.*) *n.* movement of branches and leaves in the wind. **agwirawir.** *v.* to murmur (leaves in the breeze).

wirwír: *n.* sound of the wind. **maiwirwir.** *v.* to be exposed to the wind; go against the wind. **nawirwir.** *a.* windy. (*naangin*)

wísan: **wisanwisan.** *n.* fishing tackle; antennae. [Tag. *bingwít*]

wisáwis: **wisawisan.** *n.* fishing tackle, pole and line. (*banniit*) **agwisawis.** *v.* to remove the fish from the hook, angle; sway with the wind.

wisíwis: *n.* sound of urination; (*coll.*) fiesta dance during a wedding. **iwisiwis.** *v.* to shake; swing something back and forth (in anger); attack with the mouth (dog); worry. **wisiwisan.** *v.* to sprinkle something with water. **Inton-ano ti wisiwismo?** (*coll.*) When is your wedding? [Tag. *wilíg*]

witíwit: *n.* the handle of a plow, plowtail. (*putan*)

witwít: *n.* wagging, shaking (of the finger or long object). **agwitwit.** *v.* to wag a finger. **witwítan.** *v.* to wag the finger at someone. **Nangiwitwit kaniak iti badáng a kaas-asana.** He shook the large knife he just sharpened at me. [Tag. *surot*]

Y

y-: Verbal prefix. Variant of the theme prefix *i*-used before vowels (also spelled *iy*-): **i + awat = iyawat.** *v.* to hand over. **i + amo = yamo.** *v.* to reconcile. **i + ammo = yammo.** *v.* to inform.

yaáy: (f. *ay*) *n.* the coming, arrival. (*isasangpet*)

yabáyab: *n.* imagined size (of hanging objects, etc.); direction of the smoldering tongue of the fire in a blaze. **agyabayab.** *v.* to wave, undulate; flutter; to play or sway loosely, to flap (flags, etc.); to float, drift (clouds, threatening rain). [Tag. *sikláb*]

yábe: (Sp. *llave*: key; *llave inglesa* = wrench) *n.* wrench. (*liabe*)

yabyáb₁: **yabyaban.** *v.* to fan the fire or food. (*yubyub*)

yabyáb₂: **payabyab.** *n.* wide-brimmed palm hat. **agpayabyab.** *v.* to wear the *payabyab* hat. **Nakaibarikes iti talunasan ken nakapayabyab a pimmanaw.** He had a machete dangling from his belt and was wearing a palm hat when he left.

yabyáb₃: **nayabyaban.** *a.* torn (clothes). (*pigis*)

yádi: **nayadi.** *a.* grown (rice, etc), mature, seasoned (said of *boggoong*) (*rayok*)

yadyád: *var.* of *yagyag.*

yaggá: *a.* thin, not having the constituent parts compactly arranged, said of cloth, basketwork, etc., see *utimék.*

yagyág: **yagyagan.** *v.* to insult, offend, affront (*abi*); shout at, yell. **agyagyag.** *n.* movement of the body when trying to widen a narrow receptacle, when pressing something down, when treading a treadle, etc. **Kanayon a yagyagannak, aglalo no sumangpetak a sibabartek.** He always chides me, especially when I arrive drunk. **Nakabannikes ti baket a mangyagyag kadakuada.** The old lady yelled at them with her arms akimbo. [Tag. *yagyág* = gallop, trot]

yakál: *n.* species of durable hardwood, *Hopea sp*, yacal tree.

Yákan: *n.* ethnic group living in the interior of Basilan Island, Mindanao.

yakayák: *n.* round basket sieve smaller than the *bigao*; sieve. **agyakayak.** *v.* to sieve; to wiggle the hips sexily. (*kinnikinni*) **yakayaken.** *v.* to sift, sieve, screen, bolt; to sprinkle, powder. (*yokoyok*; *gasagas*; *tar-ap*) **mayakayak.** *v.* to spill, fall or run out. [Kal. *akiyak*, Tag. *bistáy*]

yakét: **yumaket.** *v.* to creak (*ranetret*). [Tag. *laginít*]

yakúyak: **agyakuyak.** *v.* to reproduce, spread, diffuse, (skin diseases, tumors, etc.). [Tag. *dumami*]

yakyák: **agyakyak.** *v.* to wade, to ford (a river). **yakyakan.** *v.* to incite. **yakyaken.** (*obs.*) *v.* to retract, annul.

yáman: **agyaman.** *v.* to be thankful or grateful, to thank. **makapagyaman.** *v.* to be able to express one's gratitude. **panagyaman.** *n.* thanks; acknowledgement; gratitude. **yaman ta.** I am glad, pleased. **yaman pay.** Thank you. The usual answer of the inmates of a house to the greeting of a person making a call. **agyamanak (unay).** thank you (very much) **Awan ti rumbeng a pagyamanam.** There's no need to thank (me). **Nakayaman ta nagtagtagainep laeng.** He was thankful that it was only a dream. [Kal. *yaman*, Png., Tag. *salamat*]

yambán: The *shorea balangeran* (*Korth*) *Dyer*, and *S. guiso* (*blanco*) *Blume. Dipterocarpaceous* trees yielding a very valuable timber for construction. Trade names: *yacal* and *guijo*, respectively.

yammó: [*i + ammo*] *v.* to inform. (*pakaammo*; *warragawat*)

yamyám: **yumamyam.** *v.* to spread (fire) (*kayamkam*). [Tag. *kalat*]

yan: *n.* place, location (*disso*); situation; locality; spot; position. **agyan.** *v.* to stay, dwell, reside; occupy a place; be located. **agiyan.** *v.* to dwell (unseen spirits). **pagyanan.** *n.* location, situation, position; abode. **pa-yanen.** *v.* to make someone stay. **pa-yanan.** *v.* to make someone stay at a particular location. **umyan.** *v.* to spend the night, lodge. **umyanan.** *n.* place where someone spends the night. **makipagyan.** *v.* to live with. **makapagyan.** *v.* to be able to live with. **nagyan.** *n.* contents. **awan nagyan.** *a.* empty. **Ayanna?** Where is he? **No mapagustuam, pagyanennaka payen ditoy.** If you like, he will even have you stay here. [Png. *yan*, Tag. *dako*, *lugár* (Sp.)]

yanasyás: *n.* shuffling sound of slippers; sound of scraping or grating. **Nangngegnan ti yanasyas ti sinelasna.** He heard the sound of her slippers.

yáno: (Sp. *llano*: plain) *a.* plain; simple; without ornaments or decoration; *n.* plain.

yanó: from where? (*taga-ano*)

yantá: *conj.* whereas, since. (*yantangay, yata*).

yantángay: *conj.* whereas, since, for that reason (*tangay*). [Tag. *yamang*]

yantás: (Sp. *llantas*: tire) *n.* hoop or rim of a wheel.

yangyáng: **nayangyang.** *a.* clear, bright, shining (sun); strong (color); **mayangyangan.** *a.* dried properly; be laid out (to dry). **nakayangyang.** *a.* open; laid bare. **ipayangyang.** *v.* to put out to dry. **Agas-asuk ti basuraan gapu ta nasindian**

dagiti nayangyangan. The garbage dump is smoking because what was laid out caught on fire. [Tag. *yangyáng* = dry in the air]

yáong: *n.* a kind of wide, glazed china cup.

yaplág: (f. *aplag*) *v.* to spread a mat on the floor.

yápyap: *n.* (*coll.*) Mickey Mouse money; worthless currency; name given to money issued by the Japanese during occupation.

yarasáas: (f. *arasaas*) *v.* to whisper something.

yárda: (Sp. *yarda*: yard) *n.* yard. **sangayarda.** *n.* one yard.

yas: agyas. *n.* scraping, rasping sound. **agyasyas.** *v.* to rasp.

yáso: yaso a babai. *n.* pimp. (*búgaw*)

yat: mayatyat. *n.* sound of tearing paper, cloth. **agyatyat, yumatyat.** *v.* be torn; (*reg.*) to tiptoe. (*til-ay*)

yáta: *conj.* whereas, since (*yanta, yantangay*). [Tag. *yamang*; *yatà* = perhaps, maybe]

yáte: (Sp. *yate*: yacht) *n.* yacht; pleasure boat.

yatyát: agyatyat. *v.* to expand (new shoes that have been broken in); to tear (paper, cloth); (*reg.*) to tiptoe.

yáwat: (f. *awat*) *v.* to hand over.

yawyáw₁: *n.* colloquial term for eating (*tsibog*); colloquial term for dog meat. (*asosena, aw-aw, karne ti aso*).

yawyáw₂: pannakayawyaw. *n.* pilferage, stealing in small quantities. **manangyawyaw.** *n.* pilferer. **mayawyaw.** *v.* to be frustrated, foiled, baffled; confused, dumbfounded, perplexed, disconcerted, puzzled, abashed; to be lost due to constant borrowing by many people; completely consumed. **payawyawen.** *v.* to add water, dilute; weaken. **yawyawen.** *v.* to pilfer.

yáya: (Tagalog also) *n.* nursemaid, woman in charge of taking care of children, live-in babysitter.

yédra: (Sp. *hiedra*: ivy) *n.* poison ivy.

yeg: mangiyeg. iyeg. yeg. *v.* to bring, take to someone. **maiyegán.** *v.* to be provided with. **yegán.** *v.* to bring to someone. **paiyegán.** *v.* to have something brought to someone. **Kaiyegna ditoy.** He just brought it here.

yegyég: agyegyeg. *v.* to tremble, shake, shiver, quake, shudder. **yegyegen.** *v.* to grind, pulverize, triturate, comminute; shake something (*tigerger*). [Tag. *kiníg*]

yekyék: yekyeken. *v.* to choke, suffocate, smother, stifle (through coughing or sickness); to constantly cough (*kelkel; letlet*). [Tag. *ihít*]

yélo: (Sp. *hielo*: ice) *n.* ice. **kayeluan.** *n.* icy place: Arctic.

yéma: (Sp. *yema*: yolk) *n.* condensed milk; yolk of an egg.

yengyéng₁: mayengyeng. *v.* to be bothered, confused, bewildered, flurried (with noise); drunk. [Tag. *tulíg*]

yengyéng₂: *n.* buzzing sound. **agyengyeng.** *v.* to buzz.

yepyép: *n.* deep sleep. **yepyepen.** (*saguyepyepen, mayepyep*) *v.* to become calm, still quiet, (the sea). **makayepyep.** *v.* to have a soothing effect. **yepyep a kama.** *n.* comfortable bed. **Makayepyep latta ti tokar.** The music is just soothing. [Tag. *antók*]

yérba buéna: (Sp. *yerba buena*: medicinal herb) *n.* medicinal herb used against rheumatism, cough, toothaches, and stomachache.

yéro: (Sp. *hierro*: iron) *n.* galvanized iron sheet. **kaha de yero.** *n.* iron box.

yesngáw: (f. *sengngaw*) *v.* to express in words.

yetnág: *v.* to grant the request of, out of pity, love.

yetyét: *n.* the creaking sound produced by new shoes. **agyetyet.** *v.* to creak. [Tag. *laginít*]

-yo: 1. enclitic suffix. Second person plural, or second person singular polite. You, your. Attaches to transitive verbs as the actor marker: **Nakitayon.** You (pl.) saw it already. 2. enclitic second person plural, or second person singular polite possessive. Attaches to nouns. **ti asoyo.** Your (*pl.*) dog. **'diay ubingyo.** That child of yours. [Png. *yo*, Tag. *ninyó*]

yo: *n.* shark (*pating*). [Png. *yo*, Tag. *patíng*]

yubúyob: *n.* bellows, bellowing tongue of the fire. **agyubuyob.** *v.* to bellow (fire). **yubuyuban.** *n.* bellows, consisting of a hollow piece of earthenware (*ibeng*), resting on the ground, provided at one of its sides with two small iron tubes (*anguyob*) through which the air is expelled into the fire, and surmounted by two large hollow wooden cylinders through which the air is drawn into the *ibeng* by means of two pestles, whose lower ends (*topia*) are covered with feathers and which are moved up and down alternately, the operator taking hold of their handle (*alili*), one in each hand; *v.* to fan the fire. **yumubuyob.** *v.* to sound the *yubuyuban*. [Bon., Knk. *opóop*, Tag. *bulusan*]

yubyób: yumubyob. *n.* the sound of a strong fire, trees moved by the wind. **yubyuban.** *v.* to blow air at the fire to make it stronger; fan a fire to increase its intensity. **Sinindianna ti suakona sa nagpayubyob.** He lit his pipe and then blew out (the smoke).

yódo: (Sp. *iodo*: iodine) *n.* iodine.

yudyód: agyudyod. *v.* to sag, droop, sink, bend down at the middle; become flabby (muscles). [Tag. *luylóy*]

yuét: *n.* a kind of small, scaly snake.

Yógad: *n.* ethnic group from Isabela Province; language of the *Yogad* people.

yugáyog: **agyugayog**. *v.* to vibrate, shake, tremble; sway (bridges, floors, etc.), swing. [Tag. *ugóy*]

Yugoslábo: (Sp. *yugoslavo*: Yugoslav; *fem*: *Yugoslaba*) *n. a.* Yugoslav; Yugoslavian.

yugyóg: **yugyugen**. *v.* to beat (eggs, etc.); to pick (ears, etc.); shake, sway (tree). [Tag. *yugyóg*]

yúkan: see *ayukan*: honeybee.

yukáyok: **agyukayok**. *v.* to sag, droop; sink.

yúkos: *var.* of *ayyukos*: stooping.

yukót: *a.* bent; hunched; hunchbacked. (*kubbo*) **agyukot**. *v.* to hunch; bend.

yukuyók: see *yakayak*: sift; sieve. **Nayukuyok ti balitok iti kadaratan dagiti waig.** Gold was sifted from the sandy banks of the stream. (*yakayak*; *tar-op*; *sigi*; *gasagas*)

yukyók₁: *var.* of *yukayok*: sag, droop.

yukyók₂: **yukyukan**. *v.* to stab (*bagkong*). [Tag. *yukyók* = cower, duck]

yúli: (f. *úli*) *v.* to take upstairs; take up.

yúlog: (f. *úlog*) *v.* to bring down; take down.

yom: **yomén**. *v.* to close, shut (the mouth).

yummóng: (f. *ummóng*) *v.* to place something near a pile.

yúmo: **marayumo**. *n.* a variety of thin-skinned banana, resembling the *tumok* when ripe. (*tumok*)

yúmok: **marayumok**. see *yumo*, *marayumo*.

yumyóm: **yumyumen**. *v.* to roll a mouthful of rice into a ball.

yungáyong: **agyungayong**. *v.* to jut out, protrude, project, causing someone to stumble; to spread out like a canopy (tree branches) (*salumpayak*; *ruyag*). [Tag. *uslî*]

yungyóng₁: **agyungyong**. *v.* to wear the hair long in mourning, abstain from cutting the hair in mourning; see also *yengyeng*. **nakayungyong**. *a.* wearing the hair long in mourning.

yungyóng₂: **nayungyong**. *a.* shady. (*linong*) **nayungyungan**. *a.* shaded. **mangyungyong**. *v.* to shade. **Adda iti labes ti kakawayanan a nangyungyong iti nakipet a kalsada.** He is across in the bamboo field shading the narrow road. [Tag. *lilim*]

yúos: *n.* (*obs.*) stooping; hunchbacked; calling water buffalo.

yupána: *n.* a kind of creeping herb used in popular medicine.

yúrno: (f. *urno*) *v.* to bake; put in the oven.

yus: *n.* term used for sexual intercourse, a euphemism for *yot*. (*yusyus*)

yúsi: (*reg.*) *n.* pig stew with onions, tomatoes, and garlic.

yusí: (*reg.*) *n.* kidney. (*bekkél*)

yussuát: (f. *ussuat*) *v.* to begin, start; spearhead a project.

yosyós: variant of *yot* in some districts.

yot: **agyot**. *v.* to copulate. **panagyot**. *n.* sexual intercourse, coitus. **yutén**. *v.* to copulate with (a woman); to cover, serve,; to leap (a female animal); to brim (swine), to tread (birds). **yuninám**. (*vulg.*, f. *yut ni inám*) copulate your mother. [Knk. *bantók*, *yut*, Png. *yot*, Tag. *hindót*]

yúyek: *n.* earwax, cerumen (*durek*). [Bon. *táin si kóleng*, Png. *olilek*, Tag. *tutulí*]

yúyem: **nayuyem**. *a.* overcast, clouded over; gloomy (*kuyem*; *lulem*; *naulpan*). [Png. *udyem*, *lurém*, Tag. *kulimlím*]

yúyeng: *n.* abyss, abysm, gulf, chasm; the deep; shade of a tree; shade of a canopy.

yóyo: *n.* yo-yo. **agyoyo**. *v.* to play with a *yo-yo*. **Agsublisublida a kasla yoyo.** They come back and forth like yo-yos.

yúyok: **agyuyok**. *v.* to bend (ears of rice, etc.) (*deppes*); to pucker, to draw up into bulges or wrinkles (badly cut garments); sag under a heavy load. [Tag. *yukód*]

-ysa: Variant of *maysá*, used with certain prefixes: **saggaysa**. one each **kaykaysa**. only one, sole.

ENGLISH-ILOCANO

INGGLES-ILOKO

A

a: *art.* maysá nga.
aback: *n.* agpalikúd.
abandon: *v.* baybay-án, panáwan; palugodán.
abate: *v.* kissayán; agsardéng.
abattoir: *n.* pagpartián, matadéro.
abbreviate: *v.* paababaén.
abbreviation: *n.* pangyabaabaán.
abdicate: *v.* agikkát iti sáad.
abdomen: *n.* tián; pus-óng.
abhor: *v.* guráen; umsién.
abide: *v.* agyán; agtaéng.
ability: *n.* kabaelán, katun-áyan.
able: *adj.* maka-; ma-; baél, kabaelán.
abnormal: *adj.* di kadaywán.
aboard: *adj.* silulúgan.
abode: *n.* pagtaengán.
abolish: *v.* pukáwen, ikkatén, rakráken.
abomasum: *n.* pagmagaán.
abortion: *n.* alís, panangparegrég ti sikóg;
  have an ~ agpalig-ís, agparegrég; maalisán,
  agpapursíng.
abound: *v.* umatiwekwék; umadú.
about: *prep, adv.* maipanggép; maipapán.
above: *prep, adv.* (iti) ngáto; iti rabáw.
abrade: *v.* aglasílas; usaósan.
abridge: *v.* pabassitén; paababaén.
abroad: *adj.* ballasiw-taáw; ití sabáli a
  pagilián.
absence: *n.* kaawán, kinaawán.
absent: *adj.* lumángan; ~ **minded** *adj.* aleng-
  áleng; agmalmalangá; natalipanpán;
  mananglilípat.
absorb: *v.* sagepsepén; sumlép.
abstain: *v.* mangirnád, tenglén ti rikná.
abundant: *adj.* naruáy, adú, nawadwád,
  narammók.
abuse: *n.* ranggás; abúso.
abyss: *n.* dariwangwáng, lisság; yúyeng.
academy: *n.* akadémia, nangáto a pagadálan.
accelerate: *v.* papardásen; pumardás.
accent: *n.* (*mark over letter*) tuldék; (*in
  speaking*) áyug, kinalawág ti panagsaó.
accept: *v.* awáten; annugóten; ~**able** *adj.*
  maáwat.
access: *n.* surók, sumrekán.
accessory: *n.* kasangkápan; náyon; katulóngan.
accident: *n.* arámid a saán a ginagára;
  vehicular ~ disgrásia.
accommodate: *n.* pasangbáyen; isáad.
accompanist: *n.* mangdanggáy, mangkaduá,
  mangkúyog.
accompany: *v.* kumúyog, agkaduá; (*escort*)
  ikúyog, itulnóg, itulúd, itundá; (*in music*)
  danggáyan.

accomplish: *v.* leppasén; turpósen; aramíden.
accord: *n.* panagtúnos, panagbágay; **in ~ance
  with** *prep.* maidanggáy ití, mayanántup iti;
  according to *prep.* kuná ni, según.
account: *n.* (*bill*) kuénta, pakabilángan; **do
  on ~ of** *v.* igapó, ipagapó; ~ **for** *v.* idatág;
  take ~ of *v.* patgán, lukáden.
accountant: *n.* agbilbílang, kondadór.
accumulate: *v.* agtípon, agurnóng; agpaadú.
accurate: *adj.* nakanátad; agpaysó, pudnó.
accuse: *v.* pabasólen, ipúlong (*in court*) idarúm.
ace: *n.* álas.
ache: *n.* sakít, ut-ót; *v.* agsakít, agut-ót.
achieve: *v.* gun-óden, ileppás; ringpásen,
  tungpálen, tun-óyen.
achiote: *n.* atsuéte.
acid: *n.* ásido.
acknowledge: *v.* ammuén, bigbígen; akuén.
acquaintance: *n.* am-ammó, kaammó-ammó.
acquire: *v.* gun-óden.
acquit: *v.* bulósan; pakawánen.
acrobat: *n.* baligáya.
across: *prep, adv.* ballasíw, ití bángir; ití
  labés.
act: *n.* gapuánan, tignáy; arámid; (*in a play*)
  paráng; ~ **of** *n.* panag-; **catch in the** ~ *v.*
  salamaán; ~ **upon (feelings)** *v.* samáyen.
action: *n.* arámid; tignáy; gapuánan; (*in court*)
  darúm.
active: *adj.* nasiglát; (*quick*) naparták,
  nakartíng; (*diligent*) nagagét, naanép, nasaét.
activity: *n.* arámid; kinaalibták.
actor: *n.* artísta a laláki.
actual: *adj.* pudnó; itatta.
Adam's apple: *n.* ammútil.
adapt: *v.* iruám; ibágay.
add: *v.* nayónan; isílpo; dagúpen; ~**ition** *n.*
  nakadagdagúpan; ~**itional** *adj.* náyon.
addicted: *adj.* nairuám; nadekkét.
address: *n.* pagtaengán; (*speech*) bitlá.
adequate: *adj.* makaanáy.
adhere: *v.* agkapét; agkappón.
adhesive: *adj.* nakapét, napigkét.
adjacent: *adj.* kadenná, kaarúba, kasigkáy;
  bangíbang, darápat.
adjective: *n.* pangilásin.
adjoining: *adj.* kadenná, kasilpó.
adjourn: *v.* ipatinggá, isardéng.
adjust: *v.* ibága, ipagisú.
administer: *v.* taripatuén; aywánan.
administration: *n.* pagaywánan.
admiration: *n.* panagdáyaw; panagsiddáaw.
admire: *v.* dayáwen; agsiddáaw.
admiral: *n.* almiránte.
admission: *n.* panangáwat; panangpastrék;
  panangáko.

admit: *v.* pastréken, annugóten; akuén.

adopt: *v.* ampónan; taraknén; akuén.

adorable: *adj.* maay-ayát.

adore: *v.* dayáwen, ayatén.

adorn: *v.* arkósan, papintásen; adornuán.

adult: *n.* táo a nataengán, manakmán.

adultery: *n.* kamalála, ábig; **caught in** ~ *v.* matláng.

advance: *adj.* sakbáy; ~ **payment** *n.* antemáno.

advantage: *n.* gungoná; talibágok, pangatíwan; **take ~ of** *v.* gundawáyan, bulónen.

advantageous: *adj.* nakáya, naingundawáyan.

adventure: *n.* panagpádas; panangsúbok ti kabaelán.

adverb: *n.* pangkaduá.

adversary: *n.* kabúsor.

advertise: *v.* ipaskíl, iwarragáwag; iwarnák, ipakdáar; ~**ment** *n.* panangipaskíl, pakdáar.

advice: *n.* balákad, patigmaán, singásing.

advise: *v.* bagbagaán, balakádan, ipatalgéd, ipartáang; awísen; pakaammuán, patigmaanán.

advocate: *n.* abogádo, mangitakdér, mangsalakníb.

adz: *n.* pandarás.

affair: *n.* biáng; pangnó; arámid; pagbiágan; asikasuén. **state of ~s** *n.* annayásan.

affect: *v.* tignáyen, pagbalíwen; umápay; sumnék; maaríngan; ~**ed** *adj.* naaríngan.

affection: *n.* pagay-ayatán, dungngó.

affectionate: *adj.* nadungngó; nadangngó, karinióso.

affidavit: *n.* pangpasingkéd.

affiliate: *v.* kumappón; kumaduá.

affirm: *v.* paneknékan; pasingkedán.

affliction: *n.* pagsagabáan, rígat.

afford: *v.* makabáyad; kabaelán.

afraid: *adj.* mabuténg; naamák; naalumíim; **to be ~ of** *v.* kabuténg.

after: *prep.* kalpasán; ití likudán.

afterbirth: *n.* kadkaduá, súpot, bulbulluákan.

aftergrowth: *n.* sagíbo.

afternoon: *n.* malém.

aftertaste: *n.* ádat.

afterwards: *adv.* kalpasánna, no malpás.

again: *adv.* manén.

against: *prep.* maisuppiát, maikaniwás, maisungáni.

agape: *adj.* nakangangá.

agar-agar: *n.* kánotkánot.

age: *n.* tawén; **to be the same ~** *v.* agkatawén, agkasádar, agkataéb.

agency: *n.* ahénsia; sangá.

agent: *n.* pannakabagí; mangitakdér.

aggravate: *v.* (*sickness*) ilanlán.

aggressive: *adj.* nakárit, naúyong, managriríbok.

agile: *adj.* naparagsít, nasiglát, nakarantíng, nasaliwanwán, naparták.

agitate: *v.* kibúren, riribúken.

ago: *adv.* idí ugmá, idí kuá.

agony: *n.* túok; (*near death*) bugsót.

agree: *v.* umannúrot, umanámong, kumanúnong, mapasóot; ~ **with** *v.* abulúyan, buyógen, tubúyan; ~**ment** *n.* túlag; pagtunósan.

agriculture: *n.* panagtaltálon.

ahead: *adv.* umun-uná, agpauná.

aid: *n.* túlong, sadíri; *v.* tumúlong, umaráyat.

aim: *v.* paturongán; *n.* panggép, gandát.

air: *n.* ángin; **expose to** ~ *v.* iparíir, ipaángin.

airport: *n.* sangládan dagití eropláno.

ajar: *adj.* nakalukát.

akimbo: *adj.* nakabanníkes; **to stand** ~ *v.* agbanníkes, agmaníkes.

akin: *adj.* kapáris, kapáda.

albino: *n.* sárko, bugagáw.

albumen: *n.* puráw ti itlóg.

alburnum: *n.* ballagúbag.

alcohol: *n.* árak.

alert: *adj.* narídam, nakartíng, nasalawitwít; naparták, nasiglát, naalibták.

algae: *n.* arrágan, arakáyan; (*moss*) lúmot.

algebra: *n.* álhebra.

alias: *n.* sabáli a nágan; parbó a nágan.

alibi: *n.* pambár.

alien: *n.* gangannaét; tagá-sabáli a dagá.

align: *v.* itarátar; ~**ment** *n.* panangitarátar.

alight: *v.* agdissáag, bumabá ití lúgan.

alike: *adj.* padapáda; kasla.

alimony: *n.* itaraón.

alive: *adj.* sibibiág; (*lively*) nasagiksík.

all: *adj.* ámin, ísu ámin, dágup ámin; (*pure*) bíig, pásig, pulós; ~ **of a sudden** *adv.* pagam-ammuán; **give to** ~ *v* unorén, utóben; ~ **set** *adj* sikakayákay.

allege: *v.* ipasingkéd, ipaneknék, isaó; ipabásol.

alleviate: *v.* pedpedén, baw-ásen, makadepdép; ep-epén.

alley: *n.* bettáng, akíkid a dálan.

alligator: *n.* buáya.

allot: *v.* itéd.

allow: *v.* palubósan, patubóyan.

allowance: *n.* suéldo; palúbos.

allude: *v.* sagíden ití panagsaó; isalpiká.

allure: *v.* ay-aywén, alliláwen.

ally: *n.* kumaduá.

almost: *adv.* ngannganí, nagistayán.

alms: *n.* limós; **give** ~ limosán.

aloft: *adj.* nakabiráyon.

alone: *adj.* maymaysá, agwaywáyas; agpáway.

along: *adj.* agpatúloy.

alphabet: *n.* abesedário.

already: *adv.* =en, =n.

also: *adv.* met; pay; **and** ~ patí.

altar: *n.* altár, súrong; ~ **boy** *n.* sakristán.

alter: *v.* balíwan.

alternate: *v.* agsarunó; agsinnublát; agbabáles, agkasukát.

alternative: *n.* pagpilián.

although: *conj.* núpay, úray no.

altitude: *n.* kangáto ti dagá.

aluminum: *n.* alumínio.

always: *adv.* agnanáyon; kanáyon.

am: *v.* –ak, siák.

A.M.: *adv.* iti bigát.

amateur: *n.* agdamdámo.

amaze: *v.* kigtóten, pagsiddaáwen.

amazed: *adj.* masdáaw.

amazing: *adj.* nakaskasdáaw, nakakigkigtót.

ambassador: *n.* embahadór.

ambition: *n.* tarigágay, águm, agáwa.

ambush: *v.* sanebén; tambángen, saedén.

amend: *v.* tarimaánen, pasayaáten; **make ~s** *v.* alabarén.

amid: *prep.*ití tengngá ti.

amity: *n.* paggagayyemán.

ammunition: *n.* bála, pagbála.

amnesty: *n.* indúlto, pakawán (iti bálud), pammakawán.

among: *prep.* naitípon kadagití, kadagití.

amount: *n.* pakadagúpan.

ample: *adj.* nawadwád, nawatíwat.

amplify: *v.* padakkelén, papigsáen.

amputate: *v.* putdén.

amulet: *n.* antíng-antíng.

amuse: *v.* ay-ayámen, ragragsáken, lingayén, rayáwen.

an: *art.* maysá nga.

analogy: *n.* nagpadáan.

analyze: *v.* usígen, sungkáen ití ísip.

ancestor: *n.* puón, tinaúdan (a kabagián), dadakkél.

ancestry: *n.* katatáo; kaputótan; **trace one's ~** *v.* agsinggapó.

anchor: *n.* sinipéte, angklá, káwat; *v.* sumanglád, sumangrád, agbuntóg; agangklá.

anchovy: *n.* munámon.

ancient: *adj.* dáan; taga-ugmá.

and: *conj.* ken (*plural*) kadá; (*with numbers*) ket.

anecdote: *n.* ababá a saríta.

anesthesia: *n.* pangbibíneg.

anesthetize: *v.* bibinégen.

angelus: *n.* orasión, karárag ití sumipngét.

anger: *n.* gúra, pungtót.

angle: *n.* (*corner*) súli; bílid; ~ **brace** *n.* pokló, sakóbo.

angry: *adj.* makaluksáw, makaungét, maruród, naalipungét.

anguish: *n.* ladíngit, samuyéng; lidáy; sanáang.

animal: *n.* ayúp; **adult female ~** *n.* danáwan.

animate: *adj.* nabiág; *v.* biagén.

anise: *n.* anís; **star ~** *n.* sangkít.

ankle: *n.* lansalansá, lipaylípay; pingíl, píngir.

annihilate: *v.* pukáwen a talipupúsen, dadaélen.

announce: *v.* ipakaammó, ipakdáar, iballáag.

annual: *adj.* tinawén.

announce: *v.* ipadámag, ipakdáar, ibungábong, ipabláak, iwarragáwag.

announcer: *n.* parawarragáwag.

annul: *v.* waswásen.

anoint: *v.* sapsapuán, pulotán (*with oil*) lanaán; ~**ment** *n.* pulót.

anomaly: *n.* anomália, ríro.

another: *adj.*, *pron.* sabáli.

answer: *n.* sungbát; *v.* sungbáten; subalítan.

ant: *n.* kutón; **red ~** *n.* búos, ampipít, búnar, alomígas; **winged ~** *n.* simutsímot; **white ~** (*termite*) *n.* ánay; **black ~** *n.* antutúngal, kanít, rumarábak, ararásan, pangúbet; ~ **hill** *n.* buntón (dagití kutón).

antagonistic: *adj.* maisuppiát, agkaniwásiw, agkannásiw.

antagonize: *v.* busóren, paguráen.

Antarctic: *adj.* antártiko.

antennae: *n.* kaméng, rúngo.

anthem: *n.* kánta ti pagilián.

anthropology: *n.* antropolohía.

anticipate: *v.* sakbáyan, karakáren; ipakauná.

antidote: *n.* súma, súmang, dáir; ~ **maker** *n.* mannúma.

antipathy: *n.* ápas, ruród.

antique: *adj.* báak, duduógan, tagá-ugmá.

antler: *n.* sára (ti ugsa); **antlerless** *adj.* namuák, pungíl.

anus: *n.* kimmút, merrét, muríit; tatakkián, busigít, kerrét; úbet.

anvil: *n.* pasnáan, pamaksó.

anxiety: *n.* pulkók, agáwa, gágar, seggá.

anxious: *adj.* nagágar; napulkók.

any: *adj.*, *pron.* aniáman; ~**thing** *pron.* úray aniá; ~ **way** *adv.* met láeng, núpay kastá; ~**one** sínoman, uray no asíno, ~**where** sadinoman.

apart: *adv.* sinasináen.

apartment: *n.* aksesória; pagtaengán.

ape: *n.* bákes, súnggo, móno.

aphrodisiac: *n.* sustánsia a mangparásuk; gayúma.

apiece: *adv.* saggaysá.

apologize: *v.* padalánan, agpakawán, agpadispensá.

apology: *n*. dáwat ti pammakawán.
apostrophe: *n*. tuldék.
apparatus: *n*. aparáto.
apparent: *adj*. nalawág, maawátan.
apparition: *n*. al-aliá.
appeal: *v*. gumawáwa, umaráraw; umásug; agpakaási; agkiddáw.
appear: *v*. agparáng, agpakíta, rumsuá, lumtuád; lumgák; ~ **suddenly** *v*. lumtáw, tumpuár, sumngáw.
appearance: *n*. kíta, takdér, wágas, tábas.
appease: *v*. ep-epén, pagtalnáen.
appetite: *n*. gánas; gartém.
appetizer: *n*. pangpagánas (ití pannangán).
appetizing: *adj*. makapagánas.
applaud: *v*. agsipát; mangpadáyaw.
applause: *n*. panagtipát; panangitan-ók.
apple: *n*. mansánas; **Malay** ~ *n*. makúpa; **custard** ~ *n*. átis, anónas.
applicable: *adj*. maarámat, mayanátup.
apply: *v*. yapá; idangép, ikapét.
appoint: *v*. dutóken, tudingán, pusgán; ~**ment** *n*. pannakadútok; pannakaisáad, pannakaipuésto.
apportion: *v*. yallót, bingáyen.
appraise: *v*. ikeddéng ti páteg.
appreciate: *v*. dayáwen; agyáman, bigbígen ti páteg.
apprehend: *v*. tilíwen, kemmegén.
approach: *v*. umasidég, asitgán, arngián.
appropriate: *adj*. maibágay, maitutóp, maikanáda; *v*. tagikuaén.
approval: *n*. palúbos, anámong.
approve: *v*. anamóngan, pasingkedán, abulúyan, tubóyan.
approximate: *v*. asitgán; pattapattaén; ~**ly** *adv*. sumurok-kumúrang, ngannganí pumáda.
April: *n*. Abríl.
apron: *n*. bídang.
apt: *adj*. maitutóp.
aptitude: *n*. kinalaíng; kabaelán, kinasayúd ití pannakaáwat.
aquaculturist: *n*. agtartarakén ití lamés.
aquatic: *adj*. tagá-danúm, agtaéng ití danúm.
aquiline: *adj*. tundíris, napantók nga agóng.
arable: *adj*. mamuláan, tatalónen; matamnán.
arbitrate: *v*. ikeddéng, pagkappiaén.
arch: *n*. árko; **frame of an** ~ *n*. pangiapuán; ~ **mold** *n*. pagsukogán.
archaic: *adj*. kadaánan, di maarámaten.
archbishop: *n*. arsobíspo.
arched: *adj*. pakkóg, nasillók, natammóg.
archer: *n*. pumapána.
archipelago: *n*. purpúro.
architecture: *n*. panagbángon, panagpatakdér, arkitektúra.

arctic: *adj*. ártiko.
ardent: *adj*. nasgéd, nagágar.
ardor: *n*. anép, gágar.
are: *v*. ag-; see copula **be**.
area: *n*. dissó, kaláwa ti dagá.
areola: *n*. (*of nipple*) binakláy.
argue: *v*. agápa, agsuppiát, agrinnasón, agsubáng.
argument: *n*. pangsuppiát, pagrasón, panagápa.
arid: *adj*. natíkag.
arise: *v*. bumángon, tumakdér; umalsá.
ark: *n*. sasakayán, daóng.
arm: *n*. (*of body*) takkiág; (*weapon*) ármas, ígam; **cross the** ~**s** *v*. agdalikepkép; **put** ~ **on someone's shoulder** *v*. agassíbay, umassíbay; **swing the** ~**s** *v*. agwidáwid, agwayakwák; **carry under the** ~**a** *v*. igpílan; **lift the** ~**s** *v*. agkarab-ás.
armchair: *n*. butáka.
armed forces: *n*. Siiígam a Bíleg, búyot.
armistice: *n*. panangisardéng ti gubát.
armor: *n*. kalásag, kabál.
armpit: *n*. kilikilí; **smell of** ~ *n*. anglít.
armspan: *n*. demmáng, deppá, agpá, sangadpá.
army: *n*. buyótan; ~ **worm** *n*. arábas.
aroma: *n*. bangló, ayamúom, dangíir.
around: *adv*. iti lawláw; **go** ~ *v*. agíbaw; aglíbut.
arouse: *v*. parugsuén, gargarién; riingén.
arraign: *v*. idatág, isakláng (ití pangukomán).
arrange: *v*. urnósen, iságana, ipinípin, dalimanéken.
arrest: *v*. balúden, tengngelén, kemmegén.
arrive: *v*. sumangpét, dumténg; ~ **home** *v*. agáwid.
arrogance: *n*. tangsít, kuspág, pangás.
arrogant: *adj*. napangás, napasindáyaw, natangíg, napalangguád, nakuspág.
arrow: *n*. pána.
arrowroot: *n*. sagú.
arsenic: *n*. basíkut.
arson: *n*. úram nga ingagára.
art: *n*. árte.
artery: *n*. urát.
article: *n*. banag; pangiruggí; artíkulo; (*grammar*) pangipungánay.
artifice: *n*. úyam.
artificial: *adj*. nagarbó, parbó, saán a kasisígud.
artillery: *n*. artileriá.
artist: *n*. artísta, pumipínta; kumikíkir.
as: *adv*., *conj*. kas, idínto; kastá met la; (*reason clause*) gapú ta.
asbestos: *n*. asbéstos.
ascend: *v*. agpangáto, ngumáto.
ascent: *n*. sang-át, ulián.

ash: *n.* dapó; **remove ~es of (*cigar*)** *v.*
arsángan; **cook in ~es** *v.* idamdám, itemtém;
roast in ~es *v.* uttomán; **receptacle for ~** *n.*
dapogán.
ashamed: *adj.* mabainán, mabaín, maslég.
ashen: *adj.* nalusiáw, kolordapó
ashore: *n.* takdáng, nasanglád ití ígid.
ashtray: *n.* pagyarsángan.
aside: *n.* apárte; maisiási ití.
ask: *v.* saludsóden, imtuóden; **~ for** *v.*
dawáten.
askew: *adv.* agpalíg.
aslant: *adj.* naírig, impasikíg; agsálog.
asleep: *adj.* nakatúrog.
asparagus: *n.* aspárrago.
aspect: *n.* paráng, langá; kíta.
aspergillum: *n.* isópo.
asperity: *n.* gubsáng, rusangér.
asphalt: *n.* aspálto.
ass: *n.* (*donkey*) ásno; (*buttocks*) úbet.
assail: *v.* duklósen, sarangtén, kabílen.
assassin: *n.* nakapapatáy; **~ate** *v.* papatayén.
assault: *v.* duklósen, sillongén, penglán,
siblókan, arángen.
assemble: *v.* ammongén, ummongén,
urnóngen, punipónen; sukónen, tipónen.
assembly: *n.* pagtitipónan, gímong.
assent: *v.* kumanúnong, umannúrot; buyógen,
tubúyan; *n.* anámong.
assert: *v.* patalgedán, paneknekán.
assess: *v.* pategán, ikeddéng ti balór.
assiduous: *adj.* nagagét, naganetgét, nasaldét,
nargét.
assign: *v.* dutókan, patudonán, pusgán,
kedngán, ipaarámid; ipabági; **~ment** *n.*
naitudó nga aramíden.
assist: *v.* tulóngan, badángan, arayáten,
atibáyen, isalákan.
assistant: *n.* katakunaynáy, kabadángan.
associate: *n.* sósio; kaduá; tumaripnóng; *v.*
tumípon, kumaduá.
association: *n.* gungló, pagambángan;
pannakatimpúyog.
assort: *v.* lasin-lasínen.
assume: *v.* ipagarúp, pagarupén, pamayán,
ipapán.
assurance: *n.* talgéd.
assure: *v.* talgedán, ipanamnáma.
asterisk: *n.* tandá a sinambituén.
asthma: *n.* angkít.
asthmatic: *adj.* angkít, angsén.
astonish: *v.* pagsiddaáwen, rangaén; **~ment** *n.*
rangá, siddáaw; **~ing** *adj.* napasiddáaw.
astound: *v.* pagsiddaáwen.
astray: *adj.* wálang, naiwáwa, nasmá.
astrologer: *n.* astrólogo, mananglángit.

astronaut: *n.* astronáuta.
astute: *adj.* nasarírit, masírib, natarém, nasíkap.
asylum: *n.* taklín, pagtaklínan; kámang;
pakataraknán dagití nakakaási.
at: *prep.* idiáy, ití; **~ all** pulós; **~ that time** idí.
atmosphere: *n.* ángin, tangátang.
atone: *v.* alabarén.
atop: *prep.* ití ngáto.
atrocious: *adj.* makaruród, nadawél.
attach: *v.* ipidég, ináyon; (*tie*) ibaúd.
attack: *v.* penglán, bantuén, bungólan,
agdarúros; gubatén, rautén; **~ing in groups** *n.*
atibelbél, belbél.
attain: *v.* magun-ód, lak-ámen.
attempt: *v.* padásen, gayagáyen,
ipabpabáreng, isasáir, tingtíngen; *n.*
panangpádas.
attend: *v.* dumar-áy, tumabunó; tumaripnóng;
~ to *v.* asikasuén; **~ant** tumultúlong.
attention: *n.* panúnot; salúkag; imátang;
panangikaskáso; **pay ~** *v.* asikasuén,
amisígen, uppokán, agimatá; paliíwen,
matmátan.
attentive: *adj.* nasíseg, natandáan,
manangasikáso, naimátang.
attest: *v.* saksián, pabilgén.
attire: *n.* kawés, lúpot, pagan-anáy.
attitude: *n.* wágas, tingnáy, dang-ás.
attorney: *n.* abogádo; katalék,
mangikalintegán.
attract: *v.* awísen, sulisógen, guyugúyen,
paasitgén; **be ~ed** *v.* maimúyot.
attractive: *adj.* aarakén, atraktíbo,
makaguyúgoy, makaay-áyo; naguápo.
attribute: *n.* gupít; *v.* ibiáng, igapú, ipakumít,
ipabakláy.
aubergine: *n.* taróng.
auction: *n.* subásta; *v.* isubásta.
audacious: *adj.* naturéd.
audacity: *n.* kinaturéd.
audible: *adj.* mangngég.
audience: *n.* agdengdengngég.
audit: *v.* ammirísen ti kuénta.
auditor: *n.* mangsalakníb-gupít.
auditorium: *n.* taripnóngan, paggigimóngan.
auger: *n.* kulúkol, kutúkot, barréna.
augment: *n.* umadó; rumába, sumíken,
maladládan; nayónan.
August: *n.* Agósto.
aunt: *n.* íkit, tía, bápa.
auspicious: *adj.* narang-áy, naparabúran.
authentic: *adj.* napúdno, napaypaysó; **~ate** *v.*
paneknekán.
author: *n.* mannúrat, ti nangisúrat.
authoritative: *adj.* naturáy, mapagtalkán a
mangikeddéng.

authority: *n.* turáy, kalintegán, pannakabalín.

authorize: *v.* palugodán, pasingkedán, palubósan, paluspúsan.

auto: *n.* lúgan, kótse; ~ **shop** *n.* taliér.

autobiography: *n.* kabibiág ti nagsúrat.

autograph: *n.* pírma. ~ **book** *n.* pagpirmáan.

autonomy: *n.* kabukbukódan a turáy.

autopsy: *n.* panangrangkáy ti minatáy.

autumn: *n.* otónio, panawén ti panagrururós.

available: *adj.* maáwat, mabalín a gun-óden.

avenge: *v.* agbáles, ibáles iti ranggás.

average: *adj.* napipiá, taliwága, taliágum; *n.* pagtengngaán, promédio, pagpadáan.

avert: *v.* ilísi, igígir; yadayó, liklíkan.

aviation: *n.* panagpatayáb.

avid: *adj.* naganetgét, nasaét.

avoid: *v.* liklíkan, lisián, ipaliwengwéng, ikaliwengwéng; bugáwan.

avow: *v.* ipudnó, isáwang.

await: *v.* uráyen; saganáen.

awake: *adj.* nakariíng.

awaken: *v.* agriíng; (*fully and stretch out drowsiness*) agmurmuráy.

award: *n.* gunguná; *v.* gungunaán.

aware: *adj.* siammó, sisasagána, siaalibták; **be ~ of** *v.* marikná, mapusgán.

away: *adv.* iti adáyo; **carried ~ by current** *v.* maánud; **keep ~ from** *v.* makilásin; **run ~ with** *v.* agtaráy, itaráy, sakmálen; **throw ~** *v.* ibelléng.

awe: *n.* amangá; (*fright*) buténg, amák.

awesome: *adj.* makapasiddáaw.

awful: *adj.* dákes la únay; nakabutbuténg.

awhile: *adv.* apagbiít, apagkanitó.

awkward: *adj.* sulpéng, nasammukól; nakúdad, nakúlat, nanengnéng, nabannayabéd, basakbasák.

awl: *n.* lisná, kulúkol.

awn: *n.* íbo; ~**less** (*rice*) *n.* purtók.

awning: *n.* tólda, línong a lúpot, balawbáw, tambúbung, lángub.

ax(e): *n.* wásay.

axiom: *n.* annuróten, kinapudnó a naisáwang.

axis: *n.* pagtayyekán; **revolve on an ~** *v.* agtalátal, tumalátal.

axle: *n.* burayóngan, nakaubónan; éhe.

azure: *n.* máris ti lángit, asúl-lángit.

B

babble: *v.* agtanattát, agtagarí, agsaosaó.

baby: *n.* ubíng, maladága, tagíbi; **carry ~ on hip** *v.* agubbá; **breech ~** *n.* súni.

bachelor: *n.* baró.

back: *n.* búkot, likúd; *v.* tulóngan, ayúnan; umúrong; ~ **of knife** *n.* bángad; ~ **up** *v.*

andingáyen; **fall on one's ~** *v.* mapadáta; **hold ~** *v.* medmedán, tenglén, igáwid, benbenén; **look ~** *v.* tumaliáw.

backbite: *n.* agpalpalikúd, panangibabaín, padpadaksén.

backbone: *n.* dúri.

background: *n.* lugár iti likúd.

backpack: *n.* pasikíng.

backwards: *adv.* agsanúd; **bend ~** *v.* lupiáden; ~ **talk** agminamasúni, baliktád.

bacon: *n.* tosíno, príto a tabá.

bad: *adj.* dákes, nadangkés, nadangkók; ~ **luck** buísit, daksangásat; ~ **taste** ádat.

badge: *n.* úsong, medália, pagtandaánan.

baffle: *v.* im-imaén, tubngén, papaáyen, ikallaigí.

bag: *n.* súpot, bay-ón.

bagasse: *n.* úsang, ngolá, bugáso.

baggage: *n.* maléta, kargá, bagáhe.

bail: *n.* piánsa, patalgéd; *v.* karásan, limasán, piansáan.

bailiff: *n.* bilánggo.

bait: *n.* appán, pagappán, ar-árak; *v.* appanán; ar-arákan; tallangawán.

bake: *v.* yúrno; ~ **in hot ashes** *v.* idamdám, itemtém.

baker: *n.* panadéro, aglutlúto ití tinápay.

balance: *n.* gagantíngan, titimbengán; (*in account*) sáldo.

balcony: *n.* balkón, pálko.

bald: *adj.* kalbó, pulták, puridasdás, pulinangnáng, punangnáng, buldak; **half-~** *adj.* ludingás; **become ~** *v.* malpúog.

ball: *n.* bóla; (*dance*) pasála, saláan.

ballbearing: *n.* bolítas.

balloon: *n.* glóbo, palóbo.

ballot: *n.* balóta, papél a pagbutósan; ~ **box** *n.* urná.

balmy: *adj.* agsayamúsom, agsumúsum.

balsam: *n.* kamantígi.

bamboo: *n.* kawáyan, kilíng, siitán, bayúg, bólo, ánes, napnáp, bíkal; ~ **roof** *n.* talákib; **strips of ~** *n.* bambán; **very hard ~** *n.* bellangán; ~ **shoot** *n.* rabóng.

ban: *v.* ipárit.

banana: *n.* sabá; ~ **shoot** *n.* subbuál, sepláng; ~ **tree** *n.* nambaán.

band: *n.* bedbéd; (*in hats*) lingká, saríkaw; (*ribbon*) pirapír; **elastic ~** *n.* lástiko, baldíit; ~ **together** *v.* agnunumó.

bandage: *n.* alep-ép, bedbéd.

bandit: *n.* tulisán, agaágaw.

bang: *n.* panagbetták.

bangle: *n.* baládang.

banish: *v.* pukáwen; ibelléng.

bank: *n.* bánko; ~**book** *n.* libréta ti bánko.

banner: *n.* wagaywáy.
banquet: *n.* padayá, dayaán.
baptism: *n.* bunyág, bautísmo.
baptize: *v.* bunyágan.
bar: *n.* báras; (*iron*) típay; (*obstruction*) balunét, gitéb, sagipéd; (*of loom*) sapayán, síkang; (*drinking*) paginumán, kantína.
barb: *n.* sáwit, síma.
barbecue: *v.* itúno, barbakuaén; *n.* pulpóg, barbakúa.
barbed wire: *n.* bárot a siítan.
barbell: *n.* pésas.
barber: *n.* mammúkis.
bare: *adj.* lamolámo, silalábus; (*men*) butobúto, lúing, nalukdít; (*women*) nabungísan. **~foot** *adj.* sakasáka.
barely: *adv.* apáman, apagapáman, ngannganí saán, gistáy.
bargain: *n.* panagtáwar, tawáran; (*contract*) túlag.
barge: *n.* kásko.
baritone: *n.* baritóno.
bark: *v.* agtaúl; *n.* (*tree*) ukís ti káyo; (*dog*) taúl.
barley: *n.* sebáda.
barrel: *n.* baríles.
barn: *n.* sarúsar, kamálig.
barracks: *n.* kuartél.
barrel: *n.* baríles.
barren: *adj.* lúpes; di maapítan.
barrier: *n.* sarikedkéd, lappéd, bangén.
barter: *n, v.* sukatán.
base: *n.* arisadsád; (*support*) batayán, batáy.
basement: *n.* sírok (ti baláy).
bashful: *adj.* managbabaín.
basic: *adj.* kangrunáan, nakaibatayán.
basin: *n.* bakká, battiá, palanggána; (*pond*) labnéng.
basis: *n.* sarikedkéd, pangibasarán, pangikugnálan, pakaibatayán.
bask: *v.* agkagkág.
basket: *n.* (*general*) labbá; (*fishing*) alát; (*specific kinds*) allúdan, rangáya, kuríbot, karatáy, buligengén, tabidáw, babakó, kuppít, abubót, galumpápa, alúla, apiráng, bakár, balúlang, bokátot, dapílag, kágab, kalupí, kokolbén, kayyabáng, upíg, pangkiá, takará, patakbá, tallakúb, sakkúb, takkáb, batuláng, upít.
bass: *n.* kababaán a tímek.
baste: *v.* bastáen, pulupuluán.
bat: *n.* kurarapnít, úrot; **fruit ~** *n.* pannikí; (*baseball*) pang-ór.
batch: *n.* bunggóy.
bath: *n.* dígos; **~robe** *n.* báta; **~room** *n.* bánio; **~tub** *n.* batiá a pagdigúsan.

bathe: *v.* agdígos, digúsen.
bathing suit: *n.* kawés a pagdígos.
battalion: *n.* bunggóy ti buyótan.
battle: *n.* dangádang, gubát; *v.* makigubát, makidangádang; makirisíris; **~field** *n.* pagbabakálan.
bay: *n.* luék, lóok; wayáng; *v.* agtaúl.
bay leaf: *n.* laurél.
bayonet: *n.* bayonéta.
be: *v.* (Ilocano has no copular verb) (active) ag-; (stative) na-; **~ located** addá.
beach: *n.* apláya, ígid ti baybáy; *v.* itakdáng, ipaígid.
bead: *n.* abalório, kuentás.
beak: *n.* sippít ti billít.
beam: *n.* adígi, tróso; silnág, dilang.
bean: *n.* pardá, sináy, balbalíga, lubiás; **asparagus ~** *n.* palláng; **~ cake** *n.* hópia; **kidney ~** *n.* barawbáw; **lima ~** *n.* patáni; **snap ~** *n.* lúbias; **mung ~** *n.* balátong.
bear: *n.* óso; *v.* bakláyen, turdán; awitén.
bearable: *adj.* maibtúran, masawír.
beard: *n.* barbás, íming, íbo.
beast: *n.* áyup, naúyong nga animál.
beat: *v.* baúten, maluén, atíwen; (*drum*) tugtógen; (*heart*) agpitikpitík; (*defeat*) abáken; *n.* (*of music*) panagkumpás.
beautiful: *adj.* napintás.
beautify: *v.* papintásen; arkósan.
beauty: *n.* pintás; **~ parlor** *n.* pagpakulotán; **~ spot** *n.* síding, sallapíding.
because: ta, agsípud ta, gapú ta.
beckon: *v.* ayabán, payapáyan.
become: *v.* agbalín; -um-.
bed: *n.* káma; kátre; pagturógan.
bedbug: *n.* kíteb.
bedroom: *n.* siléd a pagturógan.
bee: *n.* uyókan, álig; pal-ét; **~hive** *n.* baláy ti uyókan; **beeswax** *n.* allíd.
beef: *n.* kárne ti báka; **~steak** *n.* bistík.
beer: *n.* serbésa.
beet: *n.* remolátsa.
beetle: *n.* barraírong, abal-ábal, mannárog, sibbawéng; **snapping ~** *n.* tangtang-éd, kuddó.
befall: *v.* pasamákan.
before: *adv., prep.* kasakbáyan, kasanguánan; **do ~** unaén; **same as ~** kasdí.
befriend: *v.* gayyemén, makigayyém.
beg: *v.* kumarabá, gumawáwa, agásug, agpalpalamá, makilimós.
beggar: *n.* makilimlimós, agpalpalimós, agpalpalamá.
beggar-ticks: *n.* puríket.
begin: *v.* rugián, irúsat, irukuás, serkén, wanásen; (*rain*) irábon; (*journey*) agrubbuát; **~ to walk** umádap.

beginner: *n.* agdamdámo; mangrugrugí.
behave: *v.* agsingpét, agtignáy a sitataknéng.
behavior: *n.* buát, panagkukuá, tignáy.
behead: *v.* putólan, uluén.
behind: *prep, adv.* iti likúd, malikudán, iti búkot; **look ~** *v.* tumaliáw; **trailing ~** *adj.* natúbel.
being: *n.* páda a táo; **bring into ~** *v.* parsuáen.
belch: *v.* ipugsó, agtig-áb.
belfry: *n.* tórre a pagkampanáan.
belief: *n.* pammáti, álam.
believe: *v.* patién; (*think*) ipagarúp, pamayán, panunóten, kuná, ipáto; **make ~** *v.* agpakóbas.
belittle: *v.* tagibassitén, laísen, tultuláen.
bell: *n.* kampána, kampanília.
belligerent: *adj.* makigubgubát; mannakiringgór.
bellow: *v.* agugáog, agemmák, agbugkáw, agyubúyob.
bellows: *n.* yubuyóban; **main body of ~** *n.* íbeng.
belly: *n.* tián, buksít; **~button** *n.* púseg. **with a large ~** *adj.* buttióg.
belong: *v.* maipatagikuá, maibiáng; akin-.
belongings: *n.* tagikuá.
beloved: *adj.* nadungngó, naayát.
below: *adv., prep.*ití sírok.
belt: *n.* sinturón, baríkes; (*machine*) koréa.
bench: *n.* bánko, tugáw nga atiddóg.
bend: *v.* bakkogén, killuén (*body*) agbalikutkót, agbalikuskús; (*curve*) agkebbó, kumáog; **~ backward** *v.* lupiáden; **~ under a load** *v.* matektekán; **~ forward with face to ground** *v.* agkul-ób; **~ the branches** *v.* agapdáy; *n.* (*of river*) tíkor.
beneath: *adv.*ití sírok.
benediction: *n.* bendisión, pammendisión.
beneficial: *adj.* makatúlong; makapaimbág.
beneficiary: *n.* benepisiário, umáwat ti pagimbagán.
benefit: *n.* gundáway, pagimbagán; **~ from** *v.* kamitén, maránud.
benevolent: *adj.* managayát, manangngaási.
bent: *adj.* nakilló, saán a nalintég.
bequeath: *v.* iságut, ipatáwid, ipaíma.
beriberi: *n.* ebbál, súbisúbi.
Bermuda grass: *n.* pagudpúd, galutgálut.
berth: *n.* kamaróte; pagpuestuán.
beside: *adv., prep.* iti sikigán, sidíran, arpád.
besiege: *v.* lakubén, salimpupóken.
best: *adj.* kasayaátan, kalaingán; kaimbagán; **~ man** (*at wedding*) *n.* ábay.
bestow: *v.* itdén, ipaáy; iregálo.
bet: *n.* pósta, táro, tayá; *v.* agpósta, agtayá, agtáro.

betel nut: *n.* buá, giít; **hard ~** *n.* búngil; **young ~** *n.* marabúteg, agalunét, garasigásan; **prepare ~ for chewing** *v.* agsalongsóng.
betray: *v.* lipútan, ituggúd, irúbo.
better: *adj.* nasaysayáat, naim-imbág; *v.* pasayaáten; artápan.
between: *prep.* nagbaetán, nagtengngaán.
beverage: *n.* inumén, inúm.
beware: *v.* aluádan; agannád.
bewilder: *v.* riribúken, riruén, alliláwen.
bewitch: *v.* kulámen, kayáwan, enkantuén.
beyond: *prep, adv.* iti labés, idiáy pay.
bezoar: *n.* ginammól.
bias: *n.* di nalintég.
bib: *n.* abígay, babéro.
Bible: *n.* Bíblia.
biceps: *n.* aripúyot ti takiág.
bicycle: *n.* bisikléta.
bid: *v.* mangtáwar, igay-át (ti báyad); bilínen; *n.* táwar.
bier: *n.* andás.
big: *adj.* dakkél; (*animals*) nawálat; (*wounds*) batiwáak; **~ bellied** *adj.* buy-óngan, bukíg, buntiék, buttióg; **~ dipper** *n.* dakkél nga áso.
bikini: *n.* bikíni; **~ line** *n.* sip-áng.
bilboes: *n.* tul-óng.
bile: *n.* apró, papáit.
bill: *n.* (*account*) kuénta, pakadagúpan ti útang; (*beak*) sippít.
billion: *n.* sangapúlo a riwríw, bilión.
bin: *n.* kahón.
bind: *v.* biringén, pitipítan, patapátan; (*bandage*) bedbedén; (*with rope to raise*) balukágen, batibatién; (*book*) libruén; **together** *v.* singgapolén; **~ four limbs of** *v.* punguén.
biography: *n.* biograpía, panagbiág, kabibiág.
biology: *n.* biolohía.
bird: *n.* billít, tumatayáb, manmanók; **tailless ~** *n.* túkong, úkong; **~cage** *n.* tangkál; **birdlime** *n.* píket.
birth: *n.* pannakayanák, nakapataúdan; **give ~** *v.* ipasngáy.
birthday: *n.* kasangáy, aldáw a nakayanakán.
birthmark: *n.* bálat; síding; **~ on forehead** *n.* talimúging.
bishop: *n.* obíspo.
bit: *n.* sangkabassít; pirgís; (*carpentry*) kutúkot, kulúkot.
bitch: *n.* áso a bábai.
bite: *n.* kagát; (*and tear*) agkinnít; *v.* kagatén; **~ one's lip** *v.* mangrém, agpangrém; **take a ~** *v.* agkittáb.
bitter: *adj.* napaít; **~ melon** *n.* pariá.
black: *adj.* nangísit; **~ sheep of family** *n.* lángi. **~ widow spider** terrés.

blackboard: *n*. pisárra.
blacken: *v*. pangisíten.
blackout: *n*. panangiddép ti ámin a sílaw.
blacksmith: *n*. pandáy, mammandáy.
bladder: *n*. basísaw.
blade: *n*. dápig, bulóng, tadém.
blame: *n*. pabasólen, umsién; *n*. básol, bábak.
blanket: *n*. ulés.
blaspheme: *v*. agbassáwang, agtabbáaw.
blasphemy: *n*. bassáwang, tabbáaw.
blaze: *n*. rangráng; silnág.
bleach: *v*. ikuláda, papudáwen; *n*. pangikuláda, pangpapuráw.
bleed: *v*. agdára; kaldíten, tudóken, sangráen; sutsután; ~ **at nose** *v*. agdaringóngo; ~ **to death** *v*. maubósan; **cease ~ing** *v*. malangtéd.
blemish: *n*. tukkí; (*scar*) piglát.
blend: *n*. templá, panangilímog; *v*. ináyon, ilímog, limogán.
bless: *v*. bendisiónan; pagasáten.
blessed: *adj*. bendíto, nasantuán.
blessing: *n*. bendisión; gásat.
blind: *adj*. bulsék; (*in one eye*) buldíng; (*half-blind*) nasúleng; *v*. bulsekén; **night ~ness** *n*. rádam.
blindfold: *n*. abúngot ti matá; *v*. abungótan.
blink: *v*. agkirém, agkiraykiráy, agkuridemdém, agkúyep.
bliss: *n*. ragsák.
blister: *n*. kapúyo, lapúyok, lapítog; (*mouth*) ayúma; **fever ~** *n*. ráit.
bloat: *v*. bumasísaw, lumukmég.
block: *v*. lapdén, tipdén; *n*. mutón, lappéd; **chopping ~** langdét.
blond: *adj*. olandés, bugagáw.
blood: *n*. dára; **vomit ~** *v*. agpadára; **suck the ~ of** *v*. sepsepán; **cooked in ~** *adj*. dinadaráan **bloodless** *adj*. naugútan; **bloodthirsty** *adj*. narungsót.
bloom: *v*. agsábong, bumukarkár.
blossom: *n*. sábong; *v*. agsábong.
blot: *n*. pilkát, pilták, tuláw, mulít, mantsá.
blotter: *n*. sekánte, deppél, pangpamagá.
blow: *v*. mangpuyót, agpug-áw, agpuyúpoy; ~ **a horn** *v*. agtanggúyob; *n*. (*beating*) kábil, dánog; ~ **out** *n*. panagbetták ti góma; panagpakán.
blowgun: *n*. sarbatána, sumpít.
blowpipe: *n*. anguyób.
blowtorch: *n*. sopléte.
blue: *n.*, *adj*. asúl, balbág; sammisammí.
blunder: *n*. biddút, ríro.
blunt: *adj*. rumbéb, nangudél, nasugpél; (*pointless*) teppáal; (*noses*) rúpeng.

blurry: *adj*. pusasáw.
blush: *v*. aglabbásit, agtalaín, tumarabáng.
boar: *n*. alíngo, anáping.
board: *n*. tábla, tápi; **cutting ~** *n*. langdét; *v*. agdagús, agsangbáy; **~ing house** *n*. pagdagusán, pangaseráan.
boarder: *n*. agkaséra.
boast: *v*. agpaspásaw, agpadamá, agsalawásaw, agpasindáyaw, agpalangguád, ipangaás.
boat: *n*. sasakayán, sampán, barangáy, bánka.
bobbin: *n*. kanílias, púdon, binulaló, boliós.
body: *n*. bagí; ~ **odor** *n*. payód, anglít.
bodyguard: *n*. mangsalakníb.
bog: *n*. lutúlot, lan-ák, lubnák, kalay-áb.
boil: *n*. lettég; *v*. paburkén; agburék; angrén; ~ **vegetables** *v*. dengdengén, abráwen; **~ed meat** *n*. angér.
boiler: *n*. kaldéra.
boisterous: *adj*. barisawsáw, natagarí.
bold: *adj*. naturéd.
bolt: *n*. baklíng, pasengséng, túdok, balunét, pérno.
bomb: *n*. bombá; *v*. bombáen.
bond: *n*. piánsa; *v*. isaldá.
bone: *n*. tuláng; (*fish*) siít.
bonfire: *n*. panagpúor, gayebgén.
bony: *adj*. natuláng; (*fish*) nasiít; (*skinny*) nakuttóng.
book: *n*. líbro, pagbasáan; **bookkeeper** *n*. tenedór.
boom: *n*. napardás nga irarang-áy.
boomerang: *n*. palládaw.
boost: *v*. ingáto, itag-áy; idáyaw.
boot: *n*. bótas; **~black** aglinlínis ti sapátos, limpiabótas.
booth: *n*. línong a paglakuán.
booty: *n*. samsám.
border: *n*. ígid, pagbeddengán, píngir; (*of basin*) ngárab; (*of field*) rángat; (*of hat*) lipilípi, lebléb.
bore: *v*. (*hole*) abután, kutukótan, barrenáen; (*fatigue*) makabannóg, makaúma; makaruród.
boring: *adj*. makaúma.
born: *adj*. nayanák, naipasngáy.
borrow: *v*. bulóden, angkáten; (*money*) utángan.
bosom: *n*. barúkong, saklót.
boss: *n*. pangúlo (ití trabáho).
bossy: *adj*. naingét, managturáy.
botany: *n*. botánika.
both: *pron*. isúda a duá **on ~ sides** *adj*. agsumbángir.
bother: *v*. alimuténgen, ririén.
bottle: *n*. botélia. ~ **gourd** *n*. tabúngaw.

bottom: *n.* túkok, lansád; (*buttocks*) úbet; **open ~ of** *v.* tubutóben; **sever at bottom** *v.* sipúlen, ipungét.

boulevard: *n.* akába a dálan.

bounce: *v.* agsaltó, aglagtó.

boundary: *n.* patinggá, pagbeddengán.

bounty: *n.* parangkáp, ságut; parábur.

bouquet: *n.* nareppét a raáy ti sábong.

bourgeois: *n.* burgís.

bow: *n.* (*arrow*) bái; (*violin*) udáud; (*of boat*) dúlong; (*hoop*) bakkóko; **bow net** *n.* bóbo, lása, barekbék, sallaguáng, sarípot, buráyok, sárep, binabayén, gángen; *v.* agruknóy, agrúkob, agkumbáwa; agrukbáb; **bowstring hemp** *n.* diladíla; **rain~** *n.* bullaláyaw.

bowels: *n.* bagbágis, lalaém; **move one's ~** *v.* agtakkí.

bowl: *n.* malukóng, dúyog; **bowl-shaped** *adj.* nalúsob.

bowlegged: *adj.* sallakóng, sallákup, sakáng.

box: *n.* káha, kahón, kahíta; *v.* danógen, disnógen; **~ office** *n.* takília, paglakuán ti tíket.

boxer: *n.* boksingéro.

boy: *n.* laláki; (*servant*) ubíng; (*messenger*) baonén.

boycott: *v.* iwélga, baybay-án.

brace: *n.* tengngél, sarapa, túkol.

bracelet: *n.* pulséra, kalangkáng ti punguapunguán, baládang.

bracket fungi: *n.* kudetdét, kúdit, kúlat.

brackish: *adj.* natabáng, naambál, naangbáb.

brag: *v.* agpangás, agpasindáyaw, agbusatsát; aglangsót, aglangát-langát.

braid: *n.* sallapíd; *v.* sallapidén.

brain: *n.* útek; **~less** *adj.* namáag, nakáag, nakúpa; **~pan** *n.* sabotsabót.

brake: *n.* préno; *v.* agpréno.

bran: *n.* túyo.

branch: *n.* sangá; (*of bamboo*) buraráwit, bulláwit; (*of rivers*) simáay; **young ~** *n.* tanábog; **branchy** *adj.* nasangá, narangpáya.

branchia: *n.* ásang.

brand: *n.* márka; **~-new** *adj.* kabarbaró.

brass: *n.* suér; gambáng.

brave: *adj.* naturéd, maíngel.

brawl: *v.* agápa, agsubáng, agsupápak, agríri, agringgór; *n.* ringgór, ríri.

brawny: *adj.* napunér, nabanég.

bray: *v.* baywén; taltálen.

brazier: *n.* daníkag.

breach: *v.* sawángen, giwangán; *n.* gutbáw; búong; dadaél.

bread: *n.* tinápay.

breadfruit: *n.* rímas, pakák.

breadth: *n.* lampád, dampág, kaatiddóg.

break: *v.* buóngen, bettakén, tukkolén.

breakdown: *n.* pannakabúrak, pannakapaksóy.

breakfast: *n.* pammigát.

breakpoint: *n.* pagtapliákan dagití dallúyon.

breast: *n.* súso; **~plate** *n.* kabál; **~work** *n.* írang.

breath: *n.* sang-áw; **out of ~** *adj.* mabítin ti ánges, agsung-áb; **catch one's breath** *v.* agrikabrikáb.

breathe: *v.* agánges; **~ through nose** *v.* ngesngesén.

breech baby: *n.* súni.

breeches: *n.* butárga, sarawínis; **knee ~** *n.* kalsonsílio.

breed: *n.* pulí; *v.* agpatáud, agtarakén; **half-~** *n.* mestíso.

breeder: *n.* panganakán.

breeze: *n.* pul-óy, puyúpoy; **~ fly** ngílaw ti nuáng.

bribe: *n.* suksók, pasuksók; *v.* pasuksúkan.

brick: *n.* ladrílio, ríbak.

bride: *n.* nóbia, babái a makiasáwa.

bridge: *n.* rangtáy, taytáy; **~ of nose** *n.* darangídong.

bridle: *n.* padingalngál; *v.* pakemkemán.

brief: *adj.* ababá.

bright: *adj.* naraniág; nalawág.

brilliant: *adj.* naraniág, nasilnág, nasiláp, nasiléng.

brim: *n.* ungtó; ígid.

bring: *v.* iyég, isangpét; **~ back** *v.* isublí; **~ to an end** *v.* tungpálen.

brink: *n.* ngárab, ígid, ginsáad.

brisk: *adj.* nadarás, nasagiksík; nasiglát.

bristle: *v.* sumgár, agsúngat, agsugargár.

bristling: *adj.* nasupríng, nasugargár.

brittle: *adj.* narasí, nangarasngás; (*weak*) narukóp.

broach: *n.* weswés.

broad: *adj.* akába, nasekkég; **~-chested** *adj.* nabanég.

broadcast: *v.* iwakíwak, iwarnák, iwarragáwag.

broil: *v.* itúno, isarabásab.

broken: *adj.* nabuóng, nabúrak; natukkól.

bronze: *n.* suér, gambáng.

brooch: *n.* alpilér (ti barúkong).

brook: *n.* wáig, baresbés.

broom: *n.* ságad; walís.

broth: *n.* digó, káldo.

brother: *n.* kabsát (a laláki), kabágis; **~-in-law** *n.* káyong.

brotherhood: *n.* panagkakabsát.

brow: *n.* kíday, múging.

brown: *n.* kayumanggí, madkét.

browse: *v.* agbasabása, agkibkíb.

bruise: *n.* dúnor, lítem, panagdánar, labnég.
brush: *n.* (*hair*) eskóba; (*painter's*) brútsa;
tooth~ *n.* sugígi, sipílio, gisígis; ~ **against** *v.*
agságid, agsagírad; ~ **the teeth** *v.* aggisígis,
agsipílio, agsugígi.
brutal: *adj.* nadawél, naúyong.
brute: *n.* áyup.
bubble: *n.* kabbút, síbo, luág, labútab;
(*boiling*) burék; *v.* aglabútab; agburék.
buboes: *n.* butól, pannakálen, babará.
bucket: *n.* tímba, bálde, sítaw, pagtáko.
buckle: *n.* hebília, kímit; *v.* ikímit.
bud: *n.* búsel, keppét, rúting; uggót, úbod.
buffalo: *n.* nuáng.
buffet: *n.* bánság; *v.* sipatén, danúgen.
bug: *n.* insékto, kíteb.
bugle: *n.* tanggúyob.
build: *v.* bangónen, patakdéren.
building: *n.* pasdék; bángon.
bulb: *n.* bombília.
bulge: *n.* batukót, bayokbók, baskág; bung-ór;
bulgy *adj.* nabaskág, nabakág.
bulky: *adj.* nadukáng; naragkáng; nabungkóng.
bull: *n.* tóro, báka a laláki; **young** ~ *n.* turéte.
bullfighter: *n.* matadór.
bullet: *n.* bála, pungló; ~**proof coat** *n.* kabál.
bully: *n.* nadawél a táo.
bulwark: *n.* baluárte, írang.
bum: *n.* bayanggúdaw, nasadót a táo; (*buttocks*)
úbet; *v.* agbayanggúdaw, agballóg.
bumblebee: *n.* alimbubúyog, akut-ákot,
manábung.
bump: *v.* dungpáren; matim-óg; *n.* (*swelling*)
kammúor, bung-ór.
bumper: *n.* salakníb ti lúgan.
bunch: *n.* sangabették, pungó, raáy; kerkerán.
bundle: *n.* raáy, reppét, bungón, balkút; (*of
rice*) pongó, tan-áy, binagó, binarkés, úyon,
sangarpét, sangkabesbés.
bunion: *n.* buttuán.
buoy: *n.* bóya, pátaw, tanngaltáw.
burden: *n.* awít, dagsén, kárga.
burglar: *n.* birkóg, mannanákaw, aguli-úli ití
rabií.
buri palm: *n.* sílag, burí; **fruit of** ~ *n.*
bulandáy.
burial: *n.* punpón, pannakaitábon.
buried: *adj.* nakáli, naitábon; (*dead*)
naitaném.
burly: *adj.* napunér, nabanég; nalagdá;
nasagursór.
burn: *v.* urámen, puóran, silmútan.
burner: *n.* pagseggéd; pagúram.
burnish: *v.* asáen, lidlíden, as-ásen.
burst: *v.* agbetták, lumtúog, bumták; ~ **out**
laughing *v.* bumekká.

bury: *v.* ikáli, itábon; itaném.
bush: *n.* múla.
bushy: *adj.* nasamék.
business: *n.* negósio; pagsapúlan; pangngedán.
bust: *v.* bettakén.
bustle: *v.* agdaras-darás; *n.* panagdaras-darás.
busy: *adj.* masingángar, singangáran,
makumíkom.
but: *conj.* ngem.
butcher: *n.* agpatpatáy, agparpartí, mammartí.
butler: *n.* mayordómo, agidúlot.
butt: *n.* (*of gun*) kuláta; rungróng; (*anat.*)
úbet; *v.* sangduén; idurón.
butter: *n.* mantekília; **coconut** ~ *n.* laná.
butterfly: *n.* kulibangbáng, paroparó; ~ **knife**
n. balisóng.
buttocks: *n.* úbet, kútit; **side of the** ~
kubangkúbang; **superior part of the** ~
kibongkíbong; **with protruding** ~ *adj.*
naburíri, duríri, pugíit; **raise the** ~ *v.*
agburing-át.
button: *n.* botónes, kímit; (*for pushing*)
tatalmegán; ~**hole** *n.* uháles.
buy: *v.* gatángen; ~ **at retail** *v.* agtingí.
buzz: *v.* dayamúdom, dayengdéng; ayeng-éng;
agwengwéng, agdáwang, umarimbángaw.
by: *prep.* babaén, ni, ti; asidég; gapú.
bygone: *n.* nalpás, limmábas.

C

cab: *n.* taksí.
cabbage: *n.* repólio; **Chinese** ~ *n.* petsáy.
cabin: *n.* kalapáw; (*of ship*) kamaróte.
cabinet: *n.* gabinéte, aparadór.
cable: *n.* sagáyad, talí; (*of vessle*) sayápad.
cackle: *v.* agkuták, agarakiák.
cactus: *n.* karimbuáya, kamkampílan.
cadaver: *n.* bangkáy.
cadet: *n.* agad-ádal ti kinabúyot.
café: *n.* pagkapián.
cage: *n.* tangkáy, kulúngan.
cake: *n.* tórta, bibíngka.
calamity: *n.* didigrá, púngeg, ángol,
kalamidád, péste, ganáp.
calculate: *v.* pattapattaén, panangpatáng;
lukáden.
calendar: *n.* kalendário; **lunar** ~ *n.* lunário.
calf: *n.* (*of leg*) lúlod, butóy; (*young cow*)
urbón.
call: *v.* ayabán; awágan.
callous: *adj.* buttuánan.
calm: *adj.* natalná, nasalíndeg, natánang;
namedméd, naánat, naan+nínek; (*sea*) nalínak.
calumny: *n.* pardáya.
cambium: *n.* ámag, ludlód.

camel: *n.* kamélio.
camera: *n.* kodák, mákina a pangretráto.
camouflage: *v.* parawpáwan.
camp: *n.* kámpo; *v.* agkámpo.
campaign: *n.* kampánia, basingkáwel.
camphor: *n.* alkampór.
can: *n.* láta; *v.* (*be able*) maka-, ma-, mabalín;
~ opener *n.* abreláta.
canal: *n.* paáyas, kanál.
cancel: *v.* ukásen.
candidacy: *n.* kandidatúra.
candidate: *n.* kandidáto.
candle: *n.* kandéla; ~ socket *n.* alintúbong;
~stick *n.* siriáles, kandeléro.
candy: *n.* sinam-ít; kankanén, palatípot,
palñang, kéndi.
cane: *n.* sarukód, bastón; (*bamboo*) kawáyan.
canine: *n.* áso; ~ tooth *n.* saóng.
cannery: *n.* pagidelatáan.
cannon: *n.* kanión; (*of animals*) kúkod.
canopy: *n.* balawbáw, tambúbong, lángub,
mantoreál, pabelión, lángit-lángit.
canthus: *n.* mumukátan.
canvas: *n.* mantalóna, lóna; pinintáan.
cap: *n.* góra; kalúb.
capability: *n.* kabaelán, katun-óyan.
capable: *adj.* nabaelán, mannakabaél.
cape: *n.* (*cloak*) kagáy; (*geog.*) ráwis ti dagá.
capital: *n.* (*money*) puonán; (*city*) ngúlo,
kabeséra; (*letter*) dakkél a létra;
~ punishment *n.* dúsa ití patáy, bítay,
pagbitáyan.
capricious: *adj.* agbalballukáti, agwálang,
agpapáos, agsakrár.
capsize: *v.* mapakbó, mapattóg.
capsule: *n.* kápsula.
captain: *n.* pangúlo, kapitán.
captive: *n.* kautíbo, natilíw.
capture: *v.* tiliwén, kayáwen, balúden,
kautibuén.
car: *n.* kótse, lúgan.
carabao: *n.* nuáng; ~ with short horns *n.*
atipadá.
caramel: *n.* patároy.
carbuncles: *n.* tinipáp.
card: *n.* tarhéta; (*playing*) inípis, pánid; game
of ~s *n.* pangginggí, kongkián, binnusasút.
credit ~ tarhéta ti krédito.
cardboard: *n.* kartón.
care: *n.* aluád, gágar, aywán; pannaripáto;
take ~ of *v.* aywánan, taripatuén; ~ about *v.*
ikaskáso, ikankanó.
career: *n.* karrér, pagsapúlan.
careful: *adj.* namedméd, naannád,
managtaripáto.
caress: *v.* appukuén, aglaílo, aprúsan.

cargo: *n.* awít.
caricature: *n.* karikatúra.
caries: *n.* binokbók.
carnation: *n.* klabél, rosál.
carol: *n.* biliansíko.
carpenter: *n.* allawági; ~'s horse *n.* kabaliéte.
carpet: *n.* alpómbra.
carpus: *n.* ngulayngúlay.
carriage: *n.* kalésa; karuáhe.
carry: *n.* awitén, amitén, bunágen; ~ along *v.*
itúgot; ~ in the arms *v.* sakrúyen; hand ~ *v.*
bitbíten; ~ on the shoulder *v.* bakláyen,
sakbáten, bakrúyen; ~ on head *v.* susuonén,
alindadáyen; ~ under armpit *v.* yaklíli,
isaklíli, igpílan; ~ on back *v.* sallabáyen.
cart: *n.* karetón, karesón; springless ~ *n.*
palakapák.
cartilage: *n.* kalkalannióg.
carton: *n.* kartón.
cartoon: *n.* kartún.
cartridge: *n.* kartútso.
carve: *v.* gedgedén, rangkáyen, rengsáyen,
ukíran, buríkan.
cascade: *n.* sariáp.
case: *n.* baláy, káha; pillow~ *n.* súpot.
cash: *n.* kuartá.
cashew: *n.* kasúy; ~ tree *n.* sambaldóke.
cashier: *n.* kahéro.
casket: *n.* kahíta; lungón.
cast: *v.* ipalládaw, ibató; (*nets*) agsaruág,
agdákar; ~ upward *v.* ikudduág, ampayógen.
castanets: *n.* kastaniétas, kastanuélas.
caster: *n.* toytóy.
castle: *n.* kastílio, kúta.
castrate: *v.* kaponén, ilategán.
cat: *n.* púsa; wild ~ *n.* músang, abló; young ~
n. kutíng.
catalog: *n.* katálogo, pagkitkitáan.
cataplasm: *n.* tápal, alep-ép.
cataract: *n.* busá, buskáw, kataráta.
catastrophe: *n.* didigrá, nakaladladíngit a
pasámak.
catch: *v.* tiliwén, kemmegén, sippawén; *n.* (*of
fish*) binurákan.
caterpillar: *n.* iggés; alimbúbudo, bodobódo,
samríd, sarára, timakudúg.
catfish: *n.* paltát.
catgut: *n.* bágis.
Catholic: *n.* Katóliko.
cattail: *n.* badokbádok.
cattle: *n.* báka; steal ~ *v.* agágab; ~ plague *n.*
pangók.
cauliflower: *n.* kólis, koliplór.
cause: *n.* gapú, puón, pungánay; *v.* pataúden.
caution: *n.* aluád, annád, patigmáan, salúkag.
cautious: *adj.* naannád, naaluád; naináyad.

cavan: *n.* kabán.
cave: *n.* rúkib, gukáyab, gingét, úngib.
cave-in: *n.* ludúlod.
caviar: *n.* búgi (a makán).
cavity: *n.* (*cave*) rúkib, lúngog; (*tooth*) binokbók.
cease: *v.* isardéng, sardáyan, itukéng; baybayán.
cedar: *n.* sédro, kalantás, kantíngen.
ceiling: *n.* bóbeda, kísame.
celebrate: *v.* rambákan, dayáwen (ití padayá).
celestial: *adj.* nailangítan.
cellar: *n.* bodéga, sírok (ti baláy).
cellophane: *n.* selopín.
cement: *n.* galagála, seménto.
cemetery: *n.* kamposánto.
censorship: *n.* sensúra, pannakatíped ti pannakaipabláak ti dámag.
census: *n.* sénso.
cent: *n.* sentábo (centávo); séntimos.
center: *n.* tengngá; kangitingítan; ~ **of attention** *n.* tampók; **go to the ~** *v.* agpatengngá.
centimeter: *n.* sentimétro.
centipede: *n.* gayáman.
central: *adj.* natengngá; kangrunáan.
century: *n.* sangagasút a tawén, síglo.
ceremony: *n.* ramramít, sebbáng.
certain: *adj.* agpaysó, pudnó; nalawág.
certify: *v.* paneknekán.
cerumen: *n.* dúrek, yúyek.
chafe: *v.* radrádan, lidlíden, kulilién, usaúsan; (*the groin*) asaásen.
chain: *n.* káwar; **gold ~** *n.* tanikalá; **~saw** *n.* kadéna a pagragádi.
chair: *n.* tugáw; palángka; **arm~** *n.* butáka; **rocking ~** *n.* nabuábo a palángka.
chairman: *n.* mangipangúlo.
chalk: *n.* tísa, yéso.
challenge: *v.* karíten.
chamber: *n.* kámara; siléd; **~ pot** *n.* arinóla.
chameleon: *n.* bannagáw.
chamois: *n.* gamúsa.
champion: *n.* nangábak, mangikalúya, ti nagballígi, kampeón; **~ship** *n.* kampeonáto.
chance: *n.* gundáway; gásat, gasanggásat; *v.* ipagásat; **occur by ~** *n.* mairaná.
chandelier: *n.* aránia.
change: *v.* sukatén, balíwan; agsábali; (*clothes*) agsukát; *n.* (*in a transaction*) suplí; (*coins*) sensílio; **~ one's mind** *v.* agtukkiád.
channel: *n.* pagayúsan ti danúm; *v.* ipaáyus; ipadálan.
chaos: *n.* guloguló, kusokusó, panagsasanggalá.
chaotic: *adj.* naguló.
chap: *v.* (*lips*) aglupták; (*sole*) agrangiád.

chapel: *n.* kapília.
chaplain: *n.* kapelián.
chapter: *n.* kapítulo.
character: *n.* kinatáo; kababalín.
characteristic: *n.* pakailasínan; pakaidumáan; galád.
charcoal: *n.* úring, úging.
charge: *v.* ipúlong; (*blame*) pabasólen, bilínen; (*attack*) duklósen; (*accuse*) salangáden; *n.* biáng.
charity: *n.* kaási.
charm: *n.* ánib, mutiá, al-alikámen; **herb ~** *n.* tagiráyad; *v.* kayáwan, pagrayuén.
charter: *n.* dokúmento ti lintég.
chase: *v.* kamáten; *n.* panangkámat.
chasm: *n.* yúyeng, dariwangwáng, lisság.
chaste: *adj.* nateppél.
chastise: *v.* dusáen.
chat: *v.* agpatáng.
chatter: *n.* panangsarsaríta.
chauffeur: *n.* tsupér.
cheap: *adj.* nalaká.
cheat: *v.* suitíken, imbiduén, ulbóden; (*at cards*) ampíten.
check: *v.* tubngén, lappedán, igáwid; *n.* tséke.
checkers: *n.* dáma.
cheek: *n.* pingpíng.
cheep: *v.* agpipiék, aganibáar.
cheer: *v.* liwliwaen, lingayén, linglíngen, ragragsáken.
cheese: *n.* késo.
chemise: *n.* kamisóla, kamisón.
chemist: *n.* kímiko.
cherry: *n.* serésa, mansaníta.
chess: *n.* ahedrés.
chest: *n.* lakása, baúl; (*body*) barúkong.
chestnut: *n.* kastánias.
chew: *v.* agngalngál, agmáma.
chick: *n.* piék.
chicken: *n.* manók; **young ~** *n.* piék, marapágaw; **~ pox** *n.* batúngol, tukó; **~ cholera** *n.* pangók.
chief: *n.* pangúlo, palúngo, úlo, panglakayén; *adj.* nangrúna.
chignon: *n.* pinggól.
child: *n.* anák, ubíng.
childbirth: *n.* panagpasngáy; **period after ~** *n.* tanggád.
childhood: *n.* kinaubíng, kinaagtutúbo.
childish: *adj.* inuubingán, ubing-ubíng.
chill: *n.* lammín, tayegtég; *v.* palamíisen.
chilly: *adj.* nalamíis.
chime: *n.* repíke.
chimney: *n.* pagasimbuyókan, simburión.
chin: *n.* tímid; **~ strap** *n.* paratímid; **with protruding ~** *adj.* tammí.

Chinese: *n.*, *adj.* Insík, Sangláy; ~ **sausage** *n.* longganísa.

chink: *n.* rámat, rikkí.

chip: *n.* sangkáp, sipáng, písi, pit-íng.

chirp: *v.* aganibáar, agit-ít, umariyakyák.

chisel: *n.* paét; *v.* agpaét.

chocolate: *n.* tsokoláte; ~ **porridge** *n.* tsampurádo.

choice: *n.* píli; *adj.* napíli.

choir: *n.* kóro, bunggóy a kumakánta.

choke: *v.* et-étan, irután, upíten, bekkelén.

chokoes: (*Aus.*) *n.* sayóte.

cholera: *n.* bayangúbong; **chicken** ~ pangók; **hog** ~ pangók, baládong.

choose: *v.* pilién, sarasáren, putóken; ~ **wrongly** masmáan.

chop: *v.* ilangdét, putdén, ragasragásen; (*wood*) balsígen, bilsígen; (*into pieces*) tadtáden, tegtegén, segsegén; **chopping block** *n.* langdét; **pork** ~ *n.* tsúleta ti báboy.

chord: *n.* kuérdas.

chorus: *n.* kóro.

Christian: *n.* Kristiáno.

Christmas: *n.* Paskuá.

chubby: *adj.* nalukmég, balsóg, atimbukéng.

chum: *n.* gayyém, barkáda.

church: *n.* simbáan.

cicada: *n.* andídit, kundídit, riári, nínin.

cigar: *n.* pinádis, abáno, tabáko; ~ **holder** *n.* kulísip.

cigarette: *n.* sigarílio.

cinnamon: *n.* kanéla; ~ **color** *n.* kióte.

circle: *n.* sírkulo; (*hoop*) basíkaw; (*company*) tallaóng.

circuit: *n.* lawláw.

circular: *adj.* nagtimbukél; nagbalikuskós.

circumcise: *v.* kugíten; ~**d** *adj.* kúgit; **un~** *adj.* supót.

circumference: *n.* lawláw, palíkaw.

circumflex: *n.* (*accent mark*) kapútsa.

circumstances: *n.* kasasáad, pasámak.

circumvent: *v.* ikallaigí.

circus: *n.* sírko.

citizen: *n.* umíli.

city: *n.* íli; siudád.

civet: *n.* káper ti músang.

civil: *adj.* nataknéng.

civilian: *n.* paisáno.

claim: *v.* tuntónen, gamgámen; agsingír; *n.* kalintegán; panangtuntón.

clam: *n.* kappó, kabíbi.

clammy: *adj.* napigkét, napalét.

clamor: *n.* ariwáwa, arimbángaw.

clan: *n.* sangkabagí, sangkaputótan.

clandestine: *adj.* natalímeng, nalméng.

clap: *n.* agsipát, agampák; agtipát; (*gonorrhea*) sarípit.

clasp: *n.* kímit, kalláwit, pagsangálan.

class: *n.* kláse; (*species*) sebbangán.

classic: *adj.* klásiko; nangayéd.

classified: *adj.* maidásig, nayurnós.

classify: *v.* dasigdasígen.

clatter: *n.* talakátak, padakpadák.

clavicle: *n.* aliwadáng, tuláng ti tengngéd.

claw: *n.* kukó, karámut.

clay: *n.* sekká; lutúlut, píla.

clean: *adj.* nadalús, nasin-áw; *v.* dalusán; ugásan.

cleanse: *v.* dalusán; dayasén.

clear: *adj.* nalawág, naraniág, nadalús, nalínis; nalitnáw; *v.* aglawág; agraniág; (*weather, mood*) mawaknítan; ~ **the throat** *v.* agsay-á.

cleave: *v.* beltáken; dumkét.

clemency: *n.* kaási.

clench: *v.* petpetán; agpetpét.

clerk: *n.* eskribiénte.

clever: *adj.* nasígo, nalaíng, nasarírit, nasaldét.

click: *v.* agtaklá, kumanaklíing; ~ **beetle** *n.* tangtang-éd.

client: *n.* kliénte.

cliff: *n.* derráas, rángkis, kayás, tebbáng.

climate: *n.* klíma, kasasáad ti panawén.

climax: *n.* kangitingítan, pennáak; ngálay.

climb: *v.* umúli, sang-áten, baksáyen; sumagpát.

clinic: *n.* klínika, bassít nga ospitál.

cling: *v.* kumpét, igidgíd.

clip: *n.* sigpít.

clipping: *n.* ginetténg.

clique: *n.* barkáda.

clitoris: *n.* mutíng, tamtampíra, tuldí, tunggíl.

clock: *n.* relós, pagorásan.

clod: *n.* bingkól, bingkórog.

close: *adj.* asidég; nakípet; *v.* irikép; agserrá; ~ **a book** *v.* kupinén; ~ **a hole** *v.* gaburán; ~ **woven** *adj.* nabengbéng, naimnét.

closed: *adj.* serrádo; ~ **fisted** *adj.* naímut, nakirmét, napaídam, nametmét.

closet: *n.* kasília.

clot: *n.* (*of blood in childbirth*) labonglábong; (*of blood*) pellapellá; (*in flour*) búnel.

cloth: *n.* wasíg, pessát, alipuspós, dinur-ús.

clothes: *n.* kawés, pagan-anáy, lúpot; ~**line** *n.* banténg, arténg, salapayán, salad-áyan; pagbalaybáyan.

cloud: *n.* úlep; (*of dust*) atipurápor.

cloudy: *adj.* nalúlem, nayúyem, naalibúyong, nadaguyemyém.

clove: *n.* (*spice*) klábo, klábo-de-komér; (*of garlic*) geppéng; ~ **tree** *n.* klobéra.

clown: *n.* bulbullagáw.
club: *n.* pang-ór, málo; timpúyog; *v.* pang-óren.
cluck: *v.* agkokkók.
clue: *n.* mangibagnós.
clumsy: *adj.* nasammukól, nanengnéng; pillakús.
cluster: *n.* ummóng, raáy; *v.* agtitípon.
coach: *n.* agisursúro; *v.* isúro.
coal: *n.* beggáng, karbón.
coalesce: *v.* aglalaók, agkámang, agkaykaysá; agtibnók.
coarse: *adj.* nakersáng; nasagursór; nagubsáng; nagubál; ~**-spun** *adj.* gisitgísit.
coast: *n.* ígid (ti baybáy), pantár; ~**line** *n.* apláya.
coat: *n.* amerikána, sáko; ~ **of arms** *n.* eskúdo.
coax: *v.* ulbóden; mangaliúg.
cob: *n.* ambulígan, búngas, gúmi.
cobbler: *n.* sapatéro.
cobweb: *n.* alipága, baláy ti lawwalawwá, samot-sámot.
coccyx: *n.* kimmól.
cock: *n.* kawítan, manadór; **crestfallen** ~ *n.* lupíng; ~**fighting** *n.* pallót.
cockroach: *n.* ípes, sípet.
cockscomb: *n.* taptapingár, taptapangár.
cockspur: *n.* kawwét.
cocoa: *n.* kakáw.
coconut: *n.* nióg; ~ **oil** *n.* lána; **red** ~ *n.* golímba; **soft** ~ **meat** *n.* lulukóten, kakarúyen; **hard** ~ **meat** *n.* taramusián, saramusián; **young** ~ *n.* búsel, pápeng; ~ **milk** *n.* gettá; ~ **shell** *n.* sabót; **one-half** ~ **shell** *n.* sabót, abáab, buyúboy.
cocoon: *n.* búgi (ti lawwalawwá).
coco palm: *n.* nióg; **juice of** ~ *n.* tubá; ~ **leaf** *n.* balaniúg.
cod: *n.* bakaláw.
code: *n.* kódigo.
coerce: *v.* pilíten.
coffee: *n.* kapé; ~ **pot** kapetéra.
coffin: *n.* lungón.
cogon: *n.* pan-áw.
cohesive: *adj.* nasupnét, nasuknét.
coil: *n.* kusíkos, kutíkot, kalawíkaw, putípot; (*of rope*) banáta; *v.* putipótan.
coin: *n.* kuartá; **spare** ~**s** *n.* sensílio.
coincide: *v.* maiparná, agraná; agtugmók.
coincidence: *n.* nagranaán; nagtugmókan.
coincidental: *adj.* nairanraná.
coitus: *n.* panagyót.
colander: *n.* pagsagátan.
cold: *adj.* nalamíis, nalam-ék; *n.* (*catarrh*) panaténg; (*temperature*) lam-ék, lamíis; ~ **rice** kilabbán.

cold sore: *n.* ráit.
collaborate: *v.* makitúnos, makipagarámid.
collapse: *v.* marbá, matbág, matpáng; makusbó.
collar: *n.* sanggá, ukkór; kuélio; ~**bone** *n.* aliwadáng.
collateral: *n.* panenglán.
colleague: *n.* paniéro, kaduá.
collect: *v.* singirén, urnóngen; agákup.
collection: *n.* tinípon, urnóng.
collide: *v.* agdungpár, agdinnalápus.
colloquialism: *n.* pangsarsaríta.
colon: *n.* duá a tuldék.
colony: *n.* nagtitipónan; sangkapurók.
color: *n.* máris, kulí; *v.* marísan.
colorful: *adj.* nabursí.
colt: *n.* urbón.
column: *n.* túkol, binnátong, adígi, síngit, teddék, monmón; **spinal** ~ *n.* dúri.
comb: *n.* sagaysáy; *v.* agsagaysáy; ~ **with hands** *v.* amúyen; **combing frame** *n.* pagtagúdan; (*of cocks*) ríngay, tapingár.
combat: *n.* gubát, bákal.
combination: *n.* nagtitipónan, pagkakaduaán.
combine: *v.* agkaykaysá, agkámang, agnonomó, agtatarapók, pagkaduaén.
come: *v.* umáy; dumténg; umasidég.
comedian: *n.* komediánte.
comedy: *n.* komédia.
comet: *n.* bandús.
comfort: *n.* liwliwá, nam-áy, linglingáy; *v.* lingayén; ~**able** *adj.* nanam-áy.
comical: *adj.* nakakatkatáwa, nakaang-angáw.
comma: *n.* kur-ít, kóma.
command: *v.* bilínen, ipanguluán.
commander: *n.* agbilbílin.
commemorative: *adj.* pagrukbáb.
commence: *v.* irugí, irúsat, iwáyat; irukkuás.
commerce: *n.* komérsio, panagtagtagiláko, baniága.
commit: *v.* italék, yúlo.
comment: *n.* balláag, komentário.
commission: *n.* komisión; (*market fee*) kuartáis; ~**er** *n.* komisionádo; ~ **agent** *n.* komisionísta.
commit: *v.* italék; ipakumít; ipabakláy.
committee: *n.* tínong, pagtitinóngan.
common: *adj.* sapásap, kadawyán.
commotion: *n.* guló, rápok, arimbángaw.
communicate: *v.* saritáen, ibagá; ipakaammó.
communication: *n.* pannakisaríta, pakitinnarusán, pannakitungtúngan.
communion: *n.* panagtitípon, panagkomulgár.
community: *n.* komunidád, gímong, panagkakaduá.

compact: *adj.* nasedséd, nagdedekkét.
companion: *n.* kaduá, kakúyog.
company: *n.* gímong, pagambágan; bunggóy; kompánia.
compare: *v.* idilíg, ipádis, yaspíng.
compass: *n.* brúhula, kompás.
compel: *v.* abúgen, pilíten.
compendium: *n.* pokpók.
compensate: *v.* utóken; sambútan, subadán, lunúdan, tangdánan.
compete: *v.* agsasalísal, umarták, makiinnábak, agdinnásig, agsinnúot.
competent: *adj.* mainugót, maannongán, nalaíng.
competitor: *n.* kasinnalísal, karinnisíris.
compile: *v.* gupgópen.
complain: *v.* umásug, agdarúm, agdanengdéng.
complaint: *n.* reklámo, púlong; (*in court*) darúm.
complete: *adj.* sibubukél, nalpás.
complex: *adj.* narikút; narígat; (*grammar*) naríkos.
complexion: *n.* búya, kíta ti rúpa.
complicate: *v.* parigáten, parikutén.
compliment: *n.* pangdáyaw, pangraém.
comply: *v.* agtungpál, umannúgot, agtulnóg.
compose: *v.* balabaláen, buklén, partuáten.
comprehend: *v.* maawátan.
compress: *v.* pandágan, pekkelén.
compute: *v.* bilángen, patpatangén, lukáden.
comrade: *n.* kaduá.
conceit: *n.* pangás, tangsít, pasindáyaw.
conceited: *adj.* natangsít, napangás, nadangér, naambúg, natangíg, nakuspág, napasindayág.
conceive: *v.* balabaláen; isípen, buklén; agsikóg.
concentrate: *v.* tipónen, ummongén.
concern: *n.* biáng, rebbéng, pakadanágan, pakaseknán.
concerning: *prep.* maipapán ití.
concert: *n.* panagtutúnos, panagdadanggáy ti tokár.
conciliate: *v.* sulsul-óyen.
concise: *adj.* ababá.
conclude: *v.* ipatinggá, ileppás; iturpós.
concord: *n.* tinóng, túnos, panagtumpóng.
concrete: *n.* seménto, kongkréto; *adj.* maitudtudó, nalawág.
concubine: *n.* babái, kamalála.
concur: *v.* agtúnos, agkasungdó, agtumpóng, umanámong, agkaykaysá.
condemn: *v.* ipadúlin, ipáto; pabasólen.
condense: *v.* paababaén.
condiment: *n.* rekádo.
condition: *n.* kasasáad.
condom: *n.* góma.

conduct: *n.* panagkúkua, kababalín.
conductor: *n.* bastonéro; mangipangúlo, mangituróng.
cone: *n.* balisongsóng.
confer: *v.* agtínong; isagútan.
confess: *v.* idarúm, ipudnó, ipaduyakyák.
confetti: *n.* kumpítis.
confidence: *n.* talék, inanáma.
confident: *adj.* natalgéd; natangár.
confidential: *adj.* naitalék, nailímed.
confine: *v.* ibálud.
confirm: *v.* patalgedán, pasingkedán, paneknekán.
conflict: *n.* bákal, suppiát; ringgór.
conform: *v.* umanámong; yallót; mayarkéd.
confuse: *v.* alliláwen, riruén, riribúken, itawtáw.
confused: *adj.* maríro, maríri, masakrár, matakráp, masingasingá, maringgóran, marengréng.
congeal: *v.* agbaláy.
congenital: *adj.* naikasígud.
conger eel: *n.* payó.
congratulate: *v.* kablaáwan.
congregate: *v.* aguurnóng, agtitípon.
congregation: *n.* taripnóng, tipónan.
conjunction: *n.* pangsilpó.
connect: *v.* agkámang, sangálen, idukót, isilpó, pagtipónen.
connection: *n.* silpó, nagsilpuán.
conquer: *v.* parukmáen, abáken, parmekén.
conscience: *n.* konsiénsia, rikná.
conscious: *adj.* siaammó, addaán riknâ.
consecrate: *v.* ikonsagrár.
consecutive: *adj.* agsasarunó, sumarunó.
consent: *n.* palubósan, panuynúyan; *v.* umannúgot, umanámong; ~er *n.* konsintidór.
consequence: *n.* bánag, pagbanágan; búnga, símang; **consequently** *adv.* ití kastá.
conservative: *adj.* naannád, naináyad.
conserve: *v.* idúlin; aywánan.
consider: *v.* adálen, panunóten, usígen, agpakpakinákem.
considerate: *adj.* nametmét, naánus, nasadiá, nasungdó, managtaripáto, naalumámay, nalukáy.
consideration: *n.* panangimutekték, ánus.
consign: *v.* ikumít, italék.
consist: *v.* laónen, buklén.
consistent: *adj.* maitúnos, di marúpir.
consolation: *n.* gin-áwa, liwliwá, áliw.
conspicuous: *adj.* namarangmáng, madláw.
conspiracy: *n.* pannakikumplót.
conspire: *v.* makikumplót.
constant: *adj.* naingét, kanáyon, agnanáyon; **to do ~ly** kankanayónen, nornóren.

constipation: *n.* tabbelén.
constitution: *n.* pagalagádan, batáy-lintég.
constricted: *adj.* nailét, maet-etán.
construct: *v.* bangónen, sangálen.
consulate: *n.* konsuládo.
consult: *v.* makiumán.
consume: *v.* ibusén; talipuspúsen.
consummate: *v.* leppasén, tungpálen.
consumption: *n.* sárut, dáig; pannakaíbus.
contact: *n.* panagsilpó, panaginnasidég.
contagious: *adj.* makaális.
contain: *v.* mangláon, las-úden.
container: *n.* pangikabílan.
contemplate: *v.* panunúten, imatángan.
contemplative: *adj.* managpanúnot.
contemporary: *n.* katawén, kasádar.
contempt: *n.* umsí, uyáw, rimón; ibubúsor.
contend: *v.* makisuppiát.
content: *adj.* naragsák; natalná; makakáleg; ~s *n.* nagyán.
contest: *n.* salísal, suppiát; *v.* umarták; agsalísal; agsálip.
contiguous: *adj.* kadenná, kasigkáy.
continence: *n.* parbéng.
continent: *n.* kontinénte.
continual: *adj.* awán-sardéng, agtúloy.
continually: *adv.* kankanáyon, sangsanganáyon.
continuation: *n.* kanáyon, kasilpó.
continue: *v.* agtúloy, agtagináyon.
contraband: *n.* kontrabándo, naipárit a tagiláko.
contract: *n.* túlag; *v.* agtúlag; agkaretkét, umilét.
contradict: *v.* supapákan, supiáten, tubngáren, busóren.
contradictory: *adj.* sungáni.
contrary: *adj.* kasupádi.
contribution: *n.* paráwad, namín, kanápon.
control: *v.* tengngelén; gesdán; *n.* tengngél, turáy, lappéd.
controversy: *n.* binnúsor, rinnisíris.
contusion: *n.* labnég, panaglítem.
convalesce: *v.* agpaúngar.
convene: *v.* agarák, agtaripnóng.
convenience: *n.* pakainugótan, pagnam-áyan.
convenient: *adj.* umisú.
convent: *n.* kombénto, pagtaengán dagití mádre.
convention: *n.* pagbibinnagbagaán, taripnóng.
conversation: *n.* panagsasaríta, panagtutungtóng.
convert: *v.* pagbalíwen.
convey: *v.* ipán, itultól.
convict: *n.* bálud.

convince: *v.* uyótan, ipapáti; awísen.
convulse: *v.* agarigengén; agbugsót; sumléng.
convulsion: *n.* panagbugsót, til-í, kurarét.
cook: *n.* paralúto, kosinéro; *v.* aglúto.
cookie: *n.* galiétas.
cool: *adj.* naparíir, nalamíis.
cooperate: *v.* agtinnúlong, makitúnos.
cooperative: *adj.* mannakitinnúlong.
cope: *v.* sarangtén, sanguén.
copper: *n.* gambáng.
copulate: *v.* agyót, agyosyós; (*animals*) agdakép, agmanáda, agtúon.
copy: *v.* tuláden, wadén.
coral: *n.* koráles, díli.
cord: *n.* línas, lúbid.
cordial: *adj.* naayát, naimpusuán.
core: *n.* katengngaán; búgas, unég, ámag.
cork: *n.* sullát, tapón; *v.* isullát.
corkscrew: *n.* tirabusón.
cormorant: *n.* kalamón.
corn: *n.* maís; (*of foot*) buttuán, kálio.
corncob: *n.* ambulígan.
corner: *n.* súli, píngir; *v.* ipasúli.
corporal: *n.* kábo; *adj.* maipapán ití bagí.
corporation: *n.* pagkakaduaán.
corpse: *n.* minatáy, bangkáy.
corpulent: *adj.* bukrós, nasábang, bakág.
corral: *n.* ápon, pupúkan.
correct: *v.* mangpalaíng; *adj.* apag-isú, agpaysó.
correction: *n.* panangpalaíng, tarimáan.
correspond: *v.* makipáda; makisinnúrat.
corresponding: *adj.* maitutóp.
corrode: *v.* agláti; kotkóten, murímoren; agrúnot; kurukóren.
corrupt: *v.* dadaélen, padaksén, lungsóten; *adj.* binalitungég.
corsage: *n.* korpínio.
cost: *n.* patég, ngína.
costly: *adj.* nangína.
costume: *n.* pagan-anáy.
cot: *n.* kátre.
cottage: *n.* baláy a bassít.
cotton: *n.* kápas.
couch: *n.* pápag, sopá.
councilor: *n.* konsehál.
counsel: *n.* balákad, bagbagá; *v.* bagbagaán, balakádan.
cough: *n.* uyék; ~ **repeatedly** *v.* kelkelén.
count: *v.* agbílang, dagúpen; *n.* kónde.
countenance: *n.* langá, rúpa.
counter: *n.* mostradór; *adv.* maisuppiát; *v.* maisupádi; suppiáten, salungasíngen.
counterfeit: *adj.* parbó.
counterpart: *n.* kapáda, kaaspíng.

counterpoise: *n.* kontrapéso.

countess: *n.* kondésa.

country: *n.* pagilián; (*rural area*) áway; ~ **person** mintalón, taga-áway.

coup d'état: *n.* kudetá, gólpe de estádo.

couple: *n.* paréha, pagasawáan, agasmáng, duá; *v.* silpuén.

coupon: *n.* kupón.

courage: *n.* turéd, regtá.

courageous: *adj.* naturéd, maíngel.

course: *n.* paglasátan, kabayatán, dálan, turóng.

court: *n.* husgádo, pagsaklángan, pangukomán; *v.* armén; ~**room** *n.* pagusígan, pangukomán.

courteous: *adj.* nadáyaw, naraém.

courtesy: *n.* panagdáyaw, panagraém.

cousin: *n.* kasinsín; **second** ~ *n.* kapiduá; **third** ~ *n.* kapitló; **fourth** ~ *n.* kapimpát; **fifth** *n.* ~ kapinlimá.

cover: *n.* abbóng, kelléb, kalúb, bungón; *v.* kalubán, abbongán; ilemméng.

covet: *v.* tarigagáyan, apálan.

cow: *n.* báka; ~**pea** *n.* utóng.

coward: *n.* takrót, managbutbuténg.

cowardice: *n.* kinatakrót.

cowardly: *adj.* natakrót.

cowry: *n.* buttikí, bukasít, palopagí.

cozy: *adj.* naímeng, namayengméng, nasimpá.

crab: *n.* rasá, kappí; arimbukéng; *v.* agreklámo; agpabpabásol.

crack: *n.* rikáb, birrí, buóng, ranetrét, rengngát.

cradle: *n.* indáyon, dúyan.

cram: *v.* imámel, ipápel.

cramp: *n.* kayetkét, pulíkat; bettéd, kalámbre; kissíw; (*for sawing*) grápa.

crane: *n.* babattuágan; (*bird*) típor.

crank: *n.* manikéta.

cranky: *adj.* naungét, buringetngét.

crash: *v.* dumungpár, tumupá.

crate: *n.* kuríbot, kahón; tarimbán.

crater: *n.* abút ti bulkán.

crave: *v.* tarigagáyan.

crawfish: *n.* udáng.

crawl: *v.* agkarayám, agkarádap; (*worm*) agkúyam.

crayon: *n.* krayóla; tísa a de-máris.

crazy: *adj.* bagtít, maúyong, agbulanbulánen, tawwáw, kées, sansanúong, lukarét, máit.

creak: *v.* yumakét.

cream: *n.* kulába, labútab ti gátas; luág; tabá.

crease: *n.* kupín, pliéges; *v.* tupián.

create: *v.* parsuáen, patauden.

creation: *n.* parsuá, partuát; panangpaaddá.

creature: *n.* nabiág a parsuá.

credit: *n.* talék, pammáti, útang, dáyaw; **take on** ~ *v.* angkáten.

creed: *n.* pammáti.

creek: *n.* wáig, sariáp, luék.

cremate: *v.* padapuén ti bangkáy.

creep: *v.* agkarayám, agdalapádap, agúyas.

crescent moon: *n.* immindáyon a búlan.

crest: *n.* tapingár, pantók; **crestfallen** *adj.* sitataméd, malmaldáy.

crevice: *n.* birrí, rengngát, ráta, rakká.

crew: *n.* tripulánte.

crib: *n.* kullúong, kátre ti ubíng.

cricket: *n.* kuriát; **young wingless** ~ *n.* karawkaráw; **cry of a** ~ *n.* riári.

crime: *n.* básol, labsíng, bábak.

criminal: *n.* managdakdákes, managlabsíng.

cripple: *n.* páwad; pílay, pukól.

crisis: *n.* kibaltáng, pagrigátan, didigrá.

crispy: *adj.* nasarangsáng, nangarasángas

critic: *n.* paradilláw.

critical: *adj.* managdilláw; nakaro.

criticize: *v.* uyawén, babalawén.

criticism: *n.* dilláw, uyáw.

croak: *v.* agkakkák.

crochet: *v.* aggansílio; *n.* gansílio.

crockery: *n.* damdamíli.

crocodile: *n.* buáya.

crook: *n.* kalláwit, killó; managdakdákes a táo.

crooked: *adj.* nakilló, bakkóg, kawwéng.

crop: *n.* ápit; anién; múla.

cross: *n.* krus; *v.* ballasíwen; lumásat.

cross-eyed: *adj.* pangkís.

crosswise: *adj.* nagupúgop, narupúrop.

crouch: *v.* agrúkob, agruknóy, agkul-ób.

crow: *n.* wak; *v.* agtaráok.

crowbar: *n.* barréta.

crowd: *n.* ummóng, gímong, pangén.

crown: *n.* balángat.

crucible: *n.* gángi.

crude: *adj.* nakersáng, narusangér.

cruel: *adj.* naranggás, naúlpit; nadawél, narungsót.

crumb: *n.* murkák, maregmég.

crumble: *v.* agrigírigí; remmayén, raw-áken.

crumple: *v.* lunesén, lumolumuén; kusukusuén, rumekén, burburáken.

crush: *v.* lipitén, pis-íten, lusíten, ludekén.

crust: *n.* ukís, rabáw a natangkén; (*of rice*) ittíp.

crutch: *n.* sammakéd, mulétas.

cry: *n.* sángit; (*of hungry hog*) uríris; *v.* agsángit; agikkís, agíbit.

crybaby: *n.* managsángit, mángit, anil-íl, ang-áng.

crystal: *n.* sarmíng, kristál.

cube: *n.* kúbo.

cuckoo: *n.* kakók.

cucumber: *n.* pepíno.
cuddle: *v.* kepkepán.
cue: *n.* sénias, tandá.
cuff: *n.* súlong; dánog; púnios ti bádo, bokamángga; ~ **links** *n.* mankuérna.
culinary: *adj.* maipapán ití panaglúto.
cull: *v.* imarítan, imurián, agimurí.
culprit: *n.* nakabásol.
cultivate: *v.* bangkágen, talónen, araduén.
culture: *n.* sursúro; kaannawídan; ádal.
culvert: *n.* imbornál.
cunning: *adj.* nasíkap, nasariwáwek.
cup: *n.* tása, tagayán.
cupboard: *n.* aparadór, estánte.
cupule: *n.* leppét.
curb: *n.* lappéd; ígid ti bankéta; *v.* tengngelén, lappedán, patulokén.
cure: *v.* agásan, paimbagén; *n.* ágas.
curfew: *n.* animás, kárpio.
curious: *adj.* managdadámag; usioséro, naammíris.
curl: *n.* kulót.
currency: *n.* kuartá, sapásap a pangawátan.
current: *n.* áyus; *adj.* agdamá.
curse: *n.* lunód; tabbaáw; *v.* ilunód; kadaksán.
curtain: *n.* kortínas; bengbéng, tábing; (*of a stage*) telón; ~ **ring** *n.* kandíling.
curve: *n.* killó, bakkóg.
cuspidor: *n.* pagtupráan.
custard: *n.* letseplán.
custard apple: *n.* anónas, anónang, átis.
custody: *n.* aywán, imatón.
custom: *n.* ugáli, annáwid, kannawídan.
customs: *n.* aduána; ~ **officer** *n.* aduanéro.
customer: *n.* aggatgátang; **loyal** ~ *n.* súki.
cut: *v.* putdén; gupóngen, iwáen, gupdén, iw-íwen; *n.* púted; (*of garment*) tábas; (*of meat*) sangkarangkáy; (*slice*) íwa; ~ **head of** *v.* putólan; ~ **off ears** *v.* pingásan; ~ **skin of** *v.* ukríten; ~ **hair** *v.* purtókan, pukísan; ~ **down trees** *v.* agbákir.
cutlass: *n.* kampílan.
cutlet: *n.* tsuléta.
cuttlefish: *n.* lakí; bumagtó.
cyclone: *n.* alipugpóg.
cylinder: *n.* siliniadór; silíndro.
cymbal: *n.* piangpiáng.
cynic: *n.* nasíngar.
cypress: *n.* siprés.

D

dad: *n.* táta, tátang.
dagger: *n.* puniál, dága.
daily: *adj., adv.* inaldáw.

dairy: *n.* paggatásan; *adj.* gagatásan. ~ **cow** *n.* báka a gagatásan.
dam: *n.* pennéd, kabay-án, tambák, puttót; *v.* puttotén, pennedén.
damage: *n.* dadanés, dadaél, ranggás.
damaged: *adj.* nadadaél, nadúnor, nadánar, nasíba.
damn: *v.* ilunód.
damp: *adj.* nadam-ég, nabasá.
dance: *n.* sála, pasála; *v.* agsála; ~ **in a circle** *v.* agbangibángi; ~ **vis-à-vis** *v.* agsallúpang; **martial** ~ *n.* sáyaw.
dandruff: *n.* lasí.
danger: *n.* peggád, síba, sebbáng; ~**ous** *adj.* napeggád.
dangle: *v.* agtilláyon, aguyáoy, agtallaútay, agbittáyon, agtiwatíw, agonsóy; ~ **babies** (*upwards*) *v.* timpayúgen, tippayúgen.
dare: *v.* karíten, ituréd, regtáan.
daring: *adj.* nakárit; (*defying*) arúg; (*brave*) naturéd, maíngel, nalatgán.
dark: *adj.* nasipngét, nakudrép; (*skin*) nangísit; (*cloudy*) nalúlem, nadaguyemyém; ~ **brown** madkét.
darken: *v.* sumipngét.
darling: *n.* ay-ayatén.
darn: *v.* sursién, saraíten.
darnel: *n.* maratrígo.
dash: *n.* napardás a taráy.
dart: *n.* pána, gayáng; *v.* ibkás, ibkáy, ipugsó, ibabálag; umsuát, bumkuás.
date: *n.* pétsa, aldáw; bílang; (*set for a meeting*) ragúp; ~ **plum** *n.* sapóte; ~ **stamp** *n.* petsadór.
dated: *adj.* petsádo.
daub: *v.* sapuán; pulpuluán; piltapiltákan.
daughter: *n.* anák a babái; ~**-in-law** manúgang (a babái).
dawdle: *v.* agpamayán, agbayanggúdaw; agbayág; yandoyandó.
dawn: *n.* parbángon, bannáwag, annaráar.
day: *n.* aldáw; ~ **laborer** *n.* mangmanggéd, mangmangló; **ten** ~**s** sangaparsát; **to do the whole** ~ *v.* agmalmalém; **every** ~ *adv.* inaldáw; **stay one** ~ *v.* makaysá; **return the same** ~ *v.* agkawíli; ~**break** *n.* parbángon ~**star** *n.* palpallátok, baggák, kamontála; ~**light** *n.* aglawág, agsápa.
daze: *v.* uláwen; puráren; pabutngén.
dazed: *adj.* agmalmalangá, malagáwan, maaríweng.
dazzle: *v.* puráren, rangaén.
deacon: *n.* diákono.
dead: *adj.* natáy; ~**-end road** *n.* tungéd a kalsáda.
deadlock: *n.* panagsardéng.

deadly: *adj.* makapatáy.

deaf: *adj.* túleng, sulpéng (di makangég); **pretend to be** ~ *v.* agintutúleng; **deaf-eared** *adj.* welwél, werwér; **turn a** ~ **ear** *v.* rumíreng, agpatpatúleng.

deafening: *adj.* makasisíleng.

deaf-mute: *n.* túleng ken úmel.

deal: *n.* túlag; *v.* ibúnong, bingláyen, iwáras, makitúlag, ibúray, idátar.

dean: *n.* dekáno.

dear: *adj.* (*expensive*) nangína; (*valuable*) napatég.

death: *n.* patáy; ~ **struggle** *n.* bugsót, nguy-á; **put to** ~ *v.* patayén; ~ **anniversary** *n.* pamísa.

debate: *n.* súsik, rúpir, suppiát.

debility: *n.* kinakápuy, kinakapsót.

debt: *n.* utáng; **in** ~ *adj.* siuútang.

debtor: *n.* ti nakaútang.

debris: *n.* tinumék, rugít.

debut: *n.*dámo a panagparáng.

decade: *n.* sangapúlo a tawén.

decapitate: *v.* putólan, uluén, regsén.

decay: *n.* panaglungsót, panagrupsá; (*internal*) nugúnog, nunóg; *v.* aglungsót, agrupsá; (*meat*) madersá, madur-óy, madugnóy; (*milk teeth*) agribríb; (*through moisture*) matimmíng, matmíng, matúbeg.

decayed: *adj.* (*fruits*) nalungtót, nalungsót; (*cloth*) narukóp; (*worn out*) narúnot; (*meat*) mador-óy, nadúted.

deceased: a. natáy.

deceive: *v.* alliláwen, ulbóden.

December: *n.* Disiémbre.

decency: *n.* kinatimbéng, kinangayéd, kinataknéng.

decent: *adj.* mainugót, nataknéng, nanakmán.

decide: *v.* ikeddéng, ipáto.

decimate: *v.* nasanásen; ~**d** *adj.* nanasánas.

decision: *n.* keddéng, panangipáto.

decisive: *adj.* mangikeddéng; mangipatinggá.

deck: *n.* (*of ship*) rabáw ti sasakayán, kubiérta; (*cards*) inípis, baráhas.

declaration: *n.* palawág, panangyebkás.

declare: *v.* ipalawág; ibkás, isngáw, ibkáy; ipakaammo, iparangárang, isúro; ~ **upon oath** *v.* sapataán; ~ **property** *v.* yalsá.

decline: *v.* agmadí; agapdáy; (*sun*) aglikig; (*refuse*) paíden, ipaídam, ikutát.

decorate: *v.* arkósan, pasayaáten.

decorticated: *adj.* malupdásan; ~ **wood** *n.* ir-ír.

decrease: *v.* pabassitén, kissayán.

decree: *n.* bílin, keddéng; *v.* agbílin.

decrepit: *adj.* duduúgan.

dedicate: *v.* ikúdi, isibbó, iruknóy, iságut, isangrát.

dedication: *n.* ságut, pannakaidáton, panangiruknóy.

deduct: *v.* pugáyen, kissayén.

deed: *n.* arámid; kasurátan.

deem: *v.* ipáto, ipagarúp, ipaganetgét.

deer: *n.* ugsá.

defeat: *v.* abáken, atíwen, parukmáen; parmekén; *n.* ábak.

defecation: *n.* yiibléng, itatakkí.

defecate: *v.* tumakkí, agibléng; umígid.

defect: *n.* kúrang, pakapiláwan, biddút; tukí, gannà; (*in timber*) núka.

defective: *adj.* dákes; sapsapó; ginagalimúsaw; **with** ~ **eyesight** *adj.* kurárap, arráp, kusílap; **with** ~ **pronunciation** *adj.* mútal.

defend: *v.* bantáyan, ikanáwa, kumitán, ikalúya, salakníban, isalakán.

defendant: *n.* ti mangikanáwa, ti mangsalsalakníb.

defense: *n.* salakníb.

defensive: *adj.* manangsalakníb, manangisakít.

defer: *v.* itungkuá, ikuntáng, itantán.

defiance: *n.* kárit.

deficiency: *n.* kúrang.

deficit: *n.* kúrang.

definite: *adj.* nalawág, maitudtudó.

deform: *v.* paalasén ti langá.

defy: *v.* karíten.

degrain: *v.* imurotán.

degree: *n.* grádo; rukód, kangáto.

deity: *n.* Diós, kinadiós.

delay: *n.* takták, gabay; atáday, súyat; *v.* agbayág, agtakták, agtantán, agpanpanapán.

delegate: *n.* delegádo, mangibagí.

delete: *v.* ikkatén.

deliberate: *adj.* naigagára.

delicate: *adj.* nalamí, nalúmoy, nalúba; narasí, nalap-ít.

delicious: *adj.* naímas.

delight: *n.* ragsák, rag-ó, ay-áyo; ~**ful** *adj.* makaparagsák.

delinquent: *adj.* nalabsíng, nakabásol, nalíway.

delirious: *adj.* agam-amangáw.

delirium: *n.* panagam-amangáw, tarimbángon.

deliver: *v.* yáwat; (*by lifting*) ital-ó; (*save*) isalakán; (*in childbirth*) ipasngáy.

deluge: *n.* layús.

delusion: *n.* allílaw.

demand: *v.* tontónen, sapúlen, dawáten.

demolish: *v.* rakráken, regaáyen, rebbaén.

democracy: *n.* turáy ti kaaduán, demokrásia.

demolish: *v.* rebbaén.

demon: *n.* diáblo, demónio, saíro, alán.

demonstrate: *v.* ipabúya, ipabigbíg; ibungábong; (*prove*) paneknekán, ipasinúnod.

demote: *v.* ibabá ti sáad.
den: *n.* rúkib, gukáyab; baláy.
denial: *n.* libák, panagulbód.
denounce: *v.* idarúm; pabasólen; ipúlong.
dense: *adj.* nasamék, naisék, napuskól, nasedséd.
dent: *n.* lennék, túgot, gayyét; ungáb.
dentist: *n.* dentísta (mangngágas ití ngípen).
deny: *v.* saanén, suppiáten, libakén, supapákan; ipaídam.
depart: *v.* mapán, pumánaw; agáwid.
departure: *n.* ipapánaw.
department: *n.* departaménto, bennég.
depend: *v.* agtalék; agtalgéd; agsanggír; agtalkéd, agsarikedkéd.
dependent: *adj.* agkamkammatalék, agsangsanggír; *n.* ti tartaraknén.
depict: *v.* iladáwan, iparáng.
deplete: *v.* paatianán.
depleted: *adj.* makraáyan.
depopulated: *adj.* nakumáwan.
deport: *v.* ibelléng, papanáwen, pagtaláwen.
deposit: *v.* igámit, paidúlin; itinnág; **security ~** *n.* piánsa, tanián.
depress: *v.* paladingíten.
depression: *n.* ladíngit, lidáy.
deprive: *v.* labúsan, ikkatán; agawán.
depth: *n.* kinaadálem, kinaunég.
derivation: *n.* naggapuán, nagtaúdan.
derive: *v.* aláen; alut-úten, igapú, pataúden.
descend: *v.* umúlog, agpababá.
descendant: *n.* pútot, kaputótan, anák.
descent: *n.* bumabaán.
describe: *v.* ilawlawág, ilánad, itawáng.
desert: *n.* let-áng, tay-ák; *v.* panáwan, italáwan; **go to the ~** *v.* agpáway.
deserve: *v.* rumbéng, maikarí.
desiccated: *adj.* naipriákan, namagá.
design: *n.* daremdém; (*purpose*) kananákem; *v.* isíkat, gandáten, segpén, ikarákar.
designate: *v.* dutóken, patudonán, pusgán; (*by name*) nagánen.
designer: *n.* dumidibuho.
desire: *n.* kalikágum, tarigágay, essém; *v.* kalikagúman, esmán.
desk: *n.* lamisáan a pagsurátan, eskritório.
desolate: *adj.* langálang.
despair: *n.* panagladladíngit; awanán-namnáma.
desperate: *adj.* sipupungtót, nagpagungán.
despise: *v.* uyawén, umsién, karimón.
despite: *prep.* malaksíd no, úray pay no.
dessert: *n.* sam-ít, kankanén, dúlse.
destination: *n.* papanán.
destiny: *n.* gásat; keddéng, pagtungpálan.
destitute: *adj.* napangláw, naawanán.
destroy: *v.* dadaélen, rakráken, lasángen.

destroyed: *adj.* nadadáel, nasíba; nakumáwan.
destruction: *n.* dadaél.
destructive: *adj.* naranggás.
detach: *v.* isína, ikkatén, ipusíng, suktuén.
detail: *n.* ramít, salaysáy.
detain: *v.* taktáken.
detect: *v.* duktálan, sukalán; (*perceive*) malásin, masirmataán.
detective: *n.* sekréta, agsisiím.
detention: *n.* pannakataktás, pannakaibálud.
determine: *v.* ikeddéng, ibánag, panggepén.
deter: *v.* leplepán.
deterrent: *n.* pangleplép.
detest: *v.* guráen, pakarurodán.
detour: *n.* líkaw, siási.
detriment: *n.* pakadadaelán.
deuce: *n.* duá; (*tennis*) tablá.
devastate: *v.* rebbekén, dadaélen, reggaáyen.
develop: *v.* warwáren, iparangárang; (*plants*) rumettáb; (*a place*) tan-áyen; **~ quickly** tumarúbo.
development: *n.* panagrang-áy; panangpapintás, panangpadakkél.
deviate: *v.* sumiási, agkilló; kumásiw; kumaglís, kumbásiw; (*swerve*) sumayág, sumiág.
device: *n.* síkat, paltuád, panggép; (*for picking fruits*) sarúkang; **deceptive ~** *n.* úyam.
devil: *n.* saíro, demónio, satanás.
devise: *v.* panunóten, paltuáden, isípen.
devoid: *adj.* awanán ití.
devote: *v.* ikúdi, iruknóy, ipaáy, ipamaysá, ipasnék.
devoted: *adj.* naipasnék, naitalagá.
devotion: *n.* kinapasnék; panagkarárag.
devour: *v.* ibusén, kanén, talipuspúsen.
devout: *adj.* napasnék, managkarárag, managluálo.
dew: *n.* linnáaw.
dewclaw: *n.* pakikít.
dewlap: *n.* lambilambí.
dexterous: *adj.* nalaíng, nasarírit, nasarót.
dextrose: *n.* suéro.
diabolical: *adj.* nainsairuán.
diadem: *n.* balángat.
diagnosis: *n.* panagsukímat ti puón ti sakít.
diagram: *n.* úgis-úgis.
dialogue: *n.* panagsarsaríta ti duá a táo.
diamond: *n.* briliánte, diamánte, batonsiléng.
diaper: *n.* lampín.
diarrhea: *n.* bayangúbong, burís; **sound of ~** *n.* paratipít, paratopót; **have ~** *v.* agburís, agsúyot, agibléng.
dibble: *n.* waláwal; sudsód; (*for transplanting rice*) wegwég; *v.* iwaláwal, isugkít, yásad.
dice: *n.* dádo; sukogán.

dictate: *v.* barbasáan; diktáran.

dictator: *n.* diktadór.

dictionary: *n.* pagitarusán, diksionário.

die: *v.* matáy; *n.* dádo, sukóg.

diet: *n.* diéta; *v.* agdiéta.

differ: *v.* agdúma, agsalumína, aggiddiát.

different: *adj.* maidúma, sabáli, maigiddiát.

difficult: *adj.* narígat, narikút, nasulít.

diffuse: *v.* iwáras, isaknáp; aginakbáy, agarinúor.

dig: *v.* ikáli, kutkúten.

digest: *v.* lumpa, runáwen, paluknengén.

digestion: *n.* pannakatúnaw, pannakapalpá.

dignified: *adj.* nataknéng, nadáyaw.

dignity: *n.* dignidád, kinatan-ók, dáyaw.

dike: *n.* pennéd, tambák; puttót; (*lesbian*) lakién a babái.

dilapidated: *adj.* nargáay, nadadaél.

dilate: *v.* bennatén, padakkelén; agsaripakpák; ~ **the eyes** bingatén, bulikáden.

dilemma: *adj.* narikút a kasasáad.

diligence: *n.* salúkag, agáwa.

diligent: *adj.* nagagét, naganetgét, naanép, nasaét, nasíseg.

dilute: *v.* limugén, nawnáwen; tambáan, payawyáwen, tibnókan.

dim: *adj.* nakudrép, naalibuyóng, nalidém; (*eyesight*) rituér.

dimension: *n.* rukód; kadakkél; kaláwa.

diminish: *v.* bumassít, kumúrang; kissayán, baw-ásen, ataátan.

diminutive: *adj.* bassiusít.

dimple: *n.* kallíd, kallít.

dine: *v.* mangaldáw, mangrabií (iti ruar).

dinner: *n.* mangrabii.

diocese: *n.* mítra.

dip: *v.* idennét, itáneb, irárem, ipabátok; (*in water*) yúper.

diphtheria: *n.* sakít ti karabukób.

diploma: *n.* diplóma.

diplomacy: *n.* naurnós a pannakikaduá.

diplomat: *n.* diplomátiko.

dipper: *n.* akló; pagtáko; súdo.

direct: *v.* ituróng, itudó, isúro; yáboy; *adj.* nalintég.

direction: *n.* turóng.

directly: *adv.* agtartarús, dagús.

director: *n.* mangiturturóng.

dirge: *n.* dung-áw.

dirt: *n.* rugít, dulpét, dagá; (*on skin*) kabkáb; (*spot*) pilták; *v.* rugitán; (*smear*) tapkálan, tappaálan.

dirty: *adj.* narugít; ~ **clothes** muréng.

disabled: *adj.* baldádo; pílay.

disadvantage: *n.* pakablesán, pakaatíwan, púkaw.

disagree: *v.* sumiási, di umanámong; sumarungáni; ~**ment** *n.* di pannakitúnos.

disappear: *v.* maawán, agpúkaw, maúngaw; ~ **in the distance** maitáweng.

disappoint: *v.* ikáwa, papaáyen, ilaw-án, ikallaigí, libtuán; igabís; im-imaén.

disappointment: *n.* tungdáy, uppápay.

disarrange: *v.* kusokusuén, guluén.

discard: *v.* iwaksí, iwagsák, malásen, ibelléng.

discern: *v.* malásin, masirmataán, masimudáag.

discharge: *v.* (*eyes*) agmúkat, agmirkát; (*menses*) agdaraudó; (*urine*) sarsaripíten.

disciple: *n.* agad-ádal, adálan.

discipline: *n.* dúsa; *v.* saplíten, dusáen.

disclose: *v.* irakúrak, ilátak.

disconnect: *v.* isína.

discord: *n.* suppiát, panagriríri.

discount: *n.* táwar, kissáy, púgay, rebáha, púgay.

discourage: *v.* upáyen; ublágen; patamnáyen; parítan.

discourse: *n.* balláag, bitlá.

discover: *v.* duktálan.

discredit: *v.* ikkatén ti panagtalék.

discreet: *adj.* mapagtalkán; naannád; naulímek.

discuss: *v.* agilawlawág, agsalaysáy.

disease: *n.* sakít.

disembark: *v.* dumsáag, sumanglád, aglangbás.

disgrace: *n.* baín, pannakaitulméng.

disguise: *n.* abbóng, kalupkóp, panglímo; *v.* parawpáwan; manglímo.

disgust: *n.* luksáw, ruród, gúra, surón; ikáy; **cause** ~ makasúya, makapsáw.

disgusting: *adj.* nakasursurón, nakarurruród.

dish: *n.* bandehádo; pinggán, pláto; ~ **towel** *n.* pagpúnas.

dishearten: *v.* pakapsúten.

disheveled: *adj.* warawará, nakosokosó, nagosogosó, nagorogoró; (*hair*) wakráy.

dishonest: *adj.* natákaw, dákes; ulbód.

dishonor: *v.* ibabaín.

disinfect: *v.* disimpektáran, linísen.

disintegrate: *v.* buráken, waraén, agsisína.

disjoint: *v.* lasángen, peltángen.

disk: *n.* sinanpílid.

dislike: *v.* agadí, madí.

dislocate: *v.* bulluén, peltángen; mabló; sulnóten, paglagisién.

disloyal: *adj.* nagulíb, saán a mapagtalkán.

dismantle: *v.* dupráken, warwáren, waraén, wakráen, suktuén.

dismay: *n.* buténg; *v.* kigtóten, butbutngén.

dismember: *v.* (*animals*) rengsáyen; (*people*) rangkáyen.

dismiss: *v.* likudán, malásen; pugsáyen; pagawiden, lipáten, palubósan.
dismissal: *n.* pangikkát.
dismount: *v.* dumsáag; wakráen.
disobedient: *adj.* nasúngit, nasúbeg, nasúkir; bengngég.
disobey: *v.* sukíren, supríngen, lingalíngen.
disorder: *n.* kulkól; kirokiró, riríbuk.
disorganize: *v.* guluén.
disparage: *v.* irurumén, tultuláen.
dispatch: *v.* ipaw-ít, baonén; palubósan.
dispel: *v.* iwaksí, papanáwen.
dispense: *v.* ipaáy, ibúray, laksíden.
disperse: *v.* agsisína, makakníis; maibiríndis; mawatakwaták, mabutakták, agsayyasayyá, madissodissó.
dispirited: *adj.* sidudukém, malbáy.
displace: *v.* yális, yallátiw, kutién.
display: *v.* ukraden, ipabúya, iparangárang, itanggáya, idayá.
disposal: *n.* ipaáy, panangibelléng.
dispose: *v.* isáad, ibúnong; ibelléng; (*set*) ilápag.
disposition: *n.* kababalín, ugáli, panagipáto.
dispute: *n.* súsik, suppiát, ríri; *v.* agsúsik, agsupápak, agsubáng; agtótor, agtúbar.
disregard: *v.* di ikaskáso, baybay-án.
disrobe: *v.* aglábus.
disrupt: *v.* singaén, guluén.
dissect: *v.* sinasináen, iwáen, rangkáyen.
disseminate: *v.* iwáras, ipurruák.
dissent: *v.* sumuppiát.
dissident: *n.* sumupsuppiát.
dissipate: *v.* agawán, marúnaw; agwará.
dissolve: *v.* runáwen, lunágen, waraén, nawnáwen.
dissuade: *v.* upáyen, ublágen.
distance: *n.* kaadayó, baét; **great ~** *n.* lengléng, battáway.
distant: *adj.* adayó.
distaste: *n.* pannakasúya, úma, langó.
distaff: *n.* ungkál, sukdáw.
distill: *v.* aráken, alambikién.
distillery: *n.* alambíke, pagarákan.
distinct: *adj.* maigiddiát, sabáli, naisangayán; (*clear*) nalawág.
distinction: *n.* naggiddiátan.
distinguish: *v.* ilásin, pilién, iliddíng.
distinguished: *adj.* maisalsalumína, mailiddíng, nalaták; natan-ók; nasúdi, narimbáw.
distort: *v.* rungáden; rusnién, tiritíren; riribúken.
distorted: *adj.* bakkawéng, nadíwig, nadawíris, nadaríwis; (*ears*) kupiléng; (*noses*) píwis.

distract: *v.* riribúken, singaén.
distraction: *n.* pannakaríro, pannakayaw-awán.
distress: *n.* túok, rígat, pagél.
distribute: *v.* ibúnong, iwáras.
district: *n.* purók.
distrust: *n.* di panagtalék, panagduaduá.
disturb: *v.* riribúken, singsingaén, ririén.
ditch: *n.* káli, kanál, pay-ás; abút.
divan: *n.* sopá, pápag.
dive: *v.* bumátok, agarinebnéb; *n.* bátok.
diverse: *adj.* nadumadúma.
diversify: *v.* ipasumbáliw, pagsasabalién.
diversion: *n.* aliwaksáy, siási.
diversity: *n.* nagsasabalián, nagdudumáan.
divert: *v.* lingayén; **~ water from river** *v.* simaáyen.
divest: *v.* ikkatén.
divide: *v.* bingáyen, paglasínen, sináen, atayén.
dividend: *n.* bági, bingláy.
divination: *n.* tinnugkél, tinnubkél; **practice ~** *v.* agbúyon.
divine: *adj.* nadiosan, nasantuán; nainlangítan; *v.* ipadlés, buksílan.
division: *n.* sebbangán; pasét, sangá; (*branch*) símang.
divisor: *n.* pangbingbíngay.
divorce: *n.* panagsína (ti agassáwa)
divulge: *v.* iwarnák, iwarawará.
dizzy: *adj.* maúlaw, talimudáwen.
do: *v.* aramíden.
docile: *adj.* naannúgot, naámo, natulnóg.
dock: *n.* dalukdók, puríket; pagtarimaánan iti sasakayán.
dockyard: *n.* pagsangládan.
doctor: *n.* mangngágas, doktór.
doctrine: *n.* doktrína, sursúro, pammáti.
document: *n.* dokuménto, kasurátan.
dodge: *v.* liklíkan, lisián.
dog: *n.* áso; (*with greyish hair*) ídog; (*with white hair*) paliáw; **lap~** *n.* pasakí; **whine of a ~** *n.* alang-áng; **~cart** *n.* karetéla; **~'s mange** *n.* duldóg.
dogma: *n.* patpatién.
dogvane: *n.* palaypáy.
doll: *n.* tuntúnika, tirtirís, an-anák.
dollar: *n.* doliár.
domain: *n.* sákup, kúkua, pagturayán.
dome: *n.* simborió, nagtimbukél nga atép ti pasdék.
domestic: *adj.* naámo, nagtagibaláy.
domesticate: *v.* paamuén.
domicile: *n.* pagtaengán, taéng.
dominant: *adj.* kangrunáan, mangituráy.
dominate: *v.* iturayán.

dominion: *n.* pagturayán, masakúpan.
don: *v.* ikursóng, ikawés.
donate: *v.* iságut, iparangkáp, iregálo.
donkey: *n.* ásno, borríko, búrro.
doom: *n.* dúsa; awanán-namnáma.
door: *n.* ruángan, rídaw; ~**knob** *n.*
pamusipúsan ti rídaw; **shutter** ~ *n.* rikép;
~**mat** *n.* pagpigádan.
doorbell: *n.* kampanília ti ruángan.
doorway: *n.* pagruangánan.
dope: *n.* apiáng.
dormitory: *n.* siléd a pagturógan.
dose: *n.* gatád ti ágas.
dot: *n.* tulnék; *v.* tulnekán.
double: *adj.* sukót, maminduá; kupín; *v.*
kupinén; ~ **cross** *v.* ulbóden.
doubt: *n.* duaduá, ngatangatá; *v.* agduaduá,
pagduaduaán.
doubtful: *adj.* pagduaduaán.
dough: *n.* nagamáy a bellaáy, mása.
dove: *n.* kalapáti, págaw; **wild** ~ *n.* alimúkeng.
down: *adj.* nababá; *adv.* agpababá; *n.*
(*feathers*) marasagaysáy; (*hair*) dutdút,
muldót, buldót.
downcast: *adj.* naladíngit.
downfall: *n.* panagbabá, pannakaábak.
downgrade: *v.* pagbabaén.
downhill: *adv.* agpababá.
downpour: *n.* bayakábak, napigsá a túdo.
downstairs: *adj.* ití sírok; ití babá.
downtown: *n.* púseg ti íli.
downward: *adj., adv.* agpababá.
dowry: *n.* panab-óng.
doze: *v.* agdungsá, maniwníw, mailibáy.
dozen: *n.* doséna, sangadoséna, sangapúlo ket
duá.
draft: *n.* sul-óy; ígup, súsup; ayáb ití buyótan.
drag: *v.* guyóden, ulod-ulóden, rabsúten.
dragon: *n.* bannagáw, kúmaw.
dragonfly: *n.* tuwáto; **large green** ~ *n.*
bungáw, ambungáw, alimbubungáw; **pupa
of** ~ *n.* durandúran, kolaskolás.
drain: *v.* limasán, paatianán.
drainage: *n.* pagayúsan ti danúm.
drama: *n.* pabúya, sarsuéla, dráma.
dramatist: *n.* dramatúrgo, manangipabúya.
drapery: *n.* dalingdíng.
drastic: *adj.* nadarás, nagánat, nadarasúdos.
draw: *v.* pintáan, iladáwan; ~ **out liquids** *v.*
taógen; ~ **aside** *v.* kalenkenén, irónen;
~ **water** *v.* sumakdó, sumaréb.
drawback: *n.* pakaabákan, pagkapsútan.
drawer: *n.* uyósan.
drawing: *n.* pinintáan.
dread: *n.* kigtót, buténg, aligagáw.

dream: *n.* tagtagaínep, arapáap; *v.*
agtagtagaínep; agdarepdép; agparmatá.
dreary: *adj.* nakaladladíngit.
dregs: *n.* intaér, ared-éd, arinsaéd, lissáad,
basábas, luéd; (*of vat dyes*) kió.
drench: *v.* babasaén.
dress: *n.* pagan-anáy, kawés; bestída. ~**ing
room** *n.* pamlesán.
dresser: *n.* tokadór, pagidulínan ti kawés.
dried: *adj.* nagángo; **half-~** *adj.* nabagnét;
~ **in the sun** *v.* ammaráyen; ~ **fish** *n.* dáing,
káring.
drift: *n.* gabsúon, dalúson; (*clouds*)
agyabáyab, agrayabráyab; (*ships*)
agkallaútang, agkatangkátang; (*float away*)
agánud.
driftwood: *n.* gábat.
drill: *n.* kulúkol, barréna, kutúkot; *v.* abután;
asaásan; kulukólen.
drink: *n.* inumén; *v.* uminúm; (*alcohol*)
aginúm, sumukmón.
drip: *v.* agtedtéd.
drive: *v.* agmaného; ~ **away** *v.* ipaturóng,
abúgen.
driver: *n.* tsóper, agmanmaného; **pile** ~ *n.*
martinéte.
drizzle: *n.* arimukámok, arbís; *v.* agarbís.
drone: *n.* galangúgong; *v.* agpallakáw.
drool: *v.* agkatkátay.
droop: *v.* umláy, aglay-ót, aglamuyó, aglayláy;
lumpés, agrúyag.
drop: *n.* tedtéd, ternék; *v.* agregrég; agtinnág;
maregrég.
drought: *n.* igáaw, kalgáw.
drown: *v.* malmés; lemmesén, iremrém.
drowsy: *adj.* makaturtúrog, nadungsá.
drug: *n.* gamút, pagag-ágas.
druggist: *n.* botikário.
drum: *n.* tambór, bómbo.
drunk: *adj.* nabarték, nakainúm.
drunkard: *n.* mammarték.
dry: *adj.* namagá, nagángo; (*land*) natíkag;
(*leaves*) alas-ás; (*timber*) naátir; (*cooked rice*)
naiburikayákay.
dual: *adj.* duá.
dub: *v.* birngásan, panagánan.
dubious: *adj.* tagtagiammuán,
tagtagaammuán, pagduduaán.
duchess: *n.* dukésa.
duck: *n.* páto, ítik; gakgák; **wild** ~ *n.* pápa.
duckling: *n.* piék ti páto.
dud: *n.* paliádo.
due: *adj.* rumbéng; útang; *prep.* gapú ta.
dues: *n.* báyad ti pinagkamkámeng.
duet: *n.* duéto, danggáy-dua.

dugong: *n.* dúyong.
duke: *n.* dúke.
dull: *adj.* (*blunt*) nangudél, nasugpél, nadumbér, polpól, madpér; narungbéd; (*not in demand*) nakúdad; (*overcast*) nakúnem; (*stupid*) tabbéd, namúno, nakúneng.
dumb: *adj.* úmel; **to be struck ~** *v.* masitammél, marpekán.
dummy: *n.* sinantáo.
dump: *v.* ibelléng, ipakbó, iparakúpok.
dune: *n.* karuburúban.
dung: *n.* takkí, lugít; **~ fly** *n.* pannubsúb.
dungeon: *n.* bartolína, pagbalúdan ití unég ti dagá.
duplicate: *v.* paminduaén, pagrutapén.
durability: *n.* kinalagdá, kinapáut.
durable: *adj.* nalagdá; napáut; naamnút.
duramen: *n.* búgas.
during: *prep.* báyat, iti las-úd ti.
dusk: *n.* suripét, sumipngét.
dust: *n.* tápok, manílang; (*from grinding*) tinimók.
duster: *n.* panaplíd; (*feather*) pluméro.
Dutch: *n.* Olandés.
duty: *n.* rebbéng, annóng; (*tax*) buís.
dwarf: *n.* ansisít, battít.
dwell: *v.* agnaéd, agtaéng; **~ing** *n.* pagtaengán.
dwindle: *v.* bumassít, maíbus.
dye: *v.* tináen, kolorén.
dyed: *adj.* natínta; **nicely ~** *adj.* nadketán; **poorly ~** *adj.* nabullígit.
dynamite: *n.* dinamíta.
dysentery: *n.* síka.

E

each: *adj, pron.* sag-, tunggál, tunggál maysá.
eager: *adj.* sipapágus, sirarayráy, sigagágar, sikakalayákay.
eagle: *n.* ágila.
ear: *n.* lapáyag; (*of corn*) salapí; (*of grain*) dáwa; **~drum** *n.* dedengngegán, sarmisarmíng (ti lapáyag); **drooping ~** *n.* lupíng; **groove at back of ~** *n.* tutúleng; **partly clipped ~** *n.* ríngas; **having only one ~** *adj.* píngud, ríngud; **prick up the ~s** *v.* tumingrá; **pull ~s of** *v.* lapigósen, paligósen, solsólen; **pick the ~** *v.* kuríkuren.
earlap: *n.* pipirítan.
earlobe: *n.* pipirítan, tetebbengán; **hole in ~** *n.* tebbéng, tuldó.
early: *adj.* nasápa, nadarás.
earn: *v.* teggedén, magun-ód, ragpáten, agsápul.
earnest: *adj.* napasnék, nasaét.

earnings: *n.* masapúlan, bírok.
earring: *n.* arítos, lúbay, allúday.
earth: *n.* dagá.
earthenware: *n.* damdamíli.
earthquake: *n.* ginginéd.
earthworm: *n.* alintá.
earwax: *n.* dúrek, yúyek.
ease: *n.* kinalaká, nam-áy, talná.
easel: *n.* kabaliéte.
east: *n.* dáya, leleggakán; **~ wind** *n.* kasáor.
Easter: *n.* Paskuá ti Panagúngar.
eastward: *adv.* agpadáya.
easy: *adj.* nalaká; **~ chair** *n.* butáka.
eat: *v.* mangán; kanén, sidaén; **~ secretly** *v.* agíkab; **~ between meals** *v.* agtaknáng, agsammúkat; **~ cold rice** *v.* agkilabbán.
eaves: *n.* sagumaymáy; **~ channel** *n.* kalasúgan.
eavesdrop: *v.* agalimadámad, agdengngég ití lemméng.
ebb: *v.* agbabá; **~ tide** *n.* úgot.
ebony: *n.* ballatináw, balingagtá.
echo: *n.* allíngag, anabáab, áweng, allangúgan.
eclipse: *n.* eklípse, sálip.
economize: *v.* in-inúten, timbengén, terdén; agsalimetmét.
economy: *n.* ekonomía; kinaterréd, panaginínut.
ecstasy: *n.* rag-ó.
eczema: *n.* barkés.
eddy: *n.* alinúno, alúyo.
edge: *n.* ígid, ngárab, tadém, íking; **wear out at the ~** *v.* agruyróy.
edible: *adj.* makán, masidá, malámut.
edict: *n.* bílin, keddéng.
edifice: *n.* pasdék, bángon; baláy.
edit: *v.* urnósen (iti pagmaldítan); manarawidwíd.
educate: *v.* sursuruán, adálan, taraknén, pasanúten.
educated: *adj.* de-ádal, edukádo.
educator: *n.* mangisursúro.
eel: *n.* ígat, íwet; **~ grass** *n.* ballaibá.
effect: *n.* patáud, bánag, makagapú, pagtonóyan, pagangayán; **produce an ~ upon** *v.* sumkén, sumámay.
effeminate: *adj.* binabái, baién, nalupóy.
effigy: *n.* búlto; ladáwan.
effort: *n.* ganetgét, bíleg, panagbannóg; **violent ~** purrúok.
egg: *n.* itlóg; (*of lice*) lis-á; (*with double yolk*) kambál; **skin of the ~** *n.* kuláput, kulánit; **half-cooked ~** *n.* malasádo; **~ cup** *n.* webéra.
eggplant: *n.* taróng.
egg yolk: *n.* ikgáy.

egoism: *n.* kinabuklís, kinaagum, panaginbubukódan.

egotism: *n.* panangdáyaw ití bagí, kinapasindáyaw.

egress: *n.* iruruár, ilalasút, pagruarán.

egret: *n.* kannáway.

eight: *n.* waló; ~ **o'clock** álas ótso.

eighteen: *n.* sangapúlo ket waló.

eighty: *n.* walopúlo.

either: *adj., pron.* uray asíno kadagití duá; **on ~ side** agsumbángir; **~ or** wenno … wenno …

ejaculate: *v.* yebkás; (*semen*) agkissít.

eject: *v.* paruarén, palsutén, iruár; (*from mouth*) yulá.

elaborate: *v.* pasayaáten, pagbannogán.

elastic: *adj.* mabennát, nalulók.

elate: *v.* itan-ók, daydayáwen.

elbow: *n.* síko; *v.* sikuen; duságen, sikílen, saramusóman; masídol.

elder: *n.* inauná, laklakáy, kakaén, panglakayén.

elect: *n.* pilién, dutóken.

election: *n.* panagbubutos.

electric: *adj.* nakuriénte, maipapán iti kuriénte.

electrician: *n.* elektrisísta.

electrocute: *v.* kurientién.

elegance: *n.* kinangayéd, kinadaég.

elegant: *adj.* nangayéd, naestílo, naimnás, nalibnós, nataér, nadaég, nadayág, napayús, nasadiá, naimáig.

elementary: *adj.* pangrugián.

elephant: *n.* elepánte, gádia; **~'s ear** *n.* bíga; **~ grass** *n.* tanglág.

elevate: *v.* inngáto, ipangáto, itag-áy; itan-ók.

elevation: *n.* kangáto.

elevator: *n.* mákina a pangipangáto.

eleven: *n.* sangapúlo ket maysá.

eligible: *adj.* mapíli.

eliminate: *v.* laksíden, iwálin, ikkatén.

ellipse: *n.* basíkaw nga immitlóg.

elongate: *v.* bennatén, paatiddugén.

elope: *v.* agtálaw, agtaráy.

eloquent: *adj.* nalaíng nga agbitlá.

else: *adv.* sabáli pay, sangkasabáli, pay.

elsewhere: *adv.* iti sabáli pay a dissó.

elude: *v.* lisián, liklíkan.

emaciate: *v.* kumuttóng.

emanate: *v.* agtáud, aggapó.

emancipate: *v.* wayawayaán.

embalm: *v.* embalsamarén.

embank: *v.* tambákan.

embark: *v.* sumakáy.

embarrass: *v.* lapdán, ibabaín, abbengán, kulkólen, agsipár.

embassy: *n.* embaháda, pakáda.

ember: *n.* beggáng.

embezzle: *v.* dispalkuén, takáwen.

emblem: *n.* kayarígan, tandá, pagtandaánan.

emboss: *v.* butíkan.

embossed: *adj.* nailiém; **~ ornaments** *n.* baléd.

embrace: *v.* rakepén, arakúpen; **~ from behind** *v.* tumakbá; (*include*) las-úden, sakúpen.

embroider: *v.* bordáan.

embroidery: *n.* binordáan.

embryo: *n.* pára, tumartarúbo.

emerald: *n.* esmerálda.

emerge: *v.* lumtáw, lumtungáw, rumuár; rumsuá; (*plants*) tumibnól.

emergency: *n.* emerhénsia, nariknót a pakasapúlan.

eminent: *adj.* nalaták, nangáto.

emissary: *n.* babaonén; agsisiím.

emit: *v.* ipugsó, paruarén, iruár.

emotion: *n.* rikná (ti nákem), derrép.

emotional: *adj.* managri.kná.

emperor: *n.* emperadór, ári.

emphasis: *n.* panangipeksá, panangipangrúna.

emphasize: *v.* ipapigsá, iyunay-únay.

empire: *n.* pagarián, império.

employ: *v.* (*use*) aramáten, aruáten, dakawáten, gakáten, agapáden.

employer: *n.* agpatrabáho.

employment: *n.* pagsapúlan, saád, panggedán.

emporium: *n.* pagtagilakuán.

empress: *n.* emperadóra.

empty: *adj.* kawáw, kalawákaw, awan nagyán; ubbáw; **~-handed** *adj.* siwiwidáwid. **~ pod or ear of rice** *adj.* bukáw.

enable: *v.* papigsáen, ikkán ti pannakabaél.

enamel: *n.* kalupkóp (ti pintúra), esmálte.

enameled: *adj.* napattokán, napintókan.

encase: *v.* ibaláy, ikahón.

enchant: *v.* kayáwan, enkantuén.

encircle: *v.* likmúten, lakubén, tikrópen; (*fence*) alikubkúban.

enclose: *v.* (*insert*) isapít, ilúkong; (*confine*) ipúpok, punítan, gendán; (*encompass*) likmúten, lakubén, tikrópen.

encompass: *v.* likmúten, lakubén, tikrópen.

encounter: *n.* panagdungpár, panagsárak, bákal.

encourage: *v.* patalgedén, paturdén, paregtáen, pagnamnamáen.

end: *n.* tungpál, gíbus, kaibusánan, murdóng, ungtó; aripungsán; *v.* (*stop*) agsardéng; (*finish*) malpás; **bring to an ~** *v.* tungpálen, turpúsen.

endanger: *v.* isarsárak, isagmák.

endeavor: *v.* padásen, agkagumáan, ipabpabáreng.

endless: *adj.* di agpatinggá.
endorse: *v.* lagdáan, bigbígen.
endowment: *n.* ságut.
endurance: *n.* ibtúr, andór, sagába, sákad, bíleg.
endure: *v.* maibtúr; ituréd, maandúran; (*undergo*) mapasámak, masagába; **be able to ~** *v.* masbaálan; **~ pain** *v.* matutúok, maunsóy.
enema: *n.* labatíba, sumpít.
enemy: *n.* kabúsor, kagurgúra.
energetic: *adj.* naalibták, nasiglát, nasagiksík.
energy: *n.* pigsá; siglát; enerhía.
enforce: *v.* ipapílit, ipatungpál, ipaganetgét; **law ~ment** panangipatungpál ití lintég.
engagement: *n.* nagtulágan.
engine: *n.* mákina, motór.
engineer: *n.* inheniéro, makinísta; mangipamuspúsan.
engineering: *n.* inheniería.
English: *n.*, *adj.* Ingglés.
engrave: *v.* tugótan, ibúrik, kitikítan.
engulf: *v.* ilab-óg, alun-únen, lamúten, alimúnen.
enjoy: *v.* agrag-ó, agragsák; nanámen; **~ment** *n.* rag-ó, ragsák.
enlarge: *v.* padakkelén, palawáen.
enlist: *v.* ilísta.
enmity: *n.* gurangúra.
enormous: *adj.* dakkél únay.
enough: *adj.*, *adv.* umanáy, apag-isú; básta; **not ~** kúrang, nakisáng; **be ~** umdás, umanáy, gumaw-át.
enrich: *v.* pabaknángen.
enroll: *v.* ilísta, ipadrón.
enslave: *v.* tagabuén, adipénen.
ensnare: *v.* ikalubbít, siluán.
entangle: *v.* kulkúlen, kusokusuén, ipulpulípol; (*feet*) maikánot.
enter: *v.* sumrék; **~ abruptly** *v.* sumarakúsok; **~ a net** *v.* kumná; **~ a hole** *v.* lumnék; **~ the ground** *v.* agrukíeb; **~ mouth of river (*tide*)** *v.* sumaknár, sumuknór.
entertain: *v.* sangailién, an-andingáyen, linglíngen, lingayén, sanguén.
entertainment: *n.* palpaliwá; (*spectacle*) pabúya.
enthusiasm: *n.* kinagagét; kinasiglát, kinagágar.
enthusiastic: *adj.* nagágar.
entice: *v.* sulisógen, ay-ayuén, awísen, dutdúten.
entire: *adj.* dágup, ámin.
entitle: *v.* ikkán ti kalintegán.
entity: *n.* bagí, nakabuklán.
entomb: *v.* itaném, itábon.
entrails: *n.* lalaém, bagbágis.

entrance: *n.* ruángan, serkán, iseserrék.
entreat: *v.* kararágan, dawáten.
entrust: *v.* italék, ikumít.
envelope: *n.* sóbre.
envious: *adj.* naágum, naápal, naímon.
envoy: *n.* naibaón, mangitungpál.
envy: *v.* apálan, agúman; *n.* ápal.
epidemic: *n.* péste, ángol.
epilepsy: *n.* kissíw.
epitomize: *v.* pokpóken.
equal: *adj.* maipáda; *n.* agpáda; *v.* ipáda, padáen.
equator: *n.* ekuadór.
equidistant: *adj.* nasallángad, nasallángat.
equip: *v.* ikkán ti alikámen.
equipment: *n.* aruáten, alikámen, kargá.
equitable: *adj.* nalintég, maiparbéng, nasalindég.
equivalent: *adj.* maipáda.
era: *n.* panawén.
eradicate: *v.* pukáwen, dadaélen, ungáwen.
erase: *v.* pukáwen, borraén; **~ from the mind** *v.* gudásen.
eraser: *n.* borradór.
erect: *v.* bangónen, ipasdék; *adj.* (*upright*) natangár; **become ~ (*penis*)** *v.* tumangkén, tumingrá.
erection: *n.* panaguttóg, panagultóg, panagkinód.
erode: *v.* kotkóten, manurúnor.
erogenous: *adj.* makapauttóg, aabukáyen.
erroneous: *adj.* nagbiddút, naríro.
error: *n.* biddút, ríro.
eructate: *v.* agtig-áb; **~ fetidly** *v.* rurusóken.
erudite: *adj.* masírib.
erupt: *v.* agbetták; agpugsó ti apóy.
eruption: *n.* panagbetták, panagpugsó; busáli.
escape: *v.* agtálaw, aglíbas, liklíkan; lisián.
escort: *n.* konsórte, kakúyog; *v.* ikúyog, ikalúya, itundá; (*flank*) bayabáyen.
especially: *adv.* aglálo, maysá únay.
essay: *n.* salaysáy.
essence: *n.* ánag; bangló.
essential: *adj.* masápul, naskén.
establish: *v.* bangónen, ipasdék; isungsúng; (*confirm*) patalgedán; **~ment** *n.* panagbángon; patakdér ti komérsio.
estate: *n.* asiénda, naláwa a dagá.
esteem: *v.* patgén, ilaláen; ikaskáso, ikankanó, igága.
estimate: *v.* pattapattaén, lukáden, karakáren, patpatangén.
estuary: *n.* sabángan, lúob, estéro.
et cetera: *adv.* ken daddúma pay.
etch: *v.* markáan, tugótan, kitikítan.
eternal: *adj.* agnanáyon.
eternity: *n.* kinaagnanáyon.

ethics: *n.* étika.
etiquette: *n.* urbanidád, nangayéd nga ugáli.
eunuch: *n.* yunóko, táo nga awán látegna.
evacuate: *v.* baybay-án, panawán.
evade: *v.* liklíkan, lisián.
evaporate: *v.* bumawbáw; sumngáw.
evasion: *n.* panangliklík.
eve: *n.* bísperas, rabií a kasakbáyan.
even: *adj.* nakanátad, agpátas, agtablá; páris; nasimpá.
evening: *n.* sardám, rabií.
event: *n.* pasámak, mapagténg.
eventually: *adv.* dumténgto lattá.
ever: *adv.* agnanáyon, kanáyon.
everlasting: *adv.* agnanáyon, di agpatinggá.
every: *adj.* ámin, tunggál maysá.
everyone: *pron.* ámin, tunggál maysá.
everything: *pron.* ámin; **to buy ~** *v.* buyónen; **to give ~** *v.* datdáten; **to do ~** *v.* lennebén.
everywhere: *adv.* úray sadíno man.
evidence: *n.* pamaneknék, pangipapáti.
evident: *adj.* (*manifest*) nalawág, napaták, nalaták, nabatád; adúray; (*showing in one's face*) nagindarúpa.
evil: *adj.* dákes, naranggás, nakas-áng, nadangkés; **~ spirit** *n.* lánid, di katataoán; **~doer** ballaibó.
evolution: *n.* itutúbo, irarang-áy.
evolve: *v.* ipasirmatá, parangáyen.
exact: *adj.* maitutóp, apag-isú, pudnó, nakanátad; (*unbiased*) nasalindég.
exaggerate: *v.* agpaspásaw, parawpáwan ti saó, dumaw-ás, dumukláwit; lablabsán, padakkelén, palpalausán ti manaríta.
examination: *n.* pangsúbok, eksámen.
examine: *v.* bigbigén, imatángan, sukimáten, palutpúten, pagsaludsúdan; mangbutingtíng, mangkutingtíng, mangarísit; (*by question*) untónan.
example: *n.* pagarígan, ulidán, wadán.
excavate: *v.* tukitén; **~ slantwise** *v.* irikúb.
exceed: *v.* labsán, atíwen, saliw-ánan, unaán; lumiw-ás, aglápus.
exceedingly: *adv.* aglablabés, nakapalpalálo.
excel: *v.* sagudáyan, saliw-ánan, rimbáwan, dayuán, daegén, pandágan, rupíren, parmekén.
excellence: *n.* paglaingán, pagsayaátan.
excellent: *adj.* napalunguán, napayús, naiparungbó; narimbáw.
except: *prep.* mailaksíd.
exception: *n.* laksíd.
excess: *n.* surók, labés; sawásaw, sáway; **to do to ~** *v.* surokén; **drink to ~** *v.* agrebréb; **eat to ~** *v.* agsamsammúkak; **load to ~** *v.* salensenán.

excessive: *adj.* nalabés, napalálo, napalaús; mangnibinibí; nakáro, nasurók, napalabúnan.
exchange: *n.* pattáli, sukát, sandí; tunggáli; *v.* isukát, isúno, italáli, ipásang, isúlit; sobóran.
excited: *adj.* matignáy, nakigtót.
exclaim: *v.* yesngáw, ipukkáw.
exclamation: *n.* pukkáw, láaw.
exclude: *v.* ilaksíd, saán nga iráman.
excrement: *n.* takkí, ibléng; pur-ís; (*of birds and lizards*) lugít; **small piece of ~** (*last to be evacuated*) *n.* pugtít.
excruciating: *adj.* naut-ót, natuók.
excursion: *n.* panagaliwaksáy.
excuse: *n.* pambár; pakawán; *v.* pakawanén.
execute: (*kill*) papatáyen (babaen ti linteg); (*carry out*) aramíden, tungpálen.
executive: *n.* mangipatungpál, mangimatón.
executor: *n.* ehekutór.
exempt: *adj.* mailaksíd, di maibibiáng, siwawayawayá.
exercise: *n.* panagwatwat; *v.* agwatwat.
exert: *v.* ipeksá, ipakat.
exhale: *v.* isang-áw, ipug-áw.
exhaust: *n.* pagruarán ti asúk.
exhaust pipe: *n.* túbo ti tambútso.
exhausted: *adj.* nautuyán, napaksúyan; (*weak*) nakapsút; (*used up*) naíbus.
exhibit: *v.* ipabúya, iparáng, ipakíta.
exile: *n.* pammagtálaw; *v.* pagtaláwen.
exist: *v.* panagadda; **cause to ~** *v.* parsuáen.
existence: *n.* kaaddá.
exit: *n.* ipapánaw, iruruár, pagruarán; *v.* rumuár.
exodus: *n.* itatálaw, ipapánaw (ti adu a tao).
exonerate: *v.* paawanén ti básol.
expand: *v.* pabussogén; palawáen.
expanse: *n.* kaláwa, kaatiddág.
expect: *v.* namnamáen, daánan, uráyen.
expedient: *adj.* maikanáda, masápul, mainúgot.
expedite: *v.* papardásen, palakaén.
expel: *v.* palsotén, alut-úten, pagtalawen.
expenditure: *n.* gástos.
expense: *n.* báyad, gástos.
expensive: *adj.* nangína.
experience: *n.* pádas; *v.* agpádas.
experiment: *v.* padásen, suúten; *n.* pádas.
expert: *n.* ekspérto, ansiáno, batído.
expire: *v.* agangsáb, matáy, nagsát ti ánges, maulúyan.
explain: *n.* ilawlawág, ipalawág, ipaáwat, itarusán.
explicit: *adj.* nalawág, nalitnáw.
explode: *v.* bumták, lumtúog, manablúong.
explore: *v.* sukisúken, tukóden, palutpúten.
export: *n.* komérsio iti ruár.

expose: *v.* isarsárak, isaráng, idiáya.
exposure: *n.* pannakaibílag, pakailatakán.
expound: *v.* ilawlawág.
express: *v.* yebkás, ibagá.
expression: *n.* panangisaó.
exquisite: *adj.* napalungduán, naiparungbó, napayús.
extend: *v.* bennatén, unnatén; igay-át.
extensive: *adj.* naláwa, bariwáwa, bariwakwák.
extent: *n.* kadakkél, kaláwa.
exterior: *n.* akin-ruár, akinrabáw.
exterminate: *v.* dadaélen, patayén, raríten.
external: *adj.* akinruár, akinrabáw.
extinct: *adj.* awánen, naiddépen, natáyen.
extinguish: *v.* iddepén, pukáwen, patayén.
extra: *n.* náyon, surók, sobrá; ~ **growth** *n.* síping, awaráy.
extract: *v.* yáon, uyúsen, adáwen, parúten, dutdúten; (*food from pot*) aggaó; aónen; ~ **oil by cooking** *v.* agsinglág; ~ **juice from intestines** *v.* sutsútan.
extraneous matter: *n.* rinét.
extraordinary: *adj.* naisangayán, nakaskasdáaw, namarangmáng, nakaskasdáaw.
extravagant: *adj.* barayúboy, nagásto; nalabés.
extreme: *adj.* ungtó, patinggá, maúdi.
extremity: *n.* pungtó.
extricate: *v.* subbotén.
exult: *v.* agragrag-ó.
eye: *n.* matá; (*of noose*) láog; (*of apple*) púseg, músong; ~-**ball** *n.* bukél ti matá; **inflamed ~s** *n.* bumúsel; **mote in ~** *n.* púling; **one ~ smaller than the other** *n.* kílit; **spot in pupil of ~** *n.* bundáw; **sore ~s** *n.* kamatá; **swollen ~** ballúkot; ~ **socket** *n.* sáad ti matá; ~ **stalks** (*of crustaceans*) *n.* kaméng, rúngo; **cross ~d** *adj.* pangkís; **one-~d** *adj.* buldíng; **with almond ~s** *adj.* kusipét, pingkít; **deep-set ~s** *n.* lesséb.
eyebeam: *n.* múkat.
eyebrow: *n.* kíday.
eyeglasses: *n.* sarmíng, anteóhos, antipára.
eyelash: *n.* kurimatmát.
eyelid: *n.* kalúb ti matá; **scar on ~** *n.* bírit.
eyesight: *n.* panagmatmatá, pagkíta; **with defective ~** *adj.* kurárap, arráp, kusílap, matán-manók.
eyewitness: *n.* manaksí.

F

fable: *n.* paspásaw, saríta a di napudnó, pábula.
fabric: *n.* lúpot; **woven ~** *n.* abél.
fabricate: *v.* paltuáden, pataúden, parnuáyen, parbuén.

fabulous: *adj.* parparbó, paspásaw.
façade: *n.* patsáda, rúpa ti baláy, sanguánan ti patakdér.
face: *n.* rúpa; (*forepart*) sángo; **lower part of ~** *n.* súngo; *v.* agsángo, sanguén; **make ~s** *v.* aggúyab; ~ **to ~** *v.* agsasallúpang.
facetious: *adj.* naangáw, narábak.
facilitate: *v.* palakaén.
facility: *n.* kinalaká, kinasayúd.
facing: *prep.* iti sakláng.
fact: *n.* arámid, gapuánan, kinapudnó.
faction: *n.* sangkatipónan.
factory: *n.* pábrika, baláy a pagaramídan, pagpartuátan.
fad: *n.* móda, abalbaláy, kadawyán nga aglábas, kabarbaró a partuát.
fade: *v.* umuspák, kumusnáw, mawagwág.
fail: *v.* mapáay, masáaw, agkúrang; **without ~** di sumáma.
failure: *n.* pannakaim-imá, pannakapáay, pannakasáaw.
faint: *v.* talimudáwen, mapásag, agkápuy, madapráy; (*through loss of blood*) naadásan.
fair: *adj.* nasayaat; (*complexioned*) napúdaw; *n.* péria.
fairy: *n.* duénde, aniwáas, banbánig, kaybaán.
faith: *n.* pammáti; (*confidence*) talék.
faithful: *adj.* natalék; mammáti; natulnóg.
faithlessness: *n.* ballikúg.
fake: *adj.* barengbáreng, ulbód, ubbáw, sinán-, parbó, tuklís.
fall: *v.* matnág, matuáng, agpababá; (*trip*) mailigí; *n.* pannakatnág; panagregrég; (*season*) otónio, panawén ti panagrururós; ~ **prone** maitikléb, maidaramúdom.
fallacy: *n.* allílaw, ríro, kinaubbáw.
fallow: *adj.* natangátang, malaágan; **to allow to lie ~** *v.* laegán.
false: *adj.* paspásaw, ulbód, mangikulbó.
falsify: *v.* balbaliwán, ulbóden.
fame: *n.* dáyaw.
familiar: *adj.* sapásap; am-ammó.
familiarize: *v.* ruámen.
family: *n.* pamília, kamán, kapoonán, katatáo; **found a ~** *v.* agbaláy; ~ **tree** *n.* panagsinggapó.
famine: *n.* bisín, kírang (ti kanén), gáwat.
famish: *v.* agbisín.
famous: *adj.* nalaták, nasúdi, agdindínámag, natan-ók.
fan: *n.* paíd, paypáy, abaníko.
fanatic: *adj.* napeklán, agbaglán.
fancy: *adj.* nangayéd.
fantastic: *adj.* di nakapappatí.
fang: *n.* saóng.
far: *adj., adv.* adayó; **very ~** lengléng.

fare: *n.* (*for passage*) pléte; (*food*) kanén, sidá.
farewell: *n.* pakáda; ~ **party** *n.* despedída, paskén a pammalúbos.
farm: *n.* tálon, bangkág.
farmer: *n.* mannálon, mammangkág.
fart: *n.* uttót, bisót; *v.* umuttót; bumsúut.
farther: *adj.* ad-adayó.
farthing: *n.* marabilís.
fascinate: *v.* guyugúyen, pasiddaáwen.
fascist: *n.* pasísta.
fashion: *n.* móda, ugáli, kadawyán.
fashionable: *adj.* de-móda.
fast: *adj.* napardás, nadarás; *n.* ayúno.
fasten: *v.* ipakapét, igalút, irákab, sirotén.
fastidious: *adj.* makaúma, napíli, namikkí, namitimit.
fat: *n.* tabá, lukmég; *adj.* nalukmég; (*chubby*) atimbukéng; **very** ~ *adj.* barugsóy, bakág, bukrós.
fatal: *adj.* makapatáy.
fate: *n.* gásat, keddéng, nakaikarián.
father: *n.* áma, táta; *v.* agpútot; agtarakén; **~-in-law** katugángan.
fatherland: *n.* nakayanakán a pagilián.
fathom: *n.* brása; agpá, kadeppá.
fathomable: *adj.* matúkod.
fatigue: *n.* bannóg, utóy, kettáng.
fatten: *v.* palukmegén, salegsegén, saleksekán, pardúden; (*hogs*) darupén.
faucet: *n.* grípo.
fault: *n.* biddút, básol, bábak; (*defect*) pílaw, pakababasán, tukkí.
favor: *n.* parábor.
favorite: *adj.* maay-ayát, maipangpangrúna.
fawn: *n.* kígaw.
fear: *n.* buténg, amák; *v.* bumdéng, agbuténg.
feast: *n.* rambák, padayá; *v.* agrambák.
feather: *n.* dutdót (ti billít); **showy ~s in tail of cock** *n.* lawí; **tuft of ~s** *n.* talipugóng; ~ **duster** *n.* pluméro.
feature: *n.* langá, márka a pakailasínan.
February: *n.* Pebréro.
feces: *n.* takkí.
fed: *v.* pinakán, tinaronán.
federation: *n.* tipónan ti muyóng.
fee: *n.* báyad, tangdán; (*for funerals*) límos.
feeble: nakapsút, nakápuy.
feed: *v.* pakanén, taraonán, taraknén, mamadigó.
feel: *v.* mari005kná; arikápen; tingtíngen.
feeling: *n.* rikná, pakinákem.
feet: *n.* saksáka; **wipe the** ~ *v.* agdulinát, agpolaígad.
feign: *v.* parnuáyen, agpakóbas; im-impén, panaginkukuná; agin-.
feint: *n.* síkap, pakpakuná.

felicitate: *v.* kablaáwan, paragsáken.
felicity: *n.* ragsák, rag-ó, talibágok.
fell: *v.* natnág, natuáng, napadsó.
fellow: *n.* kadduá, kapatadan a tao.
felon: *n.* (*whitlow*) ítib.
felt: *n.* samutsámut, dutdót; piéltro.
female: *adj.* babái, kabay-án.
femur: *n.* baráwas, alluás.
fence: *n.* álad, bangén, bákud; (*sword*) arnís.
fend: *v.* saripdáen, tinggáen, tipawén.
fender: *n.* salakníb ti lúgan.
fermented: *adj.* binubódan.
fern: *n.* pakó; **maidenhair** ~ *n.* dalimpakó, aroruéro; pakpakó.
ferocious: *adj.* narungsót, naranggás, naúyong.
Ferris wheel: *n.* tiobíbo, ruéda.
ferrule: *n.* palméta.
ferry: *n.* bálsa, bilóg, barangáy.
fertile: *adj.* nalamés, naagnéb, kadagaán; nabúnga; natabá; makapaagnéb.
fertilize: *v.* patabaén, ganagánan, abunuán.
fertilizer: *n.* abúno, ganágan.
fervent: *adj. adj.* nasgéd, narayráy.
fervor: *n.* bára, rayray, seggéd.
fester: *v.* umukúok; (*wounds*) umabáya, matibnág.
festival: *n.* piésta, pagragragsákan.
fetch: *v.* dagasén; aláen, iyég, sukónen.
fetid: *adj.* nabuyók, nadaép, nabangsít, naángot.
feud: *n.* ríri.
fever: *n.* gurígor, mayegmég; **mild** ~ *n.* sagabásab.
few: *adj.* sumagmamanó; bassít, manmáno.
fiancé: *n.* nóbio, kinatúlag a kakasár.
fib: *n.* salawásaw, ulbód, tíri.
fiber: *n.* sagút, lábag, urát, binggás(*in meat*) pennét, ábut; **palm** ~ *n.* píet.
fibrous: *adj.* (*sugar cane*) nangurét; (*wood*) nakulbét.
fickle: *adj.* agallaallá, agbaliwbáliw, agbalballukáti, agsakrár, agmanikuá, agtakráp.
fiction: *n.* pinarbó, binalabála.
fiddle: *n.* rabél, biolín, ing-íng.
fidelity: *n.* kinamatalék.
fidget: *v.* agbarinsawáy.
field: *n.* taltálon, tay-ák; tanáp.
fiend: *n.* saíro, demónio.
fierce: *adj.* narungsót, sumarón, naulpít, nawagnét, nawagténg.
fiery: *adj.* immapúy.
fifteen: *n.* sangapúlo ket limá.
fifth: *adj.* maikalimá.
fifty: *n.* limapúlo; ~ **cents** *n.* salapí.

fifty-fifty: *adj*. sagguguddúa.

fig: *n*. ígos, tebbég, lámay.

fight: *n*. kábil, gúbal, bákal, gubát; *v*. agápa, agkábil; gumubát.

figure: *n*. ladáwan, kíta, bílang, tábas, gayamúdaw; *v*. pattapattaén; iladáwan.

filch: *v*. takáwen, pidúten.

file: *n*. intár, urnós; (*instrument*) garugád; (*row*) bátug, pirápid; *v*. talantánen, intarén, tarataren; urnósen; **walk in single** ~ *v*. agallúdoy.

filigree: *n*. sininnabúgan.

fill: *v*. punnuén, pusekén, selselán.

filling: *n*. selsél; (*woof*) pakán, ur-áy.

film: *n*. (*movie*) pelíkula; (*membrane*) kuláput.

filter: *n*. pagsagátan; *v*. sagáten.

filthy: *adj*. narugít, namuréng, milamilát, simamalámal, simamalamála, kamulmuldít, naaributéd.

fin: *n*. pígar, palikpík, palungáping ti ikán; **dorsal** ~ *n*. páwak; **caudal** ~ *n*. kiwkíw, puypóy, puák; **pectoral** ~ *n*. palongáping, salupingpíng; **lateral** ~ **of ray** *n*. ngárab.

final: *adj*. kamaudiánan, maúdi, pangileppás.

finally: *adv*. kanungpálanna.

finance: *v*. agbusbós.

find: *n*. masarákan; maduktálan.

fine: *n*. múlta; *v*. multáen; *adj*. napíno, nalínis, nalápat; **~-toothed saw** *n*. bandíli.

finger: *n*. rámay; *v*. arikápen, abalbalayén; **index** ~ *n*. tammudó; **little** ~ *n*. kikít; **middle** ~ *n*. pattungágan; **ring** ~ *n*. pasariw-át.

fingerless: *adj*. páwad.

fingernail: *n*. kukó.

fingerprint: *n*. lemmá ti rámay.

finish: *n*. gíbus; **~line** (*in race*) *n*. kaliát; *v*. agsardéng, agsardáy; leppasén, tungpálen; (*food*) ibusén; ~ **in time** *v*. isambút.

fire: *n*. apúy, úram; **~fighter** *n*. bombéro; *v*. ikkatén ití sáad; ~ **tree** *n*. árbol; ~ **hydrant** *n*. bóka inséndio.

firearm: *n*. paltóg.

fireball: *n*. layáp, beggáng.

firebrand: *n*. alutén, átong; dapúg; **permanent** ~ patingnán.

firecracker: *n*. kuítis, labintadór, paputók.

firefly: *n*. kulalantí, kulintabá.

fireplace: *n*. temtém.

firewood: *n*. sungród, tungó.

firm: *adj*. natalinaéd, natibkér, nasikkíl, nakerdát; *n*. kompaniá; *n*. baláy ti komérsio.

firmament: *n*. lángit, tangátang.

first: *adj*. umuná; **at** ~ iti dámona; **~ born** *n*. inauná; ~ **class** *adj*. napalungduán, naiparungbó; priméra kláse.

firth: *n*. lúob, sabángan.

fish: *n*. ikán, sidá, lamés; ~ **poison** *n*. túba; ~ **eggs** *n*. búgi; ~ **paste** *n*. buggúong; ~ **sauce** *n*. patís; **~ing tackle** *n*. banníit, wisan-wísan; *v*. agkálap.

fishbone: *n*. siít; **remove the** ~ *v*. isiítan.

fisherman: *n*. mangngálap, agkalkálap.

fishhook: *n*. banníit; **baited** ~ *n*. padángal.

fissure: *n*. rengngát, betták, ukap.

fist: *n*. gemgém, petpét.

fistula: *n*. (*salivary*) lottók.

fit: *v*. umanáy; umsék; itutóp, ibágay; *adj*. apag-isú, mainugót; rumbéng; maitutóp; ~ **together** *v*. silpuén; **~ting room** *n*. pagsukatán, pagpellesán.

five: *adj*. limá; ~ **o'clock** álas-síngko; ~ **yards** *n*. anét; ~ **hundred** *adj*. kiniéntos, limá a gasút; **~fold** *adj*. maminlimá.

fix: *v*. tarimaánen, urnósen.

flabby: *adj*. nalulók, naluknéng, nalamuyó.

flaccid: *adj*. naelláy.

flag: *n*. wagaywáy, bandéra; *v*. banderáan.

flagstone: *n*. dalumpínas.

flake: *n*. pirgís, písi; (*of fire*) alipága, dalipáto.

flamboyant: *adj*. managpakíta; naadórno.

flame: *n*. gil-áyab, apóy, rangráng; *v*. aggil-áyab, umapúy.

flank: *n*. (*animal*) bakráng; (*army*) sikigán.

flannel: *n*. pranéla.

flap: *n*. paraypáy; *v*. agpayakpák.

flare: *n*. rangráng.

flash: *n*. kimát, sal-ít, kisl-áp, agíbas, kiláp; gílap; agíbas; *v*. sumiláp; sumilnóg, makasilnág; aggílap; umagíbas; (*eyes*) agpakrém.

flask: *n*. prásko, kantimplóra, redóma; botélia.

flat: *adj*. nasimpá, tumpáp, dalumpínas, nakuppít; (*noses*) pappáp, rúpeng; **~-headed** *adj*. tubabék.

flatiron: *n*. plantsá.

flatten: *v*. kuppitén, dalupitpíten, balukníten, pilpílen.

flatter: *v*. ay-aywén, mangartók; sugsugnuén, aliúgen, pasaray-ókan, pasablógan. lamióngen.

flattery: *n*. pay-ók, ambúg, pasablóg.

flatulence: *n*. kinamanaguttót.

flatulent: *adj*. managuttót.

flatus: *n*. uttót, kábag.

flaunt: *v*. agparammág, agpakíta.

flavor: *n*. ramán, nánam, ímas; *v*. templáen, paimásen.

flaw: *n*. pakapiláwan, gánná, pilták.

flay: *v*. laláten, kudílen.

flea: *n*. tímel.

flee: *v*. agtálaw, panáwan, umadayó.

fleet: *n*. plóta, eskuádra dagití bapór.

flesh: *n.* laság; (*edible*) kárne.

flexible: *adj.* nalap-ít, nalapiót, nalamí.

flick: *v.* pitíken; saplíten.

flicker: *v.* agkuridemdém, agkudre-kudrép; agpatáy-patáy.

flight: *n.* sarruád, sarruáp; panagluás; pnagtálaw; (*of stairs*) agdán.

flimsy: *adj.* narasí, naingpis, nakápuy, narukóp.

flinch: *v.* agsanúd, kumpés.

fling: *v.* ibató, ipalládaw, ibakal, iwallagés.

flint: *n.* bató-píngki.

flirt: *v.* agparammág, gargarién, ay-aywén.

flirtatious: *adj.* garampáng, ampáng.

float: *v.* agtapáw, tumpáw; *n.* (*buoy*) pátaw, tanggaltáw.

flock: *n.* pangén, purók, arbán; (*of chickens*) kumarayapán; (*of sheep*) sarruád.

flog: *v.* baúten, saplíten, basnúten.

flood: *n.* layús, lapúnos; atáb; *v.* aglayós, aglapúnos; layusén; ~**gate** *n.* aribengbéng.

floor: *n.* datár, básar; (*story*) kadsáaran; *v.* datarán.

flop: *v.* agbagsól; di agballígi.

florid: *adj.* nasábong; nalasbáng.

florist: *n.* ploréro.

flotsam: *n.* gábat.

flour: *n.* arína, bellaáy; **silag palm** ~ *n.* inaín.

flourish: *v.* agrang-áy; agtarúbo; umadú.

flow: *v.* agáyus; agkubbuár.

flower: *n.* sábong; *v.* agsábong; ~**pot** *n.* masetéra; ~ **vase** *n.* ploréra.

flu: *n.* trangkáso.

fluctuate: *v.* ngumáto-bumabá, agmokó; agallo-allón, agbaliw-balíw.

fluency: *n.* kinatarabít, kinasalawitwít.

fluent: *adj.* nasayúd, natarús (ti panagsaríta), natarabít, nasalawitwít.

fluff: *n.* (*lint*) samotsámot, sinutsót; (*of cotton*) sariwagwágen

fluid: *n.* bánag nga agáyus, líkido.

flunk: *v.* di makaruár ti pagsúbok.

flush: *v.* anúden, layásan; *n.* pasayák.

flute: *n.* píto, pláuta; **bamboo** ~ *n.* tuláli.

flutter: *v.* agpayakpák, agwayakwák, agkutikutí; (*low*) agpalaw-íng.

fly: *n.* ngílaw; *v.* agtayáb.

flying: *n.* panagtayáb; ~ **fox** *n.* pannikí.

foam: *n.* labútab, luág; *v.* aglabútab.

focus: *n.* pakipatengngaán ti ísip.

fodder: *n.* lámut ti áyup.

foe: *n.* kabúsor.

fog: *n.* angép, libbúob.

foil: *v.* tungdáyen, saáwen, im-imaén.

fold: *n.* kupín, tupí, kulpí, pliéges; *v.* kupinén, ikulpí, itupí.

foliage: *n.* bulbulóng, rukbós.

folk: *n.* tattáo.

follicle: *n.* búnga.

follow: *v.* suróten, sarunuén; tumúnos; ~ **up** *v.* surnádan.

followers: *n.* pasúrot, búyot.

folly: *n.* kinamáag, kinamaúyong.

fond: *adj.* naessém, nadekkét, naayát, nadungngó.

food: *n.* sidá, kanén, taraón.

foodstuff: *n.* pagtaraón.

fool: *n.* maúyong, natugkák a táo; *v.* ulbóden, alliláwen.

foolish: *adj.* linolóko, ampapáok, maúyong.

foot: *n.* sáka; **sole of** ~ *n.* dapán; (*of basket*) pákad; (*of hill*) arisadsád, baríkir, báwek; ~ **and mouth disease** *n.* ábas.

footfall: *n.* alimpadák.

footprint: *n.* tugót, paddák; baddék.

for: *prep.* maipaáy; gapú; ken, pára.

forbid: *v.* ipárit, páwilan, ikalúya, ipáwil.

force: *v.* pilíten; *n.* bíleg, pigsá, sarikedkéd; ~**ful** napigsá, makaguyúgoy.

forceps: *n.* sípit.

ford: *v.* agyakyák.

fordable: *adj.* nalamméd.

forearm: *n.* takkiág.

foreboding: *n.* partáang ti peggád.

forecast: *n.* padlés, padtó, panangipalnáad; *v.* padtuán, padlesán.

forefather: *n* nagtaúdan, naganák.

forefinger: *n.* tammudó.

forefoot: *n.* kamauná.

forego: *v.* laksíden, likudán, bay-án.

forehead: *n.* múging; **projection of bone in** ~ *n.* búkol.

foreign: *adj.* gangannaét; datdatlág; tao a dildilláw.

foreigner: *n.* gangannaét, tagá-sabáli a dagá.

foreman: *n.* agindég, agindáng; manarawidwíd.

foremost: *adj.* kangrunáan, kaunaán.

forerunner: *n.* mangyuná.

foreskin: *n.* lúngit.

forest: *n.* kabakíran, bákir; ~ **ranger** *n.* guardabóske.

foretell: *v.* ipakauná, ipadtó, ipakauná, ipugtó.

forever: *adv.* inggánat-inggána, agnanáyon.

forge: *v.* pandáyen, buklén, agpandáy.

forget: *v.* lipátan, liwáyan; malipátan.

forgetful: *adj.* nalídam, managtagubay-á; managlilípat; (*senile*) kábaw.

forgive: *v.* pakawanén; ~**ness** *n.* pakawán.

fork: *n.* tenedór, túdok; ~ **of tree** *n.* sápal.

forlorn: *adj.* naiwálang, nabaybay-án.

form: *n.* paráng, kíta, nakabuklán, langá.

formal: *adj.* nangayéd, pormál.
former: *adj.* dáti, akinsakbáy, umuná.
formula: *n.* pagannurótan, wadán.
forsake: *v.* baybay-án; panáwan.
fort: *n.* kóta, pagsammakedán.
fortieth: *adj.* maikauppát a púlo.
fortification: *n.* pagsammakedán.
fortify: *v.* papigsáen, sarikedkedán, lagdaán.
fortitude: *n.* bíleg, pigsá, kiréd.
fortnight: *n.* duá a láwas.
fortress: *n.* pagsammakedán, kóta.
fortune: *n.* gásat, kinabaknáng, sanikuá; **tell one's** ~ *v.* igasátan, ipudósan.
forty: *n.* uppát a púlo.
forward: *adv.* agtarús, iti masanguánan; *n.* pakauná.
foster: *v.* taraknén, patan-áyen; *n.* ~ **child** *n.* tagíbi; ~ **parent** *n.* managíbi.
foul: *adj.* nabangsít; dákes.
found: *v.* bangónen, buangáyen.
foundation: *n.* pagtaúdan, nagbatáyan, puón; pannakabángon.
fountain: *n.* ubbóg, buráyok.
four: *n.* uppát; ~**fold** *adj.* mamimpát.
fourscore: *adj.* walopúlo.
fourteen: *adj.* sangapúlo ket uppát.
fourteenth: *adj.* maikasangapúlo ket uppát.
fourth: *adj.* maikapát; *n.* pagkapát.
fowl: *n.* billít, tumatayáb.
fox: *n.* sórro; ságang.
fraction: *n.* písi ti sangabukél, kapirgís.
fracture: *n.* pannakabuóng, pannakabungtól (ti tuláng), kebradúra.
fragile: *adj.* narasí, narukóp.
frangipangi: *n.* kalatsútsi.
fragment: *n.* písi, tippíng, pedáso.
fragrance: *n.* bangló, sayamúsom.
fragrant: *adj.* nabangló, nasayamúsom.
frail: *adj.* narasí, nangarasngás; nalupóy.
frame: *n.* bastidór, sukogán, kuádro, bangkáy.
franchise: *n.* prankísia, palúbos ti panangigannuát ti negósio.
frank: *adj.* prángko, nabatád.
frantic: *adj.* agmaúyong, sirurungsót.
fraternal: *adj.* nainkakabsátan.
fraternity: *n.* pagkakabsátan.
fraud: *n.* allílaw, suítik, ulbód, kallíd.
fraudulent: *adj.* naulbód, manangallílaw, parbó.
fray: *n.* ringgór, ríri, subáng; *v.* agsuysóy, agruyróy.
freckle: *n.* pékas, turík.
free: *n.* (*liberated*) nawayá; (*gratis*) libré; *v.* wayaán.
freestyle swimming: *n.* barabára.
freedom: *n.* wayawayá.

freeze: *v.* agyélo, agbaláy (iti lamíis).
freight: *n.* kargaménto.
French: *n.*, *adj.* Pransés.
frequent: *adj.* masansán.
fresh: *adj.* nasadíwa, nalasbáng, naparíir.
freshman: *n.* primér-ánio, agdamdámo.
fret: *v.* kulilién, agalimuténg, rasrásen.
fretwork: *n.* kaládo.
friar: *n.* práyle.
friction: *n.* rasrás, risíris, radrád, gasgás.
Friday: *n.* Biérnes; **Good** ~ *n.* Biérnes Sánto.
friend: *n.* gayyém, pagáyam; (*women*) ingá.
friendship: *n.* panagpagáyam, panaggayyém.
fright: *n.* buténg, amák, aligagét.
frigid: *adj.* nalam-ek, simmikkíl (iti lamíis).
frill: *n.* kulotkulót, karkaretkét, karenkén.
fringe: *n.* barayúbay, baragúbay, parayúpay, paraypáy, rubéte.
frisk: *v.* kapkápan.
fritter: *n.* bunuélos, binuélos; **banana** ~ *n.* turrón.
frivolous: *adj.* naampáng, nagaráw.
frock: *n.* kagáy.
frog: *n.* tukák; pilát, kengkéng.
frolic: *v.* agangáw, aglangáy, umalikudóg, agsayaksák.
from: *prep.* aggapú, manípud.
front: *n.* sángo, rúpa, sanguánan.
frost: *n.* linnáaw a nagbaláy.
froth: *n.* labútab, tarabútab, luág.
frown: *n.* rupangét, sidungét, misúot, muregrég; *v.* agmuregrég, agrupangét, agmisúot.
frozen: *adj.* nagbaláy, nayélo.
frugal: *adj.* naínut, natíped; (*in eating*) namismís, nakimkím.
fruit: *n.* búnga, prútas; ~ **bat** *n.* pannikí.
fruitless: *adj.* bambannóg.
frustrate: *v.* sukálen, lapdán, abáken.
frustration: *n.* tungdáy.
fry: *v.* prituén, gisaén; babassít a lamés.
fuck: (*vulg.*) *v.* agyót.
fuel: *n.* sungród, pagtungó; (*candle*) pabílo.
fugitive: *n.* naglíbas.
fulfill: *n.* ibánag, iringpás, tungpálen.
full: *adj.* napnó, napusék, nalungpús; (*from eating*) nabság; ~ **moon** *n.* kábus.
fully: *adv.* napnék.
fume: *n.* asúk, alingásaw; *v.* umasók, sumngáw; makaungét.
fumigate: *v.* suóban, paasukán.
fun: *n.* ang-angáw, rabrábak, ragragsák, parparató.
function: *n.* opísio; rebbengén, annóng.
fund: *n.* póndo, naurnóng a pírak.
fundamental: *adj.* kangrunáan, kamasapúlan.

funeral: *n.* punpón; ~ **parlor** *n.* pagmansayágan.

fungi: *n.* úong, kudetdét, kúdit, kúlat.

funnel: *n.* imbúdo, sarangúsong.

funny: *adj.* nakaangangáw, kómiko, nakaayayát, nakakatkatáwa.

fur: *n.* dutdót a nalamúyot.

furious: *adj.* naungét, maruród, narungsót.

furl: *v.* lukóten.

furlough: *n.* bakasión.

furnace: *n.* órno; anáwang; (*underground*) tagáang, karáang.

furnish: *v.* ipaayán, ikkán ti aruáten.

furniture: *n.* alikámen, gargarét.

furrow: *n.* gúlis, gúrit; inarádo.

further: *adj.* pay, sumarunó.

furthermore: *adv.* maysá pay.

fury: *n.* pungtót, rungsót, úyong, ungét, ruród.

fuse: *n.* yéska, pagsínit, métsa; *v.* tunáwen, lunágen, pagtipónen.

fusion: *n.* lúnag, panagtípon.

fuss: *n.* arimbángaw, pakaringgóran, banggiáw.

futile: *adj.* ubbáw, away maáyna, barengbáreng.

future: *n.* masakbáyan, masanguánan.

G

gable: *n.* bayangbáyang.

gadfly: *n.* ngílaw.

gaff: *n.* (*for gamecock*) tádi; **hook in** ~ gádol.

gag: *v.* melmelán, pelpelán; *n.* tapár ti ngíwat.

gage: *n.* karí, talgéd.

gaiety: *n.* kinaragsák, pagraragsákan; kinabaién.

gain: *n.* gunguná, gánab, ganánsia; *v.* ragpáten, magun-ód, lak-ámen; agganánsia, aggunguná.

gainsay: *v.* suppiáten; ipárit.

gait: *n.* pagná, addáng.

gala: *n.* gála, rambák, piésta; *adj.* nagarbó.

galanga: *n.* langkuás.

galaxy: *n.* ariwánas.

gale: *n.* bagió, napigsá nga ángin.

gall: *n.* apró, balinawnáw.

gallant: *adj.* nataknéng, naturéd.

galled: *adj.* nalatlátan, narasrásan.

gallery: *n.* pálko.

galley: *n.* biráy.

gallon: *n.* galón.

gallop: *v.* agbuábo, agbuátit; agattuáng, agpadakpadák.

gallows: *n.* pagbitáyan.

gamble: *v.* agsugál, agpustá; ~**r** mannugál.

game: *n.* ay-áyam; pinartuát; ~**cock** pakipallót.

gang: *n.* barkáda, pangén, bunggóy.

gangplank: *n.* andámio, talaytáyan.

gangrene: *n.* kanggréna, panagnunóg.

gangster: *n.* butangéro.

ganta: *n.* salúp.

gap: *n.* abút, buáng, regkáng, sawang.

gape: *v.* agngangá, agtuyáab.

gaper: *n.* ang-áng.

gaping: *adj.* muttálat.

garage: *n.* garáhe.

garb: *n.* kawés, lúpot.

garbage: *n.* basúra, dalupitpít, baséng.

garden: *n.* minuyongán, hardín, lapóg.

gargle: *v.* agmulúmog, agalimugmóg.

garland: *n.* balángat a sabsábong.

garlic: *n.* báwang.

garment: *n.* bádo, kawés; pagan-anáy.

garnet: *n.* granáte.

garnish: *v.* arkósan, papintásen.

garrulous: *adj.* nangíwat, tarabítab.

garter: *n.* lígas, reppét ti médias.

gas: *n.* alingásaw, alibungúbong; ~ **pain** kábag.

gash: *n.* íwa (sugát); *v.* tagbáten; iwáen; laslásen.

gasoline: *n.* gasolína.

gasp: *v.* agal-ál; agtungláb; agalon-álon, aglúnos.

gate: *n.* ruángan, rídaw.

gather: *v.* urnóngen, tipónen, ummongén; (*fruits*) burásen; (*with both hands*) akúpen.

gaudy: *adj.* naarkós, napasindáyaw.

gauge: *n.* rukodén.

gaunt: *adj.* nakuttóng, narápis.

gauze: *n.* gása, aragaág.

gauzy: *adj.* nasaragásag, nasalagásag, aragaág.

gavel: *n.* máso, maliéte.

gay: *adj.* (*happy*) naragsák; (*homosexual*) baién.

gaze: *v.* agmatmát, agmuttaléng, agmulengléng, agmatamatá, agkilawkiláw.

gear: *n.* kawés; alikámen.

gecko: *n.* tekká.

gelatin: *n.* helatína.

gem: *n.* napatég a bató, mutiá, saniáta.

genealogy: *n.* kasimpuónan.

general: *adj.* sapásap, kadawyán; *n.* henerál.

generate: *v.* putóten, paaddaén, pataúden.

generation: *n.* kaputótan.

generosity: *n.* kinaparábur, kinamanagpabusóy.

generous: *adj.* naparábur, managpabus-óy; naási.

genius: *n.* sarírit, nalaíng únay.

genitals: *n.* bagí, kámeng, sángo; **wash the** ~ agkawkáw, agpawpáw.

gentle: *adj.* naalumámay, nallinaáy, nalánay, naemmá, natalná.

gentleman: *n.* nataknéng a táo.

genuflect: *v*. agkornó, agparintúmeng.
genuine: *adj*. agpaypaysó, pasingkéd, pudnó.
geologist: *n*. geólogo.
germ: *n*. mikróbio; (*of seeds*) búngag.
German: *n*. Alemán, tagá-Alemánia.
Germany: *n*. Alemánia.
germinate: *v*. tumúbo, rumúsing.
gesticulate: *v*. mamaspasápas, agkumintáng, agwágas.
gesture: *n*. tignáy, kumpás, kumintáng.
get: *v*. aláen, gun-óden.
ghastly: *adj*. nakaap-apráng.
ghost: *n*. al-aliá, pugót, di katataoán, aningáas.
giant: *n*. higánte.
giddy: **be ~** *v*. agdawengdáweng, malangenlangén; **feel ~** *v*. matalimúdaw.
gift: *n*. ságut, regálo, rangkáp, parábur.
gig: *n*. kalesín.
gigantic: *adj*. naláyog, nagdakkél.
giggle: *v*. agayek-ék, agarukikkík.
gill: *n*. ásang.
gilt: *adj*. nadorádo, nabalitók.
gin: *n*. hinébra; (*roller*) laddít, lúbang.
ginger: *n*. layá; ~ **tea** *n*. salabát; **wild ~** *n*. baséng.
girandole: *n*. alipása.
girdle: *n*. baríkes, sinturón.
girl: *n*. babái, balásang.
girt: *v*. isabikél.
gist: *n*. ánag, bagás.
give: *v*. itéd, ikkán, iságut, ipaáy ~ **birth to** ipasngáy, aganák; ~ **back** isublí; ~ **in advance** ipauná; ~ **way** agtaméd.
gizzard: *n*. battikuléng; **lining of ~** kulápot, kulánit, lapsút.
glad: *adj*. maragsákan.
glamour: *n*. kinalibnós, kinapíntas, kinangayéd.
glance: *n*. taldiáp, kisláp, palúdip; *v*. tumaldiáp, sumaldiáp; **side ~** palilítan, paludípan.
gland: *n*. salsalamági, glándula.
glans: *n*. ~ **penis** lukdít.
glare: *n*. siláp, kusílap; *v*. rumangráng.
glaring: *adj*. makapurár.
glass: *n*. sarmíng; (*drinking*) báso.
glasses: *n*. sarmíng ti matá, anteóhos.
glaze: *v*. pasilengén, palinísen.
glean: *v*. agban-á; tudtúden, adásen.
glee: *n*. ragsák, rag-ó.
glib: *adj*. mannanaó.
glide: *v*. agúyas, agáyus.
glimmer: *v*. agkudrép, agkuridemdém; rumimát, agandáp, agpagiláp.
glimpse: *n*. palúdip, taldiáp, saripatpát.
glisten: *v*. agrimát, agsiláp, agsiléng; lumiás.
glitter: *v*. agrimát, kumiláp, agraniág, agrangráng, agsiléng.

gloat: *v*. mulagátan.
globe: *n*. glóbo.
gloom: *n*. lidém, kudrép, lidáy; sipngét.
glorify: *v*. itan-ók, dayáwen, ibunannág, itandúdo.
glory: *n*. dáyaw, glória, dayág, tan-ók.
gloss: *n*. silnóg, silnág, siléng; **lacking ~** pudagdág, pugagáw.
glossary: *n*. nakatipónan dagití nalawlawág a sasaó.
glove: *n*. guántes.
glow: *v*. sumgéd, gumil-ayab; agdárang; *n*. gil-ayab.
glowworm: *n*. kulalantí, kulintabá.
glue: *n*. kóla, píket, pigkét; *v*. ikóla, ipigkét.
glutton: *n*. buklís, arsáb, naráwet a táo.
gluttonous: *adj*. nabuklís, naráwet, arsáb.
gnash: *v*. agngariét, agngaretngét.
gnat: *n*. leglég; tuktukláw, sepsép; tímel.
gnaw: *v*. kibkiban, kuríban.
go: *v*. mapán; ~ **home** agáwid; ~ **down** umúlog; (*sun*) lumnék; ~ **in** sumrék; ~ **out** rumuár; ~ **one by one** agsinsín; ~ **straight** agtarús; ~ **upstream** sumúrong; ~ **to town** agúdong; ~ **up** sumagpát, umúli.
goad: *n*. tugkík, dúros; *v*. parugsuén.
goal: *n*. pagtungpálan, kalát, patinggaán, pasuán; gandát, panggép, bagás.
goat: *n*. kaldíng.
gobble: *n*. agalukmón, alun-únen.
go-cart: *n*. lakadlákad, tangkúlong.
god: *n*. diós.
goddess: *n*. diósa.
godfather: *n*. manganák, táta ti buniág, padríno.
godmother: *n*. manganák, nána ti buniág, madrína.
going: *n*. ipapán.
goiter: *n*. ákak, bekkelán, biél, bekkák, biskél.
gold: *n*. balitók; ~ **plated** *adj*. paláda.
golden: *adj*. nabalitokán, dorádo; (*color*) duyáw.
gong: *n*. tambór.
gonorrhea: *n*. saripít.
good: *adj*. naimbág, nasayáat; nalaíng; ~ **looking** napintás, nataráki, nalangá.
good-bye: *n*. pakáda.
goodness: *n*. kinaimbág, kinasayáat.
goods: *n*. tagiláko, lakláko; sanikuá.
goodwill: *n*. naimbág a nákem.
goose: *n*. gánso.
gore: *v*. salpúten, diokén.
gorgeous: *adj*. narangá, napíntas únay, naramók; narimbáw.
gospel: *n*. ebanghélio.
gossip: *n*. tsísmis, busatsát, tarabítab, saosaó.

gouge: *v.* (*an eye*) suáten.
gourmand: *n.* arsáb.
govern: *v.* agturáy.
governess: *n.* yáya.
governor: *n.* gobernadór, pangúlo ti estádo.
gown: *n.* kamisón; tóga; báta.
grab: *v.* gammatán, rabsúten, tukmáan.
grace: *n.* grásia, ási, imnás; (*privilege*) sagúday; *v.* raemán; ~ **period** palungkít.
graceful: *adj.* nasuggóng, nangayéd; naádar.
grade: *n.* grádo, tukád, saád.
gradual: *adj.* main-ínut, naináyad.
graduate: *v.* agturpós.
graft: *n.* panangulbód.
grain: *n.* bukél; (*of wood*) binggás; *v.* agaribuábo.
gram: *n.* grámo.
grammar: *n.* gramátika, alagáden (ti pagsasaó).
granary: *n.* sarúsar, agámang, kamálig.
grand: *adj.* natan-ók, nadayág, nangayéd.
grandchild: *n.* apokó.
grandeur: *n.* kinangayéd, kinadayág.
grandparent: *n.* apó.
granite: *n.* graníto.
grant: *v.* itdén, ipaáy, ipalugód; *n.* ságut.
granule: *n.* butáy.
grape: *n.* úbas.
grapefruit: *n.* lukbán, suá, kahél.
graph: *n.* inkuri-kur-ít.
grapple: *v.* gabbuán, gemgemán, rekepén, petpetán.
grasp: *v.* tukmáan; tiliwén; sigpíten; rakmén; talián, iggamán; maawátan.
grass: *n.* rúot; **Bermuda** ~ pagudpód; **cogon** ~ pan-áw; **cut the** ~ agtabás, paraspásen; **lemon~** baraníw.
grasshopper: *n.* rumsá; sílam, kambuáw, ríried, luktón, paddúdon.
grate: *v.* agranetrét, agkaradákad, rumanadrád; agígad; **coconut ~r** *n.* ígad; **~d coconut meat** *n.* inígad a nióg.
grateful: *adj.* siyayáman, managyáman.
gratis: *adj.* líbre, awán báyadna.
gratitude: *n.* panagyáman.
gratuitous: *adj.* libré.
gratuity: *n.* ságut; tangdán.
grave: *n.* taném; *adj.* nakáro, naalidungét, nabantót, narikót.
gravel: *n.* grába, barát, dárat, baggíing.
gravity: *n.* kinadagsén, dagsén, pigsá a manggúyod.
gravy: *n.* pagsawsáwan, sársa.
gray: *adj.* nauspák, kolordapó; ~ **hair** *n.* úban.
graze: *v.* agárab.
grease: *n.* tabá, mantéka, sébo, lána; *v.* lanáan.

great: *adj.* nalaták, natan-ók, dakkél; **~-grandchild** apó ití túmeng; **~~~-grandchild** apó ití dapán; **~-grandfather** apó a báak.
greed: *n.* agáwa, águm, ápal, kinamanagim-bubukódan.
greedy: *adj.* nabukláw, naágum; (*with food*) naráwet.
Greek: *n.*, *adj.* Griégo.
green: *adj.* bérde; nalangtó; (*unripe*) naáta; ~ **pepper** gumpápeng.
gregarious: *adj.* managpapangén, managtitimpúyog.
grenade: *n.* granáda.
gridiron: *n.* parília, pariliéra.
grief: *n.* ladíngit, leddáang, tarumpíngay, lidáy.
grievance: *n.* ranggás, gulíb, reklámo, ulpít.
grieve: *v.* agladíngit, aglidáy.
grill: *v.* tunuén; *n.* parília.
grim: *adj.* nakaal-aliáw, nakabutbuténg.
grimace: *n.* rupangét, ngirsí, gílab; *v.* aggúyab; agrungsíit, agngirsí.
grime: *n.* rugít, muréng.
grin: *v.* agrungsíit, agrungíit, agpurngí, agpurngíit.
grind: *v.* gilíngen, ladditén, mulién; (*knife*) asáen.
grinder: *n.* gilíngan.
grindstone: *n.* molihón, pangasáan.
grip: *n.* petpét, kapét, iggém.
gripe: *v.* metmetán, tenglén, pislén.
grit: *v.* (*the teeth*) agkabúkab.
groan: *v.* agásug, agúngor, agunnóy.
grocery: *n.* tiendáan ti makmakán.
groin: *n.* sellóng, sep-áng.
groom: *n.* nóbio.
groove: *n.* gúrit, kanál; ~ **at back of ear** tutúleng; ~ **at back of neck** iimútan; ~ **at base of glans penis** el-él.
grope: *v.* agkarkaráwa (iti nasipngét), umapíras, arikápen; agkáwad.
gross: *adj.* narusangér, nagubsáng.
gross weight: *n.* brútos.
grotesque: *adj.* naalás, naláad.
grotto: *n.* rukíb, rukíeb, gukáyab.
ground: *n.* dagá; *adj.* (*crushed*) nabegbég, namulí, nagíling; *v.* isadsád.
group: *n.* bunggóy, pangén, sarruád, purók, pasét.
grove: *n.* kasamekán, kakaykayuán, kabarawásan.
grow: *v.* dumakkél; rumettáb; agtúbo.
growl: *n.* úngor, ngerngér; *v.* agngerngér; agngusángos, agúngor.
grub: *n.* iggés; ~ **hoe** gabión.
grudge: *n.* kátil; gúra, ruród, luksáw.

gruel: *n.* linugáw.

gruesome: *adj.* nakaar-ariék.

grumble: *v.* agtanabútob, agdayamúdom, agburingetngét, ageng-éng.

grunt: *n.* garukgók, ganukgók, rugárog; eddék; *v.* agungík, ageddék, aggarukgók, agrugárog.

G-string: *n.* baág, bayákat, anúngo.

guarantee: *n.* garantía, sadíri, piánsa, taní; *v.* ipatalgéd, paneknekán, pabilgén.

guarantor: *n.* piadór, mangpaneknék.

guard: *n.* bantáy, wanáwan; *v.* bantáyan, ikután, ispálen, ikanáwa, sakolóban.

guardian: *n.* mangay-aywán, mangsalsalakníb.

guava: *n.* bayyábas.

guerilla: *n.* gerília.

guess: *v.* ipagarúp, pattapattaén, padtuán, batabáten, pugtuám.

guest: *n.* bisíta, sangaíli; ~ **book** pagpirmáan; ~**house** pagdagusán.

guffaw: *n.* garakgák.

guidance: *n.* panangituróng; panangibagnós.

guide: *n.* bagnós; *v.* ituróng, isúro; antabáyen, ibagnós.

guild: *n.* timpúyog.

guilt: *n.* básol, babak, biddút, pílaw.

guilty: *adj.* nakabásol.

Guinea pig: *n.* kuíng.

guitar: *n.* gitára, kuriténg, kutibéng.

gulf: *n.* likkúkong ti baybáy, yúyeng, dariwangwáng, gólpo.

gullible: *adj.* mammáti, uulbóden.

gulp: *v.* tilmonén, alimónen, arurúben; *n.* ígup, tilmón.

gum: *n.* (*teeth*) gugót, gigís; (*eye*) múkat, mirkát; (*rubber*) góma.

gun: *n.* paltóg; **pop**~ palsóot.

gunpowder: *n.* polborá.

gunshot: *n.* kanalbúong, kanalbúog.

gurgle: *v.* agparukpók; agareb-éb; agbaranúbor, agbarukbók.

gush: *v.* agpussuák, agarúyot.

gust: *n.* nánam, gonés, dápag.

gusto: *n.* pagraywán, pagragsákan.

gut: *n.* bagbágis, lalaém, rakrakípa.

gutter: *n.* pagayúsan ti danúm; kalasúgan.

guy: *n.* laláki.

guzzle: *v.* agareb-éb.

gypsy: *n.* hitáno.

gyrate: *v.* agulláw, agbariwengwéng, agalipunó.

H

habit: *n.* ruám, ugáli, kadawyán.

habitual: *adj.* nadáwi, kadawyán, masná.

hack: *v.* sigpáten, rangrangkáyen, tagbáten, tadtáden.

haft: *n.* patán; padíla.

hag: *n.* brúha, mangkukúlam, naalás a bakét.

haggard: *adj.* agbebesság, nakakutkuttóng.

haggle: *v.* agtintinnáwar, agtáwar.

hail: *n.* uráro; *v.* kablaáwan.

hair: *n.* (*of head*) buók; (*of body*) dutdót, muldót; (*of nose*) parungngárong; (*of caterpillars*) búdo; **cut the** ~ **of** pukísan, purtókan.

hairpin: *n.* arípit, orkília.

hairy: *adj.* nabuók, anáping, dutdútan.

half: *n.* gudduá; ~-**breed** mestíso.

halfway: *adv.* iti tengngá.

hall: *n.* sálas; **dance** ~ saláan.

hallucination: *n.* bullabullán.

halo: *n.* (*of moon*) bákud.

halt: *v.* agsardéng.

halter: *n.* sakíma, talí a pangbítay.

ham: *n.* hamón; (*anat.*) lakkó; **kick someone in the** ~ agbansí.

hamlet: *n.* purók, karsó.

hammer: *n.* martílio; *v.* martiliwén ~**head shark** balagbágan.

hammock: *n.* indáyon; **tilted** ~ talabóng.

hamper: *v.* tipdén, tubngén, lapdán; *n.* ropéro, kanásta.

hand: *n.* íma; (*of bananas*) sápad; ~**barrow** anggarília; ~ **press** minérba; **having only one** ~ pokól; ~ **over** *v.* yáwat, yábut; **empty** ~**ed** imaíma; ~**shake** pasamáno, lamáno; ~**rail** pasamáno; ~**cloth** panio-demáno.

handcuffs: *n.* posás, putáw.

handful: *n.* gámat, sangkapetpét, sangarakém, sangkaiggém.

handicap: *n.* pakaatíwan; kakurángan.

handkerchief: *n.* pánio.

handle: *n.* pután, pangguyódan, pangiggamán; *v.* iggamán, petpetán; asikasuén.

handmade: *adj.* arámid ti íma.

handsaw: *n.* ragádi, kíkir.

handsome: *adj.* natáraki, naguápo, nataér, nalibnós, nasaldít.

handspan: *n.* dángan.

handwriting: *n.* insúrat ti íma.

hang: *v.* ibítin, isab-ít, bitáyen, ibalaybáy; (*torn cloth*) agsaluyabyáb; (*imperfectly*) agsalupaypáy; **to** ~ **oneself** agbekkél.

hanger: *n.* sasab-ítan.

hangings: *n.* bengbéng, kolgadúra.

hangman: *n.* parabítay, berdúgo.

hangnail: *n.* sasadút, laplapsí.

haphazardly: *adv.* **do** ~ barubaddután, agsáaw.

happen: *v.* mapasámak, mapagténg; maiparná; ~ **by chance** *v.* mairaná, maibatáng.

happy: *adj.* naragsák, nanam-áy.

harass: *v.* singaén, bannogén, rubuóten, riribúken, pangdásan.

harbor: *n.* sangládan, puérto, sabángan, kuála.

hard: *adj.* natangkén; (*difficult*) narígat.

harden: *v.* patangkenén; tumangkén, kumsiál.

hardly: *adv.* apagapáman.

hardwood: *n.* basangál, nammék.

hare: *n.* koného.

harelipped: *adj.* gusíng, gusáb.

harlot: *n.* pampám, balangkantís.

harm: *n.* ranggás, danar; *v.* dangrán, irurumén.

harmonica: *n.* silíndro.

harmony: *n.* túnos, timpúyog, urnós, danggáy.

harness: *v.* ipákat.

harp: *n.* árpa.

harpoon: *n.* pisgá, tarapáng; (*with at least two barbs*) sabát.

harrow: *n.* sagád, bálsa, pak-ól, karudkód, pasaratsát, parágut, súyod.

harsh: *adj.* narusangér, nagubsáng.

harvest: *n.* ápit, áni; **second** ~ darondón; *v.* burásen, anién, agápit.

has: *v.* addá.

haste: *n.* darás, pardás, allég.

hasty: *adj.* nadarás, natarabít.

hat: *n.* kallugóng, kattukóng.

hatch: *v.* pessaán.

hatchery: *n.* pagpapessaán.

hatchet: *n.* wásay.

hate: *n.* gúra, ruród, surón; *v.* guráen.

hatred: *n.* gúra, ruród.

haughty: *adj.* natangsít, napangás.

haul: *v.* guyúden, ulóden.

haunch: *n.* padingpáding; (*of horse*) angkás.

haunt: *n.* ayúyang; *v.* al-aliáen.

have: *v.* addaán; addá; agtagikuá.

haven: *n.* pagkamángan, pagsalingdán, kuála.

havoc: *n.* panagrakrák.

hawk: *n.* sáwi, kalí.

hay: *n.* garámi, sakáte; ~**stack** buntúon ti garámi.

hazard: *n.* peggád, pústa, parikút.

haze: *n.* angép, lúlem, lidém, kinakudrép.

hazy: *adj.* nakudrép, naangép.

he: *pron.* isú(na).

head: *n.* úlo; (*chief*) pangúlo; ~ **of bead** uluánan.

headache: *n.* sakít ti úlo.

headaxe: *n.* aliwá.

head cloth: *n.* dalongdóng, alidongdóng.

heading: *n.* pangrugián; paúlo.

headline: *n.* paúlo a dámag.

headman: *n.* pangúlo.

headquarters: *n.* kuartél, pagtataripnóngan.

headstrong: *adj.* nadarasúdos.

heal: *v.* agágas, agásan; aglúnit.

health: *n.* salun-át, piá, karadkád; ~**y** *adj.* nasalun-át; makapasalun-át.

heap: *n.* buntón, penpén, montón, gabsúon.

hear: *v.* mangngég, matímud; ~**say** sayanggúseng, alimámad.

hearing: *n.* panangdengngég.

hearsay: *n.* saosaó.

hearse: *n.* kárro (a pakailugánan ti natáy).

heart: *n.* púso; ~ **attack** atáke ti púso; ~ **of town** púseg ti íli; ~**sick** *adj.* nasimrón.

hearth: *n.* dapugán, dalikán, pagtaengán, temtém.

heartless: *adj.* awanán ási.

hearty: *adj.* makapapigsá.

heat: *n.* púdot, bára, dagáang; **to be in** ~ agmayá.

heave: *v.* ital-ó; ipeksá, iyesngáw.

heaven: *n.* lángit.

heavenly: *adj.* nainlangítan, tagalángit.

heavy: *adj.* nadagsén, nabantót.

Hebrew: *n.*, *adj.* Hebréo, Húdio.

heed: *v.* imdengán, imutektekán, palííwen, ikáso.

heel: *n.* múkod, takón; **sound of** ~**s** kanaktúol.

height: *n.* kangáto, katáyag; ~**en** *v.* ipangáto, padakkelén.

heinous: *adj.* nakabutbuténg, nakaal-aliáw.

heir: *n.* agtáwid.

hell: *n.* impiérno, dariwangwáng.

helm: *n.* timón, mangituróng.

helmsman: *n.* manimón.

help: *n.* túlong, bádang, aráyat; *v.* tulóngan, badángan.

helve: *n.* ugnáy, pután, tuólan.

hem: *n.* tupí, lebléb; *v.* tupián.

hematoma: *n.* bidugól.

hemorrhage: *n.* pagpadára.

hemorrhoids: *n.* almoránas, busigít, lugsót, tubél.

hemp: *n.* abaká; kaniámo.

hen: *n.* upa, dumálaga, pamusián.

henpecked: *adj.* ánder, malagabán.

hence: *adv.* ití kastá.

henchman: *n.* katulóngan.

her: *pron.* kenkuána (a babái); -na.

herald: *v.* ipadámag, ipabláak.

herb: *n.* yérba, rúot; ~ **charm** tagiráyad.

herd: *n.* pangén, sangamanadáan, sangaarbánan.

here: *adv.* ditóy.

hereditary: *adj.* pagtawintawídan, nagánab, natáwid.

herein: *adv.* kas addá ditóy.
heresy: *n.* erehía.
heretic: *n.* eréhe.
hermaphrodite: *n.* binabái.
hermit: *n.* ermitánio; ~ **crab** úmang; ~ **thrush** mammendíta.
hernia: *n.* (*scrotal*) bungáw.
hero: *n.* bannuár.
heroic: *adj.* naturéd.
heroism: *n.* kinaturéd.
heron: *n.* kannáway, teggáak, mammáboy.
herpes: *n.* tariptíp, labaít, barkés; ~ **sore** *n.* ráit.
herring: *n.* barambán.
hers: *pron.* kukuána, bágina.
hesitate: *v.* agsarimadéng, agduaduá, agtantán.
hibiscus: *n.* gumaméla, kayánga.
hiccup: *v.* agsaiddék; *n.* saiddék.
hidden: *a.* nalemméng, natalímeng.
hide: *v.* aglemméng; ilingéd; italímeng; *n.* lálat, kúdil; ~-**and-seek game** *n.* linnemméng, bibinnírok, pinnusanbaó, kinnirít.
hideous: *adj.* nakaal-aliáw, nakabutbuténg.
high: *adj.* nangáto, natáyag; ~**ness** *n.* kinangáto, karimbáwan.
highland: *n.* kabanbantáyan.
highway: *n.* dálan, kalsáda.
hilarious: *adj.* nakakatkatáwa.
hill: *n.* túrod, paduál, bantáy, bakúlud.
hillside: *n.* bakrás, ansád.
him: *pron.* kenkuána.
hind: *adj.* kútit, likúd, kamaúdi.
hinder: *v.* parítan, lapdán, tubngén.
hindrance: *n.* lappéd, arbéng, bangén.
hinge: *n.* bishágra, palaupó.
hint: *n.* singásing, pangripirípan; *v.* ipalagíp, iparipírip, iparimírim.
hip: *n.* patóng, padingpáding; ~ **rafter** solókan.
hire: *n.* tangdán, upa; *v.* tangdánan, upáan, abángan.
his: *pron.* –na; kukuána (a laláki).
hiss: *v.* sitsítan, sumarebséb.
history: *n.* pakasaritáan.
hit: *v.* kabílen, pang-óren; puntáan.
hitch: *v.* ipákat, isangól; (*hook*) ikáwit; (*to tree*) iparngéd.
hive: *n.* pagidulínan, balay dagiti uyókan.
hoard: *v.* ipagingetngét, agidúlin.
hoarse: *adj.* bángeg, agpapáraw, agrárek.
hoax: *n.* angáw, síkap a pangrabrábak; *v.* sikápan, kuógen.
hobble: *n.* simpalóng, talunggatíng; *v.* agsigkíng.
hobgoblin: *n.* aniwáas.
hobo: *n.* agalla-allá a táo.

hodgepodge: *n.* kampór, samúsam, gammogammók.
hoe: *n.* sugkít, sap-íl, suíl, suál, karudkód.
hog: *n.* báboy; ~ **cholera** baládong, pangók.
hoist: *v.* ipangáto, ibáyog, unósen.
hold: *v.* iggamán, tenglén, laónen.
hole: *n.* abút, bútaw, lussók, abbútaw, attúbaw; (*cavity*) lúngog.
holiday: *n.* piésta.
holiness: *n.* kinasánto.
hollow: *n.* lúngog, abút; *adj.* lungógan, kalawákaw.
holster: *n.* lagárna (ti paltóg).
holy: *adj.* nasantuán, nadiosán; ~ **water** *n.* bendíta.
homage: *n.* pangdáyaw, pangraém.
home: *n.* baláy, naéd, taéng.
homesick: *adj.* maíliw, siíliw, aggágar nga agáwid; ~**ness** *n.* íliw.
homicide: *n.* panagpapatáy ti táo.
hone: *n.* bató a pangasáan.
honest: *adj.* nadáyaw, nalintég, naregtá.
honey: *n.* diró; ~**bee** *n.* ayúkan, uyúkan.
honeycomb: *n.* kalába, nirára.
honk: *v.* agbusína, agpappáp, talmegán ti busína.
honor: *n.* dáyaw, taknéng; *v.* padayáwan, itanók, raemén.
honorary: *adj.* mapadayáwan.
hood: *n.* uklóp, kapútsa.
hoodwink: *v.* sikápan.
hoof: *n.* kukó (ti kabáyo).
hook: *n.* láwin, banníit, síma, káwit, kalláwit; *v.* ikáwit.
hookworm: *n.* iggés ti tián.
hoop: *n.* basíkaw, kalangkáng, kalasíkas; argólia; *v.* basikáwan.
hop: *v.* agkingkíng, aglagtó.
hope: *n.* namnáma, inanáma; *v.* namnamáen.
hopscotch: *n.* sigkíng, sigkúngbádo, kingkíng.
horn: *n.* sára; (*for signalling*) anguyób; **car ~** *n.* busína.
hornbill: *n.* kálaw.
hornet: *n.* giák, alumpipínig.
horrible: *adj.* nakakigkigtót, nakabutbuténg, nakaam-amák.
horrid: *adj.* nakaal-aliáw, nakaam-amák.
horrify: *v.* pabutngén.
horror: *n.* buténg, amák, kigtót.
horse: *n.* kabálio, kabáyo; ~**power** *n.* pigsá ti kabálio; ~**shoe** *n.* sapátos ti kabálio.
horsefly: *n.* alimbayúngan.
horseradish: *n.* marúnggay.
hose: *n.* médias; bómba.
hosiery: *n.* médias.

hospitable: *adj.* managsangaíli, managpadagús.
hospital: *n.* ospitál, pagagásan.
hospitality: *n.* kinamanagsangaíli.
host: *n.* ti mamadagús, ti agsangaíli; óstia.
hostage: *n.* bálud.
hostile: *adj.* sibubúsor, sigugúra, bumúsor.
hot: *adj.* napúdot, nabára; (*sultry*) nadagáang.
hotel: *n.* otél.
hothouse: *n.* kalnguópan.
hour: *n.* óras.
house: *n.* baláy; ~ **lizard** alutíit; ~**wife** agtagibaláy.
household: *n.* sangakabbalayán.
housekeeper: *n.* agtagibaláy, kaséra.
housewife: *n.* agtagibaláy, iná ti baláy.
housing: *n.* panagbaláy.
hover: *v.* agpaypayakpák, agalimpáyag.
how: *adv.* kasanó, an-anuén.
however: *adv.* núpay kastá.
howl: *v.* agtagúob, agúga, agpukkáw, agúngor.
hubbub: *n.* arimbángaw, ariwáwa.
huddle: *v.* agdedekkét, agdadaríson; alikumkúmen, podónen.
hue: *n.* maris, kolór.
hug: *v.* arakúpen, kepkepán.
huge: *adj.* dakkél únay.
hum: *v.* agsayengséng, agayeng-éng, umatibangráw, agtaralallay.
human: *n.* táo; *adj.* nagtagitaoán.
humanity: *n.* kinatáo.
humble: *adj.* naemmá, napakumbabá.
humid: *adj.* nadam-ég, naagnéb, nalnáab.
humiliate: *v.* paemmaén, ipababá.
humility: *n.* kinapakumbabá.
humor: *n.* dam-ég, tangátang; *v.* angawén, pagkatawáen.
hump: *n.* kubbó, písol.
hunchback: *n.* kubbó.
hundred: *n.* gasút; ~**th** *adj.* maikasangagasút.
hunger: *n.* bisín.
hungry: *adj.* mabisín, mabisinán.
hunt: *v.* aganúp; *n.* anúp; ~**er** *n.* mangnganúp.
hurl: *v.* ibarsák, ibató, ipalápal, iwallagés, basibásen, ipullásit, ipalládaw.
hurricane: *n.* bagió, alawig.
hurry: *v.* agdarás, aggánat, agparták, agapúra.
hurt: *v.* ranggásan, dangrán, saktán, danáran; (*feelings*) saíren.
husband: *n.* asáwa a laláki, lakáy.
husbandry: *n.* talónen.
hush: *v.* paguliméken, patalnáen.
husk: *n.* ukís, bunót; *v.* bunotán.
husky: *adj.* nabunót; nabarábar.
hustle: *v.* agaribungbóng, agaribúyot, sumarakúsok; ~**r** *n.* paradípad, parodípad.

hut: *n.* kalapáw, ábong.
hybrid: *adj.* mestíso.
hydrangea: *n.* milplóres.
hymn: *n.* ímno, kánta.
hypnotism: *n.* ipnotísmo.
hypnotist: *n.* ipnotísta.
hypocrisy: *n.* kinamanaginsisingpét, kina-managinkukuná.
hypocrite: *n.* managinsisingpét, managin-kukuná, ipokríto.
hypocritical: *v.* **to be** ~ agragádi, aginsisingpét.

I

I: *pron.* siák; **you and** ~ datá; ~ **think** -(n)sa.
ice: *n.* yélo.
ice cream: *n.* sorbétes; ~ **cone** ápa.
idea: *n.* panúnot, pakinákem, kananákem, kapanunótan, binukél ti panúnot.
ideal: *adj.* umnó.
identical: *adj.* agpadpáda, agpadpád, agkasúbok.
identification: *n.* pakabigbígan, pakaipakaammuán.
identify: *v.* ilásin, inagánan.
identity: *n.* kinasiasíno, kinaasíno.
idiom: *n.* pagsasaó.
idiot: *n.* máag, attít, langgóng, lóko, tungngáng.
idle: *adj.* nasadút, awan aramídna, bayanggúdaw, natamlég; ~ **talk** barisawsáw.
idol: *n.* ídolo, bannuár.
idolatry: *n.* panagrukbáb kadagití ladáwan.
idolize: *v.* tagilangíten.
i.e. (id est): kas itóy, kastá.
if: *conj.* no; no kuma; **even** ~ úray no.
ignite: *v.* silmútan, gangtán, pasgedán, solsólan.
ignorant: *adj.* nakúneng, nanengnéng, namosmós, nakáag, gonggóng.
ignore: *v.* di ikaskáso, baybay-án, di ikabilángan.
iguana: *n.* baniás.
ill: *adj.* (*bad*) dákes; (*sick*) masakít; ~**-bred** nadangkók, nakas-áng, nasayábat, naramés.
illegal: *adj.* kalílis, maisuppiát ití lintég.
illegible: *adj.* saán a mabása, kuríngkuríng.
illegitimate: *n.* ~ **child** anák ti ruár.
illness: *n.* sakít, sagubánit, sagúreng.
illogical: *adj.* saán a nasayúd a panagrasón.
illuminate: *v.* siláwan, silnágan, lawagán.
illusion: *n.* ríro, allíaw.
illustrate: *v.* iladáwan; ipangngarígan.
illustrious: *adj.* natan-ók, nadáyaw, nasúdi, nalaták, narimbáw.

Ilocano: *n., adj.* Ilokáno; (*language*) Ilóko; ~ **specialist** Ilokanísta; ~ **region** Kailokuán.

image: *n.* ladáwan, kaaspíng; aniníwan.

imaginable: *adj.* mapanúnot, mapattapattá.

imagine: *v.* panunóten, isípen; ipagarúp.

imbecile: *n.* langgóng, tungngáng, nanengnéng.

imbibe: *v.* sumagepsép, umagsép, sumlép.

imitate: *v.* tuláden; **imitation** *adj.* sinsinán.

immaculate: *adj.* napusaksák, nadarísay.

immature: *adj.* naganós, naáta.

immediate: *adj.* dumná, madagdágus, nasingdát; kaasitgán; ~ **vicinity** arubáyan, aribáyan.

immediately: *adv.* dágus, itattá, pagammuán, apagbiít.

immense: *adj.* nakalawláwa, nakadakdakkél.

immerse: *v.* ipabátok, itínep, ibuntóg, irebréb, itabnáw.

imminent: *adj.* nagarasúgas.

immortal: *adj.* saán a matáy.

immovable: *adj.* saán a magaráw.

immune: *adj.* saán a maakáran ti sakít.

impact: *n.* panagdungpár.

impair: *v.* ranggásan, rebkásen, irebréb, pakapsúten.

impale: *v.* salpúten, bakúden iti darekdék, tam-ékan.

impatience: *n.* alipúnget.

impatient: *adj.* napagél, nagatút, awán ánusna.

impeach: *v.* pabasólen, idarúm (ti pangúlo).

impede: *v.* lapdán, parítan, singaén, manapsipár, talaánan.

impediment: *n.* makatipéd, takintakín; **speech** ~ *n.* pílaw ti panagsaó.

impel: *v.* idurón, gutugóten.

impenetrable: *adj.* di makastrék.

imperative: *adj.* naingét, naskén, maipapílit; nagánat.

imperceptible: *adj.* di madláw; di marikná.

imperfect: *adj.* nanumó, sapsapó, ginagalimúsaw, agkúrang.

imperial: *adj.* tinuturáy, naarián.

imperil: *v.* isarsárak, irúbo, ipeggád, isagmák.

impersonate: *v.* tuláden ti kinatáo.

impetuous: *adj.* napalálo ti gánat.

impetus: *n.* rugsó, peggés, bíleg, siglát.

impious: *adj.* nasabrák, saán a naraém ití diós.

implant: *v.* imúla, ipasdék.

implement: *n.* maar-arámat, gargarét, ramramít, alikámen; *v.* aramáten; isayangkát.

implicate: *v.* iráman, ibiáng, tagapníden.

implore: *v.* umaráraw, kumarabá, agásug, agpakaási.

imply: *v.* ipaltíing; iparimírim, iparipírip.

impolite: *adj.* nagubál, bastós, saán a nadáyaw.

important: *adj.* importánte, nabagás, nadagsén, masápul.

impose: *v.* ipang-ál, mangallílaw, lokuén, uyóngan, pasirúkan.

impossible: *adj.* di mabalín.

impostor: *n.* managin-iisú, suítik, ballaibó, bullabullán, manangtutúlad.

impotent: *adj.* nakápuy, di makagapú, awán kabaelánna; (*penis*) elláy.

impoverished: *adj.* napangláw.

impregnate: *v.* pagsikogén.

impress: *v.* samáyen, ipaunég, ipasnék; (*influence*) seknán, talokatíken; (*stamp*) ideppél, imaldít, markáan.

impression: *n.* kapanunútan; maldít, deppél.

impressive: *adj.* nakangayngayéd, nakangay-ngayángay.

imprint: *v.* imaldít, ideppél, ibuták, imólde; *n.* maldít.

imprison: *v.* ibálud, ipúpok, ikarsél.

improbable: *adj.* pagduduaán.

impromptu: *adj.* di insagsagána.

improper: *adj.* saán a maikanáda.

imprudent: *adj.* nasaliwawá.

improve: *v.* palaingén, parang-áyen, pasayaáten, papintásen; ~**ment** *n.* pakapasayaátan, pannakapasayáat.

impudent: *adj.* nasayábat, nasarakusók.

impugn: *v.* tubngáren, tupngáren.

impulse: *n.* durón, rikná.

impulsive: *adj.* nagarasúgas, nadursók.

impulsively: *v.* **act** ~ pamráy.

impurities: *n.* (*in water*) aributéd, arituér.

in: *prep.* unég, ití unég; idiáy, ití.

inactive: *adj.* nakuyét, nasadót; agmakóy.

inappropriate: *adj.* di maiparbéng.

inattention: *n.* kinalíway.

inaugurate: *v.* rugián, isungsúng.

inborn: *adj.* naikasígud, nakayanakán, gagángay.

incapable: *adj.* awán kabaelánna.

incase: *v.* ikáha, ikahón.

incendiary: *adj.* nalaká a maúram.

incense: *n.* insiénso; *v.* subóren.

incentive: *n.* pangpapigsá, pangay-áyo.

inception: *n.* dámo, pungánay, tapóg.

incessant: *adj.* di agsardéng.

inch: *n.* pulgáda.

incident: *n.* pasámak, mapagténg.

incisor: *n.* pamaráng, ngípen a pagkinnít.

incite: *v.* durogán, sulbógen, abúgen, gargarién, parugsuén.

inclination: *n.* pagduyúsan, kanunóngan.

incline: *v.* paglikigén, agsadag; agdarapúyo.

include: *v.* iragpín, yisék, dakawáten, sakúpen, lak-ámen, sakláwen; iráman, ilakáman, iragpín.

including: *prep.* agráman; patí.

inclusion: *n.* pakairamánan; panangiragpín, pananglak-ám.

income: *n.* matgedán.

incoming: *adj.* dumténg, sumangpét; sumarunó.

incompetent: *adj.* saán a nalaíng.

incomplete: *adj.* nakúrang; gútab; sinangláw, saán a nalpás.

incomprehensible: *adj.* di maawátan.

inconsiderate: *adj.* nasalabúsab, nasarabúsab.

inconsistent: *adj.* bangkíng, bullabullán.

inconspicuous: *adj.* saán a madmadláw.

inconstant: *adj.* gutágot.

incontinent: *v.* **be ~** agpápay.

inconvenience: *n.* pagdaksán, salí, singá, dukót, pannakasipár.

inconvenient: *adj.* makasipár, makasingá.

incorporate: *v.* pagkaykaysaén, itípon, ikappón, igímong.

increase: *v.* nayónan, paaduén; tumúbo; *n.* náyon, túbo, panangpadakkél.

incredible: *adj.* di nakapappapáti.

increment: *n.* náyon, degdég, dakkelán.

incriminate: *v.* paneknekán a nakabásol.

incubator: *n.* pagpessaán.

indebted: *adj.* maútang, nakaútang.

indecent: *adj.* naalás, nakababaín.

indecision: *n.* panagalla-allá ti nákem, panagsarimadéng.

indeed: *adv.* a, pudnó, kinaagpaysóna.

indefatigable: *adj.* saán a mabannóg.

indefinite: *adj.* saán a masinunuó, awán pagtungpálanna.

indemnify: *v.* pulángan; iseguro.

indent: *v.* gergerán, ngipénan, lennekán.

independence: *n.* wayawayá, panagwaywáyas.

index: *n.* mangipatuldó, pagsurótan; **~ finger** tammudó; (*of balance*) díla.

indicate: *v.* itudó, ipatuldó, itudíng.

indication: *n.* panangipakíta, pakaammuán.

indicative: *adj.* mangipakíta.

indict: *v.* idarúm, pabasólen, isakláng.

indifferent: *adj.* naíkay, awanén anép, agmayéng; nalab-áy, di mangikaskáso.

indigent: *adj.* napangláw, marigrígat.

indigestion: *n.* lisáy; panagpalpá; **to have ~** malisayán.

indignant: *adj.* makaluksáw, makaruród.

indignity: *n.* kinagubsáng.

indigo: *n.* táyum, ngíla, anyíl, samráw; **dye with ~** samráwen.

indirect: *adj.* nalíkaw, agsikotsíkot, maikalupípis; **talk in an ~ way** *v.* ikalkalupípis, ikalkalupápis.

indiscreet: *adj.* nagarasó, managlibtó, nasaliwawá.

indispensable: *adj.* naskén, masápul.

indisposed: *adj.* nasagubánit, aglaladút.

indisposition: *n.* sagubanít, sagúreng, samuyéng; siknó; panaténg, sakít.

indisputable: *adj.* di marúpir.

indistinct: *adj.* saán a nalawág, narígat nga ilásin.

indistinctly: *v.* **hear ~** maltíing, maallínga, maalimadámad, maallíngag, maalamáam, maatíngig.

individual: *n.* máysa a táo.

individuality: *n.* kinatáo.

indivisible: *adj.* di magudduá, di mabíngay.

indolent: *adj.* nasadút.

indoors: *v.* **stay ~** agullúm.

induce: *v.* durogán, uyótan, gutugóten, idulídol.

indulge: *v.* pabus-óyan, panuynuyán.

indulgent: *adj.* napanuynúy, napabus-óy.

industrious: *adj.* nagagét, naanép, nasaldét, nargét, nasíseg, naagáwa.

industry: *n.* indústria, pamastrekán; gagét.

inebriate: *v.* bartekén, uláwen.

ineffective: *adj.* awán maibúngana.

ineffectual: *v.* **be ~** agbambannóg.

ineligible: *adj.* saán a mapíli.

inequality: *n.* sagibát, supádi, giddiát.

inert: *adj.* nakapsút, nalpáy.

inevitable: *adj.* di maliklíkan.

inexact: *adj.* saán nga apagisú.

inexcusable: *adj.* di mapakawán.

inexpensive: *adj.* nalaká, nasalimetmét.

infallible: *adj.* di maríro.

infamous: *adj.* naindaksán.

infancy: *n.* kinamaladága.

infant: *n.* maladága, tagíbi, kayyanák.

infatuate: *v.* agdarasúdos, aggaramúgam.

infect: *v.* rugitán, pagbuyokén; akáran.

infectious: *adj.* makaális.

infer: *v.* ituróng, pagarupén, ipáto.

inferior: *adj.* nabababá; nakapkapsút.

infernal: *adj.* nainsairuán.

infestation: *n.* ángol.

infested: *adj.* -in-; naángol; **~ with lice** agbungkók, kinúto.

infidelity: *n.* di pannakatalék.

infiltrate: *v.* gumampór, lumaók.

infinite: *adj.* awán inggána, awán lansádna, di kalansádan, awán patinggána.

infirmary: *n.* pangagásan.

inflame: *v.* pasgedán, parayráyen, parugsuén.

inflammable: *adj.* maúram.
inflate: *v.* bussogén iti ángin; ~ **the neck** (*snakes*) bumirkákak.
inflexible: *adj.* di mabiór, di makilló.
inflict: *v.* dusáen; ulpítan; saplíten.
influence: *v.* samáyen, talukatíken; seknán; ~ **corruptly** soksókan.
influenza: *n.* trangkáso.
inform: *v.* ipakaammó, ibagá, isaríta; agtiktík, pakdaáran.
informal: *adj.* di pormál, kadkadawyán.
information: *n.* dámag, pabláak, pakdáar, pakaammó.
infrequent: *adj.* narasáy, nabattálay, manmanó, narásay.
infuriate: *v.* paungetén, pagpungtóten.
ingenious: *adj.* nalaíng, nasarírit.
ingrained: *adj.* binalayán.
ingrate: *n.* ingráta, saán a managyáman.
ingratitude: *n.* di kinamanagyáman.
ingredient: *n.* pasét, nailimúg.
inhabit: *v.* agnaéd, agyán, agtaéng.
inhabitant: *n.* umíli.
inhale: *v.* lang-ában, say-úpen, angsén; sumang-ót.
inherent: *adj.* nakasígud, nakayanakán.
inherit: *v.* tawíden, kasigúdan; ~**ance** *n.* táwid.
inhuman: *adj.* saán a nataoán.
initial: *adj.* pangrugián; umúna a létra ti nágan.
initiate: *v.* irugí, iserrék, itápog.
inject: *v.* isumpít, ibakúna.
injunction: *n.* párit ti ukóm.
injure: *v.* dunóren, sugáten, pasaktán.
injury: *n.* dúnor, súgat.
injustice: *n.* panaglabsíng ití kalintegán.
ink: *n.* tínta.
in-laws: *n.* dagití nakaikamángan; **child-in-law** manúgang; **parent-in-law** katugángan.
inlay: *v.* ibuták, ibúrik.
inmost: *adj.* kaunegán, kaunggán.
inn: *n.* pagdagusán.
innards: *n.* lalaém.
inner: *adj.* naun-unég; ~**most** *adj.* kaunggán.
innocence: *adj.* kinaawán básolna.
innocent: *adj.* awanán básol, nasíngpet; (*naive*) ampapáok; **accuse an ~ person** *v.* agpudánir, ipatlí.
innovate: *v.* pabaruén.
innuendo: *n.* mangisingásing; panangipalláyaw, panangyanínaw.
innumerable: *adj.* saán a mabílang.
inquire: *v.* agsaludsód; agusísa, mangammíris.
inquiry: *n.* palutpót, úsig, ammíris; usísa.
inquisitive: *adj.* namutúmut, naammíris, managsaludsód.

insane: *adj.* agmaúyong, bagtít, aguúyong.
insatiable: *adj.* naráwet.
insect: *n.* insékto, agay-áyam.
insecticide: *n.* insektisídio.
insecure: *adj.* saán a natalgéd; nalukáy.
inseparable: *adj.* saán a mapagsína.
insert: *v.* isengngát, ibaét, iseksék, isigpít, yunég.
inside: *adv.* unég, laém.
insight: *n.* kinasarírit; nasayúd a pannakailásin.
insignificant: *adj.* awán kaipapanánna.
insincere: *adj.* managinkukuá, manangikulbó, natakúp, naulbód.
insinuate: *v.* ipaságid, igunamgúnam, ipaltíing, agpariknâ, yarungáing.
insist: *v.* ipapílit, irúpir, agtalinaéd.
insolence: *n.* kinarasáw, kinarabngís, kinakuspág.
insolent: *adj.* narasáw, narabngís, nakuspág.
insomnia: *n.* alimbaságen, di pannakatúrog.
inspect: *v.* imatángan, sukimáten, kitáen, usisáen.
inspector: *n.* mangusísa.
inspiration: *n.* pangparugsó, pangpabíleg; talokátik; partáan, paltíing.
inspire: *v.* pareggetén, papigsáen; talokatíken, ipartáan.
install: *v.* isimpá, isaád, ikapét; ~**ment** *n.* panagbáyad a saggabassít.
instance: *n.* pagarígan, panangidagádag, kayarígan.
instant: *n.* darikmát, kanitó, giddáto; **do in an ~** sigkíngen.
instantaneous: *adj.* apagdarikmát, apagkanitó.
instantly: *adv.* giddáto, apagdarikmát.
instead: *prep.* embés, ití sáad ti.
instinct: *n.* gagángay.
instigate: *v.* durogán, kiwkíwan, sulbógen.
institute: *v.* bangónen, isaád, ipasdék, buangáyen; *n.* pagadálan, pasdék ti sursúro.
institution: *n.* patakdér, bángon.
instruct: *v.* sursuruán, bagbagaán, adálan.
instructor: *n.* mangisursúro.
instrument: *n.* aruáten, aramáten; (*means*) pamaayán, instruménto.
insubordinate: *adj.* nasúkir, nasúbeg, nasupríng.
insufficient: *adj.* kúrang.
insult: *n.* abí, ranggás ití dáyaw, pangpabaín; *v.* ab-abién; yadyádan, yagyágan, pabainán.
insurance: *n.* segúros; talgéd, pammatián, sadíri.
insure: *v.* agisegúro; agitalgéd.
insurrection: *n.* guló, yaalsá.
intact: *adj.* sibubukél.
integrate: *v.* pagtipónen, pagkaysaén.

integrity: *n.* integridád, kinaimbág, kinamatalék.
intellect: *n.* isip, nákem, panúnot, sarírit.
intellectual: *adj.* maipapán ití ísip; *n.* nasarírit a táo.
intelligence: *n.* sarírit, kinalaíng.
intelligent: *adj.* nalaíng, nasarírit.
intelligible: *adj.* maáwatan, nalawág.
intend: *v.* panggepén, sikáten, gamdén.
intensify: *v.* papigsáen, padakkelén; kumáro, rumába.
intensive: *adj.* napeksá, nasaknáp.
intent: *n.* gandát, panggép, síkat, gágar.
intention: *n.* gagára, nákem, pakinákem, gagém, panagém, panúnot, kananákem; panggép' ~**al** *adj.* pinanggép, ginagára.
intentionally: *v.* **do** ~ gagaráen, gandáten.
intercede: *v.* sumngát, bumiáng.
intercept: *v.* tipdén, saedén, lapdán, salbátan, abáten.
interchange: *v.* isukát, agsinnukát; *n.* panangsinnukát.
intercourse: *n.* pagtitipónan, pagkakaduaán.
intercropped: *adj.* napattokán, napintókan, masal-etán.
interest: *n.* ayát, pammatég; anák, anép; rágut; *v.* pagngayangáyen.
interesting: *adj.* makaay-áyo, makaguyúgoy-riknά.
interfere: *v.* sumampítaw, bumiáng; tumabnáw.
interior: *n.* saklóp, unég; (*of house*) lóob; (*of forest*) lungngúop.
interjection: *n.* pagsidáaw.
interlace: *v.* iballaét, iballát, ibal-ét; (*vines*) agkayammét, agkemmét.
intermeddle: *v.* bumibiáng, sumagpáw, sumarakúsok, tumabbíraw, tumalaán.
intermediate: *adj.* agtengngá
interment: *n.* pumpón.
intermingle: *v.* aglalaók.
intermission: *n.* panaginaná ití pabúya.
intermittently: *v.* **appear** ~ agballaballág; **do** ~ in-inúten, ullayáten, undáen, umaánam.
internal: *adj.* nagunég, naglas-úd.
interpolate: *v.* isigpít, iballaét, isingásing, iballát.
interpose: *v.* iballaét, ibislín, isengngát, isaláng, isagpáw.
interpret: *v.* ibuksílan, ibagasán; agbarubása, agdurubása, ipatarús.
interpreter: *n.* barubása, durubása, mangipatpatarús.
interrelated: *adj.* agkabagián.
interrogate: *v.* agsaludsód, agimtúod, salaysáyen, untónan.

interrupt: *v.* tubngáren, allawáten, singasíngen; isalingbát.
interruption: *n.* pangtéd, salingbát.
intersect: *v.* baledán, krusán; *v.* agsanggalá.
intersection: *n.* pagkurosán.
intersperse: *v.* iballaballaét.
intertwine: *v.* agkayyamét, agkemmét.
interval: *n.* ballaét, baét; (*between plants*) limbáng; (*of time*) pagbayátan.
intervene: *v.* mangibabaet, tumabnáw.
interview: *n.* entrebísta, panagsaríta, sarúngkar.
intestine: *n.* lalaém, bagbágis; **small** ~ silét; **small** ~ **of chickens** konkoníkon, piníkon; **adipose tissue that cleaves to small** ~ arimungámong, arimpungápong, garimungamúngan.
intimacy: *n.* nadekkét a pannakiammo-ammó.
intimate: *adj.* nadekkét; kasimpungálan, agsandugó; ~ **friend** *n.* nadekkét a gayyém.
intimidate: *v.* butbutngén.
intimidated: *adj.* umbá.
into: *prep.* agpaunég, sumrék.
intoxicate: *v.* uláwen, bartekén; sabidóngan.
intoxicating: *adj.* makabarték, makasabídong.
intricate: *adj.* nasumonsúmon; nasulít, narikút, nasikór.
intrigue: *n.* intríga; *v.* agintríga; agsíkap.
intrinsic: *adj.* nagunég, naikasígud, sígud.
introduce: *v.* yam-ammó, ipakaammó.
introduction: *n.* panangiyammo-ammó, pangyuná.
intrude: *v.* aglabsíng, sumagpáw, bumiáng, kumalamíkam, isallín.
invade: *v.* rautén, asakén.
invalid: *adj.* imbálido, awán mabalbalínna.
invasion: *n.* panangraút, rubbúot.
invent: *v.* putáren, parnuáyen; ~**ion** *n.* parnuáy, partuát, pútar.
inventor: *n.* mamarsuá.
invert: *v.* balinsuekén, baliktáden.
inverted: *adj.* tumbangí; **wear** ~ **shirt** agballúsong; **born in** ~ **position** súni.
invest: *v.* ipaáy a puonán, makikapuonán; ~**ment** *n.* nailásin a puonán; ~**or** *n.* mangipuonán.
investigate: *v.* palutpúten, usígen, taluntúnen.
investigator: *n.* mangus-úsig, mangam-ammíris.
invigorate: *v.* papigsáen.
invincible: *adj.* saán a maábak.
invisible: *adj.* saán a makíta.
invitation: *n.* áwis, kumbidár.
invite: *v.* kumbidarén, awísen, angáyen.
invited: *adj.* kumbidádo, ináwis; **attend a party without being** ~ makilínab.

invoice: *n.* paktúra.
invoke: *v.* awágan, dawáten.
involuntary: *adj.* saán a pinanggép.
involve: *v.* laónen, sakúpen, iráman, lakmúten; **~ment** pannkairáman.
inward: *adj.* nakin-unég.
iodine: *n.* yódo.
irate: *adj.* maruród, makapungtót.
ire: *n.* pungtót, luksáw.
iris: *n.* sarmíng (ti matá); **discoloration of ~** burág, surág.
iron: *n.* (*metal*) landók; (*for clothes*) plantsá; *v.* agplantsá; **~ pot** siliási, silián; **tinned ~** ganáka.
irony: *n.* paságid, sagíbar, saáni.
irradiate: *v.* lawagán, silnágan, raniágan; agraniág.
irrefutable: *adj.* saán a madupír.
irregular: *adj.* rinángis; piníwis; tallatallá.
irrelevant: *adj.* di maitúnos.
irresponsible: *adj.* di mapagtalkán.
irreverent: *adj.* saán a naraém.
irrevocable: *adj.* di mawaswás.
irrigate: *v.* sibugán, lay-asán, pasablógan, padanumán, pasayakán.
irrigation: *n.* paayás, padanúm, pasayák.
irritable: *adj.* managpungtót, buringetngét, naungét.
irritate: *v.* gargarién, paungetén, pagpungtóten, pagluksáwen, rubrúban.
is: *v.* third person singular present tense of **be**.
island: *n.* púro.
islet: *n.* bassít a púro.
isolate: *v.* isína, ilásin, ipútong.
issue: *v.* agsayásay, rumuár, tumpuár; iruár; tumbuák; *v.* irakúrax; iruár.
it: *pron.* isú(na), daydiáy.
Italian: *n.*, *adj.* Italiáno.
italic: *n.* létra a nagíray.
itch: *n.* gaddíl, gatél; (*at mouth*) mómo; *v.* aggatél, aggaddíl; **~ mite** kágaw.
item: *n.* bensá, pasét, bánag.
its: *pron.* -na.
ivory: *n.* márpil, saóng (ti elepánte), raráng.

J

jack: *n.* pagital-ó; **~ rafter** pakikít; **~ plane** katám.
jacket: *n.* sáko, amerikána, tsakéta; kotón, bádo.
jackfruit: *n.* lángka, anángka.
jackknife: *n.* nabáhas.
jagged: *adj.* písolpísol; **~ edge** *n.* rimmagádi a tadém.
jai alai: *n.* pelóta.

jail: *n.* pagbalúdan, kársel; *v.* ibálud.
jam: *v.* idaginsén; maisangbáy; lipitén; *n.* pakarigátan.
jamb: *n.* hámba.
January: *n.* Enéro.
Japanese: *n.*, *adj.* Hapón.
jar: *n.* burnáy, karámba, putík, garapón, hárra.
jasmine: *n.* sampága, hasmín.
jaundice: *n.* kuliáw; bebesság, malmalangá.
jaunt: *n.* panagpagnapagná, pasiár.
javelin: *n.* bassít a píka.
jaw: *n.* sángi; súngo, papangalán; **with protruding upper ~** agsungáng.
jealous: *adj.* naímon, naílem; naápal.
jealousy: *n.* ílem, ímon.
jeer: *v.* katawáan; uyawén, laísen, riawán.
jelly: *n.* dudól, haléa, patatípot, duydóy.
jellyfish: *n.* karomínas.
jeopardize: *v.* ipeggád, isarsárak.
jerk: *v.* gutadén, gungónen, guttaén; *n.* gutád, guttá.
jerked: *adj.* (*meat*) pálag, pingángen.
jersey: *adj.* kamiséta.
jest: *n.* rábak, angáw, parató; *v.* angawén.
Jesuit: *n.* Hesuíta.
Jesus: *n.* Hesús; **infant ~** Sánto Níño.
jetty: *n.* wayáng.
Jew: *n.* Hudió; **~'s mallow** salúyot.
jewel: *n.* saniáta, gaméng.
jeweler: *n.* alahéro.
jewelry: *n.* aláhas.
jicama: *n.* singkamás.
jingle: *n.* agkilíling, agkaratíkit, agkalangíking.
jittery: *adj.* nerbióso, makapatakrút.
job: *n.* trabáho, panggedán, pagsapúlan; **to be new on the ~** agiraráway; **do by the ~** pakiáwen.
jocular: *adj.* manangrabrábak, naangáw, nasaramsám, nasarangsáng.
jocund: *adj.* naragsák.
join: *v.* silpuén, pagtipónen.
joint: *n.* nagsuúpan, nagsaúpan, nagsilpuán; tangép; kamángan; pagsangálan; *v.* pagsilpuén; *adj.* nagkadduán; **crack one's ~s** aglitók, agkalatokót; agrittúok, agruttúok.
joist: *n.* soléras, dellég; (*bamboo*) talagítag.
joke: *n.* rábak, angáw, parató, pásaw, pakpakatáwa.
jolly: *adj.* naangáw, nakatáwa.
jolt: *v.* gungónen, kutukotén, wegwegén, wagwagén.
jostle: *v.* idurón, sikílen, dusagén.
jot: *n.* tuldék, tulnék; *v.* isúrat.
journal: *n.* warnákan, pagiwarnák; **~ism** *n.* panagsursúrat ití

pagiwarnák; ~**ist** *n.* mannúrat ití pagiwarnák, agiwarwarnák.

journey: *n.* baniága, panagdaliásat, biáhe; *v.* agbaniága, agbiáhe; **begin a** ~ agrubbuát.

jovial: *adj.* naragsák, agsayaksák.

joy: *n.* ragsák, rag-ó; ~**ful** naragsák, narag-ó.

jubilant: *adj.* siraragsák, sirarag-ó.

jubilation: *n.* pagragragsákan.

jubilee: *n.* hubiléo, padayá tunggál limapúlo a tawén.

judge: *n.* ukóm, hués; *v.* ukomén; agiked-keddéng; ipáto.

judgment: *n.* panangipáto, pagarúp, panangukóm, keddéng.

judicious: *adj.* natánang, nalintég.

jug: *n.* gorgoríta, hárra.

juggling: *n.* salamángka.

juice: *n.* tubbóg; (*broth*) digó; (*of unripe mango*) kamíring; (*of intestines*) papáit.

juicy: *adj.* natubbóg.

July: *n.* Húlio.

jump: *v.* aglagtó, agbattúto; *n.* lagtó.

junction: *n.* pagtumpóngan ti dálan, nagsuúpan, nagsilpuán.

juncture: *n.* nagsilpuán.

June: *n.* Húlio; ~ **bug** abal-ábal, arus-árus.

jungle: *n.* bákir; ~ **fowl** abúyo.

junior: *n.* ub-ubíng.

junk: *n.* basúra; bapór ti Insík; *v.* ibelléng, ibasúra. ~ **food** *n.* sitsiriá.

junket: *n.* dayáan, baniága a pagliwliwáan.

jurisdiction: *n.* masakúpan.

jury: *n.* húrado, húnta.

just: *adj.* nalintég, umisú, apag-isú; *adv.* láeng; ka-.

justice: *n.* hustísia, kinalintég; ~ **of the peace** *n.* ukóm a mamagkakappiá.

justifiable: *adj.* nainkalintegán.

justify: *v.* paneknekán a nalintég; salakníban; itag-áy; palintégen.

jut: *n.* dawádaw, ráwis; ~ **out** agdawádaw, sumariw-át, sumipásip, agyungáyong.

juxtaposed: *adj.* agtapíl.

juvenile: *n.* ubíng.

K

katydid: *n.* sílam.

keel: *n.* dúri ti sasakyán; (*of balotó boat*) bála.

keen: *adj.* masírib; natadém, natírad, natarumámis.

keep: *v.* idúlin, aluádan, aywánan; taginayónen, salimetmetán; ~ **back** tenglén, awíden, talaánan; ~ **an eye on** sipútan; ~ **away** makilásin; ~ **up with** agtatarubák; ~ **vigil** agpúyat.

keepsake: *n.* pakalaglagipán.

keg: *n.* barríl.

kennel: *n.* úbong (ti aso).

kerchief: *n.* pánio.

kernel: *n.* bukél, bagás; **small** ~ **of rice** marapegpég.

kerosene: *n.* petróleo.

ketchup: *n.* ketsáp.

kettle: *n.* kaldéro, pagangerán.

key: *n.* tulbék; (*piano*) teklá, klábe; *v.* tulbekán.

keyboard: *n.* tekládo.

keyhole: *n.* tutulbekán.

khaki: *n.* káki.

kick: *n.* kugtár; *v.* kugtáran, kub-áyan, kusayán; ~ **sideways** patíden; ~ **in the ham** agbansí.

kid: *n.* ubíng; urbón a kaldíng.

kidnap: *v.* itaráy, itálaw.

kidnapper: *n.* kúmaw, manglanlánid.

kidney: *n.* bekkél, biél; ~ **bean** barawbáw.

kill: *v.* patayén; ~ **many at once** riputén; ~ **trees** ataátan.

kiln: *n.* paggebbaán.

kilo: *n.* kílo.

kilometer: *n.* kilométro.

kimono: *n.* kimóno.

kin: *n.* kakabagián, panagbagí.

kind: *n.* kíta, kláse, sebbangán; *adj.* naemmá, naános, naayát.

kindhearted: *adj.* naási.

kindle: *v.* gangtán, silmútan, pasgedán.

kindling: *n.* pangpúor, pangsindí.

kindness: *n.* ási, kinaánus.

kindred: *n.* kabagián.

king: *n.* ári; ~'**s evil** pasíngil, abánon, birék.

kingdom: *n.* pagarián.

kingfisher: *n.* salaksák, bíding, peskadór.

kink: *n.* kulót.

kinky: *adj.* (*hair*) kulót, margaróta.

kinship: *n.* pagkakabagianán.

kiosk: *n.* kiósko.

kiss: *n.* agék, bisíto, béso, bisong; *v.* agkán, bisuén.

kit: *n.* aruáten, gargarét.

kitchen: *n.* kusína, pagapuyán, paglutuán.

kitchenette: *n.* bassít a paglutuán.

kite: *n.* ulláw.

kitten: *n.* kutíng, bassít a púsa.

knapsack: *n.* kadáy; kalupí, karatáy (ti soldádo), tampípi.

knead: *v.* salngén, lutlóten, lubién, masáen, gamayén, gamerán.

knee: *n.* túmeng; (*of quadrupeds*) páwis; **boil on the** ~ alunít.

kneecap: *n.* lipaylípay.

kneel: *v.* agparintúmeng.
knife: *n.* kutsílio; imokó; bunéng, bólo; **pocket~** kortaplúma; **blade of a ~** dáwa; **back of a ~** bángad; **handle of a ~** pután; **two-edged ~** sikét; **worn-out ~** birút.
knight: *n.* kabaliéro.
knit: *v.* aggansílio; agikét.
knob: *n.* písol, bútol; ammútil.
knock: *n.* tugtóg; *v.* tugtógen, tiknólan, lintókan; kukkókan; agtugtóg, agkukkók; **~ out** uknógen.
knock-kneed: *adj.* kawíng, kiwíng, tipróng.
knoll: *n.* pantók.
knot: *n.* siglót, simó, silpó; bukó; *v.* siglótan.
knotty: *adj.* simósimó, silpósilpó; bukuán.
know: *v.* ammó; (*a person*) am-ammo; (*recognize*) mailásin.
knowing: *adj.* mannakaammó.
knowledge: *n.* pannakaammó.
known: *adj.* siaammó; naipakaammó.
knuckle: *n.* bukó; *v.* dikólen.
kowtow: *v.* agkumbáwa; agparintúmeng.

L

label: *n.* etikéta; tandá, márka; *v.* markáan, ikkán ti etikéta.
labia: *n.* pingpíng ti úki; **~ minora** tamantáman.
labor: *n.* trabáho, panagarámid, pananggéd; *v.* agteggéd.
laboratory: *n.* laboratório.
laborer: *n.* mangmanggéd, mangmangló, mangngarámid.
lace: *n.* gálut, singdán; puntílias, boliós, bandá; (*of curtain*) sábay, sarubaybáy; *v.* sirotén; puntelyásan.
lacerate: *v.* pigísen, sugáten, uyakén; ray-ában.
lack: *n.* kúrang; *v.* agkúrang.
lacquer: *n.* barnís, góma-láka, malapáko.
lad: *n.* bumaró.
ladder: *n.* agdán.
ladle: *n.* akló, sídok, pagkáud.
lady: *n.* balásang; nataknéng a babái.
lag: *v.* maárus; agbayág, agpapaúdi.
laggard: *adj.* nabayág, naináyad.
lagoon: *n.* álog, libtóng.
lake: *n.* dánaw, bannaáw.
lamb: *n.* karnéro, urbón.
lambent: *adj.* napúngay.
lame: a*dj.* pílay.
lament: *v.* sangítan, dung-áwan; agunnóy, agladíngit.
lamentable: *adj.* nakaladladíngit, nakakaási, nakain-inaká.

lamp: *n.* lámpara, pagsaíngan, pagsiláwan; **~ shade** pantália ti lámpara.
lamprey: *n.* ígat-berkákan.
lance: *n.* gayáng, píka, dúros.
land: *n.* dagá, dápat; pagilián; *v.* sumanglád, bumangkág, umígid; tumakdáng; agpadagá; (*set foot on*) agdappát; **high ~** tangkíg; **low ~** álog; **swampy ~** sagnéb; **to clear ~** agumá; **~ snail** birurúkong; **alluvial ~** lúsong.
landing: *n.* (*of stairs*) arusadúsan.
landlady: *n.* mangaséra.
landlord: *n.* mangaséro.
landmark: *n.* dúlon, mohón.
landscape: *n.* ladáwan ti dagá.
landslide: *n.* gueddáy, ludúlod.
lane: *n.* bet-áng; lipít; pagnaán.
language: *n.* saó, pagsasaó.
languid: *adj.* namayyét, namuyót, nauldóy, nalánay, nakismáy, nakunáil, nakapsút; agdidikkúmer.
languish: *n.* muyót.
languor: *n.* sagubanít, muyót, sagúreng.
lanky: *adj.* karantíway.
lantern: *n.* paról.
lap: *n.* saklót, sab-ók; *v.* dilpátan; **~dog** pasakí.
lapel: *n.* kulpí, lupíng.
lapse: *n.* pannakaigalís, panaglábas.
lard: *n.* mantéka, sinísi.
large: *adj.* dakkél; (*animals*) nawálat; (*clothes, nets*) naláyak, naláwa; (*wounds*) batiwáak.
lark: *n.* ruiseniór.
larva: *n.* iggés; (*different kinds*) abálen, arábas, sulsulbót, ubet-úbet, bátar, bátir, pilípig, antatáteg, takudóg, dangandángan, bokbók; (*of fly*) sur-ít; **mosquito ~** balbaltík; (*of beetle*) pusapúsa, alimpupúsa; (*of moth*) sánga.
laryngitis: *n.* sakít ti karabukób.
larynx: *n.* karabukób.
lascivious: *adj.* nauttóg, naultóg, nailubóngan, nagaramúgam; naráwet (iti laság).
lash: *v.* baúten, saplíten.
lasso: *n.* kay-óng, sílo, káka; *v.* siluán, kay-óngen.
last: *adj.* maúdi; kallabés; *v.* agbayág, agpaút, agnáyon.
lasting: *adj.* napáut.
latch: *n.* baklíng, balunét, trangká.
late: *adj.* naládaw, naúdi; (*dead*) natáy.
later: *adv.* madamdamá, intóno kuá.
latent: *adj.* malméng.
lateral: *adj.* impabakráng.
lath: *n.* talangkób, listón.
lather: *n.* labútab ti sabón; *v.* aglabútab.

latter: *adj.* naud-údi, naladládaw.

laud: *v.* idáyaw, itan-ók.

laugh: *n.* katáwa; *v.* agkátawa; umayek-ék; (*noisely*) aggaraigí, aggarakgák, pumgáak, aggarikgík; (*silently*) umkék; bumuritekték.

launch: *v.* ibákal, irúsat, irugí; *n.* lántsa.

launder: *v.* labaán.

laundry: *n.* (*dirty clothes*) muréng, labaán.

lavatory: *n.* pagbugguán, bánio.

lavish: *adj.* engránde; nabuslón; managgásto, nabarayúboy; nawadwád; nangayéd.

law: *n.* lintég, alagáden; (*field or study*) abogásia; ~ **firm** bupéte.

lawful: *adj.* nainkalintegán, mayanátupití lintég.

lawn: *n.* karuótan, solár.

lawsuit: *n.* ringgór, ríri iti pangukomán.

lawyer: *n.* abogádo, manglinlintég.

lax: *adj.* nalukáy.

laxative: *n.* pagpatakkí; pagpaburís, laksánte; (*natural ~ from tree fruit*) baliweswés.

lay: *v.* idissó, ipaiddá.

layer: *n.* túon, ap-áp, palunápin, rutáp, ratíp, aplí; **egg~** *n.* agitlóg.

layman: *n.* kadkadawyán a táo.

layout: *n.* balabála, gákat.

lazy: *adj.* nasadút, nabuntóg, napamayán; bayanggúdaw, nagínad, natamlág, nakámol, nakúdad, betbét, nakalunákol.

lead: *n.* bulí; (*of a clock*) batobató; **white ~** albayáde.

lead: *v.* ituróng, itulód.

leader: *n.* pangúlo, daúlo, mangituróng; **~ship** *n.* kinapangúlo.

leaf: *n.* bulóng; (*of book*) pánid; (*of palms*) palatángan; (*of coconut palm*) balaniúg; **discarded ~s** ubáas; **withered ~s** barakúbak, barakbák.

leafy: *adj.* nasalumpáyak, narukbós.

league: *n.* pagkakaduaán, timpúyog.

leak: *n.* úbo, tedtéd; *v.* agúbo, agtedtéd.

lean: *adj.* nalagpít; nakuttóng, kodapís; kasla tiwantíwan; *v.* agírig, agíray.

leap: *v.* aglagtó, agkulagtít.

learn: *v.* adálen, agsursúro, agraramán; ~ **by heart** ikabésa.

learned: *adj.* de-ádal, masírib, nasursuruán.

lease: *v.* ipaábang, ipaúpa; *n.* túlag ti panagúpa.

leash: *n.* singdán; *v.* singgapolén.

least: *adj.* kabassitán; kababaán.

leather: *n.* lálat.

leave: *n.* palúbos; *v.* pumánaw, umadayó; (*on a trip*) lumuás.

lectern: *n.* atríl.

lecture: *n.* pammagbagá, pammabaláw, panangilawlawág; bitlá.

leech: *n.* alimátek.

leek: *n.* kutsáy.

left: *adj.* katigíd, kanigíd; **to be ~** *v.* matdá, mabáti.

leftover: *n.* tiddá, sása.

legal: *adj.* nalintég, maitúnos ití lintég; tumutóp, nainkalintegán; ~ **document** *n.* pasingkéd.

legality: *n.* kinalintég, pannakatúnos ití lintég.

legalize: *v.* lagdáan.

legend: *n.* saríta.

legged: *adj.* **cross-~** nakasalumpáyak; **bandy-~** bákang, sallákup, tipróng, nadupakpák, piddawít; **long-~** karantíway, dangkáw.

leggings: *n.* polaínas.

legible: *adj.* mabása.

legion: *n.* reprép, sangaarbánan.

legislation: *n.* panagarámid ti lintég.

legitimate: *n.* mayanáup ití lintég; ~ **child** *n.* inyanák dagití nagkasár.

leisure: *n.* wayawayá, liwlíwa.

lemon: *n.* limón, daláyap, perrés, kabúgaw; **~grass** baraniw, baranoy.

lemonade: *n.* limonáda.

lend: *v.* ipabúlod, ipaútang.

length: *n.* kaatiddóg; **~en** *v.* paatiddogén; **~wise** *adv.* imparaatiddóg; **~y** *adj.* atiddóg.

lenient: *adj.* managitulók, naánus.

lens: *n.* lénte, anteóhos; sarmíng.

Lent: *n.* Kuarésma.

leper: *n.* agkukútel.

leprosy: *n.* kukútel, katíng.

lesion: *n.* siknó.

less: *adj.* nakurkúrang, basbassít.

lessen: *v.* pabassitén, ikkatán, kissayán.

lesson: *n.* wadén, leksión, adálen.

lest: *conj.* ta dínto ket, di la ket.

let: *v.* bay-án; palubósan; pabus-óyan.

letter: *n.* (*alphabet*) létra; (*correspondence*) súrat.

lettuce: *n.* letsúgas.

levee: *n.* tambák; (*of a rice field*) sagába.

level: *adj.* nasímpa, dalumpínas, naparánas; taradió; lansád, lessáad; *v.* simpáen; ipuntá.

lever: *n.* bassuíl, pamatuágan.

lewd: *adj.* nagaramúgam, naderrép.

liar: *n.* ulbód, salawásaw.

liberal: *adj.* naparábur, nawaywáy, naugáw, nabuslón.

liberate: *v.* wayaán, pagwayawayaén.

liberty: *n.* wayawayá, panagwaywáyas.

librarian: *n.* bibliotekário.

library: *n.* bibliotéka, penpén dagití pagbasáan.

lice: *n.* kúto; ~ **eggs** lis-á; **infested with ~** agbungkók; ~ **comb** súgod.

license: *n.* lisénsia, palúbos; *v.* palubósan ti lintég.
lick: *v.* dilpátan, silamútan, dildílan; (*beat*) baúten.
lid: *n.* kalúb, abbóng, takkáb.
lie: *v.* (*fib*) agulbod; (*recline*) agiddá, agsádag.
lieu: *n.* sandí, sukát; **in ~ of** imbés.
lieutenant: *n.* teniénte.
life: *n.* biág; **~boat** *n.* lantsá-salbabída; **~style** wágas ti panagbiág.
life preserver: *n.* salbabídas.
lift: *v.* bagkáten, ingáto, itag-áy.
light: *n.* sílaw; lawág, silnág; *adj.* nalag-án; *v.* siláwan, lawagán; **~ brown** pangalumamanién; **~ red** pangindaráen.
lighter: *n.* pagsindí.
lighthearted: *adj.* nadangér, nagarutigít, nagaratigít.
lighthouse: *n.* paróla, sílaw-taáw.
lightning: *n.* kimát, sal-ít.
like: *adj., adv.* kas, kaslá, mayaspíng, kaárig, uming-ingás, kapáda; *prep.* kas; *v.* kayát, magustuán, pagrayuán.
likely: *adj.* nalábit, segúro.
liken: *v.* ipadpád, ipáda.
likeness: *n.* panagkaingás, panagkaaspíng, panagpáda.
likewise: *adv.* kastá met.
lily: *n.* asuséna, lírio; **water ~** súkaw.
limb: *n.* takiág, kaméng ti bagí; sangá.
limber: *adj.* nalapiót, natulók, nalukáy.
lime: *n.* ápug; daláyap.
limit: *n.* patinggá, keddéng, beddéng; ígid; *v.* ikkán ti pagpatinggaán.
limp: *v.* agpilaypílay, agkingkíng.
limpid: *adj.* nalitnáw, nalit-áw, natarnáw, nasin-áw.
line: *n.* (*dash*) úged, urít; úgis, línas; (*row*) binnátog, pirápid, banténg; (*string*) lúbid; (*marking*) paltík; bartáy; *v.* ibartáy; ugísan, ukríten; (*garment*) taparán.
lineage: *n.* kapuonán, galád, katatáo.
linen: *n.* liénso; *adj.* de-líno.
linger: *v.* agtakták, agbayág, agtalinaéd.
lining: *n.* tapár, pórro, apúrro, rutáp.
link: *n.* kalangkáng ti káwar, eslabón; pakainaígan; sílpo; *v.* isílpo.
linotype: *n.* linotípia.
lint: *n.* samotsámot, sinutsót.
lion: *n.* león.
lip: *n.* bibíg; (*of fish*) ludlód; **border of the ~s** ngiwngíw; **drooping lower ~** libbí; **with sunken ~s** ngobngób, narungbéd; **bite one's ~s** *v.* agpangrém; **upper ~** dummóg.
lipstick: *n.* lipístik; pagparumpí.
liquefy: *v.* dumanúm.

liquid: *n.* danúm (aniáman nga agáyus a kas ití danúm).
liquor: *n.* árak; **~ store** pagarákan; **strong ~** sangér.
lisp: *v.* agmutal, agannawír.
list: *n.* listáan; **remove from a ~** *v.* ligsáyen.
listen: *v.* dumngég, denggén
listless: *adj.* aglaladút.
liter: *n.* lítro.
literature: *n.* literatúra, kurdítan.
litigate: *v.* ririén, ringgóren.
litter: *n.* talabóng, sangainaán a buriás; (*trash*) basúra.
little: *adj.* bassít.
live: *v.* agbiág; *adj.* sibibiág.
livelihood: *n.* pagbiágan, pagsapúlan.
lively: *adj.* nabiág, naparagsít; nakaradkád; nakartíng, naparták, nasalawitwít, nasaliwanwán, napargí, nagarutigít, nakulanggít.
liver: *n.* dálem; **~ stew** ígado.
livid: *adj.* nalítem.
living: *adj.* nabiág.
living room: *n.* sálas.
lizard: *n.* alutiít, tekká, baniás, alibút.
load: *n.* kárga, awít, amít, dagsén; *v.* kargáan; paawitán.
loadstone: *n.* batumbaláni.
loaf: *n.* tukél ti tinápay; (*round and twisted*) binalikongkóng.
loan: *v.* ipabúlod; *n.* paútang.
loathe: *v.* guraén.
lobby: *n.* paguráyan, pagtakderán.
lobe: *n.* rútong, ríting, búkol.
lobster: *n.* udáng, padáw.
locate: *v.* idissó, birókan.
location: *n.* yan, dissó, pagsaádan, pagyanán.
lock: *n.* kandádo, tutulbekán; *v.* tulbekán, kandaduán.
lockjaw: *n.* ngásib, bettéd ti sángi.
locust: *n.* dúdon.
lodge: *v.* agdagús, agsangbáy; *n.* pagdagusán.
lofty: *adj.* narimbáw; nadaég.
log: *n.* tróso.
logic: *n.* lóhika, panagrasón.
logging: *n.* panagtarikáyo; **illegal ~** taribadiók.
loin: *n.* lomolómo, síbet.
loiter: *v.* agtakták, agpamayán, agballóg, agbaliúdong.
lone: *adj.* maymaysá.
loneliness: *n.* tarumpíngay, íla.
lonesome: *adj.* matalipungáwen, natarumpíngay.
long: *adj.* atiddóg; (*noses*) napantók; (*roads*) nawatíwat; (*life*) naundáy; **~-haired** bangáw; **~-legged** karantíway, dangkáw; *v.* aggágar,

mailiw; kumaráyo; ~ **for** *v.* mail-íla, kaíliw.

look: *v.* kitáen, matmátan; ~ **down** agtan-áw, agtamdág, agdar-áw; ~ **behind** tumaliáw; *n.* kíta, tábas, takdér, púdos; gayamúdaw.

looking glass: *n.* sarmíng.

lookout: *n.* allígang.

looks: *n.* kíta, langá, itsúra.

loom: *n.* telár, pagablán.

loop: *n.* sillawíd, siló.

loose: *adj.* nalukáy; naibbét; nawayaán.

loosen: *v.* palukayán.

loot: *n.* panagsamsám.

loquacious: *adj.* mannanaó, busawsáw, saosaó, barisawsáw, nangíwat, nadarawídaw, natarawítaw.

lord: *n.* ápo; mangituráy.

lose: *v.* mapúkaw, iwágat; dadaélen.

loss: *n.* púkaw; (*in game*) ábak.

lost: *adj.* napúkaw, nayaw-awán.

lot: *n.* lóte, sangkadissó a dagá; gásat; **a lot of** adú.

lotion: *n.* losión.

lottery: *n.* rípa, lotería.

lotus: *n.* súkaw.

loud: *adj.* natebbág, naringgór, napigsá (a tímek); ~**mouthed** nabisngáw, nadalawídaw.

louse: *n.* kúto; kámay; ~ **egg** lis-á.

love: *n.* ayát, karáyo, essém; *v.* ay-ayatén; ~ **potion** *n.* gayúma, tagirúot ti ayát.

lovely: *adj.* nakaay-ayát, nakaay-áyo.

lover: *n.* agay-ayát.

loving: *adj.* nadungngó, karinióso, naayát.

low: *adj.* nababá; nanumó; ~ **pitched** nabángag; ~**-spirited** masikorán.

lower: *v.* ibabá; *adj.* nababbabá.

lowland: *n.* tanáp, álog.

lowly: *adj.* napakumbabá, nanumó

loyal: *adj.* matalék, natulnóg.

lubricant: *n.* pagpagalís; lána, grása.

lubricate: *v.* pagalisén, sapuán, grasáan.

lucid: *adj.* nalawág, nasin-áw.

luck: *n.* gásat; **good** ~ talibágok, buénas; **bad** ~ buísit, málas.

luggage: *n.* malmaléta, gargarét, al-alikámen, tamtampóng.

lukewarm: *adj.* nabáaw, apag-anem-ém, nalab-áy.

lull: *v.* pagtalnáen.

lullaby: *n.* lalláy, duayyá.

lumber: *n.* tarikáyo.

luminous: *adj.* naraniág, nasilnág.

lump: *n.* búkol, tukél, bingkól, lisdák, lisbó; (*in flour*) búnel.

lunatic: *adj.* agmaúyong, bulanbulánen.

lunch: *n.* pangngaldáw.

lung: *n.* bará.

lunge: *v.* ibagsól, duyokén.

lure: *v.* uyótan, awísen, gargarién; sairuén; *n.* pangáwis, appán, pangúyot.

lurid: *adj.* nabesság, nalidém, naalibuyóng.

luscious: *adj.* naímas, makaay-áyo.

lush: *adj.* narangpáya; narabér; nawadwád; nalasbáng.

lust: *n.* kinaderrép, gartém, tarigágay ti laság.

lustful: *adj.* nauttóg, naultóg, nailubóngan.

luster: *n.* rangráng, raniág, siláp.

luxuriant: *adj.* (*growth*) nalasbáng, nalatbáng.

luxurious: *adj.* naramén.

Lydian stone: *n.* susudián.

lye: *n.* túro.

lymph: *n.* límpa.

lyre: *n.* líra.

M

ma'am: *n.* apo a babai.

macabre: *adj.* nakabutbuténg, nakaam-amák.

mace: *n.* garróte, sarukód.

machine: *n.* mákina; ~ **gun** masinggán.

machinery: *n.* makinária.

mad: *adj.* (*crazy*) agmaúyong, agballá; (*upset*) maruród.

madam: *n.* apo a babai, senióra.

maelstrom: *n.* alipugpúg, bagió.

magazine: *n.* pagiwarnák.

maggot: *n.* sur-ít.

magic: *n.* salamángka, enkánto.

magician: *n.* salamangkéro, sumasalamángka.

magistrate: *n.* ukóm, hués.

magnet: *n.* batombaláni; ~**ic** *adj.* nabatombaláni.

magnificent: *adj.* nadaég, nangayéd. nadayág.

magnify: *v.* padakkelén, law-ásan.

magnitude: *n.* kinadakkél.

mahogany: *n.* kaóba.

maid: *n.* katúlong (a babái); balásang.

maiden: *n.* balásang.

maidenhair: *n.* kurantrílio.

mail: *n.* tinnág, korréo, súrat.

maim: *v.* pukolán, piláyan, pawádan.

main: *adj.* nangrúna, kapatgán.

maintain: *v.* taripatuén, igága, taginayónen.

maintenance: *n.* pannaripáto, pannakataginayón; saránay.

maize: *n.* maís.

majestic: *adj.* nadaég, natan-ók, nangayéd.

majesty: *n.* kinatan-ók (ti ári).

major: *adj.* nangrúna; *n.* komandánte.

majority: *n.* kaaduán.

make: *v.* aramíden; buklén; *n.* márka, modélo.

makeup: *n.* pagpapíntas ti babái.

malady: *n.* sagubánit, sakít, samuyéng.
malaria: *n.* malária, payegpég.
male: *adj.* laláki.
malediction: *n.* lunód.
malevolent: *adj.* naulpít.
malice: *n.* malísia, kinadákes, gulíb.
malign: *v.* padpadaksén, parpardayáen; pagsasaoán.
malignant: *adj.* arimpatayén.
mall: *n.* máso, martílio; pagsiapíngan.
mallard: *n.* pápa.
mallet: *n.* masíta, maliéte, bassít a pang-ór.
mallow: *n.* kastóli; **Jews'** ~ salúyot, suysúyot.
maltreat: *v.* ranggásan, labakén, lugubán, idadanés.
mamma: *n.* iná, nána.
mammoth: *adj.* nakadakdakkél.
man: *n.* táo a laláki; **young** ~ baró.
manacle: *n.* putáw, pósas.
manage: *v.* taripatuén, manarawidwíd; imatonán; ~**ment** *n.* panangituróng.
manager: *v.* mararawidwíd, mangimatón, mangituróng.
manatee: *n.* dúyong, dúgong; abáda.
mandarin: (*orange*) *n.* lolokísen.
mandate: *n.* bílin, keddéng.
mandatory: *adj.* managbílin, masápul a tungpálen.
mane: *n.* buók, pígar.
maneuver: *n.* panagtayakták, manióbra.
mange: *n.* pillútog, gudgód, duldóg.
manger: *n.* kullúong.
mangle: *v.* risangrisángen, tatkén.
mango: *n.* manggá, páo; **fiber of** ~ gunnót; **juice of unripe** ~ kamíring; **young** ~ karissábong.
manhandle: *v.* dunóren, pasakitán.
manhood: *n.* kinalaláki, kinatáo.
mania: *n.* kinaaguúyong.
manifest: *v.* ipakíta, ipamatmát, isáwang, iparáng, isngáw, ipalgák, ituyáng, ipakaammó; *adj.* nalawág.
manifestation: *n.* paltíing, panangituyáng.
manifesto: *n.* pakdáar, warragáwag.
manipulate: *v.* papagnaén, imáen, ituróng.
mankind: *n.* sangkataoán.
manly: *adj.* linalaláki, lakién; naturéd.
manner: *n.* ugáli; módo; panagwá, pamay-án, kababalín.
mannerism: *n.* kadkadawyán nga ugáli.
mannish: *adj.* lakién.
mansion: *n.* dakkél a baláy.
manslaughter: *n.* panangpapatáy ití táo.
mantilla: *n.* pandóng.
mantis: *n.* wasaywásay.
mantle: *n.* kagáy, abbóng, mánto.

manual: *adj.* arámid ti íma.
manufacture: *v.* agarámid, agpartuát.
manure: *n.* ganágan, panabá.
many: *adj.* adú, naruáy.
map: *n.* mápa.
mar: *v.* dadaelén, paalasén.
marauder: *n.* bálang.
marble: *n.* (*material*) mármol; (*playing*) korriéndo, hólen.
march: *n.* mártsa; *v.* agmártsa.
March: *n.* Márso.
mare: *n.* kabálio a babái.
margin: *n.* ígid.
marigold: *n.* marabília.
marinade: *n.* templá.
marinate: *v.* templáen.
marine: *n.* búyot ti taáw.
mark: *n.* márka, seníal, tánda; pagilasínan, urít; *v.* ugísan, ukríten.
marker: *n.* pagúgis.
market: *n.* tiendáan; ~ **fee** kuartáis.
marl: *n.* tangígi.
marooned: *adj.* nalayágan.
marriage: *n.* pannakiasáwa, panagkallaysá.
marrow: *n.* patá.
marry: *v.* mangasáwa, makikallaysá, agkasár.
marsh: *n.* lutúlut, alugúog, lugnák.
mart: *n.* tiendáan, paglakuán.
martyr: *n.* martír.
marvel: *n.* datdatlág; *v.* masdáaw.
marvelous: *adj.* nakaskasdáaw.
masculine: *adj.* laláki.
masculinity: *n.* kinamalaláki.
mash: *v.* limugén, duydúyen.
mask: *n.* abúngot.
masonry: *n.* kinamasón, kabíti.
mass: *n.* (*church*) mísa; (*of people*) tipkél; lisdák, buntón.
massacre: *n.* nadawél a panangpapatáy; *v.* agpapatáy a sidadawél.
massage: *n.* masáhe, panangílut, pekkél; *v.* ilúten, ramásen.
massive: *adj.* nabungkóng, nasábang.
mast: *n.* pálo ti sasakyán, annayásan; albór.
master: *n.* ápo, agturáy.
mastermind: *n.* mangibuángay.
masterpiece: *n.* óbra maéstra, kapíntasan nga inarámid ti maysá a táo.
masticate: *v.* agngalngál.
masturbate: *v.* agsalsál, aglaputlapút, agbatíl.
mat: *n.* (*for sleeping*) ikamén; (*for wiping feet*) pígad.
match: *n.* kasapuégo, pósporo, gurábis; (*pair*) kapáda, kaasmáng; *v.* bagáyan, parísan; ~**maker** manyalud-alúd, albasiadór.

mate: *n.* kaduá; asáwa.
material: *n.* aruáten; materiáles; *adj.* maaruát.
maternal: *adj.* maipapán ití iná; nainaán.
maternity: *n.* paganakán.
matrimony: *n.* panagasáwa, panagkasár.
matrix: *n.* matrís, aanakán.
matter: *n.* bánag, pasámak, ánag; bagí.
mattock: *n.* pandarás, gabión.
mattress: *n.* koltsón, kudsón.
mature: *adj.* nataengán, natangkenán; nalúom, napnekán.
maturity: *n.* kinalakáy; kinatangkén; kinaluóm.
maul: *n.* máso; *v.* malmaluén, sanután, satsátan, tatkén, umáren, tumekén, dunóren.
mausoleum: *n.* taném a nagarbó, pantión.
maxim: *n.* nainsiríban a sasaó.
maximum: *adj.* kadakkelán; kaaduán.
may: *v.* mabalín; maka-, ma-.
May: *n.* Máyo.
maybe: *adv.* sigúro, ngatá, nalábit.
mayonnaise: *n.* mayonésa.
mayor: *n.* alkálde, pangúlo ti íli.
me: *pron.* kaniák; -ak; siák.
meadow: *n.* karuótan, tanáp.
meager: *adj.* nakírang, narásay; napangláw; kodapís, nakiddít, natiggít.
meal: *n.* pannangán, kanén; **something eaten between ~s** saramsám, sarangsáng.
mean: *adj.* nakagúra, naúyong; *v.* kayát a sawén; kaibuksílan.
meander: *v.* agatimúrong, aglíkaw, agrikosríkos.
meaning: *n.* kaipapanán, kaibuksílan.
means: *n.* pamuspúsan, pamaayán.
meantime: *n.* kabayátan.
measles: *n.* kamúras, karibnás.
measure: *n.* rukód, súkat; **~ment** *n.* súkat.
meat: *n.* kárne, laság; **jerked ~** pálag, pindángen, katátos; **soft coconut ~** lulukóten; **hard coconut ~** taramusián, saramusián.
mechanic: *adj.* mekániko; **~al** *adj.* de-mákina.
medal: *n.* medália.
meddle: *v.* sumampítaw, tumabbíraw, bumibiáng.
meddlesome: *adj.* mannakibiáng.
medial: *adj.* namagitngá.
mediate: *v.* mamagkappiá.
medicinal: *adj.* makaágas.
medicine: *n.* ágas; **~ man** baribarí; (*field of study*) kinamangngágas.
mediocre: *adj.* nanumó, napipiá; ginagalimúsaw.
meditate: *v.* panunóten, isípen.
medium: *adj.* kalkalaingánna; *n.* pamay-án; akin-tengngá.

medley: *n.* laók, gampór, nagtitípon.
medusa: *n.* karomínas.
meek: *adj.* natulók, naemmá, napakumbabá.
meet: *v.* sabtén, sarakén; masarákan; dalapúsen; agkíta, agsábat.
meeting: *n.* típon, tallaóng, gímong, taripnóng.
melancholy: *adj.* naalidungét, naladíngit.
melon: *n.* sandiá, muród; **young ~** búsel; **bitter ~** pariá.
melt: *v.* malúag, matúnaw, dumanúm.
member: *n.* kaméng, náyon, naikappón.
membership: *n.* kinakaméng, panagkamkaméng.
membrane: *n.* kulánit, kulápot; **mucus ~** aangótan.
memento: *n.* pakalaglagipán.
memoir: *n.* naisúrat a panglaglagíp.
memorable: *adj.* nakalalagíp.
memorandum: *n.* sinúrat a mangipalagíp.
memorize: *v.* yúlo, ikabésa.
memory: *n.* lagíp, tandaán.
men: *n.* tattáo.
menace: *n.* pangamés, karián, kapeggadán, láyat.
mend: *v.* tarimaánen, tarimnén.
mendicant: *n.* agpalpalamá.
menial: *adj.* nababá.
menopause: *n.* pinggá (ti babái).
menses: *n.* régla, sangaíli, kadawyán.
menstruate: *v.* agrégla, agsangaíli, agkadawyán.
menstruation: *n.* régla, sangaíli; **beginning of ~** malibukayán; **profuse ~** daraudó.
mention: *v.* dakawáten, idukít, saritáen, ipalikpík; umagápad, agapáden; maisaó; isalpiká.
mentor: *n.* matalék a mamagbagá, mannursúro.
menu: *n.* pagtaraón, listáan ti kanén.
mercenary: *n.* mersenário.
merchandise: *n.* tagiláko.
merchant: *n.* agtagtagiláko, agbambaniága.
merciful: *adj.* naási.
mercy: *n.* kaási; parábur.
mere: *adj.* láeng.
merge: *v.* sagepsepén; lumaók.
meridian: *n.* meridiáno, kangatuán a pungtó.
merit: *n.* dáyaw, kaikarián, palungdó; *v.* maikári, kaikarián.
mermaid: *n.* siréna, abáda.
merriment: *n.* ragragsák, rambák.
merry: *adj.* naragsák, nakatáwa.
mess: *n.* wará, laók, kusokusó.
message: *n.* pakdáar, mesáhe, pakaammó.
messenger: *n.* babaonén, mensahéro, agipadpadámag.

metal: *n.* metál.
metallurgy: *n.* kinalatéro, kinapandáy.
metaphor: *n.* metápora, pangngárig.
meteor: *n.* layáp.
meter: *n.* métro; kontadór.
method: *n.* wágas, pamay-án, pamuspúsan.
mettlesome: *adj.* nadangér, bumibiáng.
microbe: *n.* mikróbio.
mid: *adj.* akintengngá.
midday: *n.* matúon.
middle: *n.* tengngá, ngálay; ~ **finger** pattungágan.
middleman: *n.* ahénte.
midget: *n.* bassít a táo.
midnight: *n.* tengngá ti rabií.
midrib: *n.* palátang.
midst: *n.* ití tengngá.
midstream: *n.* tengngá ti karayán.
midwife: *n.* mangngílut, partéra.
might: *n.* pigsá, pannakabalín; bíleg; *v.* ma-, sigúro; ngatá.
mighty: *adj.* mannakabalín; maíngel.
migrate: *v.* umákar ití pagtaengán.
mild: *adj.* naalumámay, nalanay.
mildew: *n.* búot, tarumátim; **spots of** ~ ratík.
mile: *n.* mília.
militant: *adj.* mannakigubát, nadadaán a makisuppiát.
milk: *n.* gátas; **~man** aggatgátas.
milkfish: *n.* bangós.
Milky Way: *n.* Nagririmpúok a Bitbituén.
mill: *n.* molíno; *v.* gilíngen, baywén; **wind~** molíno ti ángin.
millet: *n.* sábog, mího.
millimeter: *n.* milimétro.
million: *n.* riwríw.
millionaire: *n.* milionário.
millipede: *n.* andidikén.
milt: *n.* ballaibí.
mimic: *v.* tuláden, teldén.
mince: *v.* tegtegén, tadtáden, ilangdét, segsegén, raw-áken.
mincemeat: *n.* tinegtég, sinegség.
mind: *n.* pakinákem, panúnot, ísip; *v.* ikaskáso; timúden, annadén.
mindful: *adj.* mangikaskáso, sipapanúnot.
mine: *n.* mínas; *pron.* bágik, kukuák.
mineral: *n.* minerál.
mingle: *v.* tumípon, aglalaók, makitapkíl.
miniature: *adj.* nakabasbassít.
minimize: *v.* pabassitén.
minister: *n.* minístro.
minor: *adj.* basbassít; ub-ubíng.
minority: *n.* kinabasbassít; minoría.
mint: *n.* yerbabuéna, ménta.
minus: *adj.* kúrang, naikkatán.

minute: *n.* minúto, kanitó; ~ **hand** minutéro.
miracle: *n.* milágro, datdatlág.
mire: *n.* lúpak, lubnák, piláw, lubó.
mirror: *n.* sarmíng, paganináwan.
mirth: *n.* ragsák.
misbehave: *v.* agpalangguád, aglokolokó.
miscalculate: *v.* agríro ití panangpattapattá.
miscarriage: *n.* pannakaalís; pannakasáaw.
miscarry: *v.* maalisán, agparegrég.
miscellaneous: *adj.* naglalaók, nadumadúma.
mischief: *n.* dánar, ranggás.
mischievous: *adj.* pílio, naalikúteg, naaliwegwég, naalikád; malálo, napásig.
misdeed: *n.* dákes nga arámid.
miser: *n.* nakirmét a táo.
miserable: *adj.* nakakáasi, marigrígat, manguyapét.
miserly: *adj.* naímut, nakirmét; (*with food*) naíkab.
misery: *n.* kinakakaási, kinaay-ay-áy; kina-rigrígat, kinapangláw.
misfortune: *n.* daksangásat, buísit.
misgiving: *n.* duaduá; buténg.
misground: *v.* naarimasámas.
mishap: *n.* pakarigátan, pagél.
mishear: *v.* mabalínga.
mislaid: *adj.* maiwágat.
mislead: *v.* yaw-awán, ibaligawgáw, itawátaw, alliláwen; **~ing** *adj.* naríro, makaallílaw.
misplace: *v.* iwágat.
misprint: *n.* ríro ti pannakideppél.
miss: *n.* seniórita, balásang; *v.* labásan, libtáwan, liwáyan, saán a mapuntáan.
missing: *adj.* kúrang; napúkaw.
missionary: *n.* misionéro.
mist: *n.* angép, alibuyóng, kulláap, sengngáw, libbúob.
mistake: *n.* allílaw, ríro, biddút, maríro; *v.* agríro, agbiddút.
mistaken: *adj.* maallílaw.
mister: *n.* seniór, ápo.
mistreat: *v.* maltratuén, labakén.
mistress: *n.* kamalála, kaábig.
mistrust: *v.* aslén, tanggáden; *n.* di panagtalék.
misunderstand: *v.* di maawátan; **~ing** *n.* di panagkikinnaawátan.
mite: *n.* túngaw.
mitigate: *v.* palag-anén, pabassitén; alay-áyan.
mitten: *n.* guántes.
mix: *v.* paglaokén, itípon; templáen; ~ **colors** limugén.
mixed: *adj.* nailaók; natemplá; ~ **breed** *n.* mestíso.
mixture: *n.* kampór, gampór, bantó, samúsam, timplá.

moan: *v.* agásug, agunnóy, agsainnék.
mob: *n.* ummóng.
mobile: *adj.* nakulanggít, nakutí.
mobilize: *v.* paggarawén.
mock: *v.* rabrabáken, guyában, uyawén, laísen; *adj.* parbó, saán a pudnó.
mockery: *n.* uyáw, láis; pananggúyab.
mode: *n.* wágas; móda.
model: *n.* pagwadán, tuláden, ulidán, alágad, pangibatayán; *v.* padáen.
moderate: *adj.* natimbéng, namedméd, namismís.
moderation: *n.* kinamanagtíped, kinateppél.
moderator: *n.* mangtengtengngél, mangi-pangúlo.
modern: *adj.* baró, narang-áy.
modest: *adj.* nataknéng, nalánay.
modify: *v.* balíwan; pabaruén.
moist: *adj.* nadam-ég, naalnáab; nabasá.
moisten: *v.* ipasagepsép, pabasaén.
molar: *n.* sángi.
molasses: *n.* patáruy a tagapulót, sinayáw.
mold: *n.* búot; pagsukogán; hórma; **~board** dingdíng; *v.* damilién, sukogén, buklén.
mole: *n.* síding, sallapíding; (*mammal*) sangió, mannúkit; (*pier*) wayáng.
molest: *v.* ririén, isturbuén, ringgóren, riribúken, semsemén.
mollify: *v.* sulsul-úyen.
molt: *v.* aglúpos.
moment: *n.* darikmát, kanitó.
momentary: *adj.* apagripát.
monarch: *n.* ári, agturáy; **~y** *n.* monarkía.
monastery: *n.* monastério, pagtaengán dagití mónghe.
Monday: *n.* Lúnes.
money: *n.* kuartá, pirák; **~ order** híro postál; **counterfeit ~** kulikóg, koleró; **throw ~ to crowd** agbitór, agbríndis.
moneybag: *n.* pitáka, taggátan.
monk: *n.* mónghe.
monkey: *n.* bákes, tsónggo; **old male ~** burangén; **~ wrench** liábe inglésa.
monopolize: *v.* bukódan, tanígan, agbukbúkod.
monopoly: *n.* búkod, panagbukbúkod.
monorchid: *n.* amitáw, búdi.
monotonous: *adj.* makaumá.
monsoon: *n.* nepnép.
monster: *n.* sinampugót, nakabutbuténg nga áyup.
monstrous: *adj.* nakabutbuténg.
month: *n.* búlan.
monthly: *adj.* binúlan.
monument: *n.* monuménto, pakalaglagipán.
monumental: *adj.* nagdakkél.

moo: *v.* agúga, agugáog.
mood: *n.* pamay-án, panagwá; kasasáad ti rikná.
moon: *n.* búlan; **full ~** kábus; **new ~** kellép.
moonfish: *n.* **spotted ~** kadís.
moonlight: *n.* sellág.
Moor: *n.* Móro; **~ hen** kalá.
mop: *n.* lampáso, púnas; *v.* aglampáso, lampasuén, nasnásan.
morality: *n.* moralidád, kinadalús ti kababalín.
morass: *n.* kalubuán, lutúlut, alugúog.
more: *adj.* ad-adú; *adv.* pay, manén.
moreover: *adv.* sánto maysá, maysá pay.
morgue: *n.* mórge, pangiyuráyan dagití minatáy, pagmansayágan.
morning: *n.* bigát, agsápa; **~ star** baggák, palpallátok, kamuntatála; **~ glory** balangég.
moron: *n.* lampáy, laglág, tabbéd.
morose: *adj.* nalíday, naldáang.
morphine: *n.* morpína.
morsel: *n.* sangkakittáb, sangkasakmól, sangkakittáb.
mortal: *adj.* makapatáy.
mortality: *n.* panagpapatáy.
mortar: *n.* alsóng, paglebbekán; **deep ~** tibóng; **pound in ~** aglebbék.
mortgage: *v.* isaldá, ibalúd; *n.* saldá.
mortise: *n.* padingalngál, riáng.
mortuary: *n.* mórge, mortuário, pagmansayágan.
mosquito: *n.* lamók; **~ larva** balbaltík; **small ~** leglég, sepsép, tuktukláw; **~ net** moskitéro, kobongkóbong.
moss: *n.* lúmot.
most: *adj.* kaaduán, kadaklán, aaduán.
mote: *n.* (*in eye*) púling.
moth: *n.* sánga, burbúr, polília; **~ball** naptalína.
mother: *n.* iná; **~-in-law** katugángan (a babái); **~-of-pearl** raráng.
motion: *n.* garáw, gunáy, tignáy; **~ picture** síne, pelíkula.
motivate: *v.* paayatán, pagngayangáyen.
motive: *n.* motíbo, gapú, puón, gagém, pamuídan, pangkuátan, panggép.
motor: *n.* motór, mákina.
motorboat: *n.* bángka a de-motór.
motorcycle: *n.* motorsíklo.
motto: *n.* napíli a pagsasaó.
mound: *n.* buntón, gabór, turod.
mount: *v.* sumakáy; sumagpát.
mountain: *n.* bantáy; **~ leech** biléd.
mountaineer: *n.* tagá-bantáy.
mountainous: *adj.* nabantáy.
mourn: *v.* dung-áwan; agpanés, masnaáyan, agladíngit; **~ing** *n.* dung-áw.

mouse: *n.* baó, marabutít; (*mole*) sangió.
moustache: *n.* bigóte, bárbas.
mouth: *n.* ngíwat; (*entrance to narrow passage*) darimángan; (*of cave*) wangawángan; (*of river*) sabángan, ngawngáwan, wangawángan; (*of scoop nets*) sungában; **corner of ~** gisgís.
mouthful: *n.* sangalamdók, sangkasakmól.
mouthpiece: *n.* alintúbong, bokília.
movable: *adj.* mayális, mabagkát.
move: *v.* aggunáy, aggaráw; agkutí; (*displace*) yális, yallátiw; (*when loose*) agwáli, agluggáy; **~ment** *n.* panaggaráw, tignáy.
movie: *n.* síne, pelíkula.
mow: *v.* patpáten, anién.
much: *adj.* adú, nawadwád.
muck: *n.* rugít.
mucus: *n.* búteg, kellá, pangrés; (*dried*) duggóng.
mud: *n.* pítak, lab-ák, lubnák, lubó.
muddled: *adj.* maúlaw, malabgán.
mudguard: *n.* tapalúdo.
muffin: *n.* ensaymáda.
muffle: *v.* bungonén, abbongán, dalipenpenán.
muffler: *n.* bupánda; (*of car*) tambútso.
mulberry: *n.* móras, amúras.
mule: *n.* múla.
multiple: *adj.* adú.
multiplication: *n.* pannakapaadú.
multiply: *v.* paaduén, pamin-aduén; agadú.
multitude: *n.* reprép, ariponó, banggá, ariwátang.
mum: *adj.* naulímek.
mumble: *v.* agdayamúdum, agtanabútob, agdanengdéng, ageng-éng.
mumps: *n.* kabbí, pangál.
munch: *v.* karemkemén, ngalngálen.
mundane: *adj.* naidagaán, nailubóngan.
mungo: *n.* balátong.
municipal: *adj.* maipapán ití íli.
munitions: *n.* bála, gargarét a paragubát.
murder: *v.* patayén (ti táo); *n.* panagpapátay, pammapátay; **~er** mammapátay.
murky: *adj.* nalidém, nalibóg.
murmur: *v.* ngumangemngém, agtanabútob, agtanamítim.
muscle: *n.* piskél, laság.
muscular: *adj.* napunér, nabakéd, napinték, monnomonnó, nabanég, muskuládo.
muse: *n.* músa; *v.* pampanunóten.
museum: *n.* muséo, pakaipabuyáan dagití napatég a partuát.
mushroom: *n.* úong; *v.* dumakkél a napardás.
mushy: *adj.* naderdér, nadugnóy, nadugnóy.
music: *n.* tokár, samiwéng; **~ stand** atríl; **~ology** solpéo.

musician: *n.* umiiwéng, musikéro, tumotokár.
musk: *n.* almískle.
Muslim: *n.*, *adj.* Móro.
muslin: *n.* kóko.
mussel: *n.* káong, tahóng, kapkappó.
must: *v.* rebbéng, rumbéng, masápol.
mustache: *n.* bigóte, iming, bárbas ti súnggo.
mustard: *n.* mustása.
muster: *v.* agtitípon.
musty: *adj.* nalogó.
mute: *adj.* úmel.
mutilate: *v.* putdén.
mutiny: *n.* yaalsá ití bapór.
mutter: *v.* agtanabútob, agdayamúdum, agdanengdéng, agdayengdéng.
mutton: *n.* kárne ti kárnero.
mutual: *adj.* agsinnaránay, agtinnúlong.
muzzle: *n.* busál, pakagát, pádun, dángal.
my: *pron.* –ko, -k.
myopic: *adj.* kurárap, arráp, kusílap, matan-manók.
myriad: *n.* reprép.
myrrh: *n.* mírra.
myrtle: *n.* mírto.
myself: *pron.* bagík, siák met láeng.
mystery: *n.* palímed, palméd, mistério.
mystical: *adj.* naitalímeng.
myth: *n.* míto, paspásaw, kurintíri, saríta a di napudnó.
mythology: *n.* mitolohía.

N

nab: *v.* tukmáan.
nag: *v.* suronén, papungtóten.
nail: *n.* (*finger*) kukó; (*carpentry*) lansá.
naive: *adj.* ampapáok.
naked: *adj.* lamolámo, lábus, barin-áwas; (*from waist up*) uksób.
name: *n.* nágan; *v.* panagánan.
namesake: *n.* kanágan, tokáyo.
nap: *n.* siésta, ridép.
nape: *n.* lengngés, teltél; **hit in the ~** teltelén, sippapuén.
napkin: *n.* serbiliéta; **sanitary ~** pasadór.
narcotic: *n.* narkótiko, maipárit nga ágas.
narrate: *v.* isaríta, ipalawág.
narrative: *n.* pakasaritáan.
narrow: *adj.* nailét, akíkid, nakípet; **~ minded** *adj.* ababá ti panagísipna.
nasal: *adj.* impaagóng; **~ septum** biríng; **~ize** agbeddabéd.
nasty: *adj.* nakaar-ariék; dákes, naduldóg, naalás.

nation: *n.* pagilián; ~**al** *adj.* nailián, maipapán ití pagilián; ~**ism** *n.* ayát ití pagilián; ~**al language** *n.* nailián a pagsasaó.

nationality: *n.* pakipagilián.

native: *n.* patúbo, nayanák nga umíli.

natural: *adj.* masná, nakaisígud.

nature: *n.* kasisígud, lúbong, katutúbo.

naughty: *adj.* nawelwél, naaliwegwég, nasúkir, nasúbeg.

nausea: *n.* alidukdók, rurúsok, ulaw-úlaw.

nauseating: *adj.* nakarimrimón, makasarwá, makapadul-ó.

naval: *adj.* maipapán ití taáw.

nave: *n.* (*of wheel*) palaopó.

navel: *n.* púseg.

navigable: *adj.* mabalín a layágan.

navigate: *v.* agláyag.

navy: *n.* armáda, marína.

neap tide: *n.* alaál.

near: *adj.* asidég, adaní; síbay; bangíbang; ~**sighted** kurárap.

nearby: *adv.* ití asidég.

nearly: *adv.* nagistayán, ngannganí.

neat: *adj.* naurnós, nadalimának, nalibnos.

necessary: *adj.* naskén, masápul.

necessity: *n.* pakasapúlan, pakurángan.

neck: *n.* tengngéd; **short ~ed** ringkék; **long ~ed** tengngedán.

neckerchief: *n.* taliwaddáy.

necklace: *n.* kuentás, ukkór, gargantília; **gold ~** biniás, paligét.

necktie: *n.* korbáta.

necrophilia: *n.* panagessém ití natáy.

need: *v.* masápol, kasapúlan; **be in ~** agkúrang.

needle: *n.* dágum, pagdáit; (*large*) dúgi; **netting ~** gettáy; ~**point** landá.

needy: *adj.* makasápul.

negate: *v.* aglibák, aw-awanén.

negative: *adj.* negatíbo; sumuppiát; aglibák.

neglect: *v.* liwáyan, baybay-án, lipátan.

neglectful: *adj.* nalíway, natabiláng, managliddó, natalipanpán, managlídong.

negligence: *n.* libtáw, libtáan, kinalíway.

negligent: *adj.* managbaybay-á, nalíway, taliwaywáy.

negotiate: *v.* makitúlag, makitinnarusán.

Negrito: *n.* kulót, agtá, pugót.

neigh: *v.* aggarraígi, aggarikgík.

neighbor: *n.* kaarrúba, kabangíbang.

neighborhood: *n.* arubáyan.

neophyte: *n.* kabarbaró, agdadámo.

nephew: *n.* kaanakán a laláki.

nerve: *n.* nérbios, urát; turéd.

nest: *n.* úmok; (*of wild boar*) dugmón, ugmón; ~ **egg** ar-árak.

net: *n.* ikét, baténg; *v.* iketán; agtúbo;

mosquito ~ moskitéro, kobongkóbong; **enter a ~** kumná; **extend a ~** iwáyat; **repair ~s** agayúma.

netting needle: *n.* gettáy.

nettle: *n.* kamíring; ~ **rash** supotsúpot.

neuralgia: *n.* neurálhia, sakít ti nérbios.

neurotic: *adj.* managnérbios.

neutral: *adj.* agmangngamangngá.

never: *adj.* saán úray kaánoman.

nevertheless: *adv.* núpay kastá.

new: *adj.* baró; ~ **moon** kellép.

newcomer: *n.* kasasangpét, kabarbaró.

news: *n.* dámag, ámad; ~ **release** *n.* padámag.

newspaper: *n.* warnakán, diário, periódiko.

newt: bagangán.

next: *adj.* sumarunó, dumná, masanguánan.

nibble: *v.* kinnitén, kittibán, kuríban, agtaktaknáng, kibkíben.

nice: *adj.* nasayáat; nadalimának; napídis.

nick: *v.* pit-íngan, tippingán.

nickname: *n.* birngás, pangay-ayáb, ipampanágan.

nicotine: *n.* nikotína.

niece: *n.* kaanakán a babái.

night: *n.* rabíí; ~ **blind** *adj.* agrádam; **all ~ long** agpatnág.

nightfall: *n.* suripét, sumipngét.

nightgown: *n.* kawés a pagtúrog ti babái.

nightingale: *n.* ruiseniór.

nightly: *adv.* rinabíí.

nightmare: *n.* batíbat, bangúngot.

nightshade: *n.* am-amtík.

nil: *n.* awán.

nimble: *adj.* naparagsít, nasiglát, nakarantíng, bumalagtóng.

nine: *n.* siám.

nineteen: *n.* sangapúlo ket siám.

ninety: *n.* siám a púlo.

ninth: *adj.* maikasiám.

nip: *v.* kettelén, kittibén, gettebén.

nippers: *n.* bagingét.

nipple: *n.* (*teat*) múngay, ammútil; (*rubber*) tsupón.

nit: *n.* lis-á, liés.

no: *adv.* saán; awán.

nobility: *n.* noblésa, tangáden.

noble: *adj.* baknáng, natan-ók, nasúdi, nataknéng.

nobody: *pron.* awán táo.

nod: *v.* agtung-éd; agtaméd; (*when dozing*) agdungsá, agsugél.

node: *n.* bukó.

noise: *n.* daranúdor, tagarí, ringgór, úni, anabáab, karasákas.

noisy: *adj.* naariwáwa, naúni, natagarí.

noli me tangere: *n.* kamantígi.
nominate: *v.* inagánan, dutóken, pilién.
nonchalant: *adj.* guppápaw.
noncommittal: *adj.* saán a mangikári.
none: *pron.* awán.
nonsense: *n.* minamaúyong, minamáag, tarabítab, awán kaipapanánna.
nonstop: *adj.* awán sardéngna.
noodle: *n.* míki; **mungo** ~ sotanghón; **rice** ~ bíhon; **thin soup** ~ misuá.
nook: *adj.* napakní a yan.
noon: *n.* matúon, tengngá ti aldáw, lamésa.
noose: *n.* sílo a pagbítay.
normal: *adj.* kadawyán, kalalaingánna.
north: *n.* amiánan; **~ern** *adj.* akin-amiánan.
northeast: *n.* (*wind*) dugúdog; amiánan a dáya.
northerner: *n.* taga-amiánan.
northwest: *n.* (*wind*) panaplák; amianán a láud.
Norwegian: *n.*, *adj.* Norwégo.
nose: *n.* agóng; **bridge of** ~ bókol; **hair of** ~ parungngárong; **~bleed** agdaringúngo; **turn up the** ~ agbisngár.
noseless: *adj.* ungngób.
nostalgia: *n.* pannakaíliw, pannakail-íla.
nostril: *n.* abút ti agóng, papangresán, papangesán.
not: *adv.* saán.
notable: *adj.* nalaták, namarangmáng.
notary public: *n.* notário públiko.
notch: *n.* gergér, tikáp.
notched: *adj.* naungabán, napingawán.
note: *n.* naisúrat a pakaammó; *v.* imutektekán, dillawén, madláw, imatángan.
notebook: *n.* kuadérno.
noted: *adj.* nalaták.
noteworthy: *adj.* maikári.
nothing: *pron.* awán.
notice: *v.* madláw, maammuán; *n.* pakdáar, pabláak, pakaammó.
notify: *v.* agpakaammó, ipakaammó, ibagá; ikáad.
notion: *n.* pakinákem, panúnot, pagarúp.
notorious: *adj.* agdindinámag ti kinadákesna.
nougat: *n.* paktáal.
noun: *n.* pangnágan.
nourish: *v.* taraonán, pakanén; **~ment** *n.* pangtaraón.
novel: *n.* nobéla; *adj.* kabarbaró.
novelty: *n.* kinabaró.
November: *n.* Nobiémbre.
novice: *n.* bágo, karugrugí, agdamdámo, kaserserrék, kataldéng.
now: *adv.* itá, itattá.
nowadays: *adv.* kadagitóy nga aldáw.

nucleus: *n.* katengngaán.
nude: *adj.* lamolámo, silalábus.
nudge: *v.* idingkál, sikuén.
nuisance: *n.* sipár, pakariribúkan, alimúteng, salí.
null: *adj.* awán; awán serbína.
nullify: *v.* ukásen, rakráken.
numb: *adj.* nabibíneg, di makarikná; *v.* bibinégen.
number: *n.* bílang, número.
numerous: *adj.* adú; nawadwád.
nun: *n.* mádre, móngha.
nuptial: *adj.* maipapán ití panagkasár.
nurse: *n.* nars; **wet** ~ yáya; *v.* taraknén, aywánan; pasusuén; agtagíbi.
nursemaid: *n.* yáya.
nurture: *v.* taraonán, pasanúten, sanáyen; *n.* pannagíbi.
nut: *n.* (*edible*) bukél a makán; (*mach.*) tuérka; **betel** ~ giít, buá; **psychic nut** tagumbáw.
nutmeg: *n.* nués moskáda.
nutrient: *n.* taraón, kanén.
nutritious: *adj.* nasustánsia; makataraón.
nyctalopia: *n.* rádam.
nymph: *n.* nímpa.

O

oaf: *n.* tabbéd a táo.
oak: *n.* diráan.
oar: *n.* gáud, taguán.
oath: *n.* sapatá.
obedience: *n.* tulnóg, panagtungpál, annúgot, tudió.
obeisance: *n.* raém, panagraém.
obese: *adj.* nalukmég, barugsóy, nasábang, balsóg.
obey: *v.* tungpálen, agtulnóg; umannúgot.
object: *n.* bánag, panggép, gandát; *v.* supríngen, suppiáten, sungáten; agmadí.
objective: *n.* panggép, gagára.
obligation: *n.* rebbéng, annongén.
oblige: *v.* pilíten, pabakláyan iti annóng.
obliterate: *v.* dadaélen, pukáwen, punásen.
oblivion: *n.* tagilípat.
obnoxious: *adj.* makapagúra, makaruród.
obscene: *adj.* naalás, nadangkés.
obscure: *adj.* nalemméng, nalidém, saán a nalaták.
obsequious: *adj.* nasipsíp, natulók, natulnóg, naraém.
observance: *n.* panangsalimetmét, palíiw.
observation: *n.* palíiw, súot.
observe: *v.* palíiwen, suóten, imatángan, imutektekán.

obsess: *v.* agrágut.

obsolete: *adj.* dáanen.

obstacle: *n.* tipéd, lappéd, tubéng, sipár.

obstinate: *adj.* nasúbeg, nabángad, bengngég, napúnged, nabagnós, nablingegngég, napásig.

obstruct: *v.* tipdén; baktáden, serráan.

obstruction: *n.* lappéd, típed; (*in throat*) iddál, itdál.

obtain: *v.* gun-óden, ragpáten, lak-ámen, gawáten.

obverse: *adj.* pamaráng.

obvious: *adj.* nalaták, nalawág, napaták, masinunuó.

occasion: *n.* pasámak, gundáway, panggapuán, kanitó.

occasionally: *adv.* sagpaminsán, no daddúma.

occident: *n.* láud.

occiput: *n.* tapaktápak, pitangkók.

occult: *adj.* nailemméng.

occupation: *n.* kasasáad, annóng, trabáho, arámid, seggép.

occupy: *v.* sakúpen, akmén, aramáten, tagikuaén.

occur: *n.* mapasámak, mapagténg; mairaná; maipatáng; rumsuá.

occurrence: *n.* napasámak.

ocean: *n.* taáw, baybáy.

October: *n.* Oktúbre.

octopus: *n.* kuritá.

ocular: *adj.* maipapán ití matá.

odd: *adj.* pángis; datdatlág.

odious: *adj.* makapaluksáw, makaruród, nakarimrimón.

odor: *n.* ángot, ayamúom; ~**less** maúmag.

of: *prep.* ni, ití.

off: *adv.* iti laksíd, iti ruár; (*extinguished*) naiddép; *prep.* awán ití; **turn** ~ iddepén; ~ **switch** iiddepán.

offend: *v.* pasagídan, pagrurodén, pagluksáwen, pagpungtóten, paguráen, yadyádan.

offense: *n.* básol, biddút, labsíng, babak; pílaw; ~**ive** *adj.* makaruród, makapagúra.

offer: *v.* idáton, iságut, isingásing, igay-át, idiáya, itúkon; ~**ing** *n.* ságut, diáya, dáton.

office: *n.* opisína, pagsaádan; takém, annóng; **box** ~ takília.

officer: *n.* pangúlo.

official: *n.* opisiál, pangúlo.

officiate: *v.* mangimatón, mangipangúlo.

offset: *v.* timbengán, supapákan.

offshoot: *n.* gípi, santák; símang; sangá.

offspring: *n.* anák, pútot.

often: *adv.* masansán, nasarantá, naynáy.

oil: *n.* lána; segdén; ~ **gland** lalanáan.

oily: *adj.* natabá, nagitá.

ointment: *n.* ungénto, sapsapó.

o.k.: *adj., adv.* apagisú; *interj.* ála wen; sigé.

old: *adj.* dáan; (*ladies*) bakét; (*men*) lakáy; ~**-fashioned** *adj.* napalábas a móda; ~ **maid** nabaketán a balásang.

olive: *n.* olíbas, aseitúnas, parangípang.

Olympics: *n.* Olimpiáda.

omelet: *n.* tórta (nga itlóg).

omen: *n.* partáan, seníal.

omission: *n.* libtáan, libtáw.

omit: *v.* libtáwan, laksíden, labásan.

omnipotent: *adj.* mannakabalín.

on: *prep.* ití rabáw, idiáy.

once: *adv.* maminsán; ~ **and for all** maminpinsán.

one: *n.* maysá; sanga-.

oneself: *pron.* ití, bagína.

onion: *n.* sibúyas, lasoná.

onlooker: *n.* kumitkíta.

only: *adj.* maymaysá, bugbugtóng; *adv.* láeng.

onset: *n.* rugí.

ooze: *v.* umagnéb, tumrém, tumbóg, agsayásay.

opal: *n.* ópalo.

opalescent: *adj.* agmarismáris, agmalismális.

opaque: *adj.* agsaragásag.

open: *adj.* silulukát; duyatyát; ~ **mouthed** muttaléng; ~**-worked** minatá; *v.* lukatán; ukráden; ~ **from the bottom** *v.* lukabén; tear ~ *v.* briáten.

opening: *n.* lussók, bungánga.

operate: *v.* paggunayén, pagtrabahuén.

operation: *n.* operasión; pannakapaandár; pannakaipapagná.

operator: *n.* mangpapagná.

operculum: *n.* leppét.

opinion: *n.* pamanunótan, pangipagarupán, kananákem, panirigán, pakinákem, kapanunótan.

opium: *n.* apiáng.

opponent: *n.* kasupadi, kasúsik, kasuppiát, kabúsor.

opportune: *adj.* naingundawáyan.

opportunist: *n.* mananggundáway.

opportunity: *n.* gundáway, wayá, lugár.

oppose: *v.* suppiáten, supapákan, tubngáren, sungáten, susíken, subáen, busóren, gubsién.

opposite: *adj.* kasángo; sungáni, kasumbángir; maisuppiát.

opposition: *n.* suppiát. tinggár.

oppress: *v.* irurumén, idadanés, idagém, daginsensén, ituggúd, ilugés; ~**ive** *adj.* makairurumén, makapadagsén.

optician: *n.* óptiko.

optimism: *n.* nakanamnáma a kapanunótan.

option: *n.* kalintegán nga agpíli; panangpíli.
opulent: *adj.* nabaknáng, nasanikuá.
or: *conj.* wennó.
oracle: *n.* mammadlés.
oral: *adj.* maipapán ití ngíwat; insaó ti ngíwat; naisaó.
orange: *n.* lulukísen, lukbán, suá, barangkás, dugmón.
oration: *n.* bitlá.
orator: *n.* bumibitlá.
orbit: *n.* pagliklikmútan.
orchard: *n.* kakayuán, minuyongán.
orchestra: *n.* orkésta.
orchid: *n.* orkídia.
ordain: *v.* ibílin; ikeddéng.
ordeal: *n.* kapadásan.
order: *n.* urnós; (*command*) bílin; mandamiénto; **money** ~ híro postál; *v.* pilíten, mandáran; **put in** ~ pantágen, urnósen, pagsaganadén, ipinípin.
ordinance: *n.* bílin.
ordinary: *adj.* sapásap, samúsam, nadáwi; taliwága; bastabásta.
organ: *n.* órgano; (*instrument*) armonió.
organization: *n.* bunggóy, pagkakaduaán; urnós.
organize: *v.* urnósen; buangáyen; isungsóng.
orgy: *n.* nalabés ken nakiró a panagragragsák.
orient: *n.* dáya; ~**al** *adj.* tagá-dáya.
orifice: *n.* abút; regkáng.
origin: *n.* puón, pagtaúdan, paggapuán, pungánay; ~**ate** agtáud; agparnuáy; mangirugí.
original: *adj.* kasisígud, nakaisigúdan, kapuonán, parnuáy; ~ **sin** *n.* básol a táwid.
oriole: *n.* kiáw.
ornament: *n.* arkós, pangpasayáat, parátok.
ornate: naarkós.
orphan: *n.* ulíla; **twice** ~**ed** agdemmáng.
orthography: *n.* panagsúrat.
oscillate: *v.* ipalláyog; agindáyon; agtiwatíw, aggoyyogoyyó.
osmosis: *n.* panagagsép.
ostracize: *v.* ilaksíd.
ostrich: *n.* abestrús.
other: *adj., pron.* sabáli, daddúma; ~**wise** *conj.* wennó saán.
ouch: *excl.* annáy, aráy.
ought: *v.* rebbéng, kumá.
ounce: *n.* ónsa.
our: *pron.* -ta, -tayo, -mi.
ours: *pron.* kukuámi, kukuáta, kukuatayó.
oust: *v.* paruarén, papanáwen, pagtaláwen, pagtaláwen.
out: *adv.* ití ruár; ití laksíd.
outbreak: *n.* panagbúrak.

outburst: *n.* panagbetták.
outcast: *n.* napagtálaw, naibelléng, naiparuár.
outclass: *v.* atíwen, rimbáwan.
outcome: *n.* bánag, pagbanágan, pagmaáyan, pagangayán.
outcry: *n.* pukkáw, ikkís.
outdo: *v.* atíwen, saliw-ánan, sagudáyen, parmekén, rimbáwan.
outdoor: *adj.* ití ruár.
outdoors: *n.* kalnaáwan.
outer: *adj.* akinruár, naruruár.
outfit: *n.* gamígam, gargarét, pagan-anáy, aruáten.
outhouse: *n.* kasílias, kumón.
outing: *n.* aliwaksáy, eskursión.
outlandish: *adj.* nakadidilláw.
outlet: *n.* ruáran.
outline: *n.* tábas, balabála, bareweswés, paraígid, pamwidán.
outnumber: *v.* rimbáwan ti bílang.
outrage: *n.* damsák, ulpít, dadanés, ranggás, pagrurodén.
outset: *n.* rugí, pangrugrugián.
outside: *adj.* ití ruár.
outskirts: *n.* wayáway, áway.
outstanding: *adj.* naisangayán.
outwit: *v.* ikallaigí, atíwen, daerén.
oval: *adj.* immitlóg, maratimbukél.
ovary: *n.* iitlogán; (*of birds*) náto.
oven: *n.* órno.
over: *prep., adv.* ití rabáw; nasurók; iti ngatuén; ~ **and** ~ madagdagullít; **do** ~ **and** ~ dagullitén.
overburden: *v.* salensenán.
overcast: *adj.* nayúyem, naulpán, nalúlem, nakuyemyém, nakudrép, nakúnem, nadaguyemyém.
overcharge: *v.* sagráen.
overcoat: *n.* kapóte, sáko a parutáp.
overcome: *v.* abáken, paksiáten, latgén, addagán, rabawán, parmekén, madaerán.
overdo: *v.* palaluán, masingángar.
overdry: *v.* kumarangíkang.
overflow: *v.* aglayús, aglippiás, lumangbáy; umápaw; lumangbáy.
overhead: *adv.* ití ngáto.
overlook: *v.* taliwaywáyan; malabsán.
overpass: *v.* labásan, lipáwen.
overpower: *v.* parukmáen, abáken, paksiáten.
overripe: *adj.* naldóg.
overrule: *v.* waswásen ti keddéng.
overrun: *v.* kamakámen, labsán.
overseam: *v.* saraíten.
overseas: *adj.* ballasiw-taáw.
oversee: *v.* imatonán, aywánan, bantáyan.

overt: *adj*. nalaták a makíta, nalawág.
overtake: *v*. kamakámen, gam-úden, abúten.
overtax: *v*. singangáran.
overthrow: *v*. tuangén, rebbaén, ruppuógen, rakráken, parmekén.
overtime work: *n*. lámay.
overture: *n*. obertúra.
overturn: *v*. baliktáden, pakbuén; mapattóg, mapakbó.
overwhelm: *v*. lapunósen; umápaw; parmekén, ludon-ludónen.
overworked: *adj*. maturtúran.
owe: *v*. umútang, agútang.
owl: *n*. kulláaw, puék.
own: *v*. tagikuaén, akuén; *adj*. kabukbukódan; kukuá.
ox: *n*. laláki a báka.
oyster: *n*. tírem; kulintípay; talabá.

P

pace: *n*. addáng, akkáw, pagná; *v*. agaddáng, ageddáng.
pacific: *adj*. nalínak, natalná; nataknéng.
pacification: *n*. panagpatalná.
pacify: *v*. pagtalnáen, paglináken, ep-epén.
pack: *n*. (*of hounds*) sarruád; *v*. agmaléta; bungónen, bastáen, kabáten.
package: *n*. balkót, bungón; (*bundle*) tampóng.
packsaddle: *n*. pasangá.
pact: *n*. túlag.
pad: *n*. tapár, ap-áp; sagapá; (*on head*) dikén.
paddle: *n*. suplád, gáud, lápad.
paddock: *n*. korrál.
padlock: *n*. kandádo.
pagan: *n*. pagáno, itnég; ~ **priest** maniáblo.
page: *n*. páhina, pánid; (*messenger*) pahinánte; *v*. ipánid; ayabán.
pageant: *n*. pagpinnintásan.
paginate: *v*. ipánid.
pail: *n*. tímba, sítaw, bálde.
pain: *n*. ut-ót, sakít; **sharp** ~ apgés.
painful: *adj*. naut-ót, nasakít, natúok, naapgés.
paint: *n*. pintúra; *v*. pintáan; ~**er** *n*. mammínta, pumipínta, pintór.
painting: *n*. ladáwan, pinintáan.
pair: *n*. páris, asmáng, sangapagasawáan.
pajamas: *n*. kawés a pagtúrog.
pal: *n*. gayyém; kaduá.
palace: *n*. palásio.
palatable: *adj*. makán; naímas.
palate: *n*. ngádas, ngawngáw; ramán.
pale: *adj*. nabesság, nakusníg; (*color*) pusasáw.
palette: *n*. paléta.

palisade: *n*. bákud, pagér.
palliative: *n*. dangép.
pallid: *adj*. nalusiáw.
pallor: *n*. kinalusiáw.
palm: *n*. (*of hand*) pálad; (*tree*) anáaw, sílag; ~ **Sunday** Palaspás, Domínggo de Rámos.
palmistry: *n*. panangipálad.
palpitate: *v*. agkitebkitéb, agpitík.
palsy: *n*. kissíw.
pamper: *v*. panuynúyan.
pamphlet: *n*. poliéto.
pan: *n*. sartén; pariók, kaseróla.
pancreas: *n*. páli, dális.
pandemonium: *n*. beláak, guloguló.
panel: *n*. didíng, sangkabennég, entrepánio.
pang: *n*. ut-ót, sanáang.
panic: *n*. derráaw, pakadukotán.
pant: *v*. agngasáb, agal-ál, agkebbakebbá, agrikabrikáb.
pantry: *n*. pagidulínan ti taraón.
pants: *n*. pantalón.
papa: *n*. tátang, amá.
paper: *n*. papél; (*daily*) diário, warnakán.
par: *adj*. agpáda.
parable: *n*. pangngárig.
parachute: *n*. parakaída.
parade: *n*. paráda; *v*. agparáda.
paradise: *n*. paraíso; lángit.
paragon: *n*. wadán, pagtuládan, karimbáwan.
paragraph: *n*. párapo, bensá.
paralysis: *n*. salungayngáy.
paralyzed: *adj*. salungayngáy; (*in hands*) singkól, solpáy; (*in knees*) lugpí; (*in legs*) sapíloy; (*in legs*) piglós; (*fingers*) reppéng.
paramount: *adj*. kangrunáan; kangatuán.
paramour: *n*. kaayan-ayát a di kinakasár.
paraphernalia: *n*. kasangkápan.
parasol: *n*. páyong.
paratrooper: *n*. parakaidísta.
parboil: *v*. kelnáten; ~**ed egg** malasádo.
parcel: *n*. bungón, balkót, sangkadásig; sangkabennég.
parch: *v*. pamagaén a napúdot.
parchment: *n*. pergamíno.
pardon: *n*. pakawán, pammakawán; *v*. pakawanén.
pare: *v*. ukisán.
parent: *n*. dadakkél, nagannák; **foster** ~ managíbi; ~~**in-law** katugángan.
parenthesis: *n*. pangserrá.
parish: *n*. parrókia.
parity: *n*. pagpadáan.
park: *n*. párke; *v*. idissó; iparáda, isangbáy ti lúgan.
parliament: *n*. parlaménto, pagaramídan ti lintég.

parlor: **beauty** ~ *n*. pagpakulotán.
parole: *n*. naikondisión a wayaán ti bálud.
parrot: *n*. lóro, bullulísing, kalángay.
parry: *v*. lumiklík; lumiás.
parsimonious: *adj*. nakirmét, naímut, naámeng.
parsley: *n*. perehíl; **sea** ~ ngalugngálog
part: *n*. pasét, pirgís, písi, náyon; (*share*) bági; *v*. (*hair*) bisngáyen; (*leave*) pumánaw.
partake: *v*. makiráman; pumasét.
partial: *adj*. sangkapasét láeng.
participant: *n*. makiráman; makipasét.
participate: *v*. makibingláy, makipaglak-ám, agraránud, maikalam-ít, rumáman.
particle: *n*. tippíng, rinét.
particular: *adj*. naisangayán; maitudtudó.
parting: *n*. panagpakáda; ipapánaw; panagbisngáy.
partisan: *adj*. makitípon.
partition: *n*. bíngay, apág, bennég, mamagsína.
partner: *n*. kadúa; kaasmáng, kabúlig, kasugpón; **business** ~ sósio; (*in dancing*) kaallúp.
partnership: *n*. pagkakaduaán.
party: *n*. padayá, piésta, pagraragsákan; gúnglo; **political** ~ partído.
pass: *v*. lumábas, rumuár; lasáten; **mountain** ~ *n*. bessáng.
passage: *n*. pagnaán; pannakaanámong.
passenger: *n*. pasahéro.
passion: *n*. gartém, derrép; reggét; **~fruit** granadília.
passionate: *adj*. nasgéd, nagartém, narubrúb.
passport: *n*. pasapórte, palúbos a rumuár ití pagilián.
password: *n*. kontrasénias.
past: *adj*. nalabés, napalábas, nalpás; *n*. nalpás.
paste: *n*. kóla, píket, atóli; *v*. ipíket, ikóla, ipigkét.
pastime: *n*. pasatiémpo, palpaliwá.
pastry: *n*. kankanén, badúya.
pasture: *n*. pagarában; *v*. agárab, ipastór, ipaárab.
pat: *v*. pikpíken, aprúsan.
patch: *n*. takóp, sug-óp; *v*. takupán; **~es of discolored skin** kamánaw.
patent: *n*. paténte.
paternal: *adj*. maipapán ití amá.
path: *n*. daná, dálan, bit-áng, desdés.
pathetic: *adj*. nakakakáasi, nakalkaldáang.
patience: *n*. ánus, kinaánus.
patient: *n*. pasiénte, masakít; *adj*. naános, nasungdó, nateppél.
patriot: *n*. patrióta, managayát ití ílina; **~ism** *n*. panagayát ití ílina.

patrol: *n*. patrúlia, wanáwan.
patron: *n*. súki; **~age** *n*. pannakisúki.
pattern: *n*. wadán, pagtuládan, pagipadísan, ulidán, alágad.
paunch: *n*. rakrakípa, liblibró; bitúka.
pauper: *n*. napangláw, makilimlimós.
pause: *v*. agtukéng, agsardéng; *n*. sardéng, sarimadéng.
pave: *v*. baldosáan, kabitién.
pavement: *n*. bangkéta.
paw: *n*. dapán (ti ayúp)
pawn: *v*. isaldá, ibálud; (*in chess*) peón.
pawnbroker: *n*. agsalsaldá.
pawnshop: *n*. pagisaldáan.
pay: *n*. suéldo, tangdán; *v*. bayádan, tangdánan, supapákan.
payment: *n*. báyad.
payroll: *n*. listáan ti pagbayádan.
pea: *n*. patáni, kardís, gisántes.
peace: *n*. kappiá, talná; **~ful** *adj*. natalná.
peach: *n*. melokotón.
peacock: *n*. paboreál.
peak: *n*. rabáw, tuktók, tápaw, aringgawís, alimpatók, patokpátok, alimpapátok, ngudó.
peal: *n*. rupikí, kalangíking.
peanut: *n*. maní.
pear: *n*. péras.
pearl: *n*. pérlas, tampók; **mother-of-~** raráng.
peasant: *n*. mintálon, taga-áway.
pebble: *n*. baggíing, bató.
peck: *v*. tuktóken, sippitén.
pectoral fin: *n*. palungáping, salupingpíng.
peculiar: *adj*. naisalsalumína, naidumadúma.
pedal: *n*. babaddekán.
peddle: *v*. agláko nga agpagnapagná.
pedestal: *n*. pedestál, pagbatayán.
pedestrian: *n*. agpagpagná, mannagná.
peek: *n*. sírip; *v*. sumírip.
peel: *v*. ukisán, kulisapsápan; ~ **with teeth** agkútim.
peep: *v*. sumírip, tuman-áw; **~ing Tom** mannírip.
peer: *n*. kapáda; *v*. perngén, agtan-áw.
peevish: *adj*. naringgór, naríri.
peg: *n*. sánat, palséng.
pelican: *n*. mangngáput.
pellet: *n*. perdigónes.
pelt: *n*. kúdil, lálat; *v*. bakálen, batuén, ubóran.
pelvis: *n*. pátong.
pen: *n*. plúma, pagsúrat; (*for animals*) úbong, kubóng, pagikulóngan; *v*. ipúpok.
penalize: *v*. dusáen.
penalty: *n*. dúsa.
penance: *n*. peniténsia, panagbabáwi.
penchant: *n*. ayó.

pencil: *n.* lápis.
pendant: *n.* bitinbítin, tiltilláyon.
pending: *adj.* di pay maibánag.
penetrate: *v.* sumrék, sumarót, umunég; salpúten, lussokén.
penis: *n.* búto; **glans** ~ lukdít, lúsi; **with a small** ~ kultíp.
penitentiary: *n.* pagbalúdan.
penny: *n.* síping, sentábo; **pitch ~ies** agtanggá, agsúyo.
pension: *n.* pensión.
pensive: *adj.* sipapanúnot, agut-utób.
penthouse: *n.* pataguáb, sagumbí, duág.
people: *n.* tattáo; *v.* taoán.
pepper: *n.* síli, pimiénta.
per: *prep.* tunggál maysá.
perceive: *v.* masirmatá, makíta; malásin, masimudáag; annawágen.
percent: *n.* porsiénto; **~age** *n.* porsiénto.
perception: *n.* púot, rikná.
perfect: *adj.* nasayáat, awan kúrangna, nagannóng, nalibnós, napayós.
perforate: *v.* abután, lussokén, taldengán, butáwan; (*ears*) tub-óken.
perform: *v.* ibánag, itungpál, aramíden.
performance: *n.* pabúya; pannakaarámid.
perfume: *n.* bangbangló, ayamúom.
perhaps: *adv.* -sa, ngatá, nalábit, segúro.
peril: *n.* peggád, síba, karigátan.
perilous: *adj.* napeggád.
period: *n.* púnto, tulnék; (*of time*) pasét ti panawén; battáway, battálay; (*menses*) régla, sangaíli; **~ required for cooking** (*rice*) sangasaángan; **~ after childbirth** tanggád.
periodical: *n.* warnakán.
perish: *v.* matáy, agkanibusánan.
perjure: *v.* paglabsíngen iti sapatá.
permanent: *adj.* agnanáyon, di maik-ikkát.
permeate: *v.* salpúten, sagepsepén, samáyen, salubúngan.
permissible: *adj.* maipalúbos.
permit: *v.* palubósan, palugodán, ipalúbos; *n.* palúbos, lisénsia.
pernicious: *adj.* makadadaél.
perpendicular: *adj.* natindék, parséd.
perplex: *v.* riribúken.
persecute: *v.* ilupit-lúpit, irurumén.
persecution: *n.* pannakaidadanés.
persevere: *v.* agtalinaéd, agtalimúdok, agtagináyon, agpásil.
persist: *v.* agtalinaéd, di agsardéng, agnaynáy; ipapílit; **~ent** *adj.* mangipapílit.
person: *n.* táo; **young** ~ agtutúbo.
personal: *adj.* kabukbukódan.
personality: *n.* kinatáo.
perspiration: *n.* ling-ét.

perspire: *v.* agling-ét.
persuade: *v.* guyugúyen, sulisógen; ikámo; ulbóden, uyótan.
pertain: *v.* agtagikuá.
pertinent: *adj.* maipapán, mainumó, maipaáy, mayanátup.
perturb: *v.* riribúken.
perverse: *adj.* nadangkés, nasúkir.
peso: *n.* písos; **half** ~ salapí; **worth one** ~ mammísos.
pessimism: *adj.* dakés wennó barusngí a panagpampanúnot.
pest: *n.* péste, ángol.
pester: *v.* isturbuén, alimutngén, bannogén.
pestilence: *n.* péste.
pestle: *n.* al-ó.
pet: *n.* abalbaláy; *v.* dungdungnguén, rayray-áwen.
petite: *adj.* bassít.
petition: *n.* panagdáwat, panagkarárag.
petroleum: *n.* petrólio.
petticoat: *n.* enáguas.
petty: *adj.* bassít, nanumó.
phalange: *n.* láwas.
phantom: *n.* ulímaw, al-aliá.
pharmacy: *n.* botíka, parmásia.
pharaoh: *n.* paraón.
pharynx: *n.* dawatdáwat.
phase: *n.* paráng, pasét.
philosopher: *n.* pilósopo.
phlegm: *n.* turkák, plémas.
phone: *n.* telépono; *v.* ayabán; umáwag.
photographer: *n.* retratísta, potógrapo.
photography: *n.* potograpía.
phthisis: *n.* sárut, dáig.
physical: *adj.* maipapán ití bagí.
physician: *n.* mangngágas, doktór.
physics: *n.* písika.
physique: *n.* pammagí, kababagí.
pianist: *n.* pianísta, pumipiáno.
piano: *n.* piáno.
piccolo: *n.* oktabína.
pick: *v.* (*choose*) pilién; (*collect*) purosén; **~ up** pidúten; *n.* píli; píko.
pickle: *n.* artém, atsára.
pickpocket: *n.* agrabrabsút ti petáka, agsipdút; *n.* mannipdót.
picnic: *n.* bienkomér, dayá ití áway.
picture: *n.* ladáwan, retráto, lámina.
pie: *n.* pastél, empanáda.
piece: *n.* bukél, písi, pasét, pirgís.
pier: *n.* muélie, wayáng.
pierce: *v.* lussokén, salbágen, sarutén, tudóken; (*ears*) tub-óken.
piety: *n.* kinasingpét, kinatulnóg.
pig: *n.* báboy; **baby** ~ buriás; **guinea** ~ kuíng.

pigeon: *n.* kalapáti, págaw; (*speckled*) lagádan; ~ **pea** kardís.

pigpen: *n.* úbong.

pike: *n.* píka, darekdék; tugkél.

pile: *n.* buntón, gabsúon, penpén, montón.

piles: *n.* almoránas, tubel, lugsót.

pilfer: *v.* agtákaw.

pilgrim: *n.* peregríno.

pill: *n.* píldoras; ~ **bug** babuybáboy, simbáboy, kumbáboy.

pillage: *v.* samsámen, tulisanén.

pillar: *n.* adígi, síngit, túkol, teddék.

pillory: *n.* tul-óng.

pillow: *n.* pungán; ~**case** súpot ti pungán; ~ **lace** boliós; **side** ~ sap-ál, abrasadór.

pilot: *n.* pilóto, mangyúrit; *v.* ituróng, ipanguluán.

pimple: *n.* kamúro, taramídong.

pin: *n.* aspilí, aspilér, pasok; *v.* aspilián; ilansá.

pincers: *n.* bagingét, kaméng.

pinch: *v.* pidílen, kuddutén, ipíten.

pine: *n.* píno, sáleng; ~**nut** *n.* pinión.

pineapple: *n.* pínia.

pinion: *n.* páwis.

pink: *n.* derósas, pangindaráen.

pinnacle: *n.* kapantókan, kangatuán.

pinpoint: *v.* itudó.

pious: *adj.* nasingpét, relihióso.

pipe: *n.* suáko, píto; túbo.

piquant: *adj.* nagásang.

piracy: *n.* panagtulisánití taáw.

pirate: *n.* tiróng, tulisán ti taáw.

pirouette: *v.* agarinoknók.

pistol: *n.* bassít a paltóg.

pit: *n.* abút, kutkót, palab-óg; **cockfighting** ~ pagtadián; **ash** ~ pagkadkádan.

pitch: *n.* resína, briá, alkitrán; *v.* ipalládaw.

pith: *n.* (*medulla*) patá, búgas; (*meaning*) ámag, kababagás; *v.* ibató.

pitcher: *n.* parabató ti bóla.

pitfall: *n.* pakaitigkólan, peggád; ríro.

pitiful: *adj.* nakákaasi, nakain-inaká.

pittance: *n.* bassít a pasét.

pity: *n.* ási, kaási, panangay-áy.

pivot: *n.* pagtayyekán.

placard: *n.* paskén.

placate: *v.* pagtalnáen.

place: *n.* yan, dissó; pag- -an; *v.* ikábil, isáad; idissó; **workplace** pagtrabahuán.

placenta: *n.* kadkaduá.

placid: *adj.* natalná, naánat.

plagiarism: *n.* pláhio.

plagiarist: *n.* plahiadór.

plague: *n.* didígra, péste, pakairurumeknán; pangók.

plain: *n.* tay-ák, tanáp; *adj.* naparánas, nasimpá.

plaintiff: *n.* mangidarúm.

plait: *n.* pliéges, tupí, kupín.

plan: *n.* gandát, panggép, panúnot, daremdém; *v.* aggandát; balabaláen.

plane: *n.* katám; eropláno.

planet: *n.* planéta; ~**arium** planetário.

plank: *n.* tablón.

plant: *n.* múla; ~ **disease** aplát; **potted** ~ masétas; *v.* imúla; ~**er** *n.* agmulmúla.

plantation: *n.* minuláan; asiénda.

plaque: *n.* pláke.

plaster: *n.* tápal, yéso, mása; ~ **of Paris** eskayóla.

plastic: *n.* plastík, plástiko.

plate: *n.* pinggán, pláto; **coconut** ~ dúyog.

platform: *n.* entabládo; platapórma; ~ **scale** *n.* baskula.

platter: *n.* patilambó, bandehádo.

plausible: *adj.* makaguyúgoy.

play: *n.* ay-áyam; (*stage*) dráma, pabúya; ~**mate** kaay-áyam; *v.* agay-áyam.

player: *n.* agay-áyam; tumotokár.

playground: *n.* pagay-ayáman.

playhouse: *n.* pagpapabuyáan.

playing cards *n.* inipís, náipes.

playmate: *n.* kaay-áyam.

plaything: *n.* ay-áyam.

playwright: *n.* dramatúrgo, mannúrat ití dráma.

plaza: *n.* plása; lansángan.

plea: *n.* pagkalintegán, pambár, dáwat.

plead: *v.* agdáwat, makikalintegán; umaráraw.

pleasant: *adj.* makaay-áyo; naragsák.

please: *v.* pagustuán; *adv.* man.

pleasure: *n.* nam-áy, ayát, pagayatán, rag-ó.

pleat: *n.* ronrón, pliéges; *v.* pliegésan.

plebian: *n.* kadawyán a táo.

plebiscite: *n.* plebesíto.

pledge: *n.* saldá, tandá, karí; *v.* ikarí, isaldá.

plenty: *adj.* adú, nalabón, nawadwád.

pliant: *adj.* nalap-ít, nalappiót.

pliers: *n.* arípit; tiáni.

plot: *n.* gandát; (*of land*) áwang, áray; *v.* agpanggép, aggandát.

plow: *n.* arádo; *v.* agarádo.

plowshare: *n.* subsób, díla, lúkoy.

plowtail: *n.* witíwit.

pluck: *n.* gabnúten, rabsúten, kettelén.

plug: *n.* tapón, sullát; pakagát.

plum: *n.* sarguélas; **date** ~ sapóte; **Java** ~ lungbóy.

plumage: *n.* lawí, dutdót, plumáhe.

plumber: *n.* tubéro.

plummet: *v.* agsuék, agregrég.

plump: *adj.* nalungpó, nalukmég; **fall ~** malispók, maiparagupóg.

plunder: *v.* agsamsám, agkayaskás.

plunge: *v.* irárem, iráreb, ipabátok, irebréb; bumátok.

plural: *adj.* ad-adú ngem maysá.

plus: *prep.* nayónan ti; *adj.* pay.

pneumonia: *n.* sakít ti bará.

pocket: *n.* bólsa; **~book** kartéra; **~knife** lansíta, kortaplúma.

pockmarked: *adj.* burtóng.

podium: *n.* pagbitláan.

poem: *n.* dániw.

poet: *n.* poéta, dumadániw; **~ic** naindaníwan.

poetry: *n.* dandániw, panagdániw.

poignant: *n.* makatignáy.

point: *n.* murdóng, tudó, tírad; *v.* itudó, tuduén.

pointed: *adj.* natírad, nasarumámit; nadáwis.

pointer: *n.* paratudó, pagitudó.

poise: *n.* takdér, panaggaráw.

poison: *n.* sabídong, gámud; gamút; gíta; **fish ~** túba.

poisonous: *adj.* makasabídong.

poke: *v.* ikegsál, duyokén, dugsólen, durósen, dusagén, tukkikén.

pole: *n.* tulós, ungtó, atiddóg a sarukód, teklén.

police: *n.* pulís.

policy: *n.* pólisa, annuróten, batayán ti paglintegán.

polish: *v.* palinísen, pasilengén.

polite: *adj.* nataknéng, nadáyaw; **to be ~** agraém.

political: *adj.* maipapán ití política.

politician: *n.* polítiko.

politics: *n.* política.

poll: *n.* panagbótos.

pollen: *n.* móta, pulá ti sábong.

polliwog: *n.* bayyék.

pollute: *v.* rugitán.

pomade: *n.* pomáda.

pomegranate: *n.* granáda.

pomelo: *n.* lukbán, suá, barangkás.

pomp: *n.* rambák, pabúya, pasindayág.

pompous: *adj.* narimbáw; napangás.

pond: *n.* álog, piláw; labnéng, basáw.

ponder: *v.* usígen, ammirísen, isípen, panunóten.

poodle: *n.* burbúran.

pool: *n.* piláw, álog; pisína.

poor: *adj.* napangláw, makurkurángan, nakamlát.

pop: *v.* agbusí, agbetták.

pope: *n.* pápa.

popgun: *n.* palsúot.

popinjay: *n.* arang-aráng

poppy: *n.* amapóla.

popular: *adj.* nalaták, natan-ók, agdindinámag.

populate: *v.* taoán.

population: *n.* bílang dagití umíli.

porcelain: *n.* porselána.

porch: *n.* pataguáb, bangsál.

porcupine: *n.* anáping.

pore: *n.* bassít nga abút, abút ti kúdil.

pork: *n.* laság ti báboy.

porpoise: baboy-báboy-taáw.

porridge: *n.* linúgaw.

portable: *adj.* maitugot-túgot, maawít; nalagán, mabitbít.

porter: *n.* agaywán ti ruángan; parabitbít.

portion: *n.* písi, pirgís, apág, pasét, náyon.

portly: *adj.* nalukmég; nabiskég.

portrait: *n.* retráto.

portray: *v.* iladáwan.

pose: *v.* agtakdér, agpostúra.

position: *n.* langá, takdér, sáad, kasasáad.

positive: *adj.* positíbo, mapaneknekán.

possess: *v.* tagikuaén, ikután, tenglén.

possession: *n.* panagtagikuá.

possible: *adj.* mabalín.

possibly: *adv.* nalábit, ngatá.

post: *n.* adígi, síngit, teddék; *pref.* kalpasán ti; (*mail*) korréo; **~ office** *n.* opisína ti kórreo.

postage: *n.* báyad ti kórreo; **~ stamp** *n.* sélio.

posterior: *adj.* maúdi, taraúdi.

postman: *n.* kartéro.

postmark: *n.* tímbre ti súrat.

postpone: *n.* yallátiw, iladládaw, igábay, ikalílis, tantanén, dipáyen, itongtongkuá.

posture: *n.* takdér; langá; postúra; siríg.

postwar: *adj.* kalpasán ti gubát.

pot: *n.* bánga, bakká; **~belly** buttióg; **flower~** *n.* masetéra, pagmasetásan.

potato: *n.* patátas; **sweet ~** kamóte.

potent: *adj.* makabaél, makabalín, nabíleg.

potential: *adj.* makapatáud, adda pannakabalínna.

potsherd: *n.* gíbak, ríbak.

potter: *n.* agdamdamíli, mannamíli.

pottery: *n.* damdamíli, bangbánga.

pouch: *n.* súpot, bólsa, butsé.

poultry: *n.* billít a makán.

pounce: *v.* sumpég.

pound: *n.* líbra; *v.* taltálen, lebbekén; bayuén.

pour: *v.* ibuyát, ipattóg, isuyát, ibukbók.

pout: *v.* agumbí, aglibbí, agmisúot, agmisogsóg.

poverty: *n.* kinapangláw, kinakurápay, kinarígat ti panagbiág.

powder: *n.* pólbos, tinimók; (*dust*) manílang; (*of rice*) bábang; **~ box** polbéra.

power: *n.* bíleg, pigsá, pannakbalín, kabaelán.
powerful: *adj.* nabíleg, mannakabalín.
pox: *n.* **chicken** ~ tukó; **small** ~ burtóng; **pigeon** ~ batúngol.
practical: *adj.* naipákat, maarámat.
practice: *n.* ruám, pádas, asáas, pannaksanáy; *v.* agasáas; agarámid.
prairie: *n.* tay-ák.
praise: *n.* dáyaw; *v.* idáyaw, itan-ók.
praiseworthy: *adj.* maikári a dayáwen.
prank: *n.* kinaalikúteg, síkap.
prawn: *n.* lagdáw, kúros, ageb-éb, gaygayáman, balawbálaw.
pray: *v.* agluálo, agkarárag.
prayer: *n.* karárag, luálo.
praying mantis: *n.* wásay-wásay.
preach: *v.* mangasabá, agsermón.
preamble: *n.* pagyuná, pangirugí.
precarious: *adj.* napeggád.
precaution: *n.* annád.
precede: *v.* unaán, sakbáyan.
precinct: *n.* prisínto, lakmút, sákup, distríto, beddéng, yan a pagbotósan.
precious: *adj.* napatég, nangína.
precipice: *n.* derráas, rangkás, garangúgong, dariwangwáng.
precipitation: *n.* túdo.
precise: *adj.* apag-isú, maitumpóng.
precision: *n.* kinaapag-isú.
predecessor: *n.* ti immun-uná.
predicament: *n.* galád, dákes a kasasáad.
predict: *v.* ipakpakauná, ipadlés, ipadtó.
predominant: *adj.* mangartáp, kangrunáan.
predominate: *v.* maskír, masigkír, umartáp.
preface: *n.* balláag, pakdáar, pangirugí ití sinurátan.
prefer: *v.* kaykayát, ipangpangrúna, isagúday, idumdúma, pangrunáen.
pregnancy: *n.* sikóg.
pregnant: *adj.* masikóg.
prejudice: *n.* ílem, átap.
preliminary: *adj.* pangrugián, umun-uná.
prelude: *n.* pangrugián.
premature: *adj.* nasápa pay, di pay panawén.
premeditate: *v.* gagemén, panggepén, gandáten.
premier: *n.* kangatuán a minístro.
premium: *n.* gunguná.
premonition: *n.* arep-ép, partáan, mangipakauná.
preparation: *n.* panagsagána.
prepare: *v.* isagána, irubbuát.
preposition: *n.* pangyuná, pangisáad.
prerogative: *n.* kalintegán.
presage: *n.* pabláak.
prescribe: *v.* ipatuldó, ibílin; resetáan.

prescription: *n.* reséta.
presence: *n.* kaaddá.
present: *n.* ságut, dáton; *adj.* sisasakláng, sisasángo; agdamá, itattá; *v.* iságut, itanggayá.
presentation: *n.* panangiparáng, pannakaipabúya.
preserve: *v.* igága, igígir; taginayónen; di aramáten.
preside: *v.* ipanguluán, ituróng.
president: *n.* pangúlo, presidénte.
press: *n.* pagladditán, pagmaldítan, imprénta; **hand** ~ minérba; *v.* pespesén, pandágan; ladditén; (*a button*) talmegán; ~ **release** *n.* padámag.
pressure: *n.* presión, dagsén, talmég, pannakdagdág; **high blood** ~ altapresión.
prestige: *n.* pannakaidaydáyaw.
presume: *v.* pagarupén, atápen, ituróng.
presumption: *n.* pagarúp, atáp, panagiturturóng.
presumptuous: *adj.* managipagarúp, managipapán.
pretend: *v.* gamgámen; agin-; aginkukuná, agpakúbas, agraás.
pretense: *n.* panaginkukuná; túlad.
pretentious: *adj.* managinkukuná, mannunúlad.
pretext: *n.* pambár, umáwa.
pretty: *adj.* napintás; *adv.* kalkalaingánna.
prevail: *v.* umartáp, mangaladág; agdákor.
prevalent: *adj.* sapásap; agdamá.
prevent: *v.* atipaén, lapdán, pawílan, tubngén.
previous: *adj.* immun-uná, nasakbáyan.
prewar: *adj.* sakbáy ti gubát.
prey: *n.* samsám, ti inanupán; *v.* agkaán, sibáen, anupán.
price: *n.* patég, ngína, báyad; *v.* ipatég.
priceless: *adj.* di maigatadán ti patégna.
prick: *v.* tudóken, lussokén; *n.* dalokdók; útob, dalubdób.
prickly heat: *n.* bagás-ling-ét, balliling-ét.
pride: *n.* panagindadakkél; tangsít, pasindayág, palangguád.
priest: *n.* pádi; **pagan** ~ maniáblo.
priesthood: *n.* kinapádi.
primal: *adj.* kaunaán, umun-uná.
primary: *adj.* umuná, nangrúna, kangrunáan.
prime: *adj.* kangrunáan; umuná; *n.* kasayaátan a bagí, panawén wennó kasasáad; ~ **commodities** *n.* kamasapúlan a gatgatángen.
primer: *n.* (*spelling book*) katón, kartília; pagdamdamuán.
prince: *n.* prínsipe.
principal: *adj.* kangrunáan, kamasapúlan.
principle: *n.* pamunganáyan.

print: *v.* imólde, imaldít, ideppél; **~ing press** *n.* pagideppelán, imprénta, pagimaldítan.
prior: *adj.* umun-uná, akinsángo, kasakbáyan.
prison: *n.* pagbalúdan, karsél.
prisoner: *n.* bálud, préso.
private: *adj.* pribádo, nalímed, napakní; *n.* kababaán a búyot.
privilege: *n.* gundáway, sagúday, talibágok, talugáding.
privy: *n.* kasílias.
prize: *n.* gunguná, prémio; *v.* patgán, igága.
probable: *adj.* mabalín.
probably: *adv.* segúro, ngatá.
probe: *v.* tukóden, suúten, padásen; *n.* sundá.
problem: *n.* parikút, probléma, búong ti úlo.
procedure: *n.* pamaayán, pamusmúsan.
proceed: *v.* agpatúloy, aglayón.
proceeding: *n.* panagpatúloy.
process: *n.* panagpatúloy, panagarámid, yaaddáng.
procession: *n.* líbut.
proclaim: *v.* ipukkáw, yáwag, iwayáng, ipakdáar, ibunannág, iwarragáwag.
proclamation: *n.* warragáwag.
procrastinate: *v.* itantán, itonttongkuá, yatáday.
procure: *v.* paaddaén, gun-óden.
prod: *v.* dusnógen; tukkikén; parugsuén.
produce: *v.* pataúden, patubuén, paaddaén, paltuáden; *n.* ápit.
product: *n.* paltuád, patáud; napaaddá.
productive: *adj.* nabúnga.
profane: *adj.* nabassáwang, natabbáaw; *v.* agbassáwang.
profess: *v.* ipalawág, iparangárang, ipaduyakyák.
profession: *n.* pagsapúlan, trabáho, palawág, panangiparangárang.
professor: *n.* propesór.
proficient: *adj.* ladíno.
profile: *n.* bariweswés, bángir ti rúpa.
profit: *n.* ganánsia, gunguná; *v.* agganánsia, aggunguná; agtúbo.
profligate: *v.* nagaramúgam.
profound: *adj.* mangliwengliweng, natúkok, naunég.
profuse: *adj.* napalálo, nalabón, nabuslón.
progeny: *n.* pútot.
prognostic: *n.* labég, pakauná, eggéd.
program: *n.* prográma, pamwidán, balabála.
progress: *n.* rang-áy, panagaddáng, dur-ás; *v.* rumang-áy; dumakkél.
progressive: *adj.* narang-áy.
prohibit: *v.* ipárit, ipáwil, ipagél, ikalúya; **~ion** *n.* párit, pannakaipárit.
project: *n.* gandát, panggép, síkat.

projectile: *n.* bála.
proletariat: *n.* dagití mangmanggéd.
prologue: *n.* pangyuná.
prolong: *v.* paatiddugén, ibáyat, bennatén; iláyon.
promenade: *v.* agpasiár, agpaséo.
prominent: *adj.* nalaták, narimbáw.
promise: *n.* karí; *v.* ikarí.
promote: *v.* degdegán, ipangáto, yaddáng, iragpát.
prompt: *adj.* naparták, nasingdát, napardás.
promulgate: *v.* iwarragáwag.
prone: *adj.* sidudúyos, sipapakléb, sirurúkob, sipapakobá.
prong: *n.* tírad, siít, salungkít.
pronoun: *n.* pangsandí.
pronounce: *v.* baliksén, isaó; **~ment** *n.* pannakaisaó, pannakaibalikás.
proof: *n.* paneknék, pangipatalgéd.
prop: *n.* túkol, tongkál; súray, panigkát.
propagate: *v.* agiwarragáwag; agpaadú.
propel: *v.* idurón, papagnaén; allinén.
propeller: *n.* pangpaandár, pangpapagná.
propensity: *n.* kindúyos, gangáy, turóng ti pakinákem.
proper: *adj.* maitutóp; umisú.
property: *n.* kukuá, tagikuá, sanikuá.
prophecy: *n.* padtó, padlés, palnáad.
prophesize: *v.* ipalnáad, ipadlés, ipadtó.
prophet: *n.* mammadlés, mammadtó.
proportion: *n.* panagbágay, pannakaitutóp.
proposal: *n.* singásing, panangitúkon.
propose: *v.* igay-át, itúkon, idiáya, ibagá, isíkat, idarírag.
proposition: *n.* singásing.
proprietor: *n.* akinkuá.
prose: *n.* insúrat a saán a dániw.
prosecute: *v.* idarúm; sumakláng, yukóm.
prosecution: *n.* paraúsig; panangidarúm, isasakláng.
prospect: *n.* pamuyáan, panagkíta, manamnáma, sapúlen.
prosper: *v.* rumang-áy, umunnód.
prosperous: *adj.* narang-áy.
prostitute: *n.* pampám, púta, balangkantís, barbarrukáya.
prostrate: *adj.* sirurukbáb, sipapásag, sidudukém.
protect: *v.* salakníban, igága, saranáyen, aklónen.
protest: *v.* sumuppiát.
Protestant: *n.* Protestánte.
prototype: *n.* pagwadán, ulidán.
protrude: *v.* agdawádaw, agtungángaw, lumápos, rumútong.

proud: *adj.* managindadakkél, napasindayág, natangsít, napusóng, naambúg, nakuspág, natangár.

prove: *v.* paneknekán, pasingkedán.

provide: *v.* ikkán, ipaayán, kumitán, isaganáan.

province: *n.* probínsia.

provision: *n.* bálon, urnóng.

provocation: *n.* pakaparurodán.

provoke: *v.* paungetén, pagpungtóten, gargarién, kasíren.

prow: *n.* proá, dúlong.

prowess: *n.* pannakabalín.

prowl: *v.* agdakíwas, agballóg, agsursór.

proximate: *adj.* dumná, kaasitgán.

proximity: *n.* kinaasidég.

proxy: *n.* pannakbagí, pangikumitán, mangitakdér, palikúd.

prudence: *n.* kinaannád, kinanakmán, panagbisngár.

prudent: *adj.* naannád, nanakmán.

prune: *v.* arbásan, atúdan.

pry: *v.* sukilén, lukipén, suílen; *n.* aspíki.

psalm: *n.* sálmo.

pseudo: *adj.* parbó.

pseudonym: *n.* parbó a nágan.

psychology: *n.* sikolohía.

puberty: *n.* panagbalásang, panagbaró.

pubic: *n.* ~ **hair** urmót; ~ **region** luy-óng.

public: *adj.* públiko, maipapánití pagilián; *n.* dagití tattáo.

publication: *n.* naipabláak.

publicity: *n.* pannakaiwarnák, warragáwag.

publish: *v.* iwarnák, ibunannág, imaldít, iwasnák.

publisher: *n.* mangiwarnák, mangimaldít.

puddle: *n.* lubnák, lúpak, lubó, lugnák.

puerile: *adj.* ubing-ubíng, inuubingán.

puff: *n.* pug-áw, puyót, puyúpoy, busí; *v.* agpug-áw.

puffy: *adj.* bimmasísaw, bimsóg.

pugnacious: *adj.* mannakigubát, mannakikábil, mannakiringgór.

pull: *v.* guyóden, guttaén, rabsúten, sikdúten, awíden, yáro; *n.* gúyod; pigsá.

pulley: *n.* motón, kararét.

pulp: *n.* laság (ti prútas); ubáas; ngalá.

pulpit: *n.* púlpito.

pulsate: *v.* agpitík, agkitebkitéb.

pulse: *n.* púlso, panagpitík.

pulverize: *v.* patapúken, dikidíken, patuyuén; bayuén, yegyegén, mekmekén; ~**r** *n.* padúlang.

pumice: *n.* baggíing, búga, pomés.

pummel: *v.* baywán; danógen, bugbúgen.

pump: *n.* bómba; *v.* bombáen.

punch: *v.* lussokén; abután.

punctual: *adj.* nasingdát, saán a maládaw.

puncture: *v.* utóben, butbúten.

pungent: *adj.* nagásang, natarumamis, naíngel.

punish: *v.* dusáen; ~**ment** *n.* dúsa, pannúsa.

punitive: *adj.* pangdúsa.

puny: *adj.* bassít ken nakapsút.

pup: *n.* úken.

pupil: *n.* (*student*) estudiánte, adálan; (*of eye*) taotáo.

puppet: *n.* tirtirís, tuntúnika, bagbagáwa.

puppy: *n.* úken.

purchase: *v.* gumatáng, gatángen; *n.* gátang.

pure: *adj.* pulós; nadalús; púro; ~ **white** napusaksák.

purely: *adj.* biíg, pásig, bin-íg.

purgative: *n.* pampapurgá, purgánte, pangdalús ití bágis.

purgatory: *n.* purgatório.

purge: *v.* purgáen, dalusán ti bágis.

purify: *v.* linísan, ugásan.

purloin: *v.* agtákaw.

purple: *n.* morádo, púrpura, líla.

purpose: *n.* gagém, panggép, gandát, gagára.

purse: *n.* súpot (ti kuartá).

pursue: *v.* kamáten, suróten.

pursuit: *n.* panangkámat, panagsúrot.

pus: *n.* áno, nána, ságo.

push: *v.* idurón, dirúsen, itubbáng; (*a button*) talmegán; ~ **and pull** panagginnúyod ken panagdidinnurón.

puss: *n.* púsa.

pustule: *n.* sinnukél.

put: *v.* ikábil, idissó, isáad.

putrefy: *v.* agderdér, agrupsá; aglungsót, madur-óy.

putrid: *adj.* nabuyók, nalaés, nalungsót, nabanglés.

putty: *n.* galagála, masília.

puzzle: *n.* pakariribúkan, pakariruán, parikút; *v.* riruén, riribúken, burtiáan.

pygmy: *n.* ansisít, pandáka.

pyorrhea: *n.* pioréa, sakít ti gugót.

pyramid: *n.* pirámide.

pyramidal: *adj.* kimós.

python: *n.* beklát.

Q

quack: *v.* aggakgák, agwakwák; ~ **doctor** erbolário, sinan-doktór.

quadruple: *adj.* mamimpát.

quadruplet: *n.* nagkapát nga agkakasíngin.

quagmire: *n.* lutúlot, aluyóoy.

quaff: *v.* areb-ebén.

quail: *n.* púgo.
quaint: *adj.* karkarná, manmanó; datdatlág.
quake: *n.* ginginéd; *v.* agginginéd, aggungón, agarigengén, agkintayég, agtigergér.
qualification: *n.* galád, an-anáy, kasasáad, sagúday, kabaelán.
qualified: *adj.* maikári; kabaelánna.
quality: *n.* kíta, kababalín.
qualm: *n.* dukót, sakít ti nákem, sagubánit.
quandary: *n.* ngatangatá, duaduá.
quantity: *n.* kaadú.
quarantine: *n.* kuarenténas, pannakaipútong; *v.* kuarentenásen.
quarrel: *n.* ríri, ringgór, subáng; *v.* agríri, agápa, agringgór.
quarrelsome: *adj.* mannakiápa, naríri, managringgór.
quarry: *n.* pagbatuán.
quarter: *n.* pagkapát.
quarterly: *adj.* tunggál talló a búlan.
quash: *v.* parmekén, pukáwen.
quay: *n.* pantalán, muélie, wayáng.
queasy: *adj.* makasaruá; makaúlaw.
queen: *n.* réina, ári a babái, aribái.
queer: *adj.* baién; nakadidilláw.
quell: *v.* ep-epén, pagtalnáen.
quench: *v.* iddepén, atipaén, depdepén.
query: *n.* saludsód, usísa; *v.* agsaludsód.
quest: *n.* panagsukímat, panagsukáin.
question: *n.* saludsód, súsik, pammalutpót.
questionable: *adj.* nakaat-átap, maduaduá, nakaiílem, sospetsóso.
questionnaire: *n.* lísta dagití saludsód.
quibble: *v.* agkilló, agsiási, aglísi, agliklík.
quick: *adj.* naparták, nadarás, nasiglát, naparagsít, nasagiksík; madagdágus ~ **tempered** buringetngét, naalipúnget, narungsót, naungét.
quickly: *adv.* dágus.
quicksilver: *n.* asóge, merkúrio.
quid: *n.* maskáda, mamá.
quiet: *adj.* natalná, naulímek.
quill: *n.* dutdót a dakkél, ungkáy, tangkáy.
quinine: *n.* kinína.
quintessence: *n.* kababagás, kapipintásan.
quire: *n.* sangamanília.
quisling: *n.* manglilíput, nagulíb a táo.
quit: *v.* agsardéng, agsardáy; gupdén, ikulásay.
quite: *adv.* únay.
quiver: *v.* agpigergér, agtayegtég; *n.* (*for arrows*) tagúban.
quiz: *n.* bassít nga eksámen; *v.* pagsaludsúdan.
quoit: *n.* pása, báto.
quorum: *n.* kórum.
quota: *n.* kóta, naipabátang.

quotation: *n.* sasaó nga inádaw ití sabáli.
quote: *v.* adáwen, aónen; *n.* inádaw a sasaó.
quotient: *n.* atáy.

R

rabbit: *n.* koného.
rabid: *adj.* nalaká a makaungét; napasnék.
rabies: *n.* ballá (sakít).
race: *n.* lumbá; (*of people*) pulí.
rachitic: *adj.* nakudídit.
racial: *adj.* maipapán ití pulí.
rack: *n.* pagsab-ítan, pagsalapayán.
racket: *n.* rakéta; (*noise*) ariwáwa, riríbok.
radiant: *adj.* naraniág, narangráng, nasilnág; napúngay.
radiate: *v.* agrangráng, agraniág, agsilnág.
radio: *n.* rádio.
radiogram: *n.* radiográma.
radish: *n.* rábanos; **horse~** marúnggay.
radius: *n.* ráyos.
raffle: *n.* rípa; *v.* agrípa.
raft: *n.* rákit, bálsa, dalákit.
rafter: *n.* pasanggír, kílo; sobrekílo; **jack** ~ *n.* pakikít; **hip** ~ *n.* solókan.
rag: *n.* pagnasnás; rútay, rígis; pirgís.
rage: *n.* simrón, pungtót, rungsót.
ragged: *adj.* rigisrígis, rutayrútay.
raid: *v.* rautén; *n.* raút.
railing: *n.* barandílias.
railroad: *n.* perrokarríl, trámo.
rain: *n.* túdo; *v.* agtúdo; **stay in the** ~ *v.* agkalintuduán; **get caught in the** ~ *v.* matuduán.
rainbow: *n.* bullaláyaw.
raincoat: *n.* kapóte, annangá, bangáw.
raindrop: *n.* tedtéd ti túdo.
rainfall: *n.* panagtúdo.
raise: *v.* ingáto, itag-áy, bangónen; isáen; (*animals*) dinguén, taraknén; *n* náyon ti suéldo; pannakaingáto; panangitáyag.
raisin: *n.* pásas.
rake: *n.* karaykáy, pagkaykáy; *v.* agkaraykáy.
rale: *n.* rárek.
rally: *n.* dakkél a gimóngan.
ram: *v.* pisonén, iseksék, kugsólen, dungpáren; *n.* karnéro.
ramble: *v.* agsikawsíkaw, agtawátaw; agbariw-ás; agadák, agsaosaó.
ramie: *n.* ramí.
ramification: *n.* sangá, símang, simáay.
rampage: *v.* rautén.
rampart: *n.* sarikedkéd, pagsalingdán; kóta, írang.
ranch: *n.* rántso.

rancid: *adj.* nabanglés, nabúleg, mabunglóg, naantá.

rancor: *n.* gúra, ruród.

random: *adj.* paspasárak, padpadtó, barobaddután.

range: *v.* agsursór, agdakíwas, agbintór; *n.* sákup, beddéng; binnátog, intár.

ranger: *n.* mangbanbantáy kadagití kabakíran.

rank: *n.* ránggo, sáad, galád.

ransack: *v.* samsámen, sukisúken, sukimáten, pulinglíngen.

ransom: *n.* pangsaká, pangsubbót; *v.* subbotén.

rant: *v.* agungét.

rap: *v.* agtugtóg.

rape: *n.* ramés, pílit ití babái; *v.* ramesén, rabsúten; pilíten (ti babái); agarádas.

rapid: *adj.* napardás, nadarás, naparták.

rapids: *n.* parokpók, dimmalágan.

rapprochement: *n.* panaglantíp (ti dua a kabusor).

rapture: *n.* nalabés a panagragragsák.

rare: *adj.* narásay, manmanó; *(cooked)* nalanét.

rascal: *n.* dákes a táo.

rash: *adj.* nadursók, nadarasúdos; **nettle** ~ *n.* supotsúpot.

rasp: *v.* gadgáden, gasgásen, radrádan.

rat: *n.* baó; ~ **poison** *n.* arsinít.

rate: *n.* gatád, patég; bílang.

rather: *adv.* nga ad-addá ngem; **would** ~ *v.* kaykayát.

ratify: *v.* pasingkedán, patalgedán; lagdáan.

rating: *n.* grádo; nóta, márka.

ratio: *n.* pannakaibagí.

ration: *n.* bálon, rasión.

rational: *adj.* manákem, managpanúnot.

rattan: *n.* kulláyot, way; **hard** ~ *n.* ditáan; **fruit of** ~ *n.* littukó.

rattle: *n.* tarakaták, karadákad, karadúkod, talukátik, pakpák; *v.* agkilogkilóg, agkutokkutók, agkutukót.

rattlesnake: *n.* bárong.

rat trap: *n.* kúrod, saltók.

ravage: *v.* dadaélen; *n.* talipúpos a dadaél.

ravel: *v.* agsuysóy, agsutsót.

ravelings: *n.* samotsámot, saroysároy, sinutsót.

raven: *n.* wak.

ravenous: *adj.* naráwet, nabuklís.

ravine: *n.* raw-áng, rangkís, gungúgong, bawáng, báwek.

ravish: *v.* itálaw; gudásan.

raw: *adj.* naáta, nakiláw.

ray: *n.* annaráar, sinámar; *(skate)* pági.

raze: *v.* rakráken.

razor: *n.* nabáha, pangiskís.

reach: *v.* madánon, magaw-át; gam-úden, masagpát; pagat-.

react: *v.* sumámay; magaráw, matignáy.

read: *v.* agbása; ~**ing** *n.* panagbása.

ready: *adj.* sidadáan, sisasagána; *v.* isagána.

real: *adj.* pudnó, napaypaysó.

reality: *n.* kinapudnó.

realize: *v.* ibánag, ileppás, gun-óden.

really: *adv.* talagá; ti kinapudnóna.

realm: *n.* sákup, pagturayán.

realtor: *n.* ahénte ití panaglakuán ti dagá ken baláy.

realty: *n.* sanikuá a dagá ken baláy.

ream: *n.* resmá.

reap: *v.* anién, apíten.

reappear: *v.* *(sickness)* sumingír.

rear: *n.* likudán, taraúdi, palikúd.

rearrange: *v.* urnósen a balíwan.

reason: *n.* rasón; gapú, pamkuátan.

reasonable: *adj.* maikanadá, nanakmán, naisípan.

rebate: *n.* kissáy, paksáy; *v.* pabassitén ti kuénta.

rebel: *n.* rebélde, insurékto; immalsá; bumúsor; *v.* umalsá.

rebellion: *n.* yaalsá, panagsúkir.

rebound: *v.* agbalaték, agsublí, agallangúgan, agkallátik.

rebuff: *v.* laísen, paíden.

rebuild: *v.* bangónen a balíwan, tarimaánen.

rebuke: *v.* babalawén, tubngáren; *n.* panangpabásol, babaláw.

recalcitrant: *adj.* nasúbeg, nasúngit.

recall: *v.* lagipén; pasublién; *n.* nangpasublí.

recant: *v.* pagbabawyán ti sinaó.

recapitulate: *v.* pukpúken.

recede: *v.* agsanúd; umbáas, agsarinúnod.

receipt: *n.* resíbo; ~ **book** *n.* resibário.

receive: *v.* maáwat, anugóten, umáwat.

recent: *adj.* itay nabiít, baró; ka-; ~**ly deceased** *a.* kalnoód.

receptacle: *n.* pakaikaílan, pagikkán.

reception: *n.* pagawátan.

recess: *n.* inaná; sardéng.

recession: *n.* panagsardéng, pannakakapsút ti negósio.

recipe: *n.* reséta.

recipient: *n.* ti umáwat.

reciprocal: *adj.* agsinnupápak, agsubansubád, agsinnubálit.

reciprocate: *v.* subadán, subalítan, supapákan.

reciprocity: *n.* pagsinnubálit; panagsinnukát.

reckless: *adj.* nadarasúdos.

reckon: *v.* panunóten, pagarupén.

reclaim: *v.* subbotén, pasublién.

recline: *v.* agsádag; aginaná.

recluse: *n.* ermitánio.

recognition: *n.* pammigbíg, pakaipakaammuán.

recognize: *v.* bigbígen, ammuén; akuén; makiammo-ammó.

recoil: *v.* agpáing, tumapidéng; kumtát.

recollect: *v.* malagíp, maipalagíp.

recommend: *v.* ikalikágum, italék, ipatalkéd.

recompense: *v.* supapákan, subadán, gungunaán.

reconcile: *v.* pagamuén, pagkappiáen, pagtunósen, pagpiáen; agkinnaawátan, agkappiá.

reconstruction: *n.* panangpabaró.

record: *n.* pláka; rehístro; ti naisúrat; *v.* buangáyen.

recount: *n.* pakasaritáan.

recourse: *n.* pamuspúsan, kámang, taklín.

recover: *v.* umimbág, pumiá; (*from drunkenness*) agúngar; agpúlang; ~ **consciousness** agpúlang ti púot.

recreation: *n.* palpaliwá, panagpallaílang, aliwaksáy.

recruit: *v.* kintósen.

rectangle: *n.* rektánggulo.

rectify: *v.* lintegén, tarimaánen.

rectitude: *n.* kinalintég.

rectum: *n.* merrét, kimmút; **protruding** ~ *n* lugsót.

recuperate: *v.* pumiá, agimbág.

recur: *v.* sumró manén; malagíp manén.

red: *adj.* nalabága, nalabbásit.

redden: *v.* lumabága, lumabbásit.

redeem: *v.* subbotén, sakaén.

redemption: *n.* subbót, pannakasubbót.

redolent: *adj.* nabangló.

reduce: *v.* kissayán, pabassitén.

reduction: *n.* pakaipababaán; ikkát.

reed: *n.* róno, tanúbong, págat; (*of loom*) súgod.

reef: *n.* raw-áng, kadilián, baknád, salsalapásap.

reek: *v.* umalingásaw; bumangsít.

reel: *n.* pagpulipúlan, lalabáyan; *v.* ilábay, iputípot.

reelect: *v.* pilién manén.

refer: *v.* ituróng; itudó.

referee: *n.* umimátang, ukóm.

reference: *n.* reperénsia; maipapán ití.

refine: *v.* palinísen, pasin-áwen, papinuén; (*metals*) gugúran.

refined: *adj.* napíno, nalínis, nadalús.

reflect: *v.* agballaték; agpanúnot; ~**ion** *n.* panagballaték; panagpanúnot; annínaw, ladáwan ití danúm wennó sarmíng.

reform: *v.* balíwan, pasayaáten; *n.* pannaka-pabaró, pannakapasayáat.

refractory: *adj.* nasúbeg, nasúkir, nasupríng.

refrain: *v.* gawídan, tenglén; agtaéng; *n.* reprán, kóro.

refresh: *v.* agpalamíis.

refreshment: *n.* pagpalamíis.

refrigerator: *n.* nebéra, pagpalamiísan.

refuge: *n.* kámang, sarikedkéd, aklón.

refugee: *n.* táo a nagkámang.

refund: *v.* pasublián (ti kuartá).

refuse: *v.* agmadí; paíden, paáyen; *n.* dalupitpít.

refute: *v.* sukálen; sungbátan.

regain: *v.* sabróten; ~ **losses** *v.* bumáwi.

regal: *adj.* naarián, nadáyag.

regard: *n.* pakumustá, pammatég; *v.* raemén; ibílang; **send** ~**s** *v.* pakumustáan.

regarding: *conj.* maipapán, maipanggép.

regenerate: *v.* paungáren, paimbagén.

regiment: *n.* rehimiénto.

region: *n.* rehión, dissó.

register: *n.* pagilistáan, rehístro.

registered: *adj.* nailistáan; nairehístro; (*real estate*) nakatastrál.

registration: *n.* pannakailísta.

registry: *n.* rehístro, listáan dagití nágan.

regress: *v.* agsublí, dumákes ití dáti a kasasáad.

regret: *v.* agbabáwi; *n.* babáwi.

regular: *adj.* kadawyán; bánal.

regulate: *v.* urnósen, timbéngen.

regulation: *n.* alagáden, annuróten.

rehabilitate: *v.* isublí ití sígud a kasasáad.

rehearse: *v.* repasuén, asaásen.

reign: *v.* agturáy, agári; agdákor; *n.* panagturáy.

reimburse: *v.* talalián, sulítan, bayádan, pasublián.

rein: *n.* riénda, pangtenglán (ti kabálio).

reinforce: *v.* papigsáen.

reiterate: *v.* ulíten, sunótan, surnádan.

reject: *v.* paáyen, likudán, paíden, ipaídam, iwaksí; malasén.

rejoice: *v.* agragsák, agrag-ó.

rejuvenate: *v.* pabaruén, paubingén.

relapse: *n.* begnát; *v.* mabegnát.

relate: *v.* ibagá, ipadámag; saritáen.

related: *adj.* maikabagián.

relation: *n.* pannakibiáng; kabagián.

relative: *n.* kabagián; **collateral** ~ *n.* kabangíran; *adj.* maibiáng.

relax: *v.* aginaná, agaliwaksáy; palag-ánen.

relay: *v.* ipadámag.

release: *v.* ibbatán, warwáren; wayawayaán.

relevant: *adj.* maipaáy, maitutóp, maibiáng, maitúnos.

reliable: *adj.* mapagtalkán, matalék.
reliance: *n.* namnáma, pannakatalék.
relic: *n.* mangipalagíp, relíkia.
relief: *n.* bang-ár, gin-áwa; liwliwá.
relieve: *v.* bang-áran; (*substitute*) sandián.
religion: *n.* pammáti, relihión.
relinquish: *v.* panáwan, mawás, ikulásay.
relish: *v.* magustúan, imásen.
reluctant: *adj.* sumugkár, matartaramnáy, nakedkéd, namaredméd.
rely: *v.* agtalék; agkammatalék.
remain: *v.* agbáti, agtalinaéd.
remainder: *n.* surók; sása; ti matdá; ~ **of a** debt *n.* aptáng, lúnak.
remains: *n.* regrég, tiddá.
remark: *n.* saó; *v.* isaó, isalpiká.
remarkable: *adj.* naisangayán, namarangmáng.
remedy: *n.* ágas, pamuspúsan.
remember: *v.* malagíp; laglagipén.
remembrance: *n.* pakalaglagipán.
remind: *v.* ipalagíp; makagutád; ~er *n.* pangipalagíp.
remnant: *n.* mabáti, tiddá.
remodel: *v.* pabaruén.
remorse: *n.* panagbabáwi, panagladíngit, sakít ti nákem; *v.* agkutíkut, aggotokgotók, agladíngit.
remote: *adj.* adayó, naipatpattíway, áwar.
removal: *n.* pannakaikkát.
remove: *v.* ikkatén, yális.
remunerate: *v.* tangdánan, subadán.
renaissance: *n.* pannakapabaró.
rename: *v.* inagánan manén, ikkán ti baró a nágan.
render: *v.* ipaáy, itéd.
rendezvous: *n.* pagdadanónan, pagsinnarákan.
renegade: *n.* traidór, nagulíb a táo.
renew: *v.* pabaruén.
renounce: *v.* iwagsák, baybay-án, talikudán, mawás.
renovate: *v.* pabaruén, pasayaáten.
renowned: *adj.* nadáyaw, natan-ók, nasúdi.
rent: *n.* ábang, úpa; *v.* abángan, upáan.
repair: *v.* tarimaánen; arúben, sakában; ~ **nets** *v.* agayúma; ~ **shop** *n.* taliér.
repatch: *v.* takuápan.
repay: *v.* supapákan, subadán.
repeat: *v.* ulíten, dupágen.
repeatedly: *adv.* naynáy.
repel: *v.* paíden; abugén.
repent: *v.* agbabáwi.
repercussion: *n.* panagsublisublí.
repetition: *n.* panangúlit.
replace: *v.* sukatán, sulnítan; sandián.
replenish: *v.* punuén manén; yallúsob.

replete: *adj.* napnó.
replica: *n.* kapáda.
replow: *v.* aggogóba.
reply: *n.* sungbát; *v.* manubálit, sumungbát.
report: *v.* ipadámag; *n.* padámag.
reporter: *n.* agipadpadámag.
repose: *v.* aginaná; *n.* pannakainaná.
repository: *n.* abong-ábong, nakaikabílan.
repound: *v.* dekdekén, deg-ásen.
reprehend: *v.* babalawén, umsáen; salangáden.
represent: *v.* isáup, itakderán, sunuán; iladáwan.
representative: *n.* pannakabagí.
repress: *v.* medmedán; ep-epén; igáwid, tenglén; lapdán.
reprimand: *v.* babalawén; ungtán.
reprint: *v.* ipabláak manén; *n.* baró a pannakaipabláak.
reprisal: *n.* báles, pammáles.
reproach: *v.* umsáen; *n.* umsá.
reproduce: *v.* patubuén; alagáden; agyakúyak.
reproof: *n.* babaláw.
reprove: *v.* babalawén, ungtán.
reptiles: *n.* agay-ayám.
republic: *n.* repúblika, turáy dagití kaaduán.
repudiate: *v.* talikudán, pugsáyen; makabáwi; saán nga awátan.
repugnant: *adj.* maisuppiát; makaruród.
repulsive: *adj.* makaariék, makasugkár, makapagúra.
reputation: *n.* dáyaw, pakaidayáwan.
request: *v.* dawáten, kiddawén; *n.* dáwat.
require: *v.* tuntónen, sapúlen, dawáten.
rescind: *v.* waswásen, paawanén.
rescue: *v.* subbotén, isalákan, arayáten; alawén; *n.* panangaláw, panangsalákan.
research: *n.* panangsukísok, panangpalutpót, sukímat.
resemblance: *n.* kaarngí, kakíta, kapáda.
resemble: *v.* umaspíng, pumáda, umarngí.
resent: *v.* karuród, guráen.
resentment: *n.* ikáy, kátil.
reserve: *v.* ilatángan, isangrát, idúlin, itiddá.
reservoir: *n.* depósito, dakkél a pagurnóngan.
reside: *v.* agnaéd, agtaéng, agtalinaéd.
residence: *n.* pagtaengán, pagyanán, pagnaedán, pagindegán.
residents: *n.* umíli.
residue: *n.* natdá, sóbra.
resign: *v.* aglusúlos, aglapsót, agikkát ití sáad, agrenúnsia.
resin: *n.* tútot.
resist: *v.* agkedkéd; sukíren, sungáten, supríngen.

resolute: *adj.* naingét, aggalasúgas, nareggét, napasnék.
resolution: *n.* panangikeddéng; panangibánag.
resolve: *v.* paganamúngan; ibánag.
resonance: *n.* áweng, allangúgan.
resonant: *adj.* naáweng, naallangúgan.
resort: *n.* pagaliwaksáyan; *v.* agaywén.
resound: *v.* umáweng, agallangúgan.
resource: *n.* pamuspúsan, sanikúa; **natural ~s** *n.* rekúrsos.
respect: *n.* dáyaw, kaisiráyan; *v.* pagraemán, dayáwen.
respectable: *adj.* madaydáyaw, naraém.
respectful: *adj.* siraraém, managdáyaw.
respiration: *n.* panagánges.
respond: *v.* sumungbát, agsubálit.
response: *n.* sungbát.
responsibility: *n.* responsabilidád, biáng; rebbéng, susungbátan.
responsible: *adj.* makaammó, akinrebbéng; sumungbát.
rest: *n.* inaná; *v.* aginaná; agsádag; agidná; **~house** pakárso.
restaurant: *n.* restaurán.
restless: *adj.* nakutíkutí, naríríbuk.
restore: *v.* ipúlang, alangónen.
restrain: *v.* tenglén, tubngén, igáwid.
restrict: *v.* gawídan, pupóken, kedngán, tenglén.
result: *n.* tungpál, nagbanágan, pagtun-óyan, pagmaáyan, búnga; *v.* pagbanágan.
resume: *v.* agtúloy.
resurrection: *n.* panagúngar.
resuscitate: *v.* paungáren, biágen; agúngar.
retail: *v.* tayutáyen, patingí, iballiád.
retain: *v.* taginayónen; ikután.
retaliate: *v.* balsén, bumáles.
retard: *v.* agpaúdi; aggábay.
retch: *v.* agdul-ók.
reticent: *adj.* naulímek.
retire: *v.* agpakní; agsanúd.
retort: *n.* sungbát; *v.* sungbátan.
retouch: *v.* retokién; **~ed** *adj.* retokádo.
retreat: *v.* agsanúd; umatáng; agpakní.
retrieve: *v.* abrúten, subbotén.
retrospect: *n.* panangpanúnot ití napalábas.
return: *v.* agsublí; **~ home** *v.* agáwid.
reunion: *n.* panagtitípon.
reunite: *v.* agtípon manén.
reveal: *v.* ipalgák, ipadláw, ibutakták, ipakaammó.
revel: *v.* agrambák; *n.* ragragsák.
revelation: *n.* palgák, paltíing.
revenge: *n.* pammáles, báles; *v.* bumáles.
revenue: *n.* réntas, masapúlan, kuartá a mapastrék.

reverberate: *v.* agallangúgan, agariwáwa.
revere: *v.* pagraemán, dayáwen.
reverence: *n.* amangá, dáyaw.
reverse: *v.* baliktáden, balinsuekén; tumallikúd; *adj.* baliktád, rusngí.
review: *n.* repáso, panangasáas.
revise: *v.* balíwan.
revival: *n.* pangpaúngar, pangbiág.
revive: *v.* biágen, paungáren; agbarusbós, papigsáen.
revoke: *v.* ukásen, waswásen.
revolt: *n.* yaalsá, guló.
revolution: *n.* yaalsá; panangguló; tayyek.
revolve: *v.* aglikmút, agpusípos, agtayyék.
revolver: *n.* paltóg.
reward: *n.* prémio, gunguná; *v.* gungunaán.
rewash: *v.* balnásan.
rhetoric: *n.* retórika.
rheumatism: *n.* rayúma, reúma, álon-álon.
rhinoceros beetle: *n.* barraírong, sumusubsób; **larva of ~** pusapúsa, alimpupúsa.
rhonchus: *n.* rárek.
rhubarb: *n.* riubárbo.
rhyme: *n.* ríma.
rhythm: *n.* kumpás.
rib: *n.* paragpág.
ribbon: *n.* listón, bedbéd, pirapír, lásos.
rice: *n.* bagás, pagay; **cooked ~** *n.* innapóy; **badly cooked ~** *n.* belbél; **ground ~** *n.* binutáy; **cold cooked ~** *n.* kilabbán; **~ weevil** *n.* rekkét; **~ water** *n.* seggét; **partially husked ~** *n.* lúdang; **red ~** *n.* tarúyaw; **sweetened popped ~** *n.* kiniróg, gípang; **sweet ~** *n.* díket.
rice cake: *n.* (*kinds*) súman, badúya, bibíngka, bíko, gípang, paltáw, púto, túpig, pinuyó.
rice field: *n.* tálon; kelléng.
rich: *n.* nabaknáng; **~es** *n.* baknáng.
rickety: *adj.* nakapsót.
ricochet: *v.* agballaték.
rid: *v.* wayawayaán, lukatán.
riddle: *n.* burtiá.
ride: *v.* agsakáy, aglúgan; *n.* sakáy, panaglúgan.
ridge: *n.* pantók; pangpáng; kabaliéte; **~pole** *n.* pásag.
ridicule: *n.* rabrabaken, uyawén.
ridiculous: *adj.* nakaang-angáw.
rifle: *n.* ríple, paltúog.
rift: *n.* rengngát, betták.
rig: *n.* kalésa.
right: *n.* kalintegán; *adj.* (*just*) nalintég; (*not left*) kanawán; (*exact*) nakanátad, umisú.
righteous: *adj.* nalintég, naregtá, nasalindég.
rigid: *adj.* nasikkíl, naingét.
rigor: *n.* kinapigsá, kinaingét.

rim: *n.* íking, ngárab, lebléb, ígid, barákus.
rind: *n.* ukís; **pork** ~ *n.* sitsarón.
ring: *n.* singsíng; *v.* umáweng, agkilíng;
~ **finger** pasariw-át.
ringlet: *n.* kulót.
ringworm: *n.* kulébra, kúrad.
rinse: *n.* balbálan, barnásan, tilnógan,
ibugnáw.
riot: *n.* riríbok, yaalsá, guló; *v.* agguló, agríri.
rip: *v.* satsáten, ray-ában, gay-ában, gay-áken.
ripe: *adj.* naluóm, natangkenán.
ripen: *v.* agluóm, aglabanág.
ripple: *n.* allón; *v.* agsaraisí.
ripsaw: *n.* kíkir.
rise: *v.* bumángon; ~ **above** (*over the top*) *v.*
lipáwen.
risk: *n.* riésgo, síba, peggád.
rite: *n.* rítos, sebbáng.
ritual: *n.* rítos, seremónia.
rival: *n.* karibál, kasalísal, kaaban-ábak,
balúbal.
rivalry: *n.* panagsasalísal, panagrisíris.
river: *n.* karayán.
rivet: *n.* remátse.
rivulet: *n.* baresbés; ubbóg.
roach: *n.* ípes, sípet; alukáp.
road: *n.* dálan, kalsáda; pagnaán.
roam: *v.* agtawátaw, agalla-allá, agbintór,
agdayangdáyang, agbagilawláw, agdakíwas.
roar: *v.* agdaranúdor, agugáog, agáwer;
agúngor; *n.* úngor, daranúdor, ugáog.
roast: *v.* asarén, itúno, idamdám; *n.* tinúno.
rob: *v.* takáwan, samsámen.
robbery: *n.* panagtákaw.
robe: *n.* báta; kagáy.
robust: *adj.* nalungpó; nabanég; nakaradkád,
nalangpáw.
rock: *n.* bató; *v.* aggungón, agarigengén;
agindáyon.
rocket: *n.* kuítis.
rocking chair: *n.* nabuábo a palángka.
rocky: *adj.* nabató.
rod: *n.* sarukód, bastón; ungkáy, tangkáy.
rodent: *n.* áyup nga agkibki-kibkíb.
roe: *n.* búgi.
roiled: *adj.* nalibég.
role: *n.* papél (ití pabúya).
roll: *n.* tukél, lúkot, rólio; *v.* tulíden; agtulátid.
roller: *n.* átal, paráris, pataladtád; rodílio;
~ **gin** laddít; ~ **skate** *n.* iskéting.
rolling pin: *n.* likídan.
romance: *n.* románsa.
romantic: *adj.* romántiko, nalaílo.
romp: *n.* darangángan.
roof: *n.* atép; **gable** ~ *n.* tinúbeng; **hip** ~ *n.*
pinag-óng; **bamboo** ~ *n.* talákib; ~ **tile** *n.* téha.

room: *n.* siléd, kuárto; **bath**~ *n.* bánio.
roomy: *adj.* naláwa, nawayáng.
roost: *v.* agápon; *n.* pagapónan.
rooster: *n.* kawítan.
root: *n.* ramút; **medicinal** ~ *n.* bánay; ~**stock**
n. bagás; *v.* subsúben, ipungét, ripáten.
rope: *n.* talí; *v.* italí.
rosary: *n.* rosário.
rose: *n.* rósas; ~**bay** *n.* adélpa.
roster: *n.* lísta dagití nagnágan.
rostrum: *n.* platapórma.
rosy: *adj.* kaslá rósas.
rot: *v.* aglungsót, marúnot.
rotate: *v.* agtayyék, agbattuág, agbuttuág.
rotten: *adj.* nalungsót, nabunglóg.
rotula: *n.* lipaylípay.
rotund: *adj.* nagbukél, nagsinukél,
nagtimbukél.
rouge: *n.* koloréte.
rough: *adj.* narusangér, nagubsáng,
nakersáng; (*sea*) nadáleg.
roughly: *adv.* sumurók-kumúrang.
roulette: *n.* ruléta.
round: *adj.* natimbukél, nagbukél.
round-trip: *n.* baniága nga apán-agáwid.
roundworm: *n.* ariét, urísit.
rouse: *v.* riingén.
route: *n.* sebbáng, dálan, pagnaán.
rove: *v.* agtawátaw, agíwas, agbariw-ás.
row: *n.* intár, áray, pirápid; *v.* aggáud.
rowdy: *adj.* naguló, naríri.
royal: *adj.* naarián.
rub: *v.* radrádan, lidlíden, rasrásan; ~ **eyes** *v.*
lidlíden; ~ **against** *v.* aggidígid; ~ **off** *v.*
padílen.
rubber: *n.* góma.
rubbish: *n.* basúra; rugít.
ruby: *n.* rubí.
rucksack: *n.* makóto.
rudder: *n.* timón, pangyúrit.
rudderstock: *n.* burábor.
rude: *adj.* bastós, nagubsáng, nawagnét,
narusangér.
rudiment: *n.* pamunganáyan.
ruffle: *n.* pliéges, renrén, paraypáy, buélas.
rug: *n.* alpómbra.
rugged: *adj.* lasonglasóngan, nagubsáng;
nawagténg, saán a nasimpá.
ruin: *v.* dadáelen; *n.* dadaél.
ruined: *adj.* nadadáel, nasíba.
rule: *n.* alagáden, lintég, reglá; bílin; *v.*
agturáy.
ruled: *adj.* (*paper*) liniádo.
ruler: *n.* (*instrument*) régla; (*chief*) pangúlo, ti
agturáy.
rum: *n.* aguardiénte.

rumble: *v.* aggaradugód; *n.* ariwáwa.
rumen: *n.* liblibró, rakrakípa.
ruminant: *n.* managngalngál.
rummage: *v.* kiwáren, bukibúken, sukaínan; agdakíwas.
rumor: *n.* sayanggúseng.
rump: *n.* úbet, kibongkíbong, kútit.
rumple: *v.* agkurbób.
run: *v.* agtaráy; aglangáy; (*nose*) agluylóy, agdagútay; (*saliva*) agdagútay; ~ **away with** *v.* itaráy, itálaw; ~**ner up** *n.* sumasarunó ití immuná.
runaway: *n.* bayanggúdaw, ti naglíbas.
rung: *n.* tukád.
runt: *n.* bulilít, kuttongí.
rupture: *n.* písang, búong, bungáw, betták.
rural: *adj.* maipapán ití áway.
rush: *v.* darasén; *n.* pardás, darás.
rushing: *adj.* naapgés.
Russian: *n, adj.* Rúso.
rust: *n.* láti, takkí ti landók; *v.* agláti.
rustic: *adj.* maipapán ití áway.
rustle: *v.* agkarasákas.
rusty: *adj.* naláti.
rut: *n.* gúlis, killaóng; *v.* agkalkál.
ruthless: *adj.* naulpít, naúyong, awán kaásina, nadawél; ~**ness** *n.* kinadawél, kinaulpít.
rye: *n.* senténo.

S

Sabbath: *n.* aldáw a panaginaná ken panaglుálo.
saber: *n.* sáble, espáda, kampílan.
sabotage: *n.* pannakadadaél ti panggép.
sack: *n.* súpot, sáko, kustál, kádos.
sacrament: *n.* sakraménto.
sacred: *adj.* sagrádo, nasantuán.
sacrifice: *n.* dáton, sakripísio; *v.* ipatlí; agsakripísio.
sacrilegious: *adj.* nadamsák.
sacrum: *n.* ípel, alangaáng.
sad: *adj.* nalidáy, naldáang, naladíngit.
saddle: *n.* pústi, sília, montúra; *v.* siliáan.
saddlebag: *n.* kádos.
sadist: *n.* sadísta, managayát ití panangparígat.
safari: *n.* panagánup.
safe: *n.* káha a landók; *adj.* natalgéd; nakalásat.
safeguard: *v.* saranáyen; agdúyos; *n.* panang-salakníb.
safekeeping: *n.* panangidúlin, panagaywán.
safflower: *n.* kasabá, kasumbá.
saffron: *n.* asaprán.
sag: *v.* agbissáyot, aglusdóy, agyukyók, agyudyód, aglunggi-lunggí.

sagacious: *adj.* nasaldét, nasarót, natarém.
sage: *n.* nasírib a táo.
sago palm: *n.* kabonégro.
sail: *n.* láyag; *v.* agláyag, agbaniága ití taáw; **lower the ~s** *v.* lubágen.
sailor: *n.* marinéro, aglayláyag.
saint: *n.* sánto; **patron** ~ *n.* kasangáy, kanagánan.
sake: *n.* gapú.
salacious: *adj.* nauttóg, naultóg.
salad: *n.* ensaláda.
salamander: *n.* bannasák, bagangán.
salary: *n.* suéldo, tangdán, matgedán.
sale: *n.* pannakaláko; **first** ~ *n.* búsat.
salesman: *n.* aglakláko, ahénte.
saline: *adj.* naasín; naapgád.
saliva: *n.* kátay; tuprá.
salivary fistula: *n.* luttók.
salivate: *n.* agkátay.
sallow: *adj.* nalusiáw.
salmon: *n.* salmón.
salon: *n.* pagsasaláan.
saloon: *n.* pagtagilakuán ti árak.
salt: *n.* asín; ~ **deposit** *n.* barára; **make** ~ *v.* agsaná; **dip in** ~ *v.* isímot; *v.* asinán.
saltpeter: *n.* apáya, salítre.
salty: *adj.* naasín; (*to taste*) naapgád; (*water*) natabáng.
salubrious: *adj.* makapasalun-át.
salutation: *n.* kabláaw.
salute: *v.* kablaáwan, padayáwan, kumustáan, lugáyan.
salvage: *v.* alawén, isalakán.
salvation: *n.* pannakisalákan.
salvo: *n.* paltóog.
same: *adj.* isú met láeng, parého, agka-.
sampan: *n.* bióng.
sample: *n.* muéstra, alágad, pagtuládan; wadán, pagpakpakíta.
sanatorium: *n.* sanitário, pagpasalun-átan.
sanctify: *v.* pasantuén.
sanction: *n.* pammasingkéd, anámong, lagdáan, palúbos.
sanctity: *n.* kinasánto.
sanctuary: *n.* santuário, nasantuán a lugár.
sand: *n.* dárat, anáy, tap-óy; ~**bank** *n.* sáal; ~**box** *n.* pagtangingián; ~**stone** *n.* gúbang.
sandal: *n.* palluká, sandálias; tsinélas.
sandpaper: *n.* líha; *v.* liháen.
sandwich: *n.* emparedádos.
sandy: *adj.* nadárat, narubúrob, nalap-ók.
sane: *adj.* manákem; napiá, nasalun-át.
sanitarium: *n.* sanitário.
sanitary: *adj.* nadalús; ~ **napkin** *n.* pasadór.
sanitation: *n.* kinadalús.
sanity: *n.* kinadalús ti panúnot.

sap: *n.* tubbóg, tubá.
sapodilla: *n.* tsíko.
sapphire: *n.* sapíro.
sapwood: *n.* ballagúbag.
sarcasm: *n.* abí, umsí, pasáir, kinasagíbar; pammaságid.
sarcastic: *adj.* nasagíbar, sarkástiko, napaságid.
sardine: *n.* bilís, sardínas, tambán.
sash: *n.* bedbéd, sinturón, baríkes.
Satan: *n.* satanás, saíro.
satanic: *adj.* nainsairuán.
satchel: *n.* upít, súpot.
satiate: *v.* bussogén, pennekén, makabsóg.
satin: *n.* satín, ráso.
satire: *n.* pasáir, paságid, kinasagíbar.
satirize: *v.* angawén, tinggáren.
satisfaction: *n.* pannakapnék, talád.
satisfy: *v.* pennekén; pagustuán.
saturate: *v.* ipasagepsép, igamér, umagsép.
Saturday: *n.* Sábado.
sauce: *n.* sársa; **dip in ~** *v.* isímut.
saucepan: *n.* bassít a kasérola.
saucer: *n.* platílio, pagsanggaán, sanggá, platíto.
sausage: *n.* longganísa, saltsitsón, binatútay.
sauté: *v.* igisá.
savage: *n.* salbáhe.
savanna: *n.* tay-ák.
savant: *n.* masírib a táo.
save: *v.* (*rescue*) isalákan; ispálen; (*keep*) idúlin; (*economize*) terdén, agin-ínut; *prep.* malaksíd.
savior: *n.* mangisalákan.
savor: *n.* ánag, nánam.
saw: *n.* ragádi, kíkir, bandíli, gesgés; *v.* nakíta; **bamboo ~** gopogópen.
sawdust: *n.* nagragadián.
sawhorse: *n.* batángan, pasanggír, kabaliéte.
sawmill: *n.* pagragadián.
say: *v.* kuná, sawén, ibagá, isaó, isáwang.
saying: *n.* pagsasaó.
scab: *n.* keggáng; (*in strike*) eskiról.
scabbard: *n.* baína, kalúban.
scaffold: *n.* palapála, tabládo.
scald: *v.* lamawén, dilnákan.
scale: *n.* (*weighing*) titimbengán, gantíngan; (*of fish*) siksík; *v.* ulién; siksíkan.
scallop: *n.* baraybáy, kampís, singítan.
scalp: *n.* kúdil ti úlo; *v.* laplápen ti kúdil ti úlo, panítan.
scalpel: *n.* lansíta.
scaly: *adj.* marasiksíkan.
scamper: *v.* agbuátit.
scan: *v.* sukimáten, mingmíngan.
scandal: *n.* eskándalo; **~ous** *adj.* nakababaín.

scant: *adj.* di makaanáy.
scanty: *adj.* nanumó, nakírang, nakisáng, natakkón.
scapegoat: *n.* bullabullán, pangipulotán; langdét.
scapular: *n.* úsong.
scar: *n.* piglát, ganná; kupsiát; (*on eyelid*) bírit; (*near mouth*) gítiw.
scarce: *adj.* manmanó, narásay, nakiddít, natiggít.
scarcely: *adj.* apagapáman, nganngaáni.
scarcity: *n.* pagkurángan.
scare: *v.* kigtóten, butngén, bugáwen.
scarecrow: *n.* báir, bantí, am-amés.
scarf: *n.* ukkór, bupánda; **~ joint** *n.* pagsangálan.
scarlet: *n.* natingrá a nalabága.
scatter: *v.* iwará, iwarsí, iwarakíwak.
scene: *n.* búya; ladáwan.
scenery: *n.* ladladáwan.
scent: *n.* ángot; **lose one's ~** *v.* maúmag.
scepter: *n.* sétro.
scheme: *n.* gandát, panggép; pamuspúsan; isbangán.
scholar: *n.* agad-ádal.
school: *n.* pagadálan, eskuéla; (*of fish*) taklóng, pangén, sarruád.
science: *n.* siénsia.
scissors: *n.* kartíb, getténg, gertém.
scoff: *v.* bumiláw; rurodén, uyawén.
scold: *v.* pabasólen, ungtán, luyáan, ibir-ít.
scoop: *v.* supláden, akúpen; **~net** *n.* baringríng, batbaténg, bátok, sáyot, pamúrak.
scope: *n.* kaatiddóg.
scorch: *v.* puóran, irnitén, siráman, diráman, itúno; sinitén; *n.* síram; sinít.
score: *n.* iskór, púntos; *v.* makapúntos.
scorn: *v.* irurumén, laísen, umsién.
scorpion: *n.* manggagamá, bayáwak, tagálok, panggagamaén.
scoundrel: *n.* nasabrák a táo.
scour: *v.* radrádan, is-isuán, garugáden.
scourge: *v.* saplíten.
scout: *n.* agsáwar, eskáwt; *v.* agsáwar.
scowl: *v.* agrupangét, rumungbéd; *n.* rupangét, rungbéd.
scramble: *v.* agkarapkáp, makiinnágaw.
scrap: *n.* tiddá, písi, sóbra.
scrape: *v.* radrádan, karúsen, kuskúsen; **~ out** (*coconut meat*) *v.* sudakén.
scratch: *v.* kudkúden; karamútan; agkarúkay, karaísan, kemmengén, rasrásan; *n.* kudkúd; kuskús; karámut.
scrawny: *adj.* nakuttóng ken nakapsót.

scream: *v.* agikkís, agláaw, agpukkáw; *n.* ikkís, pukkáw; ariwáwa.

screech: *n.* ariwáwa.

screen: *n.* pantália, salingéd, tábing, línong, tábing; (*portable*) lingáling.

screw: *n.* tornílio.

screwdriver: *n.* biradór, pangwarwár ti tornílio.

scribble: *v.* kur-ikur-ítan.

scribe: *n.* eskríba, eskribiénte, parasúrat.

script: *n.* sinurátan.

scripture: *n.* nasantuán a sinurátan.

scrofula: *n.* abánon, birék, pasíngil.

scroll: *n.* nalúkot

scrotum: *n.* láteg; **scrotal hernia** *n.* ambungáw, alimbubungáw, bungáw.

scrub: *v.* ugásan, nasnásan, lampasuén; ~ **off dirt** *v.* ludlúdan.

scrutinize: *v.* bigbígen, sukimáten, mingmíngan, sukaínan, bilingén, mangbutingtíng.

scrutiny: *n.* sukímat, ammíris, imátang.

scuffle: *n.* gúbal, guloguló; *v.* agdangádong, agbibinggáw; ~ **hoe** *n.* darusdós.

scullery: *n.* kurkurí, katúlong.

sculptor: *n.* eskultór, agkitkitíkit.

sculpture: *n.* panagkitíkit.

scum: *n.* tarabútab, luág, labútab.

scurvy: *n.* eskorbúto.

scythe: *n.* kumpáy.

sea: *n.* baybáy, taáw; ~ **level** *n.* pátar ti baybáy; **~weed** *n.* rúot ti baybáy, arágan, ar-arusíp; ~ **parsley** *n.* ngalugngálog; ~ **turtle** *n.* pawíkan; ~ **urchin** *n.* maratangtáng, sagága, sabsabláy, panapána.

seagull: *n.* ágila ti taáw.

seahorse: *n.* kabáyo maríno.

seal: *n.* (*animal*) póka; (*stamp*) sélio, tímbre.

seam: *n.* saráit, pagsaípan; *v.* saípen.

seaman: *n.* marinéro.

seamstress: *n.* sástre, mannáit.

sear: *v.* siráman, diráman, sarában, puóran.

search: *v.* sukimáten, sukisúken, sapúlen, birúken, usígen.

seashore: *n.* igíd ti baybáy.

seasick: *adj.* maúlaw.

season: *n.* tiémpo; *v.* rekaduán, paimásen; templáen; **dry** ~ *n.* kalgáw, kuarésma; **hot** ~ *n.* darádar; **beginning of rainy** ~ *n.* tagidpuán; *v.* rekaduán; **in** ~ *adj.* nataengán, napnekán.

seasoning: *n.* rekádo.

seat: *n.* tugáw, sáad; **bamboo** ~ *n.* balítang.

seaward: *adj.* agpataáw.

seaweed: *n.* rúot ti taáw; (*common edible variety*) ar-arusíp.

secede: *v.* sumína, umikkát.

secession: *n.* isisína, panagikkát.

seclude: *v.* isína, ipútong, ilemméng, ipakní.

second: *adj.* maikaduá; **~hand** *adj.* segúnda máno, talibugnáy; ~ **rate** *adj.* ginagalimúsaw; *n.* segúndo; ~ **chance** *n.* palungkít.

secondary: *adj.* maikadkaduá.

secrecy: *n.* palímed.

secret: *adj.* nalímed, nalméng; *n.* palímed.

secretary: *n.* sekretário, kalímed, katúlong ití opisína.

secrete: *v.* agtubbóg, tumbóg.

sect: *n.* sékta, sangá ti relihión.

section: *n.* pasét, bíngay.

secure: *adj.* natalgéd; *v.* igálut; patalgedán; aláen.

security: *n.* talinaáy, talná; tandá; sadíri.

sedate: *adj.* natalná.

sedative: *n.* pangpatalná.

sedentary: *adj.* nakatugáw.

sedge: *n.* barisangá, balláyang, buslíg, tíker, pallupágay, tallopágay.

sediment: *n.* arinsaéd, intaér, alibudábud, burídek, basábas, lissáad, ared-éd.

seduce: *v.* sulbógen, sulisógen, sairuén.

see: *v.* makíta, masipútan, masirmataán.

seed: *n.* bukél; **~bed** *n.* pagbunubónan; **selected** ~ *n.* bin-í.

seedling: *n.* bunúbon.

seek: *v.* birúken, sapúlen; sukimáten.

seem: *v.* agarúp, kaslá.

seep: *v.* agtedtéd, umagsép.

seesaw: *n.* palláyog, battuabattuág.

seethe: *v.* agburék.

segment: *n.* písi, pasét.

segregate: *v.* isína, ipusíng, ipusísak, idásig.

seine: *n.* daklís, sayanggóng, ngaramngám, karúkod.

seize: *v.* gemgemán, kemmegén, petpetán; agáwen, sibbarutén.

seizure: *n.* panangágaw; (*lawful*) imbárgo.

seldom: *adv.* manmanó, paspasaráy.

select: *v.* pilién; *adj.* napíli; **~ion** *n.* panagpíli.

self: *n.* bagí; **~-control** *n.* parbéng; **~-defense** *n.* panangsalakníb ti bagí; **~-reliance** *n.* panagtalék ití bagí; **~-respect** *n.* panagtalék ití bagí.

selfish: *adj.* naágum, nabuklís, managimbubúkod.

sell: *v.* iláko; **~er** *n.* lumaláko.

semblance: *n.* langá, ladáwan.

semen: *n.* kissít, kapsít, semília.

semester: *n.* seméstre.

seminary: *n.* seminário.

senate: *n.* senádo.

senator: *n.* senadór.

send: *v.* ipaw-ít, ibaón; itinnág (súrat).
senile: *adj.* kábaw.
senior: *n.* panglakayén, tangáden, natangkenán a táo.
sensation: *n.* rikná.
sensational: *adj.* makapasiddáaw.
sense: *n.* púot, nákem, rikná.
sensibility: *n.* panagrikná.
sensible: *adj.* manakarikná, manákem.
sensitive: *adj.* managrikná.
sensual: *adj.* naderrép, nagartém.
sentence: *n.* keddéng; senténsia.
sentiment: *n.* panagrikná.
sentimental: *adj.* managrikná.
sentinel: *n.* bantáy, guárdia.
sentry box: *n.* írang.
sepal: *n.* sépalo.
separable: *adj.* maisína.
separate: *v.* sumína, lumásin; isína.
September: *n.* Septiémbre.
septic tank: *n.* póso négro.
septum: *n.* (*nasal*) biríng; (*of animals*) tutub-ókan.
sepulchre: *n.* taném.
sequel: *n.* sumarunó a pasét.
sequence: *n.* panagsasarunó.
sequin: *n.* antikuélas.
serenade: *n.* harána, serenáta, tapát; *v.* agtapát, agharána.
serene: *adj.* natalná, nalínak.
serf: *n.* adípen.
sergeant: *n.* sarhénto.
serial: *n.* agsasarunó.
series: *n.* pagsasarunuán dagití agpapáda.
serious: *adj.* nakáro; naskén; nadagsén; naganetgét; managpanúnot.
sermon: *n.* sermón, kasabá.
serpent: *n.* úleg.
serrate: *v.* gatában; ~**d** *adj.* nagatáb, rimmagádi.
serum: *n.* suéro.
servant: *n.* adípen, katúlong, babaonén; ubíng.
serve: *v.* agserbí, agtungpál, agtulnóg, ibúnong.
service: *n.* panagserbí; túlong.
sesame: *n.* lengngá.
session: *n.* gímong.
set: *n.* huégo; agasmáng; *v.* ikábil, idissó, isáad; yasmáng; ~ **traps** *v.* ipákat, igákat; (*sun*) lumnék; (*table*) agipuní.
setback: *n.* pakapakapsútan.
setting: *n.* (*of jewels*) montadúra; kasasáad; dissó.
settle: *v.* agrinsaéd; agtalinaéd; ikeddéng; ~**ment** *n.* pagtaengán; pannakaurnós; pannakaibánag.

seven: *n.* pitó; ~ **o'clock** álas siéte.
seventeen: *n.* sangapúlo ket pitó.
seventh: *adj.* maikapitó; *n.* pagkapitó.
seventy: *adj.* pitopúlo.
sever: *v.* bingáyen, putdén, rissingén.
several: *adj.* nadumadúma, adú.
severe: *adj.* nakáro; naingét; nadagsén.
sew: *v.* agdáit.
sewage: *n.* rugít ití pagibellengán.
sewer: *n.* alkantarília, pagarinsaedán ti rugít.
sewing: *n.* panagdáit.
sex: *n.* sékso; panagyót.
sextet: *n.* inném a síngin.
sexton: *n.* sakristán.
sexy: *adj.* nasippukél, napunggá; makapauttóg.
shabby: *adj.* rutayrutáyan, rugák.
shack: *adj.* nanumó a baláy, rutrót a baláy, kalapáw.
shackle: *n.* griliéte; káwar; *v.* isip-ól; kawáran.
shade: *n.* línong, malingdán; *v.* linóngan.
shadow: *n.* anniníwan.
shady: *adj.* nalínong, nalidém, nasalínong.
shaft: *n.* pallatíwan, tangbáw; pután.
shag: *n.* burbór.
shaggy: *adj.* burbúran, dutdútan.
shake: *v.* agarigengén, agtigergér, agpigergér; wagwágen.
shall: *v.* –(n)to.
shallow: *adj.* abábaw, narabáw.
sham: *n.* tinultúlad.
shame: *n.* baín, pakaibabaínán; *v.* pabaínán.
shampoo: *n.* siampó, gulgól; *v.* agsiampó, aggulgól.
shank: *n.* gúrong; (*animals*) kúkod.
shanty: *n.* kalapáw.
shape: *n.* tábas; sukóg, áyos ti bagí; *v.* sukogén; tabásen.
share: *n.* bingláy, bíngay, bági; (*stock*) aksión; *v.* bumági, makibingláy, makibíngay.
shark: *n.* patíng, yo.
sharp: *adj.* natadém, natírad, nasarumámit, nalaw-ít; ~**shooter** *n.* táo a nalaíng a pumuntá.
sharpen: *v.* tiráden; patademén; isáit.
shatter: *v.* tumekén; mabúrak.
shave: *v.* kiskísan, agibárbas.
shaving: *n.* panagibárbas.
shawl: *n.* mantília.
she: *pron.* isú (a babái).
sheaf: *n.* sangarpét, bették.
shear: *v.* gettengén; pukísan.
shears: *n.* kartíb, getténg.
sheath: *n.* baína; (*of muscles*) kulápot; (*scabbard*) kalúban.
sheathe: *v.* ibaína.

shed: *n.* sápaw, kalapáw; ~ **off skin** *v.* aglúpos.

sheep: *n.* karnéro.

sheepish: *adj.* natakrót.

sheer: *adj.* aragaág, nasalagásag, nasaragásag.

sheet: *n.* sábanas; ~ **metal** *n.* ganáka.

shelf: *n.* estánte, banílag; sámang.

shell: *n.* (*sea*) bató; (*gun*) kartútso ti bála; **empty** ~ ampáw.

shellfish: *n.* batbató (ti baybáy).

shelter: *n.* pagkamángan, pagsalingdán; salipengpéng; *v.* linóngan; salakníban.

shelve: *v.* ikábilití estánte.

shepherd: *n.* pastór; *v.* ipaárab, ipastóran.

sherbet: *n.* sorbétes.

sheriff: *n.* pangúlo ti pulís; alguasíl.

shield: *n.* kalásag; *v.* saranáyen, ikanáwa.

shift: *v.* sukatán, balíwan, yális; *n.* panagsinnukát.

shimmer: *n.* kilápkiláp.

shin: *n.* baráwas, balláwas, gúrong; (*animals*) kúkod.

shine: *v.* aglawág, agraniág, agsilnág, lumayáp; sumammisammí, sumiléng, sumiláp.

shingle: *n.* karátula.

shiny: *adj.* nasiléng, nasiláp.

ship: *n.* sasakayán, barangáy; ~**worm** *n.* rúsot.

shirk: *v.* lumiklík.

shirt: *n.* kamísa, kamiséta; ~**less** *adj.* siuuksób; **sleeveless** ~ *n.* sandó, páwad.

shit: (*vulg.*) *n.* takkí; *v.* tumakkí.

shiver: *n.* pigergér, tigergér, tayegtég; *v.* agpigergér, agtigergér, agtayegtég.

shoal: *n.* baknád.

shoat: *n.* buriás; **striped** ~ *n.* dágaw; **small** ~ *n.* bukiéng.

shock: *n.* siddáaw.

shocking: *adj.* makláat; makapabuténg.

shoe: *n.* sapátos.

shoehorn: *n.* kalsadór.

shoemaker: *n.* sapatéro.

shoestring: *n.* kordón ti sapátos.

shoot: *n.* sagibsíb, tarúbang; subbuál; (*from seed*) túbo; **bamboo** ~ *n.* rabóng; ~**ing star** *n.* layáp; **sweet potato** ~ *n.* lantóng.

shop: *n.* tiénda, terséna; *v.* agtiénda, aggátang.

shoplifter: *n.* mannanákaw kadagití tagtagiláko.

shore: *n.* ígid ti baybáy; ~**line** *n.* kirbáy.

short: *adj.* ababá; (*people*) pandék; ~**-necked** *adj.* ringkék; ~**cut** *n.* ápat, buntáyak, salikbáy, sakláw; **take a** ~**cut** *v.* apáten.

shortage: *n.* kakurángan.

shorthand: *n.* takigrapía.

shorts: *n.* ababá a pantalón.

shot: *n.* tíro, pammaltúog.

should: *v.* rumbéng; kumá.

shoulder: *n.* abága; *v.* ibakláy; awitén; ~**blade** *n.* akloakló; **with round** ~**s** *adj.* agpayukó.

shout: *v.* agikkís, agláaw, agdir-í, agpukkáw; birraáwan; *n.* ikkís, láaw, pukkáw, dir-í.

shove: *v.* idurón, dirósen; *n.* durón.

shovel: *n.* suplád, pála; *v.* paláen.

show: *n.* pabúya; *v.* ipakíta, isúro, ipabúya, iparáng.

shower: *n.* arbís, arimukámok, kaykayábas; (*heavy*) tagiktík; *v.* (*rain*) agarbís; (*bath*) bumuyát.

showroom: *n.* siléd a pagpabuyáan.

showy: *adj.* naramók, naparammág.

shred: *n.* pirgís, gisgís.

shrew: *n.* sangió.

shrewd: *adj.* nasíkap, nasarírit, naliklík.

shriek: *v.* agikkís, umsiág, umágal.

shrill: *adj.* nasinggít, makasisíleng, killíit.

shrimp: *n.* pasáyan, padáw; **small** ~ *n.* aramáng.

shrine: *n.* altár, nasantuán a lugár.

shrink: *v.* umrés, kumríit; agaren-én, agkaretét.

shrinkage: *n.* karetkét.

shrivel: *v.* agkarenkén, agkaretkét; agkuríteg.

shroud: *n.* mortáha, kawés ti natáy.

shrub: *n.* bassít a múla.

shrug: *v.* agkiét, agkuyét.

shudder: *v.* agpigergér, agkintayég, agkuyegyég, agyegyég; agsiddúker.

shuffle: *v.* yakar-ákar.

shun: *v.* liklíkan, lisián, samíren.

shut: *v.* rikpán, serraán; ~ **mouth** *v.* yumén, agtangép.

shutter: *n.* persiána.

shuttle: *n.* bartília, kanília, gettáy.

shy: *adj.* managbabaín, managbututéng, naátap.

sibilant: *adj.* bumanesbés.

sibling: *n.* kabsát, kabágis; **older** ~ *n.* káka; **younger** ~ *n.* áding.

sick: *adj.* masakít; ~**en** *v.* agsakít; ~**ening** *adj.* makasúya; makagúra; ~**ness** *n.* sakít.

sickle: *n.* kumpáy.

sickly: *adj.* masaksakít, agmamayó, saksakídol; delikádo.

side: *n.* bángir; sikigán, bakráng; **on either** ~ agsumbángir; **on wrong** ~ abarngís.

sideburns: *n.* patília.

sidetrack: *v.* lisián.

sidewalk: *n.* bankéta, pagnaán ti kalsáda.

sideways: *adv.* impabakráng.

siege: *v.* sillongén, lawláwen.

siesta: *n.* siésta, ridép ti malém.
sieve: *n.* yakayák, gaságas; *v.* yakayakén, gasagásen, yokoyokén.
sift: *v.* isiísen, yakayakén.
sigh: *v.* agsainnék, agsennáay; *n.* sainnék.
sight: *n.* búya, sirmatá, panagkíta; *v.* kitáen.
sightseeing: *n.* panagpasiár nga agkitkíta.
sign: *n.* seniál, tandá, pakabigbígan; (*portent*) labég, eggéd.
signal: *n.* sénias, pagilasínan; *v.* seniásan.
signature: *n.* pírma.
significance: *n.* kaipapanán, bagás, kaimudingán.
signify: *v.* kayát a saóen.
silence: *n.* ulímek, talná; kinalínak.
silent: *adj.* naulímek.
silhouette: *n.* anniníwan, balabála ti anniníwan.
silk: *n.* séda; **~-cotton tree** *n.* kapasangláy.
sill: *n.* rídaw, dapián, talangkúb, paladpád.
silly: *adj.* nakáeg, máag, sulpéng.
silt: *n.* lan-ák, anáy; **limy ~** anggápang.
silver: *n.* pirák.
silversmith: *n.* platéro, mammandáy ti pirák.
silverware: *n.* kubiértos.
similar: *adj.* umaspíng, agapíring, pumáda.
simile: *n.* simíl, kapáda.
simmer: *v.* agkubbuár, agburék.
simple: *adj.* nalaká; ampapáok; **~minded** *adj.* nanengnéng.
simpleton: *n.* langgóng, ampáw, tungngáng.
simplicity: *adj.* kinalaká; kinanumó.
simplification: *n.* panangpalaká.
simplify: *n.* palakaén.
simply: *adv.* láeng.
simulate: *v.* tuláden; aginkukuná.
simultaneously: *adj.* naigiddán.
sin: *n.* labsíng, básol, bábak, biddút; *v* agbásol.
since: *prep.* manípud idí; *conj.* yantángay, ta.
sincere: *adj.* napasnék.
sincerity: *n.* kinapasnék.
sinew: *n.* pennét, piskél; urát; ánut.
sing: *v.* agkantá.
singe: *v.* siráman, isarabásab, idalabádab.
single: *adj.* sáway, maymáysa, bugbugtóng; **~ out** *v.* pilién; **~handed** *adj.* agmaymaysá, is-isú.
singular: *adj.* maymaysá; nakaskasdáaw
sinew: *n.* pennét.
sinister: *adj.* dákes, makatigíd, mangam-amés.
sink: *v.* lumnéd, malúnod; *n.* baniéra, pagdiram-ósan, pagbugguán.
sinker: *n.* (*fishing*) bulí.
sip: *v.* sisípen, simsíman; igúpen; *n.* ígup, sísip.

siphon: *n.* kulísip a nagsikkó; pagsúsup; *v.* susúpen.
sir: *n.* ápo.
siren: *n.* tanggúyob.
sirloin: *n.* lómo.
sissy: *n.* baién; luásit.
sister: *n.* kabsát a babái; (*nun*) mádre; **~-in-law** ípag.
sit: *v.* agtugáw, agsáad.
site: *n.* dissó, sáad, pagsaádan; **mountain ~** *n.* bangéd.
situation: *n.* kasasáad.
six: *adj.* inném; **~ o'clock** álas saís.
sixteen: *adj.* sangapúlo ket inném.
sixth: *adj.* maikaném; *n.* pagkaném.
sixty: *adj.* inném a púlo.
sizable: *adj.* nakadakdakkél.
size: *n.* kadakkél, rukód.
sizzle: *v.* agsaretsét, agsarebséb; *n.* saretsét.
skate: *n.* pági, ambalangá, lulumtóg, lapés; (*roller or ice*) patín.
skein: *n.* lábay, maréhas, madéha.
skeleton: *n.* sukóg; tultuláng; ruróg.
ski: *v.* agpaúyasití niébe; *n.* pagpaúyas ití niébe.
skid: *v.* agúyas; *n.* paúyas.
skill: *n.* pádas, kinasarírit, kinasarót, kinalaíng.
skim: *v.* agsáwen.
skin: *n.* kúdil; (*of frog, squid*) kulánit; *v.* latlátan, kulatlátan, kudísan, lupdísan, kulanítan.
skimp: *v.* agmetmét.
skinny: *adj.* nakuttóng, pairpáir.
skip: *v.* laktáwen, labsán, libtáwan, layawén, libnáwan.
skirt: *n.* sáya, pandilíng, káin.
skit: *n.* ababá a pabúya.
skulk: *v.* tumapidéng.
skull: *n.* bangabánga, ruróg, búkaw.
sky: *n.* lángit. **~light** *n.* lúmbre.
skyscraper: *n.* nangáto a pasdék.
slab: *n.* tapí; tablá; baldósa.
slack: *adj.* nakámul, nalukáy, natulók.
slacken: *v.* medmedán, ataátan, lettatén, loklókan, rekkasén, waywáyan; terdén.
slam: *v.* palbaágen, panalbaágen.
slander: *n.* pammadpadákes, pardáya; *v.* padpadaksén, pardayáen.
slanted: *adj.* ríwis, bangkíng; iring, imapdalágan, nakaíray.
slap: *v.* sipatén, tungpáen, arrabisén; *n.* tungpá, sipát.
slash: *v.* tagbáten; **~-and-burn agriculture** *n.* umá.
slaughter: *v.* partién; *n.* panagpatáy, panagpartí; **~house** *n.* pagpartián, matadéro.

slave: *n.* adípen, tagábu, bag-én.

slavery: *n.* pannakaadípen.

slay: *v.* patayén.

sled: *n.* pasagád, ulnás.

sledgehammer: *n.* bettád.

sleek: *adj.* nalamúyot.

sleep: *v.* matúrog; **~lessness** *n.* púyat; **~ on floor without mat** *v.* aglubtág; *n.* túrog.

sleeper: *n.* (*railroad*) trabesánio.

sleepy: *adj.* nabannóg, saguyepyepén.

sleeve: *n.* manggás; **~less shirt** *n.* sandó; **puffed up ~s** *n.* pasargá.

sleigh: *n.* ulnás, pasagád.

slender: *adj.* nakuttóng, narápis, nalápat, nauráor; kodapís.

sleuth: *n.* agsisiím.

slice: *v.* iwáen; *n.* íwa, gerrét; (*of fish*) reggés.

slick: *adj.* nasíkap.

slide: *v.* agkaglís, maigalís, agúyas, agkuyasyás; **~ down** *v.* agkaruskús, agpapaúyas.

slight: *adj.* bassít, nanumó; apagapáman.

slim: *adj.* narápis, nakuttóng.

slime: *n.* píla, kellá; lan-ák; (*of eels*) kellá.

sling: *n.* ambáyon, pallatíbong, alimbáyong; *v.* agpallatíbong.

slink: *v.* tumapidéng.

slip: *v.* maigalís, maikaglís; *n.* kamisón; kaglís.

slipper: *n.* tsinélas, sinklétas.

slippery: *adj.* nagalís.

slit: *n.* rengngát, birrí.

sliver: *n.* rúting, bislák.

slobber: *v.* agkátay.

slogan: *n.* pagsasaó.

slop: *v.* ibokbók, iparukpók.

slope: *n.* bangkírig, sálog, ansád, arisadsád.

sloppy: *adj.* nawará; saán a naannád.

slot: *n.* sáwang.

sloth: *n.* sadút.

slough: *n.* lubó, lutúlut; aluyúoy; (*of snakes*) lúpos.

sloven: *adj.* nadungrít, nadulpét.

slow: *adj.* nabuntóg; naánat; nadágas; **~ down** *v.* agbuntóg.

slug: *n.* salúsig, birábid; diladíla, kataykátay; *v.* sintóken.

sluggard: *adj.* patikawkáw, nabuntóg.

sluggish: *adj.* nakúdad; nabantót, nasayukmó, nadágas.

sluice: *n.* aribengbéng.

slumber: *v.* rumidép; *n.* ridép.

slump: *n.* pannakakapsút; *v.* agsuék, agpababá a sipapardás.

slush: *n.* pítak, lutúlut, lan-ák.

slut: *n.* pampám, púta, dákes a babái.

sly: *adj.* nasíkap, naulbód.

smack: *v.* agsakuntáp, agsanapsáp; tungpáen.

small: *adj.* bassít.

smallpox: *n.* burtóng.

smart: *adj.* nalaíng, nasaírit; nasíkap; nasarót.

smash: *v.* rumekén, rem-ekén; pekkaén; buóngen.

smear: *v.* piltákan, milatán, sapuán, pulagídan.

smegma: *n.* káper.

smell: *n.* ángot, saép, say-óp; *v.* angóten.

smile: *n.* ísem; *v.* umísem.

smirch: *n.* tuláw.

smith: *n.* mammandáy.

smoke: *n.* asúk, asúp; *v.* suóban; agasúk; **~ tobacco** agsigarílio.

smoker: *n.* mannabáko, managsigarílio.

smolder: *v.* agkuridemdém, agaripatayán.

smooth: *adj.* nalamúyot, naparánas; nasimpá, naapíras; (*and shiny*) namuyasán.

smudge: *v.* piltáken, rugitán, idaldál.

smuggle: *v.* ikulibáw, ipuslít.

smut: *n.* pilkát, rugít.

snack: *n.* merénda.

snail: *n.* bisukól; birurúkong; leddég; **freshwater ~** *n.* susó.

snake: *n.* úleg; beklát, karasaén.

snap: *v.* agketekketék, agliték; maspák; sakbában.

snapping beetle: *n.* kuddó, tangtang-éd.

snapshot: *n.* retráto.

snare: *n.* sílo, palab-óg; **~ drum** *n.* kahabíba.

snarl: *v.* agngerngér; agpampamrít.

snatch: *v.* rabsúten, agáwen, sibbarúten; tukmáan, sipdúten.

sneak: *v.* aglíbas, aglemméng; **~ away** tumapidéng.

sneer: *v.* bumiláw; aggúyab, agdílat.

sneeze: *v.* agbaén, agbang-és, agbaéng; *n.* baén.

snicker: *v.* agayek-ék; *n.* ayek-ék.

sniff: *v.* saepén, say-úpen, saninglóten; angóten; *n.* singlót, saninglót, say-úp.

sniffle: *v.* agsinglo-singlót.

snip: *v.* pingáwan, gettengén, putdén.

snipe: *n.* tuldó.

snivel: *v.* agbúteg.

snob: *n.* isnabéro, natangsít a táo.

snooze: *v.* rumidép; *n.* ridép.

snore: *v.* agurók; umagír.

snoring: *n.* panagurók.

snout: *n.* subsób, subbók, súbil; **push forward with the ~** *v.* isarubsób.

snow: *n.* niébe.

snub: *v.* tubngáren, babalawén, laísen, papaáyen; **~~nosed** *adj.* kisáp.

snuffle: *v.* agbáed, letletén.

snug: *adj.* nasimpá, nasalikepkép, naímeng.

snuggle: *v.* kumepkép.

so: *adv.* isú nga, kastá; ~ that *conj.* tapnó.

soak: *v.* sumagepsép, yúper, isellép, rusépen.

soaked: *adj.* narúsep, nabasá, dimmagimesmés.

soap: *n.* sabón, kutabáw; *v.* sabonán; ~ opera *n.* telenobéla.

soar: *v.* tumáyok, agalindáyag, agpangáto.

sob: *v.* agsaibbék, aganug-óg, ngumogngóg, agsang-í.

sober: *adj.* natimbéng, managparbéng, saán a nabarték; ~ up *v.* mamunáwen, mausáwan.

sobriety: *n.* parbéng.

sobriquet: *n.* birngás.

sociable: *adj.* mannakikaduá, mannakigayyém.

social: *adj.* naingayemán; mannakigayyém, nalánay.

socialize: *v.* makipulápol.

society: *n.* kagimóngan, timpúyog, panagtitípon.

sock: *n.* médias; *v.* danógen, sintóken.

socket: *n.* pakailusóngan, alintúbong; eye ~ *n.* sáad ti matá.

sod: *n.* karuótan.

sodomite: *n.* managúbet.

sofa: *n.* sopá, kanapé.

soft: *adj.* naluknéng; naalumaymáy, aalumámay; nauldóy.

soften: *v.* paluknengén, palamuyóten; lumuknéng, lumamúyot.

soggy: *adj.* nadam-ég, nabasá.

soil: *n.* dagá; *v.* rugitán, mulitán.

solace: *n.* liwliwá, gin-áwa.

solder: *v.* lanángen, aglánang.

soldier: *n.* búyot, soldádo.

sole: *n.* dapán, suélas; *adj.* maymaysá.

solemn: *adj.* nadaég, narangá, nasidungét.

solicit: *v.* dawáten, kiddawén; makirangkáp, agur-ór; patipáten.

solicitor: *n.* paradáwat; abogádo.

solid: *adj.* natangkén, natibkér, naimnét; nalagdá, nasikkíl, natakéd.

solidarity: *n.* pagmaymaysáan; pannakibunggóy.

solidify: *v.* tumangkén; pagkaykaysáen.

solitary: *adj.* agwaywáyas, agwáyas.

solitude: *n.* kinmaymáysa.

solo: *adj.* maymaysá.

soluble: *adj.* marúnaw.

solution: *n.* panangilawlawág, pakailawlawágan.

solve: *v.* lawlawagán; padlesán, padtuán.

solvent: *adj.* makabáyad, adda pagbáyadna.

somber: *adj.* nasipngét, naladíngit.

some: *adj.* daddúma, sangkabassít, sumagmamanó.

someone: *pron.* maysá a táo; ~ came Addá immáy; I saw ~ Adda nakítak.

somersault: *n.* balintuág.

something: *n.* maysá a bánag.

sometimes: *adv.* sagpaminsán, no daddúma, no maminsán.

somewhat: *adv.* médio, agar-arúp.

son: *n.* anák a laláki; ~-in-law *n.* manúgang.

song: *n.* kansión, kantá, dániw, dallót; love ~ (serenade) *n.* harána.

sonnet: *n.* sonéto, kíta ti dániw.

sonorous: *adj.* naúni.

soon: *adv.* ití mabiít, madarás.

soot: *n.* úging, úring, íro.

soothe: *v.* ep-epén, sugnuén, pagtalnáen.

soothsayer: *n.* mammadlés.

sop: *v.* idennét.

sophisticated: *adj.* nataknéng ken nasírib.

soprano: *n.* sopráno.

sorcerer: *n.* mangngaráding, mangkukúlam.

sorcery: *n.* kúlam, kinamangkukúlam, enkánto.

sordid: *adj.* naduldóg.

sore: *adj.* naut-ót, nasakít; *n.* lettég; nunóg; sugát; ~head *n.* batúngol; ~ eyes *n.* kamatá.

sorghum: *n.* bukákaw.

sorrel: *n.* alasán.

sorrow: *n.* ladíngit, lidáy, leddáang.

sorry: *adj.* nalidáy, naladíngit, lumdáang.

sort: *n.* kíta, kláse; *v.* urnósen, paglalasínen.

sot: *n.* mammarték.

soul: *n.* kararuá.

sound: *n.* úni, áweng; *adj.* nasalun-át; *v.* agúni.

soup: *n.* sópas.

sour: *adj.* naalsém; ~ness *n.* kinaalsém.

source: *n.* pungánay, puón.

soursop: *n.* bayubána, guyabáno.

south: *n.* abagátan; ~ern Cross *n.* súnay.

southeast: *n.* baetán, abagátan a dáya.

southern: *adj.* agpaabagátan; maipapán ití abagátan.

southpaw: *n.* appigód.

southwest: *n.* abagátan a láud.

souvenir: *n.* pakalaglagipán.

sovereign: *adj.* naturáy.

sovereignty: *n.* pagturayán.

sow: *n.* takóng; *v.* iwáris, iwarakíwak, ipurruák.

space: *n.* lugár, limbáng; pagbaetán.

spacious: *adj.* naláwa, nawayáng, bariwakwák, nalisdák.

spade: *n.* pála, espáda.

span: *n.* dángan; kaatiddóg; sangadpá; *v.* rukodén.

spangle: *n.* antikuélas.
Spaniard: *n.* Kastíla.
Spanish: *n.*, *adj.* Kastíla, Espaniól.
spank: *v.* sipatén (ti úbet), ampáken, arrabisén; *n.* sipát ití úbet.
spanking: *n.* sipát (iti úbet), arrabís.
spare: *v.* in-inúten, ilísi, ispálen.
spark: *n.* rissík, dalipáto, alipága, kiláp.
sparkle: *v.* agalipága, agrimatrimát, rumayráy, agrangráng.
sparkplug: *n.* buhía.
sparrow: *n.* salsallapíngaw, dúrog, billíttúleng.
spasm: *n.* kuyegyég, kayetkét; (*of chest*) turtób, turtóg.
spathe: *n.* butáyong.
spatter: *v.* piltapiltákan, parsiákan.
spawn: *n.* búgi; *v.* agbúgi.
speak: *v.* agsaó, agbitlá, agsaríta.
spear: *n.* gayáng, píka.
spearhead: *v.* umun-uná.
special: *adj.* naipangpangrúna, naisangsangayán.
specialist: *n.* espesialísta.
specialize: *v.* mangipangpangrúna.
species: *n.* kíta, sebbangán.
specific: *adj.* madutókan, naisangayán, matudingán.
specify: *v.* tudingán, inagánan.
specimen: *n.* pagkitáan, muéstra, wadán.
speck: *n.* pilták, mulít, mantsá.
speckle: *n.* turík, tudík.
speckled: *adj.* labáng, butikbutikán.
spectacle: *n.* pabúya.
spectacles: *n.* anteóhos, sarmíng.
specter: *n.* anniníwan.
speculate: *v.* panunóten, isípen, pattapattáen, balabaláen.
speech: *n.* bitlá.
speed: *n.* kapardás, kaparták; *v.* dagadágen, gadagáden.
spell: *n.* pannakakáyaw, enkánto; *v.* iletráan.
spellbound: *adj.* narangá.
spelling: *n.* panangilétra.
spend: *v.* gastuén, busbósen; ~ wisely *v.* emdúken.
spendthrift: *adj.* nabuslón, managgásto; nadamsák. barasúbos, barayúboy.
sperm: *n.* kissít, semília; espérma.
spew: *v.* ipagsó; agbakuár.
sphere: *n.* glóbo, nagbukél.
spice: *n.* rekádo, pangramán; *v.* rekaduán.
spider: *n.* lawwalawwá; ~ web *n.* kátay ti lawwalawwá, sáput; ~worts *n.* kulkullaási.
spike: *n.* dáwa; bustón.

spill: *v.* maibuyát, maitedtéd, maibelléng; maibuknáy.
spin: *v.* agtayyék; ~ cotton *v.* tibbién, manbí.
spinach: *n.* kalúnay, kuantóng.
spinal column: *n.* dúri.
spindle: *n.* takbián, burayóngan.
spine: *n.* dúri; (*fish*) siít.
spinning wheel: *n.* panibbián, ruédo; sound of ~ *n.* agretrét; spindle of ~ takbián; string of ~ *n.* allítan; wheel of ~ *n.* ullaulláw.
spinster: *n.* bayóg, balásang a bakét.
spiral: *v.* agkusíkos, agkawíkaw.
spirit: *n.* kararuá; pugót; evil ~ *n.* malígno, dákes nga al-aliá.
spirited: *adj.* nagarutigit, nagaratigít.
spirits: *n.* dagití kararuá; árak.
spit: *v.* ituprá; ipugsó; *n.* tuprá; (*for roasting*) túdok, durúdor.
spite: *v.* rabrabngísen, alimutngén; in ~ of *conj.* úray no, núpay.
spittoon: *n.* pagtupráan, eskupidór.
splash: *v.* parsiákan, passiáwan; agpassiáw.
spleen: *n.* páli, ballaibí.
splendid: *adj.* nadaég, nasayáat.
splendor: *n.* raniág, kinangayéd.
splint: *n.* sangét.
splinter: *n.* bislák, sangkáp, tikáp, pangreppét ti nabló.
split: *v.* pisién, ukápen, birrién; *adj.* nabúsak, maspíg, masíwak, napísi, naúkap.
spoil: *v.* samsámen; bumanglés.
spoke: *n.* ráyos; paragpág.
spokesperson: *n.* pannakangíwat.
sponge: *n.* espóngha.
sponger: *n.* patikawkáw.
sponsor: *n.* padríno, talgéd, makasaksí, manganák; *v.* manganák.
spontaneous: *adj.* maidagdágus; sub~ plant *n.* purítak.
spook: *n.* al-aliá, pugót, aningáas.
spool: *n.* pagpulipúlan; púdon; partuát.
spoon: *n.* sidók, kutsára, ídos.
sporadic: *adj.* sagpaminsán; agsarde-sardéng.
sport: *n.* ay-áyam.
spot: *n.* dissó; pilták; turík; (*stain*) mantsá; (*on skin*) pulpulákak; (*in eye*) bundáw; (*place*) dissó; beauty ~ *n.* salláp, síding.
spotted: *adj.* labáng, turikán.
spouse: *n.* asáwa.
spout: *n.* suyát; *v.* sumuyót, tumiráyok, rumisák.
sprain: *n.* piltáng, ligós, tirítir, bulló; ping-ól; *v.* mablés, mabló.
sprawl: *v.* agúyad, agdalupakpák.
spray: *v.* warsián, barasibísan; mapuyúpoy; ~ can *n.* láta a pagpasuyót, pagpugsít.

spread: *v.* agsaknáp, agwarnák; ukráden, iwáras.

spring: *n.* (*season*) primabéra, panagsusulbód; (*of water*) ubbóg; ~ **tide** *n.* apdáy, arabáab.

sprinkle: *v.* bisibísan; barasibísan; warsián, parsiákan, iwarakíwak; agsaprí; kugmelén; ~ **water on parched earth** *v.* dalepdepén.

sprinkler: *n.* pagwáris; (*water*) regadéra.

sprint: *v.* umsiák.

sprite: *n.* kaibaán.

sprout: *n.* rúsing, saríngit, subbuál; *v.* rumúsing, agtúbo.

spume: *n.* luág, labútab, tarabútab.

spur: *n.* espuélas, kawwét; ~ **pepper** *n.* síli.

spurt: *v.* agpusísit.

sputum: *n.* tuprá; turkák.

spy: *n.* tiktík, agsisiím; tiktíkan, aridamdáman.

squab: *n.* pitsón, kalapáti.

squabble: *v.* agápa, agríri.

squad, squadron: *n.* eskuádra, kuadrília.

squalid: *adj.* narugít.

squall: *n.* gunés, bagió.

squalor: *n.* kinapangláw, kinaay-ay-ay a kasasáad.

squander: *v.* agbuslón, agbarasúbos.

square: *n.* kuadrádo; (*plaza*) plása; pasági.

squash: *n.* karabása; tabúngaw; **young** ~ *n.* búsel; *v.* duydúyen, batbáten.

squat: *v.* agmasngáad, agmasángad, agdalupakpák.

squawk: *n.* ranitrít.

squeak: *v.* agit-ít, agranitrít.

squeal: *v.* agríri, agpudnó.

squeamish: *adj.* naímis, naalumíim, namikkí.

squeeze: *v.* pespesén, upíten, et-etán, lunekén.

squid: *n.* pusít, lakí.

squint: *v.* pumalúdip, kumusipét; **with a slight** ~ *adj.* gílab, dulíng.

squire: *n.* eskudéro.

squirm: *v.* aggulágol, agkilíkil; kumalaúsig, agwásangwásang.

squirrel: *n.* mútit.

squirt: *v.* sumpíten; rumisák, pumrés, agpugsít.

stab: *n.* bagkóng, duyók; *v.* agbagkóng, dumuyók.

stabilize: *v.* isimpá, pagtalnáen.

stable: *adj.* nasimpá; natalná; *n.* kabalyerísa.

stack: *n.* penpén, talaksán, túon; *v.* kapitén, ipenpén.

staff: *n.* sarukód; uróng.

stag: *n.* ugsá a laláki.

stage: *n.* entabládo; *v.* agipabúya.

stagger: *v.* agbaríring, agtiwedtiwéd, agdaríwis, agarituangán, agibar-íbar.

stain: *n.* mántsa; pilták; *v.* mansáan.

staircase: *n.* pagagdánan.

stairs: *n.* agdán; **landing of** ~ *n.* arusadúsan.

stake: *n.* pások, darekdék; (*bet*) pústa; **at** ~ *adj.* sipupústa, sitatayá.

stale: *adj.* báak, dáan.

stalk: *n.* ungkáy; garámi.

stall: *n.* puésto; *v.* pagsardengén.

stallion: *n.* manadór.

stalwart: *adj.* naturéd; napigsá.

stamen: *n.* múta.

stamina: *n.* pigsá, sikkíl.

stammer: *v.* agbedé, agannawír, agmútal; agmará, ageng-éng.

stamp: *n.* tímbre, sélio; *v.* ideppél, ibaddék; imaldít.

stand: *v.* agtakdér; *n.* bátay; pagtakderán.

standard: *n.* pagalagádan, pamwidán; rukód; pagwadán; (*flag*) wagaywáy.

standstill: *n.* itatalná.

stanza: *n.* estrópa.

staple: *n.* pikoléte; *adj.* kangrunáan.

star: *n.* bituén; ~**fish** *n.* bituén-baybáy, limalimá; ~ **anise** *n.* sangkít; **shooting** ~ *n.* layáp; **morning** ~ *n.* baggák, kamontatála, palpallátok.

starch: *n.* almidón, atóle.

stare: *v.* agmatmát; agmuttaléng, agmuttálat, mulagátan.

starry: *adj.* nabituén, arimbituén.

start: *v.* mangrugí, irugí; agrubbuát.

startle: *v.* kigtóten, bugtáken, buttuóren; agbaláw; agtibbáyo.

starve: *v.* pabisinán.

starving: *adj.* mabisinán, manguyapét.

state: *n.* estádo; kasasáad; *v.* isaó.

statement: *n.* saríta, ti insaó.

stateroom: *n.* kamaróte.

statesman: *n.* estadísta.

station: *n.* pagsaádan, pagyanán; estasión; *v.* idestíno.

statistics: *n.* estadístika.

statue: *n.* estátua, búlto.

stature: *n.* kinatáyag.

status: *n.* sáad, kasasáad.

statute: *n.* alagáden, annuróten, lintég.

statutory: *adj.* maipapán ití alagáden.

stay: *v.* agyán, agnaéd, agtaéng; ~ **up all night** *v.* agpúyat.

stead: *n.* yan; sáad.

steadfast: *adj.* natibkér.

steady: *adj.* nasimpá, sitatalinaéd; *v.* pagsimpáen.

steal: *v.* takáwen; tikásen; ~ **food** *v.* agkallóng.

steam: *n.* alibungúbong, alingásaw, alibúob; ~ **cooker** *n.* pagsasalapusópan; ~**roller** *n.* pisón; ~**ship** *n.* bapór.

steamer: *n.* pagsasalapusópan.
steed: *n.* kabálio.
steel: *n.* paslép; **~yard** *n.* gagantígan, kakatián.
steep: *adj.* napadsók, napasdók, nasang-át.
steeple: *n.* pagkampanáan; tórre ti simbáan.
steer: *v.* ituróng; *n.* báka a laláki.
steering wheel: *n.* maníbela.
stem: *n.* tanábug, ungkáy; puón; (*bananas*) búlig.
stench: *n.* buyók, ángot.
stenographer: *n.* takígrapo.
stenography: *n.* takigrapía.
step: *n.* addáng, paddák, tukád; (*of vehicle*) payátan; *v.* agbaddék, ageddáng.
stepchild: *n.* siúman.
stepparent: *n.* agsiúman.
stepsiblings: *n.* agkasiúman.
sterile: *adj.* (*clean*) nadalús; (*unable to bear children, said of women*) lúpes; (*men*) ibbúng; (*land*) parunápon, parunápor; (*plant*) lános.
sterling: *adj.* esterlína.
stern: *adj.* naínget.
stevedore: *n.* estebedór.
stew: *n.* inangér, estopádo; **~pan** *n.* kaseróla.
steward: *n.* mayordómo.
stick: *n.* sarukód, rúting, bislák; *v.* sumkét; itúdok, itugkík; ipíket.
sticky: *adj.* napigkét, napalét.
stiff: *adj.* nasikkíl; natangkén; **~en** *v.* pasikkilén.
stigma: *n.* tuláw, pílaw.
still: *adv.* pay láeng; *adj.* natalná; *n.* (*for liquors*) buntayán.
stilt: *n.* salingkadáng, kadangkadáng, pangammadáng.
stimulant: *n.* pangparugsó, paratignáy, makapagtignáy.
stimulate: *v.* dagdágen, pakirdén, parugsuén; pagipágan; abúyan.
sting: *n.* sílud, dagumdágum; *v.* silúden.
stingray: *n.* pági.
stingy: *adj.* naímut, nakirmét, napaídam, nametmét, naámeng.
stink: *v.* agángot, agbuyók; **~bug** *n.* dángaw, nángo.
stipend: *n.* báyad; tangdán.
stipulate: *v.* itúlag, sagudáyen.
stir: *v.* kiwáren, batirén; tignáyen; kiwkíwan.
stirrup: *n.* estríbo, babaddekán.
stitch: *n.* dáit, saráit; *v.* saípen, dalubdúben.
stock: *n.* penpén; kapuonán; kaputótan; aksión; **~holder** *n.* aksionísta.
stockade: *n.* bákud.
stocking: *n.* médias.
stocky: *adj.* napunér; natibkér.

stomach: *n.* tián; bitúka; **pit of ~** *n.* rúsok.
stone: *n.* bató; batuén, ubóran.
stool: *n.* tugáw; (*feces*) ibléng; **small piece of ~** *n.* pultít, pur-ís.
stoop: *v.* agrúkob, agruknóy, agbalikuskós, kumáog.
stop: *v.* agsardéng, agsardáy; (*along the way while passing*) dumagás, dumaw-ás; *n.* sardéng.
stoppage: *n.* lappéd, panangpasardéng.
stopper: *n.* sullát, pullát.
storage: *n.* pannakaidúlin.
store: *n.* tiénda, almasén, paglakuán; *v.* agidúlin, agipenpén.
storehouse: *n.* bodéga, pagpenpenán.
storekeeper: *n.* tindéro.
storeroom: *n.* pagipenpenán.
stork: *n.* kannáway.
storm: *n.* bagió; *v.* agbagió; **~y** *adj.* nabagió.
story: *n.* saríta.
stout: *adj.* nalukmég, nabaskég, atimpék.
stove: *n.* pugón, dalikán.
stow: *v.* idúlin.
straddle: *v.* agkayáng, agakkáng, agaskáw.
straight: *adj.* natarús, nalintég.
straightaway: *adv.* dágus.
straightforward: *adj.* nalaká a maawátan.
strain: *v.* sagáten, sulnóten.
strainer: *n.* sagátan, pagbarútan.
strand: *n.* baraán, nginabrás; *v.* maisanglád, maisadsád, maisáyad.
strange: *adj.* nakaskasdáaw, datdalág, gangannaét, dildilláw.
stranger: *n.* gangannaét.
strangle: *v.* bekkelén, lemmesén.
strap: *n.* bedbéd, patápat; baríkes; surión; **chin ~** paratímid; (*for post*) brása.
strategy: *n.* síkap, úyam, estratéhia.
straw: *n.* garámi, arutáng, lugangián; (*drinking*) kulísip.
strawberry: *n.* présas.
stray: *adj.* wálang, naisiási; *v.* agallaallá; sumiási.
streak: *n.* gárit, urít; *v.* garítan.
stream: *n.* wáig, karayán.
streamer: *n.* banderília; wagaywáy.
street: *n.* dálan, kalsáda, lansángan; **~car** *n.* trambía.
strength: *n.* pigsá, bilég; (*durability*) lagdá.
stress: *v.* papigsáen.
stressed: *adj.* (*words*) nabáyat.
stretch: *v.* bennatén, bistráden; (*nets*) itagdáy.
stretcher: *n.* tarimbán, dagidági, dúyan.
strew: *v.* idukínar, iwáris, iwarakíwak.
strickle: *n.* kálus.

strict: *v.* naingét, nairút; natimbéng.

stride: *n.* addáng, akkáw; *v.* agakkáw, agaddáng; **water ~r** *n.* al-alukáp, kotokóto, kóto ti danúm.

strife: *n.* panaglában, ríri.

strike: *v.* pang-óren, kabílen, sulóngen; *n.* wélga; **go on ~** *v.* agwélga; **~breaker** (*scab*) *n.* eskiról.

striking: *adj.* makapasdáaw.

string: *n.* talí; kuérdas, singdán; lúbid, línas.

stringent: *adj.* naingét.

strip: *n.* gislá; (*of dried meat*) bánor; (*of wood*) rúting; *v.* aglábus; ukisán.

stripe: *n.* ráya, gárit, gúlis; *v.* gulísan, garítan.

strive: *v.* reggetán, gagetán, agbabatára; rupíren, dupíren.

stroke: *n.* kábil, disnóg; káwad; *v.* aprúsan.

stroll: *v.* agpasiár, agpagnápagná; *n.* pasiár.

strong: *adj.* napigsá, nabíleg; natibkér; nalagdá.

structure: *n.* balabála; bángon, patakdér.

struggle: *n.* panagsagába, panagpigsá; salísal; *v.* agsagába; (*to squirm*) aggulágol.

strum: *v.* kutengtengén.

strumpet: *n.* balangkantís.

strut: *v. v.* agsíkad, tumangár.

stub: *n.* pungól, ungél; **~ book** *n.* resibário.

stubble: *n.* palungpóng, nagpatpátan; dasdás; (*of plants*) pungét.

stubborn: *adj.* nasúbeg, nasúkir, nasúngit; napínget.

stubby: *adj.* purkéd.

stud: *n.* manadór.

student: *n.* estudiánte, agad-ádal.

studio: *n.* estúdio.

studious: *adj.* managádal.

study: *v.* agádal.

stuff: *n.* bambánag; *v.* seksekán, pusekén; selselán, gaburán.

stuffed: *adj.* estopádo; naselsél, naseksék, napekpék.

stuffing: *n.* panangseksék, panangpunnó.

stumble: *v.* agtibkól, maisugkít, maisippádong; dalapúsen.

stump: *n.* pungdól, ungél, pungpóng.

stun: *v.* sisiléngen; kelgáen.

stunning: *adj.* makatiténg.

stunted: *adj.* (*growth*) nakudídit.

stupefy: *v.* pagsiddáawen.

stupendous: *adj.* nakaskasdáaw.

stupid: *adj.* tabbéd, namúno, natuggaréng, nakúneng, nakúdag; tórpe, dagmél, betbét, nasalangá, namúneng, musmós, nasaliwawá, nanengnéng.

stupor: *n.* kinaawán ti rikná.

sturdy: *adj.* nalagdá; natibkér, natakéd.

stutter: *v.* agbedé, agngádal, agmútal, agannawír, ageng-éng, agmará.

sty: *n.* búnga ti matá.

style: *n.* móda, pamay-án, estílo, wagás; (*of pistol*) búto.

stylish: *adj.* demóda, napayús.

suave: *adj.* nasadiá, naalumámay, nasungdó, nataknéng.

subconscious: *n.* kaunggán ti ísip.

subdivision: *n.* pasét, símang.

subdue: *v.* parmekén; parángen, ep-epén; latgén, parukmáen.

subject: *n.* pamwidán, bánag; iturayán; suhéto.

subjugate: *v.* parmekén, parukmáen, pasiáen.

sublime: *adj.* natan-ók; narimbáw.

submarine: *n.* submaríno.

submerge: *v.* irebréb, irárem, ipabátok, lipúsen, irennéb.

submerse: *v.* lipúsen, irárem.

submission: *n.* panagsúko, panagparukmá.

submissive: *adj.* natulnóg, natudió, naannúgot.

submit: *v.* itulók, idatág, ipasinúnod; sumúko.

subordinate: *adj.* nababbabá.

subscribe: *v.* agsuskribír; umanámong.

subscription: *n.* suskrisión.

subsequent: *adj.* sumarunó, kasiddongán.

subservient: *adj.* agserserbí.

subside: *v.* umbáas, agtalná, agebbát.

subsidiary: *adj.* tumultúlong; naisilpó; *n.* katulóngan.

subsidize: *v.* tulóngen babaén ti kuartá.

subsidy: *n.* naitéd a kuartá a túlong.

subsistence: *n.* pagbiágen, mangbiág.

substance: *n.* bagás, ánag; sustánsia; kayamánan.

substantial: *adj.* nabagás; naramán.

substantiate: *v.* paneknekán, patalgedán.

substitute: *n.* sandí, sukát; *v.* sandián.

subterranean: *adj.* ití unég ti dagá.

subtle: *adj.* nasíkap; naliklík; nasaldét.

subtract: *v.* kissayén, ikkatán.

suburb: *n.* arrabál, subúrbio, bárrio, kabangíbang.

succeed: *v.* agballígi, agrang-áy; magun-ódan.

success: *n.* rang-áy, ballígi, talibágok, pannakagun-ód.

successful: *adj.* nagúsat, gubbuáyan, naimballigián; narang-áy.

successive: *adj.* agsasarunó.

successor: *n.* sumarunó; sumukát.

succor: *v.* tulóngan, badángan, saranáyen.

succulent: *adj.* natubbóg.
succumb: *v.* paábak; sumúko.
such: *adj.* kastá, kasdiáy, kastóy, kastáy, kasdí.
suck: *v.* susúpen, kunotén, sultúpen, sepsepán; agnotnót; ~ **up nasal mucus** *v.* bumaningrót, agsinglót.
suckle: *v.* pasusuén, tagibién.
suction: *n.* panagnotnót, panagsúsop.
sudden: *adj.* kelláat, apagdarikmát, pagam-ammuán, alibadbád, napettát.
suddenly: *adv.* pagam-ammuán, apagdarikmát, sidadarás, dágus.
suds: *n.* labútab ti sabón.
sue: *v.* idarúm, yukóm; sumakláng.
suede: *n.* gamúsa.
suffer: *v.* agsagába, aglak-ám, agtúok; sumánot; ~ **from** *v.* rigáten.
suffering: *n.* panagsagába, panagtúok; dagém, dagensén.
suffice: *v.* umdás, umanáy; makaámit.
sufficient: *adj.* umanáy, umdás, makaanáy.
suffix: *n.* suldóng, náyon.
suffocate: *v.* lemmesén, depdepén, tangepén, lungnguópen.
suffrage: *n.* kalintegán nga agbótos.
suffuse: *v.* digúsen.
sugar: *n.* asúkar, tagapulót; **brown** ~ *n.* burisangsáng; (*caramelized*) patároy; ~ **mill** *n.* dadapílan; **shaft of** ~ **mill** *n.* tangbáw.
sugarcane: *n.* unás; ~ **stalk** *n.* sebbák; **chew** ~ *v.* mang-ús; **peel** ~ *v.* kulítan; ~ **wine** *n.* bási; **harvest** ~ *v.* agtubbó.
suggest: *v.* igunamgúnam, ipaltíing; isingásing, idagádag; agparikná.
suicide: *n.* panagpapátay, panagpakamatáy; **commit** ~ *v.* agpapátay, agpakamatáy, patayén ti bagína; **commit** ~ **by hanging** *v.* agbekkél.
suit: *n.* dáwat, darúm; kawés, pagan-anáy; térno; *v.* bagáyan, tutopán; umarngí; mayarkéd.
suitable: *adj.* maibágay, maitutóp, maiparbéng, umisú.
suitcase: *n.* maléta.
suitor: *n.* agar-árem, agdawdáwat (iti babái).
sulfur: *n.* asúpre.
sulk: *v.* agpasugnód, agsidungét.
sullen: *adj.* nasidungét, makaluksáw.
sultry: *adj.* nadagáang, napúdot, sumaray-ób.
sum: *n.* dágup, pokpók.
summarize: *v.* dagdagúpen.
summary: *n.* pakapukpúkan.
summer: *n.* kalgáw, darádar.
summerhouse: *n.* gloriéta.
summit: *n.* pantók, tuktók, aringgawís, tápaw.

summon: *v.* ayabán; sonsónen, gamalén.
sumptuous: *adj.* nangayéd, nadaég; (*gaudy*) naramók.
sun: *n.* ínit; *v.* ibílag; **turn toward the** ~ *v.* isaráng.
sunbeam: *n.* lawág ti ínit.
Sunday: *n.* Domínggo.
sundown: *n.* ilelennék ti ínit.
sundry: *adj.* nadumadúma.
sunflower: *n.* mirasól.
sunken: *adj.* nalméd, nalinednéd; (*eyes*) lumiskéb; (*lips*) narungbéd, ngubngób.
sunny: *adj.* naínit.
sunrise: *n.* ileleggák (ti ínit).
sunset: *n.* lumnék diáy ínit, ilelennék; suripét.
sunshine: *n.* ínar, lawág ti ínit.
sup: *v.* mangrabíí.
superb: *adj.* nadaég, naindaklán.
supercilious: *adj.* napalálo; nakuspág.
superficial: *adj.* agpaparáng, narabáw.
superfluous: *adj.* agsubrá, nasurók, nalabés.
superimpose: *v.* itúon, isagpáw, irasúon.
superintendent: *n.* dispenséro, agindáng.
superior: *adj.* nangatngátom, naisangayán; *n.* pangúlo, palúngo.
superiority: *n.* sagúday, talugáding.
superlative: *n.* kasayaatán.
supernatural: *adj.* datdatlág; namilagruán; ~ **event** *n.* marmarná.
superstition: *n.* kaniáw; aníto.
superstitious: *v.* **be** ~ *v.* aganíto.
supervene: *v.* dumarán.
supervise: *v.* imatonán.
supervision: *n.* panangimatón.
supervisor: *n.* mangimatón, agindág, agindáng, agindég.
supine: *adj.* nakadáta.
supper: *n.* pangrabíí, pangmalém.
supplant: *v.* sumallín.
supple: *adj.* nalappiót; nalamí; nalupóy.
supplement: *n.* anáy, náyon; taraúdi.
supplicate: *v.* ikarárag, ipakaási; umaráraw.
supply: *v.* ipaáy, ikkán.
support: *v.* suráyen, saranáyen, tapayáen; taraonán; saluádan; (*a family*) isákad; *n.* panagsaránay; (*financial*) susténto.
supporter: *n.* katalék, pasúrot.
suppose: *v.* ipagarúp, pamayán, ipapán, ipáto.
supposing: *conj.* no kas pagarígan.
supposition: *n.* panangipagarúp.
suppress: *v.* lapdán, depdepén, parmekén.
supreme: *adj.* kadaklán, kangatuán.
sure: *adj.* sigurádo, natalgéd; manamnáma.
surely: *adv.* awán duaduá.
surf: *n.* katakdángan.
surface: *n.* rabáw.

surge: *v.* ngumáto (a kas dallúyon).
surgeon: *n.* siruháno.
surgery: *n.* siruhía, panagoperár.
surgical thread: *n.* sutúra.
surmise: *v.* ipagarúp, atápen, batabáten.
surmount: *v.* agballígi; dumténg ití toktók.
surname: *n.* apelyído, galád.
surpass: *v.* atíwen, saliw-ánan, sagudáyan; gumimpáw; rimbáwan.
surplice: *n.* sobrepelyís.
surplus: *n.* sóbra, surók, pakatdá.
surprise: *v.* kigtóten, labegén; mangkelláat; ~d *adj.* makláat, masdáaw.
surprising: *adj.* nakaskasdáaw.
surrender: *v.* tumulók, sumúko, rumukmá; *n.* panagsúko.
surreptitious: *adj.* nalímed.
surround: *v.* lawláwen, lakubén, likmúten; ~ings *n.* ti aglawláw.
suspect: *v.* atápen, ipagarúp; tanggáden.
suspend: *v.* atipaén, tubngén, itukéng, ibítin; (*discontinue*) liwátan.
suspense: *n.* panagsardéng; aligagét.
suspension: *n.* pannakapasardéng.
suspicious: *adj.* managátap, naílem, nakaiílem.
sustain: *v.* sarapaén, saranáyen; sarikenkedán.
sustenance: *n.* sosténto, taraón; pagbiág; saránay.
suture: *n.* panagdáit.
swaddle: *v.* lampínan.
swage: *n.* subókan, sunsíki.
swaggering: *adj.* nakáeg, natanawtáw.
swallow: *v.* alimónen, tilmónen; *n.* tilmón, sallapíngaw.
swamp: *n.* álog, aluyuóy; alugúog; sagnéb.
swan: *n.* kannáway.
swap: *v.* agsinnukát; *n.* sukát.
swarm: *n.* pangén, ariwekwék; *v.* agbangabánga, lumotolotó, agaribungbóong.
swarthy: *adj.* napugót, kayumanggí; nangísit.
swat: *v.* pang-óren, danógen.
sway: *v.* agpalláyog, agbattuabattuág; aglikíg, agpallatík, agtallayútay.
swear: *v.* agtabbaáw; agsapatá.
sweat: *n.* ling-ét; *v.* agling-ét; ~ profusely *v.* aglimdúos.
Sweden: *n.* Suésia.
Swedish: *n.*, *adj.* Suéko, tagá-Suésia.
sweep: *v.* sagáden, kaykáyen.
sweet: *adj.* nasam-ít; *n.* kankanén, dúlse; ~bread *n.* páli, dális; ~ potato *n.* kamóte, kamótig; ~sop *n.* átis; ~-toothed *adj.* natukréb.
sweeten: *v.* pasam-íten.
sweetheart: *n.* kaayan-ayát, kaingúngot.

swell: *v.* lumtég, bumsóg, umbál.
sweltering: *adj.* nadagáang.
swerve: *v.* agsikkó, agkilló; agsiási; maipálig; kumbásiw.
swidden: *n.* umá.
swift: *adj.* nadarás, napardás; naapgés.
swiller: *n.* sarangúsong.
swim: *n.* langóy; *v.* aglangóy; (*backstroke*) agtagintúdo.
swindle: *v.* suitíken, tikásen, imbiduén.
swine: *n.* báboy; ~ plague *n.* pangók.
swing: *v.* agpalláyog, agindáyon; *n.* indáyon; galonggálong.
swingletree: *n.* saudán.
swirl: *n.* alikunó, alinúno, wallagés; *v.* agwallagés, iwallagés, agalikunó.
switch: *v.* sukatán, ikalilís; yallátiw; saplíten; *n.* (*of snares*) baór.
swivel: *v.* agpusípus.
swollen: *adj.* lumtég, bumsóg; umbál; (*eyes*) ballúkot; (*breasts*) báray; (*testicles*) alimbubungáw.
swoon: *v.* agkápoy, agtalimúdaw; *n.* talimúdaw.
swoop: *v.* seppegén, sippayóten; sumpég.
sword: *n.* espáda, kampilán, badáng.
swordfish: *n.* layálay.
sworn: *adj.* nasapatá.
sycophant: *n.* sipsíp, manangaliúg, napay-ók.
syllable: *n.* sílaba.
symbol: *n.* tandá, kayarígan.
sympathize: *v.* makipagrikná, sumdáal; makipagluá.
sympathy: *n.* pannakipagrikná.
symptom: *n.* síntoma, pakadlawán.
synagogue: *n.* sinagóga.
syndicate: *n.* sindikáto.
synopsis: *n.* pakapukpúkan.
syntax: *n.* gramátika; panangurnós.
syphilis: *n.* butól.
syringe: *n.* sumpít, heringília; (*for enema*) panglabatíba.
syrup: *n.* harábe, arníbar.
system: *n.* sistéma, urnós, pamay-án.
systematize: *v.* pagaasmángen, urnósen.

T

table: *n.* lamisáan, dúlang; set the ~ *v.* agipuní.
tablecloth: *n.* mantél, abbóng ti lamisáan.
tablespoon: *n.* kutsára, sídok.
tablet: *n.* tabléta, pastílias, tápi.
taboo: *n.* pawílan, naipárit a bánag; *adj.* maipárit.
taciturn: *adj.* naulímek.

tack: *v.* agalikunnóg.
tackle: *n.* láwin, liwlíw, padokdók.
tact: *n.* síkap, sarírit.
tactics: *n.* pamuspúsan, síkap.
tadpole: *n.* bayyék, kiddokiddó; **two-legged ~** *n.* bannasák.
taffy: *n.* balikótsa.
tag: *n.* etikéta.
tail: *n.* ípus; **~less** *adj.* pugód.
tailor: *n.* mannáit; **~ bird** *n.* sawsaw-ít, mangatúday.
taint: *v.* mulitán, rugitán.
tainted: *adj.* namulitán; naan-anó; nadúted, nalaés.
take: *v.* aláen, awáten; **~ off** *n.* panagpangáto.
tale: *n.* paspásaw, sarsaríta; kuénto.
talent: *n.* talénto, talugáding, kinasírib, sagúday.
talisman: *n.* ánib, mutiá, anting-antíng.
talk: *v.* agsaó, agsaríta, agtagarí.
talkative: *adj.* nangíwat, saosaó, natarabítab, mannanaó.
tall: *adj.* natáyag; nangáto.
tally: *v.* tarkásan, rupísan, padáan.
talon: *n.* kabbéng, karámut.
tamarind: *n.* salamági; **overripe ~** *n.* kalangákang; **ripe ~** *n.* marsabá.
tambourine: *n.* panderéta.
tame: *adj.* naámo; *v.* palukmáen.
tamper: *v.* agkuditkudít, agkalbikalbít.
tan: *n.* kurtién; palabagáen; tumingrá; *adj.* abeliána.
tang: *n.* ramán.
tangible: *adj.* nabatád, maar-aríkap.
tangle: *v.* kulkúlen, kusokusuén; (*vines*) agkemmét, agkayyammét.
tank: *n.* tángke.
tantalize: *v.* ar-arákan, gargarién.
tantrum: *n.* panagalipungét.
tap: *v.* kalbíten, kutukótan, tiktíkan.
tape: *n.* síntas, bedbéd; patápat; píket; **~ measure** *n.* rukód, medída; **~ grass** *n.* ballaibá.
taper: *v.* agúngos; agkimós, agimmús.
tapestry: *n.* kolgadúra, dalingdíng.
tapeworm: *n.* apat-ápat, kuyamkúyam.
tar: *n.* briá, alkitrán; *v.* biriáan.
tarantula: *n.* kamató.
tardy: *adj.* naládaw.
target: *n.* punteriáan, gíno; **~ practice** *n.* punta-blángko.
tariff: *n.* narípa; aransél.
tarnish: *v.* agkusapó, umuspák, agpaspás, malunés, makdém.
taro: *n.* ába; **~ stalk** leppák.
tarot reader: *n.* agipadpadtó babaén ti baráha.

tarry: *v.* agtakták, agbayág; maipílot.
tart: *adj.* naalsém; makaaprád.
tartar: *n.* (*of teeth*) dikkí; **cream of ~** *n.* tártaro.
task: *n.* arámid, trabáho, akém.
tassel: *n.* bórias, buybóy, garaygáy.
taste: *n.* nánam, ramán; *v.* ramanán, parmanán; (*liquids*) simsíman, timtíman; **bad ~** *n.* ádat.
tasteful: *adj.* naramán, naímas.
tasteless: *adj.* natamnáy, nalab-áy, naluptá.
tasty: *adj.* naímas, nanánam.
tat: *v.* agayúbo.
tattered: *adj.* rutayrútay, rigisrígis; rutrót.
tattle: *v.* agtarabítab; agpúlong.
tattoo: *n.* tatú, baték.
taunt: *v.* laísen; uyawén.
tavern: *n.* pagsukmónan ti árak.
tawdry: *adj.* naparammág.
tax: *n.* buís; *v.* pagbuísen.
tea: *n.* tsá, itsá.
teach: *v.* isúro; bagbagaán.
teacher: *n.* maéstro, mannúro.
team: *n.* timpúyog, sangkakuyógan, bunggóy; *v.* umariwekwék **~ up** *v.* agbubunggóy; **~work** *n.* panagkakaduá nga arámid.
tear: *n.* (*of eye*) luá; (*cloth*) bissáng; *v.* pigísen, pisángen, ray-ában.
tease: *v.* suronén, sutilén, angawén.
teaspoon: *n.* kutsaríta.
teat: *n.* múngay, ammútil; **small additional ~ of animals** *n.* surná.
technician: *n.* tékniko.
technique: *n.* wágas, pamay-án.
tedious: *adj.* makaúma, makautóy.
teeth: *n.* ngipngípen; **tingling pain in ~** *n.* alíno; **with coupled ~** *adj.* rukapí; **brush the ~** *v.* agsugígi, agsipílio, aggisígis.
teethe: *v.* agngípen.
telecast: *v.* ipakíta ití telebisión.
telegram: *n.* telegráma; *v.* agtelegráma.
telegraph: *n.* telégrapo; *v.* agtelégrapo.
telephone: *n.* pagayabán, telépono; *v.* agayáb, umáwag, agtelépono, teleponuán.
telescope: *n.* largabísta, teleskópio.
television: *n.* telebisión.
tell: *v.* ibagá, isaó.
telltale: *adj.* nalabíd, nataribítab.
temper: *v.* (*blades*) tennebén; (*water*) tibnókan, tignópan.
temperament: *n.* rikná, pakinákem, ugáli.
temperance: *n.* panagparbéng; panagtíped.
temperate: *adj.* natimbéng, kalalaingánna.
temperature: *n.* temperatúra, kapúdot.
tempest: *n.* bagió.

tempestuous: *adj.* nabagió.
temple: *n.* témplo, simbáan, pagkararágan, paglualuán; (*of head*) pispís.
tempo: *n.* kumpás, tignáy, garáw.
temporary: *adj.* saán nga agnáyon.
tempt: *v.* sulisógen, gargarién; sairuén; ~ation *n.* sulísog.
ten: *adj.* sangapúlo; pulló.
tenacious: *adj.* napásig, napingét; nasupnét; aggalasúgas.
tenant: *n.* agup-úpa.
tend: *v.* tarawidwídan, imatonán.
tendency: *n.* gagángay, pagduyúsan.
tender: *adj.* naluknéng; naganús; managayát; (*meat*) nalumóy.
tendon: *n.* pennét; (*of foot*) ramramót; **Achilles'** ~ bebessangán.
tendril: *n.* kalawíkaw, kuriwáwet, gámat, kaméng, pakalatkát.
Tenebrae: *n.* tiniéblas.
tenet: *n.* doktrína, patpatién.
tennis: *n.* ténis.
tense: *adj.* nasikkíl; nairténg, nabennát.
tension: *n.* pannakabennát; irténg.
tent: *n.* tólda, lingáling.
tentacle: *n.* gámat.
tentative: *adj.* pangpadásan.
tenth: *adj.* maikasangapúlo; *n.* pagkapulló.
tenure: *n.* panagakém.
tepid: *adj.* apag-anem-ém, nabaáw.
term: *n.* beddéng (ti panawén); patinggá; pagsasaó, saó.
terminal: *n.* pungtó, murdóng.
terminate: *v.* ipatinggá, gibúsan; maturpós.
termite: *n.* ánay.
terrace: *n.* terása.
terrapin: *n.* pag-óng, bindóg.
terrestrial: *adj.* naindagaán, taga-dagá.
terrible: *adj.* madí; nakabutbuténg, nakaap-apráng, nakaal-aliáw.
terrify: *v.* butbutngén.
territory: *n.* território, dagá a masakúpan, kasakúpan.
terror: *n.* aligagét, aligágaw.
terrorism: *n.* panangbutbuténg.
terrorist: *n.* managbutbuténg, terorísta.
terrorize: *v.* butbutngén.
test: *n.* pádas, súot; eksámen; pangsúbok; *v.* suóten.
testament: *n.* túlag, testaménto.
testicle: *n.* bukelbukél, ukel-ukél; láteg; **animal with one** ~ *n.* amitáw; **with swollen** ~s *adj.* ambungáw.
testify: *v.* saksián.
testimony: *n.* pammaneknék, saksí.
tetanus: *n.* tétano, kurarét.

tether: *v.* iparngéd, ngedngedán; *n.* waywáy.
tetter: *n.* kúrad, labaít; kapúyo; kamúro.
textile: *n.* abél.
texture: *n.* linábag.
than: *conj.* ngem.
thank: *v.* agyáman, ag-Diós ti agngína; **Thank you.** Agyámanak, Diós ti agngína
thankful: *adj.* siyayáman.
that: *adj.* daytá, daydiáy, daytáy, daydí; **so** ~ *conj.* tapnó.
thatch: *n.* sápaw, bubóng, sukdíp, pasursór, agsít, bádok.
thaw: *v.* agrúnaw.
the: *n.* ti, dagití, diáy.
theater: *n.* pagipabuyáan, teátro.
theft: *n.* pannakatákaw, tíkas.
their: *adj.* -da.
theirs: *pron.* kukuáda, bágida.
them: *pron.* idá, kaniáda, kadakuáda.
theme: *n.* téma.
then: *conj.* ngarúd; no kastá; *adv.* sa; idí kuán.
theology: *n.* teolohía.
theory: *n.* teoría, pamanunótan.
there: *adv.* idiáy, sadiáy, ditá.
thereafter: *adv.* manípud idí.
thereby: *adv.* gapú ití daytá.
therefore: *adv.* ití kastá; ngarúd.
thermometer: *n.* termómetro, pangrukód ti púdot.
these: *pron.* dagitóy.
thesis: *n.* tésis.
they: *pron.* isúda.
thick: *adj.* napuskól; nabengbéng; nasedséd; (*liquids*) napalét; ~ness *n.* kinapuskól; kinapalét.
thicken: *v.* pumuskól; papuskólen; pumalét.
thicket: *n.* kasamekán, karikriketán, gingét, rekrék.
thief: *n.* tulisán, mannanákaw, birkóg.
thievery: *n.* panagtákaw.
thigh: *n.* luppó; (*of animals*) lápi; ~bone *n.* baráwas, alluás.
thill: *n.* (*of cart*) pallawíwan.
thimble: *n.* dedál.
thin: *adj.* (*objects*) naingpís; (*people*) nakuttóng, kuttapír, nalápat; (*scarce*) narásay; (*liquids*) nadarúy.
thing: *n.* bánag, kuá; parsuá.
think: *v.* agpanúnot; pagarupén; ipáto; **I** ~ -(n)sa; kunák.
third: *adj.* maikatló; *n.* pagkatló.
thirst: *n.* waw.
thirsty: *adj.* maawáw, mawáw.
thirteen: *adj.* sangapúlo ket talló.
thirteenth: *adj.* maikasangapúlo ket talló.

thirtieth: *adj.* maikatallopúlo; *n.* pagkatallopúlo.

thirty: *adj.* tallopúlo.

this: *adj.*, *pron.* daytóy, toy; **like** ~ kastóy.

thorn: *n.* siít, púris; ~**y** *adj.* nasiít.

thorough: *adj.* natalipúpos; mangnibnibí.

those: *adj.*, *pron.* dagitá, dagidiáy.

thou: *pron.* siká, -ka.

though: *conj.* úray, núpay.

thought: *n.* panúnot, ísip, pakinákem; I ~ **that** … Kunák no …

thoughtful: *adj.* managpanúnot, mananglagíp.

thousand: *adj.* ríbo; **one** ~ sangaríbo; **ten** ~ sangalaksá.

thousandth: *adj.* maikasangaríbo; *n.* pagkasangaríbo.

thrall: *n.* adípen.

thrash: *v.* baúten; irikén, taltágen, baywén.

thread: *n.* sinúlid, panáit; lábag; **loose ~s of a garment** *n.* saroy-sároy; ~ **of a screw** *n.* róskas.

threadbare: *adj.* rugák, narúnot; gayót.

threat: *n.* láyat, mesmés, pangtá.

threaten: *v.* ipangtá; paayapán.

three: *adj.* talló; ~ **years ago** idí katimmawén.

thresh: *v.* saksáken, irikén.

thresher: *n.* (*of rice mill*) molína.

threshold: *n.* dapián; pangrugián.

thrice: *adj.* mamitló.

thrift: *n.* panagtíped; kinaínut.

thrifty: *adj.* nasalimetmét, naínut, nakirmét, naterréd.

thrill: *v.* salbágen; sumgár; agkintayég.

thrive: *v.* sumalibúkag; rumang-áy; lumasbáng.

throat: *n.* karabukób, luludduókan; (*of hog*) ngurungóran; **glands in** ~ *n.* ásang; **clear the** ~ *v.* agsay-á, agseg-ám.

throb: *v.* agkitebkitéb, agpitikpitík, aggutokgutók, agkebbakebbá.

throne: *n.* tróno.

throng: *n.* kaaduán, reprép, pangén; sallíbad.

throttle: *n.* aangsán; *v.* bekkelén.

through: *prep.*, *adv.* aglásat, agtarús; **pass** ~ *v.* lumápus.

throughout: *adv.* ití ámin, dágup ti.

throw: *v.* ibató, ibákal, ipalládaw; ~ **upward** *v.* ikudduág, ipallátok, ipallangátok.

thrush: *n.* (*disease*) áras; **hermit** ~ *n.* mammendíta, palál.

thrust: *n.* duyók, dugsól; *v.* ikursóng; ~ **hoe** *n.* darusdós.

thud: *n.* karadúkod.

thumb: *n.* tangán (ti íma); **additional** ~ *n.* ríting, ríbing; **lower part of** ~ *n.* langkók;

part of hand between ~ **and index finger** *n.* rawayráway.

thump: *v.* maluén, kugsólen; tukbóben.

thunder: *n.* gurrúod, dullúog.

thunderbolt: *n.* sal-ít, kimát.

Thursday: *n.* Huébes.

thus: *adv.* kastá, isu nga.

thwart: *v.* atipaén, lapdán, sukálen, papaáyen, supríngen, subáen.

tibia: *n.* baráwas, alluás, dúri ti lúlod.

tick: *n.* ulmóg, ayám; talukátik; angpás; *v.* agkitekkiték.

ticket: *n.* biliéte.

tickle: *v.* kikién, kilikilién.

tide: *n.* (*flood*) atáb; (*ebb*) úgot; (*neap*) alaál; (*spring*) apdáy, arabáab.

tidings: *n.* damdámag.

tidy: *adj.* naurnós, nadalimánek; *v.* urnósen.

tie: *n.* siglót; gálut; paráut; reppét; **neck~** *n.* korbáta; *v.* igálut, siglúten, irakéd.

tiebeam: *n.* sekkég; síkang, bekkér.

tiff: *n.* panagginnúra.

tiger: *n.* tígre.

tight: *adj.* nailét; nairténg, nairút; ~**fisted** *adj.* naímot, nakirmét.

tighten: *v.* irutén, pailetén.

tile: *n.* baldósa, téha.

till: *v.* bukibúken; talónen; *prep.* inggána, aginggána.

tilt: *v.* pakbuén, battuágen, durósen.

timber: *n.* tarikáyo; tróso.

timbrel: *n.* gardáng a kawáyan.

time: *n.* panawén; kabayág, tiémpo; óras; ~**piece** pagorásan, relós; **at the** ~ agdamá; **at all ~s** kanáyon.

timely: *adj.* agtutóp.

timid: *adj.* natakrót, naátap, managbutbuténg.

tin: *n.* estánio; láta.

tincture: *n.* tintúra.

tinder: *n.* eská, pamasgedán, ammuán.

tinge: *v.* makaáli; urmáen.

tingle: *v.* agbibíneg, agpipíkel.

tinkle: *v.* agkalangíking, agkilingkilíng.

tinsel: *n.* paspasiláp, aransél.

tint: *n.* tína, kolór, máris; *v.* urmáen.

tip: *n.* ungtó; murdóng; *v.* balintuágen, pairígen, pat-ílen.

tip-off: *n.* pakdáar.

tipsy: *adj.* nakainúm, maúlaw, nabarték, naalán.

tiptoe: *v.* agtil-áy, agdanapísip, agtikláy.

tire: *n.* liánta, góma ti pilid; *v.* bannogén, mabannóg; maktangán, maúma.

tired: *adj.* nabannóg, nautoyán, napaksúyan.

tiresome: *adj.* makaúma, makabannóg.

tissue: *n.* kulápot, kulánit.
titillate: *v.* kikién, kilikilién.
title: *n.* título, galád, nágan; ~ **page** *n.* rúpa.
tittle: *n.* apagkulámaw, kundíng.
to: *prep.* ití, idiáy, ken, kadá.
toad: *n.* pilát, bat-óg, kengkéng.
toadstool: *n.* uóng.
toast: *v.* kirogén; (*in drinking*) itagáy, imulaán; **smelling of** ~ nabang-í.
toastmaster: *n.* mangipangúlo ti talontón.
tobacco: *n.* tabáko; **first leaves of** ~ *n.* túbeng.
today: *adv.* itá nga aldáw.
toddle: *v.* agardáng, agpakkapakkáw.
toe: *n.* rámay ti sáka; **little** ~ *n.* kikít.
together: *adv.* agtípon, agkúyog; -inn-.
toil: *v.* agbannóg; *n.* bannóg, nareggét nga arámid.
toilet: *n.* kasílias, siléd a pagiblengán; ~ **bowl** *n.* inodóro, lat-óng; ~ **paper** *n.* pagílo.
token: *n.* tandáan, pagtandaána; eggéd.
tolerable: *adj.* maibtúran.
tolerance: *n.* ánus, pabus-óy; panangbaybay-á; panangibtúr.
tolerate: *v.* ibtúran, turdán; ipatúboy.
toll: *n.* báyad ti panaglábas; kulitangtáng.
tomato: *n.* kamátis.
tomb: *n.* panteón, taném, túmba.
tomorrow: *adv.* intón bigát.
ton: *n.* toneláda.
tone: *n.* áweng, tímek; úni; lengngáag.
tongs: *n.* sípit, panípit.
tongue: *n.* díla; pagsasaó.
tongue-tied: *adj.* saán a makapagsaó.
tonight: *adv.* itá a rabií, intón rabií.
tonsils: *n.* salsalamági.
too: *adv.* napalálo, nalabés; met; únay.
tool: *n.* alikámen, aruáten, gamígam, gargarét.
toot: *v.* pagunién, bosináen.
tooth: *n.* ngípen; **canine** ~ *n.* saóng; **molar** ~ *n.* sángi.
toothbrush: *n.* sipílio, sugígi, gisígis.
toothless: *adj.* bungí, kabbáb.
toothpick: *n.* ingát, pagsingát.
top: *n.* rabáw, tápaw, tuktók; súnay, tarámpo; *v.* rimbáwan, ngatuán, parabawán; ~**s of vines** *n.* uggót; **cut the** ~ **off** *v.* agtáddaw.
topaz: *n.* topásio.
topic: *n.* téma, tópiko, bánag a saritáen.
topmost: *adj.* kangatuán.
topnotch: *adj.* kanunaán, kangrunáan.
topple: *v.* matumbá, margáay; matuáng, marbá.
topsy-turvy: *adj.* kusokusó, naguló.
torch: *n.* panagsílaw.
torment: *n.* túok, pagél, rígat.

torn: *adj.* napígis, naaray-áy.
tornado: *n.* alipugpóg.
torpid: *adj.* namayyét; agbibíneg; agsasadút.
torrent: *n.* águs, áyus.
torrid: *adj.* nabára, nadagáang.
torsion: *n.* tirítir.
tortoise: *n.* pag-óng.
torture: *n.* túok, dúsa, pammarparígat; *v.* tutuóken, pasakitán; pakarigátan.
toss: *v.* ipalládaw, ipallangátok, ibató.
tot: *n.* bassít nga ubíng.
total: *n.* dágup, pakadagúpan; ámin; *v.* dagdagúpen; pagtitipónen; ~**ity** *n.* pakadagdagúpan.
totter: *v.* agluggaluggád, agwaliwáli, agibaríbar, aglinggilinggí, agtiwedtiwéd, agdaríwis, agbaríring, agdawengdáweng, agbasíng, agluppaí.
touch: *v.* sagíden, arikápen, apirásen; *n.* apíras; **gentle** ~ *n.* aprós; ~ **me not** *n.* kamantígi; ~**stone** susudián.
touchy: *adj.* arsagíd, naalipúnget; managriknâ, nasentír.
tough: *adj.* nakulbét; nalagdá; napínget.
tour: *n.* panagdaliásat, panagbaniága.
tourist: *n.* turísta, biahéro, agdaldaliásat.
tournament: *n.* tornéo, pagsasalisálan.
tourney: *n.* pagsasalisálan.
tousle: *v.* guluén, kusukusuén.
tow: *v.* ulóden, guyóden, ikurná.
toward: *prep.* agturóng, agpa-.
towel: *n.* tuália, pagpunásan.
tower: *n.* tórre.
towering: *adj.* napasdók, nangáto únay.
town: *n.* íli; **go to** ~ *v.* agúdong.
toy: *n.* ay-áyam, abalbaláy; ~ **with** *v.* pulinglíngen.
trace: *n.* túgot; *v.* yúged, ilánad.
trachea: *n.* ang-anguyób.
track: *n.* alimunúmon, túgot.
traction: *n.* panaggúyod.
tractor: *n.* tráktor.
trade: *n.* komérsio, panaggátang; *v.* isukát.
trademark: *n.* márka ti pábrika.
trader: *n.* agtagtagiláko.
tradition: *n.* naipakadawyán, ugáli.
traditional: *adj.* tinawtáwid, nagallawátan.
traduce: *v.* parpardayáen, padpadkasén.
traffic: *n.* trápiko, pagdaliasátan, panagbúnag; panagtagiláko.
tragedy: *n.* didígra.
tragic: *adj.* nakalkaldáang.
trail: *n.* sebbáng; daná, wanés; (*of gown*) salinggáyad, salinggúyod; *v.* (*on floor*) agsaringgáyad, agkaraínas.

train: *n.* tren, perokaríl; *v.* isungsóng, sanayén, adálan.

training: *n.* panagsanáy.

trait: *n.* pakailiddingán, kadawyán; tandá; kababalín.

traitor: *n.* manglilípot, nagulíb, traidór; **~ous** *adj.* nagulíb.

tram: *n.* trambía.

tramp: *n.* baliúduong, birkóg, mannursór; *v.* ibaddebaddék, payáten.

trample: *v.* baddekén; ilúsit, ibaddebaddék.

trance: *n.* talimúdaw.

tranquil: *adj.* natalinaáy, natalná; **~ity** *n.* kinatalná.

transaction: *n.* panagginnátang; negósio.

transcend: *v.* ngatngatuán, artápan, saliwánan; rimbáwan, sagudáyan.

transcribe: *v.* yallátiw.

transcript: *n.* nakaisurátan.

transfer: *v.* yális, yákar, yallátiw; umákar, umallátiw.

transfix: *v.* salbágen, salpóten.

transform: *v.* balíwan.

transfusion: *n.* pannakaikábil ti dára.

transgress: *v.* aglabsíng; kaniwasén, salungasíngen.

transient: *adj.* aglábas.

transit: *n.* panaglásat, panaglábas.

transition: *n.* panaglásat, panagbáliw, panagsukát.

transitive: *adj.* mayákar.

transitory: *adj.* aglábas.

translate: *v.* yallátiw, yúlog; agbarubása, agdarubása, ipatarús.

translucent: *adj.* nalitnáw, nalit-áw; aragaág.

transmission: *n.* panangyákar.

transmit: *v.* ipatulód, ipaw-ít, yalláwat.

transom: *n.* pángal.

transparent: *adj.* masarsaráng, agsaragásag, aragaág.

transpire: *v.* aglimdúos.

transplant: *v.* iraép, kalakálen.

transport: *v.* bunágen, ipán, yális; *n.* paglugánan.

trap: *n.* palab-óg; síkap; saltók; (*for fish*) as-asád, tallakéb, balingáto, kaság, ásar, kobó, pallagtó, paéd, pasábeng, síib, patúlid, kibót, kalubkób; (*for monkeys*) paípit; (*for dogs*) kobongkóbong; **fall into a ~** *v.* kumná.

trash: *n.* basúra, mokomók.

travail: *v.* agpasíkal, agparúbang, agrígat.

travel: *v.* agbiáhe, agbaniága, agdaliásat; *n.* panagbiáhe, baniága.

traverse: *v.* ballasíwen, baliasáten.

trawl: *n.* kitáng.

tray: *n.* bandéha, battiá.

treacherous: *adj.* nagulíb, natakúp.

treachery: *n.* líput, libát, kinagulíb.

tread: *v.* baddekén, payáten.

treadle: *n.* papayátan

treason: *n.* gulíb, panaglíput, panaglib-át, ballikúg.

treasure: *n.* gámeng; *v.* patgén.

treasurer: *n.* tesoréro.

treat: *v.* (*cure*) agásan; kasuén; sanguén.

treatment: *n.* panangikáso, panangágas, tratár.

treaty: *n.* túlag, pagtulágan, tinóng.

tree: *n.* káyo; **cut down ~s** *v.* agbákir; **~less plain** *n.* tay-ák, pantár.

trek: *n.* baniága, pasiár.

trellis: *n.* pakalatkát, parsá.

tremble: *v.* agpigergér, agkintayég, agpayegpég, agkuyegyég, sumagiperpér, agarigengén.

tremendous: *adj.* nakaap-apráng, nakadak-dakkél.

tremor: *n.* ginginéd; kintayég, pigergér.

tremulous: *adj.* napigergér.

trench: *n.* paáyas, puyapúyan; trinséra; pasalingdán, dúyos.

trend: *n.* pagduyósan; turóng.

trespass: *v.* aglabsíng, aglabés.

trestle: *n.* bastidór; túkol; kabaliéte.

trial: *n.* tribunál, pamadpadásan; súot, pannakapádas.

triangle: *n.* triánggulo.

tribe: *n.* tríbu, kapuonán; pulí.

tribulation: *n.* samuyéng, pádas.

tribunal: *n.* pangukomán.

tribute: *n.* pangpadáyaw, pangraém; buís.

trick: *n.* síkap, pangallítaw; *v.* ulbóden, sikápan.

trickle: *v.* agarúyot, agarúbos, agaribásay, agtedtéd.

tricolor: *adj.* talló a máris.

trident: *n.* tarapáng.

tried: *adj.* nasúot; *v.* napádas, pinádas.

trifle: *n.* apagkulámaw, kundíng.

trigger: *n.* gatílio, kakalbítan.

trill: *n.* tayegtég; *v.* aggolósa.

trillion: *n.* sangariwríw a riwríw.

trim: *v.* arbásan, rimiríman.

trinity: *n.* trinidád.

trio: *n.* talló nga agkankánta wennó agtoktokár, bunggóy ti talló.

trip: *n.* biáhe; pannakaitibkól, pannakaitublák; *v.* maitibkól, masippádong, maipiddawíl.

tripe: *n.* liblíbro.

triple: *v.* pamitluén; *adj.* tinalló.

triplets: *n.* talló a síngin; (*of same sex*) abúroy.

triplicate: *adj.* talló a kópia.

triumph: *n.* ballígi, panangábak; *v.* agballígi.

trivial: *adj.* nanumó; barengbáreng.
trombone: *n.* trombón.
troops: *n.* búyot; bunggóy.
trophy: *n.* pakalaglagipán ti ballígi, gunguná.
trot: *n.* taltág; *v.* agpagná a naurnós.
trouble: *n.* búong ti úlo, sikór, pakaringgóran, riríbuk.
troublesome: *adj.* ririén, riribúken.
trough: *n.* kalasúgan, kullúong.
trousers: *n.* kalsón, pantalón.
trout: *n.* dalág.
trowel: *n.* barúsok.
truant: *adj.* agtagubay-á, agkaralángan.
truce: *n.* panagsardéng ti panagdangádang.
truck: *n.* pattáli, trak.
truculent: *adj.* narungsót, nawagnét, nawagténg.
trudge: *v.* manadkadapá.
true: *adj.* pudnó, napaypaysó.
trumpet: *n.* trompéta, tururót; tanggúyob; **bamboo** ~ koribáw.
truncate: *v.* putdén, pukdólan, tadáwen, tungdén.
trunk: *n.* (*chest*) lakása, baúl; (*of tree*) bungéd.
truss: *n.* baág, baríkes.
trust: *n.* pammáti, panagtalék; *v.* agtalék, agtalgéd.
trustee: *n.* mangimatón, mangigága, makaitalkán, katalék.
trusting: *adj.* managtalék.
truth: *n.* pudnó, kinaagpaysó; ~**ful** *adj.* napudnó.
try: *v.* padásen, suóten, tingtíngen; ~ **square** *n.* eskuála, síko.
T-shirt: *n.* kamiséta.
tub: *n.* bakká, baldí, batiá.
tube: *n.* túbo; singkíl.
tuberculosis: *n.* sárut, dáig.
tuberous: *adj.* rutongrutóngan, bukolbukólan.
tuck: *v.* ikupín, isalupingpíng, ikulpí, iseksék.
Tuesday: *n.* Mártes.
tuft: *n.* borlás, buybóy, talipúgong.
tug: *v.* guyóden, ulóden, alut-úten; ~ **of war** *n.* ay-áyam a ginnuyódan ití talí.
tuition: *n.* matríkula, pannakaádal.
tumble: *v.* matnág, maitublák, matuáng.
tumbler: *n.* báso, kópa.
tumefy: *v.* umbál, lumtég.
tumor: *n.* dúgol, bung-ór; lettég; (*in mouth of animals*) ábas; (*in scalp of children*) áok.
tumult: *n.* guló, riríbuk, kulkól.
tumultuous: *adj.* naríri, naariwáwa.
tune: *n.* túno, tímek; *v.* itúnos, templáen; **out of** ~ *adj.* sintunádo, nabeddáng.
tunnel: *n.* tunél, úsok.

turban: *n.* banggál, turbánte.
turbid: *adj.* nalibég.
turbine: *n.* turbína.
turbulent: *adj.* naríribuk, naríri, naguló.
turf: *n.* karuótan.
turgid: *adj.* nabanawbáw, bimmasísaw, nalubó.
turkey: *n.* pábo, burayuán.
turmoil: *n.* riríbuk, kulkól, guló.
turn: *n.* (*in game*) batáng; (*in river*) tíkor; (*in direction*) panagbuélta; *v.* pusipúsen, isikkó, pagtayyekén; agbalín; agsikkó; agbuélta.
turnip: *n.* nábo; ~ **bean** *n.* singkamás.
turnover: *n.* panangyáwat.
turpentine: *n.* aguárras, trementína.
turquoise: *n.* turkésa.
turret: *n.* ababá a tórre.
turtle: *n.* pag-óng; bindóg; **sea** ~ *n.* pawíkan; ~ **eggs** *n.* daík.
turtledove: *n.* págaw, tugtug-ó, bálog.
tusk: *n.* saóng; saw-íng.
tussle: *n.* gabbó, gabbál.
tutelage: *n.* panangisúro.
tutor: *n.* manursúro; *v.* isúro.
twang: *n.* dayyéng nga impaagóng.
tweak: *v.* kuddotén, ligusén.
tweezers: *n.* tiáni, pagikukó.
twelfth: *adj.* maikasangapúlo ket duá; *n.* pagkasangapúlo ket duá.
twelve: *adj.* sangapúlo ket duá.
twentieth: *adj.* maikaduapúlo.
twenty: *adj.* duapúlo.
twice: *adj.* maminduá; ~ **orphaned** agdemmáng.
twig: *n.* bassít a sangá, tanábog.
twilight: *n.* surípet, apagriwét, agágaw-sipngét-lawág.
twilled: *adj.* díwig, ríwis, rángis.
twin: *n.* síngin, kambál; (*of same sex*) abúroy.
twine: *v.* tiritíren, linásen, talién.
twinge: *n.* ut-ót.
twinkle: *v.* agrimatrimát, agkiremkirém; aggiraygiráy, makasilnág.
twirl: *v.* agpusípos, agtayyék; pagtayyekén, kunikónen; *n.* pusípos, tayyék.
twist: *v.* sallapidén, tiritíren.
twitch: *v.* guttaén, rabsúten; agkiét, agkayetkét.
two: *adj.* duá; ~~-**colored** sulbóngan.
twofold: *adj.* maminduá.
twosome: *n.* sinagduduá.
tycoon: *n.* nabaknáng a negosiánte.
type: *n.* típo, kíta; *v.* agmakinília.
typeset: *n.* káha; ~**ter** *n.* kahísta.
typewriter: *n.* makinília.
typhoid: *n.* típos.

typhoon: *n.* bagió; **to be caught by a ~** *v.* mailab-óng, mabagyuán.

typical: *adj.* kayarígan, mangiladáwan, taliágum.

typist: *n.* mumamakinília.

tyrannical: *adj.* naduldóg.

tyranny: *n.* kuspág, dawél, ranggás, panangidadanés.

tyro: *n.* kataldéng, agdadámo.

U

ubiquitous: *adj.* ití ámin a yan.

udder: *n.* púkal.

ugly: *adj.* naalás, naláad, nakas-áng.

ulcer: *n.* úlsera; saksakitén.

ulna: *n.* baráwas, alluás.

ultimate: *adj.* akin-ungtó, kamaudiánan.

ultra: *adv.* nalabés.

umbilicus: *n.* púseg.

umbrella: *n.* páyong.

umpire: *n.* mangikeddéng.

un- *pref.* saán, di.

unable: *adj.* di mabalín.

unaccustomed: *adj.* saán a nairuám.

unanimity: *n.* túnos, kinalimbóng.

unanimous: *adj.* agkaykaysá, nagtutúnos.

unarmed: *adj.* ima-íma (awánan ígam).

unavoidable: *adj.* di maliklíkan.

unaware: *adj.* pagammuán; di mariknâ.

unbalanced: *adj.* bangkíng; agbattúlay.

unbearable: *adj.* di maibtúran.

unbiased: *adj.* nalintég, nasalindég.

unbuckle: *v.* warwáran, palukayán (ti hebília), ukásen.

unbutton: *v.* ukásen ti botónes.

uncalled for: *adj.* saán a hústo, saán a masápul.

uncastrated: *n.* bulóg.

uncertain: *adj.* pagtagtagiammuán, maduaduá; **to be ~** *v.* agmangngamangngá, agsimpangála, agngatangatá.

uncivil: *adj.* nasabrák, saán a naraém.

uncivilized: *adj.* átap (táo).

uncle: *n.* ulitég.

uncoil: *v.* ukarkáren.

uncomfortable: *adj.* natúok; nasammukól, di nanam-áy.

uncommon: *adj.* manmanó, narásay; namarangmáng.

uncompromising: *adj.* di agbalbalíw; di mabiór.

unconcerned: *adj.* nalíway.

unconscious: *adj.* napléng, di makariknâ, awánan púot.

uncontrollable: *adj.* nasúbeg, di matngelán.

uncouth: *adj.* nagubsáng, nagubál, basakbasák, nasabrák, di nasursuruán.

uncover: *v.* lukásan, bukasán, lukatán, lukaísan.

undaunted: *adj.* saán nga agbuténg.

undecided: *adj.* maduaduá.

undeniable: *adj.* saán a malibák.

undependable: *adj.* nalangsót, natangsó.

under: *prep.*, *adv.* sírok, babaén.

underbuy: *v.* ram-óyen.

undercover: *adj.* nalímed.

undergo: *v.* agsagába, aglak-ám; aglásat, agituréd; mapagténg.

underground: *adj.* ití unég ti dagá; nalímed.

undergrowth: *n.* samsamék.

underhand: *adj.* nalméng, sinisíkap; innulbód.

underline: *v.* ugísan ití babá.

underneath: *prep.* ití sírok, ití babá.

undershirt: *n.* kamiséta.

underskirt: *n.* enáguas.

understand: *v.* maawátan; maábut, maísip; **~ing** *n.* pannakaáwat, pannakaammó.

undertake: *v.* irukuás, gayagáyen, ngayangáyen.

undertaker: *n.* agim-imatón ití punerária.

undertaking: *n.* arámid.

underwear: *n.* kaunggán a kawés; sapín.

underwrite: *v.* agiseguro.

undesirable: *adj.* di matarigagáyan.

undo: *v.* (*knots*) sarotsóten; (*hair*) wakráyen; (*unfasten*) warwáren, ukarkáren.

undoubtedly: *adv.* awán duaduá.

undress: *v.* (*take off shirt*) aguksób, uksóban; (*completely*) aglábus, labúsan.

undulate: *v.* agdaldallúyon, agkulokul-óy, agsinnó, agkitóg, agsilnó.

unearth: *v.* kutkúten, kalién, kabkában.

uneasy: *adj.* madanágan, di makatalná.

unencumbered: *adj.* nasaliwanwán.

unequal: *adj.* maigiddiát, maisupádi; bangkíng.

unequivocal: *adj.* awán duaduá; nalawág.

uneven: *adj.* pángis; di maipátas; nalikkaóng, tamból.

unexpected: *adj.* nepettát, saán a pinadpadaánan.

unexpectedly: *adv.* gúlpe, nabiglá, pagammuán; **appear ~** *v.* tumpuár, masarsáraw; **caught ~** *adj.* sibabayyát; **meet ~** *v.* maranaán, agtummó.

unfair: *adj.* di hústo, saán a nalintég.

unfaithful: *adj.* nagulíb, manglilípot.

unfamiliar: *adj.* saán nga am-ammó.

unfasten: *v.* bukaán, bukráan; warwáran, sarotsóten.

unfathomable: *v.* saán a matúkod.

unfavorable: *adj.* saán a maitúnos.
unfit: *adj.* dákes.
unfold: *v.* ukráden; bukasán; ipalgák.
unforeseen: *adj.* saán nga impagpagarúp.
unfortunate: *adj.* daksangásat, nakúdad.
unfounded: *adj.* awán nakaibatayánna.
unfriendly: *adj.* naúyong, naásir, maisungáni.
unfurl: *v.* bistráden, yaplág, ukráden, warwáren.
ungainly: *adj.* nakámol, nalampáy, nasammukól.
ungodly: *adj.* nabassáwang, nadangkés, natabaáw.
ungrateful: *adj.* saán a managyáman.
unguarded: *adj.* naliwáyan.
unguent: *n.* pagsapsapó.
unhappy: *adj.* nalidáy, nakaay-ay-áy.
unhitch: *v.* alsáan, bukráan.
unholy: *adj.* saán a nasantuán; nadangkés.
unification: *n.* pannakatípon, panagkaykaysá.
uniform: *n.* unipórme, padapáda a kawés; *adj.* agpapáda, sangsangkapáris.
unify: *v.* pagkaykaysaén; pagkakaduán.
unimportant: *adj.* nanumó.
unintentional: *adj.* di ginagára.
uninterested: *adj.* nalab-áy.
union: *n.* típon, kallaysá, kappón.
unique: *adj.* awán kapádana; bugbugtóng; is-isú; naisangsangayán.
unison: *n.* túnos; kinaurnós, pagkaykaysaán.
unit: *n.* pagbilángan; maysá, pasét.
unite: *v.* pagkaykaysáen, pagtipónen, pagsilpuán; tumípon.
unity: *n.* panagtípon, timpúyog, panag-kaykaysá.
universal: *adj.* sapásap, sangalubóngan.
universe: *n.* law-áng.
university: *n.* unibersidád, kangatuán a pagadálan.
unjust: *adj.* di nalintég, dákes.
unjustifiable: *adj.* maikaniwás, di maalángon.
unkempt: *adj.* kusokusó, saán a naurnós.
unkind: *adj.* nagubsáng, naranggás; naúyong.
unknown: *adj.* saán nga am-ammó.
unlawful: *adj.* maikaniwás iti lintég, kalílis.
unleaf: *v.* imulongán, uklápen.
unless: *conj.* malaksíd no.
unlike: *adj.* maidúma, maigiddiát, maisupádi.
unlimited: *adj.* awán pagpatinggána.
unload: *v.* deskargáen, idessáag, dissuán.
unlock: *v.* buksán, lukatán ti kandádona.
unlucky: *adj.* daksangásat, nabuísit, nakúlat.
unmanageable: *adj.* dúngis; nabánus, nadúges.
unmask: *v.* ibunannág, iwaragáwag.
unmistakable: *adj.* awanán ríro, nalawág.

unnatural: *adj.* datdatlág; ~ **growth** *n.* ríting.
unnecessary: *adj.* saán a naskén, saán a masápul.
unoccupied: *adj.* awanán aramídenna; awán nagyán.
unpack: *v.* bukasán ti maléta, ukarkáren, warwáren ti reppét.
unparalleled: *adj.* sawsáway, awán kapádana, naliw-án.
unpleasant: *adj.* makasugkár, makapagúra, makaruród.
unpretentious: *adj.* saán a natangsít; napakumbabá.
unproductive: *adj.* (*land*) parunápon, parunápor.
unquestionable: *adj.* di pagduaduaán, di marúpir, nalawág.
unravel: *v.* waswásen, ukásen.
unreal: *adj.* paspásaw, sinan-, ubbáw.
unrefined: *adj.* nagubsáng, nagubál.
unreliable: *adj.* nalangsót, nakúsit, natangsó.
unresponsive: *adj.* aglimdó.
unrest: *n.* riríbok, guloguló, kinaawán-talná.
unrestrained: *adj.* sibubúlos, di matengtengngél.
unretentive: *adj.* sarangúsong; managlilípat.
unripe: *adj.* naáta, naganús.
unrivaled: *adj.* di mapáda.
unroll: *v.* warwáren, ukráden, yaplág.
unruly: *adj.* nasúbeg, nasúkir, nasúngit.
unsafe: *adj.* napeggád, saán a natalgéd.
unsatisfied: *adj.* di mapnék.
unscrupulous: *adj.* mannábag.
unseam: *v.* saratsáten.
unseemly: *adj.* naalás, di dumkét, di maibágay, nakas-áng.
unseen: *adj.* saán a makíta.
unselfish: *adj.* naparábur, di aginbubukódan.
unsheathe: *v.* asúten, uksúten, uyúsen.
unsightly: *adj.* naalás, naláad, nakas-áng.
unskilled: *adj.* saán a sanáy.
unsociable: *adj.* di mannaskigayyém, napakní.
unstable: *adj.* saán a natalná; agallá-allá.
unsteady: *adj.* di nasimpá, naurúod.
unstrung: *adj.* maurbóy; maukbóy.
unsubstantial: *adj.* kalawákaw, ubbáw.
unsuccessful: *adj.* nawás, saán a narang-áy, nakúdad.
unswell: *v.* umpés, kumbét.
unsymmetrical: *adj.* rinángis.
untamable: *adj.* di mapaámo, naátap.
untattoed: *adj.* beddál.
untidy: *adj.* narugít, nadulpét, nawará.
untie: *v.* bukráan, bukaén, ukásen.
until: *prep.* aginggána, inggána, agpatinggá.
untilled: *adj.* nagtangátang, malaágan.

untimely 746 vale

untimely: *adj.* karábo.
untrue: *adj.* paspásaw, ulbód, naríro.
untwine: *v.* ukásen.
untwist: *v.* warwáren, bukaén ti tertérna.
unusual: *adj.* karkarná, paspasaráy;
naisangayán, saán a kadkadawyán.
unveil: *v.* lukásan, lukaísan, ikkatén ti
abúngotna.
unwell: *adj.* masakít; agmamayó.
unwilling: *adj.* agmadmadí.
unwind: *v.* warwáren, ukásen, sarutsúten,
ukarkáren.
unwise: *adj.* máag, saán a masírib.
unworthy: *adj.* di maikarí; nakas-áng.
unwrap: *v.* bukasán, warwáren ti balkótna,
ukarkáren.
unwritten: *adj.* saán a naisúrat.
unyielding: *adj.* nasúbeg, nasúngit.
unyoke: *v.* alsáan (ti sangólna).
up: *prep.*, *adv.* ití ngáto.
upbraid: *v.* tubngáren, ungtán, bir-íten.
upbringing: *n.* panangpadakkél.
upheaval: *n.* guló, yaalsá.
upheave: *v.* ingáto, ital-ó.
uphill: *adj.* nasang-át, nasulít.
uphold: *v.* sarapáen, ibáyog, iling-í,
itandúdo.
upkeep: *n.* pannakataripáto, pannakaasikáso.
upland: *adj.* tápaw, nangáto a dagá.
uplift: *v.* itag-áy, itáyag, ital-ó; itandúdo.
upon: *prep.* rabáw.
upper: *adj.* akinngáto, akinrabáw.
uppermost: *adj.* kangatuán.
upright: *adj.* natangár; (*honest*) nalintég,
naregtá.
uprising: *n.* yaalsá; ibabángon.
uproar: *n.* ariángga, arimbángaw, ariwáwa,
belláak, guló.
uproot: *v. v.* pag-úten, parúten, gabúten.
upset: *adj.* maruród; *v.* tuangén, balinsuekén,
sunganién; *n.* balinsuék.
upside-down: *adv.* balinsuék.
upstairs: *adv.* idiáy ngáto.
upstream: *adj.* ití súrong, surbók.
upward: *adv.* agpangáto.
urban: *adj.* maipapán ití siudád.
urbane: *adj.* nasungdó.
urchin: *n.* maratangtáng, pumapána,
sabsabláy, sagága.
uredo: *n.* supotsúpot.
urethra: *n.* iisbuán.
urge: *v.* dagdágen, gutugóten, guyugóyen.
urgency: *n.* gánat.
urgent: *adj.* magangánat, masápul únay.
urinal: *n.* pagisbuán; (*for women*) sayúgan.
urinary bladder: *n.* basísaw, busísaw.

urinate: *v.* umisbó; ~ **at a great distance** *v.*
pumáyud; ~ **inopportunely** *v.* agpápay.
urination: *n.* yiisbó; **painful** ~ *n.* sarsaripíten.
urine: *n.* isbó; **smell of** ~ *n.* angség; **drop of** ~
n. ternét.
urn: *n.* úrna.
urticaria: *n.* supotsúpot.
us: *pron.* kadakamí, kadatá, kadatayó.
usable: *adj.* maáramat.
usage: *n.* kadawyán, pannakaarámat.
use: *v.* usarén, aramáten; *n.* pakaaramátan,
pagserbián, paáy.
used: *adj.* usádo; talibugnáy; ~ **up** *adj.* naibús;
~ **to** *adj.* naruám.
useful: *adj.* utíl, naserbí; ~**ness** *n.* kinaserbí.
useless: *adj.* awán serbína, inútil.
usher: *n.* agipatpatugáw.
usual: *adj.* kadawyán, masansán, samúsam,
nadáwi, masná.
usurer: *n.* usoréro, mangngam-ám.
usurp: *v.* agáwen, takáwen, tagikuaén,
sumallín.
usury: *n.* am-ám.
utensil: *n.* gamígam, aruáten, longlóngan.
uterus: *n.* aanakán; **protrusion of** ~ **into**
vagina *n.* butiláw.
utility: *n.* kaes-eskán, kinaserbí, pakaaramátan.
utilize: *v.* aramáten, usarén.
utmost: *adj.* kadaklán, kapalaluán, kangatuán.
utter: *v.* yesngáw, ibalikás, yebkás; *adv.* pulós.
utterance: *n.* pannakayebkás, pannakasaó.
uvula: *n.* dawatdáwat, lalamútan.

V

vacant: *adj.* luáng, bakánte, awán nagyán,
nagpanáwan.
vacate: *v.* taláwan, pagpanáwan.
vacation: *n.* bakasión, ipapánaw (ti trabáho).
vaccinate: *v.* bakunáan.
vaccination: *n.* panagbakúna.
vaccine: *n.* bakúna.
vacillate: *v.* agmokó, agngatangatá.
vacuum: *n.* káwaw, kalawákaw.
vagabond: *n.* birkóg, bayanggúdaw,
agtawtawátaw, baligawgáw, agwálang,
basingkáwil.
vagina: *n.* úki; **wash the** ~ *n.* agkawkáw.
vagrant: *adj.* bayanggúdaw, agtawtawátaw,
baligawgáw, aliwaték.
vague: *adj.* naalibuyóng, saán a nalawág;
(*news*) aliwangáwang.
vain: *adj.* ubbáw, barengbáreng.
vainglorious: *adj.* napasindayág,
napalangguád, natangsít, napangás.
vale: *n.* gingét, lúbong.

valet: *n.* babaonén, agserserbí.
valiance: *n.* kinapusóng, kinaturéd, sarubaybáy.
valiant: *adj.* napusóng, maíngel, naturéd.
valid: *adj.* umisú, maipatég, maáwat, mausár, maarámat.
valise: *n.* maléta.
valley: *n.* gingét, lúbong.
valor: *n.* kinaturéd, íngel, pusóng, sarikedkéd.
valuable: *adj.* napatég.
value: *n.* patég, ngína.
valve: *n.* takkáb, pasngawán, bálbula.
vampire: *n.* bampíro, boróka.
vane: *n.* paligpálig, pirpír.
vanguard: *n.* akinsángo, umun-uná.
vanish: *v.* agpúkaw, agawán; (*at sea*) malúnod.
vanity: *n.* palangguád, kinaubbáw, pasindayág, kinapammarág.
vanquish: *v.* parukmaén, parmekén, abáken, paksiáten.
vapor: *n.* alingásaw, sengngáw, alibungú-bong; ~**ize** *v.* agalibungúbong.
variable: *adj.* agbaliwbáliw.
variance: *n.* suppiát.
variant: *adj.* managbalbáliw; maigiddiát.
varicella: *n.* tokó.
varied: *adj.* nadumadúma.
variegated: *adj.* buritekték; labáng, butikbutikán, matisádo.
variety: *n.* karuáy, panagdudúma.
variola: *n.* burtóng.
various: *adj.* maikamanó, nadumadúma.
varnish: *n.* barnís.
vary: *v.* agbáliw, agsukát; ipasumbáliw.
vase: *n.* putík, báso (ti sábong), ploréra.
vassal: *n.* adípen, iturayán.
vast: *adj.* nawatíwat, naláwa. nagdakkél.
vat: *n.* bálde, tánke, sinublán.
vault: *n.* kahón, aparadór a landók a pagikkán ti kuartá wennó aláhas.
vaunt: *v.* agsalawásaw; agsanéb.
veer: *v.* agsikkó, aglikkó, sumayág, lumiklík.
vegetable: *n.* naténg; **cook** ~**s** *v.* agdengdéng.
vegetation: *n.* mulmúla, kaykáyo.
vehement: *adj.* napasnék, napínget, napágus, nabíleg; narugsó.
vehicle: *n.* lúgan.
veil: *n.* abúngot, dalungdóng, abbóng.
vein: *n.* urát.
veined: *adj.* (*wood*) naurárit.
velocity: *n.* kinapardás, kinapartáka.
velvet: *n.* tersiopélo.
vend: *v.* agláko.
vendor: *n.* aglakláko.
venerable: *adj.* narangá. madaydáyaw.
venerate: *v.* dayáwen, pagraemán.

vengeance: *n.* pammáles, báles.
vengeful: *adj.* manangibáles.
venison: *n.* laság ti ugsá.
venom: *n.* sabídong ti úleg, gíta.
vent: *n.* abút, butbút; *v.* sumngáw; isaw-áy; lumsót.
ventilate: *v.* paangínan, paidán, paypáyan.
venture: *v.* agturéd, agpádas; igasanggásat; ~**some** *adj.* mannakigasanggásat, managpádas.
venue: *n.* beddéng, dissó.
Venus: *n.* baggák, kamuntatála, palpallátok.
veracity: *n.* kinapudnó, kinaagpaysó.
verb: *n.* bérbo, pangited-ánag.
verbatim: *adv.* létra por létra.
verbose: *adj.* adú ti saó.
verdant: *adj.* nalangtó, nalasbáng, nabérde.
verdict: *n.* kedddéng, panangipáto.
verdigris: *n.* takkí.
verge: *n.* ngárab, ígid; **be on the** ~ *v.* agngangábit.
verify: *v.* paneknekán, patalgedán, pasingkedán.
verity: *n.* kinapudnó.
vermicelli: *n.* pidéos; **rice** ~ *n.* bíhon.
vermifuge: *n.* pampúrga.
vernacular: *n.* nakayanakán a pagsasaó.
versatile: *adj.* adú ti arámatna.
verse: *n.* dániw, bérso.
versed: *adj.* naruám, sanáy, nalaíng.
version: *n.* bersión; kayulogán.
versus: *prep.* maisuppiát.
vertical: *adj.* agtindék, agpangáto.
vertigo: *n.* talimúdaw, ulaw-úlaw, pannakaúlaw.
very: *adv.* únay, napalálo.
vessel: *n.* sasakayán; basíha.
vest: *n.* tsáleko; *v.* bistián, kawesán.
vestibule: *n.* pataguáb, bangsál.
vestige: *n.* túgot, pakakitáan.
vestment: *n.* kawés.
veteran: *n.* beteráno.
veterinarian: *n.* mangngágas ití animál.
veto: *n.* béto, paawanén ti kalintegán.
vex: *v.* singaén, alimuténgen; pagpungtóten, karíten, saíren.
vial: *n.* práskita, ampólia.
viand: *n.* sidá, lámut.
vibrant: *adj.* natinggáw.
vibrate: *v.* agdallúyon, agpigergér; agtíbong.
vice: *pref.* bíse-; *n.* ruám a dákes.
vice-versa: *exp.* baliktáden.
vicinity: *n.* arubáya, kaarrúba, síbay.
vicious: *adj.* nadangkés, naúyong.
victim: *n.* bíktima, nadangránan.
victimize: *v.* biktimáen, sikápan.
victor: *n.* mangábak.

victorious: *adj.* nangábak, nagballígi.
victory: *n.* panangábak, ballígi.
vie: *v.* agsalísal, agsinnáit, makirinnisíris.
view: *n.* búya, imátang, kananákem; panangkíta; pamanunótan; *v.* imatángan, kitáen.
vigil: *n.* panagpúyat, panagbantáy; **keep ~** *v.* agpúyat.
vigilance: *n.* sídong, panagsíput.
vigilant: *adj.* nasíput, naalerta, narídam, managtaripáto.
vigor: *n.* bíleg, pigsá.
vigorous: *adj.* nabíleg, napigsá; nalungpó; nalapsák.
vile: *adj.* dákes; nababá; nadangkés.
vilify: *v.* ab-abién.
village: *n.* purók, íli.
villain: *n.* kontrabída, dákes a bulbullagáw.
vindicated: *adj.* naimalúsan.
vindictive: *adj.* manangibáles, manangisíkat.
vine: *n.* lánot, múla nga agkalatkát.
vinegar: *n.* suká; **season with ~** *v.* paksíwen, sukaán.
vineyard: *n.* kaubásan.
violate: *v.* labsíngen, salungasíngen; ranggásan; kaniwasén.
violation: *n.* panaglabsíng, pannakarabngís.
violence: *n.* damsák, ranggás, pammílit; labsíng.
violet: *n.* bioléta, líla, pampanúnot; *adj.* morádo.
violin: *n.* rabél, biolín, ing-íng.
violoncello: *n.* biolón.
viper: *n.* úleg, karasaén.
viperine: *adj.* narasáw.
virgin: *n.* birhén, awán tuláwna, donsélia.
virile: *adj.* napunér, aglallaláki.
virtual: *adj.* pudnó.
virtue: *n.* kinasíngpet, kinadalús; bíleg.
virulent: *adj.* rituér, makasabídong.
virus: *n.* bírus.
visa: *n.* bísa.
visage: *n.* rúpa, langá, púdos.
viscera: *n.* lalaém.
viscount: *n.* biskónde.
viscous: *adj.* napigkét, napalét.
vise: *n.* paípit, arípit.
visible: *adj.* makíta, nabatád, napaták.
vision: *n.* sirmatá, parmatá, pannakakíta.
visit: *v.* sarungkáran, suknálan; **pay a short ~** *v.* tumammídaw, dumap-áw, sumidáw.
visitor: *n.* bisíta, sangaíli.
visor: *n.* biséra.
vista: *n.* búya.
visual: *adj.* maipapánití panagkíta; **~ize** *v.* ipagarúp, pattapattaén.

vital: *adj.* makabiág, nangrúna; **~ity** *n.* kinapigsá.
vitamin: *n.* bitamína.
vivacious: *adj.* nasiglát, karantíng, salawitwít.
vivid: *adj.* napaták, nalawág.
vivify: *v.* biágen.
vocal: *adj.* insaó; **~ist** *n.* kumakánta.
vocation: *n.* pagsapúlan, panggedán; arámid, trabáho.
vociferous: *adj.* naariwáwa.
vogue: *n.* móda, ugáli.
voice: *n.* tímek, úni.
void: *adj.* dákes; kodapís.
volatile: *adj.* nalaká nga agbalbáliw.
volcano: *n.* bulkán.
volition: *n.* pakinákem, pagayatán.
volleyball: *n.* bálibol; **~ player** *n.* balibolísta.
voltage: *n.* boltáhe.
volume: *n.* tómo; kadakkél (ti danúm wenno ángin).
voluminous: *adj.* nabungkóng.
voluntary: *adj.* sitatallúgod, nadisnúdo, boluntário.
volunteer: *v.* agbulános, agdisnúdo.
voluptuous: *adj.* naderrép, nagartém.
vomit: *v.* agsaruá, agdul-ók, agkursó; *n.* saruá, balinawnáw.
voodoo: *n.* kíta ti mangkukúlam.
voracious: *n.* nasaramúsam, naráwet.
vortex: *n.* alikunó.
vote: *n.* bútos; *v.* agbútos, agpíli.
vouch: *v.* paneknekán, saksián.
voucher: *n.* resíbo ti panagbáyad, komprobánte.
vow: *n.* sapatá; *v.* agsapatá; ikarí.
vowel: *n.* bokál (létra).
voyage: *n.* panagláyag, panaglásat, panagbaniága; *v.* agbaniága.
vulgar: *adj.* nagubál, nagubsáng, nasabrák, narusangér; **~ity** *n.* kinagubál, kinarusangér, kinasabrák.
vulnerable: *adj.* madánar, masúgat.
vulture: *n.* buítre.
vulva: *n.* úki, appít; **inner lips of ~** *n.* tamantáman; **outer lips of ~** *n.* pingpíng ti úki; **large ~** *n.* bakká.

W

wad: *n.* pagseksék, nalúkot a papél.
waddle: *v.* agkinnikinní; agibar-íbar.
wade: *v.* agyakyák.
wadeable: *adj.* nalamméd, masákad.
wafer: *n.* barkílios; óstia; ápa.
wag: *v.* agkalawíkiw, aglingáling; (*index finger*) agwitwít.

wage: *v.* igubát; igákat; *n.* masapúlan, tangdán, suéldo.
wager: *n.* pústa, taén; *v.* agtáan, agpústa.
wages: *n.* tangdán, suéldo.
waggle: *v.* agkalóg.
wagon: *n.* bagón, karisón.
waif: *n.* gábat.
wail: *n.* dung-áw, unnóy; *v.* agágal, agdung-áw, agunnóy.
waist: *n.* síket, síbet; **~band** *n.* salikád, síket.
wait: *v.* agúray, agdáan.
waiter: *n.* agserserbí, kamaréro.
waive: *v.* agpayápay; iwagsák, idián.
wake: *v.* agriíng; riíngen; *n.* (*for the dead*) pinagpaluálo, lámay; (*of ship*) estéla.
waken: *v.* riingén.
wale: *n.* balegbég.
waled: *adj.* nalítem.
walk: *v.* magná; agpasiár; *n.* pannagná.
wall: *n.* didíng, taléb; *v.* talbán; bakúdan.
wallet: *n.* pitáka.
wallow: *v.* aglubnák, agaluyúoy.
walnut: *n.* nogáles.
waltz: *n.* bálse.
wand: *n.* batúta, bastón.
wander: *v.* agtawátaw, agsursór, agalla-allá, agkalkallaútang.
wane: *v.* agbabá, kumápoy, bumassít.
want: *n.* pannakasápol; *v.* kayát; agkalikágum; agkúrang, tarigagáyan.
wanting *adj.* kúrang.
wanton: *adj.* nagaramúgam, naderrép, naalikúteg, nabarayúboy, garampáng, sarampingát.
war: *n.* gubát, gérra; rúpak; **~ drum** *n.* gimbál; **tug of ~** aggiginnúyod; **world ~** *n.* gérra-mundiál.
ward: *v.* igága, aywánan; tarakén.
warden: *n.* alkálde.
wardrobe: *n.* pagan-anáy, kawkawés.
ware: *n.* tagiláko.
warehouse: *n.* bodéga; kamálig.
warfare: *n.* panagkakábil, pannakigubát.
warm: *adj.* nabára, napúdot.
warn: *v.* pakpakaunaán, patigmaánan.
warning: *n.* pakdáar, pakauná, patigmáan.
warrant: *n.* mandamiénto, bílin; **search ~** *n.* mandamiénto de rekísa.
warrior: *n.* mannakigubát, mannakidangádang.
warp: *v.* agbakkóg, agkibbó; *n.* gan-áy; **~ing frame** *n.* gagan-áyan.
warrior: *n.* soldádo, mannakigubát.
warship: *n.* pakigubát a bapór.
wart: *n.* tukaktúkak; (*on face*) bútig; **black ~** *n.* bíding.
wary: *adj.* naannád, naaluád.

wash: *v.* dalusán, ugásan, bugguán; **~ clothes** *v.* aglabá; **~ face** *v.* agdiram-ós; **~ dishes** *v.* aginnáw; **~ vegetables or rice** *v.* arasáwen; **~ genital area** *v.* agkawkáw; *n.* (*laundry*) muréng.
washer: *n.* labandéro; agdaldalús.
wasp: *n.* alumpipínig.
waste: *n.* basúra; *v.* ibelléng, sayángen; runóten.
wasteland: *n.* let-áng, luáng.
watch: *n.* relós; bantáy; *v.* buyáen; bantáyan, sipútan, pupuóten.
watchword: *n.* kontrasénias.
water: *n.* danúm; **~ buffalo** *n.* nuáng; **~ closet** kasílias; **~ lily** *n.* súkaw; **~ sprinkler** *n.* regadéra; **~ strider** al-alukáp, kotokóto; *v.* danumán, sibugán.
waterfall: *n.* buráyok, dissúor; **sound of ~** *n.* barangúbong.
watermelon: *n.* sandiá.
waterproof: *adj.* saán a serkén ti danúm.
watery: *adj.* nadanúm; nagarés.
wave: *n.* dallúyon, allón; *v.* agdallúyon; payapáyan.
waver: *v.* agsarimadéng, agibar-íbar, agngatangatá.
wavy: *adj.* kulót; nadallúyon.
wax: *n.* allíd, séra.
way: *n.* dálan, pagnaán, daná; pamay-án; panagkukuá; pamuspúsan; pamnuótan.
wayfarer: *n.* gamgámit.
waylay: *v.* saedén, sanbén; tambángan.
wayward: *adj.* nasúbeg, nasúkir, nadúgos, napúnged.
we: *pron.* (*dual*) datá; (*excl.*) dakamí, -kamí; (*incl.*) datayó, -tayó.
weak: *adj.* nakapsót, nakápoy, nalupóy; (*easily injured*) nalúba; **~-kneed** *adj.* pillakús; **~-minded** *adj.* kábaw; **~ness** *n.* kinakapsút; pagkapsútan.
weakling: *n.* kuttongí, nakapsót a táo.
weal: *n.* balegbég.
wealth: *n.* kinabaknáng, sanikuá, gámeng, gupít.
wealthy: *adj.* nabaknáng.
wean: *v.* pusotén, pugsáyen.
weapon: *n.* ígam, ármas.
wear: *v.* ikawés, aramáten; **~ out** *v.* marúnot.
wearisome: *adj.* makaúma, makabannóg.
weary: *addj.* nautoyán, naúma; nabannóg.
weather: *n.* tiémpo, panawén; **~ vane** *n.* paligpálig, pirapír.
weave: *v.* aglága, agabél **~r** *n.* mangngabél.
web: *n.* abél, lága, linága; **spider ~** *n.* sáput; **worldwide ~** *n.* sangalubóngan a sáput.

wed: *v.* agkasár, agbóda, mangasáwa; *adj.* nakasár, naasawáan.

wedding: *n.* bóda, panagkallaysá, panagkasár; **contribution to** ~ *n.* paráwad.

wedge: *n.* pasengséng, palingatngát.

wedlock: *n.* panagasáwa, panagkallaysá.

Wednesday: *n.* Miérkoles; **Ash** ~ *n.* Kurkurús.

wee: *adj.* bassít.

weed: *n.* dákes a rúot; *v.* lugáman, sarnién.

week: *n.* domínggo, láwas(na).

weekend: *n.* arinúnos ti láwas.

weekly: *adj.* lin..áwas, dinomínggo.

weep: *v.* agíbit, agsángit, agluá.

weevil: *n.* bukbók; bakábak; rekkét.

weigh: *v.* timbengén, gantínget, katién.

weight: *n.* kadagsén, káti, gantíng, timbéng; ~**y** *adj.* nadagsén.

weir: *n.* ramá.

weird: *adj.* nakabututéng.

welcome: *v.* awáten a siraragsák, kabláaw; *n.* naimbág nga isasangpét; **You are** ~ Awán ti aniámanna.

weld: *v.* lanángen, pagsaúpen, aglanáng.

welfare: *n.* nam-áy, pagimbagán, rang-áy.

well: *n.* póso, bubón; ~**-balanced** *adj.* natimbéng; ~**-being** *n.* piá; *v.* agpussuák; *adj.* naimbág, nasayáat, napiá, nakaradkád, nasalun-át; ~**-behaved** *adj.* nasingpét; ~ **formed** *adj.* naádar, nataér; ~ **off** *adj.* nabaknáng, narang-áy.

welter: *v.* aglubnák, agaluyúoy.

wench: *n.* palanggapáng.

wend: *v.* agturóng.

west: *n.* láud.

westerly: *adv.* agpaláud.

western: *adj.* akinláud, maipapánití láud.

wet: *adj.* nabasá, nadam-ég; *v.* basaán; ~ **nurse** *n.* yáya.

whack: *v.* pang-óren, basnútan, banogbógen.

whale: *n.* baliéna.

wharf: *n.* pantalán, wayáng.

what: *pron, adv.* aniá.

whatever: *pron.* aniáman, úray aniá.

whealed: *adj.* nalítem.

wheat: *n.* trígo; ~ **field** *n.* katriguán.

wheedle: *v.* aliúgen, pasablógan, ay-aywén.

wheel: *n.* pílid, lígay, ruéda, kararét; **steering** ~ *n.* maníbela; ~ **chock** *n.* kálso.

wheel-barrow: *n.* karretília.

wheeze: *v.* umanit-ít, agsinglót.

whelp: *n.* úken.

when: *adv.* kaanó, inton-anó; idí, itáy.

whenever: *conj.* tunggál; patináyon no.

where: *adv.* sadíno; ayán.

whereas: *adv.* yantá, yantángay.

whereby: *adv., conj.* isú nga.

wherefore: *adv.* ngarúd, idínto nga.

whet: *v.* asáen, patademén.

whether: *conj.* no; ~ **or not** man wennó saán.

whetstone: *n.* pangasáan.

which: *n.* aniá, siasíno.

whichever: *adj., pron.* úray aniá.

whiff: *v.* pug-áw, pul-óy.

while: *adv.* báyat.

whim: *n.* kaprítso, kaykayát.

whimper: *v.* aganang-áng, agúngol, agsanang-í, aganiíl, agunnóy.

whimsical: *adj.* managráyo.

whine: *v.* agsaning-í, agásug, agágal, agtagúob.

whinny: *v.* aggaraígi.

whip: *n.* báut, pamáut, saplít, sanút; *v.* baúten, saplíten; ~**ing boy** *n.* bullabullán, pangipulotán, langdét.

whippletree: *n.* saudán.

whirl: *v.* agpusípos, agtayyék, aguddóg.

whirligig: *n.* paligpálig, weswés.

whirlpool: *n.* alikunó, kibnór, alibnúno.

whisker: *n.* íming, bárbas.

whisky: *n.* kíta ti árak, aguardiénte.

whisper: *v.* agarasáas, agngawngáw; *n.* arasáas.

whistle: *n.* sultíp, sagawísiw; *v.* agsultíp, agsagawísiw.

white: *adj.* puráw; napúdaw; ~ **ant** *n.* ánay; **dull** ~ nalítem a puráw.

whitewash: *v.* kapóren.

whither: *adv.* sadíno.

whitlow: *n.* ítib; **to have** ~ *v.* agbabásil.

whittle: *v.* tikapán, iwáen; kayásan.

who: *pron.* síno, siasíno, asíno.

whole: *adj.* sibubukél, dágup.

wholesale: *adj.* pakiáw.

wholesome: *adj.* makapiá, nasalun-át.

whom: *pron.* siasíno, síno.

whooping cough: *n.* uyék a pugíit.

whore: *n.* púta, pampám, balangkantís.

whorl: *n.* alipuspós, aligusgús.

whose: *pron.* makimbági.

why: *adv.* ápay.

wick: *n.* pabílo; bágis.

wicked: *adj.* nadangkés, managdakdákes, nadangkók.

wickerwork: *n.* inakílis.

wicket: *n.* darimángan.

wide: *adj.* (*spacious*) naláwa; (*not narrow*) akába; ~ **shouldered** *adj.* nalapaná.

widen: *v.* paakabáen, palawáen.

widespread: *adj.* sapásap.

widow: *n.* biúda, bálo a babái.

widower: *n.* bálo a laláki, biúdo.

widowhood: *n.* kinabálo.

width: *n.* kaakába, kaláwa, sekkég, lisdák.

wife: *n.* asáwa a babái, bakét.

wig: *n.* pudós.

wiggle: *v.* agkuyamkúyam; **~ the hips** *v.* agkinníkinní.

wiggler: *n.* balbaltík.

wild: *adj.* abló, naátap.

wilderness: *n.* kabakíran, kaginggingetán, letáng, langálang.

will: *n.* nákem, pagayatán, pakinákem; testaménto; *v.* -(n)to; ikeddéng.

willing: *adj.* siaayát, sitatarigágay, sidudúyos.

willow: *n.* karawáwi.

wilt: *v.* aglayláy, makeltáy.

win: *v.* mangábak, mangátiw; *n.* panangábak.

wince: *v.* agsanúd, agkiét, agpáing.

wind: *n.* ángin, pul-óy, puyúpoy; **favorable ~** *n.* búlon; **violent ~** *n.* bagió, umarubúob; **north ~** *n.* amián; **northeast ~** *n.* dugúdug; **northwest ~** *n.* panaplák; **south ~** *n.* abágat; **southwest ~** *n.* puyúpoy; **southeast ~** *n.* baetán; **one of eight ~s** *n.* baátan.

wind: *v.* ipulípol, iputípot; katikáten; sillaudán.

windlass: *n.* battuág, luttuág.

windmill: *n.* molíno (ti ángin).

window: *n.* táwa; **ticket ~** *n.* takília; **~ shade** *n.* kortína ti táwa; **~sill** *n.* paladpád; **~ post** *n.* hámba.

windpipe: *n.* ang-anguyób, aangsán, karabukób.

windshield: *n.* akinsángo a táwa ti lúgan.

windy: *adj.* naángin.

wine: *n.* árak, bíno; **sugarcane ~** *n.* bási.

wing: *n.* payák.

wink: *v.* agkiddáy, agkirém; *n.* kirém, kiddáy.

winning: *n.* panangábak; nangabákan.

winnow: *n.* bigáo; *v.* agtaép, agtar-áp.

winter: *n.* panawén ti lam-ék, panaglalam-ék.

wipe: *v.* punásen, nasnásan; **~ nose with arm** *v.* agamlíd; **~ feet/fingers** *v.* agdulinát.

wire: *n.* bárot, alámbre; **barbed ~** *n.* bárot a siítan.

wisdom: *n.* kinasírib, kinasarírit.

wise: *adj.* masírib, manákem, nasarírit.

wish: *v.* kalikagúman, tarigagáyan; *n.* kalikágum, tarigágay.

wit: *n.* ísip, pannakaammó, pannakaáwat; tagangtáng.

witch: *n.* brúha, mangkukúlam.

witchcraft: *n.* kinabrúha, kinamanangkukúlam.

with: *prep.* ken, kadá, agráman.

withdraw: *v.* isína, yadayó, ikkatén; agsanúd.

wither: *v.* malayláy, malpés; malaláw; masnéng.

withhold: *v.* tenglén, igáwid, siparén, ipaídam.

within: *prep.*, *adv.* ití unég; ití las-úd.

without: *prep.* awanán, ití laksíd.

withstand: *v.* subáen, sukíren, rupíren, sungáten, ibtúran.

witless: *adj.* munengmúneng, nakúpa.

witness: *n.* saksí, makaimátang, mangpaneknék; *v.* agsaksí, saksián.

witticism: *n.* parparató, rábak.

witty: *adj.* nasarírit.

wizard: *n.* baglán, mangkukúlam, áran, mangngaráding.

wobble: *v.* agkalóg, agwáli, agtiliwátiw; agpadpadayég.

wobbly: *adj.* nalukáy.

woe: *n.* kinakakaási.

wolf: *n.* lóbo.

woman: *n.* babái; **old ~** *n.* bakét; **young ~** *n.* balásang.

womanly: *adj.* binabái.

womb: *n.* aanakán, matrís.

wombstone: *n.* urídeng.

wonder: *n.* siddáaw, datdatlág; *v.* agbaláw, masdáaw.

wonderful: *adj.* nakaskasdáaw.

woo: *v.* armén.

wood: *n.* káyo, tarikáyo; **~worm (borer)** *n.* bokbók, líkup; **~ louse** *n.* balbalátong, bakenbákes.

woodpecker: *n.* tukkátok, pannuktók, mannagá, tagtagá.

wool: *n.* lána; dutdót.

word: *n.* saó, balikás; **bad ~** *n.* tanawátaw.

wording: *n.* pannakaisaó.

work: *n.* arámid, trabáho; akém; *v.* agtrabáho; **hard ~ing** nagagét.

worker: *n.* mangmanggéd; **fellow ~** *n.* kanúnong.

workman: *n.* trabahadór, mangmanggéd.

workshop: *n.* pagtrabahuán, pábrika.

world: *n.* lúbong, sangalubóngan.

worldly: *adj.* nailubóngan, naindagaán.

worldwide: *adj.* ití dágup ti lúbong.

worm: *n.* iggés; **earth~** *n.* alintá; **~-eaten** *adj.* iniggés; binokbók.

wormwood: *n.* ahíngko.

worn: *adj.* (*used*) talibugnay; **~ down** *adj.* gayót, malúma; narúnot; **~ out** *adj.* nalúdap; napúno; rutrút.

worry: *n.* dukót, síkor, aburrído; *v.* madanágan, riruén, agaburrído.

worse: *adj.* dakdákes.

worsen: *v.* kumáro, dumákes, lumanlán, dumagél.

worship: *v.* dayáwen, agkarárag; *n.* panagdaydáyaw.

worst: *adj.* kadaksán.
worth: *n.* ngína, patég.
worthless: *adj.* dákes, ur-úray, awán patégna.
worthwhile: *adj.* maikanáda.
worthy: *adj.* maikanáda, mainúgot.
wound: *n.* súgat, dánar, dúnor; *v.* sugátan;
   slight ~ *n.* kiráis.
wounded: *adj.* masugátan, nasaktán; natadtád.
wrangle: *v.* agaápa, agriringgór; agbibinggáw.
wrap: *v.* balkúten, bungonén, sapútan.
wrapper: *n.* pagkalkót, bungón.
wrath: *n.* ruród, pungtót, úlay.
wreak: *v.* ipasagába, ipalak-ám, ipabáles.
wreath: *n.* balángat a bulóng.
wreck: *v.* rebbaén, dadaélen, rakráken.
wrench: *n.* biradór, liábe.
wrest: *v.* rung-áden; tiritíren.
wrestle: *v.* aggabbó, aggúbal.
wrestling: *n.* gabbó, gúbal; **finger ~** *n.* torsí;
   arm ~ *n.* sanggól.
wretched: *adj.* maum-umsí, nakakaási,
   mangalkalamáos, mangoyapét, kuránges;
   nakurápay.
wriggle: *v.* aggulágol, agkilíkil.
wring: *v.* pespesén, tiritíren, ladditén.
wrinkle: *n.* karekkét, karenkén, kuretrét;
   íren.
wrist: *n.* pungupunguán, ngulayngguláy;
   ~ bone búkol.
writ: *n.* súrat, kasurátan.
write: *v.* agsúrat, suráten.
writer: *n.* mannúrat.
writhe: *v.* agtirtirítir.
writing: *n.* panagsúrat; **sound of ~** *n.*
   kumirríis.
wrong: *adj.* allílaw, di umisú, dákes.
wronged: *adj.* agrabiádo.
wry: *adj.* awingí, tirítir, píwis, nadawíris.
wry-mouthed: *adj.* díwig, kabbíbaw.

X

xiphisternum: *n.* am-ammútil.
x-ray: *n.* ráyo-ékis.

Y

yacht: *n.* yáte.
yam: *n.* kamóte; rabók, bútir, búga, karót;
   ~ bean singkamás, kamás.

yard: *n.* inaládan; **five ~s** *n.* anét.
yarn: *n.* linábag, talí a paggansílio, sag-út;
   ~ beam pagpulipúlan ti ur-áy.
yawn: *n.* wab, suyáab; *v.* agsuyáab, agwáb.
yea: *adv.* wen.
year: *n.* tawén; **last ~** idí napán a tawén; **the ~**
   before last idí kasangatawén; **three ~s ago**
   idí katimmawén.
yearly: *adj.*, *adv.* tinawén.
yearn: *v.* gumawgawáwa, aggágar, kumaráyo,
   agkalikágum.
yeast: *n.* lebadúra, búbod.
yell: *v.* agikkís, agláaw.
yellow: *adj.* kiáw, amarílio, duyáw.
yellowish: *adj.* nakusníg, duyáw.
yelp: *n.* taúl; *v.* agtaúl.
yes: *adv.* wen.
yesterday: *adv.* idí kalmán.
yet: *adv.* (di) pay.
yield: *v.* itulók, parnuáyen; palugodán.
yielding: *adj.* natulnóg, natulók; nakdít,
   namitmít.
yoke: *n.* sangól, páko.
yolk: *n.* ikgáy, nalabága ti itlóg.
yonder: *adv.* idiáy nay.
you: *pron.* siká, dakayó.
young: *adj.* ubíng, agtutúbo; **~ unmarried**
   man *n.* baró; **~ unmarried woman** *n.*
   balásang; **~ pig** *n.* buriás; **~er sibling** *n.* ádi.
youngest: *adj.* kaubingán; **~ child** *n.* inaúdi.
youngster: *n.* agtutúbo, bumaró.
your: *adj.* -m(o); -yo.
yours: *pron.* kukuám, kukuáyo, bágim,
   bágiyo.
youth: *n.* kinaagtutúbo; **~ful** *n.* agkabannuág.
yucca: *n.* bagbagkóng, kamote-de-móro.
Yuletide: *n.* Paskuá.

Z

zeal: *n.* gagét, regtá, anép.
zealous: *adj.* nagagét, naanép.
zebra: *n.* sébra.
zenith: *n.* matúon, pantók.
zero: *n.* awán, séro.
zest: *n.* ímas, ramán, nánam.
zigzag: *v.* agsiwetsiwét, agsikkosikkó.
zit: *n.* kamúro.
zither: *n.* sakabútse.
zone: *n.* las-úd, sákup, sóna.

APPENDIXES

Grammatical Charts

Table 1. Articles

	Non-personal		Personal	
	Singular	**Plural**	**Singular**	**Plural**
Core	*ti* (neutral), *diay* (definite)	*dagití*	*ni*	*da*
Oblique	*ití*	*kadagití*	*kenní*	*kadá*

Table 2. Demonstratives

		Article	Demonstrative			
			Core		Oblique	
Visibility	Range		singular	plural	singular	plural
Neutral	Proximal	*toy*	*daytóy*	*dagitóy*	*kadaytóy*	*kadagitóy*
	Medial	*ta*	*daytá*	*dagitá*	*kadaytá*	*kadagitá*
	Distal	*diay*	*daydiáy*	*dagidiáy*	*kadaydiáy*	*kadagidiáy*
Out of sight	Recent	*tay*	*daytáy*	*dagitáy*	*kadaytáy*	*kadagitáy*
	Remote	*di*	*daydí*	*dagidí*	*kadaydí*	*kadagidí*

Table 3. Pronouns

Person			Case				
1	**2**	**3**	**Independent**	**Ergative**	**Absolutive**	**Oblique**	**Gloss**
+	-	-	*siák*	*=k(o)*	*=ak*	*kaniák*	1s
-	+	-	*siká*	*=m(o)*	*=ka*	*kenká*	2s familiar
-	-	+	*isú(na)*	*=na*	-	*kenkuána*	3s
+	+	-	*datá*	*=ta*	*=ta*	*kadatá*	1 dual incl
+	-	+	*dakamí*	*=mi*	*=kamí*	*kadakamí*	1 pl excl
+	+	-	*datayó*	*=tayó*	*=tayó*	*kadatayó*	1 pl incl
-	+	+	*dakayó*	*=yo*	*=kayó*	*kadakayó*	2 pl, (2 formal)
-	-	++	*isúda*	*=da*	*=da*	*kadakuáda*	3p

Table 4. Fused double enclitic pronouns

Actor	Patient							
	siak	sika	isu	data	dakami	datayo	dakayo	isuda
siak	RF	=ka	=k(o)	-	-	-	=kayo	=k(o) idá
sika	=nak	RF	=m(o)	-	=nakami	-	-	=m(o) idá
isu	=nak	=naka	RF/=na	=nata	=nakami	=natayo	=nakayo	=na idá
data	-	-	=ta	RF	-	-	-	=ta idá
dakami	-	=daka	=mi	-	RF	-	=dakayo	=mi idá
datayo	-	-	=tayo	-	-	RF	-	=tayo idá
dakayo	=dak	-	=yo	=data	=dakami	-	RF	=yo idá
isuda	=dak	=daka	=da	=data	=dakami	=datayo	=dakayo	RF/=da idá

RF = Reflexive = Ergative clitic + *ti bagí*. *Nakítak ti bagík* 'I saw myself'.

Table. 5 Verbal focus (voice)

Transitivity	Focus	Affix	Perfective	Example	Gloss
Intransitive	Actor	ag-	nag-	*ag*katáwa	laugh
		-um-	-imm-	*du*makkél	grow, enlarge
Detransitive		mang-	nang-	*mang*án	eat
Transitive	Patient	-en	-in-	surát*en*	write something
	Directional	-an	-in- -an	surát*an*	write to someone
	Conveyance	i-	in-; iny-	*i*súrat	write down
	Benefactor	i- -an	in(y)- -an	*i*daítan	sew for someone
	Comitative	ka-	kina-	*ka*tugáw	sit with; seat mate
	Instrumental	pag-	pinag-	*pag*íwa	slice with; knife

Table 6. Aspectual morphology of dynamic verbs

Focus	Affix	Perfective/complete	Progressive	Future
Actor	ag- agkatáwa 'laugh'	nag- nagkatáwa	agCVC- agkatkatáwa	ag- ..=(n)to agkatáwanto
	-um- tumakdér 'stand'	-imm- timmakder	CumVC- tumaktakdér	-um- ..=(n)to tumakderto
	mang-, maN- mangdáit 'sew'	nang-, naN- nangdáit	mangCVC-; maNVC- mangdàdáit	mang- ..=(n)to mangdáitto
Patient	-en suráten 'write'	-in- sinúrat	CVC- -en sursuráten	-en=..=(n)to surátento
Directional	-an adaywán 'leave'	-in- -an inadaywán	CVC- -an ad-adaywán	-an ..=(n)to adaywánto
Theme	i- iyáwid 'bring home'	in(y)- inyáwid	iCVC- iyaw-áwid	i- ..=(n)to iyáwidto
Benefactor	i- -an isurátan 'write for/on behalf of'	in(y)- -an insurátan	iCVC- -an isursurátan	i- -an..=(n)to isurátanto
Comitative	ka- kasaó 'speak to'	kina- kinasaó	kaCVC kasàsaó	ka- ..=(n)to kasaónto
Instrumental	pag- pagtugáw 'chair'	pinag- pinagtugáw	pagCVC- pagtugtugáw	pag- ..=(n)to pagtugáwto

Table 6. Potentive Verbs

Focus	Dynamic	Potentive	Example verb	Gloss
Actor	ag-, -um-, mang-	maka,	makalangóy makakíta	be able to swim see
Patient	-en	ma-	madungpár	accidentally collide
Directional	-an	ma- -an	masagádan	happen to sweep; be swept
Theme	i-	mai-	maikábil	manage to put
Benefactive	i- -an	mai- -an	maisurátan	be able to write for

Table 7. Nominalizations and Frequentatives

	Verbal affix	Gerund (Manner)	Instrum.	Locative/Reason	Perfective	Frequentative
D y n a m i c	ag-	panag-	pag-	pag- -an	nag- -an	manag-
	-um-	iCV-	-	-um- -an	-imm- -an	Cumv-
	mang-	panang-	pang-	pang- -an	nang- -an	manang-
	mangi-	panangi-	pangi-	pangi- -an	nangi- -an	manangi-
	mangipa-	panangipa-	pangipa-	pangipa- -an	nangipa- -an	manangipa-
	mangpa-	panangpa-	pangpa-	pangpa- -an	nangpa- -an	manangpa-
	mangpai-	panangpai-	pangpai-	pangpai- -an	nangpai- -an	manangpai-
	mangpag-	panangpag-	pangpag-	pangpag- -an	nangpag- -an	manangpag-
P o t e n t i v e	maka-	pannaka-	paka-	paka- -an	naka- -an	mannaka-
	makai-	pannakai-	pakai-	pakai- -an	nakai- -an	mannakai-
	makaipa-	pannakaipa-	pakaipa-	pakaipa- -an	nakaipa- -an	mannakaipa-
	makapa-	pannakapa-	-	pakapa- -an	nakapa- -an	mannakapa-
	makapai-	pannakapai-	pakapai-	pakapai- -an	nakapai- -an	mannakapai-
	makapag-	pannakapag-	pakapag-	pakapag- -an	nakapag- -an	mannakapag-
	makapagi-	pannakapagi-	pakapagi-	pakapagi- -an	nakapagi- -an	mannakapagi-
S o c i a l	maki-	pannaki-	paki-	paki- -an	naki- -an	mannaki-
	makipag-	pannakipag-	pakipag-	pakipag- an	nakipag- -an	mannakipag-
	makipagi-	pannakipagi-	pakipagi-	pakipagi- -an	nakipagi- -an	mannakipagi-

Maps

Dagiti Mapa

MAP 1. THE PHILIPPINES – TI PILIPINAS

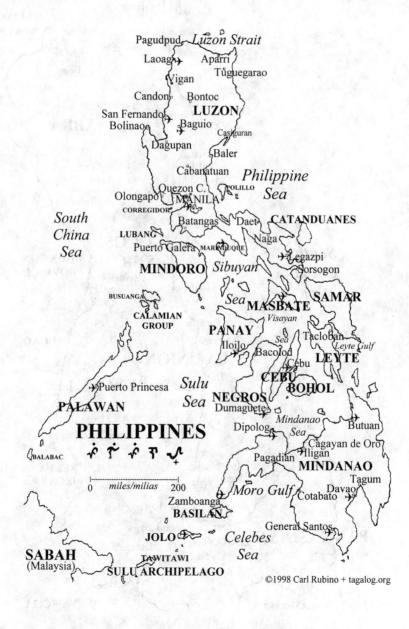

©1998 Carl Rubino + tagalog.org

MAP 2. NORTHWEST LUZON – TI KAILOKUAN

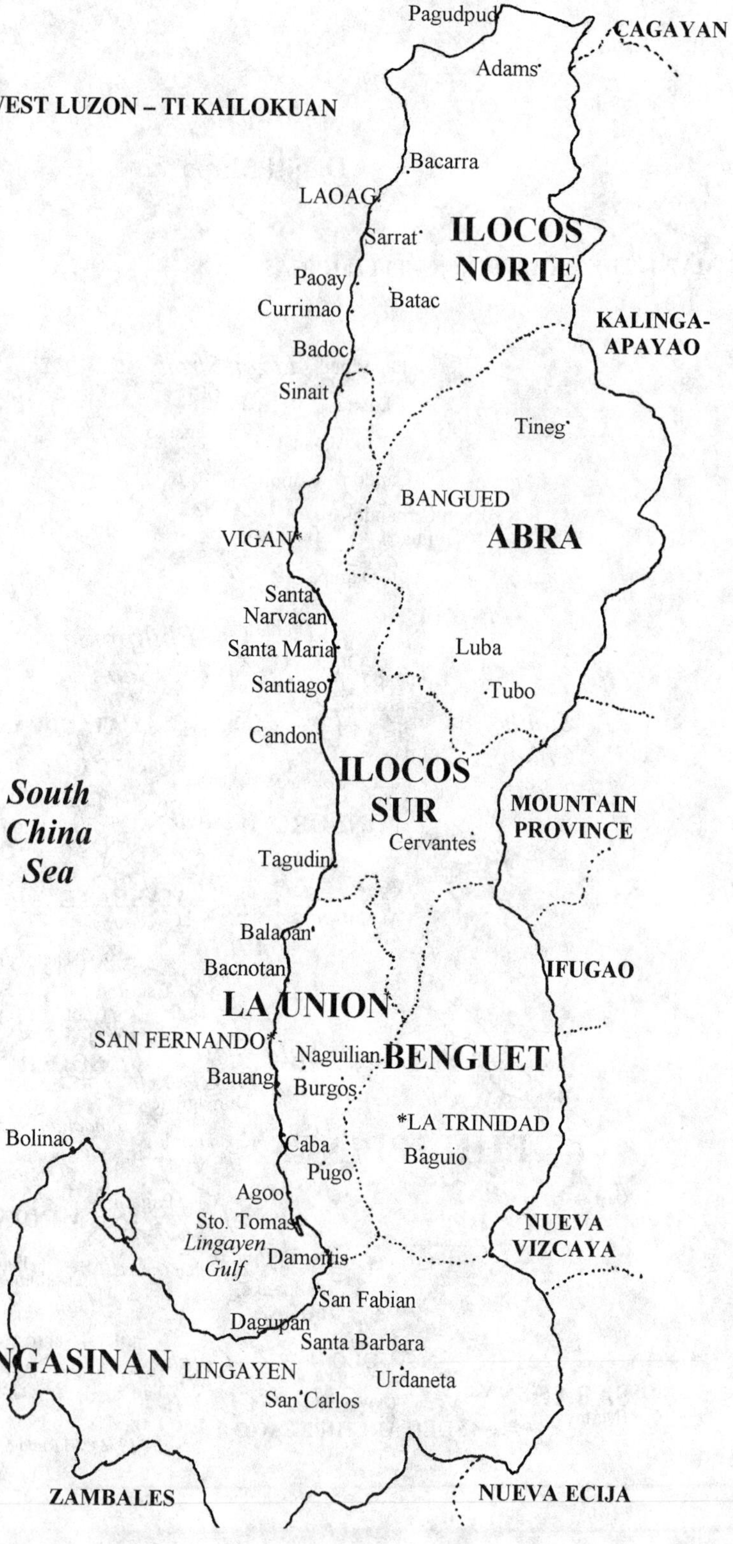

Pagudpud

CAGAYAN

Adams

Bacarra

LAOAG

ILOCOS
NORTE

Sarrat

Paoay
Currimao

Batac

KALINGA-
APAYAO

Badoc

Sinait

Tineg

BANGUED

VIGAN

ABRA

Santa
Narvacan

Santa Maria

Luba

Santiago

Tubo

Candon

South
China
Sea

ILOCOS
SUR

Cervantes

MOUNTAIN
PROVINCE

Tagudin

Balaoan

Bacnotan

LA UNION

IFUGAO

SAN FERNANDO

Naguilian

BENGUET

Bauang

Burgos

Bolinao

Caba

*LA TRINIDAD

Pugo

Baguio

Agoo
Sto. Tomas
Lingayen
Gulf

Damortis

NUEVA
VIZCAYA

San Fabian

Dagupan

Santa Barbara

PANGASINAN LINGAYEN

Urdaneta

San Carlos

ZAMBALES

NUEVA ECIJA

MAP 3. THE BATANES ISLANDS – DAGITI PURO ITI AMIANAN

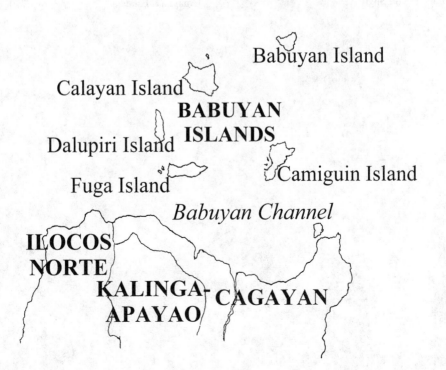

The Northern Islands
Dagiti Puro iti Amianan

Amianan Island

Itbayat Island
Diogo Island

**BATANES
ISLANDS**

Batan Island
Sabtang Island

Balintang Channel

Babuyan Island

Calayan Island

**BABUYAN
ISLANDS**

Dalupiri Island

Fuga Island

Camiguin Island

Babuyan Channel

**ILOCOS
NORTE**

**KALINGA-
APAYAO**

CAGAYAN

Traditional Ilocano Songs

Kankanta Nga Iloko

Pamulinawen (Stone-Hearted Lady)

Pamulinawen
Pusok indengam man
Toy umas-asug
Agrayo ita sadiam.
Panunotem man
Dika pagintultulngan
Toy agayat, agruknoy ita emmam.

Refrain:
Issemmo diak kalipatan
Ta nasudi unay a nagan,
(Ta) uray sadin ti ayan,
Disso sadino man,
Aw-awagak a di agsarday
Ta naganmo nga kasam-itan
No malagipka, pusok ti mabang-aran

Adu nga sabsabong, adu nga rosrosas
Ti adda't ditoy, Nena, nga mabuybuyak,
Ngem awan man laeng ti sabali nga
    liwliwak
No di la dayta sudim ken imnas.
No umulogak nga mapan magmagna
Dayta raniagmo, Neneng nga gapu kenka.

Manang Biday (Older Sister Biday)

Lalaki:
Manang Biday, ilukatmo man
Ta bentana ikalumbabam
Ta kitaem toy kinayawan
Ay matayakon no dinak kaasian

Babai:
Siasinno(ka) nga aglabaslabas
Ditoy hardinko pagay-ayamak
Ammon ngarud nga balasangak
Sabong ni lirio, dipay nagukrad

Lalaki:
Denggem ading ta bibinenka
ta inkanto diay sadi daya
agalakanto't bunga't mangga
ken lansones pay, adu nga kita

Chorus:
No nangato dimo sukdalen
no nababa dimo gaw-aten,
no naregreg dimo piduten,
ngem labaslabasamto met laeng

Babai:
Daytoy paniok no maregregko
ti makapidot ikutannanto
ta nagmarka iti naganko
nabordaan pay ti sinampuso

Lalaki:
Alaem dayta kutsilyo
ta abriem toy barukongko
tapno maipapasmo ti guram
kaniak ken sentimiento

Chorus

Naraniag a Bulan (Shiny Moon)

O naraniag a bulan
Un-unnoyko't indengam
Dayta naslag a silawmo
Dika kad ipaidam
O naraniag a bulan
Sangsangitko indengam
Toy nasipnget a lubongko
Inka kad silawan
Tapno diak mayaw-awan

No inka nanglipaten
Karim kaniak naumagen[1]
Samsam-itek ni patay
O bulan ket aklunem
Nanglaylay toy ayatkon
Inka kadi palasbangem
Un-unnoyko, darasem nga ikeddeng

Ti Ayat ti Maysa nga Ubing (The Love of a Child)

Ti ayat ti maysa nga ubing
    Nasamsam-it ngem hasmin
Kasla sabong nga apag-ukrad
Iti bulan ti Abril
Ti ayat ti maysa nga lakay
Aglalo no agkabaw
Napait, Napait,
Napait nga makasubkar

---

[1] *alt*: Karim kaniak naggibusen

Baybay-am ta ubing, Lelong
Sumapulka tay balo
A kapadpad ta ubanmo
Ken dayta tuppolmo

Baybay-am nga panunuten
Ti ayat ti maysa nga ubing
Aglalo, aglalo
No addan makin-aywanen

Aglalo, aglalo
No addan makin-aywanen

Imdengam O Imnas[2] (Listen, O Precious One)

Imdengam, O Imnas
Ta inka kad mangrikna,
Kadagitoy nga un-unnoy,
Toy gumawgawawa.
Ammuem nga toy ayatko
Rimmusing gapu kenka,
Ta siksika awan sabali[3]
Kinayawam daytoy rikna.

Apay apay dayta nakem,
Agmayeng, mangduadua,
Wenno ipagarupmo aya nga rabrabakenka?
Saan, saan, saan biagko,
Punasem kad dayta duaduam,
Ta awanen ti ay-ayatek
No di la siksika.

No duaduaem pay (If You Still Doubt— Serenade)

No duaduaem pay laeng ti pegges ni ayat
Nalawag la unayen a ranggasmo kaniak[4]
Ala man biagko, sawem ti pamuspusak
Tapno mabalinka a lipaten o imnas

Refrain:
Lipatenkanton wen
Ngem addaakton idiay tanem
Ngem no itan,
saanen nga mabalinen, ay!
Itdem ni ayat, dinak kad pagtuoken
Yantangay siksika ti innak ay-ayaten.

Refrain

Itdem ni ayat, dinak kad pagtuoken
Yantangay siksika ti innak ay-ayaten.

Bannatiran (Bannatiran Bird)

Bannatiran, ta dutdotmo't kalilibnosan
Ta panggepmo dika patuluyan
Suminakan sadino aya't papanam?
Sadino, bannatiran, ania nga kayo ti inka
    pagdissuan?

Daydiay kayo nga agsabong ken ayat
panawam man,
Ay babawyem ton kamaudianan
No ni liday ti matumpungan

Ania nga sabong ti kayatmo bannatiran,
Ta uray awan pilit nga inka isapulan.
Ta sika ti sarming nga paganninawan
Iti raniag da init ken bulan.

Duayya ni Ayat (Dungdunguenkanto) (Lullaby of Love [I Will Love You])

Dungdunguenkanto unay unay,
Indayonenkanto't sinamay
Tultuluden kanto't naalumamay
Pagammuanen inkanto mailibay

Refrain:
Annay, pusok, annay, annay,
Nasaem, naut-ut la unay.
Itdem kaniak ta pannaranay
Ta kaasiak nga maidasay.

Apaman nga inkanto makaturog
Iyabbongkonto[5] ta rupam daytoy paniok.
Tapnon dinakanto kagaten ti lamok
Ken maimasmonto't maturog.

Refrain

Apaman nga inkanto makariing
Dagdagusenkanto nga sappuyuten
Nga ililili kas maysa nga ubing
Ket nanamem sam-it ni essem

---

[2] Also referred to as *Apay Apay*.
[3] *alt*: Nagtaud gapu kenka, sika awan sabali.
[4] *alt*: Nalawag la unayen nga ulpitmo ken ranggas

---

[5] *alt*: Iyarpawkonto ta rupam daytoy paniok.

Padapadatayo (Ilocos Norte Birthday Song)

Padapadatay nga agsisiragsak
a kumablaaw – mangipaduyakyak
ta nagtengngan ti aldaw
a pannakayanak ni *(nagan)*
a napnuan gasat

Balangat nga naurnos dagiti sabsabong
nga umaymi kenka isaad ta ulom.
Kasta met nga iyawatmi kenka
ti naindayawan unay a palma
tapno isu ti mangipakita ti
ragragsakmi amin a sangapada

Sapay iti Dios ta ilayonna koma
ta salun-atmo, piam ken regtam
Ken ta singpetmo a nagpaiduma
nga ap-apalan dagiti kas kenka

Toy Karayo (This Affection)

Toy karayo nga imballaigim
dagiti un-unnoyko nga dika aklonen
Ta impagarupmon sa a barengbareng
Ulbod allilaw panangirurumen

Nairut a karik ken sapatak awan patiem
Naisnekan a panangun-unnoyko
dika pay denggen
Amin a pananggutigotko inka pay lalaisen
A panangidadanes, panangirurumen

Ania't gustuem a denggen
a pakabukayan dayta kaasim
Tapnon ayatko pasudiem
ket agbiagak a sitatalingengen

Igid Diay Baybay (Shoreline)

Idi tiempo ti igaaw
ken rabii a nalinnaaw
Intanto a dua kas natarnaw
agkanta igid diay baybay

Iti nalaus a gagarko
No dumteng daytoy a tiempo
Agtugawkanto iti takiagko
diay baybay ket matmatamto

Sadiay anian a ragsak,
Sadiay awan ti rigat
Sadiay makalinglingay
diay baybay ket nalinak

Ket intanto ikankanta
ti nalaus nga ayan-ayatta
Danggayantanto a kas gitara
diay awir ti danum a bumaba

Sadiay anian a ragsak..

Tagtagainep Laeng (Just a Dream)

Maysa a rabii tinagtagainepko
Immaymo pinasudi ti ayatta a dua
Immapay kaniak isem ken ragsak
Inamnamak nagsubli
kas man di marsaak

Datakan idi ti nagin-ayan-ayat
inggana't tungpal toy biag
Dita naglisi
Nakariingak, awanka a nakitak
Nagsennaay toy pusok
a ta di met pudno

Ayat kadagiti Ama ken Ina (Love for Father and Mother)

No ni ina't sabong ti pangyarigak
A mamunas ti adu a leddaang
Yarigko met ni ama a naayat
Manarked biagmi a dua

Nagpategen ti (dakkel nga) utang
A di mabalin a subalitan
Kada ama ken ina nagutangan
Ayat dungngoda't naruay

Ngem no sabongak ta mula ni ina
a manaraon kaniak manapaya
Ramut laeng ni Ama a napigsa
a mangted biagmi a dua

O naayat nadungngo nga inami
Awan ammomi a pagsubad kenka
Awatem ngarud toy puso ken biagmi
A pagyamanmi kenka.

Saguday[6] (Precious Gift)

Ta nagsaway a pintasmo awan umasping
No maraniagan ta lumabbaga nga pingping
Nga nakaitangpakan ti kallidmo
  nga kasla bituen
Aglalon tumamdagka iti agsapa
  wenno malem

Refrain:
No bingiem dayta bibigmo saka umisem
Agparang a dagus dayta kas marfil a ngipen
Daegen met ta buok mo pangulkuloten
Ket ta kidaymo kas bullalayaw iti malem

Awan ngatan ti kas kenkan (a nabukelen)
Nga imparabur ti Dios nga inka kaasping
Ta binukbukudam aminen nga talugading
Ta uray no agmisuotka, napintaska(nto)
  laeng

No bingiem dayta bibigmo saka umisem
Agparang a dagus dayta kas marfil a ngipen
Daegen met ta buok no pangulkuloten
Ket ta kidaymo kas bullalayaw iti malem

No Siak ti Agayat (If I Were the One to Love)

No siakto ti agayat
Kadagita nga pintasmo
Dikanto paulogen
No nalamiis ti tiempo.
Tay-akto nga payatam,
Butaka nga pagtugawam,
Ap-apakto't paniolito,
Paniolito ni Lirio.
No koma no mabalin
Agbalinak nga singsing,
Nga umay umapiring
Ta ramaymo no mabalin.
No koma no piniaka
Burasenka nga naata,
Kanenka nga naganus,
Paluomennaka toy pusok.
No makitak Ading
Napintas a pingpingmo,
Rosas nga eberlasting
panangkita toy matak.
ket uray no matayak
Duapulo't uppat oras,
No makitak isemmo,
Dagus met nga agbiagak.

(Chorus)
No sika la koma,
Maysa a kendi lemon,
Iparabawka toy dilak
Tuliden tultuliden.
Saanka a kagaten,
Saanka met alimonen,
Ket ditoy rabaw dilak
Abalbalayen.
No siakto t'agayat
Ading ta imnasmo,
Saanka a palubosan
No dakes ti tiempo.
Tay banglo pagtugawam,
Aplagak paniolito.
Ken daytay pagiddaam,
Abbungakto ay-ayat.

No Siakto ti Agayat (When I Love)

No siakto ti agayat
Siakto ti agpili
Nanumo ken nasingpet
Naemma nga babai
Ta uray no napugot
Wenno napobre
No ammona nga salimetmetan
Ti dayawmi nga lallaki

O sabong a pinili
Ay agukradka kadi
Ta yanmo nga sanga
ket sumangbaykami
Dimo kad laisen
Daytoy kinapobre
A mangidaton kenka toy bagi
Paadipen ken agserbi

Ala Kadin, Inkay Yawat (Please Give— Christmas Song)

Ala kadin, inkay yawat
Tay aginaldomi a pirak
Ta uray sisiam a sikapat
No isu't itedyo kadakam a pagayat.
Dika ket saksakiten, nanangmi
Ti magted tay aginaldomi
Di mabayag maabrotmonto
No malakoyonto daytoy baboyyo

---

[6] Also called 'Ta Nagsaway a Pintasmo'.

Dung-aw (Dirge)

Ay ama nga nageb-ebba
Dinak man kaasian aya
A panawan a sisina
Tay uneg balay a kasa.

Pakada (Farewell)

Adios, salda toy riknak.
Kalapati nga naimnas.
Biagko, panawanka,
Sayamusom nga liwliwa
Daytoy retratok ipenpenmo
Ita let-ang ta barukongmo,
Ta isunto't murmuraymo
No sumken ta ladingitmo.

Panagpakada (Farewell)

Idiak siak iti
Bassit nga tinagibi,
Diak pay nakasubalit
Ti ayatna nga nasudi
Ta narigat gayam
Iti anak nga lalaki,
No dumtengen ti gasatna,
No dumtengen ti gasatna,
Dika makalisi
Agpakada'kon
Balay a dinakdakkelak,
Ken kasta met kenka,
Paraangan nga nagay-ayamak,
Adios hardin
O hardin a nagmulmulaak
Adios Tatang ken Nanang,
Adios Manong ken Manang,
Inggat iti patay.

Panawankan Biagko (Farewell, My Love [Deathbed Song])

Itan ket umasideg ket umadani
Ti ipupusayko dita arpadmo
Biagko, agsingpetka.
Ta no itan ket panawankan.
Luluak agarubos punasem ida.

Mannamili (Potters)

Taga-awaykami nga agdamdamili
Naragsak ti biagmi
Awan dukdukotmi
Nupay aduda't manglalais kadakami

Ta napanglawkam laeng nga mannamili
Toy napigket nga daga
Pitpipitpitenmi ammona
Dangga yanmi't kankanta
Takkiagmi a napigsa
Kettang ken bannogmi dikam iginigina
Aglalo no adda ni Manong ditoy denna
Sakamto sukogen
Banga, dalikan, damilien
Linisen, pasilengen
Pitpiten a nalaing
Tapno maayo, magargari kay amin
Ket madardarasdanto nga lakuen

Lalaki:
Adingko, maluksawak
Ta nabuong tay banga

Babai:
Maisublim pay ita
tay patgek nga banga?
No dimo tinippay saan a nabuong
Agaluadka to ipulongka ken Nanang

Lalaki:
Mano, ading ti bayadna
tay damili nga banga?
Nangina ken nalaka, ituredko latta

Babai:
Nalaka, ading
Dios unay ti agngina

Duayya (Lullaby)

Maturog, duduayya
Maturogkad tay bunga
Tay lalaki nga napigsa
Ta inton dumakkel tay bunga,
isunto aya tay mammati
Tay amin nga ibagami.
Ay duayya, maturog man tay
binonga lalaki nga napigsa
Anakka nga binonga
lalaki a napigsa
Ta no dumakkel ket
sanggirkonto nga napigsa
Ket sarukodkonto nga napigsa
No kunkunak la ket tay binonga
Ta bareng dumakkel ket nalaka
Sikanto ti yan ti namnama
No maibuston daytoy pigsa.
Maturog aya ti lalaki
Nga arkos bakodtot' ili
Ta inton mapadakkelmi

Ket mapatan-aymin lalaki
Ta mapanto aya agbiahe
Tay ad-adayo nga ili.
Ngem ti kad ibilinko nay
Ket mangalakanto kadi
Tay manto kad a tamburi
Ken singsingko nga diamanti
Ken tay aritosko nga birilyanti
Ta addanto inta pangrirriri
Tay napintas nga babai.

Nasudi ni Ayat (Love Is Grand)

Nasudi unay ni ayat no dipay maumag,
Katimbengna toy biag ket puon met amin da
   ragsak
Ta na dadduma kasla awanen ti makarsaak,
Kas agnanayonto laeng
Ti langtona nga sibibiag.
Ta no ni ayat uray kasano ti kasam-itna
No gaguemna ti mangulbod ken manggulib
Nalaka unay ti inna pinangliklik
Ay awanen kaasi ti agayat no dina ipasnek.
Gapuna nga lagipen ti pateg ni annad,
Tapnon maliklikam ti sikap ni naulbod nga
   agayat,
Ta no kas agbaybay-a ket agpaay sabali nga
   biag,
Siaaddanto la da ragsak ken dalus nga awan
   pumadpad.

Da Mangngalap ken Agsansana (The Fisherman and Salt Makers)

Ipagsanaankami
Asin ti pagbiaganmi
Awan ti dukdukotmi
Naragsak ti biagmi,
Nupay aduda't manglalalis mangbabain
Ta napanglawkam la nga mangasasain.

Babai:
Diay sibay ti baybay
Kellangami nga umuna,
Danggayanmi't kankanta
Taktakiagmi a napigsa,
Kettang ken bannagmi dikam iginginga
Aglalo no adda ni Manong ditoy denna.

Lalaki:
Adingko, aganuska,
Bagim ti agsansana.

Babai:
Wen, Manong agalistoka
Agkalap ikan ken kurita,
Nakaap-apal nga agpayso't pinagbiagda
Nangngalap ken agsansana agbagayda.

Kanta ti Ulila (Song of an Orphan)

Simpuonek nga irugi
Tay pinagbiagmi nakakaasi
Anaknak ti maysa nga pobre
Nga naipalpalais ditoy ili.
Ubingak nga maladaga
Binilbilinnak daydi nana,
Anakko agsingsingpetka
Ket innakon sabali nga daga.

Tarong, Kamatis, Paria (Eggplant, Tomato, Bittermelon)

Iti bigbigat nga agsapa
Agtatamdagkam man idiay tawa
Addada tarong, kamatis, paria
Nangngegko ida nga'gsasarita
Ti kunan tarong kadakuada
Siak ti kaimasan kadakay a dua
Ni ngarud parya simmungbat ita
sika tarong napalangguadka
Siak ti mangmangted-salun-atda dagiti tattao
Ay aduda nangnangruna pay dagiti
   agbasbasa
ken dagiti ubbing nga maladaga
Ni kamatis, immisem laeng ay gagayyem
Inkay agparbeng no siak ti mailaok iti
   dinengdeng
no maluto naimas manen

Laguerta ti Langit (Door of Heaven— Humorous Song)

Laguerta ti langit agkansion ni umed
Agsigsigunda ni baed
Agdengdengngeg met ti tuleng
Aggitgitara ni pukol
Agsalsala ni pigsol
Adda met ni dulingnaka mulengleng laeng.
Ni tangad binaonda'pan
Simmukmon ti arak
Nasabatna ni singkol
Sinikolna diay botelia ket naburak.
Kinatawaan ni gusing
Kinusilapan ni gilab
Adda met ni lupoy,
Ta sipat la a sipat.

Ni kissiw isu't kosineroda
Nga'glutluto ti kanen ken sidada
No madanonanen tay oras panagkissiwna
Banga ken pariok,
ikusaykusayna.

Ilokana a Nadayag (Popular Ilocana)

O Ilokana nga nadayag
Sabongka man a napusaksak
Liwliwadaka't marigrigat
Liwliwada met aya ni ragsak
Sabongka nga ap-apalan
Kapatadam a balasang
Dayawmo ti kapatgan
Kupit a di matulawan
Ilokana a napintas
Taeng da singpet ken imnas
Talugading adda kenka
Amin a puso agrukbabda
Singpetmo pagraeman da pintasmo
Pagdayawandaka
Ilokanaka patiennak
Bagnoska nga di matulawan

Kasasaad ti Kinabalasang (Condition of Maidenhood)

Kasasaad ti kinabalasang
Paset ti biag kararagsakan,
No idiamon ket inka panawan
Aminmonton dika masublian
Adda ragsak ti makiasawa,
No ni ayat kabarbarona,
Ngem inton kamaudiananna
Rikut ti biag pasamakenna.
Ay, annadam, ti kinabalasang
Ti dana nga inka addakan,
Ta no dika makapudno ken asawam
Ay, di lumbes kugtaranna dayta rupam.

As-asug dagiti Kararua (The Complaints of the Souls)

O inami nga bumalay,
Agriingkay nga agmurmuray
Siak ita di kararua
Di minatayyo nga immununa
Addaak ti arubayan
Nga arsadanan ti agdan
Agdan nga inulogan

Idi ipandak idiay simbaan.
Ket idi indak impisok
Di abot inkay kinotkot
Luayo di agarubos
Ket sangityo ti di mabubos.
Ket idi indak gaburan
Luayo di agarubayan,
Sangityo ti di mabubusan,
Ket bangkayko ti inkay gawidan.
Ket idi indak panawan
Kamposanto nga kalawaan,
Leddaangyo ti napalaluan,
Adu nga lua di agpatinggan.
Ket idi inkay nakasangpet
Balay nagpaiduma't ngayed
Timekyo awan ti mangmangngeg
No di ti adu nga saibbek.
Nadanon ti ikakasiam,
Idi kuan ti ibubulan,
Pinagtawen di napuotan,
Sa lagipyo kaniak inaw-awan
Kasta la ti kasasaad
Ti aglak-am adu nga rigat.
Leddaang kas di malasat,
Ngem ti Apo't mangted supapak.

Bulan Sardam (Evening Moon)

Bulan sardam
Pambian ti babbalasang
Pagsunayan ti babaknang
Baknang nga i-San Juan
San Juan a i-Bamban

Tontonennaka toy Ayat (My Love Looks for You)

Tontonennaka toy ayat
Ayat biag daytoy kararuak
Sapsapulennaka toy gasat
Nga mangaklulo ken mangalasag.
O Dueña nga pagraemak,
Yetnagmo't kaasim ket indengannak,
Ta uray no pakatayak
No isu't gustuem sia' namungak.
Mangnamnamaak, mangnamnamaak,
Ngem tinsa met rigat
Nga masansan ken agdama nga kalak-amak,
Ta no ngayangayek nga idaton kenka toy
    ayat,
Diak ammo dayta kunam met nga isungbat.

Ti Dayaw (Honor)

Ti Dayaw uray bassit unay,
No ammo nga salimetmetan
Dumakkel nga di agkurang
No awan mangtunday
Ammuen met ti pateg ni ayat
Tapno malisiam ti sikap
Ni naulbod nga 'gayat
Gapuna, Neneng, dika agpuloko
Dika agriro, dimo ipalubos,
Ta dikanto mairuburob
Manipud dapan inggana't tuktok.

Toy Datonko (My Offering)

No daytoy kuma ket sabong
Napno't banglo agayumuom
Isu't innak yarkos
Pagdalanan ket muymuyong.
No daytoy koma ket bituen
Makapurar iti sileng,
Burarek nga ububonen,
Nga ikuentas kenka, Neneng.
Ikutam man wenno saan,
Toy pusok, bukodmo kukuam,
Patgem man wenno ranggasam
Kayawmo inggana't patay.
Uray pay no tutuokem,
Uray pay no rabrabakem,
Toy pusok kukuam laeng
Kayawmo inggana't tanem.

Sainita (Ideal Farmer's Wife)

Nagrigat nga agpasion
Panagbiag asawa't mannalon
Kanayon a nasapa't bangon
Lalaki mapantaltalon,
Agawitto manen ti balon
Agsikka pay iti bunubon
No malem ket agawidton
Ta daytayto man agluton.
Ngem nupay kasano't rigat
Adu a dukdukuten ti biag
No lugarmo ti agragsak
Masapul ti tumayaktak.
Ipadas nga'd ti kumanta
Ipadas met ti sumala
Padasen met nga iparang
Sainita idi kalman.

Dagiti Mulak (My Plants)

Nagmulaak ti katuday
Diay tuktok diay bantay,
Napan met kinaraykay
Ni nadawel a kannaway.
Agaluadka sika kannaway
Ta uggesek dayta ramay
Ta aramidek a sagaysay
Sagaysay ni Lela Kikay.
Nagmulaak ti tabako
Diay tuktok diay puro,
Napan met sinang-sangdo
Ni nadawel a kabalio.
Agaluadka kabalio
Tuktukkolek dayta sungo,
Ta 'ramidek nga suako
Suakonto ni Lelongko.

Agdamdamilikami (We Are Potters)

Taga-San Nicolaskami nga agdamdamili
Naragsak ti biagmi, awan dukdukotmi
Nupay aduda a manglalais kadakami
Ta napanglawkam' nga agdamdamili
Tay napigket a daga
Gamayenmi nga umuna
Warakiwakan ti darat,
Ramasen tukelen
Ta tapnon agdedeketda nga nalaing
Ket nalaklaka nga intay bibiren
Isagana't pagbibiran
Tay rigis ken danum
Tay natukel a daga
Teptepen nga umuna
Ket itan buklen tay ngarab ti banga
Pulpuligusem tapno nalinis latta.
Tay nabibir a daga
Nga inkam' inpamaga
Pitpiten a buklen
Nalaka a padakkelen
Idiiden pulaan sa ibilag manen
Santo gebbaen ading intan mangilin.

Umayka ti Eskuela (Come to School)

Umayka ti eskuela, tapno lumaingka
Adu ti masursuro
Maestra ti pangulo
Tungpalem ti bagana paginbagan ida
Ta ragsak da nanangmo
ken ni pay tatangmo

Ngaminen ta Ranggas (Because of Your Cruelty)

Ngaminen ta ranggasmo kaniak,
Ta amin nga ikikitam ket pakatayak;
Ngamin biagko ta guraem man
Ti innak kenka panagayat.
Ta siasinno kad nga parsua
Ti di sumken ti karayona,
Apaman nga inna mabuya
Ta pintasmo, tarnaw ken sadia.

Chorus:
Baliwam kad, baliwam kad,
Biagko ta pakinakem.
Yeksam ta guram,
Yeksam ta apas ken dawel.
Ta daytoy ayatko,
Ta daytoy ayatko
Saan a bareng-bareng;
Saksik ti langit
Biagko pudno patiem,
Diakto kenka babawien.

Malaglagipka Laeng (I Just Remember You)

Malaglagipka laeng,
Diak mailiwliwag dayta sudim;
Ayat koma't sabali,
Nga pagduyusak ngem awanen.

Sadsadnaka 'toy ayat,
No maikariak nga aklonem;
Ay, wen ni gasat,
Sagudayko tungpal tanem.

Refrain:
Padasek man pay ti agayat,
Itan ta diak pay matay,
Bareng ta pusom,
Ay-ayennakto pay.
No saan laeng,
Anianto kad pay;
Bumabaakton tanem a sililiday.

Biag Ken Bileg (Life and Power)

Biag ken bileg
Sam-it 'toy kararua;
Nasudi a Nena,
Sampaguita nga napusaksak.

Sika awan sabali,
ti inkarik a liwliwak;
Ditoy lubong,
nga ing-gana't tungpal 'toy biag.

Refrain:
Ay-ayatenka, ngem sika kaniak saan,
Dardarepdepenka,
ngem dinak sa met kapnekan.
Ngem uray no kasta,
Dikanton paginsasaanan,
Agpapan biagko
ti agkanibusanan.

Sabong ni Mirasol (Sunflower)

Sabong ni Mirasol a kababangluan
Sabong lirio tay kayarigko
Sabong lirio tay kayarigko
A kumarayo kadagita sadiam

Dayta pusom inyarigko't pana
Daytoy pusok ket ubonenna
Daytoy pusok ket inubonna
A kumarayo kadagita sadia

Agpilika iti gustuem
Kadakami kayatmo nga aklonen
Siak wenno ni gayyem
Wenno toy kaduak, wenno siak met laeng

Tadtadennak ti mamingasut
Igamernak darat ken tapok
Addaakto la nga maipaypayugpog
Maipalpalais kadagita likud

Ilokana a Nasudi (Noble, Renowned Ilokana)

Ilokana a napnuan sudi,
Sapatam ay nakappapati
Toy pusok innak kenka ikari
Sika laeng awan sabali
Ti innak ay-ayaten
Ken pagserbian tungpal tanem ...
Ay wen!

Koro:
Ilokana a naemma
Diakto agayaten
No dinak aklonen.
Ilokana a naregta
Diakto agbiagen
No dinak ay-ayaten.

REFERENCES

This dictionary is a compilation of Ilocano (Ilokano, Iloko) words encountered by the author from various Ilocano stories, articles, magazines (*Bannawag* and *Burnay*), and books (too numerous to mention), previous dictionaries, and a corpus of spoken Ilocano collected in various regions of the *Kailokuan*. The dictionary used as the basic reference for the skeleton of this dictionary is Morice Vanoverbergh's (1956) *Iloko-English Dictionary*, which is the translated, augmented, and edited edition of Rev. Andrés Carro's (1888) *Vocabulario Iloco-Español*. Words from ancient Ilocano texts have also been included for use by Ilocanos and linguists alike interested in deciphering older materials.

Following is a list of linguistic and literature references used in compiling this edition of the dictionary, as well as other basic references for those interested in Ilocano or basic Cordilleran topics.

Afenir, Juan O., Reynaldo de Dios, and Felix M. Manalili. 1967. *English-Tagalog-Ilocano Pocket Dictionary*. Quezon City: Pressman Printers & Publishers.

Albano, Elvira A. 1976. Some old Ilocano verses in the comic tradition. *Ilocos Review* 8:4–11.

Albano, Godofredo. 1957. Our Beautiful Iluco language. Bacarra, Ilocos Norte: St. Andrew Parish.

Azurin, Arnold M. Paoay: A profile in Ilocano folk history beliefs and practices. *Ilocos Review* 9:71–82.

Bannawag, Pagiwarnak dagiti Ilokano (weekly Ilocano magazine). Makati City: Liwayway Publishing.

Barlahan-Dagdagan, B., and Jose O. Bautista. *Trilingual Dictionary, Iloko-English-Pilipino*. Manila: National Book Store.

Benton, Richard A. 1971. *Pangasinan Dictionary*. Honolulu: University of Hawai'i Press.

Bernabe, Emma, Virginia Lapid, and Bonifacio Sibayan. 1971. *Ilokano Lessons*. PALI Language Texts. Honolulu: University of Hawai'i Press.

Blancaflor, Isidora. 1956. Philippine Folklore among the Ilocanos. *Western Folklore* 15:3:159–167.

Bloomfield, Leonard. 1942. Outline of Ilocano syntax. *Language* 18:193–200.

Buenavista, Arturo G. 1996. *Limerika-3*. Bacaca, Davao City (published by author).

Bugarin, Jose. 1854. *Diccionario ibanag-español*. Manila: Imprenta de los Amigos del País.

Carro, Andrés. 1888. *Vocabulario iloko-español*. Manila: Estab. Tipolitográfico de M. Pérez e Hijo.

———. 1895. *Gramática ilocana, corregida y aumentada por el P. Carro*. 3rd edition. Malabon: Estab. Tipog. literario del Asilo de Malabon a cargo de PP. Agustinos Calzados.

Chan, Sonja A. 1977. The Syntactico-Semantic Representations of the Ilocano Adverbial Particle *pay* and its Lexicalization in English. *Saint Louis University Research Journal* (Baguio, Philippines) 8:3–4:387–440.

———. 1981. Beyond Syntax and Semantics via Ilokano adverbial particles. *St. Louis University Research Journal* (Baguio, Philippines) 12:4:507–577.

Clausen, Josie Paz. 1990. Ilokano Verbs: Argument Structure. *Working Papers in Linguistics, University of Hawaii* 22:2.

———. 1995. *The taxonomy, semantics, and syntax of Ilokano adverbial clauses*. University of Hawai'i, PhD dissertation.

Constantino, Ernesto. 1971. *Ilokano Dictionary*. Honolulu: University of Hawai'i Press.

Domingo, Damiana L. 1996. *Philippine Folk Literature: the Folk Songs*. Manila: De la Salle University Press.

English, Leo James. 1986. *Tagalog-English Dictionary*. Quezon City: Kalayaan Press.

Espiritu, Precy. 1984. *Let's speak Ilokano*. Honolulu: University of Hawai'i Press.

Foronda, Marcelino A. Jr. 1978. Recent Ilokano Fiction in Hawaii: A Study in Philippine-American Cultural and Literary History. In Pacita Cabulera Saludes and Mario Albalos (eds.).

Foronda, Marcelino A., and Juan A. Foronda. 1972. Samtoy: Essays on Iloko History and Culture. Manila: United Publishing.

Forman, Michael Lawrence. 1971. *Kapampangan Dictionary*. Honolulu: University of Hawai'i Press.

Geeroms Henry. 1977. Treatment of Spanish Elements in Iloko. *Journal of Northern Luzon* VII:1–2:1–34.

Geladé, Rev. George P. 1993. *Ilokano-English Dictionary*. Quezon City: CICM Missionaries.

Gerdts, Donna B. 1979. Out of Control in Ilokano. *Proceedings of the Fifth Annual Meeting of the Berkeley Linguistics Society*.

———. 1988. Antipassives and Causatives in Ilokano: Evidence for an Ergative Analysis. In *Studies in Austronesian Linguistics,* ed. Richard Ginn. *Ohio University Monographs in International Studies. Southeast Asia Series* 77:295–321.

Guerrero, Angel. 1929. *English-Ilocano Manual and Dictionary*. Manila: Christian Mission. (Revised, edited and enlarged edition of Hermon P. William's dictionary)

Headland, Thomas N., and Janet D. Headland. 1974. *A Dumagat (Casiguran-English Dictionary*. Pacific Linguistics Series C, No. 28. Canberra: Australian National University.

Hendrickson, Gail R., and Leonard E. Newell. 1991. *A Bibliography of Philippine Dictionaries and Vocabularies*. Manila: Linguistic Society of the Philippines.

Herre, Albert W., and Agustin F. Umali. 1948. English and Local Common Names of Philippine Fishes. United States Department of the Interior, Circular 14. Washington: United States Government Printing Office.

Hidalgo, S. P. Juan, Jr. 1969. *Bituen ti Rosales ken dadduma pay a sarita* [Star of Rosales and other short stories]. Manila: Ilokano Publishing House.

Hidalgo, S. P. Juan, Jr. (ed.) 1968. *Napili a sarita dagiti Ilokano, umuna a libro ti GUMIL Filipinas* [Selected Ilocano short stories]. Manila: Pioneer Printing Press.

Hill, Percy A. 1931. Pedro Bucaneg—a Philippine Moses. *Philippine Magazine* 28:1:32, 42–43.

Himes, Ronald S. 1998. The Southern Cordilleran Group of Philippine Languages. *Oceanic Linguistics* 37:1:120–177.

Keesing, Felix M. 1962. *The Ethnohistory of Northern Luzon*. Stanford: Stanford University Press.

Komisyón sa Wikang Pilipino. 1992. *Diksyunaryong Filipino-English*. Quezon City, Philippines, OLPH Printers.

Laconsay, Gregorio. 1993. *Iluko-English-Tagalog Dictionary*. Quezon City: Phoenix Publishing House.

Lewis, Henry T. 1971. *Ilocano Rice Farmers*. Honolulu: University of Hawai'i Press.

Llamzon, Teodoro A. 1969. *A Subgrouping of Nine Philippine Languages*. Hague: Martinus Nijhoff.

López, Francisco. 1627. *Arte de la lengua Iloca*. Manila: Universidad de Santo Tomás. [augmented in 1793 by Fray Andrés Carro and published in its third edition in 1895]

McFarland, Curtis D. 1977. *Northern Philippine Linguistic Geography*. Tokyo: Institute for the Study of Languages and Cultures of Asia and Africa. Monograph Series #9.

———. 1980. *A Linguistic Atlas of the Philippines*. Tokyo: Tokyo University of Foreign Studies.

McKaughan, Howard, and Janette Forster. 1957. *Ilocano: an Intensive Language Course*. Grand Forks: Summer Institute of Linguistics.

Mithun, Marianne. 1995. The Implications of Ergativity for a Philippine Voice System. In P. Hopper (ed.), *Grammatical Voice: Its Form and Function*. Amsterdam: John Benjamins.

Moguet, Pamela Johnstone, and R. David Zorc. 1988. *Ilokano Newspaper Reader*. Wheaton, Maryland: Dunwoody Press.

Panganiban, Jose Villa. 1972. *Diksiyunaryong-Tesauro Pilipino-English*. Quezon City: Manlapaz Publishing.

Quisumbing, Eduardo. 1947. Philippine Plants Used for Arrow and Fish Poisons. *Science and Technology Information Instutute* 77:2.

Ramos, Maximo D. 1971. *Creatures of Philippine Lower Mythology*. University of the Philippines Press.

Rayner, Ernest A. 1923. *Grammar and Dictionary of the Pangasinan Language* [*Gramatica tan Diccionario na Salitay Pangasinan*]. Manila: Methodist Publishing House. 96 pages.

Razote, Ramon, and Geronimo L. Barba. 1977. Some Bits of Ilocano Folklore. *Ilocos Review* 9.

Reid, Lawrence A. 1971. *Philippine Minor Languages: Word Lists and Phonologies*. Oceanic Linguistics Special Publication No. 8. Honolulu: University of Hawai'i Press.

———. 1976. *Bontok-English Dictionary*. Pacific Linguistics C-36. Canberra: Dept. of Linguistics, Research School of Pacific and Asian Studies, Australian National University.

———. 1989. Arta, Another Philippines Negrito Language. *Oceanic Linguistics* 28:47–74.

———. 1992. On the Development of the Aspect System in Some Philippine Languages. *Oceanic Linguistics*. 31:1:65–91.

Reyes, Isabelo de los. 1890. *Historia de Ilocos* (2 volumes). 2nd edition. Manila: Estab. Tipog. de la Opinión.

Rosal, Mario G. R. 1977. Some Dramatic Ur Forms in Iloco Folk Tradition. *Ilocos Review* 9:4–45.

———. 1993. *Zarzuelang Iloko: Mga salin sa Pilipino kalakip ang orihinal na Iloko*. Manila: Ateneo de Manila University Press.

Rosal, Nicholas L. *Understanding an Exotic Language: Ilokano*. New Jersey: Edison Press.

Rubino, Carl. 1996. Morphological Integrity in Ilocano. *Studies in Language* 20:3:333–366.

———. 1997. A Reference Grammar of Ilocano. PhD Dissertation, University of California, Santa Barbara.

———. 1998a. *Tagalog Standard Dictionary*. New York: Hippocrene Books.

———. 1998b. *Ilocano Dictionary and Phrasebook*. New York: Hippocrene Books.

———. 1998c. The Tagalog Derivational Clitic. *Linguistics* 36:5:1147–1166.

———. 1999. Iconic Morphology and Word Formation in Ilocano. Paper presented at the First International Symposium on Ideophones, Cologne, Germany, January 1999.

———. in press. Ilocano. In *The Encyclopedia of the World's Major Languages,* Jane Garry and Carl Rubino (eds.). New York: H. W. Wilson.

———. in press. Pangasinan. In *The Encyclopedia of the World's Major Languages,* Jane Garry and Carl Rubino (eds.). New York: H. W. Wilson.

———. in press. Iloko. In *The Austronesian Languages of Asia and Madagascar,* Nikolaus Himmelmann and K. A. Adelaar (eds.). London: Curzon Press.

Saludes, Pacita Cabulera, and Mario A. Albalos. *Bullalayaw: Antolohia dagiti nangab-abak iti salip iti sarita iti 1976–1977*. Quezon City: Mafferson Printing Press.

Schachter, Paul, and Fe T. Otanes. 1972. *Tagalog Reference Grammar*. Berkeley: University of California Press.

Scott, William Henry. 1960. The *Apo Dios* Concept of Northern Luzon. *Philippine Studies* 18:4:772–788.

Silva-Corvalán, Carmen. 1978. The Ilokano Causative in Universal Grammar. *Proceedings of the Fourth Annual Meeting of the Berkeley Linguistics Society*, pp. 223–237.

Summer Institute of Linguistics. 1995. *A Topical Vocabulary: English, Filipino, Ilocano and Lubuagan Kalinga*. Manila: Department of Education, Culture and Sports.

Villamor, Ignacio. 1922. *La Antigua Escritura Filipina Deducida del Belarmino y Otros Antiguos Documentos*. Manila.

Vanoverbergh, Morice. 1927a. Iloko Games. *Anthropos* 22:216–243.

———. 1927b. Plant Names in Iloko. *Journal of the American Oriental Society* 47.2:133–173.

———. 1933. *A Dictionary of Lepanto Igorot or Kankanay as It Is Spoken at Bauco*. Vienna, Austria: Francis Chamra.

———. 1936. The Iloko Kitchen. *Philippine Journal of Science* 60:1:1–10.

———. 1937. Iloko Constructions. *Philippine Journal of Science* 62:67–88.

———. 1938. Iloko Furniture and Implements. *Philippine Journal of Science* 64:413–433.

———. 1941. Iloko Weaving Dictionary. Città del Vaticano: *Annali laternensi* 5:221–52.

———. 1948. Iloko Hunting and Fishing, Basketry and Netting. *Primitive Man (Quarterly Bulletin of the Catholic Anthropological Conference)*. 21:3:39–64.

———. 1955. *Iloko Grammar*. Baguio, Philippines: Catholic School Press.

———. 1956. *Iloko-English Dictionary*. Baguio, Philippines: Catholic School Press.

———. 1972. *Isneg-English Vocabulary*. Honolulu: University of Hawai'i Press.

Wolf, Edwin III. 1947. *Doctrina Cristiana: the First Book Printed in the Philippines*. Washington: Library of Congress.

Yabes, Leopoldo Y. *The Ilocano Epic: A Critical Study of the "Life of Lam-ang," Ancient Ilocano Popular Poem, with a Translation of the Poem into English Prose*. Manila: Carmelo & Bauermann.

———. 1936. A Brief Survey of Iloko Literature. Manila (published by author).

Yap, Gloria Chan. 1980. *Hokkien Chinese Borrowings in Tagalog*. Pacific Linguistics Series B, No. 71. Canberra: Australian National University.

Zorc, R. David. 1979. The Genetic Relationships of Philippine Languages. In *Focal II: Papers from the Fourth International Conference on Austronesian Linguistics*, ed. by Paul Geraghty, Lois Carrington, and S. A. Wurm, 147–173. Pacific Linguistics C-94. Canberra: Australian National University.